Encyclopedia of
SOCIAL MEASUREMENT

Editor-in-Chief

Kimberly Kempf-Leonard

University of Texas at Dallas
Richardson, Texas, USA

VOLUME 1

A–E

ELSEVIER
ACADEMIC
PRESS

Amsterdam Boston Heidelberg London New York Oxford Paris San Diego San Francisco Singapore Sydney Tokyo

Elsevier Ltd., The Boulevard, Langford Lane, Kidlington, Oxford, OX5 1GB, UK

First edition 2005

Library of Congress Control Number: 2004104292

A catalogue record for this book is available from the British Library

ISBN 0-12-443890-3 (set)

This book is printed on acid-free paper
Printed and bound in the United Kingdom

Contents

Volume 1

A

B

Volume 2

F

G

N

O

Volume 3

P

T

U

Contents by Subject Area

Analytical Techniques

Constructs and Variables

Data Collection

Data Sets and Websites

Data Sources and Subjects

Fields and Applications

Historical Events and Figures

Interpretation and Data Limitations

Measurement Models

Research Designs

Sampling Design

Contributors

Alberto Abadie
Harvard University, Cambridge, Massachusetts, USA

Chris Adams
Cranfield School of Management, Bedfordshire, United Kingdom

Scott Akins
Oregon State University, Oregon, USA

Faye Allard
The University of Pennsylvania, Philadelphia, Pennsylvania, USA

Garland E. Allen
Washington University, St. Louis, Missouri, USA

Micah Altman
Harvard University, Cambridge, Massachusetts, USA

R. Michael Alvarez
California Institute of Technology, Pasadena, California, USA

Duane F. Alwin
Pennsylvania State University, University Park, Pennsylvania, USA

Erling B. Andersen
University of Copenhagen, Copenhagen, Denmark

Elijah Anderson
The University of Pennsylvania, Philadelphia, Pennsylvania, USA

Leon Anderson
Ohio University, Athens, Ohio, USA

Margo Anderson
University of Wisconsin, Milwaukee, Wisconsin, USA

David Andrich
Murdoch University, Murdoch, Western Australia

Carol S. Aneshensel
University of California, Los Angeles, California, USA

Phipps Arabie
Rutgers Business School, Newark and New Brunswick, New Jersey, USA

Marc Artzrouni
University of Pau, Pau, France

Peter M. Atkinson
University of Southampton, Southampton, United Kingdom

Paul Auerbach
Kingston University, Surrey, United Kingdom

Mie Augier
Stanford University, Stanford, California, USA

Robert D. Austin
Harvard Business School, Boston, Massachusetts, USA

Kenneth D. Bailey
University of California, Los Angeles, California, USA

Christopher Baird
National Council on Crime and Delinquency, Oakland, California, USA

Robert C. Bannister
Swarthmore College, Swarthmore, Pennsylvania, USA

Kevin G. Barnhurst
University of Illinois at Chicago, Chicago, Illinois, USA

Yvette Bartholomée
University of Groningen, Groningen, The Netherlands

David J. Bartholomew
London School of Economics, London, England, United Kingdom

Jeffrey Bass
University of Missouri-Columbia, Department of Anthropology, Columbia, Missouri, USA

Nathaniel Beck
New York University, New York, New York, USA

James Beebe
Gonzaga University, Spokane, Washington, USA

Bryan Benham
University of Utah, Salt Lake City, Utah, USA

Gail R. Benjamin
University of Pittsburgh, Pittsburgh, Pennsylvania, USA

Nathan Berg
University of Texas, Dallas, Richardson, Texas, USA

Ira H. Bernstein
University of Texas, Arlington, Arlington, Texas, USA

William D. Berry
Florida State University, Tallahassee, Florida, USA

John Carlo Bertot
Florida State University, Tallahassee, Florida, USA

James J. Biles
Western Michigan University, Kalamazoo, Michigan, USA

David C. Black
The University of Toledo, Toledo, Ohio, USA

Mihai C. Bocarnea
Regent University, Virginia Beach, Virginia, USA

R. Darrell Bock
University of Chicago, Chicago, Illinois, USA

Ulf Böckenholt
McGill University, Montreal, Quebec, Canada

Hennie R. Boeije
Utrecht University, Utrecht, The Netherlands

Doug Bond
Harvard University, Cambridge, Massachusetts, USA

Marc H. Bornstein
National Institute of Child Health and Human Development, Bethesda, Maryland, USA

Avram Bornstein
John Jay College of Criminal Justice in the City University of New York, New York, New York, USA

Marcel Boumans
University of Amsterdam, Amsterdam, The Netherlands

Tony Bovaird
University of the West of England, Bristol, United Kingdom

Timothy M. Bray
University of Texas, Dallas, Richardson, Texas, USA

Chester L. Britt
Arizona State University West, Phoenix, Arizona, USA

Michael Bromwich
London School of Economics and Political Science, London, United Kingdom

Rod Buchanan
University of Groningen, Groningen, The Netherlands

C. Victor Bunderson
The EduMetrics Institute, Provo, Utah, USA

John A. Bunge
Cornell University, Ithaca, New York, USA

Annie M. Burrows
Duquesne University, Pittsburgh, Pennsylvania, USA

George W. Burruss
Southern Illinois University at Carbondale, Illinois

Ferry Butar Butar
Sam Houston State University, Huntsville, Texas, USA

Michelle Butler
University of Cambridge, Cambridge, United Kingdom

John Bynner
Institute of Education, London, United Kingdom

David Byrne
University of Durham, Durham, United Kingdom

David E. Campbell
University of Notre Dame, Notre Dame, Indiana, USA

Stephanie Carmichael
University of Florida, Gainesville, Florida, USA

Edward G. Carmines
Indiana University, Bloomington, Indiana, USA

J. Douglas Carroll
Rutgers Business School, Newark and New Brunswick, New Jersey, USA

Shannan Catalano
Bureau of Justice Statistics, Washington DC, USA

Sanjay Chawla
University of Sydney, New South Wales, Australia

Charissa S. L. Cheah
University of Maryland, Baltimore, County, USA

Peter Y. Chen
Colorado State University, Fort Collins, Colorado, USA

Oleksandr S. Chernyshenko
University of Canterbury, Christchurch, New Zealand

Mike W. L. Cheung
The university of Hongkong, Hongkong

Josef Cihlar
Canada Centre for Remote Sensing, Natural Resources Canada, Ottawa, Canada

Constance F. Citro
National Research Council of The National Academies, Washington, DC, USA

D. Jean Clandinin
University of Alberta, Edmonton, Alberta, Canada

William A. V. Clark
University of California, Los Angeles, Los Angeles, California, USA

Terry Nichols Clark
University of Chicago, Chicago, Illinois, USA

Harold D. Clarke
University of Texas, Dallas, Richardson, Texas, USA

Andrew Cliff
University of Cambridge, Cambridge, UK

Ethan Cohen-Cole
University of Wisconsin, Madison, Wisconsin, USA

Flavio Comim
St. Edmund's College, Cambridge, United Kingdom; and Universidade Federal do Rio Grande do Sul, Brazil

Wade D. Cook
Seymour Schulich School of Business, York University, Toronto, Canada

Pierre Crépel
CNRS—Université de Lyon 1, Villeurbanne, France

Kevin M. Curtin
The University of Texas at Dallas, Richardson, Texas, USA

Susan L. Cutter
University of South Carolina, Columbia, South Carolina, USA

Andrew I. Dale
University of KwaZulu-Natal, Durban, South Africa

Eric van Damme
Tilburg University, Tilburg, The Netherlands

Ton de Jong
University of Twente, Enschede, The Netherlands

Victor C. de Munck
State University of New York at New Paltz, New Paltz, New York, USA

Jamie DeCoster
Free University Amsterdam, Amsterdam, The Netherlands

Trudy Dehue
University of Groningen, Groningen, The Netherlands

Alain Desrosières
National Institute for Statistics and Economic Studies, Paris, France

Marinus C. Deurloo
University of Amsterdam, Amsterdam, The Netherlands

Robert F. DeVellis
University of North Carolina, Chapel Hill, North Carolina, USA

Karim Dharamsi
University of Winnipeg, Winnipeg, Manitoba, Canada

Carmen Diego Gonçalves
Minho University, Braga, Portugal

Don A. Dillman
Washington State University, Pullman, Washington, USA

Mustafa Dinc
The World Bank, Washington, D.C., USA

John F. Disterhoft
Northwestern University Feinberg School of Medicine, Chicago, Illinois, USA

Alesha E. Doan
California Polytechnic State University, San Luis Obispo, California, USA

Michael R. Dowd
The University of Toledo, Toledo, Ohio, USA

Laurie A. Drapela
Washington State University, Vancouver, Washington, USA

Fritz Drasgow
University of Illinois, Urbana–Champaign, Illinois, USA

William W. Dressler
University of Alabama, Tuscaloosa, Alabama, USA

Christopher S. Dunn
Bowling Green State University, Bowling Green, Ohio, USA

Peter K. Dunn
University of Southern Queensland, Toowoomba, Queensland, Australia

Steven Durlauf
University of Wisconsin, Madison, Wisconsin, USA

E. Paul Durrenberger
Pennsylvania State University, University Park, Pennsylvania, USA

Daniel R. Eignor
Educational Testing Service, Princeton, New Jersey, USA

Horst A. Eiselt
University of New Brunswick, Fredericton, New Brunswick, Canada

Joseph W. Elder
University of Wisconsin, Madison, Wisconsin, USA

Mark Elliot
University of Manchester, Manchester, United Kingdom

Charles W. Emerson
Western Michigan University, Kalamazoo, Michigan, USA

George Engelhard, Jr.
Emory University, Atlanta, Georgia, USA

Richard L. Engstrom
University of New Orleans, New Orleans, Louisiana, USA

Lee Epstein
Washington University, St. Louis, Missouri, USA

Michael T. Eskey
Troy State University, Troy, Alabama, USA

Wendy Nelson Espeland
Northwestern University, Evanston, Illinois, USA

K.J. Euske
Naval Postgraduate School, Monterey, California, USA

Michael E. Ezell
Vanderbilt University, Nashville, Tennessee, USA

David F. Gillespie
Washington University, St. Louis, Missouri, USA

George Farkas
The Pennsylvania State University, University Park, Pennsylvania, USA

Peter J. Fensham
Monash University, Victoria, Australia

Chandi Fernando
University of Toronto, Toronto, Ontario, Canada

Michel Ferrari
University of Toronto, Toronto, Ontario, Canada

Dail Fields
Regent University, Virginia Beach, Virginia, USA

Stephen E. Fienberg
Carnegie Mellon University, Pittsburgh, Pennsylvania, USA

Jeffrey A. Fine
University of Kentucky, Lexington, Kentucky, USA

Gerhard H. Fischer
University of Vienna, Vienna, Austria

Donald W. Fiske
University of Chicago, Chicago, Illinois, USA

Susan T. Fiske
Princeton University, Princeton, New Jersey, USA

Raymond J. G. M. Florax
Free University Amsterdam, Amsterdam, The Netherlands

Johnny R. J. Fontaine
Ghent University, Ghent, Belgium

John Fox
McMaster University, Hamilton, Ontario, Canada

Karen A. Franck
New Jersey Institute of Technology, Newark, New Jersey, USA

Charles H. Franklin
University of Wisconsin, Madison, Wisconsin, USA

Howard S. Friedman
University of California, Riverside, California, USA

Peter A. Furia
Wake Forest University, Winston–Salem, North Carolina, USA

Emmanuela Gakidou
Center for Basic Research in the Social Sciences, Harvard University, USA

Alison Galloway
Queen Margaret University College, Edinburgh, United Kingdom

Elizabeth Garner
Colorado State University, Fort Collins, Colorado, USA

Gilbert Geis
University of California, Irvine, Irvine, California, USA

Alan S. Gerber
Yale University, New Haven, Connecticut, USA

Arthur Getis
San Diego State University, San Diego, California, USA

Andrew S. Gibbons
Brigham Young University, Provo, Utah, USA

Jeff Gill
University of Florida, Gainesville, Florida, USA

Nicholas W. Gillham
Duke University, Durham, North Carolina, USA

Alberto Giordano
Texas State University, San Marcos, Texas, USA

Eduard Glas
Delft University of Technology, Delft, The Netherlands

Cees A. W. Glas
University of Twente, Enschede, The Netherlands

Garrett Glasgow
University of California, Santa Barbara, California, USA

Jack Glazier
Oberlin College, Oberlin, Ohio, USA

Norval D. Glenn
University of Texas, Austin, Texas, USA

Reginald G. Golledge
University of California, Santa Barbara, California, USA

Michael F. Goodchild
University of California, Santa Barbara, California, USA

Timothy R. Graeff
Middle Tennessee State University, Murfreesboro, Tennessee, USA

Jim Granato
National Science Foundation, Arlington, Virginia, USA

Louis N. Gray
Washington State University, Pullman, Washington, USA

Donald P. Green
Yale University, New Haven, Connecticut, USA

Michael J. Greenwood
University of Colorado, Boulder, Colorado, USA

Scott Greer
University of Prince Edward Island, Charlottetown, Prince Edward Island, Canada

Bhajan S. Grewal
Victoria University, Melbourne, Australia

Daniel A. Griffith
University of Miami, Coral Gables, Florida, USA

Donald A. Gross
University of Kentucky, Lexington, Kentucky, USA

John A. Grummel
West Virginia State University, Institute, West Virginia, USA

Peter Haggett
University of Bristol, Bristol, UK

John R. Hall
University of California, Davis, Davis, California, USA

Nancy S. Hall
University of Delaware, Newark, Delaware, USA and University of Maryland, College Park, Maryland, USA

W. Penn Handwerker
University of Connecticut, Storrs, Connecticut, USA

Dean M. Hanink
University of Connecticut, Storrs, Connecticut, USA

Bruce Hannon
University of Illinois, Champaign-Urbana, Champaign, Illinois, USA

Rachel Harter
National Opinion Research Center (NORC), Chicago, Illinois, USA

Kingsley E. Haynes
George Mason University, Fairfax, Virginia, USA

Linda Heath
Loyola University Chicago, Chicago, Illinois, USA

James J. Heckman
The University of Chicago, Chicago, Illinois, USA

David M. Hedge
University of Florida, Gainesville, Florida, USA

Leslie Hepple
The University of Bristol, Bristol, UK

Frederick M. Hess
American Enterprise Institute, Washington, DC, USA

David R. Hodge
University of Pennsylvania, Philadelphia, Pennsylvania, USA

Margaret Hogan
World Health Organization, Geneva, Switzerland

Herbert Hoijtink
University of Utrecht, Utrecht, The Netherlands

Søren Holm
Cardiff University, Cardiff, United Kingdom

Joop J. Hox
Utrecht University, Utrecht, The Netherlands

Lawrence J. Hubert
University of Illinois at Champaign, Champaign, Illinois, USA

John Hudson
University of Bath, Bath, United Kingdom

Casper D. Hulshof
University of Twente, Enschede, The Netherlands

Louise Irving
University of Manchester, Manchester, United Kingdom

Paul T. Jaeger
Florida State University, Tallahassee, Florida, USA

Donald G. Janelle
University of California, Santa Barbara, Santa Barbara, California, USA

Paul A. Jargowsky
University of Texas, Dallas, Richardson, Texas, USA

Jana L. Jasinski
University of Central Florida, Orlando, Florida, USA

Gayle R. Jennings
Central Queensland University, Rockhampton, Queensland, Australia

Bertram Johnson
Middlebury College, Middlebury, Vermont, USA

Robert L. Johnson
University of South Carolina, Columbia, South Carolina, USA

Renée J. Johnson
University of Florida, Gainesville, Florida, USA

Karen D. Johnson-Webb
Bowling Green State University, Bowling Green, Ohio, USA

Ron Johnston
University of Bristol, Bristol, United Kingdom

Lyle V. Jones
University of North Carolina, Chapel Hill, North Carolina, USA

Dean H. Judson
U.S. Census Bureau, Washington, D.C., USA

George Julnes
Utah State University, Logan, Utah, USA

Giora Kaplan
The Gertner Institute, Israel

Jeffrey D. Karpicke
Washington University, St. Louis, Missouri, USA

James Edwin Kee
George Washington University, Washington, DC, USA

Peter Keenan
University College, Dublin, Ireland

Jeremy T. Kerr
University of Ottawa, Ottawa, Canada

Ann H. Kim
Brown University, Providence, Rhode Island, USA

Ryuichi Kitamura
Kyoto University, Kyoto, Japan

Anastasia Kitsantas
George Mason University, Fairfax, Virginia, USA

Panagiota Kitsantas
East Carolina University, Greenville, North Carolina, USA

Amy L. Klekotka
University of Virginia, Charlottesville, Virginia, USA

Casey A. Klofstad
Harvard University, Cambridge, Massachusetts, USA

David Knoke
University of Minnesota, Minneapolis, Minnesota, USA

Ari Kohen
Duke University, Durham, North Carolina, USA

Dolph Kohnstamm
Emeritus, Leiden University, Leiden, The Netherlands

Michael J. Kolen
University of Iowa, Iowa City, Iowa, USA

John L. Korey
California State Polytechnic University, Pomona, California, USA

Autumn D. Krauss
Colorado State University, Fort Collins, Colorado, USA

Philip Kreager
Somerville College, Oxford University, Oxford, England, United Kingdom

David B. Kronenfeld
University of California, Riverside, Riverside, California, USA

John A. Kupfer
University of Arizona, Tucson, Arizona, USA

Kenneth C. Land
Duke University, Durham, North Carolina, USA

Jan de Lange
Utrecht University, Utrecht, The Netherlands

J. Stephen Lansing
University of Arizona, Tucson, Arizona, USA

Janet L. Lauritsen
University of Missouri, St. Louis, St. Louis, Missouri, USA

Danielle Lavin-Loucks
University of Texas, Dallas, Richardson, Texas, USA

Anthony C. Lea
Environics Analytics Group, Toronto, Ontario, Canada

Murray J. Leaf
University of Texas at Dallas, Richardson, Texas, USA

Raymond M. Lee
Royal Holloway University of London, Egham, Surrey, United Kingdom

Eveline S. van Leeuwen
Free University, Amsterdam, The Netherlands

James G. Lennox
University of Pittsburgh, Pittsburgh, Pennsylvania, USA

Gerty J. L. M. Lensvelt-Mulders
Utrecht University, Utrecht, The Netherlands

Charles W. Leonard
University of Texas, Dallas, Richardson, Texas, USA

Lyle E. Leritz
University of Oklahoma, Norman, Oklahoma, USA

James P. LeSage
University of Toledo, Toledo, Ohio, USA

Baruch Lev
New York University, New York, New York, USA

Mairi Levitt
Lancaster University, Lancaster, England, United Kingdom

Shlomit Levy
The Hebrew University of Jerusalem, Jerusalem, Israel

Allan J. Lichtman
American University, Washington, DC, USA

Wim J. van der Linden
University of Twente, Enschede, The Netherlands

Christy Lleras
Pennsylvania State University, University Park, Pennsylvania, USA

Stephen C. Locke
Florida Atlantic University, Boca Raton, Florida, USA

Paul A. Longley
University College London, London, UK

Sylvia Lorek
Sustainable Europe Research Institute, Cologne, Germany

Will Lowe
Harvard University, Cambridge, Massachusetts, USA

Richard M. Luecht
University of North Carolina at Greensboro, Greensboro, North Carolina, USA

Guanzhong Luo
Murdoch University, Perth, Western Australia and South China Normal University, Guangzhou, China

Scott M. Lynch
Princeton University, Princeton, New Jersey, USA

Peter J. Lynn
University of Essex, Colchester, United Kingdom

Harro Maas
University of Amsterdam, Amsterdam, The Netherlands

Cora J. M. Maas
Utrecht University, Utrecht, The Netherlands

M. Eileen Magnello
University College London/Wellcome Trust Center for the History of Medicine, London, United Kingdom

Bryan F. J. Manly
Universidade de São Paulo, Piracicaba, Brazil

Peter Kirby Manning
Northeastern University, Boston, Massachusetts, USA

Peter V. Marsden
Harvard University, Cambridge, Massachusetts, USA

Stephen W. Marshall
University of North Carolina at Chapel Hill, Chapel Hill, North Carolina, USA

Monty G. Marshall
University of Maryland, College Park, Maryland, USA

Stephen M. Marson
University of North Carolina, Pembroke, North Carolina, USA

Andrew Martin
Washington University, St. Louis, Missouri, USA

Elizabeth Martin
U.S. Census Bureau, Washington, DC, USA

Antonio Marturano
University of Exeter, Exeter, England, United Kingdom

Shadd Maruna
University of Cambridge, Cambridge, United Kingdom

Antonio Massieu
World Tourism Organization, Madrid, Spain

Geoff N. Masters
Australian Council for Educational Research, Camberwell, Australia

Richard E. Mayer
University of California, Santa Barbara, California, USA

Allyssa McCabe
University of Massachusetts, Lowell, Lowell, Massachusetts, USA

Charles R. McClure
Florida State University, Tallahassee, Florida, USA

Rose McDermott
University of California, Santa Barbara, California, USA

Michael P. McDonald
George Mason University, Fairfax, Virginia, USA

Daniel P. McMillen
University of Illinois, Chicago, Illinois, USA

Will Medd
University of Salford, Salford, Greater Manchester, United Kingdom

Scott Menard
University of Colorado, Boulder, Colorado, USA

Joel Michell
University of Sydney, Sydney, Australia

Henry L. Minton
University of Windsor, Windsor, Ontario, Canada

David L. Morgan
Portland State University, Portland, Oregon, USA

Calvin Morrill
University of California, Irvine, California, USA

Clayton Mosher
Washington State University, Vancouver, Washington, USA

Michael D. Mumford
University of Oklahoma, Norman, Oklahoma, USA

Gerardo L. Munck
University of Southern California, Los Angeles, California, USA

Darla K. Munroe
University of North Carolina, Charlotte, North Carolina, USA

David J. Murray
Queen's University, Kingston, Ontario, Canada

Andy Neely
Cranfield School of Management, Bedfordshire, United Kingdom

K. Bruce Newbold
McMaster University, Hamilton, Ontario, Canada

Frank Newport
Editor in Chief of the Gallup Poll, Princeton, New Jersey, USA

John M. Nicholas
University of Western Ontario, London, Ontario, Canada

Peter Nijkamp
Free University Amsterdam, Amsterdam, The Netherlands

Shizuhiko Nishisato
University of Toronto, Ontario, Canada

Anthony Oberschall
University of North Carolina at Chapel Hill, Chapel Hill, North Carolina, USA

Thomas R. O'Connor
North Carolina Wesleyan College, Rocky Mount, North Carolina, USA

Ayo Oyeleye
University of Central England in Birmingham, Birmingham, United Kingdom

Barnett R. Parker
Pfeiffer University, Charlotte, North Carolina, USA

Michael Quinn Patton
Union Institute and University, Minneapolis, Minnesota, USA

Dorothy Pawluch
McMaster University Hamilton, Ontario, Canada

James Penny[†]
CASTLE Worldwide, Inc., Morrisville, North Carolina, USA

Trond Petersen
University of California, Berkeley, Berkeley, California, USA

Anthony Petrosino
Nashuah, New Hampshire, USA

Thomas F. Pettigrew
University of California, Santa Cruz, Santa Cruz, California, USA

Andrew Pickles
University of Manchester, Manchester, UK

Richard J. Pike
U.S. Geological Survey, Menlo Park, California, USA

Steven Piker
Swarthmore College, Swarthmore, Pennsylvania, USA

Alex R. Piquero
University of Florida, Gainesville, Florida, USA

Alan E. Pisarski
Independent Consultant, Falls Church, Virginia, USA

Louis G. Pol
University of Nebraska, Omaha, Nebraska, USA

Carole L. Popoff
U.S. Census Bureau, Washington, D.C., USA

Carole L. Popoff
U.S. Census Bureau, Washington, D.C., USA

Eric A. Posner
University of Chicago, Chicago, Illinois, USA

Mick J. Power
University of Edinburgh, Edinburgh, United Kingdom

Ronda Priest
University of Southern Indiana, Evansville, Indiana, USA

Ram C. Rao
University of Texas, Dallas, Richardson, Texas, USA

C. Radhakrishna Rao
Pennsylvania State University, University Park, Pennsylvania, United States

Kenneth A. Rasinski
NORC, University of Chicago, Chicago, Illinois, USA

Daniel Read
London School of Economics and Political Science, London, United Kingdom

Dwight W. Read
University of California at Los Angeles, Los Angeles, California, USA

Mark D. Reckase
Michigan State University, East Lansing, Michigan, USA

Charles S. Reichardt
University of Denver, Denver, Colorado, USA

Arnold Reisman[†]
Sabanci University, Istanbul, Turkey and Reisman and Associates, Shaker Heights, Ohio, USA

Charles G. Renfro
Journal of Economic and Social Measurement, New York, New York, USA

Wilma C. M. Resing
Leiden University, Leiden, The Netherlands

Charles S. ReVelle
Johns Hopkins University, Baltimore, Maryland, USA

Christine Rider
St. John's University, Queens, New York, USA

Marc Riedel
Southeastern Louisiana University, Hammond, Louisiana, USA

Piet Rietveld
Free University, Amsterdam, The Netherlands

Violina P. Rindova
University of Maryland, College Park, Maryland, USA

Paul Robbins
The Ohio State University, Columbus, Ohio, USA

Henry L. Roediger, III
Washington University in St. Louis, St. Louis, Missouri, USA

Peter A. Rogerson
State University of New York, Buffalo, New York, USA

Robert Rosenthal
University of California, Riverside, Riverside, California, USA

Steven Rubenstein
Ohio University, Athens, Ohio, USA

Gidi Rubinstein
Netanya Academic College, Tel Aviv, Israel

Doris McGartland Rubio
University of Pittsburgh, Pittsburgh, Pennsylvania, USA

Bruce Russett
Yale University, New Haven, Connecticut, USA

Fumiko Samejima
University of Tennessee, Knoxville, Tennessee, USA

Shekhar Saxena
Mental Health: Evidence and Research, World Health Organization, Geneva, Switzerland

Erica Scharrer
University of Massachusetts, Amherst, Massachusetts, USA

Silke Schmidt
University of Hamburg, Hamburg, Germany

Ivo Schneider
University of the German Armed Forces Munich, Munich, Germany

Arthur M. Schneiderman
Independent Consultant, Boxford, Massachusetts, USA

Peter H. Schonemann
Purdue University, West Lafayette, Indiana, USA

Miriam W. Schustack
California State University, San Marcos, California, USA

Christof Schuster
University of Notre Dame, Indiana, USA

Libby Schweber
Harvard University, Boston, Massachusetts, USA

Daniel O. Segall
Defense Manpower Data Center, U.S. Department of Defense, Washington, D.C., USA

Richard J. Shavelson
Stanford University, Stanford, California, USA

Peter J. Sheehan
Victoria University, Melbourne, Australia

Shashi Shekhar
University of Minnesota, Minneapolis, Minnesota, USA

Charles Shimp
University of Utah, Salt Lake City, Utah, USA

Klaas Sijtsma
Tilburg University, Tilburg, The Netherlands

Francisco J. Silva
University of Redlands, Redlands, California, USA

Stephen G. Sireci
University of Massachusetts, Amherst, Massachusetts, USA

Maria Anne Skaates
Aarhus School of Business, Aarhus, Denmark

Garry J. Smith
University of Alberta, Edmonton, Alberta, Canada

Timothy D. Smith
Slippery Rock University, Slippery Rock, Pennsylvania, USA

Tom W. Smith
University of Chicago, Chicago, Illinois, USA

Stephen L. J. Smith
University of Waterloo, Waterloo, Ontario, Canada

J. T. Snead
Florida State University, Tallahassee, Florida, USA

David A. Snow
University of California, Irvine, California, USA

Joachim H. Spangenberg
Sustainable Europe Research Institute, Cologne, Germany

Ian Spence
University of Toronto, Toronto, Ontario, Canada

Stephen Stark
University of South Florida, Tampa, Florida, USA

David G. Steel
University of Wollongong, Wollongong, NSW, Australia

Michael Stein
Lindenwood University, St. Charles, Missouri, USA

Magnus Stenbeck
Centre for Epidemiology, National Board of Health and Welfare, Stockholm, Sweden

Mitchell L. Stevens
New York University, New York, USA

Chirayath M. Suchindran
University of North Carolina, Chapel Hill, North Carolina, USA

Joweria M. Teera
University of Bath, Bath, United Kingdom

Dawn Thilmany
Colorado State University, Fort Collins, Colorado, USA

Wendy L. Thomas
University of Minnesota, Minneapolis, Minnesota, USA

Kim M. Thompson
Florida State University, Tallahassee, Florida, USA

Kenneth W. Thompson
University of Virginia, Charlottesville, Virginia, USA

Barbara Tillmann
Université Claude Bernard Lyon 1, CNRS-UMR 5020, Lyon, France

Barbara Townley
University of Edinburgh, Edinburgh, Scotland, United Kingdom

Paul E. Tracy
University of Texas, Dallas, Richardson, Texas, USA

Lisa Troyer
University of Iowa, Iowa City, Iowa, USA

Nancy Brandon Tuma
Stanford University, Stanford, California, USA

Stephen P. Turner
University of South Florida, Tampa, Florida, USA

J. Rodney Turner
Groupe ESC Lille, Lille, France

Patricia A. Urban
Kenyon College, Gambier, Ohio, USA

Wim J. van der Linden
University of Twente, Enschede, The Netherlands

Mark van Ommeren
Mental Health: Evidence and Research, World Health Organization, Geneva, Switzerland

Carla VanBeselaere
Mount Allison University, Sackville, New Brunswick, Canada

Marina Vasilyeva
University of Chicago, Chicago, Illinois, USA

Liwen Vaughan
University of Western Ontario, London, Ontario, Canada

Marcel V. J. Veenman
Leiden University, Leiden, The Netherlands, and University of Amsterdam, Amsterdam, The Netherlands

Bernard P. Veldkamp
University of Twente, Enschede, The Netherlands

Sandra Vergari
University at Albany, State University of New York, Albany, New York, USA

Jay Verkuilen
University of Illinois, Champaign-Urbana, Champaign, Illinois, USA

D. Stephen Voss
University of Kentucky, Lexington, Kentucky, USA

Johan Wagemans
University of Leuven, Leuven, Belgium

Theodore C. Wagenaar
Miami University, Oxford, Ohio, USA

Howard Wainer
National Board of Medical Examiners, Philadelphia, Pennsylvania, USA

Lee Demetrius Walker
University of Kentucky, Lexington, Kentucky, USA

Herbert W. Ware
George Mason University, Fairfax, Virginia, USA

Noreen M. Webb
University of California, Los Angeles, Los Angeles, California, USA

Murray Webster, Jr.
University of North Carolina, Charlotte, North Carolina, USA

John R. Weeks
San Diego State University, San Diego, California, USA

Marc D. Weiner
Rutgers University, New Brunswick, New Jersey, USA

David Weisburd
Hebrew University, Jerusalem, Israel, and University of Maryland, College Park, Maryland, USA

Craig Weiss
Northwestern University Feinberg School of Medicine, Chicago, Illinois, USA

Susan C. Weller
University of Texas Medical Branch, Galveston, Texas, USA

E. Christian Wells
University of South Florida, Tampa, Florida, USA

James O. Wheeler
University of Georgia, Athens, Georgia, USA

Michael J. White
Brown University, Providence, Rhode Island, USA

Andrew B. Whitford
University of Kansas, Lawrence, Kansas, USA

Mark Wilcox
Cranfield University, Cranfield, England, United Kingdom

Willem Jan Willemse
University of Amsterdam, Amsterdam, The Netherlands

Garrath Williams
Lancaster University, Lancaster, England, United Kingdom

Phoebe D. Williams
University of Kansas School of Nursing, Kansas City, Kansas, USA

Arthur R. Williams
Mayo Clinic, Rochester, Minnesota, USA

Tamar Diana Wilson
University of Missouri, St. Louis, Missouri, USA

Gabriel K. Wolfenstein
University of California, Los Angeles, Los Angeles, California, USA

Henk Wolthuis
University of Amsterdam, Amsterdam, The Netherlands

James W. Wood
Pennsylvania State University, University Park, Pennsylvania, USA

James A. Woods
West Virginia University, Morgantown, West Virginia, USA

Richard Wright
University of Missouri, St. Louis, St. Louis, Missouri, USA

Rebecca Yang
University of Texas, Dallas, Texas, USA

Majid Yar
Lancaster University, Lancaster, United Kingdom

Paul S. F. Yip
The University of Hong Kong, Hong Kong

Yoosik Youm
University of Illinois at Chicago, Chicago, Illinois, USA

Reef Youngreen
University of Iowa, Iowa City, Iowa, USA

Chong Ho Yu
Cisco Systems/Aries Technology, Tempe, Arizona, USA

Ke-Hai Yuan
University of Notre Dame, Indiana, USA

L. A. Zander
Naval Postgraduate School, Monterey, California, USA

Richard A. Zeller
Kent State University, Kent, Ohio, USA

Pusheng Zhang
University of Minnesota, Minneapolis, Minnesota, USA

Editorial Board

Editor Biography

Dr. Kempf-Leonard is Professor of Sociology, Crime and Justice Studies, and Political Economy at the University of Texas at Dallas. Prior to her appointment at UTD in 2000, she was Associate Professor and Graduate Director of Criminology and Criminal Justice at the University of Missouri at St. Louis. She also served for ten years as a gubernatorial appointee to the Missouri Juvenile Justice Advisory Group. She received her Ph.D. at the University of Pennsylvania in 1986; M.A. at the University of Pennsylvania in 1983; M.S. at the Pennsylvania State University in 1982; B.S. at the University of Nebraska in 1980. Her book *Minorities in Juvenile Justice* won the 1997 Gustavus Myers Award for Human Rights in North America. Her publications have appeared in: *Criminology, Justice Quarterly, Journal of Criminal Law & Criminology, Crime & Delinquency, Journal of Quantitative Criminology, Advances in Criminological Theory, Punishment & Society, Corrections Management Quarterly, the Journal of Criminal Justice, Criminal Justice Policy Review, The Justice Professional, Youth and Society, The Corporate Finance Reader*, and *The Modern Gang Reader*.

Foreword

Not long ago, and perhaps still today, many would expect an encyclopedia of social measurement to be about quantitative social science. The *Encyclopedia of Social Measurement* excellently defies this expectation by covering and integrating both qualitative and quantitative approaches to social science and social measurement. The *Encyclopedia of Social Measurement* is the best and strongest sign I have seen in a long time that the barren opposition between quantitative and qualitative research, which has afflicted the social sciences for half a century, is on its way out for good. As if the Science Wars proper—between the social and natural sciences—were not enough, some social scientists found it fitting to invent another war within the social sciences, in effect a civil war, between quantitative and qualitative social science. Often younger faculty and doctoral students would be forced to take sides, and the war would reproduce within disciplines and departments, sometimes with devastating effects. This, no doubt, has set social science back. We cannot thank the editors and contributors to the *Encyclopedia of Social Measurement* enough for showing us there is an effective way out of the malaise.

This volume demonstrates that the sharp separation often seen in the literature between qualitative and quantitative methods of measurement is a spurious one. The separation is an unfortunate artifact of power relations and time constraints in graduate training; it is not a logical consequence of what graduates and scholars need to know to do their studies and do them well. The *Encyclopedia of Social Measurement* shows that good social science is opposed to an either/or and stands for a both/and on the question of qualitative versus quantitative methods. Good social science is problem-driven and not methodology-driven, in the sense that it employs those methods which for a given problematic best help answer the research questions at hand. To use a simple metaphor, asking whether social science is best served by qualitative or quantitative methods is about as intelligent as asking a carpenter whether a hammer or a saw is the better tool.

So far every effort has been unsuccessful in the social sciences at arriving at one canon for how to do science, most conspicuously the attempt at emulating the natural science model. Different explanations exist of this phenomenon, from Anthony Giddens' so-called double hermeneutic to Hubert Dreyfus' tacit skills argument. It is a great strength of the *Encyclopedia of Social Measurement* that it stays clear of the unity of science argument for social science, and of any other attempts at imposing one dominant paradigm on what social science is and how it should be conducted. The editors and most of the contributors have rightly seen that success in social science and social measurement lies with the type of methodological and epistemological pluralism, which is a distinguishing feature of the encyclopedia. Together with its impressive substantive breadth—covering the full range of social measurement from anthropology, sociology, political science, economics, and business administration over urban studies, environment, geography, demography, history, criminology, and law to neuroscience, biomedicine, nursing, psychology, linguistics, and communication—this healthy pluralism will prove the *Encyclopedia of Social Measurement* to be a robust and indispensable companion to all working social scientists for many years to come.

BENT FLYVBJERG
Professor of Planning,
Department of Development and Planning,
Aalborg University, Denmark

Preface

> *Methodology . . . [has] developed as a bent of mind rather than as a system of organized principles and procedures. The methodologist is a scholar who is above all analytical in his approach to his subject matter. He tells other scholars what they have done, or might do, rather than what they should do. He tells them what order of finding has emerged from their research, not what kind of result is or is not preferable. This kind of analytical approach requires self-awareness on the one hand, and tolerance, on the other. The methodologist knows that the same goal can be reached by alternative roads.*
>
> (Lazarsfeld and Rosenberg, 1955, p. 4)

In the social sciences we use methodology to try to answer questions about how and why people behave as they do. Some types of behavior are very common or routine, while others happen rarely or only in certain situations. When you realize that every conceivable type of behavior is within the realm of possible subjects for us to study, you can begin to appreciate the scope of social science. Beyond identifying human activities and the boundaries in which they occur, social scientists also want to explain why behaviors happen. In looking for causes, social scientists pursue all dimensions of the social world. We look at personal traits of individuals, characteristics of interactions between people, and contextual features of the communities and cultures in which they live. We study people who lived in the past, try to improve the quality of life today, and anticipate what the future will hold. It is difficult to think of a topic that involves people for which a social scientist could not investigate.

Given all we do, it is good that there are so many of us. You will find social scientists in university departments as professors of sociology, psychology, anthropology, political science, and economics. You will also find professors of geography, history, philosophy, math, management, planning, finance, journalism, architecture, humanities, and art who are social scientists. Even this multidisciplinary list is not exhaustive. There are important and prevalent social science investigations that influence decision-making in the world outside of universities too. Social scientists are world-wide and work in all branches of government, large and small organizations, and many types of businesses. Daily life for most people is influenced by social science research in marketing, insurance, and government. However, not everyone in these positions is a social scientist; the distinction involves scientific inquiry, or the approach used to try to answer questions about behavior. As the definition cited above conveys, good science includes tolerance and appreciation for many methodological paths. This encyclopedia of social science methodology provides 356 entries written by social scientists about what they do.

The entries in this encyclopedia cover many forms of measurement used by social scientists to study behavior. Eleven substantive sections delineate social sciences and the research processes they follow to measure and provide knowledge on a wide range of topics. The encyclopedia has an extensive index too, because many topics include issues that are relevant in more than one section. From many perspectives and strategies, these volumes describe the research questions social scientists ask, the sources and methods they use to collect information, and the techniques they use to analyze these data and provide answers to the important questions.

Each section includes entries that address important components of quantitative and qualitative research methods, which are dissected and illustrated with examples from diverse fields of study. The articles convey research basics in sufficient detail to explain even the most complicated statistical technique, and references for additional information are noted for each topic. Most entries describe actual research experiences to illustrate both the realm of possibilities and the potential challenges that might be encountered. Some entries describe major contributions and the social scientists who made them. The authors are accomplished methodologists in their fields of study. They explain the steps necessary to accomplish the measurement goals, as well as provide their practical advice for ways in which to overcome the likely obstacles.

Collectively, the entries in this encyclopedia also convey that no single approach, type of data, or technique of analysis reigns supreme. Indeed, plenty of disagreements exist among social scientists about what constitutes the "best" measurement strategy. Often distinctions are made between quantitative and qualitative methodologies, or are discipline-specific. Some preferences can be linked to a specific field of study or research topic; others, related to time and location, coincide with how new ideas and advances in technology are shared. Sometimes we don't even agree on what is the appropriate question we should try to answer!

Although our views differ on what is ideal, and even on what are the appropriate standards for assessing measurement quality, social scientists generally *do* agree that the following five issues should be considered:

1. We agree on the need to be clear about the scope and purpose of our pursuits. The benchmarks for evaluating success differ depending on whether our intent is to describe, explain, or predict and whether we focus extensively on a single subject or case (e.g., person, family, organization, or culture) or more generally on patterns among many cases.
2. We agree on the need to make assurances for the ethical treatment of the people we study.
3. We agree on the need to be aware of potential sources of measurement error associated with our study design, data collection, and techniques of analysis.
4. We agree it is important to understand the extent to which our research is a reliable and valid measure of what we contend. Our measures are reliable if they are consistent with what others would have found in the same circumstances. If our measures also are consistent with those from different research circumstances, for example in studies of other behaviors or with alternate measurement strategies, then such replication helps us to be confident about the quality of our efforts. Sometimes we'd like the results of our study to extend beyond the people and behavior we observed. This focus on a wider applicability for our measures involves the issue of generalizability. When we're concerned about an accurate portrayal of reality, we use tools to assess validity. When we don't agree about the adequacy of the tools we use to assess validity, sometimes the source of our disagreements is different views on scientific objectivity.
5. We also agree that objectivity merits consideration, although we don't agree on the role of objectivity or our capabilities to be objective in our research. Some social scientists contend that our inquiries must be objective to have credibility. In a contrasting view of social science, or epistemology, objectivity is not possible and, according to some, not preferable. Given that we study people and are human ourselves, it is important that we recognize that life experiences necessarily shape the lens through which people see reality.

Besides a lack of consensus within the social sciences, other skeptics challenge our measures and methods. In what some recently have labeled "the science wars," external critics contend that social scientists suffer "physics envy" and that human behavior is not amenable to scientific investigation. Social scientists have responded to "anti-science" sentiments from the very beginning, such as Emile Durkhiem's efforts in the 19th century to identify "social facts." As entertaining as some of the debates and mudslinging can be, they are unlikely to be resolved anytime soon, if ever. One reason that Lazarsfeld and Rosenberg contend that tolerance and appreciation for different methodological pathways make for better science is that no individual scientist can have expertise in all the available options. We recognize this now more than ever, as multidisciplinary teams and collaborations between scientists with diverse methodological expertise are commonplace, and even required by some sources of research funding.

Meanwhile, people who can be our research subjects continue to behave in ways that intrigue, new strategies are proffered to reduce social problems and make life better, and the tool kits or arsenals available to social scientists continue to grow. The entries in these volumes provide useful information about how to accomplish social measurement and standards or "rules of thumb." As you learn these standards, keep in mind the following advice from one of my favorite methodologists: "Avoid the fallacy fallacy. When a theorist or methodologist tells you you cannot do something, do it anyway. Breaking rules can be fun!" Hirschi (1973, pp. 171–2). In my view nothing could be more fun than contemporary social science, and I hope this encyclopedia will inspire even more social science inquiry!

In preparing this encyclopedia the goal has been to compile entries that cover the entire spectrum of measurement approaches, methods of data collection, and techniques of analysis used by social scientists in their efforts to understand all sorts of behaviors. The goal of this project was ambitious, and to the extent that the encyclopedia is successful there are many to people to thank. My first thank you goes to the members of the Executive Advisory Board and the Editorial Advisory Board who helped me to identify my own biased views about social science and hopefully to achieve greater tolerance and appreciation. These scientists helped identify the ideal measurement topics, locate the experts and convince them to be authors, review drafts of the articles, and make the difficult recommendations required by time and space considerations as the project came to a close. My second thank you goes to the many authors of these 356 entries. Collectively, these scholars represent well the methodological status of social science today. Third, I thank the many reviewers whose generous recommendations improved the final product. In particular I extend my personal thanks to colleagues at the University of Texas at Dallas, many of whom participated in large and small roles in this project, and all of whom have helped me to broaden my appreciation of social measurement. Finally, I thank Scott Bentley, Kirsten Funk, Kristi Anderson, and their colleagues at Elsevier for the opportunity and their encouragement when the tasks seemed overwhelming. Scott's insights to the possibilities of a project such as this and the administrative prowess of both Kirsten and Kristi helped make this a reality.

Good science is a cumulative process, and we hope this project will be ongoing and always improving. Despite our best efforts to identify topics and authors, sometimes we failed. If you have suggestions, criticisms, or information worth considering, I hope you will let me know.

Hirschi, Travis (1973). Procedural rules and the study of deviant behavior. *Social Problems* **21**(2), 159–173.

Lazarsfeld, Paul and Morris Rosenberg (1955). *The Language of Social Research.* The Free Press, New York.

KIMBERLY KEMPF-LEONARD

Guide to Using the Encyclopedia

The *Encyclopedia of Social Measurement* is a comprehensive and authoritative study covering the data, techniques, theories, designs, histories, and implications of assigning numerical values to social phenomena. It consists of three volumes and includes 356 articles written by leading international authorities. Each article provides a focused description intended to inform a broad spectrum of readers, ranging from research professionals to students and the general public.

In order that you, the reader, will derive the greatest benefit from the *Encyclopedia of Social Measurement*, we have provided this Guide. It explains how the *Encyclopedia* is organized and how to locate information within it.

Organization

All the articles in the *Encyclopedia of Social Measurement* are arranged in a single alphabetical sequence by title. Articles whose titles begin with the letters A to E are in Volume 1, articles with titles from F to O are in Volume 2, and articles from P to Y are in Volume 3.

Volume 3 also includes a complete subject index for the entire work along with an alphabetical list of article reviewers, whose silent contributions were essential to the success of the project.

Article Titles

Article titles generally begin with the key term describing the topic, and if necessary they have an inverted word order so the title begins with this term. For example, "Democracy, Measures of" is the article title rather than "Measures of Democracy," and "Education, Tests and Measures in" is the title, not "Tests and Measures in Education." Thus, all the articles on quantitative analysis applications appear together in the third volume of the *Encyclopedia*.

Because each article was composed for the *Encyclopedia of Social Measurement*, for the sake of simplicity we have omitted the phrase "social measurement" from article titles.

Index

The index appears as the last element of Volume 3. Subjects are listed alphabetically and indicate the volume and page number where relevant information can be found. The *Encyclopedia of Social Measurement* contains approximately 13,000 index entries. This index is the most convenient way to locate a topic, and thus it should be the starting point for any reader.

In addition, articles are also divided into key subject areas, and a contents list by area is provided for reference in each volume. The table of contents by subject area functions as an index because it lists all the topics covered in a given area; e.g., the *Encyclopedia* has 48 articles dealing with constructs and variables.

Article Format

Articles in the *Encyclopedia of Social Measurement* are arranged in this standard format:

- Title and Author
- Glossary
- Defining Statement
- Main Body of the Article
- Cross-References
- Bibliography

Glossary

The Glossary section contains terms that are important to an understanding of the article and that may be unfamiliar to the reader. Each term is defined in the context of the particular article in which it is used. The same term may appear as a glossary entry in different articles, with the details of the definition varying slightly from one article to another. The *Encyclopedia* includes approximately 2,500 glossary entries. For example, the article "Scales and Indexes, Types of" includes this entry (among others):

scale A cluster of items that taps into measurements developed on face validity and/or professional judgment of measuring what one intends to measure. The intent is to measure the relative degree, amount, or differences between variables.

Defining Paragraph

The text of each article begins with a single introductory paragraph. This introduction defines the topic under discussion and summarizes the content of the article. For example, the article "Libraries" begins with the following defining paragraph:

Social measurement in libraries involves the collection of evaluation data through social science methods. The goal is to determine the extent to which resources utilized in the management, planning, and presentation of collected sources of information, programs, and services by libraries meet the specific needs of a broad range of library users.

Cross-References

The entry list for the *Encyclopedia of Social Measurement* has been constructed so that each entry is supported by one or more other entries that provide additional information. Therefore all articles have cross-references to other articles. These appear at the end of the article, following the end of the narrative text, and preceding the further reading section. The *Encyclopedia* contains about 1,500 cross-references. The cross-references indicate related articles that can be consulted for further information on the same topic, or for information on a related topic. For example, the article "Case Study" provides the following cross-references:

- Anthropology, Psychological
- Basic vs. Applied Social Science Research
- Ethnography
- Field Experimentation
- Observational Studies
- Qualitative Analysis, Anthropology
- Quantitative Analysis, Anthropology

Bibliography

The further reading section appears next. It presents recent secondary sources that can aid the reader in locating more detailed or technical information. Review articles and research papers that are important to an understanding of the topic are also included. For example, the article "Autocorrelation" has the following references (among others):

Franses, P. H. (1998). *Time Series Models for Business and Economic Forecasting.* Cambridge University Press, Cambridge, UK.
Ghysels, E., Swanson, N. R., and Watson, M. W. (2001). *Collected Papers of Clive W. J. Granger, Volume II, Causality, Integration and Cointegration, and Long Memory.* Cambridge University Press, Cambridge, UK.
Godfrey, L. G. (1988). *Misspecification Tests in Econometrics.* Cambridge University Press, Cambridge, UK.

The further reading references do not represent a complete list of all the materials consulted by the author in preparing the article. Instead, the titles are the author's recommendations of the best and most appropriate starting points for further research.

Access

Peter Kirby Manning

Northeastern University, Boston, Massachusetts, USA

Glossary

access A working opportunity to gather data in a social unit; the process of obtaining access may be met with success, partial success, or failure.

access types Can be preexisting, worked through via a series of stages, electronic, and global in implications.

craft vs. organizational studies One to two researchers engage in craftwork, but larger teams require organization (administration, accountability, and a hierarchy).

natural history of access Stages of access: preliminary work, the approach, entry, and role relations (or secondary access).

social units A working taxonomy of what might be accessed: places, organizations, scenes, databases, or persons.

study purpose A motivational account that focuses, ideally, on a scientific and intellectual aim.

study rationale A succinct summary of the aims and purposes of the research, usually vague initially.

All science requires access of some kind. In social measurement, this includes access to socially constituted data sources and to individuals in naturalistic settings. Access must be considered as a continuous process rather than as a single deciding point, and this process should be seen as complex, not as a linear progression of entries. Access can be sought in places, organizations, scenes, interactions, databases, and persons. The efforts required are based on the foci and rationale of the research, and although these may not be firmly specified at the outset of a study, they must be developed by the time of analysis and report writing. Important issues arise prior to acquisition of access: the size and organization of the research group, preexisting or ongoing access, and power relations and access. A natural history of access (preliminaries/preparation, the approach to the unit, the entry process, role relations inside the unit, and situated and ongoing issues, or "secondary access") is important when studies must be reconstituted or when avenues of research are blocked, new foci develop, and new team members are added. In many respects, the process of access is ongoing, nonlinear, episodic, and often repetitive. Although research technique skills and methods are variables, without patience, tenacity, some distance, and humor, access may never be fully managed, reworked, or rebuilt.

Introduction

Research of socially constituted data sources and people may require access to naturalistic social life settings, rather than artificially created settings. Successful social measurement of extant social settings requires consideration of a series of access points and access levels, from the initial steps through the completion of the study.

Social Units

It is useful and perhaps necessary to subdivide the process of obtaining access, and consider first the social units, and their related patterning of interactions, to be accessed. The units to be accessed range from the most general to the most specific:

- Places. Organized interactions occur both publicly and privately. Public places that may be accessed include parks, parades, restaurants, coffee bars, lobbies, and many other easily accessed areas.
- Organizations. Authoritatively coordinated and characterized by dense interaction of collections of people in a given ecological location, organizations contain internal social units that may be studied even more intensely than the whole organizational entity.

• Scenes. Characteristic encounters, episodes, and situations that are key or thematic within the setting vary from the banal (such as making change, emptying garbage, or attending meetings or dances) to the quasi-sacred (such as baptisms, weddings, or other ritual events). The idea of scenes includes typical or characteristic interaction patterns found within the settings.

• Databases. Collections of files, manuscripts, papers, clippings, or other archived material, in electronic or paper format, provide global access.

• Persons. Access to individuals, which includes physical access (e.g., studies of tattooing, disabilities, or maladies), is circumscribed by federal, state, and committee guidelines that oversee issues of human rights and protect the privacy and dignity of individuals and study participants.

Foci

Sociologists are concerned more with access to organizations, settings, and scenes in the sense provided here, and are less likely to seek access that invades privacy. Each social unit has a front stage, so to speak, as well as a back stage. Access to these unit components for any sort of study (even a brief survey) is often nested. For example, access to organizations is one initial step in gaining access to some other unit (records or recorded and memorialized daily routines), to participants, and/or to some part of the back stage of the studied social unit. Depending on the concern of the study, there may be relevant subparts of access to front stage material (e.g., what social means are involved in occupational routines), including the setting (props and paraphernalia), appearance (status displays), and manner (expectations of performance). Social science often contrasts the ideal and the real, and contradictions of such. Consider Enron. The front stage elements, such as the accounting system, the rationale in choice of published materials, the rhetoric used, and the public expectations (stockholders), may be fruitfully contrasted with conventions for concealing losses and spreading expenditures and indebtedness and the corruption in auditing reviews. To do so, however, requires some form of access to nonpublic (back stage) information.

Generalizing about Access

Social science literature contains a rich primary and secondary literature on access, but typically as part of an article, or featured as an appendix in a monograph, rather than as the sole topic of an article or book. A few classic articles on the process of access exist; of particular note is the work of Joseph Gusfield and Gerald Berreman, in the 1950s and 1960s. The process of access and the management of role-relations during a study are so much an integral part of the fieldwork enterprise that they suffuse the narrative to the exclusion of considering other questions, such as reliability of the findings or their validity. Access is especially complex in the case of studying conflict-ridden settings and controversial people, such as the power elites, big business leaders, deviants, criminals, violent groups, and those with contact with such groups. Analytically sophisticated collections of such studies include the work of George McCall and J. L. Simmons, Howard Becker, and Robert Emerson. Notable for contrast and lessons about a crisis in the field that usually meant the project was compromised or abandoned are articles written by Rosalie Wax, Louis Yablonsky, Rik Scarce, and Richard Leo. Included here are additional examples—the often cited work by Irving Louis Horowitz on Project Camelot, a failed Central Intelligence Agency-sponsored study; Jack Douglas' study of "beautiful women"; and famous failed studies that were published nevertheless, such as *When Prophecy Fails*, by Leon Festinger and coauthors, and *Doomsday Cult*, by John Lofland. Every serious scholar has several abandoned (and perhaps much loved) projects cluttering up office and home, but few abandoned projects are deemed worthy of publication. This is odd, given that "falsification" and rejection of null hypotheses so shape social science work.

The difficulty in making sense of literature on access lies in deciding how to draw generalizations from case studies and qualitative works; this is very much shaped by the context (social, cultural, historical) in which the work was done. The case can disappear into the context. Each published field study omits details of many key matters, in part to satisfy journal reviewers and editors, in part because of space constraints and ethical obligations to informants. As a result, the oral tradition, including stories told at conferences, in bars, and at seminars, is a vibrant and salient part of teaching fieldwork. Furthermore, the classics of fieldwork, often read and referred to, are more likely to be cited and understood than are other references, and this corpus includes some famously failed, disastrous, and barely mentionable field studies. Although "semi-failed" studies contribute to the cumulative body of knowledge on access (and related issues), they are not likely to be widely known, read, and cited. Fieldwork as a craft bears an uneasy baggage, but projects that fail can provide lessons, guidance, and warning signs as well as, if not better than, completed, published (and perhaps cited) projects can. Finally, the development of university committees concerned with human "subjects" in research, and the requirement for impact statements for federal grants, have altered the terrain of what is acceptable. The differing interpretations of "risk" and "harm," and provisions for neutralizing these, are confounded with general canons of research, local traditions, and past miscues, and are often given a distinctly local twist.

Purpose or Rationale

One of the most difficult matters to articulate in the access process, and in developing the approach, before, during, and after the negotiations for access, is creating a workable purpose (a motivational account) and a brief rationale for the study. This may take some time, and is not equivalent to simply articulating a precise aim or theoretical grounding of the study, nor to the "one-liner" description that might be used in casual conversation. Clarity of purpose should go to motive and expected rewards. Ideally, such clarity might ensure that creative research and its public dissemination would govern the work, rather more than writing an expose, or seeking financial gain. The long and emotionally draining efforts by John Van Maanen, for example, to obtain access to the "Union City" (large urban) police department were finally successful through indirect sponsorship of a local professor. Van Maanen explains that he used vague terms of reference with the police chief initially, and later, as he negotiated further access. The present author used similar omissions in London in 1973, expressing simply "interest in the job" (of policing) and by implication how it differed from policing in the United States. This vagueness was sharpened after the initial entrée, and remarks informants had made about what they thought was being studied were echoed! Although these glittering generalities serve well early on, because often a field study is not precisely focused initially (or is "defocused," according to Jack Douglas), a stated rationale must be derived eventually. Mitch Duneier's candid statement of his lack of precise grounding is a good example of an implicit rationale—his aim was to gather data and write a good book. A stated research purpose is essential to the eventual completion of a project, as is honesty to self, to informants, and to respondents. This clarity of focus generally emerges, not at once, because, as Kierkegaard wrote, "life is lived forward but understood backward." If the aim is development of a grounded theory of some kind, this formulation of an account or vocabulary of motives, and specification via data, feedback, and reformulation is an intrinsic aspect of the process.

Some General Issues

A few sociological matters affect and shape the nature of access prior to explicit planning and orientation to a project. These include the size and organization of the research team, previous access, and power.

Size and Organization of the Research Unit (Individual or Group)

Access is shaped by and varies with the size of the team that is assembled to do the study. Dynamics vary, depending on whether a study is carried out by an individual, by a loosely coupled set of teammates (a group project with interlocking facets), as a tightly integrated, organized, funded, and administered project, or as an established, funded, ongoing field study. Although most field studies are done by one person, teams of fewer than four people are still engaged in craftwork. The major contrast is between small (craft) studies and those involving more than three people; the larger groups are usually funded and include a hierarchy of administration and the requisite coordination. The larger size of the study group entangles the access process in bureaucratic maneuver; the access and administration of the project may be complex, handled by administrators who are not in the field, and may not be the responsibility of the field researchers. In effect, in larger groups, craftwork in the field is no longer sufficient to manage the project, but managerial decisions will directly affect the work in the field.

Preexistant or Ongoing Access

Access may depend on previous involvement in a setting and whether the goal is to "penetrate" it further, for purposes of analysis or application to current work or projects. Access may already have been granted or obtained on grounds other than research. Robert E. Park encouraged studies grounded in personal experience. He urged his students to study something they knew or experienced directly (the same advice is given to young novel writers). Thus, he urged studies of gangs, suicide, the ecology of the city, hotel life, hobos, waitresses, and teachers to those who had previous life experiences with these matters. Donald Roy's classic articles in the 1950s, on piece work, perhaps the finest and most detailed fieldwork ever done, were carried out before, during, and after he was a graduate student at the University of Chicago. The very capable studies of Simon Holdaway, Malcom Young, and Melville Dalton followed the approach of Roy. After a period of work, they engaged in graduate work, and then gathered additional data. Some projects, such as Van Maanen's lively discussions of workers at Disneyland (*The Smile Factory*) drew on previous work, and his initial reports did not require "access." His continuing work on multiple Disneyland facilities (Toyko, Eurodisney, Epcot Center, and the original California site) required access and permission. Other variations on this approach are Erving Goffman's studies of the Shetland Islanders, in which he worked in the hotel kitchen during his fieldwork, and his studies of St. Elizabeth's Hospital, which resulted in *Asylums*, in which he acted as a recreational aide. In each case, his research role was partially secret, although he did negotiate initial entry. Another sort of research that requires no access in the formal sense is work that studies people in public settings such as bars, strip clubs, libraries, coffee bars, and other loosely coordinated scenes, and "public" events such as outdoor drug dealing. Perhaps the most ambiguous kind of access is realized when engaging semiliterate or preliterate people, where no "gatekeepers" exist, or where the approach must be indirect and relies almost entirely on subsequent in-the-field negotiations and relations.

Power Relations and Access

Power relations affect both initial access and continued access within a place or organization. The more powerful the organizations, corporations, government agencies (secret or quasi-secret parts of the Central Intelligence Agency, Federal Bureau of Intelligence, National Security Administration, and Department of Defense, including the Pentagon), higher levels of state and federal government, and secret criminal organizations, the more difficult access will be. The published studies of these organizations are few. Consider the power elite studies of the 1950s and their modest achievements, and the absence of careful and systematic studies of corporate life, especially at the highest levels (studies of Robert Jackall, W. Lloyd Warner, and C. Wright Mills are exceptions), and of the servants of men of power (the corporate and Wall Street lawyers, consultants, brokers, and accountants). Most often, studies of elites are qualitative and or interview studies. We are beholden to journalists such as Seymour Hersh, Ronald Kessler, James Bamford, and former agents of the Central Intelligence Agency, such as Phillip Agee, for the limited public knowledge about these secret and secretive organizations. Our knowledge of criminal organizations is also very weak and thin. Whereas scholars such as Dick Hobbs, Richard Wright, and Scott Decker used observations, interviews, and informants, most of their studies were based in part on confessions and interviews with former members of organized crime or on semiautobiographical books.

A Natural History of Access

There is a natural history to gaining access. There must be preparation for failures, reorganization, contingencies that were unexpected, and "lucky breaks." Many studies are never begun, or are abandoned, the oral tradition would suggest, because the investigator felt it was not possible to gain access and terminated the study. It is advisable to remain somewhat defocused on negotiating entry to the field. Yet, the more organized the approach, the easier it is to execute the study once initial access is gained. Although the logic of what follows here resembles a natural history, the stages are not linear; each step does not follow from the other but may be repeated, and the cycle begun again and again from various points. Institutional Review Boards (IRBs), committees that approve research involving humans, can delay, stop, or terminate a project, or cause it to be redesigned or essentially emptied of scientific value. It is the rare study that proceeds from conception to execution in a direct and predictable line and results in publication. Access must be negotiated and renegotiated, and in this sense, we must learn from failed projects.

Preliminaries

Preliminaries involve preparation. Preparation may involve study of the setting or organization, its history and traditions, the people interacting within it, and organizational ideology and culture. Preparation may also involve assembling a rationale and gathering sponsorship and/or and funding. After obtaining broad access, cultivating relationships and negotiating access to "targeted" persons or data may be required. Several alternative strategies for access may be required in addition to managed interactions ("in the unit," or on site), such as developing ways around obstacles to information. Generally, one or more strategies will fail to yield the necessary results. A variety of instruments are generally assembled in a field study, and these may affect access. Different approaches (use of informants; formal/informal, structured/unstructured, or face-to-face interviews; questionnaire mailings; observation); may require different modes of access.

As a general rule, within any organization, social scientists have been most successful in studying the powerless and lower level participants, e.g., small-time criminals and ex-cons, young and midlevel gang members, officers on the street, solo lawyers, and failed members of marginal groups. This is perhaps equivalent to studying academic life by interviewing only those who failed to get tenure, life-time associate professors, or those who dropped out of graduate school or were thrown out for cheating. The systematic work of Mike Useem alone has focused on the "fat cats" and the "top dogs" in recent years. Professor of sociology Jack Katz has argued that the absence of literature reports on the powerful within social organizations may be a function of lack of access, social scientists' choices of subjects, or the elites' active strategies that prevent close study.

The Approach

The published literature suggests that the more a research effort is sponsored by powerful organizations and persons, the more likely access will result. It is possible this is an artifact based on what is published (and the need to write up results as apart of the contract or grant) rather than ease of access. Seeking sponsorship is the opening move in a game. In the early days of police research, for example, it was rare that the researchers did not acknowledge the support of the Department of Justice, Police Foundation, National Institutes of Mental Health, or the National Science Foundation. An individual researcher can make an approach in a straightforward manner, seeking direct access, or through intermediaries. "Middle men" or brokers can be fellow social scientists, former students or alumni of the researcher's university, members of the sponsoring research organization (National Institute of Justice, the Police Foundation, Office of Community Oriented Police Services), neighbors, or friends. The more indirect the link leading to access (e.g., a casual acquaintance who suggests ways to open doors), the more that face-to-face negotiations will be required. The most difficult approach to gaining access is the "cold call" approach, even with some legitimate backing (indirect, or "name dropping"). Studies based on cold-call approaches are the most likely to fail, to not be published, or to be only the subject of technical reports. Thus, it is very difficult to assess the proportion of these approaches that "work." The more connected the project to a larger framework or project structure, the more that final publication will reflect some joint constraints, timetables, opportunities to publish, and even conflicts about the final product.

Entry

Entry is profoundly shaped by what is being entered. Access to public places or to organization front stages (the official greeters and receptionists in organization offices), and even to other settings of interest, may be easily available without egregious costs or efforts. Access to bars, parks, coffeehouses, and public gatherings is easily accomplished. Semipublic events such as graduations, weddings, and religious services are quite accessible. However, after the preliminaries for researching organizations have been accomplished, very often negotiations for further access flounder . For example, in a large English constabulary where the present author had personal sponsorship, a presentation, lunch, a tour of the crime analysis facility, and introductions to the Deputy Chief Constable went well, but were followed by instructions to write a letter to the Chief Constable for further access. This all looked promising until the letter of refusal came a week or so later. There was no explanation for the refusal, but an indirect inquiry revealed that the Chief Constable was about to resign, and the new deputy to be appointed and the people running the crime analysis unit were wary of criticism of a nascent undertaking. Another study involved being given initial sponsorship by a London officer visiting Michigan State University on a study bursarship; the sponsorship was linked to a friend of the London officer, i.e., a Chief Superintendent in the Metropolitan London Police (now called Metropolitan Police Services). A phone call to the Chief Superintendent (yielding the response "What took you so long to call? I've been expecting you!") led to a full round of interviews and observations with detectives, canine units, sergeants, and constables, when, previously, access had been denied by letter from the Home Office and the Metropolitan London Police Commissioner. The process of "penetrating" an organization only begins once initial entry is permitted, and is not then finished. Persistence and patience cannot be overemphasized as the basis for success.

Inside the Unit

The process of gaining initial access can alter subsequent role relations and the types of data it is possible to obtain or seek. This can be shaped by role relations in general within the unit. The entering bargain, what is promised implicitly or explicitly in order to do the study, may vary in time, because, as new contingencies arise, the researcher may have to adjust, regroup, withdraw for a time, or end the search. The promises made to those granting access, in general, will shape the nature of the access and in turn the data gathered in the resultant study. Observational data are fairly straightforward, because if there is access, there is at least one "window" into the organization. There may be backstage matters and "key scenes," those that are expressive of the culture, such as the questioning of an arrested suspect, preparation of a fine meal, or inspection of a nuclear facility, within the setting to which access is desired. For example, as described in *Narcs' Game*, this author had easy access to phone calls and meetings in public rooms, some access to raids and warrant-serving episodes, and almost no access to interviews with informants, to arrests, or to bookings and jail interviews (post-arrests or prior to trial). The study was focused on the interaction of information and action choices in drug enforcement, so lack of access to these latter scenes were not crucial. The picture of drug policing is thus partial and based on differential access. Stephen Mastroskfi's study of police–public interaction relied on interviews with ranks above sergeants and observations and interviews with those of lower rank. In short, the meaning of the organization will appear to vary, depending on the point of access to it. Access can be systematic, as when files are requested on crimes for a given time period, or more idiosyncratic and adventitious, taking opportunities when they arise (e.g., when police fieldwork goes well, researchers may be asked to go on raids, to join social occasions such as after-work drinks or lunches, or to attend informal meetings).

Most fieldworkers have sought opportunistic glances at paper files, have opened notebooks, and have deciphered things left on desks when the owner is away, but such actions constitute *bricolage* (using random findings), and are unlikely to contribute to a study in any major fashion. Because fieldwork often begins in a defocused fashion, without a clear empirical statement or hypothesis, it is best to keep alert for things on the periphery of a study, e.g., related issues in policing such as the media coverage of events, public parades and demonstrations, civic gathering places and ceremonies, and ethnic traditions of the city. This breadth of vision provides a set of connections that may in time come together and contextualize the central concern of the study, giving the work depth and breadth. Access remains something like a telescope: it must be adjusted depending on the target object.

"Occasioned" data represent yet another sort of information; examples include the marvelous detailed data Roy Rappaport gathered initially to calculate the carrying capacity of the land in New Guinea, including the weight of pigs, the acreage of taro plants, and the patterns of planting. Once inside the setting in the jungle among the Maring, systematic observations were made to support the argument. Material was gathered for later analysis. Occasioned data can also be obtained within public settings such as courthouses or employment offices; extraneous public materials can be gathered and analyzed without too much fear of retribution. The difficulty arises in gaining access to corroborative evidence or records, such as sentencing reports or background investigations by parole workers. It is crucial not to minimize the importance of the complex and changeable views of people and to accept that they may hold contradictory ideas, or may be confused, and that this confusion is data as well as that which connects in a satisfying fashion. As some scholars have emphasized, following the general orientation of capturing the actors' perspectives, the viewpoints of the actors should not be invented, but should be reported.

Situated, Negotiated Secondary Access

Qualitative work and access to settings and scenes shape the process of negotiating roles and access at other levels within an organization or scene, once initial access has been managed. The degree of focus and precision in the research plan and the required instrumentation will affect the liminal period between initial access and secondary access. These are constraints having to do with the size of the studied population and sample, the nature of the interviews, and the length and complexity of the interviews (and language skills required, as well as translation and back-translation needed). Complexity also accompanies the length of the "to get" list items, such as a floor plan, organizational chart, paper files, key scenes to observe, and so on. The resulting dynamics might thus be called "secondary access problems" and they are related to matters of establishing, negotiating, and validating roles and aims within the place, interaction, organization, scene, database, or person. Initial access to data usually comes through a higher level sponsor or person, who then directs the researcher to a secondary person (a lieutenant, middle manager, clerk, or trusted administrative assistant). Here, the usual vagueness obtains. Once negotiations ensue, those at the point of access and the access-producer, or "gatekeeper," will shape the initial roles occupied by the researcher, and hence data access to some extent. Several researchers have suggested that fieldworkers should take on a fabricated, false, and agreeable pleasant *persona* in order to gather data; others disagree with this approach. The stereotypes of academics as confused, abstracted, distant, and slightly otherworldly can be both an advantage and a disadvantage. With police, who are attuned to lies and self-serving fronts, it may be essential to disagree directly with their views, and to take positions, particularly concerning issues such as gender relations (sexism) and race bias.

As a study progresses and data are gathered (whether from interviews, observations, or questionnaires), myths, questions, curiosities, and unanticipated events will shape the study and the nature of the secondary access. In the worst-case scenario, the researcher is subpoenaed, thrown out, and the data confiscated or destroyed. These events cannot be fully anticipated, but they are common and in that sense "predictable." As access continues, the researcher takes on new depth or presence; personal features, habits, nicknames, and shared humor and jokes make data gathering more contextual and sensitive to gender, appearance, and interests. Jennifer Hunt, for example, in studies of the New York Police Department, was treated with great ambivalence by the officers, but her ability to shoot accurately and well was ultimately acknowledged and was a source of prestige. Responses to such events and patterns of interaction shape subsequent access and unfolding or closing of opportunities. One of the advantages of a multiperson team study is that people talk to researchers about the other researchers, thus facilitating role-building activities. Roles are built up over time, not immediately thrust into a setting. Some roles are a result of active decisions by a researcher, but others are beyond control. Clearly, gender, sexual orientation, and sexual preferences shape secondary access in important ways.

The question of what sort of "help" and assistance a researcher gives to the organizations' members studied also arises in fieldwork (e.g., in an ambulance, at a fight, when gang members are fleeing police). Does a researcher carry a gun, wear a bulletproof vest, engage in fights, do medical procedures, type up documents, count money or evidence seized in raids, run errands for coffee, or become a "gopher"? In general, these little duties become bases for reciprocity and obligation that exceed the narrow purpose of the research. For examples, anthropologists in Chiapas always "overpaid" their informants just enough to keep them out of debt, but not so much as to elevate the standard rate among the Zinacantecos. This encouraged the informants to depend on the anthropologists for loans, liquor, medicine, and succor. Finally, many researchers may provide feedback or agree to summarize findings to principal gatekeepers, and these meetings or brief reports in turn may lead to reactions from the organization or the people studied. Thus, exit etiquette and sensible behavior will define the current exit as well as the next one: every ending is a new beginning.

Future Issues

Global Ethics and Access

The points made in this article assume that the investigator or team has at least nominally set out a purpose and that the general purpose is known by the studied groups. Secret observers and disguised observations raise quite different questions about access, because access involving concealed observers in whole or part is patterned by their roles as they defined them within the organization, or only slightly expanded versions of these roles

When access is gained with a broad mandate and/or a secret purpose that either is not disclosed or is hidden from the people being studied (or when they do not understand what is happening, given lack of research experience or because of poor reading and language skills), then access and field tactics become fraught with ethical questions. James O'Neel and Napoleon Chagnon entered the Amazonian forest to study the Yanomamo Indians as a genetic population, seeking to establish whether the dominance of headmen shown through fighting and conquests led to a natural selection process that sustained warfare and conflict and the social structure. Holding fast to their aim, O'Neel and Chagnon would not provide medical treatments; staged, stimulated, and filmed fights; gathered genealogies that were angering and a violation of tribal traditions; and in some sense eroded an already thin and dying culture. In this research, access increased vulnerability of the tribe to diseases and outside forces and contributed to the shrinking number of the remaining isolated, preliterate groups.

Electronic Access and Fieldwork

The potential for surveillance and simulation of social control is emergent in federal, state, and local agencies. No one is quite clear on how many databases exist, or how many bytes, persons, or files they contain, and their potential, but there is a clear concern that the civil liberties may be compromised by access to the databases. The power to control the files and databanks is still under contest, as is freedom to use and access the Internet. As commercialization of the Web increases, control and access will be in the hands of large corporations or governmental bodies that will charge for or conceal modes of access. There is no doubt that in another decade, access questions will focus on manipulation, control, processing, and analyzing electronically formatted data.

From a research point of view, there are enormous advantages to the existence of and access to huge standardized, formatted, and shared databases. Three issues face future researchers concerned about these data and access to them. The first is that some "sites" and social worlds may well be electronic, or virtual. The problems and prospects of access here will be perhaps more dependent on the skills of the researchers to gain access electronically (Internet, "hacking," chat room, and individual computer technology skills). The second issue is that access to and manipulation of data via electronic files, databanks, folders, and other electronic modes of storing, transferring, and analyzing data raise new ethical questions of use, access, and distribution. Information can be stolen and used without the knowledge of the previous possessor. How to locate missing and partial information may be different when the system, the copies, and the "original" are all computer based. When accessing a series of paper files, what is physically present is obvious, unless major misfiling is involved. This is not true in electronic systems, and hidden files are accessible only by skilled computer users. It is more difficult to identify what is missing, and information can vanish (via copying) without a trace.

Comment

Fieldwork requires primary and secondary access, and some types of access are more troubling and will be negotiated more than others. Fieldwork requires diligence and open-mindedness. The shifting mandate of a project will move people in various directions, but research should always be guided by centered and peripheral concerns, i.e., the purpose of the research and the questions posed as well as the epistemological assumptions of gathering and seeking to access data. In addition, as every good research paper should state, pursuing access to new areas will produce the need for more research.

See Also the Following Articles

Field Experimentation • Units of Analysis

Further Reading

Becker, H. S. (2001). The epistemology of qualitative research. In *Contemporary Field Research* (R. Emerson, ed.), pp. 317–330. Waveland Press, Prospect Heights, IL.

Berreman, G. (1962). *Behind Many Masks.* Monograph 4. Society for Applied Anthropology, Chicago.

Dalton, M. (1962). *Men Who Manage.* John Wiley, New York.

Decker, S. (ed.) (2003). *Policing Gangs and Youth Violence*. Wadsworth, Belmont, California.

Denzin, N., and Lincoln, Y. (eds.) (1994). *Handbook of Qualitative Research*. Sage, Thousand Oaks, CA.

Douglas, J. (1976). *Investigative Social Research*. Sage, Beverly Hills.

Emerson, R. (ed.) (2001). *Contemporary Field Research*, 2nd Ed. Waveland Press, Prospect Heights.

Erickson, K., and Stull, D. (1998). *Doing Team Ethnography*. Sage, Newbury Park, CA.

Festinger, L., Reicken, H., and Schacter, S. (1956). *When Prophecy Fails*. Harper and Row, New York.

Goffman, E. (1959). *Presentation of Self in Everyday Life*. Doubleday Anchor, Garden City.

Gusfield, J. (1955). Fieldwork reciprocities in studying a social movement. *Human Org* **14**, 29–33.

Hobbs, D. (1988). *Doing the Business*. Oxford University Press, Oxford.

Holdaway, S. (1983). *Inside Police Work*. Blackwell, Oxford.

Horowitz, I. L. (1967). *Project Camelot*. MIT Press, Cambridge, MA.

Leo, R. (1995). Trial and tribulation. *Am. Sociol.* **26,** 113–124.

Lofland, J. (1966). *Doomsday Cult*. Prentice Hall, Englewood Cliffs, NJ.

Malinowski, B. (1922). *Argonauts of the Western Pacific*. Routledge, London.

Manning, P. K. (1972). Observing the police. In *Observing Deviance* (J. Douglas, ed.), pp. 213–268. Random House, New York.

Manning, P. K. (1980). *Narcs' Game*. MIT Press, Cambridge, MA.

Manning, P. K. (1997). *Police Work*, 2nd Ed. Waveland Press, Prospect Heights, IL.

Mastrofski, S., Parks, R., and Worden, R. (1998). *Community Policing in Action: Lessons from an Observational Study*. Community Oriented Police Services Agency, Washington, D.C.

McCall, G., and Simmons, J. L. (eds.) (1969). *Issues in Participant Observation*. Addison-Wesley, Reading, MA.

Rappaport, R. (1984). *Pigs for the Ancestors,* 2nd Ed. Yale University Press, New Haven.

Roy, D. (1952). Quota restriction and gold-bricking in a machine shop. *Am. J. Sociol.* **57,** 427–442.

Roy, D. (1954). Efficiency and 'the fix': Informal intergroup relations in a machine shop. *Am. J. Sociol.* **60,** 255–266.

Sanchez-Jankowski, M. (1991). *Islands in the Street*. University of California Press, Berkeley, CA.

Scarce, R. (1994). (Not) trial and tribulation. *J. Contemp. Ethnogr.* **23,** 49–123.

Staples, W. (1996). *The Culture of Surveillance*. St. Martin's, New York.

Tierney, P. (2001). *Darkness in El Dorado: How Scientists and Journalists Devastated the Amazon*. W. W. Norton, New York.

Useem, M. (1984). *The Inner Circle*. Basic Books, New York.

Useem, M. (1996). *Investor Capitalism*. Basic Books, New York.

Van Maanen, J. (1977). Watching the watchers. In *Policing: A View from the Streets* (P. Manning and J. Van Maanen, eds.), pp. 309–349. Goodyear, Los Angeles.

Van Maanen, J. (1988). *Tales of the Field*. University of Chicago Press, Chicago.

Van Maanen J. (1996). The smile factory. In *Sociology. Exploring the Architecture of Everyday Life Readings* (D. M. Newman and J. A. O'Brian, eds.), pp. 210–226. 5th Ed. Pine Forge Press Thousand Oaks, CA.

Warren, C., and Hackney, J. (2000). *Gender Issues in Field Research*. Sage, Thousand Oaks, CA.

Wax, R. (1971). *Doing Fieldwork: Warnings and Advice*. University of Chicago Press, Chicago.

Wright, R., and Decker, S. (1994). *Burglars on the Job*. Northeastern University Press, Boston.

Yablonsky, L. (1968). On crime, violence, LSD and legal immunity for social scientists. *Am. Sociol.* **3,** 148–149.

Young, M. (1991). *An Inside Job*. Clarendon Press, Oxford.

Accounting Measures

Michael Bromwich

London School of Economics and Political Science, London, United Kingdom

Glossary

accounting measurement converting physical numbers of items (such as physical quantities of sales and physical units of raw materials and components) into monetary amounts.

audit the validating of the financial reporting package and the confirmation that its contents comply with extant accounting regulations by independent qualified accountants.

free cash flow the amount of cash and financing available for future, as yet uncommitted activities.

intangible assets assets not having physical form.

internal goodwill the value of the firm over and above the total value of its net assets after deducting financing.

purchased goodwill the amount by which the price of an acquired firm exceeds its net asset value.

off-balance sheet not including some assets and liabilities in the balance sheet.

true and fair view an unbiased accounting representation of the economic situation of the business constrained by the accounting methods used.

working capital short-term assets net of short-term liabilities.

Accounting measurement has a wide range of uses both within and external to the organization. This article concentrates on external accounting measurement for profit-seeking enterprises. The theory underlying accounting and the regulation of published accounting reports has switched over time from seeking to provide information to help shareholders and creditors protect their investments to helping make investment decisions.

Introduction: Overview of the Scope of Accounting

Measurement using accounting methods is one of the oldest examples of measurement in society. Until the industrial revolution and the rise of corporations, accounting reports were a matter for organizations and especially groups of partners in commercial ventures. Here they served mainly to determine profits and their distribution as dividends. With the arrival of limited liability corporations, accounting was more regulated and aimed mainly at protecting the investment of widely based shareholders and creditors.

Generally, accounting seeks to provide measurement in quantitative and financial terms denominated in the appropriate monetary unit. Such measures may apply to projects, to parts of organizations, to nonprofit organizations, and to profit-seeking organizations. Accounting measurement may report on performance in a past period both for intraorganizational purposes, such as performance reporting on managers and on departments and divisions, and for reporting in the public domain to some or all of an organization's stakeholders. The annual financial accounting reports of companies quoted on stock exchanges provide a familiar example of a published accounting report concerning a past period. Accounting measurements may also be future-oriented, that is, quantifying future expectations in, for example, budgets and project appraisal. With future-related accounting, actual performance may be compared with plans as operations proceed. Accounting measurement is usually categorized into financial accounting and management accounting, though the two areas overlap. Other areas of accounting include auditing, taxation, and consultancy.

Financial and Management Accounting

Financial accounting incorporates accounting bookkeeping for past and actual transactions, often using highly sophisticated information systems, and external reporting of the results of a past period to stakeholders. Management accounting includes booking costs and revenues, the costing of products and sections of the organization, the developing and operating of management information systems including budgets and long-term plans, and measuring performance against these plans. The scope of accounting measurement is vast and seeking to explain accounting in nontechnical terms is space-consuming; therefore, the remainder of this article concentrates on external financial reporting, which is the accounting information most frequently used by investors, creditors, and many other accounting users.

In most commercially developed countries, the requirements for external financial reporting are strongly regulated either by law or by the private sector with legal support. Such regulation determines the financial statements that must be published, the items that must be disclosed, and the methods of measurement that must or may be used to "value" or measure (to be further discussed) accounting items. Such financial reports must be audited for, at least in companies quoted on stock exchanges by auditors external to the organization. The legislation that governs the creation and operations of large, noncorporate organizations generally requires that their published financial statements must also be audited, either by external auditors or by specially created auditing bodies, often in a way that also considers organizational effectiveness, efficiency, and economy (in what is called value for money auditing). The corporate reporting package, at least in some countries, includes reports on compliance with any corporate governance requirements.

In contrast, management accounting is a matter for the firm. Generally, there are no external requirements that are imposed in this area of accounting except that market regulators may impose such requirements, as may powerful contracting organizations, such as governments and local authorities. Much of the cost accounting area and, in some regimes, the reliability of management information will be subject to external audit but any internal audit by the organization is a matter for management.

The Use of Accounting Information by Social Scientists

Most analyses of industries and of economies refer to accounting profits, the asset bases of firms, and the financing of firms. Much work has, for example, been carried out investigating any relationship between accounting profits and asset levels with developments in the economy. Time series of published accounting information and cross-sectional information by firms and industries are available on very sophisticated databases, often with related information, such as stock prices. This allows many econometric studies to be carried out relatively easily. Examples of hypotheses that have been tested include regressing accounting profits on firm size, industry, technology, and firm type and testing the relation between accounting profits and innovation and market power. Regulators, especially in the United Kingdom, may seek to estimate whether accounting profits exhibit "above-normal" profits. Finance and accounting researchers have sought to determine any relationships between accounting information and stock prices. They have also sought to determine any information value that accounting information may have to, say, investors.

One important point for those who wish to use accounting information is that they are aware of the limitations of this information. External accounting does not provide anything like a stock market valuation for the firm and the release of some information is a matter for management; often, given information can be treated in a number of ways and some information can be released or smoothed over time. Similar firms might produce significantly different results in different countries under different accounting regimes.

The Financial Accounting Package

This section concentrates on the accounting requirements on profit-seeking enterprises. Generally acceptable accounting practices and principles (referred to as country GAAPs) differ fundamentally among countries reflecting, among other things, the country's history, its culture, its industrial organization, its financial and legal systems, its method of regulation of the financial system and of corporate governance, and its system for regulating accounting. Until the 1960s, GAAPs in most commercially developed countries consisted of either some fairly general laws and "best" accounting practice and the recommendations of the professional societies of accountants (for example, the United States and United Kingdom) or more detailed laws augmented by best practice and professional recommendations (France and Germany). Many financial crises in a number of countries led to the tightening of law and in some countries the setting up of bodies of accounting regulators to determine external accounting disclosure and valuation methods. In the face of continuing crises and the perceived softness and the vested interests of the regulators, these were given more power and more independence and especially in countries with law-based GAAP. These processes have been intensified following U.S. crises (such as Enron) in the early 2000s.

The importance of country GAAP, which incorporates any legal requirements and private sector regulations, called accounting standards, is that, at least, firms quoted on stock exchanges are generally required to follow them in preparing their accounting packages and generally the auditors must verify this. The most important GAAPs are that of the United States and that determined by the International Accounting Standards Board (IASB), which is composed of members from a number of leading commercial countries and which gains its authority from the willingness of most stock exchanges to accept accounting reports that confirm to their GAAP. The IASB accounting standards are or will be accepted in a number of countries for companies quoted on stock exchanges, including all those in the European Union by 2005.

This article is written from the perspective of U.K. GAAP (which is fairly similar to that of the IASB), which incorporates the accounting standards issued by the United Kingdom Accounting Standards Board (ASB) and which, with some exemptions, applies to all registered companies.

The Reporting Package

The reporting package in the United Kingdom and most other countries is the responsibility of the management of the firm. For details of current country GAAPs, see manuals issued by most large professional accountancy firms, for example, the 2003 manual by Wilson *et al*. The package shows comparative figures for the previous year and consists of the following elements:

The Financial Statements

The Profit-and-Loss or Income Statement for the Year This shows the revenues deriving from the firm's operations minus the cost of obtaining these revenues and the other costs of maintaining the business during the year, including interest on financing the business to obtain the profit (or earnings or income) for the year before tax. Other gains and losses not arising from operation may be added (or treated in the balance sheet). Finally, deducting tax and any planned dividends yields profits retained for the year, which can be used to finance future investments.

The Balance Sheet as at the End of the Year This contains two perspectives on the firm. First, it quantifies the firm's assets using a variety of valuation bases (see below) and second, it indicates how these assets are financed. The balance sheet normally commences with fixed assets: those held for long-term use in the business. These two major classes of fixed assets: (1) intangible assets, those with no physical form, such as patents, and (2) tangible assets. Both are shown gross and net of depreciation. Generally, net working capital (short-term assets less short-term liabilities) is then either added (if positive) or deducted (if negative), thereby yielding a measure of the firm's asset base. Deducting long-term financing (including a large variety of financial instruments) and other liabilities yields the accounting equity value in the business. Accounting equity can be analyzed into issued shares, retained profits, and reserves, which comprise either profits retained, sometimes for a specific use, or gains or losses not allowed to be or not normally included in the profit-and-loss account (for example, gains on revaluing assets to a market price as such gains have not yet been received as revenue in some form).

The Cash Flow Statement for the Year This shows the net inflow or outflow of cash during the year. It starts by showing the inflow from operations and cash from other activities including returns from investments and from financing the activities of others. From these cash inflows, cash outflows are deducted. Cash outflows could include taxation paid, interest payments, capital expenditure, the cost or receipts from acquisitions or disposals, and the payments of any dividends. The sum of inflows and outflows shows the net cash inflow or outflow during the year. The financing of this cash inflow is then shown. This financing may be long-term and may be the result of any change in the balance of current assets and current liabilities (where this change is positive, that is, where current assets exceed liabilities, this means less cash than otherwise is required to meet liabilities). The difference between the net cash flow and its financing shows the change in cash during the year. The cash flow statement allows a very important figure to be calculated: the free cash flow. This measures the firm's financial flexibility by showing any free cash remaining for further investment after allowing for all known investments and other uses of cash.

Other Items

A management review for the year (in the United Kingdom, this is called the Operating and Financial Review) applies only to quoted companies and is voluntary in the United Kingdom. This reviews current operating and financial developments and trends in these items and uncertainties that may affect the business. Additionally, for quoted companies, a corporate governance statement indicates how and to what degree the firm has complied with the corporate governance code.

All the financial figures in these statements are stated as certain amounts. Even where they can be regarded as averages, no standard deviations are given. This limits the statistical analysis that can be applied to the accounting reports of companies.

It is important to understand that the three financial statements are linked together in that the items in one statement are either derivable from one of the others or form inputs into one of the others and usually provide more details of an item in one of the other statements. Thus, profits for the year are derived in the income statement and form an entry into the balance sheet to increase the profits retained in past years. Costs incurred during the year provide another example. If paid by cash, they will affect the firm's cash flow statement and via this will change the cash balance shown in the balance sheet at the end of the year. If financed by credit and unpaid at the end of the year, this will be reflected in the amount of creditors shown in the balance sheet and any interest cost for the credit would be reflected in the income statement. This interrelationship between accounting items also indicates that the treatment of a given item must be consistent between statements.

Accounting Theory

Before examining the income statement and balance sheet in some detail and giving examples of some of the areas where care is required in interpreting their meaning, this article provides a theoretical background of accounting and briefly considers some controversies and difficulties.

Prior to the mid-1960s, accounting reports were not strongly regulated. The emphasis was on prudence (recognizing gains only when sure about them but recognizing all losses immediately and making allowances for likely future problems) and on conservatism (understate asset values and overestimate liabilities, thereby reducing the current value of the firm and current profits but increasing possible future profits). Such accounting results were seen as good for contracting purposes, which require as objective information as possible but were of little help for decision-making. The predominant accounting approach was to ensure that the revenues of any period were matched as best as possible with the costs of obtaining those revenues whenever these costs were incurred. This yields a reasonable picture of the profits earned in the period but at the expense of a balance sheet that may have little meaning (often being only collections of transactions that have not yet passed through the profit-and-loss account). In the United Kingdom, this meant that, generally, management were free to choose whatever accounting practices they wished and generally to disclose as little as they liked, subject to what was judged acceptable by the accountancy profession and the giving of a "true and fair" view. The latter is difficult to define and represents the exercise of professional judgment but relates to a reasonable representation of the economic situation of the corporation with the accounting model being used. This means there may be several degrees of freedom available in determining a true and fair view and there may be more than one true and fair view. Moreover, via conservatism and prudence, management were able to build up hidden reserves of profits in good times and release them in bad times (thus smoothing profits over time). It also meant that management, as might be expected, could choose accounting methods that favored them. Similar practices occurred in other countries. Many scandals attended this regime.

Since the 1990s, most of this accounting theory has been overthrown but the state of accounting theory is still substantially unsettled and, at least recently, the scandals have not gone away. Leading country regulators have opted for accounting that seeks to aid decision-makers, predominantly investors who are seen as wishing to value investment based on their future cash flows, their timing, and their risk. This is subject to only using reliable figures, which represent faithfully the item being measured without bias. With this view, all assets and liabilities should be defined ideally in terms of the contribution they make to corporate cash flows and ideally valued on this basis through generally either historical cost (the price when obtained) or the current market price. Given that accounting values individual assets and liabilities, it can, at best, provide only some information relevant to these issues. Many items that could be treated in the past as assets or liabilities must now be treated as expenses or gains of the year. The balance sheet is thus promoted to being the more important statement and the profit-and-loss account includes items not backed by transactions because changes in market prices are seen as producing gains or losses during the year. There is much debate over what items should be included in the balance sheet (for example, intangibles) and how assets should be valued. There is a strong drive to value all financial items at their market prices without similarly revaluing physical assets. The advantage of market prices is claimed to be that such prices are objective and not subject to managerial manipulation.

A major concern of modern theory is to stop managerial manipulation of earnings. Thus, prudence and conservatism, which allow income smoothing over periods, have been downgraded as accounting principles has the ability to make provisions for likely later costs, which can augment future profits when they are released as not needed. For example, the ability to make allowance for the cost of future enterprise restructuring has been substantially restricted in the United Kingdom and by IASB. The cost of this approach is that it might deny accounting report users information about managerial beliefs. The belief that management generally will exploit their greater knowledge for their own benefit is mainly anecdotal, although there is some empirical evidence and some current extreme examples. The ability and rationality of management in using this practice seem to be limited from an analytical perspective.

Another major controversy is whether regulation should be highly detailed (as in the United States) or based on general principles and the emphasis placed on the duty to give a true and fair view or a similar overriding objective. That in the United States companies are free to do anything that complies with the letter of the regulations (and are willing pay for advice as to how to honor the letter of regulations but not their spirit) has been argued to lay at the heart of some American financial scandals in the early 2000s. In contrast, similar things happen under other regimes and the more complex financial products that have become available need detailed rules under all accounting regimes.

Some Problems with Accounting

Space is not available to review the above accounting statements in detail. The aim is to briefly indicate some of the important contents of these statements and to give some indication of the flexibility available to management in accounting reports, which is important to understand if accounting figures are used in research and other studies.

Profit-and-Loss Account or Income Statement

The ability to recognize revenue in a given year may lead to over- or understating revenues, and therefore profits, and is being restricted by regulators. Examples of the overrecognition of revenues are the taking all revenues at the beginning of a long-term and complex contract, where, for example, a future warranty may have to be fulfilled or where later environmental clean-up work is required. Another example of the overrecognition of revenue is the recording of payments from "pseudo-independent" companies (as practiced by Enron).

Most costs in the profit-and-loss account will represent buying prices at the time of purchase, though the cost of any opening inventories used during the year may be calculated in a number of ways, which affects the costs charged to the year when items have been purchased at different prices. Depreciation represents an allocation of the cost of a long-lived asset to the year in mind. Ideally, such depreciation should reflect the loss of value of the asset in the year, but usually accounting depreciation follows an arbitrary formula of which a number are permissible, the use of which thereby generates different profits. Similarly, the cost of those intangible assets that are allowed to be incorporated into the accounts also may have to be spread over their lifetime on a reasonable basis. Provisions for future losses may also be spread over a number of years. The United Kingdom regulator and the IASB have restricted the ability to spread costs over years in order to avoid the possibility that management will use this facility to smooth profits (earnings) so that bad years are disguised using undeclared profits from better years. Such smoothing is argued to mislead investors and other users of accounts. There are some expenses that are "off" the profit-and-loss statement, as they have no obvious accounting cost, but clearly affect enterprise value. Stock options granted to employees may have this characteristic (being looked at by regulators) as may some financial instruments (again being looked at by regulators) and pension costs.

The Balance Sheet

This shows the details of the firm's assets, such as land, property, and equipment, and its liabilities in a logical sequence. An asset is an identifiable item that has been either acquired or constructed in-house in the past, is expected to yield future cash flows, and is in the control of the firm in the sense that the firm may decide whether and how to dispose of the asset or use it. The accounting approach to valuing items is a bottom-up approach with which each item is valued individually using a method appropriate to that item and these values are aggregated to obtain valuations for classes of assets and liabilities and overall asset and liability values that will generally incorporate different valuation bases for different classes of accounting items.

Intangible assets are expected to generate future cash flows but have no physical form, such as items of intellectual property, which include patents, licenses, trademarks, and purchased goodwill (the amount by which the price of an acquisition of a company exceeds the net value of all the other assets of the acquired company). Many intangibles obtained in an acquisition are allowed on the balance sheet valued at what is called their "fair value": what they would exchange for in an arm's length transaction by willing parties. Such fair values are not generally allowed to be changed to reflect changes in market prices over time. The inclusion of such intangibles is in contrast to the unwillingness to extend this treatment to either internally generated goodwill, which reflects the firm's value-added operations, or internally created intangible assets, such as brands. Often in a modern, growing, high-tech firm, the values of such intangible assets may dominate physical assets. The possibilities for inclusion would be very large, including self-created brands, information technology systems, customer databases, and a trained work force. Generally, regulators have resisted attempts to treat such items as assets. Proponents of inclusion argue that this means that many of the sources of company value go unrecognized in the accounts and must be treated as costs in the year incurred. It is argued that this is one reason the accounting value of firms may fall far below their stock exchange values, especially for high-tech companies and companies in a growth phase. This is true even today; compare the accounting and stock market values of Microsoft. This makes empirical work with accounting numbers very difficult. Where intangibles are important in such exercises, they must be estimated separately.

The value of an asset is either based on its original cost or in most accounting regimes, including the United Kingdom but not the United States, based on a revalued amount taking into account changes in prices over time. Any gains on holding assets increase the value of the firm in its balance sheet and not its operating profit, though such gains or losses are shown elsewhere in the profit-and-loss statement. Firms do not have to revalue assets and many firms may use different valuation bases for different asset classes. Any revaluation must be based on independent expert authority and such independent assessments must be obtained regularly. By not revaluing assets in the face of favorable price changes, firms build up hidden reserves of profits realized when the asset is sold or when used in production. Accounting regulators have acted to stop asset overvaluation by making assets subject to a test that their values in the accounts do not exceed either their selling value (which may be very low where assets are specific to the firm) or their value when used by the firm (an estimate by management that may be highly subjective).

It is generally agreed for useful empirical work that assets must be restated at their current market prices minus adjustments for existing depreciation and the assets' technologies relative to that currently available on the market. One example of the use of current cost is in calculating what is called Tobin's Q, the ratio between the firm's stock market value and the current cost of its net assets. One use of Tobin's Q is to argue that firms with a Q ratio of greater than 1 are making, at least temporarily, superprofits.

During the inflationary period of the mid-1970s to early 1980s, most leading accounting regimes allowed at least supplementary disclosure of generally reduced profits after allowing for current cost (adjusted replacement cost) depreciation and a balance sheet based on the increased current cost of assets. This movement fizzled out with the decline in inflation, the lack of recognition of current cost profits by tax authorities, managerial unhappiness with the generally lower profits disclosed by this type of accounting, and the need to maintain the current value of existing assets. More traditional accountants also argued that the revaluing of assets meant that profits would be reported (as an increase in the firm's value in the balance sheet) on revaluation and not when profits were realized either by use or by sale. Despite this, many experts believe that it is the intention of some accounting regulators (ASB and IASB) to move toward current cost accounting.

Regulators in most countries have acted and are planning to act further on off-balance items. Leased operating assets, such as airplanes, ships, and car fleets, do not have to appear on the balance sheet and only the annual cost of such leasing appears in the income statement. This understates the firm's capital employed often by vast amounts and thereby inflates returns on investment. This is planned to change shortly. Other ways of maintaining assets on the off-balance sheet include setting up a supposedly independent entity that owns the assets and charges the "parent" firm for their use. Similar approaches are available to keep debt and other financial liabilities out of the financial statements.

The treatment of financial assets (those denominated in monetary terms, which include financial instruments) differs between accounting regimes and classes of financial assets. Long-term loans to and investments in other companies not held for sale are generally shown at their original cost. Most other financial assets and liabilities are usually valued at their market prices, with gains and losses usually going to the balance sheet until realized by sale. Almost all regulators are agreed that all financial assets and liabilities should be shown at their market prices or estimated market prices, where such prices do not exist, which is the case for complex financial instruments (including many derivatives). Any gains and losses would go to the profit-and-loss account. Using market prices means that there will be no need for what is called "hedge accounting." This accounting means that investments to cover other risks in the firm are kept at their original cost until the event that gives rise to the risk occurs, thereby hiding any gains or losses on the hedges. The aim is to let accounting "tell it as it is," under the view that market prices give the best unbiased view of what financial items are worth. There are problems here. The approach treats some financial items differently than other items, such as physical assets and intangibles; it records gains and losses before they are realized by sale or by use, whereas this not allowed for other items; and it abandons to a degree the prudence and matching concepts and, perforce, often uses managerial estimates for complex items not traded on a good market, which conflicts with the wish of regulators to minimize managerial discretion.

Conclusion

Overall, financial reports have changed enormously over, say, the past 20 years and greater changes can be expected but care still must be taken when using accounting measurements. There is still conflict between seeking to provide reliable information and information useful for decision-making. The valuation (measurement) bases used for different items still differ. Some liabilities and many assets (especially intangibles) are not included in the balance sheet. Income is moving toward recognizing gains/losses in market prices rather than basing these on transactions. With restrictions on smoothing results, management must find other means to share their information with accounting reports users.

Accounting measurement in published financial reports seeks to be objective within its own terms and is validated in this sense by independent observers. It has the great advantage over many other measurement systems that accounting results measured at any level of the organization can be added up to give an overall view. As the measure is in financial terms, costs are automatically traded off from benefits. Thus, accounting allows the performance of areas of the corporation to be aggregated. This in contrast to other measurement systems, which measure items independently and cannot add these together because the trade-off between items cannot be easily determined other than by judgment. In contrast, published accounting reports do not provide the detailed targets common with other measurement systems, such as performance measurement systems including those that form part of management accounting. It is up to the user of accounting reports to determine the targets that they wish to use, though the literature contains much guidance.

See Also the Following Articles

Business, Social Science Methods Used in • Critical Views of Performance Measurement • History of Business Performance Measurement

Further Reading

Benston, G., Bromwich, M., Litan, R. E., and Wagenhofer, A. (2003). *Following the Money: The Enron Failure and the State of Corporate Disclosure.* AEI–Brookings Joint Center for Regulatory Studies, Washington, DC.

De Roover, R. (1956). . *The Development of Accounting Prior to Luca Pacioli According to the Account-Books of Medieval Merchants, in Studies in the History of Accounting,"* (A. C. Littleton and B. S. Yamey, eds.), pp. 114–174. Sweet and Maxwell, London.

Lewis, R., and Pendrill, (2000). *Advanced Financial Accounting.* Pitman, London.

Penman, S. H. (2001). *Financial Statement Analysis and Security Valuation.* McGraw-Hill, New York.

Wilson, A., Davies, M., Curtis, M., and Wilkinson-Riddle, G. *UK and International GAAP: Generally Accepted Accounting Practice in the United Kingdom and under International Accounting Standards.* Tolley, London.

Whittington, G. (1983). *Inflation Accounting: An Introduction to the Debate.* Cambridge University Press, Cambridge, UK.

Administrative Records Research

Dean H. Judson
U.S. Census Bureau, Washington, D.C., USA

Carole L. Popoff
U.S. Census Bureau, Washington, D.C., USA

Glossary

administrative record Data collected for an administrative purpose, as opposed to a formal research data collection effort.

coverage bias The systematic difference between the database and the population of interest.

database ontology The definition of objects that are in a database (e.g., What is a business entity? Do sole proprietors count as business entities? What is an address? Is a person living in the basement at the same address or a different address?) and the categories that are used in the database (e.g., Does race have three, five, eight, or sixty-three categories?).

microdata Information about individual persons, families, households, addresses, or similar objects, as opposed to tabulations or aggregate data.

reporting lag The systematic tendency of administrative records data to be reported in a time frame that is "behind" the actual behavior of interest. For example, a person may change addresses in one year, but that move may not be recorded in the administrative database until a later year.

response bias The systematic tendency of respondents or data collectors to respond in systematic ways that are different than the ontology intended or what was understood by the researcher.

Research with administrative records data is similar in some ways to more traditional forms of research, such as sample surveying, but it differs in several important respects. In particular, the data collection effort is not designed by the researcher, and so the researcher is "at the mercy" of the administrative agency; typically there is no sampling scheme (so that sampling variances are not easy to calculate), and there are systematic response biases and coverage biases in the data that are caused by the administrative agency and their client base. An important concept in the use of administrative data is that of a database ontology, or the structure of the objects in the database and how data on those objects is collected—in particular, a database ontology that is perfectly suitable for the administrative agency may not be at all suitable for the researcher. In such cases, the researcher can sometimes estimate coverage biases or translate data from one ontology to another; but always with care.

What are Administrative Records?

Administrative records data are typically defined (1) as being collected as a result of legal or regulatory requirements or transactions, (2) as being a result of program operations rather than intentional research data collection, and (3) as being collected without regard to their potential multiple analytic uses. Administrative records databases represent a huge potential source of data, and research into their use has exploded with the advent of inexpensive electronic storage and processing.

Two errors might be made when researchers are faced with these large, challenging databases, especially those with data problems spread throughout. The first error is simply to assume that the databases are wrong. The second mistake, made because administrative records are official, is to assume automatically that they are correct. Both assumptions are errors. The superior view is to envision a constantly changing population of interest that the database is trying to "keep up" with, "slippage" (of coverage and of individual data collection) constantly occurring; thus, a model of the relationship between the "real world" and the database is necessary.

How are Administrative Records Data Generated?

Administrative records are both the same as and different from other forms of collected data. All of the same biases occur in administrative records that might occur even in carefully controlled research data collection; however, administrative records are characterized by some additional biases that are exacerbated by the context in which data collection occurs. Thus, it is appropriate to deal with administrative records (e.g., assessor's records) and mixed administrative/research data (e.g., census forms, traffic count data), and not with secondary data generally. It is the widespread and growing use of such administrative data sets that creates this concern and focus.

Administrative records data can be generated by an agency responsible for administering a program (for example, unemployment insurance or food stamps). Similarly, administrative records data can be generated as a "side effect" of business operations (for example, address lists and sales data for a retail bookseller). Finally, administrative records data may be generated by "respondents" (for example, when a small business becomes incorporated). All of these operations generate data that can be used for analytic purposes. In no case was the data collection "planned" for research purposes—its primary purpose was different.

Figure 1 illustrates the creation, use, and potential errors in an administrative records data set. A record begins as an event or an object in the "real world" outside the database. Some of these events and objects are actually identified (note also that some are there, but do not get identified) as observed events and objects. Some of these observed events and objects get recorded (again, some do not) and become part of the administrative record. These are then arranged in some form of database. Later, when the analyst approaches these records, he or she develops analyses ("queries" in the language of databases) and makes presentation of the results.

At each step in this process, there is potential for error or misinterpretation. At the event/object level, policy changes can change the definition of an event or object (as when the program Aid to Families with Dependent Children ceased to exist, or when a mobile home is recoded from "real" property to "personal" property). As events and objects become observed, the "ontologies" (described in more detail later) that observers use to categorize the world enter in; likewise, some events and objects do not reach a threshold for official notice (as in the deviance literature, wherein the "officer on the beat" makes the call whether to identify an event as a problem or not). Some of those observed events become recorded, and there is potential for data entry errors and limitations of coding schemes for mapping the real-world events into their database representations. As data are moved from place to place in computer systems, data management problems (corruption in transit, changes in formatting, etc.) potentially arise. Finally, as the analyst uses queries of various kinds to extract data, he or she may discover that the query is either syntactically incorrect in a nonobvious way, or that the query generates results, of which the structure is spurious.

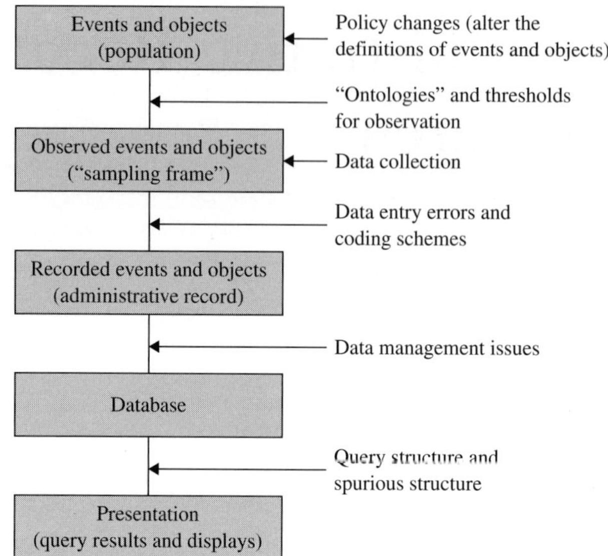

Figure 1 How administrative records data are created and used, and sources of error.

Where do We Find Administrative Records Data?

Typically, "administrative records" is a public sector term. In the private sector, transactions data are typically collected in "data warehouses" and are used for business-related analytic purposes. Both kinds of databases satisfy the preceding definition.

Private Sector Databases

A tremendous variety of business mechanisms generate data that are used by private sector firms for analytic purposes. The credit records that make up individual credit reports and ratings are the most telling example of business records. As an example of the use of these data in a context completely outside their original purpose, these credit records have been used to make small area population estimates. As a further example, consider customers' sales records. Businesses keep a database on customer buying habits; the customer data are then linked with external demographic or similar data about those same customers. Using the linked database, a firm can begin to make inferences about which kinds of customers will exhibit which kinds of buying habits.

As a final example, consider medical records. By linking medical records to demographic data obtained from a client, or by linking recorded mortality information to survey data, inferences can be made about the mortality history of certain kinds of survey respondents, or about how certain medical procedures lead to later outcomes.

Public Sector Databases

The public sector is a substantial generator of administrative data. For example, vital records (births, deaths, marriages), although of important civil use, are also very important sources of demographic information for the construction of fertility information, actuarial life tables, and the like. Tax assessor records can be used to augment other address list construction (such as the Census Bureau's Master Address File), or can be used directly to develop housing-unit-based population estimates. Unemployment insurance records are used for evaluating job-training programs, as benchmarks for survey data collected from business establishments, and as sample frames for business surveys.

At the federal level, Internal Revenue Service data collection is used to produce public use data such as the Statistics on Income. But it is also used as a comparison for survey reports of income, for small area income and poverty estimates, for net migration calculations, and for modeling the effects of welfare reform efforts.

How are Administrative Records Data Similar to Other Social Science Data?

Administrative records data are typically most similar to survey data or to secondary data analyses. It is a rare occasion when administrative data approach experimental data. Even some measurements that appear objective (e.g., diagnostic information or demographic information) can be affected by the data collector's motives. In survey research, the researcher would care about respondent's motives (for example, social desirability bias), but even though the respondent does not write a single thing on a survey form, the data collector also has motives and biases.

Administrative records data are similar to other social science data in that the unit of analysis varies across data collection needs. The term "unit of collection" is used here for the administrative unit; for research purposes, the "unit of analysis" might be something different than the unit of collection. That is, the unit of collection in an administrative database might be a person, a family, or a household, establishment, or firm. However, the unit of analysis for the researcher might be something entirely different from the unit of collection. For example, the Social Security Administration (SSA) maintains a file, the Numerical Identification (Numident) file, that is transaction based; every time a person interacts with the SSA, a new transaction record is generated. But if the researcher wishes to analyze the characteristics of persons, the researcher must somehow translate from transactions to people. As an example of translation problems, about 25% of the persons in the Numident file have transactions with different race codes, because race definitions (both official definitions and self-definitions) have changed over time. Similar variations occur in other codes (for example, gender codes change over time), and it is often not clear which transaction code is "better" for the researcher's purpose. Similarly, Internal Revenue Service 1040 forms have been proposed as a mechanism by which the U.S. population can be enumerated in lieu of a census. However, a Tax Filing Unit (the basic "object" of the 1040 form) is not a housing unit, nor is it necessarily a family, and, further, an address that might be perfectly suitable for interacting with the tax system could be entirely unsuitable for enumeration purposes (e.g., a post office box).

Administrative records data are also similar to other social science data in that, typically, the source agency has its own targeted or defined population of interest. However, again, the researcher must be careful to determine that the source agency's definition of population of interest is close enough to the researcher's population of interest to be useful. Figure 2 illustrates the problem for two examples: On the left is an attempt to capture the resident population of the United States (for example, in the Numident file); on the right is an attempt to capture all employees who work at a particular company (for example, in a company employee database).

Finally, administrative records data are similar to other social science data in that there is an important distinction between cross-sectional versus longitudinal data collection. Certain databases (for example, Internal Revenue Service 1040 forms) are necessarily cross-sectional in some aspects (e.g., number of dependents), and necessarily longitudinal in others (e.g., depreciation of capital assets). But the data collection effort is primarily cross-sectional. In contrast, the maintenance of unemployment insurance wage records (by state Employment Security agencies) is necessarily primarily longitudinal; in order to calculate unemployment insurance benefits, it is necessary to have a "wage history" for the unemployment insurance applicant. The researcher, when using administrative data, must be very careful to ascertain its nature

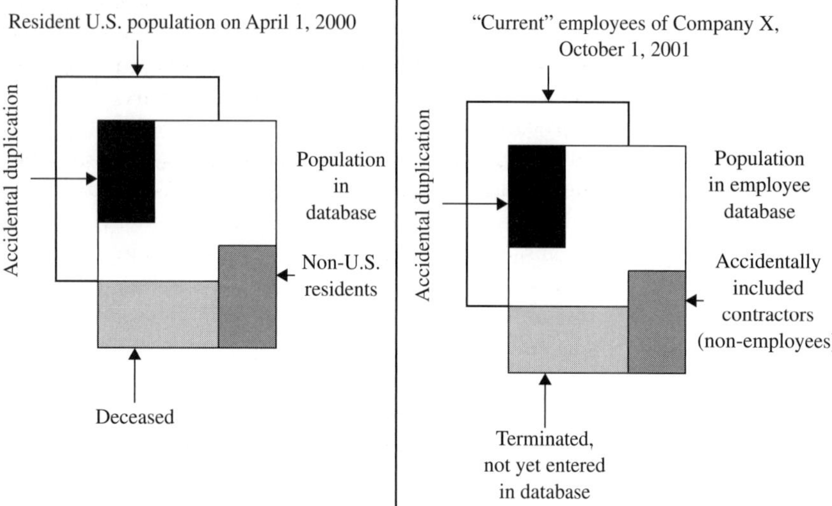

Figure 2 Illustration of coverage differentials between the database and the population of interest.

in this regard, and, of course, the researcher is completely dependent on the administrative agency's definitions.

How are Administrative Records Data Different from Other Social Science Data?

The most important distinction of administrative records data from other kinds of social science data is that the data collection mechanism is not designed by the researcher who wishes to use the data—or by any researcher at all, in most instances. This means that the researcher must become intimately familiar with the program so as to understand the coverage of the data file, unit and item nonresponse patterns in the data, and any response biases that might be present in the data. Furthermore, often there is little the researcher can do to influence the timing and often the format of data receipt.

The second distinction is related to the first: the first or primary goal of the data collected is not research. This means that the usual quality control checks that are usually put in place with the best research data collection are not necessarily in place for the administrative data. There is considerable evidence that, if a particular field is "important" to the administrative agency (either because it ties directly to the agency's funding or to its provision of services), then that field will likely be recorded with some care and some quality control. But if the field is an "add on" or is otherwise superfluous to the agency's mission, it should be used with caution because it is often neglected. (A water company economist's remark is illustrative: "I have 20 years of household level water consumption data ... all entered by people who didn't care.")

A third distinction of administrative records from research data collection is that typically there are no sampling or randomization procedures applied, and therefore statistical techniques that assume such procedures are not strictly appropriate. So, for example, because the administrative database is not a "sample" from any particular "population," it is generally not possible to estimate sampling variances for statistical tests. If the database contains groups that the researcher wishes to compare (for example, a group that received a special program or treatment and a group that did not), then the researcher most emphatically cannot assume that cases were assigned at random to the treatment and control groups.

Finally, administrative records data have systematic coverage and response biases that research databases usually attempt to address or correct. For example, in the Internal Revenue Service's 1040 Master File, families whose income does not reach the filing threshold are not required to file at all, and hence are systematically undercovered in the database. Care must be taken in using the database; for example, in one study, it was discovered that the systematic undercoverage had noticeable and systematic effects on the county-level population estimation method that used the 1040 database for net migration calculations. Similarly, systematic race response trends have been discovered in Census files; for example, between 1990 and 2000, the number of persons of "American Indian" race increased in far greater numbers than could be accounted for by natural increase. This suggested that people became more willing to indicate "American Indian" heritage in 2000.

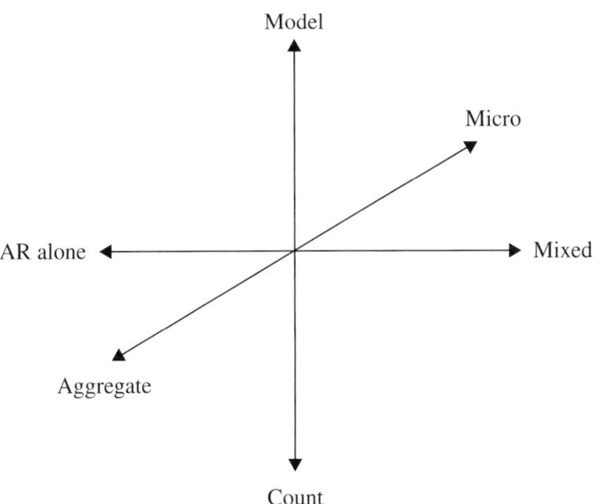

Figure 3 A diagram illustrating the strategic dimensions for using administrative records (AR) effectively.

How can Administrative Records Data be Used Effectively in Social Science?

A plethora of researchers and program evaluators have attempted to test and use administrative records. When deciding to use such a database, it is important to remain clear about how the data are to be used. Figure 3 illustrates strategic dimensions. The representation is as dimensions rather than categories because different approaches use more or less of each strategy, and there is not a clear demarcation between strategies. The vertical dimension is "count-based" versus "model-based" use. In the count-based approach, the administrative data are generally taken as a direct indicator of the phenomenon of interest. In the model-based approach, the administrative record (AR) is used as an indicator or predictor of the events of interest, so a measurement error model or a model in which the administrative data are "auxiliary variables" is more appropriate. The horizontal dimension is using administrative records "alone" or in combination with other data, or "mixed." This dimension represents the degree of mixing, calibration, or use of multiple data sources with the administrative database. The third dimension is using aggregate tabular data (e.g., counts of Medicare recipients by county) versus using microdata referring to individual records (e.g., individual Medicare recipient data).

Historically, approaches tended to be count based, AR alone, and aggregate in nature. In more modern uses, analysts have tended toward model-based, mixed data, whereby individual microdata records are put to use. A first major count-based/AR alone/micro use of administrative records is program evaluation. In the 1990s, when the Job Training Partnership Administration used performance measures to evaluate job training outcomes, unemployment insurance (UI) wage records were proposed as an alternative to a 13-week follow-up survey, and certain states determined to use UI records for performance measurement. A similar measure has been proposed for block grant evaluations under welfare reform. The immediate research question emerges: Do these different outcome measures paint the same basic picture? Can they be used interchangeably? The answer is in part "yes" and "no": although the overall pattern of outcome measures is similar for the two data sources, there are significant "slippages" in which data captured by one source are not captured by the other. A similar requirement is the required reporting under the Community Reinvestment Act (CRA) of 1977. CRA requires that each insured depository institution's record in helping to meet the credit needs of its community, especially including low-income neighborhoods, be assessed periodically by examining bank operating data on persons who receive loans.

A second major count-based/AR alone/aggregate use of administrative records data is in benchmarking other kinds of data collection or estimates. For example, the Current Employment Statistics (CES) program is a survey of establishments, with the intention of providing current information about the number of jobs in various industries. Later, when the Unemployment Insurance wage records files are complete, these CES statistics are then "benchmarked" to the UI wage records and adjusted to account for coverage differentials. A second example of benchmarking would be comparisons of survey-based or demographic estimates of phenomena (such as food stamp receipt or levels of Medicaid insurance coverage) with independent calculations of food stamp distribution or of Medicaid client data.

A third, major user of aggregate/mixed administrative records (with both count and model aspects) is the Bureau of Economic Analysis (BEA), which produces the National Income and Product Accounts (NIPA). These are the sum of all output or expenditures, or the sum of income or payments to business, government, and individuals. In a simplifying assumption, over a given period of time, one must equal the other. Expenditures (or output) are measured by the value or final price of the nation's output of goods and services or Gross Domestic Product (GDP). National Income (NI) is simply GDP minus depreciation and consumption allowances. Personal Income (PI) is NI minus indirect business taxes and other adjustments. As such, PI is composed of payments to individuals in the form of wages and salaries (including personal income taxes and nontax payments net of social insurance payments) plus income from interest, dividends, and rent, plus transfer payments (private and public).

Data for NIPA estimates come primarily from administrative records and economic census data. The census data used are primarily state estimates from the census of agriculture and the census of population and housing. The administrative records used include those originating with the income recipients or from the source, which are a by-product of the administration of various federal and state programs. The most important of these agencies include the U.S. Department of Labor, the social insurance programs of the Social Security Administration and the Health Care Financing Administration, the U.S. Department of Health and Human Services, the federal income tax program of the Internal Revenue Service, the U.S. Department of the Treasury, the veterans' benefit programs of the U.S. Department of Veterans Affairs, and the military payroll systems of the U.S. Department of Defense. The Bureau of Economic Analysis has noted that there is a trade-off to using these data—namely, the cost of collection to businesses and households is low; however, the data do not precisely "match" the series that is being estimated, thus there are adjustments made to compensate for differences in coverage, geographic detail, and definitions. Thus, although this approach is primarily count based, it does incorporate some modeling and adjustment.

A fourth major micro/AR alone/count use of administrative records data is in list construction for surveys and other frames. Two very important examples are the U.S. Census Bureau's Master Address File (MAF) and the Standard Statistical Establishment List (SSEL; now known as the Business Register). The MAF obviously serves as the frame for a decennial census and for the nascent American Community Survey. It is updated on a quarterly basis by the U.S. Postal Service's Delivery Sequence File (DSF). The Standard Statistical Establishment List is a list of all business establishments having one or more employees, including selected data such as name, address, employment size, payroll, Standard Industrial Classification code, etc. It serves as a frame for economic censuses. Prior to the 1997 census, The Census Bureau used administrative records from various federal agencies [primarily the Internal Revenue Service (IRS), the Social Security Administration (SSA), and the Bureau of Labor Statistics] to update the SSEL. Although the MAF and SSEL databases are mixed, the source files used in this example for updating them are pure administrative records sources.

A fifth major example of use of administrative records is in population accounting and similar estimates. The earliest demographic analyses of mortality by Graunt in 1662 were performed using a database of birth and death records obtained from parish registers. (Interestingly, the issues Graunt considered in his work, notably, confidentiality of the data and significant questions about data definitions and quality, are still current and highly relevant.) In evaluating coverage of a decennial census, a standard tool known as "demographic analysis" is used. Demographic analysis is an aggregate/AR (almost) alone/count approach to population accounting, whereby aggregates are generated from administrative data on births, deaths, immigration, and Medicare enrollment, combined with estimates of emigration and undocumented immigration, to generate a "hard" population estimate. A similar, but microoriented, approach was used in the Administrative Records Experiment in 2000 (AREX 2000), when administrative microdata (individual person, household, and address records) were combined, unduplicated, and allocated geographically to census blocks, generating a low-level "snapshot" of the population in a simulated Administrative Records Census. Finally, the U.S. Census Bureau's postcensal county total population estmates program uses administrative records data for virtually all components of the population estimate. A few similar efforts using private sector credit rating databases have emerged, in which the credit database was used to generate a small area estimate as a "what if" scenario.

Moving away from aggregate/AR alone/count-based uses, it is possible to see much more use of statistical modeling tools. A major example of the use of administrative data in aggregate/mixed/model-based fashion is the U.S. Census Bureau's Small Area Income and Poverty Estimates (SAIPE) program, and related small area estimates. The SAIPE program is tasked with developing estimates of persons in poverty, children in poverty, and median income levels for U.S. counties and areas as small as school districts, for funding allocation purposes. Instead of using administrative data (such as numbers of food stamp recipients) directly in the estimates, these data (and Internal Revenue Service data) are used as predictor variables in a statistical model that combines direct survey-based estimates with model-based estimates in an empirical Bayes framework. Other small area estimation techniques have proposed and/or used administrative data in a similar fashion (as "auxiliary variables" in the model rather than as "direct counts"). Similarly, administrative data have been used as a third source in a multiple-system estimate of population size.

An early example of aggregate/mixed/count- and model-based use is the Local Area Unemployment Statistics (LAUS) program by the Bureau of Labor Statistics, which generates estimates of employment and unemployment for counties. The LAUS program uses unemployment insurance claims in concert with state-level unemployment estimates from the Current Population Survey to generate these estimates. In this case, the estimate is not strictly count based, nor is it strictly model based. Instead, the Current Population Survey generates a number of employed and unemployed persons at the state level, and this number is "distributed" to counties using unemployment insurance claims in those counties (the "population-claims" method). This general approach, "distributing" a direct estimate using administrative data, appears to have great promise.

A second example of aggregate/mixed (and mostly count-based) use is actuarial life table construction. In order to construct a typical period life table, an age-specific death rate is calculated. Typically, this uses three years of administrative data on deaths, bracketing a census year. These counts are averaged and these deaths are taken as the numerator, with the census midyear population as the denominator, in the calculation of the age-specific death rate.

As the move into modern use of administrative data progresses, researchers have shown more interest in, and seen promise in, linked microdata. In these analyses, individual person, household, or address records are linked to a comparable administrative data source. This linkage has been used for comparisons of survey responses with administrative data. It has also been used for analyses of greater historical scope; for example, the National Longitudinal Mortality Survey links microdata from the Current Population Survey (CPS) to death microdata, in order to make inferences of mortality differentials from CPS characteristics.

A suite of models in use at the U.S. Census Bureau serves as an illustration of the power of linked microdata combined with statistical modeling. The race model estimates the race and ethnic origin of Social Security Number (SSN) holders on the Numident file. The model was needed because the Numident did not categorize race according to Census definitions, and the model effectively estimates what a Numident respondent would have said if their race were recorded using Census definitions. A gender model, similarly developed, estimates the gender of SSN records that do not have a gender recorded (about 6% of the Numident); this model uses first-name sex ratios and name-change flags to predict gender. Finally, a mortality model estimates the probability that a person in the Numident file is deceased, when they are not recorded as deceased on the file. The mortality model uses cohort life tables combined with Numident and other microdata to make this estimate.

What are the Major Strengths and Weaknesses in Using Administrative Records Data?

Strengths

The first major strength of administrative records databases in general is their broad coverage. It is erroneous to assume that the database represents the entire population, as is sometimes asserted (without proof), but nonetheless typically the administrative records database covers more of the population of interest than does a comparable sample survey. A second strength of administrative records databases is that, typically, the data collection is repeated on a regular basis, as, for example, the Medicare Enrollment Database collects data on new recipients over time. This is a significant advantage for longitudinal analyses. In the performance measurement use of administrative data, such repeatability means that follow-up on job-training clients can take place much later, chronologically, than would be feasible with follow-up or follow-along surveys.

A third strength of administrative records databases is that, again typically, the data collection is continued over relatively long time frames, as, for example, the Social Security Numident file covers essentially every transaction on every Social Security Number since the program's inception (ignoring the relatively minor "coverage error" caused by the transition from a paper to an electronic system). This has been used to advantage in analyses that compare the Numident file to U.S. population estimates.

Weaknesses

The first, and major, weakness of administrative records comes under the heading of "data quality." Defining data quality is in itself a challenge. For example, what does it mean for a measured data element to be "right"? How "wrong" is "too wrong"? To illustrate with a simple example, involving a relatively simple element, consider race. Prior to 1980, the Social Security Administration recorded three races (White, Black, and Other or unknown); beginning in 1980, the race codes reflected five races (White, Black, Asian or Pacific Islander, Hispanic, American Indian or Eskimo), and included the codes for Other, Blank, and Unknown. At the same time, the U.S. Census Bureau collected race data using four races (White, Black, Asian or Pacific Islander, and American Indian), which were crossed with ethnicity (Hispanic or non-Hispanic). In Census 2000, an additional race was added (Hawaiian native) and a "mark all that apply" rule was applied, resulting in 63 possible combinations. Thus, if a researcher wishes to link SSA data with Census data, the differential recording of race over time would create substantial comparability problems, but who can say which coding scheme is right?

Every preceding comment can be echoed about every conceivable data element, and the analyst must firmly keep in mind that social definitions and the uses of a database are changing, and that when a coder (either agency personnel or an individual respondent) does not have the categories that are appropriately descriptive, they will most likely choose the best fitting. Choosing the "best fitting" response, rather than choosing the "right" one, is constructing social reality, not necessarily reflecting it. Because even the simplest data elements run into definitional questions, it follows that the notion of "data quality" must follow from what database experts refer to as an ontology. At its basic level, the branch of philosophy known as ontology is the study of what is—the nature of reality. For a computer database expert, an ontology is a method for encoding the real world in a computer representation. For the analyst of administrative data, differing database ontologies are the primary challenge to proper use.

A second weakness of administrative data is timing of data receipt, especially time lag between the population of interest and delivery of a usable database. Sometimes these time lags are structural in nature; obviously, a database of wage records for a particular year requires that the calendar year is complete and also that all firms have completed reporting their wage records to the state employment security agency. Sometimes these lags are definitional; for example, a child born after December 31 of a calendar year cannot, by definition, be counted as a dependent on the tax return for that calendar year, and thus will not be recorded. Some lags are caused by limited updating of the database; for example, if a person who has a driver's license dies, that death information is typically not returned to the motor vehicle agency, resulting in systematic overcoverage of older persons.

A third weakness of administrative records data is the requirement for record linkage across databases, with the attendant potential for linkage error, both false links and false nonlinks. If the databases contain unique identifiers, such as a Social Security Number, the linkage is easier, but, even so, some studies have found that 1 in 10 SSNs may be recorded in error in public databases. Without unique identifiers, linkage can still occur, but the problem is harder by several orders of magnitude.

A fourth weakness of administrative records databases can broadly be called coverage error, both in terms of net undercoverage, net overcoverage, and duplication within the database. As noted several times in this article, the population of interest is constantly moving, and the database attempts to keep up with the population, but with slippages. Obviously, some segments of society do not wish to be captured by administrative systems (e.g., undocumented and illegal immigrants, and dedicated criminals), and some persons remain in databases when they should be removed (e.g. émigrés and the deceased).

A final weakness of administrative records databases can broadly be called data limitations. First, administrative records databases often have a very limited scope of data collection, much more limited than a researcher would normally desire. Second, for some databases, missing data are ubiquitous (this is effectively the equivalent of survey item nonresponse, except that "missing at random" and similar assumptions rarely apply). Third, often administrative data are of limited quality or suffer from systematic bias, which affects their usefulness. Fourth, inconsistent data collection strategies and quality control across different agencies can create a situation wherein a field collected by one agency does not have the same meaning as the same field collected by a different agency. Finally, policy changes may change the definition of events and objects, and the researcher or analyst must be careful to interpret the new definition properly.

A Solution to Some Weaknesses

As more and more researchers and analysts analyze administrative records databases, and discover their strengths and weaknesses, some general frameworks for their use are emerging. Probably the most important technique is "calibration" to external data. The approach is illustrated in Fig. 4. For this illustration, imagine that the administrative records database [consisting of household (HH) characteristics] is being used to make an estimate of the number and amount of food stamp (FS) recipients. In Fig. 4., begin with the initial administrative records database, which will be considered a collection of records X on households across the entire United States. A representative sample of records is chosen from the database and linked (see computerized record linkage and statistical matching) to carefully collected data. In this application, either the Current Population Survey March (Annual Social and Economic) Supplement or Survey of Income and Program Participation would serve this function. The carefully collected survey data are treated as representing "ground truth," to which the administrative records data will be calibrated. (The external data are treated as metaphorical "ground truth," recognizing that every data collection contains error.)

The next step is to estimate a model that "predicts" the carefully collected data (Y) from the data in the administrative records database for the same household. This model is crucial; it must have very strong goodness-of-fit properties. The final step is to use the fitted model to augment the database. Because the database contains the right-hand side variables X, the database can be augmented with estimated values $\hat{Y}$, using the model $\hat{Y} = f(X)$. This model can have hierarchical structure, can be Bayesian if needed, and is, by design, calibrated to the survey data. The augmented database is the best estimate of what the database would have said, if the careful data collection had taken place over the entire database. The strength of this approach is that it makes use of the best of both worlds: the high quality and content of a sample survey, and the wide coverage of the administrative records database. By no means is this model the only approach to improving data quality in administrative records databases, but it and close

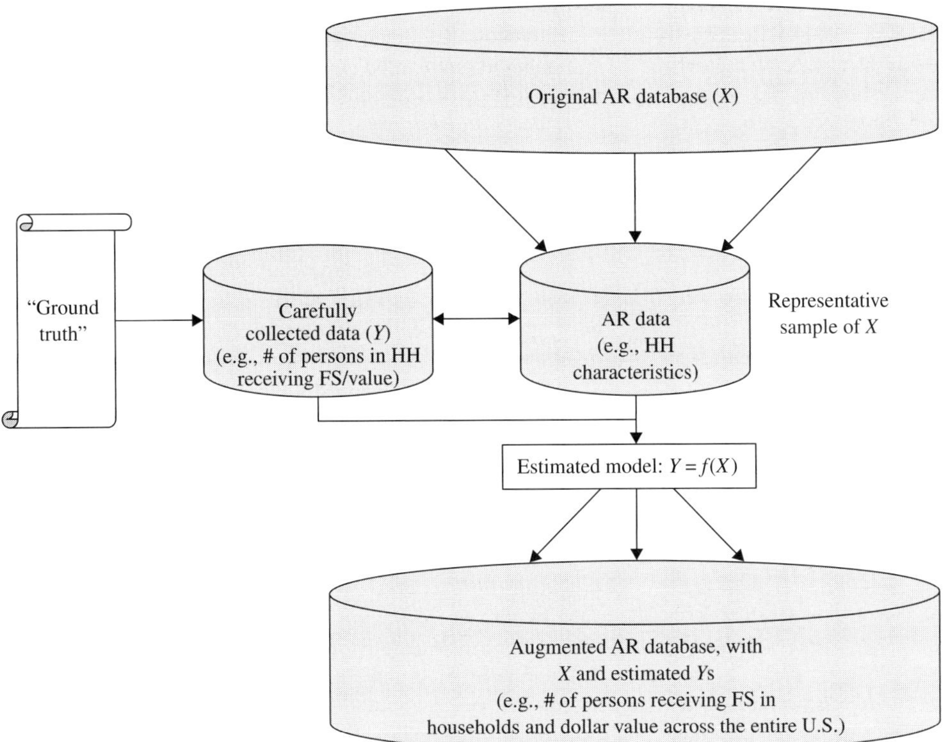

Figure 4 Illustration of "calibrating" administrative records (AR) data to an external data source. HH, Households; FS, food stamps.

relatives are currently the most common approach and appear to have the most promise.

What is the Future of Administrative Records Research?

Researchers of social measures stand on what can be described as an historical cusp: the new statistical era touted by Prevost in 1996 is coming, and a whole array of new databases will be compiled for a wide range of purposes. Many of these will be linked; others will be analyzed in a standalone fashion. No matter what the form of the analysis, decision-makers will be clamoring for information from their databases. Thus, the researcher who can work with such records and apply substantive reasoning to the results will have plenty to do over the coming decades. However, with widespread linkages of microdata from different databases, major privacy concerns have emerged. Who shall be the "data steward"? Or, more directly: Who shall watch the watchmen? No doubt the future will see greater legal definition and organizational regulation of linked administrative and mixed databases.

Acknowledgments

This article reports the results of research and analysis undertaken by Census Bureau staff. It has undergone a more limited review by the Census Bureau than have the official publications on which it is based. This report is released to inform interested parties and to encourage discussion.

See Also the Following Articles

Computerized Record Linkage and Statistical Matching • County and City Data • Federalism: Local, State, Federal and International Data Sources • Observational Studies • State Data for the United States

Further Reading

Bureau of Economic Analysis. (2002). *Updated Summary NIPA Methodologies. Survey of Current Business, October 2002*. Available on the Internet at http://www.bea.gov

Bureau of Labor Statistics. (1997). *Handbook of Methods*. Bureau of Labor Statistics. Washington, D.C. Available on the Internet at http://www.bls.gov

Bye, B. V., and Thompson, H. (1999). *Race and Ethnicity Modeling w/SSA Numident Data: Two Level Regression Model.* Administrative Records Research Memorandum Series #22, U.S. Census Bureau, Washington, D.C.

Card, D., Hildreth, A. K. G., and Shore-Sheppard, L. D. (2001). The measurement of Medicaid coverage in the SIPP: Evidence from California, 1990–1996. *JCPR Working Paper 241, 10-23-2001.* Available on the Internet at http://www.jcpr.org

Citro, C., Cohen, M., Kalton, G., and West, K. (1997). *Small-Area Estimates of Children Living in Poverty: Interim Report I, Evaluation of 1993 County Estimates for Title I Allocations.* National Research Council, Washington, D.C.

Federal Committee on Statistical Methodology. (1980). *Report on Statistical Uses of Administrative Records.* Available on the Internet at http://www.fcsm.gov

Federal Financial Institutions Examination Council. (2001). *A Guide to CRA Data Collection and Reporting.* CRA/HMDA Systems Information Technology, Board of Governors of the Federal Reserve System, Washington, D.C. Available on the Internet at http://www.ffiec.gov

Inmon, W. H. (1996). *Building the Data Warehouse.* Wiley, New York.

Judson, D. H. (2000). *The Statistical Administrative Records System: System Design, Successes, and Challenges.* Presented at the NISS/Telcordia Data Quality Conference, Morristown, New Jersey, November 30–December 1, 2000.

Judson, D. H., and Bye, B. V. (2003). *Administrative Records Experiment in 2000 (AREX 2000): Synthesis Report.* U.S. Census Bureau, Washington, D.C.

Judson, D. H., Popoff, C. L., and Batutis, M. (2001). An evaluation of the accuracy of U.S. Census Bureau county population estimation methods. *Statist. Transit.* **5,** 185–215.

Kornfeld, R., and Bloom, H. (1997). *Measuring Program Impacts on Earnings and Employment: Do UI Wage Reports from Employers Agree with Surveys of Individuals?* Available on the Internet at http://www.jcpr.org

Prevost, R. (1996). *Administrative Records and a New Statistical Era.* Paper presented at the 1996 meetings of the Population Association of America, New Orleans, Louisiana, May 9–11, 1996.

Robinson, J. G. (2001). *Accuracy and Coverage Evaluation: Demographic Analysis Results.* DSSD Census 2000 Procedures and Operations Memorandum Series B-4. Available on the Internet at http://www.census.gov

Rogot, E., Sorlie, P., and Johnson, N. J. (1986). Probabilistic methods in matching census samples to the National Death Index. *J. Chronic Dis.* **39,** 719–734.

U.S. Census Bureau. (2003). *State and County Income and Poverty Estimates: Introduction to the SAIPE Project.* U.S. Census Bureau, Washington D.C. Available on the Internet at http://www.census.gov

Wand, Y., and Wang, R. Y. (1996). Anchoring data quality dimensions in ontological foundations. *Commun. ACM* **39,** 86–95.

Zanutto, E., and Zaslavsky, A. M. (2001). Using administrative records to impute for nonresponse. In *Survey Nonresponse* (R. Groves, D. Dillman, J. Eltinge, and R. J. A. Little, eds.), pp. 403–415. John Wiley, New York.

Zaslavsky, A., and Wolfgang, G. (1993). Triple system modeling of census, post-enumeration survey, and administrative-list data. *J. Bus. Econ. Statist.* **11,** 279–288.

Age, Period, and Cohort Effects

Norval D. Glenn
University of Texas, Austin, Texas, USA

Glossary

age effect A consequence of influences that vary by chronological age.

age–period–cohort conundrum A specific case of the identification problem in which the interrelated independent variables are age, period, and cohort.

birth cohort The individuals born during a given period, such as a year or a decade (the kind of cohort usually studied in cohort analyses).

cohort The individuals (human or otherwise) who commonly experienced a significant event during a specified period of time.

cohort effect A consequence of influences that vary by time of birth or time of some other event (such as marriage) that defines a cohort.

identification problem The situation that exists when three or more independent variables that may affect a dependent variable are interrelated so that the multiple correlation of each independent variable to the others is unity.

period effect A consequence of influences that vary through time.

Age, period, and cohort effects are estimated by sociologists and other social scientists primarily to understand human aging and the nature of social, cultural, and political change.

Introduction: The Age–Period–Cohort Conundrum

In the social and behavioral sciences, there are often reasons to think that three or more independent variables simultaneously affect a dependent variable when each of the independent variables is a perfect linear function of the others. When all but one of the independent variables are held constant, the variance of the remaining variable is zero, because the multiple correlation of each variable to the others is unity. Therefore, it is impossible through any straightforward method to estimate the effects of all of the variables, and yet omitting one of them from the analysis will almost certainly render the estimates of the effects of the other independent variables inaccurate. This condition, known as the "identification problem," almost always afflicts research designed to assess the effects of a difference between two variables, as when quality of marriage may be affected by the wife's values, the husband's values, and the difference between the spouses' values.

The classic case of the identification problem, however, is the age–period–cohort conundrum, or the confounding of the effects of influences associated with chronological age, time of measurement, and date of birth (if human individuals are the units of analysis). Hypotheses abound about the effects of all three of these classes of influences. For instance, it is believed that participation in conventional crime may diminish due to declines in energy and risk-taking propensities associated with biological aging, which would be an age effect. Any changes in attitudes, behaviors, or emotions as a result of current events, such as the terrorist attacks on the United States on September 11, 2001, are period effects. And any enduring consequences of being born at a particular time, and thus of growing up during a particular era (such as the Great Depression or the Cold War) are examples of birth cohort effects. Another important kind of birth cohort effect is the result of the number of persons in the cohort relative to the numbers in earlier and later ones. For instance, members of large and small cohorts experience different degrees of competition for the good jobs when they enter the labor force, which in turn may affect several kinds of attitudes and behaviors.

The age–period–cohort conundrum can be illustrated by the use of a standard cohort table, in which multiple sets of cross-sectional data (data for one point in time) relating age to a dependent variable are juxtaposed and in which the intervals between the periods for which there are data are equal in years to the range in each age category. For instance, if 10-year age categories are used, data gathered at 10-year intervals are presented, as in Table I, in which the dependent variable is whether respondents to the 1974, 1984, and 1994 American General Social Surveys said they favored the death penalty for persons convicted of murder. In such a table, the trend within a cohort can be traced by starting with any but the oldest age category in the left-hand column and reading diagonally down and to the right. For instance, according to the data in Table I, in the cohort that was 20–29 years old in 1974, the percentage approving of the death penalty went from 58.2 in 1974 to 73.6 in 1984, to 79.5 in 1994. This increase may have been an age effect, because the cohort grew 20 years older, or it may have been a period effect reflecting general changes in society during the two decades covered. Or it may have been a combination of age and period effects. In other words, in this or any other cohort diagonal, age and period effects may be confounded. Likewise, age and cohort effects may be confounded in each column, and period and cohort effects may be confounded in each row, of a standard cohort table.

It is obvious that a simple examination of Table I cannot reveal the extent and nature of any age, period, and cohort effects reflected in the data. What has not been evident to many researchers interested in the age–period–cohort conundrum is that no routinely applied statistical analysis of the data can, by itself, be relied on to provide accurate estimates of the effects. The reason is illustrated by the different combinations of effects that could account for the data in Table II, which is a standard cohort table reporting hypothetical data. The simplest interpretation of the data is that they reflect pure linear age effects, whereby each additional 10 years of age produces a five-point increase in the dependent variable. For some dependent variables, this might be the only plausible interpretation, but, as the alternative explanations at the bottom of the table indicate, it is not the only logically possible one. Rather, an infinite number of combinations of age, period, cohort effects could produce the pattern of variation in the dependent variable shown in the table. When the pattern of variation is not as simple as that in Table II, which is usually the case, the combination of effects producing the data must be somewhat complex. It should be obvious that no mechanically applied statistical analysis can reveal which of the many possible complex combinations is the correct one. One kind of complexity, however, sometimes aids interpretation of the data. If there is an almost completely nonlinear pattern of variation by either age, period, or cohort that is uniform across the categories of the other two variables, as in Table III, there is only one reasonable explanation for the data. In the case of Table III, for instance, it is hard to imagine that any kinds of effects besides nonlinear age

Table I Percentage of Respondents to the 1974, 1984, and 1994 American General Social Surveys Who Said They Favored the Death Penalty for Persons Convicted of Murder[a]

	1974		*1984*		*1994*	
Age (years)	*%*	*n*	*%*	*n*	*%*	*n*
20–29	58.2	385	79.9	368	78.5	467
30–39	67.7	279	73.6	289	80.0	651
40–49	68.5	265	76.4	231	79.5	578
50–59	74.8	257	78.0	181	78.9	387
60–69	70.4	187	76.7	155	82.3	238

[a]To increase representativeness, data are weighted by number of persons age 18 and older in respondent's household.

Table II Pattern of Data Showing Pure Age Effects, Offsetting Period, and Cohort Effects, or a Combination of Age Effects and Offsetting Period and Cohort Effects[a]

	Year					
Age (years)	*1950*	*1960*	*1970*	*1980*	*1990*	*2000*
20–29	50	50	50	50	50	50
30–39	55	55	55	55	55	55
40–49	60	60	60	60	60	60
50–59	65	65	65	65	65	65
60–69	70	70	70	70	70	70
70–79	75	75	75	75	75	75

[a]Numbers in the cells are hypothetical values of a dependent variable. Alternative explanations: (1) Each 10 years of aging produces a 5-point increase in the dependent variable. (2) There is a 5-point per 10 years positive period effect on the dependent variable and a 5-point per 10 years negative cohort effect. (3) There is some combination of age and offsetting period and cohort effects on the dependent variable. An infinite number of combinations of such effects could produce the pattern of variation in the dependent variable shown in the table.

Table III Pattern of Data Showing Nonlinear Variation in a Dependent Variable That Can Reasonably Only Be Interpreted to Reflect Age Effects[a]

	Year					
Age (years)	*1950*	*1960*	*1970*	*1980*	*1990*	*2000*
20–29	50	50	50	50	50	50
30–39	52	52	52	52	52	52
40–49	62	62	62	62	62	62
50–59	62	62	62	62	62	62
60–69	50	50	50	50	50	50
70–79	45	45	45	45	45	45

[a]Assuming no effects from differential mortality. Numbers in the cells are hypothetical values of a dependent variable.

effects are reflected. On the rare occasions when the data fall into such a pattern, interpretation can defensibly be based on simple inspection of the data in tabular form. Usually, however, no such straightforward interpretation of cohort data is justified, which has led researchers to use statistical methods to try to disentangle age, period, and cohort effects.

Statistical Attempts to Separate Age–Period–Cohort Effects

The most widely used statistical method to try to separate age, period, and cohort effects was introduced three decades ago by Mason and co-workers. Variants of the method are still frequently used, a recent example being in Robinson and Jackson's study of trust in others. The Mason *et al.* method is a way to estimate simultaneously the effects of age, period, and cohort by making simplifying assumptions—identifying restrictions—that break the linear dependence of each variable on the other two and thus allow estimation of a regression model in which each of the variables (or occasionally just one or two of them) is entered as a set of dummy variables. The method requires only that the effects of two categories (usually two adjacent ones) of either age, period, or cohort be assumed to be equal (for examples, see Tables IV and V). Of course, when a set of dummy variables is entered as independent variables in a regression equation, one of the variables must be omitted, and the Mason *et al.* method requires only that one additional variable from one of the sets be dropped. This simple procedure allows the regression program to run and generates estimates of the effects on the dependent variable of the age, period, and cohort dummy variables. Stronger identifying restrictions can be made, and proponents of the method recommend additional assumptions if they seem justified on the basis of theory or what is already known about the phenomena being studied. If it is known with confidence that either age, period, or cohort has no effects, that variable can be omitted from the analysis and the age–period–cohort conundrum disappears.

This method has often been used as an all-purpose solution to the identification problem in cohort analysis (though Mason *et al.* essentially say in a footnote that it cannot be used to separate linear effects) that is assumed to yield reasonable estimates as long as the assumptions on which identifying restrictions are based are not gross distortions of reality. The reasoning has been that the effects of adjacent narrowly defined age, period, or cohort categories are unlikely to be very different and that the error involved in assuming equal effects is only on the order of that involved in grouping the values of a continuous variable. Use of rudimentary "side information" (information from outside the cohort data being analyzed) should, according to this point of view, assure that the estimates of effects will be about as nearly correct as the levels of sampling and measurement error allow.

Table IV Four Mason *et al.* Age–Period–Cohort Models Estimating the Effects Reflected in Table II[a]

	Model			
Variable	*1*	*2*	*3*	*4*
Constant	50.0	50.0	25.0	28.7
Age (years)				
20–29	—[b]	—[b]	0.0	—[b]
30–39	5.0	5.0	0.0	—[b]
40–49	10.0	10.0	—[b]	3.6
50–59	15.0	15.0	—[b]	6.1
60–69	20.0	20.0	0.0	8.6
70–79	25.0	25.0	0.0	11.4
Year				
1950	—[b]	0.0	—[b]	—[b]
1960	0.0	0.0	5.0	—[b]
1970	0.0	0.0	10.0	3.6
1980	0.0	—[b]	15.0	6.1
1990	0.0	—[b]	20.0	8.6
2000	0.0	0.0	25.0	11.4
Cohort (year of birth)				
1871–1880	0.0	0.0	50.0	25.0
1881–1890	0.0	0.0	45.0	23.9
1891–1900	0.0	0.0	40.0	21.5
1901–1910	0.0	0.0	35.0	19.1
1911–1920	0.0	0.0	30.0	16.8
1921–1930	0.0	0.0	25.0	14.0
1931–1940	0.0	0.0	20.0	11.8
1941–1950	0.0	0.0	15.0	9.1
1951–1960	—[b]	0.0	10.0	6.5
1961–1970	—[b]	0.0	5.0	3.9
1971–1980	0.0	—[b]	—[b]	—[b]

[a] Unstandardized regression coefficients.
[b] Reference category; value set at zero.

Applying the Mason *et al.* method to the data in Tables II and III illustrates that this reasoning is flawed (see Tables IV and V). (For these analyses, individual-level data sets were constructed, with 20 cases in each cell of the tables and identical variable values for all cases in each cell.) In each of the first three models in Table IV, the equality restriction is applied to two adjacent categories of either age, period, or cohort. Although the restrictions in the different models are equally defensible and involve equal and small distortions of reality, which restriction is used makes a huge difference. Assuming two categories of either period or cohort to have equal effects leads to a pure age-effects interpretation, whereas assuming two categories of age to have equal effects leads to an offsetting-period-and-cohort-effects explanation.

Table V Four Mason *et al.* Age–Period–Cohort Models Estimating the Effects Reflected in Table III[a]

Variable	Model 1	Model 2	Model 3	Model 4
Constant	62.0	50.0	50.0	60.0
Age (years)				
20–29	−12.0	—[b]	—[b]	—[b]
30–39	−10.0	2.0	2.0	—[b]
40–49	—[b]	12.0	12.0	8.0
50–59	—[b]	12.0	12.0	6.0
60–69	−12.0	0.0	0.0	−8.0
70–79	−17.0	−5.0	−5.0	−15.0
Year				
1950	—[b]	—[b]	—[b]	—[b]
1960	0.0	0.0	—[b]	2.0
1970	0.0	0.0	0.0	4.0
1980	0.0	0.0	0.0	6.0
1990	0.0	0.0	0.0	8.0
2000	0.0	0.0	0.0	10.0
Cohort (year of birth)				
1871–1880	0.0	0.0	—[b]	20.0
1881–1890	0.0	0.0	0.0	18.0
1891–1900	0.0	0.0	0.0	16.0
1901–1910	0.0	0.0	0.0	14.0
1911–1920	0.0	0.0	0.0	12.0
1921–1930	0.0	0.0	0.0	10.0
1931–1940	0.0	0.0	0.0	8.0
1941–1950	0.0	0.0	0.0	6.0
1951–1960	0.0	0.0	0.0	4.0
1961–1970	0.0	—[b]	0.0	2.0
1971–1980	—[b]	—[b]	0.0	—[b]

[a] Unstandardized regression coefficients.
[b] Reference category; value set at zero.

Making two equality assumptions in Model 4 leads to a three-variable solution to the age–period–cohort conundrum. It follows that it must be known *a priori* whether the one-, two-, or three-variable solution is the correct one; the Mason *et al.* method cannot be used to decide which is correct when the variation in the data is linear, as it is in Table II.

Although the Mason *et al.* method has often been applied to data in which the pattern of variation in the data is basically linear, a careful reading of the 1973 article by Mason *et al.* would prevent such use. Buried in a footnote of the article is the following statement: "These pure effects [the hypothetical effects used to illustrate the method] have deliberately been made nonlinear in form . . . . We create our data in this way because perfectly linear pure effects are inherently ambiguous to interpret, and can be estimated equally well by the pure effect variable or by the two remaining variables in cohort analysis" (p. 248). When the effects are nonlinear, the Mason *et al.* method theoretically could work well, but in practice, it is unlikely to do so. The accuracy of estimates of effects can be assessed when the method is applied to the data in Table III (Table IV), because the nature of the effects is not in doubt. The first three models in Table V use equality restrictions that are precisely correct, and each model estimates the effects correctly. The fourth model, however, uses an equality restriction when the effects of the two categories are similar but not identical. Although the assumption of equality is not a gross distortion of reality, the estimates of effects are grossly in error. Unfortunately, a researcher is almost never able to make an equality restriction based on an assumption known to be precisely correct, and precise correctness is necessary for the method to work well.

Other statistical methods to deal with the age–period–cohort conundrum have been rarely used and are even less satisfactory than the Mason *et al.* method and its variants. An example is a method developed by Japanese scholar T. Nakamura and introduced to American social scientists by Sasaki and Suzuki. Based on Bayesian statistics, the method selects the simplest combination of age, period, and cohort effects that could account for a set of cohort data, as simplicity is operationally defined by the method. Stated differently, the method is based on the invariant assumption that "successive parameters change gradually" (p. 1063). This assumption may often be correct, but because neither theory nor "side information" is used to assess its probable correctness in the case at hand, the method cannot be relied on to select the proper combination of age, period, and cohort effects. If this method is used, theory and side information should be used to assess the credibility of the estimates it yields.

An additional reason for being wary of statistical attempts to separate age, period, and cohort effects is that the Sasaki and Suzuki method and all major variants of the Mason *et al.* method are based on the assumption that the effects are additive, even though it is likely that age, period, and cohort interact in their effects on most dependent variables of interest to social scientists and psychologists. According to theory, supported by a great deal of empirical evidence, young adults tend to respond more to stimuli for change than do older adults, so that period effects generally vary by age and thus among cohorts of different ages. For instance, when major changes in attitudes occur, the change tends to be greater at the younger than at the older adult ages. Furthermore, many kinds of age effects are likely to change through time and thus to vary among birth cohorts. Social expectations for behavior at various chronological ages have shifted considerably in recent decades, an example being an increased expectation for middle-aged and older people to be sexually active. Biological aging has changed only moderately, but some aspects of social and psychological aging have changed more substantially.

If, as is argued here, age–period–cohort interactions are ubiquitous, additive age–period–cohort statistical models would not be very useful, and would often be misleading, even if they were not afflicted with other problems.

Alternatives to Age–Period–Cohort Statistical Models

The fact that age–period–cohort statistical models are rarely useful and often lead to incorrect conclusions does not mean that social and behavioral scientists must stop asking questions about the kinds of effects the models estimate. Other kinds of statistical models and informal assessments of data can often lead to defensible conclusions about the effects.

If the interest is in the effects of cohort size, for instance, an age–period–cohort-characteristic (APCC) model can be employed. Although it is impossible to control age and period and let cohort vary, it is possible to control age and period and let certain characteristics of cohorts, such as size, vary. The only requirement is that the characteristic must not bear a strong linear relationship to cohort, because, if it does, its effects will be confounded with those of age and period. O'Brien and his collaborators have used APCC models to estimate the effects of cohort size and certain family characteristics that vary by cohort on such variables as homicide commission and victimization.

Often hypotheses about age, period, or cohort effects can be made more specific, because usually it is other variables associated with these three demographic variables that are believed to have effects. For instance, it may be career progression or the taking on of family responsibility that is believed to have a particular "age effect." Or cohort effects may be attributed to differences in the sizes of communities of origin among people born at different times. If these more specific variables can be measured and incorporated into analyses, it may be possible to avoid the age–period–cohort conundrum.

Informal means of examining data for evidence of age, period, or cohort effects are varied and must be tailored to the task at hand. There is no formula, no cookbook approach, that will work well on all occasions. Often, however, examining the trend in the dependent variable among the youngest adults is useful for detecting evidence of period influences. Although period and cohort effects may be confounded in this trend, in the case of many behavioral, attitudinal, and other psychological dependent variables, both kinds of effects are likely to be rooted in changes in period influences. Consider, for instance, how the data in Table I should be interpreted. The cross-sectional data in the first column and the intracohort trends both suggest a positive age effect on approval of the death penalty; all eight 10-year intracohort changes shown are upward. However, the upward trend at ages 20–29 from 1974 to 1984 is evidence for rather strong period influences toward approving of the death penalty. Therefore, the intracohort trends could well be entirely period rather than age effects. And the positive relationship between age and support of the death penalty shown for 1974 could have resulted from earlier anti-death-penalty period influences that affected younger persons more than older ones. Of course, no serious cohort study of attitudes toward the death penalty would be based only on the data in Table I, especially because the question yielding the data has been asked on other American General Social Surveys, nor would the study stop with a simple examination of tabular data. However, given the basic evidence available, a definitive answer as to whether there has been an age effect on attitudes toward the death penalty would elude even the most sophisticated study possible.

Informal means of examining cohort data may not be satisfying to persons who have a high need for certainty, but accepting the fact that there is always some ambiguity in the evidence concerning age, period, and cohort effects is more scientific than dogmatically embracing statistical model estimates that are likely to be substantially in error.

Conclusions

Social and behavioral scientists have formulated many important hypotheses about the effects of age, period, and cohort, and research to test these hypotheses should not be abandoned. However, researchers should recognize that definitive evidence concerning many of the hypothesized effects may never be forthcoming. Belief that statistical age–period–cohort models can provide such evidence has led to much pseudorigorous research and almost certainly to many incorrect conclusions. If statistical model testing is used to estimate the effects, the credibility of the estimates should be evaluated on the basis of theory, common sense, and *a priori* knowledge of the phenomena being studied. It is important to avoid letting the model testing create an illusion of rigor that will prevent the proper application of human judgment in the research process. It is often preferable to skip the statistical model testing and proceed directly to more informal means of distinguishing age, period, and cohort effects. Although these methods are fallible, they are generally recognized as such and thus are less likely than formal model testing to lead to overly confident conclusions.

See Also the Following Article

Longitudinal Cohort Designs

Further Reading

Abramson, P. R., and Inglehart, R. (1995). *Value Change in Global Perspective.* University of Michigan Press, Ann Arbor, Michigan.

Alwin, D. F. (1991). Family of origin and cohort differences in verbal ability. *Am. Sociol. Rev.* **56,** 625–638.

Blalock, H. M., Jr. (1967). Status inconsistency, social mobility, status integration, and structural effects. *Am. Sociol. Rev.* **32,** 790–801.

Converse, P. E. (1976). *The Dynamics of Party Support: Cohort Analyzing Party Identification.* Sage Publications, Beverly Hills, California.

Glenn, N. D. (1987). A caution about mechanical solutions to the identification problem in cohort analysis: A comment on Sasaki and Suzuki. *Am. J. Sociol.* **95,** 754–761.

Glenn, N. D. (1998). The course of marital success and failure in five American ten-year marriage cohorts. *J. Marriage Family* **60,** 569–576.

Hirschi, T., and Gottfredson, M. (1983). Age and the explanation of crime. *Am. J. Sociol.* **89,** 552–584.

Mason, K. O., Mason, W. M., Winsborough, H. H., and Poole, W. K. (1973). Some methodological issues in the cohort analysis of archival data. *Am. Sociol. Rev.* **38,** 242–258.

O'Brien, R. M., and Stockard, J. (2002). Variations in age-specific homicide death rates: A cohort explanation for changes in the age distribution of homicide deaths. *Social Sci. Res.* **31,** 124–150.

O'Brien, R. M., Stockard, J., and Issaacson, L. (1999). The enduring effects of cohort characteristics on age-specific homicide rates, 1960–1995. *Am. J. Sociol.* **104,** 1061–1095.

Robinson, R. V., and Jackson, E. F. (2001). Is trust in others declining in America? An age–period–cohort analysis. *Social Sci. Res.* **30,** 117–145.

Sasaki, M., and Suzuki, T. (1987). Changes in religious commitment in the United States, Holland, and Japan. *Am. J. Sociol.* **92,** 1055–1076.

Aggregation

D. Stephen Voss
University of Kentucky, Lexington, Kentucky, USA

Glossary

aggregation bias Systematic inaccuracy induced in a method of statistical inference because of patterns in the process of grouping data.

areal units problem The recognition that the same individual-level data can produce a wide variety of aggregate-level statistics depending on the geographical areas into which the individuals are grouped.

cross-level inference When analysts attempt to generate statistics, derive estimates, or draw inferences for units of analysis at one level of measurement using data measured at a different level.

ecological inference A generic phrase describing the attempt to estimate individual-level behavior using aggregate data.

ecological regression Usually associated with Leo Goodman, refers to the use of linear regression to estimate individual-level behavior using aggregate data.

King's EI A method of ecological inference based on maximum-likelihood estimation using the truncated bivariate normal distribution. King's approach has no formal name, but it is commonly called "EI" after the software distributed to implement it.

neighborhood model An ecological inference model that assumes variations from aggregate unit to aggregate unit are entirely contextual, and therefore not compositional.

weighted average A version of the standard mean or average that is invariant to the level of aggregation because of the method of weighting each unit.

Aggregation describes a broad condition in which social indicators have been clustered together, resulting in a loss of information. Data may be clustered across time or within time periods. They may be clustered across space or within geographical boundaries. They may be clustered across social groups or across countable events. Furthermore, the method of aggregation may be through summation, through compilation into ratios or some other summary statistic, through collection in data tables such as cross-tabulations that reach across multiple variables, or through some other form of compilation. The motives for aggregation in social measurement also vary widely. Aggregation can result from an inherent limitation in how social behavior is observed and therefore must be measured, from a desire to simplify data collection and storage on the part of the researcher, or from an attempt to constrain the scope of an analysis.

The wide variety in dimensions, methods, and motives means that aggregation embraces an entire class of social measurement issues. It is not a single dilemma of data collection or analysis with its own conventional terminology or its own conventional solutions; indeed, many of them have very little in common. Aggregation is not a problem endemic to one social science discipline but one that embraces just about all of them. This article therefore lays out the conceptual issues involved with aggregation as inclusively and broadly as possible. It illustrates the problems with aggregation by concentrating on the most commonly discussed example in social science research: the ecological inference problem.

Introduction

Social science research often relies on quasi-experimentation, in which the researcher analyzes data produced incidentally by the social system rather than data produced experimentally as a direct and controlled outgrowth of the work. In fact, it is not irregular for analysts to exercise minimal control over the data available for research, aside from choosing among one or more preformed data sets to exploit in secondary analysis. Analysts therefore may not be able to select the measurement theory guiding collection of raw data.

The separability of data generation and data analysis presents a particular risk. Available information on a social phenomenon may be measured at a level distinct from the level at which relevant theories operate. The researcher may wish to theorize about the forces determining whether individuals commit crime but may have access only to neighborhood crime statistics. The researcher may wish to understand why nations protect free expression through their domestic policies, but may be stuck using survey data measured at the individual level. The researcher may wish to characterize school districts demographically, but may have data collected on zip codes. The causal process linking behavior at one level with behavior at another may be fairly complicated.

At root, determining the proper unit of analysis is a theoretical as well as a technical question. Hypothetical narratives intended to describe particular social processes may operate differently from one level of analysis to the next and may not offer any observable implications at all for some levels. A researcher, therefore, must specify theoretical claims carefully to avoid fallacious inference—that is, to avoid looking for social phenomena where a theory does not posit they ought to appear.

Awareness of this conceptual problem has a long history, although statistical attempts to escape the frustrations of "cross-level inference" have a much more recent vintage. For example, classical liberal theorists recognized that a successfully functioning economy did not need careful mercantile policymaking; it could result from the actions of individualistic profit seekers with no intent to improve social productivity or even awareness that their actions were creating that public good. Successful public policy did not require a philosopher king trained in the art of decision making; it could emerge from the multitude of highly individual and even parochial demands placed on a political system through electoral competition or legislative representation. Spiritual truth need not emerge through a religious bureaucracy dedicated to specialized theological study; it could emerge from the decentralized moral insights of a humble but literate people who read their Bible or learned the spiritual lessons of the natural world. Such a complex mechanism as the human body could function although composed of nothing more than a cluster of body parts unaware that they are sustaining life, unaware of each other, and for that matter entirely lacking in self-awareness. This was a key insight of the Enlightenment in particular: collect a large enough sample of workers or citizens or religious seekers, and their individual errors will cancel out sufficiently to bring the aggregate much closer to truth than a centralized process would. The process of aggregation could produce a whole much greater than the sum of its parts.

This central insight has remained with the social sciences as they have grown more formalized. Each social science discipline has its own language for discussing the problem of linking theory and data at the proper unit of analysis. Economists have termed the danger a "fallacy of composition." Microeconomic and macroeconomic patterns and relationships may differ sharply. Anthropologists worry that the results of etic observation (simplified, observation from the perspective of the outsider) may produce sharply different results from emic observation (again, simplified, observation from the perspective of someone within a social system). Quantitative researchers have long recognized that regressions performed on a cross-section of data will produce different results from those produced within a single panel or identifiable unit across time. In each case, the specific problem falls into this same general class: theories may have different observable implications, depending on the sort of data collected and how they are analyzed.

Cross-Level Inference

Aggregation most commonly poses a threat to inference when the theory and the data for an analysis appear at different levels. Practitioners are especially aware of the pitfalls of cross-level inference when they need to derive individual-level quantities of interest from data aggregated to a higher level. In these circumstances, it is common to fear "an ecological fallacy" caused by aggregation bias. However, the problem can be just as serious in less familiar circumstances, as when the analyst wishes to understand the phenomena driving aggregate-level patterns using only individual-level data, or when data for an analysis appear at multiple levels of aggregation.

Seeking Statistics Invariant to Aggregation: The Conceptual Problem

Regardless of the nature of any particular cross-level inference, the essential problem is the same: statistics computed at one level of analysis need not correspond to parallel statistics (or parameters) applicable at another level. Averages computed at one level of aggregation usually will not be the same as averages computed at another level of aggregation, or at the individual level. The average per capita income in the United States is not the same as the average state-level per capita income. The proportion of voters backing the Republican U.S. presidential candidate is never the same as the average level of Republican support across the various states.

Correlations also change depending on the level of statistical analysis. To take one famous example: just because literacy tended to be higher in places where immigrants were more numerous, at least during the early 20th century, literacy was not actually higher among the immigrants themselves. The correlation at the individual level went in the opposite direction from the correlation at the aggregate level. Similarly, education is highly related to political participation in the United States—educated citizens are much more likely to vote. Over time, however, the population has become more educated, but voter turnout has declined; the correlation goes in the opposite direction temporally.

As a final example, measures of dispersion can change sharply across levels of analysis. For example, the African American population varies much more widely across voter precincts or census blocs, because of patterns of residential segregation, than it does across counties or states. By contrast, during any one term the U.S. Supreme Court may vary substantially in its ideological orientation from case to case, but the typical Supreme Court justice is fairly consistent.

In theory, a set of individuals could be divided up in an infinite number of ways, making aggregate-level statistics arbitrary—more a function of the aggregation decisions than the underlying behavioral regularities. Of course, the analyst rarely makes these aggregation decisions. Indeed, if the analyst's theoretical interests lie at the individual level, the logical solution would be to avoid aggregating in the first place. The aggregation usually emerges from a process that the analyst cannot manipulate and, even worse, may not be able to observe. Various areal units—nations, states or provinces, counties or wards or cities, and neighborhoods or precincts—are defined by borders that emerge haphazardly and may change over time. Furthermore, the people who live in them can move around, which further complicates any attempt to discern the pattern sorting individuals into units. Statistics may be variant with respect to geography, in other words, a phenomenon known as the areal unit problem.

Seeking Statistics Invariant to Aggregation: The Weighted Average

The usual burden for methodologists working on cross-level inference is to identify statistics that are invariant to aggregation, which will produce quantities of interest at the proper level of aggregation even if computed from data at a different level. The best-known example of a statistic invariant to aggregation is the weighted average. A standard mean for variable x computed at the individual level takes the following form:

$$\frac{\sum_{i=1}^{n} x_i}{n} \quad \text{or} \quad \sum_{i=1}^{r} x_i \mathrm{f}(x_i),$$

where n is the number of individuals, r is the number of values that the variable takes on, i serves as the index for counting each individual, and $\mathrm{f}(\cdot)$ represents the relative frequency (in a sample) or probability (in a population) for each value x_i.

If variable x is computed at the aggregate level, the formula for its mean looks almost identical. Indeed, it is parallel except that the values of x describe quantities for an aggregate unit rather than for an individual, and the values are summed for m aggregate units across the index j:

$$\frac{\sum_{j=1}^{m} x_j}{m} \quad \text{or} \quad \sum_{j=1}^{m} x_j \mathrm{f}(x_j).$$

These two formulas may look the same, but the quantities may be quite far apart, depending on how the individual-level values of x are distributed. Let us say, for example, that x represents per capita income. If groups were divided into quartiles, with per capita income averaged for each quartile, the mean of those numbers probably would resemble the individual-level mean fairly closely. But suppose that the richest half of the population appeared in one group, whereas the remaining half of the population was divided up into nine other groups. The group-level average would be especially low, because it would include nine per capita figures below the median income level and only one above it.

The weighted average solves this problem by taking into account how many people are clustered into each group. It prevents dilution of individual-level information contained in large groups and prevents overemphasis of individual-level information contained in smaller groups. The formula for the weighted average might be expressed as such:

$$\sum_{j=1}^{m} x_j \frac{n_j}{n},$$

where n_j represents the number of individuals in group j. In short, each aggregate quantity receives a weight representing its proportion of the overall population or sample. Group the people in different ways, and their average will always be weighted according to each group's size.

While the weighted average is a useful statistic, the most common problem with cross-level inference is not so simple to solve: the ecological inference problem. Sometimes the aggregation process tosses away individual-level information such that no simple computation or weighting can restore it—yet the analyst wishes to estimate how individuals behaved. When faced with this near-intractable (if not intractable) barrier, the analyst customarily needs to make an assumption about the aggregation process or the pattern of lost information in order to derive useful quantities of interest. The next section therefore turns to this critical instance of data aggregation and its pitfalls.

Ecological Inference and Aggregation Bias

Aggregating data almost always discards information. To take one example, which will appear throughout this section: whites and blacks choose whether to register, whether to turn out, and how to vote—but analysts seldom know how racial groups differ in these forms of behavior. Instead, they usually only possess aggregated statistics that summarize the behavior observed in entire areal units. They will know how an electoral unit voted; they often know the racial breakdown of an electoral unit. Occasionally the analyst might know how groups differed in their registration rates, or even in their turnout rates. Thanks to the secret ballot, however, analysts never know for sure how groups voted. Studying racial voting behavior requires some form of estimation.

Table I summarizes the typical situation for areal unit i, with the simplifying assumption that the population is divided into only two groups, blacks and whites. One knows the totals for each row and each column, represented by the quantities appearing along the margins of the table. These quantities can be re-expressed as proportions by dividing each cell and each marginal by N_i. The ecological-inference problem is that one does not know the internal cells of the cross-tabulation, thus the question marks. Data sources seldom provide this information. Some method of inference is necessary.

It is usually helpful to think of this table as a series of discrete two-by-two cross-tabulations: the decision to register or not, to turn out or not, and to vote for one candidate or another (say, for left-wing or right-wing candidates). An analyst may choose to disregard the three-stage nature of the mobilization process, say by estimating directly the proportion of eligible adults who vote or even who select a particular candidate. However, leaving the three-stage process as a black box and simply estimating vote choices increases the likelihood of unreliable and poorly understood estimates. Analysts therefore customarily isolate portions of the three-stage process to recognize that they are politically distinct phenomena. Conceptually, if we divide eligible voters into black voters and white voters, the process for areal unit i would consist of three equations:

$$R_i = \varphi_i^b \times X_i + \varphi_i^w \times (1 - X_i),$$

where R is the general registration rate for eligible adults, X represents the proportion of the voting-age population that is African American, and φ^b and φ^w represent the registration rates among blacks and non-blacks, respectively.

$$\begin{aligned} T_i &= \beta_i^b \times \varphi_i^b/(\varphi_i^b + \varphi_i^w)X_i + \beta_i^w \times \varphi_i^w/(\varphi_i^b + \varphi_i^w) \\ &= \beta_i^b \times R_i^b + \varphi_i^w \times R_i^w, \end{aligned}$$

where T is the general turnout rate for eligible adults, R_i^b and R_i^w represent the proportion of registrants who were black and non-black, and β^b and β^w represent the turnout rates among blacks and non-blacks, respectively.

$$\begin{aligned} V_i^L &= \lambda_i^b \times \beta_i^b/(\beta_i^b + \beta_i^w) + \lambda_i^w \times \beta_i^w/(\beta_i^b + \beta_i^w) \\ &= \lambda_i^b \times T_i^b + \lambda_i^w \times T_i^w, \end{aligned}$$

where V_i^L is the general rate of left-wing voting among those who turned out, T_i^b and T_i^w represent the proportion of voters who were black and non-black, and λ_i^b and λ_i^w represent the left-wing rate of support from black and non-black voters. Customarily, analysts skip the first step and simply use X_i and $(1 - X_i)$ rather than the racial registration rates in the second identity.

These three equations are called identities because if all four quantities on the right-hand side of each equation were known, they would compute exactly to the left-hand side. There would be no error term. For example, the combined black and white registration in an electoral unit consists of the registration rates for the two groups weighted by their relative sizes. As should be clear, however, some of the terms on the right-hand side of each equation do not appear among the marginals. Those are the frequencies missing from the cross-tabulation that ecological analysis typically seeks to estimate or contextual analysis wishes to probe. They also represent the unavailable numbers that cause ecological inference techniques to dominate the evidentiary record in voting rights cases.

Table I The Ecological Inference Problem[a]

	Left-wing vote	*Right-wing vote*	*No vote*	*Unregistered*
Voting-age whites	?	?	?	?
Voting-age blacks	?	?	?	?
All races	V_i^L	V_i^R	$(R_i - T_i)$	$(1 - R_i)$

[a] Table presents the typical situation faced in areal unit i, for which marginal data is available but crosstabulations are not.

Conventional Solutions to the Ecological Inference Problem

Different researchers approach aggregate data with different motives. Some seek descriptive information about how groups behaved within an areal unit. That is, they seek across-group comparisons. For example, litigants may wish to establish the existence of racial bloc voting within a particular locale. Others would like to consider how a group's behavior shifted over various locales. That is, they seek within-group comparisons. For example, a political scientist might wish to establish that wealthier voters supported the candidate who promised tax breaks or that more-educated voters supported a gay rights referendum. These differing incentives shape the solutions that analysts prefer.

Informed Assumptions

Sometimes researchers possess such strong prior assumptions about racial behavior that they are willing to assume how one group behaved. If the right-wing candidate is a vicious race baiter, such as George Wallace or former Klansman David Duke, researchers may be willing to assume that no blacks appeared in the constituency (i.e., that $\lambda^b = 0$). If the left-wing candidate is a black Democrat, researchers may be willing to assume that no black voter crossed over to support a white Republican (i.e., $\lambda^b = 1$). Relying on informed assumptions is particularly tempting, because it allows researchers to assume that they can fill in every question mark in the cross-tabulation.

The most obvious limitation of this approach, of course, is that it is only feasible for severely polarized elections. For whatever bizarre reason, even the most extreme race baiters will draw some black supporters. Blacks never support black candidates unanimously. Once the researcher's interest expands to more mainstream elections, absolute priors of this sort become extremely difficult to defend. Furthermore, the bias introduced by incorrectly assuming behavior will be proportionate to group densities in each locale. Let us say, for example, that the true black rate of support is 0.025 but analysts assume it is 0.00. This error will throw off estimates of white behavior by 0.025 in a locale that is half black, but would not distort it much at all in a heavily white locale.

The informed assumptions approach also provides no method for considering the multilevel process that leads to voting behavior. Even in the rare case when informed assumptions about racial voting behavior are plausible, there are no defensible prior assumptions about racial turnout rates. Of course, analysts sometimes assume (implicitly or explicitly) that black and white turnout rates are the same, skipping straight to an analysis of vote choice. Research on political participation regularly contradicts this claim, however, and to assume equal turnout rates fallaciously will cause bias in the estimated white vote to vary systematically with African American mobilization rates.

Homogeneous Unit Analysis

The previous approach satisfies those who wish to study within-group variation. It requires no computer-intensive analysis and generates no measures of uncertainty. A different, but equally simple, alternative appeals to analysts who wish to compare across groups. They single out fully segregated areal units—say, those that are 90 or 95% homogeneous—and presume that the dominant group in these locales is representative of how group members behaved everywhere. This method has the virtue of certainty because we know almost exactly how blacks and white voted within the small subset of segregated units. The analyst merely looks at units that are all white, using their turnout and vote choice figures to fill in quantities for the white row of the cross-tabulation, and then similarly examines all-black units to fill in the black row.

This approach can be disastrously misleading if mixed-race communities differ from more-uniform areas. The most common name for the approach—homogeneous precinct analysis—underscores other drawbacks. It is useful only when residential patterns are highly segregated, as one often finds in urban precincts when looking at race. It is useless for county-level analysis, since counties are seldom almost entirely black. This method is also unreliable when the bulk of aggregation units fall between the extremes, such as when one wishes to study gender; only a negligible (and highly unrepresentative) selection of units will appear in the analysis.

Ecological Regression

Ecological regression is the most common approach for estimating how groups voted. It is sometimes called Goodman's ecological regression, after the scholar who developed it, but most applications of the technique stray far from Goodman's intent. The basic intuition is fairly simple. Goodman argued that ecological inference using linear regression would be possible if underlying racial vote choices were constant (e.g., $\beta_i^b = \beta_{i+1}^b = \beta_{i+2}^b = \cdots = \beta^b$) or at least constant aside from random variation. Researchers could collect data from areal units smaller than the aggregation of interest and run one or more linear regressions to estimate quantities missing from the cross-tabulation.

Consider a one-stage version of the equations introduced above, with the racial support rates expressed as constants:

$$V_i^L = \beta^b X_i + \beta^w (1 - X_i).$$

Assume a normally distributed error term e_i to make room for stochastic processes, and this equation looks like a linear regression formula with no intercept—which makes sense, given that a candidate who receives neither white nor black votes will not have any votes at all. A simple application of the distributive property provides a bivariate regression version:

$$\begin{aligned} V_i^L &= \beta^b X_i + \beta^w(1 - X_i) + e_i \\ &= \beta^b X_i + \beta^w - \beta^w X_i + e_i \\ &= \beta^w + (\beta^b - \beta^w)X_i + e_i. \end{aligned}$$

The intercept reports the white rate; adding the two coefficients together provides the black rate.

This one-stage version conflates registration, turnout, and vote choice. Conventional applications, both in research and in voting-rights litigation, use two stages—first estimating racial turnout, then plugging estimates for turnout from the first stage directly into the vote-choice equation. This ad hoc solution, which cannot produce measures of uncertainty, goes by the name double regression.

Some of the problems with ecological regression may seem obvious. Turnout and voting rates cannot be linear or normally distributed because they are bounded at 0 and 1. Areal units vary significantly in size, so coefficients that report the average properties of areal units may not parallel the individual-level behavior of interest. These are typical problems found in linear regressions; social scientists usually know how to look out for them. Weighting an ecological regression by population size can help address unequal areal units, although some scholars argue that this is an inappropriate solution.

Less obvious, perhaps, is that an identity equation cannot contain a random error term. Once we know the black population proportion and the racial voting rates, the observed vote cannot vary. Thus, if the right-hand side of the equation does not add up to the left-hand side value for any areal unit, then the noise must appear in the coefficient rather than in some separate residual. Varying coefficients violate ordinary least squares (OLS) assumptions.

The greatest barrier to ecological regression appears when group behavior varies by locale depending on the demographic context. Any contextual pattern that correlates with the independent variable, whether directly or indirectly, violates the assumption that group behavior is constant (or at least mean-independent) across units. The result is a distortion of the ecological regression results, usually called aggregation bias. Aggregation bias explains why applications of ecological regression often return impossible results. Not all instances of aggregation bias will be obvious, however.

Ecological regression can accommodate simple instances of aggregation bias. Consider a case in which white support for the left-wing candidate increases linearly as areal units become more diverse. The formula now contains a shifting parameter, $\beta_i^w = \gamma^0 + \gamma^1 X_i$, a function of racial density. Straightforward ecological regression, performed on data of this sort, will not estimate the desired quantities (i.e., β^b and the weighted average of β_i^w, presuming all other assumptions of the model were correct). Instead, it would turn up the following:

$$\begin{aligned} V_i^L &= \beta_i^w + [\beta^b - \beta_i^w]X_i + e_i \\ &= (\gamma^0 + \gamma^1 X_i) + [\beta^b - (\gamma^0 + \gamma^1 X_i)]X_i + e_i \\ &= \gamma^0 + (\beta^b - \gamma^0 + \gamma^1 - \gamma^1 X_i)X_i + e_i \\ &= \gamma^0 + [\beta^b - \gamma^0 + \gamma^1(1 - X_i)]X_i + e_i. \end{aligned}$$

The estimated intercept, assumed to represent white support for Wallace, will be γ^0 only. How does γ^0 differ from the real white rate? If the contextual effect γ^1 is positive, as hypothesized, then the missing component is also positive because X_i will never fall below zero. The estimate of white leftism will be too low. Similarly, the estimated black vote for left-wing candidates will be too high.

Fixing the aggregation bias in this case requires a simple application of the distributive property:

$$V_i^L = \gamma^0 + (\beta^b + \gamma^1 - \gamma^0)X_i - \gamma^1 X_i^2 + e_i.$$

Results generated from this equation could serve as ecological-regression estimates. Subtracting γ^0 and γ^1 from the coefficient generated by X_i, for example, would produce the black rate. The estimate for whites is more complicated, because it contains X_i and therefore requires a weighted average, but is also obtainable. The problem with this simple fix is if black behavior also changes with racial density, say by becoming more Republican in whiter communities. The second shifting parameter, $\beta_i^b = \rho^0 + \rho^1 X_i$, would produce the following:

$$\begin{aligned} V_i^L &= \gamma^0 + (\rho^0 + \rho^1 X_i - \gamma^0 + \gamma^1 - \gamma^1 X_i)X_i + e_i \\ &= \gamma^0 + (\rho^0 + \gamma^1 - \gamma^0)X_i + (\rho^1 - \gamma^1)X_i^2 + e_i. \end{aligned}$$

Now there are four constants to identify instead of three: γ^0, γ^1, ρ^0, ρ^1. Doing so is impossible, though, because the equation only produces three coefficients. The results are "underidentified."

Aggregation bias will be present in a naive ecological regression even if the coefficients are not a direct linear function of racial density (i.e., X_i), but instead change based upon some other community demographic that correlates with racial density and therefore creates an indirect relationship. For example, the poverty rate might increase as X_i increases, and poorer whites might support left-leaning candidates at a higher rate. The solution would look about the same as when racial density changed white voting behavior directly. If Z_i represents the poverty rate, then:

$$\begin{aligned} V_i^L &= \gamma^0 + (\beta^b - \gamma^0 + \gamma^1 - \gamma^1 Z_i)X_i + e_i \\ &= \gamma^0 + (\beta^b + \gamma^1 - \gamma^0)X_i - \gamma^1 Z_i X_i + e_i. \end{aligned}$$

Instead of a parabolic model with a simple squared term, the indirect form of aggregation bias simply requires an interaction term. Indeed, one could include the parabolic form plus add a whole series of interactions, each representing the product of X_i and some relevant variable that might condition the effect of race on voting behavior. These interaction terms would allow black and white voting behavior to change with relevant community demographics. Nevertheless, ecological regression provides no solution when both groups change their voting behavior with the community's racial density.

The Neighborhood Model

Ecological regression represents one extreme: the presumption that voting behavior changes systematically across groups but only changes randomly, if at all, within groups. But what if group behavior tends to converge when people live in close proximity to each other? Aggregation bias pushes estimates for each group apart, giving the appearance of greater polarization. Advocates of ecological regression quickly recognized this danger, and pointed out that the data could not rule violations of the constancy assumption: that groups behave similarly in particular locales and differ in part because their geographic distribution is unequal.

Freedman *et al.* popularized this concern when they proposed the neighborhood model. Rather than accept the extreme constancy assumption, this model goes to the opposite extreme: it supposes that groups behave identically when they reside in the same locale ($\beta_i^w = \beta_i^b$) and differ only because they reside in different locales. Presume, for example, that voting behavior shifts linearly with racial density. Assuming that the black and white responses to community density are identical (i.e., $\rho^0 = \gamma^0$ and $\rho^1 = \gamma^1$) means that:

$$\begin{aligned} V_i^L &= \gamma^0 + (\rho^0 + \gamma^1 - \gamma^0)X_i + (\rho^1 - \gamma^1)X_i^2 + e_i \\ &= \gamma^0 + (\gamma^0 + \gamma^1 - \gamma^0)X_i + (\gamma^1 - \gamma^1)X_i^2 + e_i \\ &= \gamma^0 + \gamma^1 X_i + e_i. \end{aligned}$$

This is the exact same regression required for ecological regression when conducted with the constancy (or mean-independence) assumption. The interpretations change dramatically, however. Now γ^0 represents voting behavior in all-white locales and γ^1 reports the contextual shift for each group as the community holds greater black density.

Social scientists knowledgeable about race would never accept any assumption that whites and blacks exhibit the same political preferences when they reside close to each other. They may converge somewhat, producing aggregation bias, but across-group variation clearly swamps within-group variation. The black vote for Democratic candidates varies little across geography, for example. More generally, the absurdity of each assumption—let us call it constancy versus convergence—depends upon the particular application at hand. Only theory can guide the choice; aggregate data provide no insight. In most cases neither assumption applies perfectly and the equation is underidentified. The truth lies somewhere in between, and the best an analyst can do, within the limits of linear regression, is select the assumption closest to what is known about the particular behavior under observation.

The Method of Bounds

This next solution for dealing with ecological inference is not really a method of estimation so much as a key insight that the other approaches neglect—which is that marginal quantities greatly limit the possible range of group behavior in each areal unit. Consider a locale in which the Democratic candidate wins 50% of the vote, and 25% of the voters are black. Even if every African American voted Democratic, whites must account for the remaining 25% of the Democratic candidate's votes. At least one-third of whites mathematically must have voted that way (although more may have, if some blacks voted Republican). So the possible white vote in this hypothetical example is not between 0 and 100%; the minimum is 33%.

These bounds can limit the maximum, the minimum, or both. Their helpfulness depends upon the size of each group. It is difficult to determine how a handful of blacks acted in a heavily white locale because their behavior does not make much of a dent in aggregate statistics. In heavily black locales, however, the aggregate statistics mostly reflect their choices. Bounds will be narrow on large groups and wide on small groups. The helpfulness of these bounds also depends on how extreme the outcome behavior happens to be. If almost everyone voted in a mixed-race precinct, then obviously blacks and whites both had to turn out at high levels. Added up over many small areal units, the implications for a larger electoral district can be quite informative.

The limit on the method of bounds, when used in isolation, is that the bounds identify only a range of possible behavior rather than a specific estimate. Analysts desiring to pin down a particular number cannot say whether the truth approaches one extreme or the other. Taking the midpoint may seem most sensible, since researchers familiar with the substance of their topic probably know about any phenomenon that would push rates of behavior in a consistent fashion across many small areal units (such as the strong tendency of blacks to vote for the Democratic party). But the data alone provide no guidance.

King's Solution to the Ecological Inference Problem

Gary King innovated aggregate data analysis by combining the best traits of each competing method into one relatively convenient solution to the ecological inference problem. His approach constrains estimates within the range of possible answers, consistent with the method of bounds. It selects specific quantities within those bounds through statistical inference rather than guesswork, consistent with ecological regression. For homogeneous units, his method takes advantage of the certainty about racial behavior. At the same time, it allows the possibility that behavior will differ in more diverse communities, either randomly or in some systematic contextual fashion. If the research holds particularly strong theoretical priors about how groups behave, either in general (as with the informed assumptions approach) or across particular contexts (as with the neighborhood model), then the model accommodates at least partial incorporation of those substantive insights. Best of all, King implemented his method in a convenient, and free, software package that produces estimates for the smaller areal units used as source data, not just for the electoral districts in which those smaller units are nested, and that also provides the user with a series of graphical and statistical diagnostic tools.

The method is fairly easy to describe with reference to the identities and the cross-tabulation introduced earlier. King's software, EI (or EzI), begins by identifying the complete set of values that might fill a table's cells—not for the electoral district as a whole, but for each areal unit. The method of bounds provides a range of possible behavior for both blacks and whites. However, the identity equation means that the estimate for one group must be linearly related to the estimate for the other group. Assume that one is known, the other must be known too:

$$V_i^L = \beta^b X_i + \beta^w (1 - X_i)$$
$$V_i^L - \beta^b X_i = \beta^w (1 - X_i)$$
$$\beta^w = (V_i^L - \beta^b X_i)/(1 - X_i).$$

Similarly,

$$\beta^b = [V_i^L - \beta^w (1 - X_i)]/X_i.$$

EI has reduced the range of possible estimates to a series of exclusive pairs, all within the range of possible values. The same process is possible for the observed behavior in each area unit i.

If we graph possible black and white behavior, then, the known information about each parish will be represented by a line segment, the set of all possible combinations. Figure 1 presents a "tomography plot," King's name (drawn from medical imaging) for the combined line segments of all areal units in an electoral district. It contains data for 64 Louisiana counties from 1968 and represents possible racial registration rates. This plot summarizes all deterministic information contained in the registration and demographic data available; no assumptions were required to produce it. Horizontal lines—that is, lines with very narrow bounds for white registration—correspond to almost entirely white counties. They contain so few African Americans that we know quite precisely how whites behaved (betaW), but almost nothing about blacks (which is why the slant of such a line only allows a small range of possible values on the y axis but any value on the x axis). A segment becomes more vertical, however, as the black population increases. We are less sure how many

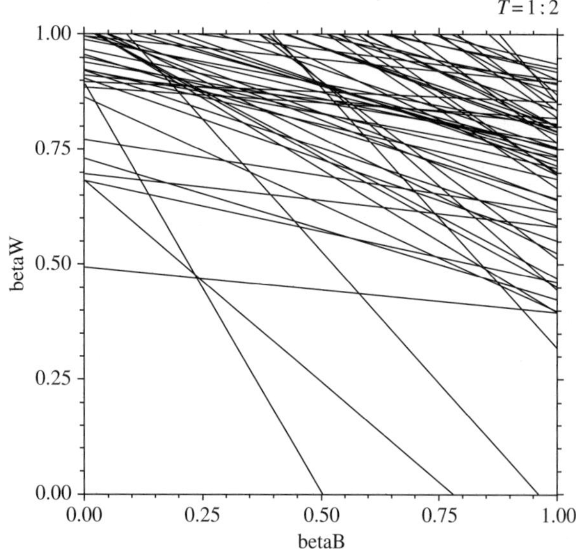

Figure 1 Tomography plot for Louisiana registration, 1968. Each line segment represents one parish (county). The vertical axis represents possible white registration rates; the horizontal axis represents possible black registration rates. Overall, this plot represents all known information about parish registration from the voting-age population and the overall registration rates. See text for more details. Plot was produced using King's EI.

whites registered in these mixed counties, because the aggregate data also include a large black population.

Somewhere on each line segment is a single point that represents the true black and white turnout rates. Deriving more specific estimates is impossible without making distributional assumptions of some kind. The usual assumption would be that the real points tend to cluster wherever the lines converge. More formally, King's proposal is to make three assumptions about the process generating racial voting behavior: (1) each areal unit's black rate and white rate together are one draw from a bell-shaped probability curve, called the bivariate normal distribution, truncated so that neither rate is outside the limits of 0 and 100%; (2) each areal unit's rates are mean independent of racial density; and (3) a racial group's behavior in one areal unit is independent of that in others. In fact, an elaborated version of King's model allows the introduction of covariates that might explain systematic variation in group behavior, therefore requiring that these assumptions hold only after controlling for the covariates.

EI estimates (using maximum likelihood) the truncated bivariate normal distribution with the greatest probability of generating an electoral district's data. Roughly speaking, it selects a bell shape that is highest where the tomography lines cluster most densely and then tapers off where the tomography lines become scarce, ending at the border of the unit square. The estimated distribution is three-dimensional, but one can imagine slicing it along any one tomography line segment to produce a simple two-dimensional (and therefore univariate) probability distribution. Where that curve is high, the pair of estimates is highly probable. Where it is low, the estimates are unlikely.

EI then takes a series of random draws from this univariate distribution, resulting in hundreds or thousands of simulations for the voting behavior in that areal unit. The mean of these simulations will represent the best estimate of how whites and blacks behaved; the variation in these simulations will represent the level of certainty. Note that, because the final estimates for each areal unit always appear on the tomography line, they will always be possible. Accumulating these estimates for each areal unit results in an estimate for the electoral arena as a whole, which also must be consistent with the known information in the data. Thus the estimate for each areal unit "borrows strength" from the other areal units. The locations of the other tomography lines determine the point estimate on any one.

This method of ecological inference is still imperfect, as indicated by early evaluations from the point of view of statistical theory, but it also has been found to operate well in actual social science data. In particular, it helps separate out contextual and compositional patterns when they are combined in an aggregation process.

Conclusion

The last section focused on one particular, and particularly intractable, example of data aggregation. It exhibits all of the traits of aggregation that appear in other methodological contexts: loss of information, statistics that vary based upon the level or unit of analysis, a search for statistics that are invariant to the level at which they are computed so that they will tap into the underlying quantities of interest. Nonetheless, there is a wide variety of examples in social measurement that represent attempts to deal with aggregated or grouped data, each with its own vocabulary and notation, but usually with the same underlying concerns.

Sometimes data are clumped across time—for example, when they are computed as five-year averages. This form of aggregation is usually considered a concern when performing time-series analysis. Often researchers attempt to combine their data into indices or scales, which often result in a loss of information at the same time they provide the researchers with relatively tidy proxies for a social phenomenon. Sometimes researchers wish to combine individual-level data with aggregate data, or for some other reason wish to work with multiple levels of data at once. Events may not be measured directly, but instead may be summed into "event counts" or recorded according to their durations—both forms of grouping. In short, aggregation as a concern in social measurement is an almost universal consideration across numerous methods and numerous disciplines.

See Also the Following Articles

Data Collection, Primary vs. Secondary • Ecological Fallacy

Further Reading

Achen, C. H., and Shively, W. P. (1995). *Cross-Level Inference.* University of Chicago Press, Chicago, IL.

Dogan, M., and Rokkan, S. (1969). *Quantitative Ecological Analysis in the Social Sciences.* Massachusetts Institute of Technology, Cambridge, MA.

Duncan, O. D., and Davis, B. (1953). An alternative to ecological correlation. *Am. Sociol. Rev.* **18,** 665–666.

Freedman, D. A., Klein, S. P., Sacks, J., Smyth, C. A., and Everett, C. G. (1991). Ecological regression and voting rights. *Eval. Rev.* **15,** 673–711.

Goodman, L. A. (1953). Ecological regression and behavior of individuals. *Am. Sociol. Rev.* **18,** 663–664.

Goodman, L. A. (1959). Some alternatives to ecological correlation. *Am. J. Sociol.* **64,** 610–625.

Grofman, B., and Migalski, M. (1988). Estimating the extent of racially polarized voting in multicandidate elections. *Sociol. Meth. Res.* **16,** 427–454.

Hannan, M. T. (1971). *Aggregation and Disaggregation in Sociology.* D. C. Heath and Co, Lexington, MA.

Hildreth, C., and Houck, C. (1968). Some estimators for a linear model with random coefficients. *J. Am. Stat. Assn.* **63,** 584–595.

King, G. (1997). *A Solution to the Ecological Inference Problem: Reconstructing Individual Behavior from Aggregate Data.* Princeton University Press, Princeton, NJ.

King, G., Rosen, O., and Tanner, M. (2004). *Ecological Inference: New Methodological Strategies.* Cambridge University Press, New York in press.

Voss, D. S. (1996). Beyond racial threat: Failure of an old hypothesis in the New South. *J. Pol.* **58,** 1156–1170.

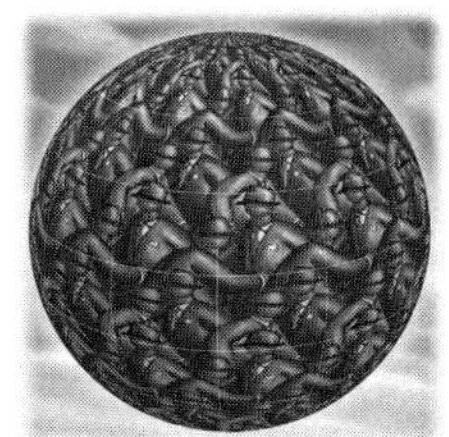

Aggregative Macro Models, Micro-Based Macro Models, and Growth Models

David C. Black
The University of Toledo, Toledo, Ohio, USA

Michael R. Dowd
The University of Toledo, Toledo, Ohio, USA

Glossary

ad hoc Improvised and often impromptu; an ad hoc model is one in which the structural equations have not been derived from microfoundations (i.e., either utility or profit maximization) but rather are postulated from the beliefs of the modeler.

aggregative model A macroeconomic model with structural equations postulated by the modeler to describe the economic relationships in the macroeconomy.

balanced growth path A rate of economic growth that has the capital-stock-per-worker and the output-per-worker growing at a constant rate. In this situation, output-per-worker is determined solely by the rate of technological progress.

break-even investment The level of investment in a growth model that is required to keep the capital-to-effective-labor ratio constant.

fiscal policy Altering government expenditures and taxes to affect the level of national income, prices, unemployment, and other key economic variables.

growth model A framework designed to examine the long-run movements in output, capital, and labor in terms of economic growth.

IS curve A curve that illustrates the combinations of interest rate and income consistent with equilibrium between investment (I) and saving (S).

IS–LM model A postulated static aggregative macroeconomic framework of aggregate demand that considers the interaction of its real side (investment–saving, or IS) with its nominal side (money demand and supply, or LM) to determine equilibrium income and interest rates.

LM curve A curve that illustrates the combinations of interest rate and income consistent with equilibrium between money demand (L) and money supply (M).

microfoundations The need for macroeconomic models to derive structural equations from utility and/or profit maximization.

monetary policy Altering the money supply and/or interest rates to affect the level of national income, prices, unemployment, exchange rates, and other key economic variables.

overlapping generations model A dynamic micro-based macro model that employs utility and/or profit maximization to determine the equilibrium consumption, saving, and employment allocations in an economy.

Phillips curve A curve illustrating the short-term negative relationship between the unemployment rate and the rate of inflation.

stabilization policy The deliberate manipulation of fiscal and/or monetary policies to affect the level of economic activity in a particular way, e.g., lessening the severity of the business cycle.

Macroeconomics analyzes the economy as a whole; the key variables macroeconomists want to explain are output, prices, interest rates, exchange rates, and unemployment. In contrast, microeconomics analyzes the behavior of individuals and firms; in this case, prices for particular products are determined by demand and supply. It is all but impossible to summarize all of the differences between macro- and microeconomic models, thus the focus here is only on three theoretic models that have had a substantial impact on economic modeling over the past 60 years. The three classes of models examined are the IS–LM, overlapping generations, and growth models. The IS–LM model is the traditional (static) aggregative macro model, which excels in short-run stabilization issues. The overlapping generations model, with production, is a general equilibrium, intertemporal micro-based macro model. It incorporates both utility and profit maximization. Growth models examine the importance of technology and human capital and convergence to equilibria; its long-run focus sharply contrasts that of the IS–LM model.

Aggregative Macro Models: IS–LM

A Simple IS–LM Model

The IS–LM model is a description of the economy's demand side; the focus of the IS–LM model is on short-run analysis of monetary and fiscal policy variables. In varying form, this model has been widely used since its introduction by Sir John Hicks in 1937. An IS–LM model is composed of a number of postulated relationships between variables, including those describing consumption demand, investment demand, and money demand. Equations (1)–(4) provide a paradigmatic version of a rudimentary IS–LM model:

Income identity $$Y = C + I + G, \quad (1)$$

Consumption function $$C = C(Y - T, r), \quad (2)$$

Investment function $$I = I(Y, r), \quad (3)$$

Money market $$M = L(Y - T, P, r). \quad (4)$$

The endogenous variables are income (Y), consumption (C), investment (I), and the interest rate (r). The exogenous variables are the money stock (M), price level (P), taxes (T), and government expenditures (G).

The IS curve is obtained by using Eqs. (2) and (3) in Eq. (1). In effect, as Eqs. (1) and (2) produce the saving curve; the IS curve portrays the interaction between saving and investment. This is commonly referred to as the goods market. The LM curve is equilibrium between money demand (L) and money supply (M) in Eq. (4). The IS is typically represented as the interest rate, being a positive function of government spending and negatively related to income and taxes; with LM, the interest rate is a positive function of income and prices and negatively related to money supply and taxes. The interaction between IS and LM determines the equilibrium income level and the interest rate, which, in turn, determines consumption, investment, and money demand. In contrast, an aggregative model with no interaction between saving and investment was provided by James Tobin.

The IS–LM model is particularly adept at providing short-run stabilization policy prescriptions, an ability that (by design) is absent in both the overlapping generations and growth models. Fiscal policy does this in the IS–LM model by driving a wedge between saving and investment. Unlike the classical model, fiscal stimuli in the IS–LM model will not necessarily alter saving and investment in the same direction nor in the same proportion (there is an overlapping generations model that assumes the contrary). The independent movements of saving and investment allow income to adjust in order for the economy to reach a new equilibrium. Monetary policy affects income by, first, altering the interest rate and, in turn, the incentives for savers and investors.

The IS–LM framework has been used to analyze the choice of how best to use monetary policy to minimize the fluctuations in the business cycle. With the central bank choosing between controlling either the interest rate or the money stock, eminently reasonable guidelines have been proposed: if disturbances originate in the money market, the central bank should choose to control the interest rate (so that no such interest rate disturbances are later transmitted to the goods market). Alternatively, if disturbances originate in the goods market, the central bank should instead control the money stock. Doing so will minimize the impact disturbances have on income. There are two reasons such a choice is not typically relevant in dynamic models such as the overlapping generations framework (OLG). First, money in an OLG model operates through different channels because it acts merely as a store of value (as opposed to the medium of exchange function in an IS–LM model). Second, in a choice-theoretic framework (such as the OLG model), utility-maximizing agents are concerned only with the real interest rate: nominal changes will not affect equilibrium consumption, saving, and labor market decisions in a dynamic model.

Two other attractive features of the IS–LM model may account for its continued use. The first is its flexibility in allowing the modeler to introduce into the theoretic model prior beliefs about the behavior of people and of the economy. For example, consider the ad hoc money demand relationship specified in Eq. (4): choosing that specification reflects the belief that the transactions' demand for money is a function of disposable income instead of gross income. As another example, it has been demonstrated that a procyclical money multiplier allows for the possibility of a downward sloping LM curve and nontraditional policy prescriptions. Over the years, this flexibility has produced innumerable variants to the relationships described in Eqs. (1)–(4), with each variant employed to emphasize the particular interests of the modeler. That said, however, it is the responsibility of the modeler to justify empirically his/her assumptions and model specification.

The second attractive feature of the IS–LM model is its rich intuitive framework. For example, consider the interaction between saving and investment, both of which are demand theories. How could IS theory be an equilibrium obtained from the interaction between two demand curves? The framework is general enough to afford the modeler the opportunity to provide the needed intuitive justification/rationalization. Saving can be interpreted as the demand for new securities: people buy an "I.O.U."—a bond—when they deposit money into their savings account. Investment can be interpreted as the supply of new securities: firms issue new securities to finance new investment spending. Using this interpretation, the IS curve is viewed as the equilibrium between the supply and demand for new securities, not two demand curves. In other words, the goods market can be viewed as the primary market for new securities. And what of LM? Because LM reflects portfolio choice between money demand and existing bonds, it can be viewed as the secondary market for securities. The particular interpretation here implies that the interest rate and national income are determined by the interaction between the primary and secondary markets of securities. As an alternative interpretation, consider that saving and investment can, respectively, be viewed as the private supply and demand of new loanable funds. Incorporating the government's budget deficit and net exports with the private supply and demand for loanable funds will determine the economy's real interest rate.

We are quick to point out that the interpretations here are not, by far, the only intuitive interpretations of the relationships behind IS–LM. As with the flexibility in model specification, so too there is flexibility in intuitive explanations of this framework. As one additional example, consider a further interpretation of the IS–LM framework: the act of saving and the act of investment are acts of accumulating wealth. In contrast, the money market determines how people would allocate their wealth (i.e., between money and bonds). This suggests that income and interest rates are determined by the interaction between the desire to accumulate wealth and the desire to allocate that wealth. As a last example of the intuitive flexibility of the IS–LM model, consider the difference between stock and flow variables. A stock variable has no reference to time. Examples of this are money and bond holdings. In contrast, flow variables, such as investment and saving, have a reference to time: they are measured in terms of \$/week or \$/year—in other words, they are measured with respect to their accumulation over time. Hence, the interaction between the IS and the LM curves yields an equilibrium that is a reconciliation between the stock and flow variables within aggregate demand.

These alternative intuitive interpretations (as well as all of those not discussed here) must be consistent with each other. This is one of the most intriguing aspects of the IS–LM framework. Its ability to lend itself to alternative explanations allows both the modeler and the reader to apply prior beliefs, interests, etc. when interpreting the structure and results of the model.

Adding Aggregate Supply to the Simple IS–LM Model

Because IS–LM models describe only the demand side of the economy, they were ill equipped to be used in modeling the supply-side shocks that occurred in the mid- and late-1970s. In response, adaptations to the IS–LM model included a "summary" of the economy's supply side, such as the Phillips curve relationship described in Eq. (5).

$$\text{Phillips curve} \qquad \frac{\dot{P}}{P} = H\left[\frac{(Y - Y^F)}{Y^F}\right] + \pi, \qquad (5)$$

where $\dot{P}/P$ and π are the actual and expected inflation rates, respectively, Y^F is full-employment output, and $H' > 0$. A complete analysis of policy prescriptions resulting from a model such as that described by Eqs. (1)–(5) is not possible here, but in general terms, appending Eq. (5) to the model in Eqs. (1)–(4) alters the role of variables and the policy prescriptions in a number of important ways. First, and probably most important, this model allows for $\dot{P}$ to be determined in the short run and P to be determined in the long run. (Whereas this attribute may now seem a prerequisite to any acceptable model, when introduced, it marked a substantial innovation from the simple demand-side IS–LM models used prior to the mid-1970s.) In terms of short-run policy analysis, endogenous prices tend to dampen the effect of well-established policy prescriptions or, in the extreme, render ambiguous the effects of such policy options. Second, with the inclusion of Y^F, a "long-run" benchmark was introduced into this short-run model. With that came discussions of the possibility of "long-run" neutrality of money and a reduced stabilization role for government policy variables within this framework. However, any discussion of the Phillips curve must include the seminal work of Milton Friedman, which contains not only a precautionary analysis of the Phillips curve models but also includes the now-famous discussion of the natural rate of unemployment, the role of monetary policy, and other issues.

As an alternative to the Phillips curve, others added slightly more realistic descriptions of the supply side. For example, combining Eqs. (1)–(4) with Eqs. (6)–(8) produces an aggregate supply–aggregate demand model that now solves for Y, r, C, I, P, W (nominal wages), and N (employment).

$$\text{Production function} \qquad Y = F(N, K), \qquad (6)$$

$$\text{Labor demand} \qquad F_N(N, K) = W/P, \qquad (7)$$

$$\text{Labor supply} \qquad S(N) = (1 - \tau)W/P. \qquad (8)$$

Here, K is the capital stock and τ is a marginal tax rate on labor. This aggregate supply–aggregate demand model added much-needed detail of the supply side of the economy and it allowed rudimentary supply-side analysis via changes in τ. However, the postulation of the supply side to the economy only exacerbated the need for microfoundations of the model specification. One example responding to the need for microfoundations on the supply side was Carl Shapiro and Joseph Stiglitz's provision of an intuitively plausible explanation for endogenously determined involuntary unemployment.

Expectations

Though "expectations" can be introduced into an IS–LM model via a number of avenues, the method most widely used has been that of specifying an adaptive expectations scheme, whereby the change in inflationary expectations ($\dot{\pi}$) is proportional (λ) to the error in expectations in the previous period:

$$\text{Adaptive expectations} \quad \dot{\pi} = \lambda\left[\frac{\dot{P}}{P} - \pi\right]. \tag{9}$$

Adding Eq. (9) to Eqs. (1)–(5) provides a mechanism for tracking the "step-by-step" movement toward "long-run" equilibrium (defined as when all expectations are satisfied). The underlying problem, of course, is that including a relationship such as Eq. (9) in an IS–LM model is an attempt to proxy dynamics in a static model.

Criticisms of the IS–LM model

Though the IS–LM model provides an intuitively rich framework, it possess other characteristics that are troublesome to many theorists. First is the fact that the IS–LM model is a static model. With no reference to time, the IS–LM model restricts in important ways the behavior of some of the variables within the model. For example, money is postulated to act as a medium of exchange. Without a reference to time, the effects of the "store of value" function of money cannot be represented in an IS–LM model. However, the most enduring criticism of the IS–LM model is that its structural equations are postulated and are not derived from utility or profit maximization. This criticism reduces to the following question: If the structural equations are ad hoc, are the policy prescriptions that follow equally ad hoc? For example, consumption in Eq. (2) is assumed to respond positively with changes in disposable income and negatively with the interest rate. Critics of IS–LM models correctly point out that important parameters such as the marginal propensity to consume (MPC) cannot be postulated. Critics could also argue as to whether saving today and, hence, whether consumption today are functions of the interest rate. Similar microfoundation arguments can be applied to the other structural equations as well.

Though the need for microfoundations in macro models is justified, the rhetorical gap between critics and defenders of IS–LM models is not unbridgeable. With regard to the preceding examples, defenders of IS–LM models would agree with the critics that the value of parameters such as the MPC, as well as the relevance of interest rates on consumption, can be determined only empirically: if empirical evidence does not support the postulated structural equation, then the postulated equation must be altered to reflect the data.

As the following discussion shows, the overlapping generations model can provide microfoundations for the examination of macroeconomic issues. In particular, the OLG model allows for an examination of whether some of the relationships postulated in IS–LM analysis can be derived from either utility or profit maximization.

The Overlapping Generations Model

The ad hoc nature of the IS–LM framework, coupled with the lack of a realistic portrayal of the economy's supply side, prompted an intense search during the 1970s and 1980s for microtheoretic macro models that could establish from first principles the behavioral relationships typically discussed in aggregative macro models. Though various models were proposed, one model that fit the dual needs of microfoundations and macro applications was the overlapping generations framework, originally suggested by Paul Samuelson in 1958.

The OLG model differs from aggregative models in a number of ways. First, it is a dynamic model: "time" matters. Agents live for two periods. They are termed "young" and "old" in their first and second period of life, respectively. In a particular period, say t, there are N_t young agents born in that period and N_{t-1} old agents that were born in the previous period. In the following period, $t+1$, the current young agents become old and the current old agents die and another N_{t+1} young agents are born. A very common assumption is that of a constant population (i.e., $N_t = N \ \forall t$). However, care needs to be given when making such an assumption, because policy prescriptions can depend critically on whether population is assumed constant in OLG models. Such assumptions impact on whether insights not available in the IS–LM framework are incorporated into the OLG model. For example, a growing population with a constant money supply results in an increase in the real interest rate, which will impact other real variables. Though this result is easy to establish in an OLG framework, it is not available to IS–LM analysis.

The second and perhaps more important structural difference is that young agents base their decisions (e.g., consumption and saving allocations) on intertemporal utility maximization. As expected, the structural differences between the OLG and IS–LM models result in a number of significantly different policy implications.

A Simple Utility-Maximizing Model

First, consider an abstraction employed in almost all OLG models: agents are endowed with a fixed income when young (W^y) and when old (W^o). In this simple OLG model, young agents at time 1 choose consumption when young $\left(C_t^y\right)$ and old $\left(C_{t+1}^o\right)$, and saving when young (S_t), which maximizes their utility function, $U\left(C_t^y, C_{t+1}^o\right)$, subject to their budget constraints in each period. Assume population is constant.

Saving when young can take many different forms: money, government bonds, land, etc. Though alternative vehicles for savings can differ (along with corresponding budget constraints), the primary characteristics of such assets do not: agents purchase these assets when young and carry them to the next period, at which time they sell the asset in order to augment second-period consumption. Hence, saving provides young agents the ability to smooth consumption over the two periods of their life.

For illustrative purposes, assume $U\left(C_t^y, C_{t+1}^o\right)$ is log-linear and saving occurs when young agents purchase money balances from old agents and/or the government. In this case, the young agent's choice problem is

$$\begin{aligned} &\underset{C_t^y, C_{t+1}^o, M_t/P_t}{\text{Max}} && U = \ln C_t^y + \ln C_{t+1}^o \\ &\text{Subject to:} && C_t^y + M_t/P_t = W^y \\ & && C_{t+1}^o = W^o + (M_t/P_t)R_t. \end{aligned} \tag{10}$$

Here P_t is the money price of the consumption good at time t. The interest rate equals the gross real rate of return on money balances, $R_t = P_t/P_{t+1}$. There are no explicit taxes in this example, though lump-sum taxes can easily be introduced into the model by way of defining $W^y = \overline{W^y} - T_t^y$ and $W^o = \overline{W^o} - T_{t+1}^o$, where T_t^y and T_{t+1}^o are lump-sum taxes when young and old. However, because such taxes are not distortionary, they do not qualitatively affect the equilibrium allocations. Therefore, with lump-sum taxes it is possible to discuss "disposable income" instead of gross income and to obtain the same qualitative results with this semantic change.

This general equilibrium model is closed by the government's budget constraint, which states that government expenditures are financed through money creation: $G_t/N = (M_t - M_{t-1})/P_t$. The young agent's equilibrium consumption and saving allocations implied by Eq. (10) are as follows:

$$C_t^y = \frac{1}{2}\left(W^y + \frac{W^o}{R_t}\right),$$

$$C_{t+1}^o = \frac{1}{2}(W^y R_t + W^o),$$

$$\frac{M_t}{P_t} = \frac{1}{2}\left(W^y - \frac{W^o}{R_t}\right).$$

These consumption and saving allocations are both intuitive and consistent with assumptions normally postulated in aggregative models. An example of such microfoundations is that an increase in the interest rate increases saving, decreases current consumption, and increases future consumption.

There are a number of general characteristics of equilibrium allocations in the OLG model. First, consumption and saving decisions are based on lifetime income (appropriately discounted). From a young agent's perspective, lifetime income is $W^y + W^o/R_t$; from the perspective of an old agent, lifetime income is $W^y R_t + W^o$. Hence, agents consume in each period half of their lifetime income. This consumption smoothing is made possible by transferring excess income in one period to the other. From a young agent's perspective, the present values of income in the two periods are W^y and W^o/R_t. Whichever income is larger, the young agent must transfer (via saving) one-half of the excess income to the other period in order to smooth consumption in each period. Because $W^y > W^o$ is typically assumed, the relationship for M_t/P_t indicates that saving in this example is chosen appropriately. The usual assumption of $W^y > W^o$ can be interpreted as the "young" period of an agent's life (the working years of that agent) and the "old" period of an agent's life (his/her retirement years). The situation of $W^y < W^o/R_t$ implies that young agents would have to borrow (perhaps from the government) in order to smooth consumption.

The second characteristic of an OLG model to note is the role that money plays. In an IS–LM model, money is postulated to act as a medium of exchange and not as a store of value. In contrast, money in an OLG model is derived from utility maximization to be a store of value and not as a medium of exchange. This makes intuitive sense because the IS–LM model is relevant for the short run and the OLG model is more applicable to long-run analysis—given its "generational" motivation. In IS–LM, short-run changes in the money supply influence real variables by first altering the nominal interest rate and then the real interest rate. In OLG, changes in the money supply (completely independent of fiscal actions) will alter the nominal interest rate, but that will not be transmitted to either the real interest rate or to other real variables.

The third OLG characteristic centers on the alternatives to holding money. The demand for money in an IS–LM model is based on transaction demand and the interest rate paid by competing assets (that is, both money and various bonds are held simultaneously). In a typical OLG model, competing assets are redundant: because competing assets all potentially serve as a store of value only, agents will demand only the asset that returns the largest interest rate and all other assets will be discarded. Attempts to model money as a medium of exchange in OLG models have included postulating utility as depending on real money balances. In such models, both money and alternative assets may be held by agents despite the fact that their respective interest rates are not identical.

Expectations

In an IS–LM model, expectations usually serve merely to provide a mechanism for moving from a short-run equilibrium toward a long-run equilibrium. In contrast, expectations play a crucial role in determining the current and future equilibrium allocations in an OLG model. The reason is straightforward: if young agents are to choose consumption now and in the future, they must form expectations of future prices to make such decisions today. In order to form expectations of prices, agents necessarily must form expectations of both fiscal and monetary policy actions now and in the future. Typically, strict government policy "rules" are imposed to facilitate expectation formation. To achieve this, OLG modelers typically assume that young agents possess complete information on all past variables, have perfect foresight of all future variables, and know with certainty all present and future government policy actions. In general terms, imposing such assumptions obtains neoclassical policy prescriptions, and relaxing any such assumptions yields neo-Keynesian results.

The common imposition of such strong assumptions has prompted an examination of rational expectations equilibria versus nonrational expectations equilibria. One reason the OLG model has been so widely used was the belief that the assumption of rational expectations in a choice-theoretic framework would deliver to the economic agent the highest level of utility obtainable. This belief has been shown to be without foundation. In a choice-theoretic framework, the utility of an agent with nonrational expectations will be higher than that of an agent with rational expectations. This results from the macro application of a micro model: what is true for an individual is not necessarily true for the group.

Adding Aggregate Supply to the Simple OLG Model

Though the IS–LM model has received substantial criticism for its lack of a realistic description of the economy's supply side, the alternative adopted by many, the OLG model, very rarely alters its specifications to address this criticism. Equation (11) represents an exception to this:

$$\begin{aligned}&\max_{C_t^y,\mathcal{L}_t^y,C_{t+1}^o,\mathcal{L}_{t+1}^o,M_t/P_t} && U=U(C_t^y,\mathcal{L}_t^y,C_{t+1}^o,\mathcal{L}_{t+1}^o)\\ &\text{Subject to:} && C_t^y+M_t/P_t=W^y, \qquad T=L_t^y+\mathcal{L}_t^y\\ &&& C_{t+1}^o=W^o+(M_t/P_t)R_t, \qquad T=L_{t+1}^o+\mathcal{L}_{t+1}^o.\end{aligned} \tag{11}$$

Here T is the total amount of time in a period, $\mathcal{L}$ is leisure, and L is labor supply. In such a model, young agents facing both budget and time constraints must choose consumption and labor supply when young and old, as well as saving. With the government budget constraint, the model is closed with the addition of the firm's maximizing profits according to the production function $I_t=f(N_t^y,N_t^o)$ and standard labor costs, where N_t^y and N_t^o are labor demand of young and old workers alive at time t. The firm's optimization problem produces a demand for labor from the current young agents and the current old agents. Equating labor demand and supply of the young and old at time t determines the equilibrium employment and real wage rate for each agent alive at time t. From this equilibrium, allocations of output, consumption, and saving are determined.

The characteristics of the simple OLG model continue, in general, to hold in models that include production. The single, general, exception is that young agents not only smooth consumption but also smooth leisure time across their lifetime. However, inclusion of the economy's supply side in a micro-based macro model allows for analyses that are not possible in the aggregative IS–LM model (for example, given unexpected disturbances, why unemployed workers choose to remain unemployed instead of negotiating a new real wage).

The OLG model is but one framework employing a microfoundation to macroeconomic analysis. Another is the representative agent model, with the most common form having the agent at time t maximize lifetime utility by choosing consumption/saving (and, perhaps labor supply) allocations in each period over an infinite time horizon (i.e., $t, t+1, \ldots, t+\infty$). Though both the OLG and the representative agent models provide microfoundations to their analysis, there are two important differences to note. First, of course, the time horizon in an OLG model is much more restrictive compared to that in the typical representative agent model. Second, though growth modeling is possible in the OLG framework, a representative agent model appears to be better suited for such analysis, given its focus on long-term equilibria. Such long-term issues are discussed in the following section.

A Growth Model

Preliminary Descriptions

The Solow growth model focuses on the long-run movements of output (Y), capital (K), labor (L), and knowledge (or the effectiveness of labor) (A). With the subscript t denoting time period, the basic model consists of the following system of equations:

$$Y_t = F(K_t, A_tL_t), \tag{12}$$

$$L_{t+1} = (1+n)L_t, \tag{13}$$

$$A_{t+1} = (1+g)A_t, \tag{14}$$

$$Y_t = C_t + I_t, \tag{15}$$

$$S_t = Y_t - C_t = sY_t, \tag{16}$$

$$I_t = K_{t+1} - K_t + \delta K_t. \tag{17}$$

Equation (12) is the production function, with A_tL_t representing effective labor. Equations (13) and (14) indicate how the stocks of labor and knowledge change over time, with n and g, respectively, representing the exogenous growth rates of labor and knowledge. Equation (15) is the income identity. Equation (16) assumes saving is a constant fraction (s) of income. Equation (17) indicates that gross investment is equal to change in the capital stock plus depreciation of the existing capital stock, with δ representing the rate at which capital depreciates.

The production function is assumed to exhibit constant returns to scale in both of its arguments. [That is, doubling K and AL leads to a doubling of output. This assumption allows us to work with the production function in intensive form: $F(K/AL, 1) = F(K, AL)/AL$.] In intensive form, the production function can be written as $y = f(k)$, where $k = K/AL$ is the amount of capital per unit of effective labor and $y = Y/AL = F(K, AL)/AL$ is the amount of output per unit of effective labor. Thus, output per unit of effective labor depends only on capital per unit of effective labor. For example, consider a particular production function that exhibits these properties, the Cobb–Douglas production function: $F(K, AL) = K^{\alpha}(AL)^{1-\alpha}$, where $0 < \alpha < 1$. Written in intensive form, this production function is $f(k) = k^{\alpha}$, where $f(0) = 0$, $df/dk > 0$, $d^2f/dk^2 < 0$.

To simplify notation, let a dot over a variable indicate the change in that variable from one period to the next (e.g., $\dot{A}_t = A_{t+1} - A_t$). Combining Eqs. (15) and (16) implies that $S_t = I_t$; this and Eq. (17) yield $K_{t+1} - K_t = sY_t - \delta K_t$. Dividing both sides of this relationship by effective labor and using $\dot{k}_t = k_t(\dot{K}_t/K_t - \dot{L}_t/L_t - \dot{A}_t/A_t)$, we can write this relationship in intensive form:

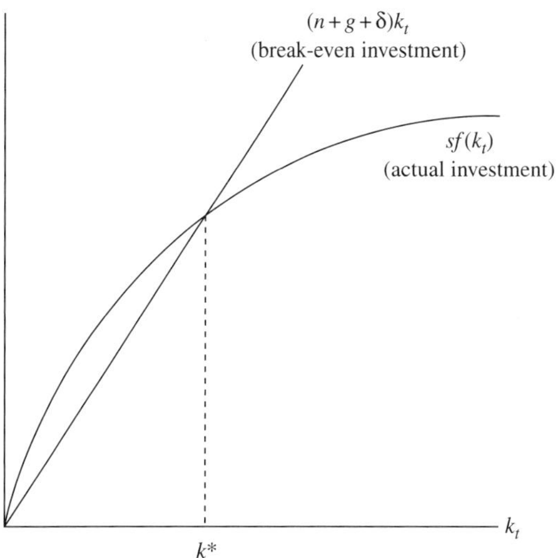

Figure 1 Determining the change in the capital stock in a Solow growth model.

$$\dot{k}_t = sf(k_t) - (n+g+\delta)k_t, \tag{18}$$

where $\dot{k}_t$ is the change in the capital-to-effective-labor ratio from time t to time $t+1$. The first right-hand-side term in Eq. (18) is saving (and, hence, investment) and the second term is referred to as break-even investment. This is the level of investment that would be needed to keep the ratio of capital to effective labor constant.

Figure 1 plots each term on the right-hand side of Eq. (18). Given the assumptions regarding the production function, actual saving in intensive form is portrayed as increasing at a decreasing rate. Break-even investment is simply a ray from the origin with slope $(n+g+\delta)$. There are two steady states: $k = 0$ and $k^* > 0$, the attracting steady state being k^*. If k_0 (the initial capital-to-effective-labor ratio) is $0 < k_0 < k^*$, then actual investment is greater than break-even investment. Equation (18) therefore implies $\dot{k}_t > 0$ (i.e., this ratio is growing). In contrast, $k_0 > k^*$ implies that actual investment is less than break-even investment and $\dot{k}_t < 0$ (i.e., this ratio is declining).

The Balanced Growth Path

Because k is constant in the long run and effective labor grows at the rate $n+g$, the capital stock (K) and, in turn, output (Y) grow at the rate $n+g$. Finally, capital per worker, K/L, and output per worker, Y/L, are growing at the rate g. Thus, all variables are growing at a constant growth rate, i.e., a balanced growth path. On the balanced growth path, output per worker is determined solely by the rate of technological progress (g). The balanced growth path in the Solow model is consistent with several of the stylized facts about economic growth. First, the growth rates of labor, capital, and output are roughly constant. Second, the growth rates of capital and output are roughly equal. Third, the growth rates of capital and output are larger than the growth rate of labor (so that output per worker and capital per worker are rising).

Remarks on the Simple Growth Model

Growth models address a fundamentally difficult question: What are the factors that influence long-term economic growth? Neither IS–LM nor OLG models can address this question. The contrasts between growth models and the IS–LM and overlapping generations models are rather sharp, due to the intended focus of each model. To some, the long run may be adequately described by the length of time between generations. However, the relevance of some variables as well as policy prescriptions that follow from a growth model indicate what is truly long-run analysis. For example, though money is a rather important policy variable in IS–LM models, and it may affect some equilibrium allocations in the dynamic OLG framework, money is not relevant in growth models.

In terms of considering the role of expectations across the three classes of models we (almost) approach a continuum with respect to its importance. The short-run IS–LM model can clumsily postulate expectational relationships, but in most cases these tend merely to adjust equilibrium allocations instead of determining them. In contrast, expectations in the longer term OLG framework play a crucial role in determining all equilibrium allocations. Finally, the long-run nature of growth models renders a discussion of expectations moot: expectations in the long run are, by definition, satisfied, so there is no point to such a discussion.

IS–LM is aggregate demand (i.e., the aggregate demand curve is derived from the IS–LM curves). Moreover, notwithstanding its dynamic framework, few OLG models specify a supply side to the economy. In contrast, the emphasis of growth models is almost entirely on the supply side of the economy: What influences an economy's long-run productive capabilities? The emphasis of these models with respect to aggregate demand versus aggregate supply is reflected in their application to monetary and fiscal policy prescriptions. When policymakers are interested in short-run impacts on the business cycle, the preferred model is IS–LM, and both monetary and fiscal options are available to policymakers. When interested in how decisions are made in a dynamic framework, the OLG model serves nicely: fiscal policy can influence equilibrium allocations while monetary policy plays a diminished role. When policymakers are interested in long-run effects, growth models provide clear guidance to appropriate policy actions. First, monetary policy is irrelevant in the long run. Second, there are two avenues that fiscal policy can use to influence the growth rate of the economy. The first avenue is to lower real interest rates in order to promote capital accumulation. The second avenue is to promote education and technological advancement (e.g., via research and development). In contrast to the policy prescriptions emanating from IS–LM and OLG models, the benefits of either of these avenues can be expected only to be reaped in the long run.

See Also the Following Articles

Aggregation • Economic Development, Technological Change and Growth • International Economics • Social Economics

Further Reading

Barro, R. J., and King, R. G. (1984). Time-separable preferences and intertemporal-substitution models of business cycles. *Q. J. Econ.* **99**(4), 817–839.

Black, D. C., and Dowd, M. R. (1994). The money multiplier, the money market, and the LM curve. *East. Econ. J.* **30**(3), 301–310.

Blinder, A. S., and Solow, R. M. (1973). Does fiscal policy matter? *J. Public Econ.* **2**(4), 319–337.

Dowd, M. R. (1990). *Keynesian Results in a Neo-Classical Framework*. Ph.D. dissertation. State University of New York, Buffalo.

Friedman, M. (1968). The role of monetary policy. *Am. Econ. Rev.* **58**(1), 1–17.

Hicks, J. R. (1937). Mr. Keynes and the classics: A suggested interpretation. *Econometrica* **5**(2), 147–159.

Holmes, J. M., and Smyth, D. J. (1972). The specification of the demand for money and the tax multiplier. *J. Political Econ.* **80**(1), 179–185.

Holmes, J. M., Dowd, M., and Black, D. C. (1991). Why real wages do not fall when there is unemployment. *Econ. Lett.* **35**(1), 9–16.

Holmes, J. M., Dowd, M. R., and Black, D. C. (1995). Ignorance may be optimal? Some welfare implications of rational versus non-rational expectations. *J. Macroecon.* **17**(3), 377–386.

Keynes, J. M. (1936). *The General Theory of Employment, Interest, and Money.* Harcourt Brace Jovanovich, New York.

Poole, W. (1970). Optimal choice of monetary policy instrument in a simple stochastic macro model. *Q. J. Econ.* **84**(2), 197–216.

Romer, D. (1996). *Advanced Macroeconomics.* McGraw Hill, New York.

Samuelson, P. A. (1958). An exact consumption-loan model of interest with or without the social contrivance of money. *J. Political Econ.* **66**(6), 467–482.

Sargent, T. J. (1987). *Dynamic Macroeconomic Theory.* Harvard University Press, Cambridge, MA.

Sargent, T. J. (1987). *Macroeconomic Theory,* 2nd Ed. Academic Press, Boston.

Scarth, W. M. (1988). *Macroeconomics: An Introduction to Advanced Methods.* Harcourt Brace Jovanovich, Toronto.

Shapiro, C., and Stiglitz, J. E. (1984). Equilibrium unemployment as a worker discipline device. *Am. Econ. Rev.* **74**(3), 433–444.

Tobin, J. (1995). A dynamic aggregative model. *J. Political Econ.* **63**(2), 103–115.

Weintraub, E. R. (1979). *Microfoundations: The Compatibility of Microeconomics and Macroeconomics.* Cambridge University Press, Cambridge.

Agricultural Statistics

Dawn Thilmany
Colorado State University, Fort Collins, Colorado, USA

Elizabeth Garner
Colorado State University, Fort Collins, Colorado, USA

Glossary

Agricultural Marketing Service (AMS) An agency that provides high-frequency, geographically delineated data and information on prices, marketing, and distribution of numerous agricultural commodities for the United States Department of Agriculture and the agricultural industry.

Economic Census The U.S. Census Bureau profile of the U.S. economy, conducted every 5 years, from the national to the local level; provides data on establishments, revenue, value of shipments, payroll, and employment.

Economic Research Service (ERS) The primary source of economic research and analysis for the United States Department of Agriculture (its department home); provides information and analysis on a broader set of agriculture, agribusiness, consumer, and rural issues.

National Agricultural Statistics Service (NASS) Primary statistics collector and information provider for the United States Department of Agriculture (its department home) and the production agriculture industry.

North American Industry Classification System (NAICS) A system that has replaced the U.S. Standard Industrial Classification system. NAICS provides more detailed classifications and new industries, reflecting the changing economy and the way business is done.

United States Census Bureau An agency of the United States Department of Commerce; collects a wide variety of data about the nation's people and economy.

United States Department of Agriculture (USDA) A cabinet-level department with seven major divisions overseeing 19 different services.

Agriculture statistics have been collected for over two centuries, but the detail and breadth of agricultural production, business, and food data have changed significantly over the years. One way to categorize agricultural statistics is by the focus of analyses and public issues they help to describe, including production, markets, trade, price levels, and behavior (of producers and consumers); emerging technologies and differentiated products (grades and certifications); rural development, demography, and social concerns; as well as food safety, security, and nutrition. The economic, social, environmental, health, and cultural aspects of farming and food influence a variety of programs, policies, and research questions related to farming and food. This article provides a summary overview of the types of data available, and an evolution of how agricultural statistics have come to include an increasingly broad set of informative data on production, natural resources, farm and food prices, economic activity, and the food sector.

Introduction to Agricultural Statistics and Data

Some of the earliest data collection in the United States was based on agriculture; the 1790 census counted 9 out of 10 Americans as living on farms. In 1791, President George Washington wrote to several farmers requesting information on land values, crops, yields, livestock prices, and taxes; this was, in effect, the first agricultural survey in the United States. According to the historical information on the United States Department of Agriculture web site (www.usda.gov), in 1840, detailed agricultural information was collected through the first Census of Agriculture, which provided a nationwide inventory of production. Yearly estimates established the general pattern of annual agricultural reports that continues to this day.

The United States Department of Agriculture (USDA) was established by Abraham Lincoln in 1862, and its first crop report was distributed in 1863 by the Division of Statistics [now the National Agricultural Statistics Service (NASS)]. Early on, the USDA helped farmers assess the value of their goods, to better negotiate with commodity buyers and get a fair price. In assessing the more recent evolution of the USDA, much of it has been guided by policy (farm bills and other price supports, data to assess market power in eras of antitrust concern, and food security and consumption data as nutrition and health have become topics of greater interest).

The importance of the agriculture sector in early U.S. history is clear: a vast majority of households were involved in the industry. However, it may be less clear why data continue to be independently collected for this industry, now that the relative importance of agriculture to the economy is diminished (less than 2% of U.S. households now operate farms). Beyond the basic need for food, and the economic activity that farming and its marketing channels create (inputs, processors, distributors, retailers, and food service), there are several potential reasons why public and private agencies prioritize agricultural statistics. First, there is the persistence of interest and institutions to serve agriculture (including the USDA); second, very few numbers of agricultural companies are publicly owned or assessed retail sales tax, so no data are available from the Security and Exchange Commission (SEC) or state Departments of Revenue; third, the nature of agriculture as an industry is complex, including its role in natural resource usage, trade activity, and government transfer programs; and finally, market outlook and production information are important factors for national food security, because short-term supply response is constrained by climate in the United States.

Still, the data and statistics discussed here, and used for analysis of agriculture, food, and rural issues, have evolved to serve a broader audience than agricultural producers and the agencies and institutions that service them. The broadening scope of agriculture and its allied sectors has led the USDA to widen its analysis and attention to a broad set of public issues. These evolving issues and the data collection efforts to provide information for analysis are discussed throughout this article. It is important to understand that this increasing complexity is likely due to the integration of food, land, and rural business activity in economic, social, and policy development and research.

Agricultural Production and Financial Statistics

As mentioned previously, the earliest scope of work for the USDA and NASS (and predecessors) was basic resource usage, production, and financial data for farms. Subsequently, early statistics included information on land in farms, market value of agricultural products (crop and animal), farm production expenses, and value of land, buildings, and, as new innovations came about, machinery and equipment.

As the agricultural industry and society evolved, so did the statistics to record structural change in food production. Every 5 years, the Census of Agriculture provides data based on over 50 reports for each state and county, with statistics on production, income, government support, inventories, and irrigation delineated by a number of enterprises and farm typologies [ethnicity of owner, tenure of operator, size in terms of sales or assets, type of legal organization, and principal occupation of operator (because nonfarm income is now such an important influence on farm households)]. The 2002 Census also allowed for the possibility of multiple operators on one farm.

In addition to more detailed data on agricultural production and structure of farms, the USDA/NASS collects annual data on acreage, production, yields, prices, and production forecasts for a set of agricultural commodities set forth by Congress this is variable by state, depending on enterprises and production in each region. A major shortcoming of these data is the limited set of agricultural commodities, but beyond congressional appropriations for the commodities that are required to be tracked, state agricultural statistics agencies must rely on industry-based financial contributions to collect data on other crops.

NASS recently began collecting data on a more diverse set of enterprises related to food production or with similar industry characteristics. The ornamental horticulture (1988) and aquaculture (1998) industries now collect census data every 5 years (similar to the agriculture census). In addition, data of broader interest to scientists and policymakers are collected in specialized surveys, including surveys on the economics of agriculture and ownership of land, farm labor usage, computer usage, agricultural practices (chemical usage; genetically modified organisms), injuries, and women's role on farms.

With the move to a new classification system, the North American Industrial Classification System (NAICS), the U.S. Census Bureau now has more detailed information on firm numbers, payroll, and employees for allied food and resource industries (timber, horticultural services, wholesale and garden centers, processors, distributors, and retailers). In addition to this information for all industrial categories, revenue, value-added, and manufacturer capital expenditure and inventory data are available, in addition to monthly revenue and inventory estimates for food service and retailers. Overall, agriculture production data is quite complete for traditional commodities and easy to disaggregate by enterprise and geography. More recently, it became a bit easier for those interested in broader issues related to food production to explore emerging technology and social and economic trends for a diverse set of agriculture, resource, and consumer topics. Yet, less frequent data gathering for some statistics (similar to the U.S. Census) makes it more difficult to assess production and finance issues relative to pricing and trade.

Agricultural and Food Prices

The availability of commodity, wholesale, and market prices for agricultural products is equaled only by data on publicly traded stocks and companies. Early on, the USDA invested money through the Agricultural Marketing Service (AMS) to place market news professionals in all major production areas of the United States. These professionals report prices being received at wholesale markets, shipping points, and terminal markets, and when possible, a sense of the relative volume, quality, and types of products moving through markets. These data are very rich in detail across time, with 400 daily, weekly, monthly, and summary annual reports covering most major foods and some ornamental horticulture products. The high frequency of the data is important because of the industry's seasonality and the perceived need for real-time information for planning by producers, shippers/distributors, and processors. The USDA now has all of these data products available on-line for researchers, and in some cases, offers compiled reports for those doing historical price analysis across a longer time period.

Beyond USDA/AMS price reports, the Chicago Board of Trade, the Chicago Mercantile Exchange, the Kansas City Board of Trade, and the Minneapolis Grain Exchange provide daily updates on futures market pricing information for most major grains (corn, soybeans, and a variety of wheat varieties) and livestock products (pork and beef). There are also some analysis-oriented organizations that track prices and provide it to industry and academic professionals. The Livestock Marketing Information Center provides prices, production, situation, and outlook data for several livestock products, and several Internet web sites offer free or reasonably priced databases for vegetables and fruits (www.todaymarket.com and www.produceforsale.com).

To track the share of consumer food dollars that return to farms, the USDA estimates the value of a market basket consisting of a fixed quantity of food at the retail and farm level, to determine the price of providing services associated with marketing foods. In recent years, the USDA has also been exploring investments in retail scanner data to get more detailed information on retail prices for differentiated meat and produce, including how feature sales pricing influences marketing margins and prices paid by consumers.

The attention to farm and retail price spreads motivates discussion of some of the limitations of available agricultural price data. As consolidation in the food retail, distribution, and food service industries has led to fewer companies making fewer public transactions, the validity of prices from remaining cash-based open markets is called into question. Still, the volume and frequency of price data for food at the farm, wholesale, and terminal market levels provide a rich informational resource for business planning and research.

Agricultural and Agribusiness Trade Data

With increased globalization, international trade is an important issue for any industrial sector, but the agricultural sector is especially influenced by trade because of related political, development, and historical issues. There are two key sources of food trade data. The USDA's Foreign Agricultural Service offers several different databases for data on international agricultural trade, including different market levels (bulk commodity, intermediate food inputs, and more fully processed food products), and breakdowns at the commodity level for both imports and exports. These data can also be disaggregated by the sending or receiving industry and country. The USDA's Economic Research Service then uses state-level historical production data from NASS to determine state export shares for crops and livestock. The FAS also provides outlook and data reports on various world markets by country and commodity.

The U.S. Census Bureau also tracks imports and exports by major product category on a monthly basis. This information is provided for imports and exports to and from each major trading partner. A fairly rich historical series is available, but these data are not delineated by commodity, so agricultural products cannot be specifically tracked. Again, these data exist for not only farm commodities, but also for agricultural inputs and processed food and textiles. There is also pertinent information from the general U.S. Census Bureau, which calculates expected world population by country, data often used when developing world food demand forecasts. The USDA's Economic Research Service reports these data, together with other macroeconomic data useful in analyzing international trade prospects, including inflation, gross domestic product (GDP), and real exchange rates for major agricultural trading partners. Following the reduction in apparent, tariff-based trade restrictions and new political economy issues, the USDA/ERS is beginning to develop typologies to measure trade barriers to agricultural trade, but there are only limited data. This is one limitation of agricultural statistics available for international trade. The other weakness of any available data is that, with increasing integration across borders, less and less information is available from public institutions.

Rural Development and Agribusiness

Agriculture tends to drive the economies of many rural areas and plays a role in rural development policy and research. Calculating the contribution of agriculture to a local or state economy can be measured many ways. Often, employment, personal income, sales, and value-added data are used as measures, but these data are not necessarily readily available from one source. Additionally, the contribution of production agriculture extends beyond the farm gate to include the input, processing, and marketing sectors (cumulatively known as "agribusiness"), which are also important to many rural economies and communities.

Employment

Data on farm labor employment are collected by four major agencies: the U.S. Department of Labor, the Bureau of Labor Statistics, the National Agricultural Statistics Survey, and the Census of Agriculture from various surveying efforts. Reliable data on farm employment are difficult to collect due to the part-time and transitory nature of the employment, as well as the number of family members working on farms. Employment data for the other industries comprising agribusiness are developed and disseminated primarily by the Bureau of Economic Analysis (BEA) and can be disaggregated to a county level and downloaded from their web site. Often, the publicly released BEA Regional Economic Information System (REIS) data cannot be disaggregated to a small enough industrial classification. Special requests for unsuppressed, more detailed county employment data are often granted through the BEA. Additionally, data from an individual state's Department of Labor and Employment can be used to supplement the BEA data.

Income

Data from the BEA are the primary source for both farm labor and proprietor income, as well as for other agribusiness industries. These data can also be supplemented by data from a state Department of Labor and Employment. Because employment and income data are available annually, they are a comparatively useful measure in determining the overall and changing impact of agriculture on a local economy in response to various shocks (policy, climatic changes such as drought or flood, and trade balance).

Sales

Production and price data for commodities leaving the farm gate were discussed in Sections II and III. Still, it is important to note that, although the data are available on an annual basis, geographic delineations of these data are more limited due to the nature of production agriculture. Sales or output data for the input, processing, and marketing sectors are somewhat restrictive to work with because they are available only every 5 years from the various economic censuses.

Multipliers

Multipliers are often used to estimate broader economic impact by estimating the indirect and imputed economic activity related to direct revenues and input expenditures. The two primary sources for regional multipliers are the Regional Input–Output Modeling System (RIMS II) by the BEA and the Impact Analysis for Planning (IMPLAN) model by the Minnesota IMPLAN Group. Sometimes the data used to create the multipliers in IMPLAN have been used to supplement employment, income, and output data needs. Using the data directly is not recommended because, in cases, local estimates can be simple adaptations of national averages, but can offer data ranges and magnitudes when other sources are limited.

Social Concerns

Indicators of rural economic and social conditions are also important when addressing the economic condition of agriculture. The Economic Research Service (ERS) branch of the USDA researches and compiles data for measuring the condition of rural America. Some of the data they monitor include farm and nonfarm rural employment, labor and education, wages and income, poverty, infrastructure (including telecommunications and transportation), federal funding, and general demographics (including age distribution and changes in ethnic and racial composition). The ERS has also worked extensively defining more detailed geographic descriptors that enable richer county-level research. This detail is especially rich for analyzing nonmetropolitan area trends that may be related to degree of rurality and metropolitan area proximity. The ERS measures the "rurality" of an area based on characteristics of the area in addition to the federal definitions provided by the Office of Management and Budget (OMB). The ERS has developed various codes and spatial aggregations useful for understanding rural areas, including typology, urban influence, rural–urban continuum, commuting zones, and labor market areas. Most of the demographic (including income and poverty) measures that the ERS monitors are collected by the U.S. Census Bureau and most of the employment, labor, and wages are collected by the Bureau of Labor Statistics.

Land Use

The number of acres planted and harvested by state and county are available annually through the National Agricultural Statistics Service, although collection is limited to the major commodities. The Census of Agriculture collects information on land use every 5 years. Variables can include land in farms, harvested cropland by size of farm, value, water use, and crop use—in essence, the productive resource base of agricultural-based rural areas. The National Resources Inventory through the Natural Resources Conservation Service (also the USDA) conducts a survey of land every 4 to 5 years as a means to monitoring the status, condition, and trends of soil, water, and other natural resources in the United States.

Food Security

The Economic Research Service leads federal research on food security and hunger in U.S. households and communities. They also provide data access and technical support to facilitate food security research in the United States. The USDA web site provides a list of publicly available national surveys on food security in the United States. Food security for a household, as defined by the ERS, means access by all members at all times to enough food for an active, healthy life. Food security includes at a minimum (1) the ready availability of nutritionally adequate and safe foods and (2) an assured ability to acquire acceptable foods in socially acceptable ways (that is, without resorting to emergency food supplies, scavenging, stealing, or other coping strategies). The Current Population Survey–Food Security Supplement (CPS–FSS) conducted by the Census Bureau for the Bureau of Labor Statistics is the primary source of national and state-level statistics on food security in the United States. The data are primarily national, with state-level data available for "food insecure" and "food insecure with hunger." Related to food security is food consumption. The ERS also annually calculates the amount of food available for human consumption in the United States. This series tracks historical national aggregate consumption of several hundred basic commodities and nutrient availability annually; the data date from 1909 and go through 2001. Although there are full time series on many foodstuffs and their subsequent nutrients, more commodities have been gradually added through the years.

Food security is also based on the availability of safe foods. The ERS provides a variety of resources and research on food safety, including estimating the costs of foodborne disease. The Centers for Disease Control, using several surveillance systems, are the primary agencies that collect data on food-related illness in the United States. Currently, only national data are available. Data on food-related illness are limited for many reasons, including nonreporting and unknown sources of transmission of pathogens. State Departments of Health are also a source for food-related illness information.

For those facing food security shortfalls, the USDA administers numerous domestic food assistance programs through the Food and Nutrition Service (FNS). Programs include the Food Stamp Program, the Special Supplemental Nutritional Program for Women, Infants, and Children (WIC), and the Child Nutrition Programs (School Lunch, School Breakfast, and Summer Food Service). These programs account for about half of total USDA outlays. Expenditures for the USDA's food assistance programs totaled $20.9 billion during the first half of fiscal 2003 (October 1, 2002, to March 31, 2003), a 7% increase over the first half of fiscal 2002. The entire USDA budget, including allocations to these programs, is available at the USDA web site.

Several organizations maintain information on food assistance programs. For research, start with the ERS data, and for data and information on the programs, consult the Food and Nutrition Service division of the USDA; the USDA web site is the source for all of this type of information. The Bureau of Census also conducts a survey on program participation, known as the Survey of Income and Program Participation (SIPP). Information on statistical sampling methods, variables, and access to the survey data is available at www.sipp.census.gov. Substate participation rate data for the food assistance programs can be difficult to acquire from the federal agencies, but state agencies administering the food assistance programs can also be sources for county-level program participation data.

The Food and Nutrition Service division of the USDA also administers food distribution programs that provide food and nutrition assistance to eligible individuals and institutions, and provides data on total participation and assistance in these programs at the USDA web site. The Farm Service Agency Commodity Operations Office provides data on purchases of basic nonperishable commodities such as cereals, grains, peanut products, nonfat dry milk, and vegetable oils for eligible outlets participating in food distribution programs. Beyond providing food assistance, the USDA also provides nutrition education through the FNS, which provides some research on usage and effectiveness of programs.

Summary Overview

The scope and detail of agricultural statistics has increased greatly since the first agricultural census of the United States. The economic, social, environmental, health, and cultural aspects of farming and food have led to a complex set of programs, policies, and research questions that are served by, and contribute to, the data resources available on agricultural issues. This article has given a very broad overview of the types of data available, and an evolution of how agricultural statistics have come to include an increasingly broad set of information. Still, the breadth of agriculture's reach does not compromise the need for heightened attention to this sector, as there are so many unique natural resource, production methods, food security, and international factors related to agriculture.

See Also the Following Articles

Census, Varieties and Uses of Data • Economic Anthropology • Economic Development, Technological Change and Growth • Economic Forecasts

Further Reading

The following entities maintain Internet web sites that publish a variety of topics of national, state, county, or local interest.

Agriculture Marketing Service (www.ams.usda.gov). Price data on crops and livestock.

Bureau of Economic Analysis (www.bea.gov). Annual state and county employment and personal income data, by industry.

Bureau of Labor Statistics (www.bls.gov). Annual, quarterly, and monthly state, county, and subcounty employment, labor force, and wage data.

Census of Agriculture (www.nass.usda.gov/census/). Every 5 years (years ending in 2 and 7), publishes state and county production, financial, land use, and demographic data.

Economic Research Service (www.ers.usda.gov). Farm labor employment and demographic data are published on an irregular basis.

Foreign Agricultural Service (www.fas.usda.gov). United States and individual state import and export data.

National Agricultural Statistics Service (www.usda.gov/nass/). Annual state and county crop and livestock production data.

Natural Resources Conservation (www.nrcs.usda.gov). Every 4 to 5 years, publishes state land use and natural resource conditions and trends.

United States Census Bureau (www.census.gov). Annual and decennial state, county, and subcounty population, age, race, poverty, and education data; a state and county economic census of employment, payroll, business establishment, and sales data is conducted every 5 years.

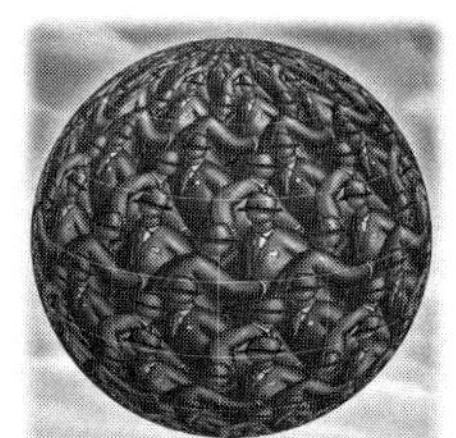

Alpha Reliability

Doris McGartland Rubio
University of Pittsburgh, Pittsburgh, Pennsylvania, USA

Glossary

coefficient alpha An index of the internal consistency of the measure. It is a lower-bound estimate of the reliability of a measure.

Cronbach, Lee The creator of the coefficient alpha or Cronbach's alpha.

Cronbach's alpha Coefficient alpha (named after the developer of the index).

correlation The degree to which two variables are related.

essential tau-equivalence The items that measure a particular factor have the same factor loadings on that factor.

homogeneity An assumption of alpha that all of the items are equally related and come from the same content domain.

internal consistency A type of reliability that indicates the extent to which the responses on the items within a measure are consistent.

items The individual questions, statements, phrases, sentences, or other word arrangements on a measure.

measurement error The amount of variance present in an item or measure that is not attributable to the construct.

multidimensional measure A measure that assesses more than one attribute of a variable.

reliability The extent to which a measure is consistent; this can be demonstrated by either stability within the measure (consistency) or stability over time.

unidimensional measure A measure that assesses only one attribute of a construct. Unidimensionality is an assumption of coefficient alpha.

Reliability is concerned with the consistency of a measure, either at one point in time or over time. When measures are administered at one point in time, the type of reliability that is of primary concern is the internal consistency of the measure. Coefficient alpha is widely used as a measure of the internal consistency. Coefficient alpha assumes that the items are homogeneous and unidimensional. A high coefficient alpha indicates that one item can be used to predict the performance of any other item on the measure. A low coefficient alpha can indicate either that the measure has poor reliability or that the items are not homogeneous. Having a high coefficient alpha does not provide any information as to the construct validity of the measure. Even if the measure has perfect reliability, this does not address what the measure is measuring. The measure must be subjected to further psychometric testing in order to ascertain its level of validity.

Introduction

Reliability is the degree to which a measure is consistent. The consistency of a measure can be shown by either the consistency of the measure over time or the consistency of the responses within a measure. When examining the consistency, we are concerned with the extent to which the responses vary (either between measures or within a measure) as a result of true variability or as a consequence of error. Reliability has been shown to represent the degree to which the variability in scores exemplifies the true variance in responses. In other words, the reliability of a measure reflects the amount of true variability, as opposed to variability attributable to error.

When assessing the psychometric properties of a measure, researchers often begin by assessing the reliability of a measure. At a minimum, the reliability provides an indication of the amount of error present in a measure. However, reliability does not address whether the measure is accurately assessing the construct. Nevertheless, an important component of validity is that the measure is reliable. In other words, reliability is necessary but not sufficient for validity.

When studying social phenomena at one point in time, researchers administer measures at one time. For this reason, the internal consistency of a measure is of paramount concern. Internal consistency assesses the reliability within a measure. It is this type of reliability that is the focus of this paper.

Definitions

Classical test theory indicates that:

$$X = T + E \quad (1)$$

where X is the observed score, T is the true score, and E is the error. Reliability is:

$$r = 1 - E \quad (2)$$

Because error and reliability directly correspond to one another, the type of reliability that we assess for a measure depends on the type of error that we seek to evaluate. When the measurement error within a measure is of concern, we seek to ascertain how much variability in the scores can be attributed to true variability as opposed to error. Measurement error within a measure manifests as a result of content sampling and the heterogeneity of behavior sampled. Content sampling refers to the sampling of items that make up the measure. If the sampled items are from the same domain, measurement error within a measure will be lower. Heterogeneity of behavior can lead to an increase in measurement error when the items represent different domain of behaviors. Other sources of measurement error within a test can occur, including guessing, mistakes, and scoring errors.

Internal consistency indicates the extent to which the responses on the items within a measure are consistent. Coefficient alpha is the most widely used reliability measure of internal consistency. Others measures of internal consistency include split-half and Kuder-Richardson 20.

Development of Alpha

Cronbach

Perhaps Lee Cronbach's most famous work stemmed from his 1951 article in which he presented coefficient alpha. Cronbach was able to demonstrate that coefficient alpha is equivalent to averaging all the split-half correlations. More specifically, if a measure consists of 20 items, the items on the measure can be split into two groups of 10 items each. Computing a correlation between the two groups provides a rough estimate of the reliability of a measure, but only for one-half of the test. If all the possible groups of two are correlated and the average of these correlations is computed, this is equivalent to the coefficient alpha. This statement is only true if (1) the measure is tau-equivalent (discussed later) or (2) the formula for split-half is computed using the 1939 Rulon method. The Rulon method for split-half reliability is based on the variance of the differences between the two halves, as opposed to correlating the two halves and then computing the Spearman-Brown prophecy formula.

Relationship to Other Measures of Internal Consistency

Coefficient alpha is the most common measure of internal consistency. It is a function of the number of items and the interrelatedness of the items. Specifically:

$$\alpha = (k/k-1)\left(1 - \sum \sigma_i^2/\sigma_y^2\right) \quad (3)$$

where k is the number of items, $\sum \sigma_i^2$ is sum of the item variances, and σ_y^2 is the variances of the total scores on the measure. Other measures of internal consistency are computed differently and are used for different purposes.

Split-Half Method

Prior to the proliferation of computers, internal consistency was computed using the split-half method. The split-half method entails splitting the measure in half, either by setting the top half versus the bottom half or by using the odd and even numbers. A correlation is computed between the halves. This estimate can then be generalized to the entire measure by using the Spearman-Brown prophecy formula (discussed later). The main limitation of the split-half method is that different splits produce different reliability estimates. How do we determine which split to use? Even more problematic is a speeded test or a test in which the items are ordered. Because most (if not all) computer packages for statistics include an option to calculate coefficient alpha, split-half method no longer is used.

Kuder-Richardson 20

As seen in formula (3), coefficient alpha is based on the variance of the item scores. With dichotomous data, a more appropriate method can be used to assess the internal consistency of a measure. This method is known as Kuder-Richardson 20 (KR20):

$$r_{\mathrm{KR20}} = (k/k-1)\left(1 - \sum pq/\sigma_y^2\right) \quad (4)$$

where $\sum pq$ is the summation for each item of the proportion of people who pass that item times the proportion of people who do not pass that item. As can be seen in formula (4), KR20 is the dichotomous equivalent to the coefficient alpha.

Characteristics and Assumptions

Measure of Internal Consistency

Coefficient alpha is a measure of the internal consistency of a measure. As such, alpha varies with the number of items and with the degree of interrelatedness between the items. The relationship among the items indicates the extent to which the responses on the items are consistent. When a measure is said to be internally consistent, the performance on one item can predict the performance on another item because the responses across items are consistent. For example, if a person is depressed, that person should consistently score high on a measure of depression. However, the internal consistency only documents that the responses are consistent and not the extent to which the items accurately measure the construct.

Not a Measure of Unidimensionality

Coefficient alpha does not assess the unidimensionality of a measure. A high coefficient alpha does not imply that the measure is unidimensional, nor does it imply that the items are homogeneous. However, if the measure is homogeneous, it will by definition be internally consistent.

Assumptions

Many people mistake the assumptions of coefficient alpha as being synonymous with the properties of the index. Coefficient alpha has three assumptions that cannot be ignored. The first assumption is that all the items have equal reliability. That is, the items contain the same amount of measurement error, indicating that the error cannot be correlated across items. Second, coefficient alpha assumes that the items are homogeneous. For items to be homogeneous, they all should measure the same latent variable. The third assumption is unidimensionality. The dimensionality of the items can be discovered by the pattern of correlations among the items. If different patterns exist, this could indicate the presence of different dimensions in the measure. In order for a measure to be unidimensional, three conditions must be present: (1) the measure must be homogeneous, (2) the measure must be internally consistent, and (3) the measure must be externally consistent. To be external consistent, all the items must correlate equally to an outside variable, taking into account sampling error. Therefore, internal consistency, as represented by coefficient alpha, is necessary but not sufficient for unidimensionality.

Properties of the Items

Number of Items

Researchers have repeatedly commented on one property of coefficient alpha, that alpha varies by the number of items in the measure. Although perceived as a weakness by some, if we accept coefficient alpha as a measure of reliability and not simply as a measure of the extent to which the items are homogenous, then this property is consistent with reliability.

If alpha were a measure of homogeneous items, we could argue that it should not vary by the number of items. As pointed out by Cronbach, a gallon of milk should be no more homogenous than a quart. Reliability, on the other hand, does increase as the number of items in a measure increases. Reliability is a function of the number of items and the reliability of the items. For example, 10 observations of a behavior are more reliable than only three observations. More items generate more information and therefore should be more reliable.

A limitation of coefficient alpha is that alpha becomes invariant as the number of items increases. Because a curvilinear relationship exists between the number of items and alpha (see Figure 1), as the threshold is reached coefficient alpha does not increase substantially. This relationship is true provided all the items have the same correlation with the total score. The threshold is dependent on several factors such as the homogeneity of the behaviors sampled. The measure may actually increase in its reliability, but this will not be manifested in the coefficient.

Direction of Relationships Between Items

In order to accurately assess the internal consistency of a measure using coefficient alpha, all the items should

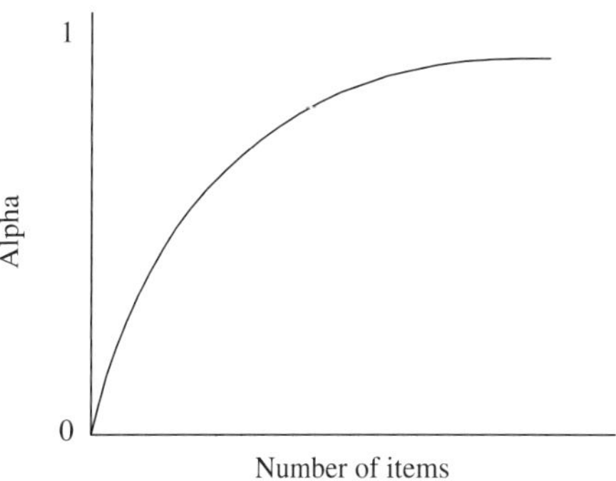

Figure 1 Relationship between the number of items and alpha citation. Adapted from Nunnally and Bernstein (1994, p. 307)

be positively related to one another. In fact, if we fail to reverse code the necessary items, a negative coefficient alpha could surface. Coefficient alpha actually ranges from $-\infty$ to 1, and it is negative if negative covariances exist between the items.

Magnitude of the Relationship Between Items

It is unlikely that all the items in the measure will be equally related to one another. However, to the extent that the items equally relate to a single common factor, we can assume the essential tau-equivalence of the items. When the items are essential tau-equivalent, the true scores of the items are the same or the items' true scores only vary by a constant. If essential tau-equivalence is met, coefficient alpha is equal to the true reliability. Without tau-equivalence, coefficient alpha is a lower-bound estimate of reliability.

Uses for Alpha

Coefficient alpha is used to assess the degree to which the items are internally consistent. A high coefficient indicates that the items are interrelated. More specifically, the performance on any one item can predict the performance on each of the remaining items.

Coefficient alpha can also be used to determine the strength of the dimensionality of a measure. This can only be done, however, if unidimensionality has been previously determined. In this sense, coefficient alpha is used as a confirmatory measure of dimensionality.

A low coefficient alpha can indicate two things. First, the measure may not be homogeneous. That being the case, coefficient alpha could be reestimated on the items that are homogeneous. Second, and more problematic, the measure may have poor reliability. It is this second reason that leads us to reevaluate the measure to determine why the measure performed so poorly in the sample.

Spearman-Brown Prophecy Formula

The Spearman-Brown prophecy formula is used to estimate the change in reliability of a measure as a function of the measure's length. If the number of items in a measure is doubled, the formula can estimate the reliability for the longer measure. Similarly, if the measure is reduced by half, the formula can estimate the reliability for the shortened form.

The formula can be used in two ways. First, the formula can be used to estimate the reliability of a measure when the split-half method is used. In order to use the formula, the measure must be split in half and the two halves correlated. Once the correlation between the halves is known, the Spearman-Brown prophecy formula can be used to estimate the reliability for the entire measure. The formula is:

$$r_{\mathrm{sh}} = \frac{2^{*}\, r_{12}}{1 + r_{12}} \tag{5}$$

where r_{12} is the correlation between the two halves.

The second application of the Spearman-Brown prophecy formula involves estimating what the reliability of a measure will be if that measure is shortened or lengthened:

$$r = \frac{k^{*}\, r_{ij}}{1 + (k-1)r_{ij}} \tag{6}$$

where k is the factor that the test will be increased by (e.g., 1/2 or 2) and r_{ij} is the reliability of the measure. For example, consider a test consisting of 50 items that has strong reliability ($r = 0.95$). If the test is reduced in half so that 25 items remain, the projected reliability of the test is $r = 0.90$:

$$r = \frac{1/2^{*}\, 0.95}{1 + (1/2 - 1)0.95} = \frac{0.475}{1 - 0.475} = 0.90$$

Conclusion

Internal consistency indicates the amount of measurement error present within a measure. This type of reliability provides useful information about the consistency of responses in a measure. If a measure has a high internal consistency, then the we can assume a high degree of interrelatedness among the items.

Coefficient alpha is a measure of reliability that represents the degree to which a measure is internally consistent. A high coefficient only indicates that the items measure something consistently. Even with a sufficient coefficient alpha, we cannot draw any conclusions as to the validity of the measure. Alpha does not provide any information about *what* the measure is measuring; the construct validity of a measure still needs to be assessed. Reliability is necessary but not sufficient for validity.

At a minimum, coefficient alpha should be computed for every measure at each administration. Given the ease with which this index is calculated, we would be remiss if we did not study the reliability of the measure given in their specific sample.

See Also the Following Articles

Inter-Rater Reliability • Measurement Error, Issues and Solutions • Reliability • Split-Half Reliability • Test–Retest Reliability

Further Reading

Cortina, J. M. (1993). What is coefficient alpha? An examination of theory and applications. *J. Appl. Psychol.* **78,** 98–104.

Cronbach, L. J. (1951). Coefficient alpha and the internal structure of tests. *Psychometrika* **16,** 297–334.

Cronbach, L. J. (1984). *Essentials of Psychological Testing.* 4th Ed. Harper & Row, New York.

Green, S. B., Lissitz, R. W., and Mulaik, S. A. (1977). Limitations of coefficient alpha as an index of test unidimensionality. *Educ. Psychol. Meas.* **37,** 827–838.

Hattie, J. (1985). Methodology review: assessing unidimensionality of tests and items. *Appl. Psychol. Meas.* **9,** 139–164.

Lord, F. M., and Novick, M. R. (1968). *Statistical Theories of Mental Test Scores.* Addison-Wesley, Reading, MA.

Miller, M. (1995). Coefficient alpha: a basic introduction from the perspectives of classical test theory and structural equation modeling. *Structural Equation Modeling* **2,** 255–273.

Nunnally, J. C., and Bernstein, I. H. (1994). *Psychometric Theory.* 3rd Ed. McGraw-Hill, New York.

Rulon, P. J. (1939). A simplified procedure for determining the reliability of a test by split halves. *Harvard Educ. Rev.* **9,** 99–103.

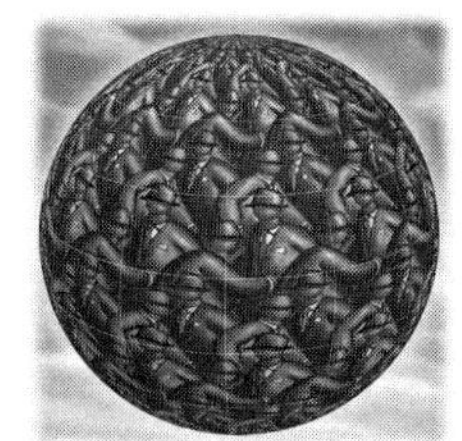

Anthropology, Psychological

Steven Piker
Swarthmore College, Swarthmore, Pennsylvania, USA

Glossary

anthropology A discipline historically dedicated to a holistic understanding of humankind, including the diversity of cultural lifeways now and in the past, the social evolution of same, language, human biology, and the relationship of humankind to its close evolutionary relatives, extant and extinct. Psychological anthropology is a part of (mainly American) anthropology.

culture, general and evolutionary The mode of adaptation of the human species, featuring, e.g., speech, learned and diversifiable social relationships, religion, technology, and material culture, all of which presuppose capacity for symbol use.

culture, specific The way of life of a specific group, including especially meaning.

evolution The processes by which species, including the human species, arise and endure and change and become extinct.

personality Enduring psychological dispositions. Psychological anthropology workers, variably, emphasize emotional or cognitive and conscious or unconscious dispositions. Sometimes the dispositions are understood in the terms of an established psychological school (e.g., psychoanalysis, cognitive psychology), sometimes not.

relativism Everything that human beings do and think is relative, to a significant extent, to the specific cultural context in which the doing and thinking occur.

Anthropology emerged as a discipline in Europe and America in the last half of the 19th century. From the outset, it was, importantly, part psychological, and it has remained so throughout its history, especially in America. This article draws on and extends previous attempts by the author to make psychological anthropology sensible to the nonanthropologist reader. The approach is broadly intellectual-historical, with emphasis given to recent and current developments.

Introduction

Psychological anthropology is a recognized subfield of (mainly) American anthropology. Its organizational focus is The Society for Psychological Anthropology, which is a branch of the American Anthropological Association, and its official journal is *Ethos*. Arguably, the central and enduring concern of psychological anthropology is the psychological mediation of the individual/culture relationship. The first organized school within psychological anthropology was culture and personality, established at about the time of World War II. Over the subsequent three decades or so, the subfield of culture and personality grew and diversified, and a number of its emphases remain active today. In part in reaction to culture and personality, and with reference to its major issues, new schools also arose, both within and outside anthropology.

Precursors (1920–1940): Anthropology and Psychoanalysis

In the first decades of the 20th century, anthropology and psychoanalysis attended to each other, and important anthropologists and psychoanalysts sometimes communicated directly with each other. For anthropologists, of course, Freud's still emerging oeuvre was the initial and main focus of attention. Significantly, attention was paid mainly not to Freud's "cultural" writings, but rather to his theory of mental symbolism and ontogenesis. And anthropologists (e.g., Bronislaw Malinowski and Margaret

Mead) began to take Freudian ideas and inspirations into the field with them in the service of understanding the psychological bases for the individual's relationship to his or her culture. This at once brought psychoanalysis into the domain of culture as lived day in and day out by natives—surely a far cry from the clinical chamber of the psychotherapist—and prompted preliminary personality/culture formulations on the part of anthropologists.

Emergence of Classical Culture and Personality: Abram Kardiner

For the study of psychology and culture, the period 1930–1945 was one of ferment and growth across the fields of psychoanalysis (e.g., Freud, A. Freud, Horney, Klein, Roheim, Erikson, Devereux, and Sullivan) and anthropology (e.g., Malinowski, Mead, Benedict, Sapir, Linton, and Hallowell). Amid this bustle, classical culture and personality took shape at Columbia University under the guidance and inspiration of the eclectic psychoanalyst, Abram Kardiner. In a series of seminars, a handful of anthropologists presented cultural material from their fieldwork, and Kardiner provided psychodynamic interpretation with suggested personality and culture relationships. From this collaboration emerged a general model of culture and personality, as well as a method for testing its validity. The model posits that basic personality, with its reality (conscious) and projective (unconscious) subsystems, mediates between primary institutions (subsistence, kinship and family, and socialization) and secondary institutions (especially religion; also, e.g., recreation, art, and folklore). Specifically, socialization practices give rise especially to the projective system of the basic personality, which expresses itself psychosymbolically, as posited by psychoanalysis, in projective institutions, in much the same manner that unconscious material is said by psychoanalysis to express itself in, e.g., the manifest content of dreams and neurotic symptoms. This model, therefore, suggests both that basic personality maintains projective institutions and that projective institutions serve important psychological functions for basic personality. Basic personality also has a collective referent. In small-scale socially relatively homogeneous cultures, Kardiner supposes there to be approximate uniformity of personalities; hence, it is possible to refer to the basic personality of a culture as well as of an individual.

The Kardinerian empirical test of this model was a culture-by-culture exercise in triangulation: For one culture, an anthropologist provided ethnographic accounts of socialization practices and religion, as well as projective test (Rorschach) protocols. From each of the first two, Kardiner attempted clinically informed inferences to basic personality; independently, a Rorschach expert interpreted the test protocols. If the personality interpretations from all three sources agreed, then, for that culture, the model was validated.

Growth and Diversification of Culture and Personality

Much, arguably most, of the midcentury growth of psychological anthropology (then more likely to be called culture and personality) pertained to issues intrinsic to Kardiner's work, or suggested by it—hence, retrospectively, Kardiner's stature as a founder. Many of the figures involved in this growth, however, were not specifically inspired by Kardiner.

The Whiting School

The Whiting school, founded by John and Beatrice Whiting in the 1950s, may properly be considered second-generation Kardiner, at least in its early stages. The school accepted Kardiner's culture and personality model (renaming it the "personality integration of culture"), but strenuously disputed Kardiner's method for testing the model. Rather than treating personality as something to be measured, Whiting and associates treated the personality terms in the model as theoretical constructs, from which hypotheses positing covariation between primary and secondary institutions were deduced, and then tested in the cross-cultural survey manner. From this Kardiner-focused beginning, the Whiting school extended the personality integration of culture model to several domains of culture and pioneered the methods for cross-cultural study of socialization that continue to set standards for the field.

Projective Tests, Modal Personality, and National Character

For psychological anthropology, the Kardiner model brought to stage center the issues of cross-cultural study of personality and the intracultural distribution of personality traits. Because of its apparent success in psychiatry in the 1930s, and because the test stimuli were culture free and did not presuppose literacy, the Rorschach test seemed to be made to order for the cross-cultural study of personality. Early culture and personality optimism about the Rorschach, however, evaporated in the face of emerging difficulties, and the test fell largely into disuse in psychological anthropology. But not quite. DeVos and Boyer provided, arguably, the strongest and best organized justification for continued use of the Rorschach for the cross-cultural study of personality.

Meanwhile, *contra* Kardiner, some culture and personality workers were not finding approximate uniformity of personalities in small-scale, socially homogeneous cultures. On several personality dimensions, rather, weak modality and much overall diversity seemed to be the pattern. Wallace, with an elegant argument, demonstrated in 1961 that this should be expected to be so in socially homogeneous small-scale cultures, and that this circumstance is consistent with and, arguably, favorable for social stability.

As a sidelight to all of this, the "national character" school projected a broadly Kardinerian understanding of personality and culture onto a vastly larger cultural screen, that of the modern nation state. However, whereas the modal personality folks made the establishment of personality traits and their distribution in a culture an empirical question, and ditto for socialization practices, the national character school did not hold itself to this standard. Not surprisingly, then, although national character often purports to explain features of culture by reference to personality traits supposedly generated by socialization practices, its interpretations are often insubstantial. Arguably, the school's greatest contribution is a number of rich and nuanced and informative depictions of national cultures. These depictions usually arise from study of the target culture through written sources (in other words, at a distance). In this methodological respect, the national character school (along with psychohistory) departs from the time-honored fieldwork, the empirical methodology of cultural anthropology, including most of psychological anthropology.

Psychoanalytic Anthropology and Psychohistory

As noted, psychoanalysis was central to the founding of culture and personality, and psychohistory is heavily dependent on psychoanalysis. So, regarding culture and personality and psychoanalytic anthropology and psychohistory, it is something of a judgment call where one leaves off and the other begins. Kardiner's debt to psychoanalysis has been noted. Perhaps the main distinction between classical (Kardinerian) culture and personality and psychoanalytic anthropology is that (mainly) the anthropologists who practice the latter are more literally psychoanalytic in interpretation of their cultural case materials than are classical culture and personality anthropologists. Perhaps the main distinction between psychoanalytic anthropologists and psychohistorians is that the former are typically anthropologists who employ fieldwork to collect their empirical materials; psychohistorians primarily perform mainly psychoanalytic interpretations of, e.g., historical figures (such as Luther, Ghandi, Hitler, and Saddam Hussein) or cultural phases (such as Nazism, racism, and reactionary politics) at a distance, relying on literature. Psychohistory is also often judgmental, and a curious feature of the field is that the same terminology is sometimes used for both analysis and insult.

Culture and Mental Health

The interest shown by psychological anthropologists in culture and mental health was evident in the writings of the pre-Kardinerians and has persisted. Recent and current workers in this field are more likely to call themselves medical anthropologists than psychological anthropologists. But recent and current work partakes of heartland psychological anthropology issues, including especially the transcultural validity of psychological (including psychiatric, or diagnostic) categories. Much of this work departs from, and criticizes, two Western biomedical postulates, which are enshrined in the *Diagnostic and Statistical Manual*, viz., that broad swaths of the emotional and experiential spectrum are properly medicalized, and that the diagnostic categories for doing so are transculturally valid.

Issues

The diversification of culture and personality in the 1970s and 1980s can be glimpsed by noting major issues treated by leading practitioners. The early work of Anthony Wallace has already been mentioned. Wallace built organically on his work to treat acculturation and revitalization, and to explore the interfaces among anthropology, psychiatry, human biology, and neuroscience. In the manner of Kardiner, Erik Erikson, also an eclectic psychoanalyst, lavishly imbibed anthropology in pursuit of an understanding of personality and culture. His conception of ontogenesis is epigenetic, life history is his method par excellence, identity his master concept, and biography his main vehicle for relating personality to culture and history. Although psychological anthropology has largely moved away from psychoanalysis, the careers of Weston LaBarre and George Devereux have remained faithful to the early charter, and to excellent effect. Nowhere is there a fuller and more psychoanalytically informed depiction of religion as a projective institution than in LaBarre's work in 1972, and Devereux, whose renaissance-like career touched so many important bases within and beyond psychological anthropology, leads the field in adapting the clinical methodology of psychoanalysis to field work. Alfred Irving Hallowell, whose brilliant and eclectic career predated and outlasted classical culture and personality, worked out, especially as regards self and culture, the basics of what cultural psychology, 30 years later, claimed to have invented. Regarding psychological functions of religion, the psychology of culture change, and psychocultural evolution, Hallowell was a pioneer. Gilbert Herdt's work in Papua showed that hypo macho masculinity and obligatory male homosexuality can co-occur. In a culture and personality framework, Herdt deployed these data to revise and vastly extend accepted wisdom on the content and development of gender identity. Gananath Obeyesekere has brilliantly employed a theoretical integration of Freud and Max Weber, tied to his own Sinhalese Buddhist case materials, to extend the concept of religion as a projective institution, and has recast "both psychoanalysis and anthropology in pursuit of a general conception which at once embraces psychoanalytic universals and . . . cultural variability, and relates the two . . . biographically and historically." Psychoanalysis and culture and personality agree in assigning analytic primacy to the universal conditions of early life. However, adult behavior, much of which projectively expresses the unconscious psychological residues of early life, is endlessly variable. Melford Spiro incisively discriminates the culturally variable from the universals, characterizes the latter, and grounds the latter evolutionarily.

Recent and Current Directions

Three current schools treat issues that have been at the heart of psychological anthropology for half a century or longer. One issue, cultural psychology, is by its affirmation a part of psychological anthropology. The others, evolutionary psychology and cross-cultural psychology, are not, but their relevance to psychological anthropology, now and in the past, is great, hence mention of them here.

Cultural Psychology

Cultural psychology, now probably the largest part of psychological anthropology, is founded on a reaction against much of the discipline of psychology as well as much of earlier psychological anthropology, and what purports to be a new and better psychological anthropology inquiry agenda. Cultural psychology dislikes four things:

1. Psychic unity conceptions, which posit central psychological processing mechanisms that can be learned about and characterized independent of any of their real-life instances, but which everywhere operate to generate thought, feeling, and behavior. Presumably these mechanisms include the perceptual processes that the psychologist studies in the laboratory, and the ontogenetic developmental processes that psychoanalysis posits and that culture and personality adopted and adapted.
2. Nomothetic interpretation, for reasons shortly to be seen.
3. The new cognitive psychology, grounded in brain science and driven by computer simulations, because of its mechanistic and deterministic implications.
4. Much of earlier psychological anthropology.

What, then, does cultural psychology favor? To begin, take "cultural psychology" literally: human psychology is irreducibly culture specific. A central emphasis is that neither culture nor the individual is analytically prior—rather, they are mutual and they interact continually. From this emerges and reemerges the "constituted self," which is the repository of the higher order mental processes that provide the psychological mediation between individual and culture. Because for cultural psychology each culture is a unique historical product, and because higher order mental processes emerge from individual/culture interaction, there can be no panhuman culturally relevant psychology. Human mental processes must be locally and particularly and variably constituted; e.g., it is not possible that depression in middle-class America and depression on the Ifaluk Atoll in Micronesia can be the same things. Cultural psychology emphasizes that human life is creative and agency driven; its writing abounds with verbs such as "negotiate," "translate," "constitute," and "construct." For the empirical domain of cultural psychology (the psychologically mediated individual/culture relationship), successful general theory is not possible; good interpretation must be idiographic. The conceptual baggage of cultural psychology purports to provide guideposts for this. For many cultural psychologists, hermeneutics is or could be the watchword; positivistic methods in search of general laws are disparaged.

With such a charter, the field's payoff could be expected to be in the case studies and the specific interpretations built on them. And this expectation is borne out by a large and growing body of admirable empirical cross-cultural studies, many but not all ethnographic. Now, just a little taste of this: The Cartesian mind/body dualism, coupled with the idea that the body houses a panhuman emotional repertoire that opposes the rational cognitive workings of the mind, suffuses Western culture and thought, including the academic disciplines that treat humankind. Cultural psychology rebuts this with well-executed studies of specific cultures. The superb study of the Ifaluk Atoll stands tall in this genre, and pays as well the traditional anthropological dividends of enabling incisive perspectives on our own culture. Ambitiously, Anna Weirzbicka has proposed, from lexical evidence, panhuman moral and emotional concepts, in seeking to reconcile the general and the culturally specific.

Identifying schools of thought can convey an overly compartmentalized view of a field, e.g., psychological anthropology. Cognitive anthropology, or culture and cognition, arguably the main focus of which is native knowledge and its relationship to culture as lived, evokes this conundrum. Cognitive anthropology is at once an important part of cultural psychology and predates it. A specific culture, understood as the body of knowledge of which natives partake to be socially competent, has been and remains a conceptual bedrock of the field. Methodologies for investigating cultural knowledge, and how it informs everyday life, have been and remain the meat and potatoes of the field.

Evolutionary Psychology

Evolutionary psychology is the child of sociobiology, in the lineage of bioevolutionary theses on human nature and cultural elaboration of same. Few psychological anthropologists study evolutionary psychology, but, along with psychological anthropology, it is centrally concerned with the psychological bases for culture and how they arise. Unlike psychological anthropology, evolutionary psychology posits evolutionary sources and draws heavily on evolutionary science to make its case, especially those parts of evolutionary science that examine how natural selection operates to maximize reproductive fitness. To cut right to the chase, as expressed by Robert Wright, "what the theory of natural selection says . . . is that people's minds were designed to maximize fitness in the environment in which those minds evolved . . . the . . . environment of evolutionary adaptation . . . .Or . . . the ancestral environment." For humans, the environment of evolutionary adaptation is the world of the foraging band, in which all of humankind lived for (conservatively) the first 90% of human history. In short, the evolved, biologically rooted human psychological and behavioral repertoire was fine tuned with reference to the adaptive exigencies of foraging band lifeways. By the evolutionary clock, it has been but the blink of an eye since human ancestors relinquished forager lifeways, and that is still basically human nature. From all of this, evolutionary psychology sets itself, *inter alia*, two large tasks: (1) to identify behavioral expressions of human forager psychologies in contemporary lifeways and (2) to illustrate the (perhaps cruel) ironies of history, viz., how historical change has consigned humans to modern lifeways that are often radically at odds with the most fundamental evolved aptitudes.

Accepting that humans are an evolved species, and that this entails that everything human is in some sense grounded in and/or an expression of an evolutionary odyssey, has evolutionary psychology advanced understanding of the specific sense in which those aspects of humanness that interest us are expressions of the nature of the evolved, biologically rooted human species? A "yes" answer includes the following dicta:

1. Evolutionary science provides the core theory (e.g., natural selection, reproductive fitness, kin selection, and reciprocal altruism) for evolutionary psychology.
2. The environment of evolutionary adaptation, which is knowable from studies of contemporary foragers and the archeological record, provides the initial empirical conditions.
3. Aligning (2) with (1), evolutionary psychology deduces a wealth of hypotheses about what to expect humankind to be like, behaviorally, and tests them against cross-cultural data. The linchpin of the system is supposition about what psychological traits made good adaptive sense in the environment of evolutionary adaptation. The hypotheses reach into many domains of human lifeways, but key domains for evolutionary psychology are the scope and content of altruistic behavior and female and male sexual behavior, or strategies.

A "no" answer might include the following statements:

1. In contrast to evolutionary psychology, it is not known in specific detail what foragers were like, behaviorally and socially, tens of thousands of years ago, and there is good reason to believe that forager lifeways then were so diverse that the taxon is valid only on a uselessly (to evolutionary psychology) high level of generality. Hence, the initial empirical conditions are not established.
2. The hypotheses that guide evolutionary psychology empirical work are not deduced. Rather, they allude to evolutionary science by positing functional "just so" stories, which arbitrarily posit an "environment of evolutionary adaptation" adaptive significance for the contemporary traits under investigation.
3. For a school of thought that purports to be evolutionary to the core, it is astonishing how little real biology is found in evolutionary psychology.

A "no" answer means that the strong and general explanatory claims of evolutionary psychology are not wrong, but rather empty. But even if this is thought, there is a lot in evolutionary psychology that merits careful attention. The inquiry agenda is of the first importance; evolutionary psychology pursues it with an intellectual rigor almost unknown in earlier bioevolutionary formulations on humankind, including especially the sound grounding of evolutionary psychology in evolutionary science, and the empirical studies are usually of interest in their own right.

Cross-Cultural Psychology

To begin, take "cross-cultural psychology" literally: it largely intends to deploy the concepts and methods of Western (positivistic) psychology in other cultures. In doing so, it has fostered lavish communication and collaboration among scholars from many nations and cultures. For (at least) two reasons, it is fitting to conclude this discussion with brief mention of cross-cultural psychology, even though it is not studied by anthropologists.

First, in its several iterations, psychological anthropology is mainly about both psychology and culture relationships, studied cross-culturally. And so, largely, is cross-cultural psychology, as the following titles from the authoritative *Journal of Cross Cultural Psychology* illustrate: "Sex differences in visual–spatial performance among Ghanaian and Norwegian adults"; "Intimacy: a cross-cultural study"; "Relationship of family bonds to family structure and function across cultures." In addition, cross-cultural psychology has taken all of the main branches of academic psychology (e.g., perception, personality, cognitive) around the world.

Second, anthropology, including psychological anthropology, often posits that culturally relevant psychology is, to a significant extent, irreducibly culturally specific. Cultural psychology, specifically, sometimes takes this to the limit by eliminating the dependent clause. Cross-cultural psychology goes in the opposite direction, viz., human psychology fundamentally comprises panhuman processes that can be measured, anywhere, with the methodologies that psychologists have developed, or may develop. Within cross-cultural psychology, this view has been extensively developed and applied by the five-factor model, which posits five panhuman personality dimensions and claims a cross-culturally valid methodology for measuring them. Given the importance of especially personality for psychological anthropology, this disagreement between cultural psychology and cross-cultural psychology is emblematic of a (perhaps the) fundamental metatheoretical issue in play here—viz., concerning the study of psychology cross-culturally, can the conceptual and empirical methodologies of a "scientific" psychology neutralize or otherwise cut through the relativizing fog of specific cultures? Within psychological anthropology as treated here, the Whiting school sides with cross-cultural psychology, albeit its concepts and methods are vastly different. Acknowledging the fundamental importance of this issue, some suppose that it may not be amenable to empirical resolution.

See Also the Following Articles

Economic Anthropology • Qualitative Analysis, Anthropology • Quantitative Analysis, Anthropology • Structural Models in Anthropology

Further Reading

Bock, P. K. (1980). *Continuities in Psychological Anthropology*. W. H. Freeman, San Francisco.

Bock, P. K. (ed.) (1994). *Handbook of Psychological Anthropology*. Greenwood Press, Westport, Connecticut, and London.

Boesch, E. E. (1991). *Symbolic Action Theory and Cultural Psychology*. Springer-Verlag, Berlin.

DeVos, G., and Boyer, L. B. (1989). *Symbolic Analysis Cross Culturally: The Rorschach Test*. University of California Press, Berkeley.

Kardiner, A., Linton, R., Dubois, C., and West, J. (1945). *The Psychological Frontiers of Society*. Columbia University Press, New York.

Kleinman, A., and Good, B. (eds.) (1985). *Culture and Depression*. University of California Press, Berkeley.

LaBarre, W. (1970). *The Ghost Dance: Origins of Religion*. Doubleday, New York.

Paul, R. (1989). *Psychoanalytic Anthropology*. (B. J. Siegel, A. R. Beals, and S. A. Tyler, eds.). Annual Reviews. Palo Alto, California.

Piker, S. (1994). Classical culture and personality. *In Handbook of Psychological Anthropology* (P. K. Bock, ed.).

Piker, S. (1998). Contributions of psychological anthropology. *J. Cross Cultural Psychol* **29**(1).

Spindler, G., and Spindler, L. (1978). *The Making of Psychological Anthropology*. University of California Press, Berkeley.

Suarez-Orozco, M. M., Spindler, G., and Spindler, L. (1994). *The Making of Psychological Anthropology II*. Harcourt Brace, Fort Worth.

Wallace, A. F. C. (1961). *Culture and Personality*. Random House, New York.

Wiggins, J. S. (ed.) (1996). *The Five-Factor Model of Personality: Theoretical Perspectives*. Guilford Press, New York.

Wright, R. (1994). *The Moral Animal. Why We Are the Way We Are. The New Science of Evolutionary Psychology*. Random House, New York.

Archaeology

Patricia A. Urban
Kenyon College, Gambier, Ohio, USA

E. Christian Wells
University of South Florida, Tampa, Florida, USA

Glossary

culture history The school of thought that dominated American archaeology prior to World War II; concerned with determining the time depth of past cultures and their spatial extent; little attention paid to explanation, group, or individual dynamics.

interpretive archaeology A subset of postprocessual archaeology; focus is on understanding past cultures, rather than explaining processes or change, and finding meaning in the material remains of the past.

postprocessual archaeology A catch-all term used for theory developed in opposition to processualist approaches; rejects fixity of knowledge, holding that all knowledge, and therefore all reconstructions of the past, are contingent on the individual and that person's social and historical context; focus is on human agency, identity, hegemony and counterhegemony, or resistance; also includes many gender/feminist and Marxist approaches.

processual (new) archaeology The school of thought dominant in American archaeology from the 1960s through the 1980s; focus is on archaeology as a science, on hypothesis testing, and on development of laws of human behavior.

This article addresses two related topics concerning the relationship of archaeology and other social sciences. First, both theory and methods are discussed, with the emphasis on theory that has been adopted from other social sciences and adapted to the specific circumstances of archaeology. The second section looks at what formal and quantitative methods archaeology shares with other social sciences.

Archaeology and Social Science Theory and Method

Introduction

In the United States, archaeology has two intellectual homes: the classics, in which the focus is Greek and Roman culture in the Mediterranean world, and anthropology, which encompasses everything else from ancient times, as well as certain approaches to more modern eras. Classical archaeology is definitely allied with the humanities, but anthropological archaeology, hereafter simply called archaeology, is firmly within the social sciences. The methods and ideas used in archaeology are drawn from the natural sciences (^{14}C dating, neutron activation studies of artifact composition, and so forth), the humanities (art historical analysis; some postmodern approaches to interpretation), and the social sciences. There is a relationship between theory in anthropological archaeology and other social science theories, i.e., cultural anthropology, sociology, economics, political science, history (arguably a social science), geography, and women's and gender studies (also a discipline that straddles the humanities and social sciences). The focus here is more on the theories derived from the social sciences than on methods, for the simple reason that archaeology shares few actual methods with other social sciences: most procedures are either unique to the field, or similar to procedures from other field-based disciplines, particularly geology.

The common roots of American archaeology and anthropology lie in the particularities of the New World, in which colonists encountered societies with demonstrable ties to prehistoric cultures. The juxtaposition of "primitive" Native Americans and "advanced" Europeans led to the development of cultural evolutionary frameworks for evaluating and classifying contemporary and extinct peoples, theories used by archaeologists and cultural anthropologists alike. For archaeology, the presence of living decedents of ancient peoples gave rise to the direct historical approach, that is, using contemporary people and their cultures as analogies for interpreting the past. Interpretation using analogy remains a common method in contemporary archaeology. In the 20th century, the evolutionary approach of 19th century practitioners withered and died, but the direct historical approach lives on, informing much current interpretation.

The earliest school of archaeological thought in the 20th century, the cultural historical approach, focused on the systematics of space (where groups were located, how they migrated through time, and how sites and regions were organized) and time (dating). To gather spatial data, archaeologists in the early 20th century developed basic methods used to this day, including ground survey (generally on foot) and recording by mapping the site and determining the geographic location. Lacking the precise dating techniques developed after World War II, culture historians in the first half of the century developed regional chronologies based on stratigraphy (the study of the natural and cultural layers found in sites) and cross-dating through artifact similarities and traded items; both of these methods are borrowed from geology, but adapt well to archaeology. Artifacts, for example, substitute for geology's type fossils in comparisons. Artifacts, botanical and faunal samples and other materials, and stratigraphic profiles are obtained through controlled excavations, a method not employed by other social sciences. The first chronologies developed were imperfect (e.g., Stonehenge was thought to date to the time of the Phoenicians, although it is 3000 years earlier), but they laid the framework for later work. Though it is unlikely that any modern archaeologists would characterize themselves as culture historians, space–time systematics are still fundamental to archaeology, as is the social science theory that cultural historians borrowed from history: the present situation of a site or area can be explained in terms of its antecedent conditions. This is sometimes known as genetic explanation, not due to any connection to biology, but because of the relationship through descent of modern and ancient cultures.

After World War II, technical dating methods, largely based on newly understood atomic decay processes, brought refinement to cultural historical sequences. At the same time, American archaeologists became dissatisfied with the normative picture of the past delineated by culture history. That approach did not deal well with behavioral variation within cultures, nor did its practitioners seek to explain change except by antecedent conditions or supposedly self-evident processes such as population migration or diffusion of objects and, to a lesser extent, ideas. The school developing in the 1960s and onward was self-named the "new archaeology" to emphasize its break with the past. The goal was explicit explanation, development of covering laws to aid both in explanation and the deduction of hypotheses and test implications, and a greater understanding of human–ecology relationships. Many of the ideas borrowed from other social sciences (see later) became part of "normal science" during the heyday of the new, or processualist, archaeology (because of its interest in the processes of cultural change and adaptations), which was considered a science modeled after natural sciences, particularly physics and chemistry.

The inevitable backlash against the excesses of processualist approaches is the unfortunately named postprocessual archaeology. This set of diverse approaches has a number of goals, among which are looking at decision making and agency; understanding sites in their particular landscapes; looking at identity, including the components of individual identity such as gender, age, sexual orientation, and ability/disability; and promoting the idea that knowledge is contingent, and that we cannot escape the ideas and language of our own era. Thus what we say about the past is as much about our times as ancient days. Inspiration is drawn from both the social sciences and the humanities.

The following discussions highlight the models and theories drawn from other social sciences that have been particularly important to anthropological archaeology since World War II. The text is telegraphic, and citations are at a minimum; nonetheless, readers should obtain enough background to follow up on particular approaches.

History

History and archaeology clearly overlap in temporal periods, methods (some archaeologists are able to use texts, whereas some historians rely on materials and goods to amplify the textual record), and societies studied (civilizations/high cultures—e.g., Egypt, Greece, China, the Aztecs). Archaeology covers the larger time span, and without written records tends to focus on long-term processes and group activities, defining societies on the basis of differences in material culture rather than in language or self-ascription. Nevertheless, both history and archaeology are concerned with diachronic and synchronic change and have similar approaches to explanation. Despite this, little conscious attention has been paid by archaeologists to history, except for recurring enthusiasms for Collingwood's contention that it is possible to think one's way into the past—that is, to understand it on its own terms. Recently, the Annales school of history, founded by Fernand Braudel, whose most influential work for archaeologists is *The Mediterranean and the Mediterranean World in the Age of Phillip II*, has affected a few archaeologists, but in different, almost opposite, ways. One objective of this school is to examine human history in the *longue duree*, the long-term relationship between humans and their environment. Such inquiry has been basic to archaeology: the current difference is a greater concordance between archaeological and historical theory about investigating these issues. The smaller scale aspects of Braudel's theory are also of interest to archaeology. These include medium-range processes such as conflict and economic change and shorter trends, such as group or individual decisions. The latter concern, agency, is of particular interest to postprocessualists, although they derive much of their inspiration not from the Annalistes, but from sociology and cultural anthropology. More recently, the Annales school has de-emphasized the extreme long term, instead providing detailed descriptions of events, with special attention to agency. The descriptive aspects are similar to thick description as defined by Clifford Geertz, again of interest in contemporary archaeological theory. Postprocessual, or interpretive, archaeologists also concur with Annalistes in rejecting the positivism of natural science. Works such as *Interpreting Archaeology: Finding Meaning in the Past*, by Ian Hodder and associates, amply illustrate the trend toward understanding and away from explanation, particularly of a positivistic sort.

Political Science

Archaeology and political science overlap in their concern for the development of the state and the forms of society leading up to it. In archaeology, this is known as the origins of social complexity, and archaeologists have drawn most inspiration from cultural anthropologists, both theorists (e.g., considerations of evolutionary stages such as bands, tribes, chiefdoms, and states) and ethnologists (for example, ethnographers working on African polities). Political science theories have been tested against archaeological data and largely found wanting; for example, humans have never lived in a state of nature. To be fair, political scientists are more concerned with modern governmental structures, international relations, and ideal types of social organization than with the pottery and stone tools of actual early states. Nonetheless, the connections between political science and archaeology are few because the overlap in subject material is more apparent than real. A classic work addressing both political science perspectives and archaeology is *Origins of the State*, edited by Ronald Cohen and Elman Service.

Economics

Manufacturing, distribution, and consumption activities are central to archaeological inquiry, because these processes leave material remains. Interpreting the remains and understanding the economic systems behind them require ideas, and here economics and archaeology have had many points of contact. The central question is whether ancient economic systems can or should be interpreted using models drawn from modern times; this is the formalist approach, where it is assumed that the ancients lived by, say, maximizing efficiency and minimizing effort. Examples of this approach are common, whether the society being examined is complex or a simple hunting and gathering society, and can be typified by the work of William Sanders and Barbara Price.

The opposite position is that of the substantivists, as exemplified by the early work of Karl Polanyi and others in *Trade and Market in the Early Empires*. Substantivists propose that ancient economic processes differ substantially from modern ones and that previous economic systems can only be understood in their own terms. Substantivist approaches appear to dominate archaeology, and practitioners have myriad models about the relationship between craft producers and elites (attached vs. independent), the location of production areas (households or distinct workshops), the level of production (part versus full time, specialized versus occasional), and the nature of exchange (market based, administrated, redistributive, tribute based).

Geography

The new archaeology movement was preceded some 10 years by similar changes in geography. The "new geography" sought to make geography more scientific, more explicit about its concepts and models, and prepared to explain, rather than just describe, geographic phenomena. The table of contents for Peter Haggett's original 1965 version of *Locational Analysis in Human Geography* is a virtual textbook of matters that concerned archaeologists interested in space: the nature of regions, describing regions and settlements, the nature and meaning of settlement hierarchies, modeling movement across space, conceiving settlements as nested in networks of interactions, and more. Much of what archaeologists saw as vibrant and new in the new geography has become internalized in contemporary archaeology. Many undergraduates learn about central places and their sustaining areas, but even at advanced levels, the fathers of central place analysis, Christaller and Lösch, may not be remembered.

There are some perduring gifts from geography to archaeology. The first is the idea of the "region," a space delimited physically or culturally that is a meaningful unit of analysis larger than the settlement, or even a site and its immediate hinterland. In archaeology, regions defined physically may be places, such as the Valley of Mexico or the Tigris–Euphrates drainage. Regions may also be defined on cultural grounds (the Levant, the Adena–Hopewell area, Mesoamerica). Whether physical or cultural, regions are likely to have smaller units nested within them, such as sites of a variety of sizes and levels of complexity, resource zones, roads or pathways, and fields and other agricultural installations.

Typically, archaeological attention has been drawn first to sites, which can be defined as any space that has been used or modified by humans. Sites are described based on surface remains and excavation information in order to grasp their plans. Natural factors, such as the location of water, certainly influence site location and internal planning, but cultural factors (social differences, craft working, religious and ceremonial practices) are equally, and at times more, important. Such factors also influence the design or internal plan of sites. To assess site spacing and interaction, techniques such as "nearest neighbor analysis" have been borrowed from geography and used by archaeologists to examine how relatively equal settlements are spaced across large territories. Methods for analyzing network characteristics, such as minimizing length, maximizing traffic, or optimizing both, as well as how cultural and natural factors impact route location and form, have been adopted and adapted by archaeologists to discuss trade routes, road systems, and traffic patterns within sites.

Another major concern of archaeologists is whether the sites within a region are uniform in size and/or complexity, or if there is some sort of hierarchy present. Geographic models have been particularly important to modeling hierarchy. Walter Christaller first proposed "central place" theory based on his studies of German cities and industries; the English version of his core work is *Central Places in Southern Germany*. His classic model has constraints that are not realistic for the real world: sites are located in a uniform plain, without edges; resources are equally distributed; and, implicitly, culture is uniform across the space. He proposed that site hierarchies were developed based on a number of basic principles, such as administration, transportation, or security; and that once a system was developed with respect to a particular principle, it remained the guideline throughout time. His model, therefore, did not adequately deal with change. Nonetheless, many archaeologists were inspired by his work to look at settlement patterns in terms of central places. Norman Hammond, among others, applied Christaller's principles to the Maya lowlands, and Henry Wright looked at lowland Mesopotamia. Wright realized that the standard hexagonal lattice presupposed by central place theory could not work in Mesopotamia, because of the linearity of the two rivers, and therefore modified Christaller's conceptions to allow for a rectangular lattice of main sites and dependencies. Other archaeologists have made similar modifications.

August Losch followed Christaller (*The Economics of Location*, a translation of his second German edition, was published in 1954), but proposed that no one basic principle defined the settlement pattern for any given area; rather, multiple principles were at work simultaneously, resulting in a heterarchical, rather than hierarchical, landscape that was richer and more complex than that of Christaller. Losch's ideas appear to be more useful in real-world situations, but his work had less of an impact on archaeologists than did his predecessor's. Nonetheless, the idea of a central place as the focus of a region, or at least a sustaining area or hinterland, is basic to contemporary archaeological analysis. These and other geographic approaches have also helped archaeologists think of sites in relation to one another—that is, as parts of networks, rather than isolated entities. Volumes such as *Network Analysis in Geography* by Peter Haggett and Richard Chorley have been heavily cited.

Three practical areas of congruency exist between archaeology and geography. First is sampling. Geographic samples often take the form of areas, for example, when a researcher is working on ground cover. At other times, the samples are point samples, such as resource locations or cities. Archaeological samples of space are similar; they are areas defined geographically, culturally, or expediently, or are specific points on the landscape, such as settlements, quarries, and so forth. Therefore, methods of sampling used by geographers can be useful in archaeology, and indeed have been adopted: transects and quadrats are two prime examples. The second area is testing or confirmation. Quantitative methods are discussed in Section II and are not covered further here. More qualitative methods are, however, shared between the fields, and the usual transmission pattern is from geography to archaeology. Nonstatistical tests can involve models (intellectual and physical) or simulations, as seen in the work of David Clarke (*Spatial Archaeology*) and Ian Hodder (*Simulation Studies in Archaeology*, and, with Clive Orton, *Spatial Analysis in Archaeology*), and in the classic articles in Kent Flannery's *The Early Mesoamerican Village*; Richard Chorley and Peter Haggett's *Models in Geography* was also highly influential. The third area of overlap is the presentation of spatial data. Both disciplines are concerned with maps and other ways of representing three-dimensional phenomena in two-dimensional media. The recent advances in geographic information systems (GIS) and computer-based mapping programs have been a boon to both fields. Beyond mapping, GIS will also be of inestimable value for analysis in archaeology, as it is in geography, because it is constructed to correlate, analyze, and visually display spatial data.

Women's and Gender Studies and Psychology

Women's/gender studies and psychology have been combined here for several reasons. First, neither is considered wholly a social science, although both have some social science aspects. Second, the subject material they share with archaeology is limited. Social psychology is the subdiscipline that shares with women's and gender studies and archaeology a concern with individual behavior, and the formation of individual and group identity. The latter—identity formation—involves both self- and other-ascription and can concern issues such as race and ethnicity. Gender is, however, the subject most often addressed by archaeologists using ideas adopted from psychology and gender studies that are reworked to fit the peculiar nature of archaeological data.

Feminism has had many influences on archaeology, although the "waves" of feminist thought so often discussed by others flow somewhat differently in the archaeological discipline, compared to others. First-wave archaeological feminists forced the field to acknowledge that women had been neglected in prehistoric studies. The contributions of "woman the gatherer" were likely more important to ancient diet than were those of "man the hunter." In the second wave, more explicitly feminist ideas were brought to the field. Archaeologists sought methods by which to see women in the archaeological record, and ideas to account for their activities as active agents, rather than as passive followers of charismatic males. Finally, the third wave has expanded archaeology's view to include a wider range of differences—age, sex, gender, disability, ethnicity, nation—and an appreciation of the active participation of all prehistoric peoples in the formation of their daily lives and choices about the future. People do not passively accept the slings and arrows of fortune, but learn how to fight back, protest, and subvert. The theoretical aspects of gender studies continue to be important, but few technical methods for recovering gender-related data, or even recognizing data, have been developed. Archaeologists, however, are learning not to project their own or their society's ideas about sex and gender onto ancient societies.

Sociology

The relationship between sociology and archaeology is not direct, and is for the most part mediated by cultural anthropology. Archaeology's recent concern with group and individual identity, as mentioned previously, is related to sociology's work with race and ethnicity. More significant are four sociologists who have had a profound influence on the postprocessual, or interpretive, school of archaeological thought: Wallerstein, Foucault, Giddens, and Bourdieu.

Emmanuel Wallerstein, an historical sociologist, developed the body of thought known as "world systems theory," which is concerned with understanding the relationships between core and peripheral states in systems made up of multiple polities; his central works are the three volumes of *The Modern World System*. In Wallerstein's view, peripheral states produce raw materials in bulk, which are shipped to the core states for processing. The manufactured goods produced in the core states are then shipped back to the peripheries, the members of which, lacking industries of their own, are forced to purchase the core's goods. Raw materials have less value than finished products, so the peripheral states are kept in perpetual subjugation to the more prosperous cores. Wallerstein's prime example of such a system, which need not literally cover the world, is the Mediterranean in the early stages of capitalism.

Because it was developed to explain relationships within capitalist economic systems, world system theory is not applicable in its original formulation to prehistoric states. The general idea of central, developed, core areas with dependent, underdeveloped peripheries has, however, been significant in much recent archaeological debate. Counterarguments have been mounted stating that dependency, "coreness," and peripherality are in the minds of the analyst, and that use of the terms "core" and "periphery" prejudge the relationships to be found within systems of interaction. Despite any specific problems with Wallerstein's ideas, the interconnectedness he posits among political units has been crucial to understanding ancient interpolity interactions, and many archaeologists focus, as does world systems theory, on the study of networks of political entities, rather than on specific political units. The 1999 edited volume of *World Systems Theory in Practice* by P. Nick Kardulias and the chapters in *Resources, Power, and Interregional Interaction* (1992) by Edward Schortman and Patricia Urban show how archaeologists have amended and/or abandoned aspects of Wallerstein's conceptions.

Wallerstein's concerns with economic patterns makes his work of natural interest to archaeologists; the attraction of the more abstract notions of Michel Foucault (who is variably considered an historical sociologist or an historian), Anthony Giddens, and Pierre Bourdieu (who is either a sociologist or an anthropologist, depending on the commentator) are often more difficult to grasp. Christopher Tilley was among the first to utilize Foucault's self-proclaimed "archaeological method" to examine not the past, but how archaeologists view and reconstruct the past. Subsequently, writers such as Julian Thomas and Trevor Kirk (e.g., in Tilley's *Interpretative Archaeology*) have shown how Foucault's work can aid in a reconceptualization of archaeology, one that recognizes the near impossibility of gaining a true understanding of the past. Because what is claimed about ancient peoples' lives is determined not by their intellectual systems, but rather by our own, we must be aware that there is no definitive past, only contingent pasts shaped by contingent presents. Finally, Foucault calls our attention to power: it is part of all social relations and actions. Individuals have "power to," that is, they can through their own agency, try to ensure that events redound to their benefit. The complementary idea of "power over" reminds us that some individuals or groups can affect activities by manipulating other people. These others need not be complacent in the face of manipulation, but may resist or subvert the actions of dominants. Thus, power, like knowledge or identity, is contingent on circumstance. Responding to evolutionary thought as applied to culture change, Giddens has adumbrated structuration theory. Humans know their history, and act in accordance with it. Their actions are reinterpretations of and reactions to social structures; as they act, they change existing conditions, but within the constraints of their own history.

Finally, contemporary archaeological theory manifests considerable influence from Bourdieu's theory of human action. In his perspective, the everyday activities that we all carry out are largely unconscious, and are passed down from earlier generations. This quotidian activity is termed *habitus*. Cultures have particular forms of habitus that characterize them, and are parts of individual and group identity. Even carrying out habitual activity, however, people make changes in their practices, and therefore engender change in the over-arching structures that generate habitus in the first place. Bourdieu's and Giddens' ideas are similar; they are subsumed under the larger rubric of practice theory, which is not confined to sociology. It has had profound influence on contemporary anthropological thought, as discussed, for example, by Sherry Orton in her 1984 article "Theory in Anthropology since the Sixties."

Sociocultural Anthropology

Earlier, the origins of archaeology in the United States were discussed as the companion science to anthropology, both united in an evolutionary perspective that stressed unilineal change through a series of fixed stages. One of Franz Boas' most enduring imprints on anthropology—and archaeology—was his debunking of unilineal cultural evolution and the racist tenets that the schema both deliberately and inadvertently promoted. Boas' work did, however, show the value of the direct historical approach for understanding prehistoric Native American societies and furthered the use of ethnographic analogy as an analytical tool—that is, using data from modern people's material culture to develop analogies about how prehistoric artifacts were used. The culture historical approach also obtained from Boas' studies the idea of particularism, that each group has its own individualistic developmental trajectory. Although Boasian particularism did much to promote respect and understanding of different cultures, it also had the unfortunate effect of dampening comparative approaches in archaeology, except for comparison of artifacts for dating purposes. Seeing each culture as totally unique inhibits us from seeing cross-cultural similarities; this is one of the aspects of culture history most reviled by the processual archaeologists from the 1960s through the 1980s. Whereas Boas and his students were not identical in their approaches to anthropology, the field in the United States was fairly uniform theoretically until after World War II. Developments in British anthropology, particularly the structural–functionalist approach that focused on the harmonious balance of parts within a society, and the resolution of conflicts in order to maintain that balance, had relatively little influence on American archaeologists.

After the war, several competing and quite different schools of thought emerged in the United States and across the Atlantic, all of which played a part in shaping archaeology as practiced today. The first, and for some time the most important for archaeology, was the neo-evolutionist group made up of Leslie White and Julian Steward, and slightly later including Elman Service, Marshall Sahlins, and Morton Fried. With the exception of Steward, these thinkers were interested in general evolution—that is, the changes in all of culture that took, and take, place through time; these alterations were/are largely caused by forces such as technological innovation, population growth, and conflict, in White's version. What developed from White's approach was a concept of stages of evolution, the now well-known bands, tribes, chiefdoms, and states of Service's formulation, and egalitarian, ranked, stratified, and state-level cultures in Fried's. Steward, on the other hand, believed that most cultural change was driven by adaptation to the environment. These adaptations are specific to a particular culture's situation, rather than being the steps on a generalized path toward social complexity. The importance of the idea of adaptation to archaeological thought cannot be overstated. The evolutionary stages of Service and Fried have been operationalized and investigated, or used as heuristic devices by generations of archaeologists, but the stronger influence came from Steward and his concept of adaptation. Under the general rubric of cultural ecology, this school of thought was the basis of theory and practice in archaeology for decades. Ecological approaches were first pioneered during the 1920s and 1930s in Great Britain, but were hampered by a lack of suitable methods for recovering the necessary data. After World War II, archaeology generated a suite of methods for finding and preserving delicate floral and faunal data; in other disciplines, researchers interested in reconstructing climate also worked on these problems, with resulting interchange between them and archaeologists. Some techniques were also imported from biology, such as pollen analysis, which helps reconstruct both climate and diet. Almost no methods important to ecological reconstruction come from social sciences, but the ideas used to interpret how humans existed in specific ecological circumstances are social theory.

A closely related offshoot of Steward and White's anthropology is cultural materialism. In distinction to cultural ecologists, who focus on how interactions between people and their environment shape culture, cultural materialists look at how specific parts of culture are developed to maintain an existing human–environmental relationship; that is, cultural ecology looks at change, whereas cultural materialism looks at balance and function, although this line of thought accommodated change when brought about from the outside (from alterations in the environment). Both intellectual strands descended from White and Steward's thinking, but also were related to functionalist anthropology, and both were central to processualist theory.

The cultural materialist concern with equilibrium is related to new archaeology's interest in culture-as-a-system. In essence, this view perceives all parts of culture as being so intimately related that a change in one (say, a new way to produce foodstuffs) will cause changes in all other segments of the system. The ecology-inclined systems archaeologist would emphasize change, while the materialist-influenced archaeologist would likely examine how a perturbed system could regain its equilibrium: a new food production technology would at first be disruptive, but a group would soon return to an essentially unchanged version of its culture that incorporated, in a nondisturbing way, the new technology. In either case, post-World War II archaeologists were better equipped intellectually than were their culture-historical predecessors to grasp both equilibrium and change or evolution.

Just as virtually no one would today claim to be a culture historian, self-identified cultural materialists or cultural ecologists are also few in the 21st century. Nonetheless, this body of theory, the methods generated to gather and interpret suitable data, and the work produced by its practitioners are central to modern archaeology. The ideas of adaptation and the significance of the environment for culture change, as well as the concept that parts of culture have specific functions in maintaining a group's existence, are now, like basic space–time systematics and the concepts of central places and peripheries, "normal science"; they are virtually unexamined parts of archaeological thinking today, via the influence of the processual archaeologists of the 1960s and 1970s. Similarly, methods developed since World War II, such as collecting soil samples (for extracting pollen and other minute remains, and studying soil composition) or screening soil and using water flotation methods (to remove soil and recover small items, such as bones, fish scales, or stone flakes from making tools), are also normal procedures today, and have been extended and refined through collaboration with natural science colleagues.

Those current practitioners who find latter-day versions of processualism congenial are in the so-called scientific subset of archaeology, whereas those who abhor positivism are today called postprocessualists or interpretive archaeologists. This latter group is not a coherent school, but rather is composed of a number of groups that may be protoschools, and they take their inspiration from very different currents in anthropology, as compared to the "scientists." Before turning to this most recent current in anthropological archaeology, the influence of Marxist thought must first be examined, for Marxism, though often occluded due to pressures and prejudices in modern Western society, was and continues to be a highly significant force in archaeological thought.

The ideas outlined in the preceding discussion, as well as others that cannot be covered due to limitations of space, often have a Marxist subtext. Sherry Ortner suggests that the predominant strain of Marxist thought in American anthropology is structural Marxism. Structural Marxists see the determinative forces behind culture change in social relations, particularly those subsumed under "modes of production," or those aspects of social organization that mediate the production of goods and services. Structural Marxists also emphasize ideas, which had no independent place in the processualist scheme. Ideas, or ideology, serve many purposes, such as legitimating the existing system, obscuring inequality, or providing a rationale for elite prominence. Thus, this variant of Marxism deals with materialism and ideas, a task not accomplished by processualists.

There are additional significant parts of a Marxist perspective that have attracted archaeologists because there appear to be material correlates for particular social situations or processes. The first of these is inequality, which can be marked by differential access to basic resources such as food and housing as well as to exotic materials such as imported goods, or to luxuries that define different social roles or statuses. Inequality leads to conflict; thus one of the crucial aspects of the past to examine is the degree of inequality, and the factions or groups engaged in conflict. This conflict may be overt, but can also be more subtle, a form of resistance rather than outright hostility.

A final Marxist-related concept salient for contemporary archaeology is hegemony. Two groups of researchers appear to take an interest in hegemony and possible counterhegemony, or resistance: those working with complex, hierarchically organized societies, with a clear, dominant elites, and those who find themselves in situations wherein a more complex, or so-called high, culture is in a position to influence smaller or less complexly organized neighboring peoples. Hegemony in the former situation indicates domination with control, but for cultural groups in contact, it may simply mean influence or even dominance without any specific controlling mechanism.

The most thorough current review of Marxism and archaeology is Thomas C. Patterson's *Marx's Ghost*. So, in sum, the methods archaeologists have obtained from Marxism are analytical ones, such as examining class structure, or looking for evidence of conflict among members of a society.

One critique of Marxist approaches is that, like processualist ones, they emphasize groups and large-scale social dynamics. Individual people, or even smaller groups, are not present, and humans appear to be buffeted by forces beyond their control, rather than being active agents making decisions and acting on their outcomes. For this reason, as Ortner has so cogently pointed out, anthropology has increasingly turned to practice theory; archaeologists have followed suit. Much of practice theory is derived from the works of Foucault and Bourdieu. Cultural anthropologists, to be sure, are making their own contributions to practice theory, but the foundation remains the French sociologists discussed earlier. Practice theory can present difficulties for archaeologists, because mental processes are not preserved in the archaeological record, only the material results of those processes. Any given material situation, however, can have many causes, and the difficulty for archaeologists is deciding among those causes. Here lies one of the problems with postprocessual thinking: in rejecting positivism, some archaeologists have rejected as well the possibility of testing or confirming any statement made about the past. In the extreme, this is a sort of radical relativism in which any interpretation is as good as another is. In more moderate guise, a number of competing ideas remain, and, if postprocessualists are correct, there are no means of deciding among them.

The preceding discussion has focused on how American archaeologists tend to approach theory borrowed from sociocultural anthropology. However, it should be remembered that the British and Continental views of the relationship between anthropology and sociology, on the one hand, and archaeology, on the other, may be quite different. Michael Shanks and Christopher Tilley evidence this in their book *Social Theory and Archaeology*. In addition, Ian Hodder, who has been highly influential in the United States for the development of both processual archaeology, with his work on spatial analysis, and postprocessual archaeology, comes from the British tradition. Thus, in the past two decades, American, British, and European strands of thought have become more closely knit as there is a convergence on structuration, practice theory, and Marxist approaches.

Conclusion

Postmodernism in general has taught us that knowledge is contingent; in an archaeological context, this means that what we say about the past is conditioned by our own present, including our considered theoretical stances and our less-considered life courses. Postprocessualists are correct to remind us that there are many pasts, depending on the beholders and their contexts. Further adoptions and adaptations of social science theory by archaeologists, as well as the development of purely archaeologically based theory, will continue to expand our conceptions of the past, while reminding us that these are firmly grounded in our own present.

Quantitative and Formal Approaches to Archaeological Data Analysis

Introduction

Inferring the nature and organization of human behavior in the archaeological record often requires the use of quantitative and formal approaches to data analysis. Many such studies carried out today employ a mix of graphic imaging with a variety of formal analyses, including descriptive and probability statistics, numerical classification and scaling, and quantitative modeling. This modern approach derives from two major developments in quantitative analysis over the past century: "statistical inference," shaped largely between 1920 and 1950, and the more recent "exploratory data analysis," devised by John W. Tukey and colleagues in the 1970s and 1980s, adumbrated in works such as Tukey's 1977 *Exploratory Data Analysis*.

Statistical Inference

Statistical inference involves hypothesis testing (evaluating some idea about a population using a sample) and estimation (estimating the value or potential range of values of some characteristic of the population based on that of a sample). Archaeologists were relatively slow to realize the analytical potential of statistical theory and methods. It is only in the past 20 or 30 years that they have begun to use formal methods of data analysis regularly. Influential essays by George Cowgill (e.g., in 1970 and 1977) and others such as David Clarke (in 1962), Hodder's 1978 *Simulation Studies in Archaeology*, Orton's 1980 *Mathematics in Archaeology*, and Spaulding (in 1953) demonstrated to archaeologists that, because most of their data represent samples of larger populations, statistical methods are critical for identifying empirical patterns and for evaluating how precisely and how accurately those patterns represent "real" trends in the broader world.

In addition to basic, descriptive statistics that summarize central tendency (what is a typical case?) and dispersion (how much variation is there?) in batches of numbers, archaeologists primarily have made use of statistical methods for sampling and for comparing data sets. For example, for nominal scale data, the chi-squared test is one of the most commonly used means of determining the probability (given relatively small sample sizes) of whether a relationship exists between cases (e.g., pottery types), although it does not inform about the strength or kind of the relationship. For interval scale or ratio scale variables, archaeologists often use tests that depend on the gaussian ("normal") distribution, although these, too, have their problems, such as sensitivity to irregularities ("outliers") in the data. Along these lines, linear regression, analysis of variance, and hierarchical cluster analysis have been important, especially for temporal seriation—building chronologies based on stylistic changes in material culture over time.

Exploratory Data Analysis

Exploratory data analysis is concerned with visual displays of data, rather than with summary statistics and statistical significance tests that are based on deductive reasoning; this is discussed by Tukey. The aim of this approach is purely inductive: to explore the data set for patterning ("smooth data"), as well as deviations from that patterning ("rough data"), relevant to some problem. One of the basic ways in which archaeologists have operationalized this approach for examining univariate and bivariate data is by constructing histograms and stem-and-leaf diagrams, box-and-whisker plots, frequency polygons, and cumulative curves. More complex considerations involving multivariate data include Tukey-line regression, *k*-means cluster analysis, principal components analysis, and correspondence analysis, to name a few. These graphic displays, especially when combined with computer visualization tools, such as geographic information systems, computer-aided design programs, and mapping software, have prompted archaeologists to work inductively and to become more intimately acquainted with their data. The new archaeology of the 1960s and 1970s required archaeologists to work within a hypothetico-deductive framework, with *a priori* models, theories, and assumptions, which were then evaluated with data. Today, with incredible advancements in computer-based imaging and graphic quality, research often begins with the discovery of patterns in graphically displayed data, which leads archaeologists to formulate new questions and to discover new relationships in an interactive process between hypothesis testing and graphic displays. The end result is that models of past human behavior often are built from the ground up, in contrast to "theory-down" approaches of the previous decades.

One example of the exploratory data analysis approach in archaeology is correspondence analysis. Pertinent works are by J. M. Greenacre (*Theory and Application of Correspondence Analysis*) and J. M. Greenacre and J. Blasius (*Correspondence Analysis in the Social Sciences*). Originally developed by Jean-Paul Benzecri in the 1960s and 1970s for linguistic applications, this multivariate analytical technique is designed to analyze data consisting of frequencies of occurrence in a two-way contingency table, with the aim of showing a graphical representation of the two-dimensional relationships (viewed on a scatterplot) between cases, those between variables, and those between cases and variables. The analysis produces a graphical display of the rows and columns of the data matrix, illustrating clusters within the rows and within the columns, as well as the association between them. Here, both cases and variables are plotted together. Importantly, the analysis reduces domination by frequency counts and focuses on relationships between groups of objects and their context. This capability helps to overcome the fact that in situations in which some variables have significantly higher frequencies than others, such as in artifact assemblages representing different activity areas, the variation in the former will tend to dominate the analysis and the variation in the latter will have very little effect on it. For interpreting the plot, if two sets of cases are similar, then they will appear close to one another on the scatterplot. Likewise, if a case and a variable are similar, then these will tend to appear close to one another on the plot as well. In this way, the relationships among cases can be compared to one another, as well as their relationships to variables. Thus, this analysis can determine the relative strength of a relationship between cases as well as the ways in which the cases are similar.

Combined Approaches

One of the more influential quantitative studies that emerged in archaeology during the 1970s, based on central-place theory, combines graphic display with statistical inference. The theory, originally developed for market economies by geographers Christaller and Lösch, proposes that a regular hexagonal distribution of hierarchically ordered central places is optimal for minimizing the cost of travel and transport and for maximizing economic profits. In central-place analysis, the hierarchy of central places is established on the basis of the sizes of centers (e.g., using rank-size measures, as discussed by Haggett in *Locational Analysis in Human Geography* and in numerous articles by archaeologists). Size is assumed to correlate positively with the number of functions the center performs such that larger centers perform more functions than do smaller centers. Rank-size analysis can be used to examine the degree of socioeconomic integration of a settlement system by plotting the sizes and ranks (based on size) of all settlements on a graph. For this study, graphic plots are produced by arranging settlement size data in descending order by size, assigning a numerical rank to each (with the largest being ranked first), and plotting size against rank using a logarithmic (base 10) scale. The idealized rank-size distribution (referred to as lognormal) is represented by a straight, negatively sloped line. Rank-size plots for particular settlement systems may approximate this line, or individual cases may lie above or below it. Distributions that lie close to the lognormal line are taken to imply a high degree of organization, cohesiveness, and interaction in a tightly integrated settlement system with a strong hierarchical structure. Deviations from the lognormal rank-size relationship (e.g., disparities in size between the first- and second-order settlements) are believed to reveal important properties of settlement structures, including the degree of centralized control or system organization.

Summary of Quantitative and Formal Approaches

In sum, quantitative and formal analyses in archaeology play an important role in evaluating patterns discovered by visual examination. As George Cowgill often has remarked, statistical analysis is not a way to arrive at certainty; rather, it is a powerful aid in discerning what the data suggest, and how strongly they suggest it. Thus, for archaeologists, quantitative methods of data analysis are often done by an estimation approach rather than by hypothesis testing. Visualization tools are essential to this effort, because simple statistics cannot convey the essence of spatial patterning in the same way that an effective graphic can. Statistical methods likewise are critical, because they provide information about the existence of tendencies or relationships (as well as the strength of those relationships) that are difficult, or even impossible, to visualize. In the future, archaeologists are likely to move beyond the statistical methods now current to nonprobabilistic methods. As their name implies, nonprobabilistic statistics are not based on probability, that is, normal distributions of data (say, random samples drawn from a known population). True archaeological populations are never knowable: no matter how thorough a surface survey, not all sites that ever existed will be found; and when working with artifacts, the sample being used consists of only those items recovered during surface collection and excavation, with the actual population remaining unknown and unknowable. Therefore, the methods discussed herein will be expanded by new approaches, ones that are relatively recent additions to the corpus of formal methods.

See Also the Following Articles

Geography • History, Social Science Methods Used in • Political Science • Sociology

Further Reading

Benzecri, J. P. (1973). *L'Analyse des Données, Tome 2: L'Analyse des Correspondances.* Dunod, Paris.

Bourdieu, P. (1977). *Outline of a Theory of Practice.* (Richard Nice, transl.). Cambridge University Press, New York.

Claassen, C. (ed.) (1992). *Exploring Gender through Archaeology: Selected Papers from the 1991 Boone Conference.* Prehistory Press, Madison, Wisconsin.

Clarke, D. L. (1962). Matrix analysis and archaeology with particular reference to British beaker pottery. *Proc. Prehistor. Soc.* **28,** 371–382.

Cowgill, G. L. (1970). Some sampling and reliability problems in archaeology. In *Archéologie et Calculateurs* (J. C. Gardin, ed.), pp. 161–172. Centre National de la Recherche Scientifique, Paris.

Cowgill, G. L. (1977). The trouble with significance tests and what we can do about it. *Am. Antiquity* **42,** 350–368.

Diehl, M. W. (ed.) (2000). *Hierarchies in Action.* Center for Archaeological Investigations, Southern Illinois University at Carbondale.

Dobres, M.-A., and Robb, J. E. (eds.) (2000). *Agency in Archaeology.* Routledge, New York.

Feinman, G. M., and Manzanilla, L. (eds.) (2000). *Cultural Evolution: Contemporary Viewpoints.* Kluwer Academic/ Plenum Publ., Madison, Wisconsin.

Foucault, M. (1972). *The Archaeology of Knowledge.* (A. M. Sheridan Smith, transl.). Pantheon Books, New York.

Giddens, A. (1984). *The Constitution of Society: Outline of the Theory of Structuration.* University of California Press, New York.

Haas, J. (ed.) (2001). *From Leaders to Rulers.* Kluwer Academic/Plenum Publ., New York.

Haggett, P., Cliff, A. D., and Frey, A. (1977). *Locational Analysis in Human Geography,* 2nd Ed. Wiley, New York.

Hodder, I. (2001). *Archaeological Theory Today.* Kluwer Academic/Plenum Publ., New York.

Hodder, I., and Hutson, S. (2003). *Reading the Past: Current Approaches to Interpretation in Archaeology,* 3rd Ed. Cambridge University Press, New York.

McGuire, R. H. (1992). *A Marxist Archaeology.* Academic Press, San Diego.

McGuire, R. H., and Paynter, R. (eds.) (1991). *The Archaeology of Inequality.* Berg, Providence.

Nelson, S. M., and Rosen-Ayalon, M. (eds.) (2002). *In Pursuit of Gender: Worldwide Archaeological Approaches.* AltaMira Press, Walnut Creek, California.

Orton, C. (1980). *Mathematics in Archaeology.* Collins, London.

Patterson, T. C. (2003). *Marx's Ghost: Conversations with Archaeologists.* Berg, Providence.

Patterson, T. C., and Gailey, C. W. (eds.) (1987). *Power Relations and State Formation.* American Anthropological Association, Washington, D.C.

Preucel, R. W. (ed.) (1991). *Processual and Postprocessual Archaeologies: Multiple Ways of Knowing the Past*. Center for Archaeological Investigations, Southern Illinois University at Carbondale.

Robb, J. E. (ed.) (1999). *Material Symbols: Culture and Economy in Prehistory*. Center for Archaeological Investigations, Southern Illinois University at Carbondale.

Spaulding, A. C. (1953). Statistical techniques for the discovery of artifact types. *Am. Antiquity* **18,** 305–313.

Trigger, B. G. (1989). *A History of Archaeological Thought*. Cambridge University Press, New York.

Willey, G. R., and Sabloff, J. A. (1993). *A History of American Archaeology*, 3rd Ed. W. H. Freeman, New York.

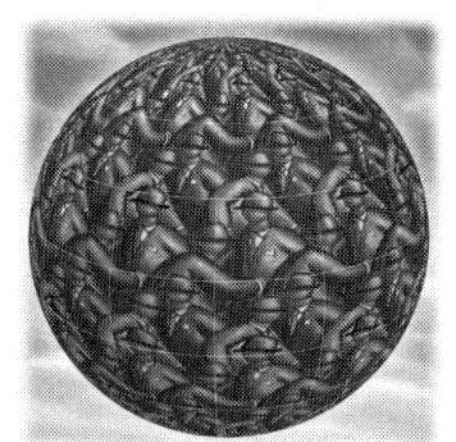

Aristotle

James G. Lennox
University of Pittsburgh, Pittsburgh, Pennsylvania, USA

Glossary

definition For Aristotle, a definition is an account of the essential characteristics of the object being defined. These essential characteristics are discovered through the use of division and causal investigation. In fact, for Aristotle, to know the fundamental cause of something is critical to having a scientifically valid definition of it. Because scientific definitions identify a thing's proper kind and the fundamental ways in which it differs from other members of the kind, a scientific definition can be represented by means of a demonstration.

demonstration A form of proof that provides scientific understanding of a fact within the domain of the science. As Aristotle defines it in his *Posterior Analytics*, such understanding comes from knowing the primary causal explanation of the fact in question.

division A method for systematically examining variation, or relations of similarity and difference, within a kind. In *On the Parts of Animals* and *History of Animals*, Aristotle criticizes the *a priori* method of dichotomous division defended by his teacher, Plato, and presents an empirical method of division that permits the systematic organization of information in scientific domains in which the objects are complex and multivariate.

polis A transliteration of the Greek word for a common method of social, political, and economic organization in classical Greece. On Aristotle's account, a polis is a natural result of the development of human society.

social animal Aristotle uses the expression *politikon zôon* ("social animal") to refer to a special subclass of gregarious animals, which includes humans and the social insects. Note that *politikon* is an adjective based on "polis," but it would be very misleading to translate it as meaning "political." Aristotle discusses social animals as a group in *History of Animals*, and, in *Politics*, he discusses human social organization as a form of animal social organization, differentiated in accordance with the characteristics that distinguish humans from other social animals.

the more and less A technical expression in Aristotle's work, along with "excess and deficiency," referring to measurable variation of a characteristic within a single kind. Forms of that kind will share all or most of the characteristics of the kind, but those characteristics will vary from one form to the next by "the more and less." Divisions within kinds will, in fact, organize information about more and less differences. Differences between kinds are, by contrast, according to analogy.

It is fair to say that Aristotle was the first person to attempt something that is recognizably a scientific study of social phenomena, certainly in the three works *Nicomachean Ethics*, *Politics*, and *Rhetoric*, but also in his zoological investigations. This is because he saw his studies of human social life as continuous in a variety of ways with his natural science, and thus, to understand his approach to the scientific study of social interaction, it is necessary to know something about his views on mankind as one among a class of "social animals." It is also interesting to explore the role of measurement in Aristotle's theory of science. He had a very clear view about the role of mathematics in the study of natural phenomena and about the limits of its uses in science. Thus, even when his scientific approach to social phenomena is very different from the modern view, his philosophical sophistication allows us to learn from those differences. It was Aristotle's view that the application of mathematics to natural phenomena was a powerful tool, but with a limited scope. He was deeply, and properly, skeptical of attempts to reduce everything to numbers, a view he saw clearly expressed by the Pythagoreans of his day.

Life and Work

Aristotle was born to Nicomachus and Phaestis of Stagira, a small town on the northern Aegean coast, in 384 BC.

Nicomachus was physician to King Amyntas of Macedon, and Phaestis was of a wealthy family from the island of Euboea. Nothing reliable is known about Aristotle's early childhood, but he was sent to Athens at the age of 17 and began a 20-year involvement with the philosophical and mathematical community gathered around Plato in the Academy. Aristotle may well have studied some medicine with his father, but there is no evidence to support this conjecture.

Aristotle's long association with Plato and the Academy ended on Plato's death in 367, by which time Aristotle had doubtless begun to develop his own distinctive philosophical ideas, including his passion for the study of nature. At the invitation of Hermias, a tyrant with connections to the Academy, Aristotle and other Academics founded a philosophical circle in Assos, a small town under Hermias' control in Asia Minor. Aristotle soon moved on to Mytilene on the island of Lesbos off the coast of Asia Minor, perhaps because he had heard of a young man with similar interests in natural science, for he there met and befriended his philosophical soul mate Theophrastus. Between the two of them, they originated the science of biology, Aristotle carrying out the first systematic scientific investigation of animals, Theophrastus doing the same for plants. This association was briefly interrupted when, in 343, Philip II of Macedon asked Aristotle to tutor his son Alexander. But by 335, Aristotle had returned to Athens, now firmly under the control of his former student. His philosophical distance from Plato was now great, and he and Theophrastus founded a rival group of scholars who spent their time in a public sanctuary known as the Lyceum. Aristotle remained at the head of this "school" until 323 BC. In that year, Alexander of Macedon died and, with anti-Macedonian feelings running high, Aristotle left Athens to live in Euboea, the birthplace of his mother. He died there in 322 BC.

The corpus of Aristotle that survives today is based primarily on manuscripts that go back only to the 10th through 14th centuries AD. There is some reason to believe that these manuscripts are based on a Roman editor's reorganization of Aristotle's writings in the 1st century BC. During the Middle Ages and Renaissance, many different manuscript editions were found, and modern printed editions are in turn based on modern editorial line-by-line choices about which of these manuscripts to trust. These works cover a remarkable range of subjects, from literary theory and rhetoric, through ethics and politics, to scientific studies of meteorology, cosmology, physics, zoology, psychology, and, finally, philosophical investigations that modern scholars classify as logic, metaphysics, and epistemology. Ancient testimony relates that Aristotle wrote a number of dialogues that rivaled Plato's, both philosophically and stylistically. Only a very few fragments of these works exist. For the most part, what survives are treatises written in a distinctively lean, unadorned, didactic style; above all else, these treatises stress rigorous argument. They also reflect a certain view of philosophical method. Nearly all begin with serious critical discussion of previous views on the subject being investigated, followed by a fresh approach to the subject using Aristotle's own philosophical categories and methods. Aristotle was quite explicit about how different areas of science were to be related to, and distinguished from, one another and about the extent to which there was a common scientific logic and method.

Theory of Science

A group of treatises known since the Middle Ages as the *Organon* present Aristotle's views on the cognitive tools necessary for thinking clearly about any subject. Aristotle's *Categories* presents a list of types of answers to fundamental questions that can be asked about any subject, and a theory about how these questions and answers can be related to one another. At the most abstract level, the answers constitute basic categories: substance, quality, quantity, place, time, relation, and so on. But it is important to note that the Greek names for these categories are nominalized interrogatives: the what is it, the what sort, the how much, the where, the when, and so on.

Aristotle also explored the basic features of the ontology behind these categories. He argued that only individuals in the "what is it" category—primary substances, he called them—are self-subsistent; everything else is inherent in these (i.e., dispositions, qualities, sizes, and changes do not exist on their own) and/or is said of them (their species and genus names, their locations, and their relationships). This is no mere grammatical point for Aristotle. In insisting on the ontological primacy of the particular substance, he is taking a stand against Platonism in all its forms—for it was Plato who argued that things like maple trees are merely fleeting and insubstantial participants in eternal forms such as goodness, unity, or equality, thus treating the particular objects encountered with the senses as inappropriate objects of scientific investigation. By arguing that being good, or being a unit, or being equal were all dependent on the existence of particular good, singular, or equal objects, Aristotle saw himself as rescuing empirical science from the Platonists.

The *Organon* also includes a small treatise that systematically investigates the different forms of propositions and their relationships (*De Interpretatione*), a much larger treatise on methods for carrying on debates on any subject whatever (*Topics*), and four books on *Analytics*, which have traditionally been divided into two units called *Prior Analytics* and two called *Posterior Analytics*, though Aristotle makes it clear that all four books constitute a single investigation. The first two are the very first formal investigation of proof—they are part formal logic and part philosophy of logic. Among the aims of these two books are to catalogue the various forms of valid proof, to show that these are the only valid forms, and to reduce them to a small number of basic forms. But Aristotle states in the opening sentence of this work that his ultimate aim is not a theory of valid proof, but a theory of demonstration, by which he means a causal explanation that provides scientific understanding: "We must first state what our inquiry is about and what its object is: it is about demonstration and its object is demonstrative understanding" (*Prior Analytics* Book I. §1, 24 a 10–11). (Note: the last element of the citation, 24 a 10–11, refers to the original two-column Greek text: page 24, column a, lines 10 and 11.) He immediately distinguishes his goals in the *Analytics* from those in the *Topics*. In the *Topics*, the interest is not in demonstrations of scientific truth, but rather in winning debates regardless of the truth of the starting premises. In either case, it will be valuable to determine the forms of valid argument. But for scientific demonstration, much more is required.

> *If to have scientific knowledge of something is what we have posited it to be, then a scientific demonstration must proceed from items that are true, primitive and immediate; moreover, they must be better known than, prior to and give the cause of the conclusions. (In this way our scientific principles will also be appropriate to what is being proved.) There can be a deduction even if these conditions are not met, but there cannot be a demonstration—for a proof without these conditions being met will not produce scientific knowledge.*
>
> [*Posterior Analytics* Book I. §2, 71b 20–26]

Each of these six additional constraints over and above logical validity deserves comment. Broadly speaking, it will be noted that the premises of a scientific demonstration have three "intrinsic" properties and three having to do with their relation to the conclusion to be demonstrated. We can go through them thinking of the following "maple tree" example (loosely based on an example in *Posterior Analytics* Book II. §16), using a standard, if anachronistic, formalization of the argument, with each subject/predicate term represented by a capital letter, and the lower case "a" representing the universal affirmative statement form:

All broad-leafed trees lose their leaves seasonally. [A a B]
All maples are broad-leafed trees. [B a C]
All maples lose their leaves seasonally. [A a C]

The premises are true; but are they primitive and immediate? Aristotle would say no. To be primitive, a premise must have no deeper explanation. Putting aside modern evolutionary accounts, even Aristotle would want an explanation for why broad-leafed plants happen to lose their leaves seasonally, but those plants with "needles" do not. A primitive premise would be obtained if it were true that all and only broad-leafed trees lose their leaves seasonally, and the basic causal explanation for that fact had been discovered. Aristotle, in fact, provides an example in the passage from which this sample demonstration is drawn—i.e., in all broad-leafed trees, sap coagulates seasonally, causing leaf shedding. A premise such as this would also be "immediate," the standard translation for a Greek term that literally means "lacking a middle." To understand this notion, look at the preceding demonstration. Notice that a term shared by both of the premises is missing in the conclusion, namely, "broad-leafed trees." Aristotle refers to this as the "middle" term of the proof, for he tended to represent the form of an argument like this one as AB, BC, AC, where B falls between A and C, the terms in the conclusion. For a premise to "lack a middle" is for it to have no more basic explanation and thus no "middle" can be inserted between A and B. "All broad-leafed plants have seasonal coagulation of sap" is, in this example, not the conclusion of a more fundamental explanation.

From what has already been said, it can be seen that the premises are both prior to and causally explanatory of the conclusion—but what about "better known"? This idea can be explicated by reference to the other five; all Aristotle has in mind is that if only the conclusion is known, insofar as it has been demonstrated from certain premises known "in themselves," and it is only scientific knowledge if those premises identify the causal explanation of the fact identified in the conclusion, then knowledge of the conclusion is conditional on the truth of the premises—those premises, then, are "better known." Without going any further into the details of his theory, there are two more claims that Aristotle makes about scientifically demonstrated conclusions, which he thinks follow from the preceding conditions on the premises. Those conclusions must identify "universal, necessary truths." That is, when a scientific demonstration shows that all broad-leafed trees lose their leaves seasonally, it is known that this is a fact about every such tree, and it is known that it could not be otherwise.

It can be seen that this is a highly demanding theory of scientific knowledge. To revert again to the example, a farmer who has noticed that olive trees lose their leaves in the winter, or a geometer who has noticed that every triangle has interior angles that add up to two right angles, is still a very long way from what Aristotle would call scientific knowledge. To know a domain of study scientifically requires penetration to a basic causal understanding of why things are so. It can also be seen that this theory of science puts a great deal of emphasis on getting the right information in the premises. Having done that, and having followed the rules of formal logic, scientific knowledge follows. It is thus frustrating that a great deal about Aristotle's theory of science is presented in the literature as axiomatic and deductive; but very little is stressed about his rich and complex account of establishing basic causal premises, the theory of scientific inquiry in *Posterior Analytics* Book II. Yet one of the most beautiful features of Aristotle's theory of science is his argument that there is an intimate relationship between determining the cause of the fact being investigated and discovering its underlying, essential nature. True understanding of why broad-leafed trees lose their leaves and those with needles do not, yields at once an understanding of what differentiates deciduous trees from conifers—it is known in fundamental terms what they are. If an understanding of what it is about three-sided rectilinear figures that accounts for their interior angles being equal to two right angles is attained, then the essence of triangles has been penetrated.

The Place of Measurement in Science

What role, if any, does measurement play in Aristotle's account of scientific knowledge? To answer this question, it is necessary to distinguish two fundamentally different notions of measurement in Aristotle, which may be called "ordinal" and "cardinal." Every form of measurement requires a standard. Greek mathematicians such as Archimedes or Heron wrote treatises on how to calculate the lengths, angles, volumes, or weights of various figures or entities, given certain measurements; they could compare incommensurable lengths by the use of the theory of ratios, and even incommensurable magnitudes (distances and times), by the general theory of proportions, newly discovered by Eudoxus (cf. *Posterior Analytics* Book I. §5, 74 b 18–24). Aristotle's discussion of Zeno's paradoxes shows him to have a sophisticated understanding of this area of mathematics. But he also had a sophisticated theory of ordinal measurement, for which the standard of measure is a norm of some sort or other, and items in the class are ranked in a series by reference to that norm. Without discussing the full range of Aristotle's theory and practice here, it is still possible to discuss his account of measuring degrees of sameness or likeness. His categories are sameness in number, sameness in form, sameness in kind, and sameness by analogy or proportion. The following extract from the opening page of the *History of Animals* provides an outline of Aristotle's theory of how to measure likeness. The *History of Animals* is a comprehensive application of that theory to a study of the similarities and differences of animals, which in turn is embedded in Aristotle's theory of differential division. All of this serves the goal of organizing information in the zoological domain in a form suitable for the discovery and presentation of causal explanation of these similarities and differences.

> *Some animals have all their parts the same as one another, some have their parts different. Some of the parts are the same in form, as the nose and eye of one human and that of another, or the flesh and bone of one in comparison with another; and the same is true of horses and of the other animals, so long as we say they are the same as one another in form—for just as the whole animal is alike to the whole, so too is each of the parts alike to each. Others—those for which the kind is the same—while the same, differ according to excess or deficiency. And by 'kind' I mean such things as bird and fish; for each of these differs according to kind, and there are many forms of fishes and birds.*
>
> *Most of the parts in these animals [those that are the same in kind] differ by way of the oppositions of their characteristics, such as their color and shape, the same parts being affected in some cases to a greater and in some cases to a lesser degree, and again by being more or fewer in number, or greater and smaller in size, and generally by excess and deficiency. For some of them will have soft flesh and some hard flesh, a long beak or a short beak, many feathers or few feathers. Moreover, some differ from others in a part that belongs to one not belonging to the other, as for example some birds having spurs and others not, and some having crests and others not. But speaking generally, the majority of the parts from which the entire body is constituted are either the same, or differ by opposition, i.e. by excess and deficiency; for we may posit the more and less to be a sort of excess and deficiency.*
>
> *The parts of some animals, however, are neither the same in form nor according to excess and deficiency, but are the same according to analogy, such as the way bone is characterized in comparison to fish-spine, nail in comparison to hoof, hand to claw or feather to scale; for what is feather in a bird is scale in fish.*
>
> [*History of Animals* 486 a 15–b 22]

Aristotle goes on to note (486 b 22–487 a 13) that similardifferentiations can be made regarding the position of a part; the same theory of sameness and difference can be applied to the uniform parts, or tissues, generally, and indeed to all of the important characteristics of animals, their ways of life (aquatic, avian, terrestrial), their activities or functions (modes of locomotion, feeding, reproduction), and their character traits (social, predatory, aggressive). It is precisely these measurable variations in shared characteristics for which scientific explanations are sought. Here is a rather typical example, from *On the Parts of Animals*, regarding the parts of birds: "Among birds, differentiation of one from another is by means of excess and deficiency of their parts, i.e. according to the more and less. That is, some of them are long-legged, some short-legged, some have a broad tongue, others a narrow one, and likewise too with the other parts" (*On the Parts of Animals* Book IV. §12, 692 b3–6). Aristotle next notes that all birds have feathers differing by more and less, but that these are analogous to scales in other kinds of animals. He goes on to make the same point about beaks: "Birds also have, on their head, the 'beak', an odd and distinctive feature in comparison with other animals; while in elephants there is a trunk in place of hands, and in some of the insects a tongue in place of a mouth, in the birds there is a bony beak in place of teeth and lips" (692 b 15–18).

Beaks differ from each other in measurable, quantitative ways, and have analogues in other animals, such as the elephant's trunk and the insect's proboscis. When Aristotle moves on to discuss the neck, he begins to note correlations among the variations in all of these parts, and offers a single, functional explanation for the correlated variations of parts:

> *Birds have a neck that is by nature stretchable, and owing to the same cause that other animals do; and in some birds it is short, in others long, generally following the legs in most cases. That is, those that are long-legged have a long neck, while those that are short-legged have a short one—setting aside those with webbed feet; for if the neck were short in those with long legs, the neck would not be of service to them for eating food off the ground; nor if it were long in those with sort legs. Again for those that eat flesh a long neck would be contrary to their way of life; while for these animals their way of life is based on overpowering prey. That is why none of the crook-taloned birds have a long neck.*
>
> [*On the Parts of Animals* 692 b 19–693 a 6]

They do, however, have a type of beak that is correlated with talons, and both are explained by their predatory way of life (see Figs. 1 and 2): "Their beaks too differ in accordance with their ways of life. Some have a straight beak, others a curved one; straight, those that have it for the sake of nourishment, curved, those that are carnivores; for such a beak is useful for overpowering prey.... But all birds whose way of life includes swamp-dwelling and plant-eating have a flat beak; for such a beak is useful both for digging up and cropping off their nourishment" (693 a 10–17).

Nature and Society

The biological example has provided a concrete picture of Aristotle's notion of division within kinds by measurable differences of excess and deficiency, or "more and less." The use of this method by Aristotle's in his discussion of social organization is pervasive. The first point to stress is that, for Aristotle, being a *politikon zôon* (a social animal) is not something that differentiates humans from all other animals. In the *History of Animals*, Aristotle begins by distinguishing gregarious from solitary animals, and then divides gregarious animals into those that are "social" (*politikon*) and those that get together "sporadically." He then comments on this distinction:

> *Social animals (politika) are those for which there is some one function or work (ergon) that is shared by all,*

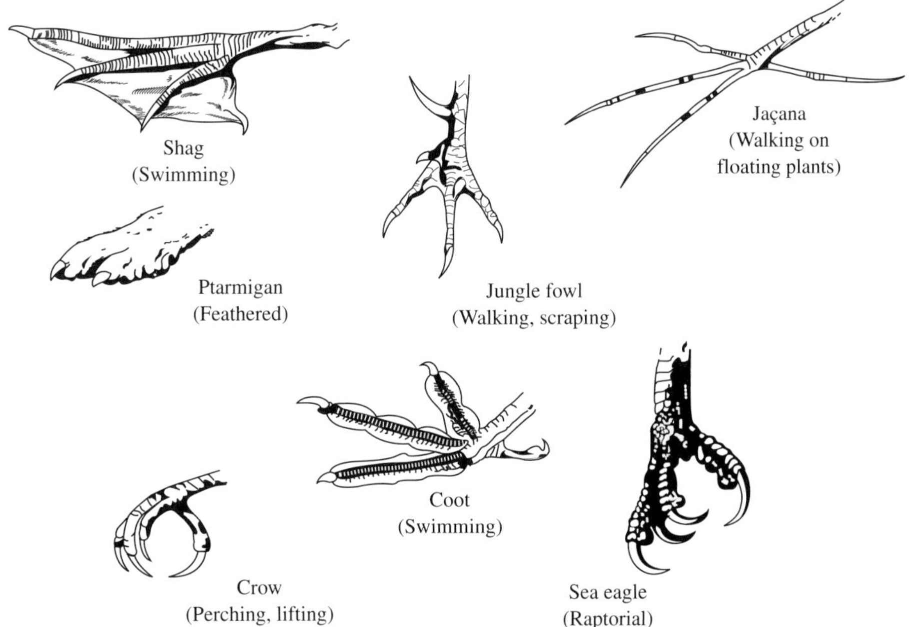

Figure 1 Kinds, forms of kinds, and the "more and the less." Types of bird feet, indicating adaptations for locomotion and predation. Reproduced with permission from Thomson, J. A. (1970), *The Biology of Birds*, in *Encyclopedia Britannica*, 14th Ed.

something not done by all gregarious animals. Such are human kind, the bee, the wasp, the ant and the crane. And among these some live under a ruler and some do not—for example, the crane and the kind consisting of the bees live under a ruler, while ants and many other kinds do not.
[*History of Animals* Book I. §1, 488 a 8–13]

Aristotle's *Politics* opens with a reminder of this theme:

Since we observe that every polis is a sort of community, and that every community is constituted for the sake of some good (for everyone does whatever they do for the sake of what seems to be good), it is clear that while all communities aim at some good, the community that both contains and is supreme over all others does so most of all; and this is the community known as the polis or the social community (he koinõnia he politike).
[*Politics* Book I. §1, 1252 a 108]

In the *History of Animals*, Aristotle differentiates social from other gregarious animals by the fact that all of the members of the social group share a common function; he here spells this out in terms of some common good each member of the community aims for. He then goes on to say that by using his preferred method of investigation, dividing the composite into its least component parts, it will be possible to discern the differences between differently constituted social organizations (1252 a 18–23). Lest there be any doubts about the zoological background to this discussion, he goes on:

But if we can somehow observe things that grow from their origin, it is best to study them in this manner, just as we do in other cases. And first of all it is necessary for those things that cannot exist without one another to couple, i.e. male and female, for the sake of generation (and this is not a matter of forethought—rather, just as in the other animals and plants, the impulse to leave behind another such as oneself is natural); next, it is natural for there to be a coupling of ruler and ruled, for the sake of security.
[*History of Animals* 1252 a 24–31]

In this manner, Aristotle traces the development of complex social organizations such as the Greek polis, concluding with a reminder that this development is not artificial, but natural.

The complete community formed from many villages is the polis, having, in a manner of speaking, reached the goal of complete self-sufficiency, coming to be for the sake of life, but being for the good life. For this reason every polis exists by nature—if, that is, the first communities do. For the polis is the goal of these communities, and the nature of something is its goal; that is, when the development of each thing has reached its goal, we say this is its nature, as with a human being a horse or a household. Again, that for the sake of

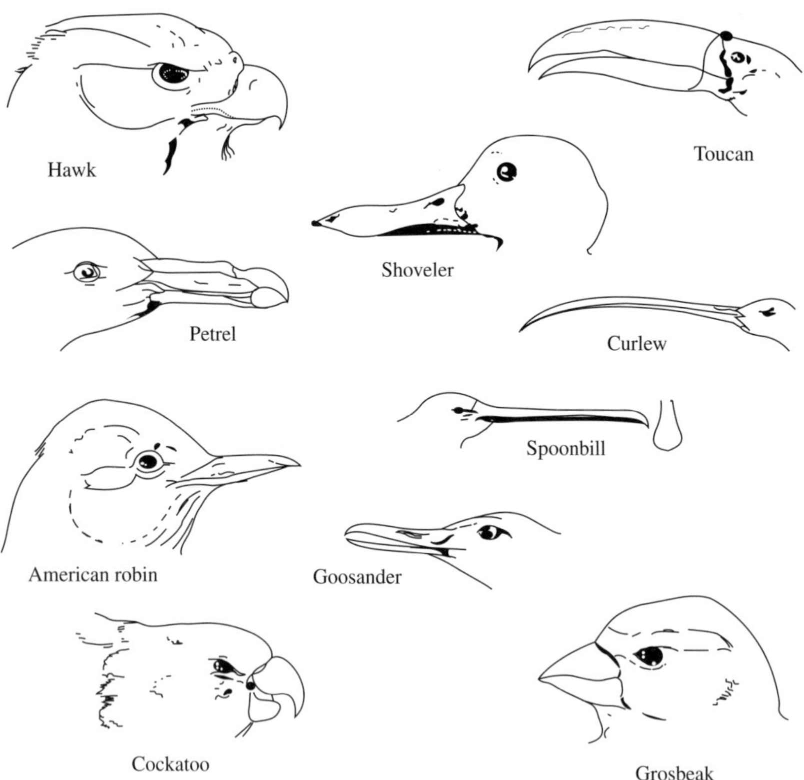

Figure 2 Matter, form, and kind. Types of bird bills, indicating adaptations for feeding. Reproduced with permission from Thomson, J. A. (1970), *The Biology of Birds*, in *Encyclopedia Britannica*, 14th Ed.

which something develops and its goal is best for it, and self-sufficiency is the goal of communities and best for them. Thus from these points it is apparent that the polis exists by nature, and that mankind is by nature a social animal.

[*History of Animals* 1252 b 28–1253 a 3]

But not only are we by nature social animals—in a conscious reminder of the discussion in the *History of Animals*, Aristotle explains why humans are the most social of animals: "The reason why mankind is a social animal more than all the bees or any of the gregarious animals is clear. Nature, as we say, does nothing in vain; and mankind is the only animal with language" (1253 a 8–10). This is not the superficial point that language is a consummately social function. In the Greek work, "language" is *logos*, and though it refers to language, it also refers to rationality. Aristotle ties the possession of language to the ability to consciously discern the differences between good and evil, justice and injustice. This is critical to the polis, for as Aristotle goes on to say, humans in the absence of law and justice are the most dangerous and savage of animals (1253 a 30–38). The remainder of the important opening chapter of the *Politics* argues for the priority of the polis over its component communities and their individuals using a biological argument—just as the parts of the whole organism exist for the sake of the organism, and in fact exist in name only unless they can serve the function of the whole organism, so too with the components of the polis (1253 a 19–29).

The Science of Political Animals

That Aristotle considers the methods of natural science to be applicable to the study of human societies should be clear by now. But does he also make use of the method of measuring similarities and differences that he so effectively deployed in biology? This can be assessed by looking at his statement in *Politics* Book IV. §4, on the proper method for investigating the similarities and differences among types of constitution:

We have noted that there are many forms of constitution (politeia) and on account of what cause; but we should add that there many more than those already mentioned, and say what they are, and why there are many, beginning by assuming what we said previously. That is, we agreed that every polis has not one part, but many. Thus, just as when we were aiming to grasp the forms of animal we would first have to determine which parts it is necessary for every animal to have (e.g., some one of the sensory organs and the parts able to take in and digest food, such as the mouth and stomach, and in addition the parts by which each of these forms of animal moves). And if there were this many necessary parts, there would be differences among them (I mean, for example, that there are many kinds of mouths, stomachs and sense organs, and in addition locomotive parts) and the number of combinations of these will of necessity produce many kinds of animals (for it is not possible for the same animal to have many different mouths, nor likewise ears). Therefore, when the possible combinations of all these different parts are grasped they will produce the forms of animal, and there will be as many forms of animal as there are combinations of necessary parts. And the same is true of the constitutions we have discussed. For in fact the various sorts of polis are not constituted from one but from a combination of many parts, as we've said often.

[*Politics* Book IV. §4, 1290 b 21–39]

As a number of commentators have noted, we have here a systematic application of the theory of differential division developed in Aristotle's biological works to the domain of the constitution of social organizations. It is applied systematically throughout the *Politics*, but this is Aristotle's clearest theoretical defense of the method, and once again, he defends it by appeal to the similarities between the constitution of society and the organism. The method is applicable under the following conditions:

1. The objects in the domain of study are made up of many parts, without which these objects cannot exist.
2. These many necessary parts each come in a variety of different forms.
3. No object will have more than one form of these necessary parts.

Assuming these conditions are met, the method, when applied to society, consists of the following empirical steps.

1. Determine the parts that are necessary to the constitution of any polis.
2. Study the measurable variations among these necessary parts.
3. Study the ways in which these variations are combined, for this will provide an exhaustive classification of constitutions.
4. Investigate the reasons behind these variations, especially the good served by each—its function, what it is for.
5. Investigate these variations as functions of the other variations with which they are combined. Just as there is a reason why a carnivorous, soaring bird has keen eyesight, crooked talons, a hooked beak, and a short thick neck, so there are reasons for the correlations among measurable variations in the constitutions of different social organizations.

Conclusion

It would not be surprising if the reader were at this point asking the question "Where is measurement?".

It is clear that Aristotle had a systematic interest in, a way of studying, variation among entities of the same kind in a domain, and that this was for him systematically connected to the sorts of differences for which causal explanations are sought. But at no point does he specify in numeric terms the exact range of curvature of a sparrow hawk's beak or the ideal range of citizenry for a constitutional democracy. It is thus reasonable to question the primacy of measurement. There are two responses.

The first response is a reminder of the distinction between "cardinal" and "ordinal" measurements. For every character about which Aristotle is concerned to give an account of its range of variation within a kind under investigation, he has an objective means of comparison. When he says beaks vary by "more and less," he means that every beak can be compared along the ranges long/short, wide/narrow, curved/straight, and so on. It is not that Aristotle did not have the means to apply an arbitrarily selected scale of numeric values to these things. Greek mathematics was at this point in history not very interested in mensuration, but the tools were certainly available. What interested Aristotle was (1) the mere fact that one bird would have a long, straight, and slender beak and another would have a short, curved, and thick one, (2) the more complicated fact that all birds with the latter sort of beak have a short rather than long neck, (3) and the search for a unified explanation for these correlated differences.

The second response points to the historical importance of this methodology. Aristotle's study of variations of forms by "the more and less" became, in the late Middle Ages, the calculation of the intension and remission of forms of the so-called Oxford calculators. They took from Aristotle the idea of studying differences in terms of measurable, continuous variation, and applied to it a quasi-geometric method for representing the differences. And though this may be considered an advance, it must be said that none of these thinkers came close to Aristotle as systematic empirical investigators of nature, nor did they deploy such methods in a systematic empirical study of society.

See Also the Following Articles

Mathematical and Statistical Approaches • Measurement Theory

Further Reading

Charles, D. (2000). *Meaning and Essence in Aristotle.* Oxford University Press, Oxford.

Cooper, J. M. (1990). Political animals and civic friendship. In *Aristoteles' Politik* (G. Patzig, ed.). Vandenhoeck & Ruprecht Verlag.

Depew, D. (1995). Humans and other political animals in Aristotle's History of Animals. *Phronesis* **40,** 156–181.

Gotthelf, A., and Lennox, J. G. (eds.) (1987). *Philosophical Issues in Aristotle's Biology.* Cambridge University Press, Cambridge.

Kullmann, W. (1991). Man as a political animal in Aristotle. In *A Companion to Aristotle's Politics* (D. Keyt and F. D. Miller, Jr., eds.). Oxford University Press.

Kullmann, W., and Föllinger, S. (eds.) (1997). *Aristotelische Biologie: Intentionen, Methoden, Ergebnisse.* Franz Steiner Verlag, Stuttgart.

Lennox, J. G. (2001). *Aristotle's Philosophy of Biology: Studies in the Origins of Life Science.* Cambridge University Press, Cambridge.

Miller, F. D., Jr. (1995). *Nature, Justice, and Rights in Aristotle's Politics.* Oxford University Press, Oxford.

Artificial Societies

J. Stephen Lansing

University of Arizona, Tucson, Arizona, USA

Glossary

agent-based Relying on the activities of individual agents who respond to events within the area of their local knowledge, but not necessarily to global events.

Boolean network A system of n interconnected binary elements; any element in the system can be connected to a series I of k other elements, where k (and therefore I) can vary. For each individual element, there is a logical or Boolean rule B, which computes its value based on the values of the elements connected with that particular element.

cellular automaton Usually a two-dimensional organization of simple finite-state machines where the next state of each machine depends on its own state and the states of some defined set of its neighbors.

dynamical systems theory The branch of mathematics devoted to the motions of systems that evolve according to simple rules. It was developed originally in the 17th century by Newton to model the motions of the solar system, evolving under the rules of his new theory of universal gravitation.

edge of chaos The hypothesis that in the space of dynamical systems of a given type, there will generically exist regions in which systems with simple behavior are likely to be found and other regions in which systems with chaotic behavior are to be found. Near the boundaries of these regions, more interesting behavior, neither simple nor chaotic, may be expected.

Feigenbaum's number A constant (4.6692...) that represents the rate at which new periods appear during the period-doubling route to chaos.

genetic algorithm An evolutionary algorithm that generates each individual from an encoded form known as a "chromosome" or "genome." Chromosomes are combined or mutated to breed new individuals. A genetic algorithm is useful for multidimensional optimization problems in which the chromosome can encode the values for the different variables being optimized.

nonlinearity The behavior of a circuit, particularly an amplifier, in which the output signal strength does not vary in direct proportion to the input signal strength.

object-oriented A kind of program structure in which conceptual objects are endowed with properties (data) and methods through which their data can be manipulated.

state space A mathematical space in which coordinates represent the variables needed to specify the state (or phase) of a dynamical system at any time.

As the philosopher Karl Popper cogently observed, social scientists who wish to take advantage of mathematical tools have the choice of two alternative approaches. The first is essentially Newtonian and is best represented by general equilibrium theories, for example, in economics. Such theories take the form of systems of differential equations describing the behavior of simple homogenous social actors. Change occurs as a result of perturbations and leads from one equilibrium state to another. The second type of theory is statistical. If one cannot write the equations to define a dynamical system, it may yet be possible to observe regularities in social phenomena. Both approaches have obvious weaknesses: the assumption of equilibrium is forced by the mathematics, not by the observation of social behavior, whereas sifting for patterns using statistical techniques is at best an indirect method for discovering causal relationships. In the 1990s, a third approach came into existence as powerful computational tools became available to social scientists. "Artificial societies" are computational models composed of populations of social agents that flourish in artificial environments. Although the behavior of the agents is governed by explicit rules, these rules may change in response to changes in the environment or as a consequence of learning and memory. In this way, the behavior of agents can become heterogeneous in ways that cannot occur in conventional equilibrium models. Repeated simulations enable the investigator to study how such model societies evolve over time and to investigate their global or macroscopic properties. A burst of such models have appeared in the social and behavioral sciences.

Origins of Artificial Societies

Experiments in simulation in the social sciences began in the 1960s as computers became available for university research. Most studies concerned either discrete event simulations, such as the passage of police cars through queues, or systems dynamics, such as the Club of Rome global forecasts that used systems of difference equations to plot the trajectory of the world economy. An early "artificial societies" approach was developed by sociologist Thomas Schelling. In a classic series of papers, Schelling used very simple agents to predict patterns of racial and ethnic segregation in American neighborhoods. At approximately the same time, European sociologists developed an approach called "microsimulation," in which samples drawn from large populations are marched forward in time (or "aged") using vectors of transition probabilities. This approach relies on linear algebra and does not attempt to model interactions between individuals or households.

In the 1990s, the concept of artificial societies seems to have been invented independently on both sides of the Atlantic by Epstein and Axtell and by Gilbert and Conte. The timing coincided with the appearance of powerful minicomputers, but the artificial societies approach was not a simple extension of preexisting techniques for social simulations. Instead, the new approach drew on earlier theoretical work in computer science, beginning with von Neumann's concept of self-reproducing automata. Von Neumann speculated that simple self-reproducing agents could be created as a set of instructions in a computer program. In 1953, he gave a series of lectures at Princeton University showing how this concept could be implemented in the form of a cellular automaton: a lattice of cells that follow local rules to update their state. Later, John Holland showed that such agents could be brought under the control of an evolutionary process. Holland's "genetic algorithm" implements evolution *in silico*, representing genotypes as computer code. As the eminent evolutionary biologist W. D. Hamilton observed, "It was a very brilliant step of John Holland to realize that he could probably do something in artificial intelligence by just importing the principles of life directly." These ideas paved the way for artificial societies models, with von Neumann agents inhabiting a lattice and evolving or interacting according to local rules. One could argue that the artificial societies research agenda came into existence when social scientists began to see the potential of von Neumannesque models for social research. A decade later, the influence of ideas from computer science remains strong. Artificial societies researchers draw models, methods, and inspiration from research in parallel fields including cellular automata, distributed artificial intelligence, evolutionary game theory, parallel distributed cognition, artificial life, and genetic programming.

Characteristics of Artificial Societies Models

Contemporary artificial societies are a specialized type of simulation model that typically employs an object-oriented, agent-based system architecture. As Epstein and Axtell observe with regard to one of the first such models, called "Sugarscape": "if the pure cellular automaton is a space with no agents living on it, and the pure adaptive agents model represents agent kinetics with no underlying space, then the Sugarscape model is a synthesis of these two research threads." In models such as Sugarscape, agents are implemented as objects that are able to perceive features of their environment, which may include messages from other agents. Typically they are able to process these perceptions and make decisions about their subsequent behavior. Agents may also possess attributes of memory and a capacity for learning. These characteristics add several dimensions of novelty to artificial societies models, in comparison with conventional equilibrium models. To begin with, the architecture of these models enables the investigator to utilize dynamical systems theory in order to investigate both equilibrium and non-equilibrium conditions. In other words, the behavior of agents and societies in state space can be studied through controlled experiments in which behavioral or environmental parameters are tuned. Agents can be as heterogeneous as the investigator chooses to make them and the model environment can be arbitrarily simple or complex. Archeologists are particularly fond of very detailed environmental models based on geographic information systems. Using parameter sweeps, they can model questions such as the effects of varying rainfall on a landscape, with respect to the growth of crops and the spatial patterning of human activities. Unlike equilibrium models in economics and sociology, artificial societies models generally involve time as a critical dimension. The usual strategy is to create a landscape with agents that are instructed to follow a set of rules. Such rules might implement evolutionary dynamics, or trading rules for an artificial stock market, or kinship rules in an anthropological study. Since the behavior of each agent depends on its local situation, in all but the simplest cases it is impossible to solve the entire system in advance. But as Stephen Wolfram observed, "One way to find out how a system behaves in particular circumstances is always to simulate each step in its evolution explicitly."

Research Themes: Contingency

As time proceeds in simulation experiments, new patterns may emerge. This phenomenon led researchers working with the first generation of models to ponder Stephen Jay Gould's famous question: "What if the evolutionary tape were run again?" Investigators found it easy to construct heterogeneous agents and environments and to observe their behavior over time. But the very ease with which such simulations could be performed could be worrisome: if an infinite number of such experiments could be performed, and analytical solutions are forever out of reach, is there any point to performing the calculations?

To answer this question required some new analytical tools. The most basic technique is dynamical systems theory, which provides methods to describe the global behavior of systems of differential equations. Systems of N variables are tracked in their passage through N-dimensional space, allowing the researcher to ask where the system spends most of its time and thus to assess its characteristic patterns of behavior. In continuous deterministic dynamical systems, all possible time series make up the vector field, which is represented by the system's phase portrait, an idea first proposed by Poincaré in 1896. Analogous questions can be asked about discrete dynamical systems, such as random Boolean networks and cellular automata. Where analytical solutions cannot be found, repeated simulations can be analyzed for their statistical properties. The initial exploration of these systems was rewarded by the discovery of unsuspected patterns of simplicity and order, from Feigenbaum's number to Langton's "edge of chaos," Wolfram's Class 4 cellular automata, and Bak's self-organized criticality. In the social sciences, political scientist Robert Axelrod reformulated the well-known "Prisoner's Dilemma" game as an artificial society simulation with a population of agents who play a series of games with their neighbors on a lattice. This turned the game into a dynamical system evolving over time. In the original game, rational choice leads to ruin, but in the artificial society model, Axelrod found that cooperation would emerge under a wide range of conditions. In further experiments, he tested the ability of Holland's genetic algorithm to evolve winning strategies and found that evolved strategies typically did as well or better as those created by game theorists. Axelrod concluded that the genetic algorithm proved to be "very good at what actual evolution does so well: developing highly specialized adaptations to specific environments." Subsequently, Kristian Lindgren embedded game-playing agents on a lattice, adding greater flexibility by making memory length an evolutionary variable. Over tens of thousands of generations, he observed the emergence of "spatial" patterns that resemble evolutionary processes and clarify preconditions for the emergence of cooperation and competition. Such simulation results have inspired behavioral ecologists to reexamine biological systems. For example, Manfred Milinski has studied stickleback fish, which enjoy "a well-earned reputation for keeping abreast of the latest trends in animal behavior." According to Milinski, cooperation in "predator inspection" by the sticklebacks follows the dynamics of the iterated Prisoner's Dilemma. The results of these simulations have also been used to model problems in political science and economics. There is a large literature on this topic.

However, cooperation is by no means the only emergent property investigated by social simulations. Philosopher Brian Skyrms has studied the "evolution of the social contract" by modeling it as a problem in the evolution of strategies. His most ambitious models tackle large questions such as the evolution of justice, linguistic meaning, and logical inference. Skyrms finds that "the typical case is one in which there is not a unique preordained result, but rather a profusion of possible equilibrium outcomes. The theory predicts what anthropologists have always known—that many alternative styles of social life are possible." But this seems a bit too modest. With respect to the evolution of meaning, for example, Skyrms shows that evolutionary processes provide a plausible answer to the fundamental question, "How do the arbitrary symbols of language become associated with the elements of reality they denote?"

Research Themes: Emergence

The study of non-equilibrium economics is well under way, for example, in the simulation of stock markets, both real and imaginary. Simulation models have facilitated a shift from equilibrium models constructed with differential equations to nonlinear dynamics, as researchers recognize that economies, like ecosystems, may never settle down into an equilibrium. A clear and readable account of this change in perspective is provided by W. Brian Arthur in a 1999 *Science* article on "Complexity and the Economy." Arthur argues that "complexity economics is not a temporary adjunct to static economic theory, but theory at a more general, out-of-equilibrium level. The approach is making itself felt in every area of economics: game theory, the theory of money and finance, learning in the economy, economic history, the evolution of trading networks, the stability of the economy, and political economy." Biologist Stuart Kauffman draws explicit parallels between biological and economic systems, viz., "the modern corporation is a collectively self-sustaining structure of roles and obligations that 'lives' in an economic world, exchanges signals and stuffs, and survives or dies in ways at least loosely analogous to those of *E. coli* ... Both *E. coli* and IBM coevolve in their respective worlds." Economists have followed up on this idea by investigating the "web structure" of economies, as, for example, in Schenkman's analysis of the relationship between the diversity of sectors and the rate of economic growth in cities.

The study of the global properties of economies has been accompanied by research on the behavior of economic actors. Economist Samuel Bowles and his colleagues have begun to work with anthropologists such as Hillard Kaplan in order to investigate, as an empirical question, how social actors make decisions in game-theoretical or economic contexts. Based on these results, they propose to supplement *homo economicus* with a larger and more diverse "family of man." Research in economics on artificial societies thus proceeds at two levels: the characteristics of individual social actors and the global dynamics of economies or societies. This research draws heavily on mathematical models of nonlinear systems; investigators keep an eye out for power-law distributions of events, such as the growth of firms or the frequency of stock market events, that may signal a system near the edge of chaos.

From Sugarscape to the Anaszazi

Artificial societies research in anthropology began with George Gumerman's pioneering collaboration with physicist Murray Gell-Mann. Gumerman became interested in Axtell and Epstein's Sugarscape, a simulation model developed to study how sociocultural phenomena such as trade, warfare, and class structures can arise from simple interactions of adaptive agents. In Sugarscape, the "environment" is very simple, consisting of the agents themselves plus some idealized resources, such as "sugar" and "spice." Gumerman and Jeffrey Dean wondered whether more realistic environments could be simulated, with heterogeneous agents and landscapes defined by real archaeological data, observing that "while potentially powerful, agent-based models in archaeology remain unverified until they are evaluated against real-world cases. The degree of fit between a model and real-world situation allows the model's validity to be assessed." They further observed that the explanatory power of mathematical models may be greatest when they fail, since such failures may expose where the researcher's underlying conceptual model or explanation is flawed. Gumerman and Dean worked with Epstein and Axtell to apply the techniques developed for Sugarscape to create an agent-based model of the Anasazi society of Long House Valley in northeastern Arizona from 1800 B.C. to 1300 A.D. The simple lattice environment of Sugarscape was replaced by paleoenvironmental data on a 96 km^2 physical landscape. The environment of "Artificial Anasazi" is populated with human households, so that spatiotemporal patterns of settlement formation and household production can be simulated and compared with the archaeological record. A similar approach was developed by Tim Kohler and Carla van West to model human settlements in Mesa Verde circa 900–1300 A.D. Such models enable their creators to test their intuitions about the complex nonlinear processes involved in human–environmental interactions. As Kohler observes, "agent-based approaches admit an important role for history and contingency (and) can also, in principle, accommodate models that invoke heterogeneity among agents, or which drive social change through shifting coalitions of agents, argued by many to be a critical social dynamic."

Critiques and Resources

There have been several critiques of the field of artificial societies. Thus, John Maynard Smith writes in the *New York Review of Books* that he has "a general feeling of unease when contemplating complex systems dynamics. Its devotees are practising fact-free science. A fact for them is, at best, the outcome of a computer simulation; it is rarely a fact about the world." Science writer John Horgan cautions that "as the philosopher Karl Popper pointed out, prediction is our best means of distinguishing science from pseudo-science ... The history of 20th-century science should also make complexologists pause. Complexity is simply the latest in a long line of highly mathematical 'theories of almost everything" that have gripped the imaginations of scientists in this century." (Here Horgan appears to be mostly concerned with the very general theories of emergence developed by Stuart Kauffman and Per Bak, among others.) A more ambitious critique was published by an anthropologist, Stefan Helmreich, who offers an "ethnographic" account of the researchers working at the Santa Fe Institute in the mid-1990s. In *Silicon Second Nature*, Helmreich argues that artificial societies models reflect the unconscious cultural assumptions and social prejudices of their creators: "Because Artificial Life scientists tend to see themselves as masculine gods of their cyberspace creations, as digital Darwins exploring frontiers filled with primitive creatures, their programs reflect prevalent representations of gender, kinship, and race and repeat origin stories most familiar from mythical and religious narratives." For example, Helmreich describes Holland's genetic algorithms as reflecting a "heterosexual" bias: "There are a number of ways we might understand the exchange of bits between strings, but the metaphor of productive heterosex is gleefully emphasized by most authors." Thus, for Helmreich, simulation models are like Rorschach tests, revealing the researcher's cultural background and psychological idiosyncrasies. All statements, especially theoretical pronouncements, are taken not as statements about the world, but as evidence about the author's beliefs and mode of thought. "That many Artificial Life practitioners are white men who grew up reading cowboy science fiction," observes Helmreich, "is not trivial." Simulation models may also be dangerous (as Helmreich suggests with reference to the author's own work), urging that "the use and abuse of computer simulations bears watching—especially in situations where there is a notable power differential between those putting together the simulation and those whose lives are the subjects and objects of these simulations."

See Also the Following Article

Computer Simulation

Further Reading

Arthur, W. B. (1999). Complexity and the economy. *Science* **284,** 107–109.

Axelrod, R. (1997). *The Complexity of Cooperation: Agent-Based Models of Cooperation and Collaboration.* Princeton University Press, Princeton, NJ.

Epstein, J., and Axtell, R. (1996). *Growing Artificial Societies: Social Science from the Bottom Up.* The Brookings Institution, Washington DC and MIT Press, Cambridge, MA.

Gilbert, N., and Conte, R. (eds.) (1995). *Artificial Societies: The Computer Simulation of Social Life.* UCL Press, London.

Gumerman, G., and Gell-Mann, M. (eds.) (1994). *Understanding Prehistoric Complexity in the Prehistoric Southwest.* Santa Fe Institute Studies in the Sciences of Complexity, Proceedings Volume XXIV. Addison-Wesley, Reading, MA.

Helmreich, S. (1998). *Silicon Second Nature: Culturing Artificial Life in a Digital World.* University of California Press, Berkeley, CA.

Hofbauer, J., and Sigmund, K. (1991). *The Theory of Evolution and Dynamical Systems.* Cambridge University Press, Cambridge, UK.

Holland, J. H. (1992). *Adaptation in Natural and Artificial Systems.* MIT Press, Cambridge, MA.

Kauffman, S. (1995). *At Home in the Universe: The Search for the Laws of Self-Organization and Complexity.* Oxford University Press, Oxford.

Kohler, T., and Gumerman, G. (eds.) (2000). *Dynamics in Human and Primate Societies: Agent Based Modeling of Social and Spatial Processes.* Santa Fe Institute Studies in the Sciences of Complexity. Oxford University Press, New York.

Koza, J. (1994). *Genetic Programming II: Automatic Discovery of Reusable Programs.* MIT Press, Cambridge, MA.

Langton, C. (1990). Computation at the edge of chaos: Phase transitions and emergent computation. *Physica D,* 12–37.

Langton, C. (1994). *Artificial Life III.* Addison-Wesley, Redwood City, CA.

Lansing, J. S. (1999). Foucault and the water temples: A reply to Helmreich. *Crit. Anthropol.* **20,** 337–346.

Lansing, J. S. (2002). Artificial societies and the social sciences. *Artificial Life* **8,** 279–292.

Levy, S. (1992). *Artificial Life: A Report from the Frontier Where Computers Meet Biology.* Vintage Books, New York.

Lindgren, K. (1994). Evolutionary dynamics of simple games. *Physica D* **75,** 292–309.

Maynard Smith, J. (1995). Life at the edge of chaos. *New York Review of Books,* **March 2,** 28–30.

Nowak, M. A., and Sigmund, K. (1998). Evolution of indirect reciprocity by image scoring. *Nature* **393,** 573–577.

Scheinkman, J., and Woodford, M. (1994). Self-organized criticality and economic fluctuations. *Am. Econ. Rev.* **84,** 417–421.

Sigmund, K. (1993). *Games of Life: Explorations in Ecology, Evolution and Behaviour.* Penguin Books, London.

Skyrms, B. (1996). *Evolution of the Social Contract.* Cambridge University Press, Cambridge, UK.

Waldrop, M. (1992). *Complexity: The Emerging Science at the Edge of Order and Chaos.* Simon and Schuster, New York.

Wolfram, S. (2002). *A New Kind of Science.* Wolfram Media, Champaign, IL.

Wuensche, A., and Lesser, M. J. (1992). *The Global Dynamics of Cellular Automata: An Atlas of Basin of Attraction Fields of One-Dimensional Cellular Automata.* Santa Fe Institute Studies in the Sciences of Complexity. Addison-Wesley, Reading, MA.

Attrition, Mortality, and Exposure Time

Alex R. Piquero
University of Florida, Gainesville, Florida, USA

Stephanie Carmichael
University of Florida, Gainesville, Florida, USA

Glossary

attrition The loss of longitudinal study participants over time.

exposure time The temporary loss of study participants due to some type of incapacitation effect.

longitudinal data Information from research that assesses people or other units during more than one time period.

missing data Information on respondents or for variables that are lost.

mortality Death of an individual during a (long-term) research project.

The study of stability and change in the social sciences requires the use of longitudinal data. Although such data are powerful for answering how key social science phenomena change over time between and within individuals, researchers are confronted with three specific challenges: attrition, mortality, and exposure time. This article provides examples of these challenges, as well as strategies that researchers could adopt for minimizing these problems before they become insurmountable and detrimentally influence the answering of important theoretical and substantive social science questions.

Introduction

Stability and change are key themes in social research, and panel, or longitudinal, data are optimal for the study of stability and change. Cohort studies examine more specific samples (e.g., birth cohorts) as they change over time; panel studies are similar to cohort studies except that the same sets of people are interviewed at two or more time periods. At their core, panel studies seek to measure the effect of age on the change in a particular outcome over a follow-up period of a certain length. Across several social science disciplines, the use of longitudinal panel design allows researchers to derive estimates of within- and between-individual change in key constructs of interest. For example, researchers can study how depression changes over the life course, how criminal activity varies with age, and so forth.

Although panel studies are well suited to examine issues of stability and change over time, they are also susceptible to three particular challenges. The first is attrition, or the loss of study participants over time. Attrition occurs when some participants either drop out of the study permanently or fail to participate in one or more of the follow-up assessments. The second is mortality, or the loss of participants due to death. Mortality is likely to be a salient problem when study participants enter old age and/or when a study includes individuals who exhibit some high-risk behavior (smoking, drug use, criminal activity, etc.). The third is exposure time, or the temporary loss of individuals due to some incapacitation effect. Exposure time is likely to be an important issue when studying change in criminal activity over time, because high-rate offenders are likely to experience differential (i.e., higher) incapacitation probabilities.

The following discussions address the usefulness of longitudinal data for assessing issues related to continuity and change in behavior over time; the three methodological challenges (attrition, mortality, and exposure time) are assessed, highlighting relevant research in this area, and approaches that researchers can take to minimize these concerns are identified. Although the issues raised herein are relevant for many social science phenomena and across several social science disciplines, the focus is on two examples that are strongly associated with age: depression and criminal activity. In addition, some preliminary data are provided on attrition in two prominent longitudinal studies, the Baltimore portion of the National Collaborative Perinatal Project (NCPP), and the National Youth Survey (NYS).

Longitudinal Data

Longitudinal studies are designed to permit observations of some specific phenomena over an extended period of time. Unlike cross-sectional studies, which permit only a snapshot of individuals or constructs at a particular point in time, longitudinal studies have the key advantage in that they can provide information describing how processes remain stable and/or change over time.

There are several ways that longitudinal research can be carried out. One of the most obvious is to identify a cohort at birth and to follow that cohort prospectively for a long period of time. Though ideal for the study of within- and between-individual changes in social science phenomena over time, prospective longitudinal designs suffer from limitations, including financial costs; history, panel, and testing effects; and sample attrition. On a practical level, human life expectancies and stakes make multidecade, longitudinal projects difficult for researchers to complete and sustain, especially because such projects require significant financial resources.

Another type of longitudinal design is retrospective. This approach avoids the long delay associated with the prospective design by defining a cohort, retrospectively. In a retrospective design, the researcher defines a cohort, such as all persons born in 1970, and then retrospectively collects various pieces of information, such as offending histories. Limitations also exist with the retrospective longitudinal design. Specifically, such a design introduces potentially serious concerns over recall errors (if self-report information is gathered).

Three Specific Challenges

Because longitudinal studies are, by definition, lengthy in nature, missing data pose a particular problem. Missing data due to nonresponse pose particularly difficult challenges. Missing data cause sample sizes to decrease over time, and may also cause biased estimates of population parameters if respondents and nonrespondents differ systematically with respect to variables involved. There are three manifestations of missing data: attrition, mortality, and exposure time.

Attrition

As noted earlier, attrition occurs when some study participants either drop out of the study permanently or fail to participate in one or more of the follow-up assessments. Although attrition does not necessarily bias the results, bias does occur when changes in an outcome differ between cases that remain in the sample and cases that drop out. In particular, when change in an outcome does relate to the probability of that change being observed, the effects observed among those who continue to participate do not equal the effects in the total sample. Because the probability of remaining in a study often depends on age, and because the changes studied often seem likely to affect the probability of remaining in the sample, panel studies are susceptible to attrition bias. In sum, it is possible that individuals who drop out of a longitudinal study differ in important ways from individuals who do not. The key issue is whether the attrition is random (i.e., attrition has nothing to do with the outcome of interest) or nonrandom (i.e., attrition has something to do with the outcome of interest).

Three examples are worth pointing out here. The first concerns the relationship between age and depression, a relationship that researchers disagree on quite often. Some report a U-shaped relationship between depression and age, with middle-aged adults feeling less depressed than younger or older adults, whereas others believe that the rise of depression in old age is more myth than fact. Mirowsky and Reynolds employed data from the first two waves of the National Survey of Families and Households, a large sample of more than 13,000 respondents ages 18 and older followed over a 6-year period, from 1988/1989 to 1994/1995. These authors analyzed the impact of attrition on estimates of the age-specific changes in depression over this 6-year period. Their findings indicated that the cross-sectional relationship of baseline depression to age differs for those who later drop out, compared to those who stay in. Interestingly, once the authors controlled for health and impairment, much of the difference vanished. In sum, these authors concluded that panel models ignoring the attrition will imply that depression decreases in old age, but models that control for attrition imply that depression rises by an amount that increases with age.

The second example comes from criminology, a discipline for which the issue of sample attrition is an important concern because high-rate offenders may fall victim to attrition more so than low-rate offenders, and thus may be less likely to remain in the later waves of longitudinal studies. Brame and Piquero used the first and fifth wave of the National Youth Survey, a national probability sample based on 1725 individuals between the ages of 11 and 17 years at the first wave, to assess how sample attrition influenced estimates about the longitudinal relationship between age and crime. In particular,

Brame and Piquero were concerned with the issue of selective, or nonrandom, attrition. Their analysis of the NYS showed that modest departures from a random drop-out model could account for a substantial proportion of the within-individual decline in offending. At the same time, they also showed how researchers might be able to use the data to impose some plausible constraints on the analysis to achieve identification. Using one set of these restrictions, their analysis suggested that within-individual declines remained while explicitly adjusting for the effects of attrition.

The third example concerns the problems created by individuals who move out of jurisdiction during the follow-up period(s) of longitudinal/panel studies. Although attrition due to such movement has not been subject to intense research scrutiny, it is clear that bias may arise if the outcomes of interest (such as depression and criminal activity) are related to individuals' frequent relocations. This is probably magnified among samples of high-rate offenders who likely will wish to avoid contact with researchers and/or criminal justice officials because of their involvement in illegal activity.

Mortality

Attrition due to mortality is also a concern for researchers using panel data to study issues related to continuity and change in social science phenomena. In several panel studies, especially those studies that include high-risk individuals and/or deal with high-risk behaviors, researchers need to be aware that some individuals may not be present on key theoretical constructs because they have died.

The issue of mortality has recently been introduced as a central feature in research on criminal activity over the life course because researchers have noticed that high-rate offenders are much more likely to die earlier (within longitudinal studies and at an earlier age) compared to low-rate offenders, and that these high-rate offenders are more likely to die via a violent death (i.e., as victims of homicide). For example, before age 40, delinquent individuals are more likely to die from unnatural causes such as accidents and homicide than are nondelinquent individuals. In a follow-up study of youthful serious offenders paroled from the California Youth Authority institutions, Lattimore *et al.* found that homicide was the prevailing cause of death for the youth. The study also revealed that a higher probability of death by murder was observed for black youth, for those from Los Angeles, for those with a history of gang involvement and institutional violence, and for those with a history of drug arrests. To the extent that such individuals are assumed to have desisted from crime in longitudinal studies, then researchers will have incorrectly identified these deceased delinquents as desisted delinquents.

The same concern regarding subject mortality may be raised for researchers who study individuals who engage in high-risk behaviors (smoking, alcohol use, etc.). Because these behaviors are related to the risk of death, researchers who are tracking these individuals in a longitudinal study need to be aware that some study participants may die throughout the course of the study. In sum, efforts to collect mortality information should be a key priority for those conducting longitudinal studies, especially concerning studies that focus on high-risk populations entering adulthood. This is especially the case for high-risk offenders, who tend to create tracking and identification obstacles.

Exposure Time

The final methodological concern deals with exposure time. This challenge deals with the temporary loss of study participants to some type of incapacitation effect, such as hospitalization, jail/prison term, etc. Unlike sample attrition and subject mortality, the issue of exposure time has been relatively under-studied because of the lack of adequate data containing information on time periods (i.e., spells) associated with exposure time.

Consider a criminological example. In longitudinal studies of crime over the life course, researchers derive estimates of individuals' offending over some period of time, typically over a 6- or 12-month period. However, during these time periods, individuals may not be "free" to commit criminal acts. The calculation of "time at risk," "street time," or "free time," then, is crucial to estimating individual offending rates, because offenders cannot commit crimes on the street while incarcerated.

Estimating an individual's offending frequency without taking into consideration their exposure time assumes that he or she is completely free to commit crimes. Under this assumption, an individual's true rate of offending is likely to be miscalculated because some offenders are not completely free. Some researchers have recognized the importance of this problem and have implemented controls for street time, but many longitudinal self-report studies do not implement controls for street time. The importance of this issue was recently demonstrated by Piquero *et al.* In their study of the recidivism patterns of serious offenders paroled from the California Youth Authority, these authors found that conclusions regarding persistence/desistance were contingent on knowledge of exposure time. For example, without controlling for street time, they found that 92% of their sample desisted; however, with controls for exposure time, only 72% of the sample desisted. In sum, variations in exposure time can affect measurements of key social science phenomena and need to be considered in panel studies.

Data Examples

The methodological challenges raised herein can be illustrated with two data examples that describe follow-up activities of two important longitudinal and panel studies. First, consider the results of a follow-up survey conducted by researchers at Johns Hopkins University in Baltimore, Maryland, who were part of the National Collaborative Perinatal Project (NCPP), a large-scale medical research project initiated in the late 1950s. In the 1990s, a team from Johns Hopkins initiated a follow-up study of a sample of the original Baltimore portion of the NCPP. Of the approximately 4000 children who were initially followed in Baltimore, 2694 were eligible to take part in the follow-up study at the point in time when the individuals would have been between 27 and 33 years old. Of the eligible 2694 individuals, 17.59% ($n = 474$) were not located, leaving 82.41% ($n = 2220$) of the individuals available. For several reasons, 28 of these individuals were not fieldable, thus leaving 2192 individuals fieldable. At the end of the follow-up study, 1758, or 80%, of the fieldable individuals received a full follow-up interview. The remaining cases (1) were still in the field at the end of the follow-up period ($n = 157$), (2) refused ($n = 135$), (3) had absent subject data ($n = 71$), (4) were deceased with data ($n = 71$), (5) were deceased with no data ($n = 17$), or (6) were unavailable ($n = 11$). Thus, the final response rate for the full follow-up interview was 65.3%, or 1758 of the originally 2694 eligible sample of individuals.

Now consider the National Youth Survey (NYS), a large-scale panel study that was administered to a national probability sample of youth ranging from age 11 to age 17 in 1976. The survey also employed multistage cluster sample techniques to produce a representative sample of United States households. Respondents were then selected from sampled households and interviewed. About 27% of the 2360 individuals who were selected to participate in the study did not participate, leaving a final sample of 1725 respondents. By the fifth wave of the survey, 1485 of these individuals had been retained and the remaining 230 respondents dropped out. This produces an overall attrition rate of about 13.4% from the first to the fifth wave of the survey. Data on mortality and exposure time have not yet been made publicly available. In sum, the methodological challenges raised here are pertinent to the follow-ups of these and other important data sources. The important question for researchers is the extent to which attrition, mortality, and exposure time are random or nonrandom.

What Can Researchers Do?

As the methodological challenges have been recognized by researchers employing longitudinal and panel data, researchers have devoted much effort to documenting their knowledge in circumventing these concerns. For example, researchers have outlined guides to detecting attrition problems and have carefully described the approaches available to finding respondents in a follow-up study. Here, the recent recommendations made by Brame and Piquero for dealing with attrition problems are underscored, and the recommended steps that researchers can take when dealing with the mortality and exposure time issues are outlined.

Regarding attrition, two practical recommendations surface. The first broad recommendation revolves around what can be done to address attrition problems in existing data sets. Currently, there are three specific strategies for handling missing data: (1) imputation of the missing values with suitable estimates, (2) analysis of incomplete data without adjustment, and (3) discarding of nonrespondents and calculation of weights for respondents to compensate for the loss of cases. The merits and demerits of these approaches must be weighed carefully before choosing which one to adopt. The second broad recommendation is the practice of partially following up on hard-to-interview respondents. For example, a researcher who has lost 150 of 1000 subjects by a later wave may wish to attempt locating all 150 missing subjects, but the outcome of this costly and time-consuming endeavor is unlikely to yield a 100% response rate. Instead, the researcher should devote resources to tracking a random sample of those 150, and then obtain valid survey-based information for those individuals. With this information, the researcher could create confidence intervals or boundaries around the estimates of interest.

With regard to mortality, perhaps the best approach is to consult the National Death Register Index, which contains information on the individual's name, date of death, and cause of death. Another approach would be to search the obituaries of newspapers. Implementation of both strategies is recommended. In terms of exposure time, two approaches are worthwhile. Regarding official data sources, researchers could obtain exposure time information regarding hospital stays and/or prison/jail stays from officially kept records at the federal, state, or local level. Because some of this information is inadequate, especially jail records, which oftentimes do not contain movement information (i.e., from jail to probation, number of days in jail, etc.), researchers could ask respondents to self-report information regarding exposure time.

Conclusion

Missing data in panel studies represent an important methodological issue that cannot be bypassed when studying continuity and change in behavior over time. The results of a recent study help to underscore the importance of the issues raised herein. Laub, Sampson, and Eggleston sought to describe the criminal activity of over 500 men from the Boston area who were followed through their early 70s. The authors showed that the shape and size of offending trajectories in the data were highly influenced by controls for street time, length of the observation window, and mortality, thereby underscoring the importance of considering such methodological issues. Future studies should visit current data sets and revisit classic data sets and explore the extent to which attrition and mortality of data and individuals influence key theoretical and substantive findings. The discussions here have described the various methodological challenges awaiting researchers employing longitudinal data as well as approaches that researchers can consider in an effort to overcome the ill effects of such data, before the challenges and effects become insurmountable.

See Also the Following Articles

Longitudinal Cohort Designs • Longitudinal Studies, Panel • Non-Response Bias

Further Reading

Allison, P. (2001). *Missing Data.* Sage, Newbury Park, California.

Brame, R., and Piquero, A. (2003). The role of sample attrition in studying the longitudinal relationship between age and crime. *J. Quant. Criminol.* **19**, 107–128.

Cernkovich, S. A., Giordano, P. C., and Pugh, M. D. (1985). Chronic offenders: The missing cases in self-report delinquency research. *J. Crim. Law Criminol.* **76,** 705–732.

Dempster-McClain, D., and Moen, P. (1998). Finding respondents in a follow-up study. In *Methods of Life Course Research: Qualitative and Quantitative Approaches* (J. Z. Giele and G. H. Elder, Jr., eds.), pp. 128–151. Sage, Newbury Park, California)

Eggleston, E., Luab, J. H., and Sanpson, R. J. (2004). Examining long-term trajectories of criminal offending. The Glueck delinquents from age 7 to 70. *J. Quant. Criminol.* **20**, 1–26.

Engel, U., and Reinecke, J. (eds.) (1996). *Analysis of Change: Advanced Techniques in Panel Data Analysis.* Walter de Gruyter & Co., Berlin.

Foster, E. M., and Bickman, L. (1996). An evaluator's guide to detecting attrition problems. *Eval. Rev.* **20,** 695–723.

Lattimore, P. K., Linster, R. L., and MacDonald, J. M. (1997). Risk of death among serious young offenders. *J. Res. Crime Delinq.* **34,** 187–209.

Laub, J. H., and Vaillant, G. E. (2000). Delinquency and mortality: A 50-year follow-up study of 1,000 delinquent and nondelinquent boys. *Am. J. Psychiat.* **157,** 96–102.

Little, R. J. A., and Rubin, D. B. (1987). *Statistical Analysis with Missing Data.* Wiley, New York.

Maxfield, M. G., and Babbie, E. (1995). *Research Methods for Criminal Justice and Criminology.* Wadsworth, Belmont, California.

Mirowsky, J., and Reynolds, J. R. (2000). Age, depression, and attrition in the National Survey of Families and Households. *Sociol. Methods Res.* **28,** 476–504.

Mirowsky, J., and Ross, C. E. (1992). Age and depression. *J. Health Social Behav.* **33,** 187–205.

Nagin, D. S., and Land, K. C. (1993). Age, criminal careers, and population heterogeneity: Specification and estimation of a nonparametric, mixed Poisson model. *Criminology* **31,** 327–362.

Piquero, A. R., Blumstein, A., Brame, R., Haapanen, R., Mulvey, E. P., and Nagin, D. S. (2001). Assessing the impact of exposure time and incapacitation on longitudinal trajectories of criminal offending. *J. Adolesc. Res.* **16,** 54–74.

Thornberry, T. P., Bjerregaard, B., and Miles, W. (1993). The consequences of respondent attrition in panel studies: A simulation based on the Rochester Youth Development Study. *J. Quant. Criminol.* **9,** 127–158.

Weis, J. G. (1986). Issues in the measurement of criminal careers. In *Criminal Careers and 'Career Criminals',* Vol. 2 (A. Blumstein, J. Cohen, J. A. Roth, and C. A. Visher, eds.). pp. 1–51. National Academy Press, Washington, D.C.

Audiovisual Records, Encoding of

Marc H. Bornstein

National Institute of Child Health and Human Development, Bethesda, Maryland, USA

Charissa S. L. Cheah

University of Maryland, Baltimore, County, USA

Glossary

audiovisual records Videotape or digital video representations of an ongoing behavioral stream.

behavior codes Operational definitions of the parameters of behaviors.

content validity The adequacy with which an observation instrument samples the behavior of interest.

continuous coding The complete and comprehensive coding of an audiovisual record.

duration The total time in which a behavior of interest occurs.

field testing The observation of behavior where it occurs and the application of a coding system for feasibility.

frequency The number of discrete times a behavior of interest occurs according to some conventional assignment of an interbehavior interval.

observation system Formalized rules for the extraction of information from a stream of behavior.

operational definitions Discrimination rules that specify target behaviors to be studied.

reactivity Atypical responses from individuals who are being observed.

sampling Behavioral coding that relies on systematic but partial coding.

This entry addresses the questions of what and how to observe about behavior. Conceptual, theoretical, practical, and ethical considerations govern the target behaviors of observation. Audiovisual record data collection procedures; coding systems, including issues related to reliability and validity; selecting and training coders; various methods of scoring observational data; and recording technologies are reviewed and two illustrations are presented.

Introduction

The Significance of Behavioral Observation

Behavioral observation involves recording the manifest activities of individuals. Direct observation is consistent with an epistemological emphasis on overt behavior, quantification, and low levels of inference. For these reasons, observational procedures are rigorous and powerful, providing measures of both behavioral frequency and duration on the basis of their occurrence in the noninterrupted natural time flow. This approach to assessment has been called the sine qua non of social science research; that is, observation is often considered the gold standard against which other kinds of assessments should be evaluated. For these reasons, observation has been employed in the vast majority of published research.

The Challenges

Social science researchers who are interested in evaluating ongoing behavior are confronted with several methodological challenges. Salient ones concern whom to observe, when to observe, where to observe, what to observe, and how to observe. The question of *whom* to observe involves participant sampling and is central to the issue of to what population the findings will generalize. The questions of *when* and *where* to observe have to do with time and place sampling and associated logistical issues. Scheduling observations is important to determining the overall character and quality of a research study; only observing at the right time will lead to representative data. Some settings promise ecological validity, for example, when participants are observed in surroundings where they are normally found. Less common or realistic situations may reflect less valid representations of the meaning and purpose for participants than actual life experiences. Finally, recording behaviors that are infrequent challenges the whole nature of observation.

Overview

The questions of what and how to observe are the main subjects of this entry. Determining the target behaviors of observation is governed by conceptual, theoretical, practical, and ethical considerations. We review audiovisual record data collection procedures. Coding systems are then discussed, including issues related to the reliability and validity of observational data, procedures for selecting and training coders, various methods of scoring observational data, and a brief review of recording technologies. After this, we present two illustrations.

Collecting Audiovisual Records

In naturalistic observation, participants are normally requested to behave in their usual manner, to do whatever they normally do, and to disregard the observer's presence as much as possible. Observational coding can be done in real time, or audiovisual records of behavior can be made using videotape or digital video technology. The presence of an observer-recorder (camera in hand) can be intrusive and may represent a kind of novelty that evokes atypical responses from those observed, a phenomenon termed reactivity. For example, observation may promote socially desirable or appropriate behaviors and suppress socially undesirable or inappropriate behaviors (e.g., adults may display higher than normal rates of positive interactions with children). Nonetheless, reactivity can be and often is successfully alleviated by observers' spending time in the situation with participants before recording to set participants at ease. Observers must be trained to make audiovisual records that have few (if any) breaks or gaps in the behavior stream, and conventions must be developed and adhered to for filming distances and angles that maximize the possibility of continuously and reliably coding behaviors of interest. Decisions must be made about which actor to focus on when multiple actors cannot be captured simultaneously on audiovisual records, and conventions must be developed to provide (future) coders with important off-camera information. Moreover, audiovisual records of naturally occurring behavior in unstructured settings suffer inherent problems and limitations, and the codes that are developed to score them must take these shortcomings into account.

Coding Systems for Audiovisual Records

For any behavior, content validity is determined by the adequacy with which an observation instrument samples the behavior of interest. Three requirements must be met to establish content validity: (1) the domain of interest must be completely defined, (2) the relevant factors must be representatively or exhaustively sampled for inclusion in the observation system, and (3) the method for evaluating and combining observations to form scores must be specified. Some observation system with formalized rules must be developed to extract information from the stream of behavior. Those rules specify a set of target behaviors, how the information is to be recorded, and how the resulting data are to be combined to form analyzable scores.

The development of a coding system initially involves extensive observations and usually involves collaborative discussion. First, narrative observational accounts of behaviors of interest are made in the field. Field testing and refinement are subsequently conducted. In this way, initial, unstructured descriptive data are shaped into more structured observations and, ultimately, quantitative data. Observation target behaviors are then identified relative to the topic(s) of interest. Next, formal operational definitions of behaviors are developed; they specify the phenomena studied and facilitate coder accuracy and consistency. These definitions represent discrimination rules for coding target behaviors, and they typically possess three main characteristics: (1) they are objective and refer to directly observable target behaviors; (2) they are clear, unambiguous, and easily understood so that (experienced) coders can accurately comprehend and follow them; and (3) they require little or no inference.

The next step in coding audiovisual records involves developing formal behavior codes, often in conceptually related groups called modes. Within each mode, component codes are best operationalized so that they are mutually exclusive and exhaustive. Exclusive observation categories apply when only one act or series of acts can be scored for each time unit of observation. In exhaustive observation systems, some behavior code must be used for each observation unit. There are numerous advantages to using mutually exclusive and exhaustive coding systems.

If a rating observational coding system is used, a system is devised according to predetermined criteria for rating each target behavior. This coding system can be used to indicate the presence or absence of the target behavior and the intensity or frequency of the target behavior. During each observational unit, a rating score is provided for each target behavior. The target behaviors rated are not necessarily mutually exclusive, which allows for the rating of more than one target behavior during each observation unit.

A target behavior may be operationally defined at different levels of abstraction. For example, a variable called "nurturant" may be globally defined at a molar level ("being attentive to a baby's physical needs"), or it can be defined in terms of more exact target behaviors at a molecular level ("holds," "feeds," or "bathes" the baby). The level of abstraction is likely to affect the pattern of the findings. Single discrete behaviors and molecular codes are often influenced by immediate interactional and contextual factors; more global responses appear to be more stable and more likely to capture similarity. Moreover, molar-level behavioral definitions require more interpretation and inference on the part of observers-coders. Molecular categories code more narrowly defined and specific behaviors or sequences of behaviors. Molecular observation categories are easier for observers-coders to learn and to apply, they require less interpretation and inference, and they can later be aggregated into molar categories for summary data analyses. Although, theoretically, the number of behavior codes in an individual mode could range from two to infinity, in practice, when coding in real time, coders cannot comfortably monitor more than six to nine behavior options, including a default code "none of the above." If rating scales are used, fewer behavior codes can be comfortably monitored in real time if the behavior modes are not mutually exclusive. To transform streams of different behaviors into appropriate quantitative data, audiovisual records are normally coded at several separate times, each time concentrating on a single behavior mode.

Reliability and Validity of Observational Data

Sampling

Before the advent of videotape and digital video technology, behavioral phenomena had to be coded in real time, and recording procedures were limited by human information-processing capacities that necessitated sampling strategies. (Indeed, even with the wider availability of new technologies and associated software, and therefore access to continuous and comprehensive coding, contemporary researchers routinely sample to make inferences to population characteristics of behavior because of the feasibility, reliability, and relative ease of sampling.) Sampling of behavior was first developed and widely applied in ethological and human developmental study.

Conventional and still popular sampling strategies include partial-interval (or time) sampling and momentary sampling. Historically, partial-interval sampling was the most common technique; an estimated one-third to three-quarters of all observational studies in psychology used partial-interval sampling. In partial-interval sampling, the observation period is divided into equal, regularly alternating observe and record periods. During each record period, the observer notes all behaviors of interest that occurred during the immediately preceding observe period. In momentary sampling, the occurrence of a behavior of interest in prespecified time slots during some or all intervals of the observation is noted. The rationale underlying these methods of data collection is that the sampling of behavior captured is a valid representation of the total behavior stream being investigated. There are many kinds of sampling measures; for example, observing and recording behaviors during alternating intervals is referred to as discontinuous partial-interval sampling; whereas observing and recording in every interval is called continuous partial-interval sampling.

Partial-interval sampling has some major advantages—for example, it permits the monitoring of a relatively large number of behaviors simultaneously. There are also, however, some major disadvantages to using partial-interval sampling. First, sampling behavior provides a valid representation of the overall phenomenon only if the behavior of interest is uniformly distributed across the observational period. Second, with partial-interval sampling, for a given observe interval, a behavior is recorded only once, regardless of whether it occurs one time, occurs many times, or extends from one interval into succeeding one(s). Thus, frequencies of behaviors are normally underestimates rather than actual counts, and these estimates vary depending on the distributional characteristics of individual behaviors. In partial-interval sampling, observers are not concerned with scoring the actual onset and offset of behaviors but more with their occurrence or nonoccurrence. In real life, all behaviors have frequencies that vary; in partial-interval sampling, all behaviors recorded in an observe interval are considered equal in terms of their quantitative and temporal characteristics. Partial-interval sampling does not yield information about duration or sequencing of behaviors. In short, using partial-interval sampling, some information about the behavior stream is lost.

By definition, sampling provides data for a subset of the population of behaviors and so is necessarily an imperfect representation of the population. All sampling methods misrepresent the source population in that sampling requires the transformation of larger numbers into smaller numbers. Because this transformation necessarily involves the loss of information, partial-interval sampling has been validly criticized for failing to accurately represent actual absolute frequency. It is fair to observe that sampling adds noise to data and in the long run diminishes power.

Continuous Coding

Videotape and digital video technology and scoring systems based on complete audiovisual records today permit the recording, documentation, aggregation, and analysis of all (rather than sampled) ongoing behaviors. In continuous comprehensive coding, behaviors of interest from an entire observation can be quantified. This strategy serves several functions: It reduces instantaneous demands on observers, it allows focused coding, and it facilitates accurate assessments and reliability. However, the amount of time necessary for data reduction increases concomitantly.

Audiovisual records coded using computer-based coding systems are applicable to a broad spectrum of behavioral data collected in a wide variety of settings. Audiovisual records enable observers to spend their time observing and recording behavior with no distractions imposed by coding requirements; reciprocally, a computer-based coding system enables coders to spend their time coding behaviors with no distractions imposed by observation requirements. With audiovisual records in hand, it is easy to succumb to the temptation to undertake highly detailed analyses.

Coders

Coders are meant to bring objectivity to evaluations of behavior; although variation in rating behaviors should decrease with training, evaluative biases may not. Shared meaning systems serve to ensure consensus among coders, and judicious observational training helps to create and consolidate shared perceptions among coders.

Nonetheless, coders may make systematic errors in assessment and hold biases based on their information-processing limitations and expectations. Coders of behavior may miss information—the human visual and auditory senses can be insensitive or unreliable in detecting certain behaviors; coders can also suffer from information overload—when a large number of target behaviors occur rapidly or frequently within a short period of time, a coder may have difficulty detecting or recording all of the behaviors. Coders sometimes see patterns of regularity and orderliness in otherwise complex and disordered behavioral data; coders sometimes harbor or develop correct or incorrect hypotheses about the nature and purpose of an investigation, how participants should behave, or even what constitute appropriate data.

To address issues of coder bias and to maintain the accuracy of quantitative measures, it is necessary to adhere to standardization procedures in observational coding:

1. Only trained and experienced but naive coders should be employed, and stringent training criteria instituted.
2. Coders should be trained prior to actual coding to a preestablished criterion performance of accuracy and consistency.
3. Observations should be assigned to coders randomly.
4. Coders should be cautioned about the potential negative effects of bias.
5. Coders should be oriented to the research issues, but remain naive to the specific scientific questions of the investigation.
6. To the degree possible, precise low-inference operational definitions should be used.
7. Coding drift should be corrected by means of regular reliability checks on coders.

Several statistical metrics of coder reliability can be employed. Cohen's kappa (κ) is preferable because it corrects for coder agreement due to chance.

Scoring

Computerized scores of continuous behavior streams normally yield measures of frequency, total and average duration, rate, and sequencing of component behavior codes. Frequency is the number of discrete times a behavior occurs according to some conventional assignment of an interbehavior interval (IBI). Frequencies obtained by continuous coding depend to a certain degree on arbitrary parameters; for example, in order to define two instances of a behavior (infant vocalization) as separate rather than as the same continuous vocalization, the time between the two instances must equal or exceed a specified minimum IBI. The standardized unit of frequency is the rate or relative frequency of occurrence per unit time. The duration is the total time that the behavior occurs. The standardized unit of duration, capturing the proportional nature of the measure, is prevalence per unit time. The mean duration of a behavior is its total duration divided by its frequency. These statistics summarize the nature of behavior occurrences within the real-time observation session. They describe quantitatively the various aspects of the behavior that are coded in a series of clock times. Continuous and comprehensive coding in real-time yields unbiased estimates of behavior frequency and duration.

A separate coding pass is normally made through each audiovisual record for each behavioral mode. When coding long audiovisual records, coding in shorter blocks helps coders to maintain the high level of concentration needed to score accurately without unduly prolonging the time needed to process each audiovisual record. Many coding software programs have built-in safeguards to eliminate coding errors (e.g., codes other than those identified in the parameters of the mode being used cannot be keyed in).

Coding behavioral data in real time (online) is efficient, but also presents a number of special challenges. Coders must make instantaneous decisions about behaviors; they cannot wait to see how a behavior unfolds or whether it recurs before deciding to code it, and they cannot stop to verify whether a decision has been made correctly. Often codes cannot depend on the outcome of an action because the outcome is not known when the behavior is first observed (e.g., measures that depend, by definition, on identifying sequences of related behaviors juxtaposed in time). Particularly challenging in working with continuous coding is the task of defining when a given behavior begins and when it ends. Coding in real time also does not allow coders to decide when an action has conceptually begun and ended (e.g., a large number of short vocalizations may actually be part of a single communication). The way in which codes are operationalized for continuous coding must take these factors into account.

A system that does not allow the coder to make decisions based on the larger context in which a behavior occurs removes much (but not all) subjectivity from the coding process. However, a new problem—that of defining an action independent of the context in which it has taken place—is introduced. One part of the solution lies in the way in which operational definitions for behavior codes are written. In addition, it is possible to set objective parameters that are then used to conceptualize the data statistically. It is also possible to derive measures (for example, "responsiveness") by examining multiple behavior streams containing the component behaviors of interest in relation to one another (that is, using "responsiveness" as an example, we define B as the response to A when B exhibits a particular distributional pattern relative to A).

Recording Technologies

Several commercially available systems for the collection, analysis, presentation, and management of observational data are now widely used to implement continuous coding of audiovisual records. The most popular include Behavioral Evaluation Strategy and Taxonomy (BEST), INTERACT, and The Observer. Ethnograph is a qualitative data version. Most programs share the same virtues. All these software packages facilitate real-time collection and analysis of real-life situations or video or multimedia recordings of observational category system data automatically. They record the start and stop times of multiple, mutually exclusive, or overlapping events. They comprehensively represent data by automatically recording response frequency, duration, intervals, time samples, latency, interresponse time, percentage of experimental time, and discrete trials, and they represent data qualitatively (using transcription methods), quantitatively, and sequentially, as well as interfacing with other software programs to effect sophisticated graphing applications. Using these systems, it is possible to identify time-based information for each category system event, including first and last event occurrence, time spans between events, the longest and shortest event occurrences, and related means and standard deviations and to conduct a sequential analysis as well as a variety of reliability analyses. These systems permit textual annotation to events and search operations to find time codes; their behavioral codes order texts in annotations and can jump directly to associated video scenes. Time codes allow coders to identify every frame of the audiovisual records. Thus, combinations of predefined codes and free-format annotation make these programs suitable for quantitative as well as qualitative observational study. They accommodate qualitative data in the form of interview transcripts, field notes, open-ended survey responses, or other text-based documents.

Audiovisual recording is now more widely available and increasingly user friendly, but it is not accessible to all and can be intrusive, it is sometimes unnecessarily detailed, and it is time and resources consuming. In general, each researcher must choose the acceptable limits of unreliability for each study. Hoping to maximize power, the researcher must consider the effect size, the N available, the acceptable experimental error, and the reliability of the measures used in overall decision making.

Illustrations

Infant-Mother Interaction

It is uncommon in research for the absolute frequencies of behaviors to be of interest (e.g., whether infants vocalize 7, 10, or 15 times). Although in certain instances population base rates convey meaningful information, researchers typically use relative frequencies to compare individuals or groups (e.g., Who vocalizes more: typically developing or Down's babies?) and to rank individuals or groups on particular variables with an eye to relating the ranks to other variables (e.g., Does infant vocalization predict child language development?). It is assumed, although not established, that continuous coding provides a more accurate reflection of reality than do sampling techniques. Do continuous recording and partial-interval sampling procedures allow investigators to reach similar conclusions regarding the relative frequency and standing of behaviors? Do partial-interval sampling procedures produce reliable estimates of actual frequencies obtained by continuous recording? To address these questions U.S. and Japanese infant-mother dyads were compared in a 2002 methodological investigation by Bornstein that directly contrasted continuous recording, in which actual frequencies of behaviors of infants and mothers were obtained, with partial-interval sampling.

Methods and Procedures

Home observations were conducted identically in all visits. Briefly, mothers were asked to behave in their usual manner and to disregard the observer's presence insofar as possible; besides the trained observer-filmer (always a female native of the country), only the baby and mother were present; and observations took place at times of the day that were optimal in terms of babies' being in awake and alert states. After a period of acclimation, hour-long audiovisual records were made of infants and mothers in naturalistic interaction.

Four infant and four maternal activities were coded in modes (i.e., groups of mutually exclusive and exhaustive behaviors) using a computer-based coding system on four separate passes through the videotapes. Two target infant activities consisted of infant visual exploration of mother or of properties, objects, or events in the environment; blank staring and eyes closed/not looking were also coded. Two other infant activities consisted of non-distress or distress vocalization; bodily sounds and silence were also coded. Two maternal behaviors consisted of the mother's active mother-oriented or environment-oriented stimulation of the infant; not stimulating was also coded. The other two mother behaviors involved vocalization, speaking to the baby in child-directed or in adult-directed speech tones; silence was also coded. Thus, behaviors within a category were mutually exclusive, and any category of behavior could occur at any time. Coding reliabilities (κ) were all acceptable.

Data were first continuously coded. Then, partial-interval sampling data of three intervals were obtained via computer programming from the continuous data set; observe intervals selected for partial-interval sampling were 15, 30, and 45 s, a common range of durations of intervals in partial-interval sampling in the developmental science literature.

Results and Discussion

First, zero-order relations between data coded by partial-interval sampling and data coded continuously were explored. To do this, the bivariate correlations between results obtained via each method were computed. The three forms of partial-interval sampling generally preserved the relative rank obtained by continuous coding. The relation between frequencies coded by partial-interval sampling and by continuous coding was approximately linear.

Second, the possibility of estimating frequencies coded by continuous coding from frequencies coded by partial-interval sampling was examined. To this end, the regression of frequencies derived by continuous coding on frequencies derived by partial-interval sampling within one data set at one time was computed. The parameters of this regression equation were then used to estimate frequencies derived by continuous coding from frequencies derived by partial-interval sampling obtained at a second time. Altogether more than 90% of estimates of frequencies derived by continuous coding were statistically equivalent to the true frequencies, where differences occurred, the difference between the estimated and true scores was never larger than one-fifth of a standard deviation. These results indicate that frequencies derived by continuous coding at the group level can be estimated relatively accurately once the relation between sampling and frequencies derived by continuous coding has been specified. Furthermore, the results of cross-cultural comparisons of infant and maternal behaviors were largely unaffected by the use of frequencies coded by partial-interval sampling as opposed to frequencies coded by continuous coding.

Beyond the insights absolute frequency and duration data can yield about population base rates, social scientists are principally interested in the relative standing of individuals or groups for two reasons: (1) Relative standing allows comparison between individuals or groups and (2) relative standing allows for the examination of predictive validity of individual or group variation over time. In other words, researchers want to know whether or not an effect exists. Most statistical inference is based on comparisons of relative ranking rather than on actual quantity. In the final analysis, using any of the data derived by partial-interval sampling in the cross-cultural comparison produced identical results, in terms of significance, to those obtained using data derived by continuous coding.

Emotion Regulation, Parenting, and Displays of Social Reticence in Preschoolers

The substantive purpose of a 2001 investigation by Rubin, Cheah, and Fox was to determine the extent to which observed social reticence–inhibition in children could be predicted by their disregulated temperament, the observed parenting behaviors, and the interaction between temperament and parenting style. This study also illustrated the use of rating scales in encoding of audiovisual records.

Methods and Procedures

Mothers of 4-year-old children completed the Colorado Child Temperament Inventory, which comprises factors that assess maternal perceptions of dispositional characteristics (e.g., emotionality, activity level, shyness, and soothability). Factors assessing emotionality (five items; e.g., "child often fusses and cries") and soothability (five items; e.g., "when upset by an unexpected situation, child quickly calms down") were composited to form an index of emotion disregulation comprising high negative emotionality and low soothability.

Children were assigned to quartets of unfamiliar same-sex, same-age peers and observed in a small playroom filled with attractive toys. Behaviors in the peer play session were coded in 10-s intervals for social participation (unoccupied, onlooking, solitary play, parallel play, conversation, or group play) and the cognitive quality of play (functional, dramatic, and constructive play; exploration; or games-with-rules). For each coding interval, coders selected 1 of 20 possible combinations of cognitive play nested within the social participation categories. The proportion of observational intervals that included the display of anxious behaviors (e.g., digit sucking, hair pulling, or crying) was also coded. Time samples of unoccupied, onlooking, and anxious behaviors were combined to obtain an index of social reticence.

The peer quartet was followed 6–8 weeks later by a visit to the laboratory by each child and his or her mother. All children and mothers were observed in two distinct mother-child situations: During an unstructured free-play session, mother and child were told that the child was free to play with anything in the room (15 min); during a second session, the mother was asked to help guide and teach her child to create a Lego structure that matched a model on the table at which mother and child were seated (15 min). Mothers were asked not to build the model for the child and to refrain from touching the materials during this teaching task, which was thought to be challenging for a 4-year-old. A maternal behavioral rating scale measure was used to assess: (1) proximity and orientation: the parent's physical location with reference to the child and parental nonverbal attentiveness; (2) positive affect: the positive quality of maternal emotional expressiveness toward the child; (3) hostile affect: negative instances of verbal and nonverbal behavior arising from feeling hostile toward the child; (4) negative affect: the negative quality of maternal expressiveness that reflects maternal sadness, fearfulness, and/or anxiety in response to the child's behavior; (5) negative control: the amount of control a mother exerts over the child that is ill-timed, excessive, and inappropriately controlling relative to what the child is doing; and (6) positive control and guidance: the amount that the mother facilitates the child's behavior or provides supportive assistance that is well-timed.

The free-play and Lego-teaching-task sessions were coded in blocks of 1 min each. For each 1-min interval, observers rated each of the maternal behaviors on a three-point scale, with higher maternal behavioral ratings indicating greater maternal expressions of proximity and orientation, positive affect, hostile affect, negative affect, positive control, and negative control. For example, with regard to positive affect, observers gave a score of 1 if no instances of parental affection, positive feeling, or enjoyment were observed; 2 if moderate positive expression or enjoyment was observed; and 3 if the mother expressed outright physical or verbal affection or positive statements of praise for the child.

A free-play solicitous parenting aggregate was created by first standardizing and then adding the following variables: free-play proximity and orientation, free-play positive affect, free-play positive control, and free-play negative control. Lego-teaching-task maternal solicitousness was measured as in free play by standardizing and then adding the following variables: Lego proximity and orientation, Lego positive affect, Lego negative control, and Lego positive control.

Results and Discussion

Socially wary and reticent preschoolers were emotionally disregulated; that is, they had relatively low thresholds for the evocation of negative affect and difficulty in being calmed once emotionally upset. However, emotional disregulation was not a significant predictor of reticence, suggesting that preschool reticence is a product of factors other than dispositional characteristics. Children with mothers who are controlling and oversolicitousness during parent-child free play and emotionally disregulated children whose mothers did not engage in such behaviors during a more stressful teaching task are thought to be more likely to display social reticence in a peer setting. Maternal oversolicitous (overprotective) behavior during the unstructured free-play situation was significantly and positively predictive of children's socially reticent, wary, and shy behaviors—behaviors known to be associated contemporaneously and predictively with anxiety, psychological overcontrol, interpersonal problem-solving deficits, and poor peer relationships. The findings also suggest that a parenting constellation of warmth, proximity, intrusive control, and joint activity was associated with shy, reticent (and inhibited) child behavior. Taken together, these findings indicate that mothers of reticent preschool-age children do not behave in ways that allow their children to develop self-initiated coping techniques.

Another significant maternal contribution to the prediction of preschoolers' socially reticent behavior was the moderating role played by mothers' solicitousness during the putatively stressful, goal-oriented Lego construction task. For children whose mothers offered limited warmth, guidance, and control during the Lego task, emotional disregulation was significantly and positively associated with the display of socially reticent behaviors among peers. The moderating role of parenting was demonstrated by the lack of a significant association between emotional disregulation and social reticence among preschoolers whose mothers provided appropriate control during the Lego paradigm. Thus, in structured situations in which parental goals are task oriented (such as the Lego teaching task), the display of maternal direction and guidance strategies may be normative and appropriate.

Conclusion

Computerized systems for the coding of audiovisual records of observation are comprehensive and versatile, with many potential applications in social science research. They can be used to code data collected in naturalistic as well as structured situations—at home, in the laboratory, and in clinical or educational settings; they can be adapted for actors of any age; they can be used to code behavior or to measure other dimensions of the environment; and they can be applied in real time or can be adapted for coding tasks that require a more prolonged or repetitive examination of the database. Regardless of the nature of the data collected, the recording system preserves most of the information available in the original data. Multiple behavior records can be juxtaposed, yielding new, composite behavior codes or information about the ways in which behaviors vary in relation to one another. This information can be used in the continual, iterative process of validating and revising the coding system. Data storage, retrieval, transmission, and manipulation are computer-based and therefore efficient, both in terms of time and space.

Acknowledgment

This article summarizes selected aspects of our research, and portions of the text have appeared in previous scientific publications (see Further Reading). We thank C. Varron for assistance.

See Also the Following Articles

Coding Variables • Content Validity • Observational Studies

Further Reading

Arcus, D., Snidman, N., Campbell, P., Brandzel, S., and Zambrano, I. (1991). A program for coding behavior directly from VCR to computer. Poster presented at the biennial meeting of the Society for Research in Child Development, Seattle, WA.

Bakeman, R., and Gottman, J. M. (1986). *Observing Interaction: An Introduction to Sequential Analysis.* Cambridge University Press, London.

Bornstein, M. H. (2002). Measurement variability in infant and maternal behavioral assessment. *Infant Behav. Dev.* **25,** 413–432.

Bornstein, M. H., Suwalsky, J. T. D., Ludemann, P., Painter, K., and Shultess, K. (1991). *Manual for Observation and Analysis of Infant Development and Mother-Infant Interaction in the First Years of Life.* Child and Family Research, National Institute of Child Health and Human Development, Bethesda, MD.

Buss, A. H., and Plomin, R. A. (1984). *Temperament: Early Developing Personality Traits.* Lawrence Erlbaum Associates, Hillsdale, NJ.

Cohen, J. (1960). A coefficient of agreement for nominal scales. *Educ. Psychol. Meas.* **20,** 37–46.

Cohen, J. (1968). Weighted kappa: Nominal scale agreement with provision for scaled disagreement or partial credit. *Psychol. Bull.* **70,** 213–220.

Fox, J. (1997). *Applied Regression Analysis, Linear Models and Related Methods.* Sage, Thousand Oaks, CA.

Hartmann, D. P., and George, T. (1999). Design, measurement, and analysis in developmental research. In *Developmental Psychology: An Advanced Textbook* (M. H. Bornstein and M. E. Lamb, eds.), 4th Ed., pp. 125–195. Lawrence Erlbaum Associates, Mahwah, NJ.

Mangold Software and Consulting. (2000). INTERACT. Munich, Germany. Available from: http://www.mangold.de

Noldus Information Technology (2002). The Observer: Professional system for collection, analysis and management of observational data. Wageningen, Netherlands. Available from: http://www.noldus.com

Rubin, K. H., Cheah, C. S. L., and Fox, N. A. (2001). Emotion regulation, parenting, and the display of social reticence in preschoolers. *Early Educ. Dev.* **12,** 97–115.

Scolari (2002). *Behavioral Evaluation Strategy and Taxonomy (BEST).* Sage, Thousand Oaks, CA. Available from: http://www.scolari.com

Scolari (2002). *Ethnograph.* Sage, Thousand Oaks, CA. Available from: http://www.scolari.com

Suen, H. K., and Ary, D. (1989). *Analyzing Quantitative Behavioral Observational Data.* Lawrence Erlbaum Associates, Hillsdale, NJ.

van de Vijver, F. J. R., and Leung, K. (1997). *Methods and Data Analysis for Cross Cultural Research.* Sage, Thousand Oaks, CA.

Autocorrelation

Harold D. Clarke
University of Texas, Dallas, Richardson, Texas, USA

Jim Granato
National Science Foundation, Arlington, Virginia, USA

Glossary

autocorrelated errors Correlations between stochastic errors ordered over either time or space in a model, typically a linear regression model.

autoregressive process A data-generating process with "memory," such that the value of the process at time t reflects some portion of the value of the process at time $t - i$.

common factor restriction A restriction on model parameters, produced in the context of linear regression analysis by the use of a quasi-differencing procedure as a generalized least-squares "correction" for autocorrelated errors.

fractionally integrated process A data-generating process with signficant autocorrelations at long lags, such that the system has long memory and shocks erode very slowly.

integrated process An autoregressive process with perfect memory, such that shocks to the system at time t are not discounted in subsquent time periods.

minimum state variable (MSV) solution A solution procedure for rational expectations models that uses the simplest, least parameterized characterization.

near-integrated process An autoregressive process where a very large portion of the value of the process at time t carries over to time $t + 1$.

rational expectations equilibrium (REE) Citizen expectations, based on all available information (in the model), about an outcome that equals the outcome on average.

stationary A time (data) series (or model) is stationary if there is no systematic change in the mean (e.g., no trend), if there is no systematic stochastic variation, and if strict periodic variations (seasonal) are stable. Time plays no role in the sample moments.

Autocorrelation exists when successive values of a random variable, ordered over either time or across space, have nonzero covariances. A variety of data-generating processes (DGPs) may produce autocorrelation. Although interest in spatial autocorrelation has grown, most analyses of autocorrelation involve the use of time series data and, accordingly, the time series case is the focus of this article. Over the past three decades, econometricians have made major advances in the analysis of one class of such data, namely, nonstationary series produced by DGPs involving stochastic trends. Particularly important have been the development of the concept of cointegration and the explication of the relationship between this concept and the specification of error correction models for analyzing nonstationary data. Related work has led to procedures for analyzing highly autoregressive and fractionally integrated data. The former manifest very strong, but imperfect, autocorrelations across adjacent time periods; the latter have statistically significant autocorrelations at very long lags and are said to have long memory. Existing side by side with these developments are a set of procedures—some now over a half-century old—that derive from a narrow (not unimportant) concern that inferences regarding parameter estimates generated by ordinary least-squares regression analysis will be thwarted by violations of the assumption that errors are uncorrelated. We argue that these traditional procedures are potentially misleading since they ignore the possibility that autocorrelated residuals constitute evidence of model misspecification. We also contend that there is a related, larger need to develop and test theories that account for the observed autocorrelation in series of interest. The argument is illustrated by the development of a theoretical model of macropartisanship.

Conventional Wisdom and Conventional Practice

Historically, interest in autocorrelation (often referred to as serial correlation) has been motivated by the use of ordinary least-squares (OLS) regression to estimate the parameters of models of the form

$$Y_t = \beta_0 + \sum \beta_{1-k} X_{1-k,t} + \epsilon_t, \qquad (1)$$

where Y_t is the dependent variable at time t; $X_{1-k,t}$ are independent variables at time t; β_0 and β_{1-k} are parameters to be estimated; and ϵ_t is the stochastic error term $\sim N(0, \sigma^2)$.

As is well known, inferences concerning OLS estimates of the parameters of this model are problematic if the stochastic errors, ϵ_t, are correlated [i.e., $\text{cov}(\epsilon_t, \epsilon_{t-1}) \neq 0$]. When errors are correlated, parameter estimates are unbiased, but standard errors are affected. Hence, t ratios (i.e., $\beta/s.e.$) are inflated or deflated (depending on the sign of the correlation) and the risk of making Type I or Type II errors is enhanced.

Generations of researchers have learned about this threat to inference and the advisability of conducting postestimation diagnostics to determine whether the threat obtains. Since the errors, ϵ_t, are not observed, these diagnostics are performed using the residuals from the regression analysis (i.e., $\hat{\epsilon}_t$). Proceeding in this fashion, analysts—either explicitly or, more frequently, implicitly—make the strong assumption that their model is correctly specified. If the assumption is invalid, autocorrelated residuals may be a consequence of model misspecification, rather than autocorrelated errors.

Some econometric texts have begun to emphasize this point, but many researchers still behave as if they were unaware of it. As a result, they continue to commit the fallacy of concluding that autocorrelated residuals constitute necessary and sufficient evidence of an autocorrelated error process.

Although various diagnostic procedures can be employed to detect autocorrelation in regression residuals, the standard one is the Durbin-Watson test. The Durbin-Watson test statistic is computed as:

$$d = \frac{\sum(\hat{\epsilon}_t - \hat{\epsilon}_{t-1})^2}{\sum \hat{\epsilon}_t^2}. \qquad (2)$$

As its formula indicates, the Durbin-Watson test considers only first-order autocorrelation (i.e., $\hat{\epsilon}_t$ and $\hat{\epsilon}_{t-1}$). The implication is that the analyst, either explicitly or implicitly, is entertaining the hypothesis that

$$\epsilon_t = \rho\epsilon_{t-1} + v_t, \qquad (3)$$

where $v_t \sim N(0, \sigma^2)$.

Noting that $\sum \hat{\epsilon}_t^2$ and $\sum \hat{e}_{t-1}^2$ are approximately equal when N is large, the formula for d implies that $d \simeq 2(1 - \rho)$. Thus, when there is perfect positive first-order autocorrelation (i.e., $\rho = 1.0$), $d = 0$, and when there is perfect negative first-order autocorrelation (i.e., $\rho = -1.0$), $d = 4$. Critical values for d vary by the number of regressors in a model and the number of data points and are characterized by an "indeterminate zone," where it is unclear whether the null hypothesis should be rejected.

Econometricians advise that the upper bound (d_u) of the critical values should be used in circumstances when regressors are changing slowly and caution that the test is not valid when one of the regressors is a lagged endogenous variable (e.g., Y_{t-1}). When a lagged endogenous variable is present, other tests (e.g., Durbin's h, Durbin's M) should be used.

If the null hypothesis of no (first-order) autocorrelation is rejected, the traditional response is to treat the autocorrelation as a technical difficulty to be "corrected," rather than evidence of possible model misspecification. The correction is to transform the data such that the error term of the resulting modified model conforms to the OLS assumption of no autocorrelation. This generalized least-squares (GLS) transformation involves "generalized differencing" or "quasi-differencing."

Starting with an equation such as Eq. (1), the analyst lags the equation back one period in time and multiplies it by ρ, the first-order autoregressive parameter for the errors [see Eq. (2) above]. Illustrating the procedure for a model with a single regressor, the result is

$$\rho Y_{t-1} = \rho\beta_0 + \rho\beta_1 X_{t-1} + \rho\epsilon_{t-1}. \qquad (4)$$

Then, (4) is subtracted from (1) to yield

$$Y_t - \rho Y_{t-1} = \beta_0 - \rho\beta_0 + \beta_1 X_t - \rho\beta_1 X_{t-1} + \epsilon_t - \rho\epsilon_{t-1}. \qquad (5)$$

This operation produces $\epsilon_t - \rho\epsilon_{t-1} = v_t$, which, by assumption, is a white-noise error process [$\sim N(0, \sigma^2)$]. The quasi-differencing operation involves computing $Y_t^* = Y_t - \rho Y_{t-1}$ and $X_t^* = X_t - \rho X_{t-1}$, and the resulting model is $Y_t^* = \beta_0 - \rho\beta_0 + \beta_1 X_t^* + v_t$, the parameters of which can be estimated by OLS.

Since the value of ρ typically is unknown, it must be estimated. Although various methods of doing so are available, the most popular (Cochrane-Orcutt) first uses OLS to estimate the parameters in model (1). The residuals then are used to estimate ρ. This $\hat{\rho}$ is used to transform Y_t and X_t to produce Y_t^* and X_t^*, respectively. The latter are then used in a second-round estimation and a new $\hat{\hat{\rho}}$ is produced. This $\hat{\hat{\rho}}$ then is used to transform the (original) data and another regression is performed. The process (called feasible GLS because ρ is estimated) continues until the value of ρ converges.

Common Factors and Dynamic Misspecification

Regardless of how ρ is estimated, the quasi-differencing procedure introduces a common factor restriction. This may be seen by rewriting Eq. (5) as

$$(1-\rho L)Y_t = (1-\rho L)\beta_0 + (1-\rho L)\beta_1 X_t + (1-\rho L)\epsilon_t, \tag{6}$$

where L is the lag operator (i.e., $LY_t = Y_{t-1}$ and $L^k Y_t = Y_{t-k}$). Thus, Eq. (6)—the model implied by the conventional wisdom that first-order autoregessive residuals entail a first-order autoregressive error process—is a restricted version of an autoregressive distributed lag model. An example of such a model is

$$Y_t = \alpha_0 + \lambda_1 Y_{t-1} + \gamma_1 X_t + \gamma_2 X_{t-1} + \nu_t. \tag{7}$$

The requirement that $\gamma_2 = -\lambda_1\gamma_1$ in Eq. (7) produces a common-factor (COMFAC) restriction similar to that in model (6)—the model implied by the quasi-differencing procedure typically utilized to deal with first-order autocorrelation in the residuals.

The validity of the restriction is an empirical question. Some econometricians stress the importance of COMFAC testing to help guard against misspecifying the dynamics in one's model. The test is easily implemented and can help one avoid the potentially misleading *non sequitur* of concluding that autocorrelated residuals imply autocorrelated errors.

Integrated, Near-Integrated, and Fractionally Integrated Processes

Modeling dynamic processes explicitly involves more than simply putting a lagged endogenous variable on the right-hand side of a regression equation. There are important theoretical and technical issues that should be addressed. One set of technical issues concerns the stationarity of the variables of interest. A variable Y_t is said to be (weakly) stationary if it has a constant mean $[E(Y_t) = \mu]$, a constant variance $[E(Y_t - \mu)^2 = \gamma_0]$, and a constant covariance $[E(Y_t - \mu)(Y_{t-k} - \mu) = \gamma_k]$ at lag $t-k$ regardless of the values of t or k.

Consider the case of a simple first-order autoregressive DGP

$$Y_t = \phi_1 Y_{t-1} + \varepsilon_t, \tag{8}$$

where ε_t is a white-noise error process and cov(ε_t, ε_{t-k})= 0 for all t and k. If $|\phi_1| < 1.0$, the process is stationary. However, if $\phi_1 = 1.0$, it is nonstationary. The defining characteristic of such a process, commonly called a random walk, is that it "never forgets." Since the ϕ_1 coefficient for Y_{t-1} equals 1.0, stochastic shocks (ε_t) are not discounted as the process evolves; rather, they accumulate over time at their full value.

One can see this by repeated recursive substitution for Y_{t-1} in Eq. (8). Doing so shows that $Y_t = Y_0 + \sum\varepsilon_i\,(i = 1, t)$, with Y_0 being the initial value of Y. This process has a nonconstant variance and is said to exhibit a stochastic trend. Modifying Eq. (8) by introducing a constant β_0 yields $Y_t = \beta_0 + Y_{t-1} + \varepsilon_t$. Repeated recursive substitution shows that this latter model, called a random walk with drift, produces nonstationary variables. After substitution, the model contains both $\sum\varepsilon_i$ and $t\beta_0$, with the latter being the "drift" component that introduces a deterministic trend.

To illustrate the behavior of these nonstationary processes, a random walk and a random walk with drift (with $\beta_0 = 0.05$) are simulated and then compared with a stationary first-order autoregression (with $\phi_1 = 0.50$). The errors for the three variables are white noise, with constant variances of 1.0. As Fig. 1 shows, the random walk and random walk with drift soon depart from their initial value (0) and never return during the 240 periods for which the data are generated. In contrast, the stationary first-order autoregressive process with an initial value of 0 repeatedly moves from positive to negative values and vice versa and shows no tendency to "trend" in any direction.

In a classic article from 1974, Granger and Newbold demonstrated that the threats to inference posed by nonstationary variables are decidedly nontrivial. Employing Monte Carlo simulation methods, they generated a large number of independent random walk variables and then performed regressions of the form $Y_t = \beta_0 + \beta_1 X_t + \mu_t$. These regressions rejected the (true) null hypothesis that $\beta_1 = 0$ at alarming rates.

Since the publication of these findings, researchers have come to appreciate the danger of such "spurious regressions." It has become routine to use unit-root tests and other, less formal, diagnostic procedures (graphs, autocorrelation functions) to determine whether variables of interest are nonstationary.

If nonstationarity is suspected, conventional practice is to difference the variables prior to conducting regression analyses. The implicit assumption is that the data-generating process producing the nonstationarity is a random walk or a random walk with drift, rather than a deterministic trend model of the form $Y_t = \pi_0 + \pi_1 t + \eta_t$, where t is time and the π values are model parameters. If the assumption is valid, the variable is said to be integrated of order 1 [$\boldsymbol{I}(1)$] because differencing it once will produce stationarity. Thus, in the random walk case, one has

$$Y_t - Y_{t-1} = 1.0Y_{t-1} - Y_{t-1} + \varepsilon_t. \tag{9}$$

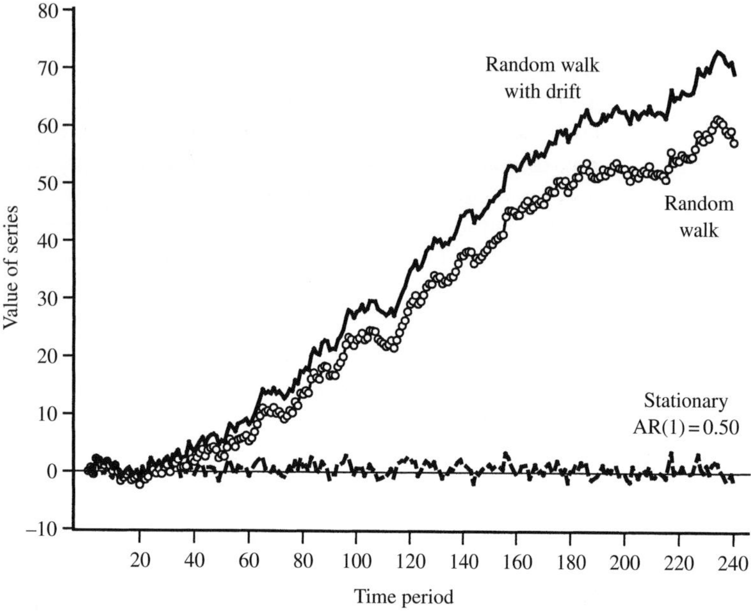

Figure 1 Simulated stationary first-order autoregressive, random walk, and random walk with drift processes.

The resulting variable $(1-L)Y_t = \varepsilon_t$ is stationary. The result for a random walk with drift is similar, except that the expected value of the differenced variable is β_0 rather than zero.

Differencing nonstationary $\boldsymbol{I}(1)$ variables solves the problem of spurious regressions, but does not take into account possible long-run relationships between Y_t and X_s. It is possible to study long-run relationships between nonstationary [$\boldsymbol{I}(1)$] variables if those variables cointegrate. For example, two nonstationary variables, Y_t and X_t, are said to cointegrate if a linear combination of the variables constitutes a stationary variable.

Cointegration cannot be assumed, but must be demonstrated empirically. In 1987, Engle and Granger proposed doing this by regressing Y_t on X_t and testing the residuals (by definition a linear combination of Y and X) for stationarity. Determining that the residuals of this "cointegrating regression" constitute a stationary series warrants the inference that Y and X cointegrate. If so, Y and X can be modeled in error correction form, with the error correction mechanism capturing the long-run relationship between them:

$$(1-L)Y_t = \beta_0 + \beta_1(1-L)X_t - \alpha(Y_{t-1} - cX_{t-1}) + v_t. \tag{10}$$

In this model, the expression $Y_{t-1} - cX_{t-1}$ constitutes the error correction mechanism. Given the negative feedback properties of error correction, the parameter α is expected to carry a negative sign. Its absolute value calibrates the speed with which shocks to the system are reequilibrated by the cointegrating relationship between Y and X. Rearranging terms shows that models such as Eq. (10) are variants of the more familiar autoregressive distributed lag form. For example, Eq. (10) may be written as:

$$Y_t = \beta_0 + (1-\alpha)Y_{t-1} + \beta_1 X_t + (\alpha c - \beta_1)X_{t-1} + v_t. \tag{11}$$

Note also that since all variables in a model such as Eq. (10) are stationary, the spurious regression problem does not arise. Thus, if other conventional assumptions hold, the parameters in model (10) may be estimated via OLS. Engle and Granger suggest a two-step process, where step 1 is to regress Y on X in levels. Assuming that the residuals from this regression are stationary, step 2 is to estimate the parameters in an error correction model such as Eq. (10). Other analysts have advocated a one-step method in which all coefficients in an error correction model are estimated simultaneously. If Y and X do not cointegrate, α will not differ significantly from zero.

An error correction model specification is attractive because it enables one to study both short- and long-run relationships among nonstationary variables. However, establishing that a variable is nonstationary in the classic sense can be difficult. This is because the principal statistical tool for this purpose, unit-root tests, has low statistical power in the face of alternative DGPs that produce highly persistent data. Two such alternatives are the near-integrated and fractionally integrated cases. A near-integrated variable is the product of an autoregressive process [e.g., model (8) above], where the ϕ_1 parameter is slightly less than 1.0 (e.g., 0.95). In this case, unit-root tests are prone to fail to reject the null hypothesis of nonstationarity, even though ϕ_1 actually is less than 1.0.

Unit-root tests also are apt to prove misleading when the DGP produces a fractionally integrated, or long-memory, variable. As its name implies, the concept of fractional integration relaxes the assumption that variables must have integer orders of integration. Rather than being integrated at orders, say 0 or 1, a variable may be generated by an autoregressive, fractionally integrated, moving average (ARFIMA) process such as:

$$(1 - L)^d Y_t = \frac{\varphi(L)}{\phi(L)} \omega_t. \quad (12)$$

This is a generalization of the familiar autoregressive, integrated, moving average (ARIMA) class of models, with ϕ and φ representing autoregressive and moving average parameters.

The fractional differencing parameter d can vary from -0.5 to 1.0. When it is ≥ 0.5, the series is nonstationary although, unlike a random walk, shocks do eventually decay. The simplest member of this model class is called fractional Gaussian noise [i.e., $(1 - L)^d Y_t = \omega_t$]. The left-hand side may be expanded as an (infinite) autoregression:

$$1 - dL - (1/2)d(1-d)L^2 - (1/6)d(1-d)(2-d)L^3 \\ - \cdots - (1-j!)d(1-d)(2-d)\cdots[(j-1)-d]L^j - \cdots.$$

Figure 2 presents simulated examples of near-integrated ($\phi_1 = 0.95$) and fractionally integrated ($d = 0.95$) data in comparison with the aforementioned typical first-order autoregressive series where $\phi_1 = 0.50$. Although the near-integrated and fractionally integrated series do not exhibit the obvious trending behavior of the random walk depicted in Fig. 1, they clearly behave much differently than the garden variety AR(1), moving away from their initial value (0) for very long periods.

The persistence (memory) in the near-integrated and fractionally integrated data means that they have significant autocorrelations at very long lags. This point is illustrated clearly by calculating autocorrelation functions (ACFs) for these series (see Fig. 3). Although the ACFs for the near-integrated and fractionally integrated series decline more quickly than does the ACF for the random walk, they are very different than the ACF for the conventional AR(1) series. For these simulated data, the latter becomes statistically insignificant ($p > 0.05$) after 2 lags, whereas the near and fractionally integrated series remain significant through 18 and 15 lags, respectively.

Near-integrated variables and fractionally integrated variables with d values in the nonstationary range (i.e., >0.5) can create threats to inference similar to those posed by random walks. In this regard, DeBoef has demonstrated that single-equation error correction models are useful for analyzing near-integrated variables. In 2003, Clarke and Lebo cited several procedures for estimating the d parameter (and associated standard error) and discussed how the ideas of cointegration and error correction may be generalized to handle the cases where variables of interest are fractionally integrated and fractionally cointegrated.

The preceding discussion has emphasized statistical issues and techniques that are relevant for the analysis of autocorrelated data. These matters are very important but, as emphasized, a crucial consideration is theoretically guided model specification. This is the topic of the next section.

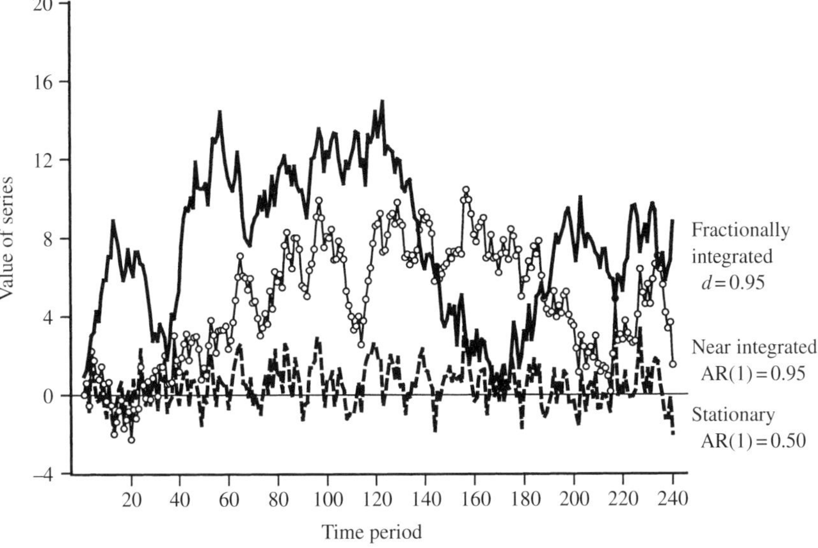

Figure 2 Simulated stationary first-order autoregressive, near-integrated, and fractionally integrated processes.

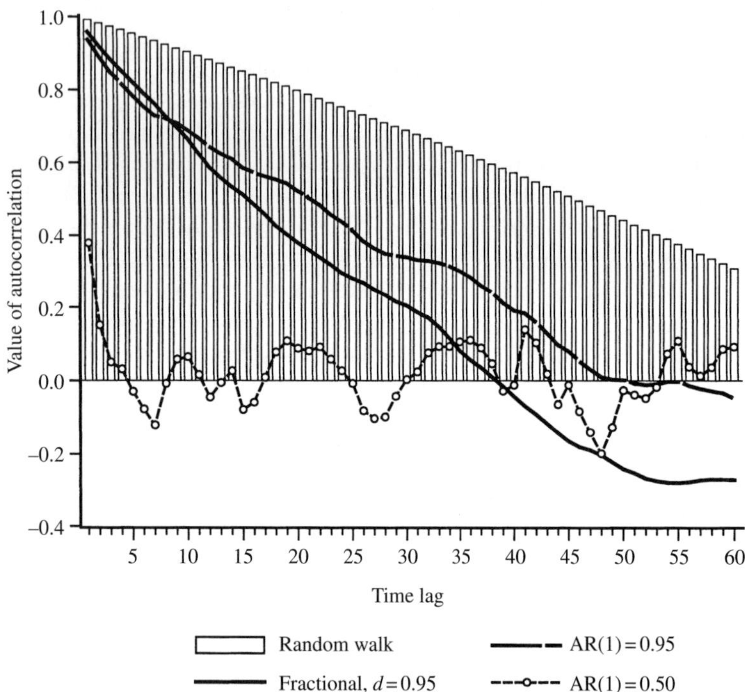

Figure 3 Autocorrelation functions for simulated autoregressive, near-integrated, fractionally integrated, and random walk processes.

From Practice to Theory: A Model of Macropartisanship

Here it is demonstrated that persistence can be explained theoretically. The example given is a simple model of party identification—so-called macropartisanship. The model makes no claim to be a powerful explanation of macropartisanship. Rather, the weaker claim is made that it serves to illustrate that its highly autoregressive behavior is a matter of specification and theoretical development. Strictly mechanical approaches, which use a variety of statistical patches, fail to address these theoretical concerns.

The behavioral assumptions are primitive, but the model does have the potential to be enriched by further theoretical (formal) revisions that would incorporate findings in, for example, economics, cognitive psychology, communications, and political science. Although these modifications are welcome, the larger point is to incorporate these modifications within a framework that merges both formal and empirical analyses. When this is achieved, persistence—autocorrelation—can be identified at its source and researchers can use theory to assist in differentiating between various types of persistence (i.e., near-integrated versus fractionally integrated processes) that may characterize an empirical realization of a time series of interest.

In the model demonstrated it is assumed that political campaign advertisments influence the public. It is argued that the persistence of rival political parties' political advisors to target and influence (through the use of political advertisement resources) rival party voters reduces the well-known persistence in macropartisanship. As a consequence, shocks to macropartisanship can either be amplified or die out quickly depending on rival political advisor behavior. Moreover, the linkage between the formal and empirical models identifies the persistence as near-integrated.

The model comprises three equations. Each citizen (i) is subject to an event (j) at time (t). The model aggregates across individuals and events so the notation will have only the subscript t. The first equation [Eq. (13)] specifies what influences aggregate party identification (M_t). The variable M_{t-1} accounts for the possibility of persistence. Citizens also have an expectation of what portion of the population will identify with the party ($E_{t-1}M_t$). It is assumed that, in forming their expectations, citizens use all available and relevant information as specified in this model (rational expectations). It is further assumed that party identification depends on how favorably a citizen views the national party (F_t). Finally, party identification can be subject to unanticipated stochastic shocks (realignments) (u_{1t}), where $u_{1t} \sim N(0, \sigma^2_{u_{1t}})$. It is assumed the relations are positive—$a_1, a_2, a_3 \geq 0$.

Macropartisanship

$$M_t = a_1 M_{t-1} + a_2 E_{t-1} M_t + a_3 F_t + u_{1t}. \quad (13)$$

Equation (14) represents citizens' impression ("favorability") of a political party (F_t). In this model, favorability is a linear function of the lag of favorability (F_{t-1}) and an advertising resource variable (A_t). There are many ways to measure political advertising resources. These measures include but are not limited to the total dollars spent, the dollars spent relative to a rival party (parties), the ratio of dollars spent relative to a rival party (parties), and the tone, content, timing, and geographic location of the advertisements (on a multinomial scale). Data have been collected for individual races but have the potential to be aggregated along partisan lines. For more details on measurement issues consult the Wisconsin Advertising Project Web site at: http://www.polisci.wisc.edu/tvadvertising. u_{2t} is a stochastic shock that represents unanticipated events (uncertainty), where $u_{2t} \sim N(0, \sigma^2_{u_{2t}})$. The parameter $b_1 \geq 0$, while $b_2 \gtreqless 0$ depending on the tone and content of the advertisement.

Favorability

$$F_t = b_1 F_{t-1} + b_2 A_t + u_{2t}. \quad (14)$$

Equation (15) presents the contingency plan or rule that (rival) political advisors use. It is argued that political advisors track their previous period's advertising resource expenditures (A_{t-1}) and react to that period's favorability rating for the (rival) national party (F_{t-1}). Political advisors also base their current expenditure of advertisement resources on the degree to which macropartisanship (M_t) approximates a prespecified and desired target (M^*). Ideally, political advisors want $(M_t - M^*) = 0$ since it is unrealistic and far too costly to make $M_t = 0$.

It is assumed that the parameters c_1 and c_3 are positive. The parameter c_2 is countercyclical ($-1 \leq c_2 \leq 0$). This reflects political advisors' willingness to increase or conserve their advertising resources depnding on whether macropartisanship is above (decrease advertising) or below (increase advertising) the target.

Rival Political Advisor

$$A_t = c_1 A_{t-1} + c_2(M_t - M^*) + c_3 F_{t-1}. \quad (15)$$

To obtain the reduced form for macropartisanship, substitute (15) into (14):

$$F_t = b_1 F_{t-1} + b_2[c_1 A_{t-1} + c_2(M_t - M^*) + c_3 F_{t-1}] + u_{2t} \quad (16)$$

and

$$F_t = (b_1 + b_2 c_3) F_{t-1} + b_2 c_1 A_{t-1} + b_2 c_2 (M_t - M^*) + u_{2t}. \quad (17)$$

Now substitute Eq. (17) into Eq. (13):

$$M_t = a_1 M_{t-1} + a_2 E_{t-1} M_t + (b_1 + b_2 c_3) F_{t-1} + b_2 c_1 A_{t-1} + b_2 c_2 (M_t - M^*) + u_{2t} + u_{1t}. \quad (18)$$

Collect terms and divide through by $(1 - b_2 c_2)$:

$$M_t = \frac{a_1}{(1 - b_2c_2)} M_{t-1} + \frac{a_2}{(1 - b_2c_2)} E_{t-1} M_t + \frac{b_2 c_1}{(1 - b_2c_2)} A_{t-1} + \frac{(b_1 + b_2 c_3)}{(1 - b_2c_2)} F_{t-1} - \frac{b_2 c_1}{(1 - b_2c_2)} M^* + \frac{u_{2t} + u_{1t}}{(1 - b_2c_2)}. \quad (19)$$

Simplifying the notation shows that there is an autoregressive component in the reduced form for macropartisanship

$$M_t = \Theta_0 + \Theta_1 M_{t-1} + \Theta_2 E_{t-1} M_t + \Theta_3 A_{t-1} + \Theta_4 F_{t-1} + \varepsilon_t^*, \quad (20)$$

where $\Theta_0 = (b_2 c_1 Y^*)/(1 - b_2 c_2)$, $\Theta_1 = a_1/(1 - b_2 c_2)$, $\Theta_2 = a_2/(1 - b_2 c_2)$, $\Theta_3 = b_2 c_1/(1 - b_2 c_2)$, $\Theta_4 = (b_1 + b_2 c_3)/(1 - b_2 c_2)$, and $\varepsilon_t^* = (u_{2t} + u_{1t})/(1 - b_2 c_2)$.

The system is now simplified to a model of macropartisanship that depends on lagged macropartisanship and also the conditional expectation at time $t - 1$ of current macropartisanship. The prior values of advertising and favorability also have an effect.

To close the model, the rational expectations equilibrium can be solved by taking the conditional expectation at time $t - 1$ of Eq. (20) and then substituting this result back into Eq. (20)

$$M_t = \Pi_1 + \Pi_2 M_{t-1} + \Pi_3 A_{t-2} + \Pi_4 F_{t-2} + \xi_t', \quad (21)$$

where

$$\Pi_1 = \left[\frac{\Theta_0}{1 - \Theta_2} - \left(\frac{\Theta_3}{1 - \Theta_2} - \frac{\Theta_4}{1 - \Theta_2} b_2\right) c_2 Y^*\right],$$

$$\Pi_2 = \left[\frac{\Theta_1}{1 - \Theta_2} + \left(\frac{\Theta_3}{1 - \Theta_2} + \frac{\Theta_4}{1 - \Theta_2} b_2\right) c_2\right],$$

$$\Pi_3 = \left[\left(\frac{\Theta_3}{1 - \Theta_2} + \frac{\Theta_4}{1 - \Theta_2} b_2\right) c_1\right],$$

$$\Pi_4 = \left[\frac{\Theta_3}{1 - \Theta_2} c_3 + \frac{\Theta_4}{1 - \Theta_2} (b_1 + b_2 c_3)\right],$$

and

$$\xi_t' = \left(\frac{\Theta_4}{1 - \Theta_2} u_{2t} + \varepsilon_t^*\right).$$

Equation (21) is the minimum state variable solution for macropartisanship. Macropartisanship (M_t) depends, in part, on the lag of macropartisanship (M_{t-1}). More importantly, the persistence of macropartisanship (Π_2) is now shown to depend on the persistence and willingness of rival political advisors to maintain a rival macropartisanship target (c_2).

This can be shown by examining the reduced form AR(1) coefficient expression Π_2:

$$\Pi_2 = \frac{a_1 + b_2c_2(c_1 + b_1 + b_2c_3)}{1 - b_2c_2 - a_2}. \quad (22)$$

The derivative of Eq. (22) with respect to (c_2) is taken and the following relationship is obtained:

$$\frac{\partial \Pi_2}{\partial c_2} = \frac{b_2[a_1(-1 + a_2)(b_1 + c_1 + b_2c_3)]}{(-1 + a_2 + b_2c_2)^2}. \quad (23)$$

The denominator is always positive since it is squared. Given the assumptions about the signs of the coefficients in the model, the numerator is positive as long as $a_2 < 1$. Therefore, under these conditions, it is known that the relationship is positive ($\partial\Pi_2/\partial c_2 > 0$).

The final step is to determine whether the model reaches an equilibrium when it starts from a point of reference that contains nonequilibrium values. Because the model presented has a first-order autoregressive component, the result is straightforward. The stability condition is summarized in the following proposition:

PROPOSITION 1. *Equation* (21) *is a uniquely stationary MSV solution if* $|\Pi_2| < 1$.

The relationship between c_2 and Π_2 is demonstrated in Fig. 4. The following values are used for Eq. (22): $a_1 = a_2 = b_1 = b_2 = c_1 = c_3 = 0.5$. The parameter c_2 ranges from 0.0 to −1.0. As the value of c_2 is varied between 0.0 and −1.0, it is found that the persistence (autocorrelation) in macropartisanship (Π_2)—all things being equal—is zero when $c_2 = -0.5$. On the other hand, macropartisanship becomes highly autoregressive ($\Pi_2 \rightarrow 1.0$) when rival political advisors fail to react ($c_2 \rightarrow 0.0$) to deviations from their prespecified target. The conclusion from this model is that negative advertisements from rival political parties can influence the persistence of their opponent's national party identification.

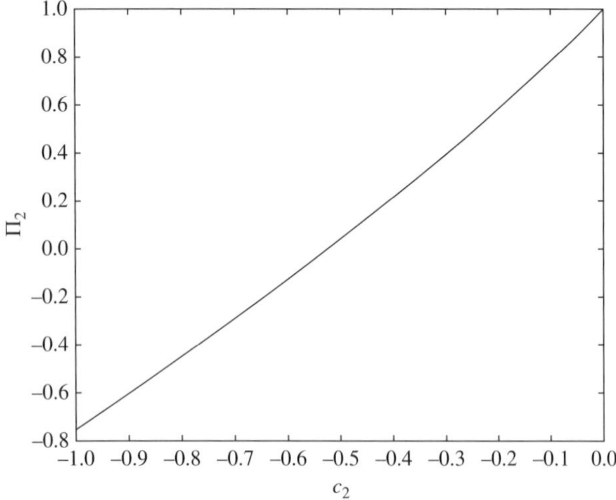

Figure 4 The relationship between Π_2 and c_2.

An Agenda for Future Research

Social scientists' interest in autocorrelation is longstanding. This interest reflects a scientifically unassailable concern to make sound inferences regarding forces driving the dynamics of a variable of interest. As discussed above, researchers historically have interpreted the remit implied by this concern very narrowly, focusing their attention exclusively on autocorrelation in the residuals of an OLS regression analysis. Construed so narrowly, autocorrelation is—to use Hendry's characterization—a "nuisance," with traditional "corrections" constituting possibly unwarranted and misleading model simplifications.

Since the early 1990s, advances in the analysis of integrated, near-integrated, and fractionally integrated data have helped to relieve this situation by explicitly articulating technical concerns with the diagnosis of various forms of autocorrelation and the implications thereof for successful inference to questions of model specification. Although these developments constitute a major step in the right direction, the analytic stance remains highly reactive. Model specification is governed by *ad hoc* inferences regarding characteristics of the data and relatively little attention is given to the theoretical foundations of the model. Above it is argued that it is desirable to redress the balance, by giving greater priority to the development of theoretical models that can generate various forms of autoregressive behavior in a variable being studied.

The argument has been illustrated by developing a small theoretical model of macropartisanship—a topic traditionally of great concern to students of voting, elections, and the stability of democratic political systems—and demonstrating how it implies autoregressive, quite possibly highly autoregressive, behavior in observed time series data. Following Granger, this model could be elaborated in various ways, for example, by specifying autoregressive heterogeneity in the electorate as a means of generating the nonstationary fractional dynamics observed in macropartisanship in mature democracies. The general point is that various forms of autocorrelation can and should be seen as empirical implications of theoretical models. Developing and testing such models constitutes a challenging agenda for future research.

See Also the Following Articles

Spatial Autocorrelation • Time-Series–Cross-Section Data

Further Reading

Beran, J. (1994). *Statistics for Long Memory Processes.* Chapman and Hall, New York.

Box, G. E. P., and Jenkins, G. (1976). *Times Series Analysis: Forecasting and Control,* revised Ed. Holden Day, Oakland, CA.

Clarke, H. D., and Lebo, M. (2003). Fractional (co)integration and governing party support in Britain. *Br. J. Polit. Sci.* **33,** 283–301.

DeBoef, S. (2001). Modeling equilibrium relationships: Error correction models with strongly autoregressive data. *Polit. Anal.* **9,** 78–94.

DeBoef, S., and Granato, J. (2000). Testing for cointegrating relationships with near-integrated data. *Polit. Anal.* **8,** 99–117.

Erikson, R. S., MacKuen, M., and Stimson, J. A. (2002). *The Macro Polity.* Cambridge University Press, Cambridge, UK.

Franses, P. H. (1998). *Time Series Models for Business and Economic Forecasting.* Cambridge University Press, Cambridge, UK.

Ghysels, E., Swanson, N. R., and Watson, M. W. (2001). *Collected Papers of Clive W. J. Granger, Volume II, Causality, Integration and Cointegration, and Long Memory.* Cambridge University Press, Cambridge, UK.

Godfrey, L. G. (1988). *Misspecification Tests in Econometrics.* Cambridge University Press, Cambridge, UK.

Gujarati, D. (2003). *Basic Econometrics,* 4th Ed. McGraw-Hill/Irwin, New York.

Hendry, D. (1995). *Dynamic Econometrics.* Oxford University Press, Oxford, UK.

Hendry, D., and Doornik, J. (2001). *Empirical Econometric Modelling Using PcGive,* Vol. 1. Timberlake Consultants, London.

Maddala, G. S., and Kim, I. M. (1998). *Unit Roots, Cointegration, and Structural Change.* Cambridge University Press, Cambridge, UK.

McCallum, B. T. (1983). On nonuniqueness in linear rational expectations models: An atttempt at perspective. *J. Monetary Econ.* **11,** 134–168.

Basic vs. Applied Social Science Research

Scott Greer

University of Prince Edward Island, Charlottetown, Prince Edward Island, Canada

Glossary

applied research Concerned with practical knowledge; outcome focused rather than theory focused, and involving the application of existing knowledge to solve problems.

applied science Knowledge directed toward producing a product for public interest, and perhaps developing its commercial value.

basic research Involves questions and investigative practices that are focused on discovering or formulating fundamental principles; generally inspired by scientific curiosity rather than by the need to solve a particular problem.

basic science Involves theories about the world that are considered foundational to human understanding.

human science Includes methods and theories based on the idea that human beings are fundamentally unlike other components of the natural world, and that methods and assumptions different from those applied to the natural sciences are necessary to understand human conduct.

ideographic research The study of a single individual case (e.g., a case study); contrasted with nomothetic research.

natural science Includes methods and theories devoted to understanding the natural world through the measurement of systematic and controlled observations.

nomothetic research The study of groups of individuals, and the search for universal generalizable laws of behavior.

paradigm A broad set of assumptions that works as a framework of knowledge.

social science The study of individual human behavior as individuals and in groups.

Although the concepts of basic and applied social sciences originated during the mid-19th century, the modern understanding of these disciplines emerged only after World War II. Basic social science research involves questions and investigative practices that are focused on discovering or formulating fundamental principles of human behavior, and are generally inspired by the scientist's curiosity rather than by an attempt to solve a particular problem. Applied social science research, by contrast, is more pragmatic and goal oriented, focusing more on practical concerns than on theory, and involves the application of existing knowledge to solve problems.

Introduction

Basic social science research involves questions and investigative practices that are focussed on discovering or formulating fundamental principles of human behavior, and is generally inspired by the scientist's curiosity rather than an attempt to solve a particular problem. Applied social science research, driven more by practicality, is outcome focused rather than theory focused. Basic research answers questions relating to the "whys" and "hows" of human behavior, and does not typically result in a product or technology. Applied research, on the other hand, is directed toward producing an improved product, or toward finding ways of making the use and delivery of the product better and easier. In short, basic research tends to improve our understanding of the world, and applied research tends to improve our ability to function and interact with it. To fully understand this distinction, however, it is important to realize that basic and applied research are sets of practices that are based on two differing conceptions of science, with differing professional interests. As a result, the relationships between them are dynamic, highly complex, and often quite ambiguous.

Although the distinction between basic science and applied science had existed in various forms since the 19th century, contemporary understanding of these terms is based on the effects of World War II, and the changes it brought about in the ways science operates within society. There is no one single definition that would be historically accurate to differentiate these approaches or the activities of social scientists, although there are some broad commonalities that serve to distinguish "basic" from "applied" science and research. It should be remembered that the definitions of and relationship between basic and applied research approaches are not static, and must be understood within their historical and social context.

Basic Science Research

Basic research refers to the activities of scientists who are investigating theoretical questions for the sake of building knowledge. Basic research is constituted by the types of investigative practices that both inform and reflect the current understanding of "basic science." These forms of research practice and scientific knowledge form a reciprocal relationship, in that knowledge informs the basis of research methods, and these methods in turn shape the questions and even the findings of scientists. Basic science involves theories about the world—and indeed the universe—that are considered foundational to human understanding. Basic social science, then, refers to the knowledge that scientists use in formulating questions and research strategies to better understand human behavior. It also involves the means by which scientists carry out these investigations, and the knowledge that is produced as a result. In the social sciences, basic science theories typically describe the essential factors believed to be involved in human behavior, and provide some explanations about the relationship of these factors to each other and to the world. Basic science therefore strives to be (1) explanatory, by developing causal theories about relationships among events in the social world, and (2) descriptive, by presenting an accurate and comprehensive portrayal of fundamental processes and structures. Ideally, basic science would be articulated in terms of causal relationships about the social world and social behavior, and these relationships would be thought of as scientific laws (or at least lawful).

Applied Science Research

Applied social science has interests that are often quite disparate from basic or pure scientific questions. As already noted, applied science is about producing a product for public interest, and perhaps developing its commercial value, whereas basic researchers are drawn to more purely theoretical questions about advancing the current state of knowledge. Applied researchers evaluate their work more in terms of its utility and public appeal, and may create instruments or measures for specific users and situations. Accordingly, applied social researchers use less technical language, and often frames their approach with a specific problem or task already in mind. A major step in the evolution of applied social science was the professionalization of applied disciplines. This development has created a much more complex picture in understanding the relationship between basic and applied social research, adding numerous other goals and interests. For example, clinical psychologists (who are specialists in psychological treatment and testing) want to maintain standards of training, restricting the job of administering mental tests only to those with the proper qualifications. Psychologists and other mental health professionals want similar standards of practice, and issues such as licensure, liability, and insurance all become highly salient and often contentious. Professional social science concerns are often economic in nature, and include ways of expanding professional horizons to include other practices and clientele (e.g., the issue of whether psychologists should be allowed to prescribe drugs). In order to accommodate the incredible proliferation of professional psychologists, the American Psychological Association (APA) was reorganized in 1945, and even altered its mission statement to reflect the presence of professional psychology. Today, over half of the psychologists in the world work in the United States, and half of American psychologists are professional, mainly clinical, practitioners.

Before addressing the relationship between basic and applied social science research, and the professionalization of social science practices, it is important to recognize there are different types of basic and applied sciences, including natural science, social science, and human science.

Types of Science: Natural Science, Social Science, and Human Science

Following the earlier writings of Vico (among others), it was typical in Germany during the 19th century to distinguish between natural scientific theories (*Naturwissenschaften*) and human scientific theories (*Geisteswissenschaften*). Natural science theories were mainly developed during the historical period known as the Enlightenment, and sought to understand the laws of nature through experimental methods. Though it has assumed many forms, the experimental method has historically emphasized objectivity, measurement, and a self-verifying cycle of deductive and inductive logical analysis: ideas (theories) yield hypotheses that are tested under controlled conditions. Measurements are taken, results are recorded, and the initial hypothesis is either supported or rejected as a possible explanation for the observed relationship.

By contrast, human science theories originated from the notion that human beings are fundamentally unlike other components of the natural world, and, although the exact nature of this difference varies and has evolved over time, different methods and assumptions are necessary to understand human conduct. Nevertheless, the principal differences between natural and human science theories revolve around the idea that human conduct is based on meaning and intentionality, factors that do not have physical referents, are not amenable to objective experimental analysis, and do not appear to follow causal laws. Where natural science theories see causal scientific laws as their essential feature, human science tends to see understanding (or *Verstand*, in the original German) as its central feature. The concept of understanding is based on the abilities of human beings to engage the world in a unique way; for instance, empathy, or the ability to understand another's point of view, is a capacity that is not found in other living things (to the best of our knowledge). Human science theories do not involve what would normally be regarded as scientific or experimental methods, but instead favor approaches that are more interpretive and discursive, emphasizing the roles of empathy, interpretation, and intentionality in framing human conduct.

The social sciences are a blend of the natural and human science orientations, although different disciplines have emphasized one over the other at various points in time. Most social sciences began during the 19th century, a time when experimental research was at its peak and widely received by both professionals and the public as unlocking the secrets of the universe. Soaring urban populations, the Industrial Revolution, and the rise of the middle class were also factors that led to new types of questions concerning the individual and the causes and processes of human behavior. Following philosophers such as John Stuart Mill, many believed it was not only possible but quite desirable to apply the highly successful experimental methods of the natural sciences to human behavior, and these burgeoning social sciences (including psychology, sociology, and economics) were founded on the natural science paradigm. Psychology, for instance, was initially conceived by its recognized founder, the German physiologist Wilhelm Wundt (1832–1920), to be a combination of natural and human sciences. However, the idea of a natural science of human behavior was eagerly embraced by North American psychologists (and the North American public) for a variety of practical and economic reasons, and "psychology" was transformed from this dual perspective into a largely singular focus on experimental approaches.

Unlike natural science theories, social science theories take human behavior as their primary object of investigation, although there are many clear links between social and natural science theories (e.g., neuroscience, physiology). The social sciences are not generally recognized as having the same type of laws as the natural sciences, principally because their subject matter is of a different nature. Nevertheless, most social scientists believe the methods of experimental analysis are an essential component of basic science knowledge. With some variation and to different degrees, the social sciences have continued to emulate the natural science method of investigation. The social sciences have developed an array of their own methodologies as well, although these are all based on the assumptions of either a natural science or a human science paradigm.

Similarly, applied social science research involves a reciprocal set of practices that are connected to the foundations of basic science on the one hand, and the practical needs and problems of society on the other. Ideally, the applied social scientist looks to the principles and advancements of basic science to meet the demands of consumers of technology and technological services. Most researchers in the social sciences, like their counterparts in the natural sciences, have assumed that there needs to be some fundamental, basic knowledge in place before progress can be made; basic research, in other words, lays the foundation for what follows. The idea that basic science necessarily precedes applied science has been traditionally accepted as the logic of scientific progress, but closer examination of the social sciences show that this is far from a set formula.

At the most fundamental level, the distinction between basic and applied social science research revolves around the purposes for which the research question is directed, not which type of knowledge was the basis for the other. In other words, knowledge itself is not essentially either basic or applied; the decisive issue concerns the context in which the research was conducted, and the ends toward which such knowledge was initially directed. It is also clear that there have been and continues to be considerable tensions between basic and applied forms of research. Examples of this complex relationship among society and basic and applied research are readily available in the social sciences: intelligence, race, genetics, abnormal behavior, and psychotherapy are but a few of the instances in which the concerns of applied research have conflicted with (and, some may argue, superseded) the foundational science of basic research.

The Case of Psychology: Basic Science, Applied Science, and Professionalization

The APA was founded in 1892, and the preamble to their bylaws stated that their mission was to "advance psychology as a science." When the APA was reorganized in 1945, the mission statement was modified to "advance psychology as a science, a profession, and as a means of promoting human welfare." This revision reflects some important and fundamental developments in the field—namely, the emergence of applied and professional psychology as dominant interests. This was, however, a complete turnaround from the notion behind the founding of psychology as a scientific discipline devoted to discovering the laws of behavior (i.e., a basic science).

Psychology as a scientific endeavor began in Germany in the late 19th century. On the heels of significant advances in physiology (e.g., Helmholtz's measurement of the speed of nerve impulses), the experimental analysis of physical movement and functioning led to attempts to measure mental functioning as well. Although there had been a long tradition of believing that mental events could not be measured, and that a scientific psychology was therefore untenable, the development of fields such as psychophysics, which looked at the relationship between changes in physical stimuli and perception, began to show that measurements of mental phenomena were indeed possible. Scientific psychology was thus dependent on the objective, experimental measurements of mental phenomena and their relationship to the world; this would be the basic science of psychology. Most German scholars in this new field would have scoffed at the idea of an "applied psychology" or any form of applied social science research—there had to be a basic set of fundamental principles in place before the practical questions of application could even be asked. Although never actually professionally aligned with psychology, Sigmund Freud started as a medical doctor, practising various treatments for hysteria. Freud wanted very much to bring relief to his neurotic patients, but he also wanted to create a new science of the mind, called "psychoanalysis," just as badly. Moreover, social sciences in Germany were relative newcomers to academic institutional stalwarts such as philosophy, physiology, and the experimental sciences. This meant that they needed first to prove themselves as bona fide disciplines, which meant creating a foundation of basic science principles.

Although generally much more practical and public oriented, some early North American psychologists also saw themselves as basic scientists. Edward Titchener and his "structuralism," for instance, sought to establish the foundational elements of conscious experience. In the long run, however, this type of psychology in North America proved to be the exception. Reflecting the American Zeitgeist (spirit of the times), most American psychologies would have a largely pragmatic philosophy of science, one that would result in a psychology of everyday life rather than a pure science. William James, one of the founders of North American psychology, noted that "the kind of psychology which could cure a case of melancholy, or charm a chronic insane delusion away, ought certainly to be preferred to the most seraphic insight into the nature of the soul." Right from the very beginnings of the field in the early 1890s, James understood that there was a great need for a practical social science, and not more grand philosophizing about the human condition, nor a purely laboratory (and thus somewhat artificial) basic science of behavior. James' *Principles of Psychology* (1890), the first American psychology text, was similarly geared toward areas of social importance and relevance, but presented itself as also dealing with scientific "principles." Similarly, John Dewey, one of the cofounders of (philosophical) pragmatism along with James, urged psychologists in the early 20th century to investigate phenomena in learning and education, areas in which basic science was needed in order to formulate new methods of application. Like Dewey and James, many early North American social scientists were trying to achieve a balance between a scientific and a public-friendly discourse. As APA's mission statement illustrates, once psychology achieved recognition as a scientific discipline, the shift toward applied psychology, and the professionalization of psychological practice, became much more pronounced and varied.

From Pseudoscience to Social Science

Early Approaches to Applied Knowledge

A variety of applied social science practices existed long before the formal disciplines were founded. One could argue that the assessment and treatment of individuals, whether for abnormal behavior or other reasons, are as old as recorded history. The witch doctor, priest, and shaman are all practitioners of assessment and intervention on the individual and society, although the means of establishing credibility and training have evolved considerably, as have the forms of treatment. Prior to the emergence of the social sciences, there were other forms of social and psychological "measurement" that would be regarded today as pseudoscience, in that they appeared to be based on empirical observation and measurement, but they often relied on untenable assumptions or failed to demonstrate a set of testable principles. Some of these included phrenology, which claimed that bumps and indentations on the skull were indications of character and aptitudes; physiognomy, which proposed that the face and facial expressions revealed the person's character and intellect; and animal magnetism, the idea that mental and physical pathologies were a result of the body's magnetic fields being out of alignment. This latter theory proposed that magnets could be applied to the body to realign the errant fields. Franz Mesmer made this treatment famous in the late 18th century, claiming that his hands alone possessed enough animal magnetism to "cure" his patients. Mesmer would pass his hands over his patients in a dramatic fashion, telling them what they would experience, and inducing a trancelike state to affect a cure. Mesmer's work is generally regarded as the beginning of modern hypnosis, a practice that has little theoretical or scientific justification, but nevertheless has maintained its presence in some therapeutic treatment.

What can be seen from such examples is that the social sciences, and the distinctions between basic and applied social science and research, evolved from earlier practices of social assessment and treatment. These early practices were a kind of applied social science, although the assessment of the individual had not yet evolved into measurement, and the forms of treatment often reflected a belief system that was a combination of the "high" (physics) and "low" (alchemy) sciences. With the emergence of psychology, anthropology, sociology, and other social sciences, the more empirical aspects of human conduct became the focus, and experimental methods became the means by which new disciplinary identities were created. For the social sciences, these new identities were formed around (1) behavior, (2) a codified set of testing and measurement practices, and (3) a new scientific vocabulary, created by and for each discipline that articulated its own perspective and findings. In other words, the role of a specialist for social assessment and intervention did not begin with the social sciences, but rather the social sciences took over existing forms of practice and transformed them. Although the social sciences were new as academic entities, they were not new in terms of their presence as specialists, now turned measurement-oriented professionals, of social assessment and intervention.

The Rise of Social Science

Social science, then, is the application of the methods originating in the natural sciences to the individual and to society. In Western thought, until the 19th century, the individual had been seen as qualitatively different from the rest of the natural world, as divine and as having a soul, thus making scientific analysis of the mind not only inappropriate but somewhat heretical. In light of Darwin and the theory of evolution through natural selection, human beings became "naturalized," or understood as just another aspect of the natural world, no different in their origins and development than any other species. Thus, the emergence of the social sciences is partly predicated on the impact of Darwin's theory on the way humans perceived themselves. This paradigm shift was also made possible by other social and economic developments during the 19th century.

In 1795, astronomer Nevil Maskelyne and his assistant David Kinnebrook were setting ships' clocks by astronomical observation: when a particular star crossed the hairline of a telescope, the time would be set. Maskelyne noticed that Kinnebrook's measurements were usually about half a second slower than his. He reprimanded Kinnebrook for sloppiness, but that only made the discrepancy greater. As a result, Kinnebrook was fired for incompetence, although as Friedrich Bessel was to discover, it was through no fault of his own. Some 20 years later, Bessel discovered what he called "personal equations": corrections to individual systematic differences in reaction time among observers. Bessel found, in other words, that such differences were a normal part of astronomical measurements, and could be adjusted by adding to or subtracting from individual measurements. A thorough understanding of the implications of this pointed to some key changes in the way we understood scientific knowledge: (1) the observer influences the observation, (2) the need to understand how the physical world was represented through human sensation and perception, and (3) the gradual realization that knowledge about the natural world deals less with certainty and more with probability (i.e., the likelihood of a particular value being true or accurate).

The Naturalistic and Probabilistic Turns

The question of how the mind works is, of course, one of the oldest questions of civilization, and theories on this topic stretch as far back as recorded history. This age-old question took on a new meaning after observations (e.g., Bessel) had revealed that mental processes take a measurable amount of time, and that the interval for these operations differed across people. The concept of "reaction time" thus provided a way to measure the mind, to compare these measurements across a population, and then to apply these findings to the calculation of scientific observations. As human behavior became increasingly connected to technology (e.g., a telescope), the differences among the users of these technologies were becoming increasingly clear; something that had not yet been salient until this point in history. However, it was becoming quite apparent that similar types of knowledge about the individual were vital to science and society. The Industrial Revolution transformed Europe in the 19th century from an agrarian society to one of urban factories and industries. The population in Europe more than doubled, from 205 million in 1800 to 414 million in 1900. Government grew even faster, with an estimated 99,000 government officials in Great Britain in 1800 to an incredible 395,000 in 1900. Growing cities and the rise of the middle class were all responses to the Industrial Revolution. This, in turn, put enormous pressure on government to manage the exploding population and the commerce of international industry. Politicians and various social leaders turned to the social sciences as a means of gaining and maintaining control. Creating personal equations out of reaction times was now replayed on the grandest scale: the need to predict and understand the behavior of populations became of paramount importance. Moreover, the individual was no longer separate from the world, but had become interwoven with not only how society functions, but with the very possibility of knowledge about the world.

The 19th century would bring great advances in the biological sciences, and the research that would figure prominently in the origins of the social sciences would be that which addressed the discrepancy between objective and subjective reality. One of the earliest research areas in psychology was the area known as "psychophysics," which was defined as the experimental investigation of the relationship between changes in the physical environment and changes in the perception of the environment. Hermann von Helmholtz, among others, laid the foundation for such research in demonstrating that nerve impulses move at a measurable rate, and in proposing a theory of color vision (known as the Young–Helmholtz theory) that shows the perception of all color is based on three types of color receptors in the body, corresponding to the primary colors of red, green, and blue-violet. In each case, it can be seen that perception is far from just a mirror of reality, but is constructed through the physiological processing of sensation and learned inferences from our environment; physical reality is not the same as psychological reality. The case of reaction times is but one example; visual perception is another. According to Helmholtz, visual perception involves "unconscious inferences" about distance and size (e.g., the image on our retina "sees" the railroad tracks converge in the distance, but the tracks are perceived as parallel).

The problems facing scientists were thus both basic and applied: how do we perceive reality (basic) and how do we address the problems arising from human–technology interactions (applied)? These questions were both pursued, initially, as essentially the same question. However, they have become differentiated over time, and scientists with interests in discovery are drawn toward basic research, and those interested in applications work in the field of applied research. In Germany, where a number of classic studies in physiology were carried out during the 19th century, there was a clear focus on basic physiological research, with the notion of applications to a market secondary. Of course, at the time, there was not the enormous complex of industry and business that there is today, nor the multitudes of professional and scientific interests that they bring.

The Language of Science and the Scientific World View

The rise of the social sciences in the 19th century resulted not only in new fields of scientific study, but also in new social roles, jobs, and forms of social behavior (e.g., filling out a questionnaire). Perhaps more than anything else, the dawn of social science, in both its basic and applied forms, entailed a new language for understanding human conduct. For example, the notion of human "behavior," now a commonplace term, was not present before the more empirical disciplinary language of social science. The concept of behavior replaced the more general notion of "conduct," because not only is it a much more discrete and measurable unit of analysis, but also because it does not deal with the moral quality of an act (something unobservable). It was for many of the same reasons that the concept of "personality" replaced the notion of "character": personality could be broken down into "traits," or predictable predispositions of behavioral consistency, and it eschewed the thorny moral implications of "character."

This shift in language and social practice represents a complex transition from prescientific language to scientific discourse. The practices of basic and applied science and research are a product of earlier attempts to perform similar functions in society—namely, the quest for knowledge about the world and the ability to apply that knowledge to people and society. Compared to earlier approaches, the scientific method emphasizes objectivity, systematic observation, and controlled conditions, allowing the experimenter to measure accurately the effects of manipulating the independent variable (i.e., the environment). The transition to the scientific method therefore shows a concern with establishing an objective way of investigating questions about the way the world works, and, at the same time, a practical concern for the ability to control and perhaps apply these observations in everyday life. We see ample evidence of this from the early experimental scientists of the Enlightenment, such as Galileo and Newton. Both were concerned with establishing the laws of nature, but both were also interested in how these laws might work for practical use, or perhaps be brought under some form of control. The telescope, for instance, not only told us about the heavens and the moons around Jupiter, but it also enabled us to see ships coming into port much more quickly and allowed for better navigation at sea. So, in other words, science, from the beginning, had this dual purpose of providing both basic and practical knowledge. These purposes were carried over and transformed from earlier prescientific theories, and part of this transformation process involved creating specialized languages about observations. It is through examining these new forms of discourse about the world that we can more fully understand the relationship between basic and applied social science research. It is here, in the language of social science, that we discover the meaning of "science" for a particular society—how scientists frame the questions and methods of their field, the process by which questions are identified, and the context in which investigations are interpreted. We also see how the professionalization of scientific interests transformed social practices that, yet again, relate to this underlying desire to know the world and to help improve our place in it.

Consider now a specific example of the ways in which applied social science differs from basic science, looking in particular at the way knowledge is transformed as it evolves from basic theoretical issues to issues of application and social practice.

The Self in Psychology: Basic vs. Applied Research

The Self and the Dawn of Psychological Testing

Among the many theories of self in the history of psychology, a distinction can be made between theories of self, addressing the person holistically (e.g., Maslow), and theories that are more fragmentary, viewing the person in terms of specific personality traits or constructs (e.g., the individual differences approach). The general trend in "self" research, since the 1950s, has been away from the holistic view of the self and toward a multidimensional perspective, which is more concretely tied to predicting specific behaviors. During and after World War II, the psychological test emerged as an important tool for both the military and the industrial and governmental complexes of North America. With the war, there were enormous numbers of decisions to be made regarding personnel: the military needed a way to screen and select soldiers for various duties, and, in the private sector, companies and industries needed to replace workers going to war. Thus, there was a tremendous need for scientifically designed tests that could be administered to large numbers of people, to determine factors such as intelligence, aptitudes, and personality traits. With regard to the self (and the person in general), prediction and application were the keys, so psychological tests defined these concepts in more objective and behavior-oriented terms to allow for better prediction. In the history of self research, then, there was a shift from theories of a single self or ego to multiple or "possible selves," as the science of the self became increasingly applied. An important part of this shift has entailed changes in the language of self research, as the theoretical self or ego became displaced by terminology with closer connections to behavior, such as is seen in the concepts of "self-concept" ("I am good at math") and "self-esteem" ("I am better looking than most of my friends").

Following World War II, the use of paper-and-pencil tests to tap such "self-report behavior" became the primary means of collecting data about the individual. The demand for psychological research on the self increased, and because large numbers of people were usually involved, it was in the form of aggregate (or group) data that information about the self was collected and disseminated. The idea that psychological tests could render mental attitudes, beliefs, and abilities in objective terms was found to be incredibly useful, and psychological research entered into the era of the questionnaire.

A central theme in our understanding of basic and applied social science research has been language and the purposes for which research is carried out; here we see that the shift toward applied research involves changes not only in how the concept is used, but in how it is defined and understood at a basic level. This difference is far from simply semantics, but represents a conceptual evolution in the meanings of scientific constructs. Similar changes were made with other personality measures during the 1940s and 1950s. For example, the early predecessors of contemporary personality testing were the projective tests, such as the Thematic Apperception Test and the Rorschach Inkblot Test. These tests purport to tap into the preconscious and unconscious forces at work within the person. Earlier examples of this same general idea resided in physiognomy, or the analysis of handwriting or other forms of personal expression. These early personality tests were based on the same basic idea: that we project parts of who we are into verbal and physical expressions, and these can be interpreted to give us insight about hidden parts of our personality. However, as psychology began to strive for more measurable and quantifiable means of measuring the person, these subjective methods fell out of favor (but by no means completely), and were replaced by more quantitative approaches.

The Self in Transition

Another clear example of the transition the self underwent as it became part of the world of applied research and testing involves the early self-concept research of Victor Raimy. For his doctoral dissertation in 1943, Raimy devised a "checklist" for describing the self-concept. As a therapist, Raimy conceived of this measure for a clinical context, and this is actually one of the early attempts to do so. To tap the self-concept, the person was asked to rate a list of self-referential statements. These were then classified by judges into one of three categories: approval of self, disapproval of self, or ambivalence toward self.

Raimy's study was groundbreaking in that it represents one of the first modern self measures in psychology. Although it drew on phenomenological theory as a conceptual basis for the self, it is also significant that it operationalized the "self-concept" into self-referential statements (i.e., behavior). This rendering of a holistic, experiential notion of self into an empirical methodological context helped bring about, and could be seen as a signal of, the rise of self-concept testing. Further efforts to understand the self along these lines soon followed with the development of the Q-sort by William Stephenson in 1953, which was quickly picked up and elaborated by Rogers and Dymond in 1954. Almost immediately afterward, there was a flash flood of self-rating methods in the early and mid-1950s, most using an adjective checklist or self-rating scale. Clearly, there was a vast and diverse audience for such a technology in schools, industry, companies, and government; the psychology questionnaire had found its place in psychology and society.

What is rather remarkable, and also quite telling about the relationship between basic and applied social science research, is that the first step toward measuring the self as a set of quantifiable component parts was made by the clinicians themselves, who at the time generally maintained a holistic and experiential understanding of the self. However, it was clear to clinicians and other mental health professionals that knowledge about the person, outside of a therapeutic context, was crucial and much needed. So, even though a fragmented, behaviorally oriented view of the self was contrary to the theoretical models they held, the decision to address applied questions substantially changed the theory of the self. In other words, issues involving the prediction of behavior are paramount in applied research, and the theory of self that emerged from these concerns represented a radical departure from the more basic question of "what is the self?" Furthermore, as the trend toward psychological testing and other applied self research grew, the self was no longer just interpreted in a clinical context by therapists who viewed the person as an organized whole. Instead, these measures became tools for more widespread consumption and application, whereby they would be increasingly used by researchers with more specific and practical questions and problems. This process proved truly transformative: self research began to be carried out within the pragmatic perspective of North American culture, and the science of the self now turned on the applied axis of psychological testing. This transformative process was thus twofold: the redefinition of self into the more behavior-focused concepts of self-concept and self-esteem, and the change in interpretative contexts from a more theoretical and clinical focus to an applied and experimental one.

Conclusion—The Future of Basic and Applied Social Science Research

The distinction between basic and applied social science is based on an evolving relationship between different forms of scientific and social practice. Basic social science, on the one hand, seeks to discover the fundamental principles of human behavior, whereas applied social science attempts to create and improve technologies that assist in the prediction, assessment, and description of behavior as it exists in society. There are numerous clashes between these perspectives, and these are also found in the natural sciences as well. Many, and perhaps most, of these conflicts have an economic basis: scientific projects with commercial value and practical utility receive a great deal more funding, and remain much more likely to be funded, than do projects that lack a commercial payoff. Today, major funding comes from public and private sources such as government agencies, universities, corporations, and industries. As a result, there is a substantial and rather lopsided monetary emphasis on applied social science research. Researchers who are interested in basic science questions are often faced with difficulties in securing funding, and may have to prove that their research has some perhaps indirect application or other economic potential. Basic social science also has as its task the rather considerable job of illustrating what the basic principles of human behavior are; as of yet, no tangible "laws of behavior" have emerged. However, the recent ascendancy of neuroscience may rejuvenate the languishing social scientist with aspirations of creating a new basic science of human behavior.

See Also the Following Articles

Case Study • Psychological Testing, Overview

Further Reading

Benjamin, L. T., and Baker, D. B. (2004). *From Séance to Science: A History of the Profession of Psychology in America.* Thomson Wadsworth, Belmont, California.

Camic, C., and Xie, Y. (1994). The statistical turn in American social science: Columbia University, 1890 to 1915. *Am. Sociol. Rev.* **59,** 773–805.

Danziger, K. (1987). Statistical method and the historical development of research practice in American psychology. In *The Probabilistic Revolution, Vol. 2: Ideas in the Sciences* (L. Kruger, G. Gigerenzer, and M. Morgan, eds.). MIT Press, Cambridge.

Danziger, K. (1990). *Constructing the Subject: Historical Origins of Psychological Research.* Cambridge University Press, Cambridge.

Easthope, G. (1974). *A History of Social Research Methods.* Longman, London.

Gigerenzer, G., Swijtink, Z., Porter, T., Daston, L., Beatty, J., and Kruger, L. (1989). *The Empire of Chance: How Probability Changed Science and Everyday Life.* Cambridge University Press, Cambridge.

Leahey, T. H. (2004). *A History of Psychology: Main Currents in Psychological Thought.* Pearson Prentice Hall, Upper Saddle River, New Jersey.

Stigler, S. (1986). *The History of Statistics.* Harvard University Press, Cambridge, Massachusetts.

Wright, B. D. (1997). A history of social science measurement. *Educat. Measure. Issues Pract.* **Winter,** 33–52.

Bayes, Thomas

Andrew I. Dale
University of KwaZulu-Natal, Durban, South Africa

Glossary

Act of Uniformity An act, passed by the anti-Puritan parliament after the Restoration, decreeing that all ministers who were not episcopally ordained or who refused to conform were to be deprived of their livings.

Bayes's Theorem A formula that allows the determination of the posterior probabilities $P[C_i \mid E]$ of the (possible) causes C_i, given the occurrence of an event E, in terms of the prior probabilities $P[C_i]$ (determined anterior to the conducting of the current investigation) and the likelihoods $P[E \mid C_i]$ of the event, given the causes C_i.

Bayesian statistics That branch of modern statistics in which Bayes' Theorem plays a fundamental role in the incorporation of past experience into the making of decisions, statistical analyses, and predictions.

fluxionary calculus Newton's development of the calculus, concerned with problems of tangency and quadrature.

prime and ultimate ratios Introduced by Newton as a rigorous justification of the methods of his fluxionary calculus, these ratios, analogous to the modern right- and left-hand limits, are concerned with the ratios of magnitudes as generated by motion.

Thomas Bayes, by profession a Presbyterian minister, presented a result in a posthumously published essay on "chances"; this work has come to play an important role in modern statistical theory and practice.

Genealogy

The family of which Thomas Bayes was a member can be traced back to the early 17th century. The city of Sheffield, in Yorkshire, England, has long been known for the manufacture of steel, iron, and brassware, and Thomas's forebears were of considerable importance in the Company of Cutlers of Hallamshire; for instance, one Richard Bayes was Master of the Company in 1643, as was his son Joshua in 1679. But the Bayes family was known not only in business circles. The 17th and 18th centuries were times during which Nonconformity and Dissent became both of importance and of concern to the Established Church, and Richard's second son, Samuel, having studied at Trinity College, Cambridge, was among those ejected in 1662 from his living because of his refusal to accept in full the doctrines of the Established Church and to take the oaths demanded of her clergy. Samuel moved to the village of Grendon St. Mary, near Wellingborough in the county of Northamptonshire, where he probably remained for some years before moving to Sankey in Lancashire.

Samuel's younger brother, Joshua, rose in the ranks of the Sheffield cutlery industry. He married Sarah Pearson on 28 May 1667, seven children issuing from this union. Ruth, Joshua and Sarah's eldest daughter, married Elias Wordsworth (who became a Town Burgess in Joshua's place on the latter's death in 1703); another daughter, Elizabeth, married John de la Rose, minister of the Nether Chapel in Sheffield. Joshua and Sarah's eldest son, Joshua, baptized on 10 February 1670 (old style), married Anne Carpenter.

The younger Joshua entered Richard Frankland's Academy at Rathmell, in Yorkshire, in 1686. Frankland, a dissenting minister, having been ejected from his living, had started the first Nonconformist academy in that town in 1669. The various laws and regulations aimed at oppressing the Nonconformists resulted in the academy having to move several times, before it ended up once again at Rathmell. Although the training provided by such dissenting academies was not restricted to those who felt they had a vocation, Joshua must have attended this academy with at least some interest in making the

Nonconformist ministry his profession, for, in 1694, he was ordained with six other candidates for the ministry. This ordination (lasting from before 10 o'clock in the morning to past 6 o'clock in the evening) was celebrated in London at the meetinghouse of Dr. Samuel Annesley and was important in being the first public ceremony of that nature held in that city after the passing of the Act of Uniformity.

Soon after his ordination, Joshua must have moved to Box Lane, Bovingdon, Hertfordshire. His signature as "clerk" is found on the trust deed by which the Bovingdon Nonconformist Chapel was entrusted by the proprietors to 12 trustees in 1697, and in 1702 he certified that the chapel was used for worship. Suitable records of that time are few and often in conflict. However, the information derived from the trust deed is probably reliable, and it may be concluded that Joshua and Anne's eldest child, Thomas, was born in Bovingdon, Hertfordshire. In all, Joshua and Ann had seven children, the others being Mary, John, Anne, Samuel, Rebecca, and Nathaniel.

In 1707, Joshua moved to London and took up a position as assistant to John Sheffield at St. Thomas's, Southwark. During this time, Joshua also became assistant to Christopher Taylor at the Presbyterian Chapel in Leather Lane, moving into a full-time position there on Taylor's death. On 24 April 1746, Joshua died, after a ministry in which he earned the respect and admiration of the London Nonconformists. He was interred in the family vault in Bunhill Fields, near Moorgate, this vault later being the repository of the remains of several of his children.

Youth and Education

Though it may thus be relatively confidently claimed that Thomas Bayes was born in Hertfordshire, the year of his birth is uncertain. It is usually derived by the subtraction of his age at death from the year of his death (both these figures being recorded on the family vault), and it would appear that he was born either in 1701 or 1702 [the doubt arises from whether dates are given in old style (o.s.) or new style]. What is clear, however, is that Thomas would have received his early education in London, though once again there is no certainty as to which school or academy he might have attended.

The British Library contains in its manuscript collection copies of letters written both from and to John Ward. One of these letters, written in 1720, is directed to Thomas, and the contents suggest that the latter had been a pupil of Ward's. Further opinion on Thomas's schooling is perhaps received from the fact that one of his sponsors for election to the Royal Society in 1742 was John Eames, who is known to have kept a school in London. There is no certainty about any of this, however, and it is possible only to attach a nonzero probability to the suggestion that Thomas had some educational connection with Eames and Ward. However, it is certain that Thomas studied later at Edinburgh University—something that makes perfect sense when it is remembered that the universities in England were closed to Nonconformists. Thomas's name is recorded in various manuscripts, still fortunately extant, showing that he was admitted to the college in 1720 on the recommendation of "Mr Bayes" (presumably his father).

Though Thomas appears to have studied both logic and theology at Edinburgh, there is no evidence of any mathematical studies; that he had perhaps some acquaintance, albeit slight, with the Scottish mathematician James Gregory is shown by the fact that the latter signed the certificate giving Thomas access to the university library in 1719 (o.s.). On completion of his theological studies, Thomas was licensed as a preacher (though not ordained), and he presumably then returned to England.

Thomas Bayes and Tunbridge Wells

Thomas's whereabouts for the years immediately following the completion of his studies in Edinburgh are uncertain. It is probable that he spent a few years in London, for his name appears in a *List of Approved Ministers of the Presbyterian Denomination* drawn up by John Evans in 1727, and he was also appointed to the Leather Lane Chapel in 1728, presumably as assistant to his father. In the early 1730s, though, we find Thomas installed as minister of the (English) Presbyterian Chapel in Tunbridge Wells, Kent. It is uncertain as to when he took up this position: the general opinion is that it was in 1730 on the resignation of John Archer, who died in 1733, but it has been suggested by Bailey and Bailey that Thomas left Tunbridge Wells in 1728 and returned in 1731. It is certainly true that the Presbyterian Chapel in Tunbridge Wells frequently enjoyed the services of visiting clergy, and Thomas could well have been of this number until his permanent appointment.

Although Presbyterianism had been supported, at first more or less covertly, in Tunbridge Wells from the late years of the 17th century, the New Chapel, with Archer as its minister, was not opened until 1720. The chapel was situated on Mount Sion, one of the hills on and around which Tunbridge Wells nestles. The salubrious air and elevation made the site most enviable, and the congregation seems to have prospered for a number of years. However, it slowly began to decline, and indeed decay set in among the Nonconformist persuasions in Tunbridge Wells in general. The Presbyterian Chapel was closed in 1814, and although the building became more and more dilapidated, it was fortunately saved from demolition and remains today as a simple but elegant secular memorial.

In the 18th century, Tunbridge Wells was regarded as one of the prime resorts for those wishing to "take the waters." The chalybeate springs were supposedly possessed of medicinal and curative powers—even the ability to cure barrenness—and royalty visited there on occasions. The Presbyterian Meetinghouse and its incumbent were as important to the Nonconformists who lived and visited there as were the Established Church's Chapel and its clergy to the orthodox; the more frivolous aspects of life were catered for by the numerous balls, card evenings, etc. organized by the Master of Ceremonies (at one time the social dandy, Richard "Beau" Nash). Visitors included members of the nobility, the clergy, and the scientific and literary community, as well, no doubt, as those of lesser ranks. Some of these visitors were certainly acquainted with Bayes. William Whiston, for instance, records that he breakfasted with Thomas on St. Bartholomew's Day in 1746, and it is also recorded (though perhaps the accuracy of the story may be doubted) that distinguished visitors from the East visited Tunbridge Wells and were introduced to Bayes, who provided them with "much useful and valuable information."

In 1752, Bayes retired. Although no longer active in the ministry, he remained in Tunbridge Wells until his death some 9 years later, his remains being taken to Founders' Hall, London, before interment in the family vault.

Bayes's Works

Tract on Divine Benevolence

In 1731, an anonymously published tract appeared. Entitled *Divine Benevolence, or, an attempt to prove that the principal end of the divine providence and government is the happiness of his creatures*, this tract, now known to be by Thomas Bayes, was a rebuttal to an earlier one by John Balguy entitled *Divine Rectitude*, and was in turn followed by Henry Grove's *Wisdom, the first Spring of Action in the Deity*. All three authors were trying in these works to find a single principle to which God's moral principles could be ascribed. Whereas Balguy maintained that God's moral attributes, such as truth, justice, and mercy, were modifications of His rectitude, Bayes found the fundamental principle to be benevolence, that is, God's "kind affection towards his creatures," leading to the conferring on the universe of "the greatest happiness of which it is capable." Bayes's argument is closely reasoned and wide ranging (the tract is some 75 pages long), critical of Balguy in some places and in agreement with him in others, but there is perhaps room for doubt as to whether it is entirely convincing.

Tract on Fluxions

Bayes's second printed work, *An Introduction to the Doctrine of Fluxions*, was also published anonymously. Its attribution to Bayes is made on the authority of the 19th-century mathematician and bibliophile Augustus de Morgan, who is most reliable in such matters. Writing in response to Bishop George Berkeley's *The Analyst*, Bayes was concerned more with the logical theory of Isaac Newton's prime and ultimate ratios than with either moments or the methods of the fluxionary calculus. Though he in general approved of the bishop's attention to fluxionary matters, Bayes could not agree with the incorporation of religious aspects, and indeed he declared in his introduction to the tract that he would restrict his attention to an "endeavour to shew that the method of Fluxions is founded upon clear and substantial principles." To this end, he set down postulates, definitions, axioms, propositions, and corollaries. The propositions are carefully proved (though the proofs may sometimes seem slightly deficient), and Bayes's defense of Newton against Berkeley seems unobjectionable. The paper shows a logical mind with concern for mathematical rigor, and the arguments adduced, without the use of limit theory and nonstandard analysis, are perhaps as sound as was possible at that time.

A Semiconvergent Series

Within a few years of Bayes's death, three posthumous papers under his name and communicated to the Royal Society by Richard Price appeared in the *Philosophical Transactions*. The first of these was little more than a note on some aspects of series, the most important being concerned with the well-known Stirling-de Moivre expansion of the series for $\log z!$ as

$$(1/2)\log(2\pi) + [z + (1/2)]\log z - [z - (1/12z) + (1/360z^3) - (1/1260z^5) + \cdots].$$

Bayes showed that the series actually failed to converge in general, a fact that he was apparently the first to note (though Leonhard Euler, some 6 years before the death of Bayes, had noted the failure for the special case $z = 1$). Comments are also found here on the divergence of similar series for $\log(2z-1)!!$ [with $n!! = n(n-2)!!$ and $n!! = 1$ for $n = 0$ or 1] and $\sum_n (k/n^r)$.

Papers on Chance

The second posthumously published paper by Bayes is the important *An Essay towards Solving a Problem in the Doctrine of Chances*. Here Bayes provided the seeds of the modern ideas of inverse, prior, and posterior probabilities, and indeed the whole theory of Bayesian statistics has its roots in this paper. The problem with which Bayes concerned himself was as follows:

> *Given the number of times in which an unknown event has happened and failed: required the chance that the probability of its happening in a single trial lies somewhere between any two degrees of probability that can be named.*

The *Essay* is set out in a way that would be quite acceptable to a modern mathematician. The given question is answered, though its solution requires the acceptance of an assumption that has generated a considerable amount of controversy since its publication—that is, in essence and perhaps somewhat crudely, the assumption of a uniform distribution as a prior when one is in a state of ignorance.

Three rules are presented for the obtaining of bounds to the exact probability required (Bayes's solution is effectively given as an infinite series), and proofs of these rules were given in a supplement to the *Essay* in a subsequent issue of the *Philosophical Transactions*, with improvements, obtained by Price, of Bayes's bounds. Price also added an appendix to the *Essay*, in which he explored the use of Bayes' results in a prospective sense. He developed a Rule of Succession (e.g., if an event is known to have occurred m times in n trials, what is the probability that it will occur on the next trial?), and discussed the place of Bayes's results in induction.

The importance of these posthumous papers on probability cannot be denied, and though it is not expedient to speculate here on the reason for Bayes not having published his results, it might be noted that this is sometimes assumed to flow from his suggested modesty.

Miscellaneous Scientific Work

Although Bayes is known mainly for his work on chances, it is clear that he enjoyed no mean reputation among the mathematical community of his time. Despite the slightness of his published work, he was elected a Fellow of the Royal Society in 1742, his proposers being men of considerable scientific weight, and including people such as Martin Folkes, John Eames, and Philip, Earl Stanhope.

David Bellhouse has recently discovered a number of manuscript papers by Bayes, in the Stanhope of Chevening papers in the Kent County archives in Maidstone, England. From certain letters in the same collection, Bellhouse has deduced that Bayes was in a sense a "referee" for mathematical papers, being consulted by Stanhope on mathematical matters. There remains to this day a notebook in Bayes's hand, now in the possession of the Equitable Life Assurance Society in London. This is a curious collection clearly kept over a number of years, with mathematical results appearing cheek by jowl with, among others, excerpta on a miracle (the cure, by the touching of a relic to the affected area, of a lachrymal fistula suffered by Blaise Pascal's niece) and from John Greaves's writings on the Great Pyramid of Cheops.

The Royal Society in London has in its possession a manuscript by Bayes on a book on electricity by Benjamin Hoadly and Benjamin Wilson. Also to be found there is a letter from Bayes to John Canton commenting on Thomas Simpson's recommendation that the error in astronomical observations could be reduced by the reliance on several measurements rather than just one. Bayes's point was that this would not do if the measuring instrument were inaccurate—and he was also unhappy with the suggestion that errors in excess, as in defect, should be taken as equiprobable.

Death and Burial

Bunhill Fields Burial Ground, the great Nonconformist cemetery, was opened in the 1660s. By 1852, more than 120,000 burials had taken place there, and the ground was then closed. It was, however, preserved as a public space, and despite its having been considerably reduced in size over the years, the visitor today can take comfort in knowing that he will find, in addition to the Bayes family vault, memorials to the Nonconformists John Bunyan, Daniel Defoe, John Eames, and Richard Price, among others. The Bayes vault has been restored a number of times over the years. Some of the original inscriptions have disappeared altogether, whereas others, presumably as a result of such restoration, have been changed. Not all these changes, however, have been for the worse: for instance, in place of the original "The Rev. Thomas Bayes, son of the said Joshua, died April 7th, 1761, aged 59 years," the vault now carries the information that it was restored "In recognition of Thomas Bayes's important work in probability . . . in 1969 with contributions received from statisticians throughout the world."

As might be expected, in view of his family's commercial success, Joshua Bayes left his family well provided for. Thomas, as the eldest child, perhaps inherited the most, and his will in turn, though showing him to be not of the wealth of his father, nevertheless proved him to have been of considerable means. His siblings were the main inheritors, though some remembrance was taken of one Sarah Jeffrey, living at the corner of Jourdans Lane in Tunbridge Wells. Roger Farthing, a modern historian of that city, has made the reasonable suggestion that Bayes, as a bachelor, might well have boarded at that address (where it is known that there was a lodging house), and might well have wished to benefit the daughter of the house in that way.

The Bayes vault had been built in 1733 (o.s.). As they in turn died, the members of the family were buried there, such burials often being of the simplest kind. The deceased having stipulated in their wills that their interment be as frugal as possible, there would have been no "singing boys" and no funeral sermon would have been preached. Thomas, too, made such a request in his will, a reflection of the modest way in which he had probably lived his life.

See Also the Following Article

Bayesian Statistics

Further Reading

Bailey, L., and Bailey, B. (1970). *History of Non-conformity in Tunbridge Wells.* Typescript copy in Tunbridge Wells Library, Kent, United Kingdom.

Bellhouse, D. R. (2002). On some recently discovered manuscripts of Thomas Bayes. *Histor. Mathemat.* **29,** 383–394.

Dale, A. I. (1999). *A History of Inverse Probability from Thomas Bayes to Karl Pearson,* 2nd Ed. Springer-Verlag, New York.

Dale, I. A. (2003). *Most Honourable Remembrance: the Life and Work of Thomas Bayes.* Springer-Verlag, New York.

Bayesian Statistics

Scott M. Lynch
Princeton University, Princeton, New Jersey, USA

Glossary

conditional probability density function A density for a random variable that is the ratio of a joint density for two random variables to the marginal density for one. For example, $f(A \mid B) = f(A, B)/f(B)$. Often simply called conditional density.

joint probability density function A probability density function that assigns probabilities to a set of random variables (see probability density function).

marginal probability density function A density for a random variable in which all other random variables have been integrated out. For example, $f(A) = \int \dots \iint f(A, B, C, \dots) dB\, dC \dots$. Often called a marginal density or marginal pdf.

normalizing constant A constant that ensures that a probability density function is proper, that is, that it integrates to 1.

probability density function (pdf) A function that assigns probabilities to random variables in a continuous parameter space. A function that assigns probabilities on a discrete parameter space is called a probability mass function, but many use pdf for both types of spaces. In both cases, the function must integrate/sum to unity to be a proper density. The pdf is often referred to as simply a density, and the term is also synonymous with distribution.

sampling density The joint probability density for a set of observations. A normalizing constant is required to make it proper (i.e., a true density). Expressing an unnormalized sampling density as a function of the parameters rather than the data yields a likelihood function.

Bayesian statistics is an approach to statistics that considers probability as the key language for representing uncertainty, including uncertainty about parameters for which inference is to be made. The Bayesian approach to statistics differs fundamentally from the classical approach, although results obtained via Bayesian and classical approaches are often numerically similar, differing only in interpretation.

Bayes's Theorem

In 1763, Reverend Thomas Bayes introduced a theorem for calculating conditional probabilities that ultimately provides a recipe for updating prior uncertainty about parameters of distributions using observed data. Bayes's theorem is simply a double application of the well-known conditional probability rule, and the mathematical basis for the theorem is thus beyond dispute. The theorem states:

$$p(B \mid A) = \frac{p(A \mid B)p(B)}{p(A)} \tag{1}$$

Proof of Bayes's Theorem and Its Extension

Bayes's Theorem is easily proven by observing that:

$$p(A \mid B) = \frac{p(A, B)}{p(B)} \tag{2}$$

Rearranging this yields:

$$p(A \mid B)p(B) = P(A, B) \tag{3}$$

Similarly,

$$p(B \mid A) = \frac{p(B, A)}{p(A)} \tag{4}$$

and

$$p(B \mid A)p(A) = P(B, A) \tag{5}$$

Given that $p(A, B)$ is equivalent to $p(B, A)$, the left-hand sides of Eqs. (3) and (5) can be set equal, and we obtain:

$$p(B|A)p(A) = P(A|B)p(B) \tag{6}$$

Dividing both sides by $p(A)$ yields Bayes's theorem. In this representation the theorem is unquestionable. However, Bayesian statisticians replace B with "parameter" or "hypothesis" and A with "data" so that the theorem appears as:

$$p(\text{parameter} \mid \text{data}) = \frac{p(\text{data} \mid \text{parameter})p(\text{parameter})}{p(\text{data})} \tag{7}$$

The denominator of the right-hand side of this equation is the marginal probability of the data (often called a normalizing constant), which is an average of the probability of the data under all possible parameter values (θ). In a continuous parameter space (S):

$$p(\text{data}) = \int_{\theta \in S} p(\text{data} \mid \theta)p(\theta)\,d\theta \tag{8}$$

In a discrete parameter space, the marginal probability of the data is:

$$p(\text{data}) = \sum_{\theta \in S} p(\text{data} \mid \theta)p(\theta) \tag{9}$$

Since the denominator typically does not provide us with any information about the parameter, Bayes's theorem is often reduced to:

$$p(\text{parameter} \mid \text{data}) \propto p(\text{data} \mid \text{parameter})p(\text{parameter}) \tag{10}$$

In Bayesian language, this expression says that the posterior probability for a parameter is proportional to the likelihood function for the data (or the sampling density for the data) multiplied by the prior probability for the parameter. The posterior is so called because it is our estimate of the probability for the parameter after having observed additional data; the prior is so called because it represents our belief about the probability for the parameter before observing data.

To provide an example of the applicability of Bayes's theorem, I demonstrate the theorem on data about prostate cancer. Suppose a 30-year-old male tests positive on the standard test for prostate cancer. Suppose also that the test has a 90% accuracy rate for people in that age group, meaning that it will give a positive test result to positive cases 90% of the time. Suppose, however, the test also produces false positive results 10% of the time; that is, among noncases 10% will receive a positive test. Obviously, the question of interest is whether, given the positive test result, the individual in fact has prostate cancer, which can be expressed as $p(\text{p.c.} \mid \text{test+})$. However, we know $p(\text{test+} \mid \text{p.c.})$, and we can obtain prostate cancer incidence rates for age 30, $p(\text{p.c.})$ (here, I use an approximate rate for people under 45). We can substitute the known information into Bayes's formula:

$$p(\text{p.c.} \mid \text{test+}) = \frac{p(\text{test+} \mid \text{p.c.})p(\text{p.c.})}{p(\text{test+} \mid \text{p.c.})p(\text{p.c.}) + p(\text{test+} \mid \text{no p.c.})p(\text{no p.c.})} \tag{11}$$

In this case, we have the following:

$$p(\text{p.c.} \mid \text{test+}) = \frac{(0.90)(0.00001)}{(0.90)(0.00001) + (0.10)(0.99999)}$$

Simplifying reveals that the actual (posterior) probability of having cancer at age 30, given a positive test, is 0.0001. Certainly our posterior probability for having cancer is greater than our prior probability, but this posterior probability is still quite small, revealing the shortcoming of a test with a modest false positive rate applied to a low-risk population.

Philosophical Foundation of Bayesian Statistics

Many researchers use Bayes's theorem for probability problems, such as the one about prostate cancer, in which the parameter values are known quantities. However, historically non-Bayesians have frowned on the use of Bayes's formula when it involves parameters whose true values are unknown. This disdain for the formula arises from the competition between two key philosophical understandings of probability. One understanding of probability defines probability in terms of the relative frequency of an event in a long series of trials. For example, the "frequentist" justification for believing that the probability of obtaining heads on a single coin flip is 0.5 is that in a long series of trials, we expect to see heads approximately 50% of the time.

The frequentist perspective grounds the classical approach to understanding probability. For virtually any statistical problem, a classical statistician will develop a likelihood function, which represents the relative frequency of a particular set of data under a particular parameter. For example, suppose a classical statistician is interested in estimating a population mean from a sample of n independently and identically distributed (i.i.d.) observations. If the statistician supposes that the data arises from a normal distribution with mean μ and variance σ^2, then the likelihood function (or sampling density) for n observations will be:

$$p(Y \mid \mu, \sigma) \propto L(\mu, \sigma \mid Y) = \prod_{i=1}^{n} \frac{1}{\sigma\sqrt{2\pi}} \exp\left\{-\frac{(y_i - \mu)^2}{2\sigma^2}\right\} \tag{12}$$

Notice that this equation presents us with the relative frequency of the data *given* a particular set of values for μ and σ. The classical statistician, interested in μ and σ, uses the notation $L(\mu, \sigma \mid Y)$ to denote that we are interested in determining the values of μ and σ that make the data *most likely* to have occurred. The classical statistician uses this likelihood notation (L) to clarify that, from his or her perspective, the data are still considered random and the parameter is assumed to be fixed. From a classical standpoint, the only random quantities in the equation are the data themselves. The parameter is fixed but unknown, and inference regarding the parameter proceeds under the assumption that $\hat{\mu}$, the estimate for μ, is a random quantity that varies if repeated samples are taken from the original probability density thought to generate the data. Classical confidence intervals around $\hat{\mu}$ are interpreted in this light, leading to expressions such as "95% of all samples drawn from this distribution would contain μ in the confidence interval around $\hat{\mu}$."

A Bayesian approach to this problem, on the other hand, begins by treating the parameters of interest as random quantities. From a Bayesian perspective, the parameter may well be a fixed quantity, but our uncertainty about the parameter's true values allows us to use the language of probability to express this uncertainty. A Bayesian approach requires us to specify a prior for the parameter, that is, a distribution representing our belief regarding the true values of the parameters (either based on prior research or prior ignorance). A Bayesian then specifies the model as:

$$p(\mu, \sigma \mid Y) \propto p(Y \mid \mu, \sigma) \times p(\mu, \sigma) \qquad (13)$$

The first expression on the right-hand side of the equation is identical to the likelihood function shown before, although the Bayesian uses the sampling density notation rather than the likelihood notation. The second term is the joint prior distribution assigned to represent our prior uncertainty about the parameter, and the left-hand side of the equation is our posterior probability distribution for the parameter after having observed the data. From this equation, it should be apparent that the posterior probability is our prior distribution updated with the new data. This posterior distribution can then be used as the prior distribution for a subsequent analysis.

Critique of Bayesian Paradigm and Responses

The classical critique of the Bayesian approach consists of two arguments: (1) treating the parameter as a random quantity is inappropriate and (2) the use of a prior distribution injects too much subjectivity into the modeling process. The first argument against the Bayesian approach is a philosophical critique with no correct answer. The classical approach is grounded in the philosophy that parameters are fixed entities, and thus attaching probability distributions to them, essentially giving them the same status as random variables, is simply wrong. [It is easy to see how the Bayesian approach gives parameters and random variables the same status. If Eq. 7 is not normalized by dividing by $p(y)$, then the left-hand side is equivalent to the joint density for both the parameters and the data: p(parameters, data).] The Bayesian response to this argument is multifaceted. Bayesians argue that probability is the natural language for representing uncertainty and, given that we do not know the true value of parameters, it is perfectly appropriate to make probabilistic statements about them. Bayesians also argue that this subjective view of probability resonates better with lay understandings of probability and thus provides for a better lay understanding of scientific analyses. Bayesians also argue (pragmatically) that the Bayesian approach works in many settings in which the classical approach does not or is philosophically unsatisfactory. For example, it is difficult to apply a frequentist approach to statements about whether a particular candidate who has never run for office will win or whether there will be a nuclear war this year, given that it is virtually impossible to conceive of these events as being part of a long series of trials. Yet laypeople always discuss these sorts of events using the language of probability. Finally, the Bayesian argues that many researchers misinterpret classical confidence intervals anyway, giving them a Bayesian interpretation, which is inappropriate under the classical paradigm.

The second argument against the Bayesian approach may seem more compelling because it implies that two researchers using the same data but different priors could draw different conclusions, something that should not occur in an objective science. However, the Bayesian has numerous responses to this criticism. First, a Bayesian points out that the entire process of statistical modeling and making inferences about parameters contains numerous subjective decisions regardless of which approach is used. We must first establish a model, which is ultimately a subjective decision. One researcher, for example, when faced with an ordinal outcome variable may specify a normal linear model, whereas another may specify a generalized linear model (GLM). Two researchers using a GLM may specify different types of GLMs—for example, an ordered logit or an ordered probit. Beyond establishing a model, researchers use subjective criteria to make inferences. The classical p value is the perfect example: the decision to declare a result statistically significant based on a p value is purely subjective. Why should $p < 0.05$ be the criterion? Is a result really less significant if $p = 0.0501$ than if $p = 0.0499$, especially if the sample sizes vary across the data sets used to obtain these p values? Finally, a Bayesian may argue that, because statistical significance and substantive significance are not equivalent, subjective criteria must ultimately be brought to bear on interpreting results in any analysis. The danger of supposing that the classical approach is objective is that we are misled into ignoring the subjective nature of the entire enterprise of statistical analysis.

As a second response to the subjectivity criticism, Bayesians argue that prior distributions can be noninformative (often called vague or diffuse priors). For example, in the normal distribution example previously discussed, we can establish independent uniform prior distributions for μ and σ over a broad enough interval (in some cases, the entire real line) that no particular value for the parameters is favored *a priori*:

$$p(\mu, \sigma) = p(\mu)p(\sigma) \propto c \times d \propto 1$$

with c and d each equal to $1/(U_{\theta_i} - L_{\theta_i})$, where L_{θ_i} and U_{θ_i} are the lower and upper bounds of the parameter space in which μ and σ (θ_1 and θ_2, respectively) can possibly lie. The use of this type of prior yields a posterior density that is equivalent to the likelihood function, and thus the results obtained under a Bayesian analysis are often equivalent to those obtained using a classical approach. For example, given that the maximum likelihood estimate (MLE), the standard estimate used by classical statisticians, is nothing more than the parameter value at the mode of the likelihood function, the mode of the posterior distribution (the maximum *a posteriori* estimate) under uniform priors is exactly equal to the MLE.

A third response is that prior distributions are often asymptotically irrelevant. The prior enters into a model only once, whereas the likelihood portion of the model contains n terms. With enough data, the prior may have little influence on the model results.

A fourth response is that priors can be made to be quite conservative in order to provide for conservative tests of hypotheses. In other words, we can establish a prior that assigns high probability to particular parameter values and see if the data are strong enough to overturn this prior expectation. Similarly, we can conduct models with different priors to determine the sensitivity of an analysis to a particular prior.

Fifth, the Bayesian approach allows for the coherent progression of science. The classical approach to hypothesis testing ultimately involves testing the same hypothesis over and over (e.g., that a particular parameter equals 0) without making any progress toward determining the true value of a parameter. The Bayesian approach readily allows us to incorporate the findings of previous studies into the current one. This approach may thus prevent us from publishing counterintuitive findings when we obtain a data set that produces such results (something that theoretically should occur on occasion).

Finally, as alluded to in some of the previous responses, a Bayesian argues that models should always be tested for sensitivity and for their fit to the data. When we assume our models are objectively based, we may be more inclined to ignore this aspect of the modeling process. Ultimately, the best test of a model's worth is how well it actually fits the data at hand—but how many classical analyses do not investigate this issue because the modeling process is assumed to be objective?

Bayesian Estimation

For decades, the two arguments against Bayesian statistics, coupled with the computational intensity required to conduct a Bayesian analysis, made Bayesian analyses of marginal use in social science. However, the recent explosion in computing capabilities, coupled with the growth in hierarchical modeling (for which the Bayesian approach is very well suited) has led to an explosion in the use of Bayesian techniques. In this section, I discuss the estimation of Bayesian models, primarily focusing on the contemporary approaches that have made Bayesian analyses more popular in the social sciences over the last decade.

Specifying a Model with a Prior Distribution

Whereas classical approaches to modeling often allow the development of canned statistical routines for particular models (e.g., multiple regression and logit models), the use of a prior distribution for parameters in a Bayesian analysis makes each modeling exercise unique. Often Bayesians use conjugate priors—priors that yield posterior distributions that have the same distributional form as the prior distribution. For example, in modeling a set of J Bernoulli outcomes, an appropriate sampling density would be a binomial density with parameters $n = 1$ and p, so that the likelihood function is a product of binomial densities:

$$p(Y \mid n = 1, p) \propto \prod_{i=1}^{J} \binom{1}{y_i} p^{y_i}(1-p)^{1-y_i} \tag{14}$$

Simplifying this expression yields:

$$p(Y \mid n = 1, p) \propto p^{\sum_{i=1}^{J} y_i}(1-p)^{J-\sum_{i=1}^{J} y_i} \tag{15}$$

A conjugate prior density for this sampling density is a beta density with parameters α and β:

$$p(p) \propto p^{\alpha-1}(1-p)^{\beta-1} \tag{16}$$

This density has a mean of $\alpha/(\alpha+\beta)$, a variance of $(\alpha\beta)/((\alpha+\beta)^2(\alpha+\beta+1))$, and a mode of $(\alpha-1)/(\alpha+\beta-2)$. For a moment, suppose we leave α and β

unspecified. Because the posterior is proportional to the multiple of the prior and the likelihood, the posterior is:

$$p(p \mid Y) \propto p^{\alpha+\left(\sum_{i=1}^{J} y_i\right)-1}(1-p)^{\beta+J-\left(\sum_{i=1}^{J} y_i\right)-1} \quad (17)$$

which is again a beta density with parameters $\alpha + \sum y_i$ and $\beta + J - \sum y_i$. In other words, our prior density is of such a form that the posterior and prior densities are the same type of density. What remains is to specify the parameters of the prior density. For the beta distribution, the parameters can be thought of as prior pieces of information. If we expect that our prior mean probability of a success on any given trial is 0.5, but we are not very certain about this, we can simply choose $\alpha + \beta$ to be small (representing a small number of prior observations) and allow $\alpha = \beta$ to represent a prior mean of 0.5. Suppose, for example, we choose $\alpha = 1$ and $\beta = 1$. In this case, our prior mean is 0.5 and the prior variance is 1/12. This yields a standard deviation of 1/3.46, which means (assuming approximate normality of the distribution, an incorrect assumption here) that the parameter p is expected to fall in the interval:

$$\left[0.5 - 2 \times \frac{1}{3.46}, 0.5 + 2 \times \frac{1}{3.46}\right] = [-0.078, 1.078]$$

with probability 0.95. This distribution is a very vague prior under the assumption of approximate normality because it says we cannot rule out any value for p within the range of [0, 1]. If we examine the density with these parameter values, it is apparent that this distribution is actually a uniform density—and hence not normal—because the exponent of p and $1-p$ is 0 and, hence, the density is flat:

$$p(p) \propto p^0(1-p)^0 = 1$$

This result demonstrates the principle that prior densities can often degenerate to a uniform density, implying that a prior density may contribute little or no information to the posterior.

In this example, the posterior mean for this distribution is $(1+\sum y_i)/(2+J)$, and the posterior mode is $\sum y_i/J$. Notice that the posterior mode in this case is identical to the MLE for a proportion. Furthermore, the posterior mean approaches the posterior mode as $J \rightarrow \infty$ because the 1 in the numerator and 2 in the denominator become asymptotically irrelevant.

In our example, we chose a prior distribution that was conjugate for the sampling density and were able to specify a closed-form solution for the mean, variance, and mode because the beta density is analytically tractable. In other words, we were able to directly compute the integrals for the mean:

$$\mu = \int_{\theta \in S} \theta p(\theta) d\theta$$

and the variance:

$$\sigma^2 = \int_{\theta \in S} (\theta - \mu)^2 p(\theta) d\theta$$

where $p(\theta)$ represents the density of interest. Often Bayesians work with prior distributions that are not conjugate, or they otherwise obtain posterior distributions that do not have analytically tractable forms. With nonconjugate prior densities or with complex multivariate posterior distributions, these integrals, which are fundamental to Bayesian inference, may be impossible to compute analytically. Also, even given any particular likelihood function, the use of different priors between researchers will lead to different values of these integrals. For these reasons, Bayesians need to use alternative methods to evaluate these functions.

Historical Approaches to Estimation

Historically, Bayesians used a number of techniques to compute such integrals or to approximate posterior distributions using known distributions, including quadrature methods (a technique for numerically integrating a density using weighted points on a grid), normal approximations based on Taylor series expansions about the mode of the posterior distribution (a technique for approximating an integral by appealing to a Bayesian Central Limit theorem regarding the normality of most posterior distributions), and other techniques (e.g., weighted normal mixture distributions for multimodal densities). These methods are computationally difficult and mathematically complex, limiting their use in mainstream social science research.

Contemporary Approaches to Estimation

Over the last decade, new methods of estimation—Markov chain Monte Carlo methods—have become popular. These methods have the advantage of being able to handle high-dimensional parameters (something that quadrature methods cannot) and being theoretically exact (something that approximation methods, by definition, are not). I focus extensively on these methods because they hold the most promise for making Bayesian analyses more accessible to social scientists.

The name Markov chain Monte Carlo (MCMC) derives from the nature of the techniques; the methods produce simulated parameter values (hence Monte Carlo), with each sampled parameter being simulated based only on the immediately prior value of the parameter (hence Markov chain). In plain English, these techniques produce sequences of random, but not independent, samples of parameters from their posterior distributions.

In order to understand the usefulness of simulated parameter values, we must discuss the linkage of a collection of random quantities to the integrals previously discussed. If we are unable to integrate a density analytically, we can simulate a large number of draws from the density and then use discrete formulas to compute summary statistics of interest, such as the mean, median, variance, and so on (this is called Monte Carlo integration). For example, suppose we are unable to integrate a normal density with mean μ and variance σ^2. We can simulate $n = 1000$ random draws $y_i, i = 1, \ldots, n$, from this density using very basic simulation algorithms. We can then compute the mean of this distribution as:

$$\hat{\mu} = \frac{\sum y_i}{1000}$$

We could also compute the variance as:

$$\hat{\sigma}^2 = \frac{\sum (y_i - \mu)^2}{n - 1}$$

For that matter, we can compute any other integral value we like. For instance, the median (M) of a distribution is defined as the value that divides the distribution in half such that one-half of the values fall below the median and one-half above, that is, it satisfies:

$$\int_{-\infty}^{M} p(\theta)\,d\theta = 0.05$$

With a large sample from the distribution, the median of the sample estimates the median of the underlying distribution. We can obtain other quantiles of interest in this fashion as well.

The Metropolis-Hastings Algorithm

With simple distributions, routines are generally available that allow us to simulate random samples directly. With complex distributions, there generally are not simple routines for generating samples. MCMC methods are techniques that enable us to conduct such simulation so that these various quantities of interest can be calculated from the iterates, thereby avoiding the necessity of analytical computation. The most basic MCMC methods are the Metropolis-Hastings (MH) algorithm and the Gibbs sampler (a special case of MH). An MH algorithm consists of the following steps, which are explained in depth later:

1. Establish starting values for the parameter $\theta^{j=0}$ (possibly at maximum likelihood estimates).
2. Sample a candidate parameter θ^c from a proposal distribution $\alpha(\theta)$.
3. Evaluate the posterior density, $p(\theta)$, at the candidate point and previous point and form the ratio $R = (p(\theta^c)\alpha(\theta^{j-1} \mid \theta^c))/(p(\theta^{j-1})\alpha(\theta^c \mid \theta^{j-1}))$. The $\alpha(a \mid b)$ terms represent the probability that a will be proposed as a candidate, given the chain is currently in state b, providing a way to compensate for asymmetric proposal densities. If the proposal density is symmetric, these terms drop from the ratio.
4. Accept the candidate parameter with probability $\min(1, R)$ by drawing a random variable $u \sim U(0, 1)$ and comparing to R. If $R > u$, then accept the candidate (set $\theta^j = \theta^c$); otherwise reject it (set $\theta^j = \theta^{j-1}$).
5. Set $j = j + 1$ and return to step 2.

As written, the parameter of interest is contained in the vector θ, and $p(\theta)$ is the density of interest (hereafter referred to as a posterior density). In step 1, we provide starting values for the parameter. These starting values could be MLEs, guesses, or some other value (e.g., for a regression model, we may choose to start all regression parameters at 0). In step 2, we simulate a candidate value for the parameter from a proposal density. This value is called a candidate because it is not automatically accepted as having come from the posterior density; it is merely a trial value. The proposal density is so called because it is any density that is easy to simulate from. The proposal need not be identical to the posterior distribution because the next steps determine whether the candidate is to be considered a draw from the posterior. In step 3, we compute R, which is a ratio of the (possibly unnormalized) posterior density evaluated at the candidate value to the (possibly unnormalized) posterior density evaluated at the previous value of the parameter, with an adjustment that accounts for possible asymmetry in the proposal density from which the candidate was drawn. We also simulate a random draw (u) from the uniform distribution on the interval $[0, 1]$. If the value of the ratio R is greater than the value of u, then we treat the candidate value as having come from the posterior distribution of interest and we update the parameter accordingly. If not, we set the current values of the parameters to the previous values. The algorithm then returns to step 2 and continues iterating until enough unique iterates have been obtained so that we can summarize the posterior density with our sampled parameters.

A few notes are in order about the algorithm. First, the ratio R obviates the need for computing the normalizing constant, often a complex integral, because the constant is contained in both the numerator and denominator. Second, the ratio R actually consists of two ratios. The first ratio, as discussed, is simply the ratio of the posterior density evaluated at the candidate versus previous values. The second ratio compensates for asymmetry in the proposal density. Often we use symmetric densities, for example, a normal proposal density with variance C centered on the previous value of the parameters; that is, $N(0, C)$. In this case, the first ratio will not oversample one value of the parameter over another (i.e., candidate versus previous) simply as a virtue of a greater probability of proposing one value over another. The probability of proposing θ^a when the previous value is θ^b will not be greater than the probability of proposing θ^b when the previous value is θ^a. To make this idea concrete, suppose we are sampling the variance parameter, σ^2, from a normal model. If we use a $U(-0.5, 0.5)$ density (centered over the previous parameter value) as our proposal density, subject to the constraint that all candidates must be greater than 0 (because variances cannot be negative), we will tend to oversample values away from 0 because whenever the previous parameter value is less than 0.5, we will automatically reject any candidate proposed below 0 for violating the boundary constraint. Over the long run, this will make the algorithm more likely to propose (and thus accept) values away from 0 out of proportion to their actual probability. The second part of the ratio compensates for this problem. Notice that in this case, the second half of the ratio will be greater than 1, boosting the overall ratio and lending a little greater probability that we may accept values closer to the boundary. In practice, with very narrow proposal densities, peaked posterior densities, or a posterior centered away from a boundary, the bounding issue is not much of a problem.

The Gibbs Sampler

In some cases, we may be able to derive the full conditional distributions for each parameter in the posterior distribution. In those cases, rather than drawing candidate parameters from proposal distributions, we can draw them from their full conditional distributions. When that occurs, the ratio R always equals 1 and every draw is accepted. This algorithm is called a Gibbs sampler. A generic Gibbs sampling algorithm with k parameters can be specified as follows:

1. Establish starting values for $\theta_2, \ldots, \theta_k$.
2. Sample $[\theta_1^{(j)} \mid \theta_2^{(j-1)}, \theta_3^{(j-1)}, \ldots, \theta_k^{(j-1)}]$
3. Sample $[\theta_2^{(j)} \mid \theta_1^{(j)}, \theta_3^{(j-1)}, \ldots, \theta_k^{(j-1)}]$
4. Sample $[\theta_3^{(j)} \mid \theta_1^{(j)}, \theta_2^{(j)}, \ldots, \theta_k^{(j-1)}]$

⋮

k. Sample $[\theta_k^{(j)} \mid \theta_1^{(j)}, \theta_2^{(j)}, \ldots, \theta_{k-1}^{(j)}]$

$k+1$. Set $j = j + 1$ and return to step 1.

This specification says that we sample the first parameter from its full conditional distribution, conditional on the previous values of the other parameters. As we work our way through the steps, we use the updated values of the parameters in drawing subsequent parameters from their conditional distributions. Because the Gibbs sampler accepts every draw, it is much more efficient than the MH algorithm. However, the price to be paid for efficiency is that we must be able to derive the full conditionals for each parameter and they must take on known forms. Otherwise, we must use some other method for simulating from the conditional distribution, including possibly using an MH step.

Fine-Tuning Markov Chain Monte Carlo Algorithms

Theory indicates that, *in the limit*, the stationary distribution of the Markov chain of iterates produced by an MH algorithm will be the distribution of interest, and so the MH algorithm and Gibbs samplers produce a random walk over the appropriate parameter space. However, convergence to this distribution is not immediate; thus, early iterations of the algorithm should be discarded (called a burn-in period). In general, checking convergence to the appropriate stationary distribution should be a primary concern when using these algorithms, and several methods for evaluating the success of an algorithm have been suggested. Some have suggested that a very long single run of the algorithm may be best. Others have suggested that several runs of the algorithm using widely dispersed starting values provide the best evidence of convergence. Diagnostic tests on the iterates from these multiple chains can help determine whether convergence has been obtained, essentially by examining the extent of the total variance in the iterates that is between-chain variance versus within-chain variance. To date, however, perhaps the most commonly used test of convergence is the ocular test—we can simply examine a trace plot of the iterates to see whether any trending exists. If so, then the algorithm has not converged; if not, then the algorithm *may* have converged.

Another key concern when using these algorithms is the acceptance rate. We have already mentioned that the acceptance rate for a Gibbs sampler is 1 because every draw is accepted. The acceptance rate for an MH algorithm, however, depends on several things. First, if the proposal density is too wide relative to the posterior density, then the algorithm tends to propose candidates that are outside the main support of the posterior. In those cases, the rejection rate will be quite high, and the Markov chain will remain in one place for a long time and will not converge rapidly. On the other hand, if the proposal density is too narrow, the acceptance rate may be quite high, but the algorithm will not explore the entire posterior density very quickly because it cannot move very far at each iteration. Obviously, a delicate balance must be reached between proposals that are too narrow or too wide, so that the algorithm mixes well. Research suggests that an acceptance rate in the range of 15% to 85% is acceptable, although most suggests a narrower range.

In high-dimensional models, establishing appropriate proposal densities becomes more difficult. For example, suppose our density of interest is a bivariate normal density with a very high correlation. In that case, the contours of the density will be a very narrow, tilted ellipse. If our proposal density is a bivariate normal with 0 correlation, most of the candidates will be drawn from regions outside the densest regions of the density. We may correct for this problem in several ways. First, we may transform the model parameters to a parameterization in which the distribution does not evidence such a high correlation. Second, we may alter our proposal density to attempt to match the relative shape of the distribution. In our example, we could, for instance, use a bivariate normal distribution with a high correlation as our proposal. These two approaches are equivalent. Third, we may update parameters one at a time rather than jointly. In high-dimensional models it is often very difficult or impossible to obtain reasonable acceptance rates without doing this. If we update parameters independently, then we have a tremendous amount of flexibility in specifying appropriate proposals for each parameter. Indeed, we can even sample some parameters from their full conditionals, yielding an algorithm that is a hybrid of Gibbs sampling and MH.

Bayesian Inference

We have already discussed some aspects of Bayesian inference, including estimating the mean, median, mode, and variance. Using simulated samples from the posterior distribution is easy, and there is virtually no limit to the statistics that we can use. For much of Bayesian inference, the variance of the posterior distribution is important. Credible intervals (the Bayesian version of confidence intervals) can be constructed based on the variance of the marginal posterior distribution for a parameter, or we can simply use the sampled iterates themselves to construct empirical intervals. That is, for a $100 \times (1-\alpha)\%$ interval for a parameter, we can simply order the simulated sample of iterates from smallest to largest and take the $n(\alpha/2)$th and $n(1-\alpha/2)$th iterates as the bounds of the interval. The interpretation of such an interval differs from the interpretation of a classical interval. From a Bayesian perspective, we simply say that the probability the parameter fell in the interval is $1-\alpha$.

The Bayesian approach also directly allows inferences for parameters that are not in the model but are functions of the parameters that are in the model. For example, suppose our MCMC algorithm generates samples from the distribution for θ, $p(\theta \mid y)$. If we are interested in making inferences for a parameter $\delta = f(\theta)$, we simply compute $\delta^j = f(\theta^j)$, $\forall j$ and use the collection of δ as a sample from $p(\delta \mid y)$. We then proceed with inferential computations as previously discussed.

Model Evaluation and Comparison

As with any statistical modeling process, after a model is estimated, we should determine whether the model actually fits the data. In addition, we may also be interested in comparing multiple models. The Bayesian approach has very flexible methods for model evaluation and comparison.

Posterior Predictive Distributions

For evaluating the fit of a model, perhaps the most flexible approach is to examine the Bayesian posterior predictive distribution. The posterior predictive distribution is the distribution of future observable data, based on the posterior distribution. It is defined as:

$$p(y^{\text{rep}} \mid y) = \int p(y^{\text{rep}} \mid \theta) p(y \mid \theta) p(\theta)\, d\theta \qquad (18)$$

In this equation, y^{rep} is future data that could be drawn from the posterior distribution, y is the current data, and θ is the model parameter. Notice that the last two terms (prior to $d\theta$) are the posterior density for the parameter. The first term is the sampling density for future data, conditional on the parameter. This equation simply specifies a form for the distribution of future data, given the model parameter and data. If a model fits the current data well, then we expect that simulated future data should look much like the current data. Thus, we can simulate data from the posterior predictive distribution, compare it to the observed data, and determine whether the model has an appropriate fit. More formally, we can conduct statistical tests that indicate a level of fit. If we define $T(y)$ to be a function of the data (a test statistic) and $\mathrm{T}(y^{\text{rep}})$ to be the same function applied to the replicated data, then we can compute a Bayesian p value as:

$$p \text{ value} = p(T(y^{\text{rep}}) \geq T(y) \mid y) \qquad (19)$$

This value can be calculated by simply computing the proportion of replicated data sets whose function values exceed that of the function applied to the original data. For example, $T(y)$ can be $T(y) = y_{\text{max}}$, that is, the maximum observed y. If we simulate 10,000 replicated data sets (of size n, where n is the original sample size) from the posterior predictive distribution, and the maximum y^{rep} value exceeds the maximum observed y value in 3500 of the replicated data sets, then the p value is 0.35. In that case, the replicated data appear consistent with the observed data.

The interpretation of tests based on the posterior predictive distribution is straightforward. It represents the probability that a future observation will exceed the existing data, given the model. An extreme p value, therefore, implies poor model fit. In addition to constructing tests that are solely functions of data, we can compute discrepancy statistics that are functions of both data and parameters.

From this brief discussion, it should be apparent that the posterior predictive distribution provides a very flexible approach to examining model fit. There is virtually no limit to the statistics that can be examined to evaluate any aspect of model fit. Furthermore, from a Bayesian perspective, this approach is more reasonable than the classical approach because it considers not only sampling variability but also parametric uncertainty, something the classical approach ignores. That is, most model fit statistics in a classical setting are predicated on the assumption that the model parameter estimates are the true values; Bayesian posterior predictive checks average over parametric uncertainty, as evidenced by Eq. (18).

Bayes Factors

Of interest for many statisticians is the comparison of multiple models that are thought to capture the processes that generate the data. Often, competing theories imply different models. The classical approach to statistics is limited to comparing nested models, but models often are not nested. A Bayesian approach to comparing nonnested discrete sets of models is based on the Bayes factor. If we have two models, M_1 and M_2, each with parameters θ, then Bayes's theorem gives the posterior probability for each model and a ratio of these probabilities can be formed:

$$\text{Posterior odds} = \frac{p(M_1 \mid y)}{p(M_2 \mid y)} \tag{20}$$

Both the numerator and denominator can be broken into their constituent parts, the Bayes factor and the prior odds for model 1 versus model 2:

$$\text{Posterior odds} = \frac{p(y \mid \theta_{M_1})p(\theta_{M_1})}{p(y \mid \theta_{M_2})p(\theta_{M_2})} \tag{21}$$

The former ratio is simply the ratio of the marginal likelihoods and is called the Bayes factor; the latter ratio is the ratio of the prior odds for the two models. The marginal likelihoods are so called because they represent the integral of the posterior density over the parameter space S_i for each model M_i (essentially averaging out parametric uncertainty within each model; notice that this is nothing more than the inverse of the normalizing constant required to make a posterior density proper):

$$p(y \mid M_i) = \int_{\theta_i \in S_i} p(y \mid \theta_i)p(\theta_i)\,d\theta_i \tag{22}$$

or, with the model explicit:

$$p(y \mid M_i) = \int_{\theta_i \in S_i} p(y \mid \theta_i, M_i)p(\theta_i \mid M_i)\,d\theta_i \tag{23}$$

The prior odds in Eq. (21) are usually set to 1. If both models are assumed to have equal prior probability, the posterior odds are equivalent to the Bayes factor. Thus, a value of 1 for the Bayes factor indicates equal support for both models, whereas a ratio greater than 1 favors model 1 and a ratio less than 1 favors model 2.

The integration required is one limitation to the use of Bayes factors; the integration is difficult. However, in 1995 Raftery proposed an approximation, termed the Bayesian Information Criterion (BIC), that can be fairly easily computed using standard output from most software packages. Perhaps a more difficult issue is that the Bayes factor is quite sensitive to the choice of priors used for parameters in each model.

Bayesian Model Averaging

Rather than comparing a discrete set of models, the researcher may be interested in making inferences about a parameter using all models in a particular class of models. Bayesian model averaging extends the notion of model uncertainty alluded to in the discussion of Bayes factors. When we conduct statistical analyses, we typically construct a single model. This approach, however, ignores model uncertainty; that is, it ignores the fact that we may not have chosen the appropriate model. Model averaging is nothing more than constructing a marginal posterior distribution for a parameter, averaging across all models in a class:

$$p(\theta \mid y) = \sum_{j=1}^{J} p(\theta \mid M_j, y)p(M_j \mid y) \tag{24}$$

The first term on the right-hand side of Eq. (24) is simply the posterior distribution for the parameter under a specific model. The second term is the posterior probability for the model. This term is the numerator of the posterior odds presented in Eq. (20). From this equation, then, it should be clear that the posterior distribution for a parameter under Bayesian model averaging is simply a weighted mixture of the probabilities under each model.

Model averaging is tricky for two reasons. First, we must assign prior distributions for each model in the model space we are examining. An obvious choice of prior may be one that assigns equal prior weight to all models, but this approach may ultimately favor models that are very similar to one another, giving them high posterior weight. Second, model averaging is computationally intensive. For example, in a normal linear regression model with J covariates there are 2^J possible models that must be examined. To date, two primary approaches to dealing with this problem have been advanced. One is to exclude models if they have low posterior probability relative to another well-fitting model using a decision rule called Occam's window. Under this approach, we can also exclude models that are supersets of better-fitting smaller models. The second approach is to sample from the posterior for all models using MCMC methods. The benefit of the first method is that it typically reduces the model space to fewer than 100 models, making Eq. (24) easier to compute; the downside is that it only provides an approximation to the true posterior probability for a parameter because numerous models are excluded. The benefit of the MCMC method is that it provides the correct posterior probability; the downside is that it is difficult to obtain convergence and that it is incredibly time intensive.

See Also the Following Articles

Bayes, Thomas • Hypothesis Tests and Proofs • Maximum Likelihood Estimation • Selection Bias

Further Reading

Box, George E. P., and Tiao, George C. (1973). *Bayesian Inference in Statistical Analysis.* Addison-Wesley, Reading, MA.

DeGroot, Morris H. (1986). *Probability and Statistics,* 2nd Ed. Addison-Wesley, Reading, MA.

Gelman, Andrew, Carlin, John B., Stern, Hal S., and Rubin, Donald B. (1995). *Bayesian Data Analysis.* Chapman and Hall, London.

Gilks, Walter R., Richardson, Sylvia, and Spiegelhalter, David J. (1996). *Markov Chain Monte Carlo in Practice.* Chapman and Hall/CRC, Boca Raton.

Hoeting, Jennifer A., Madigan, David,, Raftery, Adrian E., and Volinsky, Chris T. (1999). Bayesian model averaging: A tutorial. *Stat. Sci.* **14**(4), 382–417.

Kass, Robert E., and Raftery, Adrian E. (1995). Bayes factors. *J. Am. Stat. Assoc.* **90**(430), 773–795.

Lee, Peter M. (1989). *Bayesian Statistics: An Introduction.* Oxford University Press, New York.

Raftery, Adrian E. (1995). Bayesian model selection in social research. *Sociol. Methodology* **25**, 111–164.

Behavioral Economics: The Carnegie School

Mie Augier
Stanford University, Stanford, California, USA

Glossary

bounded rationality A phrase coined by Herbert Simon; used to describe an approach to economics that is more realistic than that of neoclassical economics.

maximization One of the assumptions of neoclassical economics and rational choice theory, assuming that all agents maximize expected utility (or profit) of all possible outcomes.

neoclassical economics A branch of economics building on very strict assumptions about economic behavior as optimizing behavior.

satisficing The idea that economic agents (and organizations) do not maximize (due to cognitive limitations and bounded rationality) but search for an outcome that is "good enough."

theory of the firm A field of economics and organization theory centered around questions relating to the existence, boundaries, and internal organization and activities of the business firm.

Behavioral economics aims at broadening the behavioral and psychological foundations of economics in order to explain phenomena, such as the firm, that are not adequately addressed in neoclassical economics. By incorporating ideas such as bounded rationality and satisficing into economic analysis, behavioral economics provides a more realistic perspective on individual and organizational decision making than does mainstream economics. Many ideas in behavioral economics began in the 1950s and 1960s around a group of researchers at Carnegie Mellon University. Herbert Simon (one of the three key figures at Carnegie in the early development of behavioral economics) won the Nobel Prize in economics in 1978. Modern developments in behavioral economics include much of the research on judgment and heuristics by Daniel Kahneman and Amos Tversky, which led to the Nobel Prize in economics in 2002. Key ideas in behavioral economics are also embedded in traditions such as transaction cost economics and evolutionary economics. Here the focus is mostly on the early development of the tradition.

History and Scope

An important part of behavioral economics is often identified with the pioneering work done by Herbert Simon, James G. March, and Richard Cyert in the 1950s and 1960s at Carnegie Mellon University. The Carnegie behavioralists are known for their interest in understanding how individuals and organizations act and make decisions in the real world, and their challenges to the neoclassical theory of optimization and maximization in decision making and organizations. Behavioral economics developed concepts such as bounded rationality and satisficing to describe individuals and organizations acting in the face of "the uncertainties and ambiguities of life." Many of these concepts were first discussed in the book *Organizations*, and none of them has lost currency. They prove their usefulness whenever actual behavior departs from the tenets of rationality (for instance, when action is rule based rather than consequence based, or when it conflicts with statistically informed strategies, as described in the prospect theory of Tversky and Kahneman).

Behavioral economics also stood out early in its aim to be interdisciplinary. Whereas mainstream economics stays within the discipline of economics to analyze behavior and decision making, behavioral economics draws on other traditions, such as political science, sociology, organization theory, and psychology, to obtain a broader understanding of human behavior and decision making.

In particular, because there are limits to rational behavior, we must deal with the psychological elements of human decision making.

The background for the Carnegie School was the Ford Foundation's mission to establish a broad and interdisciplinary behavioral social science in the late 1940s and early 1950s, and much of the efforts were directed at supporting the early setup of the Graduate School of Industrial Administration at Carnegie Mellon University (originally Carnegie Institute of Technology), where Simon, March, and Cyert worked. The Carnegie Institute of Technology had been founded in 1912 by Andrew Carnegie and had established itself as one of the best engineering schools in the country. The early president, Robert Doherty, who had come from Yale, wanted Carnegie Tech to be a leader in research and, hence, to break with the traditional mechanical engineering view of business education and include broader, social and interdisciplinary, aspects. As a result of Doherty's ambitions, the first dean of what came to be known as the Graduate School of Industrial Administration (GSIA), George Leland Bach, was hired. Bach wanted to staff his department with economists who combined intellectual skills and experience in applying theory to real-world situations and he wanted to put Carnegie at the forefront of U.S. business schools. Simon, March, and Cyert all came to Carnegie to help develop this view.

Business education at that time was not much oriented toward research, but was more focused on case studies. But Simon, Cyert, and March wanted to be different. They wanted to do research. They wanted their research to be relevant for business leaders, while at the same time emphasizing the tools of good science. Early core courses in the program included "quantitative control and business" (consisting of basically accounting and statistics), a sequence of micro- and macroeconomics, and organization theory. The vision they had was reflected in an emphasis on creating a new behavioral science that was broad enough to accommodate disciplines such as economics, sociology, and social psychology, yet precise enough to reflect the rigor and technical sophistication of mathematical models. In the end, their implementation of this vision produced significant contributions to areas such as behavioral economics, operations research, experimental economics, and theories of the firm. It also created a model for business schools that was widely adopted across the United States and (later) Europe.

The behavioral group at Carnegie was embedded in a larger group of scholars, which included innovative economists such as Franco Modigliani, John Muth, Charles Holt, and Merton Miller. The spirit at Carnegie was that everybody interacted with everybody else; discussed each other's research, and discussed science, so collaborative teams worked together as well as across each other's projects. Consisting of different people with different interests, these teams always worked together in a friendly way, despite different disciplines and despite varying degrees of admiration for the idea of rationality. It was an environment in which people were united by their deep and intense interest for doing science. And it was a unique environment where joy from work was present more than anywhere else. Several Nobel Prize winners were fostered during the golden years at Carnegie, including Robert Lucas, Franco Modigliani, Merton Miller, and Herbert Simon, and Carnegie had outstanding records on other accounts as well.

The Carnegie school tried to develop the rudiments of process-oriented understandings of how economic organization and decision making take place. They did so in an interdisciplinary way, linking economics to organization theory, cognitive science, sociology, and psychology, and centering around concepts such as uncertainty, ambiguity, norms, routines, learning, and satisficing. They used ideas from social science more broadly to advance understanding of economics and, in the process, contributed to the strands that came to be called behavioral economics. The ideas initiated by the Carnegie School helped to establish a foundation for modern ideas on bounded rationality; adaptive, behavioral, and evolutionary economics; and transaction cost theory.

Key Ideas and Theories

The behavioral research of Simon, Cyert, and March aimed at making understandable how individuals make decisions and behave in the real world. They found that neoclassical economics gave too little attention to the institutional and cognitive constraints on economic and organizational behavior and on individual decisions, and allowed too little room for human mistakes, foolishness, the complications of limited attention, and other results of bounded rationality. As a result, they proposed to include the whole range of limitations on human knowledge and human computation that prevents organizations and individuals in the real world from behaving in ways that approximate the predictions of neoclassical theory. For example, decision makers are sometimes confronted by the need to optimize several, sometimes incommensurable, goals. Furthermore, instead of assuming a fixed set of alternatives among which a decision maker chooses, the Carnegie School postulated a process for generating search and alternatives and analyzing decision processes through the idea of aspiration levels, a process that is regulated in part by variations in organizational slack. Finally, individuals and organizations often rely on routines or rules of thumb learned from experience or from others, rather than seek to calculate the consequences of alternatives.

Underlying these ideas is the emphasis on bounded rationality, bringing in a more psychological and realistic assumption to the analysis. As Simon noted early on, "the first principle of bounded rationality is that the intended rationality of an actor requires him to construct a simplified model of the real situation in order to deal with it. He behaves rationally with respect to this model, and such behavior is not even approximately optimal with respect to the real world. To predict his behavior, we must understand the way in which this simplified model is constructed, and its construction will certainly be related to his psychological properties as a perceiving, thinking, and learning animal."

The twin idea of bounded rationality is satisficing. Satisficing is the idea that decision makers interpret outcomes as either satisfactory or unsatisfactory, with an aspiration level constituting the boundary between the two. Whereas decision makers in neoclassical rational choice theory would list all possible outcomes, evaluated in terms of their expected utilities, and then choose the one that is rational and maximizes utility, decision makers in the behavioral model face only two possible outcomes, and look for a satisfying solution, continuing to search only until they have found a solution that is good enough.

Both satisficing and bounded rationality were introduced in 1955, when Herbert Simon published a paper that provided the foundation for a behavioral perspective on human decision making and introduced the ideas of satisficing and bounded rationality. The paper provided a critique of the assumption in economics of perfect information and unlimited computational capability, and replaced the assumption of global rationality with one that was more in correspondence with how humans (and other choosing organisms) made decisions, their computational limitations, and how they accessed information in their current environments. In Simon's illustration of the problem, the influence of his early ideas outlined in *Administrative Behavior* is clear, echoing the view that decisions are reasoned and intendedly rational, yet limited. He first suggests a simple and very general model of behavioral choice that analyzes choosing organisms (such as humans) in terms of basic properties to understand what is meant by rational behavior. He introduces the simplifying assumptions (such as the choice alternatives, the payoff function, possible future states, and the subset of choice alternatives considered, as well as the information about the probability that a particular outcome will lead to a particular choice). But immediately afterward, he turns to the simplifications of this model, stressing that, on careful examination, "we see immediately what severe demands they make upon the choosing organism." Whereas in models of rational choice, the organism must be able to "attach definite payoffs (or at least a definite range of payoffs) to each possible outcome," Simon suggests that "there is a complete lack of evidence that, in actual human choice situations of any complexity, these computations can be, or are in fact, performed." As a consequence of the lack of computational power, decision makers have to simplify the structure of their decisions (and thus satisfice), one of the most important lessons of bounded rationality. This idea later became important to the work on organizational behavior and decision making done by Simon and March. In addition, the idea of satisficing has been used by evolutionary and adaptive economics (such as that of Richard Nelson and Sidney Winter).

Major Early Works

One of the first major results of the Carnegie School's work was a propositional inventory of organization theory, involving Herbert Simon, James March, and Harold Guetzkow; this led to the book *Organizations*. The book was intended to provide the inventory of knowledge of the (then almost nonexistent) field of organization theory, and also a more proactive role in defining the field. Results and insights from studies of organizations in political science, sociology, economics, and social psychology were summarized and codified. The book expanded and elaborated ideas on behavioral decision making, search, and aspiration levels, and elaborated the idea on the significance of organizations as social institutions in society. "The basic features of organization structure and function," March and Simon wrote, "derive from the characteristics of rational human choice. Because of the limits of human intellective capacities in comparison with the complexities of the problems that individuals and organizations face, rational behavior calls for simplified models that capture the main features of a problem without capturing al its complexities." March and Simon also wanted to unite empirical data-gathering research with rigorous theorizing in order to create a rigorous empirical theory that could organize and so give meaning to empirical facts with legitimate theory. Science, they believed, was the product of the organization of empirical facts into conceptual schemes, and the progress of science was based on the development of more sophisticated and elegant theoretical systems, but not necessarily the discovery of new facts.

The Ford Foundation also supported a larger project on behavioral theories of organizations; this was carried out by Richard Cyert and James March (along with their students, including Julian Feldman, Edward Feigenbaum, William Starbuck, and Oliver Williamson). The project originated in the works of Cyert and March to develop improved models of oligoplogy pricing by using organization theory. The research on the behavioral theory of the firm aimed at investigating how the characteristics of business firms, as organizations, affect important business decisions. Integrating theories of organizations with existing (mostly economic) theories of the firm, they developed an empirical theory rather than a normative one, and focused on classical problems in economics (such as pricing, resource allocation, and capital investment) to deal with the processes for making decisions in organizations.

The behavioral theory of the firm is built around a political conception of organizational goals, a bounded rationality conception of expectations, an adaptive conception of rules and aspirations, and a set of ideas about how the interactions among these factors affect decisions in a firm. Whereas goals in neoclassical theory are pictured as given alternatives, each with a set of consequences attached, goals within behavioral theory are pictured as reflecting the demands of a political coalition, changing as the composition of that coalition changes. Said Cyert and March: "Since the existence of unresolved conflict is a conspicuous feature of organizations, it is exceedingly difficult to construct a useful positive theory of organizational decision-making if we insist on internal goal consistency. As a result, recent theories of organizational objectives describe goals as the result of a continuous bargaining–learning process. Such a process will not necessarily produce consistent goals." Thus, the theory treats the demands of shareholders, managers, workers, customers, suppliers, and creditors as components of the operational goals of a firm. In the behavioral view, agents have only limited rationality, meaning that behavior in organizations is intendedly rational, neither emotive nor aimless. Because firms are seen as heterogeneous, boundedly rational entities that have to search for relevant information, expectations in the behavioral theory are portrayed as the result of making inferences from available information, involving both the process by which information is made available and the processes of drawing inferences. Because information is costly, it is generated by search activity. The intensity of search depends on the performance of the organization relative to aspirations and the amount of organizational slack. The direction of search is affected by the location (in the organization) or search activity and the definition of the problem stimulating the activity. Thus, the search activity of the organization furthers both the generation of new alternative strategies, and facilitates the anticipation of uncertain futures.

Decision making in the behavioral theory is seen as taking place in response to a problem, through the use of standard operating procedures and other routines, and also through search for an alternative that is acceptable from the point of view of current aspiration levels for evoked goals. Choice is affected, therefore, by the definition of a problem, by existing rules (which reflect past learning by the organization), by the order in which alternatives are considered (which reflects the location of decision making in the organization and past experience), and by anything that affects aspirations and attention. Within this framework, four concepts were developed. The first is the quasi-resolution of conflict, the idea that firms function with considerable latent conflict of interests but do not necessarily resolve that conflict explicitly. The second is uncertainty avoidance. Although firms try to anticipate an unpredictable future insofar as they can, they also try to restructure their worlds in order to minimize their dependence on anticipation of the highly uncertain future. The third concept is problemistic search, the idea that search within a firm is stimulated primarily by problems and directed to solving those problems. The fourth concept is organizational learning. The theory assumes that firms learn from their own experiences and the experiences of others.

This view of the firm was important to modern developments such as evolutionary theory and transaction cost economics, which both bear intellectual debts to the ideas in the behavioral theory of the firm. For example, the ideas of bounded rationality and conflict of interest are now standard in the transaction cost theory of especially Oliver Williamson, and the view of the firm as a system of rules that adapt to its changing environment is important in the evolutionary theory put forward by Richard Nelson and Sidney Winter. The transactions cost approach is widely accepted as a framework for understanding economic organization. This perspective sees markets and hierarchies as alternative mechanisms for organizing transactions. In order to economize on transaction costs, production is frequently required to be organized in firms. Transaction cost economics builds on the assumptions of bounded rationality and opportunism. In the evolutionary view, the firm is seen as a profit-seeking entity, the primary activities of which are to build (through organizational learning processes) and exploit valuable knowledge assets. Firms in this view also come with "routines" or "competencies," which are recurrent patterns of action that may change through search and learning. Routines will seldom be "optimal" and will differ among agents, and behaviors cannot be deduced from simply observing the environmental signals (such as prices) to which agents are exposed. This variety drives the evolutionary process because firms articulate rent-seeking strategies on the basis of their routines and competencies, and competition in the product market constitutes an important part of the selection environment of confronting firms.

Another modern development within behavioral economics comes from the work of Daniel Kahneman and Amos Tversky. Drawing heavily on experimental psychology, they showed how rational choice theory cannot be applied to the real world and they investigated the influence of a number of human factors. One such factor is heuristics. Heuristics "reduce the complex tasks of assessing probabilities and predicting values to simpler judgmental operations." Thus, heuristics economize the limited cognitive resources of decision makers, which allows decisions to be made, but introduces errors and biases. Kahneman and Tversky's work on heuristics led them to a model of choice called prospect theory. One of the key assumptions in this model is that people's probability judgments are not attached to events but to the descriptions of events. When choices are irreversible and outcomes are time lagged, uncertainty will prevail. No objective facts will figure in the forecasts of decision makers, merely their perception of such facts. Decision making thus depends on the framing of the problem, which shapes perceptions and thus influences choices.

Closing

An important branch of behavioral economics was conceived at Carnegie Mellon University during the 1950s and early 1960s around the work of Herbert Simon, Richard Cyert, and James March. For these scholars, behavioral economics meant doing science in an interdisciplinary way, linking economics to organization theory, cognitive science, sociology, and psychology, and centering around concepts such as uncertainty, ambiguity, norms, routines, learning, and satisficing. Emphasizing the concern with the empirical validity of assumptions, Simon thus wrote that "behavioral economics is best characterized not as a single specific theory but as a commitment to empirical testing of the neoclassical assumptions of human behavior and to modifying economic theory on the basis of what is found in the testing process." He included in the behavioral economics different approaches, such as new institutional economics, transaction cost economics, evolutionary economics, and the literature on heuristics coming from Kahneman and Tversky.

See Also the Following Articles

Organizational Behavior • Organizational Psychology

Further Reading

Augier, M., and March, J. G. (2002). *The Economics of Choice, Change and Organization: Essays in Honor of Richard M. Cyert.* Edward Elgar, United Kingdom.

Augier, M., and March, J. G. (2002). A model scholar. *J. Econ. Behav. Organiz.* **49,** 1–17.

Camerer, C., Loewenstein, G., and Rabin, M. (eds.) (2004). *Advances in Behavioral Economics*. Princeton University Press, New Jersey.

Cyert, R., and March, J. G. (1992). *A Behavioral Theory of the Firm,* 2nd Ed. Blackwell, Oxford.

Day, R., and Sunder, S. (1996). Ideas and work of Richard M. Cyert. *J. Econ. Behav. Organiz.* **31,** 139–148.

Earl, P. (ed.) (1988). *Behavioral Economics*. Edward Elgar, Aldershot.

March, J. G., and Simon, H. A. (1993). *Organizations,* 2nd Ed. Blackwell, Oxford.

Nelson, R., and Winter, S. (1982). *An Evolutionary Theory of Economic Change.* Bellknap Press, Cambridge, Massachusetts.

Simon, H. A. (1955). A behavioral model of rational choice. *Q. J. Econ.* **69,** 99–118.

Simon, H. A. (1991). *Models of My Life.* MIT Press, Cambridge.

Williamson, O. E. (1985). *The Economic Institutions of Capitalism.* Free Press, New York.

Williamson, O. E. (1996). Transaction cost economics and the Carnegie connection. *J. Econ. Behav. Organiz.* **31,** 149–155.

Williamson, O. E. (2002). Empirical microeconomics: another perspective. Forthcoming in M.-S. Augier, and J. G. March (eds) *The Economics of Choice, Change and Organization: Essays in Honor of Richard M. Cyert.* Edward Elgar, Cheltenham, UK.

Behavioral Psychology

Francisco J. Silva
University of Redlands, Redlands, California, USA

Glossary

avoidance conditioning A procedure in which a particular response during a conditional stimulus prevents the occurrence of an aversive event.

conditional stimulus A stimulus that elicits a conditional response after being paired with an unconditional stimulus.

extinction In Pavlovian conditioning, when a conditional stimulus is no longer followed by an unconditional stimulus, the conditional response will return to its preconditioning level. In operant conditioning, withholding a positive reinforcer after a response it normally followed will cause the response to return to its preconditioning level.

functional relationship A description, often summarized in a graph, that shows how one variable (the independent variable) is related to another variable (the dependent variable). Knowledge of the functional relationship and of the value of the independent variable allows one to predict the value of the dependent variable.

habituation The waning of a response elicited by a usually harmless stimulus because of repeated presentations of that stimulus.

hypothetical construct Unobserved entities purported to mediate an environment–behavior relationship.

operant conditioning The procedure in which behavior is modified by its consequences.

Pavlovian conditioning The procedure in which a stimulus comes to elicit a new response after being paired with a stimulus that elicits a similar or related response.

positive reinforcer A stimulus whose occurrence after a response increases the likelihood of that response recurring.

punisher A stimulus whose occurrence after a response decreases the likelihood of that response recurring.

unconditional stimulus A stimulus that reliably and persistently elicits behavior that is resistant to habituation.

Behavioral psychology is a subdivision of psychology and an approach to the study of behavior that relates what people and animals do to the stimulus conditions before, during, and after behavior. In other words, behavioral psychology is concerned with understanding environment–behavior relationships.

Foundations of Behavioral Psychology

Historically, behavioral psychology was incorrectly identified with "rat psychology" because, at one time, its primary data were collected using laboratory rats as the subjects. It was thus assumed that its theories were most appropriate to rats and other laboratory animals. In terms of its application to humans, behavioral psychology was considered most useful for populations with developmental disabilities, autism, and the seriously and persistently mentally ill. For many critics, to modify someone's behavior is tantamount to "mind control" and evokes disturbing images from Orwell's *1984*, Huxley's *Brave New World*, and Burgess's *A Clockwork Orange*. But behavioral psychology resembles none of these any more than nuclear medicine resembles atomic bombs, meltdowns, and genetic mutations. In this section, the scope and origins of behavioral psychology are presented.

Scope

There are no restrictions on what behavioral psychologists study, as long as it is something that people and animals do. Crying during a movie, reading a book, writing a poem, counting to 10, speaking to a teacher, playing a guitar, thinking silently, feeling pain, solving a puzzle, using a tool, remembering a quote, and loving a child are examples of actions that behavioral psychologists can study, as are capturing food, attracting a mate, eluding predators, avoiding poisons, and seeking shelter. Topics such as stress, personality, learning, intelligence, creativity, and consciousness are also studied by behavioral psychologists.

There are also no restrictions on where these actions are studied. Behavior can be studied by unobtrusive observations in the natural environment, such as when a teacher observes children playing during recess or a naturalist studies ants carrying food to their nest. Behavior can also be studied by experimentation in the natural environment, such as when a coach compares the effectiveness of relaxation techniques to alleviate a tennis player's anxiety before big matches or a biologist removes pine cones and stones near the entrance of a wasp's burrow to see how this affects the insect's ability to find its home. Finally, behavior can be studied experimentally in a clinic or laboratory, such as when a therapist measures the nonverbal behavior of a married couple and then implements a counseling program to reduce their negative body language or when a psychologist presents a rat with tones of different durations to study its timing abilities.

Philosophical Origins

The origins of studying environment–behavior relationships are as old as humans themselves, for humans' earliest ancestors must have tried to understand the relationship between a season and the migration of animals, the behavior of prey animals and the noises made by those who hunt them, the ingestion of a mushroom and bodily sensations, and so on. Somewhere in the history of humans, these informal observations and understandings evolved into explicit and written musings about behavior. The intellectual roots of behavioral psychology can be traced to several sources: Francis Bacon (1561–1626), who urged an inductive approach to science; John Locke (1632–1704), who emphasized the role of experiences in the formation of knowledge; Julien de la Mettrie (1709–1751), who believed that humans and animals were machines that differed by degree and not kind; David Hume (1711–1776), who postulated several laws of association; Auguste Comte (1798–1857), who insisted that the data of science be publicly observed; Charles Darwin (1809–1882), who argued that living creatures evolved by natural selection; and many other philosophers and scientists of the late 19th and early 20th centuries who were a part of the philosophical movements known as functionalism, logical positivism, and behaviorism.

Despite these early influences and that ethologists in Europe were also studying the relationship among animals' behavior and their environments, the birth of behavioral psychology is most often attributed to Russian physiologist Ivan Pavlov (1849–1936) and American psychologists Edward Thorndike (1874–1949), John Watson (1878–1958), and B. F. Skinner (1904–1990). It was these scientists who argued most strongly that an understanding of people's and animals' actions requires discovering functional relationships between the environment and behavior. However, it is important to note that behavioral psychology is no more like associationism, positivism, or Watsonian behaviorism than modern humans are like Neanderthals. Just as humans and other species continue to evolve, behavioral psychology continues to evolve. Although once erroneously associated with stimulus–response psychology, the view that a response would reflexively occur in the presence of a particular stimulus context, contemporary behavioral psychology seeks to discover and understand several types of functional relationships between environmental conditions and behavior, such as the properties of operant and Pavlovian conditioning.

A Natural Science of Behavior: Distinguishing Features of Behavioral Psychology

Behavioral psychology is not only a subdivision of psychology it is also an approach to the study of environment–behavior relationships. There are two challenges to specifying the defining features of behavioral psychology. The first is that there is no single characteristic that distinguishes behavioral psychology from other areas of psychology. The second challenge is that there are two related but separate traditions within behavioral psychology, each with its own characteristics: laboratory research of basic mechanisms and processes in humans and other animals (termed the experimental analysis of behavior) and applied research directed toward improving people's and animals' lives (termed applied behavior analysis, behavior therapy, or behavior modification). Despite these challenges, there are features that when considered together distinguish behavioral psychology from other areas. These are described next.

Hypothetical Constructs

Hypothetical constructs are unobserved entities purported to mediate an environment–behavior relationship. Behavioral psychologists avoid the use of hypothetical constructs because these are easily misused and, hence, can hinder the scientific study of behavior. One reason for this misuse is that it is often unclear whether these constructs are real, metaphorical, or promissory notes for something that might be observed in the future. For example, it has been said that a rat navigates a maze by scanning with its mind's eye a stored cognitive map of the maze. However, proponents of this type of explanation also say that there is no actual mind's eye, no actual action of scanning, and no actual map. Behavioral psychologists, who eschew these types of explanations, then ask: If these entities and actions are not real, then how does the account explain the rat's behavior of navigating a maze? A second reason for the misuse of hypothetical constructs is that the attributes imputed to them are often poorly defined, proliferate unnecessarily, and their interconnections are unspecified. For example, "attention" can be shared, transferred, conditioned, focused or unfocused, divided or undivided, increased or decreased, conscious or unconscious, and central or peripheral. Exactly what these attributes are, how they differ, and how they relate to one another is unclear.

It is important to note that it does not follow from the information above that behavioral psychologists believe that people and animals are "black boxes" or that it is inappropriate to postulate and use hypothetical constructs. These are used in behavioral psychology and are most likely to be used when several independent and dependent variables are involved. For example, the independent variables "hours of water deprivation," "eating dry food," and "receiving a saline injection" all cause an increase in the dependent variables "lever-pressing for water," "drinking water," and "quinine tolerance." In this circumstance, some behavioral psychologists would say that an increase in thirst (the hypothetical construct) causes an increase in drinking, actions that lead to drinking, and a tolerance for unpleasant tastes in water.

Theories

Theories fall along a continuum, ranging from a set of loosely interconnected observations to precise mathematical formulations. Behavioral psychology is not atheoretical, though its practitioners believe that the best theories are those that organize facts at the same level that those facts were collected. This means that if someone has determined the functional relationship between certain environmental conditions and behavior, then it is unnecessary to appeal to physiological mechanisms or processes that were never manipulated or measured or whose own relationships to behavior are poorly understood.

Theories can also be distinguished on the basis of their use of hypothetical constructs. For behavioral psychologists, a theory with too many hypothetical constructs is sloppy because it has too many degrees of freedom. A theory that can explain everything explains nothing.

Finally, theories in behavioral psychology differ from those in other areas by using behavioral primitives—basic terms and relationships that serve as pillars of theory and therefore do not require further explanation—and then coordinating and integrating these to explain more complex behavior (see Operant–Pavlovian Interactions for an example). In the process of integration, behavioral theories stress the context of behavior and the history of experiences and iterative causes in the shaping of behavior.

Dependent Variables (Effects or Measures)

Like most areas of psychology, behavioral psychology uses behavioral dependent measures. However, unlike other areas, behavior is studied as an end in itself in behavioral psychology. It is generally not used as a means of studying other phenomena such as the brain or self-esteem. For these other areas, behavior is measured as a means toward an end: the study of something that intervenes or mediates an environment–behavior relationship.

A related difference between how the same dependent measure is used differently in behavioral psychology versus many other areas is that, for behavioral psychologists, behavior is not something apart from that which it assays. The following example clarifies the distinction. For some psychologists, low self-esteem causes people to make frequent negative self-statements (e.g., "I'm too stupid to succeed in college."). Self-esteem is a hypothetical construct. However, for behavioral psychologists, these statements express low self-esteem. That is, low self-esteem is partly defined by the behavior of making negative self-statements in specific contexts rather than resulting from low self-esteem. Viewed in this manner, self-esteem is not a hypothetical construct; it does not mediate an environment–behavior relationship because it *is* behavior.

Independent Variables (Causes or Treatments)

The ways in which psychologists conceive of the action of independent variables is yet another feature that helps distinguish behavioral psychology from other areas. Behavioral psychologists study independent variables that are lawfully related to behavior and which can be broadly categorized as ways of changing a person's environment. The rationale for this approach is that if the environment is altered, then behavior is likely to be altered. In contrast, most other areas of psychology infer that changes in an independent variable cause changes in a hypothetical construct, which then produces changes in behavior.

This is a subtle but important difference between behavioral psychology and other areas, for how psychologists conceive of the action of independent variables influences the independent variables that they use and study. Consider how a behavioral versus a cognitive sports psychologist might try to help a baseball player who is in a batting slump. Although there are many similarities between the two psychologists, the cognitive psychologist would probably attribute the player's poor batting performance to a decline in his confidence; for the behavioral psychologist, the player's slump is likely the result of poor batting mechanics and responses that interfere with batting (e.g., intrusive thoughts, tensed muscles). To help the struggling batter, the cognitive psychologist focuses on changing the player's cognitions and feelings. Thus, this psychologist might help the athlete focus on the positive ("Hey, you're swinging the bat well and making good contact!"), lower his goals ("Hitting 1 out of 4 at-bats is okay."), and challenge unrealistic statements ("You're not going to be demoted to the minor leagues because of a batting slump."). The goal is to impact the player's confidence, which will then presumably raise his batting average. In contrast, although there is nothing that prevents a behavioral psychologist from trying to change the player's confidence, this psychologist focuses on video analysis, modeling, and corrective feedback to show the player how he is gripping the bat too rigidly, dropping his right shoulder too soon, as well as how he can shorten his swing, how to steady his head, and the like. Following this instruction, the player will practice batting with these new mechanics. The goal is to change the player's batting behavior directly rather than change a hypothetical construct (e.g., confidence) that might lead to a change in batting performance.

Research Designs and Data Analysis

The research designs used in most areas of psychology are known as between-groups or large-*N* designs. In their simplest form, these designs consist of randomly assigning individuals to different groups that receive different levels of the independent variable. To assess differences in the average level of the dependent measure between the groups, researchers use inferential statistics, which are data analysis techniques rooted in probability theory that help them determine the likelihood that any differences between groups are caused by differences in the independent variable. Confidence in the differences between groups is gained by using large numbers of participants in each group. In applied settings, the dependent variable is typically measured once before and after treatment or, less desirably, once after treatment. Understanding individual differences among participants is not of particular interest; the group's mean and variance are what is important.

In contrast, the research designs favored by behavioral psychologists are known as within-subject, small-*N*, single-organism, or single-subject designs, even though studies in behavioral psychology almost always use more than one person or animal. In contrast to group designs, within-subject designs rely on measuring subjects' behavior frequently. Typically, the data are plotted in graphs that show how the dependent variable changed across time. Confidence in the effect of the independent variable relies on replicating the effects within a subject or across subjects, settings, or responses. Data from all individuals are analyzed and used to determine the effect of the independent variable.

Behavioral psychologists are interested in independent variables that consistently produce large effects relative to the amount of variation in an individual's behavior. This reduces the need for inferential statistics, for if changes in an individual's behavior are not detectable by visually inspecting the graphed data, then there was too much variation or noise in the subject's behavior and/or the effect of the independent variable was weak to nil. If the independent variable affected behavior, then the effects will be obvious. When the independent variable has not affected all individuals' behavior, behavioral psychologists try to understand this variation rather than accept it as "unexplained error."

Changing Environment–Behavior Relationships

Although there are many ways of changing environment–behavior relationships, most of these ways can be categorized into three types of procedures: habituation, Pavlovian conditioning, and operant conditioning. Whether these three procedures represent three distinct phenomena is controversial; each procedure seems to contain elements of the others. In this section, each procedure is summarized along with a few of its major properties. An understanding of these properties gives behavioral psychologists the foundation for changing environment–behavior relationships.

Habituation

If a usually harmless stimulus occurs repeatedly and there are no other events associated with it, then behavior elicited by that stimulus will diminish. This is habituation, one of the simplest ways to change behavior. By repeatedly presenting some stimuli (the environmental cause), people and animals stop responding to those stimuli (the behavioral effect). Habituation is one of the reasons that listening to the same song causes someone to lose interest in that song and a roller coaster becomes uninteresting after a few rides.

To illustrate some of the features of habituation, consider an example of a person staying in a downtown Chicago hotel along the city's famous elevated train line. Initially, trains rumbling down the track and screeching to a stop (the stimuli) elicit responses such as waking up, covering one's ears, and a set of sensations, emotions, and thoughts that collectively might be called "annoyance." However, as these trains continue to pass, say, every 20 min, these responses decline. Eventually, the trains are ignored in the sense that the person continues to sleep and is generally not bothered when the trains pass or stop.

Besides being an important phenomenon in itself, a discussion of habituation is also a starting point to introduce some features common to many environment–behavior relationships. For example, spontaneous recovery refers to the reoccurrence of a previously habituated response after the passage of time since the last stimulus presentation. If the train stops passing for a period of time (e.g., 24 h) after a person has habituated to it, a subsequent presentation of that stimulus will again elicit covering one's ears, waking up, and the like. Habituation itself wanes when the stimulus that produced it stops occurring.

Habituation also helps one to appreciate the role of a stimulus' intensity in controlling behavior. Even after a response has habituated, a more intense stimulus will elicit the (previously) habituated responses. Also, responses habituate more slowly to intense stimuli. In the preceding example, it will take longer to habituate to two loud trains stopping at the same time and the occurrence of this stimulus will again startle and annoy the guest whose behavior had habituated to the sounds of a single train.

Just as the role of time is important for spontaneous recovery, time is also a determinant of the rate of habituation. In general, habituation occurs more quickly when stimuli occur closer in time than when they are farther apart. Stimuli presented closely together also require a shorter period of nonoccurrence for spontaneous recovery than stimuli presented farther apart.

As a general rule, behavioral adaptation occurs more rapidly each time a person or animal readapts to changes in its environment. Imagine that the number of times the above hotel guest awoke during the first night she was in Chicago was recorded and it was noted that she woke up less and less as 20 trains passed during the night. Her response was habituating to the sound of the train. Then, on the second night, it was noted that she awoke only during the first 8 trains; on the third night, only the first 2 trains awoke her. These results indicate that the rate of habituation is faster each time a person or animal is presented with the stimulus series. In other words, relearning to habituate to a stimulus is quicker than learning to habituate it.

The last major feature of habituation is that a response not only habituates to the stimulus that was presented repeatedly, but also to similar stimuli. For example, once habituated to the sound of the train, a large garbage truck picking up a dumpster is also ignored. This is stimulus generalization. However, the sound of a car accident (e.g., screeching tires, crashing metal) elicits a startle response. This is stimulus discrimination. Habituation to one stimulus might (generalization) or might not (discrimination) extend to other stimuli.

Pavlovian Conditioning

If a "neutral" stimulus (e.g., a bell) reliably precedes, usually in close temporal proximity, a stimulus that reliably and persistently elicits behavior (e.g., food in the mouth), then people and animals begin reacting during the neutral stimulus (e.g., by salivating) in way that prepares them for the impending stimulus. Although few if any stimuli are neutral in the sense that they do not elicit any behavior, behavioral psychologists consider a stimulus to be neutral when any behavior it elicits readily wanes with repeated presentations of the stimulus (i.e., responding habituates). A ringing bell, for example, might initially elicit an orienting response directed toward the sound, but this action will disappear with repeated ringing.

A stimulus that comes to elicit behavior after being paired with the stimulus that elicits behavior is a conditional stimulus (CS). A stimulus that reliably and persistently elicits behavior resistant to habituation is an unconditional stimulus (US). The responses elicited by the CS and the US are the conditional response (CR) and the unconditional response (UR), respectively. The procedure for changing behavior when two or more stimuli are paired is Pavlovian, classical, or respondent conditioning.

Although many examples of Pavlovian conditioning involve biologically significant USs such as food or water, the US does not have to be biologically significant. For example, imagine that when Jane's grandparents visit each week, they give her $20 when they arrive. After several pairings between these relatives and the money, how will Jane react when her grandparents visit? She will probably be happy and expecting money at the sight of her grandparents at the door because her grandparents (CS) precede the occurrence of money (US), which normally elicits a constellation of positive emotional responses (URs) when she receives it. By reliably giving Jane $20 when they arrive, the grandparents come to elicit a set of similar responses (CRs). However, if these relatives stop giving Jane the $20 gift when they visit, then she will become less happy and less likely to expect money when she sees them. That is, when the CS no longer predicts the US, the CR weakens and might eventually disappear. Presenting a CS without the US is termed extinction.

But just as the passage of time without a stimulus causes the spontaneous recovery of a habituated response, so too does a period of time following the extinction of a CR cause spontaneous recovery of that response. If Jane's grandparents stop visiting for a few weeks after extinction had occurred, and then following this break they show up again at Jane's door, their arrival might once again elicit positive emotional responses. Extinction itself wanes when the CS on which it is based stops occurring.

Stimulus generalization and discrimination also affect Pavlovian conditioned behavior. Generalization would be evident if Jane was happy to see her grandmother when she visited without her husband. If visits by the grandmother alone did not elicit positive responses, then stimulus discrimination had occurred. Thus, a CR elicited by a CS might also be elicited by other stimuli. The more similar a stimulus is to the CS, the more likely it will elicit a strong CR; the more a stimulus differs from the CS, the weaker the CR it elicits. Explicit stimulus discrimination training could also occur when visits by Jane's grandparents together predicted a gift of $20, but visits by either the grandmother or grandfather alone were never followed by a gift. The presence of either grandparent alone would not elicit as strong a reaction as when they visited together. A stimulus that is never followed by a US becomes an inhibitory CS or CS−, a stimulus that suppresses behavior. Differential stimulus training is yet another way in which stimuli come to control behavior.

Not only is the correlation between the CS and US important, humans' and other animals' evolutionary histories predispose them to learn some stimulus associations differently from other associations. Perhaps the most well known example is taste or flavor aversion. Flavor aversion learning occurs when people and animals avoid gustatory and olfactory cues associated with gastrointestinal illness. There are two interesting facts about flavor aversions: (1) the flavor elicits illness and avoidance of the flavor after just a single pairing and (2) flavor aversion occurs even when the flavor is separated from the illness by many hours. In most circumstances, Pavlovian conditioning works best when the neutral stimulus repeatedly precedes the US by just a few seconds. The unique characteristics of flavor aversion probably evolved because most gastrointestinal illnesses are caused by the ingestion of toxins, some of which are life-threatening and have effects that might not be experienced for several hours. An organism that could associate a flavor with illness even if many hours separate this pairing has the advantage of not repeating its mistake. In this manner, natural selection could have favored organisms that learned flavor–illness associations after a single trial and when the flavor and illness were separated by many hours.

Operant Conditioning

Habituation deals with how a person or an animal's behavior is changed by repeated presentations of single stimuli. Pavlovian conditioning focuses on how someone's behavior is changed by a particular relationship among two or more stimuli. During operant conditioning, a person or animal's behavior causes a change in the environment and this change then causes subsequent changes in the organism's actions. For example, immediately after a pack of wolves kills a moose, the low-ranking (omega) wolf tries to eat but is attacked by the high-ranking (alpha) wolf. However, if the omega wolf waits until higher ranking wolves have finished eating, it will then be allowed to eat. In the future, the omega wolf is less likely to try to eat before other wolves do and is more likely to eat after other wolves have finished. Behavior that produces a consequence and is affected by that consequence is operant or instrumental behavior.

In the preceding example, the operant response produced different consequences. Behavioral psychologists classify these consequences by their effect on behavior. Consequences of an action that increase the likelihood of that action recurring are reinforcers—positive reinforcers if the consequence is the occurrence of a stimulus (e.g., allowing the omega wolf to eat) and negative reinforcers if the consequence is the cessation or avoidance of a stimulus (e.g., stopping the attack on the omega wolf). Consequences of an action that decrease the probability of that action recurring are punishers (e.g., the attack suffered by the omega wolf).

The more closely in time a consequence follows a response, the more likely that response will be affected by that consequence. Increasingly delayed consequences are relatively ineffective reinforcers and punishers. However, operant conditioning may fail to occur even when the interval between a response and a consequence is short if the correlation between the response and the consequence is low. For example, a child who is paid for completing daily chores will probably stop engaging in this behavior if she is paid once every 3 months. Similarly, a child who is paid daily regardless of whether she does any chores is also likely to stop engaging in this behavior. In both examples, the response–consequence correlation is considerably less than +1.

As with habituation and Pavlovian conditioning, changes in behavior resulting from operant conditioning are not necessarily permanent. When a response that was followed by a reinforcer is no longer followed by it, that response undergoes extinction. How quickly extinction occurs depends on how often a response was reinforced. The less often a response is reinforced relative to the number of times it occurs, the more it will persist when reinforcement no longer occurs; however, a particular behavior will cease to occur if reinforcement for that action falls below a critical value. Thus, intermittent reinforcement can increase persistence, but insufficient reinforcement will cause the response to extinguish.

The rules that specify when a response will be reinforced are termed schedules of reinforcement. Two major classes of reinforcement schedules are ratio schedules and interval schedules. In ratio schedules, the reinforcer depends solely on the occurrence of a response (e.g., a quarterback's contract that contains incentive clauses stating that he will receive a bonus each time he passes for a touchdown). In interval schedules, the reinforcer depends on the occurrence of a response and the passage of time. For example, assuming that mail is delivered at the same time daily, a person will be reinforced for checking his mailbox if he waited at least 24 h since the mail was delivered. Checking the mailbox during the 24 h period will not be reinforced because the mail will not yet have arrived.

Typically, ratio schedules support higher rates of behavior than comparable interval schedules. To see why, consider a ratio schedule in which two responses produce one reinforcer. In this schedule, how often reinforcers occur depends exclusively on how rapidly the person responds. The rate of reinforcement will always equal one-half the rate of behavior. But now consider an interval schedule in which a response is reinforced if it occurs at least 10 s since the previous reinforcer. In this situation, a person can never earn more than six reinforcers per minute regardless of how fast he or she responds. Because interval schedules have a built-in cap on the amount of reinforcement that can be earned over a period of time, people and animals generally respond slower during interval schedules than comparable ratio schedules.

Of course, all response–consequence relationships occur in a stimulus context. Just as different CSs differentially paired with a US will acquire different capacities to elicit or inhibit responding, so too do stimuli present during a response–consequence relationship come to control the operant response. Behavioral psychologists refer to this relationship among the antecedent context, behavior, and its consequences as the A-B-C of behavioral control. For example, in the presence of a red traffic light, a driver will depress the brake, stopping the car. However, once the light turns green, the driver releases the brake pedal and depresses the accelerator, moving the car forward. The color of the light (red or green) controls different actions (depressing the brake versus the accelerator) because each response is associated with different consequences (stopping versus moving the car). A stimulus in the presence of which a particular response is reinforced is an S^D (pronounced S-dee) or S+; a stimulus in the presence of which a particular response is not reinforced is an S^Δ (pronounced S-delta) or S−. Stimulus generalization occurs when a response is more likely in the presence of other, usually similar, stimuli; stimulus discrimination occurs when the response is less likely in the presence of other, usually dissimilar, stimuli. For instance, a dolphin reinforced with a fish for jumping over a red rope might also jump over a blue, yellow, or green rope, but not over a thick ribbon of any color. Which dimensions of a stimulus control behavior depends on the history of reinforcement in the presence of these dimensions (e.g., a whale that is never reinforced for splashing people in the pool, but is routinely reinforced for splashing people outside of the pool), evolutionary biases (e.g., a falcon is more likely to associate the sight than sound of a rodent with food), perceptual capabilities (e.g., a bass that is more likely to strike at silvery shad than reddish crayfish in murky water), and the like.

Operant–Pavlovian Interactions

Although habituation, operant conditioning, and Pavlovian conditioning are often discussed separately, the three procedures are almost always involved in varying proportions in learned behavior. For example, in most Pavlovian conditioning situations, the neutral stimulus usually elicits a response that undergoes habituation as this stimulus is increasingly paired with a US.

Some of the clearest examples of operant–Pavlovian interactions involve situations where people and animals avoid aversive events. A man who is afraid to speak in public will not wait to see how his audience reacts; on being asked to give a speech, he will decline the request or make an excuse. A woman who fears that an elevator she rides aboard might crash will not ride the elevator to see what will happen; she will use the stairs instead. A gang member hears gunshots and ducks for cover. In these examples, being asked to give a speech, the sight of the elevator, and the sound of gunfire predict possible aversive outcomes (e.g., an unresponsive audience, a crashing elevator, being shot) unless an avoidance response occurs (e.g., declining to give a speech, taking the stairs, diving to the ground). In these circumstances, there is a Pavlovian and an operant component that controls behavior. The Pavlovian component is the relationship between a signal and an aversive event. The operant component is the response–consequence relationship involving the avoidance response and the consequent absence of the aversive event. If someone makes a particular response during the signal that predicts the aversive event, then this event will not occur and the avoidance response is negatively reinforced.

It is worth noting that, for many people, the aversive event does not have to be probable, only possible. The probability that an elevator will crash is low. Despite this, modifying avoidance behavior is difficult. In the example of the woman who is afraid to ride in elevators, it is unlikely that this fear will disappear because she will never sample the real contingencies of safely riding in an elevator. The fear elicited by the CS (sight of the elevator) causes her to make a response (climbing the stairs) that prevents her from discovering that her fear (an elevator she rides aboard will crash) is unrealistic. To eliminate avoidance behavior related to unrealistic anxiety or fear, people must first be exposed to the fear-eliciting stimulus and prevented from making the avoidance response.

See Also the Following Article

Primate Studies, Ecology and Behavior

Further Reading

Abramson, C. I. (1994). *A Primer of Invertebrate Learning: The Behavioral Perspective.* American Psychological Association, Washington, DC.

Donahoe, J. W., and Palmer, D. C. (1994). *Learning and Complex Behavior.* Allyn & Bacon, Boston, MA.

Hearst, E. (1988). Fundamentals of learning and conditioning. In *Steven's Handbook of Experimental Psychology* (R. C. Atkinson, R. J. Herrnstein, G. Lindzey, and R. D. Luce, eds.), 2nd Ed., Vol. 2, pp. 3–109. Wiley, New York.

Kazdin, A. E. (1998). *Research Design in Clinical Psychology,* 3rd Ed. Allyn & Bacon, Boston, MA.

Martin, G. L., and Pear, J. J. (2003). *Behavior Modification: What It Is and How to Do It,* 7th Ed. Prentice Hall, Upper Saddle River, NJ.

Martin, P., and Bateson, P. (1993). *Measuring Behaviour: An Introductory Guide,* 2nd Ed. Cambridge University Press, Cambridge, UK.

Mackintosh, N. J. (1983). *Conditioning and Associative Learning.* Oxford University Press, Oxford, UK.

O'Donohue, W., and Krasner, L. (eds.) (1995). *Theories of Behavior Therapy: Exploring Behavior Change.* American Psychological Association, Washington, DC.

Pear, J. J. (2001). *The Science of Learning.* Psychology Press, Philadelphia, PA.

Pryor, K. (1999). *Don't Shoot the Dog! The New Art of Teaching and Training,* revised Ed. Bantam, New York.

Rescorla, R. A. (1988). Pavlovian conditioning: It's not what you think it is. *Am. Psychol.* **43,** 151–160.

Sidman, M. (1960). *Tactics of Scientific Research: Evaluating Experimental Data in Psychology.* Basic Books, New York.

Skinner, B. F. (1974). *About Behaviorism.* Vintage Books, New York.

Bentham, Jeremy

Gilbert Geis
University of California, Irvine, Irvine, California, USA

Glossary

felicity calculus The process by which the balance of pleasures and pains is measured; sometimes called hedonistic or hedonic calculus.

happiness For Bentham, a state measured in terms of whether an action adds to an individual's pleasure or diminishes the sum total of his or her pain. The term is generally used by Bentham to refer to the aggregate of a person's pleasures over pains.

paraphrasis Bentham's coined term for the process of demystifying words such as "liberty," by breaking them down into their constituent elements. If such a definitional breakdown is not possible, it demonstrates that the term is a "fiction," unrelated to any real thing.

pleasure and pain Bentham maintains that "nature has placed mankind under the governance of two sovereign masters, pleasure and pain." The difference between happiness and pleasure lies in the fact that the former "is not susceptible of division, but pleasure is."

utility For Bentham, the principle of utility approves or disapproves of every action whatsoever according to its tendency to augment or diminish the happiness of the party whose interest is in question.

Jeremy Bentham (1748–1832) is generally regarded as the founder of the utilitarian school, an approach still vibrant in economic and philosophical thought. Bentham was the first thinker to provide a barrage of information as well as insights and analyses that sought to make utilitarian thought approximate as closely as possible the mathematical exactitude of natural science scholarship as well as its classificatory sophistication. Bentham applied his principle of utility to ethical, legal, and constitutional issues, but, as Tom Warke observes, only after more than a century of adaptation did it become the dominant explanation within economic theory for consumer behavior and the basis for contemporary rational choice theory.

Biographical Notes

Jeremy Bentham was an eccentric, reclusive intellectual who spent the better part of his life writing tracts that sought to enlighten his fellow humans about the paths of proper thought and persuading persons with power to support the kinds of programs he believed would improve the human condition. The son and grandson of successful London lawyers, Bentham was an exceptionally precocious child. He became a boarder at the fashionable Westminster School at the age of 7 years and enrolled at Queen's College, Oxford University, when he was not yet 13. He later studied law and clerked at Lincoln's Inn, developing a deep disdain for both lawyers and lawyering, regarding the latter as a pursuit built on fictions and marked by the use of terms and concepts that only initiates could comprehend, all this being so in order to enrich practitioners and keep laymen from knowing what was going on. "Lawyers feed upon untruth, as Turks feed upon opium," was one of Bentham's caustic jabs. On his father's death in 1792, Bentham inherited a sizable fortune, realized from property investments, that allowed him the leisure to spend his days putting together a monumental outpouring of ideas that reflected his utilitarian views.

Bentham wrote tirelessly for all his adult life. James Steintrager insists that to read all that Bentham wrote would take a lifetime longer than Bentham's 84 years. Besides, Bentham's prose at times can be virtually impenetrable. The essayist William Hazlitt sarcastically observed that "his works have been translated into French—they ought to be translated into English."

Bentham's Utilitarianism

Of Pleasures and Pains

Jeremy Bentham is regarded as the father of the utilitarian school of thought that seeks to analyze human and social actions in terms of their consequences for well being. Many writers before Bentham had employed the term and some of the ideas of utilitarianism, but in a much looser sense than Bentham proposed. Bentham advocated that human action and public policy should seek to create "the greatest happiness for the greatest number." This concept, as Robert Shackleton's adroit detective work has demonstrated, was taken verbatim from Cesare Beccaria's *Dei delitti e delle pene* (1764; translated into English as *An Essay on Crimes and Punishments*). Later, Bentham would truncate the goal to "the greatest happiness," a move Mary Mack regards as mere definitional "housekeeping," though it more likely was prompted by Bentham's recognition that, from a mathematical perspective, the original definition contained one too many "greatests." Bentham finally settled on the term "the felicity maximizing principle" to describe the ideal that characterized his recommendations. Bentham also was deeply concerned not to ignore the needs of persons in the minority. This is reflected in his system of weighting, in which everyone was to count for one and no one for more than one. In modern economic welfare theory, this equal weighting defines a utilitarian principle as being specifically "Benthamite."

For Bentham, the wellsprings of human behavior reside totally in attempts to gain pleasure and to avoid pain. He maintained that "men calculate [pleasure and pain], some with less exactness, indeed, some with more: but all men calculate. And all humans voluntarily act in regard to their personal pleasure." It is difficult, Bentham granted, to prove enjoyment in the case of, say, a Japanese man who commits hari kari; but, nonetheless, the pursuit of pleasure was his goal. Bentham believed that self-interest, if enlightened, would produce socially desirable results, though he was aware that individuals at times fail to appreciate what will bring them pleasure rather than pain, in part because they cannot adequately anticipate the future.

For Bentham, present and future consequences of actions could be estimated in terms of seven considerations: (1) intensity, (2) duration, (3) certainty, (4) propinquity, (5) fecundity, (6) purity, and (7) extent, this last referring to the number of individuals affected. Bentham conceded that intensity was not measurable, but maintained that the other outcomes might be calibrated. Pleasures and pains were of various kinds, 13 of which Bentham, an inveterate maker of lists that sought to embrace comprehensively all possible ramifications of a subject, spelled out: (1) pleasures and pains of sense, (2) pleasures of wealth, with the corresponding pains of deprivation, (3) pleasures of skill and pains of awkwardness, (4) pleasures of amity and pains of enmity, (5) pleasures of good reputation and pains of ill-repute, (6) pleasures of power, (7) pleasures of piety, (8) pleasures and pains of sympathy and benevolence, (9) pleasures and pains of malevolence, (10) pleasures and pains of memory, (11) pleasures and pains of imagination, (12) pleasures and pains of expectation, and (13) pleasures and pains of association.

Bentham's aim was to teach moral agents (that is, humans) a proper arithmetic, to lay before them a satisfactory estimate of pain and pleasure—"a budget of receipt and disbursement, out of every operation of which [they are] to draw a balance of good." Vice then would be a miscalculation of pleasures and pains. Thus, "there are few moral questions which may not be resolved with an accuracy and a certainty not far removed from mathematical demonstration."

The Legislator's Task

It becomes the duty of legislators to create conditions that offer the widest potential for the personal pursuit of pleasure, so long as that pursuit does not interfere with a similar mission by others. The legislator also was to remove circumstances that would create conflicts in self-interested pursuits. Those legislating must take a scientific view of all human endeavor. Legislation was to be judged in terms of its impact on four conditions related to pleasure and pain: (1) security, (2) subsistence, (3) abundance, and (4) equality. Bentham granted that "this division has not all the exactness which might be desired" because "the limits which separate these objectives are not always easy to be determined."

A difficulty that increasingly bedeviled Bentham's blueprint concerned the question of how to reconcile the self-interest, that is, the quest for their own happiness, of those in power with his demand that they govern so as to ensure the greatest happiness of their subjects. During the latter part of his life, Bentham began to advocate widespread popular democracy so that people could seek to maximize their happiness by selecting leaders who would help them in this quest. His hope was to educate and train the citizens so that they would be better able to determine which leaders would act to increase constituent happiness.

Critiques of Bentham

Bentham's appeal was to rational argument and to what James E. Crimmins calls "consequentialist calculation." His aim was "to extend the physical branch [of science] to the moral," but it must be stressed that he was well aware that his measuring formula inevitably would provide an inexact answer: his was a roadmap without any precise mileage measurements. As Mack indicates, "the truth is that Bentham did not offer a systematic theory of ethics based on exact calculation, but a series of prudential rules . . . based on a new vocabulary and a new logic."

A Bentham scholar has pointed out that only a single dimension can be employed to measure utility as Bentham defined it because, as Warke notes, "no unique and continuous ordering exists for a multi-dimensional entity except in trivial cases where all dimensions save one remain constant or where all dimensions vary in the same proportion." Bentham's utility construct was irreducibly multidimensional, with a distinct dimension for each type of pleasure and pain. Warke further points out that faced with two outcomes, a person is likely to have a continuum of responses because preference sets tend to be fuzzy and agents often dither. Therefore, mathematical precision is likely to be elusive, if not impossible to attain: Bentham's tactics were of necessity coarse-grained; he was interested in "approximation" and in the way that the "preponderance" (two words Bentham much favored) of evidence tilted rather than in exactitude. Utility, as Mack maintains, represents in Bentham's work not a formula but an attitude.

Bentham's concept of happiness was a blunt measuring instrument. He recognized this in an early example:

> *Call the species of misery produced by any one action in a single person,* x *[say, a threat of injury], and that produced by another,* y *[say, loss of property]. Now whether* x *or* y *be the greater, is a matter of conjecture and opinion, but that* x + y *is greater than either* x *or* y *alone, is a matter of demonstration . . . . In this manner it is a matter of demonstration that Robbery is worse than Theft [since it includes both* x *and* y *while Theft includes only* y*].*

Bentham granted that more finite distinctions were out of the question and that it was only the first principles of mathematics that have anything to do with such a calculation. Therefore, whereas it is possible to rank order robbery and theft for a given loss of property, it is problematic to rank order a $100 petty theft and a $20 armed robbery.

John Plamenatz (1958) sagely notes that Bentham "often talks as if he were advising legislators and judges how to make calculations which it is plainly impossible to make. But all the misleading language can be ignored," Plamenatz adds, "and Bentham's rules can be treated as if they were rules for making possible calculations. Once this is done it is easy to see how much is really valuable."

Further Utilitarian Considerations

Motives, Punishment, and Paraphrasis

For Bentham, the motives (or "springs of action," as he labeled them) for human behavior were beside the point. There is no such thing for him as a bad motive; it is only the consequences, the pain and the pleasure created, that are significant. A man may want to eat. To satisfy his hunger he can go to a restaurant, get food at home, or steal: the motive remains the same, the behavior and its consequences are quite different.

Punishments were to be established to convince real and potential wrongdoers—that is, those who pursue pleasures by means such as stealing, acts that produce pain for others—to choose more positive paths. But the punishments should be only of such magnitude as to achieve satisfactory deterrence; harsher inflictions add an unacceptable dosage to individual and possibly to social pain. As Bentham expressed the matter, "never use a preventive means of a nature to do more evil than the offense to be prevented."

Bentham urged analysts to engage in what he called paraphrasis, that is, to tie real meanings to words that represent unanchored ideas, terms such as "natural law," "justice," "power," "duty," and "liberty." In Bentham's work, an act, once its ingredients are clearly defined, meets the standard of utility "if it tends to produce benefit, advantage, good or happiness (all this in the present case comes to the same thing) or (which again comes to the same thing) to prevent the happening of mischief, pain, evil or unhappiness to the party whose interest is considered."

Felicity Calculus

To measure the "goodness" or "badness" of an act, Bentham introduces the pseudomathematical concept of what he calls felicity calculus. Bentham offers the following vignette to illustrate how a situation might be looked at:

> *[I]f having a crown in my pocket and not being thirsty, I hesitate whether I should buy a bottle of claret with it for my own drinking or lay it out in providing sustenance for a family . . . it is plain that so long as I continued hesitating the two pleasures of sensuality in the one case, of sympathy in the other, were exactly . . . equal.*

The illustration, however, is not as straightforward as Bentham indicates, because it involves determination of the "goodness" of family considerations in contrast to that of claret. And the matter becomes a great deal more complicated if the need is to predict, as social scientists attempt to do, which of the two alternatives any given individual will adopt or, for that matter, which alternative a person will choose each time the same choice is presented.

And how are 5 minutes of exquisite pleasure to be measured against 10 minutes of routine pain? For Bentham, pains carried greater weight than did pleasures on the scale of values, and the miseries of loss outweighed those of acquisition. Despite such evaluative hurdles, Bentham pressed onward, as a further illustration demonstrates: writing about heavy gambling, he pointed out that if a person has 1000 pounds and the stake is 500, the odds are always unfavorable in regard to pleasure, even if the game is fair, because if the gambler loses, his fortune is diminished by one-half, whereas winning increases it only by a third. Besides, Bentham notes that when sums and circumstances are equal, the enjoyment produced by gain is never equal to the suffering produced by loss.

Bentham also appreciated that wealth could not be equated systematically with degrees of happiness, as the following illustration shows:

> *Put on one side a thousand farmers, having enough to live upon, and a little more. Put on the other side ... a prince ..., himself as rich as all the farmers taken together. It is probable, I say, that his happiness is greater than the average happiness of the thousand farmers; but it is by no means probable that it is equal to the sum total of their happiness, or, what amounts to the same thing, a thousand times greater than the average happiness of one of them. It would be remarkable if the happiness were ten times, or even five times greater.*

The problem of assigning satisfactory weights to different pleasures (any one of which will also vary for different persons) was overwhelming: all Bentham really asked was that responsible people ought to take the utilitarian approach as a valuable tool for directing and evaluating behaviors and public policies.

John Stuart Mill, a Bentham disciple with ambivalent views about his mentor, put the matter particularly well: "He [Bentham] introduced into morals and politics those habits of thoughts and modes of investigation, which are essential to the idea of science; and the absence of which made those departments of inquiry, as physics had been before Bacon, a field of interminable discussion, leading to no result. It was ... his 'method' that constituted the novelty and the value of what he did, a value beyond all price ... " (Mill, 1769/1838).

The issue of slavery offers a good example of Benthamite thought. Having slaves might create a good deal of happiness in those who possess them and a good deal of wretchedness in those who are enslaved. But rather than attempting to measure these consequences, Bentham points out that he knows of nobody who would voluntarily prefer to be a slave; therefore, it is apparent that the unattractiveness of the status and the pain associated with it overwhelm any advantage slavery might offer to those who benefit from it.

Bentham's felicity calculus, given his dogged analytical attempts to pin down all possible consequences of an action, usually is up to the task of differentiating what most of us would consider the "good" from the "bad," or "pleasure" from "pain." He offers, for instance, a situation of an employee of a medical research center who grabs off the street almost at random a person whose body parts are to be used to save the lives of those in need of such reinforcements. A superficial utilitarian conclusion might be that the act is commendable because, though it inflicts devastating pain on a single victim, it produces great pleasure in a number of persons whose well being is saved or improved by the transplants. But Bentham points out that the alarm created among the citizenry, that any of them might be the next person snatched off the streets by the medical team, is so painful that the act clearly falls beyond the pale of utilitarian approval. Bentham's examples often are reasonable enough, but they do not go very far toward persuading a reader that what he proposes can truly be applied to measure complex psychological phenomena mathematically. Here is another Bentham's illustration:

> *You tell me that St. Paul's is bigger than the Pantheon. I agree with you that it is so. This agreement does not hinder our ideas of the proportion of those two bodies from being very different. You may think St. Paul's ten times as big as the other building. I may think it not more than half as big again.*

The disagreement, Bentham observes, can readily be settled by obtaining a measuring stick, the accuracy of which both parties concede. The same process, Bentham maintains, can be carried out in regard to disagreements about happiness. But he never truly found an adequate measuring rod. At one point, in fact, in a not uncharacteristic manner, Bentham observed that the single honk of a goose some thousands of years earlier undoubtedly has influenced many aspects of contemporary life, and he sought to enumerate some of these consequences. His was an indefatigable pursuit of a detailed inventory of the consequences of events and actions, so that all of us could be better informed and thereby persuaded to make wiser choices.

Money as a Measure of Pleasure

Money became for Bentham one of the more readily measurable items in his felicity calculus, because its possession strongly correlates with happiness. He was well aware of what later came to be called the Law of Diminishing Marginal Utility, that is, that the more wealth an individual possesses the less total happiness an increment is likely to bring. A multimillionaire would hardly be moved greatly by the addition of $100,000 to his fortune, but a poor person undoubtedly would derive great pleasure obtaining this amount of money. Though Bentham might not be able to calculate precisely the quantities of pleasure involved in such a situation, he was able to use it to advocate public policies favoring more equitable distribution of wealth, basing his advocacy on utilitarian principles.

Conclusion

In a long life dedicated to interminable written analyses and exhortations, Bentham attempted to translate his premises regarding happiness into formulas that offered an opportunity to determine pain and pleasure. He inevitably failed by a wide margin to approximate exactitude in a mathematical sense. Nonetheless, relying on utilitarian doctrine and formulas, Bentham had remarkable success in bringing about significant number of political reforms, particularly in criminal law and in regard to the punishment of offenders. He typically did so by specifying with striking perceptiveness and in excruciating detail the consequences of the old ways and the advantages of his recommendations for creating a fairer and a happier society. In addition, Bentham's utilitarianism, scoffed at and caricatured for decades, later regained favor in the social sciences, particularly in economics, and today forms the intellectual skeleton that is being fleshed out by sophisticated analytical and empirical formulations.

Auto-Icon

Bentham's skeleton, stuffed with padding to fill it out, and seated in his favorite chair and dressed in his own clothes, is displayed in the South Cloister at University College, University of London. His head did not preserve well, so a wax replica sits atop the body (see Fig. 1). He requested in his will that his body be so preserved, but only after it furnished final utility for medical science by means of a public dissection.

A Bibliographic Note

Bentham produced a torrent of written material, much of it still unpublished. His method of work was highly disorganized. As Shackleton notes, "drafts succeeded drafts, abridgments and expansions followed each other, manuscripts were often dismantled and physically incorporated in others." Bentham's correspondence alone now occupies 11 large volumes that have been published as part of a project to move all of his manuscript material into print. Three more volumes are in process, with a possible fourth to include material that has come to light since the project began. Bentham characteristically enlisted aides to edit his material and they often took considerable liberties reorganizing and rewriting what they regarded as a sometimes impenetrable thicket of words. The best guide to the quality and reliability of Bentham's work is provided by Ross Harrison in *Bentham* (pages ix–xxiv).

The Bentham Project, housed at University College, University of London, offers a website (available at http://www.ucl.ac.uk) with up-to-date information on the

Figure 1 The wax replica of Jeremy Bentham's head, atop his skeleton at South Cloister, University College, the University of London. Photo courtesy of John Dombrink.

progress being made toward shepherding into print all of Bentham's works. The project, described by Gertrude Himmelfarb as perhaps the most ambitious publishing venture of its kind ever to be undertaken in England, is contemplated to result in at least 38 volumes. In addition, Bhikhu Parekh has edited four volumes that reprint 143 of the most important assessments of Bentham's work. Volume II is made up of pieces that focus on Bentham's ideas regarding measurement.

See Also the Following Article

Utility

Further Reading

Ben-Door, O. (2000). *Constitutional Limits and the Public Sphere: A Critical Study of Bentham's Constitutionalism.* Hart, Oxford.

Bentham, J. (1838–1843). *The Works of Jeremy Bentham* (J. Bowring, ed.). W. Tait, Edinburgh.

Bentham, J. (1996) [1789]. *An Introduction to the Principles of Morals and Legislation* (J. H. Burns and H. L. A. Hart, eds.). Clarendon, Oxford.

Crimmins, J. E. (1990). *Secular Utilitarianism: Social Science and the Critique of Religion in the Thought of Jeremy Bentham.* Clarendon, London.

Harrison, R. (1993). *Bentham.* Routledge & Kegan Paul, London.

Kelly, P. J. (1990). *Utilitarianism and Distributive Justice: Jeremy Bentham and the Civil Law.* Clarendon, Oxford.

Mack, M. (1963). *Jeremy Bentham: An Odyssey of Ideas, 1748–1792.* Columbia Univ. Press, New York.

Mill, J. S. (1969) [1838]. Bentham. In *The Collected Works of John Stuart Mill* (J. M. Robson, ed.), Vol. X, pp. 75–115. Univ. of Toronto Press, Toronto.

Parekh, B. (ed.) (1993). *Jeremy Bentham: Critical Assessments.* Routledge, London.

Plamenatz, J. P. (1958). Jeremy Bentham. In *The English Utilitarians,* 2nd Ed., pp. 59–85. Blackwell, Oxford.

Rosen, F. (1983). *Jeremy Bentham and Representative Democracy: A Study of the Constitutional Code.* Clarendon, Oxford.

Shackleton, R. (1972). The greatest happiness of the greatest number: The history of Bentham's phrase. *Stud. Voltaire Eighteenth Cent.* **90,** 1461–1482.

Steintrager, J. (1977). *Bentham.* George Allen & Unwin, London.

Warke, T. (2000). Classical utilitarianism and the methodology of determinate choice, in economics and in ethics. *J. Econ. Methodol.* **7,** 373–394.

Warke, T. (2000). Mathematical fitness in the evolution of the utility concept from Bentham to Jevons to Marshall. *J. Hist. Econ. Thought* **22,** 5–27.

Warke, T. (2000). Multi-dimensional utility and the index number problem: Jeremy Bentham, J. S. Mill, and qualitative hedonism. *Utilitas* **12,** 176–303.

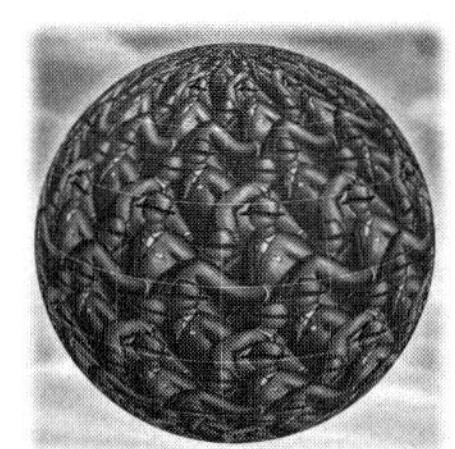

Bernoulli, Jakob

Ivo Schneider

University of the German Armed Forces Munich, Munich, Germany

Glossary

Bernoulli's measure of probability A measure of probability derived from the transformation of Huygens's value of expectation into a quantifiable concept. There are two ways of determining this measure of probability: (1) *(a priori)* for an equipossibility of the outcomes of a finite number of mutually exclusive elementary events, such as drawing a ball of a certain color out of an urn filled with balls of different colors, by the ratio of the number of cases favorable for the event to the total number of cases; (2) *(a posteriori)* for events such as a person of known age's dying after 5 years, by the relative frequency of "the frequently observed event in similar examples."

law of large numbers The theorem that the estimates of unknown probabilities of events based on observed relative frequencies of such events become the more reliable the more observations are made (also called Bernoulli's golden theorem). More precisely, Bernoulli proved that the relative frequency h_n of an event with probability p in n independent trials converges in probability to p or that for any given small positive number ε and any given large natural number c, for sufficiently large n, the inequality:

$$\frac{P(|h_n - p| \leq \varepsilon)}{P(|h_n - p| > \varepsilon)} > c$$

holds, which is equivalent to $P(|h_n - p| \leq \varepsilon) > 1 - 1/c + 1$.

mortality The quantification of human mortality.

probability The degree of certainty based either on belief depending on testimony or on evidence derived from the frequency of occurrence of an event. This is a change from earlier ideas held by Aristotle and his followers that probability was what was common opinion of most or of the majority of the best informed or what would happen "in most cases." Bernoulli's concept of probability, degree of certainty, showed at the same time subjective or epistemic and frequentist or aleatory aspects.

value of expectation According to Huygens, the payoff table in a game with a finite number of outcomes. The value of an expectation is determined the weighted average of the payoffs in terms of money.

Jakob Bernoulli (1655–1705), one of the leading mathematicians of his time with important contributions to infinitesimal calculus, is the father of a mathematical theory of probability. His posthumously published *Ars Conjectandi* influenced the development of probability theory in the 18th century up to Laplace. The basic concept in Bernoulli's art of conjecturing became probability, the classical measure of which he had derived from a transformation of Huygens' value of expectation. *Ars Conjectandi* should be applied to what we call now the social domain and what Bernoulli described as the domain of civil, moral, and economic affairs. Bernoulli distinguishes two ways of determining, exactly or approximately, the classical measure of probability. The first, called *a priori* presupposes the equipossibility of the outcomes of certain elementary events and allows us to relate the number of cases favorable for an event to all possible cases. The second, called *a posteriori*, is for the determination of the probability of an event for which there are no equipossible cases that we can count (e.g., mortality). For these cases, we can inductively, by experiments, get as close as we desire to the true measure the probability by estimating it by the relative frequency of the outcome of this event in a series of supposedly independent trials. This he justifies by his *theorema aureum*, which was called later by Poisson Bernoulli's law of large numbers.

The Role of Jakob Bernoulli in the Development of a Mathematical Probability Theory and Statistics

Jakob Bernoulli brought together in his work culminating in the *Ars Conjectandi* two hitherto largely separated domains: the calculus of games of chance as codified by Christiaan Huygens in his tract *De Ratiociniis in Ludo Aleae* and the domain of application of the word "probability" as used in the language of everyday life. By this he created a new mathematical subject that he called the "art of conjecturing" and that in the hands of his successors became the calculus or the mathematical theory of probability. The central idea in Bernoulli's art of conjecturing was the transformation of Huygens's concept of expectation into a quantifiable concept of probability applicable to what we call now the social domain and what Bernoulli described as the domain of civil, moral, and economic affairs. Bernoulli tried to justify the application of his concept of probability to the social domain by using his principal theorem, later called the law of large numbers. The problem of how to gain reliable estimates for unknown probabilities from a finite set of data became a main concern of mathematical statistics, which originated only with the biometric activities of Francis Galton in the 19th century.

Jakob Bernoulli's Scientific Career

Jakob Bernoulli, born in 1655 in Basel, came from a family of merchants. His father, Nikolaus Bernoulli, took over the drug business from his father and became a member of the town council in Basel. Jakob Bernoulli and later members of the Bernoulli family became the most prominent family in the history of mathematics, producing four generations of outstanding mathematicians.

After finishing a master's degree in 1671, Jakob Bernoulli studied theology until 1676, when he received the licentiate in theology; at the same time he studied mathematics and astronomy secretly, against his father's will. After 1676, he left Basel to work as a tutor for 4 years, which he spent in Geneva and France. In France and during a second journey in 1681 and 1682 to the Netherlands, England, and Germany, he became a Cartesian. During his second journey he also met the mathematicians Jan Hudde, John Wallis, and Isaac Barrow and natural philosophers such as Robert Boyle, Robert Hooke, and John Flamsteed. His first publication (1681) dealt with comets, based on his observations of the comet of 1680. He predicted the reappearance of this comet in the year 1719 and stated that comets belong to the solar system and reappear after a certain period.

After his return to Basel he began to give private lectures, especially on the mechanics of solid and liquid bodies. He read the mathematical works of Wallis and Barrow and the second Latin edition of Descartes's *Géométrie* with the commentaries by Frans van Schooten and his students. He became interested in problems concerning algebra and infinitesimal analysis. In 1684 Leibniz published in the *Acta Eruditorum* (founded in 1682) a short presentation of differential calculus in algorithmic form, and in 1686 he published some remarks concerning the fundamental ideas of integral calculus. These papers occupied the interest of Jakob Bernoulli and his younger brother Johann (1667–1748). Jakob tried to get further information from Leibniz in 1687, but Leibniz could answer Bernoulli's questions only 3 years later because of a diplomatic mission he had to undertake. At that time, Jakob and Johann had not only mastered the Leibnizian calculus, but also had added so considerably to it that Leibniz in a letter of 1694 remarked that infinitesimal calculus owed as much to the Bernoulli brothers as to himself. Jakob cultivated the theory of infinite series on the basis of preliminary work done by Nikolaus Mercator, James Gregory, Newton, and Leibniz. He published five dissertations on series between 1689 and 1704. He considered series to be the universal means to integrate arbitrary functions, to square and rectify curves. In 1690, Jakob had introduced the term "integral" in his solution to the problem of determining the curve of constant descent.

In the 1690s, the relationship between Jakob and Johann deteriorated and led to bitter quarrels. In 1687, Jakob had became professor of mathematics at the University of Basel, in which position he remained until his death in 1705. He was honored by the memberships of the Academies of Sciences in Paris (1699) and in Berlin (1701). He had a daughter and a son from Judith Stupan, whom he had married in 1684.

Early Work on Problems of Games of Chance and Mortality

Jakob Bernoulli's interest in stochastics began in the 1680s. His first publication on the calculus of chance dates from 1685. The development of Bernoulli's ideas leading to his art of conjecturing can be traced, at least in part, in the *Meditationes*, his scientific diary that he began in 1677. In it we can distinguish three periods in which Bernoulli worked on problems concerning games of chance and probability: (1)1684–1687, in which he was engaged in the solution of problems of games of chance; (2) in which he extended the methods for the solution of games of chance to the solution of problems concerning decisions in everyday life; and (3) approximately 1687–1689, in which he was concerned with the proof of his main theorem, the law of large numbers.

In the first period Jakob Bernoulli began with the solution of the five problems Huygens had proposed to his readers at the end of his tract *De Ratiociniis in Ludo Aleae* from 1657.

In the second period, crucial for Bernoulli's transformation of Huygens's concept of expectation to a quantifiable concept of probability was the juridical problem of a marriage contract, on which Bernoulli worked in 1685–1686. Bernoulli was concerned with a passage of the contract proposed by the groom in which it was assumed that the couple would be blessed with children and that the wife, Caja, would die before her husband, Titius, and the children; in this situation the passage governs the division of the couple's common property between the father and the children. A distinction is made among the possibilities that neither, one, or both of the fathers of the bridal couple, who were alive at the time of the conclusion of the contract, die and leave their heritage to their children. Only property that had become the common property of the couple was to be regulated, and so such distinctions needed to be drawn. The portion of the groom would be larger if he had already entered into his inheritance and smaller if not, unless both fathers die. The bride's father objected to Titius's initial proposal; this induced Titius to make a second proposal, according to which he would receive the same portion of the common property regardless of what happened to the fathers.

Here Bernoulli posed the question: Which suggestion would be more favorable for the children? To this end he had to make assumptions about the possible order of death of the three people involved, the two fathers and the bride. He first assumed that all six possible orders have equal weight. But this assumption did not satisfy him because the youth of the bride had not been taken into account. Thus, he assumes that for every two instances (e.g., diseases, symptoms, or events) that might bring about the death of either father, there is only one that would threaten Caja with death. There are thus five cases in all, each equally likely to take its victim first. Because Caja would be affected by only one of these, whereas the two fathers would be affected by four, her situation is evaluated as one-fifth of certainty of her being first to die, that is, "one probability, five of which make the entire certainty."

Here Bernoulli used the plural "probabilities," where these are equated with the no more precisely distinguished individual cases; this use does not permit the conception of probability as "degree of certainty," which is observed in the next stage. Aided by Huygens's formula for determining expectation, Bernoulli then derived a certainty of 4/15, written 4/15 c (where c stands for certitudo), or 4 probabilities out of 15 that Caja would die second and finally 8/15 c that she would die third. Bernoulli first generalized this approach to the problem and added two different models that he employed to weigh the various orders of death. In the second model, the chances of Caja dying in first, second, and third place were 2 : 5 : 11; in the third, they were 4 : 8 : 12. So each model gave different chances for Caja to survive none, one, or both fathers.

Therefore, at the end of his treatment of the marriage contract between Titius and Caja Bernoulli proposed extensive investigations into human mortality. Here he introduced the concept of a quantifiable probability with a view to making probability the main concept of the calculus of chance, extended to what we call now the social domain:

> *This we have to understand generally in civil and moral affairs, in which we of course know that one thing is more probable, better or more advisable than another; but by what degree of probability or goodness they exceed others we determine only according to probability, not exactly. The surest way of estimating probabilities in these cases is not* a priori, *that is by cause, but* a posteriori, *that is, from the frequently observed event in similar examples.*

A series of further problems underline this procedure for estimating probabilities *a posteriori*, in Bernoulli's sense of taking the average of frequently observed data as in the prediction of the number of births and deaths in a certain city in the next year or the appearance of the next epidemic. Bernoulli even wanted to determine a man's reliability from the number of times he told the truth or lied or the outcome of *jeu de paume*, a predecessor of lawn tennis, depending on estimates of the skills of the players involved. On the same basis, Bernoulli tried to solve other problems, such as whether to accept an offer for 80 bottles of light wine. In all these cases, we can find marginal notes indicating that the estimates are more reliable if based on more observations.

Bernoulli carried out the determination of probabilities *a posteriori* by adopting relative frequencies determined through observation as estimates of probabilities that could not be given *a priori*. He felt justified in proceeding in this form because of his main theorem, which at the same time served as the essential foundation of his program to extend the realm of application of numerically determinable probabilities.

In a preliminary version of the theorem, Bernoulli tried to show by induction that in a game with equal chances of winning or losing, as in the toss of a coin, the probabilities of winning more often than $2n$ times in $3n$ trials is not greater than:

$$\frac{1}{8}\left(\frac{7}{8}\right)^n$$

which tends to become smaller than any assignable small quantity for increasing n. So the probability of winning more often than $2n$ times in $3n$ trials and for reasons of symmetry the probability of winning less often than n times in $3n$ trials approaches 0 with increasing n. Accordingly, the probability of winning a number of times between n and $2n$ in $3n$ trials approaches 1 with increasing n.

After the treatment of the special case of equal chances winning or losing, Bernoulli proved in the *Meditationes* generally the equivalent of the following proposition: It is possible to make so many observations that it becomes arbitrarily much more probable that the ratio of the number of games that are won by one or the other player falls between any given narrow limits around the expected value than outside. At the end of his proof Bernoulli remarked that he valued this proposition higher than the quadrature of the circle, which even when found would be of little use.

Correspondence with Leibniz Concerning the Art of Conjecturing

Johann Bernoulli had informed Leibniz in a letter dated February 16, 1697, that his brother Jakob had been busy for many years on a work that he called art of conjecturing, that would not only treat mathematically all kinds of games but also subject to calculus probabilities in all situations of daily life. However, Johann did not know in 1697 whether Jakob was still working on the manuscript or had given up this task. Leibniz himself had developed similar ideas independently of Jakob Bernoulli. He was interested in the creation of a doctrine or a logic of degrees of probabilities motivated by the hope of quantifying things such as conditional rights. In contrast to Jakob Bernoulli, Leibniz never worked out his ideas in this field. He left only a series of partly redundant drafts and manuscripts, but no publication offering an outline of the new doctrine. He had hoped that somebody, preferably a mathematician, would indulge in the creation of this new theory of probability.

Presumably because of the many projects he was involved in, his numerous obligations, and his enormous correspondence, Leibniz took up Johann Bernoulli's information only 6 years later, when he asked Jakob Bernoulli in a letter of April 1703 to inform him about his activities concerning a theory of probability estimates. Jakob Bernoulli answered in a letter dated October 3, 1703, that he had nearly finished a book dealing with estimates of probabilities, but that it still lacked the most important part: the application to the social domain. However, he had already solved the crucial problem for such an application 12 years before; he then described his main theorem, the law of large numbers, according to which the estimates of unknown probabilities of events based on observed relative frequencies of such events become more reliable the more observations are made.

To Bernoulli's astonishment Leibniz reacted very critically. Instead of the possibility of attaining a better approximation to a sought after probability with an increasing number of observations, Leibniz suggested that the probability of contingent events, by him identified with dependence on infinitely many conditions, could not be determined by a finite number of observations. The path of a celestial body such as a comet could be determined by a finite number of observations only if we assumed that the path is a conic; otherwise infinitely many different curves could fit the finite number of observed positions of the moving body. This infinity of different curves would correspond to infinitely many estimates of probability in the same way as the finite number of observed positions would correspond to a finite number of observed outcomes of the event. In addition, the appearance of new circumstances could change the probability of an event; so the appearance of new diseases would diminish the probability of survival of a person of a certain age.

In his answer, Bernoulli attempted to clarify his main theorem, using the example of an urn containing white and black stones in the ratio of 2 : 1. In this example, Bernoulli claimed to be able to determine exactly the number of draws (with replacement) for which it would be 10 times, 100 times, 1000 times, and so on more probable that the ratio of white to black stones found by drawing would fall inside rather than outside a given interval about the true value, for example (199/100, 201/100). Although Bernoulli could only prove this assertion for probabilities *a priori*, as in the urn model, he was convinced that he had also shown with his main theorem the solubility of the reverse problem, namely, the determination of unknown, *a posteriori* probabilities. This conclusion becomes understandable through Bernoulli's belief that it would make no difference for the behavior of the observed ratio whether the person drawing the stones knew the true ratio or not. The possibility that two urns containing different ratios of white to black stones would yield the same ratio for an equal number of draws, appeared conceivable to Bernoulli only for a small number of draws; for a large number, such a result would be excluded by the "moral certainty" secured through the main theorem. In this way, Bernoulli saw no problem with applying the urn model to human mortality, with the stones corresponding to diseases with which a person could be taken ill, and so to approach by a finite number of observations the probability of dying within a certain period as close to the true value as practice affords.

Bernoulli knew of Leibniz's activities in the field and hoped that Leibniz could provide him with material relevant for the application of *a posteriori*—determined probabilities, as in certain areas of jurisprudence, or with appropriate data. Bernoulli had read of the *Waerdye*, an assessment of Jan de Witt, raadspensionaris of Holland, in which the advantage of buying and selling life annuities was determined on the basis of hypotheses about life expectations at different ages. Because Leibniz was one of the few who owned a copy of the *Waerdye*, Bernoulli asked him to send him his copy for a while. In his following letters, Leibniz disappointed Bernoulli, claiming to be unable to find the *Waerdye* or relevant papers of his own. Instead he declared that in the area of jurisprudence and politics, which seemed so important for Bernoulli's program, no such extended calculations were usually required because an enumeration of the relevant conditions would suffice. In his last letter to Bernoulli, of April 1705, Leibniz explained that the *Waerdye* contained nothing Bernoulli could not find in Pascal's *Triangle Arithmétique* or in Huygens' *De Rationciniis in Ludo Aleae*, namely to take the arithmetical mean between equally uncertain things as is done by farmers or revenue officers when estimating the value of real estate or the average income. Bernoulli, who died the following August, seemed to have ignored Leibniz's hint about Pascal's *Triangle Arithmétique*, which was not mentioned in the *Ars Conjectandi*. Astoundingly, Leibniz did not mention Edmund Halley's work on human mortality in the *Philosophical Transactions*, which was based on data from the city of Breslau that Leibniz had helped to make available to the Royal Society. The only relevant work Bernoulli mentioned in his manuscripts was John Graunt's *Natural and Political Observations* from 1662, a German translation of which appeared in 1702. However, Bernoulli took Leibniz's objections, especially those against the significance of his law of large numbers, as representative of a critical reader and tried to refute them in Part IV of the *Ars Conjectandi*.

The *Ars Conjectandi*

According to his brother's and his own statements Jakob Bernoulli had begun work on the manuscript of the *Ars Conjectandi* in the 1690s and had resumed work after some interruptions in the last 2 years of his life. When he died in 1705, the book was not finished, especially lacking good examples for the applications of his art of conjecturing to civil and moral affairs. Opinions about the time it would have needed to complete it differ from a few weeks to quite a few years, depending on assumptions about Bernoulli's own understanding of completeness. Jakob Bernoulli's heirs did not want Johann Bernoulli, the leading mathematician in Europe at this time, to complete and edit the manuscript, fearing that Johann would exploit his brother's work. Only after Pierre Rémond de Montmort, himself a pioneer of the theory of probability, offered to print the manuscript at his own expense in 1709 and after some admonitions that the *Ars Conjectandi*, if not published soon, would become obsolete did Bernoulli's son, a painter, agree to have the unaltered manuscript printed. It appeared in August 1713 together with a letter in French on the *jeu de paume* and a short preface by Nikolaus Bernoulli, Jakob's nephew. Nikolaus, who had read the manuscript when his uncle was still alive, had made considerable use of it in his thesis of 1709 and in his correspondence with Montmort. However, when asked to complete the manuscript, he declared himself to be too inexperienced.

The *Ars Conjectandi* consists of four parts. The first is a reprint of Huygens's *De Ratiociniis in Ludo Aleae*, which was published as an appendix to van Schooten's *Exercitationes Mathematicae* in 1657. Jakob Bernoulli complemented this reprint with extensive annotations that contain important modifications and generalizations. For example, in his annotations to Huygens's proposition IV, Jakob Bernoulli generalized Huygens's concept of expectation. Huygens had introduced this concept in this form:

> *that in gambling the expectation or share that somebody can claim for something is to be estimated as much as that with which, having it, he can arrive at the same expectation or share in a fair game.*

It is clear that this expectation, like the shares, is measured in terms of money. Bernoulli wanted to extend the meaning of share to include "some kind of prize, laurels, victory, social status of a person or thing, public office, some kind of work, life or death." Also, by generalizing Huygens's proposition XII, Jakob Bernoulli arrived at the binomial distribution.

In the second part of *Ars Conjectandi*, Bernoulli dealt with combinatorial analysis, based on contributions of van Schooten, Leibniz, Wallis, Johannes Faulhaber, and Jean Prestet. This part consists of nine chapters dealing with permutations, variations with and without repetitions, combinations with and without repetitions, and figurate numbers and their properties. It is probable that he did not know Pascal's *Triangle Arithmétique*, although Leibniz had referred to it in his last letter to Bernoulli. At any rate Bernoulli did not mention Pascal in the list of authors he had consulted concerning combinatorial analysis. He did repeat results already published by Pascal, among them the multiplicative rule for binomial coefficients, for which he claimed the first proof to be his own; Bernoulli's arrangement differed completely from that of Pascal and went in several instances beyond Pascal. An important result in this part is the general formula for the sums of powers of natural numbers:

$$\sum_{v=1}^{n} v^c$$

where c is a given natural number in the form of a polynomial in n of degree $c+1$, the coefficients of which were constructed with the help of certain constants, later called Bernoullian numbers. This formula played an important role in the demonstration of de Moivre's form of the central limit theorem.

In the third part of *Ars Conjectandi*, Bernoulli gave 24 problems concerning the determination of the modified Huygenian concept of expectation in various games. He solved these problems mainly by combinatorial methods, as introduced in part II, and by recursion.

The fourth part of *Ars Conjectandi* is the most interesting and original; it is also the part that Bernoulli was not able to complete. In the first three of its five chapters, it deals with the new central concept of the art of conjecturing, probability; its relation to certainty, necessity, and chance; and ways of estimating and measuring probability. Bernoulli stated on that, the one hand, at least for God, chance and with it objective probabilities do not exist in a world the functioning of which in the past, present, and future is completely known to him down to its smallest entities. Through a more precise knowledge of the parameters affecting the motion of a die, for instance, it would be possible even for humans to specify in advance the result of the throw. Chance, in his view and later in the view of Laplace, is reduced to a subjective lack of information. Thus, depending on the state of their information, an event may be described by one person as chance and by another as necessary. The entire realm of events that are described in daily life as uncertain or contingent in their outcome is such, he claimed, merely because of incomplete information; nevertheless, these too are covered by his concept of probability. However, the only way to check that the probabilities estimated *a posteriori* (in Bernoulli's sense) are reliable in practice is to make sufficiently many observations and calculate the relative frequencies of the outcome of the event in question. So the denial of objective chance and probabilities does not prevent Bernoulli's concept of probability, defined as degree of certainty, from showing at the same time subjective or epistemic and frequentist or aleatory aspects.

For the mathematical part of the *Ars Conjectandi*, this ambiguity in Bernoulli's concept of probability does not matter because the numerical value of a probability is a real (in Bernoulli's case a rational) number between 0 and 1, no matter how it is conceived. For practical applications, Bernoulli introduced the concept of moral certainty of events, "whose probability nearly equals the whole of certainty."

In chapter 3 of the fourth part, "About various kinds of arguments and how their weights are estimated for quantifying the probabilities of things," the realm of nonadditive probabilities is touched upon. In chapter 4, Bernoulli distinguished two ways of determining, exactly or approximately, the classical measure of probability. The first presupposes the equipossibility of the outcomes of certain elementary events such as drawing any 1 of n balls numbered from 1 to n out of an urn. So the probability of drawing a ball of a certain color out of an urn filled with balls of different colors is determined *a priori* by the ratio of the number of balls of this special color to the number of all balls in the urn. The second is for determining the probability of an event for which the reduction to a number of equipossible cases that are favorable or unfavorable for the event is impossible, such as a certain person's dying within the next 10 years. According to Bernoulli, we can inductively, by experiments or *a posteriori*, get as close as we desire to the true measure of such a probability. The possibility of estimating the unknown probability of such an event by the relative frequency of the outcome of the event in a series of supposedly independent trials is secured, according to Bernoulli, by his *theorema aureum*, which was called later by Poisson Bernoulli's law of large numbers. The proof of this theorem is contained in chapter 5. In it he showed that the relative frequency h_n of an event with probability p in n independent trials converges in probability to p. More precisely, he showed that, for any given small positive number ε and any given large natural number c, for sufficiently large n, the inequality:

$$\frac{P(|h_n - p| \leq \varepsilon)}{P(|h_n - p| > \varepsilon)} > c$$

holds, which is equivalent to:

$$P(|h_n - p| \leq \varepsilon) > 1 - \frac{1}{c+1}$$

This, again, is now called Bernoulli's weak law of large numbers. In an appendix to *Ars Conjectandi*, Bernoulli treats *jeu de paume* as a game of chance by taking the relative frequency of winning as a measure of the probability of winning.

The title *Ars Conjectandi* was suggested by the *Ars Cogitandi*, better known as the *Logic of Port Royal*, in the very last chapter of which the chances for future contingent events are equated with the ratios of the associated degrees of probability. We can see how Bernoulli, beginning from this notion, developed the classical concept of probability and how he became the first to set down the prerequisites for consciously formulating a program for the mathematization of all the fields of application subject to *probabilis*. The fact that he had no time to illustrate how this program could be realized with examples from the social domain was a stimulus for his successors.

The Impact of the *Ars Conjectandi*

Jakob Hermann, a student of Jakob Bernoulli who was trusted by the family, informed the authors of eloges that appeared in honor of Jakob Bernoulli of the content of the *Ars Conjectandi* and especially the law of large numbers. It can be shown that the rather short pieces of information contained in these eloges influenced Montmort, who learned from them that the main concept around which the new doctrine of chance should be built was probability. Nikolaus Bernoulli, Jakob's nephew, had tried to apply the findings of his uncle to a series of concrete problems in law in his dissertation *De Usu Artis Conjectandi in Jure*, published in 1709. Montmort included part of his extensive correspondence with Nikolaus Bernoulli on the new field in the second edition of his *Essay d'Analyse sur les Jeux des Hazard*, which appeared late in 1713. Both agreed in their judgment that the *Ars Conjectandi* had appeared too late to offer anything new for specialists, understandably in light of their own efforts to develop the subject. Their judgment has been interpreted as proof of the lack of impact of Jakob Bernoulli's work, even though both had been beneficiaries of Bernoulli's results in the *Ars Conjectandi*. Bernoulli's main theorem, the law of large numbers, stimulated Abraham de Moivre, who late in his life found the first form of the central limit theorem, which allows the approximation of the binomial by the normal distribution. Bernoulli's program to mathematize the realm of the probable, including the social domain, occupied mathematicians throughout the 18th and 19th centuries until the advent of mathematical statistics. The peak of this development was reached in late enlightenment when Condorcet and Laplace held the view that the science of the probable is the only reliable guide to deciding questions for which we have no certain knowledge, such as those concerning human mortality or the reliability of witnesses.

See Also the Following Articles

Attrition, Mortality, and Exposure Time • Descriptive and Inferential Statistics • Mathematical and Statistical Approaches

Further Reading

Bernoulli, J. (1975). *Die Werke von Jakob Bernoulli*. Vol. 3 (Naturforschende Gesellschaft in Basel, ed.), Birkhäuser Verlag, Basel.

Hald, A. (1990). *A History of Probability and Statistics and Their Applications Before 1750*. John Wiley & Sons, New York.

Schneider, I. (1984). The role of Leibniz and of Jakob Bernoulli for the development of probability theory. *LLULL* **7,** 68–89.

Shafer, G. (1978). Non-additive probabilities in the work of Bernoulli and Lambert. *Arch. Hist. Exact Sci.* **19,** 309–370.

Stigler, S. M. (1986). *The History of Statistics—The Measurement of Uncertainty Before 1900*. Harvard University Press, Cambridge, MA.

Bertillon, Louis Adolphe

Libby Schweber
Harvard University, Boston, Massachusetts, USA

Glossary

arithmetic average A term Bertillon borrowed from Laplace and Quetelet to describe an average calculated on the basis of qualitatively different types of objects. A famous example of an arithmetic average is the average height of houses on a street. As this example suggests, arithmetic averages do not give any information about the individual observations that make up the population or about the population as a whole.

demography The science of population statistics. In the 19th century, this included the study of all those features of a population that could be quantified, including measures of population size and growth such as births, deaths, and marriages, physiological measures such as height and weight, environmental measures such as the type of housing and climate, and social measures such as income and level of education.

natural averages Averages taken on (relatively more) homogenous populations, such as a racial or socioeconomic group. In contrast to arithmetic averages, natural averages were seen to provide valuable information about the characteristics of the observed population.

special rates A term coined by Bertillon to refer to what are now called "age-specific rates." They measure the likelihood of a particular event affecting a population of a particular age, generally between ages x and $x + 1$. In the case of mortality, the special rate for the population of age 20 would be the number of people between ages 20 and 21 dying in the course of a year divided by the number of people aged 20 alive at the beginning of the year.

statistical laws A term used by 19th century statisticians to refer to statistical regularities. By using the term "law," they indicated their belief that this regularity pointed to the existence of an underlying cause or force that influenced all individuals in the observed population with the same force, thus accounting for the presumed stability of the phenomena.

Louis Adolphe Bertillon (1821–1883) was one of the leading French social statisticians of the Second Empire and early Third Republic. He was highly respected internationally, in particular by administrative statisticians. He published hundreds of pages on statistical methodology, demography, and anthropological topics, such as "acclimitation" and anthropometric measurement, many of which served as standard statistical textbooks for decades thereafter. At his death, Luigi Bodio, the head of the Italian national bureau of statistics, placed Bertillon's name alongside that of Adolphe Quetelet as the two leading statisticians of the century. Bertillon's contributions to the history of social measurement can be found in his continuation of Quetelet's concern to combine mathematical and administrative statistics. More significantly, he played a major role in the education of French administrative statisticians and medical men in what he called the "correct" statistical method, moving them beyond simple forms of enumeration and sums to the construction of probabilistic rates and the use of mortality tables in the analysis of population statistics.

Bertillon and the History of Social Measurement: Primary Contributions

Historians of statistics generally focus on the development of new concepts and techniques; Bertillon's contributions, however, lie in the promotion and diffusion of what he referred to as a more "scientific" use of statistical methods among practicing statisticians. It is difficult for observers today to fully appreciate the counterintuitive character of statistical reasoning at the time and the long period of informal education necessary to transform this new way of thinking into a taken for granted aspect of political, administrative, and medical thinking. As Alain Desrosières has shown, statistical reasoning assumes the existence of statistical populations constituted by homogenous individuals. The concept was particularly difficult for French statisticians to accept, especially with regard to their own national population. Bertillon was a central figure in the diffusion of this new abstract concept of population and in the education of his colleagues in the use and interpretation of different statistical measures.

At a time when administrative statistics involved simple enumerations and general averages, Bertillon campaigned for a more sophisticated and rigorous understanding of the significance of different measures. He insisted on the use of what he referred to as "special rates," involving the number of occurrences of an event over the population at risk, rather than the general population, and on the use of serial comparisons, rather than simple averages, to identify laws and causes. Finally, he was the first French scholar to construct a mortality table combining civil registration and census data.

Whereas his methodological work focused primarily on the measurement of mortality, his empirical work laid out the contours of a new science of demography. Contemporary notions of a demographic population and the basic model of population as constituted by the entry and exit of individuals, modeled in terms of the force of natality, mortality, nuptiality, and migration, can all be traced to Bertillon's writings. At the time Bertillon wrote, the dominant national administrative statistical tradition in France treated the statistical population as an aggregate of discrete individuals, subject to the vicissitudes of history (famines, wars, epidemics) and divided along territorial lines. Bertillon, in contrast, promoted a more abstract concept of population as a collective entity (social fact) shaped by both internal and external forces, subject to discernible laws.

As this brief description of Bertillon's approach and work suggests, he was one of a group of scholars committed to using the numerical method to develop a new type of social science, one that was simultaneously empirical and devoted to the identification of an otherwise invisible, underlying reality, constitutive of the human collective. The task of statistical analysis was, first, to identify the natural laws governing society, as evidenced by statistical regularities, and second, to explain those laws by examining the parallel development of different variables two at a time. In contrast to his counterparts in England or to mathematicians engaged in the analysis of social statistics, Bertillon made no attempt to use probability calculus to measure the certainty of his statistical measures or to establish the relation between variables. For Bertillon, the innovation in his project came from its strict insistence on observation over logic or reason and in the search for constant causes or laws. In contrast with the dominant administrative tradition of the time, Bertillon called for the calculation of rates, the critique and correction of official data, the identification of statistical regularities and laws, and the search for causes.

Bertillon as Professional Methodologist

Public Hygiene and the Measure of Well-Being

Louis Adolphe Bertillon was born in Paris on April 2, 1821. Little is known about his parents, except that his mother died of cholera in 1832 and that his father subsequently placed him in a boarding school where he was destined for a career in business. Against his father's wishes, Bertillon went on to study medicine. He attended the School of Medicine in Paris, where he enthusiastically embraced the new experimental medicine, inserting himself in scientific laboratories (generally restricted to professors) and eventually gaining a position as an assistant (*préparateur*). While at the School of Medicine, Bertillon also attended the public lectures of Jules Michelet and became a devotee of the Republican historian. His Republicanism combined a strong belief in liberty—especially freedom of expression—with a socialist support of workers' associations and mutual aid societies and a strong anti-clericism. Although Bertillon opposed capitalism, he did not favor state intervention or revolutionary action. Instead, he believed that society had to be allowed to develop naturally according to its internal logic.

Bertillon's political views developed in the years leading up to the 1848 Revolution. It was during one of his many visits to political clubs that had sprung up all over Paris that he first met Achille Guillard, his future father-in-law and cofounder of demography as a discipline. These activities brought Bertillon to the attention of the authorities and he was arrested and imprisoned a number of times in the conservative backlash that followed the 1848 Revolution and the military coup of 1851. Bertillon's early political activities also introduced him to the medical researcher Paul Broca, with whom he later founded the Anthropological Society.

Arithmetic versus Physiological Averages

In 1852, Bertillon completed his medical studies with a doctoral thesis entitled *De quelques éléments de l'hygiene dans leur rapport avec la durée de la vie*. The thesis began from the classical public hygiene problem of how to measure well-being or, in this case, national prosperity. The text involves a discussion of the most commonly used measure, the average age of death. Bertillon groups the average age of death with Quetelet's search for the "average man" and criticizes both measures for failing to pay attention to the distribution around the mean. More damning, for Bertillon, is the practice of combining qualitatively distinct individuals and subgroups in the same measure. Bertillon uses the example of average age at death to expound on the difference between what he refers to as arithmetic averages and natural, physiological averages. The concept of arithmetic averages was taken from Laplace and Quetelet; it refers to an average taken on a heterogeneous population, with no natural referent, and thus no meaning or sense. In contrast, physiological averages are based on data from an existing homogenous population. They refer to real entities and thus provide valid knowledge.

The point Bertillon wishes to make is twofold. First, following Quetelet, he acknowledges cases where an arithmetic average—for example, of the heights of a group of conscripts—proves to be a physiological average as well. In this case, the average signals the fact that the different observations were taken from a single homogenous race or type. Second, in opposition to Quetelet, he warns against the tendency to treat arithmetic averages as physiological averages. His examples come from attempts to characterize the French population as a whole. National averages, Bertillon explains, combine infants and adults of all ages. Far from being probable, such measures are highly improbable; in other words, they rarely correspond to real-life individuals.

The interesting point in this exposition, from the perspective of the history of social measurement, involves the deep ambivalence that French statisticians displayed toward abstract or "improbable" statistical measures. In contrast to their English counterparts, they began from a realist approach to statistics, such that statistical indices were valid only if they corresponded to real ("natural") entities and they struggled with the assumption of homogeneity built into averages and statistical rates. This was particularly important given their insistence on statistics as certain knowledge, thereby precluding the use of hypotheses or arithmetic averages to model society. Practically, the problem was one of identifying legitimate classifications and subclassifications. This dilemma was a major subtheme in Bertillon's work throughout his career and his ability to negotiate the dilemma was one of his major contributions to the art of social measurement. Many of his methodological prescriptions—such as the use of special rates and parallel series—were directed at controlling for this problem, either by explicating the meaning of different measures or by privileging specific indices and tools. Whereas, in 1853, he focused on the different weights that infants, middle-aged, and elderly populations brought to national mortality rates, later in his career his attention shifted to the differences among single, married, and widowed persons.

The second half of the thesis reviewed different explanations for variations in longevity. This separation of the identification of statistical regularities and their explanation was characteristic of Bertillon's work throughout his life. His studies began with a documentation of statistical phenomena—either a stable trend or parallel in the development of two variables over time—and were followed by a more speculative, qualitative discussion of different types of explanation. Statistical data were sometimes used to support or discount particular trends, but no attempt was made to measure the stability of the observed trend (degree of certainty) or to discriminate between different causes. In the case of his thesis, Bertillon considered various classical public hygiene explanations, including the influence of climate, temperature, latitude, urban living, race, and profession on longevity. He concluded by supporting the well-known public hygienist, Louis René Villermé, in his then-novel arguments concerning the (nonmathematical) association of poverty with above-average death rates.

Mortality Differentials

Bertillon's political activism brought him under the suspicion of the authorities in the early years of the Second Republic. To avoid arrest, Bertillon moved his family to Montmercy, a town outside of Paris, where he practiced medicine. It was during this period that Dr. Malgaigne, a member of the Academy of Medicine and Faculty of Medicine where Bertillon had studied, asked Bertillon to participate in an ongoing debate on the efficacy of the vaccine. Bertillon intervened in the discussion as a statistical expert. The invitation led him to a study of mortality differentials in France by age and region and a first major publication entitled *Conclusions statistiques contre les détracteurs de la vaccine: essai sur la méthode statistique appliquée à l'étude de l'homme* (1857). The book was basically a methodological treatise on the construction of mortality rates in terms of the population at risk and the effect of age structure on mortality statistics, illustrated with a systematic study of mortality trends in France in the 18th and 19th centuries. In contrast to public officials who claimed that the increase in the absolute number of deaths among 20- to 30-year-olds pointed to a worsening in the health of the population, Bertillon argued the reverse. His evaluation rested on an increase in the absolute size of the cohort owing to a decline in infant mortality. The memoir received a number of prizes from the Academies of Sciences and Medicine.

This systematic study led Bertillon to the identification of an unusually high rate of infant mortality in the departments surrounding Paris. His study was the first to signal the effects of the practice of wet-nursing on infant mortality. Bertillon first submitted a report on the problem to the Academy of Medicine in 1858 in a paper entitled "*Mortalité des nouveau-nés*," but the problem was ignored. It was only a couple of years later, when other public hygienists again called attention to the phenomenon, that Bertillon's report was revived and he was credited with the discovery. Bertillon's data and testimony were subsequently used in 1874 in parliamentary hearings held on the topic and led to the passage of the *Loi Roussel* regulating the practice of wet-nursing.

Another topical issue that Bertillon's systematic study of mortality led him to address concerned the impact of Hausman's reconstruction of Paris on the well-being of the Parisian population (1869). In contrast to official claims that the public health (*salubrité*) of the city had improved, Bertillon argued that it had declined, at least for certain segments of the population. In studying the differential mortality rates within Paris, Bertillon distinguished between the mortality of the new sections of the city (where many paupers were sent to hospitals to die) and the old. In old Paris, he documented an overall increase in mortality, especially for the very young. In the new sections of the city, he found a slight decline in mortality for the very young and an overall increase for the adult and elderly population. Moreover, he demonstrated that the mortality in Paris was higher than in the rest of the country for every age. Bertillon's paper points to the central role of classification in statistical inquiry. As for the earlier public hygienists, the art of social statistics lay in the classification of the population into subgroups and the use of creative comparisons.

Bertillon's Turn to Social Science

Anthropology and Liberal Economy

In 1859, the government began to relax its strictures against public assembly and free speech. This change opened the way for the revival of scientific activity that had been suppressed in the repressive decade of the 1850s. The impact was especially striking in the moral and human sciences. In the following years, numerous new scientific societies were launched. Two, in particular, transformed Bertillon's career. The first was the Society of Anthropology. In 1859, Bertillon returned to Paris and, together with 18 other medical doctors, helped his friend Paul Broca to found the new society. Although Bertillon knew little about anthropology, he attended classes at the Natural History Museum and actively entered into the ongoing debates over monogenism versus polygenism. Bertillon's contribution lay in the application of the statistical method to anthropology. Together with Broca, he worked to develop a system for the study of skulls and skeletons and for the comparison of anthropometric characteristics. One of his most influential articles of the period was an essay entitled "*De la méthode statistique dans l'anthropologie*," which he originally presented as a memoir in 1863. The article was written in the context of ongoing debates over the influence of *milieux* on skin coloration; Bertillon used the problem to reiterate his usual insistence on the empirical method and on the need to use series of observations. This anthropological work was also the occasion for his first and only attempt to follow up on Quetelet's suggestions that the error curve could be used to establish whether a set of observations belonged to a homogenous population—in this case a single race—or not (see below).

The second society that Bertillon helped to found was the Statistical Society of Paris (1860), which brought together liberal economists and administrative statisticians. The society provided Bertillon entry into the world of quasi-official social statistics. One of his most influential papers in the Society's journal was a paper entitled "*Des diverses manières de mesurer la durée de la vie humaine*" (1866). The article had an enormous impact. It established Bertillon as a statistical expert and remained required reading for two generations of administrative statisticians, in France and abroad.

The 1866 article reviewed the 11 different measures of mortality in use by administrators at the time, discussed their construction, their significance (the phenomena they were actually measuring), and the types of problems for which they were appropriate. In terms of the history of statistical methods, the article made a strong bid for the use of age-specific rates and mortality tables as the only way to establish the "true" sanitary condition of human collectives. It also reviewed the different ways of constructing mortality tables, distinguishing between population lists (taken directly from observations) and population tables (which separated out the influence of historical causes, focusing exclusively on the effect of mortality as a force). Finally, the article provided administrators and statisticians with a manual on how to produce correct mortality tables by first using civil registration data and other comparisons to correct census data and then constructing population lists (of the mortality at each age) and finally using these lists to calculate a mortality table.

As both Michel Dupâquier and Bernard Lécuyer have noted, most of Bertillon's technical points were taken from his reading of the work of the British statistician and administrator William Farr. In contrast to Farr and in keeping with the French administrative tradition, Bertillon insisted on the total empirical grounding of his numbers at the expense of any type of hypothesis. Thus, in the conclusion to his presentation, Bertillon noted that the advantage of his procedures is that "the mortality thus determined does not depend on hypotheses of any kind; it provides the average of *a collective fact* which rests wholly on the exactitude of the empirical record" (Bertillon, 1866, p. 54). Although scholars today will quickly recognize the role of hypotheses both in the construction of Bertillon's data sets and in his qualitative explanations, Bertillon's insistence to the contrary points to the role of "reality" in the authorization of statistical claims in France at the time. This insistence on the reality of the ontological referent of statistical measures may also explain why Bertillon, and the French administrative statisticians more generally, failed to follow their English counterparts in the age standardization of mortality rates. In England, statisticians such as Neison and Farr systematically calculated the mortality of one city were it to have the age structure of another in order to assess the relative health of the two locales. In France, statisticians lacked the epistemic warrant for this type of statistical manipulation.

The Dictionnaire Encyclopédique des Sciences Médicales

Although the Society of Anthropology and the Statistical Society of Paris provided Bertillon with two distinct scientific communities, the bulk of his scientific production occurred in the context of his work for Amedée Dechambre, the editor of the *Dictionnaire Encyclopédique des Sciences Médicales*. The Encyclopedia was published between 1864 and 1889 and included over 100 large volumes. In preparing the Encyclopedia, Dechambre deliberately set out to cultivate new sciences relevant to medicine and he included demography in the list. At Dechambre's instigation, Bertillon was led to expand his statistical investigations beyond the classical public hygiene problem of mortality as a measure of well-being. Between 1864 and his death in 1878, Bertillon researched and published a series of lengthy monographs, ranging from 30 to 150 pages, on different aspects of what was to become demography. These included (1) articles on births, deaths, marriages, natality, mortality, nuptiality, migration, and population; (2) country studies, such as Austria, Bavaria, Bade, Belgium, Great Britain and her colonies; and (3) methodological entries on averages, statistics, average life, probable life, and demography. The two best known articles, which helped to make his national reputation, were the essays on France, which provided a statistical review of the state and movement of the French population (constituted as a demographic object), and his article on averages from which the Statistical Society article was taken.

In 1866, Bertillon's wife died, leaving him to raise their three sons, two of whom were to become well-known statisticians in their own right. Jacques Bertillon later took over from his father as head of the Municipal Bureau of Statistics in Paris and authored one of the leading treatises on administrative statistics and Alphonse Bertillon moved to England, where he developed the use of anthropometric measures to identify criminals. The loss of his wife affected Louis Adolphe Bertillon deeply; it also influenced his political and intellectual positions. Politically, Bertillon evoked the wrath of the religious authorities when he insisted on providing his wife with a civil burial. According to the family biography, this move led to his ostracism from a number of political and scientific societies. The attacks would also seem to have hardened his anti-clerical stance. Intellectually, they contributed to his turn to scientific materialism and his participation in the Society of Mutual Autopsy.

The personal loss also coincided with his preparation for an article on marriage—a topic that he had ignored prior to Dechambre's request. The result was a shift in his basic model of population and a new conviction that the experience of single life, marriage, and widowhood constituted one of the deepest divides structuring social life and an ontological obstacle to the construction and thus scientific legitimacy of national statistical rates. As Bertillon noted in his article on marriage, the experience of marriage creates three distinct social groups, "...which work, suffer, pleasure...live and die differently" (1872, p. 7). This concern for the differential experiences of the unmarried, married, and widowed only intensified Bertillon's already strong concern over the heterogeneity of the French population and the consequent artificiality of national population statistics.

The Promotion of Demography as a Discipline

Bertillon's reputation as a leading scientific figure only really took off in France after the fall of the Second Empire and the establishment of the Third Republic in 1871. During the siege of Paris by the Prussians in 1870, Bertillon served as mayor of the Fifth Arrondissement of Paris. He held the post until the establishment of the Republic, at which time he returned to scholarly work. The Third Republic provided a number of professional opportunities for Bertillon. In the early 1870s, the problem of depopulation was a growing concern. The decline of the French birth rate had been identified by French statisticians as early as 1857, but it was only in the last years of the Second Empire that liberal economists and administrators began to view the development with alarm; prior to that they had taken it as evidence of the Malthusian mechanism of foresight and the diffusion of civilization to the middle and lower classes. After the war, the new, Republican government actively set out to explain the defeat of France to Prussia to the French public. A slower birth rate and a lack of investment in science were presented as important causes of France's defeat. Bertillon was one of the few statisticians with the skills and data to address the problem. In 1873, he gave the opening speech at the annual meeting of the newly founded French Association for the Promotion of Science, in which he made a strong bid for the gravity of the problem of depopulation and the ability of demography, a new science devoted to the statistical study of human collectives, to address it.

For the first time in his career, Bertillon actively engaged in institution-building directed at establishing demography as a distinct discipline. In 1876, he was given a new chair of demography and medical geography in the School of Anthropology. In 1877, he launched the first specialized journal in demography, entitled *Les Annales Internationales de Démographie*, and in 1878, he organized the first International Congress of Demography in conjunction with the Universal Exposition of 1878. In 1883, Bertillon was appointed the head of the newly created statistical bureau for the city of Paris. The move was important both practically and symbolically. On a practical level, the Municipal Bureau provided Bertillon with an opportunity to shape the production of official data to suit the requisites of his new science. On a symbolic plane, the Municipal Bureau marked Bertillon's role as the carrier of Villermé and Quetelet's projects into the second half of the 19th century. The series of volumes produced by the original Municipal Bureau of Statistics for the City of Paris in the 1820s had provided both Villermé and Quetelet with the data necessary to engage in their projects. Whereas Joseph Fourier, the original director, had far more mathematical expertise than Bertillon, the two men shared with Villermé and Quetelet a commitment to overcome the strong gap between mathematical and administrative statistics.

Bertillon's project for demography can be found in his articles for Dechambre's dictionary, in his lectures at the School of Anthropology, in his contributions to *Les Annales Internationales*, and in his speeches at the first meetings of the International Congress of Demography. As the above review of his work indicates, Bertillon envisaged demography as a systematic endeavor focused on producing a demographic profile of a population, rather than a problem-oriented discipline. Most of his topical studies, such as his work on the impact of wet-nursing or on Hausman's reconstruction of Paris, emerged from his attempt to map out the differential mortality of the French nation according to a number of predefined variables. His country studies in Dechambre's dictionary were all modeled along the same grid. Each was divided into two sections: the state of the population and population dynamics, corresponding to the anatomy and physiology of the population under investigation. The first relied largely on census data to trace out the composition of the population by age, sex, language, habitat, civil state, and profession, whereas the latter mined the registration of births, deaths, and marriages for annual movements of the population. The physiology of the population was decomposed into four principal movements by which the population increases and declines: natality, matrimoniality, mortality, and the intensity of migratory movements. As this article indicates, Bertillon's approach was ultimately empiricist. The different elements of a demographic study were not tied together by any overarching theory, but instead related to one another ontologically, by their contribution to the constitution of population viewed as an abstract statistical object.

The new scientific community constituted around demography combined the earlier base of positivist Republican medical men and municipal administrators with the support of national administrators from foreign countries. For much of the second half of the 19th century, demography was treated as the applied branch of statistics. Leading statistical manuals such as the *Traité théorique et pratique de statistique* (1886) by Maurice Block and the *Cours élémentaire de statistique administrative* (1895) by Bertillon's son, Jacques, included a separate section on demography that reported on the key findings of the discipline. The term "statistics" was thus used to refer to the method (administrative or mathematics), whereas the term "demography" referred to the application of that method to population defined as an abstract statistical object. It was only after Bertillon's death in 1883 that his version of demography came to be adopted by liberal economists and mainstream statisticians and that his vision was institutionalized in national administrative bureaus.

Bertillon passed away in 1883. At the time of his death, he had the satisfaction of seeing his project for demography institutionalized in a number of specialized organizations. Although few of them survived the decade after his death, his intellectual and institutional work did contribute significantly to the "scientization" of French administrative statistics. This success was symbolized in 1885 by the creation of the *Conseil Superieure de Statistique*, an advisory committee within the administration that brought together scholars and administrators to improve the quality of official data.

Bertillon and Quetelet

One of the main themes in the little scholarly work that has been done on Louis Adolphe Bertillon concerns the relationship between his work and that of Adolphe Quetelet. The comparison is illuminating, as Bernard Pierre Lécuyer has suggested, in that it provides a vehicle to assess the impact of Quetelet's social physics on French administrative and social scientific thought. It also serves to summarize the specificity of Bertillon's own contribution to the development of social statistics in general and demography in particular. On a very general level, Bertillon took from Quetelet and others his belief that society was governed by natural laws and his faith that statistics could be used to identify them. He also shared with Quetelet the Laplacian distinction between constant and accidental causes and the association of statistical regularities with constant causes.

Problems with the Average Man

In his doctoral thesis, Bertillon refers positively to Quetelet's project to use averages to establish the characteristics of a race and to trace the (civilizational) development of the population. At the same time, he criticizes Quetelet's notion of the average man on realist grounds. In his thesis, Bertillon objects to the notion of the average man on the grounds that it is an arithmetic mean that combines values from individuals of vastly different ages or races. To illustrate his point, he considers the average height of French conscripts by combining the heights of Frenchmen in the Doubs (the department with the tallest conscripts) with those in the Corrèze and Pyrénées-Orientales (the departments with the shortest conscripts) The result, he explains, is an arithmetic mean combining individuals of different races. In contrast, the heights of conscripts from a single department tended to cluster around the departmental average in a form resembling the error curve or binomial distribution. In this case, the arithmetic mean might also be the most probable height, such that one could use a series of average heights, taken over a century, to determine the progress or decay of the population. In 1852, Bertillon failed to provide a statistical means of distinguishing between physiological and arithmetic averages. It was not until the mid-1870s that he returned to the problem.

In his course at the School of Anthropology, Bertillon explicitly distinguished his project for demography from Quetelet's social physics. According to Bertillon, Quetelet was driven by an interest in universals. His work was shaped by an *a priori* perspective directed at the identification of the average man, which he regarded as an ideal. Bertillon, in contrast, was concerned with the natural history of actual human collectivities. In his 1876 article on the theory of averages, Bertillon further developed his criticism of the average man by pointing to the failure of different average measures to adjust among themselves. The point had been made by Cournot and was supported by Bertillon's own attempts to identify the average primitive man on the basis of the collection of skulls stored at the Anthropological Society. For many years, he and Broca sought to order the collection according to multiple criteria. The attempt failed. There was no systematic relation between the five or six different measures that anthropologists used to characterize skulls.

Using the Error Curve

Although Bertillon rejected the scientific value of the concept of the average man, he accepted Quetelet's analysis of the similarities in the distribution of values around natural physiological means and certain arithmetic averages. In his article on methodology in anthropology, Bertillon returned to Quetelet's suggestion that one could use the shape of the error curve to establish the homogeneity of the population. The context for his analysis was a debate at the Society of Anthropology. The question on the table was whether climatic conditions could lead to the birth of new human species or races. More specifically, the Society was embroiled in a discussion over whether the white skin of Europeans could, over time, be transformed into the black skin of the Negro, the chocolate skin of the Ethiopian, the red skin of the Iroquois and under what influence. Underlying the discussion was a broader intellectual debate concerning the single versus the multiple origins of the human species. Bertillon and Broca were strong supporters of the polygenist position.

To counter the arguments of monogenists, Bertillon challenged the use of simple averages to establish the presence or absence of a single race. Instead he proposed that anthropologists follow Quetelet in his analysis of the circumference of the chests of conscripts in the Scottish regiment. To illustrate the value of this approach, Bertillon examined the distribution of the heights of conscripts in different departments. In the case of the Doubs, he found that the heights of 9002 conscripts, measured between 1851 and 1860, failed to cluster symmetrically around the average height. Instead, they displayed a camel-shaped distribution (see Fig. 1). According to Bertillon, this curve could be explained only by the presence of two distinct human types, with different average heights. The camel-shaped curve was the result of the superposition of two binomial distributions, corresponding to the two racial types present in the population. The absence of a binomial distribution discounted the racial homogeneity of the population.

Thirty years later, the Italian statistician Rudolfo Livi reexamined Bertillon's data and found that the observed distribution was the result of the particular way that Bertillon had converted his data from centimeters to inches. At the time, however, Bertillon used it to make his usual case for the need to move beyond simple averages to an analysis of distributions. Although this study is often cited as evidence of the connection between Quetelet and Bertillon, the study of the distribution of the heights in the Doubs was the only time that Bertillon ever attempted an analysis of this type. As such, it cannot be taken as indicative of his methodological or theoretical position.

The Theory of Averages Revisited

Bertillon did, however, use the analysis later in his career as an illustration in his article on the theory of averages. Once again, his primary focus in this article concerned the ontological referent or reality associated with a statistical measure. Whereas in 1853 Bertillon had focused on the distinction between natural physiological averages and arithmetic averages, in 1876 he refined his analysis by

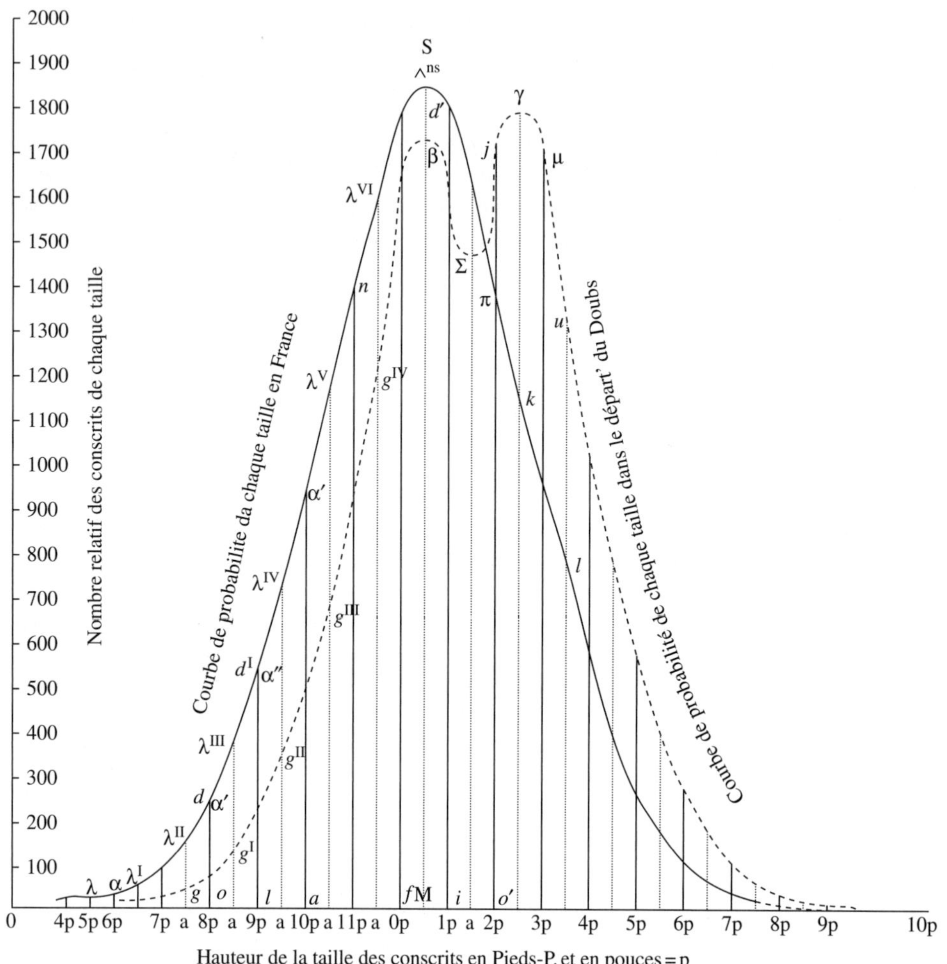

Figure 1 Camel-shaped distribution.

carving out a special conceptual space for the category of averages that were simultaneously natural and arithmetic. His point was twofold: first, to emphasize the need to move beyond simple averages to an examination of the distribution of values around the mean (what he called *mise en série*) and second, to distinguish between measures of "real" objects that could be used by scientists and artificial measures that could not. The problem, as before, concerned the reality of statistical objects or social facts.

The article on the theory of averages distinguishes between three types of averages: objective, subjective, and, within the category of subjective averages, typical and indexical. An objective average rested on a determinate (real) object, such as the series of observations taken on the same star or copies of a gladiator statue. A subjective average, in contrast, involved a summary measure of actual individual variations. It refers to an "imaginary abstraction, created by our spirit (*esprit*) to synthesize these impressions (of individual variations) and thereby direct our memory, attention and investigations" (Bertillon, 1876, p. 267). Subjective averages, he explains, were similar to the type of common-sense categories that people make every day to negotiate the complexities of social life. Within the category of subjective averages, Bertillon distinguishes between typical averages, where the individual observations were all variations of a single type or race, and indexical averages, where they rested on a purely "fortuitous and factitious agglomerations," such as the average height of houses on a street (Herschel's example) or the average height of the conscripts in the Doubs.

The challenge for statisticians was to distinguish between typical and indexical averages, the first being of scientific value, the latter not. The value of the error curve (or curve of probability as Bertillon referred to it) was that it provided a means to empirically distinguish between these types of averages. If the different values displayed a symmetrical distribution about the mean according to the binomial distribution, then the average was either objective or a typical subjective average; if not, then it was an indexical subjective average and of dubious scientific value. Bertillon's 1876 discussion suggests that, although he himself did not use the error curve to establish homogeneity (with the exception of the one above-mentioned instance), he was still attached to the prospect of a technical solution to the problem of homogeneity. Moreover, his personal reluctance to use Quetelet's method would seem to have been linked to its association with the notion of the average man.

Historians of statistics argue that Quetelet's notion of average man was essential for the conceptual slippage between a subjectivist and a frequentist interpretation of probability and thus for his entire intellectual project. To be more specific, Quetelet's social physics rested on an analogy between the distribution of observations taken from a single object, such as the copies of a single statue of a gladiator or a number of observations taken on the same star, and the distribution of a set of observations taken on different entities, such as the height of Scottish conscripts. Both the observations taken on a single real entity and the distribution of individual values taken on a group of real entities follow the binomial distribution. The concept of the average man constituted Quetelet's answer to this question of the ontological referent of a statistical series. The fact that the set of observed values clustered symmetrically about the mean was taken as evidence that the distribution was like a set of errors that converged on the true, or in this case, ideal value. The average man was the ideal type around which the characteristics of a given population tended to converge.

Bertillon recognized the explanatory work that the concept of average man accomplished in Quetelet's theory and he explicitly criticized Quetelet for using it. Instead, Bertillon appealed to the constancy of causes such as heredity and milieu over more diverse, contradictory influences belonging to subpopulations and individuals. In the case of typical subjective means, he explained, the constant causes associated with race increasingly dictated the shape of the distribution the greater the number of observations taken on the population. Like Quetelet, Bertillon argued that the sources of diversity acted like errors, balancing one another out, such that the larger the number of cases, the closer the convergence around the mean. In contrast to Quetelet, he refused to abandon a physiological notion of mechanical determinism of different types of causes for a "mystical" explanation.

See Also the following Articles

Attrition, Mortality, and Exposure Time • Data Distribution and Cataloging • Demography • Qualitative Analysis, Anthropology • Quantitative Analysis, Anthropology • Quetelet, Adolphe

Further Reading

Armatte, M. (1991). Une discipline dans tous ses etats: La statistique à travers ses traités (1800–1914). *Rev. Synth.* **2,** 161–205.

Bertillon, A., Bertillon, J., and Bertillon, G. (1883). *La Vie et les Oeuvres du Docteur L.-A. Bertillon.* G. Masson, Paris.

Brian, E. (1991). Les moyennes à la Société de Statistique de Paris (1874–1885). In *Moyenne, Milieu, Centre: Histoires et Usages* (J. Feldman, G. Lagneau, and B. Matalon, eds.), pp. 107–134. Editions de l'Ecole des Hautes Etudes en Sciences Sociales, Paris.

Cole, J. (2000). *The Power of Large Numbers: Population and Politics in Nineteenth-Century France.* Cornell University Press, Ithaca, NY.

Coleman, W. (1982). *Death Is a Social Disease: Public Health and Political Economy in Early Industrial France.* University of Wisconsin Press, Madison, WI.

Dupâquier, M. (1983). La famille Bertillon et la naissance d'une nouvelle science sociale: La démographie. In *Annales de Démographie Historique; Etudes, Chronique, Bibliographie, Documents,* pp. 293–311.

Dupâquier, J., and Dupâquier, M. (1985). *Histoire de la Démographie: La Statistique de la Population des Origines à 1914.* Librairie Academique Perrin, Paris.

Eyler, J. M. (1979). *Victorian Social Medicine: The Ideas and Methods of William Farr.* Johns Hopkins University Press, Baltimore, MD.

Lécuyer, B. P. (1987). *Probability in Vital and Social Statistics: Quetelet, Farr, and the Bertillon. The Probabilistic Revolution* (L. Kruger, ed.), pp. 317–335. MIT Press, Cambridge, MA.

See Also the following Articles

Binet, Alfred

Dolph Kohnstamm
Emeritus, Leiden University, Leiden, The Netherlands

Glossary

cephalometry Methods and scientific motives to measure the size and form of the head of individuals in order to find characteristics of specific groups of human beings, e.g., of gifted children, early forms of mankind (in evolution), criminals, and people belonging to different races. Discredited because of Nazi theories and practice. In modern times, replaced by measures of brain volume using magnetic resonance imaging scans.

conservation Jean Piaget's term for the ability of the child to recognize that certain properties of objects (e.g., mass, volume, and number) do not change despite transformations in the spatial appearance of the objects.

mental age Stage and level in cognitive (mental) development that are typical for children of a given age, as determined in large and representative samples of children in a given population.

pedagogy From the Greek words *pais* (boy; child) and *agoo* (to lead), thus the art and science of educating children. The concept currently comprises more than school education alone. It also encompasses the guidance parents give to their children, in all respects, not only their cognitive development.

suggestibility A personality trait indicating the degree to which a child or adult is susceptible to suggestions made by other children or adults.

Alfred Binet (1857–1911) found his true vocation in the new science of psychology after some years in law school and medical school. Driven by an extremely inquisitive mind, he first studied psychopathology and suggestibility before settling on experimental psychology. A warm interest in the mentally retarded led him to the invention of a wide range of tasks to test individual differences in mental capacities between retarded and normal individuals, both adults and children. Commissioned by the ministry of education to devise selection criteria for schools of special education, and assisted by his young coworker Théodore Simon, he developed the series of tasks that became known as the Binet–Simon scales for the measurement of intelligence. This invention of a practical method brought him international fame. Founder, in 1894, and long-term editor of *l'Année Psychologique*, Binet published articles and books on an unbelievably wide range of subjects. His seminal work in education bears witness to his dedication to individual differences and their standardized assessment.

Youth of Alfred Binet

Born in Nice in 1857, Alfred Binet was the only child of a physician and his wife, an amateur painter. Binet's father was not the first physician in the family: he was son of one, and so was the grandfather of his mother. The latter, Mr. Jordan, served also as mayor of Marseilles.

Little is known of Binet's childhood and adolescence. It is a pity that this great child psychologist never took the time to commit his own childhood memories to paper. Was it his characteristic modesty that prevented him from doing so? Were his memories too painful to pass on to strangers? Or did he postpone this task too long and did his deathly illness come too soon? It is known that the marriage of his parents was unhappy and that after a few years at high school in Nice, his mother took him, at age 15, to Paris for further education. There, Alfred first attended a famous lycée (Louis le Grand) before entering law school, obtaining his license degree at age 21. Dissatisfied with the prospect of a career in law or public affairs, he switched for a while to medical school. This may not have been a good choice for such an extremely inquisitive and original mind. After a year or so, he embarked on a self-study of psychology at the national library, the famous Bibliothèque Nationale, soon finding his vocation in that discipline, so new that it was not yet a field of study at the university. Binet's first enthusiasm was stirred by the then dominant current in cognitive psychology, associationism. Only 1 year later, in 1880, his first paper, on the fusion of resemblant sensations, was published in the *Revue Philosophique*.

Early Career

In 1882, a former schoolmate of Binet, the neurologist Joseph Babinski, introduced him to the psychiatrists of the famous hospital, La Salpêtrière, and Binet began work in the clinic of Professor Charcot, where hysterical patients were treated with hypnosis. Only 3 years later, young Freud came from Vienna to study Charcot's methods in this same clinic. Binet published about a dozen papers on this subject over the next 7 years, most of them in the *Revue Philosophique*. At the same time, he continued his work in cognitive psychology and published his first book, *La Psychologie du Raisonnement*, in 1886, based strictly on the premises of association psychology.

With John Stuart Mill as his "hero," the young Binet had to mitigate his extremely environmentalist beliefs that were influenced by his father-in-law, E. G. Balbiani, a professor in embryology at the Collège de France. Binet adapted his lectures on heredity for publication. All this time, Binet had no paid appointment. He must have had sufficient access to the family capital, being the only child of a wealthy father. This allowed him excursions into another new field, zoology. Studying and dissecting insects in a laboratory led him to write a doctoral thesis, entitled "A Contribution to the Study of the Subintestinal Nervous System of Insects," defended in 1894. Meanwhile, he had made yet another move by asking for and obtaining a nonpaid appointment at the Laboratory of Physiological Psychology at the Sorbonne. Being accepted as a staff member by its director, Henri Beaunis, in 1891, he was to succeed him 3 years later, when Beaunis retired. In that same year, which also brought him his doctor's title, he and Beaunis founded the first psychological journal in France, *l'Année Psychologique*, of which Binet was to remain the editor until his death, 17 years later. But that was not all. Two of his books went to print in that fruitful year, an introduction to experimental psychology and a study on the psychology of chess players and master calculators. Also, his first article on experimental child development appeared, in collaboration with his co-worker Victor Henri, foretelling what was to become the focus of his studies in child intelligence and education.

With this solid and impressive academic record, it is amazing that Binet was never offered a chair in the French universities. Notwithstanding his international recognition, even long before his scales of mental tests brought him international fame. A course of 12 lectures he gave at the University of Bucharest, in 1895, progressed so well that the number of students, professors, and interested citizens increased to the point that the course had to be continued in a larger audience hall. Also, a year before, he had been appointed member of the editorial board of the new *Psychological Review*, at a time when only American psychologists were appointed. One can imagine Binet's great disappointment about not being given a chair in Paris.

A Father Becomes a Child Psychologist

In 1884, Binet had married Laure Balbiani, daughter of an embryologist, and in 1885 and 1887, two children were born, Madeleine and Alice. The father began to observe the behavior of his little daughters, just as Piaget would do some 20 years later. Binet was struck by the differences in behavior patterns the two girls showed, especially their different styles of "voluntary attention." Madeleine always concentrated firmly on whatever she was doing, whereas Alice was impulsive. He took notes and began writing reports on his observations, using the pseudonyms Marguerite for Madeleine and Armande for Alice. He published three of these reports in the *Revue Philosophique*, when his eldest daughter was 5 years old. The following quotation from the first report (1890) described motoric behavior: "When M. was learning to walk she did not leave one support until she had discovered another near at hand to which she could direct herself . . . while A., in contrast, progressed into empty space without any attention to the consequences (of falling)." On their temperamental differences, Binet noted that M. was "silent, cool, concentrated, while A. was a laughter, gay, thoughtless, frivolous, and turbulent. . . . Now, [at their present age] the psychological differences . . . have not disappeared. On the contrary, they have disclosed a very clear character to their whole mental development."

In child psychology of the past century, long after Binet's time, people have tried to explain such individual differences between two sisters or brothers as resulting from their difference in birth order. The characteristic differences between Binet's two daughters echo the typical differences found in some of those studies between first- and second-born children. But this research has practically come to a halt because wide-scale confirmation has failed to materialize. In Binet's days, this was not yet a hypothesis known to be reckoned with and neither had Freudian psychoanalytic thinking colonized the minds of child psychologists. The explanation that Madeleine was the first to establish an oedipal relation with her father, and might be suffering from anxiety for fear of the punishment from her mother, was not yet formulated. So here we see a still-innocent investigator of child behavior, a confirmed environmentalist in his student years, who is impressed by the individual differences in personality characteristics as seen in the behavior patterns of his own children. Convinced that he and his wife had provided both girls with about the same environment and comparable experiences, no other conclusion could be inferred in these pre-Freudian decades, than differences in genetic predispositions. This unmistakable truth came to the father's mind in the same period that he edited the lectures on heredity by his father-in-law. Binet's great interest in the development of individual differences was born. So impressed was he by the differences in approaching tasks by the two girls that it seems as if he initially failed to discern the important maturational differences between young children almost 2 years apart. This amazing conclusion was derived by Binet's biographer, Theta H. Wolf, in her admirable book on Binet's professional development. This article owes much to her fine study.

Assessment of Individual Differences in Cognitive Functioning

Binet tried many cognitive tasks on his two daughters. Several tests of memory were devised, from remembering colors seen to recalling sentences spoken. Other tasks included interpreting simulated emotions in expressions (using Darwin's original pictures) asking for word definitions ("What is it? Tell me what it is?"). With answers by his daughters such as "a snail is to step on" or "a dog bites," Binet was amazed to see how "utilitarian" children are. He made discoveries that nowadays are textbook knowledge in child development. He touched on these insights in his articles, but he did not bring them into a systematic framework, e.g., by writing a book on language development or the development of memory. In this respect, he differed from other child psychologists who came after him. For example, Binet touched on the problems young children have in distinguishing between what looks like "more" and what is "more." He arranged beads of different colors or sizes on the table and asked his daughters to make judgments on quantity, much as Piaget would do two decades later with his children. But Piaget, who must have known Binet's publications, did not stop there, and devised many different tasks on number "conservation," describing meticulously how children of different ages reacted to these tasks, embedding the results in an elaborate and complex theory on the growth of logical thought.

An important change in Binet's thinking came when he and his co-worker, Victor Henri, gave cognitive tasks to school children differing much more in age than his two daughters differed. For example, he discovered how 12-year-old children could resist false suggestions made by the experimenter, as to what would be the right answer to a problem of perception, whereas most 7-year-old children could not resist. The misleading questions Binet and Henri presented to the children are similar to the tricks played by Piaget in his conservation tasks. Binet came to see the growth of children's faculty of attention, judgment, and criticism as essential in their development of intelligence. He and Henri published a book on suggestibility in 1900. In this book, they warn the reader how susceptible children are to suggestions, true or false, and that in many experimental situations, insufficient attention is given to implicit suggestions caused by the experimenter's words or acts, by the way the materials are arranged or by the behavior of other children present in the situation. This warning has not been heard or taken seriously by many researchers in cognitive development in the century following this publication. Even Piaget did not show sufficient caution against the use of "misleading" questions in the cognitive problems that he arranged for his subjects. Only since the 1980s has the suggestibility of young children come to be extensively researched, out of concern for the reliability of children's testimony in court cases.

From his earlier publications on his work in the Salpêtrière hospital, Binet was widely known as a staunch supporter of hypnosis as a method to learn more about unconscious motives and thoughts. When publishing the book on his suggestibility experiments with children, headmasters of schools in Paris closed their doors to him, fearing he was bringing their pupils under hypnosis during his experiments. Binet's pioneering work on suggestibility was seen by him as essential for the psychology of court testimony. He even saw a wider application in the courtrooms, because also the judges were subject to suggestions and let their judgments be influenced by them. Thus Binet proposed the formulation of a psychojudicial science, and if he had continued on this road he might now have been regarded as the founder of experimental forensic psychology—in particular, the validity of eyewitness testimony.

It is impossible in a short text to give a complete overview of the great variety of studies Binet undertook; among the many interests of Binet was the study of creative imagination in novelists and playwrights. In interviews and questionnaires, numerous famous authors, among whom were Edmont de Goncourt and Alexander Dumas, told Binet how inspiration appeared to come to them. Especially the "spontaneous inspirations" produced by the mind during sleep fascinated Binet. Later in his life, Binet would become an author of fiction, writing plays for the theater; one of his plays saw 30 performances in succession at the famous Sarah Bernhardt theater in Paris.

Assessment of Intelligence in Groups of Children and Mentally Retarded Adults

Not in the position to offer students grades and diplomas, nor to offer co-workers a salary, Binet was totally dependent on the enthusiasm of one or two volunteer assistants. Therefore, Theodore Simon was just the person he needed. Simon worked in a colony for retarded children and adolescents, all boys, and had permission to use them as subjects in tests. Binet first tested Simon, for his competence, persistence, and good faith, as he used to do with prospective co-workers. Luckily, Simon passed the high standards Binet had in mind for his assistants. A very fruitful period followed. Both the differences in age and the differences in mental capacities in the population of retarded children and adolescents yielded a mass of differential data on the many cognitive tasks Binet and Simon invented for them. Together with his co-worker Victor Henri, Binet joined other European investigators in studying mental fatigue in school children. The introduction of compulsory education for all children, including those from the working classes, caused concern about their endurance during long days of mental exertion. With another co-worker, Nicholas Vaschide, Binet set out to measure physical, physiological, and anatomical characteristics of the boys, to study individual differences in physique and physical force. In order to find meaningful relations between the many different measures, he invented a crude measure of correlation, using rank differences. It is fair to note that this research was met with devastating criticism, also in the *Psychological Review*, because of its many flaws in computations and the doubtful reliability of the measures used. A few years later, Binet and Simon made extensive studies of the relation between certain measures of intelligence and head size. Cephalometry was very common in those days, in psychology as well as in criminology. Both men hoped to find significant correlations between head size and intelligence. But after many years of data collection and publications, among which was Simon's doctoral thesis on mentally retarded boys, they gave up, because in the normal ranges of intelligence the correlations were too small. It is only now, with the more precise magnetic resonance imaging scans of brain volume, that some psychologists have returned to this old hypothesis. For Binet and his co-workers, it was because of their interest in the distinction between mentally retarded, normal, and gifted children that they had spent so much time on the assessment of physical and anatomical measures. When they left this track, it was because obtaining reliable measures from children was so difficult, not because they no longer believed in the relatedness of the physical measures to cognitive capacities.

One other association they saw clearly was the relatedness between intelligence and success at school, notably in reading and arithmetic. From studying cognitive development in his own two daughters, Binet was dedicated to the study of cognitive growth and to the necessity of a match between what teachers should expect from pupils and the students' developmental level. It was in fact his concern about such mismatches observed in schools Binet visited that first motivated him to create a series of age-appropriate cognitive tasks. Such an instrument would allow teachers to assess the cognitive level of each individual child and then to adapt their educational goals for each child, or group of children, according to the level of development.

A second motivation to set out on this expedition was an invitation by the French Ministry of Education to devise a test to detect those children who were too retarded to profit from ordinary schooling. For this goal, a "Ministerial Commission for the Abnormal" was appointed in 1904. Binet and Simon began to devise series of six small cognitive tasks for each age, from age 3 onward. For example, a task for a 3-year-old child was to provide the proper reaction to "show me where is your nose, your mouth, your eye," the task thus serving as a simple test of vocabulary development. Or the children were asked to copy squares and triangles, setting criteria for pass or fail. Tasks were seen as age appropriate when 75% of a given age group passed the criteria set and 25% failed. Binet framed the issue in levels of cognitive development for each individual child and in standards for groups of a given age. Thus a child of age 5 who passed all six tasks for age 5 and also three of the tasks for age 6 was deemed to have a mental level of 5 and a half years. Such knowledge would help the teacher to adapt his or her expectations for that child and to set the proper educational goals for that child accordingly. Children 2 or more years behind the standard levels for their age should be given special education in classes for the retarded. In 1905, Binet and Simon published their scales for the first time, and the title of the publication referred to the usefulness of the scales to distinguish between children of "normal" and "abnormal" intellectual level. In subsequent revisions of these scales, this "commissioned" goal was pushed into the background, as can be inferred from the change in titles, from "the development of intelligence in children" (1908) to "the measurement of intellectual level in school children" (1911).

Although Binet's first concern was with retarded children, deaf mutes, and the visually handicapped, he was probably the first to ask special attention for the gifted child, suggesting the organization of special classes for the "above-averaged." He argued that it is "through the elite, and not through the efforts of the average that humanity invents and makes progress." Though many of those who later promoted the Binet–Simon scales, such as Goddard and Terman in the United States, were ardent hereditarians, Binet held a more balanced view. As Siegler has documented in his fine biographical article, Binet strongly believed in the potential of education for increasing intelligence.

Other Offices Held in Education

In 1899, Binet was asked to become an adviser of La Société Libre pour l'Etude Psychologique de l'Enfant, a society just established by Ferdinand Buisson, occupant of the chair of the science of education at the Sorbonne University, at the request of his students, who were teachers and professors attending his courses. These students had read about child study associations abroad, notably those initiated in the United States by G. Stanley Hall. In 1901, Binet became vice-president of this society and a year later he succeeded Buisson as president. He remained president until his death. Six years later the society was renamed in La Société Alfred Binet, and after Simon's death, in 1961, it was again renamed, this time adding the name of Binet's closest ally and successor, Théodore Simon. This society exists to the present day, and publishes a bulletin that has covered more than a century in child psychology and education, under different names. The present name of the bulletin is *Eduquer. Revue de la Société Binet–Simon*, published under the direction of Bernard Andrieu of the University of Nancy.

In 1909, 2 years before his death, Binet presided over the first international pedagogical congress, held in Liège (Belgium). He was then asked to chair an international commission studying pedagogical trends in different countries.

Reception of the Binet–Simon Intelligence Scales

Both in Europe and the United States, the publication of the Binet–Simon scales in *l'Année Psychologique* did not go unnoticed. To the contrary, it was as if the profession had been waiting for this invention. All over Europe, psychologists and educators began to translate and adopt the scales. To mention only the best known names, these scholars included Alice Descoeudres in Geneva, Otto Bobertag in Breslau, and Ovide Decroly in Brussels. It was William Stern, Bobertag's colleague in Breslau, who in 1911 coined the concept "mental age" and proposed to compute an intelligence quotient (IQ) by comparing mental age and chronological age. The IQ was thus born, albeit still without the multiplication by 100. Thus, a child in those days could obtain an IQ of 0.75!

Nowhere was the reception of the 1908 revision of the scales to measure intelligence so enthusiastic as in the United States. In that same year, Henry H. Goddard of the Training School at Vineland, New Jersey, introduced to the new scales by Ovide Decroly, took them back to the States, where he published his adaptation in 1911. He was so enthusiastic about the discovery he made in old Europe that he compared the importance of the scales with Darwin's theory of evolution and Mendel's law of inheritance. The most widely known American revision became the one developed by Lewis Terman, published in 1916 and standardized on about 2000 children. This test, known as the Stanford–Binet, later revised by Terman and Merrill in 1937, used the factor 100 as a multiplier. Terman's standardization brought the normal distribution and standard deviation into Binet's invention.

Binet's biographer, Theta H. Wolf, quoted John E. Anderson when she wrote that "it is impossible, unless we lived through the period, to recapture the enthusiasm, discussion, and controversy that the Binet tests started. Clearly [Binet's work] substituted for the onus of moral blame, a measurable phenomenon within the child's resources that [was] to be studied henceforth in its own right." Wolf added that "these tests made it possible to show that measurable differences in mental levels, rather than voluntary and thus punishable 'moral weakness', could be responsible for children's [below standard] school achievement." Not everyone in the United States was charmed by the triumphal progress of the intelligence scales. Kuhlman was among the first to criticize the scales for their flaws. William Stern reported to have read in American publications about "binetists" who tried to "binetize" children and adults. Especially in France the reception of the Binet–Simon scales was met with reservation and disregard. Binet had no easy character and had been frank with many of his academic colleagues in giving his opinion on their work. After Binet's death in 1911, Simon became the director of their now world-famous laboratory. When at the end of the First World War the young biologist Jean Piaget, aged 22, came to Paris to study at Bleuler's psychiatric clinic and at the Sorbonne, Simon offered him the opportunity to work in the laboratory. Simon asked Piaget to standardize Cyril Burt's reasoning test on Parisian children. Although Piaget undertook this project without much enthusiasm, his interest grew when he began the actual testing.

He found himself increasingly fascinated with the thought processes by which the child came to his answers—in particular, the incorrect ones. Several years later, when his own children were born, he followed his predecessor Binet in probing their cognitive development by confronting them with simple problems and misleading questions. Although Piaget in his publications never explicitly recognized that he was influenced and inspired by Binet, both Wolf and Siegler concluded that circumstantial evidence clearly shows this so.

Over the next few decades, Piaget's compatriots also grew convinced of the seminal importance of Binet's work. In the early 1960s, René Zazzo and his collaborators published a new scale to measure intelligence in children. As Theta Wolf has described and explained, Zazzo discovered that Binet had never used the concept "mental age" and actually found it an inadequate notion, preferring "mental level" instead.

Acknowledgments

The author is indebted to an anonymous reviewer of this article for his critical notes and helpful suggestions.

See Also the Following Articles

Cognitive Research Methods • Education, Tests and Measures in • Psychometrics of Intelligence

Further Reading

Note: An exhaustive bibliography of Alfred Binet can be found at the website of Nancy University (www.univ-nancy2.fr).

Anderson, J. E. (1956). Child development, an historical perspective. *Child Dev.* **27,** 181–196.

Andrieu, B. (2001). Alfred Binet (1857–1911), sa vie, son oeuvre. In *Oeuvres Complètes d'Alfred Binet,* Editions Euredit. St. Pierre du Mont, Landes, France.

Bertrand, F. L. (1930). *Alfred Binet et son Oeuvre.* Librairie Felix Alcan, Paris.

Binet, A., and Simon, T. (1905). Méthodes nouvelles pour le diagnostic du niveau intellectuel des anormaux. *Ann. Psycholog.* **11,** 191–244.

Franz, S. I. (1898). Review of *l'Année Psychologique*, 1998, Vol. 4, specifically the series of articles by A. Binet and N. Vaschide. *Psychol. Rev.* **5,** 665–667.

Kuhlman, F. (1912). The present status of the Binet and Simon tests of intelligence of children. *J. Psycho-Asthenics* **16,** 113–139.

Siegler, R. S. (1992). The other Alfred Binet. *Dev. Psychol.* **28,** 179–190.

Stern, W. (1914, 1928). *Psychologie der Frühen Kindheit.* Quelle & Meyer, Leipzig.

Stern, W. (1920, 1928). *Die Intelligenz der Kinder und Jugendlichen.* Barth, Leipzig.

Wolf, T. H. (1973). *Alfred Binet.* University of Chicago Press, Chicago.

Biomedicine

Giora Kaplan
The Gertner Institute, Israel

Glossary

biomedical model Based on the dominant natural science paradigm that guides the research and practice activities of the medical enterprise.

coping with disease and treatment Viewed as either a stable coping style, reflecting a personality trait, or as a flexible, context-specific behavioral process in which an individual appraises and copes with illness.

health, disease, illness, sickness Health is as much a social and cultural as a biological issue; health standards change over time and across cultures. Disease refers to the medical practitioner's perspective as summarized in an official diagnosis. Illness is a subjective experience referring to how sick persons perceive, live with, and respond to symptoms and disability. Sickness underlines the role of the person who is ill and refers to the social aspects of illness and its consequences for wider social networks and macrosystems.

health-related locus of control A personality construct referring to an individual's perception of the locus of events as determined internally by his/her own belief that his/her outcome is directly the result of his/her behavior. This contrasts with the perception in this regard of external circumstances, the control of powerful others (doctors), or the vagaries of fate, luck, or chance.

health-related quality of life Relates both to the adequacy of material circumstances and to people's feelings about these circumstances, including feelings about how actual circumstances compare with the ideal. Quality of life is seen today as an ultimate outcome of health care and so is used for assessing the consequences of specific diseases, for characterizing the needs of those living with specific chronic conditions, or as an additional result of the evaluation of specific treatments.

holistic care Relating to or concerned with complete systems rather than with parts. Treat focuses on both the mind and the body, expanding to include the many personal, familial, social, and environmental factors that promote health, prevent illness, and encourage healing.

impairment, disability, handicap In the context of the health experience, impairment is any loss or abnormality of psychological, physiological, or anatomical structure or function. Disability is the restriction of performance of any activity within the range considered normal for a human being. A handicap is a disadvantage that limits or prevents the fulfillment of a role that is normal for a specific individual.

psychometrics The use of psychophysics methods to measure subjective judgments of psychosocial phenomena and health qualities.

reductionism Usually refers to attempts to explain all biological process by the same mechanisms (such as physical laws) that chemists and physicists use to interpret inanimate matter. Biological reductionism in the social sciences refers to interpretations that link all human phenomena exclusively to biological concepts.

the sick role Relates to the structural constraints that define the expected behavior of a sick person, transcending personalities and attitudes.

Social scientists have made very important contributions to studies of health, medicine, and the health care system. Social theorizing has elucidated some of the outer trappings of biomedicine, such as the power of the profession, its increasing impact on society, the social values often encoded in medical/scientific knowledge, and the cognitive basis of biomedicine. These perspectives are underpinned by viewing biomedicine as historically and culturally located, and afford a simple way of modeling illness. Reflecting the postmodern turn in late 20th-century thought, illness has become the object of social theorizing. However, almost all theoretic contributions have been external, independent glimpses by "outsiders," and their impact on the medical milieu has so far been minimal. This article focused on social theory rooted in the social sciences has served as conceptual support for medical enterprise, methods, specific means of measurement, and approaches that have already been incorporated and are almost integral to medical discourse.

Historical Perspective

In the conceptual relationship between social science and medicine, four important periods can be identified: the Greek and Roman holistic approach to health and disease, the "enlightenment legacy" and development of the biomedical model, the development and consequences of the epidemiological approach, and the postmodern reactions to biomedical orthodoxy.

The Greek and Roman Holistic Approach to Health and Disease

In writings as far back as Hippocrates, the father of Western medicine, health is seen as a function of a mind–body/nature equilibrium, i.e., a psychophysiological–environmental balance or harmony. The concept of fusion of psychosocial and biological factors in medicine is very old. The association of personality types with particular diseases can be found as early as the 2nd-century CE in Galen's observation that depressed women were more likely to get cancer than were happy women. Diagnoses of behavioral and biological factors interactively suggest an ongoing interest in a holistic or biobehavioral approach to medicine.

The humoral theory of disease, derived from the traditions of Hippocrates, Empedocles, and Galen, conceived the world in terms of four basic elements (fire, water, air, and earth), four qualities (hot, cold, dry, and damp), four humors (blood, phlegm, yellow bile, and black bile), and four personality types (sanguine, phlegmatic, choleric, and melancholic). In this theory, the body could be imagined as a hydraulic system in which illness represented a lack of balance. For instance, melancholia was a consequence of an excess of black bile. Greek therapeutics consisted of bloodletting, diet, exercise, and bed rest, which were designed to restore the equilibrium of the system. Medical prescriptions for good living covered a variety of activities, including leisure, nutrition, lifestyle, and sex.

The "Enlightenment Legacy" and the Development of the Biomedical Model

Two 17th-century ideas had a decisive influence on scientific thought, up to the end of the 19th century. One concept, initiated by Descartes, posited a fundamental division of reality into two separate independent realms, that of mind and that of body or matter. The other idea, converging with a manifest disjunction of mind and matter, was a novel conception of the universe stemming from Newton's *Mathematical Principles of the Natural World.* Newtonian mechanics sanctioned the idea of organized complexity, like that found in biological systems, as, in principle, reducible to the interaction of its physical parts. The influential ideas of this physical paradigm, which begot the Age of Enlightenment, had a decisive influence on the life sciences and a revolutionary impact on medical thinking. The body came to be viewed as a machine, independent of psychological and environmental factors. As such, disease, like malfunctioning in a machine, suggested the need for repair. Two defining characteristics of the Enlightenment period have had an ongoing influence to the present day, particularly on the medical sciences. These are faith in science and a belief in the human ability to exercise control over that which is understood scientifically. Both notions derive from the idea of progress. Embracing the natural science paradigm provided the foundation for the rise of biomedicine. By the mid-19th century, medicine was infused by a physicalist approach. Most notable during this period was the recognition that certain organic entities (e.g., bacteria) caused certain diseases, and their pathogenic effect could be avoided or reversed by certain substances (e.g., antitoxins and vaccines). The concepts that are at the foundation of the biomedical model surface as arguments concerning what is medically relevant. Most members of the medical profession delineate their field and their responsibility by those elements of disease that can be explained in the language of physiology, biology, and, ultimately, biochemistry and physics. They prefer not to concern themselves with psychosocial issues that lie outside medicine's responsibilities and authority. By the mid-20th century, the underlying premises of medicine were that the body can be separately considered from the mind (dualism) and that understanding the body can proceed from knowledge of its parts and how they interrelate (reductionism).

Development and Consequences of the Epidemiological Approach

Evidence of systematic epidemiological analysis can be found dating back to the 18th century. Edward Jenner, through his systematic observations during smallpox outbreaks in the 1760s through the 1780s, developed the idea of a vaccine and administered the first vaccination in 1789. John Snow, in his epidemiological work in 19th-century London, discovered that contaminated water was associated with cholera. Epidemiology as a science thus developed through studies of how disease is distributed in populations and the factors that influence or determine this distribution. A major goal of epidemiology is to identify subgroups in the population that are at high risk for disease. Most of the variables used in defining these subgroups have biological as well as social significance (for the most part, not clearly defined conceptually), such as age, sex, gender, ethnicity, or race. In fact, all early epidemiologists were at first physicians, but worked very closely with statisticians and demographers. To define population subgroups, they applied social variables, including education, occupation, socioeconomic status, religion and level of religiosity, and urban-dwelling or rural, far more so than biological parameters. Epidemiology aspires to identify the etiology or the cause of a disease and the risk factors, which are those factors that increase a person's risk for a disease. The physical and social environment to which a person is exposed determines much of his/her risk level. A person's lifestyle (residence and work environment, diet, sexual life) can determine his/her exposure to etiological factors.

After the germ theory of disease and epidemiological concepts were firmly accepted, and as countries became industrialized, changes in morbidity and mortality occurred. Medicine then had to deal with diseases characterized by multiple-causal etiology, including many psychosocial factors. Thomas McKeown's thesis led the way in demonstrating the importance of environmental and social factors in the decline of mortality rates. Social inequality and poverty are now regarded as major determinants of individual health; major differences in morbidity and mortality among social classes were demonstrated in Britain with the 1982 publication of the Black Report. Identifying the etiological or causal factors for disease allows the potential reduction or elimination of exposure to those factors through the development of prevention programs. Many public health interventions comprise changes in behavior and lifestyle, and this is the obvious territory of psychosocial disciplines.

Reactions to Biomedical Orthodoxy

Critics both within and outside the medical community have expressed concern that biomedicine is too narrowly focused in its research and practice. They charge that because biomedicine is guided by a logic that requires all meaningful data to be, in principle, reducible to a single-level physicalist vocabulary, a part of medicine will always be beyond the reach of its scientific capabilities. To recognize, for example, the placebo effect as being psychoactive, as opposed to biochemical, would violate foundational premises that recognize the primacy of the body to the exclusion of mind. Western medicine is often referred to as one of humankind's most outstanding contemporary achievements. But in the midst of success, there is the unsettling sense of "crisis." This tension is nowhere more evident than in the distinctions made between the science of medicine and the art of medicine. From the critic's point of view, the art of medicine—a euphemistic way of saying that successes cannot be explained in biomedical terms—starts where the science of medicine begins to show its limitations. Patient dissatisfaction has become an inescapable consequence of medical practice and the concept of the physician as healer has gone progressively into decline. As a result, a wide variety of health alternative approaches, cults, and sects flourish, including naturopathy, homeopathy, chiropractic, acupuncture, nutritional medicine, psychic healing, and Christian Science approaches. Common to all is an effort to meet the perceived needs of patients who feel neglected by "scientific medicine."

The marketplace has played an enormous part in the rise and fall of the popularity of alternative medicine. A strong medical counterculture emerged in the mid-1960s, debunking science and technocratic solutions to problems and exploring alternative lifestyles. There was increasing awareness of the limits to orthodox biomedicine in terms of safety and efficacy and a desire by consumers to gain greater control over their own health care and well being, especially when orthodoxy had failed to produce results for them individually. Proponents of holistic medicine argue that the proper scope of medicine is not just the "diseased body," as biomedical practitioners would propose, but rather the "sick person." Holistic proponents encourage researchers and practitioners to pursue alternative avenues, especially those involving extrasomatic, caring qualities. In particular, the holistic practitioner encourages the patient to get involved in the healing process. Holistic health recognizes the impact that attitudes and emotions can have on physiological states. Patients are appreciated as mental, emotional, social, spiritual, and physical beings.

Another counterstrategy is behavioral medicine. This movement's most basic assumption is that there is an interrelationship between the immune system, the central nervous system, and the endocrine system. The core of basic research in this field is an attempt to locate the specific neurochemical mechanisms by which subjective states, specifically those associated with emotional stress, lead to disease, by integrating biological and behavioral knowledge in a multidisciplinary approach. One conclusion is that the "insurgents" (the behavioral medicine specialists, disciplines, interest groups, and countermovements) fail to provide the medical enterprise with an alternative to the biomedical model. Unpacking the common features of the insurgents makes it clear is that the philosophical and scientific foundations of contemporary (bio)medicine go unchallenged. Despite their rather pointed criticisms, they seek only to build on the biomedical edifice. The insurgents do not follow the implications of their arguments to their logical conclusion. If they did, they would provide the basis for alternative medical foundations. Others will claim that biomedicine's success in dominating the health care field is so remarkable that its paradigm has attained virtually unique legitimacy.

In sum, medicine can be seen as a specific culture with its peculiar and distinctive perspective, concepts, rituals, and rhetoric. Medicine provides a context in which public consciousness about health and illness and about the role of medicine in society is generated.

What Methods Used in Biomedicine Can Be Ascribed to the Social Sciences?

Theoretical Recognition of Psychosocial Sciences

Biology and the social sciences have a common focal point, the human being, which gives the biologic and social sciences much common ground and differentiates them from the natural or exact sciences. August Comte (1798–1857), the creator of the first major sociological synthesis, in his theory of the hierarchy of the sciences, sees the social sciences as the most complex and the most dependent for their emergence on the development of all the other sciences. Although sociology has special methodological characteristics that distinguish it from its predecessors in the hierarchy, it is also dependent on them, especially on biology, the science that stands nearest to it in the hierarchy. The early classic sociological theories of August Comte, Herbert Spencer, and Emile Durkheim resorted many times to biological analogies, to the parallels between organic and social evolution, and to similarities in the structure and evolution of organic and social units, such as the idea of the primacy of the living entity over any particular element. This approach was to guide the functional analysis that came to dominate British anthropology under the impact of Alfred Radcliffe-Brown and Bronislaw Malinowski, and which led, somewhat later, to American functionalism in sociology under Talcott Parsons and Robert K. Merton. On the other hand, biomedicine, today's scientific medicine, has long recognized that for understanding and explaining some of its topics, it has to turn to the behavioral and social sciences, especially when trying to apply biological and other scientific knowledge to human beings. The reductionist argument claims that levels of organization do not involve ontologically new entities beyond the elements of which they are composed. As a theoretical system, pure biologism is a method that constantly and exclusively interprets all human phenomena through biological concepts; this allows no breakthrough into its preserve, no access to causal factors external to its layout causality. This theory can be found only at the margins of biomedicine. The recognition that the human is not only physiological processes, that most human behavior cannot be explained in biophysiological concepts, and that social reality cannot be wholly reduced to biology is today widely recognized in biomedicine. Emile Durkheim (1858–1917) presented a definitive critique of the reductionist explanation of social behavior. Social phenomena are "social facts" and these are the subject matter of sociology. They have, according to Durkheim, distinctive social characteristics and determinants that are not amenable to explanations on the biological or psychological level. They are external to any particular individual considered as a biological entity. Any effort to explain a physiological phenomenon such as urination in biological terms alone will never be able to succeed, because most persons can restrict urination to socially defined situations.

Despite this entire line of reasoning, the reductionist argument is still alive, receiving encouragement from sporadic discoveries of enzymes, hormones, and genes explaining some human behavior. Biology and medicine as autonomous disciplines employing *sui generis* modes of explanation will prove, in the fullness of time, that human feelings, attitudes, and states of mind are fully explicable in physiological, or even physicochemical, terms.

Concepts Based on Social Theories

Numerous biomedical concepts have strong roots in the social sciences; they are not exotic or strange to medical discourse and are routinely discussed in the professional medical literature and other contexts.

Objective and Subjective States

Health caregivers have always been interested in what patients think, know, perceive, and feel, and the meaning they attach to their own behavior. Of equal interest are issues concerning why and when people ask for care; their compliance with treatment, prevention, and health promotion directives; and the influence of feelings and attitudes on the etiology and development of disease. Ruth Wallace and Alison Wolf, in their book *Contemporary Sociological Theory*, used the words of Max Weber (1864–1920), one of the most influential and fecund masters of the art and science of social analysis:

> *Sociology is a science which attempts the interpretive understanding of social action in order thereby to arrive at a causal explanation of its course and effects. In "action" is included all human behavior when and insofar as the acting individual attaches a subjective meaning to it. Action in this sense may be either overt or purely inward or subjective; it may consist of positive intervention in a situation, or of deliberately refraining from such intervention in a passively acquiescing in the situation. Action is social insofar as by virtue of the subjective meaning attached to it by the acting individual (or individuals)*

it takes account of the behavior of others and is thereby oriented in its course. [Wallace and Wolf, 1991: 238]

Many of the attempts to understand subjective meanings in the health arena are based on a social–psychological perspective; the focus is primarily on the individual ("self") and on the interaction between a person's internal thoughts and emotions and his or her social behavior. Individuals, viewed as active constructors of their own conduct, interpret, evaluate, define, and map out their own action.

Health, Disease, Illness, Sickness

Health is a broad concept that can embody an enormous range of meanings, from the narrowly technical to the all-embracing moral or philosophical. Even today there is no clear and common definition among professionals, and social scientists have assumed a central role in challenging medical thinking, contributing additional dimensions to the phenomena, and pushing for a more systematic conceptual distinction between different states of health. Disease is what is detected as a pathology or abnormality in the body or in physiological functions. Diseases are defined medically by being included in the International Classification of Disease (ICD). Illness is the subjective experience of harm, pain, or loss of function, usually couched in terms of symptoms. Sickness is reported illness, as revealed when a person seeks care or help. Health care providers are apprised of only a fraction of illnesses, because people treat themselves, ask advice from friends, or just put up with feeling ill.

The "Sick Role"

The "sick role" relates to structural constraints that define the expected behavior of a sick person, transcending personalities and attitudes. Role expectations are at the heart of what was once the most influential schema in the sociology of medicine, that of Talcott Parsons. According to Parsons, the social structure of medical practice can be defined by the shared expectations about the "sick role" and the role of the doctor. On the one hand, the sick are exempt from normal obligations, they are not held responsible for their illness, they must try to get well, and they must seek competent help. On the other hand, the physician is expected to be "universalistic," "functionally specific," "affectively neutral," and "collectivity oriented." These complementary normative rules have a functional relation to the therapeutic process and the larger society. Critics of Parsons rejected his narrow formulation regarding the sick role and the doctor–patient relationship, as well as his assumptions of body and society as perfectly balanced harmonic systems. Parsons' sick role formulation seems to be an ideal type construct, which does not necessarily match the empirical variations of illness behaviors and doctor–patient interactions. Most sociologists have developed a more systematic and neutral typology of doctor–patient relationship based on the degree of the correspondence between the doctor's and the patient's assertion of illness. Parsons' sick role refers to only one of the many possible situations when there is an agreement between the patient's and the doctor's perception of the illness. Another major criticism of Parsons' model states that going to see the doctor is not the only component in the complex system of help-seeking behavior, so a distinction should be made between the sick role and the patient role. A large body of sociological research has demonstrated that actual doctor–patient relations can vary and do not always match the Parsonian model. Most sociologists see Parsons' model as much too oriented by the ideological claims and viewpoints of the profession. Yet, probably precisely for that reason, the concept has become bound up in the medical discourse.

Impairment, Disability, Handicap

The International Classification of Impairments, Disability, and Handicaps (ICIDH), developed in the 1970s, was issued by the World Health Organization in 1980 as a tool for the classification of the consequences of disease and of their implications for the lives of individuals. This categorization is based on a totally different approach to disease, departing from all other medical classifications, and is conceptually much more psychosocially oriented. Sickness is seen as an interference with the individual's ability to perform his/her accustomed social role and the functions and obligations that are expected of him/her. The sequence underlying illness-related phenomena can be extended as shown in Fig. 1. According to the World Health Organization, impairment from disease or injury is defined as any loss or abnormality of psychological, physiological, or anatomical structure or function. The resultant disability is any restriction or lack of ability to perform an activity in the manner or within the range considered normal for a human being. A handicap is a disadvantage for a given individual, resulting from an impairment or a disability, that limits or prevents the fulfillment of a role that is normal (depending on age, sex, and social, and cultural factors) for that individual. A handicap may result from impairment without the mediation of a state of disability (e.g., a disfigurement). On the other hand, someone with a serious disability may be living a fairly normal life without being handicapped.

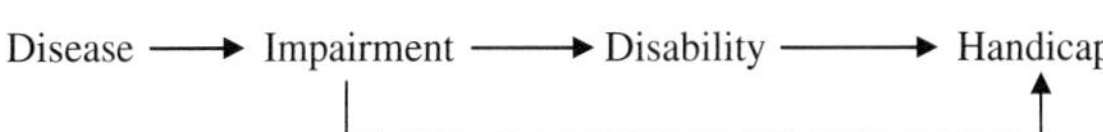

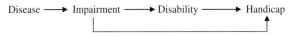

Figure 1 The extended sequence underlying illness-related phenomena.

Social, Cultural, and Personal Resources

Studies of social causes of health and illness deal with the association between stressful socioenvironmental contexts and the resources mobilized by individuals to mitigate the threats of stressful experience. Resources are classified into two broad categories: external (material or interpersonal and cultural) and internal (personal traits, skills, etc.). Resources are assumed to moderate the stressor–strain relationship (the pathogenic or salutogenic components of the stress process). Some theories emphasize the cumulative effects on health produced by the presence of social stressors and limited external or internal resources (or the presence of distinct vulnerability factors), pointing to "cycles of disadvantage" that precipitate a susceptibility to illness and adaptive breakdown.

Life Events

Illness or disability is a social experience that should be examined in the context of the life course. Critical life events can affect the etiology of illness, disease development, and personal experience with illness. Life events requiring readaptation, whether perceived culturally as "good" or "bad," increase psychological stress and can even cause acute physical symptoms and constrain daily activity. Among the most frequent stressful life events are retirement, bereavement, and severe disease of significant others.

Stigma and Labeling

The concepts of stigma and social "labeling" are well known among contemporary medical professionals and researchers. There has been much research and theory development of labeling in sociology and social psychology. Every society establishes criteria for categorizing persons, stating what the "normal" attributes are of each of the social categories. Cultural assumptions define what is normal or natural in every social situation or human condition. Sometimes individuals, or even entire social groups, possess attributes that do not match the socially defined natural states. Looking "different," or "strange" may "reduce" an individual to the single discrepant stigmatizing attribute. Sick or disabled people are often subjected to this kind of stigmatization.

In cultures with a tendency to regard the states of health and youth as normal conditions, stigmatizing and labeling are common. Health conditions differ in their capacity to be used as deeply discrediting attributes; physical abnormalities, for example, that are visible are likely to lead to labeling. Some people with evident physical "differences" may turn to plastic surgeries or other medical interventions to avoid labeling. Another factor is the social image and etiology of a disease. Health conditions may be seen as a serious cause for stigma because of their seemingly psychological and nonobjective nature. Individuals with some illnesses (e.g., sexually transmitted diseases, cancers, mental illnesses) are especially vulnerable to labeling. The sick person is often viewed as blameworthy for his or her illness. For example, people with AIDS are often assumed to have engaged in deviant and promiscuous sexual behavior. These people, who are already suffering physiological and psychological distress, have to cope with additional tensions caused by accusations, rejection, and labeling by society. Even the diagnosis process of certain diseases can unintentionally become a labeling process. In the course of the disease, the patient may internalize a label imposed by society (the "looking-glass self") and adopt behaviors and self-perceptions that match this label. This phenomenon has the nature of a self-fulfilling prophecy. In the present era of increasing medicalization (wherein social and psychological phenomena tend to be seen as primarily medical), it is especially important for medical professionals to be aware of the implications their care can have for labeling patients.

Psychosocial Measures or Indices

An influential arsenal of psychosocial measures and instruments is now widely used as health indicators of populations, as etiological factors of diseases, as interventions in disease development, as assessors of the consequences of health conditions, as estimates of the outcomes of care, as evaluators of health services, and as factors influencing the effect of treatments. This development probably has to do with the shift away from viewing health in terms of survival, toward defining it in terms of freedom from disease, and therefore to an emphasis on the individual's ability to perform his or her daily activities. The current emphasis is on positive themes of happiness, social and emotional well-being, and quality of life.

Health-Related Quality of Life

Quality of life has been studied and used from the perspectives of a variety of disciplines. Medical interest in the quality of life has been stimulated largely by modern skill and success in prolonging life, and by the growing realization that this may be a mixed blessing: patients want to live, not merely to survive. The theme, of course, is not new; what is new is the development of formal ways to measure quality of life and their application in evaluating medical outcomes. We have become bold to the point that the idea of measuring such an abstract and complex theme as quality of life no longer seems presumptuous. Although concern over quality of life in the health field is comparatively new, the social sciences have long evinced interest in measuring the quality of life in the general population. Though conceptual distinctions may be drawn among themes such as life satisfaction, happiness, morale, and anomie, progress in developing separate measurements for these concepts lags far behind. The current medical literature commonly reports the use of different quality-of-life instruments as one of the parameters for assessing the consequences of specific diseases, characterizing the needs of those living with specific chronic conditions, or as an additional result of the evaluation of specific treatments. Another use is in the estimate of medical services cost–benefit assessments.

The Quality-of-Life Index The quality-of-life instrument measures the general well-being of patients with cancer and other chronic diseases. It is intended to evaluate the effects of treatment and supportive programs such as palliative care. A measurement of quality of life considers physical, social, and emotional function; attitudes to illness; the adequacy of family interactions; and the cost of illness to the individual. The emphasis in the quality-of-life scale is on practicality: it is brief and easy to administer and yet broad in scope. It has proved acceptable to clinicians and so may come to replace the use of older and less well-validated scales.

SF-36 Health Survey The SF-36 Health Survey is probably the most extensively used tool to measure health-related quality of life. The 36-item short-form (SF-36) survey was constructed to provide a comprehensive assessment of physical, mental, and social components of health status. This tool, translated into many languages, is widely used to measure quality of life in patients with specific diseases or disabilities such as cancer, heart diseases, and diabetes, in patients in orthopedic or cardiac rehabilitation programs, and in patients after specific surgical treatments. Together with other measurements, it provides a medical tool to assess the quality of treatments or the efficiency of health services. The instrument generates a health profile consisting of 36 questions in eight subscales and two summary measures for physical and emotional well-being. Shorter versions of the tool have also been developed.

Personality Measures/Characteristics

A number of psychological instruments are used in medical research to find risk factors for disease and to classify different patient coping modes or health-related behaviors. One of the best known correlations is found between Type A personality and heart disease. Among the most widely used instruments are the Minnesota Multiphasic Personality Interview-2, the COPE Inventory, and the Health Locus of Control.

Locus of Control The "locus of control" is a personality construct referring to an individual's perception of the locus of events as determined internally by his/her belief that an outcome is directly the result of his/her behavior. This contrasts with the perception of external circumstances, by which control is in the hands of powerful others (doctors), or outcomes are due to the vagaries of fate, luck, or chance. Some research suggests that what underlies the internal locus of control is the concept of "self as agent." This means that our thoughts control our actions, and that when we apply this executive function of thinking, we can positively affect our beliefs, motivation, and performance. We can control our own destinies and we are more effective in influencing our environments in a wide variety of situations.

A health-related Locus of Control Inventory developed in the mid-1970s was derived from social learning theory. This tool was a one-dimensional scale containing a series of statements of people's beliefs that their health was or was not determined by their own behavior. A further development was the three 8-item Likert-type "internal, powerful others, chance" (IPC) scales, which predicted that the construct could be better understood by studying fate and chance expectations separately from external control by powerful others. The locus of control and IPC approaches were combined to develop the Multidimensional Health Locus of Control (MHLC) Scale. The MHLC Scale consists of three 6-item scales also using the Likert format. This tool is used to measure quality of life in patients with diseases or disabilities such as breast cancer, irritable bowel syndrome, chronic leg ulcer, and traumatic spinal cord injury. The second aspect is medical outcomes as assessment for quality of treatments (for example, for cervicogenic headache, after cardiac surgery; treatment outcome in subgroups of uncooperative child dental patients; outcomes of parent–child interaction therapy). The last aspect is efficiency of health services or planning a new service. Examples of application include prediagnostic decision-making styles among Australian women, relating to treatment choices for early breast cancer, intention to breast feed, and other important health-related behaviors and beliefs during pregnancy; predicting the ability of lower limb amputees to learn to use a prosthesis; and planning a program of awareness in early-stage Alzheimer's disease.

Sense of Coherence Sense of coherence (SOC) is a global construct expressing the degree to which a person has a pervasive and dynamic, but lasting, feeling that the internal and external stimuli and stressors in his/her environment are (a) comprehensible, i.e., predictable, structured, and explicable, (b) manageable, i.e., there are resources available to meet the demands of these stimuli, and (c) meaningful, i.e., the demands are challenges worthy of engagement and coping. It has been proposed that a strong SOC would help to mediate and ameliorate stresses by influencing coping efforts. This concept is the basis of the "salutogenetic model," i.e., explaining how people cope with stressors such as illness and how people remain in reasonably good physical and emotional health despite the stressors and environmental "insults." To explore this dimension and to explain a person's position or change on a health-disease continuum, health sociologist Aaron Antonovsky developed a 29-question self-rating scale that has been widely employed in research. Primary research dealt with the feasibility, reliability, and validity of the SOC scale in a variety of countries and settings, and then employed it as a measure of both independent and dependent (outcome) variables.

Although the SOC scale was first developed some 25 years ago, it is in wide use in a broad range of health research. A PubMed search for literature since 2000 turned up over 140 publications using this concept/instrument. These research efforts include studies on (1) general health, quality of life, and subjective well being, (2) adjustment to natural life changes such as menopause and old age, (3) coping/adjustment to illness such as chronic heart failure, stem-cell transplantation, and orthopedic injury, (4) coping with trauma such as post-traumatic stress disorder, (5) dealing with illness of a family member and/or the stress of caretaking, and (6) assessing intervention programs.

Emotional States

Psychological tests are widely used in medical research and even in medical practice to characterize states that influence the development of disease or the impact of treatment. Instruments used in medical research and settings include the Center for Epidemiological Studies Depression Scale, the Beck Depression Inventory, and the Spielberger State–Trait Anxiety Scale. Interestingly, although these instruments are decades old, they have stood the test of time and are still used extensively.

Subjective Health Requesting individuals to evaluate their general health status has become a widespread practice in health research, especially because of the correlation of subjective health status with mortality. However, conceptual/theoretical work is still needed in order to further benefit from this simple and promising parameter.

Social Measures

A person's immediate environment often has a strong impact on his/her degree of resilience or vulnerability to stresses. Examples of instruments used to measure these factors are the Multidimensional Perceived Social Support Scale and the Family Assessment Device.

Socioeconomic Status Inequalities in health are a major challenge for society and the health care system. The socioeconomic status of the individual, a central feature of the social structure of any society, is a major determinant of inequalities in health, and strong evidence exists for the association between health and socioeconomic status. The most common way to measure socioeconomic status (SES) is by education, occupation, and income, but the conceptual construction is still weak. The wide use of the indicator is almost disconnected from the large amount of theoretical work that has developed in the social sciences. Conceptualizing and measuring social status is one of the most difficult and controversial subjects in social research. The statistical findings are poorly interpreted and there is not yet a clear understanding of how education, occupation, and income influence health.

Social Support Many studies in the field of social epidemiology and gerontology have highlighted the importance of social support in attenuating the effects of stressful events and thereby reducing the incidence of disease. In addition, social support contributes to positive adjustment. Social support is generally defined in terms of the availability to the individual of trusted people, i.e., those on whom an individual can rely and who make him/her feel cared for and valued as a person. The measure of social support has become an important index and an area of growth in sociomedical studies.

Social Science Methodologies

The historical development of American social sciences led to the assiduous dedication of sociologists and social psychologists to the development and refining of their research methods. Many sociologists will claim that this investment was at the expense of the theoretical advance of the discipline. In any case, there has been a meaningful contribution by social scientists to the development and improvement of study designs, data collection methods, and statistical techniques, much of which has been adopted by other disciplines.

Survey Techniques

The collection of data through questioning people is integral to the work of clinicians, but it has largely been social scientists who have developed the query technique into a systematic survey of populations and a scientifically valid data collection method. Epidemiological surveys borrow most of their methods from the social sciences. The interview and the questionnaire methods of collecting data depend on the verbal performance of populations; what people say or write in response to stimuli presented to them is recorded by the researcher. There are different types of verbal information:

1. Statements or testimonies; these consist of "external/objective facts" known to the person being interviewed (e.g., "Have you visited a physician in the last three months?").

2. The interviewee's perceptions or comprehension of certain actions/occurrences/events/objects (e.g., "How do most parents you know react to their children's sickness?"); these perceptions can be in the form of conjectures/explanations of the interviewee's behavior or of some social event, or his/her expectations for future occurrences.

3. Attitudes, or the interviewee's evaluation or judgmental position (e.g., "Do you think it is good or bad that...?").

A distinctive feature of the measurement of subjective states (people's knowledge and perceptions, their feelings, and their judgments) is that there are, in fact, no right or wrong answers to questions. No objective criterion against which to evaluate answers exists. Although the consistency of answers with other information can be assessed, there is no direct way to know about a person's subjective states independently of what he/she says. Survey techniques have developed significantly, especially in question design, methods for question evaluation, and the study of cognitive processes and social factors that influence the way people capture/interpret/recall information, form their judgment, and respond to different types of questions. However, an unresolved problem with the questionnaire technique is that people with all manner of backgrounds, and no special training, design and administer survey questions.

Qualitative Methods

Qualitative methods are becoming more evident in health research, especially in nurses' studies. Semistructured in-depth interviews (including personal narratives of illness) explore what people say in as much detail as possible, exploring personal meaning and uncovering unanticipated data. Another widely used technique is the focus group, a kind of group interview that capitalizes on communication among the research participants. The idea behind the method is that group processes can help people explore and clarify their views in ways that would be less easily likely in a one-to-one interview. Focus groups are a popular method for assessing health education messages and examining public understanding of illness-related behaviors. In addition, the method has proved an effective technique for evaluating health services and exploring attitudes, needs, and experiences of health care users and health providers. Other qualitative methods include observation, which can supply data on what people actually do (as opposed to what they say), and consensus methods, the Delphi process and the nominal group technique, which attempt to assess the extent of agreement and to resolve disagreement by having experts (or credible lay persons) consider a problem through a self-administered mailed questionnaire (the Delphi process) or through structured meetings (nominal group). The Delphi process has been used widely in health research within the field of technology assessment, choosing outcomes for clinical trials, identifying priorities in care, developing clinical guidelines, and planning and forecasting the organization of services.

Cost–Benefit Analysis

An influential contribution of health economics has been to relate the evaluation of health treatments, services, or programs to cost accounting. In assessing benefits relative to costs, economists have succeeded in compelling the medical system to identify and systematically specify non-marketed commodities. They have developed techniques (in many cases rather controversial) to draw inferences from market data and from behavior they have observed in other contexts, as well as methods to estimate the value of life, as distasteful as such a calculation may seem. An alternative procedure widely employed is cost-effectiveness analysis, which determines the most effective way to achieve an objective.

Psychometrics

The arguments for considering subjective judgments as a valid approach to measurement derived ultimately from the field of psychophysics. Basic to the development of these techniques is the recognition that humans can make consistent, numerical estimates of sensory stimuli. The exact form of the relationship between stimulus and subjective response varies from one sensation to another. This holds important ramifications for health measurement: people can make subjective judgments in a remarkably internally consistent manner, even when asked to make abstract comparisons. Much work has been done in adapting psychophysical methods for use in measuring qualities for which there is no physical scale. Psychologists are working on applying knowledge from other psychological measurements to subjective health information.

Psychosocial Professional Partnerships in Different Areas of the Medical System

Today's complex health care system employs psychosocial professionals as members of the caregiver staff; as members of planning, priority-setting, or evaluation teams; as partners in research projects; and as consultants in many areas.

Service Delivery, Organization of Care, Organization of the Medical System

Medicine had been transformed into an industry, with a growing role of corporations and the state. Governments are assuming a major (perhaps the dominant) role in the organization of medical care. Decisions that once were exclusively professional are now often subject to public debate, and some become political issues. Whoever provides medical care or pays the cost of illness stands to win the gratitude and goodwill of the sick and their families, as well as that of the healthy public, who recognize the possibility that care may be needed in the future. Employers, unions, and insurance companies all stand to derive some advantage of goodwill, power, or profit from serving as a financial intermediary in health care. Even with wide regulatory differences between countries, physicians generally try to escape from corporate and bureaucratic control over their private practices and to channel the development of hospitals, health insurance, and other medical institutions into forms that do not intrude on the autonomy of the physician. The late 20th century, however, was a time of diminishing resources and autonomy for most physicians, hospitals, and medical schools. There is a rapidly increasing supply of physicians and a continued search by government for control over the growth of medical expenditures. These developments create severe strains throughout the medical system. Sociologist Paul Starr predicted in 1982 that these developments would lead to the rise of corporate enterprise in health services, and supply and demand are indeed already having a profound impact on the ethos and politics of medical care as well as its institutions. Emerging developments now jeopardize the medical professional's control of markets, organizations, and standards of judgment. The medical profession has benefited from state protection and political accommodation of its interests, but government is no longer so sympathetic and physicians are no longer the single, dominant claimant in the medical industry. Private corporations are gaining a more powerful position in American medicine; it has become more necessary to understand medicine as a business as well as a cultural phenomenon, and perhaps most important, to understand the relation between the two. Because medical care has become tightly arranged in bureaucratic organizations, professionals from different disciplines dealing with organizational issues have become part of the scene.

In managerial terms, the chief characteristic of most health organizations is their status as nonprofit organizations providing services. The term "service" is a vaguer, less measurable concept than "profit," and performance is even more difficult to measure. It is also more difficult to make clear-cut choices among alternative courses of action in such organizations, because the relationships between costs and benefits, and even the amount of benefits, are difficult to measure. However, the distinction between for-profit and nonprofit organizations is not black and white, and any criterion used for the distinction is certain to have gray areas, such as the sources and uses of funds, the types of services provided, or the proprietary nature of the entity. A company that manufactures and sells tangible goods has certain advantages, from a control standpoint, that a service organization does not have. Services cannot be stored; if the facilities and personnel available to provide a service today are not used today, the potential revenue from that capability is lost forever. Service organizations tend to be labor intensive, requiring relatively little capital per unit of output. It is not easy to measure the quantity of many services, and their quality cannot be inspected in advance. Medical institutions are run today like any other institution, with significant representation of organizational psychology, sociology, and economics, together with management and administration, quality control, technology assessment, marketing, jobs and production engineering.

Program/Project Evaluation

Because the delivery of health care is a social intervention, many of the approaches and methodologies used are adaptations of techniques developed in other social areas. Program evaluation is a collection of methods, skills, and sensitivities necessary to determine whether a human service is needed and is likely to be used, whether it is sufficiently intense to meet all the unmet needs identified, whether the service is offered as planned, and whether the human service actually does help people in need at a reasonable cost and without undesirable side effects. Through these activities, evaluators seek to help improve programs, utilizing concepts from psychology, sociology, administrative and policy sciences, economics, and education.

Coping with Disease and Treatment

Experiencing serious or chronic illness means much more than a feeling of physical distress, acknowledging symptoms, needing care, and confronting the inevitability of death. It also includes modifying daily routines, role changes, social status, questions of identity, the searching for new meaning, moral judgments, and ethical dilemmas. Studies have indicated that the way a person perceives his/her illness, his/her personal and social resources, and his/her coping strategy can predict his/her well being more than his/her illness and treatment. There is growing recognition in the medical field that coping is an integral part of the curative process (especially in serious illnesses), and extensive research is focused on the area. Studies have indicated that problem-focused and approach-seeking strategies (e.g., for information or social support) prove to be the best predictors for optimal management and control of the illness, whereas avoidance strategy is associated with less positive outcomes (except at certain stages of the illness). Intervention programs, such as education, behavioral training, individual psychotherapy, and group interventions, are developed and operated by health professionals to improve the health/illness outcomes. Social workers are an integral part of the hospital care team. Considering the social consequences of the patient's illness, they have acquired a major role in discharge planning and in helping the patient to cope better with the illness situation (e.g., utilizing community services, special devices, legal rights, and home care). However, there is still a need for more theoretical and methodological development of the concept of coping and its extensive application in the medical field.

Professional/Patient Communication and Relationships

Clinical work is a practice of responding to the experience of illness, and, as such, its context is a relational encounter between persons. Though the general parameters of the doctor–patient relationship have been constant throughout history, important elements vary in time and place: patient characteristics, the modes of organizing practice, and the social and economic context within which the relationship exists. With the breakdown of the paternalistic model of medical care, there is growing awareness of the importance of effective communication between the caregiver and the patient and his/her family. Obtaining the patient's compliance with medical treatment, or with instructions and recommendations given to him/her by the medical staff, has become much more difficult. The expansion of consumerism into health care, relating to the patients as "clients," has also had a strong influence. Efforts are being made to develop appropriate techniques among medical personnel, and in some cases new mediator roles have been created. There is a growing interest in better understanding patient perceptions and in techniques to manipulate patient behaviors.

Prevention, Health Promotion, Early Detection of Disease

Prevention, health promotion, and early detection of disease, or risk-factors, constitute a psychosocial arena par excellence, dealing with perceptions, motivations, persuasion, behavioral change, and lifestyle. Here psychosocial knowledge is used, and in many cases psychosocial professionals are those in charge of the programs.

Lay Perspective View

Frequently, social scientists are those responsible for presenting to the medical system the lay perspective. Social scientists are providers of feedback from clients, such as their satisfaction with services, as well as opinions relevant to health policy issues.

Research

Psychosocial variables are frequent in medical research; they take the form of independent variables in the etiology of disease or in the use of health services, of dependent variables in evaluating treatments and consequences of disease, and of intervening variables in understanding the development of disease or in the impact of treatment. Many difficulties are encountered when the premises of biomedicine attempt to explain psychosocial factors in disease causation. These premises are, in principle, if not always in practice, reductionist and dualist. The significance of these difficulties is heightened as psychosocial factors increasingly emerge as factors in today's disease burden ("afflictions of civilization"). However, social scientists are much more frequently becoming partners in health research, rising to the great challenge of influencing medical knowledge.

Psychosocial Health Specialization

The need for special expertise when dealing with psychosocial aspects of health and illness has led to the development of medical school subspecialties such as behavioral medicine and behavioral pediatrics. Conversely, most psychosocial professions have developed specializations in health, such as health psychology, health social workers, or medical sociology/sociology of health.

Critiques on the Current Situation

Quality of the Dialogue between Medicine and Social Sciences

In many cases, medicine embraces very superficially the concepts and variables from psychosocial sciences. During the absorption of these concepts into the medical professional discourse, much of their original meaning, depth, and comprehensiveness is lost. As a simple example, recall the uses of social variables in epidemiology. The associations of education or socioeconomic status with health measurements are frequently analyzed, but the impression is of a "fishing expedition," with no clear or focused hypothesis behind the effort. Explanations of the findings are usually *post factum* and superficial. Even the common characterization of population groups by ethnic origin lacks a clear and consistent rationale. Is ethnicity being used to categorize genetics, or socioeconomic or cultural groups? Considerable theoretical work done by social scientists on these issues is totally unknown to epidemiologists and other health professionals. On the other hand, social scientists are accustomed to refer exclusively to their professional colleagues, with no genuine attempt to reach other audiences. Both sides need to change their attitudes in order to improve the dialogue, not just as individuals but as a true interdisciplinary operation.

Social Scientists as Insiders or Outsiders

There are two clear positions about social scientists whose main focus of interest is health and medicine. At one extreme are those social scientists who strongly believe that in order to be a real sociologist, anthropologist, or economist, they have to be "outsiders," totally independent, autonomous academic professional intellectuals. The tenet for this is that the best and most significant research questions have to be strongly grounded in theory and must contribute directly to theory development. The main critique leveled at this position is that social scientists become a closed sect, talking only to themselves, frequently taking a one-sided critical and even scornful position. The other position is a parallel tradition of social scientists aspiring to change, improve, and in some sense modulate social reality. A modest group in this tradition consists of those social scientists who see their work as applying their perspective and knowledge to real social problems. They prefer, then, to be "insiders," in order to better identify and understand what really burdens people and social organizations, and to be able to contribute directly to social change. The major criticism brought against this position is lack of perspective, because the social scientist, like any human being, is strongly influenced by the social milieu in which he/she lives. Applied social science usually finds it far more difficult to liberate itself from the point of view and the ideology of the medical profession, and its practitioners are then criticized by colleagues for being too conformist and not critical enough in their conclusions.

Theory-Grounded Research

The development of social science as an occupation, especially in American society, carries with it some distancing from theory and submersion in survey opinion polls and experiments with strong emphasis on strict and polished techniques and methodologies. In many cases, this aspect of the social scientist's work focuses only in providing very specific data commissioned by employers or clients, with almost no significance for the broader theoretical perspective. Statistical data, even social measurements, will not "become" sociology or economics or social psychology until they are interpreted and slotted into a theoretical reference framework. Practical problems have to be translated into clear conceptual definitions, and hypotheses have to be derived strictly from theories so that when they are verified or refuted, the explanation and significance of the findings can be grounded in theory. This theoretical emphasis is not just to defend the research before academic colleagues, but to ensure in a multidisciplinary problem-solving process that the social scientist has contributed a unique point of view and body of knowledge. Social scientists, even with a strong applied or policy-oriented approach, have to always remember who they are and from where they come.

See Also the Following Articles

Cost–Benefit Analysis • Epidemiology • Interviews • Nursing • Surveys • World Health Organization Instruments for Quality of Life Measurement in Health Settings

Further Reading

Anthony, R. N., and Young, D. W. (1988). *Management Control in Nonprofit Organizations.* Richard Irwin, Homewood, IL.

Antonovsky, A. (1987). *Unraveling the Mystery of Health.* Jossey-Bass, San Francisco, CA.

Antonovsky, A. (1993). The structure and properties of the sense of coherence scale. *Social Sci. Med.* **36**(6), 725–733.

Armstrong, D. (2003). Social theorizing about health and illness. In *The Handbook of Social Studies in Health & Medicine* (G. L. Albrecht, R. Fitzpatrick, and S. C. Scrimshaw, eds.). Sage Publ., London.

Beck, A. T., Ward, C. H., Mendelson, M., Mock, J., and Erbaugh, J. (1961). An inventory measuring depression. *Arch. Gen. Psychiatr.* **4,** 551–571.

Berger, P. L. (1967). *Invitation to Sociology: A Humanistic Perspective.* Penguin Books, Harmondsworth, UK.

Carver, C. S., Scheier, M. F., and Weintraub, J. K. (1989). Assessing coping strategies: A theoretically based approach. *J. Personal. Social Psychol.* **56,** 267–283.

Coser, L. A. (1971). *Masters of Sociological Thought—Ideas in Historical and Social Context.* Harcourt Brace Jovanovich, New York.

Culyer, A., and Newhouse, J. (eds.) (2000). *Handbook of Health Economics.* Elsevier, Amsterdam.

Drummond, M. F., O'Brien, B., Drummond, O., Torrance, G. W., and Stoddart, G. L. (1997). *Methods for the Economic Evaluation of Health Care Programs,* 2nd Ed. Oxford Medical Publ., Oxford.

Foss, L., and Rothenberg, K. (1988). *The Second Medical Revolution—From Biomedicine to Infomedicine.* New Science Library, Boston, MA.

Foucault, M. (1994). *The Birth of the Clinic: An Archaeology of Medical Perception.* Vintage Books, New York.

Fowler, F. J., Jr. (1995). *Improving Survey Questions: Design and Evaluation.* Sage Publ., Thousand Oaks, CA.

Freidson, E. (1988). *Profession of Medicine: A Study of the Sociology of Applied Knowledge.* The University of Chicago Press, Chicago.

Gordis, L. (1996). *Epidemiology.* W. B. Saunders, Philadelphia, PA.

Hippler, H. J., Schwartz, N., and Sudman, S. (eds.) (1987). *Social Information Processing and Survey Methodology.* Springer-Verlag, New York.

Holland, J. (ed.) (1998). *Psycho-Oncology.* Oxford University Press, New York.

Jobe, J. B., and Mingay, D. J. (1991). Cognitive and survey measurements: History and overview. *Appl. Cogn. Psychol.* **5,** 175–192.

Kabacoff, R. I., Miller, I. W., Bishop, D. S., Epstein, N. B., and Keitner, G. I. (1990). A psychometric study of the McMaster Family Assessment Device in psychiatric, medical, and non-clinical samples. *J. Family Psychol.* **3,** 431–439.

Kaplan, G., and Baron-Epel, O. (2003). What lies behind the subjective evaluation of health status? *Social Sci. Med.* **56,** 1669–1676.

McDowell, I., and Newell, C. (1987). *Measuring Health: A Guide to Rating Scales and Questionnaires.* Oxford University Press, New York.

McHorney, C. A., Ware, J. E., and Raczek, A. E. (1993). The MOS 36-Item Short-Form Health Survey (SF-36®): II. Psychometric and clinical tests of validity in measuring physical and mental health constructs. *Med. Care* **31**(3), 247–263.

Merton, R., and Barber, E. (1963). Sociological ambivalence. In *Sociological Theory, Values and Sociocultural Change* (E. A. Tiryakian, ed.). Free Press, New York.

Nichols, D. S. (2001). *Essentials of MMPI-2 Assessment.* Wiley Publ., New York.

Parsons, T. (1951). Social structureand dynamic process: The case of modern medical practice. In *The Social System*, pp. 428–479. The Free Press, New York.

Plough, A. L. (1986). *Borrowed Time: Artificial Organs and the Politics of Extending Lives.* Temple University Press, Philadelphia, PA.

Radloff, L. S. (1977). The CES-D scale: A self-report depression scale for research in the general population. *Appl. Psychol. Measure.* **1,** 385–401.

Saks, M. (2003). Bringing together the orthodox and alternative in health care. *Complement. Therap. Med.* **11,** 142–145.

Spielberger, C. D., Gorsuch, R. L., and Luschene, R. E. (1970). *Manual for the State-Trait Anxiety Inventory.* Consulting Psychologists Press, Palo Alto, CA.

Spitzer, W. O., Dobson, A. J., Hall, J., Chesterman, E., *et al.* (1981). Measuring the quality of life of cancer patients: A concise QL-Index for use by physicians. *J. Chronic Dis.* **34,** 585–597.

Starr, P. (1982). *The Social Transformation of American Medicine: The Rise of a Sovereign Profession and the Making of a Vast Industry.* Basic Books (Harper Collins), New York.

Townsend, P., and Davidson, N. (1982). *Inequalities in Health.* Pelican Books, Harmondsworth.

Turner, B. (1995). *Medical Power and Social Knowledge.* Sage Publ., Thousand Oaks, CA.

Turner, B. (2003). The history of the changing concepts of health and illness: Outline of a general model of illness categories. In *The Handbook of Social Studies in Health & Medicine* (G. L. Albrecht, R. Fitzpatrick, and S. C. Scrimshaw, eds.). Sage Publ., London.

Wallace, R. A., and Wolf, A. (1991). *Contemporary Sociological Theory: Continuing the Classical Tradition,* 3rd Ed. Prentice-Hall, Englewood Cliffs, NJ.

Wallston, B. S., Wallston, K. A., Kaplan, G. D., and Maides, S. A. (1976). Development and validation of the Health Locus of Control (HLC) Scale. *J. Consult. Clin. Psychol.* **44,** 580–585.

Wallston, K. A., and Wallston, B. S. (1981). Health locus of control scales. In *Research with the Locus of Control Construct: Vol. 1* (H. Lefcourt, ed.), pp. 189–243. Academic Press, New York.

World Health Organization (WHO) (1980). *International Classification of Impairments, Disability, and Handicaps.* WHO, Geneva.

Zeinder, M., and Endler, N. S. (1996). *Handbook of Coping: Theory, Research, Application.* John Wiley & Sons, New York.

Zimet, G. D., Powell, S. S., Farley, G. K., Werkman, S., and Berkoff, K. A. (1990). Psychometric characteristics of the Multidimensional Scale of Perceived Social Support. *J. Personality Assess.* **55,** 610–617.

Built Environment

Karen A. Franck

New Jersey Institute of Technology, Newark, New Jersey, USA

Glossary

architectural programming The information-gathering phase that precedes architectural or interior design decisions; may include behavioral research to determine organizational goals and user needs.

behavior mapping An observational method for recording details of ongoing activities in specific locations.

behavior setting A concept referring to the regularly occurring combinations of physical features and patterns of use and meaning that constitute everyday environments.

cognitive map An internal spatial representation of the environment that takes the form of a schematic map.

participatory design A process of designing or planning an environment to be built (or modified) that includes future occupants in decision making.

personal space The zone around the body that a person, and others, recognize as that person's space; zone size varies according to activity, context, culture.

post-occupancy evaluation Research conducted in a recently built (or renovated) environment to determine how well user needs have been met.

Sanborn maps Detailed maps of cities, showing land subdivision, building forms, construction, uses, and street widths; used primarily by city governments.

spatial syntax A technique for graphically representing structure of circulation in or around the interior or exterior of a built environment.

The built environment has been the subject of social science research in the United States since the 1950s and 1960s. With the twin aims of filling a gap in the social sciences, which traditionally ignored relationships between the physical environment and human behavior and experience, and of improving the quality of built environments for occupants, members of a variety of disciplines have pursued diverse research approaches and topics, employing a variety of methods. The sources of information frequently used include occupants, environments, records and archives, architects, and building professionals. The "built environment" is understood to include buildings and interiors as well as designed open spaces such as streets and plazas, neighborhoods, communities, and cities.

Introduction

When and Why the Built Environment

Social scientists in the United States started to study the built environment and its relationship to human behavior and experience in the 1950s and 1960s. In response to inquiries from psychiatrists and architects about how to improve the design of mental wards, psychologists Humphrey Osmond and Robert Sommer in Canada, and Harold Proshansky and his colleagues William Ittelson and Leanne Rivlin in New York, began to explore how the design of these settings influences patient behavior. Psychologist Roger Barker had already been documenting the precise location, content, and sequence of everyday activities of children in small towns in the Midwest. As interest in the built environment grew among psychologists, concepts of privacy, personal space, and territoriality became useful, as evident in the research of Irwin Altman. Following earlier traditions in their discipline, sociologists, including Lee Rainwater and Herbert Gans, studied the experiences of residents in public housing, urban neighborhoods, and suburban communities. Because social scientists traditionally focus on people and their experiences, much of the research treated the built environment as the independent variable, or as context. One researcher who treated the environment as a dependent variable early on—that is, as the product of human actions—was an architect. Amos

Rapoport adopted an anthropological perspective to investigate variations in house forms resulting from differences in cultures and climates.

During the 1960s and 1970s, within the general climate of concern over solving social problems and improving urban life, architects, planners, and urban designers became aware that many of the modernist tenets of city and building design were creating serious problems for daily life; this encouraged building professionals to gain a greater understanding of human responses to the designed environment, for which they turned to social scientists and their research methods. Social science methods provided design professionals with a more systematic, empirically based and verifiable means of gaining information to make design decisions, as compared to the more personal, subjective, and anecdotal means traditionally employed in design fields.

Architects and urban designers, along with social scientists, were greatly affected by Jane Jacobs' 1961 book *Death and Life of Great American Cities* and by the 1972 demolition of the Pruitt Igoe public housing project in St. Louis. Architects and social scientists of this period began to collaborate in various ways. Professional organizations were formed, including the Environmental Design Research Association (EDRA) in the United States, the International Association of Person–Environment Studies (IAPS) in Europe, the Pacific Association for People–Environment Relations (PAPER) in Australia, and the Man–Environment Relations Association (MERA) in Japan. Over the years, journals were established (*Environment and Behavior, Journal of Environmental Psychology, Journal of Architectural and Planning Research* and *Architecture and Comportment/Architecture and Behavior*) and books and book series were published. Architecture programs hired social scientists to teach; and Ph.D. degree-granting programs were started.

Various descriptive names emerged to delineate the field, some indicating disciplinary connections, some more inclusive: environmental psychology, ecological psychology, environmental sociology, environmental anthropology, human ecology, social ecology, man–environment (and then person–environment) studies, environment behavior studies, and environmental design research. A goal among many researchers was, and continues to be, both to fill a gap in social science knowledge about the built environment, as context and as outcome, and to provide information that will improve the quality of the built environments for occupants. To do either, within a social science framework, requires the development of conceptual approaches and the invention of appropriate methods. It is clear that the foundation of this field lies in social science, not in the design disciplines. Not surprisingly then, although architects and designers have sought out, and continue to seek, education in social science disciplines, there has not been the same movement of social scientists into design.

Characteristics of Research

Research in this field is typically conducted in real-world settings and not in laboratories. Although "field research" is common in anthropology and sociology, for psychologists it was initially a disciplinary and methodological departure, which followed the legacy of Kurt Lewin's action research. Researchers may also explore people's responses to graphic representations of actual or ideal environments or may use simulated environments. These include physical models, full-scale constructions of rooms or entire buildings, and, more recently, digital modeling and virtual reality models. Studies may also be longitudinal, looking at situations before and after physical interventions have been made or before and after people move, and comparative between different kinds of environments.

Researchers acknowledge that the built environment and human behavior and experience affect each other—that the environment does not determine human behavior and experience, and that what influence it does have is very likely modified by a host of other factors. The built environment is recognized to be adaptable, to change over time, and to have both fixed and semifixed and movable features. Thus, even though any given research endeavor must, necessarily, focus on a few aspects of environment and people and often looks primarily at the environment as an independent variable (context of human action) or as a dependent variable (product of human action), the true complexity of the situation has been a key concern in the development of theories and methods. One concept that addresses this complexity, originally proposed and used by Roger Barker and further developed by Allan Wicker, is the "behavior setting." This refers to the combination of a particular type of built environment and its use, thus encompassing the regularly occurring combination of physical features, furniture and objects, patterns of use, kinds of users, and related rules of a small-scale environment. For instance, an elementary school classroom or a dentist's office is a behavior setting. Further development of this concept has emphasized the importance of meaning and cultural variations in behavior settings and the linking of both settings and activities into systems.

Both built and natural environments are subjects of study in this field, although studies of the latter are not discussed here. Research has covered all kinds of built environments (houses, housing complexes, day care centers, offices, markets, malls, schools, prisons, hospitals, post offices, courthouses, museums, zoos, parks, streets and plazas, and environments for particular groups, including housing for the elderly or those with dementia) at different scales, ranging from individual rooms or outdoor spaces to buildings to communities, neighborhoods, and entire cities. There is a strong empirical tradition in the field, and in some cases, it is possible to make quite well-controlled comparisons between environments that are similar except in only a few key respects (or even one). For the most part, however, such control is not possible. Nonetheless, a breaking down of environment and behavior/experience into discrete and measurable, or at least discernible, components is common. An alternative perspective on research in this field is found in phenomenological approaches used by David Seamon, Robert Mugerauer, and Louise Chawla.

The choice of what environments, what aspects of them, what aspects of human behavior and experience to study, and how to do so depend on the particular interests and disciplinary background and predilection of the researcher, as well as on requests for information that arise from design and planning projects. For these reasons, the kinds of research questions pursued, the conceptual approaches adopted, the methods used, the research findings, and the format and location of presentation are highly varied (and dispersed). The result is a rich array of methods, information, and insight, not a cohesive, well-structured, and centralized body of knowledge.

Research and Design

The goal of providing findings that will help to improve the built environment proves to be difficult to achieve, given the differences between the requirements and expectations of social science and those of the design professions. Designers need very specific information, quickly, regarding particular kinds of building occupants in particular kinds of buildings, in a format that allows them to make design decisions. Social scientists, however, generally conduct studies over a longer time period and generate findings that do not indicate the value of highly specific design features. For instance, a social science study of productivity in office environments may show that chairs and lighting quality are important influences on the level of productivity or worker satisfaction. On hearing this, a designer may ask "What kinds of chairs?" or even "What brand of chairs?" This degree of specificity about environmental features may well not have been recorded.

To address the differing requirements of social science research and the design process, researchers have sought, in different ways, to conduct studies that are directly addressed to contributing information that will be useful in making design decisions. One way is to use the results of research to develop guidelines, in book form, for the design and furnishing of particular types of environments, such as housing for the elderly, public plazas, or correctional facilities. Guidelines are not as specific as recommending brands of chairs, but they do contain functional information to guide design decisions (e.g., chairs with certain kinds of features, such as wheels, or with arms and a high back, that allow the elderly to use them easily). Guidelines are also likely to present examples of different design solutions, such as the size, function, and arrangement of rooms, indicating the behavioral advantages or disadvantages of the choices.

Researchers also conduct analyses of organizational goals and user needs during the information-gathering phase that precedes design; architects and interior designers call this "architectural programming." In behaviorally based programming, researchers systematically interview and observe the future occupants of the new building (possibly in their present one) and/or the occupants of similar buildings, to determine the user needs that will inform design decisions. Or the process may involve working closely with the client and the building's future occupants, including those who will manage and maintain it, to discover needs and aspirations through in-depth discussions, focus groups, and community meetings, as Henry Sanoff, Lynda Schneekloth, and Robert Shibley have done, facilitating a programming or a participatory design process.

Another form of research directly connected to design is the study of an environment after it has been built and occupied to determine how well, and in what ways, it does (and does not) fulfill the architect's intentions regarding its use and how it meets the needs of its occupants. This kind of research, often called "post-occupancy evaluation," usually takes place at least two years after the building is first occupied. The intention is that findings from the study may be used to adapt the building (or the way it is used) to make it more responsive to needs and, as importantly, to provide information for the future design of similar types of buildings. Starting with the founding in the 1970s of the Buffalo Organization for Social and Technological Innovation (BOSTI) by Mike Brill, private firms have offered research-based organizational analysis, architectural programming, and postoccupancy evaluation services to paying clients. Academics may do similar kinds of work as consultants.

Occupants

For social scientists studying the built environment, the most immediate and possibly the most obvious sources of information are the present, past, or future occupants. In contrast, given their training, designers and other building-related professionals would be more likely to look to the environments first. This was a key contribution social science made to the design disciplines early on: the recommendation to look at how environments are actually used and to talk to the occupants.

With their interest in naturally occurring behavior in everyday environments, researchers often employ methods of behavioral observation. These observations may take the form of walk-throughs of the environment being studied, possibly with the architect, staff, or occupants, during which observations may be recorded on plans, as a way to connect the observed behavior with a specific location, or with photographs or videotape. In other cases, more systematic and possibly repeated techniques may be adopted in which observers use precoded categories to record, at specific periods of the day and week, types of activities, number, and kinds of participants in each activity, location, and use of physical props. Given this noting of behaviors located in particular spaces, the technique has been called "behavior mapping." Time-lapse filming has been used as a means of recording behavior, notably by William H. Whyte in his study of public plazas in New York, work that led to revising the zoning code in New York to increase the number and quality of such places. In this type of place-centered mapping, the unit that is being observed is a given space or spaces, whereas in person-centered mapping, what is being observed is a person or group of people as they move from one space to another, a technique often used in way-finding research. Various electronic devices can now be used, by the observer and/or by the people being observed, to increase the ease and efficiency of both types of behavior mapping.

Focused interviews with individuals and groups of people and standardized questionnaires containing fixed-choice and open-ended questions are common instruments. Questions may cover environmental preferences, perceptions, and evaluations of experienced or hypothetical environments or specific features of them, uses of and experiences in given environments, adaptations of environments, and other aspects of life (such as friendships, socializing, desire to move, etc.) that the researcher may be studying in relation to the environment. Those responsible for the management, maintenance, security, or programs and activities within environments are also approached for information and insight to understand the functioning of particular buildings or outdoor spaces or of that type of environment.

Because built environments are places (actual and imagined), visual images are used in a wide variety of ways. The interviewer may present a map of a neighborhood or a simple plan of a building and ask for answers to be made on it (e.g., "Where do you feel most safe?" or "Where do you spend most of your time?" or "What route do you take to get to your house?"). This technique is often used in participatory planning and design projects. Respondents may be asked to rate photographs or drawings according to preference or other criteria, or to sort them into categories. This method has been used in studies of people's perceptions and evaluations of urban environments. In some studies, people were given cameras to take their choice of pictures of particular kinds of places, such as favorite places in their neighborhoods. Researchers have also asked respondents to give answers in the form of maps or drawings that they draw themselves. Kevin Lynch's method, described in *Image of the City*, of asking people to draw a quick sketch map as they might to describe their city to a stranger, helped initiate widespread adoption of this technique of cognitive mapping, including in way-finding research and in Donald Appleyard's planning of a planned city in Venezuela.

Environmental simulations are also used as a research method. The simulated environment may be physical (a small-scale model or a full-size mock-up of a setting) or, using computer technology, a virtual three-dimensional model that allows the participant to "move" through the simulated spaces. Whether physical or virtual, simulations are useful for getting people's feedback on environments that have not yet been built. Methods can also involve lengthier and possibly more intimate activities, such as keeping daily diaries, or writing environmental autobiographies to describe the places lived and the memorable experiences and feelings related to those places. To explore people's deepest feelings about their homes, Clare Cooper Marcus developed a role-playing method whereby respondents draw symbols to represent their homes and then speak to the drawings, as if speaking to the home. They then adopt the role of the home, speaking back.

Environments

Built environments, regardless of the presence of people, are key sources of information. One common and very useful technique is to observe environments for visual, auditory, and olfactory evidence of current or past use and for adaptations that occupants have made. With drawings, cameras, video cameras, plans of the environment, or precoded checklists, observers record the conditions of settings and a variety of physical traces. As John Zeisel has listed them, traces could include by-products of use (erosions, leftovers, missing traces), adaptations for use (props, separations, connections), displays of self (personalization, identification, group membership), and public messages (official, unofficial, and illegitimate signs). Leftovers can include items left outdoors, such as toys or lawn furniture; erosion might be shown in the way a path has been worn through the grass, and an adaptation might be the hole made in a fence.

To understand how interior space is used, and what problems may arise with the size and relationships of rooms, researchers will record on floor plans (and through photographs) the location, type, and size of furniture and other belongings, as Sandra Howell did in an early study of housing for the elderly, resulting in design guidelines for future buildings. This kind of inventory of space, furniture, and equipment is a very useful tool in architectural programming, to determine needs that should be met in a new facility. To document ongoing management philosophy, as well as the use of space, observers have recorded when and where the doors in mental wards are locked, as in research by Maxine Wolfe and Leanne Rivlin on children's psychiatric hospitals. In Harold Kayden's study of privately owned public spaces in New York, the conditions (e.g., amount of seating, quality of maintenance, presence of trees or other greenery) and accessibility of each such space was noted and documented.

All of these features are things done to the environment by people. What about the environment, as built? What features of it are important in relation to people's activities and experiences? These questions have received relatively less attention than have the activities, experiences, and attitudes of occupants. There are notable exceptions. Kevin Lynch, based on his own observations of cities and respondents' cognitive maps, found that certain urban design characteristics helped determine the imageability, or legibility, of cities. Oscar Newman drew on his own observations, as well as on crime records and resident surveys, to demonstrate that certain architectural features of buildings and public spaces in public housing affected the levels of crime, the fear of crime, and community cohesion. Each of the two latter studies contained theoretical tenets and empirical results. In other cases, researchers may adopt a more directly empirical perspective to discover which environmental features answer particular needs, or the needs of particular kinds of occupants, as in what kinds of layout, signage, and interior design enable wayfinding in hospitals, or the best features of a residential environment for people with Alzheimer disease. Or researchers determine how the view of a natural setting decreases length of hospital stay and how the presence of a green space in a residential environment affects very specific experiences and behaviors.

Built environments are also critiqued from the point of view of the behavioral needs of particular groups of people, needs that have typically been neglected. Recommendations for change and alternative environments are often presented. The needs of women in built environments, from the scale of houses to cities, have received attention, as have the needs of nontraditional households. How to meet the needs of the disabled has become an important topic with the passage of laws requiring accessibility for all.

A broad ranging, theoretically based, and systematized method of measuring built environments is spatial syntax analysis, first developed by Bill Hillier and Julienne Hanson in the 1980s. Typically, building floor plans are scrutinized to determine the structure of circulation from the entry point to all rooms. The plan is translated into a structural network of pathways represented graphically, with nodes as spaces and lines as connections; the representation illustrates the degree of accessibility to any given space as well as the overall network of connections. One of several numerical outcomes is the depth of any node (the number of lines necessary to reach all other nodes) and the average mean depth of the system as a whole. What is being analyzed is the spatial logic embodied in the plan of a building or a neighborhood. Spatial syntax analysis is used to correlate numerical outcomes of the graphs with observed patterns of use of streets and sidewalks, as Bill Hillier and his colleagues have done, as well as to demonstrate how the social and cultural ideologies behind building types is embodied in built form, as Thomas Markus and Kim Dovey have done.

Records and Archives

Records, archives, reports, the popular press, and publications of all kinds are also used. To study crime and other community conditions, researchers use police reports and management reports of turnover, vacancy, and vandalism. Hospital records on length of hospital stay or on recovery rates, which also provide information on the patient, are another useful type of record. Roger Ulrich and others have used such records to relate length of stay to environmental features of the hospital room, such as having a view of a natural setting. Similarly, student records of test scores have been related to classroom conditions such as day lighting and noise level; records of attendance and days sick were studied before and after moving to new and improved housing.

Expert reports, design guidelines, other building or zoning related documents, projects proposed but never built, or architectural plans for projects that were subsequently revised or torn down, as well as old photographs and real estate brochures, can all be used for investigation, along with popular press and newspaper articles. This kind of archival research was very useful to Galen Cranz's history of the ideas and values behind park design and to Lawrence Vale's research on the history of the building and the subsequent redesign of housing projects in Boston. In each case, the ideology, and the changes therein, that lay behind the building and the modification of environments were explored. Marketing brochures, model homes, and other sorts of advertisements for buildings provide useful documentation, along with the oral and visual presentations by architects and other building professionals. Researchers may also keep their own records of environments, as Camilo Vergara does through his documentary photographs and written comments on the changes, often the deterioration, in buildings in urban neighborhoods over time.

In studying the design process as it proceeds, researchers may collect and scrutinize sketches and initial designs, using them both as a means to query designers on what their decision-making was and as illustrations of how decisions evolved. These visual records are also used in conjunction with written records such as meeting minutes, change orders, and newspaper articles to analyze the evolution of a project. All kinds of maps of cities, neighborhoods, and individual blocks and building lots can be studied to understand changes in the built environment over time and to relate those changes to others indicators, such as census tract information. In her study of architectural change at the neighborhood level in San Francisco, Anne Vernez Moudon turned to past and current Sanborn maps that record building form, construction characteristics, internal uses, and details of land subdivision. Using the Global Information System (GIS) technology, the possibilities for using this method (layering a wide array of different kinds of digitized information, from different sources, over the same geographical area) have increased dramatically. The data can be manipulated, analyzed, and represented in a great variety of ways.

Architects and Building Professionals

For understanding the processes and factors behind the creation of particular environments, researchers often interview a variety of building professionals and their clients. This includes architects, landscape architects, interior designers, facility managers, planners, developers, municipal authorities, and members of community groups and other decision-making bodies. For understanding the design process more generally, researchers have interviewed architects and architecture students and have observed their design-related activities. For her study of professional architectural practice, Dana Cuff observed and recorded activities in architecture firms, including meetings between architects and their clients. To explore how personal memories play a role in the design process, Frances Downing interviewed students as well as established architects, incorporating sorting tasks and drawing tasks into the interview. Toby Israel used a variety of exercises and guided visualizations to explore how the personal environmental histories of several prominent architects have influenced their designs.

Current Status

The built environment in relationship to human behavior and experience continues to be studied in a variety of ways, for a variety of purposes. Although the degree of interest among individual practicing architects and architecture schools is considerably less now, at the beginning of the 21st century, than it was in the 1960s and 1970s, the use of social science methods for understanding and evaluating environments appears to be more widespread. Professional firms continue to provide the services of post-occupancy evaluation, architectural programming, and facilitation of participatory design. Public agencies, including the United States Postal Service and the General Services Administration, as well as large institutions, hire consultants or employ their own staff to develop architectural programs based on behavioral research. Post-occupancy evaluations are now routinely conducted by many public agencies, both in the United States and other countries. After each of the many new U.S. federal courthouses is completed, it receives a thorough post-occupancy evaluation, the results of which are used to revise the design guide for future courthouses.

In society at large, there seems to be greater concern for the connections between the needs and activities of individuals and the built environment. Attention is being paid to how environments can be, and often must be, designed to meet special needs, including the needs of people with disabilities. How environments can be designed to be sustainable and to support less resource-consuming lifestyles is of increasing interest. The recent design and planning movements of new urbanism and transit-oriented development make particular patterns of activity (walking, community interaction, using public transit) centerpieces of their ideology. The possibility that dependence on the car and the absence of urban design features that encourage, or even allow, walking contribute to obesity and other health problems is a recent topic of research, as well as public discussion. In general, the relationships of the built environment to health and well-being is a growing area of research. Most professional organizations, journals, and degree-granting programs established earlier continue to exist, with new research endeavors and new books in continuous production. The topic of the built environment, from the perspective of social science, social concerns, and design, is alive and well.

See Also the Following Articles

Cognitive Maps • Urban Studies

Further Reading

Baird, G., Gray, J., Issacs, N., Kernohan, D., and McIndoe, G. (eds.) (1996). *Building Evaluation Techniques*. McGraw Hill, New York.

Bechtel, R., and Churchman, A. (eds.) (2002). *Handbook of Environmental Psychology*. John Wiley & Sons, New York.

Bechtel, R., Marans, R., and Michelson, W. (eds.) (1990). *Methods in Environmental and Behavioral Research*. Krieger, Melbourne, FL.

Cherulnik, P. (1993). *Applications of Environment Behavior Research: Case Studies and Analysis.* Cambridge University Press, New York.

Groat, L., and Wang, T. (2002). *Architectural Research Methods.* John Wiley & Sons, New York.

Hershberger, R. (1999). *Architectural Programming and Predesign Manager.* McGraw Hill, New York.

Lang, J., Vachon, D., and Moleski, W. (eds.) (1996). *Designing for Human Behavior: Architecture and the Behavioral Sciences.* Van Nostrand Reinhold, New York.

Marans, R. W., and Stokols, D. (eds.) (1993). *Environmental Simulation: Research & Policy Issues.* Plenum, New York.

Michelson, W. (1976). *Man and his Urban Environment: A Sociological Approach.* Addison-Wesley, Reading, MA.

Preiser, W., and Ostroff, E. (eds.) (2001). *Universal Design Handbook.* McGraw-Hill, New York.

Proshansky, H., Ittelson, W., and Rivlin, L. (eds.) (1970). *Environmental Psychology: Man and his Physical Setting.* Holt, Rinehart & Winston, New York.

Sommer, R. (1983). *Social Design: Creating Buildings with People in Mind.* Prentice Hall, Englewood Cliffs, NJ.

Stokols, D., and Altman, I. (eds.) (1991). *Handbook of Environmental Psychology.* Krieger, Melbourne, Florida.

Wicker, A., Stokols, D., and Altman, I. (eds.) (1984). *Introduction to Ecological Psychology.* Cambridge University Press, New York.

Zeisel, J. (1984). *Inquiry by Design: Tools for Environment Behavior Research.* Cambridge University Press, New York.

Business Research, Theoretical Paradigms That Inform

Gayle R. Jennings

Central Queensland University, Rockhampton, Queensland, Australia

Glossary

axiology The study of ethics and values.

chaos theory Describes and explains a world of unstable systems (nonlinear and nonintegral) using descriptive algorithms. In the social sciences, the theory may be used metaphorically to describe a setting or organization as chaotic.

complexity theory A view of the world as being constituted of complex and open systems composed of agents, each of which interacts with the others to move from a state of disorder to order by self-organization.

critical realism A paradigm related to postpositivism in which truths, laws, and facts are fallible and theory bound to specific contexts (for example, social and historical). An objective epistemological stance recognizes that researcher biases and values may influence research projects. The methodology is primarily quantitative, although mixed methods may be incorporated. Axiology is value free and extrinsically based. Critical realism is utilized by value-based professions.

critical theory The ontology of this paradigm recognizes that there are complex, hidden power structures in the world that result in oppression and subjugation of minority groups. The researcher's role is to make visible these structures and to become the "champion" of the minority via a value-laden axiology that aims to change the world circumstances of those being studied, using a subjective epistemology and qualitative as well as some quantitative methodologies.

epistemology The science of knowledge; also the relationship between the researcher and that which is to be known. The relationship assumes either an objective or a subjective stance.

feminist perspectives A generic term used to describe a number of feminist perspectives, such as radical feminism, marxist/socialist feminism, liberal feminism, and postmodern feminism. Each perspective has its own specific ontological viewpoint regarding the subjugated position of women. Feminist researchers use a subjective epistemology and engage in primarily a qualitative methodology. Axiologically, for feminist researchers, the research process is transactional and intrinsically value laden.

interpretive social science paradigm A model associated with the terms (social) constructionism, (social) constructivism, social phenomenology, hermeneutics, and relativist approaches; also referred to as the interpretive paradigm.

ontology The world view or representation of reality particular to a specific theory or paradigm.

paradigm A set of beliefs regarding how the world operates/functions. Paradigms have specific stances in regard to ontology, epistemology, methodology, and axiology.

participatory paradigm The world view (ontology) is generated collectively and recognizes multiple realities. The research process emphasizes participant involvement, a subjective epistemology, and the use of qualitative and quantitative methodologies based on the principles of action research and an action research cycle (design, implementation, evaluation). The axiology is predicated to practical knowing as well as cooperation. The research is undertaken for its intrinsic value.

phenomenology A philosophy, a paradigmatic view of the world (social phenomenology), as well as a tradition of undertaking research in the social sciences.

positivism A theoretical paradigm with an ontological stance (world view) that assumes that universal truths and laws are able to explain and predict behaviors and events. The epistemological stance is objective, and a quantitative methodology guides research processes. Axiologically, positivism is value free and research projects are extrinsically focused.

postmodernism The ontological position of postmodernism exhibits skepticism toward knowledge. This paradigmatic view recognizes that the world is constantly changing and, subsequently, that no one position or perspective of the world should be privileged over any other. The epistemological stance involves researchers subjectively making "history"/reality via the deconstruction of texts. A qualitative methodology is used with a strong focus on the role of intersubjectivity and reflexivity. The paradigm is value laden and intrinsic in nature.

postpositivism A paradigm related to positivism. Ontologically, postpositivism assumes that the world, or "reality," may only be probabilistically and imperfectly known. Researchers maintain an objective epistemological stance. The paradigm associates with predominantly a quantitative methodology and researchers essay to be value free and adopt an extrinsically focused axiology.

qualitative methodology Provides a framework for empirical material (data) collection and analysis that enables researchers to gather empirical information in its textual entirety. The empirical materials are not substantively reduced or represented numerically.

quantitative methodology Provides a framework for data collection and analysis that enables researchers to reduce, analyze, and report the collected data numerically and statistically.

social constructivism This paradigm maintains that the world is constructed of multiple realities. These realities become subjectively known through the use of a qualitative methodology and a value-laden axiology that acknowledges the intrinsic values of undertaking research projects. The term is sometimes used interchangeably with (social) constructionism, (social) phenomenology, interpretive social science paradigm, hermeneutics, and relativism. At a general level, such interchange reflects the view that the construction of reality (the social world) is a social act. However, when considered in greater detail, each approach differs in regard to ontology, epistemology, methodology and axiology.

Business utilizes a variety of theoretical paradigms drawn from the social sciences to support its research activities. The predominant paradigms are the positivistic and postpositivistic paradigms. These paradigms have traditionally provided business with its social sciences methods. However, during the second half of the 20th century, paradigms associated with the traditions of social constructionism, social constructivism, social phenomenology, and the interpretive social science paradigm were being used (and continue to be used) by business to provide alternative methods for the conduct of business research. Related to those paradigms are critical theory, feminist perspectives, and postmodern and participatory paradigms. Essentially, the positivistically derived paradigms (positivism, postpositivism, and critical realism) are associated with a quantitative methodology. Social constructionism, constructivism, phenomenology, or interpretivism and related paradigms are associated with a qualitative methodology.

Introduction

Business incorporates a number of fields/disciplines of study, including accounting, auditing and finance, commerce, economics, entrepreneurship, human resource management, management studies, marketing, organizational studies, political sciences, public administration, strategic management and planning, and tourism, among other fields and branches of study. Each field/discipline/branch has its own specific history and predilections toward social science methods. Because the study of each field is beyond the scope of this article, the discussion here focuses on applying "business" as a generic descriptor deemed to be representative of each of the related fields. A consequence of this application is that focus is restricted to the emblematic social science methods used across the contributing fields.

Paradigms That Inform Business Research

Business disciplines have historically been predicated on the adoption of the natural or physical sciences (also known as hard sciences) model of research. Literature indicates that the adoption of this model of conducting research was assumed to increase the credibility of business disciplines/fields, as each discipline has a relatively short history compared to disciplines in the hard sciences (such as mathematics, physics, botany, and biology). The natural sciences model of research as applied to the study of people, and specifically for business, is based on positivism. Positivism (or positive philosophy) was founded by the French philosopher, Auguste Comte (1798–1857), who also coined the term "positivism." Positivism (also referred to as empiricism) has a particular ontological, epistemological, methodological, and axiological position. Specifically, positivism ascribes to universal truths and laws (ontology), an objective epistemology, a quantitative methodology, and a value-free and extrinsically based axiology. In the past (and also contemporaneously), the ontological viewpoint of positivism has been critiqued with regard to the universality or existence of such "truths" and "laws." Other critiques were concerned with the mirroring of the social world with the physical world. Karl Popper (1902–1994), for example, critiqued positivism as espoused by Comte, and later by John Stuart Mills (1806–1973), for its view that people were akin to biological entities on whom the use of scientific methods could enable predictions of the future to be made. The paradigm of postpositivism emerged in response to such and other critiques of positivism.

Postpositivism differs from positivism in that its worldview (ontology) acknowledges that truth is mutable as well as historically and socially based, rather than being universal and apprehendable. Postpositivism also incorporates mixed methods into the research design, whereas positivism does not. Specifically, postpositivism has a worldview that acknowledges that "truth" is fallibilistically determined, because humans are involved. It assumes an objective epistemology, primarily uses a quantitative methodology (incorporates mixed methods—that is, both quantitative and qualitative methods in its research design), and essays to be value free and maintains an extrinsically focused axiology. A particular branch of postpositivism that is widely used in business disciplines is critical realism. Critical realism and postpositivism have a similar ontology, epistemology, and methodology. Axiologically, however, though the critical realist paradigm essays to be value free, some proponents purport that critical realist research should also result in emancipatory outcomes.

While postpositivism developed from critiques of positivism, two other theories have emerged, chaos and complexity theories, and these also provide critiques of both positivism and postpositivism. These theories developed within the hard sciences and reflect a mathematical orientation toward theory building. Both theories challenge the linear world views of positivism and postpositivism. For chaos and complexity theorists, the world is dynamic and ever changing and requires the use of nonlinear explanations to account for such changing circumstances. Chaos and complexity theories, along with critical realism, some would argue, provide a midpoint position between positivism and the social constructionist, social constructivist, social phenomenological, and interpretive social science paradigms.

In the latter half of the 20th century, the social constructionist, social constructivist, social phenomenological, and interpretive social science paradigms began to be incorporated into research repertoires of business and business-related researchers. Some researchers positioned their research fully within social constructionist, social constructivist, social phenomenological, or interpretive social science paradigms, and others added the paradigms to their suite of research practices. Still others opposed the use of such paradigms due to the perception that the paradigms were not scientifically rigorous. Such positions continue to reflect attitudes toward paradigms that inform the conduct of business research at the commencement of the 21st century.

The paradigms of social constructionism, social constructivism, social phenomenology, and interpretive social science are concerned with the study of phenomena from an insider's perspective of the social context being studied. Constructionism is particularly associated with the work of William Thomas (1863–1947). The beginnings of social phenomenology stem from the philosophical phenomenology of Edmund Husserl (1859–1938). In particular, Alfred Schutz (1899–1959) drew on Husserl's work to fashion what has become known as social phenomenology. Several of Schutz's students, Peter Berger (1925–) and Thomas Luckmann (1927–), are recognized for their contribution to the development of social constructivism. The interpretive social science paradigm is linked to the work of Max Weber (1864–1920) and Wilhem Dilthey (1833–1911), especially their respective work in regard to *verstehen* (empathetic understanding). Hermeneutics is another related term appearing in the literature and is often described as aligned with the interpretive paradigm.

Within business literature (and other literature), there exist examples of the implicit or explicit use of these terms interchangeably and/or synonymously. At a general level, this practice recognizes that each of these approaches is associated with the social nature of the construction of social reality, as well as understanding the world from the perspective of an insider—specifically, how that insider constructs meaning in regard to the social context being studied (in this case, the business world). That being said, it must also be stressed that each term ascribes somewhat differing emphases in regard to ontological, epistemological, methodological, and/or axiological stances. To iterate, although the terms are sometimes used interchangeably, they do not in fact mean the same thing. Therefore, in the following discussions (where space permits), the four terms will be used together to remind readers that each is somewhat different from the other. Broadly speaking, then, these paradigms perceive the world as constituted of multiple realities (ontology), and assume to understand/interpret those realities through the tenets of a subjective epistemology, qualitative methodology, and value-laden and intrinsically based axiology. Associated with the paradigms of social constructionism, social constructivism, social phenomenology, and the interpretive social science are the related critical theory, feminist perspectives, postmodern, and participatory paradigms. These four paradigms are also utilized to design studies and research projects in business settings. Together with social constructionism, social constructivism, social phenomenology, and the interpretive social science paradigms; critical theory, feminist perspectives, postmodern, and participatory paradigms are associated with a "soft" science approach. The terms "hard" and "soft" sciences are used to distinguish between the scientific, objective inquiry of the natural or physical sciences and the naturalistic (as occurring in real world), subjective inquiry of the social or humanistic sciences. Critique exists in the literature regarding the use of the terms, because they are considered to be pejorative and do not effectively portray the different approaches each type of science uses for the study of business and business related phenomena.

Table I provides an overview of the differences between each of the paradigms presented in this section. This table incorporates a summary of the various paradigms in regard to their origins, associated synonyms and related terms, and overall focus of the research intent, as well as stances in regard to ontology, epistemology, methodology, and axiology. (Due to space limitations, of the social constructionism, social constructivism, social phenomenology, and interpretive social science paradigms, only social constructivism is represented in Table I.)

Current State of Practice

Business disciplines remain predicated to positivistic and postpositivistic (critical realist) paradigms in regard to the majority of research conducted. However, critical debate occurs in each of the fields of study (as per articles in academic journals and texts) as to the ability of positivistic and postpositivistic (including critical realist) paradigms to explain fully business phenomena. Subsequently, other paradigms are being included and used to study business and business-related phenomena. These paradigms include chaos and complexity theory, the previously mentioned social constructionism, social constructivism, social phenomenology, and the interpretive social science paradigm, as well as critical theory orientation, the participatory paradigm, feminist perspectives, and postmodern perspectives. These paradigms are slowly and increasingly being used to explain business phenomena. It is important to comment that debate exists regarding whether feminist perspectives and postmodern perspectives are perspectives under the rubric of social constructivism, or are paradigms in their own rights.

For business, then, a continuum of research paradigms is available. Given this continuum, commentary in the literature would indicate that the issue is not which paradigm is better, but rather which best serves the research purposes and the current world context. Having identified a suitable paradigm, the epistemological position of that paradigm will determine the choice of methodology for that business research—quantitative or qualitative or mixed. Some business researchers advocate that paradigms may be mixed. However, controversy exists in regard to the incommensurability of ontological viewpoints between positivistic paradigms, at one end of the continuum, and the social constructionist, constructivist, phenomenological, and interpretive-oriented paradigms, at the other end, albeit that business researchers recognize commensurability between like paradigms (that is, between those paradigms that are positivistic in nature, or between those that are social constructionist, constructivist, phenomenological and interpretive oriented). Furthermore, the literature suggests that methods may be mixed more readily than methodologies may be, because methodologies are informed by the ontological stance of each paradigm, and (as demonstrated in Table I) these differ across the paradigmatic continuum.

Quantitative and Qualitative Methodologies That Inform Business Research

A methodology is a set of principles that provides a guiding framework for the design of research. Each of the theoretical paradigms that can inform (business) research has a specific methodological orientation: quantitative or qualitative. The ontological, epistemological, and axiological stance of each of the paradigms will determine the methodology that will be used to design the overall research project. Positivistic and postpositivistic as well as chaos and complexity theory paradigms will align with a quantitative methodology. The social constructionist, social constructivist, social phenomenological, and interpretive social science-related paradigms will generally draw on a qualitative methodology. Research using mixed methods will utilize both quantitative and qualitative methodologies (and quantitative and qualitative methods) to varying degrees in and stages of the research project.

Due to the dominance (hegemony) of positivism and postpositivism, business research is predicated to the conduct of research using primarily a quantitative methodology. However, the use of a qualitative methodology is evident in business research reports, sector and academic publication outputs, and in the generation of qualitatively focused or inclined business journals (for example, some of the journals emanating out of Europe). Further, as a result of the critique of positivism and postpositivism in regard to their ability to explain business phenomenon adequately in its real-world contexts, and the subsequent development of midrange paradigms, a mixing of methods has resulted in order to achieve what some business researchers believe is the best of both methodologies. Essentially, a quantitative methodology, if well designed, will enable researchers to explain business phenomena deductively, systematically, and objectively, using probabilistically determined causal relationships that are generalizable and representative of wider study populations. Alternately, a qualitative methodology will enable business researchers to explain business phenomena inductively and subjectively, grounded in real-world contexts that demonstrate the multiple realities of the business phenomena ideographically in study-specific contexts that may be generalized to similar settings and contexts.

The mixing of methodologies may occur in different ways. Business researchers who mix methodologies often

Table I Overview of Paradigms That Inform Business Research[a]

Descriptors	*Positivism*	*Postpositivism*	*Critical realism*	*Critical theory*	*Social constructivism*	*Feminist perspectives*	*Postmodern*	*Participatory*
Origins	Founded in the hard/ natural sciences (*Naturwissenschaften*)	Founded on principles of hard/natural sciences (*Naturwissenschaften*)	Founded on the principles of hard/natural sciences (*Naturwissenschaften*)	Founded in human (social) sciences (*Geisteswissenschaften*)	Founded in human (social) sciences (*Geisteswissenschaften*)	Founded in human (social) sciences (*Geisteswissenschaften*)	Founded in human (social) sciences (*Geisteswissenschaften*)	Founded in human (social) sciences (*Geisteswissenschaften*)
Synonyms and/ or related terms/ comments	Empiricism, realism, naive realism objectivism, foundationalism, representationalism	New realism (note: developed as a response to critique of positivism)	Described as a midpoint between realism and relativism	A number of types: Marxist/socialist, postpositivist, postmodern critical theorists	Phenomenology interpretivism, constructivism, constructionism	A number of types: Marxist/socialist, liberal, postmodern, poststructural, critical feminist empiricism, standpoint theorists	Ludic postmodernism, oppositional postmodernism, critical postmodernism	Cooperative inquiry, participatory action research, action inquiry, appreciative inquiry
Focus	Explanation (*Erklären*), realism, objectivism	Explanation (*Erklären*), realism, objectivism	Explanation (*Erklären*), realism, objectivism	Understanding (*Verstenhen*), historical realism, perspectivism, interpretivism, intentionalism	Understanding (*Verstenhen*), relativism, perspectivism, interpretivism, intentionalism	Understanding (*Verstenhen*), relativism, perspectivism, interpretivism, intentionalism	Understanding (*Verstenhen*), relativism, perspectivism	Understanding (*Verstenhen*), relativism perspectivism, interpretivism, intentionalism
Ontology	Truth and laws are universal	Truths are fallible and a product of historical and social contexts	Truths are fallible and a product of historical and social contexts	Sociohistorical multiple realities; realities reflective of power relations	Multiple perspectives/ realities	Multiple realities mediated by gendered constructs	Multiple realities; no privileging of position; skepticism towards "truth" and "-isms"	Multiple realities collectively constructed via interactions
Epistemology	Objective	Objective: acknowledges potential for researcher bias	Objective: acknowledges potential for researcher bias	Subjective unless postpositivist critical theory (objective)	Subjective	Subjective: participants and researcher/s as coresearchers	Intersubjectivity	Subjective–objective
Methodology	Quantitative	Quantitative, (use of mixed methods)	Quantitative, inclusion of mixed methods	Qualitative, some quantitative	Qualitative	Qualitative (predominantly)	Qualitative	Qualitative, quantitative mixed method
Axiology	Value free: extrinsic purpose of research project	Essays to be value free; extrinsic purpose of research project	Essays to be value free; extrinsic purpose of research project; consideration of emancipatory role of research	Value laden; intrinsic focus of research project; political agendas, emancipatory, transformative	Value laden; intrinsic focus of the research project	Value laden; intrinsic focus of research project; political, emancipatory, transformative, educational	Skeptical of emancipation and transformation; continuous deconstruction process	Value laden; transformation

[a] Developed from texts presented in Denzin and Lincoln's 1994 and 2000 editions of the *Handbook of Qualitative Research*, particularly the work of Denzin and Lincoln (2000), Lincoln and Guba (2000), Schwandt (2000), and Guba and Lincoln (1994), as well as Guba's 1990 text, *The Paradigm dialog*, and Jennings' *Tourism Research*. The German terms used in this table are drawn from the writings of Dilthey (1833–1911).

use qualitative methodology as an exploratory phase in the overall research design, as well as a postphase to study unusual outlier cases. Alternately, each methodology may be used in its own right as a substantive part of an overall research design that is founded on an interdisciplinary and multiparadigmatic focus. The terms "methodology" and "methods" are sometimes used interchangeably; however, they are not the same. A methodology is a guiding set of principles used to frame a research design. Methods are the tools used to gather and analyze data. Methods are also linked to the overlying methodology and subsequently to the overarching theoretical paradigm, due to the latter's role in informing research designs.

Quantitative Methodology

A quantitative methodology is generally associated with the use of hypotheses to represent causal relationships as per the ontological perspective of the paradigms informing this methodology. Subsequently, a quantitative methodology is associated with hypothetico-deductive paradigms (empiricism, positivism, postpositivism), which are deductive in nature because they deduce "reality" and then establish the nature of that reality by testing hypotheses. As a consequence, researchers generally design their research projects utilizing hypotheses and *a priori* theories. The research is conducted by the researcher from an objective stance; that is, the researcher takes an outsider position (an etic position) to ensure that bias and values do not influence any research outcomes. The empirical data gathered will be used to test the hypotheses to determine whether the empirical data support or do not support those hypotheses. The overall research design will be organized and reported so that it may be repeated. Sampling methods will tend to be random or probabilistically determined. The data that are collected will be reduced numerically and analyzed using mathematical and statistical methods. The reporting of quantitative methodologically based research follows the structure of the hard sciences, i.e., introduction, literature review, methodology, findings, discussion, and conclusion. The voice used in the genre of reports is third person, passive. Findings from research projects using quantitative methodologies are usually representative and generalizable to the wider study population.

Qualitative Methodology

A qualitative methodology is associated with holistic-inductive paradigms (social constructionist, social constructivism, phenomenological, and interpretive social sciences approaches). Holistic-inductive paradigms enable researchers to study (business) phenomena in their totality and complexity, instead of focusing on sets of variables and subsequent causal relationships representing parts of the overall whole of the business or business-related phenomenon being studied. Theory development is generated inductively from empirical materials (data) rather than through the use of *a priori* theories. Researchers employing this methodology essay to understand the business phenomenon as an insider. The term "emic" is applied to describe "insider" research. Sampling methods will be nonrandom or nonprobabilistically determined. Research designs emerge and consolidate in the process of empirical materials (data) collection and concurrent analysis. Designs are context specific. Research is normally undertaken with the full understanding of the persons involved in the phenomenon, and using their knowledge bases to interpret the empirical materials (data). Research is reported using a narrative-style genre. The voice of the texts is first person and active voice. A qualitative methodology generates multiple "truths" from real-world settings, such as business environments and contexts. Findings are related to the local setting and may be generalized to other similar settings and contexts.

Mixed Methods

The term "mixed methods" is sometimes used by business researchers to describe mixed methodologies. As previously noted, some business researchers would dispute the potential for this to occur, due to the incommensurability of the ontological perspectives of some paradigms. Mixed methodologies generally occur in different phases of research design. Some research designs may include concurrent methodologies, a quantitative and a qualitative methodology to gather the data or empirical materials to illuminate business phenomena from different paradigmatic perspectives. Generally, mixed methods infer methods (data collection and sometimes analysis) within a research design that may be identified as either primarily positivistic or social constructionist, social constructivist, phenomenological, or interpretive in nature. The following examples are of mixed methods as mixed methodologies:

1. Qualitative exploratory study (phase one of design) informs quantitative data collection tool construction (phase two) in a larger quantitative research design.
2. Quantitative exploratory study (phase one of design) informs qualitative research design (phase two of design).
3. Quantitative and qualitative studies conducted simultaneously or at separate times within a larger interdisciplinary research project.

Table II provides an overview of a comparison between quantitative and qualitative methodologies. Note that mixed methods have not been included, because essentially the mixing of methods will depend on which is the dominant paradigm informing the research process and

Table II Comparison of Methodologies

Descriptors	*Quantitative*	*Qualitative*
Paradigm	Hypothetico-deductive	Holistic-inductive
Ontological perspective	Based on causal relationships	Illuminating multiple realities
Nature of reality determined by	Hypotheses, *a priori* theories	Grounding in real-world business and business-related contexts
Epistemological stance	Objective	Subjective
Purpose[a]	Explanation	Understanding and interpretation
Research position	Outsider, etic	Insider, emic
Nature of research design	Structured, replicable	Emergent/developmental, content specific
Sampling	Probabilistically determined	Nonprobabilistically determined
Analysis	Mathematical and statistically determined	Emblematic themes
Report style	Scientific report	Narrative text
Outcomes	Generalizable to the population of interest	Case specific; may be generalized to other similar cases

[a] The "Purpose" descriptors are based on the work of Dilthey (1833–1911), particularly the terms *Erklären* (explanation) or *Erklärung* (abstract explanation) and *Verstehen* (understanding or empathetic understanding) (see Table I). *Verstehen* was also used by Max Weber (1864–1920). Mixed methods will assume varying positions regarding each of the descriptors, depending on the degree of proclivity toward either the hypothetico-deductive or holistic-inductive paradigm. The potential permutations are manifold.

whether the research is multiphase, in which case the dominant or specific paradigm for that phase should be read.

Conclusion

Business research is informed by positivistic and social constructionist, constructivism, phenomenological, or interpretive paradigms. Associated with the latter cluster of paradigms are critical theory, feminist perspectives, and postmodern and participatory paradigms. Within the positivistic paradigms, a quantitative methodology informs the overall research design. Social constructionist, constructivist, phenomenological, and interpretive paradigms will inform business research primarily through a qualitative methodology.

The positivistic paradigms and their associated methods of data collection and analysis hold greater sway, compared to other paradigms. A number of business researchers critique the hegemony of the positivistic paradigms, and as a result, the use of social constructionist, constructivist, phenomenological, and interpretive paradigms informing research gradually increased in the latter half of the 20th century, a trend that continues in the 21st century. Moreover, mixed methods reflect the recognition of the advantages of both types of data collection and an attempt to better represent knowledge and truths of the world by using both approaches. Consequently, within current world circumstances at the beginning of the 21st century, business researchers continue to discuss and/or query the dominant hegemony. Some scholars assume a position that recognizes that it is not an "either/or" choice, but rather a choice of which is the best paradigm to use to achieve the information required. Still others engage in dialogue with each other to achieve greater understanding between paradigmatic positions, and some remain unmoved in regard to the dominance of positivistic paradigms for explaining business and business-related phenomena.

See Also the Following Articles

Business, Social Science Methods Used in • Complexity Science and the Social World • Ethical Issues, Overview

Further Reading

Belkaoui, A. (1987). *Inquiry and Accounting, Alternative Methods and Research Perspectives.* Quorum Books, New York.

Bhaskar, R. (1986). *Scientific Realism and Human Emancipation.* Verso, London.

Collis, J., and Hussey, R. (2003). *Business Research, A Practical Guide for Undergraduate and Postgraduate Students,* 2nd Ed. Palgrave Macmillan, Houndmills, Hampshire, UK.

Denzin, N. K., and Lincoln, Y. S. (eds.) (2000). *Handbook of Qualitative Research*, 2nd Ed. Sage, Thousand Oaks, CA.

Gummesson, E. (1999). *Qualitative Methods in Management Research*, 2nd Ed. Sage, Newbury Park, CA.

Jennings, G. (2001). *Tourism Research.* John Wiley and Sons, Milton, Australia.

Remenyi, D., Williams, B., Money, A., and Swartz, E. (1998). *Doing Research in Business and Management, An Introduction to Process and Method.* Sage, London.

Robson, C. (2002). *Real World Research*, 2nd Ed. Blackwell, Malden, MA.

Business, Social Science Methods Used in

Gayle R. Jennings
Central Queensland University, Rockhampton, Queensland, Australia

Glossary

axiology The study of ethics and values.

data Units or records of information gathered in the course of a research study/project. The term is usually associated with quantitative methodology. Data units may be derived, for example, from answers to questions in surveys, observations, or records of experiments. Data units are usually aggregated, represented in numeric form, and subsequently analyzed mathematically or statistically.

empirical materials Information gathered through the processes associated with a qualitative methodology; may include, for example, records of observations, interview transcripts, and visual images. Empirical materials are usually recorded in textual or visual form rather than being reduced to numeric representations.

epistemology The science of knowledge; also the relationship between the researcher and that which is to be known. The relationship assumes either an objective or a subjective stance.

interpretive social science paradigm Also referred to as the interpretive paradigm, this term is associated with (social) constructionism, (social) constructivism, social phenomenology, hermeneutics, and relativist approaches.

method Strategy and/or tool used by researchers to collect and analyze data or empirical materials.

methodology A set of principles that provides a guiding framework for the design of research projects/studies.

ontology The worldview or representation of reality particular to a specific theory or paradigm.

paradigm A set of beliefs regarding how the world operates/functions. Paradigms have specific stances in regard to ontology, epistemology, methodology, and axiology.

participatory paradigm The worldview (ontology) is generated collectively and recognizes multiple realities. The research process emphasizes participant involvement, a subjective epistemology, and the use of qualitative and quantitative methodologies based on the principles of action research and an action research cycle (design, implementation, evaluation). The axiology is predicated to practical knowing as well as cooperation. The research is undertaken for its intrinsic value.

phenomenology A philosophy or a paradigmatic view of the world (social phenomenology), as well as a tradition of undertaking research in the social sciences.

positivism A theoretical paradigm with an ontological stance (worldview) that assumes that universal truths and laws are able to explain and predict behaviors and events. The epistemological stance is objective, and a quantitative methodology guides research processes. Axiologically, positivism is value free and research projects are extrinsically focused.

postpositivism A paradigm related to positivism. Ontologically, postpositivism assumes that the world, or reality, may be known only probabilistically and imperfectly. Researchers maintain an objective epistemological stance. The paradigm associates with predominantly a quantitative methodology and researchers essay to be value free and adopt an extrinsically focused axiology. A form of postpositivism frequently applied in business research is critical realism. Some critical realists may assume an emancipatory axiological position.

qualitative methodology Provides a framework for empirical material (data) collection and analysis that enables researchers to gather empirical information in its textual entirety. The empirical materials are not substantively reduced or represented numerically.

quantitative methodology Provides a framework for data collection and analysis that enables researchers to reduce, analyze, and report the collected data numerically and statistically.

social constructivism Maintains that the world is constructed of multiple realities. These realities become subjectively known through the use of a qualitative methodology and a value-laden axiology that acknowledges the intrinsic values of undertaking research projects. The term is sometimes used interchangeably with the terms (social) constructionism, (social) phenomenology, interpretive social science paradigm, hermeneutics, and relativism.

Methods of data collection and analysis in business research are guided by the overall paradigm that informs the research process. Each paradigm associates with primarily a quantitative or qualitative methodology. Some mixing of methodologies may also occur. Examples of quantitative methodological forms of data collection include surveys, experimental and quasi-experimental methods, observation, forecasting, nominal group technique, focus groups, the delphic method, the documentary method, case studies, and longitudinal studies. Qualitatively informed methods of empirical materials (data) collection include semistructured interviews, in-depth interviews, observation, action research, focus groups, the delphic method, the documentary method, case studies, and longitudinal studies. A quantitative methodology incorporates various methods of data analysis, including descriptive and inferential statistics, consideration of levels of significance, and Type I and Type II errors. A qualitative methodology draws on, for example, content analysis, successive approximation, constant comparison, domain analysis, ideal types, and grounded theory analysis for empirical materials (data) analysis.

Introduction

Business research is predominantly informed by the paradigms of positivism and postpositivism, particularly critical realism. However, other paradigms—social constructionism, social constructivism, social phenomenology, and the interpretive social science paradigms—are now being included in the repertoire of business researchers. Related to this group of paradigms are critical theory, feminist perspectives, and postmodern and participatory paradigms, although there is debate as to whether feminist perspectives and "postmodernism" are independent paradigms or differing perspectives among social constructionism, social constructivism, social phenomenology, and the interpretive social science paradigms. All of these paradigms espouse specific ontological, epistemological, methodological, and axiological tenets. In particular, the tenets of each paradigm influence the methodology used to design business research projects. To be specific, positivistic and postpositivistic as well as chaos and complexity theory paradigms draw on a quantitative methodology. Social constructionist, social constructivist, social phenomenological, and interpretive social science-related paradigms generally use a qualitative methodology. Research using mixed methods incorporates both quantitative and qualitative methodologies (and quantitative and qualitative methods) in differing amounts and phases of research projects.

Methods of Data Collection Used in Business

Research on business (used here as a generic term encompassing all related disciplines, fields, and branches) draws on a wide number of social science methods, each being informed by a quantitative and/or a qualitative methodology or some mixing of methodologies within the overall research design phases.

Quantitative Methods of Data Collection

Quantitative methods of data collection reflect the methodological framework from which they are derived—that is, a quantitative methodology. A quantitative methodology is usually associated with positivistic paradigms, such as positivism, postpositivism, and critical realism. Quantitative methods (tools) are designed to enable researchers to gather data that in turn will be analyzed to test causal relationships described using variables. Specifically, data collection will enable researchers to reduce the data to numerical representations. Quantitative methods, by nature of their design, also assist in ensuring that the researcher is objective throughout the data collection phase (and analysis phase). The most frequently used quantitative methods in business are surveys (structured interviews and questionnaires), experimental and quasi-experimental methods, and observation. Other quantitative methods used include forecasting, nominal group technique, focus groups, the delphic method, the documentary method, case studies, and longitudinal studies.

Surveys

The survey is a data collection tool; a survey can be administered orally (as interviewer-conducted structured questions) and as written self-completion questionnaires. A number of modes are used for implementing business surveys: mail, telephone, face to face, intercept, and electronic. The choice of mode will determine whether the survey is subsequently classified as either an interview or a questionnaire. Another variable in survey administration is location (intercept, household, or *in situ*, such as organizational surveys). Each type of survey method has advantages and disadvantages. Table I provides an overview of the main types of surveys and a relative comparison between each in regard to administration costs, time required for data collection, and response rates.

Mail Surveys (Questionnaires) Mail surveys are postal service-delivered questionnaires that are distributed to specific population samples. Targeted respondents are requested to complete the questionnaires and return them by mail (an addressed prepaid reply envelope is usually included). To increase response rates, mail

Table I Types of Surveys[a]

Type of survey	*Implementation process*	*Cost relative to other survey types*	*Implementation time relative to other survey types*	*Response rates relative to other survey types*
By method of administration				
Mail surveys	Questionnaires distributed using postal services	Low	Long	Low
Telephone surveys	Interviewer-conducted structured interviews, conducted via telephone	Moderate	Short–medium	Moderate
Face-to-face interviews	Interviewer-completed questionnaire, conducted within businesses and business-related settings	High	Medium–long	High
e-Questionnaires	Questionnaires distributed electronically to recipients via e-mail and websites	Low	Short–long	Moderate
Self-completion surveys	Distributed to businesses and business-related contexts for completion by recipient	Moderate	Short–medium	Low (unless administrator present)
By location of administration				
In situ surveys (including organizational surveys)	Questionnaire or interview conducted within businesses and business-related settings	High	Short–long	Moderate–high
Intercept surveys	Questionnaire or interviewer-conducted structured interview or self-completion questionnaire, potential participants are contacted en route to, during, and en route from some business or business-related activity	Moderate	Short–medium	Low–moderate
Household surveys	Questionnaire or interview conducted at households (in this case, in relation to businesses and business-related issues)	High	Medium	Moderate–high
Omnibus surveys	Questionnaire or interview conducted at households (in this case, in relation to businesses and business-related issues); a number of businesses cluster together to distribute implementation costs; survey will be structured by groups of unrelated business themes	High	Medium–long	Moderate–high

[a] Although relative comparisons have been made, both implementation and response rates may vary due to the number and nature of "reminders" used.

surveys often use reminder cards and/or reminder letters. An advantage of mail surveys for business is the relative cost-effectiveness (based on postal rates) of survey distribution and receipt. Low administration costs and the ability to reach broad geographic distributions are additional advantages. Disadvantages of mail survey methods are associated with their reliance on respondents being speakers of the language used in the questionnaire and having a suitable literacy level to participate in the study. There is also reliance on respondents to return questionnaires; more importantly, there is no way of knowing whether the person targeted is the person who completes the questionnaire.

Telephone Surveys Telephone surveys are structured interviews conducted by an interviewer who records the answers to mostly closed-ended questions. Improvements in electronic technology, particularly computer-assisted telephone interview (CATI) systems, have enabled interviewers to enter responses immediately into databases that commence aggregation and analysis of the entered data. In addition to this advantage, telephone interviews are relatively inexpensive to administer (unless calling long distance) and of short duration, compared to the time taken by respondents to complete written questionnaires. Disadvantages of telephone interviews include the limited range of times available to collect data, the potential expense of long-distances, and the limited ability to use open-ended questions.

Face-to-Face Interviews Face-to-face interviews are structured interviews conducted by trained interviewers who use a standardized interview protocol and a standardized set of responses for recording participants' responses. Face-to-face interviews may be conducted *in situ* (within businesses and business-related settings), at intercept sites associated with businesses and business-related activities, and in households. Advantages of face-to-face interviews are the ability to control interactions, to ensure that the targeted participant is the respondent, to ask complex questions, and to use probe mechanisms. Disadvantages are associated with the cost of training interviewers and placing them in the field, as well as the time required to conduct interviews. In addition, despite assurance by the interviewer, and because the interview is conducted in face-to-face mode, participants may have concerns regarding confidentiality.

e-Questionnaires e-Questionnaires are electronically administered questionnaires using e-mail and websites as settings for survey administration. The advantages of e-questionnaires are related to the low cost of implementation and the relatively quick access to widely distributed geographical regions. Disadvantages are associated with low response rates and participants' concerns regarding confidentiality.

Self-Completion (Intercept, *In Situ*, and Household) Surveys Self-completion surveys are questionnaires that rely on the respondent to complete the questionnaire. This is, in fact, the case in mail surveys, but self-completion surveys also belong to a category of survey that is not mailed. Other, self-completion surveys used by businesses are intercept, *in situ*, and household (including omnibus) surveys. Intercept surveys are face-to-face interviews (sometimes self-completion questionnaires) conducted en route to or from, as well as during, a business-related activity. Intercept and face-to-face interviews have similar advantages and disadvantages. Intercept interviews tend to be shorter in length than some face-to-face interviews because participants are being interrupted at work or in the course of a business activity, and thus the researcher will design the questionnaire in order to minimize inconvenience.

Household surveys may be conducted using the telephone, by mail, or face to face, and so, depending on the mode, will have advantages and disadvantages similar to those of like survey methods. Within the household survey category, the omnibus survey is a subtype. Omnibus surveys contain questions in sections that are unrelated to other sections. The advantage of an omnibus survey is that a range of businesses may pool together to cover the cost of the administration and implementation of the survey; albeit that the survey will contain sections with questions germane to specific businesses. A major disadvantage arises when the number of businesses participating in the omnibus survey is large, thus restricting the number of questions; in this case, research design is critical to ensure that question sets are effective. All participating businesses receive information relating to their data sets as well as to the standard sociodemographic data sets collected in the survey.

Experimental and Quasi-experimental Methods

Experiments enable researchers to determine causal relationships between variables in controlled settings (laboratories). Researchers generally manipulate the independent variable in order to determine the impact on a dependent variable. Such manipulations are also called treatments. In experiments, researchers essay to control confounding variables and extraneous variables. Confounding variables may mask the impact of another variable. Extraneous variables may influence the dependent variable in addition to the independent variable. Advantages of experiments include the ability to control variables in an artificial environment. Disadvantages include the mismatch between reality and laboratory settings and the focus on a narrow range of variables at any one time. Laboratory experiments enable researchers to control experiments to a greater degree than those experiments conducted in simulated or real businesses or business-related environments. Experiments in the field (business and business-related environments) may prove to be challenging due to issues related to gaining access and ethical approval. However, field experiments (natural experiments) allow the measurement of the influence of the independent variable on the dependent variable within a real-world context, although not all extraneous variables are controllable. The classical experimental method involves independent and dependent variables, random sampling, control groups, and pre- and posttests. Quasi-experiments omit aspects from the classical experiment method (such as omission of a control group or absence of a pretest).

Observation

Within the positivistic paradigms, observations may be conducted in a laboratory setting, simulated setting, or in the field (business or business-related setting). As with experiments, laboratory or simulated settings are more controllable than are field settings. Using this paradigm within businesses or business-related settings, observations tend to focus on specific behaviors. During observation periods, the researcher may be a participant or nonparticipant and may assume an overt or hidden role.

Recording of data during observations may be undertaken using checklists of static data, which are data that will not change in the course of the observation (for example, the number of people attending a business meeting and their administrative levels, or seating patterns during a meeting), and action data, which are data that may change in the course of the recording of observations (such as the number of times a person orally participates during a meeting, or the duration of oral participation and to whom the oral participation is directed). Field notes of observations or video and other electronic recording means may also be used and later analyzed and reduced.

Observations within this paradigm take an etic approach, in order that the observations are achieved in an objective and value-free manner. As noted before, observations may also be conducted without the knowledge of the participants (subsequent to receiving ethical approval) to minimize the effect of socially desirable response sets (acting in a manner that is perceived by the participant as socially desirable, although it may not be the usual response of the participant). Observation should not be used in relation to determining levels of emotions, value-based behaviors, or opinions, because these are not able to be determined etically from observation.

Observations may also be used to record counts of a behavior occurring, the number of interactions between people, and with whom interactions occur (this is similar to the example of oral interaction in business meetings), as well as types of activity and their repetition (and who is involved) and the locations of activities. Advantages of the observation method include the possible nonintrusive nature of the observations, if undertaken in a field setting, and the acquisition of data that are not influenced by the participants having knowledge of the purpose of the observations, and subsequently changing their patterns and activities. Disadvantages are associated with not knowing why the patterns or activities are occurring (unless observations are complemented by interviews), the potential for observing people without their knowledge (ethical issues), and the lack of flexibility (because checklists predetermine observations).

Forecasting

Forecasting within a business environment is associated with drawing on past data sets and knowledge to generate predictions relating to future business patterns and trends. Three time periods are associated with forecasting, short, medium, and long term. Short term is considered to range up to 2 years, medium term ranges from 2 to 5 years, and long term is from 5 to 15 years. Making predictions beyond 15 years is considered to be futurism. Forecasting involves the use of formulae and statistical methods. In particular, time-series analysis assists business researchers in making forecasts. The two main methods are the simple additive model and the classic and more realistic multiplication model. An advantage of forecasting is that decisions are made based on historical patterns and trends. A disadvantage is associated with the inability of past trends to explain current complex, dynamic ever-changing business environments.

Nominal Group Technique

The nominal group in a positivistic framework is a method that enables businesses to determine issues and develop strategies and evaluation techniques using iterative processes. The method focuses on each of those three aspects in turn. The iterative process moves the data collection from individual standpoints to a whole-group consensus. Briefly, the process involves the researcher/facilitator organizing a group of participants. Each is asked to list factual statements/observations associated with the issue being addressed. The researcher then lists all individual responses to an issue and systematically clusters similar observations; subsequent group voting decides on a predetermined number of key statements for address by the whole group. Each statement is then processed in the same manner. Individuals brainstorm strategies to rectify the issue statements. These are listed and a smaller number for focus are identified by voting. In each phase, information is reduced and causal relationships between issues and solutions are determined by consensus and agreement, so achieving a collective and agreed worldview of the issues/problems, solutions and methods of evaluation. Advantages of the method are its systematic processing and its collective-based outcomes. Disadvantages of the method are related to its consensus-based outcomes, in which outlying statements and strategies are not considered, and to the omission of dialogue between participants regarding statements, strategies, and evaluation methods. The nominal group technique has some similarity with the delphic method (see later), a difference being that the former involves face-to-face engagements and the latter involves management of the process by questionnaire, without face-to-face engagement between participants.

Focus Groups

The use of focus groups within positivistic paradigms is predicated to a structured agenda and systematic approach to managing, recording, and analyzing the interactions associated with each of the agenda items. Focus group data and interactions are recorded in a reductionist manner using checklist categories, which are then tallied and mathematically analyzed in regard to *a priori* theory and determined variables, constructs, and categories. Within positivistic paradigms, focus groups are utilized as part of the exploratory phase of research in order to determine variables that may be utilized to construct questionnaires and structured interviews. They may also be used to check the currency of established or *a priori* theories, constructs, and categories. Depending on the management of interactions, as well as on the recording and analysis of data from the focus group (whether full text or reduced text), the method will move from either positivistic or interpretive paradigms or to mixed methods. In a positivistic framework, the facilitator will systematically focus the discussion with a strict agenda and will refocus (when necessary) participants on that agenda.

The Delphic Method

The Delphic method is an iterative process that draws on expert opinion, *a priori* theories, and the literature to predict future events. It is a forecasting method used when other trend data are not available, such as historical business and business-related data sets. The researcher uses established theories (and expert opinion) to generate a questionnaire regarding the probability of a set of events occurring in the future; these are sent (by mail or e-mail) to experts. Experts complete the questionnaire and return it, and the questionnaire data are summarized and returned to panel members by the researcher.

In the next phase, events derived from the previous questionnaire are listed and panelists are required to assign dates, probabilities, and further events. The researcher analyzes these responses and presents the individual distribution of panelist responses (anonymously). Panelists are asked to reconsider their previous position. The researcher subsequently develops interquartile response summaries from the returned data. Following another iteration, the interquartile distributions are redistributed. Exceptions in each round outside the quartile ranges are also included and reasons are provided for their positioning. Iterations continue until all panelists reach consensus.

The delphic method in the positivistic framework is based on expert responses to questionnaires and the repeated questioning and analysis of responses until consensus is achieved. Interactions between panelists are mediated by a facilitator, who analyzes the responses and disseminates the findings of each repetition to the panel members. Advantages of the Delphic method include the use of expert opinion, the anonymity and confidentiality of expert participation, and objective data gathering, because participants are not swayed by the knowledge of which expert stated which set of data. Disadvantages include the number of iterations that may occur until consensus is reached along with the possibility that face-to-face interaction of experts may reduce the time taken to reach consensus. However, this introduces subjectivity and thus does not match the paradigm that informs this approach.

The Documentary Method

The documentary method draws on secondary data sources. The diversity of sources includes company financial reports, annual reports, minutes of meetings, memorandum, e-mail correspondence, letters, position statements, policies, and addresses/speeches, among other business-related materials. Using a quantitative methodology, the researcher objectively classifies documents and/or their texts using preestablished categories or textual units. These classifications as well as the nature and number of occurrences will be reduced and recorded as numerical representations. Specifically, the researcher will determine the frequency (the number of times a text unit occurs), direction (positive or negative polarity of the text unit), intensity (level of strength in regard to negative or positive polarity), and space (measurement of the amount of physical space allocated to each text unit) of the textual units being analyzed. Advantages of the documentary method are associated with the ability to manage large textual documents into smaller manageable units and the analysis of textual units in a numeric, statistical, and objective manner. Disadvantages of the method are associated with the time it takes to amass and analyze the data and the difficulty in gaining access to all possible sources of data, because some gatekeepers may suppress some types of documentation.

Case Studies

Case studies are associated with the development of detailed information relating to a specific business phenomenon, with phenomena across similar organizations or settings, or with one specific case (person, organization, or setting). Case study method may draw on a number of methods to gather data, such as observation, experiments, structured interviews, questionnaires, and/or documentary analysis. Case study within a positivistic paradigm is subsequently guided by the tenets of a quantitative methodology. Advantages of case studies associated with case-specific detail is the obtainment of objective and use of multiple methods to gain detailed data on the case. Disadvantages are associated with resource allocation and (with field case studies) the inability to control all variables systematically.

Longitudinal Studies

Longitudinal studies (also known as panel studies) are used by researchers to measure changes over time in regard to a variable or variables being measured or a group of people being studied. A longitudinal study, for example, may assess the impact of e-mail, as the official form of organizational communication, on time allocated to all work tasks of middle management before, during, and after implementation. Experimental research involving a pre- and posttest can be classified as a longitudinal study because it contains temporal measuring points (pre- and post-). Advantages of longitudinal studies relate to how they assist in determining cause-and-effect relationships, as well as in facilitating assessment and evaluation of changes in work practices. Disadvantages of longitudinal studies are associated with the length of time it takes to conduct the research, the cost of sustaining the study over time, and the potential for participants to "drop out" in the course of the study (research mortality).

Qualitative Methods

The principles of a qualitative methodology guide qualitative methods of empirical material collection and analysis. A qualitative methodology tends to be associated with social constructionism, social constructivism, social phenomenology, and interpretive social science paradigm, as well as the related critical theory, feminist perspectives, postmodern, and participatory paradigms. A qualitative methodology focuses on gathering empirical materials holistically in real-world business settings and contexts. As a result, "theories" are inductively determined through analysis that generates ideographic (thick and depthful) insights that are specific to the study site and possibly applicable to other similar business settings and contexts. Researchers who engage in qualitatively informed research usually assume a subjective epistemological stance in relation to empirical material collection and analysis.

Some examples of qualitative social science methods of empirical materials (data) collection used in business include semistructured interviews, in-depth interviews, observation, action research, focus groups, the delphic method, observation, the documentary method, case studies, and longitudinal studies.

Semistructured Interviews

Semistructured interviews, which are less formal than structured interviews, have generic foci and/or a set of themes. The order of discussion of each of the themes may vary between interviews, depending on the response to a "grand tour" question that is used to focus the discussion. Rapport needs to be established to ensure that in-depth information will be generated in the course of the interview. Issues of reciprocity (mutual exchange of information) need to be clearly outlined. Advantages of semistructured interviews are similar to those of unstructured (in-depth) interviews; they are interactive between the participant and the researcher and reflect conversational exchange similar to that in a real-world setting. Disadvantages are the time it takes to conduct them and the volume of material generated for analysis.

In-Depth Interviews

In-depth interviews are unstructured interviews that have similarities with a conversation—albeit a conversation with a purpose, i.e., the research topic. In-depth interviews range in duration from 1 hour to upward to 5 hours and beyond. Interviews in excess of 2 hours may be conducted over a series of sessions. The keys to successful interviews are the establishment of rapport, mutual respect, and reciprocity. Advantages of in-depth interviews are that the researcher will be able to gain from the interview process information with richness and depth. Disadvantages are related to the time taken to gather and analyze information.

Participant Observation

A number of typographies describe participant observation. Generally, participant observation may be described as a continuum of roles, ranging from a complete participant to a complete observer. Participant observation, as does all research, requires the adoption of ethical practices and approval. In some instances, participants may not be aware they are being observed. The reason for not disclosing a researcher's observation role to participants is to enable the researcher to observe phenomena as authentically as possible in the everyday business or business-related setting. As a complete observer, the researcher does not participate as one of the group being studied, but observes as an outsider. At the other end of the continuum is the complete participant role. In this role, the researcher acts as an insider. Again, the identity of the researcher role may be hidden from the insiders in order not to change behaviors. Between the two end points of the continuum, researchers will adopt differing degrees of observation and participation as best suits the business research purpose.

Advantages of participant observation are that information is gathered in real-world business contexts and settings, first-hand primary information is gathered, and diverse methods may be incorporated (such as interviews, observations, and documentary analysis conducted within the context of the business study setting). Disadvantages of the method are associated with behaviors and patterns that may be influenced by the presence of the observer/participant, the difficulty in observing all interactions and events if only one observer is present in the business setting or study site, and with the fact that not all facets may be available to the observer because some contexts or interactions may be considered off-limits by the participants.

Action Research

Action research is specifically associated with the participatory paradigm, which views reality as collectively constructed from multiple realities/viewpoints. Action research is used as a method to address problems within organizations or businesses by also involving organizational or business-related personnel. In this method, groups of people from the organization or business meet to discuss problems/issues as well as ways to resolve them. Strategies are generated, implemented, and evaluated over a specific time period. Primarily, action research literature tends to use problem solving, whereas another method, appreciative inquiry, uses a less pejorative focus and envisages positive potentials for an organization by drawing on past experiences, skills, and knowledge of participants related to the achievement of those potentials. Advantages of action research are associated with how this research is conducted in real-world settings, that is, *in situ* in business and business-related settings. It uses people who are insiders as researchers to change collectively the social context of their business environment. Participants have vested interests and ownership of the process and the outcomes; so success should be high if participation is voluntary. Against this advantage are disadvantages related to setting specific outcomes and the time associated with working through the process.

Focus Groups

Focus groups involve semistructured group interviews in which interactions between participants, as well as outcomes, are important parts of the focus group process. Focus groups are used in business to elicit attitudes, opinions, values, expectations, and perspectives; they are also a tool for forecasting. Focus groups work best with group sizes that do not exceed 10–12, otherwise interactions between members become more difficult to facilitate, and it is hard to ensure that all participate and there is enough time for all to contribute. The duration of focus groups is usually 1–2 hours. Focus groups have the advantage of including the interactions of participants as part of the empirical material collection; further, researchers are able to explore unexpected issues among the group, members are able to seek clarification from each other, and members subsequently are able to adjust opinions and stances as a result of interaction. Disadvantages relate to the potential for strong personalities to dominate the discussion and to the selection of participants resulting in a biased view. The overall success of focus groups depends on the quality of the focus group design and the quality and skill of the facilitator.

The Delphic Method

The delphic method has its roots in the ancient Greek custom of using oracles or soothsayers. After World War II, this method was used as a process for forecasting. The delphic method, as a qualitative method, involves the repeated interviewing of experts by a researcher to achieve a consensus. The participants are interviewed and information is collected and analyzed. The analytical findings are then discussed with each of the experts individually. Opinions may be modified and the researcher repeats the process until a consensus is achieved regarding a number of multiple outcomes. Advantages relate to the in-depth information that is gathered and to the fact that the information is empirically sourced rather than determined by *a priori* theories. Disadvantages relate to the time taken in repeated interviewing rounds and maintaining panel participation throughout the process.

The Documentary Method

The use of the documentary method within the social constructionist, social constructivist, social phenomenological, or interpretive social science paradigms differs from use within the positivistic paradigms in that there is no *a priori* theory to guide the analysis specifically, although a process must be followed. The text documents are read and thematic units are identified, analyzed, and grouped into categories and subcategories so that a taxonomy of the materials is built up. The documents are analyzed in regard to their purpose, tone, tenor style, and explicit, implicit, and tacit texts. Advantages of this method are its unobtrusive impact and its access to temporal insights in regard to past and present businesses and business-related practices. Disadvantages relate to the need for repeated readings of texts, which results in different interpretations, and to the fact that the documents may be read without knowledge of the context of their origin.

Case Studies

Under the social constructionist, constructivist, phenomenological, or interpretive paradigms, case studies enable the extensive study of one case or similar cases across time or space using a set of methods such as interviews, focus groups, the documentary method, and participant observation. By using several methods, detailed information relating to the case or cases may be achieved. The depth of materials obtained in a case study and access to multiple sources of empirical materials (data) are distinct advantages, although the amount of time and resources required to gather details may be a disadvantage.

Longitudinal Studies

Longitudinal studies involve multiple methods of empirical material (data) collection in relation to one organization or business over time, one set of people over time, or similar organizations or sets of people over time. The purpose of longitudinal studies is to gather empirical materials in regard to changes in cultural, social, political, economic, and environmental trends concerning the research topic being studied. That temporally extended information can be gathered using a variety of methods is advantageous. The time taken to collect, analyze, and maintain the empirical materials, as well as maintenance of databases for future phases of the study, are disadvantages.

Mixed Methods

Mixed methods may be used to study businesses and conduct business-related research. For example, a phenomenological research design may include some form of quantitative data collection (a questionnaire to determine sociodemographic details of participants), or a positivistic research design may include qualitative data collection.

Table II Comparison between Methods which are Classified as Quantitative and Qualitative Methods

Examples of methods	*Quantitative*	*Qualitative*
Focus group Observation	Hypothetico-deductive approach	Holistic-inductive approach
Documentary method	Objective stance of researcher	Subjective stance of researcher
Case studies Longitudinal studies	Structured format	Semistructured or unstructured format
	Data reduced and mathematically and statistically analyzed	Empirical materials (data) maintained in their textual wholeness and analyzed in totality; textual units preserved
	Study units predominantly randomly assigned or identified	Study units identified non randomly

Quantitative and Qualitative Methods of Data Collection

As shown in Table II, some of the same terms may be used to describe both quantitative and qualitative methods of data/empirical materials collection. The alignment and influence of either a quantitative or qualitative methodology distinguish a method as either quantitative or qualitative. Table III lists quantitative and qualitative methods of data/empirical materials collection as well as those methods that may be utilized within overall research designs, which adopt mixed methods to varying degrees.

Methods of Data Analysis Used in Business

The methods of data analysis used by business researchers are varied; as with methods of data collection, the choice of method depends on the overall paradigm and methodological framework informing the research project, as well as on the purpose of the research.

Quantitative Methods of Data Analysis

A quantitative methodology as per the tenets of the positivistic paradigms ensures that causal relationships are tested. "Truth" is deductively determined using objective research methods (data collection and analysis) and the researcher remains value free throughout the entire

Table III Examples of Methods of Data Collection used in Business Research[a]

Method of data collection	*Quantitative*	*Qualitative*	*Mixed methods*
Questionnaires	✔		✔
Structured interviews	✔		✔
Experimental and quasi-experimental methods	✔		✔
Forecasting	✔	✔	✔
Nominal group technique	✔		✔
Focus groups	✔	✔	✔
Delphic method	✔	✔	✔
Observation	✔ (structured observations)	✔ (participant observations)	✔
Documentary method	✔	✔	✔
Case studies	✔	✔	✔
Longitudinal studies	✔	✔	✔
Semistructured interviews		✔	✔
In-depth (unstructured) interviews		✔	✔
Action research		✔	✔

[a] Qualitative researchers may use the terms "empirical materials" and "information" instead of "data."

research process. The stance of the researcher is an etic (outsider) one, and the research design is systematic and replicable. Data collected are represented in numerical form and are mathematically and statistically analyzed; within the postpositivistic paradigm, there is an emphasis on theory falsification over theory verification. Findings of the research are represented in tables, graphs, and models, with report texts presented in third person, passive voice. Sampling, having been random (that is, probability based), will result in findings that can be generalized to the wider population from which the sample was selected. Table IV provides an overview of a number of quantitative methods of data analysis. In addition to the methods noted in Table IV for inferential statistics, researchers also consider levels of significance (the determination of the chance that an association between variables is a product of sampling error) and Type I (rejection of the null hypothesis when it is true) and Type II (acceptance of the null hypothesis when it is false) errors.

Qualitative Methods of Data Analysis

A qualitative methodology reifies the ontological, epistemological, and axiological position of social constructionist, constructivist, phenomenological, or interpretive paradigms. This means that the methodology ensures that multiple perspectives are equally valued, that no one position is privileged over another, that the interpretation of the empirical materials (data) is subjectively informed by the researchers' emic knowledge of the research setting and the participants, as well as the participants being involved in validating the interpretations. The methodology continues to use qualitative methods that complement the empirical materials (data) collection methods used. Analysis also commences as soon as the researcher enters the field. The position of the researcher is reflexively and reflectively reviewed in the overall analysis. Subsequently, a qualitative methodology utilizes inductive practices, to illuminate "multiple realities," which are grounded in the real-world businesses and business-related settings being studied. The research design emerges in the course of the research process as concurrent analysis directs other empirical material (data) collection needs and directions. Emblematic themes arise in the course of the research. Empirical materials (data) collected is maintained as textual units that reflect the themes and motifs arising out of analysis. Reporting of the research findings should be in narrative form using first person, active voice. Because sampling practices are nonrandom, the research represents a "slice of life" from the setting and people being studied. Table V provides an overview of qualitative methods of empirical materials (data) analysis.

Table IV Examples of Methods of Quantitative Data Analysis

Type of analysis	*Examples*
Descriptive statistics	
Univariate analysis	Measures of central tendency (mode, median, mean); measures of variation (range, percentile, standard deviation)
Bivariate analysis	Cross-tabulation, scattergrams, measures of association—lambda (λ), gamma (γ), tau (τ), rho (ρ), chi-square (χ^2)
Multivariate analysis	Multiple regression analysis, path analysis, time-series analysis, factor analysis
Inferential statistics	
Statistical significance	
Nonparametric tests—nominal level	One sample: chi-squared test (goodness of fit)
	Two independent samples: chi-squared (test of independence), Fisher's exact test, z-test for proportions
	Two dependent samples: McNemar test
	More than two independent samples: chi-square test
	More than two dependent samples: Cochran Q test
Parametric tests—ordinal level	One sample: Kolmogorov–Smirnov test
	Two independent samples: Mann–Whitney U-test, Wald–Wolfowitz runs test
	Two dependent samples: Sign test, Wilcoxon test
	More than two independent samples: Kruskal–Wallis test, H-test
	More than two dependent samples: Friedman test
Interval/ratio level tests	One sample, two independent samples, and two dependent samples: t-test
	More than two independent samples, more than two dependent samples: analysis of variance

Table V Examples of Qualitative Methods of Empirical Material (Data) Analysis

Type of analysis	*Discussion*
Content analysis	Textual materials are read, annotated, and coded. Categories are generated from reading, annotating, and coding. Categories are evaluated in regard to relevance of emerging taxonomy in relation to the empirical setting from which they emerged. This involves reflection and questioning of assignment of codes and categories and the real world context
Constant comparative analysis	Constant comparative analysis involves two generic stages, coding and the comparison of codes to generate categories to build an ideographic representation of the study phenomenon. Theoretical sampling will also be applied to establish the repetitive presence of concepts. The method has similarities with grounded theory analysis
Successive approximation	The researcher will iteratively and reflectively compare codes and categories to develop concepts, relationships, and "theory." Questions in regard to "goodness of fit" with the empirical world are posed constantly throughout the process. The method has similarities with constant comparison and grounded theory analysis
Domain analysis	Categorizes study units using a "cover term," "included terms," and a "semantic relationship." Categorization is an ongoing process during data collection. Domain analysis is founded on Spradley's *Participant Observation* as well as the study of culture
Ideal types	Ideal types (models of social interactions and processes) establish a standard to which reality may be compared. Ideal types emanate from the work of Max Weber (1864–1920)
Event-structure analysis	The chronological ordering of events highlighting the causal relationships for their occurrence
Matrices	Matrices demonstrate interactions between two or more elements of phenomena
Grounded theory analysis	Grounded theory is attributed to the work of Barney Glaser (1930–) and Anselm Strauss (1916–1996). It is an inductive process, as are all of the qualitative methods of empirical material analysis. In its original form, theory is produced by identifying conditions that result in a phenomenon occurring, which establishes a specific context, concomitant actions, and related consequences
Other examples of analysis	Networks, models, typologies, taxonomies, conceptual trees, mind maps, semantic webs, and sociograms

Mixed Methods

Mixing methods for data analysis results in the relevant method of analysis being selected from either a quantitative and qualitative methodology, to match the appropriate data or empirical material collection tool. Two examples of mixed methods being associated with analysis are (1)qualitative methods of data collection and quantitative data analysis and (2) open-ended questions in a questionnaire being analyzed using qualitative methods.

Conclusion

Once the paradigm that informs the overall business research project/study has been determined, business researchers utilize quantitative, qualitative, or mixed methodologies to guide the design of research projects. Within a quantitative methodology, researchers adopt quantitative methods of data collection. Primarily surveys (interviews and questionnaires), experiments and quasi-experiments, and observation are the key business methods. Other methods used variously within businesses and business-related fields and disciplines are documentary analysis, longitudinal studies, forecasting, focus groups, the nominal group technique, and the delphic method. Some business fields and disciplines may use specific methods not utilized across disciplines or extensively due to their specific field or disciplinary nature. Examples of methods of data analysis include descriptive statistics, inferential statistics, tests of statistical significance, levels of significance, and consideration of Type I and Type II errors.

Within a qualitative methodology, empirical material (data) collection methods include semistructured and unstructured interviews, participant observation, action research, focus groups, the delphic method, the documentary method, case studies, and longitudinal studies. Analysis methods may include content analysis, constant comparative analysis, successive approximation, domain analysis, ideal types, event structure analysis, matrices, and grounded theory.

Examples of social sciences methods used in business represent a wide range of both qualitative and quantitative methods of data/empirical material collection and analysis, selected based on the relevant methodology and overarching paradigm that inform the overall research process.

See Also the Following Articles

Case Study • Data Collection, Primary vs. Secondary • Focus Groups • Longitudinal Cohort Designs • Longitudinal Studies, Panel • Mail Surveys • Participant Observation • Population vs. Sample • Quasi-Experiment • Survey Design • Survey Questionnaire Construction • Surveys • Telephone Surveys • Web-Based Survey

Further Reading

Cavana, R. Y., Delahaye, B. L., and Sekaran, U. (2001). *Applied Business Research, Qualitative and Quantitative Methods.* John Wiley and Sons, Milton, Australia.

Collis, J., and Hussey, R. (2003). *Business Research, A Practical Guide for Undergraduate and Postgraduate Students,* 2nd Ed. Palgrave Macmillan, Houndmills, Hampshire, UK.

Cooper, D. R., and Schindler, P. S. (2003). *Business Research Methods,* 8th Ed. Irwin McGraw-Hill, Boston.

Davis, D. (2000). *Business Research for Decision Making,* 5th Ed. Duxbury, Thomson Learning, Pacific Grove, CA.

Frazer, L., and Lawley, M. (2000). *Questionnaire Design and Administration.* John Wiley and Sons, Brisbane, Australia.

Frey, J. H. (1989). *Survey Research by Telephone,* 2nd Ed. Sage Library of Social Research Volume 150. Sage, Newbury Park, CA.

Hair, J. F., Jr., Babin, B., Money, A. H., and Samouel, P. (2003). *Essential of Business Research Methods.* John Wiley and Sons, Hoboken, NJ.

Jennings, G. (2001). *Tourism Research.* John Wiley and Sons, Milton, Australia.

Malhotra, N. K., Hall, J., Shaw, M., and Oppenheim, P. (2002). *Marketing Research, An Applied Orientation,* 2nd Ed. Prentice Hall, Frenchs Forest, Australia.

Marcoulides, G. A. (1998). *Modern Methods for Business Research.* Lawrence Erlbaum Associates, Mahwah, NJ.

Miles, M. B., and Huberman, A. M. (1994). *Qualitative Data Analysis: An Expanded Sourcebook,* 2nd Ed. Sage, Thousand Oaks, CA.

Sekaran, U. (2003). *Research Methods for Business, A Skill Building Approach.* John Wiley and Sons, New York.

Ticehurst, G. Q., and Veal, A. J. (2000). *Business Research Methods, A Managerial Approach.* Longman, Pearson, Frenchs Forest, Australia.

Trotman, K. T. (1996). *Research Methods for Judgment and Decision Making in Auditing.* Coopers and Lybrand and Accounting Association of Australia and New Zealand, Melbourne, Australia.

Zikmund, W. G. (2003). *Business Research Methods,* 7th Ed. Thomson/South Western, Cincinnati, OH.

Campaign Finance Data

Donald A. Gross

University of Kentucky, Lexington, Kentucky, USA

Glossary

Buckley v. Valeo U.S. Supreme Court 1976 decision that established many of the legal parameters for federal campaign finance law.

hard money Money given to political candidates and political parties that is subject to federal contribution limits and prohibitions.

independent expenditures Expenditures for campaign activities that are not coordinated with a candidate and do not expressly call for the election or defeat of a candidate.

issue advocacy Noncandidate campaign activity that does not expressly advocate the election or defeat of a candidate.

party soft money Money given to political parties for the purported purpose of party building that is not subject to federal contribution limits and prohibitions.

political action committees (PACs) Committees that collect contributions into a separate fund to support the political interest of the sponsoring organization.

soft money Money associated with federal elections that is not subject to federal contribution limits and prohibitions.

Campaign finance data encompass a wide variety of types of information that are usually defined in terms of the regulatory environment surrounding elections. As such, an understanding of systematic differences in regulatory environments is a necessary first step for any analyst. For example, in the context of the U.S. federal regulatory environment, campaign finance data are usually classified as either hard money data or soft money data. It is clear, at all governmental levels in the United States, that both the quantity and quality of campaign finance data has increased tremendously over the last 25 years. But, as regulatory environments continue to change and strategic actors continue to change their behavior, new types of campaign finance data will continue to emerge.

Introduction

Data Availability

Our understanding of the role of money in democratic elections and governance has increased dramatically in recent years. This increase in knowledge is very much tied to the ever increasing quantity and quality of campaign finance data that became available after campaign finance reform began to take hold in the mid-1970s. Prior to that, campaign finance data were difficult to obtain, generally not available for most elections, and of overall poor quality. Campaign disclosure laws for U.S. federal elections were a key component of laws passed in 1976. As the federal government continued to expand disclosure requirements, and as the states rapidly expanded their own disclosure requirements, the wealth of campaign finance data available to scholars continued to increase.

The General Use of Campaign Finance Data

To date, campaign finance data have been used to study a wide variety of social phenomena. Two general areas of research interests have formed the foci of most studies. The first focuses on issues associated with democratic elections—the impact of spending on electoral outcomes, electoral competition, voter information, participation, voter turnout, citizen engagement in the electoral process, partisan advantage, the incumbency advantage, and interest-group influence. The second group of analyses has focused on questions surrounding issues of governance: Do contributions affect how legislators vote, executives behave, or judges adjudicate? Do interest groups gain an institutional advantage as a result of contributions? Is the passage and implementation of policy affected by campaign contributions? All the numerous questions being asked by scholars interested in campaign finance and the numerous methodologies used in attempts to address these issues require different types of campaign finance data.

The Problem

Solid research requires reliable and valid data. And, even though the quantity and quality of campaign finance data have increased dramatically in recent years, a fundamental problem remains—the nature and character of almost all campaign finance data depend on the regulatory environments surrounding the phenomena of interest. This problem is compounded by the fact that regulatory environments, both state and federal, continue to evolve over time. Thus, data availability changes over time and across government units, with the likelihood of new forms of data coming to the forefront remaining a strong possibility. As such, any discussion of campaign finance data must be viewed in the context of the evolving regulatory environments governing elections.

Article Overview

An exhaustive discussion of the regulatory environments found world wide is simply beyond the scope of this essay. The focus here is on campaign finance data in the United States, especially that available for federal elections. In addition, the article examines only the most widely used types of campaign finance data, recognizing that there are other types of data that are typically classified under particular regulatory characteristics of specific states. The focus is on the data that have become available since the mid-1970s. First, the general regulatory parameters that define the characteristics of particular types of campaign finance data are examined. Next, campaign finance data that typically classified under the rubrics of hard money and soft money are discussed.

The Regulatory Environment

Because the nature of campaign finance data is heavily dependent on regulatory environments, the quantity and quality of campaign finance data differ across time and across legal jurisdictions. Five characteristics of regulatory environments are of special interest: (1) reporting and disclosure requirements, (2) limits on contributions, (3) spending or expenditure limits, (4) public financing, and (5) enforcement provisions.

Reporting and Disclosure Requirements

Perhaps no characteristic of the regulatory environment is as important to the collection of campaign finance data as reporting and disclosure requirements. Very simply, generally available records are essential to the collection of campaign finance data. Requirements are often specified in terms of the type of organizational unit involved in the expenditure of funds.

The highest quality campaign finance data typically are those for candidate committees. These are committees created for the specific purpose of electing an individual to office. At the federal level, all contributions and expenditures in excess of $200.00 must be fully disclosed. Other information that must be reported include cash on hand, loans, money transfers, dividends, and interest. Although the threshold for reporting may differ, most states now have similar laws.

When we turn our attention to leadership political action committees (PACs) and political parties, data availability lessens compared to that available for candidate committees. At the federal level, at least since 1992, all contributions to these organizations over $200.00 are fully disclosed. Their contributions given to a candidate are fully disclosed, as are all expenditures made in coordination with a candidate. However, in the case of party soft money, expenditures are not necessarily reported on a line-item basis. The transfer of monies to state parties is fully disclosed, but, because states often have weaker reporting requirements, the original source of the money and the particular use of the money are often lost.

If we consider individuals and other organizations, including PACs, the rules for reporting and disclosure change once again. Their direct contributions to candidates, political parties, and other PACs are fully disclosed. Federal law requires full disclosure of both contributions and expenditures when individuals and organizations undertake independent expenditures that directly call for the election or defeat of particular candidates, called direct advocacy ads. But when individual and organizations use issue advocacy advertisement, they generally fall outside federal regulation. They may, therefore, spend unlimited amounts of money without necessarily disclosing income or expenditures.

A similar pattern exists whenever we consider state-level reporting and disclosure requirements. Reporting requirements tend to be most extensive when evaluating candidate committees, less extensive when examining political parties, and least stringent when focusing on individuals and organizations such as PACs. However, there remains a great deal of diversity among the states in the regulatory stringency of their reporting and disclosure requirements. As such, the data that are available at the federal level and in some states, is simply nonexistent in other states.

Limits on Contributions

Other than reporting and disclosure requirements, limits on campaign contributions are the most prevalent characteristic of campaign finance regulatory environments. Limits on contributions tend to differ in terms of three basic characteristics: (1) in terms of who or what organizations that make contributions, (2) in terms of who or what organizations that receive contributions, and (3) in terms of the dollar amounts of specific types of contributions (these differ across regulatory environments as well as across different electoral offices within a given regulatory environment).

The most typical organizations and individuals that are limited in the amount that they can contribute are individuals, political parties, the candidate and his or her family, unions, corporations, foreign nationals, PACs, and regulated industries. Organizations that receive contributions that have limits placed on the size of contributions given to them typically include candidate committees, party committees, and PACs. Dollar amounts differ from a total prohibition on contributions to no limit on the size of a contribution. In addition, in some jurisdictions, dollar amounts are adjusted over time to take into account the effects of inflation.

Limits that are in place for federal elections are illustrative of the possible combinations that we may encounter in a given regulatory environment. Corporations, unions, and foreign nationals are prohibited from making contributions to candidates and political committees, whereas there are specific limits on the size of a contribution from individuals, political parties, and PACs. Until the passage of the Bipartisan Campaign Reform Act in 2002, there were no major limits on the size of contributions to party soft money accounts. And, pending the outcome of current court action, the strict limits imposed by this legislation may become nullified. When we examine the regulatory environments in the states, we see a great deal of diversity in the parameters governing contributions. States such as Texas and Illinois have almost no effective regulations limiting the size of contributions, whereas states such as Kentucky and Vermont have stringent regulations governing contributions.

Spending or Expenditure Limits

The U.S. Supreme Court's *Buckley v. Valeo* decision in 1976 found that mandatory spending limits violated First Amendment protections of freedom of expression. A consequence of this ruling is that spending limits had to be voluntary, although legal jurisdictions could use public subsidies to encourage candidates to accept spending limits. Likewise, the decision meant that expenditures by individuals or groups that spend independently of a candidate cannot be limited. The analytical consequence of the *Buckley* decision is that, with the exception of a very few legal jurisdictions for a limited number of years, we cannot analyze the effects of spending limits in jurisdictions that do not also have some form of public financing of elections.

In jurisdictions that have voluntary spending limits, the limits tend to differ in terms of the elective offices covered by spending limits, the formula used to specify the amount of the spending limit, and the mechanisms used to encourage candidates to abide by the limits. At the federal level, voluntary spending limits only exist for presidential elections. Although a limited number of states do have spending limits for state legislative races, it is the gubernatorial election that most often has spending limits associated with it.

For most elective offices, a spending limit is specified in terms of a flat sum of money that changes from year to year after being indexed for inflation. So, the spending limits for the presidential election in 1976 were set at $10,900,000 for the primary season and $21,800,000 for the general election and in 1996 rose to $30,900,000 and $61,800,000. A second way to specify the size of a spending limit is to multiply some given amount of money times a particularly relevant characteristic of the electoral district. So, for example, the limit for Hawaiian gubernatorial elections is $2.50 times the number of qualified voters.

The coercive measures used to encourage candidates to abide by spending limits differ a great deal across jurisdictions. At the presidential level, public opinion and public financing are the two prime incentives. Some states add additional incentives. In Kentucky, for example, a gubernatorial candidate who agrees to abide by the spending limits receives matching public funds at a rate of 2 to 1. And if any candidate who is not receiving public funds does exceed the spending limit, then the candidates who did originally agree to abide by the spending limits have their limit raised to be equal to the noncompliant candidate's while still receiving the 2 to 1 public funds.

Public Financing

There are two basic types of public financing schemes: those that provide funds to political parties and those that provide funds directly to candidates. At the federal level, the major political parties are given some monies to help pay for their national conventions, but public funding is only given to candidates for the presidency. At the state level, depending on the specific years we are analyzing, approximately 20 states have some type of public financing system. Some give money exclusively to political parties, some give exclusively to candidates, and some give money to both political parties and candidates.

There are two primary mechanisms for funding the state-level programs that fund political parties. Approximately one-half the states rely on a taxpayer check-off system, whereby a taxpayer can designate part of his or her tax liability (normally $1 to $5) for the public funding system. In other states, a taxpayer adds money to the fund by voluntarily adding a given amount of money to his or her tax liability. States also differ in the mechanisms for the allocation of funds to political parties. Some use a specific formula for the allocation of funds, but the majority of the states allow the taxpayer to use his or her tax form to specify which political party is to receive their contribution.

Programs designed to give money to political candidates tend to differ in terms of six basic characteristics. First, there is the issue of what type of candidate can receive funds. At the federal level, only presidential candidates receive funds. Among the 12 to 14 states that have public funding, most give it gubernatorial candidates and a few give it to legislative candidates. Second, there is the issue of whether public funding is available for the primary election or the general election or whether the state distinguishes between the two electoral periods. Third, the federal government and the states differ on the criteria for obtaining public funds, both for the major-party candidates and, especially, for third-party candidates. Fourth, differences exist in the mechanisms for allocating public funds. In some cases, candidates are given single or multiple grants of money up to a specified limit. In other cases, candidates are given matching funds, normally on a 1-to-1 or 2-to-1 basis, up to a specified limit. Fifth, there are vast differences in the amount of money given to candidates. Finally, there are differences in the requirements candidates are forced to accept in order to receive public funding, most typically, spending limits.

Enforcement Provisions

As might be expected, among the states and the federal government, there is a good deal of diversity in enforcement provisions and the implementation of campaign finance law. Malbin and Gais, in their excellent 1998 discussion of enforcement problems in the states, suggest that there are data collection errors and note that there appears to be little effort to systematically cross-check the validity of the information provided by candidates and organizations. Perhaps most important, as individuals and organizations become ever more creative in their attempts to avoid campaign finance laws, there can be ambiguities in the coding categories of data.

Even though we know that there are data collection problems, there is, at this time, no evidence to suggest that it is a serious problem for most analyses. But differences in the dissemination of information can create problems for some analysts. Often campaign finance information is only available on paper, which can become prohibitively expensive in terms of time and money. And although a number of states, like the federal government, are increasingly placing campaign finance data on the Internet, they are not always readily downloadable. Finally, states differ a good deal in the time frame for which campaign finance data are available or will remain available in paper or electronic format. In some cases, records are only kept by the state for 5 years.

This discussion of the major parameters of regulatory environments is essential because it is the regulatory environments that help define most campaign finance data. We now turn to a discussion of hard money data.

Hard Money

Hard money is a term that has specific meaning in the context of the federal regulatory environment. It is money given to candidates and political parties that is subject to federal contribution limits and prohibitions. Although there is no limit on how such money is spent, it must be fully disclosed. The definition of hard money may differ in any given state. For simplicity, campaign finance data are presented here in the context of the federal regulatory environment, recognizing the fact that similar data obtained at the state level may not necessarily fit the strict definition of hard money.

Expenditure Data

Probably the most widely used campaign finance data are aggregate candidate expenditure data. Each datum is the total amount of money spent by a single candidate for a single election or electoral cycle. The Federal Election Commission makes these data available for all federal elections since 1978. Similar types of data are generally available for many state elective offices, although there are often serious data-availability issues when we attempt to obtain data over time or across state elective offices. Aggregate candidate expenditures for gubernatorial elections are readily available for almost all states from 1978 to the present. State legislative elections are more problematic, with complete data readily available only since the mid-1990s. For earlier years, availability is much more episodic.

There are a number of readily identified potential pitfalls when using aggregate candidate data. First, there are two interrelated problems that are of special significance when analyzing the effect of candidate spending on electoral outcomes or party competition; this is called the simultaneity issue. The first way to think about the simultaneity issue involves the interactive nature of campaign spending. Jacobson established in 1980 that in many cases candidates spend money in response to spending by other candidates. Thus, spending by one candidate becomes a function of spending by the others. A second way to think about the simultaneity issue is that candidate spending can be seen as a function of anticipated outcomes. Either view of simultaneity suggests that simple ordinary least-squares regression of candidate spending on electoral outcomes will necessarily result in biased estimates for the effects of electoral spending. To resolve the problem, both two-stage least-squares regression and three-stage least-squares regression have been used.

A second pitfall in the use of aggregate expenditure data has to do with a series of problems associated with the need to ensure the comparability of the units of analysis. Any cross-temporal analysis necessitates taking into account inflationary effects. This is normally accomplished by selecting a base year and adjusting the dollar amounts for other years into constant dollar amounts. States also differ a great deal in the sizes of their population, and it is known that population size is a critical factor in determining the level of candidate spending. Spending per capita is often used to overcome this problem. In terms of political considerations, it is important to recognize that only one-third of all U.S. Senate elections occur every 2 years and the elections in any one cycle are not representative of all states. Finally, some senatorial elections occur in presidential election years and other do not; the presence of a presidential election is known to affect candidate spending.

Gubernatorial elections present a similar problem in that they are unevenly spread over a four-year cycle, differ in their population size, and may occur during a presidential election year, during off-year congressional elections, or when there are no federal elections. In addition, in some states, aggregate gubernatorial expenditures are broken down into the primary electoral season and the general election. Other states, like in U.S. Senate and House elections, make no distinction between primary and general elections when reporting expenditure data.

The very nature of aggregate candidate expenditure data prohibits the consideration of specific types of spending that can be of crucial theoretical importance. For federal candidates, however, disbursements can be broken down by functional categories such as media, travel, and administrative overhead. Similar types of data are not readily available for most state elections.

At the national level, party expenditure data are readily available for all major party committees. This is the case whether we are interested in aggregate expenditure data, transfers of funds to particular candidates and/or state parties, or expenditures for actual party activities such as media purchases and get-out-the-vote efforts. Although more difficult to obtain and often much less detailed, party expenditure data are also generally available at the state level.

Contribution Data

Perhaps the simplest type of contribution data is that which deals with the existence of the contribution limits themselves. The simplest approach is to treat each potential type of contribution limit as a dummy variable, typically coded 0 or 1 for the absence or presence of a particular type of contribution limit. But, when we use this approach, we lose all variance in the size of the contribution limits among those states that have a limit.

An alternative is to use the state's actual contribution limit for those states that have a particular limit and to assign an arbitrarily high monetary value to those states that do not have a contribution limit. Because most state contribution limits are in the range of $200 to $5000 per electoral season, experience suggests that substantive conclusions are generally not fundamentally affected whether or not we assign a value of $100,000 or $500,000 to those states that actually do not have a particular contribution limit. We must also be careful in specifying limits because some states specify the limit in terms of a given amount per election, some specify the amount per year, and others specify the amount per election cycle.

The monetary value of contributions are another type of data that is often used in analyses. The total dollar amount for all contributions and the total number of contributors are two types of data that can be especially useful. It must be recognized, however, that it is rarely possible to get a completely accurate number for the total number of contributors because most jurisdictions do not keep a count of contributors who contribute below a given dollar value, $200 for example; only the total amount of money given by all contributors below the threshold is generally available.

In many cases, we are interested in obtaining information on particular types of contributors. At the federal level, at least since the mid-1990s, it is possible to specify various categories of contribution data. We can specify the number (remembering the previous caveat) and amounts of contributions by the candidate themselves, individuals, PACs, and political parties. Standard industrial classification can be used to specify contributions by economic sectors such as union PACs, law, agriculture, construction, education, and health. At the state level, similar types of data are generally available for legislative and gubernatorial elections, at least since the mid-1990s.

Two final types of candidate contribution data that can be of interest are the timing of the contribution and whether the contribution comes from within the electoral district. Because most contribution lists provide the mailing zip code of the contributor, this generally can be used to determine whether the contribution comes from within the electoral district. The actual dates of contributions are also part of most contribution data sets and can be used to track the timing of contributions.

Soft Money

Like hard money, soft money is especially relevant in the context of the federal regulatory environment. Unlike hard money, however, the term soft money has often had a somewhat ambiguous meaning. In its broadest sense, soft money is all money associated with federal elections that is not subject to federal contribution limits. This is a broad category of monies that includes numerous types of financial transactions. Within this context, there are really three types of activities that have received significant attention in the literature: party soft money, independent expenditures, and issue advocacy money.

Party Soft Money

For many analysts, party soft money is what is really meant by soft money. Party soft money is unlimited amounts of money given to political parties for the purported purpose of party building. The only limit on contributors is a prohibition against foreign nationals. The importance of soft money began to rise in the late 1980s as a result of efforts to try and balance the federal and nonfederal roles of political parties. This includes a national party role in gubernatorial elections, state legislative elections, and party-building activities such as get-out-the-vote efforts, party-registrations efforts, and voter identification. National party money can also be used to free up the availability of state party hard money to be used in federal elections and to transfer hard money back to the national parties.

Reliable data on party soft money are effectively unavailable for most research purposes before 1991. With new federal legislation, beginning in 1992, all soft money contributions to political parties over $200 are fully disclosed. This includes funds given to the national parties and their affiliated groupings. Because there are no significant limits on who can contribute, data are available on corporate, union, PAC, and individual contributions.

Although party soft money contribution data after 1991 are quite good, expenditure data are more problematic because they are not necessarily reported on a line-item basis. Much of the difficulty results from the fact that for a number of activities parties need to meet a ratio of hard to soft money expenditures and the ratio tends to be more favorable (more soft money, less hard) when state parties do the spending. Thus, the national parties transfer much of their money to state parties. The transfer of monies to state parties is fully disclosed and so data on transfers are available. Finally, data on national party soft money expenditures for media issue ads and other types of advocacy activities, such as grassroots mail campaigns, voter contact, phone banks, and get-out-the-vote efforts, are available.

Independent Expenditures

Independent expenditures are monies spent on campaign activities that are not coordinated with a candidate and expressly call for the election or defeat of a candidate. They can be undertaken by individuals, groups, or political parties. Spending is fully disclosed and there are no limits on how much can be spent on such activities. Depending on who is expending the funds, there may or may not be relevant contribution limits. Political parties must use hard money, and contributions to nonaffiliated committees, such as PACs, are also limited.

Because full disclosure is required, data are available on who makes independent expenditures in federal elections and the costs of the expenditures. Although data on contributions to political parties and nonaffiliated committees are available, it is not possible to link specific contributions to independent expenditures.

Issue Advocacy

Issue advocacy is noncandidate campaign activity that does not expressly advocate the election or defeat of a candidate. Generally speaking, any communication activity that does not use the words specified in the *Buckley* decision (vote for, support, cast your ballot for, elect, defeat, reject, or vote against) may be considered issue advocacy. National political parties have generally been restricted to a prescribed ratio of hard and soft money when undertaking issue advocacy. However, in all other cases, costs are not considered to be either a contribution or expenditure under the federal regulatory environment. Thus, in the case of issue advocacy, there are no contribution limits or prohibitions, no expenditure limits, and no itemized reporting requirements.

The lack of reporting requirements for most issue advocacy creates serious problems for the data analyst. As previously stated, there are data on national party activities. Some organizations voluntarily publish their expenditures and records can be obtained from television and radio stations to re-create the amount of money spent on these broadcast activities by organizations. This does not guarantee, however, that we can accurately specify the nature of the organization from the name listed as the purchasing agent for the media spot. We clearly cannot specify the ultimate source of the money. Expenditure data on PACs can be used to estimate their issue advocacy monies.

Other groupings, including 501s and 527s, whose names derive from their income tax designation, have traditionally not been required to publicly disclose either their contributors or their itemized expenditures. Recent federal legislation and pending court cases may change our ability to collect more comprehensive data on these organizations. For example, new disclosure requirements on 527s began in June 2002. Nevertheless, there simply are no data sets currently available that can be considered systematic, reliable, and comprehensive when it comes to the full range of activities that fall under the rubric of issue advocacy.

Conclusion

The quantity and quality of campaign finance data are expanding every day. Entirely new categories of data are now available that were unheard of only 5 years ago or only available for a limited number of legal jurisdictions. In addition to governmental agencies, there are a number of organizations, both commercial and otherwise, that can provide campaign finance data. But, especially when we move from the federal level to the state level, we remain confronted with the possibility that data may only be available for a limited number of states or a limited time frame. In some cases, the data have been lost forever. Data availability on activities such as bundling, the use of conduits, and the use of internal communication by corporations and unions remains episodic. The multiple jurisdictions that help define the nature of campaign finance data often make direct comparisons among data sets difficult. Differences among jurisdictions can make it nearly impossible to follow the flow of funds across jurisdictions. Some data sets have reliability and validity questions associated with them. And as strategic actors change their behavior, it is likely that new types of campaign finance data will become available while other types become irrelevant.

See Also the Following Articles

Experiments, Political Science • Political Science • Politics, Use of Polls in • Qualitative Analysis, Political Science

Further Reading

Corrado, A., Mann, T., Ortiz, D., Potter, T., and Sorauf, F. (eds.) (1997). *Campaign Finance Reform: A Sourcebook*. Brookings Institution Press, Washington, D.C.

Goidel, R., and Gross, D. (1994). A systems approach to campaign finance in United States House elections. *Am. Polit. Q.* **22,** 125–153.

Goidel, R., Gross, D., and Shields, T. (1999). *Money Matters: Consequences of Campaign Finance Reform in U.S. House Elections*. Rowman and Littlefield, New York.

Gross, D., and Goidel, R. (2003). *The States of Campaign Finance: Consequences of Campaign Finance Law in Gubernatorial Elections*. Ohio State University Press, Columbus, OH.

Jacobson, G. (1980). *Money and Congressional Elections*. Yale University Press, New Haven, CT.

Jacobson, G. (1990). The effects of campaign spending in House elections. *Am. J. Polit. Sci.* **34,** 334–362.

Magleby, D. (ed.) (2000). *Outside Money*. Rowman and Littlefield, New York.

Malbin, M., and Gais, T. (1998). *The Day after Reform*. Rockefeller Institute Press, Albany, NY.

Sorauf, F. (1992). *Inside Campaign Finance: Myths and Realities*. Yale University Press, New Haven, CT.

Thompson, J., and Moncrief, G. (eds.) (1998). *Campaign Finance in State Legislative Elections*. Congressional Quarterly Press, Washington, D.C.

Campbell, Donald T.

Yvette Bartholomée
University of Groningen, Groningen, The Netherlands

Glossary

attitude Feeling or opinion about something or someone, learned in the process of becoming a member of a group, and the way of behaving that follows from this.

external validity Concerns the generalizability of a particular experimental outcome to other persons, settings, and times.

internal validity Concerns the validity of the claim that in a specific experiment the factor A, and factor A only, caused a change in factor B.

multitrait–multimethod matrix A correlational matrix measuring a set of traits by using a set of methods.

quasi-experiment A study that lacks random assignment but otherwise resembles a randomized experiment.

randomized controlled experiment A study in which subjects are assigned to either treatment or control groups at random to equal out preexisting differences between the groups.

The psychologist Donald T. Campbell (1916–1996) was one of the leading figures in American social science after the Second World War. He developed several influential concepts, such as quasi-experimentation and the multitrait–multimethod matrix, that would become widely used in the social sciences. This article discusses Campbell's work, which primarily aimed at enlarging the scope of applied social research.

Introduction

The career of the renowned American psychologist and methodologist Donald T. Campbell (see Fig. 1) developed in parallel to the ever-increasing influence of the field of psychology in the post-World War II era. Campbell acquired his first job as an army psychologist during the Second World War—a period that would become crucial in the development of psychology from an academic specialty to a profession with widespread applications. After the war, psychologists convinced others, mostly policymakers, of the practical value of their expertise. When President Johnson launched his "War on Poverty" and "Great Society" initiatives in the 1960s,

Figure 1 Donald T. Campbell (1916–1996).

psychologists and other social scientists played a pivotal role in shaping these social programs. Johnson's Great Society was an attempt to solve policy problems by appealing to the expertise of social scientists such as psychologists. By capitalizing on these societal changes, social science reflected and shaped the values and demands of the developing welfare state.

Campbell's work goes back to educational research, where randomized controlled experimentation was first developed. The unifying theme underlying of all of his work was formed by the question of how to achieve dependable knowledge of the psychological and social world. Campbell argued that "real" knowledge could be found only "in the field," outside the isolated laboratory. Even if going into the field meant that "true" (that is, randomized controlled) experimentation would not be possible, Campbell regarded the kind of knowledge that could be found in the real world so valuable that he was willing to compromise. His compromise was a range of sophisticated research designs and accompanying statistical techniques that he called quasi-experiments. Campbell's quasi-experimental methods set out to expand the scope of experimentation and became a world-famous methodological paradigm. Although these methods loosened the notion of experimentation, Campbell remained very strict in the use of quasi-experimental methods. He was committed to designing standardized methods that could rigorously test hypotheses. For Campbell, real knowledge could be achieved only by using the "right" research methods and he spent his entire life developing and continuously refining such methods.

Campbell's methods became extremely influential in evaluation research, where social scientists quantitatively tested the effectiveness and efficiency of policy measures. His work, such as the book *Experimental and Quasi-Experimental Designs for Research*, became as much as a research "bible" for evaluation researchers. Moreover, Campbell's influence was not restricted to evaluation research. His methods became the standard equipment of many Western social scientists engaged in quantitative field research. Campbell's methods were received as ways to answer questions decisively, as indisputably and objectively as possible.

The next sections show how Campbell shaped a research methodology that had to result in a trustworthy body of knowledge. The emphasis is placed on Campbell's years at Northwestern University, where he spent the largest part of his career and wrote many of his influential publications.

A Methodologist in the Making

Donald Thomas Campbell (1916–1996) was born the son of an agronomist in Grass Lake, Michigan. After finishing high school in 1934, Campbell chose to study psychology. He graduated from the University of California at Berkeley in 1939 and subsequently continued his studies for his Ph.D. degree at the same university. During the course of a traveling grant at Harvard University, the Second World War interrupted his graduate studies. In December 1941—a few days before the bombing of Pearl Harbor—Campbell decided to join his Berkeley professor Robert Tryon, who was working in Washington, DC, at what soon would become the Office of Strategic Services (OSS). Tryon was establishing a section of Social Psychology at the Research and Analysis Branch at the OSS. Here, Campbell participated in studies of social attitudes and propaganda. A year later, in 1943, he joined the U.S. Navy, where he remained in service for $2\frac{1}{2}$ years.

After the war, at the age of 29, Campbell returned to Berkeley to finish his graduate studies in social psychology. His dissertation, "The Generality of a Social Attitude," was completed in 1947. This unpublished study investigated the prejudices that five American ethnic groups ("Negro," Japanese, Jewish, Mexican, and English) held toward one another. For example, Campbell tested to what extent one minority blamed the others for problems in the country by asking whether one agreed with statements such as "Do the English in this country use their power to the disadvantage of other Americans?" or "Do the Jews in this country do very little harm to the rest of us?"

Next, Campbell accepted a job in social psychology at Ohio State University. There, one of his main projects was a study of leadership and morale among submarine crews. His central research focus, however, remained the quantitative measurement of social attitudes. Campbell kept pursuing this interest after he moved to the University of Chicago in 1950. For example, he participated in the Superior–Subordinate Orientation Project, which set out to measure the personality type and attitudes that would cause someone to favor superiors over subordinates or vice versa.

In 1953, Campbell accepted a position as associate professor at Northwestern University. In this new setting, he started developing his methodological interests. Methodology was important to Campbell before he came to Northwestern University, but now he began to develop key notions, such as the "multitrait–multimethod matrix" and "quasi-experimentation," that would make him famous.

Campbell's Prolific Years at Northwestern University

Quasi-Experimentation

One of Campbell's most cited publications—and more generally, one of the most frequently cited publications in social science—is the 84-page book *Experimental and Quasi-Experimental Designs for Research*. It was published in 1966 after it had first appeared as a book chapter in 1963 and was co-authored by the statistician Julian Stanley. In the book, Campbell and Stanley presented numerous true experimental and quasi-experimental research designs. They recommended true experimental designs, in which the experimenter had to compare at least two groups: an experimental group that received a certain treatment and a control group that did not. In order to make a comparison between the two groups—which was necessary to see whether the experimental variable had made any difference—both groups had to be the same. The best way, according to Campbell and Stanley, to ensure that the experimental and control groups were equal was randomization. Selecting people at random would dissolve differences within and between groups.

However, experimentation with randomly composed groups often is not possible. If, for example, one wants to test which teaching method would be most effective, these methods would have to be tested on existing school classes. For moral and for practical reasons, it would be impossible to just randomly select children and test several teaching methods on them. Moreover, even if randomized selection would be possible, regrouping children would be experimentally undesirable because this would create an entirely different situation, affecting the outcome of the experiment. To overcome these problems, Campbell and Stanley designed a range of so-called quasi-experiments. As the term indicates, quasi-experiments were not real or true experiments, yet they enabled experimenters to work with real groups. Sophisticated research designs and statistics had to ensure that quasi-experimental research diverged as little as possible from the ideal of randomized controlled research.

Campbell and Stanley's prime concern was with valid research results—and according to them, such results could be gained only by experimentation or, if reality put some constraints on the possibilities of experimentation, by quasi-experimentation. Only good methods could produce trustworthy results. Therefore, they assessed the quality of their research designs by scoring them on factors that could threaten the validity of their outcomes. Campbell and Stanley distinguished two types of validity: internal and external validity. Internal validity concerned the validity of the experiment itself: did the experimental treatment actually cause the outcome of the experiment or was it something else? Campbell and Stanley listed several factors that could threaten the internal validity of an experiment, such as "history," "testing," or "instrumentation." All these factors concerned events occurring during the experiment that changed the outcome of the experiment. When, for example, the effect of propaganda materials is tested and at the same time a war breaks out, the experimenter cannot tell whether the measured difference in attitude can be attributed to the effect of propaganda or is due to the outbreak of war. This is what Campbell and Stanley called the factor history: events happening outside the experimental setting influencing the experiment. This and other validity-threatening factors made it difficult, if not impossible, to discern whether the experimental treatment made any difference at all.

External validity, in contrast, had to do with the generalizability of the experiment: to which other populations or settings could the results of this particular experiment be generalized? An example of a factor threatening the external validity of an experiment are "reactive effects of experimental arrangements," which meant that certain effects could be found only under experimental conditions, when people are aware that they are in an experiment. These effects cannot be generalized to a nonexperimental setting.

In order to facilitate the use of their experimental and quasi-experimental research designs, Campbell and Stanley listed them in extensive tables where for each design plusses and minuses indicated which factor threatened its internal or external validity. With these tables in hand, researchers could work out which design would be most appropriate to test their hypotheses and generate the most valid knowledge.

The book *Experimental and Quasi-Experimental Designs for Research* became a canonical text to social scientists who wanted to do field research. More than 300,000 copies of the book have been sold, an impressive number for such a technical work. It was translated into numerous languages and is compulsory reading for psychology students as well as students in other social sciences. In 1979, Thomas D. Cook and Campbell published an update of *Experimental and Quasi-Experimental Designs for Research*, entitled *Quasi-Experimentation: Design and Analysis Issues for Field Settings*, which elaborated on many of Campbell and Stanley's concepts. Where, for example, Campbell and Stanley listed 12 factors threatening validity, Cook and Campbell extended this list to 33 factors. This book was also widely used by social scientists of various disciplines.

The Multitrait–Multimethod Matrix

Experimental and Quasi-Experimental Designs for Research was one of Campbell's most cited publications, rivaled only by an article written together with Donald Fiske, "Convergent and Discriminant Validation by the Multitrait–Multimethod Matrix." Just like *Experimental and Quasi-Experimental Designs for Research*, this was a methodological paper that focused on social measurement. Whereas Campbell and Stanley presented several experimental and quasi-experimental research designs and assessed the validity of these designs by enlisting numerous factors that could threaten their validity, Campbell and Fiske directed their attention to the validity of tests and measurements. According to them, tests should be validated in two ways, by "convergent validation" and by "discriminant validation." The validity of a test had to be examined by checking how different tests converged, that is, measured the same thing when they were intended to do so, and at the same time how those tests discriminated, that is, measured different things when they were intended to differ. In order to validate tests, Campbell and Fiske developed a so-called multitrait–multimethod matrix. In this matrix, at least two traits and at least two methods should be used to validate a test.

Campbell and Fiske's primary aim was the evaluation of tests. However, they took the view that psychologists should not evaluate tests as if they were fixed and definitive, but rather use these evaluations to develop better tests. Just like Campbell and Stanley, Campbell and Fiske submitted research methods to close scrutiny. Only after testing the tests could a researcher be sure that he had the right research instruments in hand and only with the appropriate methods could one arrive at reliable research results.

Evaluation Research

Even though the article on the multitrait–multimethod matrix was widely read and cited, its influence is rather marginal compared to Campbell and Stanley's experimental and quasi-experimental research designs, which became paradigmatic. Campbell's work was foundational for the new field of "program evaluation" or "social experimentation." This field evaluated the effectiveness of policies such as social programs. Examples of social programs are the New Jersey Negative Income Tax Experiments, Head Start, or Sesame Street, large-scale projects in the vein of President Johnson's Great Society initiatives.

The New Jersey Negative Income Tax Experiments were designed to find out whether guaranteeing an income to poor working families might be an alternative to welfare. The concept of a negative income tax was that if an income were to drop below a certain minimum level, a negative tax would be levied, which meant that the tax system would pay out cash. This negative tax would be reduced when someone again earned an income above the minimum level. The experiments were carried out from 1968 through 1972 and involved a sample of more than 1200 households. These households were randomly divided into several experimental groups, which differed in the level of guaranteed income and in the reduction rate of negative taxes when earning income above the minimum level. The experiments had to test whether or not this system of a negative income tax created an incentive to work was tested. These experiments were the first large-scale attempt to test a policy by employing randomized controlled experimentation.

Head Start and Sesame Street were compensation programs aimed at the improvement of education for disadvantaged preschool children. Head Start—a project still running in the early 2000s—started in 1964 and in its first season was already serving over half a million children. The project intended to give disadvantaged children a head start through extra training in their early childhood—the age at which they would be most receptive. Sesame Street had the same rationale: in this project, the effects of the educational television program, which was designed to teach things in a playful way to young disadvantaged children, were tested. Campbell was involved in one of the evaluations of Head Start as a member of the advisory panel for the Head Start Evaluation Design Project. He also wrote a few articles that pointed out the mistakes in previous evaluations of the program. One article claimed that one of the major quasi-experimental evaluations of Head Start—"the social experiment evaluation most cited by presidents, most influential in governmental decision-making"—mistakenly showed that the program had no or even harmful effects. These mistakes could be made because the experimental and control groups were not equal—the experimental group consisted of the neediest children, whereas the control group included untreated, on average more able, children from the same community.

Researchers evaluating the effectiveness of social programs asked causal questions—what exactly causes the success or failure of this program?—that were considered to be most decisively answered by using experimental or quasi-experimental methods. Using Campbell's methods, evaluation researchers convinced policymakers that they could provide reliable and valid answers to their questions about "what works, why it works, for whom it works, and under what conditions it works." Their experimental and quasi-experimental evaluations generated the quantitative data that policymakers needed to decide whether or not to continue a social program. At the same time, the administrative preoccupation with measuring the effectiveness and efficiency of policies advanced the rise of evaluative experimentation.

The "Experimenting Society"

Campbell not only developed the methods for the evaluation of social programs, he also had an ideal society in mind in which these methods would be used properly. This ideal society was the "Experimenting Society." Campbell drew the contours of this society in articles with compelling titles like "Reforms as Experiments," "Methods for the Experimenting Society," and "The Social Scientist as Methodological Servant of the Experimenting Society." The first article opened with the bold statement that "the United States and other modern nations should be ready for an experimental approach to social reform." New policies should be tried and tested thoroughly—preferably using experimental methods—before implementation. Most importantly, this testing would have to be consequential. When a certain program or policy proved to be ineffective, it would have to be discarded to make space for another possible solution that *did* work.

The utopian Experimenting Society would, according to Campbell, be an honest society, nondogmatic, accountable, and above all scientific—not scientific in the sense that one scientific theory established as true would be used to make policy decisions, but rather that this society would value open criticism and experimentation and would be willing to change once-advocated theories or policies in the face of experimental evidence.

Campbell considered hard-headed policy evaluation to be crucial for the proper functioning of a democratic society. In his eyes, "to be truly scientific we must be able to experiment." Evaluation by using truly scientific, experimental methods was so important to him that he argued that society should be organized in a scientific way to make this evaluation possible. Scarce resources, such as vaccinations, should be distributed among the public at random. This ensured that their effectiveness could be tested thoroughly, because randomly composed groups would be available for experimentation. And, equally important, Campbell argued that allocating scarce resources randomly was most democratic—everyone would have an equal chance of receiving the benefit.

Cross-Cultural Psychology

Campbell not only became extremely successful in the multidisciplinary field of program evaluation, his quasi-experimental research methodology also was successfully introduced in other social sciences, such as sociology and economics. He even tried to extend his standardized methodology to a discipline that predominantly used qualitative research methods: cultural anthropology. This effort retrospectively made him one of the "founding fathers" of cross-cultural psychology, a subdiscipline between psychology and cultural anthropology.

Campbell constantly emphasized the need for psychologists to test their theories in the field and he argued that his quasi-experimental research methodology enabled them to do so. Using anthropological data to test psychological theories was to him a kind of quasi-experimentation. If, for example, one wanted to investigate the effects of different modes of child-rearing on personality formation, it would be impossible to conduct a randomized experiment. In these cases, anthropological data could form a quasi-experimental alternative to true experimentation.

However, before psychologists could use these anthropological data, they had to make sure that these data were reliable—at least according to their standards. Whereas psychologists were used to testing large groups of "respondents," anthropologists relied on qualitative data gathered from small groups of people. This made anthropological data less trustworthy in the eyes of psychologists. Campbell presented his methods as most useful for standardizing anthropologists' research efforts and detecting the factors that distorted results. With the help of others, he created field manuals: ready-made research designs to gather uniform data.

An example of such a field manual is *Materials for a Cross-Cultural Study of Perception*, by the anthropologist Melville Herskovits, Campbell, and Marshall Segall, developed for their study of differences in visual perception across cultures. Fieldworkers—cooperating anthropologists actually gathering the data—received very precise research instructions through the manual, such as exactly how to phrase their questions and from what angle and distance to show the images in the manual. In total, some 1878 respondents were questioned using this standardized research design.

Campbell was so satisfied with his "field manual method" that he decided to use it for investigating another topic, together with the anthropologist Robert LeVine. This was the topic of ethnocentrism. Campbell and LeVine developed an "Ethnocentrism Field Manual" to coordinate and standardize the collection of data by anthropologists participating in their cross-cultural study. The manual prescribed strict research procedures. It gave detailed instructions on how to choose informants and how to select interpreters and presented a uniform interview schedule. An example of one of the interview questions in the manual was the "Bipolar Trait Inquiry" asking interviewees to characterize members of other ethnic groups in dichotomies, such as peaceful or quarrelsome, hardworking or lazy, filthy or clean, stupid or intelligent, handsome or ugly. After data were gathered from approximately 20 societies all over the world, Campbell and LeVine's field manual was used to interview 1500 people in East Africa.

In these cross-cultural research projects, Campbell chose subjects interesting to psychologists, and most importantly, these projects were shaped by his quantitative, standardized methodology. The field manuals were developed to make sure that the experimental conditions were as uniform as possible to ensure reliable outcomes.

Conclusion

Campbell resigned from Northwestern University in 1979 at the age of 63. By then, he had become one of the leading figures in his field. In 1970, he was granted the Distinguished Scientific Contribution Award of the American Psychological Association, the organization of which he became President in 1975; he was a member of the National Academy of Sciences and was awarded quite a few honorary doctorates. However, his resignation from Northwestern was not a retirement. He accepted a position as Albert Schweitzer Professor at Syracuse University and a few years later he became University Professor of Sociology–Anthropology, Psychology, and Education at Lehigh University. Among other things, Campbell pursued his interest in the philosophy of science there. Throughout his career, Campbell had been interested in the theory of knowledge and, in particular, his concept of an evolutionary epistemology became rather well known.

In his work, Donald Campbell addressed a variety of issues. However, the pivotal question in all of his work was how to achieve trustworthy knowledge of the world. Campbell's answer was his methodology, which enabled social scientists to experiment outside the laboratory, in the field. Moreover, in a time when policymakers increasingly appealed to scientists to justify their decisions, Campbell convinced these policymakers that what he had to offer was exactly what they needed: methods that could decisively show what policy worked. This approach vastly expanded the scope of the applied social sciences and gave Campbell's work its significance.

See Also the Following Articles

Content Validity • Cross-Cultural Data Applicability and Comparisons • Ethnocentrism • Experiments, Overview • Quasi-Experiment • Validity Assessment • Validity, Data Sources

Further Reading

Brewer, M. B., and Collins, B. E. (eds.) (1981). *Scientific Inquiry and the Social Sciences*. Jossey-Bass, San Francisco, CA. [Contains a bibliography of Donald T. Campbell, 1947–1979.]

Capshew, J. H. (1999). *Psychologists on the March: Science, Practice, and Professional Identity in America, 1929–1969.* Cambridge University Press, New York.

Dehue, T. (1997). Deception, efficiency, and random groups: Psychology and the gradual origination of the random group design. *Isis* **88,** 653–673.

Dehue, T. (2001). Establishing the experimenting society: The historical origin of social experimentation according to the randomized controlled design. *Am. J. Psychol.* **114,** 283–302.

Dunn, W. N. (ed.) (1998). *The Experimenting Society: Essays in Honor of Donald T. Campbell*. Transaction Publishers, New Brunswick, NJ.

Herman, E. (1995). *The Romance of American Psychology. Political Culture in the Age of Experts.* University of California Press, Berkeley, CA.

Oakley, A. (2000). *Experiments in Knowing: Gender and Method in the Social Sciences.* Polity Press, Cambridge, UK.

Overman, E. S. (ed.) (1988). *Methodology and Epistemology for Social Science: Selected Papers of D. T. Campbell.* University of Chicago Press, Chicago, IL. [Contains a bibliography of Donald T. Campbell, 1947–1988.]

Shadish, W. R., Cook, T. D., and Leviton, L. C. (1991). *Foundations of Program Evaluation. Theories of Practice.* Sage, Newbury Park, CA.

Wuketits, F. M. (2001). The philosophy of Donald T. Campbell: A short review and critical appraisal. *Biol. Philos.* **16,** 171–188.

Case Study

Jack Glazier
Oberlin College, Oberlin, Ohio, USA

Glossary

ethnography Used synonymously with fieldwork, or the activity of the research anthropologist; also refers to the written result, usually in book form. Ethnography focuses on human behavior and belief within a well-defined community.

fieldwork The characteristic research endeavor of cultural anthropology, involving residence of the anthropologist within a community in order to collect data based on observation and informant testimony.

holism Understanding a community as a social unit in which beliefs, values, and institutional arrangements are integrated. A holistic perspective requires that the anthropologist see any segment of behavior or belief in its natural context—in relationship to other parts of the culture and to the whole.

informants Members of a community on whom anthropologists rely for answers to questions asked in formal interviews or, more commonly, through informal interactions during fieldwork. Informant testimony can complement, support, or contradict the behavioral data the anthropologist gathers through participant observation.

participant observation A major research activity of fieldworkers that includes their immersion in the daily routines of community life. As anthropologists become increasingly familiar to their hosts over the course of many months, the effect of their presence on the data collected should be minimized. Ideally, the participant observer attempts to learn about local custom under conditions that are as "natural" as possible.

There is a relationship between case study materials and ethnographic data, on the one hand, and culture theory, on the other. Data and theory exist in dynamic tension within the field of anthropology. Textured ethnographic detail gives the case study a distinctive quality, emphasizing cultural difference and limiting generalization. Broad comparisons, by contrast, reach for a high level of abstraction that permits more sweeping theoretical statements about cross-cultural convergences and regularities.

Introduction

The distinctive features of the anthropological case study in many respects capture the theoretical and methodological qualities of anthropology as a discipline. Accordingly, any discussion of the nature of anthropological case studies can proceed only by considering the general characteristics, methods, and goals of cultural anthropology. The case study in anthropology often but not exclusively represents an extended examination of the culture, or ways of life, of a particular group of people through fieldwork. The published case study is often referred to as an "ethnography." During the first half of the 20th century, that examination often covered a wide range of topics. The breadth of early ethnographic monographs partly reflected a desire to preserve a record of historic cultures in the process of momentous change under the colonial impact. At the same time, anthropologists were documenting the range and particularly the variation in human cultures. American anthropology for the first four decades of the 20th century utilized the rich data of ethnography to point up the unique character of individual cultures, thereby undermining universal explanatory schemes based on cultural evolutionism, biology, or alleged human psychological or temperamental constants. Where early universalist theories alleged singular lines of cultural and psychological development, 20th century anthropologists, up to the 1940s, were finding endless difference and variation.

Since the 1920s, writing comprehensive ethnographies has steadily given way to more focused, problem-oriented studies within a broad ethnographic framework that continues to emphasize difference over uniformity. Classic examples of early problem-oriented case studies are Margaret Mead's *Coming of Age in Samoa* and Bronislaw Malinowski's monographic examination of Freud's oedipal theory, *Sex and Repression in Savage Society*. Both Mead and Malinowski presented case studies characteristic of their time. Their work effectively overturned widely accepted explanations of putative human universals believed to be derivative of a shared biological substrate of the human species. Instead, Mead argued that the phenomenon of adolescence was an American cultural invention alien to the experience of the people of Samoa. Likewise, Malinowski demonstrated that the supposed universality of the oedipal complex was only an expression of a particular kind of family structure—the patriarchal organization familiar in Europe—unknown in matrilineal societies, such as in the Trobriand Islands. These two cases are emblematic of anthropology's abiding interest in cultural difference and the utility of ethnographic case material in challenging universalist claims.

The term "case study" may also refer to specific case material embedded within a larger ethnographic monograph. Here, detailed examples of dispute settlement in local legal procedures, richly documented ritual performances, and the like can effectively illuminate the dynamics of social life. Especially germane is the work of Max Gluckman, his students from the University of Manchester, and their colleagues who centered their ethnographic investigations in Zambia and other areas of Central Africa. Turner's concept of the "social drama," for example, emerged from his detailed case material about social situations of crisis among the Ndembu of Zambia, where breaches of widely accepted rules create crisis conditions threatening to sever ongoing social relationships. Through formalized ritual or legal procedure, efforts at redress either may successfully avert schism, by reconciling antagonists, or may lead to social separation. Turner's "social drama" strategy focused closely on the processes of community life as it concentrated on a limited cast of players within a village, their multiplex relationships, and their shifting structural positions over time. Other Central Africanists pioneered similar detailed processual research, also referred to as the "extended case method" and "situational analysis." In all instances, the emphasis lay on close description of the behavioral dynamics of real people and their complex social relationships.

Fieldwork

Though cultural anthropologists utilize multiple theoretical orientations and study a wide range of cultural topics, disciplinary characteristics suffusing the case study tradition can nonetheless be identified. That cultural anthropology varies internally according to the practitioners' theoretical perspectives, intellectual interests, and distinctive training could hardly be otherwise in light of the large number of cultural anthropologists, now constituting approximately one-third of the nearly 11,000 members of the American Anthropological Association (Richard Thomas, personal communication, March 27, 2002). Nonetheless, the professionalization of anthropology beginning a century ago created a common universe of discourse, unifying the discipline despite its very considerable internal diversity. Over the past 15 years, however, that unity has proved very tenuous as empirically committed anthropologists have struggled with determined postmodernists, who question the fundamental assumptions of empiricism and science. Until the emergence of that recent controversy, fieldwork and empirical methods lay at the center of common understandings about the nature of anthropology.

Through intense and sustained fieldwork, case studies provide fine-grained documentation of the ethnography of everyday life. However they have defined their investigations—problem-oriented research, descriptive ethnography, extended case studies, social dramas, situational analysis—cultural anthropologists have customarily conducted their research within functioning communities. The hallmark of the fieldwork tradition is sustained residence in a community for at least a year and sometimes longer. Fieldwork is so crucial that few anthropologists have achieved professional standing without it. The self-identity of cultural anthropology—indeed, the very esprit among cultural anthropologists—is predicated on the shared experience of this characteristic mode of investigation. Consequently, it is not unusual for anthropologists to liken their initial period in the field to a rite of passage.

The day-to-day activity of the anthropologist in the field entails participant observation and working with informants. Informants are members of the community under study who provide the anthropologist with data and insights about local cultural life. Because no one controls all the information pertinent to the culture, the anthropologist must rely on those who bring particular expertise to the questions he or she is asking. For example, reconstructing the system of age sets and generation classes that once were the centerpiece of the social structure of the Mbeere people of Kenya has depended on elderly male informants. Because the age and generational systems were decidedly male institutions that still enjoyed some vitality in the 1920s, when male elders in the early 1970s were young men, the male elders have provided the anthropologist with vital sources of information. Likewise, other individuals (ritual specialists) in Mbeere have helped the anthropologist understand many of the arcane beliefs surrounding funerary practice.

Anthropologists often distinguish between immersed informants and analytical informants. The immersed informant, like people everywhere, lives his or her life with very little cultural introspection or questioning of local assumptions. Without much secondary explanation, such people can provide the anthropologist with important information. The analytical informant, on the other hand, not only answers the anthropologist's ceaseless inquiries but also provides valuable commentary and critical assessment about local custom. The analytical informant shares with the anthropologist an interest in getting beneath the surface of events and beliefs to discern meanings that cannot be immediately grasped.

Besides learning about a culture through the testimony of informants, anthropologists also gather data through participant observation. This technique is an extension of daily, local routines in which the anthropologist is caught up. Whether he or she is participating in work parties, attending rituals and ceremonies, observing dispute settlement, recording narratives, playing games, or participating in other leisure activities, the anthropologist gathers information based on the agreeable fiction that he or she is a member of the community. Indeed, over the course of many months that can stretch into a year or two, the anthropologist aims to become a familiar part of the local scene, no longer viewed as a stranger. Seeking rapport within the community, the anthropologist hopes that the trust established through his or her engagement in community activities will bring with it an understanding of culture from the inside. Accordingly, speaking the local language as a result of prior study or, if that is not possible, learning it in the course of fieldwork is extremely important; it is through language that a culture is codified and its most subtle features are expressed and apprehended. To the extent that anthropologists enter into the flow of social life and develop personal relationships with informants, the entire experience feels and appears unique.

Given the centrality of the fieldwork tradition in anthropology and the concentration on communities very far removed from the anthropologist's native experience, ethnographic documentation of diverse ways of living—a focus on differences—is an integral feature of traditional anthropology, often serving as an end in itself. Difference and certainly uniqueness are at odds with generalizations explaining multiple cases. Anthropologists have generally subordinated abstraction and theory building to the task of data collection, documentation, and description. In the case study approach, therefore, ethnographic data should lead rather than follow theory development. In other words, coming to terms with distinct personalities and individuals whom anthropologists get to know intimately predisposes seasoned fieldworkers to preserve the detail, context, and integrity of their data. The case study further induces some skepticism about predictive models of human behavior, for human agency within the broad limits of culture represents a compelling anthropological reality. Still, the explanations and interpretations that do appear in anthropological monographs depend on a minimal level of abstraction and analysis. Recognizing an inevitable tension between ethnography and generalization, Geertz observes that many anthropologists prefer to "stay rather closer to the ground than tends to be the case in the sciences."

Ethnography and Theory

The fieldwork tradition that integrates the anthropologist into the life of a community is closely connected to the kinds of data the anthropologist collects. At the same time, the relationship between method and data distinguishes anthropology from other social sciences and points to the particular strengths and weakness of the case study.

Participant observation and working with informants are ways of getting detailed information, more qualitative than quantitative, about a localized community. These fundamental fieldwork techniques aim for a sharp, ethnographically focused picture—a case study in effect—of a social order seen in the round. The material an anthropologist gathers is bound up with the intensely personal nature of fieldwork bringing the researcher into close daily contact with people in the community. He or she typically sees the cultural world in terms of distinctive individuals, not anonymous social actors playing out normative cultural scripts.

Understandings achieved through informants and participant observation contrast sharply with modes of data acquisition in other social sciences, such as sociology, dependent as they are on quantitative analysis, surveys, and other impersonal research techniques. Sociologists aim, by and large, for predictive models that will explain recurrent behaviors and beliefs. To do so, however, inevitably creates a considerable distance between the theoretical model and the reality of human lives. This discrepancy is not likely to be troublesome if the data feeding the model have been gathered through impersonal techniques. Whereas sociology has outpaced anthropology in the development of social theory, it has shown much less inclination in presenting rounded human-centered portraits of actual communities. Aside from the ethnographically oriented work of a relatively few sociologists, the discipline of sociology has valued theory over cultural fact, conceptual formulation over ethnographic reporting, and scientific explanation over description—analytical endeavors far removed from the detail of the anthropological case study.

Anthropology reverses this scale of research values. The strength of the ethnographic case study in providing richly textured descriptions of human thought and action in context immediately exposes its primary theoretical constraint—more interest in cultural difference than in cultural similarity. Illuminating the oddities of a case places considerable limits on the anthropologist's ability to construct generalizations extending his or her findings to multiple ethnographic instances. Preferring to maintain the integrity of case material, many anthropologists opt for "experience near" as opposed to "experience distant" concepts. That is, the anthropologist's article or monograph stays close to the experience of the people and therefore limits the range and scope of generalization. By contrast, the more abstract, analytical efforts of sociology facilitate theory development through comparison and the analysis of similarity and recurrence; but the results, unlike those of the anthropological case study, are far removed from any specific ethnographic reality and community of real individuals. Whereas the anthropologist's findings illuminate the particularities of the case, any reader of the anthropologist's article or monograph may legitimately ask what light the case study can shed on ways of living in other places or in other times. Is the case representative of other cases and thus to some degree generalizable, or is it idiosyncratic and unique?

Cultural Similarities or Cultural Differences

Studies that effectively contribute to culture theory and the associated construction of generalizations are necessarily comparative, because theory entails an explanation of multiple cases of cultural regularity. But in extending the reach of the single case study, theory and generalization almost exist at cross-purposes with the ethnography of the single case. On the one hand, the case study stays very faithful to detail, to native perspectives, to the subtleties of the vernacular language of the community, and to the context of events considered in holistic fashion. That fidelity to detail inevitably gives each case study a very distinct character, because the particular content and concatenation of events, activities, personalities, informant statements, and the like are singular. The detailed ethnography deriving from fieldwork may well restrict theory development and broad comparisons, if one is bent on maintaining the integrity and holism of the data. For example, anthropological accounts of peoples as diverse as Cantonese villagers, Mundurucu or Yanomamo horticulturists in Brazil and Venezuela, Mbeere farmer/herders on the Mt. Kenya periphery, and Tikopia Islanders in Polynesia characterize them as "patrilineal." This designation refers to their mode of reckoning descent through the male line, ascending to father, grandfather, and so on, to an apical ancestor. Men and women descended from that ancestor through male links belong to a patrilineal group—a lineage, a clan, or a moiety. In this respect, the five peoples cited as well as many others appear similar in regard to their construction of critical descent groups. The particular native designations of these male-descended kin groups are vastly different and the connotations of the various terms as well as the particular role the kin groups play are different in each case.

Differences between the Cantonese and the Mbeere amid the common theme of patrilineal descent are illustrative. The Cantonese lineage, a corporate patrilineal group of considerable genealogical depth, is extremely important in the death rituals of its members. The lineage represents a kind of kin-based religious congregation charged with venerating male ancestors of the lineage. By contrast, the Mbeere patrilineage in no sense constitutes a religious congregation responsible for either collective ritual at the death of a member or, subsequently, collective commemorative rites. Compared to the Cantonese, it is weakly corporate and genealogically shallow. Yet both represent examples of patrilineal descent groups organized by common principles. The Cantonese and the Mbeere are two examples among hundreds of societies that anthropologists classify as "patrilineal." Some anthropologists are, accordingly, very interested in the comparative problem of explaining the social circumstances promoting the widespread development of patrilineal descent, as documented in large cross-cultural samples. What is at play here is the chronic tension between the ethnographic case study and comparative analysis aiming for a theoretical explanation of multiple occurrences. The decision to remain close to the ethnographic facts or to integrate them into a more generalized explanation simply depends on the anthropologist's intention. A cultural system is unique and at the same time similar to other cultural systems, however self-contradictory this may seem. It all depends on the level of abstraction at which the anthropologist chooses to work. For example, the Mbeere and the Cantonese are unique among the world's cultures, because no other communities reproduce the distinct configuration of customary practices and organizational features defining each case. Indeed, even distinct Cantonese villages or Mbeere local communities assume their own individuality in the finest grained ethnographic descriptions of each people. The area inhabited by the Mbeere people is, for example, characterized by variation in local ecology based on elevation and rainfall. The arid plains constitute an ecological zone distinct from the much better watered upland areas, and these in turn lead to important internal differences in patrilineal organization.

Conclusion

The depiction of anthropology as a discipline traditionally more concerned with the uniqueness of case study material than with generalizations about culture of course requires qualification. Though ethnographic study holds a venerable place within anthropology, comparative research is very important. Comparison serves several ends that can emphasize either cultural differences or similarities. For example, the Human Relations Area Files (HRAF) developed since the 1930s have provided a vast compendium of ethnographic data for comparative research based on large cross-cultural samples. The easy accessibility of data through the HRAF depends on a coding process for classifying diverse ethnographic information into analytical categories—lineages, exchange transactions, cosmology, residence, and the like. In the process of comparing cultural features subsumed by such categories and testing hypotheses about recurrence and regularity within large samples, anthropologists necessarily lose something of the context and meaning defining the original material.

Comparison may also occur on a much smaller scale. The comparison of a limited number of societies—perhaps only three or four drawn from the same cultural area—characterized what Eggan called "the method of controlled comparison." This style of research offered very restricted, low-level generalizations that did not completely jettison either the context or the particularity of the case study materials that were compared. The particular and the general are best thought of as opposite points along a continuum marking different degrees of abstraction.

In their introduction to four ethnographic case studies of American Indian peoples, George and Louise Spindler capture the value of the case study in the terms emphasized in this article: "A student reading these four studies will understand much about the great diversity of native North America. No outline of culture patterns alone can do this. The studies . . . are complete enough so that one is not left with that unsatisfied feeling that one has gotten only the formal surface features. Each study is written with attention to living detail." Others might be more inclined to look for common cultural occurrences in the collected case studies. But whether the primary interest is in cultural differences or similarities, the ethnographic case study and theories of cultural recurrence exist in creative opposition to each other and define in part the dynamic character of anthropology.

See Also the Following Articles

Anthropology, Psychological • Basic vs. Applied Social Science Research • Ethnography • Field Experimentation • Observational Studies • Qualitative Analysis, Anthropology • Quantitative Analysis, Anthropology

Further Reading

Barrett, R. A. (1991). *Culture and Conduct,* 2nd Ed. Wadsworth, Belmont, California.

Eggan, F. (1954). Social anthropology and the method of controlled comparison. *Am. Anthropol.* **56,** 743–763.

Geertz, C. (1973). Thick description: Toward an interpretative theory of culture. In *The Interpretation of Cultures,* pp. 3–30. Basic Books, New York.

Glazier, J. (1976). Generation classes among the Mbeere of Central Kenya. *Africa* **46**(4), 313–325.

Glazier, J. (1984). Mbeere ancestors and the domestication of death. *Man* **19**(No. 1), 133–147.

Gluckman, M. (1961). Ethnographic data in British social anthropology. *Sociol. Rev.* **9,** 5–17.

Haines, D. (ed.) (1996). *Case Studies in Diversity: Refugees in America in the 1990s*. Praeger, Westport, Connecticut.

Mitchell, J. C. (2000). Case and situation analysis. In *Case Study Method: Key Issues, Key Texts* (R. Gomm, M. Hammersley, and P. Foster, eds.), pp. 165–186. Sage, London.

Spindler, G., and Spindler, L. (eds.) (1977). *Native North American Cultures: Four Cases*. Holt, Rinehart, and Winston, New York.

Turner, V. W. (1957). *Schism and Continuity in an African Society*. Manchester University Press, Manchester.

Van Velsen, J. (1967). The extended-case method and situational analysis. In *The Craft of Social Anthropology* (A. L. Epstein, ed.), pp. 129–149. Tavistock Publ., London.

Watson, J. L. (1975). *Emigration and the Chinese Lineage*. University of California Press, Berkeley.

Watson, J. L. (1982). Of flesh and bones: The management of death pollution in Cantonese society. In *Death and the Regeneration of Life* (M. Bloch and J. Parry, eds.), pp. 155–186.

Categorical Modeling/ Automatic Interaction Detection

William A. V. Clark

University of California, Los Angeles, Los Angeles, California, USA

Marinus C. Deurloo

University of Amsterdam, Amsterdam, The Netherlands

Glossary

artificial neural network A type of data mining technique, based on biological processes, for efficiently modeling large and complex problems.

chi-square automatic interaction detection A method tailored to finding structure in high-dimensional categorical spaces where the dependent variable is also categorical.

data mining A mathematical and statistical tool for pattern recognition.

decision trees Methods of representing a series of rules.

entropy A measure of diversity for nominal variables.

entropy-based relevance analysis A simple data mining method for categorical variables. It identifies variables and their categories that are highly relevant to the prediction, reduces the number of variables and their categories in prediction, and improves both efficiency and reliability of prediction.

proportional reduction in error A criterion that has been used for choosing among the various conventional measures of association between variables.

Modeling strategies for categorical data encompass a wide range of data mining techniques; these strategies use the power of modern high-speed computers to discover meaningful patterns and relationships in large data sets.

Introduction

Until the 1980s, most statistical techniques were based on elegant theory and analytical methods that worked well on the modest amounts of data being analyzed. They relied on the modeler to specify the functional form and the nature of the variable interactions. The increased power of computers, coupled with the need to analyze very large data sets, has allowed the development of new techniques based on a "brute-force" exploration of possible solutions. These new extensions of statistical methods, called data mining techniques, can approximate almost any functional form or interaction. Basically, data mining is the analysis of data and use of software techniques for discovering meaningful patterns, relationships, and trends by sifting through large amounts of data. Data mining uses pattern recognition technologies as well as statistical and mathematical techniques. The result is a description of the data that can be confidently used for valid prediction. Whereas statistical modeling produces an outcome that explains the different types of behavior of all the data, data mining identifies patterns of behavior for some (but not for all) of the data. Data mining became very popular after 1990, with the rise of accessible detailed data sets and the need of better prediction of consumer behavior.

The discussion here is restricted to methods that can be used for prediction, usually the main goal of data analysis. These methods use existing values to forecast what other values will be. Most of the numerous models of data mining can be thought of as generalizations of the statistical workhorse of prediction, the linear regression model. Unfortunately, many real-world problems are not simply linear projections of previous values. Specifically, many dependent variables are difficult to predict because they may depend on complex interactions of multiple predictor variables. This is especially true for situations with categorical variables. Though logistic regression is a powerful modeling tool that predicts the proportions of a categorical dependent variable, it assumes that the response variable is linear in the coefficients of the predictor variables. The modeler must choose the correct inputs and specify their functional relationship to the response variable. Additionally, the modeler must explicitly add terms for any interaction. It is up to the model builder to search for the right variables, find their correct expression, and account for possible interactions.

A great deal of effort in the statistics, computer science, artificial intelligence, and engineering communities has been devoted to overcoming the limitations of the basic regression model. An alternative approach with modern technologies is to use data-driven pattern-finding methods rather than user-driven approaches. In data mining, relationships are found inductively by the software, based on the existing data. The two most well-known data mining techniques are decision tree methods and artificial neural networks. Both techniques are examined here. One decision tree method, the chi-square automatic interaction detection (CHAID), is assessed because such methods are tailored to finding structure in high-dimensional categorical spaces where the dependent variable is also categorical. Furthermore, decision tree methodology appears to offer the most advantages—a competitive predictive accuracy and minimal assumptions about data. Neural network methods can handle both categorical and continuous independent variables without banding; however, the dependent variable is usually continuous, and it may be difficult to transform it to a discrete categorical outcome.

The discussion begins with a relatively little known data mining method for categorical variables; this very simple technique, entropy-based relevance analysis, needs no special software.

Entropy-Based Relevance Analysis

Creating a predictive model from a large data set is not straightforward. Most of the variables are redundant or irrelevant, so a preliminary task is to determine which variables are likely to be predictive. A common practice is to exclude independent variables with little correlation to the dependent variable. A good start perhaps, but such methods take little notice of redundancy among the variables or of any relationship with the dependent variable involving more than one independent variable. Moreover, categorical variables are often handled awkwardly. Entropy-based relevance analysis (ERA) is a simple method that identifies variables and their categories that are highly relevant to the prediction, reduces the number of variables and attributes in prediction, and improves both efficiency and reliability of prediction.

The ERA measure is based on the entropy (H) statistic as a measure of the variation of a nominal discrete variable, X:

$$H(X) = -\sum_i p_i \ln p_i, \tag{1}$$

where p_i is the probability of an observation belonging to category i of X, and $p_i \ln p_i = 0$ for $p_i = 0$. Definition (1) can be generalized to multivariate distributions by letting the index i run over all cells of the relevant multivariate cross-tabulation. For a two-dimensional table,

$$H(XY) = -\sum_{i,j} p_{ij} \ln p_{ij}, \tag{2}$$

where p_{ij} is the probability of an observation belonging to category i of X and category j of Y. It can be shown that definition (2) can be written as

$$H(XY) = H(X) + H(Y) - I(XY), \tag{3}$$

with

$$I(XY) = \sum_{i,j} p_{ij} \ln\left(\frac{p_{ij}}{p_{i\cdot} \times p_{\cdot j}}\right) \quad \text{and}$$
$$p_{i\cdot} = \sum_j p_{ij}. \tag{4}$$

$I(XY)$ is called the transmitted information between X and Y. If Y is dependent on X and if the variation of Y is measured by $H(Y)$, it can further be shown that $I(XY)$ can be considered as the variation in Y that is explained by X. The ERA of Y is defined as the ratio of $I(XY)$ to $H(Y)$:

$$\mathrm{ERA}_{XY} = \frac{I(XY)}{H(Y)}. \tag{5}$$

One of the most appealing properties of ERA is that it takes values between 0 and 1. ERA is equal to 0 if and only if the variable to be explained is independent of the explanatory variables, and ERA is 1 if and only if the dependent variable can be predicted with certainty, given the values of the observations on the independent variables. This can occur only when the dependent variable has the same or fewer categories than each of the independent variables, and then occurs when each combination of categories of the independent variables scores on just one category of the dependent variable.

There is a strong analogy between the ERA and the coefficient of determination (the square of Pearson's correlation coefficient, R^2) for continuous variables. For example, the partial ERA of Y explained by X, given Z, is

$$\mathrm{ERA}_{Y\cdot Z|X} = \mathrm{ERA}_{Y|XZ} - \mathrm{ERA}_{Y|Z}. \tag{6}$$

Like R^2, the ERA is a so-called proportional reduction in error (PRE) measure. The PRE criterion has been used for choosing among the various conventional measures of association between variables, because it always has a clear interpretation, irrespective of the distribution and the level of measurement of the data. It can also be shown that ERA is related to the likelihood ratio statistic G^2:

$$I(XY) = \frac{G^2}{2n}, \quad (7)$$

where n is the number of observations. Equation (7) is used extensively in the modeling strategy as a test of the efficacy of the process. In addition to the ERA of a particular set of variables, the associated G^2 is examined in a real-world example in Section VI to judge if there are significant differences between one set of variables and categories, and a previous set of variables and categories.

The selection of variables and the reduction of the number of categories occur stepwise. The independent variable with the highest ERA is selected and the loss in the ERA for each (permitted) combination of pairs of categories is then examined. The combination with the lowest decrease in the ERA in the table is selected. The combining process is continued until the resulting ERA drops off sharply (indicated mostly by a significant loss in G^2 at the 1% significance level). This reduced category variable is the first explanatory variable. Additional variables are selected and combined in the same manner, and finally added to the model (normally only if there is a significant increase in G^2 at the 1% significance level). This method of variable selection and category combination is one procedure for obtaining reasonable subsets of cross-tabulations. [The ERA analysis can be accomplished with the Crosstabs procedure in Statistical Package for the Social Sciences (SPSS) software. The uncertainty coefficient in the Crosstabs procedure is equivalent to the ERA.] The ERA method does not attempt to find the best selection of categories and variables. It is therefore a heuristic method, because it does not guarantee optimality. An example of the use of ERA is presented in Section VI.

Decision Trees

Decision tree methods are both data mining techniques and statistical models and are used successfully for prediction purposes. Decision trees were developed by Morgan and Sonquist in 1963 in their search for the determinants of social conditions. In one example, they tried to untangle the influence of age, education, ethnicity, and profession on a person's income. Their "best" regression contained 30 terms (including interactions) and accounted for only 36% of the variance. As an alternative to regression, they organized the observations into 21 groups. The income of an observation in a group was estimated by the group mean. The groups were defined by values on only two or three inputs. Nonwhite high school graduates had a mean income of $5005. White farmers who did not finish high school had a mean income of $3950 and so on. This method of prediction accounted for 67% of the variance. The study showed the inadequacy of regression to discern the underlying relationships in the data, how common the problem is in social research, and how easily decision trees get around it.

Decision trees are a way of representing a series of rules that lead to a class or value. For example, the goal may be to classify a group of householders who have moved to a new house, based on their choice of type of the new dwelling. A simple decision tree can solve this problem and illustrate all the basic components of a decision tree (the decision nodes, branches, and leaves). A number of different algorithms may be used for building decision trees. Some methods generate a binary tree with only two branches at each node. Other methods allow more than two branches, creating a multiway tree. Each branch will lead to another decision node or to the bottom of the tree, called a leaf node. By navigating the decision tree, it is possible to assign a value or class to a case by deciding which branch to take, starting at the root node and moving to each subsequent node until a leaf node is reached. Each node uses the data from the case to choose the appropriate branch. Decision trees are appealing because of their clear depiction of how a few inputs determine target groups.

Decision trees are "grown" through iterative splitting of data into discrete groups, where the goal is to maximize the "distance" between groups at each split. One of the distinctions between decision tree methods is how they measure the "distance." Each split can be thought of as separating the data into new groups, which are as different from each other as possible. Decision trees that are used to predict categorical variables are called classification trees because they place cases in categories or classes. Decision trees used to predict continuous variables are called regression trees. Tree size can be controlled via stopping rules that limit growth. One common stopping rule is to establish a lower limit on the number of cases in a node, allowing no splits below this limit.

The original tree program in the statistical community, automatic interaction detection (AID), created by Morgan and Sonquist in 1963, finds binary splits on ordinal and nominal independent variables that most reduce the sum of squares of an interval dependent variable from its mean. The best split is always found. AID attempts splits on nodes with the larger sum of squares first, so that the program may stop after splitting some number of nodes specified by the user. The program stops when the reduction in the sum of squares is less than some constant times the overall sum of squares.

Chi-Square Automatic Interaction Detection

The chi-square automatic interaction detection is currently the most popular classification tree method. CHAID is much broader in scope than AID and can also be applied when the dependent variable is categorical. The algorithm that is used in the CHAID model splits records into groups with the same probability of the outcome, based on values of independent variables. Branching may be binary, ternary, or more. The splits are determined using the chi-squared test. This test is undertaken on a cross-tabulation between the dependent variable and each of the independent variables. The result of the test is a "p-value," which is the probability that the relationship is spurious. The p-values for each cross-tabulation of all the independent variables are then ranked, and if the best (the smallest value) is below a specific threshold, then that independent variable is chosen to split the root tree node. This testing and splitting is continued for each tree node, building a tree. As the branches get longer, there are fewer independent variables available because the rest have already been used further up the branch. The splitting stops when the best p-value is not below the specific threshold. The leaf tree nodes of the tree are tree nodes that did not have any splits, with p-values below the specific threshold, or all independent variables are used. Like entropy-based relevance analysis, CHAID also deals with a simplification of the categories of independent variables. For a given $r \times c_j$ cross-table ($r \geq 2$ categories of the dependent variable, $c_j \geq 2$ categories of a predictor), the method looks for the most significant $r \times d_j$ table ($1 \leq d_j \leq c_j$). When there are many predictors, it is not realistic to explore all possible ways of reduction. Therefore, CHAID uses a method that gives satisfactory results but does not guarantee an optimal solution. This method is derived from that used in stepwise regression analysis for judging if a variable should be included or excluded. The process begins by finding the two categories of the predictor for which the $r \times 2$ subtable has the lowest significance. If this significance is below a certain user-defined threshold value, the two categories are merged. This process is repeated until no further merging can be achieved. In a following step, each resulting category composed of three or more of the original categories is checked; if the most significant split of the compound category rises above a certain chosen threshold value, the split is carried into effect and the previous step is entered again (this extra step ensures a better approximation of the optimal solution). Both steps are repeated until no further improvement is obtained. This procedure is executed for each predictor. For each predictor optimally merged in this way, the significance is calculated and the most significant one is selected. If this significance is higher than a criterion value, the data are divided according to the (merged) categories of the chosen predictor. The method is applied to each subgroup, until eventually the number of objects left over within the subgroup becomes too small.

The great strength of a CHAID analysis is that the form of a CHAID tree is intuitive. Users can confirm the rationale of the model. The most important predictors can easily be identified and understood. Also, a CHAID model can be used in conjunction with more complex models. As with many data mining techniques, CHAID needs rather large volumes of data to ensure that the number of observations in the leaf tree nodes is large enough to be significant. Furthermore, continuous independent variables, such as income, must be banded into categorical-like classes prior to being used in CHAID. CHAID can be used alone or can be used to identify independent variables or subpopulations for further modeling using different techniques, such as regression, artificial neural networks, or genetic algorithms. A real-world example of the use of CHAID is presented in Section VI.

Artificial Neural Networks

An artificial neural network (ANN) is another popular type of data mining technique. ANNs originate from attempts to model biological processes using computers. Neural networks offer a means of efficiently modeling large and complex problems in which there may be hundreds of predictor variables that have many interactions. Neural nets may be used for regressions (where the dependent variable is continuous), but also in classification problems (where the dependent variable is a categorical variable).

A neural network (Fig. 1) starts with an input layer, where each node corresponds to an independent variable. Each of the input nodes is connected to every node in a hidden layer. The nodes in the hidden layer may be connected to nodes in another hidden layer, or to an output layer. The output layer consists of one or more dependent variables. The input nodes (and output nodes) must have values between 0 and 1; therefore, transformations are used to convert independent categorical and continuous variables into this range.

After the input layer, each node takes in a set of inputs, multiplies them by a connection weight W_{XY} (e.g., the weight from node 1 to 3 is W_{13}; see Fig. 2), adds them together, applies a so-called activation or squashing function to them, and passes the output to the node(s) in the

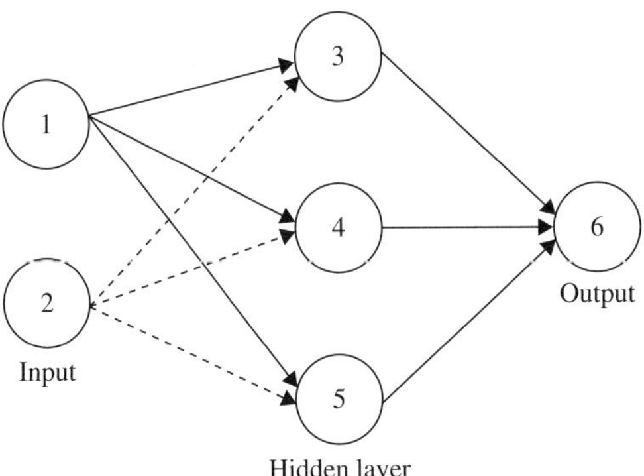

Figure 1 A neural network with one hidden layer.

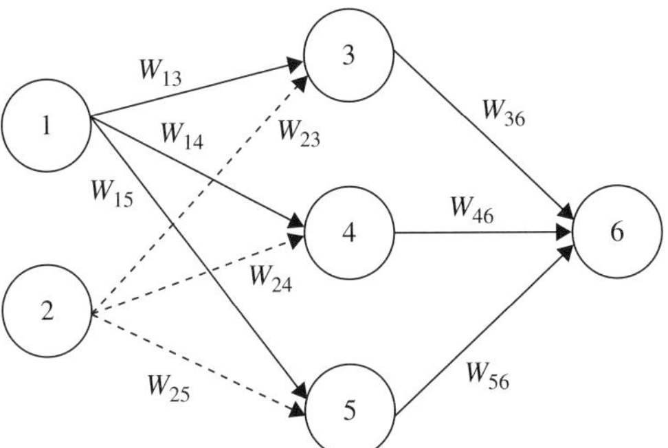

Figure 2 A neural network with weights; W_{XY} is the weight from node X to node Y.

next layer. For example, the value passed from node 4 to node 6 is as follows:

Activation function applied to $[(W_{14} \cdot \text{value of node 1}) + (W_{24} \cdot \text{value of node 2})]$.

Each node may be viewed as an independent variable (nodes 1 and 2 in this example) or as a combination of independent variables (nodes 3 through 6). Node 6 is a nonlinear combination of the values of nodes 1 and 2 because of the activation function on the summed values at the hidden nodes. In fact, if there is a linear activation function but no hidden layer, neural nets are equivalent to linear regression; with certain nonlinear activation functions, neural nets are equivalent to logistic regression. The connection weights (W values) are the unknown parameters, which are estimated by using existing data with one of the available estimation methods.

In designing a neural network, either the user or the software must choose the number of hidden nodes and hidden layers, the activation function, and limits on the weights. For simplicity of discussion here, assume a single hidden layer. One of the most common methods proceeds as follows:

1. The value of the output node is calculated based on the input node values and a set of initial weights. The values from the input nodes are combined in the hidden layer, and the values of those nodes are combined to calculate the output value.
2. The error in the output is computed by finding the difference between the calculated output and the actual values found in the data set. The error is distributed proportionally to their weights over the hidden layer nodes. The errors of the output node and the hidden nodes are used to adjust the weight coming into each of these nodes to reduce the error.
3. The process is repeated for each case in the data set. The data set will be passed through again and again, until the error no longer decreases.

Neural networks differ from many statistical methods in several ways. First, a neural network usually has more parameters than does a typical statistical model. For example, there are 13 parameters (9 weights and 4 constant terms) in the neural network shown in Fig. 2. In fact, a given result can be associated with several different sets of weights. Consequently, the network weights in general do not aid in understanding the underlying process generating the prediction. However, this is acceptable in many applications.

There are several critical issues or problems for those who use neural networks. First, neural networks are not easily interpreted. There is no explicit rationale given for the decisions or predictions a neural network makes. Second, they tend to overfit the data set unless very stringent measures are used judiciously. This is due to the very large number of parameters of the neural network, which, if allowed to be of sufficient size, will fit any arbitrary data set well. Finally, neural networks tend to work best when the data set is sufficiently large and the data are reasonably highly structured. Because they are so flexible, they will find many false patterns in a low-structured data set. Thus, on the one hand, ANNs can handle both categorical and continuous independent variables without banding, and can produce a model even in very complex situations because an ANN uses its hidden layers to estimate the forms of the nonlinear terms and interaction. On the other hand, the input requires that several parameters be set up prior to initiating processing (for instance, the number of hidden layers and the number of nodes per hidden layer). These parameters affect the model built. Furthermore, it is extremely difficult to explain the resulting set of weights, because they have no intuitive meaning.

An Application in the Social Sciences

Consider the question of understanding the variation in housing choice: the choice is between renting a single-family home, renting an apartment in a multiunit structure, and owning, for householders who have moved out of a rented house. What variables go into understanding the choices of these households? There are three choices: own, rent an apartment, or rent a house. The three choices can be influenced by variables that measure household characteristics, including income (four categories), age (four categories), and size of household (four categories). In addition, the characteristics of the previous tenure type will likely influence the new choice: previous tenure type (two categories, considering only renters in public or private rental housing), size of the previous dwelling (four categories), type of previous dwelling (two categories), and the rent of the previous dwelling (five categories). Finally, the location of the unit is important; the data from The Netherlands, summarized in Table I, cover four regions.

The abbreviated data in Table I show the steps, the ERA value, and the final derived classification. The intermediate steps in selecting the final categorization are omitted because of space limitations. The procedure is a combination of forward and backward steps. Income is selected as the first variable and various combinations of the original income categories are examined (all permitted possibilities are only shown for the first step of this first categorization). At succeeding steps, additional variables are chosen and their categories are simplified. (The simplification of additional variables is not included in this abbreviated table.) The decision-making with respect to variable choice and variable simplification rests on the change in the ERA value, and the likelihood ratio statistic G^2 can be used to assess whether further simplification should be pursued. For example, in the income case, if any simplification would involve collapsing categories 1 and 2, this would generate the lowest decrease. However, the reduction in the ERA is quite large and there is a substantial decrease in G^2. The test suggests that income should maintain all four categories. No variables are added after step 3, but further possibilities of combining income categories are explored in the "backward" step 4. The values of ERA show possible alternative combinations of categories, which marginally decrease the ERA and of course reduce the number of categories in the analysis. In this example, the original cross-tabulation of income, housing market, and size of household had 192 cells and an ERA value of 0.219. The final result after step 4 is a table with no more than 54 cells, whereas the ERA value has been only slightly reduced, from 0.219 to 0.192.

CHAID also proceeds in a step-down fashion. The variables are selected in a forward fashion as in the ERA (Fig. 3). In the CHAID procedure, categories of an independent variable are merged if they have a comparable pattern of choices and it is permitted to combine them. As said previously, the technique provides

Table I Reducing a Large Cross-Tabulation on Housing with Entropy-Based Relevance Analysis (ERA)[a]

Independent variables	*ERA*	G^2
Step 1A: Selection of the first variable		
Income (4 categories)	0.111	710.4
Age of the head of household (4 categories)	0.064	409.5
Size of household (4 categories)	0.052	330.8
Rent of previous dwelling (5 categories)	0.039	248.8
Type of housing market (4 categories)	0.035	222.5
Number of rooms in previous dwelling (4 categories)	0.024	156.2
Type of previous dwelling (2 categories)	0.015	93.7
Tenure of previous dwelling (2 categories)	0.007	43.0
Step 1B: Income category simplification		
Income 1 + 2, 3, 4	0.103	658.8
Income 1, 2 + 3, 4	0.088	561.0
Income 1, 2, 3 + 4	0.091	581.9
Step 2A: Selection of the second variable		
Housing market	0.155	995.1
Step 2B: Simplification		
Housing market 1 + 2 + 3, 4	0.152	973.2
Step 3A: Selection of the third variable		
Size of household	0.203	1301.3
Step 3B: Simplification		
Size of household 1, 2, 3 + 4	0.199	1277.7
Step 4: Further simplification of income		
Income 1 + 2, 3, 4	0.192	1230.5

[a] Adapted and modified from Clark *et al.* (1988), by permission of the Ohio State University Press.

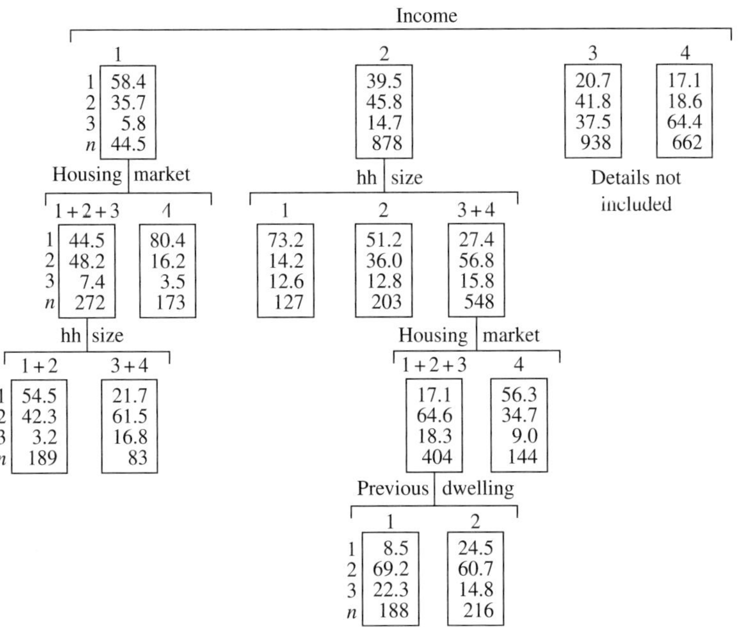

Figure 3 Chi-square automatic interaction detection dendrogram for influences on housing choice for previous renters (hh, household). Figure values are the percentages moving to each destination category: 1, multifamily rent; 2, single-family rent; or 3, owner occupied; *n* is the sample size. Adapted and modified from Clark *et al.* (1988), by permission of the Ohio State University Press.

optimal splits by maximizing the significance of the chi-square statistics at each step. For each of the categories of an independent variable selected in a previous step, the CHAID technique considers the most important predictor in the next step. Thus, the process "nests" the results and the end product can be presented as a tree (Fig. 3). As in ERA, in this example, the CHAID procedure selects income as the most important predictor and does not simplify the variable (only further splitting is shown for the first two categories of income in this presentation). Both housing market type and the size of the household are important predictors at the second and third stages for these low-income groups. Interesting additional information is contained in the way in which the two variables alternate in their contributions at different levels. Because the results from the CHAID analysis emphasize nesting of the independent variables within categories, the results suggest alternate lines of inquiry for a model of the data structure.

Observations for Data Mining

Categorical techniques have become more popular as the amount of survey data has increased, because much of those data involves measures of events that are discrete choices—moving or staying, owning or renting, a birth or marriage occurring—and so on. Such discrete nonmetric conditions require models that can relate the discrete choice to a variety of independent variables, which may also be discrete or metric. An additional important reason to examine categorical methods is that they provide a sophisticated way of parsimoniously describing large tables. Previously, such tables were often only rudimentarily analyzed, or simply described. Now, with some of the exploratory table analyses outlined here, it is possible to provide a better interpretation of large-scale data tables and to reduce the amount of information for further analysis.

The predictive relationships found via data mining should not be confused with the causes of behavior. To ensure meaningful results, it is vital that the results of a data mining exercise be imbedded in theory and that the data at hand are understood. Entropy-based relevance analysis is a simple but useful method to greatly reduce the size of a large categorical data set. It efficiently removes variables and categories that would otherwise possibly confuse the modeling process; the end result is a more interpretable model and a better understanding of the underlying processes.

Both CHAID and ANNs can be used to create predictive models. When all or most of the independent variables are continuous, ANNs should perform better than CHAID. When all or most of the independent variables are categorical, with high numbers of categories and implicitly containing relationships, CHAID should perform better than ANNs.

Software for Data Mining

In addition to the techniques discussed here, many other methods can be performed with a variety of data mining software. Such software is available from the well-known statistical software vendors, including SAS Institute Inc. and SPSS Inc.

AnswerTree is an SPSS product used to create decision trees. Four basic decision tree algorithms are used. Included are two CHAID algorithms, both of which SPSS has extended to handle nominal categorical, ordinal categorical, and continuous dependent variables.

Clementine, another SPSS product, has functions for association rules, classification, clustering, factor analysis, forecasting, prediction, and sequence discovery. Available techniques are Apriori, BIRCH, CARMA, Decision trees (C5.0; C&RT, a variation of CART), K-means clustering, neural networks (Kohonen, MLP, RBFN), regression (linear, logistic), and rule induction (C5.0, GRI). Perhaps the most unique feature of Clementine is its graphical user interface approach to data mining.

Enterprise Miner, available from SAS Institute Inc., has functions for association rules, classification, clustering, prediction, and time series. Available techniques are decision trees (CART, CHAID), K nearest neighbors, regression (linear, logistic), memory-based reasoning, and neural networks (Kohonen, MLP, RBF, SOM). An icon-based, point-and-click graphical user interface (not unlike SPSS's Clementine) creates a process flow to be performed by the data mining task.

See Also the Following Articles

Data Mining • Network Analysis

Further Reading

Abdi, H., Valentin, D., and Edelman, B. (1999). *Neural Networks, Quantitative Applications in the Social Sciences,* Vol. 124. Sage, London.

Clark, W. A. V., and Dieleman, F. M. (1996). *Households and Housing: Choice and Outcomes in the Housing Market.* Rutgers University Press, New Brunswick.

Clark, W. A. V., Deurloo, M. C., and Dieleman, F. M. (1988). Modeling strategies for categorical data: Examples from housing and tenure choice. *Geogr. Anal.* **20,** 198–219.

Deurloo, M. C. (1987). *A Multivariate Analysis of Residential Mobility.* Ph.D. dissertation. Amsterdam.

Deurloo, M. C., Dieleman, F. M., and Clark, W. A. V. (1987). Tenure choice in the Dutch housing market. *Environ. Plan. A* **19,** 763–781.

Fayad, U. M., Piatetsky-Shapiro, G., and Smyth, P. (1996). From data mining to knowledge discovery in databases. *AI Mag.; Am. Assoc. Artific. Intell.* (Fall 1996), 37–54.

Garson, G. D. (1998). *Neural Networks: An Introductory Guide for Social Scientists.* Sage, London.

Hays, W. L. (1980). *Statistics for the Social Sciences,* 2nd Ed. Holt, Rinehart and Winston, Chichester, Sussex.

Kass, G. V. (1980). An exploratory technique for investigating large quantities of categorical data. *Appl. Statist.* **29,** 119–127.

Kim, J. (1971). Predictive measures of ordinal association. *Am. J. Sociol.* **76,** 891–907.

Kim, J. (1984). PRU measure of association for contingency table analysis. *Sociol. Meth. Res.* **13,** 5–44.

Meraviglia, C. (1996). Models of representation of social mobility and inequality systems: A neural network approach. *Qual. Quant.* **30**(3), 231–252.

Morgan, J. N., and Sonquist, J. A. (1963). Problems in the analysis of survey data, and a proposal. *J. Am. Statist. Assoc.* **58,** 415–434.

Nie, N. H., Hull, C. H., Jenkins, J. G., Steinbrenner, K., and Bent, D. H. (1975). *Statistical Package for the Social Sciences,* 2nd Ed. McGraw Hill, New York.

Padraic, G. N. (1999). *Decision Trees for Predictive Modeling.* SAS Institute Inc, Cary, North Carolina.

Ripley, B. D. (1994). Neural networks and related methods for classification. *J. Roy. Statist. Soc. B* **56**(3), 409–456.

Ripley, B. D. (1996). *Pattern Recognition and Neural Networks.* Cambridge University Press, Cambridge.

Schrodt, P. A. (1991). Prediction of interstate conflict outcomes using a neural network. *Social Sci. Comput. Rev.* **9**(3), 359–380.

Sonquist, J. A., and Morgan, J. N. (1964). *The Detection of Interaction Effects.* Institute for Social Research, University of Michigan, Ann Arbor.

Two Crows Corporation (1999). *Introduction to Data Mining and Knowledge Discovery,* 3rd Ed. Two Crows Corp., Potomac, Maryland.

Causal Inference

Alberto Abadie

Harvard University, Cambridge, Massachusetts, USA

Glossary

assignment mechanism The process that determines which units are exposed to a particular treatment.

covariate A variable not affected by the treatment.

experimental study A study that uses experimental data.

observational study A study that uses nonexperimental data.

outcome The variable possibly affected by the treatment.

treatment A variable, the effects of which are the objects of study.

Causal inference comprises a set of tools that aid researchers in identifying and measuring causal relationships from data using background knowledge or assumptions about the process that generates the data to disentangle causation from association.

Introduction

Establishing causal relationships is an important goal of empirical research in social sciences. Unfortunately, specific causal links from one variable, D, to another, Y, cannot usually be assessed from the observed association between the two variables. The reason is that at least part of the observed association between two variables may arise by reverse causation (the effect of Y on D) or by the confounding effect of a third variable, X, on D and Y.

Consider, for example, a central question in education research: "Does class size affect test scores of primary school students? If so, by how much?" A researcher may be tempted to address this question by comparing test scores between primary school students in large and small classes. Small classes, however, may prevail in wealthy districts, which may have, on average, higher endowments of other educational inputs (highly qualified teachers, more computers per student, etc.) If other educational inputs have a positive effect on test scores, the researcher may observe a positive association between small classes and higher test scores, even if small classes do not have any direct effect on students' scores. As a result, observed association between class size and average test scores should not be interpreted as evidence of effectiveness of small classes improving students' scores.

This gives the rationale for the often-invoked mantra "association does not imply causation." Unfortunately, the mantra does not say a word about *what* implies causation. Moreover, the exact meaning of causation needs to be established explicitly before trying to learn about it.

Causal Models

A Model of Potential Outcomes

In our example, we want to evaluate the *causal effect* of a treatment (small classes) on some *outcome* of interest (students' scores). But how can we define causality? This section presents a causal model of potential outcomes. Let us introduce some notation first. D_i is an indicator of treatment intake for unit (individual) i. That is,

$$D_i = \begin{cases} 1 & \text{if unit } i \text{ received the treatment} \\ 0 & \text{otherwise} \end{cases}$$

For ease of exposition we consider only binary treatments (small vs. large classes). Let Y_i be the outcome variable of interest for unit i. As already argued, causality cannot be determined solely from association between D and Y. To define causality, we use the notion of *potential outcomes*:

Y_{0i}: Potential outcome without treatment for unit i. The level of outcome that unit i would attain if not exposed to the treatment (test score for student i if in a large class).

Y_{1i}: Potential outcome with treatment for unit i. The level of outcome that unit i would attain if exposed to the treatment (test score for student i if in a small class).

Potential outcomes refer to possibly counterfactual events. For a student in a large class, Y_{1i} represents test score if had been assigned to a small class. Similarly, for a student in a small class, Y_{0i} represents test score if had been assigned to a large class. For any particular unit, we cannot observe both potential outcomes (Y_{1i}, Y_{0i}); we only observe the realized outcome Y_i:

$$Y_i = \begin{cases} Y_{1i} & \text{if } D_i = 1 \\ Y_{0i} & \text{if } D_i = 0 \end{cases}$$

or

$$Y_i = D_i \cdot Y_{1i} + (1 - D) \cdot Y_{0i}$$

Once we have defined potential outcomes in this way, it is natural to define the causal effect of the treatment on the outcome for unit i as the difference between the two potential outcomes, $Y_{1i} - Y_{0i}$. Now, the fundamental identification problem of causal inference becomes apparent; because we cannot observe both Y_{0i} and Y_{1i} for the same unit, it is not possible to compute causal effects at the unit level, $Y_{1i} - Y_{0i}$. Even so, we still would like to estimate some average, such as the average treatment effect (ATE):

$$\alpha_{\text{ATE}} = E[Y_1 - Y_0]$$

or the average effect on the treated (also called the selected average treatment effect, SATE):

$$\alpha_{\text{SATE}} = E[Y_1 - Y_0 \mid D = 1]$$

where $E[\cdot]$ denotes averages over the population.

Unfortunately, comparisons of average outcomes between treated and untreated units do not usually estimate ATE or SATE:

$$\begin{aligned} &E[Y \mid D = 1] - E[Y \mid D = 0] \\ &\quad = E[Y_1 \mid D = 1] - E[Y_0 \mid D = 0] \\ &\quad = \underbrace{E[Y_1 - Y_0 \mid D = 1]}_{\text{SATE}} + \underbrace{\{E[Y_0 \mid D = 1] - E[Y_0 \mid D = 0]\}}_{\text{BIAS}} \end{aligned} \tag{1}$$

The bias term in Eq. (1) is not thought to be zero for most applications in social sciences. This is due to selection problems. Selection for treatment is usually associated with the potential outcomes that individuals would attain with and without being exposed to the treatment. I present some ways to overcome the selection problem later so that treatment effects can be estimated.

Other Causal Models

Causality has been studied using a variety of models. A structural equations model is a set of equations that describe causal relationships (i.e., potential outcomes). An alternative way to represent causation is through the use of causal diagrams. Models of potential outcomes, structural models, and causal diagrams are alternative ways of representing causal relationships. In the context of time series data, the term causality has been used to refer to predictive power; this is often referred to as Granger or temporal causality.

Identification and Estimation

Cross-Sectional Data

Randomized Experiments

Let us go back to Eq. (1). Suppose that treatment intake is independent of potential outcomes:

$$(Y_1, Y_0) \perp\!\!\!\perp D \tag{2}$$

By independence, we have that $E[Y_0 \mid D = 1] = E[Y_0 \mid D = 0]$ and therefore $\alpha_{\text{SATE}} = E[Y_1 - Y_0 \mid D = 1] = E[Y \mid D = 1] - E[Y \mid D = 0]$. Moreover, because it is also true that $E[Y_1 \mid D = 1] = E[Y_1 \mid D = 0]$, we obtain:

$$\begin{aligned} \alpha_{\text{ATE}} &= E[Y_1 - Y_0] = E[Y_1 - Y_0 \mid D = 1] \\ &= E[Y \mid D = 1] - E[Y \mid D = 0] \end{aligned} \tag{3}$$

So, $\alpha_{\text{ATE}} = \alpha_{\text{SATE}}$. In a randomized study, a randomized mechanism is used to assign experimental units to one of two groups: the treatment group and the control group. The individuals assigned to the treatment group are exposed to the treatment, whereas the individuals assigned to the control group are excluded from the treatment. That is, in a randomized study the assignment mechanism is randomized. The role of randomization is to force Eq. (2) to hold. Because the assignment mechanism is randomized, the treatment variable must be independent of potential outcomes.

Note that, although we focus the discussion on average treatment effects, randomization identifies the whole marginal distributions of Y_0 and Y_1:

$$\begin{aligned} F_{Y_0}(y) &= P(Y_0 \leq y) = P(Y_0 \leq y \mid D = 0) \\ &= P(Y \leq y \mid D = 0) \end{aligned}$$

similarly $F_{Y_1}(y) = P(Y \leq y \mid D = 1)$. So we can assess the effect of the treatment not only at the mean but also at any quantile: $Q_\theta(Y_1) - Q_\theta(Y_0)$ (here, θ is a quantile index between 0 and 1 and $F_{Y_d}(Q_\theta(Y_d)) = \theta$, for $d = 0, 1$). Note, however, that randomization does not identify the quantiles of the treatment effect: $Q_\theta(Y_1 - Y_0)$. In contrast to what happens with means, the difference of quantiles is not the quantile of the difference.

Suppose that we conduct a randomized trial with n individuals. For each individual i, the toss of a coin determines whether i is assigned to the treatment group ($D_i = 1$) or to the control group ($D_i = 0$). After the treatment group is exposed to the treatment, information is collected about some relevant outcome variable for each individual, Y_i. The estimation is carried out by using sample analogs of the population results. Letting $\alpha_0 = E[Y_1 - Y_0] (= \alpha_{ATE} = \alpha_{SATE})$, Eq. (3) suggests to estimate α_0 using a simple difference of sample averages between the treated and the untreated, $\hat{\alpha} = \bar{Y}_1 - \bar{Y}_0$, where:

$$\bar{Y}_1 = \frac{\sum Y_i \cdot D_i}{\sum D_i} = \frac{1}{n_1} \sum_{D_i=1} Y_i,$$

$$\bar{Y}_0 = \frac{\sum Y_i \cdot (1 - D_i)}{\sum (1 - D_i)} = \frac{1}{n_0} \sum_{D_i=0} Y_i$$

$n_1 = \sum_i D_i$ and $n_0 = n - n_1$. $\hat{\alpha}$ is an unbiased estimator of α_0. Usual two-sample testing methods can be applied to perform statistical inference about α_0.

Selection on Observables

In the absence of experimental data, the independence condition in Eq. (2) is rarely plausible. The reason is that treated and nontreated may differ in characteristics—other than treatment exposure—that also have an effect on the outcome variable, so Eq. (2) holds only for fixed values of those characteristics. In statistical jargon, those characteristics are called confounders. Let X be the vector of confounders, then:

$$(Y_1, Y_0) \perp\!\!\!\perp D \mid X \tag{4}$$

We say that there is selection on observables when all confounders are observed.

Following the same reasoning as shown earlier, if Eq. (4) holds, we have that $E[Y_1 - Y_0 \mid X] = E[Y_1 - Y_0 \mid X, D = 1] = E[Y \mid X, D = 1] - E[Y \mid X, D = 0]$. Therefore α_{ATE} and α_{SATE} are identified by:

$$\begin{aligned}\alpha_{ATE} &= E[Y_1 - Y_0] = \int E[Y_1 - Y_0 \mid X]\, dP(X) \\ &= \int (E[Y \mid X, D = 1] - E[Y \mid X, D = 0])\, dP(X) \end{aligned} \tag{5}$$

and

$$\begin{aligned}\alpha_{SATE} &= E[Y_1 - Y_0 \mid D = 1] \\ &= \int (E[Y \mid X, D = 1] - E[Y \mid X, D = 0])\, dP(X \mid D = 1)\end{aligned} \tag{6}$$

Matching Estimators When X is discrete and takes on a small number of values, it is easy to construct estimators of α_{ATE} and α_{SATE} based on Eqs. (5) and (6). Suppose that X takes on J different cells $\{X^1, \ldots, X^j, \ldots, X^J\}$. Let n^j be the number of observations in cell j. Let n_1^j be the number of treated observations in cell j and n_0^j be the number of untreated observations in cell j. Finally, let $\bar{Y}_1^j$ be the average outcome for the treated in cell j and $\bar{Y}_0^j$ the average outcome for the untreated. The sample counterparts of Eqs. (5) and (6) are:

$$\hat{\alpha}_{ATE} = \sum_{j=1}^{J} (\bar{Y}_1^j - \bar{Y}_0^j) \cdot \left(\frac{n^j}{n}\right)$$

$$\hat{\alpha}_{SATE} = \sum_{j=1}^{J} (\bar{Y}_1^j - \bar{Y}_0^j) \cdot \left(\frac{n_1^j}{n_1}\right)$$

When X is continuous, an obvious strategy is to divide the support of X into a finite number of cells and apply what we know for discrete X. This method is called subclassification. Subclassification works if the distribution of X can be well-approximated by a discrete distribution over a small number of cells.

Let $j(i)$ be the cell to which X_i belongs (that is, if $X_i = X^k$, then $j(i) = k$). Then, it is easy to show that:

$$\hat{\alpha}_{SATE} = \frac{1}{n_1} \sum_{D_i=1} (Y_i - \bar{Y}_0^{j(i)})$$

That is, $\hat{\alpha}_{SATE}$ matches each treated observation with an average of the untreated observations in the same cell. This suggests that when X is continuous, α_{SATE} can be estimated using

$$\hat{\alpha}_{SATE} = \frac{1}{n_1} \sum_{D_i=1} (Y_i - Y_{m(i)})$$

where $Y_{m(i)}$ is the outcome of an untreated observation such that $X_i \simeq X_{m(i)}$. This method is called matching. Matching works if for each treated observation, it is possible to find an untreated observation with close covariate values.

Matching and subclassification are both easy to carry out when X contains only one variable. However, these methods break down if the dimension of X is large. In that case, subclassification is likely to create cells of X with either no treated or no untreated observations. Similarly, when the dimension of X is large, it may be hard to find, for each treated observation, an untreated observation with similar covariate values. The next section presents propensity score methods that are useful when the dimension of X is large.

Propensity Score Methods Under selection on observables, we define the propensity score as the selection probability conditional on the confounding variables: $P(D = 1 \mid X)$. To stress the fact that the propensity score is a function of the covariates, let $\pi(X) = P(D = 1 \mid X)$. Rosenbaum and Rubin proved in their 1983 study that if Eq. (4) holds, then conditioning on the propensity score is sufficient to ensure independence between the treatment indicator and the potential outcomes. That is, if $(Y_1, Y_0) \perp\!\!\!\perp D \mid X$, then $(Y_1, Y_0) \perp\!\!\!\perp D \mid \pi(X)$.

This result suggests a two-step procedure to estimate causal effects under selection on observables: (1) estimate the propensity score $\pi(X)$ and (2) do matching or subclassification on the propensity score. The advantage of this strategy is that the dimension of the propensity score is always one, for any number of covariates in X.

Alternatively, under selection on observables, average treatment effects can be identified by weighting on the propensity score. It can be easily seen that:

$$E\left[Y\frac{D-\pi(X)}{\pi(X)(1-\pi(X))}\middle| X\right] = E[Y \mid X, D=1] - E[Y \mid X, D=0]$$

As a result, if $(Y_1, Y_0) \perp\!\!\!\perp D \mid X$, then by Eq. (5):

$$\alpha_{\text{ATE}} = E\left[Y\frac{D-\pi(X)}{\pi(X)(1-\pi(X))}\right]$$

A similar result holds for α_{SATE}. The last equation suggests a two-step procedure to estimate causal effects under selection on observables: (1) estimate the propensity score $\pi(X)$ and (2) plug the estimated values of the propensity score into the sample analog of the last equation.

$$\hat{\alpha}_{\text{ATE}} = \frac{1}{n}\sum_{i=1}^{n} Y_i \frac{D_i - \hat{\pi}(X_i)}{\hat{\pi}(X_i)(1-\hat{\pi}(X_i))}$$

This estimator weights treated observations with $1/\hat{\pi}(X_i)$ and untreated observations with $1/[1-\hat{\pi}(X_i)]$. Estimators of treatment effects that weight on functions of the propensity score originated in 1952 with Horvitz and Thompson.

Regression Regression is customarily used to control for the effect of covariates when measuring the association between two variables of interest. How can we interpret (linear or nonlinear) regression in the context of selection on observables? Consider the conditional expectation $E[Y \mid D, X]$. Under $Y_1, Y_0 \perp\!\!\!\perp D \mid X$, the conditional expectation $E[Y \mid D, X]$ can be interpreted as a conditional causal response function: $E[Y \mid D=1, X] = E[Y_1 \mid X]$ and $E[Y \mid \text{D}=0, X] = E[Y_0 \mid X]$. Therefore, $E[Y \mid D, X]$ provides the average potential responses with and without the treatment. Of course, $E[Y \mid D=1, X] - E[Y \mid \text{D}=0, X] = E[Y_1 - Y_0 \mid D=1, X] = E[Y_1 - Y_0 \mid X]$. The functional form of $E[Y \mid D, X]$ is typically unknown. Even so, it is possible to estimate a parsimonious parametric approximation to $E[Y \mid D, X]$ using least squares. To do that, specify a class of approximating functions $\mathcal{G} = \{g(D, X; \theta) : \theta \in \Theta \subset R^k\}$. Then, a least-squares approximation from $\mathcal{G}$ to $E[Y \mid D, X]$ is given by $g(D, X; \theta_0)$, where:

$$\theta_0 = \underset{\theta \in \Theta}{\arg\min} E[Y \mid D, X] - g(D, X; \theta))^2]$$

A well-known result is that θ_0 also defines the best predictor of Y within $\mathcal{G}$ under quadratic loss: $\theta_0 = \text{argmin}_{\theta \in \Theta} E[(Y - g(D, X; \theta))^2]$. An analog estimator of θ_0 is:

$$\hat{\theta} = \underset{\theta \in \Theta}{\arg\min} \frac{1}{n}\sum_{i=1}^{n} [Y_i - g(D_i, X_i; \theta)]^2$$

For example, when $\mathcal{G}$ is the set of linear functions in (D, X), then $\hat{\theta} = (\hat{\alpha}, \hat{\beta})$, where

$$(\hat{\alpha}, \hat{\beta}) = \underset{(\alpha,\beta) \in \Theta}{\arg\min} \frac{1}{n}\sum_{i=1}^{n} (Y_i - \alpha D_i - X_i'\beta)^2$$

which is the familiar linear least-squares estimator. In summary, if condition (4) holds, then least-squares regression provides a well-defined approximation to an average causal response function. Of course, this estimator will provide poor information if $E[Y \mid D, X]$ cannot be well-approximated by the functions in $\mathcal{G}$. In such a case, nonparametric regression is a useful alternative.

The functions $h_1(X) = E[Y \mid D=1, X]$ and $h_0(X) = E[Y \mid D=0, X]$ can be estimated nonparametrically (for example using kernel regression, splines, or local linear regression). Integrating $h_1(X) - h_0(X)$ over $P(X)$ we obtain α_{ATE}. Integration over $P(X \mid \text{D}=1)$ produces α_{SATE}. The propensity score result can be used to produce an estimator that conditions only on $\pi(X)$. First, the expectations $g_1(\pi) = E[Y \mid D=1, \pi]$ and $g_0(\pi) = E[Y \mid D=0, \pi]$ are estimated (where $\pi = P(D=1 \mid X)$). Then, $g_1(\pi) - g_0(\pi)$ is integrated over the distribution of π for the treated to estimate α_{SATE}.

Instrumental Variables In many relevant settings, analysts think that observed variables cannot explain all the dependence between treatment selection and potential outcomes. When there is a variable, Z, which induces selection for treatment but does not have any direct effect on the potential outcomes, instrumental variable methods can be used to estimate causal parameters (then Z is said to be an instrumental variable or instrument).

This situation is common in experiments in social sciences in which experimental units do not always comply with the treatment protocol. Let Z be a variable that takes value equal to 1 for individuals assigned to the treatment group and 0 otherwise. In this scenario, assignment for treatment, Z, is randomized, but treatment exposure, D, is not because experimental subjects may decide not to comply with the assignment. If treatment assignment only affects the outcome of interest through its effect on treatment exposure, instrumental variable techniques can be used to recover an average treatment effect (although this average treatment effect is not, in general, ATE or SATE).

For ease of exposition, we assume that Z is scalar and binary. Generalizations to multiple and nonbinary instruments have been made by Heckman and Vytlacil.

To recognize the dependence between the treatment and the instrument we use potential treatment indicators. The binary variable D_z represents potential treatment status given $Z=z$. The instrument Z is assumed to affect the outcome variable Y only through its effect on selection for treatment, D. Therefore, the potential outcomes (Y_1, Y_0) do not depend on Z.

The treatment variable can then be expressed as $D=Z\cdot D_1+(1-Z)\cdot D_0$. In practice, we observe Z and D (and therefore D_z for individuals with $Z=z$), but we do not observe both potential treatment indicators (D_0, D_1).

It is assumed that potential outcomes and potential treatments are independent of the instrument $(Y_0, Y_1, D_0, D_1) \perp\!\!\!\perp Z$, and that the instrument affects selection for treatment only in one direction: $D_1 \geq D_0$ with some units such that $D_1 > D_0$. In the context of experiments with imperfect compliance, the last condition means that some experimental subjects are induced to be treated by random assignment, but no experimental unit who will get the treatment if assigned to the control group will refuse to take the treatment if assigned to the treatment group. Units with $D_1 > D_0$, or equivalently $D_1=1$ and $D_0=0$, are called compliers because they are the subjects who always comply with the experimental protocol. Note that we cannot say who are compliers in a particular sample because we do not observe both D_0 and D_1 for the same individuals. Under these assumptions:

$$E[Y_1-Y_0\,|\,D_1>D_0] = \frac{E[Y\,|\,Z=1]-E[Y\,|\,Z=0]}{E[D\,|\,Z=1]-E[D\,|\,Z=0]} = \frac{\mathrm{Cov}(Y,Z)}{\mathrm{Cov}(D,Z)} \quad (7)$$

This result says that the average effect of the treatment for compilers is identified. This parameter is called the local average treatment effect (LATE) by Angrist, Imbens and Rubin.

Compliers are the units whose decision to take the treatment is determined by variation in the instrument. Whether compliers are an interesting group of the population depends on the particularities of each example. However, an important special case arises when $D_0=0$. This happens, for example, in randomized experiments when there is perfect exclusion of the control group from the treatment (not ruling out noncompliance in the treatment group). In such cases, $E[Y_1\,|\,D_1 > D_0]=E[Y_1\,|\,D_1=1]=E[Y_1\,|\,Z=1, D_1=1]=E[Y_1\,|\,D=1]$, and similarly $E[Y_0\,|\,D_1 > D_0]=E[Y_0\,|\,D=1]$, so LATE is the average effect of the treatment for the treated (SATE). Note also that when $D_0=0$ or $D_1=1$ for every individual, then the condition $D_1 \geq D_0$ holds trivially.

The sample analog of Eq. (7) is often called the Wald estimator:

$$\left(\frac{\sum_{i=1}^n Y_iZ_i}{\sum_{i=1}^n Z_i}-\frac{\sum_{i=1}^n Y_i(1-Z_i)}{\sum_{i=1}^n (1-Z_i)}\right)\Big/\left(\frac{\sum_{i=1}^n D_iZ_i}{\sum_{i=1}^n Z_i}-\frac{\sum_{i=1}^n D_i(1-Z_i)}{\sum_{i=1}^n (1-Z_i)}\right)$$

Abadie has extended the LATE result to the estimation of conditional average treatment responses for compliers: $E[Y_1\,|\,X, D_1 > D_0]$ and $E[Y_0\,|\,X, D_1 > D_0]$.

The Regression Discontinuity Design Sometimes assignment for treatment is determined based on whether a certain individual characteristic exceeds some threshold. That is:

$$D_i = \begin{cases} 1 & \text{if unit } X_i > \bar{X} \\ 0 & \text{otherwise} \end{cases} \quad \text{or} \quad D_i = \begin{cases} 1 & \text{if unit } X_i < \bar{X} \\ 0 & \text{otherwise} \end{cases}$$

For example, second-grade students who scored below a certain cut-off value were assigned to a compensatory reading program. Usually, the variable that determines treatment assignment is thought to be related to the outcomes of interest. Therefore, simple comparisons of outcomes between treated and nontreated do not provide valid causal estimates.

If the relationship between the covariate and the outcome is smooth, we can attribute any discontinuity in the conditional average of the outcome variable at the cut-off value, $\bar{X}$, to the effect of the treatment.

Here, we consider the case in which $E[Y_0\,|\,X]$ and $E[Y_1\,|\,X]$ are linear functions of X. The average potential outcomes conditional on X are given by:

$$E[Y_0\,|\,X] = \mu_0+\beta_0X, \quad E[Y_1\,|\,X] = \mu_1+\beta_1X$$

Therefore, the average treatment effect conditional on X is equal to $\alpha(X)=E[Y_1-Y_0\,|\,X]=(\mu_1-\mu_0)+(\beta_1-\beta_0)X$. Suppose that $D=1$ if $X>\bar{X}$, and $D=0$ otherwise. Figure 1 gives a graphical interpretation. Because D is determined given X, we have:

$$\begin{aligned} E[Y\,|\,X,D] &= D\cdot E[Y_1\,|\,X]+(1-D)\cdot E[Y_0\,|\,X] \\ &= \mu_1D+\beta_1(X\cdot D)+\mu_0(1-D)+\beta_0(X\cdot(1-D)) \end{aligned}$$

So we can run this regression and estimate the effect of the treatment at $\bar{X}$ as the analog of $\alpha(\bar{X})=(\mu_1-\mu_0)+(\beta_1-\beta_0)\bar{X}$. In practice, there is an easier way to do this. It can be shown that

$$\begin{aligned} E[Y\,|\,X,D] = {} & [\mu_0+\beta_0\bar{X}]+\beta_0(X-\bar{X})+[(\mu_1-\mu_0) \\ & +(\beta_1-\beta_0)\bar{X}]D+(\beta_1-\beta_0)((X-\bar{X})\cdot D) \end{aligned}$$

Therefore, if we run a regression of Y on $(X-\bar{X})$, D, and the interaction $(X-\bar{X})\cdot D$, the coefficient of D reflects the average effect of the treatment at $X=\bar{X}$. Even when the parametric specifications adopted for $E[Y_1\,|\,X]$ and $E[Y_0\,|\,X]$ allow us to estimate the effect of the treatment away from $X=\bar{X}$, the data per se are only informative about the effect of the treatment at $X=\bar{X}$.

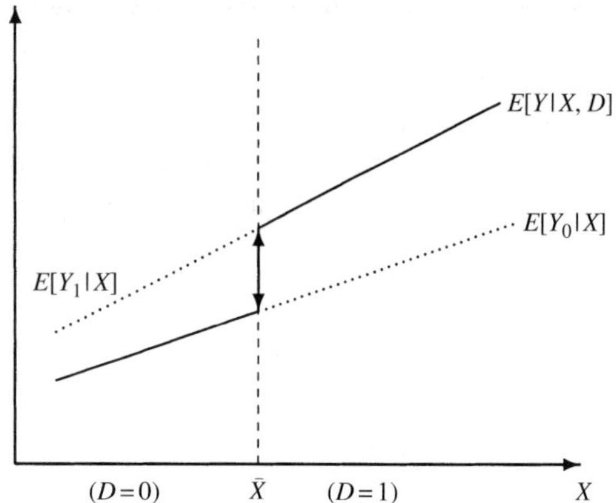

Figure 1 Regression discontinuity design, linear case.

Identification of $\alpha(X)$ for $X \neq \bar{X}$ is done by pure extrapolation of lines.

Bounds When the outcome variable is bounded (when it has lower and upper bounds), the effect of the treatment can be bounded even if no other identification condition holds.

Here we focus on a simple case, in which the dependent variable is binary, so the lower bound is 0 and the upper bound is 1. For each individual, we observe Y and D, so we can estimate $E[Y_1 \mid D=1](=E[Y \mid D=1])$, $E[Y_0 \mid D=0](=E[Y \mid D=0])$ and $P(D=1)$. We cannot estimate $E[Y_1 \mid D=0]$ or $E[Y_0 \mid D=1]$, but we know that they are in between 0 and 1. We can use this fact to bound SATE and ATE:

$$E[Y \mid D=1] - 1 \leq \text{SATE} \leq E[Y \mid D=1]$$

and

$$\begin{aligned}(E[Y \mid D=1]-1)\cdot P(D=1) - E[Y \mid D=0]\cdot P(D=0) \\ \leq \text{ATE} \leq E[Y \mid D=1]\cdot P(D=1) \\ -(E[Y \mid D=0]-1)\cdot P(D=0)\end{aligned}$$

As always, we can estimate the bounds using sample analogs. It can be easily seen that, for a binary outcome variable, the width of the bounds is 1. Manski discusses restrictions that can help narrow the bounds further.

Longitudinal Data

This section presents estimation techniques that are especially suitable for longitudinal data.

Difference-in-Differences and Fixed Effects We have studied how to control for observed differences between treated and controls. However, often there are reasons to believe that treated and nontreated differ in unobservable characteristics that are associated with potential outcomes even after controlling for differences in observed characteristics.

When there are pretreatment and posttreatment outcome data available, we can think about comparing the outcomes for the treated after the treatment to the outcomes of the treated before the treatment. Effectively, we would like to use the treated before the treatment as controls for the treated after the treatment. However, comparisons of pretreatment and posttreatment outcomes for the treated are likely to incorporate biases due to temporal trends in the outcome variable or to the effect of changes in extraneous factors between both periods.

When only part of the population is treated, an untreated comparison group can be used to identify temporal variation in the outcome that is not due to the treatment. The difference-in-differences (DID) estimator is based on this simple idea.

As in previous sections, we define the causal effect of the treatment on the outcome as the difference between two potential outcomes. In contrast with previous sections, now we are dealing with longitudinal data, so potential outcomes are also indexed by a time indicator. $Y_{0i}(t)$ represents the outcome that individual i attains at time t ($t=0, 1$) in the absence of the treatment. In the same fashion, $Y_{1i}(t)$ represents the outcome that individual i attains at time t if exposed to the treatment before t. The causal effect of the treatment on the outcome for individual i at time t is then naturally defined as $Y_{1i}(t) - Y_{0i}(t)$.

As before, for any particular individual i and time period t, we do not observe both potential outcomes $Y_{0i}(t)$ and $Y_{1i}(t)$; so we cannot compute the individual treatment effect $Y_{1i}(t) - Y_{0i}(t)$. We only observe the realized outcome, $Y_i(t)$ that can be expressed as $Y_i(t) = Y_{0i}(t)\cdot(1 - D_i(t)) + Y_{1i}(t)\cdot D_i(t)$ [$D_i(t)$ is a binary variable equal to 1 if individual i received the treatment before period t and 0 otherwise]. Because, in the simple two-period scenario considered here, the treatment is only administered after period $t=0$, we can denote $D_i = D_i(1)$, from which it follows that $Y_i(0) = Y_{0i}(0)$ and $Y_i(1) = Y_{0i}(1)\cdot(1 - D_i) + Y_{1i}(1)\cdot D_i$. Given the impossibility of computing individual causal treatment effects, researchers typically focus on estimating the average effect of the treatment on the treated: $E[Y_1(1) - Y_0(1) \mid D=1]$.

The next assumption is the crucial identifying restriction for DID. It states that average outcomes for treated and untreated will follow parallel paths over time in the absence of the treatment:

$$E[Y_0(1) - Y_0(0) \mid D=1] = E[Y_0(1) - Y_0(0) \mid D=0] \tag{8}$$

If Eq. (8) holds, then

$$\begin{aligned}E[Y_1(1) - Y_0(1) \mid D=1] \\ = \{E[Y(1) \mid D=1] - E[Y(1) \mid D=0]\} \\ - \{E[Y(0) \mid D=1] - E[Y(0) \mid D=0]\}\end{aligned} \tag{9}$$

Figure 2 shows a graphical interpretation of this result. An estimator of the effect of the treatment on the treated can be constructed as:

$$\left\{\frac{1}{n_1}\sum_{D_i=1} Y_i(1) - \frac{1}{n_0}\sum_{D_i=0} Y_i(1)\right\}$$
$$-\left\{\frac{1}{n_1}\sum_{D_i=1} Y_i(0) - \frac{1}{n_0}\sum_{D_i=0} Y_i(0)\right\}$$
$$=\left\{\frac{1}{n_1}\sum_{D_i=1} \{Y_i(1) - Y_i(0)\} - \frac{1}{n_0}\sum_{D_i=0} \{Y_i(1) - Y_i(0)\}\right\}$$

where n_1 is the number of treated individuals and n_0 is the number of untreated individuals. This estimator can be easily obtained as the least squares estimator of the coefficient on D in a regression of $\Delta Y = Y(1) - Y(0)$ on D and a constant. The regression formulation of the DID estimator is often used to introduce covariates by considering least squares estimators of:

$$\Delta Y = \delta + \alpha \cdot D + X'\beta + u \qquad (10)$$

The rationale for introducing covariates is to allow for different dynamics for treated and untreated units (as long as these different dynamics can be explained linearly by observed covariates).

Alternatively, Eq. (10) can be expressed as a fixed effect regression:

$$Y_i(t) = \eta_i + \delta(t) + \alpha \cdot D_i(t) + X_i'\beta(t) + \varepsilon_i(t) \qquad (11)$$

where η_i is a time-invariant individual fixed effect possibly correlated with $D_i(t)$. Therefore, selection for treatment is allowed to depend on time-invariant unobserved characteristics. As long as selection for treatment does not depend on the time-varying unobserved components, $\varepsilon_i(t)$, Eq. (11) can be estimated by least squares (using individual binary indicators as regressors to account for η_i). When the data set contains information on two periods only, a least-squares estimation of Eqs. (10) and (11) produces identical estimators of α. However, the fixed-effects formulation in Eq. (11) is particularly useful when the data contain information about more than two periods because Eq. (11) can accommodate multiperiod data structures.

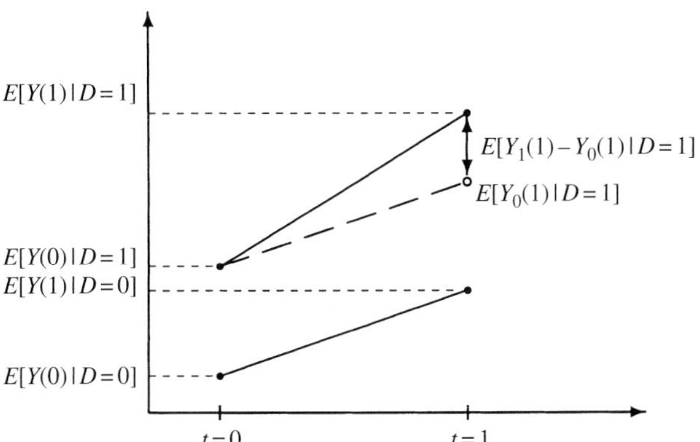

Figure 2 Graphical interpretation of difference-in-differences.

G-Formula The idea of identifying treatment effects through conditional independence has been extended to time-varying treatments. To keep the exposition simple, we only consider two periods $t = 0, 1$. As before, $D(t)$ is a binary variable that represents treatment during period t. The outcome of interest, Y, is measured after the second period. Potential outcomes are now indexed by the treatment in both periods. That is, $Y_i = Y_{d_0 d_1 i}$ if $D_i(0) = d_0$ and $D_i(1) = d_1$. In addition, let $X(t)$ represent a time-varying covariate. In this context, selection on observables can be defined in the following fashion:

$$(Y_{00}, Y_{01}, Y_{10}, Y_{11}) \perp\!\!\!\perp D(0) \mid X(0)$$
$$(Y_{00}, Y_{01}, Y_{10}, Y_{11}) \perp\!\!\!\perp D(1) \mid X(0), X(1), D(0)$$

That is, conditional on the present and past values of X and the past values of D, the treatment is independent of the potential outcomes. In other words, at every time t, the treatment assignment is “as good as random” conditional on the observed variables. Under this assumption it can be shown that:

$$E\left[Y_{d_0 d_1}\right] = \iint E[Y \mid X(0), X(1), D(0) = d_0, D(1) = d_1]$$
$$\times\, dP(X(1) \mid X(0), D(0) = d_0)\, dP(X(0))$$

for d_0 and d_1 in {0, 1}. This formula is sometimes referred to as the G-formula or G-computation formula. In principle, average potential outcomes may be estimated nonparametrically based on the G-computation formula. Comparisons of average potential outcomes inform us about different treatment effects (e.g., the average effect of one additional period of treatment given treatment in the first period is $E[Y_{11} - Y_{10}]$). Based on these ideas, Robins has developed statistical models for characteristics of the marginal distributions of the potential outcomes (marginal structural models) and models for the effects of additional periods of treatment (structural nested models).

See Also the Following Articles

Deduction and Induction • Experiments, Overview • Longitudinal Cohort Designs • Longitudinal Studies, Panel • Observational Studies • Randomization

Further Reading

Abadie, A. (2003). Semiparametric instrumental variable estimation of treatment response models. *J. Econometrics* **113**, 231–263.

Angrist, J. D., Imbens, G. W., and Rubin, D. B. (1996). Identification of causal effects using instrumental variables. *J. Am. Stat. Ass.* **91,** 444–472.

Granger, C. W. J. (1969). Investigating causal relations by econometric models and cross-spectral methods. *Econometrica* **37,** 424–438.

Hahn, J., Todd, P. E., and van der Klaauw, W. (2000). Identification and estimation of treatment effects with a regression discontinuity design. *Econometrica* **69,** 201–209.

Härdle, W. (1990). *Applied Nonparametric Regression.* Econometric Society Monograph, 19. Cambridge University Press, Cambridge, UK.

Heckman, J. J. (2000). Causal parameters and policy analysis in economics: A twentieth century retrospective. *Q. J. Econ.* **115,** 45–97.

Heckman, J. J., Ichimura, H., and Todd, P. E. (1997). Matching as an econometric evaluation estimator: Evidence from evaluating a job training programme. *Rev. Econ. Studies* **64,** 605–654.

Heckman, J. J., and Vytlacil, E. J. (1999). Local-instrumental variables and latent variable models for identifying and bounding treatment effects. *Proc. Natl. Acad. Sci. U.S.A.* **96,** 4730–4734.

Holland, P. W. (1986). Statistics and causal inference. *J. Am. Stat. Ass.* **81,** 945–960.

Horvitz, D. G., and Thompson, D. J. (1952). A generalization of sampling without replacement from a finite universe. *J. Am. Stat. Ass.* **47,** 663–685.

Imbens, G. W. (2004). Nonparametric estimation of average treatment effects under exogeneity: a review. *Rev. Econ. Stat.* **86,** 4–29.

Manski, C. (1990). Nonparametric bounds on treatment effects. *Am. Econ. Rev.* **80,** 319–323.

Pearl, J. (2000). *Causality.* Cambridge University Press, Cambridge, UK.

Robins, J. M. (1986). A new approach to causal inference in mortality studies with sustained exposure periods—applications to control of the healthy worker survivor effect. *Math. Modeling* **7,** 1393–1512.

Robins, J. M. (1999). Marginal structural models versus structural nested models as tools for causal inference. In *Statistical Models in Epidemiology: The Environment and Clinical Trials* (M. E. Halloran and D. Berry, eds.). IMA, Volume 116, pp. 119–139. Springer-Verlag, New York.

Rosenbaum, P. R., and Rubin, D. B. (1983). The central role of the propensity score in observational studies for causal effects. *Biometrika* **79,** 41–55.

Trochim, W. (1990). The Regression-Discontinuity Design. In *Research Methodology: Strengthening Causal Interpretations of Nonexperimental Data* (L. Sechrest, E. Perrin, and J. Bunker, eds.), pp. 119–139. U.S. Dept. of HHS, Agency for Health Care Policy and Research, Washington, D.C.

White, H. (1980). Using least squares to approximate unknown regression functions. *Int. Econ. Rev.* **21,** 149–170.

Census Undercount and Adjustment

Margo Anderson
University of Wisconsin, Milwaukee, Wisconsin, USA

Stephen E. Fienberg
Carnegie Mellon University, Pittsburgh, Pennsylvania, USA

Glossary

accuracy A measure of the closeness of an estimate to the true value.

contingency table A cross-classified table of counts according to two or more categorical variables.

dual systems estimation A method for combining information from two sources to estimate a population total, including an estimate for the number of individuals missed by both sources.

gross error The total error in an estimate of a population total from a census, consisting of the sum of the errors of omission and the errors of commission; also known as erroneous enumerations.

imputation A statistical method for "filling in" values for missing data. In the context of census-taking values, missing questionnaire values are imputed as is the information for entire households if the Census Bureau believed them to be occupied.

mail-out/mail-back The primary method of collecting census information in the United States. Questionnaires are mailed out to all households listed in a master address file compiled by the Census Bureau; recipients fill them out and then return them by mail.

measurement error A variety of sources of error in the census enumeration process that cause the reported enumeration values to differ from the true values.

postenumeration survey A sample survey conducted after the census to provide a second source of information on households that can be used in dual systems estimation.

The United States conducts a census of population every decade to provide information for the reapportionment of Congress and for a variety of other legal requirements. The U.S. census enumeration process both misses households and individuals within them and erroneously includes many individuals through duplication and other types of errors. Since 1940, the Census Bureau has worked to develop methods for correcting census error, primarily in the form of omissions. The size of census errors differs across population subgroups, leading to what has been known as the census differential net undercount. Statistically adjusting census enumeration counts for net undercount has been the topic of much controversy. The sources of census error and the methods that have been used to estimate the true population totals by geographic area and demographic groups are reviewed in this article.

Introduction

Taking an accurate and efficient population census of a large, rapidly growing, diverse, and mobile population such as that of the United States is fraught with difficulty. The results of the count are used to allocate political representation in Congress, tax funds to local areas, and votes in the Electoral College, and to design legislative districts at federal, state, and local levels of government. Thus, the adequacy of the census is no mere academic question. A local area overcounted or undercounted relative to others gets too much or too little political representation and tax revenue.

From the late 1960s to the early 2000s, the census faced challenges that it did not count well enough to serve its political functions, and in particular that it was biased against poor areas and minority neighborhoods. Critics charged that the census missed millions of residents and that it missed a higher proportion of minorities and the poor as compared with white middle-class residents. The differential undercount of minority communities, poor urban neighborhoods, and remote rural areas became the most difficult political and technical problem the census faced. Dissatisfied local government officials sued the Census Bureau to force improvements in counting procedures and to mandate adjustment of population estimates to correct for the known undercount. Bureau officials faced scrutiny in tense congressional committee hearings, and statisticians challenged the agency to improve its counting techniques to eliminate the undercount.

The Census Bureau began to document and measure census error systematically in the 1940s. From the late 1960s, bureau officials focused on developing techniques to measure and correct the differential net undercount of geographic areas and racial and ethnic populations. The reported net undercount rate declined from 5.4% of the population in 1940 to 1.8% in 1990. But from 1940 to 1990, the differential undercount of minorities, for example, of Blacks relative to non-Blacks, was much more recalcitrant, and remained at the 3.4 to 4.4% level. In March 2003, the Census Bureau reported a net overcount of the Census 2000 total household population of 0.49%. They also reported that there was a net overcount of 1.13% for the non-Hispanic White household population, but a net undercount of 1.84% for the non-Hispanic Black household population. As is explained in the following discussion, the 2000 results have revealed new questions about the accuracy of the census. The differential undercount debate of the 1960s to the 1990s seems to be giving way to a new census accuracy debate, the implications of which are not yet clear.

Counting vs. Estimating

The American census is an old institution, mandated by the founding fathers in the 1787 Constitution, and thus the nation has a long history of population counting and experience in dealing with problems of accuracy. That experience has led the U.S. Census Bureau to follow one fundamental counting principle: devise a procedure to locate everyone in the country at their "usual place of abode" and then count them. The decennial census process produces what is commonly referred to as a "complete count," although the completeness of the process is in fact in substantial dispute. Census officials break down the process of counting into manageable portions by devising hierarchical administrative systems that run from the national census office to the individual household. In 2000, for example, the Bureau of the Census national office in Suitland, Maryland created 12 regional census centers and 520 local census offices to collect and process the forms. The district offices were responsible for counting about 200,000 housing units each. For the households slated to get a form either by mail or a bureau enumerator, the Bureau mailed one census form to each address in the country based on its master address file. All addresses were coded by state, county, other local geography, district office, census tract, "address register area," census block, and "walking sequence" in case an enumerator had to reach a housing unit.

The final link in this chain of counting occurs at the household, in which one person reports, on the mail census form or to the enumerator, the number of people in the household. Forms are collected, edited, and tallied back to higher and higher levels of geography. The success of the system depends on the capacity of the procedures to deliver a census form or an enumerator to each household, and then to retrieve the information on one completed form from the household. Things can go wrong, from lost forms, to bad or missing addresses, to confused or suspicious respondents, to duplicate forms for a single household. The Bureau deals with such counting problems by building follow-up and checking procedures into the census process to catch errors and make sure that all households are counted once and only once. Nevertheless, the controversies surrounding the undercount have made the flaws in the counting systems painfully clear and thus have led critics to propose fundamentally new ways to count, derived from different traditions of counting.

These new methods all involve some form of systematic repeated counting, not just checking to make sure that the count obtained is accurate. The most promising method also involves using sampling methods to count households. The new methods rely on different guarantees for their efficacy. The traditional methods rely for their validity on careful bureaucratic procedures, the administrative chain of command, legal sanctions for nonresponse, and public cooperation of respondents. The new methods rely as well on the principles of statistical theory and probability for validity.

Errors and Uncertainty

Statisticians have a specialized vocabulary, and many of the terms they use have everyday meanings that differ from technical ones. For example, words such as "significant," "power," "random," "unbiased," and "independent" all have precise technical meanings that differ from the interpretations that are put on such words in everyday conversation. The word "error" presents a similar problem. No matter how carefully any scientific investigation is carried out, no measurement process is perfect and the statistician usually uses the term "error" to denote the difference between what is observed and what was intended to measure. In common parlance, error is used to denote an intentional mistake and to impute blame or even censure. Nothing could be further from the intended use of the term in the context of the work of the Census Bureau on the decennial census.

Errors in measurement contribute to the uncertainty about the quantities that researchers attempt to measure. In the case of the census, much is known about possible sources of error, and the Census Bureau workers and others have studied many, if not all, of the sources to some degree. Also, some measurement errors that occur in the implementation of a particular stage of the census process are corrected in subsequent stages, whereas others are propagated on through to the data retained as official census records. For example, the error that occurs when a house is left off of the master list of addresses can be corrected at many subsequent stages, during which the location can be added back into the address file. On the other hand, the error of omission that results when a household respondent intentionally does not include one of the occupants on the census form may never be detected and corrected.

When the measurement process is complex and measurements are aggregated, as they are in the decennial census, some of these recorded errors fortuitously cancel one another out; others are compounded to induce systematic differences or biases in the estimates of the quantities of ultimate interest. Thus, the Census Bureau might fail to enumerate every one of the 29 occupants of an apartment building in Pittsburgh, Pennsylvania, and thus distort substantially the count for the census block in which the building is situated, but that error or undercount alone will have little impact on the population totals for Pennsylvania. The omission of these 29 apartment dwellers in Pittsburgh might balance against duplicate census records for 29 individuals in 29 different blocks in nearby Wilkinsburg, Pennsylvania, yielding a net census error of 0 for the Pittsburgh metropolitan area—that is, there is no net undercount. But even if this canceling out of omissions and duplicates happens, there is an increase in the overall level of uncertainty about the total for the state of Pennsylvania and even to the total for the nation as a whole. Such uncertainty is best measured as gross error, which is the sum of all errors regardless of whether they are omissions, duplicates, or fabrications. In the example given here, 29 omissions and 29 duplicates result in a gross error of 58.

What has often been overlooked in discussions of census undercount is the array of errors in the census and how they contribute not only to the undercount estimates but also to uncertainty regarding the overall quality of the decennial census at disaggregated levels. The following list provides some examples of sources of error in the census enumeration process and indications of their possible implications for the accuracy of the census enumeration counts:

1. Missed households: Despite the enormous efforts to construct a master address file that includes all housing units in the United States, the Bureau "misses" housing units. In 1990, 30.5% of the average error came from housing units that were not enumerated at all.
2. Refusals: Some housing units and their occupants refuse to participate in the census. Some of their occupants are "included" statistically, however, by coverage-improvement programs (see later).
3. The appropriateness of census concepts and definitions: The census concepts of "housing units" and "families" are often difficult to apply in practice, especially by respondents and enumerators in minority communities where non-traditional physical and family structures may be the norm. Individuals and households are often missed as a consequence. Also, individuals who are connected with multiple households may well be counted multiple times.
4. Census day vs. census operations: Few people were enumerated at their household locations on exactly April 1. Yet many components of the census assume that people are correctly reported in the exact location where they resided on April 1.
5. Use of household respondents: One person completes the census form for each household. This person serves as a filter for information on others in the household and for household characteristics. Errors that enter into census data as a result of the "filter" applied by the household respondent are extremely difficult for anyone to correct.
6. Problems of understanding connected with the instructions and questionnaire wording: Many individuals in the population may have difficulty in interpreting the instructions on the census form. For example, the census form is quite explicit that college students should be counted where they lived while attending school. Nonetheless, many respondents believe that the students should be counted at home and thus college students are often double-counted as a result.
7. Recording error: Individuals completing the census questionnaire may check the wrong answer inadvertently.
8. Enumerator error: When a household fails to return the mailed-out census questionnaire, a census enumerator may complete the questionnaire as a result of a visit to the household location. Enumerators may record information that differs from that supplied by the household respondent.
9. Duplication error: Some households mistakenly receive two census forms. Some households provide multiple returns, either from the same household respondent or different ones. Sometimes these duplicates are easy to catch and sometimes not. This may be the result of geographic coding or other types of errors (see later).

10. Coding and processing errors: After a census questionnaire is completed and returned to the Bureau, the information must be transferred to a computer file and subsequently processed and checked for consistency. Errors creep into the official files despite the new technologically based methods for data capture.

11. Geographic coding errors: These errors occur at various stages in the process, from the compilation of initial mailing lists as part of the Topologically Integrated Geographic Encoding Reference (TIGER) system all the way through coding. In 1990, local communities complained that the census master address file missed housing units. These errors could result from geographic coding problems, thus placing an address in the wrong place. Some of these errors, presumably, lead to geographic coding errors in census records. Despite all of the "corrections" that occurred throughout the various forms of data review, residual geocoding errors place people in the wrong census blocks.

12. Fabrication: In every census, there are anecdotal reports of enumerators "curbstoning," i.e., fabricating questionnaires for real and often imaginary households, and of respondents providing fabricated information. The Bureau has a variety of methods to catch such fabrication, but inevitably, a substantial number of fabricated questionnaires are included in the official census results.

13. "Last resort" information: Some questionnaires are actually filled out as a last resort by enumerators without their directly seeing or interviewing any household occupants. The household may not submit a form, and the enumerator fails after repeated tries to contact the household. In such cases, enumerators use information from mail carriers, neighbors, or building managers, that is, proxy respondents, that may be inaccurate, incomplete, or even intentionally false.

14. Imputation: The Census Bureau uses various forms of statistical estimation (based either explicitly or implicitly on statistical models) to "fill in" values for missing data. This process of filling in is usually referred to as imputation. If the Bureau had no information about the occupancy status of a housing unit (e.g., from last-resort methods), it imputed a status to it, i.e., either occupied or vacant. If a unit was imputed as occupied, or if the Bureau otherwise believed it to be occupied, then it imputed a number of people to the household, as well as their characteristics. The current method of choice for imputation, known as the "sequential hot-deck" procedure, selects a housing unit proximate in processing as the donor of the characteristics. The assumption in the statistical "model" underlying the imputation method is that neighboring housing units are likely to have similar characteristics. In 1980, the Bureau added 3.3 million people to the census through imputation. Of these, 762,000 were added into housing units for which the Bureau had no knowledge concerning whether the units were occupied. The 1990 census had a much lower imputation rate, but it rose again to 5.7 million people in 2000. This has been the cause of serious investigation by those evaluating the census outside the Census Bureau.

The impact of each of these sources of error needs to be understood when assessing the accuracy of data from the census counts. The census process moves from addresses (i.e., labels for physical structures) to housing units, to housing units that are enumerated, either through mail-out/mail-back or some other process, to actual individuals. At each stage, there is a cumulative impact of errors leading to units or people not counted or miscounted in terms of information recorded about that unit or individual in the census files. Errors in the classification of housing units inevitably propagate into errors in enumerating housing units, and errors in enumerating housing units propagate into errors in the enumeration of individuals. As noted previously, at some levels of aggregation, the "miscounts" do not show up as errors, e.g., in determining the population total, but when discussing who makes up the population total and where they reside at the state or local level, the miscount category may be very important.

Gross error provides a measure of the total impact of these census errors. It is not as well understood or publicized as net error, and as yet has not been the subject of analysis of its impact on the distributional functions of the census. Unofficial estimates of gross error for the censuses from 1980 to 2000 are given in Table I. Erroneous enumerations include people who are counted more than once, are counted at the wrong location, or are fabricated. The estimates of erroneous enumerations given here are not especially well documented by the Census Bureau and have varied over time. In fact, reports on the errors for 2000 went through a number of revisions, shifting from a net undercount to a net overcount. Thus, important things about the values reported are (1) their order of magnitude and (2) that the level of gross error can be very high when erroneous enumerations and omissions appear to "net" out across the nation.

Two quantitative techniques have been used in the United States to estimate the undercount at a national level: demographic analysis and the dual systems (capture–recapture) technique.

Demographic analysis combines aggregate birth, death, immigration, and emigration records with other administrative records such as enrollment in Medicare,

Table I Measuring the Net Undercount (in millions)

Census year	*Erroneous enumerations*	*Omissions*	*Gross error*
1980	6.0	9.2	15.2
1990	10.2	15.5	25.7
2000	12.5	15.8	28.3

to carry forward the population from one census to the next, deriving an estimate of the overall population size to be compared with the census count. The population of 2000, for example, is estimated as follows:

$$\begin{aligned}\text{Population 2000} = {} & \text{population 1990} + \text{births since 1990}\\ & - \text{deaths since 1990}\\ & + \text{immigration since 1990}\\ & - \text{emigration since 1990.}\end{aligned}$$

The methodology can provide population and undercount figures by age, race (typically restricted to Black and non-Black, at least through 1980), and sex, but only at a national level. The approach was introduced by the demographer Ansley Coale as a check on the results of the 1950 census, and bureau demographers advanced the technique in successive censuses.

The accuracy of the demographic analysis depends on the accuracy of the inputs. Several of the statistical inputs are incomplete. For example, all births are not registered in vital statistics sources, and emigration data are generally poor. Further, the growth of illegal immigration since the 1970s poses special problems, which has led demographers to develop special estimates for this component of the population. The major strengths of the demographic analysis estimates are their use of independent data sources and their basic consistency from one census to the next. The weaknesses are that racial data are available in a reasonable form mainly for Black versus non-Black comparisons, and only at the national level. Geocoding errors of the typed described previously cannot be measured. Nor can demographic analysis identify omissions and duplications and fabrications if these "net" out in the national figures. Further, the errors and uncertainties associated with undocumented immigrants and shifting racial identification, combined with increasing intermarriage, make the numbers increasingly problematic, except as a broad coverage evaluation tool. This is, of course, what demographic analysis was created to do. In 2000, the Census Bureau released multiple versions of their demographic analysis estimates, attempting to correct the numbers of illegal immigrants and the extent of birth registration, but there was not widespread acceptance of the assumptions that lay behind the reported figures.

The second technique for estimating census error and the net national undercount, dual systems estimation (DSE), was the method of choice adopted by the methodologists at the Census Bureau in 1990 (after some 40 years of testing). It has been the subject of the ongoing controversy about methodology for a statistical adjustment. The basic premise of DSE is the use of two sources of information to arrive at a better estimate of the population than could be obtained from one source alone. In 1990, the second survey was called the Post-Enumeration Survey (PES); in 2000, the name was changed to the Accuracy and Coverage Evaluation (ACE). DSE is an old procedure, widely accepted among statisticians, and has been used for a host of different practical population estimation problems. It is most familiar in the context of estimating the size of wild life populations, where it is known as the "capture–recapture" technique.

The DSE technique can be illustrated with a hypothetical example: Suppose the task is to estimate the number of people living on a block in the Bedford–Stuyvesant neighborhood of Brooklyn. First, the population in the census is counted, yielding a list of the names and addresses of people counted. Assume that 300 people were counted by the census on this particular block. For the second count of the population, imagine a specially commissioned, independent count carried out with even greater care than the census, and yielding 400 people. In the hypothetical Bedford–Stuyvesant block, the second count will surely include many of the same 300 people counted by the census. The number of people counted both times is determined by comparing the list of names and addresses in the first count with the list of names and addresses in the second count, and matching those that are the same. Suppose that, through matching these two lists, it is found that 250 people out of 400 counted in the second count on this block were also included in the census. The three observed categories of the population, and their sizes, are thus the 250 counted both times, the 50 counted the first time but not the second, and the 150 counted the second time but not the first. Thus, 450 people have been observed. If the second count is a random sample of the population of the block as a whole, then 250 out of 400, or 5/8 of the whole population of the block, were counted in the census. The fraction of members of the second count included in the census is an estimate of the fraction of the total population of the block counted in the census. Finally, an estimate of the total population is the number of people counted in the census, or 300, divided by 5/8. This yields an estimate of the total population of 480 people. Thus, the estimated census undercount in this hypothetical block is 180 people out of 480, or 3/8 of the population.

The data can be displayed in the form of a 2×2 contingency table with rows corresponding to presence and absence in the first count and columns corresponding to presence and absence in the second count (Table II). The task at hand is to proceed from this information to an estimate of the total number in the population, including an estimate of a fourth class of people, those not counted either time. This can be done as long as the two counts are independent random samples. A random sample by its nature permits estimation of the incidence of any observable characteristic in the larger population from which the sample is drawn. In this case, the characteristic of interest is that of having been captured in the first count. The examination of the random sample—the second

Table II Dual-Systems Estimation Setup for a Hypothetical Block: 2 × 2 Contigency Table

	Day 2 count		
Day 1 count	*In*	*Out*	*Total*
In	250	50	300
Out	150	?	?
Total	400	?	??

Table III Dual-Systems Setup for Hypothetical Block by Race

Census	*Recount (Black)*			*Census*	*Recount (non-Black)*		
(Black)	*In*	*Out*	*Total*	*(non-Black)*	*In*	*Out*	*Total*
In	214	48	262	*In*	36	2	38
Out	146	?	?	*Out*	4	?	?
Total	360	?	?	*Total*	40	?	??

count—showed that 250 out of 400 people, or 5/8 of the sample, had been captured in the first count. Generalizing from the sample, the conclusion is that 5/8 of the total population was captured in the first count.

Having learned that 5/8 of the total population was covered by the first count, it is now possible to estimate the true population size, N, on the basis of the available information. The total number of people counted the first time, 300, is 5/8 of the total population, i.e., $300 = 5/8N$, where N is the estimate of true population size. To arrive at the estimate, a little high school algebra suffices: $N = 8/5 \times 300 = 480$. Of this estimated 480 total population, 450 have been observed in one or the other or both of the two counts. Thus, it is inferred that there are 30 persons who were not counted either time.

It is desirable to continue the analysis by calculating different rates of capture for different population groups in the block in Bedford–Stuyvesant, e.g., Blacks and others. This requires separate estimates for the numbers of Blacks and non-Blacks in this block. The breakdown this time might be quite different, as shown in Table III. This time, the vast majority of people in the block are Black; the estimates for the total numbers of Blacks and non-Blacks in the block are $N_{\text{Black}} = 360/214 \times 262 = 440.74$ and $N_{\text{non-Black}} = 40/36 \times 38 = 42.2$. Again, counting only the whole numbers of people, the total is $440 + 42 = 482$. The result is slightly higher than the earlier estimate of 480 from the two groups combined, and this is because the catchabilities are so different and the numbers so disproportionate. There is a very serious differential undercount in this hypothetical block, however, with $100(1 - 262/440) = 40.5\%$ of the Blacks being missed, compared with only $100(1 - 38/42) = 9.5\%$ of the non-Blacks being missed.

Because the undercount rate varies among different kinds of blocks, it is necessary to estimate separate undercount rates for each of a sample of blocks. It would not, for example, be expected that the dual-systems estimate of the undercount rate of a block in Bedford–Stuyvesant says very much about the undercount in an expensive suburb. Accordingly, in selecting the sample, it is important to start with a list of all the blocks or equivalent-size rural units in the United States, and group the blocks into categories, or "strata," according to their demographic and geographic characteristics. Such characteristics might include region, racial composition, proportion of homeowners to renters, and average household size. Rates of undercount for particular demographic groups are determined for a sample of blocks within each stratum by dual-systems estimation. Note that the original stratification applied to census blocks, but the estimates for undercount apply to individuals.

These estimates of undercount can be disaggregated further by demographic groups, forming what the Census Bureau calls poststrata. Estimates of undercount are generated for each poststratum (for example, non-Black females aged 30–49 living in a rental unit, in large metropolitan areas in the northeast). The actual correction of the census counts consists of multiplying the adjustment rate for the poststratum by the raw census count for each poststratum to compensate for the estimated undercount. Thus, the poststratification applies to individuals.

This is the basic idea and methodology underlying the dual-systems approach employed by the Census Bureau in 1990 and 2000. More formal descriptions and critiques can be found in the literature. ACE and dual-systems estimation are designed to correct for census error. Dual-systems estimation in the census context is considerably more complex in practice, and, like the census, is also subject to measurement error. In the absence of serious measurement error, ACE methodology should, in principle, improve the raw count. But there are several sources for measurement error in ACE and each contributes to both the bias and the variability of ACE-adjusted counts; these have been the focus of the evaluation of the adjustment process:

1. Erroneous enumerations: Unlike demographic analysis, dual-systems estimation in a census context measures erroneous enumerations. That is, before matching the records from the census and the survey to measure omissions, the bureau evaluates if a person is correctly counted at the current location in the census. If the person is enumerated erroneously (for example, is a duplicate enumeration), the case is removed from the file before starting the matching process. Without this procedure, the erroneous enumerations would elevate the nonmatch

rate and skew the dual-systems estimation estimates. The role of erroneous enumerations in the census is poorly understood, and became a subject of technical evaluation as a by-product of the use of dual-systems estimation in 1990 and 2000. In 2000, the dramatic differences in undercount estimates generated by demographic analysis and the ACE prompted the Bureau to conduct new evaluations of erroneous enumerations, by searching the entire census file for duplicate enumerations in the E sample of the ACE. The Bureau currently believes there were 5.8 million duplicate enumerations in Census 2000, and that the original ACE results reported in March 2001 "dramatically underestimated these duplicates."

2. Matching error: Dual-systems estimation assumes that those in the sample can be matched without error to those in the census without error. In fact, the computerized matching approaches used in 1990 led to the imputation of match status for a substantial fraction of the cases, and concern was expressed regarding the implications of this problem. Evidence from ACE evaluations suggests that the matching error rate for 2000 was substantially lower than in 1990.

3. Correlation bias: This term is used variously to describe both dependencies between the census and the sample and heterogeneity in response rates. In fact, in the dual-systems setting, the two components are not really distinguishable. Dual-systems estimation assumes that the responses to the census and the ACE are independent. The ACE survey operations were structurally separate from those of the census, but this still does not mean that the behavioral responses are independent of each other. Capture probabilities clearly vary among individuals within adjustment areas or groups, and the net effect of this variation (under relatively weak assumptions) is that it induces a positive dependence between the responses to the census and the sample in the aggregate.

4. Balancing error: Differences in search strategies for erroneous enumerations and matches lead to balancing error.

5. Synthetic error: The synthetic assumption implies that net census coverage rates do not vary within adjustment areas or groups.

6. Limitation of the ACE universe: In 2000, ACE was limited to a sample of the household population, and did not cover the roughly 8 million people living in group quarters. Insofar as there are differences in coverage for the household and group-quarters populations, the ACE cannot provide estimates of undercoverage in the group quarters, and hence the total population.

As Bureau officials modified classic dual-systems estimation methodology for the census context, they began to understand the impact of overcounts on census accuracy. They also began to develop the data that were used to construct the gross estimates in Table I. Nevertheless, until recently, officials believed that omissions loomed as a bigger numerical problem. Because the Census Bureau saw overcounts as less important as a source of coverage error, less research has been devoted to understanding and correcting for overcounts. Thus, the description of the dual-systems estimation methodology provided here is a simplified version of the Census Bureau plan for 2000. By the time it had completed its evaluation of the Census 2000 results in March 2003, the overcount errors were clearly visible, and the Bureau revised its evaluation methodology to attempt to develop estimates of duplications not detected in the ACE processes and "correcting" for some other forms of measurement error.

In both 1990 and 2000, the results of the dual-systems estimates were not used to adjust the official census results. In 1991, the Census Bureau staff and director recommended adjustment but were overruled by the Commerce Secretary. In March 2001, the Census Bureau staff recommended against adjustment, primarily because the ACE estimates and demographic analysis estimates of the population diverged sharply. The Bureau could not explain the discrepancy in time to meet the deadlines for releasing the redistricting data. Subsequent criticism of and revision to the demographic analysis estimates did not solve the problem. In October 2001, the Bureau decided not to adjust the postcensal estimates because it deemed the ACE to be too flawed for this purpose. It reaffirmed that decision in March 2003. At this writing, the Census Bureau's internal evaluation and the external critiques of Census 2000 agree that the number of erroneous enumerations in the 2000 census count may be considerably larger than previously believed, and that the 2000 ACE procedures did not capture and eliminate their impact.

Looking to the Future: Census-Taking in 2010 and Beyond

Central to the Census Bureau's plans for the future of the decennial census is the elimination of the census long form, which has gone to roughly 1 in 6 households nationwide, replacing it with a rolling national survey that has been called the American Community Survey. This action would have a variety of benefits for planning census activities and in particular would lead to what all observers hope will be a dramatic improvement in the master address file, which plays such a crucial role in a household-based census. There appears to be an expectation that this change, coupled with improvements in technology such as the field use of global positioning satellite systems, will improve census-taking sufficiently that there may not be a need for the adjustment-based approaches from the past. Nevertheless, the Bureau will likely have to plan an evaluation program to determine if the omissions and erroneous enumerations that have plagued recent decennial censuses will affect the 2010 census. The Bureau will again need careful evaluation tools and postcensal surveys to assess the accuracy of future censuses. The plans for those evaluations will of necessity draw on the experiences of the past two censuses, though at this writing, the nature of the 2010 evaluation program has yet to be determined.

Where to Learn More

The list of publications at the end of this article is an excellent source for literature on census analysis. Margo Anderson provides a comprehensive historical source on the U.S. Census. Margo Anderson and Stephen E. Fienberg describe the technical basis for census adjustment and the debates leading up to Census 2000. Harvey Choldin treats the undercount debates from the 1980 and 1990 censuses; and Barbara Everitt Bryant and William Dunn provide the perspective of 1990 Census Director, Barbara Everitt Bryant. For technical explication of census methods and history, there is also the recently published *Encyclopedia of the U.S. Census* by Anderson. For the critics of adjustment, see Freedman and Wachter, Kenneth Darga, Peter Skerry, and Lawrence D. Brown and co-workers. For responses, see Anderson, Daponte, Fienberg, Kadane, Spencer, and Steffey and Anderson and Fienberg.

Over the past decade, various panels of the Committee on National Statistics at the National Academy of Sciences have issued major reports dealing with the Census Bureau adjustment methodology and the 2000 decennial census. These subjects have been addressed by Steffey and Bradburn, Edmonston and Schultze, Cohen *et al.*, and Citro *et al.*

See Also the Following Articles

Census, Retail Trade • Census, Varieties and Uses of Data • Measurement Error, Issues and Solutions

Further Reading

Anderson, M. (1988). *The American Census: A Social History.* Yale University Press, New Haven.

Anderson, M. (ed.) (2000). *Encyclopedia of the U.S. Census.* CQ Press, Washington, D.C.

Anderson, M., Daponte, B. O., Fienberg, S. E., Kadane, J. B., Spencer, B. D., and Steffey, D. L. (2000). Sampling-based adjustment of the 2000 Census—A balanced perspective. *Jurimetrics* **40,** 341–356.

Anderson, M., and Fienberg, S. E. (2001). *Who Counts? The Politics of Census-Taking in Contemporary America.* Russell Sage Foundation, New York.

Anderson, M., and Fienberg, S. E. (2002). Counting and estimation: The U.S. 2000 Census adjustment decision. *J. Official Statist.*, (under revision).

Brown, L. D., Eaton, M. L., Freedman, D. A., Klein, S. P., Olshen, R. A., Wachter, K. W., Wells, M. T., and Ylvisaker, D. (1999). Statistical controversies in Census 2000. *Jurimetrics* **39,** 347–375.

Bryant, B. E., and William, D. (1995). *Moving Power and Money: The Politics of Census Taking.* New Strategist Publications, Ithaca, New York.

Choldin, H. (1994). *Looking for the Last One Percent: The Controversy over Census Undercounts.* Rutgers University Press, New Brunswick, New Jersey.

Citro, C. F., Cork, D. L., and Norwood, J. L. (2001). *The 2000 Census: An Interim Assessment.* Committee on National Statistics, National Research Council, National Academy Press, Washington, D.C.

Citro, C. F., Cork, D. L., and Norwood, J. L. (2004). *The 2000 Census: Counting Under Adversity.* Committee on National Statistics, National Research Council, National Academy Press, Washington, D.C.

Coale, A. J. (1955). The population of the United States in 1950 by age, sex, and color: A revision of the census figures. *J. Am. Statist. Assoc.* **50,** 16–54.

Cohen, M. L., White, A. A., and Rust, K. F. (1999). *Measuring a Changing Nation: Modern Methods for the 2000 Census.* Committee on National Statistics, National Research Council, National Academy Press, Washington, D.C.

Darga, K. (2000). *Fixing the Census Until It Breaks: An Assessment of the Undercount Adjustment Puzzle.* Michigan Information Center, Lansing.

Edmonston, B., and Schultze, C. (eds.) (1995). *Modernizing the U.S. Census.* Committee on National Statistics, National Research Council, National Academy Press, Washington, D.C.

Freedman, D. A., and Wachter, K. W. (2003). On the likelihood of improving the accuracy of the census through statistical adjustment. In *Science and Statistics: A Festscrift for Terry Speed* (D. R. Goldstein and S. Dudoit, eds.), IMS Monograph, Vol. 40, pp. 197–230. Institute of Mathematical Statistics, Bethesda, Maryland. Available on the Internet at www.stat.berkeley.edu

Kincannon, C. L. (2003). *Statement of Census Bureau Director C. Louis Kincannon on Accuracy and Coverage Evaluation Revision II.* U.S. Department of Commerce News, March 12, U.S. Census Bureau, Washington, D.C.

Skerry, P. (2000). *Counting on the Census? Race, Group Identity, and the Evasion of Politics.* Brookings Institution Press, Washington, D.C.

Steffey, D., and Bradburn, N. (eds.) (1994). *Counting People in the Information Age.* Committee on National Statistics, National Research Council. National Academy Press, Washington, D.C.

Census, Retail Trade

Louis G. Pol

University of Nebraska, Omaha, Nebraska, USA

Glossary

economic census A statistical program designed to obtain, categorize, and publish information every 5 years (in years that end in 2 and 7) for nearly all U.S. businesses.

enterprise An organization (company) that comprises all of the establishments that operate under the ownership or control of a single organization.

establishment A single physical location where business is conducted or where services or industrial operations are performed.

industry A detailed category in a larger classification system used to describe and group business activities.

merchandise line A numerical system used to group major categories of merchandise sold.

North American Industry Classification System (NAICS) A numerical classification scheme jointly developed by Mexico, Canada, and the United States to facilitate the collection, tabulation, presentation, and analysis of data on establishments.

retail trade The trade sector is made up of businesses engaged in selling merchandise, usually without transformation, and providing services incidental to the sale of the merchandise.

sector classification A numerical system used to group and describe similar businesses.

Standard Industrial Classification (SIC) A numerical scheme or code utilized to classify industries and products; superseded in 1997 by a new method, the North American Industry Classification System.

The retail trade sector (sectors 44 and 45 in the North American Industry Classification System) is made up of establishments engaged in retailing merchandise. Services that are incidental to the sale of the merchandise are also included in these sectors (e.g., warranty services on new automobiles). Retailers, in general, are the final step in the process of distributing merchandise to customers, usually following manufacturers and wholesalers. They sell products in relatively small quantities to consumers. Retailers vary greatly in employee size, from the one- or two-person "mom and pop" storefront to the hundreds of persons that make up the staff of each Super Target store. Chains of retailers often dominate local and regional markets as well as the channels of merchandise distribution (e.g., Wal-Mart). Retailers also vary with respect to the method by which customers are reached. That is, there are both store and nonstore retailers, with the latter selling merchandise using direct-response advertising, telemarketing, broadcast infomercials, catalogues, door-to-door sales, and the Internet, among other methods of reaching customers.

History of the Economic Census—Retail Trade

The history of economic censuses that focus on retail trade can be traced back to 1930, the first time retail trade data were gathered in the United States. Other economic data had been gathered in U.S. censuses as early as 1810, but the range of information was limited. The economic component of the 1930 decennial census was much broader than in previous decennial and special censuses, and was subsumed under queries related to distribution (wholesale and retail) enterprises. The 1930 census of distribution was composed of data gathered only by a field canvas, and the retail trade component covered establishments engaged in some manner of retail trade, although a limited number of service businesses were also included. Six questionnaires were utilized to gather data from 1.5 million stores. Data items such as number of stores, sales, personnel, payroll, and operating expenses were included.

Most of these items can be found 70 years later in the 1997 and 2002 economic censuses. The 1935 Census of Business covered retail trade much in the same way as it had been covered in 1930, with the exception that in this instance the Census of Business was not part of the decennial census. In 1940, retail trade data were gathered as part of decennial census activities, and with a few exceptions, the types of information gathered were identical to those collected in 1930 and 1935.

In 1948, the U.S. Congress passed Public Law 80-671, which authorized the Census Bureau to conduct an economic census in 1948 and every fifth year thereafter. The 1948 business census had a retail trade component and gathered data from a wide range of firms. To gather more detailed information, the sampling consisted of 1 in 10 of small independent firms, large retailers (sales in excess of $100,000), and multiestablishment firms. A more limited amount of data were gathered from small, single-establishment firms. Enumerators left one of two questionnaires at most single-establishment firms, and these were to be returned to the Census Bureau by mail. Enumerators completed the questionnaire on-site for most of the multiestablishment firms in the sample. Nonrespondents to the mail-back universe of establishments were mailed a reminder form, and follow-up visits to the firms were made. This census was also marked by the establishment of temporary field offices to facilitate data collection, and the collection of data via reenumeration to estimate undercoverage by the census. In 1948, it was estimated that the enumeration efforts missed 3.6% of retail establishments.

The U.S. Congress did not provide funding for the 1953 economic censuses, but after a great deal of debate and the appointment of a special commission to study such censuses, funds were appropriated to support a 1954 economic census, including a retail and wholesale trades component. This census was also noteworthy because it marked the first attempt by the Census Bureau to utilize administrative records as a method for deriving a small number of data items for retail nonemployers (retailers without paid employees). Retail employers were enumerated using a mail-out/mail-back procedure. Field offices were again established, and letters and telephone calls were utilized in follow-up activities. The 1958 and 1963 economic censuses closely resembled 1954 efforts, and once again the retail and wholesale trades were considered to be one category.

In 1967, the U.S. Congress altered the years in which economic census data were collected, changing to years ending in 2 or 7, the standard seen today. Wholesale and retail trades were still considered to be one category, and data for retail nonemployers were gathered using Internal Revenue Service income tax records. Procedural improvements were made, including reliance on computers for data processing. The 1972 economic censuses were much like those in 1967, and again administrative records were used as a source of data for a large number of businesses.

More than one-half of the enterprises enumerated in 1977 had their data extracted from administrative records. Unlike the previous censuses, retail trade and wholesale trade were treated as separate enterprise categories. Although there were a number of methodological improvements over the next decade, the census of retail trade for 1987 was very much like the 1977 version; between 1982 and 1987, however, there was a 20% increase in the number of merchandise line questions.

The 1992 economic census was characterized by the most significant expansion in over 50 years, particularly in regard to an increase in the number of businesses covered. In all, about 98% of all economic activity was covered, up from 75% for 1987. There were also surveys of minority-owned business enterprises, women-owned businesses, and characteristics of business owners. For the most part, data from the census were made available for the nation, states, metropolitan areas, counties, and places of 2500 or more population, although some retail trade data were made available only at the zip code level. A subject series report on merchandise line sales was produced along with one on major retail centers. In general, content on the questionnaire remained the same as that for 1987. Response rates were improved by emphasizing the mandatory nature of the census, standardizing the size of questionnaires, improving the quality of cover letters, utilizing more effective direct-mail techniques, and prenotifying large companies that the census questionnaire would seen be sent. In addition to making the transition from Standard Industrial Classification (SIC) codes to the North American Industry Classification System (NAICS), the 1997 economic census was marked by methodological changes. Although computer self-administered questionnaires were used in the 1992 census, their use in 1997 was much more extensive. The Internet was used to promote awareness of the census as well as to disseminate census products. The 1997 census data were available faster and in more forms (e.g., via the Internet and on compact disks) than in previous censuses. The content of the questionnaires, particularly in regard to retailing, stayed much the same.

Virtually all of the changes for the 2002 economic censuses concerned improved data availability/access and advancements in data collection methodologies. The content for retail trade businesses remained the same. Faster release of industry series (e.g., retailing) data was accomplished by producing industry-specific reports. The surveys of business owners, including minorities and women, were expanded as well as the survey of owner characteristics. In an effort to improve coverage and, therefore, data quality, establishments were divided into mail and nonmail universes. Large employers and a sample of small employers, i.e., single-establishment firms with a payroll below a fixed point, received mail surveys and the appropriate follow-up. Data for the nonmail universe were derived or estimated from administrative records of other federal agencies. Published reports in electronic format include those on merchandise line sales, establishment and firm size, and miscellaneous subjects.

Method of Data Collection

Currently, data for the Economic Census—Retail Trade are collected utilizing mail-out, mail-back surveys, with telephone follow-up, and through the examination of administrative records. More than 5 million large and medium-size firms, including firms known to operate more than one establishment, were sent questionnaires or a classification form in December 2002 for the Economic Census—Retail Trade, 2002. The forms were due back on February 12, 2003. Respondents also had the option of downloading spreadsheet-like forms and submitting data electronically. The questionnaires were tailored to the type of business in the retail sector, and in 2002 over 600 different questionnaires were utilized. For example, form NC-99510, which was sent to automobile dealers, contained questions about the location of the enterprise, sales, number of employees, and first-quarter payroll (January–March 2002) for each location if there was more than one physical location for the business. Form RT-44101, also sent to automobile dealers, contained questions on months in operation (for 2002), e-commerce sales, class of customer (i.e., individuals; other retailers and wholesalers), method sales, type of vehicle sold, and receipts from services (e.g., auto repair) rendered, among others. Some of the forms could be completed in a few minutes, but several took much longer. In the event that an establishment did not mail back a questionnaire, a remailing of the questionnaires occurred, several times in some cases. Telephone follow-ups were also utilized to maximize the response.

Data for small firms, usually with 10 or fewer employees, were gathered from administrative records (e.g., the Internal Revenue Service). These firms represent about 10% of all sales of establishments covered in the economic census. Information for the standard queries (sales, payroll, and employment) was directly extracted or estimated based on data from these records.

Several cautionary notes are appropriate at this juncture. The user of the data should be aware that rules for data disclosure affect data availability, particularly for small population areas. In addition, conversion from SIC to NAIC categories must be done carefully when making comparisons across time. A bridge table is available on the Census Bureau web site. Metropolitan statistical area (MSA) and zip code boundaries change over time due to the addition or subtraction of counties. Any time series comparisons for MSAs and zip codes must be preceded with a check on boundary changes.

Uses of the Data

Economic census data are widely used, especially in light of their ready availability via compact disk read-only memory (CD-ROM) format and on the Internet. Data are available for a wide variety of geographic units, although it is important to consider that some retail markets, e.g., health aids and books, are linked less to geography now than in the past because of purchasing via the Internet and direct advertising. Retail trade data from monthly and annual U.S. Census Bureau surveys are often combined with census data for analysis purposes. There are several broad categories of usage for economic data.

Market Conditions and Changes

Analysis of retail trade data can provide national, regional, and local information on current conditions and the aggregate effect of shifts in the structure of retail markets. The emergence of warehouse clubs, supercenters, and superstores, for example, has shifted customers toward these larger entities, which, in turn, now play a major role in local, regional, and national markets. It is possible to determine how a particular kind of business dominates a merchandise line by assembling data from two or more economic censuses. For example, in 1997, about 84% of all hardware, tools, and plumbing and electrical supplies were sold by 41,981 building materials and supply dealers in the United States. However, fewer than 10% of the stores, home centers, accounted for 23% of all sales. Comparing 1997 with 1992 and 2002 data would provide documentation of the growing concentration of sales by home centers of products in this merchandise line. Comparisons across merchandise lines would allow for a comparison of the market of home centers for a range of products sold.

Market Share

Market share refers to the percentage of sales of a product in units, dollars, or some other meaningful measure made by a business relative to all sales of that product, usually for a specific geographic unit and always for a specific time period, e.g., December 2003. It is useful to know absolute sales and trends in sales for a business, but the value of these data can be extended greatly if market share is calculated. So, if a local clothing store has experienced a recent increase in sales, e.g., a 50% rise over the past 4 years, but market share has declined, then it may be the case that even though a favorable demographic profile for the market exists, competitors, both old and new, made significant advances in the market. Additional calculations may show that if that business had held its market share for those 4 years, clothing sales would have grown 150%, not the 50% realized.

Data from the Economic Census—Retail Trade can provide the denominator for calculating market share for one or more periods of time. Data for the numerator come from a specific store or chain of stores. Market share for one areal unit, e.g., a county, can be followed for several time periods in order to better understand trends in market dominance. Market share information for one market may also be used as a benchmark or to establish expectations for a new market. For example, if Regents Sporting Goods claims 12% of the Lincoln County market, then 12% may become the expected market share in Payne County, assuming that the demographic composition, industry structure, and nature of the competition are similar. A market share of less than 12% in Payne County may be interpreted as an indicator of operational problems for Regents Sporting Goods in that location.

Assess Competition

Although the Economic Census—Retail Trade data do not make available the names and associated data for individual competing businesses, the available data can be very useful, when combined with other information, in understanding and measuring the effects of competitor strength. Telephone business listings, Chamber of Commerce memberships, and other readily available data can provide basic information on new and old competitors, including their location, within a particular market. The same sources can provide data on business expansions, e.g., new locations, as well as on closings. Figures for individual businesses (numerator) and U.S. Census Bureau retail trade data (denominator) can be used to calculate market share, but in the context of additions or exits to and from the market. If a "mom and pop" grocery store loses 30% of its market share in Jefferson County between 1997 and 2002, and in 1999 a new Wal-Mart store opens in Jefferson County, the likely reason for the decline in market share would be the presence of the new Wal-Mart store, provided that other business conditions in the market remained basically the same.

Site Location

Retail trade data can be combined with other demographic indicators as well as information on existing businesses to make decisions about where physically to locate a new business. Areas with lower than expected per capita or per household retail sales, accounting for income variations and the location of competitors, present opportunities for retail expansion. Retail grocers, for example, study the growth in population in expanding areas with respect to present and projected sales of grocery items for those places. Opportunities exist for new grocery stores in areas that are underserved, that is, have less than expected retail grocery sales. Once a market is seen as having measurable potential, then a specific site for a retail store must be found. Site location decisions are based on availability and cost of land and labor, traffic flows, the location of current competitors, and forecasts of other new competitors in that market. Sites are chosen in part to minimize the travel distance/time of potential customers. Financial analysis for competing locations is performed to determine if targeted levels of return on investment (ROI)/return on equity (ROE) are likely to be achieved.

Information to Attract Investors

Investors, i.e., venture capitalists and banks, are impressed by unique and important business ideas, but they are more impressed by business plans that include detailed financial analysis. Utilizing data from the Economic Census—Retail Trade, projected sales and market share for a given location can be produced and then used as input to present information on the profitability of the new location. In the case of small businesses, these calculations are particularly important, given the high failure rate for such establishments. Retail trade data can be used to document the size of the market (sales) for a specific retail category, e.g., furniture. Sales data can be projected, given certain growth assumptions. A specific business plan can forecast a market share, and that market share multiplied by market size will yield projected sales. It is those projected sales figures, provided that they can be justified, that drive the remaining financial indicators such as ROI. Good indicator figures can be used to attract investors.

Locate Business-to-Business Markets

Most often, retail business data are analyzed with respect to the buyers of the finished products being sold. However, retail establishments are customers for a host of products and services that are required in order to conduct business. Business-to-business marketing is an important category of economic activity. The same data on establishments, sales, and employees that can be used to calculate market share and assess market potential for retail sales can be used by other businesses to estimate the market for store fixtures, microcomputers, and cash registers, items needed by retailers to carry out business operations. Geographic areas with many establishments represent large markets for these kinds of products, and combining data for several geographic contiguous areas within a state (or contiguous states) can facilitate the creation of sales territories. Although territories vary in terms of population, population differentials are not a good predictor of variations in the number of retail establishments because those establishments can vary greatly in size. Therefore, the market for retail store products must be further differentiated based on the distribution of retail store type and size. Once the market is understood, a trained sales force can be used to fulfill market needs.

Evaluate and Compare Sales Effectiveness

Good businesses evaluate the effectiveness of sales efforts in order to allocate sales resources and determine at what level to set incentives for the sales force. Utilizing retail trade data from local, regional, or national markets, targets or sales expectations can be established for retail stores and sales quotas can subsequently be set for individual sales persons. Additional demographic and competitor data can be used to adjust expectations levels up or down. For example, sales figures for retail stores that specialize in computer equipment and software should be higher in market areas that are characterized by higher-than-average income and fewer competitors than sales figures in markets that have lower incomes and where the level of competition is greater.

Expectations for sales, and thus an assessment of sales effectiveness, are different for two stores that are part of the same retail chain but in different types of markets. In this type of situation, human and other resources can be reallocated from the established market to the burgeoning one in order to capture sales potential. Data from the Economic Census—Retail Trade can be used to estimate sales expectations, both for markets and for individual stores. Underperforming stores may require reconsideration in the recruiting and training of salespersons and/or the rewards structure designed to encourage sales productivity.

Measures of Retail Trade Activity

Change in Absolute Numbers and Percentages

Although the utilization of more complex measures of retail activity is helpful in understanding markets, it makes best sense to first examine raw data and simple percentages that describe current conditions and/or changes over two or more time intervals. To assess the current (1997) level as well as change in retail trade for the state of Nebraska between 1992 and 1997, two sets of data are needed (Table I). Simple change measures show that although the number of retail establishments in Nebraska declined by 107 (−0.9%) between 1992 and 1997, there were substantial gains in sales revenue (42.0%), annual payroll (37.6%), and number of paid employees (13.1%) over the same time interval. Comparison data for the United States show a small increase in the number of establishments (2.3%), lower increases in sales (34.4%) and payroll (30.4%), and a higher increase in paid employees (15.0%) when compared to Nebraska. These data can be used by state officials in tax revenue forecast models.

Similar analyses using specific categories of retailing (NAICS) can be used to document trends in specific types of retail activity. Table II shows establishment and sales

Table I Retail Trade Activity in Nebraska: 1997 and 1992[a]

Year	*Establishments*	*Sales ($1000)*	*Annual payroll ($1000)*	*Paid employees*
1997	11,268	16,350,932	1,799,417	149,478
1992	11,375	11,521,818	1,307,961	132,157
Nebraska change (%)	−0.9	41.9	37.6	13.1
U.S. change (%)	2.3	34.4	30.4	15.0

[a] Data from the U.S. census web site at www.census.gov

Table II Retail Trade by Establishments and Sales for Nebraska: 1982–1997

	Establishments				*Sales ($1000s)*			
Business type	*1982*	*1987*	*1992*	*1997*	*1982*	*1987*	*1992*	*1997*
General merchandise stores	328	276	300	299	784,103	1,084,413	1,567,227	2,199,033
Food stores	1229	1222	1095	1040	1,419,864	1,672,434	2,156,006	2,284,888
Automotive dealers	822	841	817	858	1,295,442	1,792,514	2,376,629	3,718,928
Apparel and accessory stores	1022	977	907	786	344,553	365,021	492,112	490,348

data for Nebraska for the period 1982 to 1997. Several patterns can be seen in these data. Although there was an increase in the number of automobile dealers over the 15-year period, the number of establishments for the remaining three categories declined. In particular, there was a more than 20% decrease in the number of apparel and accessories stores. In addition, the growth in sales for general merchandise stores and automobile dealers nearly tripled over the period. Growth in the remaining categories was much more modest. These data can be used by state and local government officials to understand the economic restructuring of the state. Persons in the private sector can use the same data to help identify market opportunities or threats.

Market Share

To calculate 1997 market share for a furniture and home furnishings store in the Omaha, Nebraska MSA, two sets of data are needed (Table III). The data in Table III show that in 1997, the Omaha Furniture Company (fictitious company) held nearly 12% of the Omaha MSA furniture and home furnishings market. An expanded analysis would help document trends in market share (i.e., comparison data for 1992 and 2002), determine what percentage of the Omaha MSA annual payroll and paid employees it took to support the 11.7% market share, and identify what percentage of the Omaha Furniture Company's sales came from outside the MSA (data from company records).

Pull Factors

One way to estimate the extent to which a community or place draws its customers from outside its boundaries is to calculate a pull ratio. Pull ratios are normally produced with a specific area of retail trade in mind. For the following example, the focus is on the extent to which Douglas County, Nebraska draws its customers for new automobiles from outside the county. Two sets of data are required to calculate the pull ratio for the scenario described (Table IV). A set of straightforward manipulations is required to arrive at the pull ratio:

$$\begin{aligned}\text{Pull factor} &= (\text{Douglas County per capita new auto sales/state per capita new auto sales}) - (\text{state per capita income/county per capita income}) \\ &= (2.284/1.904) - (19{,}613/22{,}879) \\ &= (1.199) - (0.857) \\ &= 1.027.\end{aligned}$$

The first component of the pull factor, the new auto sales ratio (county per capita sales/state per capital sales), produces an index of per capita sales using the state per capita figure as the standard or average figure. Any ratio larger than 1.0 means that Douglas County new automobile sales exceed the statewide average; in the example here, a ratio of 1.199 means that per capita sales in Douglas County are nearly 20% greater than the state average. However, the first ratio must be "adjusted" for income differences, and in this instance, state per capita income is less than that of Douglas County. That is, purchasing power for the state is lower than that for Douglas County. The new ratio, 1.027, means that Douglas County pulls 2.7% more new automobile sales than would be expected based on population and income data alone.

The analysis can be expanded to include multiple points in time to determine if pull is increasing, decreasing, or staying the same. The pull factor can be calculated for different retail NAIC systems (e.g., gasoline stations and used cars) to determine where retail pull is the greatest and least in Douglas County. Moreover, calculating pull factors for numerous NAIC systems and several counties can provide valuable information on dominant markets for different retail sectors.

Per Capita Sales, Sales per Household

Many times, analysts wish to compare retail sales figures for two or more markets when those markets differ in size.

Table III Furniture and Home Furnishing Sales Market Share for a Furniture Company, 1997[a]

Coverage	*Furniture/home furnishings sales ($1000)*
Omaha MSA[b]	566,775
Omaha Furniture Co.[c]	66,500
Market share	11.7%

[a] *Source:* U.S. Bureau of the Census (1999). 1997 Economic Census, Retail Trade, Nebraska, Table 2. U.S. Government Statistical Office, Washington, D.C.
[b] MSA, Metropolitan statistical area.
[c] Fictitious company.

Table IV Automobile Sales, Population, and Per Capita Income: Douglas County, Nebraska and the State of Nebraska[a]

Region	*Automobile sales ($1000)*	*Population*	*Per capita income*
Douglas County	1,007,465	441,006	$22,879
State of Nebraska	3,155,814	1,657,000	$19,613

[a] *Sources:* U.S. Bureau of the Census (1999), 1997 Economic Census, Retail Trade, Nebraska (Table 3) and U.S. Bureau of the Census (2002), Census 2002, Nebraska (Table DP-3), U.S. Government Printing Office, Washington, D.C.

Transforming absolute sales figures into per capita measures offers a way to make reasonable comparisons. Three sets of data are used in Table V for illustration purposes. Per capita furniture and home furnishings are $1251, $61, and $443 for Douglas County, Sarpy County, and Nebraska, respectively. Sales per household totals are $3030, $167, and $1103 for Douglas County, Sarpy County, and Nebraska, respectively. The large discrepancy in per capita figures clearly shows how dominant Douglas County is with regard to furniture and home furnishings sales. In fact, the Douglas County pull factor for furniture and home furnishings is quite high, 2.420! As it turns out, Douglas County furniture and home furnishing retailers draw customers from a five-state market area. The market is dominated by one retailer, Nebraska Furniture Mart.

Actual Versus Potential Sales

Pull factors, per capita data, and household per capita data are easily used to compare actual sales across geographic units to determine if there is market potential in one or more of those units. That is, although low values on any of these indicators suggest that a dominant retailer may exist in an adjacent county, they also show that a significant local market may be found. Caution must be emphasized in the use of these data, however. The large per capita and per household furniture and home furnishings sales figures for Douglas County, and comparison low per capita and household numbers for Sarpy County, suggest at first examination significant market potential in Sarpy County. Although some potential probably exists, the dominance of Douglas County retailers for furniture and home furnishings sales has a long history, and Douglas County competition for a new Sarpy County furniture retailer is substantial.

Focusing on a different retail category, gasoline stations, other comparisons are possible. All three of the counties have per capita sales at gasoline station figures that are substantially smaller than those found for the entire state (Table VI). All other factors being equal, if Sarpy County residents spent as much per capita as did residents statewide, there would be $106,065,000 in sales (86,232 × 1.23). The difference in the two figures, nearly $20 million, represents potential new sales. Other confounding factors, e.g., commuting patterns, drive-to-work distance, and the range of products/services offered at gas stations, that affect the demand for products sold as well as where people stop to purchase gasoline and related products and services must be accounted for before business decisions are made. It is easier to establish clear sales potential in markets that are not adjacent to others, especially if the products are not sold via the Internet or by direct sales.

An alternative way of exploring retail opportunities is to examine retail supply in one or more market areas. Table VII shows data for seven Nebraska counties with respect to food and beverage stores (NAIC 445). Although the range in the number of establishments is relatively small (11), there is substantial variation in the average number of persons employed in those stores. On average, the stores are small in Antelope and Boyd counties and they are larger in Adams and Platte counties. Extended analyses in each county would identify individual stores to determine if one or two dominate the market. By combining contiguous counties or places (cities) that were in close proximity, the market potential for a new competitor could be determined.

In conclusion, data from the Economic Census—Retail Trade are used for a wide range of business and government purposes. When combined with other U.S.

Table V Furniture and Home Furnishing Sales, Population, and Households for Douglas and Sarpy Counties and the State of Nebraska[a]

Region	*Furniture and home furnishing sales ($1000)*	*Population*	*Households*
Douglas County	552,054	441,006	182,194
Sarpy County	7278	118,571	42,426
Nebraska	734,973	1,657,000	666,184

[a] *Sources:* U.S. Bureau of the Census (1999), 1997 Economic Census, Retail Trade, Nebraska (Table 3) and U.S. Bureau of the Census (2002), Census 2002, Nebraska (Tables 1 and 3), U.S. Government Printing Office, Washington, D.C.

Table VI Gasoline Station Sales and Population for Douglas County, Sarpy County, Washington County, and the State of Nebraska[a]

Region	*Sales ($1000s)*	*Population*	*Per capita sales*	*State/county ratio*
Douglas County	306,109	441,006	$694	1.29
Sarpy County	86,232	118,571	$727	1.23
Washington County	10,826	18,470	$586	1.55
Nebraska	1,488,262	1,657,000	$898	—

[a] *Sources:* U.S. Bureau of the Census (1999), 1997 Economic Census, Retail Trade, Nebraska (Table 3) and U.S. Bureau of the Census (2002), Census 2002, Nebraska (Tables 1 and 3), U.S. Government Printing Office, Washington, D.C.

Table VII Number of Food and Beverage Stores and Number of Employees in These Stores in Seven Nebraska Counties[a]

NAIC[b] 445 (food and beverage store) location	*Establishments*	*Paid employees*	*Employees per establishment*
Adams County	16	471	29.4
Antelope County	10	73	7.3
Box Butte County	10	177	17.7
Boyd County	6	32	5.3
Phelps County	6	136	22.6
Platte County	14	472	33.7
Wayne County	5	118	23.6

[a] *Source:* U.S. Bureau of the Census (1999), 1997 Economic Census, Retail Trade, Nebraska (Table 3), U.S. Government Statistical Office, Washington, D.C.

[b] NAIC, North American Industry Classification.

Census Bureau retail trade survey data, additional economic data, population information, and private sector data, powerful sets of indicators and analyses emerge.

See Also the Following Articles

Census, Varieties and Uses of Data • Data Collection, Primary vs. Secondary • Neutrality in Data Collection • Survey Questionnaire Construction

Further Reading

Ahmed, S. A., Blum, L. A., and Wallace, M. E. (1998). Conducting the economic census. *Govt. Informat. Q.* **15,** 275–302.

Casey, D. M. (2002). *U.S. Retail Sales, Mall Sales, and Department Store Sales Review.* International Council of Shopping Centers, New York.

Dumas, M. W. (1997). Productivity in two retail trade industries: 1987–95. *Month. Labor Rev.* **120,** 35–39.

Foster, K. A. (1997). Regional impulses. *J. Urban Affairs* **19,** 375–403.

Hovland, M. A., and Gauthier, J. G. (2000). *History of the 1997 Economic Census.* U.S. Census Bureau, Washington, D.C.

Micarelli, W. F. (1998). Evolution of the United States economic censuses: The nineteenth and twentieth centuries. *Govt. Informat. Q.* **15,** 335–377.

Sieling, M., Friedman, B., and Dumas, M. (2001). Labor productivity in the retail trade industry. *Month. Labor Rev.* **124,** 3–14.

U.S. Census Bureau. (2000). *1997 Economic Census—Retail Trade—Geographic Area Series.* U.S. Census Bureau, Washington, D.C.

U.S. Census Bureau. (2001). *1997 Economic Census—Retail Trade—Merchandise Line Sales.* U.S. Census Bureau, Washington, D.C.

U.S. Census Bureau. (2002). *2002 Economic Census, Glossary of Terms for the Economic Census*. Available on the Internet at http://help.econ.census.gov/econhelp/glossary

Census, Varieties and Uses of Data

Constance F. Citro
National Research Council of The National Academies, Washington, DC, USA

Glossary

long-form items Additional items asked of a sample of households and individuals on the census long-form questionnaire (the long form also includes the short-form items).

population coverage Census count divided by the census count plus the estimated net undercount (people missed in the census minus duplicates and other erroneous enumerations).

public use microdata sample (PUMS) files Contain records for households and people sampled from census long-form records, processed to protect confidentiality.

short-form items Basic demographic items asked of everyone; short-form items are included on the short-form and long-form questionnaires.

summary (SF) files Contain census tabulations for geographic areas, down to the block level (short-form tabulations) and the block group level (long-form tabulations).

The U.S. decennial census (hereafter census) is conducted every 10 years as required by Article 1 of the Constitution. The first census in 1790 obtained minimal information for each household. The 2000 census ascertained six basic items, plus name, for everyone (short-form items) and more than 60 population and housing items for approximately one in six households on long-form questionnaires. (The number of long-form items exceeded the number of questions, some of which had multiple parts.) The data are available in tabular and microdata formats. The basic data serve constitutional purposes of reapportioning the House of Representatives, drawing new legislative district boundaries, and enforcing provisions of the Voting Rights Act. The short-form and long-form data are widely used by federal, state, and local governments, the private sector, academia, the media, and the general public. For appropriate use of census data, users should consider such dimensions of data quality as timeliness, population coverage, nonresponse error, measurement error, and sampling variability (long-form data). For analyses over time, users should consider changes in definitions, data processing procedures, and categories used in tabulations, all of which affect comparability.

Census Content and Products

Evolution

For the first census in 1790, U.S. marshals obtained for each household counts of free white males aged 16 and older and under age 16, free white females, all other free persons, and slaves. The 1820 census was the first to ask additional questions, including the number of household members engaged in agriculture, manufacturing, and commerce. Censuses in the late 19th and early 20th centuries had large numbers of questions. The 1940 census first used statistical sampling to add questions without burdening the entire population: it asked several new questions of a 5% sample of the population; it also included the first housing census. The 1960 census—the first to use the U.S. Postal Service for questionnaire delivery—introduced the concept of separate "short" and "long" forms.

Data from the earliest censuses were provided to the public in printed volumes, beginning with a single 56-page report in 1790 and growing to multiple voluminous reports. Tabulations were provided for political jurisdictions, including states, counties, places, and villages. Beginning in 1910, census data were provided for a growing number of small statistical areas defined to be useful for local analysis and planning. The first such areas were census tracts (neighborhoods), defined in eight cities in 1910. By 2000, all counties in the nation were divided into census tracts of approximately 2500 to 8000 residents each. Beginning in 1940, census data were provided for yet smaller units—namely, individual city blocks—in 191 cities. The block program expanded and, in 1990, blocks were identified nationwide—approximately 10 million in all.

Following the 1960 census — the first to use computers for data processing—the Census Bureau released machine-readable data products in addition to printed reports. These products included summary (SF) files of tabulations for geographic areas as small as census tracts, block groups, and blocks (short-form items only). SF files support small-area analyses that are not possible with other available data sources (household survey sample sizes are too small and administrative records are limited in content). Computerized products also included public use microdata sample (PUMS) files, containing anonymized records for households and persons sampled from the census long-form records. Through the initiative of the research community, PUMS files are or will be available for censuses from 1850 through 2000, except for 1890 (most of the records for that census were destroyed in a fire). PUMS files permit rich analyses over time and across population groups. Although their subject content is more limited than most household surveys, their sample size (at least 1% of the population) supports analyses for such small groups as the oldest old, which would not be possible with smaller samples.

Originally, SF and PUMS files were available on magnetic tape. Today, they are available on CD-ROM/DVD and on the Census Bureau's Web site (available at http://www.census.gov).

2000 Census Content and Products

The 2000 census used mail-out/mail-back and personal enumeration techniques to obtain information for 115.9 million housing units, of which 105.5 million were occupied, and 281.4 million people, including 273.6 million household residents and 7.8 million residents of group quarters (e.g., prisons, college dormitories, nursing homes). Six items plus name—age, race, sex, ethnicity (Hispanic origin), household relationship, and housing tenure (owner, renter)—were asked of everyone; an additional 36 population items and 26 housing items were asked of a sample of the population on the long form. (Table I compares 2000 census population content with earlier censuses.) The overall long-form sample size was about 1 in 6 (17% of the population). Four sampling rates were used—1 in 2, 1 in 4, 1 in 6, and 1 in 8—with larger rates used for people in small governmental jurisdictions and the smallest rate used for people in larger census tracts.

The 2000 census information is provided to users in several forms (see Table II). SF1 and SF2 files contain short-form tabulations for geographic areas as small as blocks; SF3 and SF4 files contain long-form tabulations for areas as small as census tracts and block groups. Two PUMS files became available in 2003: 1% and 5% samples of the population. Geographic identification varies on the files; no area is identified with fewer than 100,000 people. Compared with previous censuses, some of the 2000 PUMS file content was reduced to minimize disclosure risk, which has increased with the availability of sophisticated matching software and data on the Internet that can potentially be linked to census data.

Population Estimates

Another important census data product comprises regularly updated small-area population estimates that the Census Bureau develops based on each census. The Bureau produces estimates of total population by single years of age, sex, race, and Hispanic origin on a monthly basis for the United States and annually for states and counties as of July 1 of each year. The Bureau also produces total population estimates every 2 years for incorporated places and minor civil divisions of counties (in states that have such divisions). The Bureau has begun producing biennial estimates of total population and children aged 5 through 17 for school districts. Population estimates are produced by updating the census year figures with data from such sources as birth and death records and immigration statistics.

American Community Survey

With few exceptions, there are no sources during the decade of estimates on long-form topics for small areas, such as census tracts. The American Community Survey (ACS) is designed to fill that gap: it is planned to be a large-scale, continuing monthly sample survey of housing units in the United States, conducted primarily by mail, with content similar to that on the census long form. If the ACS is successfully implemented, there will likely be no long form in the 2010 and subsequent censuses.

From 1999 through 2003, the ACS was conducted in 31 sites, chosen to facilitate comparison with the 2000 census. In addition, from 2000 through 2003, the Census Supplementary Survey, using the ACS questionnaire, sampled approximately 700,000 households yearly nationwide. Beginning in summer 2004, contingent on funding, the full ACS will sample 250,000 housing units each month, for an annual sample size of approximately 3 million housing units spread across the nation. Over a 5-year period, the ACS sample addresses will cumulate to approximately 15 million housing units, somewhat smaller than the 2000 long-form sample size of approximately

Table I Census of Population Content

2000 Short-form population items	
Age, race, sex	Asked in every census from 1790 to 2000
Hispanic origin	Asked in 1930 (in the race question), 1970 (long form), 1980–2000
Relationship to household head	Asked in 1880–2000
2000 Long-form population items	
Ancestry	Asked in 1980–2000
Citizenship, year of immigration	Citizenship asked in 1820, 1830, 1870, 1890–2000; year of immigration asked in 1990–1930, 1970–2000; year of naturalization asked in 1920; eligibility to vote asked in 1870
Disability (several questions)	Items related to physical or mental disabilities asked in 1830–1890, 1900–1930, 1970–2000
Education (school attendance, whether public or private, educational attainment)	School attendance asked in 1850–2000; public or private school asked in 1960–2000; educational attainment asked in 1940–2000; literacy asked in 1840–1930; vocational training asked in 1970
Employment status last week	Asked in 1930–2000; duration of unemployment asked in 1880–1910, 1930–1950, 1980
Hours usually worked per week	Asked in 1980–2000; hours worked last week asked in 1940–1990
Income (total and by source)	Asked in 1940–2000; categories expanded over time
Language (whether language other than English is spoken at home, how well English is spoken)	Language spoken at home asked in 1890–1940, 1960–2000; how well English is spoken asked in 1980–2000; language of parents asked in 1910, 1920
Marital status	Asked in 1880–2000 (short form prior to 2000); other marriage-related questions asked in 1850–1910, 1930–1980; number of children living asked in 1890–1910; number of children ever born asked in 1890–1910, 1940–1990
Occupation and industry of current employment, class of worker (e.g., private, government)	Occupation asked in 1850–2000; industry asked in 1820, 1840, 1910–2000; class of worker asked in 1910–2000; occupation, industry, and class of worker 5 years ago asked in 1970; activity 5 years ago asked in 1970, 1980
Place of birth	Asked in 1850–2000; place of birth of parents asked in 1870–1970
Place of work, transportation to work (several questions)	Asked in 1960–2000
Responsibility for grandchildren in the home	New question in 2000
Prior residence (5 years ago), farm residence (housing item)	Prior residence asked in 1940–2000; farm residence asked in 1890–2000; year moved to present residence asked in 1960, 1970, 1980–2000 (housing item); whether ever farm resident asked in 1940, 1950
Veteran status (including period of service), years of military service	Veteran status asked in 1840, 1890, 1910, 1930–2000; period of service asked in 1930, 1950–2000; years of military service asked in 1990, 2000; questions on dependents of veterans asked in 1890, 1940
Weeks worked last year	Asked in 1940–2000
Year last worked	Asked in 1960–2000

Source: U.S. Census Bureau (1973); author's inspection of 1980, 1990, and 2000 questionnaires.

18 million housing units. The Bureau plans to issue annual products containing yearly averages of monthly data for areas with 65,000 or more people and multiyear averages for areas with fewer people (5-year averages for the smallest areas).

Constitutional Purposes

Reapportionment

The decennial census plays a fundamental role in the U.S. political system by providing population counts for each state once a decade for reallocation of seats in the U.S. House of Representatives. This primary role for census-taking is mandated in Article 1 of the U.S. Constitution and elaborated in Title 13 of the U.S. Code, which stipulates that the Census Bureau must provide state population counts to the president by 9 months after Census Day (December 31 of the census year) for determining the number of representatives for each state from the prescribed apportionment formula. Congress enacted this procedure in 1929 so that reapportionment would occur automatically each decade, precluding what happened after the 1920 census, when Congress could

Table II 2000 Census Data Products

Summary (SF) Files
Census 2000 Redistricting Data Summary File (P.L. 94-171 File)
Counts of the population, total and aged 18 and over, by 63 race categories, by Hispanic, not Hispanic, by state, county, place, minor civil division, voting precinct (if specified by the state), census tract, block group, block
Summary File 1 (SF1, tabulations of short-form items; file for each state unless noted)
1. Population counts for 63 race categories and Hispanic, not Hispanic—down to the block level
2. Population counts for many detailed race and Hispanic categories and American Indian and Alaska Native tribes—down to the census tract level
3. Selected population and housing characteristics—down to the block level
4. National-level file—tabulations for states, counties, and places; urban–rural tabulations
Summary File 2 (SF2, detailed tabulations of short-form items)
1. Population and housing characteristics iterated for many detailed race and Hispanic categories and American Indian and Alaska Native tribes—down to the census tract level (file for each state)
2. National-level file—tabulations for states, counties, and places; urban–rural tabulations
Summary File 3 (SF3, tabulations of long-form sample items; file for each state unless noted)
1. Population counts for ancestry groups—down to the census tract level
2. Selected long-form population and housing characteristics—down to the block group level
3. National-level file—tabulations for states, counties, places
Summary File 4 (SF4, detailed tabulations of long-form sample items)
1. Long-form population and housing characteristics iterated for many detailed race and Hispanic categories, American Indian and Alaska Native tribes, and ancestry groups—down to the census tract level (file for each state)
2. National-level file—detailed tabulations for states, counties, places
Census Transportation Planning Package Files (CTPP)
Tabulations of place of work by place of residence for traffic analysis zones
Public Use Microdata Sample (PUMS) Files
(All items for households and persons sampled from long-form records)
1-Percent Sample Files, containing ~1 million household and 3 million person records
Geographic identification: states, areas of 400,000 or more population
5-Percent Sample Files, containing ~5 million household and 15 million person records
Geographic identification: states, areas of 100,000 or more population
Printed Reports
Demographic Profiles; Congressional District Demographic Profiles
Selected population and housing short-form characteristics; demographic, social, economic, and housing long-form characteristics (3 separate tables), by state, county, place, minor civil division, census tract; congressional district (106th, 108th Congresses)
Summary Population and Housing Characteristics (PHC-1)
Short-form tabulations down to the place level
Population and Housing Unit Counts (PHC-3)
Short-form tabulations down to the place level, includes selected historical counts
Summary Social, Economic and Housing Characteristics (PHC-2)
Long-form tabulations down to the place level

Source: http://www.census.gov/population/www/censusdata/c2kproducts.html (3/5/03).
Note: SF and PUMS files and demographic profiles are available on the Internet and CD-ROM/DVD; PHC reports are available on the Internet; all files have been processed to protect confidentiality.

not agree on a reapportionment bill. The current apportionment formula, which uses the method of "equal proportions," was written into law at the time of the 1940 census.

Historically, controversies about which people to include in the reapportionment counts have involved three groups: (1) noncitizens, (2) Americans overseas, and (3) people not counted in the census who are estimated to be part of the U.S. population through a coverage estimation program, such as the 2000 Accuracy and Coverage Evaluation Program.

Noncitizens

Since 1790, the census has had a goal to count all U.S. residents, including people who are not citizens of the United States (except for tourists and other temporary visitors from abroad and foreign government representatives). With the increased numbers of illegal immigrants in the 1970s and 1980s, lawsuits were filed prior to the 1980 and 1990 censuses to exclude such immigrants from the apportionment counts. The plaintiffs argued that including illegal immigrants unfairly benefited states with larger numbers of them at the expense of states with fewer of them. The defendants countered that the Constitution did not limit the apportionment counts to citizens or potential voters but included the entire population. Defendants also argued that it was impractical to identify and exclude illegal immigrants in the census. The U.S. Supreme Court decided the cases on the narrow grounds that the plaintiffs did not have "standing" to bring the suits. In commentary the Court stated that the Constitution intended to provide representation to everyone and not just to potential voters. The 2000 census followed historical practice by striving to include all U.S. residents in the apportionment counts.

Americans Overseas

Rules for counting Americans who live overseas have varied from census to census. In 1970, 1990, and 2000, federal military and civilian employees (and their dependents) living abroad were assigned a "home" state from administrative records and included in the state reapportionment counts, but not in other data releases. This overseas population totaled 576,000 people in 2000 (0.2% of the U.S. population). Tests will be conducted in 2004 of counting private U.S. citizens who live overseas.

Population Coverage

Research on census coverage, which began with analyses of undercounts of draft-age men and young children in the 1940 census, estimated a net undercount of the population in every census from 1950 to 1990. Research also estimated higher net undercount rates for some population groups than others, such as higher rates for blacks than for nonblacks and children than for adults. Beginning in 1970, the Census Bureau made special efforts to cover hard-to-count population groups, although research showed that such efforts were only partly effective. Beginning in 1980, the Bureau worked on a dual-systems estimation (DSE) method, based on data from a post-enumeration survey and a sample of census records, that could be used to statistically adjust census counts for measured net undercount. The Bureau originally planned to use DSE methods to adjust 2000 state population totals for congressional reapportionment, but a January 1999 decision by the U.S. Supreme Court precluded such adjustment. The Bureau also planned to adjust 2000 counts for other purposes, but that was not done.

Legislative Redistricting for Equal Population Size

A second primary function of the U.S. census, deriving from its constitutional mandate for reapportionment, is to supply small-area population counts for redrawing congressional and state legislative district boundaries to meet court-mandated standards for equal population size. In the 19th century, Congress usually passed a statute at each census requiring all states to redistrict and to establish single-member districts that were contiguous, compact, and as nearly equal in population as practicable. After the 1920 census, Congress declined to reapportion the House because of the concerns of rural interests about cities' tremendous population growth, particularly from immigration. The 1929 act that provided for automatic reapportionment each decade set no standards for redistricting. The U.S. Supreme Court held that the omission was intentional and that it was up to the states to develop their own standards until and unless the courts decided to intervene.

From 1929 through the 1950s, the courts generally declined to intervene in redistricting. Many states did not redistrict after a census, unless they gained or lost seats, and those that did often paid little attention to achieving equal-size districts. Congressional and state legislative districts became increasingly unequal in population size: after the 1960 round of redistricting, the largest congressional district in the United States had over five times the population of the smallest district; disparities among state legislative districts were even greater.

The "one-person, one-vote" Supreme Court decisions, beginning in the early 1960s, changed the requirements for redistricting drastically. In *Baker v. Carr* (1962), the court held that reapportionment and redistricting matters were subject to judicial review under the equal protection clause of the 14th Amendment. In *Wesberry v. Sanders* (1964), the court held, under Article 1 of the Constitution, that congressional districts must be as nearly equal in population as practicable. In *Reynolds v. Sims* (1964), the court held, under the 14th Amendment, that both houses of a state legislature must be apportioned on a population basis and that states should strive for population equality. In *Karcher v. Daggett* (1983), the court rejected a New Jersey congressional redistricting plan in which the smallest district was only 0.7% smaller in population than the largest district. However, the courts allowed more deviation among state legislative seats than among congressional districts—deviations in state district sizes as high as 10%, and sometimes as high as 16%, were accepted.

In 1975, Congress required the Census Bureau to provide census tabulations to state officials for redistricting within 1 year after the census date [Public Law (P.L.) 94-171; section 141(c) of Title 13]. States could suggest block boundaries and specify geographic areas for which they required tabulations; if no special areas were identified, the Census Bureau provided tabulations for blocks. The P.L. 94-171 file in 2000 provided population counts for people under and over age 18 by 63 race categories, by Hispanic, not Hispanic, for states, counties, places, minor civil divisions, voting precincts (when specified), census tracts, block groups, and blocks. (The need to show 63 race categories resulted from the new option in 2000 to mark more than one race.)

Voting Rights Act and Redistricting

The 1950s and 1960s civil rights movement led to legislation, court decisions, and administrative practices that required the use of census race and ethnicity data for redistricting. The Voting Rights Act, passed in 1965 (P.L. 89-110) and amended in 1970, 1975, 1982, and 1992, is the key legislation. Its original intention was to help blacks in the South participate in elections. The 1972 and 1975 amendments extended the act's protection to all areas of the country that had voting barriers, not only for blacks, but also for language minorities—Hispanics, American Indians, Asian Americans, and Alaska Natives.

In *Allan v. Board of Education* (1969), the Supreme Court held that changes such as moving from single-member to multimember districts were "practices or procedures" subject to review under the act because they might "dilute" the black vote. The Justice Department instructed legal officers in covered jurisdictions to clear every change in voting procedure, including redistricting plans that lessened the effectiveness of minority votes—for example, by placing minority voters in as few districts as possible. Census race and ethnicity data continue to be the basis for devising districting plans that can withstand legal scrutiny.

Voting Rights Act and Bilingual Voting Assistance

Section 203 of the Voting Rights Act, adopted in the 1975 amendments and modified in 1982 and 1992, requires counties, cities, and townships to provide election materials and oral assistance in another language as well as in English for language minorities who are not literate in English. The Census Bureau makes the determination of covered areas after each census. The definition of a covered area is generally one in which 5% of the citizens of voting age speak a single minority language, do not speak English very well, and have a higher illiteracy rate in English (defined as failure to complete 5th grade) than the nation as a whole. Approximately 300 jurisdictions are required to provide bilingual voting assistance based on the 2000 census results.

Federal Program Agency Uses

Federal program agencies use data from the census for a wide range of purposes to fulfill the requirements of legislation, court rulings, and other directives. Indeed, nearly every item in the 2000 census was required in order to serve a specific federal purpose. Such purposes include implementation of sections of the Voting Rights Act, allocation of federal funds to states and localities, assessment of employment discrimination, and planning, monitoring, and evaluation of federal programs.

Fund Allocation

Over $200 billion of federal funds are allocated each year to states and localities by formulas, many of which use census data and population estimates. Examples include the following:

(1) Medicaid ($145 billion obligated in fiscal year 2002): Reimburses a percentage of each state's expenditures for medical care services for low-income elderly and disabled people and families with dependent children by a formula that uses per capita income estimates. The U.S. Bureau of Economic Analysis develops these estimates with data from administrative records, the decennial census long-form sample and other censuses and surveys, and census-based population estimates (as denominators). Other programs use the Medicaid formula.

(2) Title 1 of the Elementary and Secondary Education Act ($9.5 billion obligated in fiscal year 2002): Allocates funds to school districts to help educationally disadvantaged children by a formula that includes estimates of school-age children in families with incomes below the official poverty threshold. The estimates previously derived from the most recent census long-form sample; currently, they derive from Census Bureau statistical models, which include census poverty data as one input.

(3) Community Development Block Grants and Entitlement Grants ($3 billion authorized in fiscal year 2002): Allocates the larger amount from two formulas to states, metropolitan cities, and urban counties; the formulas use census data on total population, people living in poverty, overcrowded housing (first formula), and housing built before 1940 (second formula).

Equal Employment Opportunity

The U.S. Equal Employment Opportunity Commission and the U.S. Department of Labor's Office of Federal Contract Compliance regularly use census labor force data on occupation and industry for zip codes and other geographic areas to monitor compliance and investigate charges of employment discrimination by age, sex, race, and ethnicity. Also, federal agencies, as employers, use such data to evaluate their own recruitment and promotion systems. Recent censuses have provided special data products for equal employment opportunity analysis.

Program Planning, Monitoring, and Evaluation

Two examples of the numerous federal uses of census data for program planning and evaluation are as follows:

(1) The U.S. Department of Transportation (USDOT) uses long-form disability data for traffic analysis zones (TZAs, or groups of census blocks) to monitor compliance with the Federal Transit Act and the Americans with Disabilities Act. Since 1960, USDOT has helped develop a Census Transportation Planning Package (CTPP) for use by local governments. The CTPP provides tabulations of place of residence by place of work for TZAs. Its primary use is to describe the characteristics of commuter flows; it is also the only census product to provide data on workers at the workplace (all other tabulations are by place of residence).

(2) The U.S. Department of Housing and Urban Development uses long-form data to construct fair market rents (FMRs) for nonmetropolitan counties and most metropolitan areas. FMRs are used to determine rent subsidies to eligible families from the Section 8 Housing Assistance Payments Program; they are set at a percentile of the distribution of gross rents for recently occupied two-bedroom apartments with electricity and complete kitchen and bathroom.

Federal Statistical Agency Uses

Census long-form data and census-based population estimates serve important functions for federal statistical agencies. Four examples are as follows:

(1) Since 1950, the U.S. Office of Management and Budget has used long-form data on commuting patterns to help define metropolitan statistical areas. In turn, these areas have many uses, such as determining eligibility for fund allocations.

(2) Statistical agencies that conduct surveys of special populations often use census data to select a sample. For example, since the 1960s, the Science Resources Statistics Division of the National Science Foundation has commissioned a sample survey of college graduates drawn from the census long-form records, oversampling scientists and engineers.

(3) Census-derived population estimates are used as denominators for important national and subnational statistics, such as birth and death rates for the United States, states, and local areas, by age, sex, and race, from the National Center for Health Statistics.

(4) Federal household surveys, such as the Current Population Survey (source of official employment and poverty statistics), use census-based population estimates as survey controls—that is, the survey estimates are adjusted to agree with national population estimates by age, sex, race, and Hispanic origin. Such reweighting is needed because household surveys typically cover the population less well than the census.

State and Local Government Uses

State and local governments use small-area census data for such purposes as fund allocation, program planning and evaluation, facility planning, disaster planning, and economic development and marketing.

Formula Allocation

Examples include using census estimates of children in families with income below the poverty line in a formula to allocate state child welfare block grants to counties and using census estimates of female-headed households living in poverty with dependent children in a formula to allocate state crisis counseling funds to counties.

Program Planning and Evaluation

Examples include using long-form data on English-language proficiency, language spoken at home, and years of school completed to identify neighborhoods whose residents may need assistance in using local government services and developing socioeconomic profiles of census tracts for federal grant applications.

Facility Planning

Examples include using long-form data on commuting patterns to help redesign bus routes and plan new roads and using census socioeconomic data and administrative records data on public health needs to locate health clinics.

Disaster Planning

Examples include using long-form data on vehicle ownership and disability to estimate the numbers of people who would need to be evacuated in a disaster and how many might need transportation and using long-form place of work and place of residence data to estimate daytime populations to develop disaster plans for employment centers.

Economic Development and Marketing

Examples include using long-form data on educational attainment, occupation, and labor force participation to attract businesses by the availability of an appropriately skilled labor force and using long-form data on ancestry and language to inform businesses of opportunities to serve particular markets.

Private Sector Uses

Retail outlets, banks, media and advertising firms, insurance companies, utilities, health care providers, and other businesses and nonprofit organizations use census data. A new industry developed after 1970 to repackage census data, use them to construct lifestyle cluster systems (neighborhood types that correlate with consumer behavior), and relate them to other data through address coding and computer mapping services. Private sector uses of census data include site location, targeting of advertising and services, and compliance with government requirements. Five examples are as follows:

(1) A retail or service business uses population estimates to determine when a growing suburb will reach a threshold for opening a new store.

(2) A church compares members' characteristics to census characteristics for the surrounding community to identify similarities and differences and develop an outreach program.

(3) An insurance company sets performance standards for branches by relating small-area socioeconomic profiles to continuing and lapsed customers' characteristics for each branch.

(4) Banks use median household income and income distributions by census tract to document compliance with federal mortgage lending guidelines regarding race.

(5) Employers use census small-area data on occupation by sex, age, race, and ethnicity to assess compliance with federal equal opportunity employment and anti-discrimination laws.

Research Uses

Researchers use census data for analyses on topics such as aging, educational attainment, migration flows, environmental exposures, and concentrated poverty. Many research studies based on census data have important public policy implications.

Aging

Census summary tabulations support analyses of migration flows and concentrations of the elderly by geographic area for subgroups defined by living arrangements, income, labor force attachment, and other characteristics. PUMS files support detailed analyses of small groups of elderly, such as those with different disabilities.

Education

Researchers use census summary data on median years of school completed, average income, and unemployment to describe challenges facing communities; they use PUMS files to assess age and race group differences in educational level, income, and housing quality.

Environment

Census small-area socioeconomic information related to environmental hazards data permit analyses of the environmental effects on different population groups.

Migration

Census small-area data are an unparalleled resource for the study of migration among regions, states, counties, and places, and consequences for different parts of the country. The Census Bureau publishes data on county-to-county migration flows; the PUMS files permit detailed analysis of the characteristics of long-distance and short-distance movers and nonmovers.

Poverty

Analyses of 1970 and 1980 census summary data revealed large increases in densely populated (mainly black) urban neighborhoods with more than 40% poor families. These findings stimulated further census-based research on concentrated urban poverty.

Issues for Users

Users should learn what is known about the quality of census data, in comparison with other sources, and determine which source is best suited to their use. Quality concerns include the following:

Timeliness

Census data are collected once every 10 years and made available 1 to 3 years after collection, which may affect analyses for areas experiencing rapid change. Population estimates update the basic demographic information for small areas; the ACS is intended to provide updated long-form-type information if it is implemented.

Coverage

The census misses some people, duplicates others, and puts others in the wrong location. Although the census is the best source of population counts (it has better coverage than household surveys), recognition of coverage problems is important when using the data.

Nonresponse Error

The census strives to obtain complete data for everyone but, even after follow-up, obtains no or limited information for some households. Imputation methods use data from nearby households to supply records for whole-household nonrespondents and to fill in individual missing items on person and housing unit records. Missing data rates are high for some long-form items, such as income and housing finances, and for residents of group quarters. Imputation introduces variability in estimates and may bias estimates if nonrespondents differ from respondents in ways that the imputation procedures do not reflect.

Measurement or Response Error

People may underreport or overreport items such as age, income, and utility costs, which can introduce bias in tabulations if under- and overreports do not cancel each other out. People may also have different interpretations of questions such as ancestry.

Sampling Variability (Applicable to Long-Form Data)

Long-form estimates are based on large samples, but they can have substantial uncertainty for small areas or small groups. Sampling variability for the ACS, if implemented, will be higher than for the long form.

Definitional and Other Changes

For analyses of more than one census, changes in definitions or processing features can affect comparability across time. For example, the 2000 and 1990 race questions differ importantly, as do the education questions before and after 1990.

See Also the Following Articles

Census Undercount and Adjustment • Demography • Election Polls • Population vs. Sample

Further Reading

Anderson, M. J. (1988). *The American Census: A Social History.* Yale University Press, New Haven, CT.

Baker, G. E. (1986). Whatever happened to the reapportionment revolution in the United States? In *Electoral Laws and Their Political Consequences* (B. Grohman and A. Lijphart, eds.), pp. 257–276. Agathon Press, New York.

Citro, C. F., and Zitter, M. (2000). Population estimates and projections. In *Encyclopedia of the U.S. Census* (M. J. Anderson, ed.), pp. 300–303. CQ Press, Washington, DC.

Durbin, T. M., and Whitaker, L. P. (1991). *Congressional and State Reapportionment and Redistricting: A Legal Analysis,* Congressional Research Service Report for Congress, 91-292-A. U.S. Government Printing Office, Washington, DC.

Gaines, L. M., Gage, L., and Salvo, J. J. (2000). State and local governments: Use of census data. In *Encyclopedia of the U.S. Census* (M. J. Anderson, ed.), pp. 337–340. CQ Press, Washington, DC.

Laney, G. P. (1992). *The Voting Rights Act of 1965, as Amended: Its History and Current Issues,* Congressional Research Service Report for Congress, 92-578-GOV. U.S. Government Printing Office, Washington, DC.

McMillen, D. B. (2000). Apportionment and districting. In *Encyclopedia of the U.S. Census* (M. J. Anderson, ed.), pp. 34–42. CQ Press, Washington, DC.

National Research Council. (1995). *Modernizing the U.S. Census: Panel on Census Requirements in the Year 2000 and Beyond* (B. Edmonston and C. Schultze, eds.). Committee on National Statistics. National Academies Press, Washington, DC.

National Research Council. (2000). *Small-Area Income and Poverty Estimates—Priorities for 2000 and Beyond: Panel on Estimates of Poverty for Small Geographic Areas* (C. F. Citro and G. Kalton, eds.). Committee on National Statistics. National Academies Press, Washington, DC.

National Research Council. (2004). *The 2000 Census: Counting under Adversity: Panel to Review the 2000 Census* (C. F. Citro, D. L. Cork, and J. L. Norwood, eds.). Committee on National Statistics. National Academies Press, Washington, DC.

Naymark, J., and Hodges, K. (2000). Uses of census data by the private sector. In *Encyclopedia of the U.S. Census* (M. J. Anderson, ed.), pp. 356–358. CQ Press, Washington, DC.

Passel, J. S. (2000). Immigration. In *Encyclopedia of the U.S. Census* (M. J. Anderson, ed.), pp. 253–260. CQ Press, Washington, DC.

Rowe, J. (2000). Data products: Evolution. In *Encyclopedia of the U.S. Census* (M. J. Anderson, ed.), pp. 110–115. CQ Press, Washington, DC.

Ruggles, S. (2000). IPUMS (integrated public use microdata series). In *Encyclopedia of the U.S. Census* (M. J. Anderson, ed.), pp. 264–267. CQ Press, Washington, DC.

Spar, E. J. (2000). Private sector. In *Encyclopedia of the U.S. Census* (M. J. Anderson, ed.), pp. 309–311. CQ Press, Washington, DC.

U.S. Census Bureau. (1973). *Population and Housing Inquiries in U.S. Decennial Censuses: 1790–1970,* Working Paper No. 39. U.S. Department of Commerce, Washington, DC.

U.S. General Accounting Office. (1999). *Formula Grants—Effects of Adjusted Population Counts on Federal Funding to States,* GAO/HEHS-99-69. U.S. Government Printing Office, Washington, DC.

Chapin, Francis Stuart

Robert C. Bannister

Swarthmore College, Swarthmore, Pennsylvania, USA

Glossary

behaviorism In psychology, the study of human being in terms of observable behavior, characteristically stressing stimulus and response, without reference to values, beliefs, and attitudes.

behaviorism, pluralistic In sociology, the view that the individual and interaction among individuals constitute the basic units of analysis, and that social structures consist of externally similar acts.

cultural lag A situation where elements of a culture change at different rates causing disruption, typically when science and technology change more rapidly than social institutions.

eugenics The study of human heredity to improve humankind through selective breeding.

evolutionism, unilinear The theory that all cultures develop along similar lines from the simple to the complex, often coupled with a belief in progress.

latent function The unintended and unrecognized consequences of an activity for group adaptation, for example, the reinforcement of group identity in a Native American rain dance.

mores Binding, extra-legal social norms considered essential to a group's welfare.

objectivism A philosophical term to describe the view that objects of knowledge exist independent of human perception, often used pejoratively by humanistic sociologists who allege that positivistic sociologists treat human beings as material objects.

operationalism The view that the only valid scientific concepts are those that prescribe the means of measuring the concept.

positivism The belief that knowledge comes only from the senses and that the methods of the natural sciences thus provide the only accurate means of attaining knowledge.

positivism, instrumental The use of measurement, statistics and other quantitative techniques in formulating social policy.

scientism A term, usually pejorative, applied to positivistic social science, broadly to social evolutionism, more narrowly to the extreme sociological positivism of the inter-war years.

sociometry The study of group structure with reference to the feelings of the members of a group for one another.

synchronous cycles Parallel changes in material culture and social institutions that create changes within a larger group or nation.

Sociologist, administrator, and academic entrepreneur, F. Stuart Chapin played a key role in the creation of a quantitative, statistical sociology in the United States in the years between World Wars I and II (1920s–1940s). Moving from an early interest in social evolutionism to statistics, Chapin devised "living room scales" to measure social class by items in the home; conducted studies of civic participation as a key to social adjustment; and proposed methods for comparative study using experiment and control groups. A theorist as well as quantifier, he outlined a cyclical view of social change, and later anticipated work on latent and manifest functions. Chapin also helped professionalize American sociology, being a prime mover in the formation of the Social Science Research Council and an active participant in the American Sociological Society (Association) and other professional organizations.

Background and Early Influences

Born in Brooklyn, New York, F. Stuart Chapin (1888–1974) was reared in comfortable surroundings on Manhattan's East Side. Although not wealthy, his family enjoyed a distinguished lineage dating to early New England. One of his maternal ancestors served with Washington in the Revolution, while other forebears included merchants, lawyers, judges, and clergymen.

His father, Charles B. Chapin, a Presbyterian minister, served pastorates in Manhattan, upstate New York, and Pennsylvania. His mother, Florence Johnson, loved poetry and painting.

Chapin's youth was centered on family, the institution that was the focus of much of his later work. In 1895, he entered the Chapin Collegiate School, where his grandfather was headmaster and his father and several generations of male relatives had studied. In 1904, this comfortable world unraveled when his father left Manhattan for a pastorate in Rochester, New York. Attending the local high school for the senior year, F. Stuart suddenly developed a love of mathematics and dabbled in inventions ranging from a primitive thermostat to a new photo developing process. In 1905, he entered the University of Rochester to study engineering, dashing his father's hopes that F. Stuart would follow him into the ministry.

Chapin's life was again upended in 1906 when his mother died of a stroke. In response, he veered suddenly in a new direction, studying oil painting at a local institute. Although he did not pursue art as a career, painting, with inventing and fishing, occupied his leisure hours throughout his life. Chapin, unlike many of his contemporaries, recognized no gap between science and art, work, and leisure. Whether experimenting with oil paints or measuring and recording his fishing catches, "science" afforded standards and stability that "tradition" could no longer provide. In 1908, Chapin transferred to Columbia, where he received a Bachelor of Science degree the following year. Social science, however, was already his first love. At Rochester, he was influenced by the historian William Carey Morris and the psychologist George Mather Forbes, both members of the American Social Science Association, an organization that nurtured sociology and the other modern social sciences.

Chapin's return to Manhattan brought him in contact with his uncle, Henry Dwight Chapin (1857–1942), whom he later called "the greatest influence" in his development. A specialist in children's diseases, the elder Chapin worked tirelessly for children's welfare, tenement house reform, and sanitary legislation. In this enthusiasm for scientific reform, he also toyed with eugenics and proposed sometime-draconian solutions to social problems (for example, permanent quarantine for "all tramps, cranks, and generally worthless human beings"). Seeing no conflict between his inherited Calvinism and Darwinian science, he condemned social policies that perpetuated the "unfit." This tutelage left his nephew with a just-the-facts attitude toward reform and a suspicion of programs based on feeling.

In the graduate program in sociology at Columbia (Ph.D., 1911), Chapin studied with sociologist Franklin Henry Giddings and anthropologist Franz Boas, among others. Giddings, a social evolutionist in the tradition of Herbert Spencer and an advocate of statistics, was a major influence. In his *Principles of Sociology* (1896), Giddings described social evolution as a three-fold process of aggregation, imitation, and selection whereby useful practices are preserved and the "ignorant, foolish, and harmful" extremes are eliminated. As a quantifier, Giddings built on a Columbia tradition dating to the economist Richmond Mayo-Smith, author of *Statistics and Sociology* (1895) and a major figure in the faculty of political science until his premature death in 1901. Unlike Mayo-Smith, however, Giddings based his work on Karl Pearson's *Grammar of Science* (1892), a work that urged investigators to abandon the search for reality underlying appearances, to confine attention to observable externals, and to substitute "correlations" for "causes." From anthropologist Franz Boas, Chapin developed an interest in "primitive" societies, an appetite for facts, and a skepticism toward all "broad and beautiful" generalizations. The most important non Columbia influence was *Folkways* (1906) by William Graham Sumner of Yale.

Social Evolutionism to Statistics

In *Education and the Mores* (1911), his doctoral thesis, Chapin combined the work of these mentors with statistical analysis. The issue was whether elementary education fostered "useful tradition" and social adaptation, as urged by Columbia's John Dewey and other progressive educators, or whether it conserved "obstructive tradition and mischievous prejudice." Following Sumner, Chapin conceptualized tradition as mores—customs accepted "without attention." Chapin ranked mores in terms of their universality and rationality: tradition (general and partly rational), customs (local), and superstition and prejudice (irrational and emotional). The enemies were provincialism and passion. Adopting Giddings' theory of imitation (derived from French sociologist Gabriel Tarde), Chapin stated that the mores were "the objective products of interstimulation and response," a step beyond Sumner and toward behaviorism that reviewer Charles Ellwood criticized in 1912 in the *American Journal of Sociology*.

Although education in primitive societies fostered superstition and prejudice, Chapin argued, modern schooling introduced the scientific view, especially in the "content studies" of geography, science and history, each a potential challenge to existing mores. As taught in American schools, however, these subjects failed at this task. Using previously published data, Chapin calculated the time allotted to the "3 Rs" and to the "content studies" in schools in selected American and European cities, the time given to these newer studies at different grade levels, and the percentage of students completing each grade level. This analysis showed that, despite the rise of progressive education, the majority of students never encountered the newer subjects or else studied them at a level where they were saturated with popular prejudice (patriotic history, for example).

From 1911 to 1921, Chapin's quest for a scientific perspective took several forms. Teaching at Wellesley (1911–1912), he offered courses in economic history, conservation, and municipal socialism. In the *Independent* in 1915, he touted science and efficiency as the answers to the nation's social problems—through accident, health, and old-age insurance on the German and British models, through state-sponsored, centralized labor exchanges, and through less wasteful logging and coal mining. In *Popular Science*, he endorsed a variety of eugenic policies in language that echoed Henry D. Chapin's calls for elimination of the "unfit." In *An Historical Introduction to Social Economy* (1917), he traced the development of modern social insurance from earlier forms of charity and poor relief.

At Smith College (1912–1921), Chapin joined psychiatric social worker Mary C. Jarrett to organize the Smith College School of Social Work. In the *Scientific Monthly* in 1918, he argued that sociology and social work, if properly scientific, were complementary. Before an audience at the annual meeting of the National Council of Social Workers in 1919, he argued that work could be made more effective if investigators dispassionately and objectively applied the inductive method. As a Red Cross executive during the war, he gained further lessons in the practical applications of social theory. This path, however, led only indirectly to the statistical scales and social experiments that would soon be Chapin's trademark. In a study of voting following Woodrow Wilson's victory in 1912, he again used previously collected data to measure the variability in overall voting and in party pluralities in presidential elections since 1856. In the same journal 2 years later, he lectured readers on the uses of statistical averages (mean, mode, and median) to ascertain the representative nature of a sample. In *Scientific Monthly* in 1917, he argued that the statistical method provided the best means of overcoming problems inherent in social experimentation.

Chapin's new interest in part reflected the growing popularity of the British "new statistics" based on Karl Pearson's work with correlation coefficients, multiple correlation, and frequency curves, work Chapin first encountered in a course with statistician Henry L. Moore at Columbia. For his expositions, Chapin drew on several popularizations by English statisticians: Arthur L. Bowley's *An Elementary Manual of Statistics* (1910), George Udny Yule's *Introduction to the Theory of Statistics* (1912), and William P. and Ethel M. Elderton's *Primer of Statistics* (1909). But his interest in statistics also reflected his changing political views and a more pessimistic assessment of social evolution. Although Chapin was never as socially activist as some of his sociological colleagues, his interest in progressive education, in conservation, and in municipal socialism aligned him with many prewar progressives. His 1912 analysis of presidential elections concluded that the rise of the independent voter promised more enlightened politics. In *An Introduction to Social Evolution* (1913), a summary of unilinear evolutionism, he predicted that increasing material abundance would bring better social relations. Like Giddings, he found a model for social policy in nature's balance between stability and change.

Following the outbreak of war, however, Chapin prefaced support for eugenics with a scathing attack on the human depravity that produced "brutally unscrupulous" businessmen and the "flimsy pretext" that had ignited the "holocaust of Europe." Although his enthusiasm for eugenics proved temporary, it rested on the conviction that "societal" (psychic) evolution, such as in most social reforms, failed to "stay put," and must be supplemented by "social" (physical) evolution to improve the race biologically. In *Scientific Monthly* in 1917, he coupled the argument that statistics provided the only way to make social experimentation feasible with evidence that the history of social reform was one of unintended consequences or outright failure.

Chapin's engagement with evolutionism led indirectly to statistics. His argument that mores evolved through natural selection in a process of trial and error was inherently statistical in that the overall outcome was probabilistic in the same way as a multiple rolling of dice. Sumner, being ignorant of selectionism, did not share this view of the mores and thus remained wedded to a crudely inductive view of sociological method. Chapin, like Giddings, gravitated naturally to the new statistics, in that both questioned the optimistic assumption that social selection guaranteed moderate social change. Social evolutionism was also an obstacle to the development of scientific sociology. A staple of "armchair" theorists, it impeded empirical work. The alliance with biology undercut claims of disciplinary autonomy. It also made sociology a target of growing antievolutionist forces, as Chapin learned a few years later when some Christian fundamentalists attacked social evolution texts as among the most "sacrilegious and scornful" books in print. Chapin continued to be both quantifier and theorist, as attested by his later study of "synchronous cycles" in *Cultural Change* (1928). But, absent progress and direction, "social evolution" became "social change" and statistics the method of choice.

Field Work and Social Research (1920), a summary of lessons Chapin learned in social work during the Smith College years, was one of the first books in the United States to provide a systematic inventory of sociological methods. The presentation was in three parts: a plea for a rigorously inductive method; an analysis of case work, sampling, and total enumeration; and a discussion of the technical problems of gathering and evaluating material. Although reviewers judged the book a useful introduction, some also noted that it did little to advance the cause of statistics. The economist Frank A. Ross, writing in the *Journal of the American Statistical Association*, observed that Chapin gave readers no comprehension of the gap that separated the case study's "sympathetic and subjective" rendering of detail and the statistician's impartiality. Nor, he added, were the Pittsburgh and other prewar surveys instances of "sampling," as Chapin maintained, but rather were case studies with cities as the unit. An English reviewer in the *Journal of the Royal Statistical Society* criticized the "highly artificial" device of assigning numerical values to factors such as "care in avoiding dust" as a measure of ventilation. Informing these criticisms were inherent differences between the case study and social surveys of the social worker, on the one hand, and statistical analysis, on the other. This tension continued to shape Chapin's work as he moved from Smith College to the University of Minnesota in the fall of 1922.

Social Measurement

At the University of Minnesota, Chapin moved steadily toward behavioral analysis and scientific neutrality. The results were the "living room scales" and "social experiments" that won him a reputation as a pioneering technician of the new sociology. Although the first courses in sociology at the university dated to the early 1890s, Minnesota did not establish a formal department in the field until 1910, initially staffed by an ethnographic popularizer and two reformers in the Social Gospel tradition. In the half-dozen years before Chapin arrived, a separate department, Social and Civic Training, was established under Yale Ph.D. Arthur J. Todd; the department was subsequently merged with the Department of Sociology.

Appointed at age 33 to replace Todd, Chapin was the youngest chairman of a major sociology department in the nation. His passion for order was just what the situation demanded. The department he entered was the site of a three-way tug of war among an older generation of amateurs, social workers and social surveyors, and Luther L. Bernard, a Chicago Ph.D. who was the sole voice for what was now termed "sociological objectivism" and who made no secret of his disdain for the other factions. When Chapin appointed Russian émigré Pitirim Sorokin in 1923, Bernard feared that this distinguished theorist was being groomed as his replacement.

Chapin did not initially transform the department, partly because his own interests remained extremely broad and partly because the merger of sociology and social work gave a practical, socially oriented cast to work in both areas. As late as 1929, seminars in sociology included Applied Sociology, Social Theory, Evolution, and Rural Sociology, a subject Chapin had introduced at Smith over conservative opposition. Early doctoral theses written under his supervision reflected the reform-oriented nature of Minnesota sociology, "unscientific" by later standards; examples include Paul Perigord's *International Labor Organization* (1924) and Harold A. Phelps's *Comparative Study of Unionism* (1925). Chapin's colleagues and former students later romanticized the open and "democratic" character of these early years before the austerity of the man and his sociology became legend.

By 1925, several developments helped create a new Chapin. One was the increasing importance of educational foundations, with their emphasis on quantitative rigor. Chapin initially became involved with the Laura Spelman Rockefeller Memorial when applying for support of a bibliographical service for sociologists, *Social Science Abstracts*, which he edited during its brief existence from 1930 to 1933. A second was a personal crisis when Chapin's wife, Nellie Estelle Peck, died of peritonitis in 1925 at age 36. During their 14-year marriage, which produced three children, their relations with the world were outgoing and informal. Things changed, his colleagues later reported, following his remarriage 2 years later to a socially ambitious woman who was highly protective of her husband's reputation. Burdened with the care of three young children, Chapin had begun to show autocratic tendencies even before his remarriage. But his aloofness increased with each passing year.

Departmental affairs also demanded a firm hand. In 1925, Luther Bernard left under a cloud of scandal that absorbed much of Chapin's time. Sorokin complained that his $2000 salary was half that of most professors and disliked Chapin's increasingly autocratic ways. Chapin's strained relations with the "practical" sociologists were an open secret. One graduate student wrote Bernard that there was a set policy to get rid of anyone "who wishes to say something about Dept. and U. affairs." Although several appointments after 1926 strengthened the department, things fell apart during Chapin's 3-year absence in New York while editing *Social Science Abstracts*. Sorokin and the rural sociologist Carle Zimmerman left for Harvard and the criminologist Edwin Sutherland left for the University of Chicago. The collapse of the *Abstracts* project compounded Chapin's disappointment, completing his transformation into the formal, austere, and intensely private person that colleagues later remembered. Departures in Chapin's scholarship between 1924 and the early 1930s reflected these changes: (1) a more rigorous application of statistics, (2) an explicit rejection of unilinear evolutionism in *Cultural Change* (1928), coupled with a redefinition of social institutions in behavioral terms, and (3) the creation of "living room" and other scales to measure social status.

During 1924, Chapin returned to measuring standards of living. In *Field Work and Social Research*, he had proposed a "score card" method to standardize measures of "structural conditions," "congestion," and other variables by assigning points within an arbitrarily chosen range, much as breeder's associations and produce exchanges grade animals and grains. Now he turned to statistics to evaluate 11 studies of room crowding among Italian workmen in Chicago. He demonstrated that overcrowding in sleeping rooms in one study of 212 cases could be better stated statistically in terms of means and standard deviations than verbally; and, further, that the mean among all the studies differed less than the distributions within any one, proof that they were well-chosen samples and that statistics have practical value in demonstrating "the essential fairness of the original field work."

In *Cultural Change* (1928), Chapin described what he now called "synchronous cultural change." A variation of William F. Ogburn's theory of cultural lag (typically a lag between technology and social institutions), the theory combined Luther Bernard's work on technology, recent anthropological studies, and a cyclical conception of change derived in part from Chapin's colleague Sorokin. Cycles of change are of three orders: material, as in technology; nonmaterial, as in religion or the patriarchal family; and composite, as in nations or civilizations. When a significant number of cultural forms of the first and second order change together ("synchronously"), the larger group or nation reaches maturity and ultimately declines. Cultural change is thus "selectively accumulative in time, and cyclical or oscillatory in character." Nor, as some maintained, are these characteristics in opposition. Selective accumulation describes the "upward rise of the culture cycle," but not the stages of equilibrium, strain, and disintegration. Unilinear evolutionists erred in assuming that all societies follow a universal evolutionary path. History, in short, does not repeat itself.

Behind Chapin's countless distinctions and numerous charts lay two assumptions that reflected his postwar disillusionment. Just as unilinear evolutionism implied progress, so the cyclical view seemed to deny its possibility. The triumphs of human intelligence, whether in material or social invention, were subject to an unending cycle of growth and decay. The proliferation of material goods and new needs (consumerism, although Chapin did not use the term) created perennial "maladjustments." Danger lay in the creation of "new social machinery" and in the breakdown of common standards and shared values. A second assumption, reaffirming the lessons of Karl Pearson, was that sociology should measure differential rates of change rather than explain underlying principles. Chapin did not entirely abandon his liberal faith in progress. Statistical measurement would provide the means of controlling cultural cycles, much as a thermostat regulates heating, and allow escape from history's endless cycle of rise and decline. The book's frontispiece pictured the newly built Chicago Tribune Tower, a skyscraper with a Gothic exterior to illustrate Chapin's hopeful thesis that change is cumulative. But, as historian Dorothy Ross has observed, its jarring image of flying buttresses atop a reinforced steel structure better dramatizes his uneasy coupling of historicism and instrumental positivism.

In *Social Forces* the same year, Chapin redefined social institutions in behavioral terms, building on the work of the psychologist Floyd Allport, among others. So conceived, a social institution such as family or church consists of four relatively rigid and persistent "type parts" functioning as a unit: attitudes and behavior (affection and reverence) symbols (wedding ring and cross), utilitarian material items (home furnishings and altar), and oral and written specifications (wills and creeds). This formulation differed from his earlier view in several ways. The unit of analysis was no longer "organic society" but the products of individual behavior (wearing a ring); institutions consisted of the interrelations of individuals (being loyal to others) rather than being an inevitable expression of the collectivity, and culture was learned behavior, not an irresistible force.

This sociological behaviorism led directly to new and more ambitious social measurement. The first, begun in 1926 and published 3 years later, examined student extracurricular activities. In this study and related follow-ups, Chapin and his associates concluded that student leaders have superior ability to think symbolically and abstractly, that grades measure these abilities, and hence that there is a high correlation between leadership and grades.

Chapin's "living room scale" developed in stages, from work in seminars in 1926 through 1927 to a final revision in 1933. The initial study focused on 39 families, measuring four "objective" elements: cultural possessions (books, magazines), effective income, participation in community organizations, and "household equipment." Points were assigned within each category (one point for membership in a community organization, for example, two for attendance, and so on). Social status was then computed within each category, and the rankings compared with one another and with rankings using scales proposed by earlier investigators. When further analysis revealed that "household equipment" correlated highly with other categories, Chapin decided this scale could stand alone as measure of social status. Chapin was not the first or only social scientist to measure social status quantitatively. His "living room scale" joined related attempts to measure "social distance" (Emory Bogardus), "social adequacy" (Thomas C. McCormick), and "social attitudes" (Floyd Allport and Louis L. Thurstone). But Chapin ranked high in the diligence with which he multiplied distinctions among household items. A fireplace with three utensils or an electric light was worth 8 points, and hardwood floors, 10. A kerosene heater, sewing machine, or alarm clock in the living room cost 2 points. Chapin was aware that these judgments were culturally conditioned: a different scale would be needed for homes in China or India or for a different time in the United States. He insisted nonetheless that using objective factors to measure status avoided problems of interviewer bias and provided a valuable tool for social workers in placing children in foster homes.

Social Theory and Social Practice

Elected president of the American Sociological Society (ASS) for 1935, Chapin stood at the top of his profession. Beginning in 1923, he served on the editorial boards or as advisor to 13 scholarly journals, including the *American Sociological Review*, which he co-edited from 1944 to 1946 with his Minnesota colleague, George B. Vold. He was on the board or an officer of numerous organizations, including the American Council of Learned Societies (1919–1920), the Social Science Research Council (SSRC) (1923–1928), and the American Association for the Advancement of Science (vice-president, 1942). From 1926 to 1963, he was chief editor of *Harper's Social Science Series*.

As president of the ASS, Chapin helped launch the *American Sociological Review*, which, in 1936, replaced the Chicago-based *American Journal of Sociology* as the organization's official publication. In 1936, Chapin also led a move to found the Sociological Research Association (SRA), an invitation-only seminar of sociologists who wished to make the discipline more "scientific." Although the SRA was neither as exclusively empirical nor as elitist as some critics contended, it drew fire from dissidents who for several years had been working to make the ASS more open, democratic, and overtly reformist.

Returning to Minnesota in 1930 after the collapse of the *Abstracts* project, Chapin made quantitative work a department priority. Doctoral theses increasingly emphasized measurement rather than social movements or organizations; examples include Raymond F. Sletto's "Construction of Personality Scales" (1936) and Louis Guttman's "The Prediction of Quantitative Variates" (1942). Another graduate who earned distinction for statistical work was population expert Conrad Taeuber (Ph.D., 1931) of the U.S. Census Bureau. From the mid-1930s until his retirement, Chapin refined his earlier methods. In *Contemporary American Institutions* (1935), he expanded the institutional analysis developed in earlier articles. Repeating his distinction between "nucleated" (family, church, and local government) and "symbolically diffused" (art, mythology, and language) institutions, he focused exclusively on the former, the "core elements" of which were subject to precise measurement. He also anticipated a distinction between "manifest" and "latent" functions, although not in the meaning it would eventually assume. For Robert Merton, whom Chapin met while teaching summer school at Harvard in 1935, a "latent" function was the unintended and unrecognized consequences of an activity for group adaptation (a Hopi rain dance, for example, which reinforces group identity). As reviewer Everett Hughes commented in the *American Journal of Sociology*, Chapin sometimes defined "latent" as secretive, hidden activity (bootlegging), and at other times as something not yet formulated (children learning a language, unaware of its grammar)—neither of which was Merton's definition.

These developments in Chapin's professional life and his scholarship took place against the background of the Great Depression, a nationwide economic collapse that convulsed the still-fragile discipline of sociology. Hard times meant salary cuts and a shrinking job market. Membership in the association plunged, as did sociology enrollments at many universities. Money put an edge on discussions of the Association's annual program, because having an official role was essential in getting a member's expenses paid. For proponents of scientistic sociology, the Depression posed a special challenge. Expensive collaborative projects collapsed for lack of funds, *Social Science Abstracts* being an example. Demands for radical action from within the Association threatened to return sociology to the prewar reform tradition. Although Chapin's interest in social work and rural sociology tempered his calls for a value-neutral sociology, the narrowing of the sociologist's sphere of action became a subtext of many of his writings during the 1930s. In a 1934 symposium, he drew a sharp distinction between the "political–economic" and the "social" realms, effectively limiting sociology to the family, schools, churches, and welfare organizations. In his presidential address to the American Sociological Society in 1935, he distinguished between a "goal-directed" action and its "unintended consequences," a Weberian phrase also soon to be popularized by Robert Merton. Goal-directed action—planning—was the business of leaders; unintended consequences were the subject of social science.

By the mid-1930s, Chapin was also sympathetic to the operationalism of his former student George Lundberg. By "operationally," Chapin told colleagues at the ASS, he meant that "social concepts" must be defined "in terms of the operations and processes used in attempts to measure them or test them by experiment." Concepts not so testable were meaningless (for example the terms "social class, wage slaves, proletariat, bourgeoisie, socialite, aristocrat, plutocrat")—not by coincidence the rhetorical arsenal of the Left.

Chapin was ambivalent toward the New Deal. In *Contemporary American Institutions*, he cautiously applauded the experimentation of the "First New Deal" (1933–1935; the "planning" phase), but then analyzed without refuting a long list of criticisms. He later termed Social Security a "patchwork" that had been created by a fusion of the "unexpressed wish fantasies" of the aged with modern communications. "Unplanned results" were bound to occur. By tracing these results, "non-normative theory" could provide the necessary check.

From Statistics to Social Experiments

During and after World War II, Chapin saw new opportunities for planning: measuring national morale, gauging psychological crosscurrents that might affect peacemaking, organizing postwar conferences, and facilitating postwar demobilization. Previously confined to communities and nations, social measurement was now a global priority. Against this background, Chapin moved in two directions. From 1941 to 1951, he was a contributing editor to *Sociometry*, a journal founded by Jacob Levi Moreno to study group dynamics. Chapin evidenced an interest in sociometry in the earlier sense of "social measurement" in his studies of classroom behavior, leadership, and conference procedures. He rejected, however, narrower definitions of sociometry as the quantification of informal friendship constellations (Moreno's program), or as a therapeutic tool. An exception was an attempt in the *American Journal of Sociology* in 1950 to prove that individuals ranked sociometrically as "stars" or leaders were socially isolated and aloof, a conclusion that drew almost immediate criticism in a subsequent issue of the same journal. Chapin, the authors observed, was "an otherwise skilled social scientist who is relatively inexperienced in the sociometric field."

In *Experimental Designs in Sociological Research* (1947), Chapin revisited the problem of providing controls in social experiments, no longer convinced that statistics could give a truly "scientific" result. "Experimental designs" required "experiment" and "control" groups to be determined by frequency distributions of designated traits. Comparisons could be made at a single time ("cross-sectional design"), "before" and "after" ("projected"), or after the fact, as an effect is traced backward to previous causes" ("ex post facto"). Applying his method, he divided 102 former Boy Scouts into two groups: the first group consisted of those who dropped out of scouting after an average of 1.3 years; the second included those whose tenure averaged 4 years. These "control" and "experimental" groups were then paired by equating frequency distributions on place of birth, father's occupation, health rating, and mental ability. After 22 cases were eliminated to make the groups equal, two groups of 40 were compared for performance in later life as measured by a "Social Participation Scale." Although the methodology grew ever more complex, the issue remained social adjustment. Whether the subject was "social insight," the effects of good housing, active versus dropout scouts, or work relief, the conclusions were similar: people who join more organizations have higher social intelligence; persons affiliated with political, professional, social, and civic groups rank highest in social insight; good housing and active scouting foster adjustment; and work relief is better than the dole. Sociometry, as Chapin defined it in a 1943 article, was "essential to human adjustments in an expanding social universe."

Evaluation and Legacy

Chapin's critics increased in number as he approached retirement. Mathematicians took his "designs" to task for their statistical inadequacies and others questioned the possibility and utility of quantifying human experience. Interviewed by Chapin's biographer Ronald Althouse in 1963, Malcolm Willey confided that Chapin was inadequately grounded in statistics, "simply mechanical" in his attempts to quantify cognitive concepts, and unaware of what his subject meant in "human terms." Also speaking confidentially to the same interviewer, a second Minnesota colleague faulted the "absurdity" of attempting to understand a group through use of random sampling. A third wondered whether anyone really knew more about public housing or student extracurricular participation as a result of Chapin's studies. Although Willey also conceded that Chapin uniquely "symbolized" the movement to sociological positivism, this muted praise, like the negative assessments of the other Minnesota colleagues, underestimated Chapin's considerable influence over many decades. From the 1930s onward, studies of social status, participation and leadership, and housing policy—numbering in the dozens—routinely cited and built on his work. Among the most important were Louis Guttman's refinement of the living room scale in 1942, Stuart Queen's measurement of the relation between community disorganization and individual participation in 1949, and Robert Nash Parker's use of more sophisticated measurement techniques in 1983.

Like Chapin's contemporaries, historians of sociology have had mixed opinions regarding his work and its legacy. Writing in 1960, Minnesota sociologist Don Martindale was the first of several writers to grant Chapin a prominent role in the development of pluralistic behaviorism. In a laudatory doctoral dissertation, Ronald Althouse presented Chapin as a case study of the shift from the Protestant ethic to the scientific ethos. By the 1970s, opinion shifted. Radical sociologists Herman and Julia Schwendinger in 1974 lumped Chapin with other "liberal syndicalist" defenders of corporate capitalism, citing especially his dismissive analysis of social protest and utopian theory. In his satirical study *Class* (1983), literary critic Paul Fussell presented a humorous send-up of Chapin's living room scale ("Identifiable Naugahyde aping anything customarily made of leather—subtract 3"). Historian Dorothy Ross (1991) included Chapin among American social scientists who turned to scientism to escape the Gilded Age crisis of liberal historicism that seemed to threaten the faith in American exceptionalism.

The fact that historians on the whole have accorded Chapin a relatively minor role in the shaping of the discipline in part reflects the fact that those with quantitative tastes are less inclined to write history. Reputation in sociology, Jennifer Platt has observed, often depends less on the merit of the quantitative work than the field in which it is applied, social work being a liability in Chapin's case. Like many scholars, Chapin's short-run influence was greater than his long-term reputation. But his were shoulders on which much important later work rested. As advocate, organizer, and exemplar of the interwar movement toward sociological positivism, Chapin had few if any peers.

See Also the Following Articles

Comparative Sociology • Eugenics • Giddings, Franklin Henry • Measurement Theory • Objectivity, Quest for • Sociology

Further Reading

Althouse, R. C. (1964). *The Intellectual Career of F. Stuart Chapin.* University Microfilms, Ann Arbor, Michigan.

Bannister, R. C. (1987). *Sociology and Scientism.* University of North Carolina Press, Chapel Hill.

Camic, C. E. (1994). The statistical turn in American social science: Columbia University, 1890 to 1915. *Am. Sociol. Rev.* **59,** 773–805.

Fine, G. A., and Severance, J. S. (1985). Great men and hard times: Sociology at the University of Minnesota. *Sociol. Q.* **26,** 117–134.

Platt, J. (1996). *A History of Sociological Research Methods in America, 1920–1960.* Cambridge University Press, Cambridge, UK.

Ross, D. (1991). *The Origins of American Social Science.* Cambridge University Press, Cambridge, UK.

Classical Test Theory

Wim J. van der Linden
University of Twente, Enschede, The Netherlands

Glossary

classical test model Two-level model for observed scores on a test, one level for the score of a fixed person and another for a random person from a population, underlying all derivations in classical test theory.

measurement error Difference between an observed score and a true score.

observed score Random variable representing the test score of a person.

reliability Extent to which the true score agrees with the observed score in a population of persons, measured by the squared linear correlation coefficient between the two.

true score Expected value of an observed score over replications of the test for a fixed person.

validity The degree of success in using the observed scores on a test to predict the score on an independent criterion, measured by the linear correlation coefficient between the two.

Classical test theory is a theory of measurement error. It is customary to consider the work of Charles Spearman, published in 1904, as the origin of this theory. In his paper, Spearman adopted the model of an observed score as a sum of a true score and an error, and showed how to correct the linear correlation between observed scores for their errors. This correction is now known as Spearman's correction for attenuation. The name "classical test theory" is somewhat misleading in that it suggests a theory for test scores only. The theory applies to any type of measurement for which the notion of random variation across replications is meaningful. In fact, it shares its formal structure with most of the theory of error for physical measurements commonly used in the natural sciences, but misses its notion of systematic error as well as the platonic interpretation of the true score associated with it.

Classical Model

Charles Spearman's 1904 model of an observed score as a sum of a true score and an error seems simple, but it initially generated much controversy and confusion. Spearman viewed observed scores as random, whereas others rejected this interpretation. But even among those who accepted the idea of randomness, there was much confusion between the notions of randomness of an observed score over replications and randomness due to sampling of persons from a population. Another debate was on the nature of the true score. According to some, it represented a property existing independently of the observed score (so-called definition of platonic true score), whereas others had difficulty with such obscure properties and wanted a more formal definition.

In 1996, Melvin Novick published an axiomatization of classical test theory (CTT) based on a minimal set of assumptions, in which CTT was treated as a theory for measurement error in a hierarchical experiment with two different levels—one level at which a random person is sampled from a population and another at which his/her observed scored is obtained. Both levels involve separate model assumptions. Novick's assumptions were used in collaboration with Frederic Lord in their 1968 treatment of CTT.

Model for a Fixed Person

Let X_{jt} be the observed score of person j on test t. This score is viewed as a random variable with a distribution over replications of the test for j (sometimes referred to as propensity distribution). For most physical variables, measurements can be replicated, but for more psychological properties, replications are usually hypothetical. Humans are able to remember and learn between measurements, even though in practice it is seldom possible to maintain exactly the same conditions. For the majority of variables in the social sciences, the only realization of X_{jt} is the single observed score at hand.

An observed score X_{jt} can be used to define the following two new quantities:

$$\tau_{jt} = \mathcal{E}(X_{jt}), \tag{1}$$

$$E_{jt} = X_{jt} - \tau_{jt}, \tag{2}$$

where $\mathcal{E}(X_{jt})$ is the expected value of X_{jt}. The first definition is of the true score for examinee j on test t, the second is of the error. Observe that τ_{jt} is fixed but E_{jt} is random. The definitions of τ_{jt} and E_{jt} are based on a convention. Nothing in the distribution of X_{jt} forces us to have an interest in its mean instead of, for example, its median. The distribution of E_{jt} follows directly from the arbitrary choice of true score.

The definitions in Eqs. (1) and (2) imply the following model for the score of a fixed examinee:

$$X_{jt} = \tau_{jt} + E_{jt}. \tag{3}$$

This model is nothing else than a representation of the two definitions in Eqs. (1) and (2). No separate assumption of linearity is made; the linearity in Eq. (3) follows entirely from the definition of E_{jt} as a difference. X_{jt} is defined on the scores U_i, $i = 1, \ldots, n$, for n items in the test, often as a (weighted) sum of the scores. This definition does not need to be made for Eqs. (1) and (2). The definitions of a true score and error in CTT hold for any definition of observed score.

Model for a Random Person

At this level, the test is still considered as fixed, but the person is obtained by random sampling from a population. An extension of CTT to the case of random sampling of a test from a pool of items also exists (see below). Let J denote a random person sampled from the population and T_{Jt} be his/her true score. This true score is also random. The observed score and error of a random person, X_{Jt} and E_{Jt}, now are random due to two different sources: one source is the sampling of the person from the population, the other is the "sampling" of an observed score from his/her distribution.

Due to sampling of persons, the model in Eq. (3) therefore becomes:

$$X_{Jt} = T_{Jt} + E_{Jt}. \tag{4}$$

Again, the only additional assumptions needed to extend the model in Eq. (3) to this model for a random person is on the random status of its variables.

Summary

Let $F_{X_{jt}}(\cdot)$ be the distribution function of observed-score X_{jt} for a fixed person and $F_{T_{Jt}}(\cdot)$ be the distribution function of the true score for the population of persons. The two models in Eqs. (3) and (4) can be summarized as the following two-level model:

$$X_{jt} \sim F_{X_{jt}}(x; \tau_{jt}), \tag{5}$$

$$\tau_{Jt} \sim F_{T_{Jt}}(\tau). \tag{6}$$

It is important to note that both distribution functions are unknown. Also, the presence of the true score τ_{jt} in the argument of the function for X_{jt} in Eq. (5) should not be taken to suggest that the observed-score distribution is a member of a parametric family indexed by it. It is necessary to know the distribution to identify this parameter, not the other way around. Additional assumptions that lead to known parametric families of distributions for Eqs. (5) and (6) are discussed in the context of stronger true-score theory (see later).

The model in Eqs. (5) and (6) is equivalent to a one-way analysis-of-variance model with random person effects, albeit that the latter is usually accompanied by the extra assumption of a normal distribution for X_{Jt}. Observed scores are usually discrete and have a bounded range. The definition of the true score as an expected observed score implies the same range as for the observed score, but with real values. The error is also real valued, but its range runs between the maximum possible value of X_{jt} and its negative. Now that the score definitions in CTT have been made precise, for notational convenience, their indices, wherever possible, will be omitted.

Classical Theory

In spite of its almost tautological nature, it is amazing how many results relevant to measurement in the social sciences can be derived from the classical model in Eqs. (5) and (6). The goal of these derivations is "to derive unobservables from unobservables," that is, to express unobservable quantities defined in terms of true scores and measurement error as functions of observables. The following equations are examples of results derived directly from the model in Eqs. (5) and (6):

$$\mathcal{E}(E_{jt}) = 0, \tag{7}$$

$$\sigma^2_{E_{jt}} = \sigma^2_{X_{jt}}, \tag{8}$$

$$\mathrm{Cov}(X_{jt}, X'_{jt}) = 0, \tag{9}$$

$$\mathrm{Cov}(T, E) = 0, \tag{10}$$

$$\sigma^2_X = \sigma^2_T + \sigma^2_E, \tag{11}$$

and

$$\Pr\{X'_{jt} \le x_o\} \ge \Pr\{X'_{jt} \ge x_o\} \quad \text{for } x_o \text{ large.} \tag{12}$$

The first three results show that, for a fixed person j, the expected error is equal to zero, the variance of the error is equal to the variance of the observed score, and the covariance between the observed score and a replication X'_{jt} is equal to zero. In all three equations, the left-hand side contains an unobservable quantity and the right-hand side contains an observable quantity. The result in Eq. (10) shows that the covariance between true scores and observed scores in any population is always equal to zero. The derivation of this result is less obvious, but it follows directly from the fact that Eq. (7) implies a horizontal regression line of X on τ. The zero covariance in Eq. (10) leads directly to the equality of the observed-score variance with the sum of the true-score and error variances in Eq. (11).

The property in Eq. (12) shows that if there is a large test score x_o and the test is replicated, it is more likely that a smaller (rather than larger) second score will be observed. (By a large test score is meant a score larger than the median; a comparable statement is true for a score below the median.) This simple property, which is a trivial consequence of the assumption of a random observed score, explains the often misunderstood phenomena of regression to the mean and capitalization on chance due to measurement error.

More useful results are possible if the observed score, true score, or error is used to define new test and item parameters. Such parameters are often defined with a practical application in mind (for example, item and test analysis, choice of test length, or prediction of success in a validity study). Some results for these parameters can be derived with the model in Eqs. (5) and (6) as the only assumption; for others, an auxiliary assumption is needed. A commonly used auxiliary assumption is the one of parallel scores on two measurement instruments. Scores X_t on test t and X_r on a second test r are strictly parallel if

$$\tau_{jt} = \tau_{jr}, \tag{13}$$

$$\sigma^2_{X_{jt}} = \sigma^2_{X_{jr}}, \tag{14}$$

for each person j in the population. This definition equates the first two moments of the score distributions of all persons. Weaker definitions exist but are not reviewed here.

Reliability

A key parameter in CTT is the reliability coefficient of observed score X_{Jt}. This parameter is defined as the squared (linear) correlation coefficient between the observed and true score on the test,

$$\rho^2_{TX}. \tag{15}$$

Though this parameter is often referred to as the reliability of a test, it actually represents a property of the observed score X defined on the test. If the definition of X is changed, the value of the coefficient changes. The use of the correlation coefficient between X and T in Eq. (15) can be motivated as follows: If $\rho_{XT} = 0$, it holds that $X = T$ for each person in the population and X does not contain any error. If $\rho_{XT} = 1$, it holds that $X = E$ for each person and X contains only error. A squared correlation coefficient is used because of the standard interpretation of this square as a proportion of explained variance. From Eq. (11) it follows that

$$\rho^2_{TX} = \frac{\sigma^2_T}{\sigma^2_X}, \tag{16}$$

which allows interpretation of the reliability coefficient as the proportion of observed-score variance explained by the differences between the true scores in the population.

One of the major uses of the reliability coefficient is for calculating the standard error of measurement, which is the standard deviation of errors in the population, σ_E. From Eqs. (11) and (16), it follows that

$$\sigma_E = (1 - \rho^2_{XT})^{1/2}\sigma_X. \tag{17}$$

Internal Consistency

The internal consistency of a test is the degree to which all of its item scores correlate. If the correlations are high, the test is taken to measure a common factor. Index $i = 1, \ldots, n$ denotes the items in the test; a second index k is used to denote the same items. A parameter for the internal consistency of a test is coefficient α, which is defined as

$$\alpha = \frac{n}{n-1}\left[\frac{\sum^n_{i \ne k} \sigma_{ik}}{\sigma^2_X}\right]. \tag{18}$$

This parameter is thus equal to the sum of the item covariances, σ_{ik}, as a proportion of the total observed score variance for the test (corrected by a factor slightly larger than 1 for technical reasons).

As will become clear later, a convenient formulation of coefficient α is

$$\alpha = \frac{n}{n-1}\left[1 - \frac{\sum^n_{i=1} \sigma^2_i}{\sigma^2_X}\right]. \tag{19}$$

For the special case of dichotomous item scores, coefficient α is known as Kuder–Richardson formula 20 (KR20). If all items are equally difficult, this formula reduces to a version known as Kuder–Richardson formula 21 (KR21).

Validity

If a test score is used to predict the score on another instrument, e.g., for the measurement of future success in a therapy or training program, it is important to have a parameter to represent its predictive power. Let Y denote this other score. We define the validity coefficient for the observed test scores, X, as the correlation coefficient.

$$\rho_{XY}. \tag{20}$$

The reliability coefficient remains an important parameter in predictive validity studies, but the correlation of observed score X with Y, instead of with its true score T in Eq. (15), becomes the ultimate criterion of success for it in prediction studies.

Item Parameters

Well-known item parameters in CTT are the item-difficulty or item π value, the item-discrimination coefficient, and the item validity coefficient. Suppose that the items are scored dichotomously, where $U_i = 1$ is the value for a correct response to item i and $U_i = 0$ is for an incorrect response. The classical parameter for the difficulty of item i is defined as the expected value or mean of U_i in the population of examinees,

$$\pi_i = \mathcal{E}(U_i). \tag{21}$$

The discrimination parameter of item i is defined as the correlation between the item score and the observed test score,

$$\rho_{iX} = \mathrm{Cor}(U_i, X) = \sigma_{iX}/\sigma_i\sigma_X. \tag{22}$$

where σ_{iX}, σ_i, and σ_X are the covariance between U_i and X, and the standard deviation of U_i and X, respectively. Analogously, the correlation between its score and observed score Y defines the validity parameter for item i:

$$\rho_{iY} = \mathrm{Cor}(U_i, Y) = \sigma_{iY}/\sigma_i\sigma_Y. \tag{23}$$

Obviously, a large value for π_i implies an easier item. Likewise, a large value for ρ_{iX} or ρ_{iY} implies an item score that discriminates well between persons with a high and a low observed score X and criterion score Y, respectively. Because X is a function defined on the item-score vector $(U_1, \ldots, U_n)$, the scores on all other items than i have an impact on the correlation between U_i and X too. It is therefore misleading to view ρ_{iX} as an exclusive property of item i. This interpretation problem does not exist for the item-validity coefficient, ρ_{iY}.

It is helpful to know that the following relation holds for the standard deviation of observed score X:

$$\sigma_X = \sum_{i=1}^{n} \sigma_i \rho_{iX}. \tag{24}$$

Replacing σ_X^2 in Eq. (16) by the square of this sum of products of item parameters leads to

$$\alpha = \frac{n}{n-1}\left[1 - \frac{\sum_{i=1}^{n} \sigma_i^2}{\left(\sum_{i=1}^{n} \sigma_i \rho_{iX}\right)^2}\right]. \tag{25}$$

Using comparable relations, the validity coefficient can be written as

$$\rho_{XY} = \frac{\sum_{i=1}^{I} \sigma_i \rho_{iY}}{\sum_{i=1}^{I} \sigma_i \rho_{iX}}. \tag{26}$$

Except for the (known) test length n, these expressions for α and ρ_{XY} are entirely based on the three item parameters σ_i, ρ_{iX}, and ρ_{iY}. They allow evaluation of the effect of the removal or addition of an item to the test on the value of the internal consistency and validity coefficients. The application of CTT to test construction relies heavily on these two relations.

Key Theorems on Reliability and Validity

As examples of more theoretical derivations possible from the classical model in Eqs. (5) and (6), the following three theorems are presented:

$$\rho_{XT}^2 = \rho_{XX'}, \tag{27}$$

$$\rho_{XT}^2 \geq \alpha, \tag{28}$$

and

$$\rho_{XT} \geq \rho_{XY}. \tag{29}$$

The first theorem shows that the reliability coefficient of a test is equal to the correlation between its observed score X and the observed score X' on a replication of the test. This theorem is important in that it demonstrates again how CTT allows expression of an unobservable quantity, such as the squared relation between an observed and a true score, as a quantity that, in principle, can be observed.

Though $\rho_{XX'}$ is observable, for most psychological or social variables it is seldom possible to replicate an administration of the measurement instrument. For such cases, the second theorem is convenient. It shows that the reliability of an observed score can never be smaller than the internal consistency of the item scores on which it is calculated. Because coefficient α can be estimated from a single administration of a test, we often resort to this relation and estimate ρ^2_{TX} by an estimate of this lower bound. The bias in this estimate is only negligible if the test is unidimensional in the sense that it measures a single factor.

The third theorem shows that the predictive validity coefficient of a test can never exceed the square root of the reliability coefficient. This inequality makes sense; it implies that an observed score always correlates at least as well with its own true score as with any other observed score. It also illustrates the previous claim that, if the test is used to predict another score, the reliability coefficient remains important; high reliability is a necessary condition for high validity.

Test Length

If the length of a test is increased, its reliability is expected to increase too. A well-known result in CTT is the Spearman–Brown prophecy formula, which shows that this expectation is correct. Also, if the lengthening of the test is based on the addition of new parts with parallel scores, the formula allows calculation of its reliability in advance.

Suppose the test is lengthened by a factor k. If the scores on the $k-1$ new parts are strictly parallel to the score on the original test according to the definition in Eqs. (13) and (14), the Spearman–Brown formula for the new reliability is

$$\rho^2_{ZT_Z} = \frac{k\rho^2_{XT_X}}{1+(k-1)\rho^2_{XT_X}}, \tag{30}$$

where Z is the observed score on the new test and T_Z its associated true score.

Attenuation Corrections

As already discussed, attenuation corrections were the first results for CTT by Spearman in 1904. He showed that if we are interested in the correlation between the true scores T_X and T_Y and want to calculate it from their unreliable observed scores X and Y, the following relation can be used:

$$\rho_{T_X T_Y} = \frac{\rho_{XY}}{\rho_{XT_X}\rho_{YT_Y}}, \tag{31}$$

where ρ_{XT_X} and ρ_{YT_Y} are the square roots of the reliability coefficient of X and Y (also known as their reliability indices). If we want to correct the validity coefficient in Eq. (19) only for the unreliability of one score, Y, say, the correction is given by

$$\rho_{XT_Y} = \frac{\rho_{XY}}{\rho_{YT_Y}}. \tag{32}$$

This correction makes sense in validity studies, where we want to predict the true criterion score T_Y but always have to predict from the unreliable observed score X.

Parameter Estimation

The statistical treatment of CTT is not well developed. One of the reasons for this is the fact that its model is not based on the assumption of parametric families for the distributions of X_{jt} and T_{Jt} in Eqs. (5) and (6). Direct application of standard likelihood or Bayesian theory to the estimation of classical item and test parameters is therefore less straightforward. Fortunately, nearly all classical parameters are defined in terms of first-order and second-order (product) moments of score distributions. Such moments are well estimated by their sample equivalents (with the usual correction for the variance estimator if we are interested in unbiased estimation). CTT item and test parameters are therefore often estimated using "plug-in estimators," that is, with sample moments substituted for population moments in the definition of the parameter.

A famous plug-in estimator for the true score of a person is the one based on Kelley's regression line. Kelley showed that, under the classical model, the least-squares regression line for the true score on the observed score is equal to

$$E(T \mid X = x) = \rho^2_{XT}x + \left(1-\rho^2_{XT}\right)\mu_X. \tag{33}$$

An estimate of a true score is obtained if estimates of the reliability coefficient and the population mean are plugged into this expression. This estimator is interesting because it is based on a linear combination of the person's observed score and the population mean with weights based on the reliability coefficient. If $\rho^2_{XT} = 1$, the true-score estimate is equal to observed x; if $\rho^2_{XT} = 0$, it is equal to the population mean, μ_X. Precision-weighted estimators of this type are typical of Bayesian statistics. For this reason, Kelley's result has been hailed as the first Bayesian estimator known in the statistical literature.

Strong True-Score Models

To allow stronger statistical inference, versions of the classical test model with the additional assumption of parametric families for Eqs. (5) and (6) can be used. These models remain entirely within the framework of CTT; their main parameter and the classical true score are one and the same quantity. For this reason, they are generally known as "strong true-score models."

Binomial Model

If the item scores are dichotomous, and observed score X_{jt} is defined as the number-correct score, the observed-score distribution can sometimes be approximated by the binomial with probability function

$$f(x) = \binom{n}{x} \pi_{jt}^{x} (1 - \pi_{jt})^{n-x}, \tag{34}$$

where π_{jt} is the binomial success parameter. For the binomial distribution it holds that $\pi_{jt} = \mathcal{E}(X_{jt})$, which proves that this distribution remains within the classical model. The assumption of a binomial distribution is strong in that it only holds exactly for a fixed test if π_{jt} is the common probability of success for j on all items. The assumption thus requires items of equal difficulty for a fixed test or items randomly sampled from a pool. In either case, π_{jt} can be estimated in the usual way from the number of correct responses in the test.

The assumption of a beta distribution for the binomial true score, which has density function

$$f(\pi) = \frac{\pi^{a-1}(1 - \pi)^{b-n}}{B(a, n - b - 1)}, \tag{35}$$

with $B(a,\ n - b - 1)$ being the complete beta function with parameters a and $b - n + 1$, is natural. The beta distribution is both flexible and the conjugate of the binomial. In addition, convenient closed-form estimators for its parameters exist. Finally, the validity of the two distributional assumptions can be checked by fitting a predicted observed-score population distribution, which is known to be negative hypergeometric, to a sample estimate.

Examples of stronger statistical inferences for the beta binomial model are with respect to the standard error of measurement for a person, which is the binomial standard deviation $[\pi_{jt}(1 - \pi_{jt})]^{1/2}$, and true-score population parameters, such as the population median, variance, and interquartile range.

Normal–Normal Model

Another strong true-score model is based on the assumptions of normal distributions for the observed score of a fixed person and the true scores in the population:

$$X_{jt} \sim N[\mu_{jt}, \sigma_{jt}], \tag{36}$$

$$\mu_{jt} \sim N(\mu_T, \sigma_T). \tag{37}$$

Parameter μ_{jt} in this model is also the classical true score. Further, the model allows for inference with respect to the same quantities as the beta binomial model. The normal–normal model has mainly been used to study sampling distributions of classical item and test parameters. The results from these studies provide only a rough approximation of the empirical distributions. Observed scores are discrete and often have a bounded range; the assumption of a normal distribution cannot hold exactly for such scores.

Applications

The major applications of CTT are item and test analyses, test assembly from larger sets of pretested items, and observed-score equating.

Item and Test Analyses

Item and test analyses are based on a pretest of a set of items or a test. Such pretests yield empirical estimates of relevant item and test parameters, which can be inspected to detect possibly dysfunctional items or an undesirable feature of the test. Typical parameters estimated in item and test analyses are item difficulty and discrimination, test reliability or internal consistency, standard error of measurement, and validity coefficients.

Test Construction

If a larger set of items exists and a test of length n has to be assembled from this set, the usual goal is maximization of the reliability or validity of the test. The optimization problem involved in this goal can be formulated as an instance of combinatorial programming. Instead of optimizing the reliability coefficient, it is more convenient to optimize coefficient α; because of Eq. (28), ρ^2_{XT} is also optimized. Using the facts that n is fixed and

$$\sigma_X = \sum_{i=1}^{n} \sigma_i \rho_{iX}, \tag{38}$$

maximizing Eq. (19) is equivalent to minimizing

$$\frac{\sum_{i=1}^{I} \sigma_i^2 x_i}{\left(\sum_{i=1}^{I} \sigma_i \rho_{iX} x_i\right)^2}. \tag{39}$$

Because the denominator and numerator are based on expressions linear in the items, optimization is possible by solving a linear problem consisting of the maximization of

$$\sum_{i=1}^{I} \sigma_i \rho_{iX} x_i,$$

subject to the constraint

$$\sum_{i=1}^{I} \sigma_i^2 x_i \leq c, \tag{40}$$

with c a well-chosen constant. A comparable approach is available for the problem of optimizing the validity coefficient of the test in Eq. (20).

Test Equating

If a new version of an existing standardized test is constructed, the scales of the two versions need to be equated. The equating transformation, which maps the scores on the new version to equivalent scores on the old version, is estimated in an empirical study, often with a randomly-equivalent-groups design in which the two versions of the test are administered to separate random samples of persons from the same population. Let X be the observed score on the old version and Y be the observed score on the new version. In classical equipercentile equating, a study with a randomly-equivalent-groups design is used to estimate the following transformation:

$$x = \varphi(y) = F_X^{-1}[F_Y(y)]. \qquad (41)$$

This transformation gives the equated score $X = \varphi(Y)$ in the population of persons the same distribution as the observed score on the old version of the test, $F_X(x)$. Estimation of this transformation, which actually is a compromise between the set of conditional transformations needed to give each person an identical observed score distribution on the two versions of the test, is sometimes more efficient under a strong true-score model, such as the beta-binomial model in Eqs. (34) and (35), because of the implicit smoothing in these models. Using CTT, linear approximations to the transformation in Eq. (41), estimated from equating studies with different types of sampling designs, have been proposed.

Current Developments

The main theoretical results for the classical test model were already available when Lord and Novick published their standard text in 1968. In fact, one of the few problems for which newer results have been found is the one of finding an approximation to the conditional standard error of measurement $\sigma_{E|T=\tau}$. This standard error is the one that should be used instead of the marginal error σ_E when reporting the accuracy of an observed score. Other developments in test theory have been predominantly in item-response theory (IRT). Results from IRT are not in disagreement with the classical test model, but should be viewed as applying at a deeper level of parameterization for the classical true-score in Eq. (1). For example, it holds that

$$\mathcal{E}(U_i) = 1p_i(\theta) + 0[1 - p_i(\theta)] = p_i(\theta), \qquad (42)$$

which shows that the IRT probability of success for a dichotomous model, $p_i(\theta)$, is the classical true score at item level. Likewise, its holds for the true score at test level that

$$\tau = \mathcal{E}\left(\sum_{i=1}^{n} U_i\right) = \sum_{i=1}^{n}[\mathcal{E}(U_i)] = \sum_{i=1}^{n} p_i(\theta), \qquad (43)$$

which is the test characteristic curve (TCC) in IRT.

The IRT probability of success for a dichotomous model, $p_i(\theta)$, has separate parameters for the person and the item properties. Due to this feature, IRT is more effective in solving incomplete-data problems, that is, problems in which not all persons respond to all items. Such problems are common in test-item banking, computerized adaptive testing, and more complicated observed-score equating designs, compared to the randomly-equivalent-groups design.

See Also the Following Articles

Item Response Theory • Item and Test Bias • Measurement Error, Issues and Solutions • Reliability Assessment • Validity Assessment

Further Reading

Gulliksen, H. (1950). *Theory of Mental Tests.* Wiley, New York.

Kolen, M. J., and Brennan, R. L. (1995). *Test Equating: Methods and Practices.* Springer-Verlag, New York.

Novick, M. R. (1966). The axioms and principal results of classical test theory. *J. Math. Psychol.* **3,** 1–18.

Lord, F. M., and Novick, M. R. (1968). *Statistical Theories of Mental Test Scores.* Addison-Wesley, Reading, Massachusetts.

Spearman, C. (1904). The proof and measurement of association between two things. *Am. J. Psychol.* **15,** 72–101.

Traub, R. E. (1997). Classical test theory in historical perspective. *Educat. Psychol. Measure. Issues Pract.* **16**(4), 8–14.

van der Linden, W. J. (1986). The changing conception of testing in education and psychology. *Appl. Psychol. Measure.* **10,** 325–332.

van der Linden, W. J. (2004). *Linear Models for Optimal Test Design.* Springer-Verlag, New York.

van der Linden, W. J. (2004). Evaluating equating error in observed-score equating. *Appl. Psychol. Measure.*

von Davier, A. A., Holland, P. W., and Thayer, D. T. (2004). *The Kernel Method of Test Equating.* Springer-Verlag, New York.

Clinical Psychology

Silke Schmidt
University of Hamburg, Hamburg, Germany

Mick Power
University of Edinburgh, Edinburgh, United Kingdom

Glossary

clinical psychology The application of psychological knowledge to a range of psychological and physical problems across the life span.

life span approach The study of development and change from infancy to old age.

psychotherapy The use of verbal and behavioral methods by skilled practitioners to help individuals improve or cope more effectively with a variety of personal and interpersonal problems.

reflective practitioner model The therapist's understanding of the personal issues and needs that arise in the practice of therapy, and appropriate action taken to work on such issues.

scientist-practitioner model The application of psychological knowledge in the formulation of psychological problems following a strategy of hypothesis testing, monitoring, evaluation, and assessment of interventions and outcomes.

Clinical psychology is the application of psychological knowledge to a wide range of mental and physical problems across the life cycle, across a range of different client groups, and in a wide range of settings, with its primary focus being on the individual.

Introduction

Clinical psychology is a subject that focuses on the psychological (that is, the emotional, biological, cognitive, social, and behavioral) aspects of human functioning in varying socioeconomic, clinical, and cultural groups as well as in different age groups. This life span approach necessitates a focus on developmental psychology as well as on the dynamics of change for behavior, emotion, and cognition. The aim of clinical psychology is to understand, predict, and treat or alleviate disorders, disabilities, or any kind of maladjustment. This aim involves a variety of clinical specialities and competencies, such as the assessment of problems or impairments, the formulation of problems (which is linked to clinical judgment), and the indicated treatments for these problems. A second aim is to act on a preventative level to promote human adaptation, adjustment, and personal development, thereby placing a focus also on the prevention of mental health conditions.

In relation to the type of professional work involved, "clinical psychology" is an umbrella term that defines a collection of possible but not necessary theories and activities, akin to Wittgenstein's definition of "game." Wittgenstein argued that, although we all understand the concept, there are no essential defining criteria for "game," because there is always an example of a game to which any individual criterion does not apply. We suggest that the theory and practice of clinical psychology also have such problems of definition. Despite the plethora of evidence that has arisen from basic psychology, clinical psychology is inherently an area of applied research, which transfers findings into practice. It refers to direct work with clients and indirect work through other professionals, carers, and policy-related constructs. The professional practice of clinical psychology has now been defined in most countries to include specified training routes, registration of practitioners, and continuing professional development.

Clinical psychologists are involved in research, teaching and supervision, program development and evaluation, consultation, public policy, professional practice, and other activities that promote psychological health in individuals, families, groups, and organizations. Clinical psychology practitioners work directly with individuals at all developmental levels (infants to older adults), as well as with groups (families, patients of similar psychopathology, and organizations), using a wide range of assessment and intervention methods to promote mental health and to alleviate discomfort and maladjustment. This work can range from prevention and early intervention of minor problems of adjustment, to dealing with the adjustment and maladjustment of individuals whose disturbance requires them to be institutionalized. In terms of work settings, these include individual practice, mental health service units, managed health care organizations, counseling centers, and different departments in hospitals, schools, universities, industry, legal systems, medical systems, and government agencies.

Background

Historically, psychology was considered academically as a component of philosophy until the late 19th century; a separation arose through the application of the scientific empirical method. The scientific empirical method replaced philosophical analysis as the primary method for approaching problems and added an additional source of information linked to the hermeneutic (interpretive) method in order to gain insight. Wilhelm Wundt established the first psychological laboratory in Leipzig in 1875; his influence was widespread initially in Germany, but this spread quickly to Britain and the United States, where psychological laboratories were established along the lines of Wundt's model in Leipzig. A student of Wundt's, Lightner Witmer, coined the term "clinical psychology," which he defined in 1895 as follows: "While the term 'clinical' has been borrowed from medicine, clinical psychology is not a medical psychology. I have borrowed the word 'clinical' from medicine, because it is the best term I can find to indicate the character of the method, which I deem necessary for this work. . . . The term 'clinical' implies a method, and not a locality. Clinical psychology likewise is a protest against a psychology that derives psychological and pedagogical principles from philosophical speculations and against a psychology that applies the results of laboratory experimentation directly to children in the school room."

Strongly under Wundt's influence, Witmer founded the first psychology clinic in Philadelphia in 1896 and applied the scientific method and knowledge of psychological principles to a range of psychological problems, particularly developmental disorders. The hermeneutic approach has been revived in the emergence of psychoanalysis—less, however, in its philosophical tradition, but more in terms of its meaningfulness for inference in clinical practice. Since the beginning of the 20th century, clinical psychology has grown considerably in theoretical scope and application, and as a consequence different types of measurement have evolved.

Theory

Clinical psychology has been an area that has incorporated the approaches and perspectives of diverse, even contradictory, schools of psychology, including behaviorism, psychoanalysis, cognitive psychology, humanism, and systems approaches. Each of the schools incorporates a wide variety of theoretical models and empirical evidence from a particular domain, such as the biopsychosocial domain, the behavioral domain, the cognitive–emotional domain, and the psychodynamic domain. The models developed in these schools can best be understood as "paradigms" because they employ an exclusive language code and are based on common assumptions.

Traditionally, the most widespread paradigm in psychopathology and theory is the psychoanalytic, or psychodynamic, paradigm, originally developed by Freud. The essential assumption within psychodynamic theories is that psychopathology arises from unconscious conflict. On the other hand, the biological paradigm of abnormal behavior is a broad theoretical perspective; it assumes that mental disorders are caused by aberrant somatic or biological processes. This paradigm has often been referred to as the medical, or disease, model. The learning (behavioral) paradigm assumes that normal and abnormal behaviors are learned and acquired through experience, or shaped by environmental stimuli. Emotional and cognitive approaches have in some ways evolved as a response to these contradictory approaches, with a combination of focus both on the inner world and on the outer world. Apart from these "paradigms," a variety of internal and external processes (related to cognition and emotion) may also be used to explain the psychodynamic responses between external stimuli and inner conflicts.

In addition to the basic psychological models within each of the schools of clinical psychology, a variety of integrative approaches now span different schools, and are often pervasive in scope. For example, theories and models of emotion regulation, attachment, learned helplessness, and self-control have expanded from a distinct area of interest to the development of sets of common psychological principles. Some of these models are selectively outlined in the following discussions, in order to show how the theories of different schools can be combined into integrative models.

The first example is that of emotion regulation, which refers to the way different types of emotions are evoked in a person by different kinds of events or by actions of others, how these emotions are experienced, processed, expressed, and communicated to others, and how these emotions affect cognition. From a cross-cultural point of view, emotion theorists have long emphasized that emotion regulation is widespread among adults in different cultures. The universal aspects of emotional experience and expression are likely to be associated with biological factors and common social experience, because even very early in child development, children develop a sophisticated arsenal of emotion regulatory strategies. By adulthood, managing personal feelings would seem a natural candidate for the growing list of automatic responses that people draw on in everyday life, and would seem so overlearned that such strategies would have a strong impact on cognition and behavior. However complex the dynamics, the manner in which external responses regulate internal emotion processes also opens the way for clinical therapeutic interventions, given the fact that most emotions are elicited in the close relationships with which the therapies are concerned.

It is on the interpersonal dimension of emotions that attachment theory focuses. Attachment theory describes the propensity to form close relationships with others and the way emotions are regulated in these attachment relationships. This theory reduces the scope of emotion to those feelings that are experienced in attachment relationships. It has strong ethological underpinnings, but it has been rediscovered in psychoanalytic, interpersonal, and in cognitive behavior theories because the model can also explain key reactions in the psychotherapeutic relationship. Psychoanalysts have referred to these concepts in theories as "affect regulation," whereas "emotion regulation" is more a term used in cognitive behavioral psychology.

A third example is that of a behavioral theory, which has had quite widespread influence in the "learned helplessness" paradigm. As a behaviorist, Martin Seligman formulated the learned helplessness theory in 1975; this had a major influence on the psychological research on depression in the 1970s. Seligman identified and defined the phenomenon of learned helplessness through the laboratory study of the effects of inescapable shock on active avoidance learning in dogs. Seligman found that prior exposure to inescapable shock interfered with the ability to learn in a situation in which avoidance or escape was possible. It is important to appreciate that cognition has been at the heart of Seligman's and others' subsequent development of the theory; thus, learned helplessness affects other psychological processes, such as motivation (resulting in reduced positive motivation with no incentive to try new coping responses), cognition (resulting in an inability to learn new responses to overcome prior learning that trauma is uncontrollable), and emotion (the helpless state resembles depression). Seligman and subsequent researchers found a strong relationship between learned helplessness and human depression because there are similarities between helplessness and the symptoms of depression in humans. The theory has since been used as a paradigm for combining behavior, cognition, and emotion into integrative models.

Assessment

Assessment in clinical psychology involves determining the nature, causes, and potential effects of personal distress, types of dysfunctions, and psychological factors associated with physical and mental disorders. It involves the statistical, methodological, research, and ethical issues involved with test development and use, as well as their proper application in specific settings and with specific populations. The development, use, and interpretation of tests based on psychological theory, knowledge, and principles have seen considerable expansion and effort in the past 10 years. The ongoing advances in scientifically based assessment systems, computer technology, and statistical methodology, the increasingly sophisticated uses of psychological instruments in clinical settings, and the widespread use of psychological tests in making decisions that affect the lives of many people have created an exponentially growing body of knowledge and practice that requires the expertise of the assessment specialist. The complexity of the dimensions and tasks in clinical psychology has necessitated development of a wide range of methods of assessment, each appropriate to the different needs of basic psychology. There is no other field that utilizes such varied assessment approaches; these include unstructured and structured clinical assessment and rating approaches, observational methods (including audio/video), psychometric normative attitudinal assessment, neuropsychological standardized tests, and physiological methods. The potential strength of the diversity of methods is that rather than relying on one particular type of approach, the comparison of different sources of information allows a much more complex insight into a disorder or problem.

This variety of assessment forms has evolved from the problem that inner states are not directly observable. It is this problem that caused a dialectic between the nomothetic versus idiographic approach in clinical psychology. The nomothetic strand relies exclusively on the normative approach toward measurements—that is, by drawing references from any kind of a norm group in regard to the respective traits or state under consideration; moreover, all individuals have a score or value on a nomothetic test. The normative reference might include a variety of standardized approaches (population, subpopulation, clinical subgroups, or age groups). An example is Costa and McCrae's NEO, the most widely known nomothetic test that measures the so-called "big five" personality traits, the factors of neuroticism, extroversion, openness ("NEO"), agreeableness, and conscientiousness. In contrast, the idiographic approach rejects the potentiality of drawing normative references along traits that are applicable to all, but, instead, argues that the only method to gain insight into inner states is through the unique personalized assessment of each individual and their relevant experience. An example of an idiographic assessment method is Kelly's repertory grid technique in which bipolar constructs are elicited; these may be unique to the individual (e.g., an individual sees the world on a dimension such as "good" vs. "fat") and not applicable to others. The two empirical approaches to personality assessment, nomothetic and idiographic, are contradictory. The dialectic between the two approaches is a typical phenomenon that occurs regularly in clinical and other branches of psychology. One suggestion is that it is the interlinking of these approaches within a dialectical approach that provides the most comprehensive coverage and inclusiveness in assessment, both theoretically and practically. As an example, the repertory grid technique can be modified to include nomothetic constructs that are measurable across all respondents (e.g., "stable-neurotic"), in addition to the unique constructs elicited from a particular individual.

Interrelated with these two ways of gaining an understanding of a person's inner states are methodological issues and problems involved in clinical psychology. From a methodological point of view, quantitative approaches have been distinguished from qualitative approaches. Quantitative approaches are based on empirical methods, measurement, and statistics whereas qualitative approaches follow a heuristic empirical approach. Clinical psychology needs criteria to judge the quality of the clinical assessment obtainable from either approach. Because inner processes are not directly observable, quantitative measures can only approximate some "true state of the individual," and so qualitative criteria for the psychometric methods employed are needed. Classic psychometric theory has developed a number of criteria that indicate how objective, reliable, and valid psychometric instruments are. The reliability of a method indicates how precisely a measure assesses a construct; it refers to two types—the internal consistency of a measure and the stability of a measure when repeated across time. The validity of a measure indicates to what extent the underlying construct is genuinely measured. Validity is a complex concept and has many subtypes. A diagnosis, for instance, may have concurrent and discriminant, as well as predictive, validity. A clinician's diagnosis has concurrent validity, for instance, if other symptoms that are not part of the diagnosis substantiate the diagnosis (for example, when measured by a self-report scale or a structured interview, which act as a "criterion" for the diagnosis). Discriminant validity indicates that the measure is not related to measures of conceptually unrelated concepts. Predictive validity refers to the ability to predict similar future behavior as part of the disorder (for example, if a hopelessness scale predicts future parasuicidal behavior). The different psychometric criteria are not independent of each other, because reliable measurement is based on objective assessment and the superior criterion of validity can be achieved only with measures that are already reliable; thus, if a measure of diagnosis has poor interrater or test–retest reliability, then the measure would automatically fail to have validity.

Modern psychometric theory has provided probabilistic methods to ascertain whether sets of items that are theoretically assumed to pertain to underlying dimensions can meet the requirements of fundamental measurement (invariance across items and persons), with item and person estimates on the same continuum being the defining parameters. The theoretical field has evolved as item response theory (IRT), the most prominent model of which is the Rasch model. These models can be used with both self-report and observer report methods.

Neuropsychological testing forms another major area of development in clinical psychology. Initially, such tests tended to focus on a unitary concept of intelligence or intellectual functioning, based on the early education-based work of Alfred Binet in France. Binet introduced the concept of the intelligence quotient (IQ) at the beginning of the 20th century and it has been highly influential, albeit controversial, ever since. In relation to neuropsychological assessment, however, the concept of unitary IQ is of little value, because the same overall score can be achieved by a variety of means; thus, similar scores across a range of subtests would lead to the same overall score, as high scores on some subtests and as low scores on others, the latter pattern perhaps providing more diagnostic information from a neuropsychological assessment perspective. Modern neuropsychological assessment has therefore come to focus on increasingly specific tests of function, such as tests of attention, memory, learning, visuospatial performance, and so on. Such tests highlight the fact that some cognitive functions may be impaired while other related ones may not be, which suggests different brain organization (either structurally, functionally, or an integration of both) for such functions. When combined with recently developed neuroimaging methods such as magnetic resonance imaging (MRI), computer-assisted tomography (CAT), and positron emission tomography (PET), it is clear that significant advances will be made in the next decade in relation to understanding brain structure and function and using this information in clinical therapies.

Treatment and Intervention

The variety of theoretical approaches developed both within and in areas adjoining clinical psychology has led to a number of major treatment innovations (for example, behavior therapy, cognitive therapy, person-centered therapy, interpersonal psychotherapy, and psychodynamic approaches). One of the key generic contributions of clinical psychology across this range of interventions has been that of the application of theory-based psychological principles to individual cases, incorporating salient features of individual history and etiology. Theory-based developments in behaviorism, cognitive psychology, and psychoanalysis have led to developments in interventions based on these models.

Behavior therapy was derived primarily from the theoretical developments of Pavlov, with classical conditioning, and Skinner, with operant conditioning. The two-factor theory of Mowrer combined these two approaches in 1939 to demonstrate how fear can be acquired by classical conditioning (typically, the experience of a traumatic or aversive event) and maintained by operant conditioning (such as avoidance of trauma-related events or situations). Subsequent behavior therapy approaches, such as developed by Wolpe, sought to combine increasing trauma-related anxiety while preventing avoidance, in order to demonstrate that anxiety will decrease naturally without the need for avoidance. Although Wolpe initially focused on anxiety arousal in imagination, behavior therapists have instead come to use more direct methods of exposure to events and situations.

Limitations of behavior therapy became apparent not only from further studies of fear acquisition by Rachman and others, but also from attempts to apply behavior therapy to other disorders such as depression. For example, key aspects of depression, such as low self-esteem, suicidal ideation, guilt, and sadness, are not explicable within the behavioral approach. Cognitive and cognitive–behavioral approaches began to be developed in the 1960s and 1970s, with the major approach being the cognitive therapy approach of Beck in 1976. Cognitive therapy aims to identify and challenge depression-related thoughts and beliefs that contribute to the onset and maintenance of depression; such thoughts and beliefs typically center on the need to be loved and taken care of, and the need for achievement and success. The occurrence of critical life events that threaten these fundamental beliefs, such as the separation or loss of a love partner, or failure in an achievement-related domain, is considered to lead to depression; the aim of therapy is therefore to help the individual modify the overinvestment in these beliefs and to develop more appropriate coping strategies and deal more effectively with future adversity. The success of Beck's cognitive therapy for dealing with depression has resulted in its adaptation for the treatment of a range of other conditions, such as anxiety disorders, personality disorders, and, more recently, schizophrenia and bipolar disorders.

As noted previously, clinical psychology perhaps has made the least contribution to the development of psychodynamic approaches, in part because of the strong emphasis of the experimental psychology approach in clinical psychology, combined with Freud's dismissal of the experimental approach as being irrelevant to psychoanalysis. Notwithstanding this potential conflict, many clinical psychology practitioners in North America have been heavily influenced by psychoanalysis and have helped contribute to North American developments in understandings of self and social factors in the theory and practice of psychodynamic approaches. For example, the development of short-term approaches to therapy, as in the increasingly influential interpersonal psychotherapy approach, has stemmed from these multiprofessional North American influences. In contrast, the development of clinical psychology in the United Kingdom and other Northern European countries has focused primarily on behavior therapy and cognitive behavior therapy, so it is only more recently that psychodynamic approaches have come to play a role in those countries. Nevertheless, the practice of cognitive behavior therapies has come to recognize the need to address the therapeutic relationship and problems in this relationship, especially because these approaches have been extended to cover more long-term chronic disorders, such as those seen in individuals with personality disorders.

The initial focus in clinical psychology on individual mental health has subsequently expanded so that therapeutic interventions are now offered for a range of disabilities, including learning difficulties and physical disabilities. The life span approach now also includes a range of interventions for children and adolescents and for older adults. Moreover, there is also a diversification beyond individual approaches to include group as well as family therapy and organizational level interventions. There is, therefore, a considerable overlap in activities between clinical psychology and psychotherapy, counseling, and aspects of psychiatry, nursing, psychosomatics, and health psychology. Many of the methods developed by theorists and practitioners in each of these groupings are widely used by others. Clinical psychologists also engage in program development, evaluate clinical psychology service delivery systems, and analyze, develop, and implement public policy in all areas relevant to the field of clinical psychology. National psychological associations set the standards for clinical psychology graduate programs and recognize programs meeting these standards through an accreditation process. In all states in North America, practitioners require a license to practice clinical psychology, and most European countries either have statutory registration requirements following defined training pathways, or are in the process of implementing registration policies for clinical psychologists and psychotherapists.

Applied Research

In the spirit of Lightner Witmer's experimental influence, the so-called scientist-practitioner model was formulated at a meeting in Boulder, Colorado in 1947. The scientist-practitioner model is based on the proposition that clinical practice must be based on systematic experimental investigation into psychopathology, assessment, and intervention. It supports empirically based clinical practice as well as the training of clinical psychology students in the methods of scientific investigation and decision making, and their application to practice. Training in clinical psychology therefore has an emphasis on research skills, which now go well beyond the specifics of the behaviorally dominated Boulder model to include methods such as single-case quasi-experimental designs, longitudinal research, clinical outcome studies, randomized controlled trials, survey methods, and so on. This broad research training cuts across quantitative and qualitative methods and provides clinical psychology with an ever-increasing role in applied research, especially in North America.

Current and Future Developments

The current and future areas of development in clinical psychology are too numerous to itemize, but a few examples can be highlighted from different areas. Clinical psychology evolved primarily within the area of mental health and mental disorder, and there is a continuing advancement of methods for working with the more chronic and severe mental health problems as seen in schizophrenia, bipolar disorders, and personality disorders. However, considerable advances have also been made in the treatment and management of somatic conditions, dealt with in the fields of psychosomatics, medical psychology, and health psychology, each placing a focus on either particular diseases, the medical setting, the entire health care system, or the prevention of disorder. In general, these fields describe etiology and symptomatology, as well as diagnostic and intervention approaches in (1) psychosomatic disorders, (2) comorbid mental disorders, (3) specific psychological problems in the medical field (e.g., in dermatology and gynecology), (4) problems evolving as a consequence of the interaction with modern medical technology, (5) alleviating the coping processes with medical conditions, and (6) the area of prevention of medical conditions (e.g., through interventions on lifestyle and health behaviors). These fields are extremely important given the increasing occurrence of epidemics such as diabetes, obesity, and coronary heart disease. It has been well demonstrated that most of these conditions are related to individual risk factors, mainly associated with health behavior. It has also been recognized that these risk factors are related to certain styles of emotion regulation, which offer extensive scope for the development of further interventions. The more recent focus on prevention shifts away from the previously exclusive focus on abnormal behavior to encompass the entire spectrum of variation in behavior and attitudes toward health and well being.

Summary and Conclusions

The aim here has been to convey something of the range and diversity of theory and practice in clinical psychology. From its origins just over a 100 years ago as an experimental clinical method, clinical psychology has expanded to cover a vast range of often contradictory and conflicting methods. Sometimes the applied nature of the subject has led to pragmatic integrations, such as the originally conflicted areas of behaviorism and cognitive psychology, which are now integrated in the cognitive–behavioral therapies. However, there is no area of clinical psychology theory or practice that is not opposed in one way or another by a different viewpoint; examples include the opposition between behavioral and psychodynamic approaches, between qualitative versus quantitative research methods, between the scientist-practitioner versus other models of training and practice, and between curative versus preventative services and in regard to the format of therapy, the location of delivery of services, and so on. Although at times each of the factions has been extreme and destructive (e.g., Hans Eysenck's vitriolic attacks on psychoanalysis), nevertheless, the creative tension and energy resulting from differences in perspective have led clinical psychology to offer an increasing number of areas of innovation in both theory and practice in health care taken in its broadest sense.

See Also the Following Articles

Behavioral Psychology • Binet, Alfred • Cognitive Neuroscience • Cognitive Research Methods • Education, Tests and Measures in • Learning and Memory • Psychometrics of Intelligence • Wundt, Wilhelm

Further Reading

Beck, A. T. (1976). *Cognitive Therapy and the Emotional Disorders*. Meridian, New York.

Bowlby, J. (1969). *Attachment and Loss. Vol. 1, Attachment*. Hogarth Press, London.

Bowlby, J. (1988). *A Secure Base: Clinical Applications of Attachment Theory*. Routledge, London.

Costa, P. T., and McCrae, R. R. (1992). *Revised NEO Personality Inventory and NEO Five-Factor Inventory Professional Manual.* Psychological Assessment, Odessa, Florida.

Greenwald, A. G., and Banaji, M. R. (1995). Implicit social cognition: Attitudes, self-esteem, and stereotypes. *Psychol. Rev.* **102,** 4–27.

Harris, P. L. (1989). *Children and Emotion: The Development of Psychological Understanding.* Blackwell, Oxford.

Kelly, G. A. (1955). *The Psychology of Personal Constructs.* Norton, New York.

Kiecolt-Glaser, J. K., *et al.* (2003). Love, marriage, and divorce. Newlyweds' stress hormones foreshadow relationship changes. *J. Consult. Clin. Psychol.* **71,** 176–188.

Lezak, M. D. (1995). *Neuropsychological Assessment*, 3rd Ed. Oxford University Press, Oxford.

Marks, I. (1987). *Fears, Phobias and Rituals.* Oxford University Press, Oxford.

Mowrer, O. H. (1939). Stimulus response theory of anxiety. *Psychol. Rev.* **46,** 553–565.

Seligman, M. E. P. (1975). *Helplessness: On Depression, Development and Death.* Freeman, San Francisco.

Clustering

Phipps Arabie
Rutgers Business School, Newark and New Brunswick, New Jersey, USA

Lawrence J. Hubert
University of Illinois at Champaign, Champaign, Illinois, USA

J. Douglas Carroll
Rutgers Business School, Newark and New Brunswick, New Jersey, USA

Glossary

agglomerative algorithms Hierarchical clustering algorithms that begin with each entity as its own (singleton) cluster and then iteratively merge entities and clusters into a single cluster, constituting the entire group of entities.

divisive algorithms The reverse of agglomerative algorithms; begins with the entire set of entities as one cluster, which is then iteratively divided (usually bifurcated) until each entity is its own (singleton) cluster.

hierarchical clustering The most commonly used form of clustering in the social sciences, probably because of widely available software and the resultant dendrograms (inverted tree structures). The only form of pairwise overlap of clusters allowed is that one must be a proper subset of another.

multidimensional scaling A wide variety of techniques, usually leading to representation of entities in a coordinate space of specified dimensionality.

overlapping clustering In contrast to hierarchical clustering, entities may simultaneously be constituent members of more than one cluster. Hierarchical clustering is subsumed as a special case.

partitioning clustering Each entity belongs to exactly one cluster, and the union of these clusters is the complete set of entities.

Clustering should be among the first multivariate data analysis techniques employed in attempting to identify homogeneous groups, equivalence classes, or multimodal data. A cluster is usually a subset of the n entities under consideration, but what constitutes a cluster is generally defined, sometimes only implicitly, by the method of clustering used in the data analysis. John A. Hartigan's explanation, "Clustering is the grouping of similar objects . . . [and] is almost synonymous with classification," slightly oversimplifies the matter. Though there is no single problem or purpose that requires the development and use of cluster analysis, the empirical use of cluster analysis is overwhelmingly more exploratory than confirmatory, and as such is closely related to the approach presented in Phipps Arabie and Lawrence Hubert's *Clustering and Classification.*

Relevant Types of Data

Users of cluster analysis are often confused by compatibility between data types and types of cluster analysis. Because the literature of statistics sometimes increases the confusion, it is helpful to summarize a multidimensional scaling taxonomy developed by J. Douglas Carroll and Phipps Arabie. There are two types of matrices, (a) one with n rows and an equal number of columns, with entries depicting direct judgments of pairwise similarities for all distinct pairs of the n objects (e.g., people, products, stimuli, or other discipline-specific names), and

(b) the other matrix with n rows of objects and m columns of attributes of the objects. Although both matrices have two ways (i.e., rows and columns for the entities being clustered), the first type of matrix (a) is called "one mode," because both of its ways correspond to the same set of entities (i.e., the n objects). But the matrix (b) of objects, by their attributes, has two disjoint sets (and thus two modes of entities corresponding to the ways). It is often necessary to compute an indirect measure of proximity (e.g., Euclidean distances) between all pairs of rows/columns in a two-mode, two-way matrix to convert it to a one-mode, two-way matrix, because the method of clustering intended for the analysis can only accept a one-mode matrix. Omission of explicit statements about this distinction has clouded much of the literature of cluster analysis and has even led designers to make serious errors; in widely circulated software, John Gower devised a measure explicitly designed for mixed data (over scale types, discrete versus continuous, etc.) commonly encountered in the behavioral sciences. Unfortunately, most statistical software packages do not include a provision for computing Gower's coefficient, and consequently it has been greatly underemployed.

Hierarchical Clustering

Another important distinction is the degree of overlap allowed by the method of clustering. For "hierarchical clustering," the traditional requirement is that in any two distinct clusters, one is either a proper subset of the other ("nesting") or there is no overlap at all. Most hierarchical methods assume a one-mode, two-way input matrix; the highly popular method developed by Joe H. Ward is a major exception. In agglomerative algorithms for hierarchical clustering, the algorithm begins with each of the n objects as a singleton cluster and then begins amalgamating the objects into clusters, according to which pairs of objects or clusters are most similar if the data are similar (as in correlations) or least dissimilar (as in distances). The process continues stepwise until the result is only one cluster containing the entire set of the n objects. Divisive algorithms take the opposite route, beginning with one cluster and stepwise splitting it successively until only singleton clusters remain. Deciding on where in the resulting chain of partitions is the "right" place to claim as the final solution is generally an unsolved problem, with a solution usually dictated by the user's fiat, typically toward a comparatively very small number compared to n. The results of this iterative formation of a hierarchically nested chain of clusters are frequently represented in output from statistical software as a "dendrogram," or inverted tree, often printed in "landscape" (i.e., horizontal) format for mechanical reasons. This dendrogram can be implemented in two ways. Using the full tree is the less common way and possesses two caveats: (1) for most methods of clustering, the terminal nodes (i.e., the singleton clusters) have no preferred ordering and can readily be pivoted around the internal nodes, and (2) if the dendrogram is very complex and cannot be printed legibly, some software simply omits some of the bifurcations that give rise to the internal nodes. The user consequently receives no indication of which bifurcations were omitted or why. The most common use of a dendrogram is to find a horizontal "slice" that necessarily yields a partition with an implicit choice of the "right" number of clusters.

For decades, there was much folklore surrounding the relative advantages and disadvantages of agglomerative versus divisive algorithms for hierarchical clustering, and confusion about the topic still reigns in many textbooks. The former algorithms are more useful for pedagogical reasons, and can even be carried out manually for small data sets. For large data sets (e.g., $n > 100$), divisive algorithms can be easier to use because their graph-theoretic analogues are available in large-scale software. The choice between algorithms has always been overblown. Nicholas Jardine and Robin Sibson have introduced a useful distinction between methods of clustering and the algorithms for implementing clusters: "It is easy to show that the single-link method, for example, can be implemented by a divisive algorithm, an agglomerative algorithm, or by an algorithm which belongs to neither category." The three most commonly used hierarchical methods are complete link, average link, and single link (for which there are various synonyms across disciplines, especially in the behavioral sciences). Although the single-link method is often favored by biologists, it rarely produces substantively interpretable results in the behavioral sciences, where complete- and average-link methods have been found superior. Most of the various linkage types of hierarchical clustering can be subsumed by the classic algebraic formulation of G. N. Lance and William T. Williams that, although not computationally very efficient, nonetheless provides theoretical insights into how various types of hierarchical clustering are interrelated.

What Is the "Right" Number of Clusters?

Deciding on an appropriate number of clusters, as well as choosing the "appropriate" number of dimensions for a multidimensional scaling solution and other techniques for multivariate data analysis, are problems shared by both hierarchical and partitioning clustering. It seems apparent that the general problem for clustering will never be analytically solved (especially for large data sets), but various heuristic approaches are used and/or proposed for answering the question of what is the correct number of clusters for any given data set, for various methods of clustering. The situation is worsened by the fact that many approaches to clustering are based not on any explicit model but rather on an available algorithm. There is thus no goodness-of-fit measure to be optimized.

Additive Trees and Network Models

Some methods of hierarchical clustering have been generalized to "additive trees" and other somewhat related graph-theoretic network models. These methods often assume a one-mode, two-way matrix and entail sophisticated algorithms. Fortunately, at least one generally available software package (SYSTAT) includes such an algorithm for users' analyses when additive trees are sought.

Partitioning

For some researchers, "clustering" is (erroneously) synonymous with partitioning, which allows no overlap: each object is in exactly one cluster and no overlap is allowed among clusters. Most algorithms to implement partitioning assume a two-mode, two-way input matrix and are variations of MacQueen's K-means approach. Many applications of partitioning involve hundreds of thousands of objects and there is the major problem of finding a globally optimal representation. Few methods of clustering can guarantee a global, as opposed to a merely local, optimal solution that is computationally feasible, and the resulting partition is highly dependent on the starting configuration, which may either be random, supplied by an earlier analysis using hierarchical clustering, or based on some other strategy. It therefore sometimes becomes necessary to repeat the analysis with different starting configurations and then to attempt to decide which solution is "best" in some sense. Moreover, few methods of clustering of any kind can obtain a global optimum unless the data set is very small and/or complete enumeration (possibly implicit, as in dynamic programming) is used.

Overlapping Clustering

There is a fourth approach, overlapping clustering, which in turn has two variations: discrete versus continuous. In discrete clustering, an object may simultaneously belong to more than one cluster and membership within a cluster is all-or-none. Some of these approaches also estimate numerical weights for the clusters, the number being specified by the data analyst. Many methods of such overlapping clustering assume one or more two-way, one-mode matrices. In continuous clustering, one common approach is "mixture" models, which assume the data (generally two-way, two-mode) are inherently multimodal. Mixture methods attempt to identify these modes and then assign a probability of membership in each mode for each of the *n* objects. There are many different approaches (mostly parametric) to mixture models and consequently a burgeoning literature on that approach to clustering.

Consensus Clustering

For hierarchical and for partitioning clustering, it is common to obtain several different clusterings, using different methods, and then use logical algorithms to form a "consensus" clustering. Not surprisingly, the literature on such algorithms is often closely related to that of rules for voting or social choice.

Hybrid Approaches to Clustering and Multidimensional Scaling

Work on "hybrid" approaches simultaneously fitting both a clustering and a multidimensional scaling solution, whereby the two are interrelated in a single analysis. Extensive software is freely available for fitting hybrid and also many user-constrained structures to the kinds of data previously described, and further developments in this area of research, with both new models and extensive software for such analyses, are anticipated.

Selecting from a Large Set of Variables

As with many other techniques of multivariate data analysis, clustering is nowadays often applied to enormous data sets that would have been impossible to analyze before recent advances in computing algorithms and hardware. For two-mode, two-way data sets, the number of columns of variables depicting the characteristics of the row objects may be in the thousands, and in most applications, there can be little doubt that the great majority of the column variables are useless for the particular analysis at hand. The problem, of course, is deciding on which ones to discard. Just as in stepwise multiple discriminant analysis, researchers have sought to devise methods for weighting and possibly discarding selected variables altogether. These attempts have focused on hierarchical and on partitioning clustering, but the results have been mixed.

See Also the Following Articles

Correspondence Analysis and Dual Scaling • Quantitative Analysis, Anthropology • Sample Design • Sample Size • Surveys • Typology Construction, Methods and Issues

Further Reading

Arabie, P., and Hubert, L. (1996). An overview of combinatorial data analysis. In *Clustering and Classification* (P. Arabie, L. J. Hubert, and G. De Soete, eds.), pp. 5–63. World Scientific, River Edge, New Jersey.

Carroll, J. D., and Arabie, P. (1980). Multidimensional scaling. In *Annual Review of Psychology* (M. R. Rosenzweig and L. W. Porter, eds.), Vol. 31. pp. 607–649. Annual Reviews, Palo Alto, California. [Reprinted in Green, P. E., Carmone, F. J., and Smith, S. M. (1989). *Multidimensional Scaling: Concepts and Applications*, pp. 168–204. Allyn and Bacon, Needham Heights, Massachusetts.]

Carroll, J. D., and Klauer, K. C. (1998). INDNET: An individual-differences method for representing three-way proximity data by graphs. In *Psychologische Methoden und Soziale Prozesse* (K. C. Klauer and H. Westmeyer, eds.), pp. 63–79. Pabst Science, Berlin.

Carroll, J. D., and Pruzansky, S. (1975). Fitting of hierarchical tree structure (HTS) models, mixtures of HTS models, and hybrid models, via mathematical programming and alternating least squares. Proceedings of the U.S.–Japan Seminar on Multidimensional Scaling, pp. 9–19.

Carroll, J. D., and Pruzansky, S. (1980). Discrete and hybrid scaling models. In *Similarity and Choice* (E. D. Lantermann and H. Feger, eds.), pp. 108–139. Hans Huber, Bern.

De Soete, G., and Carroll, J. D. (1996). Tree and other network models for representing proximity data. In *Clustering and Classification* (P. Arabie, L. Hubert, and G. De Soete, eds.), pp. 157–197. World Scientific, River Edge, New Jersey.

Gordon, A. D. (1996). Hierarchical classification. In *Clustering and Classification* (P. Arabie, L. Hubert, and G. De Soete, eds.), pp. 65–121. World Scientific, River Edge, New Jersey.

Gordon, A. D. (1999). *Classification.* 2nd Ed. Chapman & Hall/CRC, Boca Raton.

Gower, J. C. (1971). A general coefficient of similarity and some of its properties. *Biometrics* **27,** 857–871.

Hartigan, J. A. (1975). *Clustering Algorithms.* Wiley, New York [Translated into Japanese by H. Nishida, M. Yoshida, H. Hiramatsu, K. Tanaka (1983). Micro Software, Tokyo.].

Hubálek, Z. (1982). Coefficients of association and similarity, based on binary (presence-absence) data: An evaluation. *Biol. Rev.* **57,** 669–689.

Hubert, L., and Arabie, P. (1994). The analysis of proximity matrices through sums of matrices having (anti)Robinson forms. *Br. J. Math. Statist. Psychol.* **47,** 1–40.

Hubert, L. J., Arabie, P., and Meulman, J. (1997). Linear and circular unidimensional scaling for symmetric proximity matrices. *Br. J. Math. Statist. Psychol.* **50,** 253–284.

Hubert, L. J., Arabie, P., and Meulman, J. (2001). *Combinatorial Data Analysis: Optimization by Dynamic Programming.* Monograph Series of the Society of Industrial and Applied Mathematics [SIAM], Philadelphia.

Hutchinson, J. W. (1989). NETSCAL: A network scaling algorithm for nonsymmetric proximity data. *Psychometrika* **54,** 25–51.

Jardine, N., and Sibson, R. (1971). *Mathematical Taxonomy.* Wiley, London.

Klauer, K. C., and Carroll, J. D. (1989). A mathematical programming approach to fitting general graphs. *J. Classification* **6,** 247–270.

Klauer, K. C., and Carroll, J. D. (1991). A mathematical programming approach to fitting directed graphs to nonsymmetric proximity measures. *J. Classification* **8,** 251–268.

Lance, G. N., and Williams, W. T. (1967). A general theory of classificatory sorting strategies. I. Hierarchical systems. *Comput. J.* **9,** 373–380.

Leclerc B. (1998). Consensus of classifications: The case of trees. In *Advances in Data Science and Classification* (A. Rizzi, M. Vichi, and H.-H. Bock, eds.), pp. 81–90. Springer-Verlag, Heidelberg.

MacQueen, J. (1967). Some methods for classification and analysis of multivariate observations. In *Proceedings of the Fifth Berkeley Symposium on Mathematical Statistics and Probability* (L. M. Le Cam and J. Neyman, eds.), Vol. 1. pp. 281–297. University of California Press, Berkeley, CA.

Milligan, G. W. (1996). Clustering validation: Results and implications for applied analyses. In *Clustering and Classification* (P. Arabie, L. J. Hubert, and G. De Soete, eds.), pp. 341–375. World Scientific, River Edge, NJ.

Sattath, S., and Tversky, A. (1977). Additive similarity trees. *Psychometrika* **42,** 319–345.

Ward, J. H., Jr. (1963). Hierarchical grouping to optimize an objective function. *J. Am. Statist. Assoc.* **58,** 236–244.

Coding Variables

Lee Epstein
Washington University, St. Louis, Missouri, USA

Andrew Martin
Washington University, St. Louis, Missouri, USA

Glossary

codebook A guide to the database that the researcher is creating—a guide sufficiently rich that it not only enables the researcher to code his or her data reliably but also allows others to replicate, reproduce, update, or build on the variables housed in the database, as well as any analyses generated from it.

observable implications (or expectations or hypotheses) What we expect to detect in the real world if our theory is right.

reliability The extent to which it is possible to replicate a measurement, reproducing the same value (regardless of whether it is the right one) on the same standard for the same subject at the same time.

theory A reasoned and precise speculation about the answer to a research question.

variable Observable attributes or properties of the world that take on different values (i.e., they vary).

variable, values of Categories of a variable (e.g., male and female are values of the variable gender).

Coding variables is the process of translating attributes or properties of the world (i.e., variables) into a form that researchers can systematically analyze. The process entails devising a precise schema to account for the values that each variable of interest can take and then methodically and physically assigning each unit under study a value for every given variable.

Introduction

Social scientists engaged in empirical research—that is, research seeking to make claims or inferences based on observations of the real world—undertake an enormous range of activities. Some investigators collect information from primary sources; others rely primarily on secondary archival data. Many do little more than categorize the information they collect; but many more deploy complex technologies to analyze their data.

Seen in this way, it might appear that, beyond following some basic rules of inference and guidelines for the conduct of their research, scholars producing empirical work have little in common. Their data come from a multitude of sources; their tools for making use of the data are equally varied. But there exists at least one task in empirical scholarship that is universal, that virtually all scholars and their students perform every time they undertake a new project: coding variables, or the process of translating properties or attributes of the world (i.e., variables) into a form that researchers can systematically analyze after they have chosen the appropriate measures to tap the underlying variable of interest. Regardless of whether the data are qualitative or quantitative, regardless of the form the analyses take, virtually all researchers seeking to make claims or inferences based on observations of the real world engage in the process of coding data. That is, after measurement has taken place, they (1) develop a precise schema to account for the values on which each variable of interest can take and then (2) methodically and physically assign each unit under study a value for every given variable.

And yet, despite the universality of the task (not to mention the fundamental role it plays in research), it typically receives only the briefest mention in most volumes on designing research or analyzing data. Why this is the case is a question on which we can only speculate, but an obvious response centers on the seemingly idiosyncratic nature of the undertaking. For some projects, researchers may be best off coding inductively, that is, collecting their data, drawing a representative sample, examining the data in the sample, and then developing their coding scheme; for others, investigators proceed in a deductive manner, that is, they develop their schemes first and then collect/code their data; and for still a third set, a combination of inductive and deductive coding may be most appropriate. (Some writers associate inductive coding with research that primarily relies on qualitative [nonnumerical] data/research and deductive coding with quantitative [numerical] research. Given the [typically] dynamic nature of the processes of collecting data and coding, however, these associations do not always or perhaps even usually hold. Indeed, it is probably the ease that most researchers, regardless of whether their data are qualitative or quantitative, invoke some combination of deductive and inductive coding.) The relative ease (or difficulty) of the coding task also can vary, depending on the types of data with which the researcher is working, the level of detail for which the coding scheme calls, and the amount of pretesting the analyst has conducted, to name just three.

Nonetheless, we believe it is possible to develop some generalizations about the process of coding variables, as well as guidelines for so doing. This much we attempt to accomplish here. Our discussion is divided into two sections, corresponding to the two key phases of the coding process: (1) developing a precise schema to account for the values of the variables and (2) methodically assigning each unit under study a value for every given variable. Readers should be aware, however, that although we made as much use as we could of existing literatures, discussions of coding variables are sufficiently few and far between (and where they do exist, rather scanty) that many of the generalizations we make and the guidelines we offer come largely from our own experience. Accordingly, sins of commission and omission probably loom large in our discussion (with the latter particularly likely in light of space limitations).

Developing Coding Schemes

Regardless of the type of data they collect, the variables they intend to code, or even whether they plan to code inductively or deductively, *at some point* empirical researchers require a coding schema, that is, a detailing of each variable of interest, along with the values of each variable—for example the variable RELIGION of a survey with, say, "Protestant," "Catholic," "Jewish," "none," and "other" as the values. With this sort of information in hand, investigators can prepare codebooks—or guides they employ to code their data and that others can use to replicate, reproduce, update, or build on the variables the resulting database contains and any analyses generated from it.

In the section that follows, we have much more to say about codebooks. For now let us home in on this first phase—developing coding schemes—and begin by reinforcing a point suggested by our emphasis on the phrase "at some point"; namely that, in terms of research design, many steps typically proceed the step developing a coding schema, such as devising research questions, theorizing about possible answers, generating observable implications, and so on. Even when it comes to coding variables, researchers may not begin with developing a coding schema. But—and this is our chief point—they almost always perform this task during the course of a project's life. This holds for those who create databases, as well as for those who work with databases developed by others, such as the General Social Survey and the American National Election Study; that is, users need to devise a plan of their own if they desire to transform variables contained in existing databases.

We also ought acknowledge at the onset that the nature of the coding task (especially its relative difficulty) varies depending on the types of variables under investigation. If we are conducting a survey of students, all of whom are between the ages of 18 and 21, then it is relatively trivial to develop a coding scheme for the variable AGE: it would take on the values "18," "19," "20," and "21." Devising the values for many other variables is not as straightforward a task. To see this, return to the deceptively simple example of the variable RELIGION, for which we listed five possible values: "Protestant," "Catholic," "Jewish," "none," and "other." This may work well for some studies, but we can imagine others for which it would not. Consider, for example, an investigation into the attitudes of individuals who belong to a Jewish synagogue wherein the researcher desires to include the variable RELIGION. Assuming that nearly all the subjects are Jews, the five values we have listed would make little sense (nearly 100% would fall into the "Jewish" category). Accordingly, the investigator would need to alter the schema, perhaps by incorporating finer divisions of "Jewish": "Jewish-Orthodox," "Jewish-Conservative," "Jewish-Reform"—or whatever schema most appropriately enables the researcher to capture the information necessary to the research task.

Other problems may exist with our original values of RELIGION; for example, what of respondents who are interdenominational in their religious preferences? They will be forced to choose among the values of RELIGION or perhaps respond with "other," even if their preference is one that combines Catholic and Protestant tenets. And, for that matter, what should we make of the "other" category? Depending on the subjects under analysis, it may be appropriate (meaning that it would be an option selected by relatively few respondents) or not. But our more general point should not be missed: Accounting for the values of the variables of interest, even for seemingly straightforward ones, may be a non-trivial task.

To facilitate the efforts of researchers to perform it, we offer the three recommendations that follow: (1) ensure that the values of the variables are exhaustive; (2) create more, rather than fewer, values; and (3) establish that the values of the variables are mutually exclusive. These guidelines reflect standard practice, along with our own experience. But there is one we presuppose: Researchers must have a strong sense of their project, particularly the piece of the world they are studying and how that piece generated the data they will be coding, as well as the observable implications of their theory that they will be assessing. Because this point is obvious, if only from the brief examples we have provided, we do not belabor it. We only wish to note that an adherence to all the suggestions that follow will be difficult, if not impossible, if researchers lack a deep understanding of the objects of their study and an underlying theory about whatever feature(s) of behavior they wish to account for.

Ensure that the Values of the Variables Are Exhaustive

Our first recommendation, simply put, is that the values for each variable must exhaust all the possibilities. To see why, consider a simple example, from a 2000 study by Frankfort-Nachmias and Nachmias, in which the values of the variable MARITAL STATUS are enumerated as "married," "single," "divorced," and "widowed." This is not an exhaustive list because it fails to include "living together but not married" and, as such, may ultimately be a source of confusion for respondents who are asked to describe their marital status or for coders who must make a decision about another's status.

To skirt the problem, investigators typically include the value "other." As a general matter, this is not only acceptable but typically necessary. It may be the case that researchers, however well they know their project and however well developed their theory, cannot anticipate every value of a particular variable. Moreover, even if they did, it may be impractical or inefficient to include each and every one. At the same time, however, because we can learn very little from a database replete with variables mostly coded as "other," researchers should avoid the overuse of this value when it comes time to code their data. Only by having a thorough understanding of their project—or at least an understanding (perhaps developed through pretesting) sufficient enough to be able to write down an exhaustive list of the likely-to-occur values—will they steer clear of this pitfall. Pretesting or conducting a pilot study when possible and is in general a useful way to detect potential problems of all sorts—including the overuse of "other." When pretesting reveals that "the 'other' response accounts for 10 percent of more of the total responses," Shi (1997) suggested in a 1997 study (as a rule of thumb) that researchers should add new values.

Create More, Rather than Fewer, Values

To some extent our second recommendation counsels "when in doubt, include a value rather than exclude it." It reinforces from our first recommendation because this will help to avoid the problem of too many "other" codes. But it suggests something else; that analysts create values that are more, rather than less, detailed.

To see why, consider the example of researchers who want to explain why lower federal appellate courts (the U.S. Courts of Appeals) sometimes reverse the decisions reached by trial courts and sometimes affirm them. For such a project investigators need to enumerate the values of the variable DISPOSITION, which they could merely list as "affirm" and "reverse" because these are the dispositions that concern her. The problem here is that appellate courts do not always simply affirm or reverse; these courts have many options available to them, as Table I indicates.

Even though our analysts are interested solely in a court's decision to affirm or reverse, the guideline of "creating more, rather than fewer, values" suggests that they start with all possible values of DISPOSITION (as listed in Table I). To be sure, the researchers should know which values of the DISPOSITION ought count as a "reverse" and which should count as an "affirm"; and we would require them to specify that (e.g., values 2, 3, 4,

Table I Possible Dispositions in Cases Decided by the U.S. Courts of Appeals

Value	*Value label*
0	Stay, petition, or motion granted
1	Affirmed; or affirmed and petition denied
2	Reversed (including reversed & vacated)
3	Reversed and remanded (or just remanded)
4	Vacated and remanded (also set aside & remanded; modified and remanded)
5	Affirmed in part and reversed in part (or modified or affirmed and modified)
6	Affirmed in part, reversed in part, and remanded; affirmed in part, vacated in part, and remanded
7	Vacated
8	Petition denied or appeal dismissed
9	Certification to another court

Source: U.S. Court of Appeals Data Base, available at: http://www.polisci.msu.edu/pljp/databases.html

6, 7 listed in Table I might be considered "reverse"). But beginning with the more detailed values has two clear advantages (both of which have even more bearing on the second phase of the coding process, discussed later). First, whoever eventually codes the data will make fewer errors. Think about it this way: If our investigators tell their coder in advance to report values 2, 3, 4, 6, and 7 as "reversals," the coder must take two steps: (1) identify the disposition by examining the court's decision and, then, (2) identify whether it is a reversal or affirmance. But if the researcher simply has the coder identify the disposition, then the coder has only one step to take. Because every step has the possibility of introducing error, researchers should seek to reduce them.

A second set of advantages accrue when the investigators turn to analyzing their data. Because they have now coded the variable DISPOSITION quite finely, they can always collapse values (e.g., they can create "reverse" from values 2, 3, 4, 6, 7 in Table I) to generate a new variable, say, DISPOSITION2, which would house the two categories of primary interest to her ("reverse" and "affirm"). At the same time, and again because they have coded DISPOSITION finely, they will be able to ascertain whether any particular coding decision affects their conclusions. Suppose, for example, that, in collapsing values of DISPOSITION, they count value 6 (in Table I) as a "reverse," even though the court affirmed in part. Because this represents a judgment on their part (although one they should record, thereby enabling others to replicate their variable) and because the converse coding (counting 6 as an "affirm") is plausible, they will be able to examine the effect of their judgment on the results. Of course, none of these advantages ensue if they initially list only two values of disposition ("reverse" and "affirm"); while researchers can always collapse values, they cannot disaggregate those coded more coarsely. This point cannot be understated; we can never go from fewer categories to many without returning to the original data source (which oftentimes, for example, in survey research, is impossible). Coding data as finely as possible allows the researcher to encode a greater amount of information.

Despite all the advantages of creating more (rather than fewer) values, limits do exist. Consider researchers who must devise values for the variable INCOME (representing survey respondents' "total family income, from all sources, fall last year before taxes"). Following the recommendation of creating detailed values might lead the investigators to ask respondents simply to report their precise income. Such, in turn, would provide them with an exact dollar figure—or the finest possible level of detail on the variable INCOME. But very few (reputable) surveyors operate in this fashion. This is because they realize that individuals may not know that exact dollar amount or may not want others to know it. Hence, rather than running the risk of reliability problems down the road, researchers typically create values that represent income categories (e.g., "under \$1000," "\$1000–2999," and "\$3000–3999").

We can imagine other projects/variables for which our recommendation of developing detailed values would not be advisable. But, in the main and depending on the project/variable, it is a general principle worth considering.

Establish That the Values of the Variables are Mutually Exclusive

Under our third guideline, researchers must be sure that they have created values such that whatever unit is under analysis falls into one and only one value. It is easy to see how the failure to follow this recommendation could lead to confusion on the part of respondents and coders alike but, unfortunately, it also easy to violate it. Consider the simple example from the 2000 study by Frankfort-Nachmias and Nachmias of a variable LIVING ARRANGEMENTS OF STUDENTS for which investigators have enumerated four values: "live in dormitory," "live with parents," "live off campus," and "live with spouse." To the extent that the values seem exhaustive and detailed, this schema meets the two other recommendations but not the third—a student could "live with parents" and "live off campus," or, for that matter, live off campus with a spouse, live with parents and a spouse, or (at some universities) live in a dorm with a spouse. The values are not mutually exclusive. Guarding against the problem requires that researchers, once again, understand their project; pretesting also may be a useful step.

Assigning Each Unit Under Study a Value

After (or perhaps concurrently with) developing a coding schema, analysts must methodically and physically assign each unit under study a value for every variable. Doing so typically requires them to (1) create a codebook to house the schema and other relevant information and (2) determine how they will ultimately enter their data into a statistical software package so that they can analyze them.

Codebooks

In line with our earlier definition, codebooks provide a guide to the database that the researchers are creating—a guide sufficiently rich that it not only enables the researchers to code their data reliably but also allows others to replicate, reproduce, update, and build on the variables housed in the database as well as any analyses generated from it. Indeed, the overriding goal of a codebook is to minimize human judgment—to leave as little as possible to interpretation.

Accordingly, while codebooks contain coding schemes (that is, the variables and the values that each can take), most contain much more—including the details about various features of the research process (e.g., information about the sample and sampling procedures, data sources, and the time period of the study). We do not provide a listing of each of these components here. (Researches should investigate the Inter-university Consortium for Political and Social Research, ICPSR, and the Data Documentation Initiative, DDI, which is "an effort to establish an international criterion and methodology for the content, presentation, transport, and preservation of 'metadata' [codebooks or, in DDI's words, "data about data"] about datasets in the social and behavioral sciences.") We instead focus on those relevant to coding variables: variables, values, missing values, and coding notes.

Variable Names

When researchers enumerate the values of their variables, those variables have (or should have) precise meanings. To return to our previous examples, investigators, may name their variable INCOME but understand that to mean "total family income, from all sources, before taxes." Likewise to researchers coding the variable DISPOSITION, this variable may signify "the rulling of a U.S. Court of Appeals."

Codebooks contain both a short variable name (e.g., INCOME) as well as the investigators' precise definition ("total family income, from all sources, last year before taxes"). The reason for the former is that many statistical software packages (into which researchers ultimately enter their data) still limit the length of the variable name, to, say, eight characters. Hence, to ensure that the variable name in the codebook corresponds to the variable name in the database, codebooks typically contain the abbreviated name. (Worth noting is that limits on length are becoming less of a concern in current versions of software packages, although being able to refer to variables using some shorthand is typically valuable for other reasons.)

Conventions for naming variables abound. But because other sources provide detailed discussions of this matter we need not delve into them here. What is worthy of emphasis is this advice, from ICPSR: "It is important to remember that the variable name is the referent that analysts will use most often when working with the data. At a minimum, it should not convey incorrect information, and ideally it should be unambiguous in terms of content."

In addition to the shortened variable name, researchers supply a longer, descriptive name for each variable (for INCOME, "total family income, from all sources, last year before taxes"), along with the form each variable takes (for INCOME, dollars). (For variables created from survey questions, the descriptive name typically is the exact question asked of respondents.) The name should convey a strong sense of the contents of the variable, and it ought be listed in the codebook and in the database (most statistical packages allow the user to enter a longer variable identifer or variable label).

Values

When researchers develop their coding schema, they create values—usually in the form of labels—for each variable, such as the nine descriptive values in Table I for the variable DISPOSITION. After (or concurrently with) doing this, they typically assign a unique number to each value (as in Table I). The codebook contains both the value numbers and the value labels (e.g., in Table I, 0 = stay, petition, or motion granted; 1 = affirmed, or affirmed and petition denied; and so on); the ultimate database houses both, but it is typically the number that the coder enters for each unit of analysis.

As is the case for variable names, conventions for assigning numbers to the values of variables abound. For example, values ought be convenient, intuitive, and consistent with the level of measurement. So, for example, even though the values of a discrete variable, say GENDER, could be 1010 = male and 5020 = female (because matters of size and order are irrelevant), this convention counsels that the researcher ought begin with 0 and increase by 1 (e.g., male = 0; female = 1). Starting with the lowest values with the fewest digits, however, need not mean that the researcher must sacrifice sophistication. Manheim and Rich in their 1995 article detailing how researchers interested in a finely coded RELIGION variable can devise a numbering system that is simultaneously simple, intuitive, and refined make this point nicely. Rather than merely assigning values 1–4 to various Protestant denominations (say, 1 = Baptist, 2 = Methodist, 3 = Presbyterian, and 4 = Lutheran), values 5–7 to various forms of Judiasim (e.g., 5 = Orthodox, 6 = Conservative, and 7 = Reform), and value 8 to Catholic, researchers can classify numbers in a logical, meaningful way (10 =Baptist, 11 = Methodist, 12 = Presbyterian, 13 = Lutheran; 20 = Jewish Orthodox, 21 = Jewish Conservative, 22 = Jewish Reform; 30 = Catholic). Under this system, each major category of religion (Protestant, Jewish, Catholic) receives the same first digit, with the second digit representing a subdivision. As Inter-university Consortium for Political and Social Research explains, "This type of coding scheme permits analysis of the data in terms of broad groupings as well as individual responses or categories."

Ease of use, intuition, and logic also should guide the assignment of values to continuous variables. This typically means that researchers should record the original value, reserving transformations for later. For example, even if the logarithm of AGE will ultimately serve as an independent variable in the analysis, the researcher ought code the raw values of AGE and do so sensibly (if a person is 27, then the value of the variable AGE for that person is 27).

Two other rules of thumb are worthy of note. One is that wherever and whenever possible, researchers should use standard values. If the ZIP CODE of respondents is a variable in the study, it makes little sense to list the codes and then assign numerical values to them (11791 = 1, 11792 = 2, 11893 = 3, and so on) when the government already has done that; in other words, in this case the researcher should use the actual zip codes as the values. The same holds for other less obvious variables, such as INDUSTRY, to which the researcher can assign the values (e.g., 11 = Agriculture, 22 = Utilities, and so on) used by the U.S. Census Bureau and other agencies.

The remaining rule is simple enough and follows from virtually all we have written thus far—avoid combining values. Researchers who create a variable GENDER/RELIGION and codes a male (value = 0) Baptist (value = 10) as value = 010 are asking only for trouble. In addition to working against virtually all the recommendations we have supplied, such values become extremely difficult to separate for purposes of analyses (but GENDER and RELIGION, coded separately are simple to combine in most software packages).

Missing Values

However carefully researchers plan their project, they will inevitably confront the problem of missing values. A respondent may have failed (or refused) to answer a question about his/her religion, a case may lack a clear disposition, information simply may be unavailable for a particular county, and so on. Investigators should be aware of this problem from the onset and prepare accordingly. This is so even if they plan to invoke one of the methods scholars have developed to deal with missing data because it might affect the analyses. That is because the various solutions to the problem assume that researchers treat missing data appropriately when they create the original database.

At the very least, investigators must incorporate into their codebook values to take into account the possibility of missing data—with these values distinguishing among the different circumstances under which missing information can arise. These can include "refused to answer/no answer," "don't know," and "not applicable," among others. Whatever the circumstances, researchers should assign values to them rather than simply leaving blank spaces. Simply leaving missing values blank can cause all types of logistical problems—for example, is the observation truly missing, or has the coder not yet completed it? Using an explicit missing-value code eliminates this type of confusion and can also provide information about why a specific variable is missing.

One final point is worthy of mention: Although in this entry our primary concern is with coding variables to be included in an initial and original database—not with imputing missing data (or recoding or otherwise transforming variables)—we do want to note that if the researcher has imputed missing data, she should indicate this in the final version of the codebook. The Inter-university Consortium for Political and Social Research suggests one of two possible approaches: "The first is to include two versions of any imputed variables, one being the original, including missing data codes, and the second being an imputed version, containing complete data. A second approach is to create an 'imputation flag,' or indicator variable, for each variable subject to imputation, set to '1' if the variable is imputed and '0' otherwise."

Coding Notes

As we have noted earlier, the overriding goal of a codebook—and indeed the entire coding process—is to minimize the need for interpretation. As far as possible, human judgment should be removed from coding, or, when a judgment is necessary, the rules underlying the judgments should be wholly transparent to the coders and other researchers. Only by proceeding in this way can researchers help to ensure the production of reliable measures.

To accomplish this in practice, analysts certainly ought be as clear as possible in delineating the values of the variables. But they also should write down a very precise set of rules for the coders (and other analysts) to follow and should include that information for each variable housed in their codebook. Such a list should be made even if investigators code the data themselves, because without it, others will not be able to replicate the research (and the measure). Along these lines, an important rule of thumb is to imagine that the researchers had to assign students the task of classifying each case by its disposition and that the only communication permitted between the researchers and the students was a written appendix to the article detailing the coding scheme. This is the way to conduct research and how it should be judged. (We do not deal with the topic of transforming original variables here, but, of course, if researchers create new variables from existing ones, they should note this.)

Coding and Data Entry

Once researchers have devised their codebook, they must turn to the tasks of (1) employing the codebook to assign a value for every variable for each unit under study and (2) entering these values into a statistical software program. They can perform these tasks concurrently or separately. Analysts making use of computer-assisted telephone interviewing (CATI) or computer-assisted personal interviewing (CAPI) programs, for example, do not separate the two; they use direct data entry. At the other extreme, researchers who are coding their data from a host of sources may record the assigned values on coding sheets and then transfer the information to a software program. To see why, let us return to the example of the analysts coding court DISPOSITIONS and suppose that, in addition to the values of this variable, they also desire data on the PARTY AFFILIATION of the judges deciding the case. Because she cannot obtain information on DISPOSITION and PARTY AFFILIATION from the same source, she may find it prudent to create a coding (or a transfer) sheet, assign values to each case on the variable DISPOSITION, and then do likewise for PARTY AFFILIATION. Once she has collected and coded all the data, she can enter the information (now on coding sheets) into her software package.

The rules covering coding sheets have been outlined elsewhere. What is important here is understanding the trade-off (often a necessary one) that researchers make when they enter data from sheets rather than directly into their computer. On the one hand, researchers must realize that every extra step has the potential to create error—recording information onto coding sheets and then transferring that information into a computer introduces a step that is not necessary in direct data entry. On the other hand (and even if data are derived from one source only), they should understand that coding and data entry typically represent two separate tasks—asking a singular person to perform them concurrently may also lead to errors in one, the other, or both.

Whatever choices researchers make, they should evaluate them. Reliability checks on the coding of variables are now standard—researchers drawing a random sample of cases in their study and asking someone else to recode them is a simple way to conduct them. So too analysts ought assess the reliability of the data entry process, even if they made use of sophisticated software to input the information. Although such programs may make it difficult, if not impossible, for investigators to key in wild or out-of-range values (e.g., a 7 when the only values for GENDER are 0 = male, 1 = female), they typically do not perform consistency or other checks. And when using multiple coders, it is necessary to have several coders code a set of the same observations to allow the researcher to assess reliability among the coders.

Researchers can undertake the process of cleaning their data set in several ways (e.g., running frequency distributions or generating data plots to spot outliers, or creating cross-tabulations to check for consistency across variables). But the key point is that they should do it, because as Babbie well states in a 2001 study, " 'dirty' data will almost always produce misleading research findings." The same, of course, is true of data that have been collected and coded via asystematic, unthinking means—that is, via means that these recommendations are designed to thwart.

See Also the Following Articles

Data Collection, Primary vs. Secondary • Data Distribution and Cataloging • Neutrality in Data Collection • Reliability

Further Reading

Babbie, E. (2001). *The Practice of Social Research.* Wadsworth, Belmont, CA.

Data Documentation Initiative. http://www.icpsr.umich.edu/DDI/ORG/index.html

Epstein, L., and King, G. (2002). The rules of inference. *University Chicago Law Rev.* **69,** 1–133.

Frankfort-Nachmias, C., and Nachmias, D. (2000). *Research Methods in the Social Sciences.* Worth, New York.

Inter-university Consortium for Political and Social Research. (2002). Guide to social science data preparation and archiving. Ann, Arbor, MI. Available at: http://www.icpsr.umich.edu/ACESS/dpm.html

King, G., Honaker, J., Joseph, A., and Scheve, K. (2001). Analyzing incomplete political science data: An alternative algorithim for multiple imputation. *Am. Polit. Sci. Rev.* **95,** 49–69.

King, G., Keohane, R. O., and Verba, S. (1994). *Designing Social Inquiry: Scientific Inference in Qualitative Research.* Princeton University Press, Princeton, NJ.

Little, R. J. A., and Rubin, D. B. (1987). *Statistical Analysis with Missing Data.* John Wiley, New York.

Manheim, J. B., and Rich, R. C. (1995). *Empirical Political Analysis,* 4th Ed. Longman, New York.

Salkind, N. J. (2000). *Exploring Research.* Prentice Hall, Upper Saddle River, NJ.

Shi, L. (1997). *Health Services Research Methods.* Delmar Publishers, Albany, NY.

Stark, R., and Roberts, L. (1998). *Contemporary Social Research Methods.* MicroCase, Bellvue, WA.

U.S. Census Bureau. http://www.census.gov/epcd/www/naics.html

U.S. Court of Appeals Data Base. http://www.polisci.msu.edu/pljp/databases.html

Cognitive Maps

Reginald G. Golledge
University of California, Santa Barbara, California, USA

Glossary

anchor point A dominant environmental cue.
bidimensional regression Regression in the spatial coordinate domain.
cognitive map The product of perceiving and thinking about environments external to one's body. It represents a store of experienced sensations that have been perceived, noticed, identified, encoded, and stored in memory for later manipulation and used in problem-solving or decision-making situations.
cognitive mapping The process of perceiving, encoding, storing, internally manipulating, and representing spatial information.
configurational matching The assessment of the degree of congruence between actual and created spatial configurations.
displacement error The absolute distance between an objective and a subjective location.
fuzziness The variance associated with a set of spatial measures.
landmark A generally well-known feature, distinct because of its physical, social, or historical properties.
multidimensional scaling An iterative procedure for finding a minimal dimensional solution for configuring spatial knowledge.
place cells Elements of the brain in which specific spatial features are stored.
pointing Use of a device or body part to identify direction from current location to a distant location.
reproduction task An act of using body-turning or locomotion to represent an experienced angle or distance.
sketch map A hand-drawn representation of what one recalls about an environment.
spatial cognition The thinking and reasoning processes used to manipulate, interpret, and use encoded spatial information.
spatial decoding errors Errors of translating encoded spatial information for manipulation in working memory.
spatial encoding errors Errors of perceiving or sensing feature or object location.
spatial product The external representation of recalled spatial information.
task environment The defined setting in which experimental procedures are carried out.
wayfinding The process of searching out a path to reach a goal.

The term "cognitive map" is generally accepted to be a hypothetical construct that refers to one's internal representation of the external world. At various times, the concept has been interpreted as a metaphor or a cartographic-like representation. It is accepted that people may think and reason by constructing images—some of which may indeed be map-like—but that the "map" portion of the term is just a convenient fiction that may facilitate the understanding of how thought processes deal with spatial and social information. A popular interpretation is that cognitive maps are the outcome of information processing that organizes places and locations and makes clear the spatial relations that connect them.

Definition and Use

Cognitive Maps and Cognitive Mapping

Although Tolman originally defined the cognitive map as an internal representation of a specific spatial area (a maze in which he was conducting learning experiments with Norwegian rats), the term has broadened considerably and generally refers to one's internal representation of the surrounding world. A narrower view of the concept refers to a level of spatial information processing in which an environment is organized as a system of interconnected locations, places, and relationships. In both views, the concept also incorporates a series of transformation

Table I Methods for Obtaining Spatial Products

- Collecting unidimensional scaling measures of spatial characteristics, such as interpoint distances or directions
- Reproducing spatial properties from memory, such as walking distances or turning angles
- Recording paths of travel
- Using sketch mapping to define what people know and recall about the structure and content of large urban environments
- Construction of latent spatial relations using indirect distance or proximity judgments and nonmetric multidimensional scaling procedures
- Using trilateration procedures to construct configurations from interpoint distance estimates
- Constructing three-dimensional table models of routes and environments that have been experienced
- Use of imagined locations at which to complete spatial tasks
- Examination of verbal reports of spatial wayfinding and layout knowledge
- Determining whether people without sight can reproduce distances, directions, and layouts
- Use of projective convergence or classical triangulation methods to determine location of obscured features
- Spatial updating after location translation
- Exploring spatial relations in virtual environments

rules and is often interpreted as a combination of declarative and procedural knowledge.

An internal representation of the world outside the body is necessarily incomplete, simply because one's senses cannot absorb all possible information about that world. The clear implication is that there is a need to balance the tension between encoding and storing as much useful information as possible and needing to be able to manage and use this information. There is strong support for the argument that a cognitive map is a valid and reliable concept that is useful for comprehending the actions of humans and some other species, but there is much less certainty whether the term "cognitive map" is an appropriate one for many other animal species, since the term "cognitive" implies directed thinking and reasoning.

Internal manipulations of spatial information take place in working memory, and the results are related to specific settings, situations, or tasks. Twenty-five years ago, O'Keefe and Nadel hypothesized that the hippocampus was one's cognitive map. Neurobiological research is examining this and other hypotheses about the storage of information in the brain by examining what have been termed "place cells." Despite growing interest in these problems, the exact location of where spatial/environmental information is stored in the brain is not known, nor is it known exactly how the mind manipulates this information internally in working memory in response to task situations. By obtaining externalized representations of recalled information, it can be inferred that certain types of information must exist in memory or that what is stored can be manipulated by natural or learned processes to produce specified outcomes. These externalizations are termed "spatial products."

The term cognitive mapping has been used to summarize the total process of encoding, storing, manipulating, and using information in task-specific and problem-solving situations that require original thinking or reproductive elaboration of experienced spatial relations among stored bits of information. Different methods for obtaining spatial products are summarized in Table I.

In designing related experiments, researchers have focused on activities such as wayfinding, direction-giving, pointing, interpoint distance estimation, configurational or layout representation of settings, neural net modeling, computational process modeling, revealed place preference analysis, protocol analysis of verbal summaries, and many other devices that illustrate that people are capable of recalling stored information and then revealing or unpacking spatial relations among bits of data in ways that conform to locational patterns, connections, or interactions in objective reality. Such matching indicates that environmental knowing occurs and that the result of such knowing can be used to help explain human actions and reactions in the spatial domain.

The Use of Cognitive Maps

Since one's senses usually constrain the space over which one can experience environments at any given moment in time, one continually supplements this information with that stored in one's cognitive maps. The information stored in long-term memory is updated constantly as one changes viewpoints or perspectives, as environments themselves change, as one develops and ages, and as one's cultural, social, economic, belief, value, and other systems are brought to bear on one's experiences. Using cognitive maps is such an integral part of everyday life that the universality of the process must be recognized. It must also be recognized that spatial relations and spatial behavior are fundamental to all human groups, regardless of ableness or impairment. The completeness, fuzziness, distortion, or other characteristics of stored information are chiefly determined by factors such as the frequency with which exposure to information has been achieved, the simplicity or complexity of the situation experienced, and the type of perceptual process that dominates encoding. It is reasonable, therefore, to assume that there are substantial individual differences in the nature, complexity, and accuracy of cognitive maps, but also that there must be a significant amount of commonality in what has been coded and stored for later use in order to communicate with other humans.

Measuring the Essence of Cognitive Maps

This section addresses the questions related to collecting evidence of and assessing the spatial nature of cognitive maps. Reviews of the different procedures for obtaining spatial products have been published elsewhere. This section focuses on measurement practices, illustrating how spatial products can be obtained and evaluated with respect to real-world settings and structures.

The Geometries

Much of cognitive map measurement has been focused on specific geometric components—depicted in terms of points, lines, simple or complex networks, sequences or strings, areas, hierarchies, and configurations or layouts of places. Information stored in long-term memory does not necessarily take the form of what is traditionally recognized to be a cartographic map. Discovering the spatial nature of stored information and the spatial relations that are embedded within it has resulted in a wide variety of experimental designs and innovative task situations including metric and nonmetric formats. Most efforts have concentrated on two-dimensional Euclidean space—although some researchers have shown that city block metric (i.e., Minkowskian space of $R = 1$) is most likely used by many people. Using a two-dimensional map metaphor to describe spatial products has the convenience of allowing access to a variety of graphic, cartographic, and geometric measurement procedures that allow comparisons to be made between the characteristics and structure of spatial products and their counterparts in objective reality.

Locating Places

In objective reality, locations are often known by several labels or identities (e.g., "the corner of High and Main"; "the bank corner"; "the center of town"). Before one can determine locational accuracy, one must find by which label a location is best known. In a designed experiment, locations can be arbitrarily identified by a single name or symbol, thus removing this ambiguity. Location is usually specified in one of two ways: absolute or relative. Absolute location requires the use of a reference frame and some type of referencing system (e.g., coordinates). Relative location often uses a fuzzy spatial preposition (e.g., "near the school"; "between Fifth and Sixth Streets"). In the case of absolute location, accuracy can be measured by examining distortion—the absolute difference between real (u, v) and estimated (x, y) coordinates. Direction of error may be equally important. By establishing the reference frame (e.g., a real or arbitrarily defined north line), directional deviation may be exposed. The angular distortion can be signed or absolute, depending on the experimenter's need, with signed directional error usually being preferred.

Identity, location, magnitude, time, and distance have at various times been suggested as the essential primitives of spatial knowledge. An occurrence is recognized as existing by giving it an identity, e.g., a label or name. Once known to exist in real or imagined space, an occurrence requires the attribute of location to be placed in that space. Since matter comes in various-sized units, a measure of magnitude needs to be attached to the locational attribute, providing a basis for differentiating between occurrences. In a dynamic universe, an occurrence may occupy a location perpetually, may exist for only a limited amount of time at a specific place before ceasing to exist, or may change locations over time. As more than one occurrence is identified, their degree of separation is determined by the concept of distance. Comprehension of environmental complexity can be enhanced by classifying occurrences into classes. In the spatial domain, spatial distributions form point patterns and acquire characteristics of density and dispersion. When occurrences are linked together, they form sequences or networks. The spaces that contain points, patterns, shapes, and networks, independently distributed or connected in some way, are said to be contained within bounded places called areas. Boundaries establish reference frames. Reference frames, in turn, allow local as well as global or universal locational and other spatial descriptors to be developed. These include distance, direction, connectivity, proximity, inclusion, sequence, association, and layout. Thus, awareness of the essential geometry of spaces and the things contained therein (usually called settings or environments) includes a host of spatial relational properties that have supported the continued use of the hypothetical construct of a cognitive map.

Defining what is known is one thing. Determining whether what is known bears a definable relationship to what exists in objective reality is another. Together, these two problems are the *prima facie* reasons for research into the measurement of cognitive maps. In the following sections, the format chosen is to proceed from simple, unidimensional measurement to more complex, multidimensional measurement procedures.

Measuring Cognitive Distances

The separation between two or more locations can be measured with varying degrees of accuracy. Interpoint distances measured in metric terms are usually the most precise, whereas nonmetric measures based on proximity, similarity, closeness, sequence, and order are less precise. Measurement of cognized interpoint distances was classified by Montello in 1991 into five categories (Table II).

Both magnitude and ratio estimation methods require estimation of cognized separation in relation to a given scale (e.g., a 1-in. line representing 10 units of measurement or a given distance between two well-known places). These measuring techniques require an understanding of the concept of a scale—i.e., that a given unit of measurement can be taken as a representative fraction of the real distance between places. Although these methods have been in common use, there is doubt concerning the ability of participants to estimate distance and to understand the idea of scale as a representative fraction. This is of particular concern when dealing with young children. Some of the most reliable results of research on cognitive distance are summarized in Table III.

Table II Cognitive Distance Measurement Categories

Psychophysical ratio scaling
Magnitude estimation
Ratio estimation
Psychophysical interval and ordinal scaling
Paired comparison
Ranking
Rating
Partition scales
Reproduction
Guided walking
Independent walking
Line length drawing
Scaled reproduction
Route definition
Segment sequencing
Route reversals or retraces
"Look back" strategies
Other measures of distance
Elapsed travel time
Estimates of travel cost

Measuring Configurations

Multidimensional Scaling

In contrast to simply matching estimated and actual data, a procedure that comes closer to the metaphorical idea of producing a map as the spatial product involves the development of a distance or similarities matrix. Assuming symmetry in judgments between pairs of places, only the top diagonal half of such a matrix is used. Typically, this is input to a metric or nonmetric multidimensional scaling algorithm; these can be found in most statistical software packages. Most of these are based on the original ideas developed by Kruskal and Wish in the 1960s. The essence of such an algorithm is to generate a set of distances that satisfy the same monotonic relationship that is expressed in the values in the data cells of the distance matrix. Starting with a random configuration, a method is used in a series of iterations to converge the two monotonic sequences. At each iteration, a badness-of-fit statistic gives an indication of whether the iterative procedure has reached a satisfactory or acceptable minimum dimensionality. When dealing with interpoint distances in the real world, the actual configuration of distances can be the starting configuration. Using this procedure, the real pattern is warped to most closely match the subjective pattern in the data matrix. Achieving best fit may involve translating or rotating the subjective configuration. When the actual configuration is used as the starting configuration, however, a fit statistic can be interpreted as an accuracy measure. In most cases, output is forced into a two-dimensional solution so that matching can occur.

Table III Outcomes of Cognitive Distance Analyses

Reliability and validity	Except for the work of Kitchin (1996), researchers have focused little attention on determining the *reliability and validity* of cognitive distance measures, and there is little evidence indicating whether any individual might give the same responses to estimating distances over various methods and at various times. Kitchin argues that, considering cognitive distance measures, both the validity and reliability of product measurements are uncertain.
Regression toward the mean	Estimates of cognitive distance usually show patterns of overestimation of short distances and underestimation of longer distances. Over a population's response set, there is a tendency to regress toward the mean.
Comparison of cognized and objective distances	Traditionally, cognized and actual distances are compared using linear regression analysis. The typical pattern of overestimating shorter distances and underestimating longer distances favors the nonlinear type (e.g., $Y = aX^b$ rather than $Y = a + bX$) (where Y is the cognitive distance, a is the intercept, X is objective distance, and b is the slope coefficient).

Interpreting Configurations

Multidimensional scaling unpacks the latent two-dimensional (or higher) structure that is embedded in a series of unidimensional distance judgments. It does so without requiring the individual to expressly know a specific distance measure (e.g., meters, kilometers, yards, miles). Although multidimensional scaling is accepted as a powerful technique to recover latent structure, criticism is sometimes leveled at the procedure because of potential impurities in the interpoint distance matrix. For example, if people are required to estimate the distances between unfamiliar pairs of points, they may guess. A good guess may be consistent with other information and allow a reasonable configuration to be estimated. A bad guess might considerably warp otherwise useful and accurate patterns of estimation.

A second criticism is that the use of similarities rather than distances may invoke functional dimensions rather than spatial dimension. Thus, appropriate low-dimensional output may exist in three or more dimensions rather than the two dimensions usually required for congruence mapping with real-world locational patterns. Like factor analysis, researchers must identify the dimensions of an output configuration. Often it is assumed that the lower dimensional configurations are most likely matched to spatial coordinate systems (e.g., traditional north, south, east, west frames). This may not be so. A necessary step before accepting such an assumption would be to regress the coordinate values along a specific dimension with the coordinate values along a particular north, south, east, or west axis. If the correlations are not high, then functional or other dimensions may be the critical ones involved in making the distance or similarity judgments. Despite these shortcomings, the production of interpoint distance matrices and analysis by metric or nonmetric multidimensional scaling procedures has become a common and useful way of measuring cognized spatial configurations.

Matching Configurations

One simple way of illustrating divergence between cognized and actual spatial data is through a grid transformation. This is achieved by first locating a standard regular square grid over an objective configuration. The same-sized grid is then applied to the cognitive configuration. The latter grid structure is warped to illustrate distortions in the cognized layout. Good matches between cognitive and real-world configurations produce very little grid distortion, whereas poor fits between the two require considerable grid distortions (Fig. 1). Distorted grids can be compiled using standard contouring or interpolation procedures. Measures are also available in most geographic information system software packages.

Measuring Accuracy and Precision in Spatial Products

Accuracy and precision can be determined from multidimensional scaling methods.

Bidimensional Regression

Comparisons between cognitive and objective configurations can be made using bidimensional regression, but only after the output configuration has been rotated to make it maximally congruent with the real-world distribution.

Accuracy

Accuracy is indirectly related to the amount of systematic bias in a measurement. In particular, it focuses on the systematic or noncompensating error. Accuracy also implies comparison with some type of norm that has been measured by independent means or, in the case of real environments, represents a selected subset of objective reality. Precision is used in reference to unsystematic error and focuses on variability over the range of values found in a set of measurements. Measuring the dispersion of the estimates requires calculating the standard deviation about the mean center. This deviation needs to be calculated along both an X axis and a Y axis and this allows the production of a standard deviation ellipse. If the ellipse is not a circle, then a dominant axis hosts the maximum value of the standard deviation of the coordinates and the orthogonal axis contains the minimum standard deviation value. This standard deviation along any X or Y axis can be calculated as follows:

$$SD(x'\text{axis}) = \sqrt{\frac{\cos^2\Theta \sum x^2 + 2\sin\Theta\cos\Theta \sum xy + \sin^2\Theta \sum y^2}{N}}$$

$$SD(y'\text{axis}) = \sqrt{\frac{\sin^2\Theta \sum x^2 - 2\sin\Theta\cos\Theta \sum xy + \cos^2\Theta \sum y^2}{N}}.$$

The major and minor axes of a standard ellipse can be found by equating the derivative of a standard deviation function with regard to Θ to zero. The maximum and minimum values are found by solving for $\Theta\mu$ and substituting them in the following pair of equations:

$$\frac{d(SD)}{d\Theta} = \frac{(\sum y^2 - \sum x^2)\cos\Theta\mu\sin\Theta\mu + \sum xy(\cos^2\Theta\mu - \sin^2\Theta\mu)}{\sqrt{\cos^2\Theta\mu \sum x^2 + 2\sin\Theta\mu\cos\Theta\mu \sum xy + \sin^2\Theta\mu \sum y^2}} = 0.$$

Alternatively, a solution to this problem can be found using the eigenvalues and eigenvectors of the covariance matrix. Here, the first eigenvalue can be interpreted as the amount of stretch along the axis representing the maximum variance and the second eigenvalue similarly serves for the minimum value along a secondary axis. The

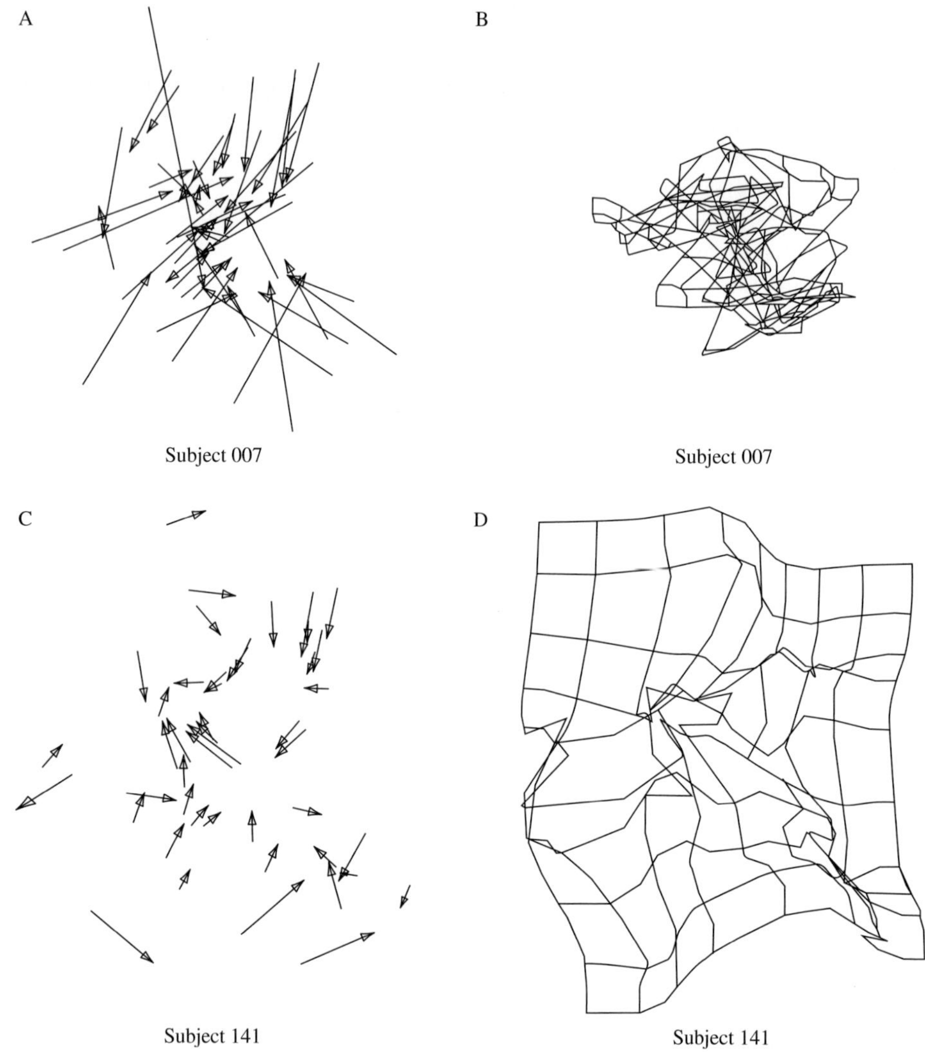

Figure 1 Examples of distorted grids. (A) Distortion vectors for a newcomer to a setting. (B) Distorted grid for a newcomer to a setting. (C) Distortion vectors for a long-time resident of a setting. (D) Distorted grid for a long-time resident of a setting.

eigenvectors will define the directions of the maximum and minimum variance. An example of the use of standard deviational ellipses is seen in Fig. 2.

Distortion and Error

Distortion and error can be measured for some spatial products, such as those produced by multidimensional scaling. Bidimensional regression has frequently been used to measure the congruence of real-world and cognitive configurations. Bidimensional regression is a combination of product moment correlation and ordinary least-squares regression procedures. It operates on two sets of coordinates and is sensitive to rotations, translations, and changes of scale. Obtaining the best correspondence between cognized and real coordinate systems may at times require reflection, which can be done prior to the calculation of the bidimensional regression coefficient. Using software such as DARCY, TRILAT, or CMAP, a series of options is available for representing the similarity of cognitive and actual configurations.

In bidimensional regression, the parameters a and b of the standard regression equation $Y = a + bX$ become

$$a = \begin{pmatrix} a_1 \\ a_2 \end{pmatrix} \quad \text{and} \quad b = \begin{pmatrix} b_{11} & b_{12} \\ b_{21} & b_{22} \end{pmatrix}.$$

The bidimensional regression equation then becomes:

$$\begin{pmatrix} u_j \\ v_j \end{pmatrix} = \begin{pmatrix} a_1 \\ a_2 \end{pmatrix} + \begin{pmatrix} b_{11} & b_{12} \\ b_{21} & b_{22} \end{pmatrix} \begin{pmatrix} x_j \\ y_j \end{pmatrix} + \begin{pmatrix} e_j \\ f_j \end{pmatrix},$$

where e_j and f_j are the residual errors, and a_1 and a_2 are analogous to the intercept terms of the standard linear regression model and are used to perform appropriate translations. Scaling and rotation are produced by the

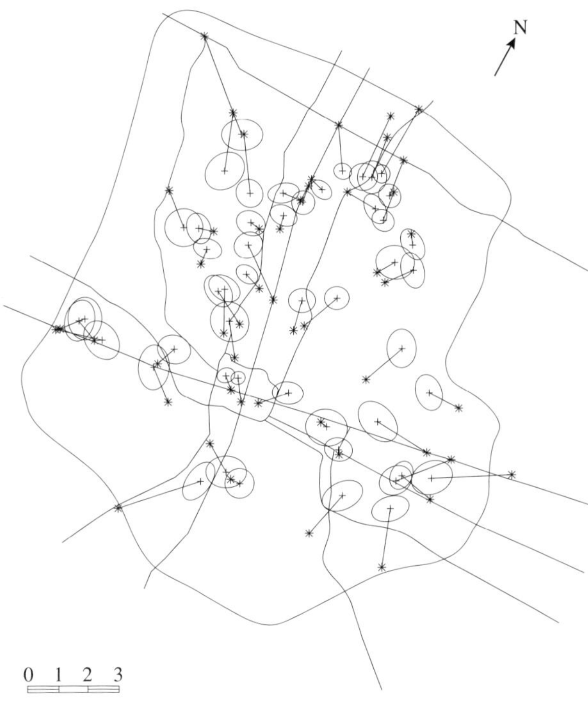

∗ Map location
+ Mean center of estimates
Ellipses represent 0.25 standard deviations

Figure 2 Standard deviation ellipses. A composite cognitive configuration for a group of long-term residents is shown.

matrix of b_{ij}, which are analogous to the slope coefficients of standard regression. Constraining b_{12} to equal $-b_{21}$ maintains a rigid Euclidean rotation and constraining $b_{22}=b_{11}$ adjusts the scale on both axes by the same amount. An r^2 equivalent ranging between 0 and 1 represents the degree of variance in the cognitive coordinates that can be explained by the objective coordinates. This measure of association is represented as:

$$R = \sqrt{1 - \frac{\sum_{i=1}^{n}(x_j - u_i)\sum_{i=1}^{n}(y_i - v_i)}{\sum_{i=1}^{n}(x_j - u)\sum_{i=1}^{n}(y_i - v_i)}}.$$

Here R equals the bidimensional regression coefficient or association measure. $(x_i,\ y_i)$ are the real-world coordinates and $(u_i,\ v_i)$ are the cognitive coordinates. This formulation was developed by Wakabayashi in 1994. R varies between zero and 1.0, with 1.0 representing a perfect fit.

To produce a best fit, scale changes of the configurations may be required. A scale value less than 1 indicates that the (u, v) space had to be contracted to fit the (x, y) space and a scale value greater than 1 would indicate that the (u, v) space had to be expanded to achieve this fit.

Measuring Cognized Directions

Direction is a spatial primitive essential for understanding configurational structures of places. In many circumstances, direction contains more relevant information than does distance. Cognitive maps incorporate directional knowledge and biases.

Self to Object and Object to Object Directions

Directional estimates usually are investigated in either of two forms: self to object or object to object. Self to object directions can be revealed by processes such as pointing with a wand, finger, nose, or other body part or by turning the entire body to face a particular place. Object to object directions often involve gridded coordinate structures or clock-face statements (e.g., "B is at 2 o'clock from A").

Direction is frequently measured using a compass oriented along the wand, arm, body part, or total body such that an angle of deviation (or turn) from an original facing direction is recorded. Directional estimates also may be given in terms of clock-face measure with the facing direction representing 12 o'clock (e.g., "shop at 4 o'clock"; "bus stop at 10 o'clock"). Alternatively, direction may be given in terms of angles referred either to an anchoring facing direction or to a standardized directional line (e.g., a north line). In the first of these two cases, the angular range is often recorded in sectors up to 180° left or right of the facing direction (e.g., 17° right or 140° left). When a standardized north line is used, directions are usually requested in 360° form (e.g., 110°, 290°). Procedures used for collecting such information may include recording a standard compass reading or providing a participant with a sheet of paper on which is drawn a circle. If an assumption is made that the individual is standing at the middle of the circle and the circle can be aligned such that the north line on paper represents the current facing direction, then vectors can be radiated out from the center of the circle to indicate the directional position of specified objects. Alternatively, the north line on the paper can be oriented with respect to compass north and the same procedure requiring radiating vectors in the direction of selected objects can be followed, but measurements are given in terms of north/south/east/west axes. As an alternative to a paper-and-pencil task, the circle can be represented on a computer screen with instructions concerning the nature of an orientation line (i.e., representing either the facing direction or a compass direction). Vectors again can be drawn toward target objects using a stylus or cursor. When paper-and-pencil or computer-based renderings of direction are obtained, angular measures of the deviation of each vector are then calculated. In the paper-and-pencil task, a protractor can be used to measure angles. In the computer-based situation, mathematical software can record direction and enter it in a data set without the need for instrumental measurement.

Research on the validity of directional estimates has indicated that whole-body pointing seems to obtain the best results. A simple way of investigating the accuracy of whole-body turning is to place a participant within a hoop that is graduated in degrees. A stopper is placed on the hoop at a particular angle. After grasping the hoop, the individual then turns the body and slides the hands until the angular block is reached. The task can be repeated several times and then the block is removed. The final task is for the individual is to turn the body and re-create the turn angle previously experienced. Estimates show that people are capable of doing this with an average of approximately 5° error.

Measuring the accuracy of directional estimates again involves comparing test results with objectively determined angular measures. As with the case of distances, association between the two can be measured using linear or nonlinear regression. There are measurement problems associated with this technique since direction estimates are constrained to a 360° range and because of this circularity, cognitive direction estimates can be no more than 180° from the objective direction value. By examining the average percentage differences between objective direction values and cognitive direction estimates, an absolute accuracy score can be obtained. Jacobson and co-workers have used the measure

$$\mathrm{RAS} = \left\{ \frac{\sum_{i=1}^{n} [(\mathrm{OAS}^i - \mathrm{CAS}^i)/180] \times 100}{n} \right\},$$

where n is the number of angle segments, RAS is the relative accuracy score, OAS is the objective angle segment, and CAS is the cognitive angle segment.

However, whereas the above measurement problems emphasize unidimensional estimation procedures, interpoint directions can be examined using multidimensional spaces.

Projective Convergence

A two-dimensional map of the location of places based on directional estimates can be obtained using a traditional surveying triangulation procedure called projective convergence. In surveying, the location of a point or an object may be estimated by using an alidade to sight on the object from a plane table placed at a known location and then drawing a projection vector toward the target location after ensuring that the plane table on which a drawing is placed is oriented in a standard direction. A convergence of three directional lines is usually subject to a small amount of error resulting from the plane table orientation errors. However, the projected lines create a triangle of error and the simple process of bisecting each angle of the triangle to define a midpoint gives a best estimate of the target point's location. In projective convergence, participants are required to point to a distant and perhaps unseen object or provide a bearing (clock-face or degrees) to that object from three different locations. The intersect of the vectors defines the triangle of error around the unseen location and determining its midpoint produces a reasonable estimate of actual location.

An abbreviated version of this technique involves drawing vectors of a standard length toward an object from three given locations, constructing a triangle from the end-points of these three vectors, and then finding the center of that triangle to give a best estimate of location. In general, projective convergence techniques are most useful when small distances are involved. Otherwise, the resulting triangles of error can be quite large and may require more complex mathematical solution procedures than the simple graphical ones suggested here.

Cognizing Layouts

This section deals explicitly with measuring cognized layouts rather than indirectly creating layouts from unidimensional judgments of spatial relations. Thus, the section starts with discussion of a two-dimensional plane instead of deriving it or assuming that one can be derived.

Anchors

As knowledge about environments is accumulated, increased understanding or familiarity allows the various structural properties of environmental layouts to be enhanced. Studies of the development of knowledge of large-scale complex environments has shown that, initially, except for a few key points labeled "anchor points," reliable information is sparse and structural information is distorted and fuzzy. Repeated excursions (e.g., journeys to work, shop, and educate) add information on a regular basis and, by so doing, assist in the process of knowing where things are and where they are in relation to other things. Given sufficient exposure, environmental knowing reaches a steady state in which a basic spatial structure becomes evident. Eventually, except for minor adjustments as better knowledge is obtained about less frequently visited places, or as new or important features are added in the environment that may grow to the stage of anchor points, the known spatial structure becomes relatively stable. For the most part, researchers have paid little attention to the development of spatial layout knowledge over time. Rather, they have assumed that cognitive maps would become stable. Indeed, Blades showed in 1991 that sketch map representation of environmental knowledge remains fairly constant over successive time periods once a stage of adequate learning has been achieved. Thus, when attempting to measure spatial layouts, it is generally assumed that people are familiar

Table IV Measuring Configurations

Freehand sketch mapping	Measurements made on sketch maps usually consist of counts of individual features, classification of such features into point, line, or areal categories, feature class counts, the imposition of traverses or profile lines to determine whether features are represented in appropriate linear sequence. Information can be obtained at both the individual (disaggregate) level and the population (aggregate) levels. The nonmetric information collected by such devices is often used as an adjunct to information collected by other procedures.
Controlled sketching	The information obtained from various controlled sketching procedures is essentially measured in terms of content classification (e.g., Lynch's elements of paths, edges, districts, nodes, and landmarks). The maps are analyzed to record how many of each type of feature occur. No *a priori* decisions of what to look for on the sketches are needed; instead, one can use panels of judges or focus groups to determine possible information classes. Sequence and ordering characteristics can be collected by referring features to relative positions with regard to the cued places.
Layout completion tasks	Measures include counts of infilled material by feature class, correct sequencing of features, correct identification of features in segments, and correct identification of nearest neighbor.
Recognition tasks	Measures include correct matching of features. Measures parallel the classic types of measurement models and represent a trend toward using forms of traditional psychometric spatial abilities tests to evaluate people's memory of specific configurations (point, line, and area). Generally called configuration tasks, they emphasize a respondent's ability to recognize which of several possible alternatives displays the same spatial relations as are displayed in a cued display. Typical tasks involve estimating which of a series of alternative building floor plans matches a recalled plan (after several learning trials).
Verbal or written spatial language	Measuring recognition of layouts may require respondents to match one of a series of statements with a verbal statement previously given or require participants to identify which of a series of layouts would be the most appropriately described by a set of logical connectives (such as "and," "or," "not or").
Placement knowledge	Classic nearest-neighbor analysis could be implemented by asking which function (e.g., named recreation area) was the closest nearest neighbor to a given function (e.g., named recreation area). Each of a set of features in turn can represent the anchor of a judgment procedure. Counts of the number of correct responses can be made. A simple rank correlation can be determined between the actual ordering of nearest neighbors and the cognized responses. If placement is determined via MDS, accuracy measures and fuzziness ellipses can be calculated.
Hierarchies	Measures include the number of matches between actual and cognized spatial neighbors.
Model building	Measures include scoring the model on completeness, the number of correct line segments, number of correct turn angles, sequencing of landmark cues, and orientation with respect to a given frame.

with the layout and that any representation they provide would be consistent with similar representations obtained at a later date.

Given an assumption of familiarity with an environment, cognized layouts can be measured in a number of straightforward ways (Table IV).

Graphic Representations

Freehand Sketching

The oldest and most widely used of these procedures is that of freehand sketching. Epitomized by the innovative work of Lynch in 1960, this procedure requires the production of a freehand sketch map of a given environment (such as a city). Although originally treated as if the resulting information was metric, it has become commonly accepted that these sketch maps relied so much on graphicacy skills and had no production controls (e.g., scales or north lines or other orienting features) that their use was very limited.

Controlled Sketching

Controlled sketching provides some information to the respondent before the sketching task takes place. This may be in the form of one or more key locations (such as current position and a significant distant landmark) or it may take the form of providing a scale bar, north line, and a keyed location. Criticisms of controlled sketch map approaches usually focus on mistakes of attributing metric properties to nonmetrically represented features, underestimating the distribution of individual differences in graphicacy skills, and confusing preferred drawing styles with content accuracy. This methodology is shown to have considerable drawbacks when dealing with children and with different disabled groups (e.g., the blind).

Completion Tasks

The extent of layout information is sometimes measured using a completion task. In this case, individuals may be given representations with selected information missing and be required to insert that information (e.g., object locations, network links, or named neighborhoods) into the incomplete task environment. For example, testing national geographic knowledge, a respondent might be given an outline map of the United States on which are located the cities of New York, Chicago, Houston, Tampa, Phoenix, and San Francisco and be asked to add in the locations of Portland, Minneapolis, Atlanta, and Washington, DC.

Recognition Tasks

Recognition tasks may involve simple shape recognition (iconic tasks), identifying which rotated, scaled, or translated figure best matches a skewed figure (e.g., the classic psychometric rotation measurement task, which is an analogue measurement), or matching layouts that are represented by different symbols (symbolic matching).

Verbal or Written Spatial Language

An increasing interest in the use of natural and technical spatial language to reveal information stored in cognitive maps has resulted in a proliferation of procedures tied to text descriptions of spatial relationships. For example, an individual may view a video, a computer scene, a photograph, or some other representation for a period of time, be distracted for some intervening period, and then be required to correctly identify answers to questions such as "The bicycle is parked to the left of the garage door—true or false?" Language interpretation tasks are often given in sets and, consequently, scored in terms of the frequency of correct answers. The number of correct answers is usually compared with chance expectations. Recognition tasks are sometimes quite useful for populations who are not able to express answers in a traditional way (e.g., blind or vision-impaired people who cannot produce sketch maps or who cannot experience visualizations of problem scenarios).

Placement Knowledge

Layout knowledge can also be tested in various recall situations by requiring people to recall relative placement of features in an environment. Here, after viewing an environmental representation (e.g., map, photo, slide, image, model), respondents may be asked to extract the layout pattern of a particular class of features.

Hierarchies in Cognitive Maps

Cognitive spatial information is apparently stored in a number of different levels. For example, individual buildings may represent nodes in one's cognitive map of a campus. However, the campus itself may appear only as a single node in one's cognitive map of the city in which the campus is located. At a higher level, the city may appear only as a node in the cognitive map of a state, and so on. In this type of structure, as the scale of the environment changes, so does the detail that is incorporated into the knowledge structure.

Model Building

Particularly useful when dealing with visually impaired or blind populations, model-building techniques can recover the configurational layout of learned or remembered environments. Replacing simple sketches with the building of three-dimensional models extends the investigation of cognitive mapping beyond the domain of the sighted. Using different symbols (e.g., blocks for objects, flexible links for paths or roads, flat solids for water bodies), it is possible to construct a three-dimensional model representation of a route or of an area experienced by following multiple routes through it. Casey successfully used this technique in 1978 to explore cognitive maps of the blind and vision-impaired. Since vision traditionally provides the greatest volume of and precision for spatial information, it is not surprising that those without vision produce models that have markedly fewer features than do those with full visual capabilities. Despite significantly smaller numbers of features that appear to be encoded in the cognitive maps of the blind or severely vision-impaired, there has been repeated evidence that such groups can develop complex and comprehensive cognitive maps of familiar environments. Such cognitive mapping capacities have also been confirmed by walking reproduction tasks for representing experienced distances and by body rotation and pointing tasks with respect to recalled directions.

Idiosyncratic and Common Components of Cognitive Maps

Cognitive maps contain some information that is somewhat unique to an individual and some that appears in the cognitive maps of many people. Usually termed "idiosyncratic" and "common," respectively, they refer to personalized spatial information needed for episodic activities (e.g., one's home location, a private place for reflection, a particular view or scene) or for more general social information (e.g., local landmarks, named ethnic districts, highways, town or city names). The former represent powerful anchors that are relevant mostly to a given individual and the latter represent equally powerful and essential cues or features that facilitate communication and interaction. Most people will not find their home boldly printed on a local city map, nor will they find the particular park bench on which they like to sit. Each person has individual likes and dislikes, so what to one constitutes a "pleasing" scene or view or what they consider to be an important neighborhood landmark, such as "the house with the barking dog" or "an unusually constructed mailbox," may not even register with another person. The idiosyncratic components of cognitive maps can rarely be aggregated. However, for social interaction, for communicating about or describing places, or for giving travel directions, commonly recognized or "familiar" features must be defined. These will appear in most people's cognitive maps. Examples might be a highly visible landmark (e.g., the Eiffel Tower), a place of worship (e.g., a cathedral), a place of historical interest (e.g., a place where a political leader lived), or a political feature (e.g., an international boundary), all of which qualify as common features readily identified by many people. When attempting to aggregate spatial products to produce "common" maps of, say, a city, usually only the common features can be explicitly counted or combined, and simple frequency counts of the number of times a feature is identified are an indication of the most familiar environmental cue or feature. For aggregation and representation purposes, these are the common anchors that allow a researcher to find out how well an environment (particularly a large geographic area such as a city) is known to residents, visitors, or information seekers by matching the cognized locational pattern of key common features to their places in objective reality.

The cognitive map, therefore, is a repository for personal and group information, includes information about places, features, and relations, and is suffused with personal and social beliefs and values.

See Also the Following Articles

Location Analysis • Locational Decision Making • Spatial Autocorrelation • Spatial Databases • Spatial Econometrics • Spatial Pattern Analysis • Spatial Sampling • Spatial Scale, Problems of

Further Reading

Blades, M. (1990). The reliability of data collected from sketch maps. *J. Environ. Psychol.* **10,** 327–339.

Gale, N. D. (1982). Some applications of computer cartography to the study of cognitive configurations. *Profess. Geogr.* **34,** 313–321.

Gärling, T., Selart, M., and Böök, A. (1997). Investigating spatial choice and navigation in large-scale environments. In *Handbook of Spatial Research Paradigms and Methodologies* (N. Foreman and R. Gillet, eds.), Vol. 1, pp. 153–180. Psychology Press, Hove, UK.

Golledge, R. G. (1992). Do people understand spatial concepts? The case of first-order primitives. In *Theories and Methods of Spatio-Temporal Reasoning in Geographic Space. Proceedings of the International Conference on GIS—From space to territory: Theories and methods of spatio-temporal reasoning. Pisa, Italy, September 21–23* (A. U. Frank, I. Campari, and U. Formentini, eds.), pp. 1–21. Springer-Verlag, New York.

Golledge, R. G. (1999). Human wayfinding and cognitive maps. In *Wayfinding Behavior: Cognitive Mapping and Other Spatial Processes* (R. G. Golledge, ed.), pp. 5–45. Johns Hopkins University Press, Baltimore, MD.

Hirtle, S. C., and Jonides, J. (1985). Evidence of hierarchies in cognitive maps. *Memory Cogn.* **13,** 208–217.

Kitchin, R. (1996). Methodological convergence in cognitive mapping research: Investigating configurational knowledge. *J. Environ. Psychol.* **16,** 163–185.

Kitchin, R., and Blades, M. (2002). *The Cognition of Geographic Space.* Taurus, London.

Montello, D. R. (1991). The measurement of cognitive distance: Methods and construct validity. *J. Environ. Psychol.* **11,** 101–122.

Silverman, I., and Eals, M. (1992). Sex differences in spatial ability: Evolutionary theory and data. In *The Adapted Mind: Evolutionary Psychology and the Generation of Culture* (J. H. Barkow, L. Cosmides, and J. Tooby, eds.), pp. 533–549. Oxford University Press, New York.

Tobler, W. R. (1994). Bidimensional regression. *Geogr. Anal.* **26,** 187–212.

Wakabayashi, Y. (1994). Spatial analysis of cognitive maps. *Geogr. Rep. Tokyo Metrop. Univ.* **29,** 57–102.

Cognitive Neuroscience

Craig Weiss
Northwestern University Feinberg School of Medicine, Chicago, Illinois, USA

John F. Disterhoft
Northwestern University Feinberg School of Medicine, Chicago, Illinois, USA

Glossary

amygdala A structure deep in the brain; coordinates autonomic and endocrine responses in conjunction with emotional states.

cerebellum A highly foliated part of the hindbrain; coordinates and modulates movement and is involved in learning motor skills.

cognitive map A representation of the spatial characteristics of an individual's environment; enables movement directly from one place to another regardless of starting point.

dendrite The structural part of a neuron; receives and conveys information to the cell body of a neuron.

galvanic skin response (GSR) A change in electric conductivity of the skin; thought to be due to an increase in activity of sweat glands when the sympathetic nervous system is active during emotional states.

hippocampus A structure deep in the temporal lobe of the brain; receives information from the association cortex, and is required for the storage of new memories.

in vitro Latin for "in glass"; refers to the technique of working with tissue that has been removed from the body and stabilized in a culture dish using physiological buffers.

neural network The structures and interconnections that comprise a functional unit within the brain.

nucleus A collection of neurons that are functionally related and located within a relatively confined area of the brain.

soma The cell body of a neuron; inputs reach the cell body via extensions known as dendrites, and the output leaves along the axonal projection.

Neuroscience is a comprehensive term that includes the study and modeling of the nervous system from the molecular–biochemical level to the behavioral level. Cognition is a more abstract notion that involves awareness, consciousness, and, perhaps, "thinking." The compound term "cognitive neuroscience" refers, then, to the study of the neurobiological mechanisms of cognition. This necessarily involves a multidisciplinary approach and involves a vast amount of research using model systems for the analysis of cognition. The model system includes the animal model (i.e., the species), the paradigm (i.e., the task that will be used to invoke and measure cognition), and the methods of analysis. The study of cognitive neuroscience includes an analysis of more than just simple sensory-response properties; it also includes an analysis of the highest orders of neural processing and the problems that arise with changes to the system, whether due to aging, disease, genetic mutation, or drug abuse. Changes in behavior due to the latter factors have an enormous impact on society, and society can thus only benefit from a better understanding of the neurobiological mechanisms underlying cognition. The discussion here concentrates on cognitive neuroscientific studies of learning and memory, the area of special expertise of the authors.

Model Paradigms

The rigorous scientific study of cognition has benefited from objective measures using well-defined tasks and situations. Subjective responses from humans can be valuable, but the responses cannot be independently verified due to the very nature of subjectivity. Furthermore, the rich experiences of human interactions confound a rigorous analysis of specific questions. The use of model paradigms, i.e., well-controlled specific tests of learning and memory, has therefore formed a keystone of cognitive neuroscience. Although most knowledge gained from these paradigms has derived from animal experimentation, many of the results have been verified in humans and have led to successful therapeutic treatments for the amelioration of impairments due to aging and disease. The most commonly used paradigms include eyeblink conditioning, fear conditioning, spatial navigation, and object recognition. These paradigms have been successful due to exquisite control of the stimuli, precise measurement of behavioral responses, and the use of adequate control groups. These reductionistic models offer the opportunity to localize the site or neural network that underlies cognition.

Eyeblink conditioning and fear conditioning are the two paradigms for which there is the most complete understanding of the required neurobiological mechanisms for acquisition, retention, and extinction of the task. The two paradigms are behaviorally very similar in that a neutral conditioning stimulus (CS) is paired with, and predicts, the presentation of an unconditioned stimulus (US) that evokes an unconditioned response (UR). The study participant eventually learns the association and exhibits a conditioned response (CR) to the CS after having experienced the paired presentations of the CS and US. The number of exposures required for an individual to exhibit CRs depends on the difficulty, or cognitive load, of the task and on the age of the individual. An advantage of these conditioning paradigms is that the stimuli can be specified precisely. A tone, for example, can be characterized by its frequency, volume, and duration; a shock can be characterized by its magnitude in amps, frequency, and duration; and a puff of air can be characterized by its pressure and duration.

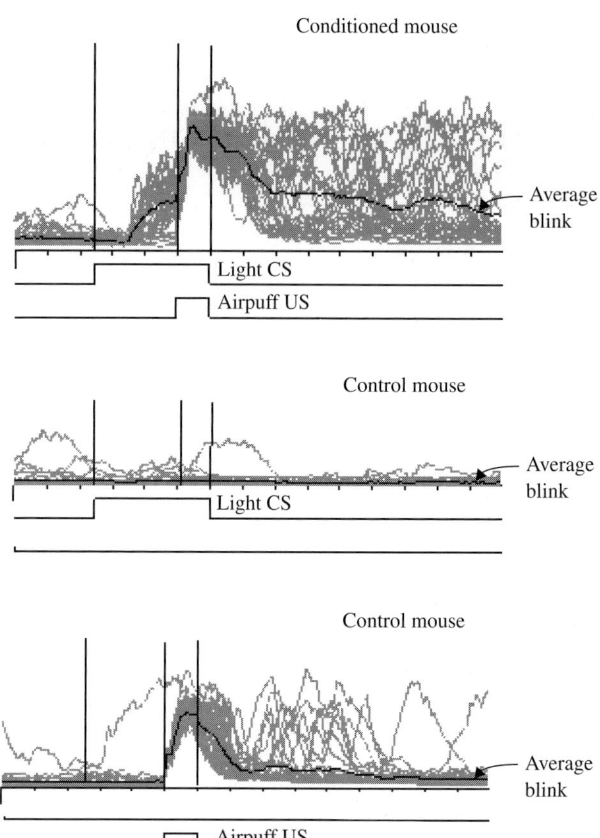

Figure 1 Mice were randomly assigned to either a conditioned or a control group (CS, conditioned stimulus; US, unconditioned stimulus). Conditioned mice were presented with a light pulse followed by a puff of air to the eye. Control mice received the same number of light pulses and puffs of air, but their stimuli were explicitly unpaired and randomly presented. The conditioned mice showed a high percentage of conditioned responses (those that start before presentation of the airpuff). Control mice responded to the light pulse with few blinks, but with robust blinks in response to the airpuff. The average blink is plotted for all of the recorded data for each trial.

Eyeblink Conditioning

Eyeblink conditioning typically pairs a tone (100–1000 ms) with a brief (100 ms) puff of air to the cornea (similar to that of a glaucoma test) or a mild shock to the side of the eye. The study participant initially has no response to the CS but blinks in response to the US. After the CS and US are repeatedly paired, the individual starts to respond prior to the onset of US such that the peak of the UR is often at the onset of the US. This is dramatic evidence that the individual has learned the temporal relationship between the two stimuli. An example can be seen in Fig. 1. The learning is relatively fast when the CS and US coterminate, and there is strong evidence, especially from Richard Thompson and colleagues, that acquisition of this task is critically dependent only on the cerebellum. For example, decerebrated animals, which have their forebrain disconnected from the brain stem, can still learn the association, whereas rabbits with cerebellar lesions as small as 1 mm^3 are unable to learn the association when the lesion is placed properly.

The cerebellar dependence of simple conditioning may suggest that the task is not cognitive in nature. However, as shown by John Disterhoft and colleagues, when the CS and US are separated in time, a memory trace of the CS must be formed to interact with the effect of US. The simple manipulation of introducing a trace interval between the CS and US appears to make the task more cognitive in nature, because the forebrain is required to learn trace eyeblink conditioning when the stimuli are separated in time beyond some critical interval. This interval may be species specific, but a trace interval of only 500 ms appears to be sufficient to require the activity of the hippocampus and forebrain for learning to occur in rabbits and humans (250 ms is sufficient for rats and mice).

Another manipulation that is often used to make the task more cognitively demanding is discrimination conditioning. This paradigm uses two different conditioning stimuli such that one CS predicts the US, and the other CS is never paired with the US. An individual that learns this task will respond to the CS+ (the stimulus that predicts the US) but not to the CS− (the stimulus that is not associated with the US). Although this task does not require the hippocampus or forebrain to be learned, an animal with such a lesion will not be able to inhibit CRs when the stimulus contingencies of the experiment are switched, i.e., the old CS+ is now the CS− and vice versa. Learning the reversal of the stimulus contingencies seems to require a flexibility of associative learning that appears to be cognitive in nature and requires that the hippocampus and associated circuitry be engaged for successful acquisition.

Fear Conditioning

Fear conditioning typically pairs a tone (3–8 sec) with a brief shock to the feet in order to evoke a fear response. The fear response of rodents appears as the cessation of normal exploration and grooming such that respiration is the only movement observed. After the two stimuli are paired together in time, the subject freezes in response to the CS. A considerable amount of evidence from investigators such as Michael Davis, Michael Fanselow, Joseph LeDoux, and Stephen Maren indicates that the association of the two stimuli is critically dependent on the amygdala, a part of the brain that is involved in modulating autonomic responses. Like eyeblink conditioning, fear conditioning can also be made more cognitively demanding by separating the tone and the foot shock in time by a stimulus-free trace interval. The presence of the trace interval adds the additional requirement of hippocampal functioning for animals to learn the association of the tone and the foot shock.

Although the two conditioning paradigms may not appear to be inherently cognitive in nature, several methodologies (e.g., neuronal recordings and lesions) indicate that those paradigms require and activate higher order brain structures that are associated with cognition. Two other widely used behavioral paradigms that also seem to be cognitive in nature are spatial navigation and object recognition.

Spatial Navigation

Spatial navigation requires the integration of numerous multimodal stimuli in order to acquire a flexible cognitive map of the environment, so that a study participant can self-direct to a goal, regardless of the starting point location in a known environment. The most widely used spatial navigation paradigm is often referred to as a Morris water maze, after Richard Morris, who developed the use of the maze. The maze, typically a pool about 6 feet in diameter, is filled with opaque water (the water is made opaque by adding either nontoxic paint or milk powder). The water serves to distribute any olfactory cues that may have been left along the swim path, and it hides a small escape platform that is submerged just below the surface of the water. The water is relatively cool, to encourage even good swimmers, such as rodents, to actively search for an escape route. Rodents typically find the escape platform in a relatively short amount of time; the platform is fixed in place relative to the visual and other contextual cues within the room. The rodents are returned to their home cage after they find, or are directed to, the escape platform and have had time to observe the room from the platform. It is during this time that they appear to form a flexible cognitive map of the room, such that they can find the escape platform from any release site. A few trials are also given with a moveable platform that is marked with a visible flag. These trials are used as a sensorimotor control to confirm that any rodent unable to locate the platform with extramaze cues (due to aging or hippocampal dysfunction) is able to swim to the goal using visual guidance. The rodents typically show a decrease over trials in the time and distance required to find the hidden platform. An example can be seen in Fig. 2. The latency and path length scores are used to assay learning.

Other motivated spatial navigation tasks include the radial arm maze and the hole-board. Those tasks are appetitive rather than aversive in nature, and rely on food or water rewards to motivate the subject to navigate the maze to find the rewards. An example of a simple maze that does not require external motivation is the Y maze. This maze is shaped as its name implies and reveals that rodents tend to alternate spontaneously their selection of which arm to explore, i.e., they tend to explore new places. Because spontaneous alternation indicates that the subjects do

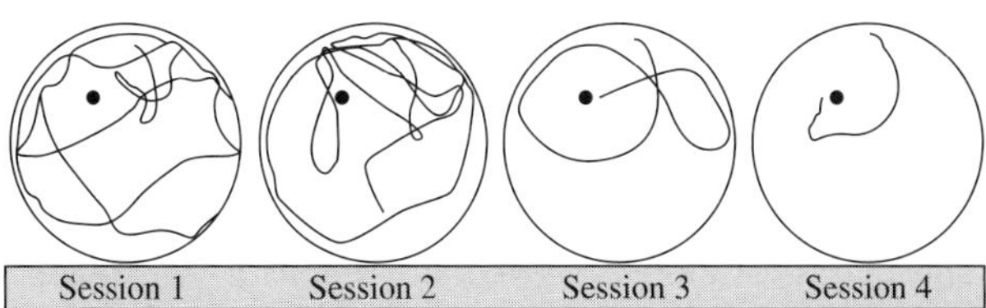

Figure 2 Rats learn the location of a submerged escape platform in a pool of opaque water by forming a cognitive map of their environment. Subjects were given four trials per session for four sessions. Each trial started from a different quadrant of the maze (chosen in random order). The single trial of each session that started from the "north" position (black dot is the target) is shown. Learning is indicated by the gradual decrease in the path length. Figure courtesy of A. Kuo with permission.

not explore randomly, they must be cognizant of their surroundings and remember where they have been.

Object Recognition

Object recognition is the ability to recognize a previously experienced object as familiar. This familiarity can be measured by recording the amount of time that a study participant appears to spend attending to the object. The object can be inanimate, or it can be another study participant, in which case the task is referred to as social recognition. Primates are often used to study object recognition, especially the task referred to as delayed nonmatching to sample. This task has trials that are separated by a delay of several seconds and the primate is rewarded for picking one of two objects that was not picked on the previous trial. This task takes advantage of the fact that primates naturally prefer to explore new objects. This task is impaired by lesions of the hippocampus and seems cognitive in nature.

Model Systems

Except for the swimming maze and hole-board, all of the paradigms discussed so far have been used with humans. However, the use of animal model systems has led to the greatest understanding of the neurobiological mechanisms that underlie the different tasks. Eyeblink conditioning was originally done with humans starting in the 1920s. The task was adapted for rabbits by Isidore Gormezano and colleagues in the 1960s. The rabbit was selected due to its tolerance for restraint and the lack of many spontaneous eyeblinks. The rabbit is also a good size for neurophysiological experiments because it can support the hardware necessary for extracellular recordings of neural activity from multiple sites. The disadvantage of the rabbit as a model system is that it has few other behaviors that can be utilized by cognitive neuroscientists, and it has a relatively long life span, impeding research on the effects of age on cognition.

More comprehensive descriptions of cognitive behaviors, including eyeblink conditioning, were attempted by adapting the eyeblink paradigm for rats. This was done by using a tether to connect the equipment to the rat so that it could move about relatively freely. The rat-based model allowed an analysis of age-related impairments and a comparison of multiple tasks such as eyeblink conditioning, fear conditioning, and water maze learning. A combination of tasks is invaluable for validating general properties of cognitively demanding tasks.

Most recently, the eyeblink conditioning paradigm was adapted for the mouse in order to determine the effects of specific genes on learning, memory, and cognition. The shift from rat to mouse is technically rather straightforward, but the selection of the conditioning stimulus needs to be considered carefully because inbred strains can be insensitive to a particular stimulus modality, such as light, or can suffer from age-related sensory impairments, such as hearing loss. Some of these details have been determined for the common C57BL/6 mouse, including the necessity of the hippocampus for trace eyeblink conditioning.

Behavioral Measurements

Eyeblink Conditioning

The parameters and methodologies used to measure cognition vary with the task being used. Eyeblink conditioning, as the name implies, relies on detecting movement of the eyelids. Many investigators who use rabbits will, however, use extension of the nictitating membrane (NM) as a measure of the response, although both responses are often collectively referred to as eyeblinks. The nictitating membrane, found, for example, in rabbits and cats, acts as a third eyelid. Animals with this membrane also have an extra set of extraocular eye muscles (the retractor bulbi muscle) that acts to withdraw the eyeball into the socket. The membrane normally rests within the inner corner of the eye and passively extends as the eyeball is retracted during a blink. Extension of the NM is often measured with either a minitorque potentiometer or a reflective sensor.

Minitorque Potentiometers

The potentiometer is usually stabilized above the head of the animal and the rotating arm of the potentiometer is connected to a loop of silk that is sutured to the distal point of the NM. This transducer can be calibrated so that there is a direct conversion of volts to millimeters of NM extension. Some researchers have also used this transducer in humans by connecting the rotating arm of the potentiometer to the eyelid with a lightweight adhesive.

Reflective Sensors

The other common method of measuring eyeblinks is to use an infrared reflective sensor that measures changes in reflected light as the NM extends and withdraws across the eye. This device combines an infrared light-emitting diode (LED) and a phototransistor into one package. The LED is used to aim invisible infrared light at the cornea and the phototransistor is aimed to detect the reflected energy. This device does not require any physical attachment to the NM or eyelids, and is often calibrated in terms of volts per maximum blink. Newer models of the minitorque potentiometer are also based on a reflective sensor, rather than wire windings, so that movement of the potentiometer spins a polarizing filter relative to a fixed polarizing filter, and the amount of light that passes through the set of polarizing filters is proportional to the movement of the potentiometer arm.

Eyeball Retraction

Because eyeball retraction is the primary mover for NM extension, it may be a more sensitive measure than NM extension is, and may be useful when looking for subtle changes in the system. This was the case when Disterhoft and colleagues determined which eye muscles regulated the conditioned response. They fitted the rabbit with a contact lens that had a thin filmstrip protruding from it. The filmstrip had an optical density grating that moved freely between an LED and a phototransistor. The output of the device was then calibrated for volts per millimeter of retraction.

Electromyographic Activity

The potentiometer and reflective sensors work well for animals that tend to be stationary. The recording of electromyographic (EMG) activity from the eyelids was introduced when freely moving rats were being used for conditioning studies. The activity can be recorded from thin, sterile wires that are implanted in the eyelid, or temporarily pasted next to the eye in the case of humans. In either case, the wires are led to an amplifier and filter so that blinks can be recorded. The EMG activity associated with a blink tends to be a very sensitive and short-latency indicator of a response, and highly correlated with simultaneous measurements using a reflective sensor. An example from studies of rabbits, rats, and humans can be seen in Fig. 3. The EMG signal is often rectified and integrated in order to produce an analog signal that can be analyzed in the same way as signals recorded from the other devices.

Fear Conditioning

As stated previously, the fear response of rodents is apparent in the cessation of normal exploration and grooming, such that respiration is the only movement observed. This measure was originally recorded with a stopwatch by trained observers. The time spent in a freezing posture relative to the total time of observation would yield a score of percent freezing. Better learning was indicated by a greater percent of freezing to the conditioning stimulus. More recently, computer software has been developed to detect movement either by video tracking or by comparisons of adjacent video frames (if the two frames are identical, there is no movement). The computer system has the advantage of being objective, extremely sensitive to small movements, vigilant in detection, and able to record and store the data accurately.

Another technique to assess fear conditioning has been to detect changes in heart rate activity. This involves the

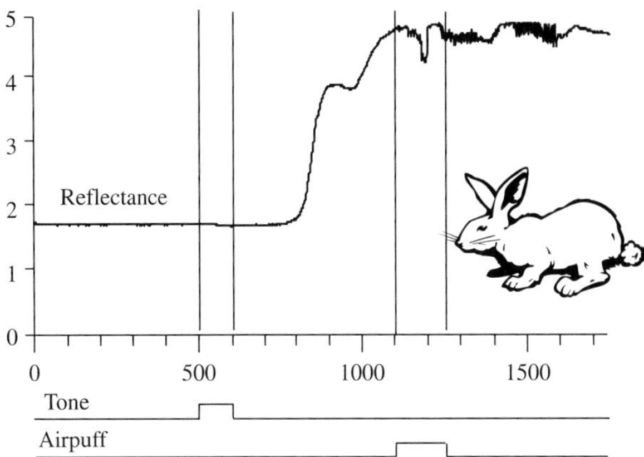

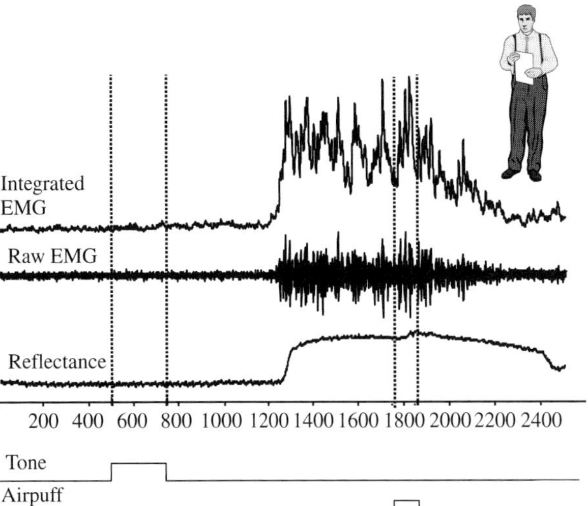

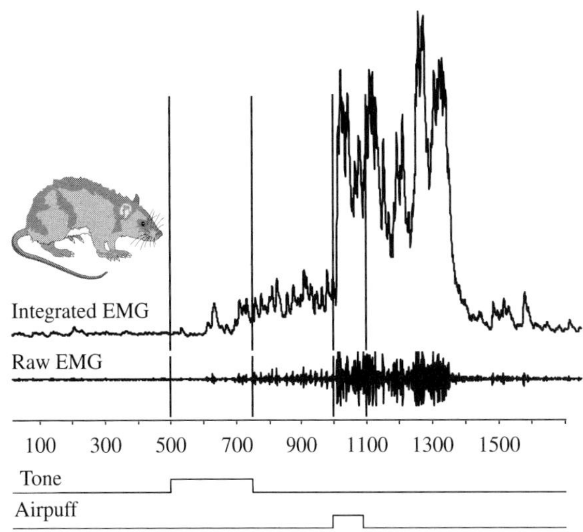

Figure 3 Examples of eyeblink data recorded with electromyographic (EMG) electrodes and infrared reflective sensors. Similar equipment can be used across species for a comparative analysis of learning using model systems. The horizontal axis represents time in milliseconds. Figure courtesy of J. Power with permission.

implantation of two subdermal electrodes. The study animal is connected by wires during each training or testing session. Heart rate measurements are especially useful for animals that have few baseline movements, such as rabbits or aged rodents. Heart rate activity can be easily recorded and presentation of the fear-eliciting stimulus is often accompanied by a transient decrease in heart rate. More recent procedures involve telemetry systems that receive a signal from a surgically implanted transponder. There are no leads connected to the animal with this system.

Fear conditioning experiments have also been done with human study participants. The individuals are usually told that they will be presented with tones and a mild shock, but they are not told that the tone predicts the onset of the shock some seconds later. They can also be instructed to use a dial to indicate their ongoing expected probability of being shocked. This methodology has been used by Fred Helmstetter and colleagues, who find that the study participants quickly learn to expect the shock at the appropriate interval after the conditioning tone. Behavioral measurement of fear conditioning in humans is done with the galvanic skin response (GSR), which is also used in lie detector tests.

Spatial Navigation

As mentioned previously, the most widely used task for spatial navigation is the water maze. Learning in this task was originally measured with a simple stopwatch, i.e., the time it took for the animal to find the escape platform was recorded. Decreases in this latency indicated learning and an awareness of the environment. Computer software that has since been developed utilizes video tracking. These computer systems not only record the time for the animal to find the target, but they also record and measure the path that the animal took to get to the target. This allows an analysis of path length, speed, and latency, as well as measures of proximity to the target. The path length measure has been a valuable tool to discriminate differences due to motor/swimming abilities from differences due to the formation of a cognitive map of the environment, i.e., recognizing the location in the environment. Many investigators will also introduce a "probe trial," in which the escape platform is removed in order to try and determine how well the location of the platform was learned.

Electrophysiological Measures of Learning

Electrophysiological correlates of learning have been sought in order to locate the sites and processing of activity that might mediate cognition. The general idea is that brain regions that exhibit task-related activity must be mediating the task. However, this is not always true, because some regions show correlated activity even though the task can be acquired after lesions of the specific region. The hippocampus provides an excellent example because it exhibits neuronal activity that is correlated with simple conditioning, even though the task can be learned after the hippocampus is removed. This finding raises the question of which regions are necessary for a task rather than just activated by the task. The answer requires either permanent or temporary inactivation of a structure to determine if the activity is essential to the function of the network. Investigations of the cerebellum provide an excellent example. Recordings from neurons within the eye zone of the cerebellar interpositus nucleus (an output of the cerebellum) during eyeblink conditioning exhibit activity that is highly correlated with the conditioned response in terms of timing and amplitude of response, and lesions of this area prevent new conditioning and abolish established conditioning.

Extracellular Recordings

The first experiments to detect electrophysiological correlates of learning and cognition used microelectrodes with an exposed tip about 0.5 mm in length. These electrodes recorded the extracellular electrical activity of numerous neurons within the vicinity of the recording tip. The activity would typically be gathered by setting a threshold and recording a time point whenever the activity crossed the threshold. This technique works well when the neuronal population is homogeneous in function, but the activities of individually isolated neurons are necessary to understand the function of a region with heterogeneous responses. Consider an example in which there are two different cell types with responses in opposite directions, i.e., one type shows increased activity and the other shows decreased activity. The net sum of this activity as recorded with a multiunit electrode would indicate no response, when in fact both cell types were responding. The solution to this problem is to record the activity of single neurons. This type of analysis often reveals that a population of neurons has heterogeneous responses, and the different response types can be quantified in terms of percent representation.

The activity of single neurons is now recorded by using electrodes or microwires with much smaller exposed tips (0.05 mm or less) or by using waveform identification techniques to cluster the activity according to groups with similar waveforms. This technique is based on the idea that each neuron exhibits a characteristic waveform based on its biophysical properties and its distance from the electrode; an analysis of subthreshold activity requires intracellular recordings (see later). More recently, a stereotrode, or closely spaced pair of electrodes (or tetrode, four closely spaced electrodes), has been used to triangulate on the activity of simultaneously recorded neurons. This technique was developed by Matthew Wilson and Bruce McNaughton. The technique increases the ability to distinguish different neurons with fairly similar waveforms, especially when recording from a region with a high density of neurons.

The characterization of large numbers of single neurons within a nucleus is necessary to gain an understanding of the function of a nucleus. Another important clue to determining the function of a nucleus is to compare the activity patterns of the main input and output of the region. This, of course, requires a knowledge of anatomical connections so that the main input and output of a region can be analyzed. This technique considers the nucleus of interest as a "black box" that converts the input function into the output function. The transformation of the signal that must have occurred identifies the function of the nucleus. This type of analysis is critical for a systems-level model of behavior.

Intracellular Recordings

Electrophysiological recordings can also be made from individual neurons by either penetrating the neuron with a sharp micropipette electrode or by attaching the tip of a micropipette to the surface of a neuron with slight suction. A few researchers use this technique in living animals. They rely on coordinates and characteristic electrophysiological signals to indicate when the electrode is near a target. A sudden drop in noise and a recorded voltage near the resting potential of neurons (about −65 mV) indicate when the electrode has penetrated a single neuron. However, most studies with intracellular recording have been done using *in vitro* brain slices. These are slices of tissue that have been cut from an extracted brain and stabilized in laboratory containers with appropriate physiological buffers. These slices remain viable for several hours under proper conditions.

In vitro slices are often used to study the hippocampus because it is involved with memory functions and because its network properties can be isolated within a single slice (consider a banana, and how each slice is similar to another). The advantage of intracellular recording is that it allows measurement of subthreshold changes in voltage or current, and the electrode can be aimed at either the soma or a dendrite when the slice is visualized with an appropriate microscope and the electrode is advanced with a micromanipulator (see Fig. 4). Furthermore, the results from these "slice" experiments can be interpreted as being intrinsic to the structure being studied because it is physically disconnected from the rest of the brain. This also applies to studies on the effects of drugs, i.e., any effect of the drug must be acting on hippocampal circuits because it is the only structure in the dish.

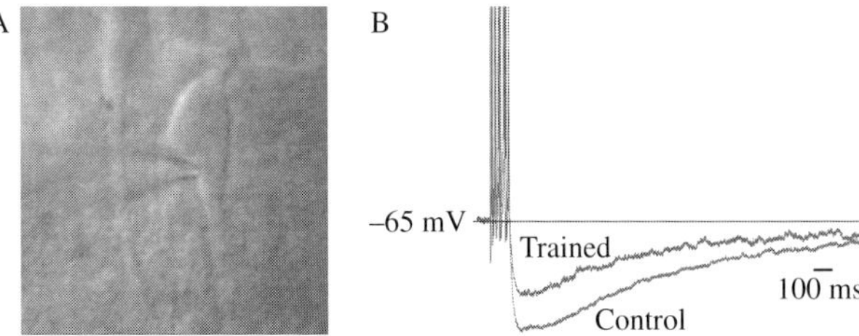

Figure 4 Intracellular recordings can be made to observe biophysical changes related to learning. (A) The photomicrograph shows two pyramidal neurons from a slice of the hippocampus. A patch pipette was attached to the neuron on the right in order to record activity. (B) The two traces show that the afterhyperpolarization following a burst of evoked action potentials is reduced in rats trained with trace eyeblink conditioning relative to rats that are given explicitly unpaired presentations of the tone and airpuff. Figure courtesy of E. Sametsky and A. Kuo with permission.

In vitro recordings from the output neurons of the hippocampus proper (area CA1) have yielded considerable insight into the mechanisms that are associated with learning and age-related impairments. John Disterhoft and colleagues discovered that the biophysical properties of individual hippocampal neurons change with learning such that the neurons become more excitable. Normally, a neuron initiates an action potential, which is a sharp rise in membrane potential followed by a sharp fall that actually exceeds the original resting potential. This afterhyperpolarization (AHP) is reduced with learning so that the neuron requires less input to respond with another action potential. This change is specific for animals that are trained on a learning task (eyeblink conditioning or water maze), because animals given control conditions do not show the increase in excitability. An example can be seen in Fig. 4. The AHP of hippocampal neurons increases with age so that neurons from aging animals are less likely to respond to a given input. This may partially explain why older subjects are slower to learn some associative tasks. Furthermore, several studies have shown that drugs (nimodipine, *d*-cycloserine, metrifonate, CI-1017, and galanthamine) that facilitate learning also reduce the AHP of hippocampal neurons, i.e., they become more excitable.

The combination of data from extracellular recording experiments and intracellular recording experiments has provided considerable insight into the mechanisms and systems-level interactions that are likely to underlie cognitive processes. A disadvantage of the techniques is that data are slowly acquired from confined regions and large numbers of neurons are necessary to make meaningful conclusions. These techniques are also only realistic if there is an *a priori* expectation for the involvement of a region in the task being studied. This information typically comes from data arising from either lesion studies or anatomical studies of neuronal interaction. The only other electrophysiological option is one of brute force mapping of the entire brain. This is sometimes referred to as a "fishing trip."

Imaging Cognition

A "fishing trip" through the brain in search of cognition could be avoided if some sort of "radar" was available to narrow down the target area. This so-called radar is now available in the form of different neuroimaging techniques. The technique that presently has the greatest spatial and temporal resolution is functional magnetic resonance imaging (fMRI), which relies on differences in the magnetic susceptibility of oxygenated and deoxygenated blood. This blood oxygen level-dependent (BOLD) response can be followed in time while a subject learns or performs a task. The response can then be superimposed on a detailed image of the brain so that functional activity (increases or decreases in the BOLD response) can be localized. The technique is most often used with human study participants because they can keep their head very still, follow directions, give verbal feedback, and indicate responses with some sort of detector (e.g., a keystroke). Some experiments have been done recently with monkeys, but they are rather precious and require lots of training, some sedation, and extreme care to maintain in good health.

A simple animal model for neuroimaging of cognition is again based on the rabbit. Alice Wyrwicz, John Disterhoft, Craig Weiss, and colleagues took advantage of the rabbit's natural tolerance for restraint and adapted the eyeblink conditioning paradigm for the MRI environment. This paradigm allows the detection of functionally active regions throughout most of the brain while the rabbit is awake, drug free, and learning a new task. The results so far have confirmed the involvement of the hippocampus and cerebellum in simple delay conditioning, and have revealed specific regions that should be explored more carefully with electrophysiological techniques to understand fully the neural mechanisms that mediate cognitive processes. An example of activation in the visual cortex and hippocampus can be seen in Fig. 5.

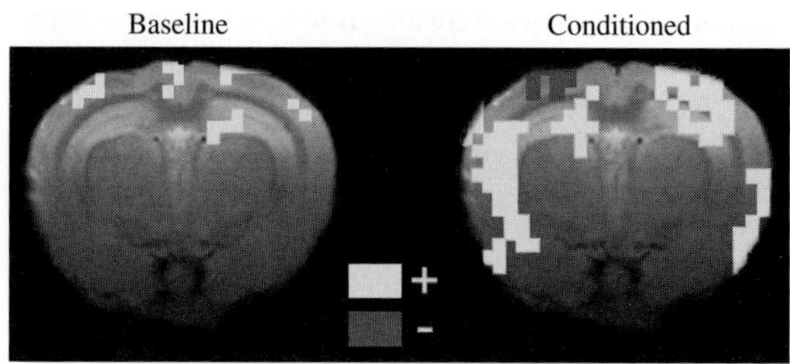

Figure 5 Functional magnetic resonance imaging of the awake rabbit brain during eyeblink conditioning. The left image shows the statistically significant blood oxygen level-dependent response to the visual stimulus during explicitly unpaired control presentations of the light and airpuff. The right image shows the activity in response to the same visual stimulus alone after the rabbit had reached a level of 80% conditioned responses on trials with paired presentations of light and airpuff. The difference in activations, especially in the visual cortex and hippocampus, represents learning. Figure courtesy of B. Tom and A. Wyrwicz with permission.

Awareness and Cognition

Although the use of the eyeblink conditioning task with animal model systems has been emphasized, the goal has always been to understand the mechanisms of human cognition. A major advantage of using humans in cognition studies is that the experimenter can get verbal feedback about the experience. The postsession interview technique has been quite revealing about interactions between awareness and conditioning. Larry Squire, John Disterhoft, Kevin LaBar, and colleagues from their laboratories have utilized questionnaires to determine whether human participants were aware that the conditioning stimulus (tone) predicted the unconditioned stimulus (airpuff). Individuals were also asked questions about the content of a silent movie that they were watching (the movie was used to keep subjects awake and alert during the experiment). All of the individuals accurately answered questions about the content of the movie, but some, especially older people, were unaware of the predictive value of the conditioning stimulus. The striking result was that only those who were aware of the stimulus contingencies exhibited conditioned responses during trace conditioning. This is strong evidence that awareness or cognition is necessary for, or occurs simultaneously with, higher forms of conditioning such as trace conditioning.

See Also the Following Articles

Behavioral Psychology • Cognitive Maps • Cognitive Psychology • Cognitive Research Methods

Further Reading

Christian, K. M., and Thompson, R. F. (2003). Neural substrates of eyeblink conditioning: Acquisition and retention. *Learn. Mem.* **10**(6), 427–455.

Disterhoft, J. F., and Oh, M. M. (2003). Modulation of cholinergic transmission enhances excitability of hippocampal pyramidal neurons and ameliorates learning impairments in aging animals. *Neurobiol. Learn. Mem.* **80**(3), 223–233.

Disterhoft, J. F., Carrillo, M. C., Fortier, C. B., Gabrieli, J. D. E., Knuttinen, M.-G., McGlinchey-Berroth, R., Preston, A., and Weiss, C. (2001). Impact of temporal lobe amnesia, aging and awareness on human eyeblink conditioning. In *Neuropsychology of Memory* (L. R. Squire and D. L. Schacter, eds.), 3rd Ed., pp. 97–113. Guilford Press, New York.

Gerlai, R. (2001). Behavioral tests of hippocampal function: Simple paradigms complex problems. *Behav. Brain Res.* **125**(1-2), 269–277.

LaBar, K. S., and Disterhoft, J. F. (1998). Conditioning, awareness, and the hippocampus. *Hippocampus* **8**(6), 620–626.

Loeb, C., and Poggio, G. F. (2002). Neural substrates of memory, affective functions, and conscious experience. *Adv. Anat. Embryol. Cell Biol.* **166,** 1–111.

Logothetis, N. K. (2003). MR imaging in the non-human primate: Studies of function and of dynamic connectivity. *Curr. Opin. Neurobiol.* **13**(5), 630–642.

Maren, S. (2003). The amygdala, synaptic plasticity, and fear memory. *Ann. NY Acad. Sci.* **985,** 106–113.

Miller, M. J., Chen, N.-K., Li, L., Tom, B., Weiss, C., Disterhoft, J. F., and Wyrwicz, A. M. (2003). fMRI of the conscious rabbit during unilateral classical eyeblink conditioning reveals bilateral cerebellar activation. *J. Neurosci.* **23**(37), 11753–11758.

Sanders, M. J., Wiltgen, B. J., and Fanselow, M. S. (2003). The place of the hippocampus in fear conditioning. *Eur. J. Pharmacol.* **463**(1–3), 217–223.

Wu, W. W., Oh, M. M., and Disterhoft, J. F. (2002). Age-related biophysical alterations of hippocampal pyramidal neurons: Implications for learning and memory. *Ageing Res. Rev.* **1**(2), 181–207.

Cognitive Psychology

Johan Wagemans
University of Leuven, Leuven, Belgium

Glossary

architecture of cognition The basic components of the cognitive system in terms of the representations and computations that are used in the different mental functions.

behaviorism Psychology as the science of behavior, limited to observable entities such as stimuli and responses, and their associations.

brain imaging The technique to visualize localized brain activity corresponding to particular mental processes.

cognitive neurosciences The multidisciplinary consortium of sciences devoted to mind–brain relationships.

cognitive sciences The multidisciplinary consortium of sciences devoted to the understanding of the mind and the mental functions.

computational (information-processing) approach The attempt to understand mental functions (e.g., perception) as processes (computations) on internal (symbolic) representations.

ecological approach The attempt to understand mental functions (e.g., perception) without intermediate processes but in relation to the behaving organism with its natural environment.

functionalism The philosophical view behind the information-processing approach, positing that mental processes can be understood at a functional level, detached from their hardware implementation in the brain.

neural network models Models of mental functions that rely on the properties of the brain as a huge network of highly interconnected simple units.

Cognitive psychology is the area of specialization within psychology that is concerned with human cognitive processes such as memory, language understanding, problem solving, thinking, and the like. This definition entails two aspects. First, cognitive psychology is a particular theoretical framework in psychology developed in the 1960s and 1970s, and is currently being subsumed under larger multidisciplinary sciences such as the cognitive sciences and the cognitive neurosciences. Second, the domain of cognition can be sketched, both in its narrow sense, including strictly cognitive phenomena, and in its broader sense, including also other phenomena such as attention and performance, perception and action, and emotion and motivation.

Origins and Rise of Cognitive Psychology

Psychology has been defined in many different ways in the past, from the science of the mind to the science of behavior and back again to the science of the mental life. The most widespread view today is that psychology is concerned with observable behavior as well as with its determining factors, both external (in the environment) and internal (within the person). Psychologists want to understand and explain why people behave the way they do. These causes are currently believed to depend on a complex interplay between external events and subjective factors such as the personal history, the desires, and the style of thinking of an individual. This has not always been acknowledged in the history of psychology.

Before Cognitive Psychology

In the early days of psychology as an independent discipline, the internal processes were studied by means of introspection: Trained observers were asked to report the contents of their own thoughts and the dimensions of their own subjective experiences. However, this method was severely criticized for its limitations: People were often not fully aware of the driving forces and internal mechanisms behind their own behavior, and even trained observers could not agree about basic aspects such as the number of dimensions that should be distinguished to describe properly the subjective experience. As a result of this, introspection was abandoned and internal processes were banned from psychology's scope.

Behaviorism defined psychology as the science of behavior. It restricted the domain of study to external factors only, which could be observed and described objectively. Psychology was thus limited to the study of stimuli (S) and responses (R) (i.e., S–R psychology), and all intermediate processes within the organism (O) were locked up in a "black box." All psychological phenomena were explained in terms of S–R connections. For example, learning was understood as the establishment of associations between stimuli and responses. In classical conditioning, Pavlov's dog started to salivate on the sound of a bell because the sound always preceded the food, the natural stimulus for the salivation response. In operant conditioning, small animals such as rats and cats learned to press a lever because this (initially random) response was rewarded by food or freedom (i.e., the opening of the cage). Skinner taught pigeons to play table tennis by sophisticated reward schemes, starting from the animal's natural repertoire of behavior and gradually shaping it into the desired behavior.

The Cognitive Revolution

By the late 1950s, psychologists became convinced that much of human behavior could not be explained in S–R terms only. Most everyday behavior is not guided by stimuli as such, but by an understanding of the stimuli. When a person smells smoke, they will not shout "fire!" if they also see their neighbor lighting a cigar; when others hear someone shouting "fire!," they will not run out of the building if they are in a movie theatre watching actors in a fire scene. In striving for objectivity, behaviorists excluded invisible entities such as understanding (and beliefs, preferences, desires, plans, strategies, and the like) from a scientific explanation of behavior, but in doing so their explanations failed to capture the real causal mechanisms behind behavior. Behaviorism thus declined and a new alternative emerged. Three interrelated factors gave rise to the so-called cognitive revolution in psychology in the 1960s. The first was definitely the widespread dissatisfaction with behaviorism's limitations, which became strongly articulated in Chomsky's vehement attack (in 1959) on Skinner's book on verbal behavior. Chomsky argued that, in principle, language cannot be explained as purely verbal behavior, determined by S–R connections. Human language production and understanding must include mental processes and representations to capture their essential characteristics of syntax and semantics, and the productivity and creativity in their usage. Language conveys meaning and meaning implies world knowledge, which is stored in memory and is activated appropriately in both the speaker and the listener. Initial behaviorist attempts to include hidden chains of S–R connections to replace the O within the black box could never solve these basic problems.

The second historically important trigger for the shift in thinking in psychology was the increased need to understand the functioning of human operators in the context of industrial processes (factories, aircraft control, telecommunication, and the like). Many instruments or machines did not function optimally or led to serious accidents because of failures at the operator level: Warning signals were missed because of limitations of attention, or were misinterpreted because of incorrect cognitive assumptions; appropriate actions were not taken because of capacity limits on short-term memory or mistakes against the principles of logical reasoning. A great deal of pioneering work was done on these topics in the 1950s. For example, Broadbent introduced the notion of a filter to understand the role of attention and selection in perception (in his 1958 book, *Perception and Communication*); Miller quantified the capacity limit of short-term memory as the "magical number seven plus or minus two" (in a famous paper, published in *Psychological Review* in 1956); and Bruner and colleagues studied thought processes by innovative experimental techniques, leading to their 1956 book, *A Study of Thinking*.

The third factor, the computer revolution in the 1950s and 1960s, provided an excellent metaphor to develop alternative theories of what happens in human language production and understanding, as well as in the case of man–machine interactions. People process information in roughly the same way as computers do: they receive and encode messages, derive their meaning by relating it to knowledge stored in memory, make decisions by following certain algorithms, and send commands to trigger appropriate responses. The information-processing stream between input (S) and output (R) devices appeared similar in the 1950s and 1960s in both cases; the underlying processes of encoding, decoding, data storage, retrieval, and transfer were considered to be at least analogous in humans and computers. The internal representations and symbol manipulations performed by the computer were considered good models of the human mind.

In 1967, Neisser wrote *Cognitive Psychology*, the first book in which this new theoretical framework was spelled out systematically. In the early 1970s, journals such as *Cognitive Psychology* and *Cognition* were initiated, and somewhat later, traditional journals were renamed to reflect a similar transition (e.g., *Journal of Verbal Learning and Verbal Behavior* was changed to *Journal of Memory and Language*). A new field was born.

The Core Program of Cognitive Psychology

Core Concepts: Internal Representations and Operations

Cognitive psychology, as an alternative approach to behaviorism and as a scientific paradigm to study mental processes, comes in different versions when applied to a variety of topics . However, all of these cognitive theories and models share a number of essential ideas. The core concept is that of internal representations and internal operations. In a classic study (reported in *Science* in 1966), S. Sternberg demonstrated that people can scan their internal representation of a stimulus display, briefly stored in so-called short-term memory, in order to find a specific target. In another *Science* paper (in 1971), Shepard and Metzler showed that the response times to determine whether two block figures are identical, despite a different orientation in space, increase linearly with the angular separation between the two images. They took this as experimental evidence for a mental rotation process, operating on the internal representations of the stimuli, analogously to the physical rotation, which would be needed to align the solid block figures in space. In 1972, Craik and Lockhart argued that what is done to the incoming information determines how well it is remembered. They provided evidence in favor of their "levels of processing" framework, when they showed that subjects who were oriented toward "shallow" aspects of the stimulus (e.g., those who were asked whether the letters of a word are printed in lowercase or uppercase letters) remembered fewer items when prompted unexpectedly in a later stage of the experiment, compared to subjects who were oriented toward "deeper," more semantic aspects of the stimulus (e.g., those who were asked to make a sentence with the word).

Core Business: The Architecture of Cognition

Theoretical and empirical research in this tradition then consists of identifying the characteristics of these internal operations, the different kinds of representations, the different stages and levels of processing, how they relate to one another, how they interact, etc. For example, classic work has divided memory into three different stages, each with its own specific properties: (1) a sensory buffer, with a very large capacity but very brief duration, which uses a veridical code, with no translation of the input format (e.g., retinal image); (2) a short-term memory system, with a very limited capacity (7 ± 2) and relatively short duration, using a phonological code (i.e., sound) to assist the internal rehearsal process that avoids the decay of the trace over time (e.g., when whispering a telephone number between hearing it and dialing it); and (3) a long-term memory system, with an unlimited capacity (lifelong learning!) and unlimited duration (reactivation of apparently forgotten material often appears possible), which is mostly based on a semantic code (i.e., the meaning is stored, not the details). A second example of this type of research concerns the format of the internal representations. This issue has given rise to one of the classic controversies in cognitive psychology, known as the "mental imagery debate." One position holds that there is a single, universal representation format for all kinds of information (i.e., encoding all information in a propositional format or "language of thought," to borrow a term introduced by Fodor in 1975). The alternative view (defended strongly by Kosslyn and Paivio) proposes that visual information is not recoded as propositions but is maintained in an analogue representation format, giving rise to the idea of "mental images" inspected by the "mind's eye" (e.g., mental rotation).

Another issue that has attracted a lot of interest and research effort is whether certain internal operations are performed sequentially (in serial stages) or simultaneously (in parallel). This type of research has lead to a wide variety of "box-and-arrow" models of the intermediate mental processes in-between input stimuli and output responses. All of these can be taken as attempts to carve up the mind into its basic building blocks or "modules" (to borrow another term introduced by Fodor, in 1983), or, more generally, to discover the basic "architecture of cognition" (i.e., the title of the 1983 book by J. R. Anderson, one of the champions of this approach).

The problem with this whole approach is, of course, that none of these cognitive mechanisms can be observed directly. Researchers must design clever experiments, with well-chosen experimental and control conditions, as well as manipulated and registered variables, to derive the internal representations and processes from observable responses such as response times and error rates. These "chronometric explorations of mind" (the title of a book by Posner in 1978) have had some success in some domains, but it is not the case that universally accepted "unified theories of cognition" have resulted from this endeavor (despite valuable attempts in that direction by pioneers such as Newell, in his last book in 1990).

Core Assumptions: The Functionalist Philosophy behind the Approach

The general theoretical framework behind most of the work in cognitive psychology is the so-called information-processing approach, that is, the notion that the human mind performs mental operations when processing the meaning of the incoming sensory signals (i.e., input) and when deciding to perform certain actions (i.e., output). In-between these peripheral input and output devices are central cognitive mechanisms that operate on internal representations. A critical assumption of this approach is that these internal representations and processes can be understood at the functional level, without consideration of the hardware level (i.e., the neural mechanisms implementing them).

This assumption constitutes the heart of the so-called computational approach to cognition, which is the idea that cognition is, literally, computation (defended strongly by Pylyshyn in his 1984 book). This approach thus goes beyond the computer metaphor in claiming that all cognitive processes can be understood as computations on internal, symbolic representations. At the functional or software level, the human mind works in just the same way as the computer; it is only at the hardware level that they differ, but that is essentially irrelevant to their operation as information processors. This philosophical position, known as functionalism (i.e., a modern version of mind–brain dualism), has implications for the relation of cognitive psychology to artificial intelligence and its position within the cognitive (neuro)sciences (see the section below).

Current Domains within Cognitive Psychology

Cognitive psychology is not only a particular theoretical approach within psychology; it also entails a particular substantive area of research, a set of phenomena that would be called "cognition" even if there were no agreement concerning all of the theoretical positions and assumptions of cognitive psychology as an approach. In a strict sense, cognition concerns only the central types of representations and processes, at the highest level of the system (using "central" as opposed to "peripheral" input and output mechanisms). However, in many textbooks of cognition (and corresponding courses within academic teaching programs), "cognition" is sometimes used in a much broader sense, implying all of the internal mechanisms (even the more peripheral ones).

Central Cognition

Problem Solving, Decision Making, and Reasoning

In their highly influential book on this topic, Newell and Simon studied human problem solving by asking people to think aloud while solving problems and by attempting to reproduce the results and the processes in computer simulations. They introduced the notion of a problem space, consisting of the initial state of the problem, the goal state, all of the intermediate states, and all of the possible operations involved in moving from one state to another. To select one of these operations, to move in the right direction in the problem space, the cognitive system relies on a means–ends analysis and other heuristics or rules of thumb (to be contrasted with algorithms, which are sequential procedures that are more complex but guaranteed to produce the correct outcome when followed accurately).

Heuristics and biases are also used quite frequently in human decision making under uncertainty. These have been studied in a flourishing line of research by Tversky and Kahneman (e.g., papers in *Science* in 1974 and 1981). Despite the fact that they sometimes introduce mistakes, these heuristics and biases also contribute to the speed and flexibility that are characteristic of human thinking but are difficult to reproduce in computers. In contrast, computers are better at applying rigid algorithms, detached from common sense and intuition (see also Dreyfus' 1972 book *What Computers Can't Do*).

Mistakes against logic are also found commonly in other forms of reasoning, such as deductive reasoning (e.g., conditional reasoning, syllogistic reasoning). Following the rules of logic, a deductive inference produces a correct conclusion if the premises are correct. According to one type of theory of deductive reasoning (e.g., that of Braine), humans use mental logic, a set of abstract, formal rules, very much like the rules of logic. According to an alternative approach, humans do not use the formal rules of logic but they represent, in so-called mental models, the different possible states of the world corresponding to the premises. Johnson-Laird is the most famous representative of this mental model approach to deductive reasoning. The latter approach has the advantage that it incorporates more of what is known of other mental processes, such as working memory and language understanding.

Memory and Language

The concept of a "working memory" was introduced by Baddeley to reflect the active, coding, and control processes in short-term memory. It is more a "workspace," to keep the code active, than a passive "warehouse" for information. It consists of a central executive system, which allocates resources to two independent subsystems, the articulatory or phonological loop and the visuospatial sketchpad (for verbal and visuospatial information).

Other memory systems have been added to the three memory systems in the traditional stage model. For example, Tulving introduced the notion of episodic memory, which encodes, stores, and retrieves facts from personal life (e.g., a person's first party or first day at college or university). This type of memory seems to operate differently than does so-called semantic memory, which stores meaning in a more abstract way, in the sense that it does not retain the spatiotemporal details of where and when the stored information was encountered. These concrete aspects of the encoding circumstances do matter for episodic memory. Semantic memory is often conceived as a network of concepts with attached properties (e.g., as slots in frames), sometimes with the nodes at different levels in a hierarchy but always with connections between the nodes. For example, in the so-called spreading activation theory of semantic processing, knowledge that is needed to answer questions such as "Can a robin fly?" or "Is a penguin a bird?" is retrieved from such a network by activating the two nodes and having the activations spread between them until they meet. These models can capture prototype effects (reported by Rosch in a famous 1973 paper in *Cognitive Psychology*) by including shorter connections between a superordinate category such as "bird" and more typical exemplars such as "robin" and longer ones for less typical exemplars such as "penguin."

Within semantic memory, a distinction is often made between declarative memory (for facts that can be stated in simple sentences, such as "Brussels is the capital of Belgium") and procedural memory (for procedures such as how to tie one's shoes). Other relevant divisions are between intentional and incidental learning (at the encoding stage), or between implicit and explicit memory (at the retrieval stage). This last dissociation has attracted a lot of interest because patients with amnesia appear to perform well on so-called implicit memory tests, in which they do not have to search in a controlled fashion for the information in long-term memory but are given the opportunity to reactivate this information automatically (e.g., in a word-fragment completion task or in a priming paradigm). This distinction between controlled and automatic processes has also been made in other contexts (e.g., expertise, attention, and performance).

In some cognitive theories, these different memory systems are made to work together. For example, in J. R. Anderson's theory of expertise, called adaptive control of thought (ACT), declarative and procedural memory are interconnected by a working memory system, which performs operations on the concepts and rules that are retrieved from the long-term memory systems. A crucial aspect of expertise development or skill acquisition in this view is knowledge compilation, a progressive shift from the use of declarative memory (serially retrieving facts) to the use of procedural knowledge (routines that can be run more automatically).

Human language is also such a complex, multileveled phenomenon, requiring the consorted activation of different subsystems and representations. On the one hand, it is useful to distinguish between syntax and semantics, and to introduce purely syntactic concepts such as a phrase structure (a tree diagram to capture the different syntactic building blocks of a sentence) and to rewrite rules (telling which components can be put together to have grammatically correct sentences). This is needed to be able to assess the grammaticality of meaningless sentences such as "Colorless green ideas sleep furiously," one of the famous examples by Chomsky, who did pioneering work on syntactic structures and on aspects of the theory of syntax and thus contributed strongly to the cognitive revolution in the 1950s and 1960s (see above). On the other hand, everyday language understanding implies the interactive activation of syntactic and semantic components from the language system. When people listen to a few sentences, they automatically draw inferences from the intended meaning. They often generate a schematic representation of the scene or scenario from their long-term memory and use that to interpret (and perhaps disambiguate) the incoming information. Making use of so-called scripts, Schank and Abelson have contributed to the construction of artificial systems for language understanding. (This work has been taken as typical for so-called strong artificial intelligence. As a consequence, it has been criticized by opponents of this type of artificial intelligence, such as Searle, in his famous Chinese room though experiment, published in a widely discussed paper in *The Behavioral and Brain Sciences* in 1980; see further discussion below.)

More recent models of text comprehension (e.g., Kintsch's "construction-integration model" published in *Psychological Review* in 1988) go even further and make use of a complicated scheme of different representations (e.g., sentence level, propositional network, and text representation) and cognitive systems (e.g., production system and semantic and episodic memory system). Likewise, Levelt's theory of speech production entails the parallel and interactive activation of representations of meaning and grammatical structure (semantics and syntax), as well as morphemes and phonemes (basic word forms and basic units of sounds).

Other Domains within "Cognition" in the Broad Sense

Attention and Performance

To the extent that information processing in complex tasks consists of different operations performed in different subsystems, an important question is how to make these subsystems work together properly. This is the issue of the control of information processing. One type of control is provided by so-called production rules. These are "if–then" rules, which automatically initiate a certain cognitive operation (or sequence of operations) when a particular stimulus triggers a particular representation in long-term memory (because they are internal, they should not be confused with behaviorist S–R connections). These production rules, which are quite central in the work of Newell and Simon and of J. R. Anderson, are rather automatic processes, but there are also more controlled ways of strategically selecting operations and assigning cognitive resources to different subsystems. These control operations are said to depend on a so-called central executive system, a kind of "big boss" that makes all the "slaves" or "assistants" do the real work (see Baddeley's model of working model, previously mentioned). One problem that has attracted a lot of attention is how to avoid the problem of infinite regression with such a command system: Who or what controls the operation of this homunculus ("little man in the head")? Another homunculus perhaps? But who controls this one then?, etc.

Control can thus be automatic and strategic. Experimental research by Shiffrin and Schneider (in a set of twin papers in *Psychological Review* in 1977) has shown that learning has strong effects on these control processes. Car driving, for example, is a complex task that requires the coordinated activity of many subsystems. Experienced drivers become so highly practiced in executing these different operations in particular sequences that they no longer require strategic control; they become automatized and the previously required resources can now be used for other tasks, such as listening to the radio or engaging in a nice discussion with another passenger. When experienced drivers need to explain all the steps to a novice whom they are teaching to drive a car, they often make mistakes because the automatized routines must now be decomposed again (which requires strategic control again). These issues also play a role in a variety of other activities such as skilled typing and piano playing. Motor control can also shift from slow and laborious complex planning to fast and automatic execution of sequential procedures.

Assigning resources is also of central importance in the domain of attention. The central processing mechanisms (e.g., short-term memory) have only a limited capacity, so a selection at the input stage is needed to avoid overload. It is not possible to pay attention to all the stimuli that are available simultaneously in a complex everyday environment. Studies of the necessary filter mechanisms were quite instrumental in the rise of cognitive psychology in the 1960s. A popular experimental paradigm to study these issues is dichotic listening with a shadowing task. In these experiments, subjects receive two different messages in the two channels of a headphone and they have to repeat the message in one (i.e., to "shadow" that target channel). They appear to be able to ignore the other (distracter) channel better when the selection is supported by acoustic or semantic differences between the channels (e.g., male versus female voice, news versus commercial). Anecdotal evidence as well as experimental results demonstrate that this selection is not always absolute; for example, while one person is listening to another person during a conversation at a cocktail party, the listener can block out effectively all of the background noise (enhancing the strength) until he/she hears his/her own name being mentioned in another group of people standing a bit further away in the room. This so-called cocktail party phenomenon implies that the background stimuli have been processed at least unconsciously, perhaps even up to the semantic level. Where exactly in the processing stream selection takes place, early or late, is one of the major distinctions between different theories and models of attention. Attention is still a very active area of research nowadays, probably even more than ever. Attention is also one of the factors that introduce a distinction between sensation and perception.

Sensation and Perception

Although sensation and perception are more peripheral functions than are attention and performance, they deserve to be covered in an overview on cognitive psychology for two main reasons. First, regardless of the theoretical approach taken, sensation and perception are the input channels through which the cognitive system acquires information about the environment and is able to behave in a well-adapted manner. Second, cognitive psychology is one of the dominant approaches of studying and understanding perception.

According to the standard view, sensation is basically the registration of stimuli from the environment, whereas perception implies the further processing of the sensations until they provide meaning. For the visual modality, the sensations are the retinal images; the perception of objects, scenes, and events in the environment strongly depends on retinal images, but is not uniquely determined by them. The same distinction applies also to other modalities such as audition (hearing), olfaction (smelling), haptics (touching), etc.

According to the standard view, incoming information is too poor to explain the richness of experience, so perception consists of the elaboration and enhancement of the stimuli by means of intermediate processes. A typical example of the poverty of the stimulus is the fact that retinal projections are two-dimensional snapshots interrupted by eye blinks and eye movements, whereas a stable, three-dimensional world is perceived. Typical examples of intermediate processes include unconscious inferences, problem solving, hypothesis testing, and memory schemata. Unconscious inference (i.e., automatic deductive reasoning) was proposed by the 19th-century physiologist and physicist Helmholtz to explain how humans recover a constant object size from the variable retinal sizes at different viewing distances. Cognitive psychologists proposed that the incoming data (i.e., the retinal images) are processed by relying on schemata in memory, which activate world knowledge in the form of hypotheses, to be tested further by checking whether the incoming data agree with them. This approach strongly defends the role of top-down processing—that is, from high-level world knowledge to low-level sensory data. Typical representatives of this cognitive approach are Gregory (*The Intelligent Eye*) and Rock (*The Logic of Perception*).

In a series of books published in 1950, 1966, and 1979, all with a strong impact on the field, J. J. Gibson revolted against this traditional view. In normal ecological circumstances, he argued, the available information is much richer than assumed in the classic, cognitive approach. When perceivers are allowed to look with their two eyes, to move their head, and to move around in their environment, new sources of information become available (e.g., retinal disparity, motion parallax, and optic flow), which often allow disambiguating the reduced projection in a single retinal image at a single instance in time. In fact, Gibson claims, perception can then be direct in the sense that no intermediate processes are then needed to further process the information (in contrast to the classic, indirect approach). The higher order invariants in this stimulation specify the surfaces, objects, and events in the world in a one-to-one fashion. The perceptual system is then required only to pick up this information or to resonate to these invariants in a direct manner, without internal representations or computations. Hence, the burden of the research is to describe and analyze the available information as such (which requires a new approach, called "ecological optics"), rather than the psychological processes. The leitmotiv here is "do not ask what is inside the head but what the head is inside of." This position has, of course, caused a great deal of controversy in the domain of perception. In fact, it has had a much larger impact than on perceptual psychology only, because this so-called ecological approach has also been applied to other domains, such as perceptual learning and development (in a 1969 book by J. J. Gibson's wife, E. J. Gibson) and coordination of motor behavior (in a 1968 book by Bernstein). Strongly influenced by J. J. Gibson's work, Neisser (one of the founders of cognitive psychology) revised his view on attention, perception, and cognition in *Cognition and Reality*, less than a decade after his first book, which had defined the domain and approach of cognitive psychology. Traditional distinctions such as those between sensation and perception, between stimuli and responses, and between perceptual and motor systems all disappear when the behaving organism is studied in relation to its environment (i.e., as an integral ecosystem).

Despite the apparent incommensurability of the different world views underlying the indirect and direct approaches, a third way has been proposed in the so-called computational approach by Marr (in his 1982 book, *Vision*). Marr acknowledges Gibson's discovery and analysis of the richness of the visual stimulation, while at the same time arguing for the need to describe and analyze the processing mechanisms that are involved. When computer or robot vision and natural or biological vision are investigated (as Marr does), it becomes immediately clear that the issue of intermediate mechanisms that detect and process the incoming information is far from trivial. The computational approach is a bottom-up approach, starting from the information, extracting as much as possible from it by some well-chosen algorithms, and representing the results in intermediate representations, before reaching the final stage of conscious perception of meaningful objects, scenes, and events. Research has shown that a whole series of intermediate processes and representations are needed to achieve tasks such as object recognition.

This comes back again to the notion of "information processing," as in traditional cognitive psychology, but with two important differences: (1) the mechanisms are now spelled out in much more detail (they are written as algorithms, implemented in a computer, to be simulated and tested as models for human vision) and (2) world knowledge stored in memory comes into play only as late as possible. In light of these similarities and differences with standard cognitive psychology, it is clear that important issues of empirical research are (1) to test the psychological plausibility of these algorithms (see Palmer's *Vision Science: Photons to Phenomenology*") and (2) to investigate when cognition penetrates perception (see Pylyshyn's paper in *The Behavioral and Brain Sciences* in 1999).

Emotion and Motivation

Emotion and motivation are normally not included as core domains within cognitive psychology, but it is useful to point out that they, too, have cognitive aspects. What humans feel is at least partly influenced by what they know, and mood has well-known influences on memory and thought processes. Regarding motivation, it is clear that knowledge is quite important in regulating and planning behavior in trying to reach goals, both lower level, physiological goals (such as satisfying hunger or sexual appetite) and higher-level, cultural goals (such as establishing a successful career and marriage, or enjoying a great novel, movie, theater play, or opera). Schank and Abelson's 1977 book (as mentioned earlier in) includes quite a bit of interesting cognitive psychology on this topic.

The Current Position of Cognitive Psychology

Within Cognitive Science

Cognitive psychology has always been a key player in the multidisciplinary cluster of sciences known as "cognitive sciences," from its emergence in the 1950s and its establishment in the 1970s (with its own journal and society starting in 1977) until today (e.g., *The MIT Encyclopedia of the Cognitive Sciences* in 2001). Along with cognitive psychology, there exists a variety of disciplines, some of which are associated also with the early pioneers of cognitive science (names in parentheses): cybernetics (Wiener), computer science (Turing, von Neumann), artificial intelligence (Newell and Simon, Minsky, McCarthy), neural networks (Hebb, McCulloch and Pitts, Rosenblatt), linguistics (Chomsky, Lakoff, Jackendoff), philosophy (Putnam, Fodor, Dretske, Dennett), cognitive anthropology (Dougherty, D'Andrade), and cognitive ethology (Griffin, Allen and Bekoff). Because cognitive psychology is a behavioral discipline, with a subject belonging to humanities but a research methodology, which is at least partly inspired by the natural sciences and engineering, it has fulfilled an important bridging function within this consortium. The functionalist philosophy and the computational framework behind most of the work in cognitive psychology have provided the foundation for this crucial role within this network of interdisciplinary collaborations.

Beyond Traditional Cognitive Science

It is fair to say that the present situation within cognitive psychology (and, in fact, cognitive science as a whole) is no longer as bright as it was in the 1980s. The past decade or so has been characterized by two tendencies, one "downward into the brain" and one "outward into the environment." These tendencies have revealed the limitations of the symbolic approach of information processing based on algorithmic computations and symbolic representations, as well as of the underlying functionalist assumptions. These tendencies have also inspired novel approaches, providing some new building blocks waiting to be integrated in a newly emerging multidisciplinary science.

Downward into the Brain

Two developments have given rise to the gradual breakdown of the functionalist assumption that mental functions can be studied independently of their hardware implementation in the brain. First, the symbolic approach, developed in collaboration between cognitive psychology and artificial intelligence, was found to miss some essential aspects of the flexibility of human intelligence. Exceptions to the cognitive models could always be found when tested experimentally, and seemingly successful computer models could not be made to generalize beyond their initial conditions (i.e., the frame problem). As mentioned earlier, Searle criticized the symbol manipulation approach for its lack of true intelligence with meaning and intentionality derived from real contact with the world. For him, applying formal rules on symbols is just like juggling with Chinese characters without understanding Chinese. Researchers started to realize that the brain's properties did matter after all. The brain is a huge network of millions of highly interconnected neurons, which are simple computational units. Early attempts to incorporate these properties into neural network models of the human mind (e.g., Hebb's 1949 book, *The Organization of Behavior*, and Rosenblatt's 1962 book, *Principles of Neurodynamics*) had lost their attraction after Minsky and Papert had criticized the limited computational powers of one-layered neural networks, known as "perceptrons" (in their 1969 book with that title). In the 1980s, however, these limitations could be solved because the computational powers emerging from large-scale networks with simple units were demonstrated (in a 1982 paper by Hopfield, a physicist) and because it was discovered how multilayered neural networks could be trained (i.e., by back-propagation, as shown in a 1986 article in *Nature* by Rumelhart and colleagues). Although neural network modeling had, in fact, always continued on a low-profile scale (e.g., Grossberg's adaptive resonance theory models), it was only with the publication (in 1986) of the two books by the parallel distributed processing research group (headed by Rumelhart, McClelland, and Hinton) that this approach, also known as the subsymbolic approach, or connectionism, emerged as a crucial and respectable player again. The properties of the brain as a dynamical system are also being taken seriously now.

The second event giving rise to breakdown of the functionalist assumption was the development of new brain imaging techniques (such as positron emission tomography and functional magnetic resonance imaging). This new technology could yield vivid images of localized brain activity corresponding to particular cognitive operations, which seemed quite attractive to a large number of cognitive psychologists for examining the brain mechanisms corresponding to their putative cognitive mechanisms. Indeed, some of the foremost cognitive psychologists from the 1970s were also pioneering these brain imaging techniques in the late 1980s and early 1990s (e.g., Posner and Kosslyn).

Thus developments in neural networks and imaging gave rise to the cognitive neurosciences, a new multidisciplinary science that has witnessed enormous growth within a rather limited period of time. Cognitive psychology now develops alongside the neurosciences, although some people fear that cognitive psychology will simply "evaporate" as a result of this, both for scientific and socioeconomic reasons (because the brain is supposed to be the real "stuff" behind the more elusive "mind" and because of the abundant funds going to the neurosciences compared to psychology).

Outward into the Environment

The tendency to break out of the laboratory into the natural environment was started by J. J. Gibson and has continued with increasing force. Within artificial intelligence, it gradually became clear that the analytic approach of decomposing intelligence into its basic building blocks and then putting the building blocks together in a computer model was doomed to failure. The radical alternative was to have "intelligence without representation" (as Brooks called it in an influential paper in *Artificial Intelligence*) or to let intelligence grow into more natural circumstances by building small, insectlike robots and studying, from a more synthetic approach, how they develop survival strategies and solve realistic problems, in interaction with their environment. In other words, rather than isolating the mind from the brain, and the cognitive system from its environment, intelligence became embodied again and cognition became situated in its context again. In artificial intelligence, this new trend has led to the emergence of a new field called "artificial life." It appears that cognitive psychology will have to collaborate more with social scientists and biologists than with computer scientists.

Conclusion

It may appear that the pendulum has started to swing back again in the direction of less internal cognition and more externally guided action, after almost half a century of dominance of cognitivism over behaviorism. However, with the experience of the disadvantages of the one-sided exaggerations of both approaches, it should be possible to achieve a better synthesis. Finally, with the increased understanding of the brain mechanisms, which mediate all of the interactions between the mind and the world, cognitive theories can now be built on firmer ground. Scientists from all of the contributing disciplines, including the social scientists, should work together to try to understand human cognition in its broadest possible sense.

See Also the Following Articles

Behavioral Psychology • Cognitive Neuroscience • Cognitive Research Methods • Heuristics • Problem-Solving Methodologies

Further Reading

Baddeley, A. D. (1999). *Essentials of Human Memory*. Psychology Press, Hove, United Kingdom.

Bechtel, W., and Graham, G. (eds.) (1999). *A Companion to Cognitive Science*. Blackwell, Oxford, United Kingdom.

Coren, S., Ward, L. M., and Enns, J. T. (1999). *Sensation and Perception*, 5th Ed. Harcourt Brace College Publ., Forth Worth.

Eysenck, M. W. (2001). *Principles of Cognitive Psychology*, 2nd Ed. Psychology Press, Hove, United Kingdom.

Gazzaniga, M. S., Ivry, R. B., and Mangun, G. R. (2002). *Cognitive Neuroscience: The Biology of the Mind*, 2nd Ed. Norton, New York.

Harnish, R. M. (2002). *Minds, Brains, Computers: An Historical Introduction to the Foundations of Cognitive Science*. Blackwell, Malden, Massachusetts.

Lamberts, K., and Goldstone, R. (eds.) (2004). *Handbook of Cognition*. Sage, London.

Osherson, D. N. (ed.) (1995). *An Invitation to Cognitive Science*, 2nd Ed. Bradford Books/MIT Press, Cambridge, Massachusetts.

Parkin, A. J. (2000). *Essential Cognitive Psychology*. Psychology Press, Hove, United Kingdom.

Pashler, H. (ed.) (2002). *Stevens' Handbook of Experimental Psychology*. Wiley, New York.

Reisberg, D. (2001). *Cognition: Exploring the Science of the Mind*, 2nd Ed. Norton, New York.

Sternberg, R. J. (ed.) (1999). *The Nature of Cognition*. Bradford Books/MIT Press, Cambridge, Massachusetts.

Styles, E. A. (1997). *The Psychology of Attention*. Psychology Press, Hove, United Kingdom.

Conclusion

See Also the Following Articles

Further Reading

Cognitive Research Methods

David B. Kronenfeld

University of California, Riverside, Riverside, California, USA

Glossary

computational Describing types of models or approaches based on actually implemented computer programs, whereby the formal representation is embodied in the computer program and the output of computer runs can be compared with empirical data.

ethnoscience Early cognitive anthropology, focused on studying the semantics of folk knowledge systems with a methodology from structural linguistics.

formal (models, features, or descriptions) Entities or statements that are explicitly and precisely specified, often via mathematical representations.

instantiation The application of an abstract but well-defined plan (such as a computer program) to a particular concrete situation (cf. "realization" in linguistics, which refers to a filled-out concrete instance of an abstract category).

kinship terminological system The kinship terms of a language, organized and analyzed as a distinct system.

reference and contrast An assessment in which "reference" refers to the semantic relationship of words or cognitive categories to phenomena in the world that the words or cognitive categories represent; "contrast" refers to the semantic relationship of words or cognitive categories to other words or categories.

semantic component A dimension of contrasting attributes, whereby the attributes distinguish members of one semantic category from another.

similarity matrix A matrix of values that represent the similarity of each item on a list to each other item. If similarity is taken as symmetric (as it usually is), then the information is all contained in half of the matrix (a half-matrix).

triads test A way of arriving at a similarity matrix by constructing a list of all possible triples from the list of items, and then having informants for each triple indicate which two out of the three items are most similar. Summing the pairwise similarity scores across triples produces a similarity matrix. Balanced block designs have been constructed that allow use of only a subset from the list of all possible triples—needed because the number of possible triples rises geometrically with the number of items on the list.

Psychology and psychological methods are basic to any study of cognition, but the shared or distributed cognition that underlies, or is embedded in, any social system presents special problems and responds to special constraints because of its extraindividual nature. Cognitive anthropology has been the research tradition most concerned with collective cognitive structures and systems, and it is work in this tradition that is emphasized herein. Cognitive anthropology initially developed, as "ethnoscience," out of an attempt to apply descriptive and analytic insights from structural linguistics—developed there for the study of phonology, morphology, and syntax—to the study of semantic systems.

Background

The study of cognitive anthropology first emerged in 1956 when Ward Goodenough challenged John Fischer's description and analysis of household composition patterns on the island of Truk. Fischer had used traditional anthropological definitions of concepts such as "matrilocal" and "patrilocal" residence (based on whether a new couple were living with the wife's or husband's parents), while Goodenough argued that, for the Trukese whose land and houses were owned by corporate matrilineal descent groups, one could understand residence decisions only in terms of the options Trukese faced and the rights that created these options (i.e., in effect, with whose matrilineage the new couple lived). Goodenough argued that Trukese decisions could be understood only in terms of the categories (and entailments of categories) they recognized as part of their language and culture. Goodenough's goal was one that goes back to Boas and his students, but his approach represented a radical departure. This approach was based on the linguistic insight most forcefully driven home by Edward Sapir (in articles on "Sound Patterns in Language" and "The Psychological Reality of Phonemes") that effective descriptions of languages (e.g., ones unknown to the linguist or the linguistic community) had to be based on the phonological (sound) and grammatical categories and distinctions used by speakers of that language, as opposed to external categories based on the linguist's own language or on some abstract or philosophic standard. The distinguishing of the "phoneme," the minimal cognitive unit of sound in a language that distinguishes one meaningful unit (e.g., word) from another, from a "phone type," a physical sound unit that linguists use to describe the sounds of a language, had an importance for linguistics comparable to the importance for physics of the distinction of "mass" from "weight"; it allowed a compact, formal, systematic characterization of the sounds of a language, and thus of the constraints on their patterning and combining into larger units. Goodenough argued that cultures, like languages, were systems that could be understood only via an analysis that was built on the conceptual units used by their members.

In linguistics, the analysis in terms of phonemes of the sound system used by speakers of a language was called "phonemic," whereas the description or analysis of a language's sounds in terms of some external classification scheme, such as the International Phonetic Alphabet (IPA), was called "phonetic." Those terms and the distinction they imply had already been generalized to culture by Kenneth Pike in 1954 as "emic" and "etic," and analyses such as that advocated by Goodenough came to be spoken of as "emic." In Pike's linguistically derived sense, "emic" referred to an analysis of knowledge and/or behavior that was structured by the categories that native participants used in making their decisions regarding distinctions or actions, whereas "etic" referred to an analysis structured by categories brought by the describer from outside the given system; the anthropologist Marvin Harris much later introduced a different and confusing—but ultimately more widely known—interpretation of the terms in which "emic" referred to a folk theory and contrasted with an "etic" or scientific theory.

The goal of the approach that grew in response to Goodenough's discussion of "residence rules" was an emic approach to the description and analysis of culture. Development of the approach began with the area of shared knowledge closest to linguistics, that of the overlap between language and culture—the semantics of word meanings. Groups of semantically related words (or the conceptual universe they referred to) were spoken of as "domains." The major structuring devices for domains were Saussure's relations of contrast (X vs. Y) and inclusion (M is a superordinate category that includes both X and Y); these semantic structuring relations were in turn to be related to the pragmatic relations among the entities the labels referred to (what X looks like, how it works, what it does, etc.). "Frame eliciting" is an ethnographic descriptive heuristic device for finding and describing emic units and emic relations among these, whereas componential analysis is an analytic heuristic for finding emic units from a pattern of etic descriptions.

Frame Eliciting

In frame eliciting, native statements on some topic of ethnographic interest are elicited, and then sentences from the statements are turned into frames by replacing meaningful entities in them with blanks; lists of potential culturally appropriate fillers of the blanks are then elicited. These statements typically came from a record of less formal questioning involving versions of "what's that?," "what is it used for?," "who does it?," and so forth. A statement such as "X is a kind of M" would then be turned into a question, as in "Is ____ a kind of M?," where other elicited entities (such as Y, C, D, etc.) would be used in the blank. Often taxonomic questions would also be involved, such as "what kinds of X are there?" and "what is X a kind of?," and sometimes attribute questions, such as "how do you tell X from Y?" or "what is the difference between X and Y?." Categories with similar privileges of occurrence are grouped together and the features on which they contrast with one another are examined, as are their differential implications for further associations or actions. Similarly, the relations between superordinate and subordinate categories (in terms of inclusion relations) are explored. The method is best described by Frake in his "Notes on Queries in Ethnography" article.

Componential Analysis

In componential analysis, an exhaustive set of referents of each of a set of contrasting terms (a domain) is assembled. Each referent is characterized on a list (ideally, a complete list) of attribute dimensions that seem relevant. The classic example was in kinship, wherein the contrasting terms were "kinterms" and the referents were "kintypes"—genealogical strings connecting "ego" (the reference person) and "alter" (the relative of ego's labeled by the kinterm); attribute dimensions included information such as "sex of alter," alter's "generation" relative to ego, and lineality (alter on, next to, or off ego's direct line of ancestors and descendants); this is discussed in Wallace and Atkins' "The Meaning of Kinship Terms." Relevance can be assessed on the basis of prior comparative experience, pertinent *a priori* assumptions, informant information, serendipity, etc. Then the analyst experiments to find the smallest set of attribute dimensions with the fewest distinctions per dimension sufficient to distinguish all of the items in the domain from one another. Those attribute dimensions are interpreted as the semantic components that structure relations among the terms in the domain. An alternative approach is to ask informants to describe the difference between one term and another or one subset of terms versus another, and build up a set of potential semantic components that way. Originally it was thought that the attribute dimensions had to come from some universal, etically specified set (modeled on a misunderstanding of the status of the IPA)—spoken of as an "etic grid"—but it has become clear that potential attributes can come from anywhere, as long as they are well defined. Within the particular domain of kinship terms, more formally explicit inductive procedures have been designed for automating the production of a componential analysis from sets of genealogically specified referents, but these methods seem specific to kinship terminologies and to depend on special, unique features of that domain.

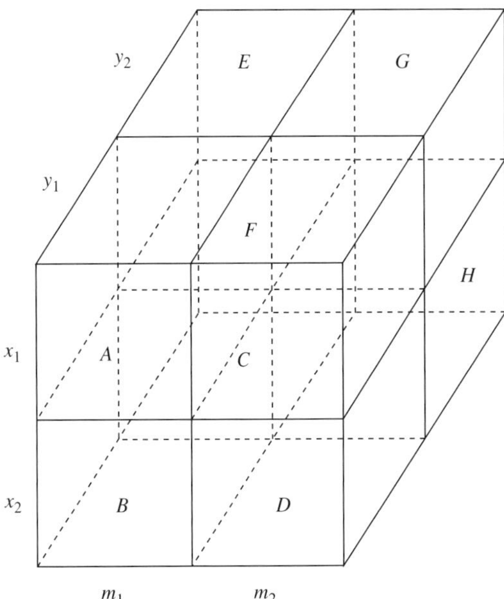

Figure 1 An abstract paradigmatic structure. Key: *A* through *G* are categories (terms), *m*, *x*, and *y* are dimensions of contrast, and m_1, m_2, x_1, x_2, y_1, and y_2 are defining attributes on the given dimensions.

Table I Tabular Presentation of a Paradigmatic Structure

	Dimension[a]		
Term	*m*	*x*	*y*
A	m_1	x_1	y_1
B	m_1	x_2	y_1
C	m_2	x_1	y_1
D	m_2	x_2	y_1
E	m_1	x_1	y_2
F	m_1	x_2	y_2
G	m_2	x_1	y_2
H	m_2	x_2	y_2

[a] As defined in Fig. 1.

Data Structures

Paradigmatic Structures

A componential analysis aims at producing one kind of cognitive structure, a "paradigm." Paradigmatic structures are composed of a set of terms (or categories), all contrasting with one another at a single level of contrast (like opposites, but with the possibility of being multinary); the terms are distinguished from one another by a set of cross-cutting semantic dimensions (i.e., sets of contrasting attributes, as in Fig. 1: m: m_1 vs. m_2, x: x_1 vs. x_2, y: y_1 vs. y_2). A paradigmatic structure is like a "cross-tabulation" in statistics. In principle, each dimension is relevant to each term. Figure 1 shows the actual structure, but the information can also be presented in tabular form, as in Table I.

Both Occam's razor and relevant psychological studies suggest that each of the categories in a paradigmatic structure should be conjunctively defined, but for folk categories the mechanism that produces conjunctivity is a probabilistic one depending on "cognitive ease," which does allow for the possibility of some disjunctivity where there exists a good functional reason and there is sufficient effort invested in relevant learning (as, e.g., with "strikes" in baseball). Cognitive ease refers in a general and loosely defined way to the mental work involved in learning and using (in this case) a category, and "conjunctivity" is one well-defined version or aspect of it. Conjunctivity refers to the intersection (as opposed to sum) of values on relevant dimensions; thus, taking "red" vs. "green" and "boxes" vs. "circles" as relevant dimensions for a restricted domain of figures, "red things," "boxes," or "red boxes" would be conjunctively defined categories, whereas a category made up of anything that was either "red" or a "box" would not be conjunctive and hence would be disjunctive.

Kinship terminological systems and pronominal systems have provided the clearest and most complete examples of semantic domains with paradigmatic structures, though cultural artifact domains (such as automobile types) can tend toward paradigms. The simplest example of a paradigm is a set of two terms contrasting with each other on a single two-valued semantic dimension (as in "black" vs. "white").

Taxonomic Structures

Another kind of structure is a "taxonomic" one. Taxonomic structures are composed of a set of terms at different levels of inclusion, related to one another by a hierarchy of contrast (e.g., "cat" vs. "dog") and inclusion relations ("cats" and "dogs" are both "carnivores") (see Fig. 2). Such structures have a head term, which includes some number of subordinate terms, which in turn may each include terms at still lower levels of contrast. Dimensions of contrast are not normally repeated; successive dimensions subdivide (rather than crosscut) prior or higher level ones. Each semantic dimension (in Fig. 2: m: m_1 vs. m_2, x: x_1 vs. x_2, y: y_1 vs. y_2) is only pertinent to the node at which it occurs in the system—that is, to the subset of items covered by the superordinate term it subdivides (e.g., whatever it is that distinguishes "cats" from "dogs" is irrelevant to "horses" vs. "cows"). Figure 2 shows the actual structure, but the information can also be presented in tabular form, as in Table II.

The clearest examples of taxonomies in the literature have been ethnobotanical and disease domains. The minimal example of a taxonomy is a set of two terms contrasting with one another under a single head term. Taxonomic categories, like other folk categories, should in the normal course of events be conjunctively defined, and the conjunctivity constraint can be a powerful tool when attempting to analyze and understand systems of folk categories.

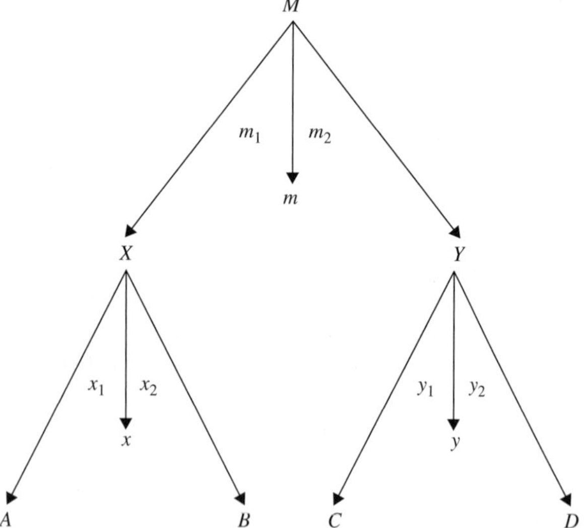

Figure 2 An abstract taxonomic structure. Key: A through D and X, Y, and M are categories (terms), m, x, and y are dimensions of contrast, and m_1, m_2, x_1, x_2, y_1, and y_2 are defining attributes on the given dimensions.

Mixed Structures

Mixed structures are possible; either of the preceding kinds of structure can, in principle, be embedded as a node in the other. That is, an item in a taxonomy could expand multidimensionally (instead of as the normal simple contrast), whereas an item in a paradigm could be the head term for a taxonomy. A fruitful research area concerns the combination of cognitive conditions, conditions of use of the terms, and nature of the pragmatic phenomena being categorized by the terms in question that lead to one or the other kind of semantic structure. Psychological issues, including concept formation strategies and constraints, short- vs. long-term memory, rehearsal time and learning, and so forth, seem relevant to the issue.

Marking

Taxonomic semantic structures are relations among named entities. But sometimes one name or label will operate at more than one level of contrast. For instance, "cow" can be opposed, as a female, to the male "bull," but "cow" can also be the cover term for bovines that includes both "cows" and "bulls." The relation between the words "cow" and "bull" is an example of a contrast between an "unmarked" term ("cow") and a "marked" term ("bull"), whereby the unmarked term is both opposed to the marked one and included by it. Such marking relations can be joined into more extensive "marking hierarchies," as "man" vs. "animal," whereby "man" includes "man" vs. "woman," which, in turn, respectively include "man" vs. "boy" and "woman" vs. "girl." The unmarked member of such an opposition represents a kind of default value for both members of the opposition when the feature on which they contrast is neutralized. For cows, the functional basis of the default is simple: the great number of cows for each bull in a dairy herd. For men and women, the basis is perhaps more interesting: having to do with women's long-time lack of civil and other rights and privileges. Marking is extensively seen in ethnobiological classifications, and indeed, according to Brent Berlin,

Table II Tabular Presentation of a Taxonomic Structure

	Dimension[a]		
Term	m	x	y
A	m_1	x_1	
B	m_1	x_2	
C	m_2		y_1
D	m_2		y_2
X	m_1		
Y	m_2		
M			

[a] As defined in Fig. 2.

provides a major mechanism via which such systems develop (a taxonomic term is used not just for its primary referents—its unmarked sense—but also as a generic cover term for other similar items; if the other items have their own specific labels, these will be rarer marked alternatives to the unmarked default, on the model of "bull"). Marking was first worked out for phonological systems by N. Trubetskoy in 1939 and translated as *Fundamentals of Phonology* in 1969, and then broadly extended by J. Greenberg 1966 to other linguistic phenomena; marking seems to show up widely, as well, in shared nonlinguistic cognitive systems. It offers a mechanism by which an existing cognitive category can be used as a kind of generic to include novel referents, and thus by which simple systems of classification can evolve into more complex ones, as the novel referents eventually get their own specific category under the older generic.

Semantic Extension

Marking provides examples, as just seen, in which not all referents of a term (or of a nonverbal cognitive category) may be equally central for their users, or as well understood. In general, for word use at least, a great amount of our usage is of words for referents that are not the primary referents of the words. A normal process in word use is "semantic extension," whereby entities (objects, actions, attributes, etc.) that do not have their own special labels are spoken of via the label of some similar entity; the choice of label depends on how the oppositional structure of the semantic domain chosen matches the relations between the target entity and other entities from which it is being distinguished. Such extension can be denotative (based on attributes of form or appearance), connotative (based on functional attributes—what makes the category useful), or figurative (metaphoric, metonymic, etc.). The referent to which the label primarily "belongs" is spoken of variously as the "focal," "core," "kernel," or "prototypic" referent. Prototypicality seems to be a result of a combination of frequency of usage (what referents learners most frequently encounter) and functional fit (what referents best fulfill, whatever it is that makes the category important enough to get its own unit or label). For instance, in English, the term "uncle" prototypically refers to a parent's brother, but it also—entirely literally and correctly—can be used for an aunt's husband (and, sometimes, as an unmarked term for a "great uncle,"—i.e., grandparent's brother). It can be used connotatively for other close males with whom there is interaction in the way interaction should occur with an uncle; these can include (depending on context and situation) a parent's cousins, family friends of the parents' generation, and so forth. Such usage is not considered "technically" correct, as can be demonstrated methodologically via native speaker use of linguistic "hedges" (such as "well he's not *really* my uncle but . . . "). Figurative usage, as when we speak of the United States government as "Uncle Sam," happens when it is not the specific functions (for uncles, avuncular behavior) that are at issue, but some more general attitude. In figurative usage, the choice of domain/paradigm (say, kinfolk in the case of "uncle") conveys something (say, for our uncle example, a close personal, solidary, and noncontingent relationship) and then the particular choice of term within that paradigm provides more specific guidance concerning what is meant ("uncle" vs. "father" signifying an affective rather than authority or provisioning emphasis; "uncle" vs. "aunt" signifying a male; "uncle" vs. "brother" signifying relative seniority).

Componential structures of relations among conceptual categories, the "defining features" of categories, in this extensionist approach apply necessarily only to the focal members or referents of categories (versus to the full ranges of members or referents); they may well apply as well to other members, but they also may not. For example, in English, a "mug" is a kind of "cup." Among other things, a prototypic mug is an extended referent of the "cup" category. English speakers also recognize that there exist some kinds of beer steins that can be called "mugs" but that these do not fall into the denotative range of the "cup" category. As this cup/mug example exemplifies, the core/extension approach applies to taxonomic structures as well as to paradigmatic ones. Basic early examples were Lounsbury's 1964 work on Crow- and Omaha-type kinship terminologies and Berlin and Kay's 1969 study of basic color terms. Eleanor Rosch, in psychology, elaborated a general descriptive model of word meanings from the Berlin and Kay base. Kronenfeld has elaborated a fuller semantic theory of extension. Marking and semantic extension are methodologically important because they strongly affect the interpretation of verbal interaction both within the study population and between the researcher and the study population. There is reason to think that nonverbal concepts might well operate in a similar manner.

Universal (cross-cultural and cross-language) patterns have been used by students of shared cognitive structures to demonstrate the force of specific kinds of cognitive patterns in the domains of color and kinship. But the universal issue has ebbed in importance. The kinds of patterns involved in marking and extension do appear to be both general and universal, but that apparent universality is a matter of form rather than of content, and depends more on general properties of human thought, memory, and communication than on any specific properties of any particular domain in which the patterns are seen; there exist particular reasons for the specific content universals that have been found in the domains of color terms and kinship terms, but marking and extension occur as well in domains that lack these particular characteristics (such as cups and glasses, pens and pencils, books, religious controversies, political factions, and men's vs. women's work in American households).

Types of Models

Taxonomic and paradigmatic structures emerged in early semantic studies as ways of descriptively organizing chunks of folk knowledge. There was and still is discussion of the psychological status of such descriptions: to what degree, or in what senses, are they to be considered psychologically "real"? The debate about psychological reality was inherited, along with the previously mentioned methodology, by cognitive anthropology from structural linguistics. When the discussion was broadened to include actual psychological data (as opposed to simple reasoning), the issue quickly became one of "real" "in what sense" and/or "under what conditions." This methodological advance was introduced by Romney and D'Andrade in 1964 in "Cognitive Aspects of English Kin Terms" (reprinted in 1969 in Tyler's *Cognitive Anthropology*). Variant versions of psychological reality emerged, *inter alia*, among folk definitions of categories, folk understandings of the connotations or implications of category membership, of differing contexts of definition and application, etc. For kinterms in particular, actual folk definitions (as in the "because he's my mother's brother" answer to "how do I know X is my uncle?") were found to be quite different in form from the definitions implied by componential analysis ["first generation, ascending, colineal (or collateral), male, kinsperson"]. On the other hand, there was found strong psychological evidence for native use of something like componential structures to reason about the attitudes and behavior that pertain to various classes of kin. (This was learned through answers to questions such as "Describe an uncle," "Why are uncles important?," "How should you treat your uncle?," etc.) Studies aimed at distinguishing psychologically "real" from unreal componential structures (among those that did the basic job of distinguishing the categories from one another reasonably succinctly) in kinship showed that interviewees were capable of applying a range of different models in different contexts, even if some models appeared more generally salient than others.

Formal Models of Cultural Knowledge Systems

Attempts to organize and formalize the description of folk definitions of kinterm categories led to a different kind of modeling and a different kind of research methodology. It was found (particularly by S. H. Gould in 2000 and by F. K. Lehman and D. Read; their articles appear in Kronenfeld (2001) that the folk definitions of different kinterm categories were systematically related to one another, and could be formally modeled as an algebraic system—i.e., via a small set of axioms and derivations from these. This breakthrough raised the possibility that other "cultural knowledge systems" (as, for example, ethnobiological classifications and kinds of property rights) could be similarly amenable to formal modeling (El Guindi and Read offered an early instance in 1979 in *Current Anthropology*). And it raised the question of whether there might exist some common properties that might run across the full set of such knowledge systems (or at least substantial subsets of them).

With the emergence of successful formal models of cultural knowledge systems, it became clear that such systems were used more for reference and communication than for actually planning or interpreting action. They were shared systems of classification and organization. They were productive systems of reasoning that could be applied by someone to new events or entities in a way that others in the culture could easily understand. They had to be fairly easily learned (because many or all members of a given culture would know them) but without being explicitly taught. They had to be structured in such a way that consistent changes in their application by users could feed back into changes in the structures. One active area in cognitive anthropology involves the construction and exploration of models of such cultural knowledge systems.

"Cultural Models" as Models of Behavioral Patterns or Interpretation

As the nature of cultural knowledge systems is better understood, it is becoming clear that there has to exist at least one other kind of culturally shared cognitive structure, which might be called a "cultural model." The term, and the kind of approach, emerged as anthropologists, on the model of schema theory in psychology and of attempts in cognitive sciences to model routine behavioral situations (such as Schank and Abelson's 1977 simulation of conversations about restaurant behavior), tried to summarize and model regularities in culturally standardized behavioral patterns or behavioral interpretations (important examples are in 1987 and 1992 collections by Quinn and Holland and by D'Andrade and Strauss; the work is summarized in D'Andrade's *The Development of Cognitive Anthropology*). The modeling task seemed to require some consideration not only of the classification of cultural entities (types of people, situations, means, etc.) but also of actors' goals and values, of understood or presumed community standards, of actors' emotions, of the aspects of situations that were understood to trigger various emotional responses (in terms of both kind and intensity), and of the cues that actors used to recognize what was in other actors' minds. The underlying task was not that different from the traditional task of ethnography, but the methodological means was radically new, based as it was on a theory of effective cognitive structures. The methodological mechanism involves constructing a model (ideally one that is computational) of the hypothesized behavioral entity, and then examining how well the model's output matches verbal data or other observations.

Individual vs. Shared Structures

Early attempts to construct such cultural models, though convincing as metaphoric accounts, seemed difficult to represent with any precision. Several different kinds of problems have emerged and are gradually being addressed. On the one hand, actual psychological schemas are dynamic structures existing only in individual minds; they are constantly adapting in response to feedback from the social and physical environments. Yet, on the other hand, cultural models are seen as shared and thus relatively stable entities that no one person can alter. Sharing and the conditions of learning a stable, shared system seem to place very different kinds of formal constraints on cultural models, compared to the constraints that shape individual schemas. Individual schemas are seen as direct producers of action, whereas cultural models, as something external to the personal psyche, have to be adapted and applied by their users. The application of cultural models to specific situations seems mediated by a number of considerations, such as whether self-behavior is being constructed or the behavior of someone else is being interpreted, how the outcome is to be interpreted, what knowledge of what set of alternative cultural models the actor or interpreter ascribes with what certainty to other relevant participants, and so forth.

Shape, Boundaries, and Content

Another kind of problem involves the shape, including, form(s), boundaries, and structure, of cultural models. Actual ethnographic conversations with interviewees suggest, on the one hand, the existence of well-known and well-shared cultural models, at least for important areas of culture (such, for example, as love and marriage). On the other hand, those conversations suggest a lot of variation in detail from one application of a given cultural model to the next, similar variance in nuances of interpretation, and a real, fuzzy line (regarding content) between where the standardized cultural model ends and where the details of some particular cognitive instantiation of it begin—and then, in turn, where the actual details of given real world events enter in. One question concerns whether cultural models are to be understood as applying directly to behavior or as providing a more abstract template, which is then used to construct a more ad hoc filled-out model (a kind of instantiated model). If the latter, then it seems possible that people have in their learned cultural repertoire not only sets of cultural models but also, perhaps, representations of the commoner instantiations of salient cultural models. Another question concerns whether cultural models are to be understood as defining complete whole classes of situations to which they apply (in the manner described earlier regarding paradigmatic definitions of semantic referent sets) or as defining prototypic situations, which then are extended by users to some variety of actual situations. If the models are prototypic, the question arises as to how much (and what kind of) detail is to be included in the prototype. The question also arises whether such included material is to be limited to what is essential to the operation of the model or, alternatively, should include as well the more common accidental attributes of typical application situations or instantiations.

Decision Theory—Models of Routine Decision Making

A third category of models of social cognition, somewhat predating the other two, was the construction (by Hugh and Christina Gladwin, James Young, Naomi Quinn, and others) of ethnographic models of routine decision making. Decisions studied included whether to fertilize fields, what kind of fertilizer to use, which market to attend for selling fish, and what kind of health care to select. This approach was based directly on Goodenough's study of residence rules. Such models differed from cultural models because their target issues came not out of the culture, but out of some externally generated conceptualization, problem, or theory, often from either standard economic theory or applied anthropological issues. The approach was limited to routine decisions for which there existed a backlog of cultural experience, clear benefits for a better vs. worse decision, and some reasonable set of alternatives from among which a choice had to be made (and any of which, in one or another context, might be best). The approach was built on insights from cognitive psychology concerning information-processing constraints. Such constraints might include overall complexity, difficulty of statistical calculations, continuous vs. discrete n-chotomous variables, or simultaneous consideration of multiple variables vs. seriatim consideration of one or two at a time. Attention was paid to standard devices for getting around those limitations. There was an attempt to develop a list of consistent attributes of such decision processes. The list included the role of preattentive processing, the use of "elimination by aspects" (in which attributes were considered sequentially in their order of felt importance, to eliminate less desirable alternatives), the conditions that determined whether decision problems were broken down into attribute-structured pieces or taken as whole gestalts, the use of "rules of thumb," and the relationship of rules of thumb to systematic framing variables (such as economic constraints, economic strategies, etc.). The ethnographic approach produced a descriptive model of actual behavior, the structure of which could then be examined for the analytic principles that structured it.

A variant of the decision-making approach was developed by Robert Randall in his 1977 dissertation, combining it with a hierarchy of decisions starting with basic cultural needs (such as "making a living") and building in marking defaults at all levels. Its organization came much closer than did other decision-making approaches to using internal (to the culture) issues to structure the decision universe. By using higher level cultural goals to define lower level goals and tasks, Randall's system paralleled Frake's approach to Subanun "Religious Behavior" (reprinted in Tyler's *Cognitive Anthropology*). Together they represented an important return to the original ethnoscience aim of describing cultures in their own terms. It was then possible to consider what universal or comparatively useful elements fell out from comparisons of such descriptions. This was an approach that had to be largely hypothetical until the emergence of modern computers and the modeling within modern cognitive sciences of emergent systems. This larger, integrated approach to cultural systems provides a frame within which cultural models can be considered, and offers an approach in which cultural models can be seen as hierarchically arranged such that more general ones include more specific ones. The cognitive sciences approach—especially the "agent-based" version—offers a way (see later) by which cultural models can be represented and evaluated for the effectiveness with which they account for relevant behavior (including conversations, actions, and interpersonal coordination).

Methods and Techniques

As indicated, frame eliciting has been a basic technique for eliciting self-conscious cultural knowledge systems (such as kinship and ethnobiological ones), and finding structure in such knowledge. Such knowledge is shared and explicit: it is what native members of the culture talk about, define for each other, use in reasoning, and so forth. The technique involves systematic exploration of statements concerning the entities in question. Relevant statements include ones involving semantic relations of contrast and inclusion and ones involving pragmatic relations such as parts and wholes, sequences, task- or context-related clusters, uses of objects, effects of actions, and so forth. The analyst then assembles the information thus gained into structures that seem of interest and that seem implicit in the data; these can be semantic structures (involving, say, the meanings of words such as "red" or "yellow") or various kinds of pragmatic ones (involving, say, the perceived structure of the interrelations among the actual hues).

One issue of debate has concerned whether the structures thus derived (for example, a taxonomic "tree diagram" derived from informant statements that C and D are kinds of Y, A and B are kinds of X, and X and Y are kinds of M) are to be ascribed to native cognition or just treated as summaries of regularities in native understanding as expressed in discussions (see Fig. 2). Because, either way, native speakers have the relevant information available to use in conversations and reasoning, the issue may not have much immediate practical importance; but the debate points up the difficulties in understanding exactly what is meant by structure, and thus in being able to consider what might constitute relevant evidence. For some kinds of structures under some conditions, as Romney and D'Andrade showed for kinterms, multidimensional scaling (MDS) of inter-item similarity data can help.

Free-Listing "Snapshots"

One kind of information that is sometimes desired about a group involves what ideas or thoughts or concerns, etc., and maybe what linkages among these, are most salient in the group in one or another context. One way of getting a quick sketch of such salient notions is to give informants a short free-listing task (e.g., "list five thoughts that come to mind when you think of 'anthropology'") or sketching task ("sketch an American high school"); it is then possible to form a composite list or picture based on responses produced by more than one or two people (used tellingly by Kevin Lynch in his 1960 *Image of the City*). The composite can be ordered so that answers produced by more people are more saliently displayed, compared to those produced by fewer people. Because the task is open-ended, and because specific responses are being counted (rather than sorted into categories or ratings), repeated answers can only represent items that are saliently associated with the stimulus concept in the relevant cultural community; the odds of two people coming up with the same response by chance (i.e., where there is no relevant shared linguistic and cultural community understanding) is exceedingly low, given the size of people's vocabularies and the varieties of ways available for describing and talking about even commonplace items. The high-frequency items provide a kind of "snapshot" of where the collective attention is directed. Such a snapshot can be used as a starting point for more careful and expensive research regarding the given issues. A comparison of such snapshots for two contrasting communities can focus a researcher quickly on salient cognitive (or behavioral) differences. The relevance of the snapshot(s) to a particular research problem is determined by the nature of the stimulus, but because the technique is inexpensive to implement, different stimuli can be experimented with in order to see what makes a difference and what responses are robust enough to come through the variants. This technique is a way of measuring collective or shared salience of concepts in some context; it does not distinguish beliefs from knowledge from incidental rumor and it does not speak to any kind of truth or falsity. Free-listing tasks can also be used for a variety of other cognitive purposes, including exploring semantic structure (as seen in Romney and D'Andrade's article in Tyler' 1969 book); Bernard (2002) has provided a useful overview.

Multidimensional Scaling

Multidimensional scaling, like factor analysis, is a computational method for taking a matrix of pairwise similarities or dissimilarities for a list of entities (e.g., color terms, kinterms, diseases, or roles) as input and finding the arrangement of points representing those entities in a space of a specified dimensionality such that the rank order of interpoint distances best matches the rank order of interentity dissimilarities. The measure of this match is called "stress." The lowest dimensionality for which the stress is still low is looked for by running the procedure for a sequence of dimensionalities. If stress gradually increases as dimensionality decreases, it suggests that the data have no clear dimensionality; on the other hand, if the stress stays more or less constant and low, down to a certain dimensionality, but spikes up below that dimensionality, it suggests that the data arrangement really has that intrinsic dimensionality. An example is the basic six primary color terms in English (with similarity measured via a triads test), whereby from 5 down through 2 dimensions stress is low, but whereby it spikes up in one dimension; an examination of the arrangement reveals the familiar red–orange–yellow–green–blue–purple color circle, sometimes with some extra distance between the cool colors and the warm ones, and sometimes with the warm colors a little more spread out than the cool ones.

MDS then offers a way of getting a metric spatial model out of ordinal (or interval) data. If the fit of the picture to the input data is good, as it was with Romney and D'Andrade's kinship data, then it suggests that the MDS spatial model is a reasonably good representation of the model that natives are using to generate the inputted similarity data (of the sort shown in Fig. 1). The picture comes in the form of a list of points with their coordinates in the given dimensional space; the axes are arbitrary in terms of the research problem, though some programs can orient them so that the first accounts for the greatest amount of interpoint distance, the second the next amount, and so forth. The analyst needs to scan the pattern of points and recognize or guess at the picture that the pattern represents. Four-dimensional pictures are hard to treat this way, and higher dimensional ones are impossible, so for higher dimensional pictures the picture has either to be simplified, by pulling out sets of points that seem odd, or indirect interpretative devices must be used. It is worth noting that, as the number of dimensions approaches the number of entities being scaled, the constraints that make the technique work break down.

Factor Analysis

Factor analysis does much the same task, but is a mathematical algorithm that generates a best arrangement of the points in relation to the inputted data. It requires ratio data. Unlike factor analysis, MDS uses a heuristic technique that can get locked into a relatively good solution while missing the optimal one, but requires only ordinal data. One by-product of the ratio/ordinal difference is that when imperfect ratio data are fed into factor analysis (as is typically the case with similarity measures), each irregularity in the data forces some extradimensionality in the picture. The effect is that factor analytic pictures can never be interpreted by direct examination of the pattern of points in the space, but always have to be attacked via indirect means, usually some attempt to orient the axes of the space (as in a "varimax" rotation) such that the resulting axes become interpretable as meaningful variables or scales.

One common data type involves a matrix of cases by data measurements, whereby data measurements are, for example, a question (e.g., "do you give money to?," "do you show respect to?," etc.) by topic (e.g., "father," "father's brother," "friend," etc.) matrix for each of a set of informants, and whereby similarity (question to question, topic to topic, or informant to informant) can be measured by correlation coefficients or by measures of the proportion of measurements (or questions), over all pairs, for which each of a pair of topics elicited the same measurement (or response) from the same informant. Another common data type is based on rating tasks (from psychology), such as paired comparisons or triads tests.

Hierarchical Clustering

Hierarchical clustering (HC) programs use the same kinds of similarity data as those used by MDS to produce hierarchical tree (or dendrogram) structures. Cladistic analysis in biology is based on such a procedure. The aim of the program is to find the best or most efficient branching structure starting with each entity separate from all others and gradually cumulatively joining entities into clusters (each new clustering being a node on the tree), until all of the entities are together in a single cluster (represented by the single apical node of the tree), with the level of similarity indicated at the point at which each new cluster is formed (i.e., previously separate clusters joined together into a new node on the tree) for each node, such that the inputted similarity values match (as well as possible) the values of the nodes on which the pair of items are split apart. Where the detailed data are less than totally or absolutely consistent with a dendrogram structure—that is, where members of one cluster have differing similarities to items in other clusters—different programs use different means of either averaging the similarity within clusters or picking the value that controls when the two clusters join. Such choices should be made in terms of an assessment of what kinds of distortions the given types of data (relative to a theory) are liable to be most vulnerable to, but commonly choices are made more capriciously. The programs thus produce tree structures even if the inputted data are to a greater or lesser degree inconsistent with such a structure. The validity of the resulting structure depends on the combination of analytic goals and the interpretative assumptions that are brought to the enterprise, and that are used to account for the inconsistent data, and on the fit of these assumptions with the method used for merging clusters. The degree to which the inputted data actually fit a tree structure can be examined by comparing the trees produced by maximal overlap and minimal overlap criteria (regarding similarity values of the separate items in the one cluster relative to items in the other cluster) for merging two clusters into a new cluster.

Both HC programs and MDS programs will produce pictures for any inputted similarity matrix. But the specific data structures they produce are logically incompatible with one another; MDS represents a many-to-many mapping of data interrelationships whereas HC represents a cumulation of many-to-one mappings, which means that they cannot both accurately represent the structure underlying the same data at the same time. But neither type of program comes with any really effective goodness-of-fit measure that tells in absolute terms how well it did.

It should be noted that MDS represents a mechanism for finding dimensional pictures (based on cross-cutting global variables) in data that look like the paradigmatic structures produced by componential analysis, hence Romney and D'Andrade's use of MDS in their test of alternative componential analyses of a set of kinship terms. On the other hand, HC programs offer a mechanism for pulling out of data tree structures that have a shape similar to that of taxonomic structures (though usually without the labeled nonterminal taxa that characterize a true taxonomy),-hence the use of such programs for cladistic analysis in biology. The intersection of cross-cutting variables, which produces a paradigm, cannot be directly represented in hierarchical structures, whereas the successive subdivisions of higher level categories by lower level features that produce a taxonomy cannot be directly represented in paradigmatic structures.

Consensus Measures

A comparable but different approach exists for evaluating answers to questions that have "right" and "wrong" answers—the consensus theory approach worked out by Romney and Batchelder. They have developed a statistical technique that can take informants' answers to a set of questions and determine whether the spread of answers to a given question represents differing degrees of knowledge about a single "correct" answer or the presence in the target community of different "correct" answers, or the lack of any consensus. When there is a single "correct" answer, the technique can tell the analyst what that answer is. "Correct" here can refer to actual facticity—say, the date on which the U.S. Civil War ended—or to a cultural consensus about what might even be a factually incorrect answer—as in beliefs in some communities about who "really" blew up the World Trade Center. Diverse "correct" answers, based on different knowledge, can be, for instance, the distinction between interpretations of ritual by priests and by laity, or the distinction for some cultural sequence, such as the "cargo system" in one Mexican pueblo (shown by Cancian in 1963), between the actual noncanonical path that some know "Joe" to have taken and the canonical path that others presume "Joe" to have taken). The method is similar to the free-listing snapshot one in that it assumes that shared answers must have a basis in shared knowledge, whereas uninformed guesses are going to be idiosyncratic. In both cases, the analyst is taking advantage of the fact that communities are characterized by shared knowledge, and thus that there are ways of pulling inferences out of shared responses from community members that could not be pulled out of answers produced by a random cross-section of strangers; the two methods represent different ways of getting at shared cognition.

Anthropology has progressed from a mechanistic view of culture in which culture was seen as unitary, whole, shared, and canonical. Formerly, everybody, at least in allegedly "simple" cultures, was presumed to know and do the same thing as everyone else, except for some variation according to age and sex. It is now realized that the kind of diversity known and experienced within our own culture characterizes the makeup of other cultures as well (even if the amount of variation is in part a function of size and contextual diversity). It is now known that the division of labor in society involves distributed knowledge as well as distributed economic activity; we are beginning to understand something of how the shared frame works that enables the coordination of diversity in everyday, un-self-consciously constructed sociocultural systems. All levels of society involve some mix of shared cultural content and diverse content, where "content" refers to some mix of knowledge, values, goals, etc. In all levels, there is a mix of enough sharing to allow coordination (whether cooperation, collaboration, competition, or avoidance) and enough diversity to provide a real division of labor. The consensus approach does not represent or entail any commitment to the monolithic view of culture; it does provide a tool for measuring some of the sharing. So far, our ways of looking at the diversity are still less formal.

Implicational Analysis

Joseph Greenberg's 1968 exploration of implicational universals in linguistics has been carried over into anthropology by Roy D'Andrade and Michael Burton, L. Brudner, and Douglass White (see below). A table is constructed showing the interaction of the presence or absence of one variable with the presence or absence of another, and then a "zero cell" is looked for in the table—that is, a logically possible combination that no empirical cases fall into (see Table III). The zero cell, if the other numbers in the table are large enough to make it statistically significant, means that there exists a logical implicational relationship between the two variables; in the example here, it means that the presence of Y implies the presence of X, but not vice versa—that is, X must be present before Y, or the presence of X is a necessary condition for the presence of Y. Depending on the data, these implicational relationships can be chained (as W → Y → X → Z) to produce, for instance, a kind of scale on which the sexual division of labor in different societies can be ranked (in Burton *et al.*'s 1977 example) or the cumulation of symptoms that go into native speakers' narrowing disease diagnoses (D'Andrade's example) or the structure of Navajo attitudes toward conditions involved in relocation (Schoepfle *et al.* in Gladwin (1984)). Such chains, based on comparisons among systems, can also provide insight into how conceptual systems can and cannot change over time (as Greenberg has shown for structural aspects of language and as Per Hage has shown for kin terminologies).

Table III A Two-by-Two Table, with a Zero Cell Implicational Relationship[a]

	Y	
X	*Present*	*Absent*
Present	Exist cases	0: no cases (hence: $Y \rightarrow X$)
Absent	Exist cases	Exist cases

[a] *X* and *Y* are features that are either present or absent in each case; "exist cases" means that there are cases in the given cell.

Network Analysis

Network analysis, though not directly cognitive, does offer considerable insight into the ways in which shared cognitive structure and content spread and into the social conditions that affect such spread. It can also provide some insight into the actual makeup of the social entities to which various shared cognitive structure or content inheres—because collective cognition, by definition, has to inhere in some social entity (whether formal or informal) and has to achieve its collective sharing, complementarity, predictability, etc. through patterns of interactions among community members. Network analysis is concerned with who communicates with whom within a group and with the analytic insights that come from considering the overall pattern of linkages within that group.

Systematic Patterns of Recall Errors

Systematic patterns of errors in informants' recall of systematic events or in calculations, when available, can be informative regarding the cognitive presuppositions shared by members of some informant community. An informant account of some event—say, who attended a particular seminar (in a 1987 study by Freeman, Romney, and Freeman) or what someone's "cargo system" trajectory in some Mexican village was (Cancian in the example mentioned earlier)—that is accurate does not necessarily speak to any underlying cognitive system; the informants could just have good memories. An erroneous account by some single given informant may not mean much—it could be bad memory, bad understanding, an attention lapse, or just plain cussedness. But any errors repeated by several informants become quite interesting, particularly in regard to what explains their agreement. Because the accounts are counterfactual, memory of what actually happened can be ruled out as an explanation for the sharing. If the questions were asked in some way such that collusion among interviewees (and picking up cues from the question or questioner) can be ruled out, then the explanation has to lie in some general knowledge that the informants bring to the question-answering task. Such general knowledge has to represent some kind of cultural/community norm or presupposition, some piece of shared cognitive structure. Thus patterned errors in responses of members of a group can give researchers a special window into the shared cognitive structures associated with group members.

How Models and Structures Get Used in Research

Verbal Models

Models of cultural knowledge systems and cultural models are not only goals of analysis, but can also (even when tentative, partial, or informal) play a useful heuristic role in research and a useful summarizing and organizing role in ethnographic reporting. Tentative and preliminary work on characterizing, for example, American student cultural models relating to love and marriage has played an important role in helping researchers to conceptualize empirical issues. These may include presentation of self, positively or negatively valued profiles or role instantiations, senses of means–ends connections, participant vs. observer perspective effects, the logic of reasoning about causality, morality, and inferential evidence, and so forth. By trying to organize their interview findings and behavioral observations into functioning agent-based (i.e. actor-oriented) models (even if still only loose verbal characterizations of such models), researchers have been led to consider questions and interrelationships that would not have occurred in more traditional ethnographic approaches.

Similarly, from the perspective of more abstract cultural descriptions, even merely verbal attempts at framing cultural categories, structures, and structural relations in terms of how native users see and reason about them (as in Frake's description of Subanun religious behavior) enable a much more coherent approach to cultural functioning than do more traditional overviews.

Formal (Explicit) Models

The next step up from verbal models is the construction of formally precise models. These can show not just classifications and strong logical entailments, but also "native" reasoning about the likely import of evidence relative to competing claims, "native" presuppositions about goals and motivations, and so forth, as in Hutchins' 1980 study of Trobriand litigation. Such explicit models allow researchers to evaluate empirically their effectiveness at accounting for data (actions, decisions, justifications of action, etc.). They allow the design of indirect psychological tests (of the sort used by Romney and D'Andrade to evaluate proposed models of kinterm systems of cultural knowledge). And they enable experimentation with realistic possible empirical situations that have not (yet) been observed but about which informants can be asked.

Formal Computational Models

Formal computer models—that is, formal models that have been implemented in computer programs, which then have been actually run—have been used in several different ways in the study of collective cognition. One of these ways is to try to model some worked out chunk of the world, including not only the relevant cognition but also the physical and social world on which the cognition is working. An example is Schank and Abelson's 1977 modeling of conversations about restaurants (including aspects that depended on knowledge of the physical world, the cultural organization of different kinds of restaurants, necessary and optional activities, and so forth); Read, in a 1998 article in the electronic *Journal of Artificial Societies and Social Simulation*, offered another example based on birth spacing decisions and marriage patterns among the !Kung san, a hunter–gatherer group in southern Africa. Other variants include attempts to model the full details of specific traffic flow patterns in specific big cities. Such models can, as in the traffic flow models, provide platforms for systematic experimentation with the effects of different arrangements, different motivations and attitudes, and so forth. They are usually too heterogeneous to constitute any coherent modeling of an actual structure. The restaurant model was systematically constructed on clear principles, knowledge structures, and reasoning processes, and so did constitute a test of the adequacy (though not the necessity) of those principles, structures, and processes for producing the behavior in question. But the complexities of interactions among simulation elements make experimentation on specific mechanisms tricky, certainly for those outside of the study group. Both kinds of simulations require major efforts by large teams, and so are not easily embarked on, nor easily criticized by outsiders.

A variant is the simulation of a single frame within which actors operate, as in Plattner's simulation of stall operation in St. Louis' Soulard market. The simulation is straightforward enough and simple enough that outsiders can consider and evaluate its actual operations, and it has a clear behavioral target that it is trying to match (the pricing decisions of stall operators). Plattner's example additionally illustrates three other important uses of such computer models. First, by bringing his informants into the development process—by trying versions out on them—he was able to use both early successes and early failures as extended ethnographic techniques for helping to raise to consciousness (both informant consciousness and researcher's consciousness) previously unrecognized aspects of the behavior being studied. Second, the developed model, once properly calibrated and accurate, became an important ethnographic tool by allowing Plattner to stop the action at key moments to discuss with informants what was going through their minds at the time, which was impossible in the hurly-burly of actual activity during active actual market operations (and which were lost from memory by the time things were quiet enough for interviews and conversations) and to experiment with novel market conditions. Third, the developed model has served as a valuable teaching tool, enabling students to get hands-on experience regarding the operation of market systems, including both the principles that drive them and the cognitive pressures that shape actor performance in them. This simulation was simple enough for one person to develop and straightforward enough that it could be examined and understood by potential critics and borrowers.

Another variant of the simulation idea involves simulating an analytic procedure used by anthropologists to make inferences from their data. In this case, the goal is to determine how well defined and complete is the given procedure, to raise to consciousness (and then include) any parts of the procedure that the analyst appears to rely on but that are not in the overt procedure, to discover any gaps in the procedure, and to look for improvements or shortcuts. An example of such a simulation was Kronenfeld's 1976 computer implementation of Romney's procedures for implementing Lounsbury's approach to the analysis of kinship terminological systems.

A very different kind of simulation involves a focus not on an output situation but on some particular (simple) mechanism. The goal is not to replicate any rich or full "reality" for some ethnographic data set, but only to implement some proposed mechanism in the context of that data set. How much of the target "reality" the given mechanism can produce can then be seen without added assumptions or mechanisms. An example of such a simulation is the 1993 *Journal of Quantitative Anthropology* article by Kronenfeld and Kaus, in which a set of computer "critters," created within a space that contained "food," were allowed to move randomly while "searching for food"; they consumed food they landed on. Parameter values included how far they could "see" food, how fast they could move, whether they could tell if another "critter" saw food, and whether they each were tied by a "leash" to the rest of the flock. One goal was to see whether a bunch of separate, independent "agents," each acting on its own, but each responding to the behavior of others (a feedback mechanism), could produce a system that clearly exhibited Durkheimian "emergent properties." A parallel goal was to evaluate the foraging effects (efficiency of cleaning out the environment, distribution of food consumption across the population, etc.) of different food distributions and different combinations of the other parameters, especially the "leash" parameter that produced the emergent system.

Algebraic Models

For systems that are well understood, and for which variability and systematicity have been well explored, the possibility arises of producing algebraic models with axioms that are clear entities and operations, and for which different ethnographic examples can be derived from such axioms. Such models are rare in anthropology, but have been constructed at least for kinship terminological systems (as in the different though not deeply dissimilar systems of Gould and Read and Lehman). Algebraic representations of other systems of cultural knowledge are perhaps in the offing However, our understanding of cultural models seems still too rudimentary for such; for these, the logically looser, though still explicit, approach involved in experimental computer modeling seems much more likely to be useful.

Conclusion

Cognitive research methods offer a particularly useful approach to an understanding of the nature of culture (and thus of society) and how it works. But such usefulness will depend on significant improvements both in our empirical knowledge of cultural models and in our ability to formally represent this knowledge. Agent-based computational models seem to offer one very promising method for addressing such goals. Our understanding of how cultural systems change and adapt will benefit from further study of the interaction of individual cognitive properties (including capabilities, constraints, mode of operation, and so forth) with shared cognitive structures (including cultural knowledge systems, cultural models, and whatever other kinds of shared cognitive structures future work may turn up).

See Also the Following Articles

Clustering • Cultural Consensus Model • Ethnography • Factor Analysis • Multidimensional Scaling (MDS)

Further Reading

Berlin, B. (1992). *Ethnobiological Classification.* Princeton University Press, Princeton, New Jersey.

Berlin, B., and Kay, P. (1969). *Basic Color Terms: Their Universality and Evolution.* University of California Press, Berkeley.

Bernard, H. R. (2002). *Research Methods in Anthropology: Qualitative and Quantitative Approaches.* Altamira Press, Walnut Creek, California.

D'Andrade, R. G. (1995). *The Development of Cognitive Anthropology.* Cambridge University Press, Cambridge.

Gladwin, C. H. (guest ed.). (1984). Frontiers in hierarchical decision modeling (1984). *Human Org.* **43**(No. 3), special issue.

Gould, S. H. (2000). *A New System for the Formal Analysis of Kinship.* University Press of America, Lanham, Maryland.

Greenberg, J. H. (1966). *Language Universals.* Mouton, The Hague.

Greenberg, J. H. (1968). *Anthropological Linguistics: An Introduction.* Random House, New York.

Hutchins, E. (1980). *Culture and Inference: A Trobriand Case Study.* Harvard University Press, Cambridge.

Kronenfeld, D. B. (1985). Numerical taxonomy: Old techniques and new assumptions. *Curr. Anthropol.* **26,** 21–41.

Kronenfeld, D. B. (1996). *Plastic Glasses and Church Fathers.* Oxford University Press, New York.

Kronenfeld, D. B. (guest ed.). (2001). Kinship. *Anthropol. Theory* **1**(No. 2), special issue.

Randall, R. A. (1985). Steps toward an ethnosemantics of verbs: Complex fishing techniques and the "unsaid" in listener identification. In *Directions in Cognitive Anthropology* (J. W. D. Dougherty, ed.), pp. 249–268. University of Illinois Press, Urbana.

Romney, A. K., Weller, S., and Batchelder, W. (1986). Culture and consensus: A theory of culture and informant accuracy. *Am. Anthropol.* **88,** 313–338.

Schank, R., and Abelson, R. (1977). *Scripts, Plans, Goals and Understanding: An Inquiry into Human Knowledge Structures.* Lawrence Erlbaum Assoc., Hillsdale, New Jersey.

Shepard, R. N., Romney, A. K., and Nerlove, S. (eds.) (1972) *Multidimensional Scaling: Theory and Applications in the Behavioral Sciences*, Vol. II. Seminar Press, New York.

Tyler, S. A. (ed.) (1969). *Cognitive Anthropology.* Holt, Rinehart and Winston, New York.

Wasserman, S., and Faust, K. (1994). *Social Network Analysis: Methods and Applications.* Cambridge University Press, Cambridge.

Commensuration

Mitchell L. Stevens
New York University, New York, USA

Wendy Nelson Espeland
Northwestern University, Evanston, Illinois, USA

Glossary

commensuration The comparison of different objects, attributes, or people according to a common metric.

cost-benefit analyses Decision-making techniques in which the benefits and costs associated with a course of action are calculated.

incommensurable Something that is not amenable to any common measurement; something unique, incomparable.

metric Any standard of measurement.

Commensuration is the expression or measurement of different entities according to a common metric. Utility, price, and cost-benefit ratios are prominent examples, but commensuration encompasses all human efforts to express value quantitatively. Commensuration entails using numbers to create relations between things, where difference is expressed as magnitude, as a matter of more or less rather than of kind. The quantitative relationships that commensuration accomplishes create new distinctions as they eliminate old ones. The logic of commensuration is built into virtually all facets of government and economic practice as well as scientific inquiry. Censuses, financial instruments such as stocks and futures, surveys, scales, and rankings all are instances of commensuration.

Theories of Commensuration

The promise and limits of commensuration have engaged thinkers since ancient times. According to Martha Nussbaum, the relationship between measurement and control, counting and knowing, has deep roots in Greek thinking about cognition.

Platonic ethics understands commensuration as essential to the determination of the "Good," which was best achieved by making all values commensurate and then prioritizing them in order to make the wisest choices. Plato believed that commensuration could simplify even the most complex ethical questions, while at the same time eliminating biases of passion from decision making. Aristotle took a contrary view, arguing that the values that make up a good human life are practical, plural, and not reducible to a common standard. For Aristotle, an ethical life requires that we attend to the distinctiveness of values, to particular cases over general rules. Living well depends on appreciating the intrinsic value of different kinds of commitments, but doing so leaves us more vulnerable to luck and passion. For Aristotle, this is the sacrifice that living in a far richer world requires.

Commensuration is a central theme in Max Weber's investigations of rationalization, which echo the dialog between Plato and Aristotle on the virtues and threat of reason rooted in calculation. For Weber, the expanding role of calculation as a strategy to manage uncertainty and make predictions was a central feature of Western rationalism and crucial for the development of capitalism. Decision making based on numbers, rather than duty, magic, or custom, represented a radically new orientation toward business. Weber argued that the development of capital accounting depersonalized business relations and fostered an objective stance toward business choices. Weber's emphasis on calculation is grounded in the technical advantage it confers to those who use it. Those who calculate more accurately or more thoroughly will outcompete those who calculate less well or less often.

The cash nexus is perhaps the most ubiquitous instance of commensuration. The rise of universal currencies both fascinated and worried many critics of modernity, who repeatedly described the relationships between money's ability to commensurate all values and human alienation. For Karl Marx, the cash nexus facilitated the appropriation of labor by capitalists by severing the natural relationship between workers and the products of their labors. For Georg Simmel, the universality of monetary valuation contributed to "the calculating character of modern times," in which people become obsessed with "measuring, weighing and calculating" while their emotional faculties wither.

More recently, rational choice theory in its various guises (game theory and utility theory are prominent examples) extends the Platonic project. Rational choice theory models all facets of human behavior on the presumption that individuals and groups calibrate their preferences and choose courses of action which maximize self-interested outcomes. Rational choice frameworks are appealing for their analytic clarity and for their generality. Scholars such as Gary Becker and Richard Posner, for example, have brilliantly applied the premise that people make choices on the basis of rational calculation to such intimate questions has how people choose mates and opt to have children. But other scholars have taken more an Aristotelian view, citing the wealth of historical and ethnographic evidence demonstrating that people often value things (such as lovers, children, or a native country) because of their singularity—that is, in qualitative rather than quantitative terms.

Commensuration as a Practical Accomplishment

Commensuration is not inevitable. It typically requires considerable human effort, political power, and large resource outlays to accomplish. The discipline, coordination, and technical expertise that commensuration demands often take a long time to establish. This partly explains why commensuration thrives in bureaucracies. Because commensuration obscures distinctive characteristics, it is also a powerful strategy for producing the impersonal authority that is the hallmark of bureaucracies. Before metrics can be used they must be invented, and some instances of their creation stand among the most enduring and consequential artifacts of human civilization. Money economies are prominent examples.

The recent transition of many European Union (EU) nations to a common currency aptly demonstrates the amount of effort required integrate disparate value systems according to a common metric. The move to the euro was in the planning stages for years and took enormous political effort to assure compliance throughout the EU. Literally all components of economic life on continental Europe had to be recalibrated to the new currency, a truly massive organizational feat. Media stories about the transition have ranged from the euro's affect on global financial markets to the Herculean task of reprogramming thousands automated teller machines, to the efforts of social workers to teach blind consumers the distinctive feel of the new bills and coins.

The rise of cost-benefit analysis in U.S. public policy provides other examples of the work commensuration requires. As Theodore Porter demonstrates, even before the Flood Control Act of 1936, when federal law first required that the benefits of federally subsidized water projects exceed their costs, bureaucracies were using cost-benefit analysis. Spurred by law and conflict, agencies invested more heavily in development of cost-benefit analysis; over time, the procedures were standardized, regulated, and eventually incorporated into economic theory. Attendant professional groups of econometricians, statisticians, and decision theorists emerged to do the job of measuring and comparing the value of such disparate objects as riparian habitats, natural vistas, flood control, Indian land claims, and revenue. Commensurative expertise became institutionalized as distinctive careers and elaborate professional industries. As a commensuration strategy, the reach of cost-benefit analysis extended far beyond decision making. It shaped what information was incorporated, how internal units interacted, relations with other agencies and with constituents, and even the terms under which government projects could be challenged or supported.

Commensuration and the Constitution of Social Things

Commensuration often creates what it purports merely to measure. But the constitutive power of commensuration is potentially threatening because its authority often hinges on its claims to be a neutral measure of existing properties. Commensuration is especially good at creating new types of people. As Ian Hacking shows, enumeration demands classification; creating new categories of individuals can fundamentally affect how we understand ourselves and others. Governments typically are key players in this creative process. Porter has noted, for example, how census officials, survey researchers, and activists have over time created "Hispanics" by aggregating people of Puerto Rican, Mexican, Cuban, Iberian, and Central and South American descent. Despite the vast cultural and historical differences represented by the peoples in this aggregate, the designation "Hispanic" has shaped the self-understanding, collective memory, and politics of millions of Americans.

Some of our most basic social units are products of commensuration. John Meyer and his colleagues have documented how the production of elaborate censuses, health-and-welfare statistics, and economic output measures do much to constitute the very idea of the modern nation-state. The global spread of standardized methods for producing these statistics has helped transform subjects into citizens and disparate peoples into comparable political entities. National measures of such attributes as infant mortality, literacy, telephone service, and GDP—easily comparable with the figures of other countries—often serve as proxies for the nation itself in global conferences and associations. Provided it has the symbolic trappings to go along with them (a flag, an anthem, a traditional costume, and a written national history), in the milieu of global diplomacy the nation *is* its numbers. Whether what emerges from commensuration is "the best colleges," "the average voter," "national productivity," or "developing economies," commensuration creates fateful categories that become embedded in institutions and acquire powerful constituencies.

Incommensurables

Incommensurables are things that are regarded as unique in ways that make them inimical to quantitative valuation. Children are perhaps the most prominent example. Feminist legal scholars have made articulate arguments against the development of markets in children and have raised concern about the rise of quasimarkets in international adoption, in which hopeful parents pay large sums to intermediate firms for the transfer of infants across national borders. Central to the feminist concern is the notion that the singular value of human life is eroded when it meets the cash nexus too directly. How to manage adoptions in a manner that sufficiently honors human integrity, alongside very real financial incentives for biological parents and the practical organizational costs of adoption transactions, remains a controversial legal and ethical question.

Sometimes people invest such singular value in particular objects that to commensurate them is tantamount to destroying them. Joseph Raz calls such objects "constitutive incommensurables." Wendy Espeland argues that for the Yavapai Indians of the U.S. Southwest, land is a constitutive incommensurable. When federal agents sought to purchase Yavapai land for a large water reclamation project, the Indians argued that their land was a part of their identity as Yavapai and so should not be the object of commensuration. In a more recent example, several member countries of the EU have refused to adopt the euro, citing the intimate relationship between national currency and national identity. These cases reveal the paradoxical way in which commensuration systems themselves can serve as constitutive incommensurables when they are imbued with singular meaning.

Commensuration Politics

Commensuration is rarely a politically neutral process because it transgresses cultural boundaries and reconfigures values in ways that variably privilege different parties. The long-standing legal debate over comparable worth pay policies, in which the pay scales of predominantly female occupations are rendered commensurate with predominantly male jobs, is a clear example. Proponents of comparable worth argue that women are systematically disadvantaged by a labor market that channels them into occupations that pay less than ostensibly equivalent jobs that are predominantly male. But the comparable worth movement has been stymied by two formidable obstacles: the expense to employers of adjusting female pay scales upward and the stubborn cultural presumption that the jobs men and women do are essentially different.

Another broad instance of commensuration politics involves the national debate over the role of standardized tests in college admissions. College entrance exams such as the SAT purport to commensurate all college-bound students with a common yardstick of college readiness. SAT scores are closely correlated with race, however. Asians have the highest average scores and African-Americans the lowest, with those of Whites and Hispanics in between. SAT scores also vary by social class. These unsettling relations are hard to reconcile with those who interpret the test as a measure of individual merit. At issue in the debates over comparable worth and the validity of test scores is the quintessential American question of how to commensurate opportunity—a political and ethical problem as well as a technical one.

Commensuration is so ubiquitous, we often fail to notice it. Yet commensuration is crucial for how we implement our most cherished ideals. Values expressed through commensuration are often associated with precision, objectivity, and rationality. Democracy has become synonymous with voting and polls. Standardized tests identify merit, assure competence, and hold educators accountable. Cost-benefit analyses evaluate efficiency. Risk assessments reassure us about uncertain futures. As a vehicle for assembling and sorting information, commensuration shapes what we attend to, simplifies cognition, and makes a complicated world seem more amenable to our control.

See Also the Following Articles

Aristotle • Cost–Benefit Analysis • Weber, Max

Further Reading

Anderson, E. (1993). *Value in Ethics and Economics.* Harvard University Press, Cambridge, MA.

Carruthers, B. G., and Stinchcombe, A. L. (1999). The social structure of liquidity: Flexibility, markets, and states. *Theory Soc.* **28,** 353–382.

Desrosieres, A. (1998). *The Politics of Large Numbers: A History of Statistical Reasoning.* Trans. C. Nash. Harvard University Press, Cambridge, MA.

Espeland, W. N. (2001). Commensuration and cognition. *Culture in Mind* (K. Cerullo, ed.), pp. 63–88. Routledge, New York.

Espeland, W. N., and Stevens, M. L. (1998). Commensuration as a social process. *Annu. Rev. Sociol.* **24,** 313–343.

Hacking, I. (1990). *The Taming of Chance.* Cambridge University Press, Cambridge, UK.

Lemann, N. (1999). *The Big Test.* Farrar, Straus and Giroux, New York.

Nussbaum, M. C. (1984). Plato on commensurability and desire. *Proc. Aristotelian Soc.* **58**(Suppl.), 55–80.

Porter, T. M. (1986). *The Rise of Statistical Thinking, 1820–1900.* Princeton University Press, Princeton, NJ.

Porter, T. M. (1995). *Trust in Numbers.* Princeton University Press, Princeton, NJ.

Stigler, S. M. (1990). *The History of Statistics: The Measurement of Uncertainty before 1900.* Harvard University Press, Cambridge, MA.

Ventresca, M. J. (1995). When states count: Institutional and political dynamics in modern census establishment, 1800–1993. Ph.D. dissertation, Stanford University, Stanford, CA.

Communication

Ayo Oyeleye
University of Central England in Birmingham, Birmingham, United Kingdom

Glossary

communication Definitions vary according to theoretical framework and focus. Media theorist George Gerbner defined the term as "social interaction through messages."

decoding The process of interpreting and making sense of the nature of messages.

discourse analysis A method for analyzing the content of mass communication; seeks to explain the ways that mass media texts are used to convey power and ideology to readers or audiences.

encoding The process of communicating through the use of codes (aural, visual, etc.) that are deemed appropriate for the objectives of the sender of a message.

group dynamics The scientific study of the behavior and interactions of people in groups.

interaction The mutual relations between people in a social context.

sociogram A chart used for illustrating the interrelations among people in groups.

sociometry A technique for identifying the structure of ties in a group based on affective interaction, as opposed to role expectations.

The term communication covers a very broad range of concepts concerned with interactions, and an enormous amount of research activity and interest is devoted to the study of the nature of communication. The focus here is the study of human communication in terms of levels of communication. This approach is useful for delineating types of communication as well as for mapping the field in terms of the subject focus and the theoretical and methodological applications entailed. Measurement and analysis of human communication encompass both scientific and humanistic traditions of inquiry and a wide range of research methods, including laboratory experiments, surveys, content analyses, semiology, discourse analyses, hermeneutics, and ethnography.

Introduction

The origin of the word "communication" has been traced back to the Latin word *communicare*, which means "to impart," i.e., to share with or to make common such things as knowledge, experience, hope, vision, thought, opinion, feeling, and belief. This historical link can be seen in the way that many contemporary dictionaries define the words "communicate" and "communication." Central to the various definitions are expressions such as "to share," "to make known," "to bestow," or "to reveal," thus conveying the concepts of imparting information and having something in common with another being. In communication studies, however the word takes on a rather more complex guise and, as such, it is not easy to offer a single definition that will encompass the various perspectives that communication scholars hold on the concept. Indeed, scholars such as J. Corner and J. Hawthorn argue that such a task is neither necessary nor desirable. They contend that the study of communication should be undertaken by reference to its essential characteristics as constituted by a variety of ideas and methods in the arts and social science disciplines. The often conflicting and contentious ideas about the nature of communication must not be seen as a drawback. Rather, they should usefully encourage students of communication to develop a critical awareness of the relative status of all contending ideas about the nature of the subject, while also engendering a sense of challenge to participate in the ongoing efforts to explore and enunciate the nature and elements of communication.

Defining Communication

Over the years, communication scholars have developed a number of definitions for communication that tend to reflect the particular perspective from which they are working. Such definitions can serve the useful purpose of providing a starting point for framing inquiries into some aspect of communication, or they can show the perspective from which scholars are studying communication. A definition of communication as framed by Berger and Chaffee, for example, inscribes it within the tradition of scientific inquiry thus: "Communication science seeks to understand the production, processing, and effects of symbol and signal systems by developing testable theories, containing lawful generalizations, that explain phenomena associated with production, processing, and effects."

Not all communication concerns or inquiries fall within this rubric, however, and as McQuail has noted, the definition represents only one of several models of inquiry into communication—an empirical, quantitative, and behavioral paradigm. In order to make some sense out of the fragmentation and coalescence that have characterized the development of communication as a field of studies, especially from the 1960s, scholars have continued to classify communication studies according to theoretical approaches, methods of inquiries, levels of communication, and so on. For instance, Sven Windahl and Benno Signitzer have identified two broad approaches to the definition of communication. There is a transmission approach whereby communication involves a sender/message/channel/receiver model. Proponents of this approach, which is also referred to as a linear model, attempt to show how an idea, knowledge, emotion, or vision is transferred from one person to another. Thus, George and Achilles Theodorson define communication as the "transmission of information, ideas, attitudes, or emotion from one person or groups to another (or others) primarily through symbols."

The second approach described by Windahl and Signitzer is one characterized by "mutuality" and "shared perceptions." This approach is referred to variously as the interactional, ritual, or humanistic model. In this approach, there is recognition that communication entails the active engagement of both the communicator and the receiver. Indeed, the proponents of this approach prefer to blur the distinctions between the roles of the communicator and the receiver of messages, stressing instead the interchangeable nature of both roles. In this regard, Gerbner defined communication as "social interaction through messages." Similarly, Wilbur Schramm, in a later review of his earlier view of communication, offers this transactional definition: "Communication is now seen as a transaction in which both parties are active. The parties are not necessarily equally active—that is more likely in the case of interpersonal communication, but less so in the case of mass media and their audiences—but to both parties the transaction is in some way functional. It meets a need or provides a gratification. To a greater or lesser degree information flows both ways." Another author has described a ritual model as one in which words and phrases such as "sharing," "participation," "association," "fellowship," and "the possession of a common faith" are linked with communication. A ritual view of communication is concerned with its role in the maintenance of society in time, rather than with the extension of messages in space.

These two broad perspectives on communication are crucial in their implications for framing the distinctive ways that scholars approach the study of communication, the sorts of questions that they pose for research exploration, and the methods used in their inquiries into the nature of communication.

The Process of Communication

From the early attempts to develop and formalize the study of human communication, scholars have conceptualized it as a process. The idea of communication as a process has come to be seen by many scholars as a crucial part of its definition. A process is an activity that has no beginning or end. It is an endless continuum with only a forward motion. That is, every new act of communication is a further development on that which it precedes. For example, news stories, by definition, are reports on new occurrences, but in many cases they are also reports of developments on previous accounts of an event. Every new account takes the original story further, to newer resolutions or developments. Likewise, in interpersonal relationships, people are always developing newer acts of communication, even when the conversation is about past events or conversations. Conversations always have a history and rarely begin from scratch. A common maxim for exploring this notion is "people cannot not communicate." They cannot "uncommunicate" either. The very attempt to not say something in a given social context does actually communicate something—a limited knowledge of the topic, a lack of interest, shyness, dislike, defiance, and so on. There is a useful Yoruba (Western Nigeria) saying that captures this forward and irreversible motion of communication so well: "A word is like an egg. Once broken, it cannot be put back together again!"

Not all communication scholars like the idea of describing communication as a process, however. Their main objection is that this view renders communication a mere product of causality, which therefore rules out the possibility of choice. Communication can be the result of both intentional and unintentional actions. Heath and Bryant have contended that the key to understanding communication does not lie in attempts to determine whether communication is intentional or unintentional, but in recognizing that communication is an endless process. One implication of seeing communication as a process is that individual events occur over time in a fairly but not totally predictable manner. Communication develops from a series of events that relate to one another for many reasons. These include causality, rule compliance, randomness, covariance, or strategic choices by each participant.

A process view of communication recognizes the twin properties of communication as a motion and an action. As motion, communication issues from linear causation, not from will or chance. As action, communication is the result of human deliberation and intentions. It is not difficult to understand these twin properties of communication if we look at our own experiences. Many human communication efforts are motivated by the need to participate in an ongoing process—at work, at home, at school, etc. This is the linear causality element of communication. Communication precedes us, it was around before we were born, and will still be there when we are gone. People participate in communication as a way of plugging into the stream of human history. Preexisting communication engenders further communication in a never-ending, forward motion. Communication is not, however, about some kind of preprogrammed reaction to events. It can also be random or unplanned. Many will recall the numerous occasions when they have said things they wish they had not said, or said things in a way that they did not intend. The extent to which communication is deliberate and intentional or spontaneous and unplanned is a key issue for scholars in all areas of communication research.

Levels of Communication

In the attempt to make sense of the expansive body of work that constitutes the communication field, a less contentious analytical approach is to distinguish between different levels of the communication process. This approach allows us to see the different communication processes involved at different levels. It also helps to map the field of human communication study in terms of the research concerns and focus, as well as the various concepts and theoretical and methodological traditions deployed for its study at each level. This explains why the study of human communication is characterized by a multidisciplinary mode of inquiry.

There are two broad categories of communication. The first concerns the locus of communication activity and the second concerns the number of people involved at any given time. The locus of communication is about whether communication takes place within a person (intrapersonal communication) or outside, i.e., between two or more people (interpersonal communication), or among a number of people linked by a form of technology (such as broadcasting) that enables the distribution of information to a large group (mass communication). When communication is classified according to the number of people that may be involved at any particular time, the individual or small groups or masses of people may be involved. The two broad categories (the locus of activity and the number of people involved) thus can be filtered into four levels of communication: intrapersonal, interpersonal, group, and mass communication.

Intrapersonal Communication

The study of intrapersonal communication involves attempts to understand how people make sense of the world around them and how this in turn impacts the way people react to the world around them. Thirteen properties have been proposed to be involved in the process of intrapersonal communication. These include perceptions, memories, experiences, feelings, interpretations, inferences, evaluations, attitudes, opinions, ideas, strategies, images, and states of consciousness. The study of intrapersonal communication draws on theoretical and methodological practices from cognitive, behavioral, and social psychology. Key questions that researchers working at this level of communication try to find answers to include how people's perceptions, feelings, and understanding affect their interaction with the world around them; how people respond to symbols; and how people store and retrieve information.

Communications scholars working at the intrapersonal level aim to understand the place of the individual in the communication process. Intrapersonal communication has been defined as "communication within the self, and of the self to the self." Communication begins and ends with the self. The individual is the basic unit of any social formation and, as such, there are important insights to be gained on the nature of human communication from understanding the role of the individual in this complex process. The self can be understood as composed of different elements. First, there is the inner self, which is made up of a number of elements such as self-perception, self-evaluation, and personality. Second, surrounding the inner self are other elements such as needs, which generate the drive to communicate with others and to interpret communications. Third, there is the element of cognition, which allows us to make sense of the external world and the communication coming from it. Because the self is a very dynamic entity that is in constant interaction with the external world, it has a fourth crucial element, a monitoring capacity that gauges the reactions of others to our communication, thus allowing us to modify our communication constantly in relation to the different contexts in which we find ourselves.

Intrapersonal communication can be said to entail two active elements, encoding and decoding. Encoding can be understood as the process by which an individual translates his/her thoughts into communicative signs (such as speech or writing) for others to interact with, or not. Decoding, by the same token, can be understood as the process of receiving signals from external sources and attempting to make sense of them.

Measurement of Intrapersonal Communication

Communication scholars working at this level are interested in finding answers to a number of questions about how communication takes place inside an individual, and how this has implications for wider concerns about human communication. The concern could be, for instance, about how individuals make sense of communication from others and what factors hamper or facilitate the process. Or it could be about understanding the factors that govern individual differences in their communicative competences.

Two fundamental properties of communication, impact and intersubjectivity, have been identified, and there has been an attempt to locate the place of the individual in the broader communication process. Impact is by far the most commonly associated property of communication. There is a huge interest, both academic and nonacademic, in the possible impact of communication (on an individual, on small or large groups of persons, on an organization, on a society, etc.). An act of communication does not necessarily guarantee an impact. Likewise, the impact of communication can range from none to total control. As such, it has been suggested that adequate accounts of human communication must identify the mechanisms that generate the degree of impact that one person's behavior has on another person's behavior or cognitive/emotive state. The contention is that such an account is necessary for communication scholars to be able to specify boundaries for their discipline.

Intersubjectivity is also an essential property of human communication. Intersubjectivity emerges out of the shared knowledge possessed by participants in a social interaction. It is based on common experience and communication. It is what makes communication between people possible, because it allows them to presume that there is a common perspective on how an event can be understood. Without the presumptions that come with intersubjectivity, communication will be frustrating or practically ineffective. In a similar vein, the existence of a shared knowledge among social actors affords them the opportunity to construct a common "world" of interconnected beliefs and inferences. Well-known communication phenomena such as coordination, coorientation, misunderstanding, emotional empathy, and identity negotiation are grounded in intersubjectivity. Because intersubjectivity exists in degrees, an adequate account of human communication must identify the mechanisms that generate degrees of intersubjectivity. Otherwise, communication scholars will be unable to explain problems associated with misunderstanding and its impact on relational definition, conflict, the sources of deception, and the lack of coordination. Conversely, by understanding the mechanisms that generate degrees of intersubjectivity, communication scholars are able to intervene and correct misunderstandings in social interactions. A good case in point is the application of social judgment theory to the study of real conflicts that have emerged from misunderstanding among social actors. By basing the method for this on an understanding of the mechanisms that generate degrees of intersubjectivity, it is possible to identify sources of misunderstanding as well as to explain the persistence of misunderstanding, even when one or both parties have sought to address the sources of that misunderstanding.

Approaches to Measuring Intrapersonal Communication

Communication scholars have developed several approaches to study communication problems. Three in particular—trait, transindividual, and cognitive/interpretive approaches—stand out for their potential for understanding the problems and measurements of intrapersonal communication.

Trait Approaches Trait approaches locate the core of communication in the individual and his/her predisposition to initiate action or to respond to behavior. Traits are understood as a stable predisposition to behavior, and, as such, trait approaches treat human beings as a complex of predispositions that are stable over long periods of time and over various contexts. Although traits are treated as constant and predictable, the behaviors they give rise to are often varied. The trait approach has been used widely to predict social behavior.

Transindividual Approaches These approaches take communication, particularly its regular features, as deriving from the evolving and ritualized practices of social aggregates such as dyads, groups, organizations, culture, and so on. Scholars working in these approaches tend to locate the center of communication away from the individual and place it instead on social collectives. They tend to place emphasis on the role that the context of communication plays in the communication process, rather than the individual. The transindividual approaches use context to explain communication behavior in two ways: behavioral contingency and conventionalized versions. In behavioral contingency, the research focus is on analyzing or measuring the interactions between individuals or among members of a group that is sufficiently stable to have a pattern. The emphasis is not on any attributes that the individuals bring to the interaction, but on the communicative acts that evolve from such interactions. The focus here is on analyzing how communication between individuals is contingent on the behavior of those individuals involved in an interaction. This approach entails the use of "relational analysis" that begins at the level of the dyad rather than at the level of the individual.

In the conventionalized versions approach, just as in the behavioral contingency approach, emphasis is on the context of communication. In this approach, emphasis is on the shared attributes of members of a linguistic community, such as knowledge of contexts, knowledge of communicative forms, and knowledge of the appropriate interpretations for them. The assumption of a communal pull of cultural resources for communicating and making sense of the world taken by this approach leads scholars away from focusing on the individual and instead, to focusing on the context of interaction. If all members of a linguistic community are assumed to share a common knowledge of communicative competence and performance, then they are culturally interchangeable. These two models within the transindividual approaches thus place emphasis on the nature of human communication as social interaction. However, these models are not very good at explaining the extent to which a message might impact on another person's behavior or state of mind, because they fail to identify the mechanisms by which such impact might occur. When such attempts have been made, they reveal the need to recognize the role of the individual in the communication process.

Cognitive/Interpretive Approaches Like the trait approaches, the cognitive/interpretive approaches are more focused on the role of the individual in the communication process. Trait approaches do this by analyzing the predispositions and peculiarities of individuals that govern the initiation of or reaction to communication. By contrast, the cognitive approaches focus on individual differences in cognitive structures that lead to differences in message interpretations and behaviors. As such, the emphasis of the cognitive approaches is on the innate, psychological processes that individuals deploy to tasks of interpretation and production of messages. The cognitive/interpretive approaches attempt to account for how individuals react subjectively to messages and behaviors. They seek to explain the degree of competences that individuals have in social interactions involving message acquisitions, such as how they tease out information from messages, how they retain and transform such information, and how they act on it.

A method of research commonly used in this area of work is discourse processing. This seeks to explain the cognitive processes and knowledge structures that individuals use to interpret and produce texts. This research method seeks to explore the ways that people in a social interaction accommodate each other's communication competences through adaptive techniques in their production and interpretation of messages. There are many approaches to the study of discourse, and the term has had a checkered history in terms of how it is defined and used in academic disciplines. Suffice it to note here that to the extent that discourse processing entails the study of the psychological processes that people deploy to communicative interactions, it can be said to be rooted in the level of intrapersonal communication. That is not to say, however, that the method of discourse processing treats messages as solely governed by psychological processes, because a considerable amount of attention is also paid to contextual factors. Work in discourse processing shows how intrapersonal communication involves a complex cognitive system that underpins the ability to interpret and produce messages in social interactions. Although much communication is social and interactional, an explanation of the mechanisms by which the twin essential elements of communication, impact and intersubjectivity, take place must incorporate an understanding of the processes that occur at the intrapersonal level (see Fig. 1).

Interpersonal Communication

Following from the work of Herbert Mead, in 1934, which showed that communication is central to the capacity of

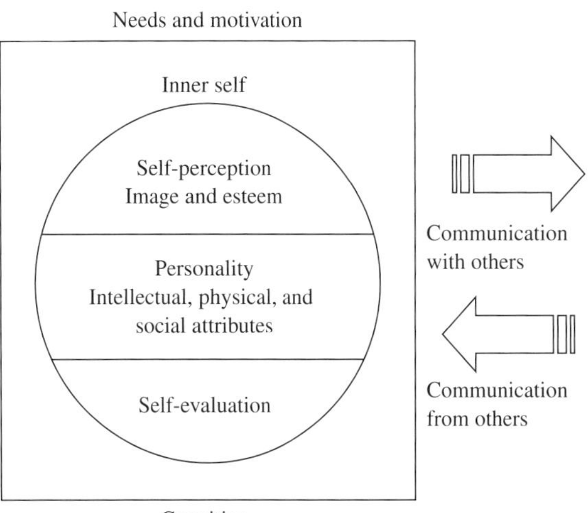

Figure 1 A model of the intrapersonal communication process.

people to grow in personality and relationships, scholars have been interested in the analysis of interpersonal communication. At the heart of the inquiry into the subject of interpersonal communication is the interest in the quality of relationships among people—loves, family, couples, peer groups, work mates, and so on. Heath and Bryant have identified four central themes among the broad range of topics that research into interpersonal communication addresses. They are (1) quality of relationships, (2) social conflict, (3) accuracy with which people understand one another, and (4) communication planning and competence. The study of interpersonal communication aims, among other concerns, to determine the variables that account for the differences in relationships. Heath and Bryant defined interpersonal communication as a "dyadic interaction in which people negotiate relationships by using communication styles and strategies that become personally meaningful as the persons involved attempt to reduce uncertainty (about themselves, their partners, and their relationships), to be self-efficacious, and to maximize rewards through interaction." They further observed that when the action or words of one person has an effect on another person, interpersonal communication can be said to have taken place.

There are two major perspectives on the motive behind interpersonal communications and relationships: uncertainty reduction and rules-based approach. Uncertainty reduction involves attempts to develop an understanding of other people, and of ourselves, by seeking and sharing information that will enhance our intelligence. Such intelligence also includes an understanding of (or a best estimate of) the communication competence of the parties involved in a relationship. In this vein, it has been pointed out that psychology, rather than sociology or culture, is the main character of interpersonal communication. By this is meant that the knowledge that people have of each other derives mainly from experiencing each other's behavior. As such, in order to understand the nature of interpersonal communication, research must examine the impacts of what people say and do during interaction, and not focus solely on the content of conversations. When people understand interactions and the relationship variables that affect their quality, they may be better able to predict how to influence relationships and to make them more rewarding. The underlying assumption of this perspective on interpersonal relationship is that it is primarily motivated by a need to reduce uncertainty in any given interaction.

By contrast, there is a rules-based approach in which participants are motivated to follow a mutually agreed interactional convention in order to achieve desirable communication outcomes. However, even in this approach, participants often break the rules in order to gain rewards, thus suggesting that perhaps uncertainty reduction is a stronger motivation for people during interpersonal communication.

Rosengren has suggested that the study of interpersonal communication must involve at least two lines of inquiry—a study of its general characteristics and how it varies according to the other known variables that come into play. He identified seven key variables: age, gender, personality, education, occupation, social class, and nationality. These variables often overlap and work in combination to influence the types of roles that people play in social interactions.

Measurement of Interpersonal Communication

Interpersonal communication research is based on the assumption that the nature of interaction between social actors derives from their mutual perceptions of words and actions. Interpersonal communication thus entails all behavior, verbal and nonverbal, that takes place during interaction. The key element in interpersonal communication is interpersonal relationship and the central focus of study in interpersonal relationship is the nature and quality of interaction between participants. Interaction is a process that develops over time and entails practices such as turn-taking, interruptions, topic shifts, disclosures, and confirmations. The quality of interaction in a given situation may be enhanced or hampered by variables such as complementarity (a reciprocal interaction in which the actions and words of one interactant suit or help to complete those of the other), divergence (whereby interaction orientates toward separate directions), convergence (whereby interaction orientates toward coming together), compensation (whereby interaction involves interactants filling in gaps, or making up for the failings of the others).

Key among the many concerns of researchers working at the level of interpersonal communication are attempts to understand the effect of the aforementioned variables on interactions and on interpersonal communications, and how each variable may enhance or hinder relationships. Some researchers focus on matters of social cognition and seek to understand the way people develop a knowledge of one another, as well as the level of communication competence that people bring to relationships and how this impacts on the quality of relationship that develops.

Group Communication

Research into the study of group influence on human behavior can be traced back to the 1950s through the work of the social psychologist Muzafer Sherif. Another social psychologist, Solomon Asch, worked on the pressures and conformity that the group can exert on individuals. A major strand of the work in group communication is that associated with Kurt Lewin and his study of group dynamics. Also, in the 1940s, Paul Lazarsfeld and his colleagues researched the influence of the group on the way that people form political attitudes and make voting decisions.

Severin and Tankard have identified three significant types of groups, primary, reference, and casual. A primary group usually comprises two or more persons in a long-standing relationship that also involves a close, face-to-face interaction. Examples of such primary groups are families, religious/social groups, work groups, teams, fraternities, classroom cohorts, military units, and so on. A reference group is a standard-bearer for the person who has so associated with such a group. A person will not necessarily belong to such a group but would have identified with the group because of some qualities, values, or principles that the group possesses, or that the person believes the group possesses. A casual group offers the loosest form of association, involving usually a grouping of people who have come together in pursuit of similar goals. Such goals may include taking a bus ride, being in an elevator, or being a spectator at a sporting event. Membership in a casual group is usually by chance, and members seldom think of themselves as belonging to any such group.

Communication processes at the level of the group are about relationships rather than attributes. The measure of communication at the group level focuses not on individual attributes, but on the relationships that emerge from the interactions of two or more people. At the heart of studies on group communication is the age-old belief that human beings are social animals, and, as such, are strongly influenced by the groups to which they belong. This belief has been reinforced by modern psychology by showing that our attitudes, behaviors, and perceptions are often strongly influenced by other people. The likelihood of being influenced by other people depends on the kind of relationship we have with those other people. As social animals, people tend to live, work, and play in groups, and it is those groups to which we belong that are more likely to influence us the most. It must be clear from the onset, therefore, that research into group communication is based on the study of relationships.

The central research activity on group communication concerns observing and analyzing what goes on in groups and how these relationships affect the nature of communication in a group. Four conceptual properties that define the nature of relationships in group communication have been identified. First is the number of people involved in the relation. The smallest number of people that can constitute a group is two. This is known as the dyad, and such a relation is referred to as dyadic. A group made up of three people is a triad, and when a communication relation involves three people, it is triadic. Although higher order relations are possible, they are rarely studied in network research. Importantly, the number of people involved in the relationship is not the same as the entire number of people that make up a group or network.

Strength or intensity of relations is the second conceptual property. Strength is the amount of interaction between the people involved in group communication. Traditionally this is measured by a binary method defined basically in terms of "present" or "absent." A recent development, however, recognizes the need to measure strength of relations in terms of the variability in the amount of interaction between pairs of people.

The third property of relations is symmetry and the fourth property of relations is transitivity. Symmetry refers to the direction of communication flow in relationships. A symmetric flow occurs when communication is equal between the people involved. There are situations when the flow of communication may be coming from only one source, or when it may be one-sided and thus asymmetric. Transitivity describes different possibilities of relationships that can occur in a group situation (see Fig. 2). In the first case, if person A is related to person B and person B is related to person C, then, by implication, person A is also related to person C. In this scenario, the relation between person A and person C is, by implication, through the relations of person A to person B, and person B to person C. In an intransitive relation, person A communicates with person B and person B communicates with person C, but person A is not, by implication, in communication with person C.

Rosengren also described the complexity that develops in groups, as the size of the group increases, by comparing a dyad to a triad. He noted that whereas in absolute terms the difference between the two is quantitatively small (being just one), in relative terms a triad is 50% larger than a dyad. This difference is qualitatively significant because a triad makes possible the formation of three coalitions within the group. This is illustrated with a scenario in which one member in a group lets slip to outsiders a secret shared by the group. In a dyad, it would be easy for both members to know who had leaked the secret, because it can only be one or the other member of

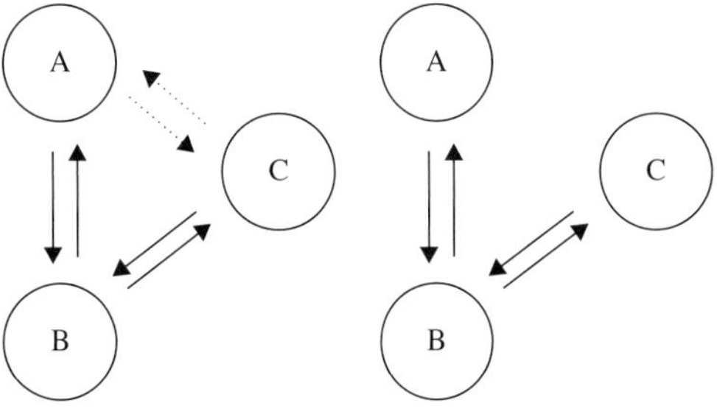

Figure 2 A model of transitive and intransitive relations in group dynamics.

the dyad. In a triad, however, only the guilty party would know who had leaked the secret. Each of the other two members would be suspicious of the other members of the triad. Thus, group membership beyond a dyad introduces increasing complexity to the relationship within such groups.

Measurement of Group Communication

A number of methods for measuring and analyzing group interaction have emerged over the past 50 years. All of the methods in use cannot be covered in detail here, but several are briefly described. The main focus here is on highlighting the key issues that the analysis of group communication raises for researchers working in this area. Two main approaches have been identified. The first is based on observation and classification of the manifest behavior of each individual member of a group. The second is based on extensive interpretation of what transpires in the relations among group members.

There are three ways in which the manifest behavior of members of a group can be measured. The most basic method simply measures the participation of group members. For instance, a group interaction can be observed with the aim of counting the number of times that each member of the group speaks. A more sophisticated method would be to measure not only the interaction between group members but to also record the actual verbal exchanges between specific members of the group. This type of analysis is useful for revealing the structure of a group, particularly in terms of differences among members. Such differences can give rise to the formation of cliques and alliances within a group. This method of measuring group dynamics uses a technique called sociometry, and the results are often presented visually as sociograms. Sociograms are diagrammatic representations of the preferences and interactions of all members of a group. In Fig. 3 for instance, the basic sociogram reveals the number of times each group member has exchanged communications, and further analysis of this pattern might lead to the observation that the pattern of exchange among the group members is uneven. This might prompt further questions: Why is there no direct communication between person A and person C? Why is it that only person C and person D have an equal amount of exchange between them? Why did person A not respond to person E?

The third method by which manifest behavior of members of a group can be measured, credited to Robert Bales, is interaction process analysis (IPA). Bales proposed three ideas about groups: first, that the small group is a social system; second, that there are fundamental problems that every group must resolve; and third, that group behavior can be observed and classified in relation to these problems. Bales distinguished between two key categories of acts, both verbal and nonverbal, that group

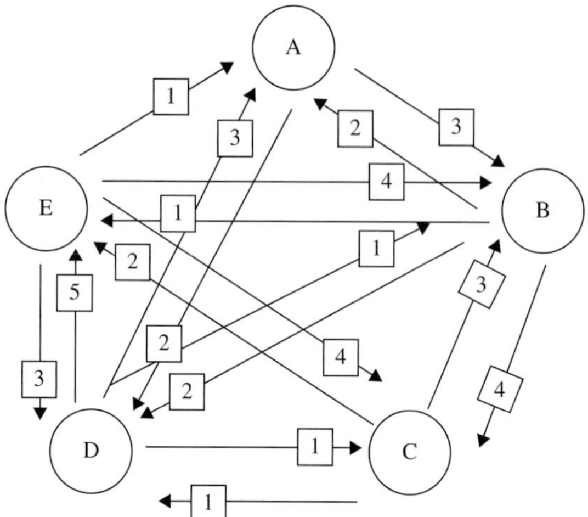

Figure 3 Participation process in a group. Arrows indicate group interaction and the number of times members spoke to each other.

members perform—the socioemotional area and task area. He further split these into two subcategories, distinguishing between positive and negative socioemotional acts and information-giving and information-seeking acts. In all, Bales identified 12 types of problems or acts that he ordered into a system for observing the behavior of members in a group. Bales' IPA has been widely used in a variety of situations, but the method has prompted discussion of a number of issues regarding its limitations for understanding what goes on in groups beyond the overt acts of group members. Some of these limitations include the problem of measuring intensity of behavior; the broad categories, which may not always distinguish between acts that ought to be treated separately; and the problem of interpreting nonverbal acts, especially with the possibility that a live coding and a video-recorded session may yield different results for the coders.

Mass Communication

Morris Janowitz defined mass communication in 1968 as "the institutions and techniques by which specialized groups employ technological devices (press, radio, films, etc.) to disseminate symbolic content to large, heterogeneous, and widely dispersed audiences." Building on the original (1959) work of Charles Wright, communication scholars have identified other characteristics of mass communication over the years:

- Mass communication involves a large, anonymous, and heterogeneous audience.
- The sources of mass communication are institutions and organizations that are primarily driven by a profit motive.

• The flow of mass communication is one-way, from the source to a multitude of receivers, with little or no opportunity of interaction for audiences.

• The content of mass communication is formulaic and standardized.

• The relations between the senders and receivers of mass communication are marked by anonymity and remoteness.

Many of these characteristics are changing, however, as a result of new communication possibilities enabled by technological innovations, changes in production practices within the media industries, different audience demands, changes in the characteristics of audiences, and other wider social changes. Thus many forms of mass communication are becoming increasingly interactive, as well as yielding more control to audiences to define the terms of their engagement with the media. As the mass media audience has become fragmented and less monolithic, media companies are tailoring their content to meet the needs of more specific groups of audiences. The new media technologies have made possible a shift from limited media sources (such as radio and television channels) to an ample supply of sources, bringing about multichannel broadcasting and other possibilities. There is also an increasing convergence of media forms and technologies, and traditionally distinct media in print, radio, television, film, music, graphics, etc. are merging on a single multimedia platform.

Mass communication media are still essentially characterized by an ability simultaneously to send either a uniform or tailored message to a large number of widely dispersed people. Also, mass communication activities are largely undertaken by large, centrally organized, and highly bureaucratic organizations. These organizations, especially in this age of globalization and conglomeration, do command a huge amount of resources, as well as economic, cultural, and political clout, which impacts on other social institutions and on the wider society. For these reasons, mass communication tends to be seen as a society-wide process. DeFleur and Ball-Rokeach have identified three critical questions entailed in the inquiry about the nature and influence of mass communication:

1. What is the impact of a society on its mass media?
2. How does mass communication take place?
3. What does exposure to mass communication do to people?

This set of questions is useful for exploring mass communication as a society-wide process, but it certainly does not exhaust the range of pertinent questions that can be asked about the nature and role of mass communication in society. A glaring omission, for instance, is a question about what people do with the media. How do people use the media and for what purpose? The study of mass communication, which began earnestly in about the 1940s through the pioneering work of Paul Lazarsfeld and his colleagues, has developed and spread out way beyond the initial preoccupation with an instrumentalist orientation, which sought to understand the effects of mass communication on people. One of the earliest attempts to define the nature and scope of mass communication was by Harold D. Lasswell. In a seminal article published in 1948, Lasswell offered this definitional statement about mass communication: "A convenient way to describe an act of communication is to answer the following questions: Who? Says what? In which channel? To whom? With what effect?" This came to be popularly known as the "Lasswell Formula" and it has been put to various applications. It has also been criticized for its limitations for understanding what mass communication entails. The main criticism of the Lasswell Formula is that, in describing the process of communication, it offers too simple a model for what is essentially a complex set of activities. Whereas this definition offers both a description of the nature of mass communication as well as a description of its scope, Lasswell seemed to have used it to describe the field in terms of the different research inquiries happening at the time, or as a prescription of the areas that research activities needed to cover. This approach, with some modification, is still useful for mapping research activities in mass communication today. The key elements in a communication process that Lasswell identified remain relevant today, even though the range of questions, and the research focus that scholars are dealing with in relation to each of them, have expanded significantly. In using his formula to describe the research activities in the field of mass communication, Lasswell identified each of the elements in his formula with a specific kind of research inquiry (see Fig. 4).

There was an attempt in 1958, by another researcher, to improve on Lasswell's original formula by adding two further questions: "Under what circumstances?"

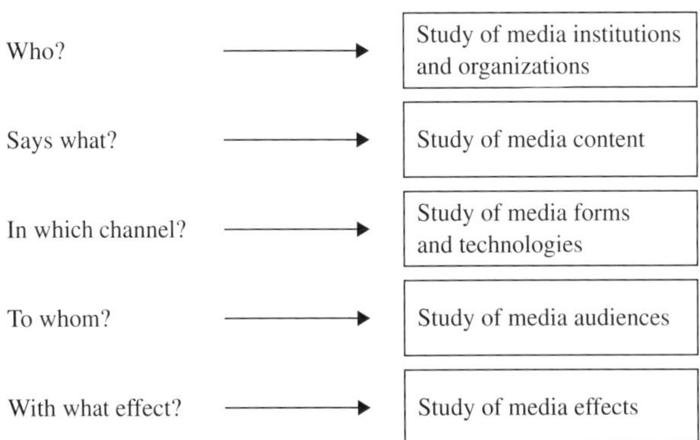

Figure 4 An adaptation of Lasswell's communication formula for mapping key research activities in the study of communication at the level of society.

(is a message sent) and "For what purpose?" These two additional questions help to refine Lasswell's original formula and can be related to both the sender and the receiver of mass communication.

Measurement of Mass Communication

Control Analysis Control studies engage with matters of organization, ownership, and regulation of the mass media, set within the broader context of the media institution. Other types of inquiry within control studies include matters of professional values and work ethics of workers in the various media industries. Scholars working in this area are interested in understanding issues such as how institutional factors shape media content, the impact of the media institution on the wider society in which it operates (as well as the impact of society on its media institution), the impact of the media institution on other social institutions (and vice versa), the internal dynamics of media organizations (particularly the relations between the various sectors inside a media organization), and how these impact on the production of media culture. Generally, control studies aim to find out how, and to what extent, these kinds of institutional factors serve to control the production of media culture. This type of study tends to involve the use of humanistic research methods such as participant observation, depth interview, and documentary analysis.

Content Analysis The study of media content emerged partly as an offshoot of the earlier preoccupation with media effects in the study of mass communication. The logic of this connection is straightforward: if the media are supposed to be able to influence audiences that are exposed to their messages, then a better understanding of how and why such effects happen can be obtained from a systematic study of media content. The need to also understand the appeal that various mass media content holds for audience members is another impetus for the development of research interest in the content of the mass media. With regard to the connection between content study and media effects, the early studies held a set of assumptions about media content:

- Media content reflect the intentions and values of those who originated them.
- Meanings encoded into messages are equally decoded by receivers of such messages.
- Once we understand the encoded meanings in media messages, we can predict the effects they will have on receivers of the messages.

Another line of inquiry into media content stemmed from the assumption about the connections between media content and dominant social values and ideology. This view holds that media content, by and large, reflects the values and preferences of dominant groups in society, leading to contentions about whether the media adequately reflect, or should reflect, social reality. Inquiries of this nature also raise critical issues with the media for being the carriers of dominant ideological values along the lines of class, race, gender, ethnicity, nation, sexuality, and so on. Media content has been studied with a variety of methods of inquiry. Lasswell referred to this area of study as content analysis, which incidentally also happens to be the title for a specific social science research method. In 1952, Bernard Berelson defined the method of content analysis as "a research technique for the objective, systematic and quantitative description of the manifest content of communication."

Scholars studying media content within the humanistic tradition have tended to use methods such as semiotics, discourse analysis, narrative analysis, genre analysis, and other methods of literary criticism. Humanistic research tends to place emphasis on the "textual" nature of media content, and the meanings that audiences get out of media texts. The word "text" suggests something that media audiences engage with, rather than something that they passively absorb. Audiences, therefore, "read" media texts, and are capable of deriving all sorts of meaning from them that are different from those intended by the producers of the texts.

Media Analysis The research tradition that comes under the media analysis section of Lasswell's formula is represented by the work of scholars such as Harold Innis and Marshall McLuhan in the 1950s and 1960s, and Alvin Gouldner, Altheide and Snow, and Eisenstein in the 1970s. Although this tradition of inquiry has a lot of internal diversity, concerning the research interests of these scholars in mass communication technologies, they are united, according to McQuail, by their emphasis on the potential of communication technology to bring about social change. Harold Innis laid the foundation for this line of inquiry in mass communication when he founded the Toronto School in the 1950s. In developing his thesis about the importance of communication technology, Innis, basing his thesis on the study of ancient civilizations and their relationship with the prevailing dominant communication technology, established the proposition that communication technologies play a crucial role in social change. This happens in two key ways, through what Innis referred to as "communication bias" and through the benefits accruing from a monopoly control of a prevailing communication technology by a dominant social group or class. He argued that communication technologies had an innate bias in relation to the dimensions of time and space, because they favor one or the other. According to this contention, a prevailing communication technology such as stone is more biased toward time and therefore allowed the Egyptian empire to exist over a long period of time. By the same token, the invention of papyrus, a much lighter substance to carry about, afforded the ancient Roman Empire to extend itself over a large territory. Also, social groups tend to fight for control of the prevailing communication technology until one ends up monopolizing its use. Because such control is essential for the production and distribution of knowledge, it also provides the group or class with power.

McLuhan extended Innis' idea about the significance of communication technology by exploring the linkages between our experience of the world and the communication technology that we use to experience it. His underlying argument here is that different communication technologies will give us different experiences of the world, hence his popular phrase that "the medium is the message." These pioneering studies, although often characterized as technological determinism, laid the foundation for contemporary inquiry into the new media technologies and their impact on existing communication and social relations.

Audience and Effects Analysis The studies of mass media audiences and effects represent two sides of a coin, and are interrelated in obvious ways. Although some effects studies relate to the impact of the mass media institution on society as a whole, or on other social institutions, much of the work in this area of media research (and the controversies it engenders) has been in relation to media audiences. Notions of a powerful media effect tend to imply a weak, malleable audience. Conversely, conceptions of a weak or limited effect of the media tend to relate to conceptions of the audience as active, obstinate, and creative. Nevertheless, the realization that media effects are not nearly as predictable as was once thought, and that the meaning of a media message cannot be predetermined at the source, led usefully to the development of audience study as an independent subject of inquiry in its own rights. This development has yielded a number of insights on the nature of the mass media audience that has enriched our understanding of mass communication.

The study of mass media effects has been a recurrent feature of theoretical and research activities in mass communication scholarship right from its inception. Although much of the body of work that constitutes the effects research is more representative of North American communication research tradition, it is only one (and for that matter a small proportion) in a wider range of subject interests covered by this tradition. Severin and Tankard identified four reasons for the continued interest in the subject of mass media effects:

1. Continued concern of the public. The widespread availability of mass media in various forms throughout the 20th century, both nationally and internationally, has meant that the public is always concerned about how some aspect of the available symbolic content will affect a section (usually children and teenagers) of the audience. Every new form of mass communication tends to engender its own public concern about its possible effect on people. Thus, in the past, such concerns had been expressed about comic books, cinema, television, radio, and popular music. Arrival of the Internet has predictably raised some concerns as well. Concerns about these media include issues about the portrayal of screen violence, bad language, explicit and gratuitous sex, and promotion of antisocial or harmful behavior.

2. The organizations that produce mass communication messages are interested in the effects of their efforts, not least because they have invested a considerable amount of time, skill, and money in producing the messages. The activities of the advertising and marketing industries are a good example of this.

3. The desire to understand causes and effects is a fundamental human trait that offers a vital source of knowledge. Such knowledge allows humans to control events and to master their environment.

4. Analysis of mass communication in terms of causes and effects is compatible with the scientific tradition of inquiry (one of the major approaches used by scholars in the field).

Jack McLeod, Gerald Kosicki, and Zhogdang Pan have characterized the media effect approach as having its primary focus on audiences; as attempting to specify the nature of influence in terms of changes or prevention of changes in the audiences in relation to other relevant variables; as aiming to locate the source of influence or effect in a particular area of the media, such as a media message system, medium, type of content, or individual message; as using the terminology of variables (e.g., independent, dependent, or intervening) as well as different notions of causality to describe the process of effects and the conditions under which they are likely to occur; and as tending to formulate propositions about effects in ways accessible to empirical testing. Denis McQuail has identified four phases in the checkered history of effects research: powerful effects (short-term, immediate effect of media), limited effects, return of powerful effects (long-term, cumulative effect of media), and negotiated media influence.

The powerful effects phase McQuail locates this phase historically between the start of the 20th century up to the late 1930s. It represents the phase when a lot of power was attributed to the mass media. The mass media were thought to be able to shape public opinion and belief and to change the behavior of people as desired and designed by those who controlled the media and their content. Crucially, McQuail noted that this phase was not marked by any actual research into the way media works and that the notions about the power of the media were based mostly on observation and speculation.

The limited effects phase This phase witnessed the arrival of empirical research into mass communication as exemplified by the Payne Fund studies in the United States in the early 1930s, and principally the work of Paul Lazarsfeld *et al.*, from the 1940s onward. This era, according to McQuail, lasted until the 1960s and involved a large amount of research into various aspects of media content and form, films, programs, political campaigns, public communication campaigns, advertising, and other marketing campaigns. The research efforts of this period were largely aimed at understanding how specific media form and content can be used to persuade or inform the public and to assess any negative effects of media that might then lead to measures to control the media. Notable among the studies of this period are Carl Hovland's study of attitude change among soldiers in the U.S. Army during World War II in the 1940s and 1950s, which showed that orientation films were not effective in changing attitudes. There was also the research by Eunice Cooper and Marie Jahoda in 1947 on the "Mr. Biggott" cartoons, which showed that the factor of selective perception could actually reduce the effectiveness of a message; Lazarsfeld also did a study of voting behavior, which showed that people were more likely to be influenced by others around them than by the mass media.

The return of powerful effects phase This phase was characterized by a shift in research focus from investigating short-term, immediate effects on individuals to investigating long-term, cumulative effects on a large number of people. Writing in defense of the research focus of this phase, Gladys and Kurt Lang argued that the conclusion about a "minima effect" of media represents only one particular interpretation, which had gained currency in media scholarship at the time. They continued: "The evidence available by the end of the 1950s, even when balanced against some of the negative findings, gives no justification for an overall verdict of 'media impotence'." Also at this time, key among the studies that attributed powerful effects to mass media are Elisabeth Noelle-Neumann's spiral-of-silence theory, which argued that three characteristics of mass communication (cumulation, ubiquity, and consonance) gave them powerful effects on public opinion. According to this theory, the opinions that people hold on any matter of significance can be influenced through a perception of such opinion as representing a minority view. People hold back on their opinion when they perceive it to be a minority one, for fear of isolation. This withholding of opinion then influences others to do the sane thing, thus creating a spiral of silence. The media are said to be a major source of defining majority views. George Gerbner's cultivation theory also ascribed a powerful influence to the mass media in terms of the effect of heavy viewing on people's perception of real conditions in the world around them. Gerbner and his associates sought to explain the effects of television viewing on people's perceptions, attitudes, and values using the survey method to explore people's view on a range of social issues, and cross-referencing these views against heavy and light viewing habits of respondents.

Negotiated media influence phase McQuail describes this phase as one characterized by an approach that saw the influence of the media in terms of their ability to "construct" social reality. By this view, the media outlets construct meanings about various aspects of the social world and present these in a systematic way to audiences. This phase is also characterized by a shift in methodological application from quantitative to qualitative methods. This phase of media effects study incorporates a view of both media power and audience power. The audience is active and participatory in a process of meaning construction that involves a continuous negotiation between the audience's worldview and the meanings offered in the mass media. In her study of the rise of the women's movement in the Netherlands, Liesbeth van Zoonen sought to assess the contribution of the media to the events. She commented that "the media image of the movement is the result of an intricate interaction between movement and media," which led to a kind of public identity and definition. It is worth noting that the latter of McQuail's four phases tend to build on, rather than cancel out, the previous ones, and that the sheer diversity of research interests in the field means that all these phases are still represented in the works of various scholars in the field.

See Also the Following Articles

Coding Variables • Linguistics

Further Reading

Berger, C., and Chaffee, S. (eds.) (1987). *Handbook of Communication Science*. Sage, London.

DeFleur, M., and Ball-Rokeach, S. (1989). *Theories of Mass Communication,* 5th Ed. Longman, New York.

Heath, R., and Bryant, J. (1992). *Human Communication Research.* Lawrence Erlbaum, New Jersey.

Lowery, S., and DeFleur, M. (1988). *Milestones in Mass Communication Research,* 2nd Ed. Longman, New York.

McQuail, D. (1994). *Mass Communication Theory,* 3rd Ed. Sage, London.

Myers, G., and Myers, M. (1992). *The Dynamics of Human Communication. A Laboratory Approach,* 6th Ed. McGraw-Hill, New York.

Rosengren, K. (2000). *Communication.* Sage, London.

Severin, W., and Tankard, J., Jr. (2001). *Communication Theories,* 5th Ed. Longman, New York.

Comparative Sociology

John R. Hall
University of California, Davis, Davis, California, USA

Glossary

analytic element A distinctive aspect of social phenomena, deemed to vary across cases.

indirect method of difference John Stuart Mill's analytic strategy based on comparison of two or more groups of cases that differ in the occurrence of basic propensities.

method of agreement John Stuart Mill's analytic strategy based on identifying propensities always found together in otherwise diverse cases.

practice of inquiry A research methodology typified on the basis of how it combines more elemental forms of discourse, including value discourse, narrative, social theory, and explanation or interpretation.

qualitative comparative analysis Charles Ragin's Boolean-algebra and fuzzy-set-theory approach to comparative analysis of potentially multiple causal configurations in a set of cases.

Comparative sociology encompasses a range of practices that focus on the juxtaposition of cases or aspects of cases, either to induce or to test theoretically derived hypotheses, to apply social theory, or to produce bounded generalizations and "rules of experience."

Introduction

Comparison occurs in social inquiry whenever observations about one or more aspects of a given case are considered in relation to observations about other cases or theoretical models. Comparisons may be formulated either by analyzing relationships among variables for multiple cases or by investigating the parallels and differences among cases. Yet similar social phenomena are often genetically connected to one another. Comparative sociology thus encounters basic issues concerning selection of cases, measurement across cases, independence versus mutual influence of cases, and logics of inference. Comparison, then, is an Archimedean point for inquiry. Issues concerning it are relevant to both quantitative and qualitative research, and to both comparisons of cases and comparisons focusing on variables. Conventionally, comparative sociology addresses similarities and dissimilarities across cases, and this article explores the issues within this domain.

Despite precursors, comparative inquiry is especially a product of modernity. Perhaps the greatest study of comparative sociology, Alexis de Tocqueville's *Democracy in America*, preceded the modern scientific delineation of comparative logic by John Stuart Mill. During the latter part of the 19th century, the *Methodenstreit* (methodological conflict) in Germany centered on issues about generalization versus the uniqueness of culture and history, and whether the natural and cultural sciences differ from one another so radically as to require different epistemologies. Max Weber developed the most influential solution. In the formative institutional developments of modern social science during the first half of the 20th century, questions about the epistemology of comparison were pushed aside. Then, beginning in the 1960s, comparative sociohistorical research underwent concerted development. Today, comparative research takes place within a broader domain of sociohistorical inquiry characterized by "integrated disparity": diverse practices invoke radically alternative logics of analysis, while nevertheless retaining sufficient points of mutual articulation to permit theoretical and substantive dialogue among them.

Classic Approaches

One enduring problem of comparative sociology concerns how to construe the object of inquiry to be studied. On the one hand, scientific positivism and, later, analytic realism suggest that research should seek to identify and study objectively discernible phenomena. Alternatively, the neo-Kantian legacy suggests that whatever the status of reality as such, investigators bring phenomena into distinctive focus by their frames of analytic interest. From these two alternatives radiate an array of issues and problems of comparative sociology that are parsimoniously framed by the contrast between two classic approaches, i.e., the scientific comparative method of John Stuart Mill and the interpretive, or *verstehende*, comparative practice of Max Weber.

Mill's Scientific Method

Overall, Mill's 1843 philosophy of scientific method structures comparisons across cases on the basis of their variable attributes. Mill specified two methods of research, both relevant to nonexperimental comparative analysis—the "method of agreement" and the "indirect method of difference."

According to the logic of the method of agreement, if two features co-occur under otherwise diverse circumstances, these features are likely to be somehow processually connected with each another. With random sampling, the very diversity of cases on other dimensions enhances the argument that similarities are patterned by whatever shared dynamic is identified. For instance, if patron–client relationships occur in the most diverse social settings, but wherever they occur, there are substantial resource inequalities, the method of agreement will produce the inference that resource inequality is somehow connected to the occurrence of patron–client relationships.

The indirect method of difference involves searching for contingent co-related variations. It is as though two different findings derived from the method of agreement were placed side by side. If a particular propensity is found only in the presence of another propensity, and never when the second propensity is absent, Mill reasoned, the propensities are causally connected. Thus, if a study of postcolonial nation-states finds that a propensity toward a particular type of state formation occurs only in former plantation slavery colonies, whereas diverse non-plantation former colonies lack the propensity, plantation slavery colonization may be identified, in Mill's words, as "the effect, or the cause, or an indispensable part of the cause."

Weber's *Verstehende* Methodology

Whereas the logic of Mill yielded a nomothetic search for general principles, an alternative, idiographic view suggests that the special character of sociohistorical phenomena makes them necessarily the subjects of a different kind of inquiry, namely, a cultural science based on understanding unique social meanings and actions. This was the central issue of the German *Methodenstreit.*

Max Weber sought to resolve this conflict by acknowledging the meaningful and cultural bases of both social life and inquiry, while retaining a rigorous method of analysis. His approach depended on two central assertions: first, that infinitely varying sociohistorical phenomena become objects of inquiry through cultural (value) interests in them, and second, that because values cannot be warranted scientifically, the objects of sociohistorical inquiry cannot be scientifically determined, even though, once determined, they may be studied by way of scientific methods. Weber thus adopted an almost heroic stance, embracing "value neutrality" as an ethical obligation, while engaging in "science as a vocation" in a way that warrants pursuit of contextualized truths.

Weber's approach was both comparative and based on the principle of *Verstehen* (interpretive understanding). Seeking a middle ground between generalization and historicism, he combined explanation and understanding by using ideal types that would be "adequate on the level of meaning" (that is, incorporate specifications of structured cultural meanings and meaningful actions). Such ideal types—what Guenther Roth calls "sociohistorical models"—serve as meaningfully coherent analogues to empirical cases, yet allow for hermeneutic and causal comparison beyond particularities.

Comparison thus becomes a multifaceted enterprise: a given case may be compared with various sociohistorical models, either to explore the degree to which one or another model subsumes the case within its explanatory orb, or to pursue refinement of the model. In addition, multiple cases may be compared with one another in relation to one or more models. Finally, models may be compared, whether they are framed at a substantive level of analysis (e.g., religious ethics of salvation in Christian Europe) or a purely conceptual one (e.g., instrumental-rational versus value-rational action).

Contemporary Issues

In the 1960s, comparative sociology began to flourish. Partly, the impetus came from increased interest during the Cold War in cross-national comparison, and partly it came from neo-Weberians, neo-Marxists, and other historically oriented social scientists interested in alternatives to social systems theory, functionalism, and positivism, which they regarded as incapable of critically engaging issues about alternative historical trajectories. Various kindred practices also took hold (initially, social science history, and later, an efflorescence of interdisciplinary research in the human sciences, broadly conceived). By the beginning of the 21st century, researchers and methodologists had confronted a set of linked problematics concerning case definitions and measurement, study design, and interdependence of cases and possibilities of generalization.

Defining Cases and Constructing Measurements

Comparison requires the existence of multiple cases that bear some formal equivalence, at least in the aspects being compared. Thus, the most general methodological problems concern the grounds on which cases can be deemed sufficiently similar constellations of social phenomena, such that knowledge could reasonably be developed through comparison.

The Ecological Fallacy Controversy

On the face of it, case definition would seem bound by some basic rules. Organizations should not be compared to people, or people to administrative governmental units. This approach posits multiple "levels of analysis" and holds that comparison must treat cases on the same level—persons with persons, organizations with organizations, and so forth. This standard of comparison is necessary, it has been argued, to avoid the "ecological fallacy," an example of which would include inferring relationships between attributes of individuals (income and political conservatism) on the basis of aggregate relationships between those same attributes found in more encompassing units (such as provinces). Recently, efforts to come to terms with the problem have yielded some fruitful procedures of ecological regression, even if the precept of avoiding inferences across levels remains a useful initial rule of thumb.

Yet there are two further issues. First, certain considerations may call for a different methodological strategy than one that defines analysis in relation to "levels." Put simply, there is no epistemological guarantee that studying cases at a given level of analysis captures the relevant social processes in a given social phenomenon. Second, as Georg Simmel pointed out long ago, a given social form (e.g., conflict) can manifest at quite different scales and within different structures of social organization. These two points imply, respectively, that comparisons may analyze cases defined as wholes that transcend levels, and that cases at radically different levels of analysis may be compared, providing there is a good theoretical rationale for doing so. Indeed, this possibility has been explicitly theorized by Charles Tilly.

Case Definition

Apart from the ecological issues, there is a wider debate, both about what constitutes a case and about whether cases are the appropriate objects of comparative sociological analysis. Sociologists are no longer so taken by the kind of "grand theory" entailed in any effort to subsume individual cases in all their nonincidental explanatory aspects within a single framework. War, for example, may involve the most diverse social processes concerning ideology, military assets, geopolitical strategies, popular mobilization, social movements, and so on. Although it is possible to compare wars with one another as "historical individuals," or wholes, there are at least two alternatives. First, "war" may be theorized as a domain so broad that it encompasses disparate subtypes that need to be compared to one another by way of alternative sociohistorical models. Second, Stinchcombe's proposal for the development of "theoretical methods" of sociohistorical analysis holds that the search for broad causal equivalences across cases is too crude; researchers are likely to achieve greater success in theorizing parallel patterns by looking for "deep analogies" about how things happen in various social phenomena that, on the face of it, might not even be considered as members of the same set. Here, comparison is not of cases, but of theoretically equivalent social processes, wherever they are found.

These considerations warrant a more general point. Contributors to Ragin and Becker have argued that "cases" come into focus on the basis of theoretical or substantive interests, and that on occasion, only during the process of research does what the case is a case of become evident. In other words, case selection is necessarily a reflexive process bound up with other research activities.

Sampling on the Dependent Variable

A connected issue about cases concerns their relation to a presumed wider universe of phenomena. Within the particular logic of variable-oriented analysis that is oriented to explaining variation across cases in outcomes measured by a dependent variable, cases need to be selected without regard to their outcome; that is, research must avoid "sampling on the dependent variable." On its face, this precept makes sense. Comparison of cases with outcomes deemed equivalent may reveal conditions necessary to the outcome, but research cannot effectively probe what conditions are sufficient for an outcome to occur unless it includes comparisons with cases that lack that outcome. To be sure, Mill's method of agreement focuses on co-occurrences of two features across cases that are otherwise diverse. But Mill's indirect method of difference has to be judged more robust, because the method of agreement provides no way of evaluating whether an outcome would occur in the absence of a putative cause.

However, as reasonable as the rule of thumb against sampling on the dependent variable seems for certain kinds of analysis, comparison with "negative" cases of a phenomenon needs to be carefully thought through.

Consider "war" again. If the analytic interest is in explaining war as an outcome, it makes obvious good sense to compare conditions under which wars occur with those in which they do not occur. However, spatially, if not temporally, "nonwar" is something of a default condition, and a question arises as to which nonwar cases to sample. Comparison of most nonwar situations with war is unlikely to be very enlightening. The goal, instead, is to include cases in which war is a serious possibility but does not occur. In this example and more generally, then, the task is to define a population broader than those with a certain value on the dependent variable but narrow enough to permit relevant comparisons of meaningfully different cases.

Moreover, how a dependent variable is defined is an open question, and explanations may be proffered even without comparison to cases in which a phenomenon is absent. Continuing with the example of war, the analytic interest may be in explaining variations across wars, rather than explaining whether war occurs. Given this interest, the dependent variable will be defined in a way that makes the exclusion of nonwars irrelevant. In short, whether sampling on the dependent variable is problematic depends on the goals of research, and whether such sampling occurs depends on how the dependent variable is defined.

Measurement across Cases

More generally, case selection is inextricably bound up with measurement. Comparisons across cases will typically take the form of noting differences and similarities in relation to certain attributes of interest (that is, "analytic elements"). The degree to which such comparisons are formalized depends on the methodology. At one extreme, a historian investigating a single case may still bring in a series of ad hoc comparisons in order to illustrate key commonalities or differences. At the other extreme, a formal methodology of comparison will require the construction of an at-least two-dimensional matrix of cases by analytic elements, or variables.

Whatever the degree of formalization, valid comparison depends on a basic assumption, namely, that a given analytic element can be meaningfully described in relation to the cases. The cultural turn in sociohistorical inquiry has brought this issue into sharper focus. To take one construct, whatever the analytic reality of "class" in material terms, it also entails a phenomenon of social construction, both of those who participate in its "making" (e.g., in E. P. Thompson's *The Making of the English Working Class*) and of sociohistorical analysts after the fact. The implications are several and significant. First, any conceptualization of class will be but a pale shadow of the phenomenon as it obtains in social processes. Analysts are thus faced with a trade-off between providing rich "measurements" of class that make comparisons across multiple cases increasingly complex, or offering relatively spartan conceptualizations that facilitate comparison, but at the expense of nuance. Second, even spartan conceptualizations will have to acknowledge different sociohistorical constructions of class, e.g., in industrializing France versus industrializing England. Third, in a postpositivist understanding of inquiry, measurement is not posited as theory free; thus, the analyst has to consider the ramifications of a particular conceptualization relative to various salient theories of a phenomenon. And fourth, even a relatively spartan approach to measurement confronts the historicity of measurement. Comparing class formations cross-nationally, for example, depends on utilizing statistical series that are products of their times, both in the definitions of occupations and in the ideas and interests that drive constructions of measures in the first place. In this instance and more generally, research is necessarily engaged in activities of "translation"—between different empirical phenomena and their historical social constructions, which may involve not only a methodological but also a social effort to establish commensuration, or equivalence among measurements of phenomena, within one or more research studies.

Advances in Study Design

The classic foundations of comparative sociology trace to positivist and *verstehende* logics of comparison. Starting in the 1960s, comparative and historical sociologists began to propose alternative methodologies across this range. During the early phases, this discussion was framed largely through reference to exemplary studies by scholars such as Reinhard Bendix, Barrington Moore, Charles Tilly, and Immanuel Wallerstein, and through inductive descriptions of institutionally established approaches, such as the *Annales* school. But no widely shared interdisciplinary enterprise emerged. Instead, practitioners operated under a mélange of competing labels such as "comparative history," "historical sociology," "social science history," and "world systems analysis," even though these labels do not identify either coherent methodologies or effectively self-contained agendas of inquiry.

How are diverse methodological practices to be construed within an overall domain of sociohistorical inquiry? One account, by Peter Burke, defines the realm as a continuum between history and social theory. Two other descriptions—those of Theda Skocpol (originally, with Margaret Somers) and of Charles Tilly—displace the idea of a continuum by specifying alternative types of interdisciplinary inquiry. Skocpol and Somers identify three alternative logics of "comparative history." One involves the "parallel demonstration of theory" in different contexts, a second approach involves a single phenomenon (such as democratization) that is studied through the "contrast of contexts" in different cases, and a third strategy, "macro-causal analysis," is concerned with testing hypotheses through comparative analysis.

Charles Tilly has taken a different tack, theorizing a two-dimensional typology that differentiates alternative kinds of propositions studied through inquiry. On the first axis, propositions about a given phenomenon (e.g., class struggle) may range in application from one to multiple forms of the phenomenon (worker resistance, social movement, or electoral politics). On the second axis, for any given form, propositions about a phenomenon could be directed to anywhere from one to all instances. Four kinds of propositions can thereby be delineated: (1) "individualizing" propositions concerned with only one instance of one form (that is, a unique case), (2) "encompassing" comparison, dealing with multiple forms of a single overall instance (such as the world economy), (3) "universalizing" analysis intended to cover all instances of a single form of a phenomenon (such as a general model of all developmental economic growth), and (4) "variation-finding" analysis that seeks to uncover the patterns of a phenomenon for all cases, whatever their alternative forms.

The other major development in methodology involves not the description of alternative types of inquiry, but the formalization and extension of one particular type, what Skocpol and Somers term macro-causal analysis. Charles Ragin uses set-theory Boolean algebra to consolidate Mill's methods of difference and agreement within an overall methodology simultaneously keyed to general problems of logic and the particular problems of sociohistorical inquiry. Ragin's qualitative comparative analysis (QCA) marks an important advance over Mill's and other formulations of comparative logic, by identifying multiple configurational patterns within an array of systematically described cases. Ragin is thus able to provide analytically for the possibility that different sets of prior conditions or conjunctures of causes may yield the same outcome. Ragin's method also may reveal "contradictory" combinations of circumstances (A, B, and C) for which a particular outcome, O, occurs sometimes but not always. This implies that general causal factor patterns do not explain everything; when they do not, their use can help focus residual puzzles to be addressed through detailed historical comparison of alternative unique outcomes. In a subsequent elaboration, Ragin confronts the problem that many social variables (e.g., ethnicity) do not have strong categorical boundaries, by developing a procedure based on the recognition of fuzzy boundaries. This modification moves the comparative method beyond restrictive classification assumptions that were poorly aligned with even the most basic social ontology.

Finally, uses of theoretical models in comparative research have been elaborated. Hall shows how theoretical sociohistorical models such as ideal types can be incorporated into even formalized comparative methodologies. In a different vein, Geoffrey Hawthorn has developed Weber's logic of the "mental experiment" into "counterfactual analysis," a procedure that sharpens the specification of conditions under which empirical cases may be compared to purely hypothetical ones. Hawthorn holds that the comparative consideration of hypothetical scenarios can deepen an analysis if the counterfactual hypotheses are neither so distant from the course of events to be irrelevant nor so unstable in their dynamics as to make prediction unreliable.

Key Issues in Contemporary Methodologies

In relation to study design, two issues that become especially important concern whether cases can be considered causally independent of one another and the relation between sample size and logic of analysis.

Independence, Genealogy, and Diffusion

One of the most formidable and intractable problems facing comparative sociohistorical inquiry concerns whether cases can be considered causally independent of one another. Any methodology that seeks to identify common patterns amenable to general explanation either has to assume independence or it has to provide a method for ascertaining the character and significance of influence across cases. Specifically, if a researcher employs Mill's "method of agreement," inquiry must assume causal independence of cases because the method cannot differentiate between independent cause–effect relationships, versus genetic or mutual influences that produce parallel outcomes. Suppose, for example, that a study of 60 panics associated with satanism in the United States showed that they developed in quite similar ways. The parallel event structures might seem to suggest a causal theoretical explanation, but alternative explanations cannot easily be excluded, because the satanism scares could have occurred through diffusion and imitation. What is the solution to this problem? In circumstances where case independence cannot be assumed (e.g., state formation in Europe, as studied by Reinhard Bendix), comparative inquiry is still possible, but it has an alternative rationale, of identifying genealogies, mutual influences, and patterns of diffusion. In such research, comparative analysis can address whether commonalities are shaped by nonindependence, and if so, how.

Number of Cases and Generalization

The other issue concerns sample size. Assuming that the problem of independence can be resolved, formal methods can be employed for comparing large numbers of cases. But Stanley Lieberson is less sanguine about using formal methods of comparison in studies with small numbers of cases, both because this situation precludes probabilistic arguments and because the number of variables of interest may overwhelm the cases analyzed. However, even if analyzing a small number of cases may not be an appropriate basis for drawing causal generalizations, it may nevertheless offer a valuable way to understand social processes in themselves and *in situ*.

The problem of sample size is most exacerbated under conditions in which the sample size is one, a situation that historians often take as their point of departure and that is also faced by world-systems theorists, i.e., when they posit a single overarching totality, the modern world system. Under these conditions, if comparison is to be maintained as a methodological enterprise, it must either compare the totality to a nonempirical sociohistorical model, or the analysis can proceed by a series of nested internal comparisons, paralleling the theoretical search for "deep analogies" proposed by Stinchcombe. The most elaborate effort in this direction for world-systems theory is "incorporated comparison" as proposed by McMichael.

Alternative Practices

By the end of the 20th century, there had been substantial development of comparative methods. Yet the differences—between inductive and deductive historical sociologists, between those interested in causal explanation versus interpretation, between historical sociologists whose methodologies are explicitly comparative and historians using comparison only implicitly—often threaten to divide practices of inquiry that nevertheless share substantive interests. It is thus important to theorize the overall domain of sociohistorical inquiry within which comparative analysis is practiced. For this project, Hall identifies the ways in which alternative "practices of inquiry" bring together various "forms of discourse," discourses that constitute interrelated moments of analyzing sociohistorical phenomena.

Four formative discourses (value discourse, narrative, social theory, and explanation or interpretation) are typically implicated both in comparative inquiry and in case studies often drawn on in comparative research. Each of these formative discourses is capable of serving as a dominant discourse that orders relations among all four discourses through internal subsumption and external articulation of them, thus consolidating a meaningfully coherent practice of inquiry. For example, if narrative discourse predominates, it will order the articulation among all four discourses in one distinctive practice of inquiry, whereas the predominance of social theory will order an articulation of discourses that constitutes an alternative practice.

In turn, generalizing versus particularizing orientations make a difference in how inquiry works. Thus, each dominant discourse, such as narrative, orders the four formative discourses in one distinctive practice when the goal is general knowledge, and a different one when the goal is detailed knowledge of a distinctive phenomenon. Given four alternative ordering discourses and two (generalizing versus particularizing) orientations of inquiry, it is possible to identify eight ideal typical practices of inquiry. In these terms, the three methodologies identified by Skocpol and Somers, theory application, contrast-oriented comparison, and analytic generalization, are the central comparative practices.

Theory Application

In the practice of theory application, the analyst seeks to bring parallel phenomena into view via narratives that apply a particular theoretical lens to the analysis of cases. The particular social theory dictates the central issues of comparative plot analysis for the narratives, and explanation (or interpretation) centers on differentiating theoretically informed versus nontheoretical accounts, and on determining whether the nontheoretical accounts require modification or disconfirmation of the theory, or are simply matters that lie outside the theory's domain. The emphasis on close and careful comparison of a small number of cases offers bases for deepening theorization of explanatory accounts and refining theory, but generalization typically is undermined by the small number of cases.

Analytic Generalization

Analytic generalization encompasses the formal methods formulated by Mill and elaborated by Ragin. Here, the researcher empirically tests or develops hypotheses deduced from theories or induced from observations. Narrative is structured to offer the basis for adjudication of hypotheses in relation to theories, and the evaluation of alternative explanations and interpretations mediates the process of theoretical adjudication. The rigor of this practice approximates the intent of positivism, but problems of measurement equivalence and sample size, discussed previously, can threaten validity.

Contrast-Oriented Comparison

Explanation and interpretation are the central discursive concerns that order inquiry oriented to the production of bounded generalizations and "rules of experience" through contingent and idiographic analysis of sociohistorical phenomena deemed kindred in relation to a theoretical theme. The focus is on how a particular social phenomenon (e.g., proletarianization, fundamentalism) plays out in different sociohistorical contexts. Narrative is used to trace the relations between contexts, processes, and outcomes. Because causal independence of cases is not assumed, analysis of genealogies, diffusion, and mutual influence is readily incorporated into comparative analysis.

Theory application, contrast-oriented comparison, and analytic generalization are part of a wider array of practices of inquiry, including a fourth generalizing one, "universal history," that persists despite postmodern condemnation of "metanarratives," and four particularizing practices (situational history, specific history, configurational history, and historicism) especially oriented to case studies. All these latter practices produce research that is implicitly comparative and that may be drawn on in comparative analysis. However, one, configurational history, is of particular importance to comparative historical sociologists.

Configurational History

The configurational history methodology operates by theoretically identifying the elements, conditions, and developments necessary for a particular ("configurational") social phenomenon to occur, e.g., modern capitalism, or a particular technology of power. The theoretically defined configuration is then used as a basis for generating questions of historical analysis about the fulfillment of conditions, creation of elements, etc. This strategy is not inherently comparative in the conventional sense, but it involves a strong use of social theory in relation to historical analysis, and is thus is favored by historical sociologists (e.g., Max Weber and Michael Mann) who seek to develop sociologically informed explanations of distinctive historical developments.

The cultural turn in epistemology, especially as underwritten by Foucault, has created conditions of substantially increased sophistication about comparative research. Once methodologies of inquiry are understood via a typology that traces their alternative relationships to more elemental forms of discourse (narrative, social theory, etc.), comparative research becomes located in relation to a broader domain characterized by a condition of "integrated disparity," in which diverse practices invoke radically alternative logics, while nevertheless retaining sufficient points of mutual articulation to permit theoretical and substantive dialogue and translation among them. Thus, although comparative research continues to be shot through with tensions between science, relativism, and constructivism, researchers may find conditions ripe for a new era in which they find themselves mediating among diverse comparative and other practices of inquiry. But to consider those possibilities would move into the realm of as-yet contingent possibility.

See Also the Following Articles

Ecological Fallacy • Qualitative Analysis, Sociology • Sociology • Weber, Max

Further Reading

Burke, P. (1993). *History and Social Theory.* Cornell University Press, Ithaca, New York.

Espeland, W. N., and Stevens, M. L. (1998). Commensuration as a social process. *Annu. Rev. Sociol.* **24,** 313–343.

Hall, J. R. (1999). *Cultures of Inquiry: From Epistemology to Discourse in Sociohistorical Research.* Cambridge University Press, Cambridge.

Hawthorn, G. (1991). *Plausible Worlds: Possibility and Understanding in History and the Social Sciences.* Cambridge University Press, New York.

Lieberson, S. (1992). Small N's and big conclusions: An examination of the reasoning in comparative studies based on a small number of cases. In *What Is a Case?* (C. C. Ragin and H. S. Becker, eds.), pp. 105–118. Cambridge University Press, Cambridge.

McMichael, P. (1990). Incorporating comparison within a world-historical perspective. *Am. Sociol. Rev.* **55,** 385–397.

Ragin, C. C. (1987). *The Comparative Method.* University of California Press, Berkeley.

Ragin, C. C. (2000). *Fuzzy-Set Social Science.* University of Chicago Press, Chicago.

Ragin, C. C., and Becker, H. S. (eds.) (1992). *What is a Case?* Cambridge University Press, New York.

Roth, G., and Schluchter, W. (1979). *Max Weber's Vision of History.* University of California Press, Berkeley.

Skocpol, T. (1984). Emerging agendas and recurrent strategies in historical sociology. In *Vision and Method in Historical Sociology* (T. Skocpol, ed.), pp. 356–391. Cambridge University Press, Cambridge.

Stinchcombe, A. L. (1978). *Theoretical Methods in Social History.* Academic Press, New York.

Tilly, C. (1984). *Big Structures, Large Processes, Huge Comparisons.* Russell Sage, New York.

Complexity Science and the Social World

Will Medd

University of Salford, Salford, Greater Manchester, United Kingdom

Glossary

complex systems Emergent open systems that are far-from-equilibric, having nonlinear and self-organized behavior.

complexity science A multidisciplinary field concerned with the analysis of complex systems.

emergent dynamics Those dynamics with properties qualitatively different from the properties of the component parts.

far-from-equilibric A state in which there is continual flow and change and yet which enables an overall structure to form and be maintained.

nonlinearity In nonlinear systems, the output of the system cannot be calculated by the sum of the results of interactions. This means that small changes within the system over time can lead to large-scale, often unpredictable, transformations in the system.

open system A system that is open to interaction in terms of the exchange of information or energy with its environment.

self-organization Emergent dynamics that are the consequence of interaction through positive and negative feedback not fully determined by the early phase of system development, the intentions of the interaction parts, nor external forces.

This article is an overview of the recent development of approaches within social sciences that understand social phenomena through the lens of complexity science. Complexity science, comprising a range of work spanning many disciplines, explicitly aims to understand the dynamics of complex systems that are open and far-from-equilibric, displaying emergent, self-organized, and nonlinear behavior. The significance of complexity science is the way it brings to the fore the interrelationships between order and chaos, stability and instability, and continuity and change. Social scientists have sought to develop the application of complexity science to social phenomena, which raises fundamental questions about what "the social" is and what are the limits to our knowledge of it.

Complexity Science

The term "complexity science" can be misleading because it implies a unified body of science. There are attempts to generate such unification, exemplified by the work of the Santa Fe Institute and more recently the United Kingdom Complexity Society. Indeed, for some, it is precisely the possibility of unification between disciplines that has generated the interest in complexity science, exemplified by the 1996 Gulbenkian Commission on Restructuring the Social Sciences. While the idea of a unified science has been very prominent in representations by popular science writers, within social science strong claims have also been made about the potential of complexity science for such unification. Social science writers argue that, now that the inherent complexity and unpredictability of nonlinear natural phenomena have been revealed, the complexity of the social world can no longer be seen as distinct due to its complexity. Both the natural and social world can, they propose, display similar complex dynamics, requiring, therefore, similar explanation according to the properties of complex dynamical systems. Though there are disputes about just what complexity science is (for example, whether it is a science of modernity or a postmodern science), there is nonetheless a shared concern, developed in recent decades, that phenomena characterized by emergent, self-organized, and nonlinear behavior share similar characteristics that render traditional linear methods of understanding limited.

Whereas there had been much initial interest in the application of chaos theory to social science during the early 1990s, interest in the implications of nonlinearity became consolidated through the notion of complexity science. Complexity science brought a focus on nonlinearity, with the limits of knowledge being understood as a consequence of the character of systems, rather than a problem of knowledge generation. Because complex systems could not be broken down into their component parts, the parts could not be analyzed to explain the whole and predict future states. Complex systems have emergent characteristics that are qualitatively different from those of their parts. Complexity science therefore incorporates an interest in understanding the emergent patterns of system behavior and in developing models that can be applied to a whole host of phenomena. It is the apparent ubiquity of the characteristics of models of complexity science that has generated the interest in complexity science, as a new science that can integrate different disciplines.

Key features can be identified to describe complex systems:

1. Self-organized emergence. Emergent dynamics typify those complex systems having properties that are qualitatively different from the properties of the component parts of the system, so that the whole is not reducible to the sum of its parts. Complexity science has been interested in how such dynamic emergence comes into being, given that such emergent differences are not inherent in the early phase of system development, nor the intentions of the interaction parts, nor is it predetermined or predictable from external forces impinging on the system. Rather the emergence is self-organized through the positive and negative feedback relationships between interacting parts, the emergent dynamics, and those parts.

2. Nonlinearity. Important to the interest in self-organized emergence has been recognition of the significance of the nonlinearity of these dynamics, in which small changes in a system over time can be iteratively amplified so that they do not necessarily lead commensurately to small effects. In nonlinear systems, recursive relationships open up the possibility that small changes over time can lead to large-scale, often unpredictable, transformations in the system. In other words, small-scale local change, in both "natural" systems and complex social or cultural fields, can lead to large-scale global transformation of the entire system. Nonlinear systems dynamics can therefore become very sensitive to the initial conditions of the system, rendering problematic specific prediction.

3. Self-organized criticality. Complexity science has a particular interest in the role of self-organized nonlinear emergence for understanding life and its evolution. The quest has been to explore how systems maintain themselves in optimum states for survival—that is, how they maintain appropriate stability, continuity, and order while at the same time nurturing the capacity for local forms of instability, change, and disorder. Particular attention has been given to systems maintaining themselves at critical points, at which they maintain an appropriate equilibrium between order and chaos (or as sometimes referred "far-from-equilibrium"), ensuring both continuity and adaptability.

4. Evolutionary dynamics. Complex systems emerge through processes that involve exchanging information and energy with their environments. Survival of the system depends on being able to learn to select and adapt to the changing environment. Such learning requires memory and therefore history. Hence, two similar systems placed in the same environment might respond in very different ways because the history of the system is important in determining the future of the system in dynamic relation to its environment. Change occurs, then, through both internal organization and an ability to take advantage of external perturbations, sometimes inducing an evolutionary leap. This means that complex systems are essentially historical and also contingent in nature.

5. Attractor states. Through the "mathematics of complexity," methods have been used to describe and visualize complex systems in "phase space." Phase space is an abstract multidimensional space with coordinates for all the variables of the system. Each point in phase space represents the system at any possible point in time. Introducing time into the system enables exploration of the system trajectory. Attractor states refers to trajectories that tend to be restricted to (attracted to) particular parts of phase space. Thus, a shift in system dynamics will often be described in terms of a shift of attractor state, i.e., a shift from one attractor to another. Such a shift can be described qualitatively.

6. Interdependent systems. Finally, to understand the dynamics of complex systems, it is important to understand their interdependence with other systems. Hence, any optimal point is subject to continual change in processes of coevolution. A related point here is the importance of scale. Patterns of system dynamics are repeated through different scales, often referred to in terms of self-similarity, and understanding their dynamics requires understanding that there are systems within systems.

Complexity Science and the Social World

Complexity science has been applied across the social sciences, including, for example, politics, economics, psychology, sociology, international relations, and organizational and management studies. The rise of complexity science across such a broad range of areas of science can be attributed to different factors, and, indeed, combinations of factors. Different extremes can be identified. For example, an essentially realist account would suggest that complexity science has gained attention because it represents a better account of the world than we have previously had—in other words, because it is right. Alternatively, an emphasis can be made on shifts in our cultural condition, in which many areas of life are becoming destabilized and hence we have developed more sensitivity toward approaches that explore instability, chaos, and change. This debate is significant for understanding the development of the application of complexity science to the social world, and gains increased prominence in the context of the infamous "Sokal" affair, in which social scientists were accused of misusing metaphors from within the sciences. That said, however, within those extremes, the strength of complexity science can be seen in terms of its ability to offer better accounts of the world in relation to shifting concerns about instabilities humans now face. Importantly then, "complexity social scientists" have wanted to do more than just use the metaphors of complexity science to describe the social world. They have wanted to show how social science can contribute to complexity science and how complexity science, applied and developed for the social world, can illuminate real processes of social dynamics, even if that knowledge is always local. The problem has been how to do this. In relation to the concerns of social measurement, are three particular areas of attempts to achieve this: mathematical modeling, simulation, and reinterpreting quantitative measurement.

Applying Nonlinear Mathematics

Though mathematicians such as Poincaré had previously considered the possibilities of nonlinear behavior, it was the advent of computer technology that really brought to light its significance. Computer technology enabled mathematicians to solve nonlinear equations numerically (by trial and error) rather than analytically (finding a formula to a solution). These new methods of numerically solving nonlinear equations enabled analysis of more complex behavior by including the possible interactive affects that linear analysis breaks down. This enabled the discovery and confirmation (for some) that ordered patterns could be hidden within what could appear quite chaotic behavior, and that ordered behavior could lead to quite chaotic outcomes. That mathematics was now recognizing the significance of nonlinearity, instability, and uncertainty and was developing techniques to understand this was particularly important to social scientists such as Kiel and Elliott writing in the mid-1990s. Previous writers had applied chaos theory to specific examples, but the edited collection of Kiel and Elliott marked an attempt to bring together the use of nonlinear techniques to the social sciences more broadly.

The core issue in these techniques was to examine graphic representations of time series data in order to expose "attractors," or forms of underlying order, pattern, and structure. The technique involved representing the system dynamic within an imaginary space called "phase space." Phase space is a multidimensional space with x number of coordinates to represent the many different aspects of the systems. A single point in phase space represents the system state at a particular point in time. Overtime, the trajectory of the system can be mapped and the emergent patterns, if, indeed, there are any, can be analyzed. Within phase space, systems that are not entirely chaotic (i.e., displaying no patterns of behavior) tend to be "attracted" to particular dynamics. The analysis of phase space enables the identification of such attractors. Whereas "point attractors" in phase space indicate a stable equilibrium and "cyclical attractors" demonstrate a stable periodic oscillation between the same points, it is "strange attractors" that researchers were interested in. Strange attractors were significant because they indicated that though the trajectory of the system never reached the same point twice (and was not therefore cyclical), an ordered pattern nonetheless emerged. Further, at particular points in time (bifurcation points), the system would suddenly switched from one side of the attractor to the other, thus generating a figure-eight pattern. Hence, though the data may appear disorderly, the geometrical representation of the data in phase space may demonstrate forms of stability. Thus, the discovery of order within chaos.

There has been much interest in the dynamics of systems in strange attractors; however, identifying that social systems are operating within strange attractors is problematic. Indeed, though the interest in nonlinearity and the language of attractor states has been quite popular, a number of problems with the application of nonlinear mathematics have meant this has remained quite marginal in the social sciences. There are three particular difficulties. First, such analysis requires large amounts of time series data that are consistent and reliable, which is difficult to achieve in the social sciences. Second, some of the emergent patterns are as much a function of the nonlinear equation as they are of the particular data being explored. Third, equations assumed deterministic relationships in their structure, meaning that the structure of the equation does not evolve; this is problematic for social analysis because underlying social structures may change in ways that the equations supposedly representing them cannot. These challenges led to much debate about the role of modeling. It was clearly the case that the models could not provide objective viewpoints of the social world, and would therefore become by necessity tools in the social world.

Developing Simulation

While computer technology led to a new interest in nonlinear equations, computer technology also enabled the emergence in the 1990s of methodologies using computer simulation. Most interest for social science has been the development of "agent-based" models for simulation. In relation to complexity science, these are models in which agents interact at the local level, producing emergent, self-organized behaviors at the collective global level. In such simulations, the agents are therefore set up to act as if they are social agents, insofar as they can process and react to information in relation to their environment. The researcher is then interested in the self-organized patterns that emerge in running the simulation, including the emergence of individual behaviors of the agents. These patterns are self-organized because they are neither the consequence of the intention of the agents nor some external force, and yet they seem to evolve in ways that are neither entirely ordered nor entirely chaotic. Indeed, some complexity scientists talk of systems at the "edge of chaos." They are emergent because the self-organized behavior displays properties that are qualitatively different from the properties of the agents and cannot be explained by aggregation of the individual agents.

Simulation has been subject to criticism. One area of criticism is that the simulations are always too simplistic—that simulation requires a simplification of the agents to rule-based behaviors, of the agents interacting in particular ways, and of what is seen as important in the environment. The problem is that when dealing with complex systems, the implication of complexity is that we do need to pay attention to detail in ways that we cannot predict. And yet simulation requires us to make various decisions about what is important. In response to this is the argument that simulation does not claim to be the real system, but instead provides a method for exploring possible dynamics that might be looked for in the real system. In this sense, certainly simulation models have brought attention to the ways in which even quite simple behaviors, distributed and recursively interacting within a system, can lead to quite complex emergent dynamics at the system level. A more problematic criticism, however, is that the problem of such simulations is that they may fail to capture a key aspect of the social world, namely, that in the social world, human beings may change their very behavior in unpredictable ways as a consequence of the emergent system. Though simulation studies have explored the adaptive behaviors of individuals in relation to the emerging system, such simulation always requires some form of programming of agent behavior or learning.

(Re)interpreting Quantitative Data

Though there have been some questions about the limits of applying nonlinear mathematics to the social world, and concerns about the extent to which simulation can capture the very complexity that complexity science is interested in, an alternative avenue of research has explored the extent to which complexity analysis can be used to interpret social science data. Particularly influential in this area of work is David Byrne, who engages with the ontological implications of complexity science for the social sciences. In particular, he built on Reed and Harvey's work, arguing that complexity science offers a definitive ontology for critical realist analysis. Byrne develops his argument through analysis of a range of phenomena, including urban dynamics, planning, health, and education. For Byrne, the implication was a call to rethink the social science agenda, and particularly the value of quantitative methodology.

The argument put forward is that the implication of complexity is a reconsideration of how we understand what we are measuring, and the key to this is "death of the variable." The notion of the variable is seen as misleading because it tends to then be taken as something that exists. Complex systems are emergent, and this means that they do not have parts that can be represented in this way. However, drawing on the notion of multidimensional phase space, in which different coordinates of the system can be represented, it becomes possible not to think of measurements as representing variables of the systems, but, instead, as representing variate traces of the underlying systems dynamic in order to identify classes of system and systems behavior. The term "variable" then comes to be used as a word referring to things outside of the system, or inputs from the environment.

The importance of this move to talk of variate traces concerns the implication of how we understand and interpret the system we are exploring. Recognizing our measurement as a trace keeps open our sensitivity to the inherent complexity of complex systems. It keeps open that within complex systems are further complex systems, nested in complex hierarchies and networks. Interpreting the system then involves exploring combinations of traces, exploring the shifting implications of different parameters of the system, and exploring subsets of relationships within the system. It represents a shift from measurement of the system to classification of systems states and of system types.

Challenges for Measuring Social Complexity

The most difficult challenge posed by complexity science for social measurement is that of complexity itself. In the case of applying nonlinear mathematical models to the social world, the difficulties of establishing determinate sets of relations to represent complex social interactions are raised. Developing simulation models requires an assumption that the boundaries of the social world under question can somehow be established, such that the interactions of agents within the simulation are clear. And in reinterpreting quantitative data, we are faced with the challenge of what counts as a variate trace and how different would the system appear if alternative measurements had been made. All of these approaches have shed light on our understanding of social measurement, and the implication is that social measurement must be undertaken as an exploratory task because modeling can never be complete. To conclude, there are two key challenges that such exploration must continue to examine, namely, the problem of the boundaries and the limits to knowledge.

First, the problem of boundaries refers to asking a pertinent question: What is the system that we are looking at? This can mean asking what are the agents of the system to include in a simulation, as well as what traces of the system we might want to measure. Similarly, this can also mean exploring the question of what constitutes the boundary of the system. Traditionally, these sorts of questions are often answered through particularly disciplinary lenses. However, in attempting to transcend disciplines, complexity science suggests that social measurement needs to involve opening up our assumptions of what is in and out of a system, to explore the processes of emergence, as well as interaction between systems and their environment (which includes other systems). Complexity science is about understanding systems as both open and closed and exploring how boundaries between the system and the environment are constituted. Particularly in a global and increasingly technological context, these questions are becoming especially pertinent and, in theory, appear to be most appropriate for the application of complexity, as exemplified in the work of John Urry.

The question of how to establish the boundaries of the system under question is significant to the second challenge, that of the role of social measurement and knowledge of the future. In establishing the boundaries of the system and hence of social measurement, we are also establishing what we assume to be the internal and external dynamics to the system. Complexity science recognizes that absolute prediction is not possible. What is less clear is the extent to which it becomes possible to shape future scenarios—that is, in complexity language, to shape the likely, desired, attractor-state of the system. If it is the case that those boundaries are dynamic, then this suggests the need for continued adjustment of interventions. One implication is that when considering strategies or planning, for example, the message is to see these as processes that are continually reflexive, in order to be adaptive to changing internal and external environments. Another implication is that it becomes necessary to involve different forms of knowledge throughout the system. For these reasons, many involved in complexity research work with those engaged in the world, exemplified by the notion, for example of "integrative method."

See Also the Following Articles

Theory, Role of • Time-Series—Cross-Section Data

Further Reading

Brockman, J. (ed.) (1995). *The Third Culture: Beyond the Scientific Revolution*. Simon and Schuster, New York.

Byrne, D. (1998). *Complexity Theory and the Social Sciences: An Introduction*. Routledge, London.

Byrne, D. (2002). *Interpreting Quantitative Data*. Sage, London.

Capra, F. (1996). *The Web of Life: A New Synthesis of Mind and Matter*. Harper Collins, London.

Cilliers, P. (1998). *Complexity and Postmodernism: Understanding Complex Systems*. Routledge, London.

Eve, R. A., Horsfall, S., *et al.* (eds.) (1997). *Chaos, Complexity, and Sociology: Myths, Models, and Theories*. Sage, London.

Gilbert, N., and Troitzsch, K. G. (1999). *Simulation for the Social Scientist*. Open University, Buckingham.

Kauffman, S. (1995). *At Home in the Universe: The Search for Laws of Self-Organization and Complexity*. Oxford University Press, Oxford.

Khalil, E. L., and Boulding, K. E. (eds.) (1996). *Evolution, Order and Complexity*. London, Routledge, London.

Kiel, L. D., and Elliott, E. (eds.) (1996). *Chaos Theory in the Social Sciences: Foundations and Applications*. University of Michigan Press, Ann Arbor.

Prigogine, I. (1997). *The End of Certainty*. The Free Press, New York.

Prigogine, I., and Stengers, I. (1984). *Order Out of Chaos: Man's New Dialogue with Nature*. Heinemann, London.

Richardson, K., and Cilliers, P. (2001). What is complexity science? *Emergence: J. Complex. Iss. Org. Mgmt.* **3**(1), special edition.

Urry, J. (2003). *Global Complexity*. Polity, Cambridge.

Waldrop, M. M. (1992). *Complexity: The Emerging Science at the Edge of Order and Chaos*. Viking, London.

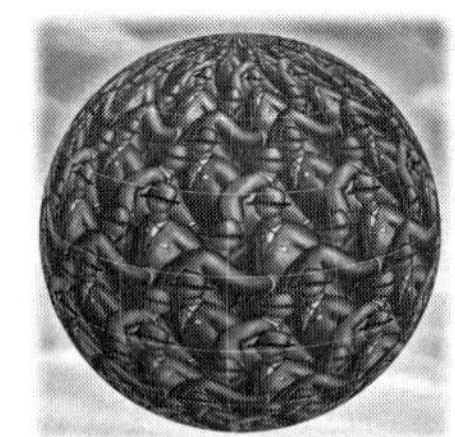

Computer Simulation

Louis N. Gray
Washington State University, Pullman, Washington, USA

Glossary

choice point A location, usually within a program, that can branch in two or more directions. The direction chosen depends on the underlying program.

compile A procedure by which a program or subroutine is translated into "machine language" (the fundamental structure of the operating system; usually binary).

endogenous variables The variables on which a system focuses; they are interrelated and may change as processes evolve within a simulation.

exogenous variables The variables external to a system; they are ordinarily set prior to simulation and cannot be altered within the simulation.

falsifiability A property of a statement (proposition or hypothesis) that makes it possible to show that the statement is false. For example, the statement "I am six feet tall" is falsifiable (given measurement assumptions); the statement "Someone is six feet tall" is not falsifiable. In science, specific empirical statements depend on the availability and applicability of appropriate measurement techniques.

flowchart A graphic depiction of elements of a simulation, with specific attention to choice points.

isomorphism A feature of a model or program that operates conceptually in a manner identical to a feature identified among humans, social groups, organizations, or social institutions.

model world The statement of a theory as specified in a simulation. The statement includes all the choice points and processes for determining outcomes.

moment-generating function A mathematical function that, with appropriate variable substitutions, produces the moments (central or raw) of a defined distribution. These functions completely specify the characteristics of a distribution.

process A procedure involving a time dimension and, thus, can result in either stability or change under specified conditions.

program Sets of instructions that control the operation of a computer.

programming language A specific symbolic language that can be used to construct a simulation or its subroutines.

real (empirical) world The processes a simulation is designed to mimic. Though some output may be available, the true underlying processes are unknown and output may also be contaminated by measurement error.

statistical test A procedure for assigning a probability to a specific hypothesis on the basis of known or hypothesized criteria.

stochastic A term generally referring to probabilistic variables; most frequently used to refer to probabilistic variables involved in processes or systems with a time dimension.

subroutine A segment of a program that performs a specific function. Subroutines are often compiled in languages different from that of the main program.

Historically, the term simulation has been used to describe procedures that attempt to mimic systems believed to exist in nature. Theory-based, simulated "model" systems must be distinguished from empirical (real-world) systems, the output of which is observable. Simulation techniques have come to replace the closed-form mathematical approaches once used to examine model systems. In particular, computer simulation forces examination of a theory in detail and requires addressing potential alternatives.

Introduction

Closed-Form Mathematics

Closed-form mathematical solutions are those that permit unique solutions to equations or systems of equations. The variables in the equations can be either exogenous or endogenous, but attention is centered on the endogenous variables. Though closed-form solutions are still sometimes preferred, they are limited in their ability to deal with large numbers of variables and/or processes involving multiple complex stochastic elements. Further, their solutions often serve to limit research questions to those that are answerable by the mathematical approach used, rather than including questions of the greatest theoretical importance. These kinds of limitations on theoretical models are removed as computer simulation techniques progress.

Early Simulation Techniques

Early techniques involved mechanical or paper-and-pencil operations that, it was hoped, behaved isomorphically with the target system as it moved from state to state. Prior to the ready availability of personal computers, a variety of procedures for randomization and for evaluating outcomes were employed. Unfortunately, these approaches were limited in their applicability due to logistical requirements and the inevitable problems with implementation.

Computer Simulation

Current simulation techniques involve the computer programming of processes analogous to those believed to characterize social systems. The speed of modern computers makes it possible to develop virtual representations of processes involving many variables and extended time periods. To some extent, computer simulation has replaced the "thought experiment" as a way of constructing, understanding, analyzing, and testing theories about social processes.

Computer Simulation Defined

Computer simulation can be defined as a program of instructions implemented by a machine that is intended to be isomorphic in output (graphic, numeric, or both) to measurement of a real or hypothetical social process.

Process The process can be one that is believed to exist or one whose existence is in question, but with implications that are being addressed. In either case, there is a theoretical assertion that the process defined in the model world "works" as if the hypothesized process was operating in the empirical world (see Fig. 1). The process may involve transitions between states of a system (as in discrete-time Markov processes), the temporal course of a system (as in continuous-time Markov process), or any alternative the theorist can envision and program. The hypothetical process, for example, may involve feedback-control processes subject to stochastic input that cannot be easily addressed in closed-form mathematics. The process is usually outlined in a flowchart.

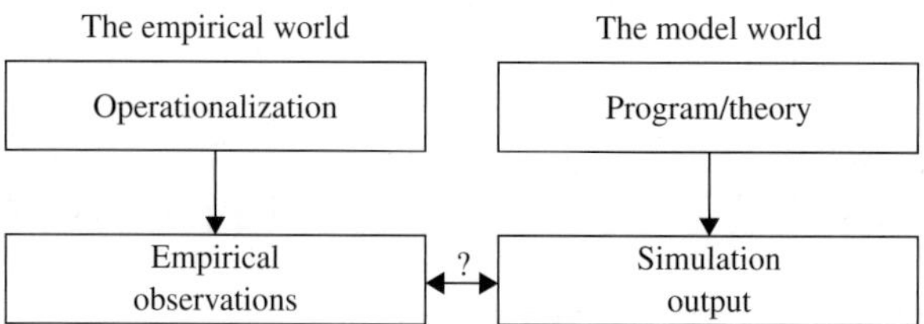

Figure 1 The relation between the empirical world and the model world. In the empirical world, operationalizations generate observations. In the model world, the program/theory generates output. In a perfect simulation, the empirical observations and simulation output should appear identical.

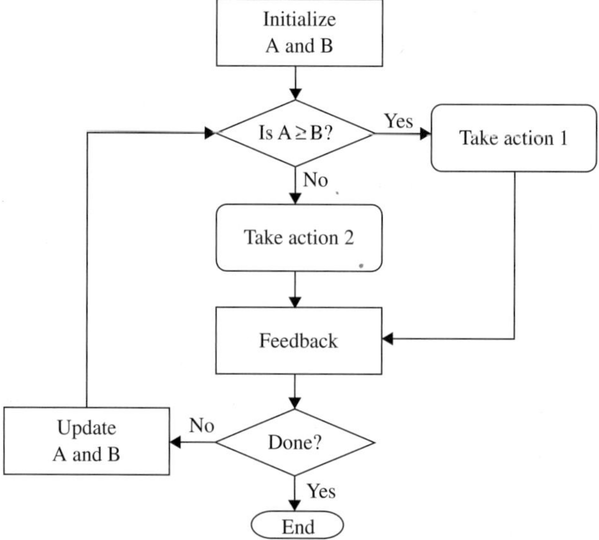

Figure 2 A generic flowchart with two registers and an undefined feedback process.

Flowchart A flowchart is a depiction of the general procedures in a simulation, including its choice points. Figure 2 provides a simple example.

Output Output refers to the kind of information that a researcher would look at (or would like to look at). For most researchers, this appears either as sets of numerical expressions or as graphical representations that depict the set of observations that could arise during, or as the result of, the hypothetical process (see Fig. 1). The range of included information depends on the focus of the research and the extent to which measurements on all aspects of the empirical process are available. The empirical or "measurement" model contains all the sources of error, known or unknown, that might be encountered. The theoretical model may, or may not, incorporate these sources of error.

Isomorphism Isomorphism refers to the extent to which a hypothetical process operates functionally as the one that is of interest—that is, the degree to which each operation of a model has, symbolically, a parallel operation in the phenomenon of interest. The abstract principles of the simulation should be logically "identical" to those of the focal phenomenon, as Fig. 1 shows. Of course, no theory achieves this ideal state, but scientific techniques are designed to approach it. When using computer simulation, the extent to which an idealized model approximates, symbolically, the target behavior can be explored.

Some Examples The range of activities generally included in computer simulation is very large. No global attempt to cover this range is made here, but potentially social examples vary from neural processes in complex learning to transportation and air quality simulations (TRANSIMS; see http://transims.tsasa.lanl.gov) based on large-scale human activities.

Two Major Applications of Computer Simulation

There are two common situations in which computer simulation is used: (1) examination of abstract theoretical claims about processes for which sufficient data are unavailable (or unobtainable) and (2) examination of observed data as the output of specific, but unknown, processes. The first approach involves theoretical propositions and their plausibility ("what would happen if . . . ?"). The second situation is one in which computer simulation is used in the empirical testing of specific theory.

Examination of Theoretical Propositions

Sometimes social scientists have ideas about segments of society and their intersections that are too controversial, prohibitively expensive, or too vaguely defined to permit clear empirical examination and the collection of all relevant data. Computer simulation offers solutions to these kinds of problems, because the simulation can be constructed in a way that shows how observations might appear should they become available.

The Inevitable Problem

Computer simulation designed to test any complicated theory will normally progress until reaching a choice point that the underlying model does not completely address. This point, and others like it, may represent the most important contribution of computer simulation to the development of theory. If, at some point in program development, the underlying theory does not specify how the process is to proceed, the programmer/theoretician is forced to make a decision unless the project is to be abandoned. Even if empirical information, or theoretical insight, is missing with respect to the choice point, the programmer/theoretician must still make a decision, or the program will not run. Before any of the other benefits of computer simulation can be realized, what may be its most important element must be noted: the programmer/theoretician must make decisions (address choice points) that may be ignored in the fundamental theory.

Unexpected Choice Points

Though theorists may believe they have fully explicated a theoretical position, it may be that they have not. In attempting a computer simulation of a set of theoretical propositions, it is usually found that there is some situation, logically arising within a computer program, that has not been addressed. It is always possible to employ a random device (e.g., a "coin-flip") to resolve such difficulties, but often it is discovered that the decision point is one that had not been considered, even though it may now appear central to the theory. Thus, computer simulation forces examination of a theory in detail and requires addressing alternatives that would otherwise have been ignored.

A Fundamental Problem A fundamental problem and potentially negative side effect is that it may not be possible to address such choice points because of inadequate prior research and/or the emerging nature of a theoretical perspective. That is, the simulation may lack fundamental empirical support and may, thus, be entirely speculative.

Determining the Theoretical Value of a Simulation The theoretical value of a simulation depends on the level of development of the theory it is designed to examine. Ordinarily, it should probably not be used just to see if there is an implementation that supports a given theory (because, eventually, one can be found). If the development of a simulation shows that important gaps exist in a theory, it seems that more empirical research is called for before a simulation can be of much scientific value or even taken seriously.

Examination of Empirical Data

Statisticians recognize that the power of a test (its ability to reject a false statistical hypothesis) is enhanced by the specificity of the theory. A theory that provides more information than another theory is, *ceteris paribus*, more powerful (and more easily falsifiable). Though researchers often concentrate on measures analogous to means and/or regression coefficients, it is also possible for a theory to specify information regarding variances or standard deviations, and, perhaps, higher moments of a distribution or sets of distributions. The more additional information supplied by a theory, the greater the likelihood of rejection of that theory and the greater the potential for its modification in ways that improve its explanatory power.

Higher Moments

A complete explanation of any social process would specify all the moments of the distribution of outcomes. That would mean that variances, skewness, kurtosis, etc. could be estimated on the basis of theoretical propositions. A good approximation of the moment-generating function should be a potential outcome of the simulation. Given sufficient sample size, this additional information permits more complete testing of theoretical formulations and, if the results so indicate, increases confidence in their predictive ability. If such additional tests seem to fail or results are mixed, then there should be less confidence in the theory, leading to a search for ways in which to improve it. Of course, because the source of such failures is not necessarily known, it is not clear which part of the simulation might be at fault. It is always possible that the entire simulation is inappropriate and that the process should be reinitiated.

Appropriate Test Structure

A theory that generates expectations for several statistics permits simultaneous tests of those statistics or even more general tests of, e.g., a moment-generating function. For example, a theory that can estimate both the mean and standard deviation (or variance) of a distribution allows use of a z-distribution rather than a Student's t-distribution for the estimated mean, and use of a chi-square distribution for the variance, with more confidence than is sometimes the case. Such a theory should also reveal whether a mean and variance are independent, and how a simultaneous test of their estimated values might be constructed. Ideally, the theoretical statement would provide instructions for a simulation that would permit answers to these questions, though that is not often the case with current theory. Statistical methods for examination of large numbers of related outcomes are not clearly understood by many theorists/researchers, and a number of developments in these areas are anticipated.

A Caveat The more quantities that a simulation can estimate, the easier it is to falsify the underlying theory. It is almost inconceivable that a simulation that is not reducible to closed-form mathematics could successfully produce a moment-generating function that exactly matches any given set of observations. The more hypotheses that are simultaneously tested, the more likely the simulation is to fail, if only because no theory is likely to be perfectly correct. Thus, it is necessary to restrict testing, at least at first, to those statistics that seem most important (e.g., the first raw and second central moments). As a simulation comes to satisfy these tests, then additional moments can be investigated.

Walking a Tightrope The point here is to make sure that a promising theory is not eliminated on the basis of tests beyond the initial interests. If the stance that any formulation is unlikely to be perfectly correct is adopted, it is also necessary to adopt a strategy that takes a middle ground. It is desirable to retain those theories that have the greatest chance of success, or modifications in them that can lead to such successes. As falsifiability is made easier, unfortunately, it is also more likely that promising models will be discarded. Because logic is pushing in two directions here, it is necessary to depend on those who use computer simulation to determine the dividing line between meaningful and meaningless levels of analysis.

Programming Languages

The programming language used for simulation requires at least two sometimes contradictory features: (1) it needs to be flexible enough to permit a variety of mathematical operations or their approximation and (2) it needs to be understandable to a focal audience of theorists and researchers without "black box" features that obscure its operation.

Flexibility and Scope

A programming language needs to have both flexibility, in terms of ease of completing operations, and scope, in terms of the range of operations it can carry out. Languages that have been used for simulation include several forms of Fortran, Basic, Pascal, C, C++, Java, and many others. Some simulations may use more than one language (e.g., compiled subroutines in C++ within True Basic) and some languages are easier to employ for some operations than others. Naturally, some languages make for efficient use of various unique computer properties and often are substantially faster than others (sometimes hours or even days faster). In addition to fundamental languages, there are also specialized languages focused specifically on simulation and related approaches. Examples of these are contained in several statistical packages plus focused software such as AMOS, GLLAMM, and Lisrel.

Programming in a Single Language

Programming completely within a language forces a programmer/theoretician to specify all the features of the simulation without resorting to any "black boxes" that are compiled in other languages. Commercial packages often make simulation easier and faster, but often contain "black box" features whose nature is not necessarily apparent to the user (though their operation may be important to the output). Realistically, it may not be efficient to exclude subroutines in more efficient languages within a simulation. Such inclusions are only problematic when a programmer/theoretician is unaware of the internal working of these modules. The important point is that the simulation remains faithful to the process it represents and that the programmer/theoretician be sensitive to failures in this respect.

Clear Operation

For a simulation to be evaluated by other theorists, researchers, and/or programmers, it is necessary that all aspects of the simulation be understandable to as many potential users as possible. To the extent that a simulation contains some kinds of "magic" (i.e., a knowingly unrealistic component of a simulation), there should be skepticism about the results. If processes are involved in the simulation that are other than those imagined to operate, or are hidden from view in such a way that problems are suspected, then the usefulness of the simulation, either for the development of theory or for the analysis of data, is suspect. The notion that "faith" should be maintained is as foreign to a scientific use of simulation as it is to other applications of science. This is not to say that elements used in simulations cannot make use of simplifications or subcomponents that are compiled separately from the main code, just that there must be some point at which these elements are accessible and can be seen to represent currently understood or hypothesized processes.

Future Directions in Computer Simulation

The range of activities that future computer simulations might include is possibly broader than can be anticipated, but two can be predicted: (1) the growth of specialized languages and/or software and (2) increased blurring of the demarcation between simulation and empirical research.

Specialized Languages

As users seek increasingly rapid ways of anticipating research and policy outcomes, the development of software to fill those needs is likely. Generally, attempts to increase the ability to respond to requests for information in these areas should be welcomed, but care should be taken that the need for information does not result in incorporation of empirically insupportable processes. It is a very human trait to take what we think we know as absolute truth, and computer simulation is no exception: The extent to which computer simulation can continue to aid us depends on our ability to represent in the simulation those features of social behavior and processes that are empirically supported. Processes that are in question need to be identified as such and their presence in simulated outcomes made clear to potential users. Fundamentally, useful simulations must be based on processes that can be empirically supported and on which there is substantial scientific agreement.

Demarcation of Simulation and Empirical Research

As empirical research expands, it is likely that various research endeavors will build on features of simulations to estimate quantities, develop measurements, or aid in quantitative analysis. As we move in these directions, the dividing line between empirical research (what we know) and our estimates of current states (what we think we know) will become increasingly blurred. As the question mark in Fig. 1 suggests, it is essential that theorists, researchers, and policymakers are clear about where the dividing line lies. In our haste to uncover solutions to real problems, we cannot afford to lose track of the difference between those things we understand and those things about which we speculate, however reasonable those speculations might be. Fundamentally, it is necessary to remember the principles of science and to refuse to be misled by technology that we may not entirely comprehend.

See Also the Following Article

Computer-Based Mapping

Further Reading

Bainbridge, W. S. (1998). *Sociology Laboratory: IBM Pc/ Manual and 256K Diskette.* Wadsworth Publ., Belmont, California.

Banks, J. (ed.) (1998). *Handbook of Simulation: Principles, Methodology, Advances, Applications, and Practice.* Interscience, New York.

Berk, R. A., Bickel, P., Campbell, K., Keller-McNulty, S. A., Fovell, R., Kelly, E. J., Sacks, J., Park, B., Perelson, A., Rouphail, N., and Schoenberg, F. (2002). Workshop on statistical approaches for the evaluation of complex computer models. *Statist. Sci.* **17,** 173–192.

Cameron, I., and Hangos, K. (2001). *Process Modeling and Model Analysis.* Academic Press, San Diego.

Casti, J. L. (1992). *Reality Rules: Picturing the World in Mathematics.* 2nd Ed. Wiley-Interscience, New York.

Donahoe, J. W., and Palmer, D. C. (1994). *Learning and Complex Behavior.* Allyn and Bacon, Boston.

Fishman, G. S. (2001). *Discrete-Event Simulation.* Springer-Verlag, New York.

Forrester, J. W. (1961). *Industrial Dynamics.* Pegasus Communications, Waltham, Massachusetts.

Law, A. M., and Kelton, W. D. (1999). *Simulation Modeling and Analysis, 3rd Ed. (Industrial engineering and Management Science Series).* McGraw-Hill, New York.

Naylor, T. H.Balintfy, J. L.Burdick, D. S.Chu, K. (1968). *Computer Simulation Techniques.* John Wiley & Sons, New York.

Perros, H. (2003). *Computer Simulation Techniques: The Definitive Introduction.* Available on the Internet at www.csc.ncsu.edu

TRANSIMS Home Page. (2003). Available on the Internet at http://transims.tsasa.lanl.gov

Computer-Based Mapping

Alberto Giordano
Texas State University, San Marcos, Texas, USA

Glossary

animated cartography The representation of movement or change on a map. An example is the representation of the path of a hurricane on a map, achieved by moving a dot across an area with velocities and directions corresponding to the ground speeds and directions of the eye of the hurricane at different times. In another example, consecutive maps of U.S. population by state at census years could be displayed at set time intervals (e.g., 10 years equals 5 s), allowing the viewer to detect change patterns. The most important aspect of an animated map is that it depicts something that would not be evident, or not as evident, if the frames were viewed individually: what happens between each frame is more important than what exists on each frame. The creation of animated (or dynamic) maps has become possible with the advent of computer cartography and the interactive map and during the 1990s dynamic maps came to be routinely used by cartographers.

computer-based mapping (computer cartography) The creation of maps with computers, made possible by specialized hardware (e.g., digitizers, scanners) and software applications. A fundamental characteristic of computer-based mapping is the separation between data management and display functionalities. This separation makes tasks such as the update and editing of maps easier than it is in traditional pen-and-ink paper cartography. Computer cartography has considerably extended the representational capabilities of traditional maps, for example, making it possible to create multimedia and animated maps. The World Wide Web has further revolutionized cartography, creating an entirely new distribution channel.

interactive map A type of computer-based map designed to allow user interaction and exploration. Functionalities implemented in interactive maps include pan, zoom in, zoom out, and the interaction with "hotspots," symbols map users can click on to access additional information related to the spot. Additionally, by turning on and off different layers, users are often able to choose which information they want displayed on the map. The interactive map is a prerequisite to the scientific visualization of cartographic data.

multimedia cartography The addition of text, images, sound, pictures, and video to the map. The creation of multimedia maps has become possible with the advent of computer cartography and the interactive map. Multimedia maps are becoming common, particularly on the Internet. For example, several tourism-related sites include maps with "hotspots" that users can click on to receive events information, see a video of the attraction, or check visiting hours.

scientific visualization In the cartographic context, the use of maps as tools for exploratory data analysis. Traditionally, maps have been used as tools for the communication of spatial information, but progress in computer-based mapping, geographic information systems technology, and spatial statistics has contributed to a shift in focus. Cartographers are becoming more and more engaged in scientific visualization, providing their expertise to other scientists to study such disparate phenomena as pollutant diffusion in a bay, environmental justice, or animal species distribution.

The introduction of computers in cartography has had profound effects on the way maps are designed, produced, distributed, and used. Maps have become easier to create and update and are more accurate. Using a computer, cartographers can easily and quickly try different cartographic designs and symbolization schemes. The World Wide Web has changed how many cartographic products are delivered to their intended final user. As a result of the introduction of computers, the distinction between mapmakers and map viewers has blurred and the roles are less defined.

Introduction

For most of its history, cartography was a highly institutionalized enterprise. Cartographers were often university or government employees or worked for a commercial company. Making maps required a highly skilled labor force and the capital investments needed for the production, reproduction, and distribution of maps were not usually available to the general public. Maps were often classified materials and, at the extreme, state secrets.

Much of this has changed. The low cost of software and hardware has made it possible for individuals to make maps and distribute them via the Internet. Geographic databases are readily available online, so that one can—at least in the United States—produce fairly sophisticated maps with data publicly available on the Internet. This democratization of the mapmaking enterprise is one of the most important and probably long-lasting effects of the computer revolution in cartography. Alternative representations of the world have become possible, often in competition with official views. Individual citizens, nonprofit organizations, and interest groups can make and distribute their own maps. On the other hand, professional cartographers often lament the poor quality of many productions, the dilettantism of several among the improvised mapmakers, and the lack of knowledge of basic cartographic principles. There is truth in these statements. Cartography is the art and science of communicating spatial information graphically and its rules, principles, and foundations should be learned and applied even by nonprofessional cartographers. For example, different cartographic projections have different properties that make them suitable for showing certain types of data and not others: an equal-area projection should be employed when representing density of population, an azimuthal projection should be employed when the map is being used for navigation, and so on. Another issue that has often surfaced concerns the reliability of the sources used in the compilation of many of the maps found on the Internet. It is often the case that these data are of uncertain origin or quality or it is not known how up-to-date they are. In other words, the maps have no reliable metadata (information about the data) or no metadata at all. In these instances, even professional cartographers might find it difficult to establish whether or not the data are fit for use. Unfortunately, the creation of metadata is often a neglected step of the cartographic process—albeit not only by the amateur cartographer.

In any case, the introduction of the computer has fundamentally changed the relationship between the map and its producer, who can more truly interact with the map, experimenting with design and symbology, modifying the map layout, and easily and readily changing scale, projection, center, and orientation. Often the map is linked to a database that can be queried by the user on the fly. Additionally, multimediality and animation have redefined the meaning of the term "map" itself. Maps have been combined with video, sound, text, and images to enhance the representation potential of the graphic media. Dynamic—or animated—maps can be used to overcome one of the limitations of paper maps, that is, the fact that they are static. A sequence of maps can be used to show time changes or symbols can be rolled on the map to represent movement (e.g., the path of a hurricane). Finally, the Internet has revolutionized the distribution of maps. Anybody with Web access can make a map and publish it for all to see at no cost.

All these topics are discussed in the next sections. The objective is to convey the basic steps in the history of computer mapping, discuss its present state, and to speculate on its possible future.

Why Maps with Computers?

"Computer-based mapping" simply means making maps with a computer. The term is synonymous with computer cartography, computer mapping, computer-assisted cartography, and digital mapping. In computer-based mapping, specialized hardware and software are employed to display and analyze a particular type of data, i.e., geographical data. Geographical data (also called spatial data) are defined by having a positional component that is measured on a coordinate system. For example, the latitude and longitude of a mountain peak are stored in a computer database and are displayed using on a monitor using a cartographic symbol, such as a cross.

The history of computer cartography can be summarized in three distinct stages. In the beginnings—the 1960s and 1970s—the focus of computer cartography was map production. Essentially, cartographers and computer scientists were interested in how to automatically draw geographical features (e.g., cities, roads, lakes) on a piece of paper using points, lines, and polygons. Computers were extremely expensive, slow, and difficult to use. Progress in software design and new and improved hardware in the 1980s made it possible to focus on incorporating analytical functionalities (such as overlay, described below) in computer mapping systems. These advances contributed to the development of Geographic Information Systems (GIS) in the same years. Since the 1990s, computer cartography has undergone a major shift toward scientific visualization. Scientific visualization refers the use of maps as exploratory tools and relies on theoretical and technical advancements in multimedia design and animation and on the development of increasingly sophisticated spatial analytical techniques.

Computer cartography has, at least in the United States, a birth date many scholars agree on. In 1959, Waldo Tobler published a paper in the *Geographical Review* titled "Automation in Cartography." In it, Tobler describes a system to automatically create map overlays. The concept of overlay is a fundamental one in spatial analysis and cartography and it is founded on another important concept, that of layers. GIS and computer mapping systems break up maps into separate layers of geographical information (a layer containing all the roads, another with all the cities, and so on.) These layers are then combined, or overlaid, to create the map. The overlay function is an important one in spatial analysis and it is performed to create, among other types, suitability maps. These are maps that show how suitable places on a map are for a certain use. For example, by overlaying geology, hydrography, soil type, and topography layers, one could identify areas where timber can be harvested. The idea of separating layers of information predates the age of computers—originally layers were combined and inspected visually by plotting geographical features on transparent sheets—but the idea perfectly fits the logic of computer databases and especially of relational databases. In a relational database, each layer is a table and each table is composed of records (rows) and attributes (columns). Relationships between tables are explicitly coded by using attributes shared by the tables. For instance, a table showing the average personal income in the counties of California in 2002 could be linked to a table showing population in the same counties in the same year through the attribute COUNTY_NAME present in both.

One of the advantages of using layers in computer cartography is that they make updating a map a relatively easy task. For example, when new data for personal income and population in the counties of California are released, making a new map simply entails updating the values, displaying the map on the monitor, and printing it (or putting it on a Web site) if needed. Updating a paper map means redoing the map altogether.

This point highlights another major difference between computer mapping systems and traditional, pen-and-ink cartography. In computer mapping systems, and also in GIS, data and the representation of data are kept separated and are handled by different software components. The data are accessed by the database management system component and are displayed by the graphic rendering component, so that, for example, the record corresponding to income in a particular county is retrieved from the table and represented with a certain shade of red at a specific location on the map depending on its value in the table. It is this separation of the stages of data management and data display that makes updating a computer map a relatively easy task.

A Brief History of Computer Cartography

As already mentioned, the first examples of the use of computers in cartography were meant to aid map production. In the *Bickmore Boyle System of Automatic Cartography*, developed in the early 1960s in the United Kingdom by D. P. Bickmore and R. Boyle, an operator would follow the coordinates of geographical features represented on a paper map and feed the coordinates to a magnetic tape. Information on the tape was coded into features such as rivers, coastlines, and contours. From the tape, the information was then plotted onto a table on which a projector was mounted. The projector would then plot the lines onto sensitized film. Worth noting is that the scale and projection could be changed by feeding the tape through a computer and that the drawing equipment was very accurate (0.07 mm). The Bickmore Boyle System is conceptually similar to a modern digitizer, a tool used to transfer geographical features from a paper map to the computer. Two other fundamental early examples of computer mapping systems were developed at the Royal College of Art in the United Kingdom and at the Harvard University Laboratory for Computer Graphics in the United States. The project developed by the Royal College of Art was to develop an automatic technique for presenting data in a cartographic form by means of a computer. It consisted of an electronic plotting table and a "lock-on" time follower, both connected to a computer. Lines traced from maps were converted into x, y coordinates and stored on magnetic tape. Later, the tape would be read to control the movement of a beam of light thrown onto photosensitive film, thereby redrawing the original. The system developed at Harvard University, called SYMAP (Synagraphic Mapping System), worked on a fundamentally different concept. In SYMAP, maps were produced by converting computer tabulations to graphic output on a coordinated basis, utilizing a grid and a standard line-printer. The program could produce different types of thematic maps, such as contour maps to show elevations and choropleth maps to show quantitative values at specified areal units (e.g., household income in the counties of Massachusetts in 2002). These early efforts were followed by more experimental systems in the 1970s and even early 1980s, but high costs severely undercut any chance of widespread use. The cost of producing digital maps on mainframe systems such as those required by early computer mapping software often ranged from $50,000 to $100,000.

Computers have become of widespread use in cartography since the late 1980s. Lower costs and technical innovations are key factors. Inexpensive raster graphics devices, digitizers, and scanners gradually came into use. The introduction of the personal computer in the early 1980s started a revolution whose last chapters are being written by the introduction of handheld digital devices, such as palmtop organizers, digital cameras, and cell phones. Interactivity, the World Wide Web, and the integration of spatial analytical functions into computer mapping systems are arguably the most important developments to occur in the field in the 1980s and 1990s. Multimediality and animation have further changed the face of cartography and will likely revolutionize the field in the future. These new developments are discussed in detail in the next sections.

Maps and Interactivity

The interactive computer as it is known today is a relatively new tool. From the 1950s until the late 1970s, computer mainframes were controlled through the use of punched cards containing instructions that were read and executed before a printout of the answers could be produced. Later, interaction with minicomputers and microcomputers occurred through a command line interface that required the use of a keyboard. In order for computers to really change the world of cartography, two major technical and conceptual advancement needed to occur: the WYSIWYG (What You See Is What You Get) principle and its implementation and the GUI (Graphical User Interface). Together, these two changed the panorama of computer cartography.

In computer systems designed according to the WYSIWYG principle, what the user sees on the screen is exactly what will appear on the paper when the document is printed. For example, a word processor software program will show formatting characteristics, such as spaces between lines, indentations, and font type, size, and style, on the screen exactly as they will be printed. The importance of the WYSIWYG principle for modern mapping systems cannot be understated. The ability to evaluate and, if needed, vary map design or symbolization choices is a very desirable function for a mapmaker. Cartographers can interactively choose the shape of a certain symbol and its size or choose where to locate a place name and immediately see on the screen how that symbol or label will look when printed or viewed on a Web site. However, the WYSIWYG principle is not fully implemented in cartography and limitations are evident, especially as concerns the use of color. This point is particularly worth discussing because it highlights one of the problems created by the use of computers in cartography. The problem lies in the difference between computers and printers when it comes to the way in which color is created. Color in computer monitors is created using light: red, green, and blue light is combined to derive all other colors in an additive process. In the RGB system, red, green, and blue are the primary additive colors. Secondary additive colors are magenta (blue plus red, with no green), yellow (green plus red, with no blue), and cyan (blue plus green, with no red). Mixing pure red with pure blue and pure green creates white. Printers create color in a very different way. The CMYK system is a subtractive color process in which cyan, magenta, and yellow (the subtractive primary colors) inks are combined to create the subtractive secondary hues red (yellow plus magenta, with no cyan), green (cyan plus yellow, with no magenta), and blue (cyan plus magenta, with no yellow). Pure cyan plus pure magenta plus pure yellow is black. In practice, however, mixing cyan, magenta, and yellow inks does not yield a pure black but rather a very dark brown. For this reason, black ink is added to the three subtractive primary colors. The difference between the RGB and the CMYK systems has a very practical implication for cartographers, in that the color seen on the screen is unlikely to be identical to the color that will be created by the printer. Tables of correspondence exist between the CMYK and RGB systems but the match is far from perfect, at least in relatively inexpensive systems. In addition to differences in how color is created, another problem is created by the fact that a computer monitor is capable of producing far more different colors than a printer. A 24-bit monitor system, for example, can create over 16 million colors (16,777,216 or 2^{24}) and no ink combination can create as many different colors. And even if it could, no human is capable of discerning 16 million colors. This limitation notwithstanding, the WYSIWYG principle has been crucial to the diffusion and adoption of computer mapping systems.

Another innovation has played a fundamental role in the evolution of computer cartography: the adoption of a GUI as the standard method for human–machine interaction. A graphical user interface employs graphic tools such as menus, windows, pointers controlled by pointing devices (such as the mouse), icons to represent files or functionalities, and a desktop where icons are grouped. Microsoft Windows and the Apple Macintosh are examples of GUI. Interaction with a computer is easier with a GUI: users do not have to learn commands as in DOS or UNIX and the point-and-click type of interaction is more intuitive and natural. In the context of cartography, a GUI has made it possible to perform tasks that were impossible on a paper map. One such functionality is zooming in and out, which is equivalent to a scale change: users can zoom in on a particular portion of the map and see it in more detail. The most sophisticated systems allow cartographers to set the amount of information that users will see at a particular scale, so that, for example, all roads are shown at a larger scale and only interstate highways are displayed at a smaller scale. In general, interactivity in cartography has provided the user with more control over how the informative content of map is displayed: using the mouse, a user can click on a symbol and retrieve information on the geographical feature that that symbol represents. The user can also choose where to display a legend and how large it should be or even if a legend should be displayed at all. These examples highlight the importance of keeping cartographic representation functionalities separated from cartographic data management functionalities. When a user clicks on a symbol, the information that pops up is retrieved from the database and displayed on the screen in a way that is similar to what was described earlier in relation to overlays. Interactivity and database connection have given the user significant freedom when it comes to making customized maps. For example, the online version of the *National Atlas of the USA* (available at http://www.nationalatlas.gov) lets the user make dozens of separate maps varying the geography and the variables mapped. This flexibility is typical of electronic atlases, a revisited version of traditional paper atlases that are becoming a prominent feature of government agencies' Web sites, especially in North America and Europe.

A final example of how computers have changed the way that users interact with the map is the case of choropleth maps. These are maps that portray the geographical variability of a quantitative variable by shading geographical units according to the value of the variable. For example, a cartographer might wish to create a map showing median household income in U.S. counties in the year 2000. The choropleth map is often used to display this type of data. Probably the most important decision a cartographer has to make when creating a choropleth map is how to subdivide the data in classes. Assigning a unique shade of color—for example, a shade of green—to all the over 3000 counties based on their household income would make it very difficult to extract information regarding individual counties from the map. A solution is to: (1) group the over 3000 values in, say, five classes ranging from the lowest to the highest value; (2) assign a shade of green from light to dark to each class so that the higher the income, the darker the shade of green; (3) color the counties a shade of green corresponding to the county's median household income. If one tries to create this same exact map at the U.S. Bureau of the Census Web site (available at http://www.census.gov) using Census 2000 data, the result is a choropleth map in which the five classes are subdivided as follows: (1) \$9243–\$23,750; (2) \$23,848–\$33,006; (3) \$33,026–\$41,183; (4) \$41,201–\$53,804; and (5) \$53,945–\$82,929. Looking at this map, the user will recognize that geographical patterns are present in the distribution of the value of median household income in the United States. For example, the corridor between Washington, DC and Boston, and the suburban counties around Atlanta, Minneapolis, Denver, and San Francisco are wealthy, with several counties in the fifth class. The southern states and parts of the southwest and the northwest have large numbers of relatively poor counties, with several counties in the first class. To obtain the five groups above, counties were first listed according to their median household income in ascending order and then grouped in five classes, each containing the same number of elements (approximately 600). This procedure is called the "quantile" method for classifying data and is one of several available methodologies used to group data. Generally speaking, the choropleth map will look slightly different depending on the classification methodology chosen, even though it is hoped that similar patterns will appear no matter which one is chosen. Computer mapping systems usually allow users to vary the methods employed to derive classes, including their number, and expert users can take great advantage of this flexibility: by varying the procedure chosen to determine classes, one can evaluate the persistence of geographic patterns. In the example regarding household income in U.S. counties, should the same spatial pattern appear using the quantile, the equal interval, and the natural breaks methods, then it would be reasonable to conclude that the pattern is a real one and not an artifact of the classification method employed. Note that in this case, the cartographer is using the software to test whether the hypotheses formulated on the spatial distribution of income in U.S. counties are robust enough to be confirmed when the classification methods are varied. This is an example of the already mentioned "scientific visualization" approach to using maps: the database is explored and hypotheses are formulated and tested. With its computational power, computers can greatly facilitate these tasks.

The Functionalities of Computer-Based Mapping Systems

It has been mentioned already that in its early history, computer cartography focused heavily on the mapmaking process, even if its potential as a tool to aid the analysis of spatial data was recognized almost immediately and even if in a sense the concept of scientific visualization—a relatively new one in cartography—was already implicit in Tobler's 1959 description of a system for overlaying layers of geographic data.

In addition to spatial analytical functionalities, such as overlay and choropleth maps, computer-based mapping systems include a wide variety of cartographic functionalities. These functionalities constitute the core of the system and are discussed in the remainder of this section. Before moving on to review them, however, it is perhaps useful to explain that in computer mapping systems and in GIS, real-world features are conceptualized and symbolized as cells or as points, lines, and polygons. When cells (usually squares) are used, the system is raster-based. The key concept in raster systems is that of resolution. In raster systems, each cell corresponds to one and only one value (e.g., "water" or "not water" in an hydrology layer). In a layer containing elevations, each squared cell is assigned one value and the topographic representation will be as accurate as the level of its spatial resolution. For example, an area of 10 by 10 km will contain 10,000 cells at a cell resolution of 100 m. So, each 100 by 100 meters cell is assigned one and only one elevation. If the resolution is increased to, say, 10 m, the resolution and the accuracy of elevation representation will increase and so will the size of the file (1 million cells). Vector systems work in a different way. Instead of being space-exhaustive as the raster systems, vector systems use points, lines, and polygons to represent real-world features. The prominent concept in vector systems is that of topology: in order to perform any cartographic or spatial functionalities, the relationships between points, lines, and polygons must be explicitly recorded. For example, a polygon is connected to other polygons by a common boundary and it is composed of a certain number of vertices or nodes. A line has an origin and an end and it might or might not cross a polygon. A point is identified by a set of spatial coordinates. The size of the files in vector-based systems is usually smaller than the size of those in raster-based systems. It is worth noting that three-dimensional representations are possible in both raster and vector systems and are generally used to show topography.

This premise is important because cartographic functionalities are implemented differently depending on the data model (raster or vector) used by the system, but in general both models include four main types of operations:

Generalization

These include functionalities to, for example, reduce the number of points in a line, smoothing its appearance, and reducing its size in bits; merging geographical units (e.g., create a map of the states of the United States from a map of the counties of the United States by merging all counties that belong to the same state); reducing the number of cities displayed on the map by using a population threshold (e.g., no cities with less than 1 million people).

Map Projections, Coordinate Systems, and Scale Transformations

This is one of the great advantages of computer mapping systems. The ability to change scale, projection, and coordinate system on the fly can be used by the cartographer to make maps that are specifically designed to fit an intended use. The example that was given earlier is that of employing an equal-area projection to show density of population. Another example would be using a conical projection with two standard parallels to represent landmasses that extend more in the East–West direction than in the North–South direction.

Cartographic Measurements

These operations include calculating the length of a line, the distance between points, the area and perimeter of a polygon, and so on. Vector and raster systems implement very different algorithms to take these types of measurements.

Symbolization

Computer-mapping systems are particularly powerful as tools to aid cartographic design. Especially in the most recent releases, cartographic and GIS software packages present the user with a wide choice of symbols and provide flexibility for designing or importing additional symbols from other sources and for varying the size, shape, and color of symbols. Additionally, the user can easily customize the layout of the map, changing the position and characteristics of the legend, the title, the scale bar, the neat line, and other cartographic elements.

However, it should be noted that there is one area in which computer-based mapping systems have thus far yielded disappointing results: the automated placement of text on a map. This is a challenging task because different and often contrasting needs must be reconciled when placing labels on a map. Text needs to be easily readable and so labels should be quite large, but at the same time space is often a scarce commodity, especially in general-purpose maps that aim at portraying all physical and human elements of a certain area. Also, labels need to be placed so that it is clear to which feature they refer to, but this is often difficult especially in areas where there are many symbols referring to the same class of features. For example, placing labels for cities in highly urbanized regions or labels for countries in Europe can be a very challenging task. The problem of automatically placing labels has been tackled in different ways. One approach that seems particular promising is artificial intelligence, perhaps one of the future directions of development of computer-based mapping.

The Future of Computer Cartography: Animation, Multimedia, and the World Wide Web

It has been said that the largest producer of maps in the history of cartography is Mapquest (available at http://www.mapquest.com), because it delivers to visitors of its Web site several hundred thousands of customized maps each day. Granted, these are virtual maps—although they can be printed—but the number is impressive nonetheless. Mapquest and several similar sites are examples of the revolution brought to the world of cartography by the World Wide Web. From the point of view of computer cartography, the revolution is one of distribution and of democratization, as already mentioned. To distribute a map to potentially millions of viewers, one simply need put it on the Internet. Compare this relatively simple action with the investments necessary to produce and distribute a map in the world of traditional print cartography. Ease of distribution has led to exponential growth in the number of maps produced and in the variety of their styles and designs and it has also facilitated the public exchange of competing views on the use of environmental and economic resources. Issues such as environmental justice and sustainable development are often discussed using maps as tools for scientific visualization.

On the other hand, the World Wide Web has not per se changed the way that maps are made. Multimedia and animated cartography, however, have. Animated cartography was pioneered by Thrower, who published a paper entitled "Animated Cartography," in a 1959 issue of *The Professional Geographer*, and by Tobler, who in 1970 developed a computer animation simulating urban growth in the Detroit region. The main advantage of animated—or dynamic—cartography is that it overcomes the traditional immobility of paper maps, in which time is kept constant (e.g., "Household income in U.S. counties in 2000"). Animated maps can show time changes, for example, by flashing a series of maps representing household income in 2000, 2001, 2002, and 2003. Animated maps can also represent another phenomenon that is problematic to deal with in traditional paper maps: movement. Traffic can be shown at different times of the day, a hurricane's path can be tracked in almost real time, and migration can be studied more effectively. When animation is combined with multimediality, the possibilities of traditional cartography increase exponentially. Multimedia cartography is the combination of maps with text, images, video, and audio. One type of map that has successfully incorporated multimedia elements is the tourist map on the Internet. Typically, these are maps in which a user clicks on a particular spot and is presented with a wide array of information. For example, clicking on a park in a city map might bring up pictures, a schedule of daily events, opening hours, and maybe a video of the park's main attractions. Multimedia and animation are perhaps only a taste of what is to come in computer cartography: virtual reality, that is, the user *in* the map.

See Also the Following Articles

Cognitive Maps • Digital Terrain Modeling • Geographic Information Systems • Geography • Land Use Mapping • Remote Sensing • Spatial Pattern Analysis

Further Reading

Cartwright, W., *et al.* (eds.) (1999). *Multimedia Cartography.* Springer-Verlag, Berlin/New York.

Clarke, K. C. (1995). *Analytical and Computer Cartography.* Prentice Hall, Englewood Cliffs, NJ.

Dodge, M., and Kitchin, R. (2001). *Mapping Cyberspace.* Routledge, London.

Kraak, M.-J., and Brown, A. (eds.) (2001). *Web Cartography.* Taylor & Francis, London.

MacEachren, A. M. (1995). *How Maps Work: Representation, Visualization, and Design.* Guilford, London.

Peterson, M. P. (1995). *Interactive and Animated Cartography.* Prentice Hall, Englewood Cliffs, NJ.

Thrower, N. (1959). Animated cartography. *Profess. Geogr.* **11**(6): 9–12.

Tobler, W. R. (1959). Automation and cartography. *Geogr. Rev.* **49,** 526–534.

Tobler, W. R. (1970). A computer movie simulating urban growth in the Detroit region. *Econ. Geogr.* **46**(2): 234–240.

Computer-Based Testing

Richard M. Luecht

University of North Carolina at Greensboro, Greensboro, North Carolina, USA

Glossary

automated test assembly (ATA) Involves the use of mathematical programming algorithms or heuristics to select optimal test forms that simultaneously meet statistical specifications as well as any number of content and other test construction constraints.

computer-adaptive testing (CAT) A test process that adapts in difficulty to the apparent proficiency of the test taker. CAT is usually more efficient than conventional fixed-item testing because it either reduces the number of items needed to achieve a prescribed level of measurement precision (reliability) and/or it achieves more precision across a broader range of the score scale with a fixed-length test.

computer-based testing (CBT) A test process delivered on a computer. Computer-based tests tend to differ in terms of the level of adaptation to the ability of examinees, the size of test administration units employed (items versus testlets), the type of connectivity required to interactively transmit data, the types of items supported, the test assembly methods employed, and the nature and extent of test form quality control mechanisms used.

multistage testing (MST) The administration of tests in stages. Multi-item modules called "testlets" are typically assigned to each stage. Examinees complete an entire testlet before moving on. Scoring and adaptive routing decisions can be employed between stages to achieve some degree of test adaptation.

test-delivery driver A software test administration application that typically performs six basic operations: (1) provides authorized navigation by the test taker, (2) selects the items to administer (fixed sequence, random, or heuristic based, such as a computer-adaptive test), (3) renders the test items, (4) captures responses, (5) timing (e.g., section time outs), and (6) real-time scoring, which may be needed for adaptive testing as well as final scoring, if a score report is immediately provided to the examinee.

testlet A collection of items administered together. Testlets are used in computerized mastery testing and can also be adaptively administered.

Large-scale computer-based testing technology is evaluated from the perspective of systems (hardware and software) and functions needed for implementation (related costs, security, and quality control). Popular computer-based testing delivery models are then defined; these include fixed forms, various computer-adaptive strategies, and multistage testing designs.

Computers in Testing

Computers have influenced almost every aspect of testing, from test development and assembly to administration, scoring, reporting, and analysis. The proliferation of personal computers (PCs), rapid improvements in network technology and connectivity, and new developments in adaptive testing technology and automated test assembly have made computer-based testing (CBT) a mainstay for virtually all types of testing, including educational tests, certification and licensure tests, psychological assessments, and even employment tests.

CBT Systems and Functions

Five core systems comprise most large-scale operational CBT systems: (1) item development and banking, (2) test assembly and composition, (3) examinee registration and scheduling, (4) test administration and delivery, and (5) postexamination processing. These systems, which are made up of hardware components, software, and varying degrees of human intervention, provide most of the functionality in the overall CBT enterprise.

Item Development and Banking

Item development and banking involve building a database of test items. The item banking development and banking system include three primary subsystems. First, an inventory control and management subsystem is needed to track the demands for items over time and to schedule new item production. Second, item authoring and prototyping subsystems are needed to actually produce the items. Item authoring tools can range from simple word processing data to elaborate item composition applications that use templates and many automated features to compose new items. Finally, an item database is needed to store the item content (text, pictures, formatting specifications, pretest item statistics, content codes, etc.).

Test Assembly and Composition

Test assembly involves two steps: (1) selecting items from a large item bank or pool for each test form and (2) packaging or publishing the selected items in the appropriate format for administration on a computer. These steps may be done off-line (that is, test forms may be prepackaged before being administered) or they can be performed in real time, on-line. Computer-adaptive tests are constructed on-line while the examinee is taking the test.

Item selection can be accomplished by database queries, by stratified sampling of items within content categories or statistically determined "bins," or by using formal item selection algorithms. CBT is gradually moving toward the latter approach, which is called automated test assembly (ATA). ATA involves the use of sophisticated mathematical optimization algorithms to select items from an item bank for one or more test forms. The ATA optimization algorithms are programmed into a computer and are used to select items from an item bank to meet large numbers of content constraints and statistical specifications for each test form. These same algorithms can be applied to many types of adaptive tests.

"Packaging" prepares the selected test items for delivery to the test takers on a computer—that is, the computerized test delivery driver administers the packaged test to the examinees. The packaging process varies for different types of CBT test delivery systems. In most CBT systems, packaging amounts to generating computer files in a data "markup" format (e.g., using a variation on the eXtensible Markup Language, or XML) that can be read by the test delivery software. Note that packaging may also include data encryption.

Examinee Registration and Scheduling

Examinee registration and scheduling are important operational activities for any CBT program. An eligibility and registration system ensures that the test applicants are eligible to take the test (e.g., have met certain educational requirements) within prescribed time frames and that they pay any appropriate fees. Multiple application access modes can be used for eligibility and registration, including mailing in hardcopy applications, telephone access, and on-line Internet-based registration.

The registration and scheduling system also needs to locate an available computer "seat" for each examinee. Many of the commercial CBT vendors use dedicated test centers with a fixed number of test workstations. Therefore, the registration and scheduling system needs to find a location and time for each applicant to take the test. Many of the scheduling systems used by the major CBT vendors work in a similar way to an airline reservation system that reserves a particular seat for each passenger on a specific flight. Due to obvious capacity limitations in any fixed testing site network, there can be enormous competition for computer seats during certain times of the year—especially at the most convenient locations in major metropolitan areas.

Test Administration and Delivery

Taking a computer-based test once implied sitting in front of a "dumb" computer terminal connected to a mainframe computer and responding with the keyboard to a sequence of test questions. The rapid increase in availability of personal computers and improvements in connectivity, including networking technology and the emergence of the Internet, have led to ever-improving distributed models for testing. Modern CBT connectivity encompasses PC local-area networks running in dedicated testing centers, wide-area networks running in multiple locations, virtual private networks built on Internet technology, and even remote wireless networks capable of administering tests on handheld personal digital assistants, "pocket PCs," and other small digital devices. Today, most computer-based testing—at least most high-stakes computer-based testing—is conducted at dedicated test centers. These testing centers have full-time test proctors and typically offer a secure, quiet, and comfortable testing environment. The actual test may be housed on a file server at the center, or the workstations at the center may connect directly to a central processing facility via the Internet or a private connection.

One of the most important components of any CBT test administration and delivery system is called the test-delivery driver, which is a software application that logs the examinee into the test, administers the test by presenting the items in some prescribed sequence, may allow the examinee to navigate around the test, carries out executive timing of the test sections, records appropriate actions or responses, and transmits the actions and responses to an appropriate storage repository. The test-delivery driver may also conduct real-time scoring and report the scores to the test taker. A test-delivery driver needs to support multiple item types. Included are multiple-choice items, open-ended response items, essays requiring word processing, computational problems, items using interactive graphics, and custom computer-based work simulations. The test-delivery driver must also support multiple CBT delivery models, some of which require sophisticated item selection activities, including using automated test assembly. These latter types of models include computer-adaptive testing and adaptive multistage testing.

Postexamination Processing

Scoring and reporting are two of the most common postexamination processing activities for CBT. Very few high-stakes computer-based examinations immediately release scores to the test takers, even though that technology is rather trivial to implement. Instead, the response data are transmitted to a central processing facility for additional quality assurance processing and to ensure the integrity of the scores. Scoring and reporting to the examinees is done from that facility.

Postexamination processing also includes conducting many types of psychometric analyses, including item analysis, item calibration and equating, and research studies meant to improve the quality of the test. These types of studies are routinely performed by most major testing organizations.

Challenges for CBT

Building a CBT enterprise is an enormous undertaking. There are five challenges facing CBT: (1) systems development and reengineering, (2) costs of CBT seats, (3) dealing with increased item production needs under a continuous testing paradigm, (4) security, and (5) quality control of test forms.

Systems Development and Reengineering

As already noted, there are numerous component systems and procedures that need to be designed from the ground up, or at least must be reengineered from existing paper-and-pencil testing systems and procedures. Facing enormous systems development costs and time lines, many testing organizations opt to contract with commercial CBT vendors that offer various types of test delivery services—principally CBT item banking software, a test-delivery driver, and dedicated, proctored testing sites.

Costs of CBT Seat Time

Using commercial testing sites adds to the cost of "seat time," at least when compared to paper-and-pencil testing. Many commercial test delivery vendors are for-profit corporations that charge premium rates for each hour of testing. For example, at $15.00 per hour of testing, a program testing 10,000 examinees per year would spend $300,000 annually in seat time, assuming 2 hours of scheduled testing time per examinee. As a possible cost-saving measure, some testing organizations are exploring the use of proctored temporary CBT sites as a lower cost alternative to dedicated testing sites (e.g., temporarily converting a university or school-based computer laboratory in to a secure, proctored test site, using encrypted Internet data transmittal to and from the workstations).

Continuous CBT and Increased Item Production

Continuous CBT—that is, scheduling tests over time to accommodate large numbers of test takers within limited-capacity computerized test delivery centers—inherently creates an ongoing demand for large numbers of new, high-quality, pretested items. The item banks can quickly become compromised and the integrity of examination scores and decisions will become suspect, especially for high-stakes examinations. The obvious solution is to increase the number of test items in the bank and establish an item-inventory management plan for renewing, rotating, and replacing item banks over time. Stepped-up item production typically means periodically commissioning and training large numbers of item designers and item writers to compose new items to meet the demands. Items must also be pilot tested on a sufficiently large sample of motivated test takers to provide the statistical data needed to evaluate the quality of the items. Item statistics are also essential for test assembly. The practical challenges of building a steady-state inventory of high-quality, pilot-tested items cannot be trivialized.

Security

Security is an integral part of CBT. There are three aspects to security. Examinee security involves verifying the identity of the examinee, authenticating his or her data, and proctoring the examination to prevent cheating. Data security relates to encryption and secure transmittal of the data. Collaboration security involves monitoring and, ideally, detecting concerted efforts by examinees using the Internet or other means to memorize and share large sections of the test or test materials.

Most commercial testing sites offer a variety of examinee security measures, including double-entry password access to the test, digital photographs of the test taker at check-in, and proctoring services to monitor the examinees while they are taking the examination. Data security is primarily handled by applying multiple encryption layers to the data for transmission to/from and for storage at the testing center. It is more difficult to contend with collaboration security. A combination of statistical, website monitoring, and informant follow-up procedures is needed to detect and prosecute collaboration efforts by examinees or organizations to steal large portions of an item bank through memorization and sharing of the item content.

Quality Control of Test Forms

Most of the early research on CBT and computer-adaptive testing viewed the challenges of CBT as strictly psychometric in nature, and almost exclusively focused on theoretical statistical issues related to measurement efficiency (issues such as achieving adequate levels of test score reliability using as few items as possible). However, testing professionals soon realized that statistical criteria and practical issues (such as overexposing test materials over time, guaranteeing content representation and test form quality for tests constructed by computers, and ensuring fairness in terms of access to and practice with CBT) were equally important; in some cases, practical issues were considered more important than statistical criteria were. With paper-and-pencil testing, content test committees functioned as the quality control (QC) experts, dealing with content-coverage issues, item or theme duplication, etc. In the CBT world, there are usually too many test forms and no opportunity for committees to review every test form before it is administered. Some CBT programs have begun to implement statistical QC and quality assurance (QA) procedures, much like those used in manufacturing and engineering. Some aspects of QC and QA can be automated (e.g., computing tolerances and flagging outliers); other aspects still require some degree of human review; carrying out test form quality checks can include a mixture of automated and human QC reviews.

CBT Delivery Models

CBT delivery models vary in the degree and nature of test adaptation provided, the type of connectivity required to transmit data interactively between testing stations or networks and central processing facilities, the size and types of testing units administered, the types of items supported, the test assembly methods employed, and the nature and extent of test form quality control mechanisms used. In most cases, a particular CBT delivery model will attempt to optimize one or two of these factors. However, there are almost always trade-offs because these factors tend to compete with one another. For example, a computer-adaptive test (CAT) almost exclusively focuses on maximizing the adaptability of the test to each test taker. There are sacrifices involved in adopting CAT, including reduced opportunities to carry out test form QC or QA, overexposure of "informative" items, and a possible degradation of system performance in large networks and Internet environments.

There are five broad classes of CBT delivery models: (1) preassembled, parallel, computerized fixed tests, (2) linear-on-the-fly tests, (3) computer-adaptive tests, (4) CBTs using testlets, and (5) computer-adaptive multistage tests. On the surface, these models may appear to differ only with respect to their use of adaptive algorithms, the size of the test administration units, and the nature and extent to which automated test assembly is used. However, at a more detailed level of evaluation, they also differ significantly with respect to parsimony of design, system performance issues, measurement efficiency, and opportunities for quality control of test forms.

Preassembled, Parallel, Computerized Fixed Tests

The category of preassembled, parallel, fixed computer-based tests includes preconstructed, intact test forms that are administered by computer to large numbers of students. Different examinees may see different forms of the test, but all examinees administered the same form will see exactly the same items (i.e., the items are fixed for each form). These models are called computerized fixed tests (CFTs). In the typical CFT implementation, a number of fixed-length test forms are constructed for active use. When an examinee sits for the test, one form is randomly selected. The different forms are typically constructed to be parallel with respect to test content and are either formally equated for difficulty (using classical test theory or item response theory) or are assumed to be randomly equivalent. A CFT is directly analogous to having a fixed-item paper-and-pencil test (PPT) form. One advantage of a CFT over a PPT is that the presentation sequence for the items can be scrambled (i.e., randomized). Scrambling the item presentation sequence prevents certain types of cheating (e.g., coming in with an ordered list of illicitly obtained answers for the test). For multiple-choice questions, distractors may further be scrambled within each item as an added measure of security.

When properly implemented, the CFT model has several attractive features. First, test assembly is rather straightforward. That is, multiple test forms can be constructed to meet a common set of statistical and content specifications. Because the test assembly is done beforehand, extensive quality control procedures can be implemented to check every test form for content balance and other critical features, before release. Second, the CFT model is simple to implement in most CBT delivery systems because it does not require the on-line test delivery software to use any special type of item selection algorithms or scoring mechanisms. CFT therefore performs well in almost any testing network or web-based environment. One limitation of the CFT model is that it is not efficient from a measurement perspective. A second possible disadvantage relates to exposure risks. Unless automated test assembly (ATA) is used to mass-produce many simultaneous CFT forms, with item overlap (exposure) controlled, there could be serious security risks.

Linear-on-the-Fly Tests

A variation on CFT is linear-on-the-fly testing (LOFT). LOFT involves the real-time assembly of a unique fixed-length test for each examinee. Classical test theory or item response theory (IRT) can be used to generate randomly parallel LOFT test forms. There are at least two variations of the LOFT model: a large number of unique test forms can be developed far in advance of test administration (which is a merely a special case of CFT, where ATA is employed, as noted previously) or test forms can be generated immediately prior to testing (i.e., in real time). A benefit of developing the test forms in advance is that content and measurement experts can review each form.

The primary advantage of the LOFT model is that numerous forms can be developed in real time from the same item pool. Furthermore, there is typically some overlap of items allowed across the test forms. When test forms are assembled just prior to administration, the current exposure levels of the items can be considered in the test assembly algorithm. At-risk items can be made unavailable for selection. For real-time LOFT, explicit item exposure controls can be used to limit the exposure of particular items, in addition to the random sampling scheme. The benefits of LOFT include all those associated with CFTs with the addition of more efficient item pool usage and reduced item exposure.

The disadvantages of LOFT are similar to those of CFTs (i.e., decreased measurement efficiency and exposure risks if test banks are relatively small, limiting the number of forms that can be produced). In addition, real-time LOFT may limit or altogether preclude certain quality controls such as test content reviews and data integrity checks. Although some quality assurance can be integrated into the live test assembly algorithm, doing so tends to complicate the functionality of the test delivery system and introduces additional data management challenges (e.g., reconciling examinee records). This latter problem can be slightly reduced in terms of risks to the integrity of the data by creative database management (e.g., using system-generated test form identifiers for every LOFT form).

Computer-Adaptive Tests

A computer-adaptive test adapts or tailors the exam to each examinee. Under the purest form of CAT, this tailoring is done by keeping track of an examinee's performance on each test item and then using this information to select the next item to be administered. A CAT is therefore developed item-by-item, in real time, by the test-delivery driver software. The criteria for selecting the next item to be administered to an examinee can range from simply choosing items that maximize the reliability of each examinee's score, to complex heuristics using automated test assembly (ATA) processes. However, as noted earlier, the primary item-selection criterion in CAT is to maximize the measurement precision for the test and, correspondingly, minimize the measurement error of the examinee's score. Presently, several successful, large-scale CAT testing programs are in use. One of the oldest and most successful CAT programs is the Armed Service Vocational Aptitude Battery.

Test Adaptation and Measurement Efficiency

Computer-adaptive testing was developed for a singular purpose—to maximize testing efficiency. CAT obtains more accurate estimates of examinees' proficiency using fewer items than are typically required on nonadaptive tests. These gains in efficiency stem directly from the CAT item selection algorithm employed, which avoids administering items that are too easy or too hard for examinees. Therefore, CATs are often significantly shorter than their paper-and-pencil counterparts—typically about half as long as a parallel nonadaptive test. Figure 1 shows the efficiency gains of a hypothetical CAT, compared to a test for which the items were randomly selected. The plot shows the average standard errors of the estimated proficiency scores over 50 items. The standard errors are averaged for examinees having different proficiency scores. How the error functions plotted in Fig. 1 decrease over the course of the two tests can be seen specifically. It is important to realize that the errors decrease for a randomly selected set of items, too. However, CAT clearly does a better job of more rapidly reducing

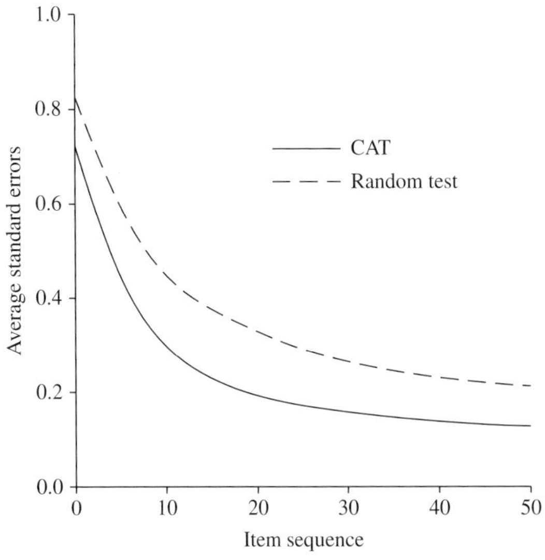

Figure 1 Average standard errors for a 50-item computer-adaptive test (CAT) vs 50 randomly selected items.

the errors. For example, at 20 items, the CAT achieves nearly the same efficiency as the 50-item random test; at 50 items, the average standard error for the CAT is approximately half as large as for the random test.

Unfortunately, measurement efficiency has often been used as the sole criterion when evaluating different CBT delivery models. Instead, the importance weight given to efficiency needs to be carefully reviewed and applied in terms of concrete benefits, considered alongside the real costs associated with system design, implementation, and maintenance, as well as costs linked to generating test materials.

CAT Item Selection Algorithms

There are several types of CAT item-selection algorithms. Two somewhat traditional approaches that are cited in the psychometric literature include maximum information item selection and maximum information item selection with unconditional or conditional item exposure controls. An interesting CAT variation reformulates the usual sequential item selection problem in CAT as a series of optimization problems that allow complex test-level constraints to be readily incorporated into the test assembly process. The serialized test assembly problem can then be solved using formal mathematical optimization procedures that include network flow and linear and mixed-integer programming algorithms. This improved methodology has been called "shadow testing." Under CAT with shadow testing, a complete test is reassembled following each item administration. This complete test, called the shadow test, incorporates all of the required content constraints and other constraints (e.g., cognitive levels, total word counts, test timing requirements, clueing across items), and uses maximization of test information at the examinee's current proficiency estimate as its objective function. Shadow testing can further incorporate exposure control mechanisms as a security measure to combat some types of cheating. The shadow test model is a powerful means for balancing the goals of meeting content constraints and maximizing test information.

Limitations of CAT

Five limitations have been identified in the research literature relative to implementing CAT in an operational setting. First, when content constraints and conditional item exposure controls are incorporated into the item selection algorithm, much of the measurement efficiency gain associated with a CAT is lost. This is especially true for longer tests that must meet extensive content specifications, because the measurement efficiency gains due to the adaptive algorithm dissipate with increasing test length. Second, subject matter experts and psychometricians are unable to review a CAT form before it is administered to an examinee. Some test development experts question the "content validity" of test forms constructed entirely by a computer algorithm, although using shadow testing and other content-balancing heuristics can mitigate some of this criticism. Third, examinees taking a CAT often complain about not being able to skip test items or review previously answered items. Using testlets (see later) helps alleviate most of these types of complaints. The final limitation relates to computer system performance issues specific to implementing CATs in Internet-based or intranet-based distributed CBT environments. A CAT is a very data intensive application and requires a fairly high degree of computation during the live test administration. When a CAT program is deployed in Internet-based testing (IBT) networks or wide-area network environments, where a central computer server needs to score and implement an item selection heuristic after every item and for every examinee, serious degradation in system performance can arise. As testing programs move toward using the Internet for real-time testing, these types of system performance issues will become more prevalent.

CBTs Using Testlets

The concept of a testlet was introduced to describe a subset of items, or a "minitest," that could be used in either an adaptive or mastery testing environment. A testlet-based CAT involves the adaptive administration of preassembled sets of items to an examinee, rather than single items. Examples of testlets include sets of items that are associated with a common reading passage or visual stimulus, or a carefully constructed subset of items that mirrors the overall content specifications for a test. After completing the testlet, the computer scores the items within it and then chooses the next testlet to be administered. Therefore, this type of test is adaptive at the testlet level rather than at the item level. This approach allows for better control over exam content and can be used to allow examinees to skip, review, and change answers within a block of test items. It also allows for content and measurement review of these sets of items prior to operational administration.

Computerized Mastery Tests

An important variation on testlet-based CAT is computerized mastery tests (CMTs). Under CMTs, parallel testlets are preconstructed to provide optimal measurement precision in the region of a pass/fail cut score (i.e., the mastery point on the score scale). The preconstructed testlets are put into a pool and are then randomly selected for each examinee. After an examinee completes a minimum number of testlets, the answers are scored by the computer and loss functions associated with "pass," "fail," or "continue testing" are calculated. Both testlet-based CAT and CMT models offer a compromise between the traditional, nonadaptive format and a purely adaptive test delivery model. Advantages of CBT using testlets include increased testing efficiency relative to nonadaptive tests, the ability of content experts and sensitivity reviewers to review the preconstructed testlets to evaluate content quality, and the ability of examinees to skip, review, and change answers to questions within a testlet or stage.

Limitations of CBT Using Testlets

One disadvantage of testlet-based CAT, relative to item-level adaptive tests, is that use of multi-item testlets sacrifices some amount of measurement precision insofar as the items are not being individually targeted to the examinees' proficiency scores. However, research suggests that the loss in efficiency may be minor, particularly in the context of classification testing such as placement, licensure, or certification. A secondary disadvantage is that testlets cannot contain any item overlap. That is, testlet-based CAT and CMT require the testlets to be unique because it is combinatorially not feasible to track testlet enemies (i.e., mutually exclusive testlets). This requirement may severely restrict the number of testlets that can be produced and may slightly increase exposure risks. A third limitation is that, despite the use of ATA to build the testlets, testlet-based CAT or CMT test forms may not meet all of the test-level specifications when various testlets are combined. Provided that all of the test specifications can be distributed at the testlet level, this is not a serious problem. However, various programs attempting to implement this model have encountered serious test form quality problems.

Computer-Adaptive Multistage Tests

Computer-adaptive multistage testing (CA-MST) is similar to testlet-based CAT, but is more structured and offers greater control over quality of the test forms and the testing data. Functionally, CA-MST can be used for adaptive testing applications or for mastery testing applications. CA-MST uses testlets as the fundamental building blocks for test assembly and test delivery. Testlets can range in size and may include discrete items, item sets that share a common stimulus (e.g., sets of 10 to 12 items, each associated with a particular reading passage), or even computer-based simulation exercises. The testlets are targeted to have specific statistical properties (e.g., a particular average item difficulty or level of precision) and all test-level content balancing is built into the test assembly process. Automated test assembly must be used to preconstruct all of the testlets so that they individually meet all relevant statistical and categorical specifications.

Computer-Adaptive Multistage Testing Panels

As part of the ATA process, the preconstructed testlets are prepackaged in small groups called "panels." Each panel is essentially a self-adapting test form. A typical panel contains four to seven (or more) testlets, depending on the panel design chosen. Each testlet is explicitly assigned to a particular stage and to a specific route within the panel (easier, moderate, or harder) based on the average difficulty of the testlet. Multiple panels can be prepared with item overlap precisely controlled across different panels. This is an important distinction from testlet-based CAT and CMT, both of which cannot share items across testlets. In CA-MST, the overlap is conditioned into the ATA process and explicitly controlled across panels.

Figure 2 presents a 1-3-3 multistage panel design. One testlet (A) is assigned to Stage 1. Three testlets are assigned to Stage 2 (B, C, D) and three more testlets are assigned to Stage 3 (E, F, G). Examinees may review and change answers within each testlet. Once the examinee completes and submits each testlet, review is not allowed on the submitted materials. The examinee's cumulative score up to that point in the test determines which testlets are administered in Stages 2 and 3. The solid line arrows in Fig. 2 denote the primary adaptive routes allowed within the panel. The four dotted arrows denote secondary routes. Routing from Stage 1 to Stage 2 is based solely on the examinee's performance on Testlet A. Lower performing examinees are routed to Testlet B. Examinees performing moderately are routed to Testlet C and top-performing examinees are routed to Testlet D. Routing to Stage 3 (Testlets E, F, and G) is based on cumulative performance for all prior testlets. As Fig. 2 also indicates, multiple panels can be simultaneously constructed. A panel can therefore be randomly selected for any examinee from within the pool of active panels. Each panel is a formal data object that "knows" how to administer itself adaptively to the examinee. Each panel has testlets at multiple levels of difficulty. The prescribed difficulty for each testlet is controlled through automated

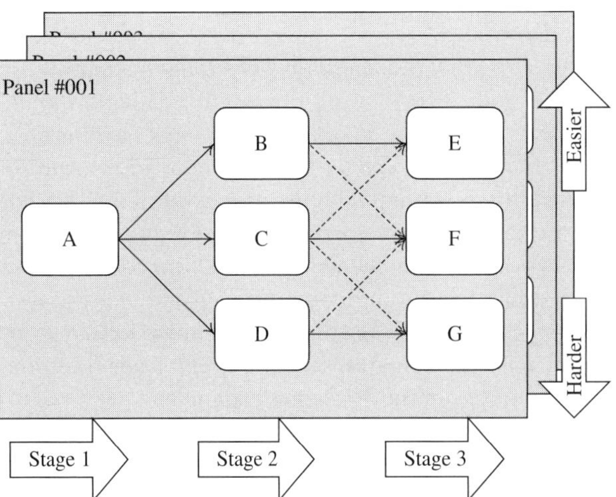

Figure 2 A sample 1-3-3 computer-adaptive multistage test panel configuration (showing three panels).

test assembly, using IRT test information functions to target the difficulty of each testlet to a specific region of the relevant score scale. This correspondingly targets the measurement precision where it is needed—achieving the same goal as CAT. There are seven explicit target test information functions underlying the 1-3-3 panel design shown in Fig. 2. There are seven viable pathways through each 1-3-3 panel: A + B + E, A + B + F, A + C + E, A + C + F, A + C + G, A + D + F, and A + D + G. Each panel is explicitly constructed so that any of those pathways provides a content-balanced test that meets all relevant test-level specifications (item counts, content balance, word counts, etc.). A large number of panels can simultaneously be constructed for operational use by mixing and matching items and testlets across panels.

In real-time, scoring and routing of the examinees within each panel can be greatly simplified by using cumulative number-correct scoring and score look-ups to mimic the maximum information criterion used in CAT. The number-correct cut-offs for each authorized route within the panel can be precomputed and packaged as part of the panel data. This feature simplifies the operational scoring and routing functionality needed by the test-delivery driver and potentially could improve performance of the test-delivery driver (i.e., involve less complex data processing and computational steps— especially in a web-enabled testing environment).

It is important to realize that the 1-3-3 panel design shown in Fig. 2 is merely one example of a CA-MST panel. Virtually any panel configuration can be custom designed to fit a particular assessment scenario by merely implementing a template for the desired configuration (number of stages, number of difficulty levels per stage, size of the testlets or modules within each stage, etc.). Some of the CA-MST panel designs proposed to date include the 1-3 (two-stage) design and the 1-2-2, the 1-3-4, the 1-3-4-5, and the 1-3-3-3 designs. More stages add to the adaptive flexibility.

The CA-MST test model is essentially a compromise solution that affords some degree of adaptation while ensuring adherence to the content specifications for every examinee as well as limiting any overexposure of the test items. Perhaps the greatest asset of CA-MST is that it contends with practical issues such as meeting test form review and other QC needs for test development, minimizing computational complexity for the test-delivery driver, and maximizing system performance by minimizing the amount of computing loads required by file servers and transmission channels.

Advantages and Disadvantages of CA-MST

CA-MST is designed to be parsimonious, to be reasonably efficient from a psychometric perspective, and to work well in most CBT environments—including Internet-based applications. One of its chief advantages is that, by preconstructing the testlets and panels, it affords numerous opportunities to implement strong quality control procedures for test forms and testing data. CA-MST, like testlet-based CAT and CMT, is not quite as efficient as CAT is, but the differences seem negligible from a practical perspective. In any case, the increased control over content and overall test form content, the simplification of the unit selection and scoring functions that need to be built into the test delivery software, and the many other operational advantages that accrue from better quality control seem to offset any very minor efficiency loss.

Conclusions

CBT was once envisioned to make testing less complex and cheaper; but the opposite tends to be true. CBT systems are complex and expensive to operate. There are also many types of CBT delivery models to consider and, clearly, no singular CBT model is ideal for every testing program. But progress is being made and each new generation of CBTs seems to improve on the previous generation. Today, testlet-based CAT, CMT, and CA-MST have emerged as highly useful test-delivery models that have attempted to reconcile some of the shortcomings of CFT and CAT. In the case of CA-MST, the use of preconstructed testlets and highly structured "panels" yields distinct improvements in test form quality control, better security, more parsimony in data management, and important system performance advantages. Yet, there is room for improvement, and there will no doubt be new CBT technologies and delivery models, as well as new issues and perspectives that should be considered in evaluating those models.

See Also the Following Articles

Computerized Adaptive Testing • Innovative Computerized Test Items

Further Reading

Folk, V. G., and Smith, R. L. (2002). Models for delivery of CBTs. In *Computer-Based Testing: Building the Foundation for Future Assessments* (C. Mills, M. Potenza, J. Fremer, and W. Ward, eds.), pp. 41–66. Lawrence Erlbaum, Mahwah, NJ.

Hambleton, R. K., and Swaminathan, H. R. (1985). *Item Response Theory: Principles and Applications.* Kluwer, Hingham, MA.

Lord, F. M. (1980). *Applications of Item Response Theory to Practical Testing Problems.* Lawrence Erlbaum Assoc., Hillsdale, NJ.

Luecht, R. M. (1998). Computer-assisted test assembly using optimization heuristics. *Appl. Psychol. Measure.* **22,** 224–236.

Luecht, R. M. (2000). *Implementing the Computer-Adaptive Sequential Testing (CA-MST) Framework to Mass Produce High Quality Computer-Adaptive and Mastery Tests*. Paper presented at the annual meeting of the National Council on Measurement in Education, New Orleans. Available on the Internet at www.ncme.org

Luecht, R. M., and Nungester, R. J. (1998). Some practical examples of computer-adaptive sequential testing. *J. Edu. Measure.* **35,** 229–249.

Parshall, C. G., Spray, J. A., Kalohn, J. C., and Davey, T. (2002). *Practical Considerations in Computer-Based Testing*. Springer, New York.

Sands, W. A., Waters, B. K., and McBride, J. R. (eds.) (1997). *Computerized Adaptive Testing: From Inquiry to Operation*. American Psychological Association, Washington, D.C.

Sheehan, K., and Lewis, C. (1992). Computerized mastery testing with nonequivalent testlets. *Appl. Psychol. Measure.* **16,** 65–76.

Stocking, M. L., and Lewis, C. (1998). Controlling item exposure conditional on ability in computerized adaptive testing. *J. Edu. Behav. Statist.* **23,** 57–75.

Swanson, L., and Stocking, M. L. (1993). A model and heuristic for solving very large item selection problems. *Appl. Psychol. Measure.* **17,** 177–186.

van der Linden, W. J. (ed) (1998). Optimal assembly of psychological and educational tests. *Appl. Psychol. Measure.* **22,** 195–211.

van der Linden, W. J. (2000). Constrained adaptive testing with shadow tests. In *Computer-Adaptive Testing: Theory and Practice* (W. J. van der Linden and C. A. W. Glas, eds.), pp. 27–52. Kluwer, Boston, MA.

van der Linden, W. J., and Boekkooi-Timminga, E. (1989). A minimax model for test design with practical constraints. *Psychometrika* **54,** 237–247.

Wainer, H., and Kiely, G. L. (1987). Item clusters and computerized adaptive testing: A case for testlets. *J. Edu. Measure.* **24,** 185–201.

Computerized Adaptive Testing

Daniel O. Segall

Defense Manpower Data Center, U.S. Department of Defense, Washington, D.C., USA

Glossary

content balancing A set of one or more ancillary item-selection constraints based on content or nonstatistical item features.

conventional testing An approach to individual difference assessment whereby all examinees receive the same items, typically (but not necessarily) in printed mode.

exposure control algorithm An algorithmic enhancement to precision-based item selection that limits the usage rates of some highly informative items for the purpose of increased test security.

information A statistical concept related to the asymptotic variance of maximum-likelihood trait estimates; it can be expressed as the sum of individual item information functions, which can be evaluated at specific points along the trait scale.

item pool A collection of test questions and associated item parameters from which items are selected for administration by the adaptive item-selection algorithm.

item response function A mathematical function providing the probability of a correct response conditional on the latent trait level θ.

measurement efficiency The ratio of measurement precision to test length. One test or testing algorithm is said to be more efficient than the other if it provides more precise scores for a fixed test length, or if it achieves equally precise scores with fewer administered items.

measurement precision An index of the accuracy of test scores, often assessed by the average or expected squared difference between true and estimated trait parameters, $E(\theta - \hat{\theta})^2$.

stopping rule The rule used to determine when to end the test; typically based on the number of administered items (fixed length), or on the precision level of the estimated trait parameter (variable length).

trait A psychological dimension of individual differences; includes ability, aptitude, proficiency, attitude, or personality characteristics.

trait estimate A test score based on item-response theory; denoted by $\hat{\theta}$, the score is typically calculated by Bayesian or maximum-likelihood estimation approaches.

trait parameter The parameter θ, based on item-response theory; denotes the examinee's standing along the latent trait dimension.

Computerized adaptive testing is an approach to individual difference assessment that tailors the administration of test questions to the trait level of the examinee. The computer chooses and displays the questions, and then records and processes the examinee's answers. Item selection is adaptive—it is dependent in part on the examinee's answers to previously administered questions, and in part on the specific statistical qualities of administered and candidate items. Compared to conventional testing, whereby all examinees receive the same items, computerized adaptive testing administers a larger percentage of items with appropriate difficulty levels. The adaptive item selection process of computerized adaptive testing results in higher levels of test-score precision and shorter test lengths.

Computerized Adaptive Testing Response Models

Modern computerized adaptive testing (CAT) algorithms are based on concepts taken from item-response theory (IRT) and from maximum-likelihood and Bayesian statistical estimation theories. Early pioneers of CAT, including Frederic M. Lord and David J. Weiss (on whose work modern CAT algorithms are based) used item response functions (IRFs) as the basic building blocks of CAT.

These functions, denoted by $P_i(\theta)$, express the probability of a correct response for an item as a function of latent trait level θ. The trait estimated from adaptive testing can be a psychological (or other) dimension of individual differences, including ability, aptitude, proficiency, attitude, and personality. For ability measurement, IRFs are generally assumed to be monotonically increasing functions. Consequently, as θ increases, so too does the probability of a correct response.

One of the most commonly used mathematical expressions for an IRF is the three-parameter logistic (3PL) model:

$$P_i(\theta) = c_i + \frac{1 - c_i}{1 + e^{-1.7a_i(\theta - b_i)}}, \tag{1}$$

where the parameters a_i, b_i, and c_i denote the slope, difficulty, and guessing parameters, respectively, for item i. The 3PL is often used to model dichotomously scored responses from multiple-choice items. The two-parameter logistic (2PL) model (often used to model attitude or personality items) is a special case of Eq. (1), where guessing is assumed to be nonexistent (i.e., $c_i = 0$). The one-parameter logistic (1PL) model (where $a_i = 1$ and $c_i = 0$) is used in cases in which the IRF associated with item i is characterized by its difficulty parameter b_i; all IRFs have identical slopes, and the probability of an examinee with infinitely low trait level correctly answering the item is zero. Other IRF models have also been used to extract information from incorrect options of multiple-choice items, or from other item-response formats (e.g., rating scales).

According to the assumption of local independence, the conditional probability of an observed response pattern is given by the product of item-specific terms:

$$P(u_1, u_2, \ldots, u_n \mid \theta) = \prod_{i=1}^{n} P_i(\theta)^{u_i} Q_i(\theta)^{1-u_i}, \tag{2}$$

where u_i denotes the scored response to item i ($u_i = 1$ if item i is answered correctly; $u_i = 0$ otherwise), $Q_i(\theta) = 1 - P_i(\theta)$ (i.e., denotes the conditional probability of an incorrect response), and n denotes the number of answered questions. One implication of Eq. (2) is that the probability of a correct response to item i is independent of the response to item j after controlling for the effects of θ.

Another important property of IRT is scale invariance. The scale of measurement along which examinees are placed, the θ-scale, is defined independently of the statistical properties of the administered items. This invariance property does not hold for scales derived from classical test theory, which are founded on number-right or percent-correct scores. A percent-correct score of 75 on a test containing easy items has a different meaning than does a score of 75 on a test containing difficult items. In contrast, an IRT-based test score (i.e., trait estimate $\hat{\theta}$) has the same meaning for tests containing either easy or difficult items (provided all item parameters have been transformed to a common scale). This IRT invariance property enables the comparison of scores from different or overlapping item sets. In the context of IRT, $\hat{\theta}$ test scores are all on a common measurement scale, even though these scores might have been estimated from tests consisting of different items.

Test Score Precision and Efficient Item Selection

Although the invariance property of IRT ensures that the interpretation of θ remains constant across tests consisting of different items, the precision with which θ can be estimated is very much dependent on the statistical properties of the administered items. Examinees with high θ-levels can be most accurately measured by tests containing many difficult items; examinees with low θ-levels can be most precisely measured by tests containing many easy items. This can be verified, for example, by an examination of the 1PL model, whereby the asymptotic variance of the maximum-likelihood estimator is given by

$$\mathrm{Var}(\hat{\theta} \mid \theta) = \left[1.7^2 \sum_{i=1}^{n} P_i(\theta) Q_i(\theta)\right]^{-1}. \tag{3}$$

It can be seen from Eq. (3) that the smallest variance is obtained when $P_i(\theta) = Q_i(\theta) = 1/2$ for each item—any other values of these conditional response probabilities lead to a larger variance. From Eq. (1), for the 1PL, this optimal condition occurs when $b_i = \theta$, which is when the difficulty parameter of each item matches the examinee trait-level parameter.

One implication of Eq. (3) is that the optimal (i.e., most precise) testing strategy chooses items solely on the basis of the examinee's true trait-level θ. But obviously this is not possible, because θ is unknown prior to testing. (If it were known, testing would be unnecessary in the first place.) It is possible, however, to use an iterative adaptive algorithm, where an estimated trait-level $\hat{\theta}_k$ is obtained after each administered item $k = 1, \ldots, n$, and the difficulty parameter of the next administered item b_{k+1} is matched to the current estimate: $b_{k+1} = \hat{\theta}_k$. In this sense, the difficulty of the next question, b_{k+1}, is adapted to the most up-to-date trait estimate, $\hat{\theta}_k$, of the examinee. By doing so, the precision level of the final estimate (obtained after the completion of the last item) is greater than that expected from conventional nonadaptive testing.

This idea of adapting the statistical properties of administered items based on responses to previous items forms the basis of all CAT item-selection algorithms. However, commonly used algorithms differ along two primary dimensions: first, in the type of statistical estimation procedure used (maximum likelihood versus Bayesian), and second, in the type of item-response model employed (e.g., 1PL, 2PL, or 3PL).

Maximum-Likelihood Approach

The maximum-likelihood (ML) approach to CAT item selection and scoring is based on the log-likelihood function

$$l(\theta) = \ln \prod_{i=1}^{n} P_i(\theta)^{u_i} Q_i(\theta)^{1-u_i}. \quad (4)$$

The estimate $\hat{\theta}_{(\mathrm{ML})}$ is defined as the value of θ for which the likelihood (or, equivalently, the log-likelihood) function is maximized. Because no closed-form expression exists for $\hat{\theta}_{(\mathrm{ML})}$, it is typically calculated using an iterative numerical procedure such as the Newton–Raphson algorithm.

The estimator $\hat{\theta}_{(\mathrm{ML})}$ is asymptotically normally distributed with mean θ and variance

$$\begin{aligned}\mathrm{Var}(\hat{\theta} \mid \theta) &= \left[-\mathrm{E}\left(\partial^2/\partial\theta^2\right) l(\theta)\right]^{-1} \\ &= \frac{1}{\sum_{i=1}^{n} I_i(\theta)},\end{aligned} \quad (5)$$

where the information function for item i, denoted by $I_i(\theta)$, is

$$I_i(\theta) = \frac{\left[P_i'(\theta)\right]^2}{P_i(\theta) Q_i(\theta)}, \quad (6)$$

and where $P_i'(\theta)$ denotes the derivative of the item response function with respect to θ. For the one- and three-parameter logistic models, these derivatives are $P_i'(\theta) = 1.7 P_i(\theta) Q_i(\theta)$ and $P_i'(\theta) = 1.7 a_i Q_i(\theta)[P_i(\theta) - c_i]/(1 - c_i)$, respectively.

From Eq. (5), it is clear that the asymptotic variance of the ML estimate $\hat{\theta}_{(\mathrm{ML})}$ can be minimized by choosing items with the largest information values. If θ were known in advance of testing, then available items could be rank ordered in terms of their information values [Eq. (6)] at θ, and the most informative items could be selected and administered. Because θ is not known (to know or approximate θ is, of course, the purpose of testing), the most informative item can be selected using item-information functions evaluated at the provisional (most up-to-date) trait estimate, $I_i(\hat{\theta}_{k(\mathrm{ML})})$. After the chosen item has been administered, and the response scored, a new provisional estimate can be obtained and used to reevaluate item information for the remaining candidate items. These alternating steps of trait estimation and item selection are repeated until a stopping rule (typically based on test length or precision) is satisfied. The adaptive item-selection and scoring algorithm is summarized in Table I.

Table I CAT Item-Selection and Scoring Algorithm

Step	*Description*
1. Calculate provisional trait estimate	Obtain a provisional trait estimate, $\hat{\theta}_k$, based on the first k responses
2. Choose item	Compute information $I_i(\hat{\theta}_k)$ for each candidate item by substituting the provisional trait estimate $\hat{\theta}_k$ (calculated in step 1) for the true parameter θ in Eq. (6); select for administration the item with the largest item-information value
3. Administer item and record response	
4. Repeat steps 1–3	Repeat until the stopping rule has been satisfied
5. Calculate final trait estimate $\hat{\theta}$	Based on all responses, including the response to the last administered item

Bayesian Approach

In instances when a prior distribution for θ can be specified, some test developers have opted to use a Bayesian framework for item selection and trait estimation. The prior density, denoted by $f(\theta)$, characterizes what is known about θ prior to testing. The most common approach to prior-specification in the context of CAT sets the prior equal to an estimated θ-density calculated from existing (or historical) examinee data. Then the assumption is made that future examinees (taking the CAT test) are independent and identically distributed, $\theta \sim f(\theta)$. Although in many cases, additional background information is known about examinees relating to θ (such as subgroup membership), this information is often ignored in the specification of individual examinee priors—to allow such information to influence the prior could lead to, or magnify, subgroup differences in test score distributions.

A Bayesian approach provides estimates with different statistical properties than are provided by ML estimates. In CAT, Bayesian estimates tend to have the advantage of smaller conditional standard errors, $\sigma(\hat{\theta} \mid \theta)$, but possess the disadvantage of larger conditional bias, $B(\theta) = \mu(\hat{\theta} \mid \theta) - \theta$, especially for extreme θ levels. Thus, the choice of estimation approach involves a trade-off between small variance (of Bayesian estimates) and small bias (of ML estimates). Bayesian procedures do, in general, provide smaller mean-squared errors (MSEs) between θ and $\hat{\theta}$ (which is a function of both conditional variance and bias) than are provided by ML estimates. This suggests that Bayesian estimates can provide higher correlations with external criteria, and a more precise rank ordering of examinees along the θ-scale. Practitioners who are concerned about the effects of bias, or who do not have precise estimates of the trait distribution, tend to favor the ML approach. Conversely, practitioners whose primary objective is to minimize MSE or conditional variance have tended to favor Bayesian approaches.

The Bayesian approach to CAT item selection and scoring is based on the posterior density function,

$$f(\theta \mid u) \propto f(u \mid \theta) f(\theta), \tag{7}$$

where $f(u \mid \theta)$ is equivalent to the probability function [Eq. (2)], $f(\theta)$ is the prior distribution of θ, and $u = (u_1, \ldots, u_n)$ is a vector of scored responses. Whereas the prior $f(\theta)$ describes what is known about θ before the data are observed, the posterior density function $f(\theta \mid u)$ provides a description of what is known about the examinee's trait level after the item-response data u have been obtained. Typically, summary statistics are used to characterize the posterior distribution: a measure of central tendency (such as the posterior mean or mode) is often taken as the trait point estimate, and the variance of the posterior distribution is typically taken as a measure of uncertainty. Small posterior variance values suggest that $\hat{\theta}$ has been estimated with a high degree of precision; large posterior variance values suggest otherwise.

One Bayesian approach to item selection chooses the next item to minimize the expected posterior variance, where the expectation is taken with respect to the yet-to-be observed response to the candidate item. This quantity is calculated by computing the values of the posterior variance if the candidate item is answered both correctly and incorrectly, and then calculating a weighted average of the two posterior variances, where the weights are equal to the probability of correct and incorrect responses based on the predictive posterior distribution. A less computationally intensive and more commonly used Bayesian item-selection method is consistent with a normal-based inference approach. According to this approach, the posterior distribution is approximated by a normal density,

$$f(\theta \mid u) = \mathrm{N}(\hat{\theta}_{(\mathrm{MAP})}, V), \tag{8}$$

with mean equal to the mode [maximum *a posteriori* (MAP)] of the posterior density, denoted by $\hat{\theta}_{k(\mathrm{MAP})}$, and variance based on the expected information evaluated at the mode:

$$\begin{aligned} V &= \frac{1}{\{-E[(\partial^2/\partial\theta^2)\ln f(\theta \mid u)]\}_{\theta=\hat{\theta}_{(\mathrm{MAP})}}} \\ &= \frac{1}{\{1/\sigma^2 + \sum_{i=1}^{n} I_i(\theta)\}_{\theta=\hat{\theta}_{(\mathrm{MAP})}}}. \end{aligned} \tag{9}$$

This approximation assumes that the prior is normal with variance denoted by σ^2. The information function for item i, denoted by $I_i(\theta)$, is equivalent to the one derived for the ML case given by Eq. (6). It is clear from an examination of Eq. (9) that the administration of the item with the largest information value (evaluated at $\hat{\theta}_{k(\mathrm{MAP})}$) will provide the greatest reduction in posterior variance V. As with the ML approach, the adaptive item-selection and scoring algorithm summarized in Table I is used, where the provisional trait estimate $\hat{\theta}_k$ is set equal to the posterior mode $\hat{\theta}_{k(\mathrm{MAP})}$. Calculation of the mode requires the use of an iterative numerical algorithm to find the maximum of the log posterior density function, Eq. (7). Alternating steps of trait estimation and item selection are repeated until a stopping rule is satisfied. The posterior variance based on observed information,

$$\mathrm{Var}(\theta \mid u) = \frac{1}{[-(\partial^2/\partial\theta^2)\ln f(\theta \mid u)]_{\theta=\hat{\theta}_{(\mathrm{MAP})}}}, \tag{10}$$

is an often-used characterization of measurement precision.

Item-Selection Enhancements

Although the adaptive item-selection algorithms form an efficient basis for precise measurement, test developers have often found it beneficial or necessary to alter these algorithms. These alterations, or enhancements, include the specification of rules used to choose the first several items; the specification of rules used to stop the test; modifications to the item-selection algorithms, intended to reduce opportunities for test-compromise and to help achieve a more balanced item content; and the use of time limits.

Item Choice Early in the Adaptive Sequence

Most commonly used adaptive item-selection algorithms require the existence of a provisional trait estimate. This provisional estimate is used to evaluate the relative information contribution of candidate items, and is specified from the responses to earlier items. But how should the first item be selected? The choice of the first item and other early items depends on the approach taken: ML or Bayesian.

ML approaches have adopted a set of heuristics for item selection early in the adaptive sequence. Typically, the first item selected is one of moderate difficulty relative to the population of examinees. If the first item is answered correctly, then a more difficult item is selected and administered; if the first item is answered incorrectly, then an easier item is selected. If necessary, selected items become successively easier or harder until at least one correct response and one incorrect response have been obtained. At this point, the ML function will typically possess a finite maximum, and the adaptive item-selection and scoring algorithm (Table I) can be used.

The Bayesian approach formalizes these heuristics by setting the initial provisional trait estimate equal to the mean of an informative prior trait density. The first item chosen is one with high, or highest, information at the prior mean. After the administration of the first item, the provisional trait estimation and item-selection algorithm (given in Table I) can be applied in a straightforward manner. Unlike the ML estimate, the provisional Bayesian estimate (taken as the posterior mean or mode) is defined for all response patterns, including those containing all correct or incorrect responses.

Stopping Rules

There are two common test termination or stopping rules used in CAT: fixed length and variable length. Fixed-length tests require that the same number of items be administered to each examinee. One consequence of fixed-length tests is that measurement precision is likely to vary among examinees. In contrast, variable-length tests continue the administration of items until an individualized index of precision satisfies a target precision level. These precision indices are often based on ML information [Eq. (5)] or Bayesian posterior variance [Eq. (10)] statistics.

Test developers have found that the choice of stopping rule is often highly dependent on the test purpose, item-pool characteristics, and operational constraints. In many instances, for example, equally precise scores among examinees are paramount, helping to ensure that decisions and interpretations made on the basis of test scores are equally precise for all examinees. In other instances, however, the occasionally long test lengths (possible with variable-length tests) might be judged too burdensome for examinees, and possibly for test administrators as well. To moderate some of the operational burdens, variable-length testing has been implemented with upper-bound constraints on the maximum number of administered items, and, in some instances, on the maximum amount of testing time allowed for each examinee. In other instances, test developers have opted for fixed-length tests to help standardized testing conditions with respect to variability in testing time and related testing fatigue.

Test Compromise Safeguards

In some instances, examinees may attempt to misrepresent their performance. This is especially likely when the test scores on the exam are used as a basis for important decisions. With CAT, the same items are typically administered on multiple occasions (spanning weeks, months, or possibly years). This repeated-item use provides examinees with an opportunity to obtain information about the questions from others taking the test before them. In these instances, one or more compromise deterrents can be implemented.

The adaptive item-selection algorithm (Table I) provides highly efficient but deterministic item selection. Consequently, two examinees providing the same pattern of responses to a set of multiple-choice questions (e.g., A, D, C, A, B, C, D, . . .) will receive the same items and the same θ estimate. An examinee could be assured a high score by simply re-entering the response pattern copied from a high-scoring examinee. This strategy can be thwarted, however, by adding a stochastic component to the item-selection algorithm. Rather than matching the difficulty parameter b_i with the provisional trait estimate $\hat{\theta}_k$, the next administered item for the 1PL model can be selected at random from among those items with difficulty parameters b_i falling in a narrow interval around $\hat{\theta}_k$ (namely, the interval $\hat{\theta} \pm \delta$, where δ is some suitably small constant). A strategy with similar intent designed for the 3PL model is based on the 5-4-3-2-1 algorithm, where the first item is selected at random from the five most informative items at the current provisional trait level, the second administered item is selected at random from the four most informative items evaluated at the current provisional trait estimate, and so forth. The fifth and subsequent items are chosen to maximize precision evaluated at the provisional trait estimate.

Although these strategies decrease or eliminate the gains associated with copied answer patterns, they do not necessarily limit the usage or exposure of the item pool's most informative items. That is, these strategies can still lead to instances in which some items are administered to nearly all examinees. An alternate method, referred to as the Sympson-Hetter exposure control algorithm, was designed specifically to place an upper ceiling on the administration rates of the most used items (typically, highly discriminating items of moderate difficulty). The Sympson-Hetter exposure control algorithm assigns an exposure control parameter, denoted by e_i, to each item i. These parameters are used in conjunction with the adaptive item-selection algorithm to screen items. For the selection of the kth item, candidate items are rank ordered by information level evaluated at the provisional trait estimate $\hat{\theta}_k$. The item with the largest information is considered first. A random uniform number r (between 0 and 1) is drawn; the item either passes or fails the exposure screen. If $r \leq e_i$, then item i passes and is administered; otherwise it fails and is not considered again for administration to the examinee. If the first evaluated item fails the exposure screen, then the next most informative item is considered for administration. A new random number is drawn, and the exposure screen is repeated. This screening process is repeated until a candidate item passes.

The exposure control parameters e_i are specified prior to testing and are calculated through a series of computer simulations. The assigned e_i values are dependent on a target ceiling exposure value T, and on an assumed trait distribution $f(\theta)$. The use of the exposure control parameters ensures (in expectation) that the exposure rates of the most used items will not exceed the target ceiling rate T in a population with trait distribution $f(\theta)$. In practice, the target ceiling exposure rate T is often set to a value between 1/10 and 1/3, ensuring that the most used items are not administered to more than 1/10 or 1/3 of the examinee population.

A conditional version of the Sympson-Hetter approach has been suggested for use in situations when it is important to maintain a target ceiling exposure rate for homogeneous subpopulations of examinees. Over narrow ranges of θ, the unconditional approach can provide higher than desired exposure rates for some items, and higher than the target T specified for the overall population. The conditional approach remedies this problem by using a vector of exposure parameters for each item (e_{i1}, $e_{i2}, \ldots$), where the exposure parameter used, e_{ij}, is specific to both the item i and to a narrow trait range indexed by the subscript j. This trait range is associated with the value of the provisional trait estimate. The conditional approach helps ensure that the exposure rates of the most used items do not exceed the target ceiling rate T; this assurance is made without requiring any specific assumption regarding the form of the trait distribution $f(\theta)$.

Other methods intended to further reduce item exposure are commonly used in conjunction with the Sympson-Hetter exposure control method. Two such methods include the simultaneous and sequential use of multiple item pools. In the case of simultaneous item-pool use, examinees are randomly assigned to two or more distinct (nonoverlapping) item pools. These item pools serve the same function as served by alternate test forms in conventional testing. In the case of sequential item-pool use, the item pool is continuously updated or replaced over a period of days, weeks, or months, thus making sharing item content among examinees less profitable.

Inevitably, the choice of any CAT exposure control method requires a consideration of the effects on measurement efficiency and test development costs. (Measurement efficiency is defined as the ratio of test score precision to test length.) In general, lower maximum item-exposure rates result in either lower measurement efficiency or in higher test development costs associated with larger or more numerous item pools. When making decisions about exposure control algorithms, including decisions about target maximum exposure rates and the number or size of simultaneous or sequential item pools, test developers have considered the unique compromise pressure placed on their exams. As part of the evaluation process, test developers typically perform extensive simulation analyses to examine the consequences of exposure control algorithms on measurement precision (for fixed-length tests), and on test lengths (for variable-length tests). These considerations have led some high-stakes developers to set low target maximum exposure levels at 0.10 and frequent item-pool replacement schedules (of just several weeks), and have led other test developers to use somewhat higher targets of 1/3 in conjunction with two or three simultaneous pools replaced at 5-year intervals.

Content Balancing

Test developers have been compelled in many cases to depart from strict precision considerations when designing and implementing CAT item-selection algorithms. These include cases, for example, in which the item pool consists of items drawn from different content areas of a more general domain (e.g., math items drawn from algebra and geometry). In such instances, item-selection algorithms that maximize precision may not administer properly balanced tests, resulting in test scores that have questionable validity. To help ensure adequately balanced content across examinees, constraints can be placed on the adaptive item-selection algorithms (e.g., constraints that ensure equal numbers of administered algebra and geometry items).

The most basic approach to content balancing spirals the sequence of item administration among key content areas. For example, math items would be administered in the following order: (1) algebra, (2) geometry, (3) algebra, (4) geometry, and so forth, where each item represents the most informative item (passing the exposure-control screen if used) at the provisional trait level among items in the given content (i.e., algebra or geometry) domain.

Although the spiraling approach is adequate for a small number of mutually exclusive content areas, this approach is poorly suited for situations in which more complex content constraints are desired. Consider the case, for example, in which items are classified along several dimensions simultaneously, and as a result do not fall into mutually exclusive categories. In such cases, methods such as the *weighted deviations* or *shadow testing* approaches can be used. These approaches are designed to maximize precision while attempting (in the case of the former method) or forcing (in the case of the latter method) adherence to specified content constraints.

Test developers have placed different levels of emphasis on the issue of content balancing. Developers of licensure and certification exams, for example, have tended to produce CAT exams in which content targets and constraints heavily influence item choice. In these exams, the direct demonstration of the understanding of key facts and concepts is considered so important that it is not sufficient to infer mastery of one concept from the correct answers to items assessing more difficult concepts. In some instances, the balanced administration of items is so important that test developers have opted for a testlet-based approach, whereby balanced groups or sets of items are selected and administered. Within each group, items are balanced for content and span a relatively narrow range of difficulty. Thus, in the testlet-based approach, the difficulty level of the testlet item group (rather than the individual item) is tailored to the level of the examinee.

The issue of content balancing is complicated not only by the question of when to balance, but also by the question of how finely to balance. Inevitably, more detailed balancing constraints will lower the measurement efficiency of the adaptive testing algorithm, with some constraints having larger effects than others. For example, in a fixed-length test of high school math skills, the forced administration of a large number of calculus items (that happened to be difficult because of their advanced content) would degrade precision over the middle and lower proficiency ranges. Examinees in these ranges would be better measured by the administration of items of more appropriate difficulty levels, such as those taken from introductory or intermediate algebra. This example illustrates that the imposition of some content constraints may actually lead to a significant decrease in precision or measurement efficiency. Unfortunately, there are no universally accepted rules regarding the optimal balance between content and measurement efficiency considerations in the construction of item-selection algorithms. Rather, to arrive at a suitable approach to content balancing, test developers routinely weigh these trade-off considerations in the context of the specific exam and its intended purpose.

Time Limits

Because the effects of time pressure are not explicitly modeled by standard item-selection and scoring algorithms, the imposition of time limits can in some instances significantly degrade CAT measurement precision. Even in spite of this undesirable consequence, most high-stakes, high-volume testing programs have implemented overall test time limits for a number of reasons, including the desire to help reduce excessive test times. In instances when time-limits have been imposed, most test developers have chosen to implement long time limits to provide most or nearly all examinees with an opportunity to answer all items without feeling rushed.

Although time limits might be desirable from an administrative standpoint, their use raises opportunities for gaming and test compromise in high-stakes testing. Low-ability examinees would be well advised to answer as few items as allowed. Under ML scoring, these low-ability examinees could capitalize on measurement error, which is greatest for short tests. Under Bayesian scoring, these same low-ability examinees could capitalize on the positive bias introduced by the prior, which is also greatest for short tests. To help discourage such test-taking strategies associated with time limits, test developers have implemented various scoring penalties applied to incomplete fixed-length tests. For variable-length tests, fair and equitable provisions must be made to help ensure that those requiring longer tests (to achieve the target precision level) are given sufficient time.

Item-Pool Development

Characteristics of the item pool (including size, item parameter distributions, and content coverage) directly impact CAT measurement efficiency and test score validity. Furthermore, particular characteristics of the adaptive algorithm (such as the stopping rule, number and type of content balancing constraints, and type and level of exposure control) can interact with key item-pool characteristics to further affect measurement efficiency and test score validity. These characteristics are listed in Table II.

Large item pools are desirable from several standpoints. First, large item pools tend to contain a larger set of highly discriminating items, which in turn can provide greater measurement efficiency (i.e., greater precision for fixed-length tests and shorter test lengths for variable-length tests). Second, large pools are more likely to satisfy content balancing constraints, or to satisfy them without severely impacting efficiency. For fixed-length tests, large pools enable lower exposure levels (for the most used items) and can satisfy these levels without severely impacting precision. Many test developers have found that high precision levels can be obtained

Table II Factors Affecting CAT Measurement Efficiency

Item-pool characteristics	*Algorithm characteristics*
Size	Stopping rule
Item parameter distributions	Content constraints
Content coverage	Exposure control

with pools of a size that is about six to eight times the test length.

In principle, the ideal item pool contains items with difficulty parameters (b_i) values uniformly distributed throughout the θ range, and for the 3PL model, contains high discrimination parameters (a_i) values and low guessing parameters (c_i) values. In practice, these ideal parameter distributions are often difficult to achieve. For some tests, highly discriminating items may be rare, or may exist only for items with difficulty values that span a narrow range or for items of specific content areas. In these cases, CAT algorithms can be very inefficient, resulting in test scores that have low precision over some trait ranges (for fixed-length tests), or resulting in long test lengths (for variable-length tests). Consequently, test developers, when possible, have tended to write and pretest large numbers of items in hopes of ending up with a sufficient number of highly discriminating items of appropriate difficulty and content.

Standard CAT item selection and scoring algorithms assume that the IRFs for all items are known in advance. In practice, these are estimated from examinee response data. For the 3PL model, large-scale testing programs have tended to use samples containing 500 or more responses per item to estimate item parameters. Programs that have based their item-selection and scoring algorithms on the 1PL model have typically relied on smaller sample sizes for IRF estimation. Test developers routinely use conditional (on $\hat{\theta}$) item-score regressions to check model fit. This model-fit analysis typically includes an additional check of dimensionality or local independence assumptions.

Many test developers have found it convenient, especially when developing the first set of pools, to collect calibration data in paper-and-pencil format. This mode of data collection is often faster and cheaper than collecting the same data by computer. In these cases, test developers have attempted to ensure that the use of item-parameter estimates obtained from paper-and-pencil data are adequate for use when the items are administered on computer in adaptive format. This assurance has been provided by several studies that have found inconsequential differences in item-response functioning due to mode of administration (computer versus paper and pencil).

Because of the complexity of the interactions between item-pool characteristics and adaptive testing algorithms, and the effects these have on measurement efficiency, test developers routinely conduct computer simulation studies to fine-tune the adaptive algorithms and to examine the adequacy of candidate item pools. These simulations take as input the item-parameter estimates of items contained in the pool (a, b, and c values), and if content balancing is proposed, the content classification of each item. Then, the consequences (on precision or test length) of using the proposed adaptive testing algorithm can be examined for examinees falling at different trait levels. The outputs of these simulations are conditional (on θ) means and variances of the estimated scores, $\hat{\theta}$. These simulation studies allow the effects of different variations of the adaptive algorithms (i.e., changes in content constraints, pool size, stopping rule, target exposure level, etc.) to be examined and compared. The outcomes of these simulations are often used as a basis for determining the suitability of candidate item pools and adaptive algorithms.

Trends in Computerized Adaptive Testing

In recent years, research on item-selection and scoring algorithms has continued. This includes work on item-selection algorithms intended to provide greater measurement precision. One class of approaches addresses the uncertainty regarding the provisional trait estimates toward the beginning of the test. These approaches include methods such as the global information criterion, weighted-likelihood information criterion, a-stratified method, and fully Bayesian approaches. Research has also continued on improved exposure control algorithms to further guard against test compromise. Another class of item-selection approaches that has been developed to further increase the measurement efficiency of CAT in the context of multidimensional IRT modeling involves items that are selected to maximize the information along several dimensions simultaneously.

As more testing programs have considered the use of CAT, more attention has been given to its cost-effectiveness. In addition to the benefits of increased measurement precision and reduced test lengths, CAT offers a host of other benefits associated with the computerized administration of test items. These include immediate and accurate scoring, minimal proctor intervention, individually timed and paced test administration, standardized instructions and test administration conditions, improved physical test security (no hard-copy test booklets are available for compromise), and provisions for handicapped examinees (large print, audio, and alternate input devices). Many of these benefits, especially when considered alongside the key benefit of increased measurement efficiency, provide compelling incentives in favor of CAT. But several obstacles have prevented many test developers from adopting CAT. In addition to specialized software requirements (necessary for test development and administration), CAT also requires considerable resources for item-pool development and for the purchase and maintenance of computer test-delivery systems.

Compared to conventional testing paradigms, many high-stakes test developers have found that CAT requires more test items and greater data demands (for item calibration). These greater demands for items and data are due in part to requirements of the adaptive branching strategy, and in part to the change in testing schedule associated with the test delivery. Conventional exams administered in high- or moderate-stakes settings are often associated with periodic test schedules, whereby substantially different items (i.e., test forms) are administered on each testing occasion to help reduce instances of cheating. Because of the large item-pool development costs and the impracticality of administering a large number of computer-delivered exams on the same day (as is the case with periodic exams), CAT exams are administered exclusively using on-demand or continuous testing schedules. According to these schedules, the same items are used over an extended time period. These continuous schedules by their nature increase the opportunity for test compromise, which is most effectively countered by large numbers of items—either contained in a few large pools or contained in a large number of smaller item pools.

It is noteworthy that increased demand for items and calibration data has been minimal for at least one major high-stakes testing program that transitioned from paper-and-pencil format to CAT. This program, the Armed Services Vocational Aptitude Battery (ASVAB) program, differed from most programs in that its conventional test version was also given on-demand, and compromise was controlled though the simultaneous use of a large number of alternate paper-based test forms. It was found that a sufficient level of CAT precision and security could be achieved by the use of a small number of moderate-sized item pools. The ASVAB experience suggests that a large part of the increase in item/data demands typically associated with high-stakes CAT may be due to the change in testing schedule (from periodic to continuous), rather than to the demands of the adaptive item-selection algorithms.

Research has also intensified on item-pool data collection and maintenance procedures. Response data required for the calibration of new items can be easily obtained by administering these items along with the operational adaptive items. This method of seeding or interspersing helps ensure that examinees will provide high-quality motivated responses, and that the item parameter estimates obtained from these response data are appropriately scaled. Depending on the mixture of tryout and operational items presented to examinees, this sort of data collection design can raise special challenges for conventional item-calibration approaches. Research has also continued on approaches for phasing items in and out of item pools, and on the effects of these approaches on precision and other important item-pool qualities.

Developers have been sensitive to computer literacy levels among their test-taking populations, and in particular to the literacy levels of select (possibly economically disadvantaged) subgroups. In large-scale test development efforts, care has been taken to ensure that aspects of the computerized test-taking experience do not place particular subgroups at an unfair disadvantage relative to corresponding subgroups taking paper-and-pencil versions. Although no consistent subgroup/medium interactions along racial or gender lines have been identified, attempts have been made to mitigate any possible disadvantage among subgroup members by the use of simple item-presentation formats and by clear test-taking instructions. As computers become even more commonplace and ubiquitous among widely diverse segments of the population, this concern is likely to dissipate.

With the proliferation of computers in recent years, it would appear that one of the last major obstacles to CAT has been removed: the availability of computer platforms for CAT test delivery. However, many high-stakes test developers have been concerned about context effects associated with different hardware and testing environments, and possible interaction effects of these with test-delivery software. For paper-and-pencil tests, test performance can be affected by subtle differences in booklet font and layout, and by subtle changes to answer sheets. These concerns about context effects have caused at least some high-stakes test publishers to go to great lengths to standardize these and other aspects of the testing experience. In the first instances of large-scale high-stakes uses of CAT, this strict adherence to standardization carried over to computers, which were also standardized so that the computer hardware and software were virtually identical across test administrations for a given exam. This strict adherence to standardization meant that testing could occur only on specially designated computers. Consequently, their cost was factored into the cost of CAT testing.

If adaptive testing could be routinely conducted on computers used for other purposes (and this could be done without loss of precision or validity), then a primary impediment of CAT testing (i.e., hardware costs) could be substantially reduced. Some test developers are, for example, considering the administration of low- or medium-stakes adaptive tests over the Internet, thus enabling CAT to be administered on a wide variety of general-purpose computer platforms. Because of the important role computer hardware plays in both the economic and the psychometric viability of CAT, necessary research on context effects is likely to intensify in the coming years. This includes research on the aspects of the computer hardware that influence test performance, and on characteristics of the exam (such as speededness) and software interface that might interact with particular hardware characteristics. Progress in these and related areas is likely to further increase the popularity of computerized adaptive testing.

See Also the Following Articles

Computer-Based Testing • Innovative Computerized Test Items • Item Response Theory

Further Reading

Drasgow, F., and Olson-Buchanan, J. B. (eds.) (1999). *Innovations in Computerized Assessment*. Lawrence Erlbaum, Hillsdale, New Jersey.

Lord, F. M. (1980). *Applications of Item Response Theory to Practical Testing Problems*. Lawrence Erlbaum, Hillsdale, New Jersey.

Sands, W. A., Waters, B. K., and McBride, J. R. (eds.) (1997). *Computerized Adaptive Testing: From Inquiry to Operation*. American Psychological Association, Washington, D.C.

van der Linden, W. J., and Glas, C. A. W. (eds.) (2000). *Computerized Adaptive Testing: Theory and Practice*. Kluwer, Boston.

Wainer, H. (ed.) (2000). *Computerized Adaptive Testing: A Primer*, 2nd Ed. Lawrence Erlbaum, Mahwah, New Jersey.

Weiss, D. J. (1982). Improving measurement quality and efficiency with adaptive testing. *Appl. Psychol. Measure.* **6,** 473–492.

Weiss, D. J. (2003). *CAT Central: A Global Resource for Computerized Adaptive Testing Research and Applications.* Retrieved December 12, 2003, from http://www.psych.umn.edu/psylabs/CATCentral

Computerized Record Linkage and Statistical Matching

Dean H. Judson

U.S. Census Bureau, Washington, D.C., USA

Glossary

blocking field/strategy A way to limit the search space by forcing certain fields to match before considering whether to link two records. Pairs that do not match on one or more blocking fields are automatically not sent to be compared.

constrained matching In statistical matching, every record from both files must be matched one and only one time, as opposed to unconstrained matching.

database A collection of records laid out in fields.

false negative/false nonlink A nonlink between two records that is in fact not correct.

false positive/false link A link between two records that is in fact not a correct link.

field A datum about the object, sometimes called a variable (for example, first name, street name, street type, owner name).

labeled data Pairs of records labeled concerning whether they already have link or nonlink decision flags on them; otherwise, they are unlabeled.

link decision A decision to join two records; a decision to not join two records is a nonlink decision.

match Two fields (in two different records) that are considered the same or sufficiently similar; two records match if they refer to the same external object.

matching field/strategy For pairs of records that satisfy the blocking strategy, the matching strategy indicates how to compare matching fields so as to determine if the two records should be linked.

record A collection of data about an individual object (for example, a person, an address, a business entity).

search space The region in which the record of interest is sought, in either record linkage or statistical matching.

statistical match Two records from different databases that have been joined together, but are not believed to refer to the same external object.

training data set Pairs of records that have been labeled as either link or nonlink by a prior (often clerical) comparison of pairs.

unconstrained matching In statistical matching, a donor record may be used more than once if it is the closest record to a target record, as opposed to constrained matching.

Computerized record linkage refers to an attempt to take two databases, each of which has records on the same collection of objects (persons and addresses are typical examples), and link each record in one database with one or more records in the other database. Record linkage is sometimes known as entity identification, list washing, data cleaning, and merge/purge. Statistical matching refers to an attempt to augment a first database with fields from a second database by finding "similar-looking" records in the second database. Using person records as an example, record linkage means linking records on the same person, whereas statistical matching means linking records on two different people who happen to look alike on certain characteristics. In record linkage, the combined database contains more information than either database separately. In statistical matching, the combined database contains more variables.

What Is Computerized Record Linkage?

Why Link Data across Databases?

Among a variety of reasons to link records across different databases, four reasons are important: to evaluate coverage overlap between two databases, to evaluate duplication in an existing database, to add new records and remove unused or unusable records, and to augment data in one database with data from another. To clarify the following discussions of database linkage, the first database will be referred to as database A, the second as database B (three-way links between databases are much less common, and typically they are composed of multiple two-way links).

Evaluating coverage overlap is important in population censuses. In censuses and vital registration (e.g., births, deaths) lists around the world, undercoverage (and occasionally overcoverage) is a constant concern. But how to evaluate undercoverage, when by definition undercoverage means that the people or addresses are missing from the list? A common solution is to use a dual system estimator, in which the census-taking organization takes the population census and follows up with a second enumeration attempt in a sample of areas. Thus, each person or address has two opportunities to be captured, and from these two captures an estimate of coverage (over or under) is constructed. But, in order to make the dual system estimate, the people and/or addresses in database A have to be linked to their equivalent record in database B. Because people write down their names, dates of birth, and their addresses with variations (e.g., William vs. Billy), linking equivalent records is not obvious.

Evaluating duplication is also important in vital registries, population censuses, marketing applications, and sample surveys. For example, immunization registries attempt to keep track of which persons have received which immunization. If the list contains duplicate records on a single person, it means that that person's actual immunization history is not accurately maintained. In vital registers, it is certainly not of demographic value to record duplicate births or to record deaths twice—both lead to estimation errors. Further afield, for direct marketing applications or sample surveys, duplication means that the household or person receives more than one solicitation, which is a waste of money at best and an annoyance to the recipient at worst.

Adding new records and removing unused or unusable records is important in list construction for sample surveys that use a list frame. In this case, database A represents the existing list, and database B represents a batch of new candidates for the list. Obviously, adding records that represent the same unit as one already existing on the database is creating duplication. Just as obviously, linking a candidate record from B with a record from A falsely, and not adding it to the list, is creating undercoverage. Thus, getting the link right is of crucial importance in list construction.

A final, important use for record linkage is to use data from database B to augment information in database A, if each database contains information not contained in the other (e.g., one is a credit card database, the other is a tax assessor's database). If the databases contain most of the same people, for example, the ability to link two records together that refer to the same person allows the analyst develop a broader "picture" of who individuals are and what they do. This has been used to compare survey responses on income components with administrative records data on those same persons. In other studies, survey data have been linked with longitudinal data to determine if respondents and nonrespondents have different profiles.

Record Linkage Terminology

A "record" can be considered as a collection of data about an external object in the empirical world. "Fields" in the record refer to individual items of information about the external object (e.g., first name, sex, street name, Federal Information Processing Standards code). In the population of all possible record pairs, two records can be said to "match" if they refer to the same external object, even if they do so with error or variation (for example, "Dean Judson", "D. H. Judson," and "Dean Harold Judson, Ph.D." all refer to the same external object); otherwise the two records are a nonmatch. Two fields can also be said to "match" if they contain the same or sufficiently similar information. After analyzing a pair of records, the records are declared "linked" if they are most likely a match; "possibly linked" if they might be a match; and "non-linked" if they are most likely not a matched pair. (Note that this terminology distinguishes "matches" in the population from "link" and "nonlink" decisions, which refer to record pairs.)

Multiple Databases, No Common Identifier

In order to construct the single record for each object, a way must be found to associate that object in database A with the same object in database B. On the surface, if the databases contain identifier information, such as a Social Security Number (SSN), this problem appears to have a simple solution: merely merge the two databases, using the SSN as the merge field. However, studies have shown that anywhere from 1 in 10 to 1 in 20 SSNs is collected or recorded with some kind of error. That means that the SSN is stored incorrectly in one or more of the databases, so that the problem of finding a common link is more challenging. Another challenge occurs when linking identical SSNs but the names (or dates of birth or some other feature) are different. Which "person" has been found? Might it be a wife using a husband's SSN, or might it be an undocumented person fraudulently using an SSN? Or is it a data entry error? Now suppose further that each database does not contain a unique identifier—i.e., there is no SSN or comparable unique identifier in each database. There are several fields that, when used together, might be sufficient to match a record uniquely in one database with the equivalent record in the other. For example, using first name, middle name, last name, and date of birth, and some geographical locator (such as an address, ZIP code, or census tract number), the pool of possible candidate records is reduced and it is likely that the two records can be linked.

False Positives and False Negatives

Unfortunately, data collection of identifying fields is never perfect. For example, consider two addresses: "2010 North Crater Road" (in database A) versus "2010 North Crater" (in database B). Are they the same address or are they different? Is "3-1402 Riverside Park Apartments, Alexandria, VA 22303" the same as "5840 Cameron Run Terrace #1402, Alexandria, VA 22303"? It is, but how is the computer to know that? Thus, the problem of false positives and false negatives must be faced. In short, there is a trade-off between being wrongly identified (a false link) and being erroneously not identified (a false non-link), which will be discussed further later.

Why Is Record Linkage a "Hard" Problem?

Classification Problem Similar to Cluster Analysis or Concept Learning

Record linkage is a special case of what are called "pattern classification" problems, which are well studied by both computer scientists and statisticians. The "record linkage as pattern classification" problem can be described very simply: given certain characteristics, should the object (a pair of records) be classified in the YES group (link them) or in the NO group (do not link them)? Consider a simplistic rule: Declare two (person) records "linked" if their first and last names match 100% on a character-for-character basis. Certainly this is a reasonable rule. However, consider the two (fictitious) records shown in Table I. The proposed simplistic rule links these records, but this is clearly a "false positive." Now consider the same rule using the records shown in Table II: "Art" is, of course, just a nickname for "Arthur." But now the simplistic rule does not link these records and a "false negative" has been created.

Table I Records That We Decide to Link (Under a Simplistic Rule)

First name	*Middle name*	*Last name*	*Suffix*	*Month of birth*	*Day of birth*	*Year of birth*
Arthur	F.	Jones	—	05	22	1971
Arthur	—	Jones	II	02	22	1988

Table II Records That We Decide Not to Link (Under a Simplistic Rule)

First name	*Middle name*	*Last name*	*Suffix*	*Month of birth*	*Day of birth*	*Year of birth*
Arthur	F.	Jones	—	05	22	1971
Art	F	Jones	—	05	22	1971

Large Search Space, Small Target Subset

Record linkage is simply finding a subset (all the pairs that are declared "linked") of a set (all possible pairs). However, record linkage problems are particularly challenging for three reasons:

1. As the number of records in either file increases, the number of possible comparisons increases as the product of the two file sizes. However, even ignoring duplication within a file, the number of matched pairs increases only as the minimum of the size of each file. Thus, for any reasonably sized record linkage problem, the size of the target subset becomes proportionally smaller and smaller relative to the size of the search space.
2. In practice, often there is no labeled training data set—that is, a collection of pairs of records that have been "hand coded" as either links or not links. This means that the problem is fundamentally a latent class problem, with the two latent classes being those pairs that indeed should be linked, and those that should not.
3. Finally, even records describing different people (or addresses) look quite a bit alike (as in Table I).

To illustrate the first reason, imagine two databases lined up in order, database A on the horizontal, database B on the vertical, as in Fig. 1. Here, an M represents a match between records that should be linked. A blank means that two records should not be linked. The target subset is the diagonal of Ms, but as the table gets larger, it should be obvious that the search space (all pairs) is growing much faster than the target subset is. To illustrate the second reason that record linkage is a problem, simply mix up the data (just like real data) and remove the Ms (as in Fig. 2). In large databases, the search space is huge. To illustrate the third reason, consider the pairs of records shown in Fig. 3; here the nearby records look a lot like matching records. Address one (101 Elm Street #1 97111) looks a lot like address two (101 Elm Court Apt.1 97111). But address two also looks a lot like address three, and, in fact, address three looks a lot like address four. But no one would like to link address one with address four.

Record #	1	2	3	4	5	...	n
1	M						
2		M					
3			M				
4				M			
5					M		
...						...	
N							M

Figure 1 Illustration of the space of all possible record pairs. Each M represents a match between records that should be linked; a blank means that two records should not be linked.

Record #	1	482	505	432	123	...	n
1							
142							
16							
4							
505							
...						...	
N							

Figure 2 Illustration of the space of all possible record pairs when the data shown in Fig. 1 are jumbled.

1	101 Elm Street #1 97111	vs.	101 Elm Court Apt.1 97111	2
2	101 Elm Court Apt.1 97111	vs.	101 Elm Street Apt.1 97111	3
3	101 Elm Street Apt.1 97111	vs.	101 Elm Street Apt.2 97111	4

Figure 3 Illustration of how "nearby" addresses look a lot like "matching" addresses.

Thus, in many cases, without a unique identifier, record linkage has been described as "searching for a needle in a haystack." This metaphor is entirely misleading, however. The record linker is not searching for a needle in a haystack, but rather for a needle in a stack of needles.

How to Perform Computerized Record Linkage?

Parsing and Preediting

A necessary pair of steps to computerized record linkage is parsing the incoming data and applying any necessary preedits. The complexity and importance of these steps are generally underappreciated; the programs needed to parse and interpret strings consistently are known as "standardizers," and they are not easy to write. Consider, as an example, the strings "3-1402 Cameron Run Terrace" and "5840 Cameron Run Terrace # 1402." Assuming that these each represent the same apartment in an apartment complex, which number in which position represents the apartment, and, more importantly, is it to possible write a computer program to pick out that number automatically? Further, can this standardizer pick out the apartment number correctly virtually every time? This is an area of very active research.

Character Matching

The most natural method of linking records, as already discussed, is some character-by-character matching of fields in the database. The primary weaknesses of character matching relate to inflexibility. Another type of weakness is nonuniqueness of the link/nonlink decision.

Sliding Windows

As an alternative to character matching, once a database has been parsed into fields, the database can be sorted according to different fields (for example, sort first by last name, then by first name, then by middle initial, then by year, month, and day of birth). Then, slide a "window" (of a predefined) size down the database, and compare all pairs of records within the window before sliding the window further.

Expert Systems

Character matching and "sliding windows" have the disadvantage that they rely only on the syntax of the fields, and not on their semantics. That is, when comparing "Arthur" to "Artie," the character matchers do not using any special intelligence about the relationship between those two strings, rather, they "blindly" compare character to character. The sliding-windows approach, though using intelligence about the relative importance of fields, also does not use any special knowledge about the contents of the fields. An expert system attacks (and partially solves) this problem. Expert systems use collections of rules or clues designed by experts. These collections of rules can accumulate over time, providing locally specific rules to account for local conditions, special situations, and the like.

Fellegi–Sunter theory

In contrast to the previously discussed approaches, the Fellegi–Sunter model is a statistically principled approach to record linkage. This model is framed as a "hypothesis test" when two records are compared. The separate fields are compared on a field-by-field basis, and the Fellegi–Sunter model uses information about the relative frequency of those fields to output one of three "decisions": the records are declared to be a positive link, the records are declared to be a positive nonlink, or the decision "possible link" is returned. The "possible link" region is then sent to presumably expensive clerical review and resolution. If the positive link is (arbitrarily) labeled with 1, the possible link with 2, and the positive nonlink with 3, and the set A is considered to be all records in the first file, and the set B is all records in the second file, then the Fellegi–Sunter model is a function from the space $A \times B$ into the space $\{1, 2, 3\}$.

In the general Fellegi–Sunter model, the problem is framed as an ordering of configurations by their "weight." For any collection of N individual fields $\vec{x}$, that configuration gets a ratio of match weight and nonmatch weight, $w(\vec{x}) = m(\vec{x})/w(\vec{u})$. The configurations are presumed ordered by this ratio (ties broken arbitrarily), indexed in order from highest weight to lowest weight, and cutoffs are chosen by defining a function $f(\vec{x})$ as follows (using the Fellegi–Sunter corollary 1 to ignore randomized choices falling exactly on a boundary):

$$f(\vec{x}) = \begin{cases} \text{Positive link} \\ \quad \text{if index for } \vec{x} \geq \text{upper cutoff.} \\ \text{Positive nonlink} \\ \quad \text{if index for } \vec{x} \text{ lower cutoff.} \\ \text{Possible link} \\ \quad \text{if upper cutoff} > \text{index for } \vec{x} > \text{lower cutoff.} \end{cases}$$

The only remaining task is to define the weights w. In the standard Fellegi–Sunter model, denoting the event "the records are in fact a match" by M and "the records are in fact a nonmatch" by $\sim M$, these weights are defined as likelihood ratios, viz.,

$$w(\vec{x}) = \frac{P[\vec{x} \text{ configuration} \mid M]}{P[\vec{x} \text{ configuration} \mid \sim M]}.$$

The Fellegi–Sunter model demonstrated that these weights are optimal in the sense that, for a fixed false link rate α and fixed false nonlink rate μ, this decision rule, using these weights, minimizes the clerical review region. Typically, in practice, researchers make the "conditional independence assumption." This assumption allows the weights in the preceding equation to be factored into

$$w(\vec{x}) = \ln \frac{P[x_1 = 1 \mid M]}{P[x_1 = 1 \mid \sim M]} \frac{P[x_2 = 1 \mid M]}{P[x_2 = 1 \mid \sim M]} \cdots \frac{P[x_N = 1 \mid M]}{P[x_N = 1 \mid \sim M]}.$$

When logarithms are taken, as is typically done in practice, this becomes a sum:

$$w^*(\vec{x}) = \ln \frac{P[x_1 = 1 \mid M]}{P[x_1 = 1 \mid \sim M]} + \ln \frac{P[x_2 = 1 \mid M]}{P[x_2 = 1 \mid \sim M]} + \cdots + \ln \frac{P[x_N = 1 \mid M]}{P[x_N = 1 \mid \sim M]}.$$

The term $P[x_i = |M]$ is typically called a "match weight" or "m-probability", and the term $P[x_i = 1 \mid \sim M]$ is typically called a "nonmatch weight" or "u-probability"; these terms are summed to construct a total score, compared to upper and lower (user-defined) cutoffs, and a decision is made.

Estimating these quantities is computationally intensive. In most applications, start values are provided by the analyst, and these start values are iteratively updated using a variant of the Expectation–Maximization (E–M) algorithm. Then, for candidate records pairs, the resulting weights are then summed and compared to the user-defined thresholds.

What Are Some Pitfalls of Computerized Record Linkage?

Like every other classification problem, computerized record linkage can sometimes link two records that should not in fact be linked. These are "false links." Similarly, computerized record linkage can fail to link records that should in fact be linked. These are "false nonlinks." Obviously, if two records are never linked, the false link rate is automatically driven to zero, at the cost of dramatically increasing the false nonlink rate. Similarly, if records that are only loosely similar are linked, the false nonlink rate is decreased at the cost of increasing the false link rate. Thus, there is a natural trade-off between these two, and the optimization problem is to balance these rates against their respective costs. If there was access to a labeled training data set, and clearly defined costs of false links versus false nonlinks, a naive Bayes classifier would be the natural choice as a classifier, although other pattern classification techniques could also be used. However, when there is no labeled training data set, the problem is exacerbated, because it is impossible to know, from the data, which links are false and which nonlinks are false, and hence how to calculate these rates. This has been a vexing problem for record linkers, and solutions in this case have been proposed, but no solution has yet been generally compelling.

A second challenge, not addressed in nonexpert system record linkage methods, is the problem of using "expert" and/or "local knowledge" about particular databases. For example, it may be well known to local planners that "Highway 1" and "Coastal Highway" are equivalent descriptions of a famous California highway, or that "Piso" and "Floor" are Spanish and English words that are approximately equivalent, or that "Susan M. Barker-Jones" has a hyphenated last name likely to be equivalent to "Susan M. Jones," but the computer, without assistance, may not know that. Expert systems and systems that use a labeled training data set may be able to make classifications based on very subtle or contextual clues. Character matching, sliding-windows, and standard Fellegi–Sunter techniques (with the exception of experimental Bayesian approaches) do not yet possess this capability.

What Is Statistical Matching?

In contrast with record linkage, statistical matching does not require, or even expect, that two records to be matched refer to the same person/address/object. Instead, typically what is desired is to "augment" (or "impute values" to) the target database with data from the "donor" database. Note that when only a single database is available, there are other techniques for imputing items, but the focus here is only on the two-database situation. The equivalent European phrase for this process is "data fusion."

What Are the Uses of Statistical Matching?

There are several reasons to use statistical matching in social science research. First, each database might contain variables that, when used jointly, provide a more complete picture of respondent behavior than either database does separately (for example, experimental poverty measures may require more information than is available in a single data set). Second, computerized record linkage might not be feasible or desirable, for practical or policy reasons, but a statistical match might be. Third, there might be item nonresponse on the first database that can be filled in with the second. Fourth, a researcher might be interested in constructing a pseudo-control group for a quasi-experimental design when random assignment between treatment and control groups is not possible.

Statistical Matching Terminology

Suppose there are two databases, one labeled the "target" database and the other labeled the "donor" database. Suppose that it is desired to add some variable Y from the donor population database to the target population database. The problem is to impute values for a variable that is missing in the target data set, but exists in the donor data set, to explore relationships between variables across the data sets. To simulate the variation in Y values that occurs in the donor population as closely as possible, an individual unique donor amount is found for each record, rather than using an average or a simple distribution. Begin by defining terminology:

- The target population has a collection of variables unique to it, labeled $\vec{Z}_1$.
- Both populations have a collection of common variables, labeled $\vec{X}_1$ for the target database and $\vec{X}_2$ for the donor database.
- Finally, the donor population has a collection of variables unique to it, labeled $\vec{Y}_2$. (If reference is made to Y values in the target database, the vector will be labeled $\vec{Y}_1$. Recall that the values do not exist in the target database; they must somehow be imputed.)
- Each population is sampled using some probability sampling mechanism, which will be ignored for the moment. Assume that the sample size of the target database is N_1 and the sample size of the donor database is N_2. To refer to the ith case in the target population, the vector will carry a subscript; i.e., $\vec{Z}_{1i}$ refers to the variables unique to the target database for the ith case, $\vec{Y}_{2j}$ refers to the variables unique to the donor database, and $\vec{X}_{2j}$ refers to the variables common to both databases, but for the jth case in the donor database.
- Treat these vectors as column vectors, e.g.,

$$\vec{X}_1 = \begin{bmatrix} x_{11} \\ x_{12} \\ x_{13} \end{bmatrix}, \text{ while } \hat{\beta} = [\beta_1, \beta_2, \beta_3].$$

The problem of finding donors in the donor data set is conceptually similar to the problem of finding distances between centroids in cluster analysis. There are essentially two proposed methods to find donors—finding the closest match and using those data, and developing a model and using the model predictions as data. The first method is to employ some distance measure algorithm typically used in clustering techniques to find the nearest neighbor or single unique donor in the donor database, then set some function of the value of the missing value Y_1 on the target database equal to some function of the amount from the donor and the target, $f(Y_1, Y_2)$. That is, the recipient on the target database gets imputed the value $f(Y_1, Y_2)$. The simplest function for a donation would simply be $f(Y_1, Y_2) = Y_2$, or simply take the donated value from the donor data set. Another function that would attempt to reflect uncertainty around the donated value would be $f(Y_1, Y_2) = Y_2 + \varepsilon$, where ε has some distribution reflecting the uncertainty around the donated value.

Another method currently in the literature is to estimate a multiple regression model $\hat{Y}_2 = \hat{\beta}\vec{X}_2$, to generate the expected value $\hat{Y}_2$ of the variable of interest from the donor data set, calculate the expected value $\hat{Y}_1$

for each record in the target data set, perform a simple match using the distance between each estimated value, then set the value of the missing variable equal to some function $f(\hat{Y}_1, \hat{Y}_2)$ of the actual amount recorded for the donor and the expected value on the target database. Of course, for either of this or the previous method to work, the predictor variables $\vec{X}$ have to exist in both databases. Furthermore, these variables common to both data sets should be reliable indicators of the missing variable.

Two Algorithms for Comparison

Two algorithms that can be compared: a nearest-neighbor centroid method and a multiple regression model-based method. These are described conceptually here, rather than mathematically (a more mathematical treatment would frame the problem in terms of covariance structure).

Nearest-Neighbor Centroid Method

In the nearest-neighbor centroid method, the centroid of a cluster (the set of indicator variables) is the average point in the multidimensional space defined by the variables chosen for matching. The difference (for example, simple or squared Euclidean distance between the two clusters) is determined as the difference between centroids. Standardized variables are used to mitigate different magnitudes of measure for each variable. The Mahalanobis distance is a standardized form of Euclidean distance wherein data are standardized by scaling responses in terms of standard deviations, and adjustments are made for intercorrelations between the variables. Using the centroid technique, each recipient would be paired to a unique donor based on the minimum Mahalanobis distance.

The nearest neighbor centroid algorithm is approximately described in pseudocode as follows:

1. Estimate the matrix S_2^{-1} (the variance–covariance matrix) from the data set in the donor population.
2. Set $i := 1$.
3. Do while $i < N_1$:.
4. Find $j \in \{1, \ldots, N_2\}$ such that $(\vec{X}_{1i} - \vec{X}_{2j})^T S_2^{-1} (\vec{X}_{1i} - \vec{X}_{2j})$ is minimized.
5. Select Y_{2j} as the donor for case i.
6. Append $f(Y_{1j}, Y_{2j})$ to the ith case in the target database.
7. Set $i := i + 1$.
8. End.

The end result of this process is that every record in the first database has been assigned a "donor" record from the second, and a function of the donor record's values has been imputed to the first record.

Model-Based Method

In the model-based method, the researcher uses multiple regression (or a generalized variant) to find the expected value of the variable of interest, to calculate the expected value for each record in both data sets, to perform a simple match using a distance measure on each estimated value, and then to set the value of the missing variable equal to a function of the value recorded for the donor. Using this technique, the match would be performed on one variable, the expected value of each case under a regression model. To pick the minimum distance, the distance measure could be among Euclidean, squared Euclidean or city-block (Manhattan) distance (absolute value), because they eliminate negative distance values. (These are not the only metrics; many others are possible.) For the purposes of this exercise, squared Euclidean distance is used as the distance measure to minimize to select donors. The model-based algorithm may be described in pseudocode as follows:

1. In the donor database, estimate the regression model $\hat{Y}_2 = \vec{\hat{\beta}}\vec{X}_2$.
2. Set $i := 1$.
3. Do while $i < N_1$:
4. Calculate $\hat{Y}_{1i} = \vec{\hat{\beta}}\vec{X}_{1i}$.
5. Find $j \in \{1, \ldots, N_2\}$ such that, $(\hat{Y}_{1i} - \hat{Y}_{2i})^T (\hat{Y}_{1i} - \hat{Y}_{2j})$ is minimized.
6. Select Y_{2j} as the donor for case i.
7. Append $f(Y_{1i}, Y_{2j})$ to the ith case in the target database.
8. Set $i := i + 1$.
9. End.

Mathematical Relationships

Each of the previously described techniques has common attributes. Mathematically, the techniques are similar in effect. The Mahalanobis distance function has two important properties: (1) the diagonal cells of the S^{-1} represent variances, and hence "scale" the individual distance calculations, and (2) the off-diagonal cells of the S^{-1} represent covariances, and "deform" the individual distance calculations. Note that the minimum value of any entry in the S^{-1} matrix is zero. There are no negative entries in the S^{-1} matrix.

In order to determine the relationship between the Mahalanobis measure and the model-based measure, begin with the function to be minimized:

$$\begin{aligned}(\hat{Y}_{1i} - \hat{Y}_{2j})^T (\hat{Y}_{1i} - \hat{Y}_{2j}) &= \left(\vec{\hat{\beta}}\vec{X}_{1i} - \vec{\hat{\beta}}\vec{X}_{2j}\right)^T \left(\vec{\hat{\beta}}\vec{X}_{1i} - \vec{\hat{\beta}}\vec{X}_{2j}\right) \\ &= \left(\vec{\hat{\beta}}\left[\vec{X}_{1i} - \vec{X}_{2j}\right]\right)^T \left(\vec{\hat{\beta}}\left[\vec{X}_{1i} - \vec{X}_{2j}\right]\right) \\ &= \left(\vec{X}_{1i} - \vec{X}_{2j}\right)^T \left(\vec{\hat{\beta}}^T \vec{\hat{\beta}}\right) \left(\vec{X}_{1i} - \vec{X}_{2j}\right).\end{aligned}$$

Now it is seen that the term $\vec{\beta}^T\vec{\beta}$ is the analogue to the S^{-1} of the Mahalanobis distance measure. Instead of scaling the space by variances and covariances, the space is scaled by the estimated coefficients of the model, and cross-products of these estimated coefficients.

Statistical Matching Considerations

When performing a statistical match, the researcher hopes that the donated data really do represent what the target record would have had, had the data been collected. Therefore, the researcher's choice of variables to be used in the match should be based on statistical evidence that they are reliable predictors or indicators of the missing variable. For model-based methods, as far as possible, fully specify the "model"; do not leave any indicators out of the set that would have an effect on the value of the missing variable, and verify that the functional form of the model is correct. Furthermore, as with any modeling exercise, the researcher needs to estimate the effect size of each of the statistical match variables. Some variables make a larger contribution to the matching of two different records, and the relative contributions of match variables should make substantive sense.

A second important consideration is whether the match should be constrained or unconstrained. In unconstrained matching, donor records are free to be reused, repeatedly if necessary, if the donor record is the closest match to more than one target record. A constrained match requires that all records are used, and thus a particular donor record, if already taken by a target record, may not be taken by a new target record.

A third consideration is the implicit assumption of conditional independence: When matching two records only on X, implicitly the researcher is assuming that Y and Z are independent conditional on their X value. Conditional independence is a feasible solution, but not the only one, and in the absence of auxiliary information that reduces the set of feasible solutions to a very narrow range, the match process should be repeated for various solutions so as to exhibit the uncertainty in the matching process.

A fourth consideration is that, like any regression-type model, a misspecified (or underspecified) set of predictor variables will bias the estimated regression coefficients $\hat{\beta}$ and thus also bias the expected value of the missing variable $\hat{Y}$; therefore, the model-based technique may not work as well when the data sets do not contain the needed predictor variables. The centroid method is nonparametric in the sense that it would simply find the match whether or not the indicator variables are good predictors. Of course, when X is not a good predictor of Y (or Z, or both), it might still be desired to perform a match, but then the procedure needs to account for the greater inherent uncertainty caused by that fact.

A final consideration relates to the populations from which each sample is drawn. The model-based technique uses only the information contained in the donor data set to estimate the value of the missing variable (as it must). If the recipient data set is drawn from a population in which the estimated model does not hold, then the match between donor and recipient will have reduced validity.

Acknowledgment

This article reports the results of research and analysis undertaken by Census Bureau staff. It has undergone a more limited review by the Census Bureau than its official publications have. This report is released to inform interested parties and to encourage discussion.

See Also the Following Articles

Data Collection, Primary vs. Secondary • Meta-Analysis • Missing Data, Problems and Solutions • Qualitative Analysis, Sociology • Secondary Data • Statistical/Substantive, Interpretations and Data Limitations

Further Reading

Belin, T. R., and Rubin, D. B. (1995). A method for calibration of false-match rates in record linkage. *J. Am. Statist. Assoc.* **90,** 694–707.

Borthwick, A., Buechi, M., and Goldberg, A. (2003). *Key Concepts in the ChoiceMaker 2 Record Matching System.* Paper delivered at the First Workshop on Data Cleaning, Record Linkage, and Object Consolidation, July 17, 2003, in conjunction with the Ninth Association for Computing Machinery Special Interest Group on Knowledge Discovery and Data Mining's (ACM SIGKDD) International Conference on Knowledge Discovery and Data Mining, Washington, D.C.

Christen, P., Churches, T., and Zhu, J. X. (2002). *Probabilistic Name and Address Cleaning and Standardisation.* Proceedings, December 2002, of the Australasian Data Mining Workshop, Canberra.

Duda, R. O., Hart, P. E., and Stork, D. G. (2001). *Pattern Classification,* 2nd Ed. John Wiley and Sons, New York.

Fellegi, I. P., and Sunter, A. B. (1969). A theory for record linkage. *J. Am. Statist. Assoc.* **64,** 1183–1210.

Gu, L., Baxter, R., Vickers, D., and Rainsford, C. (2003). *Record Linkage: Current Practice and Future Directions.* Technical Report 03/83, CSIRO Mathematical and Information Sciences. Available on the Internet at www.act.cmis.csiro.au

Hastie, T., Tibshirani, R., and Friedman, J. (2001). *The Elements of Statistical Learning: Data Mining, Inference, and Prediction.* Springer-Verlag, New York.

Hernandez, M. A., and Stolfo, S. J. (1995). *The Merge/Purge Problem for Large Databases*. SIGMOD Conference. Available on the Internet at http://citeseer.nj.nec.com

Judson, D. H. (2004). Statistical rule induction in the presence of prior information: The case of Bayesian record linkage. In *Data Mining and Knowledge Discovery Approaches Based on Rule Induction Techniques* (E. Triantaphyllou and F. Giovanni, eds.), pp. 655–689. Kluwer Academic Publ., Dordrecht.

Kadane, J. B. (2001). Some statistical problems of merging data files. *J. Official Statist.* **17,** 423–433.

Larsen, M. D.Rubin, D. B. (2001). Iterative automated record linkage using mixture models. *J. Am. Statist. Assoc.* **79,** 32–41.

Moriarity, C. (forthcoming). Statistical matching. In *Polling America: An Encyclopedia of Public Opinion* (S. Best and B. Radcliff, eds.). Greenwood Publ. Group, Westport, Connecticut.

Moriarity, C., and Scheuren, F. (2001). Statistical matching: A paradigm for assessing the uncertainty in the procedure. *J. Official Statist.* **17,** 407–422.

Rassler, S. (2002). *Statistical Matching: A Frequentist Theory, Practical Applications, and Alternative Bayesian Approaches.* Springer-Verlag, New York.

Rosenbaum, P. R. (1995). *Observational Studies.* Springer-Verlag, New York.

Thibaudeau, Y. (1993). The discrimination power of dependency structures in record linkage. *Survey Methodol.* **19,** 31–38.

Winkler, W. (1995). Matching and record linkage. In *Business Survey Methods* (B. G. Cox, *et al*., ed.), pp. 355–384. John Wiley, New York.

Condorcet

Pierre Crépel
CNRS—Université de Lyon 1, Villeurbanne, France

Glossary

calculus of probabilities A mathematical science initiated by Pascal, Fermat, and Huygens, with contributions by brothers James and Nicholas Bernoulli and, further, by de Moivre, Bayes, Price, and Laplace; These scientists thought that the nature of the calculus of probabilities changes and that it could be applied to "the functions of life and that it is the only useful part of this science, the only part worthy of serious cultivation by Philosophers."

Condorcet's effect, or "paradox" Consider the case of an election among three candidates, A, B, and C, with each voter simultaneously showing a preference by placing the candidates in order of merit. It is possible that the collective opinion gives an incoherent (or cyclical) result—for example, A is better than B, B is better than C, C is better than A. There are several interpretations of this effect (Condorcet and Kenneth Arrow, for example, are not concordant).

political arithmetic (Condorcet), or social mathematics The application of mathematics (including differential and integral calculus, the calculus of probabilities, etc.) to political sciences, involving three parts: (1) collection of precise facts such that computations can be applied, (2) derivation of consequences of these facts, and (3) determination of the probabilities of the facts and of their consequences.

political arithmetic (England, 17th century) The application of (elementary) arithmetical calculations to political uses and subjects, such as public revenues or population counts.

théorème du jury The Condorcet jury theorem proposes that n individuals, expressing their opinion independently, each have a probability p (>0.5) of giving a true decision and thus a probability $1-p$ (<0.5) of giving a false decision. The collective decision of the majority thus has a probability of truth approaching 1 when n becomes large. The name "théorème du jury" is Duncan Black's and not Condorcet's.

In the 17th century, political arithmetic was limited to elementary computations and rough previsions. It was revolutionized by Condorcet into "social mathematics"; in other words, it was changed into a genuine science dealing with all moral, political, economic, and social problems, and using all parts of mathematics, particularly the newest theories of probability.

Condorcet (1743–1794): A Biographical Sketch

Marie Jean Antoine Nicolas Caritat, Marquis de Condorcet, was born in Ribemont, Picardy, in the north of France. His father, a military man from a Dauphiné family, died when Condorcet was only a few weeks old. The boy was reared by his mother's family in Picardy in a bourgeois legal setting, accustomed to economic and political responsibilities. Following his studies with the Jesuits at Rheims, then at Collège de Navarre in Paris, Condorcet devoted himself to pure mathematics, with the direct goal of obtaining general results in integral calculus. His early work, begun toward the end of the 1750s in collaboration with his friend and first teacher, Abbé Girault de Keroudou, was both praised and criticized by Fontaine and D'Alembert, who found fault with the often confused and excessively general style. Nevertheless, Condorcet's research on integral calculus resulted in his election to the Academy of Sciences at the age of 26. His work culminated in the early 1780s in a treatise (regrettably unpublished) containing, in particular, a theorem on the integration of differential equations in terms of a finite number of explicit functions, 40 years before Liouville.

Following his participation in Turgot's ministry (1774–1776), Condorcet, already an adjunct secretary of the Academy of Sciences, took up the position of permanent secretary until the period of the most violent episodes of the French Revolution. He continued his research both in pure mathematics and in the calculus of probabilities. Strongly involved in the encyclopedic movement and a friend of D'Alembert, Turgot, and Voltaire, Condorcet was the last of the *encyclopédistes* and the only one who lived through the French Revolution. He committed himself deeply to his work, developing and illustrating his scientific vision of politics, while having little inclination to a romantic view of populist participation. This enabled him to work out some very fertile ideas on education, women, slavery, and the rights of man, but he often had little influence on current events. However, the exchange of political ideas at this time influenced developments in many countries, such as the United States, through Thomas Jefferson and James Madison, but neither of these figures understood Condorcet's social mathematics.

During the Terror, Condorcet went into hiding, writing his famous *Esquisse d'un Tableau Historique des Progrès de l'Esprit Humain*. He was arrested on 27 March 1794, and was found dead in the prison of Bourg-Egalité (Bourg-la-Reine) 2 days later. It is not known whether he committed suicide or died of apoplexy.

Early Thoughts about Measure

First Remarks on Analysis

What is measured in political arithmetic, in the old and restricted sense of the word? The answer, the number of people, quantities of products, and benefits, seems to be unambiguous, but difficulties exist; measurements (and its interpretations) appear to require refinements, and Condorcet was very aware of these subtleties. Measurement clearly involves intermediate and provisional measures of more "physical" quantities, such as lengths, surfaces, volumes, and weights. Moreover, social measurement also involves estimates of "values"; primarily, it implicates a clarification of this very concept in political economy, but it also requires getting over two additional difficulties, which Condorcet identified much better than other scholars of his time: taking in account time and random fluctuations in computations. Indeed, these problems naturally appear for life annuities and lotteries (as Condorcet's contemporaries had already noticed), but they also occur and become acute and uneasy to deal with when computing the value of land in agriculture, of future harvests, of goods transported on the sea, of feudal rights, or of the national debt. They involve risk measurement that cannot be summarized only by a probability of fatal occurrence and a monetary value of goods in peril. In several early unfinished manuscripts devoted to reflections on analysis, Condorcet laid emphasis on the following question: how to find a common measure for phenomena being studied? Two typical passages in Condorcet's writings address this, the first one being general, the second one regarding probabilities. Condorcet stated that "All over the world, everything that could be reduced to a common measure can be computed; consequently this common measure would be the only point to be determined. Measuring the nature, that is reducing everything to a number of ideas as small as possible, is the very aim of mathematics." Condorcet is saying that because uncertainty, hazard, fuzziness, and multiplicity of uncontrolled parameters are involved in social measurements, and because some of the parameters cannot be taken in account, we should solve the difficult problem of measuring probabilities. Regarding probabilities, Condorcet stated that "In every application of mathematical analysis, in order to calculate only quotients, it is necessary to get quantities that would be homogeneous with all else quantities involved in the problems.... Thus, when you try to transform the so-called calculus of probabilities into an analytical science, you have to reduce it to compute quotients and therefore first of all to find a common measure."

Early Dissertations on Philosophy and Jurisprudence

The reflections on "analysis" by the young Condorcet originated from interrogations about foundations of mathematics; the scientist had a very early concern for law and for the rights of man. Historians have often underestimated the impact of Beccaria's *Dei delitti e delle pene* on French *encyclopédistes*. In a letter to Frisi (1767), Condorcet dedicates "his last dissertation" to the Milanese thinker, and we indeed can find in his *nachlass* (deduction) at the Bibliothèque de l'Institut several texts on jurisprudence, criminal laws, etc. that are related to Beccaria; Condorcet explicitly intends there to "carry the torch of analysis" onto these topics. Therefore, the intellectual conditions were almost mature enough to undertake a far-reaching work on application of mathematics to social sciences, but still lacked a confrontation with administrative practice.

Weights, Measures, and the Mint

Under Turgot's ministry, in 1775, Condorcet was named inspector of navigation and inspector of the Mint. Shortly before (1773), he had been elected as an assistant secretary of the Académie des Sciences and became perpetual secretary in 1776. In fact, all of these public offices were very intricate: they led the scientist-administrator to a deeper (practical and theoretical) reflection on the conditions that make possible and relevant the measurement of social variables. The Controller-General's reforms were very ambitious. In an unpublished manuscript (studied by L. Marquet), Condorcet wrote that "When I was named *Inspecteur des monnaies* in 1775 by Mr Turgot, the latter said to me that he purposed to include in a general system the reform of weights and measures, the legislation of currencies and the gold and silver trade."

From the very beginning of his first plans, Condorcet aimed to solve technical problems (physical, chemical, and mechanical), to evaluate the economic stakes, and to suggest efficient administrative means for success of the reforms. He was thus led to clarify concepts, in particular to study the constancy and variability of involved phenomena, the possibility or not of measuring them with precision, the social conditions of measurement, and what may now be called examination of hidden economic variables. He also paid attention to these concepts when judging the relevance of various navigation projects (canals in Picardy, 1775–1780; in Berry and Nivernais, 1785–1786), when supporting the gauge reform proposed by Dez (an accurate means of measuring liquid content, 1776), and when refereeing plans for a new cadastre in Haute-Guyenne (1782). As a *commissaire* (referee) and also as a redactor of the *Histoire de l'Académie Royale des Sciences*, in the bosom of the Académie, Condorcet had many opportunities to deepen and perfect his reflections on numerous matters, including the controversy between Sage and Tillet on gold and metallurgy (1780) and various other problems during the French Revolution.

The Calculus of Probabilities and How to Use It

Condorcet's contributions to social measurement should not be restricted to philosophical, juridical, administrative, and technical aspects; on the contrary, some of his most original thinking consists in new mathematical theories, especially regarding the calculus of probabilities.

Calculus of Probabilities: From the Early Manuscripts to the Celebrated Memoirs

Condorcet started studying the calculus of probabilities as early as 1770. After seriously considering D'Alembert's doubts on the foundations and relevance of this science (the assumption that events are equally likely, their independence, the additivity of probabilities, and the linearity of expectation, etc.), Condorcet tried to answer the objections in a constructive way. His contributions to the mathematical theory of probability contained remarkable innovations, including a theory of mathematical expectation with a solution to the St. Petersburg problem for a finite horizon; a theory of complexity of random sequences in regard to regular arrangements; a model for probabilistic dependence, which is none other than what are now called "Markov chains"; and solutions to the problem of statistical estimation in the case of time-dependent probabilities of events. This latter contribution foreshadows, perhaps clumsily and not in a very practical way, the concept of time series. Condorcet also produced a definition of probabilities starting from classes of events, and a theory of individual economic choice in a setting of universal risk and competition. Unfortunately, he was too daring in his writing, which suggested research programs rather than concrete theorems; moreover, the exposition of ideas was so unclear and impractical that his original contributions were not understood in his lifetime or even in the two following centuries.

It is not known exactly why Condorcet did not publish his manuscript works on probability before his celebrated memoir (1784–1787) and his *Essai sur l'application de l'analyse à la probabilité des jugements rendus à la pluralité des voix* (1785). Was he unsatisfied with his own dissertations? Did he fear to displease D'Alembert? There are also questions as to what extent Condorcet's work was related to Laplace's major contributions. How did Condorcet compare his metaphysical views on probability with Hume's views? Historians and scholars can only propose hypotheses about these open questions.

Application of Probability Theory to Natural and Social Sciences

To what extent do mathematical problems and discoveries affect social measurement? An example using a discussion on agricultural insurance, published in the *Journal de Paris*; provides a sketch of an answer; the articles were published by an anonymous author, but are probably due to Condorcet.

The first obstacle to applying probability theory is related to the measurement of risk for natural catastrophes. Losses are too high, consequently, stochastic compensations are inadequate in a local space and in a local time adapted to the agricultural market and banking system of the *Ancien Régime*. The second difficulty would affect the problem of partial losses; their estimates are ambiguous, controversial, and unfeasible. How to save the partial harvest? Who (farmer or insurer) would do it? And how to convert it into money? The third obstacle is a general one for every new business: as stated in the *Journal de Paris*, "the difficulty of elaborating an insurance theory (for harvests) before the creation of insurance companies, and of creating such companies before the theory is at least approximately elaborated." The author explained that for marine, fire, and life insurance (the three existing types of insurance in Condorcet's France), the problem had so far been eluded, but that it would be impossible to avoid in the present case of agricultural insurance.

Elections and Politics

Scientific Points of View about Elections

Condorcet approached the theory of elections rather late (1783–1784) in his career, and his thinking on this subject was subordinated to other broader and more ambitious objectives. Indeed, the 500 pages of the *Essai sur l'application de l'analyse* (1785) provide at the same time a theory of knowledge and new mathematical methods for the calculus of probabilities, in addition to dealing with various topics connected to judgments (elections, decision-making, witness probabilities, etc.). The theory of elections is thus only part of the book; moreover, it is not so easy to know exactly which forms of elections are recommended in the *Essai*: specialists in the theory of social choice have considerable differences of opinion about interpreting the relevance and even the significance of Condorcet's most complicated formulas. Nevertheless, everybody does agree with the perspicacity of the author when he discovered or deepened the logical difficulties revolving around the idea of a ballot and three candidates (A, B, and C).

Condorcet examined the defaults of the "ordinary method" (admitting either an absolute or a relative majority) and of Borda's method (which consists in asking each voter to rank candidates by order of merit, giving 2 points to the best candidate, 1 point to the second candidate, and 0 to the third candidate). Condorcet indicated that the only method he thinks is natural and exact is a pair wise comparison among the candidates. For example, the order of merit, $A > B > C$, signifies the three following assertions: $A > B$, $A > C$, and $B > C$. For every possible system of assertions, Condorcet then adds the votes and takes, among the six coherent systems, the one that has the greatest number of votes. He notes the following strange situation, now called the "paradox of votes," or "Condorcet's paradox": even when individual voters are forbidden to give an incoherent (or cyclical) vote, such as $A > B$, $B > C$, $C > A$, the collective result obtained may be incoherent. Condorcet notes several examples, such as a case where $A > B$ is supported by a plurality of 18 to 13, $B > C$ has a plurality of 19 to 12, and $C > A$ is 16 to 15. What should be the good decision here, at least when an immediate choice is necessary? Condorcet's answer is the following: to exclude *a priori* the contradictory systems of propositions and to take, among the six residual coherent systems, the one that has the greatest number of votes; here, it would merely result in an inversion of the third preference ($A > C$ in place of $C > A$). But the problem becomes far more complicated when the number of candidates is greater than three, and Condorcet's position appears unclear and ill explained; it is not understood in the same manner by every interpreter.

A revival of the discoveries of the Enlightenment scientists occurred in the 1950s, and Arrow, Guilbaud, and Black later elaborated theories of social choice and summing preferences. In all his subsequent writings, Condorcet always claimed the existence and uniqueness of one rigorous method, the pair wise comparison; the few passages in which he stated that "the real preference does not exist" merely signify the logical difficulty of a cyclical result, but not the absence of a solution. Condorcet's late manuscripts were unambiguous on this point. Nevertheless, when the number of candidates is more than three, the same ambiguities as presented here could be identified in his texts.

Finally, another aspect must be emphasized. All the forms of elections recommended by Condorcet always rely on the two basic principles: (1) there are no divergent interests for all the participants in the election and (2) there is an absolute true opinion. This requires recommending the same forms for political elections and for decision-making on a purely scientific question: Condorcet did not change his point of view on this theoretical aspect. Consequently, forms of elections (familiar to modern voters) such as the proportional ballot, modification of opinion for a second round, etc. are completely beyond Condorcet's logical way of thinking: for example (with the terms used in the social choice literature), he advocates "sincere" voting and totally rejects "strategic" combinations of votes.

Condorcet and the Actual Elections

Should it be inferred from the preceding considerations that Condorcet was a sinner, that he remained unaware of the gap between theory and practice? No. Against many historians, it can be shown that Condorcet was not only conscious of the concrete difficulties of applying the best scientific methods to votes in actual politics, but that he also worked out a deep reflection in this connection about relations between theory and practice. Among the evidence is the following passage in a late manuscript (1793):

> *When putting a theory into practice, we can disregard anything which has only an imperceptible effect on the results, or which affects them only in very rare situations. A rigorous method is often impracticable. Besides, such a complicated and time-consuming method would have more disadvantages than might result from the errors in a good approximation method. Finally, a method which is rigorous in theory is not necessarily so in practice. For, by disregarding some errors without disregarding others of*

equal importance, the apparently rigorous method may lead us further from an exact result, than would a well devised approximation to that method.

In the sequel to the text, Condorcet even sketched a comparison of applying mathematics to physical and technical sciences and of applying mathematics to political and moral sciences.

The various concrete voting procedures that Condorcet proposed in his political writings, such as *Essai sur les assemblées provinciales* (1788) and *Projet de constitution* (1793), have been examined from six points of view:

- The general theory of elections.
- The main conditions to be fulfilled (that is, how to find, in some concrete cases, a form of election less satisfactory than the ideal theoretical form, but replacing the ideal and filling the main conditions required by this particular form of election).
- The pluralities (the scope and limits of the rights of the majority, conditions of equality among the voters, other types of majorities, and unanimity).
- The circumstances and preliminary operations (number of eligible people, number of candidates, number of places to be filled, how to divide the electoral body, single-stage or two-stage elections).
- How to organize the votes ("purity" of the ballot, intrigues, parties, assembling or not the voters).
- How to count the votes (cases of equality, incomplete voting papers, time consumed by counting votes).

Without giving details here, Condorcet made a clear distinction between three different ends:

1. Do we try to find one winner or to determine a total order among all the candidates?
2. Do we try first of all to choose the best candidate (as, for example, in the election of a president) or to choose only good candidates (as, for example, in the election of members of Parliament)?
3. If we know the probability of truth of each voter, does the result of the ballot give a maximum for the probability of getting the best candidate (or the best order)?

The forms proposed by Condorcet were diverse, admittedly often somewhat complicated, but the priority was always to respect the essential point (and not all the abstract possible conditions) in the concrete situation.

Political Arithmetic and Social Mathematics

A "New Science"

To sum up, Condorcet's thought about measure in political arithmetic has two sources: on the one hand, early epistemological reflections directly originated in D'Alembert's questions on probability theory and applications of mathematics to social problems; on the other hand, Condorcet had practical experience for 20 years working as an administrator, as a secretary of the Académie des Sciences, etc. During the early 1780s, the connection between both sources is established; Condorcet develops his own theory, deals precisely with an example (probabilities of judgments and decisions), and enlarges the field of social objects to be measured. In the spring of 1785, Condorcet became an activist; he wrote to the ministers and princes, in order to convince them to create a professorship in political arithmetic, treating it as a science in the full sense of the word. Finally, in the late 1780s and early 1790s, he gave to social mathematics a central role in his public education projects, advocating that it should be a basis to allow every citizen to exert consciously his own sovereignty. Shortly before he was imprisoned as a clandestine, Condorcet thought it useful to restate and to structure the project, editing the *Tableau général de la science qui a pour objet l'application du calcul aux sciences politiques et morales* (1793). This text has often been ill published and ill interpreted; the following discussion summarizes its principal elements.

In particular, Condorcet defines the new science as follows: "The Social Mathematics has men for its object, when it teaches us to work out the mortality rate in a particular area, when it calculates the advantages and or the disadvantages of an election method. It has things for its objects when it calculates the advantages of a lottery, or tries to determine the principles on which the rate of maritime premiums should be based. It has both men and things for its object when it examines life annuities and life insurance." Condorcet also gives a synopsis of its objects and its method:

Objects of social mathematics
I. Man
a) Man as an individual
b) The operations of human mind
II. Things
a) The reduction of things to a general standard
b) The calculation of values
III. Man and things
Method of social mathematics
I. Determination of the facts
a) Enumeration of the facts: 1. Observed facts, 2. Hypothetical facts
b) Classification and combinations of the facts
c) Probability of the facts
II. Appreciation of the facts
a) Formation and use of mean values
b) Their probability
III. Results of the facts
a) Probability of the results

Finally, Condorcet indicates that the five "mathematical theories" that should precede the social mathematics must be as follows:

1. The theory of quantities, which can increase in proportion to time, and includes the theory of money interest.
2. The theory of combinations.
3. That of the method for deducing from observed facts either general facts or even more general laws.
4. The theory of the calculus of probabilities.
5. And lastly that of average values.

The Social Mathematics in the Field of Human Knowledge

The separation between the social mathematics and the other branches of human knowledge, and, more broadly, its place within the classification of sciences, should not lead us to believe that it constitutes an independent field for Condorcet. As he explains in the *Tableau Général*, "the weakness of the human mind, the necessity to save time and efforts force us to divide the sciences, to circumscribe and to classify them." Condorcet insists that the last operations can be made "either according to the objects considered, or according to the methods employed." Therefore, a distinction must be made between an "objective" and a "methodological" criterion to understand the specific relationship the social mathematics has with the other fields of knowledge. Because the framework of the *Tableau Général* is built around two entries, Condorcet has to specify whether the "objects" or the "method" are the focus of the enquiry. If the "objects" are, then there is only one branch of knowledge. The social mathematics and the social sciences both have for their objects men, things, and men and things together. However, starting from their "methods," they are complementary, and not identical, which is what Condorcet shows implicitly by choosing the name "social mathematics" and not "mathematical social science." Grounded on observation and reason, the social sciences present the social mathematics with specific data and problems. Conversely, the social mathematics enlightens the social sciences by calculus.

Shortly after writing in the *Tableau Général*, in a manuscript text, *Sur les mots sciences et art* (1793–1794), Condorcet rejected the preceding classification. He explains the reasons for this: "if we choose as a foundation the methods they [the sciences] employ... we shall soon be stopped by the inconvenience of separating truths which are constantly looked into by the same men, and which are naturally connected. We would have to separate astronomy based on observation from astronomy based on calculus." This way of classifying does not come from a sudden change in Condorcet's mind, rather it is the evidence that points of view are necessarily diverse and relative: according to the natures and purposes of classifying, either criterion is equally suitable.

See Also the Following Articles

Measurement Theory • Political Science

Further Reading

Arrow, K. J. (1963). *Social Choice and Individual Values*, 2nd Ed. Wiley, New York.

Baker, K. M. (1975). *Condorcet. From Natural Philosophy to Social Mathematics.* University of Chicago Press, Chicago.

Beaune, J. C. (ed.) (1994). *La Mesure. Instruments et Philosophie*. Champ Vallon, Seyssel.

Black, D. (1958). *The Theory of Committees and Elections.* Cambridge University Press, Cambridge.

Brian, E. (1994). *La Mesure de l'Etat.* Albin Michel, Paris.

Chouillet, A. M., and Crépel, P. (eds.) (1997). *Condorcet Homme des Lumières et de la Révolution.* ENS Editions, Fontenay-aux-Roses (Lyon).

Condorcet (1994). *Arithmétique Politique Textes Rares et Inédits* (B. Bru and P. Crépel, eds.) INED, Paris.

Crépel, P. (1990). Le dernier mot de Condorcet sur les élections. *Mathémat. Informat. Sci. Hum.* **111,** 7–43.

Crépel, P., and Gilain, C. (eds.) (1989). *Condorcet Mathématicien, Economiste, Philosophe, Homme Politique*. Minerve, Paris.

Crépel, P., and Rieucau, J. N. (2004). Condorcet's social mathematics: a few tables. *Social Choice Welfare* (special issue). To be published.

Guilbaud, G. T. (1968). *Eléments de la Théorie Mathématique des Jeux.* Dunod, Paris.

Marquet, L. (1989). Turgot, Condorcet et la recherche d'une mesure universelle. *Bull. Org. Int. Métrol. Légale* **115,** 2–8.

McLean, I., and Urken, A. (1992). Did Jefferson and Madison understand Condorcet's theory of voting? *Public Choice* **73,** 445–457.

McLean, I., and Urken, A. (1992). *Classics of Social Choice.* Michigan University Press, Ann Arbor.

Perrot, J. C. (1992). *Une Histoire Intellectuelle de l'Economie Politique.* EHESS, Paris.

Rashed, R. (1973). *Condorcet. Mathématique et Société.* Hermann, Paris.

Rothschild, E. (2001). *Economic Sentiments. Adam Smith, Condorcet, and the Enlightenment.* Harvard University Press, Cambridge.

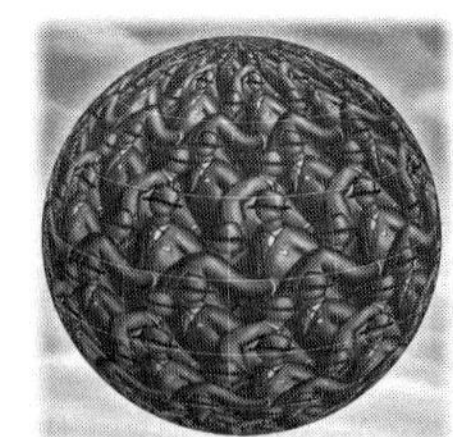

Confidence Intervals

George W. Burruss

Southern Illinois University at Carbondale, Illinois

Timothy M. Bray

University of Texas, Dallas, Richardson, Texas, USA

Glossary

alpha level Denoted as α; represents the probability that a researcher will commit a Type I error (rejecting the null hypothesis when it is true). Standard alpha levels in social science research are 0.05 and 0.01, but any level can be specified. A level of 0.01, for instance, indicates that a researcher believes they would incorrectly reject the null hypothesis only 1 in 100 times.

confidence interval The interval estimate around a population parameter that, under repeated random samples, would be expected to include the parameter's true value at $100(1 - \alpha)\%$ of the time. For instance, it is highly unlikely that the percentage of persons in a city favoring a bond issue is exactly the same as the percentage in the sample. The confidence interval builds a buffer zone for estimation around the sample percentage.

confidence level The probability that, under repeated random samples of size *N*, the interval would be expected to include the population parameter's true value. Typically, either 95 or 99% levels are chosen, but these levels are pure convention and have no scientific justification; researchers may pick any confidence interval that suits their purpose.

point estimate A sample statistic that represents an estimate of a population parameter's true value.

population parameter A number that describes some attribute of the population of interest, such as the percentage of a county's population that believes jail sentences are too lenient.

standard error of the estimate The error that results from taking a sample from a population. The standard error is derived from the sample size and the standard deviation of the distribution of samples (i.e., the distribution of repeated random samples taken from a population). Most often, the standard deviation of the distribution of samples is unknown; therefore, a sample's standard deviation is substituted in the formula.

***t* distribution (student's *t* distribution)** A theoretical distribution used for calculating confidence intervals around the mean; the *t* distribution is used for small samples. When a sample size is 120 or greater, the *t* distribution approximates the normal distribution.

***z*-score** A score that indicates how far a raw score deviates from the mean; it is measured in standard deviation units. For example, the 95% confidence level has an associated *z*-score of 1.96, or almost 2 standard deviations above and below the mean. A *z*-score is used when the distribution is normal. Estimating a mean from a small sample size requires a *t*-score rather than a *z*-score.

Most people are familiar with confidence intervals, even if they are not familiar with how to calculate them. Most everyone has heard opinion polls, early election returns, and other similar survey results, reporting a "margin of error of plus or minus 4%." Though most people do not realize it, this margin of error is actually a confidence interval. In this article, confidence intervals are defined, the calculations for several measures are demonstrated, and the presentation of uncertainty in research is discussed.

Introduction

Reports of opinion polls, election returns, and survey results typically include mention of a margin of error of plus or minus some percentage. This margin of error is actually a confidence interval. A report may state the percentage of people favoring a bond package, for instance. So why is a margin of error also reported? Let us take a moment and understand why confidence intervals (margins of error) are necessary. Then we will address how to compute one.

Suppose a researcher reported that 35% of U.S. citizens favor capital punishment, with a 5% margin of error. More than likely, that researcher did not speak with every one of the more than 250 million U.S. citizens. Instead, he or she spoke with a random sample of those citizens, say, 200 of them. Of those 200, 70 (35%) favor capital punishment. Unfortunately, the researcher is not interested in the opinions of just 200 citizens; rather, the opinions of the entire U.S. population are of interest. Therein lies the problem: from the opinions of only 200 people, how to describe the opinions of the 250 million U.S. citizens? Based on responses to the researcher's questions, it is known that 35% of the sample supports the death penalty, but what are the chances that the sample was perfectly representative of the population and that exactly 35% of the sample supports the death penalty as well? The chances are not good. What if, even though the sample was completely random, it happened by the luck of the draw that the sample was composed of a lot of conservatives? That would be an example of sampling error. In that case, even though the true percentage of the U.S. population supporting capital punishment might be only 20%, the sample is biased toward conservatives, showing 35%. The margin of error, or confidence interval, helps control for sampling error. The 5% margin of error indicates that, though 35% of the sample supports capital punishment, the true percentage for support in the U.S. population is around 35% and somewhere between 30 and 40%. This confidence interval is associated with a confidence level, which is usually expressed as a percentage, such as 95 or 99%. If, in this example, the researcher's 5% confidence interval corresponds to the 95% confidence level, that means that if an infinite number of random samples was taken, only 5% of the time would the true population parameter fail to be captured within the confidence intervals. Though the population parameter is fixed, the confidence intervals fluctuate randomly around the population parameter across repeated samples.

Reporting of a confidence interval typically includes the point estimate, the interval, and the chosen confidence level. The confidence level is the percentage of samples that, taken repeatedly, would contain the point estimate—typically either 95 or 99%. For example, a 95% confidence level would have, in the long run, 95 out of 100 samples with a point estimate that falls within the confidence interval. The most common point estimates are means, proportions, and sample differences; but other statistics, such as medians and regression coefficients, can have confidence intervals too.

In many disciplines, researchers express the uncertainty surrounding the point estimate as the result of an hypothesis test, rather than report the confidence interval. In such cases, researchers typically test what is called the null hypothesis. If, for instance, in considering differences between sentence lengths imposed by two judges, the null hypothesis (also known as the hypothesis of no difference) would state that there is no difference between the judges. The confidence level, in that case, represents the probability (or likelihood) of rejecting the null hypothesis (saying there is really a difference), when in fact it is false (there really is no difference). The similarities between the hypothesis testing approach and the confidence interval approach are apparent. For instance, if the difference in average sentences imposed by two judges is 3 years, but the margin of error is plus or minus 3 years, the judges may, on average, sentence defendants to the same number of years. The null hypothesis—both judges give the same average sentence—cannot be rejected. Hypothesis testing and confidence intervals therefore use the same logic, but hypothesis testing reports a dichotomous result based on the chosen confidence level. Some medical journals require the reporting of confidence intervals because estimated differences between control and experimental groups that lie in the null region may still indicate important effects.

Confidence Interval for a Mean

Standard Error of the Mean

Because the confidence interval represents uncertainty, measurement of the error surrounding the point estimate can be calculated through the standard error of the estimate; the error represents random variation that occurs from sampling a population. The standard error does not, however, include other types of nonsampling error, such as a biased design or improper data collection. In other words, computing a confidence interval helps a researcher overcome random error, such as randomly selecting more conservatives than liberals in an opinion survey. It will not, however, help a researcher overcome intentional bias or error, such as taking an opinion survey on citizens' support of gun control at a National Rifle Association meeting. For a mean, the standard error of the estimate is the standard deviation of the population distribution divided by the square root of the number of cases in the population. The formula for a mean's standard error is

$$\sigma_{\bar{x}} = \frac{\sigma}{\sqrt{N}},$$

where σ is the population's standard deviation and N is the population size. When the standard deviation of the parameter's distribution is known, this formula is used to calculate the standard error. If researchers know the population's standard deviation, however, chances are they also know the population mean. When the population standard deviation (σ) is unknown, the sample's standard deviation (s) can be substituted for it. Because the sample standard deviation is a biased estimator, 1 is subtracted from the sample size (n) to adjust for this substitution:

$$\text{s.e.}_{\bar{x}} = \frac{s}{\sqrt{n-1}}.$$

As a measure of uncertainty, the standard error (s.e.) is not easily interpreted; however, the confidence interval, derived by the standard error, has a clear meaning.

Confidence Interval for Mean with a Large Sample ($n \geq 30$)

With the standard error calculated, deriving the confidence interval is a simple matter of multiplying the standard error by a z-score associated with the chosen confidence level. The confidence level is the probability of rejecting the null hypothesis when it is true. The product is then added and subtracted to the mean. The formula for a mean with a sample size larger than 30 is

$$\bar{x} + z_{\alpha}(\text{s.e.}_{\bar{x}}),$$

where $\bar{x}$ is the mean for the sample (the point estimate), z_{α} is the z-score associated with the chosen confidence level (the alpha level is typically 95 or 99%, but can be any level the researcher wishes), and $\text{s.e.}_{\bar{x}}$ is the standard error of the estimate (as previously explained). The associated z-scores for the 95 and 99% confidence levels are 1.96 and 2.58, respectively. The following example demonstrates how to calculate the confidence interval at the 95% confidence level (for this example, we assume the distribution is approximately normal). In the 2000 General Social Survey, 2808 respondents said they completed an average 13.26 years of school; the standard deviation for the sample was 2.87 years. Because the standard deviation of number of years in school for the whole population is unknown, the sample standard deviation is substituted in the standard error formula:

$$\text{s.e.}_{\bar{x}} = \frac{2.87}{\sqrt{2808-1}}.$$

The standard error for the mean is 0.054 and it is used in the confidence interval formula:

$$13.26 \pm 1.96(0.054) = 13.26 \pm 0.106 \quad \text{or} \quad (13.15, 13.37).$$

Because the confidence interval is narrow (a difference of only 0.21 years), at least 13 years of school is almost certainly the average number of years of education that Americans completed in the year 2000. There is, however, a 5% chance that the average number of years reflected in this sample mean actually fell outside the confidence interval. If a researcher requires more confidence, a higher confidence level can be chosen. Using the same example of completed years of education in 2000, a 99% confidence interval would be wider than the 95% level. The 99% confidence interval has an associated z-score of 2.58:

$$13.26 \pm 2.58(0.054) = 13.26 \pm 0.140 \quad \text{or} \quad (13.12, 13.40).$$

The point estimate and the confidence interval still indicate at least 13 years of school, but the interval is slightly wider. Of course, confidence intervals can be quite large, depending on the size of the sample and the standard error.

Confidence Interval for Mean with a Small Sample

When a sample size is small, a distribution's normality can no longer be assumed: there is a greater likelihood that the point estimate will deviate from the parameter. Thus, the use of the z distribution to calculate the confidence interval is no longer appropriate. Generally, a sample size of less than 30 is considered too small. Of course, all distributions should be examined for normality, but sample sizes larger than 100 are most likely normal. When a sample is less than 30, the t distribution should be used instead of the z distribution to find the associated confidence level value. The t distribution is wider and flatter than the z distribution, producing wider confidence intervals. As degrees of freedom increase, the shape of the t distribution approaches that of the normal z distribution.

Calculating a confidence interval for a mean from a small sample is virtually the same as for a large one. The mean is added and subtracted from the confidence level's associated value multiplied by the standard error of the mean:

$$\bar{x} \pm t_{\alpha}(\text{s.e.}_{\bar{x}}).$$

The associated value for the chosen confidence level is found in a t distribution table. At the chosen confidence level, the sample's degrees of freedom (df) are cross-indexed to find the associated value. Degrees of freedom are used because the t distribution is actually a family of distributions. The degrees of freedom are calculated by subtracting the sample size from 1 (df $= n-1$).

The concept of "degrees of freedom" can seem mysterious. In reality, most of us instinctively know what degrees of freedom are. Consider the following simple equation: $a + b + c = 100$. In this equation, I know that I am going to add three numbers (a, b, and c), and those numbers will sum to 100. With no restrictions, I can pick any number I want for a. I will pick 57. I can also pick any number I want for b. I will pick 3. If $a = 57$ and $b = 3$, and $a + b + c = 100$, then I cannot simply pick any number I want for c. In other words, c is not "free to vary." If $a + b + c = 100$, and $a = 57$ and $b = 3$, then c must be 40. Now you can see why the value for degrees of freedom is entirely determined by sample size.

To illustrate how degrees of freedom are used to find the associated t-score, suppose a researcher wants to know the average number of prior delinquency referrals that juveniles have in their court record. A random sample of juvenile court files ($n = 21$) shows a mean of 3.76 referrals and a standard deviation of 5.34 referrals. First, the standard error is calculated:

$$\text{s.e.}_{\bar{x}} = \frac{5.34}{\sqrt{21-1}},$$

The standard error is 1.20. The associated value for a 95% confidence level is still required. The value for degrees of freedom for this sample is $21-1=20$. Indexing the degrees of freedom with the chosen alpha level in the t distribution table gives an associated score of 2.09. These values are plugged into the confidence interval formula and solved:

$$3.76 \pm 2.09(1.20) = 3.76 \pm 2.35 \quad \text{or} \quad (1.25, 6.27).$$

Thus, the estimated average number of prior referrals is almost four, but may be as few as two or as many as six. Using the associated z-score for the 95% confidence level would have produced a narrower confidence interval (1.41, 6.11).

Variation of Confidence Intervals through Repeated Sampling

The concept of alpha level, the accepted risk that a researcher may reject the null hypothesis when it is in fact true, can be difficult to grasp because researchers typically take only one sample from a population, not many. Nevertheless, confidence intervals are based on theoretically taking numerous samples from the same population. Figure 1 shows repeated sample confidence intervals varying around a population mean, most capturing the population mean. It also illustrates that a few samples do not contain the population mean, and relying on any of those samples, a researcher would draw the wrong conclusion. Figure 1 shows the 95% confidence interval from 100 samples with a sample size of 25 taken from a normal distribution with a population with a mean (μ) of 50 and standard deviation (σ) of 4. Note how all the sample confidence intervals vary around the mean. Solid lines (which represent a 95% confidence interval) that cross the horizontal line at 50 indicate confidence intervals that include the population mean. The

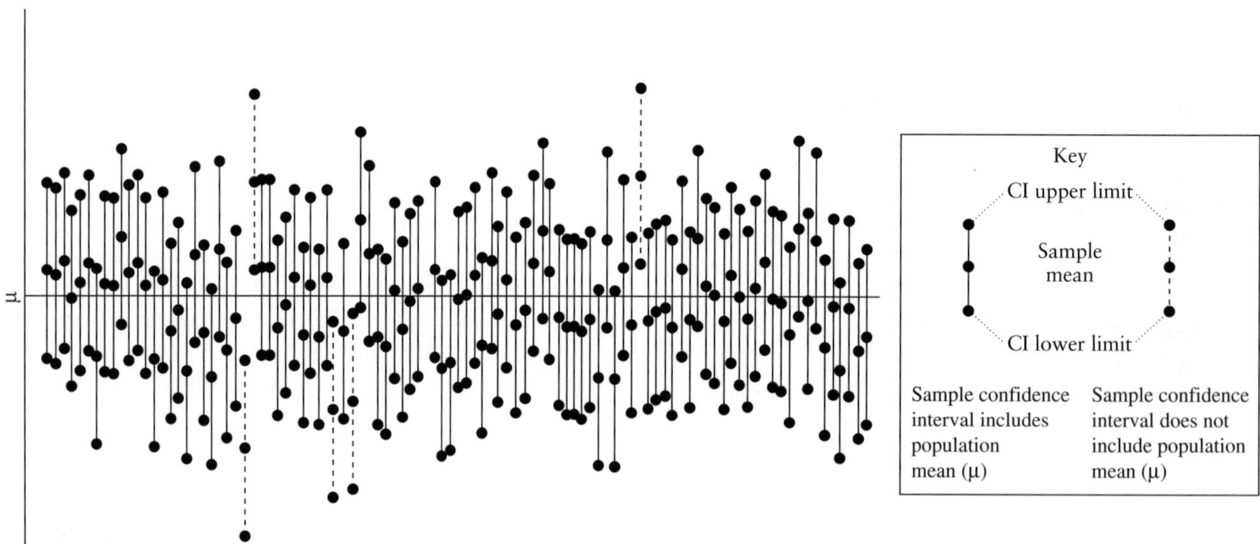

Figure 1 Confidence intervals for sample averages; 95% of the confidence intervals include the average (50). Dashed lines represent confidence intervals that do not include the population mean. This figure was generated using the Statplus Microsoft Excel add-in.

dotted lines show confidence intervals that do not intersect the horizontal line at 50; thus, 5 out of the 100 sample confidence intervals do not capture the population mean.

Figure 1 demonstrates how sampling error causes the confidence intervals of the repeated samples to vary around population mean, but would capture the value of the population 95 out of 100 random samples. Because there is always a small chance that the sample in a particular study would not actually capture the population mean, replication of research is one way that scientists guard against drawing invalid conclusions from sampling.

Confidence Interval for a Proportion

The reader should note that the standard error formula and confidence interval procedure described here are large-sample approximations that do not work when the sample is small or when the proportion is close to 0 or 1. For small samples or extreme proportions, the binomial distribution must be used as the sampling distribution.

Standard Error of the Proportion

Proportions, like means, are a common point estimate, but for qualitative data. The election poll example used previously is an estimate of a proportion. Like means, the standard error of the estimate must be calculated in order to generate the confidence interval. The standard error of a proportion has the following formula:

$$\text{s.e.}_P = \sqrt{\frac{P(1-P)}{n}},$$

where P is the sample proportion, n is the sample size, and $1-P$ is the proportion of cases that do not fall within the category of the proportion (e.g., if 35% of registered voters say they will vote for candidate X, then 65% will vote for other candidates: $1-0.35 = 0.65$).

Calculating the Confidence Interval for a Proportion

The formula to calculate a confidence interval for a proportion is similar to that of a mean:

$$P \pm z_\alpha(\text{s.e.}_P),$$

where P is the proportion (the point estimate), z_α is the chosen confidence level, and s.e.$_P$ is the standard error of the proportion. Like the formula for a confidence interval for a mean, the associated z-score is multiplied by the standard error of the estimate, then added to and subtracted from the proportion. The values for the z-scores associated with the chosen confidence intervals are the same in any confidence interval formula. For instance, the 2000 General Social Survey asked respondents whether they approved of a Supreme Court decision that ruled states cannot require the reading of the Lord's Prayer or Bible verses in public schools. Of the 1775 respondents, 38.8% said they approved of the ruling. To calculate the confidence interval for this proportion, first the standard error of the proportion is calculated:

$$\text{s.e.}_P = \sqrt{\frac{0.388(1-0.388)}{1775}}.$$

The standard error for this proportion is 0.01. To calculate the confidence interval at the 95% confidence level, the standard error of the proportion is multiplied by the associated z-score and then added to and subtracted from the proportion

$$38.8 \pm 1.96(0.01) = 38.8 \pm 0.0196 \quad \text{or} \quad (0.36, 0.41).$$

Thus, the best guess for Americans' support for this Supreme Court decision is about 39%, but can be as low as 36% or as high as 41%.

Confidence Intervals for Regression Coefficients

Regression coefficients, like means and proportions, are also point estimates and therefore can have confidence intervals. Calculating the confidence intervals for linear regression coefficients is straightforward and similar to the method for means and proportions just described. The difference lies in calculating the standard error for the coefficients.

Calculating Confidence Intervals for Linear Regression

Regression coefficients represent point estimates that are multiplied by values of variables to predict the dependent variable. Recall that the multiple linear regression equation is

$$Y = \alpha + b_1X_1 + b_2X_2 + \cdots + b_kX_k,$$

where Y is the dependent variable, X_1 through X_k are values of the independent variables, α is the intercept, and b_1 through b_k are the regression coefficients. Unlike means and proportions, regression coefficients represent their independent effect on the dependent variable after controlling for the impact of other independent variables. First, the standard error of the regression coefficient is calculated as

$$\text{s.e.}_{b_k} = \frac{\text{s.e.}_\text{R}}{sX_k\sqrt{n-1}},$$

where s.e._R is the standard deviation of the regression line (called the "standard error of the estimate" in some computer regression output data), sX_k is the standard deviation of X_k, and n is the sample size.

Once the standard error has been calculated, calculating the confidence interval is straightforward. The regression coefficient is added and subtracted from the product of the associated value from the t distribution by the standard error of the regression coefficient:

$$b_k \pm t_\alpha(\text{s.e.}_b).$$

The value associated with the chosen confidence level is found in the table for t distributions at the $\alpha - 1$ by $n - 2$ degrees of freedom.

As an example for regression coefficient confidence intervals, consider the following factors hypothesized to affect state homicide rates in 1990. Two variables are considered as correlates of homicide: percentage of a state population that has female-headed households (FEMALEHOUSE) and a state's percentage population change in the decade preceding 1990 (POPGROWTH). The standard error of the regression line (s.e._R) is 2.105. The regression coefficients and standard output are shown in Table I. For FEMALEHOUSE, the standard error for the coefficient is calculated as

$$\text{s.e.}_{b_1} = \frac{2.105}{2.004\sqrt{50-1}} = 0.150.$$

The standard error is then multiplied to the associated value from the t distribution (a 0.05 alpha level at 49 degrees of freedom, which is approximately 2). This product is then added to and subtracted from the regression coefficient to get the confidence interval:

$$1.616 \pm 2.000(0.150) = 1.616 \pm 0.300 \text{ or } (1.316, 1.916).$$

Thus, a 1% increase in a state's number of female-headed households, controlling for the preceding decade's population growth, will increase the state's number of homicides by 1.616 per 100,000 persons, plus or minus 0.30 homicides per 100,000 persons. Note in the standard output that the FEMALEHOUSE coefficient is designated statistically significant: the p-value is 0.000. This can be also be deduced from the confidence interval; it does not contain zero, the null value, within the interval. Had the lower limit of the confidence interval been negative and the upper limit positive, the coefficient would not be considered statistically significant: the percentage of female-headed households within a state may have no (that is, zero) effect on the homicide rate.

Calculating the constant would be the same as for the regression coefficients, except for using a different formula for the constant's standard error. Because the constant is seldom used in evaluating the regression model, no example is presented here. However, the constant is used in prediction with the regression model. The uncertainty that surrounds both the regression coefficients and the constant should be indicated in the presentation of any quantity of interest, such as a state's predicted homicide rate. Such presentation of statistical analysis is covered in the next section.

Presentation of Confidence Intervals in Social Science Research

The standards for presentation of uncertainty vary across disciplines and among journals within disciplines. The decision to present confidence intervals in published literature therefore seems to depend on specific editorial guidelines. If hypothesis testing is the principal goal of the analysis, the additional information provided by confidence intervals can be superfluous.

King, Tomz, and Wittenberg offer a rational for presenting uncertainty, including confidence intervals, along with the improved presentation of statistical analyses. Through the use of statistical simulation, bootstrapping,

Table I Factors Affecting State Homicide Rates in 1990[a]

					95% confidence intervals	
Variable	*b*	*s.e.*[b]	*p-Value*	*s.d.*[c]	*Lower bound*	*Upper bound*
Constant	−11.128	1.677	0.000	—	−14.503	−7.754
FEMALEHOUSE	1.616	0.150	0.000	2.003	1.314	1.918
POPGROWTH	0.070	0.026	0.009	11.527	0.018	0.123

[a] Homicide data are from the United States Federal Bureau of Investigation. The data for percentage population growth and percentage of female-headed households in the United States are from the United States Census Bureau.
[b] Standard error.
[c] Standard deviation.

or Monte Carlo simulation, King and colleagues assert that statistical results can be presented in a manner that is easily comprehensible and straightforward. They give an example of what they consider reader-friendly, candid results: "other things being equal, an additional year of education would increase your annual income by \$1,500 on average, plus or minus about \$500." The use of statistical simulation allows quantities of interest to be expressed along with the uncertainty, in this case "an additional year of education plus or minus about \$500." Typical statistical output for independent variables might include only the coefficient for education along with its standard error, the p-value, or some other indication of significance. Why use simulation instead of simply reporting the confidence interval along with the coefficient? There are two compelling reasons: to analyze small samples and to generate quantities of interest along with uncertainty. First, statistical simulation can provide analysis for small samples. The sample is treated as the population distribution by taking m number of repeated samples from the sample. The distribution from the samples is then used to compute the point estimate and the confidence interval. Regardless of sample size, the population's true parameter can be estimated as the mean from a large number of m samples, typically 1000. While the method to compute the simulation is complex, advances in computing power make it as easy as other complex statistical methods available in software packages.

Second, simulation can combine information from the regression coefficients, constants, and standard errors into a single statistic called the quantity of interest. For example, consider logistic regression coefficients from an analysis of juvenile court sentencing (note that confidence intervals for the logistic regression coefficients, the associated odds ratios, and predicted probabilities can be computed by hand, but those formulas are not reported here). The regression coefficients can be used to generate a predicted probability of being placed in an out-of-home setting (see Table II for the regression output). The predicted probability for being placed in a secure facility for one charged offense and three prior referrals to the juvenile court is calculated as follows:

$$p^\wedge = \frac{e^{b_0+b_1(\text{NOOFFENSE})+b_2(\text{PRIORS})}}{1+e^{b_0+b_1(\text{NOOFFENSE})+b_2(\text{PRIORS})}},$$

$$p^\wedge = \frac{e^{(-3.69+6.6444(1)+0.3653(3))}}{1+e^{(-3.69+6.6444(1)+0.3653(3))}},$$

$$p^\wedge = \frac{0.142}{1.142},$$

$$p^\wedge = 0.1246.$$

A juvenile with one charged offense and three prior referrals has about 12.5% chance of being placed out of home. Reporting a predicted value of the dependent variable, given specific values of the independent variables, is often the goal of statistical analysis. What is missing from this predicted probability, however, is a measure of uncertainty that accompany raw coefficients. Simulation can provide the quantity of interest and a measure of uncertainty from the distribution of simulated results. For example, the same logit regression model here was used in a Monte Carlo simulation. From a distribution of 1000 iterated models, the mean probability for secure placement was almost 13%, with a lower limit of 8% and an upper limit of about 20% at the 95% confidence level, close to the predicted value of about 12.5% calculated here. Furthermore, quantities of interest and confidence intervals can be plotted to report to laypersons statistical analysis that includes measures of uncertainty. Figure 2 shows the change in probability of an out-of-home placement as the number of prior referrals is increased. Note too that the size of the confidence intervals increases. As the probability of placement increases, the uncertainty surrounding the prediction increases as well. Thus, prediction of placement is less certain at higher levels of prior referrals in a juvenile's court record.

A researcher's decision to include confidence intervals should depend on the research question, the outlet for the research, and the target audience for the presentation of the results. Though raw coefficients and standard errors may sufficiently describe point estimates and confidence intervals to experts, more reader-friendly results can be given to the public, which are often the final consumers of research. Simulation is one method to present quantities of interest along with uncertainty. Regardless of the method, an honest presentation of statistical results should include a measure of uncertainty.

Table II Factors Affecting an Out-of-Home Placement in a Midwestern Juvenile Court

Variable	*b*	*s.e.*[a]	*Odds ratio, exp(b)*	*p-Value*
PRIORS	0.365	0.099	1.441	0.0003
NOOFFENSE	0.644	0.178	1.905	0.0002
Constant	−3.690	0.437	1.238	0.0000

[a] Standard error.

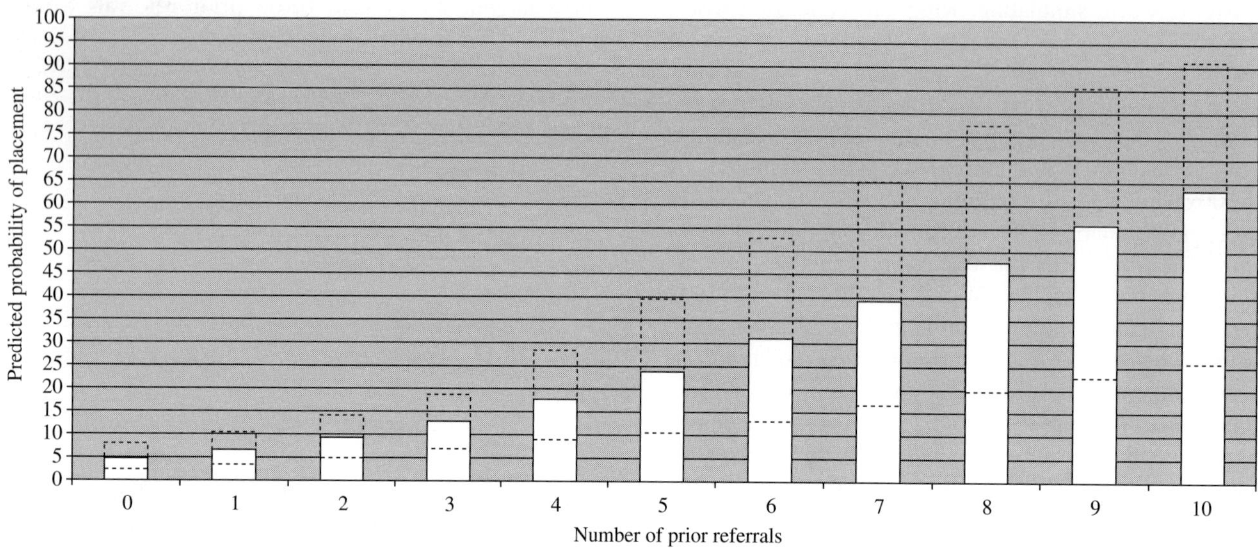

Figure 2 Predicted probability of secure placement for juvenile delinquency cases based on the number of prior referrals, holding the number of offenses constant. Dotted lines represent 95% confidence intervals.

See Also the Following Articles

Population vs. Sample • Sample Size • Type I and Type II Error

Further Reading

Altman, D. G., Machin, D., Bryant, T. N., and Gardner, M. J. (2001). *Statistics with Confidence*, 2nd Ed. BMJ Books, Bristol, England.

Federal Bureau of Investigation (1990). *Crime in the United States.* United States Government Printing Office, Washington, D.C.

King, G., Tomz, M., and Wittenberg, J. (2000). Making the most of statistical analyses: Improving interpretation and presentation. *Am. J. Pol. Sci.* **44,** 341–355.

Confidentiality and Disclosure Limitation

Stephen E. Fienberg

Carnegie Mellon University, Pittsburgh, Pennsylvania, USA

Glossary

confidentiality Broadly, a quality or condition accorded to statistical information as an obligation not to transmit that information to an unauthorized party.

contingency table A cross-classified table of counts according to two or more categorical variables.

data masking The disclosure limitation process of transforming a data set when there is a specific functional relationship (possibly stochastic) between the masked values and the original data.

disclosure The inappropriate attribution of information to a data provider, whether it be an individual or organization.

disclosure limitation The broad array of methods used to protect confidentiality of statistical data.

perturbation An approach to data masking in which the transformation involves random perturbations of the original data, either through the addition of noise or via some form of restricted randomization.

privacy In the context of data, usually the right of individuals to control the dissemination of information about themselves.

Confidentiality and privacy are widely conceived of as essential components of the collection and dissemination of social science data. But providing access to such data should also be a goal of social science researchers. Thus, researchers should attempt to release the maximal amount of information without undue risk of disclosure of individual information. Assessing this trade-off is inherently a statistical issue, as is the development of methods to limit disclosure risk. This article addresses some aspects of confidentiality and privacy as they relate to social science research and describes some basic disclosure limitation approaches to protect confidentiality. It also outlines some of the evolving principles that are guiding the development of statistical methodology in this area.

Introduction and Themes

Social science data come in a wide variety of forms, at least some of which have been gathered originally for other purposes. Most of these databases have been assembled with carefully secured consent and cooperation of the respondents, often with pledges to keep the data confidential and to allow their use for statistical purposes only. The general public disquiet regarding privacy, spurred on by the privacy threats associated with Internet commerce and unauthorized access to large commercial databases (e.g., those maintained by banks and credit agencies), has heightened concerns about confidentiality and privacy in the social sciences and in government statistical agencies. In the universities, social science and, in particular, survey data have come under increased scrutiny by institutional review boards, both regarding pledges of confidentiality and the means that researchers use to ensure them. But social scientists and government statistical agencies also have an obligation to share data with others for replication and secondary analysis. Thus, researchers need to understand how to release the maximal amount of information without undue risk of disclosure of individual information.

For many years, confidentiality and disclosure limitation were relegated to the nonstatistical part of large-scale data collection efforts; as a consequence, the methods used to address the issue of privacy were often *ad hoc* and conservative, directed more at protection and less at the usability of the acquired data. More recently, statisticians have convinced others that any release of statistical data produces a disclosure in that it increases the probability of identification of some individual in the relevant population. From this now widely recognized perspective, the goal of the preservation of promises of confidentiality cannot be absolute, but rather should be aimed, of necessity, at the limitation of disclosure risk rather than at its elimination. Assessing the trade-off between confidentiality and data access is inherently a statistical issue, as is the development of methods to limit disclosure risk. That is, formulation of the problem is statistical, based on inputs from both the data providers and the users, regarding both risk and utility.

The article covers some basic definitions of confidentiality and disclosure, the ethical themes associated with confidentiality and privacy, and the timing of release of restricted data to achieve confidentiality objectives, and albeit briefly, when release restricted data is required to achieve confidentiality or when simply restricting access is a necessity. A case is made for unlimited access to restricted data as an approach to limit disclosure risk, but not so much as to impair the vast majority of potential research uses of the data.

In recent years, many researchers have argued that the trade-off between protecting confidentiality (i.e., avoiding disclosure) and optimizing data access to others has become more complex, as both technological advances and public perceptions have not altered in an information age, but also that statistical disclosure techniques have kept pace with these changes. There is a brief introduction later in the article to some current methods in use for data disclosure limitation and statistical principles that underlie them. This article concludes with an overview of disclosure limitation methodology principles and a discussion of ethical issues and confidentiality concerns raised by new forms of statistical data.

What Is Meant by Confidentiality and Disclosure?

Confidentiality refers broadly to a quality or condition accorded to statistical information as an obligation not to transmit that information to an unauthorized party. It has meaning only when a data collector, e.g., a university researcher or a government statistical agency, can deliver on its promise to the data provider or respondent. Confidentiality can be accorded to both individuals and organizations; for the individual, it is rooted in the right to privacy (i.e., the right of individuals to control the dissemination of information about themselves, whereas for establishments and organizations, there are more limited rights to protection, e.g., in connection with commercial secrets.

Disclosure relates to inappropriate attribution of information to a data provider, whether to an individual or organization. There are basically two types of disclosure, identity and attribute. An identity disclosure occurs if the data provider is identifiable from the data release. An attribute disclosure occurs when the released data make it possible to infer the characteristics of an individual data provider more accurately than would have otherwise been possible. The usual way to achieve attribute disclosure is through identity disclosure; an individual is first identified through some combination of variables and then there is attribute disclosure of values of other variables included in the released data. However, attribute disclosure may occur without an identification. The example of union plumbers in Chicago has been used to elucidate this: for the plumbers, who all earn the same wage, attribute disclosure occurs when the Department of Labor releases the average wage of plumbers in Chicago as an entry in a table.

Inferential disclosure is basically a probabilistic notion; the definition can be interpreted as referring to some relevant likelihood ratio associated with the probability of identifying an attribute for a data provider. Because almost any data release can be expected to increase the likelihood associated with some characteristic for some data provider, the only way data protection can be guaranteed is to release no data at all. It is for this reason that the methods used to protect confidentiality are referred to in the statistical literature as disclosure limitation methods or statistical disclosure control, rather than disclosure prevention methods.

Clearly, one must remove names, addresses, telephone numbers, and other direct personal identifiers from databases to preserve confidentiality, but this is not sufficient. Residual data that are especially vulnerable to disclosure threats include (1) geographic detail, (2) longitudinal panel information, and (3) extreme values (e.g., on income). Population data are clearly more vulnerable than are sample data, and "key variables" that are also available in other databases accessible to an intruder pose special risks. Statistical organizations have traditionally focused on the issue of identity disclosure and thus refuse to report information in which individual respondents or data providers can be identified. This occurs, for example, when a provider is unique in the population for the characteristics under study and is directly identifiable in the database to be released. But such uniqueness and subsequent identity disclosure may not, of course, "reveal" any information other than that the respondent provided data as part of the study. In this sense, identity disclosure may be only a technical violation of a promise of confidentiality, but not a violation of the spirit of such a promise. Thus, uniqueness only raises the issue of "possible" confidentiality problems due to disclosure.

The foregoing discussion implicitly introduces the notion of harm, which is not the same as a breach of

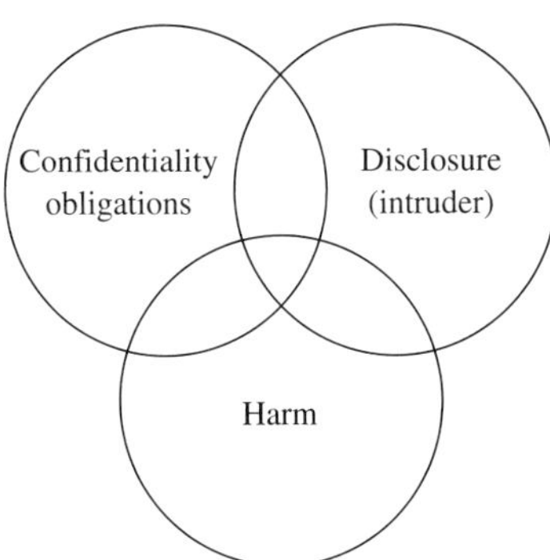

Figure 1 Relationship between confidentiality, disclosure, and harm. Adapted from Fienberg (2001).

confidentiality. As Fig. 1 depicts in a schematic fashion, not all data disclosures breach promises of confidentiality to respondents. For example, it is possible for a pledge of confidentiality to be technically violated, but for there to be no harm to the data provider because the information is "generally known" to the public at large. In this case, some would argue that additional data protection is not really required. Conversely, if an intruder attempts to match records from an external file to another file subject, and to a pledge of confidentiality, but makes an "incorrect" match, then there is no breach of confidentiality, but there is the possibility of harm if the intruder acts as though the match were correct. Further, information on individuals (or organizations) in a release of sample statistical data may well increase the information about characteristics of individuals (or organizations) not in the sample. This produces an inferential disclosure for such individuals (or organizations), causing them possible harm, even though there is no confidentiality obligation for those so harmed. For example, suppose it is possible to infer with high probability that, for a given set of variables to be released, there is a unique individual in the population corresponding to a zero cell in a sample cross-classification of these variables. Then there is a high probability of disclosure of that unique individual, even though he or she is not present in the sample of data released.

Some people believe that the way to assure confidentiality and prevent disclosures is allow participants/respondents to participate in a study anonymously. Except for extraordinary circumstances, such a belief is misguided, because there is a key distinction between collecting information anonymously and ensuring that personal identifiers are not used inappropriately. For example, survey investigators typically need personal identifier information on participants/respondents to carry out nonresponse follow-up and to perform quality control checks on collected data by reinterviewing respondents, even if such identifiers are not released to other users of the data. Moreover, as has already been noted, the simple removal of personal identifiers is not sufficient to prevent disclosures.

Yet, there remain circumstances in which the disclosure of information provided by respondents under a pledge of confidentiality can produce substantial harm, in terms of personal reputations or even in a monetary sense, to respondents, their families, and others with whom they have personal relationships. For example, in the pilot surveys for the National Household Seroprevalence Survey, the National Center for Health Statistics moved to make responses during the data collection phase of the study truly "anonymous" because of the potential for harm resulting from the "release" of information either that the respondent tested positive for the human immunodeficiency virus or engaged in high-risk behavior. But such efforts still could not guarantee that an intruder could not identify someone in the survey database. This example also raises the interesting question about the applicability of confidentiality provisions after an individual's death, in part because of the potential harm that might result to others. Several statistical agencies explicitly treat the identification of a deceased individual as a violation of confidentiality, even when there is no legal requirement to do so.

Thus there is a spectrum of types and severity of harm that might result from both nondisclosures and disclosures, and these must all be considered in some form when one develops a survey instrument, crafts a statement regarding confidentiality, or prepares a database for possible release. The present discussion restricts attention primarily to settings involving the possibility of either inferential or identity disclosure and the attendant potential harm to the data providers.

Restricted Access versus Restricted Data

Social science data, especially those gathered as part of censuses and major sample surveys or with government funding, meet two key tests that are usually applied to public goods: jointness of consumption (consumption by one person does not diminish their availability to others) and benefit to the social science enterprise and thus the nation as a whole (e.g., social science data are used to inform public policy). The only issue, then, is whether there is nonexclusivity, i.e., whether it makes sense to provide these statistical data to some citizens and not to others. If it is possible to provide access to all or virtually all, e.g., via the Internet and the World Wide Web, then the costs of providing the data to all are often less than the costs of restricting access. There are other perhaps hidden costs, however, that result from expanded use to those who produce the data. Several reports have described the costs and benefits of data sharing and data sharing in the context of confidentiality. The principal U.S. research funding agencies, the National Science Foundation and the National Institutes of Health, now require data sharing as part of the contractual arrangements for grants. These policies continue a long tradition of broad access to survey research data through archives, such as the one in the United States operated by the Inter-University Consortium for Political and Social Research.

People adopt two different philosophies with regard to the preservation of confidentiality associated with individual-level data: (1) restricted or limited information, with restrictions on the amount or format of the data released, and (2) restricted or limited access, with restrictions on the access to the information. If social science data are truly a public good, then restricted access is justifiable only in extreme situations, when the confidentiality of data in the possession of a researcher or statistical agency (in the case of government data) cannot be protected through some form of restriction on the information released.

In many countries, the traditional arrangement for data access has been limited in both senses described here, with only highly aggregated data and summary statistics released for public consumption. In the United States, there have been active policies encouraging the release of microdata from censuses and samples going back to the 1960 decennial census. Such data are now publicly available in a variety of forms, including on-line data archives. Some countries have attempted to follow suit, but others have development approaches based on limited access. In fact, many have argued that, even if cost is not an issue, access should be restricted as a means for ensuring confidentiality, especially in the context of establishment data. For example, the U.S. Bureau of the Census has now established several data centers, including one in Pittsburgh (at Carnegie Mellon University), through which restricted access to confidential Census Bureau data sets can be arranged. The process of gaining access to data in such centers involves an examination of the research credentials of those wishing to do so. In addition, these centers employ a mechanism for controlling the physical access to confidential data files for those whose access is approved, and for the review of all materials that researchers wish to take from the centers and to publish. Just imagine the difficulty the researchers would have if they are accustomed to reporting residual plots and other information that allow for a partial reconstruction of the original data, at least for some variables, because restricted data centers typically do not allow users to take such information away.

A less extreme form of restricted access, and one more consonant with the notion of statistical data as a public good, has been adopted by a number of data archives. They often utilize a "terms-of-use agreement" via which the secondary data analyst agrees to use the data for statistical research and/or teaching only, and to preserve confidentiality, even if data sets have already been edited using disclosure limitation methods. Some statistical agencies adopt related approaches of "licensing." Restricting access to a "public good" produces bad public policy because it cannot work effectively. This is primarily because the gatekeepers for restricted data systems have little or no incentive to widen access or to allow research analysts the same freedom to work with a data set (and to share their results) as they are able to have with unrestricted access. And the gatekeepers can prevent access by those who may hold contrary views on either methods of statistical analyses or on policy issues that the data may inform. In this sense, the public good is better served by uncontrolled access to restricted data rather than by restricted access to data that may pose confidentiality concerns. This presumes, of course, that researchers are able to do an effective job of statistical disclosure limitation.

Methodology for Disclosure Limitation

Many disclosure limitation methods can be described under the broad rubric of disclosure-limiting masks, i.e., transformations of the data whereby there is a specific functional relationship (possibly stochastic) between the masked values and the original data. The basic idea of data masking involves thinking in terms of transformations, to transforming an $n \times p$ data matrix Z through pre- and postmultiplication, and the possible addition of noise, i.e.,

$$Z \longrightarrow AZB + C, \qquad (1)$$

where A is a matrix that operates on cases, B is a matrix that operates on variables, and C is a matrix that adds perturbations or noise. Matrix masking includes a wide variety of standard approaches to disclosure limitation:

- Adding noise
- Releasing a subset of observations (delete rows from Z)
- Cell suppression for cross-classifications
- Including simulated data (add rows to Z)
- Releasing a subset of variables (delete columns from Z)
- Switching selected column values for pairs of rows (data swapping)

Little was one of the first to describe likelihood-based methods for the statistical analysis of masked data. Even when a mask is applied to a data set, the possibilities of both identity and attribute disclosure remain, although the risks may be substantially diminished.

It is possible to categorize most disclosure-limiting masks as suppressions (e.g., cell suppression), recodings (e.g., collapsing rows or columns, or swapping), samplings (e.g., releasing subsets), or simulations. Further, some masking methods alter the data in systematic ways, e.g., through aggregation or through cell suppression, and others do it through random perturbations, often subject to constraints for aggregates. Examples of perturbation methods are controlled random rounding, data swapping, and the postrandomization method (PRAM). One way to think about random perturbation methods is as a restricted simulation tool, and thus it is possible to link them to other types of simulation approaches that have recently been proposed.

Fienberg and colleagues have pursued this simulation strategy and presented a general approach to "simulating" from a constrained version of the cumulative empirical distribution function of the data. In the case when all of the variables are categorical, the cumulative distribution function is essentially the same as the counts in the resulting cross-classification or contingency table. As a consequence, this general simulation approach can be considered as equivalent to simulating from a constrained contingency table, e.g., given a specific set of marginal totals and replacing the original data by a randomly generated one drawn from the "exact" distribution of the contingency table under a log-linear model that includes "confidentiality-preserving" margins among its minimal sufficient statistics. If the simulated table is consistent with some more complex log-linear model, then this approach offers the prospect of simultaneously smoothing the original counts, offering room for model search and assessing goodness-of-fit, and providing disclosure limitation protection.

Rubin and others have asserted that the risk of identity disclosure can be eliminated by the use of synthetic data (using Bayesian methodology and multiple imputation techniques), because there is no direct function link between the original data and the released data. Or said another way, there is no confidentiality problem because all of the real individuals have been replaced with simulated ones. Raghunathan and colleagues describe the implementation of multiple imputation for disclosure limitation and a number of authors have now used variations on the approach, e.g., for longitudinally-linked individual and work history data. But with both simulation and multiple-imputation methodology, it is still possible that some simulated individuals may be virtually identical to original sample individuals in terms of their data values, or at least close enough that the possibility of both identity disclosure and attribute disclosure remains. Thus, it is still necessary to carry out checks for the possibility of unacceptable disclosure risk.

Another important feature of this statistical simulation approach is that information on the variability is directly accessible to the user. For example in the Fienberg *et al.* approach for categorical data, anyone can begin with the reported table and information about the margins that are held fixed, and then run the Diaconis–Sturmfels Monte Carlo Markov chain algorithm to regenerate the full distribution of all possible tables with those margins. This then allows the user to make inferences about the added variability in a modeling context. Similarly, multiple imputation can be used to get direct measure of variability associated with the posterior distribution of the quantities of interest. As a consequence, simulation and perturbation methods represent a major improvement from the perspective of access to data over cell suppression and data swapping. And they conform to a statistical principle of allowing the user of released data to apply standard statistical operations without being misled.

There has been considerable research on disclosure limitation methods for tabular data, especially in the form of multiway tables of counts (contingency tables). The most popular methods include collapsing categories (a form of aggregation) and a process known as cell suppression (developed by Larry Cox and others). Cell suppression systematically deletes the values in selected cells in the table. Though cell suppression methods have been very popular with the U.S. government statistical agencies and they are useful for tables with nonnegative entries rather than simply counts, they also have major drawbacks. First, there are not yet good algorithms for the methodology associated with high-dimensional tables. But more importantly, the methodology systematically distorts for users the information about the cells in the table, and as a consequence, it makes it difficult for secondary users to draw correct statistical inferences about the relationships among the variables in the table.

A special example of collapsing involves summing over variables to produce marginal tables. Thus, instead of reporting the full multiway contingency table, one or more collapsed versions of it might be reported. The release of multiple sets of marginal totals has the virtue of allowing statistical inferences about the relationships among the variables in the original table using log-linear model methods. What is also intuitively clear from statistical theory is that, with multiple collapsed versions, there might be highly accurate information about the actual cell entries in the original table, and thus there will still be a need to investigate the possibility of disclosures. A number of researchers have been working on the problem of determining upper and lower bounds on the cells of a multiway table, given a set of margins, in part to address this problem, although other measures of risk may clearly be of interest. The problem of computing bounds is in one sense an old one (at least for two-way tables), but it is also deeply linked to recent mathematical statistical developments and thus has generated a flurry of new research.

Consider a 2×2 table of counts $\{n_{ij}\}$ with given the marginal totals $\{n_{1+}, n_{2+}\}$ and $\{n_{+1}, n_{+2}\}$. The marginal constraints, i.e., that the counts in any row add to the corresponding one-way total, plus the fact that the counts must be nonnegative, imply bounds for the cell entries. Specifically, for the (i, j) cell,

$$\min\{n_{i+}, n_{+j}\} \geq n_{ij} \geq \max\{n_{i+} + n_{+j} - n, 0\}. \quad (2)$$

Bounds such as those in Eq. (2) usually are referred to as Fréchet bounds, after the French statistician M. Fréchet, but they were independently described by both Bonferroni and Hoeffding at about the same time in 1940. These bounds have been repeatedly rediscovered by a myriad of others. Fréchet bounds and their generalizations lie at the heart of a number of different approaches to disclosure limitation, including cell suppression, data swapping and other random perturbation methods, and controlled rounding.

Dobra and Fienberg have described multi-densional generalizations of the Fréchet bounds and explained some of the links between them and the modern statistical theory of log-linear models for the analysis of contingency tables. They analyzed a specific 6-way table and explained the extent to which easily computable bounds can be used to assess risk and data can be provided to users for model selection and assessing goodness-of-fit. Dobra and colleagues applied related methodology to a disclosure assessment of a 16-way contingency table drawn from the National Long Term Care Survey.

In the past decade, several special issues of statistical journals and edited volumes have highlighted the latest research on disclosure limitation methodology. Though many theoretical and empirical issues remain to be explored—for example, in connection with large sparse tables and longitudinal survey data—and many exciting research questions remain to be answered in this relatively new statistical literature on disclosure limitation research, the topic is receiving considerable attention and there is now a real prospect of improved disclosure limitation and increased data access in the not too distant future.

Conclusions and Further Issues

The focus here has been on the interplay between the issues of confidentiality and access to social science data. Disclosure limitation is an inherently statistical issue because the risk of disclosure cannot be eliminated unless access to the data is restricted. Complex relationships exist between promises of confidentiality to respondents in surveys or to participants in studies and the nature of disclosure of information about those respondents. Because techniques for disclosure limitation are inherently statistical in nature, they must be evaluated using statistical tools for assessing the risk of harm to respondents. This article has outlined some of the current statistical methods used to limit disclosure, especially those representable in form of disclosure limitation masks, distinguishing among suppression, recoding, sampling, and simulation approaches, on the one hand, and systematic versus perturbational approaches on the other.

Among the principles that have been the focus of much of the recent effort in disclosure limitation methodology are usability, transparency, and duality. Usability is the extent to which the released data are free from systematic distortions that impair statistical methodology and inference. Transparency is the extent to which the methodology and practice of it provide direct or even implicit information on the bias and variability resulting from the application of a disclosure limitation mask. Duality is the extent to which the methods aim at both disclosure limitation and making the maximal amount of data available for analysis. The focus here in particular has been on how these principles fit with recent proposals for the release of simulated data, the release of marginals from multiway contingency tables, and the role of marginal bounds in evaluating the disclosure limitation possibilities.

As social scientists move to study biological correlates of social phenomena such as aging, they are beginning to incorporate direct measurements of health status based on tests, including those involving the drawing of blood samples. Technology and biological knowledge have advanced sufficiently that researchers now face the prospect of including in social science databases genetic sequencing information and other nonnumeric information, e.g., functional magnetic resonance imaging or full-body scan images. These new forms of data, in principle, can uniquely identify individuals. It is essential that social scientists begin thinking about how to handle the release of such data or how to limit their disclosure, through restriction of the data they make available to others. Such issues pose enormous methodological challenges for disclosure limitation research and for social science research data more broadly.

Acknowledgments

This work was supported in part by Grant No. EIA-9876619 from the U.S. National Science Foundation to the National Institute of Statistical Sciences and Grant No. R01-AG023141 from the National Institutes of Health.

See Also the Following Articles

Contingency Tables and Log-Linear Models • Statistical Disclosure Control

Further Reading

Bishop, Y. M. M., Fienberg, S. E., and Holland, P. W. (1975). *Discrete Multivariate Analysis: Theory and Practice.* MIT Press, Cambridge.

Dobra, A., and Fienberg, S. E. (2000). Bounds for cell entries in contingency tables given marginal totals and decomposable graphs. *Proc. Natl. Acad. Sci.* **97,** 11885–11892.

Dobra, A., and Fienberg, S. E. (2001). Bounds for cell entries in contingency tables induced by fixed marginal totals with applications to disclosure limitation. *Statist. J. UN, ECE* **18,** 363–371.

Dobra, A., Erosheva, E., and Fienberg, S. E. (2003). Disclosure limitation methods based on bounds for large contingency tables with application to disability data. In *Proceedings of the Conference on New Frontiers of Statistical Data Mining* (H. Bozdogan, ed.), pp. 93–116. CRC Press, Boca Raton, Florida.

Domingo-Ferrer, J. (ed.) (2002). Inference control in statistical databases from theory to practice. *Lecture Notes in Computer Science*, Vol. 2316. Springer-Verlag, Heidelberg.

Doyle, P., Lane, J., Theeuwes, J., and Zayatz, L. (eds.) (2001). *Confidentiality, Disclosure and Data Access: Theory and Practical Applications for Statistical Agencies.* Elsevier, New York.

Duncan, G. T. (2001). Confidentiality and statistical disclosure limitation. In *International Encyclopedia of the Social and Behavioral Sciences* (N. Smelser and P. Baltes, eds.), Vol. 4, pp. 2521–2525. Elsevier, New York.

Fienberg, S. E. (2001). Statistical perspectives on confidentiality and data access in public health. *Statist. Med.* **20,** 1347–1356.

Fienberg, S. E., Makov, U. E., and Steele, R. J. (1998). Disclosure limitation using perturbation and related methods for categorical data (with discussion). *J. Official Statist.* **14,** 485–511.

Gouweleeuw, J. M., Kooiman, P., Willenborg, L. C. R. J., and Wolf, P. P. D. E. (1998). Post randomization for statistical disclosure control: Theory and implementation. *J. Official Statist.* **14,** 463–478.

Lambert, D. (1993). Measures of disclosure risk and harm. *J. Official Statist.* **9,** 313–331.

Little, R. J. A. (1993). Statistical analysis of masked data. *J. Official Statist.* **9,** 407–426.

Raghunathan, T. E., Reiter, J., and Rubin, D. B. (2003). Multiple imputation for statistical disclosure limitation. *J. Official Statist.* **19,** 1–16.

Trottini, M., and Fienberg, S. E. (2002). Modelling user uncertainty for disclosure risk and data utility. *Int. J. Uncertainty, Fuzziness Knowledge-Based Syst.* **10,** 511–528.

Willenborg L., and De Waal, T. (2001). Elements of disclosure control. *Lecture Notes in Statistics*, Vol. 155. Springer-Verlag, New York.

Consumption and Saving

Sylvia Lorek

Sustainable Europe Research Institute, Cologne, Germany

Joachim H. Spangenberg

Sustainable Europe Research Institute, Cologne, Germany

Glossary

conspicuous consumption The consumption of goods not only to meet basic needs, but also to serve as a key means of identification of status and prestige.

consumption In classical economics, the nonproductive use of savings; typified by expenditures on luxury goods and services, particularly imported precious goods, jewelry, artwork, etc. for the wealthy and upper classes.

consumption function The quantification of the positive relationship between consumption and income; it explains how much consumption increases as the result of a given increase in income. According to standard economics, total consumption is always equivalent to the level of income.

enforced saving In classical economics, the impossibility of investing available money (mainly past profits) due to a lack of investment opportunities. In socialist countries in the 20th century, the definition related to the impossibility of spending household income due to a lack of consumer goods. Recently used to describe the externally imposed need for households to save as a substitute for former public social security systems.

equimarginal principle There is always an equilibrium of production and consumption and of demand and supply because (1) the marginal utility of consumption is always declining and (2) the marginal utility of each production factor, *ceteris paribus*, declines as well.

hoarding In classical economics, holding profit, neither reinvesting it nor using it for productive consumption. For Keynes, this behavior is part of the liquidity preference; and in neoclassical economics, it is part of the planned saving. Speculation on the financial markets is based on hoarded liquidity, although the term is no longer in use.

savings In classical economics, the conversion of revenues into capital. Saving as "nonconsumption," if used "productively," equals investment. Productive use of savings by the entrepreneur is investment in productive (income-generating and capacity-enhancing) equipment and in technological improvements.

savings rate The share of income not consumed in an actual period. According to standard economics, it directly depends on the interest rate. Planned saving relies on estimations regarding income and interest and is more uncertain than real saving.

Consumption and saving have always played an important but changing role in economic reality. Consequently, since early economic theory was first framed, the relationship between saving and consumption has been a matter of dispute. As economic theory cycled from classical to neoclassical and Keynesian economics (and back to neoclassical), definitions and perceptions changed. Today, saving is considered as mostly driven by external incentives such as the rate of interest, but it is also influenced by perceptions of the need to prepare for future declines in income and by the desire to maintain a particular standard of living. For consumption, no coherent theory exists, but different approaches provide insights into the different elements that shape consumption patterns. Empirical testing of hypotheses, however, is complicated by lack of data and of standardized methodologies. Globalization and individualization will continue changing the patterns of consumption, and savings habits will be influenced by the trends to privatize government programs and to replace pay-as-you-go systems with private savings-based strategies.

Historical Development

With the evolution of the modern economic system, the role of saving and consumption has changed considerably, and so have the related theoretical analyses. In order to provide the basis for a better understanding of saving and consumption, in the following discussions, real-world developments are first briefly summarized; this is followed by descriptions of the changing role of saving and consumption in the history of economics, and the current state of the theoretical discussion. This is compared to the empirical knowledge available, illustrating the merits and limits of theoretical treatment. On this basis, measurements and future problems can be depicted.

Real-World Historical Development

Private property and market exchange are common features in economic history, back to ancient Greece, but until the mercantilist era, "economics" was restricted to household production and to limited commodity exchange. The mercantilists developed the third constitutive column of capitalist economies, the credit system, but their idea of wealth was restricted to gold, and their idea of accumulation was to trade as a zero-sum game. Up to the 18th century and until the decline of the feudal system, saving was the privilege of a few, and it was considered hoarding rather than investment. Wealth was the command of labor and land, including land improvements such as cattle or infrastructure. The wealthy had no reason to invest and the poor had no money to save. Consumption by the poor was restricted to survival needs, whereas consumption of status goods by the elite was regulated by ethics and etiquette; fashion hardly existed. Social security was provided by (large) families; nonworking phases of life constituted a need for saving, and concepts of "childhood" or "retirement" did not exist.

The situation changed with the transition from mercantilism to modern capitalism, replacing the focus on export surplus with one on capital accumulation and economic growth. Adam Smith, moral philosopher and early classical economist, has become the well-known icon of this transition. With the Industrial Revolution and the "consumption revolution" it imposed (self-sustaining households are not a suitable basis for industrial production), productive capital rather than land became the source of wealth. Dependent labor remained an essential factor, although the kind of dependency changed, and with rapid population growth and urbanization, labor supply was not scarce. Real capital follows economic rules other than those related to land; for instance, it needs permanent investment to maintain its value, making savings as the source of loans an important factor for economic development. Consequently, following the shift toward capitalism, shortage of investment capital became a prime concern, calling for more saving as the basis of credit and investment. Next, with the limited markets of the time, the lack of investment opportunities for the revenues generated was of concern, and thus the need for sufficient consumption. With growing productivity throughout the Industrial Revolution and with the adoption of minimum social standards (spearheaded by Lord Belfour in Britain and by Bismarck in Germany), the possibilities of private consumption in Europe increased slowly, with social security reducing the need for private saving. Although the proper balance of saving and consumption was long an issue of heated debate, economic growth and increasing salaries allowed for both mass consumption and saving.

Fossil fuel use and steam engines laid the ground not only for industrial expansion, but also for the mass production of consumption goods. Simultaneously, steam ships and trains revolutionized the kind and scope of domestic and international trade. Coal and machinery were exported from Europe, but raw materials such as iron ore, meat, wheat, and rubber, as well as luxury goods (e.g., coffee, spices, and cotton), were imported from the colonies. With increasing supply and decreasing prices in the centuries to follow, use of imported goods trickled down from the bourgeois class to the working population at large and from urban to rural areas. The new supply created and spread new desires and, with increasing purchasing power, new demand. Another source of the changes in consumption habits, developing in parallel, was a change in values based on secularization and the spread of Protestant ethics since the 18th century. This, and liberalization in general, contributed to a kind of individualism so far unknown. With religious values fading away and the erosion of tradition and social control, a vacuum emerged that was filled by a new habit, consumerism, defined by the shifting of the focus of consumption from subsistence goods to fashion and status goods. Consumption goods then not only served to meet the basic needs of people, but—rather than the accident of birth—became the key means of obtaining an identity associated with status and prestige. The aspirations of lower class citizens to imitate the higher class consumption patterns grew. Throughout the 19th and 20th centuries, increasing income levels and widespread savings provided the opportunity to put these aspirations into practice (a social trend that was accelerated and became all-embracing in the Fordist phase after World War II). Thanks to the Scottish political economist John Rae (1796–1872), this phenomenon is known as conspicuous consumption.

During the 20th century, in some Western countries, the development of small nuclear families, as opposed to the extended family structures of past generations, led to enforced saving to cover social risks; in the communist systems in Europe, enforced saving was basically the result of a deficit of consumption opportunities as compared to income. Comparatively high saving rates provided the resources for a loan-based investment regime and rapid economic growth. Today, the situation is characterized by the highest income levels in human history, stagnant saving rates, an unparalleled diversity and level of private consumption, and ongoing changes in the composition of goods (inferior goods are replaced by superior ones, but these categories evolve as well). Except for those in the low income brackets (the polarization of income is increasing in all Western societies), the utility from consumption is dominated by symbolism, by status seeking, and by other social functions of consuming (identity, compensation, affiliation, self-esteem, excitement, etc.). Spending patterns reflect this structural change: for instance, although spending on food declined significantly in all Organization for Economic Cooperation and Development (OECD) countries over the past four decades, the money spent on fashion, entertainment, travel, leisure in general, and other services rose dramatically. Although a minority in the northern hemispheric region and the majority in the southern hemispheric region are still restricted to consumption to meet basic needs (when possible), a global consumer class has emerged (about one-third of them living in the southern hemisphere), sharing attitudes, preferences, and consumption habits.

Unlike a quarter century ago, the sources of consumer goods and the locations of investments from national savings are no longer restricted by national economies. The share of goods originating in the southern hemispheric region has increased, and monetary flows are concentrated between the OECD countries that are no longer industrial, but service economies. The international financial markets, rather than the national savings, determine the availability of investment capital (hence the converging trend of national interest rates). On the household level, consumption and saving still represent behavioral alternatives, but the link to the level of the national economy is mediated by the globalization process. Economic theory, although developing over time (see subsection below), still struggles with this complexity (the following section); for this reason, reliable measurements and data for decision makers are all the more important (penultimate section). Nonetheless, a number of open questions remain (final section).

Saving and Consumption in Economic Theory

From the very outset of economic theory, saving and consumption have been discussed as partly antagonistic, partly synergistic phenomena. For Aristotle, consumption was part of the *oikonomia*, dealing with the use values delivered by the human economy. Saving, however, in particular in monetary terms, was possible only in the marketplace, i.e., in trade, and was analyzed by a different science, *chrematistics*. Traders and moneylenders (bankers) were the lowest class of free men in the Greek civilization, and much of this attitude remained through the ages. Much like the situation with low-esteem jobs today, suppressed minorities were forced into undesirable roles (i.e., the money-market business) and made their careers there (and in academics). Jews in Christian Europe and Christian minorities in the Arab world were among the suppressed classes that became traders and moneylenders.

Classical Economics

For the 17th-century physiocrats, living in a predominantly agrarian society, all wealth originated from nature (with land as a stand-in); the 18th-century Industrial Revolution changed the perception of wealth and prompted a labor theory of value (with capital regarded as embodied labor), and saving and consumption became an issue of heated debate. However, to avoid misunderstanding, the definitions of terms must be kept in mind: in classic economics, saving was understood to mean "the conversion of revenues into capital" (the term refers not to the process, but the result). Saving as "nonconsumption," if used "productively," equaled investment. Productive use of savings was entrepreneurial investment in productive, i.e., income-generating and capacity-enhancing, equipment and in technological improvements. Inspired by the labor theory of value, physical reproduction (procreation), improvement of living conditions, and caring for offspring were considered productive as well. Consequently, they were not classified as consumption as they would be today, but as saving/investment, contributing a minor and mostly undiscussed share to the dominant accumulation and investment regime, which created savings mainly out of previously earned profit.

The propensity to save has been explained in different, often complementary ways by different scholars. For instance, Adam Smith framed it as an institutionally and ideologically determined habit; John Stuart Mill saw it as a combination of habit, a desire to earn interest, and as investment or liquidity reserve. Because saving would be undertaken whenever possible, it was expected to be a function of the level of income and its distribution, i.e., of money availability (a hypothesis that can claim much empirical support, even in the mass-consumer society), and of investment opportunities. Of these two factors, promising investments were considered opportunities to drive the volume of saving: a shortage of investment opportunities led to (enforced) saving, stalled progress, and an increase in relative prices (thus creating new investment opportunities and providing an indirect mechanism leading to an equilibrium). Nearly two centuries after Adam Smith, J. Schumpeter suggested a similar theory, focused on innovation instead of on investment in general. Schumpeter proposed investments financed by money from savings (money, in his understanding, that was withdrawn from other productive uses) or by credits, which would create a demand for savings to balance them.

The alternative to the productive use of saving was not mass consumption, but unproductive "hoarding," withdrawing money income from current expenditures without diverting it to nonconsumptive purposes. Because the purpose of owning money was not defined to be making more money, but to buy consumer goods, stockpiling money (e.g., to gain interest) instead of investing it in the national economy was considered improbable. The economist David Ricardo has warned that hoarding, leading to shortages of investment and demand, could be a permanent problem in a growing economy. In reality, the availability of opportunities to invest in real capital, the social taboo against squandering money, and the halo of saving leave little room for interest-based saving. Remember that given the prevailing income distribution of past centuries, only nobles and business people had money to save. Consumption, i.e., the nonproductive use of savings, was perceived as typically happening in service industries catering to the demand for luxuries by the wealthy classes (as already mentioned, subsistence expenditures were not considered consumption). Expenditures on imported luxury goods, jewelry, and artwork primarily did not help the national economy, i.e., were not productive, so consumption in this sense undermined development by impinging on the financial resources available for investment. Senghaas has empirically analyzed the conditions for economic development in a comparative study, and confirms that this phenomenon, if happening on a large scale, undermines the opportunities for economic success.

The tension between saving and consumption has been dealt with by different scholars in diverging ways. Economists such as Nassau W. Senior (1790–1864) focused on the conflict by promoting an "abstinence theory," supporting the supply of saving by sacrifice of consumption for capital accumulation and for adding value to property. John Stuart Mill modified this by redefining abstinence as waiting, i.e., the sacrifice of forbearing to consume one's capital now, despite a time preference for immediate use, for the benefit of deliberate investment. Involuntary saving, then, happens in higher income brackets, if income exceeds the customary level of expenditure. Other economists, such as Smith, Ricardo, and Malthus, focused more on the cyclical flow between saving and consumption. The latter warned of overaccumulation resulting in underconsumption, stating that there was a significant risk if the propensity to save dominates the propensity to consume, as "saving, pushed to excess, would destroy the motive to production," which is consumption. Once saving is encroaching on consumption, capital accumulates but risks secular stagnation. "Without exogenous spending by unproductive consumers the process of capital accumulation leads inevitably to secular stagnation." This constitutes a permanent risk of underconsumption, i.e., the aggregate demand of consumers is not sufficient to buy all products at cost price, although the aggregate demand consists of consumption plus investment.

Adam Smith denied such a risk as a result of his perception of the economy as characterized by cyclical flows of money. His "saving-equals-consumption" theorem was based on a broader view of consumption, including household spending. It states that saving equals investment (i.e., nonconsumption) and results in salaries and income payments. These are in turn spent by consumption. Thus, saving creates effective demand as much as consumption expenditures do. Smith's theorem was formulated to undermine the diction that saving undermines consumption, assuming (1) that hoarding is a rare exemption, because money income (all!) is promptly spent, as "it is not for its own sake that men desire money, but for the sake of what they can purchase with it" (*Wealth of Nations*) and (2) that investment/saving generates purchasing power as much as luxury consumption does, i.e., the unproductive use of savings.

David Ricardo dealt with risks from saving by introducing the assumption that demands are insatiable: consumption would always rise with productivity growth. A sudden increase of saving would lead to growing capital, rising market wages, and, finally, rising consumption, and bringing consumption and saving into equilibrium again. This is rather close to Say's (Jean-Baptiste Say, 1767–1832) theorem that every supply creates its own demand (through wages spent to consume). The intention of economic actors is consumption, matching exactly the income they have gained, and entrepreneurship is considered a free service.

Neoclassical Economics

A new way of thinking arose with the "marginal revolution" in economics, first introduced to describe consumer behavior, and later extended to become "the unifying principle of economic reasoning" (William Jevons, 1835–1882). Unlike the production-centered classical economics, the neoclassical school focused on the optimal allocation of given production factors at a fixed point in time among competing use opportunities, "optimal" meaning providing maximum consumer satisfaction. Like analyzing the situation of a fixed moment, analyses of the evolution of preferences and technologies, the population growth, etc. were considered to be of no relevance for economic analysis. Consequently, with constant wants and resource endowments, it was plausible to assume that (1) the marginal utility of consumption is always declining and (2) that the marginal utility of each production factor, *ceteris paribus*, declines as well. Given this equimarginal principle, there is always equilibrium of demand and supply and of production and consumption; production and consumption are understood to be a factor of final demand, subdivided into state consumption and private consumption. Consumption is, in neoclassical economics, driven by insatiable demands, but decreasing utility of consumption permits striking a balance between consumption and the disutility of additional work. By leading to a balance of work, income, and consumption, determined by the preferences of the rational individual, equilibrium is again achieved. On the producers' side, consumer demand is the determining factor: only what is demanded is being produced, and in this sense consumption drives production.

Saving is also defined differently in neoclassical economics. "Intended saving" in modern understanding covers what had been termed "saving" plus "hoarding" in classical economics. The volume of savings realized is a function of the rate if interest; the level of income plays no role, and distribution is exogenously given. Because the economy is perceived as in a permanent equilibrium, planned saving always matches exactly planned investment. Indirect control mechanisms lead to equilibrium in free markets with full information. However, although it is easy to identify the volume of saving in monetary terms, defining its value—as Arthur Pigou (1877–1959) pointed out—causes problems under the condition of changing prices. The steady-state per capita growth rate always equals zero in the long run (with external factors constant), and is not affected by savings rate, population growth, or technology. Modern extensions, like institutional economics and endogenous growth theory, analyze the contributions from investment, skills, rules, technological innovation, etc. Although easy to formalize mathematically, this description of reality, like much of the Walrasian (Léon Walras, 1834–1910) approach, is thin in substance, stressing form at the expense of content.

Keynes

John Maynard Keynes (1883–1946), based on empirical observations, suggested changing some of the most basic assumptions of neoclassical economics. According to Keynes and his fellow scholars, saving is not a function of interest, but of income, and investment in real capital is a function of the rate of interest (financial and real investments are competing for resources). People maintain liquid reserves (similar to the classical hoarding); their liquidity preference depends on their subjective feeling of safety or insecurity, because cash is always easier to mobilize, compared to invested money. Businesses involved with turbulent consumer markets may keep a stock of cash in immediately accessible bank accounts; this reserve can be used to update the capital stock through investment, to adapt to unforeseen changes in consumer demand.

The consumption function is not directly derived from the utility maximization behavior of individuals, but is regarded as the aggregate outcome of individual choices. Oversaving is eliminated by a decline in income levels. Besides consumption, accumulation is one motive for profit generation (as suggested in classical Marxist economics). Consequently, there is no *a priori* equilibrium in capitalist economies driven by the accumulation of money, power, status, and self-esteem. Although Keynesian thinking dominated economics until the 1980s, since then neoclassical thinking, with various subtheories and extensions, is hegemonic in economic thinking.

Contemporary Knowledge on Saving and Consumption

There is no single, logically coherent theory comprising all aspects of household saving and consumption behavior. Instead, several theories and conceptual constructs exist, some of them more or less closely linked to each other. Astonishingly, academic discussions of consumption and saving often occur separately, with economists searching for the basics of consumption decisions or trying to elaborate the determinants of saving decisions. As a result, theoretical assumptions and empirical findings frequently differ among studies, although most share the basic approach.

According to modern economics, the sum of consumption spending C and savings S constitutes the total expenditure, and must be equal to the amount of total income $I: I = C + S$. This basic equation is applicable to the household level as well as to national economies. Even if, for a period, consumption expenditures are higher than income, this only refers to negative savings. Those negative savings are either paid from a stock of wealth accumulated from savings of previous periods or come from credits, establishing a negative individual capital stock. In the long run, credits have to be paid back, and the equilibrium will be reestablished. As a result, in modern (macro)economics, although defined quite differently than in the classical period, consumption and saving are still complementary ways to spend income.

Saving in Modern Economics

The motives for saving are, in general, based in a much longer term perspective than consumption decisions are. One main reason for private saving is to provide resources for the time of retirement and for certain risks of life. But as other theories point out, savings are also motivated by the attempt to smooth the availability of financial resources (from income, transfer, and the mobilization of savings) over a lifetime, long before retirement takes place. Savings plans are also implemented to finance planned or expected major expenditures, such as the purchase of a house or the education of children, or to be prepared for unexpected losses in income (precautionary saving). Aside from these explanations on the individual level, the analysis of saving trends and decisions is mostly undertaken on an aggregate national level.

The Interest Rate: Limited Explanatory Capability

As a basic assumption in basic neoclassical theory, the interest rate I is understood to explain decisions on saving S and to be the dominant incentive to increase savings: $S = s(I)$. The disconnect between saving and consumption is illustrated in this equality by the terminology: whereas in the consumption discourse I represents income, in the savings debate it characterizes the interest rate (and in Paul Ehrlich's basic $I = P \times A \times T$ formula of ecological economics related to population P, affluence A, and technology T, I represents impact). Detailed analyses and comparisons have shown, however, that although the interest rate plays a role in savings decisions, all other factors being equal, it is but one in a bundle of influencing factors. If the *ceteris paribus* assumption is abrogated, other influences are recognized as being much more important, and the interest effect is seen as not very robust. The incentive effect of a rising interest rate depends, for instance, on the inflation rate, which reduces the nominal profits, but also has a direct influence on household saving based on precautionary motives. In a similar fashion, the unemployment rate diminishes opportunities for acute saving, but the experience of unemployment increases willingness to save for precautionary reasons (if not suppressed by counteracting incentives in social security systems).

Microeconomic Effects

As opposed to the interest rate, one of the most important factors determining the propensity to save is household income. The strength of this positive correlation varies; in times of increasing income, the level of saving is strongly influenced by whether income status is perceived as permanent or subject to downward change. A decision to save a portion of income also depends on the level of uncertainty and the level of risk averseness, which is influenced by the households' optimism or pessimism about further developments (which can also change with the public mood). In addition to regular income flow, the stock of capital owned is also a decisive variable influencing the level of individual saving, partly because this decreases the level of insecurity regarding future events. Finally, slow adaptation of consumption decisions to increased income levels can result in unintended saving.

The perceived necessity to save a portion of income is also influenced by access to money via the banking system and credit institutions. Borrowing constraints can be an important motive for saving, whereas increased credit availability reduces incentives for private saving and lowers the saving rate; cultural constraints and spending habits, however, probably influence personal financial decisions more than regulations do. Nonetheless, financial deregulation has been discussed as a tool to influence saving. Finally, demographics may influence the saving rate. In aging societies, the saving rate should decline as an increasing share of households use up their financial reserves. However, household surveys, at least in OECD countries, reveal that elderly people often continue to save after retirement, whereas before retirement there is a variable but significant transfer of income to children and grandchildren. As a result of these interacting factors, the degree of saving is only marginally lower after retirement than it was during the working years.

Macroeconomic Factors

In macroeconomic terms, economic growth (and thus the growth of average incomes) is a factor that stimulates saving. Especially when comparing poorer and richer world regions, higher saving rates tend to be correlated with higher income growth, although this is not the case when comparing Germany, Japan, and the United States. Macroeconomic saving is influenced by the total wealth of all households at the aggregate level, and by the distribution of wealth within the country, because the latter determines how many households are in a position to save. Public performance, in general, greatly influences saving decisions. One factor shaping the distribution of income and thus the saving pattern is the taxation system; direct income taxes tend to lower the savings rate, compared to indirect taxes. Furthermore, private saving exhibits a strong negative correlation with public saving. This effect can be very strong, and to a certain degree household saving can even initiate changes in public saving. Explanations for this vary. According to one school of thought, in times of high levels of public spending, private households internalize the fact that government borrowing implies higher future debts and deferred taxation. Another school of thought suggests that high levels of public expenditures (mostly public services and transfers) reduce the strain on individual budgets and provide an opportunity for saving. For instance, if retirement security is one primary motive for saving, then the reliability and the generosity of the social security and welfare systems have an important impact on the perception that saving is necessary. A government-subsidized retirement income and a comprehensive system of health insurance reduce the need to set aside individual resources. Saving habits are also deeply rooted in national tradition and cultural habits. The OECD studies have found that household saving differs greatly among OECD countries, but relative attitudes in most countries are maintained over time.

Consumption in Contemporary Economics

Goods providing prestige, and those representing ambitions, fantasies, and dreams, dominate contemporary private demand. Saturation, changing preferences, and replacement of goods are the rule rather than the exception, with multiutility goods (e.g., those with use value plus status) gaining an inherent competitive advantage. Although the evolution of demand exhibits a significant inertia, because demands are learned in the socialization phases and change with generations, the instruments (what the Chilean economist Manfred Max-Neef would call the "satisfiers" used to meet needs) vary within years or even months, not only in response to income levels but also because of knowledge of and familiarity with them. Information plays a crucial role here; asymmetrical information and communication deficits on the consumers' side will restrict knowledge of and familiarity of goods, thus markets are not perfect (Joseph Stieglitz, 2002 Nobel laureate). It is not equilibrium, but rather a permanent evolution from one nonequilibrium state to another that characterizes consumer markets and keeps the consumer society going, based on savings (mostly in Europe) or on credit and loans (in the United States); in deflationary Japan and growing China, household savings do not sufficiently translate into private consumption.

Empirical economic research has shown that investment, saving, and consumption are not based on rational decisions, but instead follow social trends based on former experience, historical expectations, and rules of thumb (David Kahnemann, 2003 Nobel laureate). Empirically, increasing saving does not lead to a decrease in interest rates, which then leads to decreasing savings and thus to an equilibrium, as the dominant theory suggests. Standard economic theory still struggles to accommodate all these findings.

Utility approach

The very basic assumption of neoclassical demand theory proposes that consumers intend to maximize the utility of their consumption decisions from a given bundle of consumption goods and services. Among the necessary assumptions are that each consumer is a *homo oeconomicus*, seeking to maximize utility, deciding rationally, exclusively based on self-interest, and having complete and correct information about the commodities (mainly their price, their availability, and their ability to satisfy present and future needs). Commodities have to be uniform in quality and highly divisible to permit incremental changes in consumption. Further on, the utility has to be measurable and homogeneous with respect to all commodities consumed; consumer tastes and preferences are stable and externally determined, and consumers decide independently of other opinions, and the marginal utility decreases. These assumptions are the basis of the strength as well as the weakness of neoclassical theory. On the one hand, the assumptions are necessary for the variety of models and theories developed, having thus shown that they are enormously fruitful for theory development. On the other hand, they point to the major limitations of the theory, and they are broadly unrealistic, as demonstrated by empirical research, especially concerning commodity information and divisibility. The theory ignores the role of habit in consumer choice, the existence of multiple motives, and the dynamics of group decision making. However, regardless of the limitations, the theory has provided useful results as food for thought, and variations and extensions of the basic theory have helped to overcome some of the limitations.

Consumption Function

As the basic function $I = C + S$ illustrates (where I is income, C is consumption, and S is saving), an increase in income will lead to an increase in consumption $[C = c(I)]$ if not compensated for by increasing saving (which empirically is not justified to assume). Various hypotheses exist about the factors that influence c.

According to the absolute income hypothesis, the rate of increase in expenditures is lower than the rate of increase in income, but can change over time. It depends on several factors, such as price changes, consumer confidence, the distribution of income, and taxation. The permanent income hypothesis divides income into a permanent element and a transitory element. It assumes permanent consumption to be a fraction c from permanent income, depending on objective factors of household expectations (such as the interest rate), but no correlation is expected between transitory income and transitory consumption. The relative income hypothesis is based on a variation of the utility function. Here consumption is assumed to depend on the household's level of consumption in relation to the average consumption of a reference group. Households with an income lower than that of the reference group will spend a greater share of income on consumption, compared to households with a higher income.

Beyond Modern Economics

The analysis of household consumption and saving is not the exclusive domain of general economic approaches. Although no single comprehensive, integrated theory of household economics yet exists, several explicit theories have been derived from sociology, psychology, or anthropology. They are summarized under the term "consumer theories." Such consumer theories are (among other issues) concerned with the allocation of household income between consumption and saving. The important question they try to answer concerns the criteria by which income is divided between consumption and saving.

Within household economics, the theory of household production tries to overcome some of the limitations of neoclassical economic theory. Here the analysis of consumption decisions focuses not only on income and utility, but additionally on time aspects. Households are regarded as places where unpaid production activities are carried out to satisfy the needs of the household members. Input factors are the available time of the household members and the goods and services bought on the commodity markets. In general, household production can be replaced by purchasing decisions. The ratio of household production and market consumption will depend on income, market conditions, available time, and personal preferences.

Noneconomic approaches reflect the high level of interdependence between the economic and cultural systems of any given society. Individual needs and preferences cannot be assumed to be constant and independent, but are influenced by social and cultural values and settings. Mass media advertising and market dynamics lead to a constant search for new fashions, new styles, new sensations, and new experiences. In this way, consumption more and more becomes independent from use value of the commodity. Material goods are consumed as "communicators" rather than as simple utilities; they are valued as signifiers of taste and of lifestyle. For instance, the individual utility derived from purchase decisions may depend on the number of people possessing a specific commodity. According to the "bandwagon" effect, the utility of a product can increase with an increase in product popularity among consumers' social groups. But product utility can also decrease when individuals seek originality (snob effect), and spurn a product. In opposition to the usual assumptions of modern economics, the utility of a good can even rise with the price (Veblen effect). An elementary influence on consumption behavior is membership in a social group or the desire to belong to a next higher social group.

The life cycle hypothesis intends to integrate the otherwise separate discussions on saving and consumption, taking the broad diversity of motives, constraints, and determining factors for both into account. According to this hypothesis, people try to optimize their buying power during the lifetime of the household via cycles of saving and spending. Consumption flows are smoothed to prepare for times of financial insecurity or foreseeable phases of higher spending needs. A (long) time perspective is thus included in the utility function. Saving is regarded as a restraint on consumption in order to increase the ability to consume at a later phase.

To identify the appropriate utility-maximizing strategy, each consumer would need to know how long he/she will live, their age at retirement, what their preferences will be for goods in each time period, current assets, and the earnings in each future period. These complex data are not easily knowable in reality, making it difficult to obtain empirically valid measures to apply to the life cycle hypothesis.

Sources, Modes, and Problems of Data Collection

Data collection on saving and consumption can be undertaken on the macro level of the national economy or on the micro level of households, sectors, or individuals. On the macro level, standardized data are available from the system of national accounts, but assessing household, sector, or individual data is more challenging. Empirically, there are three possible ways to collect data on individual and household consumption of goods and services. First, the consumption activities of households or their inventory of goods can be recorded. Second, information can be collected from consumers through interviews and questionnaires. Third, data can be obtained and analyzed via reports from producers or distributors. All three methods are used in different settings, with the choice depending on the specific advantages and limitations of each methodology.

Data obtained from analyzing producer and supplier reports are likely to be more precise than those from other sources are, particularly because businesses depend on bookkeeping to maintain competitive advantage. National accounts based on aggregate data that describe income and expenditures for the nation as a whole, as well as monthly or annual retail trade reports, are based on these kinds of reports. Unfortunately, it is rarely possible to link this supply-side information with the characteristics of households, the final consumers. Therefore, for most purposes, information from business and government reports is collected. The data can be obtained at a single point in time, continuously, or periodically.

A major source of inaccuracy in household data gathering is reporting error. Error may be introduced on the reporter side by sampling limitations, but may also emerge from the study participant side. For instance, in most cases only one representative of a household is interviewed and is asked to report on behalf of all household members. Due to opinion, perspective, or lack of knowledge, the information from a single member of a household may be biased; comparative analyses of single-person interviews and separate interviews with at least two household members have demonstrated this. Of course, more interviews should yield greater precision, but are more expensive.

In addition to these problems related to methodology, a more general problem of the interview technique applies to consumption studies as well. In interviews, the interviewees often filter their opinions and tend to answer what they suppose the interviewer might like to hear. Again, the problem can be contained by sophisticated methodologies, but these come at a cost.

Another limitation of the methods based on observations and questionnaires stems from the fact that the results of individual interviews have to be aggregated to provide a meaningful result. The process of aggregation, however, has its own pitfalls. The processes used to select "representative" households, or even the definition of clusters, can be the reasons for an empirical falsification of commonly believed theories. This illustrates clearly the lack of robustness inherent in diverse current economic and noneconomic theories of saving and consumption. A similar situation prevails with data on saving. Standardized macro-level information on the rate of saving is available (although privacy regulations often restrict access to investment-related saving data); at the micro level, an analogous set of methods exists, although the borderline between saving and investment is not always easy to draw. Overall, despite efforts to assess sources, modes, and problems of data collection, what to measure as saving and what to measure as consumption remain open questions.

Open Questions

Globalization Effects

The role of saving is changing as financial systems become increasingly globalized. National saving and credit are no longer the sole source for investment, and global financial markets are providing a new reservoir. Electronic commerce and "e-money" offer consumption opportunities beyond traditional restrictions imposed by saving and credit institutions. On the macro level, savings create global flows of investment and speculation, in particular as long as the return from financial markets and stock exchanges is higher than the return from real capital investments. Such international capital flows are shifting consumption opportunities and growth potentials from capital-exporting countries (e.g., Japan, the Association of South East Asian Nations, and the European Union) to capital-importing countries (e.g., the United States). This trend has become even more pronounced in the past decade because new incentives for saving were introduced in many OECD countries (the shift of social security measures from a transfer-based system to one based on private investment at the stock exchange, mostly in globally active investment funds).

Future of Consumption Measurement

Although the commonly used methodologies are rather well suited to assess the volume of consumption, they provide no information about its value. In general, with flexible prices based on scarcity, changes in use value are hard to capture. It has been estimated that recent figures for gross domestic product growth would have been significantly higher if the increase in use value (e.g., of a new computer or car) had been expressed in the consumption statistic, rather than the price; prices for many consumer goods have decreased in the past decade, despite their increasing consumer utility.

Green Consumption and Saving

Ecologically sensitive ("green") consumption contributes to reduction of environmental damage, reducing societal costs, but this productive consumption is so far not separately accounted for. In addition, two of the consumption items enjoyed by every consumer worldwide are air and water; as far as both are public goods, their value has no price, and their consumption is not accounted for in economic statistics (although air is still a free good, water tends to be privatized). Similarly, "green investments," in addition to being attractive to investors due to their particularly good performance regarding value and annual gains, also contribute to environmental damage reduction and reduce the need for unproductive expenditures, thus increasing the volume of disposable income of a society. Nonetheless, the volume of avoided future expenditures hardly plays any role when current savings and investment patterns are discussed.

In the future, if the current debate on quantifying external costs continues, the direct external effects of consumption and the indirect external effects of saving (via investment) will play a significant role in measuring the value of saving and consumption. The situation will become even more complex if—as requested by the proponents of sustainable development paradigms—social, economic, institutional, and environmental externalities are all taken into account.

Role of the Nonmonetary Economy

A significant share (40–50%) of the work done in any industrialized economy is unpaid work (care-taking, educational roles, volunteer activities, self-employment, etc.). Although of significant relevance and potential substitutes for paid consumption, uncompensated activities are usually ignored in macroeconomic statistics. Saving of time (some "time banks" already exist) may be an alternative to saving money, but this is also not statistically accounted for. This renders the gross domestic product incomplete as a measure of welfare, and presents an incomplete picture of the standard consumption and saving measurements regarding the wealth creation process as a whole.

See Also the Following Articles

Economic Anthropology • Economics, Strategies in Social Science • Household Behavior and Family Economics • Social Economics

Further Reading

Blaug, M. (1962). *Economic Theory in Retrospect.* Richard D. Irwin, Homewood, Illinois.

Loayza, N., Schmidt-Hebbel, K., and Serven, L. (2000). What drives private saving across the world. *Rev. Econ. Statist.* **82**(2), 65–181.

Magrabi, F. M., Young Sook, C., Sanghee Sohn, C., and Se-Jeong, Y. (1991). *The Economics of Household Consumption.* Praeger Publ., New York.

Poterba, J. M. (ed.) (1994). *International Comparison of Household Saving.* University of Chicago Press, Chicago.

Reisch, L., and Röpke, I. (2004). *Sustainable Consumption, Foundations of Ecological Economics Series.* Edward Elgar, Cheltenham.

Senghaas, D. (1982). *Von Europa Lernen.* Edition Suhrkamp No. 1134. Suhrkamp Verlag, Frankfurt/Main.

Content Analysis

Doug Bond

Harvard University, Cambridge, Massachusetts, USA

Glossary

automated (or machine) coding Computer technology that "reads" text and extracts user-specified information deemed relevant to its content and/or context. Such machine processing of natural language is used to identify and then record the text-based information in structured data records for further analysis of the author or message. Typically, machine coding is used for content analysis when high volumes of information need to be processed, or when the results are needed in real-time.

coding manual The decision rules and procedural steps for creating structured data records from text-based or other media. These decision rules and procedures follow from the objectives and explicate the specific steps of a content analysis process. Coding manuals may also contain information about the assumptions underlying and purpose behind the content analysis, though sometimes these are implicit. In any case, coding manuals serve to guide and inform the coding process.

corpora Sets of tagged text or other media that are used to train or optimize a machine coding tool or technology. They may also be used for training humans to code, because they provide a measure (the tagged, marked-up or coded text) against which trial coding can be assessed. Corpora represent samples of a larger pool of information to be processed and from which certain decision rules pertaining to syntax or semantics may be inducted.

dictionaries A compilation of decision rules for various elements or parameters in a content analysis. One set of dictionary entries may pertain to entities, their attributes, and relationships, whereas others may detail actions or events, along with their characteristics. Still other entries may list alternative spellings, names, or other information needed to guide the guide and inform the coding process. When dictionaries contain multiple sets of complex and related information, they are often referred to as ontologies.

manual (or human) coding The manual equivalent to machine coding that, for content analysis, entails reading text and extracting user-specified information deemed relevant to its content and/or context. Such manual processing of natural language is used to identify and record the text-based information in structured data records for further analysis of the author or message. Typically, manual coding is used for content analysis on a narrow scope of inquiry and on limited amounts of information.

Content analysis is a method to identify, extract, and assess selected information from a form of media for use as a basis to infer something about the author, content, or message. The information may appear as text, images, or sounds, as symbolic representations of the same, or even in the context of how, and/or way in which, a message is conveyed through the media. Content analysis has been used in a wide range of applications, from analyzing print advertisements to product specifications, from patents to treaties, and from health to police records, as well as in a wide variety of literary and nonfiction texts. Over the past 70 years, the practice of content analysis has been broadening to include the investigation of information presented in audio and visual media forms, such as the monitoring of violence and sexually explicit images and language in television programs and in films. Especially with the advent of automated tools for identifying and extracting images and sounds, content analysis is no longer bound to documents, per se. Regardless of the form of media, content analysis as a field within the context of scientific inquiry seeks replicable inferences from a limited set of observations, with the goal to generalize to a larger set of the same. The scientific process of content analysis therefore is explicit and transparent in its definitions and categorizations of information, and in the independent reproducibility of its results, thereby lending an intersubjective quality to its findings, regardless of the specific procedures employed.

The Evolution of Content Analysis

Traditionally, text-based sources of information (documents) have most often been the subject of content analysis. First- or third-person documents may be analyzed for content, for different reasons. Some common first-person documents include editorials, transcripts of speeches, and responses to surveys (especially those with open-ended questions). Typical third-person documents, including news and field situation or incident reports, contain mediated observations that are often used to monitor and/or manage social, political, and economic incidents or events. Content analysis has also been used to track and assess interpersonal and intergroup interactions, typically based on transcripts of the messages exchanged.

A survey of research identified as content analysis in the social sciences and humanities by Oli Holsti in 1969 revealed a great diversity in approaches. From its ancient intellectual roots to its current practice, this diversity has remained a central characteristic of content analysis. Content analysis, then, is not monolithic; it is more accurately characterized as a collection of different techniques or methods to understand messages that spans disciplines, media, and types of analyses.

In his 1980 handbook (updated in 2004) on the methodology of content analysis, Klaus Krippendorff noted that the term "content analysis" was (then) only about 50 years old. A content analysis guidebook by Kimberly Neuendorf in 2002 documents the burgeoning popularity of the method, noting a steep rise in citations related to the terms "content" and "text analysis" over the past 20 years. Still, what qualifies as content analysis is quite ambiguous, and in some cases, contested. Many of those who use methods of computer-assisted text analysis (CATA) argue that certain long-standing traditions such as rhetorical analysis are not properly considered content analysis. Likewise, so-called postmodernist approaches such as discourse analysis are often excluded by those with a more quantitative orientation, due in large part to their explicit advocacy of multiple readings of texts.

Unfortunately, those who practice content analysis often work separately from those who, in other disciplines and professions, are working on related subject matter. Even within the social sciences, scholars have a tendency to develop idiosyncratic terminology and tools to study their respective domains of interest. For example, the protocols or conceptual frameworks used by sociologists to content analyze news reports on social movements are quite distinct from those used by political scientists to monitor the same reports from a political science perspective. And with respect to tools, divergent approaches have been taken in the rule-based and statistical approaches to natural language processing. Likewise, those who focus on text-based versus audiovisual messages typically use different tools, and rarely are the approaches integrated.

Given the disparate orientations, tools, and analytic methods of those who conduct content analyses, the evolution of content analysis may appear discontinuous or uneven, driven more by the discovery of practical applications than by a consensus of those who study messages. Still, there is a convergent sense that can be made of the evolution of content analysis. From the early academic text (manual)-coding projects used to compare documents or to determine the author of a document by using simple word counts, to the more recent (automated) data mining efforts that extract relationships among entities, their attributes, and their actions in real-time, content analysis increasingly is facilitating systematic, quantitative assessment of information in all of its forms. For text-based content analyses, much of this work is done under the rubric of a somewhat amorphous field known variously as natural language processing or natural language understanding. For other (than text-based) media, more specialized fields of audio and image analysis are leading the development of content analysis.

In any case, the capacity to conduct rigorous, real-time analyses of the ever-increasing deluge of global information has contributed to the increased visibility and expanded roles of unobtrusive content analysis. Electronic document management has become an industry, and the tools are being used for a variety of content analyses, with a premium placed on real-time monitoring of the exchange of messages and reports. The formerly solitary activity of electronic word processing has evolved to the point where it is now effectively merged into the Internet. In other words, the technologies of working with natural language to support collaborative work on shared documents are rapidly transforming content analysis from its origins in academic studies into a technique with numerous practical applications. In particular, the areas of regulatory compliance, business intelligence, and risk management offer a host of applications for content analysis tools. The pervasive use of e-mail and instant messaging, for example, has already become subject to significant governmental regulation. And more generally, a wide range of automated tools for content analysis has already found markets wherever there is a requirement for tracking, archiving, manipulating, or analyzing messages and information in virtually any form.

Manual Content Analysis

Yellow highlighter marking pens, reams of data sheets, and thick coding manuals were the dominant tools of text content analysis through the 1980s. Today, information identification and extraction algorithms have replaced the highlighters, and electronic corpora, ontologies, and dictionaries substitute for printed manuals. Nevertheless, the human element of explicating assumptions, defining terms, and specifying rules to code a word or a phrase, or the context of a message, cannot be understated in the operation of any content analysis technology.

The coding of text begins with one or more questions focused on the purpose of the analysis. For example, if assessing the personality of the author of a first-person speech is of interest, a measure of the self-reflexive pronouns "I, me, mine, my, our, ours, us, and we" might be undertaken. The usage of these pronouns can be mapped to the author as an individual (singular usage) or as a member of a group (plural usage). Such a mapping scheme might be related to a theory of the extent to which an author is self-centered, or perhaps to identifying the author in relation to a larger group. This is but a simple example of a single set of indicators (the personal pronouns) to measure one aspect of personality. Numerous other measures might be used, and each would be grounded in a theory that relates the specific indicators to the concept being measured. The questions thus anchor the investigation and serve to guide the coding of the indicators as they are found in the data. In this case, the human coder might begin by highlighting all instances of the personal pronoun indicators, and then map each of the plural forms to a group to which the author is asserting membership.

Manual coding also may be conducted to identify who is doing what to/with whom in a third-person report. This approach highlights the action or events being reported and links the source and target of the action into an event record. When applied to news reports, these event records can be tracked over time to monitor the incidence of various social, political, and economic activities. Such an approach is often used to track protest, violence, and other events deemed to be of interest. And when combined with statistical analysis of the trends, this approach has been used to provide early warnings on violence, state failure, or economic disruption. Manual-coding content analysis has two large and interrelated drawbacks. First, it is extremely laborious and expensive. Most human coders cannot code effectively for more than an hour or two, often yielding no more than a few dozen events per day. Second, human coders are notoriously inconsistent in their coding, and not just across coders, documents, or contexts, but also over time and against their own prior coding. It is not atypical for one coder to view another's "freedom fighter" as a "terrorist," and even for the same coder to see things differently in the afternoon versus the morning.

Complex coding manuals have been developed over the years within the major human coding efforts to address these shortcomings. These coding manuals are often several inches thick and provide detailed guidance to individual coders as they make the interminable number of discrete judgments involved in the coding of even a basic set of indicators within a single document. Needless to say, rigorous training and quality-control monitoring procedures are required for human coding efforts. Despite the best training and quality-control efforts, however, a reliance on human coding alone is most appropriately used for low-volume coding exercises. Nevertheless, when humans are used to code text (manually), it is possible to ignore a considerable amount of detail, particularly when dealing with seemingly trivial assumptions and distinctions removed from the objectives of the analysis. With machine coding, however, all contingencies must be specified in advance, even if only to specify predetermined defaults in the face of uncertainty. In other words, machine coding is as unforgiving as it is transparent and consistent—that is, 100%.

In sum, the basic idea is the same for most manual coding and, with some subtle but important differences, for automated coding. The process begins with hypothesized relationships between indicators and concepts to be measured. These relationships are then explicated, operationalizing the terms and outlining the scales for each measure in a detailed manual. Orientation and training with the manual is then conducted to assure consistency. Finally, the actual coding process is continually monitored and periodically tested.

Automated Content Analysis

For more generalized content analysis or natural language processing, all words, as opposed to a specific set of indicators, are typically coded and/or indexed. When all words in a text are coded, a process often referred to as "tagging," the resultant text is referred to as "marked-up text." The syntactic properties of the words, such as part of speech and their semantic attributes, are tagged in this way. Certain functional attributes might also be tagged. In addition, the same kind of indicator sets may be compiled into lists to be used as dictionaries to guide and inform the automated tools in the coding of measures beyond language attributes. In this way, automated coding has largely replaced human coding for many applications of content analysis. Even with automation, however, the basic steps of coding—explication, operationalization, scaling, and monitoring—are still fundamental to the process. The difference is that a machine rather than a human is following the instructions outlined in a manual and assigning codes to text. Virtually all of the major manual coding content analysis projects have adopted machine or automated technologies to assist humans in coding, and increasingly to replace them.

A slight difference between human and machine coding is that many automated content analyses treat text as discrete words that are statistically analyzed to identify word clusters or patterns of their covariance. In this approach, much of the coding is inducted from the text rather than being followed from a codebook. The statistical computation approach has the advantage of being language independent. In other words, the incidence of large volumes of words or symbols (for example, Chinese characters) in any language can be assessed statistically without knowing in advance their intended or referenced meaning.

The statistical computation approach often relies on the *a priori* compilation of large corpora of documents in which the individual words and phrases are catalogued along with their attributes, typically established by human or manual coding of sample texts. Thus, a key word, "nuclear," might be associated with "war" (say, 60% of the time) or with "family" (say, 30% of the time), depending on the particular substantive domain involved. The computations of content analysis tools typically account for both the distance between tokens as well as their sequence within a document.

Ontologies are also used to formalize the knowledge conveyed in words and phrases, and to represent the relationships among them. General-purpose ontologies often contain tens of thousands of fundamental facts about entities and the relationships among them. Simpler versions of these large ontologies contain nothing more than lists of words associated with a particular concept of interest to a content analyst. These lists are sometimes referred to as dictionaries, and are typically focused on a specific substantive domain. Most of the do-it-yourself automated tools in the content analysis marketplace allow for the use of standard or basic dictionaries as well as customizable lists to be compiled by individual users and tailored to their specific interests with respect to the documents being analyzed. In any case, both simple and complex ontologies facilitate the automated generation of reliable associations of selected words to other words and phrases, and create indices of the documents that contain them.

Such technology is widely used in Internet and other search engines, so that when searching for one or more terms, the documents most commonly associated with the terms will be retrieved. Other search engines are built on more sophisticated search routines that account for links across documents as well as the history of users accessing them. In addition, this technology is useful in the automated generation of summaries of documents. Coupling interactive search with automated summarizing capabilities makes the finding of specific information much easier.

Practical applications of content analysis, however, take search and summary procedures one step further by presenting the results graphically and geographically. This visualization is made possible by the computational statistics used in the content analysis tools that quantify the information and organize it in ways that are amenable to visually compelling presentations. Automated content analysis is fast and broadly usable across languages and substantive domains. In addition, the approach accounts for the common use of vague language by employing probabilistic resolution of the ambiguities. The most likely resolution of a phrase with multiple meanings can be gleaned from the domain-specific attributes listed in a corpus on which the tool has been trained. Unusual meanings may be missed with this approach, but their incidence is also likely to be rare.

The Future of Content Analysis

The optimal use of the currently available automated tools for content analysis is for high-volume, domain-specific processing. A human coder is often better able than an automated content analysis tool to discern the nuance of certain messages, and to resolve ambiguities in a given context. Unlike manual coding, however, automated coding is 100% transparent and 100% consistent. This transparency and consistency will contribute to the increased use of automated content analysis into the future.

The technology, algorithms, and models used by those who study natural language processing and content analysis are distributed across numerous communities of scholarship and practice. The diverse yet practical challenges of business and governance have garnered a convergence of skills, interests, and resources that continue to sustain large-scale projects; these endeavors are contributing to profitable, practical consumer applications as well as to pervasive and powerful unobtrusive means to monitor many public and private actions and communications deemed to be a threat. Understanding the implications and especially controlling this creeping deployment of unobtrusive content analysis technology pose critical challenges for the protection of civil liberties in an information era.

Based on explicit understandings of the relationships embedded in the content of messages, content analysis tools can acquire and analyze knowledge about beliefs, attitudes, and behavior. This knowledge is being used in content analysis tools to represent and model real-world behaviors. One of the goals of such efforts is to support practical, real-time preemptive interventions in times of impending crisis or disaster. Content analysis has a rich history of examining historical antecedents and can now automatically track reported events as they unfold. Through the real-time monitoring of global news reports, content analysis is lending more transparency to conflict processes. Computational politics, an emerging field that integrates computer science technology with social science methodology, is thus poised to acquire and analyze knowledge about human behavior and, it is hoped, to prevent, contain, or at least mitigate some of the destructive aspects of conflict.

See Also the Following Articles

Coding Variables • Computerized Record Linkage and Statistical Matching • Content Analysis and Television

Further Reading

Allen, J. (1995). *Natural Language Understanding*, 2nd Ed. Benjamin/Cummings Publ., Redwood City, California.

Bond, D., Bond, J., Oh, C., Jenkins, J. C., and Taylor, C. L. (2003). Integrated data for events analysis (IDEA): an event typology for automated events data development. *J. Peace Res.* **40,** 733–745.

Evans, W. (2003). *Content Analysis Resources*. Available on the University of Alabama web site at www.car.ua.edu/

Holsti, O. R. (1969). *Content Analysis for the Social Sciences and Humanities.* Random House, New York.

Jurafsky, D., and Martin, J. H. (2000). *Speech and Language Processing. An Introduction to Natural Language Processing, Computational Linguistics and Speech Recognition.* Prentice Hall, Upper Saddle River, New Jersey.

Krippendorff, K. (2004). *Content Analysis. An Introduction to its Methodology*, 2nd. Ed., Sage Publ., Newbury Park, California.

Neuendorf, K. A. (2002). *The Content Analysis Guidebook*. Sage Publ. Thousand Oaks, California. Available on the Internet at http://academic.csuohio.edu

Riffe, D., Lacy, S., and Fico, F. F. (1998). *Analyzing Media Messages Using Quantitative Analysis in Research.* Lawrence Erlbaum, Mahwah, New Jersey.

Roberts, C. W. (ed.) (1997). *Text Analysis for the Social Sciences*. Lawrence Erlbaum, Mahwah, New Jersey.

Schrodt, P. A., and Gerner, D. J. (2000). *Analyzing International Event Data: A Handbook of Computer-Based Techniques*. Draft book manuscript for the Cambridge University Press. Available on the Internet at www.ku.edu

Stone, P. J. (2003). *The General Inquirer*. Available on the Internet at www.wjh.harvard.edu

Weber, R. P. (1990). *Basic Content Analysis*, 2nd Ed. Sage Publ., Newbury Park, California.

West, M. D. (2001). *Theory, Method and Practice in Computer Content Analysis.* Ablex Publ., Westport, Connecticut.

West, M. D. (2001). *Applications of Computer Content Analysis.* Ablex Publ., Westport, Connecticut.

Content Analysis and Television

Erica Scharrer
University of Massachusetts, Amherst, Massachusetts, USA

Glossary

coding The process of examining content (messages and texts) in order to detect and document patterns and characteristics.

conceptual definitions Descriptions of concepts that signify their typical meaning; dictionary-type definitions.

content analysis The research methodology in which messages or texts (often but not exclusively those in the media) are examined, summarizing their characteristics by using systematic procedures to place content into carefully constructed categories.

intercoder reliability The process of establishing agreement between two or more coders in the coding of content, for the purpose of minimizing subjectivity and maximizing reliability.

operational definitions Descriptions of concepts as they will be measured in the study.

reliability The extent to which a study and its measures can be replicated by other researchers, or by the same researchers more than once, and still produce largely the same results.

sampling The process of selecting particular elements to examine from a general population about which the researcher wishes to generalize.

validity The extent to which the variables used in a study actually measure what the researcher purports or intends to measure.

The content analysis research method can be applied to the study of television content. Design of a content analytic investigation of television is accomplished in stages, which include the identification of variables, the development of a coding scheme, and the calculation of intercoder reliability. Based on the content analysis research method, data can be analyzed and interpreted to allow for valid and reliable conclusions about the nature of television content.

Introduction

Why Study Television Content?

Television has a ubiquitous presence in contemporary society, dominating the leisure time of people young and old. Recent estimates establish average viewing among adults in the United States at just over 3.5 hours/day, and children and teenagers watch about an hour less than that daily. Controversy about television content is as old as the medium. On its initial and rapid diffusion to households in the United States, television was immediately embraced as a favorite pastime but also soon sparked concern over the types of programs and messages the medium conveyed. Television was in its infancy when the first scientific analyses of its content were conducted by researchers. The results of two nearly concurrent but separate analyses by Sydney Head and Dallas Smythe in 1954 largely corroborated the concerns of early critics, with evidence that violence, gender and racial inequalities, and entertainment programming (rather than educational programming) abounded on the screen. Since those initial inquiries were undertaken, there have been hundreds of studies of television content. Researchers of television programming have documented the presence and pervasiveness of violence and sex, have investigated portrayals of gender, race, class, age, and sexual orientation, and have examined diverse topics, such as the treatment of particular occupations and the depiction of families. Analyses of television news have also been conducted and have focused on topics such as the coverage of politics, crime, health risks, natural disasters, war, and the economy. The studies have amassed an impressive body of knowledge that tracks the patterns of content that have historically been and are currently delivered to television audiences.

Systematic studies of television content are undertaken for a number of reasons. Some researchers examine television content because they are motivated by concern about the effects of viewing such content on audiences. Studies of the tendency of the news media to focus on the "horse race" aspect of presidential elections (who's ahead? who's behind?), for example, may be inspired by fear of uninformed or uninvolved voters. Studies of violence in entertainment programming have been framed according to the likelihood that such portrayals affect audiences. Another reason to study television content, however, is merely to document a cultural artifact, and studies undertaken for this reason carry no cautionary remarks about potential effects of viewing, but rather often seek to unveil relationships between television content and other social or cultural forces. An example is an analysis of the representation of women on television and what that content reveals about current cultural conditions regarding gender roles. Finally, another reason for studying television content is to compare that content to the "real world," often with the result of identifying television's distortions. In the realm of entertainment programming, such studies have assessed the number of characters on television who are African American, Latino, Asian American, or Native American and have drawn comparisons to census data showing the actual racial and ethnic composition of the nation. The most recent of such inquiries shows that of those racial and ethnic groups, only African Americans are not severely underrepresented on television, compared to population figures. Another application of this motivation is to illuminate relationships between the production process—how and by whom script writing, producing, directing, camera operating, and editing takes place—and the resulting content. An example is a study that tests whether the number of women employed behind the scenes as television producers and directors has an impact on the way that gender is presented in programs.

Defining Content Analysis

A wide variety of definitions of content analysis, the most frequently employed method for the study of television content, have been advanced. Among the most detailed is that presented by Daniel Riffe, Stephen Lacy, and Frederick G. Fico in their book, *Analyzing Media Messages: Using Quantitative Content Analysis in Research*. They say that "quantitative content analysis is the systematic and replicable examination of symbols of communication, which have been assigned numeric values according to valid measurement rules, and the analysis of relationships involving those values using statistical methods, in order to describe the communication, draw inferences about its meaning, or infer from the communication to its context, both of production and consumption." Another recent and highly inclusive definition of content analysis is provided by Kimberly A. Neuendorf in her book, *The Content Analysis Guidebook*. Neuendorf defines content analysis as "a summarizing, quantitative analysis of messages that relies on the scientific method (including attention to objectivity–intersubjectivity, *a priori* design, reliability, validity, generalizability, replicability, and hypothesis testing) and is not limited as to the types of variables that may be measured or the context in which the messages are created or presented."

The definition by Riffe and colleagues provides a compendium of many of the elements presented separately in past definitions, and it contains a number of important clauses. It identifies a research paradigm (quantitative research), raises issues of both validity and reliability, begins to reveal the process by which such studies are conceptualized and carried out, and refers to potential application and interpretation of findings. The Neuendorf definition prefers to discuss "messages" as the subject of analysis rather than "communication," and fleshes out the research priorities that attend the quantitative orientation of the method. Furthermore, Neuendorf foregrounds the flexibility of content analysis research, asserting that the variables that can be investigated are numerous and multidimensional, likely a response to other definitions that suggested they be limited to "manifest" content (discussed later). Both definitions rightly share the inclusion of the summarizing or categorizing function of the method.

Designing Studies of Television Content

Conceptualization

Like most studies, content analysis research begins with an idea of what, specifically, will be analyzed and why. In this stage, theory may be considered to support relationships between content variables and extramedia factors such as social forces, media production and distribution processes, and potential ways that audiences will receive and respond to the content. A review of the literature would most certainly take place in the conceptualization stage to determine the patterns drawn from prior, similar studies, to identify gaps in knowledge to be addressed by the present study, and to determine ways in which key concepts have been measured in the past.

Hypotheses or research questions would typically be formed to guide the inquiry. Hypotheses posed in content analysis research may include comparisons among or between media types or outlets (e.g., newspapers will report on the background of news stories more often than will television news; cartoons will contain more acts of violence than will prime-time programs). Hypotheses may also predict differences in content over time (e.g., father figures are portrayed more foolishly in contemporary sitcoms compared to in sitcoms from decades past; depictions of sexual activity in soap operas have increased in frequency over time). The hypotheses may also test relationships between television content and extramedia factors (e.g., as social indicators demonstrate increased acceptance of homosexuality, television depictions of same-sex couples will increase).

Category Construction

The next stage in designing a content analysis is defining the concepts to be studied, both conceptually and operationally. The overarching goal is to determine ways of measuring the concepts to be investigated that most closely reflect their dictionary-type denotative and connotative meanings. A close match between conceptual and operational definitions ensures validity. Operational definitions in content analysis research take the form of categories that will be used to summarize the media messages examined. For example, noting the age group of characters used in commercials requires the placement of each person that appears in the commercial into categories; these may include "children," "teenagers," "young adults," "middle-aged adults," and "the elderly." Careful attention must be paid to category construction to ensure that the summary of content is as accurate and meaningful as possible.

Many of the same rules that dictate questionnaire item construction guide the building of content analysis categories. Categories must be exhaustive and mutually exclusive. In other words, the researcher must anticipate as well as possible any and every type of content that will be encountered in the study, and must have a means of placing that content decisively into one and no more than one category. Placing the gender of reality-based program contestants into categories, for instance, provides a fairly straightforward example. The categories "male" and "female" would presumably be both exhaustive and mutually exclusive. If the researcher wanted to determine whether such contestants model stereotypical gender roles, the construction of categories to indicate such roles would be more complex but would still be guided by the exhaustive and mutually exclusive requirements.

The unit of analysis must be established. The unit of analysis is the individual entity that is actually being studied; it will be represented by one row of data in the computer file that will be used to analyze findings. The identification of the unit of analysis in content analysis research can be less straightforward than in other methods, when a single individual is often the entity studied. Does the study have television "program" as the unit of analysis? Episode? Characters within programs or episodes? Acts within programs or episodes? The researcher must clarify the unit of analysis early on.

A final consideration in the construction of categories is the richness of the information to be gleaned. Researchers should, when appropriate, attempt to measure variables at the highest possible level of measurement. Nominal-level variables are certainly of interest in content analysis research, as exemplified in the gender example as well as in studies of, for instance, the attire of music video characters (e.g., legs bare, stomach bare, tight clothing, loose clothing) or the genres of television programming (e.g., sitcoms, dramas, news, sports, "reality-based," game shows, soap operas, etc.). Yet, other studies may call for ordinal-, interval-, or ratio-level data, and their inclusion in the research design allows for a multitude of statistical tests to be used to investigate relationships between and among variables. Ordinal data may be drawn from rankings of news stories by their presentation order in a television newscast. Interval-level data may be gathered when content analysts are making judgments of the degree to which a depiction is graphically violent (e.g., on a scale of 1 to 5). Ratio-level data are often derived from counts of the presence of a particular type of content, such as the number of acts of violence, the number of jokes, or the number of characters of color. Indeed, ratio-level data do not use categories at all, but rather employ continuous measures.

After constructing categories, a coding scheme is created that provides both a coding sheet (on which a coder can readily assign television content to categories and to the numbers representing those categories) and a coding book (to provide instructions about how to make coding decisions). Because the method is quantitative, all content must ultimately be expressed in numbers, even if, as in the case of nominal-level measures, the numbers assigned to categories are arbitrary.

Sampling

Sampling decisions are also not unique to content analysis, although there are particular opportunities and challenges that arise in sampling television content. The objective is to gather a sufficient and appropriate amount and type of television content to test the hypotheses and/or examine the research questions. Therefore, content analysis samples, like other samples in social science research, are ideally fairly large and representative of the general population about which the researcher wishes to infer.

Probability sampling techniques that ensure that each unit in the population has an equal chance of being included in the sample can be utilized. A simple random sample may be generated, for instance, by compiling a list of all programs, episodes, or characters (depending on the unit of analysis) in the population and then using a table of random numbers to determine which will be selected to comprise the sample. Similarly, if such a list can be created, a systematic sample can be derived by choosing every *N*th entry in the list (e.g., every fifth, or every tenth, depending on the number of items in the list and the ultimate sample size desired).

However, restrictions concerning time, money, and access result in the fairly frequent use of nonprobability samples in studies of television content. There are two main types. First, convenience samples are selected simply because particular types of content are available to the researcher, rather than being chosen for any theoretical or methodological reason. Examples of convenience samples in television content research include sampling three episodes each of the currently running situation comedies ("sitcoms") to represent the genre, or relying on syndicated programs from decades past to investigate changes in content over time. Second, purposive samples are drawn by selecting particular content for a conceptually valid reason, but not ensuring that every element of the population had an equal likelihood of selection. A very common example in studies of television content is the use of a composite or a constructed time period to sample. Researchers interested in prime-time programming on the networks, for instance, may videotape ABC, CBS, NBC, Fox, WB, and UPN for one full week from 8 to 11 pm. If they are careful to avoid atypical weeks, such as "sweeps" week (when programming may be unusual because of heightened competition for ratings) or a period with holiday specials rather than general programming, researchers could argue for the representativeness of the week. However, as with a convenience sample, inferences about the relationship between findings in these nonprobability samples and the overall population should be couched in cautious terms.

Reliability and Validity in Studies of Television Content

Definitions

Studies that employ the method of content analysis to examine television content are guided by the ideals of reliability and validity, as are many research methods. Reliability has to do with whether the use of the same measures and research protocols (e.g., coding instructions, coding scheme) time and time again, as well as by more than one coder, will consistently result in the same findings. If so, those results can be deemed reliable because they are not unique to the subjectivity of one person's view of the television content studied or to the researcher's interpretations of the concepts examined.

Validity refers primarily to the closeness of fit between the ways in which concepts are measured in research and the ways in which those same concepts are understood in the larger, social world. A valid measure is one that appropriately taps into the collective meanings that society assigns to concepts. The closer the correspondence between operationalizations and complex real-world meanings, the more socially significant and useful the results of the study will be. In content analysis research of television programming, validity is achieved when samples approximate the overall population, when socially important research questions are posed, and when both researchers and laypersons would agree that the ways that the study defined major concepts correspond with the ways that those concepts are really perceived in the social world.

Validity: Categories and Indicators

Valid measures of general concepts are best achieved through the use of multiple indicators of the concept in content analysis research, as well as in other methods. A study of whether television commercials placed during children's programming have "healthy" messages about food and beverages poses an example. There are certainly many ways of thinking about what would make a food or beverage "healthy." Some would suggest that whole categories of foods and beverages may be healthy or not (orange juice compared to soda, for instance). Others would look at the amount of sugar or perhaps fat in the foods and beverages to determine how healthy they were. Still others would determine healthiness by documenting whether the foods and beverages contain vitamins and minerals. The content analysis codes or categories used to measure the healthiness of the foods and beverages shown in commercials would ideally reflect all of these potential indicators of the concept. The use of multiple indicators bolsters the validity of the measures implemented in studies of content because they more closely approximate the varied meanings and dimensions of the concept as it is culturally understood.

There are two major types of validity. External validity has to do with the degree to which the study as a whole or the measures employed in the study can be generalized to the real world or to the entire population from which the sample was drawn. It is established through sampling as well as through attempts to reduce artificiality. An example of the latter is having coders make some judgments by watching television content only once, rather than stopping and starting a videotaped program multiple times, in order to approximate how the content would be experienced by actual viewing audiences. The other type of validity is internal validity, which refers to the closeness of fit between the meanings of the concepts that we hold in everyday life and the ways those concepts are operationalized in the research. The validity of concepts used in research is determined by their *prima facie* correspondence to the larger meanings we hold (face validity), the relationship of the measures to other concepts that we would expect them to correlate with (construct validity) or to some external criterion that the concept typically predicts (criterion or predictive validity), and the extent to which the measures capture multiple ways of thinking of the concept (content validity).

Reliability: Training, Coding, and Establishing Intercoder Agreement

A particular strength of content studies of television is that they provide a summary view of the patterns of messages that appear on the screens of millions of people. The goal of a content analysis is that these observations are universal rather than significantly swayed by the idiosyncratic interpretations or points of view of the coder. Researchers go to great lengths to ensure that such observations are systematic and methodical rather than haphazard, and that they strive toward objectivity. Of course, true objectivity is a myth rather than a reality. Yet, content analysis research attempts to minimize the influence of subjective, personal interpretations.

In order to achieve this aim, multiple coders are used in content analysis to perform a check on the potential for personal readings of content by the researcher, or for any one of the coders to unduly shape the observations made. Such coders must all be trained to use the coding scheme to make coding decisions in a reliable manner, so that the same television messages being coded are dealt with the same way by each coder each time they are encountered. Clear and detailed instructions must be given to each coder so that difficult coding decisions are anticipated and a procedure for dealing with them is in place and is consistently employed. Most likely, many pretests of the coding scheme and coding decisions will be needed and revisions will be made to eliminate ambiguities and sources of confusion before the process is working smoothly (i.e., validly and reliably). Researchers often limit the amount of coding to be done by one coder in one sitting because the task may get tiresome, and reliable, careful thought may dwindle over time.

In addition to training coders on how to perform the study, a more formal means of ensuring reliability—calculations of intercoder reliability—is used in content analysis research. The purpose of intercoder reliability is to establish mathematically the frequency with which multiple coders agree in their judgments of how to categorize and describe content. In order to compute intercoder reliability, the coders must code the same content to determine whether and to what extent their coding decisions align. Strategies for determining how much content to use for this purpose vary, but a general rule of thumb is to have multiple coders overlap in their coding of at least 10% of the sample. If they agree sufficiently in that 10%, the researcher is confident that each can code the rest of the sample independently because a systematic coding protocol has been achieved.

A number of formulas are used to calculate intercoder reliability. Holsti's coefficient is a fairly simple calculation, deriving a percent agreement from the number of items coded by each coder and the number of times they made the exact same coding decision. Other researchers use Pearson's correlation to determine the association between the coding decisions of one coder compared to another (or multiple others). Still other formulas, such as Scott's pi, take chance agreement into consideration. There is no set standard regarding what constitutes sufficiently high intercoder reliability, although most published accounts do not fall below 70–75% agreement.

Balancing Validity and Reliability

In studies of television content, the goals of establishing validity and reliability must be balanced. Measures used in content analysis research could be reliable but not valid if they repeatedly uncover the same patterns of findings, but those findings do not adequately measure the concepts that they are intending to measure. Furthermore, often the attempts to approximate the complex understandings of concepts that occur in the social world in research designs strengthen validity at the same time that they threaten reliability, because they are more nuanced and less transparent.

Consider an example in a study of television news coverage of presidential elections. The researcher wants to determine what proportion of the newscast is devoted to coverage of the presidential candidates during election season, as well as whether those candidates receive positive or negative coverage. The former portion of the research question would be relatively straightforward to study and would presumably be easily and readily agreed on by multiple coders. All of the items in the newscast could be counted and the number of items devoted to the presidential candidates could be compared to the total number (similarly, stories could be timed). The latter part of the research question, however, is likely to be less overt and relies instead on a judgment to be made by coders, rather than a mere observation of the conspicuous characteristics of the newscast. Indeed, if the researcher were to operationalize the tone of the coverage on a scale of 1 (very negative) to 5 (very positive), the judgments called for become more finely distinct, and agreement, and therefore reliability, may be compromised. On the other hand, that type of detailed measure enhances validity because it acknowledges that news stories can present degrees of positivity or negativity that are meaningful and potentially important with respect to how audiences actually respond to the stories.

The straightforward, readily observed, overt types of content for which coders use denotative meanings to make coding decisions are called "manifest" content. The types of content that require what Holsti in 1969 referred to as "reading between the lines," or making inferences or judgments based on connotative meanings, are referred to as "latent" content. The former maximizes reliability and the latter maximizes validity. Although scholars using the method have disagreed about the best way to proceed, many suggest that it is useful to investigate both types of content and to balance their presence in a coding scheme. Coders must be trained especially well for making decisions based on latent meaning, however, so that coding decisions remain consistent within and between coders.

Analyzing and Interpreting Content Data

Statistical Analyses

Just as content analysis is best thought of as a summary of content, statistical analysis of content analytic results performs a further summary of the data gathered. The numerical values that resulted from the assignment of content to categories (or the "counts" used for ratio-level measures) are now subjected to statistical procedures to reduce the data into descriptive statistics and to investigate relationships between variables. Descriptive statistics report on the properties of the data, including the means and standard deviations of interval- and ratio-level variables and the frequencies of nominal-level variables. For instance, a study of the advertising appeals used in prime-time television commercials may report nominal-level data in the types of commercials for particular product categories that appeared in the sample (e.g., the "frequencies" of ads about cars, retail outlets, or health and beauty products). The same study may use an additional summarizing descriptive statistic to report the mean (or average) number of 30-second ads in the sample, as well as the standard deviation, which shows how widely (or narrowly) dispersed the individual values were that were used to calculate the mean.

In order to investigate variables in relationship to one another, and, therefore, to test hypotheses, bivariate (two variables) or multivariate (more than two variables) statistics are used. A full discussion of statistical analysis is well beyond the scope here, but one example is provided and a number of other commonly used tests are briefly discussed. Consider a hypothesis that predicted that male television characters, compared to female characters, would perform more physically aggressive acts. The relationship to be tested has a nominal-level measure as an independent variable (gender) and a ratio-level measure as a dependent measure (number of acts of physical aggression). The researcher would employ an independent t-test to determine mathematically whether a significant gender difference in acts of physical aggression had been found. In other research scenarios, correlations are used to look for associations between two continuous measures, analysis of variance is used to examine differences among three or more groups, and chi square is used to examine relationships between nominal-level variables.

Discussing Results

After performing statistical analyses of the data, the researcher is poised to make more general conclusions about the study and what it has discovered about the nature of television content. Limitations to the research are acknowledged when discussing the implications of the study, and connections are made to past research to determine how the new data support or refute and replicate or extend prior findings. If the motivation for the study was concern for the possible impact of watching the content that was analyzed, for children or for general audiences, then speculation and/or theoretically grounded claims about the potential effects of the content explored would be advanced.

Two particular research traditions have artfully combined content analysis research and "effects" research to determine affiliations between television messages and the thoughts or attitudes of its audiences. Agenda-setting theory, originally introduced by Max McCombs and Donald Shaw in 1972, compares topics included in news media content with the topics listed by members of the public as the most important problems facing society. Cultivation theory, initially proposed by George Gerbner in 1969, draws a link between the pervasiveness of violence on television and the perception among viewers who spend a great deal of time watching television that the world is a mean and dangerous place. Regardless of whether content findings are associated with factors pertaining to either media production and distribution processes or influence on audience members, studies of television content are immensely interesting and important. Television is a vital and pervasive part of contemporary culture, and researchers involved in documenting its patterns of content assist in furthering understanding of this highly popular medium.

See Also the Following Articles

Communication • Reliability Assessment • Validity, Data Sources

Further Reading

Berelson, B. R. (1952). *Content Analysis in Communication Research*. The Free Press, New York.

Gerbner, G. (1969). Toward "cultural indicators": The analysis of mass mediated message systems. *Audio-Vis. Commun. Rev.* **17,** 137–148.

Head, S. W. (1954). Content analysis of television drama programs. *Q. J. Film Radio Television* **9**(2), 175–194.

Holsti, O. R. (1969). *Content Analysis for the Social Sciences and Humanities.* Addison-Wesley, Reading, Massachusetts.

Kerlinger, F. N. (1973). *Foundations of Behavioral Research*, 2nd Ed. Holt, Rinehart and Winston, New York.

Krippendorff, K. (1980). *Content Analysis: An Introduction to Its Methodology.* Sage, Beverly Hills, California.

McCombs, M. E., and Shaw, D. L. (1972). The agenda-setting function of mass media. *Public Opin. Q.* **36,** 176–187.

Neuendorf, K. A. (2002). *The Content Analysis Guidebook.* Sage, Thousand Oaks, California.

Riffe, D., Lacy, S., and Fico, F. G. (1998). *Analyzing Media Messages: Using Quantitative Content Analysis in Research.* Lawrence Erlbaum, Mahwah, New Jersey.

Smythe, D. W. (1954). Reality as presented by television. *Public Opin. Q.* **18**(2), 143–156.

Content Validity

Doris McGartland Rubio
University of Pittsburgh, Pittsburgh, Pennsylvania, USA

Glossary

construct validity The extent to which an item or measure accurately represents the proposed construct.

content validity The extent to which items from measure are sampled from a particular content area or domain.

content validity index A quantitative assessment of the degree to which the item or measure is content valid by an evaluation of a panel of experts.

criterion validity The extent to which an item or measure predicts a global standard.

face validity The extent to which a measure appears to be valid.

factor The domains or categories to which a measure's individual items can be assigned.

factorial validity The extent to which the measure maintains the theoretical factor structure as assessed by factor analysis.

factorial validity index A quantitative assessment of the degree to which the factor structure hypothesized by the researcher is supported by an evaluation of the measure by a panel of experts.

interrater agreement The degree to which raters agree when evaluating something.

logical validity The extent to which a measure is deemed by a panel of experts to contain content validity.

validity The extent to which an item or measure accurately assesses what it is intended to measure.

Social science researchers often develop instruments to measure complex constructs. Before they can make conclusions based on the measure, the measure must be shown to have adequate validity. Content validity is a critical first step in the measurement process, given that most research in the social sciences involves constructs that are difficult to measure. This article discusses content validity and presents a methodology for assessing the content validity of a measure, which includes using a panel of experts to evaluate the measure. Specific techniques are demonstrated and how to calculate different indices are illustrated. These indices include a content validity index, an interrater agreement, and a factorial validity index. When an acceptable level of content validity is reached, additional psychometric testing of the measure can begin.

Introduction

Social science researchers often develop instruments to measure complex constructs. Before they can make conclusions based on the measure, the measure must be shown to have adequate validity. Validity assesses the extent to which an instrument measures the intended construct. Although all validity contributes to the construct validity of a measure, validity can be compartmentalized into three types: content, criterion-related, and construct validity.

Content validity is a critical part of measurement, given that most research in the social sciences involves constructs that are difficult to measure. Due to the complexity of constructs, single indicator items are not sufficient to measure these constructs. Rather, multiple items are needed to approximate the construct. As a result, the content validity of a construct becomes paramount to ensure that the items used in the measure all come from the same domain. Content validity is the first step in evaluating the validity of the measure. Although this subjective form of validity relies on people's perceptions, it can also be objectified with a rigorous content validity study. Such a study can inform the researcher how representative of the content domain the items are and how clear the items are, as well as providing an initial assessment of the factorial validity of the measure. Assessing validity is a never-ending process; however, the process can be advanced with the use of a content validity study.

Definitions of Validity

Traditionally, validity has been conceived as consisting of three types: content, criterion-related, and construct. Content validity generally refers to the extent to which items in a measure all come from the same content domain. Criterion-related validity indicates the extent to which the measure predicts a criterion or gold standard. Construct validity is the highest form of validity because it subsumes the other types. When we are concerned about whether the measure is measuring what it is suppose to be measuring, we are concerned with construct validity. Construct validity can be assessed by examining the measure's factorial validity, known-groups validity, and/or convergent and discriminant validity. Some would argue that construct validity is the only type of validity to which we should be referring. The differences are only in the ways of testing for validity; all the ways of testing contribute to a measure's construct validity.

Types of Content Validity

The assessment of content validity is subjective. That is, content validity relies on people's judgments of the extent to which the item and/or measure is content valid. Two methods for assessing content validity exist: face validity and logical validity. Face validity is the less rigorous method because the only process involved is reviewing the measure and making the determination of content validity is based on the face of the measure. Logical validity is a more methodical way of assessing the content validity of a measure. This type of content validity entails having a panel of experts review the measure on specific criteria. This article focuses on this second method for assessing content validity.

Ways of Testing for Content Validity

When conducting a content validity study, the researcher must follow several specific steps. These steps are germane to a content validity study and are discussed in detail next.

Devising the Content Validity Assessment

The first step in a content validity study is to develop the instrument (i.e., operationalizing the construct). Two instruments need to be developed. First, the measure of the construct must be created. This is the measure for which the content validity study is being undertaken. Second, the researcher must design the assessment tool for the content validity study. This assessment tool is the instrument that is used to assess the content validity of the measure. How to create a new measure is beyond the scope of this paper. Here we discuss the development of the assessment tool.

The assessment tool measures the representativeness and clarity of each item on a scale of 1 to 4, with 1 indicating that the item is not representative (or clear) and 4 signifying that the item is representative (or clear). For the overall measure, the tool evaluates the initial factorial validity of the measure (if more than one factor is hypothesized) as well as the comprehensiveness of the measure. The factorial validity index indicates the extent to which the factor structure as hypothesized by the creator of the measure is supported. The factors are listed for the measure. For each item, the correct factor must be identified. An example of the measure can be seen in Table I.

Selecting a Panel

Who Makes up the Panel?

In looking for a panel of experts, the researcher should consider two different populations: content experts in the field and lay experts. Content experts are people who have published in the area or who have considerable experience in working in the field. Lay experts are the people for whom the measure is being developed. For example, if the content validity for a measure of depression is to be assessed, two groups of experts should participate in the evaluation: (1) people who have published in the field and who work with people who are depressed (e.g., social workers) and (2) people who are depressed.

Sample Size

The literature is diverse with respect to the number of experts required. Some publications suggest as few as two experts, whereas others have recommended as many of 20 experts. The most consistent recommendation is to have at least three experts from each group for a minimum sample size of six. Twenty experts (10 from each group) should be the maximum sample size. More information is obtained when a larger number of experts are used.

Selection Criteria

When selecting the panel of experts, specific criteria should be used. That is, common qualifications should be present for the experts. For example, for content experts, the number of publications or the number of years of experience in the field could be the criterion. For the lay experts, how long the person has been a member of the population could serve as the criterion. That is, it is important in choosing both types of experts to take into consideration the length of time the person has experienced the construct being measured.

Table I Content Validity Assessment Form[a]

INSTRUCTIONS: This measure is designed to evaluate the content validity of a measure. In order to do that, please rate each item as follows.

- **Please rate the level of representativeness on a scale of 1–4, with 4 being the most representative. Space is provided for you to make comments on the item or to suggest revisions.**
- **Please indicate the level of clarity for each item, also on a four-point scale. Again, please make comments in the space provided.**
- **Please indicate to which factor the item belongs. The factors are listed along with a definition of each. If you do not think the item belongs with any factor specified, please circle 3 and write in a factor may be more suitable.**
- **Finally, evaluate the comprehensiveness of the entire measure by indicating if any items should be deleted or added. Thank you for your time.**

Theoretical definition	*Representativeness*	*Clarity*	*Factors*
Specify the construct measured and provide a definition	1 = item is *not representative*	1 = item is not clear	List and number the factors and provide a definition of each
	2 = item needs *major revisions* to be representative	2 = item needs major revisions to be clear	1 = factor
	3 = item needs *minor revisions* to be representative	3 = item needs minor revisions to be clear	2 = factor
	4 = item is *representative*	4 = item is clear	3 = other, specify
1. Item 1	1 2 3 4 Comments:	1 2 3 4 Comments:	1 2 3 Comments:
2. Item 2	1 2 3 4 Comments:	1 2 3 4 Comments:	1 2 3 4 Comments:

Analyzing Results (Item Level and Measure)

Interrater Agreement

Interrater agreement (IRA) can be calculated for the individual items and for the entire measure. The IRA is calculated for the representativeness of the item and measure and for the clarity of the item and measure. That is, two IRAs are calculated for each item, one for representativeness and one for clarity.

When calculating the IRA for the items, we examine the percentage of agreement among the raters. The response categories are dichotomized by combining responses 1 and 2 of the four-point scale together; likewise, 3 and 4 are combined. This creates dichotomous responses, that is, two-level variables. For example, suppose 10 raters evaluate a measure of depression. Of these 10 raters, eight agree that the first item is either not representative or clear (response 1) or that the item needs major revisions (response 2). The IRA for that item is then 0.80.

Two IRAs are also calculated for the entire measure: one for representativeness and one for clarity. To calculate the IRA for the entire measure for each domain of representativeness and clarity, the IRA needs first to be computed for each item. Following that, the average is calculated across all of the items, generating an IRA for the measure for each domain (representativeness and clarity).

Content Validity Index

The content validity index (CVI) can be calculated for each item and for the entire measure. Unlike the IRA, the CVI is only calculated for the representativeness of the items and measure. When calculating the CVI for each item, the response categories are also combined. The CVI is calculated for the item by counting the number of experts who rate the item 3 (needs minor revisions) or 4 (representative). In our example of 10 raters, where eight score the item as 1 or 2, the CVI for that item is 0.20.

The calculation of the CVI for the entire measure is similar to that of the IRA. The average is computed across all of the items, generating a CVI for the measure. A CVI of 0.80 for the measure is desired in order to consider the measure to have adequate content validity.

Factorial Validity Index

A factorial validity index (FVI) can be calculated for the entire measure. This index represents the extent to which raters are able to correctly assign the item to the respective factor. Two steps are involved when calculating the

FVI. First, the number of raters who correctly classify an item is divided by the total number of experts for that item. Second, the average is computed in order to obtain the FVI for the measure. Generally, a FVI of 0.80 is considered acceptable.

Interpreting the Results and Revising the Measure

Once the indices are computed, the information is used to modify the measure. All items should be evaluated, even if acceptable indices are obtained. However, if the overall indices for the measure are not acceptable (i.e., not at least 0.80), then the item-level information needs to be carefully examined and revisions will be necessary. The IRA for representativeness and clarity as well as the CVI and FVI are compared. The benefit of using a four-point scale is realized at this level. If the IRA is high but the CVI and FVI are low, this indicates that the item may not be acceptable. However, if the IRA is low but the CVI and FVI show some promise, the four-point scale needs to be consulted in order to determine where the discrepancies lie. This result could be a manifestation of the degree of revision needed in the item. A correction of the wording could significantly enhance the content validity of an item.

Consulting with the Panel

The panel may need to be contacted several times in order to improve the CVI of the measure. Specific panel experts might be contacted for clarification of their comments. However, if significant revisions are made to the measure, it is recommended that the entire panel of experts be consulted and that the measure be reviewed again. We may choose to conduct another content validity study in order to assess the current IRA, CVI, and FVI. For this reason, a confidential study is preferred over an anonymous study so that the original raters can be consulted as many times as necessary.

Next Steps

When the researcher is satisfied with the CVI of the measure, the next steps for the measure involve pilot testing and further psychometric testing. Different types of reliability and validity need to be assessed before the measure is used in a decision study or a study that is testing a particular theory. The measure should always be evaluated and tested prior to testing any theory. No generalizations can be made regarding the measure until we are confident that our measure accurately and consistently measures the construct of interest.

Conclusion

Testing the validity of a measure is a never-ending process. Conducting a content validity study is the first step in that process. Although content validity is a subjective form of validity, assessing content validity with a panel of experts who evaluate the measure on objective criteria enables the researcher to make significant improvements to the measure prior to pilot testing the instrument. Information can be gleaned from a content validity study that would not necessarily be realized from other forms of psychometric testing. For example, administering the measure to 200 subjects in order to assess the internal consistency and factorial validity would not provide any indication of how items could be revised in order to improve the validity of the individual items. With the exception of item response theory and structural equation modeling, most psychometric testing does not evaluate measures on an item-level analysis. A content validity study provides information on the individual items of the measure in regards to how representative and clear each item is. Raters can provide comments on each item for the researcher by offering suggestions on how the item can be revised to improve its content validity. In addition, information is obtained on the performance of the overall measure in terms of the measure's level of content validity and an initial assessment of the measure's factorial validity.

See Also the Following Articles

Organizational Behavior • Validity Assessment • Validity, Data Sources

Further Reading

Anastasi, A., and Urbina, S. (1997). *Psychological Testing,* 7th Ed. Prentice Hall, Upper Saddle River, NJ.

Davis, L. (1992). Instrument review: Getting the most from your panel of experts. *Appl. Nurs. Res.* **5,** 194–197.

Grant, J. S., and Davis, L. L. (1997). Selection and use of content experts for instrument development. *Res. Nurs. Health* **20,** 269–274.

Hubley, A. M., and Zumbo, B. D. (1996). A dialectic on validity: Where we have been and where we are going. *J. Gen. Psychol.* **123,** 207–215.

Lynn, M. (1986). Determination and quantification of content validity. *Nurs. Res.* **35,** 382–385.

Messick, S. (1989). Validity. In *Educational Measurement* (R. L. Linn, ed.), 3rd Ed., pp. 13–103. Macmillan, New York.

Nunnally, J. C., and Bernstein, I. H. (1994). *Psychometric Theory,* 3rd Ed. McGraw-Hill, New York.

Rubio, D. M., Berg-Weger, M., Tebb, S. S., Lee, E. S., and Rauch, S. (2003). Objectifying content validity: Conducting a content validity study in social work research. *J. Soc. Work Res.* **27,** 94–104.

Shepard, L. A. (1994). Evaluating test validity. *Rev. Res. Educ.* **19,** 405–450.

Contingency Tables and Log-Linear Models

Stephen E. Fienberg
Carnegie Mellon University, Pittsburgh, Pennsylvania, USA

Glossary

chi-square tests Goodness-of-fit tests designed to test the overall fit of a model to the data by comparing the observed counts in a table with the estimated expected counts associated with some parametric model; these tests involve the computation of test statistics that are referred to a chi-square distribution with a suitable number of degrees of freedom.

contingency table A cross-classified table of counts according to two or more categorical variables.

degrees of freedom Associated with a log-linear model is the number of independent parameters in a saturated model that are set equal to zero; the degrees of freedom are used as part of chi-square goodness-of-fit tests.

logit model (linear logistic model) A statistical model for the log-odds of an outcome variable associated with a contingency table as a linear function of parameters associated with explanatory variables; logit models can be given log-linear model representations.

log-linear model A statistical model for the expected counts in a contingency table, which is a linear function of parameters that measure the dependence among the underlying variables; log-linear models include models of mutual, conditional, and joint independence.

maximum likelihood A method of statistical estimation that provides efficient estimates of parameters in a model in a wide variety of circumstances.

minimal sufficient statistics Succinct data summaries associated with a parametric model; they can be used in lieu of the original data for estimation purposes. For log-linear models associated with contingency tables, these statistics are marginal totals.

multiple systems (multiple-recapture) estimation A method for combining information from two or more sources to estimate a population total, including an estimate for the number of individuals missed by all sources.

saturated model A fully-parameterized model that describes the data in a contingency table perfectly.

The analysis of contingency tables has played a central role in the evolution of statistical methodology in the 20th century. Prominent in this literature is the role of log-linear models and related methods, especially as they emerged in the 1970s. This article provides an introduction to the analysis of contingency table data using log-linear models and a discussion of selected recent developments of special interest to social scientists.

Introduction and Historical Remarks on Contingency Table Analysis

A contingency table consists of a collection of cells containing counts (e.g., of people, establishments, or objects, such as events). The cells are most often organized in the form or cross-classifications corresponding to underlying categorical variables. Contingency tables come in a variety of shapes and sizes, and their entries can be generated by a variety of different sampling models. These tables get their name from the early work of Karl Pearson, who was interested in the association between two variables, X and Y; Pearson set out to measure the contingency of Y on X by analogy with regression and correlation for continuous random variables. In the social sciences today, researchers are often interested in understanding the interrelationships among multiple categorical variables (arising, for example, in the context of sample surveys of individuals or households) and the changes among these relationships over time. Such relationships can often be represented as parameters in log-linear or logistic models.

Contingency table analysis is rooted in work at the beginning of the 20th century; George Udny Yule first introduced the cross-product ratio (or odds ratio) as a formal statistical tool. The subsequent contributions by R. A. Fisher linked the Pearson and Yule methods to basic statistical methodology and theory, but it was not until 1935 that Maurice Bartlett, as a result of a suggestion by Fisher, utilized Yule's cross-product ratio to define the notion of second-order interaction in a $2 \times 2 \times 2$ table and to develop an appropriate test for the absence of such an interaction. The multivariate generalizations of Bartlett's work form the basis of the log-linear model approach to contingency tables. Key papers in the 1960s and early 1970s, plus the availability of high-speed computers, led to an integrated theory and methodology for the analysis of contingency tables based on log-linear models, culminating in a series of books published in the 1970s. Notable contributors to this literature included Martin Birch, Yvonne Bishop, John Darroch, Leo Goodman, and Shelby Haberman.

Many statisticians and econometricians view the theory and methods of log-linear models for contingency tables as a special case of either exponential family theory or generalized linear models (GLMs). It is true that computer programs for GLMs often provide convenient and relatively efficient ways of implementing basic estimation and goodness-of-fit assessment. However, adopting such a GLM approach leads the researcher to ignore the special features of log-linear models relating to interpretation in terms of cross-product ratios and their generalizations, crucial aspects of estimability and existence associated with patterns of zero cells, and the many innovative representations that flow naturally from the basic results linking sampling schemes that can be found in books focusing primarily on the log-linear model forms.

Two-Way Tables

Table I contains a summary of University of California (Berkeley) graduate admissions data in 1973 for the six largest programs; it is essentially this information that has been used to argue that graduate admissions have been biased against women. Overall, for the six programs, 44.5% of male applicants but only 20.5% of female applicants were actually admitted to graduate school. Is this evidence of sex discrimination? Those who compiled the data in Table I argued that it is such evidence and they presented a standard chi-square test of independence to support their claims: $X^2 = 266.0$ with 1 degree of freedom (df), corresponding to a p-value $<<0.0001$. A similar conclusion appeared to hold for all 101 graduate programs.

Table II contains one version of a classical data set on social mobility in Great Britain; the data were collected by the demographer David Glass and have been analyzed by countless others. As has often been remarked by those who have analyzed these data, there is clear evidence of dependence on the status of father and son, as evidenced especially by the large counts on the diagonal of the table, and in the diagonally adjacent cells. This can be seen in a standard chi-square test of independence: $X^2 = 1199.4$ with 16 df, corresponding to a p-value $<<0.0001$. There is an extensive sociological literature on the analysis of such mobility tables using log-linear models and extensions to them that take into account the ordinal structure of the status variables.

Table I 1973 Berkeley Admissions Data for the Six Largest Programs

	Gender		
Applicants	*Men*	*Women*	*Total*
Admitted	1198	354	1552
Refused	1493	1372	2865
Total	2691	1726	4417

From Bickel *et al.* (1975).

Table II Glass Data on Social Mobility in Great Britain[a]

	Son's status				
Father's status	*1*	*2*	*3*	*4*	*5*
1 (high)	50	45	8	18	8
2	28	174	84	154	55
3	11	78	110	223	96
4	14	150	185	714	447
5 (low)	0	42	72	320	411

[a] Reported in Bishop *et al.* (1975).

The examples demonstrated in Tables I and II both rely on the well-known chi-square test for independence, which is found in virtually every introductory statistical textbook. In the first example, the comparison of two proportions was translated into a test for independence, the approach that seemed appropriate for the second example. It is actually possible to consider the models for the two situations together in common notation. For example, denote the observed count for the (i, j) cell by x_{ij} and the totals for the ith row and jth column by x_{i+} and x_{+j}, respectively. The expected value of x_{ij} (viewed as a random variable) is m_{ij}, and under the model of independence,

$$m_{ij} = \frac{m_{i+}m_{+j}}{N}, \tag{1}$$

where m_{i+} and m_{+j} are the totals for the ith row and jth column, respectively, and $N = \sum_{ij} x_{ij}$ is the total count in the table. The estimate of the expected value takes the form $\hat{m}_{ij} = x_{i+}x_{+j}/N$. Then the chi-square statistic is

$$X^2 = \sum_{ij} \frac{(x_{ij} - \hat{m}_{ij})^2}{\hat{m}_{ij}} = \sum_{ij} \frac{\left[(x_{ij} - x_{i+}x_{+j}/N)^2\right]}{(x_{i+}x_{+j}/N)}, \tag{2}$$

and the degrees of freedom are

$$\text{df} = (I-1)(J-1). \tag{3}$$

Equation (2) was used to calculate the previously reported chi-square values; the p-values come from referring the X^2 values to a chi-square distribution on the degrees of freedom in Eq. (3).

By taking logarithms of the expected value m_{ij} under independence, one can reexpress the model of independence in Eq. (1) as an additive model:

$$\log m_{ij} = u + u_{1(i)} + u_{2(j)}, \tag{4}$$

with suitable constraints on the subscripted u terms, e.g.,

$$\sum_i u_{1(i)} = \sum_j u_{1(j)} = 0. \tag{5}$$

Dependence between the row and column variables is represented by adding terms of the form $u_{12(ij)}$ (with constraints that they sum to zero across either rows or columns) to

$$\log m_{ij} = u + u_{1(i)} + u_{2(j)} + u_{12(ij)}. \tag{6}$$

Thus, there is a close similarity between this log-linear model notation and notation suitable for the analysis-of-variance or generalized linear models.

Three-Way Tables

Table I reported admissions to the six largest graduate programs at the University of California at Berkeley in 1973. Table III shows these data disaggregated by program (labeled A through E). Note that women were admitted at higher rates than men were in four of the six programs! Separate chi-square tests applied separately to each program suggest that independence is a reasonable model to characterize the admissions process, except for program A, for which the bias appears to be toward women rather than against them. Thus there appears to be little or no evidence of sex discrimination once one introduces the explanatory variable program and looks at the relationship between gender and admissions status conditional on it. A relevant overall model for this three-way table would thus be that admissions status is independent of gender or conditional on program. This is the first example of a log-linear model for three-way contingency tables.

Table III 1973 Berkely Admissions Data Disaggregated for the Six Largest Programs

	Men		*Women*	
Program	*Admitted*	*Refused*	*Admitted*	*Refused*
A	512	313	89	19
B	353	207	17	8
C	120	205	202	391
D	138	279	131	244
E	53	138	94	299
F	22	351	24	317

From Bickel *et al.* (1975)

Table IV Substance Usage for High School Seniors[a]

		Marijuana use	
Alcohol use	*Cigarette use*	*Yes*	*No*
Yes	Yes	911	538
	No	44	456
No	Yes	3	43
	No	2	279

[a] From Agresti (2002).

The data from a survey of 2276 high school seniors from a Dayton Ohio suburb, regarding use of alcohol (A), cigarettes (C), and marijuana (M), are displayed in Table IV as a $2 \times 2 \times 2$ contingency table. Exploring the dependencies among the usage of the three substances requires introduction of the notation for, and ideas behind, log-linear models in three dimensions. Let x_{ijk} be the count for the (i, j, k) cell in an $I \times J \times K$ table, where $\sum_{ijk} x_{ijk} = N$, and let m_{ijk} denote the expected value of the count for this cell. The following model generalizes that in Eq. (6):

$$\log m_{ijk} = u + u_{1(i)} + u_{2(j)} + u_{3(k)} + u_{12(ij)} + u_{13(ik)} + u_{23(jk)} + u_{123(ijk)}, \tag{7}$$

where the subscripted u-terms sum to zero over each subscript, as previously. Various special cases of the log-linear model result from setting different combinations of u-terms equal to zero, in a hierarchical fashion, e.g., setting $u_{12(ij)} = 0$ for all i and j implies that $u_{123(ijk)} = 0$ for all i, j, and k. Table V lists these models and their degrees of freedom, and interpretations of the models. The shorthand notation for referring to these models corresponds to the highest order u-terms in the model.

Sampling Models and Basic Log-Linear Model Theory

There are two standard sampling models for the observed counts in contingency tables. In the multinomial model,

Table V Log-Linear models for Three-Way Tables and Their Degrees of Freedom

Shorthand notation	*Log-linear models*	*Degrees of freedom*	*Interpretation*
[1][2][3]	$u + u_{1(i)} + u_{2(j)} + u_{3(k)}$	$IJK - I - J - K - 2$	Mutual independence of 1, 2, and 3
[1][23]	$u + u_{1(i)} + u_{2(j)} + u_{3(k)} + u_{23(jk)}$	$(I-1)(JK-1)$	Independence of 1 from 2 and 3 jointly
[2][13]	$u + u_{1(i)} + u_{2(j)} + u_{3(k)} + u_{13(jk)}$	$(J-1)(IK-1)$	Independence of 2 from 1 and 3 jointly
[3][12]	$u + u_{1(i)} + u_{2(j)} + u_{3(k)} + u_{12(ij)}$	$(K-1)(IJ-1)$	Independence of 3 from 1 and 2 jointly
[12][13]	$u + u_{1(i)} + u_{2(j)} + u_{3(k)} + u_{12(ij)} + u_{13(ik)}$	$I(J-1)(K-1)$	Conditional independence of 2 and 3 given 1
[12][23]	$u + u_{1(i)} + u_{2(j)} + u_{3(k)} + u_{12(ij)} + u_{23(jk)}$	$J(I-1)(K-1)$	Conditional independence of 1 and 3 given 2
[13][23]	$u + u_{1(i)} + u_{2(j)} + u_{3(k)} + u_{13(ik)} + u_{23(jk)}$	$K(I-1)(J-1)$	Conditional independence of 1 and 2 given 3
[12][13][23]	$u + u_{1(i)} + u_{2(j)} + u_{3(k)} + u_{12(ij)} + u_{13(ik)} + u_{23(jk)}$	$(I-1)(J-1)(K-1)$	No second-order interaction
[123]	$u + u_{1(i)} + u_{2(j)} + u_{3(k)} + u_{12(ij)} + u_{13(ik)} + u_{23(jk)} + u_{123(ijk)}$	0	Saturated model

the total count, N, fixed and the counts represent the results of a random sample from an infinite population with the underlying cell probabilities $\{m_{ijk}/N\}$. In the product-multinomial model, a marginal total (either one-dimensional or two-dimensional) is treated as fixed, and then the counts adding up to each entry in the fixed margin are taken to come from a multinomial model. As was seen in the two-way table setting, it is possible to analyze data arising from both types of sampling using the same log-linear models and methods. When product multinomial sampling is appropriate, only some of the log-linear models are interpretable, but by taking difference in the logarithmic scale, one can convert the model into what is known as a logit (or linear logistic) model, which incorporates only the interpretable parameters. For example, for the data in Table III, let admissions be variable 1, gender be variable 2, and program be variable 3. If one treats admissions as an outcome variable, the log-linear model for conditional independence of 1 and 2 given 3 is equivalent to a logit model for the log-odds of the outcome variable, which depends only on variable 3:

$$\log(m_{1jk} \mid m_{2jk}) = \log m_{1jk} - \log m_{2jk} = 2[u_{1(1)} + u_{13(1k)}] = w + w_{3(k)}. \quad (8)$$

A more technical description of this equivalence and the linked interpretation of log-linear and logit model parameters can be found in the literature.

Statisticians rely on three key statistical results for the analysis of log-linear models using the method of maximum likelihood (these are presented here in a "nontechnical" form, and the interested reader is referred to the texts listed at the end of this article for more formal versions. First, corresponding to the highest order u-term in the model, there exist succinct data summaries, technically known as minimal sufficient statistics (MSSs). For multinomial sampling, these take the form of marginal totals of the corresponding variables in the table of counts. Thus, for the no-second-order interaction model, the highest order u-term are $\{u_{12(ij)}\}$, $\{u_{13(ik)}\}$, and $\{u_{23(jk)}\}$, and the MSSs are $\{x_{ij+}\}$, $\{x_{i+k}\}$, and $\{x_{+jk}\}$, where a plus sign in the subscripts indicates summation over the corresponding subscript, i.e., the two-way marginal totals for the table of counts. Note that the shorthand notation in Table V indicates that these margins summarize the data. For product-multinomial sampling, the same minimal sufficient statistic representation can be used as long as the fixed marginal totals are included in the list.

The maximum likelihood estimates (MLEs) of the expected cell counts, $\{\hat{m}_{ijk}\}$, are the second type of statistical result; if they exist, they are unique and are found by setting the minimal sufficient statistics equal to their expectations. Conditions for the existence of MLEs are relatively complex unless all cell counts are positive, as they are in Table IV. But MLEs for log-linear models exist in many sparse situations in which a large fraction of the cells have zero counts—indeed, this is one of the virtues of using log-linear models with likelihood methods. For example, for the no-second-order interaction model, the MLEs of must satisfy the following equations:

$$\begin{aligned} \hat{m}_{ij+} &= x_{ij+}, \quad i = 1,2,\ldots,I, \quad \text{and} \quad j = 1,2,\ldots,J, \\ \hat{m}_{i+k} &= x_{i+k}, \quad i = 1,2,\ldots,I, \quad \text{and} \quad k = 1,2,\ldots,K, \\ \hat{m}_{+jk} &= x_{+jk}, \quad j = 1,2,\ldots,J, \quad \text{and} \quad k = 1,2,\ldots,K. \end{aligned} \quad (9)$$

These equations need to be solved by some form of iterative procedure, and these are now standard in most statistical packages. Many computer programs used to fit generalized linear models can also be used for this purpose. For all of the log-linear models for three-way tables other than no second-order interaction, the MLEs have a nice closed form, like those for independence in two-way tables.

The final basic result relates to assessing the fit of log-linear models. This is done using generalization of the Pearson chi-square statistic introduced previously. Let $\hat{m}_{ijk}$ be the MLE of m_{ijk} under a log-linear model. If the model is correct, then both the Pearson and the likelihood ratio goodness-of-fit statistics,

$$X^2 = \sum_{ijk} \frac{(x_{ijk} - \hat{m}_{ijk})^2}{\hat{m}_{ijk}} \tag{10a}$$

and

$$G^2 = 2\sum_{ijk} x_{ijk} \log\left(\frac{x_{ijk}}{\hat{m}_{ijk}}\right), \tag{10b}$$

have an asymptotic chi-square distribution as sample sizes tend to infinity, where the degrees of freedom vary according to the number of parameters in the log-linear model (e.g., see Table V). If the model is not correct, then the distribution of these statistics is stochastically larger than a chi-square distribution. Thus, small values of these statistics are indicators of good fits of the model to the data, i.e., there are relatively small discrepancies between the observed and estimated expected values and these can be attributed to sampling variability alone.

These results can be applied to the substance use data in Table IV. The values of two goodness-of-fit statistics and the corresponding p-values from the relevant chi-square distributions are given in Table VI. Quite clearly, there is only one log-linear model that fits the data well, that of no second-order interaction. This means that the student usage of the three substances, alcohol, cigarettes, and marijuana, exhibits pairwise dependence for the three pair of substances, but no synergistic, second-order dependence.

Table VI Log-Linear Models Fit to Substance Use Data in Table IV

Shorthand notation[a]			*df*	*p-value*
[AC][AM]	497.4	443.8	2	<0.0001
[AC][CM]	92.0	80.8	2	<0.0001
[AM][CM]	187.8	177.6	2	<0.0001
[AC][AM][CM]	0.4	0.4	1	0.54

[a] A, Alcohol; C, cigarettes; M, marijuana.

Higher Way Tables

The class of log-linear models just described for the three-way table generalizes in a direct fashion to four or more dimensions. As long as the log-linear models retain a hierarchical structure (e.g., setting a u term equal to zero implies that all of its higher order relatives must also be zero), the MSSs are sets of marginal totals of the full table, and the maximum-likelihood estimates (MLEs) are found by setting the MSSs equal to their expectations. Further, all independence or conditional independence relationships are representable as log-linear models, and these models have estimated expected values that can be computed directly. There is a somewhat larger class of log-linear models with this direct or decomposable representation. All log-linear models that are not decomposable require an iterative solution of likelihood equations.

In a multiway contingency table, the model that results from setting exactly one two-factor term (and all its higher order relatives) equal to zero is called a partial association model. For example, in four dimensions, setting $u_{12(ij)} = 0$ for all i and j, then the MSSs are $\{x_{i+kl}\}$ and $\{x_{+jkl}\}$, and the resulting partial association model corresponds to the conditional independence of variables 1 and 2 given 3 and 4. The corresponding MLEs for the expected cell frequencies are

$$\hat{m}_{ijkl} = \frac{x_{i+kl}\, x_{+jkl}}{x_{++kl}}, \tag{11}$$

for all i, j, k, and l.

One of the major innovations in log-linear model methods over the past 20 years has been the development of methods associated with a subfamily of log-linear models known as graphical log-linear models. The formulation of graphical models is due originally to John Darroch, Steffen Lauritzen, and T. P. Speed. This approach uses the vertices of a graph to represent variables, and the edges among them to represent relationships. Conditional independence relationships correspond to the absence of edges in such an undirected graph. Models defined solely in terms of such relationships are said to be graphical. For categorical random variables, all graphical models are log-linear. The subfamily of graphical log-linear models includes the class of decomposable models, but not all nondecomposable models are graphical. Various authors have used graphical log-linear models to simplify approaches to model search, and they are intimately related to an extensive literature on collapsibility and estimability of parameters via marginal tables. Although the examples presented in this article have only two or three variables and contain few zero counts, the methods can and have been applied to a broad array of social science data involving as many as 20 dimensions, and where most of the counts are small and a large fraction are zero.

Some Major Innovative Uses of Log-Linear and Related Models in the Social Sciences

Models for Social Networks

Paul Holland and Samuel Leinhardt introduced a log-linear model for representing relationships among individuals in a social network. Their model has a graphical representation, but one that is different from that discussed in the previous section, in that it links individuals instead of variables. Fienberg, Meyer and Wasserman have provided related logistic representations and have shown how to handle social network data and the Holland–Leinhardt model and its extensions in contingency table form using basic log-linear model tools. The past decade has seen renewed attention to social network models because of interest in large systems such as the World Wide Web. Although this work does have probabilistic features, it fails to utilize the interaction among individuals as a major feature.

Latent Trait and Rasch Models

In psychological tests or attitude studies, the interest is often in quantifying the value of an unobservable latent trait, such as mathematical ability or manual dexterity, on a sample of individuals. Although latent traits are not directly measurable, an attempt can be made to assess indirectly a person's value for the latent trait from his/her responses to a set of well-chosen items on a test. The simplest model for doing so was introduced by the Danish statistician Georg Rasch in the 1960s. Given responses for N individuals on k binary random variables, let X denote the $N \times k$ matrix of responses. Then the simple dichotomous Rasch model states that

$$\log\left[\frac{P(X_{ij}=1\mid\theta_i,\alpha_j)}{P(X_{ij}=0\mid\theta_i,\alpha_j)}\right]=\theta_i+\alpha_j, \qquad (12)$$

where θ_i is an individual parameter and α_j is an item parameter. This is simply a logit model for the log odds for $X_{ij}=1$ versus $X_{ij}=0$. The observed data x_{ij} can be recast in the form of an $n \times 2^k$ array, with exactly one observation for each level of the first variable. In social sciences settings, the focus is typically on the item parameters, and the individual parameters capture heterogeneity across subjects. In educational testing settings, the individual parameters are of special interest (the latent trait) and the item parameters are considered as nuisance parameters.

In the 1980s, several authors recognized an important relationship between the Rasch model and log-linear models for the corresponding collapsed 2^k contingency table. For example, Stephen Fienberg and Michael Meyer represented these models in terms of log-linear models of quasi-symmetry, but ignored the moment constraints developed in the work of Noel Cressie and Paul Holland.

Multiple-Recapture Models for Population Estimation

If the members of a population are sampled k different times, the resulting recapture history data can be displayed in the form of a 2^k table with one missing cell, corresponding to those never sampled. Such an array is amenable to log-linear model analysis, the results of which can be used to project a value for the missing cell. In the literature about animal populations, this type of modeling is often referred to as capture–recapture or multiple-recapture analysis, and for human populations, it is sometimes called multiple-systems estimation. Major recent applications of capture–recapture methodology include estimating the undercount in the U.S. decennial census, where $k=2$, and, assessing the extent of human rights violations (e.g., in Kosovo and Peru), using multiple lists. The use of standard log-linear models in this context presumes that capture probabilities are constant across the population. Fienberg, Johnson, and Junker have integrated a variation of the Rasch model into the log-linear framework to allow for special multiplicative forms of heterogeneity and explicity incorporated the Cressie-Holland moment constraints in a Bayesian implementation.

Table VI is drawn from a study of the size of the World Wide Web (WWW) in December, 1997. The investigators submitted a series of a large number of carefully structured queries to six major search engines and then used the resulting information to estimate the number of web pages missed by the search engines. The search engines play the role of lists in multiple-recapture analysis. Table VI provides the results for a single query in the study and gives the six-way cross-classification of uniform resource locators (URLs) returned by the six search engines. Notice that the last cell in the figure contails a question mark, because it corresponds to being missed by all six search engines, and it is the count for this cell that we wish to estimate. The integrated Bayesian log-linear model with heterogeneity has been used to analyze the data from the entire set of 575 queries to estimate the overall size of the WWW in terms of number of pages.

Association Models for Ordinal Variables

Log-linear models as described here ignore any structure linking the categories of variables, yet social science problems often involve variables with ordered categories

Table VI URLs retrieved by six search engines responding to a specific query in December, 1997

			Northern Light							
			Yes				No			
			Lycos				Lycos			
			Yes		No		Yes		No	
			HotBot		HotBot		HotBot		HotBot	
AltaVista	Infoseek	Excite	Yes	No	Yes	No	Yes	No	Yes	No
Yes	Yes	Yes	1	0	2	0	0	0	1	0
		No	2	0	3	2	0	0	0	2
	No	Yes	1	0	2	1	0	0	3	4
		No	1	3	0	8	2	0	3	19
No	Yes	Yes	0	0	0	1	0	0	0	0
		No	0	0	1	1	0	0	5	4
	No	Yes	0	0	0	1	0	0	4	22
		No	0	0	7	17	2	3	31	?

From Dobra and Fienberg (2004).

(e.g., the status variables in the social mobility example discussed previously). Leo Goodman provided a framework for extending standard log-linear models via multiplicative interaction terms of the form:

$$u_{12(ij)} = u^*_{1(i)} u^*_{2(j)} \tag{13}$$

to represent a two-factor u-term. This extended class of models, known as association models, have close parallels with correspondence analysis models, and both classes have been developed and extended by a number of other authors.

Bounds for Cell Entries Given Marginal Totals

The problem of assessing bounds for the entries of contingency tables, given a set of marginals, has a long statistical history, going back over 50 years ago to work done independently by the statisticians Carlo Bonferroni, Maurice Frèchet, and Wassily Hoeffding on bounds for cumulative bivariate distribution functions, given their univariate marginals. This corresponds to bounds for the entries in a 2×2 table. For the more general problem of a k-way contingency table, given a set of possibly overlapping marginal totals, Adrian Dobra and Stephen Fienberg have given explicit bounds in the case when the margins are the minimal sufficient statistics of a decomposable model. They and their collaborators have applied these bounds to the problem of statistical disclosure limitation of confidential data, including data arising from sample surveys. This is an active area of current statistical research.

New Theory and Applications for the Analysis of Categorical Data

Log-linear models for the analysis of contingency tables have played a major role in most of the social sciences of the past three decades. The methods introduced in this article should help the reader to understand some of the potential uses of such model building and analysis. As computer power and storage grow, social science researchers are attempting to work with larger and larger collections of categorical variables, especially in the context of sample surveys. At the moment, applications of the ideas introduced in this article are limited by both the size of the tables involved and their sparseness, especially the presence of large numbers of zero cell counts. New methodological approaches to model selection and the assessment of model fit are required to deal with these applications.

Graphical log-linear models gave new impetus to the developments of log-linear model theory in the 1980s and 1990s, and there were related graphical representations for social network models linking individuals. But these two graphical representations remain unconnected. Elsewhere in multivariate analysis, researchers have exploited the duality between representations in spaces for individuals and for variables. Perhaps these ideas of duality of representations might allow linking the two types of graphical structures into a new mathematical framework.

See Also the Following Articles

Maximum Likelihood Estimation • Probit/Logit and Other Binary Models • Rasch, Georg

Further Reading

Agresti, A. (2002). *Categorical Data Analysis,* 2nd Ed. Wiley, New York.

Bickel, P. J., Hammel, E. A., and O'Connell, J. W. (1975). Sex bias in graduate admissions: Data from Berkeley. *Science* **187**, 398–404.

Bishop, Y. M. M., Fienberg, S. E., and Holland, P. W. (1975). *Discrete Multivariate Analysis: Theory and Practice.* MIT Press, Cambridge, Massachusetts.

Clogg, C. C., and Shidadeh, E. S. (1994). *Statistical Models for Ordinal Variables.* Sage, Thousand Oaks, California.

Cressie, N. E., and Holland, P. W. (1983). Characterizing the manifest probabilities of latent trait models. *Psychometrika* **48,** 129–141.

Dobra, A., and Fienberg, S. E. (2000). Bounds for cell entries in contingency tables given marginal totals and decomposable graphs. *Proc. Natl. Acad. Sci. U.S.A.* **97,** 11885–11892.

Dobra, A., and Fienberg, S. E. (2004). How large is the World Wide Web? In *Web Dynamics* (M. Levene and A. Poulovassalis, eds.), pp. 23–44. Springer-Verlag.

Fienberg, S. E. (1980). *The Analysis of Cross-Classified Categorical Data,* 2nd Ed. MIT Press, Cambridge, Massachusetts.

Fienberg, S. E., and Meyer, M. M. (1983). Loglinear models and categorical data analysis with psychometric and econometric applications. *J. Econometr.* **22,** 191–214.

Fienberg, S. E., Meyer, M. M., and Wasserman, S. S. (1985). Statistical analysis of multiple sociometric relations. *J. Am. Statist. Assoc.* **80,** 51–67.

Fienberg, S. E., Johnson, M. A., and Junker, B. (1999). Classical multi-level and Bayesian approaches to population size estimation using data from multiple lists. *J. Roy. Statist. Soc. (A)* **162,** 383–406.

Goodman, L. A. (1979). Simple models for the analysis of association in cross-classifications having ordered categories. *J. Am. Statist. Assoc.* **74,** 537–552.

Holland, P. W., and Leinhardt, S. (1981). An exponential family of probability distributions for directed graphs (with discussion). *J. Am. Statist. Assoc.* **76,** 33–65.

Lauritzen, S. L. (1996). *Graphical Models.* Oxford University Press, New York.

McCullagh, P., and Nelder, J. A. (1989). *Generalized Linear Models,* 2nd Ed. Chapman and Hall, London.

Whitaker, J. (1990). *Graphical Models in Applied Multivariate Statistics.* Wiley, New York.

Conversation Analysis

Danielle Lavin-Loucks
University of Texas, Dallas, Richardson, Texas, USA

Glossary

adjacency pairs A sequence of two utterances produced by different speakers that are adjacent, where one utterance is designated the first pair part and the utterance it occasions is the second pair part.

ethnomethodology The study of the mundane activities of social life, common-sense knowledge, and methods used by social actors to produce and reproduce social order.

preference structure The notion that utterances are fashioned or designed in such a way that they "prefer" or favor a given type of response. To provide a dispreferred utterance in response requires interactional work, whereas a preferred response is one that is, by design, in line with the prior utterance.

repair A correction or change made by a speaker, a listener, or another participant in a conversation that rectifies, refines, or explains a prior utterance.

utterance A discrete unit of talk produced by a single speaker.

Conversation analysis (hereafter referred to as CA) is the study of the sequential organization of talk as a social action; as such, it offers a uniquely sociological approach to discourse practices. In placing emphasis on the orderliness of everyday verbal interaction, CA advocates the description and careful analysis of mundane interaction and the taken-for-granted activities of social life with the express purpose of uncovering social order. Thus, the study of conversation represents an approach to the problem or phenomenon of order and how order is created, sustained, and oriented to on a microinteractional level. Rather than focusing research efforts on "why" individuals behave and speak as they do, conversation analysts discover order by examining "how" participants go about interacting. With this in mind, an overview of the history, assumptions, and methodology associated with CA is presented, followed by a discussion of the relative benefits and drawbacks of such an approach to interaction.

Introduction

Why Study Conversation?

Talk pervades every aspect of social life. As a fundamental feature of social life, conversation (people talking together) forms the basis through which social identities are created and structural relationships and formal organizations are enacted and perpetuated, or literally talked into existence. Historically, those interested in social interaction and social organization relied on language and talk as a means to conduct sociological research, but gave short shrift to talk as a research topic or likewise a primary locus of social organization. Although linguists have analyzed the structure and function of language, they have not addressed the structure of social interaction or the practical actions that talk embodies, an oversight that neglected a domain of underlying social order.

Ordinary conversation provides an opportunity for studying interaction on its own terms, as opposed to imposing formal structural variables and theoretical precepts onto talk. Furthermore, the study of conversation taps into what Schegloff, in 1987, contended is a primordial site of social order and organization. More than this, for the participants involved in any given instance of interaction, conversation has meaning. Understanding how this meaning is created and altered through discourse furnishes sociologists with a study of interaction that is attentive to the context of interaction, but likewise revelatory of larger patterns of interaction that exist independently of any one instance of interaction. Talk performs actions and interactional meaning can be ascertained through an examination of the sequence of conversation.

Thus, in contrast with top-down stipulative approaches to the phenomenon of social order, the analysis of conversation provides a bottom-up approach to social life that maintains the integrity of interaction while still addressing the larger issue of social order.

Foundations of CA

In the 1960s, Harvey Sacks and Emmanuel Schegloff, and later Gail Jefferson, developed the conversation analytic perspective. However, the researchers did not set out to study language per se; the goal was to develop a new empirical approach to sociology. The quantitative techniques and large-scale grandiose theories that failed to "fit" the data that were characteristic of mainstream social research resonated as problematic with Sacks, Schegloff, and Jefferson. Hence, CA can be viewed as the outcome of a general dissatisfaction with conventional sociology.

Although it is a discourse-based approach to social interaction, CA emerged out of sociological enterprises, not entirely linguistic in nature. CA finds its roots in phenomenology, sociolinguistics, Austin and Searle's speech act theory, Wittgenstein's ordinary language philosophy, Harold Garfinkel's ethnomethodology, and the pioneering work of Erving Goffman. Below, the ethnomethodological foundations of CA as well as the contributions of Erving Goffman are discussed.

Ethnomethodology

The ethnomethodological tradition, formulated by Harold Garfinkel, had a profound impact on the development of the new radical approach to sociology. Fundamentally, Garfinkel's ethnomethodology sought to explain how people do the things they do, thereby illuminating the formal and ordered properties of the taken-for-granted details of social life. Although ethnomethodology concentrated on seemingly mundane features of interaction, it revealed something far more complex: an interaction-based social order. The interest in the mundane and taken-for-granted is mirrored in CA's approach, which takes as its starting point perhaps the most mundane of all activities, conversation.

Potentially even more profound for the development of CA, ethnomethodology endeavored to uncover the common-sense knowledge and background expectancies that allow individuals to interact with one another and make sense of the world around them. For example, Wieder's 1974 ethnomethodological study of the convict code examines deviance in a halfway house and demonstrates how residents invoke a code of conduct to explain their actions and in turn how the code serves as an interpretive framework for such deviance. What Wieder's study substantiated was the very existence of underlying social order, expectancies, and stable properties of interaction that allowed convicts to view their deviance as normal. In other words, there is a shared method or set of procedures for making sense of the world that social actors contribute to and rely on in daily interactions. Mutual understandings, then, arise in and through interaction during the enaction of these procedures and by way of achieving social order.

Goffman

The conversation analytic approach also owes a debt to Goffman's sociology of ordinary action that brought face-to-face interaction into the forefront of sociological inquiry. In examining how individuals present themselves in the ritual of face-to-face interaction, Goffman too looked at practical actions and the taken-for-granted. However, one of the most notable influences of Goffman on the development of CA is the notion of the "interaction order," constituted by the microprocesses of social interaction, which he contended existed independently of the larger social structure. Furthermore, Goffman argued, interaction embodied a social institution unto its own. The interaction order is what CA attempts to formally specify. In doing so, it responds to and radically reformulates Goffman's call for a study of interaction in natural settings.

Despite the obvious links between Goffman and CA, the crux of Goffman's work, specifically that which dealt with talk, relied on analytic formulations or theories that assigned motivations to individuals' utterances and imposed ideal types. An example helps clarify how CA departs from Goffman's approach to the sociology of ordinary action. The notion of "face" Goffman invokes to explain self-presentation assumes that individuals perform talk in such a way that revolves around a concern for maintaining face (an image rooted in socially approved attributes) or selectively presenting themselves. Thus, in this case, a concern for face takes priority over any actual talk. CA does not challenge the importance of face in interaction. However, for CA, face is a concept that, in order to verify its presence, participants in the interaction themselves must display such an orientation or alignment in their utterances. Furthermore, Goffman's reliance on ethnographic observations and detailed notes, as well as metaphors for conversation and contrived examples, stands in stark contrast to conversation analysts' use of ethnographic observations, which appears only secondarily or as a supplement to the analysis.

Methodological and Analytical Strategy

Discovery, Site Selection, and Recording

CA takes, as its starting point, data. Initially, CA investigation requires bracketing exogenous information, abandoning generalized theoretical constructs, and holding at bay preconceived notions of how things are or should rightly be organized in favor of a "neutral" process of inductive discovery. This is not to imply that researchers' interests do not guide the discovery of phenomena, but the process of discerning phenomena of interest is driven primarily by noticings and observations.

Appropriate sites for unearthing phenomena of interest include all instances of "natural" conversation. In other words, CA limits the appropriate types of data used for analysis to nonexperimental, unprovoked conversation, ranging from the everyday telephone exchange to institutional talk, such as discourse in legal trials or exchanges between doctor and patient. Thus, almost any form of verbal interaction that is noncontrived constitutes usable data. The forms of data that conversation analysts use include audio and video recordings of interaction, whether collected by the researcher or already preexisting. Supplemental data, such as observations, interviews, and ethnographic notes, constitute additional resources; however, these are generally used secondarily.

Because CA is a naturalistic science, and phenomena are unearthed using a process of "unmotivated" looking, sampling issues are somewhat different than those encountered in traditional sociological research. After a specific phenomenon has been identified, the CA approach involves gathering and assembling instances of the phenomenon within one conversation, across a number of instances of talk, and/or within varied settings. The unit of analysis or what an "instance" of a phenomenon consists of is partially dependent on the specific phenomenon. The goal is to gather as many specimens from as many different sources as possible. Many of the phenomena that CA considers are new, in the sense that they have not been fully explored or, for that matter, identified. Before the distribution of practices across social interaction can be analyzed, the practices themselves require identification. Thus, the notion of a population, or whether a sample is representative or generalizable, is not necessarily at issue. What is at issue is the endogenous organization of conversational structures, which in some cases can be ascertained with only one instance. Once a phenomenon is identified, analysts can search for instances that fall outside of the given pattern.

Transcription

After a site is selected and a recording obtained, CA research requires repeated examination of video- or audio-recorded talk. Although written transcripts can never replace audio and video recordings, they aid in satisfying the repetitive viewing constraint and additionally serve as a resource for publicly presenting data in written form. Thus, the need for a transcript is based not only on practical concerns (i.e., publishing and presenting data), but also on analytical concerns when used properly in conjunction with recordings.

Developing a detailed transcript entails not only capturing what was said, but also capturing the nuances of how it was said. However, the transcripts produced by CA practitioners are not phonetic transcripts, as is the case with discourse analysis, nor are they glosses or approximations of what participants in an interaction say, as may be the case with nonrecorded participant observation. Instead, CA practitioners write down what is said verbatim, while simultaneously attending to the details of the conversation that are normally "corrected" or omitted from records of talk. In other words, it is not sufficient to rely on accounts of conversational events or a researcher's description of a particular instance of talk; these accounts can unintentionally compromise the integrity of the data. The objective of this sort of approach is to provide as much detail as possible while still allowing a reader unfamiliar with CA access to the data and forthcoming analysis. However, despite the immense detail that goes into a transcript, even CA researchers agree that the transcript that is produced is an artifact and cannot sufficiently capture *all* of the detail that is available on a recording, which is why the focus of analysis remains on the actual recorded data.

The majority of transcripts that CA practitioners produce and rely on in their analyses utilize the transcription system developed by Gail Jefferson. Table I is a partial list of transcribing conventions and includes the most commonly used symbols and their meaning.

The purpose of the detailed notation system is to capture sounds, silences, and the character or details of the talk. As previously mentioned, ordinarily "corrected" phenomena, such as word repetitions, "uhm's," pauses, and mispronunciations, are included in the transcript and treated as important resources for accessing the nuances of conversation. A labeling system similar to the documentation that accompanies ethnographic notes is used to organize detailed transcripts. Traditionally, transcripts supply the name of the speaker(s) or pseudonym(s), the time and date that the recording was made, the date that the conversation was transcribed, the name of the transcriber, and a brief description of the setting in which the conversation occurred.

With the advent of videotaping, new conventions were necessary to capture elements of gaze, body positioning, and nonverbal gestures that were available to the participants in the conversation, but previously unavailable to the researcher. However, despite the increase in the use of videotaped data, the specific notation system used to describe actions and activities other than talk is not systematic, nor is it well developed. Although individual researchers have developed highly specialized conventions that capture the complexity of nonverbal actions,

Table I Transcribing Conventions: Symbols Common to Conversation Analysis

Symbol	*Details*	*Technical meaning*
↑↓	Arrows	Rising or falling pitch within a word or utterance
[	Right bracket	Onset of overlapping speech
]	Left bracket	Termination of overlapping speech
[[	Double brackets	Utterances begin simultaneously
( )	Empty parentheses	Inaudible speech or transcriber/listener unsure
(hello)	Parenthesized word(s)	Uncertain hearings
(( ))	Double parentheses	Transcriber notes of verbal or nonverbal elements
(0.0)	Parenthesized numbers	Pauses (measured to the tenth of a second)
(.)	Parenthesized period	Micro pause (less than 0.1 s)
HELLO	Uppercase	Volume (loudness)
<u>hello</u>	Underline	Stress or emphasis
hel(h)lo	Parenthesized (h)	Breathiness or laughter
°hhh	Raised degree and h's	Inbreath, more h's equivalent to longer breath
hhh	No degree and h's	Outbeath, more h's equivalent to longer breath
hello:::	Colon(s)	Sound stretching, more colons signify longer stretch
hel-	Dash	An abrupt stop or cut-off
hello,	Comma	A continuing level of intonation
hello?	Question mark	Rising intonation
hello.	Period	Falling intonation
hello!	Exclamation point	Animated voice quality
=	Equal sign	Latching utterances or no overlap or pause between turns
°hello°	Raised degree signs	Quieter or softer than surrounding talk
>hello<	Carets	Talk inside carets is slower than surrounding talk
<hello>	Carets	Talk inside carets is faster than surrounding talk
. . .	Ellipsis	Utterance continues beyond segment of transcript
→	Side arrow (left margin)	Calls attention to an utterance for discussion/presentation

Source: Adapted from Sacks, H., Schegloff, E. A., and Jefferson, G. (1974). A simplest systematics for the organization of turn taking for conversation. *Language* **50,** 696–735, with permission.

or in some instances provided still video images to exhibit the movements of speakers, as yet there is no universal system for dealing with the contingencies of video.

Analyzing Talk: Analytical Techniques

Conversation analysts apprehend a sense of order by examining the patterning of stable practices and generic devices present across instances of talk from different data sources, using a single-case analysis, or by examining "deviant cases" representative of conversational anomalies. The method of analysis is dependent on the phenomenon and the type of data. Since the primary mode of analysis proceeds from multiple instances of talk, this is the only technique that is elaborated here. However, single-case analyses and deviant cases often serve as pathways to collecting a corpus of instances or as powerful illustrations of the conversational pattern.

The primary order of business for analysts is the sequence of the conversation. What the analyst strives to generate is a turn-by-turn investigation of the generic conversational devices or discursive patterns in the data. Analyzing an excerpt of talk involves far more than simply summarizing what was said or how it was said. The larger question to be answered is what utterances are "doing" or what action they are performing in the conversation and how these utterances occasion responses. For example, in 1991 Maynard detailed the news delivery sequence in diagnostic consultations between doctors and patients and found a stable sequence or a set of devices whereby doctors and patients collaborate to produce "news." Furthermore, this sequence can be applied to other instances of news-giving in a variety of settings. Thus, analyzing transcripts involves two core elements: (1) uncovering patterns and (2) illuminating the significance of these patterns, on what the utterances are doing.

One way to gain access to the meaning of an utterance and the action it performs is to consider the response it occasions, which in effect can display the coparticipant's understanding of the prior turn of talk. Although portions of the transcript are broken down into smaller units or sequences, and further analyzed as discrete pieces of data, a detailed analysis necessitates a consideration of the local context or package in which the smaller sequences of talk reside. Consider the utterance "where are you going." The lexical meaning of the sentence is relatively clear. It is a question. More specifically, it is a question that requires the recipient to provide a geographic location. However, when other explanations of what this utterance is "doing" are considered and the surrounding talk is examined, it is found that it could be an invitation, a scolding, a greeting, or the solicitation of an invitation. Thus, the meaning of the utterance is dependent on the recipient's response. However, if the recipient misconstrues the utterance's intended meaning, this too can provide another resource for tapping into the meaning of the utterance. What generally ensues after a misunderstanding is a repair, which consequently provides insight into the underlying organization of the talk.

How the designer of an utterance positions and uses his or her talk provides investigators with another way to access meaning and structure. Speakers may use a device repeatedly throughout a conversational exchange. In this case, how it is arranged in relationship to other talk may be of consequence when an analysis is conducted. Although the same word or utterance may perform a variety of functions within the same conversation, the differential positioning and how the utterance is said can also serve as an analytical resource. Finally, devices that are used across multiple conversations by different speakers supply yet another way of accessing how talk is organized and what implications this has for talk as a social action.

Conversation Analysis in Practice

What Underlying Assumptions Inform the Conversation Analytic Approach?

Conversation analysts operate under a number of core assumptions that aid in defining the approach as well as specifying methods for conducting research. The most basic assumption is that talk is organized. Furthermore, talk has an ordered structure, or set of "rules." The original observation of Sacks, one of the founders of CA, helps clarify these presuppositions: individuals take turns speaking in conversation. This simplistic notion provided evidence of one of the most basic universals in conversation and further attested to a structure and logic to conversation. The sheer notion that there was a sustainable order and, furthermore, a turn-taking system consisting of rules made visible a fundamental source for order in conversation.

Although conversation analysts assume the existence of order, it is the participants in an interaction who produce and orient to that orderliness as an internal feature of the interaction or setting. Moreover, the order is generated as a real-time production or attribute of the setting. Order is not an artifact or creation of the analysts' interpretation of a conversation, nor is it derived from *a priori* theoretical models; order is observable and demonstrable as the participants themselves are generating it. It follows that this order is amenable to empirical analysis and formal analytic description. Then, it is the mission of the analyst to discover, describe, and explain the structure and order of conversation as well as attend to the actual meaning of utterances. The meaning of conversation is determined by the sequential positioning of utterances and how they respond to one another. Insofar as participants create and orient to order in conversation as a local constituent feature of that setting, they derive and generate meaning based on the sequential ordering of utterances and common-sense understanding.

Generic Devices in Conversation

Both pure and applied forms of CA aim to produce rules, or generic devices, that participants use in conversation. Although the types of findings that conversation analysts produce are as varied as the settings in which CA research has been conducted, some classic observations reveal a set of generalized conversational devices, which are outlined here. Sacks' lectures on conversation, published posthumously in 1992, defined some preliminary rules of conversation, which were consequently expanded on by numerous researchers. More than simple rules that conversants follow or blindly enact regardless of the social setting, the rules of conversation are both adaptable and at the same time stable. Although only three such devices are examined here, they are representative of the multitude of conversational practices that CA researchers have identified.

One of the most elementary rules of conversation, related to the existence of a regulatory turn-taking system, is that one party speaks at a time. This is not to say that overlap and interruption are uncommon. Yet, overwhelmingly, one party speaks at a time. Turn allocation, or who speaks next, constitutes another stable feature across conversation. Turn allocation can be explicit (as in the case of institutional talk, where speakership rights can be conditionally granted or taken away), implied by the type of utterance produced in the prior turn (as with a question/answer), or selected by the current or next speaker.

A final conversational structure is the adjacency pair. Adjacency pairs, or two contiguous utterances produced by different speakers, involve a first pair part and a second pair part. The first pair part initiates the sequence and the second pair part is elicited by and responds to the initial utterance. Common adjacency pairs include questions and answers, summons and answers, greetings, and closings, among others. Thus, the organization and structure of these utterances are dependent on the order and sequence of the utterance. The design of the first pair part can establish the form and content of the second pair part. However, the initial pair part is not necessarily determinant.

A final, but related concept within CA is preference structure, or the notion that utterances may be structured such that they prefer a certain form of response. Preference structure is not related to the interlocutor's psychological preference or other emotional states, but to the design of an utterance and the turn shape it takes. Consider the following example of an invitation sequence in which Rachael asks Anne whether she is coming to her party (see Table I for transcribing conventions):

1 RA: Yer comin' tuh my party r↑ight
2 (0.4)
3 AN:Hhh uh:::- (0.2)°I don' think I
[ca::n.°I-
4 RA:[↑O::↓h how come
5 (0.2)
6 AN:I got too much tuh do:

In this case, the preferred response is to accept the invitation to the party. In other words, the question is designed such that it prefers acceptance, or a positive "yes" response. As can be seen, to provide the dispreferred "no," and reject the invitation, requires interactional "work." The recipient of the question does not merely say no. Rather, the negative response is marked by a silence, an "uh," and a stop and restart and it is fashioned as a weak disconfirmation. In short, the response is marked by a significant amount of hesitation or interactional work. The recipient can opt to answer in a form that is not aligned with the original utterance. It is in this way that the rules and order in conversation are adaptable. Moreover, the aforementioned devices also demonstrate the sequential implicativeness of a turn of talk. Although repair of an utterance does occur, each turn can be seen as a participant's understanding of the prior turn of talk.

Types of CA

As a burgeoning approach to social interaction, CA evolved into two distinct, yet complementary trajectories, which are only moderately elaborated here. Although both trajectories attended to the phenomenon of order, and both accepted the general assumptions underlying the conversation analytic approach, the means whereby this was achieved and the goal of the analysis revealed fundamentally different approaches to social research. The first strand of CA research maintained its pure focus on structure and sequence in naturally occurring talk, concentrating on everyday conversations between friends, strangers, intimates, etc.

In contrast, the second strand of research efforts focused on the relationship between talk and social structure with the aim of generating more practical applications. Applied CA, which primarily manifested itself in the study of institutional discourse, sought to examine social structure through conversation. As a result, applied CA abandoned the more mundane program of attending to ordinary talk in favor of instances of institutional interaction. However, the institutional character of the setting is not what separated pure and applied CA, as both strands analyze talk in institutional settings. Rather, the attention or importance accorded to membership categories and the institutionality of the interaction served to distinguish the two forms. Applied conversation analysts emphasized how constraints on conversation produced potentially different patterns of interaction. The interaction of talk and social structure or, more accurately, the constitution of social structure through talk thus became the key. Along with this new focus, as the phrase "applied CA" implies, studies of talk and social structure further allowed for more "useful" applications and in some cases policy recommendations for improving communication in medical, legal, and service encounters, among others.

Conclusion: Advantages, Limitations, and Future Directions

Advantages

What is distinct about CA is its approach to the phenomenon of interest. The type of analysis that is produced can formally specify structures of talk, locate endogenous order, and systematically illuminate the patterns that characterize everyday interactions. What is most notable about the conversation analytic approach is its appreciation of and attention to detail. Each detail is treated as an analytical resource. Moreover, it is through the careful analysis of detail that conversation analysts come to an appreciation of how institutions are created, sustained, identified, conveyed, and altered and how relationships are formed through social interaction. Although conversation analysis may seem unsuited to investigations of institutions, it can identify minute details of interaction that comprise large-scale enterprises, as with the justice system or the medical field.

Limitations

The main disadvantage of CA lies in the limitations it imposes on the type of data suitable for analysis: recorded (video or audio) data. Although this constraint guarantees the veracity of the data, it severely limits the scope of examinable phenomena. In addition, some of the language surrounding CA and the related literature is highly specialized and difficult to understand for inexperienced practitioners. Although the transcription system is relatively standardized, it too can appear obscure or difficult and is likewise time-consuming to learn, sometimes giving the impression of a foreign language.

Moreover, just as other social scientific methods are suitable for answering specific types of questions, so too is CA. Researchers interested primarily in the distribution of phenomena, or large-scale macrosociological questions, find that the line-by-line analysis characteristic to CA may not be well suited to their research topic. Likewise, those large-scale macroprocesses that are not linguistically based fall outside of the realm of appropriate topics for CA research.

Future Directions

The initial findings of conversational rules and the structure present in conversation have already been extended into studies of institutional settings and workplace environments including the realms of survey research, human/computer interaction, news interviews, medical and educational settings, and justice system operations. Some researchers have used CA to examine how decisions are made, how news is delivered, how diagnoses are communicated, and how disagreements and arguments are resolved. Although CA here has been presented as a method of analysis, or analytical technique, it can also be characterized as an ideology; CA represents a way of thinking about the world and the interactions that comprise lived social experiences. As a microinteractional approach to order, CA is in its infancy. With the variation in CA research, the potential for extention into the realm of previously ignored social interaction is limitless. Although a great deal of progress has been made in describing the organization of talk, a great deal remains unexplained and unidentified.

See Also the Following Articles

Ethnography • Language Acquisition • Linguistics

Further Reading

Beach, W. A. (1991). Searching for universal features of conversation. *Res. Language Soc. Interact.* **24,** 351–368.

Boden, D. (1990). The world as it happens: Ethnomethodology and conversation analysis. In *Frontiers of Social Theory: The New Synthesis* (G. Ritzer, ed.), pp. 185–213. Columbia University Press, New York.

Clayman, S. E., and Maynard, D. W. (1995). Ethnomethodology and conversation analysis. In *Situated Order: Studies in the Social Organization of Talk and Embodied Activities* (P. ten Have and G. Psathas, eds.), pp. 1–30. University Press of America, Washington, DC.

Drew, P. (1992). Contested evidence in courtroom cross-examination: The case of a trial for rape. In *Talk at Work: Interaction in Institutional Settings* (P. Drew and J. Heritage, eds.), pp. 470–520. Cambridge University Press, Cambridge, UK.

Drew, P., and Holt, E. (1998). Figures of speech: Idiomatic expressions and the management of topic transition In conversation. *Language Soc.* **27,** 495–522.

Heritage, J. (1997). Conversation analysis and institutional talk: Analysing data. In *Qualitative Research: Theory, Method and Practice* (D. Silverman, ed.), pp. 161–182. Sage, London.

Mandelbaum, J. (1990/1991). Beyond mundane reasoning: Conversation analysis and context. *Res. Language Soc. Interact.* **24,** 333–350.

Maynard, D. W. (1997). The news delivery sequence: Bad news and good news in conversational interaction. *Res. Language Soc. Interact.* **30,** 93–130.

Pomerantz, A. M. (1988). Offering a candidate answer: An information seeking strategy. *Commun. Monographs* **55,** 360–373.

Psathas, G. (ed.) (1990). *Interactional Competence.* University Press of America, Washington, DC.

Schegloff, E. A. (1992). The routine as achievement. *Hum. Stud.* **9,** 111–152.

Silverman, D. (1998). *Harvey Sacks: Social Science and Conversation Analysis.* Policy Press, Oxford, UK.

ten Have, P. (1999). *Doing Conversation Analysis: A Practical Guide.* Sage, London.

Whalen, J., and Zimmerman, D. H. (1998). Observations on the display and management of emotion in naturally occurring activities: The case of "hysteria" in calls to 9-1-1. *Soc. Psychol. Quart.* **61,** 141–159.

Correctional Facilities and Known Offenders

Scott Akins
Oregon State University, Oregon, USA

Clayton Mosher
Washington State University, Vancouver, Washington, USA

Glossary

anonymity No identifying information is recorded that could be used to link survey respondents to their responses.

confidentiality Identifying information that could be used to link survey respondents to their responses is available only to designated research personnel, for specific research needs.

lambda (λ) The frequency with which an individual commits offenses.

National Institute of Drug Abuse (NIDA)-5 The five most commonly used illegal drugs: marijuana, cocaine, methamphetamine, opiates, and phencyclidine.

official data Information derived from the normal functioning of the criminal justice process.

probability sample A sample that relies on a random, or chance, selection method so that the probability of selection of population elements is known.

quota sample A nonprobability sample in which elements are selected to ensure that the sample represents certain characteristics in proportion to their prevalence in the population.

response rate The number of individuals participating in a survey, divided by the number selected in the sample.

selective incapacitation A policy that focuses on incarcerating individuals who are believed to be at high risk of reoffending.

self-report data Information obtained by asking people about their criminal behavior.

urinalysis A chemical analysis of a urine sample to determine if an individual has used drugs.

Social scientists frequently use data on prison and jail populations, and data on the characteristics of individuals in such institutions, in order to formulate theories about criminal behavior and the operations of the criminal justice system. Policymakers also utilize such data in order to inform criminal justice policies. Sources of data on correctional facilities and on known offenders include the Bureau of Justice Statistics (for data on prison/jail populations), the Rand studies (for data on inmates in correctional facilities), and the Arrestee Drug Abuse Monitoring Program (ADAM). Although data from each source have strengths and weaknesses, they have provided insights for many social measurement studies of the criminal justice process.

Introduction

The U.S. Department of Justice/Bureau of Justice Statistics (BJS), the Rand Corporation, and the U.S. Department of Justice/National Institute of Justice Arrestee Drug Abuse Monitoring (ADAM) program are sources of data on correctional facilities and known offenders. The BJS collects data that examine federal, state, and local correctional facilities and provides counts of inmates in such facilities; the Rand studies in 1976 and 1978 were inmate surveys of adult prisoners; and the ADAM program involved self-report data on individuals recently arrested and awaiting criminal justice processing. Because these data concerned arrested and/or incarcerated offenders, they suffer from some of the same methodological shortcomings that characterize all official crime data. The criminal justice system can be depicted using the analogy of a funnel as offenders are removed from the system at each stage of processing. Of all offenses committed, only some will come to the attention of the police through the reporting of citizens or police activity. Of all offenses known to the police, only some will result in the arrest of individuals. Only some of those arrested will be prosecuted, and only a fraction of those prosecuted will be convicted. Of those convicted, only a fraction will be incarcerated. Because prison and correctional records represent offenders at the bottom of the criminal justice system funnel, the data are particularly susceptible to biases associated with the exercise of discretion by criminal justice system officials. The data at least partially reflect the biases of police, prosecutors, and judicial officials regarding what types of crimes are particularly threatening and what types of people are most likely to be engaged in criminal acts. Though these data should thus be treated cautiously with respect to measuring and understanding criminal behavior, they provide valuable information on known offenders—a group that is not only hard to reach but also constitutes that segment of the population targeted by criminal justice policy. Thus, data on known offenders provide a vital contribution to our knowledge of crime and to development of policies to deal with crime.

Bureau of Justice Statistics Data on Prisons, Jails, and Inmates

The U.S. Bureau of Justice Statistics collects extensive data at every stage of the criminal justice system. These data and numerous publications based on them are available through the BJS web page (http://www.ojp.usdoj.gov), but the discussion here is limited to the BJS data that focus on correctional institutions and inmates. These data can be grouped in two ways: the first grouping treats the individual federal, state, and local prisons/jails as the unit of analysis, and the second focuses on the inmates incarcerated in such institutions.

Census of Jails

The Census of Jails is conducted by the Bureau of Justice Statistics approximately every 6 years and is supplemented by the more abridged Annual Survey of Jails. The most recent Census of Jails was conducted in 1999, and data have also been collected for the years 1970, 1972, 1978, 1983, 1988, and 1993. The 1999 census included all locally administered jails that detained inmates beyond arraignment (typically 72 hours, thus excluding facilities such as "drunk tanks," which house individuals apprehended for public drunkenness) and that were staffed by municipal or county employees. The 1999 census identified 3084 jail jurisdictions in the United States, and response rates of the institutions to the BJS survey were 90% in 1999 and close to 100% on critical variables such as the total number of inmates, jail capacity, number of inmates under the age of 18, and the number of staff. Data were also collected on additional variables, such as numbers of admissions and releases, overcrowding, health care issues (e.g., HIV, tuberculosis), and programs offering alternatives to incarceration. At midyear 2001, there were 631,240 inmates held in local jails, almost 90% of whom were male. From 1990 to 2001, the number of jail inmates per 100,000 U.S. residents increased from 163 to 222.

Census of State and Federal Correctional Facilities

Nationwide statistics on prisoners were collected by the United States Census Bureau decennially beginning in 1850, and the federal government has published data annually on the prisoner count in each state, the District of Columbia, and the federal prison system since 1925. In addition, the Census of State and Federal Correctional Facilities is conducted by the Bureau of Justice Statistics approximately every 5 years, enumerating all of the state and federal adult correctional facilities in the United States. This census provides detailed information on all correctional facilities, including prisons, prison hospitals, prison farms, boot camps, centers for the reception and classification of offenders, drug treatment facilities, and community-based correctional facilities such as halfway houses and work-release centers. From this census, sampling frames are generated for the surveys of inmates in state and federal correctional facilities. Data have been collected for the years 1973, 1979, 1984, 1990, and 1995 and include information on the types of inmates that are housed in the facilities, the age of the facility, the level of security of the institution, health and safety conditions, inmate programs offered, staff employment, and operating costs.

In addition to this broader and more periodic census, a supplementary count of the number of prisoners in state and federal correctional facilities is conducted every 6 months (June 30 and December 31) by the National Prisoner Statistics program. These data are particularly useful for monitoring issues such as growth in the prison population, prison expenditures, facility overcrowding, and racial disparities in incarceration rates. When combining data from federal and state prisons and local jails, it is estimated that as of December 31, 2001, there were 1,962,220 prisoners in the United States, translating to an incarceration rate of 470 inmates per 100,000 U.S. residents. In the first year in which data on sentenced prisoners were collected (1925), there were 91,669 inmates, representing an incarceration rate of 79 per 100,000 residents. It is also notable that at the end of 2001, there were

3535 sentenced Black male prisoners per 100,000 Black males in the United States, compared to 1177 Hispanic male inmates per 100,000 Hispanic males, and 462 White male inmates per 100,000 white males.

Survey of Inmates of Local Jails

Formerly referred to as the Survey of Jail Inmates, the Survey of Inmates of Local Jails was conducted by the BJS in 1972, 1978, 1983, 1989, and 1996. The surveys provide nationally representative data on persons held in local jails; survey respondents include individuals serving out their sentence in local jails, those awaiting transfer to prison, and those awaiting trial. In the 1996 survey, hour-long personal interviews were conducted with 6133 inmates in 431 jails. Nonresponse was relatively low, with approximately 10% of the inmates selected refusing to participate in the interview process. Questions included those related to demographic characteristics of inmates and those that addressed the inmates' current offense, sentence, and criminal history, the characteristics of their victims, the conditions of their confinement, their family background, and their prior drug and alcohol use and experience with substance-abuse treatment.

Surveys of Inmates in State/Federal Correctional Facilities

The surveys of inmates in state and federal correctional facilities, although separate surveys, are covered together here because they employ the same variables and because the data are often combined into a single data set. The BJS first conducted a survey of state prison inmates in 1974, and data also exist for the years 1979, 1986, 1991, and 1997. The methodology employed in these studies consists of face-to-face interviews with inmates conducted approximately every 5 years, with the most recent survey obtaining a nationally representative sample of more than 14,000 prison inmates in approximately 300 state prisons. The interviews provide information on numerous variables, including the inmates' current offense and sentence, firearms possession, criminal history, gang membership, demographic and personal characteristics, family history, prior drug and alcohol use, experience with treatment programs, and their perceptions of prison conditions.

The Survey of Inmates of Federal Correctional Facilities was first conducted in 1991 and data were collected for a second time in 1997. As mentioned, this survey and the Survey of Inmates of State Correctional Facilities collect data on the same variables. Face-to-face interviews with inmates are also carried out in these studies, with the 1997 study drawing from a probability sample of 4401 federal inmates. For both state and federal surveys, the interview completion rates exceed 90%, and key findings from these surveys are periodically reported by the Bureau of Justice Statistics.

Data on Known Offenders

Data on known offenders provide important information on crime and its correlates. This is due to the fact that self-report surveys that are drawn from the general population (even those that oversample for high-risk groups) are likely to underrepresent offenders. This problem is most pronounced for the most serious and active criminals. Because research has indicated that these relatively rare high-rate offenders are responsible for as much as half of all crime that is committed, data focusing on such offenders are especially useful from both etiological and policy perspectives.

The Rand Inmate Surveys

Perhaps the most widely known surveys of incarcerated offenders are the Rand inmate surveys. Two separate surveys were conducted at different times (1976 and 1978) and were based on different samples. However, the primary intent of both studies was the same: to obtain information about crime by studying the source—that is, known criminal offenders.

Rand I

The Rand studies began with exploratory interviews with 49 California prison inmates who had been convicted of robbery. From these preliminary data, a self-administered survey questionnaire was designed and implemented in the inmate survey, which was conducted with 624 inmates in five California prisons in 1976. Inmates completed anonymous, self-administered questionnaires; their responses provided detailed information on topics such as the crimes they committed prior to their incarceration, their frequency of offending, recidivism rates for arrest and incarceration, and the motivations that led the offender to commit the crimes as measured with social–psychological scales. Additionally, self-reported data on age, race, educational level, marital status, employment, income, and drug use were also obtained. From these data and data obtained from the exploratory interviews, it was concluded that most inmates committed crime relatively infrequently, but within the inmate population there also existed a small portion of inmates who reported offending at very high rates. However, the Rand researchers acknowledged that certain problems existed with their first study. Of greatest concern was the narrow population from which the sample was drawn (only five prisons, all of which were located in California) and the relatively low

(47%) response rate of those contacted. Because each of these problems could compromise the validity of the findings and the ability to generalize to the larger population, researchers at Rand constructed and implemented a second inmate survey in 1978.

Rand II

The second inmate survey conducted by Rand employed judgment, quota, and probability sampling in efforts to make the findings as representative as possible. Inmates were drawn from institutions in California, Michigan, and Texas, and the sample was stratified on the basis of county, age, race, previous prison record, and current conviction offense. Efforts were made to ensure that the samples were representative of a "typical" cohort of inmates, and the offenses for which the inmates were convicted covered a broad range of seriousness. In total, 2190 inmates were drawn from both prison and jail populations from the three states. The survey provided information on the inmates' criminal activity as juveniles, their criminal behavior in the two years prior to their present conviction and incarceration, the frequency of offending for a number of crimes, and past and recent use of drugs and alcohol. Information on the inmates' employment history and their demographic characteristics was also obtained. However, unlike the first Rand survey, respondents were not guaranteed anonymity (only confidentiality), which allowed the researchers to compare the inmates' self-reports of arrests and convictions with their official records to examine potential underreporting of offenses.

The concerns about inmates' underreporting of offenses proved largely unwarranted; a 1982 follow-up study by Rand researchers demonstrated that for most respondents, there were few disparities between the self-reported involvement in crime and the data obtained from official records. However, the lack of anonymity for respondents to the second survey may have contributed to the low response rates seen in some of the samples. Response rates were only 49% for inmates from California and Michigan prisons (only marginally higher than those in the initial Rand survey), but were 66 and 72%, respectively, for jail inmates from these states. In Texas, the response rates were 82% for those in prison, but the more than 300 respondents from jails in that state were excluded from the analyses because, unlike jail inmates in the other two states, they were primarily sentenced offenders awaiting a formal transfer to prison.

Similar to the 1976 Rand inmate survey, the 1978 survey identified some key findings with respect to differences in the frequency of offending (also referred to as "lambda") among inmates. To examine the frequency of offending, researchers for Rand compared the median number of crimes reported by inmates as a whole with the minimum number of crimes reported by the top 10% of inmates (i.e., the number of crimes committed by offenders in the 90th percentile of offending frequency). Their findings indicated wide disparities in offending frequency. For example, with respect to the crime of robbery, half of the active robbers reported robbing someone no more than five times in a given year, but the 10% most active robbers reported committing no fewer than 87 robberies per year. Evidence of a small percentage of highly active offenders was also reported for other types of offenses: for assault, the median number of offenses was 2.40, whereas those in the 90th percentile reported 13; for burglary, the median was 5.45, whereas those in the 90th percentile reported 232; for theft, the median was 8.59, with those in the 90th percentile reporting 425; for forgery and credit card offenses, the median was 4.50, with the 90th percentile reporting 206; for fraud, the median was 5.05, with the 90th percentile reporting 258. For crime in general, excepting drug sales, the median was 14.77 offenses, with those in the 90th percentile reporting 605. These data led researchers to conclude that most people who engage in crime, even those who are incarcerated as a result of committing crime, commit crimes at a relatively low level of frequency. However, some individuals offend so regularly that they can be considered "career criminals."

Replications of the Rand Surveys

Partially as a result of concerns regarding the methodology and low response rates in the second Rand survey, there have been three major follow-ups/replications of Rand II: a reanalysis of the original the 1978 Rand II survey data, a survey of prisoners in Colorado, and a similar survey of incarcerated felons in Nebraska. The first of these studies attempted to address the issue of incomplete or ambiguous survey responses in the Rand data. Focusing on the crimes of robbery and burglary, missing or ambiguous data were coded more conservatively than was done by the original researchers. On recoding and reanalyzing these data, the derived estimates of offending frequency were very similar to the original Rand minimum estimates, although somewhat different from the Rand maximum estimates.

The replication of Rand II in the Colorado survey involved collecting data over a 1-year period between 1988 and 1989; two separate surveys were utilized (a long and a short form). Some respondents were guaranteed anonymity, others were assured of confidentiality. These methodological strategies were used in order to examine whether the use of a particular instrument and/or the different levels of protection affected inmates' response rates. The Colorado study was also the first one of this nature to collect data on female inmates. The overall participation rate of 91% in the Colorado survey was much higher than that in the Rand surveys; this was attributed to three factors—the sample for the Colorado survey was drawn from inmates awaiting processing (with no involvement in other activities), the inmates had only recently received their sentences and were thus less likely to be influenced by peer pressure not to participate, and $5 was credited to each respondent's account for completing the interview.

Similar methodology was employed in the Nebraska inmate survey, which yielded a similarly impressive response rate and reported comparable findings. It is also important to note that although the Nebraska and Colorado replications of Rand II utilized somewhat different methods and produced much higher response rates, the findings of all three studies were quite similar with respect to offending frequency, providing support for the validity of the Rand findings.

Rand data provide an excellent resource for studying known offenders and have been used to examine a wide variety of issues. One application of these data involved the development of an offender typology. In a report entitled *Varieties of Criminal Behavior*, inmates who participated in the Rand surveys were classified into 10 different groups based on the types and combinations of crimes in which they engaged. Among these was a category of violent predators who committed a wide variety of crimes at a very high frequency. It was found that although these offenders perpetrated assaults, robberies and drug offenses at very high rates, they also committed more property crimes (e.g., burglaries and thefts) compared to offenders who specialized in these types of crimes. Partly because of these findings, research on chronic offenders and selective incapacitation was conducted using the Rand data. In one study, it was predicted that targeting highly active violent offenders could simultaneously reduce crime rates and prison populations. A correctional strategy was proposed that minimized the role of incarceration for most offenders, but emphasized long-term incarceration for offenders believed to be likely to commit crimes at a high rate in the future. The selective incapacitation approach was subsequently criticized on both methodological and ethical grounds, though research on it continues today. Of particular concern regarding this research was a proposed predictive scale that was supposedly able to identify chronic offenders; also of concern were questions about whether the prisoners in the Rand sample were characteristic of prisoners in general and the cost and likelihood of a "false positive" if selective incapacitation were put into policy—that is, incapacitating an individual based on the mistaken belief that the individual will commit future crimes.

Rand data have also been employed to investigate offender's beliefs about the financial benefits of crime and the link between drug use and crime. Indeed, such research has found that offenders tended to exaggerate the profits obtained through criminal activity in an effort to justify their current (i.e., incarcerated) situation. Further, other analyses have employed Rand data to examine the relationship between drug use and offending frequency. Results indicate that drug use cannot be said to cause crime, because predatory criminality often occurs before drug use. However, this research also found that the amount of drugs used by an offender is linked to the frequency of their offending, with rates of offending being two or three times higher when the offender is using drugs than when abstaining or in treatment.

In sum, although the Rand surveys may suffer from methodological problems associated with studying inmate populations, replications have produced similar findings, increasing confidence in their conclusions. These data have provided a significant contribution to knowledge and understanding of crime and serve as a standard for collecting and analyzing self-report data from inmates.

Arrestee Drug Abuse Monitoring Data

Another source of self-reported information on known offenders is the Arrestee Drug Abuse Monitoring program. ADAM developed out of the Drug Use Forecasting (DUF) program, which was developed by the National Institute of Justice (NIJ) and implemented in 1987 to provide information about illegal drug use among persons who had been arrested. At that time, DUF was the only source of continuously maintained data on drug use by known offenders, but serious problems with its sampling procedures resulted in the restructuring of the DUF program into the ADAM program in 1997.

As of 2002, 38 sites participated in the ADAM program, providing data on over 30,000 adult male, 10,000 adult female, and 3000 juvenile arrestees. The recent adoption of probability-based sampling by ADAM allows findings to be generalized countywide and also increases confidence in their validity. As with the DUF program that preceded it, the ADAM program uses trained interviewers to administer a structured questionnaire to arrestees within 48 hours of the arrestee arriving in a booking facility, and then collects a urine specimen from the arrestee, enabling verification of the self-reported drug use. Four times each year, research teams from local counties interview arrestees at booking facilities. Interview participation rates are quite high, with the National Institute of Justice reporting that, in most sites, over 80% of arrestees who are approached agree to be interviewed. Among the survey questions, arrestees are asked which drugs they use and how often they use them, their age at first use of each substance, what their housing situation has been in the previous year, how they have supported themselves, whether they have health insurance, and how and where they purchase their drugs. There are also measures addressing the respondents' mental health and any heavy use of alcohol and drugs, which might be useful in developing treatment programs. Basic demographic data on the subjects are also collected.

A key component of the ADAM data is that, following the interview stage, subjects are asked to provide a urine sample voluntarily; the sample can then be used to verify self-reported substance use and to estimate levels of over- or underreporting. The ADAM urinalysis can detect 10 different drugs, but focuses on the so-called National Institute of Drug Abuse (NIDA)-5, or the five most commonly used illegal drugs as identified by NIDA: marijuana, cocaine, methamphetamine, opiates, and phencyclidine (PCP). Essential to the validity of the urinalysis results is the ADAM requirement that arrestees be interviewed within 48 hours of their booking in the facility. This is due to the fact that all of the NIDA-5 drugs that ADAM tests for, with the exception of marijuana (which is detectable in the urine for up to 30 days after use), remain detectable in the urine for no more than 3 days following ingestion. The validity of ADAM data is bolstered by the fact that the vast majority of arrestees who agree to be interviewed also agree to provide a urine sample. In fact, a study recently conducted by ADAM found that most survey sites reported urinalysis completion rates above 85% and that the completion rates ranged from a respectable 79% (in Cleveland) to as high as 96% (in Atlanta, New Orleans, and New York City).

In addition to their ability to assess the validity of self-reported drug use through urinalysis, ADAM data provide invaluable information on the extent of substance use by known offenders. A key finding identified through the use of ADAM data is that a majority of male arrestees used at least one of the NIDA-5 drugs shortly before their arrest, with figures ranging from 50% of arrestees in San Antonio to 77% in Atlanta. ADAM data have also been employed to examine changes in drug use patterns by time and region. Analyses examining change over time have found use to remain relatively stable in most cities in recent years, though some cities have shown significant change. For example, between 1998 and 1999, the percentage of adult male arrestees testing positive for any one of the NIDA-5 drugs dropped 10% in Fort Lauderdale and 8% in Philadelphia. Conversely, over this same time period, the percentage of arrestees testing positive increased by 12% in Atlanta, by 11% in Anchorage, and by 9% in San Jose. Among the female arrestee population, changes were even more pronounced, with use decreasing by 20% in Birmingham and by 11% in Seattle, but increasing by 21% in San Jose and by 13% in Minneapolis.

ADAM data have also been employed to demonstrate that the use of particular substances varies by region and context. For example, a recent ADAM report concluded that arrestees in the western part of the country were frequently found to have used methamphetamine, but its use was relatively rare in the East. Indeed, ADAM findings for adult male arrestees in year 2000 found no one to have tested positive for methamphetamine use in Miami, New York, New Orleans, Philadelphia, Birmingham, Cleveland, and Atlanta. The westernmost site that identified methamphetamine use by an arrestee was Indianapolis, though the rate there was only 1%. Conversely, several cities in the West reported relatively high rates of methamphetamine use among arrestees, including Sacramento (27%), San Diego (25%), San Jose (22%), and Spokane (21%).

Unfortunately, the collection of new data by the ADAM program was discontinued by the NIJ in January 2004. However, existing ADAM data allow investigation into the relationship between substance use, crime, and the life circumstances of arrestees, such as their housing situation, means of financial support; mental health, and level of substance use/abuse. Thus, ADAM data are an excellent resource for examining substance use in the United States and for evaluating policies aimed at drug control, especially among the arrestee population.

I-ADAM

In 1998, the National Institute of Justice launched the International Drug Abuse Monitoring (I-ADAM) program, partly in recognition of the increasingly global nature of the drug trade. Efforts at understanding substance use across national borders were often confounded by the fact that laws, penalties, and recording procedures varied greatly, depending on the country in question. I-ADAM has attempted to address this problem by implementing a common survey, similar to the ADAM survey used in the United States, in a number of different countries. Currently, Australia, Chile, England, Malaysia, Scotland, South Africa, and the United States participate in the I-ADAM program. The Netherlands and Taiwan have also participated previously.

The I-ADAM program is administered similarly across the participating countries, facilitating international comparisons of substance use among arrestees. At each I-ADAM site, trained interviewers, who are not affiliated with law enforcement, conduct voluntary and confidential interviews with arrestees within 48 hours of the arrival of the arrestee in the detention facility. The survey measurement tool is standardized and common to each I-ADAM site and is administered by local researchers. Similar to ADAM in the United States, questions include those about the frequency of use of various substances, age at first use, perceptions of substance dependency, and participation in substance abuse treatment. Demographic data are also collected. Although the collection of data on female and juvenile arrestees is optional, each

I-ADAM site collects data from enough subjects to ensure reasonable statistical variation in the sample (typically at least 900 arrestees annually). As with the ADAM program, those interviewed are asked to provide a confidential urine sample following their interview, which can then be used to verify the accuracy of their survey responses and to assess the validity of the self-report data more generally. I-ADAM data thus provide researchers with another resource to study substance use and represent one of the most methodologically rigorous sources of data on substance use in a cross-national context. However, although the international nature of these data is certainly a strength, it also raises questions regarding differential levels of validity and underreporting across countries, especially at this early stage of the I-ADAM program. For example, two of the countries that have participated in the I-ADAM program (Malaysia and The Netherlands) have extremely diverse drug-control policies. The harm reduction model adopted by The Netherlands is reflected in practice by lenient enforcement of drug laws and fairly weak penalties for violation of offenses, whereas the zero-tolerance policy in Malaysia includes the death penalty for certain drug offenses. Accordingly, it is possible that rates of survey participation, truthfulness, and underreporting may vary between these countries (and others), and these issues must be kept in mind when using the data.

Conclusion

The sources of data on correctional facilities and known offenders are particularly important for understanding crime and corrections. The survey entities enable study of the correctional process and the offenders under the system's supervision, and the broad scope of their data is reflected in the wide variety of studies that have employed them. Research has been undertaken on the expansion of the correctional system in terms of prisoners, correctional officers, and cost; on racial and socioeconomic disparities in correctional populations; on offending frequency and the development of criminal typologies; and on assessments of treatment programs aimed at rehabilitating offenders. The Bureau of Justice Statistics, the Rand Corporation, and the Arrestee Drug Abuse Monitoring program have each provided a vital and unique contribution for understanding offenders and their experience with the correctional process. The federal government's Bureau of Justice Statistics collects extensive data on federal, state, and local jails as well as on the inmates incarcerated in these institutions. These data are collected regularly and allow for the constant monitoring of correctional populations, correctional resources, and inmate characteristics. The Rand inmate survey data have proved invaluable for learning about serious offenders, particularly those that offend at a very high rate, and for the development of correctional strategies. The Arrestee Drug Abuse Monitoring Program's surveys of recent arrestees in the United States and abroad have provided extensive information on criminal activity and substance use by offenders and have allowed for the verification of self-report responses through the use of urinalysis.

Each of these sources of data suffers from some of the same methodological shortcomings that characterize all official data on crime. The most problematic of these shortcomings is the extent to which official data describe offenders that were caught or incarcerated potentially as a consequence of bias on the part of police, prosecutors, and judges, rather than offenders in general. However, provided that these data are used with these issues in mind, they provide an excellent source of information on the corrections process and known offenders.

See Also the Following Articles

Criminal Justice Records • Police Records and The Uniform Crime Reports

Further Reading

Arrestee Drug Abuse Monitoring (ADAM). (2000). *1999 Report On Drug Use among Adult and Juvenile Arrestees.* National Institute of Justice, Washington, D.C.

Auerhahn, K. (1999). *Selective Incapacitation and the Problems of Prediction. Criminology* **37,** 703–734.

Bureau of Justice Statistics (BJS). (2001). *Prison and Jail Inmates at Midyear 2000.* U.S. Department of Justice, Washington, D.C.

Chaiken, J. M., and Chaiken, M. R. (1982). *Varieties of Criminal Behavior.* National Institute of Justice Report R-2814-NIJ. RAND Corporation, Santa Monica, CA.

Chaiken, J. M., and Chaiken, M. R. (1990). Drugs and predatory crime. In *Crime and Justice: A Review of Research* (M. Tonry and J. Q. Wilson, eds.), Vol. 13, pp. 203–239. University of Chicago Press, Chicago, IL.

English, K., and Mande, M. (1992). *Measuring Crime Rates of Prisoners.* National Institute of Justice, Washington, D.C.

Greenwood, P., and Abrahamse, A. (1982). *Selective Incapacitation.* National Institute of Justice Report R-2815-NIJ. RAND Corporation, Santa Monica, CA.

Horney, J., and Marshall, I. (1992). An experimental comparison of two self-report methods for measuring lambda. *J. Res. Crime Delinq.* **29,** 102–121.

Junger-Tas, J., and Marshall, I. (1999). The self-report methodology in crime research. In *Crime and Justice: A Review of Research* (M. Tonry, ed.), Vol. 25, pp. 291–367. University of Chicago Press, Chicago, IL.

Mosher, C., Miethe, T., and Phillips, D. (2002). *The Mismeasure of Crime.* Sage Publ., Thousand Oaks, CA.

Petersilia, J., Greenwood, P., and Lavin, M. (1977). *Criminal Careers of Habitual Felons.* Department of Justice Report R-2144 DOJ. Rand Corporation, Santa Monica, CA.

Tremblay, P., and Morselli, C. (2000). Patterns in criminal achievement: Wilson and Abrahamse revisited. *Criminology* **38,** 633–659.

Visher, C. (1986). The RAND Institute survey: A reanalysis. In *Criminal Careers and Career Criminals* (A. Blumstein, J. Cohen, J. Roth, and C. Visher, eds.), Vol. 2, pp. 161–211. National Academy Press, Washington, D.C.

Wilson, J. Q., and Abrahamse, A. (1992). Does crime pay? *Justice Q.* **9,** 359–377.

Correlations

Andrew B. Whitford
University of Kansas, Lawrence, Kansas, USA

Glossary

analysis of variance Method for the analysis of variation in an experimental outcome that exhibits statistical variance, to determine the contributions of given factors or variables to the variance.

cross-product Multiplication of the scores on the two variables for any single unit of observation in the data.

linear regression Method for estimating a linear functional relationship between two or more correlated variables. Regression is empirically determined from data, and may be used to predict values of one variable when given values of the others. It provides a function that yields the mean value of a random variable under the condition that one (in bivariate regression) or more (in multivariate regression) independent variables have specified values.

linear relationship Response or output is directly proportional to the input.

moment Random variables can be represented in terms of deviations from a fixed value. A moment is the expected value of some power of that deviation.

normal distribution Probability density function with the following form:

$$f(x) = \frac{1}{\sigma\sqrt{2\pi}} e^{-\frac{1}{2}\left(\frac{x-\mu}{\sigma}\right)^2}$$

polychotomous A measurement that is divided or marked by division into many parts, classes, or branches.

Correlation represents a family of methods for summarizing the strength and direction of the relationship between two variables X and Y. Pearson's correlation coefficient is the most familiar version, but is only appropriate given specific assumptions about the functional relationship between the two variables and the choices made about their measurement. Correlation as a concept serves as a basis for statements about relationships and associations, simple statistics for hypothesis testing, and more advanced methods for simultaneously assessing multiple explanations for social behavior and outcomes.

Introduction

One measure or statistical descriptor of the strength of the relationship between two variables X and Y is the correlation coefficient, which is also called the coefficient of linear correlation. As such, correlation coefficients summarize both the direction of that relationship and its strength. The most well-known means for assessing correlation is the Pearson product-moment correlation coefficient. Since its introduction in 1896, this approach has proved a useful mechanism for assessing relationships because it indexes the degree to which two variables are related. The values of this statistic are bounded between -1.0 and $+1.0$ inclusive; the negative or positive sign indicates the direction of the relationship, and the absolute value indicates magnitude (or strength of association). This statistic is also important because its construction, based on the products of moments in the data, forms the basis of extensions to other, supplementary statistics that complement the purpose of Pearson's correlation coefficient to summarize the relationship and its strength by indexing.

It is important to note throughout this discussion that a statistical description of correlation does not equate to proof of causation between two variables. A simple reason is that correlations can be deduced in single studies even without the introduction of controls. In contrast, causal statements require controlled experiments. This is a simplification of a more complicated reasoning, but signals the importance of separating statements of causality from statements about the association between two variables. In many cases, causal claims will require additional statements based on intuition or the theoretical understanding of underlying mechanisms, but more developed probability-based statements of the concordance between correlation and causality are also possible. In short, correlations can be computed without referring to dependence between two variables, even to the point of not distinguishing between independent and dependent variables.

Correlations are discussed here by emphasizing three fundamental distinctions. First, the technology used to assess correlations will depend on the measurement scale employed by the researcher. Second, the technologies available include both parametric and nonparametric choices. Third, correlation technologies are available for both linear and nonlinear relationships. Together, these patterns help separate the landscape of correlations into convenient groupings that aid the researcher in choosing the correct tool for data analysis.

Definition of Symbols

In the following discussions, X and Y are random variables; μ_x and μ_y are population means for X and Y, respectively; σ_x and σ_y are population standard deviations for X and Y, respectively; and N is the size of the population. All other symbols are defined in the context of the formulas as they are presented.

The Correlation Coefficient

Begin by considering the cross-products of the scores for two variables of interest. The cross-product is the multiplication of the scores on the two variables for any single unit of observation in the data. By summing across the N individuals, a sum of cross-products is obtained. Because the magnitude of the cross-products depends on the unit of measurement chosen for each variable, the sum of the cross-products for any two variables may not be comparable to the sum of cross-products for any other two variables. Moreover, the sum of cross-products will depend on the number of pairs considered in the experiment, and so comparability across pairs of variables and data sets is impaired. For these reasons, correlation coefficients take as their building blocks the scores in deviation form. For any two variables, the following terms form the basis for the correlation coefficient:

$$\sigma_x = \sqrt{\frac{\sum(X-\mu_x)^2}{N}}, \tag{1}$$

$$\sigma_y = \sqrt{\frac{\sum(Y-\mu_y)^2}{N}}. \tag{2}$$

Of course, σ_x and σ_y are simply the standard deviations for each variable, constructed by summing over all observations in the data, and depend on the calculated means for the variables (μ_x and μ_y, respectively). Here, z_x and z_y are built from these four components and the data for X and Y, and represent the conversion of the original scores for each distribution into z-scores.

$$z_x = \frac{X-\mu_x}{\sigma_x}, \tag{3}$$

$$z_y = \frac{Y-\mu_y}{\sigma_y}. \tag{4}$$

For a population, the correlation coefficient is calculated as follows:

$$r_{xy} = \frac{\sum z_x z_y}{N}. \tag{5}$$

The purpose of this formula is to represent the summation across the cross-products (where each variable is expressed in standard normal form) as a ratio dependent on the size of the population under consideration. This ratio accounts for the two primary considerations already mentioned: the problem of varying units of measurement across variables and the size of the population (number of pairs in the experiment). For a sample, the formula is adjusted by the degrees of freedom:

$$r_{xy} = \frac{\sum z_x z_y}{n-1}. \tag{6}$$

These technologies form the basis for the correlation coefficient as a mechanism for assessing both the direction and the strength of the association between two variables. As noted, the sign is bounded between -1.0 and $+1.0$ inclusive. The positive sign indicates that an increase (decrease) in one variable is associated with an increase (decrease) in the second variable; the negative sign indicates that an increase (decrease) in one variable is associated with a decrease (increase) in the second variable. The correlation coefficient is often represented as follows:

$$r_{xy} = \frac{\sum(X-\mu_x)(Y-\mu_y)}{\sqrt{\sum(X-\mu_x)^2 \sum(Y-\mu_y)^2}}. \tag{7}$$

This is obtained by substituting Eqs. (1)–(4) into Eq. (5). By algebraic manipulation, we obtain a computational formula for the calculation of the correlation coefficient for the original scores in the data:

$$r_{xy} = \frac{N\sum XY - \sum X \sum Y}{\sqrt{[N\sum X^2 - (\sum X)^2][N\sum Y^2 - (\sum Y)^2]}}. \tag{8}$$

The analogous formula for Eq. (6) is

$$r_{xy} = \frac{n\sum XY - \sum X \sum Y}{\sqrt{\left[n\sum X^2 - \left(\sum X\right)^2\right]\left[n\sum Y^2 - \left(\sum Y\right)^2\right]}}. \tag{9}$$

Use of Pearson's *r*

It is important to note that a number of factors affect the calculation of the correlation coefficient, whether it is calculated as z-scores, deviation scores, or by the computational formula. First, this is the coefficient of linear correlation, so the tendency of points to be located on a straight line will alter the size of the correlation coefficient. As long as the points display a random scatter about a straight line, any of these calculations will act as a statistical descriptor of the relationship between the two variables in the data. If the data are related in a nonlinear way (for example, in a U-shaped relationship), the absolute value of the correlation coefficient will suffer downward bias (will underestimate this relationship). An alteration of this basic framework for nonlinear relationships is discussed later.

For even linear relationships, as the variance for either variable shrinks (as the group becomes more homogeneous on that variable), the size of the correlation coefficient in absolute value terms is smaller. This means that for any two variables, there must be enough heterogeneity in the data for the correlation coefficient to detect the relationship. However, this caveat does not extend to the number of pairs included in the data. As long as $n > 2$, the correlation coefficient will both detect the relationship and represent its strength. If $n = 2$, the coefficient will only detect whether there is a relationship and its direction; strength in that case is expressed as one of the two end points of the correlation coefficient's scale. If $n = 1$, the coefficient fails due to homogeneity in both variables.

It is useful to note that correlation forms the basis for simple bivariate linear regression. The slope coefficient is simply

$$b_1 = r_{xy}\frac{\sqrt{\sum(Y - \mu_y)^2}}{\sqrt{\sum(Y - \mu_y)^2}}, \tag{10}$$

and the intercept is calculated as $b_0 = \bar{Y} - b_1\bar{X}$.

Interpretation of Pearson's *r*

As noted, the correlation coefficient provides information about the direction of the relationship and its strength. The range of possible values for the correlation coefficient provides an ordinal scale of the relationship's strength. In short, the correlation coefficient reveals relationships along the following ordinal scale: little to any correlation ($0.00 \leq |r| < 0.30$), low correlation ($0.30 \leq |r| \leq 0.49$), moderate correlation ($0.50 \leq |r| \leq 0.69$), high correlation ($0.70 \leq |r| \leq 0.89$), and very high correlation ($0.90 \leq |r| \leq 1.00$).

Perhaps a more intuitive and useful interpretation is in terms of the total variance in the Y variable. The total variability, noted as $\sum(Y - \mu_y)^2$, is standardized as σ_y^2. That variability can be decomposed into two parts: the variability explained or associated with the variable X and the unexplained variability associated with other factors. Just as in a linear model of $Y = f(X)$, the total variability in Y can be decomposed, and the square of the correlation coefficient (the coefficient of determination) represents the proportion of the total variability in Y that can be associated with the variability in X. That is,

$$r^2 = \frac{\sum(X - \mu_x)^2}{\sum(Y - \mu_y)^2}. \tag{11}$$

It is more difficult to extend these interpretations to the larger population as a whole. Rather than calculate Eq. (5), researchers are more likely to calculate Eq. (6) for a given sample and then seek to extend this description of the sample to the larger population. Generally, sample statistics are connected to population parameters by sampling distributions. We connect r (the sample correlation) to ρ (the population correlation) by first assuming that together the variables follow a bivariate normal distribution. There are infinitely many sampling distributions for r, each depending on the value of ρ and n (the number of pairs in the sample data), but all sharing common characteristics. The sampling distribution is not normal for small sample sizes, and only becomes more normal as sample size increases when $\rho \neq 0$. As ρ approaches ± 1, the sampling distribution is skewed for small sample sizes (negatively skewed when ρ is positive and positively skewed when ρ is negative). Fisher's transformation, published in 1921, reduces this skew and makes the sampling distribution normal as sample size increases:

$$z_r = \frac{n[(1 + r)/(1 - r)]}{2}.$$

Even so, r is an unbiased estimator of ρ, and, compared with other estimators, is best when $\rho = 0$ or 1. The standard error of r in large samples is

$$\left[\frac{(1 - \rho^2)^2}{n}\right]^{1/2},$$

and the standard error of z_r in large samples is roughly

$$\left[\frac{1}{n - 3}\right]^{1/2}.$$

Tests of the null hypothesis, $\rho = 0$, proceed by calculating the following statistic, which is distributed t with $n-2$ degrees of freedom:

$$\frac{r\sqrt{n-2}}{\sqrt{1-r^2}}.$$

Tests of the null hypothesis, $\rho = \rho_0$, proceed by calculating the following statistic, which is distributed as a normal variable:

$$\frac{z_r - z_{\rho_0}}{\sqrt{1/(n-3)}}.$$

Tests of the null hypothesis, $\rho_1 = \rho_2$, proceed by calculating the following statistic, which is also distributed as a normal variable:

$$\frac{z_{r_1} - z_{r_2}}{\sqrt{1/(n_1-3) + 1/(n_2-3)}}.$$

Chen and Popovich have developed additional tests, including those for the difference between more than two independent ρ values and the difference between two dependent correlations.

Correlation Coefficients for Various Combinations of Scales of Measurement

A primary division among types of correlation coefficients, many of which rely on the intuition present in Pearson's product-moment correlation coefficient, is best represented as resulting from the choices researchers make measuring the concepts present in their experiment. At a minimum, these may include qualitative (or categorical) and quantitative (or continuous) variables. Qualitative variables are measured in terms of the presence of a quality or characteristic, and may take either dichotomous or polychotomous forms. For quantitative variables, it is assumed that a scale underlies the measurements obtained for each variable, and that the variable, in principle, could take any number of positions on a line interval; quantitative variables are measured at the dichotomous, ordinal, or interval/ratio levels. For dichotomous measurements of quantitative data, only one of two positions is recorded for that variable. Ordinal measurements of quantitative data represent a scale of ranked values, although only a few points are recorded. Both interval and ratio level measurements of quantitative data can take any position on the line interval, with ratio level measurement schemes having a known and meaningful zero point. Of course, Pearson's r is appropriate for the situation in which both variables are interval/ratio.

Phi Coefficient (ϕ)

The distribution for two qualitative variables measured at the nominal level (or two quantitative variables measured in dichotomous form) can be represented in the 2×2 contingency table shown in Table I. The phi coefficient is the analogue of the computational formula for Pearson's correlation coefficient shown in Eq. (8). For the data described in the cells of Table I, ϕ is

$$\phi = \frac{BC - AD}{\sqrt{(A+B)(C+D)(A+C)(B+D)}}. \quad (12)$$

Here ϕ may only take maximal values ($|\phi| = 1.0$) when both $(A+B) = (C+D)$ and $(A+C) = (B+D)$. When this is not the case, the maximal value of ϕ may be substantially smaller.

If two variables are measured in dichotomous form but actually relate to concepts that could, if feasible, be measured at the interval/ratio level, we may calculate a tetrachoric coefficient instead of the point-biserial coefficient. In this case,

$$r_{\text{tet}} = \cos \frac{180°}{1 + \sqrt{(BC/AD)}}.$$

Tetrachoric coefficients are based on the notion that the variables have an underlying bivariate normal distribution. Analytical details for larger contingency tables are available.

Point-Biserial Coefficient

The point-biserial correlation coefficient is the special case of the Pearson product-moment coefficient if one variable is measured in nominal (or dichotomous) form and the second is an interval/ratio level. This statistic, which is analogous to a two-sample t test, is calculated as follows for populations:

$$r_{\text{pb}} = \frac{\mu_1 - \mu_0}{\sigma_y}\sqrt{pq}.$$

In this case, μ_1 is the mean of all the Y scores for those individuals with X scores equal to 1, μ_0 is the mean of the Y scores for those individuals with X scores equal to 0, σ_y is the standard deviation for all the scores of the variable measured at the interval/ratio level, p is the proportion of the pairs for which $X = 1$, and q is the

Table I 2×2 Contingency Table for Computing the Phi Coefficient

Variable Y \ *Variable X*	0	1	*Total*
0	A	B	$A+B$
1	C	D	$C+D$
Total	$A+C$	$B+D$	N

proportion of scores for which $X = 0$. The statistic for samples is calculated by replacing the population means and standard deviation with those for the sample:

$$r_{\mathrm{pb}} = \frac{\overline{Y}_1 - \overline{Y}_0}{s_y} \sqrt{pq}.$$

If the dichotomous measure truly has underlying continuity (an underlying interval/ratio representation), then the more general biserial coefficient is appropriate. The biserial coefficient is a transformation of the point-biserial coefficient that accounts for the height of the standard normal distribution at the point that divides the p and q proportions under the curve, which is denoted by u:

$$r_{\mathrm{b}} = r_{\mathrm{pb}} \frac{\sqrt{pq}}{u}$$

or

$$r_{\mathrm{b}} = \frac{(\mu_1 - \mu_0)}{\sigma_y} \cdot \frac{pq}{u}.$$

The biserial coefficient will always be larger than the point-biserial coefficient, and under some conditions may even be larger than 1.

Spearman Rho (ρ)

The Spearman rank-order correlation coefficient (ρ) is a special case of r for when both variables are measured quantitatively as ordinal scales. In this case, for a population,

$$\rho = 1 - \frac{6\sum d^2}{N(N^2 - 1)},$$

where N is the number of pairs of ranks and d is the difference between the paired ranks for each pair in the data. For a sample, the formula is the same with the inclusion of the sample size n instead of N. In the case of tied ranks, a correction factor is available, but r can always be calculated as an alternative.

Non-Product-Moment Coefficients

As already noted, a second dividing line between types of correlation coefficients is the weight of their reliance on Pearson's product-moment coefficient for the basis of their technology. In each of the following cases, the method significantly departs from Pearson's approach, but still operates across the first division marking various combinations of the basic measurement schemes employed by researchers.

Rank-Biserial Coefficient

The rank-biserial coefficient, proposed by Cureton in 1956 and refined by Glass in 1966, is appropriate if one variable is measured at the nominal/dichotomous level and the second is ordinal. This coefficient uses notation similar to the point-biserial coefficient:

$$r_{rb} = \frac{2}{N}(\mu_1 - \mu_0).$$

The original Cureton formula is appropriate when ties are present. For a sample, the formula is the same with the inclusion of the sample size n instead of N.

Contingency Coefficient (*C*) and Cramer's *V*

The contingency coefficient (C) and Cramer's V are appropriate when relating two variables measured on the unordered polychotomous scale. The formula for C for a population is based on the χ^2 test of independence across the cells of an $r \times c$ contingency table:

$$C = \sqrt{\frac{\chi^2}{\chi^2 + N}},$$

where

$$\chi^2 = \sum_{i=1}^{r}\sum_{j=1}^{c} \frac{\left(A_{ij} - E_{ij}\right)^2}{E_{ij}}.$$

Here, A_{ij} is the actual count of cases in the ijth cell and E_{ij} is the expected count when the null of independence is true and is calculated based on the marginals; C is not bounded +1.0, but instead depends on the number of categories for the row and column variables. This limitation makes all C values calculated across data sets incomparable unless the coding scheme for the two data sets is exactly the same.

Cramer's V is intended to limit this deficiency by ranging only from 0 to 1. The formula is again based on the calculated value of χ^2 but now adjusted by the smallest number of rows or columns in the table:

$$V = \sqrt{\frac{\chi^2}{n \cdot [\min(r,c) - 1]}}.$$

Kendall's τ

Up to this point, the non-product-moment-based coefficients offered have provided means to address combinations of measurements for which an equivalent product-moment-based coefficient is not available. Like Spearman's rank-order coefficient, Kendall's τ also addresses data in which both variables are measured at the ordinal level. This approach is intended to measure the "disarray" (extent of disagreement) in the rankings. This degree of specificity offered by τ comes at a computational cost. The formula is as follows:

$$\tau = \frac{2(\mathrm{CP} - \mathrm{DP})}{n(n-1)},$$

where CP is the number of concordant pairs and DP is the number of discordant pairs. Concordance is defined as any two pairs where, for (x_i, y_i) and (x_j, y_j), $y_i < y_j$ and $x_i < x_j$, or $y_i > y_j$ and $x_i > x_j$, or $(x_i - x_j)(y_i - y_j) > 0$; any other situation is defined as a discordant pair. Historically, this computational burden has encouraged researchers to calculate Spearman's rank-order correlation coefficient instead, but modern computing power has made this a trivial task except in the case of very large data sets. Three modified coefficients (Kendall's τ_b, Stuart's τ_c, and Goodman and Kruskal's γ) are available when there are tied ranks. Kendall's partial rank-order correlation coefficient is an analogue to the Pearson's coefficient mentioned previously.

Nonlinear Relationships

The final division among correlation coefficients addresses the question of nonlinear relationships between two variables. As noted previously, when two variables are related in a nonlinear way, the product-moment basis for Pearson's *r* will understate the strength of the relationship between the two variables. This is because *r* is a statement of the existence and strength of the linear relationship between two variables. The correlation ratio, η, addresses the relationship between a polychotomous qualitative variable and an interval/ratio level quantitative variable, but an advantage of this measure is that it also states the strength of a possible nonlinear relationship between the two variables. At the same time, it makes only a statement of the strength of that relationship, not direction, because of the polychotomous nature of the first variable. For a population, η is calculated by the following equation:

$$\eta = \sqrt{\frac{\sum(Y - \mu_c)^2}{\sum(Y - \mu_t)^2}}$$

The mean value of the interval/ratio scores (μ_c) is calculated for each category of the first variable; the grand mean (μ_t) is also calculated. Summation occurs over the differences between the score for each observational unit and these means. For a sample, the sample means are calculated instead. Generally, η^2 will be greater than r^2, and the difference is the degree of nonlinearity in the data. For two interval/ratio variables, one variable can be divided into categories of equal width and the resulting value of η will again approximate the strength of the nonlinear relationship between the two variables. In either case, η reflects the same information provided by an analysis of variance (ANOVA) about the relative contribution of the between sum of squares to the total sum of squares for the two variables.

Which Statistic to Use?

The central message of this discussion is that the choice of statistic depends on three basic selections made by the researcher. First, the researcher's choice of measurement scheme will largely determine the correlation coefficient used for data analysis. In particular, the choice to measure concepts that have an underlying continuous representation at a dichotomous or ordinal level constrains the choice of statistic, although alternative statistics are still available. This plethora of alternative coefficients should make it clear that though Pearson's *r* serves to motivate their construction, this fact does not make Pearson's *r* the best technology for all possible research designs. Second, the choice of Pearson's *r* has proceeded largely on the basis of ease of computation, but advances in modern computing have made the choice of non-product-moment (nonparametric) coefficients not just possible but preferred in many cases. Third, it remains important to emphasize the fact that most coefficients retain the focus of Pearson's *r* on linear relationships. This fact makes the choice of coefficient even sharper, in part because of the sharp distinction inherent in nonlinear versus linear thinking. To be honest, this last division is mitigated in part because of the availability of technologies such as kernel-density smoothing or nonlinear regression. However, the continuing advantage of Pearson's *r*—as well as of coefficients of nonlinear correlation—is that they provide summary indicators of relationships that are comparable across data sets. This is not the case for either graphical techniques or more regression-oriented techniques for assessing relationships.

See Also the Following Articles

Contingency Tables and Log-Linear Models • Descriptive and Inferential Statistics • Quantitative Analysis, Anthropology

Further Reading

Carroll, J. P. (1961). The nature of the data, or how to choose a correlation coefficient. *Psychometrika* **26,** 347–372.

Chen, P. Y., and Popovich, P. M. (2002). *Correlation: Parametric and Nonparametric Measures.* Sage, Thousand Oaks, California.

Cureton, E. E. (1956). Rank-biserial correlation. *Psychometrika* **1956,** 287–290.

Cureton, E. E. (1968). Rank-biserial correlation—When ties are present. *Educat. Psychol. Meas.* **28,** 77–79.

Fisher, R. A. (1921). On the "probable error" of a coefficient of correlation deduced from a small sample. *Metron* **1,** 1–32.

Glass, G. V. (1966). Note on rank-biserial correlation. *Educat. Psychol. Meas.* **26,** 623–631.

Kendall, M. G. (1938). A new measure of rank correlation. *Biometrika* **34,** 81–93.

Kendall, M. G. (1949). Rank and product-moment correlation. *Biometrika* **36,** 177–193.

Lancaster, H. O., and Hamden, M. A. (1964). Estimates of the correlation coefficient in contingency tables with possibly nonmetrical characters. *Psychometrika* **29,** 383–391.

McNemar, Q. (1961). *Psychological Statistics,* 4th Ed. John Wiley, New York.

Pearl, J. (2000). *Causality: Models, Reasoning, and Inference.* Cambridge University Press, Cambridge.

Pearson, K. (1896). Mathematical contributions to the theory of evolution—III. Regression, heredity, and panmixia. *Philos. Trans. Royal Soc. Lond., A* **187,** 253–318.

Pearson, K., and Filon, L. N. G. (1898). Mathematical contributions to the theory of evolution—IV. On the probable errors of frequency constants and on the influence of random selection on variation and correlation. *Philos. Trans. Royal Soc. Lond., A* **191,** 229–311.

Siegel, S. (1956). *Nonparametric Statistics for the Behavioral Sciences.* McGraw-Hill, New York.

Correspondence Analysis and Dual Scaling

Shizuhiko Nishisato
University of Toronto, Ontario, Canada

Glossary

duality Symmetry in quantification of rows and columns.
principal hyperspace Multidimensional space with principal axes.
singular-value decomposition (SVD) The optimal decomposition of a two-way table into row structure and column structure.
transition formulas and dual relations Mathematical relations in quantification between rows and columns.

Correspondence analysis and dual scaling are a family of multidimensional quantification methods for multivariate categorical data of both incidence and dominance types with unifying concepts, formulas, and illustrative examples.

Introduction

Historical Notes

There are a number of names for this family of scaling techniques, some of which are correspondence analysis, dual scaling, homogeneity analysis, optimal scaling, Hayashi's theory of quantification, biplot, and appropriate scoring. All of these are mathematically equivalent or closely related to one another. There are two precursors of this family of scaling techniques: (1) mathematical eigenvalue theory, developed by mathematicians in the 18th century and (2) singular-value decomposition (SVD) developed by Beltrami in 1873, Jordan in 1874, and Schmidt in 1907. The first was put into practice by Pearson in 1901 and Hotelling in 1936 under the name principal component analysis (PCA), and the second offered the computational scheme for the most efficient decomposition of a two-way table through the spacing (weighting) of rows and columns of the table. These two precursors are algebraically based on the same principle. Their first application to data analysis seems to be a study by Richardson and Kuder in 1933, which Horst called the method of reciprocal averages in 1935. It was followed by several key studies such as Hirschfeld in 1935, Fisher in 1940, Guttman in 1941 and 1946, and Maung in 1941, which together laid a solid foundation for this family of scaling methods. Among the many contributors, there are four outstanding groups of researchers: the Hayashi school in Japan since 1950 (Hayashi's theory of quantification; Hayashi, Akuto, Komazawa, Baba, Hayashi, Mizuno, Ohsumi, Sakamoto, and many others), the Benzécri school in France since the early part of 1960 (analyse des correspondances; Benzécri, Escofier-Cordier, Lebart, Morineau, Saporta, Escoufier, Pagés, Tenenhaus, Fénelon, Greenacre, and many others), the Leiden group in the Netherlands since the latter part of 1960 (homogeneity analysis; de Leeuw, Heiser, Meulman, van den Berg, van der Burg, van Rijckevorsel, van der Geer, van der Heijden, Kiers, van Buuren, Koster, and many others), and the Toronto group in Canada since the latter part of 1960 (dual scaling; Nishisato and his students, Sheu, Inukai, Lawrence, Ahn (Im), Day, Millones, Xu, Sachs, Gessaroli, Mayenga, Odondi, and many others).

In English-speaking countries, researchers have often ignored the French and Japanese studies, but we cannot overemphasize the monumental contributions to the area by many French and Japanese researchers. The Dutch contributions have also been noteworthy. In the United States, R. Darrell Bock in 1960 succeeded in disseminating the method under the attractive name optimal scaling.

Origins of Names and Classification of Data

Correspondence analysis (CA) is an English translation of French "analyse des correspondances," and the name has gained popularity in English-speaking countries since Greenacre published his book in 1984. Dual scaling (DS) is a name proposed by Nishisato in 1976 at a symposium on optimal scaling with speakers Young (United States), de Leeuw (Netherlands), Saporta (France), and Nishisato (Canada), with discussant Kruskal (United States); and it made its debut in Nishisato's 1980 book.

Categorical data can be classified into incidence data and dominance data with the following scaling properties.

Incidence data (absence or presence of a response or frequency of responses):

1. The object of scaling is to provide an approximation to the data in a reduced space.
2. The chi-square metric is used.
3. There exists a trivial solution.
4. Even if variables are perfectly correlated, the data might not be mapped in one dimension.

Dominance data (responses of inequality and equality):

1. Scaling is done so as to approximate the input ranks of objects in a reduced space.
2. The Euclidean metric is used.
3. There is no trivial solution.
4. When there is no individual difference, the data can be described in one dimension.

Traditionally, CA is used only for incidence data (e.g., contingency tables and multiple-choice incidence data), whereas DS is used for both incidence data and dominance data (e.g., paired comparison data and rank-order data). In this regard, Meulman in 1998 called DS "a comprehensive framework for multidimensional analysis of categorical data." However, it is only a matter of time until the current formulation of CA is also fully extended to dominance data, as hinted in papers by Greenacre and Torres-Lacomba in 1999 and van Velden in 2000.

Basic Rationale

Incidence Data

Data are either frequencies of responses or 1 (presence), 0 (absence) incidences. Contingency tables and multiple-choice data, expressed as (1, 0) response patterns, are examples of incidence data. For this type of data, there are a number of ways to formulate CA/DS scaling techniques, all of which, however, can be expressed in the following bilinear expansion of a data element f_{ij} in row i and column j:

$$f_{ij} = \frac{f_{i\cdot}f_{\cdot j}}{f_{\cdot\cdot}}[1 + \rho_1 y_{i1}x_{j1} + \rho_2 y_{i2}x_{j2} + \cdots + \rho_k y_{ik}x_{jk} + \cdots + \rho_K y_{iK}x_{jK}] \quad (1)$$

where $f_{i\cdot}$ is the marginal frequency of row i, $f_{\cdot j}$ is that of column j, $f_{\cdot\cdot}$ is the total frequency, ρ_k is the kth singular value ($\rho_1 \geq \rho_2 \geq \cdots \geq \rho_K$), y_{ik} is the optimal weight of row i of the kth solution, and x_{jk} is the optimal weight of column j of the kth solution. The solution, corresponding to 1 inside the bracket, is called a trivial solution (typically deleted from analysis), and is the frequency expected when the rows and the columns are statistically independent. The others are called proper solutions. For any proper solution, say solution k, there exist transition formulas or dual relations. For an $m \times n$ data matrix:

$$y_{ik} = \frac{1}{\rho_k}\frac{\sum_{j=1}^{n} f_{ij}x_{jk}}{f_{i\cdot}} \quad \text{and} \quad x_{jk} = \frac{1}{\rho_k}\frac{\sum_{i=1}^{m} f_{ij}y_{ik}}{f_{\cdot j}} \quad (2)$$

The equations are nothing more than those derived by Hirschfeld in 1935, that is, simultaneous linear regressions of rows on columns and columns on rows. It also indicates the basis for what Horst in 1935 called the method of reciprocal averages: start with arbitrary row weights to calculate weighted column means, which are in turn used as weights to calculate weighted row means, which are then used as weights to calculate weighted column means, and so on until the process converges. This reciprocal averaging scheme always converges to the optimal sets of row weights and column weights, the proportionality constant being the singular value. Nishisato calls weights y and x normed weights, and ρy and ρx projected weights, which are also referred to as standard coordinates and principal coordinates, respectively. Geometrically, y and ρx span the same space, and so do ρy and x. The angle of the discrepancy between row space and column space is given by the cosine of the singular value as shown by Nishisato and Clavel in 2003.

To arrive at a solution $[\rho, y_i, x_j]$, there are several approaches:

1. Determine y_i and x_j in such a way that the product-moment correlation between the data weighted by y_i and those weighted by x_j is a maximum; this correlation proves to be the singular value.
2. Determine y_i so that the correlation ratio (the ratio of the between-column sum of squares to the total sum of squares) is a maximum; the correlation ratio proves to be the squared singular value.
3. Determine x_j to maximize the correlation ratio (the ratio of the between-row sum of squares to the total sum of squares).
4. Determine ρ, y_i, x_j in Eq. (1) by the least squares method.

Dominance Data

Dominance data include rank-order data and paired comparison data in which the information is of the type greater, equal, or smaller. The responses are first coded as follows:

$$_if_{jk} = \begin{cases} 1 & \text{if subject } i \text{ prefers object } j \text{ to } k \\ 0 & \text{if subject } i \text{ makes a tied judgment} \\ -1 & \text{if subject } i \text{ prefers object } k \text{ to } j \end{cases} \quad (3)$$

For n objects, these are transformed to dominance numbers by

$$e_{ij} = \sum_{j=1}^{n} \sum_{k=1(j \neq k)}^{n} {}_if_{jk} \quad (4)$$

Equation (4) reduces to the following expression when dominance data are rank-order data:

$$e_{ij} = n + 1 - 2R_{ij} \quad (5)$$

where R_{ij} is the rank given to object j by subject i. This formula was used by de Leeuw in 1973 and was also derived by Nishisato in 1978.

The matrix of dominance numbers has the property that each row's elements sum to zero. Thus, to arrive at weights for subjects and weights for objects, the method of reciprocal averages, for example, is carried out with the understanding that each cell of the dominance matrix is based on $n-1$ responses (comparisons). With the new definition of row marginals, $n(n-1)$, and column marginals, $N(n-1)$, where N is the number of respondents, dominance data are now amenable to the same procedure as incidence data.

Numerical Examples

Multiple-Choice Data: An Example of Incidence Data

CA is a name for quantification of contingency tables. When CA is applied to multiple-choice data, it is called multiple correspondence analysis (MCA). Torgerson in 1958 called MCA and DS principal component analysis (PCA) of categorical data. To see the differences between PCA of categorical data and PCA of continuous data, let us look at a numerical example of the following six multiple-choice questions from a study in 2000 by Nishisato.

1. Rate your blood pressure. (Low, Medium, High): coded 1, 2, 3
2. Do you get migraines? (Rarely, Sometimes, Often): coded 1, 2, 3
3. What is your age group? (20–34; 35–49; 50–65): coded 1, 2, 3
4. Rate your daily level of anxiety. (Low, Medium, High): coded 1, 2, 3
5. How about your weight? (Light, Medium, Heavy): coded 1, 2, 3
6. How about your height? (Short, Medium, Tall): coded 1, 2, 3

Suppose we use the traditional Likert scores for PCA, that is, 1, 2, 3 as the scores for the three categories of each question, and treat the data as continuous. MCA and DS use response patterns of 1s and 0s. The two data sets from 15 subjects, one in Likert scores and the other in response patterns, are given in Table I.

The matrix of product-moment correlations based on the Likert scores (for PCA) and the correlations obtained from optimal category weight (for the first MCA/DS component) are given in Table II. Let us first look at the results on PCA of Likert scores. First we examine the correlation between blood pressure and age ($r = 0.66$) and between blood pressure and migraines ($r = -0.06$) in terms of contingency tables (Table III). We can understand why the two correlation coefficients are so different; the first pair is linearly related (i.e., the older one gets the higher the blood pressure) and the second pair is nonlinearly related (i.e., frequent migraines appear when the blood pressure is low or high). The second, nonlinear relation is clearer (stronger) than the linear relation because the nonlinear relation indicates without exception that when the migraines are frequent, blood pressure can be either low or high. This can be verified by Cramér's coefficient, which captures both linear and nonlinear relations. This coefficient is 0.63 for the blood pressure and age and 0.71 for blood pressure and migraines. Although a graphical display of PCA results is not given here, PCA identifies a cluster of blood pressure, age, and anxiety, indicating that as one gets older blood pressure tends to get higher and so does anxiety. These variables are all linearly related. Let us look at a graph of the first two DS solutions (Fig. 1). In a linear analysis such as PCA, the length of a vector indicates the contribution of the variable. In contrast, in MCA and DS, the three categories of each variable in the current example form a triangle, and the area of each triangle is generally proportional to the contribution of the variable to the first two dimensions. Here we do not look for clusters of variables but rather clusters of categories. The first two solutions can be roughly characterized as in Table IV. Notice that the associations of categories are not necessarily linear.

Rank-Order Data: An Example of Dominance Data

In a 1996 study by Nishisato, 10 subjects ranked the following six Christmas party plans according to their order of preference:

1. Pot-luck in the group during the daytime.
2. Pub-restaurant crawl after work.
3. Reasonably priced lunch in an area restaurant.

Table I Two Forms of Data[a]

	PCA						DS					
Subject	*BP Q1*	*Mig Q2*	*Age Q3*	*Anx Q4*	*Wgt Q5*	*Hgt Q6*	*BP 123*	*Mig 123*	*Age 123*	*Anx 123*	*Wgt 123*	*Hgt 123*
1	1	3	3	3	1	1	100	001	001	001	100	100
2	1	3	1	3	2	3	100	001	100	001	010	001
3	3	3	3	3	1	3	001	001	001	001	100	001
4	3	3	3	3	1	1	001	001	001	001	100	100
5	2	1	2	2	3	2	010	100	010	010	001	010
6	2	1	2	3	3	1	010	100	010	001	001	100
7	2	2	2	1	1	3	010	010	010	100	100	001
8	1	3	1	3	1	3	100	001	100	001	100	001
9	2	2	2	1	1	2	010	010	010	100	100	010
10	1	3	2	2	1	3	100	001	010	010	100	001
11	2	1	1	3	2	2	010	100	100	001	010	010
12	2	2	3	3	2	2	010	010	001	001	010	010
13	3	3	3	3	3	1	001	001	001	001	001	100
14	1	3	1	2	1	1	100	001	100	010	100	100
15	3	3	3	3	1	2	001	001	001	001	100	010

[a] Anx, anxiety; BP, blood pressure; Hgt, height; Mig, migraine; Wgt, weight.

Table II Correlation Matrices from Two Analyses[a]

	PCA						DS					
	BP	*Mig*	*Age*	*Anx*	*Wgt*	*Hgt*	*BP*	*Mig*	*Age*	*Anx*	*Wgt*	*Hgt*
BP	1.00						1.00					
Mig	−0.06	1.00					0.99	1.00				
Age	0.66	0.23	1.00				0.60	0.58	1.00			
Anx	0.18	0.21	0.22	1.00			0.47	0.52	0.67	1.00		
Wgt	0.17	−0.58	−0.02	0.26	1.00		0.43	0.39	0.08	−0.33	1.00	
Hgt	−0.21	0.10	−0.30	−0.23	−0.31	1.00	0.56	0.57	0.13	0.19	0.20	1.00

[a] Anx, anxiety; BP, blood pressure; Hgt, height; Mig, migraine; Wgt, weight.

Table III Distributions of Responses for Three Items[a]

	Age			Migraine		
	20–34	*35–49*	*50–65*	*Rarely*	*Sometimes*	*Often*
High BP	0	0	**4**	0	0	**4**
Med BP	1	**4**	1	**3**	**3**	0
Low BP	**3**	1	1	0	0	**5**

[a] BP, blood pressure.

4. Evening banquet at a hotel.
5. Pot-luck at someone's home after work.
6. Ritzy lunch at a good restaurant.

The data and the corresponding dominance matrix are shown in Table V. The relative variances of five proper solutions are 0.45, 0.27, 0.14, 0.08, and 0.06, respectively. Let us look at the first two proper solutions and at a joint plot of the normed weights y of subjects and the projected weights ρx of the party plans (Fig. 2), a practice that leads to a solution to Clyde H. Coombs's problem of multidimensional unfolding. From this graph, we can calculate the distances between the subjects and party plans and rank the distances within each subject to obtain the rank-2 approximation to the input ranks (Table VI). For example, look at Subject 2; the ranking of the distances reproduces

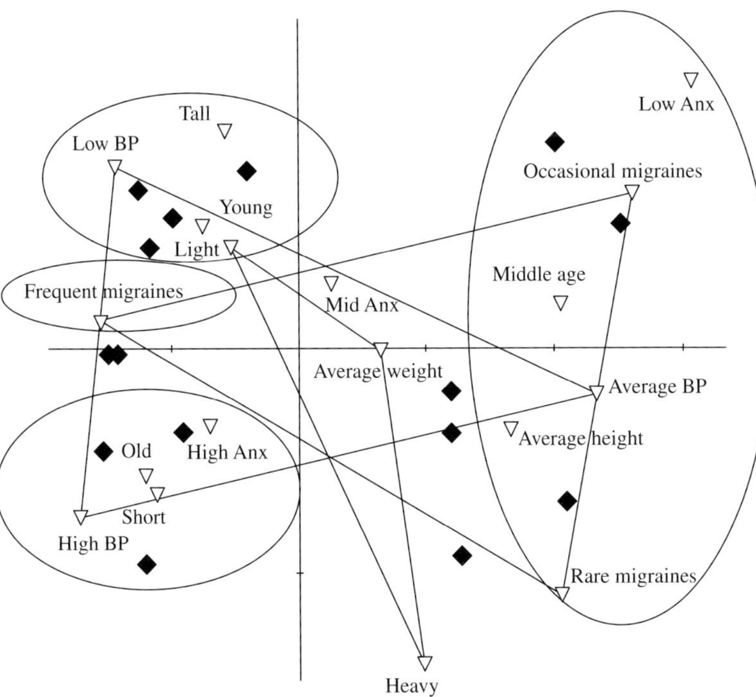

Figure 1 Dual scaling solutions 1 and 2. Anx, anxiety; BP, blood pressure.

Table IV Main Characteristics of Two DS Solutions[a]

Solution 1		*Solution 2*	
One end	*The other end*	*One end*	*The other end*
Low BP	Medium BP	High BP	Low BP
High BP	Rare migraine	Rare migraine	Occasional migraine
Frequent migraine	Middle age	Old	Young
Old	Low anxiety	Heavy	Tall
High anxiety	Medium height	Short	
Short			

[a] BP, blood pressure.

Table V Ranking and Dominance Matrix

	Party plan											
	Ranking						*Dominance matrix*					
Subject	(1)	(2)	(3)	(4)	(5)	(6)	(1)	(2)	(3)	(4)	(5)	(6)
1	6	1	5	4	3	2	−5	5	−3	−1	1	3
2	6	1	5	2	4	3	−5	1	−3	3	−1	1
3	3	5	2	4	1	6	1	−3	3	−1	5	−5
4	3	4	2	6	1	5	1	−1	3	−5	5	−3
5	5	3	1	4	6	2	−3	1	5	−1	−5	3
6	2	6	3	5	4	1	3	−5	1	−3	−1	5
7	1	2	4	5	3	6	5	3	−1	−3	1	−5
8	4	3	2	6	5	1	−1	1	3	−5	−3	5
9	2	1	4	5	3	6	3	5	−1	−3	1	−5
10	6	1	4	3	5	2	−5	5	−1	1	−3	3

Table VI Squared Distances, Rank-2 Approximation to Original Ranks

	Party plan											
	Squared distances						*Rank-2 approximation*					
Subject	*(1)*	*(2)*	*(3)*	*(4)*	*(5)*	*(6)*	*(1)*	*(2)*	*(3)*	*(4)*	*(5)*	*(6)*
1	1.94	0.73	1.72	1.06	1.67	1.37	6	1	5	2	4	3
2	2.20	0.98	2.02	1.36	1.91	1.71	6	1	5	2	4	3
3	0.67	1.75	1.21	1.53	0.81	1.98	1	5	3	4	2	6
4	0.49	1.63	1.01	1.38	0.69	1.79	1	5	3	4	2	6
5	1.72	1.58	1.18	1.27	1.77	0.54	5	4	2	3	6	1
6	1.70	2.38	1.37	1.95	1.96	1.51	3	6	1	4	5	2
7	1.10	1.42	1.55	1.45	0.89	2.14	2	3	5	4	1	6
8	1.61	1.70	1.07	1.33	1.71	0.76	4	5	2	3	6	1
9	1.40	1.28	1.74	1.45	1.11	2.18	3	2	5	4	1	6
10	2.13	1.02	1.79	1.21	1.91	1.25	6	1	4	2	5	3

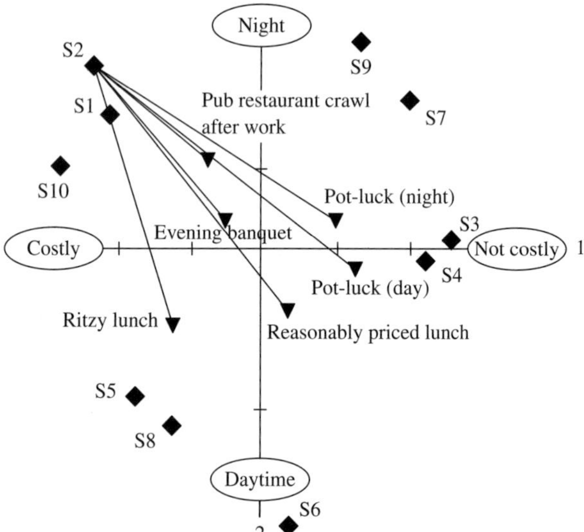

Figure 2 Joint plot of respondents and party plans. S, subject.

exactly the subject's ranking of the plans. Other cases require more dimensions than two to provide the exact rankings. Overall, the rank-2 approximation is close to the rank-5 data. The graph in Figure 2 reveals individual differences in ranking as affected by the party cost and the party times. Observe their closeness to particular plans, and the ability of the method to capture individual differences in preference.

See Also the Following Articles

Contingency Tables and Log-Linear Models • Correlations • Prevalence and Incidence • Ranking

Further Reading

Benzécri, J.-P., *et al.* (1973). *L'Analyse des Données: II. L'Analyse des Correspondances [Data Analysis II: Correspondence Analysis].* Dunod, Paris.

Gifi, A. (1990). *Nonlinear Multivariate Analysis.* John Wiley, New York.

Gower, J. C., and Hand, D. J. (1996). *Biplots.* Chapman & Hall, London.

Greenacre, M. J. (1984). *Theory and Applications of Correspondence Analysis.* Academic Press, London.

Greenacre, M. J., and Blasius, J. (eds.) (1994). *Correspondence Analysis in the Social Sciences.* Academic Press, London.

Lebart, L., Morineau, A., and Warwick, K. M. (1984). *Multivariate Descriptive Statistical Analysis.* John Wiley, New York.

Meulman, J. J. (1986). *Distance Approach to Multivariate Analysis.* DSWO Press, Leiden.

Nishisato, S. (1980). *Analysis of Categorical Data: Dual Scaling and Its Applications.* University of Toronto Press, Toronto.

Nishisato, S. (1994). *Elements of Dual Scaling.* Lawrence Erlbaum Associates, Hillsdale, NJ.

Nishisato, S. (1996). Gleaning in the field of dual scaling. *Psychometrika* **61,** 559–599.

Cost–Benefit Analysis

James Edwin Kee
George Washington University, Washington, DC, USA

Glossary

discount rate The interest rate used to convert future benefits and costs to their present value in year 1.

marginal benefits/marginal costs Marginal cost is defined as the incremental (additional) cost of producing one more unit of output. Marginal benefit is the incremental benefit generated by that one unit of output.

net present value (NPV) The conversion of a stream of future benefits less future costs to their equivalent benefits and costs in year 1, at the beginning of the project or program.

opportunity cost The value of using a resource (land, money, etc.) for one thing instead of another.

shadow pricing An attempt to value a benefit or a cost where no competitive market price exists.

sunk cost Investments previously made in a program or project—such as original research and development costs that cannot be recouped—compared to ongoing costs.

Cost–benefit (or benefit–cost) analysis is a useful quantitative tool for policy analysts and program evaluators. It is used to analyze proposed programs, to conduct evaluations of existing programs (to assess their overall success or failure), to help determine whether programs should be continued or modified, and to assess the probable results of proposed program changes.

Introduction

The Use of Cost–Benefit Analysis

Cost–benefit analysis is an applied economic technique that attempts to assess a government program or project by determining whether societal welfare has or will increase (in the aggregate more people are better off) because of the program or project. At its greatest degree of usefulness, cost–benefit analysis can provide information on the full costs of a program or project and weigh those costs against the dollar value of the benefits. The analyst can then calculate the net benefits (or costs) of the program or project, examine the ratio of benefits to costs, determine the rate of return on the government's original investment, and compare the program's benefits and costs with those of other programs or proposed alternatives.

Description of the Process

Cost–benefit analysis has three rather simple-sounding steps: (1) Determine the benefits of a proposed or existing program and place a dollar value on those benefits; (2) calculate the total costs of the program; and (3) compare the benefits and the costs.

These simple steps, however, are challenging for the analyst. Even when benefits can be calculated in unit terms, e.g., so many lives saved, it is often quite difficult to place a dollar value on each unit. For many intangibles (national security, wilderness values, quality of life), both determining the unit of analysis and determining its dollar value are problematic. Nevertheless, even when the analyst cannot capture all of the benefits and costs in quantitative terms, the procedure can uncover important issues for judging a program's success or failure.

In many respects, cost–benefit analysis of government programs is similar to financial analysis conducted in the private sector as existing and potential investment opportunities are considered. Government and its taxpayers are investing funds to achieve certain societal benefits, just as a firm is investing to achieve profit. Public agencies and their evaluators must ask:

- Is a proposed program expected to create net benefits to society?
- For an existing program, is it a success; that is, has it improved societal welfare?
- Finally, at any given decision-making point, should the program be continued when weighed against alternative uses for the government's funds?

Benefits and costs seldom occur simultaneously. For government programs, there are start-up costs, such as expenditures on studies or consultants, and capital costs. There may be costs associated with advertising the program and developing the constituency for the program. And there are the continuing costs of operating the program. Most government programs are not priced (at least not to maximize profits); thus, benefits are broader than any monetary return to the government—even though revenue may be important from a budgetary perspective—and may occur over decades. In assessing the success or failure of the project, a government must consider the opportunity cost of using the funds in the proposed project. Governmental policymakers have alternative uses for tax dollars or borrowing capacity, such as other programs or returning the money back to its citizens in the form of tax reductions and thus allowing more spending in the private sector.

Cost–Benefit Illustration

Analysis of a 5-Year Project

Table I provides an illustration of a cost–benefit analysis. The illustration is a 5-year project, designed to achieve certain benefits to society. Those may include both direct benefits (such as services to citizens) and indirect benefits (such as cost-savings to society). Costs (which are sometimes grouped into cost ingredients or objects of expenditure) also may be direct, such as personnel (salaries and benefits), equipment, materials, and capital costs (land, buildings, or other major purchases with an extended life), and indirect, such as government central administrative costs and mitigation of unintended consequences of the program (e.g., damage to the environment).

At the end of the 5-year period, the agency has spent $20.5 million and reaped total benefits of $21.25 million for (what seems to be) a 5-year net benefit (benefits less costs) of $750,000. From the agency's perspective, was the project a success? Because of the project's front-end costs, including start-up costs, and expenditures on mitigation of possible adverse effects, the agency's costs exceeded benefits during the first 2 years of the project. Benefits do not exceed costs until the third year. The agency or the government financing the agency also has alternative investment opportunities for its funds. If it loses $2.68 million in the first year of the project, it loses the opportunity to use

Table I Cost–Benefit Illustration (in Thousands of Dollars)

	Year					
	1	2	3	4	5	*Totals*
Benefits						
Direct	1000	1750	3000	4750	5000	15,500
Indirect		750	1250	1750	2000	5750
Total benefits	1000	2500	4250	6500	7000	21,250
Costs						
Direct						
Start-up	250					250
Personnel	400	700	900	1500	1500	5000
Equipment and materials	250	500	500	500	500	2250
Capital	2000	1925	1850	1775	1700	9250
Indirect						
Overhead	580	625	650	755	740	3350
Mitigation	200	50	50	50	50	400
Total costs	3680	3800	3950	4580	4490	20,500
Benefits less costs	(2680)	(1300)	300	1920	2510	750
5-Year Total	750					
5-Year NPV @ 5%	78					
Benefit–cost ratio (5 years)	1.0042					
Benefit–cost ratio in year 5	1.5590					

those funds elsewhere. The \$2.68 million loss in year 1 is more costly than the same amount in later years because the loss of the potential gain. The apparent \$750,000 in benefits over costs does not take into account this important consideration. In order to incorporate the concept of opportunity cost, cost–benefit analysis employs net present value analysis that converts all costs and benefits to their present value at the beginning of the project, in year 1.

The opportunity costs to the agency are expressed as the real rate of return—r—available to the agency at the beginning of the project. The benefits (B) less costs (C) in year 2 can be expressed as $B - C/(1+r)$; those in year 3 can be expressed as $B - C/(1+r)(1+r)$ or $B - C/(1+r)^2$; those in year 4 can be expressed as $B - C/(1+r)^3$; and those in year 5 can be expressed as $B - C/(1+r)^4$. For the 5-year period, the net benefits less costs of the project can be calculated using the following formula:

$$\mathrm{NPV} = B^{y1} - C^{y1} + \frac{B^{y2} - C^{y2}}{1+r} + \frac{B^{y3} - C^{y3}}{(1+r)^2} \cdots \frac{B^{yx} - C^{yx}}{(1+r)^{x-1}}.$$

Using a present value function in a spreadsheet, such as Excel, yields net benefits of \$78,000 using a 5% "real" interest rate—the project barely breaks even. The benefit–cost ratio is the net present value of the stream of benefits over the 5 years divided by the net present value of the costs. In the illustration, the benefit–cost ratio is slightly more than 1 (1.0042). Present value analysis is often extremely sensitive to the choice of the appropriate interest rate (usually referred to as the discount rate) for the agency. If, instead of 5%, the agency's opportunity costs were reflected by a 7% interest rate, then the net present value turns to a negative \$151,000. The higher the discount rate, the greater future benefit streams are discounted. An alternative approach is to determine the return on investment (ROI), sometimes referred to as the internal rate of return (IRR) on the investment. The IRR is the discount rate that would make the present value of the project just equal to zero. In the illustration, the IRR is approximately 5.6%. The government agency or political decision maker can then assess the success or failure of the project based on whether a 5.6% rate of return is satisfactory given other opportunities the agency might have had in year 1.

Continuing or Not Continuing the Project

Should the agency continue the project in the illustraion? By year 5, the project is yielding total benefits of \$7.0 million and net benefits of \$2.51 million on expenditures of \$4.49 million—a benefit–cost ratio of 1.559. Certain costs incurred by the agency are now sunk costs; that is, funds have already been spent and resources used. They have no relevance for decisions about whether to continue the project. They have achieved (or not achieved) benefits. Thus, the previously spent funds on start-up and on capital costs are not considered by the agency in deciding whether to continue the project. The agency is concerned only with its current and future costs and expected continued benefits. Will it need to spend additional dollars to modify the program? Will it need to upgrade its facilities and equipment? What is the salvage value of current capital involved in the project or its opportunity costs for alternative uses, if any? Is there still a need or demand for the agency's product? Thus, the project's continuation faces a different evaluation than either a prospective or retrospective analysis of the project's net benefits. One of the challenges for the analyst is determining whether agency projections are realistic. Agency policymaker support for a project may lead to an underestimation of future costs and an overestimation of future benefits.

The cost–benefit illustration reveals an important distinction for the analyst—the difference between total and marginal benefits and costs. In assessing the overall "profitability" (or net benefits) of a proposed or existing project, an agency will consider the total costs involved in getting the project started through its operation's cycle. But at any point in time, when an agency is deciding whether to continue or discontinue a project or program, it should consider only its marginal costs and benefits.

Framework for Analysis

In conducting a cost–benefit analysis as part of a program evaluation, the first step is to identify all of the known benefits and costs of the program, to the government, to the program clients or beneficiaries, and to others not directly involved in the program. There are several distinct categories of benefits and costs: real versus transfers; direct and indirect; tangible and intangible. Each of these categories is explained and examples are given to assist the analyst.

For each benefit or cost—direct or indirect—it is important to clearly state its nature, how it is measured, and any assumptions made in the calculations of the dollars involved. The statement of the assumptions is particularly critical because the dollar values often hinge on an analyst's assumptions. Those assumptions need to be made clear to the decision maker and also subjected to a sensitivity analysis to determine to what extent the outcome of the analysis is controlled by certain assumptions made.

Real Benefits and Costs versus Transfers

Real benefits and costs represent net gains or losses to society, whereas transfers merely alter the distribution of resources within society. Real benefits include dollars saved and dollars earned, lives saved and lives enriched, increased earnings and decreased costs to the taxpayers, and time saved and increased quality of life. In contrast, some societal gains are directly offset by other losses. For example, a local tax abatement program for the elderly will provide a tax-saving benefit to some but a cost (of equal amount) to others (higher taxes or lower services). Transfers also occur as a result of a change in relative prices of various goods and services as the economy adjusts to the provision of certain public goods and services. Transfers are often important to policymakers. Many government programs involve subsidizing of one group by another in the society and thus should be clearly identified where possible. But from an overall societal perspective, transfers do not increase total welfare; they merely redistribute welfare within society.

Direct and Indirect Benefits and Costs

Direct benefits and costs are those that are closely related to the primary objective(s) of the project. Indirect or secondary benefits and costs are by-products, multipliers, spillovers, or investment effects of the project or program. An oft-cited example of indirect benefits from space exploration is the spin-off of numerous technologies benefiting other industries. Direct costs include the costs of personnel, facilities, equipment and materials, and administration. Indirect costs are intended (such as overhead) and unintended costs that occur as a result of a government action. For example, a dam built for agricultural purposes may flood an area used by hikers who would lose the value of this recreation. This loss would have to offset by benefit gains to those using the lake created by the dam for recreation. In all cases, the benefits and costs must be traced to the government action. For example, if a claimed benefit is the creation of new jobs, the benefit is the new jobs created at the margin, over what new jobs would have occurred without the government action.

Tangible and Intangible Benefits and Costs

Tangible benefits and costs are those that the analyst can readily convert to dollars or find an approximate valuation for. Intangible benefits and costs are those that one cannot or chooses not to put a price on in an explicit fashion, e.g., the value of wilderness or increased "sense of community." The process of valuation of costs and benefits and various methods of approaching the intangibles are discussed below; however, this is perhaps the most problematic area of benefit–cost analysis. It is especially difficult to place a dollar value on many intangible benefits.

Determining the Geographic Scope of the Analysis

Although the focus of an analysis may be within a certain geographical area (e.g., a political jurisdiction, such as a state), there may be benefits or costs that spill over to neighboring areas (another jurisdiction). One method of dealing with these spillovers or externalities is through transfer pricing, or estimating the value of the subsidy or cost prevention measure, if deemed important for the analysis. There is a tendency for evaluators of existing projects to ignore spillover costs and benefits if they are not costed in some fashion; however, these spillovers often have political consequences. Thus, by attempting to measure their benefits or costs, one gains insight into the total effects of the project.

Valuing the Benefits

Most economists argue that, despite their imperfections, market prices are the best valuation of a benefit. Therefore, the evaluator should use a market value when one is available or a surrogate, such as willingness to pay. For most government programs, the recipients are not fully paying for the benefits received; therefore, the evaluator must make an alternative assessment of value. For example, the value or shadow price of a "free" outdoor swimming pool might be the amount that people are willing to pay for a similar swimming experience in a private or nonprofit pool. In addition, particularly in developing nations, there often are market distortions (e.g., tariffs, monopolies, and subsidies) and no true competitive market. In this case, attempts are made to find a shadow price, such a world price, that approximates a competitive market value.

Cost avoidance or cost savings are also benefits. Thus, an anti-crime program analyst could measure dollars saved from avoided burglaries. An anti-flood program analyst could measure dollars saved from avoiding flood damage. A health program analyst could measure avoided costs such as medical care expenditures and loss of productivity.

Time saved is a tangible benefit. However, measurement of its value is more subjective. Each person may value his or her time differently. A common method of estimating the value of time is by using the economists' theory of work–leisure tradeoff. When people have control over the hours they are working, they will work (including overtime) until their subjective value of leisure is equal to the income they would gain from one more hour of work—their after-tax wage rate.

Lives saved are clearly a real, tangible benefit—an inestimable value to the person whose life was saved—and the justification for many government health and safety programs. Economists have developed two principal methods to value a human life. The first, which is often used in civil court cases, estimates an individual's lost earnings for his/her remaining life. A second approach looks at people's acceptance of higher risk jobs and the related higher salaries paid for a higher probability of death. If the chief benefit of a government program is to save lives, a cost–benefit analysis is extremely sensitive to the analyst's choice of a dollar figure per life saved. In such a case, it is not clear that a cost–benefit analysis is superior to a cost-effectiveness analysis that would simply calculate the cost of the program per life saved, without making a judgment on the value of life.

Increased productivity is a common benefit goal of many government investment programs, either capital investments, such as roads, bridges, water projects, and other infrastructure developments, or human capital investments, such as education and job training. Typically, these benefits might be measured in increased profits or lifetime earnings.

Cost Categories

In examining various types of program costs, both direct and indirect, the following categories are often used:

- one-time or up-front costs: planning, research and development, pilot projects, and computer software;
- on-going investment costs: land, buildings and facilities, equipment and vehicles, and initial workforce training;
- recurring costs: operations and maintenance; salaries, wages, and fringe benefits for personnel; materials and supplies; overhead costs;
- compliance costs: time of citizens to fill out forms; cost to business of new health and safety or Environmental Protection Agency regulations; and
- mitigation measures: preventing a cost to government or to others, such as pollution control equipment or relocation costs for affected persons or animals.

Table II provides a framework for cost–benefit analysis with examples and generally accepted approaches to valuation of the benefits and costs.

Key Issues and Concerns

Spillovers and Unintended Effects of Government Actions

Private firms are unconcerned with costs or benefits to third parties (nonbuyers). For example, if a local community has built a new road to a plant or if effluent from the plant pollutes the downstream locality or places strains on the government's wastewater treatment plant, these spillover costs (or externalities) are not taken into account by a private firm when it analyzes its profit margin. The firm will "internalize" these costs only if the government taxes, regulates, or otherwise holds the firm accountable. Regardless of government action, however, any program evaluation must consider these spillover costs to society.

Unfortunately, government actions do not have only beneficial effects; some adversely impact the environment and others may have unintended consequences on certain populations. A new dam may flood a wildlife habitat; an urban renewal program may displace low-income housing. Often government tries to mitigate the adverse consequences of their actions and those costs are considered in the analysis. However, even if the government has not taken actions to mitigate damages to others, those damages should be counted. If it is impossible to calculate the dollar value of the damage (e.g., certain environmental consequences), one method of evaluating the damage is to calculate what it would have cost the government to mitigate the damage had it chosen to do so.

Other Cost Issues

The costs of capital assets should be spread out over their expected useful life. There are many standard depreciation schedules for buildings and other capital equipment—sometimes there are different rates used for accounting or tax purposes. For government programs, an estimate needs to be made of the useful life of the asset considering physical deterioration, potential for obsolescence, salvage value at the end of the program, and other factors. Normally, the asset (less its final salvage value) is depreciated equally per year over the life of the asset (straight-line depreciation). In addition to depreciation, the government loses the opportunity to use the money that is tied up in the undepreciated asset—this opportunity cost is expressed as an interest rate times the undepreciated portion. Spreadsheets and numerical tables also provide an annualized cost of amortization plus interest. Land is not consumed as other capital facilities and equipment and it is not depreciated; however, it has alternative uses. Land used for one activity cannot be used for another and it cannot be sold to raise funds for other activities. Its value for a particular program is its opportunity cost to the government—normally expressed as the market value of the land times the prevailing rate of interest for government investments (e.g., long-term U.S. Treasury bill rate).

The cost of interest payments is sometimes counted as a program or project cost if the project required the issuance of debt to finance it. This is particularly true if the program or project is designed to be self-sufficient with revenues paying for total costs (for example, a specific recreational facility or a water or sewer project). From a budgetary perspective, interest payments are clearly a cost. Some economists, however, argue that interest

Table II Cost–Benefit Framework

	Illustration of Benefit–Cost	*Valuation approaches*
Benefits		
Direct: Tangible	Goods and services	Fair market value or willingness to pay
	Increased productivity/earnings	Increased production or profits/lifetime earnings
	Time saved	After-tax wage rate
Direct: Intangible	Lives saved	Lifetime earnings (if valued)
	Healthier citizens	(Implicit or contingent valuation using survey data or other techniques)
	Quality of life	
	Aesthetics	
Indirect: Tangible	Cost savings	Difference between before and after action
	Spillover impacts to third parties	Estimated impact or mitigation of impact
	Multiplier effects	Additional indirect jobs created by proposal
Indirect: Intangible	Preservation of community	
	Increased self-esteem	
Costs		
Direct: Tangible	Personnel	Wages and benefits
	Materials and supplies	Current expenses
	Rentals (facilities/equipment)	Fair market rents
	Capital purchases	Depreciation plus interest on undepreciated part or annualized cost of depreciation and interest
	Land	Next best use or market value times interest rate
	Volunteers	Market or leisure value
Direct: Intangible	Fear if harm	
Indirect: Tangible	General overhead	Standard allocation formula or activity-based costing
	Spillover costs to third parties	Estimation of impact or mitigation cost
	Environmental damage	
	Compliance/client costs	Resources required of others (money, time, etc.)
Indirect: Intangible	Loss of aesthetics	Surveys of valuation
Transfers	Taxes and subsidies	(While pure transfers result in no net gains or loses to society, they may be important for decision-makers because of their distributional consequences)
	Changes in profitability of businesses/industries	
	Changes in relative land value	

payments on borrowing should not be counted—that including both borrowing interest cost and opportunity interest cost double-counts this cost to government. If the analyst is doing a comparison of programs across jurisdictions, the inclusion of interest payments from borrowing, although representing a real budget cost to the jurisdictions that are borrowing, would give a faulty comparison of program efficiency.

The choice of an appropriate discount rate for government is subject to considerable debate. Many economists argue for the use of a before- or after-tax private sector interest rate based on the theory that government expenditures require taxation or borrowing that takes money out of the private sector and therefore government should be held to a similar investment standard. Others argue that government exists to operate programs that the private sector will not. Therefore, a low social discount rate, 2 to 3%, is the appropriate standard. Still others suggest using the rate at which government can borrow funds, such as the "real" long-term Treasury bill rate or municipal bond rate for state–local projects. Unless mandated otherwise, analysts should use a range of discount rates to determine how sensitive the net benefits or benefit–cost ratio is to the choice of a particular discount rate.

It is important for the analyst to recognize that conducting a present value analysis is not the same as adjusting for inflation. Most cost–benefit analysts use constant dollars. But a decision to use current (nominal) or constant (inflation adjusted out) dollars does affect the choice of an appropriate discount rate. If benefits and costs are discounted for inflation, then the discount rate should reflect a real market rate, i.e., the full market rate less anticipated inflation. If future benefits and costs include inflation, the discount rate must reflect the full market rate, which includes an inflation factor.

Analysis of Benefits–Costs

Presenting the Results

Net present value of benefits minus costs or costs minus benefits is the most traditional format for government agencies to present the results of the analysis; however, a benefit–cost ratio is sometimes used when comparing similar programs. The benefit–cost ratio is determined by dividing the total present value of benefits by the total present value of costs. For example, if benefits equal $20 million and costs equal $10 million, the program is said to have a benefit–cost ratio of 2 to 1 or 2.0. Any project with a benefit–cost ratio of less than 1.0 should not be undertaken because the government's opportunity cost (its discount rate) is greater than that returned by the project.

Unlike the private sector, government evaluators usually do not conduct ROI or IRR analysis; however, such an analysis also can be computed. It is the discount rate that would yield total present value benefits equal to costs. It is important for the analyst to conduct a sensitivity analysis of key assumptions to see which have the greatest impact on the analysis. What is the probability that those assumptions will occur? The analyst should examine a range of alternative assumptions and determine how they impact the analysis.

Intangibles

No matter how creative the analyst, there are some benefits and costs that defy quantification. Even if an analyst can value the cost of an injury, that dollar figure will not fully capture the pain and suffering involved, and financial savings from burglaries prevented does not fully capture the sense of security that comes with crime prevention. These are often important components of the cost–benefit equation and should be identified and explained as clearly as possible. Cost–benefit analysis may sometimes draw attention to an implicit valuation of some intangibles that may hitherto have been hidden in rhetoric. For example, if the costs of Program X exceed the "hard" benefits (i.e., those that are quantifiable in dollar terms) by an amount y, the intangibles must be worth at least y to the public and their decision makers or the program should be reconsidered.

Equity Concerns

It is not just the total benefits and costs but also who benefits and who pays that are of concern to policymakers. This is not always easy to determine, but where there are strong distributional consequences to the program, they should be noted. In general, government taxpayers subsidize the beneficiaries of specific government programs. One approach to dealing with distributional issues is to weight the benefits and costs. For example, the analyst could weight a benefit or cost to a low-income family as twice the value of a similar benefit and cost to a middle-income family and three times as much as a similar benefit to an upper-income family. The issue is the appropriate weights—one more subjective factor that must ultimately become a judgment by policymakers. Perhaps a better alternative is to attempt to identify the costs and benefits to each significant group that is impacted by the project.

Comparison with Cost-Effectiveness Analysis

The major alternative to cost–benefit analysis is cost-effectiveness analysis, which relates the cost of a given alternative to specific measures of program objectives. A cost-effectiveness analysis could compare costs to units of program objectives, for example, dollars per life saved on various highway safety programs. Cost-effectiveness analysis is sometimes the first step in a cost–benefit analysis. It is especially useful when the program's objectives are clear and either singular or sufficiently related so that the relationship between the objectives is clear and the evaluator cannot place a dollar value on program benefits. For example, if the goals of certain education programs are to prevent high school dropouts, alternative programs can be compared by analyzing the costs per dropout prevented (or per increase in the percentage of students graduating) without valuing those benefits in dollars.

The major advantage of cost-effectiveness analysis is that it frees the analyst from expressing all benefits in monetary terms. The analyst can simply present the benefits per x dollars and allow the decision maker to assess whether the benefits equal the costs. However, government programs often generate more than one type of benefit. Therefore, the analyst would have to weight the various benefits to achieve a common "denominator," whereas in cost–benefit analysis it is dollars that are the common denominator. Nevertheless, when valuing in dollars is impossible or impractical, or where the program objectives are singular, cost-effectiveness analysis provides an alternative economic technique. Other alternatives to cost–benefit analysis include cost–utility analysis, risk analysis, and a variety of decision-making grids that value and weight various aspects of program alternatives.

Conclusion: The Uses and Limitations of Cost–Benefit Analysis

Cost–benefit or cost-effectiveness analyses are not panaceas that will provide decision makers with "the answer." However, if the analyst provides an accurate framework of benefits and costs—attempting to identify them, measure them, and value them—the decision maker is provided with a wealth of information, on the basis of which a better decision can be made.

The greatest danger in such analysis is the "black box" syndrome. Instead of laying out the relevant issues, assumptions, and concerns, the analyst may be tempted to hide the messiness of the analysis from the decision maker, presenting a concise answer as to net benefits, net costs, or cost-effectiveness. However, two honest, careful analysts might arrive at opposite conclusions on the same set of facts if their assumptions about those data differ. A Scotsman once proclaimed that the "devil is in the detail" and it is the details—the assumptions and the sensitivity of the analysis to particular assumptions—that may be of most use to the decision maker in judging the value and usefulness of the evaluator's work.

See Also the Following Articles

Commensuration • Epidemiology • Intangible Assets: Concepts and Measurements

Further Reading

Adler, M., and Posner, E. (eds.) (2001). *Cost–Benefit Analysis: Legal, Economic, and Philosophical Perspectives*. University of Chicago Press, Chicago, IL.

Boardman, A. E., Greenberg, D. H., Vinning, A. R., and Weimer, D. L. (1996). *Cost–Benefit Analysis: Concepts and Practices*. Prentice Hall, Upper Saddle River, NJ.

Kee, J. E. (2004). Cost-effectiveness and cost–benefit analysis. In *Handbook of Practical Program Evaluation* (J. Wholey, H. Hatry, and K. Newcomer, eds.), 2nd Ed., pp. 506–541. Jossey-Bass, San Francisco, CA.

Levin, H. M., and McEwan, P. J. (2001). *Cost-Effectiveness Analysis*, 2nd Ed. Sage, Thousand Oaks, CA.

Mishan, E. J. (1988). *Cost–Benefit Analysis: An Informal Introduction*. Unwin Hyman Press, London.

Nas, T. F. (1996). *Cost–Benefit Analysis: Theory and Applications*. Sage, Thousand Oaks, CA.

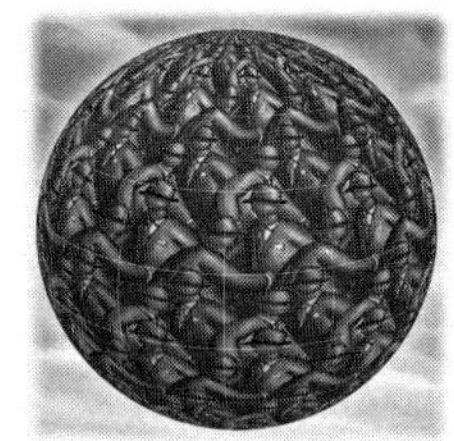

County and City Data

Karen D. Johnson-Webb

Bowling Green State University, Bowling Green, Ohio, USA

Glossary

annexation Changing the boundaries of two municipalities by decreasing the land area of one and increasing the land base of the other; extending the boundaries of a municipality by incorporating the territory of an adjacent unincorporated area.

borough The primary legal division in Alaska; in other states, treated by the U.S. Census Bureau as statistically equivalent to a county.

census area One of several types of areas demarcated by the U.S. Census Bureau specifically for data collection purposes.

central city Usually the largest city in a metropolitan statistical area or consolidated metropolitan statistical area. Additional cities qualify as central cities if requirements specified by the Office of Management and Budget are met concerning population size and commuting patterns.

city A type of incorporated place in all U.S. states and the District of Columbia.

county The primary legal division in every U.S. state except Alaska and Louisiana.

incorporated place A type of governmental unit legally incorporated as either a city, town, borough, or village. These entities are created to provide government services for a place that has legally delineated boundaries.

independent city An incorporated place that is not part of any county.

metropolitan area (MA) A core area with a large population nucleus, usually of about 50,000 people, together with adjacent communities that have a high degree of economic and social integration with that core. In New England, the total MA population must number at least 75,000.

parish The primary legal subdivision of the state of Louisiana.

place A location where population is concentrated in sufficient numbers to be either an incorporated place, or a location that is delineated by the U.S. Census Bureau for statistical purposes.

County and city data can be very useful to policymakers, researchers, academics, practitioners, and the general public. The data that are collected for these entities are often the basis for public policymaking, economic development, and formation of social programs. Therefore, a clear understanding of what these geopolitical units encompass is important. It is also essential to understand the benefits and difficulties associated with the data collected at these scales. A wide array of important data is collected and disseminated for counties and cities—for example, vital statistics and economic, demographic, fiscal, and social data. The Census Bureau, a part of the U.S. Department of Commerce, oversees the collection of a wide range of data. It also compiles data and information about the geographical extent of these entities. Therefore, census data will be a major focus of this article. In the United States, the Census Bureau is the primary agency for the collection of data for counties and cities.

Overview of Counties

In the United States, each state is generally divided into counties, which are smaller administrative districts. According to the U.S. Census Bureau, "counties are the primary legal division of states." The Census Bureau also recognizes several county equivalents. A large quantity of data is collected and published for counties, which makes them a good scale for local analysis. The boundaries of counties remain relatively stable and this fact makes county data ideal for comparisons from one time period to another. However, the boundaries of counties do change periodically, and this has implications for comparison of data across time periods. The National Association of Counties (NACo) reports that there are 3066 counties in the United States. However, the U.S. Census Bureau recognized 3219 units as counties or county equivalents in 2000. This figure includes municipios in Puerto Rico and county equivalents in other U.S. territories.

County Equivalents

County equivalents are treated as counties by the Census Bureau for data collection purposes (Table I). For historical and cultural reasons, counties are called parishes in Louisiana. Before the 2000 census, Alaska was composed of boroughs; the primary legal division in Alaska is now called a "city and borough," which is considered to be a county equivalent.

Independent Cities

Independent cities are the most common type of county equivalent. Independent cities are considered cities in every sense of the word. However, for the purposes of this discussion, they are treated as counties because they are considered by the Census Bureau to be county equivalents. There are now 39 independent cities in the states of Virginia, Maryland, Missouri, and Nevada. Using Virginia as a case study, the concept of an independent city may be aptly illustrated (Fig. 1). Most of the independent cities in Virginia are completely enclosed by an adjacent county. Some independent cities collect and report data independently of their surrounding county; in others, data are collected for both the independent city and its surrounding county and are reported by that county.

When working with county data in states that have independent cities, a number of pitfalls can be encountered. Those who wish to utilize county data must first be made aware of how the independent cities are situated. For example, in assessing the correct figure for the population of Albemarle County, the population that has been enumerated in Charlottesville City must be taken into consideration. Even residents of these independent areas often assume they reside in a county when in fact they reside in an independent city.

Changes to County Boundaries

County level is a good scale of analysis because for most of the 50 states in the United States, these boundaries have remained relatively stable or unchanged over the past several decades. Changes do occur, however. In most states, county or county equivalent boundary changes may be made by majority vote of the electorate of the jurisdictions involved. The Census Bureau is then notified of the changes, which will be reflected in future data collection. Since 1970, most of the changes in counties or county equivalents have taken place in the states of Virginia or Alaska. County name changes also sometimes occur for various reasons. One county may be split into two counties and all or parts of counties may be merged into a new county. An independent city may be absorbed by its surrounding or adjacent county. Prominent examples of this include the name change for Dade County, Florida in 1996. It was changed to Miami-Dade County by a majority vote of the electorate. Also, Cibola County, New Mexico was created from part of Valencia County in 1981. The city of Louisville, Kentucky and Jefferson County, Kentucky were combined in 2003. Changes such these must be taken into consideration when using data for these entities. This is especially true when comparing data for counties or their equivalents over time.

Table I Census-Designated County Equivalents[a]

County equivalent	*Geographical area*	*New designation for 2000?*
City and borough	Alaska	Yes
Borough	Alaska	No
Municipality	Alaska, Northern Mariana Islands	Yes
Municipio	Puerto Rico	No
Parish	Louisiana	No
Independent city	VA, MD, MO, NV[b]	No

[a] Adapted from the *Glossary of Basic Geographic and Related Terms*, Census 2000, U.S. Census Bureau. Data available at http://www.census.gov

[b] Virginia, Maryland, Missouri, and Nevada.

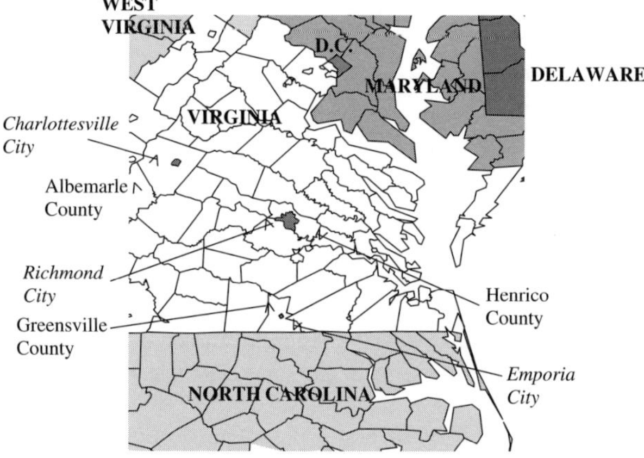

Figure 1 Illustration of independent cities in the state of Virginia.

Overview of Cities

A city is a legally defined geographic entity that is incorporated. Incorporated places provide a range of public services to the population situated within its bounds.

A variety of data are also collected for cities. Cities as a unit of analysis, however, can be complex. Cities are more fluid in their extent than are counties. The boundaries of cities often cross county boundaries. City boundaries are more subject to change through processes such as annexation. These factors make comparison of city data over time more problematic.

Metropolitan Areas

Cities are often a part of larger metropolitan areas (MAs). MAs are designated by the federal Office of Management and Budget (OMB) according to standards published in the *Federal Register* and were designed to be used solely for statistical purposes. Metropolitan areas are urban areas that are composed of cities and counties (or county equivalents) that are closely connected economically and socially. To date, several types of metropolitan areas have been designated.

Metropolitan Statistical Areas

A metropolitan statistical area (MSA), also designated by the OMB, has been developed for use by federal statistical agencies. These areas are utilized for data collection and dissemination on the state, county, and municipal levels. A type of metropolitan area, the MSA is one that is not closely associated with another MA in terms of economic and social interaction and integration. It is usually surrounded by nonmetropolitan counties. Counties are the building blocks for MSAs in states that designate counties as the primary legal division. Each MSA must contain either a place with a minimum population of 50,000 or a Census Bureau-defined urbanized area and a total MA population of at least 100,000. Additionally, in MSAs, the county (or counties) that contain(s) the largest city becomes the "central county" (or counties). Any adjacent counties that have at least 50% of their population in the urbanized area that surrounds the largest city also become part of the MSA. If additional "outlying counties" exist, they are included in the MSA if they meet specified requirements for population density and for the percentage commuting to the central counties. The title of each MSA consists of the names of up to three of its central cities and the name of each state into which the MSA extends. Central cities with less than 250,000 population and less than one-third the population of the MSA's largest city are not usually included in an MSA title. The exception to this convention is if local opinion supports the inclusion of the smaller central city in question. The titles and composition of MSAs are altered by the OMB fairly regularly, and new MAs and MSAs are also designated from time to time. These changes must be considered when comparing metropolitan data over time.

In New England, slightly different criteria are used for classifying metropolitan areas. MSAs in New England are defined in terms of county subdivisions, such as towns and cities. However, the Office of Management and Budget has also developed standards for county-based entities in New England, called New England county metropolitan areas (NECMAs). Central cities of a NECMA are those cities in the NECMA that qualify as central cities of an MSA or a consolidated metropolitan statistical area (CMSA). NECMA titles derive from names of central cities. NECMAs, which are defined for an MSA or a CMSA, include the county containing the first-named city in that MSA or CMSA title. The first-named cities of other MSAs or CMSAs may be used as well. In addition to these entities, each additional county having at least half its population in the MSA or CMSA whose first-named cities are in the previously identified county is also included. There are 12 NECMAs, including the Boston-Worcester-Lawrence, MA-NH-ME-CT CMSA and the Connecticut portion of the New York-Northern New Jersey-Long Island, NY-NJ-CT-PA CMSA.

An area that qualifies as an MSA and has more than 1,000,000 population may have primary metropolitan statistical areas (PMSAs) defined within it. An example of a PMSA is Milwaukee PMSA or New York PMSA. Titles of PMSAs typically are also based on central city names, but in certain cases consist of county names. Once PMSAs have been established, the larger MA, of which they are a part, is designated as a consolidated metropolitan statistical area (which must have at least 1,000,000 population). An example of this is Chicago-Gary-Lake County, IL-IN-WI CMSA. PMSAs are not required to contain at least 1,000,000 population. CMSAs and PMSAs are composed of entire counties. New England is an exception, where CMSAs are composed of cities and towns. NECMAs are not identified for individual PMSAs. Generally, titles of CMSAs are based on the titles of their component PMSAs. Figure 2 illustrates these concepts.

Core-Based Statistical Area System

As part of its periodic review of metropolitan area standards, the OMB has revised its standards for defining MAs. The OMB adopted a set of standards that replaced its previous system of classifying MAs with the core-based statistical area (CBSA) system in June 2003. These changes addressed, as a first priority, the concerns that data users had about the complexity of the current standards, both conceptually and operationally, as they have evolved since 1950.

CBSAs use counties and county equivalents as building blocks (and cities and towns in New England; these are called New England city and town areas, or NECTAs). Designation of CBSAs is based on geographic areas that contain at least one core area of at least 10,000 population.

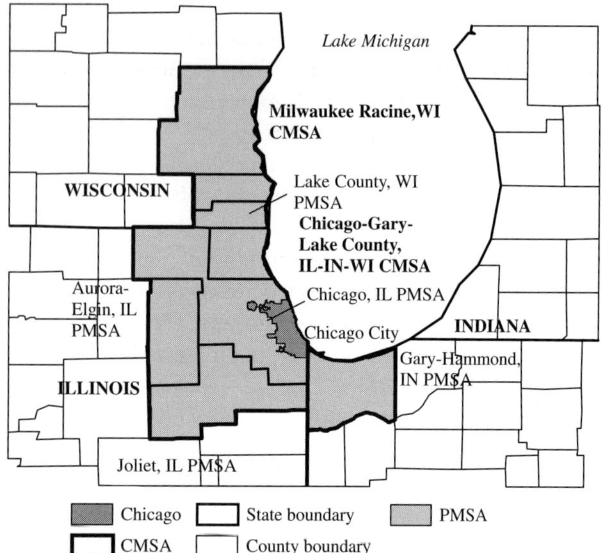

Figure 2 Illustration of county, city, metropolitan statistical area, primary metropolitan statistical area (PMSA), and consolidated metropolitan statistical area (CMSA), around Chicago, Illinois. Note that the city of Chicago is part of the Chicago-Gary-Hammond, Illinois CMSA.

High measures of social and economic integration also continue to be used as criteria to designate outlying territory to the CBSA. Two categories of CBSAs have been defined: metropolitan statistical areas and micropolitan statistical areas. Metropolitan statistical areas are based on urbanized areas of at least 50,000 population. Micropolitan statistical areas are based on urban clusters of at least 10,000 but less than 50,000 population. NECTAs are referred to as either a metropolitan NECTA or a micropolitan NECTA. Counties that fall outside these criteria are designated as outside core-based statistical areas. These designations provide definitions for collecting, tabulating, and publishing federal statistics that are nationally consistent for geographic areas. The OMB stipulates however, that these geographic entities, like those described in the previous section, are to be used for statistical purposes only and are not designed for other uses, such as implementation or administration of nonstatistical federal programs. A complete description of this new classification system can be found in the *Federal Register*.

Coding and Identification

Each county and city is assigned a unique Federal Information Processing Standards (FIPS) code by the National Institute of Standards and Technology (NIST). NIST, a part of the U.S. Department of Commerce, is responsible, among other functions, for the setting and maintenance of standards for government data.

FIPS codes are a standardized set of numeric or alphabetic codes used to ensure uniform identification of geographic entities throughout all federal government agencies. The objectives of this standard are to improve the utilization of data resources of the federal government and to avoid unnecessary duplication and incompatibilities in the collection, processing, and dissemination of data. FIPS codes are useful in facilitating the accurate transfer and utilization of data between government agencies. Among many other legal or geographic entities, states, counties, county equivalents, MAs, and cities have all been assigned a unique FIPS code by NIST.

County FIPS codes are a five-digit number assigned on the basis of state and county. For instance, the first two digits of a county FIPS code represent the state of which that county is a part. For example, the FIPS code for California is 06; the FIPS code for Los Angeles County is 037. Therefore, the FIPS code for Los Angeles County, California is 06037. Note that the FIPS code for Darke County, Ohio is also 037. However the FIPS code for Ohio is 39, thus Darke County, Ohio has a unique FIPS code of 39037.

Geocoding is a method of referencing data for spatial analysis, and geocodes are particularly useful to those who map their data. FIPS codes are commonly used for geocoding county data.

Data Sources

County and city data are available through several sources. Most city and county data are considered to be secondary data because they are collected by an entity other than the user. The most commonly used secondary data sources can be divided into two basic categories: public domain data and data collected by private or nongovernmental organizations or businesses. The federal government of the United States is the largest and most comprehensive source of public domain demographic and economic data for cities and counties. Within the federal government, the U.S. Census Bureau is the most important data source and the entity that is most familiar to the public at large.

The U.S. Census Bureau

The Census Bureau provides a wide array of data on the U.S. population. Data are collected by the Census Bureau through decennial censuses, through provision of population projections and estimates, and through other surveys that are conducted between censuses. Census data are probably the most widely utilized source of city and county data. Currently, a large proportion of

Census 2000 is available for counties and cities and more datasets and variables are scheduled for release in 2003–2004.

There are several benefits to using census data. Census data are widely available to the public through a variety of means; they are usually available at most public and scholarly libraries either in hard copy or in compact disk read-only memory (CD-ROM) format. However, use of census and other secondary data has limitations. Such data are a snapshot in time. This can be problematic, especially if the user is considering a population or variable that changes rapidly in quality or quantity over a short period of time. Also, underrepresented populations, such as the homeless, undocumented immigrants, and ethnic and race minorities, often the very populations that require the services provided by agencies and prescribed by policymakers, tend to be significantly undercounted in the decennial censuses. Intercensal population estimates can be helpful here, especially in urban areas; however, estimates for underrepresented groups may contain undercounts as well.

Two other frequently used federal data sources are the Bureau of Labor Statistics (BLS) and the Bureau of Economic Analysis. The BLS, a part of the U.S. Department of Labor, is the principal federal agency for collecting and disseminating a broad range of data in the field of labor economics and statistics. The BLS provides an array of variables, such as employment data and data on productivity and price indexes, among many, many others. BLS also provides the local area unemployment statistics (LAUS), a database of monthly and annual employment, unemployment, and labor force data for various geographic scales, including counties, metropolitan areas, and cities. The Bureau of Economic Analysis (BEA), an agency of the U.S. Department of Commerce, provides data estimates and analyses of personal income, population, employment, and gross state product for counties, MSAs, and other local areas through its regional economic information system (REIS). These are the only detailed, broadly inclusive economic time series data for local areas currently provided in the United States.

State Data Centers

Since 1978, the Census Bureau has made much of its data available to the public through the State Data Center Program. This program is a cooperative effort between the Census Bureau and a network of state agencies, libraries, universities, and governments, both regional and local. Each state in the union has a memorandum of understanding with the Census Bureau through one or more of these outlets. A second program, called the Business and Industry Data Center (BIDC), was created in 1988 to provide local businesses easier access to economic data. These census data are made available to users (the general public) at little or no cost. The Census Bureau provides a list of all the State Data Centers and BIDCs on its website (http://www.census.gov).

Print Sources

City and county data are provided in print, in several important publications. The best known sources are *The County and City Data Book*, the *State and Metropolitan Data Book*, and *USA Counties*. The U.S. Census Bureau publishes each of these reference books. *The County and City Data Book* has been published since the 1940s and contains population and economic data for all U.S. counties and for cities with 25,000 or more inhabitants, and places of 2500 or more inhabitants. *The State and Metropolitan Data Book*, which has been published since 1979, is a supplement to the *Statistical Abstract of the United States*. *The State and Metropolitan Book* summarizes social, economic, and political statistics for states and metropolitan areas. It also serves as a guide to other publications and data sources. *USA Counties*, which includes data from 1982 on, provides over 5000 data items for counties. These data are gathered from nine different federal and private agencies.

Internet Sources

Since the advent of the World Wide Web, city and county data have become more widely available and much easier to procure and manipulate for those with access to and knowledge of the Internet. From the Census Bureau's website for the Census 2000, American Fact Finder, county or city data can be downloaded for any number of variables. The reports that can be generated may be designed by the user to make geographical comparisons, and a user may also generate a data report for a variety of scales in the same report. For instance, a report can be designed to provide data on the race and ethnicity breakdown of Chicago City, Cook County, Illinois, Chicago MSA, and the state of Illinois. The same variables (and others) could be generated for all the counties in Illinois as well.

Most public libraries are equipped with Internet access, and may even have a librarian who is trained to assist patrons with accessing census data from the World Wide Web. State data centers may also make data available over the Internet on their websites. There are countless other sources of county and city data available on the Internet. One of the easiest methods of "diving in" is to use a gateway of some sort to narrow down or organize the data sets. A gateway is a website that provides access to a larger range of data or information from other Internet sources.

Information and Data Gateways

One of the most comprehensive gateways to federal statistical data is FED-STATS. It is a gateway to over 100 government agencies and their data. The types of data that can be found on FED-STATS range from census data, to statistics from the Immigration and Naturalization Service, to agricultural and economic censuses, to housing data, to vital statistics through the National Center for Health Statistics.

Another selected gateway includes the Census Bureau's American FactFinder, which was mentioned previously. Ameristat, a program of a nongovernmental organization called the Population Reference Bureau, provides summaries of various U.S. census data to the general public. Another example is the United States Historical Census Data Browser, which is maintained by the Fisher Library at the University of Virginia (UVA). The Fisher Library, like many other university-based libraries, obtains data from the Inter-University Consortium for Political and Social Research (ICPSR). ICPSR, a data gateway for member institutions, compiles data from a variety of sources that would be of interest to social science researchers. Member institutions are able to provide their patrons with a vast array of data sets and technical assistance.

Spatially referenced data are also available through both public and private organizations. The Census Bureau provides its Topologically Integrated Geographic Encoding and Referencing (TIGER) system files through its Census Bureau Geography gateway. The U.S. Geological Survey (USGS) and the Center for International Earth Science Information Network (CIESIN) at Columbia University are just two of the better known resources for geographic city or county data. These are but a small subset of the various information and data gateways that have become available on the World Wide Web.

See Also the Following Articles

Census, Varieties and Uses of Data • Federalism: Local, State, Federal and International Data Sources • State Data for the United States

Further Reading

Center for International Earth Science Information Network (CIESIN). (2003). Columbia University website. Available at http://www.ciesin.columbia.edu

Fisher Library. (2003). United States Historical Census Data Browser. Available at http://fisher.lib.virginia.edu

Gaquin, D., and Littman, M. (eds.) (1998). *1998 County and City Extra: Annual Metro, City, and County Data Book.* Bernan, Lanham, Maryland.

Office of the Federal Register. (2002). *Federal Register OMB BULLETIN NO. 99-04.* National Archives and Records Service, General Services Administration, Washington, D.C.

Office of Management and Budget. (2000). Standards for defining metropolitan and micropolitan statistical areas; notice. *Fed. Reg.* **65**(249), 82228–82238.

Population Reference Bureau. (2003). Ameristat website. Available at http://www.ameristat.org

U.S. Bureau of Census. (1996). *USA Counties 1996* (on CD-ROM). U.S. Department of Commerce, Washington, D.C.

U.S. Bureau of Census. (1998). *County and City Data Book. 1949.* U.S. Government Printing Office, Washington, D.C.

U.S. Bureau of Census. (1998). *State and Metropolitan Data Book 1997–98*, 5th Ed. U.S. Government Printing Office, Washington, D.C.

U.S. Bureau of Census. (2002). *About Metropolitan Areas.* Available at http://www.census.gov

U.S. Bureau of Census. (2003). *Census Bureau Geography.* Available at http://www.census.gov

U.S. Bureau of Census. (2003). *Guide to the State and Metropolitan Data Book.* Available at http://www.census.gov

U.S. Bureau of Census. (2003). *Guide to USA Counties.* Available at http://www.census.gov

U.S. Bureau of Census. (2003). *Significant Changes to Counties and County Equivalent Entities: 1970–Present.* Available at http://www.census.gov

U.S. Bureau of Census. (2003). *State & County QuickFacts.* Available at http://quickfacts.census.gov

U.S. Bureau of Economic Analysis. (2003). *Regional Economic Information System (REIS).* Available at http://www.bea.doc.gov

U.S. Bureau of Labor Statistics. (2003). *Local Area Unemployment Statistics (LAUS).* Available at http://stats.bls.gov

U.S. Geological Survey. (2003). *USGS Geospatial Data Clearinghouse.* Available at http://mapping.usgs.gov

Criminal Justice Records

Clayton Mosher
Washington State University, Vancouver, Washington, USA

Glossary

European Law Enforcement Organization (Europol) The European Police Office.

International Criminal Police Organization (Interpol).

self-report surveys Surveys in which individuals are asked to report on their commission of a variety of criminal acts.

United Nations Crime Surveys (UNCSs) Surveys conducted every 5 years (since the early 1970s) that collect data on crime and criminal justice system operations in certain member nations of the United Nations.

victimization surveys Surveys in which individuals are asked to report on their experiences as victims of crime.

Social scientists frequently use criminal justice system data in order to formulate theories about crime and to examine the operations of the system. Given increasing globalization and an interest in analyzing crime trends cross-nationally, international data sources on crime have been refined in recent years. This entry examines the history of the collection of data on crime in the United States and other countries, with a specific focus on data collected by the International Criminal Police Organization, and the United Nations Crime Surveys. After addressing some of the problems in using these sources of crime data, comparisons of crime rates for selected countries are presented.

Introduction

Since the early 1800s, social scientists and policy makers have been interested in measuring the amount of crime in society in order to examine trends in crime over time and differences in crime across jurisdictions, address the correlates of crime and develop theories on the causes of crime, and create policies to deal with the crime problem. This entry examines criminal justice records, which consist of data on crime collected and compiled by police agencies, courts, and correctional institutions. In addition to their use as measures of criminal activity, these data also reflect the activities of agents and organizations in the criminal justice system, including police, prosecutors, judges, and corrections officials.

The entry examines the history of the collection of criminal justice records; given increasing globalization and concerns with examining crime trends cross-nationally, it focuses on the collection of criminal justice records by international agencies. Particular attention will be paid to data collected by the International Police Agency (Interpol) and the United Nations through their World Crime Surveys. The entry examines the strengths and weaknesses of these data as measures of crime and the activities of components of criminal justice systems and what these data reveal about differences in crime and its correlates cross-nationally.

In using records derived from the criminal justice system as measures of crime in a particular society or jurisdiction, it is important to note that, in the aggregate, crime data are the product of two different conditions. One of these conditions is behavioral, that is, the volume of criminal acts committed in the society or jurisdiction; the other is institutional, that is, the activities of the agencies responsible for defining and maintaining public order. When we interpret data on crime trends, the practical task is to disentangle the social reality of behavioral change from the political and administrative reality of change in the institutions that respond to crime.

The History of Criminal Justice Records

European Countries

The first known publication of statistics derived from criminal justice records were based on individuals appearing in criminal courts in England in 1805, and more standardized judicial statistics recording indictments and convictions for indictable (more serious) offenses were collected annually in that country beginning in 1834. Early commentators on these statistics emphasized the importance of exercising caution in interpreting them and using them as measures of crime. For example, discussing an alleged increase in crime in England and Wales in the late 1800s, Morrison asserted in 1892 that it was not possible to determine through the examination of such statistics whether crime was increasing or decreasing in England due to the erratic and haphazard manner in which criminal statistics were collected and analyzed. Morrison further noted that a primary cause of increases in crime revealed by judicial statistics was changes in legislation that added offenses to criminal codes. At the same time, decreases in crime could be attributed to the abolition of certain laws and to the greater reluctance of the public and police to set the law in motion against trivial offenders by reporting their offenses. The influence of legislative changes on crime rates was also addressed by duCane, who noted in 1893 that offenses against the British Education Acts (which required parents to send their children to school), which were not legislatively mandated in England until 1870, totaled over 96,000 in 1890. In his work *The Decrease of Crime*, duCane thus argued that an uninformed comparison of crime rates over the 1870–1890 period in England might conclude that crime had increased, when in reality the increase was attributable to an expansion in the definition of crime.

France published crime statistics, based on judicial data, in 1827 (covering the year 1825). These early crime statistics were part of the moral statistics movement that emerged in several Western countries in the early 1800s. The collection of these statistics was also related to the belief that the quantitative measurement techniques that were being applied in the physical sciences could be applied to the measurement of human phenomena. Based on judicial statistics from France, Quetelet in 1842 examined the correlates of crime, with a particular focus on gender and age. He also attempted to explain the causes of crime, examining factors such as the relationship between the consumption of alcohol and violent crime rates, the relationship between poverty and relative inequality and crime rates, and the relationship between the racial composition of the population and crime rates.

The United States

The earliest criminal justice records published on a statewide basis in the United States were judicial statistics from the state of New York in 1829; statewide statistics on prisons were first collected in Massachusetts in 1834. By 1905, 25 states had enacted legislation requiring the collection of statistics on the number of people prosecuted in their courts.

Prior to the development of the Uniform Crime Reporting (UCR) system in the United States in 1930, the closest thing to national crime statistics were data on individuals committed to jails, houses of correction, and penitentiaries. These statistics were compiled by the United States Census Bureau beginning in the 1850s, and collection continued in the years 1860, 1870, 1880, and 1890, with separate enumerations in 1904, 1910, 1923, and 1933. These data counted the number of offenders serving sentences on the date the census was taken, and information was collected on the sex, race, age, and length of sentence received by offenders, among other things.

Federal government attention to more refined criminal justice records began in 1870, when Congress passed a law creating the Department of Justice. One aspect of this legislation was a requirement that the attorney general make an annual report to Congress on the statistics of crime under the laws of the United States, and, as far as practicable, under the laws of the individual states. However, this provision was basically ignored by law enforcement officials, with the result that reliable measures of crime in the United States remained unobtainable.

In the 1920s, certain jurisdictions and states conducted surveys of their criminal justice systems. The first of these was conducted in Cleveland in 1922, and surveys at the state level were subsequently administered in Illinois, Pennsylvania, California, Virginia, Minnesota, Michigan, and Oregon. Although these studies provided important insights into the administration of criminal justice in the jurisdictions they examined, they too were not particularly useful for the purposes of crime measurement and cross-jurisdictional comparisons.

It is generally agreed that of all official sources of criminal justice system data, crimes reported to the police provide the best measure of the amount of crime occurring, but such statistics were not widely published in the United States until the 1930s. In 1929, with the exception of Massachusetts, no state printed any statistics concerning the total number of arrests made and only one state published figures on crimes known to the police. Almost the sole source of information in the field of police statistics was the annual reports of city police departments, and in 1929 only 14 cities in the United States published such data.

The UCR program was initiated in 1930, and in that year reports were received from 1127 cities and towns having a combined total population of approximately 46 million. In 1940, reports were received from 2747 cities and towns with a total population of more than 70 million people.

Today, along with the UCR program, which addresses offenses known to the police, the federal government also publishes criminal justice records that are derived from court proceedings, correctional facilities, and probation and parole. These data are available at the U.S. Bureau of Justice Statistics Web site. Although participation in the UCR program is voluntary, the proportion of U.S. law enforcement agencies participating is remarkably high. A total of 16,788 state, county, and city law enforcement agencies, covering more than 272 million inhabitants, submitted crime reports under the UCR system in 1999.

In considering the use of UCR data to understand crime and crime trends, it is important to note that this source undercounts crime to a certain extent. For example, police are unlikely to uncover all victimless crimes such as illegal drug use and prostitution, and victims do not report all crimes to the police. Victimization surveys, which question individuals about their experiences of crime, indicate that approximately two and half times as many crimes occur in the United States as appear in official data. Self-report surveys, which ask individuals about their own involvement in criminal activities, similarly reveal a great amount of hidden crime that does not appear in official statistics. Further, there is evidence that at least some police departments manipulate and even fabricate their official crime reports for political purposes and that there may be race and social-class biases in the structure of policing.

Criminal Justice Records in International Context

The earliest known occasion at which the collection of criminal justice records at the international level was considered was at the General Statistical Congress held in Brussels in 1853; this was followed by another effort at the International Congress on the Prevention and Repression of Crime in London in 1872. A major problem identified in this early period, and one that continues to frustrate efforts to collect international data, was that definitions of crime are not consistent across all nations.

Interpol Data

The International Criminal Police Organization (Interpol) has collected international crime statistics based on crimes known to the police annually since 1950. The European Law Enforcement Organization (Europol), formed in 1999, also serves to facilitate the sharing of crime information among countries of the European Union. Interpol crime data are accessible at the organization's Web site. Interpol's first report was issued in 1954 and included data for only 36 countries; subsequently, data were published every 2 years and every year since 1993, with the inclusion of data on a greater number of countries. The most recent data available, for the year 2000, includes information from 70 countries. Interpol reports are published in four languages (Arabic, English, French, and Spanish) and the statistics relate to the major categories of crime brought to the attention of the police in Interpol member countries: murder, sex offenses (including rape), serious assault, theft, aggravated theft (robbery and violent theft, and breaking and entering), theft of motor cars, fraud, counterfeit currency offenses, drug offenses, and the total number of offenses contained in national crime statistics.

In discussing the use of these data, Interpol cautions that the statistics are not intended to be used for comparisons among different countries. This is due to the fact that the statistics cannot take into account the differences in the definitions of crime in different countries, the diversity of methods used by different countries in compiling the statistics, and the changes in laws or data collection methods over time. Interpol further notes that police statistics reflect reported crimes, but this only represents a fraction of the real level of crime. Furthermore, the volume of crime not reported to the police actually depends, to a certain extent, on the action of the police and can vary with time, as well as from country to country. As a result, Interpol notes that these statistics should be treated with caution.

So, there are two basic weaknesses with respect to Interpol data: (1) There are variations across nations in their definitions of crime, particularly property crimes; (2) there are differences in crime-reporting tendencies among countries. As the International Victimization Survey has demonstrated, the proportion of crime not reported to the police varies considerably across nations and across different types of crime. The access that people have to and trust they have in, police vary across nations and can thereby influence the proportion of crimes that are reported to the police. Generally, violent crimes are more likely to be reported to the police than personal thefts, female victims are more likely to report crimes than male victims, and older people are more likely to report crimes than younger people. In addition, countries in which a higher percentage of households have access to telephones tend to report a higher rate of crime, and countries in which household insurance is more developed similarly report a higher proportion of crime. As a result, cross-national comparisons using Interpol data are best done for crimes of extreme violence such as homicide, which are most likely to come to the attention of the police. In addition to these concerns regarding potential weaknesses in Interpol statistics, due to the fact that many crimes are committed against commercial enterprises, crime rates that are calculated using police statistics in the numerator and population in the denominator will be higher in countries with a larger number of commercial enterprises than in countries with fewer commercial enterprises, even when the risk of victimization to private citizens is the same.

United Nations Crime Surveys

An additional source of international data on crime is the United Nations Crime Surveys (UNCSs). Data from these surveys are accessible at the United Nations Web site. In the early years of the organization, the United Nations expressed interest in the collection of criminal justice statistics at the international level, with resolutions concerning this issue emanating from the UN Economic and Social Council in 1948 and 1951. However, with the exception of one limited cross-national crime survey conducted over the 1937–1946 period, international crime data were not compiled systematically until the early 1970s, when the current series of surveys was initiated by a resolution passed in the General Assembly.

The more recent UNCSs were initiated in 1977, covering 5-year intervals from 1970 (as of 2002, seven UNCSs had been conducted). The original rationale for collecting and comparing statistics at the international level was to provide social scientists with additional data to examine the correlates and causes of crime, and the first UNCS received responses from 64 nations, providing crime data for the years 1970–1975. The second UNCS covered the years 1975–1980 and represented an explicit change in rationale, with the emphasis moving from a focus on the causes of crime to issues surrounding the operations of criminal justice systems cross-nationally. This survey included data from 80 nations, but data from the first two surveys are not directly comparable due to the fact that approximately 25% of the countries that responded to the first survey did not complete the second. Similarly, approximately 30% of countries responding to the second survey did not respond to the first. The second UNCS also included a number of questions that were not asked in the first survey. The third UNCS covered the years 1980–1985, with 78 countries responding; the fourth UNCS covered the years 1986–1990, with 100 countries responding. In the fourth survey, data were also collected from major cities of the world, with 67 responding. The number of countries responding to the fifth and sixth UNCSs was somewhat lower than for the fourth, and as of 2002, 82 countries had responded to the seventh UNCS, which covered the years 1998–2000.

Variables included in the more recent UNCSs include information from each responding country on the combined police and prosecution expenditure by year; the number of police personnel by gender; the total number of homicides (intentional and unintentional); the number of assaults, rapes, robberies, thefts, burglaries, frauds, and embezzlements; the amount of drug crime; the number of people formally charged with crime; the number of individuals prosecuted and the types of crime they were prosecuted for; the gender and age of individuals prosecuted; the number of individuals convicted and acquitted; the number sentenced to capital punishment and various other sanctions; the number of prisoners, the length of sentences they received, and prison demographics. It is important to note, however, that these data are not complete for all countries responding to the surveys for all years.

Problems in Using International Crime Data

When making comparisons of criminal justice records across countries using Interpol and UNCS data, it is important to be cognizant of a number of problems. The first is the issue of differences in the categorization of criminal offenses. For example, in contrast to all other Western nations, the Netherlands has no category for robbery; an uninformed examination of data from that country might conclude that no serious property crime occurs. Similarly, in contrast to other countries, Japan classifies assaults that eventually result in the death of the victim as an assault rather than as a homicide.

It is generally agreed that homicide is the most similarly defined and classified crime across nations, whereas rape and sexual offenses are probably the least similarly defined and classified. But caution must be exercised even when examining data on homicides. For example, although the UNCS collects information on the total, intentional, and unintentional homicides for each country, there are extreme differences in the proportion of homicides classified as intentional across countries, with a range from 10% to (inexplicably) over 100%. This clearly indicates the use of diverse criteria across nations in defining intentional and unintentional homicides. In the Netherlands, many nonserious offenses are first recorded by the police as attempted murders, for example, a situation in which the driver of a car almost hits a pedestrian. At least partially as a result of such coding, in 1990 the Netherlands reported a homicide rate of 14.8/100,000 to Interpol, which, on the surface, makes it appear to have a higher homicide rate than the United States. However, a closer perusal of the data indicate that over 90% of the offenses coded as homicide in the Netherlands were attempts. The importance of recognizing these distinctions between actual and attempted homicides cannot be understated; an uninformed comparison of statistics cross-nationally can be very misleading. For example, in 1998, in his criticism of Dutch drug policy, the United States drug czar, General Barry McCaffrey, asserted that drug problems in the Netherlands were responsible for the fact that the murder rate in Holland was double that in the United States.

However, McCaffrey had arrived at the Dutch figure by combining homicides and attempted homicides, which he had not done for the U.S. figure. In fact, the correct Dutch homicide rate was less than one-quarter of the U.S. rate.

The classification of casualties as homicides can be particularly problematic in nations that are experiencing war, rebellion, or serious political and civil conflicts. For example, for Rwanda the 1994 Interpol report indicated a total of exactly 1 million homicides, which translates into a rate of 12,500 homicides per 100,000 population. Clearly, this figure for Rwanda's homicide rate, which is overly exact and incredibly high, includes deaths resulting from war and civil conflict.

Errors in international crime data and its interpretation can also result from problems with coding and the calculation of rates. For example, in the 1994 Interpol report, Belgium was indicated to have a homicide rate of 31.5/100,000 population, a figure that was 25 times greater than the figure for previous years. It turns out that a zero was left off the reported population of Belgium when calculating the homicide rate, with the result that the rate (which was based on a total of 315 homicides, 195 of which were attempts) was calculated based on a population of 1 million rather than the actual population of 10 million.

Similar coding problems and problems related to misinterpretations of the questions by reporting officials in some countries have been revealed in the data reported from the 2002 UNCS. For example, data from South Africa indicated that there were 24,238 female prisoners in that country in the year 2000, compared to 2390 in 1999. This increase was not due to a sudden surge in female crime in South Africa but was instead due to the fact that a stray 2 had crept in (i.e., the actual figure for female prisoners was 2438). UNCS data from Hong Kong from the seventh survey were also questionable, given that the total number of prisons reported for the year 2000 was 10,593, even though the total number of prison beds was only 9107. Clearly, what had occurred in this case, as also was the case for Malaysia, was that the people reporting the data misinterpreted the question as asking for the total number of *prisoners*, as opposed to the number of *prisons*. Data from Maldive were even more problematic. In that country, the 2000 data indicated that there were 775 adult prisons, 775 prison beds, 775 staff in prisons, and a total of only six individuals incarcerated. The United Nations report noted that all year 2000 data for the country of Maldive should be rejected.

An additional weakness of the UNCSs with respect to measuring the amount of crime is that they do not address the issue of corporate and white-collar crime. In its summary of the fourth survey, the United Nations noted that injuries stemming from white-collar crime, such as bad environmental management of factories or personal misery caused by financial speculation or the manipulation of international money transactions may be far greater than that of all recorded homicides. These types of crimes are not recorded in most countries.

Although these weaknesses in both Interpol and UNCS data should be kept in mind, the danger in emphasizing the problems involved in comparing crime data across countries is that an inference could be made that nothing can be gained from gathering and analyzing such information. On the contrary, although crime survey results cannot be reliably used to rank countries with respect to their levels of crime, they are appropriate for assessing the direction of change in crime over time and across nations.

The Uses of International Crime Data

Researchers using international criminal justice records in combination with social structural data have presented a number of interesting findings that provide insight into cross-national differences in crime and some of the factors related to these differences. Van Dijk and Kangaspunta in a 2000 study examined data from 49 countries in three regions of the world: Central and Eastern Europe, Western Europe, and North America. They found that the most important predictor of crime rates was the percentage of the population who were young males, 16–29 years of age, who were dissatisfied with their income or unemployed. They also found that the motivation for committing crime appears to be greater in the countries of Central and Eastern Europe, which were in transition to market-based economies, than in Western Europe. Not surprisingly, Van Dijk and Kangaspunta found that countries, such as England, that primarily rely on cars for transportation experience higher rates of vehicle-related crimes. Conversely, countries, such as the Netherlands and Sweden, in which bicycles are more commonly used for transportation experience higher rates of bicycle theft. They also found that violent crimes have been exhibiting an upward trend in several member states of the European Union, an increase they attribute to the emergence of a large underclass in the larger cities of Western Europe. Perhaps most important in the context of prevailing beliefs about crime, Van Dijk and Kangaspunta noted that crime in the United States differs less from other countries than is commonly assumed. For example, both the United States and Canada have relatively high rates of burglaries and car-related crimes in urban settings. The most important difference between the United States and the other countries examined by van Dijk and Kangaspunta is the relatively higher level of homicide and robbery in the United States. These offenses frequently involve the use of firearms, and the higher rates of homicide and robbery in the United States are primarily attributed to the greater ease of access to firearms in that country.

Relying on Interpol data from 1998, Lynch, in a 2002 study, also focused on comparisons between the United States and other countries and emphasized that the United States experiences considerably lower levels of serious property crime than other similar nations. Burglary is a crime that is fairly similarly defined across nations, and a comparison of data on burglaries indicates that the burglary rate in Australia was 2.7 times higher than in the United States and in Canada it was 1.3 times higher; in England and Wales it was twice the U.S. rate. Even the Netherlands, which has the reputation of being a relatively low-crime country had a 1998 burglary rate that was 2.45 times greater than the U.S. rate.

Other studies using international crime data have focused on the ratio of male to female offenders and the commission of crimes against women. Newman in a 1999 study found that the ratio between adult male suspects and suspects of other age-gender groups varies considerably among countries. In Western Samoa there were 91 adult male suspects for each adult female suspect, whereas in Bolivia there were only two adult male suspects for each adult female suspect. Generally speaking, in countries where women have more rights, crimes involving violence against them are lower—these crimes are most prevalent in countries in Latin American and Africa.

Although the caveats discussed here should be kept in mind when assessing research using cross-national criminal justice records, more recent research conducted by the European Institute for Crime Prevention and Crime Control has attempted to reduce the possibility of misinterpretation by compiling crime data from a variety of different sources (including Interpol, UNCSs, International Victimization Surveys, and International Self-Report Surveys) to determine whether they point in the same direction. Future research on cross-national crime comparisons should attempt to use these multiple sources of data along with other structural-level data.

Conclusion

Criminal justice records have been collected and compiled since the early 1800s and have been used by social scientists to study trends in crime and the correlates and causes of crime. They have also been used by legislators to inform policies on crimes. More recently, especially given concerns about the increasing globalization of crime and the possible lessons that can be learned from cross-national comparisons of crime rates, statistics have been compiled and published by agencies such as Interpol and the United Nations. In addition to serving as indicators of the relative levels of crime in particular countries, these records can also be construed as measures of how certain countries respond to crime and they allow policy makers to place crime in their own countries into a larger cross-national perspective. Although there are certainly weaknesses in criminal justice records in general and international crime statistics in particular, in combination, they provide a valuable source for charting cross-national trends in crime and the operations of criminal justice systems.

See Also the Following Articles

Correctional Facilities and Known Offenders • Criminology • Experiments, Criminology • National Crime Victimization Surveys • Police Records and The Uniform Crime Reports

Further Reading

du Cane, E. (1893). The decrease of crime. *Nineteenth Century* **33,** 480–492.

Gurr, T. (1977). Contemporary crime in historical perspective: A comparative study of London, Stockholm, and Sydney. *Ann. Am. Acad. Polit. Soc. Sci.* **434,** 114–136.

Interpol. (2003). International Crime Statistics. Available at: http://www.interpol.int

Lynch, J. (2002). Crime in international perspective. In *Crime* (J. Wilson and J. Petersilia, eds.), pp. 5–41. ICS Press, Oakland, CA.

Maltz, M. (1977). Crime statistics: A historical perspective. *Crime Delinquency* **23,** 32–40.

Morrison, W. (1892). The increase of crime. *Nineteenth Century* **31,** 950–957.

Mosher, C., Miethe, T., and Phillips, D. (2002). *The Mismeasure of Crime.* Sage, Thousand Oaks, CA.

Neapolitan, J. (1997). *Cross-national crime: A research review and sourcebook.* Greenwood Press, Westport, CT.

Newman, G. (ed.) (1999). *Global Report on Crime and Justice.* Oxford University Press, New York.

Quetelet, L. (1842). *Treatise on Man and the Development of His Faculties.* S. W. and R. Chambers, Edinburgh, Scotland.

Reichel, P. (2002). *Comparative Criminal Justice Systems: A Topical Approach.* Prentice-Hall, Upper Saddle River, NJ.

United Nations. (2002). The United Nations Crime Survey. Available at: http://www.uncjin.org

U.S. Bureau of Justice Statistics Web site. http://www.ojp.usdoj.gov.bjs

van Dijk, J., and Kangaspunta, K. (2000). *Piecing Together the Cross-National Crime Puzzle.* National Institute of Justice Journal, Washington, D.C.

Criminology

Chester L. Britt
Arizona State University West, Phoenix, Arizona, USA

Glossary

crime An act committed that violates a law and for which there is a state-imposed sanction upon conviction.

criminal justice system The agencies responsible for the enforcement of criminal laws, including the police, courts, and corrections.

delinquency An act committed by a minor that violates a law and for which the state may impose a sanction upon adjudication.

domestic violence Causing or threatening harm to a member of the family or household.

victimization Physical, psychological, or monetary harming of an individual victim in a criminal incident.

Social science methods used in the field of criminology represent a broad array of approaches and techniques aimed at gathering information about the causes and consequences of crime, the operation of the criminal justice system, and the impact of criminal justice policy. Although there is no single, best method for all of criminology, some methods are better suited to answering different types of research questions.

Introduction

Criminology is a wide-ranging interdisciplinary field that encompasses the study of crime and the criminal justice system. Criminological research focuses on issues related to the causes and consequences of crime, delinquency, and victimization, as well as the operation of the criminal justice system, with an emphasis on police, courts, and corrections. Because of the wide range of topics studied within criminology, researchers have required a variety of different methods to address various topics. At the outset, it is important to establish that there is no single, best method for studying crime and the criminal justice system in all its various dimensions. Rather, as the discussion herein explains, the type of method used should be the one best suited to answer the research question.

The primary focus of this article is to illustrate examples of methods used to study crime and the criminal justice system. The article is organized so that the methods used to measure crime, delinquency, victimization, and the operation of the criminal justice system are discussed first. Since the assessment of a particular program or policy is often contingent on the measurement of criminal behavior or some dimension to the operation of the criminal justice system, the discussion of the methods used to assess the impact of programs, policies, and legal changes builds on the description of the methods used to measure crime and criminal justice activity. Finally, the discussion turns to more qualitative and mixed methods of studying crime and criminal justice.

Methods Used to Measure Crime, Delinquency, Victimization, and Dimensions of the Criminal Justice System

Measuring Crime, Delinquency, and Victimization

The two primary ways of gathering information on criminal and delinquent behavior are self-reports and official records. Each method has strengths and weaknesses in its ability to elucidate the causes and consequences of crime, but may, at times, provide complementary findings, which further reinforce the validity of the observed relationships.

Self-Reports

Crime and Delinquency Self-report studies of crime and delinquency were pioneered in the mid-1950s by researchers interested in examining the link between family characteristics and delinquent behavior. A decade later, Travis Hirschi systematically linked the testing of theories of crime and delinquency to the collection and analysis of self-reported delinquency data. The central feature of self-report surveys of crime and delinquency is the expectation that respondents to a questionnaire will respond to one or more questions about criminal or delinquent acts that they may have committed. In the early work by Hirschi, questions about delinquency were fairly simple and focused on less serious forms of crime. Hirschi's original delinquency scale, for instance, consisted of six items that asked whether the person had stolen something of little value (less than $2), stolen something of moderate value ($2 to $50), stolen something of great value (more than $50), hit or attacked another person, taken someone's car for a ride without the owner's permission, and damaged property that did not belong to them. In the years following Hirschi's work, many other large-scale self-report delinquency surveys that expanded on the list of criminal or delinquent acts were conducted. These surveys included much more serious offenses, such as robbery and sexual assault, than were found in Hirschi's original scale. Self-report surveys have become a staple in criminological research. In addition to investigator-initiated surveys specifically designed to test one or more theories of crime and delinquency, government agencies also conduct surveys. For example, the National Institute of Drug Abuse conducts the annual Household Survey of Drug Use, which is designed to provide annual and national estimates of drug use that can be linked to other background characteristics of the respondent.

Although it strikes many people as odd that respondents to a questionnaire would tell a stranger about crimes that they had committed, a rather large body of evidence indicates that people are generally quite willing to self-report their own illicit behavior. This willingness to self-report crime and drug use appears to hold regardless of the manner in which the questionnaire is administered. For example, questionnaires administered in face-to-face interviews and self-administered questionnaires administered anonymously and nonanonymously have shown the same general patterns of responses. In other words, there is no evidence of differential truthfulness that systematically varies by the format in which a questionnaire is administered. Checks on the accuracy of responses also indicate that respondents tend to be truthful in self-reporting the behavior in question, although it may not be with perfect accuracy or recall.

One of the primary benefits to using the self-report method is that it allows the researcher to gather extensive data on other characteristics of the respondent that allow the researcher to test one or more theories about the causes of criminal behavior. For example, a researcher who was particularly interested in the effects of peers on delinquency among adolescents would likely include numerous questions that assess multiple dimensions of the respondent's peer relationships, such as the number of close friends, the level of personal attachment to these close friends, how time is spent with these friends, and estimates about whether their friends commit crimes. In most of the commonly reported large-scale self-report surveys, the researchers conducting the study have typically included questions that have the potential to test multiple theories and would likely include several questions that assess various aspects of peer and family relationships, school activities and performance, and employment activities, as well as psychological inventories that measure the level of characteristics such as anger and depression.

Victimization A related way of measuring crime is by asking respondents questions about their victimization experiences. In the same way that respondents to a self-report delinquency survey are asked about behaviors that they have committed, a self-report victimization survey asks respondents to self-report crimes that they have experienced. Again, similar to delinquency surveys, victimization surveys allow for the inclusion of multiple follow-up questions that can give the researcher a fuller understanding of the circumstances surrounding any given victimization experience.

Since 1973, the Census Bureau has conducted the National Crime Victimization Survey (NCVS). Prior to 1992, this survey was known as the National Crime Survey. The Census Bureau interviews approximately 50,000 households annually; each household selected for the NCVS is interviewed a total of seven times over a 3-year period. The NCVS obtains detailed characteristics of a criminal event after the respondent (or another member of the household) claims to have been a victim of a crime. The survey is organized in such a way that a series of screening questions is used to identify any victimization experiences. Once the respondent (or other household member) reports a victimization, there is an additional series of questions that is asked to provide detailed information on the context of the victimization experience. These follow-up questions focus on characteristics such as the time and the location of the crime, the level of physical harm (if any), the value of property damaged or stolen (if any), and the perceived characteristics of the offender (e.g., age, sex, and race) if the offender was viewed by the victim.

One of the key benefits to the use of victimization survey data is that it has allowed researchers to gain a better understanding of the conditions or the circumstances that make a crime event more or less likely. As victimization data have become more accessible to researchers, analyses have helped to further develop theoretical frameworks for understanding victimization risk. Newer research relying on victimization survey data has focused on the dynamics of crime, with a particular interest in the interactions among the victim, the offender, and the social and physical space of the criminal event.

Life-History Calendars Researchers have begun including life-history calendars to expand on the self-report method. Respondents are asked to review a calendar that contains a designated number of days, weeks, months, or years and to note the date or time when different events occurred. One of the key advantages in the use of life-history calendars is the possibility for the researcher to establish causal order, although the researcher is clearly dependent on the accuracy of the respondent's memory. Clearly, if the time period covered by the life-history calendar is too great, the possibility of error is considerable. For example, one would not expect a respondent to be able to remember specific dates several years in the past. However, using a calendar that covered the past 6 to 12 months, one would have a reasonable expectation that the respondent would correctly pick the month in which some event (e.g., birth of a child, separation from a spouse) occurred, which could then be compared to the timing of a crime and/or arrest. For longer time periods, or events that may have taken place in the more distant past, a calendar simply using years of events would provide the researcher with a rough approximation of the timing of different events.

Official Sources

An official source of data on crime refers to information collected by a government agency. The level of government may range from the city to the county, state, or national level. In the United States, the primary source of official data on criminal behavior is collected by the Federal Bureau of Investigation (FBI) and published in its annual Uniform Crime Reports (UCR). The UCR contains two different types of information on crimes that researchers frequently use: crimes known to the police and arrest reports. Crimes known to the police are used to calculate the official crime rate and are based on monthly reports submitted by thousands of police precincts across the United States. These are crimes that have either been reported to the police by citizens calling for police service (either as a victim or as a witness to a crime) or been discovered by the police while on duty. Arrest statistics are based on arrest reports submitted by the arresting agency to the FBI. Arrest statistics provide information on the demographic characteristics (e.g., age, sex, and race) of the person arrested for a crime. Both crimes known to the police and arrest statistics are broken down by type of offense, such as homicide, robbery, burglary, aggravated assault, and motor vehicle theft.

One of the difficulties with using the official statistics published by the FBI in the annual Uniform Crime Reports is that the data have been aggregated to the level of the city, county, state, or nation. It is not possible to examine the effects of individual characteristics on crime using the data published in the UCR. As an expansion of the UCR reporting system, the FBI has released more detailed information on criminal behavior through its National Incident-Based Reporting System, where participating agencies provide detailed event data to the FBI. Although these data are not as rich in regard to the kinds of personal background characteristics that are found in self-report surveys, they do include information on the demographic characteristics of offenders and victims (if any), as well as detailed information on the crime and the circumstances of arrest. The ability to analyze individual events using official FBI data represents a significant improvement over the aggregated UCR data for testing theories of individual criminal behavior and should provide a wealth of information to researchers in the near future as these data are analyzed more systematically.

Beyond data collected by the FBI, researchers have also used arrest and criminal event data collected and managed at the local or state level. These data often contain more detailed information on the offender and the victim than might be found in the FBI's Uniform Crime Reports, but also require special permission by the law enforcement agency to access the data. Where this kind of data has been especially useful in the study of crime and delinquency is in tracking the official criminal behavior of a group of individuals. For example, Wolfgang and co-workers' 1972 study of a cohort of Philadelphia adolescents born in 1945 traced the arrest histories for a group of several thousand youths from age 10 to age 18. These data continue to be analyzed by other researchers to try to understand the possibility of patterning or sequencing that may be found in official criminal behavior. Alternatively, Hindelang *et al.*'s 1981 assessment of the validity of the self-report method used official arrest records to validate the self-reported levels of crime reported by the respondents in the study, finding a broad consistency in individual self-reported rates of crime and individual official rates of crime.

Measuring the Criminal Justice System

Archival records provide the main source of data for studying the operation of the police, courts, and prisons. Researchers, for example, have used records on individuals who have been arrested, who have had their cases processed through a particular court jurisdiction, or who have been confined to a particular prison. Until recently, much of this kind of data collection required researchers to gather data from paper documents that were maintained or stored by some agency within the criminal justice system. The researcher would then have to transcribe the information from the original source for input into a computer file. Since most agencies have begun to keep computerized records, the amount of time required to gather original data and the chances for error have been greatly reduced. Studies relying on archival records to test hypotheses about the operation of the criminal justice system have tended to focus on a small number of agencies, jurisdictions, facilities, or organizations, because of the demands of collecting this kind of data.

The collection and use of archival records have become much easier since the mid-1990s, with many criminal justice agencies posting basic archival data or records online so that anyone with an Internet connection may access the information. Some of this data availability is mandated by the state where the agency is located. Other agencies that routinely collect data may not post it on a local Web site, but instead forward it to the National Archive of Criminal Justice Data (NACJD), located at the University of Michigan (http://www.umich.edu/NACJD). The NACJD, with the financial support of the National Institute of Justice, provides free access to hundreds of crime and criminal justice data sets. Most of the data sets archived were originally collected with federal funding, whereas many of the newer additions reflect ongoing data collection efforts by various state agencies. For example, the Pennsylvania Commission on Sentencing has posted annual sentencing data for Pennsylvania for 1996 and 1998. Each year of sentencing data contains information on more than 50,000 cases. At a local level, many police departments post data on different crimes in the particular city. Sometimes, the department will even provide online mapping opportunities that depict crime throughout the city. An excellent example of this type of Web site is provided by the San Antonio (Texas) Police Department (available at http://www.sanantonio.gov/). Users have access to an interactive mapping program that allows them to plot the location of serious crimes (i.e., homicide, rape, robbery, assault, burglary, larceny, and motor vehicle theft) on a map of San Antonio. Features are also available to overlay other maps of the San Antonio area to see what patterns may exist in the spatial distribution of crime. Court records are also easily accessible, so that an interested person may track a given case through a local court, learning what an individual was arrested for and charged with and the final disposition of the case, such as having the case dismissed or having a plea of guilty entered, and the length of the sentence received. An example of this type of publicly available information is provided by the Maricopa County (Arizona) Superior Court's Web site (http://www.superiorcourt.maricopa.gov), where individual cases may be accessed and provide a brief history of the case. Although there is relatively little personal background information on the individual whose case is being processed, precluding a detailed multivariate analysis, the information provided makes tracing the history of a case quite easy.

Methods Used to Assess Program, Policy, and Legal Impact

The study of crime and the criminal justice system leads to many different designs for assessing the impact of the system on the behavior of individuals or groups. Researchers are often interested in whether a particular treatment is effective at reducing subsequent criminal behavior or whether a change in law will alter the behavior of individuals living in the jurisdiction where the law was changed. Experimental and quasi-experimental methods provide the most direct and effective ways of assessing program effectiveness and policy or legal impact and also rely on self-report and official records to measure crime and criminal justice outcomes.

Experimental Methods

Experimental methods allow the researcher to manipulate the treatment or intervention and the assignment of cases to treatment and control groups. Although many disciplines routinely use experiments to test theories of behavior, the study of crime and criminal justice presents a more challenging venue in which to conduct experimental research. Often, it is not ethical or practical to conduct experimental research in the study of crime. For example, a theory might suggest that family environment is an important cause of criminal behavior, but it is not realistic to think that one could randomly assign children to families in order to test the impact of various family characteristics on crime and delinquency. Yet, researchers have devised a number of other creative ways of testing criminological theory using experimental designs, even those that highlight the importance of family dynamics. It is more common to find the applications of experimental methods in criminology to focus on some aspect of the criminal justice system, where cases can be randomly assigned to different treatments and to a control group without there being concern for violating an individual's rights or raising concerns about ethics violations or even public safety.

Experimental Research in Criminal Justice

Perhaps the most widely known use of experimental methods in criminology comes from the 1984 work of Sherman and Berk on the effect of arrest on domestic violence in Minneapolis, Minnesota. In their study, officers were asked to randomly assign the male partner involved in a domestic violence call to one of three conditions: verbal warning, physical separation (removed from the premises for a short time), or arrest. A follow-up interview then attempted to measure whether rates of domestic violence changed after intervention by the police. Sherman and Berk concluded that arrests had a deterrent effect on the individual who had been arrested and that individuals who had been arrested were less likely to commit new domestic violence offenses than those who had received only a verbal warning or been separated. In the years since the Sherman and Berk paper was published, there have been many reanalyses of their data that call into question their conclusions, but their basic design has provided the framework for a series of replication studies in other jurisdictions. The use of experimental methods has also been common in the examination of the effectiveness of different types of supervision for defendants on pretrial release or individuals serving community-based punishments, police intervention into areas with perceived higher rates of crime (so-called "hot spots"), and jury decision-making.

Design Sensitivity in Criminal Justice Experiments

Unfortunately, many of the experimental studies in criminal justice fields show a lack of an effect—the treatment condition does not appear to reduce the incidence of crime or to affect the outcome measured by the researcher. The lack of statistically significant effects of the treatment on the outcome measure has been a source of frustration for criminological researchers, because the design of many of these different studies is usually sound and should provide a convincing and straightforward way to test the validity of a theory. Weisburd explains that experiments in the study of some dimension of the criminal justice system are generally not sensitive enough to detect effects. In part, this is due to the small samples used in many evaluation studies, resulting in concerns about the statistical power of studies. Unfortunately, criminal justice agencies often do not have the personnel and other resources to perform a large-scale experiment. A related issue concerns the administration of the treatments. Weisburd notes that it is usually a small number of individuals working within an agency who are responsible for administering the treatment. Thus, when one particularly highly motivated employee works hard at accomplishing the goals of the program, the final analysis may show an effect. Yet, if the entire staff is not so motivated, or does not consistently administer the treatment in the way expected by the researcher, the chances of detecting a significant effect are low. The inconsistency of treatment also helps to explain why a program may appear to be effective in one jurisdiction but fail in another. Although these concerns about experimental research could be expressed about research in any discipline, experimental criminological research seems to be particularly susceptible to these weaknesses.

Quasi-experimental Methods

One of the most common ways to assess the impact of a change in policy or in the law is through the use of quasi-experimental methods. In contrast to experimental methods, where the treatment is manipulated by the researcher and the control (no treatment) group has been randomly assigned, quasi-experimental methods use a nonequivalent control group: it was not randomly assigned. Researchers will try to ensure that the control—really a comparison—group is similar to the treatment group on as many dimensions as possible, but there is no assurance that the control group in a quasi-experimental study would react in the same way as a true control group. Although the use of a nonequivalent control group may appear to be problematic, in 1979 Cook and Campbell described the properties of a number of different quasi-experimental designs that have the potential to be just as convincing as a true experiment.

Assessing the Impact of a Change in Laws

The quasi-experimental approach is particularly useful in assessing the impact of a law or policy change, because one may compare two or more cities, states, or nations that are similar, except for a change in law or policy that went into effect in one location. For example, Britt and co-workers examined the effectiveness of a change in a gun law in Washington, DC in the late 1970s. According to those who pushed for passage of the law, it was expected to reduce the number of gun homicides in the DC metro area. Britt *et al.*'s test of the impact of the change in the DC gun law used Baltimore as a control site, since Baltimore was demographically similar to DC. Also important was that the two cities exhibited similar historical trends in rates of homicides. Britt *et al.* concluded that the change in gun law had no effect on homicides, since a virtually identical pattern of homicides occurred in Baltimore, where no change in gun laws had occurred. Other research has used a similar approach to determine the impact of changes in drunk-driving legislation on drunk-driving fatalities.

Qualitative Methods to Study Crime and the Criminal Justice System

Alternative methods for studying crime and the criminal justice system may involve the use of qualitative methods, such as observational or ethnographic techniques. In the same way that the other methods are differentially able to answer research questions about crime and criminal justice, qualitative methods also allow the researcher to frame the research question in an alternative way, facilitating yet another way to understand criminal behavior and the operation of the criminal justice system. When survey or archival data are inadequate for understanding individual behavior, the use of systematic observations and/or ethnographic techniques may help the researcher to gain a fuller understanding of *why* people behave in the ways that they do.

Observational Methods

Observational methods typically require the researcher to follow along with the individual(s) being studied in order to gain a fuller understanding of each person's behavior. The researcher might take notes, conduct unstructured or structured in-depth interviews, tape conversations, or videotape activities. The close and regular contact between the researcher and the subject of the research allows for a relationship to develop that permits the researcher access to information that would otherwise be unavailable in a more standard survey or in archival data. For example, a researcher who has spent several hundred hours riding along with police officers in a given department will build a rapport, and presumably trust, with the officers over time. This allows the researcher to ask "why questions" after some event that provide the researcher with some insight as to the motivations of the officers being studied. Observational methods, usually combined with in-depth interviewing, have helped to produce some of the richest research on the criminal justice system that continues to affect the way that researchers view the operation of different agencies.

Police Behavior

In the area of policing research, the study of police behavior, with its emphasis on the use of discretion, often requires researchers to spend many hours of "ride-alongs" with police. During the many hours spent with police, researchers are able to collect detailed information about the conditions that place police and citizen decision-making in a broader theoretical context. The ability to observe repeated police–citizen encounters has allowed researchers to identify patterns in these encounters, which in turn has helped to generate theoretical explanations for the use of police discretion. Research continues to explore the links among characteristics of the suspect, the officer, the apparent victim, and the context of the police–citizen encounter and how these affect the chances of an officer making an arrest in any given situation.

Courts

One of the classic studies of courtroom operations is provided in Eisenstein and Jacob's 1977 analysis of courts in Baltimore, Chicago, and Detroit. In addition to using official archival data on cases processed in each of these three jurisdictions, they spent many hours in courtrooms taking notes on the activities and interactions occurring in the courtroom. They followed their detailed observations by interviewing judges, prosecutors, and defense attorneys to have each explain what was taking place in the courtroom and why. Thus, where prior research and Eisenstein and Jacob's own analysis of archival data had been able to document statistical regularities in courtroom decision-making, such as the effect of pleading guilty on the severity of punishment, the use of systematic observation and in-depth interviewing was able to provide an explanation for why this link existed.

Ethnographic Methods

An ethnography is essentially an attempt by the researcher to understand another world view or culture. In contrast to the methods described above, ethnographic research does not try to use information on one characteristic or variable to predict the value of another characteristic or variable. Instead, the intent is to try to understand the reasons for behaviors, norms, and customs. The information gathered in an ethnography may come from many different sources, including in-depth interviews that may be structured or unstructured, content analysis of documents or other cultural forms, and participant observation.

Examples of Ethnographic Research on Crime and Criminal Justice

The use of the ethnographic technique has a long history in the study of crime and delinquency. Much of the classic research on gangs in the mid-20th century was based on ethnographic methods, which has continued with more recent ethnographies of gangs, some of which have also focused on female adolescents participating in gangs. Ethnographic methods are rarely used in the study of the criminal justice system, because of the legal constraints often associated with the positions of the individuals being studied, such as a judge or a police officer. That said, a small number of fascinating ethnographic studies of the criminal justice system have been published. For example, in a 1986 study, Marquart was able to work as a prison guard in the Texas Prison System and in a 1973 study, Harris entered a police academy to experience the recruit socialization and training process.

Mixed Methods

There may be situations where one is interested in the relationship between two different concepts or variables and has the opportunity to use multiple methods. Although earlier criminological studies used mixed methods, it is only since the late 1980s that their use in criminology has been taken seriously. When researchers use both quantitative and qualitative methods to test hypotheses, the validity of the results is strengthened considerably if the answers to the research questions appear to be similar. In those situations where the answers appear to be different, the use of qualitative methods is likely to point to important gaps in the quantitative method or the extant theory on an issue. In light of these gaps, the qualitative methods then help to explain the observed pattern of results or how the theory could be modified. Ulmer's 1997 study on the use of sentencing guidelines in three different counties in Pennsylvania helps to illustrate how in-depth interviews can inform quantitative findings. After noting that conformity to sentencing guidelines varied significantly across the three counties, even after controlling statistically for predictors of sentence decisions, he used in-depth interviews with key courtroom actors to discover why there was a greater (or lesser) emphasis on complying with the guidelines.

Summary

The range of topics and issues in the field of criminology has required researchers to use a wide range of methods to gain a fuller understanding of crime and the criminal justice system. Again, it is important to note that there is no single best method to use for the study of crime and criminal justice; each method is aimed at answering a different kind of question. Fundamentally, the most important concern related to the use of different methods in the study of crime and criminal justice is for the research question to match the method used. The qualitative and quantitative methods outlined above have the potential to answer different research questions or to answer the same research question in different ways. Consider the link between family structure and crime. Using the self-report method, a researcher could gather detailed survey data on characteristics of the respondent's family and self-reported criminal behavior and test for a link between family structure and crime. A researcher could also use data from the Uniform Crime Reports to examine the link between crime rates and rates of divorce or single-parent households at the city, the county, or the state level. Alternatively, a researcher could conduct in-depth interviews with individuals confined in correctional facilities, asking for detailed life histories and for information about the person's family, possibly also interviewing family members. Although the research question is conceptually the same in all three studies—the link between family structure and crime—the methods used to gather data on the phenomena have the potential to generate different answers to the question. The criminological research that has had the greatest impact on the field is work that has paid careful attention to the nature of the research question as well as to the limits and strengths of the method used.

See Also the Following Articles

Correctional Facilities and Known Offenders • Criminal Justice Records • Domestic Violence: Measurement of Incidence and Prevalence • Experiments, Criminology • National Crime Victimization Surveys • Police Records and The Uniform Crime Reports

Further Reading

Agar, M. (1996). *The Professional Stranger.* Academic Press, San Diego, CA.

Britt, C., Kleck, G., and Bordua, D. (1996). A reassessment of the D.C. gun law: Some cautionary notes on the use of interrupted time series designs for policy impact assessment. *Law Soc. Rev.* **30,** 361–380.

Cook, T., and Campbell, D. (1979). *Quasi-Experiments: Design and Analysis for Field Settings.* Houghton Mifflin, Boston, MA.

Eisenstein, J., and Jacob, H. (1977). *Felony Justice.* Little Brown, Boston, MA.

Fleisher, M. (1998). *Dead End Kids: Gang Girls and the Boys They Know.* University of Wisconsin Press, Madison, WI.

Harris, R. (1973). *The Police Academy: An Inside View.* Wiley, New York.

Hindelang, M., Hirschi, T., and Weis, J. (1981). *Measuring Delinquency.* Sage, Newbury Park, CA.

Hirschi, T. ([1969] 2002) *Causes of Delinquency.* Transaction Publishers, New Brunswick, NJ.

Marquart, J. (1986). Prison guards and the use of physical coercion as a mechanism of social control. *Criminology* **24,** 347–366.

Sherman, L., and Berk, R. (1984). The specific deterrent effects of arrest for domestic assault. *Am. Sociol. Rev.* **49,** 261–272.

Ulmer, J. (1997). *Social Worlds of Sentencing.* SUNY Press, Albany, NY.

Weisburd, D. (1991). Design sensitivity in criminal justice experiments. *Crime Justice Annu. Rev.* **17,** 337–379.

Wolfgang, M., Figlio, R., and Sellin, T. (1972). *Delinquency in a Birth Cohort.* University of Chicago Press, Chicago, IL.

Yablonsky, L. (1959). The delinquent gang as near-group. *Soc. Problems* **7,** 108–117.

Critical Views of Performance Measurement

Barbara Townley
University of Edinburgh, Edinburgh, Scotland, United Kingdom

Glossary

discourse An accepted way of viewing or talking about a subject or issue; a "framing" process operating culturally that circumscribes what may be said or thought about a particular issue.

epistemology The study and theory of the nature, origins, objects, and limitations of knowledge.

New Public Management A generic term for changes in public administration in many Organization for Economic Cooperation and Development (OECD) countries at the end of the 20th century; involves the introduction of markets into public bureaucracies and monopolies, the contracting out of public services and their management through performance contracts and oversight agencies, and the increased use of management and accounting controls.

ontology Theory of the nature of being or existence.

performance indicators Statistics, ratios, and other forms of information that illuminate or measure progress in achieving aims and objectives of an organization. They are indicative rather than precise and unambiguous and alert the need to examine an issue further.

performance measures Benchmarks designed to indicate the economy (minimize cost of resources with regard to quality of inputs), efficiency (e.g., relationship between output of goods and services, in relation to resources used to produce them), or effectiveness (relationship between the intended and actual results) of a current or past activity, unit, organization, etc. Measures should reflect consistency (over time and between units), comparability (comparing like with like), clarity (simple, well defined, and easily understood by those being measured), comprehensiveness or centrality (reflecting those elements important to the organization or program, but also needing to be parsimonious, because too many measures are problematic), and control (should measure only those elements over which the individual or unit has control).

Some of the problems that may be encountered in the introduction and operation of performance measurement in organizations, with particular reference to their role in public sector, are discussed in this article. In considering some of the usual explanations for difficulties with performance measures, in relationship to their organizational consequences and implications for individual behavior, it is suggested that explanations need to delve deeper into some of the epistemological and ontological assumptions that underlie their operation.

Introduction: The Move to Performance Measurement

The gain in preeminence of the role of performance measurement has placed emphasis on the Balanced Scorecard for private sector organizations, and their introduction as part of moves to New Public Management in the public sector. New Public Management strongly emphasizes the role of performance measurement and output indicators in reporting government and public sector performance. As a result, strategic performance measurement systems are now recommended as important components of managing organizations. Within this, the organization (and every level within it) identifies its mission or purpose, and clearly identifies strategic and operational objectives linked to the organizational mission. For every level, key functions are identified, each having a number of key targets, and within these a number of operational targets. Performance targets are set for each function or objective and performance is measured against target. A results-based budgeting system may provide the link between performance and funding. Performance measurement is thus designed to provide an indication of the effectiveness of activities, by performing a mediating role between the complexities of organizational activities and decision-making centers.

Performance measures are designed for institutional, managerial, and technical purposes. Institutionally, they indicate to external bodies that the organization is making responsible use of resources allocated to it and is therefore acting legitimately. Managerially, they monitor activities; inform decisions on internal structure, process, and allocation; and influence formation and implementation of policy and planning. Technically, they indicate the quality of services and products. They are used to make comparisons, of performance against targets, previous periods or similar departments, trends over time, etc., and as the basis for developing norms, targets, and local benchmarks.

Several different and sometimes conflicting discourses sustain the appeal of performance measurement. Primarily, however, the use of performance measures reflects a belief in the efficacy of rational management systems in achieving improvements in performance. The identification and setting of quantifiable targets are seen as an essential component of monitoring the successful outcome of activities. Performance measures also inform rational decision making, acting as a mechanism for improving allocative decisions and technical efficiency.

This rationale is also pertinent for public sector organizations. Within the public sector, however, two other interrelated arguments are used to justify the increased reference to performance measures. The first is the democratic imperative, i.e., that government must be accountable to its electorate. One of the arguments in favor of performance measures is that accountability that relies solely on voting in general elections in a 4- or 5-yearly cycle does not provide an adequate accountability to the electorate for decisions and activities that take place within cycles. Citizens need to be informed of the performance of public sector bodies, hospitals, schools, etc., in order to make informed choices as consumers of their services and to call these bodies to account under circumstances in which their performance is inadequate.

A second strand of this argument is the questioning the logic of good faith. The professional delivery of public sector services in health and education, for example, relies on professional knowledge that, by definition, is not easily accessible to those who rely on these services and who are thus not in a position to evaluate or question decisions. The logic of good faith that sustained these services, i.e., that professionals are dedicated to a code of good conduct and the application of knowledge is guided by a concern for the public good, welfare, or benefit, is increasingly being questioned. Concern is raised about the protection of privilege, professional judgment being used to hide errors, and organizational practices being determined by their benefit to service deliverers, rather than for the benefit of service consumers or clients. In this sense, performance measures are designed to enhance citizen confidence in producer and professional delivery. However, rather than seeing the introduction of performance measures as the progressive refinement of management techniques, a critical perspective on their use poses a different set of questions: Why the current concern with performance measurement? What are performance measures a problematization of, or an answer to? Within the public sector, the focus on performance measures has accompanied state restructuring, with an increased market component to public sector delivery, including privatization and outsourcing. This is accompanied by a discourse that emphasizes the importance of outcomes of government activity, a refocus from process or procedural compliance, as the main criteria of organizational effectiveness. Within this framework, performance measures are designed to act as substitutes for market forces, to achieve organizational decentralization and managerial flexibility while at the same time ensuring there is effective service delivery. Thus a critical perspective alerts us to the economic and political contexts in which appeals to the use of performance measures have more salience. It does so in the belief that an awareness of these issues helps in understanding the reception of, and responses to, their introduction.

Behavioral and Organizational Implications of Performance Measurement

One difficulty with performance measures is that they have many potential uses for organizations (for example, strategic planning, program management and monitoring, internal reporting, external reporting, monitoring, and resource allocation). They may be used to motivate, compensate, compare, look back, look ahead, and "roll up" or "cascade down" organizational hierarchies. These different uses prompt different responses from those who must report measures. Though individuals and organizational units may be willing to report measures in order to improve the operation of a particular program, there will be greater circumspection or even resistance when it is thought that measures have a direct impact on individual or unit resource allocation or budgets, or will be used for individual monitoring, or in other ways have impacts on jobs, status, and ambitions. Equally, responses may vary according to whether reviews are internal or are for external consumption.

Other difficulties with the design and implementation of performance measures relate to the nature of the organization and its activities. The following factors influence the ease with which performance measures may be identified:

1. The degree of organizational homogeneity versus organizational heterogeneity in terms of the number of products and services provided.
2. The ease with which objectives can be identified or whether these are many and conflicting.
3. The extent to which there are tangible versus more nebulous outcomes.
4. The extent to which the organization can "control" its own outcomes or is dependent on other organizations and bodies to secure its objectives.
5. Organizational complexity in terms of the number of different skills, and their degree of interdependence, drawn on to deliver goods and services required, and the degree of standardization of work tasks.
6. The specificity of the causal relationship with regard to the input of resources and stated organizational outcomes, or delivery of a service and its impact.

A failure to ground performance measures in the everyday activity of the workforce is likely to see them dismissed for being irrelevant, unwieldy, arbitrary, or divisive. Another danger is that the time and resources taken to collect measures may outweigh the benefits of their use, or may be perceived to outweigh any benefits, particularly when measures are subsequently reviewed and audited by other bodies. It is not surprising, therefore, that one of the most frequently reported difficulties with performance measures is their underutilization, in the sense that it is sometimes difficult to get staff to use them. Often measures are either not developed, are developed but only selectively, or are developed but not used or used only selectively.

A number of organizational responses may be made to address performance measures that are deemed to be too intrusive and disruptive of the complexity of organizational activity. Organizations may engage in decoupling, whereby the normal activity of the organization continues, with limited engagement of those involved with the collection and reporting of performance measurement, such that the latter becomes the responsibility of a specialist unit or section. Such a response leads to performance measures being seen as being ritualistic and their introducing another layer of bureaucracy. In this sense, performance measures remain at the level of "performance," i.e., at the level of data collection, rather than providing useful information or knowledge that affects activity.

Explanations for some of these undesirable consequences make reference to the "usual suspects" that are often cited for organizational failures—lack of senior management or political support, lack of resources, an incorrect implementation process, time constraints on devising measures and their implementation, or not choosing the right measure. Though each reason has been used to explain lack of success, implicit in these analyses is the assumption that if there were changes in the choice of measures and the nature of their introduction or implementation, then performance measurement may be able to work well within organizations. Unfortunately, studies of performance measures over several decades indicate that there are some serious and recurring drawbacks with their use.

Unintended Consequences

The act of measurement is designed to influence behavior. Performance measures do indeed influence behavior, but their introduction does not necessarily ensure that the behavior that results is the desired behavior, hence the reference to their "unintended consequences." Problems arise with an implicit assumption that "influence" is synonymous with eliciting desired behavior, or control. The following discussions present some of the dysfunctional consequences (tunnel vision, goal displacement, suboptimization, myopia, ossification, gaming, and misrepresentation) that have been observed with the introduction of performance measures at both individual and organizational levels.

Tunnel vision occurs when there is a focus on the measures to the exclusion of other aspects of operations or organizational functioning. This sometimes results in goal displacement, whereby individuals focus on behavior that tries to affect the measure of the performance, rather than the performance. For example, maintaining a "good record" becomes more important than any notion of service to clients, and managerial activity is directed to the appearance, rather than the substance, of good performance. Suboptimization is characterized by a focus on the unit to which the measures apply in order to achieve these, regardless of whether a unit focus may detract from the effectiveness of the organizational performance as a whole or, indeed, cause problems for the achievement of organizational objectives. Similarly, myopia is the focus on achieving short-term objectives or measures at the expense of longer term needs.

Once performance measures have been established for an organization or unit there is a danger that these measures then constrain behavior to the extent that new or innovative methods or practices are eschewed for fear that measures may not be reached. This can lead to ossification of practices and ossification of measures, because they reflect criteria that were important at the time of their creation but may not reflect current concerns or objectives. Performance measures may also introduce a climate of competitiveness and fear, which may in turn introduce an element of gaming, or the search for strategic advantage as units attempt to achieve their targets, even if this is to the detriment of other groups or units within the organization. Concerns with achieving targets, and more importantly concerns with the consequences of not achieving targets, may lead to misrepresentation, or "creative accounting." When this occurs, inaccurate data are fed into subsequent operational and policy decisions, with consequent problems.

As is recognized with the problems of perverse incentives, performance measures may induce behavior that is both unwanted and the direct opposite of that which is desired. An extreme example would be where crime-solving targets for the police induce unethical behavior such as tampering with evidence.

With the increase in the numbers of precise and detailed performance indicators, especially when these are designed and monitored at an aggregate level, in addition to goal distortion and data manipulation, there is danger of an increased inflexibility at the local level and restraints on a local, practical response. For example, in the United Kingdom, patients admitted to hospital through accident/emergency departments are to be given a bed within 2 hours. Due to bed shortages, using bed assignment to meet this target may result in hospitals missing targets for the maximum waiting times allowed for nonemergency surgery admissions. This example reflects some of the unplanned and unintended consequences of sets of decisions designed to achieve one target conflicting with other areas of activity and other targets. Other problems arise when the unit to which measures are applied is individualized (for example, when a department or unit objective is the successful resolution or handling of 100 cases per month being disaggregated to individualized measures of completing 10 cases per month each). In the former, the differences between time-absorbing difficult cases and relatively simple, quick cases can be canceled out. In the latter, the advantages of aggregation are more difficult to achieve, with the result that the need to meet targets may result in inattention to detail and failure to follow up on cues. In certain areas of public sector provision—for example, child welfare and protection services—the potential for tragedies is great.

Combined, these responses to performance measurement may have serious consequences for the effectiveness of organizations. Rather than acting as convenient proxies that give a general indication of the efficiency and effectiveness of organizations, measurement may seriously distort and damage organizational objectives.

System Effects: Performance Measures—A Life of Their Own?

Any system of management necessarily relies on a system of representation—a pattern, a picture, or model of some aspect of an organization or "the environment." Representations condense, simplify, and translate an activity located in a specific time and space and enable it to be controlled at a distance. A three-dimensional world is reduced to a two-dimensional representation. Any organization needs to use performance measures as a form of organizational intelligence, but as with any system of representation, a distinction must be drawn between an abstract representative system and that which it is claimed to represent.

One danger lies in the reification of the proxy or model, i.e., the model, or that which is measured, is then assumed to be "the real." The reliance on measurement implies that the measurement is of something that is an intrinsic or objective property of the system, rather than a construct of the measurement process. For example, the construction of performance measures tends to focus on those things that are most easily demonstrated and measured, especially if measures are designed to be comparable and conform to ideals of replicability (i.e., they can be reproduced over time), portability (they can be transmitted or reported to other locations or organizations), and calculability (the ease with which they may be combined with other measures to give overall measures). Because something is easily demonstrated and measured, it does not necessarily capture what is considered to be important in the organization, or give a complete picture of organizational activities. For example, an emphasis on traditional crime statistics (measures of crimes committed, detection and arrest, etc.) focuses specifically on law enforcement and downplays police service roles in crime prevention and victim support, both of which are more difficult to measure.

Because of the failure to capture the "whole picture" in a few measures, there is a tendency for performance measures to expand to take into account all phases of operations, an inevitable tendency for performance measures to grow in complexity. An already burgeoning bureaucratization grows as systems are introduced to ensure that all activities that are engaged in are recorded. As these become too complicated for a clear-cut view of performance, some pieces of information are disregarded and others are singled out. Core functions become the things that get measured, others may get downgraded. Over time, however, this can lead to a shift in, or loss of, organizational capabilities and a redefinition of organizational identity. Activities conform to the constructions demanded by the management technique. These changes are subtle over time, but they are introduced through measures, not through debate and agreement.

A degree of discrepancy can emerge between managerial and practitioner models, between official knowledge and practice. Measures, simplified versions of specialist knowledge and complex practice, come to represent the "real." A "shadow rationalization," an abstracted form of representation that reflects institutional definitions, takes precedence over socially recognized and acknowledged meanings of what is going on. Investing too heavily in abstract representations at the expense of other forms of organizational intelligence is in danger of producing a "learned ignorance." In tightly coupled systems, i.e., when the activity of one unit or department impacts directly and closely on others (rather than there being a degree of independence between them), or when there is tight monitoring and control between units, minor measurement errors cease to be trivial errors, but may be magnified into major inaccuracies, as they are "rolled up" or "cascaded down" the organization.

Some of the unintended consequences of performance measures are reflected in the double-edged nature of some of the mantras that accompany their introduction, as, for example, in "what gets measured gets done" or "what you measure is what you get." References to unintended consequences, however, seem an inadequate explanation for these outcomes, given that the difficulties with performance measures are well documented (knowledge of which, however, does not seem to have influenced their design and introduction over a period of time). This prompts the need to address a deeper question of whether the epistemological foundations of performance measurement may mitigate against their successful operationalization.

Performance Measures—Epistemological and Ontological Foundations

It is useful to examine in more depth some of the assumptions that sustain performance measures, by addressing two questions: What is the underlying model that supports them and what are the epistemological assumptions that need to be in place to sustain performance measurement as a reasonable practice?

There is a heavy reliance on analysis, the reduction of entities to their component parts. Implicit within this model is a reductionism and decomposition, an assumption that elements can be reduced to their component parts, that an analysis of component parts will lead to their synthesis, and that the whole is the sum of its parts. Some of the difficulties with this model are illustrated by the practical problems of trying to identify performance measures. Mention has already been made of the bureaucratic impact of performance measures. This in part because of a plethora of terms that are available to capture activities. Reference may be made to outputs, intermediate outputs, final outputs, outcomes, intermediate outcomes, etc. These may be supplemented by core measures, management measures, indicators, activity-based measures, efficiency measures, etc. It is this that leads to a reported proliferation of measures that accompany these systems over a period of time.

It also, in part, reflects a confusion as to what "performance" is, whether it is economy, efficiency, effectiveness, outputs, quality, customer service, social results, etc. The balanced scorecard, for example, was devised in response to dissatisfaction with reliance solely on accounting measures in organizations, on the grounds that these did not give an adequate reflection of organizational performance. Measures should therefore reflect a broader range of considerations, not only financial ones, and should thus incorporate customer perspectives, internal business perspectives, innovation, and learning. There is, however, no limit as to what may be reported.

This proliferation is the inevitable outcome of trying to stabilize what are after all complex organizational and social interactions occurring through time and space. As Mintzberg observed, "organizations can certainly define on paper whatever they choose . . . but what have these labels to do with real phenomena and working processes?" Mintzberg continues that it is a major fallacy of this approach that "a phenomena has been captured because it is written down, labeled, and put in a box, ideally represented by numbers."

There is concomitantly a high degree of formalization attached to the operation of performance measures: the assumption of carefully delineated steps—mission statements, objectives, targets, performance measures—executed in sequential order, and their integration secured through rules and procedures. This, however, assumes a degree of tight coupling between the various elements of organizational activities and their overall objectives. In many areas, this degree of tight coupling is difficult to identify, as, for example, school activity and educational levels and hospitals and general health. It is for these reasons that often identified targets may not relate to organizational plans. A related assumption is that organizational units and interorganizational networks stay tied together by means of controls in the forms of incentives and measures. Undue emphasis on this, of course, is in danger of underestimating the role of values in securing organizational objectives and integration.

Performance measures place a heavy emphasis on both objectivity, i.e., measures reflect what is "out there," and quantification, i.e., the importance of facts' and hard data. There is sometimes the assumption that this may substitute for, rather than guide, social and political issues in judgment and decision making. Imagine the following vignette: Two states or governments want to measure the effectiveness of public schools in relation to the educational attainment of students. The performance measures in both states indicate poor educational attainment by students in state schools in comparison to private sector education. With the same information, the decision-making process may be diametrically opposed.

The government of one state decides to allocate more money to the state education systems on the grounds that state schools need more investment to improve educational attainment. The second state decides to reduce the school budget on the grounds that state schools are underperforming in relation to private education, and that resources should be directed to the most "efficient" organizations. Both policy decisions can be justified by reference to the performance measures. The point of the vignette is not just to recognize that there are powerful groups within organizations that influence the interpretation of measures. The principal point is that measures are not embedded in the actions that they describe. Hence they do not, and cannot, indicate what should be done or how to behave.

Performance measurement assumes and facilitates detachment, i.e., the thinking that it is not necessary to be immersed in the details of the task (that the separation of strategic from operational management, or policy formulation from policy implementation, may be easily made and achieved), and aggregation, i.e., the denial of the importance of local knowledge. Apart from very routine levels of implementation (and even here it is not excluded), this denies the reality that engaging in administration inevitably also involves an aspect of policymaking, because administrative issues often highlight areas that are not covered by a predetermined policy, given that the latter can never be specified in sufficient terms to cover all eventualities. Policy is often adapted and changed according to experiences with implementation.

These epistemological assumptions in turn are sustained by a number of deeper ontological assumptions that are required in order to sustain the practice of performance measurement:

- That the world is knowable through observation and the recording of objective reality.
- That there is an objective reality to be known independent of the knower. This presumes a distinction or separation between the subjective knower and the object to be known.
- That verification of claims about the social world is based on observations that give accurate and reliable information.
- That order takes cause-and-effect form, with a linear progression along a causal chain of one thing following another in a determined form. Cause-and-effect links can be identified so that actions can be selected according to long-term outcomes.
- That measurement is a transparent reflection of that which is observed.

It would appear that performance measurement is sustained by a specific epistemological tradition, the assumptions of which are historically and culturally specific. Historically, some of the assumptions identified herein reflect what has been referred to as the methodological style of "Enlightenment" thought, or a 17th-century rationalism. These assumptions may not be an adequate model for the reality of organizational behavior and interaction, and indeed some current thinking in organizational analysis that is influenced by developments in new science and complexity theory would indicate that such models are inadequate.

Performance Measures: A Technical or Political Tool?

A critical perspective on performance measures has a guiding axiom: "it is not that everything is bad, it is that everything is (potentially) dangerous." Any socially coordinated system requires some mechanisms that can act as proxies for activities between their location and decision-making centers. In this sense, measures provide an invaluable coordinating role, notwithstanding some of their obvious drawbacks. However, there is a danger of viewing organizations and the managerial techniques within a rational or technocratic framework; that is, that organizations are rational systems and that procedures or systems used in their coordination are purely a technical mechanism. Perhaps a main conclusion that may be drawn from the studies of their use is that there is a danger in seeing performance measures as merely technical devices, a transparent snapshot of activity. Rather, it becomes important to be aware of their political role, not in a self-interested sense as politics is so often understood, but in terms of a recognition of the values and perspectives that measures represent.

It seems important when using and interpreting performance measures to be cognizant of several questions:

- What are the origins of the criteria used in the measures? That is, what are the measures and how were they devised?
- Who chose or set the measures, and to what purpose?
- Which groups or whose perspectives are being served by the measures? Which groups or whose perspectives are being silenced by these particular measures?
- What is it hoped to achieve by recourse to these measures?

An awareness of these questions should have two effects. First, acknowledging these questions should guard against an unreflective use of measures that reduces them to a technical artifact. Second, when the legitimacy of the measures is contended, these questions should direct debate, encourage democratic engagement, and inform learning to secure, if not agreement, then at least an awareness of the objectives that measures are designed to represent.

See Also the Following Articles

History of Business Performance Measurement • Public Sector Performance

Further Reading

Carter, N., Klein, R., and Day, P. (1992). *How Organizations Measure Success.* Routledge, London.

De Bruijn, H. (2002). *Managing Performance in the Public Sector.* Routledge, London.

Kaplan, R. S., and Norton, D. P. (1992). The balanced scorecard: measures that drive performance. *Harvard Bus. Rev.* **70**(1), 71–79.

Kaplan, R. S., and Norton, D. P. (1996). *The Balanced Scorecard.* Harvard Business School Press, Boston.

Kaplan, R. S., and Norton, D. P. (2001). *The Strategy-Focused Organization.* Harvard Business School Press, Boston.

Kerr, S. (1995). On the folly of rewarding A while hoping for B. *Acad. Manage. Exec.* **9**(1), 7–16.

Meyer, M. (2002). *Rethinking Performance Measurement.* Cambridge University Press, Cambridge.

Mintzberg, H. (1994). *The Rise and Fall of Strategic Planning.* Free Press, New York.

Osborne, D., and Gaebler, T. (1993). *Reinventing Government.* Plume, New York.

Smith, P. (1993). Outcome-related performance indicators and organizational control. *Br. J. Manage.* **4,** 135–151.

Cross-Cultural Data Applicability and Comparisons

Murray J. Leaf
University of Texas at Dallas, Richardson, Texas, USA

Glossary

cross-cultural comparison Similar cultural ideas, behaviors, or institutions compared across different communities.

culture The ideas, values, artifacts, and organizational arrangements that human beings develop interactively and disseminate by means of communication and example.

cultural information system A system of mutually interrelated ideas established in a community and referred to in communications and symbolic interactions.

information In the mathematical theory of information, the information potential of a message is the inverse of its probability; the lower its probability, the higher its information potential. The information potential of a message source corresponds to its entropy or degree of randomness.

system A collection of elements in which each element has a determinate relation to every other element.

A clear understanding of cross-cultural data applicability and comparisons requires a clear understanding of the underlying concept of "culture." The term has different uses in different social science fields, often more than one in each, and the most widespread uses consistently lack empirical justification. Accordingly, we begin by providing a concept that is factually justified. We then relate this to theoretical issues in the several fields concerned with cross-cultural data applicability and to current issues in data interpretation.

The General Concept of Culture

The most widespread view of culture at the present time, originating in anthropology, is that "a culture" can be thought of as equivalent to a total social community—the totality of "all" patterns "of and for behavior" in a community. Alternatively, in economics, comparative politics, and to some extent sociology, culture is not treated as what is studied, but rather what is not studied, a kind of total local externality that surrounds and distorts what is really of interest, which seems to be thought of as something more universal.

No conception of culture as a totality has ever been justified by an analysis that is at once factual, consistent, and comprehensive. No community has ever been shown to have only one comprehensive and consistent set of patterns of and for behavior. Culture alone is not found, but rather, cultural systems exist, and no community has just one system.

Cultural Systems

Although anthropologists commonly describe culture as "learned," better operational guidance is achieved by thinking of culture as "taught." The idea of "learned" directs attention to what is largely personal and subjective. "Taught" directs attention to what is observable and public. If what the people in a community teach each other is traced out, it can be seen to fall into a number of quite distinct bundles. Each bundle involves a distinctive set of interrelated ideas. Some of these bundles are shared by everyone within a community, some by most in the community, and some by very few. For a small community, such as a New Guinea tribe or a Punjab village, the total number of systems is commonly small, perhaps six to eight in general consensus and 20 to 30 overall. For a nation-state, the total number of systems shared by absolutely everyone may be smaller, just two or three, but the total number in circulation is enormous. But whatever the number may be, such systems are always of just three major types: languages, systems of ideas that define social relations, and systems of ideas that define technologies (technical knowledge systems).

Each cultural system has the formal properties and functions of an information system or a message source as defined by Shannon and Weaver in 1954 in their mathematical theory of information. The systems are organized and their elements are used in the construction of communicative behavior. There are different degrees of firmness in the associations of their elements with each other, and these translate into the different probabilities of co-occurrence in communicative action that Shannon and Weaver described. Although Shannon and Weaver were clear about the mathematical properties of message sources, they were not clear about what actual things had those properties. They recognized language as a message source, but did not distinguish between a language in a strict linguistic sense (phonetics, phonemics, morphology, and grammar) and all that can be said in it. Rather, they tended to speak of it as an omnibus message source, much in the same naive way others speak of omnibus culture.

In fact, language is one cultural message source among many, but it serves a very distinct type of function. Linguistic messages, in the sense of messages that fulfill our probabilistic expectations about language as such, serve as a channel for other messages. If there is in addition something like a telephone system linking speaker and hearer, as Shannon and Weaver were concerned with, that is an additional channel. The ideas that make up the cultural information systems that language conveys are best thought of as systems of definitions. Definitions, in turn, are most precisely thought of as systems of linked ideas. When "mother" is defined as a female progenitor and the wife of a person's father, what is observably being accomplished by this definition is linkage of the ideas of mother, female, progenitor, wife, father, and, implicitly, self, into a specific configuration. Similarly, when "apple" is defined as the fruit of a tree of the rose family, a different and obviously unrelated configuration is created. That is all that is being done—nothing more mysterious.

If it is not known what the linked elements are, the definition will not be understood. Understanding some but having only a rough idea of others allows a configuration that will add precision to all. No idea can be learned in isolation; no idea can exist in isolation. Ideas can exist only in systems, and such systems, insofar as they are communicated, are cultural. The ideas in human cultural information systems are the means by which attention is focused on others and on aspects of the surrounding world, for purposes of coordinated action. Such selected aspects count as "observations." Collected observations are "data."

Types of Cultural Systems

Although it is, in principle, possible to establish the content and organization of cultural systems with a probabilistic content analysis, the most direct way is by field elicitation. Start with any one idea that seems important in a community and in a series of appropriate settings (such as family gatherings for kinship ideas, or religious gatherings for religious ideas) and ask how it is defined. Look for the absolutely consistent and firm elements in the responses, and query them in turn in the same way in further gatherings that the participants recognize as being of the same sort. This will yield additional associations that should also be queried, and so on until no new concepts are derived and all of the *prima facie* occasions that these concepts define have been connected together. After appropriate checking, this is then set aside as one system, and the process begins again with another idea current in the community, but that did not come up as part of this system. This process is repeated until all the concepts that are encountered in normal activity are accounted for by being placed in one or another such system. Although the idea of multiple cultural systems has not been established in explicit social theory, it has been widely acted on in practice, every time anyone describing a community has been compelled to divide the description into "conventional" chapters such as economy, ecology, kinship and the family, and, perhaps, leadership or religion.

Cultural idea systems are of two major types: those that define systems of social relationships and those that define technologies and natural systems. The ideas that define systems of social relations have the logical properties of ideologies. Each such system is closed, logically circular, and normative. Normative means that although a system seems to refer to observable realities, it will not be held to be falsified if these realities do not behave as described. When pressed, they are treated as descriptions of what reality should be rather than what it is. The cultural idea systems having definitions that shape the data of modern comparative studies fall into four reasonably well-recognized broad types: kinship, government, professional associations, and voluntary associations. Although they vary endlessly in detail, each major type has also has a generally distinctive set of logical properties that are formally interrelated with their distinctive conceptual content.

Kinship systems exist in all communities and all individuals have positions in them. They are the first major system of organizational ideas each person learns, and the vehicle through which they learn the basic conceptual forms for social relationships that they carry over into the others. Kinship utilizes ideas of relations established by birth and marriage and, usually, persisting throughout life. Such relationships are always defined in reciprocal pairs: "if I am an X to you, you must be a Y to me." As a logical concomitant of the reciprocal character of kinship definitions, kinship systems are usually described and can always be graphically represented as "ego centered." That is, the definitions of a position to be occupied by all possible relatives are framed in relation to a specific "I" or "self." A kinship system does not provide a definition for "a" father or father in general, but for "my" father; not uncle in general, but "my" uncle, and so on. "The person who is my father at birth will remain my father till death" (in most systems), and "if X is father to me, then I am son or daughter to him." The specificity of the definitions permits precise reasoning from one set of relations to others in the system. For example, brothers (in the English/American system) will have exactly the same people as uncles and exactly the same person as father. But cousins will have all but one uncle in common, and one cousin's uncle will be the other cousin's father—among other things. Additional kinship ideas are attached to the basic relational ideas. These commonly include rules for marriage, adoption, inheritance, marital residence, and definitions of what constitutes a household.

Organizations that are viewed as governments, professional associations, or voluntary associations are not usually defined by the idea of relationships from birth, relations as reciprocal pairs, or a central self or ego. They use instead the basics of an "office." An office is position that a given individual may occupy for a time but can or must leave, to be replaced. Unlike the ideas of kinship relations, this requires making an absolute separation between the social position and the person who occupies the position, and in this sense, a much more fully developed cognitive logic is embodied in Piaget's sense. Offices are defined in such a way as to be the same for all comers. The President of the United States is not "president" only in relation to "citizen," for example, but also in relation to all other defined or possible political roles or relations.

Systems of ideas that define government are more standardized around the world than are those that define kinship, and hence lend themselves more readily both to holistic comparison ("constitutional" analysis) and to comparison of selected items of data created by the application of the definitional categories. The feature that most marks such systems as governmental is lawful power. The positions are defined in such a way that the one can command the many. One or a few people occupying certain positions may properly give orders to any or all of those occupying other positions, and may command force (which is to say, people occupying other positions) to compel obedience.

By contrast, the distinguishing feature of professional associations is that their offices are divided between members or experts and "clients" in some form or the other. Professional associations provide for a division between one class of offices, occupied relatively permanently by a cadre of experts who maintain the ideas by which the system is defined, and a second smaller set of offices, occupied by nonexperts who come under the authority of the experts for a short period and then leave. Like government officers, such experts often act with some sort of public authority, but unlike government, their power extends only to those in the client position at that place in time. They cannot issue orders in general. Professional associations in this sense include universities, administrative bureaucracies, military training programs, courtrooms, lawyers' offices, medical practices, shops and other places of business, and places of worship of the world's main literary religions.

Voluntary associations are like professional associations but without a "client" relation. In Western societies, these include business associations: partnerships, corporations, cooperatives, and, most importantly, the relationships that define economic transactions. Although economics as a discipline does not recognize its subject matter as a particular type of cultural system, the core of every real-world economic system is a very specific idea of an economic transaction in which numerically denominated money is exchanged for a right, and appropriate records are made to indicate what has happened. Money differs from similarly important ideas in kinship and governmental systems in that it is not a conventionalized role but a conventionalized object, but the relations created by handing it over in the proper way are roles: buyer and seller, lessee and lessor, and so on. Such systems are now found in every region in the world, and the even though many of the conventions differ from place to place, the prices created through their use have effects worldwide.

The boundaries between these types of systems are not constant across locations. Sometimes religion is closely associated with government, sometimes businesses can take on the qualities of professional associations, and professional associations can assimilate to religions. There are also localized systems of ideas associated with types of social relations that do not readily fit any of these major types, such as the idea of factions and factional conflict in South Asia or "outfits" among the Navaho. Cross-cultural comparisons of such definitions or of data collected under them are meaningful only to the extent that the systems are genuinely similar.

Technical knowledge systems differ organizationally from the systems that describe social relations, in being much more complex and open ended. They differ semantically in the way in which individual ideas or representations may be taken as true or false and in the consequences of such an evaluation on the rest of the system. Theirs is the logic of description. The most accessible practical examples of such systems are technological tool kits such as those associated with various occupations and trades around the world: the equipment of an Egyptian farmer, of an Icelandic fisherman, or of a French electrician. The ideas that make up such systems are held by those who use them to apply to real material artifacts and things in nature, and what holds them together as conceptual systems are these objects, to which they pertain. The semantics of such systems are descriptive rather than normative. If a son does not act like a son is supposed to, argument is very likely to be used with him to make him do so. If a wheat plant, however, does not act according to the common definition of a wheat plant, it is more likely (assuming rationality) that the definition will be changed.

Other important technical information systems are the theories of the various sciences and applied sciences: natural selection, the structure of the atom, plate tectonics, and materials science as used in engineering, hydrodynamic models, and so on, each with their associated instrumentations and operationalizations. However, although these specific theories are technical cultural systems, the sciences as disciplinary communities are not. Rather, like communities of any other sort around the world, they are groupings or associations of people who establish relations among themselves using cultural systems of all three sorts: social, economic, and technical. Generally, the ideas of technical systems around the world are more readily translated into one another than are the ideas of the social ideologies, and this is the kind of information that makes up most useful international databases.

Consequences for Cross-Cultural Comparisons and Data

Most comparisons thought of as "cross-cultural" are actually monocultural but cross-community, such as comparing party activity and governmental stability in several countries, or comparing the relation between savings and economic growth or between agricultural yields. Aspects of two or more such systems across communities may be compared, but comparisons of two or more cultural systems as such, whether within communities or across them, are exceedingly rare. The reason for this is not that those who design such studies have a clear understanding of the general idea of a cultural system and make a considered choice to examine them in this way, but rather that comparative studies are usually narrowly disciplinary and the major academic disciplines correspond to major cultural systems.

In every country, there are real systems of economic conventions and real institutions charged with supporting them: central banks or treasury departments that issue money, government and private banks and credit institutions, and various kinds of market-making institutions. Economics as an academic discipline extracts and elaborates the logic of these institutions and serves as a training facility for those who will staff them. There are real systems of adjudication, and academic lawyers and law teachers try to explain and codify the principles. There are real systems of governmental ideas, and the academic discipline of political science seeks, develops, and trains people to use their assumptions. Theology does the same for religious institutions. Sociology has a similar relation to social work and police organizations, and sociocultural anthropology has had a historical relationship with governmental relations with indigenous peoples in the new world and with colonialism in the old world.

The physical sciences similarly correspond to naturally evolved systems of technical ideas and the productive systems that incorporate them, even though we do not normally think that there might be local variants of physical or chemical idea systems that we would want to study as we would study local variants of law or government. In certain applied areas, however, such as agronomy, civil engineering, and botany, there has been a growing awareness that much of what has been taken as true everywhere is in fact true only "somewhere," and that any serious practical application of such knowledge, such as the introduction of new cropping technologies or the design of an irrigation system, must incorporate "local knowledge" or "time and place knowledge."

Limitations and Cautions

The utility of data for cross-locality or cross-cultural comparisons depends on the extent to which the variables taken as the same in different localities are the same in fact. There are four main ways in which they may not be. First, the theoretical ideas that motivate the comparison may be so confused that nothing in the localities of interest can be consistently related to them. Second, the cultural ideas that the observations reflect may differ. Third, the institutional apparatus for operationalizing the cultural ideas may differ. Fourth, the social values attached to the ideas may differ.

As an example of the first comparative default, government and academic economics departments in India have been doing farm budget analyses since the turn of the 20th century using Ricardian assumptions to frame what is considered to be a scientific model of the farm as a firm. Such studies do not conceptualize inputs as farmers do, but try to apply "objective" categories in order to amortize what they consider to be all the "economic" costs of the farm, including the farmer's own labor, maintenance of tools, depreciation on equipment, and the like, over all the farming activities. For example, the economic model assigns one rate for family labor and another rate for hired labor, and the most constrained and "rational" accounting method assumes that all are being paid for with borrowed funds at the current interest rates. In fact, laborers have different relative bargaining power for the different operations, and wages vary accordingly. Weeding is less crucial than harvesting and does not have to be done in such a short time span. So the daily rate for weeding usually comes out to less than the daily rate for harvest. Some work is also more difficult. Men commonly do the heavier work; women do the work that is lighter but more repetitious. Men usually get a higher daily rate, but also work longer days. Similarly, the farmer buys fertilizer by type and calculates the cost per unit of land per crop. The model breaks the fertilizer into its chemical components, assigns a charge to the active ingredient, and applies it to the entire farm. The model ignores fodder, because it is not grown for sale. The farmer calculates fodder production very carefully, because if he does not grow it, he will have to buy it and the price is very volatile.

On the economists' calculations, most farms have been losing money most years since the studies began, and the farms that lose the most are in fact the largest and most prosperous. The result of these and other similar distortions is that it is not only impossible to use the economic model to predict what farmers or laborers will do, it is also impossible to work back from the economic data to what they actually did. The economic parameters are so unlike those of the farmers that there is no way a field investigator can predictably move from one to the other.

Unemployment rates are an example of an important idea that differs significantly across locations, even though it tends to be operationalized in the same way institutionally. The statistic is commonly derived from registrants in unemployment offices or labor exchanges. As such, it has approximately the same cultural significance in the North America, Western Europe, and Central Europe, where a person without employment is usually a person without income and represents a definite societal liability. In South Asia, however, most of those registered with employment exchanges are actually already working in a family enterprise, usually a village household. The purpose of the registration is to seek a salaried position as a way to add additional cash to the family income mix. Hence "unemployed" does not mean without income and the unemployment statistics are in many ways better viewed as a kind of societal asset. Recognizing this, the International Labor Organization generally confines its published unemployment rates to the developed countries and Central Europe, and considers unemployment rates for countries such as India and China to be uncertain.

By contrast, a vote is a datum that represents the same idea everywhere but differs because of the way it institutionalized. In the United States, candidates and voters alike must meet local residency requirements. In Britain, anyone can run from any constituency, or even from more than one. In Austria, the vote is tallied for the party rather than for the individual candidate; in some one-party states, the only possible vote is "for," and the government has ways to retaliate against those who do not cast it. A vote obviously means something different in each of these situations.

Another example is birth and death statistics. In America, Europe, and China there are elaborate institutional arrangements to assure that every birth and death is an "official" birth and is officially recorded. In South Asia, by contrast, people are usually born and die with no official record. Hence, figures on birth rates, death rates, infant mortality, and losses of life in disasters necessarily have an entirely different empirical status in the two systems.

The kind of problem that springs solely from different social evaluations is represented by the ongoing inability to arrive at a universal definition of poverty. The idea of poverty is universally recognized and so is the general method for estimating it: the cost of a package of what are considered basic necessities. In 2001, this allowance in the United States came to just over $12.06/day. On this basis, however, only about a third of Americans in poverty are "food insecure." For international comparisons, the World Bank uses a figure of $1/day (in 1985 dollars adjusted for subsequent price shifts). As applied to India, this makes the portion of the population in poverty over 52%, most of whom are in rural areas. To the Indian government and most of the public, this does not make social sense. Poverty generally implies a kind of desperation and is commonly associated with social instability and crime. This does not characterize the population that would be included under this label in India. Certainly an Indian earning $1/day will lack many things that the American will have at $12.06/day, but he or she will also have many things the American will lack. Among others, the Indian is very likely to own his own house and have a secure and recognized place in a society. Accordingly, India uses a figure of about $0.73/day, based wholly on the cost of a minimum diet.

Conclusion

International comparative studies now have available a great deal of data. National censuses are increasingly available on-line. Numerous international governmental and nongovernmental agencies are supervising the collection of large amounts of internationally standardized data on a wide range of important matters including law, labor, health, agriculture, the environment, and virtually all commercial activities important for international trade. Although the work of creating these databases is academically informed, it is not primarily theoretically motivated. Generally, the data are kept when it seems to make practical sense and not kept when it does not. The interactive power of the Internet enormously facilitates the process of deciding what is useful. The central problem is not how to manipulate information, but how to understand it.

Anyone using such information should recognize its limitations. These lie in the cultural meaning of each datum at the point of generation, the institutional arrangements through which the observations are aggregated, and the purposes that the collecting agency expects it to serve. If the underlying bases are understood, worldwide or regional data are the only way to see worldwide or regional trends. It is not alarming that, according the World Bank measure, over 52% of the Indian population is in poverty. It is alarming, however, that according to data from the Food and Agriculture Organization of the United Nations, world foodgrain production per capita increased from 1961 to 1990 but has since begun to decline.

It is extremely unlikely that comparative studies of present data sets will yield general "laws" of economics, government, or other such social systems. Such laws could only be regularities of system structure or process, and this is not the way to discover them, any more than fish anatomy can be understood by comparing different features in a large pile of chopped up fish. To the extent that these social systems are indeed systematic in any strong sense that they can only be analyzed by tracing out the relations among their elements one system at a time. It is only after this is done that will be possible to assert rational control over the selection of data for comparative study; when that can be done, far more immediate reasons for making such comparisons are likely to become apparent.

See Also the Following Articles

Census, Varieties and Uses of Data • Data Collection in Developing Countries

Further Reading

Bernard, H. R. (1994). *Research Methods in Anthropology. Qualitative and Quantitative Approaches.* Sage, Beverly Hills.

Brokensha, D., Warren, D. M., and Werner, O. (1980). *Indigenous Knowledge Systems and Development.* University Press of America, Lanham, Maryland.

Feinberg, R., and Ottenheimer, M. (eds.) (2001). *The Cultural Analysis of Kinship: The Legacy of David M. Schneider.* University of Illinois Press, Urbana.

Fischer, M. (2002). Integrating anthropological approaches to the study of culture: The "hard" and the "soft." *Cybernetics and Systems, Vol. 1. Proc. 16th Eur. Mtg. Cybernet. Syst. Res., Vienna* (R. Trappl, ed.), pp. 3767–3772. Austrian Society for Cybernetic Studies, Vienna.

Krippendorff, K. (1980). *Content Analysis: An Introduction to its Methodology.* Sage, Beverly Hills.

Leaf, M. J. (1972). *Information and Behavior in a Sikh Village.* University of California Press, Berkeley and Los Angeles.

Neale, W. C. (1990). *Developing Rural India: Policies, Politics and Progress. Perspectives on Asian and African Development #3.* Riverdale Publ., Maryland.

North, D. C. (1990). *Institutions, Institutional Change and Economic Performance.* Cambridge University Press, Cambridge.

Ostrom, E., Shroeder, L., and Wynne, S. (1993). *Institutional Incentives and Sustainable Development: Infrastructure Policies in Perspective.* Westview Press, Boulder.

Salzman, P. C. (2001). *Understanding Culture: An Introduction to Anthropological Theory.* Waveland, Prospect Heights, Illinois.

Shannon, C. E., and Weaver, W. (1949). *The Mathematical Theory of Communication.* University of Illinois Press, Urbana.

Werner, O. (1993). Short take 11: Constructed folk definitions from interviews. *Cult. Anthropol. Methods J.* **5**(3), 4–7.

Cultural Consensus Model

Susan C. Weller

University of Texas Medical Branch, Galveston, Texas, USA

Glossary

competence Knowledge; the probability of knowing a correct answer (without guessing and not by chance).

cultural beliefs Learned and shared beliefs.

cultural competence How much an individual knows or shares group beliefs. In the formal model, this is the proportion of answers an individual knows; in the informal model, this is the correspondence between the responses of an individual and those of the group.

formal model A formal process model of how questions are answered. The model proceeds from axioms and uses mathematical proofs to arrive at estimates of competence and answers to a series of questions. It can only accommodate categorical-type responses.

informal model A variation of the consensus model that estimates the relative level of competency in a sample from the pattern of correlations between individuals' responses. It can accommodate interval-scale or fully ranked responses.

performance The probability of a correct answer due to knowledge and chance/guessing.

The cultural consensus model is an aggregative method that facilitates the estimation of answers to a series of related questions, when the answers are unknown, and also estimates individual cultural competence in answering those questions. The model applies only when the homogeneity in responses (agreement) across subjects is sufficient to assume that a single set of answers exists. The agreement between pairs of subjects is used to estimate individual "cultural competence." Answers are estimated by weighting responses of individuals by their competence and then combining responses.

Introduction

Cultural beliefs are beliefs that are learned and shared across groups of people. Because the amount of information in a culture is too large for any one individual to master, individuals know different subsets of the cultural knowledge and thus can vary in their cultural competence. Varying access to and participation in cultural knowledge also contribute to variation and specialization in cultural competence. Given a set of questions, all on the same topic, shared cultural beliefs or norms regarding the answers can be estimated by aggregating the responses for each question across a sample of culture members. When agreement on the answers approaches either 100 or 0%, the conclusion is straightforward: when all individuals provide identical answers (100% agreement), there is complete consensus and sharing of beliefs regarding the culturally correct answers to the questions. When each individual provides a different answer to each question (0% agreement), there is a lack of consensus and no shared beliefs. The problem is to estimate beliefs when some degree of heterogeneity is present in responses. The cultural consensus model provides a framework for determining if responses to a set of questions are homogeneous. If the answers are sufficiently homogeneous (defined later), then the model estimates the shared beliefs and individual cultural competencies across the set of questions.

When the answers to a series of questions are unknown, as is the case when estimating beliefs, the answers can be estimated with a variety of aggregation techniques. One such method is to use the majority opinion of a panel of experts, such as a "consensus panel." Although this method may have content validity, the estimated answers may be biased due to the interpersonal dynamics of interaction and status among the panel members (nonindependence). Another method is to ask the questions of a sample of subjects and then use a simple aggregation or majority rule to combine independent responses across subjects to estimate the answers. The combined, independent responses will be more accurate than will the responses of each individual included in the aggregation. Reliability theory from psychology (specifically, the reliability coefficient), may be applied to aggregations across subjects, rather than questions, to estimate the accuracy or validity of the aggregated responses. Validity of an aggregation is a function of the number of units being combined and the level of agreement among the units. In this case, the accuracy of the aggregated responses in estimating the "true" answers can be calculated from the number of subjects and the average Pearson correlation coefficient between all pairs of subjects.

The cultural consensus model is designed to estimate the answers to a series of questions, when the answers are unknown. The model has an advantage over simple aggregation: it provides estimates of individual competencies as well as estimates for the answers and the degree of confidence in each answer. In general, individual competence for answering a series of questions is estimated by comparing the answers to the true or correct answers. When the answers to a series of questions are known (as in the typical "yes/no" or multiple-choice examination in school), this is straightforward. Each answer is compared to the answer key, with one point scored for each correct answer. The consensus model, however, estimates individual competence from the agreement between pairs of subjects. Answers are estimated by "weighting" the responses of individuals by their competencies and then combining responses. The formal consensus model can accommodate multiple-choice data and uses Bayesian adjusted probabilities to provide a confidence level for each answer. An informal version of the model can accommodate interval-scale or fully ranked response data and uses a linear combination of competencies and responses to estimate the answers.

The consensus model was developed in the social sciences. It is known as the cultural consensus model in anthropology, but is also known as "grading without an answer key" in psychology, as a method to assess rater accuracy without a "gold standard" in medical decision making, and as the Condorcet, or jury, problem in political science. The model has been used most widely in anthropology to study beliefs about the causes, symptoms, and treatments for illnesses. Examples include studies of autoimmune disease syndrome (AIDS), asthma, diabetes, the common cold, and causes of cancer and death. The model has been used to study indigenous plant knowledge and has been applied to psychological constructs such as personality and social support. In medicine, it has been used to study rater accuracy in judging X rays. In sociology, it has been used to measure social class rankings of occupations.

The Formal Cultural Consensus Model

The cultural consensus model proceeds from three axioms (Romney, Weller, and Batchelder 1986; Batchelder and Romney 1988). First, it is assumed that one set of correct answers (one answer for each question) is applicable to all subjects. This assumption requires that there be relatively homogeneous responses (consensus) across the subjects. (This assumption is tested as part of a consensus analysis.) Second, the responses of subjects should be independent of one another. This means that the responses given by any one person should not influence, or be influenced by, another person; questions and their answers should not be collected in a setting that allows them to be discussed with others. The agreement between individual responses, then, is a function of the degree to which each person knows the culturally correct answer to each of the questions. Third, all of the questions should be on a single topic and at the same level of difficulty. Although competence can vary across individuals, it is assumed that individual competence is constant across questions. In practice, this means that the ordering of people by their competence should be similar on different subsets of the total set of questions being asked. These three assumptions allow for a formal mathematical derivation of individual cultural competence and procedures for estimating the answers to the questions.

The model applies to the case when N people answer M questions and the set of correct answers, Z, is unknown. The model is currently limited to categorical response data, with L possible responses for each question. The model can accommodate open-ended questions that request a single word or short phrase, and close-ended, multiple-choice questions. All questions should be in the same format. The response data are contained in the matrix $\mathbf{X}$, where X_{ik} refers to person i's response to question k. It is assumed that all respondents answer all questions. This discussion focuses on multiple-choice questions with two response categories ($L = 2$), where a positive response ("true" or "yes") is coded as a "1" and negative response ("false" or "no") is coded with a "0."

Estimating Cultural Competence

The cultural consensus model is a cognitive model and includes parameters relevant to the process of answering questions. First, in estimating competence, knowledge is differentiated from performance. When the answers are known and responses are scored as correct or incorrect, the percentage correct is the observed performance score. When performance is corrected for chance/guessing, the score estimates knowledge. Competence is the underlying, unobservable knowledge level. Competence is synonymous with knowledge and is defined as the probability (D_i) that individual i knows the correct answer. Performance is the proportion of correct answers (P_i) obtained through knowledge plus those answered correctly through guessing or chance: $P_i = D_i + (1 - D_i)/L$. Because competence is not directly observable and performance is, performance scores may be corrected for chance and knowledge can be estimated: $D_i = (LP_i - 1)/(L - 1)$. Such corrections are used on standardized tests, such as college entrance exams and aptitude tests.

A second consideration is that the consensus model incorporates a parameter for guessing or response bias. When someone knows an answer to a question, it is assumed that they will provide it, and if they do not know an answer, it is assumed that they will guess without bias. Guessing without bias means that there is no preference for any particular response category and that each response category is equally likely to be picked (probability $= 1/L$). For example, someone with no knowledge ($D_i = 0.0$) would be expected to get approximately half of the answers correct ($P_i = 0.50$) on a true/false test ($L = 2$) due to chance $[(1 - D_i)/2]$. When an individual tends to choose a particular category more than another, bias is present. For dichotomous data, response bias is the probability (g_i) that an individual will respond with a "1," when he or she does not know the correct answer ($0 \leq g_i \leq 1.0$). When g_i is greater than 0.50, a positive bias is present (the tendency to agree or say "yes" to questions), and when g_i is less than 0.50, a negative bias is present (the tendency to disagree or say "no" to questions). When $g_i = 0.50$, no bias is present and $P_i = D_i + (1 - D_i)$, $g_i = D_i + (1 - D_i)/2$.

When the correct answers (Z) are known, performance (and bias) can be calculated directly and competence can be estimated. When the correct answers are unknown, competence can be estimated from the similarity in responses between all pairs of subjects. Because the agreement between a pair of respondents is a function of their individual competencies, observed agreement coefficients can be used to estimate competencies. Specifically, the consensus model uses either the probabilities of matched responses (the match method) or the probabilities of different response combinations (the covariance method) to estimate competence. A matrix of observed agreement coefficients (match or covariance) between each pair of subjects is used to solve for the individual competencies. These individual competence values then are used to weight the responses and estimate the answers with Bayesian adjusted probabilities for the confidence in each answer.

The observed proportion of matches between each pair of subjects can be used to estimate individual competencies, when no response bias is present. The proportion of matches is defined as the number of identical answers divided by the number of questions asked. The expected proportion of matching responses between two people is the sum of the probabilities of the four ways that a match can occur (both say "0" or both say "1," e.g., "00" or "11"): (1) both individuals know the correct answer and answer the same (D_iD_j); (2) person i knows the correct answer (D_i) and person j guesses it $[(1 - D_j)/L]$, so the probability of a match is $D_i(1 - D_j)/L$; (3) person j knows the answer (D_j) and person i guesses $[(1 - D_i)/L]$, so the probability of a match is $D_j(1 - D_i)/L$; and (4) neither knows the correct answer but both guess the same (not necessarily the correct) response $[(1 - D_i)(1 - D_j)/L]$. The sum of these four probabilities (assuming no response bias, guessing $= 1/L$) simplifies to

$$\mathrm{E}[M_{ij}] = D_iD_j + \left(1 - D_iD_j\right)/L, \tag{1}$$

where $\mathrm{E}[M_{ij}]$ is the expected proportion of matching responses between individuals i and j. Thus, competence is related to the observed proportion of matching answers (M_{ij}):

$$D_iD_j = (LM_{ij} - 1)/(L - 1). \tag{2}$$

Using this transformation to correct the observed proportion of matches allows for estimation of competence:

$$\begin{aligned} M^*_{ij} &= \frac{(LM_{ij} - 1)}{(L - 1)} = \widehat{D_iD_j} \\ &= 2M_{ij} - 1 = \widehat{D_iD_j} \qquad \{\text{when } L = 2\}. \end{aligned} \tag{3}$$

where M^*_{ij} is the corrected match coefficient, M_{ij} is the observed proportion of matches, and $\widehat{D_iD_j}$ is the estimated product of the competencies of individuals i and j.

Competence can also be estimated from the covariance between pairs of subjects' responses. With dichotomous data, the probabilities of the four possible response combinations ("11," "10," "01," and "00") can be expressed in terms of competence, guessing, and the proportion of ones (π) in the correct answers:

$$\begin{aligned}
\Pr(X_{ik} = 1, X_{jk} = 1) &= \pi[D_i + (1 - D_i)g_i][D_j + (1 - D_j)g_j] + (1 - \pi)[(1 - D_i)g_i][(1 - D_j)g_j], \\
\Pr(X_{ik} = 1, X_{jk} = 0) &= \pi[D_i + (1 - D_i)g_i](1 - [D_j + (1 - D_j)g_j]) + (1 - \pi)[(1 - D_i)g_i](1 - [(1 - D_j)g_j]), \\
\Pr(X_{ik} = 0, X_{jk} = 1) &= \pi\{1 - [D_i + (1 - D_i)g_i]\}[D_j + (1 - D_j)g_j] + (1 - \pi)\{1 - [(1 - D_i)g_i]\}[(1 - D_j)g_j], \\
\Pr(X_{ik} = 0, X_{jk} = 0) &= \pi\{1 - [D_i + (1 - D_i)g_i]\}\{1 - [D_j + (1 - D_j)g_j]\} + (1 - \pi)\{1 - [(1 - D_i)g_i]\}\{1 - [(1 - D_j)g_j]\}.
\end{aligned} \tag{4}$$

Covariance can be calculated from the cross-products of these probabilities and simplified to $E[C_{ij}] = \pi(1-\pi)D_iD_j$, where $E[C_{ij}]$ is the expected covariance between subjects i and j. Thus, competence can be estimated from the observed covariance,

$$C^*_{ij} = \frac{C_{ij}}{\pi(1-\pi)} = \widehat{D_iD_j}, \tag{5}$$

where C_{ij} is the observed covariance between subjects i and j and C^*_{ij} is the observed covariance corrected for π. Because π is unknown, it can be conservatively estimated as 0.50 (as long as the true value of π is between 0.30 and 0.70).

The observed agreement (C° or M°) between pairs of subjects can then be used to solve for competence. The previous equations can be re-expressed with the following equation:

$$\begin{bmatrix} D_1^2 & C^*_{12} & C^*_{13} & \cdots & C^*_{1n} \\ C^*_{21} & D_2^2 & C^*_{23} & \cdots & C^*_{2n} \\ C^*_{31} & C^*_{32} & D_3^2 & \cdots & C^*_{3n} \\ \vdots & \vdots & \vdots & & \vdots \\ C^*_{n1} & C^*_{n2} & C^*_{n3} & \cdots & D_n^2 \end{bmatrix} = \begin{bmatrix} D_1 \\ D_2 \\ D_3 \\ \vdots \\ D_n \end{bmatrix} [D_1, D_2, D_3, \ldots, D_n]. \tag{6}$$

Estimating the Culturally Correct Answers

A confidence level is obtained for each answer from the pattern of responses and the individual competence scores. Using Bayes' theorem, the prior probabilities are adjusted using the observed pattern of responses and the competence scores. For dichotomous responses, the prior probability of a correct answer of "1" or "0" is 0.50: $\Pr(Z_k = 1) = \Pr(Z_k = 0) = 0.50$. The probability of the responses across subjects, for question k, given that the correct answer is "1" $[\Pr(\langle X_{1k}, \ldots, X_{nk}\rangle | Z_k = 1)]$ or "0" $[\Pr(\langle X_{1k}, \ldots, X_{nk}\rangle | Z_k = 0)]$ is the product of the probabilities that each rater answered correctly $[D_i + (1 - D_i)g_i]$ or incorrectly $[(1 - D_i)g_i]$. Thus, the conditional probability for a correct answer of "1" is

$$\prod_{i=1}^{N} \Pr(\langle X_{1k}, \ldots, X_{nk}\rangle | Z_k = 1) = \prod_{i=1}^{N} \{X_{ik}[D_i + (1-D_i)g_i] + (1-X_{ik})(1-D_i)g_i\}, \tag{7}$$

and for a correct answer of "0" is

$$\prod_{i=1}^{N} \Pr(\langle X_{1k}, \ldots, X_{nk}\rangle | Z_k = 0) = \prod_{i=1}^{N} \{(1-X_{ik})[D_i + (1-D_i)g_i] + X_{ik}(1-D_i)g_i\}. \tag{8}$$

Bayes' theorem can then be used to estimate the posterior probability that an answer is "1," for the given responses:

$$\Pr(Z_k = 1 | \langle X_{1k}, \ldots, X_{nk}\rangle) = \frac{\Pr(\langle X_{1k}, \ldots, X_{nk}\rangle | Z_k = 1)\Pr(Z_k = 1)}{\Pr(\langle X_{1k}, \ldots, X_{nk}\rangle | Z_k = 1) + \Pr(\langle X_{1k}, \ldots, X_{nk}\rangle | Z_k = 0)\Pr(Z_k = 0)}. \tag{9}$$

The person-by-person agreement matrix may be factored with a minimum residual factoring method ("principal axis factoring" or "iterated principal factor analysis" without rotation) to solve for the unknown competence values on the main diagonal. Because there are two unknowns (D_i and D_j) in each equation, three or more subjects are required to find a solution. A goodness-of-fit rule is used to determine the dimensionality of the solution. If the ratio of the first to second eigenvalues is at least three 3 : 1, then it is assumed that the data contain only a single dimension. This is equivalent to testing the first assumption of the consensus model, namely, that there is only a single answer key applicable to all the subjects. Also, all competencies should be positive ($0 \le D_i \le 1.0$).

The posterior probability that the answer is "0" $[\Pr(Z_k = 0, \langle X_{1k}, \ldots, X_{nk}\rangle)]$ may be found by subtraction, because the two posterior probabilities sum to one.

Sample Size

Sample size determination in a consensus analysis is similar to other types of analyses; namely, when variability is low, power is high and small samples will suffice. Here, variability is a function of the concordance (competence) among subjects. Three parameters are needed in order to estimate the number of subjects necessary: the average competence level of the group being studied, the minimum proportion of items to be correctly classified, and the desired confidence level (Bayesian posterior probability) in those classifications. When planning a study, it is advisable to use conservative estimates for these parameters. For example, with relatively low agreement (average competence level of 0.50), a high proportion of items to be correctly classified (0.95), and high confidence (0.999), a minimum sample size of 29 is necessary. For higher levels of competence and lower levels of accuracy and confidence, smaller sample sizes are necessary.

Other Related Analyses

Signal Detection Theory

Performance and competence also can be expressed in terms of signal detection theory. The hit rate (true positive rate, TPR_i) is defined as rater *i*'s positive response when the correct answer is positive ($X_{ik} = 1$ and $Z_k = 1$), and the false alarm rate (false positive rate, FPR_i) is defined as a positive response when the correct answer is negative ($X_{ik} = 1$ and $Z_k = 0$). Competence can be calculated from the hit and false alarm rates or from the true positive and true negative rates: $D_i = TPR_i - FPR_i = TPR_i + TNR_i - 1$. Bias can be calculated from true positive and true negative rates, or the hit and false alarm rates: $g_i = (1 - TNR_i)/(2 - TPR_i - TNR_i) = FPR_i/(1 - TPR_i + FPR_i)$. When there is no response bias, the true positive and true negative rates are equal, and the true positive and false positive rates sum to one.

Latent Class Analysis

Maximum-likelihood latent class models provide the general solution to the problem of how to classify questions and estimate subject competence. An advantage of latent class analysis is that it provides TPR and TFN estimates for each subject. However, the application of latent class analysis is limited, because it is limited to few subjects with a large number of questions (or vice versa). Latent class analysis examines the frequency of each of the 2^n possible combinations of responses across N subjects (similar to a log-linear analysis of subjects). The number of questions is a function of the number of response combinations, and some recommend a minimum of three questions per combination (3×2^n) to test the goodness of fit of the observed data to the model. Thus, five subjects must answer at least 96 questions and six subjects would need to answer a minimum of 192 questions. By restricting the number of parameters that are estimated (specifically, by limiting $TPR_i = TNR_i$ or $g_i = 1/L$), the consensus model provides an approximation of the latent class solution without examining the distribution of all possible combinations of responses and requires fewer questions.

The Informal Cultural Consensus Model

Given a series of related questions, an informal version of the model estimates individual cultural competence and estimates the answers to the questions when responses are rank or interval data (Romney, Batchelder, and Weller, 1987). In contrast to the formal version of the model, this version does not mathematically derive competence, but instead estimates the relative level of competence among the subjects from the correlation in responses between pairs of subjects. As before, the true answers and each person's knowledge of those answers are unknown and the goal is to estimate both. The model is a data model or an application of general principles from the cultural consensus model to extend it to fully ranked response data.

As before, cultural competence is calculated from agreement. A key assumption is that the observed agreement between the responses of a pair of subjects is due to each one's correlation with the true answers. In this case, agreement between each pair of subjects is calculated with a Pearson correlation coefficient and the answer key is the correct scale or ordering of the items. The correlation between subjects i and j can be expressed as $R_{ij} = C_{ij}/s_i s_j$, where C_{ij} is the covariance between subjects i and j. The competence estimates are obtained by factoring the subject-by-subject correlation matrix. The recommended algorithm is the maximum-likelihood factor analysis specifying a single factor solution with use of the squared multiple correlations to begin iterations. However, when the solution is close to a single factor solution or there are fewer questions than there are subjects, the algorithm cannot find a unique solution. In this case, the minimum residual (principal axis) factoring algorithm (without rotation) can be used. The competence values appear as the loadings on the first factor. As with the formal model, the goodness-of-fit criteria should indicate that the solution is a single factor solution (the eigenvalue ratio for the first to the second eigenvalues should be three or greater) and all the competence values should be positive ($0.0 \leq D_i \leq 1.0$). In this application, the answers also are obtained from factoring the correlation matrix. The answers (Z_k) are estimated from the sum of the weighted responses of the subjects: $Z_k = \sum\{B_i[(X_{ik} - X_i)/s_i]\}$, where the B_i are the individual competence scores used to weight the standardized response data. Because this is the same procedure for weighting and combining variables within factor analysis, the solution and the estimated answers can be obtained from the first set of factor scores.

Related Analyses

This model closely parallels the psychometric test model, with some exceptions. First, the focus of a consensus analysis is on the subjects as the unit of the analysis and not on the items. Second, the answers are unknown, and so the analysis estimates the answers and correspondence with the answers. Third, the answers are estimated with a weighted aggregation: a linear combination of subject competencies and responses is used. As with test data, responses may be dichotomous, interval scale, or ranked. Instead of a confidence level for each answer, the reliability (and validity) of the overall set of answers is given by the reliability coefficient. The reliability coefficient is calculated from the average Pearson correlation coefficient across all pairs of subjects and the number of subjects.

In a reliability analysis of subjects, the square root of the reliability coefficient estimates the validity of the aggregated responses, e.g., the correlation between the averaged responses and the true answers. The average Pearson correlation coefficient across all pairs of subjects estimates competence: the square root of the average Pearson correlation coefficient approximates the average competence. Thus, a 0.25 average correlation is equivalent to an average competence level of 0.50. The correspondence between each individual and the set of answers (the aggregated responses) is provided by the item-to-total correlation—that is, the correlation between each individual's responses and the aggregated responses of the other subjects.

Sample Size Estimation

An estimate of the required sample size can be obtained from reliability theory. The Spearman–Brown prophesy formula (applied to people instead of items) formally describes the relationship between the level of agreement among subjects, the number of subjects, and the validity of their averaged responses. When planning a study, the sample size requirements are similar to those for the consensus model. Thus, for a relatively low level of agreement (average competence of 0.50 or an average correlation of 0.25) and a high degree of desired validity (0.95 correlation between the averaged responses and the true answers), a study would require a sample size of at least 30 subjects.

Summary

The cultural consensus model provides estimates for the answers to a series of questions, when the answers are unknown, and estimates individual competence on the questions. The formal model can accommodate multiple-choice type questions and the informal version can accommodate fully ranked or interval response data. The formal version of the consensus model proceeds from axioms and uses mathematical derivations to solve for competence from observed agreement. The confidence (probability) in each answer is calculated using the competence scores to adjust the prior probabilities. In the informal version of the model, a subject-by-subject correlation matrix is factored to estimate both the competencies (the first factor loadings) and the answers (the first factor scores). Although many aspects of the model are similar to scale construction and attitude measurement in psychology, the consensus model instead focuses on agreement between subjects rather than between questions.

A limitation of the model is that it applies only to simple response scenarios. The model also cannot handle missing data or "I don't know" responses, because chance/guessing is incorporated into the model. Currently, a missing response must be replaced with a randomly selected response. The model is restricted to the case of no response bias, an assumption that often is violated in field research. With the formal model, the match method is sensitive to response bias. The presence of response bias inflates competence estimates by inflating the proportion of matches. The covariance method is insensitive to response bias, but is sensitive to the proportion of positive answers in the set of true answers. Although the true answers are unknown and the purpose of a consensus analysis is to estimate them, the covariance method may be used by providing an estimate of the proportion of positive answers (π). Because the researcher develops the interview materials, an attempt should be made to balance the proportion of positive and negative items. If the proportion of positive cases is assumed to be 0.50 and the true proportion is between 0.30 and 0.70, then competence estimates will be underestimated by less than 10%. It is not known, however, how robust estimates would be under more complex conditions. Estimates may be less accurate as both π and bias deviate from 0.50, but the model may not be appropriate for extreme conditions, and this may be signaled by the failure of solutions to meet the goodness-of-fit criteria.

Aside from these limitations, consensus theory provides a viable option to assessing competence when no standard is available. Estimates provided by the model are both reliable and accurate. In studies that have compared model estimates for questions when the true answers are known, and in simulation studies when competence has been systematically varied, the results show high accuracy in estimating the answers and individual competencies. Furthermore, when model assumptions are violated, specifically when simulation studies have introduced varying degrees of bias into the response scenarios previously described, the estimates remain relatively accurate. Extensions to the model now focus on estimating more than one answer key (between group differences) and estimating bias as well as competence for each individual.

The model, however, is appropriate only for high-concordance data. When there is less than 0.50 competence (0.25 average Pearson correlation among subjects), the data may not fit the model. At lower levels of agreement, the goodness-of-fit criteria may not be met. The model includes a procedure for estimating sample sizes based on the level of competence (agreement) and the desired accuracy for estimating the answers.

See Also the Following Articles

Aggregation • Cross-Cultural Data Applicability and Comparisons

Further Reading

Baer, R. D., Weller, S. C., Pachter, L. M., Trotter, R. T., de Alba Garcia, J. E., *et al.* (1999). Beliefs about AIDS in five Latin and Anglo-American populations: The role of the biomedical model. *Anthropol. Med.* **6,** 13–29.

Baer, R. D., Weller, S. C., Pachter, L. M., Trotter, R. T., de Alba Garcia, J. E., *et al.* (1999). Cross-cultural perspectives on the common cold: Data from five populations. *Human Org.* **58,** 251–260.

Batchelder, W. H., and Romney, A. K. (1986). The statistical analysis of a general Condorcet model for dichotomous choice situations. In *Information Pooling and Group Decision Making* (G. Grofman and G. Owen, eds.), pp. 103–112. JAI Press, CT.

Batchelder, W. H., and Romney, A. K. (1988). Test theory without an answer key. *Psychometrika* **53**(1), 71–92.

Boster, J. S. (1986). Exchange of varieties and information between Aguaruna manioc cultivators. *Am. Anthropol.* **88,** 429–436.

Chavez, L. R. H., Hubbell, F. A., McMullin, J. M., Martinez, R. G., and Mishra, S. I. (1995). Structure and meaning in models of breast and cervical cancer risk factors: A comparison of perceptions among Latinas, Anglo women, and physicians. *Med. Anthropol. Q.* **9,** 40–74.

Dressler, W. W., Balieiro, M. C., and Dos Santos, J. E. (1997). The cultural construction of social support in Brazil: Associations with health outcomes. *Cult. Med. Psychiatr.* **21**(3), 303–335.

Magana, J. R., Burton, M., and Ferreira-Pinto, J. (1995). Occupational cognition in three nations. *J. Quant. Anthropol.* **5,** 149–168.

Pachter, L. M., Weller, S. C., Baer, R. D., Garcia de Alba, J. E., Trotter, R. T., *et al.* (2002). Variation in asthma beliefs and practices among mainland Puerto Ricans, Mexican-American, Mexicans, and Guatemalans. *J. Asthma* **39**(2), 119–134.

Reyes-García, V., Godoy, R., Vadez, V., Apaza, L., Byron, E., Huanca, T., Leonard, W. R., Pérez, E., and Wilkie, D. (2003). Ethnobotanical knowledge shared widely among Tsimane' Amerindians, Bolivia. *Science* **299,** 1707.

Romney, A. K., Batchelder, W. H., and Weller, S. C. (1987). Recent applications of cultural consensus theory. *Am. Behav. Scientist* **31,** 163–177.

Romney, A. K., Weller, S. C., and Batchelder, W. H. (1986). Culture as consensus: A theory of culture and informant accuracy. *Am. Anthropol.* **88**(2), 313–338.

Trotter, R. T., Weller, S. C., Baer, R. D., Pachter, L. M., Glazer, M., *et al.* (1999). A consensus theory model of AIDS/SIDA beliefs in four Latino populations. *AIDS Educ. Prevent.* **11,** 414–426.

Webster, C. M., Iannucci, A. L., and Romney, A. K. (2002). Consensus analysis for the measurement and validation of personality traits. *Field Meth.* **14,** 46–64.

Weller, S. C. (1987). Shared knowledge, intracultural variation, and knowledge aggregation. *Am. Behav. Scientist* **31,** 178–193.

Weller, S. C., and Mann, N. C. (1997). Assessing rater performance without a "gold standard" using consensus theory. *Med. Decision Making* **17,** 71–79.

Weller, S. C., Baer, R. D., Pachter, L. M., Trotter, R. T., Glazer, M., *et al.* (1999). Latino beliefs about diabetes. *Diabetes Care* **22,** 722–728.

Data Collection in Developing Countries

Emmanuela Gakidou
Center for Basic Research in the Social Sciences, Harvard University, USA

Margaret Hogan
World Health Organization, Geneva, Switzerland

Glossary

administrative data Information on indicators of performance and service delivery reported by governments or government agencies at a national or subnational level.

census An enumeration of people, houses, firms, or other important items in a country or region at a particular time. Used alone, the term usually refers to a population census.

developing country Generally, a country that has a per capita income below a certain threshold; this is usually the case in Latin America and the Caribbean, Africa, Europe (not including member states of the European Union or European Free Trade Area), the Middle East, and Asia (not including Japan, Australia, and New Zealand).

microdata Information from surveys or censuses at the individual level, i.e. unaggregated original data; not always available due to confidentiality concerns.

There are four major sources of data in developing countries: censuses, household surveys, administrative data, and vital registration systems. Each source has built-in advantages, biases, and problems. Censuses, the preferred source of microdata, are the most commonly available data source but are conducted infrequently, making social measurements somewhat difficult. Household surveys are most important in developing countries. Administrative data may be complicated by a variety of biases, and complete vital registration systems exist in only a small number of developing countries. Meaningful analyses of all of the data sources require thorough assessment of the problems and usefulness of each type.

Introduction

In developing countries, the data required for basic social measurements are often not collected in a systematic manner. Where available, censuses, household surveys, and administrative and vital registration systems all offer the potential for rigorous investigation of a broad range of social issues. In many developing countries, it is encouraging to note that microdata are becoming increasingly available, facilitating more advanced social measurement.

Existing data sources offer a rich base of evidence, but it is essential that any analysis using these sources takes into account, wherever possible, the wide range of biases that can affect them. New data collection efforts, particularly in the form of specific survey programs, provide opportunities to address biases through improved instrument design.

Census Availability

In both developed and developing countries, censuses are the foundation of microdata analysis for many social measurement tasks. Almost every country has some sort of census initiative; in the period from 1995 to 2004, approximately 85% of countries around the world had or planned to have a census. The U.S. Census Bureau has a complete record of the censuses that have been conducted in countries and areas of the world since 1945.

Because of the magnitude of the undertaking, there are sometimes significant time lags associated with the dissemination of data collected in censuses. Despite the tremendous quantity of data contained in census microdata sets, many developing countries, for various reasons, have not routinely released the entire samples, leaving untapped a vast wealth of data. To facilitate the dissemination of census data, various international initiatives have been undertaken. Some of the most significant projects include the African Census Analysis Project, the Integrated Public Use Microdata Series, the Centro Latinoamericano y Caribeno de Demografia partnership, and the Population Activities Unit Demographic Database.

The African Census Analysis Project

The African Census Analysis Project (ACAP) is a collaborative effort between the University of Pennsylvania in the United States and several African institutions (such as the Statistical Committee of the Southern African Development Community and the Union for African Population Studies), as well as the census bureaus or statistical offices of nearly 30 African countries. At the time of writing, ACAP had archived some 40 censuses from 16 countries on the continent, with the intent of making the data sets available for academic and policy research and to prevent this valuable microdata from being lost. Censuses available from the ACAP project, for specific years, are from the following countries: Botswana, 1981 and 1991; Burkina Faso, 1985; Cameroon, 1987; Gambia, 1973, 1983, and 1993; Kenya, 1969, 1979, and 1989; Lesotho, 1986 and 1996; Liberia, 1843 and 1974; Malawi, 1977 and 1987; Nigeria, 1991; Senegal, 1976 and 1988; South Africa, 1970 and 1996 (and several individual states); Sudan, 1973; Swaziland, 1986; Tanzania, 1988; Uganda, 1980 (partial) and 1991; and Zambia, 1980 and 1990.

The Integrated Public Use Microdata Series

The Integrated Public Use Microdata Series (IPUMS)—International project is a new undertaking at the University of Minnesota in the United States. It is based on the successful IPUMS—USA project, which has compiled 25 samples of the U.S. population drawn from U.S. censuses from 1850 to 1990. The new IPUMS—International project collects census data from countries around the world, along with important documentation from international organizations such as the United Nations, and converts microdata into a format consistent across countries. The project intends to make these comparable data sets available via the World Wide Web. Although still a new project, IPUMS has made available preliminary microdata and documentation from Colombia, France, Kenya, Mexico, the United States, and Vietnam; Brazil, Hungary, and Spain are expected to be released in 2004. Over a dozen countries in Central and South America have also agreed to participate in a new IPUMS—Latin America project.

Centro Latinoamericano y Caribeno de Demografia

Centro Latinoamericano y Caribeno de Demografia (CELADE) is a partnership between the United Nations and the Economic Commission for Latin America and the Caribbean to compile and make available census microdata for the Latin American and the Caribbean region of the world. There are 19 countries (Argentina, Bolivia, Brazil, Chile, Colombia, Cost Rica, Cuba, Dominican Republic, Ecuador, Guatemala, Haiti, Honduras, Mexico, Nicaragua, Panama, Paraguay, Peru, Uruguay, and Venezuela) in the region; in each, a 2000-round census has been completed, is underway, or is planned for completion by 2005. Once available, the microdata will be distributed via the software made available by CELADE, to enhance comparability across countries.

The Population Activities Unit Demographic Database

The Population Activities Unit Demographic Database (PAU-DB) of the United Nations Economic Commission for Europe (UNECE) draws on statistical sources, primarily national statistics offices and selected international organizations, to compile demographic data for, at this stage, approximately 50 countries in Central and Eastern Europe, as well as a growing number of countries in Western Europe. The indicators generated by PAU-DB, from both census microdata and other sources, are comparable across countries. The European countries with available data are Albania, Armenia, Austria, Azerbaijan, Belarus, Belgium, Bosnia and Herzegovina, Bulgaria, Croatia, Cyprus, Czech Republic, Denmark, Estonia, Finland, Former German Democratic Republic, Former Yugoslav Republic of Macedonia, France, Georgia, Germany, Greece, Hungary, Iceland, Ireland, Israel, Italy, Kazakhstan, Kyrgyzstan, Latvia, Lithuania, Luxembourg, Malta, Netherlands, Norway, Poland, Portugal, Republic of Moldova, Romania, Russian Federation, Serbia and Montenegro, Slovakia, Slovenia, Spain, Sweden, Switzerland, Tajikistan, Turkey, Turkmenistan, Ukraine, United Kingdom, and Uzbekistan.

Limitations of Census Data Analysis

Although census microdata offer a wealth of information for analysis, there are some drawbacks associated with the data sets. Most national censuses are undertaken only every 10 years, thereby limiting the types of social measurement that are possible. Many social programs may require regular monitoring, and data may be needed on a much more frequent basis than can be fielded and disseminated by a census. However, the wide coverage of populations is a major advantage of censuses as measurement tools, even though this also means that the census format must be restricted in size and scope. There is always a trade-off in social measurement between coverage of the population and length of individual interviews. In addition, staff members involved in census administration often have limited training in interviewing, and interview quality may suffer as a result. The broad-based coverage provided by censuses does afford a unique opportunity to explore local area variations in social patterns. For those indicators that can be measured from a short-format instrument, the comprehensive coverage of a census offers a more finely grained measurement opportunity, allowing community-level comparisons that otherwise would not be feasible based on smaller sample sizes.

Within a census database, comparisons can be made among small geographical areas or among sociodemographic groups, but further comparisons can be complicated. Comparative analyses using census data are often limited by the fact that items in censuses often change between census rounds (i.e., from one census to another), thereby making within-country comparisons over time difficult. In addition, despite efforts by cooperative projects, census items are very often different across countries, making cross-country comparisons a significant challenge.

Household Surveys

The most important source of data for developing countries is household surveys. When implemented with an appropriate sampling plan, household surveys can overcome the significant challenges of selection bias inherent in most administrative data systems. Contrasted with censuses, the smaller scale of household surveys allows for longer interviews and smaller pools of more thoroughly trained interviewer staff, which can result in higher quality data on a more comprehensive set of topics. The smaller sample size of household surveys also means that the surveys can be carried out regularly, allowing for more immediate feedback on program effectiveness for policymakers. National statistical offices often carry out household surveys on an annual or other frequent periodic basis.

The national household surveys are often part of multicountry efforts using common instruments. Some of the major programs are the World Fertility Survey, the Living Standards Measurement Study, the Multiple Indicator Cluster Surveys, the Demographic and Health Surveys, the Labor Force Survey, the Pan-Arab Project for Child Development and the Pan-Arab Project for Family Health, and the World Health Surveys.

The World Fertility Survey

The World Fertility Survey was implemented in 41 developing countries between the years 1974 and 1982, primarily in Africa, the Americas, and Asia. The data are available in the public domain. The surveys were implemented by various agencies in different countries, but the result was a collection of high-quality, internationally comparable survey data sets on fertility. The standard survey instrument included sexual union histories, number of children born and in which union, contraception use and intended use, and a birth history. Other questions were country specific, including parental survival, sources of contraception, travel mode to source, and other fertility-related topics.

The Living Standards Measurement Study

The Living Standards Measurement Study (LSMS) is a project initiated by the World Bank in 1980. Approximately 30 countries have implemented household surveys designed in the format of the LSMS, with several countries having repeat rotations of surveys over a period of years. The World Bank is not directly involved in the implementation of all the surveys, which collect a variety of data. Multitopic questionnaires include questions on consumption, income, savings, employment, health, education, fertility, nutrition, housing, and migration. Sample sizes for LSMS surveys tend to range between 1600 and 3200 households, which is relatively small for household surveys, in order to keep costs down and teams consistent. The data sets are available on the LSMS web site, though some data sets require government permission to access.

The Multiple Indicator Cluster Surveys

The Multiple Indicator Cluster Surveys (MICS) were initiated by the United Nations International Children Emergency Fund (UNICEF) in an effort to help monitor the progress of countries on the goals set by the World Summit for Children. A first-round, mid-decade assessment implemented MICS (or elements of MICS) in 100 countries, and a second, end-decade assessment is underway. MICS have three sections: a household questionnaire, a questionnaire for women who are mothers of children under 5 years of age, and a questionnaire for children under 5 years. The surveys include questions related to water and sanitation, iodized salt, education, tetanus toxoid, care of acute respiratory illness, pregnancy history, diarrhea, vitamin A, breastfeeding, immunization, and anthropometry. The data sets have not yet been released in the public domain, but country reports summarizing the key findings for each survey have been published by UNICEF.

The Demographic and Health Surveys

The Demographic and Health Surveys (DHS) were initiated in 1984 by The Institute for Resource Development, Inc., modeled largely on the World Fertility Surveys and Contraceptive Prevalence Surveys, with additional questions related to maternal and child health and nutrition. The surveys are now run by Macro International Inc. in cooperation with governmental or nongovernmental agencies, and are available to registered users on their web site. The DHS can be implemented in several separate surveys, with sample sizes ranging from 3000 respondents to 90,000 respondents. The core questionnaire is directed to a nationally representative sample of women aged 15–49 years, and includes questions on basic sociodemographic characteristics, reproduction, contraception, breastfeeding, nutrition, children's health, and antenatal, birth and postpartum care. A separate household questionnaire collects information on household characteristics and nutritional status of household members (including, in some cases, a hemoglobin test), and records a household roster. A men's questionnaire is also included in some countries, generally with a smaller sample size than the women's questionnaire, and relating to sociodemographic characteristics, reproduction, sexual behavior, tobacco use, autoimmune deficiency syndrome (AIDS) knowledge, and other major categories.

The Demographic and Health Surveys have been initiated in four major waves (I, II, III, and DHS+), with changes to the instrument in each wave. Several additional optional modules to the core questionnaires have been added over the years, including, but not limited to, questions on malaria, anemia, AIDS knowledge and testing, sibling survival, vitamin A status, status of women, and tobacco use. The DHS program has provided the technical assistance necessary to implement more than 100 surveys in over 60 countries in the developing world, in Africa, Asia, the Near East, Latin America, and the Caribbean.

The Labor Force Survey

The Labor Force Survey is a standard survey of work-related statistics; it can be implemented as a stand-alone survey or incorporated into a national population survey. These surveys are implemented either in face-to-face, mail, or telephone interviews, and contain questions on several indicators, including occupation (which are generally processed in terms of the national occupational classification), work status, wages and earnings, industry, and education. The availability of these surveys is dependent on a government's desire to put them in the public domain, but the International Labor Office makes available via the Internet all Labor Force Surveys that governments have released.

The Pan-Arab Project for Child Development and the Pan-Arab Project for Family Health

The Pan-Arab Project for Child Development (PAPCHILD) and the Pan-Arab Project for Family Health (PAPFAM) together represent a concerted effort by the League of Arab States to collect demographic and reproductive information on the population of its member states. A PAPCHILD or PAPFAM survey has been carried out in some 20 countries, including Algeria, Djibouti (in process), Egypt, Lebanon, Libya, Mauritania, Morocco, Oman, Saudi Arabia, Sudan, Syria, Tunisia, and Yemen, with another six surveys planned over the next 2 years. The main PAPFAM survey (called the Arab Family Health Survey) and the PAPCHILD instrument (called the Arab Mother and Child Health Survey) contain questions on housing and household characteristics, health status, and reproductive health, with sample sizes of approximately 6000 to 7000 households. Additional optional modules include questions on maternal mortality, female genital cutting, husband's role in reproductive health, post-reproduction health, and status of women and the elderly.

The World Health Surveys

The World Health Surveys (WHS) consist of a new program of household surveys designed by the World Health Organization; they are implemented in and in cooperation with approximately 70 countries. The WHS is intended to monitor the performance of health systems and to provide low-cost and cross-country comparable evidence for policymakers, based on nationally representative surveys in all regions of the world. The surveys are implemented via face-to-face, postal, or computer-assisted telephone interviews. The modules of the WHS can be selected by countries based on need, with a choice among the following modules: health states of populations, risk factors, responsiveness of health systems, coverage, access and utilization of key health services, and health care expenditures. The first wave of

WHS was completed in 2003 and data are expected to be available in the public domain in 2004.

Household Survey Limitations

Although household surveys can be the main source of timely, high-quality information for social measurement in developing countries, they present a number of important challenges that must be addressed. In the following discussions, these problems are grouped into three major categories: sample design and implementation, psychometric properties of items, and cross-population comparability.

Sample Design

Expertise in designing a sample frame and sampling is essential to the successful implementation of a household survey. Many household surveys, particularly in countries without recent national censuses, must deal with fundamental challenges in the design of the sample. The science of survey sampling is well developed, with widely recognized standards of quality, but the implementation of the sample design may be problematic. In the process of implementation, there are several opportunities for creating selection bias. Older members of the household may not want to be the primary interview respondent even if chosen by Kisch tables or a similar approach. For reasons of cost, interviewer teams may not be able to return to households multiple times in remote areas if respondents were not available or if follow-up is required.

Post-hoc evaluation of the sample age, sex, and education distribution for many surveys can reveal how far away a sample is from the actual age and sex distribution of the population. This problem is particularly pronounced in conflict or postconflict settings, but may be an important issue in all low-income countries as well. It is an unfortunate situation that these countries are perhaps most in need of reliable demographic data. For middle-income developing countries as for developed countries, there is also the problem of institutionalized individuals; this can be very important, particularly because individuals are often institutionalized because they are not like the rest of the population. The absence of elderly, sick, or mentally handicapped household members in a household sample can bias population figures dramatically.

Psychometric Properties of Items

The psychometric properties of items included in the survey instrument pose another major challenge in the use of household surveys to generate data for social measurement. In some fields of social measurement, items or questions are included in surveys only after rigorous psychometric evaluation. This is particularly true in the field of educational testing. Despite this standard in many areas of survey work, items that have not undergone quantified psychometric evaluation are included in several types of survey instruments. Test–retest data are rarely available, and validation studies are usually not conducted. This means that it is often impossible to test whether respondents understood the questions as they were intended.

Cross-Population Comparability

Comparability has become an important challenge in modern survey instrument development. Comparability is required not only across countries, but also within countries over time, or across different subpopulations delineated by age, sex, education, income, or other characteristics.

The fundamental challenge in seeking cross-population comparable measures is that the most accessible sources of data are categorical self-reported data. When categorical data are used as the basis for understanding quantities that are determined on a continuous, cardinal scale, the problem of cross-population comparability emerges from differences in the way different individuals use categorical response scales. Efforts to ensure linguistic equivalence of questions across different settings may improve the psychometric properties of these questions in terms of traditional criteria such as reliability and within-population validity, but they will not resolve problems stemming from noncomparability in the interpretation and use of response categories. Thus, cross-population comparability represents a more stringent criterion for evaluation of measurement instruments, beyond the traditional concepts of reliability and validity.

Recent advances in survey design, including work at the World Health Organization, have resulted in two main strategies to correct the problem of differential use of categorical response scales. The first strategy is to establish a scale that is strictly comparable across individuals and populations. Measurements on the comparable scale can then be used to establish the response category cut-points for each survey item. The second approach is to get categorical responses from different groups for a fixed level on the latent scale. If the level is fixed, variation in the responses provides information on the differences in cut-points across individuals and populations. This strategy usually involves the introduction of short stories ("vignettes") into survey instruments that allow analysts to calibrate people's responses to their perceived "cut-points" on a latent variable scale. Vignettes are (usually brief) descriptions of hypothetical people or situations that survey researchers can use to correct otherwise interpersonally incomparable survey responses. This approach has recently been implemented in questionnaires on health, health systems, state effectiveness and corruption, and school or community strength, among others.

Administrative Data

Some areas of social measurement depend heavily on administrative data collected by service providers. Well-known examples include primary school enrollment data collected from primary schools and aggregated up to the national level, and extensive information collected from public health service providers on the delivery of various interventions, such as immunizations or the Directly Observed Treatment Short course (DOTS) for tuberculosis. These types of data can often be useful, especially because they may be the only source of data for a particular field of social measurement for several countries.

Administrative data, however, have to be used with caution, and there are at least four fundamental problems associated with them. First, there is the problem of denominators: the groups in need of service may not access the service in the first place (e.g., the poor or marginalized groups). For some measures, the problem of denominators may not be a significant issue when census data can be used to define the target group, but for other areas, such as health, defining who needs a service in an area may be much more challenging. The second problem involves selection bias: the individuals who receive an intervention or service in a community are likely to be a nonrandom sample of the population. This creates many analytical challenges for using such data to understand what is happening in a population. Third, there are problems of collation and aggregation: data from different levels of an administrative systems often do not get communicated, or get partially communicated to the next level up in the system. The result is that aggregations for provinces or for the entire country are often based on incomplete returns from various levels. This limits comparability across years and across units of study. A final problem is that, in many countries, financial incentives are paid based on the administrative data performance results. Even when incentives are not paid, other nonfinancial incentives may lead to inflated figures. This often means that administrative data tend to exaggerate service delivery. An important challenge for social measurement is to figure out how to deal with these issues in data analysis and how to correct administrative data for known biases.

Conclusions

Although there are many possibilities for data analysis in developing countries, there are several problems associated with each data source; these difficulties must be minimized, corrected for, and acknowledged before meaningful analysis can be completed. Developing countries have incredible need for accurate data at the population level, and yet struggle with the collection of consistently useful and complete data sets. International efforts at collating and dispersing microdata may lead to more cross-country comparability and access to what could be important information related to welfare in developing countries.

See Also the Following Articles

Census Undercount and Adjustment • Census, Varieties and Uses of Data • Demography • Election Polls • Population vs. Sample • Surveys

Further Reading

Abu-Libdeh, H., Alam, I., Dackam-Ngatchou, R., Freedman, H. A., and Jones, G. C. (2003). *Counting the People: Constraining Census Costs and Assessing Alternative Approaches.* Population and Development Strategies Series No. 7. United Nations Population Fund (UNFPA), New York. Available on the Internet at www.unfpa.org

African Census Analysis Project (www.acap.upenn.edu).

Centro Latinoamericano y Caribeno de Demografia (CELADE) (www.eclac.org/celade).

Demographic Database of Population Activities Unit (PAU-DB) of the United Nations Economic Commission for Europe (UNECE) (www.unece.org).

Demographic and Health Surveys (DHS) (www.measuredhs.com).

Integrated Public Use Microdata Series (IPUMS)—International project (www.ipums.umn.edu).

Labor Force Survey (www.ilo.org).

Living Standards Measurement Study (LSMS) (www.worldbank.org).

Multiple Indicator Cluster Surveys (MICS) (http://childinfo.org).

Murray, C. J. L., *et al.* (2003). Cross-population comparability of evidence for health policy. In *Health Systems Performance Assessment: Debates, Methods, and Empiricism* (C. J. L. Murray and D. Evans, eds.), pp. 705–714. World Health Organization, Geneva.

Pan-Arab Project for Child Development (PAPCHILD) and the Pan-Arab Project for Family Health (PAPFAM) (www.papfam.org).

U.S. Census Bureau. Census dates for countries and areas of the world: 1945 to 2004 (www.census.gov).

World Fertility Survey (http://opr.princeton.edu).

World Health Surveys (WHS) (www.who.int).

Data Collection, Primary vs. Secondary

Joop J. Hox
Utrecht University, Utrecht, The Netherlands

Hennie R. Boeije
Utrecht University, Utrecht, The Netherlands

Glossary

codebook A description of the variables, the possible values, and their location in the data file. In many cases, there is a second section detailing the original studies methods and procedures.

data archive An organization that acquires, archives, and disseminates data for secondary research.

data structure The organization of the data. This can be simple (e.g., rectangular data matrices in which rows are objects and columns are cases) or complex (e.g., hierarchical and relational databases).

meta-information The description of a data file, usually in the form of a codebook.

primary data Original data collected for a specific research goal.

qualitative data Data involving understandings of the complexity, detail, and context of the research subject, often consisting of texts, such as interview transcripts and field notes, or audiovisual material.

quantitative data Data that can be described numerically in terms of objects, variables, and their values.

secondary data Data originally collected for a different purpose and reused for another research question.

Data collection, primary vs. secondary, explains the advantages and disadvantages of collecting primary data for a specific study and reusing research material that was originally collected for a different purpose than the study at hand. After a brief discussion of the major data collection strategies in primary research, we discuss search strategies for finding useful secondary data, problems associated with retrieving these data, and methodological criteria that are applied to evaluate the quality of the secondary data.

Introduction

To collect data, social scientists make use of a number of different data collection strategies. First, experiments and quasi-experiments are important because they typically involve a research design that allows strong causal inferences. Second, surveys using structured questionnaires are another important data collection strategy because they typically involve collecting data on a large number of variables from a large and representative sample of respondents. Third, within a qualitative research design the data collection strategy typically involves collecting a large amount of data on a rather small, purposive sample, using techniques such as in-depth interviews, participant observation, or focus groups.

Primary data are data that are collected for the specific research problem at hand, using procedures that fit the research problem best. On every occasion that primary data are collected, new data are added to the existing store of social knowledge. Increasingly, this material created by other researchers is made available for reuse by the general research community; it is then called secondary data. Data may be used for (1) the description of contemporary and historical attributes, (2) comparative research or replication of the original research, (3) reanalysis (asking new questions of the data that were not originally addressed), (4) research design and methodological advancement, and (5) teaching and learning.

Data sets collected by university-based researchers are often archived by data archives; these are organizations set up chiefly for the purpose of releasing and disseminating secondary data to the general research community. In addition to universities, other organizations such as national and regional statistical institutions also collect data. More and more, such data are also archived and made available, usually via the statistical agency itself. Finally, universities, research institutes, and individual researchers themselves may decide to make their data available. For data archives and, to a smaller extent, the large statistical agencies, the systematic preservation and dissemination of data are part of their institutional mission. For individual researchers and small research units, this is not the case. Nevertheless, the Internet holds several interesting Web sites where individuals or research units offer access to their data sets.

Most of the secondary data sets contain quantitative data; that is, the information consists of studied objects whose characteristics are coded in variables that have a range of possible values. A qualitative database consists of documents, audiocassette or videocassette tapes, or the transcripts of these tapes. Increasingly, qualitative researchers share their data for secondary analysis.

Social scientists who intend to study a particular theoretical problem or a specific policy issue have the choice to collect their own data or to search for existing data relevant to the problem at hand. The most important advantage of collecting one's own data is that the operationalization of the theoretical constructs, the research design, and data collection strategy can be tailored to the research question, which ensures that the study is coherent and that the information collected indeed helps to resolve the problem. The most important disadvantage of collecting one's own data is that it is costly and time-consuming. If relevant information on the research topic is accessible, reusing it gains benefits. The data can serve to answer the newly formulated research question, smooth the pilot stage of a project, or provide the researcher with a wider sample base for testing interpretations at far less cost and with greater speed.

This nicely sums up the advantages and disadvantages of using secondary data. The disadvantage is that the data were originally collected for a different purpose and therefore may not be optimal for the research problem under consideration or, in the case of qualitative data, may not be easy to interpret without explicit information on the informants and the context; the advantage of using secondary data is a far lower cost and faster access to relevant information.

Primary Data Collection

The Experiment

One major primary data collection strategy is the experiment. In an experiment, the researcher has full control over who participates in the experiment. The researcher manipulates one or more independent variables following a planned design and observes the effects of the independent variables on the dependent variable, the outcome variable. The essence of an experiment is that the research situation is one created by the researcher. This permits strong control over the design and the procedure, and as a result the outcome of an experiment permits causal interpretation. This is referred to as the internal validity—the degree to which the experimental design excludes alternative explanations of the experiment's results. At the same time, the fact that the experimenter creates the research situation, often in a laboratory setting, implies that the situation is to some degree artificial. The problem here is the ecological validity—the extent to which we can generalize the results of our study to real-life situations. Experimental laboratory studies put emphasis on those variables that are easily manageable rather than on variables that reflect the everyday activities of people coping with real-life situations. Typically, because an experiment involves setting up experimental situations and exposing subjects to different stimuli, experiments involve a relatively small number of subjects and variables. However, because there is strong control over the design, most experiments make an effort to manipulate several variables, using designs that permit conclusions about both their individual and their combined effects. Several handbooks describe a variety of experimental designs, including designs for longitudinal research and case studies.

The Social Survey

A second established primary data collection strategy is the interview survey. In a survey, a large and representative sample of an explicitly defined target population is interviewed. Characteristically, a large number of standardized questions are asked and the responses are coded in standardized answer categories. A survey is carried out when researchers are interested in collecting data on the observations, attitudes, feelings, experiences, or opinions of a population. Information on subjective phenomena can be collected only by asking respondents about these. Surveys are also used to collect information about behavior. Behavior could in principle be studied by observation, but this is often expensive, or impossible, as in questions about past behavior. Social surveys are usually targeted at a household population, but they can also aim at a specific subpopulation. A specific form of survey is interviewing key informants from communities or organizations. These individuals are purposively selected because they are formal or informal nodes of information and therefore in a position to provide the researcher with informative responses to the survey questions or to point the researcher to other sources of information. The strong point of survey research is that it can provide information about subjective and objective characteristics of a population. The major methodological problems in interview surveys are obtaining a representative sample and the validity of the responses given by the respondents. Obtaining a representative sample is usually accomplished by drawing a random sample from the population, using scientific sampling methods. However, in most Western countries survey nonresponse is considerable and increasing, which may threaten the representativeness of the sample. In addition, both respondent and question characteristics can affect the responses. To ensure valid responses, interview questions must be carefully designed, evaluated, and tested.

Qualitative Research

Qualitative researchers examine how people learn about and make sense of themselves and others and how they structure and give meaning to their daily lives. Therefore, methods of data collection are used that are flexible and sensitive to the social context. A popular method of data collection is the qualitative interview in which interviewees are given the floor to talk about their experiences, views, and so on. Instead of a rigidly standardized instrument, interview guides are used with a range of topics or themes that can be adjusted during the study. Another widely used method is participant observation, which generally refers to methods of generating data that involve researchers immersing themselves in a research setting and systematically observing interactions, events, and so on. Other well-known methods of qualitative data collection are the use of focus (guided-discussion) groups, documents, photographs, film, and video.

Settings, events, or interviewees are purposively sampled, which means guided by the researcher's need for information. Provisional analyses constantly change this need, and therefore sampling takes place during the research and is interchanged with data collection. Contrary to probability sampling, which is based on the notion that the sample will mathematically represent subgroups of the larger population, purposive sampling is aimed at constructing a sample that is meaningful theoretically; it builds in certain characteristics or conditions that help to develop and test findings and explanations. Sampling strategies include aiming at maximum variation, snowball sampling, critical case, and stratified purposeful.

The intense role of the researcher brings about issues with regard to reliability and validity. That the researchers are their own instrument is necessary to gain valid knowledge about experiences or the culture of a specific individual or group; to reduce the reactivity of the research subjects, prolonged engagement is recommended. Another issue is the lack of control over the researchers' activities; therefore, researchers should keep detailed notes of their fieldwork and the choices they make in order to increase replication and reproducibility. Many other quality procedures have been developed, such as triangulation, member checks, peer debriefing, and external audits.

Solicited and Spontaneous Data

A distinction that involves all primary data collection techniques is that between data that are solicited and data that are spontaneous. In experiments, surveys, and much qualitative research, the researcher uses a stimulus (experimental variable, survey question, or open question) to elicit information from the research subjects. Explicitly soliciting information has the advantage that the researcher can design the data collection to optimally provide data given the research question. However, the disadvantage is that the research subjects are aware that they are taking part in a scientific study. As a consequence, they may react to the announcement of the study topic, the institution that sponsors the study or carries it out, the individual experimenter or interviewer, and so on. It is not clear whether the recorded behavior or response is the "true" behavior, that is, whether it is the same behavior that would have occurred naturally, if it had not been elicited.

The possible reactivity of research subjects can be circumvented by observing natural activities or the traces they leave behind, without disturbing the research subjects in any way. Nonreactive or nonintrusive primary data collection methods include (covert) observation and monitoring. Observation, which can be done in the actual location or remotely using video technology, can lead to both quantitative and qualitative data. Increasingly, technological advances make it possible to monitor activities without disturbing the subjects. For instance, media research in general no longer relies on a panel of respondents who report on their television viewing; instead, in selected households a monitoring device is installed in the television that monitors the television use and transmits the information to the researchers without disturbing the respondents. Scanning devices are used to monitor consumer behavior. Internet behavior can also be monitored. For instance, when people visit a specific Web site, it is simple to monitor which banners and buttons they click on, how long they stay on the page, where they come from, and where they go to when they leave the site. All this provides information without directly involving the subjects in any way.

Summary of Primary Data

Table 1 lists the types of data in primary data collection. The list is not intended to be exhaustive; rather, it is indicative of the primary data collected in social research.

Table 1 Examples of Primary Data in Social Research

	Solicited	*Spontaneous*
Quantitative	Experiment	(Passive) observation
	Interview survey	Monitoring
	Mail survey	Administrative records
	Structured diary	(e.g., statistical records,
	Web survey	databases, Internet archives)
Qualitative	Open interview	(Participant) observation
	Focus group	Existing records (e.g.,
	Unstructured diary	ego-documents, images, sounds, news archives)

Secondary Data Collection

For some social research questions, it is possible to use data collected earlier by other researchers or for other purposes than research, such as official statistics, administrative records, or other accounts kept routinely by organizations. By virtue of being archived and made available, any type of primary data can serve as secondary data.

Using secondary data presents researchers with a number of characteristic problems. First, researchers must locate data sources that may be useful given their own research problem. Second, they must be able to retrieve the relevant data. Third, it is important to evaluate how well the data meet the quality requirements of the current research and the methodological criteria of good scientific practice.

Finding Useful Secondary Data: Search Strategy

The main sources of information are the official data archives. These organizations are established for the precise purpose of acquiring, archiving, and disseminating data for secondary research. For example, the described aim of the Qualitative Data Service (Qualidata) at the U.K. Data Archive is providing research, learning and teaching communities with significant real-life data that can be reanalyzed, reworked, and compared with contemporary data and that will, in time, form part of the cultural heritage as historical resources. Nowadays, archives usually store electronic data. Important data archives maintain Web sites that describe the data in the archive and coordinate information about the existence of available sources of data wherever they are housed. These catalogs usually contain information on the subject of the original study, the data collection mode used, the number of variables, and the number of subjects.

After a data set that looks attractive has been located, the next step is to obtain a more detailed description of the study. Well-documented data sets come with a detailed description of the methods and procedures used to collect the data. For example, if the original study is a large-scale survey conducted by an official statistical agency, the detailed description of the study will describe the interview procedures, the sampling design, whether sampling weights are to be used, and any transformations performed by the original researchers on the data set. In addition, the text of the questionnaire will be available. All this information may be needed to judge whether the secondary data suit the present research problem.

In addition to official data archives, many other data sets are available. The problem here is twofold: tracing them and judging their usefulness. National and regional statistical agencies sometimes make data available for secondary analysis. Also, several universities and research institutes offer data files, and there are individual researchers who maintain Web sites about topics of special interests. However, data that are not part of an official data archive are typically poorly documented. This makes it much more difficult to evaluate whether they are useful and whether their methodological quality is good enough so that the researcher can trust the results of the original analysis.

The Internet is a vast but extremely disorganized source of information. To use it effectively, we must be able to formulate a search strategy using appropriate keywords. Some Internet search machines support logical expressions, which allows searching for combinations of keywords. Because no individual search engine covers all of the Internet, the best approach is to use a metasearch program such as Copernic. Metasearch programs send a search request to a collection of search engines, combine the results into one list, and sort this list on the basis of estimated relevance. If relevant secondary data files are available on the Internet, such a procedure has a reasonable chance of finding them.

The projected ability to assess the data quality is part of the search strategy. Before the methodological quality is assessed (which may mean retrieving the codebook and sometimes even the data), potential secondary data sources must be screened for practicality or feasibility. The criterion of practicality means that the data must be promising because they appear to cover the topic (contents and variables), are described in a language that the researcher can read, and are readily obtainable. The availability of meta-information, that is, information that describes the data and thus enables methodological quality assessment, is an important requirement in selecting potentially interesting secondary data sets.

Retrieving Secondary Data

Secondary data contained in an official data archive are easy to retrieve. They may be available as files obtained via the Internet or as data files on CD-ROM or DVD data discs. Because of the widespread use of email and the World Wide Web, it has become easier to retrieve data in a usable format (i.e., in a form that can be input simply into the appropriate analysis software). Different archives set different conditions for delivering data to individual researchers, and these terms may also differ according to the specific data set asked for. Some data sets are freely available, without cost. Others may be expensive, either because the original data collector wants to recover part of the expense of the primary data collection or because of the cost of offering the existing data sets in a reusable format for new research purposes. Conditions can sometimes involve the use of the data itself. In most cases, use of the data is restricted to the researchers who request them. Therefore, if secondary data are needed for teaching purposes, and therefore must be supplied to classes of students, special permission for this use is usually needed. In some cases, the only requirement is that the original study and the data archive be cited; in others, the original investigator must be informed of the purpose of the secondary analysis and must give explicit permission for the data to be reused for that purpose. However, for the majority of secondary data sets in official archives it is straightforward to obtain them at a reasonable cost.

If data sets are found that are not part of an official archive, locating the original investigator might be part of the research process. Even if the data are simple to obtain, locating information about the original data collection procedures may be difficult. Nevertheless, if the secondary data are to be used for research, this additional information is vital to evaluating the methodological quality of the data. Again, it may be necessary to locate the original investigator or research agency in the hope that a research report is available that describes the methods and procedures of the original study.

If data are stored in an archive, they are usually available in several different formats. The lowest common denominator is a text or ASCII file, meaning the numeric values are available in a raw data file without additional information. Usually, the data are organized as a rectangular data matrix, with fixed columns for the variables and one or more lines (records) per subject. In addition, there usually is a codebook, which describes the variables in the data set, what values they may legitimately take, and their location in the raw data file. The recipients of the data can use this information to input the data into the statistical package they use. In many cases, the data are also available in the format of the major statistical packages such as SPSS or SAS, so the variables already have appropriate names, the variable values are labeled, and missing data indicators are set.

The rectangular data structure is the simplest structure. Other data structures are hierarchical and relational data structures. In a hierarchical data structure, multiple hierarchical sources of information are combined. For example, an educational study may have data both on pupils and on their schools, with a number of pupils belonging to the same school. Such data can exist as two separate files, linked by a school identification variable, or as a single file, containing both pupil and school variables. In a relational data structure, there are several files that are connected on the basis of a predefined variable or structure. For instance, an educational study might have data on pupils and schools, but also data on the pupils, their families, and the neighborhoods they live in. This does not fit a tidy hierarchical structure, but all the data are related through the pupils.

Although it is common practice to analyze survey material collected for other researcher's projects, earlier qualitative research data are considered to be less of a source and are scarcely used, except by social historians. Sharing qualitative data generates mixed feelings that have to do with practical, methodological, and ethical issues. The value of secondary qualitative data is questioned because much of the meaning is supposed to be lost when, for instance, tone of voice and interviewees' gestures are ignored. There is also concern that the original fieldwork context cannot be recovered, which is necessary for adequate interpretation and understanding. Ethical issues have to do with confidentiality and obtaining consent for the preservation and future reuse of the raw materials by those other than the original researcher.

Qualitative data can be of all kinds. Open interviews generally result in long transcriptions, which can be stored as a text file. Again, the lowest common denominator is the simple text or ASCII file. However, qualitative data can contain many different information sources, such as video tapes and audiocassette tapes, photographs, diaries, and so on. The most valuable qualitative data sets for future reanalysis are likely to have three qualities: (1) the interviewees have been chosen on a convincing sampling bases, (2) the interviews follow a life-story form rather than focusing on the researcher's immediate themes, and (3) recontact is not ruled out.

Evaluating the Methodological Quality of Secondary Data

If the secondary data set stems from previous research, it should be considered that each research project is undertaken with a view to answering a specific set of research questions. Choices are made regarding which information is going to be collected, how sampling will proceed, and specifically how the information is collected. In quantitative research, these generally involve deciding on a general strategy of data collection—carrying out a survey and subsequently deciding on specific survey instruments or scales to be used and a specific mode of surveying respondents, such as a face-to-face survey. In qualitative research, similar decisions are made about the general strategy—carrying out a qualitative interview study and subsequently on the sample, instruments, data analysis, and structure of the report. In both cases, (small) differences in definitions, classifications, and concepts among studies may have an impact on the reusability of the data.

How well the choices and limitations of the original study fit the current research problem is a matter of judgment. Secondary researchers must consider carefully whether the data appropriately fit their research question. In general, it is acceptable if the limitations of the available data limit the secondary analysis to some extent, for instance, by impeding tests of some specific hypothesis. However, it is not acceptable if the limitations of the data make it necessary to change the research question in order to be able to use them at all.

In any case, when secondary data are used it is very important to evaluate the quality of the data closely. This requires that additional information be archived with the data itself. Such information should at least include the study purpose, operationalization, data collection details (who, when, and where), entities being studied and sampling criteria, and any known biases. Because searching for suitable secondary data and retrieving them in usable form can be time-consuming, an integral part of the search strategy is to make certain that such additional metadata describing the data and their quality are in fact available. This is also important because the data sets deemed sufficiently interesting to be archived are usually very large. Typically, secondary researchers need to select specific subsets of variables or groups of cases. Some providers of secondary data offer a proprietary interface to select subsets from the data; others provide a huge data file from which the customers must select what they need. Again, all this demands a good description of the data.

For the purpose of protecting the confidentiality of the respondents, the data that are made available are sometimes purposively altered. When data are available on a microlevel, combining information from different sources may make it possible to identify individual respondents. For instance, by combining information on job (librarian), age (42), gender (female), and town (San Diego), it may be possible to identify a specific respondent with reasonable probability. For reasons of disclosure control, secondary data providers sometimes transform the data by adding random numbers from a specified statistical distribution. This makes it impossible to identify individual respondents. And, obviously, it will also impede the analysis; however, statistical procedures exist to obtain correct results when the data have been deliberately contaminated this way.

The analysis of quantitative data often starts with a process in which the data are cleaned—incomplete records may be edited or automatically imputed, nonnormal data may be transformed, aggregated scores may be calculated, and so on. This is all based on the assumptions and interpretations of the primary researcher. Researchers who reanalyze the data for another research purpose may not always agree with the assumptions implied in the data cleaning and coding. Instead, they may prefer to use other methods that are more in line with their own research purpose. If the secondary data contain all the original variables and if the codebook documents all data manipulations, researchers can apply their own data-cleaning process. However, tracing the preliminary data-cleaning process can be a difficult and very time-consuming process. At the very least, researchers should be alerted and aware of changes to and recodings of the original raw data when secondary data are used.

If meta-information on the secondary data is incomplete or even totally lacking, it becomes impossible to assess the reliability and validity of the original procedures. Such data, however, can still be useful for teaching purposes, for use as example data or as practice data for students. In fact, there are several data archives and other organizations that make data available specifically for teaching purposes; some of these are general, whereas others aim at a specific analysis technique.

See Also the Following Articles

Focus Groups • Interviews • Surveys

Further Reading

American Statistical Association. http://www.amstat.org/

Berg, B. L. (2001). *Qualitative Research Methods for the Social Sciences.* Allyn & Bacon, Boston.

British Library National Sound Archive. Oral history collection. http://www.cadensa.bl.uk

Copernic. Available at: http://www.copernic.com/

Council of European Social Science Data Archives (CESSDA). http://www.nsd.uib.no/cessda/

Cresswell, J. W. (1998). *Qualitative Inquiry and Research Design: Choosing among Five Traditions.* Sage, Thousand Oaks, CA.

Dbmscopy. Available at: http://www.dataflux.com

De Leeuw, E. D., and de Heer, W. (2002). Trends in household survey nonresponse: A longitudinal and international comparison. In *Survey Nonresponse* (R. M. Groves, D. A. Dillman, J. L. Eltinge, and R. J. A. Little, eds.), pp. 41–54. Wiley, New York.

De Vaus, D. (2001). *Research Design in Social Research.* Sage, Thousand Oaks, CA.

Doyle, P., Lane, J., Theeuwes, J., and Zayatz, L. (2002). *Confidentiality, Disclosure and Data Access: Theory and*

Practical Applications for Statistical Agencies. Elsevier, Amsterdam.

Experimental-data Archive. http://www.radcliffe.edu/murray/data

Fink, A. (1998). *Conducting Research Literature Reviews.* Sage, Thousand Oaks, CA.

Hammersley, M., and Atkinson, P. (1995). *Ethnograph: Principles in Practice.* Routledge, London.

International Consortium for Political and Social Research (ICPSR). http://www.icpsr.umich.edu/

Kerlinger, F. N., and Lee, H. L. (2000). *Foundations of Behavioral Research.* Harcourt, Fort Worth, TX.

Library of Statistical Problems. http://lib.stat.cmu.edu/DASL/

Lyberg, L., Biemer, P., Collins, M., de Leeuw, E., Dippo, C., Schwarz, N., and Trewin, D. (eds.) (1997). *Survey Measurement and Process Quality*. John Wiley, New York.

Maxwell, J. A. (1996). *Qualitative Research Design: An Interactive Approach.* Sage, Thousand Oaks, CA.

Maxwell, S. E., and Delaney, H. D. (1990). *Designing Experiments and Analyzing Data.* Brooks/Cole, Pacific Grove, CA.

Qualidata. Qualicat. http://www.qualidata.essex.ac.uk/search/qualicat.asp

Seale, C. (1999). *The Quality of Qualitative Research.* Sage, London.

Silverman, D. (2000). *Doing Qualitative Research: A Practical Handbook.* Sage, London.

StatTransfer. Available at: http://www.stattransfer.com

Stewart, D. W., and Kamins, M. A. (1993). *Secondary Research: Information Sources and Methods.* Sage, Newbury Park, CA.

Thompson, P. (2000). Re-using qualitative research data: A personal account. Forum: *Qual. Soc. Res.* [Online Journal], **1**(3), Available at: http://qualitative-research.net/fqs/fqs-eng.htm

UK Data Archive (UKDA). http://www.data-archive.ac.uk/

Weiss, R. S. (1994). *Learning from Strangers: The Art and Method of Qualitative Interview Studies.* Free Press, New York.

Data Distribution and Cataloging

Wendy L. Thomas
University of Minnesota, Minneapolis, Minnesota, USA

Glossary

aggregate data The result of analyzing or totaling microdata for a group of respondents. Statistical publications normally group by geographic areas, but may also group by discrete subpopulations.

cataloging The process of classifying items to form a catalog or list; describing items or characteristics of items.

data discovery The part of the search process where the existence and location of the data set are determined.

Dublin Core A standard set of elements considered to be the base level of information needed to locate an information object. The contents of the Dublin Core resemble the contents of a standard bibliographic record, like those found in a library catalog.

metadata All-encompassing term meaning data about data. In terms of social science data files, it generally refers to all of the material normally found in a complete codebook and related documents.

microdata Respondent-level data.

Data distribution and cataloging cover the full postcollection production stream from storing the data, creating the documentation, determining the level of access to be provided, preserving the data and supporting documentation, and providing the means for the discovery, acquisition, and intelligent secondary analysis of the data. The decisions made during this process, as well as how thoroughly it is accomplished, have a direct bearing on the availability and usability of social science data for secondary analysis. Distribution of data refers to the format of publication, access restrictions imposed on the data, archival considerations, and the network chosen for providing access to the data. Cataloging is viewed in its broadest sense: how extensively and exhaustively the data collection is described and how well it facilitates discovery of and access to the data for the secondary user.

The Issue of Access

Secondary analysis of social science data has a long tradition in the quantitative social sciences. Major collections of data have been made accessible over the years through libraries and archives as well as by the original investigator. These collections consist of microdata or microdata samples and published statistical tables of aggregated data. Academic researchers, practicing demographers and analysts, and the general public use these data. The usability of any of these data collections has been a function of the means of data distribution and the quality of data description or cataloging. As the ease of access has improved, heavily used or broadly applicable data collections have been incorporated into both teaching and research at the undergraduate level. However, an ever-increasing body of data has lain dormant and unused due to lack of awareness and difficulty in gaining access. Changes in technology and description during the past 30 years have radically changed the face of data distribution, making the discovery, acquisition, and use of social science data easier than ever before.

The most obvious change in distribution over the years has been in publication formats. The implication of this change for both the amount of data available and its usability has been profound. New formats are cheaper to create, are easier to distribute, increase the amount of data available to the user, raise new issues in data confidentiality, make old distribution and support networks obsolete, and raise new challenges in determining who is responsible for supporting access to the data, both physical and functional, over time.

Cataloging practices are encompassing more material, moving further into the details of the documentation, expanding standards to improve shared access, and ensuring the preservation of both physical and functional access long into the future. These emerging descriptive standards are beginning to drive a variety of search engines and analysis tools. In addition, the integration of the descriptive material and the object being described into a single electronic package of information raises the possibility of dramatic improvements in research tools in the next decade.

The changes in distribution and cataloging practices are reflected in new data discovery engines, improved data access and manipulation tools, and broader in-depth access to data for secondary analysis. The implications for the data user are clear. For the social science researcher, improved access through new means of data dissemination and cataloging practices means that more attention must be paid to the preparation, documentation, distribution, and preservation of primary data sets so that future researchers can fully benefit from these new innovations.

Development of Distribution Methods

Social and economic data have been recorded and distributed for as long as written materials have been accumulated. Some of the earliest clay and stone tablets record economic transactions, population censuses, and storehouse inventories. Although the media and extent of content have changed over time, the means of distribution has stayed essentially the same until the mid-1960s and the introduction of the computer into daily life. Up until this point, the distribution of social science data depended on recording information on some medium that could be stored, copied, and physically delivered in an inflexible format for interpretation by the end user. Generally, the data were integrated into the metadata either as an inclusion in a line of text or in a formal table with column headers and row stubs. In order to transfer the information into another format or another work, researchers had to copy and transfer the image of the original data or hand-entered the individual data items into a new format.

Access to computing resources brought changes to the distribution process that are still emerging. The first step was the creation of a data file that could be processed electronically by the end user. Initially, the storage medium continued to require copying and physically transporting the file to the end user. These storage media were primarily off-line and included things such as paper tape, punch cards, and 9-track or round tapes. However, if one had the right reader and the right equipment, one could process the data without additional hand-entry. As on-line methods of storage became cheaper and Internet transfer speed improved, data could be downloaded directly to the end user's computer ready to use.

This not only opened up opportunities for secondary data analysis, but also resulted in the separation of data from their surrounding metadata. The metadata that described the storage structure of the data, as well giving them context and meaning, remained in the traditional formats. Archives, such as the Inter-University Consortium for Political and Social Research (ICPSR), stored, copied, and distributed data on rapidly changing media, but continued to store, copy, and distribute print versions of the accompanying metadata. Even when the metadata information, or parts of it, was put into an electronic format, there was little consistency in its structure. The noted exceptions were set-up files for heavily used statistical packages, such as Statistical Package for the Social Sciences (SPSS) and Statistical Analysis System (SAS). However, these files contained only a small portion of the metadata available for accurately interpreting data. Even the switch to electronic images of metadata material simply improved the access and transfer rate for obtaining metadata; it did not radically change how the information could be processed. Human intervention and interpretation were still required.

Advances in data storage and transfer changed user expectations. Statements such as the following, made in reference to the extremely large electronic summary data files from the 1990 Census, were common: "If it's electronic, you just need to put it in the computer and look at it." This statement reflects the disjoint between a user's understanding of the structure of electronic data and the realities of presenting data in an understandable manner through the incorporation of data and metadata. The data referred to here resided on hundreds of 9-track tapes, stored in files with hundreds of thousands of records up to 150,000 characters in length. Without the information provided by the printed metadata, it was, in essence, just a bunch of numbers. Clearly, in order to meet the rising expectation of users to be able to locate, access, AND interpret data on-line, the quality, consistency, and manageability of the metadata would have to improve to the level of the data files themselves.

Levels of Description

Descriptive material, or metadata, for social science data files can be extensive. For example, the printed metadata for the National Longitudinal Survey creates a stack over 5 ft high. This may seem excessive, but the metadata for any single data item should provide information on how, when, why, and by whom it was collected, how it was processed, the decisions made in editing it, and the resulting analysis, as well as its relation to other data. This information may be well defined, scattered in a variety of documents and formats, or missing altogether. It helps to think of metadata as layers of description related to a data item.

The top layer is the standard bibliographic citation including title, author (or equivalent), producer, date, geographic coverage, and basic subject identifiers (subject headings or keywords). The second layer gives a fuller description or abstract that provides additional detail as to the content and coverage of the data file. This is generally provided as unstructured text. Next is detailed information about the gross structure of the data set: the number of data files, records, and variables included in the data set. This is followed by detailed information about the variables themselves, including the questions they were derived from, the ordering of those questions, the variables' names, response categories, response frequencies, and how the individual variables are arranged within a record. In addition, there are related materials covering methodology for data collection, questionnaire or source layout, data collection and encoding instructions, editing processes, term definitions, and structured coding schemes. In essence, each data item should have the full hierarchy of information attached to it as well as carry information regarding its relationship to other data items within the data set.

The amount of detail that is available in a uniformly structured set of metadata directly affects the level of data search and retrieval that can be accomplished. The level of description that can reasonably be applied to any piece of information, be it a number, a document, or an object, is related to the format of the original piece of information and one's ability to integrate the metadata description with the information itself. This may sound a bit strange, but consider a handwritten document, say a letter. In its original form, it is difficult to incorporate it into an electronic search system. Instead, a brief description complying with a common, widely used structure is used. If well constructed, this description can provide a broad clue as to whether the letter is of interest to a researcher. The more detailed the description, the better able one is to determine the letter's value. If one can create an image of the letter to accompany the description, one can tell whether it is of value simply by viewing it. If one has hundreds of such letters, one needs a better means of locating those of interest. One needs, in fact, to be able to search directly against the contents of the letter. A fully electronic copy of the letter can be created that will allow one to do just that. Even then, one would need to "tag" the text, providing additional information that would allow the searcher to differentiate, say, the color green from the name Green.

Next, consider social science metadata. It is much more complex than a letter or even a simple book. The term "Germany," if found in different places, can mean a variety of things. It could be the geographic coverage of the data set, a place of residence, a place of birth, a military station, or a number of other things. The ability to link the term to its structural location becomes increasingly important as one tries to narrow down the information one wants to retrieve from an ever-growing pile of social science data. For example, category labels such as "Under 5 years" or "5 to 9 years" mean little unless the searcher knows that they are category labels for AGE or YEARS OF RESIDENCE.

Clearly, the increased use of computers to store and display a range of information objects has resulted in a concept of cataloging that is much more encompassing than the traditional bibliographic citation. This is true for all forms of information, not just social science data sets. However, unlike many other forms of information (images, books, museum objects, music, etc.), data make little sense without their accompanying descriptive material. Because of this, data archivists, librarians, and producers have worked for years to develop a means of structuring metadata so that it is not only something a human can process, but that a machine can process as well.

One system, the Data Documentation Initiative (DDI), is gaining prominence as a hardware-, software-independent model for marking up social science metadata in a consistent and discrete manner. The DDI grew out of an international collaborative effort, promoted by ICPSR. It includes the major archives, national data producers, and researchers in Europe and North America and has been in existence since 1995. The DDI developed a specification in eXtensible Markup Language (XML) for describing all the elements of social science metadata in a consistent and persistent format. Structured around the major components of the traditional codebook and accompanying materials, the DDI specification covers bibliographic information on the XML codebook itself, source materials for the creation of the XML codebook, study description and methodology, physical file description, and the intellectual content of the data file (the variables and the questions that produced them). By using both the hierarchical structure of XML and the ability to link to information both inside and outside of the XML codebook, the DDI creates a navigatable path between a single data item and all of its related metadata.

Implications for Discovery Tools

Discovery tools form the first line of access to data sets. Discovery simply means identifying the existence and location of needed information. Dissemination tools allow the researcher to obtain a full copy of the data, an extraction of a subset of the data, or the results of an analysis of the data. It is similar to the idea of an interlibrary loan service with book material. In the discovery phase, one locates the item in the on-line catalog and determines where it is located. Then, in the dissemination phase, one obtains a copy of the book (full copy), a copy of a chapter (extraction), or a synopsis or analysis of the content by a research service (analysis). Whereas dissemination tools tend to be designed for specific types of information, discovery tools can provide general discovery access to a wide array of information types or be designed to provide in-depth discovery access to specific types of information.

What does this detailed level of description mean in terms of data discovery? First and foremost, it means that the entire range of metadata, including internal relationships between the parts of the metadata, can be used for data discovery. With the right search engine, a user can do things that were previously impossible. For example, a researcher can search across a collection of data sets for those that include age variables with detailed age groupings for person 65 years of age or older, such as "65 to 69 years," "70 to 74 years," "75 to 79 years," "80 to 84 years," and "85 years and over." This may sound like a simple issue, but a large number of aggregate data sets prior to 1980 use an upper age grouping of "65 years and over" with no further breakdowns, making the data set useless for many studies on aging. Earlier, generalized descriptions of content would simply state that a data set included "age reported in 5-year cohorts" without noting the top code field. Only by searching at the category level within variables dealing with age can the answer to the query be found quickly. Alternatively, a researcher could search for the data sets whose variables most closely match a list of desired variables or easily discover what surveys asked a particular question, including variations in phrasing or position within the questionnaire. With in-depth description, locating a single data item could put the researcher on a path to all types of related data, both within the same data set and outside of that data set.

Well-structured description also facilitates linking social science data to other forms of information. In the DDI, the component parts of the metadata are described through a hierarchical structure of elements and attributes. These elements are tightly defined and can be mapped to similar elements in other descriptive systems for other forms of information. At the highest level, the citation or bibliographic information can be mapped to the elements that make up the Dublin Core record or the MARC record commonly found in library catalogs. Mapping between elements means that the contents of element X in descriptive system A are the conceptual equivalent of the contents of element Y in system B. Therefore, if one's search engine is designed to search system B, one can easily instruct it how to search at least some levels of system A by telling it which elements are equivalent.

The ability to search between metadata structures for different forms of information is particularly important given that different forms of data (social science, biological, geographic, etc.) have specialized metadata structures that are designed for the needs of a particular discipline. If one wanted to discover what social and biological data were available for a particular area, and then wanted to analyze the data spatially, one would need to search for all three file types and determine their compatibility. By carefully crafting fields that retain closely similar contents, or providing information in a form that is understood by related search systems, metadata producers increase the ease of quickly locating a variety of material in a single search. For example, DDI has an element field, "Geographic Coverage," that uses the same name as a field in the descriptive structures for geographic files, but the element content description from Dublin Core. The Dublin Core description is much broader in scope than what the geographic search system would expect. By providing alternative means of determining the geographers' definition of Geographic Coverage, DDI allows a means of mapping to both systems.

An additional problem for search systems is that, as detailed as the metadata might be, it simply cannot replicate all the information in the data file itself. By integrating the metadata with an object (in this case, the data set) either physically or virtually, information found only in the object becomes searchable. For example, metadata for a particular data set may say that it includes data for the following geographic levels: United States, State, County, and Places with Population over 10,000. If one has a general sense of the size of certain places such as Blackduck or Sauk Rapids, Minnesota, one might suspect that a small place such as Blackduck, Minnesota would not be found in this file. However, one may be unsure about a medium-sized place such as Sauk Rapids, Minnesota. The metadata generally will not list the names of each state, county, and place in the file, particularly those files that are large or have complex geography. Unless one knows the size of the place that one is looking for, the only way to discover whether there are data for Sauk Rapids would be to query the data set. Good metadata would include information on how a foreign search system could query the data directly using an abbreviated search string that is understood by the local system supporting the data set.

Implications for Data Distribution Tools

The development of distribution tools is generally dependent on there being a known and significant pool of potential users for the system, as well as a critical mass of relevant material. Without these two elements, the cost of developing and maintaining a system is not feasible. This is the reason that many of the data distribution tools that are available are specific to particular, heavily used studies, such as the General Social Survey, the U.S. Census, and the National Longitudinal Survey. It is also the reason that, in the past, the focus was to create very limited descriptions of large numbers of materials. One increased access to a large amount of material that was formerly inaccessible even though it was only very basic discovery access.

Study-specific tools also took the process of data distribution to the level of extraction and on-line analysis. The ability to extract only the variables or cases needed for a specific study relieved the researcher of the burden of downloading, managing, and subsetting large, unwieldy data files. Early analysis tools could not always handle the size and complex structures of these data files. Researchers required the assistance of computing and data specialists to help them understand and extract data and put it into a file in a format and size that they could handle. The ability to perform this type of selection on-line placed more control with the researcher. Similarly, the ability to analyze data on-line meant that those looking for quick answers or a relatively straightforward analysis of the data could avoid both the download time and the local set-up and processing time formerly required. In order to make any of these extraction or analysis tools work, however, the metadata had to be created in a format that the computer could process. These were often created in proprietary or unique formats that did not facilitate sharing of the metadata or the wider application of the extraction or analysis tool. By developing uniform and persistent structures for describing data, the potential is created not only for the discovery and basic distribution of an ever-growing mass of relevant material available, but for extraction and on-line analysis as well.

Uniform and persistent metadata structures mean that developers of distribution tools can focus on addressing the needs of users as opposed to the peculiarities of specific data sets. They can address variations in users' preferred approaches to data, specialized needs for access or processing, and the skill level of individuals. There are trade-offs in every system and, in general, system developers focus on meeting the needs of the majority of users. If one happens to be in the minority, one either finds a way to "make" the system do what one needs or learns to live within the limitations of the system as designed. Because multiple search and distribution tools can, in theory, access the same data files, a single tool does not need to be all things to all users and can concentrate on performing a limited number of things very well. It also means that even when a highly specialized distribution tool is developed for a specific data set, the user is not limited to this tool as a sole means of discovery access to the data.

Even those data producers who wish to retain control of access to the data could provide broader access to the metadata by allowing external systems to run queries against their metadata. This would be particularly useful for search engines that were not designed specifically for social science data.

The movement of social science data to an electronic format at an earlier date than many other forms of information commonly distributed through a general library also resulted in its being treated similarly to materials in archives. Such materials often were not included in library catalogs, or if so, not in a sufficiently detailed manner. Users of these materials tended to do their research "outside" of the traditional library catalog systems. Improvements in detailed cataloging methods and the widespread switch to electronic catalogs during the 1980s resulted in the descriptions of these materials being integrated into the general library cataloging systems. This means that a wider range of users is being informed of a greater variety of potentially useful information. The ability of search engines to "virtually" search other collections in other metadata formats by mapping to similar fields in the foreign metadata not only increases the potential user pool, but offers multiple means of access without the development of additional specialized search engines.

Detailed metadata provides additional support for directly accessing data files. This direct access can facilitate searching, as noted in the example of geographic information not available in the metadata. It also means that specific item searches, for example, the population of a particular location, can be extracted from the data file and provided to the user. It can be thought of as the functional equivalent of being told that the information one is seeking is located in a specific book and then having the book virtually opened and the sought after passage being directly provided for one. Specific item searches need not be limited to data sets providing statistical information preaggregated to identified locations or groups. Specific item searches could trigger algorithms that would be run against the microdata to produce the needed piece of information. In short, new forms of metadata provide the hooks used to develop a previously unavailable level of access to a large collection of materials.

The metadata also supports the development of a range of extraction and transformation tools that can be applied to multiple data sets. Systems built on a single format of metadata could include all three levels of services: discovery, extraction, and transformation. In this way, the user would have a number of options after discovering a data set. The user could stop at that point and acquire the entire data set and its metadata to work with on his or her own system. The user could extract the subset of data needed as well as the related metadata (altered to reflect the contents and format of the extracted subset) or analyze or transform the data on-line, taking only the results away. The versatility of the metadata allows for the support of all of these options. The uniform structure of the metadata encourages the development of systems with these capabilities by expanding both the pool of potential users and the volume of source materials available to the system.

Implications for Researchers

As a data creator, the individual researcher has a major role to play in providing adequate metadata to support the systems described above. Metadata is not something that should be created after the fact nor should it be totally left to catalogers and other information specialists. Good metadata tracks the process of data creation and should be something that is added to throughout the life of the project. Metadata specifications, such as the DDI, can help the researcher identify those pieces of information that need to be recorded, or recorded in a particular way, and actually help organize and track the research process. By not "requiring" any fields except for title, the DDI allows the researcher to begin filling in the structure at any point.

For example, one could start by entering information about the principal investigator, the organization, the funding source, and the citation for the proposal. The study description section can hold notes on the methodology and the question section can provide elements to hold information on the conceptual base of each question, question text, pre- or postquestion text, response categories, question order, and other relevant information. The methodology section covers all aspects of data collection, sample information, accuracy, and response rate. Even when information is held outside of the DDI structure in other forms, the DDI can be used to store pointers to these documents, serving as an information map to the project during its development. Elements that require the knowledge and expertise of trained catalogers can be added as the project nears completion and is being prepared for release. Catalogers base their descriptions and subject assignments on the materials they are provided. Receiving these materials in a uniform manner allows catalogers to quickly identify the information relevant to their work and to complete the sections that will relate to other cataloged materials in a way that enhances their use in discovery tools.

Entry tools have been developed with the intent of assisting data archivists and librarians in converting existing metadata in other formats to the DDI specification. Other tools are being developed to capture information from survey development tools and output it in DDI. Additional tool development work needs to be performed in order to provide a flexible interface for the researcher to capture development information, store it in a way that facilitates interactive use during the project, and then output completed metadata in DDI at the end of the project. Although such a tool is not yet available, the very existence of the DDI specification has provided researchers with an outline of the specific pieces of information that should be recorded and preserved along with their data. A brief survey of the wide variety of metadata provided for data in the past makes it clear that even this small accomplishment is a major step in improving access to data files.

For the researcher performing secondary analysis or researching previous work done in a particular area, the value of improved cataloging is immense. Metadata is the only means of making sense of a pile of numbers. It is the gateway for discovering what data exist, determining whether the data are of value, and locating, obtaining, and working effectively with the data.

See Also the Following Article

Neutrality in Data Collection

Further Reading

Cruse, P., Fanshier, M., Gey, F., and Low, M. (2001). Using DDI extensions as an intermediary for data storage and data display. *IASSIST Quart.* **25**(3), 5–12. Available at http://iassistdata.org/publications/iq/iq25/iqvol253cruse.pdf

Dodd, S. (1982). *Cataloging Machine-Readable Data Files: An Interpretive Manual.* American Library Association, Chicago, IL.

Data Documentation Initiative. Available at http://www.icpsr.umich.edu/DDI

Green, A., Dionne, J., and Dennis, M. (1999). *Preserving the Whole: A Two-Track Approach to Rescuing Social Science Data and Metadata.* Council on Library and Information Sciences, Washington, DC.

Mayo, R. (2000). Metadata in international database systems and the United Nations Common Database (UNCDB). *IASSIST Quart.* **24**(1), 4–14. Available at http://datalib.library.ualberta.ca/publications/iq/iq24/iqvol241mayo.pdf

Musgrave, S., and Ryssevik, J. (1999). The Social Science Dream Machine: Resource Discovery, Analysis and Data Delivery on the Web. Available at http://www.nesstar.org/papers/iassist_0599.html

National Archives and Records Administration, Archival Research and Evaluation Staff. (1990). *A National Archives Strategy for the Development and Implementation of Standards for the Creation, Transfer, Access, and Long-Term Storage of Electronic Records of the Federal Government.* National Archives and Records Administration, Technical Information Paper No. 8. Available at http://www.archives.gov/research_room/media_formats/strategy_for_electronic_records_storage.html

Ryssevik, J. (1999). Providing Global Access to Distributed Data Through Metadata Standardisation—The Parallel Stories of NESSTAR and the DDI, Working Paper No. 10, UN/CEC Work Session on Statistical Metadata. Available at http://www.nesstar.org/papers/GlobalAccess.html

Thomas, C. (ed.) (2002). *Libraries, the Internet, and Scholarship: Tools and Trends Converging*. Dekker, New York.

Treadwell, W. (1999). Maximizing the search potential of social science codebooks through the application of the codebook DTD. *IASSIST Quart.* **23**(4), 10–13. Available at http://datalib.library.ualberta.ca/publications/iq/iq23/iqvol234treadwell.pdf.

Treadwell, W. (2002). DDI, The Data Documentation Initiative: An introduction to the standard and its role in social science data access. In *Cataloging the Web: Metadata, AACR, and MARC 21* (L. Jones, J. Ahronheim, and J. Crawford, eds.), pp. 155–168. Scarecrow Press, Lanham, MD.

Data Envelopment Analysis (DEA)

Kingsley E. Haynes

George Mason University, Fairfax, Virginia, USA

Mustafa Dinc

The World Bank, Washington, D.C., USA

The findings, interpretations and conclusions are entirely those of the authors and do not represent the views of the World Bank, its executive directors, or the countries they represent.

Glossary

allocative efficiency The efficiency of a production process in converting inputs to outputs, where the cost of production is minimized for a given set of input prices. Allocative efficiency can be calculated by the ratio of cost efficiency to technical efficiency.

decision-making unit (DMU) The designator for units (firms, organizations, production elements, service delivery agents, etc.) being analyzed in a data envelopment analysis model. Use of this term redirects emphasis of the analysis from profit-making businesses to decision-making entities; i.e., the analysis can be applied to any unit-based enterprise that controls its mix of inputs and decides on which outputs to produce (the enterprise is not dependent on having profit as an output, although in the private sector, this is likely to be one of the outputs).

efficiency frontier The frontier represented by the "best performing" decision-making units; made up of the units in the data set that are most efficient in transforming their inputs into outputs. The units that determine the frontier are those classified as being 100% efficient, usually with a value of 1; any unit not on the frontier has an efficiency rating of less than 100%.

efficiency score/relative efficiency A score allocated to a unit as a result of data envelopment analysis. This score is between 0 and 1 (i.e., 0 and 100%). A unit with a score of 100% is relatively efficient; any unit with a score of less than 100% is relatively inefficient (e.g., a unit with a score of 60% is only 60% as efficient as the best performing units in the data set analyzed). The efficiency score obtained by a unit will vary depending on the other units and factors included in the analysis. Scores are relative (not absolute) to the other units in the data set.

input Any resource used by a unit to produce its outputs (products or services); can include resources that are not a product but are an attribute of the environment in which the units operate, and they can be controlled or uncontrolled.

output The products (goods, services, or other outcomes) that result from the processing and consumption of inputs (resources); may be physical goods or services or a measure of how effectively a unit has achieved its goals, and may include profits where applicable.

productive efficiency Often just referred to as efficiency; a measure of the ability of a unit to produce outputs from a given set of inputs. The efficiency of a decision-making unit is always relative to the other units in the set being analyzed, so the efficiency score is always a relative measure. Unit efficiency is related to unit radial distance from the efficiency frontier; it is the ratio of the distance from the origin to the inefficient unit, to the distance from the origin to the reference unit on the efficiency frontier.

reference set The reference set of an inefficient unit is the set of efficient units to which the inefficient unit has been most directly compared when calculating its efficiency rating; contains the efficient units that have input/output orientations most similar to that of the inefficient unit, therefore serving as a model of good operating practice for the inefficient unit.

scale efficiency An optimal unit size of operation, the reduction or increase of which will decrease efficiency; calculated by dividing aggregate efficiency by technical efficiency. A scale-efficient unit operates at optimal returns to scale.

slack The underproduction of outputs or the overuse of inputs; represents the improvements (in the form of an increase/decrease in inputs or outputs) needed to make an inefficient unit become efficient.

targets The values of the inputs and outputs that would result in an inefficient unit becoming efficient.

technical efficiency Unit maximization of output per unit of input used; the efficiency of the production or conversion process, which can be calculated independently of prices and costs. The impact of scale size is ignored because decision-making units are compared only with units of similar scale sizes.

virtual input/output A value calculated by multiplying the value of the input (output) with the corresponding optimal weight for the unit as given by the solution to the primal linear programming model. Virtual inputs/outputs define the level of importance attached to each factor. The sum of the virtual inputs for each unit always equals 1; the sum of the virtual outputs is equal to the unit's efficiency score.

weights Within data envelopment analysis models, weights are the '"unknowns" that are calculated to determine the efficiency of the units. The efficiency score is the weighted sum of outputs divided by the weighted sum of inputs for each unit. The weights are calculated to solve the linear program in such a way that each unit is shown in the best possible light. Weights indicate the importance attached to each factor (input/output) in the analysis.

Data envelopment analysis is a nonparametric technique used for performance measurement and benchmarking. It uses linear programming to determine the relative efficiencies of a set of homogeneous (comparable) units. It is a "process-based" analysis; in other words, it can be applied to any unit-based enterprise, regardless of whether a "profit" figure is involved in the evaluation. The use of data envelopment analysis also overcomes some of the problems with traditional performance measurement methods, such as simple ratio analysis and regression models.

What Is Data Envelopment Analysis?

Data envelopment analysis (DEA) is concerned with the evaluation of the performance of organizations in converting inputs to outputs. In DEA, such organizations are usually called decision-making units (DMUs). DEA is a powerful methodology that measures the efficiency of a DMU relative to other similar DMUs by identifying a "best practice" frontier, with a simple restriction that all DMUs lie on or below the efficiency frontier. DEA is a mathematical programming model that uses a set of non-parametric, linear programming techniques to estimate relative efficiency. The underlying assumption behind DEA is that if the most efficient DMU can produce Y amount of output by using X amount of input, then it is expected that other DMUs should also be able to produce the same, if they are efficient. DEA combines all efficient DMUs and forms a virtual DMU_0 with virtual inputs and outputs. If the virtual DMU_0 is better than DMU_k by either making more output with the same input or making the same output with less input, then DMU_k is considered inefficient.

A DEA study can have the following objectives:

- Identify the efficiency frontier and efficient units, and rank other units by their relative efficiency scores.
- Identify an efficiency measure that reflects the distance from each inefficient unit to the efficient frontier.
- Project inefficient units to the efficient frontier (efficient targets for the inefficient units).
- Identify efficient input–output relations.
- Evaluate the management of compared units for potential benchmarking.
- Evaluate the effectiveness of comparable programs or policies.
- Create a quantitative basis for reallocation of resources among units under evaluation.
- Identify sources and amounts of relative inefficiency in each of the compared units.
- Identify technical and allocative inefficiencies.
- Identify scale problems of units and determine the most productive scale size.
- Identify achievable targets for units under evaluation.
- Identify an individual unit's progress over time.

Differences between DEA and Other Efficiency Measurement Models

There are two basic approaches to quantify productive efficiency of a unit or entity: parametric (or econometric) and nonparametric (mathematical programming). These two approaches use different techniques to envelop a data set with different assumptions for random noise and for the structure of the production technology. These assumptions, in fact, generate the strengths and weaknesses of both approaches. The essential differences can be grouped under two characteristics: (a) the econometric approach is stochastic and attempts to distinguish the effects of noise from the effects of inefficiency and is based on the sampling theory for interpretation of essentially statistical results; (b) the programming approach is nonstochastic, lumps noise and inefficiency together (calling this combination inefficiency), and is built on the findings and observation of a population and only projects efficiency relative to other observed units. The econometric approach is parametric and confounds the effects of misspecification of the functional form of production with inefficiency. The programming model is nonparametric and population based and hence less prone to this type of specification error.

Weaknesses and Strengths of DEA

There have been arguments made that the traditional parametric methods fail to measure productive efficiency satisfactorily because of the following reasons: (a) most of the traditional approaches are based on process measures with little or no attention to important outcome measures; (b) such outcome measures as well as some input factors are qualitative and it is difficult to quantify them, and to assign them their proper relative weights is usually problematic; (c) it is very difficult to formulate an explicit functional relationship between inputs and outputs with fixed weights on the various factors; and (d) averaging performance across many DMUs, as in regression analysis, fails to explain the behavior of individual DMUs, particularly leaders and laggards. DEA has several characteristics that make it a powerful tool: (a) DEA can model multiple input and multiple output situations and it does not require an assumption of a functional production form in relating inputs to outputs; (b) DMUs are directly compared against a peer or combination of peer units; and (c) DEA can have inputs and outputs with very different measurement units (for example, X_1 could be in units of lives saved and X_2 could be in units of dollars without requiring *a priori* monetization or prespecifying a trade-off between the two). There are other key aspects of DEA:

- The ability of DEA to incorporate environmental factors into the model as uncontrollable inputs or outputs or by assessment of after-the-fact results.
- DEA is a nonparametric method not requiring the user to hypothesize a mathematical form for the production function.
- DEA measures performance against efficient performance rather than average performance.
- DEA can identify the nature of returns to scale at each part of the efficient boundary area (facet).
- DEA can identify the sources of inefficiency in terms of excessive use of particular input resources or low levels on certain output generation.
- DEA offers accurate estimates of relative efficiency because it is a boundary method.
- DEA offers more accurate estimates of marginal values of input or outputs, provided it offers no negligible marginal value for any variable.
- DEA allows for variable marginal values for different input–output mixes.

On the other hand, econometric approaches have some advantages over DEA:

- Econometric approaches offer a better predictor of future performance at the collective unit level if the assumed inefficiencies cannot be eliminated.
- Econometric approaches offer the ability to estimate confidence intervals for unit-related point estimates.
- Econometric approaches offer the ability to test assumptions about mathematical relationships assumed between input and output variables.
- Econometric approaches may offer more stable estimates of efficiency and target input–output levels because the estimates are not dependent on only a small subset of directly observed input–output levels.
- Econometric approach estimates of marginal input–output values and of efficiency are more transparent and can be more readily communicated to the layperson.
- Because DEA is an extremal value method, noise (even symmetrical noise with zero mean) such as measurement error can cause significant problems.
- DEA is good at estimating "relative" efficiency of a DMU, but it converges very slowly to "absolute" efficiency. In other words, it can tell you how well you are doing compared to your peers, but not compared to a "theoretical maximum." The latter is a strength of the econometric approach.

Use of DEA

Since it was first introduced in 1978, DEA has become a widely used analytical tool for measuring and evaluating performance of organizations. It has been successfully applied to different entities operating in various areas in many contexts worldwide. In many cases, evaluations of these entities by using traditional approaches have been very difficult because of complex and multidimensional aspects of production processes in which input–output relations were poorly understood. Some examples of the areas in which DEA has been used are health care, education, banking and finance, manufacturing, benchmarking, and management evaluation. In addition to these relatively narrow and focused areas, DEA techniques have been applied to evaluations of local governments, cities, regions, and even countries. Studies incorporating a wider scope include assessments of social and safety-net expenditures as inputs and various quality-of-life dimensions as outputs.

In other applications, analysts have employed DEA to get new insights about business activities and methods and to evaluate these activities. Examples of these applications are benchmarking studies of organizations and evaluations of the relative efficiencies of mutual vs. corporate forms of organization in the U.S. insurance sector. Analysts have also used DEA to evaluate governmental and community activities. The underlying reason DEA has been used in such a wide variety of activities is its ability to handle multiple inputs and outputs without having to specify a production relationship and weighting system.

Fundamentals of DEA

The application of a DEA model involves a three-stage process. The first stage is involved with the definition and selection of DMUs to be analyzed. In a DEA analysis, all units under consideration should perform similar tasks with similar objectives under the same set of "technological" and "market" conditions. These units should use the same kind of inputs to produce the same kind of outputs. The second stage is the determination of input and output variables that will be used in assessing the relative efficiency of selected DMUs. The final stage is the application of one of the DEA models and analysis of results.

After selecting DMUs to be investigated, the analyst needs to choose a DEA model appropriate to the analysis. This process has two important aspects; one is related to the returns-to-scale assumption and the other is related to the orientation of the model. The returns-to-scale issue is relatively easy. If the production process is observed to have constant returns to scale, then an additive model would be appropriate; otherwise, a multiplicative variable return-to-scale model should be selected. An additive model ratios outputs to inputs; the model developed by Abraham Charnes, William Cooper, and Edwardo Rhodes (the CCR model) is probably the most widely used and best known DEA model. It is used when a constant returns-to-scale relationship is assumed between inputs and outputs. This model calculates the overall efficiency for each unit, where both pure technical efficiency and scale efficiency are aggregated into one value. A multiplicative variable return-to-scale model measures technical efficiency. The convexity constraint in the model formulation of Rajeev Banker, Charnes, and Cooper (the BCC model) ensures that the comparable unit is of a scale size similar to that of the unit being measured. The efficiency score obtained from this model gives a score that is at least equal to the score obtained using the CCR model.

Determining the orientation of the model depends on the purpose of the analysis. Most decision-making processes have two major aspects: administrative and policy. An input minimization model addresses the administrative aspect of the problem on hand by addressing the question "how much input (cost) reduction is possible to produce the same level of output?" This information gives decision makers an opportunity to reallocate excess inputs to more needed areas. However, there is also a policy aspect of the efficiency assessment of institutions. Because many inputs used are fixed or quasi-fixed, it is very difficult to reduce them in the short run. Moreover, particularly in public policy-related studies, these inputs are largely financed by taxpayer money and involve equity and equality issues. Therefore, policymakers often want to answer the question "how much output increase is possible by using available inputs to serve more people?" An output maximization model is run to address this question. Comparison of targeted and actual values of inputs and outputs obtained from both models provides valuable information about the administrative and policy-related concerns of decision makers.

Variable selection is the most important step in a DEA application and it is seen as one of the weak spots of DEA. This process is delicate, difficult, sometimes controversial, and most open to misspecification. In some cases, there is no clearly definition of or consensus on the input/output relationship and functional production direction for units that use multiple inputs and produce multiple outputs. Some scholars have suggested that initially all relevant variables should be included in the list. From this larger list (following a three-step process—judgmental screening, non-DEA quantitative analysis, and DEA based analysis), the number of the variables is reduced to include only the most relevant ones.

In the judgmental screening process, the researcher needs to make a proper distinction between variables determining efficiency and variables explaining efficiency gaps among DMUs. For example, labor input may help in determining efficiency whereas the scale of the unit under examination may be the explaining factor of the different efficiency scores. In this process, the following questions need to be addressed: Is the variable related to or contributing to the objective of the analysis? Does the variable have needed information not included in other variables? Are data on the variable readily available and reliable? With the help of expert knowledge at the end of this process, the initial list could be shortened significantly.

Having reduced the number of variables via judgmental screening, the next step is the non-DEA quantitative analysis, in which numerical values are assigned to each variable that represents the physical units by which the variable is measured. This will give the researcher an opportunity to consider, depending on the objectives of the analysis, whether to aggregate some variables. The next step within this stage is to classify variables into inputs and outputs. Resources utilized by the DMU are typically inputs, whereas measurable benefits generated constitute the outputs. This, in most cases, is a straightforward procedure, but some variables may be interpreted as both input and output, depending on the researcher's point of view, or may have feedback effects. A practical solution to this may be to carry out some regression or correlation analyses, in which a weak relation to inputs and strong relation to outputs indicate that this variable could be classified as an input. The reverse outcome suggests it is an output. Another approach may be factor analysis. Depending on the factor loading of variables, the researcher can often determine which variables will be classified as inputs and which ones are outputs, and the degree of potential multicolinearity among inputs and among outputs. In the DEA-based analysis, the selected variables are examined by running the DEA, preferably by the strictest CCR model. When variables are consistently associated with very small multipliers, the implication is that they have little impact on the efficiency scores, and potentially may be dropped from the analysis.

Formulation of a Basic DEA Model

Consider first the relatively simple fractional programming formulation of DEA. Assume that there are n DMUs to be evaluated. Each consumes different amounts of i inputs and produces r different outputs, i.e., DMU_j consumes x_{ij} amounts of input to produce y_{rj} amounts of output. It is assumed that these inputs, x_{ij}, and outputs, y_{rj}, are nonnegative, and that each DMU has at least one positive input and output value. The productivity of a DMU can then be written as follows:

$$h_j = \frac{\sum_{r=1}^{s} u_r y_{rj}}{\sum_{i=1}^{m} v_i x_{ij}}. \tag{1}$$

In this formulation, v_i and u_r are the weights assigned to each input and output. By using mathematical programming techniques, DEA optimally assigns the weights subject to the following constraints: (1) The weights for each DMU are assigned subject to the constraint that no other DMU has an efficiency greater than 1 if it uses the same weights, implying that efficient DMUs will have a ratio value of 1, and (2) the derived weights, u and v, are not negative.

The objective function of DMU_k is the ratio of the total weighted output divided by the total weighted input:

$$\text{Maximize}\, h_k = \frac{\sum_{r=1}^{s} u_r y_{rk}}{\sum_{i=1}^{m} v_i x_{ik}} \tag{2}$$

subject to

$$\frac{\sum_{r=1}^{s} u_r y_{rj}}{\sum_{i=1}^{m} v_i x_{ij}} \leq 1 \qquad \text{for} \quad j = 1, \ldots, n, \tag{3}$$

$v_i \geq 0$ for $i = 1, \ldots, m$, and $u_r \geq 0$ for $r = 1, \ldots, s$. This is a simple presentation of a basic DEA model.

The CCR model generalizes the single-output/input technical efficiency measure to the multiple-output/multiple input case by constructing a single virtual output to single virtual input relative efficiency measure. This CCR ratio model is the principal form of the DEA model. For a given DMU, this ratio provides a measure of efficiency that is a function of multipliers. The objective is to find the largest sum of weighted outputs of DMU_k while keeping the sum of its weighted inputs at the unit value, thereby forcing the ratio of the weighted output to the weighted input for any DMU to be less than or equal to 1.

It is possible to create and estimate models that provide input-oriented or output-oriented projections for both constant returns-to-scale and variable returns-to-scale envelopments. An input-oriented model attempts to maximize the proportional decrease in input variables while remaining within the envelopment space. On the other hand, an output-oriented model maximizes the proportional increase in the output variables while remaining within the envelopment space. Varying inputs and outputs systematically and examining the impact of these variations on the efficiency score result in a common approach to sensitivity analysis of DEA results.

DEA Softwares

Several commercially available DEA software packages are powerful enough to handle thousands of DMUs and a large number of input and output variables by using different extensions of DEA.

Warwick DEA Software

The DEA software developed at Warwick University (Coventry, United Kingdom) is sold on a commercial basis. The software requires input in the form of an American Standard Code for Information Interchange (ASCII) file containing the input/output levels of the unit assessed. Any spreadsheet or a word processor can create this file. The output from the package can be read directly into a spreadsheet or a word processor. The package facilitates the following processes:

- Assessment of units by the constant returns-to-scale model.
- Assessment of units by the variable returns-to-scale model.
- Assessment of units with restrictions to the estimated weights over inputs/outputs.
- Assessment of targets when priorities over specific inputs/outputs are expressed.
- Assessment of units when some variables are exogenously fixed and returns to scale are variable.
- Table of efficiencies (fixed and/or spreadsheet format).
- Table of targets (fixed and/or spreadsheet format).
- Table of efficient peer units (fixed and/or spreadsheet format).

- Table of virtual inputs/outputs.
- Information on whether increasing or decreasing returns to scale hold for the input/output mix of a unit.

The software can run on any IBM-compatible machine. The size of problem it can solve depends on the random access memory (RAM) of the machine. For a 640-RAM machine, the number of units that can be assessed is the ratio of 20,000 to the sum of the inputs and outputs plus 1. The hardware requirement is an IBM personal computer (PC) with a math coprocessor; the computational precision is double precision; the models it solves are CCR, BCC, and additive; other features include super-efficiency, weight restrictions, and handling target models, nonradial models, mixed-target models, and nondiscretionary variables for BCC (see the related website at www.deazone.com).

BYU DEA Software

This Brigham Young University (BYU) software was developed at the Marriott School of Management, Brigham Young University (Provo, Utah). The hardware requirement is an IBM-compatible PC; the computational precision is 10E-6; the models it solves are CCR, BCC, and multiplicative; other features include handling nondiscretionary variables and categorical variables (for information, contact Donald L. Adolphson or Lawrence C. Walters, Marriott School of Management, Brigham Young University, Provo, Utah).

Frontier Analyst Software

Frontier software is a commercial DEA software developed by Banxia Software (Glasgow, United Kingdom). It is aimed primarily at identifying opportunities to improve operational productivity. The software easily computes data envelopment analysis solutions for business and public sector applications. The software identifies best performers to locate best practice, identifies underachievers, sets realistic, peer-based improvement targets, uncovers greatest potential efficiency gains, allocates resources effectively, visualizes important information, and informs strategy development (see the Banxia website at www.banxia.com).

OnFront Software

EMQ has developed OnFront software for measuring economical productivity and quality. The software was developed by Rolf Fare and Shawna Grosskopf, the originators of the Malmquist productivity index. [The Malmquist total factor productivity index is defined using distance functions. Distance functions allow descriptions of a multi-input/multi-output production technology without the need to specify a behavioral objective, such as cost minimization or profit maximization. Input distance functions and output distance functions can be defined and used in the same manner. The distance functions that constitute the Malmquist index are calculated using the linear programming approach. The data for this aspect of the research are the same as those utilized for the DEA analysis.] The OnFront program is a 32-bit menu-driven Windows application. The current version includes the following features: data handling, spreadsheet layout, input- and output-based analysis, weak and strong disposability, decompositions, flexible specifications of variables, simulation capability, and Malmquist productivity, including decomposition into efficiency and technical change. OnFront requires Windows 95/98/2000/NT, 16 Mb of RAM, and 8 Mb of disk space (see the website at www.emq.com).

Efficiency Measurement System Software

Efficiency Measurement System (EMS) software was developed by Holger Scheel; it contains various models for efficiency measurement. EMS is free of charge for academic users and can be downloaded from the Internet (www.wiso.uni-dortmund.de). Features of Version 1.3 include convex and nonconvex technologies; constant, nonincreasing, nondecreasing, variable returns to scale; radial, additive, maxAverage (also known as Färe-Lovell), minAverage, and super efficiency measures; input, output, or nonoriented; weights restrictions; nondiscretionary inputs/outputs; support for program efficiency, Malmquist indices, and Window analysis; and reports scores, shadow prices/weights, intensities ("lambdas"), benchmarks, and slacks. The operating system is Windows 9x/NT and accepted data files are Excel 97 or ASCII.

DEAP Software

DEAP Version 2.1 was written by Tim Coelli from the Centre for Efficiency and Productivity Analysis (CEPA). CEPA was established in 1995. It is located in the School of Economic Studies at the University of New England (Armidale, Australia). This program is used to construct DEA frontiers for the calculation of technical and cost efficiencies and for the calculation of Malmquist total factor productivity (TFP) indices. The DEAP program can be downloaded from the University of New England website (www.une.edu) free of charge (interested parties may contact Tim Coelli at the University of New England to discuss bugs or new versions).

The DEAP program has three principal DEA options: (1) standard constant returns-to-scale (CRS) and variable returns-to-scale (VRS) DEA models that involve the calculation of technical and scale efficiencies (where applicable), (2) the extension of these models to account for cost and allocative efficiencies, and (3) the application of Malmquist DEA methods to panel data to calculate indices of TFP change, technological change, technical efficiency change, and scale efficiency change. All methods are available in either an input or an output orientation (with the exception of the cost-efficiencies option). The output from the program includes, where applicable, technical, scale, allocative and cost-efficiency estimates, slacks, peers, and TFP indices. The program is compiled using a Lahey F77LEM/32 compiler for an IBM-compatible PC. The program package includes the executable program, data files for four simple examples, and a 47-page user's guide in portable document format (pdf) format. Features include a DEA Excel Solver and Microsoft Excel DEA add-in; DEA Excel Solver is a DEA software developed by Joe Zhu, author of *Quantitative Models for Evaluating Business Operations: DEA with Spreadsheets and Excel Solver*. The software is available free of charge and can be downloaded from the Worcester Polytechnic Institute (Worcester, Massachusetts) website (www.wpi.edu). The license allows use of the DEA Excel Solver for educational and research purposes only, not for commercial purposes. DEA Excel Solver requires Excel 97 or later versions and uses Excel Solver, and does not set any limits on the number of DMUs, inputs, and outputs. However, users are advised to check www.solver.com for problem sizes that various versions of Solver can handle. DEA Excel Solver includes the following 32 DEA models:

- Envelopment models (CRS, VRS, and nonincreasing and nondecreasing returns to scale; input oriented, output oriented—8 models).
- Multiplier models (CRS, VRS, and nonincreasing and nondecreasing returns to scale; input-oriented, output-oriented—8 models).
- Slack-based models (CRS, VRS, and nonincreasing and nondecreasing returns to scale; weighted, nonweighted—8 models).
- Measure-specific models (CRS, VRS, and nonincreasing and nondecreasing returns to scale; input-oriented, output-oriented—8 models).

DEA-Solver-PRO 2.1 Software

DEA-Solver-PRO is designed on the basis of the textbook *Data Envelopment Analysis—A Comprehensive Text with Models, Applications, References and DEA-Solver Software*, by W. W. Cooper, L. M. Seiford, and K. Tone (further information about this software is available at www.saitech-inc.com).

Conclusions

DEA is an exciting flexible method of assessing relative efficiency among decision units using the same technology and in the same or very similar organizational circumstances. One of the reasons that DEA is an important management tool for diagnosis among decision-making units is its ability to provide guidance for how nonefficient units can become more efficient. In addition to the DEA aspects covered here, several other issues may be of interest to performance analysts, ranging from different formulations of the DEA model, to bounding the relative weights, to the use of discretionary vs. nondiscretionary variables, to parametric alternatives to DEA. One of the most important contributions to the technique is the incorporation of the Malmquist index, which, in a way, involves the time dimension in the model. In order to obtain reliable results from DEA applications, the technique should be used with a series of sensitivity assessments.

See Also the Following Article

Regional Input–Output Analysis

Further Reading

Arnold, V. L., Bardhan, I. R., Cooper, W. W., and Kumbhakar, S. C. (1996). New uses of DEA and statistical regressions for efficiency evaluation and estimation—with an illustrative application to public sector secondary schools in Texas. *Ann. Op. Res.* **66,** 255–277.

Banker, D. R., and Thrall, R. M. (1992). Estimation of returns to scale using data Envelopment analysis. *Eur. J. Op. Res.* **62,** 74–84.

Banker, R. D., Charnes, A., and Cooper, W. W. (1984). Some models for estimating technical and scale inefficiencies in data envelopment analysis. *Mgmt. Sci.* **30**(9), 1078–1092.

Banker, R. D., Chang, H., and Cooper, W. W. (1996). Simulation studies of efficiency, returns to scale and misspecification with nonlinear functions in DEA. *Ann. Op. Res.* **66,** 233–253.

Bjurek, H., Hjalmarson, L., and Forsund, F. R. (1990). Deterministic parametric and nonparametric estimation of efficiency in service production: A comparison. *J. Econometr.* **46,** 213–227.

Charnes, A., Cooper, W. W., and Rhodes, E. L. (1978). Measuring the efficiency of decision making units. *Eur. J. Op. Res.* **2**(6), 429–444.

Charnes, A., Cooper, W. W., Lewin, A. Y., and Seiford, L. M. (eds.) (1994). *Data Envelopment Analysis: Theory, Methodology and Applications*. Kluwer Academic Publ., Boston, MA.

Cooper, W. W., Kumbhakar, S., Thrall, R. M., and Yu, X. (1995). DEA and stochastic frontier analysis of

Chinese economic reforms. *Socio-Econ. Plan. Sci.* **29**(2), 85–112.

Cooper, W. W., Seiford, L. M., and Tone, K. (2000). *Data Envelopment Analysis.* Kluwer Academic Publ., Boston, MA.

Golany, B., and Roll, Y. (1989). An application procedure for DEA. *Omega* **17**(3), 237–250.

Hjalmarson, L., Kumbhakar, S. C., and Hesmathi, A. (1996). DEA, DFA and SFA: A Comparison. *J. Productiv. Anal.* **7**(2/3), 303–328.

Data Mining

John A. Bunge
Cornell University, Ithaca, New York, USA

Dean H. Judson
U.S. Census Bureau, Washington, D.C., USA

Glossary

cross-validation In statistics, the process of selecting (random) fractions of the data set, using one fraction for training and the remaining fractions for test or validation.

data mining The process of using computational and statistical tools to discover usable information in large databases.

labeled data Records that have been labeled with the classification outcome, as opposed to unlabeled data, for which the classification outcome is not available.

latent variable An outcome or a variable that is presumed to exist and to be causally important for the model, but is not observed by the researcher.

supervised learning Statistical learning based on a labeled data set.

test or validation data set The portion of the data set, or a new data set, on which the model fit on the training data set is tested or validated.

training data set A data set (typically labeled) to which the data mining model is fit.

unsupervised learning Statistical learning based on an unlabeled data set.

The term data mining covers a wide variety of data analysis procedures: statistical, mathematical, computational, logical, and ad hoc. In this article, the focus is on opportunities, benefits, challenges, and trends in data mining and on methods that are widely used in practice and for which commercial software is currently available. Supervised learning, for which there is a target variable along with a large number of input variables, is first discussed: the objective is to characterize the target in terms of the inputs. The main procedures here are discriminant analysis, logistic regression, neural networks, classification trees, support vector machines, and Bayesian networks. Unsupervised learning, for which there is a search for patterns in a data set without a specific known target variable, is then discussed with respect to clustering and latent class analysis.

Data Mining Defined

Old versus New Definitions

The term data mining covers a wide variety of data analysis procedures with roots in a number of domains, including statistics, machine learning, pattern recognition, information retrieval, and others. There are probably as many definitions as there are practitioners. At one time, the term had a pejorative connotation similar to "data snooping," which means allowing the data to define the research hypotheses, or even reanalyzing the same data until some hypothesis test becomes significant, regardless of the original research question. Statisticians object to this because it violates a certain paradigm of scientific objectivity. In modern usage, though, data mining is simply a metaphor for certain kinds of analyses, and no value judgment is implied.

The idea is that there is a large quantity, a mountain, of data, and this mountain is mined for nuggets of valuable information. In one common application, a credit-card company retains complete information on all of its customers (demographic characteristics, history of card use, etc.) and seeks to identify, among its customers, good prospects for a new product offering. In another application, Federal law requires all manufacturers using toxic chemicals to report such usage each year at each facility, along with a large amount of related information (chemical characteristics, location of plant and disposal facilities, waste management strategies, etc.); researchers wish to characterize best-practice facilities that perform especially well in toxic-waste reduction. Data miners may apply a variety of analytical procedures, separately or in conjunction, to solve such problems.

In this article, there is no attempt to discuss every kind of analysis that might be considered data mining. Rather, the focus is on methods that are judged to be the most-used and most important, and that will be most useful to the practitioner. They are classified in the following ways. First, "supervised" and "unsupervised" learning, terms that come from the machine learning literature, are distinguished. In supervised learning, there is a target (response, dependent) variable, along with a typically large number of input (predictor, independent) variables: The objective is to characterize the response in terms of the predictors, that is, to find a function, rule, or algorithm that relates the predictors to the response. Doing this requires a learning or training sample, i.e., a data set in which a case or observation consists of a large list or vector of independent variables (called the feature vector in the pattern recognition literature) and a known response. A data mining procedure analyzes the learning sample, generates or "builds" the desired function or rule, and assesses its performance. Supervised learning is further subdivided according to the nature of the target variable, which may be binary (dichotomous), categorical with several unordered categories (polytomous or multinomial), ordered (such as a Likert scale), or quantitative (discrete or continuous). The first is arguably the canonical data mining situation, as in the credit-card marketing example, in which the customers are classified either as buyers or nonbuyers. On the other hand, in the example of toxic chemicals, there is a quantitative response, namely, the amount of toxic waste released by a given facility in a given year; this is more readily related to classical statistical procedures such as multiple regression.

Unsupervised learning is also considered. In this situation, the search is for patterns in a data set without a specific known target variable or response. The data set now consists only of feature vectors without an observed target variable, and data mining must search for clusters, connections, trends, or patterns in an open-ended way. Thus, unsupervised learning tends to be more computationally intensive. Both methods may be used in conjunction: For example, clusters in the data may first be searched for and defined, and then characterized using supervised learning.

Opportunities and Benefits

The most important goal of data mining is to discover relationships without human preknowledge. This is becoming more important as high-dimensional data sets and high-volume data delivery outpace human ability to process and perceive patterns in the data. Thus, the data mining tools described herein seek patterns that are not obvious to a human observer. For this purpose, the computer, although still not up to the task of fully emulating human contextual understanding, has one significant advantage: it can use rapid computational techniques to outperform human searching by orders of magnitude. In the time a human might take to sift through hundreds of records in search of a pattern, a computer can search billions, or can run complex and sophisticated algorithms.

Furthermore, the data mining tools described herein attempt to achieve high-dimensional understanding that is beyond most humans. Although some people can conceptualize (or perhaps visualize) high-dimensional relationships, it is easier for the mathematical formalism of the computer to do so, provided the formalism is effective. As an example, consider all the possible relationships, and how to represent them, among variables in a 2^4 experimental design.

Challenges

The challenges to data mining are effectively the converse of the benefits. Certainly computers can discover patterns in data: But do the patterns discovered by the computer make sense? "Making sense" is a contextual concept, and computers have not yet achieved the intuitive ability that a human has. A second challenge is the problem of "multiplicity": in a statistical sense, multiplicity refers to the fact that, in 20 tests of hypotheses with an α-level of 0.05, a single test is expected to result in significant findings just by chance. If the computer is instructed to pursue classically significant results, 5% of the time, a random phantom will be chased. A third challenge to the data miner is selection bias and representativeness of the training data set: does the database, however large it may be, represent the population of interest? In many databases currently subject to data mining techniques, the relationship between the database available to the analyst and any population of interest is questionable, due to factors such as imprecise population definition, nonrandom sampling, or temporal drift of the phenomenon in question since the sample was taken. If the database depicts a nonrepresentative portion of the population, how can the results of the analysis accurately reflect that population? A final crucial challenge to the data miner is the "curse of dimensionality." This refers to the fact that, as the numbers of observations and measured variables increase, the volume of the possible data space increases rapidly, but the volume of the populated data space (that is, the portion of the possible space that actually has data in it) increases at a slower rate. In sum, the space is getting more and more empty as the number of observations and data elements increase.

There are intensive research efforts underway to address these challenges and others. Here, a (partial) picture of current practice is provided; for information on cutting-edge research, the reader may consult the literature and the many web sites devoted to data mining in its various forms.

Supervised Learning: Binary Response

The problem of binary response, also known as "statistical classification," is a special case of pattern recognition and machine learning. Observations are partitioned into two groups or classes, and often one class is smaller and more interesting than the other. Examples include buyers versus nonbuyers of a product or service, persons receiving unemployment benefits versus persons not receiving benefits, fraudulent credit-card transactions versus nonfraudulent ones, and so on. The objective is to classify the individuals based on their "features," or more specifically, to characterize the class of interest in terms of available observed information. More technically, suppose there is a "learning" or "training" sample consisting of some (often large) number of cases, and each case has a known class and a (large) number, say k, of recorded feature variables or covariates. When a new (hitherto unobserved) case is confronted, its class will not be known—this is the essence of the problem—so the classifier must be constructed based solely on the observable feature variables.

The range of all possible values of all the feature variables defines a k-dimensional space called the feature space. The initial objective of statistical classification is to partition or subdivide this feature space into two subsets, one corresponding to each class. When a new observation is obtained, where it falls in the feature space is checked and it is classified accordingly. The problem is to define the boundary between the two subsets in an optimal way—that is, to find the optimal classification boundary or classifier. Statistical theory states that, given (1) the distributions of the data in the two classes, (2) the relative population sizes (or "prior probabilities") of the classes, and (3) the costs of misclassification, an optimal classifier exists and can, in principle, be approximated. To find it, some method is applied—mathematical, statistical, logical, computational, or some combination thereof—that relates the values of the feature variables to the known classes of the observations in the learning sample.

Although, in principle, the entire feature space is partitioned, in fact, often only a small proportion of the feature variables will be effective for classification. The problem of selecting the optimal subset of available variables (that is, of reducing the dimension of the operative feature space) is called "feature selection," "variable selection," or "model selection." Feature selection is an integral part of some data mining procedures, but in others it can be done only *ex post facto* as a kind of workaround. In modern large-scale or production data mining, when thousands or tens of thousands of variables are available, there are often two stages of variable selection. First, a simple routine is used to reduce the number of variables by some orders of magnitude; this may be as simple as sorting the variables by correlation with the response, or clustering the variables into highly correlated subsets and then selecting a representative from each subset. After arriving at a manageable number of candidate feature variables (perhaps in the hundreds), more formal variable selection procedures can then be applied, whether embedded in the data mining algorithm, as in the case of tree-structured classifiers, or external, such as stepwise regression.

Having constructed the classifier, its performance must be assessed. The basic tool for this is the misclassification table, which is a cross-tabulation of the counts of true vs. predicted classes. Clearly it is desirable to maximize the number of correctly classified cases and minimize the number of incorrectly classified cases. However, care must be taken: the classifier will perform best on the learning sample that was used to construct it. This is not necessarily a good predictor of misclassification rates on hitherto unknown data; indeed, the misclassification table of the learning sample is optimistically biased. (This is called the "resubstitution estimate" of misclassification because it is found by resubstituting the learning sample into the classifier.) To obtain less biased estimates of the misclassification rates, the training sample is ideally split into (at least) two parts: the classifier is then constructed on the first part and its predictive accuracy is tested on the second part. If the data for this are insufficient, some form of cross-validation can be used. The simplest version of this is "leave-one-out": the first case from the data is deleted, the classifier is built on the remaining data, and it is tested on the held-out case, then cycled through case-by-case so as to test the classifier on each case in the learning sample in a relatively unbiased fashion. Alternatively, a similar algorithm can be used, but some fixed number of cases (greater than 1) is omitted on each iteration.

Note that it is natural to suppose that comparing or combining the results of several classifiers in the same problem might lead to improved or "boosted" performance. Two important methods for this are "boosting" and "bagging" (bootstrap aggregation). These are very active areas of current research, and specialized software is available, but as of this writing, implementations of these methods are just beginning to appear in generally used data mining software. The reader may consult the literature or on-line resources (e.g., www.kdnuggets.com/) for more information.

The discussion now turns to various specific methods or procedures for the two-class problem. All of these methods have been generalized for classification into several classes (the polytomous or multinomial problem); this situation is not discussed here, but the reader can readily find information in the references or in software documentation.

Discriminant Analysis

The oldest method of statistical classification, dating back to the 1940s, is discriminant analysis, classically based on the multivariate normal distribution. In this method, the assumption is that the feature variables follow a multivariate normal distribution in both classes. Note that this is generally not realistic, because (among other considerations) typically there are different types of feature variables, such as the binary variable "sex," whereas the multivariate normal assumes that everything is quantitative and continuous. Nevertheless, discriminant analysis is often employed as part of a suite of analyses, whether or not the multivariate-normality assumption is met.

Assume that the distribution of the features in both classes is the same multivariate normal except for location (multivariate mean); the resulting classification boundary, then, is linear, so the procedure is called "linear discriminant analysis." This boundary is a line in two-dimensional space, a plane in three-dimensional space, and a hyperplane in higher dimensional feature spaces. If the feature distribution in the two classes differs both in location and in dispersion (multivariate mean and covariance matrix), then the classification boundary is quadratic (that is, a parabola or paraboloid sheet) and is called "quadratic discriminant analysis." It is possible to test for equality of covariance matrices to decide which to use.

The effectiveness of linear or quadratic discriminant analysis is often limited by the underlying distributional assumptions and the simplicity of the classification boundary. "Nonparametric discriminant analysis" attempts to address this by allowing a nonparametric (relatively unspecified) form for the feature distributions in the two classes, and hence a highly flexible shape for the classification boundary. However, in this case, it can be difficult to understand or characterize the fitted distributions and boundary, especially in high-dimensional data, and overfitting the learning sample, and consequent lack of generalizability, may be of concern.

Feature selection is less than straightforward in discriminant analysis. The user may test all possible subsets of the variables, looking at (for example) overall misclassification rate as the objective function; in some software implementations, there are various iterative routines modeled on stepwise regression.

Logistic Regression

Logistic regression is a well-known procedure that can be used for classification. This is a variant of multiple regression in which the response is binary rather than quantitative. In the simplest version, the feature variables are taken to be nonrandom. The response, which is the class, is a binary random variable that takes on the value 1 (for the class of interest) with some probability p, and the value 0 with probability $1 - p$. The "success probability" p is a function of the values of the feature variables; specifically, the logarithm of the odds ratio or the "log odds," $\log[p/(1-p)]$, is a linear function of the predictor variables. To use logistic regression for classification, a cutoff value is set, typically 0.5; a case is assigned to class 1 if its estimated or fitted success probability is greater than (or equal to) the cutoff, and it is assigned to class 0 if the estimated probability is less than the cutoff. Because of the nature of the functions involved, this is equivalent to a linear classification boundary, although it is not (necessarily) the same as would be derived from linear discriminant analysis.

Like standard multiple regression, logistic regression carries hypothesis tests for the significance of each variable, along with other tests, estimates, and goodness-of-fit assessments. In the classification setting, the variable significance tests can be used for feature selection: modern computational implementations incorporate several variants of stepwise (iterative) variable selection. Because of the conceptual analogy with ordinary multiple regression and the ease of automated variable selection, logistic classification is probably the most frequently used data mining procedure. Another advantage is that it produces a probability of success, given the values of the feature variables, rather than just a predicted class, which enables sorting the observations by probability of success and setting an arbitrary cutoff for classification, not necessarily 0.5. But wherever the cutoff is set, logistic classification basically entails a linear classification boundary, and this imposes a limit on the potential efficacy of the classifier. Some flexibility can be achieved by introducing transformations (e.g., polynomials) and interactions among the feature variables.

Neural Networks

Neural networks have attracted a vast amount of theoretical research and commercial software development. The discussion here is confined to their application in the classification problem. The basic purpose of introducing neural networks in this problem is to allow a flexible classification boundary: in fact, mathematical theory states that, under certain conditions, neural networks can approximate an arbitrarily complex boundary. However, this flexibility comes with two main costs. First, complex models require complex computation. Neural network models are typically nonlinear, with hundreds or thousands of parameters, and fitting these models to data presents a formidable computational challenge. Indeed, more research effort has been devoted to fast computing for neural networks than to their theoretical properties. Even with modern computers and software, convergence of the iterative routines used to fit these models on large data sets can take significant time. Second, neural network models do not admit a mathematical or computational description that is at once transparent and precise, so it is difficult to understand their behavior except phenomenologically, by looking at results such as misclassification tables. In a sense, a neural network is a black box, and it is hard to open the box. Nevertheless, they sometimes dramatically outperform other methods.

In a very simple example, illustrated in Fig. 1, a neural classifier consists of input nodes, which accept the feature variables as inputs; a hidden layer of nodes, each of which accepts a differently weighted sum of the inputs and applies a nonlinear transfer function to it; and an output layer, which accepts a weighted sum of the outputs of the hidden layer nodes and applies a nonlinear transfer function to it. The result is a highly nonlinear function of the feature variables, which returns a probability of success and also typically the corresponding probability of failure. As in logistic regression, a case is assigned to class 1 if the estimated success probability is greater than or equal to some cutoff value (or simply greater than the failure probability), and to class 0 otherwise.

The "architecture" of the neural network refers to the number of layers, especially the number of hidden layers, and the number of nodes in each layer. Methods

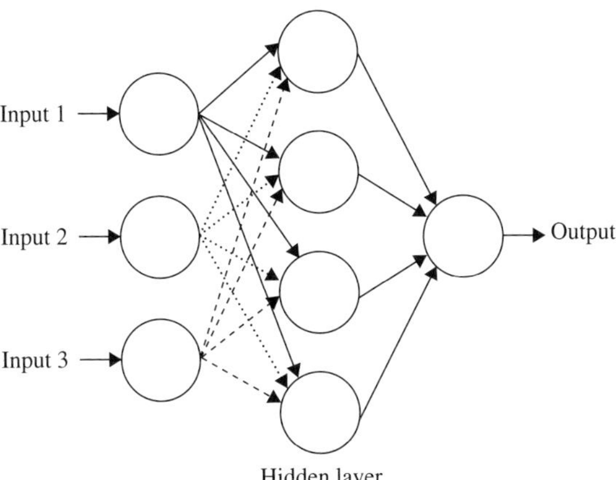

Figure 1 Illustration of the input nodes, hidden layer, and output layer of a neural network.

for specifying the architecture of a network for a given problem are largely heuristic at present, although, in general, a more complex architecture implies a more complex classification boundary (in fact, logistic classification is a very simple case of neural classification). In addition, the user must select the particular nonlinear transfer functions to be applied at the nodes, and there are many choices for these as well.

Given a specific architecture, transfer function, etc., the computing task is to train the network on the existing data. Essentially this means to compute optimal values for the many weight parameters (coefficients); this is done iteratively, by comparing the network's output to the known classifications of cases in the learning sample, and then adjusting the coefficients until the closest possible match is obtained. The goal is to complete this process in a reasonable amount of time on large data sets; this is a major problem in numerical analysis and has attracted a great deal of attention. This is not elaborated here except to mention that there are now a number of inexpensive commercial neural network software packages available that perform well.

Just as there is currently no transparent way to design the network architecture, there is no universally agreed-upon method for feature selection in neural classifiers, although commercial software implementations typically include algorithms (sometimes proprietary) for this purpose. In particular, it is not obvious how to carry out statistical hypothesis tests of significance for the various weights (coefficients) in a network, or what the meaning of such tests would be, so feature selection based on statistical testing is not straightforward.

Tree-Structured Classifiers

These classifiers, also known simply as "decision trees," have several advantages: they are easy to understand and interpret, they are nonparametric (depending on no distributional assumptions), and they incorporate feature selection as an integral part of the algorithm. They are of relatively recent date, but there are nonetheless a number of variants and competing procedures within the family. In production data mining, a tree may be used as a primary model-building procedure or as an independent analysis (for example, as a check on logistic regression results), or for automated feature selection.

Arguably, the most well-established decision tree algorithm is Classification and Regression Trees (CART); although there are a number of competitors, for simplicity, the focus here is on CART. The objective is to subdivide the data into decreasing subsets, according to the descending branches of a decision tree, in such a way that the resulting "nodes" or "leaves" are as pure or unmixed as possible (that is, so that the subsets of cases represented by the final nodes are almost entirely in one class or the other). This is done as follows:

1. Start with the entire learning sample. Sort the entire sample according to the values of the first variable.
2. Take the lowest value of the first variable. Split the learning sample into two parts: a left descendant node for cases in which the first variable is less than or equal to this value and a right descendant node for cases which the first variable exceeds this value. Assess the purity of this split (according to some standardized measure).
3. Repeat for each value of the first variable, in order.
4. Repeat for each variable, in order.
5. Select the best of the best (that is, the value and variable that gives the overall purest split).
6. Repeat for each descendant node.

This will ultimately lead to a large and complex tree with one case in each "terminal" node, which overfits the data. To arrive at a tree of reasonable size and simplicity, the maximal tree is grown and then pruned back according to some optimality criterion (which is not elaborated here). Although this may seem to be a purely logical procedure, it can be characterized in statistical terms. Indeed, the decision tree is equivalent to a classification boundary constructed from (hyper)planes at right angles to the axes of the feature space. As with neural networks, it is, in principle, possible to approximate a highly complex boundary in this way.

For concreteness, consider Fig. 2, which is a fictional tree based on the authors' work. The context for this tree was jury selection in a lawsuit against a tobacco company, and the company's goal was to find jurors to strike from the jury. The plaintiffs claimed that the company intentionally addicted them to tobacco, causing their cancer. The response variable in this case is "bad juror" (those jurors that were particularly hostile to the company and would likely vote in favor of the plaintiff). As can be seen in Fig. 2, "bad jurors" made up about 20% of the jury pool. The tree for current smokers exits to the left, and is omitted. The tree for current nonsmokers proceeds to the right. Of those who had never smoked, the next split was a general measure of political liberality, with those self-identifying as liberal more likely to be hostile. But here a particular interaction is illustrated: of the current nonsmokers, former smokers were quite a bit more likely to be hostile to the company (50%). In particular, those former smokers who found it "difficult to quit" were particularly likely to be hostile (90% of them). This is the kind of "interaction effect" that tree-based analyses are good at finding.

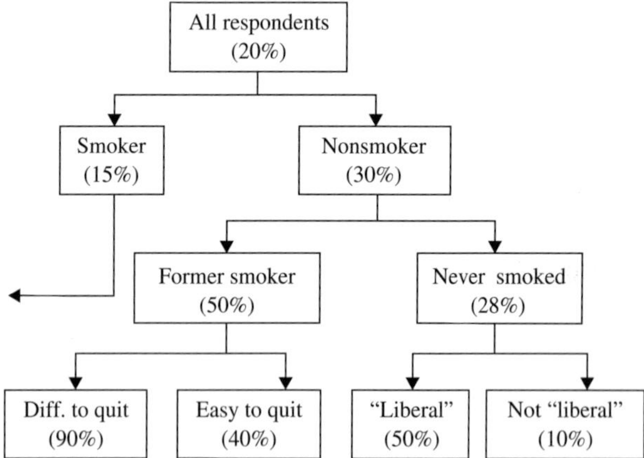

Figure 2 Illustration of a classification tree detecting the percentage of "bad jurors" (from the point of view of the corporate defendant) in a fictional lawsuit against a tobacco company. Each box represents the percentage of jurors with the specified characteristics.

In tree-structured classification, feature selection is an integral part of the algorithm; those features (variables) that have not been used to make any splits can be safely ignored. However, in some cases, several variables may lead to almost equally good splits. Taking the collection of these possible "surrogate" splitting variables, a collection of possible alternative trees is obtained. This does not, however, amount to a true statistical confidence set for the true tree: the ramifications of tree-structured classifiers in terms of classical statistical paradigms have not been fully worked out.

Support Vector Machines

Support vector machines (SVMs) are a relatively new and popular set of classification tools that integrate many features of separate existing tools. Like discriminant analysis, SVMs begin with the notion that the data are "separable" (that is, that they can be split into groups by a functional separator). However, SVMs significantly generalize this separability notion based on several principles:

- When fitting a linear separator to data; the points closest to the separator in the data space completely determine the separator.
- The problem of finding the linear separator can be treated as an optimization (quadratic) program with relaxed constraints (to account for imperfectly separated data).
- For data that are not separable by a linear separator, the data can be mapped into a higher dimension, and in the higher dimension, the linear separator might be appropriate.
- For data that are not linearly separable in the higher dimension space, a transformation of the data can be used to construct a nonlinear separator in the higher dimensional space.

These principles are combined, and solved computationally, in support vector machine software.

Bayesian Networks

Bayesian networks are graphical tools for representing causal relationships between variables. A Bayesian (or belief) network is represented by a directed acyclic graph that encodes the dependencies between variables. At each point in the graph, the structure of the graph, prior knowledge, and data are used to update conditional dependencies. The strength of a Bayesian network is that it encodes causal and probabilistic information and provides an updating mechanism for adding new data as they come into a learning system.

Supervised Learning: Continuous Response

If the response is a quantitative, continuous variable, as in the previously stated toxic-waste-reduction example, classical multivariable statistical methods, such as multiple regression, are often used. There exist continuous-response variants of neural networks and classification trees, hence the terms "classification" and "regression trees" (but these are far beyond the scope here).

Unsupervised Learning

Until now the discussion has focused on situations in which a collection of records is labeled; that is, the value of the response variable is known (e.g., it is known whether a particular credit card transaction in question was fraudulent or valid). In the unsupervised learning situation, the records are not labeled; instead, there is a collection of data, but, *a priori*, there is nothing to indicate in what class the particular record is located. In unsupervised learning, the analysis technique imposes more structure on the data by searching for that structure (and not some other kind of structure). Of course, if the structure imposed by the analysis technique is incorrect, the results will be fallacious.

Cluster Analysis

A classical approach to discovering structure in unlabeled databases is cluster analysis. In cluster analysis, it is presumed that the cases or units can be grouped into meaningful groups, called "clusters," based on the observed data. Cluster analysis was used in the natural sciences in early attempts to classify species, and it was called numerical taxonomy.

Nonhierarchical

The basic form of cluster analysis is nonhierarchical. In nonhierarchical cluster analysis, we merely attempt to form groups, but there is no ordering between the groups. For example, when comparing crude death rates and crude birth rates for nations of the world, often three groups appear to emerge: countries with high crude birth and high crude death rates (developing nations, labeled "1"), countries with high crude birth and low crude death rates (nations passing through the "demographic transition", labeled "3"), and countries with low crude birth and rising crude death rates (the developed nations, labeled "2"; the rising crude death rate is caused by aging of the population). Figure 3 illustrates this kind of clustering (the labels 1, 2, and 3 are arbitrary).

Hierarchical

In contrast to nonhierarchical cluster analysis, hierarchical cluster analysis forms clusters iteratively, by successively joining or splitting groups. There are two kinds: divisive, which starts with the entire data set in one large group and then successively splits it into smaller groups until each observation is its own group; and agglomerative, in which each observation starts in its own group, and groups are successively paired until at the end every observation is in the same large group. Divisive methods are computationally intensive and have had limited applications in the social sciences. Agglomerative methods have been implemented in many standard software packages.

In hierarchical cluster analysis, a problem arises when two (or more) observations have been placed in a group: If I am comparing a new observation with the group, do I choose the observation (in the group) that is closest to my new observation, do I choose the observation (in the group) that is farthest from my observation, or do I choose some middle point (say, an average value) to compare to my new observation? The first choice is known as single linkage, the second is known as complete linkage, and the third is known as average linkage.

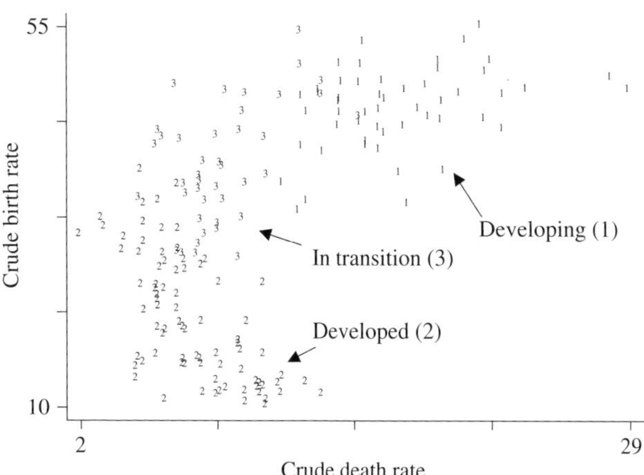

Figure 3 Crude birth and death rates in nations worldwide in 1988, with a three-class clustering solution depicted.

Latent Class Analysis

The final technique for unsupervised learning is known as latent class analysis. Latent class analysis is more statistically principled than either of the standard nonhierarchical and hierarchical clustering techniques, in that the statistical inference is built from a probability model assumed to hold in the data. In latent class analysis, which applies to categorical observed data, the observed patterns are presumed to be "caused" by each observation's relationship to an unmeasured variable. The value of this unmeasured variable is the latent classification, and may consist of two or more actual classes. The observed data are a function of which latent class the observation comes from—so that the observed patterns in class one will differ from those in class two, and from class three, and so on. Latent class analysis has been effectively used, for example, to perform record linkage, to analyze response error in surveys, and to analyze erroneous enumerations in a census environment (in which the two latent classes were "true census day resident" and "true census day nonresident").

The Future of Data Mining

If the past 20 years are a guide, then data mining has a bright future. The growing size, complexity, and varieties of data representation in databases, and their availability for analysis, generate demand for data mining tools. These additional tools aid the most impressive data analysis tool nature has yet invented—the human mind—and impressively leverage that mind. Theoreticians and technicians have been responding to the demand, developing applied methods and theory, laying the foundation for this collection of tools. This is a far cry from the derisive "data dredging" appellation of an earlier, more naive time.

In terms of specific developments, continuing improvement in computing hardware and speed should be expected, with enhanced ability to handle mining of large, complete databases, such as those collected by the U.S. government (or customer-level businesses), as opposed to subsamples. The "trickle-down" availability of user-friendly software implementing more advanced procedures, such as boosting and support vector machines (this has already happened with neural networks), can be anticipated. Most importantly, though, it is possible to foresee the expansion of data mining from the almost classical statistical or computational tasks discussed here, to the ability to mine directly immense quantities of relatively unstructured data that are not (at present) amenable to classical statistical analysis, including text, image, bioinformatic, and Internet mining. These capabilities are presently in their infancy.

Acknowledgments

The authors wish to thank three anonymous reviewers for their valuable comments, which improved the content and readability of the article.

This article reports the results of research and analysis undertaken by Census Bureau staff. It has undergone a more limited review by the Census Bureau than its official publications. This report is released to inform interested parties and to encourage discussion.

See Also the Following Articles

Clustering • Type I and Type II Error

Further Reading

Bellman, R. (1961). *Adaptive Control Processes.* Princeton University Press, Princeton, New Jersey.

Bennett, K., and Campbell, C. (2000). Support vector machines: Hype or hallelujah? *SIGKDD Expl.* **2,** 1–13.

Fayyad, U. M., Piatetsky-Shapiro, G., and Uthurusamy, R. (eds.) (1996). *Advances in Knowledge Discovery and Data Mining.* AAAI Press, Menlo Park.

Hastie, T., Tibshirani, R., and Friedman, J. H. (2001). *The Elements of Statistical Learning.* Springer-Verlag, New York.

Heckerman, D. (1995). *A Tutorial on Learning with Bayesian Networks.* Microsoft Research Technical Report MSR-TR-95-06. Available on the Internet at ftp://ftp.research.microsoft.com

Mitra, S., and Acharya, T. (2003). *Data Mining: Multimedia, Soft Computing, and Bioinformatics.* Wiley, New York.

Pearl, J. (1997). *Probabilistic Reasoning in Intelligent Systems.* Morgan Kaufman, New York.

Deduction and Induction

Karim Dharamsi
University of Winnipeg, Winnipeg, Manitoba, Canada

Glossary

argument Sets of statements that support a conclusion. An argument is designed to persuade.

inference The evidentiary relationship maintained between premises and conclusions.

logic A normative discipline that studies the forms of reasoning; seeks the criteria by which to differentiate good from bad arguments.

soundness A quality of an argument if and only if it contains all true premises.

validity If the premises of an argument are taken as true and the conclusion drawn is compelling, the argument is considered valid. A valid argument is sound if and only if all the premises are in fact true. Invalid arguments cannot be sound.

Deduction and induction are two different forms of argument. In a deductive argument, the conclusion necessarily follows from premises. In an inductive argument, the premises support a conclusion to varying degrees. Part of the challenge of the inductive argument is to establish criteria by which to determine which conclusion is best supported. In this article, deductive and inductive inferences are examined with the aim of showing how to establish the criteria by which to differentiate between good and bad arguments.

Logic and Validity

William and Martha Kneale begin their book, *Development of Logic*, with the claim that "logic is concerned with the principles of valid inference." Their contention is that logic is not simply valid argument but involves "reflection upon the principles of validity." In other words, we are concerned with determining the criteria by which we decide whether an argument is good or bad. It is also by way of such reflection that we can properly identify the basic differences between induction and deduction.

Logic studies forms of thought, and this distinguishes it from other disciplines. For example, sociologists study human society and physicists study the physical universe. Both the sociologist and the physicist are concerned with formulating good arguments and somehow distinguishing, in light of their specific interests and research, between good arguments and bad ones. Hence, we can understand logic as being, at its core, a normative discipline that is concerned with providing the proper criteria for differentiating good arguments from bad ones. In calling logic normative, we are contrasting it with the descriptive or the empirical. Whereas we might subject our descriptive claims to logical analysis, our aim in logic is to ask what it is that makes a good argument "good." Indeed, we might also ask what it is about a compelling argument that makes rejecting it very difficult, or perhaps impossible. Understanding, even in a general way, what arguments are and how to distinguish between good and bad forms are essential to understanding the differences between deduction and induction. These two central categories of logic designate forms of arguments that are basic to understanding the nature of the claim or claims being made in a given argument. Examination of some distinctions will help to understand what this means.

Stating that "the car will not start," for example, would not be making an argument; rather, it would be stating a fact. On the other hand, stating that "you ought to take a course with Professor Keenan because he is a good professor" would be trying to persuade someone to do something. An indispensable part of argumentation is persuasion. Suggesting that someone should act in a certain way for a specific reason is making a claim that aspires to persuade, resulting in belief and action. This is also making an argument.

Typically, when a claim of the sort suggested is made, an interlocutor will ask for qualification ("why do you think that I should take a course with Professor Keenan?"). In asking this question, the interlocutor is asking for the set of sentences that bring the original speaker to maintain the claim that has been made. We can say of arguments, again in a rough and ready sense, that they are sets of sentences that are designed to persuade a reader, a listener, indeed any interlocutor, to believe some conclusion. So, to say of the city that it is beautiful is not to make an argument; the intent is not to persuade or to change someone's mind. In contrast, claiming that "Professor Keenan is a good professor and you ought to take a course with him" is arguing and not merely stating a fact.

Take the example of the following argument:

1. All coffee at the neighborhood coffeehouse is either dark or light roast.
2. Andy has a cup of coffee from the neighborhood coffeehouse.
3. Therefore, Andy's coffee is either dark or light roast.

The conclusion (the claim) is that Andy's coffee is either dark or light roast. If the supporting sentences are true, if we accept that (1) and (2) are true, can the argument (3) be anything but valid? No. If the supporting sentences are true, then the argument is valid. In the case of this argument, we are compelled to believe that Andy's coffee is either dark or light roast. Take the example of another argument:

1. Kevin is an archaeology student.
2. Some archaeology students love underwater archaeology.
3. Therefore, Kevin loves underwater archaeology.

The supporting sentences (1) and (2) in this argument are true, but are we compelled to accept the conclusion (3)? No. Why not? Whereas in the former argument, the conclusion followed from the supporting sentences, in this argument, it is clear that Kevin may not love underwater archaeology and that claming he does is not secured by the supporting sentences (1) and (2).

Given what has been said so far, it is possible to discriminate between two parts of any argument. The first part provides the claim or the conclusion of the argument. This is what we would like our interlocutor to believe. The second part concerns the reasons why we should believe the conclusion. These are the argument's premises, or supporting sentences. If we take the premises to be true, then the conclusion should follow; the deduction is valid. Logic, then, in its broadest sense, involves establishing criteria by which to judge good arguments. Deductive arguments and inductive arguments typically separate two fundamentally distinct forms of argument. How we go about establishing the criteria for judging whether a given argument is good or bad also depends on the kind of argument we are scrutinizing.

Deduction

Consider the following argument (a traditional example of a deductive argument):

1. All humans are mortal.
2. Socrates is human.
3. Therefore, Socrates is mortal.

The conclusion (3) in this argument is established by the premises (1) and (2). It is a valid argument; (1) and (2) have to be true, but apart from whether this is a good or bad argument, we can recognize this argument as expressing the standard form of a deduction, i.e., it is a deductive argument.

Deductive arguments are unique in that the claims of such arguments are conclusive. When, as in the preceding argument, the conclusion follows from the premises, we have validity. If the conclusion did not follow, we would say of this argument that it is invalid. For deductive arguments, when it is not possible for the premises to be true at the same time that the conclusion is false, we say that the conclusion follows from the premises. Note well that the premises need not actually be true. The requirements of deductive validity require only that it is not possible for the conclusion to be false while at the same time the premises are true. The conclusion of a valid deductive inference is never false.

Oftentimes it is suggested that deductive arguments move from the general to the particular, as in the claim that Socrates is mortal. In this case, talk of the particular simply refers to the conclusion having to do with "Socrates" as a single object of the deduction's focus. Irving Copi and Keith Burgess-Jackson suggest that this way of thinking of deduction and deductive arguments is more than slightly misleading. "The difficulty lies," they write, "in the fact that a valid deductive argument may have universal propositions for its conclusion as well as for its premises." For example, consider the argument that Copi and Burgess-Jackson provide to substantiate their claim:

1. All animals are mortal.
2. All humans are animals.
3. Therefore, all humans are mortal.

This argument is valid; (3) follows from (1) and (2). But the conclusion (3) is not about a particular object; the conclusion (3) quantifies over all objects that fall into the class of mortals (2). Copi and Burgess-Jackson add that "a valid deductive argument may have particular propositions for its premises as well as for its conclusion." They consider the following example as exemplifying this type of contrasting argument:

1. If Socrates is human, then Socrates is mortal.
2. Socrates is human.
3. Therefore, Socrates is mortal.

What can be said, then, of deductive arguments (or of deductive inference) is that conclusions of this sort follow from their premises, and so long as we take the premises to be true, the conclusions cannot be false. The conclusion is a necessary consequence of the true premises.

Truth and Soundness

Suppose that the following argument is made:

1. All trucks have seven wheels.
2. Anna's vehicle is a truck.
3. Therefore, Anna's truck has seven wheels.

If we accept the premises as true in this deductive argument, are we also compelled to accept the conclusion? If yes, then we have to accept that this argument is valid. So it can be said that the premises are taken as true in a valid argument; they establish the conclusion and the validity of the argument. The problem is that validity guarantees the truth of the conclusion only on the grounds that the premises are in fact true. Validity is only the first step in evaluating deductive arguments. Once we have determined if an argument is valid, we then wish to know if it is sound—that is, if the premises of the valid argument are in fact true. A sound deductive argument is an argument in which the truth of the conclusion is guaranteed. Validity is not enough to secure truth. We require further criteria to establish truth and we require a further distinction.

An argument is thought to be sound if and only if it is valid and it contains all true premises. Take the following argument (it is valid but not sound):

1. Lou is a secretary.
2. All secretaries are female.
3. Lou is female.

Although the premises (1) and (2) in this argument are true, we are compelled to question its conclusion (3). Valid arguments do not secure true conclusions (even if we later find out that "Lou" is short-form for "Louise." In contrast, consider the following argument (it is sound, which implies that it is already valid):

1. All medical students are in the Faculty of Medicine.
2. Nafisa is a medical student.
3. Therefore, Nafisa belongs to the Faculty of Medicine.

Not only does (3) follow from the true premises (1) and (2), we are compelled to believe that (3) is true and so the argument is sound.

So far, we have been considering arguments that are deductive; the contents of the conclusions lie entirely within the domain of the contents of the premises. In such arguments, it seems relatively straightforward to think about the differences between validity, truth, and soundness. Matters get more complicated when these principles of logic are applied to induction, or to inductive arguments.

Induction

Take the example of the following argument from Copi and Burgess-Jackson:

1. Most corporation lawyers are conservatives.
2. Barbara Shane is a corporation lawyer.
3. Therefore, Barbara Shane is probably a conservative.

This kind of argument is different from the kinds we have considered. In this inductive argument, the conclusion lies at least partially outside the content of the premises, though we can say of this argument that premises (1) and (2) are true and that its conclusion (3) is more than likely to also be true. Interestingly, we can strengthen or weaken this argument by adding premises. We might add the premise that Barbara Shane is an officer of the American Civil Liberties Union (ACLU). We might also add that most officers of the ACLU are not conservatives. These additions would no doubt cast some level of suspicion about the likelihood of the conclusion (3) being true. Our inference (our having moved from the premises to the conclusion) is in this case nondemonstrative insofar as the conclusion does not necessarily follow from the premises. As noted of deductive arguments, the conclusions do necessarily follow from their premises and so the conclusions are guaranteed. What is especially noteworthy of inductive arguments is that the evidence is compatible with several hypotheses. We depend on better reasons to accept one conclusion over another. How we go about deciding on good reasons is part of the riddle of induction.

There are generally thought to be two kinds of inductive inference, namely, enumerative and hypothetical. The former is often attributed to David Hume (1711–1776). In his famous *An Enquiry Concerning Human Understanding*, Hume questions the commonplace understanding of causation. He first makes an important distinction between relations of ideas and matters of fact. Hume thinks that geometry, algebra, and arithmetic are species of the former; he notes that "every affirmation" involved in these "sciences" is "either intuitively or demonstratively certain." In short, Hume understands relations of ideas as being species of deductive inference. On the other hand, Hume thinks that matters of fact present especially difficult challenges to certainty:

> *Matters of fact, which are the second objects of human reason, are not ascertained in the same manner; nor is our evidence of their truth, however great, of a like nature with the forgoing. The contrary of every matter of fact is still possible; because it can never imply a contradiction, and is conceived by the mind with the same facility and distinctness, as if ever so conformable to reality. That the sun will not rise to-morrow is no less intelligible a proposition, and implies no more contradiction, than the affirmation, that it will rise. We should in vain, therefore, attempt to demonstrate its falsehood. Were it demonstratively false, it would imply a contradiction, and could never be distinctly conceived by the mind.* [Steinberg, 1977, pp. 15–16]

Hume is saying that the inference that the sun will rise tomorrow is nondemonstrative; the conclusion does not follow necessarily from the evidence. Hume is further claiming that there is no noncircular justification to a general or particular knowledge of things that have not been observed. We are inclined to accept inductive arguments on the grounds of past experience, but this in itself is an inductive argument; hence the circularity.

Consider another example of an enumerative induction (this one comes from the American philosopher, Gilbert Harman):

1. All peaches have pits.
2. *X* is a peach.
3. *X* has a pit.

Suppose that we have a basket of 100 peaches. We have now examined 99 peaches; the evidence of the peaches in the basket does not guarantee that the next peach will also have a pit. The conclusion (3) does not provide a guarantee as it would in a deductive inference. Still, there does seem to be something reliable in thinking that the last peach in the basket will have a pit. Why? It seems that we might be adding on a hidden premise, the uniformity premise. This premise suggests that the unobserved will resemble the observed. Take the following example, which looks a great deal like the argument we have just considered:

1. All observed *X*s are *Y*s.
2. Therefore, all *X*s are *Y*s.

Now reconstruct this argument with the uniformity principle:

1. All *X*s are *Y*s.
2. The unobserved resembles the observed (the uniformity principle).
3. Therefore, all *X*s are *Y*s.

The problem is still whether we are entitled to believe the uniformity principle. It seems that our experience of the world tells us that the uniformity principle obtains, but in accepting the principle, we are making an inductive inference. The crux of Hume's problem with induction is that any attempt to justify an inductive inference is circular. Even the uniformity principle is unhelpful. But why, in spite of Hume's logical attack on induction, should we worry about circularity? The problem arises, in part, because we are taking the uniformity principle for granted, without justification. Using empirical evidence to justify recourse to the principle is doing what Hume is warning against. Calling forth "deeper reasons," cashing out the laws of physics or chemistry that seem to "guarantee" uniformity of nature, is recoiling into a former induction to justify the present one.

One way to cope with the problem of induction is to agree with the skeptic that the future never exactly resembles the past. But the future is, on balance, something that more likely than not resembles the past. Consider the following argument:

1. Previously observed *X*s are *Y*.
2. Therefore, future and other unobserved *X*s are probably *Y*.

Any observed evidence is only a sample; we have not seen every crow to determine whether all crows are black. But in the second kind of inductive inference, the hypothetical induction, a hypothesis is inferred as the best explanation for the given evidence. Imagine hearing a knock at the window. You are likely to think that there is someone there, but on moving the curtains, you realize that a branch is banging at the window. Your original inference is nondemonstrative. You might have settled on "someone being at the window" or on "the branch is banging at the window." You did settle for what you took to be the best explanation.

Matthew Ginsberg has suggested that we think of induction in its widest sense, such that it constitutes our default assumptions about our experience. For instance, imagine that you are asked if you need a lift from campus to your hotel when you are attending a conference. You simply assume that the person asking you can drive. This is a default assumption, because it could be the case that your colleague cannot drive, but it is unlikely. In cases of nondemonstrative inductive inferences, the given evidence is compatible with many hypotheses; the aim is to determine which hypothesis best explains the phenomena in question. Harman, as recounted in Dancy and Sosa's *A Companion to Epistemology*, reminds us that this is workable for induction, but we should proceed with caution: "Consider Sam's evidence that several peaches have been found not to have pits.

That evidence is compatible with Sam's hypothesis that all peaches have pits and also with the hypothesis that only some peaches have pits but Albert has been removing all the peaches without pits before Sam sees them."

See Also the Following Articles

Causal Inference • Falsification in Social Science Method and Theory

Further Reading

Copi, I. M., and Burgess-Jackson, K. (1996). *Informal Logic.* Prentice Hall, Upper Saddle River, New Jersey.

Dancy, J., and Sosa, E. (1992). *A Companion to Epistemology.* Blackwell Reference, Oxford, United Kingdom and Cambridge, Massachusetts.

Ginsberg, M. L. (1987). *Readings in Nonmonotonic Reasoning.* M. Kaufmann Publ., Los Altos, California.

Kneale, W. C., and Kneale, M. (1962). *The Development of Logic.* Clarendon Press, Oxford.

Steinberg, E. (ed.) (1977). *Hume, David. 1777. An Enquiry Concerning Human Understanding and A Letter from a Gentleman to His Friend in Edinburgh.* Hackett Publ. Co., Indianapolis.

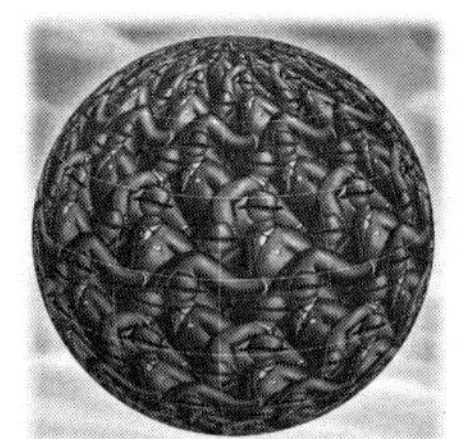

Deming, William Edwards

Mark Wilcox
Cranfield University, Cranfield, England, United Kingdom

Glossary

common cause The description given to variation in a stable process; can also be described as natural variation in a system, when nothing unusual is happening (e.g., no special causes). However, common cause variation is also present in processes that are out of control and are constant over time and throughout the system.

deadly diseases and obstacles The term used by Deming to describe the things that stand in the way of transformation.

Plan, Do, Study, Act (PDSA) model In its original form, this was the Plan, Do, Check, Act model for continual improvement, depicted in the form of a four-spoke wheel. Though many refer to this as the Deming wheel, Deming always referred to this as the Shewhart cycle. Deming had taken this four-step approach from Shewhart's method for continually improving processes, to achieve a "state of statistical control." In fact, Shewhart intended the wheel to be drawn as spiral, to represent the continual nature of the improvements taking place.

prediction For Deming, "management is prediction." The premise, if a process is in statistical control, is that the future behavior of that process is predictable for the foreseeable future. The notion of prediction comes from theory. The construction of a chart allows the evidence to be interpreted, using theory to predict what may happen next. Data alone do not provide a prediction. Deming stated that "rational prediction requires theory and builds knowledge through systematic revision and extension of theory based on comparison of prediction with observation."

Shewhart control chart A two-axis chart, used to plot data taken from processes and products. The plotted data points on the chart illustrate "variation" in the entity being measured. The chart will also show the mean and upper and lower control limits. Charts are an operational definition of the distinction between common and special causes of variation. Charts can be used for judgment of the past, stability of the present, and prediction of the future by looking back on a set of results from a process, and as an operation to attain and maintain an ongoing process.

special causes Events outside natural variation in the process. In manufacturing, these could be some faulty material, an untrained employee making a mistake, or a worn machine tool, for example. Special causes are often sporadic and may have a local impact on the process as a whole. Process instability is shown on the control chart as evidence of special causes, which the operator or engineer will have to find, remove, or correct to get the process back into control.

subgroups Sets of measurements collected at specific times or points in a process to monitor the process. Each subgroup is treated as a sample and will display a pattern of behavior that may be treated as part of a population. If the patterns of behavior are consistent, then the process may be assumed to be in control.

system As Deming defined it, "a network of interdependent components that work together to try to accomplish the aim of the system."

system of profound knowledge (SoPK) Deming's last major theory based on four elements: (1) appreciation of systems, (2) knowledge about variation, (3) theory of knowledge, and (4) psychology.

transformation The term used by Deming to describe the changes required to halt the decline of Western industry. He developed 14 points for managers to use to achieve transformation.

variation A result of common and special causes; variation in a system is based on the premise that no matter how hard we try to do something, there will always be some variation in the process and the outcome.

Dr. William Edwards Deming was invited to Japan in the period immediately following World War II to help in the improvement of Japanese manufacturing. Several years later, his work received the accolade it deserved in his native United States, and he became a legend in the field of quality management. Deming's work was based on the application of statistical methods to different types of organizations. His theories required a paradigm shift from the traditional "control and command" methods of management, based on the work of Frederick Taylor and the like. Subsequently, Deming was known for his diatribe against what he called "Western-style" management. Not surprisingly, Deming's work is still inadequately understood and continues to meet a great deal of resistance. He listed 14 points for the transformation of Western-style management, citing what he called the "diseases and obstacles" that would get in the way. His "Plan, Do, Study, Act" model became the trademark for those less familiar with the minutiae of his work. Deming always referred to this as the Shewhart cycle because it came from W. A. Shewhart's method for continual improvement. Deming's final contribution was his "system of profound knowledge," published in 1993, the year of his death. His work covered many topics both within and outside of statistics and he commented several times near the end of his life that it would take a lifetime to work out all the consequences of his concept of a system.

Introduction

Dr. William Edwards Deming's (1900–1993) most notable achievement in his long life was probably the impact he had on Japanese manufacturing in the post-World War II period. Deming, a statistician from the United States, was asked by General MacArthur to visit Japan to help train the industrialists on how to improve the quality of their products in the rebuilding process (in Japan, MacArthur was frustrated with the poor-quality telephone systems, which he was finding very unreliable). MacArthur was familiar with the work on improving the quality of telephone manufacture by Dr. W. A. Shewhart, who famously invented the control chart when he applied statistical methods to mass production. Deming had followed Shewhart's teachings and developed the application of statistical quality control to an increasing number of sectors and processes outside of manufacturing. It was this "new philosophy" that Deming taught the Japanese.

Deming's impact on Japanese manufacturing remained relatively unknown until the 1960s, when the Western economies started to notice and feel the impact of superior Japanese products. It was only when Western journalists, academics, and industrialists started to investigate the "secrets" of Japan's success that they came across Deming's name, along with the names Juran, Sarashon, Prossman, and Ishikawa, for example. The Japanese Union of Scientists and Engineers (JUSE) recognized the impact of Deming's work and in 1951 named their annual quality award after him (the Deming Prize). This prize is arguably still the most sought after quality award in the world.

Deming taught and consulted in statistics in many countries throughout his long life. He published many academic papers in this field, plus a considerable number of books on statistics. It was only after his rapid rise to fame, following his "discovery" by his native Americans, that he published what was arguably his first management text book, *Out of the Crisis*, in 1986. Deming continued to develop his ideas right up till his death. His final book, *The New Economics for Industry, Government, Education*, first published in 1993, is considered to be an unfinished work. In this work, he introduced his theory of a system of profound knowledge (SoPK). (Those who knew Dr. Deming well say that he was never comfortable writing management textbooks, preferring to focus on statistical papers for academic journals, because he was often misunderstood, misquoted, or misinterpreted by so many people in the quality management arena.)

Deming's SoPK has four elements. In essence, the application of statistical techniques to run/manage an organization requires first viewing the organization as a system. To view the organization as a system requires a particular way of thinking about how processes interconnect and support one another. With that view in mind, the second step is to understand the notion of variation in a system. If the goal of having all the processes in a system "in control" (stability) can be achieved, then the future behavior of the organization is potentially predictable. The view of an organization as a set of processes working (in harmony) as a system, allowing the prediction of the behavior of that system, requires the third element, an understanding of the principles of the philosophy of science and theories of knowledge. Fourth, to manage people in an organization requires a knowledge of psychology. The interaction of these four elements amount to the basis of Deming's theory on management.

A Potted Biography

Deming, born 14 October 1900, died 20 December 1993. His first degree, in 1917, was at the University of Wyoming, where he was studying mathematics. He then read for a Masters degree in mathematics and physics from the University of Colorado in 1922 and earned a Ph.D. in physics from Yale University in 1928. During his summer vacation work (1925–1926) at the Hawthorne, Illinois plant of Western Electric, he met Dr. W. A. Shewhart, who was conducting a research project to find a more economic way of controlling quality. This meeting was an important event in the history of quality management. Deming learned the theory of statistical quality control from Shewhart, and it was these ideas that were developed over the next 65 years.

Deming always acknowledged the enormous debt owed to Shewhart's contribution to this field of work and study.

Deming worked with the National Bureau of Statistics between 1930 and 1946. During that time, Deming studied statistics at University College in London under R. A. Fisher. In addition, he invited Shewhart to give a series of lectures at the Department of Mathematics and Statistics of the Graduate School, U.S. Department of Agriculture. These lectures formed the basis of a short book edited by Deming, published in 1939 and still available in the 21st century.

During World War II, Deming had the opportunity to develop and practice statistical quality control in supplying the Army, which served to show the benefits to be gained from statistical quality control. Deming then developed training courses for ordinance workers and their suppliers. It is also reputed that he accomplished a sixfold productivity increase by applying quality control methods to the processes being employed at the National Bureau of the Census. Deming became a full professor at New York University in 1946 and undertook specific projects, including a trip to Japan in 1947. The significant trip to Japan came in 1950, when Deming talked to about 100 top industrialists. The following year, he talked to another 400, by which time he had "ignited Japan."

Deming also tried to promote statistical quality control in the United States at this time, but the managers and engineers would not listen to what he had to say. He felt they were indulging in a "boom sellers" market and not focusing on quality and the customer. It was 1968 before people started to see what was going on in Japan, and it was not till 1980, when Clare Crawford-Mason was researching a documentary called *If Japan Can Why Can't We?*, to be televised by the National Broadcasting Corporation (NBC), that she uncovered the stories about Deming from the Japanese. Crawford-Mason tracked Deming down and interviewed him for a total of 25 hours. She has recalled how he emphasized that business leaders in the United States would not take his work seriously during the postwar years.

After the NBC documentary was broadcast, Deming's phone never stopped ringing and he was suddenly to become an American folk hero. By 1981, he was a consultant with Ford and was no doubt responsible for precipitating their drive for statistical process control (SPC) throughout the supply chain, a policy that still exists today. From the early 1980s, Deming developed his legendary 4-day seminars, during which he taught the principles of his work with the now-famous "Red Beads Experiment" and the "Funnel Experiment." These exercises cleverly demonstrate the principles of his work and (much to the embarrassment of Western business leaders) emphasize many failings in Western-style management (e.g., blaming workers for poor quality; tampering with the system, making things worse). Deming traveled the world conducting his seminars, continuing to work until about 1990, when ill health started to take its toll on his output. When he died in 1993, glowing obituaries appeared in newspapers and journals in all four corners of the world, showing the impact he had made in his long and prolific life. Will Hutton, writing in *The Guardian*, provided a balanced view of Dr. Deming's work with some of his quotes. Deming's view of American managers was not untypical of his criticisms: "American management on the whole has a negative scrap value . . . it's like a an old refrigerator—you can't sell it off. You have to pay someone to cart it off." On how he would like to be remembered in his native United States, Deming said "Well maybe [as] someone who spent his life trying to keep America from committing suicide."

Deming and many of his followers were convinced that the benefits of systemic thinking and all its implications had yet to be fully realized. Writing the foreword for Shewhart's 1939 published lectures, Deming said, in 1986, that "another half-century may pass before the full spectrum of Dr Shewhart's contribution has been revealed in liberal education, science and industry." It is to Deming's credit that the remnants of his work and ideas still provoke much interest and debate [the ongoing Internet discussions at the Deming Electronic Network (DEN) web pages provide current discourse on Deming's ideas].

An Overview of Deming's Work

Deming had a substantial education, covering mathematics, engineering, physics, and statistics. Nevertheless, he learned his core theory from Dr. W. A Shewhart, with whom he worked in his holidays as a Ph.D. student in the 1920s. Deming always acknowledged the debt that both he and society as whole owed to Shewhart's contribution, as Deming developed his own work over the next 60 years.

Shewhart's theories were developed in the context of high-volume mass production, to which statistical methods were probably well suited. Deming, Juran, and others took Shewhart's ideas to a wider audience and developed them into more comprehensive theories for running entire organizations. Deming's work, while following this path to some extent, never lost sight of Shewhart's statistical method in developing "the new philosophy." As already noted, Deming's work took some time to be established in his native United States. Deming's notion of "transformation" and "deadly diseases" indicates the extent of change required to make his modus operandi work. So what was so radical about his work? To answer this question would take far more space than can be afforded here, but an outline of the implications of applying statistical method to managing organizations can begin with Deming's application of Shewhart's statistical method, which led to the expression of Deming's 14 points and the "system of profound knowledge."

Variation

First, consider Shewhart's 1939 invention of the control chart and his notions of common and assignable (Deming called these "special") causes of variation. The purpose of the control chart is to detect the presence of special causes in a process. This concept is at the root of reducing variation to provide stable and predictable processes.

The control chart is a unique invention, illustrating variation in a process or product. There are many types of charts for different processes. The example given in Fig. 1 shows a simple but effective individuals-moving-range chart, with the mean, upper, and lower control limits all calculated from the data from measuring specific features of a process. The chart shows data taken from a typical management report on weekly overtime. If these data were presented in the form of a table of figures, as is often the case in monthly management reports, the discussion around the meeting room might be quite exciting around week 12, with a high of nearly 400 hours. The managers would return to their departments and warn about excessive overtime, and low and behold, the next 2 weeks would show a reduction! Then, the managers would celebrate getting the overtime down to 150 hours. But, surprise, surprise, the figure would go up again. If, however, the data are presented in a different format, on a chart, the flows of the weekly trends are seen more clearly. It is apparent that though the data appear variable, when the mean and the 3σ control limits are calculated and drawn on the chart, the process is shown to be stable and predictable. This is the application of Shewhart's theory of variation and presentation of data, which Deming followed. So, it can be seen that there are no data points outside the control limits and probably no special causes in this process.

If the managers of the organization represented by the control chart in Fig. 1 were not happy with the level of overtime being worked, they would have to look elsewhere in the system to reduce the overtime. It would be no use reacting to "bad" weeks shown on the chart, because within the current system, those levels of overtime can be expected. Managers that react to such figures on a weekly basis may not understand the notion of variation in a system, and may thus be guilty of tampering with the system and making things worse. Understanding variation is only one element of Deming's SoPK. Reflecting on the immediate impact of this approach in Japan in 1948 and 1949, Deming observed that "the results were exciting, showing that productivity does indeed improve as variation is reduced, just as prophesied by the methods and logic of Shewhart's book."

Knowledge of Systems

There are many processes in an organization. Collectively, they form a system. Deming defined a system as a network of interdependent components that work together to try to accomplish the aim of the system. The interdependent components can be conceived as processes. An orchestra is an example of how a network of individuals may choose to cooperate, combine, and communicate in order to produce a piece of music for the listeners to enjoy. Deming points out that there are no prima donnas in an orchestra; the players are there to support one another.

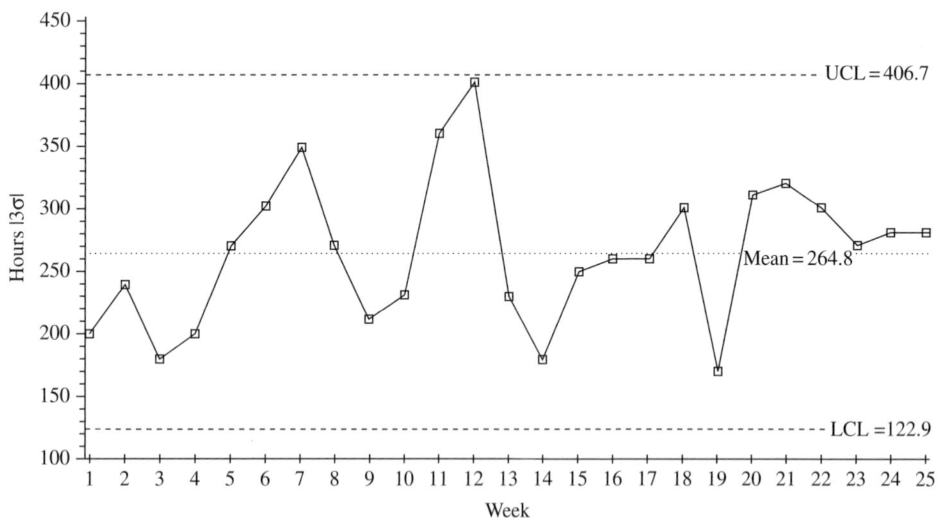

Figure 1 A Shewhart control chart, showing weekly overtime data. UCL, Upper control limit; LCL, Lower control limit.

Such is the problem with management by objectives (MBO), which can cause divisions in an organization as one function succeeds (with prima donnas) at the expense of another (In the 14 points, number 11 states "eliminate slogans, exhortations, and numerical targets"; deadly disease number 5 is "management by use only of visible figures, with little or no consideration of unknown and known figures.") Deming's conception of an organization as a system was quite radical when compared to the more traditional "command and control" structures found in many organizations. It is therefore not surprising that the process of transforming organizations into a systems way of operating required considerable upheaval and change.

A Theory of Knowledge

The third element of SoPK is a theory of knowledge. In his writings on this, Deming begins the section with the subheading "Management is Prediction," with a footnote to C. I. Lewis' 1929 publication *Mind and the World-Order*, which is a theory of knowledge, based on the notion of "conceptualistic pragmatism." It is a little-known fact outside the community of those who know Deming's and Shewhart's work that they were both influenced greatly by Lewis' book. Shewhart was reputed to have read it first and recommended it to Deming. He apparently read it 14 times and Deming a mere seven!

So why was this important? First, Shewhart had read widely as he developed his work in the 1920s. His reading included several books from the philosophy of science. Those reading Shewhart's work carefully will find that he talks consistently about prediction, so that if a process is in control, it is predictable—all things remaining equal. Second, a systems view of an organization (or, for that matter, the universe) progresses into a theory of knowledge that goes back to the pre-Socratic philosophy of Heraclitus, famous for claiming that we cannot step in the same river twice. This theory suggests that the universe is in a state of flux, or motion, e.g., a nonstatic universe. Therefore, the application of the statistical method to organizations requires being able to view the world as if it was in flux, because control charts show the variation of data over time. So, for variation, apply the concept of "flux."

The organization is therefore a dynamic entity with the future unfolding before us. The control chart provides a means of capturing this process, and we have to learn to interpret the charts from this perspective. This is where pragmatism comes into the equation. Lewis provided a theory of knowledge that would help to understand the "world-order" with our minds, based on a theory of "conceptualistic pragmatism," which incorporated prediction. Lewis' work gave both Shewhart and Deming a theory that in many ways supported what they were trying to do—in effect, it was post-hoc rationalization. The fact that the development of statistical method was underpinned with a pragmatic theory of knowledge is one of the best-kept secrets in the history of management.

The Fourth Element: Psychology

Psychology features in Deming's work in several ways. He was concerned with continual improvement and how we learn, and was passionate about creating the right environment for people to fulfill their need for learning in the work environment. "One is born with a natural inclination to learn," he proclaimed. Hence, when this does not happen, he blames managers for their shortcomings in failing to provide an environment where learning can flourish.

Perhaps Deming's most contentious ideas are around the notion of ranking, rating, and rewarding people. He believed that extrinsic motivation may eventually lead to the destruction of the individual, and argued against monetary rewards based on the notion of "overjustification," suggesting that "appreciation" may be a far more meaningful approach. "An award in the form of money for a job well done for the sheer pleasure of doing it is demoralizing, overjustification. Merit awards and ranking are demoralizing. They generate conflict and dissatisfaction. Companies with wrong practices pay a penalty. The penalty can not be measured." With the combination of systems thinking and his views on psychology, it is obvious that Deming was drawn to favor cooperation rather than competition. Even organizations, he argued, that are in the same sector can learn to cooperate on things such as research and development. Not everyone shared this view; in a harsh competitive environment, the survival of the fittest may be the mantra for many companies.

Plan, Do, Study, Act

The PDSA cycle is a methodology developed by Deming from Shewhart's work. Plan, do, study, act is a four-stage process of continual improvement. The overall aim is to get the key processes of the organization (viewed as a system) into a state of statistical control. This is achieved with the PDSA cycle, to reduce variation to a stage where it is no longer economical to remove special causes of variation in a process. Shewhart had compared mass production to the scientific method. Here the specification equals the hypothesis, the production equals the experiment, and the inspection equals the test of the hypothesis. Link these together into a cycle and you have the foundations of continual improvement with the aim of achieving a state of statistical control.

See Also the Following Article

Shewhart, Walter

Further Reading

Deming, W. E. (1950). *Some Theory of Sampling.* John Wiley and Sons, New York (reprinted in 1984 by Dover, New York).

Deming, W. E. (1953). On the distinction between enumerative and analytic surveys. *J. Am. Statist. Assoc.* **48**(262), 244–255.

Deming, W. E. (1986). *Out of the Crisis.* MIT Press, Cambridge, Massachusetts.

Deming, W. E. (1991). *A Tribute to Walter Shewhart on the Occasion of the 100th Anniversary of His Birth.* SPC Press, Knoxville.

Deming, W. E. (1994). *The New Economics for Industry, Government, Education,* 2nd Ed. MIT Press, Cambridge, Massachusetts.

Lewis, C. I. (1929/1956). *Mind and the World-Order: Outline of a Theory of Knowledge.* Dover, New York.

Neave, H. (1989/1994). *A Brief History of W. Edwards Deming.* British Deming Association, Salisbury.

Politz, A., and Deming, W. E. (1953). On the necessity of presenting consumer preferences as predictions. *J. Marketing* **XVIII**(1), 1–5.

Shewhart, W. A. (1931). *Economic Control of Quality of Manufactured Product.* Van Nostrand, New York (republished in 1980 as a 50th anniversary commemorative reissue by ASQC Quality Press, Milwaukee).

Shewhart, W. A. (1939/1986). *Statistical Method from the Viewpoint of Quality Control* (W. E. Deming, ed.). Dover, New York.

Wheeler, D. J. (2000). *Understanding Variation: The Key to Managing Chaos,* 2nd Ed. SPC Press, Knoxville.

Wilcox, M. (2003). Management by prediction. *J. Quality* **1**(1), paper no. 101.

Democracy, Measures of

Jeffrey Bass
University of Missouri-Columbia, Department of Anthropology, Columbia, Missouri, USA

Glossary

civil society The social space created by institutions and civil associations, autonomous of the state and its institutions.

consensus democracy A form of democracy in which political power is shared and decentralized so as to accommodate enduring regional, religious, ethnic, and linguistic social cleavages; the alternative to majoritarian democracy.

illiberal democracy A political system with regular elections, but in which civil liberties are severely restricted and the rule of law is routinely violated by the state.

liberal autocracy A political system without elections, but in which the state respects and maintains the rule of law and guarantees partial, but significant, civil liberties.

liberal democracy A political system marked not only by free and fair elections, but also by the rule of law and the protection of basic civil liberties, such as freedom of speech, assembly, and religion.

majoritarian democracy A form of democracy in which political power tends to be centralized and concentrated so as to reflect the will of the majority, or even a bare plurality; associated with a strong centralized government, single-party cabinets, and a first-past-the-post plurality electoral system; the alternative to consensus democracy.

polyarchy An operational definition of political democracy divorced from democratic ideals; used to describe objectively the procedures and institutions associated with contemporary liberal democracies.

social democracy A democracy that emphasizes socioeconomic equality and the creation of certain social rights, such as education, health care, and extensive social services.

In measuring the degree to which modern states are democratic, most social scientists currently evaluate democratic performance using some type of "procedural" measure that focuses on the state's democratic institutions and practices. Alternatively, some scholars have begun to develop measures of democracy that more fully take into account the roles that civil society, culture, and socioeconomic factors play in creating "substantive" democracy and in influencing the quality of democracy in modern societies.

Introduction

Social scientists have developed a range of approaches to measure the degree to which modern states are democratic. Although dictionaries commonly define democracy very simply as "rule by the people," this definition alone has proved too vague to be used as an operational measure. Historically, "rule" and "the people" have been very broadly defined. For example, the Soviet Union used its claim to have achieved relative socioeconomic equality to refer to itself as a "people's democracy," even though it was a one-party dictatorship. Alternatively, the United States strongly identified itself as a political democracy, even though slavery and later segregation in southern states politically disenfranchised a large segment of its African-American population. In both historical cases, local understandings of democracy differed from those commonly accepted by social scientists today.

This article begins by briefly outlining various conceptions of democracy, and how it is understood by most social scientists. It then examines attempts by social scientists to develop "procedural" indices to compare political democracies and measure the degree to which democratic ideals are realized in modern states. It also explores how some scholars have created measures of democracy that more fully take into account the roles that civil society, political culture, and socioeconomic forces have in creating a substantive democracy. In the concluding section, I argue that future research on democracy should take into account an even broader range of cultural factors that have influenced the texture and quality of democracy in modern societies.

Liberal Democracy Briefly Defined

The foundational essence of democracy consists of a political community in which there is some form of political equality among its members. The classical form of democracy that developed in ancient Athens was a form of direct participatory democracy in which citizens directly voted on important political issues during assemblies. Rather than elect officials, citizens were chosen by lot to serve as judges and legislators. Although this form of direct democracy was possible in the context of relatively small city-states, it has proved unfeasible to fully adapt this system to the political realities of larger states. Only in the 18th century was the term democracy first used to describe a political system in which enfranchised citizens elected a government of representatives.

Modern representative democracy differs from classical forms of democracy in other significant ways. In classical Athenian democracy, citizen assemblies had unlimited sovereignty, and individual rights could be abrogated simply by a majority decision. Only when democratic principles were combined with liberalism were civil rights first considered to be essential to democracy. Liberal political philosophy can trace its genealogy to theorists such as John Locke and John Stuart Mill, who conceived of civil liberties and individual rights as a way of limiting monarchal absolutism and religious intolerance, by creating a public sphere outside the control of the state. During the 18th century, democratic theorists integrated liberalism with democratic theory and practice, so as to limit the powers of the state and to prevent "a tyranny of a majority." Today, political democracy in contemporary states is typically built on both representational and liberal democratic principles.

Whereas the term "political democracy" commonly refers to political equality, the term "social democracy" generally denotes degrees of socioeconomic equality. Social democrats argue that democratic citizenship includes social rights, such as a right to education and other social services. Although some Marxists have argued that socioeconomic equality should take priority over political liberty and equality, most social democrats conceive of social democracy as something that is achievable even within a liberal democratic framework. Social democracy (with its emphasis on social rights) has been contrasted to liberal democracy (with its emphasis on civil and political rights). Nevertheless, in contemporary formulations, social democracy is usually conceived of as a form of liberal political democracy.

Procedural Approaches

Joseph Schumpeter: Basic Premises of the Procedural Approach

Joseph Schumpeter has been widely credited with pioneering the influential procedural approach toward measuring democratic performance. He argued in 1947 against understanding democracy as rule by a general will that achieves a common good, and in favor of what he called a "realist" model, in which democracy is defined as "an institutional arrangement for arriving at political decisions in which individuals acquire the power to decide by means of a competitive struggle for the people's vote." Schumpeter viewed democracy as a set of political institutions and procedures divorced from any broader ideal conceptions of democracy. Later, social scientists augmented Schumpeter's minimalist procedural standard by adding additional criteria for identifying and measuring political democracy. The following discussions review some of these augmented procedural standards.

Robert A. Dahl: Polyarchy and Democracy

Robert A. Dahl refined the procedural approach in 1971 by coining a new term, "polyarchy," which he used for the purpose of empirically describing and measuring democratic political systems. He restricted his use of the word "democracy" to describe a separate normative ideal (not yet achieved in modern states) in which a political system is equally responsive to all of its citizens. He identified a series of eight essential conditions necessary for a government to be identified as a polyarchy. In its most basic form, a polyarchy is a political system in which leaders are not only chosen within a free, fair, competitive, and a relatively inclusive electoral system, but it must also be a political system that ensures freedoms (such as freedoms of expression and organization) that make these elections meaningful.

These conditions can be understood to reflect two different dimensions in the measurement of liberal representative democracy: first, degrees of inclusiveness and, second, degrees of public contestation. That is, political regimes can be measured based on the extent to which they guarantee democratic citizenship to the whole population. But they can also be measured on how well they permit and empower these citizens to participate as political equals. Dahl's approach and assumptions have exerted considerable influence over subsequent studies of liberal democratic performance by such scholars as Kenneth Bollen and Axel Hadenius. These studies generally mirror the democratic criteria outlined by Dahl, carry the same implicit democratic normative range as his own study, and, like his own study, they tend to aggregate their scores into a single democratic performance scale.

Freedom House: Survey of Freedom

One of the most utilized contemporary measures of political democracy is the yearly Survey of Freedom, produced since 1973 by the nonprofit organization Freedom House. The Freedom House survey has several features that distinguish it from some other procedural democratic measures. First, because the survey's focus is on "freedom" (rather than narrowly on political democracy), it has been less concerned with institutional arrangements and more concerned with the realities of daily life, than have some other procedural measures of liberal democracy. Second, this comparative survey was one of the first measures clearly to identify and distinguish between two conceptual dimensions of liberal democracy. The survey is made along two equally weighted scales, that of political rights and that of civil liberties. The survey's checklist for political rights focuses on the electoral process, whereas the civil liberties checklist evaluates the development of a free and independent media, freedom of expression, the rule of law, the use of torture and state terror, and the rights of citizens to organize trade unions, cooperatives, and religious societies within civil society.

Although Dahl's measure includes many of the political rights and civil liberties found on the Survey of Freedom, he does not identify them as being conceptually distinct. The Freedom House survey, however, in keeping these features conceptually distinct, has been better able to reveal how societies can develop political systems that are unevenly democratic. Although there is usually a high degree of correlation between the political and civil dimensions measured, significant divergences do sometimes occur. A recent trend in much of Latin America and Eastern Europe, for example, is for political rights to be fairly secure, but for civil liberties to be far from complete. The term "illiberal democracy" has been coined recently to describe electoral democracies such as these, which typically lack respect for the rule of law, checks and balances among the branches of government, and protections of civil rights. The Freedom House survey data has also made it somewhat easier to identify the more rare inverse phenomenon, "liberal autocracy," in which citizens have few political rights, but have access to the rule of law and some civil liberties. Most liberal autocracies are either small (e.g., Singapore), are monarchies (e.g., Jordan and Morocco), or share both of these characteristics (e.g., Tonga, Barbuda, and Antigua).

Additional Dimensions of Liberal Democracy

Recently, many of the traditional procedural measures of liberal democracy have been challenged on the grounds that they do not take into account important, but less commonly recognized, liberal democratic values. Contemporary debates concerning the importance of minority rights and the democratic implications of different types of representational institutions reveal dimensions of liberal democracy not yet taken account of by most procedural democratic measures.

Minority Rights

Liberal democratic theorists since World War II have traditionally tended to argue that democratic freedom and equality can best be ensured through the provision of individual political rights and civil liberties. But recently some theorists have resurrected a tradition of liberal democratic thought that argues that for freedom and equality to prosper in multinational (or even multicultural) societies, it is necessary to also require some group-differentiated or minority rights. This has been justified on the grounds that these group-differentiated rights ensure that members of national minorities can participate as equals in the greater society. For example, laws that ensure the use of bilingual ballots or allow the use of minority languages in the court system help to ensure the protection of the political and civil rights of minority groups. It has been argued that an additional measure of the degree to which minority interests are protected should be included in any comprehensive measure of liberal democratic performance.

The introduction of this additional measure of liberal democracy, however, creates a paradox, namely, that as minority rights are expanded, it is possible that some individual political and civil rights might be restricted. For example, "special representation rights" in which historically marginalized groups are ensured a certain number of seats in national legislatures can be interpreted as limiting the individual political rights of other citizens. Additionally, legislation that prioritizes the employment of members of historically disadvantaged groups can be seen to restrict the individual civil rights of citizens who are not members of these groups. Not all democratic values are necessarily mutually reinforcing. Nevertheless, multidimensional measures of democratic performance that distinguish differences among these value dimensions better identify and measure these types of potential democratic trade-offs.

Consensual and Majoritarian Principles

It has also been argued that much of the Anglo-American writing on liberal democracy (and its measures) is biased toward majoritarian political institutions and values. Majoritarian democracies tend to share a cluster of institutional traits, such as first-past-the-post plurality electoral systems, only two major political parties, single-party cabinets, and a unitary centralized government.

Great Britain shares all of these characteristics, and the United States most of them. In contrast, consensus democracies (such as Switzerland and Belgium) are typically characterized by proportional electoral systems with multiple major political parties, coalition cabinets, and federalist systems of decentralized government.

Significantly, a majoritarian bias seems to be evident in some measures of liberal democracy. For example, Arend Lijphart has pointed out that several measures of democracy stipulate that political parties should periodically alternate in government and opposition. This turnover test implies the existence of a two-party system. Furthermore, it penalizes multiparty systems in which changes in government usually lead only to a partial change in the composition of the ruling party, rather than in a wholesale takeover of the government by the opposition.

It has also been argued forcefully that democracies constructed out of consensual institutions better reflect liberal democratic ideals and values than do those democracies based on majoritarian institutions. Consensus democracies tend to disperse or limit power, whereas majoritarian democracies often lead to the concentration of power in the hands of a majority or even a bare plurality. Additionally, majoritarian institutions tend to promote an exclusive, competitive, adversarial winner-take-all approach to politics, whereas consensual practices such as proportional representation encourage cross-party compromise and cooperation. In fact, it appears to be the case that consensual institutions are better suited to fostering a political culture of compromise, bargaining, and cooperation that is essential in ensuring the endurance of democratic institutions. For these reasons, a comprehensive measure of liberal democracy should indeed take into account the values that different types of systems of democratic representation tend to promote.

Methodological Issues

Determining the exact point along any procedural measure of democracy at which a country should be designated as democratic (or polyarchic) is ultimately subjective. In fact, from a historical perspective, identifying what exactly a political democracy consists of has proved to be a moving target. In the 19th-century United States, political elites (and elites in most other "democracies" of the time) typically assumed that the limited voting rights of women, Blacks, and the poor did not compromise the democratic credentials of their governments. By these typical 19th-century democratic standards, countries such as apartheid South Africa, for example, could be described as fully functioning liberal democracies. Since this time, however, both popular and scholarly democratic standards have evolved. In fact, since the 18th century, there has not only been a gradual deepening and broadening of democratic practices within societies identifying themselves as democratic, but also in the criteria scholars and politicians use to define democracy. Although some scholars evaluated apartheid South Africa as a fully functioning political democracy in the 1950s, few scholars of democracy did so by the 1980s.

Objective and Subjective Indicators of Democracy

The procedural measures that Dahl, Freedom House, and other researchers have developed to evaluate democratic political systems consist of both objective and subjective indicators. Objective indicators include indicators such as whether there are elections for the chief executive and legislature, whether constitutional separation of powers is guaranteed, and whether there exist laws ensuring individual rights. Subjective indicators generally rely on the judgments of outside evaluators to determine to what extent existing elections are in fact free and fair, and whether laws protecting political rights and civil liberties are consistently enforced. The extent to which the "rule of law" is enforced and to which a state acts in accordance with the law involves subjective evaluations based on media reports, the reports of human rights organizations, and the claims of opposition groups. The main disadvantage of subjective indicators is that they may reflect biases found in source materials and in the idiosyncrasies of the researcher. Nevertheless, although subjective indicators lack the precision of objective indicators, they can gauge many key traits of political democracy that otherwise would escape detection.

How Indicators and Measures of Democracy Are Weighed

Subjective judgments also play a role in considering how much to weigh each of the specific indicators that make up these measures of political democracy. In the case of Freedom House, for example, the specific weight given to each of the more than a dozen indicators of political rights and civil liberties has not been defined. Furthermore, the equal weight that Freedom House gives to the two dimensions of liberal democracy it measures (political rights and civil liberties) seems to have been largely decided for reasons of ease of statistical presentation, rather than because of any specific understanding of the relative importance of these dimensions to the functioning of liberal democracy.

Additionally, although many measures of liberal democracy frequently combine distinct scores into a single index, this may be too simplistic to capture the democratic reality of these contexts. The Freedom House survey is one of the few measures that produces separate measures for political rights and civil liberties. But this is just a start. Separate disaggregated measures could be made for other dimensions of liberal democracy. A more fully disaggregated approach would better reveal any potential trade-offs among these distinct values, as appears to be the case in relation to minority rights and individual rights.

Substantive Approaches to Measuring Democracy: Economics, Culture, and Civil Society

Critics of the procedural approach point out that these measures typically overlook those components of democracy that exist largely outside of state structures. Liberal democratic political institutions do not exist in a vacuum. Socioeconomic conditions, cultural attitudes, and independent mutual-interest associations within a country's civil society all influence the nature and quality of political democracy in modern societies.

The Socioeconomic Dimension of Democracy

Perhaps the most penetrating critique made about procedural measures of liberal democracy is that they have generally excluded socioeconomic considerations. Although social democracy is a concept distinct from political democracy, this does not mean that socioeconomic factors do not influence how a political democracy functions. Critics of a purely procedural approach toward defining and measuring democracy often point out that conditions of extreme poverty and illiteracy make it impossible for citizens to participate fully in democratic government or to enjoy fully its civil liberties and protections. Scholars of democracy have also noted that extreme, cumulative socioeconomic inequalities also promote undemocratic attitudes and practices. For example, societies with extreme inequalities tend to have social relations based on "patron–client" relationships that tend to inhibit the development of independent civil associations correlated with democratic governance. These societies tend to not only have electoral systems in which elites maintain "clientelistic control" over poor voters, but also tend to inhibit the development of broader social values conducive to political participation, tolerance, and cooperation.

Democratic Political Culture

Another legacy of the contemporary dominance of "procedural" approaches toward measuring democracy has been a relative inattention to "idealist" approaches that take into account people's political attitudes and ideals. Although the procedural approach is now dominant, scholars of democracy have long recognized that citizens of stable democracies tend to hold certain enduring political beliefs and values. In their seminal five-country comparative study on political culture and democracy, Almond and Verba identified a framework by which political beliefs could be classified into three different types of orientations: a cognitive orientation, involving knowledge of and beliefs about the political system; an affective orientation, consisting of feelings about the political system; and an evaluational orientation, which includes judgments about the performance of a political system and its adherence to certain values.

Scholars of democracy have further identified a series of related cultural values that most agree are critical to the stable functioning of any political democracy. The first is tolerance, a willingness to accept the articulation of opposing political views, but also more generally a tolerance for social and cultural difference. On an interpersonal level, this tolerance includes a readiness to participate in adversarial relationships without allowing feelings of aggression to take over.

Another related democratic value is trust. The ability to trust others, and the social environment more generally, is crucial in promoting cooperation and compromise. Skepticism about the integrity of leaders is acceptable as long as it does not reach the level of cynicism and alienation that leads to the end of participation (and a sweeping distrust of political institutions). On a larger political level, tolerance and trust allow for the development and acceptance of the notion of a "loyal opposition": instead of being viewed as traitors who conspire to overthrow the government, the opposition is trusted to play by the rules of the democratic game.

Another important quality of a democratic political culture is pragmatism, as opposed to a rigid ideological approach to politics. Pragmatism facilitates bargaining and compromise by rendering political goals as being negotiable and opinions as being open to new information. Pragmatism restrains the role of ideology in politics and, hence, the dangers of political polarization. Tolerance, trust, and pragmatism are mutually reinforcing values that promote moderation, bargaining, and accommodation, all of which have been identified as parts of a dense "pro-democratic" political culture.

Finally, in order for a democracy to be stable, it is important for a political culture to develop in which citizens have strongly internalized the exclusive legitimacy of democratic institutions. Citizens in recently democratized countries may support their democratic institutions, but unless democracy is viewed as the only legitimate political option, this support may be fragile. At some point, a democratic government is likely to experience a crisis, and if democratic legitimacy is not strongly internalized this can lead to democratic instability and the adoption of nondemocratic political practices. Throughout the twentieth century, democracies have disintegrated due to the persistence of authoritarian values and the lack of internalized democratic legitimacy. In some cases, citizens have simply voted democracy out of existence. The classic example is that of the democratic Weimar Republic. Facing economic distress and political insecurity, Germans voted the antidemocratic Adolf Hitler and the National Socialist Party into power. More recently, democratically elected leaders, such as Peru's Alberto Fujimori and Venezuela's Hugo Chavez, have received massive popular support (at least initially) in their systematic dismantling of democratic procedures and institutions.

These cases of democratic "devolution" indicate the importance of developing measures of liberal democracy that take into account political values, especially when democratic stability and endurance are some of the variables being measured. Democratic measures, such as those of Freedom House, currently rank some newly democratized countries (e.g., Slovenia) as achieving the same level of democracy as much more established democracies (e.g., France). Nevertheless, the reality that stable democratic institutions have survived for decades in France (and their legitimacy firmly internalized) and for less than a decade in Slovenia should influence any prediction of future democratic stability in these countries.

Recently, the World Values Survey, first carried out in 10 Western European countries in 1981 and later expanded to more than 43 societies in the early 1990s, has made available data on political values; the data can be used to create comparative measures of democratic political culture. Ronald Inglehart has used these surveys to demonstrate a strong correlation of high degrees of interpersonal trust, tolerance, and participatory values, with high rankings on other procedural measures of liberal democracy. Inglehart has also used this data to demonstrate that countries within certain cultural zones corresponding to religious traditions (Protestant, Catholic, Islamic, Confucian) or recent historical experiences (e.g., Communism) tend to share distinctive political value traits. For example, historically Protestant countries generally rank slightly higher on scales of social trust than do historically Catholic countries. These differences persist even after controlling for economic development. Interestingly, within these historically Protestant or Catholic countries, members of both of these denominations generally rank equally high on measures of interpersonal trust. It appears that it is not the contemporary beliefs of these religions that influence such social attitudes, but rather the shared cultural experiences of countries historically permeated by these religions.

The Role of Civil Society

Recently, democratic theorists have increasingly recognized the important role that independent civil associations play in the functioning of liberal political democracies. In his ground-breaking work on Italy's decentralized democracy, Robert Putnam found evidence that regional differences in effective local democratic government could be traced directly to regional differences in the density of civil associations, ranging from farmers' mutual aid societies to bird-watching clubs. A rich nexus of civil associations, through which people independently organize to manage their own affairs, creates both direct and indirect channels for citizens to influence their government. Some independent civil associations directly mobilize their members to influence specific political issues. But even those civil associations that never directly engage in politics do foster among their participants certain skills of negotiation, cooperation, and compromise, all of which are important for the smooth functioning of democratic politics. Although some scholars have argued that a developed civil society should mainly be seen as an important condition for promoting democracy, others propose that it should be seen as an essential part of it. David Beetham, for example, has created a democratic measure that takes into account not only political rights and civil liberties, but also the diversity of civil associations within a society, as central dimensions by which liberal democracies should be measured.

A Direction for Future Research

During the past 30 years, social scientists have formulated increasingly sophisticated measures of democracy. Procedural measures of liberal democracy have been expanded so as to take into account a greater range of institutions and democratic practices. Scholars have rediscovered the influence of citizens' political attitudes and beliefs in determining the quality of democratic institutions and in ensuring democratic endurance. Nevertheless, despite these advances, social scientists studying democracy have tended to define too narrowly those attitudes and beliefs that are relevant components of a "democratic political culture." Too often, there is a tendency to restrict the concept of political culture to ideas about political legitimacy, trust, tolerance, and participation.

Some recent anthropological studies of modern societies highlight how a broader range of attitudes and beliefs can directly influence the functioning and quality of democracy. Teresa Caldeira, for instance, examines the uneven development of democracy in Brazil, where social and political rights are fairly secure but civil liberties and the rule of law remain evasive. She does so by tracing how

Brazilian beliefs about crime, evil, and the "unbounded body" have all influenced the texture of Brazilian democratic citizenship. For example, the way in which Brazilians generally conceive of the human body as violable has led not only to general support for the corporal punishment of children, but to massive popular support for police and vigilante groups that commit extrajudicial executions of suspected criminals. In a very different context, John and Jean Comaroff reveal how the unique texture of democratic political participation in Botswana can be traced back to political ideals associated with the *kgotla* chieftainship system, in which traditional understandings of authority have promoted a form of nonparticipatory delegative democracy. These ethnographic studies reveal important political attitudes that are typically missed in more narrowly focused surveys on value orientations. And although these studies may not lend themselves as easily to comparison as do surveys, they do identify some of the multiple sociocultural sources for the uneven configurations of democracy found across the globe.

See Also the Following Articles

Election Polls • Election Polls, Margin for Error in

Further Reading

Beetham, D. (1999). *Democracy and Human Rights.* Polity Press, Cambridge.

Bollen, K. (1993). Liberal democracy: Validity and method factors in cross-national measures. *Am. J. Pol. Sci.* **37**(4), 1207–1230.

Caldeira, T. P. R. (2000). *City of Walls: Crime, Segregation, and Citizenship in Sao Paulo.* University of California Press, Berkeley.

Comaroff, J., and Comaroff, J. (1997). Postcolonial politics and discourses of democracy in Southern Africa: An anthropological reflection on African political modernities. *J. Anthropol. Res.* **53,** 123–146.

Dahl, R. (1971). *Polyarchy: Participation and Opposition.* Yale University Press, New Haven.

Foweraker, J., and Krznaric, R. (2000). Measuring liberal democratic performance: An empirical and conceptual critique. *Pol. Stud.* **48,** 759–787.

Hadenius, A. (1992). *Democracy and Development.* Cambridge University Press, Cambridge.

Inglehart, R. (1997). *Modernization and Postmodernization: Cultural, Economic, and Political Change in 43 Societies.* Princeton University Press, Princeton.

Inglehart, R. (2000). Culture and democracy. In *Culture Matters: How Values Shape Human Progress* (L. Harrison and S. Huntington, eds.). Basic Books, New York.

Karatnycky, A. (ed.) (2003). *Freedom in the World: The Annual Survey of Political Rights and Civil Liberties 2001–2002.* Freedom House, New York.

Kymlicka, W. (1995). *Multicultural Citizenship: A Liberal Theory of Minority Rights.* Clarendon Press, Oxford.

Lijphart, A. (1999). *Patterns of Democracy: Government Forms and Performance in Thirty-Six Countries.* Yale University Press, New Haven.

Putnam, R. (1993). *Making Democracy Work: Civic Traditions in Modern Italy.* Princeton University Press, Princeton.

Schumpeter, J. A. (1947). *Capitalism, Socialism, and Democracy,* 2nd Ed. Harper and Brothers, New York.

Zakaria, F. (2003). *The Future of Freedom: Illiberal Democracy at Home and Abroad.* W. W. Norton, New York.

Demography

John R. Weeks

San Diego State University, San Diego, California, USA

Glossary

age pyramid A graph of the number (or percentage) of people in a population distributed by age and sex, in which the ages are represented by bars stacked horizontally.

age and sex structure The distribution of a population according to age and sex.

cohort data Data referring to people who share something in common that is tracked over time; in demography this is most often the year of birth, thereby producing age cohorts.

demographic balancing (or estimating) equation The formula expressing that the population at time 2 is based on the population at time 1 plus births minus deaths plus the net migration between times 1 and 2.

fecundity The physiological capacity to reproduce.

fertility Reproductive performance rather than the mere capacity to do so; one of the three basic demographic processes.

infant mortality rate The number of deaths of infants under 1 year of age divided by the number of live births in that year (and usually multiplied by 1000).

life expectancy The average duration of life beyond any age of people who have attained that age, calculated from a life table.

longevity The length of life, typically measured as the average age at death.

migration The process of permanently changing residence from one geographic location to another; one of the three basic demographic processes.

period data Population data that refer to a particular year and represent a cross section of the population at one specific time.

population projection The calculation of the number of people who could be alive at a future date, given the number now alive and given reasonable assumptions about future mortality, fertility, and migration.

sex ratio The number of males per the number of females in a population.

standardization The adjustment of rates, such as the crude death rate and crude birth rate, so that differences in age structure between two populations are taken into account.

Demography is the science of population. It is the study of the causes and consequences of population size, growth (or decline), spatial distribution, structure, and characteristics. It is a field that is highly quantitative because an understanding of demographic processes can arise only from intensive and extensive measurement. Many of the methods have underlying biological principles, and the combination of biological and social science applications have helped to popularize many of the techniques commonly used in demography.

Introduction

Population growth is determined by the combination of mortality, fertility, and migration, so all three processes must be measured if we are to understand what kind of demographic change is occurring in a given region. However, because each of these three demographic processes varies by age and sex, we must also know how to measure the population structure according to those characteristics. Change in population processes and in the spatial distribution of the population are influenced especially by changes in the social and economic structure of a society, which means that we must also know the basic measures by which we track the demographic characteristics of the population. Population change underlies many, if not most, of the social changes occurring in the world today—it is both evolutionary and revolutionary. For this reason, methods of projecting the population are important tools for assessing alternate scenarios for the future of human society. Because population projections can employ all of the other demographic methods, the methods for doing projections are discussed last.

Basic Descriptors of Population Growth

Human populations, like all living things, have the capacity for exponential increase rather than simple straight-line increase. We can express this growth in terms of the ratio of the population size at two different dates:

$$\frac{p_2}{p_1} = e^{rn} \tag{1}$$

where p_2 is the population at time 2 (e.g., 2000), p_1 is the population at time 1 (e.g., 1990), e is the exponential function (a mathematical constant), r is the rate of growth between the two dates, and n is the number of years between the two dates. For example, in 1990 (time 1), there were 248,709,873 people enumerated in the U.S. census, and in 2000 (at time 2, which is 10 years later, so n is 10) the census counted 281,421,906. The average annual rate of growth r between those two dates can be calculated by rearranging formula (1), as follows:

$$r = \frac{\ln(p_2/p_1)}{n} \tag{2}$$

Plugging in the numbers given, the rate of growth in the United States between 1990 and 2000 was 0.0124 per year, which is usually multiplied by 100 to make it 1.24% per year.

Equation (2) can itself be rearranged to allow us to calculate the doubling time for a population, the time required for a population to double in number if the current rate of growth continues. A doubling of the population means that the ratio of the population at time 2 to that at time 1 is 2, so the numerator of Eq. (2) becomes the natural logarithm (ln) of 2, which is then divided by the rate of growth r to yield the number of years n that it would take for the population to double at the given rate of growth. Because the natural logarithm of 2 is 0.69, you can calculate this easily for yourself by remembering the rule of 69. The doubling time is approximately equal to 69 divided by the growth rate (in percent per year).

$$n = \frac{\ln(p_2/p_1)}{r}$$

so,

$$\text{Doubling-time} = \frac{\ln(2)}{r} \tag{3}$$

So, if the population of the United States is growing at a rate of 1.24% per year, we can calculate the doubling time to be 69 divided by 1.24 or 55 years. Similarly, if we want to know how long it would take a population to triple in size, we first find the natural logarithm of 3, which is 1.10, or 110 when multiplied by 100. At its current rate of growth, the U.S. population will triple in 89 years.

The rate of growth tells us nothing about the components of that growth, which represent some combination of people being born (fertility), people dying (mortality), people moving in (in-migrants), and people moving out (out-migrants). The demographic balancing (or estimating) equation provides that information:

$$p_2 = p_1 + b - d + \text{im} - \text{om} \tag{4}$$

This equation says that the population at time 2 is equal to the population at time 1 plus the births between time 1 and 2 minus the deaths between time 1 and 2 plus the in-migrants between time 1 and 2 minus the out-migrants between time 1 and 2. Thus, if we know the number of people from the previous census, we can add the number of births since then, subtract the number of deaths since then, add the number of in-migrants since then, and subtract the number of out-migrants since then to estimate what the total population count should be. This is useful for estimating population totals between censuses, and it is the cornerstone of the demographic analysis (DA) method of evaluating the accuracy of a census. A comparison of this number with the actual census count provides a clue to the accuracy of the census, as long as we have an accurate assessment of births, deaths, and migrants. Before the results of Census 2000 were known, the Census Bureau had calculated that between the 1990 census in April 1990 and the census in April 2000 there were 39,845,588 babies born, 22,733,741 people who died, and the net number of international migrants (immigrants minus emigrants) was 8,281,974. When these numbers are added to the 248,709,873 people counted in the 1990 census, the demographic balancing equation estimates a total population of 274,103,694. However, as already noted, Census 2000 counted a total of 281,421,906 people—7,318,212 more than expected. Some of that difference was due to underenumeration in the 1990 census (that count should have been higher), some might have been due to the overcount of some groups in the Census of 2000, and some was almost certainly due to a greater number of undocumented immigrants than had been estimated to be entering the country.

If the migration component is ignored in Eq. (3), the remaining component is called the natural increase if the difference between births and deaths is positive (more births than deaths) and the natural decrease if the difference is negative (fewer births than deaths). Natural increase is associated with population growth (or even population explosions), whereas natural decrease is associated with population implosion. The crude rate of natural increase (CNI) can be defined as the difference between the crude birth rate (CBR, see Eq. 17) and the crude death rate (CDR, see Eq. 6):

$$\text{CNI} = \text{CBR} - \text{CDR}. \qquad (5)$$

Measuring Mortality

Demographers generally are interested in more than just the total count of vital events such as birth and death, and a variety of rates have been developed to evaluate the risk of death. The ability to measure accurately varies according to the amount of information available, and as a consequence the measures of mortality differ considerably in their level of sophistication. The least sophisticated and most often quoted measure of mortality is the crude death rate.

Crude Death Rate

The CDR is the total number of deaths in a year divided by the average total population. In general form:

$$\text{CDR} = \frac{d}{p} \times 1000 \qquad (6)$$

where d represents the total number of deaths occurring in a population during any given year, and p is the total average (mid-year) population in that year. It is called crude because it does not take into account differences by age and sex in the likelihood of death. Nonetheless, it is frequently used because it requires only two pieces of information, total deaths and total population, which often can be estimated with reasonable accuracy, especially in developing countries where the cost of censuses and vital registration systems may limit their availability.

Differences in the CDR between two countries could be due entirely to differences in the distribution of the population by age, even though the chance of dying is actually the same. Thus, if one population has a high proportion of old people, its crude death rate will be higher than that of a population with a high proportion of young adults, even though at each age the probabilities of death are identical. For example, in 2000 Mexico had a crude death rate of 4 per 1000, scarcely one-third of the 11 per 1000 in Lithuania in that year. Nonetheless, the two countries actually had an identical life expectancy at birth of 72 years. The difference in crude death rates is accounted for by the fact that only 5% of Mexico's population was aged 65 and older, whereas the elderly accounted for 13% of Lithuania's population. Mexico's crude death rate was also lower than the level in the United States (9 per 1000 in 2000). Yet in Mexico a baby at birth could expect to live 5 fewer years than a baby in the United States. The younger age structure in Mexico puts a smaller fraction of the population into the older high-risk ages, even though the actual probability of death at each age is higher in Mexico than in the United States.

Age- and Sex-Specific Death Rates

To measure mortality at each age and for each sex we must have a vital registration system (or a large survey) in which deaths by age and sex are reported, along with census or other data that provide estimates of the number of people in each age and sex category. The age- and sex-specific death rate (${}_nM_x$ or ASDR) is measured as follows:

$${}_nM_x = \frac{{}_nd_x}{{}_np_x} \times 100{,}000 \qquad (7)$$

where ${}_nd_x$ is the number of deaths in a year of people of a particular age group in the interval x to $x + n$ (typically a 5-year age group, where x is the lower limit of the age interval and n is the width of the interval in years of age) divided by the average number of people of that age, ${}_np_x$ in the population (again, usually defined as the mid-year population). It is typically multiplied by 100,000 to get rid of the decimal point.

In the United States in 2000, the ASDR for white males ages 65–74 (denoted as ${}_{10}M_{65}$) was 2955 per 100,000, whereas for white females it was 1900 per 100,000, approximately two-thirds that for males. In 1950 the ASDR for white males ages 65–74 was 4865 per 100,000, and for white females 3243. Thus, over the last half of the twentieth century, the death rates for males ages 65–74 dropped by 39%, whereas for females the decline was 41%, keeping women well ahead of men in terms of survival at these ages. If the death data are sufficiently detailed, it is possible to be even more specific in the calculation of rates. Thus, it is possible to calculate rates that are, for example, specific to causes of death, specific to marital status, or specific to racial/ethnic groups.

Age-Adjusted Death Rates

It is possible to compare CDRs for different years or different regions, but it is analytically more informative if the data are adjusted for differences in the age structure of the populations prior to making those comparisons. The usual method is to calculate age-specific death rates for two different populations and then apply these rates to a standard population. For this reason, this method is also known as standardization. The formula for the age-adjusted death rate (AADR) is as follows:

$$\text{AADR} = \sum_i {}_n\text{ws}_x \times {}_nM_x \qquad (8)$$

where ${}_n ws_x$ is the standard weight representing this age group's proportion in the total population and ${}_nM_x$ is the age-specific death rate as calculated in formula (6). We can apply this methodology to compare the CDR in Egypt in 1996 (6.19 deaths per 1000 in population) with the United States in that same year (8.70 deaths per 1000 in population). We use the United States population as the standard weight and apply the age-specific death rates for Egypt to the United States age-sex structure in 1996 to see what the CDR would be in Egypt if its age-sex structure were identical to that in the United States. The result is that the AADR for Egypt in 1996 was 15.08 deaths per 1000—nearly twice that of the United States.

Life Tables

Another very useful way of standardizing for age is to calculate the expectation of life at birth, also known as life expectancy. This measure is derived from a life table, which was first used in 1662 by John Graunt to uncover the patterns of mortality in London. Life expectancy can be summarized as the average age at death for a hypothetical group of people born in a particular year and being subjected to the risks of death experienced by people of all ages in that year. An expectation of life at birth for U.S. females in 1999 of 79.4 years does not mean that the average age at death in that year for females was 79.4. What it does mean is that if all the females born in the United States in the year 1999 have the same risks of dying throughout their lives as those indicated by the age-specific death rates in 1999, then their average age at death will be 79.4. Of course, some of them would have died in infancy whereas others might live to be 120, but the age-specific death rates for females in 1999 implied an average of 79.4. Note that life expectancy is based on a hypothetical population, so the *actual* longevity of a population is measured by the average age at death. Because it is undesirable to have to wait decades to find out how long people are actually going to live, the hypothetical situation set up by life expectancy provides a quick and useful comparison between populations. One of the limitations of basing the life table on rates for a given year, however, is that in most instances the death rates of older people in that year will almost certainly be higher than will be experienced by today's babies when they reach that age. This is especially true for a country that is in the midst of a rapid decline in mortality, but even in the United States in the twenty-first century, current life tables are assumed to underestimate the actual life expectancy of an infant by 5 or more years.

Life-table calculations, as shown in Table I for U.S. females for 1999, begin with a set of age- and sex-specific death rates, and the first step is to find the probability of dying during any given age interval. Table I is called an abridged life table because it groups ages into 5-year categories rather than using single years of age. The probability of dying (${}_nq_x$) between ages x and $x+n$ is obtained by converting age/sex-specific death rates (${}_nM_x$) into probabilities. A probability of death relates the number of deaths during any given number of years (that is, between any given exact ages) to the number of people who started out being alive and at risk of dying. For most age groups, except the very youngest (less than 5) and oldest (85 and older), for which special adjustments are made, death rates (${}_nM_x$) for a given sex for ages x to $x+n$ may be converted to probabilities of dying according to the following formula:

$$ {}_nq_x = \frac{(n)({}_nM_x)}{1+(a)(n)({}_nM_x)} \tag{9} $$

This formula is only an estimate of the actual probability of death because the researcher rarely has the data that would permit an exact calculation, but the difference between the estimation and the "true" number will seldom be significant. The principal difference between reality and estimation is the fraction a, where a is usually 0.5. This fraction implies that deaths are distributed evenly over an age interval, and thus the average death occurs halfway through that interval. This is a good estimate for every age between 5 and 84, regardless of race or sex. At the younger ages, however, death tends to occur earlier in the age interval. The more appropriate fraction for ages 0–1 is 0.85 and for ages 1–4 (shown in Table I as 1–5) is 0.60. Another special case is the oldest age group. Deaths tend to occur later rather than earlier in the interval at the oldest ages. However, Table I uses 85+ as the oldest age group and so avoids the specific age detail at the very oldest ages. Note that because the interval 85+ is open-ended, going to the highest age at which people might die, the probability of death in this interval is 1.0000—death is certain.

In Table I the age-specific death rates for females in 1999 in the United States are given in column (4). In column (5) they have been converted to probabilities of death from exact age x (for example, 10) to exact age $x+n$ (for example, $10+5=15$). Once the probabilities of death have been calculated, the number of deaths that would occur to the hypothetical life-table population is calculated. The life table assumes an initial population of 100,000 live births, which are then subjected to the specific mortality schedule. These 100,000 babies represent what is called the radix (l_0). During the first year, the number of babies dying is equal to the radix (100,000) times the probability of death. Subtracting the babies who died (${}_1d_0$) gives the number of people still alive at the beginning of the next age interval (l_1). These calculations are shown in columns (7) and (6) of Table I. In general:

$$ {}_nd_x = ({}_nq_x)(l_x) \tag{10} $$

Table I Calculation of Life Expectancy for U.S. Females, 1999

(1) Age interval, x to $x+n$	(2) Number of females in the population, $_nP_x$	(3) Number of deaths in the population, $_nD_x$	(4) Age-specific death rates in the interval, $_nM_x$	(5) Probabilities of death proportion of persons alive at beginning who die during interval, $_nq_x$	Of 100,000 hypothetical people born alive: (6) Number alive at beginning of interval, l_x	(7) Number dying during age interval, $_nd_x$	Number of years lived: (8) In the age interval, $_nL_x$	(9) In this and all subsequent age intervals, T_x	(10) Expectation of life Average number of years of live remaining at beginning of age interval, e_x
0–1	1,867,649	12,291	0.00658	0.00654	100,000	654	99,444	7,939,099	79.4
1–5	7,383,117	2274	0.00031	0.00123	99,346	122	397,089	7,839,655	78.9
5–10	9,741,935	1510	0.00016	0.00077	99,223	77	495,924	7,442,566	75.0
10–15	9,538,922	1593	0.00017	0.00083	99,146	83	495,525	6,946,642	70.1
15–20	9,587,530	3998	0.00042	0.00208	99,064	206	494,802	6,451,117	65.1
20–25	8,841,667	4244	0.00048	0.00240	98,857	237	493,694	5956,315	60.3
25–30	9,150,709	5161	0.00056	0.00282	98,620	278	492,407	5,462,621	55.4
30–35	9,959,530	7629	0.00077	0.00382	98,343	376	490,773	4,970,213	50.5
35–40	11,332,470	13,123	0.00116	0.00577	97,967	566	488,419	4,479,440	45.7
40–45	11,231,542	19,015	0.00169	0.00843	97,401	821	484,953	3,991,021	41.0
45–50	9,855,838	24,817	0.00252	0.01251	96,580	1208	479,879	3,506,068	36.3
50–55	8,447,622	32,498	0.00385	0.01905	95,372	1817	472,316	3,026,188	31.7
55–60	6,692,991	41,443	0.00619	0.03049	93,555	2852	460,643	2,553,872	27.3
60–65	5,546,089	54,812	0.00988	0.04822	90,702	4374	442,577	2,093,229	23.1
65–70	5,110,451	79,166	0.01549	0.07457	86,328	6437	415,549	1,650,652	19.1
70–75	4,909,038	118,514	0.02414	0.11384	79,891	9095	376,719	1,235,103	15.5
75–80	4,272,506	163,496	0.03827	0.17463	70,796	12,363	323,074	858,384	12.1
80–85	3,003,063	194,124	0.06464	0.27824	58,433	16,259	251,520	535,310	9.2
85+	2,934,837	436,152	0.14861	1.00000	42,175	42,175	283,790	283,790	6.7

Source: Death rate data from the U.S. National Center for Health Statistics; other calculations by the author.

and

$$l_x + n = l_x - {}_nd_x \qquad (11)$$

The final two columns that lead to the calculation of expectation of life are related to the concept of number of years lived. During the 5-year period, for example, between the 5th and the 10th birthdays, each person lives 5 years. If there are 98,000 people sharing their 10th birthdays, then they all have lived a total of $5 \times 98{,}000 = 490{,}000$ years between their 5th and 10th birthdays. Of course, if a person dies after the 5th but before the 10th birthday, then only those years that were lived prior to dying are added in. The lower the death rates, the more people there are who will survive through an entire age interval and thus the greater the number of years lived will be. The number of years lived ($_nL_x$) can be estimated as follows:

$$_nL_x = n(l_x - a_nd_x) \qquad (12)$$

The fraction a is 0.50 for all age groups except 0 to 1 (for which 0.85 is often used) and 1 to 5 (for which 0.60 is often used). Furthermore, this formula will not work for the oldest, open-age interval (85+ in Table I) because there are no survivors at the end of that age interval and the table provides no information about how many years each person will live before finally dying. The number of years lived in this group is estimated by dividing the number of survivors to that oldest age (l_{85}) by the death rate at the oldest age (M_{85}):

$$L_{85+} = \frac{l_{85}}{M_{85}} \qquad (13)$$

The results of these calculations are shown in column (8) of Table I. The years lived are then added up, cumulating from the oldest to the youngest ages. These calculations are shown in column (9) and represent T_x, the total number of years lived in a given age interval and all older age intervals. At the oldest age (85+), T_x is just equal to ${}_nL_x$. But at each successively younger age (e.g., 80 to 85), T_x is equal to T_x at all older ages (e.g., 85+, which is T_{85}) plus the number of person-years lived between ages x and $x+n$ (e.g., between ages 80 and 85, which is ${}_5L_{80}$). Thus, at any given age:

$$T_x = T_{x+n} + {}_nL_x \tag{14}$$

The final calculation is the expectation of life (e_x), or average remaining lifetime. It is the total years remaining to be lived at exact age x and is found by dividing T_x by the number of people alive at that exact age (l_x):

$$e_x = \frac{T_x}{l_x} \tag{15}$$

Thus for U.S. females in 1999, the expectation of life at birth (e_0) was 7,939,099/100,000 = 79.4, whereas at age 55 a female could expect to live an additional 27.3 years.

Other Widely Used Death Rates

There are several other mortality rates that are routinely and widely used in demographic research. The infant mortality rate (IMR) is actually the first line of the life table, but it can be calculated on its own. It is the number of deaths during the first year of life (d_0) per 1000 live births (b):

$$\text{IMR} = \frac{d_0}{b} \times 1000 \tag{16}$$

The IMR is extremely sensitive to overall levels of health and well-being and is highly correlated with life expectancy, so on its own it provides a good index of a population's mortality situation. As recently as the nineteenth century, IMRs of 500 (meaning that one-half of all babies born died before reaching their first birthday) were not unheard of. As of the beginning of the twenty-first century, the lowest rates were in Japan and Sweden (3 per 1000) and the highest rates were in several West African countries (such as Sierra Leone with 153 per 1000).

Although IMR measures infant deaths from birth through the first year of life, the most dangerous time for infants is just before and just after birth. There are special measures of infant death that take these risks into account. For example, late fetal mortality refers to fetal deaths that occur after at least 28 weeks of gestation. Neonatal mortality refers to deaths of infants within 28 days after birth. Postneonatal mortality, then, covers deaths from 28 days to 1 year after birth. In addition, there is an index called perinatal mortality, which includes late fetal deaths plus deaths within the first 7 days after birth. All of these values are typically divided by the number of live births. Technically, they should be divided by the number of conceptions in order to measure the risk of various pregnancy outcomes, but the data on conceptions are generally not available or are not very reliable even if they are available.

Maternal mortality refers to those deaths that are associated with complications of pregnancy and childbearing. The maternal mortality ratio measures the number of maternal deaths per 100,000 live births. At the end of the twentieth century, the world average was estimated by the World Health Organization to be 400 per 100,000. Another way of measuring maternal mortality that takes into account the number of pregnancies that a woman will have is to estimate a woman's lifetime risk of a maternal death. As a woman begins her reproductive career by engaging in intercourse, the question that is asked is: What is the probability that she will die from complications of pregnancy and childbirth? This risk represents a combination of how many times she will get pregnant and the health risks that she faces with each pregnancy, which are influenced largely by where she lives. For the average woman in the world, that probability is 0.013 or 1 chance in 75, but for women in sub-Saharan Africa, the risk is 1 in 11.

Measuring Fertility

Demographers use the term "fertility" to refer to actual reproductive performance and use the term "fecundity" to refer to the biological capacity. This can lead to some confusion because the medical profession tends to use the term "fertility" to refer to what demographers call "fecundity." For example, couples who have tried unsuccessfully for at least 12 months to conceive a child are usually called "infertile" by physicians, whereas demographers would say that such a couple is "infecund." A woman is classified as having impaired fecundity if she believes that it is impossible for her to have a baby, if a physician has told her not to become pregnant because the pregnancy would pose a health risk for her or her baby, or if she has been continuously married for at least 36 months, has not used contraception, and yet has not gotten pregnant.

Among women who are normally fecund and who regularly engage in unprotected sexual intercourse, the probability is very close to 1.0 that she will become pregnant over the course of 12 months. This varies somewhat by age, however, with the probability peaking in the early 20s and declining after that. Furthermore, women who are lactating are much less likely to conceive than nonlactating women.

The measures of fertility used by demographers attempt generally to gauge the rate at which women of reproductive age are bearing live births. Because poor health can lead to lower levels of conception and higher rates of pregnancy wastage (spontaneous abortions and stillbirths), improved health associated with declining mortality can actually increase fertility rates by increasing the likelihood that a woman who has intercourse will eventually have a live birth. Most rates are based on period data, which refer to a particular calendar year and represent a cross section of the population at one specific time. Cohort measures of fertility, on the other hand, follow the reproductive behavior of specific birth-year groups (cohorts) of women as they proceed through the childbearing years. Some calculations are based on a synthetic cohort, which treats period data as though they referred to a cohort. Thus, data for women ages 20–24 and 25–29 in the year 2000 represent the period data for two different cohorts. If it is assumed that the women who are now 20–24 will have just the same experience 5 years from now as the women who are currently 25–29, then a synthetic cohort has been constructed from the period data.

The CBR is the number of live births (b) in a year divided by the total midyear population (p). It is usually multiplied by 1000 to reduce the number of decimals:

$$\mathrm{CBR} = \frac{b}{p} \times 1000 \tag{17}$$

The CBR is "crude" because (1) it does not take into account which people in the population are actually at risk of having the births and (2) it ignores the age structure of the population, which can greatly affect how many live births can be expected in a given year. Thus, the CBR (which is sometimes called simply "the birth rate") can, on the one hand, mask significant differences in the actual reproductive behavior between two populations and, on the other hand, can imply differences that do not really exist. For example, if a population of 1000 people contains 300 women who were of childbearing age and one-tenth of them (30) had a baby in a particular year, the CBR would be (30 births/1000 total people) = 30 births per 1000 population. However, in another population, one-tenth of all women may also have had a child that year. Yet, if out of 1000 people there were only 150 women of childbearing age, then only 15 babies would be born, and the CBR would be 15 per 1000. CBRs in the world at the start of the twenty-first century ranged from a low of 8 per 1000 (in Bulgaria and Latvia) to a high of 51 per 1000 in Niger. The CBR in Canada was 11, compared with 14 in the United States, and 23 in Mexico.

Despite its shortcomings, the CBR is often used because it requires only two pieces of information: the number of births in a year and the total population size. If, in addition, a distribution of the population by age and sex is available, usually obtained from a census (but also obtainable from a large survey, especially in less-developed nations), then more sophisticated rates can be calculated.

The general fertility rate (GFR) uses information about the age and sex structure of a population to be more specific about who actually has been at risk of having the births that are recorded in a given year. The GFR (which is sometimes called simply "the fertility rate") is the total number of births in a year (b) divided by the number of women in the childbearing ages (${}_{30}F_{15}$, denoting females starting at age 15 with an interval width of 30, i.e., women ages 15–44):

$$\mathrm{GFR} = \frac{b}{{}_{30}F_{15}} \times 1000 \tag{18}$$

Smith has noted that the GFR tends to be equal to about 4.5 times the CBR. Thus, in 2000 the GFR in the United States of 67.5 was just slightly more than 4.5 times the CBR of 14.7 for that year.

If vital statistics data are not available, it is still possible to estimate fertility levels from the age and sex data in a census or large survey. The child–woman ratio (CWR) provides an index of fertility that is conceptually similar to the GFR but relies solely on census data. The CWR is measured by the ratio of young children (ages 0–4) enumerated in the census to the number of women of childbearing ages (15–44):

$$\mathrm{CWR} = \frac{{}_{4}p_{0}}{{}_{30}p^{\mathrm{f}}_{15}} \times 1000 \tag{19}$$

Notice that there is typically an older upper limit on the age of women for the CWR than for the GFR because some of the children ages 0–4 will have been born up to 5 years prior to the census date. Census 2000 counted 19,176,000 children ages 0–4 in the United States and 61,577,000 women ages 15–44; thus, the CWR was 311 children ages 0–4 per 1000 women of childbearing age. By contrast, the 2000 census in Mexico counted 10,635,000 children ages 0–4 and 23,929,000 women ages 15–49 for a CWR of 444.

The CWR can be affected by the underenumeration of infants, by infant and childhood mortality (some of the children born will have died before being counted), and by the age distribution of women within the childbearing years; researchers have devised various ways to adjust for each of these potential deficiencies. Just as the GFR is roughly 4.5 times the CBR, so it is that the CWR is approximately 4.5 times the GFR. The CWR for the United States in 2000, as previously noted, was 311, which was slightly more than 4.5 times the GFR in that year of 67.5.

As part of the Princeton European Fertility Project, a fertility index has been produced that has been useful in making historical comparisons of fertility levels.

The overall index of fertility (I_f) is the product of the proportion of the female population that is married (I_m) and the index of marital fertility (I_g). Thus:

$$I_f = I_m \times I_g \tag{20}$$

Marital fertility (I_g) is calculated as the ratio of marital fertility (live births per 1000 married women) in a particular population to the marital fertility rates of the Hutterites in the 1930s. Because they were presumed to have had the highest overall level of "natural" fertility, any other group might come close to, but is not likely exceed, that level. Thus, the Hutterites represent a good benchmark for the upper limit of fertility. An I_g of 1.0 means that a population's marital fertility was equal to that of the Hutterites, whereas an I_g of 0.5 represents a level of childbearing only half that. Calculating marital fertility as a proportion, rather than as a rate, allows the researcher to readily estimate how much of a change in fertility over time is due to the proportion of women who are married and how much is due to a shift in reproduction within marriage.

One of the more precise ways of measuring fertility is the age-specific fertility rate (ASFR). This requires a rather complete set of data: births according to the age of the mother and a distribution of the total population by age and sex. An ASFR is the number of births (b) occurring in a year to mothers ages x to $x + n$ (${}_nb_x$) per 1000 women (p^f) of that age (usually given in 5-year age groups):

$$\text{ASFR} = \frac{{}_nb_x}{{}_np^f_x} \times 1000 \tag{21}$$

For example, in the United States in 2000 there were 112 births per 1000 women ages 20–24. In 1955 in the United States, childbearing activity for women ages 20–24 was more than twice that, as reflected in the ASFR of 242. In 2000 the ASFR for women ages 25–29 was 121, compared with 191 in 1955. Thus, we can conclude that between 1955 and 2000 fertility dropped more for women ages 20–24 (a 54% decline) than for women ages 25–29 (a 37% drop).

ASFRs require that comparisons of fertility be done on an age-by-age basis. Demographers have also devised a method for combining ASFRs into a single fertility index covering all ages. This is called the total fertility rate (TFR). The TFR employs the synthetic cohort approach and approximates how many children women have had when they are all through with childbearing by using the age-specific fertility rates at a particular date to project what could happen in the future if all women went through their lives bearing children at the same rate that women of different ages were bearing them at that date. For example, as previously noted, in 2000 American women ages 25–29 were bearing children at a rate of 121 births per 1000 women per year. Thus, over a 5-year span (from ages 25 to 29), for every 1000 women we could expect 605 (= 5 × 121) births among every 1000 women if everything else remained the same. Applying that logic to all ages, we can calculate the TFR as the sum of the ASFRs over all ages:

$$\text{TFR} = \sum \text{ASFR} \times 5 \tag{22}$$

The ASFR for each age group is multiplied by 5 only if the ages are grouped into 5-year intervals. If data by single year of age are available that adjustment is not required. The TFR can be readily compared from one population to another because it takes into account the differences in age structure and its interpretation is simple and straightforward. The TFR is an estimate of the average number of children born to each woman, assuming that current birth rates remain constant and that none of the women die before reaching the end of the childbearing ages. In 2000, the TFR in the United States was 2.13 children per woman, which was well below the 1955 figure of 3.60 children per woman. A rough estimate of the TFR (measured per 1000 women) can be obtained by multiplying the GFR by 30 or by multiplying the CBR by 4.5 and then again by 30. Thus, in the United States in 2000, the TFR of 2130 per 1000 women was slightly more than, but still close to, 30 times the GFR of 67.5.

A further refinement of the TFR is to look at female births only (because it is only the female babies who eventually bear children). The most precise way to do this would be to calculate age-specific birth rates using only female babies; then the calculation of the TFR (Eq. 22) would represent the gross reproductive rate (GRR). Because there is not much variation by age of mothers in the proportion of babies that are female, it is simpler to use the proportion of all births that are female, and the formula is as follows:

$$\text{GRR} = \text{TFR} \times \frac{b^f}{b} \tag{23}$$

In the United States in 2000, 48.8% of all births were girls. Because the TFR was 2.130, we multiply that figure by 0.488 (the percentage converted to a proportion) to obtain a GRR of 1.039. The GRR is generally interpreted as the number of female children that a female just born may expect to have during her lifetime, assuming that birth rates stay the same and ignoring her chances of survival through her reproductive years. A value of 1 indicates that women will just replace themselves, whereas a number less than 1 indicates that women will not quite replace themselves and a value greater than 1 indicates that the next generation of women will be more numerous than the present one.

The GRR is called "gross" because it assumes that a person will survive through all her reproductive years. Actually, some women will die before reaching the oldest age at which they might bear children. The risk of dying is taken into account by the net reproduction rate (NRR). The NRR represents the number of female children that a female child just born can expect to bear, taking into account her risk of dying before the end of her reproductive years. It is calculated as follows:

$$\mathrm{NRR} = \sum \frac{{}_nb_x^{\mathrm{f}}}{{}_np_x^{\mathrm{f}}} \times \frac{l_x}{500{,}000} \qquad (24)$$

where ${}_nb_x^{\mathrm{f}}$ represents the number of female children born to women between the ages of x and $x+n$, which is divided by the total number of women between the ages of x and $x+n$ (${}_np_x^{\mathrm{f}}$). This is the age-sex specific birth rate which, in this example, assumes a 5-year age grouping of women. Each age-sex specific birth rate is then multiplied by the probability that a woman will survive to the midpoint of the age interval, which is found from the life table by dividing ${}_nL_x$ (the number of women surviving to the age interval x to $x+n$) by 500,000 (which is the radix multiplied by 500,000). Note that if single year of age data were used, then the denominator would be 100,000 rather than 500,000.

The NRR is always less than the GRR because some women always die before the end of their reproductive periods. How much before, of course, depends on death rates. In a low-mortality society such as the United States, the NRR is only slightly less than the GRR—the GRR of 1.039 is associated with a NRR of 1.023. Thus, in the United States the ratio of the NRR to the GRR of is 0.985. By contrast, in a high-mortality society such as Ethiopia, the difference can be substantial (the ratio of the NRR of 2.600 to the GRR of 3.700 is 0.700). As an index of generational replacement, an NRR of 1 indicates that each generation of females has the potential to just replace itself. This indicates a population that will eventually stop growing if fertility and mortality do not change. A value less than 1 indicates a potential decline in numbers, and a value greater than 1 indicates the potential for growth unless fertility and mortality change. It must be emphasized that the NRR is not equivalent to the rate of population growth in most societies. For example, in the United States the NRR in 2000 was almost exactly 1 (as I have just mentioned), yet the population was still increasing by more than 2.6 million people each year. The NRR represents the future potential for growth inherent in a population's fertility and mortality regimes. However, peculiarities in the age structure (such as a large number of women in the childbearing ages), as well as migration, affect the actual rate of growth at any point in time.

Measuring Migration

Migration is defined as any change in usual residence. Although definitions of migration have a certain arbitrariness to them, the change is usually taken to mean that you have stayed at your new residence for least 1 year, and implicit in the concept of migration is the idea that a person has moved far enough so that the usual round of daily activities in the new location does not overlap with those of the old location. A person who changes residence within the same area has experienced residential mobility, but is not a migrant. In the United States, a person who moves across county lines is typically considered to be a migrant, whereas a move within county boundaries is classified as residential mobility but not migration.

When data are available, migration is measured with rates that are similar to those constructed for fertility and mortality. Gross or total out-migration represents all people who leave a particular region during a given time period (usually a year), and so the gross rate of out-migration (OMigR) relates those people to the total mid-year population (p) in the region (and then we multiply by 1000):

$$\mathrm{OMigR} = \frac{\mathrm{OM}}{p} \times 1000 \qquad (25)$$

Similarly, the gross rate of in-migration (IMigR) is the ratio of all people who moved into the region during a given year to the total mid-year population in that region:

$$\mathrm{IMigR} = \frac{\mathrm{IM}}{p} \times 1000 \qquad (26)$$

The gross rate of in-migration is a little misleading because the mid-year population refers to the people living in the area of destination, which is not the group of people at risk of moving in (indeed, they are precisely the people who are *not* at risk of moving in because they are already there). Nonetheless, the in-migration rate does provide a sense of the impact that in-migration has on the region in question, and so it is useful for that reason alone.

The difference between those who move in and those who move out is called net migration. If these numbers are the same, then the net migration is 0, even if there has been a lot of migration activity. If there are more in-migrants than out-migrants, the net migration is positive; and if the out-migrants exceed the in-migrants, the net migration is negative. The crude net migration rate (CNMigR) is thus the net number of migrants in a year per 1000 people in a population and is calculated as follows:

$$\text{CNMigR} = \text{IMigR} - \text{OMigR} \tag{27}$$

The total volume of migration also may be of interest to the researcher because it can have a substantial impact on a community even if the net rate is low. This is measured as the total migration rate (TmigR), which is the sum of in-migrants and out-migrants divided by the mid-year population:

$$\text{TMigR} = \text{IMigR} + \text{OMigR} \tag{28}$$

Migration effectiveness (E) measures how effective the total volume of migration is in redistributing the population. For example, if there were a total of 10 migrants in a region in a year and all 10 were in-migrants, the effectiveness of migration would be 10/10, or 100%; whereas if four were in-migrants and six were out-migrants, the effectiveness would be much lower: (4 − 6)/10, or −20%. In general, the rate of effectiveness is as follows:

$$E = \frac{\text{CNMigR}}{\text{TMigR}} \times 100 \tag{29}$$

There is no universally agreed-on measure of migration that summarize the overall levels in the same way that the TFR summarizes fertility and life expectancy summarizes mortality. However, one way of measuring the contribution that migration makes to population growth is to calculate the ratio of net migration to natural increase (the difference between births and deaths), and this is called the migration ratio (MigRatio):

$$\text{MigRatio} = \frac{\text{IM} - \text{OM}}{b - d} \times 1000 \tag{30}$$

The U.S. Immigration and Naturalization Service (INS) estimates that between 1990 and 2000 there were 9,095,417 legal immigrants admitted to the United States and that an additional 1,500,000 people entered the country illegally, for a total of 10,595,417 immigrants. The INS also estimates that 2,674,000 people migrated out of the United States. Thus, the net number of international migrants was 7,921,417. During this same 10-year interval there were 39,865,670 births and 22,715,464 deaths, so the natural increase amounted to the addition of 17,150,206 people. Dividing the net migration by the natural increase produces a ratio of 462 migrants added to the American population during the decade of the 1990s for each 1000 people added through natural increase. Looked at another way, migrants accounted for 32% of the total population growth in the United States during that period of time.

We can also calculate intercensus net migration rates for each age group and gender by combining census data with life-table probabilities of survival—a procedure called the forward survival (or residual) method of migration estimation. For example, in 1990 in the United States there were 17,996,033 females ages 15–24. Life-table values suggest that 99.56% of those women (or 17,916,850) should still have been alive at ages 25–34 in 2000. In fact, Census 2000 counted 20,083,131 women in that age group, or 2,166,281 more than expected. We assume, then, that those extra people (the residual) were immigrants. This assumption of course ignores any part of that difference that might have been due to differences in the coverage error in the two censuses. If one census undercounted the population more or less than the next census, then this could account for at least part of the residual that is otherwise being attributed to migration. Conversely, if we knew the number of migrants, then the difference between the actual and expected number of migrants would tell us something about the accuracy of the census.

Measuring the Age and Sex Structure of a Population

Births occur only at age zero and only to women; deaths can occur at any age, but are concentrated in the youngest and oldest ages and tend to occur with greater frequency among men than women; and migration can occur at any age, although it is concentrated among young adults, and especially among men. These variations in the three demographic processes affect the age and sex structure of every society, which in turn affects how the society works. Changes in any of the demographic processes influence the age and sex structure and thus affect the social structure.

Sex Structure

Migration, mortality, and fertility operate differently to create inequalities in the ratio of males to females, and this measure is known as the sex ratio (SR):

$$\text{SR} = \frac{M}{F} \times 100 \tag{31}$$

A sex ratio that is greater than 100 thus means that there are more males than females, whereas a value of less than 100 indicates that there are more females than males. The ratio can obviously be calculated for the entire population or for specific age groups.

Age Structure

At any given moment, a cross section of all cohorts defines the current age strata in a society. Figure 1 displays the

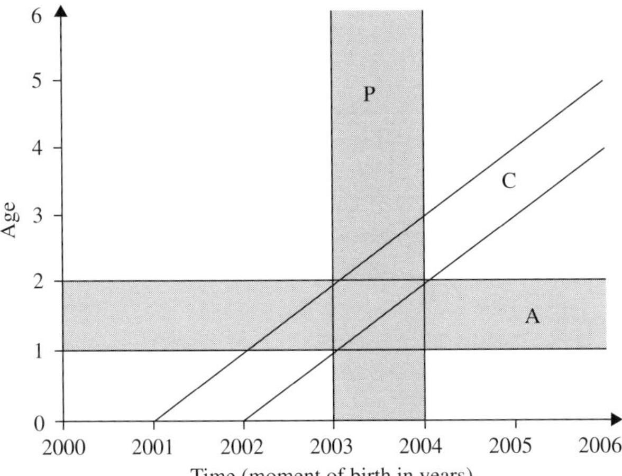

Figure 1 Lexis diagram. A, age (area represents children age 1, between their first and second birthdays); C, cohort (area represents aging over time of people born in 2001, between January 1 and December 31); P, period (area represents people of all ages in 2003, between January 1 and December 31). Permission to Population, An Introduction to Concepts and Issues (Non-InfoTrac Version) 8th edition, by Weeks, copyright © 2002 Wadsworth, a division of Thomson Learning, has been granted to John Weeks for class use. All rights reserved. Aside from this specific exception, no part of this book may be reproduced, stored in a retrieval system, or transcribed in any form or by any means—electronic, mechanical, photocopying, recording or otherwise—without permission in writing from Thomson Learning Global Rights Group: www.thomsonrights.com. Fax 800 739-2215.

Lexis diagram, a tool often used in population studies to help discern the difference between period data (the cross-sectional snapshot of all ages at one time) and cohorts (of which there are many at any one point in time). The diagram is named for a German demographer, Wilhelm Lexis, who helped to develop it in the nineteenth century as an aid to the analysis of life-table data. Age is shown on the vertical axis and time (the moment of birth in years) is shown along the horizontal axis. The cohort of people born in 2001 (starting at 2001 and ending just at 2002) advances through life along an upward (increasingly older) trajectory, which is represented by the area C in Fig. 1.

In Fig. 1, the period data, cross-cutting many cohorts but including all ages, is illustrated by the shaded area P, whereas a comparison of people at the same age across many cohorts over time is represented by the shaded area. Researchers use the Lexis diagram to visualize and interpret the calculation of age-period-cohort (APC) rates that disentangle the combination of influences of things that are specific to a particular age, things are unique to a time in history (the period effect), and things that are unique to specific birth cohorts (the cohort flow effect). Lung cancer, for example, is more likely to kill people at older ages (the age effect), but death rates from it will depend partly on when a person was diagnosed (the period effect influenced by the timing of new treatments for the disease) and partly on cohort effects (cohorts born in the 1920s through the 1940s were more likely to be cigarette smokers than were earlier or later cohorts).

A population is considered old or young depending on the proportion of people at different ages. In general, a population with approximately 35% or more of its people under age 15 is considered to be "young," and a population with approximately 12% or more of its people aged 65 or older is considered to be "old." Further, as the proportion of young people increases relative to the total, we speak of the population as growing younger. Conversely, an aging population is one in which the proportion of older people is increasing relative to the total.

Age Pyramids

An age pyramid (also known as a population pyramid) is a graphical representation of the distribution of a population by age and sex. It can graph either the total number of people at each age or the percentage of people at each age. It is called a pyramid because the classic picture is of a high-fertility, high-mortality society (which characterized most of the world until only several decades ago) with a broad base built of numerous births, rapidly tapering to the top (the older ages) because of high death rates in combination with the high birth rate. Nigeria's age and sex structure as of the year 2000 reflects the classic look of the population pyramids, as shown in Fig. 2A. Developed countries such as the United States have age and sex distributions that are more rectangular or barrel-shaped (see Fig. 2B), but the graph is still called an age pyramid.

Average Age and Dependency Ratio

The average age and dependency ratio are two measures that summarize the age structure in a single number. The average age in a population is generally calculated as the median, which measures the age above which is found one-half the population and below which is the other half. In Fig. 2, the population pyramids of Nigeria and the United States reflect median ages of 17.4 and 35.7, respectively. Thus, the obvious differences in the shapes of the age distributions for less-developed and more-developed countries are reflected in the clear differences in median ages.

The dependency ratio (DR) is an index commonly used to measure the social and economic impact of different age structures—it is the ratio of the dependent-age population (the young and the old) to the working-age

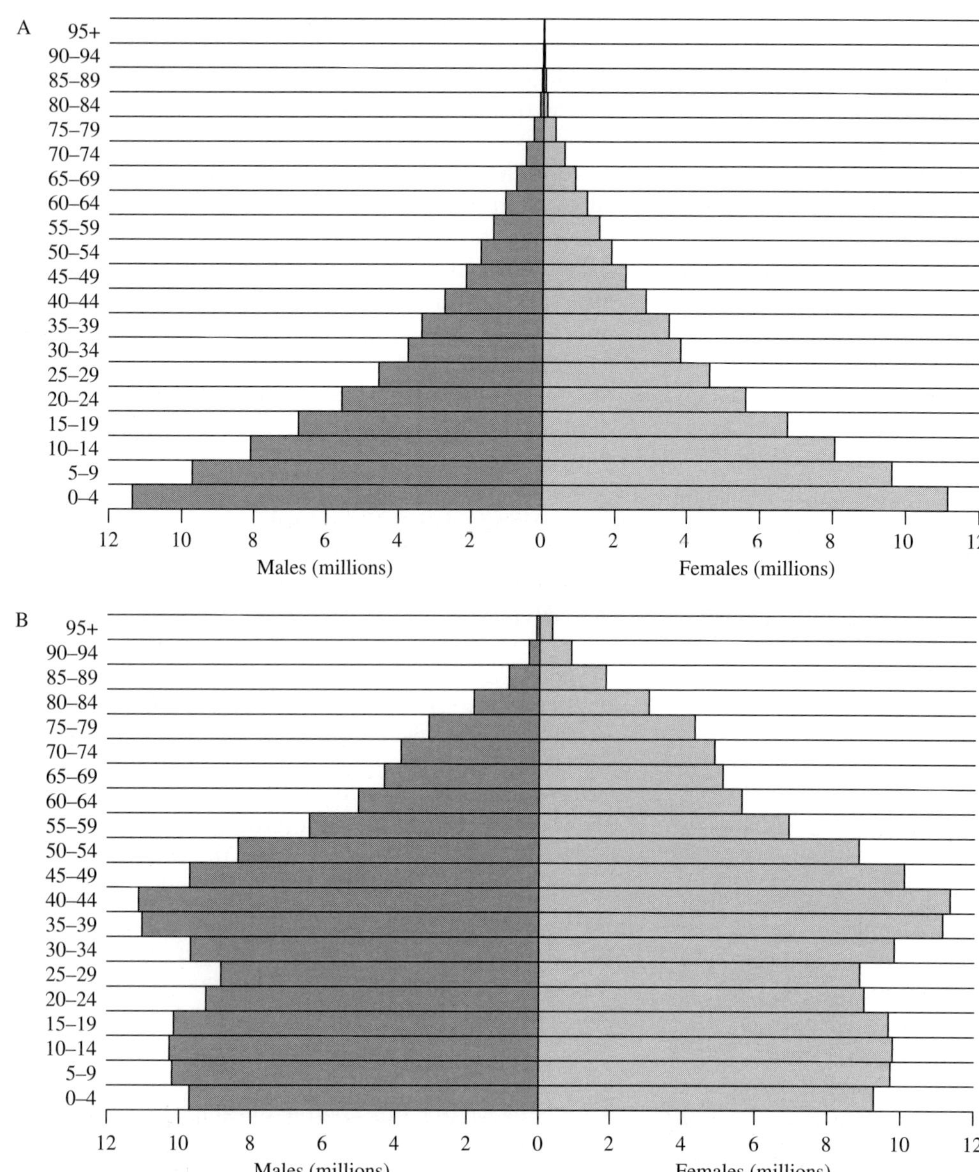

Figure 2 Age pyramids. (A) Nigeria 2000. (B) United States 2000. Permission to Population, An Introduction to Concepts and Issues (Non-InfoTrac Version) 8th edition, by Weeks, copyright © 2002 Wadsworth, a division of Thomson Learning, has been granted to John Weeks for class use. All rights reserved. Aside from this specific exception, no part of this book may be reproduced, stored in a retrieval system, or transcribed in any form or by any means—electronic, mechanical, photocopying, recording or otherwise—without permission in writing from Thomson Learning Global Rights Group: www.thomsonrights.com. Fax 800 739-2215.

population. The higher this ratio is, the more people each potential worker has to support; conversely, the lower it is, the fewer people each worker has to support. The DR is calculated as follows:

$$\mathrm{DR} = \frac{{}_{15}p_0 + {}_{\infty}p_{65}}{{}_{50}p_{15}} \times 100 \qquad (32)$$

where ${}_{15}p_0$ denotes the population between the ages of 0 and 14, ${}_{\infty}p_{65}$ denotes the population ages 65 and higher, and ${}_{50}p_{15}$ denotes the population from ages 15 to 64 (e.g., a lower limit of 15 and an interval width of 50). Nigeria, for example, has 48% of the population of dependent age (0–14 and 65+) compared with the remaining 52% of working age. Thus, the DR is 48/52 or 0.92, which, when multiplied by 100 means that there are 92 dependents per 100 working-age people. By contrast, in the United States, 19% are under 15, 13% are 65 or over, and the remainder (68%) are of working age. This produces a DR of 32/68 or 0.42, which when multiplied by 100 means that there are only 47 dependents per 100 working-age people.

The long-term dynamics of an age structure are conveniently laid out by formal demographic models called stable and stationary populations. A stable population is one in which neither the age-specific birth rates nor the age-specific death rates have changed for a long time, assuming that there is neither in- nor out-migration. A stable population is stable in the sense that the percentages of people at each age and sex do not change over time. However, a stable population could be growing at a constant rate (that is, the birth rate could be higher than the death rate), it could be declining at a constant rate (the birth rate could be lower than the death rate), or it could be unchanging (the birth rate could equal the death rate). This last is the case of zero population growth (ZPG), and if it prevails we call this a stationary population. Thus, a stationary population is a special case of a stable population—all stationary populations are stable, but not all stable populations are stationary.

Population Projections

A population projection is the calculation of the number of people who could be alive at a future date given the number now alive and given assumptions about the future course of mortality, fertility, and migration. In many respects, population projections are the single most useful set of tools available in demographic analysis. By enabling researchers to see what the future size and composition of the population might be under varying assumptions about trends in mortality, fertility and migration, it is possible intelligently to evaluate what the likely course of events might be many years from now. Also, by projecting the population forward through time from some point in history, it is possible to speculate on the sources of change in the population over time. It is useful to distinguish projections from forecasts. A population forecast is a statement about what the future population is expected to be. This is different from a projection, which is a statement about what the future population could be under a given set of assumptions. There are two principal ways to project populations: (1) extrapolation methods and (2) the cohort component method.

Extrapolation

Extrapolation methods are an adaptation of Eq. (1). It assumes that some rate of growth will hold constant between the base year (P_1—the population in the beginning year of a population projection) and the target year (the year to which a population is projected forward in time). We then calculate the projected population at time 2 (P_2) as follows:

$$p_2 = p_1 \times e^{rn} \qquad (33)$$

If P_1 is the population of the United States in 2000 (281,421,916) and it is assumed that the rate of population growth between 1990 and 2000 (1.2357% per year) will continue until 2050, then the projected population in the year 2050 (P_2) will be 522,014,164. Actually, we would rarely use this method for national projections, but it can be used for local areas where data are not available on births, deaths, and migration.

Cohort Component Method

The extrapolation methods of population projection do not take into account births, deaths, or migration. If assumptions can be made about the trends in these demographic processes, then the population can be projected using the more sophisticated cohort component method. This method begins with a distribution of the population by age and sex (in absolute frequencies, not percentages) for a specific base year. The method also requires age-specific mortality rates (that is, a base-year and intermediate-year life table); age-specific fertility rates; and, if possible, age-specific rates of in- and out-migration. Cohorts are usually arranged in 5-year groups, such as ages 0–4, 5–9, 10–14, and so on, which facilitates projecting a population forward in time in 5-year intervals. The projection then is undertaken with matrix algebra.

See Also the Following Articles

Age, Period, and Cohort Effects • Attrition, Mortality, and Exposure Time • Longitudinal Cohort Designs • Mathematical Demography • Population vs. Sample

Further Reading

Chiang, C. (1984). *The Life Table and Its Applications.* Krieger, Melbourne, FL.

Hinde, A. (1998). *Demographic Methods.* Oxford University Press, New York.

Murdock, S. H., and Ellis, D. R. (1991). *Applied Demography: An Introduction to Basic Concepts, Methods, and Data.* Westview Press, Boulder, CO.

Palmore, J., and Gardner, R. (1983). *Measuring Mortality, Fertility, and Natural Increase.* East-West Population Institute, Honolulu, HI.

Plane, D., and Rogerson, P. (1994). *The Geographical Analysis of Population: With Applications to Planning and Business.* John Wiley & Sons, New York.

Preston, S. H., Heuveline, P., and Guillot, M. (2001). *Demography: Measuring and Modeling Population Processes.* Blackwell Publishers, Oxford.

Shryock, H., Siegel, J., *et al.* (1976). *The Methods and Materials of Demography.* Condensed by E. Stockwell. Academic Press, New York.

Siegel, J. S. (2002). *Applied Demography: Applications to Business, Government, Law, and Public Policy.* Academic Press, San Diego, CA.

Smith, D. P. (1992). *Formal Demography.* Plenum, New York.

Smith, S., Tayman, J., and Swanson, D. (2001). *Population Projections for States and Local Areas: Methodology and Analysis.* Plenum Press, New York.

Weeks, J. R. (2005). *Population: An Introduction to Concepts and Issues,* 9th Ed. Wadsworth, Belmont, CA.

Descriptive and Inferential Statistics

Paul A. Jargowsky

University of Texas, Dallas, Richardson, Texas, USA

Rebecca Yang

University of Texas, Dallas, Texas, USA

Glossary

bootstrapping A resampling procedure to empirically estimate standard errors.

central tendency The dominant quantitative or qualitative trend of a given variable (commonly measured by the mean, the median, the mode, and related measures).

confidence interval A numeric range, based on a statistic and its sampling distribution, that contains the population parameter of interest with a specified probability.

data A plural noun referring to a collection of information in the form of variables and observations.

descriptive statistics Any of numerous calculations that attempt to provide a concise summary of the information content of data (for example, measures of central tendency and measures of dispersion).

dispersion The tendency of observations of a variable to deviate from the central tendency (commonly measured by the variance, the standard deviation, the interquartile range, etc.).

inferential statistics The science of drawing valid inferences about a population based on a sample.

level of measurement A characterization of the information content of a variable; for example, variables may be qualitative (nominal or interval) or quantitative (interval or ratio).

parameter The true value of a descriptive measure in the population of interest.

population The total collection of actual and/or potential realizations of the unit of analysis, whether observed or not.

sample A specific, finite, realized set of observations of the unit of analysis.

sampling distribution A theoretical construct describing the behavior of a statistic in repeated samples.

statistic A descriptive measure calculated from sample data to serve as an estimate of an unknown population parameter.

unit of analysis The type of thing being measured in the data, such as persons, families, households, states, and nations.

There are two fundamental reasons for analyzing data: the first is to describe a large number of data points in a concise way by means of one or more summary statistics; the second is to draw inferences about the characteristics of a population based on the characteristics of a sample. Descriptive statistics characterize the distribution of a set of observations on a specific variable or variables. By conveying the essential properties of the aggregation of many different observations, these summary measures make it possible to understand the phenomenon under study better and more quickly than would be possible by studying a multitude of unprocessed individual values. Inferential statistics allow one to draw conclusions about the unknown parameters of a population based on statistics that describe a sample from that population. Very often, mere description of a set of observations in a sample is not the goal of research. The data on hand are usually only a sample of the actual population of interest, possibly a minute sample of the population. For example, most presidential election polls sample only approximately 1000 individuals and yet the goal is to describe the expected voting behavior of 100 million or more potential voters.

Descriptive Statistics

A number of terms have specialized meaning in the domain of statistics. First, there is the distinction between populations and samples. Populations can be finite or infinite. An example of the former is the population of the United States on April 15, 2000, the date of the Census. An example of the latter is the flipping of a coin, which can be repeated in theory *ad infinitum*. Populations have parameters, which are fixed but usually unknown. Samples are used to produce statistics, which are estimates of population parameters. This section discusses both parameters and statistics and the following section discusses the validity of using statistics as estimates of population parameters.

There are also a number of important distinctions to be made about the nature of the data to be summarized. The characteristics of data to be analyzed limit the types of measures that can be meaningfully employed. Some of the most important of these issues are addressed below.

Forms of Data

All statistics are based on data, which are composed of one or more variables that represent the characteristics of one or more of the type of thing being studied. A variable consists of a defined measurement. The type of thing on which the measurements are taken is called the unit of analysis. For example, the unit of analysis could be individual people, but it could also be families, households, neighborhoods, cities, nations, or galaxies.

The collection of all measurements for one realization of the unit of analysis is typically called an observation. If there are n observations and k variables, then the data set can be thought of as a grid with $n \times k$ total items of information, although more complex structures are possible.

It is absolutely central to conducting and interpreting data analysis to be clear about the unit of analysis. For example, if one observes that 20% of all *crimes* are violent in nature, it does not imply that 20% of all *criminals* are violent criminals. Crimes, though obviously related, are simply a different unit of analysis than criminals; a few really violent criminals could be committing all the violent crimes, so that less than 20% of criminals are violent in nature.

Levels of Measurement

A variable is something that varies between observations, at least potentially, but not all variables vary in the same way. The specific values that a variable can take on, also known as attributes, convey information about the differences between observations on the dimension measured by the variable. So, for example, two persons differ on the variable "income" if one's income is \$100,000 and the other's is \$200,000. They also differ on the variable "sex" if one is male and the other is female. But the nature of the information conveyed by the two variables is quite different. For one thing, the incomes can be ranked, but the individuals' sexes cannot be ranked. One can say that one individual has twice as much income as the other but there is no comparable statement regarding the individuals' sexes. There are four main types of variables, in two distinct categories, ordered from the highest level of measurement to the lowest.

- Quantitative variables are measured on a continuous scale. In theory, there are an infinite number of potential attributes for a quantitative variable.
    - Ratio variables are quantitative variables that have a true zero. The existence of a true zero makes the ratio of two measures meaningful. For example, one can say that for the example given above, one individual's income is twice the other individual's income because \$200,000/\$100,000 = 2.
    - Interval variables are quantitative as well, but lack a true zero. Temperature is a common example: the zero point is arbitrary and in fact differs between the Centigrade and Fahrenheit systems. It does not make sense to say that 80°F is twice as hot as 40°F; in Centigrade, the ratio would be 6; neither ratio is meaningful.
- Qualitative (or categorical) variables are discrete; that is, a measurement consists of assigning an observation to one or more categories. The attributes of the variable consist of the finite set of potential categories. The set of categories must be mutually exclusive and collectively exhaustive. That is, each observation can be assigned to one and only one category.
    - In ordinal variables, the categories have an intrinsic order. Sears and Roebuck, for example, classifies its tools in three categories: good, better, and best. They have no numerical relation; one does not know if better is twice as good as good, but they clearly can be ordered.
    - In nominal variables, the categories have no intrinsic order. A variable for Religion, for example, could consist of the following set of categories: Catholic, Protestant, Hindu, Muslim, and "Other." Note that a category like Other often needs to be included to make the category set collectively exhaustive. Of course, a far more detailed set of categories could be devised depending on the needs of the researcher. One could rank these categories based on other variables, such as the number of adherents or age since inception, but the categories themselves have no intrinsic order.

The issue of coding of categorical variables merits further discussion. Frequently, the attributes of a categorical variable are represented numerically. For example, a variable for region may be coded in a data set as follows: 1 represents north, 2 represents south, and so on. It is essential to understand that these numbers are arbitrary and serve merely to distinguish one category from another.

A special type of categorical variable is the dummy variable, which indicates the presence or absence of a specified characteristic. A dummy variable is therefore a nominal variable containing only two categories: one for "yes" and one for "no." Female is one example; pregnant is an even better example. Typically, such variables are coded as 1 if the person has the characteristic described by the name of the variable and 0 otherwise; such coding simplifies the interpretation of analyses that may later be performed on the variable. Of course, other means of coding are possible, since the actual values used to indicate categories are arbitrary.

The level of measurement describes how much information is conveyed about the differences between observations, with the highest level conveying the greatest amount of information. Data gathered at a higher level can be expressed at any lower level; however, the reverse is not true.

Time Structure

Data always have a time structure, whether time is a variable in the data or not. The most fundamental distinction is between cross-sectional data and longitudinal data. In cross-sectional data, there is one set of measurements of multiple observations on the relevant variables taken at approximately the same point in time.

In longitudinal data, measurements are taken at multiple points in time. Longitudinal data can be further divided into several types.

- Trend data are data on one object, repeated at two or more points in time, for example, a data set consisting of the inflation, unemployment, and poverty rates for the United States for each year from 1960 to 2003.
- Cohort data are data consisting of observations from two or more points in time, but with no necessary connection between the individual observations across time, for example, a data set consisting of the incomes and ages of a sample of persons in 1970, a different sample of persons in 1980, and so on. With such a data set, one could compare the incomes of 20 to 29 year olds in one decade to the same age group in other decades. One could also compare the incomes of 20 to 29 year olds in 1970 to that of 30 to 39 year olds in 1980, 40 to 49 year olds in 1990, and so on, if one wanted see how the incomes of a single group changed over time.
- Panel data consist of measurements conducted at multiple points in time on two or more different realizations of the unit of analysis, for example, one can observe the income and marital status of a set of persons every year from 1968 to 2003. "Panel" is a metaphor for the grid-like structure of the data: there are n persons observed at t different points in time, forming a panel with $n \times t$ cells, and each of these cells consists of k variables. Panel data are very powerful, because they enable a researcher to observe the temporal order of events for individual persons, strengthening causal inferences that the researcher may wish to draw.

With these basic concepts in hand, the most common descriptive statistics can be explored.

Measures of Central Tendency

The term "average," as it is used in common discourse, is imprecise. Nevertheless, individuals can communicate perfectly well despite this imprecision. For example, the following exchange is perfectly clear:

"Is he a good student?"
"No, he's just average."

For data analysis, however, the concept of average must be defined more precisely. The concept of average refers to the central tendency of the distribution of scores on a given variable.

There are three main measures of central tendency:

- The mode is simply the most frequently occurring single value. For example, the modal racial group in the United states is white, because there are more whites than any other racial group.
- The median is the value of the middle observation, when the observations are sorted from the least to the greatest in terms of their value on the variable in question. The median is not at all sensitive to extreme values. One could multiply all values above the median by a factor of 10, and the median of the distribution would not be affected. For this reason, the median is often used to summarize data for variables where there are extreme outliers. Newspapers typically report the median value of home sales.
- The arithmetic mean, indicated by μ for a population and by $\bar{X}$ for a sample, is the most common measure of central tendency and is the sum of the variable across all the N observations in a population or across all n observations in a sample, divided by the number of observations:

$$\mu_X = \frac{\sum_{i=1}^{N} X_i}{N}, \qquad \bar{X} = \frac{\sum_{i=1}^{n} X_i}{n}.$$

Because each observation's value is included in the calculation, the mean is sensitive to and reflects the presence of extreme values in the data. The formulas for a population and the sample are identical from a computational standpoint, but the former is a population parameter and the latter is a statistic based on a sample.

The level of measurement of the variable determines which of the many measures of central tendency can be calculated. A mode may be calculated for any variable, whether nominal, ordinal, interval, or ratio. However, it is most useful for nominal variables, in that it indicates which of the categories occurs the most frequently. In contrast, the median requires a ranking of all observations, so that it is not possible to calculate a median of a nominal variable. The lowest level of measurement for which a median can be calculated is ordinal. The mean requires quantitative values that can be summed over all observations.

Note that the actual level of measurement is the limiting factor on which statistics are meaningful, not the coding system. If a variable for the day of the week that a crime is committed is coded as 0 = Sunday, 1 = Monday, and so on, it is still a nominal variable. Any computer will happily calculate that the mean of the variable is approximately 3.5; however, this number is meaningless. The average crime is not committed on a Wednesday and a half. Although this example is clear, it is fairly common that researchers calculate the means of ordinal variables, such as Likert scales, which are coded 1 for "strongly disagree," 2 for "disagree," and so on up to 5 for "strongly agree." Strictly speaking, this is an invalid calculation.

One interesting exception is that one can calculate the mean for dummy variables. Because they are coded as 1 if the characteristic is present and 0 otherwise, the sum of the variable—the numerator for the calculation of the mean—is simply the count of the observations that have the characteristic. Dividing by the total number of observations results in the proportion of observations sharing the trait. Thus, the mean of a dummy variable is a proportion.

There is no one right answer to the question of which measure of central tendency is correct. Each conveys slightly different information that may be more or less useful or appropriate depending on the question being addressed.

There is a variety of real-world complications that must be taken into account when calculating any descriptive statistic. It is paramount to correctly identify the complete universe of the statistic to be calculated. For example, in calculating the mean wage, how should people who do not work be handled? For some purposes, one might treat them as having a wage of zero, but for other purposes, this could be quite misleading, because one does not know what their wages would have been if they had been working.

There is a number of variations on the concept of mean that may be useful in specialized situations, for example, the geometric mean, which is the nth root of the product of all observations, and the harmonic mean, which is the reciprocal of the arithmetic mean of the reciprocals of the values on the variable. There are numerous variations of the arithmetic mean as well, including means for grouped data, weighted means, and trimmed means. Interested readers should consult a statistics textbook for further information on these alternative calculations and their applications.

Measures of Variability

Variety may be the spice of life, but variation is the very meat of science. Variation between observations opens the door to analysis of causation and ultimately to understanding. To say that variation is important for data analysis is an understatement of the highest order; without variation, there would no mysteries and no hope of unraveling them. The point of data analysis is to understand the world; the point of understanding the world is the differences between things. Why is one person rich and another poor? Why is the United States rich and Mexico poor? Why does one cancer patient respond to a treatment, but another does not?

It is no accident, therefore, that this most central pillar of science has a variety of measures that differ both in the details of their calculations and, more importantly, in their conceptual significance.

In the world of measures of variability, also called dispersion or spread tendency, the greatest divide runs between measures based on the position of observations versus measures based on deviations from a measure of central tendency, usually the arithmetic mean. A third, less common, group of measures is based on the frequency of occurrence of different attributes of a variable.

Positional measures of variation are based on percentiles of a distribution; the xth percentile of a distribution is defined as the value that is higher than $x\%$ of all the observations. The 25th percentile is also known as the first quartile and the 75th percentile is referred to as the third quartile. Percentile-based measures of variability are typically paired with the median as a measure of central tendency; after all, the median is the 50th percentile.

Deviation-based measures, in contrast, focus on a summary of some function of the quantitative distance of each observation from a measure of central tendency. Such measures are typically paired with a mean of one sort or another as a measure of central tendency. As in the case of central tendency, it is impossible to state whether position-based or deviation-based measures provide the best measure of variation; the answer will always depend on the nature of the data and the nature of the question being asked.

Measures of Variability Based on Position

For quantitative variables, the simplest measure of variability is the range, which is the difference between the maximum and minimum values of a variable. For obvious reasons, this measure is very sensitive to extreme values. Better is the interquartile range, which is the distance between the 25th and 75th percentiles. As such, it is completely insensitive to any observation above or below those two points, respectively.

Measures of Variability Based on Deviations

The sum of the deviations from the arithmetic mean is always zero:

$$\sum_{i=1}^{N}(X_i - \mu) = \sum\left(X_i - \frac{\sum X_i}{N}\right)$$
$$= \sum X_i - N\left(\frac{\sum X_i}{N}\right) = 0.$$

Because the positive and negative deviations cancel out, measures of variability must dispense with the signs of the deviations; after all, a large negative deviation from the mean is as much of an indication of variability as a large positive deviation.

In practice, there are two methods to eradicate the negative signs: either taking the absolute value of the deviations or squaring the deviations. The mean absolute deviation is one measure of deviation, but it is seldom used. The primary measure of variability is, in effect, the mean squared deviation. For a population, the variance parameter of the variable X, denoted by σ_X^2, is defined as:

$$\sigma_X^2 = \frac{\sum_{i=1}^{N}(X_i - \mu)^2}{N}.$$

However, the units of the variance are different than the units of the mean or the data themselves. For example, the variance of wages is in the units of dollars squared, an odd concept. For this reason, it is more common for researchers to report the standard deviation, denoted by σ_X, which for a population is defined as:

$$\sigma_X = \sqrt{\frac{\sum_{i=1}^{N}(X_i - \mu)^2}{N}}.$$

Unlike the formulas for the population and sample means, there is an important computational difference between the formulas for the variance and standard deviation depending on whether one is dealing with a population or a sample. The formulas for the sample variance and sample standard deviation are as follows:

$$S_X^2 = \frac{\sum_{i=1}^{n}(X_i - \bar{X})^2}{n-1}, \qquad S_X = \sqrt{\frac{\sum_{i=1}^{n}(X_i - \bar{X})^2}{n-1}}.$$

Note that the divisor in these calculations is the sample size, n, minus 1. The reduction is necessary because the calculation of the sample mean used up some of the information that was contained in the data. Each time an estimate is calculated from a fixed number of observations, 1 degree of freedom is used up. For example, from a sample of 1 person, an estimate (probably a very bad one) of the mean income of the population could be obtained, but there would be no information left to calculate the population variance. One cannot extract two estimates from one data point. The correction for degrees of freedom enforces this restriction; in the example, the denominator would be zero and the sample standard deviation would be undefined.

The variance and the standard deviation, whether for populations or samples, should not be thought of as two different measures. They are two different ways of presenting the same information.

A final consideration is how the variability of two different samples or populations should be compared. A standard deviation of 50 points on a test means something different if the maximum score is 100 or 800. For this reason, it is often useful to consider the coefficient of relative variation, usually indicated by CV, which is equal to the standard deviation divided by the mean. The CV facilitates comparisons among standard deviations of heterogeneous groups by normalizing each by the appropriate mean.

Measures of Variability Based on Frequency

The calculation of interquartile ranges and standard deviations requires quantitative data. For categorical data, a different approach is needed. For such variables, there are measures of variability based on the frequency of occurrence of different attributes (values) of a variable.

The Index of Diversity (D) is one such measure. It is based on the proportions of the observations in each category of the qualitative variable. It is calculated as

$$D = 1 - \sum_{k=1}^{K} p_k^2,$$

where p_k is the proportion of observations in category k, and K is the number of categories. If there is no variation, all the observations are in one category and D equals 0. With greater diversity, the measure approaches 1.

Other Univariate Descriptive Statistics

Central tendency and variability are not the only univariate (single variable) descriptive statistics, but they are by far the most common. The skewness of a distribution indicates whether or not a distribution is symmetric. It is calculated using the third power of the deviations from the mean, which preserves the sign of the deviations and heavily emphasizes larger deviations. When skewness is zero, the distribution is said to be symmetric. A distribution with a long "tail" on one side is said to be skewed in that direction. When the distribution is skewed to the right, the skewness measure is positive; when it is skewed to the left, skewness is negative. Kurtosis, based on the 4th power of the deviations from the mean, gauges the thickness of the tails of the distribution relative to the normal distribution.

Association between Variables

All of the measures described above are univariate, in that they describe one variable at a time. However, there is a class of descriptive measures that describes the degree of association, or covariation, between two or more variables. One very important measure is the correlation coefficient, sometimes called Pearson's r. The correlation coefficient measures the degree of linear association between two variables. For the population parameter,

$$\rho = \frac{\sum_{i=1}^{N}(X_i - \mu_X)(Y_i - \mu_Y)}{\left(\sqrt{\sum_{i=1}^{N}(X_i - \mu_X)^2}\right)\left(\sqrt{\sum_{i=1}^{N}(Y_i - \mu_Y)^2}\right)}.$$

For the sample statistic,

$$r = \frac{\sum_{i=1}^{N}(X_i - \bar{X})(Y_i - \bar{Y})}{\left(\sqrt{\sum_{i=1}^{N}(X_i - \bar{X})^2}\right)\left(\sqrt{\sum_{i=1}^{N}(Y_i - \bar{Y})^2}\right)}.$$

Because both terms in the denominator are sums of squares and therefore always positive, the sign of the correlation coefficient is completely determined by the numerator, which is the product of the deviations from the respective means. These products are positive either when both deviations are positive or when both are negative. The product will be negative when the deviations have opposite signs, which will occur when one variable is above its mean and the other is below its mean. When there is a positive linear relationship between the variables, their deviations from their respective means will tend to have the same sign and the correlation will be positive. In contrast, when there is a negative linear relationship between the two variables, their deviations from their respective means will tend to have opposite signs and the correlation coefficient will be negative. If there is no linear relationship between the variables, the products of deviations with positive signs will tend to cancel out the products of deviations with negative signs and the correlation coefficient will tend toward zero.

Another feature of the correlation coefficient is that it is bounded by -1 and $+1$. For example, if $X = Y$, then they have an exact positive linear relationship. Substituting $X = Y$ into the formula yields $\rho = 1$. Similarly, if $X = -Y$, they have an exact negative linear relationship, and the correlation coefficient reduces to -1. Thus, the interpretation of the correlation coefficient is very simple: values close to 1 indicate strongly positive linear relationships, values close to -1 indicate strongly negative linear relationships, and values close to zero indicate that the variables have little or no linear relationship.

Inferential Statistics

On October 7, 2002, the *New York Times* reported that "Two-thirds of Americans say they approve of the United States using military power to oust [Iraqi leader Saddam] Hussein." This is an extraordinary claim, since it is obviously impossible to know precisely what 290 million people say about anything without conducting a full-scale census of the population. The claim by the *Times* was based on a telephone survey of only 668 adults nationwide, meaning that the times did not know what the remaining 289,999,332 Americans actually had to say about the impending war. To claim to know what is on the mind of the country as whole from such a small sample seems like utter madness or hubris run amok, even if they admit that their poll has "a margin of sampling error of plus or minus four percentage points."

In fact, they have a very sound basis for their claims, and under the right conditions they can indeed make valid inferences about the population as whole from their sample. Much of what one thinks one knows about this country's people and their attitudes—the poverty rate, the unemployment rate, the percentage who believe in God, the percentage who want to privatize Social Security, etc.—is information based on surveys of tiny fragments of the total population. This section briefly describes the essential logic of sampling theory and subsequent sections illustrate some of the most important applications.

Sampling Theory

Suppose one has a large population and one wishes to estimate the value of some variable in that population. The problem is that for financial or practical reasons, one can draw only a small sample from the population. There are parameters of the population that are unknown, such as the population mean, μ, and the population standard deviation, σ. Even the total size of the population, N, may not be known exactly. Through some selection process, one draws a sample. Based on the sample, one calculates the sample statistics, such as the sample mean and the sample standard deviation. The sample size, n, is known, but typically is minuscule compared to the population size.

The key question, as illustrated in Fig. 1, is how can one make a valid inference about the population parameters from the sample statistics? One usually does not care at all about the sample itself. Who cares what 668 individual people think about the prospect of war? Only the population values are of interest.

The first step is to understand the process for drawing the sample. If the sample is drawn in a biased fashion, one will not be about to draw any inference about the population parameters. If one's sample is drawn from

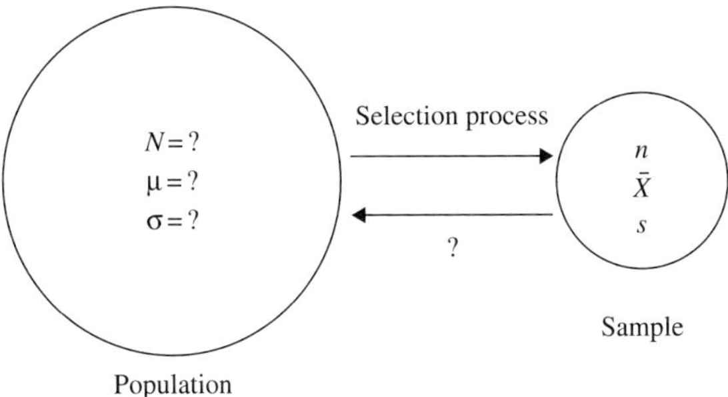

Figure 1 The inference problem.

West Point, or from a Quaker Meeting House, or is the result of a self-selection process where people vote on a Web site, it will not be possible to generalize to the population at large. At best, such a sample would allow one to generalize about cadets, or Quakers, or people who participate in Internet surveys.

One needs a sample that is representative of the population of interest. The easiest way to obtain one is to draw a truly random sample, in which each member of the population of interest has an equal chance of being selected. Even then, in any given sample, there is the possibility that one's sample statistic might be high or low relative to the true population parameter just by chance. Rarely, if ever, will the sample statistic be exactly the same as the population parameter. In order to make use of sample statistics, then, one must understand how sample statistics behave, that is, how often will they be too high or too low and by how much will they vary from the true value. Sampling theory provides the answers to these questions.

As a example, imagine that 55 students in a graduate statistics class are the population. The mean age of these students is the parameter one wishes to estimate. Each student writes his or her age on a 3 in. by 5 in. card and places the card in a box. The box is shaken and three of the cards are drawn at random. One obtains a value for the sample mean. Clearly, one does not know whether the sample statistic is too high or too low, but it seems doubtful that one would be so lucky that it is exactly right. Even if it was, one would not have any way of knowing it. One could draw a second sample, and a third. Each time, one would obtain a different sample mean, depending on which cards one happened to pick. Typically, if one actually tries this, the values will be quite different. At this point, one might be tempted to decide that sampling is utterly useless.

One might also be tempted to take the average of the three sample means and that leads to the solution. The key is to see that the sample mean is a random variable. The value of the sample mean depends on the outcome of a random process. Any random variable has a probability distribution, with a mean (or expectation) and a variance. In the case of the age example, if there are 55 students in the class, there are exactly 26,235 different combinations of

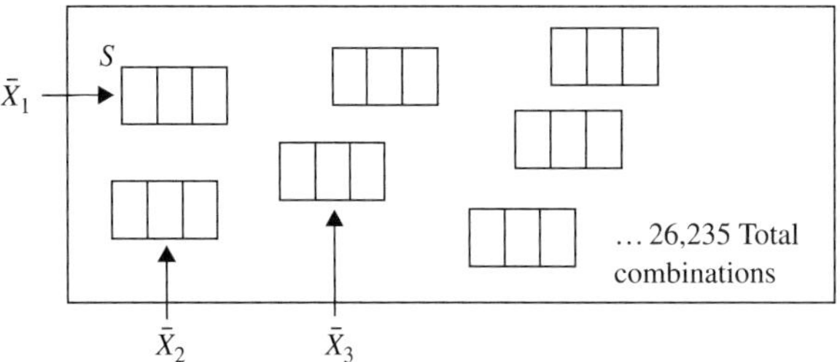

Figure 2 Samples of 3 drawn from a class of 55.

3 cards that can be drawn from the box. Figure 2 shows the sample space, containing all possible outcomes of the process of drawing 3 cards; each is equally likely and each outcome has a sample mean associated with it. All of these possible outcomes, considered together, make up the sampling distribution of the sample mean, that is, the probability distribution for the variable that records the result of drawing 3 cards from the box of 55 cards.

What is the mean of the distribution of these potential sample means? The Central Limit Theorem, the most important finding in all of statistics, provides the answer. The mean of the sample means is the population mean. Symbolically,

$$\mu_{\bar{X}} = \mu.$$

On the one hand, this is very good news. It says that any given sample mean is not biased. The expectation for a sample mean is equal to the population parameter one is trying to estimate. On the other hand, this information is not very helpful. The expectation of the sample mean just tells one what one could expect in the long run if one could keep drawing samples repeatedly. In most cases, however, one is able to draw only one sample. This one sample could still be high or low and thus it seems that no progress has been made.

However, progress has been made. The sample mean, as a random variable, also has a variance and a standard deviation. The Central Limit Theorem also states that:

$$\sigma^2_{\bar{X}} = \frac{\sigma^2}{n}; \quad \text{therefore,} \quad \sigma_{\bar{X}} = \frac{\sigma}{\sqrt{n}}.$$

This formula states that the degree of variation in sample means is determined by only two factors, the underlying variability in the population and the sample size. If there is little variability in the population itself, there will be little variation in the sample means. If all the students in the class are 24 years of age, each and every sample drawn from that population will also be 24; if there is great variability in the ages of the students, there is also the potential for great variability in the sample means, but that variability will unambiguously decline as the sample size, n, grows larger. The standard deviation of the sample means is referred to as the standard error of the mean. Note that the size of the population does not matter, just the size of the sample. Thus, a sample size of 668 out of 100,000 yields estimates that are just as accurate as samples of 668 out of 290 million.

The Central Limit Theorem provides one additional piece of information about the distribution of the sample mean. If the population values of the variable X are normally distributed, then the distribution of the sample mean of X will also be normally distributed. More importantly, even if X is not at all normally distributed, the distribution of the sample mean of X will approach normality as the sample size approaches infinity. As a matter of fact, even with relatively small samples of 30 observations, the distribution of the sample mean will approximate normality, regardless of the underlying distribution of the variable itself.

One thus has a complete description of the probability distribution of the sample mean, also known as the sampling distribution of the mean. The sampling distribution is a highly abstract concept, yet it is the key to understanding how one can drawn a valid inference about a population of 290 million from a sample of only 668 persons. The central point to understand is that the unit of analysis in the sampling distribution is the sample mean. In contrast, the unit of analysis in the population and the sample is, in this case, people. The sample mean, assuming a normally distributed population or a large enough sample, is a normally distributed random variable.

This property of the sample mean enables one to make fairly specific statements about how often and by how much it will deviate from its expectation, the true population mean. In general, a normally distributed random variable will take on values within 1.96 standard deviations of the variable's mean approximately 95% of the time. In this case, the standard deviation of sample means is called the standard error, and the mean of the sample means is equal to the underlying population mean.

Concretely, the normality of the sampling distribution implies that the probability is 0.95 that a randomly chosen sample will have a sample mean that is within 1.96 standard errors of the true population mean, assuming that the conditions for normality of the sampling distribution are met. And therefore it follows, as night follows day, that the probability must also be 0.95 that the true population mean is within 2 standard errors of whatever sample mean one obtains in a given sample. Mathematically,

$$\Pr\left[\left(\mu - 1.96\frac{\sigma}{\sqrt{n}}\right) < \bar{X} < \left(\mu + 1.96\frac{\sigma}{\sqrt{n}}\right)\right] = 0.95$$

implies that

$$\Pr\left[\left(\bar{X} - 1.96\frac{\sigma}{\sqrt{n}}\right) < \mu < \left(\bar{X} + 1.96\frac{\sigma}{\sqrt{n}}\right)\right] = 0.95.$$

One can derive the second formula from the first mathematically, but the logic is clear: if New York is 100 miles from Philadelphia, then Philadelphia is 100 miles from New York. If there is a 95% probability that the sample mean will be within 1.96 standard errors of the true mean, then the probability that the true mean is 1.96 standard errors of the sample mean is also 95%. The first statement describes the behavior of the sample mean as a random variable, but the latter statement provides truly useful information: an interval that includes the unknown population mean 95% of the time. This interval is known as the 95% confidence interval for the mean. Other levels of confidence, e.g., 90% and 99% may be selected, in which case the 1.96 must be replaced by a different figure, but 95% is by far the most common choice.

A simpler and more common way of writing the 95% confidence interval is to provide the point estimate (PE) plus or minus the margin of error (ME), as follows:

$$\text{PE} \pm \text{ME}, \qquad \text{for example, } \bar{X} \pm (1.96)\frac{\sigma}{\sqrt{n}}.$$

The point estimate is simply an unbiased sample statistic and is the best guess about the true value of the population parameter. The margin of error is based on the distribution of the sample statistic, which in this example is a normal distribution. Thus, a distributional parameter of 1.96, based on the normal distribution, and the standard error of the estimator generate the margin of error.

One practical issue needs to be resolved. If the mean of the variable X is unknown, then it is quite likely that the standard deviation of X is also unknown. Thus, one will need to use the sample standard deviation, s, in place of the population standard deviation, σ, in calculating the confidence interval. Of course, s is also a random variable and introduces more uncertainty into the estimation and therefore the confidence interval will have to be wider. In place of the normal distribution threshold of 1.96, one will have to use the corresponding threshold from the t distribution with the same degrees of freedom that were used to calculate s—that is, the sample size minus 1. One can think of this as the penalty one must pay for being uncertain about the variance of the underlying variable. The fewer the degrees of freedom, the larger the penalty. For samples much greater than 30, the Student's t distribution effectively converges to the normal and the penalty becomes inconsequential.

Figure 3 summarizes the theory of sampling. One has a population with unknown parameters. One draws a single sample and calculates the relevant sample statistics. The theoretical construct of the sampling distribution, based on the Central Limit Theorem, is what enables one to make an inference back to the population. For any estimator of any population parameter, the sample by itself is useless and would not support inferences about the population. Only by reference to the sampling distribution of the estimator can valid inferences be drawn. Thus, one must understand the properties of the sampling distribution of the statistic of interest. The following section describes some of the most commonly encountered statistics and their sampling distributions.

Common Sampling Distributions

All statistics are estimators of population parameters that are calculated from samples and therefore all statistics are random variables. Table I describes the essential features of the sampling distributions of the most common estimators.

The expected value, variance, and shape of some estimators are not known. For example, there is no known analytic solution for the sampling distribution of a difference of two medians. Yet it is easy to imagine a scenario in which this would be the preferred estimator, for example, in an experimental trial where there are small samples, many extreme values drawn from an unknown but highly skewed distribution, and unreliable measurement instruments. The viral load of AIDS patients in a clinical trial is one example.

In such cases, it would seem that no valid inference can be drawn from a sample, because the sampling distribution is not known. When the parameters of a sampling distribution are not known analytically, they may be estimated empirically using a technique known as bootstrapping. In this procedure, numerous samples are drawn with replacement from the original sample and the measured variability of the statistic of interest across these samples is used as the estimate of the statistic's standard error.

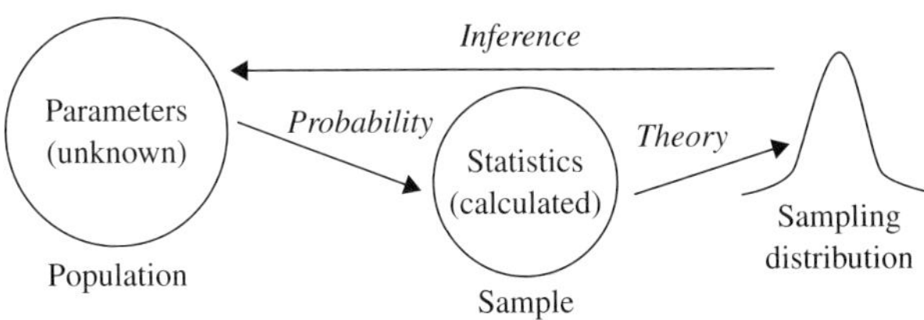

Figure 3 Sampling theory.

Cautions and Conclusions

Statistics, as a discipline, is a bit schizophrenic. On the one hand, given a specific set of observations, there are precise formulas for calculating the mean, variance, skewness, kurtosis, and a hundred other descriptive statistics. On the other hand, the best that inferential statistics can tell one is that the right answer is probably between two numbers, but then again, maybe not. Even after the best statistical analysis, one does not know the truth with complete precision. One remains in a state of ignorance, but with an important difference: one has sharply reduced the degree of one's ignorance. Rather than not knowing a figure at all, such as the poverty rate for the United States, one can say that one is 95% confident that in 2002 the poverty rate was between 10.1 and 10.5%.

A number of caveats are in order. The arguments above assume random, or at least unbiased, samples. The margin of error, based on sampling theory, applies only to the random errors generated by the sampling process and not the systematic errors that may be caused by bad sampling procedures or poor measurement of the variables. If the variables are poorly conceived or inaccurately measured, the maxim "garbage in, garbage out" will apply. Moreover, there is a tendency, in the pursuit of mathematical rigor, to ignore variables that cannot be easily quantified, leading to the problem of omitted variable bias.

Table I Common Sampling Distributions

Estimator	*Mean*	*Standard error*	*Distribution*
Sample mean: $\bar{X}$	$\mu_{\bar{X}} = \mu$	$\sigma_{\bar{X}} = \frac{\sigma}{\sqrt{n}}$	~Normal if X is normal or n is large
Sample proportion: $\hat{P}$	$\mu_{\hat{P}} = P$	$\sigma_{\hat{P}} = \sqrt{\frac{(P)(1-P)}{n}}$	~Normal if n is large
Difference of means from 2 independent samples: $\bar{X}_1 - \bar{X}_2$	$\mu_{\bar{X}_1 - \bar{X}_2} = \mu_1 - \mu_2$	$\sigma_{\bar{X}_1 - \bar{X}_2} = \sqrt{\frac{\sigma_1^2}{n_1} + \frac{\sigma_2^2}{n_2}}$	~Normal if both variables are normal in the population or if both samples are large
Difference of proportions from 2 independent samples: $\hat{P}_1 - \hat{P}_2$	$\mu_{\hat{P}_1 - \hat{P}_2} = P_1 - P_2$	$\sigma_{\hat{P}_1 - \hat{P}_2} = \sqrt{\frac{(P_1)(1-P_1)}{n_1} + \frac{(P_2)(1-P_2)}{n_2}}$	~Normal if both samples are large

Note: For most purposes, samples of 30 or more may be considered large.

In a sense, statistics has the potential to be the refutation of the philosophical doctrine of solipsism, which says that, because the data of one's senses can be misleading, one has no true knowledge of the outside world. With statistics, one can compile evidence that is sufficient to convince one of a conclusion about reality with a reasonable degree of confidence. Statistics is a tool and an extremely valuable one at that, but it is neither the beginning nor the end of scientific inquiry.

See Also the Following Articles

Confidence Intervals • Units of Analysis

Further Reading

Blalock, H. M., Jr. (1972). *Social Statistics*. McGraw-Hill, New York.

Everitt, B. S. (1998). *The Cambridge Dictionary of Statistics*. Cambridge University Press, Cambridge, UK.

Fruend, J. E., and Walpole, R. (1992). *Mathematical Statistics*, 5th Ed. Prentice-Hall, Englewood Cliffs, NJ.

Fruend J. E., and Walpole, R. (1992). *Mathematical Statistics*, 5th Ed. Prentice-Hall, Englewood Cliffs, NJ.

Hacking, I. (1975). *The Emergence of Probability: A Philosophical Study of Early Ideas about Probability, Induction, and Statistical Inference*. Cambridge University Press, London.

Kotz, S., Johnson, N. L., and Read, C. (eds.) (1989). *Encyclopedia of Social Statistics*. Wiley, New York.

Krippendorf, K. (1986). *Information Theory*. Sage, Newbury Park, CA.

Pearson, E. S., and Kendall, M. G. (eds.) (1970). *Studies in the History of Statistics and Probability*. Hafner, Darien, CT.

Stigler, S. M. (1986). *The History of Statistics: The Measurement of Uncertainty before 1900*. Harvard University Press, Cambridge, MA.

Tukey, J. W. (1977). *Exploratory Data Analysis*. Addison-Wesley, Reading, MA.

Vogt, W. P. (1993). *Dictionary of Statistics and Methodology: A Nontechnical Guide for the Social Sciences*. Sage, Newbury Park, CA.

Weisberg, H. F. (1992). *Central Tendency and Variability*. Sage, Newbury Park, CA.

Digital Terrain Modeling

Richard J. Pike
U.S. Geological Survey, Menlo Park, California, USA

Glossary

adaptive (surface specific) Close correspondence of digital elevation model pattern and density to critical ground-surface features.

critical feature Any of the six fundamental elements of ground-surface geometry: a peak, pit, pass, pale, ridge, or course (channel).

digital elevation model (DEM) Any set of terrain heights defining a topographic surface; commonly arranged in a square grid, but also a triangulated irregular network or digitized contour or slope lines.

facet A planar or moderately curved area of sloping terrain, especially where delimited by explicit rules or procedures.

geometric signature A set of measures describing topographic form sufficiently well to distinguish different landscapes or landforms.

geomorphometry (morphometry) The numerical characterization of topographic form.

shaded relief (analytical hill shading) A depiction of topography by varied intensity of reflected light calculated from slope gradient, aspect, and the location of a simulated sun.

slope line (flow line) A topographic path of steepest descent, normal to height contours.

triangulated irregular network (TIN) A digital elevation model comprising heights located at the vertices of triangles that vary in size and shape commensurate with terrain complexity.

viewshed The ground area, computed from a digital elevation model, visible from a specified location.

Digital terrain modeling (DTM), or simply terrain modeling, is a modern approach to the measurement of Earth's surface form. Loosely applied to any computer manipulation of terrain height (elevation), the term is variously defined (for example, as the representation of continuous topography from finite measurements of height and plan). DTM involves the activities and applications of collection, refinement, or analysis of height data; terrain visualization; and numerical description of ground-surface shape.

Introduction

An amalgam of Earth science, computer science, engineering, and mathematics, digital terrain modeling (DTM) is a comparatively new field, paralleling the development of digital cartography and geographic information systems (GIS). DTM provides hydrologic analyses, base maps for plotting nontopographic information, and other visual and numerical representations of the ground surface for civil engineering, national defense, agriculture, resource management, and education.

Cognate Disciplines

Geomorphometry, the overarching practice of terrain measurement, includes landforms; discrete features such as watersheds, landslides, and volcanoes; and landscapes, or continuous topography. DTM principally automates the quantification of landscapes. Originating in the descriptive geometry of curved surfaces by 19th-century French and English mathematicians and the measurement of mountain ranges (orometry) by German geographers, DTM evolved from disciplines that predate the electronic computer. Two of these are the engineering-directed quantitative terrain analysis and the process-oriented quantitative geomorphology. DTM includes the computer animation of topographic display, or terrain rendering; operationally, it resembles metrology, the measurement of industrial surfaces.

Terrain Geometry

The continuous surface that DTM must approximate from a finite sample of discrete heights is complex but not without order. Topography consists of repeated occurrences of a few geometric elements (Fig. 1), six of which (four points and two lines) are known as critical features. A peak is a height maximum; a pit is a local minimum, or closed depression; a pass, or saddle, is a low point between two peaks; a pale is a high point between two pits. Two operational constructs—contours, intersections of the terrain with a surface of constant height, and slope lines, paths of steepest descent (normal to contours)—help define two critical features: ridge, a slope line linking peaks via passes (or pales), and course (channel), a slope line linking pits via pales (or passes).

Additional elements that outline the geometry of the surface include break in slope, a linear discontinuity formed by a flat area, terrace, escarpment, or similarly noncritical feature; facet, an area of uniform planar or slightly curved slope (Fig. 2); hill, an elevated area where slope lines fall from the same peak or peaks; valley, a low area where slope lines fall to the same pit(s) or course(s); and watershed (also drainage basin or catchment), an area enclosed by ridge lines and occupied by one stream or stream network.

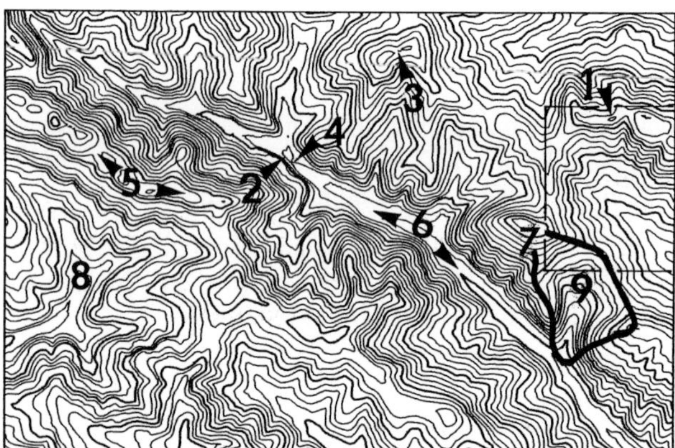

Figure 1 Some elements of surface form in terrain recontoured to a 10-m interval (source-map interval, 20 ft) from a square-grid 10-m digital elevation model. 1, Peak; 2, pit; 3, pass; 4, pale; 5, ridge; 6, course; 7, hill; 8, valley; 9, watershed. A 3.3-km × 2.1-km area near Oakland, California, prepared in GIS software. Northwest trend reflects local geologic structure and fault lines. Rectangle locates Fig. 3.

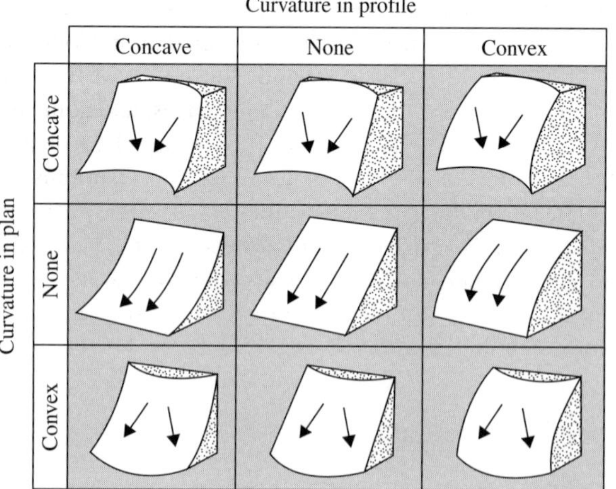

Figure 2 The nine possible configurations of a terrain facet, as defined by surface curvature in plan and profile. Arrows indicate convergent, parallel, or divergent drainage.

Digital Terrain Data

To represent the geometric elements, DTM requires abundant measurements in machine-readable form. A digital elevation model (DEM; rarely digital height or digital ground model) is any spatial array of terrain heights, most commonly a square grid. DEM spacing (resolution) varies from fine (<1 m) to coarse (≥10 km), depending on the chosen application, desired level of detail, and data storage and processing limitations. Confusingly, the term "digital terrain model" not only is a common synonym for a DEM, but also is used freely for any derivative rendering of topography by computer, rather than for just the height array.

DEM Structures

Terrain heights usually are arranged in a data structure for efficient manipulation and display (Fig. 3). As in GIS generally, the spatial arrangement is either raster (grid cell) or vector (point–line–polygon). A DEM may be arrayed in a square grid (hexagons or equilateral triangles are rare), a triangulated irregular network (TIN), and as height contours or slope lines. All data structures are compromises, each with advantages and drawbacks.

Square (actually rectangular) grid DEMs mimic the file structure of digital computers by storing height Z as an array of implicit X and Y coordinates (Fig. 3A). Although a grid facilitates data processing, algorithm development, and registration with spacecraft images, its discretized (discontinuous) structure and regular spacing do not accommodate the variable density of terrain features. Many data points are redundant. Grids can adapt somewhat to topography by recursively subdividing squares in complex areas, but at a loss of computational efficiency. The TIN structure (Fig. 3B) is a DEM interpolated from critical features that are extracted manually from maps or by computer from a grid or contour DEM. The irregularly distributed heights are vertices of triangles

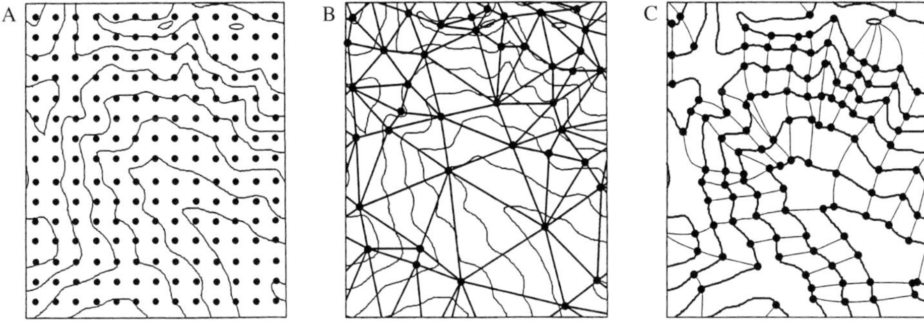

Figure 3 Digital elevation model structures for the 780-m × 640-m rectangle in Fig. 1. Dots are height locations. (A) Square grid (every fifth point); (B) triangulated irregular network; (C) intersections of 20-m contours (heavy lines) with slope lines (light).

that vary in size and shape. The TIN is adaptive—it follows ridge and course lines and generates many heights for intricate areas while minimizing redundant heights in planar terrain. Offsetting these advantages is the storage and processing burden imposed by each value of *Z* requiring explicit *X*, *Y* coordinates.

The spatial structure of the ground surface is neither triangular nor rectilinear. The DEM arrangements best reflecting the formational processes of erosion and deposition follow paths of steepest descent. Terrain heights located at intersecting contours and interpolated slope lines (Fig. 3C) constitute an adaptive DEM that defines quadrilateral facets of varied size and shape—most important among them the hillside convergences (Fig. 2) sought out by surface water. Explicit *X*, *Y*, *Z* coordinates are required.

DEM Sources

Most DEMs are produced and distributed as square grids. Early DEMs were created by field survey, visual interpolation of topographic maps, or semiautomated tracing of contours coupled with computer interpolation. These methods were replaced by photogrammetric profiling and then by optical scanning and automated interpolation of map contours (Fig. 1). DEMs now cover all of Earth, Earth's seafloor, and the planet Mars. The global GTOPO30, compiled from many maps and several raster and vector sources, has a 30' ($\approx$ 1 km) spacing. The digital terrain elevation data (DTED) system is the U.S. military equivalent. Global coverage also exists at 5- and 10-km spacing. The U.S. National Elevation Dataset (NED) is a seamless 1" (30 m) DEM (Alaska is at 2") assembled from all 55,000 1 : 24,000- and 1 : 63,360-scale topographic maps. Japan is gridded at 50 m, Australia is at 9" (250 m), and other areas are at various resolutions.

Remote sensing bypasses contour maps and generates DEMs from direct measurement of terrain height. Among current technologies are the Global Positioning System (GPS), digital photogrammetry, synthetic-aperture radar interferometry (InSAR or IfSAR), laser light detection and ranging altimetry (LiDAR), Advanced Spaceborne thermal emission and reflection radiometry (ASTER), and (for bathymetry) deep-towed sound navigation and ranging (SONAR). The 3" (90 m) DEM recently compiled for 80% of Earth's land surface (60°N–56°S) from results of the February 2000 Shuttle Radar Topography Mission (SRTM) supplements GTOPO30 (the 1" SRTM data are not available outside the United States).

DEM Preprocessing

Data Limitations

Regardless of source or spatial structure, all DEMs contain systematic or random flaws. Most error in DEMs derived from contours originates in the maps, which were not intended to provide heights of the high density and accuracy desirable for DTM. Because contour maps are approximations of terrain, just as DEMs are of the maps, the level of quality guaranteed by official map standards is only statistical. Locally, contour accuracy can be low; precision in most level terrain is poor. Contour-to-grid processing is a second source of error. All interpolation procedures are compromises, and some algorithms add spurious pits (feature 2 in Fig. 1), terracing, and linear artifacts. Advanced technology does not insure DEM quality; the U.S. 1" SRTM data are no more accurate than the 1" National Elevation Dataset (NED). InSAR, LiDAR, and other remote-sensing techniques all introduce errors, some of them severe, that are unique to their technologies.

Data Refinement

DEMs generally must be calibrated, amended, or otherwise prepared for subsequent analysis. Computer processing can create a TIN or grid DEM from scattered heights, convert from one map projection or data structure to another, and recontour a map to a different interval (Fig. 1). A DEM may be interpolated to finer (within limits, to avoid creating artifacts) or coarser grids for compatibility in merging or joining DEMs and registering terrain height to other data. Point-by-point editing or bulk processing corrects errors or replaces parts of a DEM with data of higher quality. Removing long- or shortwave variation from a DEM by digital filtering can enhance detail or reduce systematic and random error by smoothing the heights. A method of drainage enforcement, which incorporates ridge and course lines and other slope discontinuities into a grid DEM, minimizes artifacts of digitizing and ensures the stream-channel continuity essential to hydrologic analysis.

Modeling Landscapes

DTM represents continuous topography by a spatial calculation shared with digital image processing, the neighborhood operation, in which a result is computed from adjacent input values. The input from a grid DEM is a compact array of heights (a subgrid or window) moved through the data in regular increments. The default subgrid is 3 × 3 (the result is assigned to the central cell), but may be any size or shape. The result is assigned to each triangle in a TIN or to each quadrilateral facet in a DEM defined by contour and slope lines (Fig. 3). Neighborhood operations characterize topography in three, broadly overlapping, domains—vertical, or relief (*Z*); horizontal, or spatial (*X*, *Y*); and three-dimensional (*X*, *Y*, *Z*). The spatial pattern and frequency distribution of the derived attributes can vary greatly with DEM resolution.

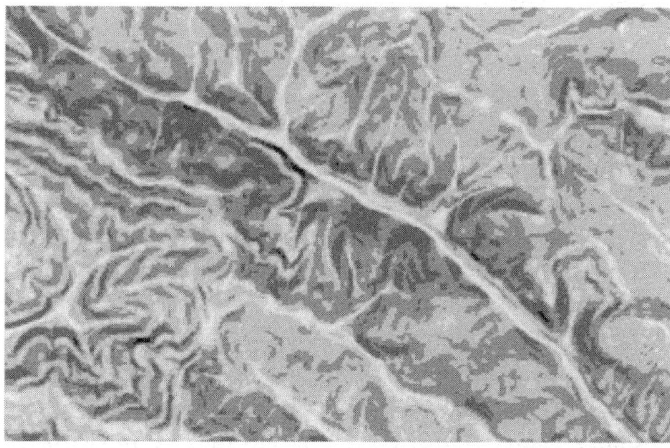

Figure 4 The two most common height derivatives (10-m digital elevation model). (Top) Slope gradient, mapped on grid cells in six (unequal) intervals from 0° to 5° (white) to >45° (black). (Bottom) Slope aspect, modeled as a triangulated irregular network; compass direction, in 12 30° intervals, varies clockwise from 346° to 15° (black) to 316° to 345° (white). A 3.3-km × 2.1-km area near Oakland, California, prepared in GIS software.

Relief Measures

Because terrain height is measured from an absolute datum, Z-domain calculations are the most straightforward. Standard statistics describe height and its first and second derivatives, slope gradient (Fig. 4), and profile curvature (Fig. 2). The higher derivatives require very accurate DEMs. Mean, median, and modal height express central tendency; height range, or local relief, and standard deviation describe dispersion. Skewness and its approximation, the elevation-relief ratio (the hypsometric integral), express height (and volume) asymmetry. Kurtosis, a measure of distribution peakedness or the influence of extreme values, is rare in modeling height and of uncertain significance for slope or curvature.

Spatial Measures

Parameters of terrain pattern and texture, unreferenced to an absolute datum, are more abstract. Derivatives of orientation, distance, and connectivity, three fundamental qualities of location, include shape, elongation, spacing, sinuosity, parallelism, adjacency, sequence (relative position), and containment (a feature within another). Among common *X*, *Y* measures computed from neighborhood operations are aspect (Fig. 4), the compass direction faced by a slope, and plan curvature (Fig. 2). Nearest-neighbor statistics and other metrics express qualities such as uniformity of features (clustered, regular, or random), to which standard statistics do not apply. Some spatial properties are independent of distance and thus topologic rather than geometric. Not only are these non-Euclidean properties difficult to quantify, but the *X*, *Y* topology imprinted on most terrain by hierarchically ordered drainage is random. Analysis of critical features by graph theory, equally applicable where the fluvial overprint is absent or faint, offers an approach to quantifying topologic attributes.

Three-Dimensional Measures

Processing DEMs in the X, Y, Z domain captures the most complex properties of terrain. Among them are roughness, which comprises both relief and spacing; intervisibility, which quantifies line-of-sight and calculates a viewshed—the area visible to an observer; openness, the exposure or enclosure of a location; and anisotropy, the variance of terrain complexity with azimuth. All Z-domain attributes vary with the size of the area over which they are measured. This scale dependence is quantified by the power spectrum, a technique of waveform analysis; by semivariance, the correlation of relief with distance; and by the fractal dimension, a measure of the proportion of fine- to coarse-scale relief.

DTM Applications

Measures of surface form calculated from DEMs yield topographic displays and input to further analysis. The results are used to engineer infrastructure for transportation and communications, predict natural hazards, plan urban land use, improve crop yields, model regional climate, inventory water resources, delimit physical regions, conduct military operations, explore seafloor and planetary surfaces, understand changes in Earth's surface, and for many other purposes.

Visualization

Diagrams, tables, profiles, and maps all display DTM results. Histograms show the frequency distribution of terrain measures, and semivariograms and spectral functions show their scale dependence. Tables that are output from correlation and factor analysis reveal redundancy among measures. Though topography may be illustrated in cross-section, by profiles, it is best displayed as thematic maps in color or gray tone (Figs. 4 and 5). The most elementary DTM map, showing height contoured in wide intervals, can be enhanced substantially by adding three-dimensional perspective or land-cover detail from an aerial photo or satellite image. Height maps are used widely as a base for nontopographic information, and vast resources are committed to the video rendering of height for computer games and military simulations. The technique of relief shading creates a particularly effective base map by combining slope gradient and aspect (Fig. 4) to portray topography as the varied intensity of reflected illumination (Fig. 5).

Aggregation

DTM may combine several maps of terrain measures or may incorporate nontopographic data. The likelihood of deep-seated landsliding, for example, can be mapped statistically over large areas from a synthesis of terrain geometry, rock structure, and evidence of past slope failure (Fig. 6). Computing a geometric signature, or set of diagnostic measures, from a DEM identifies occurrences of terrain types (mountain, hill, plain, plateau). Clusters of terrain types divide an area into unique terrain regions, which reveal both the spatial extent of surface-shaping processes and their relation to nontopographic phenomena. To simulate broad-scale landscape evolution, maps of terrain parameters are combined with longitudinal stream profiles and mathematical expressions for diffusion processes.

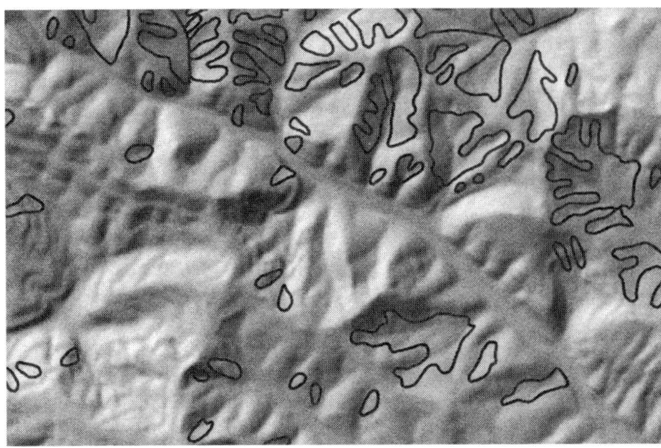

Figure 5 Shaded-relief base map computed on 10-m digital elevation model cells; steep terrain is light or dark in tone, low-sloping terrain is intermediate. Overlaid polygons are areas of known landsliding. A 3.3-km × 2.1-km area near Oakland, California, prepared in GIS software.

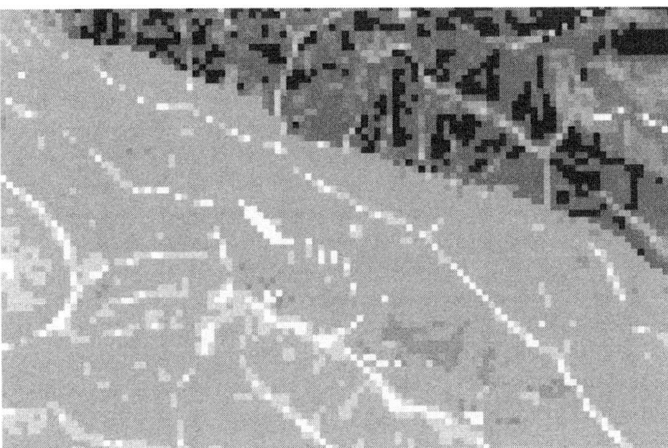

Figure 6 Digital terrain modeling applied to hazard mapping. Likelihood of deep-seated landsliding, from low (white) to high (black), estimated on 30-m grid cells. A fine-scale measure, slope gradient (Fig. 4) in 1° intervals, was employed to refine the coarser scale criteria, areal density of existing landslides (Fig. 5) in different geologic-map units (not shown). Reproduced from Pike *et al.* (2001). A 3.3-km × 2.1-km area near Oakland, California, prepared in GIS software.

Hydrologic Modeling

Ecology and water resources drive much current DTM. Parameters of hydrologic behavior that are mapped from DEMs include watershed area (Table I), specific catchment area (A_s, the upslope area between slope lines, per unit contour width), the topographic wetness index [$\ln(A_s/S)$, an estimate of soil moisture], and the stream power index (A_sS, an estimate of erosive force, where S is slope gradient). Drainage networks extracted from a DEM help simulate watershed hydrographs, measure stream flow, forecast the extent of flooding, and estimate sediment delivery. The automated techniques delineate stream channels, by sequentially recording DEM grid cells along convergent flow paths (Fig. 2) to accumulate drainage area with decreasing elevation, and then identify the enclosing ridges (Fig. 7). Fidelity of the resulting drainage net depends on the algorithm and DEM quality and structure. Where these procedures organize continuous terrain into a mosaic of watersheds (Fig. 7), the extracted landforms can be analyzed further as discrete entities.

Modeling Landforms

DTM of watersheds and other landforms can reveal correlations with physical processes that explain their origin and morphologic evolution. Linking recognition of a landform with its physical understanding requires defining the feature, sampling its population, choosing and measuring descriptive parameters, analyzing the data, and interpreting the results. A sample of landforms extracted from a DEM, by rule-based procedures, must be large enough to include all sizes and morphologic subtypes. Descriptive measures should reduce landforms to basic dimensions of height, breadth, area, and their derivatives (slope, curvature, and symmetry). Additional rules maintain objectivity in measuring dimensions and recording presence or absence of qualitative attributes. Though symmetric forms such as volcanoes and impact craters are captured by a few measures, watersheds, landslides, and other irregular landforms may require many parameters (Table I).

Table I Some Morphometric Parameters of a Landform—A Fluvial Watershed

Parameter	*Description*
Watershed area	Area of horizontally projected watershed surface
Total drainage length	Length of horizontal projection of all channels
Drainage density	Total drainage length/watershed area
Plan symmetry	Area of largest inscribed circle/area of smallest circumscribed circle
Mean height	Average of $\geq$30–50 digital elevation model heights
Relief	Maximum height−minimum height
Ruggedness number	Relief/drainage density
Elevation-relief ratio	(Average height−minimum height)/relief

Because interpreting landforms in the automated environment of DTM risks losing insight from the measurements through their uncritical manipulation by computer, the data should be explored in different ways. Where landforms vary in shape with size or relative age, analysis by subgroups may strengthen correlations and quantify contrasts in morphology. Identifying redundancy among parameters, transforming skewed distributions, and screening data graphically before fitting regression lines or making other calculations also can clarify landform interpretation.

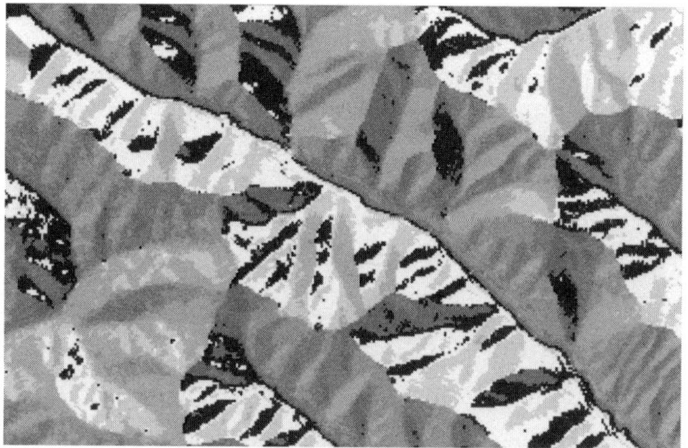

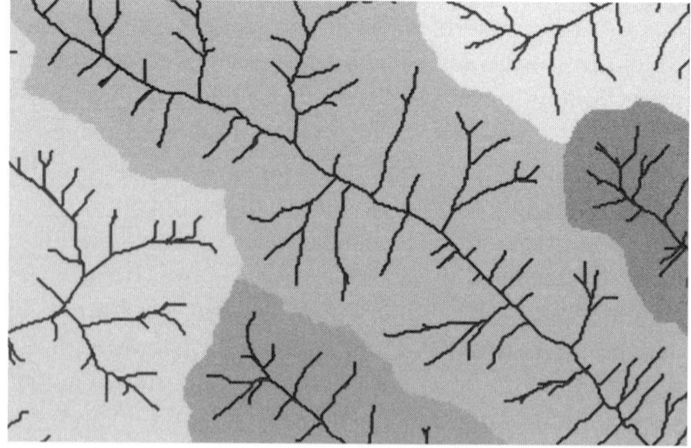

Figure 7 Automated extraction of hydrologic networks from a digital elevation model. (Top) An intermediate result: drainage direction at each 10-m grid cell, mapped as one of eight azimuths, varies with gray tone clockwise from 90° (white) to 45° (black). (Bottom) The end result: a landscape divided into landforms, the five large watersheds and their principal drainageways. Triangulated irregular network- and contour-based algorithms also perform this operation. A 3.3-km × 2.1-km area near Oakland, California, prepared in GIS software.

See Also the Following Articles

Geographic Information Systems • Land Use Mapping • Remote Sensing • Spatial Pattern Analysis

Further Reading

Brooks, S. M., and McDonnell, R. A. (eds.) (2000). Geocomputation in hydrology and geomorphology. *Hydrol. Proc.* **14,** 1899–2206.

Discoe, B. (2002). *The Virtual Terrain Project.* Available on the Internet at http://www.vterrain.org

Evans, I. S. (2003). Scale-specific landforms and aspects of the land surface. In *Concepts and Modeling in Geomorphology—International Perspectives* (I. S. Evans, R. Dikau, E. Tokunaga, H. Omori, and M. Hirano, eds.), pp. 61–84. Terrapub, Tokyo.

Guth, P. L. (2002). MicroDEM+ package, for Windows 95 and NT. Available on the Internet at http://www.nadn.navy.mil/users/oceano/pguth/website/microdem.htm

Hengl, T., Gruber, S., and Shrestha, D. P. (2003). *Digital Terrain Analysis in ILWIS*. Available on the Internet at http://www.itc.nl/personal/shrestha/DTA/

Hutchinson, M. F., and Gallant, J. C. (1999). Representation of terrain. In *Geographical Information Systems* (P. A. Longley, M. F. Goodchild, D. J. Maguire, and D. W. Rhind, eds.), 2nd Ed., Vol. 1, pp. 105–124. Wiley, New York.

Kumler, M. P. (1994). An intensive comparison of triangulated irregular networks (TINs) and digital elevation models (DEMs). *Cartographica* **31**(2, monogr 45).

Lane, S. N., Richards, K. S., and Chandler, J. H. (eds.) (1998). *Landform Monitoring Modelling and Analysis*. Wiley, New York.

Maune, D. (ed.) (2001). *Digital Elevation Model Technologies and Applications, the DEM Users Manual.* American Society for Photogrammetry and Remote Sensing, Bethesda.

Pike, R. J., Graymer, R. W., Roberts, S., Kalman, N. B., and Sobieszczyk, S. (2001). Map and map database of susceptibility to slope failure by sliding and earthflow in the Oakland area, California. U.S. Geological Survey Miscellaneous Investigations Series Map MF-2385. Available on the Internet at http://geopubs.w.usgs.gov/map-mf/mf2385/

Pike, R. J., and Dikau, R. (eds.) (1995). Advances in geomorphometry. *Z. Geomorph.* (Suppl. 101).

Rana, S. S. (ed.) (2004). *Topological Data Structures for Surfaces*. Wiley, Chichester.

Rodríguez-Iturbe, I., and Rinaldo, A. (1997). *Fractal River Basins, Chance and Self-organization.* Cambridge Univ. Press, Cambridge.

Wilson, J. P., and Gallant, J. C. (eds.) (2000). *Terrain Analysis, Principles and Applications*. Wiley, Chichester.

Discrimination, Measurement in

Trond Petersen
University of California, Berkeley, Berkeley, California, USA

Glossary

allocative discrimination Occurs in the employment setting when there is unequal access to jobs at the point of hiring, promotion, and firing.

disparate impact discrimination Occurs when rules and procedures that should be irrelevant to a situation confer advantage to one group over another (for example, minimum height requirements that do not affect job performance but give males an advantage).

disparate treatment discrimination Occurs when treatment of people depends on race, gender, or other characteristics that should be irrelevant to a situation.

valuative discrimination Occurs in the employment setting when female-dominated occupations command lower wages than male-dominated occupations do, even though there are no differences in relevant requirements in the jobs, such as skills and work effort.

within-job wage discrimination Occurs in the employment setting when wages for doing the same work for the same employer are unequal.

The measurement of discrimination involves collecting data on and assessing (1) disparate treatment by sex, race, and other illegitimate characteristics, as occurs in several arenas, including employment, education, housing, health care, and retail markets, and (2) disparate impact by sex or other characteristics, whereby rules and procedures that are irrelevant in a given setting (for example, performance in a job) advantage one group over another.

Introduction

Discrimination may occur in many settings, including employment, housing, schools and universities, retail trade, health care, legal systems, and law enforcement. The agents and institutions that may discriminate are even more varied; examples include owners in housing markets; salespersons in retail markets; and employers, managers, co-workers, and customers in businesses. The bases for discrimination and those discriminated against also vary, by sex, race, age, social status, religion, sexual orientation, and health, for example.

Discrimination has been most thoroughly studied in the employment setting, and it is here that it is most heavily regulated, with considerable attention given to discrimination according to sex and race, but also to age, health status, and other factors. The issues raised in the employment setting are the most varied and are of relevance in all other settings. A first step in an analysis of the issues of employment discrimination is to identify the discriminatory agents and institutions, as well as the parties who are targeted by discriminatory practices. Three central questions should then be asked: Why, how, and where do the discriminators discriminate?

Why do discriminators discriminate? This concerns the motives for discrimination; the principal motives are based on prejudice, stereotypes, and statistical discrimination.

How discriminators discriminate concerns the methods of discrimination. Methods can be categorized as two distinct types: (1) disparate treatment discrimination occurs when two or more people, who are otherwise equal in what is relevant in a given setting, are treated differently because of their sex, race, or other characteristics that should be irrelevant in the situation in which the treatment occurs; (2) disparate impact, or structural, discrimination occurs when two groups are treated equally within a given set of rules and procedures, but the rules and procedures are in reality irrelevant to the situation to which they are applied (for example, irrelevant for job performance), and, as such, are constructed so that they favor one group over another.

Where discriminators discriminate concerns the arenas for discrimination. In the employment setting, there are three broad arenas: (1) allocative discrimination concerns unequal access to positions at the point of hiring, promotion, and firing, (2) within-job wage discrimination concerns unequal pay for the same work for the same employer, and (3) valuative discrimination concerns lower pay in female-dominated occupations. The third arena arises only in discrimination based on gender, not in racial or other forms of discrimination. Each of the three arenas is covered by legislation and public policy in most developed countries, and each requires different measurement strategies.

In measuring discrimination, the central concern, more so than measuring variables correctly, should be to collect what can be called, to use a legal term, admissible evidence—that is, relevant kinds of data. It is necessary to measure discriminatory actions and their outcomes, especially how "likes" are treated as "unlikes." It is not sufficient to observe that, for example, men and women experience different employment outcomes. What is also required is observing how those differential outcomes were caused by discrimination of men and women when they faced the same employer, either at the point of hiring or during later employment. Not all differences between employment-related behaviors toward men and women are caused by discrimination. Differences are also caused by the differential choices made by men and women, especially due to differences in burdens that arise from treatment by agents other than employers, such as parents, spouses, and children. So when inequality in outcomes between groups is observed, there is no automatic presumption that those were caused by discrimination.

It is always difficult empirically to assess whether employment discrimination has occurred, but when it has, the researcher should expect to observe differences in hiring rates, wages, and promotions. Given the difficulty of measurement, there are wide variations in how well measurement is accomplished, and the distance can be wide, between practice in research and what would count as sufficient evidence regarding discrimination within organizations and the courts.

Why: Motives for Discrimination

Why do employers and others discriminate? The motives vary, but the principal ones are prejudice, stereotyping, and statistical discrimination. Prejudice occurs when an employer or other agent has a dislike for a specific group, such as women or ethnic minorities. Such prejudice is usually irrational. It is based on dislike of group members, not on objective characteristics that could be relevant in a specific employment situation. For example, an employer may refuse to hire Hispanics, not because they are less suitable employees, but because of distaste for associating with Hispanics. This is sometimes referred to as taste discrimination.

Stereotyping occurs when an employer views some groups as less suitable employees than other groups are, even though there are few solid grounds for holding such a view. Relying on stereotypes in hiring and promotion decisions, for example, would incorrectly deny opportunities to some groups. This is different from acting with prejudice, in that stereotyping is not based on dislike, but rather on erroneous information or an incorrect assessment of the situation. Stereotyping is often about every member of a group, making no allowance for variations among individuals within a group. Stereotyping has been referred to as error discrimination.

Statistical discrimination arises when groups differ statistically in their distributions on characteristics relevant in a given situation. For example, men may on average take fewer sick days than women do. An employer, faced with hiring either a man or a woman, may treat the man and the woman as representative of their groups, rather than trying to make an assessment of how many sick days the specific man versus the specific woman is likely to take. If this results in hiring the man, the employer has engaged in statistical discrimination. Such discrimination may be rational. It is not based on prejudice, but on a correct assessment of average or other statistical characteristics of groups. As compared to ignoring group information and assessing individual characteristics, better average outcomes may result when simple decision rules are used, i.e., an employer does not take the time to assess each person separately, but assesses only their group membership. Such decision making is a simple and often inexpensive way to act when facing uncertainty. An informed employer knows that not everyone within a group is the same, but, given that there are known statistical differences between groups, expediently chooses not to take the time to evaluate members within groups on an individual basis. This is different from stereotype discrimination in that it is based on correct information about group characteristics, though often incorrect assessments of individuals within a group.

There is the question of whether motives for discrimination are conscious or nonconscious, and thus whether the ensuing discrimination is conscious. Many researchers hold the view that most prejudice today is nonconscious, and that particularly the most important forms of discrimination occur nonconsciously. Much of the discrimination-related literature focuses on what leads employers and others to discriminate. This is difficult to research and measure, because it concerns motivations, intentions, and desires. Discriminatory actions are the outcome of motivations and intentions, but it is often easier to observe the outcomes of the actions.

The difficulties of measurement get compounded when discrimination is nonconscious rather than conscious.

How: Methods of Discrimination, Disparate Treatment, and Disparate Impact

How do employers discriminate? There are two broad methods, disparate treatment discrimination and disparate impact discrimination. In the employment setting, both may occur in each of three arenas—allocative, within-job wages, and valuative. Disparate treatment discrimination occurs when equally qualified people are treated differently because of their gender, race, religion, or other illegitimate characteristics. This usually requires a discriminatory motive, conscious or nonconscious. Disparate impact, or structural, discrimination occurs when two groups are treated equally within the given set of organizational rules and procedures, but the rules and procedures confer advantages to one group over another, and at the same time are irrelevant for job or organizational performance. This may, but need not, require a discriminatory motive. The discriminating agent or institution can even be unaware that there is discrimination. The rules and procedures may be residues from past practices, such as carefully negotiated and difficult-to-change union contracts constructed for an historically male-dominated labor force. It is often difficult to identify agents, motives, and responsibility in disparate impact discrimination. This can make it harder to analyze and understand.

An example of disparate impact discrimination in hiring would be a physical height or strength requirement unrelated to job performance. This would favor men over women. Such requirements have been important in hiring of fire fighters, for example, and it has been claimed that the amount of strength often required is excessive. Similarly, rewarding military service with better hiring chances or higher wages would advantage men over women. In the United States, if the employer can show that a job requirement is a so-called bona fide occupational qualification, then there is no discrimination in a legal sense. There are many variations on this. For example, if women have higher accident rates in some jobs, compared to men, would it be discriminatory to have hiring requirements that would theoretically lower accident rates, thus giving men an advantage? Many would argue that it would be discriminatory, and in a legal sense, it often is. Conversely, in many settings, including the employment setting, men on average take more risks than women do, which can lead to higher accident rates. A job requirement that would favor hiring "safer" employees, i.e., women, could then be viewed as disparate impact discrimination.

There is also concern over disparate impact (structural) discrimination at a broader societal level. Child care provisions, access to part-time work and over-time hours, health benefits, pension rules, etc. may have disparate impacts on men and women. For example, the degree of wage inequality in a society may be especially detrimental to women. Women may be at the bottom of an occupational hierarchy in most societies, but the actual experience of being at the bottom, and its impact on, say, the overall gender wage gap, depend on how wide the distance is between the bottom and the top. These broader features of entire societies necessitate comparative analyses. They are very important but are rarely directly relevant for understanding the discriminatory aspects of actions taken by employers within a given society.

Measuring disparate treatment discrimination requires assessing whether equally qualified people are differentially treated by the same discriminator (i.e., employer), due, for example, to their race or sex. Measuring disparate impact discrimination requires investigating employment rules and procedures. It is necessary to establish that these are unrelated to job performance, and a correlation between sex and race, on the one hand, and the rules and procedures, on the other, must be established. If there is such a correlation, it can be concluded that the rules have disparate impact for men and women or for ethnic groups.

Admissible Evidence

Specific types of data are needed in order to measure whether discrimination has occurred. The main difficulty in assessing within-job wage and allocative discrimination arises from the fact that it is employers or their representatives who discriminate, ignoring here co-worker or customer discrimination. An essential requirement of obtaining relevant data, making them equivalent to "admissible evidence," is access to specific information on employer behaviors (for example, how employers handle hiring and promotions related to gender, wages, etc.). The relevant sampling unit is therefore the employer and the decisions the employer makes regarding groups. This is the case in both disparate treatment discrimination and disparate impact discrimination.

Relevant data usually come from personnel records, testimonies, interviews, in-depth case studies, and employment audits. A large and mostly quantitative research streams comparing the outcomes of men and women who have worked for different employers, but not for the same employer, are problematic in this regard, not because this type of research lacks value, but because it is typically inconclusive in assessing possible discrimination. Standard sample employee surveys do not usually reveal whether differential outcomes among groups were caused by (1) unequal opportunity, through employer discrimination, (2) equal opportunity unequally taken, through employee preferences for different kinds of work and work schedules, or (3) a combination thereof. To identify the role of employer discrimination, it is necessary to have access to the actions taken by employers and by the agents that make employment decisions, and how these agents, when faced with equally qualified employees, may have discriminated on the basis of race, sex, or other characteristics irrelevant to job performance.

Measuring employee perceptions of discrimination, instead of outcomes, either in qualitative interviews or using survey data, can provide a correct record of whether employees believe they have experienced discrimination. Although perceptions are real, they need not match discriminatory action by the employer. Measuring the latter requires recording the actions of employers and how treatment may have differed by sex or race. Outcomes of discriminatory actions, such as who gets job offers and who does not, usually can be assessed. This should include data on who carried out the action (i.e., an employer or an agent), who was affected by it (i.e., applicants or employees), whether there was disparate treatment discrimination or disparate impact discrimination, based on gender or race, and when decisions were made. Direct observations of actions and motives are rarely available. The focus is thus typically on outcomes.

General Approach for Measuring Discrimination

In assessing employment discrimination in quantitative studies, the first step is usually to identify an outcome (a "reward") that may be differentially given to employees or potential employees. The reward can be getting hired, getting promoted, job assignments, wages, or fringe benefits, for example. The next step is to identify the relevant qualifications for getting the reward; these can be specific to a given work setting and may include education, experience, productivity, or work effort. In some lines of work, the only qualification may be productivity, as in piece-rate and sales work. The third step is to identify individual "illegitimate" characteristics such as sex, race, and religion that may be the basis for discriminatory actions. It is illegitimate to use sex, race, or religion as a basis for making employment decisions, and discrimination legislation clearly bars such action in most countries; social science analyses, however, include a wider array of additional characteristics. The final step is to identify irrelevant rules, i.e., workplace rules or procedures unrelated to job performance but that could favor women over men, or vice versa. An example is a physical height requirement that is irrelevant for job performance. This would correlate statistically with gender, and would advantage men over women. Irrelevant rules are important in assessing disparate impact discrimination. (In some settings, a normally illegitimate characteristic could be a legitimate qualification; for example, for some jobs in religious institutions, religious faith could be a requirement.)

Consider how to model disparate treatment discrimination, assuming, for the moment, that disparate impact is not an issue. The typical approach in social science analysis is to model, in a regression framework, rewards as a function of qualifications and illegitimate characteristics. Suppressing the effect of coefficients of variables and functional form for the effects, the relationship can be specified as follows:

$$\text{Rewards} = \text{Qualifications} + \text{Illegitimate characteristics} + \text{residual}. \quad (1)$$

Here the rewards received depend on qualifications, on illegitimate characteristics, and on a "residual," or the idiosyncratic factors that influence the outcome but that are not taken account of in the analysis. This often gets modeled in a linear regression framework. For example, the wages of employees in a company can be regressed on qualifications, such as education and experience, and on illegitimate characteristics, such as sex and race. Or, in the case of hiring, the dependent variable, getting an offer or not from a company, can be regressed on the same variables using a logit model. If the impact of illegitimate characteristics, net of qualifications, is different from zero, then there is evidence for discrimination in the disparate treatment sense, assuming for the moment no disparate impact discrimination: one group receives better rewards than another, even though their qualifications are the same.

The thinking in qualitative studies is similar. An assessment is made of whether differences in rewards can be justified by differences in qualifications, in which case there is no discrimination, or whether the differences also depend on illegitimate characteristics, in which case there is discrimination. There are variations on this general formulation, but this captures what often is done in discrimination studies. An important problem is whether the relevant qualifications have been measured. It is easy to measure education, experience, and similar factors, but difficult to measure less tangible factors such as punctuality, cooperativeness, level of initiative, leadership potential, fit between person and job, etc. Employers to varying degrees care about these too, and try, at least in a qualitative manner, to assess them. Social scientists or the courts almost never have access to information on such variables. Failing to account for these in the analysis may result in finding differences according illegitimate characteristics, but differences that would disappear if all the relevant qualifications were measured.

The procedure in Eq. (1) would be good for assessing disparate treatment discrimination. But there is also disparate impact discrimination. In this case, there are rules or procedures at the workplace that matter for rewards, but that are irrelevant for job performance; when these irrelevant rules are correlated with illegitimate characteristics, such as sex and race, thus giving one group an advantage over other groups, there is disparate impact discrimination. Disparate impact discrimination is not frequently modeled, but one possibility is to specify as in Eq. (2), again suppressing parameters and functional form:

$$\text{Rewards} = \text{Qualifications} + \text{Illegitimate characteristics} + \text{Irrelevant rules} + \text{residual}. \tag{2}$$

Evidence for disparate impact discrimination now obtains from comparing Eqs. (1) and (2). There would be such discrimination under the following conditions: there is (a) an effect on rewards due to illegitimate characteristics in Eq. (1), (b) no net effect due to illegitimate characteristics in Eq. (2), (c) an effect due to irrelevant rules in Eq. (2); from (b) and (c), it follows that (d) illegitimate characteristics correlate with irrelevant rules, thus women and minorities are at a disadvantage with respect to the rules. If in Eq. (2) there are effects on rewards due to both illegitimate characteristics and irrelevant rules, and the two are correlated, then there would be evidence of both disparate treatment discrimination and disparate impact discrimination. But the effect of illegitimate characteristics should be lower in Eq. (2) than in Eq. (1).

As previously mentioned, to assess employment discrimination requires data at the workplace level, comparing men and women as they face the same employer in terms of hiring, promotions, and wages. It is not sufficient to have only data from a random sample or census of men and women, with no information on what occurred once they faced the same employers. There are two parties to any discriminatory act, those that discriminate and those discriminated against, and data on both are needed. As Alfred Marshall once said, "To analyze a market from only one side is like trying to cut with one blade of a scissors."

The formulation in Eq. (2) can be viewed in entirely conceptual terms, but if it is going to be the starting point for statistical analysis, then it requires that an organization has several different irrelevant rules, so that there is variation in these at the organizational level (for example, by job or by organizational unit).

Where: Employment Arena 1, Allocative Discrimination

Allocative discrimination occurs in three settings: in hiring, in promotion, and in dismissal or firing. There may be both disparate treatment discrimination and disparate impact discrimination. A variety of motives for discrimination may be present. Allocative discrimination leads to racial and gender segregation, by which is meant, in the context here, to unequal distribution of races and genders in occupations, firms, and jobs. In the United States, there has been much discussion of the impact of affirmative action, whereby employers make special efforts to hire and promote women and ethnic minorities. The fear of some (especially White males) is that this may lead to reverse discrimination. Others claim that reverse discrimination, to the degree that it exists, might counteract already existing and widespread discrimination.

Hiring

Discrimination at the point of hiring entails an intricate set of issues, and three processes need to be analyzed. The first concerns the recruitment process (for example, through newspaper ads, employment agencies, or social networks). The second concerns who gets offers and who does not when a job is being filled. The third concerns the conditions (pay, job level, etc.) under which those hired get hired, or the quality of the offers given.

Assessing the recruitment process requires observing and measuring how it occurs, whether due diligence was given when placing employment ads, whether information about the jobs reached potential applicant pools in a nonbiased way, etc. These processes are difficult to document. Disparate impact discrimination may easily arise in recruitment procedures. For example, if recruitment to a large extent takes place through information networks (say, referrals from male employees or male job networks), there may be a disparate impact on women or minorities. In terms of who gets offers or is hired, discriminfation is also difficult to document. Information on the applicant pool is rarely available and all that may be accessible to outsiders is information on those hired. Even in large firms, information on the hiring process is often incomplete, or if complete, often is not computerized or is available only in an incompletely documented format. And when the relevant information is available, it likely is ambiguous and open to many interpretations.

Data on who gets offers and who does not may come from personnel records kept by firms on all of their applicants. With information about the qualifications of the applicants, and their fit relative to the job, it is possible to assess whether there is disparate treatment in making job offers. Audit studies provide another source of data on who gets hired. If matched pairs of equally qualified men and women apply for the same jobs with same employer, a higher rate of success by men, compared to women, in getting job offers is evidence of discrimination.

To assess the quality of offers made and the placements at hire requires measuring the conditions for all offers made, accepted, and rejected; it is not necessary to have information on the entire applicant pool. It is often easy to document the conditions in accepted offers, but it is more difficult for rejected ones. As in who gets an offer, there is usually a subjective element in deciding which conditions to offer, simply because less is known at the point of hire than is known at later stages when promotions are considered. Thus, unless an employer determines the conditions offered exclusively on the basis of formal qualifications, such as degree, grades, and experience, there is much scope for subjective elements, and these can be difficult to measure.

Promotion

Allocative discrimination in the promotion process, compared to hiring, is easier to measure and analyze. Although deciding which employee is more qualified for promotion usually involves some amount of subjective judgment, on which there may be disagreements among various assessors, the relative qualifications of those promoted and those passed over can be documented in a comparatively unambiguous manner, given the promotion rules of the organization. Assessment of allocative discrimination thus requires measuring the relevant job performance and qualifications of employees, and whether they were subsequently promoted from one evaluation period to the next. If women or minorities with qualifications equal to those of men or nonminorities are promoted at a lower rate, then there is evidence of disparate treatment.

Disparate impact discrimination can also occur at the promotion stage. For example, if an employer requires geographic mobility for an employee to advance, this may, on average, be more difficult for women than men to satisfy. A requirement of geographic mobility in order to be promoted, unless mobility would lead to acquiring a bona fide occupational qualification, such as experience in different units of an organization, could be classified as disparate impact discrimination.

A major difficulty arises in measuring discrimination in promotion to, or hiring into, top positions, often referred to as the glass-ceiling problem. For top positions, a considerable amount of intangible information always goes into a decision; highly qualified people make judgments about highly qualified candidates, and the judgment to a large extent not only assesses past performance, but also future potential. Investigating statistical data is rarely sufficient in such cases, and what is needed is the supplementary "thicker" description that can be acquired from observing the hiring or promotion process, how candidates were selected, job interviews, and so on. Social scientists rarely have access to information on these processes.

A similar measurement problem arises when the groups discriminated against are small. For example, an employer may not have hired any people with visible handicaps (e.g., in wheel chairs), but may not have had many qualified applicants with such handicaps. Assessing whether a failure to hire was due to discrimination would require investigating quite carefully the relevant applicant files. A more equal representation of various groups should be expected with large employers, simply because large employers usually get many applicants, hire more, and hence have better opportunities to achieve numerical equality along various dimensions.

Firing

To assess discrimination in firing and layoffs requires collecting data on the grounds for termination and workforce reductions, and whether there is disparate treatment (for example, say two women were fired, but two equally or less qualified men were kept). In the United States, most employment discrimination lawsuits relate to firing, but that need not mean that this is the most prevalent form of discrimination. It may only reflect that it is a form that is easy to pursue in the courts. In many work settings, layoffs have been tied to seniority; the last hired is the first to be laid off. This may disadvantage women, who often have lower seniority, and can thus be construed as disparate impact discrimination. Discrimination by age and health status may also be a factor in firing.

Where: Employment Arena 2, Within-Job Wage Discrimination

For assessing within-job wage discrimination, primarily an instance of disparate treatment discrimination, it is necessary to obtain information on the wages of men and women who do the same work for the same employer. The "same" work can be defined as same job title or same narrow occupation description. The "same" employer is defined as the same workplace (i.e., establishment). In some instances, the actual work tasks may be the same, but job titles can differ and wages can also differ. Disproportionate employment of men within a job title with a higher wage may be evidence of discrimination. This is termed "within-job wage discrimination," because the two different job titles only reflect different wages, not different work tasks. It can also be considered allocative discrimination, because the problem in part lies in the allocation to job titles. If the job title with the higher wage is given as reward for experience, past productivity, or acquired qualifications, the situation may be considered nondiscriminatory.

The main difficulty in measurement arises when pay depends not only on the job occupied but also on the qualifications, merit, or productivity of the employee. These parameters can justify wage differences even within jobs, but they can be hard to measure. If the pay depends on factors unrelated to job performance, and the factors are correlated with gender, then there is disparate impact discrimination. Sometimes it may also be difficult to identify whether two jobs are substantially equal, and hence whether the U.S. Equal Pay Act or similar legislation in other countries applies. Historically, there have been particularly transparent examples of within-job wage discrimination. In Sweden, Australia, and Britain, for example, union contracts for each job title specified separate wages for men and women, with female wages sometimes set as much as 50% below male wages. Many justifications for such discrimination were given; one was that men needed to earn a wage sufficient to support a family. The practice was abolished in most countries in the 1960s. It was certainly a form of within-job wage discrimination that was easy to measure.

Researchers often use sample surveys of individuals and then a regression analysis to relate wages to qualifications, occupation, and illegitimate characteristics. Finding that women on average earn less than men, net of qualifications and occupation, the conclusion is sometimes drawn that there is within-job wage discrimination. But survey data provide no evidence that employers pay different wages to men and women in the same occupation. The observed differential may simply reflect that men and women work for different employers who pay different wages. It may also reflect crude occupational codes, with comparisons of employees in broad occupational groups within which there is much heterogeneity.

Where: Employment Arena 3, Valuative Discrimination

In valuative discrimination, the discrimination is not against any specific individual but rather is against classes of jobs held primarily by women; this is often referred to as comparable worth discrimination. Classification as either disparate treatment discrimination or disparate impact discrimination can be difficult here; sometimes valuative discrimination falls between the two. The classification problem reflects the disputed status such discrimination has. In its pure form, men and women are paid the same wages when working in the same occupation in the same firm, but wages are lower in occupations with a high percentage of females. Framed this way, valuative discrimination may be viewed as disparate impact discrimination. This is especially the case when male-dominated jobs require characteristics that are typically male, such as physical strength, but are irrelevant for job performance, yet are rewarded in the market. The U.S. courts have also approached this as disparate treatment discrimination, as when an organization pays females in certain job catgories lower wages only because the category is female dominated, without there being any other characteristics of the job that could justify lower wages.

Valuative discrimination has so far arisen only in connection with gender, not in connection with racial or other kinds of discrimination. It is not necessarily related to any prejudice against women or to any statistical differences between the sexes. The employer's sole motive may be to minimize wage costs, paying lower wages by taking advantage of occupational categorizations as "female dominated." This is an "easy" (legally blameless) way to minimize wage costs, compared to, say, within-job wage discrimination, because in the latter case, an employer would be in blatant violation of the law. Legislation regarding valuative discrimination varies across countries. It is not illegal in the United States, and though it is illegal in Canada, it is not enforced.

Documentation of valuative discrimination is difficult and the evidence is often ambiguous. There are two principal ways to measure it. One approach, which can be called the market approach, is based on use of sample or census data on individual employees, their wages, occupations, and qualifications. To each occupation is imputed a "value" or "job worth." This can be obtained from measuring how hard the occupation is to perform, the skills it requires (such as technical versus people skills), and so on. This is sometimes obtained from separate sources, developed for assessing aspects of occupations, and then matched to individual-level data. An index of the factors may be created or each factor may be considered by itself. A low versus high score on a factor or the index indicates a low versus high job worth. Jobs or occupations with equal scores on an index are said to be of equal value. The final step is to regress the individual wages on the index for job worth (or on the separate factors entering into an index), on individual qualifications, illegitimate characteristics such as gender, and, particularly, the percentage of females in the occupation. If there is a negative effect on the wage due to the percentage of females in the occupation, then the conclusion is that female-dominated jobs are undervalued in the market, because, even for same job worth, as measured by the index or the factors, and for same individual qualifications, wages in female-dominated occupations are lower than they are in male-dominated ones. Many such studies have been undertaken in North America, Europe, and elsewhere.

The market-based approach establishes the extent to which female-dominated occupations earn lower wages, even when they have the same value as measured by a job-worth index or the separate job-worth factors. The job-worth index or factors capture what is valued in the market. Some factors here that perhaps ought to be highly valued, such as nurturing skills, which are more common among women than men, are nevertheless given a low value in the market. That would indicate a bias in what the market values. This bias would come in addition to the devaluation of female-dominated occupations that occurs net of the characteristics that the market actually values. The market-based approach does not document whether the lower pay in female-dominated occupations occurs in a way that could be considered illegitimate at the workplace level, and it does not identify a discriminatory agent. All it documents is that the market values female-dominated occupations less than it does male-dominated ones.

In the second approach, the case study approach, single organizations are investigated. This is especially easy when an organization has assigned worth to jobs using a tool called job evaluation, as is often done in the United States. Then, as in the market-based approach, the researcher assesses whether wages in the jobs, net of their value as measured by the job-worth index, are negatively related to the percentage of females in the job or occupation. A negative relationship is evidence of valuative discrimination in the organization. This can be classified as disparate impact discrimination; i.e., wages in jobs are set so that they disadvantage females more than males. It is sometimes also classified as disparate treatment discrimination. Again, which factors enter into a job-worth index, and how these are weighed, can reflect typically male traits more than female ones, in which case, it can be argued, there is discrimination in the job evaluation procedure, clearly an instance of disparate impact discrimination.

This kind of evidence concerning valuative discrimination is controversial. Not only is the legal status of such discrimination unclear, there is also ambiguity as to how to measure this type of discrimination. Many researchers, policymakers, and judges consider the lower pay in female-dominated occupations not to be discrimination at all, but rather as arising from market processes that, in principle, should be viewed as fair. Others are of the view that the lower wages in female-dominated jobs reflect biases in society at large. These values may have become embedded in wage systems and are simply passed on by inertia by employers and due to historically male-dominated unions.

It should be noted that the various forms of discrimination in the employment arena do not always operate independently. For example, there is a subtle connection between allocative and valuative discrimination. It is sometimes claimed that without allocative discrimination, occupational gender segregation would vanish, and hence that valuative discrimination would cease to be a factor; the former is thus a necessary condition for the latter. But this claim requires two other processes to occur: first, that gender segregation in education ceases (which is clearly not happening), and second, that gender differences in preferences for occupations, work schedules, and the like cease (also not happening, in part due to the unequal distribution of labor in the household). With gender differences in educational choices and in preferences, occupational gender segregation will persist, even in the absence of allocative discrimination, and valuative discrimination will hence persist. But because two forms of discrimination are connected, it does not follow that they cannot be separated for measurement purposes. As previously discussed, documentation of the two requires different types of data and measurement strategies.

Summary

In measuring employment discrimination, the central difficulty is in assembling admissible evidence. This is evidence on how employers treat people differentially by gender, race, or other illegitimate factors, or how rules and procedures irrelevant for job performance advantage one group over another. Evidence of discrimination in hiring, promotions, and setting of wages needs to be assembled primarily at the workplace level. The type of measurement needed varies with the kinds of discrimination.

Discrimination may occur in a number of settings other than employment. In housing markets, discrimination against specific ethnic groups can arise as a result of pure prejudice or from statistical discrimination, as when some groups are correctly considered to be worse or better tenants. In retail markets, such as in car sales, discrimination may arise from knowledge of bargaining behaviors of various groups, which then can be exploited in order to extract higher sales prices. Regardless of the setting, the central requirement of a measurement strategy is that the discriminatory actions are measured on the basis of how "likes" are treated as "unlikes" at the level at which discrimination occurs.

See Also the Following Articles

Behavioral Psychology • Organizational Behavior • Social Interaction Models

Further Reading

Bloch, F. (1994). *Antidiscrimination Law and Minority Employment.* University of Chicago Press, Chicago, IL.

England, P. (1992). *Comparable Worth: Theories and Evidence.* Aldine de Gruyter, Hawthorne, New York.

Nelson, R. L., and Bridges, W. P. (1999). *Legalizing Gender Inequality. Courts, Markets, and Unequal Pay for Women in America.* Cambridge University Press, New York.

Reskin, B. F. (1998). *The Realities of Affirmative Action in Employment.* American Sociological Association, Washington, D.C.

Rhoads, S. E. (1993). *Incomparable Worth. Pay Equity Meets the Market.* Cambridge University Press, Cambridge, MA.

Valian, V. (1998). *Why So Slow? The Advancement of Women.* MIT Press, Cambridge, MA.

Domestic Violence: Measurement of Incidence and Prevalence

Jana L. Jasinski
University of Central Florida, Orlando, Florida, USA

Glossary

alpha coefficient A measure of internal validity, ranging from 0 to 1, that indicates how much the items in an index measure the same thing.

common couple violence Occasional outbursts of violence from either partner in an intimate relationship.

incidence Frequency of occurrence of a phenomenon.

patriarchal terrorism Systematic male violence based on patriarchal control.

prevalence Presence versus the absence of a social phenomenon.

Domestic violence began to be recognized, by researchers and the general public alike, as a serious social problem in the late 1960s and early 1970s. Since then, the term has been used to describe a variety of violent relationships, including intimate partner violence, child abuse, elder abuse, and stalking. Although there exists a general understanding about the meaning of the term, there remains a considerable debate regarding its definition and measurement. Consequently, estimates of the occurrence of domestic violence range widely and empirical research has been hindered. It is these methodological issues, particularly their inconsistencies, that may make it more difficult to understand the true nature and extent of the problem. In addition, the highly politicized nature of domestic violence has contributed to controversy over the prevalence of omestic violence, the identities of the victims and perpetrators, and the nature of the risk factors.

How Prevalent is Domestic Violence?

Early estimates of intimate partner violence suggested that male violence against women occurred in one out of eight couples. Much more controversial, however, was the finding that violence by women occurred at nearly the same rate. More recently, the National Violence Against Women Survey estimated in 2000 that almost 2 million women were physically assaulted and more than 300,000 women experienced a completed or attempted rape in the year prior to the survey. This same survey estimated that more than 50 million women were physically assaulted and almost 20 million experienced an attempted or completed rape in their lifetime. Also used to understand the prevalence of domestic violence in the United States, the National Crime Victimization Survey (NCVS) estimated that slightly more than 800,000 women and 160,000 men were victims of intimate partner violence in 1998. Each of these surveys has been cited as a reliable source of domestic violence figures in the United States, yet each has arrived at different, sometimes widely divergent, estimates of both the extent of the problem and gender differences in the rates of victimization and perpetration. Why are there such large discrepancies between studies? Certainly there are a number of explanations for differences in research results, but it has been suggested that perhaps the most likely explanation has to do with issues of definition and measurement.

Issues in Definition

What Is Domestic Violence?

Research on domestic violence has almost a 30-year history and there exists a general understanding of the meaning of the term. At the same time, however, when pressed to indicate exactly which actions and relationships should be considered as domestic violence, there is little consensus. According to the Model Code on Domestic and Family

Violence of National Council of Juvenile and Family Court Judges, domestic violence is defined as the occurrence of one or more of the following acts by a family or household member, but does not include acts of self-defense:

- Attempting to cause or causing physical harm to another family or household member.
- Placing a family or household member in fear of physical harm.
- Causing a family or household member to engage involuntarily in sexual activity by force, threat of force, or duress.

This definition was designed to provide a model for state lawmakers in their development of state codes. As such, it is a relatively broad definition that covers several different types of violent relationships, including partner abuse, parent abuse, child abuse, and sibling abuse. The definition also excludes certain relationships, specifically dating partners who are not living together. Researchers, however, have often been more specific when defining domestic violence for the purposes of a particular empirical study. For example, perhaps the most common use of the term "domestic violence" in research refers to intimate partner violence, and, even more specifically, to violence against women. The choice of what to include under the broad term of domestic violence is particularly important because it has ramifications for estimates of the prevalence and incidence of domestic violence.

How Is Domestic Violence Defined?

Although there are literally thousands of studies on "family or domestic violence," the field as a whole has yet to reach any type of consensus on what exactly constitutes family or domestic violence. This is most likely due to the interdisciplinary nature of domestic violence research. Different disciplines focus on different areas with respect to domestic violence and as a result there are variations in definitions. Defining a problem, however, is a vital first step in any empirical study because it shapes every aspect of research on the problem. Moreover, the debate about how to define and measure domestic violence has resulted in serious divisions within the field of violence research.

Definitions of domestic violence can be grouped into two main categories, with wide-ranging results. Narrow, legalistic definitions, for example, may result in lower estimates of the extent of the problem, whereas broader definitions may elicit larger numbers. One difficulty with using broad definitions, however, may be the perception that, by including so many different types of behaviors, most individuals are then defined as victims. It also makes it more complicated to isolate risk factors that may or may not be the same for different types of behavior. At the same time, limiting definitions to only one or two acts ignores the possibility of interconnected multiple forms of abuse in a relationship. This said, definitions of domestic violence do vary widely. Some, for instance, are based on legal codes, some include different types of abuse (such as physical, emotional, sexual, and psychological), and others include only one type.

In many cases, acknowledging that individuals differ in how they define the concept of domestic violence, researchers have used behaviorally specific measures that ask respondents if certain acts have been perpetrated against them, rather than asking if they have been a victim of domestic violence. It has also been suggested, however, that the concept of domestic violence is multidimensional and that, in order to design quality research studies and ultimately more effective prevention and intervention efforts, it is necessary to consider the possibility that there are multiple types of violence that should be defined and measured differently. For example, some researchers have made the distinction between common couple violence and patriarchal terrorism, two distinct forms of violence with different dynamics and consequences. Although the consequence of using different types of definitions (resulting in different estimates of the extent of the problem) provides an interesting intellectual debate, it also has practical consequences. Policymakers, for example, may be more likely to allocate resources for a particular social problem if the numbers suggest its significance.

In addition to the issues regarding definition, there are other research design-related issues that have great consequences for the study of domestic violence. Unfortunately, even if researchers in the field all used the same definition, incidence and prevalence rates would still differ as a result of using different samples (e.g., college students, shelter residents, or health professionals) and different modes of research (phone surveys, in-person interviews, or self-administered questionnaires). For example, it has been suggested that the context of the study can also influence the rates of violence obtained. Studies presented in the context of a study on criminal behavior will tend to produce higher rates of assault by men, whereas in family conflict studies, equal rates of assault by both men and women are observed.

Issues in Measurement

How Do We Measure Domestic Violence?

Although the debate about how to define domestic violence is essential, equally important to consider is how to measure the phenomenon. The most common assessment of domestic violence focuses on physical assaults, including slapping, hitting, and punching, among other actions. There is, however, some agreement that domestic violence includes more than simply physical assaults, and measurement strategies should include some assessment of emotional abuse, sexual violence, and verbal aggression as well as physical abuse. Differences in the type of behaviors measured may account for much of the variation in rates of violence. For example, rates of violence that include only physical assaults are likely to be lower than rates that include physical and sexual assaults.

In addition to the particular assessment used to measure domestic violence, it is also important to consider the methodological strategy employed. Information gathered from individuals via a self-administered survey instrument is likely to be different from that gathered from police reports. Moreover, even different types of instrument administration may result in very different responses. Self-administered surveys, for instance, may produce different results than produced by interviewer-administered surveys. In addition to the influence of the research design, sample differences may also result in different types of data. For example, research using information obtained from a sample of victims in shelter will be decidedly different than that obtained from a convenience sample of college students. Also debated is the potential difference in rates of intimate partner violence when reports are obtained from both partners in a couple or only one.

Issues Related to Measurement Strategies

Given the variety of decisions that must be made in any research design, a number of issues need to be considered for research on domestic violence. For example, perhaps the first question any researcher must ask is "What is it we really want to know?" In addition, researchers must decide on the purpose of the research. Research designed to estimate how much violence exists in a certain area (the United States, for example) will look very different from research designed to assess the impact of violence on a sample of victims. The scope of the issue to be addressed must also be decided. In other words, decisions must be made regarding definitions of what behaviors will constitute violence, as well as what relationships between the perpetrator and victim (e.g., dating partner, cohabitant, or spouse) will be evaluated.

Incidence vs. Prevalence

How much domestic violence occurs in the United States? This question is fundamental to understanding the significance of this social problem. The results from research designed to answer this question are often presented in terms of an incidence or prevalence rate. However, some scholars argue that researchers are inconsistent when referring to prevalence versus incidence. Incidence has been used to refer to both the extent and the frequency of violent events. Similarly, the term "prevalence" has also generally been used to measure the extent to which violence occurs. At the same time, regardless of which term is used (prevalence or incidence), most studies have presented rates in terms of either the presence or absence of violence. It has also been argued that it is very common for researchers to make the distinction between prevalence and incidence based on the reference period used. Most often, researchers using a 1-year referent period refer to rates as incidence rates, whereas others using reference periods greater than 1 year refer to rates as prevalence rates. Regardless of what terminology is used, it is apparent that readers of these studies must be clear on the definition of the concepts of prevalence and incidence as they are used in particular studies. To aid in this process, standardized meanings should be used. Specifically, prevalence should be used to indicate how much violence occurs in the population (presence vs. absence) and incidence should indicate how much violence occurs among those who are violent (frequency of violence). Although researchers are inconsistent in the use of terminology, they are in greater agreement regarding the particular instruments used to measure domestic violence. Some of the most commonly used instruments are given in Table I.

Common Measures of Domestic Violence

Conflict Tactics Scales

The Conflict Tactics Scale (CTS) is perhaps the most widely used and accepted instrument to assess assaults by intimate partners. It is also the subject of a great deal of controversy. The original CTS was based on the theoretical framework provided by conflict theory and was developed as a way to measure overt actions used as a response to a conflict of interest. Specifically, this instrument measures the extent to which specific tactics have been used by either partner in an intimate relationship. The original design of the CTS was to begin with the less coercive items and move toward the more aggressive items so that the socially acceptable items were presented first to the respondents. The CTS is designed to measure three methods for dealing with conflict: reasoning, verbal aggression, and physical force. The alpha coefficients for reliability ranged from a low of 0.50 for the reasoning scale to 0.83 for the physical assault scale.

Table I Common Measures of Domestic Violence

Measure	*Definition*
Conflict Tactics Scale	Both CTS and CTS2 measure the extent to which specific tactics are used by individuals in an intimate relationship
CTS	Measures reasoning, verbal aggression, and physical force (19 items, form R)
CTS2	Measures sexual coercion, physical injury, physical assault, psychological aggression, and negotiation (39 items)
Composite Abuse Scale	Measures different types of abuse and frequency of abuse; includes four scales (emotional abuse, physical abuse, harassment, and severe combined abuse)
Severity of Violence Against Women Scales	Measures symbolic violence, threats of physical violence, actual violence, and sexual violence (46 acts are included)
Abusive Behavior Inventory	Measures frequency of physical, sexual, and psychological abuse (30 items)
Index of Spouse Abuse	Measures severity or magnitude of both physical and nonphysical abuse (30 items)
Propensity for Abuse Scale	Nonreactive measure of propensity for male violence against a female partner (29 items)
Measure of Wife Abuse	Measures frequency of verbal, physical, psychological, and sexual abuse, and emotional consequences of abuse for the victim (60 items)

The more recently developed Revised Conflict Tactics Scales (CTS2) is also based on the theoretical foundation of conflict theory. The 39-item CTS2 includes measures of sexual coercion and physical injury in addition to scales measuring physical assault (formerly violence), psychological aggression (formerly verbal aggression), and negotiation (formerly reasoning). In addition, changes have been made to the language of each item, from "his/her" to "my partner," and the format has been simplified to make self-administration easier. The item order was also revised in the CTS2. Rather than a hierarchical order of items, from most socially acceptable to least, the CTS2 uses an interspersed item order. Alpha coefficients for reliability ranged from 0.79 (psychological aggression) to 0.95 (injury).

Results from the 1975 National Family Violence Survey indicating that women were equal to men, if not more, in violent behavior started a debate that continues today. The results from this study, using the Conflict Tactics Scale, directly contradicted what other researchers and advocates had seen in the criminal justice system and in shelters. Perhaps the most common critique of the CTS is that by focusing on actions used to resolve conflict, there is no attention given to the context and meaning of the actions for the individuals involved in the incident and gendered power imbalances are excluded. For example, the scale begins by asking respondents to think of situations in the past year when they had a disagreement or were angry with their spouse or partner and to indicate how often they or their partner engaged in each of the acts included in the CTS. It has been argued that the context of a disagreement may serve to minimize abusive actions. Additionally, the exclusive focus on physical violence has often been considered too narrow, because it excludes other forms of interpersonal violence, such as sexual violence. The revised CTS has addressed some critiques by including measurements for injury and sexual assault and coercion, but the scale still treats all actions the same. Additionally, the criticisms surrounding the lack of context for violent actions remain.

Composite Abuse Scale

The Composite Abuse Scale was designed to measure different types of abuse, the frequency of abuse, and the consequences. It is a comprehensive measure including items from previously established measures of violence, including the Conflict Tactics Scale, the Measure of Wife Abuse, the Inventory of Spouse Abuse, and the Psychological Maltreatment of Women Inventory. Four scales measuring emotional abuse, physical abuse, harassment, and severe combined abuse were developed from the pool of items from the established measures. Alpha coefficients were used to assess the reliability of this measure. For each scale, coefficients were greater than 0.90.

Severity of Violence Against Women Scales

The Severity of Violence Against Women Scales were developed as a more sensitive measure of intimate violence. The creators of the scale wanted to include in their measure of physical violence seriousness, abusiveness, aggressiveness, violence, and threat value. To accomplish this, items were chosen from the violence literature to represent symbolic violence, threats of physical violence, actual violence, and sexual violence. The scale includes 46 acts that can distinguish between nine dimensions of violence by men against women: symbolic violence (e.g., drove dangerously with her in the car), threats of mild violence (e.g., shook a fist at her), threats of moderate violence (e.g., destroyed something belonging to her), mild violence (e.g., pushed or shoved her), minor violence (e.g., twisted her arm), moderate violence (e.g., slapped her with the back of his hand), serious violence (e.g., beat her up), and sexual violence (e.g., physically forced her to have sex). The scales can be used to examine one incident of violence or to compare several incidents to find out if violence is increasing. One of the advantages of using this scale is that it allows for the differentiation of nine different forms of violence. It may also address some of the common critiques of the Conflict Tactics Scale in that it is able to assess some of the dimensions of violent relationships that are not included in the CTS. It is also a reliable scale, with alpha coefficients ranging from 0.89 to 0.96.

Abusive Behavior Inventory

The Abusive Behavior Inventory (ABI) is a 30-item measure designed to assess the frequency of physical, sexual, and psychological abuse as well as psychological abuse including emotional violence, isolation, intimidation, and threats. In contrast to the CTS, which is based on conflict theory, the ABI focuses on the concepts of power and control derived from feminist theory. Its focus, therefore is on violence as a means of maintaining power and control over a victim. The instrument can be administered both to batterers and to their partners and measures the frequency of abuse experienced within a 6-month time frame. Reliability coefficients ranged from 0.70 to 0.92 using samples of nonabusive and abusive men and nonabused and abused women.

Index of Spouse Abuse

The Index of Spouse Abuse was designed for use in clinical settings for monitoring and evaluating treatment progress. It is a 30-item scale designed to measure severity or magnitude of abuse, including a scale for physical violence against women and a scale for nonphysical violence against women. It is not designed to measure prevalence or incidence. The self-reported scale scores on each scale range from 0 to 100; a low score indicates relative absence of abuse. Examples of items include "my partner belittles me," "my partner slaps me around my face and head," and "my partner acts like he would like to kill me." In the initial validation of the scale, three samples were used (female university students in ongoing relationship with a male partner, university students and faculty, and a female community sample in which some women were classified by therapists as victims and others were classified as free of victimization). Alpha coefficients for both scales were greater than 0.90. The authors of the scales also developed clinical cutting scores for each of the two scales. For the physical abuse scale, a score of 10 was the cutoff; for the nonphysical abuse scale, a score of 25 was used. Although psychometric testing indicated that the Index of Spouse Abuse was a reliable measure of the degree and magnitude of abuse by men of women, the authors also point out that the abused women in their sample were primarily from shelters and may only represent severely abused women.

Propensity for Abuse Scale

The propensity for abuse scale is composed of 29 items selected from other scales. It was designed to be a nonreactive measure of the propensity for male violence against a female partner, and as a result does not include any overt items about abuse. The scale is completed by the perpetrator and can be corroborated with victim reports. It contains items from a variety of established scales, including the Self-Report Instrument for Borderline Personality Organization (a 30 item measure of identify diffusion, primitive defenses, and reality testing), the Multidimensional Anger Inventory (an assessment of various dimensions of anger response), and the Trauma Symptom Checklist (to assess symptoms and consequences associated with experiences of trauma). Other items assess memories of parental behavior, attachment patterns, and psychopathology. Initial validation of the scale suggested that it correctly classifies men into high or low abusiveness categories. The scale has also been correlated with the Power and Control Wheel, a conceptual measure of the dynamics of abusive relationships, and significantly predicted intimidation tactics, emotional abuse, and use of male privilege. Cross-validation of the scale suggested that it predicts abuse across different groups, including clinical samples, college males, and gay couples. The authors suggest that the Propensity for Abuse scales, because of their nonreactive nature, may be very useful in prevention programs as well as to assess the severity and frequency of men whzo have already been identified as abusive.

Measure of Wife Abuse

The Measure of Wife Abuse (MWA) is a 60-item instrument that measures the type of abuse enacted by a man toward his wife. Similar to the Abusive Behavior Inventory, the MWA uses a reference period of 6 months and contains questions regarding the number of times various abusive acts occurred in a couple's relationship. In addition to assessing the frequency of verbal, physical, psychological, and sexual abuse, the MWA also measures the emotional consequences for the victim by asking how much the particular action hurt or upset her. Alpha coefficients ranged from 0.73 to 0.94 for the subscales.

Conclusion: What Is the Impact of Measurement?

The manner in which domestic violence is defined, measured, and presented is extremely important. Establishing that domestic violence is a social problem paves the way for the development and funding of prevention and intervention programs. At the same time, however, disagreements about how to define and measure domestic violence, and the use of a wide variety of instruments and samples, produce differences in incidence and prevalence rates, making policy and program creation more difficult. Certainly lower bound estimates of domestic violence may influence the quantity of programs available. Furthermore, intervention programs may also be affected because, as different definitions of domestic violence are used, diverse risk factors are identified. Understanding how important defining and measuring any social problem is, the Centers for Disease Control has compiled a set of uniform definitions and recommended data elements for the surveillance of intimate partner violence. This represents one of the first steps toward establishing some consistency with regard to measurement. Regardless of how deep the impact of measurement is, it is certainly an issue that deserves greater attention now that the field of domestic violence research is moving beyond its infancy.

See Also the Following Article

National Crime Victimization Surveys

Further Reading

Brownridge, D. A., and Halli, S. S. (1999). Measuring family violence: The conceptualization and utilization of prevalence and incidence rates. *J. Fam. Violence* **14,** 333–349.

DeKeseredy, W. S. (2000). Current controversies on defining nonlethal violence against women in intimate heterosexual relationships. *Violence Women* **6,** 728–746.

DeKeseredy, W. S., and Schwartz, M. D. (2001). Definitional issues. In *Sourcebook on Violence against Women* (C. M. Renzetti, J. L. Edelson, and R. K. Bergen, eds.), pp. 23–34. Sage Publ., Thousand Oaks, California.

Dobash, R. P., Dobash, R. E., Wilson, M., and Daly, M. (1992). The myth of sexual symmetry in marital violence. *Social Probl.* **39,** 71–91.

Dutton, D. G. (1995). A scale for measuring propensity for abusiveness. *J. Fam. Violence* **10,** 203–221.

Hegarty, K., Sheehan, M., and Schonfeld, C. (1999). A multidimensional definition of partner abuse: Development and preliminary validation of the composite abuse scale. *J. Fam. Violence* **14,** 399–415.

Hudson, W. H., and McIntosh, S. R. (1981). The assessment of spouse abuse: Two quantifiable dimensions. *J. Marr. Fam.* **43,** 873–885, 888.

Johnson, M. P. (1995). Patriarchal terrorism and common couple violence: Two forms of violence against women. *J. Marr. Fam.* **57,** 283–294.

Marshall, L. L. (1992). Development of the severity of violence against women scales. *J. Fam. Violence* **7,** 103–123.

National Council of Juvenile and Family Court Judges. (1994). *Family Violence: A Model State Code.* Conrad N. Hilton Foundation, Reno, Nevada.

Rennison, C. M., and Welchans, S. (2000). *Intimate Partner Violence.* U.S. Department of Justice No. NCJ 178247. Bureau of Justice Statistics, Washington, D.C.

Rodenburg, F. A., and Fantuzzo, J. W. (1993). The measure of wife abuse: Steps toward the development of a comprehensive assessment technique. *J. Fam. Violence* **8,** 203–228.

Saltzman, L. E., Fanslow, J. L., McMahon, P. M., and Shelley, G. A. (1999). *Intimate Partner Violence Surveillance: Uniform Definitions and Recommended Data Elements (Version 1.0).* Centers for Disease Control and Prevention, National Center for Injury Prevention and Control, Atlanta, Georgia.

Saunders, D. G. (1988). Wife abuse, husband abuse, or mutual combat? In *Feminist Perspectives on Wife Abuse* (K. Yllo and M. Bograd, eds.), pp. 90–113. Sage Publ., Newbury Park, California.

Shepard, M. F., and Campbell, J. A. (1992). The abusive behavior inventory: A measure of psychological and physical abuse. *J. Interpers. Violence* **6,** 336–344.

Straus, M. A. (1999). The controversy over domestic violence by women: A methodological, theoretical, and sociology of science analysis. In *Violence in Intimate Relationships* (X. B. Arriage and S. Oskamp, eds.), pp. 17–44. Sage Publ., Thousand Oaks, California.

Straus, M. A., and Gelles, R. J. (eds.) (1990). *Physical Violence in American Families: Risk Factors and Adaptations to Violence in 8,145 Families.* Transaction Publ., New Brunswick, New Jersey.

Straus, M. A., Gelles, R. J., and Steinmetz, S. K. (1980). *Behind Closed Doors: Violence in the American Family.* Doubleday/Anchor, New York.

Straus, M. A., Hamby, S. L., Boney-McCoy, S., and Sugarman, D. B. (1996). The Revised Conflict Tactics Scales (CTS2): Development and preliminary psychometric data. *J. Fam. Iss.* **17,** 283–316.

Tjaden, P., and Thoennes, N. (2000). *Full Report: Prevalence, Incidence, and Consequences of Violence against Women: Findings from the National Violence against Women Survey.* Research Brief. U.S. Department of Justice, Washington, D.C.

Duncan, Otis Dudley

Magnus Stenbeck
Centre for Epidemiology, National Board of Health and Welfare, Stockholm, Sweden

Glossary

contingency table A multivariable table with cross-tabulated data.

Likert scale A rating scale to measure attitudes by quantifying subjective information.

quasi-symmetry A generalization of the contingency table model symmetry corresponding to the generalized multidimensional Rasch model.

Rasch model A model providing a formal representation of fundamental measurements.

Otis Dudley Duncan is a leading figure in social science and in social measurement. In the 1980s, he adapted and introduced Georg Rasch's measurement theory and models for the evaluation of social surveys. Prior to this, Duncan developed several important methods and strategies for data collection and sociological data analysis. He laid the foundation for the United States General Social Survey, he developed the Duncan Socioeconomic Index for measuring the social standing of individuals, and he introduced structural equation models into sociology. These instruments and methods became established as standard tools for empirical sociologists worldwide. Duncan's work also contributed to methodological developments in other disciplines, including social statistics, political science, economics, epidemiology, and public health. Furthermore, his empirical work in occupational sociology, stratification, social mobility, and urban sociology provided points of departure and defined the research agendas for several generations of empirically oriented sociologists. Duncan's most important contributions to social measurement are his development of Rasch models for the evaluation and development of social surveys and his work on the sociology of measurement. He eventually developed a very critical attitude toward both the overemphasis on data analysis, particularly the frequent applications of advanced structural equation models, and the lack of fundamental work on design and measurement problems in sociology.

Introduction

Otis Dudley Duncan (1921–) is a leading figure in 20th-century social science. Duncan's academic career encompasses over 40 years of groundbreaking contributions to social science theory and methods. Duncan's contribution to the scientific literature includes 16 authored and 6 edited books, as well as over 200 articles in scientific journals and other publications.

Duncan was born in Texas in 1921 and grew up in Stillwater, Oklahoma, where his father headed the Department of Sociology at the Oklahoma A&M College (subsequently Oklahoma State University). He started his training as a sociologist before World War II, but was drafted immediately after completing his Master of Arts. After the war, Duncan went to the University of Chicago, where he was trained by William F. Ogburn and Philip M. Hauser. He took his doctorate in Chicago in 1949. His long career includes professorships at the universities of Chicago, Michigan, Arizona, and Santa Barbara. Short appointments as a visiting scholar to Oxford, England and Vienna, Austria in the 1970s were important for his contributions to social measurement. Since his retirement in the fall of 1987, he has been Professor Emeritus at the University of California at Santa Barbara.

Throughout his career as a sociologist, Duncan introduced many methods of data analysis, and often developed them to suit the needs of social science. His focus on analyzing actual empirical data, and his inventiveness in adapting methodological tools to sociological research problems made his work useful for several generations of empirically oriented social scientists. He defined research agendas for several lines of empirical social research, such as human ecology, social stratification, urban sociology, occupational sociology, and social mobility. In his own words, he has gained a reputation as a "'methodologist' (a term that I dislike) because I have so frequently been in the position of offering a more rigorous and more quantitative approach to research on topics where the significant insights have already been attained by sociologists using less formal techniques." Duncan has dealt with all phases of social measurement and has made contributions to all of them. This includes designing social survey instruments, developing social "scales," creating analytical tools for social science, developing measurement models, and outlining the agenda for a sociology of measurement. Even though his early contributions have gained greater attention than has his later work, the latter is more important from a measurement perspective.

After having introduced structural equation models into social science, in his late career, Duncan turned to Georg Rasch's measurement models and applied them to sociological survey measurement. The work included introducing and illustrating the usefulness of Rasch models for sociological measurement problems as well as developing and extending the models to multidimensional latent structures, extended response formats, and various other design characteristics. Duncan simultaneously developed a "historical and critical" sociological perspective on social measurement, which is best described in his 1984 book *Notes on Social Measurement: Historical and Critical*. He became critical of the general development of North American empirical social science, including much of his own previous work and the research traditions based on it, particularly the work on structural equation models. In the 1980s, he spent the concluding years of his career combining the recently developed methods of log-linear contingency table analysis with Rasch's development of item response theory and measurement theory.

Contributions to Data Collection, Data Analysis, and Methods of Analysis

In general, Duncan's contributions include designing large data collection efforts, creating tools for data analysis, and defining measurement models for social science. With respect to data collection, Duncan's most important contribution is laying the foundations for the United States General Social Survey (GSS). In his small book *Toward Social Reporting: Next Steps*, Duncan outlined the design of a national sample survey for the purpose of monitoring social change on a national basis. This resulted in the GSS, which, since 1972, has served as the baseline social survey of the United States. The GSS provides publicly available annual social data for the benefit of the research and policymaking communities. Similar national social surveys have been developed in several other Western countries, partly with Duncan's model for the national survey as a basis for social reporting in mind. This work also had important consequences for the development of the social indicator movement of the 1970s, which promoted the use of social indicators in social policymaking, and to which Duncan also contributed by showing how to analyze social change within the framework of the 1971 Detroit Area Study.

In the field of data analysis, Duncan developed several strategies and methods, some of which, if the term "measurement" is used in a broad sense, may be regarded as measurement instruments. Perhaps Duncan's best known data analysis that resulted in a measurement scale is the 1961 socioeconomic index (SEI) for all occupations. The index was created by combining the 1947 North–Hatt study of occupational prestige with national census data on occupation, education, and income. Duncan subsequently showed that the occupational prestige ratings were stable across different populations of raters and measurement designs. Furthermore, they could be predicted by using already available census information on the average income and education for different occupations. Based on these analyses, Duncan computed an algorithm whereby all occupations could be prestige rated based on available registry information in the census.

Duncan's analysis of social stratification using an SEI score based on income and education has caught on internationally. The SEI, albeit sometimes constructed in slightly different ways compared to the original index, has become an international standard for measuring the social standing of individuals. Although the connection to prestige ratings frequently has been dropped, the SEI score has often served as the only available empirical data on social class. It is therefore widely used in the health sciences as well as in social research to measure social inequality.

In the late 1960s and early 1970s, Duncan introduced into social science the advanced statistical techniques of path analysis, originally proposed and developed by the population geneticist Sewall Wright in 1921 and 1934. Duncan's 1966 paper "Path Analysis: Sociological Examples" became a classic; it was used by several generations of sociologists as the point of departure for empirical work and further development of structural equation modeling techniques. It was reprinted in a book edited by Blalock in 1971 and was translated into German in 1976. Duncan's 1975 book *Introduction to Structural Equation Models* eventually became a standard textbook for all students of causal modeling.

The topics analyzed by Duncan in collaboration with others included occupational achievement, stratification, and social change. Duncan's work on path analysis was of pivotal importance for the ways in which causal analysis was approached in all the social sciences after 1970. When they subsequently were developed into LISREL models (programs for estimation of recursive and nonrecursive structural equation models), the methods became regarded as important tools in the construction of social measurements. Duncan's work with structural models is therefore a major contribution to social measurement in the social sciences. In his late career, Duncan became increasingly critical of the applications of structural equation models, especially with respect to the claim that they are measurement models. The view that measurements can be constructed by the advanced causal modeling techniques offered by LISREL is at odds with Duncan's more recent thinking about measurement.

During several periods of his career, Duncan returned to the analysis of occupational mobility and achievement, employing structural equation regression methods as well as contingency table analysis. He clarified the mutual relationships in the analysis of these problems and used components from both approaches in creating new models. In the late 1970s, Duncan increasingly turned to the new methods for sociological contingency table analysis developed by Shelby J. Haberman, Leo A. Goodman, and others. The mobility table models developed by Goodman and published along with Duncan's paper in 1979 makes possible the separation of the individual and structural components of social change. This in turn makes it possible formally to separate structural change from patterns of occupational inheritance over time (for instance, between fathers and sons). In Goodman's mobility model, the row and column marginals of the square table formed from two measurements of the same occupational categories are allowed to differ by mutually unconstrained sets of row and column (RC) parameters. The associations inside the table are accounted for by parameters describing, for instance, inheritance of occupational status across generations or similarity in status across time for the same individual. Goodman's mobility model is a log-linear parameterization of quasi-symmetry (QS), first described by Caussinius in 1966. Duncan (1979) showed how the contingency table model could be constrained with regression-like parameters to create more parsimonious and substantively interesting mobility models. The regression-type scoring he used has subsequently become common in log-linear modeling of causal relationships.

Later, in collaboration with Hout and Sobel, Duncan returned to the mobility analyses by comparing Goodman's association models with the Rasch model. A interesting alternative parameterization of QS is the generalized n-dimensional Rasch model. This model focuses not on the similarity of individual positions across time, but on the dissimilarity between individuals and between items. Items can be realizations of measurements on the same individual over time, across pairs of individuals, or across survey questions intended as components of a measurement scale. The dissimilarity results from the specific form of quantitative differences proposed by Rasch between the units of observation (e.g., persons) and between items. This work exemplifies how Duncan, albeit not developing the original formal aspects of each model, rearranged and rewrote models and combined thinking from different fields to provide important links between sociological theory and formal methods. In his own words, he thereby showed how to achieve a "a more rigorous and quantitative approach" to important research questions.

Rasch Measurement

In 1973, Duncan spent time at the Institute of Advanced Studies in Vienna teaching path analysis and structural equation modeling. There he was introduced by one of his students to the work of Georg Rasch. Until then, Rasch's work had largely been applied to psychological and educational tests. According to Duncan's own recollection, he did not pursue the idea immediately, but only after having learned about log-linear contingency table analysis in the late 1970s. In the early 1980s, Duncan chaired the Panel on Survey Measurement of Subjective Phenomena of the National Research Council. In the final report from the panel, he introduced the idea of Rasch measurement as a way of evaluating social survey measurement. He used a log-linear contingency table model to demonstrate the model. The work was more or less contemporaneous with Tue Tjur's work in 1982 and Henk Kelderman's, in 1984, and contributed along with these to the identification of Rasch models as a special class of log-linear models.

Theoretical Foundation

Many texts on Rasch focus on the mathematical and statistical properties of the models. For Duncan, the theoretical foundation of Rasch's perspective was of major importance. He emphasized the scientific meaning of Rasch's term "specifically objective measurement," used by Rasch in 1966 and 1977 in describing the unique properties of the model. In particular, Duncan cared about its potential consequences for social science. In 1960, Rasch had given his definition of objective measurement an exact formal representation in what was later called the one-parameter Rasch model. Duncan pointed out that social survey measurements must adhere to the one-parameter Rasch model in order to justify quantitative comparisons between objects measured on any proposed social scale. The measurement instrument is independent of the measured objects ("specifically objective"), and thereby valid as an instrument, only if the one-parameter model holds.

In view of the difficulty in satisfying the Rasch model, modern psychometric developments defined the two- and three-parameter item response theory (IRT) models, relaxing Rasch's basic invariance criterion. In contrast to this, Duncan emphasized the importance of empirically verifying the one-parameter Rasch model on any given set of empirical data. Only when the data fit this model were the estimates invariant measurements in Rasch's sense. Such a strong test of the quality of social measurement had in Duncan's view hitherto not been available, and its potential for the advancement of quantitative social science was important. Instead of the IRT models Duncan developed models that retained Rasch's criterion of specific objectivity in a multidimensional context. The models draw on earlier work by, for instance, Louis Guttman in the 1950s; Guttman had suggested the possibility of two-dimensional response structures for the deterministic Guttman response model. The multidimensional Rasch model is based on the same idea of a noninteractive multidimensional response structure, but allows for a probabilistic rather than a deterministic relationship between the unmeasured latent variables and the manifest response.

The Unidimensional Rasch Model as a Log-Linear Model

In 1961, Rasch applied his model to tests of reading ability in Danish grade-school children. Proper measurement of children's reading ability is achieved when only two parameters enter into the response process independently—namely the individual ability α_i and the item difficulty β_j. The individual ability was conceived independent of other children's abilities. Hence, the estimate of individual ability must be independent of the group or sample of children participating in the test. The item difficulty should also be independent of other items that are part of the reading test. It follows from this that proper measurement requires the item difficulty to be equal across individuals and the individual ability to be equal across items. Log-linear contingency table methods provided a solution on how to use Rasch models in the survey context. The one-parameter unidimensional model was written by Duncan as in Table I, which shows the response probabilities for two dichotomous items, A and B, each with possible responses {no, yes}. The probability expressions for person i follow the stipulated noninteractive relationship between persons and items. If item A is used as a baseline ($\beta_A = 1$), the item parameter for item A cancels out of the expressions (Table II). The joint probabilities of possible responses for two dichotomous

Table I Response Probabilities for Two Items

Response	*Item A*	*Item B*
Pr(no)	$1/(1+\beta_A\alpha_i)$	$1/(1+\beta_B\alpha_i)$
Pr(yes)	$\beta_A\alpha_i/(1+\beta_A\alpha_i)$	$\beta_B\alpha_i/(1+\beta_B\alpha_i)$

Table II Response Probabilities for Two Items (β_A deleted)

Pr(Response)	*Item A*	*Item B*
Pr(no)	$1/(1+\alpha_i)$	$1/(1+\beta_B\alpha_i)$
Pr(yes)	$\alpha_i/(1+\alpha_i)$	$\beta_B\alpha_i/(1+\beta_B\alpha_i)$

items are then as shown in Table III. In Table III, β_B represents the person invariant item effect for the second item compared to the first. In a data set containing many sets of responses to the two items, it is now possible to estimate the item parameter independently of the distribution of the latent trait α in the sample. The person variability inherent in the data is completely contained in the ratio expressions involving the α_i for person $i = \{1, \ldots, n\}$. The clue to the effectiveness and power of the Rasch model is that the sum scores S_k for $k = \{0, 1, 2\}$ represent sufficient statistics for this person parameter. They are

$$\begin{aligned} S_0 &= 1/(1+\alpha_i+\beta_B\alpha_i+\beta_B\alpha_i^2), \\ S_1 &= \alpha_i/(1+\alpha_i+\beta_B\alpha_i+\beta_B\alpha_i^2), \\ S_2 &= \alpha_i^2/(1+\alpha_i+\beta_B\alpha_i+\beta_B\alpha_i^2). \end{aligned} \tag{1}$$

With the subscript on β_B omitted, the resulting expressions rewritten as a log-linear model are as in Table IV. The sample independent parameter for the contrast between the items is estimated using conditional maximum likelihood (CML). The CML estimate in the simple model for the 2×2 table is directly given by the difference between the logarithms of the observed joint frequencies f_{ab} for the responses {a, b} = {no, yes}, within score group S_1, i.e.,

$$\ln\widehat{\beta} = \ln(f_{01}) - \ln(f_{10}). \tag{2}$$

For the cross-classification of two dichotomous items, the model has zero degrees of freedom, providing an estimate of β, but no test of how the data fit the Rasch model. For more than two items, alternative ways of estimating β exist within several score groups. The invariance of these estimates can be tested using conventional model fit statistics. Because the score group parameters are sufficient statistics for person variability, the test of similarity of the item effect across score groups entails checking the invariance of the effect across individuals. Unlike in the latent class theory, no grouping of persons with the same value on the latent trait must be assumed. The grouping of persons into the observed sum score groups S_0, S_1, and S_2, does not impose any

Table III Joint Probabilities for Two Items

Response *Item A\Item B*	*No*	*Yes*
No	$1/(1+\alpha_i+\beta_B\alpha_i+\beta_B\alpha_i^2)$	$\beta_B\alpha_i/(1+\alpha_i+\beta_B\alpha_i+\beta_B\alpha_i^2)$
Yes	$\alpha_i/(1+\alpha_i+\beta_B\alpha_i+\beta_B\alpha_i^2)$	$\beta_B\alpha_i^2/(1+\alpha_i+\beta_B\alpha_i+\beta_B\alpha_i^2)$

Table IV Log Linear Rasch Model for Two Items

Response *Item A\Item B*	*No*	*Yes*
No	$\ln S_0$	$\ln \beta + \ln S_1$
Yes	$\ln S_1$	$\ln \beta + \ln S_2$

restrictions on individual variability on the underlying latent trait. Duncan pointed out that this model provides a strong (in fact, complete) test of how well the survey instrument works for comparing individuals on a proposed quantitative scale. He gave examples of the application of such survey measurement tests by reanalyzing several data sets from sociology and political science.

Multidimensional Rasch Models

Unlike psychological tests, few sociological surveys are limited to dichotomous response formats. Therefore, it was important to extend the model to the multicategory response formats. The extension to polytomous items was described by Rasch in 1966. Further work was done by David Andrich in 1978 and 1979 and by Geoffrey Masters in 1985. They described unidimensional rating scale and "partial credit" models allowing for ordered multicategory response formats. In contrast, Duncan focused a great deal of his attention on the possibility of discovering more than one latent dimension in the response process, and on comparing unidimensional with multidimensional Rasch models.

In a couple of such examples Duncan worked with the hypothesis that a common latent trait can pertain not only to individuals but also to families. He found that survey data from both husband and wife on spousal sexual fun fitted a Rasch model, including common latent traits for the couple and couple-invariant gender effects. The general format for extending the one-dimensional model into several dimensions is described in a 1990 publication concerning effects of family and birth order on educational attainment. In this work, Duncan reanalyzed 1967 data first used in the classic *The American Occupational Structure*. In 1990, Duncan assumed that the similarity within the pair of siblings is a multidimensional function of family kinship, and that the difference between siblings in the number of years of schooling is a function of birth order. The generalized Rasch model on the expected frequencies of the 6×6 table of the attained years of schooling of the younger and older siblings was described as a five-dimensional model, with

$$F_{ij} = a^{j-1} b_j T_{ij} \quad (b_1 = b_2 = 1; T_{ij} = T_{ji} \text{ when } i \neq j), \tag{3}$$

where F_{ij} represents the expected frequency in row i and column j of a cross-classification of the number of years of schooling of both siblings. The T_{ij} are the score group parameters for five latent variables (analogous with the S parameters described previously) and represent diagonal ($i = j$) and nondiagonal ($i \neq j$) family effects, whereas a and b_j represent birth-order effects. The latent traits are assumed to distinguish each pair of siblings from each other pair. In contrast, the birth-order effects are constrained to be the same across all pairs. The T values are sufficient statistics for the family effects. The five birth-order effects, a and b_j, must be equal across T groups, but in the current example, no restrictions were put on them across the six levels of education (from 0 to 7 up to 16 or more years of schooling). This makes up a multidimensional latent structure, where each latent dimension corresponds to a separate level of education. Each latent dimension operates independently of each and all of the other dimensions. The multidimensional family and birth-order model turned out to be equal to quasi-symmetry (QS) parameterized so as to account for the Rasch model components, unconstrained family effects (latent traits), and common birth-order effects. The general observation illustrated in this example is that QS corresponds to a generalized Rasch model. As described in Duncan's paper, the number of underlying latent traits in QS cannot be empirically verified, but even though it includes more than one parameter for family kinship, the specific objectivity of the unidimensional Rasch model is retained. In contrast, the IRT multi-parameter models lack this property. In Duncan's view, this result combined with earlier applications makes QS the natural point of departure in the analysis of square contingency tables, much as the model of independence provides an appropriate baseline for regression-like log-linear models on contingency table data.

Local Independence and Heterogeneity Bias

The condition of local independence plays a major role in QS. It generates local symmetry of the associations in any 2×2 subtable such that the condition $T_{ij} = T_{ji}$ holds when $i \neq j$. The association in the table is completely described as relationships between the T values. This means that association is generated solely by heterogeneity between families. But the expected frequencies F_{ij} are not symmetric, because they also contain the effects of birth order. The presence of birth-order effects account for marginal heterogeneity, and the estimates of birth-order effects are unbiased only when controlling for family heterogeneity. A model in which all birth-order effects equal zero would be symmetric. Here and elsewhere, Duncan pointed out that estimates of change computed by the direct comparison of marginal distributions for different time periods, such as in comparative cross-section estimates, ignore the confounding effects of population heterogeneity. Comparative cross-section estimates are therefore "heterogeneity biased." The Rasch estimates of change, based on the panel table, are heterogeneity unbiased if the model holds. An important implication of this is that analysis of social change can avoid heterogeneity bias in estimates of change only by using cohort (panel) data. The finding accounts for some of the difference frequently seen between cross-section and panel estimates of change.

Heterogeneity bias can be compared with the biases resulting from ignoring confounding effects in regression-type models. In regression analysis, the effects of confounders are removed only to the extent that they are included in the model. Unknown sources of confounding bias remain. In the panel table, the heterogeneity is completely accounted for by including sufficient statistics for the person parameters. This is done without measuring, or perhaps even without knowing about, all the possible sources of person heterogeneity.

Research on Response Formats

Duncan attempted to develop substantively meaningful parameterizations of multidimensional latent structures and apply them to test the quality of survey instruments. In one example, drawing on Louis Guttman's understanding of the response process, Duncan defined a response model whereby Guttman's two dimensions, direction and intensity, were interpreted as two latent dimensions operating independently on the response (Table V). Direction indicates negative or positive loading (for instance, with respect to an attitude item), whereas intensity assesses the propensity to use the middle rather than the extreme response categories. The intensity trait should be independent of the direction of the attitude. In a probabilistic context, this corresponds to Rasch measurement.

Table V Coding of Content and Intensity as Latent Dimensions in the Response Process

Attitude response	*Direction* (α_i)	*Intensity* (ζ_i)
Negative	0	0
Neither negative nor positive	1	1
Positive	2	0

For cross-classifications extending beyond two three-category responses (e.g., $3 \times 3 \times 3$ tables), it is possible to write models that test Rasch-like multidimensional invariance. Duncan and Stenbeck examined the use of Likert response formats in opinon research (e.g., "strongly agree," "agree," "neutral," disagree, "strongly disagree"). They found evidence of multidimensionality corresponding to the presence of the qualifying intensity labels (e.g., "*strongly* agree," "*strongly* disagree"), as well as the neutral response alternatives. This questions the general opinion among survey methodologists that Likert scales may increase the precision of unidimensional measurement. It may instead introduce unintended additional sources of variation in the response process. If the additional sources can be estimated as additional traits operating independently of the content dimension, then multidimensional Rasch measurement is achieved. But the evidence seemed to suggest that the introduction of the intensity labels on response categories confound the measurements in a way that renders the Rasch model untenable, a result that spoke against the application of the Likert response format in social survey measurement.

Hierarchical Systems of Rasch models

In using Rasch-like tools for measurement work, Duncan developed hierarchical systems of Rasch and Rasch-like contingency table models with the one-parameter rating scale model as the most restrictive model and QS as the least restrictive model. The number of empirically detectable latent dimensions depends on the size of the table. In the case of two items and two response categories, QS and the rating scale model are identical and have zero degrees of freedom. Increasing the number of items and the number of response categories increases the number of Rasch-type models that can be tested and compared.

Duncan's Critique of Contemporary Sociology

Duncan's late work on Rasch models as applied to survey data repeatedly produced results that questioned the validity and reliability of a large body of research tools and empirical results derived from social science surveys. Duncan's critique of social science was eventually delivered in an explicit way. In his short paper "What If?," written in 1992, after the conclusion of his active career, Duncan called for a complete reorientation of the way in which social scientists approach scientific inquiry. He asks the social scientist to pay more serious attention to the problems involved in translating sociological thinking and conceptualisation into relevant study designs and proper measurement. In contrast, less attention ought to be paid to "numerology," i.e., the mindless production of numbers with little or no relation to quantification and measurement. Duncan argued that measurement cannot be achieved by fiat, but only by repeated empirical efforts to achieve proper measurements based on sound theory. He therefore believed that methodological science ought to be preoccupied more with the development of proper study designs than with matters of data analysis: "What if, in other words, some younger quantitative sociologist repudiates our Faustian bargain which gave us instant, voluminous, and easy results—but results that often were mischievous or meaningless when they were not both?" Duncan's critique was delivered from within the paradigm of empirical science. It was directed against empiricist approaches to empirical science, but it advocated empirical research. Hence, while being critical of the current state of affairs, Duncan proposed an empirical approach to theory building and the design of measurement instruments. He thereby retained the empirical perspective of the Chicago school of which he may be counted as a member.

The theoretical and methodological implications of Duncan's late work may have been too profound to catch on. Fifteen years after the conclusion of Duncan's work in this area, relatively little has come out of his efforts. Few followers seem to be active within the social science community. This stands in stark contrast to Duncan's strong impact on other fields of quantitative social science. At the late point of his career when Duncan devoted his work to Rasch measurement, he was in no position to organize survey design experiments with the Rasch model in mind. Hence, his work took on a more critical and less constructive orientation than it may have had if he had run into the Rasch models at an earlier age.

See Also the Following Articles

Contingency Tables and Log-Linear Models • Likert Scale Analysis • Rasch, Georg • Sociology

Further Reading

Blau, P. M., and Duncan, O. D. (1967). *The American Occupational Structure.* Wiley, New York.

Duncan, O. D. (1961). A socio-economic index for all occupations. Chapters 6–7 in Reiss, Albert J. and collaborators. *Occupational and Social Status.* The Free Press of Glencoe, New York.

Duncan, O. D. (1966). Path analysis: sociological examples. *Am. J. Sociol.* **72,** 1–16. Reprinted with Addenda, in H. M. Blalock, Jr. (ed.) (1971). *Causal Models in the Social Sciences.* Aldine-Atherton, Chicago, pp. 115–138.

Duncan, O. D. (1969). *Toward Social Reporting: Next Steps.* Social Science Frontiers No. 2. Russell Sage, New York.

Duncan, O. D. (1979). How destination depends on origin in the occupational mobility table. *Am. J. Sociol.* **84,** 793–803.

Duncan, O. D. (1983). On a dynamic response model of W. F. Kempf. *Soc. Sci. Res.* **12,** 393–400.

Duncan, O. D. (1984a). *Notes on Social Measurement: Historical and Critical.* Wiley, New York.

Duncan, O. D. (1984b). The latent trait approach in survey research. The Rasch measurement model. In *Surveying Subjective Phenomena* (C. F. Turner and E. Martin, eds.) Vol. 1, sect. 6, pp. 211–227. Russell Sage Foundation, New York.

Duncan, O. D. (1984c). Rasch measurement in survey research: further examples and discussion. In *Surveying Subjective Phenomena* (C. F. Turner and E. Martin, eds.) Ch. 12, pp. 367–403. Russell Sage Foundation, New York.

Duncan, O. D. (1990). Family and birth order effects on educational attainment. In *Structures of Power and Constraint. Papers in honor of Peter M Blau* (C. Calhoun, M. W. Meyer, and W. R. Scott, eds.), Ch. 5. Cambridge University Press, New York.

Duncan, O. D. (1992). What if? *Symposium: The American Occupational Structure: Reflections after Twenty-Five Years. Contemporary Sociology* **21,** 5.

Duncan, O. D., and Stenbeck, M. (1987). Are Likert scales unidimensional? *Social Sci. Res.* **16,** 245–259.

Duncan, O. D., and Stenbeck, M. (1988a). No opinion or not sure? *Public Opinion Quarterly* **52,** 513–525.

Duncan, O. D., and Stenbeck, M. (1988b). Panels and cohorts: design and model in the study of voting turnout. *Sociological Methodology* **18,** 1–35.

Duncan, O. D., Stenbeck, M., and Brody, C. J. (1988). Discovering heterogeneity. continuous versus discrete latent variables. *Am. J. Sociol.* **93,** 1305–1321.

Hout, M., Duncan, O. D., and Sobel, M.E. (1987). Association and heterogeneity: structural models of similarities and differences. *Sociological Methodology* **17,** 145–184.

Jöreskog, K. G. (1973). A general method for estimating a linear structural equation system. In *Structural Equation Models in the Social Sciences* (A.S. Goldberger and O. D. Duncan, eds.), pp. 85–112. Academic Press, New York.

Rasch, G. (1960/1980). *Probabilistic Models for Some Intelligence and Attainment Tests.* Second Edition. University of Chicago Press, Chicago.

Sobel, M. E., Hout, M., and Duncan, O. D. (1985). Exchange, structure, and symmetry in occupational mobility. *Am. Sociol. Rev.* **48,** 721–727.

Durkheim, Émile

Stephen P. Turner

University of South Florida, Tampa, Florida, USA

Glossary

anomie An absence or diminution of the effective power of social facts, such as obligations, over the individual, or underregulation.

collective consciousness The source of causes, corresponding to individual consciousness, which constrain individual thinking, typically through feelings of obligation.

generality and externality The two definitional properties of social facts: "general," meaning appearing throughout society (which may also refer to such societies as the family), and "external," meaning exercising constraints on the individual.

social fact A collective cause that is manifested as a constraint on individuals and is general or collective in origin, or an effect of such a cause.

social realism The doctrine that collective causes are real forces or that collective entities, such as society, are real.

The French sociologist Émile Durkheim is generally regarded as one of the two major founding figures of sociology (along with Max Weber) and the primary source of the central ideas of this discipline about the scientific significance of statistical facts. An intellectual leader who built up a school around the journal he edited, *L'Année Sociologique*, Durkheim exercised influence on educational policy in the Third Republic and was a supporter of secularism and the spiritual or moral Socialism of the time. His major quantitative work, *Le Suicide*, published in 1897, is regarded as *the* classic work of quantitative sociology. His shorter methodological treatise, *The Rules of Sociological Method*, contains many of the standard arguments for understanding statistical facts as indicators of latent causal processes, which Durkheim directed at the received tradition of social science methodological thought represented by John Stuart Mill's *System of Logic* and the tradition of Adolphe Quetelet. Durkheim himself did little statistical work after this, although some of his followers, notably Maurice Halbwachs, continued to. Nevertheless, the efforts of his journal to review statistical work and interpret it sociologically had a powerful effect on the formation of the discipline. The reception of his thought in later years, especially in the United States after World War II, extended his reputation by treating him as a progenitor of the model of theory-driven empirical research that was adopted by American sociology.

Background and Early Influences

Born into a rabbinical family in Épinal, Lorraine, France, Émile Durkheim was an outstanding student at the local Collège de Épinal, from which he achieved a *baccalauréats* in letters in 1874 and sciences in 1875. His father became ill while he was studying in Paris in preparation for the École Normale Supérieure; this was a time of financial difficulty for the family, which was a source of anguish for Durkheim. During his preparations, he became interested in philosophy. He was admitted in 1879 on his third try to the École, where he joined an especially brilliant group of students, including Henri Bergson and the future psychologist Pierre Janet. His close friend at the École, Victor Hommay, apparently committed suicide, which deeply affected Durkheim. As a student, he was influenced by the French neo-Kantian philosopher Charles Renouvier and personally by the philosopher of science Émile Boutroux and the historian Fustel de Coulanges, both of whom were his professors. He began his academic career with a teaching license in philosophy and briefly taught the subject in the schools in Sens and Saint-Quentin, a normal start to an academic career. He soon began to climb the academic ladder of the university system, with an appointment in Bordeaux, where he was to stay from 1887 to 1902, rising to the rank of professor in 1896. During this time he wrote his dissertation, *The Division of Labor in Society* (1933 [1893]), and the two works on which his reputation as a methodological and statistical thinker rests, *The Rules of Sociological Method* and *Suicide*.

In 1898, Durkheim founded the *Année Sociologique* and published a series of important papers on anthropological topics: the origins of the incest taboo, totemism, and marriage among the Australian aborigines. His subsequent writings continued in this direction, reflecting his idea of religion as the basis of social life and the source of the sacred character of its institutions. He was appointed to the Sorbonne in 1902, in charge of a program of pedagogy and sociology, and gave an inaugural lecture on education and sociology; in 1905, he became professor at L'École des Hautes Études Sociales. His major work, *The Elementary Forms of the Religious Life*, was published in 1912, and his lectures were published as a book after his death. At the end of his life, he was writing on the nature of morality, directly addressing the topic that had concerned him throughout his career.

Although Durkheim's primary work using statistics dated from the early part of his career, the significance of his contribution to the transformation of the subject matter of social statistics into sociology continued in a different form. His journal, the *Année Sociologique* (published 1898–1913) reviewed and critically surveyed the literature of the social sciences from the perspective of Durkheim's own conception of the division of intellectual labor among the various fields of social science. Social statistics, which by the beginning of the twentieth century had a changing and somewhat insecure base in the universities, was a major topic of Durkheim's and his students' reviews of the contemporary literature. Their efforts did much to both legitimate statistical study as a part of sociology and to strengthen the identification between sociology and social statistics; this was in contrast to the way in which the relation was defined in Germany, where "pure" sociology was distinguished from statistics by such thinkers as Ferdinand Tönnies.

Several of his devoted students, and his son, died in World War I, and the remaining students devoted considerable effort to preserving and publishing the work of this lost generation. The Durkheimian school was thus cut off in the flower of its youth; its historical influence came through its appropriation by other thinkers, frequently in quite different intellectual traditions, such as American quantitative sociology and British social anthropology, as well as serving as an inspiration for the Annales school of historians in France.

Early Work and Intellectual Context

Durkheim's earliest writings included an essay on German thinkers about morality, considering prominent figures such as the psychologist Wilhelm Wundt for his *Völkerpsychologie*, and Rudolph Ihering, the philosopher of law and historian of Roman law, for his *Der Zweck im Recht*. He was also intensely engaged with Herbert Spencer and evolutionary thought, a concern that appears as early as his introductory lectures on philosophy to his students at Sens. These concerns were, characteristically, related by Durkheim to French sources, notably Auguste Comte. In his Latin dissertation of 1892, Durkheim developed a protosociological critique of Montesquieu and Rousseau. These early commentaries focused on the problem of the basis of obligation, a typically Kantian theme. Durkheim already had by this time come to see obligations as relative to society and, therefore, explicable only on the basis of an understanding of society. Thus, his critique of Montesquieu was a denial that law makers produced obligation by legislating and an argument that the nature of a given society determined the kind of law that a society developed.

Durkheim's dissertation, *The Division of Labor in Society*, published in 1893, was his first effort to systematize these ideas and at the same time to formulate an account of the nature of a science of society that could answer questions about the basis of morality. The book was historical and anthropological; he argued that the characteristically different forms of law in modern and primitive societies reflected characteristically different forms of social solidarity. He was occupied with one of the great nineteenth-century intellectual problems, the division of labor, but the evidence that he employed in this work was, broadly, evidence of comparative law, in particular the demise of the guild system of the legal organization of labor in Europe, and with the contrast between legal and moral regulation in primitive societies and advanced societies. The primitive form, which he designated "mechanical," applied equally to all members of the society; the modern form, which he called "organic" was exemplified by the different professional moralities that operated together to govern the relations between the parts of the division of labor that is characteristic of modern societies. He saw mechanical solidarity as producing punitive ideas of justice (e.g., for the violation of taboos), whereas organic solidarity was associated with forms of justice that redressed wrongs and sought equity.

The Division of Labor introduced some key ideas that Durkheim later used differently, including the idea of collective consciousness, which he applied here only to primitive societies; later he used this to mean the collective component of the causes that combine to produce individual feeling, action, and thought. The guiding idea that social morphology determines social consciousness undergoes a parallel change, as do Durkheim's ideas about explanation, which in *Division* still reflect an ambiguity between the idea that social facts were causes and the idea that they were adaptations. These changes begin to appear in a series of articles in 1894 and then as a book, *The Rules of Sociological Method*, in 1895. The importance of this methodological work is disputed, but with respect to Durkheim's methodological legacy, its importance is in its clear formulation of the concept of social fact and in its clarification of Durkheim's position on teleological explanation, which he explicitly rejected.

Social Fact

Durkheim took a great deal of his rhetoric about treating social facts as things from Adolphe Quetelet; the idea of treating collective statistics as measures of underlying social phenomena is Quetelet's as well. Quetelet, however, conceived these claims in terms of an analogy between statistical variation and the perturbations of the planetary paths, both of which could be understood as variations around stable curves, or laws, which in the social case were typically represented as the curves that could be fit to a tabular presentation of rates, such as age-specific rates of marriage. As a consequence, Quetelet focused his attention on the theoretical embodiment of societal means or central tendencies, which led to his theory of the *homme moyen* (the average individual), who was understood to represent the center of gravity produced by social influence on the individual in a given society.

Durkheim's problem in *The Rules of Sociological Method* was to provide an alternative account of the significance of these more or less stable rates within a society that did not depend on this dubious analogy and that allowed other kinds of evidence, such as the evidence of fixed and stable phenomena (such as laws) to be understood in the same terms. Accordingly, Durkheim urged that collective statistics be treated as things and that many other stable features of social life, such as laws and customs and even proverbs, be understood in the same way. Durkheim's argument is that these social facts are the visible by-products of hidden causal processes, and he locates these causal processes in the collective consciousness. Social facts are by definition general and external, meaning that they operate in a collective consciousness that is part of the mental life of all individuals in a society and impose themselves on the individual as though from outside.

The concept of social fact that he employed in *Suicide* and defended in his methodological manifesto *The Rules of Sociological Method* reflected this basic argument: Social statistics of certain kinds, particularly stable rates for a collectivity or social group, are indirect measures of latent causal structures that produce their effects on and through this group. This was an idea that he advanced significantly from the form in which it had appeared in such predecessors as Quetelet by transforming its relation to causation and laws. Quetelet was wedded to the analogy between the forces producing statistical uniformities and gravitational forces and, thus, saw the average man as a summation of the causal results of social forces. Durkheim sought underlying causal laws in which quantities covaried and in which both quantities were understood to be representations of social facts, facts of a mental kind that operated in the collective consciousness. In retrospect, this idea seems to be simple enough, but in fact it was quite complex.

Collective Consciousness

By collective consciousness, Durkheim now meant something different than what he had meant in *The Division of Labor in Society*. It now indicated a kind of mental cause that lives within each individual mind, so that the individual is a duplex, with psychological impulses originating from the individual, but also from what Durkheim called collective currents or causal forces that are the product of the pooling of the causal powers of the many minds that join together in a collective social relationship such as a society. Durkheim thought that such forces were produced by any society and considered a national society, a classroom, and a single family to be collective entities with their own social forces. Individual conscious experience reflected, but only imperfectly, the operations of these causal forces. An individual's sense of obligation, for example, is experienced as external, and for Durkheim the externality is genuine in that the force of obligation is a real causal force arising in the collective consciousness. Introspection, however, is an inadequate guide to the actual causal processes at work in the case of the production of a feeling of obligation, and similarly the manifestations in values of underlying collective consciousness processes are imperfect guides to these processes. But there are circumstances under which rates can serve as good indices of latent lawlike causal relations.

The novelty of this argument, but also its closeness to widely expressed ideas about the relationship between observed social statistics and underlying causal laws, must be understood if we are to consider it as an attempt to solve the puzzle that in many ways represented an intellectual dead end for the older social statistics tradition at the time Durkheim was writing. Texts of this and earlier periods routinely reported results in the form of tabular data, often of rates (such as Halley tables) or visual representations of statistical facts (particularly through maps based on statistics) that were apparently stable and thus could be (and were) assumed to represent not the free choices of individuals but underlying unknown causal processes presumably governed by laws. The problem faced by these statisticians was that no plausible account of underlying processes, much less identifiable underlying laws, corresponded to these relatively stable tables of rates. Suicide rates, the subject of Durkheim's most famous study, exemplified this problem, and his study of the subject exemplifies his distinctive approach.

Suicide

Suicide rates were routinely invoked in the nineteenth century as evidence of the power of collective forces, however this idea might be understood, and suicide seems to embody the problem and the promise of the quest for underlying laws in its most extreme and dramatic form. Individual decisions to commit suicide are deeply private and paradigmatically individual. They do not directly arise from obligation, law, or any other ordinary external compulsion; nevertheless, suicide rates are stable in a way that makes it appear that they are compelled. The problem of suicide in the collection of suicide statistics and their analysis was a major concern of mid-nineteenth-century statisticians, and their studies produced quite extraordinary collections of analyses of the diurnal, seasonal, and other periodicities of suicide, showing that they decreased in times of revolutionary ferment and varied with latitude, light, and temperature, as well as with religion, marital status, age, and so forth. Jacques Bertillon, in an encyclopedia article, estimated the interaction between age and marital status in order to estimate the preservative effect of marriage when the preservative effect of age had been taken into account, an early form of the reasoning that G. U. Yule was to develop as partialling, but this was unusual. Most of the analyses concerned tables of rates and their secular trends, in particular to answer the question of whether suicide was increasing.

One theorist of suicide who attempted to make sense of the tables, Enrico Morselli, an Italian psychiatrist, collected a vast number of published studies of suicide in order to give a social account of the causes of secular increase in suicide and distinguished patterns in the statistical explanations that could be given different explanations in terms of different social processes. Morselli introduced the notion of egoism, by which he meant unregulated desire, as a cause of suicide in order to explain the higher suicide rates of the richer areas of Italy. But Morselli believed that the intermingling of causes in these cases limited the value of statistical analysis. Nevertheless, he had no technique to deal with this problem and presented tables of rates. Durkheim reanalyzed some of these tables and, with the help of his nephew Marcel Mauss, also analyzed data on France supplied to him by his main intellectual rival, Gabriel Tarde.

The first part of Yule's classic paper on pauperism was published in 1895, and this paper transformed the analysis of intermingled causes. Durkheim acknowledged, but did not employ, Bertillon's methods for controlling for the contributions of marriage (although they influenced his discussion of the preservative effects of marriage) and was unaware of Yule's methods. Neither, indeed, was relevant to the point he wished to make. In keeping with his notion that the statistical imperfectly represented underlying or latent processes, he looked instead for cases in which the statistical patterns pointed most directly to the underlying processes, and this meant in practice that he operated with tables of rates, typically suicide rates by category or region and argued that only cases in which the patterns were absolutely consistent indicated the presence of law. Thus, he eliminated as failing to point to a law a huge number of well-established statistical relationships in which the monotonic progression of rates was imperfect and constructed tables that showed perfect monotonically increasing relationships that he then interpreted as indicating genuine relationships. In theory, this was a stringent standard. In practice, the method was somewhat arbitrary in that one could produce imperfections or perfection in the monotonic increases in the "law" of the table by manipulating the intervals. The problem of arbitrariness of selection of intervals was known at the time, and it was also discussed in relation to mapping, in which shadings were determined by intervals.

The very backwardness or peculiarity of Durkheim's analytical technique was recognized at the time, even by his associates, but ignored by his American admirers. The book was read by them as a primitive kind of correlational analysis using aggregate variables, a technique that was widely deployed in early quantitative sociology, in part as a result of the computational difficulties in dealing with data for large numbers of individuals and in part because the unit of analysis both for Durkheim and for many of these early studies was a collectivity. In most early nineteenth-century American studies, statistics were used on communities (such as per person rates of church giving). This style of analysis was subsequently criticized on the grounds of the ecological fallacy, but for Durkheim, and indeed for many subsequent studies following him and using these aggregate statistics, the criticism was misplaced because, as Durkheim himself understood, the statistics that were being analyzed were measures of collective currents rather than surrogates for data about individuals.

Durkheim's basic reasoning in *Suicide* was that increased rates of suicide were a result of imbalances between over- and underregulation and excessive or inadequate social connectedness. In Durkheim's terminology, anomie designates underregulation and egoism designates lack of social connectedness or integration, which he understood as excessive individuation. Insufficient individuation he called altruism, and he suggested that there was a form of suicide common in primitive societies that corresponded to it. Overregulation, in theory, produced suicide as well, and he speculated that suicides among slaves might be explained in this way, but he treated this possible form of suicide as rare and did not even examine the well-known statistics on suicides under different prison regimes. Egoism can be most easily seen in relation to religion. The well-known fact that suicide rates were higher for Protestants than for Catholics he interpreted as a result of the role of free inquiry and its effect on groups. Protestantism, he argued, produces less integration; Judaism, as a result of anti-Semitism, produces more integration and consequently less suicide. The product of less integration is excessive individualism, and this produces a higher suicide rate. A family life with children preserves from suicide by integration as well. At the other extreme from excessive individuation was insufficient individuation, which resulted in what he called altruistic suicide, marked by an insufficient valuation of one's own life, which he considered to be common in primitive societies and to account for the statistical differences between military suicide and civilian suicide. Marriage has a more complex effect, on which Durkheim spent much effort; he argued that family life with children produced an integrative effect separate from the regulative effect of marriage itself. He knew that whereas married men are less suicide-prone than unmarried men of the same age, women generally do not benefit as much from marriage. So he explained the effect of marriage itself in terms of regulation or anomie and observed that the preservative effect of marriage on men was stronger where divorce was legally difficult, but more favorable to women where divorce was easier. Durkheim's explanation for this difference relied on a claim about feminine psychology, namely that the desires of women are more limited and less mental in character, so that regulation that benefits men is excessive for wives. This explanation might be thought to violate his own methodological principle of explaining social facts solely by reference to social causes, but it also overlooked an obvious possible social cause—fatalism resulting from overregulation. This Durkheim, who was opposed to radical divorce-law reform was predisposed to ignore, although he acknowledged in passing that there might be some examples of this kind of suicide in modern life among childless young married women or very young husbands.

Durkheim's Later Work

The relation of *Suicide* to Durkheim's thought as a whole is ambiguous. It had the effect of establishing the reality of social forces—vindicating his social realism (his idea of the reality of superindividual causal forces) and his specific version of it (the idea of the collective consciousness as the source of currents that produced action, such as suicide). The argument was also a powerful corrective to a certain view of morality because by establishing the laws of sociology governing suicide rates, the idea of suicide as a pathological phenomenon was diminished; particular rates of suicide were normal at given stages of societal life. But Durkheim's interests increasingly turned in other directions, notably to the problem of the origin and nature of society as a moral phenomenon. Suicide statistics provided one of the most developed sets of data for nineteenth-century social science and handling them in a novel theoretical manner was a means of turning one of the famous mysteries of nineteenth-century statistics—the stability of suicide rates—into an argument for the science of sociology, understood in a particular way. But it was not a demonstration that he attempted to build on with studies of other social statistical phenomena.

During this same period, some new data became available, notably through ethnographic studies of the Australian aborigines, but also through publications of the Bureau of Indian Ethnology of the Smithsonian Institution. These new materials had the potential for enabling a transformation of the understanding of the origins of society. The Australian data concerned the simplest societies then known. Durkheim used the American data to support a thesis about the socially determined character of classifications and fundamental concepts, such as causation, which he argued needed to be understood as social in origin. With the Australian material, he pursued the idea that religion was the *fons et origo* of human society, that in religion the primitive thinker was worshiping society itself—thinking through, in a symbolic way, the problem of the relation of utter dependence between the individual and society and arriving at a collective solution to this problem through rituals of respect to the sacred core of society.

Some of Durkheim's most compelling insights appear in the course of his discussions of ritual and his claim that they celebrate and give force to social bonds. He applied this kind of analysis to the classroom as well in his pedagogical writings, showing how the rituals of deference to symbols are a means of defining the sacred areas of life that represent the social and how physical objects, such as the national flag, are used in rituals whose significance is to define social relationships. This kind of analysis could be carried through to illuminate the ritual character of various social phenomena, such as punishment.

The progress of Durkheim's thought is a continuing puzzle. His earliest writings, notably *The Division of Labor*, seemed to affirm the methodological idea that social forms and collective ideology were to be accounted for materially, as a matter of the manner in which individuals were grouped, and by such facts as social density. Later on, this picture changed, and, although the terms and emphases did not shift completely, the later emphasis tended to be on the ideational aspects of collective life, particularly on representations, which Durkheim understood collective life to consist in. The representations of a society were formed in moments of collective flux and then crystallized, much as a period of revolutionary enthusiasm and fervor was followed by a more or less stable set of symbols, national rituals, and sacralized forms of public action.

Reception

The legacy of Durkheim's ideas, and of the general strategy of measurement and quantitative analysis that Durkheim established in *Suicide*, as I have indicated, is somewhat peculiar for a work that was widely read and studied as a classic. The concept of anomie had a long subsequent history in American sociology, but as a measure applied to the individual, not, as Durkheim had conceived it, to the social milieu. In anthropology, the basic dimensions of Durkheim's account were recharacterized by Mary Douglas as the features of institutions and of perception, especially in her notion of group-grid analysis, which defined group and grid axes as Cartesian coordinates into which institutions could be placed (thus, the Nazi party is considered high in group and high in grid, i.e., high both in integration and in regulation). This use of Durkheim's basic concepts in anthropology, however, has generally not been associated with either measurement or quantitative analysis. During the middle part of the twentieth century, anomie was a widely used concept. Robert Merton's paper on anomie, designed as an explanation of criminal behavior as sharing societal goals and aspirations but indifferent as to the legality of the means, was one of the most widely cited texts in social research during this period. Within Durkheim's own camp, his protegé Maurice Halbwachs, who continued to write on the statistics of suicide, notably in the 1930 book *The Social Causes of Suicide*, modernized the statistical approach and sought to treat social causes as a variable contributing to the suicide rate and to reinterpret Durkheim's achievement as having pointed out these causes—which of course had actually been amply done by his predecessors, especially Morselli for whom the social causation of suicide was his central thesis.

Durkheim's reputation as a theorist has been affected by the rise and fall of the influence of an American sociologist, Talcott Parsons, who used some of Durkheim's ideas in his own synthesis of the classical tradition, which associated Durkheim with systems theorizing about society, emphasizing the confused appeal to adaptation found in *The Division of Labor in Society* and deemphasizing his subsequent rejection of teleological thinking. Unfortunately for Durkheim's reputation, this led to a popular misunderstanding of his work among sociologists and anthropologists, especially in the United States, which 40 years of Durkheim scholarship has done little to erase. He was seen as a conservative thinker of the organic school, and the polemical association of positivism with conservatism in the 1960s combined with this reputation to make him a target of critiques and hostility.

See Also the Following Articles

Qualitative Analysis, Sociology • Sociology

Further Reading

Besnard, P., Borlandi, M., and Vogt, P. (eds.) (1993). *Division du Travail Social et Lien Social: La Thèse de Durkheim un Siècle Après*. Presses Universitaires de France, Paris.

Borlandi, M., and Mucchielli, L. (eds.) (1995). *La Sociologie et Sa Méthode: Les Règles de Durkheim un Siècle Après*. L'Harmattan, Paris.

Jones, R. A. (1999). *The Development of Durkheim's Social Realism*. Cambridge University Press, New York.

Stedman-Jones, S. (2001). *Durkheim Reconsidered*. Polity Press, Oxford.

Lukes, S. (1972). *Émile Durkheim: His Life and Work, a Historical and Critical Study*. Harper & Row, New York.

Pickering, W. S. F. (ed.) (2001). *Émile Durkheim: Critical Assessments*. 3rd series. Routledge, New York.

Schmaus, W. (1994). *Durkheim's Philosophy of Science and the Sociology of Knowledge: Creating an Intellectual Niche*. University of Chicago Press, Chicago, IL.

Schmaus, W. (ed.) (1996). Durkheimian sociology. *J. Hist. Behav. Sci.* (special issue) **32**(4).

Turner, S. P. (ed.) (1986). *The Search for a Methodology of Social Science*. D. Reidel, Dordrecht.

Turner, S. P. (ed.) (1995). Celebrating the 100th anniversary of Emile Durkheim's 'The Rules of Sociological Method.' *Sociol. Perspect.* (special issue) **38**(1).

Dynamic Migration Modeling

K. Bruce Newbold

McMaster University, Hamilton, Ontario, Canada

Glossary

cohort A group of like-aged individuals born in the same calendar year or group of years.

Cross-sectional data Data that provide the characteristics of a population at a particular point in time (i.e., census data).

discrete choice models A family of models developed using utility theory to represent choices between finite, discrete alternatives.

gravity model A model used to account for a variety of spatial interactions, including migration movements, based on an analogy to Newton's gravity equation.

gross migration The number of in-migrants to a region or out-migrants from a region, expressed either as an absolute number or as a migration rate.

longitudinal data Data that include a history of migration and residences.

Markov property The probability of migrating between two areas is dependent only on the current location.

migrant An individual who makes a permanent change of residence that alters social and economic activities.

multiregional cohort models Models that project a population into the future subject to constant birth, death, and migration rates.

net migration The difference between the number of in- and out-migrants to a region.

Dynamic migration models encompass statistical methods incorporating changing migration events, behavior, and determinants over time, in contrast to a static interpretation of migration. As a representation of testable hypotheses, migration models incorporate data that typically measure population movement based on the comparison of place of residence at two points in time. This means, in essence, that the dynamic processes of migration, as revealed by such indicators as return migration, the lag between employment opportunities and migration, or the increasing importance of amenity effects, are reduced to a static representation. Instead, past residential locations, previous migration experiences, and shifting economic opportunities, among other variables, continuously influence individual migration decisions and reshape migration flows. The challenge, therefore, is how to model the dynamic or temporal nature of migration while acknowledging the known limitations of migration analysis.

Introduction

Populations in Motion

Since the first settlements along the Atlantic seaboard, the geographic center of the American population has consistently shifted west and south as the population expanded across the country. Defined by five major periods including western settlement, movement from rural to urban areas, movement from the city to the suburbs, movement from the rustbelt of the Northeast and Midwest, and counterurbanization, the directions and reasons that Americans move has changed over time. In fact, the seemingly restless nature of the American population is translated into a continuously changing population distribution, with the large volume of migration partly attributable to an apparent lack of rootedness within the population, but which also underlies deeper economic, cultural, or social issues. Indeed, Americans are one of the most mobile populations in the world, leading Long (1988, p. 57) to comment that "Americans have a reputation for moving often and far away from home, for being committed to careers and life-styles, not places." Americans are not the only highly mobile population, with approximately 20% of the Canadian population changing residence each year and with similarly large proportions found in other developed countries such as Australia, whereas the European Union allows its citizens ease of movement across its internal borders. Given that birth and death processes are relatively stable over time and space in most developed countries, internal migration therefore assumes increased importance as the primary vehicle for short-term population change at the subnational scale.

The Problem

The migration literature is full of examples regarding the dynamism and temporal aspects of migration, including the impact of life cycle effects such as marriage, divorce, empty-nesting, and failing health on migration propensities, return and "chronic" migration (multiple migrations by the same person), the lag between opportunities and migration as information diffuses over space, and the changing economic and social determinants of migration. For instance, the migration literature has noted the declining importance of distance. Whereas distance was once a formidable barrier to long-distance migration due to the physical costs of relocation and costs associated with attaining information on distant opportunities, it has become much less so as enhancements to telecommunications and transportation have eased its burden. Likewise, the importance of amenity effects has likely increased in the past two decades, as individuals and corporations alike are able to "vote with their feet," highlighted by the rapid population and economic growth of states such as Colorado, Utah, and Arizona and the Canadian province of British Columbia.

In simple terms and given such highly mobile societies, the problem is how to accurately capture the nature of population movement within migration models. Representing the mathematical, conceptual, or statistical representations of testable hypotheses, models frequently try to identify the factors that explain migration behavior by identifying statistical relationships and selecting the dependent and independent variables to operationalize the model. Based loosely on Newtonian physics, the gravity model, for instance, has a long and rich history within the migration literature but is conceptually and empirically limited. Instead, given the propensity to migrate within most populations, there is a need to understand how migration into and out of an area is likely to evolve over time with respect to both personal factors, such as age and education, and regional effects, such as changing employment opportunities. Yet, much of the data utilized within migration models are cross-sectional in nature, relying on a static image or "snapshot" of a population system at a particular point in time. As a consequence, many models typically rely on a single period to capture what is an inherently dynamic process. The problem, therefore, is how to adequately represent this dynamism within migration models.

Data Issues: Dynamism in a Cross-Sectional World

Migration Definition and Measurement

The mobility of a population is typically defined by a variety of terms, with the population literature differentiating between international (i.e., immigration, emigration, refugees, and illegal migration) and internal (within the same country) migration. If one is interested in modeling internal migration, the literature distinguishes between temporary migrations such as the seasonal movement of "snow-birds" between colder and warmer climates, circular migrations including commute-to-job or extended vacations, local residential moves (mobility), or long-distance migrations that cross some defined political unit and involve changes in the permanent place of residence and labor market. The following discussion focuses on modeling of the latter.

Although internal migration is an important avenue of population change and redistribution over space, how migration is defined alters the empirical measurement of migration and the derived conclusions. Typically, measures of migration rest on three basic premises. First, the length of the migration interval, whether it is 1 year, 5 years, or some other period, impacts on the number of migrants captured and the derived measures of migration such as net migration or migration rates. Most developed countries, for example, gather migration data based on place of usual residence 5 years before the census. Although data based on a 5-year interval provide a clear picture of the spatial impacts of migration and captures permanent migrants rather than temporary movers, they also typically undercount migration events by missing multiple moves that occur within a census period. For instance, if migration is measured over a 5-year interval, then the individual migrating from region A to B and back to A before the end of the interval would be defined as a nonmigrant (stayer).

Although too long an interval risks missing migration events, the converse is also true. That is, too short an interval may add "noise" to the overall system by capturing short-term perturbations to the system and nonpermanent relocations, including extended vacations, short-term employment transfers, and circulation. The disparity between too short and too long an interval is revealed in the "1- and 5-year" problem, where the observed number of 5-year migrations is much less than the number of migrations recorded in a single year. That is, the number of 1-year migrations cannot simply be multiplied by a factor of 5 in order to arrive at the number of 5-year migrants. Instead, multiplication by 5 implicitly assumes that a different set of people migrate each year, while failing to account for multiple moves, a phenomenon described by return migration and chronic mobility.

Second, the size, shape, and characteristics of the spatial units will influence the number of migrants captured within an analysis. That is, the use of alternate spatial units, such as counties, states, or regions, will alter the count of migrants (along with the reason for migration). Additionally, the fraction of the population measured as migrants will be affected by the size, shape, and population distribution within the chosen spatial units. In general, the larger the areal aggregation, the fewer migrants will be counted. For this reason, one sees fewer individuals making long-distance migrations than local, residential moves.

Third, the composition of the sample population is of particular importance when studying specific population groups, such as the foreign-born, that may display a high degree of social and economic heterogeneity. Among the foreign-born, for example, composition reflects a set of issues including period of arrival, immigrant status (i.e., legal immigrant or refugee), changing immigration laws, and the national origin of new arrivals, all of which may contribute to important between-group differences with respect to migration propensities, economic advancement, or social incorporation. Failing to control for such effects may lead to potentially erroneous measures and conclusions owing to the differences between groups.

What Migration Quantity Should be Used?

Prior to selecting an analytical technique to model migration, an analyst must first decide how to measure migration, with several options available. Though the choice might be constrained by insufficient or pretabulated data (rather than individual "microdata"), the increasing availability and quality of migration data typically mean that the modeler is faced with a choice of the type of data to utilize. Data options include net migration (the number of out-migrants from region j subtracted from the number of in-migrants to j), gross in- and out-migration flows (the number of in- or out-migrants to/from a region, denoted by IM_j and OM_j, respectively), or region-to-region streams (the number of migrants from i to j, m_{ij}). Although one of the simplest measures to use, net migration is subject to the volatility of in- and out-migration flows, masking the typically more important variations associated with gross migration flows and/or changing origins and destinations. Using the net migration rate, derived by dividing the number of net migrants to region k by the population of k, is equally problematic, producing biased projections.

In fact, there are no "net migrants." Instead, net migrants are a statistical creation meant to portray movement into and out of a place. It is therefore preferable to base models on gross in- and out-migration flows. Even better is the use of detailed origin and destination migration streams (i.e., state to state), with both measures adding increased detail to the model. Commonly, migration is expressed as a rate, calculated by dividing the number of migrants by an appropriate "at-risk" population to standardize the measures. For example, the at-risk population for out-migration from region j (OMR_j) is the population of j (P_j), such that the gross out-migration rate from j is defined as

$$OMR_j = \left(\frac{OM_j}{P_j}\right) \times 1000. \tag{1}$$

Likewise, transition rates are defined as

$$P_{ij} = \frac{m_{ij}}{P_i} \tag{2}$$

where P_i is the population of origin i at time t. The at-risk population for in-migration is somewhat more problematic. Frequently defined as

$$IMR_j = \left(\frac{IM_j}{P_j}\right) \times 1000, \tag{3}$$

the at-risk population is the population of region j, or where migrants have just moved to. Yet, those at-risk to migrating to j are really those residing outside of j at the beginning of the time period, leading to the more appropriate definition of in-migration,

$$IMR_j = \left(\frac{IM_j}{\sum_{i \neq j} P_i}\right) \times 1000. \tag{4}$$

In other words, the in-migration rate to j is really the destination-specific out-migration rate of the rest of the system, with the destination being j.

Data Sources and Limitations

In modeling migration, two types of data are commonly used: longitudinal and cross-sectional. Longitudinal data, such as the Panel Survey of Income Dynamics (PSID), the National Longitudinal Survey on Youth, or the Current Population Survey (CPS), provide temporal depth and typically measure migration over short periods of time (commonly 1 year), allowing a migration history to be constructed and linked to events such as employment or life cycle changes. Their usefulness, however, is frequently limited by their relatively small sample size (particularly of specific populations such as Aboriginals or immigrants) and lack of geographical detail, limiting their ability to provide insight into the spatial processes of migration. Alternate longitudinal data sources include IRS (or comparable) records that compare place of residence from one tax year to the next. However, historical records extend back to 1976 only and do not include age–sex detail.

One of the most common sources of migration data is derived from census questionnaires. Most countries, including the United States, Canada, and Australia, collect information on place of residence 5 years prior to the census and on census day, with comparison of the current and prior residences providing insight into migration over the period. Although lacking temporal depth and providing only limited information on trends and changes in migration over time, census data typically provide much larger data sets that are based on 100% of the population. Alternatively, microdata files, such as the U.S. Census Bureau's Public Use Microdata Sample, are increasingly common and represent a sample of the population. In addition, census data typically provide a high degree of geographic detail and can be disaggregated by age, sex, race, and other demographic indicators. However, census data are a cross-sectional representation of the population, providing locational information at two points in time only (residence at the time of the census and 5 years prior). Missing from 5-year measurements of mobility are intervening moves, with cross-sectional data sources typically undercounting the number of migrations. Moreover, the census does not provide any information on prior residences or locations, although the return migration literature has detailed the importance of place of birth or a "home" region as a motivator of migration.

Although census information has provided the basis for numerous analyses, the U.S. Census Bureau is moving to phase out the decennial census, replacing it with a continuing monthly survey called the American Community Survey (ACS). Unlike the census, the ACS will ask about place of residence 1 year ago (rather than 5 years ago), creating problems for modelers who need information on migration within, for example, cohort projection models with specified time intervals of 5 years. Moreover, although the survey will be national, small coverage at local scales may limit local area analyses.

Dynamic Modeling Methods

An examination of the migration literature provides the analyst with multiple ways to incorporate dynamic or temporal components within migration models. Transition matrices, for example, can be used to describe the probability of migrating from one region to another during a time period (i.e., the probability of migrating from New York to California during 1995–2000). The comparison of migration probabilities over multiple periods (i.e., 1975–1980, 1985–1990, 1995–2000) provides a descriptive account as to how migration probabilities change through time, but provides relatively little insight into the underlying causal determinants of migration, how they change, and potential consequences.

More complex approaches to incorporate the dynamic aspects of migration include Plane's spatial shift-share analysis, which provides an understanding of changes in the volume of flows between regions over time, rather than for a specific period. Analogous to shift-share analysis used by economists to study changes over time in the sectoral structure of employment, spatial shift-share argues that differences in migration flows from one period to the next can be similarly analyzed. Alternatively, temporal changes in the structure of interregional flows can be examined through causative matrix models, such that migration data for one period are related in some way to migration information for a subsequent period. Pooled migration probabilities, for instance, could be used to derive an average pattern, which could then be used for projection purposes under the assumption that average probabilities would remove the cyclical effects or consequences associated with economic shocks or other period-specific effects. More complex methods are suitable when the assumption of fixed rates is not tenable. One choice, for example, is to assume that migration is a function of independent explanatory variables (i.e., economic measures), with parameters estimated via a choice model. Once estimated, the parameters are assumed to be constant and changes to migration patterns occur as the independent variables are altered.

Although these and other methods have been utilized to capture or model the dynamic nature of migration, four general methodological areas reflect the majority of research within the realm of dynamic migration modeling. These include multiregional cohort projection models, econometric methods, longitudinal (panel) analysis, and pseudo-cohort analysis, each of which is presented in the following discussion.

Cohort Projection Models

Cohort models project populations into the future via the extrapolation of existing birth, death, and migration rates, enabling a researcher to answer the question of "what will the distribution of the population across a series of regions be like if individuals move in the future as they did in the past?" Two principal concepts underlie the cohort component method. First, the population is divided into cohorts of like individuals, usually defined by age and sex, but also perhaps by race, ethnicity, or some other demographic indicator. Second, the models focus on components of change, with the population of each cohort subjected to fertility, mortality, and migration that, in effect, introduce a dynamic into the model.

Assuming first a single-region cohort component model with no migration, the model can be defined using matrix notation as

$$\mathbf{p}(t+n) = \mathbf{G}^n\mathbf{p}(t), \tag{5}$$

where $\mathbf{p}(t)$ is a column vector of a age–sex groups within the population at time t, $\mathbf{p}(t+n)$ is the projected population at time $t+n$, and $\mathbf{G}$ is a "growth" matrix containing birth rates and survival probabilities obtained from vital statistics. Note that birth rates are associated only with the childbearing age groups and all rates are assumed to remain constant throughout the projection. Multiplication of $\mathbf{G}$ by $\mathbf{p}(t)$ projects the population forward in time, thus "aging" and "surviving" a population over time via extrapolation.

Clearly, what is missing from the above model is migration. Developed by Rogers, multiregional cohort projection models use the cohort survival concept to age individuals from one age group to the next and extending the basic model by introducing interregional migration. In a three-region system, for example, each region is linked to the others via migration flows, such that out-migration from two regions defines in-migration to the third. Like basic cohort projection models, multiregional population projection models typically involve determining the starting age-region distribution and age-specific regional schedules of mortality, fertility, and migration to which the multiregional population has been subjected during the past period. Based on the initial population, the projection procedure is identical to that described above, with fertility, mortality, and migration rates applied to the initial population and projected into the future.

Although the matrix equation remains unchanged from that presented above [Eq. (5)], each of the matrices become increasingly complex as additional regions are added. For instance, the population vectors are subdivided into age groups, with each age group subdivided by region. The structure of the growth matrix is also altered so that the age and location of individuals can be simultaneously modeled. As in the single-region model, the growth matrix is assumed to remain constant throughout the projection period. Commonly, the length of the projection period is equated with the width of the age group. That is, if the migration interval is 5 years (the interval used in the U.S., Canadian, and Australian censuses), the age group is defined by an interval of 5 years, as is the projection period. Therefore, the present number of 10- to 14-year-olds who are subjected to the appropriate rates defines the expected number of 15- to 19-year-olds in a population 5 years hence. Repeated multiplication of the matrix equation projects the population further into the future, so that projecting the population 15 years into the future ($n=3$) may be written as

$$\mathbf{p}(t+5n) = \mathbf{G}^3\mathbf{p}(t). \tag{6}$$

Key to the success or accuracy of the model is how migration is measured. Whereas inclusion of net migration rates is one of the most straightforward ways to include migration in projection models, the measure is problematic since net migration rates are not based on the proper at-risk population, as noted earlier. In fact, using net migration will result in growing regions continuing to grow via in-migration, despite the fact that the population supply in other regions is diminishing. Likewise, declining regions will continue to decline despite a growing population elsewhere. Moreover, using net migration fails to account for regional interactions inherent within migration flows. Consequently, the use of properly defined transition rates (P_{ij}) is preferable. In this case, out-migration from a declining region will continue, but the absolute number of out-migrants will decline as the population at-risk to migration is reduced.

Whereas these models are useful short-term projection devices, projections associated with longer-time horizons are questionable given the assumptions inherent within the models. Most models assume, for instance, that (1) the probability of movement between regions does not change over time; (2) the population is homogenous, with each individual governed by the same set of probabilities; (3) the probabilities apply to a fixed time; and (4) the Markov property holds.

Clearly, most of these assumptions are unrealistic. First, the return migration literature, for example, is well documented, with returns to a "home" region invoking the role and importance of prior migration experiences and representing an important component of total interregional migration flows. Second, the stationarity of migration rates over the life of the projection is unlikely, given that different groups (i.e., blacks and whites, immigrants and the native born) will have differential migration probabilities. Moreover, migration probabilities should reflect shifting economic opportunities or amenities and the general aging of the population. Finally, the Markov property assumes that the probability of migrating is dependent only on the current location. In other words, previous locations and behavior do not influence current migration decisions. Although it simplifies the modeling task, the Markov assumption is problematic given the high mobility of most individuals. In essence, therefore, multiregional cohort models are not truly dynamic, in that migration rates (along with other demographic processes of birth and death) do not evolve over time, but are constant for the projection period.

Still, long-term projections utilizing this method offer insight as to where the population is headed, if present demographic rates were to hold over the longer term. Moreover, if fertility, mortality, and migration are held constant over a sufficiently long period of time, the population will ultimately converge to a stable age structure that does not change over time. An additional feature of the long-run stable population is that it is entirely dependent on the growth matrix and independent of the initial age structure.

Econometric Methods

Given that migration is typically motivated by economic concerns, it is only logical that analysts have attempted to link both economic and demographic components and their interrelationships with a single model or set of models. In 1986, Kanarolgou *et al*., for example, described discrete choice models, where potential migrants choose between a finite set of migration options. Rooted in utility theory, the probability of migration from i to j is assumed to be an outcome of a utility maximization process. Migration is treated as a random phenomenon and probabilities are used to describe migration propensities due to uncertainties on the part of the observer and the migrant. A set of variables representing the economic, geographic, or social characteristics of the regions (i.e., regional wage rates, employment, population effects) along with observed personal attributes (i.e., selectivity measures such as age, level of education, gender of the migrant) operationalizes the model, with the utility function written as

$$U_{in} = V_{in} + \varepsilon_{in}. \quad (7)$$

The first component, V_{in}, is the deterministic component, describing utility via a set of observed characteristics (i.e., employment growth rate, wage levels, unemployment level, and personal attributes). The second, stochastic component, ε_{in} represents all unobserved differences in utility, making the model a random utility model.

Using the random utility concept, the migration decision can be formalized such that the probability that an individual will choose to migrate to j is

$$P(M_{ij}) = \Pr[U_j > U_i], \quad \text{for all } j \text{ not equal to } i. \quad (8)$$

Assuming that all ε_{in} are independent and identically distributed yields the multinomial logit model defined by

$$P_i = \frac{\exp(V_i)}{[\sum \exp(V_j)]}. \quad (9)$$

The unknown parameters may be estimated using standard techniques such as maximum-likelihood estimation.

Perhaps some of the best known applications of random utility models include the nested logit model, which provides a number of theoretical and empirical advantages. Theoretically, such models "bridge" the microbehavioral determinants of migration (i.e., the selectivity of individual migrants with respect to age, education, marital status, or other personal attributes) and the macroeffects (i.e., regional employment rates, income, or amenities). Empirically, although it is possible (and methodologically straightforward) to apply logit models to any binary (i.e., move/stay) or multinomial (i.e., choice of destination out of a set of k options), the strength of the nested logit model lies in its ability to evaluate the departure and destination choice components of the migration decision in a systematic way. Assuming that the migration decision is the outcome of a two-level decision process, the "upper level" (departure choice) is influenced by the migration interval. Longer intervals, *ceteris paribus*, increase the likelihood of migration, associated with a greater likelihood of life cycle changes or other residential stresses. The "lower level" is defined by the destination choice, with the migrant choosing among a series of competing destinations (i.e., states or provinces). Mathematically, these two levels are linked through what is referred to as the "inclusive variable," which measures the utility or attractiveness of the system at the destination choice level.

Although random utility models have assumed a central place within migration modeling, their dynamic representation of migration is limited. Temporal information can, for example, be captured via the linkage of subsequent census periods and the introduction of variables to capture period-specific effects within the model. Alternatively, time-series techniques may be used to capture the dynamics of migration, including moving average (MA) or autoregressive models. The q-order MA model, for example, defines migration as an outcome generated by a weighted average of a finite number of previous and current random disturbances, such that the error term is

$$u_t = \varepsilon_t + \theta_1\varepsilon_{t-1} + \theta_2\varepsilon_{t-2} + \cdots + \theta_q\varepsilon_{t-q}. \quad (10)$$

Alternatively, the error term of a p-order autoregressive scheme is expressed as

$$u_t = \phi_1 u_{t-1} + \phi_2 u_{t-2} + \cdots + \phi_p u_{t-p} + \varepsilon, \quad (11)$$

such that migration is a weighted average of past observations and a random disturbance reflecting the current period. Used together, an autoregressive-moving average (ARIMA) scheme models migration as an outcome of previous migration plus current and previous random disturbances. Although limited by their inability to incorporate additional explanatory information, such models have been applied to migration analysis. In 1983, Clark, for instance, investigated migration flows using ARIMA models, arguing that both autoregressive and moving average processes were at work. In particular, he found that autoregressive models were inappropriate for rapidly growing regions. Instead, these were better described through a moving average model that implied considerable volatility to the in-migration process influenced by exogenous shocks rather than previous flows of in-migrants. Alternatively, Clark noted that autoregressive models represented declining regions best.

Distributed lag models allow the incorporation of temporal information in the explanatory variables, typically represented by a variable (i.e., unemployment rate, employment growth, or wages) that is measured over a series of prior time periods. This allows the analyst to account for the noninstantaneous relationship between migration and other variables. That is, there is frequently some time lag between economic change and its consequences for migration flows. The migration equation may be specified as

$$Y_t = \alpha + \beta_0 X_t + \beta_1 X_{t-1} + \beta_2 X_{t-2} + \beta_3 X_{t-3} + \varepsilon, \quad (12)$$

where Y_t is a measure of migration at time t, X_t is a measure of unemployment at time t, X_{t-1} is unemployment in the previous period, etc. Though the distributed lag model may be estimated through ordinary least-squares regression, modelers need to be aware of potentially serious problems associated with multicollinearity in the explanatory variables and a reduction in the degrees of freedom with large lag structures.

Although these models are dynamic in nature in that they use information from multiple periods to model migration, they do not directly link the economic and demographic systems in a recursive manner, such that the economic component informs the demographic component, or vice versa. Yet, it is clear that population change is affected by economic conditions and has a concurrent effect on economic conditions through changes to the labor force and participation rates, consumer demand, employment, unemployment, and other economic activities. More specifically, if a regional population expands, in-migrants will take advantage of new employment opportunities (i.e., "people follow jobs"), whereas "jobs follow people" as increasing consumer demand attracts new industry and promotes the growth of trade and services.

Arguably, demo-economic models provide the analyst with some of the most complex tools available to represent the dynamism of the system. For the modeler, the linkage of economic and demographic systems within a demo-economic model offers a number of advantages. More generally, demo-econometric models are important, general-purpose tools, drawing on economics, geography, statistics, and demography, that enable the concurrent analysis of regional phenomena. With a large supporting literature, a rigorous method to test the validity of theory, the ability to forecast a dependent variable under different conditions, and the ability to predict the effects of policy decisions, they provide an important approach to modeling migration.

The basic structure of the model takes the form of a linear multiple regression equation representative of underlying theory relating a dependent variable to a set of independent variables, with the relationship estimated using ordinary least-squares regression. The complex interrelations of the economic and demographic systems typically mean, however, that a set of interrelated equations is needed. Known as simultaneous equation models, variables may appear on both the left- and right-hand sides of the equation, with the structure of the equations derived from economic and migration theory along with the realities of data availability. For example, migration may be determined by a set of economic variables, including (for example) the unemployment rate. In return, the unemployment rate may be modeled as a partial function of the demographic makeup of a region, with out-migration expected to reduce unemployment. The ECESIS model, for example, represents each U.S. state, with economic and cohort-component models linked through a system with 7400 endogenous (model-forecasted) and 884 exogenous (external to the model) variables, along with matrices of state-to-state migration flows for 10 age–sex groups. One of the greatest advantages of simultaneous models is their nonreliance on fixed coefficients, a problem that plagues cohort methods, as already noted.

Although the existence of these economic–demographic relationships is obvious, the direct linkage of economic and demographic systems and how best to achieve it have proven more problematic. By and large, demo-economic models have taken multiple routes in their linkage of economic and demographic change. Economists, for example, have often incompletely modeled the migration system, relying on net migration or incorporating only limited age–sex detail to portray changing migration propensities with age. Demographers, on the other hand, have historically focused on projection methods but neglected the economic component. In some cases, population may be treated as exogenous to the model, with models incorporating the consequences of population change, but not the causes. Others ignore the causes and model the consequences. The actual, statistical representation of the linkage between the economic and demographic components is also open to interpretation. Various models have, for example, utilized input–output techniques, cohort component methods, or simultaneous equations to represent and link the various components. Whereas the former two methods rely on fixed demographic and economic effects, the latter has sought to simultaneously determine economic and demographic variables. By and large, such differences in methodology, and in particular how migration or population structures are constructed within models, reflect disciplinary boundaries. Fortunately, these have been minimized and models have shown increasing complexity.

Longitudinal (Panel) Analysis

It is arguable as to whether or not cross-sectional data, which are typically used in cohort projection and other migration models, adequately capture the dynamic properties of migration. Instead, what is needed is a sequence of cross sections or panel data, involving successive waves of individual or household interviews that give histories of the sequence of residences over time so that the duration of residence before moving can be derived. Longitudinal analyses allow the interrelationships between specific life-course events, representing some identifiable and quantitative change, such as leaving school, marriage, or divorce, to be statistically related to migration. Therefore, the event occurs at a discernable point in time, with the event history represented by a longitudinal record of when events occur to a sample of individuals or households. Longitudinal data files, such as the PSID, represent a particularly rich source of migration information. The added advantage of longitudinal files is the enriched ability to examine the dynamic properties of migration, with the files providing histories of migration and linkages to other events correlated with migration. By using the sequence of residences and the duration of residence prior to the move, the determinants of migration can be empirically derived and tested. Ideally, the times associated with migration are accurate, so that a discrete time approximation to the continuous process is not needed.

Migration is therefore viewed as a transition from one region (residence in i) to region j, which terminates the episode. Key to the analysis is the length of the episode, with the resulting methodology reflecting either "continuous" or "discrete" events. Although both may be based on longitudinal data, differences in model definition arise over whether the timing of an event (migration) is measured exactly (continuous) or whether it occurred over some interval t (discrete). In both cases, an important concept is the hazard function. In the case of discrete data, the hazard rate is defined as the probability of migrating from region i at time t, such that

$$h_{it} = \Pr[T_i = t \mid T_i \geq t,\ X_{it}]. \quad (13)$$

In this formulation, the hazard rate is the probability that individual i will migrate at some moment in time given that they have not migrated before that time, t is the time of migration, and X_{it} is a set of exogenous variables that vary over time, such as wage or employment rate differentials. It should be noted that the hazard rate is similar to the survival rate, which would represent the probability of a person with characteristics X_{it} not migrating by time t. Although the hazard is unobserved, it controls both the occurrence and timing of migration and is therefore the dependent variable within any model. It should be noted that the hazard rate is similar to the survival rate, which would represent the probability of a person with a defined set of characteristics not migrating by time t.

Ideally, the timing of migration is accurate, so that a discrete time approximation to a continuous process is not needed. In this case, the modeler is interested in the instantaneous probability that migration occurs in the interval from t to $t+s$, where s is infinitesimally small, such that the hazard rate is defined as

$$h(t) = \lim_{s \to 0} P(t, t+s)/s. \quad (14)$$

Although potentially providing important insights into the dynamic nature of migration, the construction of continuous history data is time-consuming and costly, with such data sets typically "one-of-a-kind" and created for a particular need. Indeed, dynamic data on migration are typically more available for discrete time intervals than for continuous time histories as employed in event history analyses.

Although there is no single methodology for the analysis of either discrete or continuous events, most approaches have focused on regression (or similar) models, allowing the event of interested (the dependent variable) to be expressed as a function of independent explanatory variables. Methods typically represent straightforward generalizations of static models applied to cross-sectional data, such as regression techniques or the random utility model discussed earlier.

Regardless of whether discrete-time or continuous models are used, the principal problem of all longitudinal studies is the need to separate "state dependence" from "unobserved heterogeneity." The former includes how migration behavior is influenced by previous migration experience (i.e., return migration and the importance of a home region), whereas the latter reflects the fact that some people migrate due to unobserved characteristics and will therefore move more than others (i.e., "chronic" migrants). Both effects produce similar behavioral patterns but have different implications with respect to methodology and the derived conclusions. Care should also be taken in the analysis of panel data, since different survey methods and designs, such as the timing and duration of waves, will alter derived conclusions.

In addition to suffering from the problems of small sample size and spatial representation, as already discussed, longitudinal surveys suffer from two additional problems. First, attrition of sample members through death or for other reasons will reduce sample size over time as well as reduce model power. Second, longitudinal data suffer from problems associated with the "initial condition." That is, panel data must start and stop at some point in time, therefore interrupting the process of interest (migration) at some intermediate point rather than its true start or end. It is therefore reasonable to assume that panel data may miss important information pertaining to migration or residential history that occurred before that start of the sampling frame. Statistically, this results in "censored" information, with the application of ordinary least-squares techniques to censored data leading to potentially biased estimates. Various econometric techniques, including maximum-likelihood estimation and techniques such as TOBIT models, have been derived in order to overcome problems associated with censoring.

Pseudo-cohort Analysis

Although longitudinal data files offer significant advantages when modeling migration, information relating to relatively small populations such as the foreign-born or Aboriginal populations is often limited by small sample sizes. More generally, detailed geographical information may be limited given the relatively small sample size of many longitudinal data files. Reliance on a single census interval, on the other hand, is also imperfect, given that it is a cross-sectional representation of a population at a particular point in time. Ultimately, information derived from a single census tells us little about the dynamics of the population—how it evolved over time, where it evolved from, or the differential directions and paths through which it evolved.

One option is to link consecutive census files (or other cross-sectional sources), creating "pseudo" or "artificial" panels. The advantage of linking census files is the ability to follow groups and changes to those groups over time. In particular, the analyst can define cohorts that may be followed through time as they artificially age and make spatial (i.e., by migrating) or other (i.e., economic, occupation, social) adjustments. Cohort definition should rest on the issues that are most salient to the study, with samples defined with respect to age. For example, a cohort aged 25 to 34 in 1980 would be aged 35 to 44 in 1990. In addition to changes in their age profile, other social, economic, and demographic characteristics of the cohort will evolve over the interval. Clearly, although individuals cannot be followed, this methodology can trace aggregate changes in groups or group behavior over time.

Pseudo-cohort analysis has proven particularly useful as a tool to examine the immigrant population where key questions continue to revolve around their assimilation and settlement, both of which occur across a relatively long time frame. Although it may be tempting to compare immigrant populations and measures of their adjustment over consecutive census periods, compositional effects embedded within the immigrant population will likely result in biased or misleading conclusions. Such effects are particularly important when investigating questions pertaining to the assimilation of immigrants. When comparing the immigrant population in 1990 and 2000, for example, the total group of immigrants in 2000 is not the same as that observed in 1990, given the continued arrival of new immigrants and the death or return migration of previous arrivals. At the regional scale, the noncomparability of the immigrant population is even more relevant, given in- and out-migration. Even after controlling for national origin, the two measures will differ, with the attributes of new arrivals superimposed on the existing immigrant population, the effect of which may be to obscure measures of adjustment, such as English language proficiency, level of education, or home ownership, or other complementary measures.

Pseudo-cohorts can be used to minimize these compositional effects. Typically, immigrant cohorts are defined by age at the time of the census and period of arrival, as well as national origin, therefore controlling for "compositional effects" noted above. As before, changes in group characteristics, migration behavior, migration selectivity, or concentration may be evaluated through both descriptive and multivariate techniques, including discrete time and econometric models as discussed above.

Summary: Capabilities and Limitations of Dynamic Models

Plane and Rogerson (1994, p. 227) noted that "migration is typically one of the most difficult components of population change to model and forecast," a comment that is perhaps particularly valid when attempting to model the dynamic nature of migration. In this article, several complementary methods of dynamic migration modeling have been highlighted. Unless one is working with event history data, one's best attempt must make basic assumptions regarding how migration is to be modeled. Although numerous options exist for the migration analyst to extend static models of migration to incorporate a dynamic component, the ultimate form of the migration model is defined as much by the nature of the data as its overall purpose (i.e., explanation or forecasting), with the lack of appropriate data a common problem. Surveys such as the CPS generate data at the individual level and record place of residence at time t and $t - 1$. Alternatively, longitudinal surveys, such as the PSID, provide a more continuous record of residences, duration of residence, and other socioeconomic or sociodemographic variables over time, whereas cross-sectional data sources, such as the census, measure migration between two fixed points in time, with relatively little insight into previous or intervening migrations. In general, the greater the detail in the data source, the more sophisticated and rigorous the models that can be fitted. Regardless of whether cross-sectional or longitudinal data are selected, models tend to reveal complementary findings, with longitudinal analyses tending to enrich the cross-sectional results.

See Also the Following Articles

Census, Varieties and Uses of Data • Demography • Longitudinal Cohort Designs • Mathematical Demography • Modeling Migration

Further Reading

Beaumont, P. M. (1989). *ECESIS: An Interregional Economic–Demographic Model of the United States.* Garland, New York.

Clark, G. (1983). *Interregional Migration, National Policy, and Social Justice.* Rowman and Littlefield, Totowa, NJ.

Kanaroglou, P. K., Liaw, K. L., and Papageorgiou, Y. Y. (1986). An analysis of migration systems. 2. Operational framework. *Environ. Planning A* **18,** 1039–1060.

Long, L. (1988). *Migration and Residential Mobility in the United States.* Russell Sage, New York.

Myers, D., and Lee, S. W. (1996). Immigration cohorts and residential overcrowding in Southern California. *Demography* **33,** 51–65.

Newbold, K. B., and Bell, M. (2001). Return and onwards migration in Canada and Australia: Evidence from fixed interval data. *Int. Migration Rev.* **35,** 1157–1184.

Plane, D. A. (1987). The geographic components of change in a migration system. *Geogr. Anal.* **19,** 283–299.

Plane, D. A., and Rogerson, P. A. (1994). *The Geographical Analysis of Population with Applications to Planning and Business.* Wiley, New York.

Rogers, A. (1995). *Multiregional Demography: Principles, Methods and Extensions.* Wiley, New York.

Ecological Fallacy

Paul A. Jargowsky

University of Texas, Dallas, Richardson, Texas, USA

Glossary

aggregation The process of grouping data on individual units of analysis, such as calculating neighborhood-level means of individual-level variables.

bias The difference between the expected value of an estimator and the value of the parameter being estimated.

correlation A measure of the linear association between two variables.

ecological fallacy The assumption that relationships between variables at the aggregate level imply the same relationships at the individual level.

ecological inference A conclusion about associations or causal relationships among individual observations at one level, based on the analysis of data aggregated to a higher level.

omitted variable bias The bias in an estimator, resulting from the omission of a relevant variable when the omitted variable is correlated with one or more of the explanatory variables.

Abstract

In many important areas of social science research, data on individuals are summarized at higher levels of aggregation. For example, data on voters may be published only at the precinct level. The ecological fallacy refers to the incorrect assumption that relationships between variables observed at the aggregated, or ecological, level are necessarily the same at the individual level. In fact, estimates of causal effects from aggregate data can be wrong both in magnitude and in direction. An understanding of the causes of these differences can help researchers avoid drawing erroneous conclusions from ecological data.

Origins of the Ecological Fallacy

The ecological fallacy has a long history spanning many disciplines, particularly sociology and political science. It is closely related to what economists tend to call aggregation bias. Stated briefly, an ecological fallacy exists if it is assumed that relationships observed at an aggregated level imply that the same relationships exist at the individual level. For example, observing that the percentage of Blacks and the crime rate are correlated at the level of police precincts does not necessarily imply that Black persons are more likely to commit crimes. Indeed, it is possible that the correlation of two variables at the aggregate level can have the sign opposite that of the correlation at the individual level. As a result, it can be quite difficult to infer individual-level relationships from aggregated cross-sectional data, an issue known as the problem of ecological inference.

Social science is mostly about understanding the behavior of individuals. Quite often, however, researchers find that the only data available to address certain empirical questions are aggregate data. For example, a researcher may wish to know whether a specific racial group is more inclined to vote for a particular party. However, because balloting is secret, the researcher does not have access to the individual-level data. Instead, he or she may know the vote total for two parties in each election precinct and the demographic characteristics of the voting-age population in each of these precincts. Ecological inference refers to this process of attempting to draw an inference about individual relationships from aggregate data. In this example, the researcher would attempt to draw a conclusion about the relationship between the race of an individual and his or her voting propensity from the relationship between two precinct-level variables: the precinct proportion in the racial group, and the precinct proportion voting for a particular party.

More generally, ecological inference is the drawing of a conclusion about how X affects Y, in some population of interest, from data that consists of the means of X and Y for subgroups of the population.

Robinson's Critique of Ecological Inference

Although not the first to draw attention to the problems of ecological inference, William S. Robinson, in 1950, had the most dramatic impact. Robinson cited a number of famous studies from several disciplines that were based on what he called "ecological correlations" (pp. 351–352). That is, the cited studies relied on ordinary Pearsonian correlation coefficients between two variables calculated from the averages of those variables for spatially defined groups of individuals, such as neighborhoods, cities, states, or regions. These studies had assumed, often implicitly, that the implications that could be drawn from the sign, magnitude, and significance of the ecological correlations applied equally to the relationship between the two variables at the level of individuals, which in almost all cases was the primary role of the research.

Robinson subjected this practice to a withering critique, by contrasting individual and ecological correlations in cases in which data were available at both levels. He showed that the individual-level correlation between race and illiteracy in the United States in 1930 was 0.203, but the correlation between percentage Black and percentage illiterate at the state level was far higher, 0.773. Robinson showed that not even the sign of ecological correlations could be trusted. The correlation between having been born abroad and being illiterate was a positive 0.118 at the individual level (again using 1930 data for the United States), probably reflecting the lower educational standards of the immigrants' countries of origin. However, the correlation at the state level between the corresponding ecological aggregates (percentage foreign born and percentage illiterate) was a counterintuitive −0.526, the opposite direction of the individual correlation! Robinson concluded that "there need be no correspondence between the individual correlation and the ecological correlation" (p. 354). Moreover, he said he provided "a definite answer as to whether ecological correlations can validly be used as substitutes for individual correlations." His answer: "They cannot" (p. 357).

The impact of Robinson's condemnation of ecological inference was profound. Indeed, as discussed by Selvin in 1958, inferences about individual relationships from aggregate data came to be regarded not just as problematic, but—though Robinson's seminal article did not use this word—as a fallacy. And though Robinson's critique was stated in terms of simple bivariate correlation coefficients, his critique is a challenge to regression analysis on aggregate data as well. All slope coefficients in bivariate and multiple regressions can be expressed as functions of either simple or partial correlation coefficients, respectively, scaled by the standard deviations of the dependent and independent variables. Because standard deviations are always positive, the sign of any regression coefficient reflects the sign of the correlation coefficient on which it is based, whether simple or partial. Thus, regression analysis on aggregated data, a common practice in several disciplines, runs the risk of committing the ecological fallacy as well.

Limitations of Robinson's Critique

Seen in retrospect, Robinson's analysis seems to ignore the presence of confounding variables. For example, using Robinson's second example, immigrants tended to flock to industrial states in search of jobs, and these states were wealthier and had higher literacy rates than did poor (jobless) Southern states that failed to attract as many immigrants. To a modern reader, Robinson's analysis seems to lack appropriate controls for socioeconomic status, regional dummy variables, or a fixed-effects model to isolate the effect of illiteracy from other covariates. Indeed, Hanushek *et al.* revisited Robinson's data in 1974 and showed that the sign of his correlation was a reflection of omitted variable bias; in other words, Robinson's model was underspecified.

If the anomalous results attributed to the ecological fallacy actually result from model misspecification, then the ecological fallacy, according to Firebaugh in 1978, is a "near fallacy." On the other hand, if the divergence between individual- and aggregate-level estimates is more subtle and intractable, then ecological inference is a dangerous business. Illustration of the mathematical bases of the ecological fallacy gives some guidance as to how it can be avoided.

Understanding the Mathematical Structure of the Ecological Fallacy

To understand the ecological fallacy, it is necessary to understand what causes the differences between estimators generated by data at different levels. Graphical illustrations establish how ecological inference can go wrong, and the two mathematical conditions that cause such aggregate estimates of relationships between variables to differ from their individual-level counterparts can then be developed.

Graphical Illustration of the Problem with Ecological Correlations

First, consider a few simplified scenarios using scatterplots, following Gove and Hughes' 1980 example. Suppose the interest is in a dichotomous dependent variable such as dropping out of high school, coded as either 1 if a person is a dropout or 0 if a person is not. Further, suppose there are two groups, White and Black, and the basic question of interest is whether members of one group or the other are more likely to drop out. Data on individuals are lacking, but the overall proportion of persons who are dropouts in three different neighborhoods is known. Also known is the proportion of Black persons in each of the three neighborhoods, which for the purpose of illustration is set to 0.20, 0.50, and 0.80.

Figure 1 shows how ecological inference is supposed to work. The figure shows the separate rates for Whites and Blacks as dashed lines, because the researcher does not observe these data. The Black group has a higher dropout rate than does the White group, and so as the proportion of Black persons in the neighborhood rises, the overall dropout rate also rises. In this case, it is possible to infer correctly from the aggregate data that Blacks are more likely to drop out.

Figure 2 shows how the ecological data can give misleading results. In this case, Whites have a higher dropout rate than do Blacks in each neighborhood. However, the dropout rate of both groups rises as the percentage of Blacks in the neighborhood rises, perhaps because the percentage of Blacks in the neighborhood is correlated with some other variable, such as family income. Even though higher rates exist for Whites than for Blacks in every neighborhood, the ecological regression coefficient will have a positive slope, because the overall dropout rate rises as the percentage of Blacks rises. In this case, the ecological regression would correctly report that the dependent variable (DV) is positively associated with the percentage of Blacks in the neighborhood, but the inference that individual Blacks are more likely to drop out than individual Whites would be wrong (this is an example of what is known as Simpson's paradox).

Other scenarios are possible. Suppose the Black and White dropout rates are exactly the same within each neighborhood, but the rates for both groups rise as the percentage of Blacks in the neighborhood rises. At the ecological level, the observed dropout rates will slope upward, even though there is no effect of race at the individual level. Figure 3 shows a case in which the dropout rate rises as the percentage of Blacks rises solely because the Whites drop out at higher rates in the neighborhoods in which they are the minority. Again, an inference from the ecological level that Blacks drop out more often would be incorrect.

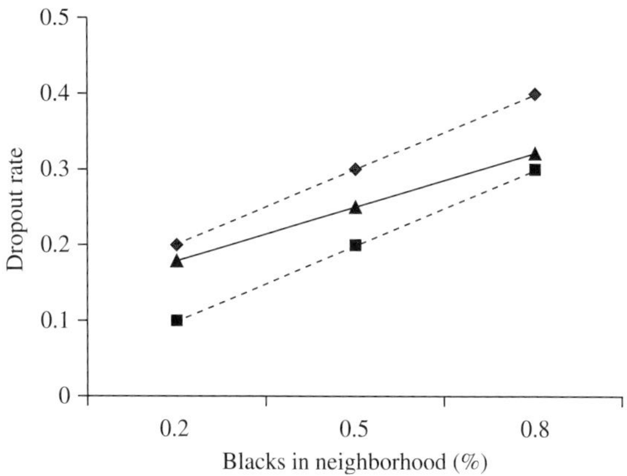

Figure 2 High school dropout rate. Incorrect inference from ecological data. ▲ Total observed; ◆ Whites (unobserved); ■ Blacks (unobserved).

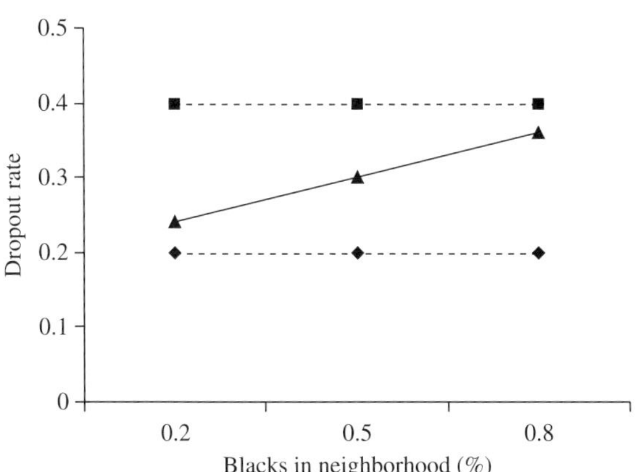

Figure 1 High school dropout rate. Correct inference from ecological data. ▲ Total observed; ◆ Whites (unobserved); ■ Blacks (unobserved).

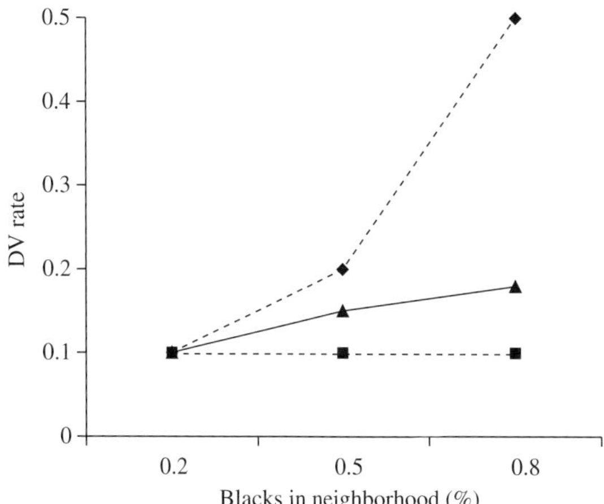

Figure 3 Incorrect inference from ecological data. DV, Dependent variable. ▲ Total observed; ◆ Whites (unobserved); ■ Blacks (unobserved).

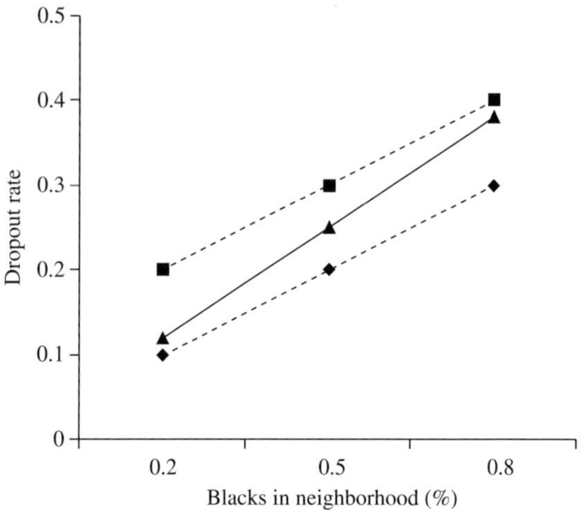

Figure 4 High school dropout rate. Correct inference, but for the wrong reason. ▲ Total observed; ◆ Whites (unobserved); ■ Blacks (unobserved).

In Fig. 4, Blacks do have higher dropout rates, compared to Whites, in each neighborhood, and the rates of both groups rise as the percentage of Blacks increases. Regression on the aggregate data produces a positive slope, but virtually all of that slope is driven by the common dropout increase in both groups in the more heavily minority neighborhoods. Only a small fraction of the slope reflects the influence of the race of individuals on the dropout rate. In this case, the direction of the ecological inference would be correct, but the magnitude of the effect would be substantially overestimated.

How Aggregation Produces Bias

The problem just described can be restated as a form of aggregation bias, as shown by Freedman in 2001, Irwin and Lichtman in 1976, Stoker in 1993, and Theil in 1955. The goal is to understand how one variable affects another in the population. In other words, the aim is to know the slope parameter that tells us how the dependent variable changes in response to changes in the independent variable. An estimate of the effect can be obtained by applying ordinary least squares (OLS) to the following regression equation:

$$Y_{ij} = \alpha + \beta X_{ij} + u_{ij}, \tag{1}$$

in which j indexes neighborhoods and i indexes individuals within neighborhood j. The OLS estimate of the slope, b, has the following expected value:

$$E[b|X] = \beta + E\left[\frac{\sum_j \sum_i X_{ij} u_{ij}}{\sum_j \sum_i (X_{ij} - \overline{X})^2}\right]. \tag{2}$$

This result is analogous to the standard proof that OLS coefficients are unbiased, found in any econometrics textbook, except for the double summation signs. However, in view of the associative property of addition, the double summation signs do not affect the sums or the conclusion. If the second term in Eq. (2) is zero, which will occur if and only if X and u are uncorrelated, then b is an unbiased estimate of β. The disturbance term, however, implicitly includes the effect of all other variables as well as random influences. If the net effect of these omitted variables and influences is correlated with X, the assumption is violated, the second term does not reduce to zero, and the estimator is biased.

By summing up to the neighborhood level and dividing by the number of observations in each neighborhood, Eq. (1) implies that

$$\overline{Y}_j = \alpha + \beta \overline{X}_j + \overline{u}_j. \tag{3}$$

The β that appears in Eq. (3) is algebraically identically to the β in Eq. (1). Thus, in principle, an estimate of the effect can be obtained from either the individual- or the aggregate-level regressions. However, the expected value of the slope estimate from the aggregate regression, b^*, is

$$E[b^*|X] = \beta + E\left[\frac{\sum \overline{X}_j \overline{u}_j}{\sum (\overline{X}_j - \overline{X})^2}\right]. \tag{4}$$

At the aggregate level, the condition for the unbiasedness is that the mean disturbance term is not correlated with the mean value of the independent variable. It is quite possible that in a given set of data, the criteria for unbiasedness are met at the individual level [Eq. (2)], but are violated at the aggregate level [Eq. (4)]. According to Freedman in 2001, such a correlation could arise if the grouping process is related to some variable Z, not included in the regression, which is correlated with the outcome variable. Thus, the ecological fallacy can arise from a particular kind of omitted variable bias, one that is introduced or exacerbated because of the aggregation process. In addition, a correlation between X and u at the aggregate level could arise if the grouping process is based on the values of the dependent variable, Y; in that case, either extreme values of X or extreme values of u would produce extreme values of Y, which would then tend to be grouped together.

Although these ideas have been explicated in the context of a bivariate regression, they apply equally well in the multiple regression context. In fact, in the world of social phenomena, where there are always correlations among explanatory variables, it is highly unlikely to be the case that a bivariate regression would be correctly specified at either the individual or the aggregate level.

In the multivariate context, however, one additional problem arises. As described by Firebaugh in 2001, an outcome variable for an individual may be affected both by the individual's value of X and by a contextual variable that is a function of the aggregated values of X, such as the mean of X. When the individual data are aggregated, the individual and contextual values of X may not be separately identified. This problem is discussed further in the next section.

The first implication of the foregoing discussion is that if both the individual and ecological regressions are correctly specified, both types of analyses will provide equally unbiased estimates of the true slope parameter. In symbolic terms,

$$E[b|X] = E[b^*|X] = \beta. \quad (5)$$

The second implication is that both regressions can be misspecified, and in the latter case, there is no guarantee that the individual regression is the better of the two. In 1960, Grunfeld and Griliches, referring to individual regressions as micro equations and ecological regressions as macro equations, argued that ecological regressions may be better in certain circumstances:

> *[I]n practice we do not know enough about micro behavior to be able to specify micro equations perfectly. Hence empirically estimated micro relations . . . should not be assumed to be perfectly specified. . . . Aggregation of economic variables can, and in fact frequently does, reduce these specification errors. Hence, aggregation does not only produce aggregation error, but may also produce an aggregation gain.* (p. 1)

It is not hard to think of examples whereby aggregation could reduce correlation between the disturbance term and X. For example, persons may choose their neighborhoods on the basis of unobserved characteristics that affect their wages. In that case, neighborhood characteristics will be correlated with the disturbance term in a wage regression, resulting in biased estimates of the neighborhood effect on wage. Aggregating to the metropolitan level would sharply reduce this source of bias, by subsuming all neighborhood-to-neighborhood selection in the metropolitan averages.

The third implication is that is possible to think about the conditions under which the bias term in Eq. (4) has an expectation different from zero. Assume that a well-specified individual model based on individual-level variables can be written down, as in Eq. (1), but that the data to estimate it are lacking. If the same equation estimated at the aggregate level produces biased estimates, then there must be something about the grouping mechanism that leads to correlation between the relevant X variables and the disturbance term. In other words, it matters how the data were aggregated. It is useful to consider the following possibilities and their implications:

1. Random grouping is not very likely to arise in practice, but it is instructive to consider the possibility. If the data are aggregated randomly, and the model was correctly specified at the individual level, there will be no aggregation bias. The expected value of mean X and mean u for all groups will be the grand mean of X and u, respectively, and they will not be correlated.
2. If the grouping is based on the X (or multiple Xs), there will be no aggregation bias. This follows because the conditional mean of the disturbance term is zero for all values of X if the individual model is correctly specified.
3. If the grouping is based on Y, aggregation bias is very likely. For example, if Y and X are positively related, in the groups with higher levels of Y, both high values of X and larger than average disturbance terms would be found, and at lower levels of Y, the opposite would occur. Clearly, the aggregate levels of X and u will be correlated and the ecological regression is misspecified.
4. Grouping based on geography, the most common method, is also the most difficult to evaluate, because neighborhood selection may be based on a complex set of factors operating at different levels. However, if the dependent variable is something like income, the danger exists that neighborhood aggregation is more like case 3. If the dependent variable is less likely to be involved in the residential choice function, then sorting by neighborhood will be more like cases 1 or 2.

When data are provided in an aggregate form, the researcher must understand and evaluate how the groups were formed. Then the researcher must try to ascertain whether the procedure is likely to introduce aggregation biases or aggregation gains in view of the specific dependent variable and explanatory models under consideration.

Problems Related to Group-Level Effects

The foregoing discussion is based on Eq. (1); like most empirical literature in social science, this equation does not take into account the possibility of group-level effects on individuals. That is, the individual-level equation includes only individual-level variables. But it is possible, indeed likely, that the mean value of X in a neighborhood could have an independent effect on Y even after controlling for the individual's own level of X. Firebaugh described several possibilities in 1980. An intelligent student may well learn more in the presence of more intelligent fellow students. On the other hand, a mediocre student might be discouraged in such an environment and may do better if he was "a big fish in a small pond." Group effects include or are related to neighborhood effects, peer group effects, and social network effects.

In general, these models can be characterized as including some measure of a group level variable in an individual model:

$$Y_{ij} = \beta_1 + \beta_2 X_{ij} + \beta_3 \overline{X}_j + u_{ij}. \tag{6}$$

At the aggregate level, this model becomes

$$\begin{aligned} \overline{Y}_j &= \beta_1 + \beta_2 \overline{X}_j + \beta_3 \overline{X}_j + \overline{u}_j \\ &= \beta_1 + (\beta_2 + \beta_3)\overline{X}_j + \overline{u}_j. \end{aligned} \tag{7}$$

Clearly, even if there is no bias of the type discussed in the previous section, the individual and group effects are not identified, only their sum. In the absence of individual data or outside information on the magnitude of one or the other of the two effects, the lack of identification in the aggregate models poses a formidable obstacle.

Fortunately, in certain cases, the sum of the two effects may itself be of interest. For example, suppose the dependent variable is a measure of children's health, and X is a measure of insurance coverage through a public program. A direct impact of the child's own coverage status might be expected, as well as an effect of the level of coverage in his or her area, through reduction of contagious diseases and increased availability of medical service providers (a supply response). Both effects are real benefits of the program, and both are included in the coefficient from the ecological regression.

Solutions to the Ecological Inference Problem?

Though Robinson's critique sent shock waves through the social science community and undoubtedly influenced some researchers to eschew aggregate data, it also spawned a literature on "solutions" to the ecological inference problem. Goodman addressed the problem in 1953 and 1959 in terms of dichotomous variables. He noted that the dependent variable at the aggregate level is a proportion, which must be the weighted sum of the unobserved proportions of the two groups formed by the independent variable. This is just an accounting identity. In the case of voting, we observe the overall proportion voting for a given party and wish to make inferences about the votes for specific individuals depending on their racial group. The weighted average of the two groups' voting must add to the observed total proportion in each neighborhood:

$$T_i = (1 - P_i)W_i + P_i B_i, \tag{8}$$

where T_i is the observed proportion, P_i is the percentage of Blacks, and W_i and B_i are the unobserved rates for the White and Black subpopulations, respectively.

Algebraic manipulation yields an equation that can be estimated from the aggregate data:

$$T_i = W_i - (W_i + B_i)P_i = \alpha + \beta P_i + u_i. \tag{9}$$

The constant term in the regression is the average proportion voting for the party in the White population, and $\beta - \alpha$ produces the estimate of the Black proportion. The disturbance term is introduced because α and β are fixed, whereas in actuality W_i and B_i vary from neighborhood to neighborhood. The validity of this approach depends on the "constancy assumption"; in other words, as discussed by Goodman in 1953 and 1959 and by Freedman in 2001, the voting proportions do not depend on the ethnic composition of the neighborhood. Figure 1 illustrated a case of the constancy assumption, because the White and Black dropout rates were unrelated to the percentage of Blacks.

A second basic approach, described in a 1953 study by Duncan and Davis, is based on establishing bounds for the minimum and maximum possible for each cell of a cross-tabulation in each of the aggregate units. By summing these extrema up over the data set, it is possible to determine with 100% confidence the minimum and maximum bounds of the correlation that could obtain in the individual-level data.

In 1997, King proposed a "solution" to the ecological inference (EI) problem, the EI technique. It was also developed in the context of dichotomous dependent variables. The EI technique combines the method of bounds with the Goodman regression technique, and estimates the system using maximum likelihood and numerical simulation, assuming a bivariate normal distribution for the parameters. Critics, however, have pointed out a number of flaws with King's technique, a review of which is beyond the scope of this essay. Important critiques were done by Anselin in 2000, Anselin and Cho in 2002, Freedman in 1998, and McCue in 2001.

The debate on the statistical underpinnings and empirical performance of the EI method will likely continue for some time, even as the technique is being widely adopted within the field of political science. However, the most important issue concerning King's approach is that it is developed within and justified for a very narrow range of problems that are not fully representative of the range of issues and types of data historically associated with the ecological fallacy and the problem of ecological inference. King dismisses the argument that ecological inference is mainly a matter of model specification, and in doing so reveals the most serious problem in his proposed methodology. He argues that the

> *concept of a "correctly-specified" individual-level equation is not helpful in this context, since individual data contain the answer in ecological inference problems with certainty. That is, with individual data, we would not need to specify any equation; we would merely construct the cross-tabulation and read off the answer. Having the extra variables around if individual-level data are available would provide no additional assistance* (p. 49).

In other words, the narrow focus of King's technique is reconstructing a description of the individual data, not evaluating a causal model. This is an adequate goal in King's motivating example, ascertaining voting patterns by race for the purpose of redistricting litigation. But in virtually any other social science application, our interest is in a causal model that cannot be reduced to a contingency table. Even in voting analysis, there are substantively interesting questions about whether racial identity affects voting net of other factors, such as income, occupation, and so on. Further, King readily acknowledges that his method will be less effective when the dependent variable is continuous, because no information is gleaned from bounds. These are rather important limitations.

Further discussions of approaches to reduce bias in ecological inference were provided by Achen and Shively in 1995, Cho in 2001, and Freedman in 1991 and 2002.

Conclusion, or Learning to Live with Aggregate Data

Anselin, in a 2000 review of King's work, put it best: "There is no solution to the ecological inference problem" (p. 589). There are only estimates based on assumptions, but this is also true about regressions on individual-level data. No single procedure can claim to be the solution to the ecological inference problem. In the absence of data about individuals, estimates can be derived about individual relations only by carefully specifying a model, and these assumptions must be guided by theory, experience, and consistency with observable relations.

When social scientists attempt to analyze aggregate data, the best course of action is to parameterize the variables relevant to the grouping process as well as possible. As noted previously, in 1974 Hanushek *et al.* were able to show that the real problem with Robinson's data was an underspecified model, not aggregation. For example, it is particularly important to control for race and income if the data are neighborhood aggregates. If there are contextual effects, these need to be modeled as well, perhaps using multilevel models, as discussed by Brown and Saks in 1980 and Firebaugh in 1978. In 1999, Firebaugh proposed adding additional independent variables that explain and hence control for contextual effects.

It is possible to be misled by ecological correlations or by regressions on aggregate data, but also equally misled by simple correlations or regressions based on individual data, and for some of the same reasons—omitted variables, model misspecification, and false assumptions about the process under study. Robinson's 1950 article generated five decades of productive debate over the ecological fallacy and related topics, such as ecological inference, aggregation bias, and contextual effects. With multivariate analysis, advanced modeling techniques, and an understanding of the aggregation process, researchers can mostly avoid falling victim to the ecological fallacy. Indeed, in certain specific situations, aggregate data may be better than individual data for testing hypotheses, even if those hypotheses are about individual behavior. The "ecological fallacy" has lost some of its sting, and should not cause researchers to abandon aggregate data.

See Also the Following Articles

Aggregation • Omitted Variable Bias • Ordinary Least Squares (OLS) • Units of Analysis

Further Reading

Achen, C. H., and Shively, W. P. (1995). *Cross-Level Inference.* University of Chicago Press, Chicago.

Anselin, L. (2000). The alchemy of statistics, or creating data where no data exist. *Ann. Assoc. Am. Geogr.* **90,** 586–592.

Anselin, L., and Cho, W. K. T. (2002). Spatial effects and ecological inference. *Polit. Anal.* **10,** 276–297.

Brown, B. W., and Saks, D. H. (1980). Economic grouping and data disaggregation. In *New Directions for Methodology of Social and Behavioral Science, Vol. 6, Issues in Aggregation* (K. Roberts and L. Burstein, eds.) Jossey-Bass, San Francisco.

Cho, W. K. T. (2001). Latent groups and cross-level inferences. *Electoral Stud.* **20,** 243–263.

Duncan, O. D., and Davis, B. (1953). An alternative to ecological correlation. *Am. Sociol. Rev.* **18,** 665–666.

Firebaugh, G. (1978). A rule for inferring individual-level relationships from aggregate data. *Am. Sociol. Rev.* **43,** 557–572.

Firebaugh, G. (1980). Groups as contexts and frog ponds. In *New Directions for Methodology of Social and Behavioral Science, Vol. 6, Issues in Aggregation* (K. Roberts and L. Burstein, eds.) Jossey-Bass, San Francisco.

Firebaugh, G. (2001). Ecological fallacy, statistics of. In *International Encyclopedia of the Social and Behavioral Sciences* (N. J. Smelser and P. B. Baltes, eds.), pp. 4023–4026. Elsevier, Oxford.

Freedman, D. A. (2001). Ecological inference. In *International Encyclopedia of the Social and Behavioral Sciences* (N. J. Smelser and P. B. Baltes, eds.), pp. 4027–4030. Elsevier, Oxford.

Freedman, D. A., Klein, S. P., Ostland, M., and Roberts, M. R. (1998). A solution to the ecological inference problem. *J. Am. Statist. Assoc.* **93,** 1518–1522.

Freedman, D. A., Klein, S. P., Sacks, J., Smyth, C. A., and Everett, C. G. (1991). Ecological regression and voting rights. *Eval. Rev.* **15,** 673–711.

Goodman, L. (1953). Ecological regressions and the behavior of individuals. *Am. Sociol. Rev.* **18,** 663–664.

Goodman, L. (1959). Some alternatives to ecological correlation. *Am. J. Sociol.* **64,** 610–625.

Gove, W. R., and Hughes, M. (1980). Reexamining the ecological fallacy: A study in which aggregate data are critical in investigating the pathological effects of living alone. *Social Forces* **58,** 1157–1177.

Grunfeld, Y., and Griliches, Z. (1960). Is aggregation necessarily bad? *Rev. Econ. Statist.* **42,** 1–13.

Hanushek, E., Jackson, J., and Kain, J. (1974). Model specification, use of aggregate data, and the ecological correlation fallacy. *Pol. Methodol.* **1,** 89–107.

Irwin, L., and Lichtman, A. J. (1976). Across the great divide: inferring individual level behavior from aggregate data. *Pol. Methodol.* **3,** 411–439.

King, G. (1997). *A Solution to the Ecological Inference Problem: Reconstructing Individual Behavior from Aggregate Data.* Princeton University Press, New Jersey.

McCue, K. F. (2001). The statistical foundations of the EI method. *Am. Statist.* **55,** 106–110.

Robinson, W. S. (1950). Ecological correlations and the behavior of individuals. *Am. Soc. Rev.* **15**, 351–357.

Selvin, H. C. (1958). Durkheim's suicide and problems of empirical research. *Am. J. Sociol.* **63,** 607–619.

Stoker, T. M. (1993). Empirical approaches to the problem of aggregation over individuals. *J. Econ. Lit.* **XXXI,** 1827–1874.

Theil, H. (1955). *Linear Aggregation of Economic Relations.* North-Holland, Amsterdam.

Economic Anthropology

E. Paul Durrenberger

Pennsylvania State University, University Park, Pennsylvania, USA

Glossary

formalism An approach based on methodological individualism.

institutional economics A theory of economics that holds that people create institutions to minimize the costs of information gathering and transactions.

methodological individualism The assumption that institutional forms emerge from individual decisions.

practice theory The theory that knowledge is a function of everyday activity.

substantivism The assumption that all economic systems are unique and understandable in their own terms.

Economic anthropology is not the importation of economics to exotic locales, but anthropological understandings of all human systems of production, exchange, and consumption. This paper, is a discussion of measurement issues in economic anthropology. I discuss how theoretical approaches shape our understanding of systems; how our understanding of systems forms our view of which variables to operationalize and measure; the relationships among mental and material phenomena; and issues of measurement of both material and mental phenomena.

Introduction

Anthropology is different from other social science and humanities disciplines because it is at the same time holistic, comparative, and ethnographic. Anthropologists think in terms of whole systems rather than part systems. We think as much of the interconnections among economics, politics, religion, demography, ecology, and other systems as we do about the variables that modern scholarship isolates for separate study by different disciplines such as sociology, political science, economics, demography, and biology. Because we seek to generalize our conclusions, we situate our findings within a matrix of findings from many times and places. We attempt to expand our historic coverage, and thus our range of comparison, by the recovery and interpretation of archaeological remains. Where we can observe social life, we are ethnographic—we base our findings on the meticulous observation of everyday life in particular locales. Although ethnography may be theory-driven, theory in anthropology is highly constrained by ethnographic observation and archaeological findings. There are a plethora of issues and problems that center on the measurement and interpretation of archaeological remains that I do not address here.

Issues of measurement arise from anthropology's being holistic, comparative, and ethnographic—but perhaps most directly in ethnography when we describe the workings of concrete economic systems. Because we must strive for reliability and validity, measurement issues are paramount in comparative studies as well. How can we recognize an economic system in a society that is radically different from the ones with which we are familiar? How can we compare different economic systems? What kinds of samples allow cross-cultural generalization? The holistic approach also relies on measurement to the extent that we wish to be able to show relationships among different aspects of cultures—for instance, security of land tenure and the allocation of labor.

Because the assumptions we bring to a problem determine what and how we measure, all questions of measurement start with questions of theory. In economic anthropology, the technical problems of how to measure variables are almost trivial compared to the theoretical problems of what to measure and which units to use in making observations and measurements. On the other hand, the details of measurement are always important because on them rest our assessments of validity and reliability. If we are not measuring what we think we are measuring, the measurement is invalid. If others cannot repeat it, it is not reliable.

In the next section, I briefly discuss some issues of theory in economic anthropology to show how our theoretical assumptions shape our conceptualization of what and how to measure. In the third section, I discuss concepts of systems and how our understanding of systems shapes our view of which variables we operationalize and measure, the topic of the fourth section. Throughout, I contrast economic anthropology with the discipline of economics. Economic anthropology is not simply the transportation of economics to exotic locales. It is, rather, a different way of conceptualizing the phenomena of economics, a different set of theoretical traditions, and, hence, a different set of issues of operationalization and measurement. One of the assumptions of economics is that institutional structures emerge from the aggregate of individual rational decisions. Decisions are mental phenomena, whereas their consequences are often material. One of the questions anthropologists debate, discuss, and study is the relationship between the mental and the material. In the fifth section, I discuss this issue; in the last section, I return to the discussion of some measurement issues entailed in studying decision making as a mental and cultural phenomenon. Here we move from the measurement of material phenomena to the measurement of mental ones, culture.

Theory

Economic theory proceeds from the cautionary assumption that we hold all other things equal and from an orientation toward natural science. Does a feather fall faster or slower than a cannonball? If we abstract away atmosphere and weather and think of them in a vacuum, they fall at the same rate. This is fine for physics, but engineers know there are no vacuums in practice, so, while the insight might be of interest to the formulation of theory, it is of little practical importance. In their aspiration to achieve the same abstract level of theory as physicists, economists define similar uniform, if imaginary, all-things-equal environments. They then proceed to derive the logical implications of the set of assumptions about human nature. Anthropologists build their discipline on the fact that things are never equal.

Neoclassical economists assume that ideal economic individuals know all the alternatives available to them, can assess the results of one decision relative to another, and thus can chose rationally among possibilities. Economic anthropologists dare to challenge this assumption and suggest that human beings not only do not operate in this fashion, they cannot.

In the pristine theoretical world of neoclassical economists, Garrett Hardin can argue that self-interested herders increase their livestock to extract as much from a common resource as possible for their short-term benefit before others, acting according to the same logic, do so and leave them with nothing. The inevitable and tragic result is overgrazing the common pasture until it is useless to everyone. But real people are not so rational. Since Hardin's article, numerous ethnographic examples have shown that such a tragedy is not inevitable. No matter how much theoretical sense Hardin's model may make, it is not an accurate description of the experience of people who depend on resources that are not privately owned.

We might assume that the realm of the economic is defined by decisions that individuals make to allocate their limited resources among competing needs or demands. Marshall Sahlins discusses this assumption as a peculiarly Western cultural construct. This fundamental assumption, this culturally given ideological axiom of economics, is called methodological individualism, the assumption that institutional forms and structures emerge from the aggregate of individual decisions. Decisions are, then, the independent variables and institutions are the dependent variables. In economic anthropology, approaches based on this assumption are called formalist or the formalist approach.

An alternative view is that individual decisions are highly constrained or determined by institutional forms. This rests on the idea that there is a social and institutional order of experience beyond the individual. Social constraints are the independent variables and individual decisions are the dependent variables. These social forms are widely variable and define different economic orders and different rationalities. In anthropology, approaches based on this notion are called substantivist.

A third school of economists, institutionalists, observe that as soon as we introduce one note of reality into the neoclassical economists' system of assumptions, the whole theoretical groundwork shifts. People are in fact not equally well informed. Information is costly; people have to allocate resources to gain information. Making any decision entails costs. The time it takes to make one decision detracts time from other possible decisions. Thus, the cost of making any decision is not making another that we might have made with the same time and effort. A story has it that a wealthy financier quit smoking cigars after he weighed the minute-by-minute gains of his ventures against the time it took to unwrap and light a cigar. At the rate of return on his time, it was not worth his effort to smoke a cigar.

Institutional economics assumes that institutions emerge from individual decisions, but that the decisions are constrained. This view recognizes that people do not have perfect knowledge, that they are deceitful and self-interested, and that incomplete information or disinformation increases uncertainty. Thus, people try to gain more information, but the effort to get information is costly. Even in terms of economic assumptions, it is costly to use markets. People therefore create alternatives that short circuit the process to gain more certainty—these are institutions. These institutions then guide further decisions.

A major response of economic anthropology to such abstract theoretical formulations has been to ignore them in favor of detailed ethnographic accounts of people in locales. This approach so characterizes American anthropology that it is called American particularism or historical particularism. Barrett sums up the features of this approach. There is a limited interest in history, and because this approach assumes that habit and custom, rather than individual decisions, guide social life, it emphasizes values, norms, and emotions. This leads researchers to emphasize interior views rather than external ones. The emphasis on relativism and the associated assumption that cultures are loosely organized and unique imply that little generalization is possible. The emphasis on ethnographic description of individual examples means, as Robin Fox put it in 1991, that fieldwork replaces scholarship and thought.

The substantivist approach assumes that all economic systems are unique and understandable in their own terms. The formalist approach assumes that all people share the mentality that economists attribute to people—that they allocate scarce means among competing ends with perfect knowledge of alternatives and hierarchically ranked objectives. In his 1982 study of domestic production among Oaxacan metate producers and their relationships to a larger capitalist system of which they are part, Scott Cook came to appreciate a number of limitations in economic anthropology that both these approaches share as a consequence of their adherence to the underlying assumption of particularism. He summarizes the limitations as:

1. A tendency to reduce explanations of complex processes involving interrelated and contradictory variables to descriptions of isolated events.
2. A tendency to explain economic process at the empirical level and a failure to develop any conceptual framework to expose underlying social dynamics.
3. A pervasive focus on individual agents.
4. An almost completely circulationist view of the economy.

He finds that economic anthropologists see events as unique and unrelated because they stay close to the empirical; do not analyze systems; and do not understand, appreciate, or develop theories. They are more concerned with the exchange rather than the production of objects. This is in keeping with a long tradition of empiricism in American anthropology.

The decision of what to measure depends on understandings of what the variables are and how they are related. The problem of measurement is more than simply operationalizing measures for variables. Nicola Tannenbaum's 1984 study of anthropologists' use of A. V. Chayanov's concepts in the United States underscores Cook's conclusion.

Chayanov argues that Russian peasants did not employ wage workers and they were not engaged in business; and, without a category of wages, standard economics could not apply. The annual household product less production costs was the end product, and this could not be divided into wages, capital, and rent because there were no such categories in the system. In Chayanov's view, this net product is determined by the interaction of several variables: the size and composition of the working family, the number of workers, the productivity of labor, and how much people worked. The composition of the household is only one variable in the system that contributes to the household's total demand. Household composition changed over time with the developmental cycle from a married couple to a couple with nonworking children to a couple with working children to an older couple with working children and their spouses. Households with more consumers to support worked more land and had larger household incomes than those with fewer consumers. Chayanov considers this to be a major, but not the only, factor that determined economic differentiation among peasant households.

Many have considered family composition or the demographic cycle to be the key element in Chayanov's analysis. Chayanov, in contrast, holds that the key factor in determining household production is the balance between the marginal utility of value produced and the disutility of labor to produce it. The fertility of land, distance to markets, market situations, and availability and costs of labor and technology all contribute to the determination of the productivity of labor and its inverse, the disutility of labor. The marginal utility of value produced is determined by factors such as rates of taxation, rents or other costs of access to means of production, debt, costs of labor and technology, and the ratio of consumers to workers. Nor does he make any assumptions about whether peasants were producing for markets. The value produced could be in rubles or potatoes.

Tannenbaum concludes that misuses of Chayanov's ideas are part of a more general trend of conceptual distortion—the preference for method over theoretical reflection and an empiricist outlook that equates statistical summaries with theory and attempts to develop theories from "data" rather than to understand systems of relationships in theoretical terms and to develop relevant methods of measurement from them.

Issues of measurement depend in large part on our understandings of how to describe systems and how they operate.

Systems

The first problem of measurement is to specify a system. Our assumptions may provide the answer—but, from the global to the household, the definition of the system, its parts, and their relations with one another will determine the variables of interest. These assumptions specify the relationships we can possibly see among events and individuals. This kind of analysis is qualitative, but it specifies the variables and relationships that raise the questions of measurement.

From an ecological perspective, we can say that it is always important to trace energy flows. If the inputs are greater than the outputs, as, for instance, in industrial agriculture, we know immediately that the system is not sustainable. This approach does not tell us why anyone would engage in activity that has no possible future, but our observations show us without a doubt that, for instance, modern states and corporations do engage in such nonsustainable agricultural practices.

From a purely economic perspective, if we look at only market transactions, we ignore the institutional systems that support the market. For instance, people may sell their labor on markets, but a commodity approach cannot ask or answer questions about the source of the labor. The people are created somehow. Furthermore, markets require vast legal and institutional structures to support them. They are not natural. They are costly to maintain, and someone must bear the costs. Seeing economic systems in this way is a consequence of anthropology's insistence on holism—seeing the relationships among demography, markets, law, and households.

As Marshall Sahlins points out, if we only ask questions about production, we ignore the uses to which people put the things they obtain, their reasons for valuing them. So cultural questions have material consequences even if we argue that material relations determine cultural awareness.

Eric Wolf argues that anthropology, like the other social sciences, straddles the reality of the natural world and the reality of people's organized knowledge about that world. This is the distinction between the exterior view of what is and the interior views of different people at different places and times—what they think or know about external realities. Some analysts treat the problem that this poses by disregarding the impasse between the interior and the exterior realms. Others discount the mental and consider behavior in the material world as primary. Still others focus on the mental schema that people define for themselves and consider behaviors in the material world as epiphenomenona or irrelevant. And still others assign equal importance to both spheres, but do not discuss how to reconcile them. Wolf argues that the key to the resolution is in focusing on the intersection of material and mental events by paying close attention to the exterior relations of power that mobilize labor and the internal patterns of thought that define who does what. This challenges us to show how tasks and mental constructs are distributed among genders, age categories, and classes. Such questions call for the measurement of mental artifacts (an issue to which I return later). Wolf asks how knowledge is built and used to accumulate power and how some forms of knowledge come to dominate others. This is the program he carried out in his 1999 book, *Envisioning Power*.

Wolf defines the units of observation as modes of production or different means by which people have organized production with their concomitant institutions, social relations, tools, and forms of knowledge. The units of observation are as important as the systems we define and are equally dependent on the questions we ask. If our units are villages, firms, modes of production, or nations, we cannot compare households. If we focus on households or villages, we may lose sight of modes of production, nations, and global relations.

Gwako, for example, summarizes research that finds no relationship between the security of land tenure and the productivity of agriculture. In this 2002 work, households are the units of analysis. In Africa, men may own land and be heads of households, but it is women, not men, who do most of the agricultural work. Gwako finds that if we look at security of property rights per cultivated plot rather than per household, it does predict the level of agricultural output. Women put more into those plots whose product they control. Using households as units obscures this relationship between security of property rights and allocation of effort.

Diane Wolf challenges the validity of households as units of decision making, as well as the concept of strategic decision making itself. Her 1992 qualitative work among rural Indonesian households whose daughters work in factories shows that in the context of factory jobs, people in poor households make decisions experimentally and *ad hoc*. They do not have strategies; they do not enjoy the luxury of being able to plan into the future. There may be household coping mechanisms or household practices, but no strategies or planning.

Her meticulous quantitative data on landholdings and household budgets allow her to conclude that there is a relationship between the resources available to households and the likelihood that their daughters will work in factories. However, she also shows that although households of factory workers are poor in land, women from the poorest families that have a high number and ratio of dependents do not work in factories because their presence is needed for the daily work of maintaining the household or taking care of their own children. She insists that, rather than assuming that households have strategies and rather than assuming a relationship between resources and availability for wage labor, we must describe the details of household budgets and individual decisions. These fine-grained observations allow for wider conclusions that are devastating to the theoretical assumptions that inform the concept of household strategies.

Diane Wolf's quantitative data do support the expectations of household models about access to resources and factory work, but the qualitative data do not support the inferences of the models about reasons. The Chayanovian, Marxist, and neoclassical models do not indicate process. In isolating and measuring variables such as access to resources and household cycle, Diane Wolf was able to ask questions about the relationships among the inferences of various models and the processes she could observe ethnographically.

In contrast, Mary Beth Mills argues in her 1999 study that cultural and ideological factors bring rural Thai women to work in factories. But the lack of any quantitative data on household budgets or access to resources makes the assessment of her conclusions impossible. Diane Wolf empirically assesses the implications of various theoretical models, whereas Mills simply asserts relationships without any data. This contrast suggests the importance of measurement for ethnographic description and the importance of ethnographic description for testing assumptions.

If we assume that all economic activity is market directed and profit oriented, then we measure only those transactions that leave some historical trace in the records of transactions. For instance, we could measure money paid in wages, rent, and capital to determine the profitability of various enterprises. But if we use this concept of economic activity, we must confine our empirical enquiries to one sector of capitalist economies. With this definition of the economic, we will not see unremunerated activity or production or any activity that is off the books in the informal sector. Work in households to raise children, produce food, and process or sell food or other commodities is invisible. Any segment of any economy that does not work according to the principles of firms is also invisible. Thus, the range of our empirical enquiries becomes either very distorted or very limited.

One response to such limitations is to assume that all economic activity follows the logic of firms. But such an assumption is not ethnographically or historically supportable. It introduces even further distortions into the characterization of economies.

If we single out one economic phenomenon for attention, we may lose sight of the system of which it is a part. If we trace only money, we are likely to overlook other important kinds of value such as unremunerated work. If we look only at production, we may ignore the circulation of goods and the reasons for their production. If we look only at exchange, we may ignore the organization of production.

The technical problems of measurement vary from place to place and from one problem to another. This is as it should be because if we only work from a single perspective we will not be able to admit the considerable detail that empirical observation demands and on which anthropology rests. On the other hand, the cost of such eclecticism, as Cook points out, is that there is little in economic anthropology that is cumulative. Studies do not build on one another. The dialectical and critical relationship between theoretical and empirical work is underdeveloped.

Variables

Each set of assumptions suggests different units of analysis and different variables to measure. The first technical methodological question is how to operationalize each variable so that we can recognize it. The second related methodological question is how to measure each variable. These decisions and categories do not depend on or necessarily reflect locally relevant systems of thought.

If we assume that economic activity is that which produces, exchanges, or uses something, we measure the amounts of time and goods as people produce, exchange, and use them. This opens all realms of activity to our analysis. The invisible labor of households and the informal economy can become the subjects of inquiry, and we can develop less distorted and more realistic descriptions of economic systems.

One method of measuring the allocation of labor is time allocation studies. The objective of the method is to record what a sample of people are doing at a sample of places and moments of time. From this information on the number of times people do specific activities, we can infer the amount of time they spend doing different things. Bernard discusses the problems and potentials of this method. One problem is that observers affect the behavior of the people they are observing; it is difficult to control for this reaction effect of people being observed. The method assumes answers to the questions of whom to observe, how frequently to observe them, how long to observe them, when to observe them, and where to observe them. A truly random sampling strategy would have to consider each dimension, except perhaps duration. A less than truly random sampling strategy introduces questions of bias that can never be answered after the fact. Another problem is the validity of the categories of observation. How do observers categorize the actions to count them? What counts as an instance of a given category of activity? Such studies can produce valuable data if they are integrated with participant observer accounts, but without due consideration to the problem of classifying activities and sampling, they may be exercises in spurious precision.

In 1972 Marshall Sahlins based his notion of the original affluent society—the idea that people adjust their needs to their resources and do not work incessantly to supply insatiable demands—on such data from hunting and foraging peoples. The Dobe of the Kalahari Desert in South Africa work an average of 2 hours and 9 minutes each day to support themselves and their dependents, an observation that led Sahlins to challenge the assumption that hunters and foragers spend most of their time working to feed themselves.

Sol Tax suspects, based on his observations in 1936, that the Guatemalan Indians of Panajachel worked "more than is typical either of primitive tribesmen or of urbanites." He classifies activities as community service (time for church and state including "military service, sporadic assistance on public works . . . and service in the formal political-religious organization"), personal and social (including personal hygiene, sickness—when people call shamans—nursing infants, birthing children, baptisms, marriages, funerals), and economic activities (including time devoted to different crops and animals as well as hunting and fishing, household tasks, weaving, sewing, providing firewood, and marketing). On the basis of his observations, he prepared a time budget for all men, women, and children of the village. Given the computational apparatus at his disposal in 1953 when he made this analysis, this was a major statistical accomplishment.

The units of analysis are significant. Because he aggregates the figures for the village, it is not possible to check for variation among households. This effectively removes households as units. Tax does preserve distinctions between women's work and men's work and between ethnic groups, so it is possible to draw conclusions on the basis of gender and ethnicity. Here, household work is very visible, but not on a per household basis.

These approaches assume that people move from one meaningful category of activity to another. One challenge is to understand the categories (e.g., sickness characterized by calling a shaman), and another is to adequately measure the allocation of time to each activity. Time allocation studies have the problems of sampling and observer effect, but Tax's approach fills in the gaps with observation, measurement, and assumption. He observes and measures the time that specific individuals spent doing specific tasks and then generalizes on the basis of age, gender, and ethnicity to estimate a time budget for the entire community. This approach may be less technically sophisticated than time allocation studies, but, given the problems with them, it is probably just as adequate a representation of realities.

When Tannenbaum and I became interested in similar questions of household labor and resource allocation among Shan in northwestern Thailand, we developed a third method of measuring time use. Like Tax, we relied heavily on participant observation for the definitions of locally relevant categories of effort, expenditure, and return. We measured effort and expenditures by visiting interviewing members of every household once each week to determine their weekly expenditures and work. We cross-checked these reports against other reports and against our own observations.

Researchers interested in markets and economic transactions have shown how they cover great areas via periodic markets, traveling merchants, and relationships of credit. Skinner shows in studies published in 1964 and 1977 that the Chinese villages clustered within 3 miles of a market town formed a meaningful unit of kinship, marriage, and culture. These units themselves clustered around larger ones related through the literate elite. This example provides an apt illustration of central place theory.

Von Thunen explains the intensity of agricultural production in terms of central place theory as a function of distance to market centers. Boserup explains it in terms of demographic pressure as a function of population density. Carol Smith tests both of these approaches in western Guatemala, where there is considerable variability in production intensity, population density, and distance from market centers. Peasants may produce most of their subsistence goods, produce some specialized goods for the market, and buy goods on the market or specialize in nonagricultural occupations such as handicraft production or long-distance trading. Because Carol Smith does not have data on the allocation of effort or time for these alternatives, she ranks them from lowest to highest based on observations that she and other anthropologists have made. To measure the importance and size of the 250 local marketplaces, she developed an index based on the number of different kinds of goods each market offered and the number of sellers. Using census data, she estimates the sizes of peasant holdings and population densities.

Her empirical work suggests that Von Thunen's central place theory and Boserup's demographic approaches are compatible and that each is incomplete. Although they are reasonable when all things are equal, all things are never equal. Boserup assumes that farmers will consume their own production and Von Thunen assumes that farmers have only a single market center. Both assumptions are wrong. Following Skinner, Smith discusses central place theory in her analyses of regional economic and political structures that global forces influence. She differentiates different market functions and sizes in her meticulous empirical study of the types and locations of Guatemalan rural markets to show the dynamic relations in the regional systems that enmesh villages. Others have expanded these concepts of regional and central place analysis to different geographic areas.

In her 1994 study of the California strawberry industry, Miriam Wells develops quantitative data on many variables from many sources, including government documents, observation, and interviews. This allows a meticulous comparison of areas within the state and illustrates the historical forces at work so she can assess the causal factors at work, for instance, in the re-emergence of share-cropping arrangements after they had all but disappeared. She finds that different factors affected different regions in different ways, something that a theoretical approach, neoclassical or Marxist, could never have shown because it would have assumed a uniformity that was unrealistic.

In his 1965 assessment of the civil-religious hierarchy the Mayan community of Zinacantan, Frank Cancian meticulously measures the wealth and prestige of individuals to understand how they are related to participation in the system over time.

These examples, and others like them, show that how the anthropologist defines the system indicates the variables to measure and that this sets the problems of operationalization and measurement that the anthropologist must then solve. The solutions are different for different units of analysis—from agricultural plot to household to village to market area to nation to global system; from production to consumption to exchange; and from questions of marketing to questions of prestige.

Mental vs. Material Variables

Is there any empirical way to investigate the relationship between the material and the mental or must it forever remain in the realm of speculative philosophy or assumption? Parallel to the distinction that Eric Wolf draws between the mental and the material is Malinowski's 1922 differentiation between the internal views of the people he was trying to understand, which he called "ethnographic," and his own external constructions, which he called "sociological." Marvin Harris's 1999 distinction between the emic and the etic captures another difference, which Alan Sandstrom and Pamela Sandstrom discuss at some length—the people we are trying to understand build emic statements from discriminations *they* make.

If Sahlins is correct that what people think affects their economic action and if Wolf is correct that relations of power affect people's patterns of thought, then our study of economics necessitates the measurement of cultural artifacts—patterns of thought as well as patterns of action. If we attempt to put active people into the equation, individuals making decisions, we must consider the question of agency. Again, we can either assume rationality or we can investigate it empirically. Our concern for understanding agency shifts our attention to the relationships between thought and action and our concern for culture focuses our attention on the relationship of thought to structures such as class. Posing the question "culture is related to what, how?" Roy D'Andrade agrees with Clifford Geertz's critique of symbolic analysis:

> *The danger that cultural analysis, in search of all-too-deep-lying turtles, will lose touch with the hard surfaces of life—with the political, economic, stratificatory realities within which men* [sic] *are everywhere contained . . . is an ever present one. The only defense against it . . . is to train such analysis on such realities . . . in the first place.*

D'Andrade continues, commenting that the solution is not to add to the stack of turtles with further analyses of cultural meanings, social exigencies, and cognitive capacities but to understand the relationships among social and economic systems, cultural forms, and action, a program congenial to Eric Wolf's 1999 work, which explores the connection between ideas and power to describe the ways cultural configurations articulate with the power that arranges the settings and domains of social and economic life, especially the allocation and use of labor. Casting his eyes back some hundreds of years to understand varied social formations, Eric Wolf analyzes the ways relations that organize economic and political interactions shape patterns of thought that make the world intelligible to the people that we are trying to understand. In cultures as diverse as Kwakuitl, Nazi Germany, and Aztec, he answers D'Andrade's question by describing the workings of class and power, analyzing the relations among power, ideology, stratification, and the allocation of labor to show the role of power in defining the cultures that determine how people understand their situations and lives.

Ulf Hannerz reviews the literature on these topics and recognizes that people's views of things depend on the positions from which they see them. People construct meanings in their location in social structures from the flow of available experiences and intentions. "Through the interaction of perspectives, culture is produced. How many people have to be involved in order for us to see culture as a collective phenomenon? As few as two, or as many as millions." Concrete personal experiences are the basis for generalized understandings and generalized understandings are frameworks for interpreting experiences. Shared meanings are tied to the specific shared experiences of people in settings. Because Christoph Brumann has reviewed the literature and arguments about culture, there is no need to repeat this here. The question is how to operationalize these insights and incorporate them into the practice of ethnography.

Decision Making

In 1956, Ward Goodenough argued that if anthropologists impose outside categories such as Malinowski's "sociological" or Harris's "etic" on a culture they cannot understand how people make the important decisions that guide their lives. He was discussing residence rules that specify where newlywed couples live after they get married. The categories were some of the most precisely defined in anthropology, yet Goodenough found that they did not guarantee reliable interpretations of data. Another anthropologist had collected census data that were similar to Goodenough's, but had arrived at different conclusions about postmarital residence. Goodenough argued that the problem was that neither anthropologist had understood how people actually decided where to live after they married. He proceeded to outline the factors that were relevant to the people and how they balanced them in making residence decisions. His more general conclusion is that accurate ethnography depends on describing how people think about and decide things—the internal, "ethnographic" or "emic" view—rather than on imposed exogenous categories.

This paper informed ensuing work in cognitive anthropology, much of it collected in Steven Tyler's 1969 book, *Cognitive Anthropology*. When Roger Keesing returned to the issue of how to understand how people make allocative decisions, he distinguished between statistical models that describe the observed frequencies of possible outcomes and decision models that specify how people decide on allocations in terms of their own categories and judgments of salience and importance.

In 1987, Christina Gladwin and Robert Zabawa agreed with anthropologists' rejections of neoclassical economists' explanations of increasing farm sizes and decreasing number of farmers in the United States. This critique rejects the idea that such social phenomena were the net result of the decisions of rational self-seeking individuals and argues in favor of a more institutional, sociological, structural, or materialist view that emphasizes social relations, class structures, patterns of ownership, and conflict among sectors, regions, and countries. Like Keesing, they argue that these structures do not themselves account for changes but that changes in international markets, technology, monetary policies, and inflation shape farmers' decisions. They argue that people change structures by their decisions. This is consistent with Gladwin's other work.

More recently, Joseph Henrich argues that although we can understand phenomena in terms of individual decision making, people do not in fact base their decisions on the weighing of costs and benefits. It is incorrect to assume, he argues, that people use their reasoning abilities to develop strategies to attain goals. In fact, people have to operate in terms of limited information, cognitive capacities, multiple goals, and constraining social structures. He argues that the way people learn creates changes in the frequencies of ideas, beliefs, values, and behaviors without cost-benefit decisions. Thus do cultures change.

The notion that thought determines action is widespread. From advertising to education, there are modern institutional structures dedicated to the proposition that the way to change people's actions is to change their minds. When Jean Lave, attempting to understand how people learn and use that most cerebral of cognitive skills—mathematics—challenged transference theory, the notion that we can isolate abstract properties of systems and communicate them to others via symbols, she advocated expanding our understanding of cognition from something that happens in the mind to a process that stretches through the environment as well as through time into past experiences and future expectations. In doing so, she offers a new definition to a movement that Sherry Ortner detected in the attempts to synthesize and sort out anthropological theorizing since the 1960s, a trend that she tentatively calls practice theory.

Some who call themselves cognitive anthropologists describe well-structured patterns of thought that they understood by talking to people. In a precursor of the now-fashionable linguistic turn, some even argued that because cultures were things of the mind embodied in language anthropologists had only to talk to people to understand their cultures.

Other cognitive anthropologists question the salience of such language-centered patterns. Van Esterik shows that there are no static taxonomies of spirit-ghosts in Thailand and concludes that, "the process of creating guardian spirits is continuous . . . . " Durrenberger and Morrison expand on this finding. Challenging language-centered analyses, Gatewood discusses the complex patterns of cultures that are not encoded linguistically, not available for labeling, and not accessible to language or language-centered investigative techniques. People learn some things not by hearing about them but by doing them; actions speak louder than words. A decade later Gísli Pálsson (1994), reflecting on similarly nautical experiences, reaches a similar conclusion.

Few today would argue that any structures—cognitive, political, or economic—endure. We have seen too much change in patterns of economic, political, and cultural relations for the premise of systems in equilibrium, even dynamic equilibrium, to be persuasive. The riddle repeats an earlier one: What are the directions of causality? From thought to action, as structuralists and cognitivists would have it? Or from structures of power and other relationships to thought, as materialists would have it?

One solution to this riddle is the extreme postmodernist one, which argues that structures of meaning are not anchored in the outside world. Another solution might be extreme holism—to affirm that everything affects everything else and that we cannot sort it all out because it is too complex. At best, this view suggests, we can provide an appreciation for the complexity by some attempt to recapitulate it in another mode. In the postmodern view, the explication of reality needs no mediation, only experience (not reflection, analysis, or depiction). This is counter to the principles of both art and science, which highlight some dimensions and underplay others to organize and filter reality rather than replicate it. Although it may be true that everything is related, we do not see hurricane forecasters watching butterflies to detect how the beat of their individual wings will impact El Nino.

Here I return to a practical issue and to the work of Jean Lave. If patterns of thought are situational, determined by changing social structures, then it is not effective to try to change social patterns by changing minds. The prevalent model of education in the United States seems to be the transference of abstractions from teachers to students. Alternatives to this involve learners in practice and more or less resemble apprenticeship programs. Lave challenges the currently popular view of education as transference of knowledge that centers on the idea that scientific research abstracts the principles underlying phenomena, teachers transfer these principles to students in classrooms, and students then apply them in their work and lives. The idea of transference is that people learn by assimilating abstractions that are transferred to them in classrooms. This is the logic of safety courses that have no relationship to accident rates and the classroom education of fishermen that has no relationship to their subsequent success. Lave centers her account on computation, mathematics in practice, to show that the principles that teachers teach are not the ones that people use—that the knowledge of mathematics that teachers transfer in classrooms is not used or useful beyond classrooms.

She goes on to argue that schooling has become a means of legitimizing hierarchy in terms of, to use Katherine Newman's phrase, meritocratic individualism, the ideology of ranking individuals according to their merit and attributing their success, failure, prestige, status, income, and other characteristics to some measure of individual merit or achievement. Schooling is a way of establishing an individual's merit for such rankings. Thus, it becomes its own end, its own objective, and loses references to the outside world of practice. In the process, schooling becomes the measure of merit and becomes rationalized as the means of transferring knowledge so that schooling or education becomes identified with knowledge. Thus, when people want to change someone's behavior, it seems obvious that education is the answer.

Lave and Wenger argue that people do not learn by transference in classrooms but by practice, by moving from peripheral participation to more and more central and expert roles in what they call a community of practice, people who recognize and validate a certain kind of practice. They suggest that the transference of abstractions does not change people's minds or behavior, but that changing the nature of people's everyday lives to involve them continuously and progressively in communities of practice does effect such changes.

Analyses of this kind indicate the problem of measuring mental constructs. How can we know what ideas people use, how they define them, and to what extent they share them? Moore, Romney, and colleagues developed a means to explore, characterize, and quantify similarities and differences in shared patterns of thought. They illustrate their method by examining terms for emotion in Chinese, English, and Japanese. Culture, they argue, resides in the minds of people as pictures that are cognitive representations of semantic domains (organized sets of words at the same level of contrast that refer to single conceptual spheres). Using judgments of similarity, they use scaling and visualization procedures to make precise comparisons among what is in the minds of different individuals, and they measure the extent to which these pictures correspond or differ.

One important dimension of culture is the shared aspects of mental pictures people create of related sets of words. People's judgments of similarities among an organized set of words or a semantic domain is an ethnographic means to construct individual mental pictures and measure their similarities to others'. As Romney and Moore put it, "the meaning of each term is defined by its location relative to all the other terms." This requires some way to measure people's ideas of similarity among the items of an organized set of words. A triads test does this by asking informants to indicate which of three items is least like the other two for all possible combinations of three items in the set of words. In selecting one item as least similar, informants indicate that the remaining two are somehow similar.

Thus, I was able to assess awareness of union membership using a test that asked respondents to select which was most different in each combination of "steward," "union representative," "manager," "supervisor," and "co-worker." Consider the triad: supervisor, co-worker, union representative. If a person selected "supervisor" as the most different, indicating similarity between workers and union reps, it would imply a union model; they would be distinguishing in terms of union vs. non-union affiliation. The choice of "co-worker" would indicate a conceptual scheme based on hierarchy because co-workers are less powerful than supervisors and union reps. Picking "union representative" would indicate a workplace proximity scheme because this is the feature that supervisors and co-workers share.

Ethnographic observation and interviews might indicate other criteria of classification such as gender (if all co-workers are women and all supervisors are men), race or ethnicity, or age.

Empirical work in this vein indicates that among the American working class, at least, everyday realities are more powerful in determining patterns of thought than patterns of thought are in determining the everyday realities. Thus, working-class cultural constructs do not always agree with those of others in different structural positions. If their consciousness can be said to be false, it is at least realistic—it reflects the realities of power at their workplaces. If their consciousness is false, it may not be so much because of the hegemony of another class over the cultural apparatus, their ability to shape ideas that form culture, but their power to shape the daily lives of workers in their workplaces, realities that become encoded as patterns of thought.

If patterns of thought reflect realities as Moore, Romney, A. K. Hsia, and G. D. Rusch suggest, then it behooves us to understand the realities that shape cultures, to understand in some detail what determines culture and how. Among the most powerful determinants of social and economic realities are class practices. By understanding the relationships among class practices and patterns of thought we can keep in touch with the hard surfaces of life that Geertz rightly predicted we would ignore when we turned to the analysis of ever-deepening piles of cultural turtles.

Conclusion

The theories that we use define the systems that we observe. The systems that we observe define the variables that we can measure. Some variables are material; some are mental. We operationalize these variables and measure them in order to compare our theoretical understandings with the empirical realities we can observe. We use the insights we gain from such work to refine our theoretical understandings, our understandings of systems, and our measurements. By measuring and using a scientific approach, we can break out of the endless rounds of other-things-equal speculation and develop reliable and valid understandings of the variety of economic systems that characterize humanity today and through history.

See Also the Following Articles

Behavioral Economics: The Carnegie School • Behavioral Psychology • Cognitive Psychology • Household Behavior and Family Economics • Social Economics

Further Reading

Acheson, J. M. (2002). Transaction cost economics. In *Theory In Economic Anthropology* (Jean Ensminger, ed.), pp. 27–58. Altamira, Walnut Creek, CA.

Bernard, H. R. (1988). *Research Methods in Cultural Anthropology*. Sage, Newbury Park, CA.

Cancian, F. (1965). *Economics and Prestige in a Maya Community*. Stanford University Press, Stanford, CA.

Cook, S. (1982). *Zapotec Stone Workers*. University Press of America, Washington, D.C.

Durrenberger, E. P. (2000). Explorations of class and consciousness in the U.S. *J. Anthropol. Res.* **57,** 41–60.

Durrenberger, E. P. (2001). Structure, thought, and action. *Am. Anthropol.* **104,** 93–105.

Durrenberger, E. P., and Erem, S. (2000). The weak suffer what they must. *Am. Anthropol.* **101,** 783–793.

Durrenberger, E. P., and King, T. D. (eds.) (2000). *State and Community in Fisheries Management*. Bergin and Garvey, Westport, CT.

Durrenberger, E. P., and Tannenbaum, N. (1990). *Analytical Perspectives on Shan Agriculture and Village Economics*. Yale University Southeast Asia Studies, New Haven, CT.

Hannerz, U. (1992). *Cultural Complexity*. Columbia University Press, New York.

Lave, J. (1988). *Cognition in Practice*. Cambridge University Press, New York.

Malinowski, B. (1922). *Argonauts of the Western Pacific*. Waveland, Prospect Heights, IL.

McCay, B. M., and Acheson, J. M. (eds.) (1987). *The Question of the Commons*. University of Arizona Press, Tucson, AZ.

Moore, C., Romney, A. K., Hsia, T.-L., and Rusch, G. D. (1999). Universality of the semantic structure of emotion terms. *Am. Anthropol.* **101,** 529–546.

Romney, A. K., Weller, S. C., and Batchelder, W. H. (1986). Culture as consensus. *Am. Anthropol.* **88,** 313–338.

Wells, M. J. (1994). *Strawberry Fields*. Cornell University Press, Ithaca, NY.

Wolf, D. L. (1990). *Factory Daughters*. University of California Press, Berkeley, CA.

Wolf, E. R. (1997). *Europe and the People without History*. University of California Press, Berkeley, CA.

Wolf, E. R. (1999). *Envisioning Power*. University of California Press, Berkeley, CA.

Economic Development, Technological Change, and Growth

Paul Auerbach
Kingston University, Surrey, United Kingdom

Glossary

economic growth The growth rate in national income.

economic income The maximum amount that an individual, firm, or nation can consume without causing a deterioration in the value of that individual, firm, or nation's capital stock or assets.

human capital Human beings viewed as productive assets. Education enhances the value of human capital.

Human Development Index (HDI) An index of development aggregating measures of income per capita, life expectancy, and education.

national income Commonly measured as Gross Domestic Product: the value of output produced within a nation in a given year.

Paretian criterion Economic growth takes place in a society only when at least one member of the society is made better off (by his or her own reckoning) and none made worse off.

Economic development connotes the complex process of structural and institutional changes by which poor countries attain the standard of well-being associated with the rich nations of the world. It has been described by the Nobel laureate Armatya Sen "...as a process of expanding the real freedoms people enjoy." The measurement of economic development will begin with economic growth (the growth rate in national income) as a basis and then proceed with a series of modifications. Technological change, improvements in human capital, and the quality of state governance are key determinants of economic development. The Human Development Index is the most prominent example of an attempt at a unitary measure of economic development.

Introduction

Why Economic Development and Growth are Important

For the greater part of its history, humankind has lived in poverty. The long tenure of even the greatest civilizations of the past—the Egyptians, the Romans—evidenced, by contemporary standards, little change in the material existence of the vast majority of the population. By contrast, the exceptional nature of the experience of the past few hundred years in the richer, more privileged parts of the world may be illustrated with the numerical example given in Table I. It is presumed that, at the beginning of the period, the population has a material claim on resources at a low level of subsistence. This claim on resources will be set as equivalent to $50 per year per capita.

One may note the following results from this simple hypothetical calculation. First, it is clear that the long-lived civilizations mentioned above never approached monotonic increases in per capita expenditure of even 1% per year, since even this level of growth would, after a few hundred years, have resulted in material standards for their populations unknown in the ancient world. Second, seemingly small differences between societies in per capita growth rates that are sustained over periods of more than 100 years can evidently cause dramatic changes in their relative fortunes. One may conclude that the past few hundred years mark a new period in the material

Table I Per Capita Annual Expenditure of $50 and Its Increase over Time for Annual Rates of Growth of 1%, 1.25%, 1.3%, and 1.5%

	1%	*1.25%*	*1.3%*	*1.5%*
After 10 years	$55	$56	$56	$57
After 50 years	$81	$92	$94	$104
After 100 years	$134	$171	$180	$218
After 150 years	$220	$318	$343	$460
After 200 years	$362	$592	$654	$968
After 250 years	$596	$1102	$1247	$2037
After 300 years	$980	$2052	$2378	$4289
After 350 years	$1611	$3818	$4536	$9029
After 400 years	$2650	$7105	$8652	$19,007
After 450 years	$4358	$13,223	$16,505	$40,016
After 500 years	$7167	$24,609	$31,484	$82,241

Table II National Income Accounts

Expenditure	*Income*
Consumption	Wages
Investment	Profits
Government expenditure	Interest
Exports minus imports	Rent

history of humankind—one characterized by economic growth and development.

Linking Development and Growth

A common starting point in trying to measure economic development is to consider the rate of economic growth. In pure economic theory, economic growth takes place in a society only when at least one member of the society is made better off (by his or her own reckoning) and none made worse off (the Paretian criterion). But for many reasons, including the impracticality of the latter approach, economic growth is usually straightforwardly measured as the growth rate in national income, a statistic that is readily available, in principle, for practically every nation in the world. Starting with this statistic, one can then modify it to approach a notion of economic development, first by satisfying some of the strictures of the Paretian criterion and then by developing a suitable notion of "economic income."

Economic Growth and Economic Development

Economic Growth as Change in National Income

The term "economic growth" is not a natural or biological process, but one that measures the rate of change of a particular accounting measure, i.e., national income. The accounting system for national income is linked to a double-entry bookkeeping identity of the form expenditure = income. The most common measure is Gross Domestic Product (GDP), the value of output produced within a nation in a given year. (Alternative measures of national income, such as Net Domestic Product, in which a deduction is made for depreciation on the capital stock, are unlikely to effect important changes in the economic growth measure.) Total expenditure is divided between consumption of goods and services, gross capital formation (business investment), government expenditure, and net exports. The income side of the ledger indicates how this expenditure is disbursed as wages, profits, interest, or rent (see Table II).

When measured in per capita terms, the rate of change of this economic statistic has an obvious intuitive appeal as an indication of the improvement or the deterioration in the overall well-being of the population.

Economic Growth: Paretian Critiques

There are several well-recognized problems associated with this measure of the change in the population's well-being, many of which are linked to violations of the Paretian criterion specified above:

Inflation

Rises in national income that are merely due to price rises may not signal real improvements in the population's well-being. National income in any given year can be adjusted by a deflater constructed from a "basket" of representative goods so that changes in *real* income may be calculated. Controversy has surrounded these adjustments, with the claim being made that improvements in the quality of goods produced have led to an overestimation of inflation and therefore an understatement of the rises in real income.

Nonmarketed versus Marketed Goods

A typical by-product of economic growth, most especially in traditional societies, is the rise in the share of goods and services devoted to market exchange. To the extent that these marketed goods merely replace others, for instance, those produced in the home (and therefore not counted as part of national income), rises in measures national income may overstate economic growth.

Income Distribution

The gap between high and low incomes often widens in the growth accompanying the transition from a traditional to a market economy (as in the early stages of the Industrial Revolution in Great Britain). Furthermore, wide gaps between rich and poor can distort investment priorities (e.g., a priority in pharmaceutical research may be given to the "diseases of the rich").

Changes in the Work–Leisure Ratio

Rises in national income merely due to increases in the amount or intensity of work being performed by the population should not enter into a "true" measure of economic growth.

Problems of Market Failure

Rises in consumption in the national income accounts will indicate the increasing benefits to the population of the goods purchased. But if such goods (e.g., automobiles) manifest negative externalities in consumption (commuting times to work do not decrease due to enhanced congestion on the roads), any increase in the well-being of the nation may be overstated. In contrast, the increased provision of nonexclusionary public goods, such as public parks, may yield true increases in national income not captured in the national accounts.

Outputs Measured as Inputs

The price paid for most goods and services is usually taken to be an accurate reflection of the benefits that they yield. Thus, if, for instance, expenditures on medical care and education rise, measured national income will increase. This statistical increase will take place even in the absence of improvements in the health and the educational standard of the population if the efficiency in these sectors has declined due, for instance, to increasing levels of corruption.

Economic Growth and the True Nature of Income

National Income versus Economic Income

Increases in national income should accurately register the augmentation in a nation's capacity to fulfill various tasks, its "economic power." In formal economic theory, the closest approach to a measure of overall economic power is economic income, defined as the maximum amount that an individual, firm, or nation can consume without causing a deterioration in the value of that individual, firm, or nation's capital stock or assets. Thus, for a firm, its economic income or profit, properly calculated, will provide a "snapshot" of its economic health in a sustainable, nontransitory way. By contrast, national income, as conventionally calculated, is not a measure of a nation's economic income and therefore does not give a proper indication of its overall economic power.

To clarify the concept of economic income, the case of a firm is used, since, unlike both individuals and nations, firms make some attempt to measure the value of their capital. This case exists in a simple world, with no inflation and zero interest rates. The firm's annual revenue, net of wages and materials—its cash flow—is $150,000 per year if it runs its fixed capital for 8 h per day and $225,000, or 50% more, if it runs the fixed capital for 12 h per day. The purchase price of the capital good is $1.2 million. This machine will last for 10 years if it is run for 8 h per day and this is considered to be "normal practice" for this particular capital good. If, however, the capital good were to be run for 12 h per day, it would last for only 5 years.

One can thus compare the net revenues of the two regimes, as shown in Tables III and IV.

Clearly, running the capital good for 12 h per day is advantageous from the point of view of net revenue compared with the 8 h per day regime.

Now economic income or profit is calculated. To make this calculation, one must account for the deterioration in the capital stock under each regime. For the 8 h per day regime, one calculates the deterioration of the capital stock on the basis of its normal life of 10 years. Thus, for the capital good costing $1.2 million, one would deduct, using so-called straight-line depreciation, $120,000 per year (one-tenth of the value of the capital good) from net revenues each year. This will yield an economic income or profit of $30,000 each year. And this number is indeed a true calculation of the economic income, if one goes back to the given definition: $30,000 can be

Table III Net Revenue of the Firm (8 h day)

	Year 1	*Year 2*	. . .	*Year 5*	*Year 6*	. . .	*Year 10*
Net revenue (thousands of dollars)	$150	$150		$150	$150		$150

Table IV Net Revenue of the Firm (12 h day)

	Year 1	*Year 2*	. . .	*Year 5*	*Year 6*	. . .	*Year 10*
Net revenue (thousands of dollars)	$225	$225		$225	?		?

consumed each year and not cause a deterioration in the capital stock, since at the same time $120,000 will be put away every year for 10 years and this restriction in consumption will pay for the new capital good, priced at $1.2 million, at the beginning of year 11 (see Table V).

By contrast, one can calculate this firm's economic income if the capital were to be run for 12 h per day. First, one assumes that the firm mechanically calculates its economic income under the delusion that the capital good will last 10 years, when indeed it will last for only 5 years. The firm will find itself living in a fool's paradise. For the first 5 years, the 12 h per day regime seems to outperform the 8 h per day regime, with an apparent economic income of $105,000 per year, as opposed to $30,000 for the 8 h per day regime. But then, at the beginning of year 6, a new machine must be purchased for $1.2 million and the depreciation fund has accumulated only one-half of that sum, that is to say, $600,000 ($120,000 per year times 5 years) (see Table VI).

There is a shortfall of $600,000 at the beginning of year 6. Clearly, this mechanical or inappropriate calculation of the depreciation of the capital stock can lead to disastrous estimates of the true level of economic income.

If, in this simple case, the depreciation had been calculated in a realistic fashion, then economic income calculations would have served much better as an indication of the true economic health of the firm. For the 8 h per day regime, the calculations are already satisfactory, yielding a true economic income of $30,000 per year. For the 12 h per day regime, in order to calculate the depreciation of the capital stock in a realistic fashion, one must subtract $240,000, and not $120,000, from net revenue each year, because the capital good will last only 5 years, and not 10 years. The true estimate of economic income shows a *loss* of $15,000 per year under the 12 h per day regime and therefore indicates that this regime is not sustainable. The very regime that had looked so attractive in terms of net revenues and in terms of economic income when falsely calculated simply ceases to exist, as is indicated by the dashes after year 5 (see Table VII).

Table V Economic Income of the Firm (8 h day)

	Year 1	*Year 2*	...	*Year 5*	*Year 6*	...	*Year 10*
Net revenue (thousands of dollars) (the capital good lasts 10 years)	$150	$150		$150	$150		$150
minus							
Accounting depreciation charge (10-year basis)	$120	$120		$120	$120		$120
Economic income	$30	$30		$30	$30		$30

Table VI Economic Income of the Firm (12 h day): Falsely Calculated

	Year 1	*Year 2*	...	*Year 5*	*Year 6*	...	*Year 10*
Net revenue (thousands of dollars) (the capital good lasts 5 years)	$225	$225		$225	$225		$225
minus							
Accounting depreciation charge (10-year basis)	$120	$120		$120	$120		$120
Economic income	$105	$105		$105	?		?

Table VII Economic Income of the Firm (12 h day): Correctly Calculated

	Year 1	*Year 2*	...	*Year 5*	*Year 6*	...	*Year 10*
Net revenue (thousands of dollars) (the capital good lasts 5 years)	$225	$225		$225	—		—
minus							
Accounting depreciation charge (5-year basis)	$240	$240		$240	—		—
Economic income	($15)	($15)		($15)	—		—

Economic Income and Economic Development

National Income and the Natural Environment The example above examines the concept of economic income using a firm, rather than an individual or a nation, because the concepts of "capital stock" and "depreciation" are well known for firms. In principle, a calculation of a nation's economic power (and therefore true economic income at a national level) must employ the concepts outlined here. National income accounts do indeed incorporate the depreciation charges made by firms on their own capital (when one, for instance, calculates Net Domestic Product as opposed to Gross Domestic Product), but make no other adjustments of this kind.

One context in which this issue is subject to widespread discussion is the fact that national income measures make no deductions for the running down of a society's natural resources that are common property (e.g., the atmosphere in the context of global warming), a key element of its collective capital stock. Thus, if they are to be used as indicators of economic power, national income calculations must be modified to take into consideration the deterioration in the natural environment with, for instance, appropriate deductions for increased pollution of the air and water.

Economic Income and Human Capital Another key element of a nation's capital stock is its human capital. A nation's human resources are largely an immobile, fixed asset. This may be especially true, relatively speaking, in the present period, with its very high mobility of capital and technology. Existing national income accounts make no adjustments for the "accelerated depreciation" of the human capital stock, such as that that took place in Great Britain during the Industrial Revolution. Even if national income accounts had existed at the time, they would not have registered this accelerated depreciation in the stock of "human capital" of a goodly section of the population. As a result, periods of intense development in industry and agriculture will overestimate any reasonable calculations of the true growth in national economic income if there is an accompanying deterioration in the "human capital stock."

Economic Income and the Problem of Irreversibilities

There is one further way in which increases in measured national income may not correspond to increases in economic power—in society's potential to make alternative decisions in the future. The problem is that many decisions are irreversible, or at least very difficult to reverse. In the context of the natural environment, this is a central consideration. Societies may also abort the intergenerational transmission of skills and knowledge. It is, for instance, a typical aspect of the process of economic development and urbanization that many folk traditions in music, art, and literature will die out. Another prominent example of irreversibility may be seen in the context of an automobile-oriented society. A social decision to remove trams, buy up rights of way for highways, and zone residential living conditions to low-density, car-oriented living precludes the possibility of having viable public transport systems at any time in the future and illustrates that many decisions of this kind can be irreversible.

Technological Change and the Factors Contributing to Growth and Development

Technological Change and Growth

Economists have devoted much attention to identifying the sources of economic growth. A pioneering study by Robert Solow in 1957 studied the determinants of economic growth in the United States from 1909 to 1949. He reached the surprising conclusion that only a small fraction of the rise in output per unit of labor could be accounted for by rises in the stock of capital per unit of labor. The statistical residual accounted for 90% of this increase and was dubbed "exogenous technical change."

In subsequent investigations, the relationship between technological change and growth has proved to be more complex than that postulated above. Technological change may well be generated "endogenously," i.e., through the very expansion in the capital stock discussed above. Firms and nations that proceed in this direction may well gain "first mover" advantages in the use of these technologies through a process of "learning by doing." Success in the use and implementation of new technologies may result in further efficiency gains as a result of economies of scale consequent on market expansion, resulting in a "virtuous cycle" of growth. Central to this process is investment in the form of research and development, which leads to the discovery and elaboration of new processes and products. Technological change is thus not a "magic bullet" that, of its own accord, leads to economic growth and development.

Human Capital and Growth

Education and Income Inequality

The augmentation of the quality of human capital is seen as a key aspect of economic development, including the ability of nations to absorb and implement new technologies. In prominent examples of a successful transition from low-wage, low-skill economies to high levels of development such as Japan or South Korea, rapid growth was accompanied by the maintenance of a limited dispersion between the incomes of the rich and poor. Raising educational standards is seen to promote both economic growth and the narrowing of income inequality; in the opposite direction, a low level of income inequality itself promotes the likelihood of rising educational standards.

Education and Positive Externalities

Investment in education is seen as a social priority in the context of economic development, since it is seen to yield positive external benefits—beneficent spillovers to others in the society. The positive external benefits to education include the following:

Improvements in Communication These improvements can be linked to the most fundamental and important invention of the human species, *Homo sapiens*—the invention of language. In the modern world, the ability of individuals to communicate and absorb information in writing is an inherent aspect of development.

Emulation Improvements in the education and skills of an individual can hardly be kept secret and emulation by others is a fundamental aspect of human history. Since individuals can rarely lay claim and then capture the full value of the benefits gained by others as a result of their example, there are bound to be positive spillover effects from an individual's acquisition of improvements in education and skills.

Inherently Interactive Activities A simple example of an inherently interactive activity is the driving of an automobile. The legal requirement that drivers must pass a test of proficiency is linked to the notion that the probable benefits to society as a whole are greater than those that accrue to any one individual: the likelihood of an individual avoiding a car accident is a function not only of his or her own proficiency, but that of the other drivers on the road.

State Governance

Great emphasis has been placed on the quality of state governance as a key variable affecting economic development. Two aspects have been emphasized.

Democratic Rule

Democracy has been held to be important, not only for its own sake, but because it can facilitate the process of development. Democratic governments may often have short time horizons, focusing on the next election, and their resultant behavior may have deleterious effects on the nation's long-term development. However, the positive aspects of democratic rule appear to be of much greater weight:

The Free Flow of Information Dictatorships find it easier to cover up economic mistakes for long periods of time, such as the ecological disasters in the former Soviet Union, than do democracies.

The Need for Consensus Extreme and arbitrary policies, such as the Great Leap Forward in China, which led to mass famine, are less likely to exist in democracies.

The Level of Corruption

State corruption is seen as a major obstacle to a nation's economic development, both in terms of the misallocation of domestic resources that corruption generates and in the discouragement of international involvement in the nation's economy.

The Human Development Index

The Components of the Human Development Index

The most prominent example of an attempt to construct a unitary measure of economic development as an alternative to standard economic growth measures is the Human Development Index (HDI) of the United Nations. Some see it as a measure of an even broader concept than "economic development." Three "dimensions" are specified:

GDP per capita. This variable is corrected for local pricing conditions, such as low prices for domestic foodstuffs, to permit comparisons between countries (purchasing power parity in U.S. dollars). The use of a logarithmic measure of GDP reduces the weight given to high incomes in the index.

Life expectancy at birth.

Education. The adult literacy rate is given a weight of two-thirds and the combined primary, secondary, and tertiary gross enrollment ratio is given a one-third weight.

The Calculation of the HDI

To aggregate these dimensions into the HDI, an index ranging between 0 and 1 is created for each dimension using the following formulation:

$$\frac{\text{actual value} - \text{minimum value}}{\text{maximum value} - \text{minimum value}}$$

The maximum and minimum values for the variables used are as follows:

	Maximum value	*Minimum value*
Life expectancy at birth (years)	85	25
Adult literacy rate (%)	100	0
Combined gross enrollment ratio (%)	100	0
GDP per capita (PPP $US)	40,000	100

One may then proceed to calculate the HDI for Albania in 2001. Life expectancy is 73.4 years. The life expectancy index is thus

$$\frac{73.4 - 25}{85 - 25} = 0.807.$$

The Education Index

The adult literacy rate in Albania in 2001 was 85.3% and the combined gross enrollment ratio was 69%. One must first calculate the subindices:

The adult literacy index is

$$\frac{85.3 - 0}{100 - 0} = 0.853.$$

The gross enrollment index is

$$\frac{69 - 0}{100 - 0} = 0.690.$$

The education index is then

$$2/3(\text{adult literacy index}) + 1/3(\text{gross enrollment index}) = 2/3(0.853 + 1/30.690) = 0.798.$$

The GDP Index

Albania's per capita GDP in 2001 was $3680. The GDP index is thus

$$\frac{\log(3680) - \log(100)}{\log(40000) - \log(100)} = 0.602.$$

The HDI for Albania in 2001 can then be calculated as

$$1/3(\text{life expectancy index}) + 1/3(\text{education index}) + 1/3(\text{GDP index}) = 1/3(0.807) + 1/3(0.798) + 1/3(0.602) = 0.735.$$

The HDI as a Measure of Development

This index is obviously only an approximate measure of economic development and each of the components used may be subject to criticism.

1. Life expectancy at birth is an amalgam of two conceptually different statistics of interest. First, among very poor countries, this measure will be importantly affected by the level of infant mortality. Second, it also reflects the extent to which members of the population of a nation have the opportunity to live "long and healthy lives." The latter is conceptually a different issue from that of infant mortality and in principle should be measured separately.

2. The education measure is also an amalgam of two different conceptualizations. The adult literacy component is a measure of a society's accomplishment in achieving the goal of literacy, its *output* of the desired result. The gross enrollment measure, by contrast, is an indication of the level of *inputs* devoted to this purpose.

3. GDP per capita in the index "serves as a surrogate for all the dimensions of human development" not reflected in the life expectancy and education indices. It therefore serves as a catchall for all excluded variables in the development measure.

In principle, an ideal index of development would deal with all the Paretian and the economic income critiques of the GDP growth variable suggested above and monitor developments in gender equality, access to clean water, political freedom, and other key variables. The limitations on the HDI in its present form are imposed by the absence of more detailed data for the various countries of the world and the conceptual difficulties of formulating a single measure that encapsulates the process of development.

Even with these limitations, however, the HDI rankings for the countries of the world often show dramatic deviations from their GDP rankings, as can be seen in

Table VIII GDP per Capita (PPP US$) Rank Minus HDI Rank for 2001 (Selected Countries)

High human development	
Sweden	+15
United States	−5
Italy	−5
Poland	+17
Medium human development	
Panama	+23
Saudi Arabia	−33
Philippines	+19
Dominican Republic	−26
Low human development	
Zimbabwe	−18
Kenya	+14
Yemen	+21
Angola	−32

Source: Data taken from "United Nations Development Programme Human Development Report 2003," pp. 237–240. Oxford University Press, Oxford, UK.

Table VIII. For all its weaknesses, the HDI helps to focus attention away from a one-sided emphasis on GDP growth as a measure of economic progress.

See Also the Following Articles

Aggregative Macro Models, Micro-Based Macro Models, and Growth Models • Business Research, Theoretical Paradigms That Inform • Economic Forecasts • Economics, Strategies in Social Science • Quantitative Analysis, Economics

Further Reading

Dasgupta, P. (1993). *An Inquiry into Well-Being and Destitution.* Clarendon Press, Oxford, UK.

Ghatak, S. (2003). *Introduction to Development Economics,* 4th Ed. Routledge, Andover, MA.

Maddison, A. (2001). *The World Economy: A Millennial Perspective.* Organisation for Economic Cooperation and Development, Paris.

Sen, A. (1999). *Development as Freedom.* Oxford University Press, Oxford, UK.

Streeton, P. (1999). On the search for well-being. *Econ. Dev. Cult. Change* **48,** 214–245.

Economic Forecasts

Charles G. Renfro

Journal of Economic and Social Measurement, New York, New York, USA

Glossary

business cycles Perceptible, regular periods of expansion and contraction of an economy, often graphically represented as an undulating pattern around an upward trend.

forecast or prediction An attempt to make a statement, based on a set of observations, about an event or thing not yet observed.

macroeconometric model A mathematical–statistical representation of an economy; generally contains from 25 to 2500 equations, depending on the detail and complexity of the representation.

measurement The attempt to assess as a quantity a specific, defined set of characteristics.

time series A sequence of observations on a variable, referring to particular intervals of chronological time, such as weeks, months, quarters, or years; each variable may or may not have the property of being statistically a random variable.

The process of making and evaluating economic forecasts or predictions, from the measurement perspective, must take into consideration the implications of the context in which the forecasts are made, both in terms of public forecasts pertaining to an entire economy and of individual forecasts that might be made privately. The issues relevant to the after-the-fact evaluation of forecasting must also be considered. The primary forecast methodologies utilized by economists are considered briefly here, with the principal focus being the statistical aspects of that methodology, rather than the economic theoretic motivation. The emphasis is on the ways in which the economic measurement problem affects the forecasts made by economists.

Introduction

Forecast, prediction, and prophecy are words that imply the ability, or at least denote an attempt, to describe or suggest what will happen in the future. However, these three words are not synonymous. In the specific case of the economic future, the distinction usually made is that "prophesy" implies a mystical, possibly god-given, ability to foretell, whereas the concepts behind the terminology "forecast" and "prediction" are much more commonplace in origin. For this reason, prophesies, when they are wrong, are often labeled as false. In contrast, forecasts and predictions, when they fail to be realized, are normally either characterized as being simply inaccurate or at worst incorrect. One of the benefits of being incorrect rather than false is that, although economic forecasters can suffer some degree of obloquy from time to time for their sins, they are seldom put to death for their presumption, at least in modern times.

The distinction just drawn between economic prophesy and forecasts or predictions essentially resides in the characteristic that prophesies are fundamentally independent of any past observations or measurements, whereas forecasts and predictions necessarily rely on the connectedness of the past and the future. This connectedness is, in fact, a double-edged sword: journalists and others often deride economic forecasts for being (simply) extensions of the past, as if prophesy were an option, but a more thoughtful response to the retrospective evaluation of any forecast is to ask "Why was this result obtained: what are the circumstances of both the forecast and the actual outcome?" In a world in which governments and individual economic actors, be they organizations or people, act on the basis of their expectations about the future, actual outcomes may be the result of forecasts.

A macroeconomic forecast, in particular, if believed, might lead to a particular outcome if governments, consumers, and businesses all react to the prediction by changing aspects of their behavior. Indeed, because of this possibility of reaction, in at least some cases, it is the economic forecasts that are not believed (or not made publicly) that could have the best chance to be realized. Believed forecasts, as just indicated, can be self-falsifying: for example, a forecasted recession might never occur if, as a result of this prediction, the "right" governmental policies are put into place sufficiently well in advance. In contrast, if the "wrong" policies are adopted, the forecast could then possibly be self-realizing—particularly in the case of recession, because, almost by definition, "wrong" policies are those that precipitate negative economic consequences. There is even an economic school of thought that holds that, because of people's ability to forecast, governmental economic policies will tend to be self-frustrating, especially to the degree that individual consumers and businesses compensate by consciously adopting behaviors that neutralize the impact of those policies. In effect, according to this logic, economic policy and associated forecasts can generally be expected to be self-defeating.

These are, of course, general statements, rather broadly made. The issue of forecast accuracy can also be considered more specifically. The evaluation of a single forecast can be made in terms of its overall general characteristics; however, particularly when alternative forecasts are compared, the question commonly asked is one of relative quantitative accuracy. At first sight, it might seem that, in principle, such accuracy is easy to assess, but in fact, there are a number of difficulties lying in wait. At one level, there is the issue of simply measuring that accuracy, which becomes increasingly complex when forecasts involve the simultaneous prediction of two or more economic variables. For example, a given forecast might simultaneously involve the prediction of values of gross domestic product, one or more interest rates, and various measures of employment, unemployment, and price inflation. In this instance, it is not immediately obvious how to evaluate alternative forecasts for a given time period if, as is usually the case, the measured relative accuracy ranking of each competing forecast differs, depending on the individual variable or variables considered. For example, one forecast might be quantitatively more accurate in its prediction of gross domestic product; another, in its prediction of interest rates; and yet another, in its inflation predictions. In addition, when considering predictive accuracy, there is also the question whether overprediction of a realized value should be treated on equal footing with an underprediction. And, of course, proceeding in this way seemingly sets aside the problem mentioned earlier, of the possible impact of any of the considered forecasts on the actual measured outcomes; taking this possibility into account when evaluating predictive accuracy obviously can further muddy the water.

At a deeper level, apart from the forecast values, there is also the fact that the apparent measured outcomes are not necessarily determinate. Specifically, the first published estimates of the realized values of many macroeconomic variables, including gross domestic product, employment, and even price measures, are subject to revision. They may change significantly in the next month after the first estimates are made, and then one or more times in the year after that. They may change multiple times in succeeding years. For example, for the United States, the aggregate estimates of nonfarm employment published during or immediately after the 1992 presidential election are not even approximately the same as the estimates published today for that same 1992 time period. A forecast of employment made at the beginning of 1992, which at the end of 1992 might then have appeared to be a wild overestimate of employment, could today be assessed in retrospect as an underprediction of what is now believed to be the contemporaneous actual level of employment. Obviously, today's U.S. employment measurements can have no impact on the 1992 U.S. presidential election, but they are pertinent to today's evaluations of forecast accuracy then. In short, in as much as the estimated, realized values of many economic variables are subject to multiple revisions, the measurement of forecast accuracy for these variables is not simply a matter of applying once, or even twice, some formula to measure the prediction error.

It should be apparent from what has been said so far that economic prediction, as an activity, involves inherent complexities that can far exceed those associated with other types of prediction. For example, the prediction of the relative movement of the planets around the sun, based on the laws of physical motion, differs in nature from economic prediction in several ways. Most fundamentally, the prediction of planetary motion obviously has no effect on the motion: what is predicted is independent of the subject of the prediction. However, in addition, once the prediction is made, the process of evaluating the accuracy of that prediction involves also a much less complex measurement problem. The inference to be drawn from these considerations is not that the laws of physical motion are better understood than is the nature of economic processes, although this could be true, but rather that, in the case of large-body physical motion, the predictive context is a much simpler context. Notice also that it is only at this point that any specific mention has been made of the qualitative basis on which an economic forecast might be made—that is, the model or other representation of the economic process that generates the values that are predicted. Obviously, as a matter of scientific consideration, the adequacy of this representation is important and this issue will need to be investigated carefully later, but it should be evident from the foregoing that the several complexities that have been briefly considered so far are inherently characteristic of the act of making and evaluating economic forecasts, and are not at all dependent on nor necessarily a result of the specific forecasting methods used. Indeed, in a given instance, a good forecasting method, with "good" as an intrinsic quality, might produce an apparently, or even actually, inaccurate prediction. Likewise, a bad forecasting method, interpreting "bad" as an intrinsic quality, might result in an accurate or seemingly accurate prediction. However, when contemplating this seeming paradox, it should also be recalled that before Galileo and Newton, there were now-discredited methods of predicting the movements of planets that achieved quite a high degree of predictive accuracy, so that obtaining "good" predictions using what can be later seen as a flawed methodology is not in itself particular to economic forecasting.

Methodology of Economic Prediction

The preceding discussion presumes a general familiarity with the concept of a forecast, but so far, neither have the specific methods of making economic predictions been considered nor have many of the terms used been defined. Considered generally, the methods commonly used to make economic forecasts range from those that have no apparent logic, to those that possess a logic that can, at least at first sight (or even after careful evaluation), appear to be farfetched, to defensible statistical methodologies that may be capable of being generally replicated and may or may not be grounded in economic theory. The first type of method includes simply "guesses" that can be made by anyone, in much the same sense that it is not necessary to be a meteorologist to predict that it will rain tomorrow; furthermore, a given prediction of the weather might or might not be made with reference to any immediately available meteorological evidence. An example of the second type of methodology is the sunspot theory of the economist and logician, William Stanley Jevons (1835–1882). Jevons attempted to relate economic activity—particularly the trade cycle—to the observed pattern of solar flares; on first consideration, this theory appears quite tenuous, but it gains a degree of logic, particularly for an agricultural economy, from the idea that crop yields can be affected by changes in the intensity of the sun's energy. The well-known argument put forward by Thomas Malthus at the beginning of the 19th century, that bare subsistence would be the inevitable lot of mankind in general, because the food supply increases arithmetically whereas population growth is exponential, is also a type of forecast. Its logical methodology relies on observation of the world combined with recognition of aspects of the dynamic that exists between economic and population growth, as well as some of the effects of imbalances between supply and demand. However, in the case of Jevons and Malthus, these are now simply examples of attempts to explain observed phenomena in a general way, and early examples at that.

During the 20th century, explanations of economic behavior and of the reasons for particular outcomes became much more varied and prescriptive in nature—and ostensibly more capable of being made operationally precise. Especially with the publication in 1936 of John Maynard Keynes' *General Theory of Employment, Interest, and Money*, economists began to consider—as an increasingly widely accepted idea—that government policies might systematically affect the economy's performance, even to the point that this performance could be managed actively. Whether because of this perception that an economy could be controlled, or possibly because of a general sentiment that democratic governments should at least attempt to do this, by the middle of the 20th century, governments began to take responsibility, to at least some degree, for ensuring economic prosperity. Out of this came both specific proposals for targeted economic policies and methodologies for the creation of precisely specified forecasting "models" that could be used to choose between alternative policies at a particular moment in time. In this process, the particular theories that provide logical substance to general explanations of economic behavior also became differentiated from the essentially statistical methodologies of forming and "estimating" equations to make forecasts: the content of the equations might be suggested by economic theory, but the particular statistical technique of obtaining specific parameter estimates became almost its own specialty. It is the abstract characteristics of these equations that are primarily considered here, because replicable, statistically based methodologies that are commonly used by professional economists—in part because of their replicability, among other traits—are thus arguably scientific in motivation and basis.

Viewed broadly as polar examples, there are two commonly employed methods of making economic predictions. The first of these is primarily statistical in nature and relies on the regular behavior of economic variables as a sequence, or series, of observations over time, rather than on a representation of these variables in terms of their relationship to each other, as might be proposed by economic theory. At one extreme, this time-series methodology is an economic forecasting methodology only by virtue of the fact that it can be applied to the explanation of the behavior of economic variables over time, seen as statistical time series. At this extreme, often no attempt is made by practitioners to provide any justification, based on any economic behavioral concepts, in order to explain the series' behavior over time, either before or after the development of the forecasting model. The statistical methods can be, and regularly are, applied in many other contexts as well.

A statistical time series variable, Y_t, generally can be conceived as characterized by the following expression:

$$Y_t = a_0 + a_1 Y_{t-1} + \cdots + a_k Y_{t-k} + u_t, \quad (1)$$

where the $a_0, a_1, \ldots, a_k$ are constants and u_t is a random disturbance term. The subscript t refers to observation intervals of time that might, in a particular case, be identified as days, weeks, months, or years for which past values of Y_t are historically observed. Particularly for macroeconomic variables (such as gross domestic product, consumption expenditures, employment by industry, and the like), historical observations are commonly available for at least 10 to 50 or more past years. Thus the expression given by Eq. (1) characterizes the relationship between the value of the variable Y_t, at some time t, its past values at times $t-1$, $t-2, \ldots,$ $t-k$, and the values of u_t, at each time t, with u_t being a random error or disturbance term, the actual values of which are unknown and the general statistical properties of which therefore must be assumed. The specific properties of this characterization depend on the values taken by the constants and the properties of the disturbance term. If, for instance, it is specified that

$$\begin{aligned} a_1 &= 1, \\ a_i &= 0 \quad \text{for all} \quad i \neq 1, \end{aligned} \quad (2)$$

the expression immediately simplifies to

$$Y_t = Y_{t-1} + u_t. \quad (3)$$

Given certain assumptions about the properties of the disturbance term u_t, this representation, or model, is known as a random walk process. The model essentially specifies that over time, the change in Y_t at each time t is directly a function of the disturbance term u_t; in this context, this disturbance is usually assumed to be a purely random, so-called white-noise process with a constant mean and constant variance.

The characterization of economic variables as obeying a random walk is normally limited to the prices of financial securities in organized markets. These prices arguably reflect in their behavior that the moment-to-moment observed changes are due to the accretion of new information about their economic circumstances, which arrives randomly. The fundamental conceptual basis for this statistical model is that, at each point in time, the prices fully reflect what is known by all participants in the market for these securities, thus it is the advent of new information that causes the prices to change. In order to predict the moment-to-moment behavior of such a price, it is necessary to explain, or "model," how and when this new information occurs, obviously a difficult, if not impossible, task. Operationally, in this case, simply knowing the pattern of past price behavior does not provide a valid basis on which to predict future price behavior. In contrast, if it is true that, instead, $a_1 < 1$, the current value of the variable Y_t depends systematically on both its previous values and the random effects of the disturbance term, u_t. Nonzero values of a_0 and the other a_i constants ($i = 2, 3, \ldots, k$) will affect the particular pattern of the behavior of the variable Y_t over time, but clearly do not change the basic assertion that future values of this variable are systematically related to its past values. Obviously, in practice, a number of issues arises, including such things as the value of k, the maximum number of lagged values of Y_t, and which of the a_i take nonzero values, as well as what specific values. In addition, the properties of the disturbance term can be characterized in a variety of ways, leading to much more complex mathematical–statistical expressions as potential models, including the approach taken by George Box and Gwilym Jenkins. To examine, even in general terms, the various aspects of this type of statistical model would easily take several hundred pages, and there are many books devoted to the ways in which time-series variables can be characterized in order to then attempt to forecast their future values. A further extension is to consider not one single variable Y_t, but instead a set of economic variables $Y_{1t}, Y_{2t}, \ldots, Y_{nt}$ in order to form a multivariate forecasting model, but this extension does not change the nature of the methodology variable by variable, if each time series is treated as being independent of the others as a process.

All such characterizations of the behavior of time series are based on the idea that it is a fixed pattern of past behavior of the variables that provides the means to produce forecasts of future values. This is not to say that the potential patterns of behavior cannot be very complexly represented: practically any regular, and even some seemingly highly irregular, patterns of behavior can be modeled, in principle. However, these patterns will depend on the specific values taken by the constants, a_0 and the a_i ($i = 1, 2, \ldots, k$), as experimentation with a graphing calculator will easily demonstrate. Moreover, as indicated previously, for a real-world example, these values are *a priori* unknown. Consequently, they must be estimated using appropriate statistical estimation methods, given the observed past values of the Y_t (or the set of variables $Y_{1t}, Y_{2t}, \ldots, Y_{nt}$). The capability to estimate these reliably depends on, among other things, the available quantity (and their quality as measurements) of past observations. Furthermore, during this estimation process, tests must also be made to assess the validity of any hypotheses adopted concerning certain critically important values, such as which, if any, of the a_i have a value of zero—the occurrence of which particular value evidently implies that certain lagged values of Y_t should not appear in the estimated equation. And, of course, operationally, as a forecasting method, this methodology obviously relies on the persistence of the estimated behavioral patterns over time, at least throughout the time for which the forecasts are made. For its validity, therefore, the methodology does not necessarily require any knowledge as to why economic variables behave as they do, but this is not to say that it does not require instead a possibly immense amount of acquired knowledge concerning the representation of the patterns of that behavior, and not a little faith that these patterns will persist in the future.

Forecast methodologies of the type just briefly described clearly have the property of requiring a statistical characterization of the variable to be predicted. For this reason, they are commonly employed in those instances in which the person making the forecast either lacks knowledge as to why a particular economic variable might behave in a particular way, or lacks the time to attempt a particular detailed study of the whys and wherefores of that behavior. One of the reasons to adopt the approach in a particular case might be the need to provide forecasts for a substantial number of variables. For example, an employee of large firm, particularly a firm producing a variety of products that are sold in various different markets or in a range of container sizes, might choose to employ a statistical methodology of this type as a sales forecasting technique. This decision may be buoyed, in part, by the belief that among many forecasted variables, the prediction errors made might, in the aggregate, cancel to at least some degree, in the end providing a satisfactory composite result. As a normative consideration, it is important to recognize that the choice between methodologies can depend on a great variety of circumstances, so that the particular choices made do not always need to be justified on the basis of individual predictions. It is, for example, difficult to predict the length of a given human life, but the life expectancy characteristics of large populations are known to be quite predictable, at least under normal circumstances.

As just indicated, the choice of methodology for economic forecasts is obviously, in part, a question of the particular application, as well as what is meant by "an economic forecast." Prior to the work in the later 1930s of Jan Tinbergen, who is generally credited with the construction of the first macroeconometric models, economic forecasts almost always took the form of predictions of individual prices, as well as a variety of other individual economic, generally microeconomic, variables. Beginning in about 1954, with the creation of the first macroeconometric model to be used to make economic forecasts, known as the Klein–Goldberger model, the prediction of the performance of entire economies began to take center stage. It is such macroeconomic forecasts that many people today commonly consider to be "economic forecasts." These predictions have the characteristic that what is predicted is a set of variables, including those such as gross domestic product, consumption, investment, interest rates, and industry employment. In addition, these variables as a group are treated as being interrelated in their behavioral patterns. Moreover, not only are these variables generally covariant in their behavioral patterns, but they may also have the property of being simultaneously determined: for instance, consumption and income not only have a presumed causal relationship, but the causality may be mutual. When relationships between economic variables are thought to be thus jointly determined, it is plausible to argue that the methodology used to forecast future values of these variables should take this characteristic into account.

Such simultaneity also involves increased computational complexity. The development of the electronic computer during the past 60 years, together with the creation of the necessary computer software, began to make the construction and use of macroeconometric models increasingly feasible during the 1960s and subsequently. To use these models requires the solution of a set of hundreds or even thousands of simultaneous equations, which is a practical impossibility in the absence of a high-speed computer. A further important aspect of this type of model is that it includes among its equations the statement of economy-wide accounting relationships, using government statistical agency-produced national income and product accounts data, as well as industry-specific and aggregate data on employment, wages, and a variety of other such economic variables. Although individual economists have in the past occasionally constructed such data sets on their own, sometimes as a pathbreaking research activity for which Nobel Prizes have been awarded, such efforts are increasingly exceptional. As a practical matter, it is essentially a precondition to the active use of (if not the building of) such models that a multiyear data-gathering and accounts-construction activity first be undertaken, on a scale likely to require, in each case, the participation of multiple governmental agencies, trade groups, and other organizations. Even for governments, ongoing construction and elaboration of these data sets only became feasible with the development of computers and related data-processing equipment.

Since the late 1960s, macroeconomic models have commonly consisted of as many as 300 or more equations, with a few containing as many as 5000 or more. In general, such models attempt to account for categories of aggregate expenditures by consumers, businesses, and governments, acting as both domestic and foreign purchasers of goods and services produced by one or more economies. The sum of such expenditures on new goods and services produced domestically by a given economy is gross domestic product (GDP). Many of the equations are devoted not only to explaining how various types of expenditures arise, but also employment and income originating by industry (originating in the form of wages and profits), among other classifications. As a rule of thumb, the more detailed the individual industry representation in a given model, the greater the number of equations. Added to these equations are other equations to account for interest rates, the money supply, and related aggregate financial variables. A typical equation, represented in somewhat simplified form, can be stated as follows:

$$Y_t = a_0 + a_1 Y_{t-1} + \cdots + a_k Y_{t-k} + b_1 X_{1t} + \cdots + b_n X_{nt} + u_t. \qquad (4)$$

The presence of the X_{jt} $(j = 1, 2, \ldots, n)$ variables here signifies that a variable Y_t depends for its behavior not only on the past self-values but also on other variable values; some of the X_{jt} could be past values of these other variables, but in the interest of simplicity, this complication is not shown here. The b_j $(j = 1, 2, \ldots, n)$, as well as the a_i $(i = 0, 1, 2, \ldots, k)$, are unknown constants that must be statistically estimated, based on the past values of the model's variables. As before, u_t should be regarded as a random error or disturbance term. The estimation of the constant values involves a number of the same or similar considerations as in the case of the statistical univariate model discussed previously, although the specific estimation methodologies generally differ in detail.

Equation (4) is only a single representative equation, and is a linear equation, but as a predictive device, a macroeconometric model almost always consists of a nonlinear system of equations that must be solved for the values that are to be predicted. Even when the individual equations are estimated as linear equations, as a composite, the system can be highly nonlinear in its form and characteristics. An additional difference, in comparison with the univariate time-series model, is that certain of the variables in a macroeconometric model are not predicted by the model. Their values are instead provided by the economic forecaster, who will state these as assumptions. For example, whereas it is usual for a macroeconometric model to predict consumption expenditures, the amount of government expenditures within each forecast time period will often be stated as assumed values. In the near term, these may represent planned government expenditures. In the longer term, such expenditure values may be provided on a "what-if" basis. The degree to which particular variable values appear as forecast assumptions or are predicted by the model depends on the particular model. For instance, the immigration of people into a country (treated as an economy) presumably will depend on opportunities for employment, hence will be affected by the relative economic performance of that country, but some models may instead require the forecaster to assume the immigration rates, rather than to predict them endogenously.

Statistical and macroeconometric models will produce predictions that depend on the estimated values of the constant parameters they include (the a_i and the b_j, $i = 0, 1, 2, \ldots, k, j = 1, 2, \ldots, n$), so that arguably both types of models produce conditional forecasts, when used as predictive devices. However, ignoring this somewhat esoteric point, a fundamental difference between the statistical model and the structural macroeconomic model lies in the ability of the latter to incorporate in its forecasts specific variable assumptions. In contrast, forecasts of the former do not permit different assumptions to be made about such things as changes in various governmental economic policies, including levels of government expenditures or tax rates or monetary policy. Once a statistical model has been estimated, its predictions are essentially determined and are produced mechanically. In contrast, the estimation of a macroeconometric model only partially determines (by the estimated values of its constant parameters) the predictions that might be made subsequently using the model. The capability to make alternative forecasts is therefore a characteristic property of such a model.

A more comprehensive and detailed description of econometric forecast methodology would consider hybrid methodologies, but at the moment, it may be more useful to focus on the strong distinction between the statistical methodologies as described: the statistical model, which produces forecasts that depend on prior behavioral patterns of the time-series variables, versus the structural macroeconometric model, which emphasizes the relationships between economic, demographic, and other relevant variables. Using the estimated relationships between these variables provides the capability to predict future values. Both methodologies depend on the persistence of the estimated relationships into the future, but obviously in a somewhat different way.

The conceptual characteristics of an historical pattern-based approach (versus relationships between contemporaneous variables as predictive concepts) actually transcend the specifics of these particular economic forecasting methodologies. For, instance stock market prices are commonly predicted by analysts either using a methodology that attempts to infer from past patterns of behavior of particular prices and price indices the future performance of these variables, or using a methodology that focuses on the relationship between stock prices and variables that either relate to the economy as a whole or to the characteristics of the company to which the particular financial securities refer.

Other Measurement Aspects of the Economic Prediction Process

Considering economic predictions, it is possible to focus progressively on several different aspects of the individual variables. For example, gross domestic product can be considered in terms of its level values, expressed in dollars, euros, pounds, yen, or other currency units, reflecting the economy considered in a given instance. Alternatively, it is possible to measure the predicted rate of change from one time period to another or the difference in value between one point in time and another. In addition, the level values may refer to gross domestic product stated as the current value of all newly produced goods and services or as a measure of the value produced stated as real values (that is, ostensibly independent of the effect of changes in the prices of those goods and services). Each of these alternatives can be predicted directly, or else computed later from directly predicted values. These alternatives can also have a particular inferential meaning individually; for instance, it is the rate of change in real gross domestic product that is usually viewed as a summary measure of the performance of an economy in terms of its growth or decline, and thus is often given prominence in newspaper headlines and in political debates.

Interestingly, it is generally not true that the same final predicted values will be obtained, whichever variable representation is used to actually make the predictions. As time series, the alternative representations present individual and different patterns of behavior: rates of change of GDP vary greatly from time period to time period, and the value in one quarter or one year can be quite different than that in the next quarter or year. In contrast, the level values of GDP generally do not appear radically different from one time period to the next. The time graph of GDP takes the form of a rather gently fluctuating curve, whereas the graph of its rate of change tends to be somewhat spiky. Represented as a time series, it is therefore generally much more difficult to model the period-to-period changes than it is to model the level performance of GDP. A similar statement can be made about the decomposition of GDP into its price and real value components:

$$\text{GDP\$}_t = \text{GDP}_t \times \text{PGDP}_t \quad (5)$$

where $\text{GDP\$}_t$ is the dollar value of gross domestic product, GDP_t is the real value, and PGDP_t is the price level component, known as the price deflator. Note that both GDP_t and PGDP_t can both, in turn, be converted into percent change variables, in order to express respectively the economy's rate of growth and a measure of the overall rate of price inflation or deflation.

Taking into account that the modeling of period-to-period changes or rates of change will involve the time-series process expressed as a systematic component and a random disturbance, attempts to model such variables tend to result in models that express average behavior over time, thus any predictions made with such models inherently tend to be predictions of average changes or average rates of change. It is the period-to-period variability that tends to be represented by the random disturbance and that is then not predicted, and is perhaps not even predictable. An economic variable expressed in difference form may be related to the systematic, or persistent, component of past differenced values of itself, conceived as a statistical time-series variable, or it could even exhibit the previously described properties of a random walk. The inference to be drawn is not that something definite or profound can be stated at this level of generality, but rather that such considerations help to explain why it is difficult to both model and predict in a context in which the variables used vary decidedly from period to period. As suggested earlier, the problem of predicting the motion of planetary bodies may be a much simpler prediction problem, in part because of the regular period-to-period change that is involved, as well as the greater simplicity in the statement of the physical laws of their motion.

Business Cycle Measurement: An Exception?

The techniques considered, although considered briefly and somewhat at arm's length, because a more detailed treatment might involve multiple hundreds of pages, nonetheless encompass the statistical techniques generally applied today by economists in their attempts to predict the behavior of economic processes. However, the question does arise whether this quick survey is sufficiently inclusive. Anyone, who is not an economist, who follows newspaper reports on the economy's performance is likely to wonder how the leading indicators and the measurement and mapping of what is variously called "business cycles," or sometimes the "economic cycle," fit into the picture that has been painted. Employment, unemployment, residential construction (also known as "home building"), and the behavior of the securities markets are commonly spoken of as being among the leading, lagging, and coincident indicators. Surveys of consumer and business sentiment, particularly the former, receive a good deal of press and political attention. In contrast, "time series" is an expression that has seldom, if ever, been heard on the television evening news. Jevons' attempt to relate economic cycles to sunspots was mentioned previously as a more or less aberrant case. However, it has been perceived by economists, since even early in the industrial revolution, that industrial economies generally experience somewhat regular, roughly cyclical periods of expansion and contraction. Beginning in the 19th century, various attempts began to be made to map and classify these cycles, essentially in order to determine those aspects of the process that might possess predictive content. During the early years of the 20th century (in fact, before governments began to collect and publish detailed data on an economy's performance), a group of economists, generally associated with Wesley Mitchell, began to use stock market and other data then available in order to attempt to identify the essential characteristics of the business cycle. These characteristics were seen as being exhibited by sets of variables that had the property of being, in their behavior, either indicative of the early phase of the expansion or contraction, coincident with these phenomena, or "lagging." Such variables could also be characterized as being individually procyclical, countercyclical, and even acyclical. Such a classification of various individual economic measures required, first, the definition of a regular "reference" cycle, but once the general characteristics of this had been identified, the role of the individual indicator variables could be determined in relation to it.

The central evaluative question that arises from this work as a predictive methodology is that of precision. There is no question that characteristic patterns of economic performance exist. It is, for example, generally true that residential construction characteristically begins to increase during the depths of a recession, and can be viewed as a harbinger of recovery. There is a reason for this behavior: this construction is interest rate sensitive, inasmuch as it is generally funded by short-term bank loans. All other things equal, interest rates are lowest during times such as the depths of recession, when borrowing is otherwise at its least. Similarly, during the expansion toward boom, interest rates characteristically rise, and residential construction consequently falters. But is this enough to set one's watch by? Various regularities have been deduced, ranging from cycles of approximately 50–54 years (the famous Kondratiev longwave cycle) to short cycles (months in duration), but it is not clear that an economy's behavior is actually sufficiently determined by anything approaching immutable "laws of economics," so as to make it possible to use reliably and uniquely the insights obtained from business cycle analyses to predict and manage an economy's performance. In any case, the variables that populate these analyses are often the same time series discussed previously, with the same properties as measurements, including in many cases that of being subject to revision. Similarly, the same statistical techniques, and the same ways of characterizing the time-series behavior of economic variables, when estimating the (constant) parameters of an equation, are used in business cycle analysis as in other economic quantitative analyses. The inference to be drawn from such considerations is that the varieties of logical explanation of economic processes do not individually change the measurement context of the prediction problem.

The central concept that underlies and distinguishes the dyed-in-the-wool measurement of business cycles can be seen as being essentially the same as that which motivates the development of a predictive model for an economic variable, viewed as an individual time series, by estimating a statistical model based on the historical record of that variable's behavior: in each case, an attempt is made to erect a predictive methodology on the basis of the patterns of the economy's behavioral characteristics. However, there is a qualifying distinction to be made, inasmuch as Wesley Mitchell and others who have mapped and characterized business cycles have attempted to link the behavior of multiple economic variables in order to provide a seemingly more heuristic model of the business cycle—in contrast to the statistical estimation of the parameters of a univariate or multivariate representation of a time series. Nevertheless, in both cases, it is the characteristics of behavior that are represented, rather than any logical explanation of the reasons for that behavior.

Other predictive approaches adopted by economists have focused on the explanation of economic behavior as the motivation for and method of defining the relationships that are embodied in a model used to predict future behavior. Such an approach can also absorb the analysis of the business cycle. Especially when this structural approach is used to model and predict the behavior of entire economies, it is possible to view it generally as a means to both characterize and predict periods of economic contraction and expansion—but on the basis of explanation, rather than pattern similarity. In fact, a structural model of an economy is not only a predictive device, but can also much more generally be used to simulate that economy's behavior on a "what-if" basis, in order to attempt to consider the particular nature of economic expansions and contractions as phenomena.

It is important to observe behavioral patterns, as a first investigative step, but ultimately it is the explanation that matters. It is this idea that provides the deeper philosophical motivation behind the structural approach. Broadly stated, economists who have adopted it have often tended to see the causes of contraction as reflecting in each particular case a specific example of failure in the economic system: as a general proposition, during an expansion and boom, businesses may reach a point at which more has been produced than can be sold, which then leads to a contraction of production and the layoff of workers. This, in turn, may become contractively cumulative, because unemployed workers—in their role as consumers—find themselves less able to afford to purchase what has been produced. In a somewhat similar progression, from the depths of recession, new expansions in turn require, in chicken-or-egg fashion, either an increase in production or an increase in purchases in order to then interactively and cumulatively sustain that expansion. In effect, from this perspective, it is imbalances in supply and demand, or, in a slightly different terminology for the same thing, the failure of markets to clear, that can be seen as the general cause of economic contractions and expansions. However, even as a general characterization, this is not the only possible cause: for example, today certain economists hold that, in fact, markets do clear, that contractions and expansions are instead directly related to and rooted in changes in the rate of technological change. The immediate question that then naturally arises concerns what determines and explains this change.

Either explanation leads to further questions in order to account for the particular timing of the underlying causes, as well as, ideally, to pinpoint the ultimate reasons, but at present it is not necessary to pursue these obviously tantalizing questions. Instead, the point to be made is that the existence of various alternative explanations for an economy's performance, not to mention the evident complexities of that performance, call into question the idea that the secret to predicting that performance can be captured simply by a precise representation of historical patterns of behavior. It is necessary only to point to jet planes, computers, mobile phones, digital cameras, and other appurtenances of modern economic life to confirm its evolutionary nature, and, in the process, immediately raise questions about the reliability of earlier historical patterns of the behavior of individual variables as predictive touchstones. Simplicity is not the solution.

Conclusion

Economic prediction, as a subject on its own, might be approached by first considering, in particular, the question of the degree to which a particular predictive model is or is not a good representation of the economic process being modeled. The second issue addressed might then be the degree to which the characteristics of the process remain essentially the same over time. If the model is inherently a good representation and if the characteristics of the process do not change between the past and the future, it might logically be expected that any attempt at prediction would be likely to yield good results. However, here, these topics have only been considered toward the end of the narrative. The reason is that when the prediction of economic variables is considered as a measurement problem, there may be certain other aspects of this particular context that also need to be taken into account and given an equal weight.

It has been accepted, as a first principle, that any forecast of the future must be rooted in the observation of the past. Whereas a single guess about the future can possibly be realized independently of such observation, as a matter of consistent performance, it is only to the degree that the past provides the raw materials of the future that scientifically based prediction is possible. In this context, it is not strictly necessary that no changes take place between now and the future, for it may be possible to model that change successfully. But within this qualification, persistence of the characteristics of the forecasted process would seem to be required: more or less by definition, unpredictable change makes scientific prediction impossible. However, what also appears to be true is that the economic prediction problem has two other aspects that give it particular properties that are not universally shared. The first is that economic forecasts can, and often do, affect the realization of the predicted event or process. This statement appears to be most true in the case of widely disseminated macroeconomic forecasts, and much less true of private, independently made microeconomic forecasts. The other aspect is that the economic measurement process involves a degree of uncertainty beyond that of measurement problems in other disciplines, particularly the physical sciences. Obviously, these properties can, in turn, affect the ability of the economist to represent adequately the underlying economic process, because the more difficult something is to observe, the harder it generally is to describe or represent it precisely. Thus, the simple fact of a less precisely defined representation argues for worse predictions. But if, in turn, the future keeps changing, even once it is no longer the future, but as a varying series of views of the realized past, it obviously becomes difficult to assess the quality of previous predictions. These complexities may be enough to call into question the very attempt to forecast the economic future. On the other hand, they pose a challenge to the intrepid.

See Also the Following Articles

Aggregative Macro Models, Micro-Based Macro Models, and Growth Models • Business Research, Theoretical Paradigms That Inform • Economic Development, Technological Change and Growth • Economics, Strategies in Social Science • Quantitative Analysis, Economics

Further Reading

Bodkin, R. G., Klein, L. R., and Marwah, K. (1991). *A History of Macroeconometric Model-Building.* Edward Elgar, Brookfield, VT.

Box, G., and Jenkins, G. (1984). *Time Series Analysis: Forecasting and Control.* Holden Day, San Francisco, CA.

Clements, M. P., and Hendry, D. F. (1998). *Forecasting Economic Time Series.* Cambridge University Press, Cambridge.

Hogg, R. V., and Craig, A. T. (1978). *Introduction to Mathematical Statistics.* Macmillan, New York.

Keynes, J. M. (1936). William Stanley Jevons 1835–1882: A centenary allocation on his life and work as economist and statistician. *J. Roy. Statist. Soc.* **99**(3), 516–555.

Klein, L. R. (1971). *An Essay on the Theory of Econometric Prediction.* Markham Publ., Chicago, IL.

Klein, L. R., and Goldberger, A. S. (1955). *An Econometric Model of the United States, 1929–1952.* North-Holland Publ., Amsterdam.

Malkiel, B. G. (1981). *A Random Walk Down Wall Street.* Norton, New York.

Mitchell, W. C. (1927). *Business Cycles: The Problem and Its Setting.* National Bureau of Economic Research, New York.

Renfro, C. G. (2004). Econometric software: The first fifty years in perspective. *J. Econ. Social Measure* **29,** 9–108.

Tinbergen, J. (1939). *Statistical Testing of Business Cycle Theories.* League of Nations, Geneva.

Economics, Strategies in Social Sciences

Marcel Boumans
University of Amsterdam, Amsterdam, The Netherlands

Glossary

accurate measurement A measurement in which the difference between a true value of a measurand and the measurement result is as small as possible.

calibration The adjustment of the model parameters to obtain the best match between stable properties of the set of observations and those of the model generated outcomes.

filter A model that accomplishes the prediction, separation, or detection of a random signal.

graduation The process of securing, from an irregular series of observed values of a variable, a smooth, regular series of values consistent in a general way with the observed series of values.

index number A measure of the magnitude of a variable at one point relative to a value of the variable at another.

passive observation An observation of a quantity, influenced by a great many factors that, in two ways, cannot be controlled: it is not possible to insulate from those factors that fall outside the theoretical domain, and those factors falling within the theoretical domain cannot be manipulated systematically.

precise measurement A measurement in which the spread of the estimated measurement errors is a small as possible.

The strategies that have been developed in economics can and do play an important role in other social sciences, when there is a concern with building and estimating models of the interconnections between various sets in a predominantly nonexperimental situation. Accurate measurements are obtained by controlling the circumstances in which the measurements are taken. The lack of the possibilities of control in most cases studied in the social sciences necessitates a shift of the requirement of accuracy to the requirement of precision, which is a feature of the model. Widely used economic methods of measurement are reviewed here by discussing them in terms of how they deal with the problem of precision.

Introduction

To discuss and compare various measurement strategies in economics, it is helpful to have a framework to indicate more precisely the kinds of problems encountered in economics and the kinds of strategies developed to treat them. To make comparisons of these, at first sight, quite different strategies possible and transparent, the scope of these strategies is reduced to the common aim of finding the true values of the system variables, denoted by the $(K \times 1)$ vector x_t. (see Table I). Throughout this article it is assumed that these system variables are independent. Because all systems discussed are dynamic systems, t denotes a time index. For all strategies, it is assumed that x_t is not directly measurable. In general, the value of x_t is inferred from a set of available observations y_{ti} $(i = 1, \ldots, N)$, which always involve noise ε_{ti}:

$$y_{ti} = f(x_t) + \varepsilon_{ti}. \tag{1}$$

This equation will be referred to as the observation equation.

Some strategies of economic measurement require *a priori* knowledge about the performance of the vector x_t. The discussion will be limited to models in which the behavior of x_t follows a difference equation, called the system equation. In some cases, it is assumed that this equation is subject to random disturbances. To measure x_t, a model, denoted by M, has to be specified, of which the y_s vectors, $s \in T_t$, function as input and $\hat{x}_t$, the estimation of x_t, functions as output:

$$\hat{x}_t = M\big(y_s,\ s \in T_t;\ \ \alpha_1, \alpha_2, \ldots\big), \tag{2}$$

Table I Symbols

Symbol	*Description*
K	Number of system variables
N	Number of observations
t	Time index
x_t	$(K \times 1)$ vector of system variables
y_t	$(N \times 1)$ vector of observations
$\hat{x}_t$	Measurement of x_t
$\hat{x}_{t\mid t-1}$	Estimate of x_t made at time t using the information available up to time $t-1$
OC	Background conditions
M	Measurement model
T_t	Time domain relevant for the measurement of x_t
ε_t	$(N \times 1)$ vector of observation errors
η_t	$(K \times 1)$ vector of system noise
ε'_t	$(K \times 1)$ vector of measurement errors
ε^M_t	$(K \times 1)$ vector of estimated measurement errors
A_t	$(K \times N)$ matrix of model parameters (α_{tij})
H_t	$(N \times K)$ observation matrix
F_t	$(K \times K)$ system matrix
Q	Variance–covariance matrix of η_t
R	Variance–covariance matrix of ε_t (σ^2_{tij})
$\| \; \|$	Norm

where $\alpha_1, \alpha_2, \ldots$ are the parameters of the model. The set T_t is the time domain relevant for the measurement x_t and is determined by the purpose of the model. For example, if $T_t = \{1, \ldots, t-1\}$, the aim is prediction. The term "model" is used here in a very general sense; it includes various measuring devices in economics, such as econometric models, filters, and index numbers.

Substituting Eq. (1) into model M [Eq. (2)], it is possible to derive that (assuming that M is a linear operator)

$$\begin{aligned}\hat{x}_t &= M[f(x_s) + \varepsilon_s, \quad s \in T_t; \;\; \alpha_1, \alpha_2, \ldots] \\ &= M_x(x_s, s \in T_t; \;\; \alpha_1, \alpha_2, \ldots) \\ &\quad + M_\varepsilon(\varepsilon_s, s \in T_t; \;\; \alpha_1, \alpha_2, \ldots). \end{aligned} \tag{3}$$

A necessary condition for $\hat{x}_t$ to be a (indirect) measurement of x_t is that model M must be a representation of the observation equation [Eq. (1)], in the sense that it must specify how the observations are related to the values to be measured. This specification also implies a specification of the error term. A common feature of the strategies is that they all are developed to deal with the problem of taking measurements under circumstances that cannot be controlled. To explore this problem of (lack of) control, it is useful to rewrite Eq. (1) as an empirical relationship, f, between the observations y, the system variables x, and background conditions OC:

$$y = f(x, OC), \tag{4}$$

where OC represents "other circumstances" and the subscript t has been dropped for convenience. The observed quantities y can only provide information about the system variables, x, when these variables do influence the behavior of the y. To express more clearly how x and possible other factors (OC) influence the behavior of the observed quantities, the relationship is transformed into the following relation:

$$\Delta y = \Delta f(x, OC) = \sum_{i=1}^{K} \frac{\partial f}{\partial x_i} \Delta x_i + \frac{\partial f}{\partial OC} \Delta OC. \tag{5}$$

Comparing this relation with Eq. (1), it is easily seen that the second term, $\partial f / \partial OC \cdot \Delta OC$, is associated with the noise term, ε, that goes along with every observation.

To achieve reliable measurement results, the following problems have to be dealt with:

1. Invariance problem: $\partial f / \partial x_i$ is the element of Eq. (5) that expresses the relation between the observed quantity y and the ones to be measured, x_i. This element should be, as much as possible, invariant—that is to say, it has to remain stable or unchanged for, and to be independent of, two kinds of changes: variations over a wide range of the system variables, Δx_i, and variations over a wide range of the background conditions, ΔOC.

2. Error problem: $\hat{x}_t - x_t = \varepsilon'_t$ is the measurement error, the measurement result minus the true value of the measurand. The aim is to reduce this error term—in other words, to attain an accurate measurement. However, a true value is a value that would be obtained by a perfect measurement, so is by nature indeterminate. To deal with this error problem, the measurement error is split into two parts: $\varepsilon'_t = \hat{x}_t - M_x + M_x - x = M_\varepsilon + (M_x - x)$. Here M_ε is the estimated measurement error term $\varepsilon^M_t = M_\varepsilon\ (\varepsilon_s, s \in T_t; \alpha_1, \alpha_2, \ldots)$ and $M_x - x$ is the systematic error, which, like true value, cannot be completely known. Therefore, in practice, the aim is to reduce the error term ε^M_t as much as possible.

Invariance Problem

To find out about $\partial f / \partial x_i$ and whether it is stable for, and independent of, variations in x and other conditions, the aim, whenever possible, is to carry out controlled experiments. To simplify the notation, $\partial f / \partial x_i$ will from now on be denoted by f_{x_i}. The idea behind a controlled experiment is to create a specific environment, a laboratory, in which the relevant variables are manipulated in order to take measurements of particular parameters, with the aim to discover the relationship, if any, between these variables. In a laboratory, a selected set of factors would be artificially isolated from the other influences; in other words, care would be taken that *ceteris paribus*

(CP) conditions are imposed: $\Delta OC = 0$, so that a simpler relationship can be investigated:

$$\Delta y_{CP} = f_{x_1}\Delta x_1 + \cdots + f_{x_K}\Delta x_K. \quad (6)$$

By a systematic variation of x (assumed to be possible in a controlled experiment) and comparing this with the results, y, it is possible to find out about the nature of relationship between both:

$$f_{x_i} = \frac{\Delta y_{CP}}{\Delta x_i}, \quad \Delta x_j = 0 \quad (j \neq i). \quad (7)$$

The problem typically faced in economics is that real economic phenomena cannot be investigated insulated from other influences falling outside the theoretical domain, and by manipulating the relevant factors. Passive observations (*PO*) have to be dealt with, and these are influenced by a great many factors not accounted for in theory and which cannot be eliminated by creating a *ceteris paribus* environment. To clarify the nature of passive observations, Haavelmo made a helpful distinction between factual and potential influence. The factual influence of a quantity, say x_i, is defined as $f_{x_i}\,\Delta x_i$. A factor x_i has potential influence if f_{x_i} is significantly different from zero. What is passively observed is that a large part of the factors have a negligible influence, $f_{x_i}\Delta x_i \approx 0$, and that only a limited number of factors have a nonnegligible influence:

$$\Delta y_{PO} = f_{x_1}\Delta x_1 + \cdots + f_{x_K}\Delta x_K. \quad (8)$$

The problem, however, is that it is not possible to identify the reason for the factual influence of a factor, say $f_{x_{K+1}} \cdot \Delta x_{K+1}$, being negligible. It cannot be distinguished whether it has no potential influence, $f_{x_{K+1}} \approx 0$, or whether the factual variation of this factor over the period under consideration is too small, $\Delta x_{K+1} \approx 0$. In the first case, it is legitimate to discard this influence; in the latter case, it is not.

The variation of x_{K+1} might be determined by other relationships within the system. In some cases, a virtually dormant factor may become active because of changes in the economic system elsewhere. However, whether the potential influence of the relevant quantity is found to be significant and stable should be independent of structural changes elsewhere. This can be clarified by rewriting Eq. (5) as follows:

$$f_{x_i} = \frac{\Delta y}{\Delta x_i} - f_{OC}\frac{\Delta OC}{\Delta x_i}, \quad (9)$$

where it is assumed for convenience that, for a specific set of observations, the other $K-1$ factors were rather stable, i.e., $\Delta x_j \approx 0$ $(j \neq i)$. (This is of course not always the case, and then another set of problems has to be solved by the appropriate statistical techniques, but this discussion is beyond the scope of this article.) Equation (9) shows that in the case of passive observations, the nature of f_{x_i} can be determined only if the potential influence of changes elsewhere in the system is negligible, $f_{OC} \approx 0$. Then, the empirical determination of f_{x_i} is comparable with measurements in a *ceteris paribus* environment ($\Delta OC = 0$), expressed by Eq. (7). However, suppose it is found that f_{x_i} is stable for a certain set of observations because, for this set, the factual influence of the "other conditions," OC, is negligible. Then there is never certainty about for what reason the factual influence of the other conditions is negligible: $f_{OC} \approx 0$ or $\Delta OC \approx 0$. Thus, there will never be certainty as to whether the empirically determined f_{x_i} remains stable for another set of observations.

Error Problem

In general, it is desirable that the measurement results, $\hat{x}$, are accurate. Accuracy is a statement about the closeness of the agreement between the measurement results and the true values of the measurand. Closeness means that the results should be concentrated near the true value x in the sense of location and spread: It might be required that measurement results have their mean close to x (i.e., are unbiased) and have little spread (i.e., are precise). Precision is a statement about the closeness of the individual measurement results of the same measurement procedure. The difference between precision and unbiasedness is illustrated in Fig. 1 by an analogy of measurement with rifle shooting. A group of shots is precise when the shots lie close together. A group of shots is unbiased when it has its mean in the bull's-eye.

In an ideal laboratory, accurate measurements can be achieved by controlling the circumstances such that $\Delta OC = 0$. Then y would be an accurate measurement of x, in the sense that y is an observation of x without noise. Whenever it is not possible to control the circumstances, which is usually the case in economics, accurate

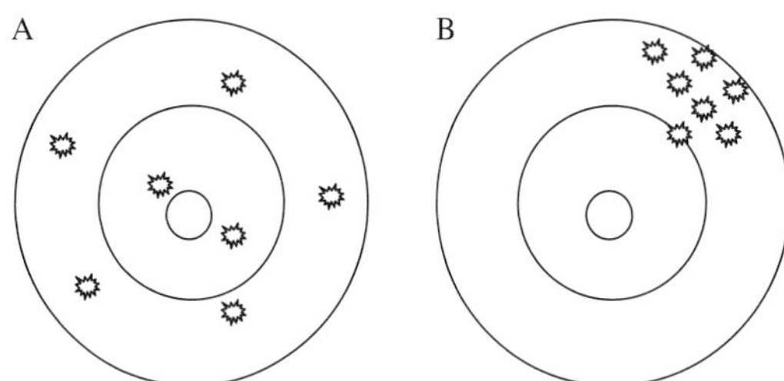

Figure 1 Rifle shooting illustrates the concepts of precision and unbiasedness. (A) The group is imprecise, but because the mean lies in the center, the group is unbiased. (B) A precise group of shots lies close together, but the group is not as unbiased as could be; the mean is not in the center. Adapted from Sydenham (1979).

measurement can be attempted by aiming at reduction of the estimated error term M_ε (ε_s, $s \in T_t$; $\alpha_1, \alpha_2, \ldots$). To simplify the discussion of accuracy, the custom in economics is to prefer linear models:

$$\hat{x}_t = \sum_{s \in T_t} A_s y_s, \tag{10}$$

where y_s is an $(N \times 1)$ vector of observations and $A_s = (\alpha_{sij})$ is a $(K \times N)$ matrix of model parameters. Substitution of the linearized version of the observation equation [Eq. (1)],

$$y_t = H_t x_t + \varepsilon_t, \tag{11}$$

where x_t is a $(K \times 1)$ vector of system variables, H_t is an $(N \times K)$ observation matrix, and ε_t is an $(N \times 1)$ vector of observation noise, into this model [Eq. (10)], obtains

$$\hat{x}_t = \sum_{s \in T_t} A_s H_s x_s + \sum_{s \in T_t} A_s \varepsilon_s. \tag{12}$$

For some approaches, *a priori* knowledge about the system is required. This means that sometimes a system equation must be specified:

$$x_t = \sum_{s \in T_t} (F_s x_s + \eta_s), \tag{13}$$

where F_s is a $(K \times K)$ system matrix and η_s is a $(K \times 1)$ vector of system noise.

To complete the model specification, assumptions about the noise terms η_t and ε_t are required. Their means and variance–covariance matrices may be written as follows:

$$Q = \text{Var}(\eta_t) = E\left[\eta_t\, \eta_t^T\right], \tag{14}$$

$$R = \text{Var}(\varepsilon_t) = E\left[\varepsilon_t\, \varepsilon_t^T\right]. \tag{15}$$

It is assumed that the system and observation noises have zero means:

$$E[\eta_t] = 0 \quad \text{and} \quad E[\varepsilon_t] = 0. \tag{16}$$

It is further assumed that the noise processes are not serially or cross-dependent; in particular,

$$E\left[\eta_t\, \eta_s^T\right] = 0, \quad E\left[\varepsilon_t\, \varepsilon_s^T\right] = 0, \quad t \neq s, \tag{17}$$

and

$$E\left[\eta_t\, \varepsilon_s^T\right] = 0 \qquad \text{for all } t, s. \tag{18}$$

In this linearized framework, accuracy is achieved by reducing the estimated measurement error term,

$$\varepsilon_t^M = \sum_{s \in T_t} A_s \varepsilon_s, \tag{19}$$

as much as possible, but at least the estimated measurement error is smaller than the observation error, $\varepsilon_t^M < \varepsilon_t$. In the strategies discussed next, this inequality will have different meanings. If not further specified, it means that $|E[\varepsilon_t^M]| < |E[\varepsilon_t]|$ (reducing unbiasedness), or $\text{Var}(\varepsilon_t^M) < \text{Var}(\varepsilon_t)$ (increasing precision). Because it is assumed that $E[\varepsilon_t] = 0$, accuracy will generally be obtained by aiming at precision—that is, reducing $\text{Var}(\varepsilon_t^M)$. In other words, most error-reducing strategies discussed herein are based on the principle of minimizing the squared error $\|\varepsilon_t^M \cdot \varepsilon_t^{M^T}\|$, where $\|\ \|$ is a norm that each strategy is defined in a specific way. Because unbiasedness is assumed, these strategies aim at precision.

An example of an old and very simple strategy to achieve accuracy is by taking the average. In this strategy, it is assumed that all errors taken together will nullify each other. Suppose that $y_i = x + \varepsilon_i$ $(i = 1, \ldots, N)$, then $\hat{x} = (1/N)\sum_{i=1}^N y_i$ is considered to be an accurate measurement of x because it is assumed that $\sum_{i=1}^N \varepsilon_i \approx 0$.

Econometric Modeling

In general, economists believe that theory can solve the problem of invariance; theory tells us which factors have potential influence and which do not. One of the reasons for believing this is that Haavelmo, who had advanced this problem, had pointed out the possibility that the empirically found relationships may be simpler than theory would suggest. This could lead researchers to discard potential influences that could explain shifts in these relationships.

A standard econometric textbook describes the basic task of econometrics: to put empirical flesh and blood on theoretical structures. This involves three steps of specification. First, the theory must be specified in explicit functional form. Second, the econometrician should decide on the appropriate data definitions and assemble the relevant data series for the variables that enter the model. The third step is to bridge theory and data by means of statistical methods. The bridge consists of various sets of statistics, which cast light on the validity of the theoretical model that has been specified. The most important set consists of the numerical estimates of the model parameters, A. Further statistics enable assessment of the precision with which these parameters have been estimated. There are still further statistics and diagnostic tests that help in assessing the performance of the model and in deciding whether to proceed sequentially by modifying the specification in certain directions and testing out the new variant of the model against the data.

Predictive Performance

With the generally shared belief among economists that theory functions as a reliable guide, one of the strategies of attaining precise measurement is the method of adding a variable, suggested by theory, to the model, each time the model predictions are not precise enough. In this strategy, two models, I and II, are compared with each other, and the one that provides the best predictions is chosen:

$$\text{Model I:}\quad \hat{x}^{\text{I}}_{t+1,i} = \sum_{s\leq t}\sum_{j=1}^{K}\alpha^{\text{I}}_{sij}y_{sj} \quad \text{and}$$

$$\varepsilon^{\text{I}}_{t+1,i} = \|y_{t+1,i} - \hat{x}^{\text{I}}_{t+1,i}\| \quad (i{:}\ 1,\ldots,K);$$

$$\text{Model II:}\quad \hat{x}^{\text{II}}_{t+1,i} = \sum_{s\leq t}\sum_{j=1}^{K+1}\alpha^{\text{II}}_{sij}y_{sj} \quad \text{and}$$

$$\varepsilon^{\text{II}}_{t+1,i} = \|y_{t+1,i} - \hat{x}^{\text{II}}_{t+1,i}\| \quad (i{:}\ 1,\ldots,K+1);$$

where each observation y_{sj} is a proxy variable of the unobservable x_{sj}, thus $N = K$ and $H_t = I$ (the identity matrix): $y_{sj} = x_{sj} + \varepsilon_{sj}$. If $\varepsilon^{\text{II}}_{t+1,i} < \varepsilon^{\text{I}}_{t+1,i}$ for the majority of these error terms (i: 1, ..., K), choose model II. Note that for each additional variable, the model is enlarged with an extra (independent) equation. As a result, the prediction errors are assumed to be reduced by taking into account more and more variables.

In this strategy, it assumed that the estimation techniques lead to the true system parameters: $A_t = F_t$.

$$x_{t+1} = \sum_{s\leq t}(A_s x_s + \eta_s) = \sum_{s\leq t}A_s x_s + \sum_{s\leq t}\eta_s$$

$$= \sum_{s\leq t}A_s x_s + \eta, \qquad (20)$$

where η represents all other quantities influencing the performance of x. Then, the estimated measurement error can be described as (dropping the time index for convenience):

$$\varepsilon^{\text{M}} = \hat{x} - \sum A_s x_s = \hat{x} - x + \eta = \hat{x} - y + \varepsilon + \eta, \quad (21)$$

or, in terms of prediction errors:

$$\|\varepsilon^{\text{M}}\| \leq \varepsilon^{\text{I}} + \|\varepsilon\| + \|\eta^{\text{I}}\|. \qquad (22)$$

Precision can now be obtained by improving prediction (reduction of ε^{I} to ε^{II}) by taking into account more economic variables and thus reducing the term $\|\eta^{\text{I}}\|$ to $\|\eta^{\text{II}}\|$. In this strategy, it is assumed that by building structural models that are as comprehensive as possible, preciseness can be achieved. However, this assumption has been attacked by empirical research showing that large-scale models failed to be better predicting devices, compared to very simple "naive models":

$$\text{Naive model I:}\quad \hat{x}^{\text{NI}}_{t+1,i} = y_{t,i};$$

$$\text{Naive model II:}\quad \hat{x}^{\text{NII}}_{t+1,i} = y_{ti} + \left(y_{ti} - y_{t-1,i}\right).$$

These two naive models belong to a more general class of autoregressive (AR) models and are used to study time series. Their naivety is that they are atheoretical. The better prediction performance of these simple models was a blow to forecasters who used large models. In defense of these results, builders of structural models have argued that at least with a structural model the source of forecasting errors is more easily identified. With naive models, forecast errors are just random events, and thus not very informative.

A consequence of these results is that applied modelers shifted their interest in macro modeling away from a whole economy, to parts of economic activities in which economic theories were relatively well developed. In this kind of empirical research, the strategy is to start with simple models and to investigate for which domain this model is an accurate description. In other words, empirical research is guided by the rule to search for those phenomena for which the estimated measurement error remains small or can even be made smaller. To illustrate how econometric research has changed due to the predictive failure of large-scale models, two opposite strategies are now discussed.

Zellner's Structural Econometric Modeling, Time-Series Analysis Approach

Zellner's structural econometric modeling, time-series analysis (SEMTSA) approach starts with selecting a key variable and modeling it as a simple, low-order autoregressive process, say of order three, denoted by AR(3):

$$y_{ti} = \alpha_{0i} + \alpha_{1i}y_{t-1,i} + \alpha_{2i}y_{t-2,i} + \alpha_{3i}y_{t-3,i} + \varepsilon^{\text{M}}_{ti}. \quad (23)$$

This simple model is improved each time in the direction indicated by all kinds of diagnostic checks on the forecasting properties of the model.

Hendry's General-to-Specific Modeling Strategy

Hendry's strategy is neatly summarized by Pagan, who also discusses two other competing econometric methodologies, as consisting of the following steps:

1. Formulate a general model that is consistent with what economic theory postulates are the relevant variables, and which restricts the dynamics of the process as little as possible:

$$y_{ti} = \sum_{s=1}^{p}\alpha_{si}y_{t-s,i} + \sum_{s=0}^{q}\sum_{\substack{j=1\\ j\neq i}}^{K}\alpha_{sj}y_{t-s,j}, \qquad (24)$$

where p and q are as large as practicable in view of the type of data.

2. Simplify the model to the smallest version that is compatible with the data. If it turns out that the data can be accounted for by a smaller set of $y_{t-s,j}$ variables, with the others being insignificant, then these others should be excluded.

3. Evaluate the resulting model by extensive analysis of residuals and predictive performance, aiming to find the weakness of the model designed in the previous step.

Calibration

A second alternative response to the preceding naive model results is to retain to the modeling a whole economy, nevertheless with simple models, but to change the strategy of achieving precision. This strategy can be captured by the term "calibration." The introduction of calibration techniques was also a response to the critique that the estimated econometric models could be interpreted as structural, i.e., the estimated parameters are invariant. Lucas published in 1976 a very influential paper in macroeconomics, showing that the estimated so-called structural parameters were not invariant under changes of policy rules. This put the problem of invariance back on the econometric research agenda.

The problem is that the system equations in the social sciences are often behavioral relationships. Lucas has emphasized that agents form expectations of the future and that these expectations play a crucial role in the economy because they influence the behavior of economic actors. People's expectations depend on many things, including the economic policies being pursued by the government. Thus, estimating the effect of a policy change requires knowing how people's expectations will respond to the policy change. Lucas has argued that the preceding estimation methods do not sufficiently take into account the influence of changing expectations on the estimated parameter values. Lucas assumed that economic agents have rational expectations—that is, the expectations are based on all information available at time t and the model M, is known, which they use to form these expectations.

The classic example is the so-called Philips curve, which describes a trade-off between inflation and employment. Assume that employment, y_t, and inflation, x_t, follow the relation

$$y_t = \alpha(x_t - \hat{x}_{t|t-1}) + \varepsilon_t, \tag{25}$$

where α is a positive constant and $\hat{x}_{t|t-1}$ denotes agents' rational expectations in period $t-1$, using information available in period $t-1$, about inflation in period t. Assume now that a given monetary policy results in the following stochastic process for inflation:

$$x_t = \bar{x} + \eta_t, \tag{26}$$

where $\bar{x}$ is a given constant average inflation rate. Then the expected inflation is given by $\hat{x}_{t|t-1} = \bar{x}$, and employment will fulfill

$$y_t = \alpha x_t - \alpha\bar{x} + \varepsilon_t. \tag{27}$$

This relation might be interpreted as showing a stable trade-off between inflation and employment to be used for policy aims. Policymakers may try to increase the employment level by an inflationary policy. This results in a new stochastic process for inflation,

$$x_t = \tilde{x} + \eta_t, \tag{28}$$

where $\tilde{x} > \bar{x}$. Now expected inflation is given by $\hat{x}_{t|t-1} = \tilde{x}$; inflation expectations are adjusted upward. Employment will obey

$$y_t = \alpha x_t - \alpha\tilde{x} + \varepsilon_t. \tag{29}$$

The Phillips curve will shift downward, and the policy would not work.

Structural parameters should be obtained in an alternative way. Either they could be supplied from microeconometric studies, accounting identities, or institutional facts, or they are chosen to secure a good match between the behavior of the actual macrodata and simulated data from the model along limited dimensions of interest. In general, calibration works as follows: use stable facts about a phenomenon to adjust the parameters to get as far as possible preciseness. Two different methods of obtaining parameter values are now considered: first, the method of simulated moments, and second, a method that comes down to gauging.

Method of Simulated Moments

The first method of calibration is a method of estimation, which entails simulating a model with ranges of parameters and selecting from these ranges those elements that best match properties of the simulated data with properties of historical data. In other words, this kind of calibration is a simulation-based estimation method—the operation of fitting model parameters to the observations. It is assumed that the observations' y_i values are measurements of x with error:

$$y_i = x + \varepsilon_i \quad (i \in N). \tag{30}$$

An often-used calibration criterion is to measure the difference between some empirical moments computed on the observed variables and its simulated counterpart. The estimator derived by calibrating some empirical moments based on observations and simulations is the so-called method of simulated moments (MSM) estimator. This kind of parameter estimation is based on the sample moments of some of the observable variables. These sample moments are represented by the $(L \times 1)$ vector of sample moments m_y, where m_y could include the sample means and variances of a selected set of observable variables. Here $m(A)$ is the $(L \times 1)$ vector of simulated moments—that is, the moments of the simulations $\hat{x}(A)$. Then the estimation of the parameters is based on

$$\hat{A}_{\mathrm{MSM}} = \arg\min_{A} \|m_y - m(A)\|. \tag{31}$$

Gauging

When some facts about one of the system components are known, the information can be used to adjust the model parameters. This strategy can be clarified by rewriting and simplifying Eq. (12) as a difference equation ($K = 1$):

$$\Delta\hat{x}_t = A\Delta x_t + A\Delta\varepsilon_t. \tag{32}$$

When there are circumstances in which it is expected that quantity x is stable ($\Delta x = 0$), the parameters of A can be adjusted such that $\Delta\hat{x} = A\Delta\varepsilon$ is as small as possible. However, preciseness attained for these circumstances does not guarantee an accurate result for other circumstances, though preciseness for specific circumstances does argue for the validity of results for other circumstances.

Methods of Graduation

London has defined graduation as the process of securing, from an irregular series of observed values of a continuous variable, a smooth regular series of values consistent in a general way with the observed series of values. This method assumes that some underlying law gave rise to an irregular sequence of values, that these should be revised, and that the revised sequence should be taken as a representation of the underlying law. There are two main classes of graduation methods: the moving weighted average method and the Whittaker–Henderson method.

Moving Weighted Average Method

The moving weighted average (MWA) method determines a graduated value by taking a weighted average of a certain number of consecutive observed values. The basic formula is as follows:

$$\hat{x}_t = \sum_{s=-m}^{m} \alpha_s y_{t+s}. \tag{33}$$

In most cases, the MWA formulas are symmetric: $\alpha_s = \alpha_{-s}$. Each observation is assumed to consist of a true component and an error component:

$$y_t = x_t + \varepsilon_t. \tag{34}$$

Substituting Eq. (34) into Eq. (33) obtains

$$\hat{x}_t = \sum_{s=-m}^{m} \alpha_s x_{t+s} + \sum_{s=-m}^{m} \alpha_s \varepsilon_{t+s}. \tag{35}$$

The problem is to find α_s so that x_t is reproduced,

$$x_t = \sum_{s=-m}^{m} \alpha_s x_{t+s}, \tag{36}$$

and the residual error, which is

$$\varepsilon_t^{\mathrm{MWA}} = \sum_{s=-m}^{m} \alpha_s \varepsilon_{t+s}, \tag{37}$$

is substantially smaller than ε_t, the observation error component of y_t. The assumption used in this method is that the sequence x_t over the limited range $[t-m, t+m]$ is closely represented by a low-degree polynomial, such as a cubic. This assumption leads to a first set of conditions that the α_s values should satisfy. The second set of conditions is derived from reducing the residual estimated measurement error. Because it is assumed that y_t is unbiased, then $\varepsilon_t^{\mathrm{MWA}}$ given by the MWA method is also unbiased, so that $E[\varepsilon_t^{\mathrm{MWA}}] = 0$. Thus there is no merit in trying to minimize estimated residual error. Instead, the estimated squared model error, $E[(\varepsilon_t^{\mathrm{MWA}})^2]$, which is the variance of the model error, $\mathrm{Var}(\varepsilon_t^{\mathrm{MWA}})$, is minimized. But because $\hat{x}_t = x_t + \varepsilon_t^{\mathrm{MWA}}$, it follows that $\mathrm{Var}(\varepsilon_t^{\mathrm{MWA}}) = \mathrm{Var}(\hat{x}_t)$. Note that this is based on an assumed polynomial form for x_t. If it is assumed that each observation error has the same variance, σ^2, Eq. (38) can be can derived:

$$\mathrm{Var}(\hat{x}_t) = \sigma^2 \sum_{-m}^{m} \alpha_s^2. \tag{38}$$

Defining

$$R_0^2 = \sum_{-m}^{m} \alpha_s^2, \tag{39}$$

it can now be said that the coefficients α_s sought for Eq. (33) are those that minimize R_0^2 and satisfy the polynomial form constraints. An MWA formula with coefficients so derived is called a minimum-R_0 formula.

Because $\mathrm{Var}(y_t) = \mathrm{Var}(\varepsilon_t) = \sigma^2$, then it follows that

$$R_0^2 = \frac{\mathrm{Var}(\hat{x}_t)}{\mathrm{Var}(y_t)}. \tag{40}$$

In other words, R_0^2 is a ratio of variance. Unfortunately, graduations using the minimum-R_0 formula seldom prove to be satisfactory, frequently resulting in neither good fit nor an acceptable degree of smoothness. For practical criteria of fit and smoothness, a generalization of the minimum-R_0 formula is preferred. The ratio being minimized is

$$R_z^2 = \frac{\mathrm{Var}(\Delta^z \hat{x}_t)}{\mathrm{Var}(\Delta^z y_t)}. \tag{41}$$

As in the $z = 0$ case, it can be derived that

$$\mathrm{Var}(\Delta^z \hat{x}_t) = \sigma^2 \sum_{-m-z}^{m} (\Delta^z \alpha_s)^2. \tag{42}$$

The uncorrelated and equivariance assumptions lead to

$$\mathrm{Var}(\Delta^z y_t) = \binom{2z}{z}\sigma^2. \quad (43)$$

The R_z^2 can be interpreted as the rate of roughness in $\hat{x}_t$ to that in y_t, as measured in the zth order of differences. If it is desired that $\hat{x}_t$ is smoother than y_t, it is preferred to find that $R_z^2 < 1$. R_z is the "smoothing coefficient" of the MWA formula.

Whittaker–Henderson Method

According to the Whittaker–Henderson method, graduation should be such that two criteria are taken into account. First, the graduated values should not deviate overly much from the original observed values. This criterion is referred to as "fit." A numerical measure of fit might be defined as follows:

$$\mathrm{Fit} = \sum_s w_s(\hat{x}_s - y_s)^2, \quad (44)$$

where the w_s values indicate the weights. Second, it is assumed that the underlying law is smooth, regular, and continuous. So, to get a better representation of the underlying law, "smoothness" is the second criterion at which the graduation should aim. A numerical measure of smoothness might be defined as follows:

$$\mathrm{Smo} = \sum_s (\Delta^z \hat{x}_s)^2, \quad (45)$$

where parameter z establishes the degree of polynomial $(z-1)$ inherently being used as a standard of smoothness.

The Whittaker–Henderson method adopts the numerical measures of fit and smoothness defined by Eqs. (44) and (45), and combines them linearly to produce Eq. (46):

$$G = \mathrm{Fit} + \lambda\mathrm{Smo} = \sum_s w_s(\hat{x}_s - y_s)^2 + \lambda \sum_s (\Delta^z \hat{x}_s)^2. \quad (46)$$

The minimization of Eq. (46) is referred to as a Type B Whittaker–Henderson graduation; a Type A graduation is the special case of Eq. (46) in which $w_s = 1$ for all s.

When $\lambda = 0$, then, because $\mathrm{Fit} \geq 0$, G is minimized at $\mathrm{Fit} = 0$, which implies $\hat{x}_s = y_s$ for all s, the no-graduation case. Thus, in general, as λ approaches 0, $\hat{x}_s$ approaches y_s, and fit is emphasized over smoothness. Conversely, as λ is set very large, the minimization process inherently emphasizes Smo to overcome the influence of the large λ. This, in the limiting case, constrains $\hat{x}_s$ toward the least-squares polynomial of degree $z-1$, thereby reducing the magnitude of Smo, and securing a least-squares fit.

Type A with the linear trend as the standard of smoothness $(z = 2)$ is in macroeconomics better known as the Hodrick–Prescott filter. The observed time series, y_t, is viewed as the sum of a cyclical component, c_t, and a growth component, g_t. This filter has been widely adopted in current business cycle literature to make the business cycle visible.

Kalman Filter

A handbook definition of Kalman filtering is a method of predicting the behavior of a signal x_t given observations y_t that are subject to error ε_t, so that $y_t = H_t x_t + \varepsilon_t$. The term filtering refers to the removal as much as possible of the error term ε_t to give a prediction of the true signal x_t. A prerequisite to the application of the Kalman filter is that the behavior of the system under study be described by a system equation:

$$x_{t+1} = F_t x_t + \eta_t. \quad (47)$$

Let $\hat{x}_{t|t-1}$ denote an estimate of x_t based on an estimate of x_{t-1}, where the subscript $t|t-1$ denotes the estimate made at time t using the information available up to time $t-1$, and assume for a moment that this estimate is available. A new measurement y_t now becomes available; this constitutes an estimate of x_t but it is, of course, subject to noise. To obtain the best unbiased linear estimate of x_t, a weighted linear sum of the two available estimates is formed to yield

$$\hat{x}_{t|t} = L_t \hat{x}_{t|t-1} + K_t y_t, \quad (48)$$

where L_t and K_t are time-varying weighting matrices to be specified by imposing on the filter the conditions that the estimate of the system variables at each time point should be unbiased and of minimal variance.

The condition of unbiasedness is first imposed. If the measurement errors of the system variables are defined as

$$\varepsilon'_{t|t} = \hat{x}_{t|t} - x_t \quad \text{and} \quad \varepsilon'_{t|t-1} = \hat{x}_{t|t-1} - x_t, \quad (49)$$

then $\hat{x}_{t|t}$, $\hat{x}_{t|t-1}$, and y_t can be replaced in Eq. (48) to give

$$\varepsilon'_{t|t} = [L_t + K_t H_t - I]x_t + L_t \varepsilon'_{t|t-1} + K_t \varepsilon_t, \quad (50)$$

where I is the identity matrix. By definition $E[\varepsilon_t] = 0$, and if $E[\varepsilon'_{t|t-1}] = 0$, the updated estimator will be unbiased; that is $E[\varepsilon'_{t|t}] = 0$, if the quantity $[L_t + K_t H_t - I] = 0$. An unbiased estimate of x_t is therefore ensured by having

$$L_t = I - K_t H_t, \quad (51)$$

which, when substituted into Eq. (48), gives

$$\hat{x}_{t|t} = \hat{x}_{t|t-1} + K_t[y_t - H_t \hat{x}_{t|t-1}], \quad (52)$$

with corresponding estimation error

$$\varepsilon'_{t|t} = [I - K_t H_t]\varepsilon'_{t|t-1} + K_t \varepsilon_t. \quad (53)$$

Equation (52) gives the relation between the updated estimate $\hat{x}_{t|t}$ and the previous estimate $\hat{x}_{t|t-1}$. It may be written in the form

$$\hat{x}_{t|t} = \hat{x}_{t|t-1} + K_t \nu_t, \tag{54}$$

in which the weighting matrix K_t is referred to as the Kalman gain, and the quantity

$$\nu_t = y_t - H_t \hat{x}_{t|t-1} \tag{55}$$

is referred to as the filter innovation, because it represents the new information incorporated in the observation y_t, which is potentially of use in estimating x_t. The Kalman gain clearly plays a crucial role in the operation of the filter, and so an optimum choice of K_t is clearly desirable to ensure a minimum variance estimate of the state x_t.

To describe the uncertainty in the measurements of the system variables, the variance–covariance matrices of $\varepsilon'_{t|t}$ and $\varepsilon'_{t|t-1}$ are required; these are defined as follows:

$$P_{t|t} = \mathrm{Var}(\varepsilon'_{t|t}) = E[\varepsilon'_{t|t}\varepsilon'^{T}_{t|t}] \quad \text{and}$$
$$P_{t|t-1} = \mathrm{Var}(\varepsilon'_{t|t-1}) = E[\varepsilon'_{t|t-1}\varepsilon'^{T}_{t|t-1}]. \tag{56}$$

By minimizing the variances of the measurement errors ε', thus by minimizing the variances of $\hat{x}$, the optimum choice of the Kalman gain K_t is obtained:

$$K_t = P_{t|t-1}H_t^T\left[H_t P_{t|t-1} H_t^T + R\right]^{-1}. \tag{57}$$

Then,

$$P_{t|t} = [I - K_t H_t]P_{t|t-1}, \tag{58}$$

which is the variance–covariance matrix of the measurement errors corresponding to the optimum value of K_t given by Eq. (57). This equation also provides a convenient computational means of updating the variance–covariance matrix of the system variables to take account of the observation made at time t.

In accord with Eq. (47), the forecast at time t of the state at time $t+1$ is taken to be

$$\hat{x}_{t+1|t} = F_t \hat{x}_{t|t}. \tag{59}$$

By subtracting the system Eq. (47) from this, the error of prediction, $\varepsilon'_{t+1|t}$, is obtained as

$$\varepsilon'_{t+1|t} = F_t \varepsilon'_{t|t} + \eta_t, \tag{60}$$

from which the variance–covariance matrix $P_{t+1|t}$ of the prediction error can be derived as

$$P_{t+1|t} = F_t P_{t|t} F_t^T + Q. \tag{61}$$

The recursive cycle of filter operations may be summarized as follows (see Fig. 2): given an observation at time t, calculate the innovation vector ν_t [Eq. (55)], the Kalman gain K_t [Eq. (57)], the filtered or updated state vector $\hat{x}_{t|t}$ [Eq. (54)], and the updated state error covariance matrix $P_{t|t}$ [Eq. (58)].

Index Numbers

An index number measures the magnitude of a variable at a point relative to its value at another point. Here, the limit is to comparisons over time. The values of the variable are compared with the value during a reference base period

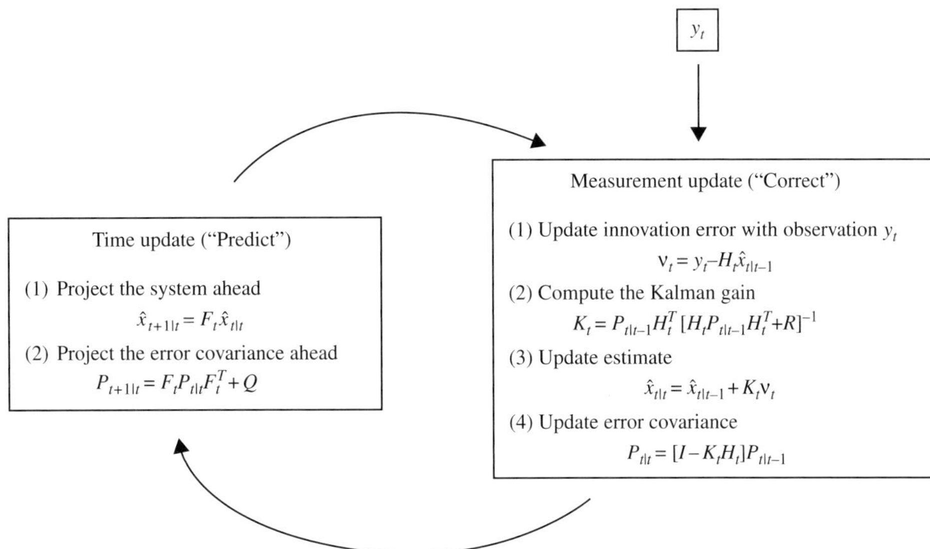

Figure 2 The recursive Kalman filter cycle. Adapted from Welch and Bishop (2002).

around, say, t_0. The index number may be phrased as follows. Suppose there are observations (usually prices) at two points of time, y_t and y_0. The ratios y_{ti}/y_{0i} could be considered as elements having a certain distribution, the central measure of which is sought:

$$\frac{y_{ti}}{y_{0i}} = x_{0t} + \varepsilon_{0ti}. \tag{62}$$

Then x_{0t} is measured by taking a weighted arithmetic, harmonic, or geometric average over the ratios. To simplify the discussion, only arithmetic averages are considered:

$$\hat{x}_{0t} = \sum_{i=1}^{N} \alpha_i \left(\frac{y_{ti}}{y_{0i}}\right). \tag{63}$$

By choosing the weights α_i in different ways, it is possible to arrive at many types of indexes. The problem is how to combine the relative changes y_{ti}/y_{0i} (i.e., to choose the most appropriate weight system) into a single measure that can be interpreted as a measure of the relative change in the aggregate level of the y values.

In economics, index numbers are most often discussed in terms of a consumer price index. The object is to measure the changes in the cost of living of a person. Therefore, it is necessary to define a utility function, U, which is associated with every combination of quantities of goods, q, that is under consideration. The person chooses the set of quantities that minimizes the cost of achieving at least a given utility u. The cost function C is defined as the solution to this minimization problem:

$$C(u, y_t) \equiv \min_q \{y_t \cdot q_t : U(q_t) \geq u\}. \tag{64}$$

Then the cost of living index is defined as follows:

$$x_{0t}(u) = \frac{C(u, y_t)}{C(u, y_0)}. \tag{65}$$

If U is known, the cost function C can be constructed and thus the cost of living index $x_{0t}(u)$. However, generally, U is not known. Thus $x_{0t}(u)$ is estimated by developing bounds that depend on observable price and quantity data but do not depend on the specific functional form of U. To obtain these bounds, it is assumed that the observed quantity vectors for the two periods, q_i ($i = t$, 0) are solutions to the cost minimization problems; i.e., assume

$$y_i \cdot q_i = C(u_i, y_i). \tag{66}$$

There are now two natural choices for the reference quantity vector q that can be used in the weight system of index number Eq. (63). The Laspeyres index, $\hat{x}_{0t}^{\mathrm{L}}$, is defined as $y_t q_0 / y_0 q_0$ (thus $\alpha_i^{\mathrm{L}} = y_{0i} q_{0i} / \sum_{j=1}^{N} y_{0j} q_{0j}$) and the Paasche index, $\hat{x}_{0t}^{\mathrm{P}}$, is defined as $y_t q_t / y_0 q_t$ (thus $\alpha_i^{\mathrm{P}} = y_{0i} q_{ti} / \sum_{j=1}^{N} y_{0j} q_{tj}$). Under the assumption of cost-minimizing behavior [Eq. (66)], both indexes provide the following bounds:

$$\begin{aligned} \hat{x}_{0t}^{\mathrm{L}} &\geq x_{0t}(u_0), \\ \hat{x}_{0t}^{\mathrm{P}} &\leq x_{0t}(u_t). \end{aligned} \tag{67}$$

If a reference vector $q \equiv \lambda x_0 + (1 - \lambda) x_t$ is chosen, and it can be shown that there exists a λ between 0 and 1 such that $\hat{x}_{0t}^{\mathrm{P}} \leq \hat{x}_{0t}^{\mathrm{L}}$, then

$$\hat{x}_{0t}^{\mathrm{P}} \leq x_{0t}(u_\lambda) \leq \hat{x}_{0t}^{\mathrm{L}}, \tag{68}$$

or if $\hat{x}_{0t}^{\mathrm{P}} > \hat{x}_{0t}^{\mathrm{L}}$, then

$$\hat{x}_{0t}^{\mathrm{L}} \leq x_{0t}(u_\lambda) \leq \hat{x}_{0t}^{\mathrm{P}}. \tag{69}$$

The bounds given by Eqs. (67)–(69) are the best bounds that can be obtained without making further assumptions on U. In the time series context, the bounds given by Eqs. (68) and (69) are quite satisfactory: the Paasche and Laspeyres price indexes for consecutive time periods will usually differ by less than 1%, thus the measurement error ε' is smaller than 1%.

See Also the Following Articles

Quantitative Analysis, Economics • Time-Series–Cross-Section Data • Weighting

Further Reading

Gouriéroux, C., and Monfort, A. (1996). *Simulated-Based Econometric Methods.* Oxford University Press, Oxford.

Haavelmo, T. (1944). The probability approach in econometrics. *Econometrica* **12**(suppl).

Hodrick, R., and Prescott, E. (1997). Postwar U.S. business cycles: An empirical investigation. *J. Money Credit Banking* **29,** 1–16.

Jazairi, N. (1983). Index numbers. In *Encyclopedia of Statistical Sciences* (S. Kotz and N. Johnson, eds.), Vol. IV, pp. 54–62.

Johnston, J. (1984). *Econometric Methods.* McGraw-Hill, Singapore.

London, D. (1985). *Graduation: The Revision of Estimates.* ACTEX, Winsted, Connecticut.

Lucas, R. (1976). Econometric policy evaluation: A critique. In *The Phillips Curve and Labor Markets* (K. Brunner and A. Meltzer, eds.), pp. 19–46. North-Holland, Amsterdam.

O'Connell, P. (1984). Kalman filtering. In *Handbook of Applicable Mathematics* (W. Ledermann and E. Lloyd, eds.), Vol. VI, pp. 897–938.

Pagan, A. (1987). Three econometric methodologies: A critical appraisal. *J. Econ. Surveys* **1,** 3–24.

Sydenham, P. (1979). *Measuring Instruments: Tools of Knowledge and Control.* Peter Peregrinus, Stevenage.

Welch, G., and Bishop, G. (2002). *An Introduction to the Kalman Filter.* Available on the Internet at http://www.cs.unc.edu

Zellner, A. (1994). Time-series analysis, forecasting and econometric modelling: The structural econometric modelling, time-series analysis (SEMTSA) approach. *J. Forecast.* **13,** 215–233.

Edgeworth, Francis Ysidro

Andrew I. Dale
University of KwaZulu-Natal, Durban, South Africa

Glossary

calculus of variations The calculus concerned in general with the choice of a function so as to maximize (or minimize) the value of a certain integral. An example is finding a curve that joins two fixed points in a plane with the minimum distance.

contract curves As introduced by Edgeworth, a mathematical investigation into the degree to which matters such as utility functions and boundary conditions restrict the possibility of exchanges between people.

hedonism An ethical theory of conduct whose criterion is pleasure. Such happiness, however, is nowadays seen as that of society rather than that of an individual person.

index numbers Numbers used in the measurement of things such as relative price levels and the changes in price levels. They can be calculated over months or even years, attention being focused on their variation in time or space.

subjective probabilities The numerical representation an individual's own beliefs in the chances of occurrence of events.

utility A number indicating a thing's value or the numerical representation of individuals' preferences.

Francis Ysidro Edgeworth's writings ranged from comments on Matthew Arnold's interpretation of Butler to the statistical law of error, including items as different as the theory of banking, the behavior of wasps, examination statistics, index numbers, utility, and the theory of correlation and of the multivariate normal distribution. Edgeworth made important contributions to the moral sciences, economics, probability, and statistics. He was, in the best sense of the word, a scholar.

Genealogy

Francis Ysidro Edgeworth, born on February 8, 1845, in Edgeworthstown, County Longford, Ireland, was a member of a family distinguished in both the arts and the sciences. The family's social circle included the luminaries Jeremy Bentham, Sir William Rowan Hamilton, Sir John Herschel, Thomas Malthus, David Ricardo, and Sir Walter Scott.

His paternal grandfather, Richard Lovell Edgeworth (1744–1817), was deeply interested in mechanical science. This interest manifested itself materially in inventions that resulted in his being awarded both silver and gold medals by the Society for the Encouragement of Arts; a Fellowship in the Royal Society followed in 1781. He also wrote several works on education, a number in collaboration with his eldest daughter Maria, who was perhaps better known as a successful novelist.

Richard's boundless energy was not entirely dissipated on machinery. He married four times (once more than his own father, Francis) and had 22 children in just under half a century. Such fecundity naturally resulted in a breadth of close connections, and the Edgeworths were related to both scientific and humanitarian notables, for example, Sir Francis Galton, Sir George Gabriel Stokes, Thomas Lovell Beddoes, and (more distantly) the Abbè Henry Essex Edgeworth De Firmont, confessor to Louis XVI.

But just as a surfeit often prompts a desire to dine with Duke Humphrey, so excessive fertility in one generation is often followed, at least in the human species, by a decline in the perpetuating passion in a later one, and the death of Francis Ysidro on February 13, 1926, saw the extinction of the male Edgeworth line in Europe.

Francis Ysidro's father, Francis Beaufort, was the son of Richard and his last wife, Frances Anne Beaufort (whose brother invented the Beaufort scale). At the relatively young age of 22, Francis Beaufort married the 16-year-old Catalan refugee Rosa Florentina Eroles. After some time in Florence and an unsuccessful attempt at running a private educational establishment near London, the couple returned to the family estate in

Ireland, and here Francis Ysidro (registered at birth as Ysidro Francis) was born some 18 months before his father's death during the Irish famine.

Education and Career

Privately taught until he was 17, Francis Ysidro had his first taste of higher learning at Trinity College, Dublin. Here he studied classics with marked success for some 5 years before being transferred to Oxford (first Magdalen Hall and later Balliol College), where he took a First in *Literae Humaniores*. He then moved to London and was called to the bar by the Inner Temple in 1877; he never practiced, although he did describe himself as a barrister-at-law in some of his early writings.

His formal training in mathematics having apparently been somewhat rudimentary, Edgeworth spent some time while studying for the bar in furthering himself in this discipline. His first book, *New and Old Methods of Ethics,* was published during this period.

Edgeworth occupied various lecturing positions in logic in the capital before accepting a lectureship in that subject at King's College, London, in 1880. He was appointed Tooke Professor of Political Economy at King's in 1890 and succeeded Thorold Rogers as Drummond Professor of Political Economy at Oxford in 1891.

Edgeworth's Works

Edgeworth's work is neither easily nor comfortably compartmentalized; even Edgeworth himself, in preparing his *Papers Relating to Political Economy* for publication, admitted to difficulty in classifying his economics papers appropriately (he ended up placing them in the following sections: value-and-distribution, monopoly, money, international trade, taxation, mathematical economics, and reviews). The early work in ethics (and mathematics) flowed naturally into that in economics and that in turn gave rise to the work in probability and statistics.

Writers on Edgeworth have usually, at least until relatively recently, made much of the difficulty and obscurity of his style, qualities that to a large extent have been responsible for the comparative neglect (which Stigler's 1978 paper did a great deal to remove) of his work. Part of the problem lies in his terminology and notation. For example, in considering a random variable X having a normal distribution with

$$P[a \leq X \leq b] = \frac{1}{\sqrt{2\pi\sigma^2}} \int_a^b \exp[-(x-\mu)^2/(2\sigma^2)]\, dx$$

he uses "fluctuation" for twice the variance (our $2\sigma^2$), "modulus" for its square root, "precision" for the reciprocal of the modulus, and "weight" for the reciprocal of the fluctuation. As Bowley has noted, "In the individual papers the mathematical style varies from complete lucidity to very involved work set out verbally and with insufficient explanation of terms." And somewhat more poetically Keynes writes, as only he can, of Edgeworth's "building up his lofty constructions with beautiful bricks but too little mortar and no clear architectural design."

To be perfectly frank, Edgeworth's writings, while undeniably important, are often thin in both rigor and detail. Classical allusions abound, and a dry wit is often glimpsed lurking among some mathematical details. Edgeworth had no compunction about the use of Latin and Greek quotations in his work; indeed, in the introductory description to the 1925 reprint of his 1890 presidential address to Section F (Economics) of the British Association he in fact wrote, "Mathematics are described as a useful, though not an indispensable adjunct to economic studies; a finish to the training of an economist comparable with a knowledge of the Classics as part of a general education." Difficult though it may be, however, the perseverator will find the time spent in reading Edgeworth both profitable and pleasurable, not only as regards the statistical and economic gems to be found, but also for the insight into the character of the author himself.

In 1877, *New and Old Methods of Ethics* was published. Here, in one of the first books to use the calculus of variations in the social sciences, Edgeworth began the development of his hedonical calculus. Here too we find the assertion that quantification of pleasure does not necessarily require precise numerical values; Edgeworth's version of utility called merely for a mathematical ordering, a similar notion being used profitably by Keynes in his *A Treatise of Probability* of 1921 (although, while Edgeworth asserted that all pleasures are commensurable, Keynes did certainly not accept that such was true of probabilities).

Economics

Edgeworth's first contribution to political economy, *Mathematical Psychics: An Essay on the Application of Mathematics to the Moral Sciences*, was published in 1881. Containing the application of mathematical techniques to economics and sociology, this work may be seen as an extension of the *New and Old Methods of Ethics*. Here Edgeworth not only presented, for the first time, his contract curves, but also declared his intent to attempt to "illustrate the possibility of Mathematical reasoning without *numerical* data . . . ; without more precise data than are afforded by estimates of *quantity of pleasure*." He also suggested an analogy between the "*Principles of Greatest Happiness*, Utilitarian or Egoistic" and the

"*Principles of Maximum Energy* which are among the highest generalizations of Physics."

Later in the book the "greatest possible happiness" is defined as "the greatest possible integral of the differential 'Number of enjoyers × duration of enjoyment × degree thereof.' " Here we see an early occurrence of the modern decision theorist's principle "Maximize expected utility."

Whether the book would be incontrovertibly received today is debatable. Sentiments such as (1) "Equality is not the whole of distributive justice" and (2) "Concerning the classification of future society, common sense anticipates no utopia of equality" may perhaps be unacceptable to those whose zeal outstrips their reason. Nevertheless, there is much to be read, marked, learned, and inwardly digested here.

Three notable papers on economics were published in the 1890s. In the first of these, "The Pure Theory of International Values" (1894), Edgeworth restates the first principles of the subject, both classically and mathematically, and then offers criticism of other writers on the matter. In the second, "The Pure Theory of Taxation" (1897), he discusses the incidence of taxes and "the rule according to which the burden of taxation ought to be distributed among the tax-payers." He concludes by advocating minimum aggregate sacrifice as the criterion of good taxation. The third paper, "The Pure Theory of Monopoly" (1897), is concerned with the incidence of taxation in a monopolistic regime dealing with competitive individuals.

Bowley draws special attention to Edgeworth's important work on index numbers. In his 1887 paper "Measurement of Change in Value of Money," Edgeworth proposed to define the meaning and measure the magnitude of variations in the value of money. Given the prices of commodities and the quantities purchased at different times, it required incorporating these data into one formula that would represent the appreciation or depreciation of money.

In 1925, scarcely a year before Edgeworth's death, the Royal Economic Society published a three-volume collection of his writings on political economy (a subject that Edgeworth described in his "The Philosophy of Chance" of 1884 as "an arbitrarily selected fragment of the Calculus of Hedonics"). The choice of papers reprinted was the author's own, and he took the opportunity afforded him by the Society to avail himself of a number of alterations, including changes in titles.

Probability and Statistics

Edgeworth's third book, *Metretike, or the Method of Measuring Probability and Utility*, was published in 1887; the main purpose of this work was the finding of a technique for the determination of probability and utility. Here Edgeworth presented utilitarian arguments in favor of equality contrasted with an approach using probability and discussed the connection between assumptions of equal frequency and those of equal utility. Edgeworth was perhaps not altogether successful in what he attempted to do here, although he concluded by writing "There is established then, upon a rough yet sufficiently sure basis, the calculation both of Probability and Utility; and the more fundamental of these is Utility."

In his obituary for Edgeworth, Keynes wrote, "[*Metretike*] is a disappointing volume and not much worth reading (a judgment with which I know that Edgeworth himself concurred)." Although Keynes may have been right in his statement, later work by F. P. Ramsey in the 1920s showed the fecundity of Edgeworth's ideas; however, the simultaneous axiomatization of probability and utility had to wait until L. J. Savage's work in the 1950s. The statistician may be interested to note that we also find here something similar to R. A. Fisher's advocation of the rejection of a hypothesis if an observation equal to or greater than some specified value is obtained.

Edgeworth's early thoughts on probability, prompted by John Venn's *The Logic of Chance*, were published in his "The Philosophy of Chance" in *Mind* in 1884. Here he examines the "metaphysical roots rather than the mathematical branches of the science." Probability is described as "importing partial incomplete belief"; also, "the object of the calculus is probability as estimated by statistical uniformity."

In 1922, in a paper again in *Mind* and with the same title as that just discussed, Edgeworth gave his final thoughts on probabilities, this time in response to Keynes's *A Treatise on Probability*. Here he makes the important observation, often ignored by modern writers, that there are applications in which "the use of *à priori* probabilities has no connexion with inverse probability." Here he also discusses some objections to commonly made assumptions about *a priori* probability and shows that these are of little practical importance in the theory of errors. Once again he notes that the effects of the *a priori* probabilities are very often masked by evidence conveyed by observations when the latter are sufficiently numerous.

Another of Edgeworth's wide-ranging and important papers is his article on probability published in the 11th edition of the *Encyclopædia Britannica*. This article, a summary not only of Edgeworth's original work but also of that of other statisticians, covers topics such as the probability of causes and future effects, the measurability of credibility, the binomial distribution, the rule of succession, Buffon's needle problem, the normal law of error and other laws, regression, and correlation. We find here too, in his discussion of prior probabilities, the statement "in general the reasoning does not require the a priori probabilities of the different values to be very nearly equal; it suffices that they should not be very unequal." Compare the modern Bayesian requirement that a prior probability density (in certain circumstances) should be relatively flat in a region where the likelihood is considerable.

Edgeworth published papers on the law of error over a period of 40 years. In the first of these, "The Law of Error," published in 1883, he shows quite cogently that nonexponential laws of error do in fact occur in nature (perhaps, more accurately, that they occur on very much the same hypotheses as do exponential ones). This paper contains the first explication of the Edgeworth series (a series providing an expansion of a continuous density in terms of the normal density). There is also work on the method of translation, which, crudely put, is concerned with the finding of probability laws for observations that are not normally distributed but are functions of a normally distributed variable.

As time passed, Edgeworth perhaps grew less interested in probability and more interested in statistics. This Keynes attributes to an increased skepticism toward philosophical foundations combined with a pragmatic attitude toward the practical applications that rested on these foundations.

Edgeworth's most important statistical paper was perhaps the 1885 "Methods of Statistics," a paper whose principal aim was "the practical application of the Law of Error." Not inconsiderable theoretical discussion is followed by examples pertaining to (1) anthropometry; (2) births, deaths, and marriages; and (3) miscellaneous matters, including such recondite items as bankruptcies in the second months in each quarter, the statistics of a wasp's nest, fluctuation in the attendance at a club dinner, and numbers of dactyls in the hexameter as a criterion of Virgil's style. Early versions of hypothesis tests may be found here.

Applications

The third volume of McCann's 1996 collection is devoted to Edgeworth's papers on applications in economics, the social sciences, physics, chemistry, biology, education (mainly to do with examinations, and perhaps sometimes carried out with his paternal grandfather and aunt in mind), and psychical research. Even this classification by no means covers all the topics; there is a paper detailing the behavior of various species of hymenoptera, based on observations made over 11 years, and a single paper is concerned with matters as widespread as bimetallism, bees, and "the preponderance of one sex in our nurseries and one party in our parliaments." We also find in the more applied papers contributions to analysis of variance, stochastic models, multivariate analysis, and (multiple) correlation.

Conclusion

Edgeworth occupied various honorable positions in learned societies; he was, at various times, president of Section F (Economics) of the British Association for the Advancement of Science, president of the Royal Statistical Society, vice-president of the Royal Economic Society, and a fellow of the British Academy. Edgeworth was the founding editor of *The Economic Journal* and essentially retained this post from March 1891 until his death in 1926.

There is no complete bibliography of Edgeworth's writings. In 1928, Bowley published an annotated bibliography (in itself, no mean feat), with summaries of the papers (and reviews) grouped in a number of classes, of most of Edgeworth's writings on mathematical statistics. Further lists, with considerable overlap, may be found in the collections by Edgeworth (1925) and McCann (1996).

What sort of man was Edgeworth? Most of those who wrote about him after his death did not know him as a young man. Arthur Bowley, long-time friend and sole disciple of Edgeworth, became acquainted with him only in his middle-age. Beatrice Webb (then Potter) described him as "gentle natured . . . excessively polite . . . diffident," and Keynes, joint editor for some time with Edgeworth of *The Economic Journal*, found him to be "modest . . . humorous . . . reserved . . . angular . . . proud . . . unyielding."

The many facets of Edgeworth's personality were perhaps best summarized by Alfred Marshall, who said "Francis is a charming fellow, but you must be careful with Ysidro"; nevertheless, I think I should like to have known them both.

See Also the Following Articles

Qualitative Analysis, Political Science • Utility

Further Reading

Bowley, A. L. (1928). *F. Y. Edgeworth's Contributions to Mathematical Statistics.* Royal Statistical Society, London.

Edgeworth, F. Y. (1925). *Papers Relating to Political Economy.* 3 vols. Macmillan, for the Royal Economic Society, London.

Keynes, J. M. (1972). *The Collected Writings of John Maynard Keynes. Vol. X. Essays in Biography.* Macmillan, for the Royal Economic Society, London.

McCann, C. R., Jr. (ed.) (1996) *F Y. Edgeworth: Writings in Probability, Statistics and Economics.* 3 vols. Edward Elgar, Cheltenham, U.K.

Mirowski, P. (ed.) (1994). *Edgeworth on Chance, Economic Hazard, and Statistics.* Rowman & Littlefield, Lanham, MD.

Savage, L. J. (1954). *The Foundations of Statistics.* John Wiley & Sons, New York.

Stigler, S. M. (1978). Francis Ysidro Edgeworth, statistician. *J. Royal Statist. Soc.* **141,** 287–322.

Education, Tests and Measures in

Daniel R. Eignor
Educational Testing Service, Princeton, New Jersey, USA

Glossary

achievement test A sample of an examinee's behavior, allowing inferences about the extent to which the examinee has succeeded in acquiring knowledge or skills in a content domain in which the examinee has received instruction.

adaptive test A sequential form of individualized testing in which successive items in the test are chosen based on psychometric properties and test content, in relation to the examinee's responses to previous items.

aptitude test A sample of an examinee's behavior; intended to allow inferences about how successful the examinee will be in acquiring skills.

certification Voluntary process by which examinees demonstrate some level of knowledge or skill in a specified area, typically an occupational area.

constructed response item An exercise for which examinees must create their own responses or products, rather than choose a response from a specified set of responses.

criterion-referenced test An assessment instrument that allows its users to make score interpretations as to how well an examinee has performed with respect to the content measured by the test. Such tests often provide an indication as to where the examinee is with respect to a specified performance level or cut score. These interpretations can be distinguished from those that are made in relation to the performance of other examinees.

formative evaluation Concerned with judgments made during the administration of an instructional program; directed toward modifying or otherwise improving the program or the status of students taking the program before it is completed.

licensing The granting, usually by a governmental or supervisory agency, of authorization or legal permission to practice an occupation or profession.

norm-referenced test An assessment instrument that allows its users to make score interpretations in relation to the performance of a defined group of examinees, as distinguished from those interpretations made in relation to a specified performance level.

performance assessment Measurements based on settings designed to emulate real-life contexts or conditions in which specific knowledge or skills are actually applied and a product is produced.

placement A purpose for testing that results in a decision as to which educational treatment is most appropriate for a student.

portfolio A systematic collection of educational or work products that have been compiled or accumulated according to a specific set of principles.

selection A purpose for testing that results in the acceptance or rejection of applicants for a particular educational or occupational opportunity.

standardization In test administration, maintaining a consistent testing environment, test content, test scoring procedures, and conducting the test according to specified detailed rules, so that the testing conditions are equivalent for all examinees.

summative evaluation Concerned with making judgments about the merits of an instructional program that has been completed, or the status of students who have completed the program.

Tests and measures in education encompass the wide variety of assessment instruments used in the field of education. Tests or measures are assessment instruments typically used to measure cognitive or psychomotor skills. They may also be used to tap into interests or attitudes that are part of the affective domain. Distinctions among tests are best made at the level of the kind of use to be made of the resulting test scores. A test is an evaluative device or procedure in which a sample of an examinee's behavior or skill in a specified domain is obtained and subsequently interpreted.

Introduction

The use of tests is pervasive in the field of education. Before children attend kindergarten, tests may be administered to them to assess their readiness to undertake the normal activities of their age group. Tests may be administered to examinees who have completed their educational programs and want to engage in teaching others. Tests may be given to senior citizens interested in getting their high school equivalency diplomas. However, by far, the bulk of the testing done in the educational arena is related to the evaluation of student progress, as when a teacher has completed a unit of instruction and wants to see if the students have sufficiently mastered the content. There are, however, many other uses made of tests in the field of education. In the material that follows, the varieties of tests used in education are first discussed. Delineation of these varieties helps in the ensuing discussion of the various uses made of tests in education. Some attention is then paid to the delivery modes used with educational tests, given the current rapid influx of computers into everyday lives around the world. The final section provides information on how and where to locate many of the existing tests in education.

Varieties of Tests and Measures in Education

The varieties of tests used in education may be described through the use of a number of sets of contrasting terms or definitions. Typically, a test falls within or under one of the terms in the set. The sets are not mutually exclusive, however, and a particular test may have characteristics related to terms in a number of these sets.

Formative and Summative Tests

Tests of a formative nature are typically given during the administration of a course of instruction and may be used to modify elements of the instructional program. For instance, a classroom teacher typically administers a test following a unit of instruction in a course. Any of a number of outcomes of a formative nature are possible based on the test results. The teacher may decide to revise subsequent lesson plans, to reconsider subsequent learning material, to recycle to reteach critical subareas of the unit not mastered by the students, or, in the extreme, to start all over again with the unit. Summative tests, on the other hand, are given after an instructional program has been completed. This can range temporally from immediately after the course of instruction, as is the case with a final exam on a subject, to some time after instruction has taken place, as would be the case with a placement test given to an individual at the beginning of college.

Norm-Referenced and Criterion-Referenced Tests

Norm-referenced tests are made up of test items that have the effect of spreading examinees out along a score continuum. An examinee's status can then be determined by seeing where along this continuum the examinee is located in relation to a well-defined group of examinees. Many of the commercially available achievement tests given in elementary/secondary schools are of this nature. Criterion-referenced tests, on the other hand, are not used to compare a particular examinee to a well-defined group of other examinees, but rather to provide an indication of how well an examinee has performed with respect to the content measured by the test. Often such tests provide an indication as to where the examinee is with respect to a specified performance level. This requires that a cut score, or passing score, is established so that the examinee's score can be compared to this cut score, to judge whether the material being tested has been mastered. With criterion-referenced tests, items are selected that measure as well and as completely as possible the domain being tested. However, if the passing score has been set prior to actual test construction, items may be selected to be content representative and to separate students at the passing score.

With the expanded amount of testing now being done on a statewide level in the United States, and with recent federal mandates with respect to statewide testing, a new kind of testing, standards-based testing, is often described. Standards-based tests are, however, really just a type of criterion-referenced test. They are used to determine the extent to which examinees have mastered state content standards, indicating what students should know or be able to do at different grade levels. Such tests are not intended to be used to compare the rank ordering of one examinee with another. However, normative information is often used for groups of examinees, as when the percentage of proficient students in a particular school is compared with the percentage in a district or state. Critical to this sort of testing is the degree of match of content specifications, and resulting test content, to the state standards. With many commercially available achievement tests of a norm-referenced nature, a suitable level of match does not exist, and many states have consequently engaged in the construction of standards-based tests particular to the given state.

Cognitive, Psychomotor, and Affective Tests or Measures

In very brief terms, cognitive tests measure what people know; psychomotor tests measure what people can do. Affective measures are used to assess how people feel about or perceive something, although they may also be used to measure attitudes. A test of high school geometry qualifies as a cognitive test. A test in physical education that measures how adept students are on the parallel bars qualifies as a psychomotor test. Finally, an activities questionnaire, which assesses students' preferences for in-school, out-of-class activities, qualifies as an affective measure. Typically, tests are said to measure only one of the cognitive, psychomotor, or affective domains, but sometimes the lines of demarcation are not completely clear and sometimes a test can measure more than one of the domains. For example, a test of the ability to speak a foreign language can be viewed as both a cognitive and a psychomotor test.

Psychomotor tests and affective measures typically have problems not usually associated with cognitive tests. Psychomotor tests are usually more costly and time consuming to administer, and because test tasks are typically scored by human raters, may be less reliable than cognitive tests are. Affective measures suffer from the problem that students often select the most socially acceptable response, rather than the response that best reflects truth. In addition, depending on the nature of the affective measure, students or other stakeholders may view the questions as an invasion of privacy.

Achievement and Aptitude Tests

Achievement tests allow inferences about the extent to which an examinee has succeeded in acquiring knowledge or skills in a content area in which the examinee has, at some point, received instruction. An aptitude test, on the other hand, is intended to allow inferences as to how successful the examinee will be in acquiring knowledge or skills in the future. Often it is extremely difficult to distinguish items used in an aptitude test from those used in an achievement test. Because aptitude tests are often mistakenly thought to measure innate abilities, such as the potential to learn, such tests are now more often referred to as tests of "developed abilities." As already mentioned, the boundary that distinguishes the two types of tests is often difficult to establish with certainty. This has led some educators to question the aptitude/achievement dichotomy, and aptitude tests are sometimes simply viewed as achievement tests, wherein the content of the test is widely accessible outside of a specific course of instruction.

Selected Response and Constructed Response Tests

With a selected response test, the examinee has to choose a response from a set of responses that have been provided. With a constructed response test, the examinee must create a response or product. Closely related to the selected response/constructed response dichotomy are the contrasting terms, "objectively scored" and "subjectively scored." With an objectively scored test, the scoring can be done by simply matching the examinee's responses to a key (list of correct answers). Subjectively scored tests are tests that require human intervention in the scoring process. The process of human intervention typically relies on structured professional judgment with agreed-upon criteria, and hence the use of the terminology "subjectively scored" should not be viewed as implying there is a great deal of subjectivity in the scoring process. Finally, not all constructed response tests need to be subjectively scored. For instance, a grid-in item, whereby the examinee grids in a response, can be objectively scored by matching the examinee's response to a key that contains a list of all possible acceptable responses.

Performance assessment is a measurement concept now used to describe certain sorts of educational and occupational tests of a constructive response nature. Performance assessments are product-based measurements based on settings designed to emulate real-life contexts and conditions. All tests in the psychomotor domain qualify as performance assessments. Tests in the cognitive domain can sometimes also qualify if the sort of thinking or reasoning involved can be closely linked to that demanded in real-life situations. Finally, a portfolio constitutes a systematic collection of work products, i.e., a "work sample." Such a collection of work products can be compiled all at once or accumulated over time. Portfolios may be used to assess both cognitive and psychomotor domains, and along with performance assessments, almost always have to be scored in a subjective fashion.

Standardized and Unstandardized Tests

The designations "standardized" and "unstandardized" usually refer to the conditions under which a test is administered, but they can also be used in describing test content and test scoring procedures. When a test is given under standardized conditions, a constant testing environment is maintained based on a set of detailed rules, so that testing conditions are equivalent for all examinees, regardless of when or where they are tested. Commercially available tests are almost always standardized, with the exception of certain tests that may have been used for research purposes or used for testing examinees with special needs (such as disability accommodations). Classroom tests are typically unstandardized, but may have some elements of standardization. For instance, a teacher who has three classes of algebra may ensure that examinees in all three classes have a full 40 minutes for a classroom test.

Individual and Group-Administered Tests

The conditions under which a test is administered may relate to individuals or to groups. A direct measure of speaking ability in a foreign language, in which an examinee interacts one-on-one with an examiner, is an example of an individually administered test. Most commercially available educational tests are group-based in nature.

Linear and Adaptive Tests

Whether a test is linear or adaptive is a distinction that has really only become meaningful with the advent of computers. A linear test is one in which all examinees take the same questions in exactly the same, fixed order. Such a test could be delivered in either paper-and-pencil or computer format. With an adaptive test, examinees do not receive the same questions, and in some instances, may not even receive the same number of questions. With an adaptive test, successive items to be administered to an examinee are chosen based on psychometric properties and test content, in relation to the examinee's responses to previously administered items. In other words, with such a test, items are chosen to be "tailored" to an individual's ability, but, at the same time, in their totality, to satisfy content specifications. With a very few exceptions, such adaptive tests are given via computer.

Uses Made of Tests and Measures in Education

Educational tests and measures are used for a fairly large number of identifiable purposes. In the material that follows, nine general uses are discussed. These are not mutually exclusive, however, and often a particular test can be used for a variety of purposes. The issue of test misuse comes to the forefront any time scores from a particular test have not been validated for all uses to which they are applied.

A convenient way to separate tests by use is to group them by the level at which scores derived from these tests are considered. Scores are typically considered at either the individual level or the group level. With an achievement test in geometry, individual scores are generally the focus. For certain of the national and international surveys, such as the National Assessment of Educational Progress (NAEP), group-level scores are the focus. In fact, with NAEP, only group-based scores are reported and individual examinees do not receive scores. For six of the nine uses that follow (the first six), test scores for individual examinees are the focus of attention; for the other three uses, with one exception, the focus is on the use of scores for groups of individuals.

Evaluation of Student Progress and Management of Instruction

By far the largest use made of individual test scores is in the evaluation of student progress. Changes in instructional techniques may sometimes follow if progress is viewed as less than adequate. The tests may be from the cognitive or psychomotor domains, although cognitive tests, which are typically of an achievement nature, are clearly more prevalent. Examples range from formative use (administration by a teacher of an unstandardized test of a criterion-referenced nature that follows a unit of instruction in geometry) to a standardized summative final examination in a subject area, administered at the school, district, or even state level. The Regents examinations given in New York State are an excellent example of such tests given at the state level. In New York, every examinee who has studied Regents-level geometry takes the Regents exam at the end of the school year. It is a summative, criterion-referenced achievement examination that tests elements of the formal state curriculum in this subject area. The Regents tests contain questions requiring selected responses, short constructed responses (i.e., the examinee provides a numerical answer), and more expansive constructed responses (i.e., the examinee needs to provide a proof for a particular theorem). A somewhat comparable example that measures the psychomotor domain (along with the cognitive domain) occurs when a teacher of French (as a foreign language) includes a tape-recorded speaking component on the final exam in second-year French.

Diagnosis

Tests are used extensively to evaluate the special needs of individual students, both in planning for individualized educational programs and for determining the need for special services, such as individualized counseling sessions. For the former use, the tests are typically of the variety that measures basic academic skills and knowledge in the cognitive domain. It is clearly better if the tests are criterion referenced in nature, with a close match between the test content and the basic skills, but sometimes norm-referenced tests can prove useful. For the latter use (that is, determining the need for special services), measures employed often assess within the affective domain. However, intelligence quotient (IQ) tests, which measure within the cognitive domain, may also be employed. With these tests, which are typically standardized and administered on an individual examinee basis, special skills are often needed to interpret the results. Hence, such tests are typically administered, and the scores interpreted, by school or clinical psychologists.

Self-Discovery

Self-discovery is a test use area that is underemployed, particularly at the elementary/secondary school level. Most often measures of this sort are interest inventories that tap the affective domain, but these tests may also measure other attributes in the affective domain, such as attitudes. Of particular importance are the interest inventories administered toward the end of secondary school that can assist an individual who is trying to make a decision with respect to career choice.

Selection

Selection tests measure within the cognitive domain and are used to select individuals for admission to an institution or special program. Such tests are standardized and almost always are of a selected response nature. An example is the Scholastic Achievement Test (SAT) I Reasoning Test, which is a test of developed verbal and mathematical skills given to high school juniors and seniors in a group-based setting. Another example is the Academic College Test (ACT) assessment battery, a set of standardized achievement tests of cognitive abilities also given in a group setting. Such tests are norm referenced in nature and are used to rank examinees on the cognitive attributes being assessed. The test scores are typically combined with high school grade point average to predict success in college.

For a variety of reasons, selection testing has been written about extensively. A major reason is because different groups of examinees receive different average scores on such tests. For example, in the United States, African-American and Hispanic examinees tend to score lower than do Caucasian and Asian-American examinees, and the issue is whether the differences are construct relevant, i.e., whether the differences are related to what is being measured and are not due to extraneous variables. The other major reason for the attention paid to these tests has to do with the perceived susceptibility of these tests to coaching (i.e., short-term instruction on non-construct-related attributes such as test-taking skills and strategies). Finally, it should be noted that scores on such tests are used, albeit on an infrequent basis, to select younger students for "gifted and talented" programs. At issue with certain of these programs is whether this constitutes an appropriate use of the test score.

The distinction between linear and adaptive testing comes to the forefront with selection testing because two prevalent existing admissions testing programs (in this case, for admission to graduate or professional school) are computer adaptive in nature. These tests are the Graduate Record Examinations (GRE) General Test and the Graduate Management Admission Test (GMAT).

Placement

Placement tests are standardized tests in the cognitive domain, usually of a criterion-referenced nature, that are used in deciding which educational treatment or level is most appropriate for a student. Placement tests are used with greatest frequency with students who are transitioning between high school and college. An example of a well-known placement testing program is the Advanced Placement (AP) Program. The AP tests, which presently number upward of 30, are given after completing instruction in a specified subject in a high school course that is comparable to a course the examinee would take in college. The AP tests are given under standardized conditions in a group setting, and almost all the tests contain both selected response and constructed response components. Based on the score, the examinee may be granted advanced placement, in which case the examinee receives college credit for the course and is placed in the next more advanced course in the curriculum sequence during the freshman year in college. This typically happens in courses in or closely related to the student's declared major field of study. For AP courses taken that are of lesser importance to the declared major, the examinee is granted college credit and is exempted from taking the course in college, thereby freeing up a spot on the examinee's schedule to take another college course of interest. Finally, certain placement testing systems in the United States have now been computerized, and may be adaptive in nature.

Licensure, Certification, and Qualification

Licensure, certification, and qualification tests are grouped together because all three are designed to allow inferences about whether an examinee has sufficient knowledge and skill to meet certain needs. As such, these tests are typically criterion referenced, with a clearly articulated cut score or scores specified. Licensure tests are required tests established by governing boards to protect the public. Passing such a test and being awarded a license means that the recipient has demonstrated a minimum level of competence in the cognitive or psychomotor domain, necessary to avoid harming the public when the examinee begins working in a professional capacity. Licensure exams are common in a number of professional fields; in the field of nursing in the United States, the licensure exams are adaptive in nature.

Certification exams are voluntary in nature. Certification is typically granted by professional organizations that choose to recognize certified members as being at a specified level of competence above the minimum level required to protect the public. Finally, qualification exams are often required by institutions such as colleges to demonstrate that examinees have an acceptable level of knowledge or skills to function successfully. The Test of English as a Foreign Language (TOEFL) is viewed by many as being a qualification exam. Foreign students who want to study in the United States must attain a certain score on TOEFL in order to be considered for admission into the U.S. university of their choice.

Monitoring Trends

Monitoring tests are used to evaluate group performance over time. Such monitoring can be done using either a cross-sectional approach, whereby the performances of successive cohorts of students (i.e., fourth graders in two successive years) are monitored, or longitudinally, whereby the same cohort's performance is measured over time (i.e., fourth graders in year one and the same group of students, now fifth graders, in year two). A good example of such a test in the United States is the National Assessment of Educational Progress, which makes use of a cross-sectional approach.

Program Evaluation

Program evaluation tests have been implemented to see how well a particular program has been progressing or functioning. At the district level, for instance, such a test would be used to see how well students in the schools in that district are functioning with respect to state curriculum standards. Typically, cut points are set on such exams, and students are separated into descriptive categories based on their scores, such as "proficient" or "partly proficient." The grouped results of fourth grade tests in math and language arts considered in successive years can provide a macro-level indicator of how well a particular district has been performing. When tests are used for program evaluation purposes, strong sanctions are typically not imposed for schools or districts that may not have met expectations.

Accountability

Accountability testing in education is carried out with the express purpose of holding schools, districts, and states accountable for student performance. Such testing programs set explicit performance standards, often with some form of reward for those schools or districts in states that meet standards, and sanctions for those that do not meet standards. In the spotlight in the United States is testing of this sort related to the "No Child Left Behind" Act, which provides a federal-level imperative that states must meet certain specified performance standards to continue to receive federal funding (e.g., the states must demonstrate "Adequate Yearly Progress"). At present, the imperative holds for the areas of mathematics and language arts for grades 3–8 and for certain of these grades for science, although these grades have yet to be specified. As an outcome of this, states are presently studying closely, or even overhauling, their state testing programs to ensure that the assessments are aligned with the state performance standards. Further, most state testing programs presently do not have tests that measure these skills for all consecutive grades from grade 3 to grade 8. Given the costs of developing such tests, certain states are considering whether commercially available standardized norm-referenced achievement tests are sufficiently aligned to the state's performance standards so that they can be used.

Although tests used for accountability purposes typically involve group-based uses of scores, high school graduation exams are an exception. In this case, the individual student is held accountable, and any student who does not pass the test at the end of high school is not eligible to graduate. However, students are given multiple opportunities to pass the test, and in some cases, are allowed to demonstrate that they are eligible to graduate through alternative means tailored to particular individual needs.

Delivery Modes Used for Educational Tests

For years, the bulk of the tests and measures administered to examinees in the cognitive and affective domains were exclusively paper-and-pencil based. That is, the stimulus to be responded to was presented in writing in a paper format and the responses were collected via the use of a pencil for writing the response on paper; the response was recorded by filling in a "bubble" corresponding to one of the options for a multiple-choice question or was the written response to an essay question. Tests in the psychomotor domain, whereby examinees were asked to perform or do something, were typically administered in as direct a manner as possible, with the score on the performance recorded on paper. For example, in the direct testing of foreign language speaking ability, which measures within the psychomotor domain along with the cognitive domain, the examiner interacted in a one-to-one fashion with the examinee. The examinee listened to a stimulus spoken by the examiner, responded directly to that stimulus, and then the examiner recorded the score on the response via paper-and-pencil. Because of the individual nature of such speaking tests and the associated costs, many of today's tests of foreign language speaking ability are carried out in an indirect fashion, making use of a specialized mode of administration (e.g., the electronic tape medium), rather than depending on the presence of an examiner. The spoken stimuli may be recorded and delivered via audiotape and the examinee's responses to these stimuli may also be recorded via audiotape. If it is felt that the facial expressions and body movements of the examinee are important components of the speech act, audiovisual tape may be used in capturing the responses for later scoring. Clearly, delivery and capture of responses can be more complicated for the psychomotor domain than for the cognitive and affective domains.

With the advent of computer test delivery and computer-capture of test responses, a whole range of new testing possibilities has opened up. A variety of innovative item types in the cognitive domain have become possible, such as the "click and drag" item, whereby an examinee uses a computer mouse to insert a phrase of provided text in the appropriate spot in a paragraph of text on a computer monitor. In the language ability test, the stimulus would be delivered via computer using sound functionality, likely with accompanying context-setting visuals on the computer screen, and the spoken response would be recorded via computer and stored for later distribution to scorers, perhaps at individual remote scoring sites. Such a delivery scenario circumvents many of the problems associated with presentation of stimuli via audiotape, typically in a large group setting. At this point in time, investigations into the use of the computer for creating innovative item types and for delivery of stimuli and collection of responses are still in the beginning stages, and a number of possibilities, yet to be tried, can be envisioned. Availability of a significant number of computers, or at least computer terminals, will be a major stumbling block to the replacement of traditional paper-and-pencil testing with computer testing.

Sources of Information on Existing Educational Tests

For most educational testing contexts, likely one or several commercially available tests can be considered. One exception is in classroom testing for the management of instruction; a teacher-made test is often preferable in this case, if only to ensure an exact match between what has been taught and what is being tested. Even in this context, however, a commercially available test or an item pool from which the teacher can build the test may often prove to be sufficient. There are a number of good sources for finding out about existing tests and for getting additional information on any of the tests that may prove to be of interest. For those individuals interested in searching or checking online, a good place to start is at www.ericae.net. Clicking on the "Test Locator" link will reveal a number of good source sites, such as the ERIC Clearinghouse on Assessment and Evaluation, the Library and Test Collection at Educational Testing Service (ETS), and the Buros Institute of Mental Measurements. Alternatively, direct access to information on tests available from ETS can be obtained by going to www.ets.org and making use of the relatively new service called "TestLink." The TestLink database has archived descriptions of over 20,000 tests, including tests available from U.S. test publishers and individual test authors, and for unpublished tests that have been used for research purposes. Finally, information is available on a number of tests from publishers and authors outside the United States.

If printed materials are preferred, two sources can be obtained from the Buros Institute of Mental Measurements, housed at the University of Nebraska in Lincoln. One of the sources, *Tests in Print*, provides a listing of published tests, broken down into a number of different relevant categories. *Tests in Print* contains minimal information on the tests, but more detailed information can typically be obtained from the *Mental Measurements Yearbook*. The fourteenth yearbook was published in 2001. These yearbooks contain material on available tests, but perhaps the most important contributions are the reviews of individual tests provided by measurement professionals. Although not every test listed in *Tests in Print* is reviewed, typically the most important, widely used, new, and revised tests have associated review information. Finally, the numerous introductory texts in educational testing are another excellent source of information, particularly for detailed discussions on varieties and uses of tests. Many of these texts contain separate discussions for the cognitive, psychomotor, and affective domains, and frequently mention or discuss the important tests in each of these domains.

See Also the Following Articles

Classical Test Theory • Computer-Based Testing • Computerized Adaptive Testing • Innovative Computerized Test Items • Item and Test Bias • Optimal Test Construction • Psychometrics of Intelligence • Test Equating

Further Reading

American Educational Research Association, American Psychological Association, and National Council on Measurement in Education. (1999). *Standards for Educational and Psychological Testing.* American Psychological Association, Washington, D.C.

Buros Institute of Mental Measurements. (2001). *The Fourteenth Mental Measurements Yearbook.* Buros Institute of Mental Measurements, Lincoln, Nebraska.

Educational Testing Service. (2003). *TestLink, the ETS Test Collection.* Princeton, New Jersey. Available on the Internet at www.ets.org

ERIC Clearinghouse on Assessment and Evaluation. (2003). *Test Locator.* College Park, Maryland. Available on the Internet at www.ericae.net

Joint Committee on Testing Practices. (1988). *Code of Fair Testing Practices in Education.* Washington, D.C. Available on the Internet at www.apa.org

Murphy, L., Impara, J., and Plake, B. (1999). *Tests in Print V: An Index to Tests, Test Reviews, and the Literature on Specific Tests.* Buros Institute of Mental Measurements, Lincoln, Nebraska.

Elaboration

Carol S. Aneshensel

University of California, Los Angeles, California, USA

Glossary

extraneous variable Source of spurious covariation between two other variables; also known as a control variable.

focal relationship The one cause-and-effect type of relationship that is pivotal to the theory being tested.

internal validity The extent to which cause-and-effect-type inferences can be drawn.

intervening variable Operationalizes the causal mechanism by linking an independent variable to a dependent variable; a consequence of the independent variable and a determinant of the dependent variable.

redundancy Covariation due to correlated independent variables.

spuriousness Two variables appear to covary because they depend on a common cause.

suppressor variable Conceals a true relationship or makes it appear weaker.

test factor Variable added to a bivariate analysis to clarify the connection between the other two variables.

The elaboration model is a set of data analytic techniques designed to enhance the inference of cause and effect for correlational data. Causal inference is of utmost importance to social science research because theory usually specifies how one or more constructs affect the occurrence of one or more outcomes, such as exposure to stress influencing emotional well being. However, the data used to test social theory often come from observation of natural occurrences, as distinct from experimental manipulation, which makes the inference of causality problematic, especially when data are cross-sectional in design. This situation arises because ethical or practical constraints place many areas of social research outside the realm of experimental manipulation. The techniques contained in the elaboration model strengthen causal inference by examining the range of possible meanings for an observed association, asking why this association exists, and specifying the conditions under which the association appears. The elaboration model is discussed here as it was originally formulated, and its recent revision for multivariate analysis is then detailed.

Overview of the Elaboration Model

The elaboration model dates from the early days of quantitative survey analysis, following World War II; the model builds on the work of Paul Lazarsfeld and others. Its components and principles were presented in detail by Morris Rosenberg in 1968 in the now classic *The Logic of Survey Analysis*. The elaboration model entails the systematic introduction of "third variables," or test factors, into analysis to examine the nature of a bivariate association between two other variables. The core issue is whether the estimate of the initial bivariate association is altered by the introduction of various types of test factors—that is, whether a third variable accounts for the observed association. The overarching objective is to differentiate theoretically meaningful relationships among constructs from inconsequential empirical associations.

The elaboration model can be seen as a method for evaluating the internal validity of a theory. Internal validity refers to the extent to which conclusions about cause and effect can be drawn. It is very strong in experimental research, where it is achieved through design. Specifically, the random assignment of subjects to experimental and control conditions holds constant factors that could otherwise influence the outcome of interest in the experiment. In contrast, internal validity is achieved in large part through data analysis in nonexperimental research designs. In quasi-experimental research (a hybrid type), threats to internal validity are controlled by design to the extent possible, and then by data analysis. Data analysis is used to establish internal validity because nonexperimental and quasi-experimental research are typically conducted within naturally occurring settings, where it is not possible to achieve the strict control of experiments in laboratory-type settings. In this regard, Rosenberg argued that introduction of test factors into survey analyses enables exploitation of some of the virtues of the experimental design, while avoiding the inappropriateness of experimentation for many research questions.

In the elaboration model approach to internal validity, the first step is the operationalization of theory as an association between an independent variable and a dependent variable. Threats to internal validity are then evaluated by ruling out alternative explanations—that is, explanations other than those set forth by the theory being tested, such as ruling out spuriousness due to extraneous variables. Additional evidence of internal validity is then sought by examining the causal mechanisms that generate the observed associations (for example, identifying intervening variables). Finally, the conditions under which the relationship operates are specified.

Components of the Elaboration Model

The elaboration model concerns relationships that reflect an inherent connection between two variables: An independent variable exerts an influence on a dependent variable. This type of causal connection is one of three possible types of relationships. In the language of the original elaboration model, asymmetrical relationships entail causal influence that is unidirectional; effects flow from one construct to a second construct, but not in the reverse direction. In contrast, reciprocal relationships entail causal influence that is bidirectional; one construct influences a second construct, and the second construct, in turn, influences the first construct. In symmetrical relationships, the two constructs are empirically associated with one another, but no causal influence flows from either construct to the other. In the elaboration model, the primary emphasis is on asymmetrical relationships; reciprocal relationships are treated as "alternating asymmetry." However, the analysis of putative causality rests, in part, on ruling out the possibility that the relationship is symmetrical (noncausal) in nature.

Types of Symmetrical Relationships

Rosenberg identified five types of symmetrical or noncausal relationships. The first type—the two variables are alternative indicators of the same construct—is a measurement misspecification, not an issue of cause and effect. The second type concerns effects of a common cause: the two variables do not influence each other, but empirically covary because each variable depends on the same causal agent; this is the classic meaning of the term "spurious." Third, the two variables are parts of a common system or complex, whereby the parts are often arbitrary because they are not functionally interdependent, such as practices associated with being a member of the middle class. Fourth, and very similar, is the joint complex, whereby the elements of a whole hang together for essentially normative reasons, such as cultural complexes. Finally, some symmetrical relationships are simply fortuitous; empirical associations that occur by chance.

These five types of symmetrical relationships have different consequences for data analysis. Three pertain to measurement issues of separating the parts of a whole: alternative indicators, parts of a common system, and joint complex. The remaining two types of symmetrical relationships are especially consequential because they commonly emerge as alternative explanations for a hypothesized cause-and-effect type relationship: spurious and fortuitous relationships. Establishing internal validity relies on ruling out these two alternatives.

Types of Test Factors

To establish that an association between two variables is indicative of an asymmetrical relationship, six types of test factors are introduced into analysis: extraneous, component, intervening, antecedent, suppressor, and distorter variables. An extraneous variable reveals that an apparently asymmetrical relationship is instead symmetrical because the introduction of the test factor into the analysis diminishes the observed association. This result occurs because the test factor is associated with both the independent and the dependent variables. When a relationship is extraneous, there is no causal connection between independent and dependent variables. The most common case is spuriousness: independent and dependent variables appear to be associated with each other because both depend on a common cause. Figure 1 illustrates an instance of spuriousness in which the joint dependency of the independent variable and the dependent variable on the test factor explains some or all of the original empirical association between these variables. Spuriousness occurs because changes in the "third variable" produce changes in both the focal independent variable and the focal dependent variable; because the latter two change in unison, they appear to be related to each other, whereas they are actually related to the "third variable." Component variables are subconcepts of global or complex concepts. From the perspective of

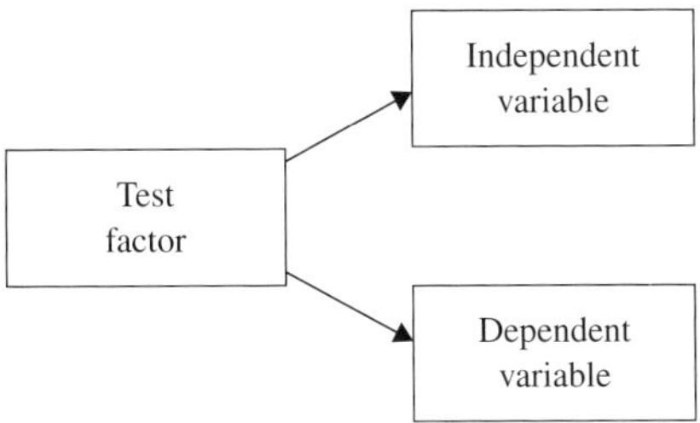

Figure 1 Spuriousness between independent and dependent variables due to a test factor. Reprinted from Aneshensel (2002), with permission.

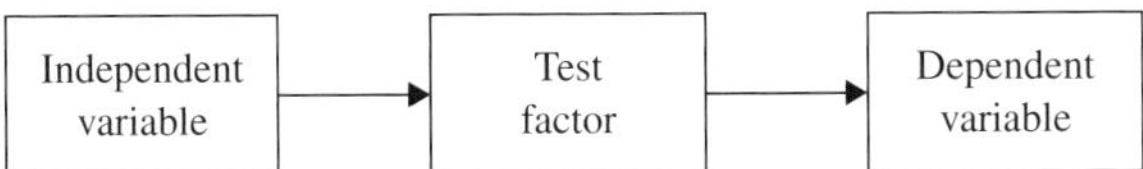

Figure 2 The test factor as an intervening variable between an independent variable and a dependent variable. Reprinted from Aneshensel (2002), with permission.

the elaboration model, the purpose of these test factors is to determine which of the components is responsible for the observed effect on a dependent variable.

The intervening variable is a consequence of the independent variable and a determinant of the dependent variable, as shown in Fig. 2. A test factor that is an intervening variable requires three asymmetrical relationships: the original relationship between the independent and dependent variables, a relationship between the independent variable and the test factor (acting as a dependent variable), and, a relationship between the test factor (acting as an independent variable) and the dependent variable. If the test factor is indeed an intervening variable, then its introduction into the analysis accounts for some or all of the original relationship between the other variables.

According to Rosenberg, the antecedent variable logically precedes the relationship between an independent variable and a dependent variable. Its introduction into the analysis does not explain the relationship, but clarifies the influences that precede the relationship. As shown in Fig. 3, the test factor acting as an antecedent variable is assumed to be directly responsible for the independent variable, which, in turn, influences the dependent variable; the independent variable now acts as an intervening variable. Thus, analysis of antecedent variables is derivative of intervening variable analysis. For antecedent variables, the causal chain is carried as far back in the process as is theoretically meaningful.

A suppressor variable conceals a true relationship or makes it appear weaker than it is in fact: the full extent of an association emerges only when the suppressor variable is taken into consideration. In this instance, negative

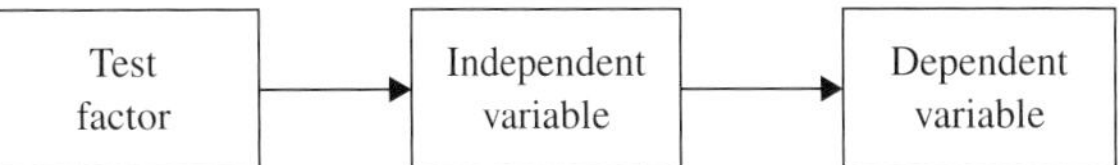

Figure 3 The test factor as an antecedent variable to an independent variable and a dependent variable. Reprinted from Aneshensel (2002), with permission.

findings are misleading because the real association is concealed at first by the suppressor variable; the absence of the bivariate association is spurious. The suppressor variable is a threat to validity because it attenuates the full extent of a true relationship. A distorter variable, however, produces a relationship that is the reverse of that originally observed: this reversal becomes apparent only when the distorter variable is included in the analysis.

The elaboration model, according to Rosenberg (1968), is designed to deal with two dangers in drawing conclusions from two-variable relationships: accepting a false hypothesis as true, and rejecting a true hypothesis as false. Extraneous, suppressor, and distorter variables are designed to reduce the likelihood of making these mistakes. In addition, the elaboration model enables the analyst to explicate a more precise and specific understanding of a two-variable model. Component, intervening, and antecedent variables serve this purpose.

Revised Multivariate Elaboration Model

The original development and most textbook discussions of the elaboration model limit its application to cross-tabular analytic techniques for simple two-variable models stratified on the "third variable." Although this approach serves an expository purpose, it is of limited value to research applications that employ numerous variables in one simultaneous multivariate model. A revised elaboration model has recently been presented, with application to multivariate analysis. This revision starts by introducing the concept of the focal relationship, which is implicit in the original version of the model. The focal relationship is the one relationship that is pivotal to the theory being tested. It serves as an anchor for the remainder of the elaboration analysis, which is dedicated to evaluating its internal validity. In addition, the revised model organizes the various test factors of the elaboration model into two strategies for establishing internal validity: an exclusionary strategy that rules out alternative explanations, and an inclusive strategy that connects the focal relationship to a theory-based causal nexus.

The focal relationship is the one relationship of primary significance to the theory being tested, the linchpin that holds the remainder of the model in place. It has two main components, an independent variable and a dependent variable, terms that imply a cause-and-effect type of relationship. From this perspective, other independent variables serve a single purpose, establishing the internal validity of the focal relationship (that is, evaluating whether it is legitimate to interpret the focal relationship in a causal manner). This emphasis on one relationship is distinctly different from empirical approaches that emphasize maximizing the amount of explained variance in the dependent variable. Instead, a theory-based bivariate association takes center stage, and other variables serve to establish the relatedness of these two variables through the strategic manipulation of various "third variables."

Elaboration: The Exclusionary Strategy

The revised elaboration model pairs two strategies for evaluating the focal relationship as a cause-and-effect type of relationship. The first is the exclusionary strategy, which rules out other explanations (that is, explanations other than relatedness) for the observed association between the focal independent and dependent variables. The analytic goal is to show that at least some of the focal relationship cannot be attributed to factors other than the hypothesized cause-and-effect type of relationship. The major alternatives to be ruled out are chance, spuriousness, and redundancy. This strategy is exclusionary in the sense that it concerns the covariation between the focal independent and dependent variables that remains when other potential sources of this covariation have been analytically excluded. The focal relationship is supported when residual covariation remains at the end of exclusionary analysis; it not supported when little or no covariation remains.

Happenstance

The first possibility to be ruled out is that the two variables have been observed to co-occur simply by chance. This possibility is usually addressed with tests of statistical significance, although some researchers use confidence intervals instead. In many applications, this is a simple regression of the following form:

$$\hat{Y} = c + b_f X_f, \tag{1}$$

where $\hat{Y}$ is the estimated value of the focal dependent variable; c is a constant; and b_f is the unstandardized regression coefficient—the effect on Y of a unit increase in the focal independent variable X_f.

At this juncture, the central concern is the total association between the focal independent and dependent variables, given as b_f in Eq. (1); specifically, this is the null hypothesis H_0: $b_f = 0$, the value indicative of no linear relationship between Y and X_f. This null hypothesis is evaluated with the t-test for b_f. If the null hypothesis cannot be rejected, there usually is no need to proceed with the other aspects of the elaboration model because there is no statistically meaningful focal relationship to be elaborated. Exceptions to this generalization include suppression and effect-modification; both can produce the illusion of independence at the bivariate level of analysis. If the null hypothesis is rejected, however, the analysis proceeds by considering extraneous sources of covariation.

Spuriousness

As already mentioned, with spuriousness, the values of the two focal variables coincide because they share a common cause. When a spurious "third variable" is added to the analysis, the covariation between the focal independent and dependent variables is partly or completely eliminated. "Third variables" that generate spuriousness are referred to as control variables. For a control variable to produce spuriousness, it must be related to both the focal independent variable and the focal dependent variable. If both of these conditions are not met, the variable cannot be a source of spurious covariation. To test for spuriousness, one or more control variables (X_c) are added to the simple regression that was given by Eq (1):

$$\hat{Y} = c + b_f X_f + b_c X_c. \tag{2}$$

The regression coefficient b_f is now the expected change in Y with each unit increase in X_f when the control variable is held constant. In other words, b_f is now the partial effect of the focal independent variable net of the effects of the control variable. (Although this treatment is developed for single variables of each type, multiple variables would typically be included in an elaboration analysis, e.g., multiple control variables.)

For the analysis of spuriousness, the key consideration remains the null hypothesis H_0: $b_f = 0$. If this null hypothesis cannot be rejected, it means that the original bivariate association between X_f and Y can be entirely attributed to their joint dependence upon X_c. If instead, the assertion that $b_f = 0$ can be rejected, it means that at least some of the covariation between X_f and Y is separate and distinct from the effects of this control variable; that is, some of the covariation appears to be nonspurious.

Although b_f in Eq. (2) gives the partial effect of the focal independent variable net of the control variable, the elaboration model is best seen by comparison across regression equations—in this instance, by comparison to the simple regression in Eq. (1). This comparison reveals the impact on the focal relationship of adding the control variable. The ratio of these two estimates of b_f gives the proportion of the zero-order association between X_f and Y that can be attributed to X_f in isolation from the control variable. (This fraction subtracted from 1 yields the proportion of the zero-order association that can be attributed to the joint dependency of X_f and Y on X_c.) If the relationship is not spurious, then the regression coefficient b_f will remain essentially unchanged from the simple regression to the expanded regression, and the ratio of regression coefficients will approach 1.00. The ratio will approach 0 if the relationship is completely spurious.

Redundancy

"Third variables" that generate redundancy can be referred to simply as other independent variables, although in the language of the original elaboration model, these are labeled "conjoint." In a redundant association, the other independent variable covaries with the focal independent variable; it also influences the dependent variable. Consequently, the focal independent variable appears to be related to the focal dependent variable when this variable is not included in the analysis. As with control variables, other independent variables must be associated with both focal independent and dependent variables to produce redundancy. If these conditions are not both met, then the association between the two focal variables cannot be due to redundancy. Redundancy is the result of correlated independent variables.

To assess redundancy, the model presented in Eq (2) is expanded by the addition of another independent variable (X_i):

$$\hat{Y} = c + b_f X_f + b_c X_c + b_i X_i. \qquad (3)$$

As before, we are interested in whether b_f continues to differ from 0, and in the ratio of b_f across equations. A reduction in the size of this coefficient indicates that at least some of the impact of the focal independent variable is redundant with the added independent variable. Typically, several independent variables would be considered in an analysis of redundancy. It should be noted that control variables and other independent variables are indistinguishable in the regression equation. They are differentiated conceptually, not empirically. In spuriousness, the focal independent and dependent variables serve as dependent variables to the control variable. In contrast, in redundancy, only the focal dependent variable is dependent.

Elaboration: The Inclusive Strategy

Whereas the exclusionary strategy follows a negative form of validation (covariation that is not ruled out may be indicative of a relationship), the inclusive strategy follows a positive form of validation (covariation with other theory-based constructs is evidence of relationship). Specifically, the inclusive strategy seeks to establish internal validity by connecting the focal relationship to a network of relationships with other constructs, explicating the functioning of the causal system of which the focal relationship is part. These other relationships are operationalized by antecedent, intervening, and consequent variables. These additional variables clarify the focal relationship by explaining, respectively, the occurrence of the independent variable, the connection between the independent and dependent variables, and the outcomes of the dependent variable. The inclusion of these variables in the analytic model strengthens the inference of relatedness by demonstrating that the association between the independent variable and the dependent variable fits within a set of relationships anticipated by theory.

Antecedent Variables

Analysis of the antecedent variable is isomorphic to analysis of control and other independent variables. It logically follows the exclusionary analysis, but often these variables are considered in one simultaneous step with control and other independent variables. The cumulative regression is

$$\hat{Y} = c + b_f X_f + b_c X_c + b_i X_i + b_a X_a, \qquad (4)$$

where X_a is an antecedent variable. If the variable performs this role, b_f should be essentially unchanged from its previous value [Eq. (3)]. The function of the antecedent variable is to explain the occurrence of X, not its relationship to Y. Therefore, a complete analysis would estimate an additional regression equation with X_f as the dependent variable and X_a as the independent variable, i.e., $X_f = c + b_{a^*} X_a$, where b_{a^*} is expected to have a nonzero value (see Fig. 3).

Intervening Variables

Intervening variables are, by far, the most important of the inclusive set of variables, because they specify the causal mechanisms that generate the observed focal relationship. The intervening variable (X_v) is added to the cumulative Y-regression:

$$\hat{Y} = c + b_f X_f + b_c X_c + b_i X_i + b_a X_a + b_v X_v. \qquad (5)$$

Once again, the focus is on b_f (whether it continues to differ from 0, and if so, how much of the original association remains). However, the analytic goal is reversed insofar as the intent is to explain some or all of the empirical association between the focal independent and dependent variables. Typically, multiple intervening variables would be evaluated. The inclusion of intervening variables should reduce the magnitude of the focal relationship, ideally fully accounting for it. In other words, when intervening variables fully capture the causal processes, b_f should approach 0. The focal relationship is diminished in magnitude because the pathways through which its influence is exerted have been specified. To the extent that these causal mechanisms are consistent with the theoretical model, the inference of relatedness for the observed association is enhanced. To complete the analysis of the intervening variable, an additional equation is necessary, one in which it serves as the dependent variable, $X_v = c + b_{f^*}X_f$, where b_{f^*} is expected to have a nonzero value (see Fig. 2).

Consequent Variables

Consequent variables were not part of the original elaboration model, but have been added to the inclusive strategy because they perform a function isomorphic to that of antecedent variables. Whereas antecedent variables extend the causal sequence backward to the conditions producing the focal independent variable, consequent variables extend the causal sequence forward to the conditions that follow from the focal dependent variable. Consequent variables help to establish the validity of the focal relationship by demonstrating that Y produces effects anticipated by the theoretical model. Consequent variables logically succeed the dependent variable and clarify the continuation of the causal sequence within which the focal relationship is embedded. Like the antecedent variable, the consequent variable does not alter the focal relationship but rather enhances our understanding of it. The consequent variable functions as a dependent variable and is therefore not part of the cumulative regression previously developed. Instead, it requires an additional regression equation in which the consequent variable is the dependent variable, and the focal dependent variable acts as an independent variable, e.g., $\hat{Y}_c = c + Y_f$.

Elaboration: Specification

Thus far, the focal relationship has been discussed as if it is universal, operating at all times and for all persons. Some relationships, however, are found only under some conditions and other relationships affect only some types of persons. Therefore, the final component of the elaboration model concerns specification of the focal relationship—that is, examining the possibility that the focal relationship is conditional. A conditional relationship varies across the values of the test factor. It may be present for only some values, and otherwise absent, for example, or positive in sign for a range of values and negative for another range of values. Specification is also referred to as "effect modification," or the analysis of moderators or moderating variables. In the original elaboration model, specification was achieved through stratified analysis, which is estimating the bivariate association across the various values of the test factor. In the multivariate elaboration model, specification is also achieved by examining interaction terms that embody the expected conditional relationship. For example, the preceding analysis of the intervening variable could be expanded to include the possibility that this variable modifies the effect of the focal independent variable on the focal dependent variable:

$$\hat{Y} = c + b_f X_f + b_c X_c + b_i X_i + b_a X_a + b_v X_v + b_x (X_f \times X_v), \quad (6)$$

where b_x represents the conditional nature of the association. Suppose that X_v represents membership in a subgroup of the population (say, gender), and it is coded 1 for females and 0 for males. Under these circumstances, b_f is the impact of X_f among males and the corresponding value is $b_f + b_x$ for females. If b_x is significantly different from 0, it means that the focal relationship is conditional on gender. In other words, the analysis has specified the focal relationship for females versus males. Identifying particular circumstances and specific subgroups that modify the focal relationship is the final step in testing how well the data align with theoretical expectations.

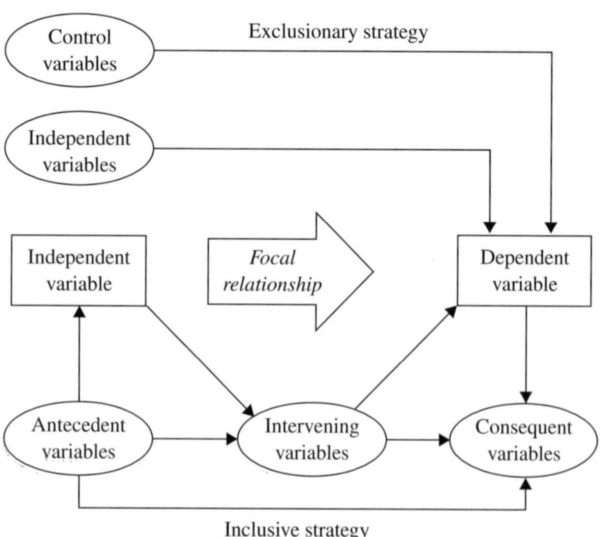

Figure 4 Exclusionary and inclusive strategies for establishing internal validity of the focal relationship. Reprinted from Aneshensel (2002), with permission.

Summary

To recap, the elaboration model is a method of analysis for drawing causal inferences from correlational data by systematically adding test factors or "third variables" to the analysis of a bivariate association. In multivariate analysis, two strategies are used to assess the internal validity of the focal relationship, as illustrated in Fig. 4. In the exclusionary phase of analysis, covariation that is accounted for by control variables and other independent variables is indicative of spuriousness and redundancy, respectively, whereas residual covariation may be indicative of relatedness. If no residual covariation remains at the end of the exclusionary analysis, there is no need to proceed to the inclusive strategy because there is no relationship to be elaborated. Otherwise, the analysis turns to a consideration of the causal system within which the focal relationship is embedded. The inclusive strategy elaborates the meaning of the focal relationship. When expected patterns of association with the focal relationship do indeed materialize, the inference of relatedness is supported. This analysis entails antecedent, intervening, and consequent variables. This is an inclusive approach to internal validity in that it includes other explanatory variables in the analysis of the focal relationship.

See Also the Following Articles

Experiments, Overview • Lazarsfeld, Paul

Further Reading

Aneshensel, C. S. (2002). *Theory-Based Data Analysis for the Social Sciences.* Pine Forge Press, Thousand Oaks, CA.

Clogg, C. C., Petkova, E., and Haritou, A. (1995). Statistical methods for comparing regression coefficients between models. *Am. J. Sociol.* **100,** 1261–1293.

Converse, J. M. (1987). *Survey Research in the United States: Roots and Emergence 1890–1960.* University of California Press, Berkeley, CA.

Davis, J. A. (1985). *The Logic of Causal Order.* Sage, Newbury Park, CA.

Kenny, D. A. (1979). *Correlation and Causality.* John Wiley & Sons, New York.

Rosenberg, M. (1968). *The Logic of Survey Analysis.* Basic Books, New York.

Election Polls

Marc D. Weiner
Rutgers University, New Brunswick, New Jersey, USA

Glossary

benchmark survey An election poll conducted early in the campaign season that (1) provides a starting point from which a campaign may measure its progress and/or (2) informs a campaign or media organization about the public's attitudes, interests, and preferences on issues relevant in the campaign.

election poll An information-gathering effort that uses survey research techniques during a political campaign to assess public opinion on a particular topic or candidate.

exit poll Election day polls sponsored by media organizations, conducted as in-person interviews predominantly about vote choice, outside the polling place immediately after the voter has cast his or her ballot; exit polls are used to inform election day news coverage, including analysis of how particular groups are voting, and projections of winners.

horserace journalism The practice of news reporting predominantly or exclusively on which candidate is winning, as opposed to reporting on the candidates' positions on issues in the election.

push poll A form of political telemarketing to disseminate campaign propaganda under the guise of conducting a legitimate public opinion poll; its purpose is to "push" voters toward a particular candidate or issue position.

tracking poll One in a series of election polls that are used over the course of a campaign to track changes in support for a candidate, likely voting patterns, and related items of electoral interest.

trial heat A preelection poll, or part of a preelection poll, that forces respondents to choose between candidates in order to assess the viability of a potential candidate or the immediate strength of an existing candidate.

An election poll is an information-gathering effort that uses survey research techniques during a political campaign to assess public opinion on a particular topic or candidate. There is a variety of different procedures for election polls and different organizations and individuals can sponsor them for several different purposes. Election polls are distinguished from other instances of survey research by their relationship to politics, in both their timing and their content vis-à-vis a given election. By permitting political actors and the media to assess public opinion, these information-gathering exercises can play an important role in democratic elections.

Introduction

An election poll is an information-gathering effort that uses survey research techniques during a political campaign to assess public opinion on a particular topic or candidate. There is a variety of different procedures for election polls and different organizations and individuals can sponsor them for several different purposes. Election polls are distinguished from other instances of survey research by their relationship to politics, in both their timing and their content vis-à-vis a given election. By permitting political actors and the media to assess public opinion, these information-gathering exercises can play an important role in democratic elections.

Whereas the concept and purposes of election polls are essentially straightforward, they are operationally complex because the population to be sampled—a given electorate—exists only on the given election day. This makes determining and weighting the sample to accurately reflect the true voting population for the upcoming election both difficult and fraught with political implications. In addition, the publication of election polls may have an effect on the composition and behavior of the electorate, and so in addition to the operational complications, there are normative political and ethical considerations.

Types of Election Polls

Election polls are best categorized on three sets of criteria: Who is sponsoring the poll and why? What is the timing of the poll; i.e., when in the campaign season is it being conducted? What is the methodological approach; i.e., how was the sample determined and weighted and what is the mode of interviewing?

At the most basic level, election polls are sponsored either by political actors—those with political affiliations such as candidates, political consultants, political parties, or interest groups—or by media organizations—such as newspapers, magazines, television networks, or consortiums of those organizations. Political actors sponsor election polls in order to inform strategic decisions, such as which issues to stress during a campaign and what issues constitute weak spots for the opponent, or to determine the demographic groups and/or geographic areas in which a candidate has a likely chance of winning. Media organizations use election polls to provide information content for their political campaign reporting.

Election polls are also effectively characterized on the basis of timing, which is determined by the poll's purpose. Preelection polls are conducted before and during all stages of a political campaign, whereas exit polls are conducted only on election day. Both political actors and media organizations conduct several different types of preelection polls, but typically only media organizations conduct exit polls.

Benchmark surveys are conducted early in the campaign season to provide a starting point from which a campaign may measure its progress, in terms of its candidate's name recognition, electoral strength, and issue-position identification. The benchmark survey may also inform a campaign's decision makers about the public's attitudes, interests, and preferences on issues relevant in the campaign. As the election season progresses, candidates' organizations and political parties will use tracking polls to compare the more recent results against the benchmark survey findings in order assess the success of the campaign and make adjustments in campaign strategy.

Toward the end of the campaign season, the media also sponsor tracking polls, often daily, in order to publish the most current election projections. Although there are a variety of different methodologies for these polls, they often use "rolling samples," or small, overnight samples of approximately 100 to 200 interviews. Typically, each day's poll results are combined with consecutive days' results to produce 3-day "rolling averages," each of which is then based on an aggregate of 300 to 600 interviews. Usually, respondents for these samples are screened on the basis of "likely to vote" so that the poll results are generalizable to the likely electorate, as opposed to the general population. In practice, it is generally very difficult to determine who will actually vote and since a sample that does not reflect the composition of that particular election day's electorate is likely to be biased, the composition of the sample for these smaller sample polls is extremely important. Not only is there often a meaningful difference between the results for a sample of "registered voters" and a sample of "likely voters," but also partisanship—the number of Democrats and Republicans in the sample—is extremely important. That factor, like many others, will skew the results if the sample is not correctly weighted.

Another type of preelection poll is the trial heat, an approach that requests a respondent to force a vote selection. Political parties and candidate organizations frequently use the trial heat approach during the primary season to assess the viability of a potential party nominee against her likely opposite party opponent. Similarly, both political and media sponsors can use the trial heat to force a selection prior to election day. When constructed for that purpose, the question typically begins with the phrase, "If the election were held today..." Very often, a trial heat may be included as a component in a larger tracking poll.

The practice of candidates changing their electoral strategy on the basis of benchmark/tracking poll results has been criticized as contributing to campaigns that merely pander to voters. On the other hand, the selection of question content by partisan pollsters to promote issues that their candidates want to discuss, rather than issues the electorate would spontaneously raise, has also been subject to criticism. On the media side, the frequent use of tracking polls and trial heat polls has been criticized as leading to "horserace journalism," i.e., a journalistic obsession with who's winning, as opposed to reporting on the candidates' positions on issues in the election, to better inform the electorate. Although the use of these types of election polls by candidates and political parties to ensure that voters' concerns are addressed in the campaign arguably has a positive effect on the electoral democratic dialogue, the media's use of these types of election polls appears less defensible.

Exit polls, sponsored almost exclusively by media organizations, are generally in-person interviews conducted only on election day outside the polling place immediately after the voter has cast his ballot. The core information sought at an exit poll is the vote, i.e., for whom the voter voted. In addition, the polls will ask about issue positions, other items on the ballot, such as referenda, as well basic demographic information. These types of polls avoid the potential difficulties of all other preelection polls vis-à-vis sample selection. Because the sample is composed of known voters, the demographic and partisan composition and likelihood of voting are predetermined. As such, the exit-poll sample very accurately reflects the true electorate, in terms of both demographic and partisan composition as well as vote choice. However, media outlets that report winner projections on the basis of exit polls have been the subject of bitter criticism on the basis that publishing known election outcomes in real time affects electoral results in voting jurisdictions in later time zones where the polls have not yet closed.

In the American national context, coordinating the conduct, aggregation, and reporting of in-person interviews over a 1-day period in a set of voting precincts sufficient to represent all voting jurisdictions is a logistically enormous and extraordinarily expensive undertaking. As a result, since 1990 the major media networks and large news organizations have banded together to form an exit-polling consortium to conduct nationwide exit polling and winner projections. This type of consortium takes advantage of the economy of scale, in terms of both the aggregation of information and the minimization of costs. For the 1996 presidential election, the consortium conducted approximately 150,000 in-person interviews in 1 day at over 1500 voting precincts across the country. The newest incarnation of the exit-polling consortium, the National Elections Pool, was formed in 2003 to replace Voter News Service, the organization that performed the function from 1994 through 2002. Voter News Service, formed in 1994 as an extension of a similar consortium, Voter Research and Surveys, was disbanded in 2003 after failing to produce accurate data on the 2002 midterm election and providing flawed information on the 2000 presidential election. Its performance on the 2000 presidential election was particularly poor, most notably as to the news networks' predictions of the Florida results.

Election polls can also be characterized on the basis of their method. There are four well-developed basic methods of conducting survey research—person-to-person telephone interviews, written interviews by mail, personal interviews, and person-to-machine telephone interviews (also known as "interactive voice response" interviews). Since telephone interviewing is the quickest and most immediate method, most preelection polls are conducted that way, whether sponsored by political actors or media organizations. On-line Web interviews show promising potential, but there are still concerns about respondent accessibility as well as ensuring representative samples.

A comprehensive typology must also consider what is not an election poll, such as focus groups, push polls, and the use of simulated polls to market goods or services or to raise funds for political and nonprofit organizations. Although focus groups are legitimate research techniques, push polls, marketing and solicitation, and fundraising are not and often serve to undermine the legitimacy of the polling industry.

Because they are often used in a campaign setting, focus groups are sometimes considered a form of election polling. The focus group is a qualitative research technique in which a small group of people is brought together with a facilitator who stimulates and guides otherwise informal discussion around a given set of topics. The content of the discussion is in the nature of a group interview, can provide in-depth insight into issues, and can be used to supplement quantitative research with a level of detail that could not be obtained through conventional survey interviewing. Focus groups cannot, however, be considered surveys because they do not employ probability sampling to permit inferences to be made to the larger population. Although the participants are sometimes selected on the basis of demographic characteristics, because of the size the group—typically ranging from 8 to 20—the results are not generalizable. Focus groups are, however, useful to campaigns to permit the pretesting of themes and approaches and to explore how the conversation about issues takes place among potential voters. Similarly, focus groups can help both campaign and media pollsters to determine the best content for an election survey and to pretest survey instruments.

Another phenomenon often appearing during election campaigns is the "push poll." The push poll, however, is not a legitimate poll but rather a campaign technique designed to affect, rather than measure, public opinion with regard to a candidate or issue. This technique has been referred to as both a "pseudo-poll" and as a "negative persuasion strategy." The American Association of Public Opinion Researchers described push polling as "a form of political telemarketing [designed] to disseminate campaign propaganda under the guise of conducting a legitimate public opinion poll." A push poll appears to be something that it is not; as such, it is an unethical practice.

In a typical push poll operation, a campaign approaches potential voters in a manner that simulates a legitimate public opinion poll and provides negative information about an opposing candidate or issue. The push poll sponsor then asks opinion and preference questions using wording designed to "push" respondents away from the opposition and toward the sponsor's position or candidate. Although push polling has been used by political parties, individual candidate organizations, and interest groups, it is an insidious activity that undermines the public's confidence in the both the polling industry and the electoral process. As a result, several state legislatures, as well as the House of Representatives, have entertained bills to ban push polling. Constitutional free speech considerations, however, have prevented the adoption of such legislation.

Much in the same way that sponsors of push polling use the legitimacy of the polling industry to sway public opinion, marketing organizations may use the appearance of a public opinion poll to sell products and services, and political parties, candidates, and special-interest groups may use the appearance of an election poll to raise funds. In the marketing context simulation of legitimate public opinion polling is known as SUGging—selling (or soliciting) under the guise of polling—and in the fundraising setting it is known as FRUGing (fund-raising under the guise of polling). As with push polling, both SUGging and FRUGing are patently unethical in that they are predicated on a deception.

Complexities of Election Polls

There are two methodological concerns that distinguish election polls from other instances of survey research—particular difficulties in probability sampling and the treatment of undecided voters. The goal of drawing any probability sample is to accurately reflect the larger population of interest. In the case of election polls, the population of interest is the subset of all registered voters in a given voting jurisdiction that actually votes on election day. Because that subset is never known for certain until after election day, the determination of a sample that is composed of those who actually vote—in proportions that accurately reflect the electorate's true demographic and partisan composition—is a difficult endeavor. Moreover, this task is compounded by the fact that it is the very purpose of campaigns to affect the composition of the electorate, as well as the substantive vote choice. In that respect, the population of interest is dynamic in terms of demographic and partisan composition and with regard to its individual members' attitudes, interests, and preferences.

The first step in determining an accurate election poll sample is to draw respondents that have the franchise, i.e., the legal right to vote. This group, known as "potential voters," includes only those with a legal residence within the voting jurisdiction and excludes those too young to vote, convicted felons who have lost the right to vote, and those who have not registered to vote during the required period prior to the election. Typically, pollsters use lists of registered voters as the sample frame. However, as voting requirements are loosened with, e.g., the availability of same-day registration, even the use of registered voter lists may be inadequate to determine who is—or more accurately, who will be—registered to vote on the given election day. In addition, there is the practical problem that in most jurisdictions there is no list of registered voters that both is accurate and contains up-to-date telephone numbers. As a result, additional efforts must be taken as part of the questioning sequence to determine likely voters.

Once the sample frame has been determined and the sample has been drawn, pollsters continue to make efforts to ascertain likely voters by including relevant questions in the election poll. Whereas the exact content and order of these questions varies from pollster to pollster, typically included items are whether the respondent says that he will vote, whether he knows where his polling place is, how often he reports having voted in the past (often validated by public voting records), his level of interest in the election, the intensity of his reported vote choice, and the intensity of his partisanship. Based on historical responses to these questions, pollsters develop an index of likely voting and report that together with the substantive election polls results. In this way, consumers of the election poll results—candidates, campaign strategists, political consultants, political journalists, commentators, and ultimately the public—can carve out from the overall results the attitudes, interests, preferences, and vote choice of those most likely to actually vote. It is the substantive results for that category that best predict the likely election results.

For most polls, the important characteristics of the population of interest are known and thus the weighting process is fairly straightforward. For election polls, however, although the population is often reasonably predictable, it cannot be completely known until after the election. This uncertainty is compounded by the fact that the purpose of the campaign is to affect the composition of the electorate in a manner favorable to one of the candidates. In addition, substantive results can be significantly affected by weighting decisions, particularly adjustments for the number of "strong" Democrats or Republicans. Thus, in addition to determining likely voters, election poll results are weighted to adjust the sample results to the results that probably would have been obtained had the sample accurately reflected the true population of interest.

Typically, the key considerations in sample-to-population weighting are partisanship and demographic composition. Political party support and certain demographic characteristics, such as age, income, race, ethnicity, and sex, are often significant determinants of vote choice. As a result, a critical goal is to draw a sample that is made up of the same proportion of political party supporters and the same demographic proportions as the true electorate. This is particularly important because even if the sample is composed entirely of likely actual voters who do, in fact, go the polls on election day and vote, if one political party is overrepresented in that sample, the results will be skewed in the direction of the oversampled political party.

In addition to sampling accuracy, a vital concern for producing accurate election poll results is the treatment of undecided voters. Whether undecided voters are truly undecided or merely reluctant to share their vote intention, they may well constitute the critical category necessary to predict accurately the election results. To illustrate, assume an election where there are only two major party candidates running for an open political office. Assume that an accurately sampled and weighted election poll produces results whereby 300 likely voters report that they will vote for the Democratic candidate, 300 likely voters report a vote intention for the Republican candidate, and 50 likely voters report that they are undecided. The 300 likely Democratic votes cancel out the 300 likely Republican votes. As a result, the critical determining category for the election is the undecided. Depending on how the undecided vote is treated, a pollster could report a statistical tie, a victory for the Democratic candidate, or a victory for the Republican candidate. For this fairly common reason, the treatment of the undecided vote in election polls results is extremely important.

There are two key strategies pollsters may deploy to address the issue of undecided voters. On the one hand, they may not make efforts to further develop a substantive response. Under that strategy, the illustration above would be reported as a statistical tie, an undesirable poll result, and an unlikely election result. On the other hand, they may take some effort to distribute the undecided vote. The difficult part of that strategy is developing an accurate algorithm for that distribution. Some pollsters will distribute the undecided vote in the same proportions that the decided vote is distributed. In the illustration above, the 50 undecided voters would be distributed 25 each to the Democratic and Republican candidates. In the absence of external considerations, this strategy is likely to be effective. However, the illustration assumes that the candidates are vying for an open office. If that assumption is changed so that the Democratic candidate is given as a four-term incumbent, that candidate will have the benefit of the extensive name recognition that incumbency affords. Under these conditions, the development of a distribution algorithm for the undecided category is more difficult as it must take the incumbency advantage into account.

Poll Results and Effects/ Democratic Implications

Election polls are a useful technique for both campaigns and journalists. Political campaign strategists use election polls to craft an initial campaign strategy and to adjust that strategy to address changes in the electoral environment brought about by the campaign dialectic, external electoral factors (such as the success of candidates in other races on the ballot on election day), and external nonpolitical factors (such as economic and social conditions, both domestic and international). To the extent that the results help candidates and the media covering them to address issues that the public considers important, election polls play a meaningful, positive role in democratic campaigns and elections.

There are, however, two overarching categories of concerns about the reporting and use of election poll results that observers of democratic elections have raised. One category addresses the effect of election poll results on mass voting behavior; the other category is concerned with the effect of election poll results on the behavior of elite political actors, typically, candidates (and, most notably, candidates who are incumbents in a position to affect public policy).

The effect on mass voting behavior can manifest itself during the campaign in two opposing ways: the bandwagon effect or the underdog effect. Under the conditions of the former, voters are believed to support the candidate who is ahead in the polls, generally speaking, because people prefer to be associated with a winner. Under the conditions of the latter, voters associate with the candidate who is behind in the polls, generally speaking, out of sympathy or the desire to level the playing field. Ultimately, which of the two effects occurs is a difficult empirical question; the explanation for its occurrence, however, is an even more difficult question requiring a complex understanding of political sociology. The greater weight of the research shows that these effects are more likely to be manifested in those voters with weaker partisan identification and weaker candidate preferences. In addition, it has been shown that "both the bandwagon and underdog effects are present simultaneously ... offsetting each other in estimating the outcome of the 'real' election" (Traugott and Lavrakas, 2000).

Whereas the bandwagon and underdog effects are operative during the campaign, the "early returns" effect manifests itself on election day. The nature of the news media industry provides an incentive for media organizations to be the first to report an election result. It is often possible, based on exit polls, to project the winner of an election prior to the polls closing. The critical question is whether the making of that projection, particularly in close elections, affects late-day turnout. This question is particularly relevant in presidential elections where the main set of voting jurisdictions, the continental United States, spans four time zones. This problem is compounded when it is considered that there is a pattern to time of voting. Very often, blue-collar workers, who have less flexibility in the time they report to work than white-collar workers, will vote later in the day after their shifts have finished. If those voters are told by otherwise reputable media outlets that the election has been determined, it is at least an arguable possibility that they will not expend the time or energy required to cast a ballot. To the extent that it may prevent voters from exercising the right to vote, and especially to the extent that the effect may be systematic in depressing certain demographic groups' turnout, concerns about the early returns effect are valid.

An additional objection about early projections of the winner in presidential elections is that it affects races for Congress and other lower offices in the states that are not yet finished voting. Supporters of the projected presidential loser's party may decide to stay home when they hear the projections, causing candidates of that party in the other races on the ticket to lose the "coattail" support they would otherwise have had.

In the American context, the possibility of legislation to prevent the publication of any polls, even if laudable to protect the electoral process from these effects, is extremely limited by the First Amendment's guarantees against restrictions on freedom of the press and freedom of speech. Generally, the type of legislation proposed makes it more difficult either to conduct exit interviews themselves or to temporally restrict the publication of the results. In the international context, according to a late 1990s survey by the European Society of Opinion and Market Research and the World Association for Public Opinion research, 30 of 78 countries have "embargoes" or "moratoriums" on the publication of election polls. Typically, these types of restrictions take the form of "publication bans during a specified period prior to the election, for example, 7 days in France or 3 in Canada" (ESOMAR, 2001).

The second concern speaks to the quality of the democratic dialogue between the candidates. The operative assumption under this concern is that political parties will alter the content of their platforms and that candidates will alter which issues they address and/or the position they will take on those issues simply to curry favor with the electorate. Ultimately, an assessment of this concern must speak to complex normative issues of political representation, i.e., whether or how in a representative democracy a political leader should be affected by public opinion.

See Also the Following Articles

Election Polls, Margin for Error in • Polling Industry • Polling Organizations

Further Reading

American Association of Public Opinion Research. (AAPOR) (1997). *Best Practices for Survey and Public Opinion Research and Survey Practices AAPOR Condemns.* University of Michigan Press, Ann Arbor, MI.

Asher, H. (2001). *Polling and the Public: What Every Citizen Should Know,* 5th Ed. CQ Press, Washington, DC.

Foundation for Information. (2001). *Who's Afraid of Election Polls? Normative and Empirical Arguments for the Freedom of Pre-Election Surveys.* European Society for Opinion and Marketing Research, Amsterdam.

Traugott, M. W., and Lavrakas, P. J. (2000). *The Voter's Guide to Election Polls,* 2nd Ed. Chatham House, New York.

Traugott, M. W., and Kang, M. (2000). Push Polls as Negative Persuasion Strategies. In *Election Polls, the News Media, and Democracy* (P. Lavrakas and M. Traugott, eds.), pp. 281–300. Chatham House, New York.

Election Polls, Margin for Error in

Charles W. Leonard

University of Texas, Dallas, Richardson, Texas, USA

Glossary

confidence level The likelihood that a sample's results will fall within the statistical margin for error of a given sample size. Most large, national survey samples are calculated so that they have a margin for error at plus or minus 3 percentage points at the 95% confidence level, meaning that the results normally would vary within plus or minus three percentage points 19 out of 20 times.

hypothesis testing A systematic attempt to verify research assumptions by testing a hypothesis against the "null hypothesis."

measurement error The error introduced into survey results that comes from question wording, question order, faulty sampling design, or other logistics. Any error that is not a statistical sampling error counts as measurement error.

null hypothesis A statement that is the opposite of the research hypothesis. In hypothesis testing, the researcher attempts to disprove the null hypothesis before proceeding to verify the research hypothesis.

population The entire body of units being studied—the group from which the sample is drawn. For example, national presidential election polls attempt to choose a sample of voters from the population of all those who will vote in the election.

push poll A persuasive, usually negative, campaign message delivered over the phone and disguised as a polling call. Its purpose is to "push" voters' preferences away from one candidate and toward another.

random digit dialing A technique used by researchers to ensure that unlisted phone numbers as well as listed numbers are included in the sample of voters called.

randomness Accurate polling requires a random sample of voters. Random sampling requires that every member of the population being studied (for example, voters in a given jurisdiction) should have an equal chance of being chosen for the sample.

refusal rate The percentage of people who refuse to participate in a survey.

sample A systematically selected group of the population being studied.

sampling error The percentage-point difference between the result obtained in a sample and that likely to exist in the whole population being studied.

subgroups Survey samples are drawn to approximate representative results for an entire population—likely voters, for example. Groups within that population (for example, women voters or those under age 35) are "subgroups" whose smaller sample sizes are subject to larger margins for error.

What does it mean for one candidate to be "ahead" of another in an election poll? How large would a lead have to be to regard that lead as "statistically significant"? What is the statistical theory behind polling and sampling, and is it understandable to a nonprofessional audience? This article clarifies some of the most common questions about margin for error—or, more precisely, sampling error—in modern election polling.

Margin for Error—What Does It Mean?

Though national public opinion polls have generally been improving in their ability to "predict" the outcome of U.S. presidential elections, the public's confidence in the utility and impartiality of the polls has been declining. Certainly much of this disparity between perception and performance can be lain at the feet of confusion in the mass media, which in turn creates confusion in the minds of voters and other members of the public. Perhaps some of the confusion comes from the reporting and interpreting of the statistical "margin for error" that is inherent in any modern, professional, random-sampled public opinion poll. The common perception of margin for error would lead even a careful reader to think that polls are more accurate than they really are.

The *New York Times*, which devotes more time and resources to its coverage of election surveys than most papers can afford to allocate, cautions readers of poll stories that in theory, in 19 cases out of 20, the results based on such samples will differ by no more than 3 percentage points in either direction from what would have been obtained by seeking out all American adults. After reading the *Times'* explanation, imagine a story on an election poll telling readers that Candidate A leads Candidate B 52% to 48% in a poll with a 3-point margin for error. Because A's lead is 4 points—greater than the 3-point margin—readers or viewers might regard that lead as statistically significant. But is it? What the *Times'* explanation of margin for error should make more explicit is that each number may vary by 3 points "in either direction," so that A's proportion might be as little as 49, and B's might be as much as 51 points. By the same token, A could be enjoying a 10-point, 55/45% lead over B. A careful interpretation of the result—presuming ahead of time the poll is a large-sample survey conducted by a reputable polling firm—would tell us that in all likelihood A was enjoying a slim lead at the time the survey was conducted, but that it is possible A is either tied with B or might even be a little behind.

Simple Sampling Theory

Hypothesis Testing

What readers want to know from an election poll is simple: who is ahead? Implicit in the question—and in the answer—is a hypothesis: In order for a candidate to be "ahead," that person has to be receiving more support than the other. To have confidence in the implied hypothesis, the null hypothesis must first be eliminated; in other words, it is necessary to disprove the opposite of the hypothesis. The opposite of "one candidate has to be receiving more support than the other" is "neither is receiving more support than the other." In other words, the null hypothesis is "the two candidates are tied."

The election poll, thinking about it as social scientists, is the research organization's attempt to gain support for the hypothesis that one candidate is ahead of another by falsifying the null hypothesis that the two are tied. So, to believe there is a difference in the proportions of support between the two candidates there has to be (1) a lead by one candidate over another that is (2) larger than the statistical sampling error.

Statistical Sampling and Sampling Error

A pollster chooses a sample of voters to survey because there is neither the time nor the money to speak to every voter in the electorate—whether the race is for the city council or the presidency of the United States. One important decision the pollster has to make is how many voters to sample. The more voters contacted, the greater the confidence in the results of the poll, generally speaking. On the other hand, the more voters sampled, the greater the expense in interviewing costs. At some point, the pollster reaches a point of diminishing returns—at which the ever-smaller increments in precision are not worth the costs to achieve them. This is why the large, national surveys typically sample somewhere between 1000 and 1200 voters.

The value of greater sample size is easy to see conceptually. Take the old statistics-class example of a pickle barrel full of red and green marbles. Given the task of calculating the proportion of red to green marbles in the barrel, the simple but time-consuming method is to dump out the barrel and count the red vs. green marbles. The less time-consuming—though less precise—method is to take a random sample of marbles from the barrel, count the red vs. the green marbles in the sample, and extrapolate from the results of the sample to the true "population" of marbles in the barrel. Assume a random distribution of marbles and a continually mixed-up barrel. If 10 marbles—6 red to 4 green—are selected, this small sample gives no more confidence in an estimate of the proportions of colored marbles than does 10 coin flips indicate that a penny is 60% "heads" and 40% "tails." The greater the number of randomly drawn marbles, the greater is the confidence in the estimate derived from the samples. In visualizing the barrel as the boundary around an electorate (Cleveland or Ohio or the United States of America) and the marbles as voters (red for Candidate A and green for Candidate B), it is easy to see how this analogy relates to election polling.

Randomness, Survey Sampling, and Statistical Theory

It is easy to imagine randomness in the proverbial barrel of marbles, or in the rotating hopper of ping-pong balls used for televised lottery drawings. How is a concept like this extrapolated to living, breathing voters (or individual human beings representing other social strata, such as parents of public schoolchildren or drivers of sport-utility vehicles)? A common complaint of news consumers regarding election polls ("they never say what I and my friends think about politics") reflects the importance of randomness in a well-done election poll. "Friends" never constitute a random sample of any population. Statistical randomness, whether in the pickle barrel, in the Lotto ball hopper, or in the electorate, means that every member of the population from which the sample is drawn has an equal chance of being picked for the sample.

Though pollsters cannot precisely satisfy this condition with people—as the statistician could with the barrel of marbles—they can come close enough to it, given the penetration of the telephone into almost all American households. Of course, it is true that not all households have phones, but homes without phones tend to be younger and lower income households that have very low probabilities of being part of the population of actual voters. A potentially larger issue for statistical reliability is the "problem" of unlisted phones, owned by households whose members do not wish to be contacted by solicitors (or even pollsters). Those with unlisted phones tend to be higher income voters who, in fact, are, overall, more likely to vote than are those with listed phone numbers. Pollsters overcome this statistical hurdle, and improve their approximation of the condition of randomness, with a technique known as random-digit dialing (RDD), which uses computers or slightly more cumbersome manual techniques to ensure that households with unlisted numbers are contacted, without relying on directories or published lists.

Calculating the Margin for Error

Statisticians have calculated a sample's margin for error at a given size. In other words, if 400 voters are surveyed, candidate A's 52-to-48% margin has a sampling error of plus or minus 5 percentage points, giving less confidence in her 4-point lead over candidate B. A fairly common sample size in big, important surveys—1200 voters sampled—gives a margin for error of about 3 percentage points. At this sample size, there is the beginning of a feeling of comfort that A was ahead of B at the time the survey was taken. If the sample size is increased to 3000 voters, the margin for error is about 2 percentage points. One of the beauties of the statistical theory behind sampling error is that the margin depends on the number sampled, regardless of the size of the population from which the sample is drawn. That is to say, 1200 voters sampled have a margin for error just under plus or minus 3 percentage points, whether the population in question is Nacogdoches, Texas, or the United States of America.

Another statistical factor to take into account is the confidence level. Virtually all error margins in election polls are reported at the 95% confidence level, which means that 95% of the time—or 19 times out of 20—in a survey sample drawn at random, the results will differ from the results of the survey in question by no more than X percentage points, depending on sample size. Most political scientists prefer to use the 95% confidence level in interpreting statistical data. This presents an acceptable balance between statistical precision and cost of interviewing voters. Error margins also can be calculated at the 90% confidence level, requiring fewer interviews to get to the 3 percentage-point level, or the 99% confidence level, requiring more interviews. Many social science statistics textbooks publish tables of the sample sizes required to produce particular margins for error. A condensed version of sample sizes and attendant sampling error at the 95% confidence level has the following values:

- 100, $\pm$9.8 percentage points
- 200, $\pm$6.9 percentage points
- 400, $\pm$4.9 percentage points
- 500, $\pm$4.3 percentage points
- 750, $\pm$3.6 percentage points
- 1000, $\pm$3.1 percentage points
- 1200, $\pm$2.8 percentage points
- 1500, $\pm$2.5 percentage points

It can be seen that beyond 1000 voters sampled, relatively large numbers of additional interviews will bring relatively small improvements in precision. For a news organization or a political campaign, the added three-tenths of a percent precision provided by moving, for example, from 1200 to 1500 interviews will not likely be worth the extra cost of conducting 300 more interviews.

With any sample size of more than a couple dozen, it is easy to use the following formula to calculate a margin of error at the 95% confidence level:

$$1.96\sqrt{P(1-P)/N-1}$$

The value 1.96 represents the first standard deviation from the mean, in either direction, at the 95% confidence level; P represents the 50% standing probability of a vote for Candidate A (all things being equal), $1-P$ represents the probability of a vote for B, and N is the number of respondents in the sample. To find the sampling error, divide 0.25 [which is the result of $P(1-P)$, or 0.5×0.5] by the sample size minus one. Calculate the square root of that. Now multiply the product by 1.96. The formula can be manipulated to match different sample sizes and different assumptions. Using the example of Candidate A's 52% versus Candidate B's 48%, the product of $P(1-P)$ changes things very little (from 0.25 to 0.249), which also would most likely be the case with other reasonable manipulations of the formula. Most researchers are content to leave the formula more or less alone for the purpose of calculating margin for error.

The formula also presumes there are only two alternatives from which to choose—two candidates, two public policy alternatives, two brands to purchase, etc. To the extent that there are more than two meaningful alternatives, the formula becomes more complex and interpretation of margin for error becomes more problematic. In national presidential polls, for example, this issue does not receive much serious treatment, because it is presumed that only the Democratic and Republican candidates represent meaningful choices at the ballot box.

Interpreting the Results for Subgroups

Even in large-sample surveys done by experienced pollsters, there remain pitfalls for misinterpretation. In election polls, one such danger comes from subsamples of the voters interviewed. For example, if, in a 1000-person survey, Candidate A leads Candidate B 52% to 48%, there is a 3.1 percentage-point margin for error. If A's lead among Black voters is examined and is found it to be 54% to B's 46%, does that mean Black voters are more supportive of A than are Whites? The answer is "not necessarily." Assume there are 200 Blacks in that random sample of 1000 voters. The margin for error in a sample size of 200 is 6.9 percentage points, so Black voter support for the candidate could be anywhere from 47% to 61%. Similarly, if in the same 1000-person sample, Asian voters favor Candidate A 58% to 42%, how much confidence can there be that this is a real difference? If Asian voters were only a tenth of the 1000-person sample, their number would be reliable at the 95% confidence level plus or minus 9.8 percentage points. These and similar results from subsamples need to be evaluated in terms of the smaller size of the number from which they are taken, not from the size of the total sample.

Measurement Error vs. Statistical Error

Even the best public opinion surveys will have the potential to introduce lots of their own sources of error in addition to the cold, hard statistical error that is built into the sample size. Reputable news organizations should provide their readers with some warning about these possibilities. For example, statistical margin for error assumes a truly random sample; real-world polling approaches this ideal to a greater or lesser degree. To the extent that a sample is drawn with inherent flaws, this will skew the data.

Question wording and question order effects also can influence the answers of survey respondents in ways that the greater body of voters who do not participate in phone interviews do not hear. The wording of a question, for example, can make respondents consider a candidate or an issue in a way that would not occur to them otherwise. Similarly, the order in which questions are posed can influence respondents' answers in ways that would not happen in the absence of such a survey.

Large-sample surveys can be conducted over a period of days, during which big news events change voter perception. This can make for a very different set of views collected on day 1, before a big event happens, compared to day 2, when it occurs, and days 3 and 4, when news coverage and analysis might shape public perceptions of the event. It also is possible that refusal rates—that is, the percentage of individuals reached who refuse to participate in the poll—will have a detrimental effect on the extent to which it is possible to generalize from the findings of an election poll and extrapolate to the real attitudes of the electorate at large. The refusal rate poses a substantial theoretical and practical problem for pollsters, because it threatens the condition of randomness, on which the entire sampling theory rests. This assumption is especially under threat if nonrespondents are different in some important way from those who respond. This, in turn, is problematic because it is not possible to tell whether nonrespondents are different—they do not respond!

These examples of measurement error are ways in which the practical logistics of an individual survey introduce bias into the results. These will present their own problems in interpretation, but they have nothing to do with the statistical margin for error, which would occur even in the hypothetical "perfect" opinion poll.

The 2000 Presidential Election Polls

An analysis by Michael Traugott of the performance of the 2000 presidential election polls in the United States shows that, as a group, the polls performed better than did polls in the 1996 election, in terms of predicting the percentage of the two-party vote received by each candidate. Though polls in 1996 correctly showed a Clinton victory over Bob Dole, most significantly overestimated the size of the Clinton victory. Most polls in 2000 showed George Bush with a very narrow lead over Al Gore. Although Gore actually won the popular vote, the national polls got much closer to Bush's actual percentage of the vote than they got to Clinton's 4 years earlier. The problem with the year 2000 presidential election poll was that the statistical models could not overcome the null hypothesis; the national vote total was a virtual tie. With each candidate receiving 50% of the vote, the race was indeed a tie, and no poll of an achievable size would have a margin for error of less than a percentage point!

There are lots of reasons to be concerned about the use of election polling in the media; overnight tracking polls, so-called push polls, instant polls, and Internet polls are among the methodologies that have inherent problems. In particular, the push poll, in which a negative campaign message is disguised as a polling call, is downright dishonest. The traditional, large-sample preelection poll, however, is based on sound social science and statistical theory. Despite its flaws, the modern telephone poll is the best, and cheapest, way to get a snapshot of public opinion in a dynamic election campaign.

Improving Reporting of Margin for Error

There might be less confusion about the accuracy (or relative lack of accuracy) in election polls if news organizations more precisely explained how margin for error is to be interpreted. If, like the *New York Times*, they explained that each percentage in a two-person race varies by plus or minus *X* percentage points, perhaps it would help news consumers have a more realistic notion of what polls can and cannot do. One of the problems in this misinterpretation is the tendency of news organizations to report that a lead is statistically significant if the percentage-point difference between the two candidates' levels of support is greater than the statistical margin for error, given its particular sample size. As in the example previously given, a 4-point lead in a sample with a 3-point margin for error does not represent a "statistically significant" lead, even before considering measurement error on top of sampling error.

News consumers can only hope that academic pollsters, professional pollsters, candidates, and news organizations can put their collective minds and resources together to improve understanding and reporting of these important tools in the measurement and understanding of electoral politics.

See Also the Following Articles

Confidence Intervals • Election Polls • Hypothesis Tests and Proofs • Polling Industry • Polling Organizations • Randomization

Further Reading

Asher, H. (2001). *Polling and the Public: What Every Citizen Should Know.* CQ Press, Washington, D.C.

Shively, W. P. (1997). *The Craft of Political Research.* Prentice Hall, Saddle River, New Jersey.

Traugott, M. W. (2001). Trends: Assessing poll performance in the 2000 campaign. *Public Opin. Q.* **65**(3), 389–419.

Traugott, M. W., and Lavrakas, P. J. (2000). *The Voter's Guide to Election Polls.* Chatham House Publishers, New York.

Van Evera, S. (1997). *Guide to Methods for Students of Political Science.* Cornell University Press, Ithaca, New York.

Epidemiology

William W. Dressler
University of Alabama, Tuscaloosa, Alabama, USA

Glossary

buffering effect A moderating effect in which some factor reduces the impact of a risk factor on a health outcome.

cultural constructivism A theoretical orientation in social science emphasizing the study of subject-defined meaning of events and circumstances.

generalized susceptibility A condition of heightened risk of falling ill.

relative risk The probability of disease among a group of people exposed to a risk factor divided by the probability of disease among people not exposed to that risk factor.

social epidemiology The study of the distribution of disease and health-related issues in relation to social factors.

social inequality Differential access to resources within a society, based on membership in one of several ranked social statuses.

social integration The degree to which an individual is linked to others by a variety of social relationships.

qualitative methods Nonnumeric methods of observation for the description and analysis of meaning and patterns of association among concepts.

quantitative methods Numeric methods of observation for the description and analysis of patterns of association among variables.

Epidemiology is the study of the distribution of disease and health-related issues in populations. The term epidemiology literally refers to the study of epidemic disease in human populations, but it has come to be applied much more widely. In its current use, the term can refer to monitoring the health of populations, to a specific area of study (e.g., psychiatric epidemiology or social epidemiology), to research on a health-related topic that might not assess actual health (e.g., rates of insurance coverage in economically marginal populations), or as a shorthand way of referring to a particular set of research methods used to accomplish all of these. In short, the referents of the term can vary widely. The focus on populations, however, places epidemiology squarely among the social sciences because social categories are powerfully associated with the distribution of disease within a population. Indeed, the evidence is persuasive that social factors are causally implicated in the differential risk of disease observed within and between population groups. Given the focus on populations, in certain respects the methods of epidemiology differ little from general social survey methods. At the same time, there are particular qualities in the study of the distribution of disease that have led to a specialized vocabulary and emphases in research design that set the area somewhat apart from survey research per se.

Epidemiology: An Overview

The conceptual framework for epidemiologic research grew out of its original focus on infectious disease. In that framework, there are three important elements: (1) the agent, or the virus, bacteria, or parasite responsible for the disease; (2) the host, or the person infected; and (3) the environment or setting in which the agent can flourish and encounter the host. Because of this broad perspective on people in their environments, some writers like to refer to epidemiology as a part of a larger field of medical ecology. This ecological perspective has been very useful for locating the production of disease in human-environment transactions.

The nature of the environment, of disease-producing agents, and of person-environment transactions have come to be viewed quite differently in the convergence of the social sciences and epidemiology. Although many of the conditions studied by social scientists do not involve the classic host-agent-environment triad, the general model involving the exposure of individuals to risk-producing features of the environment has been adapted as a guide in much research. But instead of a focus on the physical and biotic environment, the focus is on the social environment and how membership in various social statuses or how exposure to various social processes influences disease risk in individuals and population subgroups. In general, this area of study is referred to as social epidemiology.

The beginnings of social epidemiology can be found in the 19th century. In 1897, Durkheim employed a social epidemiological framework in his classic study of suicide in 19th-century France. In doing so, he established social-survey research methods as a fundamental tool in social scientific research and he demonstrated how social processes could be examined through a focus on disease outcomes. Durkheim's work also illustrates the basic logic of epidemiologic inference. Durkheim was concerned with how the study of suicide could illuminate points of distress in social structures, points of distress so profound that they could lead not only to mortality but to the death of an individual by his or her own hand. Although suicide occurs with a particular frequency within a population, it remains a relatively rare event. Therefore, in order to study trends in suicide, Durkheim had to amass extensive population statistics from throughout France. In order to compare the frequency of occurrence of suicide from populations of different sizes, he calculated suicide rates, or the frequency of occurrence per unit of population. This rate could then be calculated for different population subgroups, such as French Catholics versus French Protestants. When Durkheim found that suicide rates for Protestants were much higher than those for Catholics, he formulated an argument for, or an interpretation of, what social processes would differentially affect the two groups and hence result in this difference in mortality rates.

Although conducted well over a century ago, Durkheim's work on suicide remains a classic example of the process of epidemiologic research and inference. Several issues are noteworthy. First, health problems are relatively rare events in populations. For example, despite coronary artery disease continuing as the leading cause of death in the United States, in any given year fewer than 300 people out of every 100,000 will die from it. For a psychiatric disorder such as true bipolar depression, the number of people afflicted in any given year may only be 1–2/100,000. Thus, epidemiologists have traditionally worked with disease rates as their outcome variable. Given the small number of cases of disease that might occur, these rates have traditionally been standardized to a relatively large population base (ranging from 1000 to 100,000 people). Hence, conventionally, epidemiologic research has meant studying relatively rare events in large populations.

Second, the logic of inference in epidemiology has involved comparing the rates of disease in one population or segment of a population to another. This comparison of rates, or the calculation of rate ratios, provides an estimate of the relative probability of falling ill in one segment versus the other. Typically, population segments are defined by their exposure to some set of conditions thought to be conducive to the development of a disease versus those not exposed. The classic rate ratio is then a relative risk, or the relative probability of disease for those exposed to a risk factor versus those unexposed.

Third, epidemiologists have traditionally relied on secondary data for their research. The costs of mounting an epidemiologic survey can be prohibitive, especially when dealing with a rare disorder. Therefore, epidemiologic surveillance systems have been established, both for monitoring the public health and for providing data for epidemiologic research. Much of these data come in the form of mortality statistics, which means that often etiologic arguments are based not on who is at risk of a particular disease, but who is at risk of dying from a particular disease. As a result, notions of reliability and validity in epidemiology have often revolved around how death certificates and other public records are kept. Also, reliance on existing or public data has limited the range of factors studied in epidemiology because investigators must rely on data already collected.

Finally, as a way of coping with the relatively rare occurrence of certain disorders and with the limitations of data available in public data sets, particular specialized research designs for the collection of primary data in epidemiology have been developed, especially the retrospective case-control design.

The foregoing is hardly exhaustive of the distinctive features of an epidemiologic approach but, rather, illustrates some of the issues giving rise to a specialized vocabulary and set of measurement and data analytic procedures in epidemiology that sets it apart from conventional social science survey methods. At the same time, this separation is only relative and is a function of some of the unusual qualities of studying health outcomes. Any standard text in epidemiology provides the fundamentals of this specialized lexicon.

As Durkheim demonstrated, studying disease outcomes has proven to be remarkably productive in social science research as a way of illuminating social and cultural processes. In the remainder of this entry, some examples of this research are reviewed, both to outline what has been learned in the process and to highlight how some fundamental methodological issues have led to new insights into the study of society.

Social Epidemiology

Social Inequality and Health

There is probably no more widely replicated finding in social epidemiology than the inverse association of socioeconomic status and health outcomes. Across a wide variety of acute, chronic, and traumatic health outcomes, those lower in the socioeconomic hierarchy are at higher risk than those in higher strata. This association has been replicated widely in western European and North American societies. There is some evidence that there is a direct association between socioeconomic status and disease risk in developing societies, although as a nation develops economically the association becomes inverse. The pattern of the association between socioeconomic status and health outcomes differs only slightly using different measures of socioeconomic status. In general, the same results are obtained using occupational class, income, or education as a measure of socioeconomic status.

The typical pattern can be illustrated by data collected on the relationship between occupational class and coronary heart disease mortality for men in the industrial state of São Paulo, Brazil, by Duncan and colleagues in 1995. Men who are unskilled laborers die at a rate of 57.8/100,00 population from coronary artery disease. For men in semiskilled and skilled occupations the rate declines sharply to 14.2/100,000. Men in service and professional occupations have death rates of 8.0/100,000 population.

There are several basic issues to be noted about these results. First, in virtually any epidemiologic analysis, the inclusion of control variables or covariates is essential. There are differences in disease rates between genders and age groups, associations which, under some circumstances, can be of social epidemiologic interest in and of themselves. In many circumstances, however, these are confounding variables (or variables that limit the analyst's ability to discern patterns if those variables are left uncontrolled) to be removed from the analysis. Therefore, in these data, gender is controlled for by including data only for men, and the data have been adjusted for differences among men in the age of death.

Second, there is a gradient evident in the relationship. Whereas there is a sharp decline from unskilled to skilled occupations, the decline continues from skilled to service and professional occupations. Epidemiologists traditionally refer to this kind of gradient as a dose-response relationship (i.e., varying doses of a factor lead to corresponding differences in the outcome), which is often considered to be stronger evidence of a causal relationship.

Third, and related to the previous point, these data are cross-sectional. That is, data were collected from death certificates, indicating the cause of death and the person's occupation at the time of death. As such, the direction of causality cannot be established from these data.

From a strictly social scientific perspective, the impulse at this point might be to proceed directly to research designed to unpack which more precise factors (e.g., occupational exposure to hazards, diet, access to health care, or economic stresses) might be more proximally associated with health status. The epidemiologic response to these kinds of results has been more to try to disentangle alternative explanations for this association that could have resulted from the research methods used. For example, the precise definition of coronary artery disease employed to code death certificates could be an issue here, as well as the reliability with which death certificates are completed in São Paulo. Similarly, the question of how accurately an occupation reported at an individual's death reflects his working life can be posed.

The most important question from the standpoint of methods, however, revolves around the issue of temporal ambiguity in the association and hence causality. Does lower occupational class somehow predispose individuals to poorer health status, or does poor health status result in the differential selection of individuals into lower occupational strata? This question can only be answered by the most expensive (in the sense of both time and money) research design in social epidemiology, the community-based prospective study. In this type of study, an epidemiologic survey of a community is undertaken. Cases of a disease existing at that point in time, referred to as prevalent cases, are then removed from the study, leaving only people free of disease. Also, the risk factors of interest are measured at that point in time. Then, this cohort is followed over time (for studies of coronary artery disease, this is typically a period of 8–10 years), after which the study participants are reexamined to determine what new (or incident) cases of the disease have developed. Although this does not entirely remove issues of temporal ambiguity (e.g., this can depend on how old the study participants are at the outset), this research design goes far in reducing that ambiguity.

Probably the most famous of prospective studies examining the association of socioeconomic status and health outcomes is the 1978 Whitehall Study led by Michael Marmot. "Whitehall" is a generic term used to refer to the civil service in the United Kingdom. A large cohort ($n = 18{,}403$) of male civil servants was enrolled in a prospective study of coronary heart disease. Although not, strictly speaking, community-based, the study did include a gradient of occupational classes that could be ranked in terms of income and educational qualifications. At follow-up, it was found that members of the lowest occupation class (including clerks and custodial staff) had four times the risk of developing coronary artery disease during the course of the study compared to the highest occupational class (i.e., a relative risk of 4.0).

The nature of the study rules out a number of competing hypotheses. First, the data are prospective, making the differential selection hypothesis less likely. Second, differential access to health care seems an unlikely alternative because the civil service is covered by a national health scheme (although this does not rule out differential use of health care). Third, other relevant control variables were measured at the beginning of the study. These included known risk factors for coronary artery disease, including cholesterol, blood pressure and glucose levels. These factors could then be adjusted for at follow-up, statistically removing their effects.

This combination of methods goes far in increasing our confidence that the association between socioeconomic status is not an artifact of the design of the study or of confounding with other, unmeasured variables. At the same time, despite its methodological sophistication, this research only slightly increases our insight into the social processes involved.

Social Integration and Health

The relationship between social integration and health ranks with the associations explored in the previous section as one of the most widely replicated findings in social epidemiology. Investigation of this association actually began with Durkheim's finding that Protestants committed suicide at rates higher than Catholics in 19th-century France. He argued that the norms governing social life were clearer, which increased social solidarity and cohesion, among Catholics. Protestants, on the other hand, were exposed to more competitive and individualistic tendencies than Catholics, which lowered social solidarity and increased the risk of suicide.

Modern investigations of social integration and health have many foundations, including the early studies of psychiatric epidemiology carried out by Leighton and associates in the 1950s, as well as Srole in that same time period. But a general source for this hypothesis stems from basic descriptive epidemiology. It has been shown repeatedly, for example, that people who are married die at lower rates from all causes than do people who are single, widowed, or divorced/separated. What is particularly intriguing about the relationship is that it applies equally to deaths from coronary artery disease and to vehicular accidents. In other words, there must be some kind of generalized effect of living with other people that can influence a wide variety of health outcomes in much the same way as being higher in the socioeconomic hierarchy can.

Unlike the association with socioeconomic status, however, this relationship has been more difficult to investigate because data on social relationships (beyond marital status) are rarely encountered in public data sets (e.g., death certificates). Therefore, research intended to examine this association had to be designed. In many countries, there are ongoing population-based studies of health, studies intended to monitor changes in the public health and hence to inform policy decisions. One of the oldest of these in the United States is the Alameda County, California, study. For several decades, beginning in the 1960s, a representative sample of residents of this county in northern California have been followed in order to determine which factors influence their health and longevity. Periodically, new data are collected, and there is a system that links California death certificates to the study.

A landmark study on social integration and health came out of the Alameda County study in 1979. Data had been included in the survey that recorded marital status, church membership, and amount of social interaction with friends and relatives. Berkman and Syme combined this into an index of social networks, although few contemporary researchers would use this term for that measure, "social network" having a much more precise operational referent. In its current use, the Berkman-Syme measure is generally referred to as a measure of "social integration," or the degree to which an individual is linked in a set of social relationships, regardless of the quality of those relationships.

Berkman and Syme found that those with the lowest social integration (i.e., few social relationships) had four to six times the risk of dying at follow-up, compared to people with the highest social integration. Although this is a prospective study, there are a number of characteristics of it that complicate the findings. Because it is a study of total mortality, there is no way to eliminate prevalent cases at the outset and the selection hypothesis, that sicker people have less opportunity for social interaction, looms large. But this is a situation in which controlling for variables measured at the outset of the observation period is extremely important, which the investigators were able to do. The association of low social integration and higher mortality was unaffected by controlling for initial health status, functional status, socioeconomic status, smoking, overweight, and preventive health behaviors. As noted previously, this association has been widely replicated in other prospective studies.

Implications

As S. V. Kasl once noted, epidemiologic findings tend to be quite reliable, but opaque. That is, given the methodological emphases in epidemiology, great care is usually taken to deal with issues of confounding, temporal ambiguity in associations and certain kinds of measurement error (especially having to do with public data sources such as death certificates), among others. At the same time, given that large-scale surveys are often undertaken that require long-term follow-ups, the nature of the data collected is frequently such that hypotheses of greater interest to social and culture theory cannot be adequately evaluated. Therefore, the integration of epidemiological and social scientific thinking has developed along a couple of lines in the past 20 years. First, a great deal of consideration has been given to theoretical development. This theoretical development has followed the fundamental findings presented thus far; namely, that social inequality and social integration contribute to the prediction of health outcomes. Considerable effort has been devoted to trying to understand, in a more refined and theoretically satisfying way, what the social processes are underlying these associations. Second, and closely related to the first point, research in social epidemiology that more fully satisfies questions of social and culture theory is difficult to carry out in the context of large-scale epidemiological surveys. This has meant that social scientists have had to adapt epidemiological research design to their own aims.

Social Stress, Social Support, and Health

Buffering Model of Stress and Social Support

Epidemiology and the social sciences converge most completely in research on social stress and health. The hypotheses linking stress and health have been generated (not exclusively, but in a very important way) out of the observations regarding social inequality, social integration, and health. Basic research in social epidemiology has demonstrated nearly conclusively that the associations of these factors are not an artifact of research design. When subjected to the most rigorous prospective designs, incorporating relevant control variables from other domains (e.g., other risk factors, access to medical care, and diet), both social inequality and social integration contribute independently to the risk of disease.

At the same time, from the standpoint of a refined social theory, both the concepts of social inequality and social integration are rather blunt instruments; neither concept specifies very well the precise kinds of social processes that influence disease risk in individuals. In 1976, an influential paper appeared that provided a conceptual foundation for work that was ongoing and for work that was to follow over the next 2 decades. John Cassel, an epidemiologist, had been criticizing conventional epidemiological models for over 20 years, arguing that a narrow focus on biological risk factors had led researchers to ignore the degree to which social factors influenced the risk status of groups. This critique reached fruition with his 1976 paper, "The Contribution of the Social Environment to Host Resistance." The key concept here, host resistance, is a brilliant rhetorical appeal to ideas fundamental to basic infectious-disease epidemiology. In the classic triad of agent-host-environment, the interaction of the agent and host in a particular environment does not automatically lead to the illness of the host; rather, there are factors (e.g., nutritional status) that enable the host to resist the invasion of a pathogen. Cassel drew the analogy with human social life. Individuals are exposed to certain kinds of stressful events and circumstances, often as a result of being disadvantaged in the socioeconomic hierarchy. There are, however, resources that individuals can bring to bear to withstand these psychosocially noxious events and circumstances, resources that are social in nature. Higher social integration can provide individuals a greater opportunity to obtain the help and assistance of others, as well as their emotional support, in times of crisis. This support, in Cassel's term, "buffers" the effects of social stressors on the risk of disease. By buffering, Cassel means that under conditions of low support from others increased exposure to stressors is associated with a substantial increase in the risk of disease, but that under conditions of high social support increasing exposure to stressors has little association with health outcomes. People with greater access to social support are thus protected from the harmful effects of stressors.

There was also a second component to Cassel's argument that was crucial to the development of research on social factors and health. That was his suggestion that social factors were not specific in their etiologic effects but rather created a state of "generalized susceptibility" to disease. Cassel based his argument on the observation that social inequality and social integration are associated with a wide range of disease outcomes, not with a few or even a category of health outcomes. Therefore, research on social processes can take any of a number of health outcomes as its object of study because of the creation of a state of generalized susceptibility.

It is difficult to underestimate the influence that this model of the stress process has had on research on social factors and disease risk. Also, in true epidemiological fashion, this research depends in an important way on a complex linkage of research literatures. To use an analogy, explaining the association of elevated serum cholesterol with coronary artery disease mortality does not rest on the epidemiologic observation of association, but also requires evidence from pathological studies of victims of heart disease showing the buildup of plaque on the walls of the main coronary arteries. Similarly, studies of the stress process do not rest solely on the observation of associations in population studies, but depend in an important way on laboratory research on psychophysiology and psychosocial processes, as well as basic social research. But community-based research is fundamental in examining the distribution of health outcomes.

Therefore, social scientific research on disease risk has had to cope with a number of problems in adapting social epidemiologic approaches. First and foremost has been the problem of sample size to study rare events. The resources to mount the large-scale studies traditionally required by epidemiology are less-frequently encountered in the social sciences. Similarly, incorporating meaningful social measures into existing epidemiologic surveillance studies is problematic because measuring social phenomena in a useful way is often a time-consuming process, a process incompatible with the extensive data collection required in surveillance systems.

One way around this problem is a traditional epidemiologic solution, the case-control design. In this design, the investigator obtains cases of a disorder from a local health-care facility. These cases are then matched to a control group on a variety parameters, and then the two groups are compared to determine if they differ on the etiologic factors of interest. In many respects, the case-control design, despite its obvious flaws with respect to the representativeness of subjects, has been the mainstay of traditional epidemiologic research, and it has been used with some success in social scientific research.

Defining the Outcome Variable

An alternative approach in the social sciences, however, has been to change the nature of the operational definition of health outcomes. Epidemiology has, historically, been wedded to clinical medicine. It looks to clinical medicine for its conceptual and operational definitions of major variables, especially health outcomes (hence, the narrow concern with validity and reliability in traditional epidemiology; their measures arrive prepackaged). These outcomes are measured as they would be in clinical diagnosis, which is typically a binary decision—either the patient has a disease or not—which facilitates decisions about treatment. This view of disease conflicts with the conventional social scientific view of variables of interest being distributed continuously within a population. Furthermore, it considerably increases sample size requirements because the statistical power needs are greater with a dichotomous outcome.

Therefore, in much research in psychosocial or behavioral epidemiology (as this area is sometimes called), health outcomes are measured in a way that can be employed in extensive social surveys and applied by interviewers who are not trained technicians and that return a level of measurement that enables the investigator to order subjects along a continuum assessing the degree to which they deviate from a level of optimum health. Much of the research in this area (including some of Cassel's own early work) has relied on symptom checklists to assess an overall degree of psychiatric impairment. The impact of social factors on the expression of psychological distress could be taken as an indicator of the importance of those factors in all areas, under the assumption of generalized susceptibility.

The shift in the definition of health outcomes is evident in other areas as well. Although many researchers in the area of cardiovascular disease continue to use clinical definitions as outcome variables, substantial contributions have been made by social scientists using the direct measurement of blood pressure as an outcome variable. Blood pressure is particularly suited to this kind of research because it is conveniently measured and has a wide continuous distribution in human populations. Many investigators working cross-culturally have employed blood pressure as an outcome variable for this reason.

Another example of shifting the definition of health outcomes can be seen in the 2001 study of low birth weight done by Oths, Dunn, and Palmer. These investigators examined the contribution of job stressors to the risk of low birth weight in a sample of predominantly low-income women in the rural South. Due to the time-limited nature of the process (i.e., 9 months) the investigators were able to use a prospective research design, measuring job stressors at the beginning and in the third trimester of pregnancy, and then obtaining birth weights after delivery. Even with a sample of 500 women, however, statistical power was low when treating the outcome as a conventional clinical assessment (i.e., less than 2500 grams at birth). Using the direct measurement of birth weight as a continuous variable, however, enabled the investigators to detect an effect of job-stressor exposure during pregnancy on birth weight (an effect of 190 grams or over 7 ounces of birth weight, after controlling for known covariates).

Such a strategy in measurement can lead to disagreements with researchers who place greater stock in biomedical systems of nosology, but this has been an effective strategy for increasing the quantity and quality of social scientific research on health outcomes.

Measuring Stressors and Supports

Without doubt, the most extensive methodological developments in this area have come from the creation of measures of stressors and social supports. A relatively complete review of these measures was carried out in 1995 by Cohen, Kessler, and Gordon. From the standpoint of more general methodological issues, a continuing tension in this area of measurement revolves around the relative importance of the exposure of individuals to actual social events or circumstances that are stressful versus the way in which the meaning of those events and circumstances is constructed by the individual. Ever since the influential work of Richard S. Lazarus in the 1960s on the concept of psychological stress, it has been axiomatic that the perception of the stressful nature of an event or circumstance by an individual is fundamental in determining the impact of the event. This has led to the development of numerous measurement scales in which the individual respondent is asked to define the degree of stress provoked by an event or circumstance. Indeed, such a view is so fundamental to the basic western European conception of the autonomous individual that to challenge this view would seem absurd,

Yet there are several reasons, all of them having direct methodological implications, for questioning this view. In the first place, it may be that psychological processes for coping with a stressful event or circumstance are set in motion so quickly that, when questioning an individual about the perceived impact, it becomes difficult in practice, if not in principle, to distinguish between the impact of the event and the person's coping response. For example, an extremely stressful or threatening event (e.g., hearing that one's child has been diagnosed with leukemia) may elicit an immediate response of denial or intellectualization, either of which may lead a person to downplay the impact of the event. Stress and coping may be so completely packaged in cognition that to try to disentangle them after the event is to ask the wrong question.

The methodological responses to this issue have been of two types. One is to ask individuals about the occurrence of events or circumstances thought to be stressful and then simply to assume the cognitive processing that goes on. This can be illustrated by the use of life-event scales. These are inventories of common social events (e.g., marriage, birth of a child, death of a family member, and unemployment) that, independent of their occurrence, have been rated as requiring substantial efforts at adaptation or readjustment (one concept of stress). Then, rather than asking people their individual perception of the stressfulness of the event, investigators simply note their occurrence and look for associations with outcomes, thus bypassing the problems of individual information processing. The other response has been a belief that through careful questioning, investigators can disentangle perceived stress from coping style, resulting in extensive inventories of events or circumstances with equally extensive ways for respondents to rate various aspects of each event (e.g., was it anticipated? was it experienced as a loss? what emotions accompanied its occurrence? what responses were attempted?).

There is, however, a quite different approach to this issue that is based in a theory of social or cultural constructivism, with quite different methodological implications. This approach was developed by George Brown in his 1978 research on depression in England. Brown argues that the stressfulness of an event or circumstance is not individually, but rather socially, defined. He poses the question: Why would, for example, unemployment be stressful? To be sure, the loss of a job has very concrete economic and material implications for the survival for some people. Yet, other people might be only slightly affected economically by job loss, as in situations in which other sources of family income are high or reemployment is highly likely. Yet, for these latter people, job loss remains a potent risk factor for depression. Brown argues that the stressfulness of job loss lies not in individual perception, but rather in the way in which productive employment is socially constructed as an essential feature of an individual's social and personal identity in a modern western European society. To be seen and understood by others as an economically productive member of society is fundamental to a definition of personhood. To have that identity removed, regardless of the concrete economic implications, is to be seen to fail in a social sense. Therefore, whatever an individual may report regarding the stressful or nonstressful nature of the event, Brown argued that it is a potent stressor based on the social meaning of the event.

Brown developed a system for assessing the impact of stressors on an individual, termed the Life Events and Difficulties Schedule (LEDS). Using the LEDS requires the collection of a relatively large amount of information regarding the context of an event or circumstance in an individual's life, as well as information about the individual himself or herself. Then, a basic phenomenological question is posed: Would a reasonable person in this society, in the position of the respondent, feel distressed at the occurrence of this event or circumstance? If the answer to that question is yes, based on discussion among a panel of raters, then that event or circumstance is designated as a stressor. Brown has found stressful events and circumstances, assessed using these procedures, to be powerful risk factors for depression.

Although not as extensively developed, similar arguments have been made for social supports. The general approach to measuring social supports has involved two assumptions. First, that perceived support is more important than whether or not actual support has been received. And second, that support can come from anyone. When viewed outside the context of western European and North American society, however, these assumptions, especially the latter, can be questioned. The analysis of social structure teaches us that there are norms governing the relationships among individuals that involve the reciprocal rights and obligations that adhere to those relationships. Certain kinds of requests between individuals standing in a particular relationship are socially appropriate, whereas others are not. The appropriateness of interactions are defined by social convention. Therefore, it seems likely that an individual's ability to seek help, advice, counsel, or material support from others, the kinds of transactions that are essential in giving and receiving social support, is dependent on these cultural constructions of social relationships. Support cannot come from "anyone" but, rather, is more likely to come from "someone," that someone being socially defined. Using this approach, a number of investigators have found that the stress-buffering effect of social support is found only within those culturally defined relationships.

Collective and Individual Terms

These issues lead directly to a long-term vexation in social science methods; implicit here is the idea that there is a quality to stress and social support that transcends individual respondents and hence leads to the question of the relationship between individual terms and collective terms. The issue here is the extent to which a concept refers to an individual or some collection of individuals. For example, take the concept of socioeconomic status. Is the referent of this term an individual, with a particular income and occupational status? Or is the referent of this term an aggregate of individuals who, by virtue of their similar educational and occupational background, share certain characteristics that influence life chances above and beyond what specific individuals may or may not do? The point is far from merely academic because a growing body of empirical work shows that factors referring to aggregates have effects on the health of individuals apart from the characteristics of those individuals.

Two classes of aggregate terms have been identified: integral and nonintegral. Integral aggregate terms are terms that refer exclusively to groups. Perhaps the best example of an integral aggregate term comes from the growing literature on economic inequity and health. It has been shown that the degree of inequality in a system, as measured by the percentage of income received by the upper 20% of an income distribution, is associated with the mortality rates and life expectancy in that society. Economic inequity cannot refer to individuals because it is based on the distribution of income. It can only refer to the social environment.

A nonintegral aggregate variable refers to a variable that applies to individuals, but is being used to describe a group. For example, the proportion of smokers in a community is a nonintegral aggregate variable.

One of the more interesting developments in analytic models in recent years has been the development of hierarchical models (not to be confused with the entry of blocks of variables in multiple regression analysis) in which individual-level variables and aggregate variables are introduced simultaneously into a model. For example, Haan and colleagues showed that residence in a census tract that carried the designation of "poverty area" was associated with mortality beyond the risk associated with individual-level socioeconomic status. These theoretical and methodological developments promise new ways of connecting macrolevel concepts of culture and social structure with microlevel concerns of individual disease risk.

Cultural Dimensions of Population Health

The epidemiologic transition refers to the shift in patterns of morbidity and mortality within a population from one dominated by infectious and parasitic diseases (compounded by nutritional deficiencies) to one dominated by chronic diseases (compounded by nutritional imbalances and excessive caloric intake). The use of this descriptive term followed decades of cross-cultural research on health, research that has documented the changing patterns of health accompanying social and cultural change.

Many of these observations were based on studies of blood pressure because (as previously noted) the measurement of blood pressure could be conveniently done under relatively difficult field conditions. By the 1970s, literally dozens of studies had accumulated on societies around the world, ranging from peoples still leading a hunting and gathering way of life to peoples in the throes rapid industrialization. In an interesting integration of social science and epidemiology, Waldron and colleagues in 1982 combined data on sample blood pressure, body mass, and age and sex distributions with data from the Human Relations Area Files, a compendium of sociocultural data on world societies. When examined in relation to subsistence economy, they showed that there were no blood pressure differences and no increase of blood pressure with age in societies based on simpler technologies and economies (i.e., foraging, pastoralism, and intensive agriculture). When compared to societies practicing extensive agriculture (i.e., plantation societies) and industrialized societies, however, there was a sharp and dramatic increase in community average blood pressures (independent of differences in age, sex, and body mass distributions).

This study provides a useful context for understanding research on modernization (or acculturation; the terms are often used interchangeably) and disease. In most of this work, research has been carried out in which communities have been ordered along a continuum of modernization. Traditional communities are those in which the local economy is still based on production for local consumption, there is little formal education, national languages are not frequently used, the social structure emphasizes extended family relationships, and there is little penetration by global supernatural belief systems. Modern communities are those in which wage-labor has replaced local production, formal education is present, the national language has supplanted local dialects, the nuclear family is a more important unit of social structure, and individuals have adopted one of the global supernatural belief systems. There is a gradient of increasing risk of chronic disease, as indicated by increasing blood pressure, serum glucose, serum cholesterol, obesity, and symptoms of psychiatric disorder, that is associated with a gradient of increasing modernization. Furthermore, careful methodological research has shown that this is not a function of changing diets or patterns of energy expenditure (although both of these factors have a role to play); nor is it a function of increased access to biomedical care and hence increased life expectancy.

Like the evidence on social inequality and social integration, this research is consistent with a process in which sociocultural change has a direct effect on health outcomes. The stress of acculturation has been offered as the explanation of these findings, but this is really just another term to describe the findings. More interesting work in the area has attempted to theoretically define and operationalize the relevant stressors operating in any given situation, as well as the resources available that enable individuals to cope with those stressors. This has led to a small but important literature in which ethnographic methods have been integrated with epidemiological methods. This is a particularly interesting area because at first glance these methodological traditions appear to have little to offer one another. Epidemiology is rigorously quantitative, based on large and representative samples. Ethnography is resolutely qualitative, with an intensive focus on the meaning of events and circumstances to the participants, and substitutes an in-depth description of a few respondents for surveys of representative samples. If epidemiology is all about extensive results with little context, ethnography is all about context with few results.

Nevertheless, in cross-cultural research, as well as in research on ethnic groups within industrialized nations, the two methods have been combined fruitfully. A good example of this is Janes's 1990 research on Samoan migrants to northern California. In order to understand the precise kinds of challenges this migration created, Janes carried out traditional ethnographic research in the community, consisting of intensive qualitative interviews and participation in community activities. He discovered that, far from abandoning traditional ideas about social status and social relationships, Samoan migrants struggled to adapt these ideas to the urban context of the United States. Therefore, some migrants sought to remain essentially Samoan. At the same time, American culture offered its own set of status aspirations and its own models of social relationships, ways of living that other Samoans followed. Using these insights from ethnography, Janes constructed relevant measures and carried out a small-scale ($n = 100$) epidemiologic survey. He found that status aspirations in either direction could be stressful and associated with higher blood pressure if the individual could not match a precise set of skills or resources necessary for success in that particular cultural context. Similarly, he found that support systems that buffered these stressors were still anchored in the traditional Samoan social structure, but were altered to fit the local context. In other words, without careful ethnography to understand that social and cultural context, it is likely that the wrong variables could have been measured and erroneous conclusions reached. Nor is the adequacy of the analysis to be based solely on the characteristics of the survey sample. Rather, the adequacy of the analysis depends on the way in which the survey work and the ethnography converge.

The linkage of the ethnographic and the epidemiological has been extended by integrating traditional ethnography, more systematic ethnographic methods, and epidemiological methods. Systematic ethnographic methods refer to a set of data-collection and data-analytic techniques that enables investigators to define the distribution and content of cultural models more precisely. Cultural models are schematic representations of the world shared within a society that define meaning and direct behavior. Social life is made possible because members of a society share this understanding of the world. Systematic ethnographic techniques can be used in concert to define with a fair degree of precision what these meanings are and hence provide a more direct way of linking traditional ethnographic data with measurement in epidemiologic surveys. Using these methods, Dressler and Santos found in 2000 that the greater the degree to which individuals are able to approximate in their own behaviors the culturally appropriate behaviors defined in these shared cultural models (which they call cultural consonance), the lower their blood pressure, level of depressive symptoms, and perceptions of stress. These systematic ethnographic methods thus provide a new avenue for the integration of ethnography and epidemiology.

Another area in which epidemiologic methods have been adapted to the goals of social science is in the study of culture-bound syndromes. A culture-bound syndrome (or, more simply, a cultural syndrome) is an illness that is localized in space and hence found in only particular cultural contexts. For example, there are a number of disorders found in Latin America, including *susto*, *nervios*, and *debilidad*, that have distinctive profiles of symptoms (often having fatigue, lassitude, headaches, and stomach disorders at their core) that do not fit biomedical systems of nosology. Yet these illnesses are easily recognized and diagnosed in their local cultural context, and they have well-defined etiologic theories and treatments. Traditionally, these illnesses have been investigated using only ethnographic methods. But a number of epidemiological studies of these disorders have been carried out, of which Guarnaccia's 1993 study of *ataques de nervios* in Puerto Rico is a prime example. Guarnaccia was able to add a single question regarding a history of *ataques* (a disorder characterized by extreme anxiety and seizurelike symptoms) to a psychiatric epidemiology study in Puerto Rico. By doing so, he was able to precisely estimate the prevalence of the disorder (16%); show that it was comorbid with biomedically defined psychiatric disorder, but not explained by any one disorder; and show that there was a distinctive profile of social factors that defined the risk of *ataques*. Then, he carried out a follow-up study to more intensively investigate the cases of *ataques* identified, which added substantially to an understanding of the phenomenology of the illness. The reconciling of ethnographic and epidemiologic goals in this research add value to the research within each approach.

Summary

At one level, the convergence of social science research and epidemiological research is uncontroversial because both approaches share many things in common. Indeed, social scientists exposed to epidemiological methods for the first time may wonder why they would be regarded as distinctive. At the same time, special features of studying health and disease have led to a distinctive approach with an attendant set of concerns in epidemiology that social scientists will come to appreciate. By the same token, epidemiologists incorporating social scientific sensibilities into the study of health and disease have open to them a distinctive way of thinking about the subject matter and a novel set of solutions for research on social processes of clear relevance.

There are, however, compromises to be made in moving in either direction. For example, epidemiologists may be dismayed by the labor-intensive nature of social scientific measurement and the way that this measurement process places limits on sample size. Anthropologists (for example) may be equally dismayed at the thought that something as subtle and nuanced as a cultural syndrome could be studied by including a single question on a survey. But by stepping back from their usual conventions and appreciating the theoretical insights to be gained by this methodological rapprochement, researchers in these varied fields will find much to be gained.

See Also the Following Articles

Durkheim, Émile • Ethnography • Event History Analysis

Further Reading

Adler, N. E., Boyce, W. T., Chesney, M., Folkman, R., and Syme, S. L. (1993). Socioeconomic inequalities in health. *JAMA* **269,** 3140–3145.

Berkman, L. F., and Kawachi, I. (2000). *Social Epidemiology.* Oxford University Press, New York.

Berkman, L. F., and Syme, S. L. (1979). Social networks, host resistance and mortality. *Am. J. Epidemiol.* **109,** 186–204.

Brown, G. W., and Harris, T. W. (1978). *Social Origins of Depression.* Free Press, New York.

Cassel, J. C. (1976). The contribution of the social environment to host resistance. *Am. J. Epidemiol.* **104,** 107–123.

Cohen, S., Kessler, R. C., and Gordon, L. U. (1995). *Measuring Stress.* Oxford University Press, New York.

Dressler, W. W (1994). Cross-cultural differences and social influences in social support and cardiovascular disease. In *Social Support and Cardiovascular Disease* (S. A. Shumaker and S. M. Czajkowski, eds.), pp. 167–192. Plenum Publishing, New York.

Dressler, W. W., and Santos, J. E. D. (2000). Social and cultural dimensions of hypertension in Brazil: A review. *Cadernos de Saúde Pública* **16,** 303–315.

Duncan, B. B., Rumel, D., Zelmanowicz, A., Mengue, S. S., Santos, S. D., and Dalmaz, A. (1995). Social inequality and mortality in São Paulo state, Brazil. *Int. J. Epidemiol.* **24,** 359–365.

Durkheim, E. (1951 [1897]). *Suicide* (J. Spaulding and G. Simpson, trans.). Free Press, New York.

Guarnaccia, P. J. (1993). Ataques de nervios in Puerto Rico. *Med. Anthropol.* **15,** 157–170.

Haan, M. N., Kaplan, G. A., and Camacho, T. (1987). Poverty and health: Prospective evidence from the Alameda County study. *Am. J. Epidemiol.* **125,** 989–998.

Janes, C. R. (1990). *Migration, Social Change and Health.* Stanford University Press, Stanford, CA.

Marmot, M., Rose, G., Shipley M., and Hamilton, P. J. S. (1978). Employment grade and coronary heart disease in British civil servants. *J. Epidemiol. Community Health* **32,** 244–249.

Mirowsky, J., and Ross, C. E. (1989). Psychiatric diagnosis as reified measurement. *J. Health Soc. Behav.* **30,** 11–25.

Oths, K. S., Dunn, L. L., and Palmer, N. S. (2001). A prospective study of psychosocial strain and birth outcomes. *Epidemiology* **12,** 744–746.

Waldron, I., Nowotarski, M., Freimek, M., Henry, J. P., Post, N., and Witten, C. (1982). Cross-cultural variation in blood pressure. *Soc.l Sci. Med.* **16,** 419–430.

Wilkinson, R. G. (1996). *Unhealthy Societies—The Afflictions of Inequality.* Routledge, London.

Equivalence

Johnny R. J. Fontaine
Ghent University, Ghent, Belgium

Glossary

construct bias Generic term used to refer to the cultural specificity of the theoretical variable and/or domain underrepresentation.

construct equivalence Generic term used to refer to functional and/or structural equivalence.

cultural specificity of the theoretical variable Occurs when a theoretical variable can be used validly only within a specific cultural context.

domain underrepresentation Occurs when important aspects of the domain that a theoretical variable is assumed to account for are not represented in the measurement instrument.

full score equivalence Occurs when scores that can be directly compared between cultural groups.

functional equivalence Occurs when the same theoretical variable accounts for measurement outcomes across cultural groups.

item bias Occurs when scores on a specific item cannot be compared across cultural groups.

method bias Occurs when method factors have a differential impact on measurements across cultural groups, leading to noncomparability of scores.

metric equivalence Occurs when relative comparisons, for instance, between experimental conditions, are valid between cultural groups.

structural equivalence Occurs when the same measurement instrument forms a valid and sufficient indicator of a theoretical variable across cultural groups.

Introduction

Intensified intercultural exchanges and mass migrations leading to multicultural societies have also influenced the behavioral sciences. These sciences have become more cross-culturally oriented and the types of societal and individual problems with which practitioners are confronted increasingly require attention for cultural diversity. It is against this background that the question to which extent measurements are comparable across cultural groups has become relevant from both theoretical and applied perspectives.

Measuring across cultural groups adds a major complexity to behavioral science measurement. In 1970, Przeworksi and Teune expressed this as follows: "For a specific observation a belch is a belch and nepotism is nepotism. But within an inferential framework, a belch is an 'insult' or a 'compliment' and nepotism is 'corruption' or 'responsibility.'" Identical questions can have different meanings across cultural groups. In order to deal conceptually with comparability or noncomparability of data, the two twin concepts of equivalence and bias have been developed. Although both concepts have a more or less opposite meaning—with equivalence pointing to comparability and bias to noncomparability—historically they have somewhat different roots. Equivalence mostly refers to the question whether scores can be compared, whereas bias mostly refers to causes leading to distortion of comparability.

Since the conceptualization of bias and equivalence is embedded in and builds on general concepts developed for behavioral science methodology and measurement, an overview of these concepts is presented here followed by a discussion of the major levels of equivalence. Then, various factors that can bias cross-cultural measurement are examined followed by a discussion of commonly applied research and data-analytic methods that are used to justify cross-cultural equivalence of data or to detect bias.

Equivalence and Bias: A General Framework

Measurement within the behavioral sciences can be conceptualized as an interplay between three types of variables, namely, observed, latent, and theoretical variables. The term "observed variables" refers to the concretely observed test behaviors, such as the correct or incorrect answers to a set of items in an inductive reasoning test. According to some implicit or explicit rule, the observed test behaviors are transformed into an estimate of an underlying characteristic, called the latent variable. For example, by coding any wrong answer as zero and any correct answer as 1 and taking the sum of the correct answers, the position of a person on the latent variable can be estimated. The name "latent" variable is used since it is not directly observed; one observes only the correct and incorrect answers. Subsequently, estimated scores on the latent variable are interpreted in terms of a theoretical variable. In a test of inductive reasoning, the test scores are interpreted as referring to an ability for inductive reasoning.

The adequacy of inferences in terms of a theoretical variable based on latent variable score estimates derived from observed variables forms the subject of analysis in the validity framework. The validity of the inferences depends on the links that can be demonstrated between each of the three types of variables. It should be noted that it is not the measurement instrument as such but the behaviors elicited by it within a specific measurement context that determine the validity. Even if prior knowledge or research has established the relevance and representativeness of the items used in an instrument, it is always possible that the items do not elicit the intended behavior. For instance, due to a complex wording of items in an inductive reasoning test, the test may tap verbal abilities rather than inductive reasoning. Moreover, the same stimuli can elicit different behavior in different contexts. For instance, social desirability is likely to have a larger impact on an attitude questionnaire used in a selection context than in a survey context where anonymity is guaranteed. Thus, the adequacy of the inferences derived from an instrument must be demonstrated separately for the various contexts, including cultural contexts, in which that instrument is applied.

Relevance and Representativeness

The items or stimuli of an instrument usually form a limited subset of the domain of phenomena that the theoretical variable is assumed to account for. The aim is to generalize the results of this small subset to an entire domain. Thus, the score on an inductive reasoning test will be generalized to other situations, beyond the testing situation, where inductive reasoning is assumed to play a role. For this generalization to be justified, the observed variables should be both relevant to and representative of the entire domain of phenomena. Irrelevant items would introduce some other theoretical domain(s) into the measurement and lead to systematic noise. If items of an inductive reasoning test contain unfamiliar words, verbal abilities have a systematic, additional impact on the measurement. Moreover, an instrument cannot give any information about aspects of the domain that are not represented in the items. For example, the results of an inductive reasoning test do not give an indication for intellectual functioning in general, since the latter theoretical variable refers to a much broader domain than represented in the test. Although evidence for the relevance and representativeness of the stimulus material forms a necessary condition for a valid interpretation of the test scores, it does not form a sufficient condition; other unintended factors, such as response styles, may interfere. As already mentioned, it must be demonstrated that the selected stimuli elicit the intended behavior in the specific contexts where they are applied.

Psychometric Modeling

Analysis of the relationships between observed and latent variables provides a first possibility for investigating whether the intended psychological phenomena are elicited by a set of stimuli. In psychometrics (but also in sociometrics and in econometrics), mathematical and statistical models have been developed that relate observed item behavior to a position on a latent variable. By specifying precise relationships between items and the latent variable, a psychometric model also makes predictions about how the scores on the items should interrelate. Thus, it can be tested whether a psychometric model adequately accounts for the observed interrelationships. If this is the case, the psychometric model allows estimates of the position of an individual test taker on the latent variable.

The most common psychometric models use two basic parameters to describe the relationship between an observed and a latent variable, namely, an association or weight parameter and a level or intercept parameter. Since these parameters play an important role further on in this article when the levels of equivalence and types of bias are distinguished, these two parameters are presented in somewhat more detail for two prototypical psychometric models, namely, confirmatory factor analysis and the two-parameter logistic model.

Confirmatory factor analysis (CFA) is often used with the measurement of attitudes and personality traits. In this model, it is assumed that both the observed and the latent variables are measured at interval level. The relationship between observed and latent variable can be represented by a regression model, $X_{ij} = a_i + b_i Y_j$, where X_{ij} is the expected score on the observed variable i and Y_j is the position on the latent variable for subject j. The association parameter, or weight, b_i, indicates the expected change in the observed score when there is one unit change in the latent variable. The stronger the association between observed and latent variable, the higher is the weight. The level parameter or intercept, a_i, is a constant corresponding to the expected score on the observed variable when the score on the latent variable is zero. The higher the intercept of an item, the higher the item scores across positions on the latent variable.

A quite different model is the two-parameter logistic model. This model is used in achievement and ability testing where the observed variables can be scored dichotomously (correct or incorrect) and the latent variable is at interval level. It models the probability of success on a specific item $[P_i(\theta)]$ as a logistic function of the position on the latent variable, namely, $P_i(\theta) = \exp[x_i(\theta - y_i)]/1 + \exp[x_i(\theta - y_i)]$, with y_i representing the item difficulty and x_i the item discrimination. The item difficulty corresponds to the position on the latent trait where the probability of success is 50%. The item discrimination corresponds with the steepness of the logistic curve. It indicates how well correctly responding to the item discriminates between subjects situated below and above the item difficulty level. Although this model may look very different from the CFA model, the natural logarithm of the odds of a correct versus an incorrect answer to an item can be described by the same regression equation that was presented for CFA, namely, $\ln[P_i(\theta)/1 - P_i(\theta)] = a_i + b_i\theta$. In this equation, the weight b_i is equal to x_i and the intercept a_i is equal to $-y_i x_i$. The weight and the intercept parameter have the same interpretation as the association and level parameters in the CFA model.

Nomological Network

A fundamental question in scientific research concerns the interpretation of latent variable scores in terms of the intended theoretical variable, while excluding other theoretical variables. An important source for the meaning of a theoretical variable is the network of predicted positive, zero, and negative relationships with other theoretical variables, called the nomological net. It reflects major information on the scientific theory about that variable. The interpretation of a measurement gains in credibility to the extent that this network of relationships can be empirically confirmed. For instance, the credibility of a score interpretation in terms of inductive reasoning increases if the measurement relates in the theoretically predicted way to other measures, such as tests of deductive reasoning and school success or failure.

Multitrait–Multimethod Approach

One of the major practical concerns in measurement lies in controlling for the possible impact of the specific method that is used on the estimates of a theoretical variable. For example, working with Likert scales can introduce an acquiescent response style. Method variance can be detected by varying the method that is used to measure a theoretical variable. In the validity literature, a multitrait–multimethod research paradigm has been proposed in which each of several theoretical variables is measured by more than one method. By comparing relationships between the measurements of the same theoretical variable using different methods with relationships between the measurements of different theoretical variables using the same method, it is possible to disentangle the variance introduced by a specific method from valid variance that is accounted for by the theoretical variable.

Levels of Equivalence

When the measurement context is extended to more cultural groups, three basic questions can be asked within the general measurement framework presented, namely, whether across these groups (1) the same theoretical variables can account for test behavior, (2) the same observed variables can be used for measurement, and (3) comparisons can be made based on the same latent variables. Since two basic parameters can be distinguished in the relationship between observed and latent variables, these questions lead to four different levels of equivalence. These are as follows: (1) functional equivalence, which implies that a theoretical variable has the same psychological meaning across the cultural groups; (2) structural equivalence, which implies that an observed variable refers to the same latent variable, or—in measurement terms—that the weight parameter linking observed and latent variables differs (nontrivially) from zero in each of the groups; (3) metric equivalence, which implies that the weight parameter between an observed and a latent variable has the same value in the cultural groups and thus that cross-cultural comparisons of score patterns can be made; and (4) full score equivalence, which implies the same value for both the weight and the intercept parameters between observed and latent variables across the groups. This allows for cross-cultural comparisons of scores at face value. Note that these four types are hierarchically ordered in the sense that a higher level of equivalence requires that the conditions for the lower levels are met. Each of these four levels of equivalence is presented in greater detail here (see also Table I).

Functional Equivalence

The first and most fundamental question is whether the same explanatory concept can account for (test) behavior across cultural groups. A valid measurement instrument has to be constructed within each of the cultural groups satisfying the general methodological and measurement requirements as presented previously. Since this level of

Table I Four Levels of Equivalence, with Corresponding Types of Bias and Research and Data Analytic Methods

Level of equivalence	*Answer to question*	*Major conditions*	*Types of bias*	*Type of research and data analytic methods*
(1) Functional equivalence	Can the same theoretical variable account for test behavior across cultural groups?	Similar network of convergent and discriminant relationships with other theoretical variables across cultural groups	(1) Cultural specificity of the theoretical variable	(1) Analysis of nomological network and context variables
(2) Structural equivalence	Can the same observed variables be used across cultural groups?	Stimuli should be relevant and representative for the content domain across cultural groups	(2) Domain under-representation	(2) Analysis of domain via expert judgments or qualitative research
		Stimuli should have a non-trivial weight parameter across cultural groups (= same internal structure)	(3) Method bias • Instrument bias • Administration bias • Sample bias	(3) Multitrait–multimethod measurements
(3) Metric equivalence	Can patterns of scores be compared between cultural groups?	Identical weight parameters across cultural groups	(4) Item bias • Non uniform item bias	(4) Psychometric models for studying relationships between observed and latent variables
(4) Full score equivalence	Can scores be directly compared between cultural groups?	Identical intercept parameters across cultural groups	• Uniform item bias	

equivalence does not require that measurement procedures, and thus observed variables, are the same in each cultural group, only patterns of convergent and discriminant relationships with other theoretical variables can be compared across cultural groups. This means that the measurement should demonstrate the same functional interactions in a network of convergent and discriminant relationships with other variables. Hence, cross-cultural comparability for this level of equivalence is called functional equivalence.

An example of functional equivalence can be found in the work of Ekman and Friesen. For their investigation of emotion recognition in facial expressions among the illiterate Fore in East New Guinea, they could not rely on measurement procedures used in literate societies. Literate respondents were asked to select the emotion term from a written list of terms that best described the emotion displayed in each of a series of photographs of facial expressions. Fore respondents were told three emotional stories and were then asked to mention which story corresponded best with the facial expression. Also, Fore participants were asked to display the facial expression that would correspond to the emotion they would feel in various emotional situations presented by the researchers. Although the measurement procedures were different for the Fore, it can be considered functionally equivalent with the procedure with literate samples.

Structural Equivalence

The second question is whether the same theoretical variable can be operationalized by the same observed variables across cultural groups. Since such observed variables reflect the reactions of respondents to specific stimuli, two conditions that are often treated separately in the literature must both be met. First, the items or stimuli of the instrument should be relevant to and representative of the content domain within each of the cultural groups. Second, it should be demonstrated that the items or stimuli indeed elicit the intended behavior in each of the cultural groups. This implies that each item response should refer to the same latent variable in each of the cultural groups. In terms of psychometric modeling, this means that the latent variable should have positive (nontrivial) weight parameters for each of the observed variables in each of the cultural groups. No further restrictions are imposed on the weight and intercept parameters. Since the relationships between observed and latent variables are referred to as the "structure" of a test, cross-cultural comparability at this level is called structural equivalence. For instance, in 1995, Schwartz and Sagiv found that 44 of the 56 value items of the Schwartz Value Survey shared a highly stable position in a two-dimensional representation across cultural groups based on the rank order of their mutual conflicts and compatibilities. Although the analyses gave no information about the exact size of weight and intercept parameters (they were based on rank orders), the stable positions pointed to cross-culturally stable nontrivial weights of these 44 items with respect to the underlying dimensions.

In the literature, structural equivalence and functional equivalence are often discussed together as construct equivalence. They both imply the use of the same theoretical variables across cultural groups. However, empirical support for these two levels of equivalence is insufficient to justify quantitative comparisons of scores or patterns of scores between cultural groups.

Metric Equivalence

The third question is whether it is possible to make quantitative comparisons between cultural groups on the basis of the latent variable. The type of comparisons that can be made depends on the restrictions that hold on the intercept and weight parameter in the psychometric model. If only the values of the weight parameter are the same across cultural groups, then it is possible to compare patterns of scores between cultural groups. Equal weight parameters imply that a change in the latent variable leads to the same expected change in the observed variables in each of the cultural groups. The restriction of equal weight parameters implies that the observed and latent variables are measured on the same metric scale across cultural groups. Since the origin of the scale can still differ across cultural groups, only patterns of scores, referring to, for instance, experimental conditions or subgroups, can be directly compared across cultural groups. This level of equivalence is called metric equivalence or measurement unit equivalence in the literature. It can be compared with measuring temperature on a Celsius scale in one cultural group and on a Kelvin scale in another cultural group. The temperatures cannot be directly compared between the two groups; however, relative differences can be compared, such as the difference between the average temperature in summer and in winter.

In a study on information processing comparing Kpelle (Liberian) with U.S. children, metric equivalence was assumed. Children were asked to report the number of dots they had seen on short-term (0.25 s) displays. In one condition, the array of dots was random; in the other, there was patterning. According to the authors, the observed differences in average achievement between Kpelle and U.S. children could have been caused by factors such as motivation and familiarity with the testing procedure. However, it was assumed that these would affect both conditions to the same extent. Only the relative differences between the conditions were compared between the two cultural groups and interpreted in terms of information processing.

Full Score Equivalence

The final and last question is whether scores on a measurement instrument can be compared directly (i.e., at face value) across cultural groups. In addition to the requirements for functional, structural, and metric equivalence, this level of equivalence requires equal intercepts across cultural groups in the regression functions linking the observed and latent variables. This means that if two persons have the same position on the latent variable, exactly the same observed score is to be expected independent of cultural membership. This level of equivalence is therefore called full-score equivalence. Differences between cultural or ethnic groups on a test can be validly interpreted only if there is full score equivalence. In the literature, the term "impact" has been coined to refer to such differences.

Authors who take the stance that differences between ethnic groups on intelligence tests reflect genuine and even genetic differences in intelligence assume full-score equivalence for the instruments measuring intelligence. However, there is a vigorous debate as to whether such an assumption is justified. The next section focuses on possible causes of distortion of equivalence.

Types of Bias

Complementary to the three basic questions for equivalence, there are three basic questions for bias: across cultural groups (1) what can cause bias in theoretical variables, (2) what can cause bias in the observed variables, and (3) what can cause bias in the direct comparisons of score patterns or scores based on the same latent variables? Taking into account that method factors can have an impact on both the whole instrument and specific items of the instrument, four major types of bias can be distinguished. These are as follows: (1) cultural specificity of the theoretical variable, (2) domain underrepresentation, (3) method bias, and (4) item bias. Each of these four types of bias is discussed here in more detail (see also Table I).

Cultural Specificity of the Theoretical Variable

The first question asks what can cause bias theoretical variables. Here, the answer here lies in the cultural specificity of the theoretical variable itself. When the theoretical variable and the framework in which it is embedded refer to phenomena that are culturally constructed, the use of that variable is limited to the culture concerned. This implies that there is no functional equivalence. For instance, "reading disabilities" make sense only in literate societies. This concept cannot be transported to illiterate societies. However, it is often not clear whether or not theoretical variables refer to culturally constructed aspects of psychological functioning, especially if they refer to the traits and processes that may be rooted in biological dispositions. Cultural relativists and universalists differ widely in the estimated *a priori* likelihood of culture-specific theoretical variables. According to the relativists, basic human traits and processes are fundamentally culturally constructed and show at best an echo of underlying biological processes. According to the universalists, these traits and processes are universal in human behavior, with the cultural context having an impact on the specific behavior manifestations in which they emerge.

Domain Underrepresentation

The second question asks about sources of bias in the use of the same instrument across cultural groups. Since the observed variables form the interplay between the stimuli of the measurement procedure and the behavior that is elicited by it, the causes might be situated (1) in the stimulus material or (2) in the fact that the intended behavior is not elicited by the stimulus material. Here, the first problem is examined. The second problem is discussed as method bias.

As has been made clear in the presentation of the general framework, the stimuli must be relevant to and representative of the domain to which they are supposed to refer. Since cultural groups can differ widely in their behavioral repertoire, this can pose serious problems. A set of stimuli that is relevant to and representative of the target domain in one cultural group need not be relevant and representative in another cultural group. An instrument constructed in one cultural group might contain items that are irrelevant for the corresponding domain in another group. For instance, an item about systematically locking one's windows and doors might be a good indicator of psychoticism in cold countries but not in warm countries, where windows must be opened at night to let in the fresh air. In addition, it is possible that the stimuli of an instrument designed in one cultural group are relevant, but not representative of the target domain in another cultural group. This is called domain underrepresentation. It means that the results of the measurement cannot be generalized to the whole domain. This implies that the same observed variables are insufficient or cannot be used across cultural groups to measure the same theoretical variable. For instance, in 1996, Ho demonstrated that the domain of behaviors relevant to the theoretical variable of filial piety is much broader in China than in the United States. Merely translating a U.S. instrument for filial piety seriously underrepresents the domain in China.

When the behavioral repertoire turns out to be very different between cultural groups, the question arises as to whether this points to noncomparability of the underlying theoretical variable. For instance, the question has arisen as to whether or not filial piety has a different meaning in a Chinese context than in a U.S. context and thus is not comparable between the two cultural groups. Hence, cultural specificity of the theoretical variable and domain underrepresentation are often discussed together under the umbrella term of construct bias.

Method Bias

The third and last question asks which factors can cause bias in quantitative comparisons of scores or score patterns between cultural groups. If cultural specificity of the theoretical variable and domain underrepresentation can be excluded, then the remaining type of bias is method bias. The possible threats to full score and metric equivalence are discussed together, because the factors that have been described in the literature to cause bias in the full comparability of scores (causing a lack of full score equivalence) also affect comparability of score patterns (causing a lack of metric equivalence). Moreover, the factors can also affect structural equivalence (see also Table I). Method bias refers to all those biasing effects that are caused by the specific method and context of the measurement. It must be noted that method bias does not affect cross-cultural comparisons, if it operates in the same direction and to the same extent within each cultural group. From a cross-cultural perspective, the problem lies in a differential impact of method bias across cultural groups.

In the literature, method bias is restricted to those factors that have a biasing effect on all or substantial parts of a measurement instrument. Method factors that have an effect only on specific items are treated separately as item bias. Although, conceptually, item bias is just a form of method bias, there is a good reason to distinguish the two. As seen in the next section, item bias can often be straightforwardly detected by applying adequate psychometric methods, whereas the detection of method bias requires additional research using different methods. According to a 1997 paper by Van de Vijver and Tanzer, factors that cause method bias relate to the stimulus material, how it is administered, and to whom it is administered. These are called, respectively, instrument bias, administration bias, and sample bias.

Instrument Bias

Instrument bias is caused by specific item content, specific response format, and specific response styles. Differential familiarity across cultural groups with either the item content or the response format can be considered a major source of method bias. Lack of familiarity with the stimulus material or the response format may cause unintended difficulties, whereas familiarity can lead to test-wiseness and unintended test-easiness. For instance, it has been demonstrated that the direction of writing the alphabet (from the left to the right for Latin languages or from the right to the left for Arab languages) has an impact on the difficulty of items in a figural inductive reasoning test that are presented in a horizontal way. The differential impact of the response format was demonstrated in a 1979 study by Serpell. British children outperformed Zambian children in a pattern reproduction task with a paper-and-pencil response format, but not when plasticine or configurations of hand positions were used to present the items. The cultural difference in performance was even reversed when respondents had to reproduce patterns in iron wire; making toys in iron wire is a favorite pastime in Zambia.

Another form of instrument bias is caused by differences in response style. Specific response formats may have a differential impact on response styles, such as social desirability, extremity scoring, and acquiescence. For instance, Hispanics tend to use more the extremes of the scale than Anglo-Americans, but only when a 5-point scale is used, and not when a 10-point scale is used.

Administration Bias

Administration bias refers to all biasing effects that are caused by the way in which a test is administered. This bias may be due to a lack of standardization across cultural groups or by different interpretations of standardized administration procedures. A lack of standardization in test administration between cultural groups may be caused by (1) differences in physical conditions (such as temperature or luminosity) and social environment (such as class size when subjects are tested in groups); (2) different instructions for the respondents due to ambiguous guidelines or differential expertise of the test administrators; and (3) problems in the communication between tester and testee due to differences in language, the use of an interpreter, or culture-specific interpretation of the instructions.

Even if the test administration is perfectly standardized from an objective point of view, a differential meaning of the characteristics of the test administration may lead to bias. Effects have been reported in the literature of (1) the use of measurement or recording devices that arouse more curiosity or fear in cultural groups less acquainted with them and (2) differential tester (or interviewer or observer) effects. In particular, when the tester is of a different ethnic background as the testee, all kinds of unintended social processes can be elicited, such as defensive or more socially desirable responding.

Sample Bias

Sample bias is due to the noncomparability of cultural samples on other characteristics than the target variable. Sample bias threatens comparability, especially if it interacts with other forms of method bias. For instance, if cultural groups differ systematically in the motivation to respond to cognitive tests, the interpretation of differences in mean scores is ambiguous. These could point to differences in motivation, ability, or both. The differential impact of the nuisance factors across groups leads to a lack of full-score equivalence. However, even if the measurement instrument generates fully score-equivalent scores, sample bias can have an adverse impact on the interpretation of the results. For instance, if the cultural samples strongly differ in terms of their average educational level, observed differences on cognitive tests could be interpreted in terms of such educational factors, rather than in terms of cultural differences in cognitive functioning.

Item Bias

Item bias refers to those causes of noncomparability that are due to responses on specific items. The most obvious reason for item bias lies in a poor translation of the item. For instance, in an international study, the original English item used the term "webbed" feet for water birds. In the Swedish version, this item was translated as "swimming" feet, which caused an unintended easiness of this item for Swedish pupils. The impact of a poor translation may increase when the original item has an ambiguous meaning. Another problem is that items can cause nuisance variance by invoking unintended traits or processes. For instance, the word "dozen" in a numerical ability item might introduce additional verbal abilities. In addition, individual items might be more appropriate for the domain of interest in one cultural group than in another.

Psychometrically, the item bias can affect the intercept, the weight, or both parameters in the relationship between the observed and latent variable. Item bias that affects only the intercept is called uniform item bias. Within a particular cultural group, the item score (or log odds of a correct versus an incorrect answer) is systematically higher than in another cultural group independently of (or uniform across) the position on the latent variable; the bias is the same for all persons. Item bias that affects the weight parameter is called nonuniform item bias. If the weight parameter differs, the size of the bias for a respondent in a group depends on her or his position on the latent variable. The bias is thus not uniform across the possible positions on the latent variable.

Bias and the Level of Inference

If item bias is limited to a few items in a test, it can be detected in a fairly straightforward manner by means of psychometric modeling. Expected consistencies in item responses specified by the psychometric model will not hold for biased items across cultural groups. However, no evidence of bias will be detected if all items are uniformly biased in the same direction for a particular cultural group. Such a generalized uniform bias will be modeled psychometrically by an average difference in position on the latent variable between the cultural groups, rather than by a similar uniform bias in each of the items. It depends on the intended level of inference whether generalized uniform bias forms an alternative explanation for observed differences between cultural groups.

At a low level of inference, a measurement is basically focused on behavioral manifestations. This means that inferences stay close to the observed behavior. If item bias can be excluded by psychometric modeling, then differences between cultural groups can be interpreted in a straightforward way. Suppose one is interested only in whether children can solve correctly the type of items used in intelligence tests. After item bias has been ruled out psychometrically, a lower score in one cultural group means that the children of that group know less well how to solve the items.

At a higher level of inference, the measurement is focused on the traits and processes that underlie the concrete behavior, rather than on the behavior as such. Items are selected because they are assumed to form privileged phenomena where the underlying traits and processes manifest themselves clearly. At this level of inference, uniform bias forms a plausible alternative hypothesis for observed differences between cultural groups, even if psychometrically no item bias can be detected. Cultural groups can differ widely in their repertoire of behavior and thus also in the extent to which underlying processes and traits underpin concrete behavior in each of the groups. For instance, observed cultural and ethnic differences in scores on intelligence tests strongly relate to group differences in schooling and socioeconomic status and thus to group differences in behavioral repertoire. Factors relating to the differences in repertoire, such as stimulus unfamiliarity, may well have a generalized effect across items in an intelligence test. This is illustrated by the decrease during the past century of the gap in intelligence scores between Afrikaans- and English-speaking white South Africans as these two groups were growing closer together in schooling and socioeconomic status.

It can be concluded that higher level inferences are more susceptible to generalized bias factors than low-level inferences that focus on specific behavioral manifestations. Paradoxically, the absence of any form of item bias is usually easiest to establish if there are no observed differences at all between cultural groups.

Research and Data-Analytic Methods for Detecting Bias and Justifying Equivalence

This section presents some major methods that can be used to detect bias or justify an assumption of equivalence in cross-cultural measurement. Going back to the general framework, the question is how can one justify the use of the same theoretical, observed, and latent variables across cultural groups or how one can detect bias. Four major approaches follow from the framework on equivalence and bias, namely, (1) investigating the nomological network in order to justify functional equivalence or to detect cultural specificity of the theoretical variable; (2) focusing on the domain in order to justify relevance and representativeness of the items or to detect irrelevance and underrepresentation; (3) applying psychometric methods in order to justify structural, metric, and possibly full score equivalence or to detect differences in weight and intercept parameters; and (4) applying a multimethod approach in order to further justify structural, metric, or full score equivalence or to detect method bias (see also Table I).

Nomological Network

As already discussed, the network of convergent and discriminant relationships of a theoretical variable with other theoretical variables is one of the main sources of information on the scientific meaning of a theoretical variable. Therefore, the empirical study of the nomological network within each cultural group forms one of the important strategies to exclude cultural specificity of the theoretical variable and support functional equivalence.

The study of the nomological network, however, is interesting not only for justifying the identity of theoretical variables cross-culturally. It can also contribute to elucidating the meaning of cross-cultural differences obtained with full score equivalent measurements. In 1987, Poortinga and Van de Vijver compared the study of the impact of culture on behavior with the peeling of an onion. The variables from the nomological network that account for the cultural differences are like the layers of an onion. The impact of culture has been fully grasped when all cultural differences have disappeared after the effects of those variables are controlled for. For instance, in 1989, Earley found that a difference in social loafing (working less hard in a group than alone) between a U.S. sample and a Chinese sample disappeared when the allocentric versus idiocentric orientation of the individual respondents participating in the study was controlled for. Thus, cultural differences in social loafing could be attributed to differences in allocentric versus idiocentric orientations.

Even if there are no clear *a priori* hypotheses about the explanation of observed cross-cultural differences, inclusion of variables that possibly belong to the nomological network, such as social, political, or economic context variables, can considerably strengthen cross-cultural research. Consistent relationships with these variables make an interpretation of cross-cultural differences in terms of mere method artifacts less likely to occur. Moreover, they can offer a rich source for generating new hypotheses about the meaning of the cross-cultural differences.

Domain

In the context of achievement testing, judgment methods are frequently used to detect irrelevance of items for specific ethnic or cultural groups. Expert judges who are familiar with the ethnic or cultural group screen items for inappropriate content. These items can then be deleted from the instrument.

In other research fields, relevance and representativeness of the stimuli can also be studied by means of key informants who are well acquainted with the local culture and language. For instance, in 1992, Schwartz asked local researchers to add culture-specific value items that they thought were not represented in the original instrument. Later analyses indicated that these culture-specific value items did not lead to culture-specific value dimensions, which supported the comprehensiveness of the original model.

Another approach is to study the domain of investigation in a rather open and unstructured way, such as performing content analysis on responses to open questions. For instance, in a 2002 comparative study of the cognitive structure of emotions between individuals from Indonesia and from The Netherlands, Fontaine and co-workers first asked subjects to write down as many emotion terms as they could think of in 10 minutes. Thus, they ensured that the emotion terms used were relevant to and representative of the domain of emotion terms in each of these groups.

Internal Structure of the Instrument

If only a few items in an instrument are biased, psychometric modeling of the internal structure of the item responses offers a powerful tool for identifying bias. Here, six prototypical data-analytic and psychometric models that allow for detection of item bias are presented, namely, (1) two-factorial analysis of variance (ANOVA), (2) exploratory factor analysis, (3) confirmatory factor analysis, (4) the Mantel-Haenszel statistic, (5) logistic regression, and (6) the two-parameter logistic model. Which of these models can be applied in order to detect uniform or nonuniform bias or to justify structural, metric, or full-score equivalence is also briefly mentioned.

These models can be classified according to two criteria. The first criterion is whether or not observed and latent variables are related to one another by means of a formal measurement model. The two-parameter logistic model, exploratory factor analysis, and confirmatory factor analysis all rely on a formal measurement model. If no formal measurement model is used, the position on the latent variable is estimated by a so-called proxy. ANOVA, the Mantel-Haenszel statistic, and logistic regression all rely on the sum of the individual item scores as a proxy for the position on the latent variable. The second criterion is the assumed measurement level of the observed and the latent variables (nominal, ordinal, interval, or ratio level). ANOVA, exploratory factor analysis, and confirmatory factor analysis can be used when both the observed and the latent variables are assumed to be measured at the interval level. The Mantel-Haenszel statistic, logistic regression, and the two-parameter logistic model can be used when the observed variables are measured at the nominal (dichotomous, correct–incorrect) level and the latent variable is assumed to be at the interval level.

ANOVA

If both the observed and the latent variables are supposed to be measured at the interval level, and the sum score is used as a proxy for the position on the latent variable, ANOVA with both the proxy and the cultural group as independent variables can be used to detect uniform and nonuniform item bias. First, the sum score is reduced to a limited number of score levels. Then, an ANOVA is performed for each item separately with score level and group as independent variables. The main effect for the score level gives information about the strength of the relationship between proxy and observed variable across cultural groups. If only this effect is significant, the item demonstrates full score equivalence. If the main effect for cultural group is significant, there is uniform bias; independent of the score level, the item has a higher mean in one cultural group than in the other cultural group. If only the main effect for score level and the main effect for cultural group are significant, the item still demonstrates metric equivalence. If the interaction effect between score level and cultural group is significant, then there is nonuniform bias.

Exploratory Factor Analysis

Exploratory factor analysis (EFA) is a classical formal measurement model that is used when both observed and latent variables are assumed to be measured at the interval level. Characteristic of EFA is that the observed variables are first standardized (mean of zero and standard deviation of 1). EFA is executed on the correlation matrix between the items. In EFA, a latent variable is called a factor and the associations between latent and observed variables are called factor loadings. Factor loadings are standardized regression weights. Since EFA is an exploratory technique, there is no expected distribution of loadings; hence, it is not possible to test statistically whether or not factor loadings are the same across cultural groups. However, congruence measures, such as Tucker's ϕ, have been developed to indicate whether the pattern of factor loadings across items on a factor is the same across cultural groups. Sufficient congruence for structural equivalence is usually taken to be found if Tucker's ϕ exceeds 0.95. Values below 0.90 are taken to indicate that one or more items show deviant factor loadings and thus show bias. Bootstrap procedures have been developed to test the identity of factor loadings in EFA.

EFA is used to investigate structural equivalence. However, since it works on standardized variables (mean of zero and standard deviation of 1), this model is not suited to detect nonuniform and especially uniform item bias.

EFA is often used in the multidimensional situation where more than one latent variable is measured at the same time. Before evaluating congruence in this case, the factor structures should be rotated toward a target structure.

Confirmatory Factor Analysis

CFA offers a measurement model based on structural equation modeling. It is related to EFA (latent variables are called factors and item weights are factor loadings), but does not suffer from several of the limitations of EFA for bias research. It is executed on the means and variance–covariance matrix instead of on the correlation matrix. It can thus detect both nonuniform and uniform bias. Moreover, it is an inferential model that allows for statistical testing of the model parameters. With CFA, structural, metric, and full-score equivalence can be modeled elegantly. Structural equivalence holds if the same factor model applies in each of the cultural groups. This means that each of the items has a significant loading on the predicted factor. Metric equivalence holds if the factor loadings are the same across cultural groups per item. Full score equivalence holds when both the factor loadings and the intercepts are the same per item. Like EFA, CFA is often used when there is an array of variables measuring more than one dimension.

Mantel-Haenszel Statistic

The Mantel-Haenszel statistic (MH) can be used for comparing two cultural groups when the observed item scores are dichotomous (correct–incorrect) and the sum score is used as a proxy for the latent variable. In a first step, the sum score is reduced to a limited number of score levels. Within each score level, the odds of correctly versus incorrectly responding are computed within each of the two groups and the ratio of these odds is taken. Then, the odds ratios are averaged across score levels. If there is no uniform bias present, the average odds ratio should equal 1. This means that the probability of correctly responding is on average the same in each group for subjects with the same position on the proxy. If the odds ratio deviates significantly from 1, there is a case for uniform bias. It means that in one cultural group the probability of correctly answering the item is systematically higher than in the other cultural group with the same position on the proxy. Because the MH is robust and easy to use, it is one of the most frequently used psychometric methods in item bias research.

The MH is useful only to demonstrate full score equivalence if structural equivalence and metric equivalence have already been demonstrated by means of other psychometric analyses. The MH as such gives no information about the relationship between item score and proxy within each group. Moreover, the MH is not powerful in detecting nonuniform bias, because it is based on the average odds ratio across score levels.

Logistic Regression

When the observed variables are dichotomous (correct–incorrect) and the sum score is used as a proxy for the latent variable, logistic regression can be used to detect both uniform and nonuniform bias. Per item a logistic regression analysis is executed. In this regression, the sum score across items is the independent variable and the logarithm of the odds of correctly versus incorrectly responding on a single item is the dependent variable. Equal intercepts and equal-weight parameters across cultural groups indicate full score equivalence of the item. Unequal intercepts across cultural groups point to uniform bias. If the weight parameters are the same across cultural groups, the item is characterized by metric equivalence. Unequal weights across cultural groups point to nonuniform bias.

Two-Parameter Logistic Model

The two-parameter logistic model has already been presented. It models the probability of success on a specific item as a logistic function of the position on the latent variable. For each item, there is an item-characteristic curve defined by two parameters, namely, the item difficulty (y_i), which corresponds to the position on the latent trait where the probability of success is 50%, and the item discrimination (x_i), which represents the steepness of the logistic curve. If both the difficulty and the discrimination parameters are the same across cultural groups, then conditions for full score equivalence have been met. If the item difficulty parameter is not equal across cultural groups, there is uniform item bias. If only the item difficulty parameters are different across cultural groups, but not the item discrimination parameters, there is a case for metric equivalence. If the item discrimination parameters are significantly different across cultural groups, then there is nonuniform item bias. However, if the two-parameter logistic model holds within each of the cultural groups separately, then there is still a case for structural equivalence.

Multimethod Approach

In addition to the problem of generalized uniform bias for higher level inferences, which was discussed in the previous section, there is the difficulty that method factors can have a biasing effect on all item responses in a particular cultural group. For instance, the same items might be more susceptible to social desirability in one cultural group than in another. These systematic method effects may go unnoticed if only the internal structure of the instrument is analyzed. However, this type of bias can be detected by applying multiple methods or, more preferably, a multitrait–multimethod design. Only by applying different methods for measuring the same theoretical variable can systematic effects associated with a specific method be revealed.

Conclusions

Cross-cultural measurements can be distorted in many different ways and this leads to noncomparability of scores. The tenet of the entire bias and equivalence literature is that one cannot simply assume full score equivalence in cross-cultural measurement and interpret cross-cultural differences at face value. In reaction to the recognition of the plethora of possible biasing effects, extensive psychometric, methodological, and theoretical tools have been developed to deal with these effects. This arsenal of tools offers a range of possibilities to empirically justify the intended level of equivalence and draw valid conclusions from cross-cultural measurements.

See Also the Following Articles

Item and Test Bias • Measurement Error, Issues and Solutions

Further Reading

Berry, J. W., Poortinga, Y. H., Segall, M. H., and Dasen, P. R. (2002). *Cross-Cultural Psychology: Research and Applications,* 2nd Ed. Cambridge University Press, Cambridge, UK.

Camilli, G., and Shepard, L. A. (1994). *Methods for Identifying Biased Test Items.* Sage, Thousand Oaks, CA.

Cole, N. S., and Moss, P. A. (1989). Bias in test use. In *Educational Measurement* (R. L. Linn, ed.), 3rd Ed., pp. 201–219. Macmillan, New York.

Harkness, J. A., Van de Vijver, F. J. R., and Mohler, P. P. (2003). *Cross-Cultural Survey Methods.* Wiley, Hoboken, NJ.

Holland, P. W., and Wainer, H. (eds.) (1993). *Differential Item Functioning.* Erlbaum, Hillsdale, NJ.

Messick, S. (1989). Validity. In *Educational Measurement* (R. L. Linn, ed.), 3rd Ed., pp. 13–103. Macmillan, New York.

Millsap, R. E., and Everson, H. T. (1993). Methodology review: Statistical approaches for assessing measurement bias. *Appl. Psychol. Measur.* **17,** 297–334.

Poortinga, Y. H. (1989). Equivalence of cross-cultural data: An overview of basic issues. *Int. J. Psychol.* **24,** 737–756.

Reynolds, C. R. (1995). Test bias and the assessment of intelligence and personality. In *International Handbook of Personality and Intelligence* (D. H. Saklofske and M. Zeider, eds.), pp. 543–573. Plenum, New York.

Steenkamp, J.-B.E.M., and Baumbartner, H. (1998). Assessing measurement invariance in cross-national context. *J. Consum. Res.* **25,** 78–90.

Tanzer, N. K. (1995). Testing across cultures: Theoretical issues and empirical results [Special Issue]. *Eur. J. Psychol. Assess.* **11**(2).

Van de Vijver, F. J. R., (ed.) (1997) Cross-cultural psychological assessment [Special Issue]. *Eur. Rev. Appl. Phychol.* **47**(4).

Van de Vijver, F. J. R., and Leung, K. (1997). Methods and data analysis of comparative research. In *Handbook of Cross-Cultural Psychology, Vol. 1, Theory and Method* (J. W. Berry, Y. H. Poortinga, and J. Panday, eds.), 2nd Ed., pp. 257–300. Allyn and Bacon, Boston, MA.

Van de Vijver, F. J. R., and Leung, K. (1997). *Methods and Data Analysis for Cross-Cultural Research.* Sage, Thousand Oaks, CA.

Van de Vijver, F. J. R., and Tanzer, N. K. (1997). Bias and equivalence in cross-cultural assessment: An overview. *Eur. Rev. Appl. Psychol.* **47,** 263–279.

Ethical Issues, Overview

Mairi Levitt
Lancaster University, Lancaster, England, United Kingdom

Garrath Williams
Lancaster University, Lancaster, England, United Kingdom

Glossary

bias The distortion of results; may be deliberate or unwitting. Bias can occur either by neglect of some relevant factor(s) or overestimation of others; it can also take place at any stage of research—in the selection and definition of a topic, in research design, in the conduct of the study, or in the interpretation and publication of results.

ethics May have a descriptive or a normative sense; ethics may offer a description of standards by which a group or community regulates its behavior and distinguishes what is legitimate and acceptable as aims, or means of pursuing these. Normative ethics (the main concern of this article) offers evaluation, vindication, or critique of such standards.

fabrication, falsification Two important ways in which research can be undermined. Fabrication is the artificial creation of data, invariably of data that support a researcher's hypothesis. Falsification is the altering of data, again usually so as to make a chosen result or hypothesis appear more strongly supported.

informed consent The voluntary participation of a person in any transaction with another; guards against both coercion and deception. There is a high potential for ignorance or false belief when much research is conducted. Speaking of consent as "informed" draws attention to the need for relevant knowledge if participation is indeed to be voluntary.

plagiarism The copying of another's intellectual endeavors without appropriate acknowledgment, probably leading to incorrect attribution of work; can sometimes occur unwittingly (for instance, by forgetting to reference a source).

research misconduct A relatively narrow category, by convention covering only a subset of forms of unethical research conduct. Different funding and regulatory bodies adopt varying definitions, usually with the aim of specifying behaviors that should attract formal investigation and penalty. In most definitions, fabrication or falsification of data and plagiarism of others' research constitute standard examples of misconduct.

validity, reliability Two important criteria for the meaningfulness and truthfulness of research. For validity, the measures devised must measure what they are intended to measure and the relationships found must reflect actual causal relationships. Findings that are reliable would be found by another researcher repeating the study—that is, they stem from a robust methodology.

Ethical issues surrounding research are complex and multifaceted. There are issues concerning methods used, intended purpose, foreseen and unforeseen effects, use and dissemination of findings, and, not least, what is and what fails to be researched. In this article, the issues are broken down into two main categories: first, how research is done, and second, how it is determined by and in turn affects a wider context. Familiar issues are discussed, such as the need for methodologically sound investigation and appropriate protections for human research participants, as well as issues arising in collaborative research. The second set of issues is less well investigated and, indeed, particularly difficult to address; these are issues that extend well beyond the control of the researcher or, quite often, any one individual or organization. Also discussed are research topic selection, research funding, publication, and, finally, the role of external ethical guidelines and their institutional setting.

Introduction: the Scope of Research Ethics

Ethical issues around social measurement arise from many different directions. In the most general terms, an ethical overview needs to take account of the impacts of social research on the welfare or respect accorded to its practitioners and their peers, those who are investigated, those to whom the research is disseminated or by whom its results are used, and those who are apparently or in fact excluded from all these categories. In this article, social measurement is approached in a broad sense, to include some issues pertaining to qualitative research. The main focus, however, is on quantitative research.

Importantly, ethical issues extend considerably beyond the field conventionally known as research ethics. In a standard sense, research ethics focuses on the need for accurate investigation and reporting, proper treatment of research participants (human and animal), and fairness as regards credit for the work done. It thus excludes responsibilities regarding proper use of resources, or the uses to which findings might foreseeably be put. Likewise, the pressures arising from competition for research funds or commercialization may not attract scrutiny. More generally, research ethics is largely and understandably concerned with the foreseeable (if not intended) impacts made by individual researchers or small teams. Yet many of the most significant effects of social research arise from the relatively uncoordinated work of very many individuals or teams. Thus, in an overview of the ethical issues per se, "research ethics" represents only one part of the field.

The focus of this article is first on the most significant issues in the conduct of research, issues that may be more within the control of individual researchers or teams. The discussion then turns to the context, dissemination, and use of research, whereby the issues very quickly leave the hands of individuals and become matters requiring coordinated policy solutions or, indeed, political debate. Finally, it should be noted that discussions of ethical issues are notorious for their failure to generate concrete conclusions or firm rules of conduct. An attempt is made here to tackle the broad issues that arise in the field of social measurement, but the aim is not to provide specific policy guidance. For this, readers are referred to the guidelines of the relevant professional association or the codes of practice issued by their host institutions or both.

Conduct of the Research

In terms of the conduct of the research, it is useful to isolate three particular areas of concern. The first relates to the need for "good science" and responsible analysis. The second issue, historically the most well rehearsed, involves proper conduct toward human research participants. Finally, there are the thorny issues that arise in collaborative work.

Methods and Analysis

It is a truth universally acknowledged that bad science is bad ethics. If the science is unsound—and there are numerous ways in which research may fail to produce valid, reliable, or meaningful results—the research will be a waste of time and effort. (The obvious exception is research performed by trainee researchers, who need to gain a practical as well as theoretical grasp of what constitutes sound research.) Most likely, wasteful research will detract from the possibilities for better research, inasmuch as researchers tend to be in competition for scarce resources. It may even happen that a preponderance of bad research can discredit a whole subdiscipline, as a long history of obviously biased and tendentious work on race differences might be thought to have done. It is therefore a matter of moral as well as scientific importance that appropriate methods be used. Moreover, the criteria of appropriateness are not simply scientific, because the matter is also one of effective use of resources and time. Though it may often be the case that findings of better quality can be obtained by greater use of resources and longer investigation, there will be questions of proportionality and practicality: is the research topic sufficiently worthwhile to merit a "Rolls Royce" investigation? And what does the research context realistically permit? When findings are important for human life and death, there will be decisions with no easy resolution: "belt and braces" research may seem the only responsible option, yet results may be needed swiftly. This is most obviously an issue in medical research, for instance in epidemiological work.

Many imperatives of scientific procedure also have clear ethical overtones or implications, two in particular: the need for honesty in investigation and reporting and the quest for value-neutral inquiry and freedom from bias.

Honesty in Research

Dishonesty in research represents the most obvious ethical violation of scientific procedure, and has attracted increasing attention over the past two decades, often under the relatively narrow rubric of "research misconduct" or "fraud." These terms tend to focus on behaviors that are open to formal or even legal investigation, particularly fabrication or falsification of data or plagiarism (whether these take place in making proposals, during the research process, or in reporting or reviewing). But many more subtle sorts of dishonesty may threaten the integrity of research findings: distortion or selectivity with regard to data, for example. Often such activities will be seen in a quite different light by researchers—for instance, as means to ensure that the "right" result is achieved, or to eliminate ambiguities that could be seized on by challengers, or to compensate for limited resources. Naturally, subtle sorts of dishonesty may also arise through inadvertence or negligence. Though these factors might affect our judgments of those who perpetrate such fraud, and should caution us to take account of the wider pressures to which researchers are subject, they cannot and do not alter the fact that such practices are fundamentally unethical. They violate canons of respect for truth, and threaten several harmful consequences: of findings that perpetuate bias and will be less effective or harmful if used; if discovered, they naturally undermine both findings and researcher, and generate wider costs to colleagues and sponsoring institutions.

Social Science and Values

Perhaps more common than deliberate fraud, being an inescapable peril of the social scientific process, is the danger of bias. Findings and even procedures in the human sciences naturally and inevitably raise issues for particular ethical, political, or religious perspectives. One tempting response to the ideological contestation that may ensue is to insist on the importance of "value neutrality" on the part of researcher(s), a position historically associated with the work of Max Weber. However, it is now generally accepted that such a position is naive, neutrality being not only an impossible ideal, but sometimes even questionable in itself. In the first place, there are strong evaluative forces at work in researchers' choice of research topic and methods: these will concern the interest and importance of the topic, and its delimitation. Particular methods will likewise have different strengths in revealing various aspects of the phenomenon under investigation. A structured questionnaire administered by mail can reveal general concerns about the health care system among a large representative population. But it would not be suitable for revealing the concrete reasons for and experiences behind such concerns; for this, individual contact and a skilled interviewer would be necessary. Second, we come to social phenomena with at least some preconceptions and commitments, which inevitably go beyond a belief that they are worth studying. Whether these precommitments concern the usefulness of the knowledge or belief in a cause, they manifest moral concerns, which it would be senseless to expect researchers to abandon and unrealistic to demand that they be put wholly to one side (a sure recipe for self-deceit). What can be asked of researchers, however, is that they try to be explicit about their commitments and extend other interlocutors the courtesy of acknowledging these nondogmatically. In an academic context, at least, this represents one important way of alerting both themselves and others as to likely directions of bias. (It is, however, of very limited use when the researcher conducts a project not of his/her own choosing, when the issues are more likely to relate to what sponsors seek and how the project is situated—its context, its potential impacts—than what the researcher intends.)

Finally, and not least, it must be remarked that a commitment to neutrality represents a very strong value commitment, one that is by no means self-evident. Justifying her mode of historiography, Hannah Arendt once said she had aimed "to describe the totalitarian phenomenon as occurring, not on the moon, but in the midst of human society. To describe the concentration camps *sine ira* [without anger, as in the historian's creed, *sine ira et studio*] is not to be 'objective,' but to condone." The case is extreme, but the point is general: commitments to finding out about human phenomena are always informed by particular human purposes. Whether these are acknowledged or even whether they are intentional will not alter the fact that different purposes will be more or less amenable to different human agendas. The pollster who sees no political agenda in asking about attitudes related to a public figure's sex life may indeed have no particular political opinions; nonetheless, and to some extent regardless of particular findings, the work is doomed to be of more use to some political groupings than to others. (Discussed later is the fact that researchers' intentions may diverge considerably from the effects of their activity, in considering the context in which research takes place.)

This suggests that unwitting bias is an ever-present danger in experimental conduct or data gathering, as it is in data analysis and reporting. Such bias may show in a failure to acknowledge the limitations of a methodology, or failure to properly acknowledge findings obtained via different methodologies. These issues have plagued the human sciences, most obviously via crude or dismissive attitudes toward quantitative or qualitative research methods, where polemics and the (often implicit) attitudes they reveal are by no means harmless to the quality of findings and their synthesis. At a less global level, inexperienced researchers may be particularly likely to bias findings through badly constructed and therefore unclear questions, or via a selective reporting of qualitative findings when overwhelmed with data.

There is a further question about the bias that may arise through overall patterns of research activity (for instance, should there occur an undue preponderance of work on the criminal behavior of African-Americans). This issue is discussed later.

Different Issues Raised by Qualitative and Quantitative Research

The use of quantitative methods modeled on research in the natural sciences demands particular skills in devising the research instrument (e.g., questionnaire, structured observation, or clinical trial) and selecting the sample to ensure the validity and reliability of the findings, as well as care in interpreting findings. Quantitative methodologies are less likely to reveal differences in understandings between researcher and the researched, and thus researchers' assumptions may easily lead to misinterpretation of data. Qualitative research is often thought to be less ethically problematic because the researcher does not remain a neutral gatherer of information but is involved with the research participants, seeks to establish a rapport, and wants to learn from them. However, qualitative social research is likely to be more intrusive for the participants and the researcher's sympathy and involvement is usually limited because he/she will leave the situation having completed the study. Confidentiality is an ethical issue in all research, but will often be more problematic with regard to qualitative work insofar as data reveal more about the person studied. For instance, when detailed case studies are reported, care has to be taken to ensure that individuals are not identifiable.

Respecting Individuals in Human Research

Respect for the participants in human research has long been the most debated area of research ethics. The well-known background for these concerns resides in Nazi experiments on concentration camp inmates during World War II, gruesome in degrees right up to prolonged torture and deliberate killing. The Nuremberg code of 1946 and the World Medical Association Declaration of Helsinki, first promulgated in 1962, presented an explicit disavowal of such "science" and affirmed the importance of both the welfare of each person who was to be the subject of research, and of each individual's free and explicit consent.

Though this background is medical, the same issues apply to all social research that poses potential risks to the interests or welfare of individuals. When the research does not pose risks to welfare, there may also be a case for thinking considerations of consent are irrelevant. However, this is by no means necessarily the case: people have, and take, an interest in their privacy, which is generally not reducible to welfare considerations. Individuals care deeply about how they are seen by others, so that even the most innocuous research that touches on the privacy of those researched must raise the matter of consent. Here the focus is on three issues—welfare, consent, and privacy; the discussion then briefly touches on some possible conflicts that arise when the public interest seems to contradict these rights of research participants.

Welfare

Welfare is a consideration in regard of all research participants—adult or child, well or infirm, of sound-mind or affected by mental disturbance or degeneration (indeed, it is also a matter of concern with regard to research animals). It is usually taken as the first priority that research must not pose undue risks to research participants. Often this may be a relatively marginal issue in social research (as opposed to, say, medical research); it will nonetheless be relevant in some psychological work (recall, for instance, the famous Stanford prison experiment, whereby volunteers playing roles of guards and inmates became brutalizers and victims within a space of days), or in anthropology (whereby the presence of outsiders may have unpredictable effects on previously closed societies). Likewise, special consideration must be given to research on those who are vulnerable for various reasons: the very young, the infirm, and those belonging to groups who experience prejudice or systematic injustices such as poverty.

Consent

Consent poses an obvious problem for social measurement. Though it is a straightforward ethical requirement that researchers not interfere with people's lives without their consent, the fact remains that someone who knows they are being observed will almost certainly act differently than if they believed they were unobserved by evaluating strangers. Even pollsters have found a problem here: in Britain in the 1980s, polls consistently underpredicted the proportion of the electorate that would vote Conservative. The usual explanation is that people were reluctant to admit to voting Conservative, this being perceived by many as the party of not-so-enlightened self-interest.

There are several obvious methods of avoiding this sort of problem. In the first place, research might be designed so as to leave people's lives untouched, so that there is neither risk nor manipulation nor invasion of privacy. In some disciplines, this may be straightforward: very many economic statistics can be gathered without raising any of these problems; historical research, except of the recent past, is even less likely to raise such issues. Retrospective use of data gathered for other purposes is another technique, though it may nonetheless pose privacy and consent issues, depending on how the data were initially gathered. In other areas, it may often be impossible not to affect people's lives. Much sociology, for example, will wish to get close to people's lived experience, which requires direct contact between researched and researcher. Observers who do not declare themselves as such are effectively manipulating other participants, and if discovered would almost certainly be perceived to have betrayed their trust.

Direct, nonmanipulative contact inevitably gives rise to observer effects. Withholding information about the particular purpose of the study is one strategy to minimize these. This means, however, that individuals will not know, to a greater or lesser extent, what they are consenting to; in research, as in ordinary life, this naturally renders their "consent" less meaningful. In some cases, even the vaguest indication of the general purpose might be enough to skew behavior, so that deception of one form or another may be necessary to obtain meaningful data. Some very famous experimentation in psychology has proceeded on this basis; Milgram's work on obedience, for instance, among the most significant (and contentious) of social psychological research, involved individuals being told to administer severe electric shocks to someone; in fact, the "recipient" was acting, and no such shocks were given. Debate continues as to when such extreme deception might be justified, if ever.

In the case of research on, or pertaining to, particular communities (geographical, ethnic, religious, or particular minorities), some form of "community consent" may also be important, especially if that community has been exposed to social injustice or prejudice. This might involve prior consultation with recognized leaders (though this in turn raises questions about whether they can legitimately speak for the community) or some sort of more open consultative process being conducted. When seeking individual consent would not be practical, some such consultation or at least public information process may well be crucial.

When proxy consent is obtained because the participants are deemed incapable of giving informed consent, through age or mental incapacity, it might also be thought that the researcher should still attempt to take the participants' feelings into account. For example, in research on those suffering from severe Alzheimer's, a patient may appear distressed by the questions or tests. Just because consent has been given by the caregiver, this does not relieve the researcher of a responsibility to consider whether to continue with the research or to stop the interview because of the apparent feelings of the participant.

In practice, a need for individual consent may be overridden in instances for which there is specific national legislation, although it is, naturally, not a matter of course that such legislation is justified. Examples that have attracted some degree of controversy include legal obligations to fill in census forms, or the collection of DNA samples by the police from those charged with certain sorts of offenses. And, of course, governments regularly require information for taxation purposes, which is used in both government and public research. Here there are complex questions concerning what sort of public interests justify overriding consent or obliging citizens to participate in data collection, and such complexities are a matter for political as much as ethical debate.

Privacy and Confidentiality

The concept of privacy has a vexed philosophical and legal history, much of which is beyond the scope here. Many justifications have been advanced regarding privacy rights, as have many different notions of their extent and defeasibility. For most practical purposes, the relevant considerations will be (1) whether research participants are likely to take the activity or space in question as a private one, or (2) whether the law has stipulated this to be private, as well as (3) whether the research is conducted on anonymous, statistical basis (clearly research that homes in on a very few people tends to invade privacy, as does research in which individual identities are taken to be relevant). Many people may be unaware that supermarkets scrutinize their shopping behavior. However, that space is not considered private, and behavior in stores is already adjusted to the presence of many anonymous onlookers; moreover, individuals are not singled out from the mass in such research. There is thus no significant privacy issue here, and because there are also no welfare implications for individuals, consent is also not a relevant issue. (Of course, it is possible to argue that such research increases retailers' ability to manipulate their customers in various ways, and is therefore of ethical concern. But this is not an argument that concerns just those who happen to be observed, rather it concerns all those who use or even depend on supermarkets.) Note that simply because behavior is open to observation does not make considerations of privacy necessarily irrelevant: Internet chat rooms may be accessible to all, but—recurring to the first item previously mentioned, i.e., whether research participants are likely to take the activity or space in question as a private one—participants might reasonably object to their exchanges being used by a researcher without their agreement.

Various points are important to ensure ethical research on a small group of individuals, or of respect for private spaces. In the first place, there must be some clear point to the research: mere curiosity is clearly insufficient motivation. Second, the informed consent of research participants will be crucial. (Some sort of community consent, as already mentioned, might also be important when a particular group is singled out for research.) Third, the anonymity of individuals needs to be protected, or at least stands under a very strong presumption of needing this. In some cases, it may appear that there is a duty to preserve anonymity, regardless of whether individual research participants are concerned about it, inasmuch as the trust a participant invests in the researchers cannot be assumed to be appropriate with regard to wider audiences. In general, it remains the researchers' responsibility to anticipate and guard against possible harmful consequences of their work for the participants, particularly when participants are vulnerable because of age, disability, health, poverty, or social status.

In the context of social measurement, the duty of confidentiality that applies to researchers and their coworkers is a means to ensure the privacy of research participants, and raises no additional issues. Note, however, that there is an important tension between preserving confidentiality and allowing scrutiny of research findings and interpretations. This reflects a more general tension between respecting privacy and sharing data and results. As a final point, it may be worth emphasizing that there will be a strong duty of care with regard to data: carelessness in storage (for instance, the use of a computer system without adequate security protections) can obviously lead to significant breaches of the privacy of research subjects.

Conflicts with the Public Good or the Law

Many social investigations can or do touch on activities that are illegal or on the fringes of legality, or that damage public goods. Here, of course, the research can often be claimed to be in the public interest: to reduce criminal or antisocial behavior, it may be helpful to understand it better. (Indeed, it may turn out that such behavior is not damaging or is at least less so than supposed. The use of illegal drugs might be thought a case in point, insofar as the legal context of the activity is much more of a problem than is the activity.) Nonetheless, when there is a real, apparent, or claimed injury to the public, state agencies may take an interest in the research in ways that threaten research subjects' privacy and undermine or vitiate their consent. (A useful analogy is to compare the protection of sources in journalism.) There is no straightforward way to deal with such dilemmas, or even to prevent their arising, because apparently innocuous research may uncover unpleasant surprises. Institutional measures can, however, help protect the integrity of researchers and foster trust on the part of research participants. A recent case in the United Kingdom illustrates the difficulty. In 1997, a study was published of human immunodeficiency virus (HIV) transmission in a Scottish men's prison. By including one case of sexual transmission to a female nonprisoner, the study provided concrete evidence of how a particular strain of HIV could be transmitted by different pathways. The infected woman subsequently approached the police, however, and via a complicated chain of events, blood samples from the study were seized by police and used to convict one research participant of "culpable and reckless conduct." Now, the legality of such police activity clearly varies with jurisdiction, and, of course, there may be cases when the privacy accorded to research participants ought, morally speaking, to be overridden. The point, however, is that such cases are often open to dispute, so that researchers may find themselves under pressure from state agencies and may be doubtful whether compliance is ethical or indeed legal. In the case given, no protection was offered by the institution where the research had taken place, and individual researchers had effectively no choice but to comply with police requests. In the United States, by contrast, it would be much more likely that the sponsoring institution would take a strong interest in defending the data or study materials. Whether research confidentiality is likely to be supported by institutions or is liable to be undermined by state bodies may, then, be a salient factor in deciding whether particular sorts of research should be done at all.

Collaborative Issues

As social research has become more and more of a collaborative endeavor, and the size of research teams has tended to increase, so the significance of issues posed by collaboration has grown. These are first and foremost questions about clarity and fairness in the demarcation of responsibilities, questions that may be posed prospectively (who will do what?) and retrospectively (who should be credited, or blamed, for what?). These questions concern not just intellectual division of labor, but also resource allocation, legal and contractual responsibilities, and intellectual property rights (IPRs). Confusion about any of these can clearly generate grave practical and moral problems, and so the first issue will be to ensure, prospectively, as much clarity and fairness as possible.

If there is a lack of clarity regarding responsibilities for validating data, for instance, it is easy to see that inaccuracies may enter into analysis and reporting, inviting doubt concerning the honesty of the research and damaging its integrity. Standards of fairness will to a large degree be conventional, as in researchers' salary payments, or contractual regulation of IPRs. However, conventions may compass significant injustices, the salary gap between male and female academics being a notorious case in point. Moreover, changing circumstances or unexpected findings may alter the division of labor; prospective arrangements will need to be revisited and clear management will thus be vital to maintaining the integrity of collaborative work. Here the institutional context may help or hinder significantly—for instance, by providing clear channels for oversight and review, straightforward mechanisms to adjudicate disputes, or clear and fair policies regarding remuneration (or their opposites).

One important subset of issues arises with regard to publication and authorship in research teams. Different contributors may have different expectations as to who should, and should not, be included as an author, particularly in multidisciplinary teams wherein participants are used to different conventions. Differing levels of seniority pose obvious problems, especially because they are unlikely to correspond directly to the extent of responsibility for the work or, obviously, to the amount contributed to the project. Junior researchers are also most likely to be excluded from authorship if, for example, they are no longer employed on the project when papers are published. In addition, "honorary" authors who have not made a direct contribution to the work are sometimes included, whether because they wield influence in the field or with regard to a particular project or over a more junior researcher.

Context, Dissemination, and Use of the Research

The proper treatment of human research participants has attracted huge ethical debate, and issues of intellectual property have drawn a great deal of legal attention, but the same cannot be said for wider sociopolitical issues involved in the context of research. Publication and sponsorship issues are attracting increased attention, however, and issues such as institutional support and the role of external ethical review are live and pressing issues for researchers.

In the first place, there is the choice of research topic: what gets researched and what is ignored is a matter of great moral and political significance. This leads naturally to the second aspect, how research is funded, and (in particular) how it is sponsored by firms or other bodies. Such bodies will often set limits regarding dissemination, and publication issues are thus the third aspect to consider. Finally, there is the role of external ethical guidelines, and the need to go beyond instituting an ethics committee if such guidelines are to have a serious impact on an organization's internal and external ethics.

Choice of Research Topics

Here the issue is not so much what individual researchers choose to research or even what sponsoring organizations choose to fund, so much as the overall pattern of research that emerges from these more local decisions. There is more than inefficiency at stake in the excess research of some areas, if this implies that other areas are neglected. On the other hand, excess scrutiny may be as questionable as neglect: if the deviance of a particular group is studied and studied again, this embodies a clearly pejorative judgment about its members.

Important areas of social life may be under- or over-researched for all sorts of reasons, but the general tendency seems to be for these problems to overlap with existing injustices. For instance, the criminality of the poor may attract far greater attention than that perpetrated by the privileged, be it fraud or domestic violence. Problems facing some communities may attract political attention, funding, and thence research more quickly and more sympathetically, compared to other problems. This has been especially clear in medicine—the early lack of research into autoimmune deficiency syndrome (AIDS), the lack of research into tropical diseases, the focus on pharmaceutical products rather than other means of relieving disease or suffering, and so on. (One interesting reverse case is the relative lack of attention to diseases specific to men, such as prostate cancer.) But, as the example of criminological research suggests, social research is by no means exempt from such patterns of bias. Consider how historians have, until the past 20 years or so, almost entirely neglected the experiences of women. Maslow famously complained of how psychologists focus on the average human being, in the search for validity on the model of the natural sciences, thus ignoring those human beings whose moral and personal qualities transcend the average. Repetitive investigation of welfare fraud and African-American criminality provide obverse examples.

Such patterns of bias raise questions about the intellectual independence of disciplines, and even the political role they may occupy, be it unwittingly or not. Of course, social science also has an honorable tradition of questioning the status quo, in particular uncovering inequality and discrimination. The responsibilities of the sociologist were summed up by C. Wright Mills: "Do not allow public issues as they are officially formulated, or troubles as they are privately felt, to determine the problems that you take up for study." The social scientist is expected to maintain some intellectual distance from individual problems and those of the government. In deciding whether to take on someone else's issues or troubles, the researcher might ask several questions: Why is this research is being funded now? What are the interests that mean these research questions are being asked? Will this research legitimate a particular solution to a problem and cut off alternative approaches? For example, there has been controversy over research into the genetics of aggression and antisocial behavior, because it might be seen as legitimating biological or genetic explanations and take resources away from other known "causes," such as inequality and racism. C. Wright Mills wrote at the end of the McCarthy era, during which there was an attempt to root out "anti-Americanism" in public life; Mills' message remains pertinent—that the researcher should beware of being sucked into the agendas of government or public opinion (or indeed of commercial bias that goes against the public interest).

There is a further important issue here, about peer pressure. Discipline, as Foucault famously noted, has two senses. As well as defining a respectable area of intellectual inquiry, a discipline sanctions those who go beyond this area. There is nothing mysterious about this process, and it need (though it may) involve no conspiracy. Innovative work is less likely to meet with comprehension by peers or external funding bodies. It is likely to challenge certain precepts that are currently taken for granted among peers, appearing to threaten established work. And indeed, it is not unreasonable to think that those who chart new intellectual territory might be less likely to succeed in their work. The upshot, however, is that research tends to follow established routes, and that the proponents of almost every advance and breakthrough in a discipline will have spent time being marginalized, be it from funding or publication opportunities, promotions, or other forms of recognition. (Many times, such pressure has gone much farther, to patently unethical behaviors such as ostracism or manipulation of grant award processes.) How a discipline can maintain healthy diversity and promote innovation, while protecting its intellectual standards, is surely one of the more intractable issues in the organization of research. One thing is clear: without diversity and innovation, the intellectual standards within a discipline will fall and its research will cease to confront society with significant findings.

How Research Is Funded

The preceding problem is, of course, tightly bound up with the question of how research is funded. Not only will governments have particular political agendas, but, as large bureaucracies, some sorts of research are simply more likely to be of interest to them than are others. Funding bodies that distribute support for research often effectively insulate researchers from the pressure of political agendas, which is an important achievement; they are less likely to do so with regard to bureaucratic bias. The "effectively insulated" researcher receiving funds will probably encounter little pressure to demonstrate particular outcomes (unlike a researcher funded by a right-wing think-tank to look at the "problem" of single mothers, for example). The researcher will, however, often have to conform to particular methods, or work on some topics rather than others, especially when large sums of money are at stake. Whether this finally results in undesirable bias is of course a contingent matter, and a question of fine political judgment: a system of support for socially useful research is not only legitimate but appropriate, the question being (of course) how, and by whom, "socially useful" is defined.

Grant-giving bodies obviously need to ensure fairness in the distribution of monies, in terms of research priorities and merits of researchers and proposals. Fairness is particularly difficult to institutionalize here. On the one hand, there is a clear imperative to simplify the review and competition process, to minimize the time, resources, and effort it demands of researchers and funder. On the other hand, careful scrutiny of credentials and of the merits of proposals is labor and time intensive, and requires some process of peer review. Peer review, essential for the knowledgeable assessment of expertise and projects, in turn raises difficult issues. It tends not to favor originality. Reviewers are exposed to unfortunate temptations: to take ideas from proposals, to denigrate competitors, or to favor persons known over unknown (anonymization may be difficult in specialized areas, and hinders assessments of expertise). On the applicants' side, pressure to win funding may tempt researchers to claim expertise they do not have, to be unrealistic about what can be done within the required time scale and budget, or to write proposals that seem more likely to win favor but do not accord with actual intentions.

Once funding is secured, it will be important that researchers and funders are clear about their respective obligations, preferably in the form of a written contract that does not conflict with professional obligations or ethical principles. This is clearly of especial importance where work is funded by a commercial body or a special interest group. Areas in which clarification may be necessary include the researchers' rights over publication and dissemination of the findings, and confidentiality of information provided by the sponsor. It should also be recognized that there is a duty on the part of researchers to disclose sources of funding or of benefits received from organizations that might have a stake in the research outcomes. Failure to clarify rights of publication and dissemination has resulted in the suppression of findings that do not promote the sponsor's interests. In general, it would be naive to expect unbiased research to survive the combination of pressures involved in commercially funded work, unless there are strong institutional safeguards to separate researcher and funder.

Publication Issues

Publication is increasingly recognized as an area posing many ethical problems. As already noted, serious issues may arise in commercially sponsored work, when findings are disliked by the sponsor. In the academic context, more subtle difficulties arise. In the first place, publication shares in the problem mentioned previously, that of allowing innovation in the institutional context of research. Some sorts of research may be easier to publish, or at least easier to publish in officially recognized or prestigious places, thus supporting the conventional at the price of the original.

None of this would be quite so serious, however, were researchers not exposed to an environment in which extreme weight is placed on publication, both as regards quantity of publications and, because quality is extremely difficult to assess objectively, the prestige of the publishing journals. The very idea of publication as an end in itself, which tends to emerge from this pressure, represents a basic distortion of research ethics. Publication is fundamentally a means to the most effective and concise reporting of research and findings; the quantity of publications is no indicator of the significance of research or the ability of a researcher to produce sound, innovative research. The pressure to publish creates an obvious incentive to overpublish, or to publish work sooner than might be desirable from the point of view of intellectual development. "Splintering," breaking up the results of research into more publications than is intellectually justified, violates the needs for concision and effectiveness in reporting, as does duplication, be it subtle or not.

There are, of course, issues about what is accepted for publication by journals. Usually the acceptance process is governed by peer review, with prefiltering by editors. This raises the same issues discussed with regard to fairness in grant application processes, though the results are not usually so severe. Space limitations may represent a constraint on full reporting of methods, or of the complications of coauthorship responsibilities; they may even operate as an excuse not to declare interests or funders. Negative findings naturally tend to appear of less interest than positive ones, so there tends to be overall publication bias.

Finally, there are serious issues about access to publications. The ever-increasing quantity of research makes it extremely difficult for researchers in all but the most specialized fields to keep up with the activities of their peers. The use of summaries and abstracts is one compensating technique, but these obviously do not allow assessment of overall validity or methods. Actually accessing the increasing number of journals is also problematic, especially given the sharp price increases publishers have made in recent years. In this situation, it is not surprising that many have wondered about the logic of pursuing ever-increasing amounts of research: who is in a position to digest the findings and actually make use of them?

External Ethical Guidelines and Institutional Setting

As recognition of the many ethical issues surrounding social research has grown, it has become increasingly common for the social sciences to follow the example of medicine, not only by establishing guidelines of professional ethics (see Table I), but also by instituting "institutional review boards" (United States) or "research ethics committees" (United Kingdom). Though generally welcome, especially as a means to ensure that research participants can trust researchers, this process is not without its own costs and dangers. In particular, such measures can only operate as intended if they reflect a wider commitment on the part of the researcher's institution to promote good practice and to deal with nonideal practice in an impartial and constructive manner. This judgment reflects the belief that almost all research-related ethical issues are shaped and sometimes sharpened by the context in which research takes place. Pressures to conform to the conventions of the discipline, to publish, to gain funding, and to undertake commercial partnerships are felt by researchers at almost every level, whether it be in terms of criteria for a first academic post, for promotion, or for peer recognition. Nonetheless, how strongly these forces operate depends on the structure, ethos, and management of the institution and the sector in which it operates. Likewise, whether it is relatively "safe" or acutely dangerous to draw attention to possible breaches of ethics is a matter of great importance, which is strongly determined by the policies, procedures, and leadership of research institutions. For example, when conflicting or even unethical pressures come from different parts of an institution, it is not difficult to see how many researchers can feel that they "can't do right for doing wrong."

In contrast with ethics committees, professional ethical codes are not so liable to generate counterproductive effects. They might occasionally be used, perhaps as the nearest tool at hand, as a way to exert pressure on innovative or merely quirky researchers. Generally, however, as they are typically "aspirational" and are enforced by no institutional mechanisms; their role is one of providing guidance to those individual researchers

Table I American Sociological Association: Summary of Five General Principles of Research Ethics[a]

Principle	*Description*
A	Professional competence: stresses the importance of the "highest levels of competence"; sociologists should recognize the limits of their expertise, pursue on-going training to maintain competence, and consult with other professionals
B	Integrity: stresses the importance of honesty, fairness, and respect for others in all professional activities
C	Professional and scientific responsibility: sociologists should adhere to the highest scientific and professional standards and accept responsibility for their work; they should show respect for colleagues but "must never let the desire to be collegial outweigh their shared responsibility for ethical behavior"
D	Respect for people's rights, dignity, and diversity: emphasizes the importance of trying to eliminate bias in professional activities and not tolerating discrimination "based on age, gender, race, ethnicity, national origin, religion, sexual orientation, disability, health conditions, or marital, domestic, or parental status"; asks sensitivity to cultural, individual, and role differences, and acknowledgment of the rights of others to hold different values and attitudes
E	Social responsibility: demands awareness of professional and scientific responsibility to the communities and societies where researchers live and work; sociologists should strive to advance the science of sociology and to serve the public good

[a] Summary of the principles of the ASA Code of Ethics originally agreed on in 1997.

who are particularly concerned about issues their work might raise. (Even then, however, they might be too vague to be helpful, for the simple reason that the more specific a code is, the more likely it is to inadvertently restrict unobjectionable work.) For example, the American Sociological Association sets out five general ethical principles "which should be considered by sociologists in arriving at an ethical course of action" (together with some more specific guidance entitled "ethical standards"). Professional bodies emphasize that the ethical implications of research should be the subject of active discussion and reflection with colleagues throughout the course of a project. This is only to make the basic point that guidelines are neither self-interpreting, self-enforcing, nor self-implementing. When, however, a code or set of guidelines is accompanied by institutional enforcement measures, the likelihood is that these measures will also have unintended and indeed undesirable consequences. This is not to say that, on balance, institutional enforcement is undesirable—far from it; but it is necessary to point out that simply adding one more committee to an organization's structure is unlikely to be enough to alter significantly the values that it puts into practice. In other words, if an institution takes an ethics committee to be adequate to discharge its responsibility for ensuring ethical research, then it has not taken its responsibility seriously enough.

The most basic danger is that the ethics committee will become just one more bureaucratic hurdle for researchers or grant applicants to leap. Should it work in this way, or be perceived to do so (and especially if committee members share this perception), then ethics will be seen as a hindrance to research; even if the letter of guidelines is respected, there can be little hope that the spirit will be respected. In general, the picture will be that ethics is the researcher's responsibility, with the institution scrutinizing to make sure unethical projects are not undertaken. Yet given the pressures already described, this is not good enough. If researchers face unmitigated imperatives to publish, get grant funding, and so on, they are placed under the standing temptation to cut corners. It will often be the case that more responsible research requires more thought, effort, and time. Unless greater responsibility is taken seriously as a criterion by the institution, researchers are simply in a double bind: damned it they do (cut corners and get caught), damned if they do not (less likely to be promoted, have their contract renewed, etc.).

Thus ethics committees need to be located within a culture that values responsible research, so that ethical review processes are not seen simply as a hindrance to research: a clear framework can promote trust and be enabling for researchers. This is partly a question of leadership and example, but also a question of institutional design. Negatively speaking, there will be a need for clear, prompt, and open procedures that penalize bad practice. When individuals have clearly transgressed recognized standards, this must be challenged and some appropriate form of action taken, otherwise the status of those standards is fogged with ambiguity and the danger of selective (hence unfair) enforcement arises. This is notoriously difficult for institutions to achieve: openness will always seem risky, procedural fairness demands a careful (time-consuming) process and certain standards of evidence, and the tendency will be for only one or a few people to be singled out, even when many people had a share of responsibility. Positively speaking, organizations can institute positive educative measures to ensure that researchers and their co-workers are aware of their shared responsibility for responsible research. They can create systems and procedures for the mentoring and support of more junior researchers, thus making them less vulnerable to pressure to cut ethical corners. They can be more or less active in emphasizing purely quantitative measures as regards research output. They can do much to ensure (or to hinder) secure data storage, or to encourage clarity as regards management, allocation of responsibilities, and accountability in large collaborative projects. Not least, they can play an important role in seeing that commercial agreements do not threaten the integrity of researchers or, indeed, of the organization.

Conclusion

The most important general considerations that need to be taken into account in the conduct and context of social measurement have been discussed. It is clear that many of the issues are complex and usually require that researchers weigh a number of competing and potentially conflicting factors. A general overview will not necessarily be immediately helpful in providing specific guidance in any concrete situation; nonetheless to make appropriate and ethical decisions across a professional career, a wide awareness of the issues is vital.

See Also the Following Articles

Confidentiality and Disclosure Limitation • Research Ethics Committees in the Social Sciences

Further Reading

American Psychological Association (APA). (2004). *Ethical Principles of Psychologists and Code of Conduct*. Available via the APA website at www.apa.org

American Sociological Association (ASA). (2004). *Code of Ethics*. Available via the ASA website at www.asanet.org

Barnes, J. A. (1979). *Who Should Know What? Social Science, Privacy and Ethics.* Penguin, Harmondsworth, England.

British Sociological Association. (2001). *Guidelines on Publication*. Available via the Internet at www.britsoc.org.uk

DeLaine, M. (2000). *Fieldwork Participation and Practice: Ethics and Dilemmas in Qualitative Research.* Sage, London.

Dresser, R. S. (2001). *When Science Offers Salvation: Patient Advocacy and Research Ethics.* Oxford University Press, Oxford.

Hudson Jones, A., and McLellan, F. (eds.) (2000). *Ethical Issues in Biomedical Publication*. Johns Hopkins University Press, Baltimore.

Kimmel, A. J. (1996). *Ethical Issues in Behavioral Research: A Survey.* Blackwell, Cambridge, Massachusetts.

Lee, R. (1993). *Doing Research on Sensitive Topics.* Sage, London.

Shamoo, A. E., and Resnik, D. B. (2002). *Responsible Conduct of Research.* Oxford University Press, Oxford.

Sieber, J. E. (1992). *Planning Ethically Responsible Research: A Guide for Students and Internal Review Boards.* Sage, London.

Ethnocentrism

Thomas F. Pettigrew

University of California, Santa Cruz, Santa Cruz, California, USA

Glossary

acquiescence bias The systematic bias caused by respondents of surveys and questionnaires who agree with whatever is presented to them. The bias is enhanced when a scale's items are unidirectional, that is, measure the phenomenon in the same form.

authoritarian personality A personality syndrome of traits that is highly associated with outgroup prejudice characterized by submission to authorities and rigid adherence to conventional standards.

ingroup A group of people who share a sense of belonging and a feeling of common identity.

ingroup bias A systematic tendency to favor one's own group.

outgroup All groups outside of the ingroup. Especially salient outgroups are those that are perceived as distinctively different from the ingroup.

Ethnocentrism is a basic social science concept that refers to the widespread belief in the cultural superiority of one's own ethnic group or, more loosely, an unusually high regard for one's own ethnic group. The central research question concerning the concept involves the hypothesis that ethnocentrism universally involves a rejection of outgroups. Studies in various disciplines seriously question this contention and exemplify the various measures that researchers have employed to gauge this elusive concept.

Introduction

The Need for the Concept

From Africa and Northern Ireland to the Middle East, wars, sectarian strife, and intergroup conflict are major concerns of the world in the twenty-first century. Not surprisingly, then, intergroup relations are now one of the major realms of study in the social sciences and, like any domain of study, this work requires fundamental concepts and their accurate measurement to capture basic intergroup processes. Ethnocentrism is one of these concepts that have proven highly useful.

Definition of Ethnocentrism

In popular language, ethnocentrism refers to a belief in the cultural superiority of one's own ethnic group. In this sense, ethnocentrism involves cultural provincialism. More recently, the concept has come to signify simply an unusually high regard for one's ingroup.

William Graham Sumner, a Yale University Professor of Political and Social Science, coined and introduced the concept in 1906 in his classic volume *Folkways*. It soon gained wide use throughout the social sciences. At the same time, Sumner also introduced the invaluable concepts ingroup and outgroup—a social differentiation that is universal among human beings. These three concepts are still widely employed in social science even though social science long ago dismissed Sumner's larger theoretical positions as invalid.

The positive functions of ethnocentrism for the ingroup are obvious. High morale, group cohesiveness, patriotism, pride, and loyalty are often linked to a sense of ingroup superiority. But there are negative consequences of ethnocentrism as well. In addition to making harmonious intergroup relations with other groups possibly more problematic, such a belief can lead to arrogant inflexibility and blindness, which prevent actions needed for the ingroup's own welfare.

Sumner's definition was broader than the now-standard use. He held ethnocentrism to describe a view by "... which one's own group is the center of everything, and all others are scaled and rated in reference to it." Note that this conception of ethnocentrism has two components: (1) an exaggeration of the ingroup's position and cultural superiority and (2) a disparagement of all outgroup cultures. These components form the core of Sumner's hypothesis.

The Sumner Hypothesis

Sumner held the two components—ingroup aggrandizement and outgroup denigration—to be universally two sides of the same coin. Thus, the Sumner hypothesis maintains that hostility toward outgroups is a direct reciprocal function of an ingroup's sense of superiority. He stated his proposition in blunt terms: "The relation of comradeship and peace in the we group and that of hostility and war towards other-groups are correlative to each other. The exigencies of war with outsiders are what make peace inside. . . . Loyalty to the group, sacrifice for it, hatred and contempt for outsiders, brotherhood within, warlikeness without—all grow together, common producers of the same situation." In short, the hypothesis holds that ingroup love is invariably linked with outgroup hatred. Numerous other, more recent theories make the same prediction.

Because Sumner also believed virtually all groups felt themselves to be superior, the hypothesis holds intergroup hostility and conflict to be natural and inevitable. Intergroup competition for scarce resources exacerbates the process. Such contentions were a critical part of his general position of Social Darwinism. A political reactionary, he agreed with Herbert Spencer that society advanced by "the survival of the fittest" of human beings. He viewed social reforms to be destructive of society's advances because they interfered with the natural selection process that led to superior human beings. Although ordained as an Anglican clergyman, he scoffed at "the absurd effort to make the world over."

Thus, Sumner viewed societies, like individuals, as organisms evolving, as Darwin had posited for animal life. And the greater the society's inequality, the more likely ". . . the steady growth of civilization and advancement of society by and through its best members." Conflict is inherent in such a process, he believed, and ethnocentrism entered into his sweeping theory at this point.

In this context, Sumner cast his ethnocentrism hypothesis in the broadest terms. He saw each of the components—ingroup preeminence and outgroup hostility—as syndromes with numerous attributes. In addition, he intended the hypothesis to apply at both the individual and societal levels of analysis. The sense of ingroup attachment includes such individual-level phenomena as patriotism, nationalism, loyalty, group pride, and strong ingroup identification. At the group level, ingroup preeminence assumes such forms as strong intragroup cohesion, the absence of intragroup conflict, and numerous cross-cutting ties within the ingroup. Similarly, the syndrome of outgroup rejection consists of various attributes. For individuals, it includes prejudice and negative stereotyping of the outgroup, as well as refusal to interact with outgroup members and other personal acts of discrimination. For groups and societies, outgroup rejection can include institutionalized systems of discrimination and open warfare directed at the outgroup. The sweeping scope with which Sumner endowed the two components of his ethnocentrism hypothesis has led to a great variety of research designs and empirical measures in studies attempting to test the hypothesis; indeed, the breadth of the hypothesis has attracted tests of Sumner's hypothesis throughout the social sciences.

Tests of the Sumner Hypothesis

Tests at the Individual Level of Analysis

Psychologists have frequently tested Sumner's hypothesis at the individual level. Of special interest are tests made with children by developmental psychologists, and with college students by personality psychologists and social psychologists.

A Developmental Study of Children

Aboud conducted two investigations in 2003 of Canadian children between the ages of 3 and 7 years. She used measures that attempted to measure both ingroup favoritism and outgroup prejudice. In her first study, Aboud tested 80 young white children in all-white suburban settings. These children had little or no contact with the black and native Indian people about whom they were questioned. Consistent with the Sumnerian hypothesis, the ingroup and outgroup evaluations of this sample were negatively correlated ($r = -0.37$). But the two types of evaluations differed in important ways. For example, ingroup favoritism formed earlier in life than outgroup prejudice.

Aboud's second study took place in a racially mixed kindergarten, and its results failed to support the hypothesis. In this sample, the two variables did not covary significantly ($r = -0.08$), and again they revealed contrasting correlates. Thus, children who were more favorable toward their ingroup were not more prejudiced toward outgroups.

Why the difference between the two samples? Aboud suggests that the children in the all-white setting had no experience with the racial outgroups on which to base their outgroup evaluations. So they had to use their ingroup attachment as a referent comparison by which to evaluate the other groups. By contrast, the second sample did have extensive and direct experience with outgroup children and could base their outgroup evaluations independent of their ingroup attachments.

These developmental data with children indicate that the validity of the Sumnerian hypothesis is context dependent rather than universalistic as Sumner assumed. Aboud's research suggests that favorable, face-to-face intergroup contact is one factor that moderates the hypothesized relationship between ingroup favorability and outgroup prejudice. With intergroup contact, it is possible to possess positive attitudes toward the ingroup and outgroups.

A Personality Test of College Students

During the 1940s, personality psychologists took up Sumner's contentions and broadened the ethnocentrism concept further. The co-authors of the classic 1950 study of the authoritarian personality viewed ethnocentrism as an ideology that closely related to the personality syndrome of authoritarianism. Further, they held this ideology contained both pro-ingroup and anti-outgroup elements. Their definition of ethnocentrism embraced the Sumnerian hypothesis, defining ethnocentrism as "... a tendency in the individual to be 'ethnically centered,' to be rigid in his acceptance of the culturally 'alike' and in his rejection of the 'unlike.'"

From this definition, the personality researchers devised a measure that captured both the positive ingroup and negative outgroup components in the same scale. The Ethnocentrism Scale (E-scale) consisted of three subscales measuring white American prejudices against black Americans and American minorities in general, as well as rigid patriotism. A sample anti-black item in the 12-item subscale reads: "Most Negroes would become officious, overbearing, and disagreeable if not kept in their place." The subject chose one of six responses for each item: "agree strongly, agree, agree slightly, disagree slightly, disagree, and disagree strongly."

The antiminority subscale of 12 items had the same format, but it tested attitudes against an array of outgroups ranging from "zootsuiters" and criminals to Japanese and Filipinos. A sample item reads: "We are spending too much money for the pampering of criminals and the insane, and for the education of inherently incapable people."

For the ingroup favorability indicator, the authoritarian personality researchers devised a 10-item subscale of a type of rigid patriotism that is better labeled a *pseudo*-patriotism scale. A sample item reads: "Patriotism and loyalty are the first and most important requirements of a good citizen." The full E-scale combines all three of these subscales and provides a rough test of the Sumnerian hypothesis. Just as Sumner predicted, the two prejudice scales correlate highly and positively with the patriotism scale (+0.76 and +0.83) for a sample of white American college women.

Several methodological factors, however, limit the significance of these correlations. First, there was an overlap in the content of the scales. For example, one of the antiminority items explicitly invokes a rigid patriotism set: "Certain religious sects whose beliefs do not permit them to salute the flag should be forced to conform to such a patriotic action, or else be abolished." Second, all three of the E-scale's subscales as well as the authoritarianism scale itself have an absolutist tone—a quality that is consistent with authoritarian thinking. Third, all the items in these scales have the same six-point response categories; and all the items present statements that are worded in the same direction of indicating increased prejudice, pseudo-patriotism, or authoritarianism. These similarities across items mean that both format covariance and acquiescence bias artificially inflate the relationships among the subscales.

Not surprisingly, then, later research using different measures failed to replicate the relationship between patriotism and aggression against outgroups. Measures of nationalism, however, do consistently relate to increased indicators of anti-outgroup hostility. Nonetheless, the lasting contribution of this research is that the Sumnerian hypothesis is more likely to receive support among authoritarians.

Social Psychological Experiments

Favoring your ingroup not only develops in children before negative attitudes toward outgroups, but it is easily aroused in experimental situations. Social psychologists have shown repeatedly that mere arbitrary classification into groups (called a minimal intergroup situation) can invoke a systematic ingroup bias in the distribution of positive resources. But further experiments cast doubt on the Sumnerian hypothesis. When investigators repeat these same experiments and ask subjects to distribute negative outcomes between the ingroup and outgroup, the ingroup bias is virtually eliminated. In conflict with Sumner's assumptions, people appear quite willing to favor their ingroup, but they are reluctant to hurt outgroups more blatantly.

Tests at the Societal Level of Analysis

An Anthropological Study in East Africa

Studies of preindustrial societies test the Sumnerian hypothesis at the societal level. One 1971 study collected individual data from 30 different tribes in East Africa. Averaging the individual data, the tendency to view their ingroup in a positive light was widespread across the groups. Hence, almost all the tribes systematically considered themselves more trustworthy, obedient, friendly, and honest than other tribes. But this ingroup bias did not correlate at all with their trait ratings of the other tribes or their willingness to interact with the other tribes.

A Test with the Cross-Cultural Area Files

Cashdan provided the most extensive test of the Sumnerian hypothesis at the societal level. In 2001, she used the invaluable data file of published codes on 186 preindustrial societies developed by Murdock and White. Two independent sets of ratings for ethnic loyalty and outgroup hostility strengthened her analysis. Two additional independent measures tapped the amount of internal warfare. And five further measures tapped the degree of threat to the group: two independent ratings of the threat of famine and three of external conflict. All independent ratings of the same concept proved significantly and positively correlated.

Catastrophic food shortages, but not routine food shortages, were consistently associated with stronger ingroup loyalties. External warfare also consistently related to greater ingroup loyalty. The latter finding can be interpreted in several ways. Cashdan saw it as evidence that external warfare led to enhanced loyalty. But the causal paths could go in both directions. As the Sumnerian hypothesis holds, greater loyalty could be contributing to the increased external warfare.

Other tests, however, failed to support the universality of Sumner's hypothesis. Cashdan found that none of the four Spearman rank correlations between the ratings of group loyalty and outgroup hostility attained statistical significance. With varying numbers of societies in the tests, the correlations ranged from +0.08 to −0.25. Indeed, three of the relationships were in the opposite direction from that predicted by Sumner. Similarly, the degree of internal warfare was positively related with hostility toward outgroups—not negatively as predicted by the hypothesis.

Measures of Ethnocentrism

Measures at the Individual Level of Analysis

This selective review provides an overview of the type of measures that researchers throughout the social sciences have employed to measure ethnocentrism. At the individual level, studies have relied heavily on scales. But, as we have noted, the only scale explicitly named as a measure of ethnocentrism—the E-scale—has many problems. It shares with the other scales of the authoritarian personality research numerous methodological problems. For instance, all the E-scale's statements are worded in the same direction so that agreeing with the statements always adds to the respondent's ethnocentrism score. This procedure risks a strong acquiescence bias—that is, regardless of content, some respondents will agree with all the statements (yea-sayers) and a few others will disagree with all the statements (nay-sayers). When a scale contains an equal number of positively and negatively worded statements, these responses are moved toward the center of the distribution of responses.

In addition, the E-scale has a fundamental conceptual problem. By combining two prejudice subscales with a subscale of rigid patriotism, it simply assumes the universal validity of the Sumnerian hypothesis. And our review of relevant studies demonstrates that such an assumption is not justified. Ethnocentrism at the individual level of analysis is best tailored to the concept's basic definition of markedly high regard for one's own ethnic group. Whether ethnocentrism relates positively with hostility toward outgroups must remain an empirical question. Consequently, independent measures of attitudes and actions toward outgroups are needed.

Most studies of ethnocentrism at the individual level have followed this procedure. Researchers have used various measures of ingroup regard while placing increasingly less emphasis on the cultural component of ethnocentrism. One popular measure is to ask how identified the subject is with the ingroup, for example, the question "How close do you feel toward other Xs?"

Working with children, Aboud in 2003 used the same measures to tap both positive and negative evaluations of the ingroup (whites) and outgroups (blacks and Native Indians). The ratings of whites by her subjects constituted her ethnocentrism measure, whereas the other ratings constituted her outgroup measures. Similarly, other studies assess ingroup bias by testing for ingroup preference in evaluations. Such preferences can be determined not only by questionnaires but in laboratory experiments as well by measuring the differential allocations of resources to the ingroup and outgroup.

Measures at the Group Level of Analysis

Two types of group measures of ethnocentrism appear in the research literature. One type simply combines individual data on ingroup evaluations and preferences to get a group-level index. Brewer and Campbell used this procedure in their 1971 study of 30 East African tribes. The other type of measure involves group ratings. This method is commonly used when such valuable data collections as the Cross-Cultural Area files are used. We have seen how effective this procedure can be in the study by Cashdan. Of particular importance in this study is its use of multiple ratings for each variable. Given the breadth of meaning given to ethnocentrism by social science, multiple indicators at both the individual and group levels of analysis are appropriate. Such a procedure allows the researcher to measure ethnocentrism as a latent variable in structural equation models and other similar analyses.

Summary and Conclusion

Ethnocentrism is an important concept in the study of intergroup relations. William Graham Sumner introduced it, and he advanced the central theorem concerning the concept. In its simplest terms, he held that ethnocentrism—defined broadly as extreme attachment to the ingroup—led to outgroup hate. Moreover, he believed that this link was universal, ingroup attachment and outgroup hate being simply two sides of the same coin.

Research in the social sciences, however, fails to confirm Sumner's hypothesis. Both at the individual and societal levels of analysis, tests of the hypothesis demonstrate repeatedly that ethnocentrism and outgroup hatred are separable phenomena. Ethnocentrism develops first and has different correlates than outgroup hatred. To be sure, the two phenomena are closely related under certain conditions. External warfare and other forms of threat such as extreme famine typically enhance ingroup unity. The lack of contact between the groups also can connect the two phenomena. Similarly, those with authoritarian personalities are more likely to combine ingroup favoritism with outgroup rejection. But Sumner's assumption that the two processes are invariably and universally correlated is not correct.

The breadth of the general concepts involved in the Sumerian hypothesis invites a wide range of indicators for both ingroup and outgroup reactions. The present review suggests the use of multiple indicators for each of the key parts of the Sumnerian hypothesis. For direct indicators of ethnocentrism itself, numerous measures exist at both the individual and societal levels of analysis.

See Also the Following Articles

Campbell, Donald T. • Cross-Cultural Data Applicability and Comparisons

Further Reading

Aboud, F. E. (2003). The formation of in-group favoritism and out-group prejudice in young children: Are they distinct attitudes? *Dev. Psychol.* **39,** 48–60.

Adorno, T. W., Frenkel-Brunswik, E., Levinson, D. J., and Sanford, R. N. (1950). *The Authoritarian Personality.* Harper, New York.

Brewer, M. B. (1999). The psychology of prejudice: Ingroup love or outgroup hate? *J. Soc. Issues* **55**(3): 429–444.

Brewer, M. B., and Campbell, D. T. (1976). *Ethnocentrism and Intergroup Attitudes: East African Evidence.* Sage, Beverley Hills, CA.

Cashdan, E. (2001). Ethnocentrism and xenophobia: A cross-cultural study (1). *Curr. Anthropol.* **42,** 760–765.

Feshbach, S. (1994). Nationalism, patriotism and aggression: A clarification of functional differences. In *Aggressive Behavior: Current Perspectives* (L. Huesmann, ed.), pp. 275–291. Plenum, New York.

Levine, R. A., and Campbell, D. T. (1972). *Ethnocentrism: Theories of Conflict, Ethnic Attitudes, and Group Behavior.* John Wiley, New York.

Mummendey, A., and Otten, S. (1998). Positive-negative asymmetry in social discrimination. In *European Review of Social Psychology* (W. Strobe and M. Hewstone, eds.), Vol. 9, pp. 107–143. John Wiley, New York.

Murdoch, G. P., and White, D. R. (1969). Standard cross-cultural sample. *Ethnology* **8,** 399–460.

Struck, N., and Schwartz, S. H. (1989). Intergroup aggression: Its predictors and distinctness from in-group bias. *J. Pers. Soc. Psychol.* **56,** 364–373.

Sumner, W. G. (1906). *Folkways.* Ginn, New York.

Ethnography

Faye Allard
The University of Pennsylvania, Philadelphia, Pennsylvania, USA

Elijah Anderson
The University of Pennsylvania, Philadelphia, Pennsylvania, USA

Glossary

analytic induction Both a theoretical and a research approach that aims to uncover causal explanations. This is done inductively, by testing, redefining, and refining hypothesized concepts and relationships throughout the research process until no new data contradicts the researcher's explanation.

ethnographic interview An in-depth interview conducted with the aim of understanding the worldview, beliefs, and social reality of the respondent. This type of interview is often open-ended and typically not does adhere to a strict set of predetermined questions.

field notes The primary way in which ethnographic research data are recorded; this may include thick descriptions of observations (dialogue, gestures, facial expressions, body movements, use of space, and physical surroundings), the researchers' responses to these observations, and the hypotheses that emerge from the data.

folk ethnography A term coined by Elijah Anderson which describes the process through which individuals construct and maintain everyday understanding about their social world by continually observing and interpreting the behavior around them. An individual's interpretations of these observations are shaped by a personal ideological framework, which develops over time through socialization and experiences and provides the lenses through which an individual tries to understand the people encountered in daily life.

grounded theory A theoretical approach that places emphasis on the construction of theory, which is grounded in data and is generated through inductive reasoning.

local knowledge A term developed by Clifford Geertz that describes the shared ideologies, norms, and values, etc. that are transmitted, learned, and maintained by a specific cultural group.

naturalistic ethnography Ethnographic research that develops its questions, concepts, and theory after entering the field site. This stands in contrast to ethnography that establishes its research questions or theoretical frameworks before entering the field site.

participant observation A research method in which the researcher becomes actively immersed in a group in their natural setting in order to gain experience and deep understanding of the community being studied.

symbolic interaction A theoretical approach developed by Herbert Blumer that focuses on the meanings that shape society and human behavior. This approach posits that meanings are social products that shape, and are shaped by, the social interaction of individuals.

thick description A concept pioneered by Clifford Geertz, who argues that in order to uncover a more nuanced understanding of behavior, interpretation must be based on "thick description." This is done by immersion of the researcher into the setting, to uncover the different meanings given to the behavior by the actors involved, and then describing these interpretations in a rich, layered (thick) manner.

The term ethnography is derived from the Greek *ethnos* (a people, race or cultural group) and *graphos* (denoting a thing written or drawn). Ethnography is best defined as the systematic study of culture—which can in turn be defined as the artifacts, values, norms, and the shared and learned understandings of a given group. Although these definitions appear broad, studying any culture systematically commonly requires posing questions concerning how people meet the exigencies of everyday life, how social groups form, function, and maintain themselves, and how shared ideologies, rules, and values are negotiated and transmitted by people. Ethnography often addresses these questions.

Introduction

Ethnography is the systematic study of culture. Ethnography is an inductive, qualitative research method, in which the researcher, or ethnographer, immerses himself or herself into the field (the social reality of the subjects of investigation) to study and describe local culture. Typically, the ethnographer uses two main techniques to collect data—participant observation, which is recorded in the form of field notes, and in-depth, or ethnographic, interviews. Ethnographic data can also be collected from historical records and artifacts, journals, and other written material. Ethnographic data are usually, but not necessarily, derived from the process of ethnography and are characterized by thick description, a term coined by Clifford Geertz in 1973 to describe rich, layered descriptions of the field. The way in which ethnographic data are presented is not, however, limited to the written form; photographs, films, audio recordings, and poetry have been used to render local settings ethnographically. It is impossible to distinguish between ethnographic theory and method, because data analysis is a continual process that is developed as fieldwork progresses. Thus, ethnographic methodology comprises not only the physical processes of conducting ethnography, but also the logical procedures of analysis and the presentation of data.

Ethnographic Evolution and Major Contributions

Early Anthropologists

Ethnography had its beginning in the early 20th century, at which time British anthropologists were grappling to align their cross-cultural studies with the emerging scientific paradigms that were dominating intellectual thought. Until this point, anthropology had been characterized by speculative, unsystematized travel accounts, which were indistinguishable from the ethnocentric amateur writing often produced by missionaries documenting their observations from abroad. The individual work of Bronislaw Malinowski and Reginald Radcliffe-Brown in 1922 marked the full initiation of fieldwork into anthropology, reconciling anthropologists' need to obtain a holistic overview of culture, while simultaneously meeting the demands for academic rigor. By immersing themselves in the groups they were studying and acting as participant observers, Malinowski and Radcliffe-Brown strived to construct their theories and representations inductively—in other words, to base their theory on their observations. Both presented their findings in very detailed monographs, favoring impersonal description over personal narrative.

In the United States, anthropologists employed by government agencies to study Native Americans usually reflected the ideology of their employers, who perceived Native Americans as "problem people" in need of integration into American life. However, this attitude did not always prevail; anthropologist Franz Boas, as detailed in Ronald P. Rohner's *The Ethnography of Franz Boas*, and ethnologist Frank Hamilton Cushing reported their findings from the Native American perspective, resulting in higher levels of objectivity and validity. Through studying Native Americans, Boas and Cushing also helped to legitimize fieldwork completed "closer to home," which was then an unconventional field site.

Early Sociologists

As the distinctive fieldwork techniques pioneered by Malinowski and Radcliffe-Brown gained popularity within their discipline, other academics in Europe and America were also taking an increasing interest in field methods. In the late 19th century, Charles Booth, a prominent London businessman, hybridized field techniques with more traditional quantitative techniques, such as descriptive statistics, surveys, and mapping data, to produce a detailed study of London's impoverished population. On the other side of the Atlantic, the American philanthropist Jane Addams also adopted, albeit unwittingly, the anthropological methods being pioneered by Boas to describe Hull House, a racially and ethnically diverse working-class settlement in Chicago. Addams hoped to influence social reform by informing a wider segment of society about the harsh conditions faced by the urban poor. This distinguished Addams from her anthropological forefathers, whose political motivations were limited to those who were sent by governments to study how to "civilize primitive people."

One of the first sociological studies to utilize field methodology to conduct a comprehensive and scientific community study was *The Philadelphia Negro*, by William Edward Burghardt Du Bois in 1899. Drawing heavily on the hybrid methods forged by Booth, Du Bois' study involved systematically mapping, surveying, interviewing, and studying the history of Philadelphia's black population. This pioneering work resulted in the first systematic study of the African-American community. In the late 1920s, at the University of Chicago, William I. Thomas and Florian Znaniecki's *The Polish Peasant in Europe and*

America also embraced fieldwork. Thomas and Znaniecki paid particular attention to "social disorganization," laying the foundations for a theme that would come to characterize much prewar fieldwork. Like Booth and Du Bois, Thomas and Znaniecki integrated a variety of data into their study, such as letters, papers, and, notably, a detailed life history of a Polish man, this being one of the first examples of a case study. The early use of field methods, though innovative, suffered from a lack of systematization and, in some cases, was terribly impressionistic. As compared to today's standards, Booth's methods of measuring poverty were crude and hazy, Thomas and Znaniecki's theoretical framework would not be proved by their data, and few social scientists kept systematic and detailed field notes. Despite their shortcomings, these social scientists were critical in the development of ethnographic methodology, because without their contributions, the foundations on which the eminent Chicago School was built would not have been laid.

The Early Chicago School

Robert Ezra Park's arrival at the University of Chicago's Department of Sociology marked a great leap for field methods. Park was one of the first sociologists to write explicitly about methodology, in 1915, in the seminal piece *The City: Suggestions for the Investigation of Human Behavior in the Urban Environment.* Park sought to bring objectivity, organization, and precision to the unsystematic, haphazard, and "journalistic" methods of his predecessors, by advocating a scientific framework through which the forces and processes driving social problems could be studied and generalized. Along with his colleague Ernest Burgess, Park went on to write perhaps the first textbook on methodology, *Introduction to the Science of Sociology.* In this book, Park placed great emphasis on doing fieldwork, advocating "the first thing that students in Sociology need to learn is to observe and record their own observations."

Having been invited to the department by W. I. Thomas, Park came to Chicago with a great interest in the city, stating that Chicago was not merely a geographical phenomenon, but that it could be viewed as a kind of social organism. Park was particularly concerned with the inequality, social organization, and social control that were characteristic of cities, and these interests were reflected in the two broad areas of study pursued by the Early Chicago School sociologists, i.e., community studies and social disorganization. Furthermore, Park and his colleagues wrote with reform in mind and actively sought to correct the problems of their day.

Though Park was heavily influenced by the anthropologist Boas, and grounded his methods on the early anthropologists' belief that social phenomenon should be directly observed in its natural setting, he rejected their belief that social life was fixed, instead positing that the social world was ever changing. In order to study such a dynamic entity, Park argued that fieldworkers should take a pragmatic approach. This notion was heavily influenced by Park's colleagues John Dewey, George Mead, and William James, who belonged to the first American philosophical movement, known as Pragmatism, which explained meaning and truth in terms of the application of ideas or beliefs to the performance of actions and their outcomes. Based on the theoretical ideas of the Pragmatists and the methodology of the anthropologists, Park believed that the researcher should actively participate in the social world in order to understand the culture in the context of the setting. Park further stressed that the fieldworkers should remain in the setting for an extended period of time, and must enter without prior assumptions in order to understand the true meaning of the behavior being observed. Park's principles of studying social life in the natural setting formed the beginnings of naturalistic ethnography.

Advances in Ethnographic Methodology

Park and Burgess meticulously trained their students, who included sociologists from the "Second" Chicago School, notably, Everett C. Hughes, Herbert Blumer, and Louis Wirth. Park taught by example and strongly encouraged his students to go into the field to conduct empirical research, even advising them to forgo the library in favor of "getting [their] hands dirty in real research." Fieldwork at the Chicago School was characterized by informal and somewhat unstructured procedures. Drawing on the eclectic methods of Thomas, Park insisted that his students should utilize a range of research techniques. Participant observation was one of the major components of the early Chicago School's methodological repertoire, and Park expected his students to enter a field site and assume a role within it. Participant observation was sometimes done covertly, as exemplified by Nels Anderson's study *The Hobo* and Frederick Thrasher's research on gangs. By shedding their identity as a researcher, participant observers were able to gain entry to and infiltrate a social group in order to participate in and observe interaction in its natural form, thus improving the validity of data collected. Yet, covert participant observation demands a great deal from the researcher, requiring them to learn how to "speak the speak" of those being studied and to conform to patterns of behavior that can be unfamiliar, illogical, and sometimes illegal. Until Park and his followers advocated the process, there had been little attempt to conduct covert participant research, as anthropologists had primarily tended to be physically conspicuous to the groups they studied. In Chicago, on the other hand, sociologists generally looked like the populations they were researching and so could observe covertly.

Although participant observation was the primary method used by fieldworkers, map making was also characteristic of the early Chicago school. Park also encouraged the inclusion of public and personal documentation, and, contrary to popular belief, some fieldworkers even incorporated statistical analysis into their studies. Importantly, Burgess oversaw the development of Thomas and Znaniecki's life history analysis and likened the method to a microscope, stating it permitted the researcher to see "in detail the total interplay of mental processes and social relationships." Studies such as Harvey Zorbaugh's *The Gold Coast and the Slum* (1929) and Paul Cressey's 1932 *Taxi Hall Dance* embraced life history methodology and successfully used it to supplement data collected via observations, to give a fuller depiction of the cultures they were studying. Clifford Shaw's 1930 work, *The Jack-Roller*, was a unique example of the life history method, in that it consisted entirely of a monologue written by a delinquent teenager, the lone subject of the study, proving to be one of the first oral narratives. In this study, Shaw's input was limited to making suggestions about the structure of the piece, and the teenager's exact words were used for the monologue in an effort to avoid introducing researcher bias into the study. Shaw did, however, attempt to confirm the validity of the boy's life history by cross-checking his story with official documentation and conducting in-depth interviews with the boy. Shaw heralded his life history method as scientific, if tested and validated by other case studies.

Another important development made by the Early Chicago School was the movement toward the methodical construction of classifications and the systematic recording of field experiences. Park encouraged his students to document their interpretations of their field experiences carefully, and to record their perceived effects on the social world they were studying. In demanding such standards, Park lessened the likelihood that researchers would introduce their own cultural biases into their data, and thus Park elevated field methods to a new level of accountability.

Critiques of Early Ethnographic Methodology

As a result of the efforts of Park and others, the Chicago School became synonymous with interpretive research and subsequently dominated American sociology well into the 1930s. However, the rise of positivism (especially that emerging from the Harvard School, spanning the early 1930s and peaking in the late 1950s) marked a period of stultification and intense criticism of field methods, particularly for being "too impressionistic." During this time, William Ogburn, a Chicago sociologist, strongly advocated the use of quantitative methods for governmental research and successfully fostered the association between quantitative, scientific work and reliability. However, some progress was made in qualitative methodology in this period; the focused interview, initially developed by quantitative sociologist Paul Lazarsfeld and later refined by Robert Merton, was being developed, forming the basis of what is now a common ethnographic technique, the focus group.

The "Second" Chicago School

Between 1946 and the mid-1950s, great progress in evolving field methods was accomplished by the Second Chicago School, comprising an eclectic set of students, including Howard Becker, Erving Goffman, and Anselm Strauss, under the leadership of Everett C. Hughes and Herbert Blumer. This new generation of fieldworkers sought to correct the weaknesses of the early Chicago School, while simultaneously attempting to address the dominant positivistic paradigms. Community studies continued to flourish, with St. Clair Drake and Horace Cayton's *Black Metropolis* exemplifying, the trademark Chicago School mixed methodological approach utilizing historic documents, census data, social statistics, archival data, and traditional systematic observations and in-depth interviews to render a holistic representation of African-American urban enclaves in Chicago.

Strides were made by Buford Junker in the 1950s to formalize the processes of participant observation by identifying four distinct types of observation, each having different effects on the nature of the data produced. In the first category, a "complete participant" fully engages in the activities of those being studied, at the same time conducting a covert investigation, producing more accurate data and heightening understanding; this was utilized in William Whyte's classic 1943 study of street corner culture. In contrast, a "participant as observer" conducts research overtly and is not bound to act as one of the group; however, participants as observers often have to "act" in a way that makes those being observed comfortable, and must strive to maintain the field site in a natural way as much as possible, as exemplified by the work of sociologist Ned Polsky in the late 1960s.

Junker's third category, "observers as participants," defines researchers as not being overly concerned with participation, tending to be more formal in their approach. Compared to participant observers, observers as participants spend less time in the field, mainly because they do not have to establish high levels of rapport with those being observed, and in some cases make just a single visit to the field site. A final type of participant observation is the "complete observer," who remains completely uninvolved and records data from a distance, sometimes by "eavesdropping." The distinction between types of observation was further considered in 1977 by Victor Lidz, who distinguished between participant observers and observing participants by the depth of the relationship with those being studied. He argued that the relationships developed by participant observers tend to be tentative and incipient, and deeper empathetic relationships are typical of an observing participant. In the 1950s, other researchers addressed the problems of establishing rapport with subjects and further refined Junker's categorizations by examining the demands that each type of "participation observation" placed on the researcher and the roles that they must assume to collect data successfully.

Howard Becker's seminal work, *Problems of Inference and Proof in Participant Observation*, published in 1958, did not directly answer the criticisms of his positivistic peers, but it did embody the "Second" Chicago School's commitment to the further formalization and systematization of field methods. In this piece, in a very scientific, yet clear manner, Becker explains "the basic analytic operations carried on in participant research," in order to generate a comprehensive set of systematized field methods, outlining the analytic processes associated with these systematic operations. The high level of commitment to methodological issues shown by Becker was very much characteristic of the Second Chicago School and proved invaluable in the advancement of field methods.

Symbolic Interactionism

Building on the theoretical discourse of Mead, Dewey, and other early Chicagoans, Herbert Blumer, developed a theoretical framework that has come to be known as symbolic interactionism. Symbolic interactionism served to rejuvenate and legitimate fieldwork at the Chicago School by responding to many of the positivistic critiques. Blumer openly criticized sociologists' fixation on establishing "scientific" causal relationships. He argued that many sociologists, including some early Chicagoans, held a superficial knowledge of the social world they studied, and consequently their data had been forced into preconceived categories and concepts that bore little relation to the social reality being investigated. Blumer insisted that social interaction was the sociologists' primary subject matter. To Blumer, the social world was composed of an infinite number of social interactions, taking place in an infinite number of settings, involving an infinite number of individuals, thus every social interaction was a completely unique event. He argued that humans do not merely react to social events; they interpret, define, and give meaning to behavior, based on their experiences. Blumer criticized those who depicted individual actors as involuntary pawns of social structures, and argued that the role of social forces should be explained in terms of the process of interpretation engaged in by the individuals as they encounter situations. To do so, Blumer argued that it is imperative to grasp an individual's view of social reality, by engaging in participant observation and attempting to assume the role of the individual in order to understand his/her interpretive processes and meanings.

Despite his criticisms of positivistic methodology, Blumer believed that data derived from fieldwork should be subject to the test of the empirical world and validated through such testing, and he went so far as to claim that symbolic interactionism was the only method that could fully satisfy scientific procedures. Blumer strongly warned against the formation of theory without sufficient data, and recommended revealing theory to those being studied and also checking it against new observations to increase validity. Whereas these verification mechanisms had been done sporadically by fieldworkers prior to Blumer, they had never been so clearly verbalized and were a clear rebuttal against claims of impartiality in field methods.

Though they did not label themselves symbolic interactionists, Howard Becker and Erving Goffman exemplified Blumer's theoretical framework. In order to understand how marijuana users became labeled deviant, Becker used participant observation and in-depth interviews to generate data, and then contextualized the data in historical analysis, which he maintained was essential for comprehensive understanding. Unlike fieldworkers before him, Becker looked specifically at how power structures influenced labels, meanings, and interpretations of the social world. Becker assumed that meanings permeate every level of social life, from drug users to the judiciary, and all are relevant in the understanding of social reality.

Erving Goffman has been called "the ethnographer of the self," which is a revealing description of his contribution to the social sciences. Among his seminal works, his 1959 book, *The Presentation of Self in Everyday Life*, was notably influential in the development of theory that has facilitated fieldworkers to explain the processes and meanings behind the everyday social interactions they have observed. In this work, Goffman proposed the use of a dramaturgical approach to understand social interaction, likening social life to a staged drama in which social actors are constantly "performing." He posits that actors consciously foster, produce, and maintain their self-image, but the generation of "the self" is also contingent on teamwork from those involved in the interaction, who allow an individual's self to emerge, and from the audience, who interpret the presentation of "the self." With time, an actor will perform in a standardized way for a specific audience, which is consistent with the self they have been cultivating for, and is recognized by, that specific audience. Goffman deemed this repeated performance a "front," which, in turn, helps to establish the role of the social actor to whom it belongs. In comparison to the "front stage" on which performances take place, the "back stage" is characterized by spontaneous behavior, which oftentimes can contradict the "front" self that is carefully managed for others. In this sense,

Goffman presented fieldworkers with the notion that the self is a dynamic, plastic entity that should not be studied in isolation. Goffman provided the theoretical tools through which social interaction could be understood in light of the social situation within which it is embedded.

Neonaturalism

Though Robert Park made strides toward naturalistic ethnography, some early Chicagoans entered the field with assumptions that divisions between different groups were inherently problematic, and required reintegrating the "other" into the "normal." This contradicts true naturalistic ethnography because of the researchers' *a priori* assumptions that these social group divisions were necessarily dysfunctional. This problem was somewhat tempered by Everett Hughes, who urged his students to look beyond the disenfranchised, the main subject matter for the Early Chicago School. Hughes advocated the investigation of individuals in traditional positions of power, such as those working in the medical profession, a suggestion subsequently adopted by other researchers, many of whom contributed to the growth of a new area of fieldwork; the study of work.

Eliot Freidson, in particular, made a very strong case regarding the important contribution that fieldwork could make to the study of work, which had been previously characterized by statistical analysis, arguing that the "direct, systematic qualitative study of the everyday settings of work or practice" was the most appropriate manner in which to understand the everyday experience of "concrete people doing work in their own way." Exemplifying Freidson's argument, Donald Roy conducted covert participant observation in a steel factory in order to understand "loafing." Contrary to the findings of other researchers, Roy found that loafing was a far more complex activity than commonly thought, and involved two distinct strategies, "quota restriction" and "goldbricking," both of which were carefully calculated levels of efficiency that reflected the economic payoffs for the job at hand.

David Matza was a major advocate of the naturalistic fieldwork that was introduced by Robert Park. Though positivistic inquiry had been the dominant methodological paradigm since the end of the Early Chicago School, the 1960s saw a movement away from positivistic inquiry toward naturalistic research. Matza argued that naturalistic methodology was committed "to phenomena and their nature; not to Science or any other system of standards." He placed great emphasis on remaining true to the nature of the culture being studied, rather than the theoretical or methodological beliefs of the researcher. Matza felt that if a researcher entered the field site with ideological assumptions, he or she would subconsciously seek data to support these assumptions, instead of documenting phenomena as they really were. To prevent this, Matza contends that instead of entering the field site with predefined concepts, theory, or even research questions, the researcher should generate all three—theory, concepts, and questions—from first-hand observations made in the field site. To garner such observations, Matza suggested using participant observation "to comprehend and to illuminate the subject's view and to interpret the world as it appears to him."

Ethnomethodology

In the mid-1960s, Harold Garfinkel developed ethnomethodology, a radical micro-level qualitative methodology that drew on the work of Georg Simmel and capitalized on the developments made by symbolic interactionists. Unlike the interactionists, however, Garfinkel argued that there were no meanings waiting to be discovered and documented by researchers. Instead, Garfinkel maintained that the role of the fieldworker is to understand the processes through which observable and reportable reality are organized, produced, and managed by individuals. Around the same time, Aaron Cicourel posited that field data is not only a reflection of the external reality of the respondent, but also the internal reality of the data collection process. Thus, he argued that both the researcher and respondent influence the creation of data. Contrary to previous methodological ideals, ethnomethodologists do not consider the influence of the researcher on the data to be detrimental to the validity of the data collected. Instead, ethnomethodologists believe that the joint creation of data by the researcher and the observed simply exemplifies the normal processes of social interaction.

As well as using participant observation, ethnomethodologists developed other techniques to deal with the microinteractions in which they were specifically interested. These new methods included Garfinkel's breaching experiments, in which the social reality of an individual is temporarily disrupted and observed in order to reveal their underlying assumptions, beliefs, and understandings. Ethnomethodologists also introduced conversational and discourse analyses, which focus on patterns of speech and other forms of communication, such as gestures and expressions, that comprise social interaction. By adapting existing methodology to investigate systematically the processes that individuals use to construct their social reality, Garfinkel hoped to evade detrimental common sense procedures that he believed to be inherent in standard empirical research practices.

Analytic Induction and Grounded Theory Approach

Fieldworkers were criticized for lacking a systematic method through which to generate, refine, and validate generalizations. Without having adequate means to generalize, fieldworkers were forced to formulate and present their theories in a way that would facilitate the identification of negative cases and potential tests of their theory. Analytic induction addressed these shortcomings, and was first conceived by Florian Znaniecki in 1934, and further developed by W. S. Robinson and Alfred Lindesmith in the early 1950s. Znaniecki argued that researchers should use inductive, rather than deductive, reasoning to create generalizations. To do so, the fieldworker should search not for cases that confirm their theory; rather they should search to find "a decisive negative case" in order to refute the theory. By finding negative cases, the fieldworker can continually refine, or if need be, completely restructure a preliminary theory at any time during fieldwork. At the point at which no more negative cases can be found to refute the developing theory, Znaniecki believed that the researcher would achieve the most realistic depiction of social reality. Making sound generalizations is an important goal of analytic induction, though it is acknowledged that no analysis can ever be considered absolutely final because it is assumed that the social world is constantly changing.

Analytic induction particularly lends itself to the study of deviance. Because deviant behavior often challenges the ideological assumptions of the ethnographer, the constant questioning of personal beliefs, which is an implicit process of analytic induction, helps to eliminate these biases. Lindesmith, in his 1947 study on opiate addiction, illustrates how analytic induction challenges *a priori* assumptions. By continually searching for negative cases and constantly questioning his assumptions, Lindesmith found that his initial theories about drug addiction, which were grounded in his prior understandings of drug use were incorrect. Lindesmith then modified his theory based on the data he had collected, and concluded that drug addiction was dependent not on the positive feelings drugs users experience, his initial theory—rather, addiction hinged on the unpleasant withdrawal symptoms drug users suffer when drug use is stopped.

Barney Glaser and Anselm Strauss, with their grounded theory approach, further formalized strategies for constructing theory. Echoing the objectives of analytic induction, Glaser and Strauss argued that those conducting fieldwork should concern themselves with the generation of theory from the ground up. Blumer argued that this approach permits the development of "sensitizing concepts." These are concepts that are grounded in the empirical world of the individuals being studied, as opposed to what Blumer describes as "definitive concepts," which are concepts that are developed and imposed onto the data by the researcher, thus are often irrelevant and distorting. In order to achieve truly grounded theory, Glaser and Strauss advocated a four-stage constant comparative method of coding and analyzing data. This process begins by comparing all the data that have some relevance to categories that have emerged during fieldwork, coding data into as many categories as necessary. Second, these categories are refined by combining any categories that overlap, a process that Glaser and Strauss argued should be shaped by the emerging properties of each category. Third, theory must be delimited by removing redundant categories. Finally, when these steps are complete, the theory can be written.

Glaser and Strauss encouraged the use of theoretical sampling, which they defined as "the process of data collection for generating theory whereby the analyst jointly collects, codes, and analyzes his data and decides what data to collect next and where to find them, in order to develop his theory as it emerges." This strategy is intended to encourage a comprehensive investigation of the research question, because cases will be selected based on their theoretical relevance to the emerging categories. When data no longer aid the construction of categories, Glaser and Strauss claim that the categories have become saturated and at this point theory can be constructed. Two types of theory can be generated via grounded theory, substantive and formal. Substantive theory is applicable only in specific situations, but from this, formal theory can be developed, which can be generalized across broader contexts.

Current Status; Moving Beyond the Chicago School

Despite the progression made in the systematization of field methods made by the Second Chicago School, the 1960s saw the continuation of positivistic criticisms against fieldwork. Questions were being raised regarding the role and function of field methods; for example, some researchers deemed participant observation as an "exploratory" method only. However, by the early 1970s, field methods were being rejuvenated through the leadership of Morris Janowitz and Gerald Suttles at the University of Chicago, and also through the work of Howard Becker and his colleagues at Northwestern University. This period saw the publication of important fieldwork, which demonstrated that field methods need not be confined to "exploratory" purposes, such as Suttles' *Social Order of the Slum*, William Kornblum's, *Blue Collar Community*, and Elijah Anderson's *A Place on the Corner*.

The 1970s marked the beginnings of a gradual shift in the self-identification among qualitative workers in sociology, from fieldworkers doing fieldwork to ethnographers doing ethnography—in particular, urban ethnography. Prior to this time, the term "ethnography" was primarily associated with anthropologists and was seen as a methodology appropriate for the study of "exotic" or "primitive" societies only, not the modern industrialized setting. Scandinavian anthropologist Ulf Hannerz's 1969 study of a racially tense ghetto in Washington, D.C. began to challenge these perceptions of what anthropologists considered an ethnographic field study to be. In his book *Reinventing Anthropology*, Dell Hymes underscored the potential value of using the ethnographic methods usually reserved for traditional anthropological subject matter, to study urban culture, thus helping to legitimize the term "ethnography" in the manner in which we now recognize it. Increasingly, this term caught on, becoming somewhat of catch-all label for anyone not engaged in strictly quantitative work, from middle-range theorists, to social historians, to survey researchers who paid an extraordinary amount of attention to the qualitative interviews with, and by implication, to the social lives of, the survey participants. Progressively, all have been grouped together to be called "ethnographers," despite the fact that not all deal with the inherent concern of ethnography, i.e., culture.

From the 1970s onward, ethnographic methods were adopted by a wide range of disciplines, including nursing, cultural studies, organizational behavior, education, and film making. Great advances in technology, such as software for coding and analyzing data, voice-activated transcription programs, and unobtrusive but sophisticated audio and visual recording devices, have increased the viability of fieldwork, making it accessible to disciplines that would not usually spend as much time conducting research. Furthermore, as the traditional boundaries between quantitative and qualitative became less distinct; data derived from fieldwork has been increasingly used alongside statistical analysis. Typically, these mixed-method studies employ fieldwork as an exploratory tool before quantitative data are collected, or as a means to investigate meaning and culture after quantitative data are collected or to construct typologies out of traditional survey data.

Postmodern Ethnography and the "Crisis of Representation"

Between the 1980s and the 1990s, ethnography underwent a significant period of critical self-reflection. The "New Ethnography," a radical, postmodern movement derived from cognitive anthropology, challenged common conceptions of fieldwork, questioning if these methods were able to produce accurate representations of those being studied. The New Ethnography suggested that ethnographers should not only be concerned with how they influence and interpret the social world they are studying, but they should also pay equal attention to how respondents generate and influence the image they give to others. Norman Denzin stated that an ethnographer should consider the many factors that shape an individual's self-image, such as the mass media, religion, and the family. Elijah Anderson's "folk ethnography" further explores how individuals construct and maintain understanding about their social world. Anderson argues that all individuals are continually observing and interpreting the social world in accordance with their own ideological frameworks, which have been developed over time through their socialization and experience. These frameworks provide the lenses through which individuals try to understand "others." Through observation and interaction, most people seek to reaffirm their system of "folk taxonomies," namely, the classifications, categories, and concepts used to negotiate their social world. Those observations that fall outside their folk taxonomies are often seen as threatening, and consequently are interpreted in such a way as to maintain the individual's existing framework. Thus, ethnographers should consider individuals as dynamic beings who are constantly creating and reaffirming their socially constructed realities.

Another way ethnographers have addressed problems associated with representation is through collaborative ethnography. Collaborative ethnography helps eliminate misrepresentation and increase validity by involving informants in the research process. In this approach, data are negotiated between the researcher and the informants. Snow and Anderson used collaborative ethnography to investigate homeless people; in the study the participants were viewed not only as a source of data, but were also actively seen as part of the research team, giving them sufficient status to question the data and theory of the ethnographers.

Ethnographers have also become increasingly concerned with how their own voices are depicted in their data. Reflexive ethnography can be defined as ethnography that strives to include the voice of the researcher, and in so doing, allows others to assess the authority of the ethnographer. For reflexive ethnographers, their role in the social setting becomes an intrinsic part of the data analysis. Ethnography has increasingly served as a means through which historically unheard voices, such as those of feminists, ethnic minorities, and gays and lesbians, can be vocalized. This has rendered a more comprehensive view of the social worlds that have been studied, by adding to, or in some cases challenging, the dominant beliefs expressed in ethnography.

The 1980s and 1990s also saw growing interest in writing, a fundamental, yet relatively unexplored, element of ethnography. John Van Maanen identifies three types of ethnographic "tales" (realist, confessional, and impressionist) were proposed in order to illustrate the various effects different rhetorical tools had on ethnography. Others focused their inquiry on field notes, questioning what field notes actually were, how they were produced, what their specific role in the construction of ethnography was, and their availability to others to inspect and utilize for further study. Thus, in their attempts to amend "the crisis of representation," ethnographers are continuing to evolve useful theoretical and methodological tools that aid understanding of how respondents and researchers shape the production of data to ensure that representations are as accurate as possible.

Urban Ethnography Reconsidered

The urban "laboratory" continues to be as popular a site for fieldwork as it was in Park's era. However, urban ethnography has become progressively comprehensive, focusing not only on conventional issues such as race, class, and subculture, but increasingly on the wider influences on the urban setting, such as de- and reindustrialization, migration, immigration, and globalization. How these broad structural changes influence the culture of city residents is a consideration of much urban field work. The work of Elijah Anderson, for example, documents how socioeconomic forces have resulted in escalating urban poverty, illustrating how many people are unable to develop the human and social capital necessary to overcome this hardship. Mitchell Duneier is one of a number of ethnographers who have studied vendors and homeless people in the urban metropolis. Taking a holistic approach, a characteristic feature of modern urban ethnography, Duneier grounds his explanations for the behavior of panhandlers, scavengers, and vendors in the cultural and historical context of their social situation.

Redefining the Ethnographic Interview

Whereas in-depth interviews were once seen as just one part of a repertoire of techniques needed to be used in conjunction with each other to conduct ethnography, in-depth interviews now are legitimately used alone to complete field studies. This has been in part due to an increased theoretical interest in the interview process. Drawing on Erving Goffman's theoretical work on interaction and conversation rituals, James Holstein and Jaber Gubrium have reconsidered the process of interviewing. They suggest that the interview process is active, and both the interviewer and informant are equally involved in the generation of data that, in turn, are contingent on the meaning given to the interview procedure. Thus, Holstein and Gubrium believe that data are not discovered per se, rather they are produced. It follows that understanding how data are produced in an interview is essential to understanding social reality. Holstein and Gubrium's emphasis on data generation is echoed in other researchers' consideration of the various types of interview techniques, for example, examinations of the effectiveness of focus group interviews, extended interviews, and the theory and practice of oral history interviews.

Survey Ethnography

The way in which interviews have been utilized in ethnography has expanded over the past decade. One particularly important progression has been the development of survey-style ethnography. Survey-style ethnography consists of a large number of in-depth interviews and frequently requires interviewing over 100 informants. Typically, in order to expedite this process, data are collected by a team of collaborative ethnographers, a methodological process originally cultivated in 1941 by Lloyd Warner in the *Yankee City Series*, an epic multivolume, mixed-approach study of Newburyport, Massachusetts, and also through the individual work of Howard Becker and Reneé C. Fox, whose collaborative field teams investigated student physicians. Usually, those who are interviewed are drawn from a nonrandom sample of individuals whom the ethnographer has reason to believe can shed light on the topic being investigated. Survey-style interviews are generally conducted only once with each participant, who are encouraged to speak frankly and at length in his or her own terms regarding the topic being investigated.

Aided by over 30 research associates, sociologist Kathryn Edin and anthropologist Laura Lein interviewed 379 single mothers in Chicago, Boston, San Antonio, Charleston, and rural Minnesota. The interviews were conducted in order to study the efficacy of welfare reform. Edin and Lein compared the in-depth interview data for those mothers who held low-wage, unskilled employment with data for those mothers who were on welfare, to ascertain the financial well being of both groups, and concluded that mothers who worked were worse off than those on welfare. In her bid to understand morality among the working class, in 2000, sociologist Michèle Lamont singlehandedly interviewed over 300 blue-collar men, each for approximately 2 hours, the information from which comprised the entire data set. Katherine Newman, in an attempt to gain a comprehensive understanding of the working poor, mobilized a large multiethnic research team in 1999 in order to conduct 300 in-depth interviews. Supplementing the data generated by these interviews, Newman's team completed 150 life history interviews, shadowed 12 individuals for a year, and completed 4 months of participant observations at fast-food restaurants. To overcome problems of consistency with multiple interviewers, many survey-style ethnographers extensively train their team of interviewers, which has contributed to growing trend in the formal teaching of ethnographic methods. Whereas Park taught by example and much of what his students learned about methods was through first-hand experience in the field, ethnographic methodology now forms the basis of classes at academic institutions and is the focus of a great number of books. The formal teaching of ethnographic techniques has resulted in a generation of introspective and reflexive ethnographers, and a renewed interested in methodological issues.

Although survey-style ethnography does not result in the thick description generated by ethnography that is based on extended periods of observation and interviews, the survey-style method can produce a broader, more universal set of generalizations in a greatly reduced amount of time. Because survey-style ethnography relies on the identification of the social issue being investigated prior to data collection, in order to identify suitable participants and plan interviews, it can be distinguished from naturalistic ethnography, which develops research questions in the field site in order to mitigate any ideological bias. Due to the predetermination of research questions and the nature of interviews, survey-style ethnographic data tend to be more in-depth, but focuses on fewer aspects of the social world being investigated, compared to naturalistic ethnography, which is more holistic in approach.

Alternative Ethnographic Forms

Ethnographic methods have undergone a particularly rapid transition over the past few decades. This is in part due to ethnography having been embraced by a broad array of researchers from many disciplines; it has thus been used to investigate an increasingly diverse range of subject matter, which has placed different demands on the function of ethnographic methods.

One of the newest forms of ethnography to evolve is autoethnography, which builds on oral narrative techniques and consists of highly personal, self-conscious, first-person accounts describing the ethnographers' experience. Autoethnographers do not concern themselves with generalizations; rather, they focus on cultural differences between themselves and their subjects. This frequently involves analyzing how the ethnographer dealt with entering and navigating their field site, how they may have been "othered" by subjects, and how they overcame these problems. By focusing on these aspects of their fieldwork, those conducting autoethnography counter common criticisms, i.e., that ethnographers rarely consider their influence on the field site. Because of its focus on subjective experience, autoethnography provides a means through which muted voices and stories can be heard. Autoethnography has been used, for example, to explore the issue of how women experience the academic system.

Ethnographic poetics is another radical form ethnography that has recently emerged. Hailing from anthropology, ethnographic poetics uses the same procedures as used in a traditional ethnography, but data are presented in the form of poetry. Those using this method believe it permits a greater freedom to reflect the voice of the ethnographer and this in turn promotes a deeper understanding of the research process. Ethnoperformance, or performance ethnography, has been defined as "ethnography in a kind of instructional theater." Drawing on the work of Goffman, performance ethnographers believe that because culture is an ongoing "performance," and individuals are constantly "acting," the only way a researcher can fully grasp the social reality of the actors involved is by actually participating in the drama. Another art form, photography, has long been used to enhance written ethnographic accounts. However, over the past few decades, visual ethnography has become a distinct method in itself, and data composed only of images have been collected, as exemplified by the work of Douglas Harper and Howard Becker.

Toward the Future and a Renewed Ethnography

Recent ethnographic studies have placed much emphasis on a more comprehensive understanding of the social world of those who are studied. There has been some concern regarding the manner in which macro forces shape the micro-level interactions that are typically observed in ethnographic studies. Michael Burawoy advocates that ethnographers use "the extended case method" to uncover the links between the subject matter and the social structure within which it lies, and focus particular attention on how forces of domination and resistance shape patterns of behavior in the field sites. Moreover, with concerns over issues of reliability and validity, there have been calls to revisit, deconstruct, and reevaluate classic ethnographic studies to identify how the methodological, theoretical, and ideological paradigms of the past have contributed to current trends in representation. Additionally, Michael Burawoy has suggested that ethnographers engage in "focused revisits," which involve attempts to replicate earlier ethnographic studies in order to ascertain their reliability and validity. Mitchell Duneier has suggested that ethnographies should present rival hypotheses and contradictory evidence that permit others to draw their own conclusions from the data.

Conclusion

Ethnography can be considered a fundamental methodology of the social sciences. Over the past century, ethnographic methodology has led to the discovery of some of the most valuable concepts, theory and data produced in the social sciences. Without ethnography and its attendant fieldwork, the development of labeling theory, the level of understanding about the plight of the urban poor, and the appreciation of the subjective complexity of social interaction would have gained less ground.

Once marginalized by positivistic paradigms, ethnography has now evolved into multiple flourishing branches of social science methodology, each of which holds great potential for the investigation of an ever-expanding range of subject matter. Though some of this evolution can be attributed to researchers' aims to address ethnography's shortcomings, much of the recent methodological development is inherent within the methodology. Ethnography is an inherently flexible method and can be easily adapted to a variety of disciplines and their related interests. As a result, ethnography has been able to burgeon into a number of distinct forms that are well adapted to investigating specific social and cultural phenomena. As it divides into these increasingly specialized branches, the next hurdle ethnography may have to overcome is to determine what actually constitutes ethnographic study, as indicated by the important theoretical divisions that are emerging between naturalistic ethnography and survey-style ethnography.

As the world experiences wide-scale changes such as globalization, deindustrialization, and migration, ethnography has the capacity to adapt to dealing with these broader social trends. The rapid evolution of ethnography is very evident in the fact that ethnography was not long ago relegated to micro-level exploratory study, but is now gaining respect as a methodology that can generate first-rate data that can straddle both micro and macro levels. Perhaps ethnography's enduring feature is that it can be adjusted and adapted while data collection is taking place to produce better data. As such, all ethnographers can easily address Becker's warning that "methodology is much too important to leave to the methodologists."

See Also the Following Articles

Anthropology, Psychological • Cross-Cultural Data Applicability and Comparisons • Qualitative Analysis, Anthropology • Quantitative Analysis, Anthropology

Further Reading

Anderson, E. (2001). Urban ethnography. *International Encyclopedia of the Social and Behavioral Sciences*, pp. 16004–16008. Elsevier.

Anderson, E. (2003). *A Place on the Corner.* University of Chicago Press, Chicago, IL.

Anderson, E. (2004). *The Cosmopolitan Canopy.*

Becker, H. (1968). Social observation and social case studies. In *International Encyclopedia of the Social Sciences*, pp. 232–238. Macmillan, New York.

Becker, H. (1970). *Sociological Work: Method and Substance.* Aldine, Chicago, IL.

Becker, H. (1998). *Tricks of the Trade; How to Think about Your Research While You're Doing It.* University of Chicago Press, Chicago, IL.

Burawoy, M., *et al.* (1991). *Ethnography Unbound. Power and Resistance in the Modern Metropolis.* University of California Press, Berkeley, CA.

Denzin, N. K. (1997). *Interpretive Ethnography: Ethnographic Practices for the 21st Century.* Sage, London.

Duneier, M. (1999). *Sidewalk.* Farrar Straus & Giroux, New York.

Farris, R. E. L. (1967). *Chicago Sociology 1920–1932.* University of Chicago Press, Chicago, IL.

Fine, G. A. (1995). *A Second Chicago School: The Development of a Postwar American Sociology.* University of Chicago Press, Chicago, IL.

Geertz, C. (1983). *Local Knowledge: Further Essays in Interpretive Anthropology.* Basic Books, New York.

Glaser, B. G., and Strauss, A. L. (1967). *The Discovery of Grounded Theory: Strategies for Qualitative Research.* Aldine de Gruyter, Berlin.

Holstein, J. A., and Gubrium, J. F. (1995). *The Active Interview.* Sage Press, Thousand Oaks, CA.

Lamont, M. (2000). *The Dignity of Working Men: Morality and the Boundaries of Race, Class and Immigration.* Harvard University Press, Cambridge, MA.

Newman, K. S. (1999). *No Shame in My Game: The Working Poor in the Inner City.* Knopf and the Russell Sage Foundation, New York.

Robinson, W. S. (1951). *The Logical Structure of Analytic Induction. Am. Sociol. Rev.* **16,** 812–818.

Eugenics

Garland E. Allen
Washington University, St. Louis, Missouri, USA

Glossary

allele One of several forms of a gene for a particular trait; for example, tall (symbolized T) in pea plants is one form of the gene for height and dwarf (symbolized t) is another allele; there can be more than two alternative alleles for a given trait within a population.

dominant gene A gene whose effects mask those of its recessive counterpart (for example, tallness in pea plants is dominant over shortness, or dwarf).

eugenics An ideology and movement of the early 20th century aimed at improving human social conditions by preventing those deemed genetically unfit from having few, if any, offspring, and encouraging those who are deemed fit to have more offspring.

gene A unit of heredity (known to consist of a specific segment of DNA) that is passed on from parent to offspring during reproduction; in sexually reproducing organisms such as humans, offspring inherit two genes for each trait, one from the male parent and the other from the female parent.

genetics The science of heredity in the biological sense.

genotype The particular set of genes any individual carries for a given trait (TT, Tt, tt); genotype determines the genes that an individual can pass on to his or her offspring.

heterozygous The condition in which an individual has two different alleles for a given trait (in Mendelian notation given as Aa, Tt, Bb, etc.).

homozygous The condition in which an individual has the same alleles for a given trait (in Mendelian notation given as AA or aa, TT or tt, BB or bb).

phenotype The appearance or expression of a trait, regardless of genotype; thus, in pea plants individuals that are TT or Tt look alike (they are tall) but have different genotypes.

recessive gene A gene whose effects are masked by a dominant gene (for example, blue eye color in humans is recessive to brown eye color).

unit-character hypothesis The idea that most traits are controlled by a single gene or group of alleles (i.e., a gene for "tallness" or for "purple flower color").

Eugenics refers to an ideology and a social movement that was widespread in the early years of the 20th century. On the scientific front, eugenics was initially framed in terms of the biometrical principles of Francis Galton, such as regression to the mean (in which offspring of parents at either extreme of a distribution tend to resemble the mean of the population) and ancestral heredity (where the two parents contribute 50% of the inheritance of each offspring, the four grandparents contribute 25%, the eight great-grandparents contribute 12.5%, etc.) but as these were statistical values only, they did not allow predictions in given cases. After 1900, eugenics became based on the then-new science of Mendelian genetics and attempted to place human breeding on the same scientific principles as those applied to animal and plant husbandry. A subset of eugenicists, particularly in France, adopted a neo-Lamarckian theory of inheritance based on the inheritance of acquired characteristics. Eugenicists were motivated by what they saw as the disturbing increase in social problems in industrialized countries, claiming that social problems such as criminality, alcoholism, prostitution, aggression, pauperism, and nomadism were caused by defective genes. Eugenics movements flourished in the United States, Great Britain, Germany, and Scandinavia, though there were visible movements in several Asian countries (Japan and China), Russia, and Latin America (especially Brazil and Cuba). In the United States and Germany, eugenics was associated with repressive legislation for compulsory sterilization, immigration restriction, and anti-miscegenation laws for those deemed to be genetically "unfit." After the Nuremberg trials in 1945, revelation of Nazi atrocities carried out in the name of eugenics gave the term a negative connotation that it still carries.

The Origin and Basic Principles of Eugenics

The Origin of Eugenics

The term "eugenics," derived from the Greek ευγενεσ, or *eugenes*, was first coined by English mathematician and geographer Francis Galton (1822–1911) (Fig. 1) in his book *Inquiries into Human Faculty and Its Development* (1883) to refer to one born "good in stock, hereditarily endowed with noble qualities." As an intellectual and social movement in the early 20th century, eugenics came to mean, in the words of one of its strongest American supporters, Charles B. Davenport (1866–1944), "the improvement of the human race by better breeding." For both Galton and Davenport, better breeding implied improving the hereditary quality of the human species by using the known scientific principles of heredity. Eugenics was the human counterpart of scientific animal and plant husbandry. It seemed ironic to eugenicists that human beings paid such careful attention to the pedigrees of their farm and domestic stock, while ignoring the pedigrees of their children:

> *[the purpose of eugenics] is to express the science of improving stock, which is by no means confined to questions of judicious mating, but which, especially in the case of man, takes cognizance of all influences that tend in however remote a degree to give the more suitable races or strains of blood a better chance of prevailing over the less suitable than they otherwise would have had.*

In this brief definition, Galton lays out all the dimensions that came to characterize eugenics as an ideology and social/political movement during the first half of the 20th century: (1) a clear belief in the methods of selective breeding from early 20th century animal and plant breeding as applied to the improvement of the human species; (2) a strong belief in the power of heredity in determining physical, physiological, and mental (including personality) traits; (3) an inherent ethnocentrism and racism that included belief in the inferiority of some races and superiority of others (a view extended to ethnic groups and social classes as well); and (4) a belief in the power of science, rationally employed, to solve social problems, including ones so seemingly intractable as pauperism, crime, violence, urban decay, prostitution, alcoholism, and various forms of mental disease, including manic depression and "feeblemindedness" (retardation).

Although the term eugenics and the idea behind it were Galton's, he himself did not found a movement to either develop eugenics as a "science" or to put its principles into practice. Eugenics movements did not begin to arise in various countries of Europe or the United States until the first decade of the 20th century, nor did they become generally effective in promoting social and political programs nationally or internationally until after 1910. The earliest eugenics movements were founded in Germany in 1904, in Great Britain in 1907, and in the United States in 1908–1910. Other eugenics movements appeared subsequently around the world: in western Europe (France, Norway, Sweden, Denmark), Russia, Latin America (Cuba, Brazil, Mexico), Canada, and Asia (Japan). However, it was in the United States, Great Britain, and Germany where eugenics as an intellectual and social movement reached its greatest strides and, from the eugenicists' point of view, achieved its greatest ideological and political effects.

Figure 1 Sir Francis Galton. From the Cold Spring Harbor Laboratory Archives, with permission of the American Philosophical Society.

Basic Principles of Eugenics

Variety of Eugenic Views

Because eugenics developed in a variety of national contexts with a wide range of ideological and political programs, its content and style varied from one country to another, and over time, from the early 1900s until the period just before the onset of World War II. For example, British eugenicists were particularly concerned with the high fecundity and inherited mental degeneracy of the urban working class, particularly those labeled as "paupers." By contrast, American eugenicists were more concerned with the number of feebleminded who filled the prisons and insane asylums and, after World War I, with the supposed genetic deficiencies of immigrants. In Germany, mentally ill, psychotic, psychopathic, and psychiatric patients in general, along with the congenitally deaf, blind, and feebleminded, were of greatest concern. German eugenicists were also particularly interested in increasing the number of "fitter" elements in society (positive eugenics)—where prior to the National Socialist takeover in 1933 "fitness" was understood more in terms of class rather than "race." In France and Russia, where ideas of the inheritance of acquired characteristics held more sway than in other countries, eugenicists concentrated more on public health reforms than on selective breeding. Although eugenics was not a monolithic movement, certain core principles and beliefs did link various eugenics movements together and the three major international eugenics congresses, held in 1912 (London) and in 1921 and 1932 (New York), emphasized the similarities among the various movements while also revealing the differences.

Core Principles of Eugenics

The core principles of eugenics as they came to be understood by the mid-1930s were summarized in a report, Eugenical Sterilization: A Reorientation of the Problem, published in 1936 by the Committee for the Investigation of Eugenical Sterilization of the American Neurological Association. Among documents stemming from the period of the eugenics movement itself, this report summarizes clearly and succinctly the major principles and goals of eugenics:

1. The belief that a number of social and behavioral problems, such as "insanity, feeblemindedness, epilepsy, pauperism, alcoholism, and certain forms of criminality are on the increase . . . ."
2. People bearing these various defective traits "propagate at a greater rate than the normal population." Thus, the number of defective or degenerate people in society is increasing at a faster rate than ordinary, nonpathological stocks.
3. Such defects in mental function and behavior are "fundamentally and mainly hereditary," so that it was common "to speak of insanity, feeblemindedness, epilepsy, pauperism, and criminality, as if they were unitary traits and at the same time were linked together as a psychopathic set of trends." Most of the hereditarian arguments put forward in the United States were couched in terms of the Mendelian theory of heredity, where various adult traits were often spoken of as being transmitted via discrete units, called genes, from parents to offspring. This was sometimes referred to as the unit-character hypothesis, in which an adult character or trait (e.g., feeblemindedness) was thought to be determined by a single Mendelian gene (e.g., in this case a recessive gene, i.e., one whose effects could be masked by its dominant allele, or alternative form of the gene).
4. Coupled with point (3) above, eugenicists argued that the environment in which a person was raised was of much less importance than the germ plasm inherited from their parents (i.e., biological inheritance) as the cause of "adverse social status," criminality, or general "social maladjustment." A corollary of the latter two points is that such behaviors, including feeblemindedness, were so strongly determined by biological factors that they were virtually unchangeable. Significantly improving the cognitive ability of the feebleminded or making the criminal into a model citizen was deemed virtually impossible. Biology was destiny.

The Historical Development of Eugenics: 1904–1950

Biologists' Involvement with Eugenics

Major Leadership

In most countries, eugenics movements combined theory (about the nature and pattern of inheritance) with various forms of social and political programs (from education committees to lobbying political leaders). For example, the acknowledged leader of American eugenics, Charles B. Davenport (1866–1944), was inspired by spending part of a sabbatical year (1899–1900) in London with Galton and his protégé Karl Pearson (1857–1936) to develop eugenics as the "quantitative study of evolution." Indeed Davenport, like Galton and Pearson, first applied biometrical principles to the evolution question and only secondarily to eugenics. In the years before 1925, most eugenicists were well-respected members of the scientific community and the eugenic ideas they espoused were not considered eccentric or bizarre. Davenport received his Ph.D. from Harvard in 1891, taught at the University of Chicago, and then obtained funds from the Carnegie Institution of Washington to establish his own research laboratory, the Station for the Experimental Evolution (SEE) in 1904 at Cold Spring Harbor, Long Island, New York, to promote the study of heredity (soon to become known as "genetics") and its relationship to selection and evolution. He was a member of the National Academy of Sciences (United States) and the National Research Council. In

Great Britain, Davenport's equivalent was Karl Pearson, director of another Eugenics Record Office and Galton Professor of Eugenics at University College, London. In Germany, Eugen Fischer (1874–1967), the acknowledged academic leader of *Rassenhygiene* (racial hygiene) (often interpreted as a synonym for eugenics in the German context, but a term employed by German practitioners who tended to harbor "pro-Aryan" sympathies), had received an M.D. from the University of Freiburg where he taught until, in 1927, he was appointed Director of the newly founded Kaiser-Wilhelm Institute for Anthropology, Human Genetics, and Eugenics (KWIA) in Berlin-Dahlem. In the Soviet Union, Solomon Levit (1894–1938), who had held a postdoctoral fellowship to study genetics with Herman J. Muller (1890–1967) at the University of Texas, was Director of the prestigious Maxim Gorky Scientific Research Institute of Medical Genetics in Moscow. Along with other colleagues, these investigators contributed solid work on aspects of human inheritance including the genetics of blood groups, albinism, brachydactyly (shortened digits), polydactyly (extra digits), Huntington's chorea, achondroplastic dwarfism, diabetes, ulcers, and cancer, as well as more tenuous studies on inheritance of feeblemindedness, mental capacity, and social traits.

Broad-Based Support for Eugenics among Rank-and-File Biologists

In addition to such conspicuous national leaders, many well-known, rank-and-file biologists, especially in the period 1910–1925, enthusiastically endorsed the aims of eugenics. Thus, all of the following biologists supported the goals of eugenics at one time or another: in England, J. B. S. Haldane (1892–1964) (Professor of Biochemistry at Cambridge, and after 1928 at the John Innes Horticultural Institution), Lancelot Hogben (1884–1976), and C. D. Darlington (1903–1981); in Germany, botanist Erwin Baur (1875–1933) and human geneticist Fritz Lenz (1887–1976); in Russia, *Drosophila* geneticist Aleksandr S. Serebrovsky (1892–1948) (Timiriazev Institute in Moscow); and in the United States, mammalian geneticist W. E. Castle (1867–1962), plant geneticist E. M. East (1879–1938) (Harvard), protozoologist H. S. Jennings (1868–1947), geneticist Raymond Pearl (1879–1940) (Johns Hopkins), paleontologist Henry Fairfield Osborn (1857–1935) (Columbia University and President of the American Museum of Natural History), and embryologist turned geneticist Thomas Hunt Morgan (1866–1945) (Columbia University). The attraction for these biologists was that the new science of genetics appeared to offer a solution to recurrent social problems—crime, feeblemindedness, alcoholism, manic depression, and violence, among others—that had eluded social workers and charitable organizations for so long. Eugenics was seen as the efficient, rational, and scientific way to solve social problems, by eliminating the cause—in this case, what was considered to be defective heredity ("bad genes")—rather than treating just the symptoms. Though the activities in which these eugenics supporters engaged varied from technical research to popularization, administration, and fund-raising, all contributed in some way or another to spreading the eugenics message to a broader public.

Funding Support for Eugenics

Major academic figures such as Davenport, Pearson, and Fischer were able to garner considerable funds to initiate and expand eugenics work in their respective countries. Davenport obtained a major gift in 1910 and again in 1916 from the wealthy Harriman family of New York to establish the Eugenics Record Office (ERO), next door to the SEE at Cold Spring Harbor (Fig. 2). It was the first major research institution anywhere devoted solely to eugenics. On Galton's death in 1911, his will left a bequest to set up a similar office at University College, London, with Pearson as its Director. The KWIA was funded largely by the German and Prussian governments, with only very marginal support supplemented by private industry. It always stood as one of the state-supported Kaiser Wilhelm Institutes (Fig. 3). Fischer became an adept politician in persuading the government to increase his allocations almost every year after the KWIA was opened in 1927. Eventually, it became one of the largest eugenics institutions in the world, with a staff of over 30. Eugenics in Germany, as something separate from *Rassenhygiene* (in the openly racist sense of the term), was all but eliminated after the "Nazi seizure of power." Practitioners who remained active in the German racial hygiene movement after 1933 tended to be right-wing nationalists, if not outright Nazis. As such, it is hardly surprising that racial hygiene became a major ideological basis for the new Nazi "racial state." In addition to carrying out research, such institutions also served, both in their own countries and internationally through ties with one another, as clearinghouses for exchange of eugenic information, as repositories of eugenic data, especially family case study and pedigree charts, and as organizational centers for eugenic education and propaganda.

Whereas eugenics research and propaganda in most countries was carried out by middle-class and upper middle-class practitioners (scientists, teachers, reformers), financial support came from the economic, political, and social elite (especially the "captains of industry") and clearly served several special interests. First, was economic efficiency: it was expensive to let defective people be born and then spend taxpayers' money to keep them in institutions for much of their lives. Second, the eugenic argument that social problems originated in bad

Figure 2 The Eugenics Record Office, new building constructed in 1912. From the Harry H. Laughlin Papers, Cold Spring Harbor Laboratory Archives, courtesy of Truman State University Archives.

Figure 3 The building that housed the Kaiser-Wilhelm Institute for Anthropology, Human Genetics and Eugenics, as it looks today. Photo courtesy of Garland Allen.

genes deflected criticism of social policies (low wages, long working hours, intolerable working and living conditions) and placed the blame for social problems on individuals. For example, labor unrest, growing in the industrial countries in the first decades of the 20th century, was claimed to be the result of an increase in genetically defective individuals. In the United States, eugenics was very much a product of progressivism, a popular movement that emphasized efficiency and the control of society by scientifically trained experts. Eugenics was merely the rational control of human evolution by geneticists.

Research Methods in Eugenics: 1900–1950

Defining and Measuring Traits

Defining Traits

Eugenicists were faced with the problem of defining and measuring the traits whose patterns of inheritance they wanted to determine. Definition posed a considerable problem when the traits were complex behaviors that were often defined in different ways in different cultures or different historical periods. What counted as an alcoholic or a criminal? How was feeblemindedness defined? Recognizing that such conditions are culturally defined, Davenport, for example, lumped all such individuals into the category of "social defectives" or "socially inadequate persons." Although eugenicists would have liked to have had what they could refer to as objective and quantitative measurements, for most of the behavioral and mental traits in which they were interested, no such definitions or measurements existed. For the most part, they had to rely on highly qualitative, subjective methods of defining traits and categorizing individual behavior.

Measuring the Trait of Intelligence

One trait that could be expressed quantitatively was intelligence, tests for which were developed particularly in the United States. In 1912, Davenport arranged for his long-time friend, Henry H. Goddard (1856–1962), then Director of the Training School for Feebleminded Boys and Girls at Vineland, New Jersey, to administer versions of the French Binet-Simon test to immigrants arriving at Ellis Island. Although the Binet-Simon test was intended to measure only an individual's mental functioning at a given point in time, Goddard and a host of American psychometricians considered that it also measured innate, or genetically determined intelligence. Goddard coined the term feeblemindedness to refer to those people who scored below 70 on his tests and claimed that it "was a condition of the mind or brain which is transmitted as regularly and surely as color of hair or eyes." Because Goddard was convinced that feeblemindedness was a recessive Mendelian trait, he reformulated the concept of intelligence from a continuous character to that of a discrete character. And it was Goddard who carried out the famous study demonstrating the supposed inheritance of mental deficiency in a New Jersey family known by the pseudonym Kallikak.

For psychometricians and eugenicists, the belief that their tests measured innate capacity rather than merely accumulated knowledge meant that the tests could be used as an instrument for carrying out educational and social policy, not merely as a measure of an individual's progress at a specific point in time. For eugenicists, the new mental tests, especially the Stanford-Binet test first published in 1916, were seen as a precise, quantitative tool for measuring an otherwise elusive, but fundamental human trait. The fact that much of the material, including terminology, on which the tests were based was culture-bound did not deter psychometricians or eugenicists from claiming that the tests measured only innate learning capacity. Even when results from the U.S. Army tests during World War I showed that the longer recruits from immigrant families had lived in the United States, the better they did on the tests, Carl C. Brigham (1890–1943), a Princeton psychologist who analyzed the data, argued

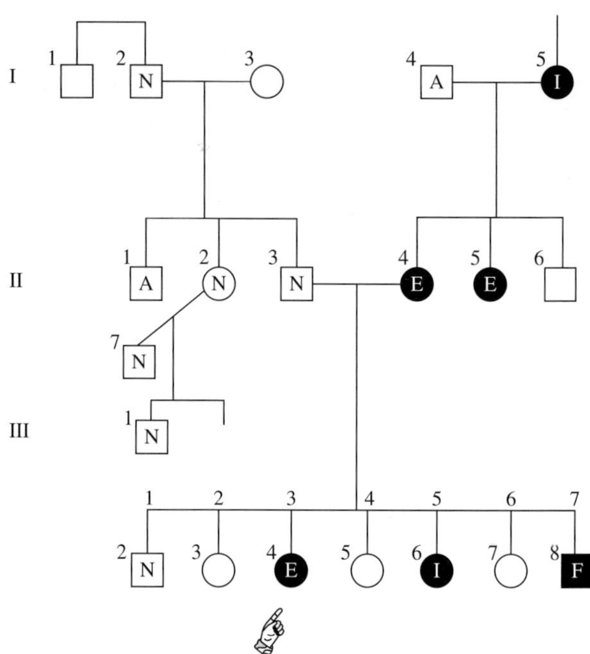

Figure 4 A generalized pedigree chart showing the various symbols used and the methods of display. Squares are males and circles are females; black squares or circles represent individuals who show the trait in question, white squares or circles represent individuals who are unaffected. Roman numerals indicate generations; horizontal (or in some cases diagonal) lines connecting two individuals indicate parents (whether legally married or not), and vertical lines indicate offspring from a parental pair. In any one generation, the individuals are designated by an Arabic number (1, 2, 3, etc., at the top of the line; the superscript numbers to the left of each individual indicate the birth order for that individual); in the first family from the left in generation I, individual 2 is the second husband of individual 3. Letter symbols are as follows: E, epileptic; F, feebleminded; I, insane; C, criminalistic; A, alcoholic; N, normal. The finger symbol at III, 3, 4 indicates the individual ("Propositus") who was institutionalized and with whom the study began. Reprinted from Davenport, C. B. (1911). "The Study of Human Heredity. Methods of Collecting, Charting and Analyzing Data," Eugenics Record Office, Bulletin No. 2, Cold Spring Harbor, New York.

that the trends showed a decline in the quality of immigrants over time, not their degree of familiarity with the cultural content of the tests.

The Family Pedigree Method

The family pedigree chart was one of the main analytical means of displaying and analyzing data on the heredity of one or another behavioral trait (Fig. 4). The data that went into constructing pedigree charts, and on which strong hereditarian claims were based, were often anecdotal, subjective, and many times obtained from second- and third-hand sources. Typical examples are the family studies carried out through the auspices of the Eugenics

Record Office at Cold Spring Harbor, by their trained field workers. Starting with an individual, known as the "propositus," usually incarcerated in a state institution (for the feebleminded, insane, or a prison), the field workers would interview not only that individual, but as many members of the family as possible. Where possible, medical records would be obtained, but in most cases detailed examples of the latter were simply not available. In some cases, questionnaires would be filled out by the family members themselves when direct interview was not practical. The data were then organized into pedigree charts to suggest how heredity influenced many behavioral, personality, and mental traits. For example, in a study published in 1919, Davenport claimed that thalassophilia, or "love of the sea," was due to a sex-linked Mendelian recessive appearing in the families of prominent U.S. naval officers (Fig. 5). That the condition must be sex-linked was clear to Davenport, since in pedigree after pedigree, only males showed the trait. Davenport dismissed criticism that such complex behaviors could not be reduced to the effects of single genes as "uninformed." Similar simplistic arguments were also extended to explain the differences between racial, ethnic, and national groups, for example, the claim that blacks showed genetic tendencies toward "shiftlessness" and the Irish toward "alcoholism."

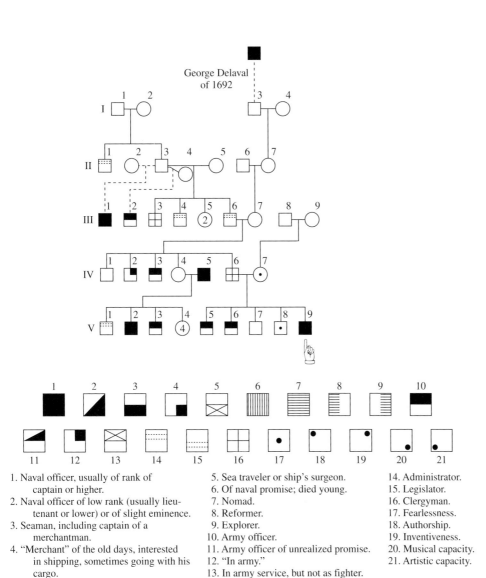

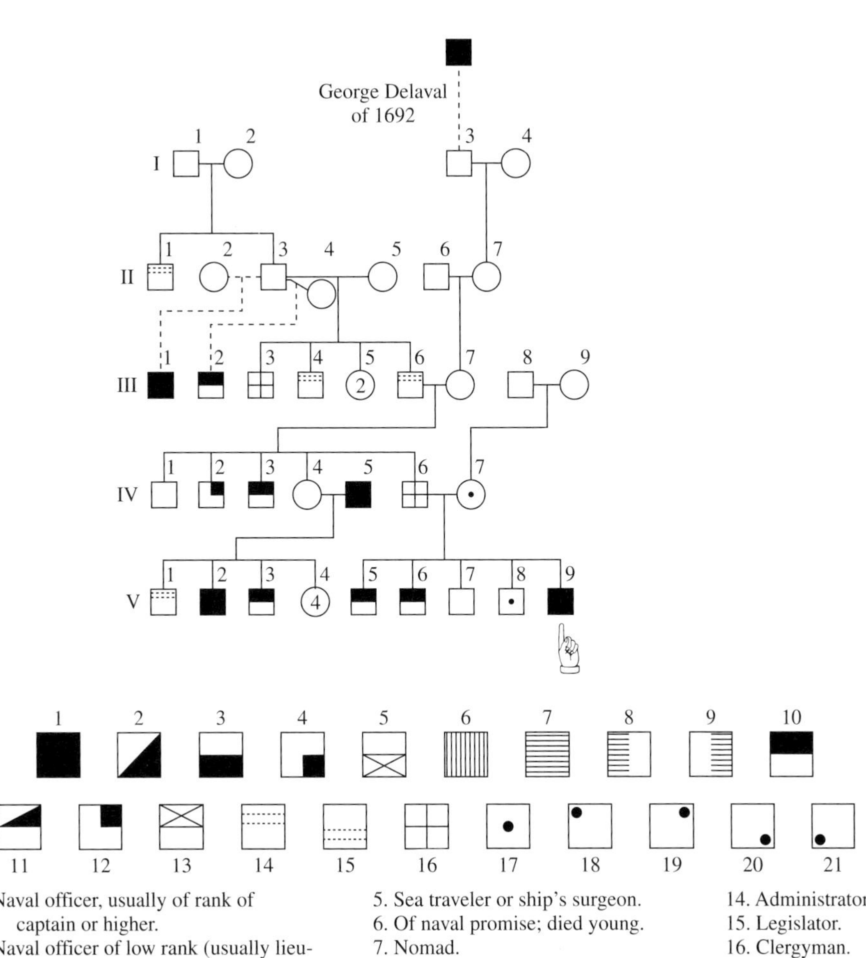

Figure 5 A family pedigree chart for "thalassophilia" (love of the sea), in the family of Charles William de la Poer Beresford. Davenport interpreted the fact that the trait appears only in males (squares) and can skip generations to indicate that it was a sex-linked Mendelian recessive. Reprinted from Davenport, C. B. (1919). "Naval Officers, Their Heredity and Development," p. 43. Carnegie Institution of Washington, Washington, DC.

Eugenics in the Public Arena

Eugenics and Popular Culture: Magazine Articles, Popular Books, and Textbooks

Eugenics ideology was spread not only through scientific but also popular channels, including the press, exhibits, the eugenicists' own popular journals such as *Eugenical News* (published by the American Eugenics Society), various movies (including a feature film, *The Black Stork*, based on a true story of the decision to let a seriously deformed baby die), Fitter Family Contests at State Fairs, and even, in the 1920s, a Eugenical Sermon Contest. The number of articles on eugenics in popular magazines rose precipitously between 1910 and 1914, and again in the 1920s, especially concerning the immigration restriction issue being debated in Congress between 1921 and 1924. Most high school biology textbooks carried some discussion, often a chapter or more, on eugenics. Through these sources, the general public was made aware of the claim that many segments of society were genetically unfit for anything but the most menial and physically exhausting work. Although it is difficult to assess the impact of such publicity, it seems reasonably clear that by the early to mid-1920s many segments of the American, British, and wider European public were at least aware of a claim, made in the name of modern science, that many social, especially mental, traits were genetically determined and that in these respects blacks, Native Americans, and many non-Nordic or non-Anglo-Saxon groups were genetically the most inferior groups in the human species.

Political Activity

From the start, most eugenicists were anxious to play a role in the public arena—in what today would be called formation of public policy (Karl Pearson in England was an exception in maintaining caution in this regard, and for that and other reasons related to the structure of British politics, eugenicists did not influence much legislation in Parliament). A good deal of eugenicists' efforts in other countries, however, focused on lobbying for compulsory sterilization laws for the "genetically unfit" and, especially in the United States, for eugenically informed immigration restriction.

Passage of Eugenical Sterilization Laws

The United States pioneered in the passage of eugenical sterilization laws. After the ERO was launched in 1910, Laughlin became particularly active in lobbying for the passage of a number of such sterilization laws at the state level. Indeed, Laughlin drew up a "Model Sterilization Law" that served as a prototype from which each state could derive its own modified version. The majority of such laws were passed by state legislatures in the United States during the interwar period (1920–1940). Eugenical sterilization was aimed specifically at those individuals in mental or penal institutions who, from family pedigree analysis, were considered likely to give birth to socially defective children. Sterilization could be ordered only after a patient had been examined by a eugenics committee, usually composed of a lawyer or family member representing the individual, a judge, and a doctor or other eugenic "expert." Like most eugenicists, Laughlin felt that sterilization was an example of "social efficiency."

Eugenic sterilization reached astounding proportions worldwide in the first half of the 20th century. In the United States, between 1907, when the first law was passed in Indiana and the summary calculations of Jonas Robitscher in 1963, over 60,000 eugenical sterilizations were performed, with California leading all other states. A similar number was estimated for Sweden between 1928 and the early 1960s, whereas the Germans, who passed their first law (at the national level) in July 1933, just months after the Nazis came to power, ultimately sterilized over 400,000. In the United States, the most publicly visible sterilization case was that of Carrie Buck in Virginia in 1925. When Virginia passed its eugenical sterilization law in 1924, based on Laughlin's "model law," a test case (known as "Buck vs Bell") was set up the next year to determine whether the law was constitutional. Carrie Buck, then in a Virginia home for the feebleminded, was sterilized as the daughter of a feebleminded woman and mother of a feebleminded child. When the lower court ruled in favor of the law, an appeal was sent to the Supreme Court of the United States, where Justice Oliver Wendell Holmes wrote the majority opinion. In upholding the lower court ruling, Holmes made his oft-repeated assertion, "Three generations of imbeciles are enough." Laughlin's model sterilization law also served as the basis for Germany's 1933 "Law for the Prevention of Hereditarily Defective Offspring." For this effort, as well as for his enthusiastic support of other Nazi eugenic programs, Laughlin was awarded an honorary doctorate (M.D.) from Heidelberg University on the occasion of its 550th anniversary celebration in 1936.

Eugenics and Immigration Restriction in the United States

In the United States under Laughlin's leadership, eugenicists were instrumental in the passage of the 1924 Immigration Restriction Act (The Johnson-Reed Act). Immigration from Europe, especially from eastern and southern Europe, the Balkans, Poland, and Russia (including many of Jewish origin), had increased significantly since the 1880s, replacing the traditional immigrant groups from northern Europe and the British Isles. As various political and economic groups poised to oppose further immigration after World War I, Laughlin was appointed "Expert Eugenics Witness" to the House Committee on Immigration and Naturalization. He testified twice before the Committee, using I.Q. test scores, data on institutionalization of various immigrant groups for feeblemindedness, insanity, criminality, blindness, etc., to support the claim that recent immigrants were less genetically fit than the older, northern European stock. Laughlin provided an air of scientific objectivity for what various nativist groups wanted to accomplish for reasons of economics or prejudice. The Johnson-Reed Act was passed by both houses of Congress and was signed into law in 1924.

Criticisms of Eugenics

Almost from the beginning, many of the basic premises of eugenics were brought under critical scrutiny by biologists, medical doctors, social workers, and laypersons from all walks of life. Criticisms emerged in most countries by the mid-1920s, though the reasons differed widely.

Criticism in Catholic Countries

In Catholic countries, criticism of eugenics was made official by the Papal Encyclical, *Casti connubi*, of 1930. Prior to the encyclical, however, in countries such as France eugenic claims were tempered by the prevailing theory of inheritance of acquired characters (sometimes referred to as neo-Lamarckism after the French zoologist Jean-Baptiste de Lamarck (1744–1829), who had emphasized the influence of the environment as a cause of adaptations acquired by organisms during their lifetime and passed on to their offspring). If such adaptations could be inherited, then the environment had a much larger role to play in changing human behavior than eugenicists had thought. Consequently, in France prior to 1930, and in the countries whose scientific culture it influenced (particularly in Latin America), eugenics was always coupled with programs for public health reforms and attention to improving environmental conditions. In addition, few French biologists adopted the Mendelian paradigm ("hard" heredity, not influenced by the environment) when it was reintroduced into the scientific community in 1900. Their view of heredity was thus a "soft" one, that is, whereas traits were obviously transmitted between parents and offspring, modifications to the body tissues allowed for corresponding modification of the parents' germ plasma and thus of the characteristics of the offspring. Genetics was not so much destiny for French eugenicists as it was for biologists elsewhere.

Criticism in the Soviet Union

Russia had a small, but flourishing eugenics movement before the Bolshevik revolution of 1917. With the advent of the communist regime, there was initial hope among biologists that the application of scientific principles to reproductive policies, as to agriculture, would receive official support. Although such official support did not materialize—there were far more pressing problems in the early years of the revolution—eugenics was also not prohibited. Especially after H. J. Muller visited the Soviet Union in 1921, bringing with him cultures of *Drosophila melanogaster*, a whole school of experimental geneticists developed, accompanied by expanding interest in eugenics. Several eugenicists worked out eugenic pedigrees for many members of the aristocracy who had fled the revolution, arguing that the exodus of so many of "good stock" was draining off the best genes from the population. Such claims came under increasing criticism as bourgeois, anti-working-class science. In addition, the influence of "Michurinism," a variety of neo-Lamarckism put forward by agronomist Trofim Lysenko (1898–1976) starting in the late 1920s, and the claim that Mendelian genetics represented western mechanistic science conspired to oppose eugenics as a legitimate science. Recognizing that complex human behaviors and social values cannot be ascribed to genes in any clear way, many Soviet biologists found the claims of western eugenicists to be naive and class-based. Moreover, the hard hereditarian line promoted by most western eugenicists was at odds with the communist views of the malleability of human nature and thus appeared to provide no role for the environment in shaping human destiny. These recognitions became official when the Central Committee of the Communist Party outlawed work on eugenics in 1930. Much of what was carried out as eugenic research before that time was either abandoned or recast as medical genetics. Solomon Levit's institute, founded in 1929, was carefully named the Maxim Gorky Biomedical Scientific Research Institute to avoid any apparent link with eugenic work. Only in the Soviet Union was eugenics officially denounced by governmental legislation.

Criticism in the United States and Great Britain

In western countries such as the United States and Great Britain, where eugenics had flourished, criticisms began to arise over the sloppiness of many eugenicists' research methods: definition of phenotypes, methods of collecting and analyzing data, the frequent lack of control groups, and the strong racial and ethnic biases that surfaced in many eugenicists' writings. Among the first and most important critics in the United States was Thomas Hunt Morgan, the *Drosophila* geneticist at Columbia

University and, prior to 1915, a moderate supporter of eugenics. Morgan felt that the movement had become more propagandistic than scientific and criticized eugenical claims in print, starting with his 1925 book *Evolution and Genetics*. He chastised eugenicists for lumping many mental and behavioral conditions together under a rubric such as feeblemindedness and treating it as if it had a single underlying cause (i.e., a single gene):

> *The case most often quoted is feeblemindedness that has been said to be inherited as a Mendelian recessive, but until some more satisfactory definition can be given as to where feeblemindedness begins and ends, and until it has been determined how many and what internal physical defects may produce a general condition of this sort, . . . it is extravagant to pretend to claim that there is a single Mendelian factor for this condition.*

Morgan went on to argue that because environmental influences on mental and nervous development are so strong, and since it is impossible to raise humans under controlled conditions like fruit flies, no rigorous claims could be made about a genetic basis for such traits.

Echoing similar concerns, English mathematician, geneticist, and sometime eugenicist Lancelot Hogben made one of the clearest statements at the time about the oversimplified concept of genetics that informed much of the eugenics movement: "No statement about a genetic difference has any scientific meaning unless it includes or implies a specification of the environment in which it manifests itself in a particular manner." Furthermore, as Reginal C. Punnett (1875–1967), one of Bateson's collaborators in England noted, the fact that even if a trait were found to be controlled by a single Mendelian gene, unless it was a dominant, it would take hundreds of generations of rigorous selection to eliminate it from the population.

A more public attack on eugenics came in 1926 from Raymond Pearl at Johns Hopkins University, himself a one-time eugenics supporter. Pearl, and his Hopkins colleague Herbert Spencer Jennings, both agreed with the basic principles and aims of eugenics, but felt that propagandists such as Laughlin and others made claims that went far beyond any reasonable biological evidence. During the congressional debates, both Pearl and Jennings were struck by the pejorative tones used to describe the supposed biological inferiority of new immigrants. Jennings was so appalled by the kind of arguments put forth by Laughlin's testimony before the House Committee that he wrote a series of rebuttals of Laughlin's claims and a small book (*Prometheus, or Biology and the Advancement of Man*, 1925), condemning the vulgarization and racism of some eugenic writers. H. J. Muller, a student of Morgan's, and in the early 1930s a professor at the University of Texas, delivered a searing attack on "old style" eugenics, titled "The Dominance of Economics over Eugenics," at the Third International Eugenics Congress in New York City in 1932. Muller, who harbored strong eugenical beliefs as well as socialist leanings, argued that until the economic and social environment could be equalized it would be impossible to know how much of any individual's "social inadequacy" was due to heredity and how much to environment.

Eugenics in Germany: 1933–1945

The Period of Ascendancy: 1933–1940

Because racial policy and eugenics formed one of the cornerstones of National Socialism, eugenics research and policy found considerable support in Germany after 1933. Although the KWIA was founded in 1927, prior to the Nazi takeover, after 1933 Fischer quickly turned it into a major research institution serving both the ideological and practical needs of the new government. In addition to studies on the "racial" basis for legislation such as the sterilization and marriage laws, members of the KWIA taught courses for doctors on heredity and eugenics, testified in eugenic courts and in regular civil courts regarding paternity issues, and in other ways provided much technical assistance to the government. A similar trajectory was enjoyed by Ernst Rüdin's KWIA for Psychiatry in Munich, beginning with its founding in 1928 and much-expanded funding in 1931. In return, support from the government (and the Rockefeller Foundation) (for both Fischer's and Rüdin's institutes) catapulted German eugenics well above eugenic movements elsewhere. By 1933, many eugenicists in the United States complained that overnight the Germans had already surpassed American efforts in both research support and legislative accomplishment.

Eugenics as a "Murderous Science" (1940–1945)

When Fischer retired as Director of the KWIA in 1942, he was succeeded by his protégé Ottmar von Verschuer (1896–1969), one of the pioneers in the use of identical twins in genetic and eugenic research (identical, or monozygotic, twins share the same genes, so they can be used to try and separate the effects of genes and environment). Whereas Fischer had relied on state hospitals and asylums as a source of subjects for study, during his own directorship of the KWIA (1942–1945) Verschuer eventually took the institute's research into extermination and slave-labor camps, where his assistant and former doctoral student, Josef Mengele (1911–1984), made pairs of twins available, especially for research on pathological conditions. For example, twins (with nontwins as controls) were infected with disease agents to study the effects of the same and different hereditary constitution on the course of disease. After the twins died or were killed, their body organs were sent back to the KWIA for analysis. Such procedures, when brought to light at the Nuremberg trials, not only shocked the world, but indicated the extent to which eugenic work could so easily transgress the bounds of acceptable scientific practice. Long before these extreme forms of unethical research were undertaken at Auschwitz and "euthanasia" hospitals, those KWIA scientists who remained at their posts (some left because they were Jewish, or Catholic, or not in sympathy with the direction of the institute's research) had all made the "Faustian bargain" with the Nazi state. This was especially true of the first and second institute Directors, Fischer and Verschuer.

The Decline and Transformation of Eugenics: 1935–1950

The United States and England

Except for Germany and the countries it influenced or occupied, by the mid-1930s eugenics began to experience a decline in general popularity and in political effectiveness. Scholars have suggested several possible reasons for this change of fortune. Clearly, both the depression of 1929–1933 and reports of Nazi eugenics activity played some part in a general disaffection with eugenical principles. During the Depression, people without jobs became paupers and social inadequates overnight with no change in their genetic make-up, whereas in Germany the sterilization and infamous Nuremberg Laws (1935) showed the extent to which eugenical legislation under a powerful central government could erode personal liberties. An additional factor may have been the recognition that eugenicists were increasingly out of touch with the most recent findings of laboratory genetics. Davenport's and Laughlin's simple unit-character concept did not square with experimental data suggesting that most traits were produced by the interaction of many genes and that evidence for a clear-cut genetic basis of complex human social behaviors was almost nonexistent.

Whatever the exact causes, what has been labeled "mainline" eugenics was losing favor in the United States and Great Britain by the late 1930s. The older generation of eugenicists were retiring or had died and a younger generation, though sharing some of the earlier ideals, took the movement in different directions. For example, in the United States, from the mid-1930s on, the center of eugenic activity shifted from older organizations such as the ERO and the Race Betterment Foundation, to the American Eugenics Society under its then-new Secretary, Frederick Osborn, retired railway executive and nephew of American Museum of Natural History President, Henry Fairfield Osborn. Frederick Osborn has been described as a "moderate" or "reform" eugenicist, perhaps a misleading term but nonetheless signaling the different approach he was to give to eugenics ideas especially in the postwar period. Osborn did not invoke a rejection of eugenic ideology or goals, but a toning down of the overtly racist and simplistic genetic claims of the previous generation. Osborn was the first secretary and later President of the Pioneer Fund, set up by millionaire Wycliffe Draper of New York, with Harry Laughlin and Madison Grant as advisors, to demonstrate that biologically as well as sociologically blacks were inferior to whites (in the 1950s and 1960s, Draper funded, through other channels, a number of citizens' groups in the southern United States to oppose the civil right movement and school integration; the Fund exists in the early 21st century under the Presidency of psychologist J. Philippe Rushton). As a major figure after the war in the Rockefeller-funded Population Council, Osborn expanded eugenicists' goals from controlling the fertility of individual (what he considered "inferior") families to whole groups and nations: that is, control of population growth, especially among the poor at home and Third World nations abroad. Concern about the high birth rate of non-whites was the central underlying issue of the population control movement, although its mission was stated in less directly racist terms as "saving the planet from overpopulation." Centered primarily in the United States, the population control movement (represented by organizations such as the Population Council, Zero Population Growth, and Planned Parenthood) was the direct heir to the social mission of the older eugenics movement.

France

In France, eugenics was based from the outset of the soft hereditary concepts associated with the inheritance of acquired characteristics and so placed less emphasis on Mendelian interpretations, i.e., the unit-character hypothesis. The French were never able to pass any significant eugenic-based legislation and, in 1930, with promulgation of the Papal Encyclical *Casti connubi*, which directly criticized eugenical sterilization, the movement took a serious setback. As a result, throughout the 1930s eugenics became much more a public health movement than a biological determinist movement.

The Soviet Union

Although eugenics flourished in Russia both before and immediately after the revolution of 1917, in the post-revolutionary period it was viewed as both one of the most important applications of Marxist science to human society (Marxism gave high priority to science and scientific thinking applied to societal issues) and potentially as a class-based and racist ideology that denied the possibility of human improvement. Several factors conspired to temper and finally eliminate eugenics as a science in the U.S.S.R. One was the increased influence of neo-Lamarckian biology in the U.S.S.R., promoted by Trofim D. Lysenko, an agronomist with little or no biological training. Lysenko attacked Mendelian genetics as an example of Western bourgeois idealism (in the philosophical sense that genes were figments of theoreticians' imagination), having no application to the country's pressing agricultural needs. Since eugenics was largely based on Mendelian principles, it was seen as purely mechanical and philosophically naive. In addition, and more serious, was the fact that some eugenicists, such as Solomon Levit's mentor, A. S. Serebrovsky, proposed outlandish schemes such as artificially inseminating women with the sperm of superior men, an idea that was attacked as bourgeois by Party leadership and ridiculed publicly. By 1930, the Central Committee banned all work on eugenical issues and Levit's Institute was reorganized, focusing solely on medical topics.

Eugenics Today

The history of the older eugenics movement raises many issues relevant to the expanding work in genomics, especially the Human Genome Project (HGP). Since the advent of new technologies associated with test-tube babies, sequencing the human genome, cloning new organisms from adult cells, stem cell research, genetic testing, and the prospects of gene therapy, the term eugenics has once again come into popular culture. Since it is possible, through *in utero* testing, to determine whether a fetus is male or female, has Down's syndrome (trisomy 21), or a mutation for Huntingon's disease, cystic fibrosis, thalassemia, or Tay-Sachs, should these tests be required for all pregnant women? And if so, who should have access to the results? Can medical insurance companies refuse to cover families or their children if the mother does not undergo genetic testing of the fetus? Some medical ethicists argue that the outcome—controlling births in order to reduce the number of "defective" people in society—is identical to that issuing from the old eugenics movement, only the means and the agency are different. According to this view, it makes little difference whether state legislation or social and economic pressure force people to make reproductive decisions that they might not otherwise make. Other ethicists, however, argue that state coercion, as in the old eugenics movement, is qualitatively different from various forms of social pressure, since the latter still gives the individual some range of choice. In addition, it can be argued that modern genetic decisions are made on a case-by-case basis and do not involve application of policies to whole groups defined racially, ethnically, or nationally.

Clearly, it is in the interests of insurance companies to reduce as much as possible the medical costs incurred by their clients. And some would argue that it is also in the interest of individual families to avoid bringing a seriously disabled child into the world. But ethicists raise the question of what is "disabled" and who should be the judge? What economic, social, and psychological factors are conspiring to make families today seek what medical ethicist Glenn McGee calls "the perfect baby"? These issues have become more pressing, the more costly that medical care has become and the more that ancillary social services (e.g., support groups for families of disabled children, special education and training programs) are cut back. Ironically, as a result of sequencing the human genome, the project that carried with it funds for ethical considerations, geneticists know that there is no one-to-one correspondence between genotype and phenotype and that the reading out of the genetic code is far more plastic than previously believed. Individuals with the same identical mutation in the cystic fibrosis gene, for example, can have quite different phenotypes (some are seriously affected and others are not, or the effects manifest themselves in different organs and at different stages in development). Thus, *in utero* genetic testing may reveal a mutant gene but will provide little information on how the child will turn out phenotypically.

Although these various ethical issues are problematical with well-defined clinical conditions, they are infinitely more so when mental, behavioral, and personality traits are the center of discussion. From the last quarter of the 20th century to 2004, many claims have been made for identifying genes that affect human behavior or personality (alcoholism, manic depression, criminality, homosexuality, shyness, aggression, etc.). No gene or group of genes has ever been isolated or shown clearly to affect any of these conditions, yet the belief that the conditions are to a significant degree genetically determined has become widespread throughout the media and in the public. Reproductive decisions based on circumstantial or nonexistent data add another level of ethical considerations in the growing debate about reproductive technologies. Recognizing the consequences of policies put forward under the guise of the old eugenics movement can help avoid some of the more obvious errors of the past.

See Also the Following Articles

Chapin, Francis Stuart • Fisher, Sir Ronald • Galton, Sir Francis • Human and Population Genetics • Psychometrics of Intelligence

Further Reading

Adams, M. B. (ed.) (1990). *The Wellborn Science: Eugenics in Germany, France, Brazil and Russia*. Oxford University Press, New York.

Allen, G. E. (2001). Mendel and modern genetics: The legacy for today. *Endeavour* **27,** 63–68.

Allen, G. E. (1986). The eugenics record office at Cold Spring Harbor, 1910–1940: An essay in institutional history. *Osiris* **2,** 225–264.

Barkan, E. (1992). *The Retreat of Scientific Racism. Changing Concepts of Race in Britain and the United States between the World Wars.* Cambridge University Press, New York.

Broberg, G., and Roll-Hansen, N. (eds.) (1996). *Eugenics and the Welfare State. Sterilization Policy in Denmark, Sweden, Norway and Finland*. Michigan State University Press, East Lansing, MI.

Carlson, E. A. (2001). *The Unfit: History of a Bad Idea.* Cold Spring Harbor Laboratory Press, Cold Spring Harbor, New York.

Chase, A. (1977). *The Legacy of Malthus.* Alfred A. Knopf, New York.

Kevles, D. J. (1985). *In the Name of Eugenics.* Alfred A. Knopf, New York.

Kühl, S. (1993). *The Nazi Connection. Eugenics, American Racism and German National Socialism.* Oxford University Press, New York.

Lombardo, P. A. (1985). Three generations of imbeciles: New light on Buck v. Bell. *N. Y. Univ. Law Rev.* **60,** 30–62.

Mazumdar, P. M. H. (1992). *Eugenics, Human Genetics and Human Failings. The Eugenics Society, Its Sources and Its Critics in Britain.* Routledge, London.

Müller-Hill, B. (1988). *Murderous Science. Elimination by Scientific Selection of Jews, Gypsies and Others, Germany 1933–1945.* Oxford University Press, New York.

Paul, D. (1995). *Controlling Heredity.* Humanities Press, Montclair, NJ.

Proctor, R. (1989). *Racial Hygiene: Medicine under the Nazis.* Harvard University Press, Cambridge, MA.

Selden, S. (1999). *Inheriting Shame: The Story of Eugenics and Racism in America.* Teachers College Press, New York.

Tucker, W. H. (2003). *The Funding of Scientific Racism: Wickliffe Draper and the Pioneer Fund.* University of Illinois Press, Urbana, IL.

Event History Analysis

Nancy Brandon Tuma
Stanford University, Stanford, California, USA

Glossary

censoring Happens when the timing of events for members of a sample are observed incompletely because events do not occur within the observation period.

competing risks Two or more distinct possible changes in a discrete outcome (e.g., someone may leave a job because she quits, retires, dies, or is fired).

event An essentially instantaneous change in the value of a discrete random variable, or of some outcome measured by such a variable.

hazard rate The limit, as Δt shrinks to zero, of the probability that an event occurs between t and $t + \Delta t$, divided by Δt, given that the event did not occur before t.

risk set Sample members at risk of a certain event at a particular time (e.g., only currently married people are at risk of divorce).

spell A continuous interval of time between a change in the value of the discrete outcome; it may be partitioned into subspells (shorter continuous intervals of time) to record changes in predictor variables or changes in their effects.

survival analysis The special case of event history analysis that examines a single nonrepeatable event (e.g., death, first birth).

transition rate Analogous to a hazard rate, but focuses on transitions to a particular state of the discrete outcome (i.e., a transition to one of several competing risks).

truncation Occurs when event histories of certain cases are excluded from the sample because their event occurred before data collection began or after it ended.

Event history analysis refers to the analysis of data on the timing of events for a sample of cases during a continuous time period of observation. An event is a change in the value of a discrete random outcome that is defined during some time interval (which may not coincide with the observation period used in data collection) and that has a countable number of exhaustive and mutually exclusive values. The values of the discrete outcomes may be unordered or ordered; if ordered, the values may or may not have metric properties.

Introduction

Empirical Applications

Social scientists in many fields collect event histories. The usual goals are to understand the timing, spacing, and order of events and the factors that influence them. For example, demographers collect fertility histories, marital and cohabitation histories, and migration histories. Demographers, economists, and sociologists assemble work histories of people. Sociologists also gather histories of riots, strikes, and other forms of collective action. Both political scientists and political sociologists compile histories of wars and other international conflicts and, contrastingly, of various efforts of nation-states to solve world problems (e.g., accession to treaties, joining of international organizations). Political scientists also examine histories of various legislative actions and of political party changes. Organizational scientists accumulate histories of organizational foundings, mergers, and failures, and of various actions of organizations (e.g., changes in organizational strategy, replacement of an organization's chief officers, shifts in its linkages to other organizations). Social psychologists sometimes collect histories of the behaviors and interactions of individuals (e.g., who talks to whom) in both experimental and nonexperimental settings.

Social scientists may use event history analysis to address the following types of questions: Do marriages tend to end in divorce more often and/or sooner if preceded by the couple cohabiting? What types of workers and jobs lead to more rapid job turnover? Which kinds of individuals are especially slow to leave unemployment? How does police intervention in a riot affect the timing and nature of subsequent collective action in the same locality? Which types of countries are quick (or slow) to accede to various kinds of treaties? What attributes of businesses are associated with a business failing or being acquired by another firm?

An Example of an Event History

Figure 1 illustrates an event history for a hypothetical man starting at his birth at t_0. During his lifetime, he has a series of jobs, eventually retires, and finally dies. The object of social scientific interest here is the interrelated processes of entering and leaving jobs. The discrete outcome, $Y(t)$, describes a person's status at time t. For completeness, "retirement" and "death," along with "jobless," are included as possible statuses, as well as various types of jobs. In this example, "jobless" is coded as 0, "retirement" as 4, and "death" as 5. Three types of jobs are distinguished, coded as 1, 2, and 3 (e.g., blue collar, lower white collar, and upper white collar jobs, respectively).

In Fig. 1, the hypothetical man is jobless until he starts his first job at time t_1. His first job is in status 1. He leaves his first job at t_2 and is again jobless (status 0) until starting his second job at t_3, which is also in status 1. At time t_4, he leaves his second job and moves immediately to his third job, which is in status 2. He remains in his third job until t_5, when he switches to a fourth job, which is in status 3. He remains in his fourth job until he retires at t_6. He dies at t_7. Because death is an absorbing state that cannot be left, there are no events after t_7. This hypothetical man has seven events, four jobs, and five statuses. Various other people may experience more or fewer events and occupy more or fewer statuses. The timing and sequence of the events of other people may also be different.

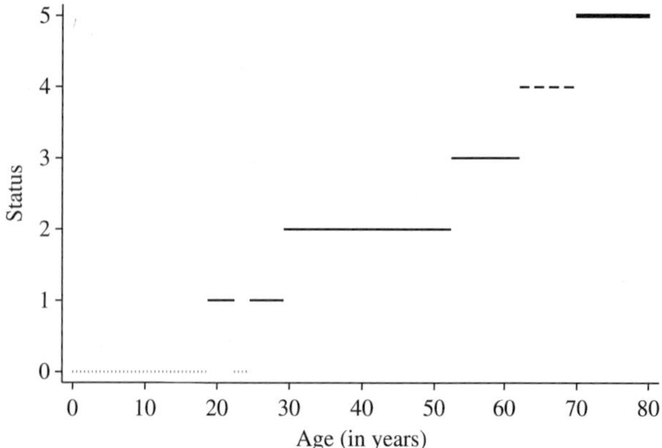

Figure 1 A hypothetical job history. Zero status is joblessness (dotted line); 1–3, jobs of varying status (solid lines); 4, retired (dashed line); 5, deceased (bold solid line).

Conceptualization of the Change Process

In event history analysis, a time path like the one in Fig. 1 is customarily assumed to represent reality for a member of the sample. But a specific conceptualization of the change process—in this example, of starting and stopping jobs—influences the picture in important ways. In particular, analysts may differ as to which statuses should be distinguished and which ones should be combined. For example, some might distinguish various kinds of jobs (e.g., in terms of occupation) and treat "unemployed" and "not in the labor force" as distinct ways of being out of work. Others might combine "never worked" with "out of work" into one status called "not working."

Further, transitions from one status to another are not always instantaneous. If changes are not instantaneous, analysts may make different decisions about the time of each event. For example, an analyst might decide that the date of a divorce occurs when a couple ceases to live together, files for divorce, or is officially divorced. Such decisions should be grounded in social scientific theory, but practical considerations also play a role. Available methodological tools give limited guidance concerning the consequences of making one decision rather than another. Making finer (coarser) distinctions about statuses tends to increase (decrease) the number of events and to shorten (lengthen) the time between events. Consequently, these kinds of decisions can profoundly affect overall findings.

Data

Information like that shown graphically for a single case in Fig. 1 must be converted into a form of data suitable for statistical analysis of event histories. How information is coded and put into machine-readable form depends on the computer software that will be used for the event history analysis. A wide variety of software is available, and new software and new extensions of existing software appear intermittently.

There is no single standard way of organizing event histories as data. From a statistical viewpoint, one way is not intrinsically better than another, but some ways yield data that are easier to manipulate and require less storage space. One common way is to subdivide each case's event history into a series of spells. A spell refers to a continuous interval of time when the value of the discrete outcome does not change. It ends when an event occurs or when the observation period ends so that the spell is censored on the right. A spell that begins with an event and terminates either with another event or with the end of the observation period may be subdivided further into a series of subspells (shorter time intervals), in which covariates or their effects may change. Splitting spells defined in terms of events into subspells defined by changes in covariates or their effects is a very helpful way to study time variation in a process.

Essential information about a spell (or a subspell) is the time when it starts, t_s; the value of the discrete outcome when it starts, $y(t_s)$; the time when it ends, t_e; and the value of the discrete outcome at its end, $y(t_e)$. There needs to be some indicator of whether the spell (or the subspell) ends with an event or is right-censored at t. This indicator may be a separate variable, $c(t)$, or it may be specified by a unique value of the discrete outcome. For instance, $y(t) = -1$ might be used to designate a right-censored spell if all meaningful values of the discrete outcome are nonnegative. If multiple events can occur (e.g., a person has a series of jobs over time), it is also useful to record the number of the event (e.g., job number) for each spell. Typically, the data also furnish the values of predictor variables, which are best measured continuously or, if this is impossible, at the start of each spell or subspell.

Another common way of storing event histories is to convert them into a series of discrete-time observations on the value of the outcome and the covariates. In essence, the analyst transforms information for a continuous time interval into a panel history for a series of discrete times. For example, information on six spells in a 10-year period might be converted into data on the discrete outcome and associated relevant covariates during the 120 months covering the 10-year period. The number of points included in the series of discrete times depends on how precisely time is measured in the data. How precisely time should be measured (as contrasted with how precisely it is measured) depends on how rapidly events occur. If there is a relatively short length of time from t_0 to an event, or from one event to the next event for any given case, then time needs to be measured rather precisely. In contrast, when there is a relatively long length of time from t_0 to an event, or between successive events, then relatively little information is lost if time is measured less precisely. Creating a data file suitable for event history analysis can be laborious. But, once the data file is created, most tasks in the actual analysis resemble those in other types of quantitative analysis.

Statistical Concepts

Survival Probability (Survivor Function)

Consider an event in an individual's lifetime, assumed to begin at t_0, when the individual may first become at risk of the event. For simplicity, t_0 is assumed to be zero and is omitted from subsequent equations. The time of the first event is a random variable, T_1, or simply T for a single nonrepeatable event, such as death or having a first child. A basic concept that describes the timing of this event is the survival probability, also known as the survivor function:

$$S(t) \equiv \Pr(T > t), \tag{1}$$

where $S(t)$ is the probability of survival to time t (that is, the probability of no event before time t). At the starting time, t_0, the survival probability is $S(t_0) = 1$.

Normally, $S(\infty) = 0$, meaning that an event eventually occurs. If $S(\infty) > 0$, the probability distribution of the time of the event is said to be defective. Defective probability distributions are fairly common in empirical applications. For example, because some individuals never marry, never have a child, and never have a job, the probability distributions of age at a person's first marriage, first birth, and first job are defective. On the other hand, because death is inevitable, and because people with jobs eventually leave them, the probability distributions of the length of a person's lifetime and the length of a job are not defective.

Cumulative Distribution Function

The cumulative distribution function (CDF) of T is the complement of $S(t)$:

$$F(t) \equiv \Pr(T \le t) = 1 - S(t), \tag{2}$$

where $F(t)$ is the probability that the event occurs before time t. The CDF and the survival probability give equivalent information, but traditionally the survival probability is reported more often than the CDF in event history analysis. Ordinarily, $F(\infty) = 1$; eventually the event occurs. If the probability distribution of the event time is defective, there is a nonzero probability that the event does not occur, even after an infinite amount of time has elapsed. Then $F(\infty) < 1$.

Probability Density Function

Associated with $F(t)$ is a probability density function (PDF),

$$f(t) \equiv dF(t)/dt \equiv -dS(t)/dt. \tag{3}$$

The unconditional probability that the event occurs between time t and $t + \Delta t$ is obtained by integrating $f(t)$ over the interval from t to $t + \Delta t$.

Hazard Rate

A particularly important concept is the hazard rate, also called the failure rate (especially in the engineering literature):

$$\begin{aligned} h(t) &\equiv \lim_{\Delta t \downarrow 0} \frac{\Pr[t < T < t + \Delta t \mid T > t]}{\Delta t} = f(t)/S(t) \\ &= -d \ln S(t)/dt. \end{aligned} \tag{4}$$

The probability that an event occurs between time t and $t+\Delta t$, as Δt shrinks to zero, conditional on the event not occuring before t, is measured by the hazard rate. A noteworthy difference between the hazard rate and the PDF is that the hazard rate conditions on being at risk at time t whereas the PDF does not. Note that Eq. (4) implies that the PDF is

$$f(t) = h(t)S(t). \qquad (5)$$

Equation (5) can be used to estimate the PDF when there is extensive censoring in the available data.

As the limit of the ratio of two nonnegative quantities, a hazard rate cannot be negative. However, it is not a probability, and it may exceed 1. Further, a hazard rate is measured "per unit of time" (e.g., per year, per month). Altering the units of time (e.g., years to days) induces a proportional change in the units of the hazard rate. For example, a hazard rate of 2.4 per year is equivalent to a hazard rate of 0.2 per month.

Integrated (Cumulative) Hazard Rate

The integral of the hazard rate is known as the integrated or cumulative hazard rate, $H(t)$. It can be shown to equal minus the natural logarithm of $S(t)$:

$$H(t) \equiv \int_{t_0}^{t} h(u)\,du = -\ln S(t). \qquad (6)$$

Conditional Transition Probability

When there are K different types of events (i.e., K competing risks), another concept is the conditional transition probability, $m_k(t)$, the probability of event type k between time t and $t+\Delta t$, as Δt shrinks to zero, conditional on the occurrence of one of the K types of events in this interval.

Transition Rate

An especially important concept when there are competing risks is the transition rate (also known as the transition intensity, or as the instantaneous rate of a transition) to k,

$$r_k(t) \equiv h(t)m_k(t). \qquad (7)$$

Some authors do not use a distinct term for the transition rate and instead refer to the "hazard rate of a transition to k." Like a hazard rate, a transition rate is always nonnegative, may exceed 1, and is measured per unit of time. When there are competing risks, explanations usually focus on transition rates rather than on the hazard rate of any specific event, because the transition rates may have very different predictors and patterns of variation over time.

Exploratory Analyses

Exploratory analyses rely primarily on estimating the statistics defined in the previous section and then examining how the estimates vary over time and across subgroups of cases distinguished on the basis of proposed predictor variables. These methods are especially useful in event history analysis because patterns of variation over time and across cases are complex and are not easily captured by a single statistic.

Survival Probability

When right-censoring occurs and is independent of the occurrence of the event being studied, the product-limit estimator of $S(t)$ proposed by E. L. Kaplan and Paul Meier (KM) in 1958 is unbiased and asymptotically consistent:

$$\hat{S}_{\mathrm{KM}}(t) = \prod_{t_{(i)}<t}\left[1-\frac{d_{(i)}}{n_{(i)}}\right], \quad t_{(i-1)}<t<t_{(i)}, \qquad (8)$$

where (i) denotes the ith event when events are arranged in nondescending temporal order, $t_{(i)}$ refers to the time of the (i)th event, $d_{(i)}$ is the number of events occurring at $t_{(i)}$, and $n_{(i)}$ is the number at risk just before $t_{(i)}$, which, by convention, includes those right-censored at $t_{(i)}$. Although $\hat{S}_{\mathrm{KM}}(t)$ is a step function, connecting the estimates for successive time points by line segments usually yields a picture that better reflects the true survivor function, assuming it is continuous.

Greenwood's formula gives the asymptotic variance of $S(t)$ at time t:

$$\mathrm{Var}\left[\hat{S}_{\mathrm{KM}}(t)\right] = \left[\hat{S}_{\mathrm{KM}}(t)\right]^2 \sum_{t_{(i)}<t} \frac{d_{(i)}}{n_{(i)}\left[n_{(i)}-d_{(i)}\right]},$$

$$t_{(i-1)}<t<t_{(i)}. \qquad (9)$$

Equation (9) is often used to estimate a two-sided $(1-\alpha)\cdot 100\%$ pointwise confidence interval of the survival probability at time t:

$$\hat{S}_{\mathrm{KM}}(t) \pm z_{\alpha/2}\sqrt{\mathrm{Var}[\hat{S}_{\mathrm{KM}}(t)]}, \qquad (10)$$

where z has a standard Gaussian distribution. This formula implicitly assumes that the Kaplan–Meier estimator has a Gaussian distribution, and asymptotically it does. However, Eq. (10) underestimates the width of the confidence interval when the number at risk at time t is too small for asymptotic properties to apply.

A pointwise confidence interval is the confidence interval at a single time t. Usually a simultaneous confidence band around $S(t)$ for a time interval is preferable. The pointwise confidence intervals of $\hat{S}_{\mathrm{KM}}(t)$ and $\hat{S}_{\mathrm{KM}}(u)$ at times t and u, respectively, are not statistically independent when estimated from the same data. Consequently, repeated application of Greenwood's formula to a set of time points using the same data set overstates the true confidence level and underestimates the real width of the confidence band. Several authors have proposed ways to estimate a simultaneous confidence band for $\hat{S}_{KM}(t)$.

All survivor plots [i.e., graphs of $S(t)$ versus time t] tend to look similar; $S(t)$ equals 1 at the starting time and tends to decline toward zero as t increases. All survivor plots have an approximately backward S shape. Because of their broadly similar shape, survivor plots rarely give much insight into a process being studied. Analysts may identify selected percentile values for survival, such as the time at which $S(t) = 0.5$ (the half-life). If the observation period is long enough, a survivor plot may also give a good indication of whether the CDF is defective. At the highest observed times, $S(t)$ approaches zero if the probability distribution is not defective, and it approaches a nonzero asymptote if the distribution is defective.

Cumulative Distribution Function

Because the survival probability is the complement of the CDF, an unbiased and asymptotically consistent estimator of the CDF is $1 - \hat{S}_{KM}(t)$.

Probability Density Function

A relative frequency distribution or histogram of event times gives an empirical approximation to the probability density function of the time of events. When censoring is extensive, a relative frequency distribution gives a biased estimate of the PDF. It is then preferable to estimate the PDF another way. For example, the PDF might be estimated as the product of estimates of the hazard rate and the survival probability that consider censoring [see Eq. (5)].

Integrated Hazard Rate

An estimator of $H(t)$ with good asymptotic properties was first proposed by Wayne Nelson in 1972 and proved to be asymptotically unbiased by Odd Aalen in 1978. This estimator, usually termed the Nelson–Aalen (NA) estimator, is

$$\hat{H}_{NA}(t) = -\ln \hat{S}_{NA}(t) = \sum_{t_{(i)}<t} \frac{d_{(i)}}{n_{(i)}}, \qquad t_{(i-1)} < t < t_{(i)}. \tag{11}$$

Except when the number at risk at time t is small, $\hat{H}_{NA}(t)$ differs only slightly from $-\ln \hat{S}_{KM}(t)$. The pointwise confidence interval of the integrated hazard rate can be computed using an estimate of its asymptotic variance:

$$\mathrm{Var}\left[\hat{H}_{NA}(t)\right] = \sum_{t_{(i)}<t} \left[\frac{d_{(i)}}{n_{(i)}[n_{(i)} - d_{(i)}]}\right]^2, \quad t_{(i-1)} < t < t_{(i)}. \tag{12}$$

Examining a plot of estimates of the integrated hazard versus time t gives useful information about time variation in the likelihood of an event. If the likelihood of an event does not vary with time, the integrated hazard plotted against time should approximate a straight line. If the integrated hazard increases at an increasing rate as time increases (i.e., is upward bending), it suggests that the likelihood of the event is increasing as time increases (the mortality rate of elderly adults has this pattern). If the integrated hazard increases at a decreasing rate as time increases (i.e., is downward bending), it suggests that the likelihood of the event is decreasing as time increases (the rate of marital break-up usually has this pattern). If the integrated hazard increases at an increasing rate as time increases but then shifts and increases at a decreasing rate as time increases, it suggests that the hazard rate is a nonmonotonic function of time (the rate of first marriage has this pattern). If the integrated hazard increases at a decreasing rate and then shifts and increases at an increasing rate, it also suggests that the hazard rate is a nonmonotonic function of time, and that it has a "bathtub" shape.

In many instances, broad tendencies can be discerned in how a hazard rate varies over time by estimating it directly and plotting it versus time, as described in the next section. However, empirical plots of estimates of hazard rates versus time tend to be very jagged unless the number of cases at risk and the number of events are fairly large. When plots of the hazard rate are jagged, broad tendencies in time variation in the hazard rate can often be identified more easily by examining a graph of the integrated hazard rate versus time, rather than a graph of the hazard rate versus time.

Hazard Rate

There is no unambiguously "best" estimator of hazard rates. One estimator is based on the Kaplan–Meier estimator of the survival probability at time t:

$$\hat{h}_{KM}(t) = \frac{1}{\Delta t_{(i)}} \ln\left(1 - \frac{d_{(i)}}{n_{(i)}}\right), \qquad t_{(i-1)} < t < t_{(i)}. \tag{13}$$

Another corresponds to the Nelson–Aalen estimator of $H(t)$:

$$\hat{h}_{NA}(t) = \frac{1}{\Delta t_{(i)}} \frac{d_{(i)}}{n_{(i)}}, \qquad t_{(i-1)} < t < t_{(i)}. \tag{14}$$

An older estimator, traditional with demographers, is the life-table (LT) estimator:

$$\hat{h}_{\mathrm{LT}}(t) = \frac{1}{\Delta t_{(i)}} \frac{d_{(i)}}{n_{(i)} - 0.5d_{(i)}}, \qquad t_{(i-1)} < t < t_{(i)}. \quad (15)$$

The life-table estimator was originally developed for applications containing information on the number at risk and the number of events in a series of time intervals, but not the exact times of events. In the classical application to mortality, there are data on the number alive at the start of an interval (e.g., at age a) and on the number who die before the end of that interval (e.g., in the 5-year interval from age a to age $a+5$). The adjustment to $d_{(i)}$ in the denominator of Eq. (15) is intended to correct for the fact that not all $n_{(i)}$ cases are at risk for the entire interval.

Plots of estimated hazard rates versus time tend to be jagged, especially when the number at risk and the number of events are small. Smoothing the empirical estimates gives a better representation of the underlying hazard rate if it is a continuous function of time. The life-table estimator smooths by computing the hazard rate for a time interval rather than at a time point. Alternatively, smoothing algorithms may be applied to estimates of the hazard rate at a set of adjacent time points in a manner analogous to computing a running mean.

Conditional Transition Probability

When there are competing risks (i.e., when multiple kinds of events can occur), the conditional transition probability to state k, $m_k(t)$, can be estimated like other probabilities. For example, it may be estimated as the relative frequency of event k among all events occurring at or around time t.

Transition Rate

The transition rate to state k, $r_k(t)$, is estimated using analogues to Eqs. (13)–(15), except that $d_{(i)}$ in those equations is replaced by $d_{k(i)}$, the count of the events consisting of a transition to state k at time $t_{(i)}$. For example, the Nelson–Aalen estimator of the transition rate to state k is:

$$\hat{r}_k(t) = \frac{1}{\Delta t_{(i)}} \frac{d_{k(i)}}{n_{(i)}}, \qquad t_{(i-1)} < t < t_{(i)}. \quad (16)$$

Confirmatory Analyses

Exploratory analyses are usually followed by confirmatory analyses in which researchers seek to model the process generating events in terms of proposed explanatory variables and some basic underlying pattern of time dependence. After formulating a model, they want to estimate it and test it against plausible alternatives. In principle, any of the previously defined statistical concepts could be the primary focus of a model. For various reasons, the most appropriate statistic is often the hazard rate, or the transition rate if there are competing risks. Another popular choice is the mean time between events, or the mean logarithm of the time between events.

Modeling the Hazard Rate or Transition Rate

This approach is particularly useful because the hazard rate and transition rate are analogous to the probability that those at risk of an event experience it in a specified small interval of time. Thus, researchers can develop behavioral arguments about why the event is more or less likely to occur in this time interval, and hence why the hazard (or transition) rate is relatively high or low, or increases or decreases at that time. In addition, hazard and transition rates can have widely varying shapes over time. They can be flat, declining, increasing, declining and then increasing, and so on. The wide variation in possible time patterns differentiates hazard and transition rates from the survivor function, CDF, and integrated hazard, all of which are monotonic functions of time. It is usually easier to differentiate among groups and the processes generating the occurrence of events when very different time patterns are possible in principle.

Modeling the Mean

Some models focus on the mean duration between events or on the mean logarithm (log) of this duration. The major advantage of a multivariate model of the mean (log) of an observed variable is its similarity to an ordinary linear regression model. Many people find that this similarity facilitates the interpretation of results. If some durations are right censored, ordinary least-squares estimation of a model of the mean duration (or mean log duration) yields biased results. Right censoring is a relatively minor problem, however, requiring only use of a more complex method of estimation, such as maximum-liklihood estimation (see later).

Basing a model on the mean (log) duration has more important disadvantages, one of which is conceptual. A model based on a hazard (or transition) rate fits naturally with a conceptualization of the occurrence of the event as a result of a contingent, dynamic process that causal factors influence but do not determine. Values of the causal factors may change over time, making the event more or less likely to occur than it had been. A model based on the mean (log) duration discourages viewing the change process in this way. A second, related disadvantage is methodological. Many explanatory variables of scientific interest can change over time, and extending a model of the mean (log) duration to include time-varying explanatory variables is not straightforward. In addition, it is also difficult to deal with competing risks when modeling the mean (log) duration.

Basic Issues in Modeling

Two main issues arise in event history analysis: (1) time dependence (how does the process generating events vary over time?) and (2) population heterogeneity (how does this process vary with characteristics of the cases at risk of an event and with characteristics of their environment?). Two main empirical approaches are used to study each issue—a nonparametric approach and a parametric approach.

Analysts adopting a nonparametric approach cross-classify key variables and then estimate the quantities of interest within cross-classifications. For example, if time refers to age, analysts may discretize age (a continuous variable) into year-of-age (ignoring fractional ages) and estimate a discrete-time model. Likewise, they may categorize proposed explanatory variables and estimate a model using cross-classifications of the resulting categorical variables. This approach is especially popular with analysts who routinely use log-linear or log-multiplicative models of cross-tabulations and who like to apply models with which they are already familiar to the analysis of event histories. This approach generates the usual problems that arise in modeling cross-tabulations, such as the occurrence of numerous empty (or nearly empty) cells when many variables are cross-classified, especially if variables are categorized finely. In addition, it can be hard to detect trends or patterns over time or with predictor variables when truly continuous variables are treated as categorical. Further, it can be hard to communicate results when there are numerous cells in a cross-tabulation.

Analysts adopting a parametric approach postulate a specific functional form for various relationships and then estimate it from the data. Ideally the postulated functional form is assessed empirically, but this is not always done.

Models for Time Dependence

Table I gives some of the most common functional forms used in parametric approaches to modeling time dependence in a hazard or transition rate. In this table, $h(t)$ may stand for the hazard rate, the transition rate, or a time-dependent baseline function of either of these rates. Note

Table I Selected Common Specifications of $h(t)$ and Its Integral[a]

Specification	$h(t)$	$H(t) = \int_0^t h(u)\,du$
Constant		
Exponential	α	αt
Monotonic		
Gamma[b]	$\dfrac{\alpha(\alpha t)^{\beta-1}e^{-\alpha t}}{\Gamma(\beta)-\alpha\int_0^t(\alpha u)^{\beta-1}e^{-\alpha u}du}$	$-\ln\left[\dfrac{\alpha}{\Gamma(\beta)}\int_t^{\infty}(\alpha u)^{\beta-1}e^{-\alpha u}du\right]$
Gompertz	$\beta\, e^{\gamma t}$	$(\beta/\gamma)(e^{\gamma t}-1)$
Makeham	$\alpha+\beta\, e^{\gamma t}$	$\alpha t+(\beta/\gamma)(e^{\gamma t}-1)$
Rayleigh	$\alpha+\beta t$	$\alpha t+\beta t^2/2$
Pareto	$\alpha/(t+\beta)$	$\alpha\,[\ln(t+\beta)-\ln\beta]$
Weibull	$\beta(t+\delta)^{\gamma}$	$\dfrac{\beta}{\gamma+1}\left[(t+\delta)^{\gamma+1}-\delta^{\gamma+1}\right]$
Nonmonotonic		
Generalized Rayleigh	$\alpha+\beta t+\gamma t^2+\cdots$	$\alpha t+(\beta\, t/2)t^2+(\gamma/3)t^3+\cdots$
Log-logistic	$\delta\gamma(\delta t)^{\gamma-1}/[1+(\delta t)^{\gamma}]$	$\ln[1+(\delta t)^{\gamma}]$
Log-Gaussian[c]	$\dfrac{\frac{1}{\sigma t\sqrt{2\pi}}\exp\left[-\frac{(\ln t-\mu)^2}{2\sigma^2}\right]}{1-\Phi\left(\frac{\ln t-\mu}{\sigma}\right)}$	$-\ln\left[1-\Phi\left(\dfrac{\ln t-\mu}{\sigma}\right)\right]$
Sickle	$\beta\, te^{\gamma t}$	$(\beta/\gamma)^2[(\gamma t-1)\,e^{\gamma t}+1]$

[a] In terms of time t, $t_0=0$, and parameters (denoted by Greek letters) chosen so that $h(t)\geq 0$.
[b] $\Gamma(\beta)$ denotes the gamma function, $\int_0^{\infty}u^{\beta-1}e^{-u}du$.
[c] $\Phi(x)$ denotes the cumulative standard Gaussian distribution function, $\int_{-\infty}^{x}\frac{1}{\sqrt{2\pi}}\exp(-u^2/2)du$.

that $h(t)$ may be constant (i.e., not varying with time), may change monotonically (either increasing or decreasing with time), or may change nonmonotonically (typically having only one inflection point).

Models of Population Heterogeneity

Models of hazard and transition rates that include population heterogeneity are conveniently divided into three main types: (1) ones including only observed covariates having time-invariant effects (proportional models), (2) ones including only observed covariates but allowing covariates' effects to vary over time (nonproportional models), and (3) ones allowing unobserved as well as measured variables to have effects. To date empirical applications have fallen mainly in the first category and to a lesser extent in the second category.

Proportional Models of Rates

Proportional models of rates assume that

$$h[t, \mathbf{x}(t)] = q(t)\theta[\mathbf{x}(t)], \tag{17}$$

where $\mathbf{x}(t)$ is a vector of covariates and $q(t)$ is a function of time t but does not depend on the covariates. The model in Eq. (17) is termed a proportional model because the function of the covariates, $\theta[\mathbf{x}(t)]$, multiplies the time-varying baseline, $q(t)$. Consequently, the ratio of the hazard rates for two cases i and j with different values of the covariates at a given time t depends only on the values of the covariates at that time:

$$h[t, \mathbf{x}_i(t)]/h[t, \mathbf{x}_j(t)] = \frac{q(t)\theta[\mathbf{x}_i(t)]}{q(t)\theta[\mathbf{x}_j(t)]} = \frac{\theta[\mathbf{x}_i(t)]}{\theta[\mathbf{x}_j(t)]}. \tag{18}$$

One issue is how to specify $\theta[\mathbf{x}(t)]$. Because hazard and transition rates must be nonnegative for all feasible values of $\mathbf{x}(t)$ and time, $\theta[\mathbf{x}(t)]$ must be nonnegative for all values of $\mathbf{x}(t)$ and time. This constraint argues against a linear specification because it could lead to negative values of $\theta[\mathbf{x}(t)]$ unless parameters are constrained so that $\theta[\mathbf{x}(t)] > 0$ for all possible values of $\mathbf{x}(t)$. A functional form that automatically leads to positive values of $\theta[\mathbf{x}(t)]$ is generally preferred because it conveniently imposes nonnegativity constraints. The most popular specification is

$$\ln \theta[\mathbf{x}(t)] = \boldsymbol{\beta}'\mathbf{x}(t), \tag{19a}$$

$$\theta[\mathbf{x}(t)] = \exp[\boldsymbol{\beta}'\mathbf{x}(t)] = \prod_{j=1}^{J} \gamma_j^{x_j(t)}, \tag{19b}$$

where $\gamma_j \equiv \exp(\beta_j)$ and J is the number of covariates. In this specification, a covariate has an additive effect on the log hazard rate (or log transition rate) and a multiplicative effect on the hazard rate (or transition rate).

"No effect of a covariate j" means that $\beta_j = 0$ and, equivalently, that $\gamma_j = 1$. Similarly, if $\beta_j = 0.3$, then $\gamma_j = \exp(0.3) = 1.35$, implying that a one-unit increase in covariate j increases the hazard rate (or transition rate) by 35%. If $\beta_j = -0.3$, then $\gamma_j = \exp(-0.3) = 0.74$, implying that a one-unit increase in covariate j decreases the hazard rate (or transition rate) by 26%. The percentage change in the hazard rate (or transition rate) associated with a one-unit change in covariate j is calculated as $(\gamma_j - 1) \cdot 100\%$. A particularly popular proportional model of hazard and transition rates was proposed by David Cox in 1972. In the Cox model, $q(t)$ is unspecified but is assumed to be the same for all members of a certain population. This model is estimated by the method of partial likelihood that Cox proposed in 1975. Researchers interested in the pattern of time dependence ordinarily specify $q(t)$ to have a particular functional form [e.g., one of those specified for $h(t)$ in Table I] and estimate the resulting model by the method of maximum likelihood.

The assumption that a covariate has an additive effect on the log hazard rate can be assessed by plotting the log hazard rate versus time for selected values of the covariate. If the curves for various values of a certain covariate differ by amounts that do not vary with time, it suggests that the effects of the covariate on the hazard rate are log-linear and proportional. If the curves for different values of the covariate cross one another or differ by an amount that fluctuates a great deal over time (and, in particular, does so systematically), it suggests that the effects of the covariate on the hazard rate are not proportional (i.e., are time varying), in which case a nonproportional model is preferable.

Nonproportional Models of Rates

If hazard or transition rates appear to be nonproportional, the analyst can let the parameters in a parametric model (e.g., parameters in one of the common functional forms of time dependence given in Table I) depend on covariates as well as on time. For example, suppose that the hazard rate of leaving unemployment appears to decline exponentially with time, suggesting a Gompertz model of time dependence (cf. Table I):

$$h(t) = b\exp(ct), \tag{20a}$$

$$\ln h(t) = \ln b + ct, \tag{20b}$$

where b and c are substituted for β and γ in Table I for clarity in the equations that follow. A proportional Gompertz model usually assumes that

$$\theta[\mathbf{x}(t)] = \exp(\boldsymbol{\beta}'\mathbf{x}), \tag{21a}$$

$$\ln \theta[\mathbf{x}(t)] = \boldsymbol{\beta}'\mathbf{x}, \tag{21b}$$

where the covariates $\mathbf{x}(t)$ are assumed not to depend on time t in Eqs. (21)–(23) for simplicity of expression.

Then the proportional Gompertz model is

$$h(t) = \exp(\boldsymbol{\beta}'\mathbf{x})\exp(ct) = \exp(\boldsymbol{\beta}'\mathbf{x} + ct), \tag{22a}$$

$$\ln h(t) = \boldsymbol{\beta}'\mathbf{x} + ct. \tag{22b}$$

In the proportional Gompertz model, the parameter c controlling time variation in the hazard rate is assumed not to depend on covariates. A nonproportional Gompertz model allows the parameter c to be a function of covariates, $c = \boldsymbol{\gamma}'\mathbf{z}$:

$$h(t) = \exp(\boldsymbol{\beta}'\mathbf{x} + \boldsymbol{\gamma}'\mathbf{z}t), \tag{23a}$$

$$\ln h(t) = \boldsymbol{\beta}'\mathbf{x} + \boldsymbol{\gamma}'\mathbf{z}t. \tag{23b}$$

In Eq. (23), time variation in the hazard rate depends on the covariates $\mathbf{z}$, which may or may not overlap with the covariates $\mathbf{x}$.

A nonproportional hazard rate model that has proved especially useful in empirical applications is a piecewise constant hazard (transition) rate model originally proposed by Holford in 1976 without covariates and by Tuma, Hannan, and Groeneveld in 1979 with covariates:

$$h(t) = \exp\left(\boldsymbol{\lambda}_p'\mathbf{x}_p\right), \qquad \tau_{p-1} < t \leq \tau_p; \tag{24a}$$

$$\ln h(t) = \boldsymbol{\lambda}_p'\mathbf{x}_p, \qquad \tau_{p-1} < t \leq \tau_p; \tag{24b}$$

where p denotes a time period running from τ_{p-1} to τ_p. This model allows the rate both to vary with time in a fairly flexible way and also to vary nonproportionally with covariates. In Eq. (24), the hazard rate is assumed to be time invariant within a given time interval p but to depend on covariates $\mathbf{x}_p$ in ways that may vary from one time interval to another. Indeed, different covariates may be included in different time intervals.

A piecewise Gompertz model has been used with considerable success by Lawrence Wu and colleagues. Parameters are constrained so that the rate at the end of one time interval equals the rate at the beginning of the next time interval, thereby avoiding discontinuities (sudden jumps) in the hazard rate from one time interval to the next. A constrained piecewise Gompertz model can give a good approximation to a hazard rate that varies nonmonotonically with time and that has nonproportional effects of covariates. It is also possible to construct a nonproportional hazard rate model in other ways, but alternative approaches have been rarer than the approach described here.

Models with Unobserved Heterogeneity

A researcher rarely includes all covariates that influence the change process in any model that is estimated empirically. That is, in addition to observed heterogeneity due to the measured covariates included in a model, there is zusually also unobserved heterogeneity due to influential covariates that are omitted from the model. The omission of unobserved variables from linear models does not cause bias if the omitted variables are uncorrelated with the included variables. Unfortunately, an analogous conclusion cannot be drawn for event history models. Unobserved heterogeneity leads to spurious time dependence because the cases with a lower unobserved propensity to experience the event tend to have events later (a longer time to the event). Consequently, as time passes, those with a lower unobserved propensity become a rising proportion of those still at risk of the event, causing the hazard rate to appear to decline with time, even if it is a constant over time for every member of the population.

Both parametric and nonparametric models with unobserved heterogeneity have been proposed. A parametric model relies on strong assumptions about the true time dependence and nature of unobserved heterogeneity (e.g., that it is a single fixed effect that does not change over time, but only varies across cases). If these strong assumptions are not met, a parametric model may not give better estimates of the effects of observed variables, compared to a similar model that ignores unobserved heterogeneity. Nonparametric approaches tend to be computationally intensive, but this fact per se does not lead to intractable difficulties in the present era of high-speed computers. A more challenging requirement is the unusually large samples that are necessary to allow relationships to be estimated nonparametrically. Because of both types of stringent requirements, the usage of event history models incorporating unobserved heterogeneity has languished.

Models of the Mean: Accelerated Failure Time Models

Accelerated failure time models (AFT), sometimes called accelerated life models, are based on modeling the mean or average time to an event rather than modeling the hazard or transition rate. Let T_0 be a random variable describing the time of an event; assume that it has the associated hazard rate

$$h_0(t) = \frac{f_0(t)}{S_0(t)}, \tag{25}$$

where $f_0(t)$ and $S_0(t)$ refer to the PDF and the survival probability associated with T_0. In Eq. (25), the subscript 0 indicates that the quantities refer to the baseline. In an AFT model, it is assumed that the CDF of the time of an event T_i for a case i with covariates $\mathbf{x}_i$ equals the CDF for T_0 (the baseline) multiplied by some function of the covariates, $g[\mathbf{x}_i]$. It is usually assumed that $g[\mathbf{x}_i] = \exp(\boldsymbol{\beta}'\mathbf{x}_i)$; consequently,

$$T_i = \exp(\boldsymbol{\beta}'\mathbf{x}_i)T_0. \tag{26}$$

Note that in an AFT model, there is an underlying baseline random variable for time, T_0 in contrast to the underlying baseline hazard rate, $q(t)$, found in a proportional hazard model. Equation (26) means that T_i tends to be shorter than T_0 if $\boldsymbol{\beta}'\mathbf{x}_i < 0$ and that T_i tends to be longer than T_0 if $\boldsymbol{\beta}'\mathbf{x}_i > 0$. It is called an "accelerated failure time" model because the covariates for case i are conceptualized as speeding or delaying the time of the event for case i, T_i relative to T_0, in a multiplicative way. Given this conceptualization of the underlying process, a series of mathematical manipulations yields

$$\begin{aligned} h(t \mid \mathbf{x}_i) &= f(t \mid \mathbf{x}_i)/S(t \mid \mathbf{x}_i) \\ &= \frac{f_0(\exp[-\boldsymbol{\beta}'\mathbf{x}_i]t)\exp[-\boldsymbol{\beta}'\mathbf{x}_i]}{S_0(\exp[-\boldsymbol{\beta}'\mathbf{x}_i]t)} \\ &= h_0(\exp[-\boldsymbol{\beta}'\mathbf{x}_i]t)\exp[-\boldsymbol{\beta}'\mathbf{x}_i]. \end{aligned} \tag{27}$$

After the hazard rate implied by a particular AFT model has been deduced, the AFT model can then be estimated by the method of maximum likelihood.

Finally, define $U_i \equiv \log T_i$. Then

$$\begin{aligned} \mathrm{E}(U_i) &= \boldsymbol{\beta}'\mathbf{x}_i + \mathrm{E}(\log T_0) \\ &= \boldsymbol{\beta}'\mathbf{x}_i + \theta. \end{aligned} \tag{28}$$

Hence, an AFT model is equivalent to the following model:

$$U = \boldsymbol{\beta}'\mathbf{x}_i + \theta + \epsilon, \tag{29a}$$

$$\epsilon = \log T_0 - \mathrm{E}(\log T_0). \tag{29b}$$

Usually the random disturbance or error term in a linear model is assumed to have a Gaussian distribution, and this is indeed a possibility here. But other assumptions can be made about the probability distribution of ϵ, thereby generating other forms of AFT models.

The exponential and Weibull models (Table I) are special cases of models that are both proportional hazard models and AFT models. No other model falls into both classes of models. For example, the model in which the time of the event has a log-Gaussian distribution is not a proportional hazard rate model. The log-logistic model is an example of a model that may be specified either as a proportional hazard rate model with covariates or as an AFT model with covariates; however, the two versions of a log-logistic model have different parameterizations as well as different underlying conceptualizations and interpretations.

Model Estimation

Maximum-Likelihood Estimation

The method of maximum likelihood (ML) is usually used to estimate parametric models of hazard and transition rates, as well as models based on the mean (log) duration between events. For a simple random sample of I event histories with a single nonrepeatable event, the log likelihood is

$$\ln \mathcal{L} = \sum_{i=1}^{I}(1-c_i)\ln f(t_i, \mathbf{x}_i) + c_i \ln S(t_i, \mathbf{x}_i) \tag{30a}$$

$$= \sum_{i=1}^{I}(1-c_i)\ln h(t_i, \mathbf{x}_i) + \ln S(t_i, \mathbf{x}_i), \tag{30b}$$

where c_i is 1 if case i is censored and 0 if it is uncensored; $\mathbf{x}_i$ is case i's values on the covariates included in the model, and t_i is the time of the event for uncensored cases and the end of the observation period for censored cases. Equation (30b) follows from Eq. (30a) because $\ln S(\cdot)$ equals $-H(\cdot)$, the integrated hazard rate [see Eq. (6)]. For event histories that have multiple origins, multiple destinations (i.e., competing risks), and repeatable events, the log likelihood is a somewhat more complex version of Eq. (30).

Estimating an event history model by ML has the standard advantages. The ML estimators are asymptotically unbiased, efficient, and normally distributed under fairly general conditions. Further, it is possible to perform likelihood ratio tests on nested models. If $\mathcal{L}_1$ is the likelihood for a model with $k_0 + k_1$ parameters, and $\mathcal{L}_0$ is the likelihood for the nested model with only k_0 parameters, then $-2 \ln \mathcal{L}_0/\mathcal{L}_1$ is χ^2 distributed with k_1 degrees of freedom under the null hypothesis. In addition, the inverse of the Hessian matrix, usually estimated as the matrix of second derivatives of the log likelihood with respect to the parameters in the model, gives an estimate of the asymptotic variance–covariance matrix of the parameters. Hence, the square root of the diagonal elements of the asymptotic covariance matrix provides an estimate of the asymptotic standard errors of parameters, allowing use of Wald tests of hypotheses about whether given parameters differ significantly from specified values. For example, if β_0 is the value of a parameter under the null hypothesis, $\hat{\beta}$ is the ML estimate of the parameter, and $\hat{se}(\hat{\beta})$ is its estimated standard error, then $(\hat{\beta} - \beta_0)/\hat{se}(\hat{\beta})$ is the estimated test statistic. To perform a two-sided test at the α level of significance based on an analysis of a large sample, the null hypothesis β_0 can be rejected if the absolute value of the estimated test statistic is greater than the critical value of $z_{\alpha/2}$, where z has a standard Gaussian distribution.

Partial-Likelihood Estimation

The method of partial likelihood (PL) can be used to estimate the proportional hazard rate model in which $q(t)$ is taken to be a nuisance function that is not directly estimated. The partial likelihood is

$$\mathcal{L}_p = \prod_{i=1}^{I^*} \left\{ \theta[\mathbf{x}_{(i)}(t_{(i)})] \Big/ \sum_{v \in R(t_{(i)})} \theta[\mathbf{x}_v(t_{(i)})] \right\}, \qquad (31)$$

where I^* is the number of events, and the risk set $R(t)$ is the set of cases at risk of an event at a given time t. Usually $\theta[\mathbf{x}(t)]$ is assumed to be $\exp[\boldsymbol{\beta}'\mathbf{x}(t)]$. Although time-varying covariates are easily incorporated in principle, there is one practical problem with including them. Equation (31) assumes that $\mathbf{x}(t)$ is observed at the time of every event for every case at risk, but few data sets have such complete information on time-varying covariates. A common approximation is to substitute the most recent value of the covariates. This approximation is likely to be satisfactory in practice as long as the covariates are not undergoing rapid and marked change over time.

See Also the Following Articles

Hazards Measurement • Maximum Likelihood Estimation

Further Reading

Blossfeld, H.-P., and Rohwer, G. (2002). *Techniques of Event History Modeling: New Approaches to Causal Analysis,* 2nd Ed. Lawrence Erlbaum, Mahwah, New Jersy.

Cox, D. R., and Oakes, D. (1984). *Analysis of Survival Data.* Chapman and Hall, London.

Petersen, T. (1991). The statistical analysis of event histories. *Sociol. Methods and Res.* **19,** 270–323.

Tuma, N. B., and Hannan, M. T. (1984). *Social Dynamics: Models and Methods.* Academic Press, Orlando.

Wu, L. L. (2003). Event history models in life course analysis. In *Handbook of the Life Course* (J. Mortimer and M. Shanahan, eds.), pp. 477–502. Plenum, New York.

Experimenter Effects

Robert Rosenthal
University of California, Riverside, Riverside, California, USA

Glossary

biosocial effects The experimenters' biological characteristics predicting the responses of study participants.

expectancy effects The experimenters' research hypotheses functioning as self-fulfilling prophecies.

intentional effects Experimenter falsification of research results.

interpreter effects Individual differences among experimenters in how they interpret specific data.

modeling effects Experimenters unintentionally influencing research participants to respond as the experimenter would respond.

observer effects Individual differences among experimenters in how the same events are perceived and/or recorded.

psychosocial effects Psychological characteristics of experimenters that predict the responses of study participants.

situational effects The experimenters' transient states affecting the responses of study participants.

Experimenter effects are those sources of artifact or error in scientific inquiry that derive from the person of the experimenter. It is useful to think of two major types of effects, usually unintentional, that psychologists or other behavioral researchers can have on the results of their research. The first type operates, so to speak, in the mind, in the eye, or in the hand of the scientist. It operates without affecting the actual response of the human or animal study participants. It is not interactional. The second type of experimenter effect is interactional. It operates by affecting the actual response of the participants in the experiment. It is a subtype of this latter type of effect, the effects of the investigators' expectancy or hypothesis on the results of their research, that has been of greatest interest to behavioral and social scientists.

Noninteractional Effects

Observer Effects

In any science, the experimenter must make provision for the careful observation and recording of the events under study. It is not always so easy to be sure that an accurate observation has, in fact, been made. That necessary lesson was learned early in the field of psychology, but it was not the psychologists who first focused attention on it—it was the astronomers.

Just near the end of the 18th century, the royal astronomer at the Greenwich Observatory, a man called Maskelyne, discovered that his assistant, Kinnebrook, was consistently "too slow" in his observations of the movement of stars across the sky. Maskelyne cautioned Kinnebrook about his "errors," but the errors continued for months. Kinnebrook was fired. The man who might have saved that job was Bessel, the astronomer at Königsberg, but he was 20 years too late. It was not until then that he arrived at the conclusion that Kinnebrook's "error" was probably not willful. Bessel studied the observations of stellar transits made by a number of senior astronomers. Differences in observation, he discovered, were the rule, not the exception. That early observation of the effects of the scientist on the observations of science made Bessel perhaps the first student of the psychology of scientists. More contemporary research on the psychology of scientists has shown that although observer errors are not necessarily serious, they tend to occur in a biased manner. This means that, more often than would be expected by chance, when errors of observation do occur, they tend to give results more in the direction of the investigator's hypothesis.

This matter can be made more concrete using an illustration of the probable rate at which observer or recording errors are made in the behavioral sciences. On the basis of 21 studies involving 314 observers recording a total of 139,000 observations, it was found that about 1% of the observations are in error and that errors are in the direction of the observer's hypothesis about two-thirds of the time.

Interpreter Effects

The interpretation of the data collected is part of the research process, and a glance at any of the technical journals of the contemporary behavioral and social sciences will suggest strongly that researchers only rarely debate each other's observations, but they often debate the interpretation of those observations. It is as difficult to state the rules for accurate interpretation of data as it is to define accurate observation of data, but the variety of interpretations offered in explanation of the same data implies that many interpreters must turn out to be wrong. The history of science generally, and the history of psychology more specifically, suggest that more observers and interpreters are wrong longer than is necessary because theories are not held quite lightly enough. The common practice of theory monogamy has its advantages, however. It does maintain motivation to make more crucial observations. In any case, interpreter effects seem less serious than observer effects. The reason is that the former are public whereas the latter are private. Given a set of observations, their interpretations become generally available to the scientific community. There is freedom to agree or disagree with any specific interpretation. This is not so with observations. Often these are made by a single investigator, so others are not simply free to agree or disagree. Instead, it can only be hoped that no observer errors occurred, and the observations can and should be repeated by others.

Some kinds of common interpreter effects in the behavioral and social sciences may be reducible by means of improved research and data analytic methodology. For example, the interpretations by many psychotherapy researchers of the literature on psychotherapy outcome, i.e., that psychotherapy does not work, held sway for a long time until, in 1980, Smith, Glass, and Miller showed on the basis of quantitative, comprehensive analyses of all the literature that the interpretation that psychotherapy did not work was not only in error but was in error to a large and specifiable degree.

As recently as 25 years ago, bodies of literature were little more than massive inkblots on which the interpreter could impose a wide range of interpretations. Now, however, the variety of meta-analytic procedures that have been evolving make more objective, more systematic, and more quantitative the summarizing of entire research domains. As more behavioral researchers employ these newer procedures of meta-analysis, the rate of overlooking real effects, a common error of interpretation, should drop noticeably.

Intentional Effects

It happens sometimes in undergraduate laboratory science courses that students "collect" and report data too beautiful to be true. (That probably happens most often when students are taught to be scientists by being told what results they must get to do well in the course, rather than being taught the logic of scientific inquiry and the value of being quite open-eyed and open-minded.) Unfortunately, the history of science tells us that not only undergraduates have been dishonest in science. Fortunately, such instances are rare; nevertheless, intentional effects must be regarded as part of the inventory of the effects of investigators. Four separate reports on important cases of scientific error that were very likely to have been intentional have been authored by Hearnshaw, Hixson, Koestler, and Wade, respectively. The first and last of these, of greatest relevance to behavioral researchers, describe the case of the late Cyril Burt, who, in three separate reports of over 20, over 30, and over 50 pairs of twins, reported a correlation coefficient between intelligence quotient (IQ) scores of these twins, who had been raised apart, of exactly 0.771 for all three studies! Such consistency of correlation would bespeak a statistical miracle if it were real, and Wade credits Leon Kamin for having made this discovery on what surely must have been the first careful critical reading of Burt. Although the evidence is strong that Burt's errors were intentional, it is not possible to be sure of the matter. That is often the case also in instances when fabrication of data is not the issue, but when there are massive self-serving errors of citation of the literature.

Intentional effects, interpreter effects, and observer effects all operate without experimenters' affecting their subjects' responses to the experimental task. In those effects of the experimenters to be described next, however, the subjects' responses to the experimental task are affected.

Interactional Effects

Biosocial Effects

The sex, age, and race of the investigator have all been found to predict the results of his or her research. It is not known, but is necessary to learn, however, whether participants respond differently simply in reaction to experimenters varying in these biosocial attributes or whether experimenters varying in these attributes behave differently toward the participants; in the latter case, experimenters obtain different responses from participants because the experimenters have, in effect, altered the experimental situation for the participants. So far, the evidence suggests that male and female experimenters, for example, conduct the "same" experiment quite differently, so the different results they obtain may well be due to the fact that they unintentionally conducted different experiments. Male experimenters, for example, were found in two experiments to be more friendly to participants. Biosocial attributes of participants can also affect experimenters' behavior, which in turn affects participants' responses. In one study, for example, the interactions between experimenters and the participants were recorded on sound films. In that study, it was found that only 12% of the experimenters ever smiled at the male participants, whereas 70% of the experimenters smiled at the female participants. Smiling by the experimenters, it was found, predicted the results of the experiment. The moral is clear. Before claiming a sex difference in the results of behavioral research requires first ensuring that males and females are treated identically by experimenters. If the treatment is not identical, then sex differences may be due not to genic, or constitutional, or enculturational, or other factors, but simply to the fact that males and females are not really in the same experiment.

Psychosocial Effects

The personality of the experimenter has also been found to predict the results of his or her research. Experimenters who differ in anxiety, need for approval, hostility, authoritarianism, status, and warmth tend to obtain different responses from experimental participants. Experimenters higher in status, for example, tend to obtain more conforming responses from participants, and experimenters who are warmer in their interaction with participants tend to obtain more pleasant responses. Warmer examiners administering standardized tests of intelligence are likely to obtain better intellectual performance than are cooler examiners, or examiners who are more threatening or more strange to the examinees.

Situational Effects

Experimenters who are more experienced at conducting a given experiment obtain different responses from study participants as compared to their less experienced colleagues. Experimenters who are acquainted with the participants obtain different responses than do their colleagues who have never previously met the participants. The things that happen to experimenters during the course of their experiment, including the responses they obtain from their first few participants, can influence the experimenters' behavior, and changes in their behavior can predict changes in the participants' responses. When the first few study participants tend to respond as they are expected to respond, the behavior of the experimenter appears to change in such a way as to influence the subsequent participants to respond too often in the direction of the experimenter's hypothesis.

Modeling Effects

It sometimes happens that before experimenters conduct their study, they try out the task they will later have their research participants perform. Though the evidence on this point is not all that clear, it would seem that at least sometimes, the investigators' own performance becomes a predictor of their subjects' performance. For example, when interviewers speak in longer sentences, their research participants tend also to speak in longer sentences.

Expectancy Effects

Some expectation of how the research will turn out is virtually a constant in science. Psychologists, like other scientists generally, conduct research specifically to test hypotheses or expectations about the nature of things. In the behavioral sciences, the hypothesis held by the investigators can lead them unintentionally to alter their behavior toward their participants in such a way as to increase the likelihood that participants will respond so as to confirm the investigator's hypothesis or expectations. This is essentially describing, then, the investigator's hypothesis as a self-fulfilling prophecy. An event is prophesied and the expectation of the event then changes the behavior of the prophet in such a way as to make the prophesied event more likely. The history of science documents the occurrence of this phenomenon, with the case of Clever Hans serving as a prime example.

Hans was the horse of Mr. von Osten, a German mathematics instructor. By tapping his foot, Hans was able to perform difficult mathematical calculations and he could spell, read, and solve problems of musical harmony. A distinguished panel of scientists and experts on animals ruled that no fraud was involved. There were no cues given to Hans to tell him when to start and when to stop the tapping of his foot. But, of course, there were such cues, though it remained for Oskar Pfungst to demonstrate that fact. Pfungst, in a series of brilliant experiments, showed that Hans could answer questions only when the questioners or experimenters knew the answer and were within Hans' view. Finally, Pfungst learned that a tiny forward movement of the experimenter's head was a signal for Hans to start tapping. A tiny upward movement of the head of the questioner or a raising of the eyebrows was a signal to Hans to stop his tapping. Hans' questioners expected Hans to give correct answers, and this expectation was reflected in their unwitting signal to Hans that the time had come for him to stop tapping.

Thus, the questioner's expectations became the reason for Hans' amazing abilities.

Experiments conducted in later decades are considered next. These will show that an investigator's expectation can come to serve as self-fulfilling prophecy.

Some Early Studies of Expectancy Effects

To demonstrate the effects of the investigator's expectancy on the results of his or her research, at least two groups of experimenters are needed, each group with a different hypothesis or expectancy as to the outcome of its research. One approach might be to do a kind of census or poll of actual or potential experimenters in a given area of research in which opinions as to relationships between variables are divided. Some experimenters expecting one type of result and some experimenters expecting the opposite type of result might then be asked to conduct a standard experiment. If each group of experimenters obtained the results expected, i.e., results opposite to those expected by the other group of experimenters, it could be concluded that the expectation of the experimenter does indeed affect the results of his or her research. Or could it? Probably not. The problem would be that experimenters who differ in their theories, hypotheses, or expectations might very well differ in a number of important related ways as well. The differences in the data they obtained from their participants might be due, then, not to the differences in expectations about the results, but to other variables correlated with expectancies.

A better strategy, therefore, rather than trying to find two groups of experimenters differing in their hypotheses, would be to "create" two groups of experimenters differing only in the hypotheses or expectations they held about the results of a particular experiment. That was the plan employed in the following research.

Animal Experiments

Twelve experimenters were each given five rats that were to be taught to run a maze with the aid of visual cues. Half of the experimenters were told their rats had been specially bred for maze-brightness; half of the experimenters were told their rats had been specially bred for maze-dullness. Actually, of course, rats had been assigned at random to each of the two groups. At the end of the experiment, the results were clear. Rats that had been run by experimenters expecting brighter behavior showed significantly superior learning compared to rats run by experimenters expecting dull behavior. The experiment was repeated, this time employing a series of learning experiments, each conducted on rats in Skinner boxes. Half of the experimenters were led to believe their rats were "Skinner box bright" and half were led to believe their animals were "Skinner box dull." Once again, rats had been assigned at random to the "bright" and "dull" conditions. However, by the end of the experiment, the allegedly brighter animals really were brighter and the alleged dullards really were duller.

If rats became brighter when expected to by their experimenter, it seemed possible that children might become brighter when expected to by their teacher. Educational theorists had, after all, been saying for a long time that culturally disadvantaged children were unable to learn because their teachers expected them to be unable to learn. True, there was no experimental evidence for that theory, but the two studies employing rats suggested that these theorists might be correct. The following experiment was therefore conducted.

The Pygmalion Experiment

All of the children in an elementary school were administered a nonverbal test of intelligence, which was disguised as a test that would predict intellectual "blooming." There were 18 classrooms in the school, three at each of the six grade levels. Within each grade level, the three classrooms were composed of children with above-average ability, average ability, and below-average ability, respectively. Within each of the 18 classrooms, approximately 20% of the children were chosen at random to form the experimental group. Each teacher was given the names of the children from his or her class who were in the experimental condition. The teacher was told that these children had scored on the test of "intellectual blooming" such that they would show remarkable gains in intellectual competence during the next 8 months of school. The only difference between the experimental group and the control group children, then, was in the mind of the teacher.

At the end of the school year, 8 months later, all the children were retested with the same IQ test. Considering the school as a whole, those children from whom the teachers had been led to expect greater intellectual gain showed a significantly greater gain in IQ than did the children of the control group.

The Generality and Implications of Interpersonal Expectancy Effects

Generality

In this article there has been space to describe only a few experiments designed to investigate the idea that one person's expectation can come to serve as a self-fulfilling prophecy for the behavior of another person. However, the basic issue is no longer in doubt. There are now nearly 500 experiments investigating this phenomenon, and the cumulative results of all show an essentially zero probability that these results could have been obtained if there were no such phenomenon as interpersonal expectancy effects. More important than an extraordinarily low p value, however, is having available a stable estimate of the typical magnitude of the effect. That estimate is an r of about 0.30, which translates in practical terms to improving success rates from about 35% to about 65%, a very large effect indeed.

Implications

Three kinds of implications flow from the work on interpersonal self-fulfilling prophecies. The first are the methodological implications for the conduct of scientific inquiry to minimize the effects of experimenter expectancy effects (and other effects of the experimenter). For example, the use of double-blind research designs flows directly from the need to control a variety of experimenter effects, including the effects of experimenter expectancy. More indirect consequences of a methodological sort flowing from this research are some of the work focusing on newer procedures for the analyses of scientific data, including work on meta-analysis, on contrast analysis, and other developments in significance testing and effect size estimation.

A second line of implications involves those for the study of nonverbal communication. For some 35 years, there have been strong reasons to suspect that the mediation of interpersonal expectancy effects depends heavily on unintended nonverbal communication, and this has generated a good deal of work on that topic. A third line of implications involves those for the practical consequences of these phenomena—for example, in classrooms, clinics, corporations, courtrooms, and, in particular, interpersonal contexts, such as those involving gender and race.

All three types of implications have been investigated intensively, but much of what needs to be known is not yet known. It seems very likely, however, that efforts to fill these gaps in knowledge will be repaid by noticeable progress in the methodological and the substantive development of the sciences.

See Also the Following Articles

Experiments, Overview • Focus Groups

Further Reading

Ambady, N., and Rosenthal, R. (1992). Thin slices of expressive behavior as predictors of interpersonal consequences: A meta-analysis. *Psychol. Bull.* **111,** 256–274.

Blanck, P. D. (ed.) (1993). *Interpersonal Expectations: Theory, Research, and Applications.* Cambridge University Press, New York.

Cooper, H. M., and Hedges, L. V. (eds.) (1994). *The Handbook of Research Synthesis.* Russell Sage, New York.

Goring, E. G. (1950). *A History of Experimental Psychology,* 2nd Ed. Appleton-Century-Crofts, New York.

Harris, M. J., and Rosenthal, R. (1985). The mediation of interpersonal expectancy effects: 31 meta-analyses. *Psychol. Bull.* **97,** 363–386.

Hearnshaw, L. S. (1979). *Cyril Burt: Psychologist.* Cornell University Press, Ithaca, New York.

Hixson, J. (1976). *The Patchwork Mouse.* Anchor Press/Doubleday, Garden City, New York.

Koestler, A. (1971). *The Case of the Midwife Toad.* Random House, New York.

Lipsey, M. W., and Wilson, D. B. (2001). *Practical Meta-analysis.* Sage, Thousand Oaks, California.

Pfungst, O. (1907). *Clever Hans.* Barth, Leipzig. (Translated in 1911 by C. L. Rahn; Henry Holt, New York.).

Rosenthal, R. (1976). *Experimenter Effects in Behavioral Research.* Irvington Publ., Halsted Press, Wiley, New York.

Rosenthal, R. (1991). *Meta-analytic Procedures for Social Research.* Sage, Newbury Park, California.

Rosenthal, R. (1994). Interpersonal expectancy effects: A 30-year perspective. *Curr. Direct. Psychol. Sci.* **3,** 176–179.

Rosenthal, R., and Jacobson, L. (1968). *Pygmalion in the Classroom.* Holt, Rinehart and Winston, New York.

Rosenthal, R., and Rubin, D. B. (1978). Interpersonal expectancy effects: The first 345 studies. *Behav. Brain Sci.* **3,** 377–386.

Rosenthal, R., Rosnow, R. L., and Rubin, D. B. (2000). *Contrasts and Effect Sizes in Behavioral Research: A Correlational Approach.* Cambridge University Press, New York.

Smith, M. L., Glass, G. V., and Miller, T. I. (1980). *The Benefits of Psychotherapy.* Johns Hopkins University Press, Baltimore.

Wade, N. (1976). IQ and heredity: Suspicion of fraud beclouds classic experiment. *Science* **194,** 916–919.

Experiments, Criminology

David Weisburd

Hebrew University, Jerusalem, Israel, and University of Maryland, College Park, Maryland, USA

Anthony Petrosino

Nashuah, New Hampshire, USA

Glossary

block randomization A type of random allocation that is stratified in order to maximize equivalence of experimental groups on key indicators. Block-randomized experiments also allow examination of interactions between blocking factors and outcomes in an experimental context.

control group The group in an experiment that does not receive the proposed intervention; often defined as a comparison group because it usually receives some form of traditional criminal justice intervention that is compared to the experimental condition.

cluster randomized trials A type of experiment in which large units, such as drug markets, schools, police beats, or prison living units, are randomly assigned.

eligibility pool The cases or units of analysis that are eligible for inclusion in an experiment.

experimental criminology The application of randomized studies to understand crime and justice issues.

experimental group The group in an experiment that receives the innovative intervention or treatment.

external validity A measure of the extent to which findings or results from a study sample are seen to represent the characteristics of the larger population of interest.

evidence-based policy An approach that encourages the development of public policy based on research findings. Randomized experiments are generally considered an important component of strong evidence-based policy.

internal validity A measure of the extent to which an evaluation design can rule out alternative explanations for the observed findings; a research design in which the effects of treatment or intervention can be clearly distinguished from other effects is defined as having high internal validity.

post-test measures Post-test or follow-up measures are the outcomes examined after an experiment is completed, in order to assess the impacts of the innovation examined.

random allocation A process whereby cases are assigned to treatment and control groups through the play of chance, thereby ensuring that each person or unit of analysis in a study has an equal probability of being selected for the experimental or control group. Random allocation of subjects into treatment and control conditions is the main procedure used in an experiment, to ensure high internal validity.

randomized experiments Studies that employ randomization of study units (individuals or places) in order to isolate the effects of specific treatments or interventions; also referred to as randomized field trials, randomized controlled trials, or true experiments.

In common usage, "experiments" can refer to any test or study that is carried out using systematic methods. Criminologists, however, generally use the term only when referring to studies that randomly allocate individuals or cases into treatment and control conditions. Experiments are used most often in criminology to evaluate the impact of programs, policies, or practices (interventions) on subsequent criminal behavior.

Introduction

In criminology, experiments involving programs, policies, or practices are an important research design because, when implemented with full integrity, they provide the most convincing evidence about the impact of an intervention. Compared to other research designs, experiments provide more confidence that all possible alternative explanations for any observed findings—except the impact of the intervention—have been ruled out. Nonetheless, the application of experimental methods in crime and justice has met with significant controversy, and experimental designs are much less commonly used in evaluation research in criminology than are nonexperimental designs.

Rationale

The major problem that faces evaluation researchers in criminology, and indeed in the social sciences more generally, is that causes and effects are extremely difficult to isolate in the complex social world in which treatments and programs are implemented. The finding that some people, institutions, or places do better after treatment is always confronted with the challenge that improvement was not because of treatment, but because of some other confounding factor that was not measured. Sometimes that confounding factor derives from the nature of the selection processes that lead some people to gain treatment. For example, if a program relies on volunteers, it may recruit people who are likely to improve in regard to drug use, crime, or other measures, simply because they were ready and motivated to improve when they volunteered. Or if an evaluation compares program completers to those who dropped out, the results may be confounded by differences (other than prolonged exposure to the program) between those who stay and those who do not. Sometimes the confounding is simply a matter of the natural course of events. For example, when sites for intervention are chosen, it is often because of the need to address existing serious crime problems. Though choosing sites with very serious problems makes sense in terms of distributing scarce criminal justice resources, it may be that the unusually high crime rates observed would naturally decline even if there was no intervention (the technical term for this phenomenon is "regression to the mean").

An evaluation design's ability to rule out alternative explanations for observed findings is measured in terms of internal validity. A research design in which the effects of treatment or intervention can be clearly distinguished from other effects is defined as having high internal validity. A research design in which the effects of treatment are confounded with other factors is one in which there is low internal validity. For example, suppose a researcher seeks to assess the effects of a specific drug treatment program on recidivism. If, at the end of the evaluation, the researcher can present study results and confidently assert that the effects of treatment have been isolated from other confounding causes, the internal validity of the study is high. But if the researcher has been unable to assure that other factors, such as the seriousness of prior records or the social status of offenders, have been disentangled from the influence of treatment, he or she must note that the effects observed for treatment may be due to such confounding causes. In this case, internal validity is low.

In randomized experimental studies, high internal validity is gained through the process of random allocation of the units of treatment or intervention to an experimental condition (that receives the designated treatment) or a control condition (that either receives "no treatment" or an alternative treatment). When units of analysis (such as participants in the program) are randomly assigned, each has the same probability of being selected for the treatment group as well as for the control or comparison group. This process of random assignment theoretically produces groups that are equivalent on both known and unknown factors that could confound evaluation results. Although the groups are not necessarily the same on every characteristic—indeed, simply by chance, there are likely to be differences—such differences can be assumed to be randomly distributed and are part and parcel of the stochastic processes taken into account in statistical tests.

Comparing Experimental and Nonexperimental Studies

Randomization of subjects to treatment and control groups distinguishes experimental from nonexperimental studies. In nonrandomized studies, two methods can be used for isolating treatment or program effects. In the first, generally defined as "quasi-experimentation," researchers either intervene in the research environment to identify valid comparisons or rely on naturally occurring comparisons for assessing treatment or program impacts. For example, subjects, institutions, or areas that have and have not received treatment may be matched based on data available to the researcher. In a "natural experiment," researchers capitalize on a naturally occurring event to allow for valid comparisons, such as the introduction of new legislation or sanctions in particular jurisdictions but not in other similarly situated jurisdictions. In the second method, sometimes defined as an "observational" approach, multivariate statistical techniques are used to isolate the effects of an intervention or treatment from other confounding causes. For example, offenders sentenced to imprisonment might be compared with those not sentenced to imprisonment in a court system controlling for other confounding causes (such as seriousness of the crime or seriousness of prior record) using multivariate regression techniques. In practice, these two methods are often combined in an attempt to increase the level of a study's internal validity.

The main difficulty that nonexperimental studies face is that they require that the researcher use existing knowledge to identify and then control for potential competing explanations of the outcomes observed. In randomized experiments, the researcher can take a "naive" approach to such explanations, because the process of random allocation ensures high internal validity for a study. In contrast, in ensuring high internal validity in a quasi-experimental study, the researcher must use knowledge about groups or individuals under study to identify or create equivalent treatment and no-treatment comparison groups. Similarly, in an observational study, knowledge about potential confounding causes must be used to identify factors that may bias the estimate of a program or treatment effect for their inclusion in a statistical model. The problem with these approaches is that some competing explanations for study outcomes may be unmeasured or even unknown, and thus it is never certain that the comparison groups are alike on every relevant factor, or that all such factors have been taken into account through statistical controls. For this reason, Kunz and Oxman noted in 1998 that randomized experiments are "the only means of controlling for unknown and unmeasured differences between comparison groups as well as those that are known and measured."

There is considerable debate both among criminologists and across other fields, including education and medicine, as to the type of bias that results from relying on nonrandomized, as opposed to randomized, studies to determine treatment or program effects. Some scholars (e.g., Lipsey and Wilson) have argued that the differences between well-designed nonrandomized studies and randomized experiments are not large. However, a 2001 review of a large number of criminal justice evaluations, conducted by Weisburd, Lum, and Petrosino, suggests that nonrandomized studies are likely to overestimate program success systematically.

Barriers to Experimentation in Crime and Justice

Despite the theoretical benefits of experimental study in terms of internal validity, some scholars (e.g., Clarke and Cornish, in 1972, and Pawson and Tilley, in 1997) have argued that practical and ethical barriers limit the use of randomized experiments in real crime and justice contexts. Ordinarily, such concerns relate to the question of whether the random allocation of sanctions, programs, or treatments in criminal justice settings can be justified on the basis of the benefits accrued to society. Or conversely, the concern is whether the potential costs of not providing treatment to some offenders (either in terms of harm to them or to the principles of equity and justice in the criminal justice system) are outweighed by those benefits. Over the past two decades, criminal justice researchers have illustrated that randomized experiments can be carried out across a wide variety of settings and across a number of different types of criminal justice institutions. As described by Weisburd in 2000, researchers have overcome barriers to randomization of criminal justice innovations in a number of different ways. For example, it is common that there are not enough resources to provide treatment to all eligible subjects. In such cases, researchers have argued successfully that random allocation provides a fair method for choosing those who will gain treatment and those who will not. One objection often raised to experimentation in crime and justice is that it is unethical and sometimes illegal to create control conditions in which individuals receive no treatments or sanctions. In practice, most experiments in crime and justice involve comparison groups that receive either conventional treatment or some alternative type of treatment. The most serious barriers to experimental research have been encountered in studies of criminal justice sanctions such as arrest or imprisonment. However, even here, a number of studies have been developed. In general, fewer ethical objections are raised in studies in which the innovation proposed involves a less punitive sanction than that conventionally applied.

Practical barriers to experimentation have also hindered the development of randomized studies in criminal justice. It is generally assumed that it is more difficult to gain cooperation for randomized experimental approaches than for nonrandomized methods. This has led some scholars to argue that the "external validity" of experimental research is often lower than that of nonrandomized studies. External validity refers to the degree to which the findings or results from a study sample represent the characteristics of the population of interest. If experimental studies are to be carried out only in select criminal justice jurisdictions or institutions, or only among specific subjects, then the external validity of experimental studies can be questioned. Though the external validity of randomized studies, like nonrandomized studies, will vary from study to study, a number of recent trends have contributed to the expansion of the experimental model in criminal justice evaluation. First, the wide use of randomized experiments in medicine, and public exposure to such studies, have led to wide acceptance among the public and policymakers of the value of experimental methods. Second, there is a growing recognition of the importance of evaluating criminal justice treatments and programs as part of a more general movement referred to as "evidence-based policy," which seeks to track the effectiveness and efficiency of government. Finally, in the United States, and more recently in

Europe, public support for partnerships between criminal justice researchers and criminal justice professionals has grown. Such collaboration has led to a greater understanding of experimental methods among practitioners.

Structure of a Typical Criminological Experiment

Though the substantive area and measurements can be different, experiments in criminology do not differ structurally from other randomized experiments. Criminological experiments typically have an eligibility pool, randomization, experimental and control groups, and post-test or follow-up measures relevant to crime and justice (Fig. 1). The eligibility pool is composed of those cases or units of analysis that are eligible for the experiment. For example, in an experimental test of sex offender treatment, the eligibility pool may consist of only those sex offenders who volunteered for treatment, have a certain percentage of time left on their sentence, and have no prior sexual crime history. The eligibility pool is thus composed of all sex offenders who meet these criteria for inclusion in the study. Researchers then randomly assign members of this eligibility pool to the study conditions. Randomization often follows a simple division between treatment and control or comparison conditions. However, some studies use stratification procedures in randomization; this ensures greater equivalence between study groups on the characteristics used for stratification. Such stratification is called blocking, and criminal justice experiments may block on characteristics such as gender, education, or criminal background. "Block randomization" procedures not only enhance equivalence on the traits used in stratification, they also allow experimental analysis of interactions between those traits and outcomes. For example, in a block-randomized experiment in which randomization has been stratified by gender, the researcher can examine not only the average difference in outcomes between treatment and control groups, but also whether the treatment works differently for men or women. Importantly, the use of block randomization requires adjustments in the statistical analysis employed by the researcher.

There are many ways in which researchers randomize to treatment and control or comparison conditions, though computer programs are the most common way used today. Before computer technology was developed, researchers would use the toss of die, a lottery system, or the toss of a coin to assign members to each group. Use of alternate procedures, such as assigning every other case to a group (or all odd numbers), is often referred to as quasi-random assignment. The important principle is to ensure that each case has the same probability of being selected for the control group as the experimental group has, and that the actual assignment is left only to chance.

In the typical criminological experiment, eligible cases are assigned to either of two conditions or groups. Of course, randomized experiments may have more than two groups. But usually there is an experimental group that receives the intervention and a control group that does not. As already noted, it is fairly common in criminological experiments for the control group to receive something other than no intervention or a placebo. For example, in the sex offender example, the control group (or what may be defined as the comparison group) may receive treatment as usual, or the standard prison regime.

One advantage of experimental studies is that that they generally do not require complex statistical manipulation in identifying the effects of a treatment or intervention. Because of random assignment, there is not a need to develop cumbersome multivariate statistical models to control for potential competing explanations for the outcomes observed. At the same time, as in quasi-experimental and observational studies, it is important to develop valid and reliable outcome measures. Outcome measures gained to assess the impacts of a study are called "post-test measures." Though in a randomized experiment, the investigators could conduct a simple post-test on the outcome measure to determine if an intervention "worked," it is generally recognized that stronger results will be gained if the researcher also collects "pre-test" measures of the outcomes of interest. It is often costly to conduct follow-up measurements, and so many criminological experiments do not extend follow-up beyond 6, 12, or 24 months. This is unfortunate, because it restricts

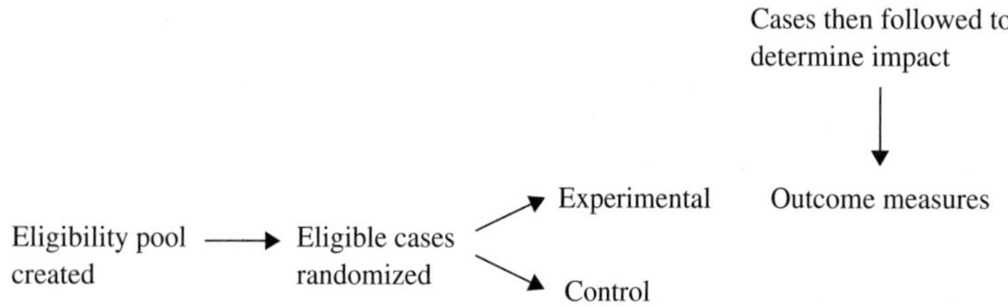

Figure 1 Diagram of the typical criminological experiment.

learning about the potential long-term impacts of many interventions.

An Illustrative Example: The Minneapolis Hot Spots Experiment

Most experiments in criminal justice involve the random assignment of individuals. When larger entities such as schools, police beats, or prison living units are randomly assigned, they are sometimes referred to as "cluster randomized trials." The Minneapolis Hot Spots Experiment described by Sherman and Weisburd in 1995 provides a well-known example of a cluster randomized trial. In that study, the investigators wanted to determine in the least equivocal manner whether intensive police patrol in clusters of addresses that produced significant numbers of calls for service to police, also known as "hot spots," would reduce the levels of crime calls or observed disorder at those places. To conduct the experiment, the investigators established a pool of 110 hot spots that were eligible for random assignment. This pool of eligible hot spots was then randomly assigned to the experimental group receiving intensive police patrol or to a control group that received normal police services. In the Minneapolis study, the investigators randomly assigned the hot spots within statistical blocks, or grouped cases that were like one another based on characteristics measured before the experiment. Such block randomization is not required in randomized experiments, but, as noted earlier, is a method for further ensuring the equivalence of treatment and comparison (control) groups.

The strength of the randomized experiment, if it is implemented with full integrity, is that it permits the investigators to make a direct causal claim that the innovation was responsible for the observed results. If the researchers had simply looked at changes over time at the treated hot spots, it would have been difficult to claim that the observed changes were due to treatment rather than to a natural change in levels of crime or disorder over time. Similarly, if the hot spots researchers had tried to control statistically for other potential causes in order to isolate the effect of treatment, it could be argued that some unknown or unmeasured factor was not taken into account. In the Minneapolis study, the researchers found a statistically significant difference in crime calls to the police and in observed disorder between the treatment spots and the control hot spots. The investigators concluded that hot-spots patrols could reduce crime and disorder in crime hot spots. Random allocation of subjects to treatment and control conditions allowed the assumption that other factors had not systematically confounded the results.

A Brief History of Criminological Experiments

The statistician Sir Ronald Fisher, in his 1935 treatise entitled *Design of Experiments*, is often credited with publishing the first discussion of using randomization to ensure equivalent groups. The first randomized experiment reported in a journal was probably the test of streptomycin for pulmonary tuberculosis in 1948, a study that led the *British Medical Journal* to celebrate the first 50 years of the randomized clinical trial in a special issue in 1998. The first criminological trial was likely the Cambridge–Somerville Youth Study, reported in 1951 by Edwin Powers and Helen Witmer. In this experiment, investigators first pair-matched individual participants (i.e., youths nominated by teachers or police as "troubled kids") on certain characteristics and then randomly assigned one to a counseling group and the other to a no-treatment control group. Investigators (e.g., McCord, in 1978) have consistently reported that the counseling program had no positive impact and likely caused more harm than doing nothing. Although the first major report did not get published until 1951, the first child was likely assigned randomly sometime during 1937.

Randomized trials were used selectively in criminology and elsewhere in the 1960s. Interest in such studies was stimulated after the publication in 1963 of the book *Experimental and Quasi-Experimental Designs for Social Research*, by Donald Campbell and Julian Stanley. Evaluators were now armed with an arsenal of tools for implementing randomized and quasi-experimental designs, but the book clearly recognized a hierarchy of techniques based on how well they controlled internal validity. Because of their high internal validity, randomized trials soon became an important research design across the social sciences in the 1960s. This was particularly true in the United States, where randomized trials were frequently used to evaluate social programs during President Lyndon Johnson's effort to launch a "great society." Oakley noted in 1998 that randomized studies fell out of favor and were less frequently used after the 1960s because they consistently questioned the efficacy of government programs. Undeterred, Donald Campbell went on to describe how the "experimenting society" could take advantage of randomized studies to promote evidence-based policy; in the journal *American Psychologist* in 1969, Campbell wrote that "The United States and other modern nations should be ready for an experimental approach to social reform, an approach in which we try out new programs designed to cure specific social problems, in which we learn whether or not these programs are effective, and in which we retain, imitate, modify, or discard them on the basis of apparent effectiveness on the multiple imperfect criteria available."

Randomized studies again appeared on the radar screen of criminologists in the mid-1980s. An important influence on the reemergence of experimental methods was David Farrington, Lloyd Ohlin, and James Q. Wilson's influential 1986 book, *Understanding and Controlling Crime*, which recommended the use of randomized studies whenever possible to test criminological interventions. Another influential factor was the Minneapolis Domestic Violence Experiment reported by Sherman and Berk in 1984. In this study, the investigators were able to gain police cooperation for a design that took away police discretion and instead randomly assigned misdemeanor domestic violence cases at the scene to one of three conditions: arrest, mediation, or separation of suspect and victim for 8 hours. The investigators reported that arrest reduced subsequent violence in a 6-month follow-up. This study not only influenced the adoption of mandatory arrest policies by police departments across the nation, as noted by Binder and Meeker in 1988, but also increased the visibility and legitimacy of randomized trials in criminology. In the 1980s, under the leadership of Director James "Chips" Stewart, the National Institute of Justice embarked on an ambitious plan to fund criminal justice trials, including several replications of the Minneapolis study, as reported by Garner and Visher in 1988, though Garner and Visher pointed out in 2003 that the National Institute of Justice did not maintain this interest through the 1990s.

The rise of evidence-based policy has generated more attention than ever to the randomized trial in social policy and justice settings. Boruch and colleagues documented in 2000 a surge of international interest, and countries such as Japan, Sweden, England, and the United States held conferences with full or partial focus on randomized trials. In 2000, the policy journal *Crime & Delinquency* devoted two entire issues to randomized trials in criminal justice. The first issue, edited by Barry Krisberg and Karl Schuman, focused on randomized trials in an international context and included papers presented at a conference on experimentation held in Germany in 1998. The second issue was edited by Lynette Feder and Robert Boruch and included further discussion on the conduct of trials. Interest in the randomized trial in journal publications is matched by interest among professional societies. The Academy of Experimental Criminology, a professional society to promote the use of randomized trials in justice settings, was created in 1998. It will promote experiments by honoring as Fellows those who conduct randomized field trials or promote their use in other important ways.

The surge of interest has been matched by a dramatic upswing in the number of reported experiments relevant to crime and justice issues. For example, in 2000, Robert Boruch and his colleagues marshaled evidence from a number of sources to show that criminal justice and other social experiments were increasing, at least according to the publication dates of reported studies. Figure 2 also demonstrates an increase in crime reduction experiments that targeted individuals, at least through 1993. Paradoxically, despite the documented increase in randomized experiments over the past few decades, experiments remain a small proportion of all outcome or impact evaluations conducted in criminology. For example, the Campbell Collaboration, an international organization with special interest on preparing scientific reviews of experimental and other studies with high internal validity, has now identified approximately 11,000 studies that used randomization (or may have used it) in areas relevant to social and educational intervention. As Petrosino *et al.* noted in 2000, only 700 or so of these could be described as criminological. Even if the register dramatically underestimates criminological trials, the number of randomized studies, compared to all evaluative studies reported, must be extremely small. These findings are confirmed in recent reviews (e.g.,Weisburd *et al.*, in

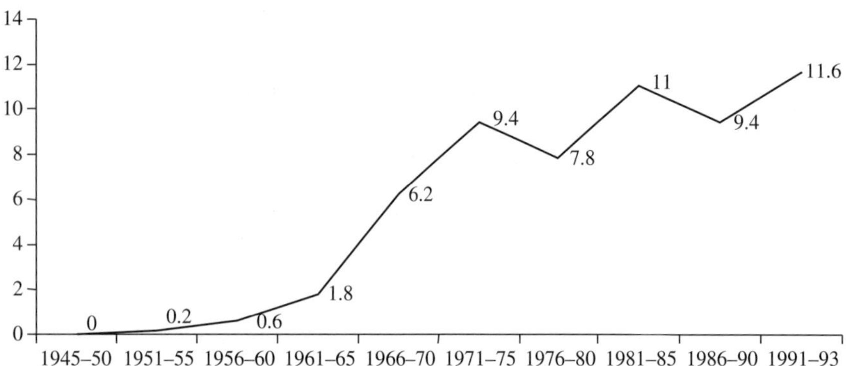

Figure 2 Surge of reported studies in crime reduction experiments targeting individuals, showing the average number of reports/year ($N = 267$). Reprinted from Petrosino *et al.* (2003), with permission.

2001) of criminal justice evaluation studies, which suggest that randomized experiments make up only between 10 and 15% of such investigations.

The Future of Randomized Experiments in Criminology

There is a growing consensus among scholars, practitioners, and policymakers that crime control practices and policies should be rooted as much as possible in scientific research. This would suggest that randomized experiments, sometimes termed the "gold standard" of evaluation design, will become an ever more important component of criminological study. Nonetheless, both Shepherd and Weisburd argued in 2003 that a full-scale experimental criminology cannot be developed without the creation of a series of new institutional arrangements in criminology. The present disjuncture between academic criminology and criminal justice and clinical practice will have to be altered if large numbers of successful trials are to be carried out in crime and justice settings. The priorities of criminal justice funders, who have often considered experimental studies too expensive or too difficult to implement, will also have to be shifted in support of an experimental criminology. Finally, a more comprehensive infrastructure for supervising the conduct of randomized experiments in crime and justice, and dealing with methodological problems specific to this field, would have to be created.

See Also the Following Articles

Criminology • National Crime Victimization Surveys • Randomization

Further Reading

Binder, A., and Meeker, J. W. (1988). Experiments as reforms. *J. Crim. Just.* **16,** 347–358.

Boruch, R. F. (1997). *Randomized Experiments for Planning and Evaluation. A Practical Guide.* Sage, Thousand Oaks, California.

Boruch, R. F., Snyder, B., and DeMoya, D. (2000). The importance of randomized field trials. *Crime Delinq.* **46,** 156–180.

Campbell, D. T. (1969). Reforms as experiments. *Am. Psychol.* **24,** 409–429.

Campbell, D. T., and Stanley, J. (1963). *Experimental and Quasi-Experimental Designs for Research.* Houghton-Mifflin, Boston.

Clarke, R., and Cornish, D. (1972). *The Controlled Trial in Institutional Research: Paradigm or Pitfall for Penal Evaluators?* H. M. Stationery Office, London.

Cullen, F., and Gendreau, P. (2000). Assessing correctional rehabilitation: Policy, practice, and prospects. In *Policies, Processes, and Decisions of the Criminal Justice System: Criminal Justice 3* (Julie Horney, ed.). U.S. Department of Justice, National Institute of Justice, Washington, D.C.

Farrington, D. P., Ohlin, L., and Wilson, J. Q. (1986). *Understanding and Controlling Crime.* Springer-Verlag, New York.

Feder, L., and Boruch, R. (eds.) (2000). The need for experimental research in criminal justice settings. *Crime Delinq.* **46**(3), special issue.

Fisher, R. A. (1935). *The Design of Experiments.* Oliver and Boyd, London.

Garner, J., and Visher, C. A. (2003). The federal role in experimentation. *Eval. Rev.* **27**(3), 316–335.

Garner, J., and Visher, C. (1988). Experiments help shape new policies. *NIJ Rep.* **211,** 2–8.

Krisberg, B., and Schumann, K. F. (eds.) (2000) *Crime Delinq.* **46**(2).

Kunz, R., and Oxman, A. (1998). The unpredictability paradox: Review of empirical comparisons of randomized and non-randomized clinical trials. *Br. Med. J.* **317,** 1185–1190.

Lipsey, M. W., and Wilson, D. B. (1993). The efficacy of psychological, educational, and behavioral treatment: Confirmation from meta-analysis. *Am. Psychol.* **48,** 1181–1209.

MacKenzie, D. (2000). Evidence-based corrections: Identifying what works. *Crime Delinq.* **46,** 457–471.

McCord, J. (1978). Thirty year follow-up of treatment effects. *Am. Psychol.* **33**(3).

Oakley, A. (1998). Experimentation and social interventions: A forgotten but important history. *Br. Med. J.* **317**.

Pawson, R., and Tilley, N. (1997). *Realistic Evaluation.* Sage, London.

Petrosino, A. (2004). Estimates of randomized controlled trials across six Areas of childhood intervention. *Ann. Am. Acad. Pol. Social Sci.* [Special issue on experimentation and social science (L. W. Sherman, ed.).]

Petrosino, A. J., Boruch, R. F., Rounding, C., McDonald, S., and Chalmers, I. (2003). The Campbell Collaboration Social, Psychological, Educational and Criminological Trials Register (C2-SPECTR) to facilitate the preparation and maintenance of systematic reviews of social and educational interventions. *Eval. Res. Edu.* **14**(3/4), 293–307.

Petrosino, A., Boruch, R. F., Farrington, D., Sherman, L. W., and Weisburd, D. (2003). Toward evidence-based criminology and criminal justice: Systematic reviews, the Campbell Collaboration, and the Crime and Justice Group. *Int. J. Compar. Criminol.*

Powers, E., and Witmer, H. (1951). *An Experiment in the Prevention of Delinquency: The Cambridge-Somerville Youth Study.* Columbia University Press, New York.

Shepherd, J. P. (2003). Explaining feast or famine in randomized field trials: Medical science and criminology compared. *Eval. Rev.* **27**(3), 290–315.

Sherman, L. (1998). *Evidence-Based Policing.* Police Foundation, Washington, D.C.

Sherman, L., and Berk, R. (1984). The specific deterrent effects of arrest for domestic assault. *Am. Sociol. Rev.* **49**(2), 261–272.

Sherman, L., and Weisburd, D. (1995). General deterrent effects of police patrol in crime "hot spots": A randomized controlled trial. *Justice Q.* **12**(4), 625–648.

Sherman, L., Farrington, D., Welsh, B., and MacKenzie, D. (eds.) (2002). *Evidence Based Crime Prevention*. Routledge, New York.

Weisburd, D. (2000). Randomized experiments in criminal justice policy: Prospects and problems. *Crime Delinq.* **46**(2), 181–193.

Weisburd, D. (2003). Ethical practice and evaluation of interventions in crime and justice: The moral imperative for randomized trials. *Eval. Rev.* **27**(3), 336–356.

Weisburd, D., Lum, C., and Petrosino, A. (2001). Does research design affect study outcomes in criminal justice. *Ann. Am. Acad. Pol. Social Res.* **578**.

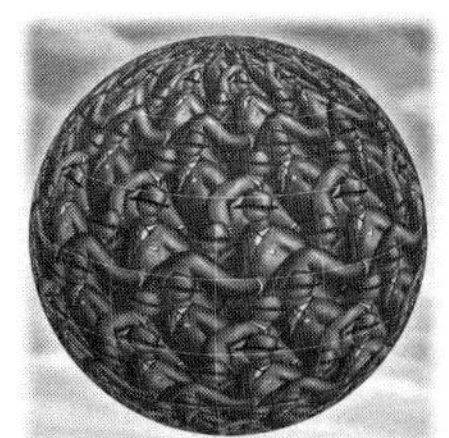

Experiments, Overview

George Julnes
Utah State University, Logan, Utah, USA

Glossary

context-confirmatory inquiry Quantitative or qualitative research in which initial hypotheses are tested as in a traditional deductive experiment, but then subsequent hypotheses (e.g., of moderated relationships not entailed by the main effects studied first) are developed and subjected to a confirmatory test using the same data or other information available in that context.

controlled experiment Inquiry in which the researcher manipulates the independent variable(s), with some control over other factors, in order to observe the effects on the dependent variable(s).

critical experiment An experiment that provides a definitive test of two or more competing theories.

experiment A deliberate intervention guided by and in service of promoting our understanding of the structures and causal processes of our world.

falsificationism An epistemological and methodological stance in which knowledge is viewed as advancing by subjecting the implications of theories to empirical tests and dismissing as falsified those theories not supported.

hypothetico-deductive inquiry Confirmatory research guided by deducing implications of preferred theories and then testing whether those implications are consistent with the observed patterns.

INUS (insufficient but necessary element of an unnecessary but sufficient package) **conditions** Causation conceived in terms of an insufficient but necessary element achieving a causal impact by virtue of being part of an unnecessary but sufficient package.

natural experiment Observations around an event uncontrolled by the researcher but believed to be sufficiently powerful as to reveal a causal relationship between the event and changes in outcomes associated with the event.

randomized experiment A controlled experiment in which the assignment of levels of the independent variable(s) is performed based on a random process; ideally, this involves matching subjects into pairs (or triads, etc.) and randomly assigning one to the treatment group and the other to the control group.

thought experiment A deductive exercise in which the implications of a theory are used to predict what must be found if the theory were true.

Experiments are central to social science methodology, but our understanding of the experimental method has been evolving. This overview of experiments examines this evolution, describes the modern view, considers criticism of the modern view, and speculates on future directions in the development of our understanding of experiments. Specifically, by tracing this development from early roots, including Galileo and Newton, we can see the increasing formalization of the method, particularly under the influence of logical positivism and empiricism. Around fifty years ago the positivist view was countered by a more naturalistic interpretation of the experiment as a pragmatic tool for managing our conclusions in the face of complexity and uncertainty. The naturalistic view tries to answer not "what is the proper definition of an experiment?" but rather the more nuanced "what view of the experiment is most useful in particular contexts?" From this view, if we are to make informed decisions in guiding the future definitions of the experiment in social science, we need to develop and organize empirical information on which features of the experiment are necessary for supporting valid conclusions in different contexts.

Introduction

Experiments have been central to the development of the social sciences. What we understand as the experimental method, however, (1) has evolved over centuries, (2) is somewhat different in different social sciences, and (3) continues to evolve. Accordingly, we must acknowledge several definitions of "experiment," beginning with an inclusive view and then considering more restrictive views that are based on design features of the studies in question. The inclusive definition of experiment, often promoted by philosophers of science, is of a deliberate intervention, guided by our current understanding, that probes the structures and causal processes of our world. What makes this definition inclusive is that it is not limited to interventions that involve manipulating independent variables, but also includes those that are active efforts at observation. For example, Abraham Kaplan makes no mention of manipulating variables in defining experiment as "a process of observation, to be carried out in a situation especially brought about for that purpose." Kaplan's definition highlights that it is the intentional strategy of acting on, or intervening in, the world that defines the experiment as much as the specific designs that are employed.

This overview of the experiment in the social sciences addresses the differing definitions but also focuses on some of the conceptual themes and foundations common across more specialized and applied topics in experimental methodology (e.g., field experiments, laboratory experiments, and quasi-experiments) and across disciplines. We begin by considering different views of what constitutes a social science experiment and then tracing the development of the modern theory of the social science experiment. After presenting the standard view of the experiment in social science, we examine some of the alternative views and use the insights from these other views to suggest some future trends in developing a more useful approach to social science experimentation.

Varieties of Research Experiments

What we accept as the proper definition of experiment matters to both practice and theory. Because of the particular challenges of social science methodology, definitions of experiment in this field have tended to differ from those in the natural sciences.

Social Science Definitions of Experiment

In contrast to the broad philosophy of science definition, many social scientists define experiment based on more restrictive design features. For Campbell and his colleagues, an experiment involves the manipulation of an independent variables in order to explore the effects on dependent variables. Thus a study is considered an experiment only if the experimenter has control over some presumed causal influences. Some describe this as a "controlled experiment," and it is the traditional notion of experiment as taught in social science.

Another tradition in social science (see the writings of Michael Scriven and Donald Campbell) is to distinguish between randomized experiments (involving random assignment to treatment and relevant control groups) and quasi-experiments (designs that approximate the strength of an experimental design by offering some control over specific threats to internal validity). This distinction gives primacy to a particular type of control—random assignment to treatment and control groups. The value of random assignment is that it is able to counter most sources of bias and can generate something akin to true knowledge.

Moving away from controlled experiments, many define natural experiments as situations in which some event uncontrolled by the researcher (yet also fairly random with respect to the outcomes of interest) is seen as sufficiently potent that outcomes before and after the event will differ enough to indicate a causal relationship between the event and the changes. A typical example of this type of design is monitoring outcomes before and after a law is passed, such as a change in automobile speed limits or a change in welfare policy.

Finally, researchers from ancient times to the present have made use of thought experiments in which the implications of theories are used to predict what must be found if the theories were true. Although their use is perhaps not as central as in the natural sciences, thought experiments in social science nonetheless form the basis for developing hypotheses.

Natural Science Experiments and Their Implications

The definitions presented emphasize experimental control and random assignment as essential features of experiments in social science. Revisiting the natural science perspective will help us to appreciate the implications of the social science definitions. Consider the example of setting up a telescope (choosing the type of telescope, aiming it, selecting the appropriate filters, employing a particular technology to record solar radiation, etc.) before a solar eclipse to test Einstein's prediction about the effect of gravity on light. This constitutes an experiment for both physicists and astronomers, but would not satisfy most definitions of experiments as involving manipulations of independent variables.

Indeed, when readers of *Physics World* voted in the September 2002 issue to identify the "most beautiful" scientific experiments in human history, several of the top 10 experiments involved no manipulation of anything resembling a traditional independent variable. For example, Eratosthenes, in the third century B.C., used measurements of the angle of the sun in two towns at noon on the summer solstice to estimate the circumference of the Earth (voted the seventh most beautiful experiment). Similarly, Newton placed a prism in a beam of sunlight to decompose light into a spectrum, refuting Aristotle's conclusion that white light was pure and colored light was some alteration of it (voted the fourth most beautiful experiment). Neither of these experiments involves the manipulation of a variable as part of the study. Or, rather, if placing a prism in a stream of light is understood as manipulating a variable, then almost any systematic observational methodology can be viewed as experimental.

It remains an open question whether it would be productive in the social sciences to view similar systematic observations as experiments. It seems clear, however, that the social science definition is not universal across the sciences and that the more restrictive view common in social science is motivated by the greater likelihood of reaching the wrong conclusions in complex situations. Failure to manipulate causal factors in social settings generally leaves important questions unanswerable.

Of course, even in the inclusive sense, not every observation, or set of observations, qualifies as an experiment. As with Kaplan's, all definitions of experiment refer to some degree of active organization of the observations, with the experiments generally inspired by theories and with the results used to inform theories. Indeed, the common, although perhaps unfair, criticism of the inductive approach associated with Francis Bacon is that observation is too indiscriminate and of limited use unless guided by some conceptual framework. Among social scientists, there may be some (e.g., B. F. Skinner) who claim never to have tested an hypothesis, but most would recognize their efforts as being guided by a paradigm and devoted to elaborating that paradigm.

Examples of the Experiment in Social Science

To understand these views of what constitutes an experiment in social science, it is useful to consider some examples. The following three examples of classic experiments, in addition to their contributions to their areas within social science, provide useful referents when addressing the basic functions and structures of experiments.

Gestalt Experiment on Phi Phenomena

Max Wertheimer, one of the three original Gestalt psychologists, designed his study of what was to be called the phi phenomenon in order to confront Wundt's view of consciousness and perception. Wertheimer's investigation was designed as a critical experiment, one intended to provide unambiguous support for one theory and rejection of a competing theory. In brief, he was able to demonstrate that stationary lights being turned on and off will, when spaced and timed correctly, lead subjects to see "induced motion" when real motion was not occurring. The significance of this finding is that Wundt had attempted to develop an account in which immediate experience was understood as a function of a set number of elements of consciousness. Although Wundt presumed the active organization of experience by respondents and also studied cultural psychology, his approach appeared mechanistic to the Gestalt psychologists, who intended to discredit the larger Wundtian view by identifying a flaw in its basic assumptions about perception.

Smith's Experimental Economics

Vernon Smith, a 2002 Nobel laureate, was among the pioneers in developing the experimental study of economics. Rather than simply derive laws based on a passive observation of patterns in the marketplace, he and others simulated (a word that Smith used, but "simulation" now has the different meaning of mathematical modeling) market dynamics in laboratory studies of groups of subjects. In a typical study, volunteer subjects (usually college students) were divided into two groups, buyers and sellers, with the buyers being told the maximum price that they would pay for a unit of some commodity and the sellers being told the minimum price that they would accept for a unit of that commodity. The independent variable that is manipulated in these experiments relates to features that are expected to make economic markets more or less efficient, such as the nature of the information available to the buyers and sellers. The immediate point of this type of experiment is to establish quantitative laws that relate experimental conditions with outcomes. The larger point is to use findings in controlled settings to inform our understanding of real-life market dynamics.

Milgram's Studies of Obedience to Authority

Stanley Milgram began his famous series of studies by exposing people to a situation in which they were instructed to apply what they believed might be dangerous electric shocks to a third person, actually a confederate playing the role of the "learner" in what was described as a learning experiment. The explicit impetus for these studies on obedience to authority was the awareness of social situations, such as the Nazi-designed Holocaust, in which people follow immoral orders. Not being able to study these social dynamics directly, the goal was, as with Smith and others in social science, to create and study a parallel setting in the laboratory.

Many of Milgram's findings are important in themselves (e.g., a high percentage of subjects continued to obey the experimenter in raising the voltage of the shocks up to what was supposedly 450 volts despite the concerns expressed by these same subjects, who often protested against the experimenter's orders). What is most relevant here, however, is that Milgram designed a series of studies with the deliberate aim of testing the mechanisms involved in yielding high obedience rates. For example, one of the causal factors considered by Milgram concerned the degree of identification subjects felt with the experimenter. Accordingly, one set of studies varied the exposure to the experimenter, with some subjects having the experimenter present during the experiment and others only meeting the experimenter at the beginning of the experiments. As expected, the greater the exposure to the experimenter, the greater the overall obedience rate. Similarly, other studies examined the degree of proximity to the confederates and the personality features of the subjects that were suggested by theory and experience as being relevant to the mechanisms affecting subject decisions to continue shocking confederates.

Development of the Theory of the Experiment

The examples just presented highlight some of the important uses for experiments and emphasize the importance of using the design of the experiment as a way to strengthen our confidence in its conclusions. As various commentators have pointed out, our understanding of the experiment in science did not emerge complete but, rather, evolved over centuries. In considering the value of this evolution, it is helpful to recognize that, despite the role of experiments in addressing questions of both structure and process, the development of the social science experiment has been guided primarily by a single motive—the desire to design experiments to strengthen our confidence in the causal conclusions that result.

Theories of Experimental Method

There were many ancient Greek contributors, such as Aristotle, to the empirical approach that now defines science. For our purpose in understanding the modern theory of the experiment, we can begin much later, with the scientists of the Middle Ages through the Renaissance who advocated variations of what came to be known as the *probatio duplex*, or double method.

Double Method of Resolution and Composition

As an example of the understanding of the double method, Robert Grosseteste (working around 1200 at Oxford) followed Aristotle in differentiating between a knowledge of facts and knowing the reasons for facts. The double method for Grosseteste involved first using induction to identify causes (resolving the observed composite into its elements) based on the study of the effects. The resulting understanding became scientific when researchers could then recompose the abstracted elements to conform to other observed patterns. Recognizing the need for some discipline in making causal claims, Grosseteste and colleagues developed experiments designed to confirm or falsify theories. Highlighting the broad scope of their inquiry method, in addition to work on optics, they also used their observational methods to verify and falsify theories of comets and heavenly phenomena that were not subject to experimental manipulation.

Several centuries later, Agostino Nifo (1473–1545) and Jacopo Zabarella (1533–1589) followed Grosseteste in arguing that science seeks to discover the causes of observed effects. The double method that they advocated for pursuing this object of science was also sympathetic to Grosseteste's views. As before, the first step, resolution or analysis, seeks to abstract out patterns in order to infer causes. Then, with the second step of composition or demonstration, the implications of these inferred causes are developed and compared with additional phenomena.

In sum, the double method of these early scientists begins with an exploratory analysis to infer causes. This first step may be nonrigorous with only limited probative value, meaning that it supports little confidence that the causal relationships are as inferred. This limitation is overcome by the strength of the second step of the double method, in which the inferred causes are put to the test by developing their implications and judging these implications in light of the effects then observed.

Galileo (1564–1642) developed these notions of the double method and applied this method to identify and confirm quantitative laws of motion. Consistent with earlier scholars and with the hypothetico-deductive approach of our times, the analytic (or resolution) step involves exploratory approaches that suggest a conclusion. In the synthesis step, this conclusion is then demonstrated, which can be done either by showing that the conclusion entails something already known or by testing the conclusion through experiment. Distinctive in Galileo's treatment is that the first step, analysis, based on an active manipulation of something, is seen as offering more confidence in the causal inferences than was presented by earlier scientists.

Newton's Experimental Method

During the seventeenth century many of the earlier advances were brought together into a more sophisticated view of the experiment. For example, Newton (1642–1727) selected aspects from these available views to create an approach to conducting inquiry that remains relevant to modern science. Specifically, he took the concepts of the analytic and synthetic aspects of the double method and proposed a single method that tested hypotheses, particularly hypotheses about causality.

> "[P]roceeding alternately from experiments to conclusions and from conclusions to experiments untill you come to the general properties of things, [and by experiments and phaenomena have established the truth of those properties.] Then assuming those properties as Principles of Philosophy you may by them explain the causes of such Phaenomena as follows from them: which is the method of Composition."

Several points follow from this view of the experiment. First, for Newton, the goal of the experiment is to explain the causes of observed phenomena, even when the emphasis is on, as with his experiments on the nature of light, understanding the structure of phenomena. Second, rather than viewing the experiment as a two-step sequence that leads to conclusions, Newton recognized a continuing iteration between theory and inquiry such that experiments are both inspired by, and the source of, evidence for hypotheses.

Third, building on this last point, the analysis phase of the cycle, although still a method of discovery, is also independently probative, which is to say that the resulting evidence is appropriate for making causal claims. In other words, the synthesis aspect of experimentation does not carry the whole weight of strengthening our convictions. A fourth point relates to the importance that Newton placed on experiments functioning as critical experiments (*experimentum crucis*, a phrase Newton borrowed from Bacon by way of Hooke) or as well-designed efforts to decide between two (or more) alternatives.

These four points have important implications for our current view of experiments and how they are defined. For example, in contrast to the previous emphasis on confirmatory research in assessing causality (including when it is presented as falsifying a straw-man null hypothesis), more recent views of experimentation have returned to recognizing that exploratory work need not be devoid of probative support for causal claims.

Theories of Causation

We have seen that for Newton and his predecessors the goal of experimentation was to reveal the causes of observed effects. To understand how the modern view of the experiment came about it is necessary to understand how causation has been viewed over the past few centuries. We begin with the skeptical critique of Hume and then highlight some of the ways that people have responded to his skeptical challenge.

Hume's Skeptical Critique

David Hume (1711–1776), the last of the three major British Empiricists, sought to offer a theory of knowledge that remained true to the core empiricist belief that all knowledge was derived from experience. From this view, to assert that a claim is true, it must be supported either by experience or from valid deductions that are derived from experientially validated premises. One of the problems he faced, however, is that much of what we would like to claim as true has no necessary justification. For example, if we wish to claim that "all swans are white," we are struck by the recognition that we cannot derive this conclusion from logic and we can never see enough white swans to be sure that the next one we see will not be another color.

More important for our purposes, Hume was drawn to the same skeptical conclusions about causality. Whereas we see actions that are presumed to be causal, such as seeing a window break after it is hit by a stone, we do not see the causation directly. How then do we know that being hit by the stone caused the window to break? According to Hume, all that we experience are two observed events—the stone hitting the window and the window breaking. Accordingly, all that a consistent empiricist can do is to apply criteria based on what can be observed. The now-familiar criteria that Hume proposed were:

1. Did the presumed cause precede the observed effect?
2. Was the presumed cause contiguous, or in contact with, the observed effect? and
3. Does the presumed cause display a constant conjunction with the observed effect, such that the effect does not occur without the cause and always occurs when the presumed cause is present?

Modern scientists recognize several limitations in Hume's view, particularly the inability of Hume's framework to distinguish between likely causes and unlikely causes that nonetheless satisfy his simple criteria. For example, without supporting evidence, we are no longer inclined to take the covariation of a presumed cause with an effect as strong evidence that the causal relationship is as believed. This modern critique, however, does little to blunt the core skepticism of Hume's account. And yet, the commonsense position is that we cannot be as challenged in developing appropriate causal inferences as Hume believed. Thus, there is a tension that we see in most subsequent accounts of causality. Each theory can be understood in terms of the balance that it chooses between, on the one hand, attempting to remain faithful to the empiricist directive to consider only what can be observed and, on the other, defending the more optimistic view that supporting valid causal conclusions is primarily a matter of following agreed-upon procedures.

Methods of J. S. Mill

Accepting that the potential for unwarranted causal claims is great, John Stuart Mill (1806–1873) elaborated Hume's basic insight by developing the criteria to be met before asserting causality. First, as with Hume, what is presumed to be a cause must precede in time the observed effects. Second, beyond mere contiguity, there needs to be some sense that the presumed cause and the effects might indeed be related. This is understood as requiring that we need to be able to conceive of some mechanism by which the effect might have been caused as presumed.

The third criterion has particular relevance to modern views of internal validity: "eliminating other explanations of the presumed causal relationship." To address this third criterion, Mill presented several methods, including the method of agreement, method of difference, and method of concomitant variation (Mill also offered a method of combined agreement and disagreement). The method of agreement requires that the observed effects occur whenever the presumed cause is present; the method of difference entails that the effects not occur without the presence of the presumed cause.

Concomitant variation is observed when the nature of the effects is found to be a function of variation in the causes. For example, muscle tissues are observed to twitch when electric current is applied, to not twitch when the current is not applied, and to vary in the level of twitching depending on the level of current applied. Each of these methods employs a comparison of some sort, with the point of the comparison being to provide some protection against the potential for fallacious conclusions. There is also the emphasis, as in the muscle example, on the importance of the researcher's active control of the causes, so that the methods of agreement, differences, and concomitant variation might be applied intentionally.

Logical Positivism

The urge to be rigorous in applying the lessons of Hume's critique contributed to the logical positivist movement in the beginning of the twentieth century. In attempting to cleanse philosophy of speculative metaphysics, members of this movement sought to restrict their claims about the world to only what could be directly observed and to the direct deductions from this observational knowledge. In consequence, there was no effort to address the unseen mechanisms that might be responsible for observed covariation. One result was that some, like Bertrand Russell, attempted to deemphasize the importance of making judgments about causality. Based on a somewhat selective reading of the natural sciences, Russell argued for placing greater importance on discovering laws that can reveal something important about nature without making claims about causation. This position comes from the recognition that most scientific laws can be "solved" in either direction. For example, we can calculate the increase in pressure of a gas that will result when it is heated; similarly, we can calculate the increase in temperature that will result from applying more pressure. In neither case need we presume anything about the direction or mechanisms of causality.

A different response to this reliance only on what is observed was the effort to use Mill's methods of agreement and disagreement to talk about causality in terms of a presumed cause being necessary and sufficient for particular effects to occur. Without needing to presume unobservable dynamics, researchers could conclude, for example, that reinforcement led to a change in behavior if such a change never occurred without the reinforcement (reinforcement is necessary for the change) and the change always followed the reinforcement (reinforcement is sufficient for the change). If a cause is necessary and sufficient for yielding a particular effect, there is a constant conjunction between cause and effect.

Mackie's INUS Conditions

The problem with requiring constant conjunction in making claims about causes is that causality now appears to us to be more complicated than this approach assumes. For example, whereas the notion of a cause being necessary and sufficient may seem adequate when turning on a light switch or in the classic example of billiard balls hitting one another, it is of less use when describing the outcomes associated with complex dynamics, such as interpersonal or social causes. With complex social phenomena it becomes difficult to make explicit predictions that always hold, that display constant conjunction. Rather, acknowledging the importance of contextual factors, we tend to make probabilistic judgments.

In consequence, the old positivist approach of looking for necessary and sufficient conditions has been rejected, but we still need some way of thinking about the regularities that experiments are to help us understand. J. L. Mackie developed what he called the INUS framework (standing for an insufficient but necessary element of an unnecessary but sufficient package) with this goal in mind. The thrust of his approach is to think of causality in terms of bracketed packages that include elements operating in particular contexts.

Let us illustrate this abstract formulation. We might agree that a particular glass windowpane was broken when it was hit by a thrown stone. And yet the stone would not have broken the glass if someone had not opened the shutters moments before or, perhaps, if the glass had not been cracked by previous contact with wind-blown branches. In this analysis, the stone was necessary for the windowpane to break when it did (nothing else would have broken it at that time), but, by itself, the stone was not sufficient (the shutters had to be open and the glass had to be damaged by prior assault). On the other hand, the total package of the stone in that context was sufficient for breaking the glass, but it was not necessary (other packages of causes could have yielded that effect).

Thus, the stone was an insufficient but necessary element of an unnecessary but sufficient package of causal factors.

In a social science context, we might find that being laid off from work is associated with later suicide; in the individual case, being laid off is, by itself, an insufficient factor to cause the suicide (many of those who are laid off go on to lead long and productive lives), but it may have been necessary in the particular case (suicide would not have occurred if the individual had not been laid off). The total package of background factors and experiences, however, turns out to have been sufficient (the individual did commit suicide) but not necessary, as other packages of experiences (e.g., relationship problems) might have led to an effectively identical outcome, even if the individual had remained employed.

Scientific Realism

Bertrand Russell deemphasized casual claims, and Mackie considered probabilistic relationships in terms of causal elements in packages. Another major response to Hume's skeptical critique has been to relax the strictures of positivism to allow for some unobservable concepts, such as believing that there are unobservable atoms and subatomic particles responsible for what we observe in physics experiments. Support for this approach grew as Hans Reichenbach's scientific realism took hold within the positivist movement and the label of the movement switched from logical positivism to logical empiricism. Thus, instead of taking a nominalist stance about relationship between theory and what was being studied, logical empiricists who adopted scientific realism allowed that there were unobserved underlying causal mechanisms responsible for all observable patterns, and they sought to represent these causal mechanisms using the methods of science. For these scientists and scholars, molar-level descriptions (observed patterns), even those involving Mackie's INUS model, are superficial representations that are of limited scientific interest except as they prepare for inquiry about the underlying mechanisms.

This emphasis on underlying mechanisms highlights the retention by scientific realists of the positivist goal of unity of science, wherein a small set of basic concepts can be used to account for the phenomena of all sciences. In practice, this requires (at least as a working hypothesis worthy of being pursued) that the phenomena of interest be reduced to concepts that apply at more basic levels. In the standard formulation, the social sciences can be reduced to the concepts of biology, biology can be understood in terms of chemical concepts, which can, in turn, be micro-reduced to the concepts of physics. This presumes that there are underlying mechanisms responsible for the observed effects at higher levels.

In sum, the scientific realist approach made it acceptable to talk about underlying entities, such as atoms, as real and not simply linguistic conventions. On the other hand, by emphasizing underlying mechanisms, scientific realism encouraged the view that causality operated only at an underlying molecular level and so the causal relationships studied in social sciences are at the level of epiphenomena, superficial patterns caused by the real underlying mechanisms. Scientists who study brain chemistry as the source of the mechanisms that result in psychological patterns provide an example of this belief in the primacy of underlying mechanisms (revealingly, few argue that their neurological mechanisms are epiphenomena that would be better studied using the mechanisms of quantum physics).

Modern Theory of the Social Science Experiment

Having reviewed some of the roots of the experiment, we now consider in more detail what has become the received, or standard, view of the experiment in social science. We begin by relating our examples of social science experiments to the functions of experiment identified by Thomas Kuhn. We then present some of the contributions to the modern theory of the structure, or design, of experiments in social science.

Functions of Experiments

The examples presented so far suggest that there are several functions of experiments. Using categories suggested by Kuhn in 1962, one function is the verification or weakening of theories by comparing theory-based predictions with observations of the phenomena of interest. The studies conducted by Wertheimer to counter Wundt's theory illustrate this effort to put theories to empirical test. Despite this being the central role of the critical experiment as presented by Newton, Kuhn did not believe that it is common or easy to find unequivocal points of contact between theories and nature. Indeed, the Quine-Duhem corollary recognizes that typically there are so many ancillary assumptions involved in translating theory into hypotheses that results inconsistent with theory-based predictions can usually be explained away.

As such, Kuhn emphasized two other functions of experiments. A particularly common function has been the use of experiments to develop more precise measurements of important facts, such as speed of light, the speed of signals sent along neurons, or the mass of a particular particle. Other than in areas like physiological psychology, the social sciences do not have many facts or constants that need to be confirmed or established. Milgram's initial study, however, provides a parallel to this concern with facts or constants in establishing the percentage of people who obey authority in a morally ambiguous setting.

The third function, the focus of much of Kuhn's work, is the use of experiments in the normal science mode to articulate the concepts of a paradigm. This is not a matter of testing the validity of a theory but of exploring the unknowns that the theory indicates to be important. In addition to the previous function of measuring facts or constants, the articulation can involve using experiments to identify quantitative laws (e.g., establishing the universal gas law or Fechner's law in psychophysics) and also to apply the theory to new areas not previously understood in terms of the given theory (this corresponds to Kaplan's notion of extrinsic development, in contrast to the intrinsic development involved in reestimating constants and identifying laws). In the process, researchers often test the boundary conditions of the relationships previously observed, establishing the generality of what is being studied.

Smith's work in relating changes in experimental market conditions to changes in market outcomes provides an example of the experiment in service of establishing quantitative social science laws. Similarly, subsequent studies by Milgram were intended to articulate his paradigm, relating obedience to both situational and personality factors. But his work also highlights Newton's emphasis on conducting experiments that are designed to distinguish the causes of the relationships. An emphasis on distinguishing causes leads naturally to a concern with identifying the underlying mechanisms responsible for the observed effects. This concern was deliberately deemphasized by the logical positivists and might be underappreciated in that an experiment can be conducted without an interest in underlying mechanisms. And yet, even if not labeled as such, it is the interest in identifying underlying mechanisms that guides most decisions about what to study. In Milgram's case, the personality and situational variables were studied because they allowed the testing of presumed psychological mechanisms.

Structure of Experiments

Given that experiments are employed to serve different functions, we can expect them to vary somewhat in how they are structured. And yet there are only a few basic forms that constitute the domain of design for most social science experiments. This is perhaps because the structure of experiments is the result of the overriding function of advancing our conceptual understanding of our world.

Interestingly, in the natural sciences, understanding the causes of phenomena often involves understanding the structure of what is being studied. Thus, Rutherford's experiment explained deflected particles as evidence of the dense nuclei of atoms (ranked ninth of the ten most beautiful experiments in the history of physics). Similarly, the thought experiment carried out early in the twentieth century that established the wave model of the electron explained phenomena yet to be observed in terms of its basic structure (ranked first of the ten most beautiful physics experiments; when the actual experiment was conducted, in 1961, to confirm the thought experiment, the conclusion was so little in doubt that it generated little interest). In contrast, social science experiments rarely seek structural causal explanations (as discussed later, Wundt and Titchener were frustrated in their efforts to identify the structures of consciousness), focusing instead on mechanisms implied by observed relationships. This has meant an evolution of social science experimental design to provide stronger support for valid causal conclusions by being less susceptible to challenges of spurious effects due to other mechanisms. We discuss this evolution in terms of the methods used to strengthen experimental control and in terms of the conceptual logic that was believed to strengthen the validity of conclusions.

Development of Experimental Control

If the experiment were to be a reliable source of valid conclusions about causal relationships, early social scientists recognized, the many causal dynamics that operate in most real world conditions must be separated. In that sense, the development of experimental control is about ways of isolating specific, or small sets of, causal factors.

Controlled Laboratory Experiments and Isolation

The first challenge for social science experimentation was to replicate the kinds of experiments that had proven to be so important in the natural sciences. Just as scientists used experiments to derive the universal gas law, so early efforts in the social sciences conducted laboratory experiments to derive laws. Among the social sciences, psychology was notable for its emphasis on controlled laboratory experiments, tracing its methodological heritage back to the studies of physiology by the likes of Helmholtz and Weber in the beginning of the nineteenth century. For example, Fechner was a major figure responsible for applying the methods used in physiology to psychological issues, in particular relating changes in physical stimuli, via sensations, to changes in perceptions.

From these beginnings, an interest in laboratory methodology continued in psychology. Wundt, and then later Titchener, conducted controlled experiments that used introspection to reveal the basic elements of experience. The failure of Wundt and Titchener to establish the structures of consciousness became in part a cautionary tale that dissuaded other social scientists from seeking structural explanations of causal relationships, but it was also a cautionary tale about methods. Other psychologists were critical of these methods because they did not go far enough in isolating causal factors and so appeared open to subjective bias. For example, Thorndike began with animal experiments because they allowed greater control; this greater control made it easier for him to derive his law of effect and law of exercise. Tolman disagreed with several aspects of Thorndike's theories, but he agreed on the importance of conducting controlled experiments with considerable attention given to ruling out other explanations for the observed behavior. This tradition of laboratory research, often with single-subject designs, was accepted even by researchers from opposing paradigms, as evidenced by subsequent laboratory research that ranged from Wertheimer's perception experiments to Skinner's operant conditioning experiments with graphs of single-subject responses.

Aggregation and Control Group Designs As the subject matter of social science diversified, away from the comparatively simple phenomena of perception and animal conditioning, it became more difficult to demonstrate experimental outcomes on single subjects. For example, not all subjects displayed changes in racial attitudes after exposure to an experimental manipulation; not all subjects reacted equally to changes in the market information made available in laboratory studies of economics. As a result of this more probabilistic effect of manipulations, many social science experiments were structured with the classic aggregated experimental and control groups design. Evidence of causal relationships changed from observations of changes in an individual (as emphasized by Skinner) to differences in group averages. This focus on aggregate relationships led to a need for more sophisticated ways of analyzing the data.

Statistical Inference and Experiments Many of these group-comparison experiments took place under laboratory conditions (e.g., the experimental study of economics), but others took place in real-world conditions (such as randomized experiments of teaching methods in actual schools). In either event, the statistical methods developed by Karl Pearson, Sir Ronald Fisher, Egon Pearson, and Jerzy Neyman provided the analytic tools that allowed experimenters to demonstrate the covariation that was taken as evidence for causal relationships. The preferred way of using what was called the statistical control approach (not to be confused with the statistical modeling that is often promoted as an adequate replacement for experimental control) is to make use of random assignment to yield, within a known statistical likelihood, equivalent groups that should not have any meaningful differences not related to the independent variable(s).

These techniques are particularly important when the experimental manipulation is only one of many important causal factors that vary naturally across subjects. Perhaps the ultimate challenge for understanding the effects of causal factors in applied social science is in trying to understand the impact of policy changes intended to improve social conditions. This was the goal that Campbell put forward in promoting the experimenting society, and it remains an attractive goal for many. Although some are skeptical of our ability to carry out randomized experiments in policy settings, the economist Larry Orr has written persuasively on the merits and practicality of randomized social experiments. He points out that randomized experiments are particularly important for understanding the policy effects that result from a known policy change.

Development of the Logic of Experimental Design

The developments described so far represented tactics to control threats to the validity of causal conclusions. This emphasis on strengthening causal conclusions also led to the development of the logic of experiments, with each step in this development intended to reduce the likelihood of reaching invalid conclusions.

Hypothetico-Deductive Logic Wanting to be as scientific as the natural sciences, many social scientists, such as the psychologist Clark Hull, promoted a version of the hypothetico-deductive method that we discussed as having been developed by Galileo and Newton. This formal model guided the design of experiments by requiring confirmatory research in which the implications of a theory are developed through deduction and then tested. Implications that are supported, or confirmed, by experimental results are accepted as theorems, and our belief in the theoretical postulates, or axioms, that generated them is strengthened. The logic of this confirmatory approach was seen as being scientific in that the testing of implications appeared to be a fair way of testing theories.

As such, although the axioms and theorems of Hull's behavioral theory were ultimately judged not to be of lasting value, the method was accepted as a standard for how experiments were to be designed. This reinforced the dichotomy of exploratory work that generates hypotheses and confirmatory inquiry that tests the implications of those hypotheses.

Falsification and Null Hypotheses The confirmatory approach of the hypothetico-deductive method, however, involved the willing acquiescence to what is known as *modus tollens*, the fallacy of the excluded middle, or affirming the consequent. Basically, this involves the logical error of moving from the premise of "If my theory is true, Outcome A will be observed" and the empirical result of "Outcome A is observed" to the conclusion, "My theory is true." To avoid this obvious error (Outcome A might be predicted by a host of conflicting theories), all researchers need to do is follow the appropriate rules of logic and make the valid move from the premise of "If Theory X is true, then Outcome A will be observed" and the observed result that is inconsistent with Outcome A ("Not Outcome A") to the conclusion that "Theory X is not true." Popper's 1935 program of falsificationism made use of this valid syllogism to fashion an entire approach to science. This elaboration of formal logic was so compelling that the official object of experiments became not to confirm one's own theory but to falsify, or disprove, other theories.

Although this approach is supported by the logic of valid inference, falsificationism has had an uncertain impact in the social sciences. In that it presumes the possibility of falsifying one or more of the alternative theories vying for acceptance, falsificationism as a formal, or reconstructed, logic emphasizes the critical experiment function we have described. Critical experiments are, as Kuhn noted, difficult to design even in the natural sciences. In the social sciences it is rarer still to find theories that yield contrasting predictions; instead, we attempt to falsify null hypotheses.

Consequently, instead of making precise predictions (in effect the composition stage of the early double-method theories) and rejecting theories when the data deviate from such predictions, we articulate null hypotheses that typically are not associated with any viable theory and then proclaim support for our theory when the null hypothesis is rejected. As Paul Meehl observed (in an article subtitled, "Sir Karl, Sir Ronald, and the Slow Progress of Soft Psychology"), the typical null hypothesis in psychology that is subjected to a two-tailed statistical test is "quasi-always false" (a one-tailed alternative hypothesis would not share this particular defect, nor would a confidence interval, but their use in a falsification paradigm is still weak) and so its rejection carries with it little advance in knowledge. Nonetheless, falsificationism is an accepted element of the modern experiment and is represented in the official logic reported in most social science research texts and many journal articles.

Alternative Views of Experimental Inquiry

The standard, or modernist, model of the social science experiment developed so far has not gone unchallenged. Alternative views of what experimentation is and should be have been offered from several perspectives. In considering these critiques, it is useful view each as a criticism of one or more consequences of the single-minded focus in the standard model of experiment on strengthening causal conclusions.

To frame this presentation of alternatives, recall the description of the series of experiments by Stanley Milgram. As presented, Milgram's first study of obedience to authority attempted to confirm and explore in the laboratory the observation that ordinary people seemed capable of following what might be thought of as immoral orders. After documenting the frequency with which people continued to follow objectionable requests (applying what they believed were electric shocks to another participant), Milgram then set out to understand the factors that contributed to this obedience to authority. One study examined situational factors (e.g., degree of interaction with the experimenter); another study looked at personality factors. For each of these studies, certain psychological mechanisms were identified as potentially responsible for the observed causal patterns, and then these posited mechanisms were used as a basis for developing hypotheses to be tested in other contexts.

Naturalistic Critique

One of strengths of the standard model is that, with its reliance on hypothetico-deductive logic and falsificationism, it offers a foundation for valid inference. However, Kuhn's early critique of the modern model of the experimental method concluded that the model did not correspond well to what real scientists actually do. Instead of the systematic development and testing of hypotheses, scientists seemed to be more opportunistic in conducting experiments.

In particular, actual research does not seem to follow the falsificationist logic emphasized as the ideal for social science experiments. Milgram's research, for example, makes no real effort to falsify any theory. At most, falsification in Milgram's work, and most social science, is represented by rejecting, or falsifying, a null hypothesis. But, as previously noted in regard to Meehl's criticism, the null hypothesis in most research reports is not a position claimed by any meaningful alternative theory. As such, there is the appearance of following the rigorous standard model of the experiment in service of the falsificationism agenda, but the actual practice is different.

This discrepancy between formal model and practice is an example of Kaplan's distinction between the reconstructed logics that are reported in journals and the logic in use that is employed by scientists in their everyday scientific lives. According to this view, Milgram's series of studies appear to reflect a rational unfolding of research questions, but the actual process was less tidy. In addition to the chance elements that might have led to some personality factors or environmental conditions being studied before others, there is the issue of a maturation in understanding occurring as the series of studies is conducted, with the later understanding then being used to represent the logic of the earlier studies. More generally, experiments designed with one purpose in mind are recast in terms of a different logic once the results are understood.

One implication of this naturalistic view is that it calls into question the value of the standard model of experiment as a prescriptive framework. If practicing scientists conduct their experiments using an implicit logic that differs somewhat from the formal logic described in the textbooks (i.e., the hypothetico-deductive approach with an emphasis on falsifying theories), one possibility is that some of their deviations from the standard model are useful and constructive (another possibility, of course, is that all of these deviations are bad and we would be better off if the standard model were accorded more loyalty).

Contextualist Critique

One reason why deviations from the standard model might be constructive is that the context confronting researchers may be different from what is presumed by the standard model. Consistent with this, a second criticism of the modern experiment has been that efforts to isolate single causal factors, one of the strengths of the modern experiment, are misguided and destined for disappointment. In this view, causation is much more contextual in that the impact of one factor is dependent on the levels of other factors in a specific context. If causation is so context-dependent, the general laws that experiments are so often designed to discover become ideals that are difficult to achieve in social science. Furthermore, the deductive stance reported in most accounts of experimentation has the difficulty of being useful only if we are able to make meaningful predictions. If the situation being studied is sufficiently complex, there will always be caveats in our predictions, resulting in either post hoc explanations of why the predicted outcomes did not occur or post hoc revisions of the predictions. Furthermore, if the reality of causal relationships is too complex for meaningful predictions, the result of the hypothetico-deductive method will be an overemphasis on those trivial predictions that will hold true in almost all contexts (e.g., "Students receiving an experimental form of instruction will learn more than students receiving no instruction").

One response to this recognition of contextual factors has been to incorporate moderated relationships into the deductive frameworks used to make predictions. Lee Cronbach had in 1957 argued for this use of moderated relationships but later, in 1975, realized that all efforts to incorporate interaction effects in service of developing general laws would be of only limited value. In a 1986 article entitled "Social Inquiry by and for Earthlings," he distinguishes a hypothetical world of constant truths from the more complex real world that he views us as confronting. In the hypothetical world, the hypothetico-deductive method is rational: The timeless truths that social scientists could attain through this approach to experimentation are worth the effort. If, however, the truths discovered in social science experiments are so contingent on a myriad of contextual factors that findings do not generalize even to fairly similar contexts, then it is not clear what the point is of expending the effort.

This problem of context raises the larger issue of the value of nomothetic (belief in and search for general truths) and ideographic (belief that every context is unique and needs to be represented as such) approaches to knowledge. The controversy between those who pursue nomothetic knowledge and those who value ideographic knowledge has become more acute as social science has become increasingly tied to resolving social problems. If Cronbach is correct in his assessment, methodology in social science should be directed not at distilling general causal laws but rather toward understanding the interaction of causal influences in particular cases. This same emphasis has led other social scientists and philosophers of social science (e.g., Robert Fishman and Rom Harre) to promote forms of inquiry that focus on the analysis of specific cases. Because specific cases will differ in many ways, there will be only limited value in making deductive predictions based on findings in other cases. More emphasis should be given to learning the process of understanding specific cases and maintaining an inductive openness to the unique combinations of dynamics in particular settings.

Constructivist Critique

A third critique of the standard model is concerned not with the generality of the truths that result from experiments but rather with the question of whether our conclusions from experiments are a function of the reality that we are studying or more a function of the constructs and operations that we use to make sense of what we are observing. In this view, different people with different constructs will interpret the results of an experiment differently. More formally, Kuhn emphasized how the use of different constructs leads naturally to the incommensurability of different paradigms coexisting within science.

Like the contextualist critique, the constructivist view questions the value of the search for general laws. It is not that constructivists deny that experimentalists could come up with general laws; they merely dismiss the laws as regularities that result from imposing researchers' constructs on a more complex reality. The focus instead for constructivists is to use methodologies that emphasize our interpretative abilities in making sense of the world around us. Theory is still possible in the constructivist view (see Karl Weick's seminal work in the areas of organizational behavior and theory), but the generality of our understanding is opposed by our giving priority to developing meaningful representations of specific settings. As with the contextualists, the constructivist critique claims that induction from exposure to specific settings is of greater value than is presumed in the traditional experimental framework.

Future Trends

The critiques of experimental methods just summarized challenge the standard model of experiment, but the experiment, in some form, will remain central to social science. In considering changes in the function and structure of experiments that might strengthen their usefulness, we can talk with some confidence about minor refinements and speculate about more fundamental changes.

Tactics for Refining the Social Science Experiment

Some of the refinements that are evident in experimental methodology involve the use of statistical techniques that better fit our theories of the dynamics that concern us (e.g., the use of hierarchical linear modeling when studying embedded units). Other refinements will come from the increased use of meta-analysis in making sense of the results of a whole field of experiments (e.g., the work of Mark Lipsey and his colleagues in making sense of experimental evidence of the efficacy of psychotherapy).

Still other refinements are coming from studies of the psychology of experiments (see the work of Martin Orne), through which we better understand how subjects in experiments view what they are experiencing. The use of double-blind experiments in drug studies (when neither the patient nor the health professionals interacting with the patient know which drug the patient is receiving) is an example of an adjustment made based on our understanding of the psychological factors, such as unconscious cues, that can moderate the apparent effectiveness of a treatment.

More generally, investigators are studying the strengths and limitations of different research designs in particular contexts. The psychologist William Shadish has called for more empirical research on the qualities of different research designs for different contexts. As an example of work on this agenda, LaLonde and Maynard documented in 1987 the superiority of true experiments over quasi-experiments when estimating the impacts of employment and training policies. Heckman and Hotz countered in 1989 by demonstrating that more sophisticated use of statistical controls could improve the inferences from quasi-experiments in these research contexts.

Another approach to improving our use of experiments involves clarifying the task at hand. The statistician A. P. Dawid contends that the proper application of statistical techniques for causal inference requires distinguishing between trying to identify the causes of observed effects (often important in developing theory and emphasized in nonexperimental methods) and understanding the effects of a known cause (the central task for policy analysis and one for which the social experiments promoted by Larry Orr are particularly useful). Many journal articles in social science include efforts to accomplish both of these tasks without distinguishing them. The work of Judea Pearl is contributing alternative mathematical foundations of causal modeling and its relationship to experimentation.

Beyond Hypothetico-Deductive Formalism

In addition to these tactical refinements of better statistical methods and more empirical knowledge about the strengths and weaknesses of the different experimental designs, there is a notable trend to reframe the role of the experiment in advancing our understanding. In general terms, the trend associated with a commonsense realist philosophy of science involves viewing the experiment as an evolved methodology that allows us to pose questions to nature and, when done right, increases our chances of receiving meaningful answers. This pragmatic turn is behind Kaplan's abovementioned distinction between logic in use and reconstructed logic, with the implication that the reconstructed logic is useful but is not an ideal that we must restrict ourselves to in conducting science.

Rom Harre, a realist philosopher of science, amplifies this point in referring to the fallacy of logical essentialism, which involves the disastrous assumption that formal logic should be given primacy as the preferred form of discourse in science. Hilary Putnam, another realist philosopher of science, refers to antiformalism as describing a stance in which we value the insights from the formal theories associated with logic and the experimental method but do not expect or allow these theories to dictate practice (he speaks instead of the primacy of practice). To provide a flavor of this realist trend in the future of the experiment, we consider two examples of methodological issues associated with experiments that are increasingly being viewed in pragmatic terms.

Experimental Methodology and Ramification Extinction

Donald Campbell was one of the major scholars concerned with experimental and quasi-experimental inquiry. Whereas his early work was focused on the advantages of true randomized experiments and ways to approximate those advantages with weaker designs, he came to appreciate the larger task of scientific method and even the role of case studies in addressing that larger task. In writing the forward to Robert Yin's book on case study research he noted, "More and more I have come to the conclusion that the core of the scientific method is not experimentation per se, but rather the strategy connoted by the phrase 'plausible rival hypothesis'.... The plausibility of these rivals is usually reduced by 'ramification-extinction,' that is, by looking at their other implications on other data sets and seeing how well these fit." In addition to the reference to the double-method and falsificationism, Campbell's statement highlights the importance of recognizing the particular the rival hypotheses that need to be countered in specific contexts. Whereas random assignment may not be a necessary part of the definition of experiment in some fields, in other fields it can be critical in isolating causal influences.

Consistent with this more general focus on filtering out rival plausible hypotheses, there is a move away from the deduction/induction dichotomy that has been the source of much controversy in social science. Recall that in the hypothetico-deductive framework, exploratory inquiry is important, but only the deductive approach can be relied on to avoid spurious conclusions. This corresponds to the early views of the double method, in which only the demonstration, or composition, stage provides confidence about causal conclusions.

On the other hand, the contextualist and constructivist critiques question our ability to make such deductions when dealing with real-world phenomena. Instead, predictions that are complex enough to be interesting are unlikely to hold up when tested in different contexts. Because the deductive method is not realistic, these critics of the standard model of experiment argue that an inductive approach is a better way to develop an appreciation of the complexity of the phenomena of interest to social sciences.

In the commonsense realist reframing of this issue, having to choose between a rigorous deductive approach and an open-minded inductive approach now appears to be a false choice. Instead, quantitative researchers are becoming adept at the types of context-confirmatory inquiry long used by qualitative researchers (see Robert Yin's work on case study methodology). In context-confirmatory inquiry, researchers begin with some hypotheses to be tested, based on prior inquiry, and then, after testing these hypotheses, continue with the exploration of more complex relationships. Rather than stopping with this exploratory work, leaving for later research with new subjects the task of testing the predictions from the exploratory phase, researchers continue the cycle between deduction and induction that Newton described. That is, the hypotheses that result from the exploratory analyses can then be tested with additional aspects of the same set of data.

For example, if exploratory analyses suggest that an innovative teaching approach is effective because it helps students visualize complex statistical relationships, we could attempt to confirm this interpretation with further analyses of the data available about these same students. One way to approach this confirmation would be to predict which students, perhaps based on measurements of how gifted they are in visualizing quantitative relationships, might benefit most and least from the intervention and then to examine the moderated relationship (e.g., using interaction terms in regression analysis) to assess the prediction. Another way to confirm the hypothesis in the same context that generated, it is to obtain additional outcome variables, predict patterns in which some of the outcomes measured would be affected more by the intervention than others, and then conduct the analyses to assess that prediction.

In that this testing of an interaction effect occurs after the data are in hand, it is less vulnerable to the limits of rationality highlighted by the contextualist critique. However, to the extent that the interaction terms to be tested cannot be derived in any direct manner from the analyses already conducted (as is true with tests of the interaction terms when only the main effects were analyzed previously), this approach satisfies the confirmatory intent of the hypothetico-deductive model. Interestingly, this emphasis on the iteration between gathering evidence and developing theoretical implications is consistent with the method developed by Newton and also promoted 100 years ago by pragmatic social scientists who preceded the ascendence of logical positivism. As such, we might talk of a prepositivist emancipation wherein we are now free to make better use of the insights of the early pragmatists. The current emphasis on using pattern-matching to strengthen internal validity is an example of this pragmatic orientation.

Satisfying the Superego versus Supporting Cognitive Management

Adherence to good practice in applying quantitative methods is intended to yield a better understanding of the phenomena being studied. There are, however, multiple paradigms available for guiding statistical analyses as applied to experiments. The hypothetico-deductive model is typically framed in terms of only one of these alternative paradigms, the Neyman-Pearson paradigm. Referred to as forward-looking, this approach dominates statistical textbooks in social science and involves the traditional emphasis on deciding before the data are collected what criteria will be used to reach conclusions once the analyses are carried out (e.g., the null hypothesis will be rejected if $p < 0.05$).

Although the Neyman-Pearson approach seems reasonable, we need to ask whether this paradigm is really suited for the task at hand when interpreting experimental results. Specifically, Gerd Gigerenzer has argued that the Neyman-Pearson approach is a statistical parallel of the psychodynamic superego in that it specifies correct behavior but is out of touch with the demands of everyday living. Instead, Gigerenzer promotes Fisher's statistical framework as being more consistent with our task of making sense of experimental data. Referred to as a backward-looking approach, the Fisherean experimenter first collects and analyses the data and then (looking back at these data as analyzed) comes up with what appear to be the best interpretations (Teddy Seidenfeld and Henry E. Kyburg are recent mathematical philosophers who have sought to rehabilitate Fisher's approach).

Viewing the development of understanding as less a matter of making decisions and more a matter of supporting interpretations, a pragmatic stance on applying statistical analyses to experimental results emphasizes a backward-looking approach to guiding our beliefs. This distinction between forward- and backward-looking approaches to statistical inference brings to mind again the distinction that Kaplan made between the formal reconstructed logic that is used to explain results and the logic in use that reflects actual practice. Most of the criticisms of the use of statistical inference in social science (including both hypothesis tests and confidence intervals; see the work of psychologist Charles Reichardt for more on advantages of confidence intervals) concern their failings in terms of a presumed reconstructed logic. In contrast, statistical inference can be useful from the vantage point of supporting a logic in use.

Taking the superego-ego metaphor more broadly, an additional step in moving beyond hypothetico-deductive formalism is the view that the role of the experiment in social science is as a tool for cognitive management, meaning that it is valued primarily not as an arbiter of truth but as a means of screening the beliefs that we are willing to hold. The philosopher Jerry Fodor makes this point in arguing that the notion of observation in the empiricist account of the experiment is becoming increasingly abstract. Pointing out that the use of technology means that observation by humans may be nothing more than observing computer printouts, Fodor argues that the essence of the experiment is neither formal deduction nor direct observation but rather a process of posing questions to nature. Accordingly, what constitutes an effective tool for cognitive management in one field might differ from what is effective in other fields. This, along with Campbell's notion of context-dependent ramification extinction, argues for a flexible definition of what constitutes an experiment in social sciences. In some fields, such as neuropsychology, random assignment may not be as important as other forms of experimental control. On the other hand, in fields such as anthropology, it may be useful to conceive of experiments in very different ways, including the use of qualitative methods and other methods not based on aggregate covariation, to assess the impacts of deliberate interventions.

Conclusion

The design and use of experiments in social science is evolving. The critiques of the standard model from other perspectives have highlighted limitations that can be overcome. A consideration of the variety of physical science experiments reminds us that we need not restrict ourselves to a narrow definition. Instead of viewing the experiment solely as an instrument for the particular form of empiricism promoted by logical empiricists, a prepositivist emancipation allows us to view experiments as tools in the pragmatic task of guiding our efforts to make sense of our world.

In particular, we can consider the standard model of the social science experiment, with its design-based definition (i.e., requiring active, preferably random, manipulation of causal factors) and its role in promoting falsificationism, as *one* valuable model rather than the *only* viable model. A more inclusive definition of the experiment as a deliberate intervention designed, based on current understanding, to probe the nature of our world (to pose questions in ways that we can expect meaningful answers) has several advantages. Of greatest import, such an inclusive definition can avoid most of the limitations raised by the naturalistic, contextual, and constructivist critiques while still allowing us to focus on the rigor necessary to counter the rival alternatives that Campbell and others have identified as the crucial task of scientific inquiry.

See Also the Following Articles

Experiments, Political Science • Experiments, Psychology • Explore, Explain, Design • Field Experimentation • Laboratory Experiments in Social Science • Quasi-Experiment • Randomization • Research Designs

Further Reading

Cook, T. D. (1985). Postpositivist critical multiplism. *Social Science and Social Policy* (L. Shotland and M. M. Mark, eds.), pp. 21–62. Sage, Thousand Oaks, CA.

Cook, T. D., and Campbell, D. T. (1979). *Quasi-Experimentation: Design and Analysis Issues for Field Settings.* Rand McNally, Skokie, IL.

Cronbach, L. J. (1986). Social inquiry by and for earthlings. *Metatheory in Social Science* (D. W. Fiske and R. A. Shweder, eds.), pp. 83–107. University of Chicago Press, Chicago, IL.

Guerlac, H. (1973). Newton and the method of analysis. *Dictionary of the History of Ideas* (P. P. Weiner, ed.), pp. 378–391. Charles Scribner's Sons, New York.

Harre, R. (1986). *Varieties of Realism.* Blackwell, Oxford.

Julnes, G., and Mark, M. (1998). Evaluation as sensemaking: Knowledge construction in a realist world. *Realist Evaluation: An Emerging Theory in Support of Practice* (New

Directions for Evaluation, no. 78) (G. Henry, G. Julnes, and M. Mark, eds.), pp. 33–52. Jossey-Bass, San Francisco.

Kaplan, A. (1964). *The Conduct of Inquiry*. Chandler, San Francisco, CA.

Kuhn, T. S. (1962). *The Structure of Scientific Revolutions*. University of Chicago Press, Chicago, IL.

Mohr, L. B. (1996). *The Causes of Human Behavior: Implications for Theory and Method in the Social Sciences.* University of Michigan Press, Ann Arbor, MI.

Orr, L. L. (1998). *Social Experiments: Evaluating Public Programs with Experimental Methods.* Sage, Thousand Oaks, CA.

Putnam, H. (1987). *The Many Faces of Realism.* Open Court, LaSalle, IL.

Shadish, W., Cook, T. D., and Campbell, D. T. (2002). *Experimental and Quasi-Experimental Designs for Generalized Causal Inference.* Houghton Mifflin, Boston.

Wallace, W. A. (1973). Experimental science and mechanics in the Middle Ages. *Dictionary of the History of Ideas* (P. P. Weiner, ed.), pp. 196–205. Charles Scribner Sons, New York.

Yin, R. K. (1994). *Case Study Research: Design and Methods*, 2nd Ed. Sage, Thousand Oaks, CA.

Experiments, Political Science

Rose McDermott
University of California, Santa Barbara, California, USA

Glossary

artifact An exogenous variable that is created by some aspect of the experimental manipulation and which can vary with the independent variable. The effects of these variables can then become confounded with the experimental findings.

between-subjects design An experimental design in which each person is exposed to only one of the experimental manipulations. Differences are then measured between groups.

control condition The condition of subjects in an experiment who receive no treatment or manipulation.

direct replication Repeating an experiment as closely as possible to determine the reliability of results.

experiment A method of investigation with an independent variable, a dependent variable, high levels of control on the part of the investigator, and the random assignment of subjects to treatment conditions.

experimental condition The condition of subjects in an experiment who are exposed to the manipulated variable or treatment.

interaction effect When the outcome or effect of one variable varies with the outcomes or effects of a second variable. This occurs in factorial design experiments.

systematic replication Repeating an experiment in such a way that certain aspects, measures, or protocols of the original experiment are systematically varied. These replications serve to clarify or extend aspects of the original experiment.

within-subjects design An experimental design in which each person is exposed to all treatment conditions. Thus, each person serves as his or her own control and differences are found within each individual.

Experiments constitute the gold standard of many forms of scientific inquiry in a variety of fields, including hard sciences, such as biology and physics, as well as social sciences, such as psychology and behavioral economics. Because of the methodological demands of experimental control and the randomization of subjects, the experimental method offers unparalleled leverage in determining causation. Experiments can be used to great effect in uncovering causal relationships in political science as well, although they have not yet been as widely employed as other forms of methodological inquiry, such as formal or quantitative work. This article explores why experiments offer a potentially useful form of social measurement and investigation. Various basic aspects of experimental design will be covered, along with potential sources of error. The advantages of experimental design, as well as nonexperimental alternatives, will be discussed. Finally, the ethics of experimentation require mention.

Why Experiments? Advantages of Experimentation

Experiments offer the best scientific method available for finding out whether or not one thing causes another thing. All other methods can offer interesting, important, and persuasive arguments about causality, but only experiments can actually prove causality. For example, many people knew that smoking caused lung cancer as a result of all the correlational data showing the relationship between smoking and lung cancer. However, the tobacco companies could still engage in plausible deniability because these relationships were correlational and they could argue that these associations were spurious and that other factors, such as genetic predisposition, could cause both smoking and lung cancer. However, once experimental work at the cellular level took place and demonstrated that tar, nicotine, and other components of smoke caused lung tissue to die under controlled conditions, the causal link was established and it became much more difficult for the tobacco companies to argue that the relationship was spurious in origin. This causal link remains critical in addressing many questions of great importance in political and social life as well.

There are at least three ways in which experiments differ from other forms of social measurement. First, many political scientists begin their inquiries by looking for naturally occurring phenomenon in which they are interested and then seeking to examine them in a variety of ways. Thus, if a scholar was interested in military coups, he could find states where they occurred and then study them in some systematic fashion. In these cases, methods of inquiry can include field work, interviews, surveys, archival exploration, and so on. On the other hand, an experimentalist tends not to wait for events to occur. Rather, an experimentalist goes about creating the conditions that produce the events of interest.

Thus, if a scholar is interested in how leaders make decisions under conditions of stress, he can design an experiment in which he asks subjects to make various decisions and then imposes stress on them while they are completing these tasks. Experimentally induced stress can take many forms, depending on the interest of the investigator. One can turn up the heat in the room, impose a tight time limit, give an impossible task with false-negative feedback, make the room too loud or too bright, or simply create a crisis in the midst of the task, such as a fire or medical emergency. Obviously, some issues and questions of concern lend themselves more readily to experimental creation and manipulation than others, but clever experimentalists can gain a great deal of control by creating their own conditions of interest. The real advantage of this opportunity lies in the experimentalists' ability to measure and capture exactly what they are interested in studying. Because of this, experimenters are not easily led astray by irrelevant forces. In other words, experimentalists do not need to test or replicate every aspect of the real world in order to investigate their areas of interest. Rather, they need only examine the key relationships between variables that they suspect have causal impact on the outcomes of interest. In this way, an experimentalist draws on theoretical ideas and concepts to derive hypotheses and then designs a test, or multiple tests, to explore the variables and relationships that appear to be causal in nature. Therefore, experimentalists do not need to re-create the external world in their laboratories in order to achieve meaningful results; by carefully restricting their observation and analysis to those variables deemed central to the relationships of interest, they can test competing alternative causal hypotheses within controlled conditions.

Second, and related, experimentalists can control and systematically manipulate the treatment conditions to which their subjects are exposed. This ability to control the events and measures allows an investigator to expose subjects under different conditions to exactly the same situation except for the variable being tested and manipulated. Therefore, if the scholar observes a systematic difference between groups, he knows exactly what caused the change because only one thing varied between conditions. In less controlled conditions in the real world, it can often prove extremely difficult, or even impossible, to find events that vary systematically enough to allow for such comparisons to be made. Two different dictators, for example, certainly differ in more ways than they are similar and thus systematic comparisons may prove difficult and dangerous. Yet analogies between them remain accessible and powerful nonetheless, as when Saddam Hussein was compared with Adolf Hitler by members of the Bush administration. Although such comparisons can prove strongly evocative, problems arise because real systematic comparisons between actors remain impossible.

Third, experimenters can decide who gets exposed to what treatment condition. The ability to randomize subjects to manipulations provides the single most powerful tool available to experimenters. Random assignment to condition ensures that observed differences do not result from preexisting systematic differences between groups or individuals. Because of this procedure, subjects cannot self-select into a particular condition due to personal proclivities or systematic environmental pressures. With random assignment, condition should be determined by chance alone. The best experimenters tend to use random number tables or some other systematic method to ensure truly random assignment of subject to condition. When this happens, any preexisting systematic differences between subjects should cancel each other out. As Aronson *et al.* (1990, p. 38) explain: "In an experiment, the experimenter both has control over what treatment each subject receives and determines that treatment by assigning subjects to conditions at random. If the subject receives a treatment that has truly been determined at random, it is virtually impossible for a third variable to be associated with that treatment. Consequently, such a third variable cannot affect the dependent variable."

These elements of control and randomization, along with the ability to create the experimental environment, allow investigators to determine whether certain factors really do cause other ones or are merely correlated with them. The null hypothesis in these circumstances typically assumes that the independent variable or variables of interest have no effect on the dependent variables of interest. When systematic observed differences are found between conditions, investigators can feel confident that these discrepancies were actually caused by the manipulations they created. In this way, the primary benefit of experiments lies in their unparalleled ability to uncover causal relationships. As Aronson *et al.* (1990, p. 39) sum up, "the major advantage of an experimental enquiry is that it provides us with unequivocal evidence about causation. Second, it gives us better control over extraneous variables. Finally, it allows us to explore the dimensions and parameters of a complex variable."

Experimental Design and Potential Sources of Error

Variables

As Aronson *et al.* (1990, p. 114) write, "experimental design refers to the selection and arrangement of conditions." Experimentalists typically structure particular experimental protocols that outline what subjects are expected to do and indicate which measures will be used to record outcomes of interest. Typically, as in many other methods of social inquiry, experimenters start with a hypothesis about the relationship between two or more variables. These hypotheses, as in other methods of inquiry, can come from a variety of different sources. They can derive from theoretical understandings, problems in the real world, previous research, and so on. The experimenter then seeks to determine whether the independent variable, or putative cause, influences the dependent variable, or effect, in the manner expected. Experiments then seek to explore how and in what way these variables are related. As Underwood (1957, p. 87) noted, the most basic goal of experimentation is to "design the experiment so that the effects of the independent variables can be evaluated unambiguously." The design of experiments is often extremely time-consuming because it can be hard to figure out how to operationalize the conceptual variables of interest into an engaging and coherent activity for subjects. This process of transforming ideas into concrete events is called empirical realization.

Conditions

Several specific aspects of experimental design deserve mention. First, perhaps the most important aspect of experimental design relates to the creation of the experimental conditions themselves. Experiments require at least two conditions in which to measure the independent variable in order to see whether it has had any effect on the dependent variable; obviously, one condition simply constitutes a constant and no effect can be demonstrated. Typically, an experiment is designed with a control condition and an experimental one. This means that in one treatment group, the control condition, subjects engage in some benign but related task, which should take a similar amount of time, require the same kind and amount of information, involve the same experimenters, and engage a similar amount of interest as the experimental condition. In particular, it remains critical that subjects in the control condition receive the same background information as those in the experimental condition, so that ostensible findings do not simply result from differences in the information provided to the two groups at the outset. In practice, this equivalency of experience can often be very difficult to achieve. In the other group, the experimental condition, subjects receive the experimental manipulation. In practice, the control and experimental conditions often translate into the presence or absence of the independent variable. The control condition does not have the independent variable of interest, but the experimental condition does. Recall that the null hypothesis usually assumes that no relationship between independent and dependent variables exists, until proven otherwise.

Although random assignment of subjects to conditions allows the investigator to rid himself of systematic sources of error, random error, or background noise, can still pose a problem. In order to avoid this problem, experimenters often hold as many variables as possible constant. Another option for investigators is to allow certain variables, hopefully the less important ones, to vary randomly. The third alternative is to introduce systematic variation by adding a second (or more) independent variable for examination. When this occurs, two experimental treatment conditions exist, rather than one control and one experimental condition.

This strategy of using two experimental conditions, rather than one treatment and one control condition, occurs, for example, in medical experiments, where no treatment would constitute an unethical option. The control condition then becomes the standard treatment of care, compared with the experimental condition provided by a new medication or procedure. Similarly, in political science, many settings would not lend themselves to ethical experimentation. For example, it would not be ethical to try to examine the impact of torture on prisoners of war by re-creating such techniques in a laboratory. Similar examples of unethical experimentation could be imagined in field settings, such as investigating the impact of suicide bombing on policy preferences. More will be said about field experiments later.

Between- and Within-Subjects Designs

Experiments can take the form of within- or between-subjects designs. Both types offer certain advantages and disadvantages. There is no one right way to conduct an experiment; investigators decide whether to use a within- or between-subjects design depending on the circumstances, based on how and what they want to study. In between-subjects designs, each subject is exposed to only one condition and the differences between groups are then examined. Because each subject is exposed to only one condition in this design method, observed differences exist between groups or individual subjects. Randomization should prevent the introduction of systematic bias into the subject pool, but there remains a very small possibility that some systematic personality differences underlying each population can introduce some kind of systematic error. In within-subjects designs, each subject serves in effect as his or her own control. In this design, each subject encounters every condition in sequence. Thus, the same group of people constitute the entire experimental variance.

The advantage of a within-subjects design is that it prevents the introduction of any underlying systematic individual differences from contaminating the experimental findings. The problem lies in the risk of potential contamination of experimental results in one condition from the subject's prior experience of another condition in the same experiment. These within-subjects designs prevail in experiments that ask subjects to make judgments about hypothetical scenarios or individuals. They remain a very cost-effective option for collecting large amounts of data relatively quickly.

The disadvantages of within-subjects designs lie in their potential for interexperimental contamination. When an investigator examines an issue or topic that has great impact, because it appears quite vivid, concrete, or emotional in nature, within-subjects designs risk the threat of a so-called carryover effect, in which exposure to one condition unduly affects or contaminates a subject's response to the other condition.

Overall, if an investigator is interested in examining how people make judgments in particular situations or contexts, a within-subjects design can be ideal. However, as Greenwood warns, if a scholar wishes to see how a particular person, event, or condition affects people in isolation, certain precautions should be used to make sure that within-subjects designs remain valid. For example, making sure that stimuli are counterbalanced in their order of presentation will help avoid systematic contrast effects that might produce artifacts in the experimental results. In other words, if an experimenter wants to examine the effect of fear versus anger on decision-making, some subjects should be presented with the fear condition first, while others receive the anger condition first. This strategy ensures that the contrast between the most recent mood state does not systematically contrast with, and affect, the subject's performance on the dependent measures in a way that produces systematic, but confounded, results.

In addition, some experimenters will combine within- and between-subjects designs to avoid the pitfalls inherent in either one. A final technique that can be used to help overcome the contamination effects of a within-subjects design without invoking the difficulties of potential underlying personal similarities inherent in a between subjects design is called matching. In matching, experimenters try to closely match subjects based on particular criteria, such as age, race, sex, and then expose one subject to the experimental condition and one subject to the control condition. This strategy works best when the dimension on which subjects are matched is similar to the dependent variable. Intelligence, education, and profession provide examples of such categories in which people can be matched because these factors can influence a wide variety of other behaviors and outcomes in systematic ways. Sometimes, particularly in medicine, matching can take place based on the dependent variable. If someone wants to examine factors that led to a certain disease, he might match individuals who are similar in terms of age, sex, race, education, and occupation, but who differ in their disease status, where one might be infected with hepatitis and the other not, to examine the differences between them. To be clear, matching in no way substitutes for the random assignment of subjects to condition; indeed, in matching, subjects are still assigned to treatment conditions at random within paired blocks. For example, one could not take groups of people who naturally differ on some dimension such as race, construct two new groups based on party identification, and then treat one group as an experimental group and another as a control group. Rather, matching provides an additional control, typically used in within-subjects designs, that can further protect against the impact of systematic personal variations on experimental results.

Interaction Effects

In an experiment, investigators typically look for main effects, that is, the direct effect of the independent variable on the dependent variable. One of the potential methodological advantages of introducing more than one experimental condition at a time, however, lies in the ability to uncover interaction effects between variables that might have been hidden if only one variable were examined at a time. Interaction effects occur when one independent variable has different effects depending on the impact of a second independent variable. For example, an interaction effect would be discovered if one found that party identification had a different impact on voting behavior depending on race.

Obviously, many variables can affect social and political behavior. Therefore, depending on the topic under investigation, sometimes an experimenter will hold certain things constant, sometimes he will allow certain variables to vary at random, and sometimes he will introduce a systematic variation in independent variables. When such a systematic variation exists, precautions must be taken to avoid artifactual findings, those results that may appear to look like real interaction effects, but in fact result from systematic sources of error that occur when other exogenous variables shift with the independent variables of interest. When this happens, it can appear that those exogenous factors influence outcomes in a systematic way, but in fact those findings remain spurious. Such variables can confound the results of the experiment.

Two kinds of artifacts pose relatively consistent potential problems for experimenters in general. The first concerns demand characteristics, whereby subjects change their behavior either because they know they are in an experiment and are being watched or because they want to please or impress the experimenter in some way. This can bias results in systematic, but irrelevant, ways. Second, experimenter bias can produce another kind of systematic artifact. This occurs when subjects change their behavior either because they think they are given certain cues about what the experimenter wants or because the experiment is designed in such a way that they actually are given such cues. This creates particularly problematic effects when these subtle pressures actually encourage subjects to behave in inauthentic ways that nonetheless support the experimenter's hypotheses.

Replication

Obviously, repeating experiments constitutes a fundamental part of the scientific method in order to determine the reliability of results. Replication also means that results remain falsifiable. However, the reasons for, and forms of, replication shift depending on the purpose.

Replication means only that an investigator repeats an experiment. In a direct replication, the experimenter tries very hard to reproduce closely as many elements of the original experiment as possible. Similar results typically confirm the reliability of the findings. These kinds of replications are unusual, however. More common is a replication of some elements of the original experiment coupled with some kind of extension into a new and different aspect of the original work. Typically, this occurs when some aspect of the original experiment stimulates some additional hypotheses about the phenomenon under investigation.

Another type of repetition takes the form of systematic replication. In this situation, an experimenter systematically varies some aspect of the original experiment. Most commonly, this takes places to clarify some unexpected or unexplained aspects of the original experiment or to seek some additional information about some previously unconsidered feature of the original study. This can occur, for example, when a new alternative explanation, which did not occur to anyone beforehand, presents itself after the first experiment is complete. Even though it can seem time-consuming and expensive at the time, pilot testing almost always ends up saving time, money, and enormous amounts of aggravation by helping to reduce these kinds of last-minute complications. Sometimes, further experimental replications are planned from the outset because many variables of interest exist, but any one experiment that includes every factor would be too complex or confusing. As a result, a sequence of experiments may be planned in order to address each variable systematically in relation to other variables of interest.

Cross-cultural replications no doubt present the most difficult challenge to experimenters. The difficulty with cross-cultural replications lies in the fact that exact replications do not always translate directly into another culture, either linguistically or socially. Although cross-cultural work is becoming increasingly important and common, it can be difficult to translate stimulus materials from one culture to another without introducing tremendous variations. Because subjects in different cultures may not interpret materials the same way, identical manipulations may prove meaningless because experimenters cannot assume that what would constitute, say, self-determination in the United States would mean the same thing to the Kurds in northern Iraq and southern Turkey. However, changing experimental materials, even with simple language translations, can profoundly alter the experimental question, technique, and findings. The question becomes: are differences found true differences—do they result from different interpretations of the same materials, the same interpretation of different materials, or, most likely, an entirely different understanding of the meaning and purpose of experimentation itself?

This does not mean that cross-cultural research should not be pursued. Rather, experimentalists should remain cautious in designing materials. They should try as best as possible to ensure that materials used in different cultures stay conceptually similar in terms of the perspective of the subjects themselves. The subjects' experience should be as similar as possible, even if the stimulus materials differ somewhat. Furthermore, cross-cultural research might benefit from the knowledge of comparativists who can help translate materials across cultural boundaries in conceptually similar ways. Finally, experimentalists can feel more confident about their results to the extent that they can replicate their studies both within and across different cultures. Similar results from different studies in the same culture add credibility to the findings, as do consistent cross-cultural differences across experiments. Wide variation in results may indicate that the differences in materials and techniques simply overwhelm any true differences that might exist.

Subjectivity in Design

The best and most clever experimentalists put a lot of time and energy into designing successful experiments.

At least two factors really enhance the ability of an experimentalist to design experiments of high quality and impact. First, strong experimentalists do their best to put themselves in the place of their subjects. They try to imagine what it would be like to enter their experimental condition blind, for the first time, without a clear sense of the purpose or the working hypothesis. In undertaking this fantasy, it can be helpful to assume that although subjects may be cooperative and want to help, they will nonetheless most probably be trying to figure out what the experimenter wants. A further step in this process involves careful debriefing of subjects after early or pilot testing. They should be asked what they experienced, what made sense to them, and what was confusing. It should be ascertained whether they were able to determine the purpose, if they were not told outright, or, if not, was there any pattern to what they thought was going on that differed from the real intention of the experiment?

A second way to help improve experimental design is to try to imagine how a different potential pattern of responses might appear. If the results were not what was wanted or expected, why might that be the case? What other potential patterns might emerge? How can new tests be designed to examine these alternative hypotheses? Being able to anticipate alternatives prior to actual large-scale testing can really help clarify and improve experimental designs beforehand.

Nonexperimental Alternatives

Why?

In many cases, experiments may not be the optimal form of investigation in political science. There may be other forms of inquiry that are better suited to the problem under investigation. However, when this happens, there may be other forms of nonexperimental research that nonetheless remain related to experimental work that might be worth considering.

There are several reasons that researchers might want to seek nonexperimental alternatives to experimental work. The first and most important lies in the fact that many questions of interest are not causal questions. For example, in trying to predict the outcome of a particular election, pollsters may not need to know why certain people vote in particular ways; they just want to be able to survey people in such a way as to obtain an accurate prediction. Other issues that are important to political scientists also fall outside the causal realm. For example, sometimes investigators merely want to demonstrate that a particular phenomenon exists, such as incipient democracy in a formerly communist country.

Second, there are many situations in which experimental work would be impossible to conduct or unethical to perform and thus a researcher will look to alternative methods. Sometimes it is simply impossible to impose the variable of interest on people randomly, as it would be with race or sex. Other times, it would be immoral and unethical to do so. For example, no one would want to start a war or induce a famine or plague in order to examine the effect of these phenomena on economic structures. People can study these things after a naturally occurring event, of course, but, again, such work will not constitute experimental work.

Finally, nonexperimental work can supplement experimental work and vice versa. In this way, nonexperimental work does not constitute a substitute but rather an addition to experimental work. This occurs frequently in behavioral economics, for instance, when formal models are tested with experiments and then further refined. There is no reason that similar kinds of interplay cannot take place between game theoretic models in political science and experimental validation and refinement of such models.

Correlational Work

Correlational work does not involve the administration of any experimental treatment manipulation or condition. As noted previously, correlational work can offer useful, interesting, and important hypotheses about the relationship between variables, but it cannot demonstrate causality. Partly this results from the possibility of a third spurious cause influencing both factors. On the other hand, correlational work can establish that no causal relationship exists. If there is no correlation between variables, there is no causation. Occasionally, some very complicated relationship that depends on several mediating factors may exist, but at least a direct or simple causal relationship is ruled out if no correlation exists. In other words, it cannot prove, but it can disprove, a causal relationship between variables.

A second problem with correlational work results from confusion about directionality. In correlational work, it can be difficult to determine what the cause is and what the effect is in many circumstances. Some techniques that seek to partially ameliorate the problem of directionality exist. The cross-lagged panel technique collects correlational data on two separate occasions. Thus, in other words, investigators obtain information on variables 1 and 2 at times 1 and 2. By looking at the same variables in the same populations over time, some element of directionality might be illuminated.

Pseudo-Experimental Designs

Pseudo-experimental designs represent nonexperimental designs in which the investigator nonetheless maintains some control over the manipulation and the collection of data. In other words, an investigator does create and administer an independent variable to subjects and then measures its effect on some dependent variable of interest. However, because it is either not possible or not desirable to have a control group, proper comparisons across conditions are not possible. Without such appropriate comparison groups, any one of a wide array of factors could have led to the observed results. Because of this, researchers are not able to fully determine the effects of their intervention.

Several types of pseudo-experimental designs exist. The one-shot case study design, often referred to as the posttest-only design, examines a single group on a single occasion. These kind of tests appear common after particular disasters, in order to examine their effects on a particular population. Such tests might be conducted after an earthquake, a terrorist event such as 9/11, or other man-made disasters such as the explosion of the space shuttle *Columbia*.

Other types of pseudo-experimental designs include one-group pretest–posttest design studies that examine a group of people both before and after a particular event. As Campbell and Stanley warn, the trouble with this design is that it still poses a number of threats to the internal validity of the study, including problems presented by preexisting history, maturation, testing, instrumentation, and mortality. The static group comparison design constitutes a final type of pseudo-experimental design. In this design, researchers compare two different groups on the same variables at the same time. This design also poses selection threats to the internal validity of the study.

Quasi-Experimental Designs

A quasi-experiment allows an investigator to assign treatment conditions to subjects and measure particular outcomes, but the researcher either does not or cannot assign subjects randomly to those conditions. To be clear, in pseudo-experimental design, the study lacks a control condition, whereas in quasi-experimental design, the researcher does not or cannot assign subjects to treatment conditions at random. This feature actually makes quasi-experiments much easier to use and administer in field and applied settings outside of the laboratory. However, what is gained in flexibility and external validity may be lost in being able to make unequivocal arguments about causality. However, quasi-experiments do allow scholars to make some causal inferences and interpretations, just not fully dependable arguments about causality.

In general, two types of quasi-experimental designs predominate: the interrupted time series design and the nonequivalent control group design. In the former, a within-subjects design is employed to examine the effects of particular independent variables on the same group of subjects over time. Typically, subjects are measured both before and after some kind of experimental treatment is administered. In the latter, a between-subjects design is invoked to measure the impact of the independent variable on different groups of subjects. What remains common to both types of quasi-experiments is the fact that investigators do not or cannot assign subjects to treatment condition at random.

Field Experiments

Field experiments are those that take place outside a laboratory, in a real-world setting. Goznell published the first field experiment in political science in the *American Political Science Review* in 1927. In conducting a field experiment, an investigator typically sacrifices control in order to achieve increased generalizability. In psychology, nonexperimental field testing early in a research program often helps generate novel hypotheses. Once these ideas are tested and refined in laboratory settings, psychologists often then return to field testing to validate their findings. In this way, field studies can prove extremely helpful in specifying the level of generalizability of laboratory results to the real world.

Two important points should be made about field experiments. First, successful field experiments rarely constitute a simple transfer of a laboratory study to a field setting. Investigators have less control in the field; they cannot always control the nature of the treatment, the comparability of subjects, or the impact of unplanned, extraneous factors on outcomes of interest. Most importantly, often subjects cannot be assigned to treatment conditions at random. Second, results from a single field study, no matter how large the population, can rarely be taken on their own, because there are often so many extraneous and potentially confounding factors occurring during the completion of the field study. Figuring out what is actually causing the outcome of interest can be challenging. Such findings typically need to be interpreted within the context of similar studies conducted using other formats, including laboratory experiments, interviews, surveys, or other methods. Results that demonstrate convergent findings across methods allow for greater confidence in accuracy.

Despite these concerns, field experiments can prove quite beneficial for a variety of reasons. Often, behaviors of interest cannot be induced in a laboratory, but can easily be observed in the real world. In addition, experimental findings that replicate in the field increase people's sense of confidence in the generalizability of the results. Obviously, trade-offs between laboratory and field experiments exist and the nature of the research question of interest often determines the appropriate setting for a study.

Rather than creating a setting as experimenters do in a laboratory setting, those who conduct field experiments seek to find the best environment in which to examine their issue of concern. Experimenters should seek out settings that possess the variables and relationships of interest, but as few extraneous factors as possible. Effective field experiments usually share certain characteristics. Settings should involve events or processes that subjects find meaningful and impactful. Experimenters should be able to intervene in some way to test and measure the phenomenon of interest. These settings should contain the elements of coherence, simplicity, and control to the greatest extent possible. Coherence requires that experiments be defined and limited to a specific time and place or event. Focusing on a single main event often increases the likelihood that the setting is both coherent and as simple as possible; in this way, the impact of extraneous factors can be reduced. Field experimenters can often benefit by using a naturally occurring event as a variable of interest. This can happen, for example, by taking advantage of a change in the law to examine before-and-after effects of processes such as segregation, busing, and affirmative action. Often, field researchers who are not able to assign subjects to condition at random can select comparable control groups to try to extricate the impact of extraneous factors on outcomes. When this occurs, investigators need to be careful to ensure the comparability of the control and the treatment groups.

A critical factor to remember in field experiments is that if the experimenter is not able to intervene in such a way as to assign subjects randomly to conditions, then the study is no longer a true experiment, but rather a field study. In these cases, conclusions about causal relationships cannot be justified and results should be interpreted as suggestive at best.

Experimental Ethics

When conducting any experimental work, ethics remain an important consideration. The U.S. Department of Health and Human Services imposes certain guidelines on the ethical treatment of human subjects. Most universities have human subjects institutional review boards to oversee the administration and implementation of these guidelines. These guidelines encompass four aspects.

First, subjects must be able to give their informed consent before participating in an experiment. Experimenters should provide subjects with a clearly written, simple statement explaining the potential risks and expected gains from their participation in the experiment. They should be told that they can stop their participation at any time without penalty. And they should be given contact information about who to go to in case they have any concerns about the ethics of experiments in which they participate.

Second, experimenters are required to take every reasonable precaution to avoid harm or risk to their subjects as a result of their participation. Third, experimenters should provide a debriefing opportunity to all subjects, in which they are told as much as possible about the experiment in which they just participated. In particular, subjects should be told that their information will be kept confidential and that no identifying information will be released without their prior written consent. Often, subjects are told how they can receive copies of the results at the conclusion of the experiment if they are interested in doing so.

Finally, the issue of deception remains a controversial topic. Psychologists continue to employ deception more than behavioral economists. Deception may prove necessary in those instances in which a subject's prior knowledge of the working hypotheses would influence his or her behavior in systematic or inauthentic ways. This bias can hinder the discovery of important processes and dynamics. However, when investigators employ deceptive techniques, institutional review boards remain particularly vigilant to ensure that the use and value of such experiments are carefully monitored.

Conclusion

Experiments provide a valuable tool for the measurement of social variables and processes. They provide unequaled purchase on causal inference through experimental control and the random assignment of subjects to treatment conditions. And careful design can ensure the ethical treatment of subjects during the experimental process, so that the benefits of discovery continue to outweigh the risks posed to subjects.

Experiments provide an unparalleled ability to clarify causality in ways that can reduce confusion about important processes and relationships. By showing the true direction of the casual link, human beings can learn something important about themselves, and possibly, take steps to change environments and institutions that can cause ill. In his famous experiment, Stanley Milgram attempted to try to understand what it was about the German national character that would lead ordinary citizens to become complicit in the atrocities surrounding the Holocaust. Before he tested his hypotheses about the nature of obedience to authority in Germany and Japan, where he expected high levels of compliance, he ran his control group of presumed individualist Americans at Yale. All the experts agreed that less than 1% of subjects would shocks "learners" to their assumed death. Yet, the majority of subjects did so. As the films show, these subjects were not obvious sadists nor did they delight in being cruel to their fellow man. They did not easily or readily comply; they argued, cried, walked around the room, tried to talk their way out of the situation, and were inordinately relieved when they found out their partner was not dead, but they obeyed nonetheless. After Milgram's experimental findings, those observers who discarded Nazi defenses that claimed that they were "just following orders" were forced to confront results that proved that the power of the situation could overcome personal dispositions. One may not be comfortable knowing this, but this insight teaches one the importance of deviance when morality is compromised, the critical significance of opposition to inappropriate authority, and the transcendent knowledge that removing oneself from the situation can provide the best defense against self-destruction.

See Also the Following Articles

Correlations • Cross-Cultural Data Applicability and Comparisons • Experiments, Overview • Explore, Explain, Design • Field Experimentation • Political Science • Quasi-Experiment

Further Reading

Aronson, E., Ellsworth, P., Carlsmith, J. M., and Gonzales, M. (1990). *Methods of Research in Social Psychology.* McGraw-Hill, New York.

Brody, R., and Brownstein, C. (1975). Experimentation and simulation. In *Handbook of Political Science* (F. Greenstein and N. Polsby, eds.), Vol. 7, pp. 211–263. Addison-Wesley, Reading, MA.

Campbell, D., and Stanley, J. (1966). *Experimental and Quasi-Experimental Designs for Research.* Rand McNally, Chicago, IL.

Greenwald, A. (1976). Within-subjects design: To use or not to use? *Psychol. Bull.* **82,** 1–20.

Iyengar, S., and McGuire, W. *Explorations in Political Psychology*. Duke University Press, Durham, NC.

Kagel, J., and Roth, A. (1995). *Handbook of Experimental Economics.* Princeton University Press, Princeton, NJ.

Kinder, D., and Palfrey, T. (1992). *Foundations of an Experimental Political Science.* University of Michigan Press, Ann Arbor, MI.

McConahay, J. (1973). Experimental research. In *Handbook of Political Psychology* (J. Knudson, ed.), pp. 356–382. Jossey-Bass, San Francisco, CA.

McDermott, R. (2002). Experimental methodology in political science. *Polit. Anal.* **10,** 325–342.

McDermott, R. (2002). Experimental methods in political science. *Annu. Rev. Polit. Sci.* **5,** 31–61.

McGraw, K. (1996). Political methodology: Research design and experimental methods. In *A New Handbook of Political Science* (R. Goodin and H. Klingeman, eds.), pp. 769–786. Oxford University Press, Oxford, UK.

McGraw, K., and Hoekstra, V. (1994). Experimentation in political science: Historical trends and future directions. *Res. Micropolit.* **4,** 3–29.

Palfrey, T. (1991). *Laboratory Research in Political Economy.* University of Michigan Press, Ann Arbor, MI.

Plott, C. (1979). The application of laboratory experimental methods to public choice. In *The Application of Laboratory Experimental Methods to Public Choice* (C. Russell, ed.), pp. 14–52. Johns Hopkins Press, Baltimore, MD.

Sniderman, P., Brody, R., and Tetlock, P. (1991). *Reasoning and Choice: Explorations in Political Psychology.* Cambridge University Press, New York.

Underwood, B. (1957). *Psychological Research.* Appleton-Century-Crofts, New York.

Experiments, Psychology

Peter Y. Chen
Colorado State University, Fort Collins, Colorado, USA

Autumn D. Krauss
Colorado State University, Fort Collins, Colorado, USA

Glossary

construct validity Inferences about the extent to which operations of variables are similar to their correspondent constructs.

dependent variables Those variables that are affected by the independent variables.

external validity Inferences about the extent to which a causal relationship found in an experiment generalizes across people, settings, time, etc.

extraneous variables Nuisance variables that remain uncontrolled and are confounded with either the independent or dependent variables.

independent variables Presumed causal variables that are deliberately manipulated by experimenters.

internal validity Inferences about the extent to which the observed causal relationship between an independent and a dependent variable is accurate.

random assignment A process to allow all participants an equal chance of being selected and/or placed in experimental conditions.

reliability Consistent responses to a measure.

variables Quantitative or qualitative attributes of an object of interest.

An array of methods, including observation, interview, survey, quasi-experiment, field experiment, and laboratory experiment, can be utilized to advance understanding of human behavior. Among all of these, laboratory and some field experiments are by far the most robust methods when examining the causes and effects of psychological constructs. Their unique strength is attributed to the fact that "causes" are deliberately manipulated and their subsequent "effects" are systematically observed in a highly controlled setting, particularly for the laboratory experiment.

Survey of Psychological Experiments

Virtually every psychological discipline uses laboratory experiments to investigate hypotheses derived from theory or reasoning. For example, some investigators have examined how different types of cognitive processing tasks activate different areas of the brain. By manipulating the type of cognitive processing task (such as repeating presented words aloud or generating a use for each of the same words), it has been substantiated that different areas of the brain are activated.

In another laboratory experiment that simulated an organization, the effects of belief about decision-making ability on multiple performance measures were investigated. While participants played the roles of managers, researchers manipulated beliefs about decision-making ability by including information in the instructions for the task that described the ability either as a stable trait or as an acquirable skill. Compared to participants who believed that decision-making ability was a stable trait, those who received information conveying that decision-making ability was an acquirable skill perceived higher levels of self-efficacy throughout the simulation, set increasingly difficult organizational goals, and subsequently achieved higher levels of productivity.

Considerable research in psychology has examined eyewitness testimony and the factors that can affect the recall of events. Evidence has shown that people are less able to discriminate between accurate event details and misleading information when the misleading information is presented shortly after the actual event, compared to when it is presented a considerable time after the event. In one of the experimental conditions, participants listened to a postevent narrative immediately following a sequence of slides depicting an event. Another group of participants listened to the same postevent narrative 48 hours after watching the slide sequence. After the participants were informed that the postevent narrative contained some inaccurate information, they then completed a memory test containing questions about the event described on the slides. Participants' memory test scores in the delayed-narrative condition outperformed those in the immediate-narrative condition.

Experiments are also the common method to investigate the beneficial effects of interventions on psychological disorders. In a study that examined the effects of a treatment program for people checked into substance-abuse facilities, participants either received the treatment of interest or a placebo control treatment. The former treatment consisted of a coping-skills training program specifically designed to aide cocaine users in coping with the emotions they experience during abstinence; the latter consisted of a meditation–relaxation training program that had no history of providing therapeutic effects for cocaine abusers. Participants receiving the treatment reported using cocaine on significantly fewer days for the first 6 months, compared to those who received the placebo treatment; however, the treatment effect diminished when the participants were retested 12 months after the interventions.

Basic Components in Psychological Experiments

Although the topics of the preceding examples are diverse, the basic structures of the experiments are similar. Each experimental structure contains three critical elements: variables of interest, control, and measurement. A thorough understanding of these elements and other related concepts, such as validity, is paramount for successfully conducting an experiment.

Variables

A variable represents a quantitative or qualitative attribute of an object of interest. In a psychological experiment, the object can be a person, an animal, a time period, a location, an institution, or almost anything else . There are three types of variables involved in any psychological experiment: independent variables, dependent variables, and extraneous variables.

Independent variables (IVs) generally refer to the presumed causes that are deliberately manipulated by experimenters. Examples of IVs based on the studies surveyed earlier are the type of cognitive processing task, belief about decision-making ability, the timing of the postevent narrative, and the type of treatment. In contrast, dependent variables (DVs) are viewed as outcomes that are affected by the independent variables, such as, respectively, the activated areas of the brain; level of self-efficacy, difficulty of organizational goals set, and amount of productivity; memory test score; and days of cocaine use.

Both IVs and DVs are considered the foci of scientific inquiries. They are equally important, and neither can be overlooked because both variables are attempts to represent correspondent constructs, which are "theoretical constructions, abstractions, aimed at organizing and making sense of our environment." Specifically, independent and dependent variables are merely snapshots of what the causal relationship between the constructs may look like within a theoretical framework. As shown in Fig. 1, an IV (e.g., number of peers present) and a DV (e.g., arguing with people) capture very small fractions of their correspondent constructs, peer pressure and aggression, as shown in paths 1 and 2. By observing changes in the DV after the IV is manipulated by experimenters, the effect of number of peers present on arguing is substantiated (path 3), which allows the inference of the causal relationship between peer pressure and aggression (path 4), assuming all extraneous variables are controlled.

Extraneous variables or nuisance variables are variables that remain uncontrolled and are confounded with either the independent or dependent variables. It is possible that the number of peers present increases the level of anxiety, which in turn affects the extent that participants argue with others, as shown in paths 9 and 10 in Fig. 1. Furthermore, social desirability or other unknown factors might affect whether participants argue with others (as shown in path 8 in Fig. 1). Failure to control extraneous variables results in experimenters being unable to eliminate other equally plausible explanations about why IVs relate to DVs, thus allowing little faith in the internal validity of an experiment. Internal validity refers to inferences about the observed causal relationship between an independent and a dependent variable (path 3 in Fig. 1). The observed relationship is employed to infer the underlying causal relationship between constructs (path 4). Note that a variable can be viewed as an independent or a dependent variable contingent on the theoretical perspective of a study; it can also be considered an extraneous variable that needs to be controlled in another study.

Recognize that it is path 4 rather than path 3 that is interesting to experimenters, although path 4 is almost

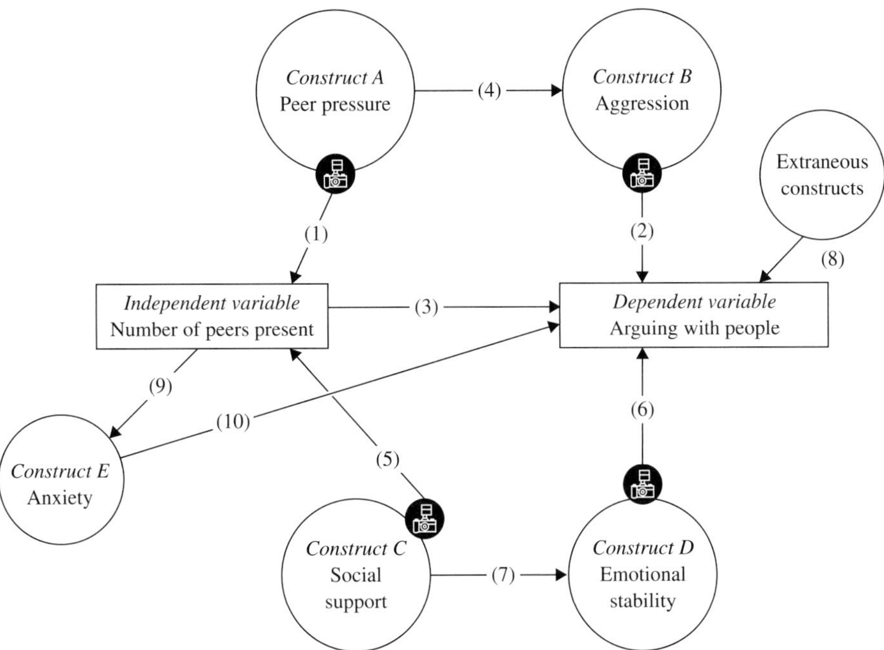

Figure 1 Snapshot of the causal relationship between peer pressure and aggression from an independent variable and a dependent variable.

never observed in psychological experiments. Before experimenters can be certain about the existence of path 4, they need to provide evidence about path 3, which still only serves as a necessary but not sufficient requirement. Three conditions should be considered when evaluating the legitimacy of path 3. First, the IV must precede the DV in time. Second, the IV must relate to the DV. Finally, no extraneous variables can cause these two variables to covary. The former two conditions are relatively easy to meet by means of research designs as well as statistical analyses. It is the violation of the last condition that presents the greatest threat to the internal validity of an experiment.

Various factors may directly challenge the veracity of path 3. These factors, also referred to as threats to internal validity, include selection, history, and maturation. For instance, selection bias occurs when participants in different experimental conditions are dissimilar at the beginning of the experiment. History refers to an external event (e.g., tragedy of September 11, 2001) occurring during the period of experimentation and potentially altering the DV. In contrast to history, maturation threatens internal validity because some internal changes (e.g., more experience) occur during the period of experimentation. The preceding examples clearly show that a DV can be changed even in the absence of any effects caused by the IV. To reduce threats to the internal validity of an experiment, it is imperative that experimenters exercise rigorous experimental controls and use adequate research designs.

Experimental Controls

An experiment conducted without three types of control (i.e., manipulation, elimination or inclusion, and randomization) is technically not considered a true experiment. Although statistical control is widely practiced in data analysis, it should not be confused with the concept of experimental control. Statistical control is an application of statistical techniques (e.g., analysis of covariance or hierarchical regression analysis) to remove the effects of presumed extraneous variables. It is a type of control that is performed at the stage of data analysis.

Manipulation

Control by manipulation refers to the procedure when researchers systematically change the properties of IVs (e.g., different types of cognitive processing tasks presented to participants, as described earlier) in a consistent and standardized manner. Consistency and standardization are met when the properties of the IV (e.g., strength of the manipulation) are identical for participants within the same experimental condition and different across experimental conditions. It is safe to say that definite causal conclusions cannot be made without a systematic manipulation, although a systematic manipulation does not necessarily guarantee causation. There are several critical points regarding manipulation.

First, to qualify as a true experiment, the properties of an independent variable need to be deliberately changed by experimenters. The common pitfall is to treat characteristics of participants, such as different types of patients (e.g., eating disorder or insomnia) or different levels of psychological attributes (e.g., high or low anxiety), physical characteristics (e.g., old or young), or employment status (e.g., unemployed, temporary workers, or permanent workers) as "independent variables." These variables are merely characteristics of participants and cannot be deliberately influenced by experimenters for practical as well as ethical reasons. For instance, it has been reported that patients with a somatic disorder are characterized by significantly higher levels of heart rate compared to symptom-free participants. Although differences of heart rate can be clearly demonstrated, it would be erroneous to conclude that the somatic disorder increases the heart rate, because the higher heart rate among somatic disorder patients may be attributed to numerous unknown variables such as type of diet, hours of sleep, or amount of air inhaled, which were not manipulated (or controlled).

Second, operationalization may differ for the same construct or be similar for different constructs. Specifically, different researchers may use different manipulation procedures to operationalize the same construct. To study the effects of social exclusion on aggressive behavior, social exclusion has been manipulated by providing participants with bogus feedback on a personality test, specifically telling them that they would end up alone in life. In another experiment also designed to manipulate social exclusion, participants were first asked to choose two people they would most like to work with from a group of four to six people. Participants in the social exclusion condition were told "no one chose you as someone they wanted to work with."

On the other hand, different researchers might use similar manipulation procedures to operationalize two distinct constructs. For instance, in one study it was hypothesized that people perceive a consistency between a negotiator stereotype (e.g., assertive, rational, decisive, constructive, or intelligent) and the classic gender stereotype. To induce the gender stereotype about negotiation ability, participants were told that "this negotiation . . . serves as a helpful diagnostic tool for students to assess their negotiating skills at the beginning of the course. We have selected this particular negotiation for you to complete because it is an extremely challenging one for novice negotiators. As such, it is an accurate gauge of your genuine negotiating abilities and limitations. In the past, we have found that how untrained students do on this negotiation is particularly diagnostic of their performance in negotiation courses and real-world negotiations. Because this negotiation is diagnostic of your ability, you should use this negotiation as a learning tool." Surprisingly, a somewhat similar manipulation procedure was used to manipulate the belief about decision-making ability as a stable trait. In this case, participants were told that "decision making reflects the basic cognitive capabilities that people possess. The higher their underlying cognitive-processing capacities, the better is their decision making . . . the simulation provided a vehicle for gauging the underlying cognitive capacities." Although the statements used in the two studies are not literally the same, the underlying meanings are arguably similar because both statements attempt to manipulate participants' beliefs that their abilities (in negotiating or decision making) are diagnosed and gauged, respectively.

The importance of examining both the intended and the unintended effects of a manipulation has also been emphasized. The accuracy of the operationalization of a variable in representing the correspondent construct, referred to as construct validity, is the cornerstone of science and practice. Unlike physical attributes such as height, psychological constructs such as social exclusion are difficult to operationalize and manipulate. Incidentally, an IV may reflect a snapshot of not only the construct of interest, but also of other constructs. For example, "number of peers present" may reflect peer pressure and also capture a portion of social support (path 5), and "arguing with people" may capture aggression and a portion of emotional stability (path 6). Therefore, even if there is strong evidence supporting path 3, experimenters cannot be sure whether path 3 represents the causal relationship of path 4 or path 7.

Including a manipulation check to validate the manipulation of social exclusion (e.g., Do participants feel that they are excluded? Do participants care about being excluded?) could have ruled out other constructs that might be responsible for the occurrence of path 3, making it possible to conclude the causal relationship of path 4 with more confidence.

Elimination or Inclusion

To control directly the extraneous variables that are suspected to be confounded with the manipulation effect, researchers can plan to eliminate or include extraneous variables in an experiment. Control by elimination means that experimenters remove the suspected extraneous variables by holding them constant across all experimental conditions. In the treatments-effect study described earlier, researchers examined the effects of a treatment program for people checked into substance-abuse facilities. If the researchers suspected that the gender of the therapist might be confounded with the effects of the treatment, they could use the same male (or female) therapist in both treatment conditions. As a result, any potential effect caused by the gender of the therapist is converted to a constant in both conditions.

In contrast to control by elimination, researchers can include the suspected extraneous variables in an experiment. If researchers suspect the gender of the therapist is an extraneous variable, they can include the gender of the therapist as an additional independent variable. Specifically, participants can be assigned to one of four experimental conditions: a treatment with a male therapist, a treatment with a female therapist, a placebo control with a male therapist, and a placebo control with a female therapist. This experimental design enables consideration of the effect of the treatment, the effect of the therapist's gender, and the interaction of both independent variables.

Random Assignment

Practically speaking, not all extraneous variables can be directly controlled by elimination or inclusion. It is random assignment that indirectly controls extraneous variables. Random assignment refers to a process by which all participants have an equal chance of being selected and/or placed in experimental conditions. This randomization process works under the assumption that the threats of extraneous variables are equally distributed over all experimental conditions in the long run, thereby reducing the likelihood that IVs are confounded with extraneous variables. As a result of random assignment, changes in a DV can be attributed to variations in an IV. There is considerable evidence that nonrandom assignment and random assignment often yield different results. In practice, researchers can accomplish random assignment by using random number tables provided by most statistics books, or by using statistical software produced by various companies (e.g., by SPSS Inc., Minitab Inc., and SAS Institute Inc.) to generate random numbers.

Random assignment should not be confused with random selection or random sampling. In contrast to random assignment, which facilitates causal inferences by equating participants in all experimental conditions, random selection is a process to select randomly a sample of participants from a population of interest as a way to ensure that findings from the sample can be generalized to the population. Although researchers can use various probability sampling strategies such as systematic sampling to select a sample from a population, most published psychological experiments rely on nonprobability or convenience samples. Therefore, results of an experiment using random assignment based on a convenience sample may or may not be similar to those found for another group of participants who are randomly selected from the population.

The distinction between the process of random assignment and the outcome of random assignment is also very important, although it is often overlooked or misunderstood. The process of random assignment, in theory, equates participants across experimental conditions prior to any manipulations of IVs. In other words, randomly assigned participants are expected to be equal on every variable across all conditions in the long run. However, the actual outcome of random assignment does not often reflect the expected result. Imagine tossing 100 coins; it rarely results in 50 heads.

Measurement

As mentioned earlier, adequate construct validity is vital for both IVs and DVs, though the construct validity of the DV is often neglected. Having a valid DV, which is often assessed by an instrument (e.g., measures or records) in psychological experiments, allows the intended inference about a construct to be made, compared to other plausible inferences (path 2 vs. path 6 in Fig. 1).

The major factors that threaten the construct validity of independent and/or dependent variables have been delineated, including inadequate explication of the construct, construct confounds, mono-operation bias, monomethod bias, reactivity to the experimental situation, experimenter expectancies, and resentful demoralization. For instance, mono-operation bias and monomethod bias are biases that arise when only one operationalization or one method is used to assess independent or dependent variables. If results are similar when the same construct is operationalized differently or measured by different methods, greater confidence about construct validity is obtained.

Contrary to the factors that may threaten construct validity, other characteristics, such as reliability, may provide evidence to support the construct validity of both the IV and the DV. Reliability is a necessary piece of this type of evidence, and it is an indication of the relative amount of random fluctuation of individual responses on the measure. A measure cannot be valid if it is not reliable, although a reliable measure does not ensure validity. Suppose that aggression in Fig. 1 was not assessed by the amount of arguing with others but instead by a questionnaire containing several queries about the participant's desire to quarrel and fight with others. If this measure possessed low reliability, it would imply that participants' responses to the items would be inconsistent. Inconsistent responses can be attributed to one or more sources of measurement error, such as the items on the measure, the time or location of administration, and the motivation or fatigue of the participants. The magnitude of these measurement errors can be evaluated by different types of reliability indices, including test/retest reliability, internal consistency, alternate form reliability, intercoder (or interrater) reliability, or generalizability coefficients.

Experimental Designs

In this section, the discussion centers on five experimental designs, and their variations, that are often utilized in psychological research. These designs can be used either in a laboratory or in the field. The laboratory setting tends to be more artificial and the phenomenon of interest tends to be more contrived in comparison with the field setting. The advantage of conducting an experiment in a laboratory over a field setting is the ability to control more extraneous variables. However, laboratory experiments possess less mundane and experimental realism than do field experiments. Mundane realism refers to the extent to which independent variables manipulated in an experiment resemble reality, and experimental realism refers to the extent to which the participants both believe and are affected by the experimental manipulation.

To illustrate the following designs, conventional terminology and notations are used. Specifically, O stands for one or more than one quantitative observations or outcome measures pertaining to the DV, X represents the manipulation of an IV (i.e., treatment), and R indicates that the random assignment approach is employed. Several one-group designs, such as the one-group posttest-only (X O) or one-group pretest–posttest (O_{pre} X O_{post}), are often used for practical reasons. However, these designs suffer from many threats to internal validity. For instance, the absence of a pretest in the one-group posttest-only design prevents researchers from determining if changes have occurred. Similarly, the absence of a control group in the one-group pretest–posttest design prevents researchers from stating if changes between O_{pre} and O_{post} are a result of the independent variable. In the next section, the focus is on stronger designs that include pretests, control groups, and random assignment.

Basic Design

The basic design, also referred to as a treatment–control posttest design, consists of two groups, a treatment group and a control group. Only participants in the treatment group receive a manipulation. Although the control group generally receives no manipulation, other types of control groups (e.g., placebo control or wait-list control) receive manipulations for either ethical or practical reasons. An assessment of dependent variables from both groups will be conducted after an IV is manipulated. Part of the treatments-effect study described earlier used the basic design. This design can be depicted as having the following structure:

R	X	O	Treatment group
R		O	Control group

There are other variations of the basic design:

R	X_1	O	(Variant 1.1)
R	X_n	O	

or

R	X_1	O	
R	X_n	O	(Variant 1.2)
R		O	

Variant 1.1 consists of multiple treatment groups, and participants in each group receive different treatments from X_1 to X_n. In contrast, variant 1.2 consists of a control group in addition to multiple treatment groups.

Pretest/Posttest Control Group Design

Without having a pretest in the basic design, any results may be tenuous if attrition is a problem. Attrition occurs when participants drop out of an experiment or fail to complete outcome measures. Without the pretest information, experimenters are not able to determine if those who drop out are different from those who complete the experiment. Furthermore, the pretest information can be used to examine if all groups are similar initially, which should be the case if random assignment is employed. Researchers are also able to examine if there are differences between scores on the pretest and posttest measures. Note that although the following example includes the pretest (O_{pre}) after random assignment occurs, another potential design structure involves the pretest administration before random assignment.

R	O_{pre}	X	O_{post}
R	O_{pre}		O_{post}

In general, the measures at pretest (O_{pre}) and posttest (O_{post}) should be identical. For practical reasons, the measures are sometimes different. Assuming both measures assess the same underlying construct (e.g., cognitive ability), the underlying construct (or latent trait) of each participant can be estimated from both pretest and posttest measures according to item response theory (IRT). By substituting the pretest and posttest scores with the correspondent latent trait scores, the newly calibrated O_{pre} and O_{post} become identical.

There are two variations of the pretest/posttest control group design; once again, these designs may be altered by administering the pretest before conducting random assignment:

R	O_{pre}	X_1	O_{post}	(Variant 2.1)
R	O_{pret}	X_n	O_{post}	

or

R	O_{pre}	X_1	O_{post}	
R	O_{pre}	X_n	O_{post}	(Variant 2.2)
R	O_{pre}		O_{post}	

Factorial Design

When describing manipulation by inclusion, it was shown that more than one independent variable can be included in an experiment. Such a design is referred to as a factorial design, in which IVs are labeled as factors (e.g., treatment and gender of therapists), and each factor has at least two levels (e.g., types of treatments or male and female therapists). The structure of the design varies contingent on the number of factors and the number of levels within each factor. The number of experimental conditions in the factorial design is equal to the product of the number of levels of each factor, although experimenters can employ fewer conditions if some have no theoretical interest or are difficult to implement. If there are four factors and two levels within each factor, the number of experimental conditions is 16 ($2 \times 2 \times 2 \times 2$).

The simplest structure can be shown to consist of four experimental conditions created by two factors (A and B) and two levels (1 and 2) within each factor. Based on the combination of factors and levels, participants in the experiment receive one of four treatments: X_{A1B1}, X_{A1B2}, X_{A2B1}, or X_{A2B2}:

R	X_{A1B1}	O
R	X_{A1B2}	O
R	X_{A2B1}	O
R	X_{A2B2}	O

Variations of the design can include the addition of a pretest measure after random assignment, such as shown below, or a pretest measure before random assignment (not depicted):

R	O_{pre}	X_{A1B1}	O_{post}	
R	O_{pre}	X_{A1B2}	O_{post}	(Variant 3.1)
R	O_{pre}	X_{A2B1}	O_{post}	
R	O_{pre}	X_{A2B2}	O_{post}	

One major advantage of the factorial design is to examine the interactive effect of the independent variables. It is likely that neither independent variable solely causes a change in the dependent variable; however, the dependent variable is affected when both independent variables are jointly manipulated.

Solomon Four-Group Design

The Solomon four-group design is a combination of the basic design and the pretest/posttest control group design. The design is specifically useful to control for instrument reactivity, a threat to internal validity that cannot be eliminated by the aforementioned designs. Instrument reactivity refers to when participants react to pretest measures, which subsequently distorts their performance on posttest measures. It occurs if the pretest measure influences participants' subsequent responses on the posttest measure (i.e., a main effect of the pretest measure), or the pretest measure interacts with the treatment and then influences participants' responses on the posttest measure (i.e., an interaction effect). The structure of the design is depicted as follows:

R	O_{pre}	X	O_{post}	Group 1
R		X	O	Group 2
R	O_{pre}		O_{post}	Group 3
R			O	Group 4

According to the Solomon four-group design, the mean of group 1 and group 3 on the pretest measure, assuming they are equal, enables researchers to estimate the pretest performance of group 2 and group 4. Furthermore, researchers can examine the change of the posttest performance in group 2 by comparing it to the mean of the pretest measure obtained from groups 1 and 3. Comparisons on the posttest measure between group 1 and group 2 as well as between group 3 and group 4 allow researchers to examine the main effect of the pretest measure. Interactions between the pretest measure and the experimental treatment can be investigated by the divergence between two sets of differences on the posttest measure (group 1 vs. group 2 and group 3 vs. group 4). Assuming there is a positive effect from the treatment (i.e., the posttest measure increases after the treatment), further evidence for the treatment effect exists if (1) the posttest measure in group 1 is higher than the pretest measure in group 1, (2) the posttest measure in group 1 is higher than that in group 3, (3) the posttest measure in group 2 is higher than that in group 4, and (4) the posttest measure in group 2 is higher than that in group 3.

Longitudinal Design

Compared to the prior designs, a longitudinal design provides stronger evidence for internal validity. Recall from the substance-abuse study that participants receiving the treatment reported using cocaine on significantly fewer days for the first 6 months, as compared to those who received the placebo treatment; however, the treatment effect diminished when the participants were retested 12 months after the interventions. Without the longitudinal design, the lack of a long-term benefit of the treatment would not have been known. The design consists of multiple pretests and posttests over a period of time. The numbers of pretests and posttests do not need to be the same, and generally there are more posttests than pretests. An example of the structure of the longitudinal design is as follows:

$$\begin{array}{llllllll} R & O_{pre} & O_{pre} & X & O_{post} & O_{post} & O_{post} & O_{post} \\ R & O_{pre} & O_{pre} & & O_{post} & O_{post} & O_{post} & O_{post} \end{array}$$

Practical constraints are often encountered when attempting to implement a study using a longitudinal design. For instance, attrition is common in longitudinal designs, so data for some participants are often incomplete. Furthermore, it is not clear from a theoretical viewpoint how long a longitudinal design should be conducted; as such, requiring participant involvement for an extended period of time may pose ethical concerns.

Criteria to Evaluate a Psychological Experiment

All of the characteristics of an experiment described herein can be used as criteria to evaluate the findings of a study. Specifically of interest are the reliabilities of the measures, the internal validity, the construct validity, the experimental design, and the external validity. Note the intimate relationships among these criteria. In the case of internal and external validity, it may be necessary to compromise the generalizability of an experiment's results to the world outside the laboratory (external validity) in order to ensure causation with a strong manipulation (internal validity). Realize that although the experiment is a useful tool to further knowledge about human behavior, it is rare that any one experiment can possess all characteristics at optimum levels (e.g., internal validity, construct validity). Therefore, when conducting an experiment, it is appropriate to acknowledge the stronger features of the design (e.g., manipulation and random assignment) and the weaker aspects (e.g., weak experimental realism and mundane realism) so that later experiments can build on the solid components and strengthen the limitations. Experiments can be conceptualized as small pieces of a larger puzzle whereby each study provides a small understanding of a larger overarching human phenomenon. Other designs, such as the field experiment, quasi-experiment, or correlational design, would complement traditional experiments by offering different pieces of the same puzzle.

See Also the Following Articles

Experiments, Overview • Explore, Explain, Design • Longitudinal Cohort Designs • Randomization • Reliability Assessment • Validity Assessment • Validity, Data Sources

Further Reading

Abdullaev, Y. G., and Posner, M. I. (1997). Time course of activating brain areas in generating verbal associations. *Psychol. Sci.* **8,** 56–59.

Aronson, E., Ellsworth, P. C., Carlsmith, J. M., and Gonzales, M. H. (1990). *Methods of Research in Social Psychology,* 2nd Ed. McGraw Hill, New York.

Chen, P. Y., and Krauss, A. D. (2004). Reliability. In *Encyclopedia of Research Methods for the Social Sciences* (M. Lewis-Beck, A. Bryman, and T. F. Liao, eds.). Sage Publ., Newbury Park, California.

Chen, P. Y., and Popovich, P. M. (2002). *Correlation: Parametric and Nonparametric Measures.* Sage Publ., Newbury Park, California.

Hambleton, R. K., Swaminathan, H., and Rogers, H. J. (1991). *Fundamentals of Item Response Theory.* Sage Publ., Newbury Park, California.

Holland, P. W. (1986). Statistics and causal inference. *J. Am. Statist. Assoc.* **81,** 945–960.

Kray, L. J., Thompson, L., and Galinsky, A. (2001). Battle of the sexes: Gender stereotype confirmation and reactance in negotiations. *J. Personal. Social Psychol.* **80,** 942–958.

Lindsay, D. S. (1990). Misleading suggestions can impair eyewitnesses' ability to remember event details. *J. Exp. Psychol. Learn. Mem. Cognit.* **16,** 1077–1083.

Lyskov, E., Sandstroem, M., and Mild, K. H. (2001). Neurophysiological study of patients with perceived "electrical" hypersensitivity. *Int. J. Psychophysiol.* **42,** 233–241.

Pedhazur, E. J., and Schmelkin, L. P. (1991). *Measurement, Design, and Analysis: An Integrated Approach.* Lawrence Erlbaum, Hillsdale, New Jersey.

Rohsenow, D. J., Monti, P. M., Martin, R. A., Michalec, E., and Abrams, D. B. (2000). Brief coping skills treatment for cocaine abuse: 12-month substance use outcomes. *J. Consult. Clin. Psychol.* **68,** 515–520.

Shadish, W. R., Cook, T. D., and Campbell, D. T. (2002). *Experimental and Quasi-experimental Designs for Generalized Causal Inference.* Houghton Mifflin, Boston.

Shavelson, R. J., and Webb, N. M. (1991). *Generalizability Theory: A Primer.* Sage Publ., Newbury Park, California.

Solomon, R. L., and Lessac, M. S. (1968). A control group design for experimental studies of developmental processes. *Psychol. Bull.* **70,** 145–150.

Twenge, J. M., Baumeister, R. F., Tice, D. M., and Stucke, T. S. (2001). If you can't join them, beat them: Effects of social exclusion on aggressive behavior. *J. Personal. Social Psychol.* **81,** 1058–1069.

Wood, R., and Bandura, A. (1989). Impact of conceptions of ability on self-regulatory mechanisms and complex decision making. *J. Personal. Social Psychol.* **56,** 407–415.

Wortman, P. M. (1992). Lessons from the meta-analysis of quasi-experiments. In *Methodological Issues in Applied Social Psychology* (F. B. Bryant, J. Edwards, R. S. Tindale, E. J. Posavac, L. Heath, E. Henderson, and Y. Suarez-Balcazar, eds.), pp. 65–81. Plenum Press, New York.

Expert Witness Testimony

Richard L. Engstrom
University of New Orleans, New Orleans, Louisiana, USA

Glossary

abuse of discretion The standard that an appellate court uses when reviewing a trial court judge's decision whether to allow a particular expert witness to testify.

Daubert/Kumho Tire test The Supreme Court's guidelines concerning factors to examine in assessing the reliability of expert witness testimony.

ecological fallacy The reliance on aggregate level data to draw inferences about the behavior of individuals.

expert witness Someone qualified by knowledge, skill, training, or education to express opinions about facts in dispute in a case.

general acceptance test The guideline that expert analyses and testimony must be based on principles and practices generally accepted as reliable by others working in the same field.

In court proceedings, an expert witness is distinguished from a fact witness by the latitude with which he or she may express opinions. Although these are sometimes opinions about the causes of things, they are often simply opinions about facts that are crucial to claims made by parties to a case, facts that must be inferred from an examination rather than observed directly. Social scientists testify about numerous issues in courts. Political scientists, for example, are called on to assess the extent to which voting in a particular political jurisdiction is racially polarized. Sociologists may be questioned about the extent to which the locations of hazardous waste facilities reflect environmental discrimination against minority groups. And geographers may be asked to assess the extent to which legislative districts are compact. The adversarial environment within which expert witness testimony occurs often results in battles over the definition and measurement of social science concepts such as these.

Standards Governing Expert Witness Testimony

The admissibility of expert testimony is governed in federal courts by Rule 702 of the Federal Rules of Evidence (FRE). This rule states:

> *If scientific, technical, or other specialized knowledge will assist the trier of fact to understand the evidence or to determine a fact in issue, a witness qualified as an expert by knowledge, skill, experience, training, or education, may testify thereto in the form of an opinion or otherwise, if (1) the testimony is based upon sufficient facts or data, (2) the testimony is the product of reliable principles and methods, and (3) the witness has applied the principles and methods reliably to the facts of the case.*

This threshold for admissibility is designed to allow novel approaches to addressing issues in litigation, yet to preclude testimony based on "junk science."

Daubert v. *Merrell Dow Pharmaceuticals*

Rule 702 was interpreted by the United States Supreme Court in *Daubert* v. *Merrell Dow Pharmaceuticals* (1993). Prior to *Daubert*, the dominant test for the admissibility of expert testimony was the general acceptance standard (*Frye* v. *United States*, 1923). Under this test, an expert's analysis has to be based on principles and practices generally accepted as reliable by others working in the same field as the expert. In *Daubert* the Court held that under the FRE this general acceptance test could no longer function as the sole test for admissibility.

The Court in *Daubert*, in which the ultimate issue was whether the use, during pregnancy, of a prescription antinausea drug had caused birth defects in children, held that federal trial court judges are to serve as gatekeepers on the admissibility of scientific evidence. The Court stated that "the trial judge must ensure that any and all scientific testimony or evidence admitted is not only relevant, but reliable." The reliability or "trustworthiness" of scientific evidence, the Court further noted, is to be based on "scientific validity." The Court did not provide an exhaustive checklist of things that a trial judge needs to consider in making such a determination, but did identify some pertinent considerations. These are whether a theory or technique used by an expert "can be (and has been) tested," whether it has been "subjected to peer review and publication," whether there is a "known or potential rate of error" in the methodology, and whether there are "standards controlling the technique's operation." The Court further added that the notion of "general acceptance" remains a relevant consideration. The inquiry, the Court stated, was to be "a flexible one," although "The focus, of course, must be solely on principles and methodology, not on the conclusions that they generate."

In deciding *Daubert*, the Court made it clear that its holding was limited to the "scientific context" presented by the case, and left for another day the issue of standards applicable to "technical, or otherwise specialized knowledge." This was a substantial limitation because testimony by experts with scientific specialties constitutes only a small part of the expert testimony presented in courts. A 1998 study of civil cases in federal courts involving expert testimony reports that only 7.3% of the experts testified on the basis of a scientific specialty.

Kumho Tire Company v. *Carmichael*

The relevance of *Daubert* to nonscientific expert testimony, including that based on the soft sciences (many of the social sciences), was clarified 6 years later in *Kumho Tire Company* v. *Carmichael* (1999). The issue in *Kumho Tire* was whether a tire on a minivan that had blown out had been defective. In this case, the Supreme Court held that the responsibility of a federal trial judge to ensure that expert testimony is relevant and reliable applies to "all expert testimony."

Although trial court judges continue to function as gatekeepers on relevance and reliability under *Kumho Tire*, how they perform that role is even less constrained than under *Daubert*. The *Daubert* list of pertinent considerations regarding reliability, appropriately described by a dissenting justice in that case as "vague and abstract," was recognized as not directly transferable to most types of expert inquiry. Its utility depends on "the nature of the issue, the expert's particular expertise, and the subject of his testimony." No similar list of considerations was provided in *Kumho Tire*. The decision on admissibility is a flexible, case-specific determination, in which the trial judge is granted "considerable leeway" and "broad latitude," subject to the very deferential "abuse-of-discretion" standard of review by appellate courts. Not surprisingly, one appellate court judge, in a case (*United States* v. *Smithers*, 2000) involving expert testimony concerning eyewitness identifications, after referring to "a *Daubert* test" commented, "whatever that may be."

Post-*Daubert* and -*Kumho Tire*

There are no bright line tests for the admissibility of expert testimony. The objective of the gatekeeping role assigned trial judges in *Daubert* and *Kumho Tire*, however, was clearly expressed in the *Kumho Tire* opinion:

> *It is to make certain that an expert, whether basing testimony upon professional studies or personal experience, employs in the courtroom the same level of intellectual rigor that characterizes the practice of an expert in the relevant field.*

Since *Daubert*, judges have devoted more attention to assessing the reliability of the analyses and testimony of expert witnesses, although whether such assessments have resulted in "better outcomes" is still an open question. The extent to which this increased attention has heightened concerns about "intellectual rigor" among attorneys is certainly questionable. As a federal Court of Appeals judge noted recently (in *United States of America* v. *Hall*, 1999): "Many lawyers think that the best (=most persuasive) experts are those who have taken acting lessons and have deep voices, rather than those who have done the best research."

The Adversarial Context

Expert witness testimony occurs in an adversarial environment. Litigation is not a process in which the parties themselves are neutral and mutually seek to discover the truth. It is a process in which facts, as well as law, critical to the outcome of a case are almost always disputed. The parties compete to persuade a decision maker (judge or jury) that their version of the fact or facts is the accurate one. Expert testimony on behalf of one party therefore is typically challenged through cross-examination and the testimony of the experts for the opposing party or parties. These challenges sometimes entail serious objections to the methods and procedures employed. This no doubt occurs often when the expertise of an expert is in a multiparadigmatic field of scholarship, such as many of the social sciences. But often these attacks unfortunately degenerate into what has been described as blowing smoke and nit-picking, in other words, efforts at obfuscation rather than enlightenment. When an expert analysis withstands such attacks, it is also not uncommon for the attacks to become focused on the messenger rather than the methods in an effort to discredit the expert, separate from the analysis, as biased, incompetent, or otherwise untrustworthy.

The disputes between or among experts often take the form of disagreements over the definitions and measurements of concepts. In order to make these abstract points more concrete, I focus on disputes that commonly occur among experts testifying about racially polarized voting, a key concept in voting rights litigation. These disagreements concern the definition and appropriate statistical procedures for measuring the presence of this type of voting behavior. Sociologists and historians, as well as political scientists, have testified as experts assessing the extent to which voting is polarized. These disputes have not divided experts by disciple but, rather, by the party for which they testify, plaintiffs or defendants. The differences among experts on this issue provide good illustrations of the types of definitional and measurement disputes that play a major role in expert testimony by social scientists more generally.

Definitions and Measures

Disputes about the definitions of key concepts, which directly affect the measurement of these concepts, are a common dimension of litigation. The type of evidence considered relevant typically varies by the definition chosen. Voting rights litigation today almost always involves the issue of minority vote dilution rather than vote denial. Under the federal Voting Rights Act, protected minorities (African Americans, Latinos, Asian Americans, Native Americans, and Native Alaskans) are to have an opportunity to elect "representatives of their choice" equivalent of that of "other members of the electorate." When voting is racially polarized, minorities complain that their ability to elect representatives of their choice is diminished and sometimes cancelled out completely, by the manner in which electoral competition is structured. Most of these allegations concern the use of jurisdictionwide (e.g., city, county, or school district) at-large elections or the delineation of representational district lines. Dilution cases are tried before judges, not juries, and a necessary condition for plaintiffs to prevail is a factual finding that voting in the respective area is "racially polarized" (*Thornburg* v. *Gingles*, 1986). Disputes over how racially polarized voting should be defined and how it should be measured therefore play a central role in many of these cases.

We might expect, given that racial divisions in candidate preferences in biracial elections are so prevalent in the United States, that this factual issue would usually be a matter stipulated to by the parties. Indeed, upon being told that he would be presented with testimony by experts about racially polarized voting, a federal judge in Georgia stated from the bench, "Blacks vote for blacks and whites vote for whites. . . . I don't know that I need anybody to tell me that. I mean, I didn't just fall off the turnip truck." Another federal judge, this one in Virginia, commented from the bench while an expert presented evidence of racially polarized voting that no one would deny "that black precincts by and large support—overwhelmingly support—black candidates or that white precincts by and large generally support white candidates" and asked the witness, "when we're talking about polarization, you know, you are just beating the obvious aren't you?" Plaintiffs in voting rights cases argue that bench comments such as these reflect the common understanding of what "racially polarized voting" entails—consistent racial divisions in candidate preferences.

The Plaintiffs' Evidence

The plaintiffs' experts typically analyze past elections in which voters have been presented with a choice between or among minority and other candidates. The racial divisions in candidate preferences in these elections are often striking and reveal a preference among minority voters to be represented by people from within their own group. When this is the case, it is then argued that if the opportunity to elect is to be considered equal, it must provide the opportunity, at least, to elect minority candidates.

The secret ballot precludes information on how each person voted in an election. Expert witness testimony about racially polarized voting therefore involves estimates of the percentages of support that candidates have received from different groups of voters. These analyses identify the candidates of choice of different groups and indicate the magnitude of the differences in these preferences between or among groups.

Polls and Surveys

Data on the candidate preferences of even samples of individual voters in past elections are rarely available. In some jurisdictions, exit polls may have been taken, but these data are usually for only one or a few elections and these elections are typically not for the office at issue (e.g., mayoral elections when the office at issue is city council member). And even then a host of methodological issues are likely to arise as to how a poll was conducted and how representative the respondents were of the voters participating in the election or elections. Exit polls tend to have higher nonresponse rates than other polls, and these rates tend to vary between or among types of voters. Sampling frames from which to select replacements randomly for those who have declined to participate are not available in exit polls.

Other types of polls and surveys have problems as well. The reliability of preelection surveys obviously suffers from an analyst not knowing whether the respondents did or did not ultimately vote and, if they did, whether they voted the way they indicated they would. The reliability of postelection surveys suffers from voters memories not being accurate and from the tendency of respondents to overreport not just voting itself but also voting for the winning candidates. In general, there is considerable skepticism about the reliability of poll or survey data concerning racially sensitive matters, as elections involving choices between or among minority and other candidates often are.

Ecological Inference

The experts' estimates of racial divisions in past elections, therefore, are almost always based on ecological inference. They rely on records of voting within the smallest groupings in which votes are aggregated, the precincts in which the votes are cast. The independent variable in the analysis is a measure of the relative presence of the particular protected minority in the precincts. This is usually that group's share of the voting age population in each precinct, as reported in the U.S. Census. In a few jurisdictions, better measures of the racial composition of precinct electorates may be available, such as voter registration by race within each precinct or, even more rarely, voter turnout within precincts by race. When the minority at issue is Latinos, counts of the number of people registered to vote or receiving ballots with a Spanish surname are often employed.

Simple scatter plots showing the relationship between the racial composition of precinct electorates and the vote for a minority candidate or candidates typically create a strong presumption that voting is along group lines (see, Fig. 1, which shows how the vote for an African-American candidate across precincts varied with the relative presence of African Americans among those voting in those precincts). These are supplemented, however, by specific point estimates of the percentage of the votes cast by the protected minority that are cast for the various candidates and the percentage of votes cast by the other voters. These estimates often become a major subject of dispute.

Several measurement techniques, which vary greatly in complexity, are commonly used to derive the estimates of candidate-support levels from the aggregate-level data identified. Two of these, homogeneous precinct analysis and ecological regression, met with the approval of the U.S. Supreme Court in *Thornburg* v. *Gingles* (1986). Since *Gingles*, a third technique, called ecological inference (EI), has been developed specifically for this purpose (although it can be applied more generally to data based on aggregates).

In a homogeneous precinct analysis, the precincts in which the electorate consists predominately of a protected class and those consisting predominately of other voters are identified and the support levels for candidates within each set are compared. This simple procedure rarely contains sufficient coverage of a group's voters to constitute a valid jurisdictionwide estimate of the divisions, however, and therefore experts also perform analyses that are based on all of the precincts.

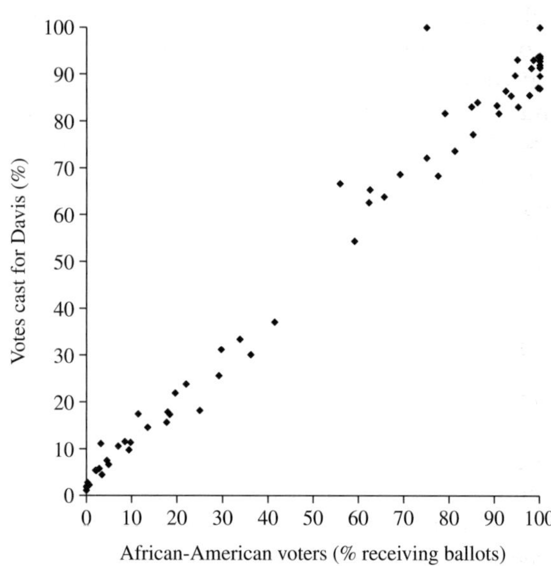

Figure 1 Percentage of votes for the African-American candidate, Louisiana House of Representatives, District 21, 1995 run-off election, in all of the voting precincts in the district.

The standard procedure for deriving estimates from all of the precincts has been regression, typically the ordinary least squares type, in which the measure of the vote for a candidate is regressed onto the measure of the minority presence in the precincts. The intercept and slope coefficients provide the information from which the respective estimates of group support are derived. When an election analyzed is a contest in which only one person may win and voters have only one vote to cast, the particular variant of regression most often employed is the two-equation method, commonly called double regression.

The EI method developed by Gary King is the most complex of the three. It supplements the information employed in regression analyses by adding information about the empirical limits, or bounds, in group support within every precinct. It also does not assume that the group divisions in the vote are constant across precincts, as do the regression analyses. Maximum likelihood estimation is employed to derive a bivariate normal distribution, truncated by the bounds, of possible combinations of support levels for a particular candidate by each group. Tomography lines that reflect the racial composition of precincts are inserted through the bivariate distribution to identify the possible values for each specific precinct. Point estimates for the respective precincts are randomly derived along the tomography line of possible values through numerous iterations of simulations. These are then combined to provide an estimate of each group's support across all the precincts. Although more experts continue to rely on regression rather than on EI, no doubt because EI is difficult to explain to lawyers and judges and because the use of regression was approved in *Gingles*, EI is now becoming the more popular approach to aggregate-based measures of group divisions in the scholarly literature.

The Defendants' Response

The defendants' response to the plaintiffs' evidence takes several forms. One is to argue that precinct-level data are not a valid basis for deriving the estimates reported. This often entails little more than a recitation of the ecological fallacy, which in this context states that we cannot draw inferences about the distributions of candidate preferences of the individuals within groups from data based on heterogeneous aggregations (precincts) of these groups. This response is rarely successful, however, in light of the pronounced differences usually observed across these aggregates.

A far more frequent response is to offer a different definition of what racially polarized voting entails, a definition under which such divisions are, by themselves, treated as irrelevant. Defendants often argue that if voting is to be considered polarized, it must be based on racial animus. Voting, in short, must be more than racially divided; it must also be racially motivated. Under this definition, group divisions in candidate preferences, no matter how acute or consistent, are not sufficient to establish polarized voting. Rather, additional evidence showing that these preferences were motivated by racial animus is required. This necessary condition, given this definition, is normally introduced by the testimony of an expert. At times, the jurisdictions simply argue that the burden of proving that racism is the causal factor, or at least a pronounced causal factor, rests with the plaintiffs. Experts called by defendants testify that the plaintiffs' evidence of group divisions, no matter how pronounced and persistent the divisions may be, is simply descriptive and establishes at best correlation not causation. Without evidence of racial motivations behind the racial divisions, defendants argue, the plaintiffs must lose.

Racial divisions in voting patterns could be viewed, however, as establishing a reasonable presumption of polarized voting, even if racial animus is a definitional criterion. If this is the case, then a defendant jurisdiction must rebut this presumption through evidence of its own that shows the absence of racial animus. This requires that the defendants themselves provide evidence that demonstrates nonracial explanations for the divisions. This approach involves identifying variables other than the relative presence of a minority group's voters across the precincts that might relate to the voters' choices. Variables suggested to have this explanatory power include the party identifications of the voters, their incomes, the issues that concern them, and the geographical distance between the residences of candidates and the precincts within which voters reside—variables that themselves typically relate to the racial composition of the precincts.

These actual multivariate analyses deviate from the precinct-based analyses used to demonstrate racial divisions. Although some of the suggested variables can be directly measured at the precinct level for past elections, others such as the party identifications and issue concerns of voters cannot. The actual analysis therefore shifts to an examination, across elections, of the characteristics of candidates and their campaigns. The unit of analysis becomes elections, not precincts. Variables such as the party affiliation of the candidates (rather than the voters), their incumbency status, their name identification, the relative cost of their campaigns, and the race of the candidates are related to the outcomes of elections, measured by the overall percentage of the votes the various candidates received or simply whether the candidates won or lost. These analyses do not reveal whether or not the voters are divided along racial lines but, rather, whether the race of the candidate has a separate, independent effect on the outcome measures when the other variables are included. If it does not, it is argued, the divisions in candidate preference are cleansed of any racial content.

Another approach to the nonracial explanation argument has been employed recently. This approach does rely on the precinct as the unit of analysis. It involves attempting to measure the party identification of the voters in past elections at the precinct level and then comparing the bivariate correlation coefficient between that variable and the vote for candidates with that between the minority composition of the precincts and the vote. Reliable party identification measures are not usually available for precincts in past elections, however. In the recent applications, the measure of party identification has been based on the votes cast for the candidates of the political parties in a previous election. If the correlation between party, as measured, and the vote tends to be higher than that between the minority composition and the vote, it is argued that party is the more important determinant of the vote and therefore that voting is not racially polarized.

Another common approach to minimizing the impact of the plaintiffs' evidence of racial divisions is to include in the analysis elections in which there are no minority candidates. These are almost always white-on-white elections, in terms of candidates, and the estimated divisions in the vote are derived through the same measurement techniques that the plaintiffs employ. Without a biracial choice of candidates, racial differences in candidate preferences will usually appear less often. Even when the preferences are split, the divisions are typically not as intense as in biracial elections, which may result in the white candidates preferred by minority voters in these elections winning. Despite the evidence of racial divisions varying greatly between the two types of elections, the defendants' experts treat all elections as equally probative. Given that the white-on-white elections are typically much more numerous than biracial elections in challenged jurisdictions, the findings for these elections dilute the evidence from the biracial contests, leading to the conclusion that voting is not polarized or, if it is, that minority votes are not diluted because the candidates preferred by minority voters win a sufficient number of elections.

The Plaintiffs' Rebuttal

The plaintiffs' experts rebut these analyses by arguing that the issue of racially polarized voting is correctly viewed as a descriptive one. If minority voters prefer representation from within their own group and the minority candidates preferred by them are usually vetoed by the other voters, then the minority's voting strength is diluted and their opportunity to elect representatives of their choice is impaired, regardless of the motivations behind the vetoes. An inability to elect candidates from within their own group cannot be ignored because minority voters may be on the winning side in some, even many, white-on-white elections.

They may also criticize the measurements of many of the variables used in the defendants' analyses, such as the party identification measure. This measure assumes that all the votes cast for candidates affiliated with a party are motivated by a party preference. It is argued that this is not a valid assumption when campaigns, as so many are today, are candidate-centered rather than party-centered. They may also point out that the nonracial variables that the defendants' experts find in their multivariate analyses to be related to election outcomes are themselves highly correlated with race. Incumbency status, for example, is a variable that often has a major impact on the outcome variables. Empirically, however, incumbency status is often not a race-neutral variable. In some settings, all the past incumbents have been white, and therefore it is difficult to disentangle incumbency status from the race of the candidates. In other settings, only one or a few minority individuals have been incumbents, and an examination of the racial divisions in the support for incumbents might reveal that the pull of incumbency is itself racially selective. Voter support for incumbents, the evidence may show, varies with the race of the incumbent. If minority voters (but not the other voters) prefer the minority incumbent and the other voters (but not the minority voters) prefer the white incumbents, then, again, incumbency can hardly be considered to be a race-neutral variable. Multivariate analyses such as these, it has been argued, may result in judges being "bamboozled by misleading fancy statistics."

The *Gingles* Decision

The only time the Supreme Court has intervened in these disputes was the *Gingles* case, which involved a challenge by African Americans to multimember state legislative districts in North Carolina. A five-member majority of the Court sided with the plaintiffs on the definitional issue, holding that the concept of racially polarized voting concerns racial divisions, not motivations. The majority, as did the three-judge district court that initially heard the case, adopted the definition offered by an expert for the plaintiffs, that "'racial polarization' exists where there is 'a consistent relationship between [the] race of the voter and the way in which the voter votes . . . 'or to put it differently, where 'black voters and white voters vote differently.'" (Due to the voter registration data available, the comparisons in the case could be made only between nonwhite and white voters; the more appropriate comparison, as previously noted, is between the protected minority or minorities at issue in the case and all the other members of the electorate.) Racial divisions in candidate preferences, according to the Court, is all that needs to be shown to conclude that voting is polarized. The plaintiffs evidence, based exclusively on homogeneous precincts and bivariate regression analyses of elections involving a biracial choice of candidates, was found to demonstrate those divisions.

Causal arguments were not completely dismissed, however. Whereas four justices rejected them, four others stated in a concurring opinion that although evidence of nonracial causes for the voting patterns does not rebut the presence of racially polarized voting, such evidence may be considered in "the overall vote dilution inquiry." The discussion was completely conceptual, however, because no evidence of this type was presented in *Gingles*. The ninth justice joined neither group on this issue. Arguments about nonracial causes therefore continue to be heard in dilution cases, and empirical attempts to demonstrate them continue to be presented.

Conclusion

Litigation is an adversarial process in which critical concepts under the law, such as racially polarized voting, often become the subjects of great dispute. Social scientists serving as expert witnesses are engaged in a form of applied research. This does not usually involve the theory building and testing prevalent in their basic research, but it does entail issues of definition and measurement common to all empirical work. These issues are often at the center of their analyses and testimony.

A survey of federal trial court judges in 1998–1999 inquired about their experiences with expert testimony in civil cases. The responses send a clear message to those who may serve as expert witnesses. The number one problem with expert testimony, the judges reported, was that "Experts abandon objectivity and become advocates for the side that hired them." The adversarial process can trigger competitive emotions. While dealing with issues of definition and measurement, experts need to remember that it is not their responsibility to win cases—that is the lawyers' responsibility! It is their job to reach opinions objectively or, as expressed in *Kumho Tire*, to do so using "the same standard of intellectual rigor" that is expected of them in their other scholarly pursuits. If they do so, their opinions should carry greater weight with judges and juries. (Practical advice about the demeanor and candor of experts while testifying is the subject of a 1984 report by Wuffle.)

See Also the Following Articles

Ecological Fallacy • Law • Surveys

Further Reading

Daubert v. *Merrell Dow Pharmaceuticals*, 509 U.S. 579 (1993).

Dixon, L., and Gill, B. (2001). *Changes in the Standards for Admitting Expert Evidence in Federal Civil Cases since the* Daubert *Decision* Rand Institute for Civil Justice, Santa Monica, CA.

Engstrom, R. L. (1985). The Reincarnation of the intent standard: Federal judges and at-large election cases. *Howard Law Rev.* **28,** 495–514.

Frye v. *United States*, 54 App DC 46 (1923).

Grofman, B. (2000). A primer on racial bloc voting analysis. In *The Real Y2K Problem* (N. Persily, ed.), pp. 43–81. Brennan Center for Justice, New York.

Johnson, M. T., Krafka, C., and Cecil, J. S. (2000). *Expert Testimony in Civil Rights Trials: A Preliminary Analysis.* Federal Judicial Center, Washington, DC.

King, G. (1997). *A Solution to the Ecological Inference Problem.* Princeton University Press, Princeton, NJ.

Kumho Tire Company v. *Carmichael*, 526 U.S. 137 (1999).

Thornburg v. *Gingles*, 478 U.S. 30 (1986).

United States v. *Hall*, 165 F.3d 1095, (1999).

United States v. *Smither*, 212 F.3d 306 (2000).

Wuffle, A. (1984). A Wuffle's advice to the expert witness in court. *PS: Polit. Sci. Polit.* **17,** 60–61.

Explore, Explain, Design

Andrew S. Gibbons

Brigham Young University, Provo, Utah, USA

C. Victor Bunderson

The EduMetrics Institute, Provo, Utah, USA

Glossary

design experiments Exhibit all aspects of a design study, except that, in seeking explanatory and design theories, reliance on narrative methods is supplemented with invariant measurement of the growth or change constructs spanning the domain. The measurement instruments evolve over the cycles of design; they implement, evaluate, redesign, and come to embody an increasingly adequate descriptive theory of the processes operative in the domain. In addition, the technological devices designed to introduce and control the treatment effects are forthrightly described using the emerging layers and languages of technology in that domain. In experimental terminology, design experiments are quasi-experiments, but may include mini-randomized experiments within a larger cycle.

design research Includes design studies and design experiments, both of which build domain-specific descriptive theories as well as design theories. Design research also includes research on design methods or design theory, as applied across two or more domains.

design studies Seek two kinds of theoretical knowledge: first, a descriptive explanation of the processes operative in a domain, and second, technological or design knowledge about how to create and implement the tools—both measurement instruments and the treatment control technologies. These studies are attempts to discover new artifact- and intervention-related principles or to improve the effectiveness of existing artifacts or intervention plans. Design studies take place in live settings, and are iterative, cyclical applications of a process of principled design, implementation, evaluation, and redesign. Design studies often aid in exploring a domain and possible treatments, and thus may be largely qualitative, producing narrative accounts. These accounts may not provide adequate warrant for causal claims, nor do they fully rule out alternate explanations.

invariant measurement A careful and extended design, development, and validation process may obtain technological devices (measurement instruments) that produce measures approaching the ideal of invariance. The measures produced are invariant to the sample of subjects or the set of tasks selected, have an agreed-upon zero point and a standard unit used by many practitioners and scientists across national boundaries, and have a widely accepted interpretive framework based on a theory of the operative constructs of change or growth being measured in the domain spanned by the instrument's scales.

natural history A knowledge-producing process in which natural phenomena are observed, described, measured, and collected to amass a body of facts from which patterns and trends can be detected through study of the facts in the presence of each other. This type of knowledge seeking is equated here with exploratory research. A benefit of attention to this type of knowledge seeking is the growth of collections, which can be studied and restudied as evidence to support or question new models and hypotheses as they are advanced.

science A knowledge-producing process in which questions are asked, primarily of an explanatory nature, and research is carried out to answer them. The questions asked seek to describe authoritatively the nature of underlying operations that lead to observed phenomena. This type of research attempts to discover the single best coherent description of observed phenomena that is consistent with all observations; here, explanatory research and science are equated.

technology A knowledge-producing process in which questions are asked, primarily to learn principles for connecting human intentions with the form and function of human-made artifacts, and research is carried out to answer these questions. The questions asked seek ways of structuring time and space with information, forces, and materials in such a way that a particular prespecified outcome is achieved. Here, this activity is placed under the heading of design. Rather than a single explanation of observed phenomena, this type of knowledge seeking attempts to discover efficient structuring principles and processes that will produce a variety of solutions to a problem, from which the most suitable may be selected on the basis of problem-specific criteria.

The explore, explain, and design concept designates three synergistically related knowledge-producing enterprises. "Explain" denotes the familiar goal of scientific research, which is to explain why and explain how. In this type of research, the single best explanatory principle is sought. "Design" denotes the goal of design research, which is to discover and apply structuring and synthesizing principles in order to satisfy a set of criteria. In this type of research, classes of increasingly desirable artifacts (or structuring principles) are sought so that they may be used to satisfy target criteria. "Explore" denotes a type of research aimed at producing observations that can lead to category formation and formation of hypotheses of relationships relevant to both of the other research enterprises. Within emerging domains of human knowledge, the questions concern what is there and what are possible groupings and relationships among what is there.

Distinguishing Explore, Explain, and Design

The three knowledge-producing enterprises—explore, explain, and design—are necessary conditions for each other, each producing results that become mutually and self-inputting, providing a continuous stream of research questions in all three areas. The three enterprises are discriminated on the basis of the kinds of questions they address and the types of knowledge they produce, but not definitively on the research techniques employed. The focus here is to place these three knowledge-producing activities into context with each other, and to highlight design research. Throughout this encyclopedia, the word "design" appears in only a handful of titles, referring, for instance, to experimental design, sampling design, survey design, and longitudinal cohort design. These are methods of setting up data- gathering opportunities for exploration- and explanation- centered observations, but design as a synthetic process by which knowledge can be gained is not featured. This is the domain here. Moreover, though measurement foundations and models are discussed in the literature, little attention is paid to the fact that the practice of research through synthesis requires measurement, and that measurement instruments are technological products—tools both for research and for practical purposes. These tools, however, have unique properties of scientific interest. Even prior to the existence of adequate theory, the development and use of new measurement instruments has repeatedly, in the history of science, led directly to discovery and then to new theory. As instruments and theory evolve together, the instruments are used to test, confirm, or discredit and replace theory with better theory. Measurement instruments are thus inextricably linked as products of—and as precursors to—the advancement of theory.

Social measurement requires extensive and disciplined design and development to design, produce, validate, and maintain scientifically, socially, and economically valuable measurement instruments. Examining the relation of explore, explain, and design and their relationship to measurement is important because valuable measurement instruments produce social, economic, and scientific capital. Producing this capital is the work of natural history and technology as much as it is the work of science, a distinction elaborated herein. Explore, explain, and design activities are mutually sustaining, and no one of them can proceed far without producing questions to be answered by the other two. Figure 1 illustrates this relationship. The two-way arrows in Fig. 1 indicate that influence between activities can act in either direction. In the graphical depiction, the explore activity is situated above the explain and design activities, indicating that exploration often tends to provide a starting point, stimulating the other two activities.

New concepts about invariant and computer-administered instrumentation make possible research methods in the social sciences that offer new and promising opportunities for all three knowledge-producing activities. Computers and networks can support introduction of both treatments and metrics into live settings where real phenomena of interest are found, though it requires far greater engineering and scientific investment. Extended efforts to achieve broad acceptance (efforts far beyond what is usually attempted in the social

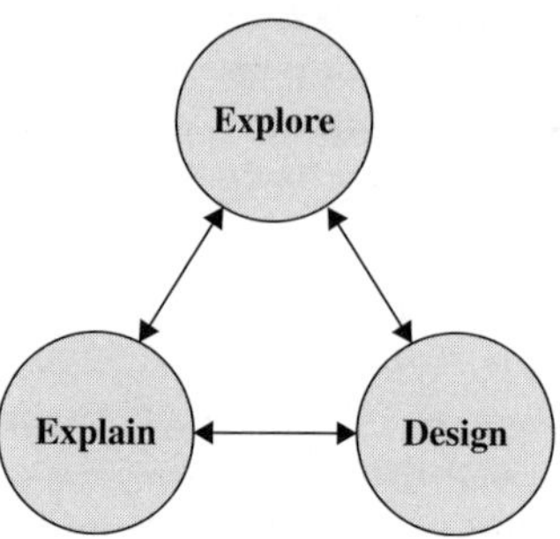

Figure 1 Mutually sustaining relationship between three knowledge-creation activities: explore, explain, and design.

sciences) can then approach the ideal of invariant measurement, providing comparability from occasion to occasion and from group to group, so that unprecedented progress can be made. However, progress will continue to be limited in the human sciences and in design so long as the metrics are incommensurable from study to study.

Explore

Early Scientific Exploration—Natural History

Before it is possible to create theories, we must have some description of nature and the content to which theories pertain. Natural history has been described as a type of research involving the collection and cataloguing of specimens as an inventory of "what we've got." This becomes a register of facts and a compilation of the contents of the world. This way of knowing is contrasted with experimental inquiry into cause, which originated as natural philosophy, i.e., an explanation of causes rather than an inventory.

Natural history studies have historically embraced anything that can be named and collected, though it is a common misperception today that naturalistic studies are confined to animals and plants. One of the most famous collectors, the founder of the British Museum, Sir Hans Sloane (1660–1753), collected thousands of plant and animal specimens, at the same time amassing collections of coins, medals, spoons, goblets, rings, minerals, weaponry, combs, and a huge library of manuscripts. Today, similar collections of human-made objects from around the world compete in size with those of naturally occurring phenomena. Sloane's collections, donated to government, formed an important core of the British Museum. Sloane considered his major contribution to science the "collection and accurate arrangement of these curiosities."

Natural history explorations have a long history of rich collectors assembling collections of oddities, gathered mainly as conversation pieces and enhancements to social status. However, natural history research expanded greatly from approximately 1800 to 1900 and changed in character. More serious and systematic collectors emerged to gather and catalogue with the purpose of arranging specimens in orderly tableaux that emphasized gradation of similarities, suggested regular underlying patterns, and identified gaps that supplied targets for further collection. The method of natural history research became wide search, collection, description, cataloging, preservation, preparation for display, and archiving. This, of course, required that systems of measurement be devised for describing the magnitude of the different qualities of specimens. The search of natural historians became guided by empty positions in collections: places where something ought to be. The sense-making of natural historians was to find the patterns and gradations of difference that might give hints about underlying relationships. These motives continue in today's natural history research. Researchers today work with all possible speed to catalogue Brazilian tribes still untouched by modern civilization, dying native languages, mutant viruses, and evolving forms of computing machinery. Though the subjects of observation, collection, measurement, and inventory have changed, as have the means of measuring, what has not changed is the necessity of measuring observed phenomena. The formation of categories that result from this type of research depends on ordering along presumed dimensions, leading to measurement. The constant refinement of categories goes hand in hand with the constant refinement of all parts of measures: constructs, dimensions, observable indicators, rubrics, scales, instruments, and inference/analysis methods.

Many Exploratory Methods Exist and Often Lead to Explanation

Natural history collections lead to the formation of named categories, and subsequently to order relationships. In the mathematical theory of measurement, this empirical achievement provides the basic definitions needed to construct theorems of representation from the empirical world into the real number system. Theorems of representation must be anchored in the empirical world. First, the categories of objects are defined as sets, and order relations among them are defined as relations on those sets. When these sets and relations meet certain axioms, it can be shown that a mathematical structure (usually the real number system with its many desirable properties) can be used to represent or model the real-world observations. Mathematical models yield predictions of consequences (often otherwise unexpected) that can be tested using methods much stronger than natural history or other largely exploratory methods. Useful explanatory theories can result, with warrant to claims that the causal connections proposed in the theory operate as claimed, and warrant to claims that other competing explanations are not the causal agents. This path from exploration through category formation through measurement, which enables crucial and rigorous testing, is typical in science. Discussion of theorems of representation, based on the fundamental work of David Krantz and co-authors, in three volumes published in 1971, 1989, and 1990, shows the fundamental contribution of exploration to further progress toward explanation. Exploration leads to the formation of the categories (sets) of empirical observations, and relations among them. These lead in turn to measurement, and then to strong tests of causal predictions and relations among them.

The intent of some methods is initially exploratory, but may lead to hypotheses testable by stronger methods. Exploratory narrative methods include case studies, field and observational studies, naturalistic inquiry, some of the cognitive methods, focus groups, participant observation, unobtrusive methods, and others. In all these cases, experts in these methods point out a linkage to theories in their domains of interest, which increasingly guide and shape the plans for their otherwise exploratory observations. Thus, it may perhaps more properly be said that a method is exploratory when it is used in an early phase of observation in a relatively new area. In a later phase, when constructs and relations have been observed, named, and documented, beginning explanatory theories come into being and guide explanatory research. The example of the "empty space" on the shelf in a natural history collection is a case in point. Even the beginnings of relational constructs can direct the search for interesting observations. A method used early to explore a new domain may be used later to investigate a theory-based prediction.

In addition to narrative methods, quantitative methods are also used in exploratory phases. Exploratory factor analysis, cluster analysis, latent class analysis, and Q methods produce sets of possible groupings—possible constructs with varying explanatory value and potential utility. After further development, the quantitative methods give way to confirmatory analyses, structural equation models, hierarchical models, and causal models. Other more quantitative exploratory methods include data mining, computerized record linkage, and statistical matching.

Exploratory Research Leads Also to Design Research

Just as exploratory research leads naturally to research into causes, it leads also to research into outcomes and the means of predictably producing them. Exploration leads to measurement instruments, which are technological devices, the products of design. "Design" is a term that describes intentional structuring of artifacts and intervention plans to bring about predictable outcomes. Design is both a subject of research and a method of research and knowledge production. As a subject of research, it poses many interesting questions:

- How can knowledge about how things work be converted into principles for making things work in a particular way to reach specified goals?
- What generalizable structuring principles guide synthesis and dimensioning of artifacts?
- What generalizable principles guide the formation of intervention plans using artifacts?
- How can practices that currently produce desirable results be refined to meet ever higher, ever more specific criteria?
- How can new measurement constructs, measurement instruments, and constructs be created that permit better measurements of artifact properties, intervention points, intervention progress, and attainment of criterial end points?

As a method of research, design involves principles of search, analysis, problem re-representation, discovery of abstract operational principles, principled proliferation of configurations, means-end matching, optimizing, and testing—all of which requires constant, continuous measurement. Herbert Simon has attributed recent rapid growth of interest in design research to "the fact that all who use computers in complex ways are using computers to design or to participate in the process of design. Consequently, we as designers or as designers of design processes, have had to be explicit as never before about what is involved in creating a design and what takes place while the creation is going on." The domain of design can be illustrated as in Fig. 2. As shown, natural processes involving the transfer and translation of energy and information proceed independently of human agency. Even matters as complex as human learning and forgetting are natural processes, and either one may proceed in a natural but less desirable path than if instructional interventions are introduced. Natural processes are the subject of much exploratory (natural history) and explanatory (scientific) research. Humans, in the exercise of technology designs, identify measured intervention points at which they impress energy (force) or information (structure) on natural processes, using artifacts and intervention plans in a way calculated to deflect the natural processes toward the achievement of desired, measured outcomes. Attaining the desired outcomes may require multiple interventions, multiple intervention artifacts, and multiple, often continuous, measurements.

Intervening in different processes at different measured points using different artifacts is an important

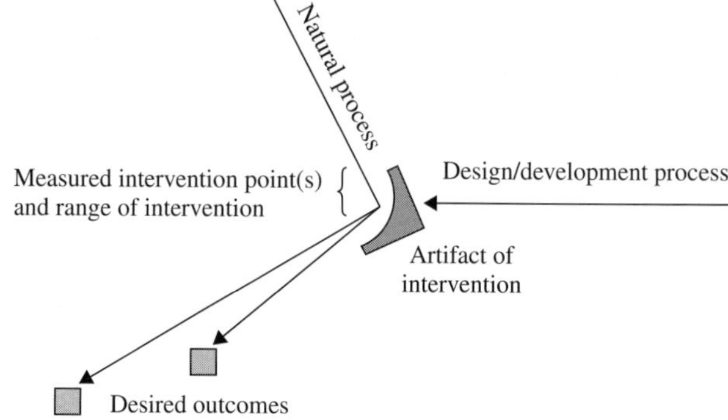

Figure 2 The domain of design.

method of knowledge production through design. It can rely on random permutation, which results in occasional success, or it can proceed deliberately, according to generative design principles that promise a higher rate of success and predictability. Of interest here are the many ways in which the technology of measurement is not just involved in, but makes possible, other technologies. Measurement is therefore a central topic in design research. Design research produces knowledge that is nontrivial, and according to Walter Vincenti, consists of several distinct types:

1. Fundamental design concepts—principles for structuring designs.
2. Criteria and specifications—means of expressing problems and designs.
3. Theoretical tools—concepts that relate scientific to technological knowledge and that support the formulation of design theories.
4. Quantitative data—data on properties and ranges, constants, data for prediction.
5. Practical considerations—how things work in real and messy settings.
6. Design instrumentalities—design process reasoning and procedural knowledge.

These categories interact with knowledge from other sources, especially from science, to enable the design of new things, processes, and events. However, it is not always practical to separate out sources of knowledge, because science and design operate hand in hand in everyday problem solving, Vincenti underscores the importance of beginning to see design research as a knowledge-producing activity on a par with explanatory research.

Design

What Is Design?

Design research is historically the least well known and least well understood of the triad in Fig. 1, but interest in design research is increasing. Tough-minded experimental, sampling, and survey designs are used, and other aspects of the design of measurement instruments, including new types of items or questions, and computer-administration, are increasingly common, but the bulk of these works take their perspective from the framework of scientific research; the focus here is on discussing design research in more detail to provide an alternative viewpoint. Design research is emphasized here as a distinct knowledge-producing activity that discovers processes, principles, and structural concepts essential for the production of the technological tools and devices used in explorational research, explanatory research, and in design research.

For a long time, design has been deemphasized among other ways of knowing. Aristotle, in *Nichomachean Ethics*, described five kinds of "intellectual virtues," for which he used the term knowledge. Considering the first three of these, scientific knowledge is analytical, deductively provable, and teachable, whereas art and design, or "making," were regarded as chancy, variable, and intuitive, thus not teachable. Practical knowledge, including ethics, was also variable, not deductively demonstrable, and a virtue, not an art. Aristotle dealt much with practical knowledge or political science, which he claimed was that kind of knowledge most related to the most good for the most people.

The axiomatic method of deductive proofs developed and stressed by Aristotle became associated with science, but modern writers such as Herbert Simon and Buckminster Fuller have reasserted it and other mathematical methods in efforts to establish the foundations of a design science. It is through mathematical, logical, and conceptual rigor that Simon hopes that design will be accepted within academic circles: "In terms of the prevailing norms, academic respectability calls for subject matter that is intellectually tough, analytic, formalizable, and teachable. In the past, much, if not most, of what we knew about design and about the artificial sciences was intellectually soft, intuitive, informal and cookbooky."

The term "design" here thus refers to knowledge-producing studies and experiments into (1) the act of designing, (2) the design processes and generative principles for design, and (3) study of the structural properties of designed things. Design consists of the structuring of time and/or space in order to achieve specified purposes within the bounds of given constraints and to the level of given criteria. This involves the arrangement of materials and/or events to transfer or translate energy or information with the intention of producing a specific, measured result. The varieties of design knowledge previously described are produced through design research. Simon emphasizes the importance of giving design research equal standing with explanatory, or scientific, research: "The proper study of those who are concerned with the artificial is the way in which that adaptation of means to environments is brought about—and central to that is the process of design itself. The professional schools will reassume their professional responsibilities just to the degree that they can discover a science of design, a body of intellectually tough, analytic, partly formalizable, partly empirical, teachable doctrine about the design process."

Some social scientists have puzzled over why many graduate students and advisors prefer to engage in hypothesis testing rather than instrument design and development. Warren Tryon, in 1996, noted that such investigators may recognize that defective instrumentation limits their inferences, but that nevertheless, they continue to engage in hypothesis testing without prior instrument development. Tryon explains this phenomenon by pointing out that test development is not as scientifically respected as hypothesis testing is, even though test development entails construct validation, which is a highly theoretical enterprise. The neglect of design as a knowledge-producing activity has been changing slowly. An Internet search on the term "design science" shows that it has been incorporated forthrightly in fields as disparate as engineering design, public administration, and education.

Establishment of a Science of Design

Simon lists the "tough-minded, analytic, formalizable, and teachable" subjects he thought might become a part of a design science curriculum. He encourages rigor and discipline by associating design research with techniques for utility theory and statistical decision theory for evaluating designs; linear programming, control theory, and dynamic programming for choosing optimal alternatives; imperative and declarative logics for a formal logic of design; heuristic search for design alternatives, theory of structure, and organization of designs; and alternate representation of design problems. The term "design science" has more often been used in disciplines influenced by his work than has the term "artificial science." Simon emphasizes that natural science is knowledge about natural objects and phenomena, so an "artificial" science would contain knowledge about artificial objects and phenomena—and the disciplined activities by which artifacts are designed and developed. Simon believed that design is central, and should be at the core of every liberal education: "If I have made my case . . . the proper study of mankind is the science of design, not only as a technical discipline but as a core discipline for every liberally educated person."

Another influential 20th-century design scientist, Buckminster Fuller, promulgated the concept of a "comprehensive anticipatory design science" to seek solutions for global problems and to preserve life and progress on "spaceship earth." As does Simon, Fuller points to rigorous theory of structure and organization at the heart of design. Unlike Simon, he invented synergetic geometry as the heart of his theory of structure. To Fuller, the idea was not to set out to invent or design something. As quoted by a colleague and interpreter, Amy Edmonson, in 1987, he "did not set out to design a geodesic dome." Rather, he sought to "tap into the exquisite workings of nature," to "discover the principles operative in universe," and then to apply "generalized principles to produce artifacts useful to humankind." Fuller's observations of nature and explorations into a geometry of space different from what he (and we) learned in school reveal a geometry of spatial forms that is practical and empirical. Fuller's attention to "universe" and its general principles and constraints on what can exist therein guides his designs, and has been amplified in the *Design Science Series* of books on natural structural principles in design. Many other writers besides Simon and Fuller provide ample evidence that design is not restricted to the chancy, the variable, and the intuitive as Aristotle stated, nor is it unteachable.

Relationships among Explore–Explain–Design

It is customary for scholarly writers to end their works with the statement that more research is needed to answer questions generated by the results of the research being reported. Figure 1 illustrates the relationship of the three knowledge-producing activities—explore, explain, and design—as a set of two-way arrows, to show that the results of any one type of research can lead to questions answerable by any of the other types. A few examples are given at this point to show that this relationship has important implications for research of each type.

Exploratory Research Leads to Explanatory Research

As the activities of natural history measure and catalog natural phenomena, patterns become evident, requiring explanations of causal relationships, origins, and interdependencies. For example, when paleontological research on both sides of the Atlantic revealed the types of prehistoric animal and plant life that had once inhabited those regions, a pattern of relationship became evident to the scientist Alfred Wegener, and to others, that ran directly contrary to the prevailing explanatory theories of the time regarding the origin and history of the continents. To Wegener, the only explanation that fit all of the observations was that the separate continents had been joined at one point in the past but had drifted apart. Though his explanatory theory of continental drift was dismissed by opinion leaders, additional evidence that supported Wegener's theory appeared many years later when the Atlantic sea floor was being mapped for the first time. Clear signs of sea-floor spreading gave a new relevance to Wegener's theory. What is important here is not that Wegener's theory triumphed, but that it was the description—the sea-floor mapping—of natural phenomena that led to the ultimate reconsideration of Wegener's theory.

Exploratory Research Leads to Design Research

When humans find patterns in nature's mechanisms that they can copy, they do so even if the details of the pattern's internal operations are not fully understood. For thousands of years of recorded history, humans have created and used artifacts and intervention processes that mimic natural phenomena, with little or no prior research that could produce an explanation of the effect. The discovery of medicines and medical procedures through the ages has tended to follow this route. Even today, folk remedies and natural healing concoctions derived from locally found substances supply the beginning point for the refinement of pharmaceuticals. Until recently, serendipity, or dogged persistence in trial-and-error, was a major source of new drug discovery. Interestingly, this is being replaced with principled anticipatory design research.

Early in the industrial revolution, some manufacturers proceeded by trial-and-error in the absence of direction from explanatory science. The excellence of early Wedgwood china traces its origins to tireless design experiments involving clay and various minerals from Wedgwood's own farm. Writer Jenny Uglow has ascertained that "ceramics has always been a mix of science, design, and skill, and every good potter was in a sense an experimental chemist, trying out new mixes and glazes, alert to the impact of temperatures and the plasticity of clay." This, along with various patterns of aging, working, and firing using a variety of glazes, ultimately produced formulas that looked attractive and survived in their environment of use better than did the products of competitors. In some cases, then, exploratory research turns up useful structures and processes that become fundamental technologies. For example, the transistor effect was discovered by chance because of studies on the impurities in crystal substances.

Explanatory Research Leads to Exploratory Research

As explanatory theories gain support through scientific research, inferences using the theory lead to the expectation of finding as-yet undetected natural phenomena. The early stages of success of a theory constructed and initially supported through explanatory research often require additional exploratory research to develop further support. Armed with predictions of theory, researchers can go in search of specific phenomena that are predicted but as yet not observed. Exploratory research motivated by the explanatory theory of Mendeleyev's periodic table of the elements led to the discovery of several elements, most notably the trans-uranium elements, one of which was named after Mendeleyev, in honor of his discovery. Likewise, improved astronomical instruments developed decades after Einstein's relativity theory allowed astronomers to observe the phenomenon of gravitational lensing, just as Einstein's theory had predicted.

Explanatory Research Leads to Design Research

As descriptive theories gain support through scientific research, using principles from the theories to exercise control to produce specific outcomes becomes a possibility. Though the ideal of science is often expressed as seeking knowledge for the sake of knowledge, it is also true that the foundation of our technology-based economy relies on the ability to turn principles into products. Examples of this transfer are common. One of the most interesting and little recognized examples, however, is the basing of the modern technology of surgery on John Hunter's realization that the human body's own healing powers could be relied on following surgery, or what Sherwin Nuland has described as a "controlled injury" to the body. By determining what injury to inflict on the self-healing system, surgeons today recruit the body's natural processes to correct painful and deadly conditions. The study of surgery can be seen in this light as the design of injuries to inflict for given unhealthy body conditions.

The pattern of transfer from explanatory research to design research is so common that what is being described here as design research is often referred to as "applied science." It is the unquestioning acceptance of this belief and a lack of awareness of the complexities of bridging the science–technology gap that has, until recently, given technology an image subordinate to, and as simply a receiver of, the benefits of science. One of Simon's main points is that the image of applied science has obscured the knowledge-producing nature and complexities of design research and has masked the full range of technological knowledge that is required for the design of artifacts and intervention plans. Historically, this has placed design research in the shadow of science, rather than giving it equal regard and proportionate study.

Design Research Leads to Explorational Research

Design research leads to exploratory research when a design study or a design experiment produces results that are unexpected and even undescribed. The first objective after such an event is to explore the region around the undescribed phenomenon, in search of an entire class of similar new phenomena. This occurred in the 1980s when chemists examined the residue produced by intense laser heating of small sections of graphite, or pure carbon. What was found was a family of pure carbon compounds containing up to 60 or more atoms per cluster in the shape of a sphere—a form of carbon never before recognized. Philip Ball has described the process of discovering the compound's shape: "Smalley [one of the chemists] located a book on Buckminster Fuller's work, *The Dymaxion World of Buckminster Fuller* by Robert W. Marks, which he took home on the Monday evening to ponder. It is remarkable to find that, despite what we like to think of as the sophistication of modern science, some of the most significant insights can still be obtained by sitting down with a can of beer and fiddling with cardboard or ball-and-stick models. Yet this is how the structure of C_{60} was deduced." Once the structure of sixty-carbon compounds had been recognized and confirmed, and the C_{60} cage of hexagonal and pentagonal sides with 60 vertices was named "Bucky Ball," in Fuller's honor, more exploratory research was launched. An entire family of pure carbon compounds containing geometrically determined numbers of carbon atoms had to be explored. This included the "stable and cagelike" clusters of C_{32}, C_{50}, and C_{70}. This additional period of exploratory research was initiated by the unexpected discovery of previously unrecognized design research.

Design Research Leads to Explanatory Research

Design research leads to explanatory research when phenomena result from design studies or design experiments that cannot be explained. As methods for producing the buckminsterfullerines (as the class of chemicals became named) in quantity were perfected and published, the question of their chemical behavior became paramount, particularly the manner in which they encapsulate other atoms within a spherical cage, and the arrangements they take on under different conditions of creation. According to Ball, an entire subdiscipline of fullerene chemistry has formed just around the study of one class of these forms, the nanotubes.

Design Studies and Design Experiments

Definitions and a Brief History

The design study/design experiment movement has been growing rapidly in educational research, and the examples that follow will largely be drawn from that domain, but surely Simon was correct in stating that design methods cut across the professional schools of many disciplines. Education is but one of many social science and engineering professions that can use design studies and design experiments, and it is the one closest to the experience of the present authors. In the glossary at the beginning of this article, brief definitions were given of the terms "design studies" and "design experiments." More extended definitions are given here.

Design Studies

Two kinds of theoretical knowledge are sought in a design study; the first is a descriptive explanation of the processes operative in a domain (e.g., learning, growth, reversal of a disease state, improvement of an environmental condition), and the second is technological or design knowledge about how to create and implement the technological tools that control the treatment effects. Design studies take place in live settings, and are iterative, cyclical applications of a process of design, implement, evaluate, redesign. Design studies often aid in exploring a domain and possible treatments, and thus may be largely qualitative, producing narrative accounts of intense, iterative, often ideographic observations over each cycle. These accounts may perform the functions of exploration discussed in this article, and may begin to use theory to guide both the design interventions and the explanations of the processes operative in the domain. However, they may not provide adequate warrant for causal claims, nor do they fully rule out alternate explanations. For these research goals, design experiments are needed.

Design Experiments

All aspects of a design study are shared by a design experiment, except that heavy reliance on narrative methods in seeking the explanatory and design theories is supplemented with research using (and improving) the invariant measurement instruments designed to assess and track the learning or growth constructs spanning the domain. Because measurement in live settings has typically been very costly in time and attention, design experiments are becoming practical primarily because of new adaptive measurement technologies that can be implemented in live settings and can measure progress unobtrusively, seemingly as a fully integrated part of learning and instruction, not as separate events. Moreover, the perception of measurement as a separate accountability activity for grading, sorting, rewarding, and punishing can change to a useful helping function owned by the participants in pursuing valued attainment goals. All the time, the measurements are being used for research, and the teachers and others are participant evaluators in this research, not unknowing subjects. They are the ones who, in concert with researchers and developers having additional expertise, will participate in the redesigns, then will implement them during the next cycle. The measurement instruments evolve over the cycles of design, implement, evaluate, redesign, and come to embody an increasingly adequate descriptive theory of the processes operative in the domain. In addition, the technological devices designed to introduce and control the treatment effects are forthrightly described using the emerging layers and languages of technology in that domain. In addition, both quasi-experimental designs and randomized experiments may be used to warrant causal claims and rule out alternative explanations.

Some History

The roots of the idea of a design experiment in education can be traced back to the time before the accelerating growth of interest in the previous decade; documentation of this was provided by John Dewey in 1916 and

Robert Glaser in 1976, for example. Despite this longer history, most proponents writing today cite Ann Brown's 1992 paper on design experiments and Allan Collins' 1992 paper on a design science of education; the term "design experiment" was introduced in the latter paper. Both of these authors, as well as Glaser, cite Herbert Simon's work. There has been a substantial growth of interest in, and publications dealing with, design studies and design experiments since the 1990s. An entire issue (January/February 2003) of the *Educational Researcher* has been devoted to the design research movement.

How a Design Study or Experiment Proceeds

A study begins by selecting one or more live settings in which the phenomenon of interest may be observed. The setting may be one or more classrooms, or nonconventional learning settings, or it may be a medical treatment facility studying treatment options and ways to implement them, or a management initiative in a group setting, repeated with different groups at later times. A repeating cycle is selected. A semester or block schedule may be used for education, an end point in a medical treatment, or natural assessment points for the management activity. The repeating cycles are essential, because the earlier cycles serve as controls for later ones. (There may also be additional control or treatment groups in rigorous design experiments.) The goals of the research depend on the stage of maturity of the study in the domain of interest. The researchers may seek exploratory, explanatory, or design knowledge in any mixture. Good research design will, as usual, set forth the questions in advance. To be called a design study or experiment, design knowledge will be central among the research questions. In exploratory studies, the questions concern what design interventions exist already and which seem to be working well. As three examples of explanatory studies, the questions may concern the nature of the descriptive progression of learning or growth (in education), the progression of the disease state (in medicine), or the propagation of employee behaviors and associated results (in management). In all design research studies, design knowledge is sought, along with the implementation conditions that enable the designed treatments to yield their best results.

The procedure is to design four aspects of the study: (1) the measurement instruments to assess the progression (of learning, disease states, effective employee performance, and results), (2) the treatment properties (technology), (3) the evaluation/research design for the next cycle, and (4) the implementation plan for the next cycle. Once the measurement instruments are in place, even before a new treatment is introduced, a cycle can be run to collect baseline data. When all four designs are in place, subsequent cycles can be run, involving implementation of the latest version of the designs, then evaluation, followed by seeking improvements in the next cycle through design. Anything may be improved, including the measurement instruments, the treatment, the implementation methods, or the evaluation/research plan. If measurement instruments are changed, equating must be performed to assure comparability with measures taken during previous cycles, or a new series of cycles launched. Because new technologies are making possible continuous measurements all along the way—that is, along the explanatory theory of progression of learning, disease progression or improvement, or employee performance (keeping to our three examples)—evaluation and research data collection are also continuous, and their effects (good and bad) can be attributed to stages along the path of progression. The outcomes of a series of cycles investigated in this type of research are answers to the knowledge-seeking questions stated at the outset of each study, whether explore, explain, or design. An outcome of substantial importance is a documented argument for the validity of a total treatment method, including the technology used and "best practices," i.e., the manner of implementing it to get the best results. When design experiments are used, this validity argument may include evidence to back causal claims for the efficacy of the treatment in leading to desirable outcomes.

Terminology is still in flux. The term "design experiment" has often been appropriated by those interested in intuitive and reflective types of action research in education, in which the teacher takes the lead role, rather than in a partnership role with researchers. The teacher journals personal reflections on possible designs and outcomes as a way to improve practice. Theory, measurement, and the validity of causal inferences are not often important in such studies, but are very important issues in research generalizable beyond single practitioners. For this reason, the term "design studies" can be used to avoid the term "experiment" so as not to confuse these studies with randomized trials in social and behavioral science. This usage was suggested by Richard Shavelson and co-authors, in the previously mentioned issue of *Educational Researcher* focusing on design research, to distinguish single-practitioner studies from true experiments. Influential writers on experimental methods define and emphasize two main types of experiments, i.e., the randomized experiment and the quasi-experiment. Both types of experiments are designed to test descriptive causal hypotheses about manipulable causes. Thus, when the definition of experiment or quasi-experiment holds in a design study, it may justly be called a design experiment.

Design Experiments and Experimental Design

It is useful to consider the nature of experimental design to appreciate fully what can be accomplished with a principled design experiment using invariant measurement scales. In publications extending back to 1963, Donald Campbell and Julian Stanley, and later Thomas Cook, William Shadish, and many others, have given guidance much used over the years in how threats to the validity of causal inferences can be reduced by employing good experimental design. Classically, three pre-experimental designs, three true experimental designs, and 10 quasi-experimental designs have been discussed. There has been a shift away from significance testing in fairly recent times in favor of effect sizes, but the need to consider threats to the validity of inference has not abated. The simplest inference is that the introduction of treatment X did indeed cause the change in observation (measure) O. The emphasis here is that there is a need for design disciplines to assure both that measurement O and treatment X do indeed involve the constructs of learning progression along the pathway to greater expertise. Design theories to guide the development of instructional treatments can succeed far better to the extent that they have a descriptive account of the progress that learners typically follow in moving to higher levels of knowledge and expertise. Figure 2 depicts a design intervention into a natural process. In learning and instruction, the most useful explanatory account would describe the sequence of progressive attainments in the particular learning domain of interest. This descriptive knowledge guides the design of both the measurement instruments, to determine outcome effects (O), and the instructional treatments (X). Instructional-design theories (a term elaborated in a series of books by Charles Reigeluth) are now available to guide the development of controlling technologies for the treatment. Designing X and O in a principled manner can help give this design the six aspects of construct validity discussed in numerous publications by validity theorist Samuel Messick. The descriptive account (or theory) of progressive attainments in learning the increasingly difficult tasks in a learning domain, along with construct-linked measurement scales of learning and growth, along with a validity argument, can assure that the O indeed measures valid levels of progress in the construct. For simplicity, designs that require adaptation to individual difference measures are not discussed here. It is sufficient to note that good quasi-experimental and experimental designs exist for examining hypotheses of how treatments might differ for subgroups of individuals receiving the treatment differentially, depending on their individual profiles.

To understand the sequential nature of a design experiment, and how results from prior cycles can serve as controls for later cycles, consider a simple pretest/post-test design, one of Campbell and Stanley's three true experimental designs. It can be diagrammed as follows, where R means random assignment to either group, and the sequence of events in a single row (e.g., $R \rightarrow O \rightarrow X \rightarrow O$ for row one) is the temporal sequence of events for the experimental group:

$R \quad O \quad X \quad O$ Experimental group

$R \quad O \quad \quad\; O$ Control group

A gain score can be calculated as $O_{\text{post-test}} - O_{\text{pretest}}$ if the measurement scale O supports equal intervals, and other precautions in using gain scores have been followed. Then we may graph the gain for the experimental group and compare it to the gain for the control group.

Consider a series of such experiments, each with a well-documented change in the design specifications for treatment X, or perhaps only changes in the implementation procedures for the treatment.

The design experiment in Table I assumes that all repeating cycles of principled design intervention, X_1–X_5, take place in the same class in an educational institution (or group of similar classes using the same treatments and outcome measures, X and O). The designers of the experiment in Table I altered the treatment condition X_i each time, being careful to conform each design change to a prescriptive theory and assuring that each version of X was well documented. No R for random assignment is shown in this table, because it is neither possible nor necessary for random assignment to occur in these classes. Assume that both the registration procedures of the educational institution and the ethical considerations bar such a practice. Thus we must depend on the sample-invariance and interpretive invariance properties of outcome measure O, and on repeated near-replications with other groups in additional studies, presumably from the same or similar population to substitute for random assignment. The construct-linked variable of interest, O, has the appropriate properties to reduce the risks to internal validity that randomization was assumed to reduce.

Table I Repeating Cycles of a Principled Design Experiment Using Invariant Scale O

Parameter	*Cycle* 1	*Cycle* 2	*Cycle* 3	*Cycle* 4	*Cycle* 5
Baseline measure O_0	X_1	X_2	X_3	X_4	X_5
	O_0	O_1	O_2	O_2	O_3
Control for cycles 1–5	Control for cycles 2–5	Control for cycles 3–5	Control for cycles 4–5	Control for cycle 5	Control for future cycles

Repeated measurements of subsequent groups over the cycles of a design experiment give further basis for ruling out the effects due to peculiarities of one group of students during one semester. But the students who flow through the classes of any one institution are unique and slanted in their own way, so population representativeness has not been obtained. For this function, randomization is a poor tool as well. To obtain evidence of generalizability to other groups, with other language, gender, racial, and special conditions, it is necessary that design experiments be set up in other locations wherein samples of students with subsets of these other characteristics abound. Nevertheless, it is no small benefit to causal inference to be assured that each semester's group was either equivalent on the highly interpretable pretest/post-test measure O, or of known deviation. It is of no small benefit to know that the use of a gain score is appropriate because we have achieved a close approximation to equal interval properties in the measurement scale(s) O. Finally, the quest for the validity of causal inference is, in the framework of a design experiment, set in a larger context similar to the quest for total quality management. After all, there are many aspects to treatment X and its procedures for implementation. To which specifically is the causal inference to be made? An outstanding result is a tribute to the entire group of people and the roles they assumed, the rules they followed, and the tools they used to administer the treatment. An outstanding result is evidence of the possibility that such results can be obtained by managing the implementation of the treatment well, and if in one group, why not in another?

In addition to substituting known starting positions on an invariant scale for random assignment, the design experiment in Table I also replaces the control group, using a series of comparisons to previous groups. Starting with the baseline measurement on O_0, each succeeding cycle can compare its outcome not only to this baseline measure, but also to each of the preceding outcomes, using invariant scales O_0–O_2 (the subscripts indicate that, in this experiment, it was necessary to modify the outcome measure only twice, by adding or deleting tasks, whereas during the same five cycles, the treatment X was modified five times, after each cycle and before the next one). By the specific objectivity property of scale invariance, we can add or subtract questions or tasks from the most recent version of the instrument each semester. Then, after assuring that the versions are equated to the same meaningful scale each semester, we can make inferences that the version of X used that semester was likely the main cause of whatever improvement in gain score was observed.

New guidelines to update good experimental design prescriptions must be developed for principled design experiments. Scientists writing in Campbell and Stanley's era could not have foreseen today's opportunities for unprecedented control of a complex interplay of many treatment variables, possible in live settings through interactive technology. Neither could they have envisioned sophistication of online measurement, nor new measurement methods that can provide close approximations to the invariance properties needed to realize the design experiment scenario. Certain of Campbell and Stanley's quasi-experimental designs are similar to parts of this design experiment scenario, but scientists of their day could not have anticipated the full extent of reliable replication (using technology) with well-documented design changes. Advances in the technology of learning, measurement, and management of complexity changes how well we can control each of the 12 common threats to validity, of concern to these pioneering scientists. Moreover, these advances both introduce new threats to validity and help to find the means to reduce their effects.

It is interesting that the use of the term "validity" by experimental design writers and validity concepts from psychometrics, such as Messick's unified validity concept, do not coincide. For example, the idea of "external validity" is used in entirely different ways. By bringing these two views together through validity-centered design and the methods of principled design experiments, perhaps we are taking a step toward bridging the gap between the "two disciplines of scientific psychology" described by Lee Cronbach.

Conclusion

The three knowledge-producing activities—explore, explain, and design—have been placed into a common context in this article in hopes of distinguishing among the different types of question each activity addresses; at the same time, it has been shown that it is not research methodology that allows them to be separated. Contributions of each form of knowledge-seeking to the other forms have also been described, and examples have been given to show that though exploratory research and explanatory research have longer formal histories than design research has, all three forms of research continue today to contribute to unanswered questions, and none has outlived its usefulness, especially not exploratory research, which continues today at what might be considered an accelerated, rather than a diminished, rate.

The types of research and knowledge-seeking have been described in proportion to the measurement theory and technique concerns addressed in this volume. In particular, measurement has been related to the health and progress of design research and exploratory research to correct what can be viewed as a current underemphasis in those areas caused by living in the shadow of science. The intent here has not been to isolate the three enterprises from each other, but to show their essential contribution to each other: each produces results in the form of answers that stimulate a continuous stream of research questions in all three areas. The three are discriminated on the basis of the kinds of questions they address and the types of knowledge they produce, but not definitively on the research techniques employed.

Progress will continue to be limited in the human sciences and in design as long as metrics used in research are incommensurable from study to study. In discussing design studies and design experiments, the emphasis here is that rigorous design experiments are now possible using well-designed instrumentation for administering both experimental treatments and measurements in live settings. This depends not only on development of commensurable measure-building techniques, but also on use of emerging technologies that give access to data collection and analysis tools previously not available.

See Also the Following Article

Research Designs

Further Reading

Brown, A. L. (1992). Design experiments: Theoretical and methodological challenges in creating complex interventions in classroom settings. *J. Learn. Sci.* **2**(2), 141–178.

Campbell, D. T., and Stanley, J. (1963). *Experimental and Quasi-Experimental Designs for Research.* Hougton-Mifflin, Boston, MA.

Collins, A. (1992). Toward a design science of education. In *New Directions in Educational Technology* (E. Scanlon and T. O'Shea, eds.), pp. 15–22. Springer-Verlag, New York.

Cronbach, L. J. (1957). The two disciplines of scientific psychology. *Am. Psychol.* **12,** 671–684.

Cronbach, L. (1975). Beyond the two disciplines of scientific psychology. *Am. Psychol.* **30,** 116–127.

Dewey, J. (1916). *Democracy and Education.* Free Press, New York. [Cited in Tanner, L. N. (1997) *Dewey's Laboratory School: Lessons for Today.* Teachers College Press, New York.]

Edmondson, A. C. (1987). *A Fuller Explanation: The Synergetic Geometry of Buckminster Fuller.* Barkhauser, Boston, MA.

Glaser, R. (1976). Components of a psychology of instruction: Toward a science design. *Rev. Edu. Res.* **46**(1), 1–24.

Hubka, V., and Eder, W. E. (1996). *Design Science: Introduction to Needs, Scope and Organization of Engineering Design Knowledge.* Springer, Berlin and New York.

Kelly, A. E. (ed.) (2003). Theme issue: The role of design in educational research. *Edu. Res.* **32**(1).

Krantz, D. H., Luce, R. D., Suppes, P., and Tversky, A. (1971). *Foundations of Measurement: Additive and Polynomial Representations.* Vol. 1., Academic Press, New York.

Luce, R. D., Krantz, D. H., Suppes, P., and Tversky, A. (1990). *Foundations of Measurement: Representation, Axiomatization, and Invariance.* Vol. 3., Academic Press, San Diego, CA.

Messick, S. (1989). Validity. In *Educational Measurement* (R. L. Linn, ed.), pp. 13–103. Macmillan, New York.

Messick, S. (1995). Validity of Psychological Assessment. *Am. Psychol.* **50**(9), 741–749.

Messick, S. (1998). Test validity: A matter of consequence. *Social Indicat. Res.* **45,** 35–44.

Pickstone, J. V. (2001). *Ways of Knowing: A New History of Science, Technology, and Medicine.* University of Chicago Press, Chicago, IL.

Reigeluth, C. M. (ed.) (1999). *Instructional-Design Theories And Models: A New Paradigm of Instructional Theory.* Lawrence Erlbaum Assoc., Mahwah, NJ.

Shadish, W. R., Cook, T. D., and Campbell, D. T. (2002). *Experimental and Quasi-Experimental Designs for Generalized Causal Inference.* Houghton-Mifflin, Boston, MA.

Simon, H. (1969). *The Sciences of the Artificial.* MIT Press, Cambridge, MA.

Suppes, P., Tversky, A., Krantz, D. M., and Luce, R. D. (1989). *Foundations of Measurement: Geometrical, Threshold, and Probabilistic Representations.* Vol. 2., Academic Press, San Diego, CA.

Tryon, W. W. (1996). Instrument-driven theory. *J. Mind Behav.* **17**(1), 21–30.

Vincenti, W. G. (1990). *What Engineers Know and How They Know It: Analytical Studies from Aeronautical History.* Johns Hopkins University Press, Baltimore, MD.

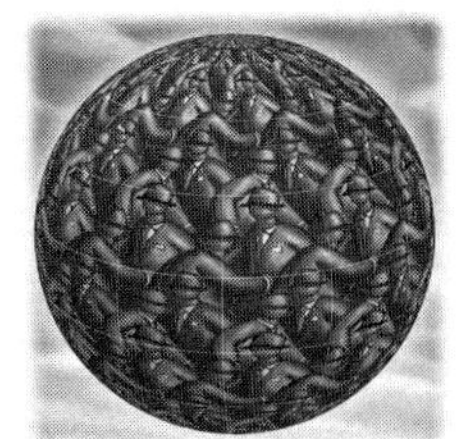

Eysenck, Hans Jürgen

Rod Buchanan
University of Groningen, Groningen, The Netherlands

Glossary

classical conditioning Also known as Pavlovian conditioning; a form of learning that transfers or extends an existing response to a stimulus to that of a new stimulus via the temporal and/or spatial association of the two stimuli.

correlation A measure of covariation, measured on a scale from +1.00 (perfect positive association) through 0.00 (no association) to −1.00 (perfect negative association).

cortical arousal The level of activity in the brain, with high levels of arousal indicative of mental alertness or readiness.

covariation The extent that two variables are associated, that is, vary together.

dimension A continuous psychological variable.

electroencephalography Measures of electrical activity of the brain, involving the analysis of various forms of brain waves.

excitation–inhibition The action and counteraction of cortical activity.

factor-analysis A statistical tool for summarizing the covariation between sets of variables; the patterns it yields may point to underlying dimensions in the data.

genes The physical unit contained within the cells of living organisms by which particular characteristics may be passed from one generation to the next.

genetic That pertaining to genes.

hereditary Refers to characteristics passed from one generation to the next via genes.

limbic system A section of the midbrain associated with the regulation of emotions, memory, feeding, and sexuality.

neurosis A term loosely applied to a relatively mild set of mental disorders, often involving anxiety, phobias, compulsions, and depression.

psychosis A term loosely applied to the more severe mental disorders, including schizophrenia and manic depression.

Hans Eysenck was a founding figure in postwar British psychology, noted for the audacity of his theorizing, the expansive scope of his empirical research, and the forthright, often controversial views that he expressed. He developed a distinctive personality psychology that married descriptive statistics with physiological experimentation and collapsed any firm distinction between pure and applied science. The author of 85 books and over 1000 scientific papers, Eysenck was also renowned as a popularizer of psychological science.

Introduction: Life and Career

Eysenck was born in Berlin in 1916. After graduating from secondary school in 1934, he fled Hitler's Germany and settled in London the following year. Without the necessary prerequisites to do his first choice, physics, he enrolled in psychology at University College, London, where he was taught by J. C. Flügel, S. J. F. Philpott, and Cyril Burt. He rapidly took a degree and then completed a Ph.D. that focused on the experimental analysis of aesthetic preferences, supervised by Burt.

The outbreak of war saw Eysenck declared an enemy alien and he found it difficult to obtain work. After a spell as a firewatcher, he landed a job at the Mill Hill hospital in 1942. Headed by the imposing psychiatrist Aubrey Lewis, Mill Hill functioned as the relocated Maudsley psychiatric hospital. Soon after the war, plans were drawn up for a new Institute of Psychiatry (IoP), a training and research facility to be affiliated with the Maudsley and Bethlem hospitals. Eysenck turned down offers at several other universities to head psychology there. Eysenck was given an unusual degree of bureaucratic freedom to organize research around his vision of an experimental psychology of individual differences. The IoP provided a stable institutional environment where he spent the rest of his career. By 1955, he had become a full Professor in an independent psychology department. After he retired in 1983, his research activities and writing were undiminished and his interests were even more diverse.

The Dimensional Approach to Personality

Theoretical Assumptions and Methodological Approach

Eysenck advocated and adopted what he saw as the methods characterizing the physical sciences. For Eysenck, human behavior could be studied like any other natural phenomenon. Throughout his career, he searched for laws and regularities that might provide a deeper-level, causative structure for human behavior. He took Thorndike's notion of the primacy of measurement as a starting point—anything psychologically real and scientifically important could and should be made measurable. Without measurement, there could be no hope of precise, testable theory. Eysenck combined the pragmatic, rule-bound operationism of correlational methods with experimental work that utilized the continuous measurement scales and instrumental techniques of the physical sciences.

Eysenck remained suspicious or dismissive of aspects of psychology that did not meet his criteria of good science. His antipathy to psychoanalysis was legendary; it was, he thought, insular and subjective, imprecise and untestable. Those parts of psychoanalysis that could be rendered predictive seldom did so successfully. In short, Freudian psychology was a fiction—made all the more damaging by its widespread influence and uncritical application.

Eysenck believed that humans were clearly biosocial organisms. He rejected any notion of a dualism of mind and body in favor of a continuum. It was an assumption that he felt was "too obvious to require supporting argument" and he seldom gave one. However, he was an interactionist rather than a biological reductionist, consistently arguing that behavior was both biologically and socially determined.

The Structure of Personality

Eysenck's most significant contribution was in personality psychology. Early in his career, he put forward a decisive vision of human personality, original as a synthesis of disparate ideas and results and distinguished by its vast investigative potential. Eysenck began with little in the way of equipment or research funds and was drawn to psychometric description of personality. He factor-analyzed the data sheets Lewis kept on new hospital arrivals, correlating the results with questionnaire and experimental data. He published his results and interpretations in 1947 in *Dimensions in Personality*. It was Eysenck's first book and probably his most important.

Dimensions of Personality outlined two main personality factors—that of Neuroticism (N) and Introversion–Extraversion (I–E). Eysenck deliberately contrasted these bipolar continuums with the confused typological thinking that had dominated psychiatry and attempted to clear up the vague and speculative trait lists of personality psychology. It was a work unprecedented in Britain, but drew inspiration from personality trait research of Allport and Cattell in the United States and the typological theories of Jung and Kretschmer on the Continent. However, Eysenck went beyond descriptive level theory—since various factor-analytic solutions might be seen to be mathematically equivalent—by investigating the predictive relationship of his dimensions to specific behavior and by attempting to anchor them in biology.

Dimensions of Personality set out the future direction of Eysenck's research, although the details of his theoretical position shifted over the years. In 1952, *The Scientific Study of Personality* introduced a third dimension, that of Psychoticism (P). Eysenck spent much of the remainder of his career attempting to back the claim that these three independent dimensions represented the underlying structure of personality. An individual's position on these dimensions was indicative of a cluster of more specific traits. These traits, in turn, determined habitual response patterns made up of particular acts. Eysenck's dimensions were, he further claimed, culturally universal, with a continuum from humans to animals.

For Eysenck, personality differences were directly related to constitutive differences in the brain that were largely hereditary. Utilizing what now appear to be the limited techniques of functional neurology of the 1950s, Eysenck searched for these constitutive differences in studies of animal behavior. In his landmark 1957 book *The Dynamics of Anxiety and Hysteria*, N was related to the level of instinctual activity in the midbrain, whereas I–E was linked to a simplified version of Pavlov's notion of excitation and inhibition. Not all agreed that the evidence Eysenck gathered convincingly supported the scope of his theorizing. Yet it remained the most sustained and ambitious attempt to combine trait description with neurological subsystems defined in terms of their behavior control function and their place in the economy of the nervous system.

Eysenckian personality theory became an elaborate feed-forward model. Basic differences in neurobiology lay at the root of broader differences in complex cerebral capacities that dictated the rate and pattern of learning in any particular situation. However, Eysenck never maintained that personality was fully determined by biology. Instead, he viewed behavior as the sum effect of genes and environment. This framework enabled Eysenck to explore the genetic basis of personality differences, the way in which these differences determined conditioned learning, and the net effects of this interaction. For example, introverts were thought to be far more responsive than extraverts, learning quicker, better, and for longer; as a consequence, Eysenck suggested that introverts also tended to have a more developed sense of morality and a greater capacity for academic achievement.

Eysenck drew many other implications from his personality theories, suggesting that various forms of social distress were related to extreme positions on at least one of these dimensions. Since the early 1950s, he collaborated with a number of other researchers on pioneering twin and family studies on the inheritance of personality—indicating a hereditability of at least 50%—as well as writing on the genetic basis for intelligence, sexual behavior, crime, and political attitudes. As the implications were tested, the results served to elaborate or modify an evolving theoretical framework. By the mid-1960s, the formalism of Hull that inspired earlier work had fallen out of favor. After some disappointing results in experimental conditioning work, Eysenck revised the biological basis of I–E by linking it to cortical arousal thresholds in the brainstem's activation systems, with N related to limbic system activity.

Several shifts were made to the content of Eysenck's three personality dimensions in order to maintain their theoretical coherence, independence, and explanatory power. High N was finally made up of traits such as anxiety, depression, guilt, and tension, with the opposite pole being stability. The extraversion end of I–E was characterized by sociability, assertiveness, and sensation-seeking and the introversion end by low levels of these traits. High P was defined by aggression, coldness, and impulsivity, with the opposite being control. Eysenck made an initial distinction between dysthymic and hysteric neuroticism that related to introversion–extraversion. However, this distinction was later dropped as these terms disappeared from psychiatric discourses. The P dimension was less theoretically driven and never enjoyed a clearly articulated biological basis. At the extreme, P was initially associated with schizophrenia and manic–depressive illness. However, P was empirically reworked so that high P became more indicative of the sociopathy of current psychiatric nomenclature. The high ends of the N and P dimensions were associated with psychopathology. Neither extreme on the I–E dimension per se carried quite the same implications, although scores on this dimension helped characterize the kind of psychiatric symptomology that extreme scores on the other scales indicated.

In a bid to provide standardized measures for his personality dimensions, Eysenck developed successive versions of a relatively short, accessible questionnaire. It first appeared in 1959 as the Maudsley Personality Inventory (measuring I–E and N). With considerable input from his wife, Sybil, the 1975 version was renamed the Eysenck Personality Questionnaire and included a measure of P as well. These inventories became some of the most widely used of their type in the world and served as valuable research tools for those attempting to confirm or extend the Eysenckian paradigm.

Other Major Contributions

Clinical Psychology and Behavior Therapy

When Eysenck was placed in charge of psychology at the IoP, part of his brief was to develop the profession of clinical psychology in Great Britain. There were no formally recognized training courses at the time, though other programs would start up around this time at the Tavistock in London and the Crichton Royal in Dumfries. Eysenck hired Monte Shapiro to head the clinical section soon after the war. However, Eysenck dominated as the professional spokesperson, even though he had little to do with clinical training and never treated patients.

In his writings on clinical psychology in the early 1950s, Eysenck initially argued for an independent, research-based discipline. He saw the American model for clinical psychology as an imitation of the medical model that was accompanied by subservience to psychiatry and a misplaced enthusiasm for psychotherapy. According to Eysenck, clinical psychologists should respond only to the problems thrown up by their science, not to social need. These attacks were accompanied by a program of research that highlighted the inadequacies of psychiatric practices. He and his clinical colleagues attacked the reliability of psychiatric diagnosis and the validity of tests such as the Rorschach. He also, famously, questioned the efficacy of psychotherapy, especially psychoanalytic psychotherapy.

Maudsley psychologists had begun treating patients in the mid-1950s with a new form of behavior therapy—disguising it as case-based research because psychologists were officially discouraged from treating patients. They borrowed from work done in Europe, the United States, and South Africa (especially Joseph Wolpe's), but were mindful to put in a Pavlovian learning perspective. Importantly, it was a form of treatment that fitted in well with the Eysenckian perspective of the detached scientist. Behavior therapy was less talk and more a planned course of remedial training. As "the scientific application of learning principles," it demanded no empathy from the therapist, Eysenck claimed.

By the late 1950s, Eysenck began to openly advocate that psychologists practice this form of treatment. It provoked a furious and largely unsuccessful backlash from psychiatrists, led by Aubrey Lewis. Lewis eventually conceded the weakness of his position by instructing a number of psychiatrists to study and practice behavior therapy. The 1960s became the era of behavior therapy in British clinical psychology. Eysenck edited several books on the subject, linking up diverse practices into a seemingly coherent international movement. He also started the journal *Behaviour Research and Therapy* (BRAT) in 1963. The Maudsley nexus dominated clinical training in Great Britain in this period, supplying the dominant rationale and most of the trained personnel for a small but growing profession. Maudsley graduates came to head many of the clinical courses started in the late 1950s and 1960s across the United Kingdom.

The sense of unity that characterized both the behavior therapy movement and the Maudsley model for clinical training started to break down by the early 1970s. At an intellectual level, Maudsley insiders acknowledged that Eysenck's framework did not translate easily into clinical practice. Ascertaining a patient's location on Eysenck's personality dimensions had few treatment implications and often did not furnish much new information. In other ways, Eysenck's professional strategy became a victim of its success. As the most visible and dominant psychological treatment, behavior therapy also proved vulnerable to the radical social critiques of the period. As in America, advocates of behavioral interventions were obliged to soften their style. Moreover, Eysenck's vision of the clinical psychologist as the applied scientist did not map easily onto the structure of British health care. The National Health Service never fully embraced a research-based role for psychologists. The strict Maudsley formula of diagnostics and behavior therapy gave way to an uncertain eclecticism in the mid-1970s, boosted by humanistic and cognitive approaches to theory and practice.

Eysenck shifted his position only slightly in the ensuing years, conceding that cognitive factors were important but redescribing them in a manner that backed his contention that behavior therapy always allowed for them. Although he bemoaned the lack of theoretical cohesion in latter-day therapeutics, Eysenck still claimed to be amazed at how quickly behavior therapy had taken hold.

Intelligence

Eysenck's interest in intelligence research started late in his career, partly because his mentor Burt had already carved out the area so assiduously. As a result, his contribution was bound to be overshadowed by his earlier, more definitive work on personality. In the late 1960s, Eysenck proposed a structural model for intelligence similar to Guildford's model that aimed to avoid the circular problems of its psychometric derivation. Throughout his career, he remained committed to a version of the "g" concept, a notion originated by his intellectual forefather, Charles Spearman. For Eysenck, intelligence was a general cognitive factor rather than a set of distinct abilities, although there were lesser components to it. Although it was not an entity in itself, general intelligence was a useful construct reflecting a general property of the cerebral cortex. Psychometric tests were a good if not perfect measure of general intelligence. Moreover, Eysenck suggested that it was largely innate and heritable—accounting for up to 80% of the variance—with this figure depending on the statistical model used and the homogeneity of particular environments. Until recently, it was a position in general accord with most of those who accepted the assumptions of the twin-study paradigm.

An important component of Eysenck's work in this area was to define concepts and arbitrate debates. Eysenck attempted to clarify what he saw as the three main understandings of intelligence. First and most narrowly, there was biological intelligence, dependent on genetic potential and expressed by various biological and neurological indices. Next was psychometric intelligence, which was highly dependent on genetic endowment but also influenced by environmental factors. Most generally, there was social intelligence, reflecting success in those aspects of life that required intelligent behavior. Social intelligence was dictated by psychometric intelligence but also enhanced or hindered by personal events, practical habits, and emotional propensities.

Most of Eysenck's original contribution focused on the interface between biological and psychometric intelligence. Eysenck picked up a thread from the late 1950s work of his colleague Desmond Furneaux, namely, that there are three almost orthogonal components to intelligence: speed, persistence, and error-checking. The former was a strictly cognitive property and the latter two were more features of personality. In the 1980s, Eysenck urged psychologists to have another look at Galton's contention that mental speed was a central factor in intelligence. Utilizing his own and other reaction-time results, Eysenck concluded that intelligent people were faster in their intake and processing of information, partly because they were more efficient and less prone to transmission error. In his later experiments in this area, he explored more direct measures of brain activity—using electroencephalography—producing some promising but not robust correlations with psychometric tests. In reintroducing the notion of mental speed, Eysenck tried to account for individual differences in performance, rather than elucidate the component mechanisms of intelligence that characterized the work of the equally prolific Robert Sternberg.

Eysenck's public reputation stemmed largely from his research and writing on intelligence—comparatively limited as it was—since it touched on some sensitive areas. Most notorious was his attempt to give a popular explanation for Arthur Jensen's contention that racial differences in IQ distributions were probably hereditary and could not be substantially affected by educational interventions. The breezy, popular book he published on the subject saw him publicly hounded and cost him the support of some of his more liberal-minded peers. Through it all, he strongly defended his position on the nature versus nurture question, most famously against Leon Kamin. Although he tended to equivocate on the cause of race differences, opponents saw him as a wholehearted advocate of the hereditarian position and the issue is still a divisive one inside and outside the discipline.

When a fraud charge was launched against Cyril Burt in the mid-1970s, Eysenck staunchly defended his old mentor. As the evidence against Burt mounted, he felt obliged to distance himself from Burt's questionable practices but not his general ideas. In the latter part of his postretirement career, he also played a key role in attempts to raise intelligence with vitamins. The suggestive results of these studies were, however, contested by competing researchers with data countering the IQ boost Eysenck's team claimed. This issue remains open.

Political Attitudes

Eysenck extended his success in getting a grip on personality via factor-analysis into the political realm. Although he published several more papers in the 1960s and 1970s, his 1954 book *The Psychology of Politics* remained his major statement in the area. According to Eysenck, social and political attitudes can be organized into two bipolar dimensions. One dimension followed the traditional means for differentiating left—right political ideology—Radical versus Conservative. However, Eysenck labeled the second dimension Tough versus Tender-Mindedness (T), following the classic distinction of William James. This produced a four-quadrant space, the most provocative implication being that the political extremes of Fascism and Communism were separated by ideology but were similar in terms of personal style. Eysenck linked this conclusion with postwar research on Authoritarianism, controversially arguing that Adorno *et al.*'s F concept was practically synonymous with T. For Eysenck, this balanced out the political picture, explaining the "same but different" paradox he had witnessed in the volatile politics of prewar Germany.

Eysenck's work on political attitudes met with considerable hostility from liberal researchers, especially in the United States. He engaged in a somewhat acrimonious, highly technical debate with Rokeach and Hanley, and with Christie, over the reality of left-wing authoritarianism and the adequacy of his factor-analytically derived measures. As he struggled to obtain a pure, independent measure of T, critics doubted that he had demonstrated that left-wing authoritarianism existed—at least in Western democratic societies. However, Eysenck redirected political attitudes research by introducing constitutional personality factors. Having linked T with the personality dimension of extraversion, he later assimilated it within a reconceptualized P dimension. Redolent of Cold War thinking, Eysenck stopped short of applying his analyses to the political environment on the other side of the (former) Iron Curtain.

Physical Disease and Drug Use

With his biosocial perspective, Eysenck took seriously the folk wisdom linking temperament with physical health—now a more mainstream idea within medical epidemiology and immunology. An early collaboration with oncologist David Kissen suggested an association between cancer and personality. Eysenck attracted more attention by claiming that the causal role of cigarettes in cancer had not (yet) been convincingly proven and that personality was probably a mediating variable in this equation. He argued that certain types of people smoked, some of who were also susceptible to cancer. Although opponents later acknowledged some of his methodological criticisms of epidemiological research, Eysenck took a welter of criticism from public health advocates as the anti-smoking message became more visible and forceful.

Eysenck published very little in this area again until 1980, when he revisited the issue and presented new genetic evidence linking personality, smoking, and disease. He then took up with a little-known Yugoslav researcher with longitudinal data on personality and disease. In a series of papers in the late 1980s and early 1990s, Eysenck and Ronald Grossarth-Maticek reported a variety of results demonstrating a strong association between particular personality types and cancer, coronary heart disease, and other ailments. Although these were mostly write-ups of studies set in train more than a decade earlier, Eysenck's input helped fine-tune the presentation, theoretical explanations, and analyses. A number of intervention studies were also carried out, with Eysenck more actively involved in the design and analysis of some of these. They suggested that particular forms of psychotherapy that targeted cancer sufferers or those with unhealthy personal styles could have remarkable therapeutic or prophylactic effects. Though the scope and ambition of these studies were applauded, critics complained of lack of detail in the descriptions of the methods used and a lack of controls ensuring the integrity of the data sets. Some even suggested that the results were "too good to be true." Health psychologists and medical epidemiologists appeared to suspend judgment on the value of these studies until replications appear.

Crime, Social Behavior and Astrology

During his long career, Eysenck also took time to research and write on a variety of other topics, including crime and personality, marriage and sex. In the mid-1960s, he raised eyebrows by suggesting that criminality was related to personality and was therefore partly hereditary. For Eysenck, conscience was a conditioned reflex rather than the result of rational learning. Certain personality types, those with a lower capacity for conditioned learning (i.e., extraverts), were slower to develop prosocial behavior. Moreover, emotionally labile persons (i.e., high N) with antisocial tendencies were more likely to act out than emotionally stable people with similar tendencies. He backed up this contention with data suggesting that prisoners, psychopaths, and unwed mothers tended to lie in the extraverted-neurotic quadrant. High P scorers also came to be associated with the persistence and severity of criminality and the external attribution of blame. Eysenck drew several key implications from this work, notably that punishment by itself will seldom work as deterrent and that any attempt at rehabilitation should take personality into account. Less than influential outside an academic context, Eysenck's suggestions helped stimulate research into the psychological causes of crime rather than its prevention or control.

Eysenck made various contributions to many other topics—collaborating with a wide range of colleagues and always attempting to integrate new findings within his increasingly elaborate, tightly defined dimensional model. Studies of sexual behavior linked individual preferences to different personality types; for example, certain gender specific traits complement each other, whereas other traits in either sex predicted marital unhappiness. Eysenck also took a serious look at astrology, defending various suggestions and results up to a point and championing Gauguelin's finding that planetary positions at birth and professional eminence were correlated. One last set of writings looked at genius, creativity, and madness, exploring their link with P and their biological underpinnings. Over the years, Eysenck authored a number of extremely popular paperbacks explaining psychology as he saw it to a lay audience. He also made numerous media appearances discussing issues relevant to his expertise.

Wider Reception and Influence

Intellectual Legacy and Current Reputation

Eysenck's three-dimensional view of personality was always countered by more complex descriptive systems in the United States, particularly the 16 personality factors of Raymond Cattell. However, Eysenck never compromised on his view that three dimensions were sufficient. Prolonged attempts by others to reconcile the two systems have led to a synthesis of sorts. Currently, 5 factors are seen as the most defensible, 2 of which are similar to Eysenck's I–E and N.

Eysenck mapped out an integrated set of research that continues to inspire, especially in the search for a genetic basis for personality disorders and psychiatric distress. He dominated the study of the biological basis for personality and introduced testable theoretical accounts into an area that had appeared to avoid them. Within this tradition have come several major challenges, notably from his successor at the IoP, Jeffrey Gray. Gray has shifted the axes of Eysenck's factors and hypothesized a basis in neurological subsystems that mediate reactions to reinforcing stimuli rather than arousal.

In hindsight, Eysenck was only partially successful in bridging Cronbach's two schools of psychology. The physiological aspects of his work repulsed the social psychologists, and experimentalists did not appreciate his insistence on accounting for individual variation in their search for averaged mechanisms. Although a handful of researchers still share his integrative vision, these two schools are still largely segregated at an intellectual and institutional level.

Eysenck also shaped much of the initial history of clinical psychology in Great Britain and ushered in a new form of psychological therapy in the process. Nonetheless, his vision of clinical psychology as the rigorous application of learning theory has been swamped by a more service-oriented profession wielding a variety of therapeutic techniques. Although psychoanalysts quickly learned to ignore his attacks, he helped ensure that clinical psychology became a more accountable, empirically based practice.

The Outsider as Insider

Without qualification, Eysenck was the most prominent psychologist in postwar Great Britain. Yet he received only belated acknowledgment in the United States and was never truly honored in his adopted homeland. He was, his supporters remarked, a foreigner in many senses—too ambitious, too controversial, and too much the nonconformist. Eysenck was a pronounced introvert who was largely uninterested in the more usual forms of social networking. Ever the realist, he came to forego the difficult and uncertain task of dominating or remodeling existing disciplinary bodies and instead created his own. People joined him rather than the other way round. He cared little for the polite niceties of traditional authority, a stance partly deliberate, partly forced on him. It radicalized Eysenck's intellectual message but limited his acceptance in established circles.

With his all-embracing, programmatic research setup, Eysenck trained hundreds of research students, many of whom subsequently took up key positions in universities in the United Kingdom and abroad. Although he was reluctant to push the idea of a dogmatic "Eysenckian school," his ideas and research approach continue to evolve in the hands of an international network of admirers. This network centers around journals such as *Personality and Individual Differences* and BRAT, and the International Society for the Study of Individual Differences—all of which Eysenck was pivotal in founding.

Eysenck's reputation as a controversial figure derived in part from his involvement in issues that were already controversial—the psychology of political extremism, the hereditary basis of black–white differences in IQ scores, the scientific potential of astrology, and the link between smoking and cancer. However, his notoriety predated and went beyond these interventions. His attempt to unite entrenched factions within the discipline, along with his appetite and facility for combative debate, served to divide support and generate motivated opposition. To insiders—those who accepted the major assumptions of his work—he was stimulating, supportive, inclusive, and trusting. To outsiders, his style was less than conciliatory, resembling that of a prosecuting lawyer selectively marshalling data and arguments for a preferred point of view.

Eysenck claimed that he never deliberately provoked or relished debate for its own sake. Certainly he could not have enjoyed the more vituperative attacks that he (and his family) endured. However, he clearly wished to have his ideas taken seriously and to have them actively discussed. Perhaps rooted in his memory of the Nazi era of his youth, Eysenck greatly valued the freedom to express unpopular views and saw something sinister in any kind of enforced consensus. Speaking out was, to him, almost always worth the risk.

See Also the Following Articles

Behavioral Psychology • Clinical Psychology • Correlations • Factor Analysis • Intelligence Testing

Further Reading

Claridge, G. (1998). Contributions to the history of psychology. CXIII. Hans Jürgen Eysenck (4 March 1916–4 September 1997), an appreciation. *Psychol. Rep.* **83,** 392–394.

Corr, P. J. (2000). Reflections on the scientific life of Hans Eysenck. *History Philos. Psychol.* **2,** 18–35.

Eaves, L. J., Eysenck, H. J., and Martin, L. J. (1989). *Genes, Culture and Personality: An Empirical Approach.* Academic Press, New York.

Eysenck, H. J. (1991). Personality, stress and disease: An interactionist perspective (with commentaries and response). *Psychol. Inquiry* **2,** 221–232.

Eysenck, H. J. (1997). *Rebel with a Cause: The Autobiography of Hans Eysenck.* Transaction, New Brunswick, NJ.

Eysenck, H. J., and Kamin, L. (1981). *The Intelligence Controversy.* Wiley, New York.

Eysenck, H. J., and Nias, D. K. B. (1982). *Astrology: Science or Superstition?* Temple Smith, London.

Furnham, A. (1998). Contributions to the history of psychology. CXIV. Hans Jürgen Eysenck, 1916–1997. *Percept. Motor Skills* **87,** 505–506.

Gibson, H. B. (1981). *Hans Eysenck: The Man and His Work.* Peter Owen, London.

Gray, J. (1997). Obituary: Hans Jürgen Eysenck (1916–97). *Nature* **389,** 794.

Jones, G. (1984). Behaviour therapy: An autobiographic view. *Behav. Psychother.* **12,** 7–16.

Modgil, S., and Modgil, C. (eds.) (1986). *Hans Eysenck: Consensus and Controversy.* Falmer Press, London.

Nyborg, G. (ed.) (1997). *The Scientific Study of Human Nature: Tribute to Hans J. Eysenck at Eighty.* Pergamon, Oxford, UK.

Pelosi, A. J., and Appleby, L. (1992). Psychological influences on cancer and ischaemic heart disease. *Br. Med. J.* **304,** 1295–1298.

Wiggins, J. S. (ed.) (1996). *The Five-Factor Model of Personality: Theoretical Perspectives.* Guilford, New York.